$\mathcal{E}$ntrepreneur and the Law

Expanded Ethics Coverage in Chapter 8 "Ethics and Social Resposibility of Business"

"Turn to the inside back cover for information on International
Coverage and Contemporary Business Applications"

BUSINESS LAW

ETHICAL,

INTERNATIONAL,

&

E-COMMERCE

ENVIRONMENT

FOURTH EDITION

HENRY R. CHEESEMAN

Clincial Professor of Business Law
Director of the Legal Studies Program
Marshall School of Business
University of Southern California

Prentice Hall

Upper Saddle River, New Jersey 07458

Library of Congress Cataloging-in-Publication Data

Cheeseman, Henry R.
    Business law : ethical, international & e-commerce environment / Henry R.
    Cheeseman.—4th ed.
        p. cm.
    Includes bibliographical references and index.
    ISBN 0-13-087913-4
    1. Business law—United States. I. Title.

KF889.C433 2001
346.7307—dc21   00-022497

Senior Editor: Linda Schreiber
Assistant Editor: Jennifer Surich
Media Project Manager: Michele Faranda
Senior Marketing Manager: Debbie Clare
Associate Managing Editor (Production):   Judy Leale
Production Editor: Cindy Spreder
Production Coordinator: Keri Jean
Manufacturing Supervisor: Arnold Vila
Manufacturing Buyer: Diane Peirano
Senior Prepress/Manufacturing Manager: Vincent Scelta
Design Manager: Patricia Smythe
Interior Design: Jill Little
Cover Design: Jill Little
Cover Art/Photo: Henry Cheeseman
Senior Print/Media Production Manager: Karen Goldsmith
Print Production Manager: Christina Mahon
Page Formatter: Ashley Scattergood
Composition: UG / GGS Information Services, Inc.

Photos courtesy of Henry Cheeseman

10 9 8 7 6 5 4 3 2
ISBN 0-13-087913-4

Like oceans, we have spent
  this time together before.
In galley slave pits you fed me
  water and removed my slivers.
Riding Ch'u dynasty chariots
  we perished on Mongol swords.
We toiled rocks in chains
  and built Stonehenge,
drank with King Arthur
  and danced with Black Elk.
We fled, hand-in-hand, dodging
  Hitler's bullets, and
I carried you over the border
  to have our baby in freedom.
During past full moons, the sun set
  the seas in orbit
and as driftwood we tumbled
  onto the shores of Los Angeles.
Another life together, my love?

Henry Cheeseman

Contents in Brief

Contents

Preface

— To the Students —

Each semester, as I stand up in front of a new group of business majors in my business law class I am struck by the thought that, cases and statutes aside, I know two very important things that they have yet to learn. The first is that I draw as much from them as they do from me. Their youth, enthusiasm, questions, and even the doubts a few of them hold about the relevance of law to their futures, fuel my teaching. They don't know that every time they open their minds to look at a point from a new perspective or critically question something they have taken for granted, I get a wonderful reward for the work that I do.

The other thing I know is that both teaching and learning the law are all about stories. The stories I tell provide the framework on which students will hang everything they learn about the law in my class. It is my hope that long after the facts about the specific language of the statutes have faded, they will retain that framework. Several years from now, "unintentional torts" may draw only a glimmer of recognition with business managers who learn about them as students in my class this year. However, they will likely recall the story of the man who sued Pepsi as a result of impotence caused by a vending machine. The story sticks and gives students the hook on which to hang the concepts.

I remind myself of these two facts every time I sit down to work on writing and revising *Business Law*, as well. My goal is to present the law in a way that will spur students to ask questions, to go beyond rote memorization. Business law is an evolving outgrowth of its environment, and that environment keeps changing. In addition to the social, ethical, and international contexts I have incorporated in previous editions of **Business Law**, this edition adds coverage and emphasis on the Internet and entrepreneurship as two vital catalysts to the law and a key part of its environment.

It is my wish that my commitment to these goals shines through in this labor of love, and I hope you have as much pleasure in using it as I have had in creating it for you.

Henry Cheeseman

Making the Most of the Fourth Edition

These boxes focus on the business challenges and legal issues businesses face as they either launch new Internet ventures or rise to the challenge of incorporating on-line technologies into their existing business models.

The Internet and the Law

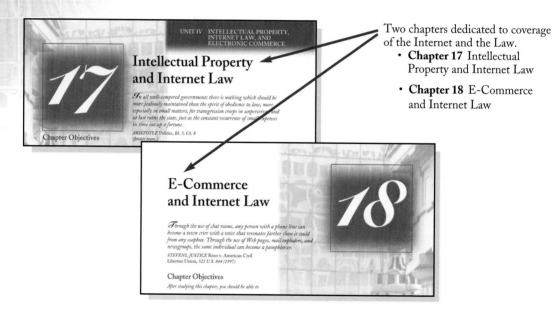

Two chapters dedicated to coverage of the Internet and the Law.
- **Chapter 17** Intellectual Property and Internet Law
- **Chapter 18** E-Commerce and Internet Law

Over 60 **E-Commerce** and **Internet Law Boxes** focus on the legal issues businesses face as they either launch new Internet ventures or rise to the challenge of incorporating on-line technologies into their existing business models.

Chapter 32 Law for Entrepreneurs, recognizes the explosion of entrepreneurial ventures as an important factor in contemporary American business and investigates the legal issues unique to them.

Law for Entrepreneurs

Commerce never really flourishes so much, as when it is delivered from the guardianship of legislators and ministers.
WILLIAM GODWIN *Enquiry Concerning Political Justice (1798)*

Chapter Objectives

After studying this chapter, you should be able to

1. Describe the role of entrepreneurs in starting and operating businesses.
2. List and describe the forms of conducting domestic business.
3. Describe sole proprietorships and the liability of sole proprietors.
4. Distinguish between general and limited partnerships.
5. Describe limited liability partnerships.
6. Describe limited liability companies.
7. Describe corporations.
8. Describe the taxation of the major forms of conducting business.
9. Describe the use of agents, representatives, and distributors in conducting international business.
10. Explain the difference between using a branch and a subsidiary to conduct international business.

Chapter Contents

- **Entrepreneurial Forms of Conducting Business**
  Entrepreneur and the Law *The Entrepreneurial Spirit: The Creation of Amazon.com*
  Entrepreneur and the Law *VA Linux IPO Soars*

- **International Perspective** *Conducting International Business Through a Branch Office or a Subsidiary Corporation*
  Entrepreneur and the Law *AOL Acquires Time-Warner in Megamerger*

Entrepreneur and the Law

THE ENTREPRENEURIAL SPIRIT: THE CREATION OF AMAZON.COM

In 1994, Jeff Bezos, the son of a Cuban immigrant to the United States, had made it big. After graduating from Princeton University, he had gone on to Wall Street where he worked for a hedge fund. But Bezos saw an even greater opportunity: on-line commerce. So he quit his job, jumped in the car with his wife, MacKenzie, and headed west. While she drove, he typed on his laptop computer. Bezos drew up a list of 20 products that he figured he could sell on-line but then narrowed it to two—books and music. Bezos settled on books for two reasons. First, there are more to sell (about 1.3 million books in print versus 300,000 music titles). Second, the Goliath's of publishing seemed less imposing than the six record companies that dominated music; there were thousands of bookstores, the largest being Barnes & Noble with 12 percent of the industry's $25 billion annual sales.

After checking out Colorado and Oregon, Bezos and his wife settled in Seattle, Washington. They rented a house, hired four employees, and started Amazon.com out of their garage. Bezos and his family incorporated the business, sold some stock to friends and other investors, and kept the rest of the stock for themselves. Bezos took a traditional business—bookselling—on-line. He reasoned that books were fungible—everyone sold the same product—and that a portion of a traditional bookseller's cost represented the real estate on which the store sat. So Bezos lined up a distribution center in Oregon and began taking orders in cyberspace. Amazon.com sold its first book in July 1995.

Amazon.com became a success, at least at selling books. However, it was not a success at making a profit, losing

customers and getting the Amazon.com brand name to be recognized by over one-quarter of Americans. Like most start-ups, Amazon.com needed more seed money. Underterred by the company's unprofitability, the venture capitalist firm Kleiner Perkins Caufield & Byer put up $10 million for preferred stock, which represented a 15 percent stake in Amazon.com.

Following on the heels of its book-selling success, Amazon.com began selling other products over the Internet, including CDs, videos, gifts, greeting cards, and thousands of other items. Amazon.com entered the world of on-line auctions; linked with other companies selling pet supplies, drugstore goods, and more; and agreed to pay fees of 4 to 8 percent to other Web site owners who linked a purchaser to Amazon.com. Purchasers pay Amazon.com by credit card, submitted over the telephone or the Web, and the transaction is guarded by encryption. Amazon.com offers one-click ordering, which lets buyers store credit cards and addresses after their first purchase.

After several years of operation and quick growth, Amazon.com needed more money to reach its goals. In May 1997, Amazon.com went public, raising over $40 million by selling stock for $18 per share. The price of Amazon.com doubled on the first day of trading and reached $200 per share over the next year before retreating. Bezos became a billionaire by the age of 34. Bezos and his family own about 40 percent of Amazon.com. In the span of less than five years, Bezos had taken his business plan and created the largest, most recognized e-commerce company in the world. This entrepreneur's dream became

Over 40 **Entrepreneur and the Law** boxes examine the legal implications of entrepreneurial successes and failures.

Chapter 4 Comparative and International Law, is devoted exclusively to coverage of international laws, courts, organizations, dispute resolution, and regional trade agreements.

Comparative and International Law

International law, or the law that governs between nations, has at times, been like the common law within states, a twilight existence during which it is hardly distinguishable from morality or justice, till at length the imprimatur of a court attests its jural quality.
JUSTICE CARDOZO
New Jersey v. Delaware, 291 U.S. 361, 54 S.Ct. 407, 78 L.Ed. 847 (1934)

Chapter Objectives

After studying this chapter, you should be able to

1. Explain the U.S. government's role in foreign affairs.
2. List and describe the sources of international law.
3. Explain the principle of comity.
4. List and describe the major international organizations.
5. List and describe the major international courts.
6. Describe the forum-selection and choice of law clauses.
7. Describe the act of state doctrine.
8. Describe the doctrine of sovereign immunity.
9. Describe the arbitration of international disputes.
10. Describe criminal prosecutions in the international arena.

Chapter Contents

International Perspective

CHINA AND THE UNITED STATES REACH LANDMARK TRADE PACT

For the past 50 years, China and the United States have pursued divergent paths. China became the world's largest communist country and the United States the leading democracy. China maintained its agricultural base, while the United States pursued industrialization. China's businesses were state-owned, while those in the United States were privately owned under a capitalist system. So what do these countries have in common? A new landmark trade pact. For over a decade, these two countries engaged in on-again, off-again trade negotiations. Then in November 1999 the two countries reached a compromise.

Prior to the agreement, the United States annually granted China "most favored nation" status which permitted China to import most goods and services into the United States. The new trade pact eliminates the need for this annual ritual. In exchange for being granted the right to import most goods and services into the United States, China, which had substantially restricted imports into its country, agreed to open its markets to foreign goods and services in the following ways:

- **Telecommunications** Foreign telephone companies may own up to 50 percent of Chinese telephone companies.
- **Entertainment** China will double the number of U.S.

- **Services** Foreigners may establish their own repair and maintenance service businesses in China.
- **Vehicle sales** China will permit foreign automobile manufacturers to sell and finance sales to Chinese customers.
- **Farm products** China will eliminate subsidies to Chinese exports.
- **Internet** Foreign investors may own up to 50 percent of Chinese Internet businesses.

The China-U.S. trade agreement was a prelude to China's application to join the World Trade Organization (WTO). China's entry into the WTO makes China a full partner in the world's trading system. The integration of China into the global economy sets the stage for the eventual entry of the other 16 non-market economies into the WTO, from Russia to Vietnam.

The China-U.S. trade agreement is not without its critics. In the United States, labor unions criticize the agreement for its potential to ship U.S. manufacturing jobs to China, while environmentalists complain that little is being done to protect the environment from an industrialized economy the size of China. In China, workers at state-owned enterprises might lose their jobs to foreign capitalist companies that can produce goods and services more efficiently, and China's already impoverished farmers may be

More than 40 **International Perspective** boxes provide students the opportunity to draw comparisons between the American system of justice and various other systems abroad.

Ethics and the Law

Chapter 8 Ethics and Social Responsibility, is just the beginning of the ethics coverage in the fourth edition.

8

Ethics and Social Responsibility of Business

Ethical considerations can no more be excluded from the administration of justice, which is the end and purpose of all civil laws, than one can exclude the vital air from his room and live.

JOHN F. DILLON *Laws and Jurisprudence of England and America* Lecture 1 (1894)

Chapter Objectives

After studying this chapter, you should be able to:

1. Describe ethical fundamentalism.
2. Describe utilitarianism as a moral theory.
3. Describe Kantian ethics.
4. Describe Rawls's social justice theory.
5. Describe ethical relativism.
6. Describe maximizing profits as a theory of social responsibility.
7. Describe the moral minimum theory of social responsibility.
8. Describe the stakeholder interest theory of social responsibility.
9. Describe the corporate citizenship theory of social responsibility.
10. Describe corporate social audits.

More than 40 **Ethical Perspectives** boxes use ethical issues from real companies to highlight the importance of ethics in making business decisions.

Consider This Example Suppose a professional football team enters into a five-year employment contract with a "superstar" quarterback. The quarterback breaches the contract and enters into a contract to play for a competing team. Here, the first team can seek an injunction to prevent the quarterback from playing for the other team.

Ethical Perspective

STATE FARM: NOT SUCH A GOOD NEIGHBOR

Most car drivers purchase automobile insurance to cover themselves from liability for accidents. Many drivers also purchase collision insurance, which means that the insurance covers the cost of repairing an insured's damaged automobile. Collision insurance policies routinely provide that replacement parts be of "like kind and quality" to the original damaged parts. But what if the replacement parts are "after-market" parts, that is, parts manufactured by companies other than the original automobile manufacturer. Do these generic parts qualify "like kind and quality?" Many insureds (and their lawyers, of course) did not think so and sued their insurance company, State Farm Mutual Automobile Insurance Company, the largest insurance company in the United States, for breach of contract for including replacement parts in their vehicles without telling them.

The plaintiffs' class-action lawsuit on behalf of all similarly situated insureds of State Farm included all those who had their automobiles repaired by State Farm over the past 10 years. The plaintiffs presented evidence that State Farm required body shops to use replacement parts made by

aftermarket manufacturers and not by the automobile's original manufacturer. State Farm said it did this to save costs. For example, a replacement hood for a 1995 Pontiac Grand Am cost $307 from General Motors but only $154 from an after-market manufacturer.

The plaintiffs argued that the replacement parts were inferior to original parts, were less safe and had not been

chest, breaking three of his ribs and his collarbone and severely bruising his lungs. Bryan's parents sued the Club for negligence to recover damages for injuries suffered by Bryan and the loss of consortium for themselves. The Club moved for summary judgment, asserting that the exculpatory agreement signed by Bryan's mother barred the claims. The trial court agreed and granted the Club's summary judgment motion. The court of appeals affirmed. The plaintiffs appealed to the Supreme Court of Ohio.

ISSUE
Did the exculpatory agreement signed by Mrs. Zivich on behalf of her son release the Club from liability for the child's claims and the parents' claims?

IN THE LANGUAGE OF THE COURT
Sweeney, Justice With respect to adult participants, the general rule is that releases from liability for injuries caused by negligent acts arising in the context of recreational activities are enforceable. Here, however, the exculpatory agreement was executed by a parent on behalf of the minor child.

It cannot be disputed that volunteers in community recreational activities serve an important function. Organized recreation

Therefore, we conclude that although Bryan, like many children before him, gave up his right to sue for the negligent acts of others, the public as a whole received the benefit of these exculpatory agreements. Because of this agreement, the Club was able to offer affordable recreation and to continue to do so without the risks and overwhelming costs of litigation Bryan's parents agreed to shoulder the risk. Public policy does not forbid such an agreement. In fact, public policy supports it.

DECISION AND REMEDY
A parent's signature on an exculpatory agreement on behalf of his or her child releases the other party from liability to the child, the parent who signed the agreement, and the other parent. Affirmed.

Case Questions

Critical Legal Thinking Do exculpatory agreements serve any valid purpose? Should exculpatory agreements be enforceable?

Ethics Was it ethical for Mrs. Zivich to sign the exculpatory agreement and then bring this lawsuit?

Business Application What would have been the consequences if the court had found the exculpatory agreement to be invalid in this case?

Every case in the text ends with an ethics question for discussion

sales representative for Hardware/Software that the PerFinPlan III software does not meet his described business needs. Harold returns the copy of the software to

program to Metatag stating that he is canceling the license. Metatag sues Bates to recover the unpaid license fees. Who wins?

ETHICS CASES

18.13. BluePeace.org is a new environmental list group that has decided that expounding its environmental causes on the Internet is the best and most efficient way to spend its time and money to advance its environmental causes. To draw attention to its Web sites, BluePeace.org comes up with "catchy" Internet domain names. One is "macyswearus.org," another is "exxonvaldezesseals.org," and another is "generalmotorscrashesdummies.org." The "macyswearus.org" Web site first shows beautiful women dressed in mink fur coats sold by Macy's Department Stores and then goes into graphic photos of minks being slaughtered and skinned and made into the coats. The "exxonvaldezesseals.org" Web site first shows a beautiful pristine bay in Alaska with the Exxon Valdez oil tanker quietly sailing through the waters and then shows photos of the ship breaking open and spewing forth oil and then seals who are good with oil suffocating and dying on the shoreline. The Web site "generalmotorscrashesdummies.org" shows a General Motors automobile involved in normal crash tests with dummies followed by photographs of automobile accident scenes where people and children lay bleeding and dying after an accident involving General Motors automobiles. Macy's Department Stores, the Exxon Oil Company,

Act. Who wins? Has BluePeace.org acted unethically in this case?

18.14. Apricot.com is a major software developer that licenses software to be sold over the Internet. One of its programs called "Match" is a search engine that searches personal ads on the Internet and provides a "match" service for potential dates and possible marriage partners. Norlan Bates subscribes to the Match software program from Apricot.com. The license fee is five years at $200 per month license fee. For each subscriber, Apricot.com produces a separate Web page that shows photos of the subscriber and personal data. Bates places a photo of himself with his mother with the caption, "Male, 30 years old, lives with mother, likes quiet nights at home." Bates licenses the Apricot.com "Match" software and uses it 12 hours each day searching for his Internet match. Bates does not pay Apricot.com the required monthly licensing fees for any of the three months he uses the software. After using the Match software but refusing to pay Apricot.com its licensing fee, Apricot.com activates the disabling bug in the software and disables the Match software on Bates's computer. Apricot.com did this with no warning to Bates. It then sends a letter to Bates

Each chapter ends with additional ethics cases.

(1712–1778) proposed a **social contract** rson is presumed to have entered into oral rules that are necessary for people states, "I will keep the rules if everyolve conflicting interests in society. ce theory is John Rawls, a contemporary's *distributive justice theory*, fairness is

Rawls's social contract
A moral theory that says each person is presumed to have entered into a social contract with all others in society to obey moral rules that are necessary for people to live in peace and harmony.

Contemporary Business Applications

Contemporary Business Application

SOMETIMES VIAGRA STIRS THE HEART TOO QUICKLY

The anti-impotency drug Viagra, introduced in 1997, was heralded as the most important drug to hit the market since the birth control pill. Viagra is prescribed by doctors to male patients who cannot have or have trouble getting erections and helps such men have intercourse. It became wildly successful and is now used by millions of men worldwide. In the United States, the Food and Drug Administration (FDA) approved the drug for use by the general public. A black market for Viagra has developed in countries where the drug has not been given government approval. Pfizer, the manufacturer of the drug, is receiving a financial bounty from its now-famous drug.

It seems that Viagra not only gets men's hearts stirring again, but it may also cause their hearts to explode, literally. After hundreds of deaths of men taking the drug were reported, the FDA investigated and found that men with certain health predispositions may be at risk of death if they take Viagra. Therefore, the FDA now requires Viagra labels to warn individuals with

the following conditions to be careful when taking the drug:

- Men who have had a heart attack or an irregular heartbeat in the past six months
- Men who have a history of cardiac failure or coronary artery disease that caused angina
- Men who have significant high or low blood pressure

Viagra causes visual disturbance—particularly the ability to distinguish between blue and green—in about 3 percent of the men who use it. And Viagra sometimes works too well, causing priapism, or painful erections that last up to four hours. Doctors and consumers must also be warned against these conditions.

Pfizer asserts that its explosively popular drug was not the culprit in the reported deaths, but that the drug was taken by men with health problems who should have not used the drug. By requiring the new warnings, the FDA wants men with the noted risk factors to first ask, "Is sex a good idea for me?" before taking Viagra.

The 40-plus **Contemporary Business Applications** boxes recognize that not all of the modern challenges facing businesses are Internet-related. These boxes explore other types of legal issues currently confronting businesses.

Cases

Each chapter includes 3 to 5 interesting and lively cases presented in an edited format, retaining the language of the court. The format of each case is: Fact, Issue, Language of the Court, Decision. Three questions follow each case to promote active learning.

---

if he or she personally guarantees repayment of the debts of the LLC.

to such a new LLC unless the members personally guaranty the loan. To obtain the loan, Patricia, Arnold, and Emory sign personal guarantees with the bank agreeing to repay the loan if the LLC does not. In this case, if the LLC fails to repay the loan, the bank may enforce the personal guarantees and recover the amount of the loan from the members.

In the following case, the court enforced a personal guaranty against a manager of a limited liability company.

Creative Resource Management, Inc. v. Soskin
1998 WL 813420 (1998)
Court of Appeals of Tennessee

CASE 35.2

FACTS
Nashville Pro Hockey, LLC, was a limited liability company organized under the laws of Tennessee. The LLC owned and operated the Nashville Nighthawks, a minor league professional hockey team. On September 4, 1996, Nashville Pro Hockey, LLC, contracted with Creative Resource Management, Inc. (CRM), whereby CRM, for fees and other consideration, would provide employee leasing services to Nashville Pro Hockey, LLC. The contract was signed by Barry Soskin, the president of Nashville Pro Hockey, LLC. A paragraph in the contract provided

By affixing my hand and seal to this agreement, I personally guarantee any and all payments payable as represented and outlined in this agreement.

Nashville Pro Hockey, LLC, failed, owing CRM $29,626. CRM sued Nashville Pro Hockey, LLC, and Barry Soskin to recover the unpaid compensation. Soskin defended, alleging that his signature on the contract was in

his representative capacity only and not in his individual capacity as a guarantor. The trial court agreed and granted summary judgment to Soskin. CRM appealed.

ISSUE
Did Soskin's signature on the contract constitute a personal guarantee for the payment of the debt of Nashville Pro Hockey, LLC, to CRM?

IN THE LANGUAGE OF THE COURT
Cain, Judge The well settled precedent in Tennessee suggests that a corporate officer's signature preceded by a corporation's name and followed by a designation of the signer's corporate capacity is evidence that the signer was acting as an agent of the corporation rather than individually.

This rule, however, must yield where the language of the contract compels a different conclusion. The language of the contract involved in the case at bar distinguishes this case from the general rule. This case concerns a contract which contains personal guarantee language in the body of the contract.

---

the purported sender in a false light in the eyes of the receiver. Falsely attributing beliefs or acts to another can also form the basis of a lawsuit.

Misappropriation of the Right to Publicity
Each person has the exclusive legal right to control and profit from the commercial use of his or her name and personality during his or her lifetime. This is a valuable right, particularly to well-known persons such as sports figures and movie stars. Any attempt by another person to appropriate a living person's name or identity for commercial purposes is actionable. The wrongdoer is liable for the **tort of misappropriation of the right to publicity** (also called the **tort of appropriation**). In such cases, the plaintiff can (1) recover the unauthorized profits made by the offending party and (2) obtain an injunction against further unauthorized use of his or her name or identity. Many states provide that the right to publicity survives a person's death and may be enforced by the deceased's heirs.

In the following case, the court found that there had been a misappropriation of the right to publicity.

tort of misappropriation of the right to publicity
An attempt by another person to appropriate a living person's name or identity for commercial purposes.

Hoffman v. Los Angeles Magazine, Inc.
33 F.Supp.2d 867 (1999)
United States District Court, C.D. California

CASE 5.2

FACTS
Dustin Hoffman is one of the most successful and recognizable motion picture actors. He has appeared in such movie classics as *The Graduate* and *Rainman* and has won two Academy Awards, a Golden Globe Award, and an Emmy Award for his work. In 1982, Hoffman appeared as the main character in the movie *Tootsie*, where he played a male actor who dressed as a woman to get acting jobs as an actress. In the movie, Hoffman appeared in a woman's bright red dress posing in front of the American flag, which was used as a still shot in advertising for the movie. The movie was a great commercial success.

In 1997, the Los Angeles Magazine, a glitzy regional magazine, decided to rev up sales by including more celebrity photos in the magazine. The March 1997 issue included a feature called "Grand Illusions" where celebrity figures were dressed in clothes, shoes, and accessories of fashion designers who advertised in the magazine. One photo was the full-figured shot of Dustin Hoffman from *Tootsie* that had been digitally altered to remove the red dress and heels and replace them with a silk gown designed by Richard Tyler and high-heel shoes designed by Ralph Lauren. *Los Angeles Magazine* did not ask Mr. Hoffman for permission to use his name and likeness. After the magazine was published, Mr. Hoffman sued Los Angeles Magazine, Inc., in federal court to protect his name from commercial exploitation and recover damages.

ISSUE
Did Los Angeles Magazine, Inc. misappropriate Dustin Hoffman's right to publicity?

IN THE LANGUAGE OF THE COURT
Tevrizian, District Judge The right to use Plaintiff Dustin Hoffman's name and likeness is an extremely valuable commodity and privilege not only because of Mr. Hoffman's stature as an actor, but because he does not knowingly permit commercial uses of his identity. Since appearing in the film The Graduate, Mr. Hoffman has scrupulously guided and guarded the manner in which he has been shown to the public. Mr. Hoffman maintains a strict policy of not endorsing commercial products for fear that he will be perceived in a negative light by his peers and motion picture industry executives, suggesting that his career is in decline and that he no longer has the business opportunities or the box office draw as before.

Defendant, Los Angeles Magazine, Inc., did not seek or obtain permission from Mr. Hoffman to use his name or likeness in the March 1997 issue of Los Angeles Magazine and, in particular, did not obtain Mr. Hoffman's consent to commercially endorse or "skill" for any fashion designer or advertiser in the magazine. The reason permission was not sought is because Los Angeles Magazine knew, or should have known, that the celebrities either would not consent or, alternatively, would demand payment for the fair market value for their right to utilize their names and likenesses in this manner for commercial

(case continues)

M.A. Mortenson Company, Inc. v. Timberline Software Corporation
970 P.2d 803 (1999)
Court of Appeals of Washington

CASE 18.1

e-biz

FACTS
The Timberline Software Corporation (Timberline) produces software programs that are used by contractors to prepare bids to do work on construction projects. The M.A. Mortenson Company (Mortenson), a contractor, had been using Timberline software for some time without any problem. In 1993, Timberline introduced an advanced version of its bidding software program called "Precision." Mortenson, as the licensee, entered into a license agreement with Timberline, the licensor, to license the use of the Precision software. Timberline delivered the software to Mortenson and a Timberline representative installed the software on Mortenson's computer. The software license agreement contained the following terms, which were printed on the outside of the envelope in which the software disks were packaged and on the inside cover of the user's manual, and they also appear on the introductory computer screen each time the software program is executed:

CAREFULLY READ THE FOLLOWING TERMS AND CONDITIONS BEFORE USING THE PROGRAMS. USE OF THE PROGRAMS INDICATES YOUR ACKNOWLEDGEMENT THAT YOU HAVE READ THIS LICENSE, UNDERSTAND IT, AND AGREE TO BE BOUND BY ITS TERMS AND CONDITIONS. IF YOU DO NOT AGREE TO THESE TERMS AND CONDITIONS, PROMPTLY RETURN THE PROGRAMS AND USER MANUALS TO THE

BERLINE'S LIABILITY FOR DAMAGES IN NO EVENT SHALL EXCEED THE LICENSE FEE PAID FOR THE RIGHT TO USE THE SOFTWARE.

On December 2, 1993, Mortenson used the Precision software and prepared a bid to do contracting work for the Harborview Hospital project. While preparing the bid, the program aborted at least five times before Mortenson's employees finished the bid. Subsequently, Mortenson claimed that its bid was $2 million under what it should have been had the Precision software program worked correctly. Mortenson sued Timberline to recover consequential damages, arguing that the Precision software calculated an inaccurate bid. Timberline defended, alleging that the limitation of remedies clause in the software license prevented Mortenson's lawsuit. Mortenson countered that the limitations of remedies clause was unconscionable and therefore unenforceable. The trial court granted summary judgment to Timberline and dismissed the lawsuit. Mortenson appealed.

ISSUE
Was the limitation of remedies clause in the Timberline software license unconscionable?

IN THE LANGUAGE OF THE COURT
Webster, Judge Mortenson makes much of the fact that Timberline never mentioned the license agreement or any of its terms during the negotiations. But the negotiations between the

Exhibits help clarify legal formats and documents that may be foreign to students.

Margin notes include a running **glossary of terms, Business Briefs,** and **relevant historical quotes**

Concept Summaries appear periodically within each chapter to give students a chance to pause and be sure they have mastered the preceding material.

At the end of each chapter, **Working the Web** exercises require students to work through interactive web-based activities; **Critical Legal Thinking Cases** encourage the application of students' analytical skills; and **Critical Legal Thinking Writing Assignments** give students experience in briefing cases.

An Integrated Supplements Package

To ensure consistency of style, approach, and coverage among the key print supplements, these critical pieces were created by a single author team working in conjunction with Henry Cheeseman.

The *Instructor's Manual* provides bulleted chapter outlines, answers to text questions and cases, as well as lecture suggestions linked directly to PowerPoint slides.

PowerPoint slides provide complete lecture support.

The *Study Guide* includes the same bulleted outline found in the *Instructor's Manual* along with a variety of objective questions and critical thinking legal essays to effectively reinforce the concepts introduced in the corresponding text chapter.

The *Test Item File* contains over 30 percent new questions to this edition and closely mirrors the content stressed in the *Instructor's Manual* and *Study Guide*.

Other Valuable Supplements and Technology Options:

The *Surfing for Success in Legal Studies* Internet guide covers frequently asked questions and offers concrete discipline-specific advice on navigating the Internet. It is available free to your students and is updated annually.

The **Business Law Custom Video Series** provides ten 5-10 minute segments designed to foster discussion on key business law topics. Each segment revolves around the activities of a single company and its employees, suppliers, customers, and other associates.

The *TotaLaw* **CD-ROM** is available free with the purchase of each student text and includes the complete text of 30 acts that are important and relevant to business. A built-in feature allows users to search by keyword. This extensive resource is easy to load, convenient to use, and includes the U.S. Constitution, the United Nations Charter, the Uniform Commercial Code, and much more.

Prentice Hall's Learning on the Internet Partnership (PHLIP) Companion Web Site (**www.prenhall.com/cheeseman**) lets students log on to have a dialogue with their peers, talk to a tutor, take a quiz with immediate feedback, and read articles about current events—all with the click of a mouse.

Adopters of *Business Law, Fourth Edition* are eligible to receive 10 free hours of **LEXIS,** the legal, on-line database service used by law professionals. This offer is valid each semester the text is in use and applies to adoptions where new books are purchased. Contact your Prentice Hall sales representative for more information.

Prentice Hall offers **WebCT,** an on-line course to provide you with a learning option in legal studies. The content has been preloaded into the popular WebCT course management software. Contact your Prentice Hall sales representative for more information.

Acknowledgments

When I first began writing this book, I was a solitary figure researching cases in the law library and writing text at my desk. As time passed, others entered upon the scene—editors, research assistants, reviewers, production personnel—and touched the project and made it better. Although my name appears on the cover of this book, it is no longer mine alone. I humbly thank the following persons for their contributions to this project.

THE PROFESSIONALS AT PRENTICE HALL

For this fourth edition of *Business Law* a special group of people from Prentice Hall have come together: Linda Schreiber, acquisitions editor, who brought wonderful new ideas to revision who was the guiding light during the entire production, and whose imprint is everywhere in the new edition; Cindy Spreder, production editor, whose design suggestions I accepted wholeheartedly, and who was a joy to work with through the patient task of shepherding the manuscript from first manuscript pages to the final bound book; Deb Clare, senior marketing manager, who is the most creative marketing person in the industry and who has more energy than anyone I know; Jim Boyd, vice president/editorial director, who authorized all the resources necessary to make this fourth edition possible; Sandy Steiner, president of Prentice Hall Business Publishing, who was the marketing manager on the first edition of *Business Law* and whose influence is still part of this revision.

THE SUPPLEMENTS TEAM

Jennifer Surich, supplements editor, is in charge of producing the extensive supplements that support this fourth edition of *Business Law*. The supplements themselves have been produced by a remarkable team of authors: Rhonda Carlson, lecturer, University of Denver School of Law; Ed Gac, professor of business law, School of Business, University of Colorado; and Jay Ballentine, professor of business law, School of Business, University of Colorado. I have worked closely with this team in producing the *Instructors Manual*, *Student Guide*, *Test Bank*, and PowerPoint slides to support this edition. Michele Faranda, media project manager, has been in charge of putting together the Prentice Hall Web Site to support this edition, as well as the *Totalaw* CD-ROM that accompanies the book.

The Prentice Hall "family" has come together and produced a book and supplements package that I believe is the best available. My success is theirs, and theirs' mine. They are my friends.

The reviewers. I would like to particularly thank the following reviewers, who have spent considerable time and effort reviewing the manuscript, and whose comments, suggestions, and criticisms are seen in the final project.

David Austill	Union University
Ed Gac	University of Colorado
Gregory McCann	Stetson University
Scott Sandstrom	College of the Holy Cross
Allen Simonson	Montclair State University

The following research assistants: Shou-Yi Kang at the Marshall School of Business at the University of Southern California; Jon Reiter and Chris Hopkins at the University of Southern California Law Center.

My family: My parents—Henry B. and Florence, deceased; my twin brother Gregory; my sister Marcia; my aunt Georgina Gustafson; and my cousins George, Albert, Howard, and Ronald Gustafson.

The students at the Marshall School of Business at the University of Southern California. Their spirit, energy, and joy is contagious, and I love teaching them (and as important, they teaching me).

While writing this Preface, I have thought about the thousands of hours I have spent researching, writing, and preparing this manuscript. I loved every minute, and the knowledge gained has been sufficient reward for the endeavor.

I hope this book and its supplementary materials will serve you as well as they have served me.

With joy and sadness,
emptiness and Fullness,
honor and humility,
I surrender the fruits of this labor

Henry R. Cheeseman

Nature of Law and Critical Legal Thinking

*W*here there is no law, there is no freedom.

*JOHN LOCKE Second Treatise
of Government, Sec. 57*

Chapter Objectives

After studying this chapter, you should be able to

1. Define *law*.
2. List and describe the functions of law.
3. Describe the flexibility of the law.
4. List and describe the schools of jurisprudential thought.
5. Explain the development of the U.S. legal system.
6. Explain how English common law was adopted in the United States.
7. List and describe the sources of law in the United States.
8. Define the doctrine of *stare decisis*.
9. Apply critical legal thinking in analyzing judicial decisions.
10. Describe the civil law legal system.

Chapter Contents

- **What Is Law?**
  Contemporary Business Application *Feminist Legal Theory*
  E-Commerce and Internet Law *Students Plug Into the Internet
  and the Law*
- **Schools of Jurisprudential Thought**
  Contemporary Business Application *The Law and Economics
  School of Jurisprudential Thought*
- **History of American Law**
  International Perspective *Adoption of English Common Law
  in America*
  International Perspective *The Civil Law System*

- **Sources of Law in the United States**
  Contemporary Business Application *Regulations and Orders
  of Administrative Agencies*
- **Critical Legal Thinking**
- **Case for Briefing**
- **Working the Web**
- **Critical Legal Thinking Cases**
- **Ethics Cases**
- **Critical Legal Thinking Writing Assignment**

Every society makes and enforces laws that govern the conduct of the individuals, businesses, and other organizations that function within it. In the words of Judge Learned Hand, "Without law we cannot live; only with it can we insure the future which by right is ours. The best of men's hopes are enmeshed in its success."[1]

Although the law of this country is primarily based on English common law, other legal systems, such as Spanish and French civil law, also influenced it. The sources of law in this country are the U.S. Constitution, state constitutions, federal and state statutes, ordinances, administrative agency rules and regulations, executive orders, and judicial decisions by federal and state courts.

Businesses that are organized in the United States are subject to its laws. They are also subject to the laws of other countries in which they operate. Businesses organized in other countries must obey the laws of the United States when doing business here. In addition, businesspeople owe a duty to act ethically in the conduct of their affairs, and businesses owe a responsibility not to harm society.

This chapter discusses the nature and definition of law, the history and sources of law, and "critical legal thinking" as applied by the U.S. Supreme Court in deciding an actual case.

*W*hat is Law?

The law consists of rules that regulate the conduct of individuals, businesses, and other organizations within society. It is intended to protect persons and their property from unwanted interference from others. In other words, the law forbids persons from engaging in certain undesirable activities.

Consider the following passage.

> *Hardly anyone living in a civilized society has not at some time been told to do something or to refrain from doing something, because there is a law requiring it, or because it is against the law. What do we mean when we say such things? Most generally, how are we to understand statements of the form "x is law"? This is an ancient question. In his* Memorabilia *(I,ii), Xenophon reports a statement of the young Alcibiades, companion of Socrates, who in conversation with the great Pericles remarked that "no one can really deserve praise unless he knows what a law is."*
>
> *At the end of the 18th century, Immanuel Kant wrote of the question "What is law?" that it "may be said to be about as embarrassing to the jurist as the well-known question 'What is truth?' is to the logician."[2]*

Definition of Law

law

That which must be obeyed and followed by citizens subject to sanctions or legal consequences; a body of rules of action or conduct prescribed by controlling authority, and having binding legal force.

The concept of **law** is very broad. Although it is difficult to state a precise definition, *Black's Law Dictionary* gives one that is sufficient for this text:

> *Law, in its generic sense, is a body of rules of action or conduct prescribed by controlling authority, and having binding legal force. That which must be obeyed and followed by citizens subject to sanctions or legal consequences is a law.[3]*

Functions of the Law

The law is often described by the functions it serves within a society. The primary *functions* served by the law in this country are:

1. Keeping the peace, which includes making certain activities crimes
2. Shaping moral standards (e.g., enacting laws that discourage drug and alcohol abuse)
3. Promoting social justice (e.g., enacting statutes that prohibit discrimination in employment)
4. Maintaining the status quo (e.g., passing laws preventing the forceful overthrow of the government)

5. Facilitating orderly change (e.g., passing statutes only after considerable study, debate, and public input)
6. Facilitating planning (e.g., well-designed commercial laws allow businesses to plan their activities, allocate their productive resources, and assess the risks they take)
7. Providing a basis for compromise (approximately 90 percent of all lawsuits are settled prior to trial)
8. Maximizing individual freedom (e.g., the rights of freedom of speech, religion, and association granted by the First Amendment to the U.S. Constitution)

The Law, in its majestic equality, forbids the rich as well as the poor to sleep under bridges.

Anatole France

Fairness of the Law

On the whole, the American legal system is one of the most comprehensive, fair, and democratic systems of law ever developed and enforced. Nevertheless, some misuses and oversights of our legal system—including abuses of discretion and mistakes by judges and juries, unequal applications of the law, and procedural mishaps—allow some guilty parties to go unpunished.

In *Standefer v. United States*[4] the Supreme Court *affirmed* (let stand) the criminal conviction of a Gulf Oil Corporation executive for aiding and abetting the bribery of an Internal Revenue Service agent. The agent had been acquitted in a separate trial. In writing the opinion of the Court, Chief Justice Burger stated, "This case does no more than manifest the simple, if discomforting, reality that different juries may reach different results under any criminal statute. That is one of the consequences we accept under our jury system."

Business Brief
Sometimes the law, because of error or misuse, does not reach a fair result.

Contemporary Business Application _____ SKip

FEMINIST LEGAL THEORY

In the past, the law treated men and women unequally. For example, women were denied the right to vote, could not own property if they were married, were unable to have legal abortions, and could not hold the same jobs as men. The enactment of statutes, the interpretation of constitutional provisions, and the courts have changed all of these things. The Nineteenth Amendment gave women the right to vote. States have repealed constraints on the ability of women to own property. The famous U.S. Supreme Court decision in *Roe v. Wade*, 410 U.S. 959 (1973), gave women the constitutional right to an abortion.

Title VII of the Civil Rights Act of 1964 prohibits employment discrimination based on sex. In addition, the equal protection clause of the U.S. and state constitutions provides that women cannot be treated differently than men (and vice versa) by the government unless some imperative reason warrants different treatment.

But is it enough for women to be treated like men? Should the female perspective be taken into account when legislators and judges develop, interpret, and apply the law? A growing body of scholarship known as **feminist legal theory**, or **feminist jurisprudence**, is being created around just such a theory.

The so-called "battered woman's syndrome" illustrates how this type of theory works. It has been introduced into evidence to prove self-defense in homicide cases where a woman is accused of killing her husband or another male. This defense asserts that sustained domestic violence against a woman may justify such a murder. Although rejected by many courts, some courts have recognized battered woman's syndrome as a justifiable defense.

Some other areas of the law where a woman's perspective might differ from a man's include male-only combat rules in the military, rights to privacy, family law, child custody, surrogate motherhood, job security for pregnant women, rape, sexual assault, abortion, and sexual harassment.

Even the traditional "reasonable man standard," so prevalent in American law, is being attacked as being gender-biased. The supporters of this theory argue that merely renaming it the "reasonable person theory" is not enough. They assert that women will be judged by the reasonable actions expected of men until this standard is redefined to take into account females' unique values.

(box continues)

This view seems to be gaining ground. For instance, in a recent sexual harassment case, the court recognized that a "reasonable woman standard" should be used to determine whether a male's conduct toward a female coemployee violated Title VII. The court stated, "We prefer to analyze harassment from the victim's perspective. A complete understanding of the victim's view requires, among other things, an analysis of the different perspectives of men and women. Conduct that many men consider unobjectionable may offend many women" [*Ellison v. Brady*, 924 F.2d 872 (9th Cir. 1991)].

One of the major disappointments to the feminist legal movement was the defeat of the Equal Rights Amendment in 1981. This proposed constitutional amendment, which would have forbidden the denial of rights based on sex, was not ratified by the number of states needed for approval.

Critics of feminist legal theory argue that existing laws adequately protect the equal rights of females in society. Feminist legal theorists counter that justice for women will remain elusive until the female perspective is recognized by the law.

Flexibility of the Law

One of the main attributes of American law is its *flexibility*. It is generally responsive to cultural, technological, economic, and social changes. For example, laws that are no longer viable—such as those that restricted the property rights of women—are often repealed.

Landmark Decision

In *Brown v. Board of Education,* the U.S. Supreme Court overturned precedent and held that providing separate schools for black children and white children was unconstitutional.

Sometimes it takes years before the law reflects the norms of society. Other times, society is led by the law. The Supreme Court's landmark decision in *Brown v. Board of Education*[5] is an example of the law leading the people. The Court's decision overturned the old "separate but equal" doctrine that condoned separate schools for black children and white children.

U.S. law evolves and changes along with the norms of society, technology, and the growth and expansion of commerce in the United States and the world. The following quote of Judge Jerome Frank discusses the value of the adaptability of law.

> The law always has been, is now, and will ever continue to be, largely vague and variable. And how could this be otherwise? The law deals with human relations in their most complicated aspects. The whole confused, shifting helter-skelter of life parades before it—more confused than ever, in our kaleidoscopic age.

Business Brief

Laws cannot be written in advance to anticipate every dispute that could arise in the future. Therefore, *general principles* are developed to be applied by courts and juries to individual disputes. This flexibility in the law leads to some uncertainty in predicting results of lawsuits.

> Men have never been able to construct a comprehensive, eternalized, set of rules anticipating all possible legal disputes and formulating in advance the rules which would apply to them. Situations are bound to occur which were never contemplated when the original rules were made. How much less is such a frozen legal system possible in modern times?

> The constant development of unprecedented problems requires a legal system capable of fluidity and pliancy. Our society would be straightjacketed were not the courts, with the able assistance of the lawyers, constantly overhauling the law and adapting it to the realities of ever-changing social, industrial, and political conditions; although changes cannot be made lightly, yet rules of law must be more or less impermanent, experimental and therefore not nicely calculable.

> Much of the uncertainty of law is not an unfortunate accident; it is of immense social value.[6]

E-Commerce & Internet Law

STUDENTS PLUG INTO THE INTERNET AND THE LAW

e-biz

Every year millions of students arrive on college campuses and unpack an array of items—clothes, books, furniture, decorations, and their computers. College students used to be judged by the size of their stereo speakers; today it is their computer and their

Internet savvy. Ninety percent of college students now own personal computers.

The Internet has revolutionized campus life. Computer kiosks abound around college campuses, occupying more space in libraries, dorm rooms, and hallways of athletic departments. Traditional libraries have become obsolete for many students as they conduct almost all of their research on-line. More than 60 percent of college students check out the Web daily, while others communicate through e-mail, pick up course assignments, download course notes, and socialize on-line. Current university and college students are wired to modern technology and will lead their parents, employers, and sometimes even their professors, into the new world of high technology. Today's college students are the leaders of the e-generation.

Universities and colleges are now rated on not only how well they are connected with alumni, but also on how well they are connected to computer technology. Some universities have installed software that allow their students to sit anywhere on campus with their laptops and "plug" into the school's computers. The computer is no longer just a study tool, it has become totally integrated into the lives of college students. The new generation of students study on-line, shop on-line, and even date on-line.

With this new technology comes one other thing that a student should know about: E-commerce and Internet law. The use of new computer technology has developed so rapidly that much of the law has not kept up. For example, purchase of goods and items over the Internet is exploding, but state and federal governments are struggling to develop laws to handle these transactions. How is the contract formed? What

about signatures? Is a purchaser's credit card information protected? What laws protect privacy over the Internet? Can an Internet user crack a wrapper and use certain software? What criminal laws apply to fraud over the Internet? The number of legal questions pertaining to this new technology is endless.

To help the student understand his or her legal rights and duties, this business law book is the first to fully integrate e-commerce and Internet law. The book does this in several ways. First, there are three chapters that specifically cover the law of e-commerce and computer law. Chapter 17 covers intellectual property rights, which include copyright, patent, and trademark law. Chapters 18 and 19 are two new e-commerce chapters, which cover the law of the Internet, use of domain names, contracting over the Internet, licensing agreements, criminal law, and consumer protection law applicable to e-commerce and the Internet. Second, most chapters contain a special feature titled "E-Commerce and Internet Law." These featured items discuss special legal issues that relate to the subject matter of the chapter. For example, the Securities Regulation and Investor Protection chapter includes a special feature item that discusses selling securities and taking a company public over the Internet. Through this total integration of e-commerce and Internet law, a student will not only learn traditional business law topics, but will also be well versed in his or her legal rights while using the Internet. Good luck in studying business and Internet law.

e·biz

Schools of Jurisprudential Thought

The philosophy or science of the law is referred to as **jurisprudence**. There are several different philosophies about how the law developed. They range from the classical natural theory to modern theories of law and economics and critical legal studies. Legal philosophers can generally be grouped into the major categories discussed in the paragraphs that follow.

Jurisprudence
The philosophy or science of law.

The Natural Law School

The **Natural Law School** of jurisprudence postulates that the law is based on what is "correct." Natural Law philosophers emphasize a **moral theory of law**—that is, law should be based on morality and ethics. Natural law is "discovered" by man through the use of reason and choosing between good and evil. Documents such as the U.S. Constitution, the Magna Carta, and the United Nations Charter reflect this theory.

The Historical School

The **Historical School** of jurisprudence believes that the law is an aggregate of social traditions and customs that have developed over the centuries. It believes that changes in the norms of society will gradually be reflected in the law. To these legal philosophers, the law is an evolutionary process. Thus, Historical legal scholars look to past legal decisions (precedent) to solve contemporary problems.

Human beings do not ever make laws: it is the accidents and catastrophes of all kinds happening in every conceivable way, that make law for us.
Plato Laws IV. 709

The Analytical School

The **Analytical School** of jurisprudence maintains that the law is shaped by logic. Analytical philosophers believe results are reached by applying principles of logic to the specific facts of the case. The emphasis is on the logic of the result rather than on how the result is reached.

Skip

The Sociological School

> Law must be stable and yet it cannot stand still.
>
> Roscoe Pound
> Interpretations of Legal History (1923)

The **Sociological School** of jurisprudence asserts that the law is a means of achieving and advancing certain sociological goals. The followers of this philosophy, who are known as *realists*, believe that the purpose of law is to shape social behavior. Sociological philosophers are unlikely to adhere to past law as precedent.

The Command School

The philosophers of the **Command School** of jurisprudence believe that the law is a set of rules developed, communicated, and enforced by the ruling party rather than a reflection of the society's morality, history, logic, or sociology. This school maintains that the law changes when the ruling class changes.

The Critical Legal Studies School

The **Critical Legal Studies School** proposes that legal rules are unnecessary and are used as an obstacle by the powerful to maintain the status quo. Critical Legal theorists (the "*Crits*") argue that legal disputes should be solved by applying arbitrary rules that are based on broad notions of what is "fair" in each circumstance. Under this theory, subjective decision making by judges would be permitted.

Contemporary Business Application

THE LAW AND ECONOMICS SCHOOL OF JURISPRUDENTIAL THOUGHT

Should free market principles, like the supply and demand and cost-benefit theories, determine the outcome of lawsuits and legislation? U.S. Court of Appeals Judge Richard Posner thinks so, and so do a growing number of other judges and legal theorists. These people are members of the **Law and Economics School** (or the "Chicago School") of jurisprudence, which had its roots at the University of Chicago.

According to the Law and Economics School, which is unofficially headed by Judge Posner, promoting market efficiency should be the central goal of legal decision making. In the area of antitrust law, for example, Law and Economics theorists would not find corporate mergers and takeovers to be illegal simply because they resulted in market domination. Instead, they would find this practice to be illegal only if it rendered the overall market less efficient.

Focusing on cold economic categories like market efficiency may seem appropriate when making decisions in cases that involve businesses. However, proponents of Law and Economics theory use this type of analysis in cases involving everything from freedom of religion to civil rights. For example, in a 1983 dissenting opinion, Judge Posner suggested that the practice of appointing counsel, free of charge, to prisoners who bring civil rights cases should be abolished. If a prisoner cannot find a lawyer who will take the case on a contingency fee basis, it probably means that the case is not worth bringing.

Despite the naysayers who warn that the morality of certain rights and liberties must be safeguarded even if it is unpopular or costly from an economic point of view, proponents of Law and Economics are gaining increased acceptance in law schools and increased appointments to the judiciary.

CONCEPT SUMMARY SCHOOLS OF JURISPRUDENTIAL THOUGHT

School	Philosophy
Natural Law	Postulates that law is based on what is "correct." It emphasizes a moral theory of law—that is, law should be based on morality and ethics.
Historical	Believes that law is an aggregate of social traditions and customs.

School	Philosophy
Analytical	Maintains that law is shaped by logic.
Sociological	Asserts that the law is a means of achieving and advancing certain sociological goals.
Command	Believes that the law is a set of rules developed, communicated, and enforced by the ruling party.
Critical Legal Studies	Maintains that legal rules are unnecessary and that legal disputes should be solved by applying arbitrary rules based on fairness.
Law and Economics	Believes that promoting market efficiency should be the central concern of legal decision making.

History of American Law

When the American colonies were first settled, the English system of law was generally adopted as the system of jurisprudence. This was the foundation from which American judges developed a common law in America.

English Common Law

English **common law** was law developed by judges who issued their opinions when deciding a case. The principles announced in these cases became *precedent* for later judges deciding similar cases. The English common law can be divided into cases decided by the law courts, equity courts, and merchant courts.

common law
Developed by judges who issued their opinions when deciding a case. The principles announced in these cases became precedent for later judges deciding similar cases.

Law Courts   Prior to the Norman Conquest of England in 1066, each locality in England was subject to local laws as established by the lord or chieftain in control of the local area. There was no countrywide system of law. After 1066, William the Conqueror and his successors to the throne of England began to replace the various local laws with one uniform system of law. To accomplish this, the king or queen appointed loyal followers as judges in all local areas. These judges were charged with administering the law in a

Red bus, London. *The legal system of most states in the United States is primarily based on the English common law. Some state legal systems, because of their French and Spanish heritage, reflect the European civil law as well.*

law court
A court that developed and administered a uniform set of laws decreed by the kings and queens after William the Conqueror; legal procedure was emphasized over merits at this time.

Court of Chancery
Court that granted relief based on fairness. Also called *equity court.*

Merchant Court
The separate set of courts established to administer the "law of merchants."

uniform manner. These were called **law courts**. Law at this time tended to emphasize form (legal procedure) over the substance (merit) of the case. The only relief available at law courts was a monetary award for damages.

Chancery (Equity) Courts   Because of the unfair results and the limited remedy available in the law courts, a second set of courts—the **Court of Chancery** (or **equity court**)—was established. These courts were under the authority of the Lord Chancellor. Persons who believed that the decision of the law court was unfair or that the law court could not grant an appropriate remedy could seek relief in the Court of Chancery. The Chancery Court inquired into the merits of the case, rather than emphasizing legal procedure. The Chancellor's remedies were called *equitable remedies* because they were shaped to fit each situation. Equitable orders and remedies of the Court of Chancery took precedent over the legal decisions and remedies of the law courts.

Merchant Courts   As trade developed in the Middle Ages, the merchants who traveled about England and Europe developed certain rules to solve their commercial disputes. These rules, known as the "law of merchants" or the **Law Merchant**, were based upon common trade practices and usage. Eventually, a separate set of courts was established to administer these rules. This court was called the **Merchant Court**. In the early 1900s, the Merchant Court was absorbed into the regular law court system of England.

International Perspective

ADOPTION OF ENGLISH COMMON LAW IN AMERICA

All the states except Louisiana base their legal systems primarily on the English *common law.* Because of its French heritage, Louisiana bases its law on the *civil law* (see discussion of international legal systems later in this chapter). Elements of California and Texas law, as well as other southwestern states, are rooted in civil law. In the United States, the law, equity, and merchant courts have been merged. Thus, most U.S. courts permit the aggrieved party to seek both law and equitable orders and remedies.

The importance of common law to the American legal system is described in the following excerpt from Justice Douglas's opinion in the 1841 case of *Penny v. Little* [4 Ill. 301 (Ill. 1841)]

The common law is a beautiful system, containing the wisdom and experiences of ages. Like the people it ruled and protected, it was simple and crude in its infancy, and became enlarged, improved, and polished as the nation advanced in civilization, virtue, and intelligence. Adapting itself to the conditions and circumstances of the people and relying upon them for its administration, it necessarily improved as the condition of the people was elevated. The inhabitants of this country always claimed the common law as their birthright, and at an early period established it as the basis of their jurisprudence.

International Perspective

THE CIVIL LAW SYSTEM

One of the major legal systems that has developed in the world in addition to the Anglo-American common law system is the **Romano-Germanic civil law system**. This legal system, which is

commonly called the **civil law** dates to 450 B.C., when Rome adopted the Twelve Tables, a code of laws applicable to the Romans. A compilation of Roman law, called the *Corpus Juris Civilis* (the Body of Civil Law), was completed in A.D. 534. Later, two national codes—the French Civil Code of 1804 (the Napoleonic Code) and the German Civil Code of 1896—became models for countries that adopted civil codes.

In contrast to the Anglo-American common law, where laws are created by the judicial system as well as by congressional legislation, the Civil Code and parliamentary statutes that expand and interpret it are the sole sources of the law in most civil law countries. Thus, the adjudication of a case is simply the application of the Code or the statutes to a particular set of facts. In some civil law countries, court decisions do not have the force of law.

Today, Austria, Belgium, Greece, Indochina, Indonesia, Japan, Latin America, the Netherlands, Poland, Portugal, South Korea, Spain, Sub-Saharan Africa, Switzerland, and Turkey follow the civil law.

✓ SOURCES OF LAW IN THE UNITED STATES

In more than 200 years since the founding of this country and the adoption of the English common law, the lawmakers of this country have developed a substantial body of law. The *sources of modern law* in the United States are discussed in the paragraphs that follow.

Constitutions

The **Constitution of the United States of America** is the *supreme law of the land*. This means that any law—whether federal, state, or local—that conflicts with the U.S. Constitution is unconstitutional and, therefore, unenforceable.

The principles enumerated in the Constitution are extremely broad since the founding fathers intended them to be applied to evolving social, technological, and economic conditions. The U.S. Constitution is often referred to as a "living document" because it is so adaptable.

The U.S. Constitution established the structure of the federal government. It created the following three branches of government and gave them the following powers:

- **Legislative (Congress)** Power to make (enact) the law.
- **Executive (President)** Power to enforce the law.
- **Judicial (courts)** Power to interpret and determine the validity of the law.

Powers not given to the federal government by the Constitution are reserved to the states. States also have their own constitutions. These are often patterned after the U.S. Constitution, although many are more detailed. State constitutions establish the legislative, executive, and judicial branches of state government and establish the powers of each branch. Provisions of state constitutions are valid unless they conflict with the U.S. Constitution or any valid federal law.

> **Constitution of the United States of America**
> **The supreme law of the United States.**

> *Two things most people should never see made: sausages and laws.*
>
> *An old saying*

Treaties

The U.S. Constitution provides that the President, with the advice and consent of the Senate, may enter into **treaties** with foreign governments. Treaties become part of the supreme law of the land. With increasing international economic relations among nations, treaties will become an even more important source of law that will affect business in the future.

> **treaty**
> **A compact made between two or more nations.**

Codified Law

Statutes are written laws that establish certain courses of conduct that must be adhered to by covered parties. The U.S. Congress is empowered by the Commerce Clause and other provisions of the U.S. Constitution to enact *federal statutes* to regulate foreign and interstate commerce. Federal statutes include antitrust laws, securities laws, bankruptcy laws, labor laws, equal employment opportunity laws, environmental protection laws, consumer protection laws, and such. State legislatures enact *state statutes*. State statutes include

> **statute**
> **Written law enacted by the legislative branch of the federal and state governments that establishes certain courses of conduct that must be adhered to by covered parties.**

ordinances

Laws enacted by local government bodies such as cities and municipalities, counties, school districts, and water districts.

corporation laws, partnership laws, workers' compensation laws, the Uniform Commercial Code, and the like. The statutes enacted by the legislative branches of the federal and state governments are organized by topic into code books. This is often called *codified law*.

State legislatures often delegate lawmaking authority to local government bodies, including cities and municipalities, counties, school districts, water districts, and such. These governmental units are empowered to adopt **ordinances**. Examples of ordinances are traffic laws, local building codes, and zoning laws. Ordinances are also codified.

Contemporary Business Application

REGULATIONS AND ORDERS OF ADMINISTRATIVE AGENCIES

The legislative and executive branches of federal and state governments are empowered to establish **administrative agencies** to enforce and interpret statutes enacted by Congress and state legislatures. Many of these agencies regulate business. For example, Congress has created the Securities and Exchange Commission (SEC) and the Federal Trade Commission (FTC), among others.

Congress or the state legislatures usually empower these agencies to adopt **administrative rules and regulations** to interpret the statutes that the agency is authorized to enforce. These rules and regulations have the force of law. Administrative agencies usually have the power to hear and decide disputes. Their decisions are called *orders*. Because of their power, administrative agencies are often informally referred to as the "fourth branch" of government.

Executive Orders

executive order

An order issued by a member of the executive branch of the government.

The executive branch of government, which includes the President of the United States and state governors, is empowered to issue **executive orders**. This power is derived from express delegation from the legislative branch and is implied from the U.S. Constitution and state constitutions. For example, in 1993, President Clinton issued an executive order that lifted the so-called "gag" rule forbidding abortion counseling in federally funded family planning clinics.

Judicial Decisions

judicial decision

A decision about an individual lawsuit issued by federal and state courts.

When deciding individual lawsuits, federal and state courts issue **judicial decisions**. In these written opinions the judge or justice usually explains the legal reasoning used to decide the case. These opinions often include interpretations of statutes, ordinances, administrative regulations, and the announcement of legal principles used to decide the case. Many court decisions are printed (reported) in books that are available in law libraries.

The Doctrine of Stare Decisis

precedent

A rule of law established in a court decision. Lower courts must follow the precedent established by higher courts.

Based on the common law tradition, past court decisions become **precedent** for deciding future cases. Lower courts must follow the precedent established by higher courts. That is why all federal and state courts in the United States must follow the precedents established by U.S. Supreme Court decisions.

The courts of one jurisdiction are not bound by the precedent established by the courts of another jurisdiction, although they may look to each other for guidance. For example, state courts of one state are not required to follow the legal precedent established by the courts of another state.

stare decisis

Latin: "to stand by the decision." Adherence to precedent.

Adherence to precedent is called *stare decisis* ("to stand by the decision"). The doctrine of *stare decisis* promotes uniformity of law within a jurisdiction, makes the court system more efficient, and makes the law more predictable for individuals and businesses. A court may later change or reverse its legal reasoning if a new case is presented to it and change is warranted. The doctrine of *stare decisis* is discussed in the following excerpt from Justice Musmanno's decision in *Flagiello v. Pennsylvania*.[7]

> *Without* stare decisis, *there would be no stability in our system of jurisprudence.* Stare decisis *channels the law. It erects lighthouses and flies the signals of safety. The ships of jurisprudence must follow that well-defined channel which, over the years, has been proved to be secure and worthy.*

Priority of Law in the United States

As mentioned previously, the U.S. Constitution and treaties take precedence over all other laws. Federal statutes take precedence over federal regulations. Valid federal law takes precedence over any conflicting state or local law. State constitutions rank as the highest state law. State statutes take precedence over state regulations. Valid state law takes precedence over local laws.

CONCEPT SUMMARY   SOURCES OF LAW IN THE UNITED STATES

Source of Law	Description
Constitutions	The U.S. Constitution establishes the federal government and enumerates its powers. Powers not given to the federal government are reserved to the states. State constitutions establish state governments and enumerate their powers.
Treaties	The President, with the advice and consent of the Senate, may enter into treaties with foreign countries.
Codified law: Statutes and ordinances	Statutes are enacted by Congress and state legislatures. Ordinances are enacted by municipalities and local government agencies. They establish courses of conduct that must be followed by covered parties.
Administrative agency rules and regulations	Administrative agencies are created by the legislative and executive branches of government. They may adopt rules and regulations that regulate the conduct of covered parties.
Executive orders	Issued by the President and governors of states, executive orders regulate the conduct of covered parties.
Judicial decisions	Courts decide controversies. In doing so, a court issues decisions that state the holding of the case and the rationale used by the court in reaching that decision.

✓ CRITICAL LEGAL THINKING

Judges apply *legal reasoning* in reaching a decision in a case. That is, the judge must specify the issue presented by the case, identify the key facts in the case and the applicable law, and then apply the law to the facts to come to a conclusion that answers the issue presented. This process is called **critical legal thinking**. Skills of analysis and interpretation are important in deciding legal cases.

Key Terms

Before you embark upon the study of law, you should know the following key legal terms.

    Plaintiff   The party who originally brought the lawsuit.
    Defendant   The party against whom the lawsuit has been brought.

critical legal thinking
The process of specifying the issue presented by a case, identifying the key facts in the case and applicable law, and then applying the law to the facts to come to a conclusion that answers the issue presented.

Petitioner or *Appellant*   The party who has appealed the decision of the trial court or lower court. The petitioner may be either the plaintiff or defendant, depending on who lost the case at the trial court or lower court level.

Respondent or *Appellee*   The party who must answer the petitioner's appeal. The respondent may be either the plaintiff or defendant, depending upon which party is the petitioner. In some cases, both the plaintiff *and* the defendant may disagree with the trial court's or lower court's decision, and both parties may appeal the decision.

Briefing a Case

It is often helpful for a student to "brief" a case in order to clarify the legal issues involved and to gain a better understanding of the case.

The procedure for briefing a case is as follows. The student must summarize, or brief, the court's decision in no more than 400 words (some professors may shorten or lengthen this limit). The assignment's format is highly structured, consisting of five parts, each of which is numbered and labeled:

Part	Maximum Words
1. Case name and citation	25
2. A summary of the key facts in the case	125
3. The issue presented by the case, stated as a one-sentence question answerable only by *yes* and *no*	25
4. The court's resolution of the issue (the "holding")	25
5. A summary of the court's reasoning justifying the holding	200
Total words	*400*

case brief

A summary of each of the following items of a case:

1. Case name and citation

2. Key facts

3. Issue presented

4. Holding of the court

5. Court's reasoning

Briefing a case consists of making a summary of each of the following items of the case.

1. **Case Name and Citation**

   The name of the case should be placed at the beginning of each briefed case. The case name usually contains the names of the parties to the lawsuit. Where there are multiple plaintiffs or defendants, however, some of the names of the parties may be omitted from the case name. Abbreviations are also often used in case names.

   The case citation, which consists of a number plus the year in which the case was decided, such as "126 L.Ed.2d. 295 (1993)," is set forth below the case name. The case citation identifies the book in the law library in which the case may be found. For example, the case in the above citation may be found in volume 126 of the *Supreme Court Reporter Lawyers' Edition (Second)*, page 295. The name of the court that decided the case should be set forth below the case name for the case.

2. **Summary of the Key Facts in the Case**

   The important facts of a case should be stated briefly. Extraneous facts and facts of minor importance should be omitted from the brief. The facts of the case can usually be found at the beginning of the case, but not necessarily. Important facts may be found throughout the case.

3. **Issue Presented by the Case**

   It is crucial in the briefing of a case to identify the issue presented to the court to decide. The issue on appeal is most often a legal question, although questions of fact are sometimes the subject of an appeal. The issue presented in each case is usually quite specific and should be asked in a one-sentence question that is answerable only by a *yes* or *no*. For example, the issue statement, "Is Mary liable?" is too broad. A more proper statement of the issue would be, "Is Mary liable to Joe for breach of the contract made between them based on her refusal to make the payment due on September 30?"

4. **Holding**

   The "holding" is the decision reached by the present court. It should be *yes* or *no*. The holding should also state which party won.

5. **Summary of the Court's Reasoning**

When an appellate court or supreme court issues a decision, which is often called an *opinion*, the court will normally state the reasoning it used in reaching its decision. The rationale for the decision may be based on the specific facts of the case, public policy, prior law, or other matters. In stating the reasoning of the court, the student should reword the court's language into the student's own language. This summary of the court's reasoning should pick out the meat of the opinions and weed out the nonessentials.

Following is a U.S. Supreme Court opinion for briefing. The case is presented in the language of the U.S. Supreme Court.

Case for Briefing

Harris v. Forklift Systems, Inc. 126 L.Ed.2d. 295 (1993) United States Supreme Court

OPINION, O'CONNOR, JUSTICE   Teresa Harris worked as a manager at Forklift Systems, Inc., an equipment rental company, from April 1985 until October 1987. Charles Hardy was Forklift's president. Throughout Harris's time at Forklift, Hardy often insulted her because of her gender and often made her the target of unwanted sexual innuendos. Hardy told Harris on several occasions, in the presence of other employees, "You're a woman, what do you know" and "We need a man as the rental manager"; at least once, he told her she was "a dumb-ass woman." Again in front of others, he suggested that the two of them "go to the Holiday Inn to negotiate Harris' raise." Hardy occasionally asked Harris and other female employees to get coins from his front pants pocket. He threw objects on the ground in front of Harris and other women, and asked them to pick the objects up. He made sexual innuendos about Harris' and other women's clothing.

In mid-August 1987, Harris complained to Hardy about his conduct. Hardy said he was surprised that Harris was offended, claimed he was only joking, and apologized. He also promised he would stop and based on this assurance Harris stayed on the job. But in early September, Hardy began anew: While Harris was arranging a deal with one of Forklift's customers, he asked her, again in front of other employees, "What did you do, promise the guy some sex Saturday night?" On October 1, Harris collected her paycheck and quit.

Harris then sued Forklift, claiming that Hardy's conduct had created an abusive work environment for her because of her gender. The United States District Court for the Middle District of Tennessee found this to be "a close case," but held that Hardy's conduct did not create an abusive environment. The court found that some of Hardy's comments "offended Harris, and would offend the reasonable woman," but that they were not "so severe as to be expected to seriously affect Harris' psychological well-being." A reasonable woman manager under like circumstances would have been offended by Hardy, but his conduct would not have risen to the level of interfering with that person's work performance. The United States Court of Appeals for the Sixth Circuit affirmed in a brief unpublished decision.

We granted certiorari to resolve a conflict among the Circuits on whether conduct, to be actionable as "abusive work environment" harassment, must "seriously affect an employee's psychological well-being" or lead the plaintiff to "suffer injury."

Title VII of the Civil Rights Act of 1964 makes it "an unlawful employment practice for an employer . . . to discriminate against any individual with respect to his compensation, terms, conditions, or privileges of employment, because of such individual's race, color, religion, sex, or national origin." 42 U.S.C. §2000e-2(a)(1).

When the workplace is permeated with discriminatory intimidation, ridicule, and insult that is sufficiently severe or pervasive to alter the conditions of the victim's employment and create an abusive working environment, Title VII is violated. This standard takes a middle path between making actionable any conduct that is merely offensive and requiring the conduct to cause a tangible psychological injury. Mere utterance of an epithet which engenders offensive feelings in an employee does not sufficiently affect the conditions of employment to implicate Title VII. Conduct that is not severe or pervasive enough to create an objectively hostile or abusive work environment—an environment that a reasonable person would find hostile or abusive—is beyond Title VII's purview. Likewise, if the victim does not subjectively perceive the environment to be

*Sidebar labels:*
- Case name, Citation, and Court
- Opinion of the Court
- Facts
- Lower Courts' Opinions
- Issue
- Statute Being Interpreted
- U.S. Supreme Court's Reasoning

abusive, the conduct has not actually altered the conditions of the victim's employment, and there is no Title VII violation.

But Title VII comes into play before the harassing conduct leads to a nervous breakdown. A discriminatorily abusive work environment, even one that does not seriously affect employees' psychological well-being, can and often will detract from employees' job performance, discourage employees from remaining on the job, or keep them from advancing in their careers. Moreover, even without regard to these tangible effects, the very fact that the discriminatory conduct was so severe or pervasive that it created a work environment abusive to employees because of their race, gender, religion, or national origin offends Title VII's broad rule of workplace equality.

Holding

We therefore believe the district court erred in relying on whether the conduct "seriously affected plaintiff's psychological well-being" or led her to "suffer injury." Such an inquiry may needlessly focus the factfinder's attention on concrete psychological harm, an element Title VII does not require. So long as the environment would reasonably be perceived, and is perceived, as hostile or abusive, there is no need for it also to be psychologically injurious. This is not, and by its nature cannot be, a mathematically precise test. But we can say that whether an environment is "hostile" or "abusive" can be determined only by looking at all the circumstances.

We therefore reverse the judgment of the Court of Appeals, and remand the case for further proceedings consistent with this opinion.

Concurring Opinion

CONCURRING OPINION, GINSBURG, JUSTICE   The critical issue, Title VII's text indicates, is whether members of one sex are exposed to disadvantageous terms or conditions of employment to which members of the other sex are not exposed. The adjudicator's inquiry should center, dominantly, on whether the discriminatory conduct has unreasonably interfered with the plaintiff's work performance. To show such interference, the plaintiff need not prove that his or her tangible productivity has declined as a result of the harassment.

𝓔XHIBIT 1.1   *Brief of the Case*

1. **Case Name, Citation, and Court**
   Harris v. Forklift Systems. Inc
   126 L.Ed.2d. 295 (1993)
   United States Supreme Court

2. **Summary of the Key Facts**
   A. Teresa Harris worked as a manager at Forklift Systems, Inc. (Forklift). Charles Hardy was Forklift's president.
   B. While Harris worked at Forklift. Hardy continually insulted her because of her gender and made her the target of unwanted sexual innuendos.
   C. This conduct created an abusive and hostile work environment, causing Harris to terminate her employment.
   D. Harris sued Forklift, alleging sexual harassment in violation of Title VII of the Civil Rights Act of 1964, which makes it an unlawful employment practice for an employer to discriminate in employment because of an individual's sex.

3. **The Issue**
   Must an employee prove that she suffered severe psychological injury before she can prove a Title VII claim for sexual harassment against her employer?

4. **The Holding**
   No. The Supreme Court remanded the case for further proceedings consistent with its opinion.

5. **Summary of the Court's Reasoning**
   The Supreme Court held that a workplace that is permeated with discriminatory intimidation, ridicule, and insult so severe that it alters the conditions of the victim's employment creates an abusive and hostile work environment that violates Title VII. The Court held that the victim is not required to prove that she suffered tangible psychological injury to prove her Title VII claim. The Court noted that Title VII comes into play before the harassing conduct leads the victim to have a nervous breakdown.

Working the Web

The Great American Web Site The U.S. Government is the largest source of information anywhere in the world, and it belongs to you! The mission of the Great American Web Site is to highlight the most useful information in our government's domain and to help you navigate the maze of government agencies. This site has something for everyone.

Visit at **www.uncle-sam.com**

The White House Beginning with the Clinton administration, our government made a serious commitment to provide access to government information via the Internet. Through this site, you can find out about the President and Vice President and their families and send them electronic mail, find out what is happening at the White House, take a tour of the White House, search White House documents, and even listen to speeches or view photos (with the right computer equipment).

Visit at **www.whitehouse.gov**

The U.S. House of Representatives Do you want to read the full text of bills introduced into the House of Representatives? Do you want to find out how each member voted? Do you want to find out how a bill becomes a law? Maybe you want to find out who your representative is (you can search by state and zip code), visit his or her Web page, and send him or her some electronic mail. You can do all this and much more on the House of Representatives' Web site. There are up-to-the-hour committee hearing schedules as well as an annual congressional schedule.

Visit at **www.house.gov**

The U.S. Senate Do you want to find out what is happening in the U.S. Senate? Then visit its Web site. You can get information on recent legislative actions, scheduled activities, committee information, senators and Senate leadership, Senate history, procedures, terminol-

ogy, and links to other information. This site is less comprehensive than its House counterpart.

Visit at **www.senate.gov**

Critical Thinking Community This site is a resource center that provides the latest information on critical thinking, a bookstore that informs users of materials that are available on-line, a conference center that gives detailed information about upcoming events of interest to the critical thinking community, and a library that holds a growing collection of articles and reference materials on critical thinking.

Visit at **www.criticalthinking.org**

CYBER EXERCISES

e-biz

1. You are interested in a bill that was introduced into the U.S. House of Representatives last month. You want to read the full text of the bill and find out what happened to it (its legislative history). Using the U.S. House of Representatives Web site, retrieve a current House bill and its legislative history.

2. You want to find out who your representative is in the House of Representatives. Using the U.S. House of Representatives Web site, determine who your representative is. Print out the biographical material about him or her. Find out what his or her e-mail address is.

3. You want to find out what is on-line from the Internal Revenue Service. Using the Great American Web Site, navigate your way to the Internal Revenue Service's home page.

4. Send a message to the President or Vice President on an issue of importance to you. Using the White House Web site, navigate to the page that lets you send e-mail to the President or Vice President.

5. You want to find out more about critical thinking. Using the Critical Thinking Community Web site, click on *college and university*, then click on *library*. From the library, find the *Glossary of Critical Thinking Terms* and print or write out the definition for *dialogical thinking*.

CASES AND EXERCISES

CRITICAL LEGAL THINKING CASES

1.1. In 1909, the state legislature of Illinois enacted a statute called the "Woman's 10-Hour Law." The law prohibited women who were employed in factories and other manufacturing facilities from working more than 10 hours per day. The law did not apply to men. W. C. Ritchie & Co., an employer, brought a lawsuit that challenged the statute as being unconstitutional in violation of the Equal Protection Clause of the Illinois constitution. In upholding the statute, the Illinois Supreme Court stated,

> It is known to all men (and what we know as men we cannot profess to be ignorant of as judges) that woman's physical structure and the performance of maternal functions place her at a great disadvantage in the battle of life; that while a man can work for more than ten hours a day without injury to himself, a woman, especially when the burdens of motherhood are upon her, cannot; that while a man can work standing upon his feet for more than ten hours a day, day after day, without injury to himself, a woman cannot; and that to require a woman to stand upon her feet for more than 10 hours in any one day and

> perform severe manual labor while thus standing, day after day, has the effect to impair her health, and that as weakly and sickly women cannot be mothers of vigorous children.

> We think the general consensus of opinion, not only in this country but in the civilized countries of Europe, is, that a working day of not more than ten hours for women is justified for the following reasons: (1) the physical organization of women, (2) her maternal function, (3) the rearing and education of children, (4) the maintenance of the home; and these conditions are, so far, matters of general knowledge that the courts will take judicial cognizance of their existence.

> Surrounded as women are by changing conditions of society, and the evolution of employment which environs them, we agree fully with what is said by the Supreme Court of Washington in the Buchanan case: "Law is, or ought to be, a progressive science."

Is the statute fair? Would the statute be lawful today? Should the law be a "progressive science"? [*W. C. Ritchie & Co. v. Wayman, Attorney for Cook County. Illinois* 91 N.E. 695 (Ill. 1910)]

ETHICS CASES

1.2. In 1975, after the war in Vietnam, the U.S. government discontinued draft registration for men in this country. In 1980, after the Soviet Union invaded Afghanistan, President Jimmy Carter asked Congress for funds to reactivate draft registration. President Carter suggested that both males and females be required to register. Congress allocated funds only for the registration of males. Several men who were subject to draft registration brought a lawsuit that challenged the law as being unconstitutional in violation of the Equal Protection Clause of the U.S. Constitution. The U.S. Supreme Court upheld the constitutionality of the draft registration law, reasoning as follows:

> The question of registering women for the draft not only received considerable national attention and was the subject of wide-ranging public debate, but also was extensively considered by Congress in hearings, floor debate, and in committee. The foregoing clearly establishes that the decision to exempt women from registration was not the "accidental by-product of a traditional way of thinking about women."

> This is not a case of Congress arbitrarily choosing to burden one of two similarly situated groups, such as would be the case with an all-black or all-white, or an all-Catholic or all-Lutheran, or an all-Republican or all-Democratic registration. Men and women are simply not similarly situated for purposes of a draft or registration for a draft.

Justice Marshall dissented, stating that "The Court today places its imprimatur on one of the most potent remaining public expressions of 'ancient canards about the proper role of women.' It upholds a statute that requires males but not females to register for the draft, and which thereby categorically excludes women from a fundamental civic obligation. I dissent."

Was the decision fair? Has the law been a "progressive science" in this case? Is it ethical for males, but not females, to have to register for the draft? [*Rostker, Director of the Selective Service v. Goldberg*, 453 U.S. 57, 101 S.Ct. 2646, 69 L.Ed.2d 478 (1981)]

CRITICAL LEGAL THINKING WRITING ASSIGNMENT

Read Case A.1 in the Case Appendix [*Anheuser-Busch Incorporated v. Schmoke Mayor of Baltimore City*]. This case is excerpted from the court of appeals opinion. Review and brief the case. In your brief, be sure to answer the following questions.

1. What law was at issue in this case and what was the source of the law?

2. Who challenged the law? On what grounds did the plaintiff challenge the law?

3. Do you think the challenged law was fair? Explain.

4. How did the court of appeals decide the case? Was this an easy case for the court to decide?

NOTES

1. *The Spirit of Liberty*, 3d ed (New York: Alfred A. Knopf, 1960).
2. "Introduction," *The Nature of Law: Readings in Legal Philosophy*, ed. M.P. Golding (New York: Random House, 1966).
3. *Black's Law Dictionary*, 5th ed (St. Paul, MN.: West, 1979).
4. 447 U.S. 10, 100 S.Ct. 1999, 64 L.Ed.2d 689 (1980).
5. 347 U.S. 483, 74 S.Ct. 686, 98 L.Ed. 873 (1954).
6. *Law and the Modern Mind* (New York: Brentano's, 1930).
7. 208 A.2d 193 (PA 1965).

Judicial and Alternative Dispute Resolution

I was never ruined but twice; once when I lost a lawsuit, and once when I won one.

VOLTAIRE

Chapter Objectives

After studying this chapter, you should be able to

1. Describe the state court systems.
2. Describe the federal court system.
3. Explain how a justice is chosen for the U.S. Supreme Court.
4. Explain subject matter jurisdiction of federal and state courts.
5. Describe in personam jurisdiction of courts and service of process.
6. Describe venue.
7. Describe the pretrial litigation process, including pleadings, discovery, dismissals and pretrial judgments, and settlement conference.
8. Describe how a case proceeds through trial.
9. Describe how a trial court decision is appealed.
10. Explain the use of arbitration and other nonjudicial methods of alternative dispute resolution.

Chapter Contents

There are two major court systems in the United States: (1) the federal court system and (2) the court systems of the 50 states and the District of Columbia. Each of these systems has jurisdiction to hear different types of lawsuits. The process of bringing, maintaining, and defending a lawsuit is called **litigation**. Litigation is a difficult, time-consuming, and costly process that must comply with complex procedural rules. Although it is not required, most parties employ a lawyer to represent them when they are involved in a lawsuit.

Several forms of *nonjudicial* dispute resolution have developed in response to the expense and difficulty of bringing a lawsuit. These methods, collectively called **alternative dispute resolution**, are being used more and more often to resolve commercial disputes.

This chapter discusses the various court systems, the jurisdiction of courts to hear and decide cases, the litigation process, and alternative dispute resolution.

> *The law, wherein, as in a magic mirror, we see reflected, not only our own lives, but the lives of all men that have been! When I think on this majestic theme, my eyes dazzle.*
>
> *Oliver Wendell Holmes*
> The Law, Speeches *17 (1913)*

THE STATE COURT SYSTEMS

Each state and the District of Columbia has a separate court system. Most state court systems include the following: *limited-jurisdiction trial courts, general-jurisdiction trial courts, intermediate appellate courts,* and a *supreme court.*

Limited-Jurisdiction Trial Court

State **limited-jurisdiction trial courts**, which are sometimes referred to as **inferior trial courts**, hear matters of a specialized or limited nature. In many states, traffic courts, juvenile courts, justice-of-the-peace courts, probate courts, family law courts, and courts that hear misdemeanor criminal law cases and civil cases involving lawsuits under a certain dollar amount are examples of such courts. Because these courts are trial courts, evidence can be introduced and testimony given. Most limited-jurisdiction courts keep a record of their proceedings. Their decisions usually can be appealed to a general-jurisdiction court or an appellate court.

Many states have also created **small claims court** to hear civil cases involving small dollar amounts (e.g., $5,000 or less). Generally, the parties must appear individually and cannot have a lawyer represent them. The decisions of small claims courts are often appealable to general-jurisdiction trial courts or appellate courts.

limited-jurisdiction trial court
A court that hears matters of a specialized or limited nature.

small claims court
A court that hears civil cases involving small dollar amounts.

General-Jurisdiction Trial Court

Every state has a **general-jurisdiction trial court**. These courts are often referred to as **courts of record** because the testimony and evidence at trial are recorded and stored for future reference. They hear cases that are not within the jurisdiction of limited-jurisdiction trial courts, such as felonies, civil cases over a certain dollar amount, and so on. Some states divide their general-jurisdiction courts into two divisions, one for criminal cases and another for civil cases. Evidence and testimony are given at general-jurisdiction trial courts. The decisions handed down by these courts are appealable to an intermediate appellate court or the state supreme court, depending on the circumstances.

general-jurisdiction trial court
A court that hears cases of a general nature that are not within the jurisdiction of limited-jurisdiction trial courts. Testimony and evidence at trial are recorded and stored for future reference.

Intermediate Appellate Court

In many states, **intermediate appellate courts** (also called **appellate courts** or courts of appeal) hear appeals from trial courts. They review the trial court record to determine if there have been any errors at trial that would require reversal or modification of the trial court's decision. Thus, the appellate court reviews either pertinent parts or the whole trial court record from the lower court. No new evidence or testimony is permitted. The parties usually file legal *briefs* with the appellate court stating the law and facts that support

intermediate appellate court
An intermediate court that hears appeals from trial courts.

their positions. Appellate courts usually grant a brief oral hearing to the parties. Appellate court decisions are appealable to the state's highest court. In less populated states that do not have an intermediate appellate court, trial court decisions can be appealed directly to the state's highest court.

Highest State Court

state supreme court

The highest court in a state court system; it hears appeals from intermediate state courts and certain trial courts.

Each state has a highest court in its court system. Most states call this highest court the **supreme court**. The function of a state supreme court is to hear appeals from intermediate state courts and certain trial courts. No new evidence or testimony is heard. The parties usually submit pertinent parts of or the entire lower court record for review. The parties also submit legal briefs to the court and are usually granted a brief oral hearing. Decisions of state supreme courts are final, unless a question of law is involved that is appealable to the U.S. Supreme Court.

Exhibit 2.1 portrays a typical state court system.

Exhibit 2.1   A Typical State Court System

Entrepreneur and the Law

SPECIALIZED COURTS HEAR COMMERCIAL DISPUTES

In most states, business and commercial disputes are heard by the same judges that hear and decide criminal, landlord-tenant, matrimonial, medical malpractice, and other nonbusiness-related cases. The one major exception to this standard has been the state of Delaware, where a special Chancery Court hears and decides business litigation. The court, which mainly deals with cases involving corporate government disputes, has earned a reputation for its expertise in handling and deciding corporate matters. Perhaps the existence of this special court and a corporation code that tends to favor corporate management are the primary reasons that more than 60 percent of the corporations listed on the New York Stock Exchange are incorporated in Delaware.

New York is one state that is following Delaware's lead in this area. New York has designated four courts within its general court system to hear commercial disputes. These courts, which began operating in 1993, hear contract, sales, insurance, unfair competition, libel and slander, shareholder, business-related tort, and other commercial cases. Other states are expected to establish courts that specialize in commercial matters in the near future.

Businesses tend to favor special commercial courts because the judges presiding over them are expected to have the expertise to handle complex commercial lawsuits. Also, the courts are expected to be more efficient in deciding business-related cases, thus saving time and money for the parties.

THE FEDERAL COURT SYSTEM

Article III of the United States Constitution provides that the federal government's judicial power is vested in one "Supreme Court." This court is the **U.S. Supreme Court**. The Constitution also authorizes Congress to establish "inferior" federal courts. Pursuant to this power, Congress has established special federal courts, the U.S. district courts, and the U.S. courts of appeal. Federal judges are appointed for life by the President with the advice and consent of the Senate (except bankruptcy court judges, who are appointed for 14-year terms).

U.S. Supreme Court
Court created by Article III of the U.S. Constitution.

Special Federal Courts

The **special federal courts** established by Congress have limited jurisdiction. They include the following courts:

- **U.S. tax court** Hears cases involving federal tax laws
- **U.S. claims court** Hears cases brought against the United States
- **U.S. Court of International Trade** Hears cases involving tariffs and international commercial disputes
- **U.S. bankruptcy court** Hears cases involving federal bankruptcy laws

special federal courts
Federal courts that hear matters of specialized or limited jurisdiction.

U.S. District Courts

The **U.S. district courts** are the federal court system's trial courts of general jurisdiction. There is at least one federal district court in each state and the District of Columbia, although more populated states have more than one district court. The geographical area served by each court is referred to as a *district*. There are presently 96 federal district courts. The federal district courts are empowered to impanel juries, receive evidence, hear testimony, and decide cases. Most federal cases originate in federal district courts.

U.S. district courts
The federal court system's trial courts of general jurisdiction.

U.S. Courts of Appeals

U.S. courts of appeals

The federal court system's intermediate appellate courts.

The **U.S. courts of appeals** are the federal court system's intermediate appellate courts. There are 13 circuits in the federal court system. The first 12 are geographical. Eleven are designated by a number, such as the "First Circuit," "Second Circuit," and so on. The geographical area served by each court is referred to as a *circuit*. The twelfth circuit court is located in Washington, DC and is called the "District of Columbia Circuit."

As appellate courts, these circuit courts hear appeals from the district courts located in their circuit as well as from certain special courts and federal administrative agencies. The courts review the record of the lower court or administrative agency proceedings to determine if there has been any error that would warrant reversal or modification of the lower court decision. No new evidence or testimony is heard. The parties file legal briefs with the court and are given a short oral hearing. Appeals are usually heard by a three-judge panel. After a decision is rendered by the three-judge panel, a petitioner can request a review *en banc* by the full court.

Court of Appeals for the Federal Circuit

A court of appeals in Washington, DC, that has special appellate jurisdiction to review the decisions of the Claims Court, the Patent and Trademark Office, and the Court of International Trade.

The thirteenth court of appeals was created by Congress in 1982. It is called the **Court of Appeals for the Federal Circuit** and is located in Washington, DC.[1] This court has special appellate jurisdiction to review the decisions of the Claims Court, the Patent and Trademark Office, and the Court of International Trade. This court was created to provide uniformity in the application of federal law in certain areas, particularly patent law.

Exhibit 2.2 shows the 13 federal circuit courts of appeals.

*ℰ*XHIBIT 2.2   *The Thirteen Federal Judicial Circuits*

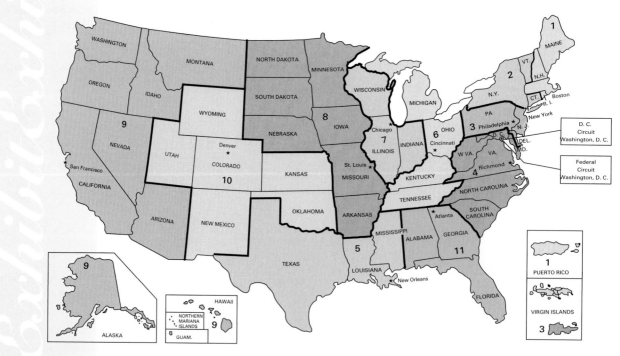

The U.S. Supreme Court

The highest court in the land is the **Supreme Court of the United States**, located in Washington, DC. The Court is composed of nine justices who are nominated by the President and confirmed by the Senate. The President appoints one justice as *chief justice*, responsible for the administration of the Supreme Court. The other eight justices are *associate justices*.

The Supreme Court, which is an appellate court, hears appeals from federal circuit courts of appeals and, under certain circumstances, from federal district courts, special federal courts, and the highest state courts. No evidence or testimony is heard. As with other appellate courts, the lower court record is reviewed to determine whether there has been an error that warrants a reversal or modification of the decision. Legal briefs are filed, and the parties are granted a brief oral hearing. The Supreme Court's decision is final.

The federal court system is illustrated in Exhibit 2.3.

U.S. Supreme Court
The highest court in the land. It is located in Washington, DC.

Pieces of evidence, each by itself insufficient, may together constitute a significant whole, and justify by their combined effect a conclusion.

Lord Wright
Grant v. Australian Knitting Mills. Ltd. (1936)

℮XHIBIT 2.3   *The Federal Court System*

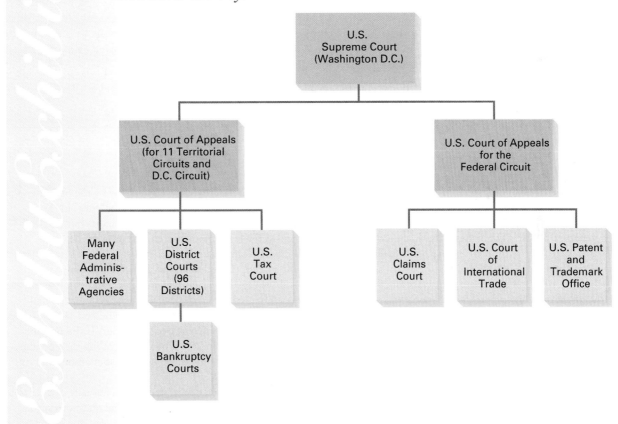

Decisions by the U.S. Supreme Court

The U.S. Constitution gives Congress the authority to establish rules for the appellate review of cases by the Supreme Court, except in the rare case where mandatory review is required. Congress has given the Supreme Court discretion to decide what cases it will hear.[2]

petition for certiorari
A petition asking the Supreme Court to hear one's case.

writ of certiorari
An official notice that the Supreme Court will review one's case.

Sancho: But if this is hell, why do we see no lawyers?

Clarindo: They won't receive them, lest they bring lawsuits here.

Sancho: If there are no lawsuits here, hell's not so bad.

Lope de Vega
The Star of Seville. Act 3, Scene 2

A petitioner must file a **petition for certiorari** asking the Supreme Court to hear the case. If the Court decides to review a case, it will issue a **writ of certiorari**. Because the Court issues only about 150 to 200 opinions each year, writs are usually granted only in cases involving constitutional and other important issues.

Each justice of the Supreme Court, including the chief justice, has an equal vote. The Supreme Court can issue the following types of decisions:

- **Unanimous decision** If all of the justices voting agree as to the outcome and reasoning used to decide the case, it is a unanimous opinion. Unanimous decisions are precedent for later cases.
- **Majority decision** If a majority of the justices agrees to the outcome and reasoning used to decide the case, it is a majority opinion. Majority decisions are precedent for later cases.
- **Plurality decision** If a majority of the justices agrees to the outcome of the case, but not as to the reasoning for reaching the outcome, it is a plurality opinion. A plurality decision settles the case but is not precedent for later cases.
- **Tie decision** Sometimes the Supreme Court sits without all nine justices being present. This could happen because of illness, conflict of interest, or a justice has not been confirmed to fill a vacant seat on the Court. If there is a tie vote, the lower court decision is affirmed. Such votes are not precedent for later cases.

A justice who agrees with the outcome of a case, but not the reason proffered by other justices, can issue a *concurring opinion* that sets forth his or her reasons for deciding the case. A justice who does not agree with a decision can file a *dissenting opinion* that sets forth the reasons for his or her dissent.

Contemporary Business Application

I'LL TAKE YOU TO THE U.S. SUPREME COURT!—NOT!

As textbooks say, in the United States you can appeal your legal case all the way to the U.S. Supreme Court. In reality, however, the chance of ever having your case heard by the highest court is slim to none.

Each year, over 7,000 petitioners pay the $300 filing fee to ask the Supreme Court to hear their case. In addition, these petitioners usually pay big law firms from $30,000 to $100,000 or more to write the appeal petition. In recent years, the Supreme Court has only accepted about 100 of these cases for full review each term.

Each of the nine Supreme Court justices have three law clerks—recent law school graduates usually chosen from the elite law schools across the country—who assist them. The justices rarely read the appellate petitions but instead delegate this task to their law clerks. The clerks then write a short memorandum discussing the key issues raised by the appeal and recommend to the justices whether they should grant or deny a review. The justices meet once a week to discuss what cases merit a review. The votes of four justices are necessary to grant an appeal and schedule an oral argument before the Court. Written opinions by the justices are usually issued many months later.

So what does it take to win a review by the Supreme Court? Often it requires that there be a "split" in the circuit courts of appeal, that is, several circuit courts have decided the legal issue differently. For example, the Supreme Court recently decided a case where several courts of appeal had held that Title VII, which prohibits sex discrimination in employment, prohibited same-sex discrimination, whereas several other circuit courts had held that Title VII did not apply to same-sex discrimination. The Supreme Court decided Title VII did prohibit same-sex discrimination. The Court's ruling then became the "law of the land" and resolved the split among the circuit courts.

In addition, the U.S. Supreme Court usually decides to hear cases involving major constitutional questions such as freedom of speech, freedom of religion, and due process. The Court, therefore, rarely decides such day-to-day legal issues as breach of contract, tort liability, or corporations law unless it involves a more important constitutional or federal law question. So the next time you hear someone say, "I'll take you to the U.S. Supreme Court!" just say, "Not!"

Jurisdiction of Federal and State Courts

Article III, Section 2, of the U.S. Constitution sets forth the jurisdiction of federal courts. Federal courts have *limited jurisdiction* to hear cases involving:

1. **Federal questions** Cases arising under the U.S. Constitution, treaties, and federal statutes and regulations. There is no dollar-amount limit on federal question cases that can be brought in federal court.[3]
2. **Diversity of citizenship** Cases between (a) citizens of different states, (b) a citizen of a state and a citizen or subject of a foreign country, and (c) a citizen of a state and a foreign country where the foreign country is the plaintiff. A corporation is considered to be a citizen of the state in which it is incorporated and in which it has its principal place of business. The reason for providing diversity of citizenship jurisdiction was to prevent state court bias against nonresidents. The federal court must apply the appropriate state's law in deciding the case. The dollar amount of the controversy must exceed $75,000.[4] If this requirement is not met, the action must be brought in the appropriate state court.

Federal courts have **exclusive jurisdiction** to hear cases involving federal crimes, antitrust, bankruptcy, patent and copyright cases, suits against the United States, and most admiralty cases. State courts cannot hear these cases.

State and federal courts have **concurrent jurisdiction** to hear cases involving diversity of citizenship and federal questions over which federal courts do not have exclusive jurisdiction (e.g., cases involving federal securities laws). If a case involving concurrent jurisdiction is brought by a plaintiff in state court, the defendant can remove the case to federal court. If a case does not qualify to be brought in federal court, it must be brought in the appropriate state court.

Exhibit 2.4 illustrates the jurisdiction of federal and state courts.

federal question
A case arising under the U.S. Constitution, treaties, or federal statutes and regulations.

diversity of citizenship
A case between (1) citizens of different states, (2) a citizen of a state and a citizen or subject of a foreign country, and (3) a citizen of a state and a foreign country where a foreign country is the plaintiff.

exclusive jurisdiction
Jurisdiction held by only one court.

concurrent jurisdiction
Jurisdiction shared by two or more courts.

*Ɛ*XHIBIT **2.4**   *Jurisdiction of Federal and State Courts*

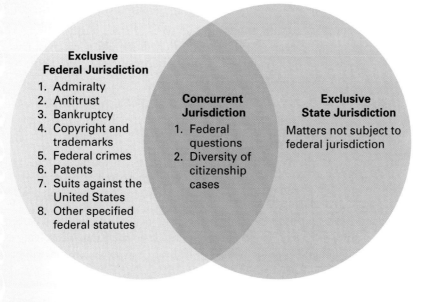

Exclusive Federal Jurisdiction
1. Admiralty
2. Antitrust
3. Bankruptcy
4. Copyright and trademarks
5. Federal crimes
6. Patents
7. Suits against the United States
8. Other specified federal statutes

Concurrent Jurisdiction
1. Federal questions
2. Diversity of citizenship cases

Exclusive State Jurisdiction
Matters not subject to federal jurisdiction

Contemporary Business Application

THE PROCESS OF CHOOSING A SUPREME COURT JUSTICE

In an effort to strike a balance of power between the executive and legislative branches of government, Article II, Section 2 of the U.S. Constitution gives the President the power to appoint Supreme Court justices "with the advice and consent of the Senate." In recent years, however, many conservative and liberal critics have charged that this process has become nothing more than a political tennis match in which the hapless nominee is the ball.

Some of the most notorious fights over Supreme Court nominations in U.S. history took place during the Reagan administration. President George Bush was given the chance to cast a conservative shadow over the Court's decisions when Justice Thurgood Marshall retired in 1991. Marshall, who served 24 years, was one of the most liberal members of the Court. Also, he had been the only black person to serve on the Supreme Court. In 1991, Bush nominated Clarence Thomas, a black conservative serving as a judge of the U.S. court of appeals in the District of Columbia, to replace Marshall. Thomas grew up in rural Georgia and graduated from Yale Law School.

Thomas was hardly an unknown quantity. He had a paper trail that clearly showed he preferred individual rights to group rights, opposed affirmative action, and favored the right-to-life side of the abortion issue. During his confirmation hearings, Anita Hill came forward with charges that Thomas had sexually harassed her when she was his subordinate at the Equal Employment Opportunity Commission. Thomas vehemently denied the charges. After a heated political debate, Clarence Thomas was confirmed by the U.S. Senate with a 52–48 vote in October 1991.

The election of Bill Clinton as President swung the pendulum back to the Democrats. President Clinton got an early opportunity to nominate a candidate when Justice Byron R. White, the only Democrat-appointed member of the Court, retired. President Clinton nominated Judge Ruth Bader Ginsburg to serve on the Supreme Court. Judge Ginsburg, who is considered a moderate liberal, had ruled in favor of abortion rights and was a pioneer in the area of women's rights. Ginsburg was approved by a bipartisan vote of the Senate and took office for the Supreme Court's 1993–1994 term. She is the second woman to serve on the Court, joining Sandra Day O'Connor, who was nominated by President Ronald Reagan. Ginsburg is also the first Jewish person to serve on the Court since Justice Abe Fortas resigned in 1969.

THE JURISDICTION OF COURTS

Not every court has the authority to hear all types of cases. First, to bring a lawsuit in a court the plaintiff must have *standing to sue*. In addition, the court must have *jurisdiction* to hear the case, and the case must be brought in the proper *venue*. These topics are discussed in the following paragraphs.

Standing to Sue

standing to sue
The plaintiff must have some stake in the outcome of the lawsuit.

To bring a lawsuit, a plaintiff must have **standing to sue**. This means that the plaintiff must have some stake in the outcome of the lawsuit.

Consider This Example   Linda's friend Jon is injured in an accident caused by Emily. Jon refuses to sue. Linda cannot sue Emily on Jon's behalf because she does not have an interest in the result of the case.

A few states now permit investors to invest money in a lawsuit for a percentage return of any award or judgment. Courts hear and decide actual disputes involving specific controversies. Hypothetical questions will not be heard and trivial lawsuits will be dismissed.

Jurisdiction

jurisdiction
The authority of a court to hear a case.

A court must have **jurisdiction** to hear and decide a case. There are two types of jurisdiction: (1) subject matter jurisdiction and (2) in personam, in rem, or quasi in rem jurisdiction.

1. **Subject Matter Jurisdiction** To hear and decide a case, a court must have **subject matter jurisdiction** over the subject matter of the case. Some courts have only limited jurisdiction. For example, federal courts have jurisdiction to hear only certain types of cases (discussed later in this chapter). Certain state courts, such as probate courts and small claims courts, can hear only designated types of cases. If a court does not have subject matter jurisdiction, it cannot hear the case.

2. **In Personam, in Rem, and Quasi in Rem Jurisdiction** Jurisdiction over the person is called **in personam jurisdiction**, or **personal jurisdiction**. A *plaintiff*, by filing a lawsuit with a court, gives the court in personam jurisdiction over themselves. The court must also have in personam jurisdiction over the *defendant*, which is usually obtained by having that person served a summons within the territorial boundaries of the state (i.e., **service of process**). Service of process is usually accomplished by personal service of the summons and complaint on the defendant. If this is not possible, alternative forms of notice such as mailing of the summons or publication of a notice in a newspaper may be permitted. A corporation is subject to personal jurisdiction in the state in which it is incorporated, has its principal office, and is doing business. A party who disputes the jurisdiction of a court can make a *special appearance* in that court to argue against the imposition of jurisdiction. Service of process is not permitted during such an appearance.

A court may have jurisdiction to hear and decide a case because it has jurisdiction over the property of the lawsuit. This is called **in rem jurisdiction** ("jurisdiction over the thing"). For example, a state court would have jurisdiction to hear a dispute over the ownership of a piece of real estate located within the state. This is so even if one or more of the disputing parties live in another state or states.

Sometimes a plaintiff who obtains a judgment against a defendant in one state will try to collect the judgment by attaching property of the defendant that is located in another state. This is permitted under **quasi in rem**, or **attachment, jurisdiction**.[5]

Long-Arm Statutes In most states, a state court can obtain jurisdiction over persons and businesses located in another state or country through the state's **long-arm statute**. These statutes extend a state's jurisdiction to nonresidents who were not served a summons within the state. The nonresident must have had some *minimum contact* with the state. In addition, the maintenance of the suit must uphold the traditional notions of fair play and substantial justice.

The exercise of long-arm[6] jurisdiction is generally permitted over nonresidents who have (1) committed torts within the state (e.g., caused an automobile accident in the state), (2) entered into a contract either in the state or that affects the state (and allegedly breached the contract), or (3) transacted other business in the state that allegedly caused injury to another person.

Parties to a contract may include a **forum-selection clause** that designates a certain court to hear any dispute concerning nonperformance of the contract. In the following case, the U.S. Supreme Court upheld a forum-selection clause in a contract.

---

subject matter jurisdiction
Jurisdiction over the subject matter of a lawsuit.

in personam jurisdiction
Jurisdiction over the parties to a lawsuit.

service of process
A summons is served on the defendant to obtain personal jurisdiction over him or her.

in rem jurisdiction
Jurisdiction to hear a case because of jurisdiction over the property of the lawsuit.

quasi in rem jurisdiction
Jurisdiction allowed a plaintiff who obtains a judgment in one state to try to collect the judgment by attaching property of the defendant located in another state.

long-arm statute
A statute that extends a state's jurisdiction to nonresidents who were not served a summons within the state.

forum-selection clause
Contract provision that designates a certain court to hear any dispute concerning nonperformance of the contract.

Carnival Cruise Lines, Inc. v. Shute
499 U.S. 585, 111 S.Ct. 1522, 113 L.Ed.2d 622 (1991)
United States Supreme Court

CASE 2.1

FACTS
Mr. and Mrs. Shute, residents of the state of Washington, purchased passage for a seven-day cruise on the *Tropicale*, a cruise ship operated by the Carnival Cruise Lines, Inc.

(Carnival). They paid the fare to the travel agent, who forwarded the payment to Carnival's headquarters in Miami, Florida. Carnival prepared the tickets and sent them to the Shutes. Each ticket consisted of five pages, including

(case continues)

contract terms. The ticket contained a forum-selection clause that designated the state of Florida as the forum for any lawsuits arising under or in connection with the ticket and cruise. The Shutes boarded the *Tropicale* in Los Angeles, which set sail for Puerto Vallarta, Mexico. While the ship was on its return voyage and in international waters off the Mexican coast, Mrs. Shute was injured when she slipped on a deck mat during a guided tour of the ship's galley. Upon return to Washington, she filed a negligence lawsuit against Carnival in U.S. district court in Washington seeking damages. Carnival filed a motion for summary judgment contending that the suit could be brought only in a court located in the state of Florida. The district court granted Carnival's motion. The court of appeals reversed, holding that Mrs. Shute could sue Carnival in Washington. Carnival appealed to the U.S. Supreme Court.

ISSUE

Is the forum-selection clause in Carnival Cruise Lines' ticket enforceable?

IN THE LANGUAGE OF THE COURT

Blackmun, Justice   As an initial matter, we do not adopt the court of appeals' determination that a nonnegotiated forum-selection clause in a form ticket contract is never enforceable simply because it is not the subject of bargaining. Including a reasonable forum clause in form contract of this kind may well be permissible for several reasons: First, a cruise line has a special interest in limiting the fora in which it potentially could be sub-

ject to suit. Because a cruise ship typically carries passengers from many locales, it is not unlikely that a mishap on a cruise could subject the cruise line to litigation in several different fora.

Additionally, a clause establishing the forum for dispute resolution has the salutary effect of dispelling any confusion where suits arising from the contract must be brought and defended, sparing litigants the time and expense of pretrial motions to determine the correct forum, and conserving judicial resources that otherwise would be devoted to deciding those motions. Finally, it stands to reason that passengers who purchase tickets containing a forum clause like that at issue in this case benefit in the form of reduced fares reflecting the savings that the cruise line enjoys by limiting the fora in which it may be sued.

DECISION AND REMEDY

The forum-selection clause in Carnival's ticket is fair and reasonable and therefore enforceable against Mrs. Shute. If she wishes to sue Carnival, she must do so in a court in the state of Florida, not in a court in the state of Washington. The U.S. Supreme Court reversed the decision of the court of appeals.

Case Questions

Critical Legal Thinking   Should forum-selection clauses be enforced? Why or why not?

Ethics   Did Carnival Cruise Lines act ethically by placing the forum-selection clause in their tickets?

Business Application   Do forum-selection clauses serve any legitimate business purpose? Explain.

Venue

venue

A concept that requires lawsuits to be heard by the court with jurisdiction that is nearest the location in which the incident occurred or where the parties reside.

Venue requires lawsuits to be heard by the court with jurisdiction nearest the location in which the incident occurred or where the parties reside.

Consider This Example   Harry, a Georgia resident, commits a felony crime in Los Angeles County, California. The California Superior Court located in Los Angeles is the proper venue because the crime was committed there, the witnesses are probably from the area, and so on.

Occasionally, pretrial publicity may prejudice jurors located in the proper venue. In such cases, a *change of venue* may be requested so that a more impartial jury can be found. The courts generally frown upon *forum shopping* (i.e., looking for a favorable court without a valid reason).

Entrepreneur and the Law

COST-BENEFIT ANALYSIS OF A LAWSUIT

In most civil lawsuits each party is responsible for paying its own attorney's fees, whether the party wins or loses. This is called the "American rule."

The court can award attorney's fees to the winning party if a statute so provides, the parties have so agreed (e.g., in a contract), or the losing party has acted maliciously or pursued a frivolous case. Accused parties in criminal cases are responsible for paying their own attorney fees if they can afford to do so. If the accused is indigent, the government will provide an attorney (e.g., a public defender) free of charge.

An attorney in a civil lawsuit can represent the plaintiff on an hourly, project, or contingency fee basis. Hourly fees usually range from $75 to $500 per hour, depending on the type of case, the expertise of the lawyer, and the locality of the lawsuit. Under a *contingency fee arrangement*, the lawyer receives a percentage of the amount recovered for the plaintiff upon winning or settling the case. Contingency fees normally range from 20 to 50 percent of the award or settlement, with the average being about 35 percent. Lawyers for defendants in lawsuits are normally paid on an hourly basis.

The choice of whether to bring or defend a lawsuit should be analyzed like any other business decision. This includes performing a **cost-benefit analysis** of the lawsuit. For the plaintiff, it may be wise not to sue. For the defendant, it may be wise to settle. The following factors should be considered in deciding whether to bring or settle a lawsuit:

- The probability of winning or losing.
- The amount of money to be won or lost.
- Lawyers' fees and other costs of litigation.
- Loss of time by managers and other personnel.
- The long-term effects on the relationship and reputations of the parties.
- The amount of prejudgment interest provided by law.
- The aggravation and psychological costs associated with a lawsuit.
- The unpredictability of the legal system and the possibility of error.
- Other factors peculiar to the parties and lawsuit.

𝒯HE PRETRIAL LITIGATION PROCESS

The bringing, maintaining, and defense of a lawsuit are generally referred to as the **litigation process,** or **litigation**. The pretrial litigation process can be divided into the following major phases: *pleadings, discovery, dismissals and pretrial judgments,* and *settlement conference.* Each of these phases is discussed in the paragraphs that follow.

litigation
The process of bringing, maintaining, and defending a lawsuit.

The Pleadings

The paperwork that is filed with the court to initiate and respond to a lawsuit is referred to as the **pleadings**. The major pleadings are the *complaint,* the *answer,* the *cross-complaint,* and the *reply.*

pleadings
The paperwork that is filed with the court to initiate and respond to a lawsuit.

Complaint and Summons To initiate a lawsuit, the party who is suing (the **plaintiff**) must file a **complaint** with the proper court. The complaint must name the parties to the lawsuit, allege the ultimate facts and law violated, and contain a "prayer for relief" for a remedy to be awarded by the court. The complaint can be as long as necessary, depending on the case's complexity. A sample complaint appears in Exhibit 2.5.

plaintiff
The party who files the complaint.

Once a complaint has been filed with the court, the court issues a **summons**. A summons is a court order directing the defendant to appear in court and answer the complaint. The complaint and summons are served on the defendant by a sheriff, other government official, or a private process server.

complaint
The document the plaintiff files with the court and serves on the defendant to initiate a lawsuit.

summons
A court order directing the defendant to appear in court and answer the complaint.

Answer The defendant must file an **answer** to the plaintiff's complaint. The defendant's answer is filed with the court and served on the plaintiff. In the answer, the defendant admits or denies the allegations contained in the plaintiff's complaint. A judgment will be entered against a defendant who admits all of the allegations in the complaint. The case will proceed if the defendant denies all or some of the allegations. If the defendant does not answer the complaint, a *default judgment* is entered against him or her. A default judgment establishes the defendant's liability. The plaintiff then has only to prove damages.

answer
The defendant's written response to the plaintiff's complaint that is filed with the court and served on the plaintiff.

*E*XHIBIT 2.5 *A Sample Complaint*

In the United States District Court for the District of Idaho

John Doe   Civil No. 2-1001
     Plaintiff

     v.   COMPLAINT

Jane Roe
     Defendant

The plaintiff, by and through his attorney, alleges:

1. The plaintiff is a resident of the State of Idaho, the defendant is a resident of the State of Washington, and there is diversity of citizenship between the parties.
2. The amount in controversy exceeds the sum of $75,000, exclusive of interest and costs.
3. On January 10, 2000, plaintiff was exercising reasonable care while walking across the intersection of Sun Valley Road and Main Street, Ketchum, Idaho when defendant negligently drove his car through a red light at the intersection and struck plaintiff.
4. As a result of the defendant's negligence, plaintiff has incurred medical expenses of $104,000 and suf-fered severe physical injury and mental distress.

WHEREFORE, plaintiff claims judgment in the amount of $1,000,000 interest at the maximum legal rate, and costs of this action.

             By _____
                Edward Lawson
                Attorney for Plaintiff
                100 Main Street
                Ketchum, Idaho

In addition to answering the complaint, a defendant's answer can assert *affirmative defenses*. For example, if a complaint alleges that the plaintiff was personally injured by the defendant, the defendant's answer could state that he or she acted in self-defense. Another affirmative defense would be an assertion that the plaintiff's lawsuit is barred because the *statute of limitations* (time within which to bring the lawsuit) has expired.

cross-complaint
Filed by the defendant
against the plaintiff to seek
damages or some other
remedy.

Cross-Complaint and Reply A defendant who believes that he or she has been injured by the plaintiff can file a **cross-complaint** against the plaintiff in addition to an answer. In the cross-complaint, the defendant (now the *cross-complainant*) sues the plaintiff (now the *cross-defendant*) for damages or some other remedy. The original plaintiff must file a **reply** (answer) to the cross-complaint. The reply, which can include affirmative defenses, must be filed with the court and served on the original defendant.

reply
Filed by the original plaintiff
to answer the defendant's
cross-complaint.

Intervention and Consolidation If other persons have an interest in a lawsuit, they may **intervene** and become parties to the lawsuit. For instance, a bank that has made a secured loan on a piece of real estate can intervene in a lawsuit between parties who are litigating ownership of the property.

intervention
The act of others to join as
parties to an existing lawsuit.

If several plaintiffs have filed separate lawsuits stemming from the same fact situation against the same defendant, the court can **consolidate** the cases into one case if it would not cause undue prejudice to the parties. Suppose, for example, that a commercial airplane crashes, killing and injuring many people. The court could consolidate all of the lawsuits against the defendant airplane company.

consolidation
The act of a court to combine
two or more separate law-
suits into one lawsuit.

E-Commerce & Internet Law

e-biz

E-FILINGS IN COURT

When litigation ensues, the clients, lawyers, and judges involved in the case are usually buried in paper. These papers include pleadings, interrogatories, documents, motions to the court, briefs, and memorandums; the list goes on and on. By the time a case is over, reams of paper are stored in dozens, if not hundreds, of boxes. In addition, court appearances, no matter how small the matter, must be made in person. For example, lawyers often wait hours for a 10-minute scheduling or other conference with the judge. In addition is the time it takes to drive to and from court, which in an urban area may amount to hours.

Some forward-thinking judges and lawyers envision a day when the paperwork and hassle are reduced or eliminated in a "virtual courthouse." The technology is currently available for implementing electronic filing—**e-filing**—of pleadings, briefs, and other documents related to a lawsuit. E-filing would include using CD-ROMs for briefs, scanning evidence and documents into a computer for storage and retrieval, and e-mailing correspondence and documents to the court and the opposing counsel. Scheduling and other conferences with the judge or opposing counsel could be held via telephone conferences and e-mail.

Some courts have instituted e-filing. For example, in the Manhattan bankruptcy court, e-filing is now mandatory. Other courts around the world are doing the same. Companies such as Microsoft, West Group, and LEXIS-NEXIS have developed systems to manage e-filings of court documents.

Some court personnel are resisting the advancement of the electronic courthouse because they perceive it as a means of reducing personnel needs and court funding. Some lawyers are resisting e-filing because they have to learn how to deal with new technology and because it might reduce their billable hours when they no longer get paid for shuffling paper or sitting and waiting to appear before a judge. But eventually—albeit slowly—courts and lawyers will be brought into this new technological age.

Statute of Limitation

A **statute of limitation** establishes the period during which a plaintiff must bring a lawsuit against a defendant. If a lawsuit is not filed within this time period, the plaintiff loses his or her right to sue. A statute of limitations begins to "run" at the time the plaintiff first has the right to sue the defendant (e.g., when the accident happens, or when the breach of contract occurs).

> **statute of limitations**
> **A statute that establishes the period during which a plaintiff must bring a lawsuit against a defendant.**

Federal and state governments have established statutes of limitation for each type of lawsuit. Most are from one to four years, depending on the type of lawsuit. For example, a one-year statute of limitation is common for ordinary negligence actions. Thus, if on July 1, 2000, Otis negligently causes an automobile accident in which Cha-Yen is injured, Cha-Yen has until July 1, 2001, to bring a negligence lawsuit against Otis. If she waits longer than that, she loses her right to sue him.

In the following case, the court held that the statute of limitations barred the plaintiff's lawsuit.

Norgart v. the Upjohn Company
21 Cal.4ᵗʰ 383, 87 Cal.Rptr.2ⁿᵈ 453 (1999)
Supreme Court of California

CASE 2.2

FACTS
Kristi Norgart McBride lived with her husband in Santa Rosa, California. Kristi suffered from manic-depressive mental illness (now called bipolar disorder). In this disease, the person cycles between manic (ultrahappy, expansive, extrovert) episodes to depressive episodes. The disease is often treated with prescription drugs. In April 1984, Kristi attempted suicide. A psychiatrist prescribed an antianxiety

(case continues)

drug. In May 1985, Kristi attempted suicide again by overdosing on drugs. The doctor prescribed Halcion, an hypnotic drug, and added Darvocet-N, a mild narcotic analgesic. On October 16, 1985, after descending into a severe depression, Kristi committed suicide by overdosing on Halcion and Darvocet-N. On October 16, 1991, exactly six years after Kristi's death, Leo and Phyllis Norgart, Kristi's parents, filed a lawsuit against the Upjohn Company, the maker of Halcion, for wrongful death based on Upjohn's alleged failure to warn of the unreasonable dangers of taking Halcion. The trial court granted Upjohn's motion for summary judgment based on the fact that the one-year statute of limitations for wrongful death actions had run. The court of appeals reversed, and Upjohn appealed to the Supreme Court of California.

ISSUE

Is the plaintiffs' action for wrongful death barred by the one-year statute of limitations?

IN THE LANGUAGE OF THE COURT

Mosk, Justice   *Statute of limitations is the collective term commonly applied to a great number of acts that prescribe the periods beyond which a plaintiff may not bring a cause of action. It has a purpose to protect defendants from the stale claims of dilatory plaintiffs. It has as a related purpose to stimulate plaintiffs to assert fresh claims against defendants in a diligent fashion. Inasmuch as it necessarily fixes a definite period of time, it operates conclusively across the board and not flexibly on a case-by-case basis.*

Under the statute of limitations, a plaintiff must bring a cause of action from wrongful death within one year of accrual. The limitations period is thus defined by the Legislature. We believe that, at least as a usual matter, the general rule for defining the accrual of a cause of action should govern a cause of action for

wrongful death. That means that the date of accrual of a cause of action for wrongful death is the date of death. Under the statute of limitations, the Norgarts had to bring the cause of action for wrongful death within one year of accrual. They did not do so. Pursuant to this rule, the Norgarts were too late, exactly five years too late.

Finally, we reject any argument by the Norgarts that Upjohn was not entitled to judgment as a matter of law based on the statute of limitations because of the asserted meritoriousness of their cause of action for wrongful death. But, as stated, the statute of limitations necessarily fixes a definite period of time, and hence operates conclusively across-the-board. It does so with respect to all causes of action, both those that do not have merit and also those that do. That it may bar meritorious causes of action as well as unmeritorious ones is the price of the orderly and timely processing of litigation, a price that may be high, but one that must nevertheless be paid.

DECISION AND REMEDY

The supreme court of California held that the defendant, the Upjohn Company, was entitled to judgment as a matter of law based on the fact that the one-year statute of limitations for wrongful death actions had run, thus barring the plaintiffs' lawsuit. Reversed.

Case Questions

Critical Legal Thinking   What is the public policy behind having statutes of limitations? What is the public policy against having such statutes? Which policy should dominate and why?

Ethics   Was it ethical for the Upjohn Company to avoid facing the merits of the lawsuit by asserting the one-year statute of limitations?

Business Application   What are the business implications for having statutes of limitations?

---

discovery

A legal process during which both parties engage in various activities to discover facts of the case from the other party and witnesses prior to trial.

deposition

Oral testimony given by a party or witness prior to trial. The testimony is given under oath and is transcribed.

deponent

Party who gives his or her deposition.

Discovery

The legal process provides for a detailed pretrial procedure called **discovery**. During discovery, both parties engage in various activities to discover facts of the case from the other party and witnesses prior to trial. Discovery serves several functions, including preventing surprise, allowing parties to thoroughly prepare for trial, preserving evidence, saving court time, and promoting the settlement of cases. The major forms of discovery are as follows:

1. **Depositions**   A **deposition** is the oral testimony given by a party or witness prior to trial. The person giving the deposition is called the **deponent**. The *parties* to the lawsuit must give their depositions, if called upon by the other party to do so. The deposition of a *witness* can be given voluntarily or pursuant to a subpoena (court order). The deponent can be required to bring documents to the deposition. Most depositions are taken at the office of one of the attorneys. The deponent is placed under oath and then asked oral questions by one or both of the attorneys. The questions and answers are recorded in written form by a court reporter. Depositions can also be videotaped. The deponent is given an opportunity to correct his or her answers prior

to signing the deposition. Depositions are used to preserve evidence (e.g., if the deponent is deceased, ill, or is not otherwise available at trial) and impeach testimony given by witnesses at trial.

2. **Interrogatories** Interrogatories are written questions submitted by one party to a lawsuit to another party. The questions can be very detailed. In addition, it might be necessary to attach certain documents to the answers. A party is required to answer the interrogatories in writing within a specified time period (e.g., 60 to 90 days). An attorney usually helps with the preparation of the answers. The answers are signed under oath.

interrogatories
Written questions submitted by one party to another party. The questions must be answered in writing within a stipulated time.

3. **Production of Documents** Often, particularly in complex business cases, a substantial portion of the lawsuit may be based on information contained in documents (e.g., memoranda, correspondence, company records, and such). One party to a lawsuit may request that the other party produce all documents that are relevant to the case prior to trial. This is called a **production of documents**. If the documents sought are too voluminous to be moved, are in permanent storage, or would disrupt the ongoing business of the party who is to produce them, the requesting party may be required to examine the documents at the other party's premises.

production of documents
Request by one party to another party to produce all documents relevant to the case prior to trial.

4. **Physical and Mental Examination** In cases that concern the physical or mental condition of a party, a court can order the party to submit to certain **physical or mental examinations** to determine the extent of the alleged injuries. This would occur, for example, where the plaintiff has been injured in an accident and is seeking damages for physical injury and mental distress.

physical or mental examination
A court may order another party to submit to a physical or mental examination prior to trial.

Contemporary Business Application

CALENDARS ORDERED INTO THE DAYLIGHT

Most executives keep some form of calendar that contains lists of things to do, where to be, and what I've done notes. If a calendar contains business-related information exclusively, it is discoverable by the prosecution in a criminal case. If the calendar is personal in nature, its owner can shield it from discovery under the Fifth Amendment's self-discrimination privilege. What if an executive's calendar contains both business and personal information? Is it discoverable or not? The court had to decide this issue in the following case.

John Doe I and John Doe II are two executives of a company that is the subject of an ongoing grand jury investigation into possible illegal price fixing in a certain industry. Both executives kept calendars that contained both business and personal notes. The grand jury sought production of the calendars, but the executives refused to produce them, alleging Fifth Amendment protection. After examining the evidence, the district court determined that the calendars were corporate in nature and ordered them disclosed. The court also issued an order holding the executives in contempt for their failure to turn over their calendars. The executives appealed.

The court of appeals decided that where a calendar contains a mixture of business and personal notes, a multifactor approach should be applied to determine if they are discoverable. The court will look at ownership, preparation, access, content, purpose, and ratio of business to personal entries in determining whether a document is corporate or personal in nature. This balancing test asks, What is the essential nature of the document? No single factor is dispositive, and the final determination whether the calendar is business or personal in nature is a question of fact.

Applying this multifactor approach to the instant case, the court found that the executives' calendars contained a majority of business-related entries. There were notes concerning business travel, job-related "to do" lists, and compensation at work. The court found that the executives' self-serving affidavits to the contrary were not credible. The court of appeals stated, "In the totality of these circumstances, the district court's conclusion that the daytimers were prepared, maintained, and used for business, not personal purposes, is not clearly erroneous." The court held that the executives' calendars were discoverable and were not protected by the Fifth Amendment's privilege against self-incrimination. [*In Re Grand Jury Proceedings*, 55 F.3d 1012 (1995)]

E-Commerce & Internet Law

DIGITAL DISCOVERY

E-mail has made it faster and easier to communicate with others, whether for business or personal reasons. E-mail messages have also become a source of evidence to be used at both criminal and civil trials. Consider the following case.

Karen Strauss worked for Microsoft Corporation as an assistant editor for the *Microsoft Systems Journal.* When she was passed over for a promotion and then subsequently dismissed from her job, she brought a sex discrimination case against Microsoft. She alleged that her supervisor, Jon Lazarus, sexually harassed her by making certain remarks and sending messages to her by e-mail. She alleged that Lazarus referred to another woman in the office as "Spandex Queen," told another woman that he would pay her $500 if he could call her "Sweet Georgia Brown," and referred to himself as the "president of the Amateur Gynecology Club." Strauss also wanted to introduce e-mail evidence that Lazarus followed these remarks with e-mail messages to Strauss containing a satirical essay entitled "Alice in UNIX Land," an advertisement for the replacement of "Mouse Balls," and a parody on a play entitled *A Girl's Guide to Condoms.*

The e-mail messages had been erased, but the plaintiff retrieved them from backup tapes automatically made by the company's computer network.

Microsoft made a motion to the court to preclude this evidence, including the e-mail messages, from being introduced at trial. The district court denied Microsoft's motion. The court stated that the e-mail messages, when viewed in light of Strauss's other evidence, could lead a reasonable jury to conclude that Microsoft engaged in the challenged conduct. The court noted that although the e-mail messages may be embarrassing to Microsoft, such evidence is admissible. The court stated, "The Federal Rules of Evidence favor placing even the nastier side of human nature before the jury if to do so would aid its search for the truth." The court permitted Strauss to sue Microsoft for sexual harassment using the e-mail messages as evidence.

As e-mail continues to increase in use, it will become a greater—and very tangible—source of evidence at criminal and civil trials. [*Strauss v. Microsoft Corporation*, 68 Fair Empl. Prac. Cases (BNA) 1576 (S.D.N.Y. 1995)]

---

pretrial motion

A motion a party can make to try to dispose of all or part of a lawsuit prior to trial.

motion for judgment on the pleadings

Motion that alleges that if all the facts presented in the pleadings are taken as true, the party making the motion would win the lawsuit when the proper law is applied to these asserted facts.

motion for summary judgment

Motion that asserts that there are no factual disputes to be decided by the jury; if so, the judge can apply the proper law to the undisputed facts and decide the case without a jury. These motions are supported by affidavits, documents, and deposition testimony.

Dismissals and Pretrial Judgments

There are several **pretrial motions** that parties to a lawsuit can make to try to dispose of all or part of a lawsuit prior to trial. The two major pretrial motions are:

1. **Motion for Judgment on the Pleadings**   A **motion for judgment on the pleadings** can be made by either party once the pleadings are complete. This motion alleges that if all of the facts presented in the pleadings are true, the party making the motion would win the lawsuit when the proper law is applied to these facts. In deciding this motion, the judge cannot consider any facts outside the pleadings.

2. **Motion for Summary Judgment**   The trier of the fact (i.e., the jury, or, if there is no jury, the judge) determines *factual issues.* **A motion for summary judgment** asserts that there are no factual disputes to be decided by the jury and that the judge should apply the relevant law to the undisputed facts to decide the case. Motions for summary judgment, which can be made by either party, are supported by evidence outside the pleadings. Affidavits from the parties and witnesses, documents (e.g., a written contract between the parties), depositions, and such are common forms of evidence. If, after examining the evidence, the court finds no factual dispute, it can decide the issue or issues raised in the summary judgment motion. This may dispense with the entire case or with part of the case. If the judge finds that a factual dispute exists, the motion will be denied and the case will go to trial.

Settlement Conference

Federal court rules and most state court rules permit the court to direct the attorneys or parties to appear before the court for a **pretrial hearing**, or **settlement conference**. One of the major purposes of such hearings is to facilitate the settlement of the case. Pretrial conferences are often held informally in the judge's chambers. If no settlement is reached, the pretrial hearing is used to identify the major trial issues and other relevant factors. More than 90 percent of all cases are settled before they go to trial.

pretrial hearing
A hearing before the trial in order to facilitate the settlement of a case. Also called a *settlement conference.*

Gold Phoenix, Indonesia. Religious beliefs are often reflected in a nation's laws. For example, the Jewish, Hindu, and Islamic religions provide the basis for many nations' laws, such as those of Israel, India, and Egypt, respectively.

THE TRIAL

Pursuant to the Seventh Amendment to the U.S. Constitution, a party to an action at law is guaranteed the right to a *jury trial* in cases in federal court.[7] Most state constitutions contain a similar guarantee for state court actions. If either party requests a jury, the trial will be by jury. If both parties waive their right to a jury, the trial will be without a jury. The judge sits as the **trier of fact** in nonjury trials. At the time of trial, the parties usually submit **trial briefs** to the judge that contain legal support for their side of the case.

Trials are usually divided into the following phases:

1. **Jury Selection** The pool of the potential jurors is usually selected from voter or automobile registration lists. Individuals are selected to hear specific cases through the process called **voir dire** ("to speak the truth"). Lawyers for each party and the judge can ask prospective jurors questions to determine if they would be biased in their decision. Biased jurors can be prevented from sitting on a particular case. Once the appropriate number of jurors is selected (usually 6 to 12 jurors), they are *impaneled* to hear the case and are sworn in. The trial is ready to begin. A jury can be *sequestered* (i.e., separated from family, etc.) in important cases. Jurors are paid minimum fees for their service.

2. **Opening Statements** Each party's attorney is allowed to make an **opening statement** to the jury. In opening statements, attorneys usually summarize the main factual and legal issues of the case and describe why they believe their client's position is valid. The information given in this statement is not considered as evidence.

trier of fact
The jury in a jury trial; the judge where there is not a jury trial.

trial briefs
Documents submitted by the parties' attorneys to the judge that contain legal support for their side of the case.

voir dire
Process whereby prospective jurors are asked questions by the judge and attorneys to determine if they would be biased in their decision.

opening statements
Statements made by the attorneys to the jury in which they summarize the factual and legal issues of the case.

burden of proof
The plaintiff bears the burden of proving the allegations made in his complaint.

plaintiff's case
Process by which the plaintiff introduces evidence to prove the allegations contained in his or her complaint.

defendant's case
Process by which the defendant (1) rebuts the plaintiff's evidence, (2) proves affirmative defenses, and (3) proves allegations made in a cross-complaint.

closing arguments
Statements made by the attorneys to the jury at the end of the trial to try to convince the jury to render a verdict for their client.

jury instructions
Instructions given by the judge to the jury that informs them of the law to be applied in the case.

jury deliberation
Process by which the jury retires to the jury room and deliberates its findings.

verdict
Decision reached by the jury.

judgment
The official decision of the court.

judgment notwithstanding the verdict (j.n.o.v.)
In a civil case, the judge may overturn the jury's verdict if he or she finds bias or jury misconduct.

3. **The Plaintiff's Case**   Plaintiffs bear the **burden of proof** to persuade the trier of the fact of the merits of their case. This is called the **plaintiff's case**. The plaintiff's attorney will call witnesses to give testimony. After a witness has been sworn in, the plaintiff's attorney examines (i.e., questions) the witness. This is called *direct examination*. Documents and other evidence can be introduced through each witness. After the plaintiff's attorney has completed his or her questions, the defendant's attorney can question the witness. This is called *cross-examination*. The defendant's attorney can ask questions only about the subjects that were brought up during the direct examination. After the defendant's attorney completes his or her questions, the plaintiff's attorney can ask questions of the witness. This is called *redirect examination*. The defendant's attorney can then again ask questions of the witness. This is called *recross examination*.

4. **The Defendant's Case**   The **defendant's case** proceeds after the plaintiff has concluded his or her case. The defendant's case must (1) rebut the plaintiff's evidence, (2) prove any affirmative defenses asserted by the defendant, and (3) prove any allegations contained in the defendant's cross-complaint. The defendant's witnesses are examined in much the same way as the plaintiff's attorney cross-examines each witness. This is followed by redirect and recross examination.

5. **Rebuttal and Rejoinder**   After the defendant's attorney has completed calling witnesses, the plaintiff's attorney can call witnesses and put forth evidence to rebut the defendant's case. This is called a *rebuttal*. The defendant's attorney can call additional witnesses and introduce other evidence to counter the rebuttal. This is called the *rejoinder*.

6. **Closing Arguments**   At the conclusion of the evidence, each party's attorney is allowed to make a **closing argument** to the jury. Both attorneys try to convince the jury to render a verdict for their client by pointing out the strengths in the client's case and the weaknesses in the other side's case. Information given by the attorneys in their closing statements is not evidence.

7. **Jury Instructions**   Once the closing arguments are completed, the judge reads **jury instructions** (or **charges**) to the jury. These instructions inform the jury about what law to apply when they decide the case. For example, in a criminal trial the judge will read the jury the statutory definition of the crime charged. In an accident case, the judge will read the jury the legal definition of *negligence*.

8. **Jury Deliberation**   The jury then retires to the jury room to deliberate its findings. This can take from a few minutes to many weeks. After deliberation, the jury will announce its **verdict**. In a civil case, the jury also assesses damages. The judge assesses penalties in criminal cases.

9. **Entry of Judgment**   After the jury has returned its verdict, in most cases the judge will enter **judgment** to the successful party based on the verdict. This is the official decision of the court. The court may, however, overturn the verdict if it finds bias or jury misconduct. This is called a **judgment notwithstanding the verdict** or **judgment n.o.v.** or **j.n.o.v.** In a civil case, the judge may reduce the amount of monetary damages awarded by the jury if he or she finds the jury to have been biased, emotional, or inflamed. This is called *remittitur*. The trial court usually issues a *written memorandum* setting forth the reasons for the judgment. This memorandum, together with the trial transcript and evidence introduced at trial, constitutes the permanent *record* of the trial court proceeding.

In the following case, the court was asked to grant a judgment notwithstanding the verdict.

Ferlito v. Johnson & Johnson Products, Inc.
771 F.Supp. 196 (1991)
United States District Court, E.D. Michigan

CASE 2.3

FACTS
Susan and Frank Ferlito were invited to a Halloween party. They decided to attend as Mary (Mrs. Ferlito) and her little lamb (Mr. Ferlito). Mrs. Ferlito constructed a lamb costume for her husband by gluing cotton batting manufactured by Johnson & Johnson Products, Inc. (JJP), to a suit of long underwear. She used the same cotton batting to fashion a headpiece, complete with ears. The costume covered Mr. Ferlito from his head to his ankles, except for his face and hands, which were blackened with paint. At the party, Mr. Ferlito attempted to light a cigarette with a butane lighter. The flame passed close to his left arm, and the cotton batting ignited. He suffered burns over one-third of his body. The Ferlitos sued JJP to recover damages, alleging that JJP failed

to warn them of the ignitability of cotton batting. The jury returned a verdict for Mr. Ferlito in the amount of $555,000 and for Mrs. Ferlito in the amount of $70,000. JJP filed a motion for judgment notwithstanding the verdict (j.n.o.v.).

ISSUE
Should defendant JJP's motion for j.n.o.v. be granted?

IN THE LANGUAGE OF THE COURT
Gadola, District Judge If after reviewing the evidence, however, the trial court is of the opinion that reasonable minds could not come to the result reached by the jury, then the motion for j.n.o.v. should be granted. In this action no reasonable jury could find that JJP's failure to warn of the flammability of cotton batting was a proximate cause of plaintiffs' injuries because plaintiffs failed to offer any evidence to establish that a flammability warning on JJP's cotton batting would have dissuaded them from using the product in the manner that they did. In addition, both plaintiffs testified that they knew that cotton batting burns when it is exposed to flame.

Susan Ferlito testified that the idea for the costume was hers alone. As described on the product's package, its intended uses are for cleansing, applying medications, and infant care. Plaintiffs' showing that the product may be used on occasion in classrooms for decorative purposes failed to demonstrate the foreseeability of an adult male encapsulating himself from head to toe in cotton batting and then lighting up a cigarette.

DECISION AND REMEDY
The trial court granted defendant JJP's motion for j.n.o.v. By doing so, the court vacated the verdict entered by the jury in favor of Mr. and Mrs. Ferlito.

Case Questions
Critical Legal Thinking Should trial courts have the authority to enter a j.n.o.v., or should jury verdicts always be allowed to stand? Explain your answer.

Ethics Did the Ferlitos act ethically in suing JJP in this case? Were they responsible for their own injuries?

Business Applications What would have been the business implications had JJP been found liable?

THE APPEAL

In a civil case, either party can **appeal** the trial court's decision once a *final judgment* is entered. Only the defendant can appeal in a criminal case. The appeal is made to the appropriate appellate court. A *notice of appeal* must be filed within a prescribed time after judgment is entered (usually within 60 or 90 days). The appealing party is called the **appellant**, or **petitioner**. The responding party is called the **appellee**, or **respondent**. The appellant is often required to post a bond (e.g., one-and-one-half times the judgment) on appeal.

The parties may designate all or relevant portions of the trial record to be submitted to the appellate court for review. The appellant's attorney may file an *opening brief* with the court that sets forth legal research and other information to support his or her contentions on appeal. The appellee can file a *responding brief* answering the appellant's contentions. Appellate courts usually permit a brief oral argument at which each party's attorney is heard.

An appellate court will reverse a lower court decision if it finds an *error of law* in the record. An error of law occurs if the jury was improperly instructed by the trial court judge, prejudicial evidence was admitted at trial when it should have been excluded, prejudicial evidence was obtained through an unconstitutional search and seizure, and the like. An appellate court will not reverse a *finding of fact* unless such finding is unsupported by the evidence or is contradicted by the evidence.

appeal
The act of asking an appellate court to overturn a decision after the trial court's final judgment has been entered.

appellant
The appealing party in an appeal. Also known as *petitioner*.

appellee
The responding party in an appeal. Also known as *respondent*.

Business Brief
Trial court decisions are overturned on appeal only if there has been an error of law or the decision is not supported by the evidence.

E-Commerce & Internet Law

OBTAINING PERSONAL JURISDICTION IN CYBERSPACE

Obtaining personal jurisdiction over a defendant located in another state has always been a difficult issue for the courts. States have enacted long-arm statutes that permit the courts located in one state to reach out and make people in another state come to court and defend themselves. To make sure this is not

(box continues)

overly burdensome, the U.S. Supreme Court has held that out-of-state defendants must have had certain "minimum contacts" with the state before they are made to answer to a lawsuit there [*International Shoe Co. v. Washington*, 326 U.S. 310, 66 S.Ct. 154 (1945)]. Today, with the advent of the Internet and the ability of persons and businesses to reach millions of people in other states electronically, the application of the *International Shoe* minimum contacts standard is even more difficult.

Several courts have decided cases involving the reach of a state's long-arm statute to obtain jurisdiction over someone in another state because of his or her Internet activities. In one case, Zippo Manufacturing Company (Zippo) sued Zippo Dot Com, Inc. (Dot Com) in federal district court in Pennsylvania. Zippo manufactures its well known line of Zippo tobacco lighters in Bradford, Pennsylvania, and sells them worldwide. Dot Com, a California corporation with its principal place of business and its servers located in Sunnyvale, California, operates an Internet Web site that transmits information and sexually explicit material to its subscribers. Three thousand of Dot Com's 140,000 paying subscribers worldwide are located in Pennsylvania. Zippo sued Dot Com in federal district court in Pennsylvania for trademark infringement. Dot Com alleged that it was not subject to personal jurisdiction in Pennsylvania. The district court applied the *International Shoe* "minimum contacts" standard and held that Dot Com was subject to personal jurisdiction under the Pennsylvania long-arm statute and

e·biz

ordered Dot Com to defend itself there. [*Zippo Manufacturing Company v. Zippo Dot Com, Inc.*, 952 F.Supp. 1119 (W.D.Pa. 1997)]

In another case, the court held that maintaining a passive Web site that merely provides advertising and other information is not sufficient to draw the Web site operator into another state's courts. The case involved Circus Circus Hotel (Circus Circus), a hotel and casino located in Las Vegas, Nevada, which maintains an Internet Web site advertising its services. Janice and Robert Decker, two New Jersey residents, brought a lawsuit against Circus Circus in federal district court in New Jersey for alleged personal injuries suffered at the Las Vegas hotel. On Circus Circus's motion, the district court dismissed the action, finding that Circus Circus's passive Web site did not subject it to personal jurisdiction in New Jersey even though its advertisements were seen by the Deckers in New Jersey. The court held that mere Internet advertising, without selling products or services over the Internet, does not meet *International Shoe's* minimum contacts standard necessary to haul a defendant into court. [*Decker v. Circus Circus Hotel*, 49 F.Supp.2d 743 (D.N.J. 1999)].

Courts will be faced with thousands of lawsuits that involve the issue of when a state's long-arm statute can reach into cyberspace and make an out-of-state Web site owner respond to a lawsuit in that state. The *International Shoe* "minimum contacts" standard is in for a whole new application.

*A*LTERNATIVE DISPUTE RESOLUTION

The use of the court system to resolve business and other disputes can take years and cost thousands, if not millions, of dollars in legal fees and expenses. In commercial litigation, the normal business operations of the parties are often disrupted. To avoid or lessen these problems, businesses are increasingly turning to methods of **alternative dispute resolution (ADR)** and other aids to resolving disputes. The most common form of ADR is *arbitration*. Other forms of ADR are *mediation, conciliation, minitrial, fact-finding*, and a *judicial referee*.

Arbitration

In **arbitration**, the parties choose an impartial third party to hear and decide the dispute. This neutral party is called the *arbitrator*. Arbitrators are usually selected from members of the American Arbitration Association (AAA) or another arbitration association. Labor union agreements, franchise agreements, leases, and other commercial contracts often contain **arbitration clauses** that require disputes arising out of the contract to be submitted to arbitration. If there is no arbitration clause, the parties can enter into a *submission agreement* whereby they agree to submit a dispute to arbitration after the dispute arises.

alternative dispute resolution (ADR)
Methods of resolving disputes other than litigation.

arbitration
A form of ADR in which the parties choose an impartial third party to hear and decide the dispute.

arbitration clause
A clause in contracts that requires disputes arising out of the contract to be submitted to arbitration.

Evidence and testimony are presented to the arbitrator at a hearing held for this purpose. Less formal evidentiary rules are usually applied in arbitration hearings than at court. After the hearing, the arbitrator reaches a decision and enters an *award*. The parties often agree in advance to be bound by the arbitrator's decision and award. If the parties have not so agreed, the arbitrator's award can be appealed to court. The court gives great deference to the arbitrator's decision.

Congress enacted the **Federal Arbitration Act** to promote the arbitration of disputes.[8] About half of the states have adopted the **Uniform Arbitration Act**. This act promotes the arbitration of disputes at the state level. Many federal and state courts have instituted programs to refer legal disputes to arbitration or another form of alternative dispute resolution.

> **Business Brief**
> Litigation is expensive and time-consuming. Businesses should consider ADR to solve their disputes.

Contemporary Business Application

THE FEDERAL ARBITRATION ACT

The **Federal Arbitration Act (FAA)** was originally enacted in 1925 to reverse the long-standing judicial hostility to arbitration agreements that had existed as English common law and had been adopted by American courts. The act provides that arbitration agreements involving commerce are valid, irrevocable, and enforceable contracts, unless some grounds exist at law or equity (e.g., fraud, duress) to revoke them. The FAA permits one party to obtain a court order to compel arbitration if the other party has failed, neglected, or refused to comply with an arbitration agreement.

Since the FAA's enactment, the courts have wrestled with the problem of which types of disputes should be arbitrated. Breach of contract cases, tort claims, and such are clearly candidates for arbitration if there is a valid arbitration agreement. In addition, the U.S. Supreme Court has enforced arbitration agreements that call for the resolution of disputes arising under federal statutes. For example, in *Shearson/American Express, Inc. v. McMahon*, 482 U.S. 220 (1987), and *Rodriguez de Quijas v. Shearson/American Express, Inc.*, 490 U.S. 4777 (1990), the Court held that certain civil claims arising under federal securities laws and the Racketeer Influenced and Corrupt Organizations Act (RICO) were arbitrative. In these cases, the Court enforced arbitration clauses contained in customer agreements with the securities firm.

In another case, *Gilmer v. Interstate/Johnson Lane Corporation*, Ill. S.Ct. 1647 (1991), the Supreme Court upheld an arbitration clause in an employment contract. In that case, a 62-year-old employee who was dismissed from his job sued his employer for alleged age discrimination in violation of the federal Age Discrimination in Employment Act (ADEA). The employer countered with a motion to compel arbitration. The Supreme Court upheld the motion and stated, "By agreeing to arbitrate a statutory claim, a party does not forgo the substantive rights afforded by the statute, it only submits to their resolution in an arbitral, rather than a judicial, forum."

The Court did not find any reason to revoke the contract. There was no indication that the employee was coerced or defrauded into agreeing to the arbitration clause at issue in the case.

Because the Supreme Court has placed its imprimatur on the use of arbitration to solve employment disputes, it is likely that such clauses will appear in more employment contracts. Critics contend that this gives the advantage to employers. Employers argue that arbitration is the only way to combat skyrocketing jury verdicts.

Mediation and Conciliation

In **mediation**, the parties choose a neutral third party to act as the *mediator* of the dispute. Unlike an arbitrator, a mediator does not make a decision or award. Instead, the mediator acts as a conveyor of information between the parties and assists them in trying to reach a settlement of the dispute. A mediator often meets separately with each of the parties. A

> **mediation**
> A form of ADR in which the parties choose a *neutral* third party to act as the mediator of the dispute.

conciliation
A form of mediation in which the parties choose an *interested* third party to act as the mediator.

settlement agreement is reached if the mediator is successful. If not, the case proceeds to trial. In a **conciliation**, the parties choose an interested third party, the *conciliator*, to act as the mediator.

Minitrial

A *minitrial* is a session, usually lasting a day or less, in which the lawyers for each side present their cases to representatives of each party who have authority to settle the dispute. In many cases, the parties hire a neutral person (e.g., a retired judge) to preside over the minitrial. Following the presentations, the parties meet to try to negotiate a settlement.

Fact-Finding

We're the jury, dread our fury!
William S. Gilbert
Trial by Jury

Fact-finding is a process whereby the parties hire a neutral person to investigate the dispute. The *fact-finder* reports his or her findings to the adversaries and may recommend a basis for settlement.

Judicial Referee

If the parties agree, the court may appoint a *judicial referee* to conduct a private trial and render a judgment. Referees, who are often retired judges, have most of the powers of a trial judge, and their decisions stand as a judgment of the court. The parties usually reserve their right to appeal.

International Perspective

COMPARISON OF THE JAPANESE AND AMERICAN LEGAL SYSTEMS

Businesses often complain that there are too many lawyers and too much litigation in the United States. There are currently more than 800,000 lawyers and over 20 million lawsuits per year in this country. On the other hand, in Japan, a country with about half the population, there are only 15,000 lawyers and little litigation. Why the difference?

Much of the difference is cultural: Japan nurtures the attitude that confrontation should be avoided. Litigious persons in Japan are looked down upon. Thus, companies rarely do battle in court. Instead, they opt for private arbitration of most of their disputes.

Other differences are built into the legal system itself. For example, there is only one place to go to become a *bengoshi*, or lawyer, in Japan—the government-operated National Institute for Legal Training. Only 2 percent of 35,000 applicants are accepted annually, and only 400 new *bengoshi* are admitted to Japan's exclusive legal club per year.

There are other obstacles, too. For example, no class actions or contingency fee arrangements are allowed.

Plaintiffs must pay their lawyers a front fee of up to 8 percent of the damages sought, plus a nonrefundable filing fee to the court of one-half of 1 percent of the damages. To make matters even more difficult, no discovery is permitted. Thus, plaintiffs are denied access before trial to an opponent's potential evidence. And, even if the plaintiff wins the lawsuit, damage awards are low.

Some experts argue that Japan has more legal practitioners than the statistics reveal. For example, there are approximately 5,000 non*bengoshi* patent specialists who perform services similar to U.S. patent attorneys. Another 50,000 licensed tax practitioners offer services similar to U.S. tax attorneys. Many non*bengoshi* legal experts handle tasks such as contract negotiation and drafting. In addition, sales personnel and front-line managers often act as problem solvers.

The Japanese bias against courtroom solutions remains strong. The current system is designed to save time and money and to preserve long-term relationships. The belief that disputes can be solved amicably without litigation is a concept American businesses are starting to embrace.

Working the Web

U.S. Supreme Court   The U.S. Supreme Court does not have its own Web site at this time. Cornell University maintains a site that features recent decisions and selected historic decisions of the U.S. Supreme Court. You can search for decisions by date, party, and subject.

Visit at **supct.law.cornell.edu/supct**

U.S. Courts of Appeals   The U.S. Courts of Appeals do not have their own Web sites at this time. The Emory School of Law is your gateway to various circuit courts whose Web sites are located at different universities. Most include a syllabus and summaries of decisions for recent cases and one or more ways to search for the decisions.

Visit at **www.law.emory.edu**

U.S. District Courts   Some U.S. District Courts publish their opinions on the Internet. The Villanova Center for Information Law and Policy is also a gateway to those decisions.

Visit at **www.vls.law.vill.edu/Locator/fedcourt.html**

State Courts   State courts are far ahead of the federal government when it comes to creating and maintaining their own Web sites. There are a number of places with links to state court information. Many state courts have their own Web pages.

Visit at **www.vls.law.vill.edu/Locator/statecourt.htm**

> **Note**: Although many sites are adding retrospective cases all the time, most cases that can be found on the Internet are *current decisions*. To find older decisions, you will have to use traditional research methods, i.e. books, or computer-assisted legal research databases such as LEXIS and WESTLAW.

> **Note**: Many lower state court decisions and municipal court decisions are not reported anywhere including the Internet. Some information about these decisions on "hot" topics can be found in news archives on the Internet and by using news-based databases such as NEXIS.

American Arbitration Association   Information on alternative dispute resolution can be found on the American Arbitration Association Web site. This site contains information on labor relations, employment, commerce, and international disputes. It includes rules, forms, and articles about alternative dispute resolution.

Visit at **www.adr.org**

CYBER EXERCISES

1. Using the Cornell Web site, click on the *Gallery of Current Justices*. Read the biography of Justice Ginsburg.

2. Using the Emory gateway, find the U.S. Court of Appeals for the circuit in which your state is located. Find a recent decision.

3. Using the Emory gateway, find out if any U.S. District Courts for your state publish opinions on the Internet. List the courts and dates of coverage for each court.

4. Find the home page for courts in your state. Which courts in your state are reporting cases on the Internet? What are the dates of coverage for each court in your state?

5. Using the American Arbitration Association Web site, click on *Customer Service*. Find a form for *Submission to Dispute Resolution*.

*C*ASES AND *E*XERCISES

CRITICAL LEGAL THINKING CASES

2.1. Nutrilab, Inc. (Nutrilab), manufactures and markets a product known as "Starch Blockers." The purpose of the product is to block the human body's digestion of starch as an aid in controlling weight. On July 1, 1982, the U.S. Food and Drug Administration (FDA) classified Starch Blockers as a drug and requested that it be removed from the market until the FDA approved of its use. The FDA claimed that it had the right to classify new products as drugs and prevent their distribution until their safety is determined. Nutrilab disputes the FDA's decision and wants to bring suit to halt the FDA's actions. Do the federal courts have jurisdiction to hear this case? [*Nutrilab, Inc. v. Schweiker*, 713 F.2d 335 (7th Cir. 1983)]

2.2. James Clayton Allison, a resident of the state of Mississippi, was employed by the Tru-Amp Corporation as a circuit breaker tester. As part of his employment, Allison was sent to inspect, clean, and test a switch gear located at the South Central Bell Telephone Facility in Brentwood, Tennessee. On August 26, 1988, he attempted to remove a circuit breaker manufactured by ITE Corporation (ITE) from a bank of breakers, when a portion of the breaker fell off. The broken piece fell behind a switching bank and, according to Allison, caused an electrical fire and explosion. Allison was severely burned in the accident. Allison brought suit against ITE in a Mississippi state court, claiming more than $50,000 in damages. Can this suit be removed to federal court? [*Allison v. ITE Imperial Corp.*, 729 F.Supp. 45 (S.D. Miss. 1990)]

2.3. Saul and Elaine Mozuck borrowed money from the Peoples Trust Company of Bergen County (Peoples Trust) and cosigned a promissory note promising to repay the money. When Peoples Trust contacted the Mozucks about payment, they denied liability on the grounds that the bank improperly filled in the due date on the note. Peoples Trust filed suit against the Mozucks in a New Jersey state court. A process server went to the Mozucks' home in New Jersey to serve the summons. The process server rang the bell at the home and a woman appeared at the upstairs window. The process server asked her if she was Mrs. Mozuck, and the woman replied in the affirmative. When the process server identified himself, the woman denied that she was Mrs. Mozuck and refused to come out of the house. The process server told the woman that he would leave the papers in the mailbox if she refused to open the door. When the woman did not reappear, the process server placed the summons in the mailbox and left. Is the service of process good? [*Peoples Trust Co. v. Mozuck*, 236 A.2d 630 (N.J.Super. 1967)]

2.4. Sean O'Grady, a professional boxer, was managed by his father, Pat. Sean was a contender for the world featherweight title. On January 30, 1978, Pat entered into a contract with Magna Verde Corporation (Magna Verde), a Los Angeles-based business, to copromote a fight between Sean and the current featherweight champion. The fight was scheduled to take place on February 5, 1978, in Oklahoma

City, Oklahoma. To promote the fight, Pat O'Grady scheduled a press conference for January 30, 1978. At the press conference, Pat was involved in a confrontation with a sportswriter named Brooks. He allegedly struck Brooks in the face. Brooks brought suit against Pat O'Grady and Magna Verde in Oklahoma state court. Court records showed that the only contact Magna Verde had with Oklahoma was that a few of its employees had taken several trips to Oklahoma in January 1978 to plan the title fight. The fight was never held. Oklahoma has a long-arm statute. Magna Verde was served by mail and made a special appearance in Oklahoma state court to argue that Oklahoma does not have the personal jurisdiction over it. Does Oklahoma have jurisdiction over Magna Verde Corporation? [*Brooks v. Magna Verde Corp.*, 619 P.2d 1271 (Okla.App. 1980)]

2.5. The National Enquirer, Inc., is a Florida corporation with its principal place of business in Florida. It publishes the *National Enquirer*, a national weekly newspaper with a total circulation of more than 5 million copies. About 600,000 copies, almost twice the level of the next highest state, are sold in California. On October 9, 1979, the *Enquirer* published an article about Shirley Jones, an entertainer. Jones, a California resident, filed a lawsuit in California state court against the *Enquirer* and its president, who was a resident of Florida. The suit sought damages for alleged defamation, invasion of privacy, and intentional infliction of emotional distress. Are the defendants subject to suit in California? [*Calder v. Jones*, 465 U.S. 783, 104 S.Ct. 1482, 79 L.Ed.2d 804 (1984)]

2.6. On May 9, 1983, attorneys for Ronald Schiavone filed a lawsuit against *Fortune* magazine in U.S. district court in New Jersey. The complaint claimed that *Fortune* had defamed Schiavone in a cover story entitled "The Charges against Reagan's Labor Secretary," which appeared in the May 31, 1982, issue of the magazine. The complaint named *Fortune* as the defendant. *Fortune*, however, is only a trademark owned by Time, Incorporated, a New York corporation. Time, Incorporated, refused to accept service of the complaint because it had not been named as a defendant. Has there been proper service of process? [*Schiavone v. Fortune*, 477 U.S. 21, 106 S.Ct. 2379, 91 L.Ed.2d 18 (1986)]

2.7. Dennis and Francis Burnham were married in 1976 in West Virginia. In 1977, the couple moved to New Jersey, where their two children were born. In July 1987, the Burnhams decided to separate. Mrs. Burnham, who intended to move to California, was to have custody of the children. Mr. Burnham agreed to file for divorce on grounds of "irreconcilable differences." In October 1987, Mr. Burnham threatened to file for divorce in New Jersey on grounds of "desertion." After unsuccessfully demanding that Mr. Burnham adhere to the prior agreement, Mrs. Burnham brought suit for divorce in California state court in early January 1988. In late January, Mr. Burnham visited California on a business trip. He then visited his children in the San Francisco Bay area, where his wife resided. He took the older child to San Francisco for the weekend. Upon returning the child to Mrs. Burnham's home, he was served with a California court summons and a copy of Mrs. Burnham's divorce petition. He then returned to New Jersey. Mr. Burnham made a special appearance in the California court and moved to quash the service of process. Is the service of process good? [*Burnham v. Superior Court of California*, 495 U.S. 604, 110 S.Ct. 2105, 109 L.Ed.2d 631 (1990)]

2.8.   Captain Conrad was a pilot for Delta Airlines. In 1970, Conrad was forced to resign by the airline. He sued, alleging that he was discharged due to his prounion activities and not because of poor job performance as claimed by Delta. During discovery, a report written by a Delta flight operations manager was produced that stated: "More than a few crew members claimed that Conrad professed to being a leftist-activist. His overactivity with the local pilots' union, coupled with inquiries regarding company files to our secretary, lead to the conclusion that potential trouble will be avoided by acceptance of his resignation." Conrad claims that the report is evidence of the antiunion motivation for his discharge. Delta made a summary judgment motion to the trial court. Should its summary judgment motion be granted? [*Conrad v. Delta Airlines, Inc.*, 494 F.2d 914 (7th Cir. 1974)]

2.9.   Robert Schlagenhauf worked as a bus driver for the Greyhound Corporation (Greyhound). One night the bus he was driving rear-ended a tractor-trailer. Seven passengers on the bus who were injured sued Schlagenhauf and Greyhound for damages. The complaint alleged that Greyhound was negligent for allowing Schlagenhauf to drive a bus when it knew that his eyes and vision "were impaired and deficient." The plaintiffs petitioned the court to order Schlagenhauf to be medically examined concerning these allegations. Schlagenhauf objected to the examination. Who wins? [*Schlagenhauf v. Holder*, 379 U.S. 104, 85 S.Ct. 234, 13 L.Ed.2d 152 (1964)]

2.10.   Haviland & Company filed suit against Montgomery Ward & Company (Ward) in U.S. district court claiming that Ward used the trademark "Haviland" on millions of dollars' worth of merchandise. As the owner of the mark, Haviland & Company sought compensation from Ward. Ward served notice to take the deposition of Haviland & Company's president, William D. Haviland. The attorneys

for Haviland told the court that Haviland was 80 years old, lived in France, and was too ill to travel to the United States for the deposition. Haviland's physician submitted an affidavit confirming these facts. Must Haviland give his deposition? [*Haviland & Co. v. Montgomery Ward & Co.*, 31 F.R.D. 578 (S.D.N.Y. 1962)]

2.11.   Cine Forty-Second Street Theatre Corporation (Cine) operates a movie theater in New York City's Times Square area. Cine filed a lawsuit against Allied Artists Pictures Corporation (Allied Artists) alleging that Allied Artists and local theater owners illegally attempted to prevent Cine from opening its theater, in violation of federal antitrust law. This suit also alleged that once Cine opened the theater, the defendants conspired with motion picture distributors to prevent Cine from exhibiting first-run, quality films. Attorneys for Allied Artists served a set of written questions concerning the lawsuit on Cine. Does Cine have to answer these questions? [*Cine Forty-Second Street Theatre Corp. v. Allied Artists Pictures Corp.*, 602 F.2d 1062 (2d Cir. 1979)]

2.12.   On November 9, 1965, Mr. Simblest was driving a car that collided with a fire engine at an intersection in Burlington, Vermont. The accident occurred on the night on which a power blackout left most of the state without lights. Mr. Simblest, who was injured in the accident, sued the driver of the fire truck for damages. During the trial, Simblest testified that when he entered the intersection, the traffic light was green in his favor. All of the other witnesses testified that the traffic light had gone dark at least 10 minutes before the accident. Simblest testified that the accident was caused by the fire truck's failure to use any warning lights or sirens. Simblest's testimony was contradicted by four witnesses who testified that the fire truck had used both its lights and sirens. The jury found that the driver of the fire truck had been negligent and rendered a verdict for Simblest. The defense made a motion for judgment n.o.v. Who wins? [*Simblest v. Maynard*, 427 F.2d 1 (2d Cir. 1979)]

2.13.   AMF Incorporated and Brunswick Corporation both manufacture electric and automatic bowling center equipment. In 1983 the two companies became involved in a dispute over whether Brunswick had advertised certain automatic scoring devices in a false and deceptive manner. The two parties settled the dispute by signing an agreement that any future problems between them involving advertising claims would be submitted to the National Advertising Council for arbitration. In March 1985, Brunswick advertised a new product, Armor Plate 3000, a synthetic laminated material used to make bowling lanes. Armor Plate 3000 competed with wooden lanes produced by AMF. Brunswick's advertisements claimed that bowling centers could save up to $500 per lane per year in maintenance and repair costs if they switched to Armor Plate 3000 from wooden lanes. AMF disputed this claim and requested arbitration. Is the arbitration agreement enforceable? [*AMF Incorporated v. Brunswick Corp.*, 621 F.Supp. 456 (E.D.N.Y. 1985)]

ETHICS CASES

2.14.   One day Joshua Gnaizda, a three-year-old, received what he (or his mother) thought was a tantalizing offer in the mail from Time, Inc. (Time). The front of the envelope contained a see-through window that revealed the following statement: "Joshua Gnaizda, I'll give you this versatile new calculator watch free just for opening this envelope before February 15, 1985." Beneath the offer was a picture of the calculator watch itself. When Joshua's mother opened the envelope, she realized that the see-through window had not revealed the full text of Time's offer. Not viewable through the see-through window were the following words: "And mailing this certificate today." The certificate required Joshua to purchase a subscription to *Fortune* magazine to receive the free calculator watch. Joshua (through his father, a lawyer) sued Time in a class action, seeking compensatory damages in an amount equal to the value of the calculator watch and $15 million in punitive damages. The trial court dismissed the lawsuit as being too trivial for the court to hear. Joshua appealed. Should Joshua be permitted to maintain his lawsuit against Time, Inc.? Did Time act ethically? Should Joshua's father have sued for $15 million? [*Harris v. Time, Inc.*, 191 C.A.3d 449, 237 Cal.Rptr. 584 (Cal. App. 1987)]

2.15.   For some years prior to 1972, Robert C. Vesco engaged in a fraudulent scheme whereby he misappropriated hundreds of millions of dollars from investors in the United States. On June 7, 1973, International Controls Corporation (ICC) filed a lawsuit in U.S. district court in New York against Vesco, alleging violations of federal securities laws. By that time, Vesco had moved to Nassau, the Bahamas. ICC's New York counsel, Lois S. Yohonn, applied to Judge Stewart of the U.S. district court for an order permitting her to personally serve Vesco in Nassau. If personal service could not be effected, she sought an alternative order that would permit service by leaving the summons and complaint at Vesco's last-known address in the Bahamas and then mailing a copy of the papers to that address. Judge Stewart signed both orders.

Miss Yohonn proceeded to Nassau on July 28, 1973. She spent two days searching for Vesco at various locations but was unsuccessful in finding him. On July 30, she drove to Vesco's residence, where she found a bolted gate protected by two bodyguards. They refused to let her in and chased her away. She went back to her hotel and telephoned Judge Stewart, who authorized her to effect service according to the terms of the ancillary order. Miss Yohonn returned to Vesco's residence. There, she threw a copy of the summons and complaint folded and tied with a blue ribbon over the fence and photographed the papers as they remained on the lawn in front of the house. The two guards, one armed with a pipe and the other with a stick, chased her. As she drove away, the guards got in their car and pursued her until she managed to lose them. Miss Yohonn returned to the United States on July 31, and on August 1 mailed a copy of the summons and complaint to Vesco at his Bahamas residence. Vesco challenged the service of process. Is the service of process good? Is it ethical to "dodge" service of process? [*International Controls Corp. v. Vesco*, 593 F.2d 166 2d Cir. (1979)]

CRITICAL LEGAL THINKING WRITING ASSIGNMENT

Read Case A.2 in the Case Appendix [*Gnazzo v. G.D. Searle & Co.*]. This case is excerpted from the court of appeals opinion. Review and brief the case. In your brief, be sure to answer the following questions.

1. What is a statute of limitations? What purposes are served by such a statute?

2. What was the Connecticut statute of limitations for the injury alleged by the plaintiff?

3. What is summary judgment? When will it be granted?

4. What was the decision of the trial court? Of the court of appeals?

5. Was the decision fair? Should the plaintiff have been granted her day in court against the defendant?

NOTES

1. Federal Courts Improvement Act of 1982. Pub. L. 97–164, 96 Stat. 25, 28 U.S.C. § 1292 and § 1295.

2. Effective September 25, 1988, mandatory appeals were all but eliminated except for reapportionment cases and cases brought

under the Civil Rights and Voting Rights Acts, antitrust laws, and the Presidential Election Campaign Fund Act.

3. Prior to 1980, there was a minimum dollar amount controversy requirement of $10,000 to bring a federal question action in federal court. This minimum amount was eliminated by the Federal Question Jurisdictional Amendment Act of 1980, Public Law 96-486.

4. The amount was raised from $50,000 to $75,000 by the 1996 Federal Courts Improvement Act.

5. Under the **Full Faith and Credit Clause** of the U.S. Constitution, a judgment of a court in one state must be given "full faith and credit" by the courts of another state. Article IV, Section 1.

6. *International Shoe Co. v. Washington*, 326 U.S. 310, 66 S.Ct. 154, 90 L.Ed. 95 (1945).

7. There is no right to a jury trial for actions in equity (e.g., injunctions, specific performance).

8. 9 U.S.C. §§ 1 et seq.

3

Constitutional Authority to Regulate Business

The nation's armour of defence against the passions of men is the Constitution. Take that away, and the nation goes down into the field of its conflicts like a warrior without armour.

HENRY WARD BEECHER
Proverbs from Plymouth Pulpit, 1887

Chapter Objectives

After studying this chapter, you should be able to

1. Describe the concept of federalism and the doctrine of separation of powers.
2. Define and apply the Supremacy Clause of the U.S. Constitution.
3. Explain the federal government's authority to regulate foreign commerce.
4. Explain the federal government's authority to regulate interstate commerce.
5. Explain how speech is protected by the First Amendment.
6. Describe how commercial speech may be regulated by proper time, place, and manner restrictions.
7. Describe how the Internet is protected by the Freedom of Speech Clause.
8. Describe the freedom of religion provided by the First Amendment.
9. Describe substantive and procedural due process.
10. Explain the doctrine of equal protection.

Chapter Contents

Prior to the American Revolution, each of the 13 original colonies operated as a separate sovereignty under the rule of England. In September 1774, representatives of the colonies met as a Continental Congress. In 1776, the colonies declared independence from England and the American Revolution ensued. In 1778, the Continental Congress formed a *federal government* and adopted the **Articles of Confederation**. The Articles of Confederation created a federal Congress composed of representatives of the 13 new states.

The Articles of Confederation was a particularly weak document that gave limited power to the newly created federal government. For example, it did not provide Congress with the power to levy and collect taxes, to regulate commerce with foreign countries, or to regulate interstate commerce among the states.

The **Constitutional Convention** was convened in Philadelphia in May 1787. The primary purpose of the Convention was to strengthen the federal government. After substantial debate, the delegates agreed to a new **U.S. Constitution**. The Constitution was reported to Congress in September 1787. State ratification of the Constitution was completed in 1788. Many amendments, including the **Bill of Rights** have been added to the Constitution since that time.

This chapter examines the major provisions of the U.S. Constitution and the amendments that have been adopted to the Constitution. Of particular importance, this chapter discusses how these provisions affect the operation of business in this country. The Constitution, with amendments, is set forth as Appendix A to this book.

The Constitution of the United States is not a mere lawyers' document: it is a vehicle of life, and its spirit is always the spirit of the age.

Woodrow Wilson
Constitutional Government in the United States *69 (1927)*

U.S. Constitution
The fundamental law of the United States of America. It was ratified by the states in 1788.

*T*HE CONSTITUTION OF THE UNITED STATES OF AMERICA

The U.S. Constitution serves two major functions:

1. It creates the three branches of the federal government (i.e., the executive, legislative, and judicial branches) and allocates powers to these branches.
2. It protects individual rights by limiting the government's ability to restrict those rights.

The Constitution itself provides that it may be amended to address social and economic changes.

The American Constitution is, so far as I can see, the most wonderful work ever struck off at a given time by the brain and purpose of man.

W. E. Gladstone
Kin Beyond Sea *(1878)*

Basic Constitutional Concepts

Federalism and Delegated Powers   Our country's form of government is referred to as **federalism**. That means that the federal government and the 50 state governments share powers.

When the states ratified the Constitution, they *delegated* certain powers to the federal government. They are called **enumerated powers**. The federal government is authorized to deal with national and international affairs. Any powers that are not specifically delegated to the federal government by the Constitution are reserved to the state governments. State governments are empowered to deal with local affairs.

federalism
The U.S. form of government; the federal government and the 50 state governments share powers.

enumerated powers
Certain powers delegated to the federal government by the states.

The Doctrine of Separation of Powers   As mentioned previously, the federal government is divided into three branches:

1. **Article I** of the Constitution establishes the **legislative branch** of government. This branch is bicameral; that is, it consists of the Senate and the House of Representatives. Collectively, they are referred to as *Congress*.[1] Each state has two senators. The number of representatives to the House of Representatives is determined according to the population of each state. The current number of representatives is determined from the 1990 census.

legislative branch
The part of the government that consists of Congress (the Senate and the House of Representatives).

The United States is the world's leading democracy. The country, however, has had many blemishes on its citizens' constitutional rights. For example, during World War II Japanese Americans were involuntarily placed in camps. During the McCarthy hearings of the 1950s, citizens who were communists or associated with communists were "blackballed" from their occupations, most notably in the film industry. And it was not until the mid-1960s that equal opportunity laws outlawed discrimination in the workplace based on race and sex.

executive branch

The part of the government that consists of the President and Vice President.

judicial branch

The part of the government that consists of the Supreme Court and other federal courts.

Business Brief

Checks and balances is the way the U.S. Constitution prevents any one of the three branches of the government from becoming too powerful.

Supremacy Clause

A clause of the U.S. Constitution that establishes that the federal Constitution, treaties, federal laws, and federal regulations are the supreme law of the land.

preemption doctrine

The concept that federal law takes precedent over state or local law.

2. **Article II** of the Constitution establishes the **executive branch** of government by providing for the election of the President and Vice President. The President is not elected by popular vote but instead is selected by the *Electoral College*, whose representatives are appointed by state delegations.[2]

3. Article III establishes the **judicial branch** of the government by establishing the Supreme Court and providing for the creation of other federal courts by Congress.[3]

Checks and Balances   Certain **checks and balances** are built into the Constitution to ensure that no one branch of the federal government becomes too powerful. Some of the checks and balances in our system of government are

1. The judicial branch has authority to examine the acts of the other two branches of government and determine whether these acts are constitutional.[4]

2. The executive branch can enter into treaties with foreign governments only with the advice and consent of the Senate.

3. The legislative branch is authorized to create federal courts and determine their jurisdiction and to enact statutes that change judicially made law.

The Supremacy Clause

The **Supremacy Clause** establishes that the federal Constitution, treaties, federal laws, and federal regulations are the supreme law of the land.[5] State and local laws that conflict with valid federal law are unconstitutional. The concept of federal law taking precedent over state or local law is commonly called the **preemption doctrine**.

Congress may expressly provide that a particular federal statute *exclusively* regulates a specific area or activity. No state or local law regulating the area or activity is valid if there is such a statute. More often, though, federal statutes do not expressly provide for exclusive jurisdiction. In these instances, state and local governments have *concurrent jurisdiction* to regulate the area or activity. However, any state or local law that "directly and substantially" conflicts with valid federal law is preempted under the Supremacy Clause.

In the following case, the U.S. Supreme Court held that a state law was unconstitutional because it conflicted with a valid federal statute.

Capital Cities Cable, Inc. v. Crisp, Director, Oklahoma Alcoholic Beverage Control Board
467 U.S. 691, 104 S.Ct. 2694, 81 L.Ed.2d 580 (1984)
United States Supreme Court

CASE 3.1

FACTS

The Federal Communications Act (Act) authorizes the Federal Communications Commission (FCC) to regulate television and radio broadcasts in this country. The FCC adopted a regulation that requires cable television operators to transmit all signals "in full, without deletion or alteration of any portion," including commercials. A provision in the Oklahoma state constitution prohibited the advertising of alcoholic beverages within the state. Many out-of-state cable broadcasts contain alcoholic beverage commercials. When the director of the Oklahoma Alcoholic Beverage Control Board (Board) threatened to criminally prosecute cable operators that televised out-of-state alcoholic beverage commercials in the state, Capital Cities Cable, Inc., and other cable operators sued the Board, alleging that the Oklahoma law was preempted by federal law. The U.S. district court held for the cable operators, but the U.S. court of appeals reversed. The cable operators appealed to the U.S. Supreme Court.

ISSUE

Is the provision in the Oklahoma constitution that prohibits the advertising of alcoholic beverage commercials by cable operators preempted by federal law?

IN THE LANGUAGE OF THE COURT

Brennan, Justice Under the Supremacy Clause, the enforcement of a state regulation may be preempted by federal law when compliance with both state and federal law is impossible, or when the state law stands as an obstacle to the accomplishment and execution of the full purposes and objectives of Congress.

The Oklahoma advertising ban plainly conflicts with specific federal regulations. Consequently, those Oklahoma cable operators required by federal law to carry out-of-state broadcast signals in full, including any alcoholic beverage commercials, are subject to criminal prosecution under Oklahoma law as a result of their compliance with federal regulations. Since the Oklahoma law, by requiring deletion of a portion of these out-of-state signals, compels conduct that federal law forbids, the state ban clearly stands as an obstacle to the accomplishment and execution of the full purposes and objectives of the federal regulatory scheme.

In the FCC's view, uniform national communications policy with respect to cable systems would be undermined if state and local governments were permitted to regulate in piecemeal fashion the signals carried by cable operators pursuant to federal authority. On the other hand, application of Oklahoma's advertising ban to out-of-state signals carried by cable operators in that state is designed principally to further the state's interest in discouraging consumption of intoxicating liquor. When this limited interest is measured against the significant interference with the federal objective of ensuring widespread availability of diverse cable services throughout the United States—an objective that will unquestionably be frustrated by strict enforcement of the Oklahoma statute—it is clear that the state's interest is not of the same stature as the goals identified in the FCC's rulings and regulations. The balance between state and federal power tips decisively in favor of the federal law, and enforcement of the state statute is barred by the Supremacy Clause.

DECISION AND REMEDY

In a unanimous opinion, the U.S. Supreme Court held that the provision in the Oklahoma constitution directly and substantially conflicted with a valid federal regulation and was therefore unconstitutional under the Supremacy Clause of the U.S. Constitution.

Case Questions

Critical Legal Thinking Should federal law preempt state and local law? Why or why not? What would be the effect if the Supremacy Clause were not part of the U.S. Constitution?

Ethics Should state law, such as Oklahoma's ban on alcoholic beverage advertising on television, be used to promote a moral view?

Business Application What would have been the economic consequences to cable operators if the Oklahoma law in this case had been upheld?

Ethical Perspective

CIGARETTE COMPANIES ASSERT SUPREMACY CLAUSE

Business persons often complain that there are too many laws. In some cases business executives actually like a law because it works in their favor, however. Consider the following case.

Rose Cipollone began smoking cigarettes in 1942, when she was 17 years old. She continued to smoke between one and two packs of cigarettes per day until the early 1980s. Cipollone first smoked Chesterfield cigarettes, manufactured by Liggett Group, Inc., because they made her feel "glamorous," like the "pretty girls and movie stars" depicted in Chesterfield advertisements. She then switched to L&M filter cigarettes, also made by Liggett Group, because the "miracle tip" filter "was the new thing and I figured it was better—the bad stuff would stay in the filter." Cipollone subsequently switched to Virginia Slims cigarettes manufactured by Philip Morris, Inc., "because [the product] was very glamorous and had very attractive ads." Finally, she smoked Parliament cigarettes, also made by Philip Morris, because they had a "recessed" filter that she thought made them healthier than other brands.

In 1981, Cipollone was diagnosed with lung cancer. Even though her doctor advised her to quit smoking, she was unable to do so. Cipollone continued to smoke heavily until June 1982 when her lung was removed, but even after that she smoked in secret. She only stopped smoking in 1983, after she had become terminally ill with cancer. On August 1, 1983, she sued those cigarette manufacturers for personal injuries. Cipollone died on October 21, 1984, but her heirs continued to prosecute the case.

Since 1965, the Federal Cigarette Labeling and Advertising Act has required cigarette manufacturers to place on cigarette packages a warning of the dangers of smoking. The act requires one of the following warning labels, which must be rotated every quarter, to be placed on each cigarette package after the words "SURGEON GENERAL'S WARNING":

1. *Smoking Causes Lung Cancer, Heart Disease, Emphysema, and May Complicate Pregnancy*
2. *Cigarette Smoke Contains Carbon Monoxide*

3. *Quitting Smoking Now Greatly Reduces Serious Risks to Your Health*
4. *Smoking by Pregnant Women May Result in Fetal Injury, Premature Birth, and Low Birth Weight*

The cigarette company defendants argued that the warnings on cigarette packages—which are mandated by the Federal Cigarette Labeling and Advertising Act—preempted Cipollone's state tort action against them. The district court ruled in the defendants' favor, and the court of appeals affirmed. Cipollone's heirs appealed to the U.S. Supreme Court.

The Supreme Court held that the act preempted Cipollone's state law claims based on failure to warn of the dangers of smoking. The Court held that the Federal Cigarette Labeling and Advertising Act was a valid federal law that, under the Supremacy Clause of the U.S. Constitution, took precedent over conflicting state law failure to warn claims. The Supreme Court affirmed the court of appeals as to this issue.

The Supreme Court did, however, rule that the act did not bar lawsuits against cigarette companies for claims based on fraudulent misrepresentation or conspiracy among cigarette companies to misrepresent or conceal material facts about the dangers of cigarette smoking. Therefore, if they can prove fraud—that is, intentional conduct whereby the cigarette companies knew of the dangers of cigarette smoking and either lied to the public or concealed this information—smokers can win against cigarette companies. The Supreme Court reversed the court of appeals and allowed Cipollone's heirs to proceed against the defendants on this issue. Worn down, Cipollone's heirs dropped the lawsuit after this U.S. Supreme Court ruling. [*Cipollone v. Liggett Group, Inc.*, 112 S.Ct. 2608 (1992)]

1. Do you think cigarette companies knew of the dangers of smoking during the time period that Cipollone smoked? Did they conceal this information from her?
2. What would be the economic consequences if courts held cigarette companies liable to injured smokers? Who would gain? Who would suffer?

Commerce Clause

A clause of the U.S. Constitution that grants Congress the power "to regulate commerce with foreign nations, and among the several states, and with Indian tribes."

THE COMMERCE CLAUSE

The **Commerce Clause** of the U.S. Constitution grants Congress the power "to regulate commerce with foreign nations, and among the several states, and with Indian tribes."[6] Because this clause authorizes the federal government to regulate commerce, it has a greater impact on business than any other provision in the Constitution. Among other things, this clause is intended to foster the development of a national market and free trade among the states.

Federal Regulation of Foreign Commerce

The Commerce Clause gives the federal government the exclusive power to regulate commerce with foreign nations. Direct and indirect regulation of *foreign commerce* by local governments is a violation of this clause. For example, the federal government could prohibit the sale of music and video CDs from the People's Republic of China because of that country's lax enforcement of intellectual property laws (e.g., copyright law), but the state of California could not take the same actions.

Federal Regulation of Interstate Commerce

The Commerce Clause also gives the federal government the authority to regulate **interstate commerce**. Originally, the courts interpreted this clause to mean that the federal government could only regulate commerce that moved *in* interstate commerce. The modern rule, however, allows the federal government to regulate activities that *affect* interstate commerce.

Under the **effects on interstate commerce test**, the regulated activity does not itself have to be in interstate commerce. Thus, any local (*intrastate*) activity that has an effect on interstate commerce is subject to federal regulation. Theoretically, this test subjects a substantial amount of business activity in the United States to federal regulation.

For example, in the famous case of *Wickard, Secretary of Agriculture v. Filburn*,[7] a federal statute limited the amount of wheat that a farmer could plant and harvest for home consumption. Filburn, a farmer, violated the law. The U.S. Supreme Court upheld the statute on the grounds that it prevented nationwide surpluses and shortages of wheat. The Court reasoned that wheat grown for home consumption would affect the supply of wheat available in interstate commerce.

> **Business Brief**
> The Commerce Clause gives the federal government the exclusive power to regulate commerce with foreign nations.

> **interstate commerce**
> Commerce that moves between states or that affects commerce between states.

> **Business Brief**
> The federal government may regulate:
> 1. *Interstate* commerce that crosses state borders.
> 2. *Intrastate* commerce that affects interstate commerce.

Contemporary Business Application

SUPREME COURT IMPOSES LIMITATIONS ON THE FEDERAL GOVERNMENT'S COMMERCE CLAUSE POWERS

In 1990, the Congress enacted the Gun-Free School Zone Act (Act), a federal statute that made it a crime "for any individual knowingly to possess a firearm at a place that the individual knows, or has reasonable cause to believe, is a school zone." On March 10, 1992, Alfonso Lopez, Jr., a 12th-grade student at Edison High School in San Antonio, Texas, arrived at school carrying a concealed .38 caliber handgun and five bullets. After being caught and arrested, he was charged with violating the Act. The trial court found the defendant guilty and sentenced him to six months' imprisonment. The court of appeals reversed, holding that the Act did not regulate "interstate commerce" and was therefore an unconstitutional exercise of the federal government's power under the Commerce Clause of the Constitution. The U.S. Supreme Court agreed to hear an appeal.

Is the possession of a gun in a local school zone a commercial activity that substantially affects interstate commerce? No. The U.S. Supreme Court held that the Act neither regulates commercial activity nor requires that the possession of a firearm be connected in any way to interstate commerce.

Although in the past the Supreme Court has permitted expanded congressional power under the Commerce Clause, in this case the Court held that the federal government had exceeded the outer limits of this power. The Supreme Court noted that under the Commerce Clause the federal government can regulate the channels and instrumentalities of interstate commerce and activities having a substantial effect on interstate commerce. The Supreme Court found that the activity of carrying a gun in a local school zone does not involve a channel or instrumentality of interstate commerce or have a substantial effect on interstate commerce. The Court concluded that the Act was invalid as beyond the power of Congress under the Commerce Clause. [*United States v. Lopez*, 115 S.Ct. 1624 (1995)]

police power

The power of states to regulate private and business activity within their borders.

Business Brief

States may enact laws that protect or promote the public health, safety, morals, and general welfare as long as the law does not unduly burden interstate commerce.

Business Brief

State and local governments may regulate:

1. *Intrastate* commerce.

2. *Interstate* commerce not exclusively regulated by the federal government.

State and Local Government Regulation of Business—State "Police Power"

The states did not delegate all power to regulate business to the federal government. They retained the power to regulate *intrastate* and much interstate business activity that occurs within their borders. This is commonly referred to as states' **police power**.

Police power permits states (and, by delegation, local governments) to enact laws to protect or promote the *public health, safety, morals, and general welfare*. This includes the authority to enact laws that regulate the conduct of business. Zoning ordinances, state environmental laws, corporation and partnership laws, and property laws are enacted under this power.

State and local laws cannot **unduly burden interstate commerce**. If they do, they are unconstitutional because they violate the Commerce Clause. For example, if the federal government has chosen not to regulate an area that it has the power to regulate (*dormant Commerce Clause*), but the state does regulate it, the state law cannot unduly burden interstate commerce.

In the following case, the court had to determine whether an action by a local government constituted an undue burden on interstate commerce in violation of the Commerce Clause.

Fort Gratiot Sanitary Landfill, Inc. v. Michigan Department of Natural Resources
112 S.Ct. 2019, 119 L.Ed.2d 139 (1992)
United States Supreme Court

CASE 3.2

FACTS

In 1988, the state of Michigan added the Waste Import Restrictions to its Solid Waste Management Act. These restrictions prohibited privately owned landfills in the state from accepting solid wastes (e.g., garbage, rubbish, sludges, and industrial waste) from any source outside the county in which the landfill was located unless the county expressly permitted it. Fort Gratiot Sanitary Landfill, Inc. (Fort Gratiot), submitted an application to the county government to allow it to accept up to 1,750 tons per day of out-of-state solid waste. The county rejected the application. Fort Gratiot sued the county and state, alleging that the Waste Import Restrictions violated the Commerce Clause of the U.S. Constitution. The U.S. district court concluded that the restrictions did not discriminate against interstate commerce. The U.S. court of appeals agreed. The U.S. Supreme Court granted review.

ISSUE

Do Michigan's Waste Import Restrictions violate the Commerce Clause?

IN THE LANGUAGE OF THE COURT

Stevens, Justice Solid waste, even if it has no value, is an article of commerce. The Commerce Clause thus imposes some con-

straints on Michigan's ability to regulate these transactions. The "negative" or "dormant" aspect of the Commerce Clause prohibits states from advancing their own commercial interests by curtailing the movement of articles of commerce, either into or out of the state. A state statute that clearly discriminates against interstate commerce is therefore unconstitutional unless the discrimination is demonstrably justified by a valid factor unrelated to economic protectionism.

Michigan and St. Clair County assert that the Waste Import Restrictions are necessary because they enable individual counties to make adequate plans for the safe disposal of future waste. Although accurate forecasts about the volume and composition of future waste flows may be an indispensable part of a comprehensive waste disposal plan, Michigan could attain that objective without discriminating between in- and out-of-state waste. Michigan could, for example, limit the amount of waste that landfill operators may accept each year. There is, however, no valid health and safety reason for limiting the amount of waste that a landfill operator may accept from outside the State, but not the amount that the operator may accept from inside the State. Of course, our conclusion would be different if the imported waste raised health or other concerns not presented by Michigan waste.

The Waste Import Restrictions enacted by Michigan authorize each of its 83 counties to isolate itself from the national *economy. The Court has consistently found parochial legislation of this kind to be constitutionally invalid. For the foregoing reasons, the Waste Import Restrictions unambiguously discriminate against interstate commerce and are appropriately characterized as protectionist measures that cannot withstand scrutiny under the Commerce Clause.*

DECISION AND REMEDY

The Supreme Court held that the Waste Import Restrictions discriminated against interstate commerce in violation of the Commerce Clause of the U.S. Constitution.

Case Questions

Critical Legal Thinking Do you think some states will "export" their wastes to other states rather than provide landfills within their own boundaries?

Ethics Is it ethical for a state to prohibit wastes from other states to be dumped within its boundaries? Was the state of Michigan acting in "good faith"?

Business Application What effect will the Supreme Court's ruling have on landfill operators? Would your answer be different if the restriction had been found constitutional?

E-Commerce & Internet Law

FEDERAL TELECOMMUNICATIONS ACT PREEMPTS STATE AND LOCAL LAWS

Congress enacted the **Federal Telecommunications Act of 1996 (FTA)** to increase competition within the telecommunications industry. In addition to deregulating the telephone industry, the FTA prohibits state and local governments from blocking freedom of entry into the burgeoning telecommunications industry. To accomplish this goal, **Section 253** of the FTA prohibits any state or local government laws that "prohibit or have the effect of prohibiting the ability of any entity to provide any interstate or intrastate telecommunications service." Because the FTA is federal law, under the Supremacy Clause of the U.S. Constitution, it preempts any state or local law that conflicts with its provisions. Consider the following case.

Prince George's County, Maryland, enacted a county ordinance that required telecommunications firms to obtain a franchise from the county to use its rights-of-way, imposed a $5,000 application fee, charged three percent of the franchisee's gross revenues, and gave the county sole discretion to deny the franchise. Bell Atlantic-Maryland, Inc. (Bell Atlantic), a telecommunications company, sued Prince George's County in federal district court, alleging that the county ordinance violated the FTA and was preempted by the Supremacy Clause.

The court agreed with plaintiff Bell Atlantic. The court held that the county's ordinance went way beyond the county's authority to recover legitimate costs of maintaining the county's rights-of-way and instead was a general rev-enue-raising tax statute. The court also determined that the local government did not have the authority to keep out telecommunications companies because that authority was granted by Congress to the Federal Communications Commission (FCC), a federal administrative agency that oversees telecommunications for the nation. In finding that the county's ordinance was preempted by the FTA, the court stated:

It was Congress's intention that market competition, rather than state or local regulations, would primarily determine which companies would provide the telecommunications services demanded by consumers. To carry out this goal, Congress adopted sweeping restrictions on the authority of state and local governments to limit the ability of telecommunications companies to do business in local markets. Congress's intent was to remove all barriers to entry in the provision of telecommunications services by preempting all state and local requirements that directly or indirectly prohibit market entry.

Thus, the federal government under its Commerce Clause powers choose to regulate the national telecommunications industry by the passage of the FTA. In doing so, the federal government preempted any state or local laws that conflict with this federal law. [*Bell Atlantic-Maryland, Inc. v. Prince George's County, Maryland*, 49 F.Supp.2d 805 (D.Md. 1999)]

e-biz

THE BILL OF RIGHTS AND BUSINESS

Business Brief

The first 10 amendments to the Constitution are called the Bill of Rights. They were added to the U.S. Constitution in 1791.

In 1791, the 10 amendments that are commonly referred to as the **Bill of Rights** were approved by the states and became part of the U.S. Constitution. The Bill of Rights guarantees certain fundamental rights to natural persons and protects these rights from intrusive government action. Most of these rights have also been found applicable to so-called artificial persons (i.e., corporations).

In addition to the Bill of Rights, 17 other amendments have been added to the Constitution. These amendments cover a variety of things. For instance, they have abolished slavery, prohibited discrimination, authorized a federal income tax, given women the right to vote, and specifically recognized that persons 18 years of age and older have the right to vote.

Originally, the Bill of Rights limited intrusive action by the *federal government* only. Intrusive actions by state and local governments were not limited until the **Due Process Clause of the Fourteenth Amendment** was added to the Constitution in 1868. The Supreme Court has applied the **incorporation doctrine** and held that most of the fundamental guarantees contained in the Bill of Rights are applicable to state and local government action. The amendments to the Constitution that are most applicable to business are discussed in the paragraphs that follow.

incorporation doctrine

A doctrine that says that most fundamental guarantees contained in the Bill of Rights are applicable to state and local government action.

Freedom of Speech

freedom of speech

The right to engage in oral, written, and symbolic speech protected by the First Amendment.

One of the most honored freedoms guaranteed by the Bill of Rights is the **freedom of speech** of the First Amendment. Many other constitutional freedoms would be meaningless without it. The First Amendment's Freedom of Speech Clause protects speech only, not conduct. The U.S. Supreme Court places speech into three categories: (1) *fully protected*, (2) *limited protected*, and (3) *unprotected speech*.

I disapprove of what you say, but I will defend to the death your right to say it.

Voltaire

Fully Protected Speech   **Fully protected speech** is speech that the government cannot prohibit or regulate. Political speech is an example of such speech. For example, the government could not enact a law that forbids citizens from criticizing the current administration. The First Amendment protects oral, written, and symbolic speech.

offensive speech

Speech that is offensive to many members of society. It is subject to time, place, and manner restrictions.

Limited Protected Speech   The Supreme Court has held that certain types of speech have only *limited protection* under the First Amendment. The government cannot forbid this type of speech, but it can subject this speech to **time, place, and manner restrictions**. The following types of speech are accorded limited protection:

commercial speech

Speech used by businesses, such as advertising. It is subject to time, place, and manner restrictions.

1. **Offensive Speech**   **Offensive speech** is speech that offends many members of society. (It is not the same as obscene speech, however.) The Supreme Court has held that offensive speech may be restricted by the government under time, place, and manner restrictions. For example, the Federal Communications Commission (FCC) can regulate the use of offensive language on television by limiting such language to time periods when children would be unlikely to be watching (e.g., late at night).
2. **Commercial Speech**   **Commercial speech**, such as advertising, was once considered unprotected by the First Amendment. The Supreme Court's landmark decision in *Virginia State Board of Pharmacy v. Virginia Citizens Consumer Council, Inc.,*[8] changed this rule. In that case, the Supreme Court held that a state statute prohibiting a pharmacist from advertising the price of prescription drugs was unconstitutional because it violated the Freedom of Speech Clause. However, the Supreme Court held that commercial speech is subject to proper time, place, and manner restrictions.

Business Brief

The U.S. Supreme Court has held that a federal statute prohibiting beer producers from displaying alcoholic content on labels violated their commercial free-speech rights under the First Amendment [*Rubin v. Coors Brewing Company*, 115 S.Ct. 1585 (1995)].

In *Rubin v. Coors Brewing Company,*[9] the Supreme Court held that a state ban on the disclosure of the alcohol content on beer labels violated a beer producer's commercial speech rights.

However, the Supreme Court held that commercial speech is subject to proper *time, place, and manner restrictions*. For example, a city could prohibit billboards along its highways for safety and aesthetic reasons as long as other forms of advertising (e.g., print media) was available.

Unprotected Speech The Supreme Court has held that the following types of speech are not protected by the First Amendment and may be totally forbidden by the government:

- Dangerous speech (including such things as yelling "fire" in a crowded theater when there is no fire)
- Fighting words that are likely to provoke a hostile or violent response from an average person[10]
- Speech that incites the violent or revolutionary overthrow of the government; the mere abstract teaching of the morality and consequences of such action is protected[11]
- Defamatory language[12]
- Child pornography[13]
- Obscene speech[14]

The definition of **obscene speech** is quite subjective. One Supreme Court justice stated, "I know it when I see it."[15] In *Miller v. California*, the Supreme Court determined that speech is obscene when

1. The average person, applying contemporary community standards, would find that the work, taken as a whole, appeals to the prurient interest.
2. The work depicts or describes, in a patently offensive way, sexual conduct specifically defined by the applicable state law.
3. The work, taken as a whole, lacks serious literary, artistic, political, or scientific value.[16]

States are free to define what constitutes obscene speech. Movie theaters, magazine publishers, and so on are often subject to challenges that the materials they display or sell are obscene and therefore not protected by the First Amendment.

> **unprotected speech**
> Speech that is not protected by the First Amendment and may be forbidden by the government.

> **obscene speech**
> Speech that (1) appeals to the prurient interest, (2) depicts sexual conduct in a patently offensive way, and (3) lacks serious literary, artistic, political, or scientific value.

E-Commerce & Internet Law

Broad Free-Speech Rights Granted in Cyberspace

On February 1, 1996, President Clinton signed into law the **Computer Decency Act**, which was passed by Congress as part of the broader Telecommunications Act of 1996. The Computer Decency Act (Act) made it a felony to knowingly make "indecent" or "patently offensive" materials available on computer systems, including the Internet, to persons under 18 years of age. The Act provided for fines and prison terms for anyone convicted of violating the Act.

Immediately, over 50 cyberspace providers and users filed a lawsuit challenging the Act as a violation of their free-speech rights granted under the First Amendment to the Constitution. Proponents of the Act argued that it was necessary to protect children from indecent materials.

The three-judge panel of the U.S. district court in Philadelphia agreed with the plaintiffs, declared the Act an unconstitutional violation of the Freedom of Speech Clause, and issued a restraining order prohibiting the federal government from enforcing the Act. The court held that the terms "indecent" and "patently offensive" were too vague to define and enforce. On appeal, the U.S. Supreme Court held that the Act was an unconstitutional violation of free-speech rights.

The Court reasoned that limiting the content on the Internet to what is suitable for a child resulted in unconstitutionally limiting adult speech. The Court noted that children are far less likely to trip over indecent material on the Internet than on TV or radio because the information must be actively sought out on the Internet. The Court also stated that less obtrusive means for protecting children are available, such as requiring parents to regulate their children's access to materials on the Internet. The Court's

(box continues)

e-biz

decision will spur the development of filtering and blocking software programs to enable parents to control what their children do and see on the Internet.

As a policy, the Court stated that the Internet and on-line communication should be accorded greater free-speech protection than TV and radio. The Court did not apply earlier court decisions that place more restrictions on electronic speech delivered over TV and radio.

The Court concluded that the Internet allows an individual to reach an audience of millions at almost no cost, setting it apart from TV, radio, and print media, which are prohibitively expensive to use. The Court stated, "As the most participatory form of mass speech yet developed, the Internet deserves the highest protection from government intrusion." The Court also reasoned that because the

Internet is a global medium, even if the Act was upheld, there would be no way to prevent indecent material from flowing over the Internet from abroad.

Once or twice a century a new medium comes along that presents new problems for applying freedom of speech rights. This time it is the Internet. The Court in this case declared emphatically that the Internet must be given the highest possible level of First Amendment free-speech protection. The district court stated, "Just as the strength of the Internet is chaos, so the strength of our liberty depends upon the chaos and cacophony of the unfettered speech the First Amendment protects." [*Reno v. American Civil Liberties Union*, 1997 WL 348012 (1997)]

[*Note:* It still remains a crime under existing laws to transmit *obscene* materials over the Internet.]

Contemporary Business Application

RAP MUSIC: WHEN IS IT OBSCENE?

Every older generation believes that the music young people are listening to is louder and more obnoxious than the music they listened to during their youth. Today, this criticism goes even further: Some people are accusing modern music of being obscene. Consider the following case.

A Florida statute outlaws the production, distribution, or sale of any obscene thing, including a recording. Skyywalker Records, Inc. (Skyywalker), is a Florida corporation headquartered in Miami, Florida. Luther Campbell, Mark Ross, David Hobbs, and Chris Wongwon constitute a rap group known as 2 LIVE CREW. Campbell is president, secretary, sole shareholder, and sole director of Skyywalker. In 1989, the group released the *As Nasty as They Wanna Be* (Nasty) record album. Public sales totaled approximately 1.7 million copies in various formats. The lyrics and titles to many of the songs explicitly refer to sexual conduct. A Florida judge issued an order finding that the recording was obscene. The Sheriff's Department distributed the order to music stores to warn the stores as a matter of courtesy rather than make initial arrests. The warnings were effective: Within days, all retail stores in Broward County ceased offering the Nasty recording for sale.

Skyywalker and members of 2 LIVE CREW brought a declaratory relief action against Broward County Sheriff Nicholas Navarro, seeking an injunction. The trial court judge found the music to be obscene and held for the sheriff. The judge stated:

This is a case between two ancient enemies: Anything Goes and Enough Already. Justice Oliver Wendell Holmes, Jr., observed in *Schenck v. United States*, 249 U.S. 47 (1919), that the First Amendment is not absolute and that it does not permit one to yell "Fire" in a crowded theater. Today, this court decides whether the First Amendment absolutely permits one to yell another "F" word anywhere in the community when combined with graphic sexual descriptions.

The appellate court reversed, however [*Skyywalker Records, Inc. v. Navarro*, 960 F.2d 134 (11th Cir. 1992)].

Other courts presented with the same issue could reach a different result. Musicians, singers, and other performers face uncertainty as to whether their work is obscene. Work that is found to be obscene loses its constitutional protection.

Establishment Clause
A clause to the First Amendment that prohibits the government from either establishing a state religion or promoting one religion over another.

Freedom of Religion

The U.S. Constitution requires federal, state, and local governments to be neutral toward religion. The First Amendment actually contains two separate religion clauses. They are:

1. **The Establishment Clause** The **Establishment Clause** prohibits the government from either establishing a state religion or promoting one religion over another. Thus, it guarantees

that there will be no state-sponsored religion. The Supreme Court used this clause as its reason for ruling that an Alabama statute that authorized a one-minute period of silence in schools for "meditation or voluntary prayer" was invalid.[17] The Court held that the statute endorsed religion.

2. **The Free Exercise Clause**   The **Free Exercise Clause** prohibits the government from interfering with the free exercise of religion in the United States. Generally, this clause prevents the government from enacting laws that either prohibit or inhibit individuals from participating in or practicing their chosen religion. For example, in *Church of Lukumi Babalu Aye, Inc. v. City of Hialeah, Florida*,[18] the U.S. Supreme Court held that a city ordinance that prohibited ritual sacrifices of animals (chickens) during church services violated the Free Exercise Clause. Of course, this right to be free from government intervention in the practice of religion is not absolute. For example, human sacrifices are unlawful and are not protected by the First Amendment.

> **Free Exercise Clause**
> **A clause to the First Amendment that prohibits the government from interfering with the free exercise of religion in the United States.**

𝒞ONCEPT SUMMARY   FREEDOM OF RELIGION

Clause	Description
Establishment Clause	Prohibits the government from either establishing a government-sponsored religion or promoting one religion over other religions.
Free Exercise Clause	Prohibits the government from enacting laws that either prohibit or inhibit individuals from participating in or practicing their chosen religion.

𝒪THER CONSTITUTIONAL CLAUSES AND BUSINESS

The **Fourteenth Amendment** was added to the U.S. Constitution in 1868. Its original purpose was to guarantee equal rights to all persons after the Civil War. The provisions of the Fourteenth Amendment prohibit discriminatory and unfair action by the government. Several of these provisions—namely the *Equal Protection Clause*, the *Due Process Clause*, and the *Privileges and Immunities Clause*—have important implications for business.

> **Fourteenth Amendment**
> **Amendment that was added to the U.S. Constitution in 1868. It contains the Due Process, Equal Protection, and Privileges and Immunities clauses.**

The Equal Protection Clause

The **Equal Protection Clause** provides that a state cannot "deny to any person within its jurisdiction the equal protection of the laws." Although this clause expressly applies to state and local government action, the Supreme Court has held that it also applies to federal government action.

> **Equal Protection Clause**
> **A Clause that provides that a state cannot "deny to any person within its jurisdiction the equal protection of the laws."**

This clause prohibits state, local, and federal governments from enacting laws that classify and treat "similarly situated" persons differently. Artificial persons, such as corporations, are also protected. Note that this clause is designed to prohibit invidious discrimination; it does not make the classification of individuals unlawful per se.

The Supreme Court has adopted three different standards for reviewing equal protection cases. They are:

1. **Strict Scrutiny Test** Any government activity or regulation that classifies persons based on a *suspect class* (i.e., **race**) is reviewed for lawfulness using a **strict scrutiny test**. Under this standard, most government classifications of persons based on race are found to be unconstitutional. For example, a government rule that permitted persons of one race, but not of another race, to receive government benefits would violate this test.

2. **Intermediate Scrutiny Test** The lawfulness of government classifications based on *protected classes* other than race (such as **sex** or **age**) are examined using an **intermediate scrutiny test**. Under this standard, the courts determine whether the government classification is "reasonably

> **strict scrutiny test**
> **Test that is applied to classifications based on *race*.**

> **intermediate scrutiny test**
> **Test that is applied to classifications based on protected classes other than race (e.g., *sex* or *age*).**

related" to a legitimate government purpose. For example, a rule prohibiting persons over a certain age from serving in military combat would be lawful, but a rule prohibiting persons over a certain age from acting as government engineers would not be.

3. **Rational Basis Test** The lawfulness of all government classifications that do not involve suspect or protected classes is examined using a **rational basis test**. Under this test, the courts will uphold government regulation as long as there is a justifiable reason for the law. This standard permits much of the government regulation of business. For example, providing government subsidies to farmers but not to other occupations is permissible.

rational basis test

Test that is applied to classifications not involving a suspect or protected class.

In the following case, the Supreme Court applied the rational basis test and upheld a government classification.

Nordlinger v. Hahn
112 S.Ct. 2326, 120 L.Ed.2d 1 (1992)
United States Supreme Court

CASE 3.3

FACTS
In the late 1960s and early 1970s, real estate prices in California increased dramatically. In many instances, this caused property taxes to triple and quadruple because the tax was based on assessed valuation. In 1978, the voters in California approved Proposition 13, an amendment to the state's constitution that fixed property taxes at 1 percent of a property's value as of the 1975–1976 tax year. Real estate that changed ownership or was built after 1978 was taxed at 1 percent of its appraised value at the time of transfer or construction. In November 1988, Stephanie Nordlinger purchased a house in the Baldwin Hills area of Los Angeles for $170,000. In early 1989, she received a tax bill for $1,701 for the 1988–1989 fiscal year. When Ms. Nordlinger discovered that she was paying about five times more in taxes than some of her neighbors who had owned their homes in 1978, she sued the tax assessor. She alleged that California's real property tax system violated the Equal Protection Clause of the U.S. Constitution because new landowners were charged higher taxes than old landowners. The California trial court dismissed her complaint, and the court of appeals affirmed. The California Supreme Court denied review. The U.S. Supreme Court granted certiorari.

ISSUE
Does Proposition 13 violate the Equal Protection Clause of the U.S. Constitution?

IN THE LANGUAGE OF THE COURT
Blackmun, Justice   Unless a classification warrants some form of heightened review because it jeopardizes exercise of a fundamental right or categorizes on the basis of an inherently suspect characteristic, the Equal Protection Clause requires only that the classification rationally further legitimate state interest. The appropriate standard of review is whether the difference in treatment between newer and older owners rationally furthers a legitimate state interest. In general, the Equal Protection Clause is satisfied so long as there is a plausible policy reason for the classification.

We have no difficulty in ascertaining at least two rational or reasonable considerations of difference or policy that justify denying the petitioner the benefits of her neighbors' lower assessments. First, the state has a legitimate interest in local neighborhood preservation, continuity, and stability. The state therefore legitimately can decide to structure its tax system to discourage rapid turnover in ownership of homes and businesses. Second, the state legitimately can conclude that a new owner at the time of acquiring his property does not have the same reliance interest warranting protection against higher taxes as does an existing owner. If a new owner thinks the future tax burden is too demanding, he can decide not to complete the purchase at all. By contrast, the existing owner, already saddled with his purchase, does not have the option of deciding not to buy his home if taxes become prohibitively high. In short, the state may decide that it is worse to have owned and lost, than never to have owned at all.

DECISION AND REMEDY
The U.S. Supreme Court held that Proposition 13 does not violate the Equal Protection Clause because the difference was rationally justified. The Supreme Court held that Proposition 13 was lawful and affirmed the judgment of the California court of appeals dismissing Ms. Nordlinger's suit.

Case Questions

Critical Legal Thinking What public policy is served by Proposition 13? Do you think that these reasons justify the classification of real property taxes in California?

Ethics Should homeowners who owned their homes prior to 1978 accept the benefit of lower taxes? Should they voluntarily pay the higher taxes if they can afford to do so?

Business Application Proposition 13 also applies to real property owned by businesses. What effect, if any, does this have on business competition?

Due Process Clause

The Fifth and Fourteenth Amendments to the U.S. Constitution both contain a **Due Process Clause**. These clauses provide that no person shall be deprived of "life, liberty, or property" without due process of the law. The Due Process Clause of the Fifth Amendment applies to federal government action; that of the Fourteenth Amendment applies to state and local government action. It is important to understand that the government is not prohibited from taking a person's life, liberty, or property. However, the government must follow due process to do so. There are two categories of due process: *substantive* and *procedural*.

Substantive Due Process   This category of due process requires that government statutes, ordinances, regulations, or other laws be clear on their face and not overly broad in scope. The test of whether substantive due process is met is whether a "reasonable person" could understand the law to be able to comply with it. Laws that do not meet this test are declared *void for vagueness*. Suppose, for example, that a city ordinance made it illegal for persons to wear "clothes of the opposite sex." Such an ordinance would be held unconstitutional as void for vagueness because a reasonable person could not clearly determine whether his or her conduct violates the law.

Procedural Due Process   This form of due process requires that the government must give a person proper *notice* and *hearing* of the legal action before that person is deprived of his or her life, liberty, or property. The government action must be fair. For example, if the government wants to take a person's home by eminent domain to build a highway, the government must (1) give the homeowner sufficient notice of its intention and (2) provide a hearing. Under the **Just Compensation Clause** of the Fifth Amendment, the government must pay the owner just compensation for taking the property.

Due Process Clause
A clause that provides that no person shall be deprived of "life, liberty, or property" without due process of the law.

substantive due process
Requires that government statutes, ordinances, regulations, or other laws be clear on their face and not overly broad in scope.

procedural due process
Requires that the government must give a person proper notice and hearing of the legal action before that person is deprived of his or her life, liberty, or property.

*C*ONCEPT SUMMARY   DUE PROCESS

Type of Due Process	Description
Substantive due process	Requires government laws to be clear and not overly broad. The test is whether a reasonable person could understand the law.
Procedural due process	Requires the government to give a person proper notice and hearing before depriving that person of his or her life, liberty, or property.

Ethical Perspective

WHEN ARE PUNITIVE DAMAGES TOO BIG?

Punitive damages are damages that can be awarded to plaintiffs in civil cases. These damages are assessed against defendants who have engaged in fraud, intentional misconduct, or other egregious conduct. They are intended to (1) punish the defendant, (2) deter the defendant from similar conduct in the future,

and (3) set an example for others. Punitive damages are awarded in addition to actual damages.

U.S. businesses have argued for years that the award of punitive damages has gotten out of hand. They point to hundreds of multimillion-dollar punitive damage awards to back up their claim. Plaintiffs, on the other hand, argue

(box continues)

that punitive damages serve a useful purpose and that without them businesses could engage in reprehensible conduct with impunity.

The U.S. Supreme Court addressed the issue of punitive damages in two recent cases. The first case was *Pacific Mutual Life Insurance Company v. Haslip*, 499 U.S. 1, 111 S.Ct. 1032, 113 L.Ed.2d 1 (1991). In that case, Cleopatra Haslip sued Pacific Mutual Life Insurance Company (Pacific Mutual) for fraud for denying her health insurance coverage.

The jury found in favor of Haslip and awarded her $4,000 out-of-pocket medical expenses, $196,000 for emotional distress and other compensatory damages, and $840,000 in punitive damages. When several appeals of the verdict in Alabama's state courts proved unsuccessful, Pacific Mutual took its case to the U.S. Supreme Court. There it argued that unbridled jury discretion in assessing punitive damages violates the Due Process Clause of the U.S. Constitution.

The business community, which eagerly watched the case, was disappointed when the Supreme Court announced its decision in favor of Haslip. The Supreme Court refused to rule that the award of punitive damages is per se unconstitutional, citing the fact that such damages have been a part of the legal landscape of this country for over 200 years. The Supreme Court did state that punitive damages would violate due process if they were unreasonable.

The second case is *BMW of North America, Inc. v. Gore* [1996 WL 262429 (U.S.)]. In that case, Dr. Ira Gore, Jr., purchased a black BMW sports sedan for $40,470 from an authorized BMW dealer. Later, Dr. Gore discovered that several panels on the car had been repainted by BMW because of damage suffered while the car was being transported from Germany to the United States. BMW failed to disclose this fact to Dr. Gore when he purchased the car. Dr. Gore sued BMW for fraud. The jury found BMW liable and awarded Dr. Gore $4,000 in compensatory damages and $4 million in punitive damages. The Alabama Supreme Court reduced the punitive damages to $2 million. BMW appealed to the U.S. Supreme Court.

In a 5–4 decision, the Supreme Court found that the punitive damage award was "grossly excessive" and therefore violated the Due Process Clause of the U.S. Constitution. The Court based its determination on the fact that the harm was purely economic, the repainting had no effect on the car's performance, BMW's conduct evinced no reckless disregard for the health and safety of others, and the amount of the punitive damages—500 times actual damages—was excessive. The Supreme Court remanded the case to the Alabama supreme court for a determination of reasonable punitive damages. On remand, the award was reduced to $50,000 by the Alabama court.

The business community hailed the *BMW v. Gore* decision as the death knell to oppressive and excessive awards of punitive damages by juries. Plaintiffs' lawyers and consumer groups argue that the case reduces an important lever against businesses that engage in unethical and illegal conduct.

1. What purposes are served by the award of punitive damages?
2. Do you think that the specter of punitive damage awards forces companies to act more ethically?
3. Should punitive damages be awarded to charities or other worthy causes rather than to the plaintiff?

International Perspective

JEWISH HALAKHAH ADMINISTERED BY THE BEIS DIN

Jewish law, which has existed for centuries, is a complex legal system based on ideology and theology of the Torah. The Torah prescribes comprehensive and integrated rules of religious, political, and legal life that together form Jewish thought. Jewish law is decided by rabbis who are scholars of the Torah and other Jewish scriptures. Rabbinic jurisprudence, known as **Halakhah**, is administered by rabbi-judges sitting as the **Beis Din**, Hebrew for the "house of judgment." As a court, the Beis Din has roots that go back 3,000 years.

Today, Jews are citizens of countries worldwide. As such, they are subject to the criminal and civil laws of their host countries. But Jews, no matter where they live, abide by the principles of the Torah in many legal matters such as marriage, divorce, inheritance, and other family matters. Thus, the legal principles imbedded in the Torah coexist with the secular laws of Jews' home countries.

In modern times, the influence of the Beis Din as a court has diminished, however, the Beis Din is making a comeback in several Jewish areas of the United States as an alternative dispute resolution mechanism. The first Beis Din in the United States was set up about 100 years ago on the East Coast. There are now about three dozen Beis Dins across the country, with the most active being located in Los Angeles. Modern Beis Dins deal with such civil matters as divorces, child custody, and inheritances. Importantly, many business disputes are also being presented in Beis Din arbitration proceedings. Beis Dins do not administer criminal laws.

To have a legal dispute heard and decided by the Beis Din, both parties must agree to the proceeding and sign a binding arbitration contract agreeing that the decision of the Beis Din is binding; that is, there can be no proceeding in a civil court. As in other forms of alternative dispute resolution (ADR), each side gets to present his or her side of the case, call witnesses, and introduce evidence. However, in a Beis Din hearing, proceedings are less adversarial and less formal than a normal civil court or even other forms of ADR. The rabbinical judges tend to be more actively involved in the case. True to its roots, the Beis Din is more a search for the truth than it is an adversarial process.

The Beis Din offers a cost-effective and timely way of obtaining the resolution of business and other disputes that will be in compliance with the Torah. The modern Beis Din and its rabbinical scholar-judges will be called upon to rule in many more cases in the future.

The Privileges and Immunities Clause

The purpose of the U.S. Constitution is to promote nationalism. If the states were permitted to enact laws that favored their residents over out-of-state residents, the concept of nationalism would be defeated. Both Article IV of the Constitution and the Fourteenth Amendment contain a **Privileges and Immunities Clause** that prohibits states from enacting laws that unduly discriminate in favor of their residents. For example, a state cannot enact a law that prevents residents of other states from owning property or businesses in that state. Only invidious discrimination is prohibited. Thus, state universities are permitted to charge out-of-state residents higher tuition than instate residents. Note that this clause applies only to citizens; corporations are not protected.

> **Privileges and Immunities Clause**
> A Clause that prohibits states from enacting laws that unduly discriminate in favor of their residents.

Working the Web

Thomas The Library of Congress began the Thomas Web site, in the spirit of Thomas Jefferson, in 1995. It is a collection of legislative information on the Internet. You can find out about floor activities of the House and Senate; bills (by topic, short title, or bill number), bill summaries and status, and public laws; text of the *Congressional Record*, committee information, historical documents, and links to other U.S. government Internet resources.

Visit at **thomas.loc.gov**

Constitution Finder This index, published by the University of Richmond, offers constitution charters, amendments, and other related documents. Nations of the world and states are listed alphabetically, and each nation's or state's name is linked to its constitutional text posted somewhere on the Internet.

Visit at **www.urich.edu/~jpjones/confinder**

Supreme Court Historical Society The Supreme Court Historical Society was incorporated in 1974 for the purpose of expanding public awareness of the history and heritage of the Supreme Court. All sorts of information about the Supreme Court are available from this site.

Visit at **www.supremecourthistory.org**

The Constitution of the United States of America The full constitution of the United States is on-line at this site.

Visit at **www.law.cornell.edu/constitution/constitution.overview.html**

CYBER EXERCISES

1. Using Thomas, find the Senate committee hearing schedule.

2. Using the Constitution Finder, can you find the constitution of Belarus?

3. Using the Supreme Court Historical Society site, find a picture of the current justices of the Supreme Court.

4. Using the Constitution of the United States of America site, find the subject matter of Article VII.

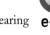

CASES AND EXERCISES

CRITICAL LEGAL THINKING CASES

3.1. In 1951, a dispute arose between steel companies and their employees about the terms and conditions that should be included in a new labor contract. At the time, the United States was engaged in a military conflict in Korea that required substantial steel resources from which to make weapons and other military goods. On April 4, 1952, the steelworkers' union gave notice of a nationwide strike called to begin at 12:01 A.M. on April 9. The indispensability of steel as a component in weapons and other war materials led President Dwight D. Eisenhower to believe that the proposed strike would jeopardize the national defense and that governmental seizure of the steel mills was necessary to ensure the continued availability of steel. Therefore, a few hours before the strike was to begin, the President issued Executive Order 10340, which directed the Secretary of Commerce to take possession of most of the steel mills and keep them running. The steel companies obeyed the order under protest and brought proceedings against the President. Was the seizure of the steel mills constitutional? [*Youngstown Co. v. Sawyer, Secretary of Commerce*, 343 U.S. 579, 72 S.Ct. 863 (1952)]

3.2. Article I, Section 8, clause 8 of the U.S. Constitution grants Congress the power to enact laws to give inventors the exclusive right to their discoveries. Pursuant to this power, Congress enacted federal patent laws that establish the requirements to obtain a patent. Once a patent is granted, the patent holder has exclusive rights to use the patent. Bonito Boats, Inc. (Bonito), developed a hull design for a fiberglass recreational boat that it marketed under the trade name Bonito Boats Model 5VBR. The manufacturing process involved creating a hardwood model that was sprayed with fiberglass to create a mold. The mold then served to produce the finished fiberglass boats for sale. Bonito did not file a patent application to protect the utilitarian or design aspects of the hull or the manufacturing process. After the Bonito 5VBR was on the market for six years, the Florida legislature enacted a statute prohibiting the use of a direct molding process to duplicate unpatented boat hulls and forbade the knowing sale of hulls so duplicated. The protection afforded under the state statute was broader than that provided for under the federal patent statute. Subsequently, Thunder Craft Boats, Inc. (Thunder Craft), produced and sold boats made by the direct molding process. Bonito sued Thunder Craft under Florida law. Is the Florida statute valid? [*Bonito Boats, Inc. v. Thunder Craft Boats, Inc.*, 489 U.S. 141, 109 S.Ct. 971 (1989)]

3.3. The Heart of Atlanta Motel, located in the state of Georgia, has 216 rooms available to guests. The motel is readily accessible to interstate highways 75 and 85 and to state highways 23 and 41. The motel solicits patronage from outside the state of Georgia through various national advertising media, including magazines of national circulation, and it maintains more than 50 billboards and highway signs within the state. Approximately 75 percent of the motel's registered guests are from out of state. Congress enacted the Civil Rights Act of 1964, which made it illegal for public accommodations to discriminate against guests based on their race. Prior to that, the Heart of Atlanta Motel had refused to rent rooms to blacks. After the act was passed, it alleged that it intended to continue not to rent rooms to blacks. The owner of the motel brought an action to have the Civil Rights Act of 1964 declared unconstitutional, alleging that Congress, in passing the act, had exceeded its powers to regulate commerce under the Commerce Clause of the U.S. Constitution. Who wins? [*Heart of Atlanta Motel v. United States*, 379 U.S. 241, 85 S.Ct. 348 (1964)]

3.4. In 1972, Congress enacted a federal statute, called the Ports and Waterways Safety Act, that established uniform standards for the operation of boats on inland waterways in the United States. The act coordinated its provisions with those of foreign countries so that there was a uniform body of international rules that applied to vessels that traveled between countries. Pursuant to the act, a federal rule was adopted that regulated the design, length, and size of oil tankers, some of which traveled the waters of the Puget Sound area in the state of Washington. Oil tankers from various places entered the Puget Sound area in the state of Washington to bring crude oil to refineries located in Washington. In 1975, the state of Washington enacted a statute that established different designs, smaller lengths, and smaller sizes for oil tankers serving Puget Sound than allowed by the federal law. Oil tankers used by the Atlantic Richfield Company (ARCO) to bring oil into Puget Sound met the federal standards but not the state standards. ARCO sued to have the state statute declared unconstitutional. Who wins? [*Ray, Governor of Washington v. Atlantic Richfield Co.*, 435 U.S. 151, 98 S.Ct. 988, 55 (1978)]

3.5. Most trucking firms, including Consolidated Freightways Corporation (Consolidated), use 65-foot-long "double" trailer trucks to ship commodities on the highway system across the United States. Almost all states permit these vehicles on their highways. The federal government does not regulate the length of trucks that can use the nation's highways. The state of Iowa enacted a statute that restricts the length of trucks that can use highways in the state to 55 feet. This means that if Consolidated wants to move goods through Iowa it must either use smaller trucks or detach the double trailers and shuttle them through the state separately. Its only other alternative is to divert its 65-foot doubles around Iowa. Consolidated filed suit against Iowa alleging that the state statute is unconstitutional. Is it? [*Kassel v. Consolidated Freightways Corporation*, 450 U.S. 662, 101 S.Ct. 1309 (1981)]

3.6. During the 1970s, a period of a booming economy in Alaska, many residents of other states moved there in search of work. Construction work on the Trans-Alaska Pipeline was a major source of employment. In 1972, the Alaska legislature enacted an act entitled the "Local Hire" Statute. This act required employers to hire Alaska residents in preference to nonresidents. Is this statute constitutional? [*Hicklin v. Orbeck, Commissioner of the Department of Labor of Alaska*, 437 U.S. 518, 98 S.Ct. 2482 (1978)]

3.7. Satiric humorist George Carlin recorded a 12-minute monologue entitled "Filthy Words" before a live audience in a California theater. He began referring to "the words you couldn't say on the public airwaves—the ones you definitely couldn't say, ever." He proceeded to list those words and repeat them over and over again in a variety of colloquialisms. At about 2:00 P.M. on October 30, 1973, a New York radio station owned by Pacifica Foundation broadcast the "Filthy Words" monologue. A man who heard the broadcast while driving with his young son complained to the Federal Communications Commission (FCC), the federal administrative agency in charge of granting radio licenses and regulating radio broadcasts. The FCC administers a statute that forbids the use of any offensive language on the radio. The FCC found that Carlin's monologue violated this law and censured the Pacifica Foundation for playing the monologue. Can the FCC prohibit Pacifica Foundation from playing the Carlin monologue on the radio? [*Federal Communications Commission v. Pacifica Foundation*, 438 U.S. 726, 98 S.Ct. 3026 (1978)]

3.8. The city of San Diego, California, enacted a city zoning ordinance that prohibited outdoor advertising display signs—including billboards. On-site signs at a business's location were exempted from this rule. The city based the restriction on traffic safety and aesthetics. Metromedia, Inc., a company that is in the business of leasing commercial billboards to advertisers, sued the city of San Diego, alleging that the zoning ordinance is unconstitutional. Is it? [*Metromedia, Inc. v. City of San Diego*, 453 U.S. 490, 101 S.Ct. 2882 (1981)]

3.9. Eddie C. Thomas, a Jehovah's Witness, was initially hired to work in a roll foundry at Blaw-Knox Company. The function of the department was to fabricate sheet steel for a variety of industrial uses. On his application, Thomas listed that he was a Jehovah's Witness. Approximately one year later, the roll foundry closed and Blaw-Knox transferred Thomas to a department that fabricated turrets for military tanks. On the first day at this new job, Thomas realized that the work he was doing violated his religious beliefs because it was weapon-related. Because there were no other jobs available, Thomas quit and filed for unemployment compensation. The state of Indiana denied his claim on the ground that Thomas quit his job for personal reasons. Thomas sued, alleging that the government's denial of unemployment benefits violated his right to freedom of religion. Who wins? [*Thomas v. Review Board of the Indiana Employment Security Division*, 450 U.S. 707, 101 S.Ct. 1425 (1981)]

3.10. On February 20, 1978, the village of Hoffman Estates, Illinois (Village), enacted an ordinance regulating drug paraphernalia. The ordinance makes it unlawful for any person "to sell any items, effect, paraphernalia, accessory or thing which is designed or marketed for use with illegal cannabis or drugs as defined by Illinois Revised Statutes, without obtaining a license therefore." The license fee is $150. A violation is subject to a fine of not more than $500. The Flipside, a retail store located in the Village, sold a variety of merchandise, including smoking accessories, clamps, roach clips, scales, water pipes, vials, cigarette rolling papers, and other items. On May 30, 1978, instead of applying for a license, Flipside filed a lawsuit against the Village, alleging that the ordinance was unconstitutional as a violation of substantive due process because it was overly broad and vague. Who wins? [*Village of Hoffman Estates v. Flipside, Hoffman Estates, Inc.*, 455 U.S. 489, 102 S.Ct. 1186 (1982)]

3.11. The state of Alabama enacted a statute that imposed a tax on premiums earned by insurance companies. The statute imposed a 1 percent tax on domestic insurance companies (i.e., insurance companies that were incorporated in Alabama and had their principal office in the state). The statute imposed a 4 percent tax on the premiums earned by out-of-state insurance companies that sold insurance in Alabama. Out-of-state insurance companies could reduce the premium tax by 1 percent by investing at least 10 percent of their assets in Alabama. Domestic insurance companies did not have to invest any of their assets in Alabama. Metropolitan Life Insurance Company, an out-of-state insurance company, sued the state of Alabama, alleging that the Alabama statute violated the Equal Protection Clause of the U.S. Constitution. Who wins? [*Metropolitan Life Insurance Co. v. Ward, Commissioner of Insurance of Alabama*, 470 U.S. 689, 105 S.Ct. 1676 (1985)]

Ethics Cases

3.12. The McLains were involved in the sale of a home in the Greater New Orleans area. A real estate broker was paid a commission on the transaction. The real estate brokers in the New Orleans area belonged to the Real Estate Board of New Orleans (Board), a trade association that required all member brokers to charge the same percentage commission on the sale of real estate. The McLains sued the Board and several real estate brokers for engaging in price fixing in violation of federal antitrust law. The U.S. district court dismissed the case, finding that federal antitrust law did not apply because no interstate commerce was involved. The U.S. court of appeals affirmed the decision. The McLains appealed to the U.S. Supreme Court. Who wins? Did the defendants act ethically? [*McLain v. Real Estate Board of New Orleans, Inc.*, 444 U.S. 232, 100 S.Ct. 502 (1980)]

3.13. The "Oakland Raiders" is a professional football team and a National Football League (NFL) franchise. Each NFL franchise is independently owned. Al Davis is an owner and the managing general partner of the Raiders. The NFL establishes schedules, negotiates television contracts, and otherwise promotes NFL football, including conducting the "Super Bowl" each year. The Raiders play home and away games against other NFL teams.

Up until 1982, the Raiders played their home games in Oakland, California. The owners of the Raiders decided to move the team from Oakland to Los Angeles, California, to take advantage of the greater seating capacity of the Los Angeles Coliseum, the larger television market of Los Angeles, and other economic reasons. The renamed team was to be known as the "Los Angeles Raiders." The city of Oakland brought an eminent domain proceeding in court to acquire the Raiders as a city-owned team. Can the city of Oakland acquire the Raiders through eminent domain? Is it socially responsible for a professional sports team to move to another location? [*City of Oakland, California v. Oakland Raiders*, 174 C.A.3d 414, 220 Cal.Rptr. 153 (Cal.App. 1985)]

3.14. In 1989, Congress enacted the Flag Protection Act (Act), which made it a crime to knowingly mutilate, deface, physically defile, burn, or trample the U.S. flag. The law provided for fines and up to one year in prison upon conviction [18 U.S.C. § 700]. Certain individuals set fire to several U.S. flags on the steps of the U.S. Capitol in Washington, DC, to protest various aspects of the federal government's foreign and domestic policy. In a separate incident, other individuals set fire to a U.S. flag to protest the Act's passage. All of these individuals were prosecuted for violating the Act. The district courts held the Act unconstitutional in violation of the defendants' First Amendment free speech rights and dismissed the charges. The government appealed to the U.S. Supreme Court, which consolidated the two cases. Who wins? Does the flag burner exhibit any morals? [*United States v. Eichman*, 496 U.S. 310, 110 S.Ct. 2404 (1990)]

Critical Legal Thinking Writing Assignment

Read Case A.3 in the Case Appendix [*Lee v. Weisman*]. This case is excerpted from the U.S. Supreme Court's opinion. Review and brief the case. In your brief, be sure to answer the following questions.

1. Who are the plaintiff and defendant?
2. What does the Establishment Clause provide?

3. Was the fact that the prayer was nonsectarian important to the Supreme Court's decision?
4. What argument did the dissenting opinion make in support of allowing prayer at high school graduation ceremonies?
5. How close was the vote by the justices in this case?

Notes

1. To be elected to Congress, an individual must be a U.S. citizen, either naturally born or granted citizenship. To serve in the Senate, a person must be 30 years of age or older. To serve in the House of Representatives, a person must be 25 years of age or older.
2. To be President, a person must be 35 years of age or older and a natural citizen of the United States. By amendment to the Constitution (Amendment XXII), a person can serve only two full terms as President.

3. Federal court judges and justices are appointed by the President with the consent of the Senate.
4. The principle that the U.S. Supreme Court is the final arbiter of the U.S. Constitution evolved from *Marbury v. Madison*, 1 Cranch 137 (1803). In that case, the Supreme Court held that a judiciary statute enacted by Congress was unconstitutional.
5. Article VI, Section 2.
6. Article I, Section 8, clause 3.
7. 317 U.S. Ill, 63 S.Ct. 82 (1942).

8. 425 U.S. 748, 96 S.Ct. 1817 (1976).

9. 115 S.Ct. 1585 (U.S.).

10. *Chaplinsky v. New Hampshire*, 315 U.S. 568, 62 S.Ct. 766 (1942).

11. *Brandenburg v. Ohio*, 395 U.S. 444, 89 S.Ct. 1827 (1969).

12. *Beauharnais v. Illinois*, 343 U.S. 250, 72 S.Ct. 725 (1952).

13. *New York v. Ferber*, 458 U.S. 747, 102 S.Ct. 3348 (1982).

14. *Roth v. United States*, 354 U.S. 476, 77 S.Ct. 1304 (1957).

15. Justice Stewart in *Jacobellis v. Ohio*, 378 U.S. 184, 84 S.Ct. 1676 (1963).

16. 413 U.S. 15, 93 S.Ct. 2607 (1973).

17. *Wallace v. Jaffree*, 472 U.S. 38, 105 S.Ct. 2479 (1985).

18. 113 S.Ct. 2217 (1993).

Comparative and International Law

*I*nternational law, or the law that governs between nations, has at times, been like the common law within states, a twilight existence during which it is hardly distinguishable from morality or justice, till at length the imprimatur of a court attests its jural quality.

JUSTICE CARDOZO
*New Jersey v. Delaware, 291 U.S. 361,
54 S.Ct. 407, 78 L.Ed. 847 (1934)*

Chapter Objectives

After studying this chapter, you should be able to

1. Explain the U.S. government's role in foreign affairs.
2. List and describe the sources of international law.
3. Explain the principle of comity.
4. List and describe the major international organizations.
5. List and describe the major international courts.
6. Describe the forum-selection and choice of law clauses.
7. Describe the act of state doctrine.
8. Describe the doctrine of sovereign immunity.
9. Describe the arbitration of international disputes.
10. Describe criminal prosecutions in the international arena.

Chapter Contents

International law, important to both nations and businesses, has many unique features. First, there is no single legislative source of international law. All countries of the world and numerous international organizations are responsible for enacting international laws. Second, there is no single world court that is responsible for interpreting international law. There are, however, several courts or tribunals that hear and decide international legal disputes of parties that agree to appear before them. Third, there is no world executive branch that can enforce international laws. Thus, nations do not have to obey international law enacted by other countries or international organizations. Because of these uncertainties, some commentators question whether international law is really "law."

As technology and transportation bring nations closer together and American and foreign firms increase their global activities, international law will become even more important to governments and businesses. This chapter introduces the main concepts of international law and discusses the sources of international law and the organizations responsible for its administration.

THE UNITED STATES AND FOREIGN AFFAIRS

The U.S. Constitution divides the power to regulate the internal affairs of this country between the federal and state governments. On the international level, however, the Constitution gives most of the power to the federal government. The following two constitutional provisions are the ones that establish this authority.

> **Commerce Clause** Article I, Section 8, clause 3 vests Congress with the power "to regulate commerce with foreign nations."

> **Treaty Clause** Article II, Section 2, clause 2 states that the President "shall have power, by and with the advice and consent of the Senate, to make treaties, provided two-thirds of the senators present concur."

The Constitution does not vest exclusive power over foreign affairs in the federal government, but any state or local law that unduly burdens foreign commerce is unconstitutional under the Commerce Clause. Under the Treaty Clause, only the federal government may enter into treaties with foreign nations. Under the Supremacy Clause of the Constitution, treaties become part of the "law of the land" and conflicting state or local law is void. The President is the agent of the United States in dealing with foreign countries.

international law
Law that governs affairs between nations and that regulates transactions between individuals and businesses of different countries.

Business Brief
International trade is increasing in importance for the United States and other countries of the world. The development of a uniform body of law and the creation of tribunals to peacefully settle disputes between nations and commercial enterprises are necessary for the further development of international trade.

Commerce Clause
Clause of the U.S. Constitution that vests Congress with the power "to regulate commerce with foreign nations."

Treaty Clause
Clause of the U.S. Constitution that states the President "shall have the power . . . to make treaties, provided two-thirds of the senators present concur."

International Perspective

FOREIGN COMMERCE CLAUSE BARS STATE'S ATTEMPT TO REGULATE INTERNATIONAL COMMERCE

The military regime of the country of Myanmar (formerly known as Burma) has been accused of major civil rights violations, including using forced labor, imprisoning and torturing political opponents, and harshly repressing ethnic minorities. These inhumane actions have been condemned by human rights organizations around the world.

The state legislators in Massachusetts were so appalled at these actions that they enacted a state statute banning

the state government from purchasing from any company that did business in Myanmar. The National Foreign Trade Council—a powerful Washington-based trade association—filed suit against Massachusetts to have the state law declared unconstitutional. Many of the council's 580 members, which include such giants as Citibank and Unocal, wanted to do business in Myanmar and with Massachusetts, but the state statute prevented them from doing both.

(box continues)

The council alleged in its lawsuit that the Massachusetts state law violated the **Foreign Commerce Clause** of the U.S. Constitution, which grants the federal government and not state or local governments the authority to regulate foreign commerce. The council argued that the U.S. system of government was not designed to allow each of the 50 states and thousands of cities to have their own foreign policies. The council pointed out that under the U.S. Constitution, only the federal government has this power.

The court agreed with the council and found that the Massachusetts selective-purchase statute interfered with the federal government's power to regulate foreign affairs. The court stated, "Massachusetts' concern for the welfare of the people of Myanmar may well be regarded as admirable," but because the federal government has exclusive power to make foreign policy, "the proper forum to raise such concerns is the U.S. Congress." This court decision will lead to challenges to similar selective-purchasing statutes and ordinances adopted by several states and cities across the country. [*National Foreign Trade Council v. Massachusetts*]

SOURCES OF INTERNATIONAL LAW

sources of international law
Those things that international tribunals rely on in settling international disputes.

The **sources of international law** are those things that international tribunals rely on in deciding international disputes. **Article 38(1) of the Statute of the International Court of Justice** lists the following four sources of international law: *treaties and conventions, custom, general principles of law*, and *judicial decisions and teachings*. Most courts rely on the hierarchy suggested by this list; that is, treaties and conventions are turned to before custom, and so on. Each of these sources of law is discussed in the following paragraphs.

China's trade agreements with the United States, Canada, and other countries paved its way for entry into the World Trade Organization (WTO). Such trade agreements will have a monumental effect on the future of China and the rest of the world.

Treaties and Conventions

treaties and conventions
The first source of international law, consisting of agreements or contracts between two or more nations that are formally signed by an authorized representative and ratified by the supreme power of each nation.

convention
Treaty that is sponsored by an international organization.

Treaties and conventions are the equivalents of legislation at the international level. A **treaty** is an agreement or contract between two or more nations that is formally signed by an authorized representative and ratified by the supreme power of each nation. *Bilateral treaties* are between two nations; *multilateral treaties* involve more than two nations. **Conventions** are treaties that are sponsored by international organizations, such as the United Nations. Conventions normally have many signatories.

Treaties and conventions address such matters as human rights, foreign aid, navigation, commerce, and the settlement of disputes. Most treaties are registered with and published by the United Nations.

E-Commerce & Internet Law _____

WORLD INTELLECTUAL PROPERTY ORGANIZATION (WIPO) INTERNET TREATIES

In 1967, the United Nations (UN) created the **World Intellectual Property Organization (WIPO)**. WIPO is a special agency of the UN that administers international intellectual property conventions and treaties. Over 160 nations are members of WIPO. WIPO administers over 20 major conventions and treaties affecting intellectual property, including the Paris Convention of 1883 that provides international patent and trademark protection and the Berne Convention of 1886 that provides international copyright protection. The United States is a signatory to both of these conventions. In addition to administering existing conventions and treaties, WIPO develops and adopts new conventions and treaties.

WIPO convened its members in 1996 to address the impact that the new digital technologies and the Internet were having on intellectual property rights. The goal of the delegation was to conclude new conventions that would cover and expand copyright and intellectual property protection in the digital environment. After much negotiation,

WIPO issued two new conventions collectively called the **Internet Treaties**. The two conventions are:

- **Copyright Treaty** This treaty grants copyright protection to computer programs and data compilations, protects the rights of copyright holders to make their works available on the Internet or by any other wire or wireless means, and extends copyright protection to rentals and means of distribution in addition to sale transactions.
- **Phonogram Treaty** This treaty provides protection to performers and producers by giving them exclusive rights to broadcast, reproduce, distribute, and rent copies of their performances using any type of media including video recordings, satellite transmissions, digital sound, and encrypted signals.

These two WIPO treaties go far to create new intellectual property rights and to grant protection to copyright holders over the Internet and in the digital marketplace. The United States signed the final act of the convention. Selected provisions of the WIPO Copyright Treaty appears as Exhibit 4.1.

e·biz

---

*E*XHIBIT **4.1** *Selected Provisions From the World Intellectual Property Organization Copyright Treaty Adopted December 20, 1996 Geneva, Switzerland*

Preamble

The Contracting Parties,

Desiring to develop and maintain the protection of the rights of authors in their literary and artistic works in a manner as effective and uniform as possible,

Recognizing the need to introduce new international rules and clarify the interpretation of certain existing rules in order to provide adequate solutions to the questions raised by new economic, social, cultural, and technological developments,

Recognizing the profound impact of the development and convergence of information and communication technologies on the creation and use of literary and artistic works,

Emphasizing the outstanding significance of copyright protection as an incentive for literary and artistic creation,

Recognizing the need to maintain a balance between the rights of authors and the larger public interest, particularly education, research and access to information, as reflected in the Berne Convention,

Have agreed as follows:

Article I

Relation to the Berne Convention

This Treaty is a special agreement within the meaning of Article 20 of the Berne Convention for the Protection of Literary and Artistic Works, as regards Contracting Parties that are countries of the Union established by that Convention.

(Exhibit continues)

Article 2
Scope of Copyright Protection
Copyright protection extends to expressions and not to ideas, procedures, methods of operation or mathematical concepts as such.

Article 4
Computer Programs
Computer programs are protected as literary works within the meaning of Article 2 of the Berne Convention. Such protection applies to computer programs, whatever may be the mode or form of their expression.

Article 5
Compilations of Data (Databases)
Compilations of data or other material, in any form, which by reason of the selection or arrangement of their contents constitute intellectual creations, are protected as such. This protection does not extend to the data or the material itself and is without prejudice to any copyright subsisting in the data or material contained in the compilation.

Article 6
Right of Distribution
Authors of literary and artistic works shall enjoy the exclusive right of authorizing the making available to the public of the original and copies of their works through sale or other transfer of ownership.

e·biz

Article 7
Right of Rental
Authors of:
(i) computer programs;
(ii) cinematographic works; and
(iii) works embodied in phonograms, as determined in the national law of Contracting Parties, shall enjoy the exclusive right of authorizing commercial rental to the public of the originals or copies of their works.

Article 8
Right of Communication to the Public
Without prejudice to the provisions of Articles 11 (1) (ii), 11bis (1) (i) and (ii), 11ter (1) (ii), 14 (1) (ii) and 14 bis (1) of the Berne Convention, authors of literary and artistic works shall enjoy the exclusive right of authorizing any communication to the public of their works, by wire or wireless means, including the making available to the public of their works in such a way that members of the public may access these works from a place and at a time individually chosen by them.

Article 11
Obligations concerning Technological Measures
Contracting Parties shall provide adequate legal protection and effective legal remedies against the circumvention of effective technological measures that are used by authors in connection with the exercise of their rights under this Treaty or the Berne Convention and that restrict acts, in respect of their works, which are not authorized by the authors concerned or permitted by law.

Article 12
Obligations concerning Rights Management Information
Contracting Parties shall provide adequate and effective legal remedies against any person knowingly performing any of the following acts knowing, or with respect to civil remedies having reasonable grounds to know, that it will induce, enable, facilitate or conceal an infringement of any right covered by this Treaty or the Berne Convention:
(i) to remove or alter any electronic rights management information without authority;
(ii) to distribute, import for distribution, broadcast or communicate to the public, without authority, works or copies of works knowing that electronic rights management information has been removed or altered without authority.

Article 14
Provisions on Enforcement of Rights
(1) Contracting Parties undertake to adopt, in accordance with their legal systems, the measures necessary to ensure the application of this Treaty.
(2) Contracting Parties shall ensure that enforcement procedures are available under their law so as to permit effective action against any act of infringement of rights covered by this Treaty, including expeditious remedies to prevent infringements and remedies which constitute a deterrent to further infringements.

Article 16
International Bureau
The International Bureau of WIPO shall perform the administrative tasks concerning the Treaty.

e-biz

Article 18
Rights and Obligations under the Treaty
Subject to any specific provisions to the contrary in this Treaty, each Contracting Party shall enjoy all of the rights and assume all of the obligations under this Treaty.

Article 24
Languages of the Treaty
This Treaty is signed in a single original in English, Arabic, Chinese, French, Russian and Spanish languages, the versions in all these languages being equally authentic.

Article 25
Depositary
The Director General of WIPO is the depositary of this Treaty.

Custom

Custom between nations is an independent source of international law. Custom describes a practice followed by two or more nations when dealing with each other. It may be found in official government statements, diplomatic correspondence, policy statements, press releases, speeches, and the like. Two elements must be established to show that a practice has become a custom:

1. Consistent and recurring action by two or more nations over a considerable period of time
2. Recognition that the custom is binding—that is, followed because of legal obligation rather than courtesy

International customs evolve as mores, technology, forms of government, political parties, and other factors change throughout the world. Customs that have been recognized for some period of time are often codified in treaties.

General Principles of Law

Courts and tribunals that decide international disputes frequently rely on **general principles of law** that are recognized by civilized nations. These are principles of law that are common to the *national* law of the parties to the dispute. They may be derived from constitutions, statutes, regulations, common law, or other sources of national law. In some cases, however, the countries' laws may differ concerning the matter in dispute.

Judicial Decisions and Teachings

A fourth source of law to which international tribunals can refer is **judicial decisions and teachings** of the most qualified legal scholars of the various nations involved in the dispute. Although international courts are not bound by the doctrine of *stare decisis* and may

custom
The second source of international law, created through consistent, recurring practices between two or more nations over a period of time that have become recognized as binding.

general principles of law
The third source of international law, consisting of principles of law recognized by civilized nations. These are principles of law that are common to the national law of the parties to the dispute.

judicial decisions and teachings
The fourth source of international law, consisting of judicial decisions and writings of the most qualified legal scholars of the various nations involved in the dispute.

decide each case on its own merits, the courts often refer to their own past decisions for guidance. Court decisions of national courts do not create precedent for international courts.

Principle of Comity

principle of comity
Courtesies between countries based on respect, goodwill, and civility rather than law.

In addition to the four sources of international law discussed above, countries often grant courtesies to other countries that are not obligations of law but are based on respect, goodwill, and civility. The extension of such courtesies is referred to as the **principle of comity**.

E-Commerce & Internet Law

e-biz

GERMANY BECOMES THE WORLD'S E-COMMERCE POLICE

E-commerce—selling of products and services over the Internet—is exploding! American marketeers, who are already used to compiling, maintaining, and selling lists of detailed information about customers and potential customers, welcome the ability not only to sell over the Internet but also to collect more detailed information about customer profiles. Now they can target sales pitches more accurately. Today, soon after a person subscribes to a magazine, he or she is inundated with advertising from myriad companies, often related to the subject of the new magazine. What has happened? The magazine has sold the new subscriber's name to companies, without the subscriber's permission. Compiling and selling customer lists is a very lucrative side business for many retailers. Companies also use "cross-marketing" to reach potential customers. For example, airlines commonly try to sell customers everything from car rentals, hotel services, and even luxury goods.

In the United States, the compilation and selling of customer databases is all very legal. In the European Union, however, as of October 25, 1998, the compilation and selling of consumer databases became highly regulated. Led by Germany, the European Union, the world's largest economy comprised of many nations of Europe and surrounding areas, has adopted the **European Union Directive on Data Protection**. This directive, which is law, establishes the following rules:

1. If a company wants personal information on an individual, it must get that person's permission after explaining what the information will be used for. For example, an airline would have to explain why it wants birth dates to distinguish one John Smith from another. A person can refuse to give the data.

2. Companies will have to show customers their complete data profiles on demand, correct a profile if it is wrong, and delete it if it is objectionable

3. Web site owners will not be able to use "cookies," the data tags that hook into a log-in name, track the Web sites the user has explored, and send back consumer profiles

4. Companies cannot engage in cross-marketing without customer permission

5. A company cannot transmit personal data about European Union citizens to users in other countries whose privacy laws do not meet European Union standards

Any company wanting to do business in any European Union country will have to abide by the law. Police from European Union countries investigate companies to ensure that they abide by the directive, and companies and individuals may be prosecuted criminally for violating it. Companies like Citicorp, which issues credit cards in Europe, permits the Datenschutz—the German data police—to pay regular visits to its giant data-processing center in Sioux City, South Dakota, to ensure compliance with the new law. Other companies that wish to do business in the European Union must do the same or be denied access to do business there.

This concerted directive from the European Union attempts to dictate a norm for protecting privacy and e-commerce on the Internet to the rest of the world. The Germans argue that a global system requires global regulation to protect privacy rights, and they believe that the new directive accomplishes this goal. Regardless of whether or not the directive establishes a world standard, companies that want to do business in the European Union must abide by its requirements.

THE UNITED NATIONS

One of the most important international organizations is the **United Nations**, which was created by a multilateral treaty on October 24, 1945.[1] Most countries of the world are members of the United Nations. The goals of the United Nations (U.N.), which is headquartered in New York City, are to maintain peace and security in the world, promote economic and social cooperation, and protect human rights (see Exhibit 4.2).

United Nations
An international organization created by a multilateral treaty in 1945.

EXHIBIT 4.2   *Selected Provisions from the Charter of the United Nations*

Our respective Governments, through representatives assembled in the city of San Francisco, who have exhibited their full powers found to be in good and due form, have agreed to the present Charter of the United Nations and do hereby establish an international organization to be known as the United Nations.

Chapter I. Purposes and Principles

Article I The Purposes of the United Nations are:

(1) To maintain international peace and security, and to that end: to take effective collective measures for the pre- vention and removal of threats to the peace, and for the suppression of acts of aggression or other breaches of the peace, and to bring about by peaceful means, and in conformity with the principles of justice and interna- tional law, adjustment or settlement of international disputes or situations which might lead to a breach of the peace;

(2) To develop friendly relations among nations based on respect for the principle of equal rights and self-determi- nation of peoples, and to take other appropriate measures to strengthen universal peace;

(3) To achieve international co-operation in solving international problems of an economic, social, cultural, or humanitarian character, and in promoting and encouraging respect for human rights and for fundamental free- doms for all without distinction as to race, sex, language, or religion; and

(4) To be a centre for harmonizing the actions of nations in the attainment of these common ends.

Article 2 The Organization and its Members, in pursuit of the Purposes stated in Article I, shall act in accor- dance with the following Principles.

(1) The Organization is based on the principle of the sovereign equality of all its Members.

(2) All Members, in order to ensure to all of them the rights and benefits resulting from membership, shall fulfill in good faith the obligations assumed by them in accordance with the present Charter.

(3) All Members shall settle their international disputes by peaceful means in such a manner that international peace and security, and justice, are not endangered.

(4) All Members shall refrain in their international relations from the threat or use of force against the territorial integrity or political independence of any state, or in any other manner inconsistent with the Purposes of the United Nations.

(5) All Members shall give the United Nations every assistance in any action it takes in accordance with the present Charter, and shall refrain from giving assistance to any state against which the United Nations is taking preven- tive or enforcement action.

(6) The Organization shall ensure that states which are not Members of the United Nations act in accordance with these Principles so far as may be necessary for the maintenance of international peace and security.

Governance of the United Nations

The United Nations is governed by

- **The General Assembly** composed of all member nations. As the legislative body of the United Nations, it adopts resolutions concerning human rights, trade, finance and economics, and other matters within the scope of the U.N. Charter. Although resolutions have limited force, they are usually enforced through persuasion and the use of economic and other sanctions.

- **The Security Council** composed of 15 member nations, five of which are permanent members (China, France, Russia, the United Kingdom, and the United States) and ten other countries chosen by the members of the General Assembly to serve two-year terms. The Council is primarily responsible for maintaining international peace and security and has authority to use armed forces.

- **The Secretariat** which administers the day-to-day operations of the United Nations. It is headed by the *Secretary-General*, who is elected by the General Assembly. The Secretary-General may refer matters that threaten international peace and security to the Security Council and use his office to help solve international disputes.

The United Nations is also composed of various autonomous agencies that deal with a wide range of economic and social problems. These include UNESCO (United Nations Educational, Scientific, and Cultural Organization), UNICEF (United Nations International Children's Emergency Fund), the IMF (International Monetary Fund), the World Bank, and IFAD (International Fund for Agricultural Development).

Ethical Perspective

CAUX ROUND TABLE **Principles for International Business**

Ethics is a function of history, culture, religion, and other factors. It differs from culture to culture and person to person. The social responsibility of business also differs considerably, depending on the corporation's philosophy and the influence of the home country's mores.

Recognizing that laws are necessary but insufficient guides for conduct, a group called the Caux Round Table—a collaboration of leaders from various multinational corporations—promulgated an international ethics code called the *Principles for International Business.* These principles are unique because they are based on transnational values from the East and West: the Japanese concept of *kyosei* (living and working together for the common good) and the Western concept of the dignity of the human person. Since they were first introduced in 1994, the *Principles* have been adopted by many multinational corporations around the world.

The Caux Round Table *Principles* that international businesses should take into consideration when making business decisions are:

- **Principle 1** *The Responsibilities of Businesses: Beyond Shareholders Toward Stakeholders* The value of a business to society is the wealth and employment it creates

and the marketable products and services it provides to consumers at a reasonable price commensurate with quality. To create such value, a business must maintain its own economic health and viability, but survival is not a sufficient goal.

Businesses have a role to play in improving the lives of all their customers, employees, and shareholders by sharing with them the wealth they have created. Suppliers and competitors as well should expect businesses to honor their obligations in a spirit of honesty and fairness. As responsible citizens of the local, national, regional, and global communities in which they operate, businesses share a part in shaping the future of those communities.

- **Principle 2** *The Economic and Social Impact of Business: Toward Innovation, Justice, and World Community* Businesses established in foreign countries to develop, produce, or sell should also contribute to the social advancement of those countries by creating productive employment and helping to raise the purchasing power of their citizens. Businesses also should contribute to human rights, education, welfare, and vitalization of the countries in which they operate.

Businesses should contribute to economic and social development not only in the countries in which they operate but also in the world community at large, through effective and prudent use of resources, free and fair competition, and emphasis upon innovation in technology, production methods, marketing, and communications.

• **Principle 3** *Business Behavior: Beyond the Letter of Law Toward a Spirit of Trust* While accepting the legitimacy of trade secrets, businesses should recognize that sincerity, candor, truthfulness, the keeping of promises, and transparency contribute not only to their own credibility and stability but also to the smoothness and efficiency of business transactions, particularly on the international level.

• **Principle 4** *Respect for Rules* To avoid trade frictions and to promote freer trade, equal conditions for competition, and fair and equitable treatment for all participants, businesses should respect international and domestic rules. In addition, they should recognize

that some behavior, although legal, may still have adverse consequences.

• **Principle 5** *Support for Multilateral Trade* Businesses should support the multilateral trade systems of the GATT/World Trade Organization and similar international agreements. They should cooperate in efforts to promote the progressive and judicious liberalization of trade and to relax those domestic measures that unreasonably hinder global commerce, while giving due respect to national policy objectives.

• **Principle 6** *Respect for the Environment* A business should protect and, where possible, improve the environment, promote sustainable development, and prevent the wasteful use of natural resources.

• **Principle 7** *Avoidance of Illicit Operations* A business should not participate in or condone bribery, money laundering, or other corrupt practices; indeed, it should seek cooperation with others to eliminate them. It should not trade in arms or other materials used for terrorist activities, drug traffic, or other organized crime.

*I*NTERNATIONAL REGIONAL ORGANIZATIONS

There are several significant regional organizations whose members have agreed to work together to promote peace and security as well as economic, social, and cultural development. The more important of these organizations are discussed in the following paragraphs.

The European Union

One of the most important international regional organizations is the **European Union (EU),** formerly called the **European Community**, or **Common Market**. The EU was created in 1957. The EU is composed of many countries of Western Europe, including Belgium, France, Italy, Luxembourg, The Netherlands, Germany, Denmark, Ireland, the United Kingdom, Greece, Portugal, and Spain, which represent more than 300 million people and a gross community product that exceeds that of the United States and Canada combined.

The EU's **Council of Ministers** is composed of representatives from each member country who meet periodically to coordinate efforts to fulfill the objectives of the treaty. The Council votes on significant issues and changes to the treaty. Some matters require unanimity, whereas others require only a majority vote. The member nations have surrendered substantial sovereignty to the EU. The EU **Commission**, which is independent of member nations, acts in the best interests of the union. The member nations have delegated substantial powers to the Commission, including authority to enact legislation and take enforcement actions to ensure member compliance with the treaty.

The EU treaty creates open borders for trade by providing for the free flow of capital, labor, goods, and services among member nations. Under the EU, customs duties have been eliminated among member nations. Common customs tariffs have been established for EU trade with the rest of the world. A single monetary unit, the EURO, and common monetary policy have been introduced. An EU central bank equivalent to the U.S. Federal Reserve Board has been established.

European Union (Common Market)
Comprises many countries of Western Europe; created to promote peace and security plus economic, social, and cultural development.

We need to have the spirit of science in international affairs to make the conduct of international affairs the effort to find the right solution, the just solution of international problems, not the effort by each nation to get the better of other nations, to do harm to them when it is possible

Linus Carl Pauline
No More War (1958)

A unanimous vote of existing EU members is needed to admit a new member. Other Western European and some Eastern European countries are expected to apply for and be admitted as members of the EU.

Latin, Central, and South American Economic Communities

Countries of Latin America and the Caribbean have established several regional organizations to promote economic development and cooperation. These include (1) the **Central American Common Market**, comprised of Costa Rica, El Salvador, Guatemala, Honduras, Nicaragua, and Panama; (2) the **MERCOSUR Common Market**, created by Argentina, Brazil, Paraguay, and Uruguay; (3) the **Caribbean Community**, whose member countries are Barbados, Belize, Dominica, Grenada, Jamaica, St. Kitts-Nevis-Anguilla, St. Lucia, St. Vincent, and Trinidad-Tobago; and (4) the **Andean Common Market (ANCOM)**, with current members being Bolivia, Colombia, Ecuador, and Venezuela.

Mexico, the largest industrial country in Latin America and the Caribbean, has entered into a free trade agreement with all the countries of Central America as well as Chile, Colombia, and Venezuela.

African Economic Communities

Several regional economic communities have been formed in Africa. They include (1) the **Economic Community of West African States (ECOWAS)**, created by Dahomey, Gambia, Ghana, Guinea, Guinea-Bissau, Ivory Coast, Liberia, Mali, Mauritania, Niger, Nigeria, Senegal, Sierra Leone, Togo, and Upper Volta; (2) the **Economic and Customs Union of Central Africa**, comprised of Cameroon, Central African Republic, Chad, Congo, and Gabon; and (3) the **East African Community (EAC)**, created by Kenya, Tanzania, and Uganda. In 1991, 51 African countries of the **Organization of African Unity** signed a **Treaty Establishing the African Economic Community**. This wide-ranging treaty with its large organization of countries is expected to wield more power than the smaller African regional organizations.

Middle Eastern Economic Communities

The most well-known Middle Eastern economic organization is **OPEC**, the **Organization of Petroleum Exporting Countries**. This organization—which is composed of the Middle Eastern countries of Iraq, Iran, Kuwait, Libya, and Saudi Arabia, as well as Venezuela—sets quotas on the output of oil production by member nations. The **Gulf Cooperation Council** was established by Bahrain, Kuwait, Oman, Qatar, Saudi Arabia, and the United Arab Emirates to establish an economic trade area.

International Perspective

THE NORTH AMERICAN FREE TRADE AGREEMENT

Mexico is a poor country with a population of about 90 million people. In the past, Mexico was dominated by government-run industries and protectionist laws. In the late 1980s, however, Mexico began a program to privatize its government-owned industries and to embrace capitalism.

In 1990, Mexican President Carlos Salinas de Gortari asked President George Bush to set up a two-country trade pact. Negotiations between the two countries began. Canada joined the negotiations eight months later, largely to make sure the United States did not undercut the earlier U.S.-Canada trade pact.

On August 12, 1992, after 14 months of arduous negotiations, the **North American Free Trade Agreement (NAFTA)** was signed by the leaders of the three countries. The treaty creates a free-trade zone stretching from the

Yukon to the Yucatan, bringing together 360 million consumers in a $6.5-trillion market.

NAFTA eliminates or reduces most of the duties, tariffs, quotas, and other trade barriers between Mexico, the United States, and Canada. Agriculture, automobiles, computers, electronics, energy and petrochemicals, financial services, insurance telecommunications, and many other industries are affected. The treaty contains a safety valve: A country can reimpose tariffs if an import surge from one of the other nations hurts its economy or workers.

Some of the major features of the treaty are:

- Mexican tariffs on vehicles and light trucks were cut in half immediately. Mexican trade barriers and restrictions on autos and auto parts are to be phased out over 10 years
- All North American trade restrictions on textiles and apparel will be eliminated within 10 years
- Banks and securities firms are allowed to establish wholly owned subsidiaries in all three countries
- Mexican import licenses, which cover about 25 percent of U.S. exports, were dropped immediately, and remaining Mexican tariffs will be phased out over 15 years
- Tariffs on import-sensitive American industries will be phased out over 15 years

- Intellectual property rights, such as patents, trademarks, and copyrights, will receive increased protection

Like other regional trading agreements, NAFTA allows the bloc to discriminate against outsiders and to cut deals among themselves. For example, only automobiles that consist of 62.5 percent North American content benefit from the treaty's tariff cuts.

NAFTA also includes special protection for favored industries with a lot of lobby muscle. For example, Mexico's oil industry, far and away its most lucrative, may keep out U.S. companies except on the most minimal basis. The U.S. sugar industry is protected by a quota system. Thus, many economists assert that NAFTA is not a "free trade" pact, but a *managed* trade agreement.

Proponents allege that NAFTA forms a supernational trading region that can more effectively compete with Japan and the European Community. Consumers in all three countries can expect lower prices on a wide variety of goods and services as trade barriers fall and competition increases.

Critics contend that NAFTA will shift American jobs—particularly blue-collar jobs—south of the border where Mexican wage rates are about one-tenth of those in the United States. Environmentalists criticize the pact for not doing enough to prevent and clean up pollution in Mexico.

THE WORLD TRADE ORGANIZATION (WTO)

In 1995, the **World Trade Organization (WTO)** was created as part of the Uruguay Round of trade negotiations on the *General Agreement on Tariffs and Trade (GATT)*. GATT is a multilateral treaty that establishes trade agreements and limits tariffs and trade restrictions among its more than 130 member nations.

The WTO is an international organization located in Geneva, Switzerland. WTO members have entered into many trade agreements among themselves, including international agreements on investments, sale of goods, provision of services, intellectual property, licensing, tariffs, subsidies, and the removal of trade barriers.

World Trade Organization (WTO)
An international organization of more than 130 member nations.

WTO Dispute Resolution

One of the primary functions of the WTO is to hear and decide trade disputes between member nations. Before the creation of the WTO, GATT governed trade disputes between signatory nations. This system was inadequate because any member nation that was found to have violated any GATT trade agreement could itself veto any sanctions imposed by GATT's governing body. The WTO solved this problem by adopting a "judicial" mode of dispute resolution to replace GATT's more politically based one.

A member nation that believes that another member nation has breached one of these agreements can initiate a proceeding to have the WTO hear and decide the dispute.

The dispute is first heard by a three member **panel** of the WTO, which issues a "panel report." The members of the panel are professional judges from member nations. The report is the decision of the panel and contains its findings of fact and law and orders a

Business Brief
One of the primary functions of the WTO is to hear and decide trade disputes between member nations.

panel
A panel of three WTO judges that hears trade disputes between member nations and issues a "panel report."

dispute settlement body

A board comprising of one representative from each WTO member nation that reviews panel reports.

appellate body

A panel of seven justices selected from WTO member nations that hear and decide appeals from decisions by the dispute settlement body.

remedy if a violation has been found. The report is then referred to a newly created **dispute settlement body** of the WTO. This body is required to adopt the panel report unless the body, by consensus, agrees not to adopt the report. Because each member nation has a representative on this settlement body, it can be presumed that panel reports will automatically be adopted because the winning nation to the dispute will almost assuredly vote to adopt it. This is a radical change from the former GATT settlement procedure. Under GATT, unanimity was required to enforce a panel report, and the losing party usually voted to "block" the implementation of a panel's findings against it. One of the most important features of the WTO is the elimination of this blocking power of member nations.

The WTO creates an **appellate body** to which a party can appeal a decision of the dispute settlement body. This appeals court is comprised of seven professional justices selected from member nations. Appeals are heard by panels composed of three members of the appellate body. Appeals are limited to issues of law, not fact. The entire dispute proceeding is completed within nine months when a panel report is not appealed, and in 12 months when there is an appeal. A shortened period is available if the parties agree or if there is an urgent matter that must be decided quickly.

If a violation of a trade agreement is found, the general report and appellate decision can order the offending nation to cease from engaging in the violating practice and to pay damages to the other party. If the offending nation refuses to abide by the order, the WTO can order retaliatory trade sanctions (e.g., tariffs) by other member nations against the noncomplying nation.

International Perspective

WTO TAKES A BITE OUT OF JAPANESE APPLES

Japan produces and sells over $1.6 billion of apples annually, the majority of which are consumed there. The United States, which produces over 100 varieties of apples, would like to export apples to Japan and compete for a share of this market. There's a problem, however. Although Japan has removed tariffs on United States apples, in accordance with WTO rules, the Japanese government has frustrated foreign apple growers with time-consuming apple-testing regulations that have in effect prevented the sale of most varieties of U.S. apples in Japan. Japan insists that these regulations are necessary to ensure the safety of apples imported into their country. U.S. apple growers argue that Japan's complex inspection, fumigation, quarantine, and handling regulations are calculated to accomplish what old tariffs used to do: block another country's goods from entering the market.

After attempts at negotiation failed to resolve the issue, U.S. apple growers took their case to court, the court of the World Trade Organization (WTO). There, the U.S. growers presented evidence that the Japanese rules lacked scientific merit and were blatant protectionist measures designed to shield local farmers from global competition. The Japanese government argued that its rules were required to protect against pests that could travel on the apples.

After hearing presentations by both sides, the Geneva-based WTO concluded that the Japanese apple-testing regulations lacked scientific merit and improperly impeded entry of foreign-grown apples into Japan. The WTO ordered that the apple-testing regulations be disbanded to allow the importation of foreign-grown apples into Japan.

Business Brief

By enforcing trade agreements among its more than 130 member nations, the WTO has become the world's most important trade organization.

The Future of the WTO

The WTO, which has been referred to as the "Supreme Court of Trade," has become the world's most important trade organization. The WTO has jurisdiction to enforce the most important and comprehensive trade agreements in the world among its more than 130 member nations. Some critics argue that the WTO has been granted powers too great and will impinge upon the sovereignty of individual nations. Others herald the WTO as a much needed world court that can peaceably solve trade disputes among nations.

International Perspective

CHINA AND THE UNITED STATES REACH LANDMARK TRADE PACT

For the past 50 years, China and the United States have pursued divergent paths. China became the world's largest communist country and the United States the leading democracy. China maintained its agricultural base, while the United States pursued industrialization. China's businesses were state-owned, while those in the United States were privately owned under a capitalist system. So what do these countries have in common? A new landmark trade pact. For over a decade, these two countries engaged in on-again, off-again trade negotiations. Then in November 1999 the two countries reached a compromise.

Prior to the agreement, the United States annually granted China "most favored nation" status which permitted China to import most goods and services into the United States. The new trade pact eliminates the need for this annual ritual. In exchange for being granted the right to import most goods and services into the United States, China, which had substantially restricted imports into its country, agreed to open its markets to foreign goods and services in the following ways:

- **Telecommunications** Foreign telephone companies may own up to 50 percent of Chinese telephone companies.
- **Entertainment** China will double the number of U.S. films that can be imported into the country to 20 annually; the content of these films must be approved by the Chinese government.
- **Banking and financial services** Foreign banks may offer financial services to Chinese customers. China will allow foreign companies to own up to 49 percent of banks, insurance companies, and other financial-service companies.
- **Distribution** Foreigners may establish their own product distribution systems and sell directly to Chinese customers.
- **Services** Foreigners may establish their own repair and maintenance service businesses in China.
- **Vehicle sales** China will permit foreign automobile manufacturers to sell and finance sales to Chinese customers.
- **Farm products** China will eliminate subsidies of Chinese exports.
- **Internet** Foreign investors may own up to 50 percent of Chinese Internet businesses.

e·biz

The China-U.S. trade agreement was a prelude to China's application to join the World Trade Organization (WTO). China's entry into the WTO makes China a full partner in the world's trading system. The integration of China into the global economy sets the stage for the eventual entry of the other 16 non-market economies into the WTO, from Russia to Vietnam.

The China-U.S. trade agreement is not without its critics. In the United States, labor unions criticize the agreement for its potential to ship U.S. manufacturing jobs to China, while environmentalists complain that little is being done to protect the environment from an industrialized economy the size of China. In China, workers at state-owned enterprises might lose their jobs to foreign capitalist companies that can produce goods and services more efficiently, and China's already impoverished farmers may be harmed by cheap farm products imported from other countries. But leaders from both countries thought the entry of China as a full member of the international trading community was worth these risks.

In recent years, entering into trade agreements has replaced military actions as a new organizational device for the United States and other countries in their international relationships. The landmark China-U.S. trade pact may be only one of many such agreements that underscores the importance that trade and commerce now plays in international politics.

International COURTS

Various international courts have jurisdiction to decide cases involving international disputes. These courts are discussed in the following paragraphs.

International Court of Justice

International Court of Justice
The judicial branch of the United Nations that is located in The Hague, the Netherlands. Also called the *World Court.*

The **International Court of Justice (ICJ)**, also called the **World Court**, is located in The Hague, the Netherlands. It is the judicial branch of the United Nations. Only nations, not individuals or businesses, may have cases decided by this court. The ICJ may hear cases that nations refer to it as well as cases involving treaties and the U.N. Charter. A nation may seek redress on behalf of an individual or business that has a claim against another country. The ICJ is composed of 15 judges who serve nine-year terms; not more than two judges may be from the same nation. A nation that is a party to a dispute before the ICJ may appoint one judge on an ad hoc basis for that case.

The ICJ's jurisdiction is limited by two factors: (1) Nations must voluntarily agree to allow the court to hear a case and (2) nations are not bound by a decision rendered by the court. The court's decision may award monetary damages or injunctive relief and may authorize the Security Council to take further action, including military action. The court's decision applies only to the case at hand and has no precedential value. The ICJ may issue advisory opinions on international law if requested by the United Nations or one of its specialized agencies.

European Court of Justice

European Court of Justice
The judicial branch of the European Community located in Luxembourg. It has jurisdiction to enforce European Community law.

The **European Court of Justice**, located in Luxembourg, has jurisdiction to enforce European Community law. Each EC member country appoints one judge to the court for a six-year term. The court decides disputes concerning member nations' compliance with EC law. The court follows civil law (rather than common law) traditions. Thus, the court may call witnesses, order documents produced, and hire experts.

Member nations, EC institutions, and interested persons and businesses may bring actions before the court. Although national courts may interpret and enforce EC law, the European Court of Justice is the final arbiter of EC law. The court may give preliminary rulings on EC law questions on the motion of a member nation. The highest national courts must refer EC matters to the court. National courts are responsible for enforcing judgments of the European Court of Justice. Although the court's decisions are given great respect, the court has no means of enforcing its decisions against member nations.

An amendment to the Treaty of Rome created the **European Court of First Instance (CFI)**, which is attached to the European Court. It has jurisdiction to hear actions brought by individuals and businesses. The purpose of the court is to relieve some of the European Court's caseload. The CFI started to hear cases in 1989.

Other International Courts

Only when the world is civilized enough to keep promises will we get any kind of international law.

Julius Henry Cohen (1946)

Various other treaties have created regional courts to handle disputes among member nations. For example, the ANCOM and the African Economic Community treaties have each established a Court of Justice to enforce provisions of their respective treaties and to solve disputes among member nations. Regional courts, however, usually do not have mechanisms to enforce their judgments.

National Courts

national courts
The courts of individual nations.

The majority of cases involving international law disputes are heard by the **national courts** of individual nations. This is primarily the case for commercial disputes between private litigants that do not qualify to be heard by an international court. Some countries have specialized courts that hear international commercial disputes. Other countries permit such disputes to proceed through their regular court system.

In the United States, commercial disputes between U.S. companies and foreign governments or parties may be brought in federal district court. The *Alien Tort Statute*[2] allows a noncitizen to sue another noncitizen in federal district court if a tort that occurred outside the United States has been committed in violation of a U.S. treaty or the law of nations.

Most often, a case involving an international dispute will be brought in the national court of the host country or the plaintiff's home country. Jurisdiction is often a highly contested issue.

International Perspective

NATIONALIZATION OF PRIVATELY OWNED PROPERTY BY FOREIGN NATIONS

When a company invests capital in a foreign country in plant, equipment, bank accounts, and such, it runs the risk that that country may **nationalize** (seize) its assets. International law recognizes the right of nations to nationalize private property owned by foreigners if done for a public purpose. Nationalization of assets occurs more often in underdeveloped or developing countries than in developed countries. Nationalization can be classified as

- **Expropriation** The owner of the property is paid just compensation by the government that seized the property.
- **Confiscation** The owner receives no payment or inadequate payment from the government that seized the property.

When a foreign government confiscates property of U.S. firms, there are few legal remedies available to the owners.

The U.S. government may try to recover payment for the firms through diplomatic means, but this is often not successful.

The United States has created the **Overseas Private Investment Corporation (OPIC)**, a government agency, which insures U.S. citizens and businesses against losses incurred as a result of the confiscation of their assets by foreign governments. This is often called **political risk insurance**. Low-cost premiums are charged for the insurance. Those insured that receive a payment under this insurance program must assign their claim against the foreign government to OPIC. The **United States Export-Import Bank (Eximbank)** also offers insurance protection against confiscation to U.S. firms engaged in exporting. Political risk insurance is also available through several private insurance companies.

JUDICIAL RESOLUTION OF INTERNATIONAL DISPUTES

In hearing international disputes, national courts, including those in the United States, may have difficulty securing jurisdiction over the parties and discovering evidence. In addition, national courts are limited by two principles of judicial restraint—the *act of state doctrine* and the *doctrine of sovereign immunity*. These issues are discussed in the following paragraphs.

Judicial Procedure

A party seeking judicial resolution of an international dispute faces several problems, including which nation's courts will hear the case and what law should be applied to the case. Many international contracts contain a **choice of forum** (or **forum-selection**) **clause** that designates which nation's court has jurisdiction to hear a case arising out of the contract. In addition, many contracts also include a **choice of law clause** that designates which nation's laws will be applied in deciding the case. Absent these two clauses, and without the parties agreeing to these matters, an international dispute may never be resolved.

choice of forum clause
Clause in an international contract that designates which nation's court has jurisdiction to hear a case arising out of the contract. Also known as a *forum-selection clause*.

choice of law clause
Clause in an international contract that designates which nation's laws will be applied in deciding a dispute.

To facilitate the deposition of international law disputes, the United States has entered into several treaties concerning legal procedure. The **1965 Convention on the Service Abroad of Judicial and Extra Judicial Documents in Civil and Commercial Matters**[3] establishes a procedure for serving judicial papers on parties located in other countries. The **1970 Hague Convention on the Taking of Evidence Abroad in Civil or Commercial Matters**[4] provides a procedure for conducting discovery in other countries.

𝒞ONCEPT SUMMARY   INTERNATIONAL CONTRACT CLAUSES AFFECTING JURISDICTION AND CHOICE OF LAW

Clause	Description
Forum-selection	Designates the judicial or arbitral forum that will hear and decide the case.
Choice of law	Designates the law to be applied by the court or arbitrator in deciding the case.

Act of State Doctrine

act of state doctrine
States that judges of one country cannot question the validity of an act committed by another country within that other country's borders. It is based on the principle that a country has absolute authority over what transpires within its own territory.

A general principle of international law is that a country has absolute authority over what transpires *within* its own territory. In furtherance of this principle, the **act of state doctrine** states that judges of one country cannot question the validity of an act committed by another country within that other country's own borders. In *United States v. Belmont*,[5] the U.S. Supreme Court declared, "Every sovereign state must recognize the independence of every other sovereign state; and the courts of one will not sit in judgment upon the acts of the government of another, done within its own territory." This restraint on the judiciary is justified under the doctrine of separation of powers and permits the executive branch of the federal government to arrange affairs with foreign governments.

In the following case, the U.S. Supreme Court was called on to decide whether the act of state doctrine barred a civil lawsuit.

W. S. Kirkpatrick & Co., Inc. v. Environmental Tectonics Corporation, International
493 U.S. 400, 110 S.Ct. 701 (1990)
United States Supreme Court

CASE 4.1

FACTS
In 1981, Harry Carpenter, a U.S. citizen and chairman of the board and chief executive officer of W. S. Kirkpatrick & Co., Inc. (Kirkpatrick), learned that the Republic of Nigeria was interested in contracting for the construction of an aeromedical center at Kaduna Air Force Base in Nigeria. He made arrangements with Benson "Tunde" Akindale, a Nigerian citizen, whereby Akindale would help secure the contract for Kirkpatrick by paying bribes to Nigerian officials. In accordance with the plan, the contract was awarded to a wholly owned subsidiary of Kirkpatrick; Kirkpatrick paid the agreed-upon funds to Akindale, which were dispersed as bribes to Nigerian officials. Environmental Tectonics Corporation, International (Environmental), an unsuccessful bidder for the Kaduna contract, learned of the bribes and informed the U.S. embassy in Lagos, Nigeria. In a criminal action, Carpenter and Kirkpatrick pleaded guilty to violating the U.S. Foreign Corrupt Practices Act. Environmental then brought this civil action against Carpenter, Kirkpatrick, and Akindale seeking damages under federal and state racketeering and antitrust laws. The district court held that the action was barred by the act of

state doctrine and dismissed the complaint. The court of appeals reversed. The defendants appealed to the U.S. Supreme Court.

ISSUE

Does the act of state doctrine bar the plaintiff's civil suit against the defendants?

IN THE LANGUAGE OF THE COURT

Scalia, Justice   In every case in which we have held the act of state doctrine applicable, the relief sought or the defense interposed would have required a court in the United States to declare invalid the official act of a foreign sovereign performed within its own territory. In the present case, by contrast, neither the claim nor any asserted defense requires a determination that Nigeria's contract with Kirkpatrick was, or was not, effective.

Act of state issues arise only when a court must *decide*—that is, when that outcome of the case turns upon—the effect of official action by a foreign sovereign. When that question is not in the case, neither is the act of state doctrine. That is the situation here. Regardless of what the court's factual findings may suggest as to the legality of the Nigerian contract, its legality is simply not a question to be decided in the present suit, and there is thus no occasion to apply the rule of decision that the act of state doctrine requires.

The short of the matter is this: Courts in the United States have the power, and ordinarily the obligation, to decide cases and controversies properly presented to them. The act of state doctrine does not establish an exception for cases and controversies that may embarrass foreign governments, but merely requires that, in the process of deciding, the acts of foreign sovereigns taken within their own jurisdictions shall be deemed valid. That doctrine has no application to the present case because the validity of no foreign sovereign act is at issue.

DECISION AND REMEDY

The Supreme Court held that the act of state doctrine did not apply to the case and therefore did not bar plaintiff Environmental's civil lawsuit against the defendants.

Case Questions

Critical Legal Thinking   Should the act of state doctrine be followed by the United States?

Ethics   Did Carpenter act ethically in obtaining the contract with the Nigerian government?

Business Application   What implications does the act of state doctrine have for businesses? Explain.

The Doctrine of Sovereign Immunity

One of the oldest principles of international law is the **doctrine of sovereign immunity**. Under this doctrine, *countries* are granted immunity from suits in courts in other countries. For example, if a U.S. citizen wanted to sue the government of China in a U.S. court, he or she could not (subject to the exceptions discussed below).

Originally, the United States granted absolute immunity to foreign governments from suits in U.S. courts. In 1952, the United States switched to the principle of *qualified* or *restricted immunity*, which was eventually codified in the **Foreign Sovereign Immunities Act of 1976 (FSIA)**.[6] This act now exclusively governs suits against foreign nations in the United States, whether in federal or state court. Most Western nations have adopted the principle of restricted immunity. Other countries still follow the doctrine of absolute immunity.

Exceptions   The FSIA provides that a foreign country is not immune from lawsuits in U.S. courts in the following two situations:

1. The foreign country has waived its immunity, either explicitly or by implication.
2. The action is based upon a *commercial activity* carried on in the United States by the foreign country or carried on outside the United States but causing a direct effect in the United States.

What constitutes "commercial activity" is the most litigated aspect of the FSIA. If it is commercial activity, the foreign sovereign is subject to suit in the United States; if it is not, the foreign sovereign is immune from suit in this country. In the following case, the Supreme Court had to decide whether a foreign sovereign had engaged in commercial activity that would subject it to suit in the United States.

doctrine of sovereign immunity
States that countries are granted immunity from suits in courts of other countries.

Foreign Sovereign Immunities Act
Exclusively governs suits against foreign nations that are brought in federal or state courts in the United States; codifies the principle of *qualified* or *restricted* immunity.

Business Brief
A foreign nation may be sued in a court in the United States if that nation has engaged in a *commercial activity* that either (1) is carried on in the United States or (2) is carried on outside the United States but causes a direct effect in the United States.

Republic of Argentina v. Weltover, Inc.
112 S.Ct. 2160 (1992)
United States Supreme Court

CASE 4.2

FACTS
In an attempt to stabilize its currency, Argentina and its central bank, Banco Central (collectively Argentina), issued bonds called "Bonods." The bonds, which were sold to investors worldwide, provided for repayment in U.S. dollars through transfers on the London, Frankfurt, Zurich, and New York markets at the bondholder's election. Argentina lacked sufficient foreign exchange to retire the bonds when they matured. Argentina unilaterally extended the time for payment and offered bondholders substitute instruments as a means of rescheduling the debts. Two Panamanian corporations and a Swiss bank refused the rescheduling and insisted that full payment be made in New York. When Argentina did not pay, they brought a breach of contract action against Argentina in U.S. district court in New York. Argentina moved to dismiss, alleging that it was not subject to suit in U.S. courts under the federal Foreign Sovereign Immunities Act (FSIA). The plaintiffs asserted that the "commercial activity" exception to the act applied, subjecting Argentina to suit in U.S. court. The district court denied Argentina's motion for dismissal and the court of appeals affirmed. Argentina appealed to the U.S. Supreme Court.

ISSUE
Does the doctrine of sovereign immunity prevent the plaintiffs from suing Argentina in a U.S. court?

IN THE LANGUAGE OF THE COURT
Scalia, Justice   The dispute pertains to whether the unilateral refinancing of the Bonods was taken "in connection with a commercial activity" of Argentina, and whether it had a "direct effect in the United States." When a foreign government acts, not as regulator of a market, but in the manner of a private player within it, the foreign sovereign's actions are "commercial" within the meaning of the FSIA.

The issue is whether the particular actions that the foreign state performs are the type of actions by which a private party engages in "trade and traffic or commerce." Thus, a foreign government's issuance of regulations limiting foreign currency exchange is a sov-

ereign activity, because such authoritative control of commerce cannot be exercised by a private party; whereas a contract to buy army boots or even bullets is a "commercial" activity, because private companies can similarly use sales contracts to acquire goods.

The commercial character of the Bonods is confirmed by the fact that they are in almost all respects garden-variety debt instruments: they may be held by private parties; they are negotiable and may be traded on the international market (except in Argentina); and they promise a future stream of cash income. We conclude that Argentina's issuance of the Bonods was a "commercial activity" under the FSIA.

We have little difficulty concluding that Argentina's unilateral rescheduling of the maturity dates on the Bonods had a "direct effect" in the United States. Respondents had designated their accounts in New York as the place of payment, and Argentina made some interest payments into those accounts before announcing that it was rescheduling the payments. Because New York was thus the place of performance for Argentina's ultimate contractual obligations, the rescheduling of those obligations necessarily had a "direct effect" in the United States: Money that was supposed to have been delivered to a New York bank for deposit was not forthcoming.

DECISION AND REMEDY
The Supreme Court held that Argentina's issuance of the bonds was a commercial activity that had a direct effect in the United States. Therefore, the commercial activity exception to the Sovereign Immunities Act applied, which allowed the plaintiffs to sue Argentina in a U.S. court.

Case Questions

Critical Legal Thinking   Should the United States recognize the doctrine of absolute sovereign immunity or qualified immunity? Explain.

Ethics   Did the government of Argentina act ethically in not paying the bonds when due and unilaterally rescheduling the debt?

Business Application   Is there more risk for investors who invest in obligations of foreign countries than in obligations of the U.S. government?

*C*ONCEPT SUMMARY   ACT OF STATE DOCTRINE AND SOVEREIGN IMMUNITY COMPARED

Doctrine	Description
Act of state	Act of a government in its *own country* is not subject to suit in a foreign country's courts.
Sovereign immunity	Act of a government in a *foreign country* is not subject to suit in the foreign country. Some countries provide absolute immunity, whereas other countries (such as the United States) provide limited immunity.

INTERNATIONAL ARBITRATION

As an alternative to litigation, the parties to an international contract may agree that any dispute that arises between them regarding the transaction will be decided by mandatory arbitration. **Arbitration** is a nonjudicial method of dispute resolution whereby a neutral third party decides the case. The parties agree to be bound by the arbitrator's decision. Generally, arbitration is faster, less expensive, less formal, and more private than litigation.

An **arbitration clause** should specify the arbitrator or the means of selecting the arbitrator. Several organizations conduct international arbitrations, including the American Arbitration Association, the International Chamber of Commerce, the International Center for the Settlement of Investment Disputes, and the United Nations Commission on International Trade Law. International arbitrators are usually businesspeople or lawyers experienced in worldwide commercial transactions. An arbitration clause should also specify the law to be applied by the arbitrator. Arbitration clauses are appearing in an increasing number of international contracts.

An arbitrator issues an *award*, not a judgment. An arbitrator does not have the power to enforce the award it renders. Therefore, if the losing party refuses to pay the award, the winning party must petition a court to enforce the award. More than 50 countries that conduct the bulk of worldwide commercial transactions are signatories to the **United Nations Convention on the Recognition and Enforcement of Foreign Arbitral Awards** (Convention).[7] The United States adopted the Convention in 1970 and amended the Federal Arbitration Act to reflect this international law.[8] The recipient of an arbitral award subject to the Convention can attach property of the loser that is located in any country that is a signatory to the Convention.

arbitration
A nonjudicial method of dispute resolution whereby a neutral third party decides the case.

arbitration clause
A clause contained in many international contracts that stipulates that any dispute between the parties concerning the performance of the contract will be submitted to an arbitrator or arbitration panel for resolution.

Contemporary Business Application

ARBITRATION OF INTERNATIONAL BUSINESS DISPUTES

Arbitration clauses often appear in international commercial agreements signed by U.S. companies that designate that a foreign country's arbitration system will hear and decide the dispute. Consider the following case.

Mitsubishi Motors Corporation (Mitsubishi) is a Japanese corporation that manufactures automobiles and has its principal place of business in Tokyo, Japan. Soler Chrysler-Plymouth, Inc. (Soler), is a Puerto Rican corporation with its principal place of business in Puerto Rico. On October 31, 1979, Soler entered into a sales and distributor agreement that gave Soler the right to sell Mitsubishi-manufactured automobiles within a designated area, including metropolitan San Juan. The agreement included an arbitration clause that stipulated, "All disputes, controversies, or differences which may arise between the parties out of this Agreement or for the breach thereof, shall be finally settled by arbitration in Japan in accordance with the rules and regulations of the Japan Commercial Arbitration Association." Initially, Soler did a brisk business in Mitsubishi-manufactured vehicles. In early 1981, the new-car market slackened, and Soler ran into serious difficulties in meeting the agreed-upon minimum sales volume. Soler repudiated its agreement with Mitsubishi. Mitsubishi requested arbitration before the Japan Commercial Arbitration Association and brought an action in U.S. district court in Puerto Rico for an order compelling arbitration. Soler filed a cross-complaint alleging that Mitsubishi violated U.S. antitrust laws. The district court held that all claims were subject to arbitration. The court of appeals reversed as to the **antitrust claims**. Mitsubishi appealed to the U.S. Supreme Court, arguing that issues involving U.S. antitrust laws are subject to arbitration by an arbitration panel located in a foreign country.

The U.S. Supreme Court agreed with Mitsubishi and held that issues involving U.S. antitrust laws may be arbitrated by a foreign arbitration panel and ordered the arbitration agreement between Soler and Mitsubishi enforced. The Supreme Court noted that by agreeing to arbitrate a statutory claim, a party does not forgo the substantive

(box continues)

rights afforded by the statute; it only submits to their resolution in an arbitral, rather than a judicial, forum. It trades the procedures and opportunity for review of the courtroom for the simplicity, informality, and expedition of arbitration. In upholding international arbitration of the antitrust claims, the Supreme Court noted, "The expansion of American business and industry will hardly be encouraged if, notwithstanding solemn contracts, we insist on a parochial concept that all disputes must be resolved under our laws and in our courts. We cannot have trade and commerce in world markets and international waters exclusively on our terms, governed by our laws, and resolved in our courts. We conclude that concerns of international comity, respect for the capacities of foreign and transnational tribunals, and sensitivity to the need of the international commercial system for predictability in the resolution of disputes require that we enforce the parties' arbitration agreement." [*Mitsubishi Motors Corporation v. Soler Chrysler-Plymouth, Inc.*, 473 U.S. 614, 105 S.Ct. 3346 (1985)]

CRIMINAL PROSECUTIONS IN THE INTERNATIONAL ARENA

extradition

Sending a person back to a country for criminal prosecution.

A nation has authority to criminally prosecute individuals or businesses that commit crimes within its territory or that violate that nation's laws, as well as its citizens (including businesses) that commit crimes elsewhere. One of the main problems of criminal prosecution, however, is that the perpetrator may be taking refuge in another country. In such cases, the person may be **extradited** (sent back) to the country seeking to criminally try him or her. The United States has entered into *extradition treaties* with many countries. If the perpetrator is not extradited, the crime may go unpunished.

International Perspective

MEXICO BECOMES AN INTERNATIONAL BUSINESS JUGGERNAUT

For decades the economy of Mexico was stagnant compared to the United States. But in 1992, Mexico joined the United States and Canada to create the North American Free Trade Agreement (NAFTA), effective January 1, 1994. By reducing tariffs and eliminating most protectionism, the Mexican economy improved steadily under the new NAFTA rules.

There was one major problem: As of 1999, 85 percent of Mexico's exports went to the United States. Once Mexico saw that the regional trade pacts were good for its economy, it started seeking out new trading partners to balance its exports and reduce its reliance on the United States. Mexico also feared the consequences of China increasing its exports to the United States under the new China-U.S. trade pact. To boost its export trade, Mexico entered into individual trade treaties with over a dozen Central and South American countries, including Chile and Columbia.

But Mexico decided to exploit its unique position and sought an even bigger deal. After much negotiation, in November 1999 Mexico signed an international trade agreement with the 15-member European Union (EU).

This international trade agreement gave Mexico access to the markets of the United Kingdom, Germany, France, Spain, Greece, and the other European nations that represent over 300 million people. The pact called for Europe to grant duty-free entry to most Mexican products beginning in 2000, and for Mexico to gradually open its markets to EU goods and services by 2007. The pact reduced tariffs and duties from an average of 12 percent to two percent or lower, depending on the type of goods and services.

With the creation of this new trade pact, Mexico became the only country other than Israel to have international trade agreements with both the United States, Canada, and the European nations of the EU. This new position encourages European firms to establish factories in Mexico so that they can more cheaply sell goods in the United States, and for U.S. firms to establish factories in Mexico as well so they can directly export goods more cheaply to the EU. The new trade pact with the EU assures that Mexico, already the world's eighth-largest trading country, will continue the growth in its industrial-export economy.

Working the Web

U.S. State Department   The U.S. State Department has a great Web site. You can find out all about where the secretary of state is traveling. You can even get situation updates, testimony, and briefings.

Visit at **www.state.gov**

ASIL Guide to Electronic Resources for International Law   This guide is a development project of the American Society of International Law. It has links to materials on all aspects of international law.

Visit at **www.asil.org/resource/home.htm**.

Research Guide to International Law on the Internet—International Environmental Law   From this site, you can find treaties, documents and annotated Web sites.

Visit at **www.spfo.unibo.it/spolfo/ ENVLAW.htm**

Eye on International Law   This is a great site for links to all sorts of materials on international trade law and commercial arbitration.

Visit at **www.uni-muenster.de/Jura.iwr/english/berger/linkse/linkse.html**

Legal Research on International Law Issues Using the Internet, by Lyonette Louis-Jacques   This is just about the greatest Internet site there is for finding links to all aspects of international law. Professor Louis-Jacques has outdone herself by including major Web sites, international organizations, government agencies, publishers and vendors, databases, library catalogs, discussion groups, news sources, research guides, and more. Many of the links are annotated.

Visit at **www.lib.uchicago.edu/~llou/forintlaw.html**

CYBER EXERCISES

1. From the U.S. State Department Web site, can you find materials on Cuba?

2. Make a list of the materials you find on human rights from the ASIL Guide.

3. From the *Research Guide to International Law on the Internet*, find the North American Agreement on Environmental Cooperation.

4. From the Eye on International Business Law, visit the home page and find information on the Vienna Sales Convention.

5. From the Lyonette Louis-Jacques list, can you link to the home page for the United Nations?

CASES AND EXERCISES

CRITICAL LEGAL THINKING CASES

4.1.   Prior to 1918, the Petrograd Metal Works, a Russian corporation, deposited a large sum of money with August Belmont, a private banker doing business in New York City under the name of August Belmont & Co. (Belmont). In 1918, the Soviet government nationalized the corporation and appropriated all of its property and assets wherever situated, including the deposit account with Belmont. As a result, the deposit became the property of the Soviet government. In 1933, the Soviet government and the United States entered into an agreement to settle claims and counterclaims between them. As part of the settlement, it was agreed that the Soviet government would take no steps to enforce claims against American nationals (including Belmont) and assigned all such claims to the United States. The United States brought this action against the executors of Belmont's estate to recover the money originally deposited with Belmont by Petrograd Metal Works. Who owns the money? [*United States v. Belmont*, 301 U.S. 324, 57 S.Ct. 758 (1937)]

4.2.   Banco Nacional de Costa Rica (Bank) is a bank wholly owned by the government of Costa Rica. It is subject to the rules and regulations adopted by the Minister of Finance and Central Bank of Costa Rica. In December 1980, the Bank borrowed $40 million from a consortium of private banks located in the United Kingdom and the United States. The Bank signed promissory notes agreeing to repay the principal plus interest on the loan in four equal installments due on July 30, August 30, September 30, and October 30, 1981. The money was to be used to provide export financing of sugar and sugar products from Costa Rica. The loan agreements and promissory notes were signed in New York City and the loan proceeds were tendered to the Bank there.

On July 30, 1981, the Bank paid the first installment on the loan. The Bank did not, however, make the other three installment payments and defaulted on the loan. The lending banks sued the Bank in U.S. district court in New York to recover the unpaid principal and interest. The Bank alleged in defense that on August 27, 1981, the Minister of Finance and the Central Bank of Costa Rica issued a decree forbidding the repayment of loans by the Bank to private lenders, including the lending banks in this case. The action was taken because Costa Rica was having trouble servicing debts to foreign creditors. The Bank alleged the act of state doctrine prevented the plaintiffs from recovering on their loans to the Bank. Who wins? [*Libra Bank Limited v. Banco Nacional de Costa Rica*, 570 F. Supp. 870 (S.D.N.Y. 1983)]

4.3. Zapata Off-Shore Company (Zapata) is a Houston, Texas-based American corporation that engages in drilling oil wells throughout the world. Unterweser Reederei, GMBH (Unterweser) is a German corporation that provides ocean shipping and towing services. In November 1967, Zapata requested bids from companies to tow its self-elevating drilling rig "Chaparral" from Louisiana to a point off Ravenna, Italy, in the Adriatic Sea, where Zapata had agreed to drill certain wells. Unterweser submitted the lowest bid and was requested to submit a proposed contract to Zapata, which it did. The contract submitted by Unterweser contained the following provision: "Any dispute arising must be treated before the London Court of Justice." Zapata executed the contract without deleting or modifying this provision.

On January 5, 1968, Unterweser's deep-sea tug *Bremen* departed Venice, Louisiana, with the Chaparral in tow, bound for Italy. On January 9, while the flotilla was in international waters in the middle of the Gulf of Mexico, a severe storm arose. The sharp roll of the Chaparral in Gulf waters caused portions of it to break off and fall into the sea, seriously damaging the Chaparral. Zapata instructed the *Bremen* to tow the Chaparral to Tampa, Florida, the nearest port of refuge, which it did. On January 12, Zapata filed suit against Unterweser and the *Bremen* in U.S. district court in Florida, alleging negligent towing and breach of contract. The defendants assert that suit can be brought only in the London Court of Justice. Who is correct? [*MIS Bremen and Unterweser Reederei, GMBH v. Zapata Off-Shore Company*, 407 U.S. 1, 92 S.Ct. 1907 (1972)]

4.4. Alberto-Culver Company (Alberto-Culver), an American company incorporated in Delaware with its principal office in Illinois, manufactures and distributes toiletries and hair products in the United States and other countries. Fritz Scherk owned three interrelated businesses organized under the laws of Germany and Liechtenstein that were engaged in the manufacture of toiletries. After substantial negotiations, in February 1969, Alberto-Culver entered into a contract with Scherk to purchase his three companies along with all rights held by these companies to trademarks in cosmetic goods. The contract contained a number of express warranties whereby Scherk guaranteed the sole and unencumbered ownership of these trademarks. The contract also contained a clause that provided that "any controversy or claim that shall arise out of this agreement or breach thereof" was to be referred to arbitration before the International Chamber of Commerce in Paris, France. The transaction closed in June 1969 in Geneva, Switzerland.

Nearly one year later, Alberto-Culver allegedly discovered that the trademark rights purchased under the contract were subject to substantial encumbrances that threatened to give other parties superior rights to the trademarks and to restrict or preclude Alberto-Culver's use of them. Alberto-Culver sued Scherk in U.S. district court in Illinois, alleging fraudulent misrepresentation in violation of Section 10(b) of the federal Securities Exchange Act of 1934. Scherk asserts in defense that the case is subject to mandatory arbitration in Paris. Who is correct? [*Scherk v. Alberto-Culver Co.*, 417 U.S. 506, 94 S.Ct. 2249 (1974)]

ETHICS CASES

4.5. Bank of Jamaica (Bank) is wholly owned by the government of Jamaica. Chisholm & Co. (Chisholm & Co.) is a Florida corporation that is owned by James Henry

Chisholm, a Florida resident. The Export-Import Bank of the United States (Eximbank) provides financial services and credit insurance to export and import companies. In January

1982, the Bank and Chisholm & Co. agreed that Chisholm & Co. would arrange lines of credit from various banks and procure $50 million of credit insurance from Eximbank to be available to aid Jamaican importers. Chisholm & Co. was to be paid commissions for its services.

Chisholm & Co. negotiated and arranged for $50 million of credit insurance from Eximbank and lines of credit from Florida National Bank, Bankers Trust Company, and Irving Trust Company. Chisholm & Co. also arranged meetings between the Bank and the American banks. Unbeknownst to Chisholm & Co., the Bank went directly to Eximbank to exclude Chisholm & Co. from the Jamaica program and requested that the credit insurance be issued solely in the name of the Bank; as a result, Chisholm & Co.'s Eximbank insurance application was not considered. The Bank also obtained lines of credit from other companies and paid them commissions. Chisholm & Co. sued the Bank in U.S. district court in Miami, Florida, alleging breach of contract and seeking damages. The Bank filed a motion to dismiss the complaint, alleging that its actions were protected by sovereign immunity. Who wins? Did the Bank of Jamaica act ethically in trying to avoid its contract obligations? [*Chisholm & Co. v. Bank of Jamaica*, 643 F. Supp. 1393 (S.D. Fla. 1986)]

4.6. Nigeria, an African nation, while in the midst of a boom period due to oil exports, entered into $1 billion of contracts with various countries to purchase huge quantities of Portland cement. Nigeria was going to use the cement to build and improve the country's infrastructure. Several of the contracts were with American companies, including Texas Trading & Milling Corporation (Texas Trading). Nigeria substantially overbought cement, and the country's docks and harbors became clogged with ships waiting to unload. Unable to accept delivery of the cement it had bought, Nigeria repudiated many of its contracts, including the one with Texas Trading. When Texas Trading sued Nigeria in a U.S. district court to recover damages for breach of contract, Nigeria asserted in defense that the doctrine of sovereign immunity protected it from liability. Who wins? Was the conduct of the parties ethical in this case? [*Texas Trading & Milling Corp. v. Federal Republic of Nigeria*, 647 F.2d 300 (2nd Cir. 1981)]

CRITICAL LEGAL THINKING WRITING ASSIGNMENT

Read Case A.4 in the Case Appendix [*OHG v. Kolodny*]. This case is excerpted from the court's opinion. Review and brief the case. In your brief, be sure to answer the following questions.

1. In the German action, who was the plaintiff? Who was the defendant?

2. Who was the plaintiff in the New York action? Who was the defendant?

3. What was the decision of the German court? Would the decision under New York law have been different? Explain.

4. What was the plaintiff's argument to the New York court? Explain.

5. Did the enforcement of the German judgment violate New York's public policy?

NOTES

1. The Charter of the United Nations was entered into force October 24, 1945; it was adopted by the United States October 24, 1945 [59 Stat. 1031, T.S. 993, 3 Bevans 1153, 1976 Y.B.U.N. 1043].
2. 28 U.S.C. § 1350.
3. 20 U.S.T. 361 et seq., T.I.A.S. 6638.
4. 23 U.S.T. 2555 et seq., T.I.A.S. 7444.
5. 301 U.S. 324, 57 S.Ct. 758 (1937).
6. 28 U.S.C. §§ 1602–1611
7. 21 U.S.T. 2517, T.I.A.S. 6997.
8. 9 U.S.C. §§ 201-208.

Intentional Torts, Negligence, and Strict Liability

Negligence is not actionable unless it involves the invasion of a legally protected interest, the violation of a right. Proof of negligence in the air, so to speak, will not do.

C. J. CARDOZO *Palsgraf v. Long Island Railroad Co. (1928)*

Chapter Objectives

After studying this chapter, you should be able to

1. List and describe intentional torts against persons and against property.
2. Define the tort of false imprisonment and apply merchant protection statutes.
3. Describe the *torts of defamation of character* and invasion of privacy.
4. List and explain the elements necessary to prove negligence.
5. Define and distinguish between the torts of intentional and negligent infliction of emotional distress.
6. Apply special negligence doctrines such as negligence per se and *res ipsa loquitur.*
7. List and describe defenses to tort liability.
8. Describe and list the elements to prove the tort of fraud.
9. Define *racketeering* under the civil RICO statute and the remedies that are awarded to successful plaintiffs.
10. Describe and apply the doctrine of strict liability.

Chapter Contents

Tort is the French word for a "wrong." Tort law protects a variety of injuries and provides remedies for them. Under tort law, an injured party can bring a *civil lawsuit* to seek compensation for a wrong done to the party or to the party's property. Many torts have their origin in common law. The courts and legislatures have extended tort law to reflect changes in modern society.

Tort damages are monetary damages that are sought from the offending party. They are intended to compensate the injured party for the injury suffered. They may consist of past and future medical expenses, loss of wages, pain and suffering, mental distress, and other damages caused by the defendant's tortious conduct. If the victim of a tort dies, his or her beneficiaries can bring a *wrongful death action* to recover damages from the defendant. *Punitive damages*, which are awarded to punish the defendant, may be recovered in intentional tort and strict liability cases. Other remedies, such as injunctions, may be available, too.

This chapter discusses various tort laws, including intentional torts, negligence, and strict liability.

Intentional Torts Against Persons

The law protects a person from unauthorized touching, restraint, or other contact. In addition, the law protects a person's reputation and privacy. Violations of these rights are actionable as torts. ***Intentional torts against the person*** are discussed in the paragraphs that follow.

Assault

Assault is (1) the threat of immediate harm or offensive contact or (2) any action that arouses reasonable apprehension of imminent harm. Actual physical contact is unnecessary. Threats of future harm are not actionable. For example, suppose a 6-foot-5-inch, 250-pound male makes a fist and threatens to punch a 5-foot, 100-pound woman. If the woman is afraid that the man will physically harm her, she can sue him for assault. If she is a black-belt karate champion and laughs at the threat, there is no assault because the threat does not cause any apprehension.

Battery

Battery is unauthorized and harmful or offensive physical contact with another person. Basically, the interest protected here is each person's reasonable sense of dignity and safety. For example, intentionally hitting someone is considered battery because it is harmful. Note that there does not have to be direct physical contact between the victim and the perpetrator. If an injury results, throwing a rock, shooting an arrow or a bullet, knocking off a hat, pulling a chair out from under someone, and poisoning a drink are all instances of actionable battery. The victim need not be aware of the harmful or offensive contact (e.g., it may take place while the victim is asleep). Assault and battery often occur together, although they do not have to (e.g., the perpetrator hits the victim on the back of the head without any warning).

Transferred Intent Doctrine   Sometimes a person acts with the intent to injure one person but actually injures another. The *doctrine of transferred intent* applies to these situations. Under this doctrine, the law transfers the perpetrator's intent from the target to the actual victim of the act. The victim can then sue the defendant.

False Imprisonment

The intentional confinement or restraint of another person without authority or justification and without that person's consent constitutes **false imprisonment**. The victim may be restrained or confined by physical force, barriers, threats of physical harm, or the

---

tort

A wrong. There are three categories: (1) intentional torts, (2) unintentional torts (negligence), and (3) strict liability.

Thoughts much too deep for tears subdue the Court When I assumpsit bring, and godlike waive a tort.

*J. L. Adolphus
The Circuiteers (1885)*

intentional tort

A category of torts that requires that the defendant possessed the intent to do the act that caused the plaintiff's injuries.

assault

(1) The threat of immediate harm or offensive contact or (2) any action that arouses reasonable apprehension of imminent harm. Actual physical contact is unnecessary.

battery

Unauthorized and harmful or offensive physical contact with another person. Direct physical contact is not necessary.

false imprisonment

The intentional confinement or restraint of another person without authority or justification and without that person's consent.

merchant protection statutes

Statutes that allow merchants to stop, detain, and investigate suspected shoplifters without being held liable for false imprisonment if (1) there are reasonable grounds for the suspicion, (2) suspects are detained for only a reasonable time, and (3) investigations are conducted in a reasonable manner.

perpetrator's false assertion of legal authority (i.e., *false arrest*). A threat of future harm or moral pressure is not considered false imprisonment. The false imprisonment must be complete. For example, merely locking one door to a building when other exits are not locked is not false imprisonment. A person is not obliged to risk danger or an affront to his or her dignity by attempting to escape.

Merchant Protection Statutes   Shoplifting causes substantial losses to merchants each year. Almost all states have enacted **merchant protection statutes**, also known as the **shopkeeper's privilege**. These statutes allow merchants to stop, detain, and investigate suspected shoplifters without being held liable for false imprisonment if

> There are reasonable grounds for the suspicion,
> Suspects are detained for only a reasonable time, and
> Investigations are conducted in a reasonable manner.

Contemporary Business Application

WAL-MART SHOPPER WINS $3.2 MILLION

On Christmas Eve 1995, LaShawna Goodman went to the local Wal-Mart store in Opelika, Alabama, to do some last minute holiday shopping. She brought along her two young daughters and a telephone she had purchased earlier at Wal-Mart to exchange. She presented the telephone and receipt to a Wal-Mart employee, who took the telephone. Unable to find another telephone she wanted, Goodman retrieved the previously purchased telephone from the employee, bought another item, and left. Outside, Ms. Goodman was stopped by Wal-Mart security personnel and was accused of stealing the phone. Goodman offered to show the Wal-Mart employees the original receipt, but the Wal-Mart employees detained her and called the police. Ms. Goodman was handcuffed in front of her children. Wal-Mart filed criminal charges against Ms. Goodman.

At the criminal trial, Ms. Goodman was acquitted of all charges. Now it was Ms. Goodman's turn: She filed a civil lawsuit against Wal-Mart Stores, Inc., to recover damages for falsely accusing her of stealing the telephone. She pre-

sented the evidence as outlined above. Wal-Mart asserted the defense that it was in its rights to have detained Ms. Goodman as it did and to prosecute Ms. Goodman based on its investigation. Wal-Mart asserted that the merchant protection statute protected its actions in this case. Wal-Mart alleged that it had reasonable grounds to suspect Ms. Goodman of shoplifting, that it conducted the investigation in a reasonable manner, and that it had sufficient grounds to have Ms. Goodman prosecuted criminally based on its investigation.

But the jury did not accept Wal-Mart's plea that it had acted reasonably. The jury rejected Wal-Mart's defenses, including the shopkeeper's privilege and its allegations that it had not maliciously prosecuted her. The jury determined that Ms. Goodman should be awarded $200,000 in compensatory damages for her suffering. The jury then decided that Wal-Mart had acted so badly in this case that it tacked on $3 million in punitive damages in its award to Ms. Goodman just to teach Wal-Mart a lesson. [*Goodman v. Wal-Mart* (AL 1999)]

defamation of character

False statement(s) made by one person about another. In court, the plaintiff must prove that (1) the defendant made an untrue statement of fact about the plaintiff and (2) the statement was intentionally or accidentally published to a third party.

Defamation of Character

A person's reputation is a valuable asset. Therefore, every person is protected from false statements made by others during his or her lifetime. This protection ends upon a person's death. The tort of **defamation of character** requires a plaintiff to prove that (1) the defendant made an *untrue statement of fact* about the plaintiff and (2) the statement was intentionally or accidentally *published* to a third party. In this context publication simply means that a third person heard or saw the untrue statement. It does not just mean appearance in newspapers, magazines, or books.

The name for an oral defamatory statement is *slander*. A false statement that appears in a letter, newspaper, magazine, book, photograph, movie, video, and the like is called *libel*. Most courts hold that defamatory statements in radio and television broadcasts are considered libel because of the permanency of the media.

The publication of an untrue statement of fact is not the same as the publication of an opinion. The publication of opinions is usually not actionable. "My lawyer is lousy" is an opinion. Because defamation is defined as an untrue statement of fact, truth is an absolute defense to a charge of defamation.

Public Figures as Plaintiffs In *New York Times Co. v. Sullivan*,[1] the U.S. Supreme Court held that *public officials* cannot recover for defamation unless they can prove that the defendant acted with "actual malice." Actual malice means that the defendant made the false statement knowingly or with reckless disregard of its falsity. This requirement has since been extended to *public figure* plaintiffs such as movie stars, sports personalities, and other celebrities.

In the following case, the court found the defendant liable for defamation of character.

> Whatever a man publishes he publishes at his peril.
>
> Lord Mansfield C.J.R. v. Woodfall (1774)

Sommer v. Gabor
40 Cal.App.4th 1455, 48 Cal.Rptr.2d 235 (1996)
Court of Appeals of California

CASE 5.1

FACTS
Elke Sommer, who was born in Germany in 1940, is an actress who played romantic leads in over 70 films in Europe and the United States from 1958 to 1991. She also played many lead roles in live theater and TV productions. She obtained an international reputation as a sexy leading lady. Zsa Zsa Gabor is an actress who starred in films in both Europe and the United States. In the February 22, 1990, issue of *Freizeit Revue*, a German-language woman's publication with a worldwide circulation of over one million, including 310 in southern California, Gabor said that Sommer "is broke, had to sell her house in Hollywood, now lives in the worst section, hangs out in the sleaziest bars, and lives from handknit pullover sweaters that she now sells for $150." Gabor also stated that no one wants to have anything to do with Sommer anymore.

Sommer sued Gabor for defamation of character. At trial, Sommer proved that Gabor's statements were untrue. Sommer proved that knitting was just a hobby, that she had assets worth over 30 million marks, and she did not frequent bars. Sommer also proved that she suffered sleeplessness, headaches, upset stomach, and had to see a psychiatrist because of Gabor's comments. Gabor defended, alleging that her comments were only opinions and therefore not actionable. The trial court held in favor of Sommer and awarded her $800,000 in compensatory damages and $450,000 in punitive damages against Gabor. Gabor appealed.

ISSUE
Were Gabor's comments statements of opinion or statements of fact?

IN THE LANGUAGE OF THE COURT
Lillie, Presiding Justice *Without merit is appellant Gabor's contention that all of the statements attributed to her are subjective opinions and not provably false as a matter of law. Gabor's claim is that "sleazy" and "worst" express subjective opinions that are not actionable. However, the import of Gabor's statements were not so limited.*

The evidence in this case established that Sommer did not frequent bars of whatever nature, was not broke, did not have to sell her house in Hollywood, and did not move, whether to the "best" or "worst" part of town. Thus, the statements were indeed proven to be false in their broad sense, so that it did not matter what kind of bars were described or to what part of town she was alleged to have moved. Thus, taken in context, the statements were defamatory not because of the adjectives used in the statements, but because even without the adjectives they attributed characteristics to Sommer's lifestyle which exposed her to contempt, ridicule and disgrace. Thus, Gabor has not established that any of the statements attributed to her were not actionable as a matter of law.

DECISION AND REMEDY
The court of appeals held that Gabor's comments about Sommer were misleading and malicious statements of fact

(case continues)

and not statements of opinion. The court affirmed the trial court's judgment in favor of Sommer.

Case Questions

Critical Legal Thinking   What is the difference between statements of opinion and statements of fact? Which do you think Gabor's statements were in this case?

Ethics   Do you think Gabor acted ethically in making the statements about Sommer? Why do you think she did it? Do you think Sommer was warranted in suing in this case?

Business Application   How can a newspaper or magazine prevent defamatory statements from appearing in their publications? Explain.

E-Commerce & Internet Law

e-biz

AOL LEFT OFF THE HOOK FOR USER'S DEFAMATION

Under the common law concept of defamation, publishers of newspapers, magazines, newsletters, and such are liable for defamatory statements made by writers whose material appear in these publications. A distributor of defamatory material, such as a newsstand that sells a magazine that contains a defamatory statement, is liable for defamation if it has knowledge of the defamation yet still sells the publication. But these common law doctrines of *publisher* and *distributor* liability pose particular problems for Internet providers.

Many firms, such as America Online, Inc. (AOL), provide interactive computer services to which tens of millions of users worldwide subscribe to gain access to the Internet. Users may transfer information privately via e-mail or may communicate publicly by posting messages on bulletin boards. But what if a user transfers a defamatory statement over the Internet using an on-line provider's service? Should the on-line provider be held liable for defamation as a publisher or distributor of the information?

Congress expressly addressed this issue by passing **Section 230 of the Communications Decency Act of 1996**, which states, "No provider or user of an interactive computer service shall be treated as the publisher or speaker of any information provided by another information content provider" [47 U.S.C. § 230 (c) (1)]. By its plain language, Section 230 creates a federal statutory immunity against liability of on-line service providers for defamatory statements made by users of its services. This policy recognizes that interactive service providers have millions of users and that the specter of imposing tort liability on service providers for defamatory statements of users would impose a chilling effect on free speech.

The court applied Section 230 in *Zeran v. America Online, Inc.* In that case, some unidentified AOL user posted a message on an AOL bulletin board advertising T-shirts featuring offensive and tasteless slogans relating to the bombing of the federal building in Oklahoma City. Those interested in purchasing the shirts were instructed to call "Ken" at Ken Zeran's home number in Seattle, Washington. Zeran received a high volume of calls, including angry and derogatory messages, as well as death threats. Zeran sued AOL for defamation. The trial court applied Section 230 and held that AOL was immune from liability and dismissed the case. The court of appeals affirmed. [*Zeran v. America Online, Incorporated*, 129 F3d 327 (4th Cir. 1997)]

Invasion of the Right to Privacy

invasion of the right to privacy

A tort that constitutes the violation of a person's right to live his or her life without being subjected to unwarranted and undesired publicity.

The law recognizes each person's right to live his or her life without being subjected to unwarranted and undesired publicity. A violation of this right constitutes the tort of **invasion of the right to privacy**. Examples of this tort include reading someone else's mail, wiretapping, and such. In contrast to defamation, the fact does not have to be untrue. Therefore, truth is not a defense to a charge of invasion of privacy. If the fact is public information, there is no claim to privacy. However, a fact that was once public (e.g., the commission of a crime) may become private after the passage of time.

Placing someone in a "false light" constitutes an invasion of privacy. For example, sending an objectionable telegram to a third party and signing another's name would place the purported sender in a false light in the eyes of the receiver. Falsely attributing beliefs or acts to another can also form the basis of a lawsuit.

Misappropriation of the Right to Publicity

Each person has the exclusive legal right to control and profit from the commercial use of his or her name and personality during his or her lifetime. This is a valuable right, particularly to well-known persons such as sports figures and movie stars. Any attempt by another person to appropriate a living person's name or identity for commercial purposes is actionable. The wrongdoer is liable for the **tort of misappropriation of the right to publicity** (also called the **tort of appropriation**). In such cases, the plaintiff can (1) recover the unauthorized profits made by the offending party and (2) obtain an injunction against further unauthorized use of his or her name or identity. Many states provide that the right to publicity survives a person's death and may be enforced by the deceased's heirs.

In the following case, the court found that there had been a misappropriation of the right to publicity.

tort of misappropriation of the right to publicity
An attempt by another person to appropriate a living person's name or identity for commercial purposes.

Hoffman v. Los Angeles Magazine, Inc.
33 F.Supp.2d 867 (1999)
United States District Court, C.D. California

CASE 5.2

FACTS
Dustin Hoffman is one of the most successful and recognizable motion picture actors. He has appeared in such movie classics as *The Graduate* and *Rainman* and has won two Academy Awards, a Golden Globe Award, and an Emmy Award for his work. In 1982, Hoffman appeared as the main character in the movie *Tootsie,* where he played a male actor who dressed as a woman to get acting jobs as an actress. In the movie, Hoffman appeared in a woman's bright red dress posing in front of the American flag, which was used as a still shot in advertising for the movie. The movie was a great commercial success.

In 1997, the Los Angeles Magazine, a glitzy regional magazine, decided to rev up sales by including more celebrity photos in the magazine. The March 1997 issue included a feature called "Grand Illusions" where celebrity figures were dressed in clothes, shoes, and accessories of fashion designers who advertised in the magazine. One photo was the full-figured shot of Dustin Hoffman from *Tootsie* that had been digitally altered to remove the red dress and heels and replace them with a silk gown designed by Richard Tyler and high-heel shoes designed by Ralph Lauren. *Los Angeles Magazine* did not ask Mr. Hoffman for permission to use his name and likeness. After the magazine was published, Mr. Hoffman sued Los Angeles Magazine, Inc., in federal court to protect his name from commercial exploitation and recover damages.

ISSUE
Did Los Angeles Magazine, Inc. misappropriate Dustin Hoffman's right to publicity?

IN THE LANGUAGE OF THE COURT
Tevrizian, District Judge   The right to use Plaintiff Dustin Hoffman's name and likeness is an extremely valuable commodity and privilege not only because of Mr. Hoffman's stature as an actor, but because he does not knowingly permit commercial uses of his identity. Since appearing in the film The Graduate, *Mr. Hoffman has scrupulously guided and guarded the manner in which he has been shown to the public. Mr. Hoffman maintains a strict policy of not endorsing commercial products for fear that he will be perceived in a negative light by his peers and motion picture industry executives, suggesting that his career is in decline and that he no longer has the business opportunities or the box office draw as before.*

Defendant, Los Angeles Magazine, Inc., did not seek or obtain permission from Mr. Hoffman to use his name or likeness in the March 1997 issue of Los Angeles Magazine *and, in particular, did not obtain Mr. Hoffman's consent to commercially endorse or "shill" for any fashion designer or advertiser or the magazine. The reason permission was not sought is because* Los Angeles Magazine *knew, or should have known, that the celebrities either would not consent or, alternatively, would demand payment for the fair market value for their right to utilize their names and likenesses in this manner for commercial*

(case continues)

exploitation. The photographs were manipulated and cannibalized to such an extent that the celebrities were commercially exploited and were robbed of their dignity, professionalism and talent. To be blunt, the celebrities were violated by technology.

Plaintiff, Dustin Hoffman, has been damaged by Defendant, Los Angeles Magazine, Inc., *for the unauthorized use of his name and likeness to endorse and promote articles of clothing designed by Richard Tyler and Ralph Lauren. In addition, Mr. Hoffman has been damaged by* Los Angeles Magazine *for the unauthorized use of his name and likeness as a "runway model." The fair market value of Plaintiff's damages is the value that a celebrity of Mr. Hoffman's reputation, appeal, talent and fame would bring in the open market for this type of one-time use in a publication in a regional magazine, in the Los Angeles area. This Court finds the fair market value of plaintiff's name and likeness used for endorsement purposes to be $1,500,000. The Court also finds that Plaintiff has established by clear and convincing evidence that Plaintiff is entitled to an award of punitive damages of $1,500,000.*

DECISION AND REMEDY

The federal district court held that Los Angeles Magazine, Inc. had misappropriated plaintiff Dustin Hoffman's right to publicity and awarded Mr. Hoffman $1.5 million in compensatory damages and $1.5 million in punitive damages.

Case Questions

Critical Legal Thinking Should the right to publicity be a protected right? Why or why not?

Ethics Did *Los Angeles Magazine* act ethically in using Dustin Hoffman's celebrity status without getting his permission or paying him?

Business Application What kind of message does this case send to parties who intend to commercially exploit a celebrity's name and likeness?

Intentional Infliction of Emotional Distress

intentional infliction of emotional distress

A tort that says a person whose extreme and outrageous conduct intentionally or recklessly causes severe emotional distress to another person is liable for that emotional distress. Also known as the *tort of outrage.*

Negligence is the omission to do something which a reasonable man would do, or doing something which a prudent and reasonable man would not do.

B. Alderson Blyth v.
Birmingham Waterworks Co.
(1856)

In some situations, a victim may suffer mental or emotional distress without first being physically harmed. The Restatement (Second) of Torts provides that a person whose *extreme and outrageous conduct* intentionally or recklessly causes severe emotional distress to another is liable for that emotional distress.[2] This is called the tort of **intentional infliction of emotional distress**, or the **tort of outrage**. The plaintiff must prove that the defendant's conduct was "so outrageous in character and so extreme in degree as to go beyond all possible bounds of decency, and to be regarded as atrocious and utterly intolerable in a civilized society."[3] An indignity, an annoyance, rough language, or an occasional inconsiderate or unkind act does not constitute outrageous behavior. However, repeated annoyances or harassment coupled with threats are considered "outrageous."

The tort does not require any publication to a third party or physical contact between the plaintiff and defendant. For example, a credit collection agency making harassing telephone calls to a debtor every morning between 1:00 and 5:00 A.M. is outrageous conduct.

The mental distress suffered by the plaintiff must be severe. Many states require that this mental distress be manifested by some form of physical injury, discomfort, or illness, such as nausea, ulcers, headaches, or miscarriage. This requirement is intended to prevent false claims. Some states have abandoned this requirement. The courts have held that shame, humiliation, embarrassment, anger, fear, and worry constitute severe mental distress. The tort of outrage was asserted in the following case.

Roach v. Stern

675 N.Y.S.2d 133 (1998) Supreme Court, Appellate Division, New York

CASE 5.3

FACTS

Howard Stern is a famous television talk show host who emcees an irreverent daily show on the radio. The show is syndicated by Infinity Broadcasting, Inc. (Infinity), and is listened to by millions of people across the country. Deborah Roach, a self-described topless dancer and cable-access television host, was a perennial guest on the Howard Stern radio show. She was famous for her stories about encounters with aliens. Roach died of a drug overdose at the age of 27. Roach's sister, Melissa Driscoll, had Roach's body cremated and gave a portion of the remains to Roach's close friend, Chaunce Hayden. Driscoll said she did so with the understanding that Hayden would "preserve and honor said remains in an appropriate and private manner."

On July 18, 1995, Hayden brought a box containing Roach's cremated remains to Stern's radio show. Hayden said she did so as a memorial to Roach because "the only happiness Debbie had was the Howard Stern show." Thereafter, Stern, Hayden, and other participants in the broadcast played with Roach's ashes and made crude comments about the remains. The radio show was videotaped and later broadcast on a national cable television station. Roach's sister and brother sued Stern, Infinity, and Hayden to recover damages for intentional infliction of emotional distress. The trial court dismissed the complaint. The plaintiffs appealed.

ISSUE

Have the plaintiffs sufficiently pleaded a cause of action to recover damages for the intentional infliction of emotional distress?

IN THE LANGUAGE OF THE COURT

Memorandum by the Court   Upon our review of the allegations in the case at bar, we conclude that the Supreme Court erred in determining that the element of outrageous conduct was not satisfied as a matter of law. Although the defendants contend that the conduct at issue was not particularly shocking, in light of Stern's reputation for vulgar humor and Tay's actions during her guest appearances on his program, a jury might reasonably conclude that the manner in which Tay's remains were handled, for entertainment purposes and against the express wishes of her family, went beyond the bounds of decent behavior.

DECISION AND REMEDY

The court held that the complaint and the facts of the case as pleaded sufficiently stated a cause of action to recover damages for intentional infliction of emotional distress. Reversed.

Case Questions

Critical Legal Thinking   Should the tort of intentional infliction of emotional distress be recognized by the law? What difficulties arise in trying to apply this tort?

Ethics   Was Stern's and the other participants' conduct on the radio show tasteless? Did it amount to "outrageous conduct" for which legal damages should be awarded?

Business Application   If Stern and Infinity are found liable, will a chilling effect on future broadcasts result?

INTENTIONAL TORTS AGAINST PROPERTY

There are two general categories of property: real property and personal property. *Real property* consists of land and anything permanently attached to that land. *Personal property* consists of things that are movable, such as automobiles, books, clothes, pets, and such. The law recognizes certain torts against real and personal property. These torts are discussed in the paragraphs that follow.

Trespass to Land

Interference with an owner's right to exclusive possession of land constitutes the tort of **trespass to land**. There does not have to be any interference with the owner's use or enjoyment of the land; the ownership itself is what counts. Thus, unauthorized use of another person's land is trespass even if the owner is not using it. Actual harm to the property is not necessary.

Examples of trespass to land include entering another person's land without permission, remaining on the land of another after permission to do so has expired (e.g., a guest refuses to leave), or causing something or someone to enter another's land (e.g., one person builds a dam that causes another person's land to flood). A person who is pushed onto another's land or enters that land with good reason is not liable for trespass. For example, a person may enter onto another person's land to save a child or a pet from harm.

trespass to land
A tort that interferes with an owner's right to exclusive possession of land.

trespass to personal property
A tort that occurs whenever one person injures another person's personal property or interferes with that person's enjoyment of his or her personal property.

conversion of personal property
A tort that deprives a true owner of the use and enjoyment of his or her personal property by taking over such property and exercising ownership rights over it.

Trespass to and Conversion of Personal Property

The tort of **trespass to personal property** occurs whenever one person injures another person's personal property or interferes with that person's enjoyment of his or her personal property. The injured party can sue for damages. For example, breaking another's car window is trespass to personal property.

Depriving a true owner of the use and enjoyment of his or her personal property by taking over such property and exercising ownership rights over it constitutes the tort of **conversion of personal property**. Conversion also occurs when someone who originally is given possession of personal property fails to return it (e.g., fails to return a borrowed car). The rightful owner can sue to recover the property. If the property was lost or destroyed, the owner can sue to recover its value.

Entrepreneur and the Law

LIABILITY FOR FRIVOLOUS LAWSUITS

Entrepreneurs and others often believe they have a reason to sue someone to recover damages or other remedies. If the plaintiff has a reason to bring the lawsuit and does so, but the plaintiff does not win the lawsuit, he or she does not have to worry about being sued by the person whom he or she sued. A losing plaintiff does have to worry about being sued by the defendant in a second lawsuit for **malicious prosecution** if certain elements are met, however.

In a lawsuit for malicious prosecution, the original defendant sues the original plaintiff. In this second lawsuit, which is a *civil* action for damages, the original defendant is the plaintiff and the original plaintiff is the defendant. The courts do not look favorably on malicious prosecution lawsuits because they feel they inhibit the original plaintiff's incentive to sue. Thus, to succeed in a malicious prosecution lawsuit, the courts require the plaintiff to prove all of the following:

- The plaintiff in the original lawsuit (now the defendant) instituted or was responsible for instituting the original lawsuit
- There was no *probable cause* for the first lawsuit; that is, it was a frivolous lawsuit
- The plaintiff in the original action brought it with *malice*. [Caution: This is a very difficult element to prove.]
- The original lawsuit was terminated in favor of the original defendant (now the plaintiff)
- The current plaintiff suffered injury as a result of the original lawsuit

A successful case of malicious prosecution involves proof of malicious conduct, which is an intentional tort. Therefore, punitive damages can be awarded in a malicious prosecution case. The moral of the story is simple: Make sure you have probable cause for instituting an action before bringing a lawsuit.

UNINTENTIONAL TORTS (NEGLIGENCE)

unintentional tort or negligence
A doctrine that says a person is liable for harm that is the foreseeable consequence of his or her actions.

Under the doctrine of **unintentional tort**, commonly referred to as **negligence**, a person is liable for harm that is the *foreseeable consequence* of his or her actions. Negligence is defined as "the omission to do something which a reasonable man would do, or doing something which a prudent and reasonable man would not do."[4]

Consider This Example   A driver who causes an automobile accident because he or she fell asleep at the wheel is liable for any resulting injuries caused by his or her negligence.

Elements of Negligence

To be successful in a negligence lawsuit, the plaintiff must prove that (1) the defendant owed *a duty of care* to the plaintiff, (2) the defendant *breached* this duty of care, (3) the plaintiff suffered *injury*, and (4) the defendant's negligent act *caused* the plaintiff's injury. Each of these elements is discussed in the paragraphs that follow.

Duty of Care   To determine whether a defendant is liable for negligence, it must first be ascertained whether the defendant owed a **duty of care** to the plaintiff. Duty of care refers to the obligation we all owe each other—that is, the duty not to cause any unreasonable harm or risk of harm. For example, each person owes a duty to drive his or her car carefully, not to push or shove on escalators, not to leave skateboards on the sidewalk, and the like. Businesses owe a duty to make safe products, not to cause accidents, and so on.

The courts decide whether a duty of care is owed in specific cases by applying a *reasonable person standard*. Under this test, the courts attempt to determine how an *objective, careful, and conscientious person would have acted in the same circumstances*, and then measure the defendant's conduct against this standard. The defendant's subjective intent ("I did not mean to do it") is immaterial in assessing liability. Certain impairments do not affect the reasonable person standard. For instance, there is no reasonable alcoholics standard.

Defendants with a particular expertise or competence are measured against a *reasonable professional standard*. This standard is applied in much the same way as the reasonable person standard. For example, a brain surgeon is measured against a reasonable brain surgeon standard, rather than a lower reasonable doctor standard. Children are generally required to act as a *reasonable child* of similar age and experience would act.

Breach of Duty   Once a court finds that the defendant actually owed the plaintiff a duty of care, it must determine whether the defendant breached this duty. A **breach of the duty of care** is the failure to exercise care. In other words, it is the failure to act as a reasonable person would act. A breach of this duty may consist of either an action (e.g., throwing a lit match on the ground in a forest and causing a fire) or a failure to act when there is a duty to act (e.g., a fire fighter who refuses to put out a fire). Generally, passersby are not expected to rescue others gratuitously to save them from harm.

duty of care
The obligation we all owe each other not to cause any unreasonable harm or risk of harm.

No court has ever given, nor do we think ever can give, a definition of what constitutes a reasonable or an average man.

Lord Goddard C.J.R. v. McCarthy (1954)

Business Brief

Domino's Pizza canceled its 30-minute delivery guarantee after juries concluded in several cases that Domino's drivers, trying to meet this deadline, negligently caused accidents.

breach of the duty of care
A failure to exercise care or to act as a reasonable person would act.

Contemporary Business Application

OUCH! THE COFFEE'S TOO HOT!

Studies have shown that people care less about how good their coffee tastes than if it is hot. So restaurants, coffee shops, and other sellers make their coffee hot. McDonald's, however, discovered that it was in hot water for making their coffee *too* hot. Consider this case.

Stella Liebeck, an 81-year-old resident of Albuquerque, New Mexico, visited a "drive-through" window of a McDonald's restaurant with her grandson. Her grandson, the driver of the vehicle, placed the order. When it came, he handed a hot cup of coffee to Liebeck. As her grandson drove away from the drive-through window, Liebeck took the lid off the coffee cup she held in her lap. The coffee spilled all over Liebeck, who suffered third-degree burns on her legs, groin, and buttocks. She required medical treatment, was hospitalized, and suffers permanent scars from the incident.

Liebeck sued McDonald's for selling coffee that was too hot and for failing to warn her of the danger of the hot coffee it served. McDonald's rejected Liebeck's pretrial offer to settle the case for $300,000. At trial, McDonald's denied that it had been negligent and asserted that Liebeck's own negligence—opening a hot coffee cup on her lap—caused her injuries. The jury heard evidence that McDonald's enforces a quality-control rule that requires its restaurants and franchises to serve coffee at 180 to 190 degrees Fahrenheit. Evidence showed that this was 10 to 30 degrees hotter than coffee served by competing restaurant chains, and approximately 40 to 50 degrees hotter than normal house-brewed coffee.

Based on this evidence, the jury concluded that McDonald's acted recklessly and awarded Liebeck $200,000 compensatory damages (reduced by $40,000 for her own negligence), and $2.7 million punitive damages. After the trial court judge reduced the amount of punitive damages to $480,000, the parties reached an out-of-court settlement for an undisclosed amount. Because of this case, McDonald's and other purveyors of coffee have reduced the temperature at which they sell coffee and have placed warnings on their coffee cups.

injury

The plaintiff must suffer personal injury or damage to his or her property to recover monetary damages for the defendant's negligence.

Injury to Plaintiff Even though a defendant's act may have breached a duty of care owed to the plaintiff, this breach is not actionable unless the plaintiff suffers **injury**. For example, a business's negligence causes an explosion and fire to occur at its factory at night. No one is injured and there is no damage to the neighbors' property. The negligence is not actionable.

The damages recoverable depend on the effect of the injury on the plaintiff's life or profession. Now suppose two men injure their hands when a train door malfunctions. The first man is a professional basketball player. The second is a college professor. The first man can recover greater damages.

In the following case, the court held the defendant liable for the injuries caused to the plaintiff.

Fischer v. Pepsi Cola Bottling Company of Omaha, Inc.
972 F.2d 906 (1992)
United States Court of Appeals, Eighth Circuit

CASE 5.4

FACTS
On March 4, 1987, Robert J. Fischer was in Omaha, Nebraska, attending a seminar and was a guest at the Red Lion Inn. At the end of the seminar's first day, Fischer took a swim in the inn's pool. Following his swim, Fischer stopped to purchase a pop from a vending machine on the inn's eleventh floor. The machine was owned and operated by Pepsi Cola Bottling Company of Omaha, Inc. (Pepsi). Fischer was still wearing his wet swimming trunks and was barefoot. As he inserted his money into the vending machine, an electrical current passed through his body.

After Fischer reported the accident, a service technician inspected the machine and found that the power cord connecting the rear of the machine to the electrical socket was resting underneath the machine's metal cabinet. He noticed that the power cord's metal conducting wires were exposed and came into contact with the machine's cabinet. After the accident, Fischer suffered pain while having sexual relations with his wife and became impotent. According to expert testimony, Fischer's impotence resulted from the electrical shock. He sued Pepsi for damages for alleged negligence in not inspecting and correcting the problem with the vending machine. The trial court found in favor of Fischer and awarded him $324,000. Pepsi appealed.

ISSUE
Is Pepsi liable for negligence?

IN THE LANGUAGE OF THE COURT
Beam, Circuit Judge *Pepsi's service foreman, Gruebel, testified that he saw damaged power cords on Pepsi's vending machines about nine or ten times a year, and that the service department received complaints that a vending machine was causing electri-*

cal shocks about once or twice a month. Gruebel also testified that on the day Fischer was electrically shocked, Pepsi had no policy for periodically inspecting the electrical parts of vending machines. Given this testimony, the jury could reasonably conclude that Pepsi was aware that its machines could cause injury, and that Pepsi was negligent in not inspecting its machines.

It is unnecessary that the particular injury or precise form of the injury be perceived or foreseen, but if there is some probability of harm sufficiently serious that an ordinary reasonable person would take precautions to avoid it, then failure to take such care is negligence.

For a supplier to be liable for failing to exercise reasonable care, it is not necessary for the supplier to know that a particular chattel is dangerous. Where the chattel supplied is part of a lot, it is sufficient that the supplier knows some of the chattels in the lot are dangerous. Nebraska law imposed a duty of inspection on Pepsi.

DECISION AND REMEDY
The court of appeals held that Pepsi had been negligent for failing to inspect the vending machine and correct the problem associated with electrical shocks caused by the machine. Affirmed.

Case Questions

Critical Legal Thinking Should the law recognize the type of injury claimed in this case? Is it hard to prove (or disprove) the injury alleged?

Ethics Was it ethical for Pepsi to deny liability in this case?

Business Application How could Pepsi have protected itself from liability in this case?

Causation   A person who commits a negligent act is not liable unless this act was the **cause** of the plaintiff's injuries. Courts have divided causation into two categories—*causation in fact* and *proximate cause*—and require each to be shown before the plaintiff may recover damages.

1. **Causation in Fact** The defendant's negligent act must be the **causation in fact** (or **actual cause**) of the plaintiff's injuries. For example, suppose a corporation negligently pollutes the plaintiff's drinking water. The plaintiff dies of a heart attack unrelated to the polluted water. Although the corporation has acted negligently, it is not liable for the plaintiff's death. There was a negligent act and an injury, but there was no *cause-and-effect* relationship between them. If instead, the plaintiff had died from the pollution, there would have been causation in fact, and the polluting corporation would have been liable. If two (or more) persons are liable for negligently causing the plaintiff's injuries, both (or all) can be held liable to the plaintiff if each of their acts is a substantial factor in causing the plaintiff's injuries.

2. **Proximate Cause** Under the law, a negligent party is not necessarily liable for all damages set in motion by his or her negligent act. Based on public policy, the law establishes a point along the damage chain after which the negligent party is no longer responsible for the consequences of his or her actions. This limitation on liability is referred to as **proximate cause** (or **legal cause**). The general test of proximate cause is *foreseeability*. A negligent party who is found to be the actual cause—but not the proximate cause—of the plaintiff's injuries is not liable to the plaintiff. Situations are examined on a case-by-case basis.

The landmark case establishing the doctrine of proximate cause is *Palsgraf v. Long Island Railroad Company*.[5] Helen Palsgraf was standing on a platform waiting for a passenger train. The Long Island Railroad Company owned and operated the trains and employed the station guards. As a man carrying a package wrapped in a newspaper tried to board the moving train, railroad guards tried to help him. In doing so, the package was dislodged from the man's arm, fell to the railroad tracks, and exploded. The package contained hidden fireworks. The explosion shook the railroad platform, causing a scale located on the platform to fall on Palsgraf, injuring her. She sued the railroad for negligence. Justice Cardoza denied her recovery, finding that the railroad was not the proximate cause of her injuries.

---

causation

A person who commits a negligent act is not liable unless his or her act was the cause of the plaintiff's injuries. The two types of causation that must be proven are (1) *causation in fact (actual cause)* and (2) *proximate cause (legal cause)*.

causation in fact or actual cause

The actual cause of negligence. A person who commits a negligent act is not liable unless causation in fact can be proven.

proximate cause or legal cause

A point along a chain of events caused by a negligent party after which this party is no longer legally responsible for the consequences of his or her actions.

Business Brief

A negligent party who is found to be the actual cause but not the proximate cause of the plaintiff's injuries is not liable.

Contemporary Business Application _____

IS A SINGER LIABLE WHEN SOMEONE ACTS UPON HIS LYRICS?

Many people, particularly youths, are influenced by singers, musicians, sports figures, movie stars, and other celebrities. Some listeners, readers, or watchers will be moved to love; others to tears; some to creativity, spirituality, or fear. But what happens when a person is so moved by a song, a movie, or a book that he or she commits a crime or engages in other dangerous conduct? Is the songwriter, singer, author, scriptwriter, or movie company liable for this conduct? This question was posed to the court in *McCollum v. CBS, Inc., and Osbourne*.

John "Ozzie" Osbourne is a well-known singer of rock and roll music and has become a cult figure. The words and music of his songs demonstrate a preoccupation with unusual, antisocial, and even bizarre attitudes and beliefs, often emphasizing such things as satanic worship, the mocking of religious beliefs, death, and suicide. CBS Records (CBS) produced and distributed Osbourne's albums.

On Friday night, October 26, 1984, John Daniel McCollum (John) listened over and over again to certain music recorded by Osbourne. He was a 19-year-old youth who had a problem with alcohol abuse as well as serious emotional problems. John was in his bedroom using headphones to listen to the final side of Osbourne's two-record album, *Speak to the Devil*, when he placed a .22 caliber handgun next to his right temple and took his own life.

(box continues)

One of the songs that John had been listening to was called "Suicide Solution." Three of the verses of the song stated:

Wine is fine but whiskey's quicker
Suicide is slow with liquor
Take a bottle drown your sorrows
Then it floods away tomorrows
Made your bed, rest your head
But you lie there and moan
Suicide is the only way out
Don't you know what it's really about
Ah know people
You really know where it's at
You got it
Why try, why try
Get the gun and try it
Shoot, shoot, shoot

John's relative, Jack McCollum, and John's estate sued Ozzie Osbourne and CBS for negligence, alleging that the lyrics of Osbourne's music incited John to commit suicide. When the trial court dismissed the action, the plaintiffs appealed. The appellate court held that although Osbourne's lyrics might have been an actual cause of John's suicide, they were not the proximate cause of the suicide. The court stated:

> John's tragic self-destruction, while listening to Osbourne's music, was not a reasonably foreseeable risk or consequence of defendant's remote artistic activities. It is simply not acceptable to a free and democratic society to impose a duty upon performing artists to limit and restrict their creativity in order to avoid the dissemination of ideas in artistic speech that may adversely affect emotionally troubled individuals. Such a burden would quickly have the effect of reducing and limiting artistic expression to only the broadest standard of taste and acceptance and the lowest level of offense, provocation, and controversy. [*McCollum v. CBS, Inc., and Osbourne*, 202 Cal.App.3d 989, 249 Cal.Rptr. 187 (Cal.App. 1988)]

Professional Malpractice

professional malpractice

The liability of a professional who breaches his or her duty of ordinary care.

Professionals, such as doctors, lawyers, architects, accountants, and others, owe a duty of ordinary care in providing their services. This duty is known as the *reasonable professional standard*. A professional who breaches this duty of care is liable for the injury his or her negligence causes. This liability is commonly referred to as **professional malpractice**. For example, a doctor who amputates a wrong leg is liable for *medical malpractice*. A lawyer who fails to file a document with the court on time, causing the client's case to be dismissed, is liable for *legal malpractice*. An accountant who fails to use reasonable care, knowledge, skill, and judgment when providing auditing and other accounting services to a client is liable for *accounting malpractice*.

Professionals who breach this duty are liable to their patients or clients. They may also be liable to some third parties.

Negligent Infliction of Emotional Distress

negligent infliction of emotional distress

A tort that permits a person to recover for emotional distress caused by the defendant's negligent conduct.

Some jurisdictions have extended the tort of emotional distress to include the **negligent infliction of emotional distress**. The most common examples of this involve bystanders who witness the injury or death of a loved one that is caused by another's negligent conduct. The bystander, even though not personally physically injured, can sue the negligent party for his or her own mental suffering under this tort.

Generally, to be successful in this type of case, the plaintiff must prove that (1) a relative was killed or injured by the defendant, (2) the plaintiff suffered severe emotional distress, and (3) the plaintiff's mental distress resulted from a sensory and contemporaneous observance of the accident. Some states require that the plaintiff's mental distress be manifested by some physical injury; other states have eliminated this requirement.

In the following case, a plaintiff recovered damages for negligent infliction of emotional distress.

Estrada v. Aeronaves de Mexico, S.A.
967 F.2d 1421 (1992)
United States Court of Appeals, Ninth Circuit

CASE 5.5

FACTS

On the morning of August 31, 1986, Theresa Estrada left her home near Cerritos, California, to go shopping at a nearby grocery store. She left her husband at home reading the newspaper, and her three children were still in bed. Returning from the store, Estrada saw, heard, and felt a big explosion. Within minutes, she maneuvered her way through burning homes, cars, and debris to find her home engulfed in flames. Her husband and children died in the house. Although she did not know it at the time, an Aeromexico passenger airplane had crashed into her home after colliding with a privately owned plane. Estrada suffered severe emotional distress from the incident. She sued Aeromexico, the owner of the private plane, and the U.S. government for the wrongful death of her family. Aeromexico was found not responsible for the accident. The jury found the private pilot 50 percent liable, and the United States 50 percent liable because air traffic controllers had failed to detect the private plane's intrusion into commercial airspace and to give a traffic advisory to the Aeromexico flight. The jury awarded Estrada $5.5 million for the death of her family and $1 million for negligent infliction of emotional distress. The U.S. government appealed the $500,000 judgment against it for negligent infliction of emotional distress.

ISSUE

Was Estrada entitled under the law to recover damages for negligent infliction of emotional distress?

IN THE LANGUAGE OF THE COURT

Hug, Circuit Judge   A plaintiff may recover damages for emotional distress caused by observing the negligently inflicted injury of a third person if, but only if, said plaintiff: (1) is closely related to the injury victim; (2) is present at the scene of the injury-producing event at the time it occurs and is then aware that it is causing injury to the victim; and (3) as a result suffers serious emotional distress—a reaction beyond that which would be anticipated in a disinterested witness and which is not an abnormal response to the circumstances.

Estrada clearly satisfies the first and third requirements. The second requirement is the one at issue here. The Government argues that Estrada was neither present at the scene of the injury-producing event nor aware that it was causing injury to her family. The plaintiff need not visually perceive the injury while it is being inflicted. The district court concluded that the disaster was still occurring while Mrs. Estrada was driving to her home and after she arrived to see her house in flames. The injury-producing event was the fire. The district court correctly found that Estrada knew her husband and children were being injured by the fire. Estrada understandably experienced great emotional distress as a result of watching helplessly as flames engulfed her home and burned her family to death.

DECISION AND REMEDY

The court of appeals held that Estrada had established the elements necessary to recover damages for the negligent infliction of emotional distress.

Case Questions

Critical Legal Thinking   Should the law recognize the doctrine of negligent infliction of emotional distress? Should the elements be expanded so that they are easier to meet?

Ethics   Did the U.S. government act ethically in arguing against paying Mrs. Estrada the award assessed by the jury?

Business Application   What economic effects does the doctrine of negligent infliction of emotional distress have on businesses?

SPECIAL NEGLIGENCE DOCTRINES

The courts have developed many *special negligence doctrines*. The most important of these are discussed in the paragraphs that follow.

Negligence Per Se

Statutes often establish duties owed by one person to another. The violation of a statute that proximately causes an injury is **negligence per se**. The plaintiff in such an action must prove that (1) a statute existed, (2) the statute was enacted to prevent the type of injury suffered, and (3) the plaintiff was within a class of persons meant to be protected by the statute.

negligence per se
Tort where the violation of a statute or ordinance constitutes the breach of the duty of care.

Consider This Example Most cities have an ordinance that places the responsibility for fixing public sidewalks in residential areas on the homeowners whose homes front the sidewalk. A homeowner is liable if he or she fails to repair a damaged sidewalk in front of his or her home and a pedestrian trips and is injured because of the damage. The injured party does not have to prove that the homeowner owed the duty, because the statute establishes that.

Res Ipsa Loquitur

If a defendant is in control of a situation where a plaintiff has been injured and has superior knowledge of the circumstances surrounding the injury, the plaintiff might have difficulty proving the defendant's negligence. In such a situation, the law applies the doctrine of ***res ipsa loquitur*** (Latin for "the thing speaks for itself"). This doctrine raises a presumption of negligence and switches the burden to the defendant to prove that he or she was *not* negligent. *Res ipsa loquitur* applies in cases where the following elements are met:

1. The defendant had exclusive control of the instrumentality or situation that caused the plaintiff's injury.

2. The injury would not have ordinarily occurred "but for" someone's negligence.

Consider These Examples Haeran goes in for major surgery and is given anesthesia to put her to sleep during the operation. Sometime after the operation it is discovered that a surgical instrument had been left in Haeran during the operation. She suffers severe injury because of the left-in instrument. Haeran would be hard pressed to identify which doctor or nurse had been careless and left the instrument in her body. In this case, the court can apply the doctrine of *res ipsa loquitur* and place the presumption of negligence on the defendants. Any defendant who can prove he or she did not leave the instrument in Haeran escapes liability; any defendant who does not disprove his or her negligence is liable. Other typical *res ipsa loquitur* cases involve commercial airplane crashes, falling elevators, and the like.

Good Samaritan Laws

In the past, liability exposure made many doctors, nurses, and other medical professionals reluctant to stop and render aid to victims in emergency situations, such as highway accidents. Almost all states have enacted **Good Samaritan laws** that relieve medical professionals from liability for injury caused by their ordinary negligence in such circumstances. Good Samaritan laws protect medical professionals only from liability for their *ordinary negligence*, not for injuries caused by their gross negligence or reckless or intentional conduct. Most Good Samaritan laws protect licensed doctors and nurses and lay persons who have been certified in CPR. Lay persons not trained in CPR are not generally protected by Good Samaritan statutes—that is, they are liable for injuries caused by their ordinary negligence in rendering aid.

Consider This Example Sam is injured in an automobile accident and is unconscious in his automobile alongside the road. Doctor Pamela Heathcoat, who is driving by the scene of the accident, stops, pulls Sam from the burning wreckage, and administers first aid. In doing so, Pamela negligently broke Sam's shoulder. If Pamela's negligence is ordinary negligence, she is not liable to Sam because the Good Samaritan law protects her from liability; if Pamela was grossly negligent or reckless in administering aid to Sam, she is liable to him for the injuries she caused. It is a question of fact for the jury to decide whether a doctor's conduct was ordinary negligence or gross negligence or recklessness. If Cathy, a lay person not trained in CPR, had rendered aid to Sam and caused Sam injury

---

res ipsa loquitur
Tort where the presumption of negligence arises because (1) the defendant was in exclusive control of the situation and (2) the plaintiff would not have suffered injury but for someone's negligence. The burden switches to the defendant(s) to prove they were not negligent.

Good Samaritan law
Statute that relieves medical professionals from liability for ordinary negligence when they stop and render aid to victims in emergency situations.

because of her ordinary negligence, the Good Samaritan law would not protect her and she would be liable to Sam.

Dram Shop Acts

Many states have enacted **Dram Shop Acts** that make a tavern and bartender civilly liable for injuries caused to or by patrons who are served too much alcohol. The alcohol must be either served in sufficient quantity to make the patron intoxicated or served to an already intoxicated person. Both the tavern and the bartender are liable to third persons injured by the patron and for injuries suffered by the patron. They are also liable for injuries caused by or to minors served by the tavern, regardless of whether the minor is intoxicated.

Dram Shop Act
Statute that makes taverns and bartenders liable for injuries caused to or by patrons who are served too much alcohol.

Guest Statutes

Many states have enacted **guest statutes** that provide that if a driver voluntarily and without compensation gives a ride in a vehicle to another person (e.g., a hitchhiker), the driver is not liable to the passenger for injuries caused by the driver's ordinary negligence. However, if the passenger pays compensation to the driver, the driver owes a duty of ordinary care to the passenger and will be held liable. The driver is always liable to the passenger for wanton and gross negligence, for example, injuries caused because of excessive speed.

guest statute
Statute that provides that if a driver of a vehicle voluntarily and without compensation gives a ride to another person, the driver is not liable to the passenger for injuries caused by the driver's ordinary negligence.

Fireman's Rule

Under the **fireman's rule**, a fireman who is injured while putting out a fire may not sue the party whose negligence caused the fire. This rule has been extended to policemen and other government workers. The bases for this rule are (1) people might not call for help if they could be held liable; (2) firemen, policemen, and other such workers receive special training for their jobs; and (3) these workers have special medical and retirement programs paid for by the public.

"Danger Invites Rescue" Doctrine

The law recognizes a **"danger invites rescue" doctrine**. Under this doctrine, a rescuer who is injured while going to someone's rescue can sue the person who caused the dangerous situation. For example, a passerby who is injured while trying to rescue children from a fire set by an arsonist can bring a civil suit against the arsonist.

"danger invites rescue" doctrine
Doctrine that provides that a rescuer who is injured while going to someone's rescue can sue the person who caused the dangerous situation.

Social Host Liability

Several states have adopted the **social host liability** rule. This rule provides that a social host is liable for injuries caused by guests who are served alcohol at a social function (e.g., a birthday party, a wedding reception, etc.) and later cause injury because they are intoxicated. The injury may be to a third person or to the guest himself. The alcohol served at the social function must be the cause of the injury. A few states have adopted statutes that relieve social hosts from such liability.[6]

social host liability
Rule that provides that social hosts are liable for injuries caused by guests who become intoxicated at a social function. States vary as to whether they have this rule in effect.

Liability of Common Carriers and Innkeepers

The common law holds common carriers and innkeepers to a higher standard of care than most other businesses. Common carriers and innkeepers owe a **duty of utmost care**—rather than a duty of ordinary care—to their passengers and patrons. For example, innkeepers must provide security for their guests. The concept of utmost care is applied on a case-by-case basis. Obviously, a large hotel must provide greater security to guests than a "mom-and-pop" motel. Some states and cities have adopted specific statutes and ordinances relating to this duty.

duty of utmost care
A duty of care that goes beyond ordinary care that says common carriers and innkeepers have a responsibility to provide security to their passengers or guests.

Liability of Landowners

Owners and renters of real property owe certain duties to protect visitors from injury while on the property. A landowner's and tenant's liability generally depends on the status of the visitor. Visitors fall into the following categories:

1. **Invitees and Licensees** An *invitee* is a person who has been expressly or impliedly invited onto the owner's premises for the *mutual benefit* of both parties (e.g., guests invited for dinner, the mail carrier, and customers of a business). A *licensee* is a person who, *for his or her own benefit*, enters onto the premises with the express or implied consent of the owner (e.g., the Avon representative, encyclopedia salesperson, Seventh-Day Adventists). An owner owes a **duty of ordinary care** to invitees and licensees. An owner is liable if he or she negligently causes injury to an invitee or licensee. For example, a homeowner is liable if she leaves a garden hose across the walkway on which an invitee or a licensee trips and is injured.

2. **Trespassers** A *trespasser* is a person who has no invitation, permission, or right to be on another's property. Burglars are a common type of trespasser. Generally, an owner does not owe a duty of ordinary care to a trespasser. For example, if a trespasser trips and injures himself on a bicycle the owner negligently left out, the owner is not liable. An owner does owe a **duty not to willfully or wantonly injure a trespasser**. Thus, an owner cannot set traps to injure trespassers.

A few states have eliminated the invitee-licensee-trespasser distinction. These states hold that owners and renters owe a duty of ordinary care to all persons who enter upon the property.

duty of ordinary care
The duty an owner owes an invitee or a licensee to prevent injury or harm when the invitee or licensee steps on the owner's premises.

duty not to willfully or wantonly injure
The duty an owner owes a trespasser to prevent intentional injury or harm to the trespasser when the trespasser is on his or her premises.

Arch, St. Louis, Missouri.
Private and public owners of real estate usually purchase liability insurance to cover payments for any injuries caused by their negligence on the premises.

*D*EFENSES AGAINST NEGLIGENCE

A defendant in a negligence lawsuit may raise several defenses to the imposition of liability. These defenses are discussed in the following paragraphs.

Superseding or Intervening Event

Under negligence, a person is liable only for foreseeable events. Therefore, an original negligent party can raise a **superseding** (or **intervening**) **event** as a defense to liability. For example, assume that an avid golfer negligently hits a spectator with a golf ball,

superseding event
A defendant is not liable for injuries caused by a superseding or intervening event for which he or she is not responsible.

knocking the spectator unconscious. While lying on the ground waiting for an ambulance to come, the spectator is struck by a bolt of lightning and killed. The golfer is liable for the injuries caused by the golf ball. He is not liable for the death of the spectator, however, because the lightning bolt was an unforeseen intervening event.

Assumption of the Risk

If a plaintiff knows of and voluntarily enters into or participates in a risky activity that results in injury, the law recognizes that the plaintiff assumed, or took on, the risk involved. Thus, the defendant can raise the defense of **assumption of the risk** against the plaintiff. This defense assumes that the plaintiff (1) had knowledge of the specific risk and (2) voluntarily assumed that risk. For example, under this theory, a race car driver assumes the risk of being injured or killed in a crash. Assumption of the risk was raised as a defense in the following case.

assumption of the risk
A defense a defendant can use against a plaintiff who knowingly and voluntarily enters into or participates in a risky activity that results in injury.

Knight v. Jewett
3 Cal.4th 296, 11 Cal.Rptr.2d 2 (1992)
Supreme Court of California

CASE 5.6

FACTS
On January 25, 1987, the day of the 1987 Super Bowl football game, Kendra Knight and Michael Jewett, together with a number of other social acquaintances, attended a Super Bowl party at the house of a mutual friend. During halftime, several guests decided to play an informal game of touch football on an adjoining vacant lot, using a "peewee" football. Each team included four or five women and men. Knight and Jewett were on different teams. Five minutes into the game, Jewett ran into Knight during a play. She told him to be more careful. On the next play, Jewett tried to intercept a pass to Knight and in doing so collided with her, knocking her down. When Jewett landed, he stepped backward onto Knight's hand. Because of the injury, Knight had to have her little finger amputated. Knight sued Jewett for damages. The trial court applied the doctrine of assumption of the risk and granted defendant Jewett's motion for summary judgment. The court of appeals affirmed. Knight appealed.

ISSUE
Does the doctrine of assumption of the risk bar recovery?

IN THE LANGUAGE OF THE COURT
George, Justice   The overwhelming majority of the cases, both within and outside California, that have addressed the issue of coparticipant liability in a sport have concluded that it is improper to hold sports participants liable to a coparticipant for ordinary careless conduct committed during the sport—for example, for an injury resulting from a carelessly thrown ball or bat during a baseball game—and that liability properly may be imposed on a participant only when he or she intentionally injures another player or engages in reckless conduct that is totally outside the range of the ordinary activity involved in the sport.

In the heat of an active sporting event like baseball or football, a participant's normal energetic conduct often includes accidentally careless behavior. The courts have concluded that vigorous participation in such sporting events likely would be chilled if legal liability were to be imposed on a participant on the basis of his or her ordinary careless conduct. The cases have recognized that, in such a sport, even when a participant's conduct violates a rule of the game and may subject the violator to internal sanctions prescribed by the sport itself, imposition of legal liability for such conduct might well alter fundamentally the nature of the sport by deterring participants from vigorously engaging in activity that falls close to, but on the permissible side of, a prescribed rule. As applied to the present case, the foregoing legal principle clearly supports the trial court's entry of summary judgment in favor of defendant.

DECISION AND REMEDY
The state supreme court held that, under the doctrine of assumption of the risk, summary judgment was properly entered barring recovery in this case. Affirmed.

Case Questions

Critical Legal Thinking   Do you think the law should recognize the doctrine of assumption of the risk? Why or why not?

Ethics   Did Jewett act properly in playing hard during the touch football game? Should Knight have sued him?

Business Application   Should the doctrine of assumption of the risk be applied when spectators are injured at professional sports events?

Contributory Negligence

contributory negligence
A doctrine that says a plaintiff who is partially at fault for his or her own injury cannot recover against the negligent defendant.

Under the common law doctrine of **contributory negligence**, a plaintiff who is partially at fault for his or her own injury cannot recover against the negligent defendant. For example, suppose a driver who is driving over the speed limit negligently hits and injures a pedestrian who is jaywalking. Suppose the jury finds that the driver is 80 percent responsible for the accident and the jaywalker is 20 percent responsible. The pedestrian suffered $100,000 in injuries. Under the doctrine of contributory negligence, the pedestrian cannot recover any damages from the driver.

There is one major exception to the doctrine of contributory negligence: The defendant has a duty under the law to avoid the accident if at all possible. This rule is known as the *last clear chance rule*. For example, a driver who sees a pedestrian walking across the street against a "Don't Walk" sign must avoid hitting him or her if possible. When deciding cases involving this rule, the courts consider the attentiveness of the parties and the amount of time each has to respond to the situation.

Comparative Negligence

comparative negligence
A doctrine under which damages are apportioned according to fault.

As seen, the application of the doctrine of contributory negligence could reach an unfair result where a party only slightly at fault for his or her injuries could not recover from an otherwise negligent defendant. Many states have replaced the doctrine of contributory negligence with the doctrine of **comparative negligence**. Under this doctrine, damages are apportioned according to fault. When the comparative negligence rule is applied to the previous example, the result is much fairer. The plaintiff-pedestrian can recover 80 percent of his damages (or $80,000) from the defendant-driver. This is an example of *pure comparative negligence*. Several states have adopted *partial comparative negligence*, which provides that a plaintiff must be less than 50 percent responsible for causing his or her own injuries to recover under comparative negligence; otherwise, contributory negligence applies.

*C*ONCEPT SUMMARY CONTRIBUTORY AND COMPARATIVE NEGLIGENCE COMPARED

Situation	Doctrine	Liability of the Defendant
Defendant liable for causing injury to plaintiff, but plaintiff partially at fault for causing his own injuries	Contributory negligence	Defendant not liable Exception: Last clear chance rule
	Comparative negligence	
	1. Pure comparative negligence	Defendant liable for plaintiff's injuries according to fault
	2. Partial comparative negligence	
	a. Plaintiff less than 50 percent responsible	Defendant liable for plaintiff's injuries according to fault
	b. Plaintiff 50 percent or more responsible	Defendant not liable

*B*USINESS TORTS

Although many of the torts previously discussed are committed by or against businesses, certain other torts commonly involve businesses. Several of these torts are discussed in the following paragraphs.

Entering Certain Businesses and Professions Without a License

There are government restrictions and prohibitions on the freedom of entry into certain businesses and professions. These restrictions are intended to protect the public from unqualified practitioners and to promote the efficient operation of the economy.

For instance, a person cannot simply erect a television or radio transmitter and start broadcasting: The Federal Communications Commission grants television and radio station licenses for assigned frequencies. In addition, many occupations, such as lawyers, physicians, dentists, real estate brokers, hairdressers, and the like, require state licenses. In some states, even palm readers and astrologists must be licensed. To obtain the necessary license, an applicant must (1) meet certain educational requirements and (2) demonstrate a certain level of proficiency in the subject matter through examination, experience, or both. Entry into these industries or professions without permission subjects the violator to various civil and criminal penalties. In many states, a licensed professional can bring an action to prevent an unlicensed person from practicing.

Intentional Misrepresentation (Fraud)

One of the most pervasive business torts is **intentional misrepresentation**. This tort is also known as **fraud** or **deceit**. It occurs when a wrongdoer deceives another person out of money, property, or something else of value. A person who has been injured by an intentional misrepresentation can recover damages from the wrongdoer. The elements required to find fraud are

1. The wrongdoer made a false representation of material fact.
2. The wrongdoer had knowledge that the representation was false and intended to deceive the innocent party.
3. The innocent party justifiably relied on the misrepresentation.
4. The innocent party was injured.

Item 2 above, which is called **scienter**, includes situations where the wrongdoer recklessly disregards the truth in making a representation that is false. Intent or recklessness can be inferred from the circumstances.

intentional misrepresentation
Intentionally defrauding another person out of money, property, or something else of value.

There are some frauds so well conducted that it would be stupidity not to be deceived by them.

C. C. Colton
Lacon *Vol. 1 (1820)*

Civil RICO

In an effort to combat organized crime, Congress enacted the **Racketeer Influenced and Corrupt Organizations Act (RICO)**.[7] The act outlaws a pattern of "racketeering activity," including arson, counterfeiting, gambling, dealing in narcotics, bribery, embezzlement, mail and wire fraud, and other enumerated criminal activities. (For a discussion of criminal RICO, see Chapter 7.)

Persons injured by a RICO violation can bring a private civil action against the violator. RICO permits recovery only for injury to business or property. Recovery for personal injury is not permitted under RICO. The plaintiff can sue to recover **treble damages** (three times actual loss), plus attorney fees.[8] A defendant in a civil RICO case does not have to first be found guilty of criminal RICO.[9]

Because by definition commercial fraud is a racketeering activity, many fraud cases are now being brought as RICO cases. Thus, insurance companies, banks, and other businesses are being sued in RICO treble damage actions.

Racketeer Influenced and Corrupt Organizations Act (RICO)
Federal statute that authorizes civil lawsuits against defendants for engaging in a pattern of racketeering activities.

treble damages
Civil damages three times actual damages may be awarded to persons whose business or property is injured by a RICO violation.

*S*TRICT LIABILITY

Strict liability is another category of torts. Strict liability is *liability without fault*. That is, a participant in a covered activity will be held liable for any injuries caused by the activity even if he or she was not negligent. This doctrine holds that (1) there are certain activities

strict liability
Liability without fault.

Business Brief

Whereas intentional torts and negligence require the defendant to have been at fault, strict liability imposes liability without the defendant's having been at fault.

that can place the public at risk of injury even if reasonable care is taken, and (2) the public should have some means of compensation if such injury occurs.

Strict liability was first imposed for *abnormally dangerous activities*, such as crop dusting, blasting, fumigation, burning fields, storage of explosives, and keeping wild animals as pets. In the following case, the court applied the doctrine of strict liability to a dangerous activity.

Klein v. Pyrodyne Corporation
810 P.2d 917 (1991)
Supreme Court of Washington

CASE 5.7

FACTS

Pyrodyne Corporation (Pyrodyne) is a licensed fireworks-display company that contracted to display fireworks at the Western Washington State Fairgrounds in Puyallup, Washington, on July 4, 1987. During the fireworks display, one of the mortar launchers discharged a rocket on a horizontal trajectory parallel to the earth. The rocket exploded near a crowd of onlookers, including Danny Klein. Klein's clothing was set on fire, and he suffered facial burns and serious injury to his eyes. Klein sued Pyrodyne for strict liability to recover for his injuries. Pyrodyne asserted that the Chinese manufacturer of the fireworks was negligent in producing the rocket, and therefore Pyrodyne should not be held liable. The trial court applied the doctrine of strict liability and held in favor of Klein. Pyrodyne appealed.

ISSUE

Is the conducting of public fireworks displays an abnormally dangerous activity that justifies the imposition of strict liability?

IN THE LANGUAGE OF THE COURT

Guy, Justice Section 519 of the Restatement (Second) of Torts *provides that any party carrying on an "abnormally dangerous activity" is strictly liable for ensuing damages. Anytime a person ignites rockets with the intention of sending them aloft to explode in the presence of large crowds of people, a high risk of serious personal injury or property damage is created. We therefore*

hold that conducting public fireworks displays is an abnormally dangerous activity justifying the imposition of strict liability.

Pyrodyne argues that even if there is strict liability for fireworks, its liability under the facts of this case is cut off by the manufacturer's negligence. We hold that intervening acts of third persons serve to relieve the defendant from strict liability for abnormally dangerous activities only if those acts were unforeseeable in relation to the extraordinary risk created by the activity. In the present case, negligence on the part of the fireworks manufacturer is readily foreseeable in relation to the extraordinary risk created by conducting a public fireworks display. Therefore, even if such negligence may properly be regarded as an intervening cause, it cannot function to relieve Pyrodyne from strict liability.

DECISION AND REMEDY

The Washington Supreme Court held that the public display of fireworks is an abnormally dangerous activity that warrants the imposition of strict liability. Affirmed.

Case Questions

Critical Legal Thinking Should the law recognize the doctrine of strict liability? What is the public policy underlying the imposition of liability without fault?

Ethics Did Pyrodyne act ethically in denying liability in this case?

Business Application Does the doctrine of strict liability increase the cost of doing business? Explain.

International Perspective

ISRAELI TORT LAW

David Ben Gurion proclaimed the establishment of the State of Israel on May 14, 1948. Historically, the Jewish people have been governed by biblical law. With the advent of a national state, secular laws were developed and coexist with religious law. One of the laws developed by the State of Israel was *tort* law. Israeli

tort law is based on the theory that monetary compensation is awarded to promote justice and to ensure fair compensation when a tort occurs.

American tort law allows juries almost unlimited discretion to evaluate injuries and award damages. Under Israeli tort law, there is no right to trial by jury. Instead, all actions are tried by a panel of three judges or three lay people who decide both questions of fact and law. In essence, they are closer to arbitrators than judges.

Also, under Israeli tort law, all damages awarded must be assessed under one of these categories of damages:

1. *Medical expenses (ripui)* actually incurred and those expected to be incurred in order to cure the victim or return him or her as close as possible to preinjury state.
2. *Loss of earnings (shevet)* incurred during the time of the victim's injury and recovery.
3. *Loss of income (nezek)* for the long-term decrease in the victim's market value as a worker and skills he or she will never recover.
4. *Pain and suffering (tza'ar)* for short-term pain and suffering incurred at the time of the injury and their immediate consequences.

5. *Embarrassment (boshet)* for long-term pain and suffering caused from such things as permanent disfigurement, emotional distress, and such.

Israeli law limits the assessment of noneconomic damages (categories 4 and 5) to cases of willful, intentional, or grossly negligent infliction of harm.

Medical malpractice is one area of tort law where American and Israeli systems differ. Under American law, doctors are liable for their negligent conduct unless a Good Samaritan law relieves them of liability. Jewish law goes one step further. It excuses doctors from liability for their negligence in most situations. This is based on the public policy that the fear of such liability would otherwise discourage people from going into the medical profession.

 ## *Working the Web*

ABA Tort and Insurance Practice Section (TIPS) This 30,000 member American Bar Association section brings together plaintiffs' attorneys, defense attorneys, and insurance company counsel for the exchange of information and ideas in a unique non-adversarial setting. TIPS members can interact on a personal basis with nationally renowned experts in tort and insurance matters.

Visit at **www.abanet.org/tips/home.html**

Law Journal Extra Torts Page Law Journal Extra's Torts Page contains a table of contents, practice areas, news, resources, and links to law firms. This is a great place to get information on current torts cases of national interest.

Visit at **www.ljextra.com/practice/negligence/index. html**

Georgetown University Torts Page Georgetown University has a torts page that links to primary legal materials, associations and organizations, journals and newsletters, and specific subjects.

Visit at **www.ll.georgetown.edu/lr/rs/torts.html**

CYBER EXERCISES

e-biz

1. Visit the home page of the ABA Tort and Insurance Practice Section. Click on *Books and More*. Then click on *Ethics and Practice Issues*. What is the price of a publication called *Making Rain: Business Development and Professionalism Commercial Torts*?

2. Using the Law Journal Extra Torts Page, check out malpractice memos.

3. From the Georgetown University Torts Page, find and read the Consumer Law Page.

*C*ASES AND *E*XERCISES

CRITICAL LEGAL THINKING CASES

5.1. On September 16, 1975, the Baltimore Orioles professional baseball team was at Boston's Fenway Park to play the Boston Red Sox. Ross Grimsley was a pitcher for the visiting

Baltimore club. During one period of the game, Grimsley was warming up in the bullpen, throwing pitches to a catcher. During this warmup, Boston spectators in the stands heckled

Grimsley. After Grimsley had completed warming up and the catcher had left from behind the plate in the bullpen, Grimsley wound up as if he were going to throw the ball in his hand at the plate, then turned and threw the ball at one of the hecklers in the stand. The ball traveled at about 80 miles an hour, passed through a wire fence protecting the spectators, missed the heckler whom Grimsley was aiming at, and hit another spectator, David Manning, Jr., causing injury. Manning sued Grimsley and the Baltimore Orioles. Are the defendants liable? [*Manning v. Grimsley*, 643 F.2d 20 (1st Cir. 1981)]

5.2. At about 7:30 P.M. on September 8, 1976, Deborah A. Johnson entered a Kmart store located in Madison, Wisconsin, to purchase some diapers and several cans of motor oil. She took her small child along to enable her to purchase the correct size diapers, carrying the child in an infant seat, which she had purchased at Kmart two or three weeks previously. A large Kmart price tag was still attached to the infant seat. Johnson purchased the diapers and oil and some children's clothes. She was in a hurry to leave because it was 8:00 P.M., her child's feeding time, and she hurried through the checkout lane. She paid for the diapers, the oil, and the clothing. Just after leaving the store she heard someone ask her to stop. She turned around and saw a Kmart security officer. He showed her a badge and asked her to come back into the store, which she did. The man stated, "I have reason to believe that you have stolen this car seat." Johnson explained that she had purchased the seat previously. She demanded to see the manager, who was called to the scene. When Johnson pointed out that the seat had cat hairs, food crumbs, and milk stains on it, the man said, "I'm really sorry, there's been a terrible mistake. You can go." Johnson looked at the clock when she left, which read 8:20 P.M. Johnson sued Kmart for false imprisonment. Is Kmart liable? [*Johnson v. Kmart Enterprises, Inc.*, 297 N.W.2d 74 (Wis.App. 1980)]

5.3. On December 15, 1956, Marvin Briscoe and another man hijacked a truck in Danville, Kentucky. They were caught and convicted, and Briscoe served a term in prison. After release from prison, Briscoe established a life of respectability. In 1967, *Reader's Digest* published an article entitled "The Big Business of Hijacking," stating that the looting of trucks had reached a rate of more than $100 million per year. Without indicating that the Briscoe hijacking had occurred 11 years earlier, the article contained the following sentence: "Typical of many beginners, Marvin Briscoe and another man stole a 'valuable-looking' truck in Danville, Ky., and then fought a gun battle with the local police, only to learn that they had hijacked four bowling pin spotters." After publication of the article, Briscoe brought an action for damages against Reader's Digest Association, Inc., for the inten-

tional tort of invasion of the right to privacy. The complaint alleged that as a result of the *Reader's Digest* publication, the plaintiff's 11-year-old daughter, as well as the plaintiff's friends, learned of his criminal record for the first time and thereafter scorned and abandoned him. Did Briscoe's complaint state a cause of action for invasion of the right to privacy? [*Briscoe v. Reader's Digest Association*, Inc., 4 Cal.2d 529, 93 Cal.Rptr. 866 (Cal. 1971)]

5.4. In January 1984, George Yanase was a paying guest at the Royal Lodge-Downtown Motel (Royal) in San Diego, California. Yanase was a member of the Automobile Club of Southern California (Auto Club). The Auto Club publishes a "Tourbook" in which it lists hotels and motels and rates the quality of their services, including the cleanliness of rooms, quality of the restaurant, level of personal service, and the like. Yanase had selected the Royal from the Tourbook. On the night of his stay at the Royal, Yanase was shot in the parking lot adjacent to the motel and died as a result of his injuries. Yanase's widow sued Auto Club for negligence. Is the Auto Club liable? [*Yanase v. Automobile Club of Southern California*, 212 Cal.App.3d 468, 260 Cal.Rptr. 513 (Cal.App. 1989)]

5.5. In February 1973, W. L. Brown purchased a new large Chevrolet truck from Days Chevrolet (Days). The truck had been manufactured by General Motors Corporation (General Motors). On March 1, 1973, an employee of Brown's was operating the truck when it ceased to function in rush-hour traffic on Interstate Highway 75 in the Atlanta suburbs. A defect within the alternator caused a complete failure of the truck's electrical system. The defect was caused by General Motors's negligence in manufacturing the truck. When the alternator failed to operate, the truck came to rest in the right-hand lane of two northbound lanes of freeway traffic. Because of the electrical failure, no blinking lights could be used to warn traffic of the danger. The driver, however, tried to motion traffic around the truck. Some time later when the freeway traffic had returned to normal, the large Chevrolet truck was still motionless on the freeway. At approximately 6:00 P.M. a panel truck approached the stalled truck in the right-hand lane of traffic at freeway speed. Immediately behind the panel truck, Mr. Davis, driving a Volkswagen fastback, was unable to see the stalled truck. At the last moment the driver of the panel truck saw the stalled truck and swerved into another lane to avoid it. Mr. Davis drove his Volkswagen into the stalled truck at freeway speed, causing his death. Mr. Davis's wife brought a wrongful death action based on negligence against General Motors. Was there causation linking the negligence of the defendant to the fatal accident? [*General Motors Corporation v. Davis*, 233 S.E.2d 835 (Ga.App. 1977)]

5.6. On March 21, 1980, Julius Ebanks set out from his home in East Elmhurst, Queens, New York, en route to his employment in the downtown district of Manhattan. When Ebanks reached the Bowling Green subway station, he boarded an escalator owned and operated by the New York City Transit Authority (Transit Authority). While the escalator was ascending, Ebanks's left foot became caught in a two-inch gap between the escalator step on which he was standing and the side wall of the escalator. Ebanks was unable to free himself. When he reached the top of the escalator he was thrown to the ground, fracturing his hip and suffering other serious injuries. The two-inch gap exceeded the three-eighths-inch standard required by the city's building code. Ebanks sued the Transit Authority to recover damages for his injuries. Who wins? [*Ebanks v. New York City Transit Authority*, 70 N.Y.2d 621, 518 N.Y.S.2d 776 (N.Y.App. 1986)]

5.7. Elsie Mack was admitted as a patient to the Lydia E. Hall Hospital for a surgical procedure for the treatment of rectal cancer. Dr. Joseph Jahr was the surgeon in charge of the operation. An anesthesiologist, nurses, and other hospital personnel assisted with the operation. An electrical instrument called an electrocoagulator was used during the surgery to coagulate Mack's blood vessels and stop the bleeding. A component part of the electrocoagulator known as a grounding pad was placed on Mack's left thigh and remained there throughout the surgery. While under anesthesia, Mack sustained third-degree burns on the side of her left thigh during the course of surgery because the pad came in full contact with Mack's skin tissue. When the grounding pad was removed at the conclusion of the operation, a burn more than one-half inch deep and over two inches in diameter was discovered where the pad had been. The burn was excised along with the nerves and a two-and-three-quarter-inch scar remains. Mack sued the hospital, Dr. Jahr, and other medical personnel to recover damages caused by their negligence. Does the doctrine of *res ipsa loquitur* apply to this lawsuit? [*Mack v. Lydia E. Hall Hospital*, 503 N.Y.S.2d 131 (N.Y.Sup.Ct. 1986)]

5.8. George and Beverly Wagner own a 1.6-acre parcel of land upon which they operate "Bowag Kennels," which caters to training, boarding, and caring for show dogs. The property is entirely surrounded by land owned by Reuben Shiling and W. Dale Hess. In August 1964, Shiling and Hess granted the Wagners an easement right-of-way over their land that connected the kennel to Singer Road, a rural, unlit two-lane public road running through a wooded area. The right-of-way is an unpaved, unlit narrow road that crosses an uninhabited wooded area leading to the Bowag Kennels. On numerous occasions, unauthorized motorcyclists drove upon the right-of-way. On several occasions, the bikers had loud parties along the right-of-way. In September 1982, the Wagners stretched a large metal chain between two poles at the

entrance of the right-of-way. The Wagners testified that they marked the chain with reflectors and signs. Just before midnight on October 2, 1982, William E. Doehring, Jr., and his passenger, Kelvin Henderson, drove their motorcycle off Singer Road and turned onto the right-of-way. The motorcycle they were riding was not equipped with a headlight and the riders were not wearing helmets. Doehring and Henderson had not been granted permission by the Wagners or Shiling or Hess to use the right-of-way. The motorcycle struck the chain and the riders were thrown off. Doehring died several hours later at a hospital. Doehring's father filed a wrongful death and survival action against the Wagners. Who wins? [*Wagner v. Doehring*, 553 A.2d 684 (Md.App. 1989)]

5.9. David Andres was a 19-year-old student at Northeast Missouri State University. He was a member of Alpha Kappa Lambda Fraternity and lived in the fraternity house. During the evening of December 11, 1979, and the early morning hours of December 12, 1979, the fraternity sponsored a mixer at its house with the Delta Zeta Sorority at which alcoholic beverages were furnished without restriction as to age. Missouri's lawful age for drinking alcoholic beverages was 21. Andres was observed drinking before, during, and following the mixer. During the early morning hours of December 12, he was sitting at the bar in the fraternity house, matching straight shots of whiskey with a fraternity brother. After watching them for some time, another fraternity brother took the bottle from them. Several fraternity brothers helped Andres into the television room, where a pillow and blanket were obtained for him. He was left to "sleep it off" on the television room floor. At about 10:00 A.M. on December 12, when Andres could not be awakened, he was taken to a local hospital but could not be revived. The autopsy showed Andres's blood alcohol level measured 0.43 percent, and the cause of death was acute alcohol intoxication with aspiration. Andres's parents brought a wrongful death action against the fraternity. Who wins? [*Andres v. Alpha Kappa Lambda Fraternity*, 730 S.W.2d 547 (Mo. 1987)]

5.10. The Southern California Rapid Transit District (RTD) is a public common carrier that operates public buses throughout the Los Angeles area. Carmen and Carla Lopez were fare-paying passengers on an RTD bus when a group of juveniles began harassing them and other passengers. When the bus driver was notified of this problem, he failed to take any precautionary measures and continued to operate the bus. The juveniles eventually physically assaulted Carmen and Carla, who were injured. The RTD was aware of a history of violent attacks on its bus line. Carmen and Carla sued the RTD to recover damages for their injuries. Who wins? [*Lopez v. Southern California Rapid Transit District*, 40 Cal.3d 780, 221 Cal.Rptr. 840 (Cal. 1985)]

5.11. Virginia Rulon-Miller began working for International Business Machines Corporation (IBM) in 1967. Over the course of several years she was promoted to a marketing-representative position, selling typewriters and office equipment in San Francisco's financial district. She became one of the most successful salespersons in the office and received money prizes and awards for her work. She also received the highest merit rating an employee could receive under the IBM rating system. In 1976, Rulon-Miller met Matt Blum, who was an account manager for IBM. They began dating shortly thereafter and became involved in a romantic relationship. This fact was widely known at IBM. In 1977, Blum left IBM to work at QXY, a competitor of IBM. Rulon-Miller and Blum continued their relationship. About one year later, Phillip Callahan, who was Rulon-Miller's immediate manager, called her into his office. He told her that her dating Blum constituted a "conflict of interest," told her to stop dating Blum, and told her he would give her a "couple of days to a week" to think about it. The next day, however, Callahan called Rulon-Miller in again and told her he had "made up her mind for her" and dismissed her. Rulon-Miller suffered severe emotional distress because of this incident. She sued IBM for intentional infliction of emotional distress. Who wins? [*Rulon-Miller v. International Business Machines Corporation*, 162 Cal.App.3d 241, 208 Cal.Rptr. 524 (Cal.App. 1985)]

5.12. On August 10, 1983, Gregory and Demetria James, brother and sister, were riding their bicycles north on 50th Street in Omaha, Nebraska. Spaulding Street intersects 50th Street. A garbage truck owned by Watts Trucking Service, Inc. (Watts), and driven by its employee, John Milton Lieb (Lieb), was backing up into the intersection of 50th and Spaulding streets. The truck backed into the intersection of 50th and Spaulding streets, through a stop sign, and hit and ran over Demetria, killing her. Gregory helplessly watched the entire accident but was not in danger himself. As a result of watching his sister's peril, Gregory suffered severe emotional distress. Gregory sued Watts and Lieb to recover damages for his emotional distress. Who wins? [*James v. Watts Trucking Service, Inc.*, 375 N.W.2d 109 (Neb. 1985)]

ETHICS CASES

5.13. On the night of June 13, 1975, the New York Yankees professional baseball team played the Chicago White Sox at Yankee Stadium, New York. Elliot Maddox played center field for the Yankees that night. It had rained the day before, and the previous night's game had been canceled because of bad weather. On the evening of June 13 the playing field was still wet, and Maddox commented on this fact several times to the club's manager but continued to play. In the ninth inning, when Maddox was attempting to field a ball in center field, he slipped on a wet spot, fell, and injured his right knee. Maddox sued the City of New York, which owned the stadium, the Metropolitan Baseball Club, Inc., as lessee, the architect, the consulting engineer, and the American League. Maddox alleged that the parties were negligent in causing the field to be wet, and that the injury ended his professional career. Who wins? Did Maddox act ethically in suing the defendants? [*Maddox v. City of New York*, 496 N.Y.S.2d 726 (N.Y.App. 1985)]

5.14. Radio station KHJ was a successful Los Angeles broadcaster of rock music that commanded a 48 percent market share of the teenage audience in the Los Angeles area. KHJ was owned and operated by RKO General, Inc. (RKO General). In July 1973, KHJ inaugurated a promotion entitled "The Super Summer Spectacular." As part of this promotion, KHJ had a disc jockey known as "The Real Don Steele" (Steele) ride around the Los Angeles area in a conspicuous red automobile. Periodically KHJ would announce to its radio audience Steele's location. The first listener to thereafter locate Steele and answer a question received a cash prize and participated in a brief interview on the air with Steele. On July 16, 1973, one KHJ broadcast identified Steele's next destination as Canoga Park. Robert Sentner, 17 years old, heard the broadcast and immediately drove to Canoga Park. Marsha Baime, 19 years old, also heard the broadcast and drove to Canoga Park. By the time Sentner and Baime located Steele, someone else had already claimed the prize. Without the knowledge of the other, Sentner and Baime each decided to follow Steele to the next destination and to be first to "find" him.

Steele proceeded onto the freeway. For the next few miles Sentner and Baime tried to jockey for position closest to the Steele vehicle, reaching speeds of up to 80 miles per hour. There is no evidence that the Steele vehicle exceeded the speed limit. When Steele left the freeway at the Westlake off-ramp, Sentner and Baime tried to follow. In their attempts to do so, they knocked another vehicle driven by Mr. Weirum into the center divider of the freeway, where it overturned. Mr. Weirum died in the accident. Baime stopped to report the accident. Sentner, after pausing momentarily to relate the tragedy to a passing police officer, got back into his car, pursued and successfully located Steele, and collected the cash prize. The wife and children of Mr. Weirum brought a wrongful death negligence action against Sentner, Baime, and RKO General. Who wins? Did RKO General, Inc., act responsibly in this case? [*Weirum v. RKO General, Inc.*, 15 Cal.3d 40, 123 Cal.Rptr. 468 (Cal. 1975)]

5.15. Guy Portee, a seven-year-old, resided with his mother in an apartment building in Newark, New Jersey. Edith and Nathan Jaffee owned and operated the building. On the afternoon of May 22, 1976, Guy became trapped in the building's elevator between its outer door and the wall of the elevator shaft. When someone activated the elevator, the boy was dragged up to the third floor. Another child who saw the accident ran to seek help. Soon afterward, Renee Portee, the boy's mother, and officers of the Newark Police Department arrived. The officers worked for four and one-half hours trying to release the boy, during which time the mother watched as her son moaned, cried out, and flailed his arms. The police contacted the Atlantic Elevator Company (Atlantic), which

was responsible for the installation and maintenance of the elevator, and requested the company to send a mechanic to assist in the effort to free the boy. Apparently no one came. The boy suffered multiple bone fractures and massive internal hemorrhaging. He died while still trapped, his mother a helpless observer.

After her son's death, Renee became severely distressed and seriously self-destructive. On March 24, 1979, she attempted to take her own life. She survived and the wound was repaired by surgery, but she has since required considerable physical therapy. She has received extensive counseling and psychotherapy to help overcome the mental and emotional problems associated with her son's death. Renee sued the Jaffees and Atlantic to recover damages for her emotional distress. Who wins? Did either of the defendants act unethically in this case? [*Portee v. Jaffee*, 417 A.2d 521 (N.J. 1980)]

CRITICAL LEGAL THINKING WRITING ASSIGNMENT

Read Case A.5 in the Case Appendix [*Braun v. Soldier of Fortune Magazine, Inc.*]. This case is excerpted from the court of appeals opinion. Review and brief the case. In your brief, be sure to answer the following questions.

1. Who are the plaintiffs? What are they suing for?

2. When does a magazine owe a duty to refrain from publishing an advertisement?

3. Was the advertisement the proximate cause of the plaintiff's injuries?

4. Should the award of punitive damages have been reduced?

NOTES

1. 376 U.S. 254, 84 S.Ct. 710 (1964).
2. *Restatement (Second) of Torts*, Section 46.
3. *Restatement (Second) of Torts*, Section 46, comment d.
4. Justice B. Anderson, *Blyth v. Birmingham Waterworks Co.*, 11 Exch. 781, 784 (1856).
5. 248 N.Y. 339, 162 N.E. 99 (1928).
6. For example, see Cal. Civil Code, Section 1714(c).
7. 18 U.S.C. §§ 1961–1968.
8. 18 U.S.C. § 1964(c).
9. *Sedima, S.P.R.L. v. Imrex Co., Inc.*, 473 U.S. 479, 105 S.Ct. 3275, 87 L.Ed.2d 346 (1985).

Product Liability

A manufacturer is strictly liable in tort when an article he places on the market, knowing that it is to be used without inspection for defects, proves to have a defect that causes injury to a human being.

GREENMUN v. YUBA POWER PRODUCTS, INC.,
59 Cal.2d 57, 27 Cal.Rptr. 697 (1963)

Chapter Objectives

After studying this chapter, you should be able to

1. Describe and distinguish among the various legal theories of product liability.
2. Define the *doctrine of strict liability*.
3. Identify the parties who are liable for injuries caused by defective products.
4. Identify and distinguish defects in manufacture, design, and packaging.
5. Identify and distinguish defects caused by failure to warn and failure to provide adequate instructions.
6. List and describe defenses to product liability lawsuits.
7. Describe the damages recoverable in a product liability action.
8. Distinguish between contributory negligence and comparative negligence.
9. Define and describe the doctrine of market share liability.
10. Describe product liability law in Japan.

Chapter Contents

If a product defect causes injury to purchasers, lessees, users, or bystanders, the injured party may be able to recover for his or her injuries under certain *tort* theories. These include negligence, misrepresentation, and the modern theory of strict liability. The liability of manufacturers, sellers, lessors, and others for injuries caused by defective products is commonly referred to as **products liability**.

The various tort principles that permit injured parties to recover damages caused by defective products are discussed in this chapter.

𝒯ORT LIABILITY BASED ON FAULT

Depending on the circumstances of the case, persons who are injured by defective products may be able to recover damages under the tort theories of *negligence* and *misrepresentation*. Both theories require the defendant to be *at fault* for causing the plaintiff's injuries. These theories are discussed in the paragraphs that follow.

Negligence

A person injured by a defective product may bring an action for **negligence** against the negligent party. To be successful, the plaintiff must prove that the defendant breached a duty of due care to the plaintiff that caused the plaintiff's injuries. Failure to exercise due care includes failing to assemble the product carefully, negligent product design, negligent inspection or testing of the product, negligent packaging, failure to warn of the dangerous propensities of the product, and such. It is important to note that in a negligence lawsuit only a party who was actually negligent is liable to the plaintiff.

The plaintiff and the defendant do not have to be in privity of contract.[1] For example, in the landmark case *MacPherson v. Buick Motor Co.*,[2] the court held that an injured consumer could recover damages from the manufacturer of a product even though the consumer was only in privity of contract with the retailer from whom he had purchased the product. The plaintiff generally bears the difficult burden of proving that the defendant was negligent.

Consider This Example   Assume that the purchaser of a motorcycle is injured in an accident. The accident occurred because a screw was missing from the motorcycle. How does the buyer prove who was negligent? Was it the manufacturer, who left the screw out during the assembly of the motorcycle? Was it the retailer, who negligently failed to discover the missing screw while preparing the motorcycle for sale? Was it the mechanic, who failed to replace the screw after repairing the motorcycle? Negligence remains a viable, yet difficult, theory upon which to base a product liability action.

Misrepresentation

A buyer or lessee who is injured because a seller or lessor fraudulently misrepresented the quality of a product can sue the seller for the tort of **intentional misrepresentation** or **fraud**. Recovery is limited to persons who were injured because they relied on the misrepresentation.

Intentional misrepresentation occurs where a seller or lessor either (1) affirmatively misrepresents the quality of a product or (2) conceals a defect in it. Because most reputable manufacturers, sellers, and lessors do not intentionally misrepresent the quality of their products, fraud is not often used as the basis for product liability actions.

In the following case, the court held a defendant manufacturer liable for negligence in a product liability lawsuit.

products liability
The liability of manufacturers, sellers, and others for the injuries caused by defective products.

negligence
A tort related to defective products where the defendant has breached a duty of due care and caused harm to the plaintiff.

Business Brief
In *MacPherson v. Buick Motor Co.*, the court held that an injured consumer could recover damages from the manufacturer of a product even though he or she was only in privity of contract with the retailer from whom he or she had purchased the product.

intentional misrepresentation
When a seller or lessor fraudulently misrepresents the quality of a product and a buyer is injured thereby.

Benedi v. McNeil-P.P.C., Incorporated
66 F.3d 1378 (1995)
United States Court of Appeals, Fourth Circuit

CASE 6.1

FACTS

Antonio Benedi consumed three to four glasses of wine a night during the week and sometimes more on the weekend. On February 5, 1993, Benedi began taking Extra-Strength Tylenol in normal doses for flu-like aches. On February 10, 1993, Benedi was admitted to the hospital in a coma and near death due to liver and kidney failure. On the night of February 12, 1993, Benedi underwent an emergency liver transplant. Because of the transplant, Benedi will have to undergo kidney dialysis in the future. Blood tests performed shortly after Benedi's admission to the hospital revealed that he suffered from acetaminophen (Tylenol) toxicity, which is caused by a combination of Tylenol and too much alcohol. The bottle from which Benedi took the Tylenol did not contain a warning of the dangers of the combination of Tylenol and excessive alcohol consumption. Benedi sued McNeil-P.P.C., Incorporated (McNeil), the manufacturer of Tylenol, for negligent failure to warn. The jury found McNeil negligent and awarded Benedi $7,850,000 in compensatory damages. McNeil appealed.

ISSUE

Is McNeil liable for negligent failure to warn?

IN THE LANGUAGE OF THE COURT

Anderson, District Judge   At trial, Benedi called two liver disease specialists who both testified that a warning of the possible danger to heavy drinkers from combining alcohol and acetaminophen should have been placed on the Tylenol label since the mid-1980s. These experts described exactly how the alcohol-acetaminophen mixture can become a toxin in the liver. They cited numerous treatises and articles published in medical journals prior

to 1993 that describe the increased risk of liver injury when acetaminophen is combined with alcohol. One of plaintiff's experts referred to sixty reports that McNeil had received by the end of 1992 documenting cases of liver injury associated with combining therapeutic doses of Tylenol with alcohol. Because Benedi's experts presented sufficient evidence on the issue of causation, the district judge properly submitted that issue to the jury. It was the jury's role to assess the weight and credibility of the evidence, and the jury found that Benedi proved causation. We find that ample evidence existed from which a reasonable jury could find for Benedi.

DECISION AND REMEDY

The court of appeals affirmed the jury's verdict awarding plaintiff Benedi $7,850,000 against McNeil for negligent failure to warn.

Note: In the summer of 1993 (after Benedi's injury), McNeil included a warning on Tylenol that persons who regularly consume three or more alcoholic drinks a day should consult a physician before using Tylenol.

Case Questions

Critical Legal Thinking   What elements are necessary to prove negligence? Do you think that McNeil was negligent in this case? Do you think jurors are sophisticated enough to evaluate and judge scientific evidence?

Ethics   Did McNeil act ethically in failing to put a warning on Tylenol? Do you think a warning was warranted?

Business Application   What will be the implication of this case to manufacturers of pain-killing drugs? Will consumers be better off because of this decision? Explain.

---

doctrine of strict liability in tort

A tort doctrine that makes manufacturers, distributors, wholesalers, retailers, and others in the chain of distribution of a defective product liable for the damages caused by the defect *irrespective of fault.*

Business Brief

In *Greenmun* v. *Yuba Power Products, Inc.*, the California Supreme Court adopted the doctrine of strict liability in tort for product liability actions.

*T*HE DOCTRINE OF STRICT LIABILITY

In the landmark case *Greenmun v. Yuba Power Products, Inc.*,[3] the California Supreme Court adopted the **doctrine of strict liability in tort** as a basis for product liability actions. Most states have now adopted this doctrine as a basis for product liability actions. The doctrine of strict liability removes many of the difficulties for the plaintiff associated with other theories of product liability. The remainder of this chapter examines the scope of the strict liability doctrine.

The Restatement of Torts

The doctrine of strict liability is not part of the Uniform Commercial Code (UCC). The most widely recognized articulation of the doctrine is found in **Section 402A** of the **Restatement (Second) of Torts**, which provides

> *(1) One who sells any product in a defective condition unreasonably dangerous to the user or consumer or to his property is subject to liability for physical harm thereby caused to the ultimate user or consumer, or to his property, if*

(a) the seller is engaged in the business of selling such a product, and
(b) it is expected to and does reach the user or consumer without substantial change in the condition in which it is sold.
(2) The rule stated in Subsection (1) applies although
(a) the seller has exercised all possible care in the preparation and sale of his product, and
(b) the user or consumer has not bought the product from or entered into any contractual relation with the seller.

Liability Without Fault

Unlike negligence, strict liability does not require the injured person to prove that the defendant breached a duty of care. *Strict liability is imposed irrespective of fault.* A seller can be found strictly liable even though he or she has exercised all possible care in the preparation and sale of his or her product.

The doctrine of strict liability applies to sellers and lessors of products who are engaged in the business of selling and leasing products. Casual sales and transactions by nonmerchants are not covered. Thus, a person who sells a defective product to a neighbor in a casual sale is not strictly liable if the product causes injury.

Strict liability applies only to products, not services. In hybrid transactions involving both services and products, the dominant element of the transaction dictates whether strict liability applies. For example, in a medical operation that requires a blood transfusion, the operation would be the dominant element and strict liability would not apply.[4] Strict liability may not be disclaimed.

> **Business Brief**
> Strict liability law imposes liability without fault on manufacturers, sellers, and lessors who make and distribute defective products that cause injury to users and others.

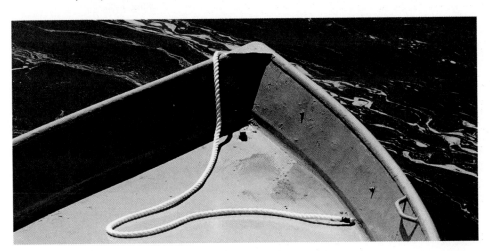

The sale or lease of goods, such as this boat, are subject to product liability laws. Strict liability is a modern tort concept that only applies to transactions in goods, and not to service contracts or contracts for the sale of real estate.

All in the Chain of Distribution Are Liable

All parties in the **chain of distribution** of a defective product are strictly liable for the injuries caused by that product. Thus, all manufacturers, distributors, wholesalers, retailers, lessors, and subcomponent manufacturers may be sued under this doctrine. This view is based on public policy. Lawmakers presume that sellers and lessors will insure against the risk of a strict liability lawsuit and spread the cost to their consumers by raising the price of products.

> **chain of distribution**
> All manufacturers, distributors, wholesalers, retailers, lessors, and subcomponent manufacturers involved in a transaction.

Consider This Example Suppose a subcomponent manufacturer produces a defective tire and sells it to a truck manufacturer. The truck manufacturer places the defective tire on one of its new model trucks. The truck is distributed by a distributor to a retail dealer. Ultimately, the retail dealer sells the truck to a buyer. The defective tire causes an accident in which the buyer is injured. All of the parties in the tire's chain of distribution can be sued by the injured party, in this case, the liable parties are the subcomponent manufacturer, the truck manufacturer, the distributor, and the retailer.

A defendant who has not been negligent but who is made to pay a strict liability judgment can bring a separate action against the negligent party in the chain of distribution to recover its losses. In the preceding example, for instance, the retailer could sue the manufacturer to recover the strict liability judgment assessed against it.

Exhibit 6.1 compares the doctrines of negligence and strict liability.

*&*XHIBIT **6.1**   *Doctrines of Negligence and Strict Liability Compared*

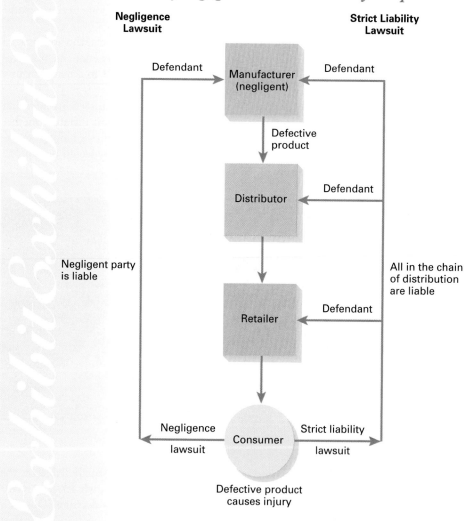

Parties Who Can Recover for Strict Liability

Business Brief

Privity of contract is not required for a plaintiff to sue for strict liability.

Because strict liability is a tort doctrine, privity of contract between the plaintiff and the defendant is not required. In other words, the doctrine applies even if the injured party had no contractual relations with the defendant. Under strict liability, sellers and lessors are liable to the ultimate user or consumer. Users include the purchaser or lessee, family members, guests, employees, customers, and persons who passively enjoy the benefits of the product (e.g., passengers in automobiles).

Most jurisdictions have judicially or statutorily extended the protection of strict liability to bystanders. The courts have stated that bystanders should be entitled to even greater protection than a consumer or user. This is because consumers and users have the chance to inspect for defects and to limit their purchases to articles manufactured by reputable manufacturers and sold by reputable retailers, whereas bystanders do not have the same opportunity.[5]

Damages Recoverable for Strict Liability

The damages recoverable in a strict liability action vary by jurisdiction. Damages for personal injuries are recoverable in all jurisdictions that have adopted the doctrine of strict liability, although some jurisdictions limit the dollar amount of the award. Property damage is recoverable in most jurisdictions, but economic loss (e.g., lost income) is recoverable in only a few jurisdictions. *Punitive damages* are generally allowed if the plaintiff can prove that the defendant either intentionally injured him or her or acted with reckless disregard for his or her safety.

> **Business Brief**
> **Punitive damages are often awarded in strict liability lawsuits if the plaintiff proves that the defendant either intentionally injured him or her or acted with reckless disregard for his or her safety.**

Entrepreneur and the Law

SO, IF YOU DID NOTHING WRONG, WHY ARE YOU PAYING?

Entrepreneurs often own small and medium-size retail stores as well as many wholesale and distributor businesses. In this capacity, they distribute and sell products made by manufacturers. Many of these products are sold in their original boxes or are otherwise sold without individual inspection by the retailer, wholesaler, or distributor. But what happens if the product has been produced defectively by the manufacturer and a purchaser or user is injured by the product? Who is liable?

In the past, when negligence was the major legal theory asserted by the injured victim to recover damages, the negligent manufacturer paid, but the retailer, wholesaler, and distributor did not pay because they did nothing wrong. Gone are those days, however. With the advent of the legal theory of **strict liability**, all in the chain of distribution of a defective product are liable for any injury caused by the product even though some of the parties are not at fault. Today, entrepreneurs and others who sell and distribute products made by others have to worry about being named in a products liability lawsuit and paying for injuries caused by the product.

To protect against such liability, retailers, wholesalers, and distributors should purchase products liability insurance. If the seller is embroiled in a products liability lawsuit, the insurance company will pay the costs of the defenses (e.g., attorney's fees, court costs) as well as any settlement amount or judgment, up to the policy limits. The insured business is liable for any amount beyond the policy limit. Paying for products liability insurance raises the cost of doing business.

THE CONCEPT OF DEFECT

To recover for strict liability, the injured party must first show that the product that caused the injury was somehow **defective**. (Remember that the injured party does not have to prove who caused the product to become defective.) Plaintiffs can allege multiple product defects in one lawsuit. A product can be found to be defective in many ways. The most common types of defects are *defects in manufacture, design,* and *packaging* and *failure to warn.* These defects are discussed in the following paragraphs.

> **defect**
> **Something wrong, inadequate, or improper in manufacture, design, packaging, warning, or safety measures of a product.**

defect in manufacture
A defect that occurs when the manufacturer fails to (1) properly assemble a product, (2) properly test a product, or (3) adequately check the quality of the product.

DEFECT IN MANUFACTURE

A **defect in manufacture** occurs when the manufacturer fails to (1) properly assemble a product, (2) properly test a product, or (3) adequately check the quality of the product. The following case is a classic example involving a defect in the manufacture.

Shoshone Coca-Cola Bottling Co. v. Dolinski
420 P.2d 855 (1967)
Supreme Court of Nevada

CASE 6.2

FACTS
Leo Dolinski purchased a bottle of "Squirt," a soft drink, from a vending machine at a Sea and Ski plant, his place of employment. Dolinski opened the bottle and consumed part of its contents. He immediately became ill. Upon examination, it was found that the bottle contained the decomposed body of a mouse, mouse hair, and mouse feces. Dolinski visited a doctor and was given medicine to counteract nausea. Dolinski suffered physical and mental distress from consuming the decomposed mouse and possessed an aversion to soft drinks. The Shoshone Coca-Cola Bottling Company (Shoshone) manufactured and distributed the Squirt bottle. Dolinski sued Shoshone, basing his lawsuit on the doctrine of strict liability. The state of Nevada had not previously recognized the doctrine of strict liability. However, the trial court adopted the doctrine of strict liability and the jury returned a verdict in favor of the plaintiff. Shoshone appealed.

ISSUE
Should the state of Nevada judicially adopt the doctrine of strict liability? If so, was there a defect in the manufacture of the Squirt bottle that caused the plaintiff's injuries?

IN THE LANGUAGE OF THE COURT
Thompson, Justice   We affirm the verdict and judgment since, in our view, public policy demands that one who places upon the market a bottled beverage in a condition dangerous for use must be held strictly liable to the ultimate user for injuries resulting from such use, although the seller has exercised all reasonable care. Though appellant Shoshone suggests that only the legislature may declare the policy of Nevada on this subject, the weight of the case authority is contra. As indicated, most states approving the doctrine of strict liability have done so by court declaration.

Our acceptance of strict tort liability against the manufacturer and distributor of a bottled beverage does not mean that the plaintiff is relieved of the burden of proving a case. He must still establish that his injury was caused by a defect in the product and that such defect existed when the product left the hands of the defendant. The concept of strict liability does not prove causation, nor does it trace cause to the defendant.

In the case at hand, Shoshone contends that insufficient proof was offered to establish that the mouse was in the bottle of "Squirt" when it left Shoshone's possession. The plaintiff offered the expert testimony of a toxicologist who examined the bottle and contents on the day the plaintiff drank from it. It was his opinion that the mouse "had been dead for a long time" and that the dark stains (mouse feces) that he found on the bottom of the bottle must have been there before the liquid was added. The jury apparently preferred the latter evidence that traced cause to the defendant.

DECISION AND REMEDY
The Supreme Court of Nevada adopted the doctrine of strict liability and held that the evidence supported the trial court's finding that there was a defect in manufacture. Affirmed.

Case Questions

Critical Legal Thinking   Should the courts adopt the theory of strict liability? Why or why not?

Ethics   Was it ethical for Shoshone to argue that it was not liable to Dolinski?

Business Application   Should all in the chain of distribution of a defective product—even those parties who are not responsible for the defect—be held liable under the doctrine of strict liability? Or should liability be based only on fault?

DEFECT IN DESIGN

defect in design
A defect that occurs when a product is improperly designed.

A **defect in design** can support a strict liability action. Design defects that have supported strict liability awards include toys that are designed with removable parts that could be swallowed by children, machines and appliances designed without proper safeguards, and trucks and other vehicles designed without a warning device to let people know that the vehicle is backing up.

In evaluating the adequacy of a product's design, the courts apply a risk-utility analysis and consider the gravity of the danger posed by the design, the likelihood that injury will occur, the availability and cost of producing a safer alternative design, the social utility of the product, and other factors.

The following design defect case demonstrates the application of the risk-utility analysis.

Lakin v. Senco Products, Inc.
925 P.2d 107 (1996)
Court of Appeals of Oregon

CASE 6.3

FACTS

Senco Products, Inc. (Senco), manufactures and markets a variety of pneumatic nail guns, including the SN325 nail gun, which discharges 3.25 inch nails. The SN325 uses special nails designed and sold by Senco. The SN325 will discharge a nail only if two trigger mechanisms are activated; that is, the user must both squeeze the nail gun's finger trigger and press the nail gun's muzzle against a surface, activating the bottom trigger or safety. The SN325 can fire up to nine nails per second if the trigger is continuously depressed and the gun is bounced along the work surface, constantly reactivating the muzzle safety/trigger.

On December 1, 1990, John Lakin was using a Senco SN325 nail gun to help build a new home. When attempting to nail two-by-fours under the eaves of the garage, Lakin stood on tiptoe and raised a two-by-four over his head. As he held the board in position with his left hand and the nail gun in his right hand, he pressed the nose of the SN325 up against the board, depressed the safety, and pulled the finger trigger to fire the nail into the board. The gun fired the first nail and then, in a phenomenon known as "double firing," immediately discharged an unintended second nail that struck the first nail. The gun recoiled violently backward toward Lakin and, with Lakin's finger still on the trigger, came into contact with his cheek. That contact activated the safety/trigger, causing the nail gun to fire a third nail. This third nail went through Lakin's cheekbone and into his brain.

The nail penetrated the frontal lobe of the right hemisphere of Lakin's brain, blocked a major artery, and caused extensive tissue damage. Lakin was unconscious for several days and ultimately underwent multiple surgeries. He suffers permanent brain damage and is unable to perceive information from the left hemisphere of the brain. He also suffers partial paralysis of the left side of his body. Lakin has undergone a radical personality change and is prone to violent outbursts. He is unable to obtain employment. Lakin's previously warm and loving relationship with his wife and four children has been permanently altered. He can no longer live with his family and instead resides in a supervised group home for brain-injured persons. Lakin and his wife sued Senco for strict liability based on design defect. The trial court found Senco liable and awarded $3.6 million to Lakin, $457,000 to his wife, and $4 million in punitive damages against Senco. Senco appealed.

ISSUE

Is Senco liable to Lakin for strict liability based on a design defect in the SN325 that allowed it to double fire?

IN THE LANGUAGE OF THE COURT

Haselton, Judge   *Defendant Senco's failure to effectively address the SN325's double firing problem was conscious and was motivated, at least in part, by a profit motive. The evidence disclosed that defendant earned substantial profits from the sale of nails used in its products and that the waste of nails from double firing—the SN325 double-fired once in every 15 firings—generated additional sales for defendant. Indeed, the most prevalent complaint about double-firing from users of the SN325 was the resultant waste of nails. Thus, defendant generated greater profits by failing to address and remedy the double-fire defect. Moreover, defendant rushed the SN325's production in order to maintain its position in the market, modifying an existing nail gun model so that it could shoot longer nails, without engaging in additional testing to determine whether the use of longer nails in that model would increase the prevalence of double fire. Again, a reasonable juror could plausibly infer that conscious profit/market share motives underlay the failure to engage in adequate product research, development, and testing.*

After reviewing the entire record, we conclude that the amount of damages awarded was within the range that a rational juror would be entitled to award. Before John Lakin's injury, defendant knew from numerous complaints that it was highly probable that the SN325 would "double fire." Thus, it was foreseeable—indeed, highly likely given the SN325's recoil and "bump fire" potential—that serious injury could occur to someone when the nail gun double fired. Finally, the evidence indicates that defendant had a net liquidation value of $82,076,000. The $4 million punitive damages award equals approximately five

(case continues)

percent of defendent's net value. In the light of the evidence, and given the jury's award of approximately $6.2 million in compensatory damages, we cannot say that a $4 million punitive damages award is outside the range that a rational juror would be entitled to award in this case. The award of punitive damages was not unconstitutionally excessive.

DECISION AND REMEDY
The court of appeals applied the risk-utility analysis and held that the SN325 was defectively designed. The court affirmed the award of damages to Lakin and his wife.

Case Questions

Critical Legal Thinking   Do you think the utility served by the nine-nail-per-second SN325 outweighed its risk of personal injury?

Ethics   Did Senco act in conscious disregard of safety factors when it designed, manufactured, and sold the SN325 nail gun?

Business Application   Do you think the award of punitive damages was warranted in this case?

Crashworthiness Doctrine

crashworthiness doctrine
A doctrine that says automobile manufacturers are under a duty to design automobiles so they take into account the possibility of harm from a person's body striking something inside the automobile in the case of a car accident.

Often, when an automobile is involved in an accident, the driver or passengers are not injured by the blow itself. Instead, they are injured when their bodies strike something inside their own automobile (e.g., the dashboard or the steering wheel). This is commonly referred to as the "second collision." The courts have held that automobile manufacturers are under a duty to design automobiles to take into account the possibility of this second collision. This is called the **crashworthiness doctrine**. Failure to design an automobile to protect occupants from foreseeable dangers caused by a second collision subjects the manufacturer and dealer to strict liability.

Ethical Perspective

GENERAL MOTORS HIT WITH BILLION DOLLAR JUDGMENT

On Christmas Eve, Patricia Anderson was driving her Chevrolet Malibu automobile, which was manufactured by the General Motors Corporation (GM), home from church. Her four young children, ages one through nine, and a neighbor, were also in the car. The Chevy Malibu was stopped at a stoplight at 89th Place and Figueroa Street in Los Angeles when a drunken driver plowed his car into the back of the Malibu at 50 to 70 mph. The Malibu burst into flames as its gas tank ruptured and ignited. Although no one died in the crash, the occupants of the Malibu were severely burned. Many required substantial and multiple skin grafts.

The two injured women and four injured children sued GM for product liability. They alleged that the fuel tank of the Chevy Malibu was defectively designed and placed too close to the rear bumper. GM countered that the tragic accident was the fault of the driver who struck the Malibu. The accident victims produced evidence that showed that GM knew that the car's fuel-tank design was unsafe but had not changed the design because of cost. The Chevy Malibu was one of GM's A-Class cars, which also include the Pontiac Grand Am, the Oldsmobile Cutlass, and the Chevrolet Monte Carlo, all of which have similar fuel-tank designs. The plaintiffs produced GM memos that said it would cost GM $8.59 per vehicle to produce and install a safer fuel tank design, but that it would only cost the company an estimated $2.40 per car to not fix the cars and pay damages to injured victims.

After a 10-week trial, the jurors returned a verdict of $107 million in compensatory damages to the plaintiffs for injuries, disfigurement, and pain and suffering caused to them by the accident. The jury then tacked on $4.9 billion as punitive damages to punish GM. This was the largest amount ever awarded in a personal-injury lawsuit. GM, the world's largest automobile company, reported annual earnings of $3 billion in 1998, the year of the verdict. After the trial one juror stated: "We're just like numbers. Statistics. That's something that is wrong."

GM asked the trial judge to throw the trial out. GM claimed that it was not given a fair trial because the trial court judge refused to allow the jury to hear evidence that (1) the driver of the other car was drunk and went to jail and (2) crash-test data that showed the safety history of the vehicle. GM also claimed that the jury was prejudiced by repetitive personal attacks on GM as a "soulless company" and its lawyers as "hired guns" who consumed "cappuccinos and designer muffins." GM did not convince the judge that such animosity influenced the jury. GM also alleged that the jury was allowed to hear evidence that it should not have heard, namely, that GM had lobbied Congress in the 1970s to not adopt tougher standards for protecting fuel tanks in crashes.

In its post-trial motions, GM argued that the award of damages, specifically the $4.8 billion of punitive damages, was the result of bias and prejudice of the jury, and asked the trial court judge to reduce the award of damages. This the trial court judge did do: He let the compensatory dam-

age award stand but reduced the award of punitive damages to $1 billion. The revised award is equivalent to two percent of GM's net worth and 10 times the compensatory damages. GM faces over 30 other lawsuits involving fuel tank explosions in its A-Class cars.

1. Should a company follow the results of a cost-benefit analysis in making decisions to design or not design safer products?
2. Was GM prejudiced by the nonadmission of evidence that the driver of the other automobile was drunk and sent to prison for his crime?
3. Do you think the award of punitive damages was warranted? Why or why not?

*D*EFECT IN PACKAGING

Manufacturers owe a duty to design and provide safe packages for their products. This duty requires manufacturers to provide packages and containers that are tamperproof or that clearly indicate if they have been tampered with. Certain manufacturers, such as drug manufacturers, owe a duty to place their products in containers that cannot be opened by children. A manufacturer's failure to meet this duty subjects the manufacturer and others in the chain of distribution of the product to strict liability. In the following case, the court had to decide whether there was defective packaging.

defect in packaging
A defect that occurs when a product has been placed in packaging that is insufficiently tamperproof.

Elsroth v. Johnson & Johnson
700 F.Supp. 151 (1988)
United States District Court, S.D. New York

CASE 6.4

FACTS
On February 4, 1986, Harriet Notarnicola purchased a box of Extra-Strength Tylenol capsules from a Bronxville, New York, grocery store owned by The Great Atlantic & Pacific Tea Co. (A&P). The Tylenol was manufactured by McNeil Consumer Products Co., a division of McNeilab, Inc. (McNeil), under the name Johnson & Johnson. Diane Elsroth was visiting her boyfriend, Michael Notarnicola, for a week at the home of Michael's parents. Late on the night of February 7, Diane complained of a headache. Michael went to the kitchen, opened the box and plastic container of Extra-Strength Tylenol purchased by his mother at the A&P store and returned with two capsules and a glass of water for Diane. A short time after ingesting the capsules, Diane retired. Her dead body was found the next day. The medical examiner concluded that the Tylenol capsules ingested by Diane were contaminated by a lethal dose of potassium cyanide. The murder remains unsolved, but evidence shows that the Tylenol bottle had been tampered with

after the product left the manufacturer's control. An unknown third party purchased the Tylenol, breached the packaging, substituted cyanide for some of the medicine contained in several of the gelatin capsules, somehow resealed the container and box in such a way that the tampering was not readily detectable, and placed the contaminated box on the shelf of the A&P store. John Elsroth, administrator of Diane's estate, brought this strict liability action against McNeil and A&P seeking $1 million in compensatory damages and $92 million in punitive damages.

ISSUE
Was there a defect in packaging that would support an action for strict liability?

IN THE LANGUAGE OF THE COURT
Goettel, District Judge   In late September of 1982, this country was shocked by a series of murders in the Chicago area stemming from cyanide tampering of Extra-Strength Tylenol capsules. In swift response to those tragedies, the pharmaceutical industry, in

(case continues)

concert with the federal government, moved to protect consumers from the perils and random madness of product tampering. On November 5, 1982, barely one month after the Chicago tragedies were made public, the Food and Drug Administration (FDA) issued a final rule on tamper-resistant packaging applicable to most over-the-counter drugs, such as Tylenol. As a result of that rule, manufacturers of over-the-counter drugs were given a timetable in which to take steps to improve product integrity by virtue of a tamper-resistant package. The rule defines a tamper-resistant package as "one having an indicator or barrier to entry that, if breached or missing, can reasonably be expected to provide visible evidence to consumers that tampering has occurred."

Following issuance of the rule, the makers of Tylenol have marketed the product in tamper-resistant packaging with the following features: (1) a foil seal glued to the mouth of the container or bottle, (2) a "shrink seal" around the neck and cap of the container, and (3) a sealed box (the end flaps of which are glued shut) in which the product and container are placed.

McNeil, through its research, knew that this package could be violated by a determined tamperer using sophisticated means and that no evidence of this kind of sophisticated tampering would be visible to the average consumer. As one McNeil official put it, tampering by "the Rembrandt kind of criminals" could not be prevented by this type of packaging. McNeil was also operating under the constraint, however, as recognized by the FDA when it drafted the 1982 regulations, that no packaging could prevent this kind of "exotic" tampering—tamperproof packaging is not possible.

The packaging alternative designed by McNeil employed not one, not two, but three of the tamper-resistant features listed as alternatives in the 1982 FDA regulations. When all of these factors are thrown into the mix, we find, as a matter of law, that under a utility/risk analysis this packaging was in a condition reasonably contemplated by the ultimate consumer and was not unreasonably dangerous for its intended use. Moreover, plaintiff has presented no evidence of what other steps might feasibly have been taken to ensure a higher degree of safety. If there are better tamper-resistant features available that would be feasible for use here, plaintiff has not described them. We return, however, to the fundamental premise: no packaging can boast of being tamper-proof.

DECISION AND REMEDY

The court held that there was not a defect in packaging. The defendants are not therefore strictly liable for Ms. Elsroth's death.

Case Questions

Critical Legal Thinking   Should manufacturers be forced to make tamperproof packaging for their products? Is this possible? What would be the expense?

Ethics   Did any of the parties in the case act unethically?

Business Application   Do you think the plaintiff's seeking $92 million in punitive damages was warranted?

FAILURE TO WARN

failure to warn

A defect that occurs when a manufacturer does not place a warning on the packaging of products that could cause injury if the danger is unknown.

Certain products are inherently dangerous and cannot be made any safer and still accomplish the task for which they are designed. For example, certain useful drugs cause side effects, allergies, and other injuries to some users. Many machines and appliances include dangerous moving parts which, if removed, would defeat the purpose of the machine or appliance. Manufacturers and sellers of such products are under a *duty to warn* users about the product's dangerous propensities. A proper and conspicuous warning placed on the product insulates the manufacturer and others in the chain of distribution from strict liability. **Failure to warn** of these dangerous propensities is a defect that will support a strict liability action.

The court found an inadequate warning in the following case.

Nowak v. Faberge USA Inc.
32 F.3d 755 (1994)
United States Court of Appeals, Third Circuit

CASE 6.5

FACTS

Faberge USA Inc. (Faberge) manufactures Aqua Net, a hair spray that is sold in an aerosol can. In addition to the hair-holding spray, Aqua Net contains a mixture of butane or propane as the aerosol propellant and alcohol as a solvent. Alcohol, butane, and propane all are extremely flammable. Aerosol cans of Aqua Net carry a warning on the back stating, "Do not puncture" and "Do not use near fire or flame."

Alison Nowak, a 14-year-old girl, tried to spray her hair with a newly purchased can of Aqua Net. The spray valve would not work properly, so she cut open the can with a can opener. She thought she could then pour the contents into an empty aerosol bottle and use it. Nowak was standing in the kitchen near a gas stove when she punctured the can. A cloud of hair spray gushed from the can and the stove's pilot light ignited the spray into a ball of flame. She suffered severe, permanently disfiguring burns over 20 percent of her body.

Nowak sued Faberge for damages under strict liability, alleging that Faberge failed to warn her of the dangers of the flammability of Aqua Net. The jury held against Faberge and awarded Nowak $1.5 million. Faberge appealed.

ISSUE
Did Faberge adequately warn the plaintiff of the flammability of Aqua Net?

IN THE LANGUAGE OF THE COURT
Roth, Circuit Judge *A product is considered to be defective where the product left the supplier's control lacking any element necessary to make it safe for its intended use or possessing any feature that renders it unsafe for the intended use. Under Pennsylvania strict liability law, a defect may be in the warnings given for the use of the product as well as in the design of that*

product. A product can be held to be defective if it is distributed without sufficient warning to notify the ultimate user of the dangers inherent in the product.

The threshold decision concerning whether a product is defective can be difficult to make: In making this determination, the judge acts as a combination social philosopher and risk-utility analyst. We find that the district court made the threshold risk-utility determination that Faberge's product was defective under the facts by sending this case to the jury. We conclude that this is a sufficient determination under Pennsylvania law. We will, therefore, affirm the verdict and judgment of the district court.

DECISION AND REMEDY
The court of appeals affirmed the district court's judgment that Faberge had failed to warn the plaintiff of the dangers of flammability of its product and is therefore strictly liable.

Case Questions

Critical Legal Thinking   Should the law recognize a failure to warn as a basis for imposing strict liability on manufacturers and sellers of products? Why or why not?

Ethics   Did Faberge violate its duty of social responsibility in this case? Explain.

Business Application   Do you think this case was decided properly? What else could Faberge have done to avoid liability?

OTHER PRODUCT DEFECTS

Other product defects can prove the basis for a strict liability action. *Failure to provide adequate instructions* for either the safe assembly or safe use of a product is a defect that subjects the manufacturer and others in the chain of distribution to strict liability.

Other defects include inadequate testing of products, inadequate selection of component parts or materials, and improper certification of the safety of a product. The concept of "defect" is an expanding area of the law.

E-Commerce & Internet Law

PRODUCT LIABILITY LIMITED BY THE Y2K ACT

Many computer programs written in the 1900s were written without thought that the twenty-first century was coming. Computer software designers made their programs go up to and recognize the year 1999 but not beyond. This problem developed because the codes of computer software programs did not recognize the change to the numbers of the year 2000. Companies around the world spent hundreds of millions of

dollars to correct this year 2000 issue, dubbed the "Y2K" problem. Because computer software is a product, computer software companies faced state-law negligence and strict liability lawsuits based on the Y2K bug.

Prior to the changeover to the year 2000, software companies began lobbying Congress for a federal statute that would save them from liability. After much debate, Congress enacted the **Y2K Act**, which was signed into law

e-biz

(box continues)

on July 20, 1999. As a federal law, the Y2K Act supercedes state product liability laws where there is a conflict between the Y2K Act and state law. The Y2K Act regulates any civil product liability lawsuit brought in state or federal court. The Act does not absolve software companies from product liability, but it made it harder for such a lawsuit to be brought and limited the damages that could be recovered. The main provisions of the Y2K Act provide that

1. Any warranty, exclusion of liability, or warranty disclaimer in software licenses and contracts shall be strictly enforced. Such warranties, exclusions, and disclaimers, which are drafted by software companies, appear in most software licenses and contracts.
2. Damages for breach of contract are limited to those allowed by the terms of the software license or contract. Most software licenses and contracts contain liquidated damage clauses that limit liability for breach of contract to a fixed dollar amount.
3. Plaintiffs asserting tort claims cannot recover for "economic loss" caused by a Y2K defect unless it is so provided in the software license or contract. Thus, a plaintiff cannot recover for such consequential damages as loss of customers or business caused by a Y2K defect. Software licenses or contracts, which are drafted by software companies, very seldom provide for this kind of recovery.

4. Punitive damages against small software companies—those with net worth less than $50,000 or fewer than 50 employees—are capped at the lesser of (1) three times compensatory damages or (2) $250,000.
5. Any judgment for Y2K liability is proportionate; that is, it is limited to the percentage responsibility of each individual defendant. Therefore, a "deep pocket" defendant will not be made to pay the entire judgment against multiple defendants but will only have to pay its proportionate share of the judgment based on its fault.
6. Before bringing a lawsuit, a plaintiff must notify a defendant of the alleged specific defect and give the defendant 30 days to remedy the defect. This time period gives the plaintiff time to "cool off" and the defendant time to "cure" the defect before a lawsuit is commenced.

The Y2K Act does not entirely eliminate product liability of software companies for the Y2K bug, but it does make it harder for plaintiffs to sue and limits the damages that can be recovered for the Y2K product defect. The passage of the Y2K Act also demonstrates how businesses sometimes lobby Congress for laws that will absolve them of, or limit, their liability exposure.

*D*EFENSES TO PRODUCT LIABILITY

Defendants in strict liability or negligence actions may raise several defenses to the imposition of liability. These defenses are discussed in the paragraphs that follow.

Supervening Event

supervening event
An alteration or modification of a product by a party in the chain of distribution that absolves all prior sellers from strict liability.

For a seller to be held strictly liable, the product it sells must reach the consumer or user "without substantial change" in its condition.[6] Under the doctrine of **supervening** or **intervening event**, the original seller is not liable if the product is materially altered or modified after it leaves the seller's possession and the alteration or modification causes an injury. A supervening event absolves all prior sellers in the chain of distribution from strict liability.

Consider This Example A manufacturer produces a safe piece of equipment. It sells the equipment to a distributor, who removes a safety guard from the equipment. The distributor sells it to a retailer, who sells it to a buyer. The buyer is injured because of the removal of the safety guard. The manufacturer can raise the defense of supervening event against the imposition of liability. However, the distributor and retailer are strictly liable for the buyer's injuries.

Generally Known Dangers

generally known dangers
A defense that acknowledges that certain products are inherently dangerous and are known to the general population to be so.

Certain products are inherently dangerous and are known to the general population to be so. Sellers are not strictly liable for failing to warn of **generally known dangers**. For example, it is a known fact that guns shoot bullets. Manufacturers of guns do not have to place a warning on the barrel of a gun warning of this generally known danger. However, the manufacturer would be under a duty to place a safety lock on the gun.

Government Contractor Defense

Many defense and other contractors manufacture products (e.g., rockets, airplanes, and such) to government specifications. Most jurisdictions recognize a **government contractor defense** to product liability actions. To establish this defense, a government contractor must prove that (1) the precise specifications for the product were provided by the government, (2) the product conformed to those specifications, and (3) the contractor warned the government of any known defects or dangers of the product.

Correction of a Defect

A manufacturer that produces a defective product and later discovers said defect must (1) notify purchasers and users of the defect and (2) **correct the defect**. Most manufacturers faced with this situation recall the defective product and either repair the defect or replace the product.

The seller must make reasonable efforts to notify purchasers and users of the defect and the procedure to correct it. Reasonable efforts normally consist of sending letters to known purchasers and users and placing notices in newspapers and magazines of general circulation. If a user ignores the notice and fails to have the defect corrected, the seller may raise this as a defense against further liability with respect to the defect. Many courts have held that reasonable notice is effective even against users who did not see the notice.

Assumption of the Risk

Theoretically, the traditional doctrine of **assumption of the risk** is a defense to a product liability action. For this defense to apply, the defendant must prove that (1) the plaintiff knew and appreciated the risk and (2) the plaintiff voluntarily assumed the risk. In practice, the defense of assumption of the risk is narrowly applied by the courts.

Misuse of the Product

Sometimes users are injured when they **misuse** a product. If they bring a product liability action, the defendant-seller may be able to assert the misuse as a defense. Whether the defense is effective depends on whether the misuse was foreseeable. The seller is relieved of product liability if the plaintiff has **abnormally misused** the product—that is, there has been an *unforeseeable misuse* of the product. However, the seller is liable if there has been a *foreseeable misuse* of the product. This reasoning is intended to provide an incentive for manufacturers to design and manufacture safer products.

Statute of Limitation and Statute of Repose

Most states have **statutes of limitation** that require an injured person to bring an action within a certain number of years from the time that he or she was injured by the defective product. This limitation period varies from state to state. Failure to bring an action within the appropriate time relieves the defendant of liability.

In most jurisdictions, the statute of limitations does not begin to run until the plaintiff suffers an injury. This subjects sellers and lessors to exposure for an unspecified period of time because a defective product may not cause an injury for years, or even decades, after it was sold. Because this may be unfair to the seller, some states have enacted **statutes of repose**. Statutes of repose limit the seller's liability to a certain number of years from the date when the product was first sold. The period of repose varies from state to state.

---

government contractor defense
A defense that says a contractor who was provided specifications by the government is not liable for any defect in the product that occurs as a result of those specifications.

assumption of the risk
A defense in which the defendant must prove that (1) the plaintiff knew and appreciated the risk and (2) the plaintiff voluntarily assumed the risk.

misuse
A defense that relieves a seller of product liability if the user *abnormally* misused the product. Products must be designed to protect against *foreseeable* misuse.

statute of limitation
A statute that requires an injured person to bring an action within a certain number of years from the time that he or she was injured by the defective product.

statute of repose
A statute that limits the seller's liability to a certain number of years from the date when the product was first sold.

CONCEPT SUMMARY — COMPARISON OF STATUTES OF LIMITATION AND STATUTES OF REPOSE

Statute	Begins to Run
Statute of limitation	When the plaintiff suffers injury
Statute of repose	When the product is first sold

Contemporary Business Application

RESTATEMENT (THIRD) OF TORTS DEFINES *DEFECT* FOR PRODUCT LIABILITY

Soon after Section 402A of the Restatement of Law (Second) of Torts first recognized the doctrine of strict liability in 1965, most states adopted this new doctrine. Section 402A did not define *defect*, however. Courts in each state have wrestled with the issue of what constitutes a defect for product liability purposes, and a substantial body of case law has developed around this definition. In 1997, the American Law Institute (ALI) adopted the **Restatement of the Law (Third) of Torts: Product Liability**. This new Restatement includes the following definition of *defect*:

A product is defective when, at the time of sale or distribution, it contains manufacturing defect, is defective in design, or is defective because of inadequate instructions or warnings. A product:

(a) contains a manufacturing defect when the product departs from its intended design even though all possible care was exercised in the preparation and marketing of the product;

(b) is defective in design when the foreseeable risks of harm posed by the product could have been reduced or avoided by the adoption of a reasonable alternative design by the seller or other distributor, or a predecessor in the

commercial chain of distribution, and the omission of the alternative design renders the product not reasonably safe;

(c) is defective because of inadequate instructions or warnings when the foreseeable risks of harm posed by the product could have been reduced or avoided by the provision of reasonable instructions or warnings by the seller or other distributor, or a predecessor in the commercial chain of distribution, and the omission of the instructions or warnings renders the product not reasonably safe.

Subsection (a) defines a manufacturing defect as one that includes a physical deviation from what the manufacturer intended the product to be. Subsection (b) requires a court to consider any "reasonable alternative design" when determining whether there has been a design defect. In determining whether there has been a failure to warn or failure to provide adequate instructions, subsection (c) looks at the foreseeable risks of harm and whether they could have been reduced or avoided by reasonable warnings or instructions.

There is obviously no easy or bright-line test that can define when a product is defective, however, the new Restatement (Third) definitions of *defect* may be helpful to courts hearing product liability lawsuits.

CONTRIBUTORY AND COMPARATIVE NEGLIGENCE

contributory negligence

A defense that says a person who is injured by a defective product but has been negligent and has contributed to his or her own injuries cannot recover from the defendant.

Sometimes a person who is injured by a defective product is negligent and contributes to his or her own injuries. The defense of **contributory negligence** bars an injured plaintiff from recovering from the defendant in a negligence action. This doctrine generally does not bar recovery in strict liability actions, however.

Many states have held that the doctrine of **comparative negligence** (or **comparative fault**) applies to strict liability actions. Under this doctrine, a plaintiff who is contributorily negligent for his or her injuries is responsible for a *proportional share* of the damages. In other words, the damages are apportioned between the plaintiff and the defendant.

comparative negligence

A doctrine that applies to strict liability actions that says a plaintiff who is contributorily negligent for his or her injuries is responsible for a proportional share of the damages.

Consider This Example Suppose an automobile manufacturer produces a car with a hidden defect and a consumer purchases the car from an automobile dealer. Assume that the consumer is injured in an automobile accident in which the defect is found to be 75 percent responsible for the accident and the consumer's own reckless driving is found to be 25 percent responsible. If the plaintiff suffers $1 million worth of injuries, the plaintiff may recover $750,000 from the defendant manufacturer and car dealer.

Contemporary Business Application

MARKET SHARE LIABILITY

Some products that are produced by different manufacturers are *fungible*; that is, they are made from the same chemical base or are otherwise identical. The only variation is that they are sold under different brand names by different manufacturers. In some situations, persons who are injured by fungible products cannot identify the specific manufacturer who produced the product that caused their injury. This happened to Judith Sindell. Consider her case.

Between 1941 and 1971, many drug companies manufactured and marketed drugs containing diethylstilbestrol (DES). This was a fungible chemical compound that was sold under various manufacturers' brand labels. DES, which was a synthetic compound of the female hormone estrogen, was taken by pregnant mothers to prevent miscarriages. The drug prevented miscarriages, but it also caused cancer in many children (particularly female children) of the mothers who took the drug. These daughters suffer from a form of cancer called adenocarcinoma, a fast-spreading and deadly disease that may not manifest itself for 10 to 30 years. The treatment for the cancer is cauterization, surgery, or cryosurgery. Women who suffer from this condition must be monitored by biopsy or colposcopic examination twice a year, a painful and expensive procedure. It is estimated that up to 30 percent of the children of the 2 million or so pregnant mothers who took DES will contract the disease.

In 1971, the federal Food and Drug Administration (FDA) ordered manufacturers to cease producing and marketing DES and to warn physicians and the public of the dangers of the drug.

Judith Sindell, whose mother had taken DES when she was pregnant with Judith, contracted cancer from the DES. After seeing the public notices, she sought to sue the manufacturer of the DES that her mother took. There was only one problem: Because many years had passed, she could not identify the specific manufacturer of the DES that her

mother had taken. Not thwarted, Judith sued *all* the manufacturers of DES that could have produced the DES her mother had taken. These manufacturers filed motions to be dismissed from the case, alleging that the traditional requirement of *causation* was lacking; that is, Sindell could not identify the specific manufacturer that produced the product that injured her.

The case reached the California Supreme Court. The court adopted the novel theory of **market share liability** and permitted Sindell to pursue her lawsuit against the named defendants. In adopting this theory, the court stated, "In our contemporary complex industrialized society, advances in science and technology create fungible goods which may harm consumers and which cannot be traced to any specific producer. We acknowledge that some adaptation of the rules of causation and liability may be appropriate in these recurring circumstances."

The court held that the burden of proof in such cases switches to the defendants and that any defendant that can prove it did not manufacture the defective product that caused the plaintiff's injuries can be dismissed from the case. This, of course, is a difficult task. Of the remaining defendants, liability is apportioned based on the *market share* of the industry that each defendant had at the time the defective product was sold. The court noted, "Some minor discrepancy in the correlation between market share and liability is inevitable. It is probably impossible, with the passage of time, to determine market share with mathematical exactitude."

There are thousands of California DES daughters who have benefited from the "market share" liability theory. Several other states have also adopted this theory, which is also called **enterprise liability, industry-wide liability**, and **horizontal liability**. The theory has been applied to other fungible products. [*Sindell v. Abbott Laboratories*, 26 Cal.3d 588, 163 Cal.Rptr. 132 (Cal. 1980)]

International Perspective

PRODUCT LIABILITY LAW IN JAPAN

Japanese manufacturers sell many of the same products in Japan and the United States. In the United States, the products are subject to the same product liability laws as are American companies. In Japan, they enjoy near-immunity from product liability claims. For example, in almost 50 years, consumers have won only 150 product liability cases in Japan and recovered meager damages. In the same period, companies in the United States have lost tens of thousands of such suits and have paid out hundreds of millions of dollars in damages.

Product liability claims are rare in Japan for several reasons:

1. The plaintiff has the difficult burden of proving that the company was negligent. Japan has not adopted the U.S. doctrine of strict liability.
2. Japanese courts do not allow discovery. It is often impossible to prove a product was defective if the plaintiff cannot obtain access to the defendant's files.
3. Win or lose, claimants must pay a percentage of any damages requested (not won) as court fees. This keeps damage requests low.
4. Awards that are granted by courts are small (at least by U.S. standards), and punitive damages are not available.

Consider the case of Japanese chemical maker Showa Denko. The company faces more than 1,000 lawsuits in the United States. The suits allege that the company's food supplement L-tryptophan causes injuries. In one of those cases, Showa settled out of court with Randy Simmons, a 43-year-old Wichita, Kansas, resident who alleged that the food supplement caused him to become a quadriplegic. The same company has few Japan-based cases pending against it alleging similar claims. There, the company currently offers only to reimburse Japanese customers the purchase price of the supplement.

The docile attitude of Japanese consumers is changing, and more injured consumers are suing to recover damages for their injuries. There is even a move by the Japanese government to adopt new consumer protection laws. However, the Diet, which has shown a probusiness sentiment in the past, is unlikely to expand the laws to anything near those in the United States.

Critics argue that the Japanese system leaves injured consumers unrecompensed for injuries caused by defective products. Some argue that the near-immunity from product liability claims at home gives Japanese manufacturers an edge in selling goods in international markets. Proponents of the Japanese system argue that it promotes the development and sale of products free from the oppressive liability costs that manufacturers face in the United States. They point to the fact that liability insurance costs are sometimes 20 times higher in the United States than in Japan.

Working the Web

U.S. Food and Drug Administration The U.S. Food and Drug Administration links you to information about foods, human drugs, animal drugs, cosmetics, and many other subjects.

Visit at **www.fda.gov**

Occupational Safety and Health Administration The U.S. Department of Labor has a Web site that links you to all the publications, programs, and services of OSHA.

Visit at **www.osha.gov**

American Medical Association The American Medical Association links you to all sorts of medical information.

Visit at **www.ama-assn.org**

Products Liability Law Page This Web page has all kinds of links to products liability information including information about asbestos, silicone breast implants, tobacco, medical malpractice, and more.

Visit at **www.productslaw.com**

CYBER EXERCISES

1. Use the FDA site to find information about the dietary supplement Herbal Fen-Phen.

2. Use the OSHA site to find a definition and description of ergonomics.

3. Use the AMA site to find AMA's Patient Bill of Rights.

4. Using the Products Liability Law Page, read the current news.

*C*ASES AND *E*XERCISES

CRITICAL LEGAL THINKING CASES

6.1. Jeppesen and Company (Jeppesen) produces charts that graphically display approach procedures for airplanes landing at airports. These charts are drafted from tabular data supplied by the Federal Aviation Administration (FAA), a federal agency of the U.S. government. By law, Jeppesen cannot construct charts that include information different from that supplied by the FAA.

On September 8, 1973, the pilot of an airplane owned by World Airways was on descent to land at the Cold Bay, Alaska, airport. The pilot was using an instrument approach procedure chart published by Jeppesen. The airplane crashed into a mountain near Cold Bay, killing all six crew members and destroying the aircraft. Evidence showed that the FAA data did not include the mountain. The heirs of the deceased crew members and World Airways brought a strict liability action against Jeppesen. Does the doctrine of strict liability apply to this case? Is Jeppesen liable? [*Brocklesby v. Jeppesen and Company*, 767 F.2d 1288 (9th Cir. 1985)]

6.2. To reduce the risk of miscarriage, Christine Murphy's mother took diethylstilbestrol (DES) while she was pregnant with Christine in 1951 and 1952. As a result of her mother's taking DES, Christine developed adenocarcinoma (a form of cancer) at the age of 23. Although the pharmacy (Exclusive Prescription Pharmacy Corp.) where Christine's mother purchased the DES was proven, the drug manufacturer could not be identified. Christine sued the pharmacist who sold her mother the DES for strict liability. The pharmacist asserted that he provided a service, and therefore the doctrine of strict liability does not apply. Is the pharmacist liable? [*Murphy v. E. R. Squibb & Sons, Inc.*, 40 Cal.3d 672, 221 Cal.Rptr. 447 (Cal. 1985)]

6.3. Robert Lovitz was competing in a trapshooting competition at the McCaun Gun Club near Newman, Illinois, using a Remington Model 1100 shotgun, manufactured by the Remington Arms Co., Inc. (Remington). While he was shooting at clay targets, the shotgun barrel exploded in his hands. He suffered injuries to his left hand and thumb. Lovitz brought suit against Remington, claiming that a manufacturing defect in the shotgun made the company strictly liable for his injuries. Remington employees testified that shotguns are tested prior to shipment, but that the tests do not reveal whether any cracks developed during the testing itself. At the trial, an expert witness stated the following: (1) the steel from which the shotgun barrels are made includes tiny particles of manganese sulfide, (2) these particles—known as inclusions—are the cause of the tiny cracks that may develop during the testing of the shotgun, (3) each time the shotgun is fired, these cracks slowly expand, and (4) eventually, the shotgun may explode. Is Remington liable for Lovitz's injuries? [*Lovitz v. Remington Arms Co., Inc.*, 532 N.E.2d 1091 (Ill.App. 1988)]

6.4. At 11 P.M. on April 10, 1968, Verne Prior, driving on U.S. 101 under the influence of alcohol and drugs at a speed of 65 to 85 miles per hour, crashed his 1963 Chrysler into the left rear of a 1962 Chevrolet station wagon stopped on the shoulder of the freeway for a flat tire. Christine Smith was sitting in the passenger seat of the parked car when the accident occurred. In the crash, the Chevrolet station wagon was knocked into a gully, where its fuel tank ruptured. The vehicle caught fire and Christine Smith suffered severe burn injuries. The Chevrolet station wagon was manufactured by General Motors Corporation (General Motors). Evidence showed that the fuel tank was located in a vulnerable position in the back of the station wagon outside of the crossbars of the frame. Evidence further showed that if the fuel tank had been located underneath the body of the station wagon between the crossbars of the frame, it would have been well protected in the collision. Smith sued General Motors for strict liability. Was the Chevrolet station wagon a defective product? [*Smith v. General Motors Corporation*, 42 Cal.App.3d 1, 116 Cal.Rptr. 575 (Cal.App.3d 1974)]

6.5. Virginia Burke purchased a bottle of "Le Domaine" champagne that was manufactured by Almaden Vineyards, Inc. (Almaden). At home, she removed the wine seal from the top of the bottle but did not remove the plastic cork. She set the bottle on the counter, intending to serve it in a few minutes. Shortly thereafter, the plastic cork spontaneously ejected from the bottle, ricocheted off the wall, and struck Burke in the left lens of her eyeglasses, shattering the lens, and driving pieces of glass into her eye. The champagne bottle did not contain any warning of this danger. Evidence showed that Almaden had previously been notified of the spontaneous ejection of the cork from its champagne bottles. Burke sued Almaden to recover damages for strict liability. Is Almaden liable? [*Burke v. Almaden Vineyards, Inc.*, 86 Cal.App.3d 768, 150 Cal.Rptr. 419 (Cal.App. 1978)]

6.6. Talbott purchased a gas space heater from Manito Hardware Company (Manito) in Manito, Illinois. The space heater was manufactured by Martin Stamping and Stove Co. (Martin). Talbott installed the gas heater in his cabin at Anderson Lake. The four-page pamphlet of instructions contained one cutaway drawing showing that a vent pipe should be connected to the heater to allow carbon monoxide and other gases generated by the heater to escape out-of-doors. Talbott installed the gas heater and vent pipe pursuant to these instructions. Sometime later, he allowed Harly Wallinger and four other guests to use the cabin. When they did not return, an investigation found all of the guests dead at the cabin. They had died in their sleep from carbon monoxide poisoning caused by the space heater. Evidence showed that to install the vent properly to allow the escape of carbon monoxide gases, the vent had to be installed above the peak of the roof. The instruction pamphlet, however, did not mention this fact. The heirs of Wallinger and the other deceased guests sued Martin for strict liability. Is Martin strictly liable? [*Wallinger v. Martin Stamping and Stove Co.*, 236 N.E.2d 755 (Ill.App. 1968)]

6.7. On the morning of February 25, 1980, Elizabeth Horton (name changed to Ellsworth) wore a lady's flannelette nightgown inside out. As a result, two pockets on the sides of the nightgown were protruding from the sides of the nightgown. Ellsworth turned on the left front burner of the electric stove to "high" and placed a tea kettle of water on the burner. The kettle only partially covered the burner. As Ellsworth reached above the stove to obtain coffee filters from one of the cupboards, the nightgown came in contact with the exposed portion of the burner and ignited. Ellsworth was severely burned and suffered permanent injuries. Ellsworth sued Sherme Lingerie, the seller of the nightgown, and Cone Mills Corporation, the manufacturer of the textile from which the nightgown was made, for strict liability. Is there a misuse of the product that would relieve the defendants of liability? [*Ellsworth v. Sherme Lingerie and Cone Mills Corporation*, 495 A.2d 348 (Md.App. 1985)]

6.8. The Wilcox-Crittendon Company (Wilcox-Crittendon) manufactures harnesses, saddles, bridles, leads, and other items commonly used for horses, cattle, and other ranch and farm animals. One such item was a stallion or cattle tie, a five-inch-long iron hook with a one-inch ring at one end. The tongue on the ring opened outward to allow the hook to be attached to a rope or other object. In 1964, a purchasing agent for United Airlines, who was familiar with this type of hook because of earlier experiences on a farm, purchased one of these hooks from Keystone Brothers, a harness and saddlery wares outlet located in San Francisco, California.

Four years later, on March 28, 1968, Edward Dosier, an employee of United Airlines, was working to install a new grinding machine at a United Airlines maintenance plant. As part of the installation process, Dosier attached the hook to a 1,700-pound counterweight and raised the counterweight into the air. While the counterweight was suspended in the air, Dosier reached under the counterweight to retrieve a missing bolt. The hook broke and the counterweight fell and crushed Dosier's arm. Dosier sued Wilcox-Crittendon for strict liability. Who wins? [*Dosier v. Wilcox-Crittendon Company*, 45 Cal.App.3d 74, 119 Cal.Rptr. 135 (Cal.App. 1975)]

6.9. Mrs. Kearl took her four-month-old daughter Elizabeth to the Contra Costa County health clinic for an oral polio vaccination. Mrs. Kearl was provided an extensive information sheet that described the oral vaccine as a live vaccine and warned of risks. The warning specifically stated that 1 in 4 million persons who received the vaccine actually contracted polio and that the side effects could include paralysis. Evidence showed that the vaccine could not be made in any safer manner nor was there any alternative design that would have accomplished the same purpose with less risk. The vaccine was administered after Mrs. Kearl gave her approval. The vaccine was manufactured by Lederle Laboratories (Lederle). Elizabeth suffered severe side effects from taking the vaccine, including paralysis. She currently walks with leg braces. Kearl sued defendant Lederle for strict liability. Is Lederle liable? [*Kearl v. Lederle Laboratories*, 172 Cal.App.3d 812, 218 Cal.Rptr. 453 (Cal.App. 1985)]

6.10. Pennwalt Corporation (Pennwalt) is a bulk manufacturer of sodium chlorate. It sells the chemical in 100-pound drums that contain elaborate warnings of its risks and dangers. In this case, Pennwalt sold 100-pound drums of sodium chlorate to Van Waters & Rogers, an experienced wholesaler, which in turn sold them to Student Science Services (Student Science), an experienced retailer of chemicals. Student Science repackaged the sodium chlorate in small jars that contained only the following warning: "Oxidizer. Use of this material is at the sole risk of the purchaser." Gregory Evangelatos, an 18-year-old, purchased a jar of the chemical from Student Science. The chemical exploded when Evangelatos was mixing the sodium chlorate with other chemicals to make homemade fireworks. Evangelatos suffered severe injuries. He brought this strict liability action against Pennwalt, Van Waters & Rogers, and Student Science. Who is liable to Evangelatos? [*Pennwalt Corporation v. Superior Court (Evangelatos)*, 218 Cal.Rptr. 675 (Cal.App. 1985)]

6.11. Jamie Camacho purchased a Hawk motorcycle that was manufactured by Honda Motor Co., Ltd. (Honda). Several months later, while driving through an intersection, Camacho collided with an automobile. He sustained serious injuries to both of his legs. Camacho and his wife sued Honda for strict liability to recover for personal injuries and loss of consortium. They alleged that Honda failed to warn them of the dangers of riding a motorcycle. Is Honda liable? [*Camacho v. Honda Motor Co., Ltd.*, 701 P.2d 628 (Colo.App. 1985)]

6.12. From 1942 to 1975, Lee Copeland worked as a boilermaker. During his work, he was exposed to various asbestos-containing products, particularly the insulation used to make the boilers. The asbestos insulation Copeland handled was manufactured by Celotex Corporation and 15 other manufacturers. Each type of insulation was made from a different formulation of asbestos and other chemicals. During the early 1970s, Copeland developed respiratory problems. These problems forced him to quit his job in 1975. He was diagnosed as having both asbestosis and cancer. Copeland brought a strict liability lawsuit against all 16 insulation manufacturers. Copeland claimed that liability should be extended to each through application of the market share theory of liability. Is that theory applicable to this situation? [*Celotex Corporation v. Copeland*, 471 So.2d 533 (FL 1985)]

ETHICS CASES

6.13. The Emerson Electric Co. (Emerson) manufactures and sells a product called the Weed Eater Model XR-90. The Weed Eater is a multipurpose weed-trimming and brush-cutting device. It consists of a handheld gasoline-powered engine connected to a long drive shaft at the end of which can be attached various tools for cutting weeds and brush. One such attachment is a 10-inch circular saw blade capable of cutting through growth up to 2 inches in diameter. When this saw blade is attached to the Weed Eater, approximately 270 degrees of blade edge is exposed when in use. The owner's manual contained the following warning: "Keep children away. All people and pets should be kept at a safe distance from the work area, at least 30 feet, especially when using the blade."

Donald Pearce, a 13-year-old boy, was helping his uncle clear an overgrown yard. The uncle was operating a Weed Eater XR-90 with the circular saw-blade attachment. When Pearce stooped to pick something up off the ground about 6 to 10 feet behind and slightly to the left of where his uncle was operating the Weed Eater, the saw blade on the Weed Eater struck something near the ground. The Weed Eater kicked back to the left and cut off Pearce's right arm to the elbow. Pearce, through his mother, Charlotte Karns, sued Emerson to recover damages under strict liability. Under ethical principles, should Emerson's warning have been clearer and stronger? Is Emerson liable? [*Karns v. Emerson Electric Co.*, 817 F.2d 1452 (10th Cir. 1987)]

6.14. Lillian Horn was driving her Chevrolet station wagon, which was designed and manufactured by General Motors Corporation (GM), down Laurel Canyon Boulevard in Los Angeles, California. Horn swerved to avoid a collision when a car coming toward her crossed the center line and was coming at her. In doing so, her hand knocked the horn cap off the steering wheel, which exposed the area underneath the horn cap, including three sharp prongs that had held the horn cap to the steering wheel. A few seconds later, when her car hit an embankment, Horn's face was impaled on the three sharp exposed prongs, causing her severe facial injuries. Horn sued GM for strict liability. GM asserted the defense of assumption of the risk against Horn. Does the doctrine of assumption of the risk apply to the facts of this case? Is it ethical for GM to assert this defense in this case? [*Horn v. General Motors Corporation*, 17 C.3d 359, 131 Cal.Rptr. 78 (Cal. 1976)]

CRITICAL LEGAL THINKING WRITING ASSIGNMENT

Read Case A.6 in the Case Appendix [*Johnson v. Chicago Pneumatic Tool Company*]. Review and brief this case. In your brief, be sure to answer the following questions.

1. Who was the plaintiff? Who was the defendant?

2. What law did the plaintiff assert was violated by the defendant?

3. What was the defendant's defense? Explain.

4. Was this defense effective in this case?

NOTES

1. Restatement (Second) of Torts, § 395.
2. 111 N.E. 1050, 217 N.Y. 382 (N.Y. App. 1916).
3. 59 Cal.2d 57, 27 Cal.Rptr. 697, 377 P.2d 897 (1963).
4. Some states have enacted statutes that provide that the doctrine of strict liability does not apply to transactions involving the sale of blood or blood products.
5. See, for example, *Elmore v. American Motors Corporation*, 70 Cal.2d 578, 76 Cal.Rptr. 652 (1969).
6. Restatement (Second) of Torts, § 402A(1)(b).

Criminal Law and Business Crimes

It is better that ten guilty persons escape, than that one innocent suffer.

SIR WILLIAM BLACKSTONE
*Commentaries on the Laws
of England (1809)*

Chapter Objectives

After studying this chapter, you should be able to

1. Distinguish between felonies and misdemeanors.
2. Define and list the essential elements of a crime.
3. Describe criminal procedure, including arrest, indictment, arraignment, and the criminal trial.
4. List and describe crimes against persons and property.
5. Define major white-collar crimes, such as embezzlement, mail fraud, and bribery.
6. Explain the elements necessary to find criminal fraud.
7. Describe the scope of the Racketeer Influenced and Corrupt Organizations Act (RICO).
8. Explain the constitutional safeguards provided by the Fourth, Fifth, Sixth, and Eighth Amendments to the U.S. Constitution.
9. Explain the scope of the Foreign Corrupt Practices Act.
10. List and describe laws involving computer and Internet crimes.

Chapter Contents

crime

A crime is a violation of a statute for which the government imposes a punishment.

For members of society to peacefully coexist and commerce to flourish, people and their property must be protected from injury by other members of society. Federal, state, and local governments' **criminal laws** are intended to accomplish this by providing an incentive for persons to act reasonably in society and imposing penalties on persons who violate them.

The United States has one of the most advanced and humane criminal law systems in the world. It differs from many other criminal law systems in several respects. A person charged with a crime in the United States is *presumed innocent until proven guilty.* The *burden of proof* is on the government to prove that the accused is guilty of the crime charged. Further, the accused must be found guilty "beyond a reasonable doubt." Conviction requires unanimous jury vote. Under many other legal systems, a person accused of a crime is presumed guilty unless the person can prove he or she is not. A person charged with a crime in the United States is also provided with substantial constitutional safeguards during the criminal justice process.

Business Brief

In the United States, a person accused of a crime is *presumed innocent until proven guilty.* The government has the burden of proving that the accused is guilty of the crime charged.

This chapter discusses the definition of a crime, criminal procedure, crimes affecting business, white-collar crime, computer crime, inchoate crime, criminal penalties, and constitutional safeguards afforded criminal defendants.

*D*EFINITION OF A CRIME

A **crime** is defined as any act done by an individual in violation of those duties that he or she owes to society and for the breach of which the law provides that the wrongdoer shall make amends to the public. Many activities have been considered crimes through the ages, whereas other crimes are of recent origin.

Penal Codes and Regulatory Statutes

penal codes

A collection of criminal statutes.

Statutes are the primary source of criminal law. Most states have adopted comprehensive **penal codes** that define in detail the activities considered to be crimes within their jurisdiction and the penalties that will be imposed for their commission. A comprehensive federal criminal code defines federal crimes.[1] In addition, state and federal regulatory statutes often provide for criminal violations and penalties. The state and federal legislatures are continually adding to the list of crimes.

The penalty for committing a crime may consist of the imposition of a fine, imprisonment, both, or some other form of punishment (e.g., probation). Generally, imprisonment is imposed to (1) incapacitate the criminal so he or she will not harm others in society, (2) provide a means to rehabilitate the criminal, (3) deter others from similar conduct, and (4) inhibit personal retribution by the victim.

Parties to a Criminal Action

No! No! Sentence first—verdict afterwards.

Lewis Carroll
Alice in Wonderland Ch: 12

In a criminal lawsuit, the government (not a private party) is the **plaintiff.** The government is represented by a lawyer called the *prosecutor.* The accused is the **defendant.** The accused is represented by a *defense attorney.* If the accused cannot afford a defense lawyer, the government will provide one free of charge.

Classification of Crimes

All crimes can be classified in one of the following categories.

felony

The most serious type of crime; inherently evil crime. Most crimes against the person and some business-related crimes are felonies.

Felonies   **Felonies** are the most serious kinds of crimes. Felonies include crimes that are *mala in se,* that is, inherently evil. Most crimes against the person (e.g., murder, rape, and the like) and certain business-related crimes (e.g., embezzlement and bribery) are felonies in most jurisdictions. Felonies are usually punishable by imprisonment. In some jurisdictions, certain felonies (e.g., first-degree murder) are punishable by death. Federal law[2] and some state laws require mandatory sentencing for specified crimes. Many statutes define different degrees of crimes (e.g., first-, second-, and third-degree murder). Each degree earns different penalties.

Misdemeanors **Misdemeanors** are less serious than felonies. They are crimes *mala prohibita*; that is, they are not inherently evil but are prohibited by society. Many crimes against property, such as robbery, burglary, and violations of regulatory statutes, are included in this category. Misdemeanors carry lesser penalties than felonies. They are usually punishable by fine and/or imprisonment for one year or less.

misdemeanor

A less serious crime; not inherently evil but prohibited by society. Many crimes against property are misdemeanors.

Violations Crimes such as traffic violations, jaywalking, and such are neither felonies nor misdemeanors. These crimes, which are called **violations**, are generally punishable by a fine. Occasionally, a few days of imprisonment are imposed.

violation

A crime that is neither a felony nor a misdemeanor that is usually punishable by a fine.

Window, the Bahamas.
Federal law provides for the forfeiture of money and property obtained through illegal gambling, securities fraud, and other illegal activities. Sometimes the money cannot be discovered if it has been deposited in banks in the Bahamas and other countries that have bank secrecy laws.

Essential Elements of a Crime

The following two elements must be proven for a person to be found guilty of most crimes:

1. **Criminal Act** The defendant must have actually performed the prohibited act. The actual performance of the criminal act is called the ***actus reus*** (guilty act). Killing someone without legal justification is an example of *actus reus*. Sometimes, the omission of an act constitutes the requisite *actus reus*. For example, a crime has been committed if a taxpayer who is under a legal duty to file a tax return fails to do so. However, merely thinking about committing a crime is not a crime because no action has been taken.

2. **Criminal Intent** To be found guilty of a crime, the accused must be found to have possessed the requisite state of mind (i.e., specific or general intent) when the act was performed. This is called the ***mens rea*** (evil intent). *Specific intent* is found where the accused purposefully, intentionally, or with knowledge commits a prohibited act. *General intent* is found where there is a showing of recklessness or a lesser degree of mental culpability. The individual criminal statutes state whether the crime requires a showing of specific or general intent. Juries may infer an accused's intent from the facts and circumstances of the case. There is no crime if the

actus reus

"Guilty act"—the actual performance of the criminal act.

mens rea

"Evil intent"—the possession of the requisite state of mind to commit a prohibited act.

requisite *mens rea* cannot be proven. Thus, no crime is committed if one person accidentally injures another person.

strict or absolute liability
Standard for imposing criminal liability without a finding of *mens rea* (intent).

Some statutes impose criminal liability based on **strict** or **absolute liability**. That is, a finding of *mens rea* is not required. Criminal liability is imposed if the prohibited act is committed. Absolute liability is often imposed by regulatory statutes, such as environmental laws.

Criminal Acts as the Basis for Tort Actions

Business Brief
The same act may be the basis for both a criminal lawsuit and a civil lawsuit.

An injured party may bring a *civil tort action* against a wrongdoer who has caused the party injury during the commission of a criminal act. Civil lawsuits are separate from the government's criminal action against the wrongdoer. In many cases, a person injured by a criminal act will not sue the criminal to recover civil damages. This is because the criminal is often *judgment proof*—that is, the criminal does not have the money to pay a civil judgment.

CONCEPT SUMMARY CIVIL AND CRIMINAL LAW COMPARED

Issue	Civil Law	Criminal Law
Party who brings the action	The plaintiff	The government
Trial by jury	Yes, except actions for equity	Yes
Burden of proof	Preponderance of the evidence	Beyond a reasonable doubt
Jury vote	Judgment for plaintiff requires specific jury vote (e.g., 9 of 12 jurors)	Conviction requires unanimous jury vote
Sanctions and penalties	Monetary damages and equitable remedies (e.g., injunction, specific performance)	Imprisonment, capital punishment, fine, probation

Ethical Perspective

SHOULD CRIME PAY?

To satisfy the public's seemingly endless thirst for tales of crime, publishers have eagerly paid large sums of money to acquire criminal defendants' rights to tell their sensational stories. Convicted murderers Caryl Chessman, Juan Corona, James Earl Ray, Sirhan Sirhan, and other convicted felons, such as the Watergate burglars, have all reaped substantial profits from selling the publication rights to their stories.

Beginning in the late 1970s, however, the public's distaste at rewarding crime fueled the passage by state legislatures of laws that prevented enterprising criminals from pocketing megabucks from selling their stories. Many of these so-called Son of Sam laws, which were passed by 40 states, were patterned on New York's statute. New York's

law was enacted in 1977 while New York City's "Son of Sam" killer held the population hostage by continuing a highly publicized killing spree despite one of the most intense manhunts in the city's history.

To preclude the Son of Sam and other criminals from cashing in on crime, the New York law required publishers and movie companies to deposit any profits earned by criminals with the state's victim's compensation agency. If there was a conviction, the money went to the victim or the victim's heirs. If the accused was acquitted, the money was used to pay the defense attorney's bills and any remainder was paid to the defendant.

The enactment of Son of Sam statutes quieted the public's outcry. However, the statutes were challenged by criminals and publishers as an unconstitutional abridgment of free-speech rights. In 1991, the U.S. Supreme Court agreed that the Son of Sam laws were unconstitutional. In a case brought by publisher Simon & Schuster, which had published a book by a convicted criminal, the Supreme Court held that the Son of Sam law violated the Freedom of Speech Clause of the U.S. Constitution.

Opponents of this decision argue that the potential of lucrative book and movie contracts will provide an incentive for people to commit heinous crimes. They also continue to argue that "crime should not pay." Proponents of the U.S.

Supreme Court's decision assert that even criminals should be accorded full free-speech rights guaranteed by the Constitution. [*Simon & Schuster, Inc. v. Members of the New York State Crime Victim's Board*, 112 S.Ct. 501 (1991)]

1. Should a person who commits a crime be permitted to profit from that crime?
2. Will the U.S. Supreme Court's decision lead to more or fewer crimes? Explain.
3. Is it ethical for publishers, movie companies, and other entertainment firms to pay criminals for their stories?

CRIMINAL PROCEDURE

The court procedure for initiating and maintaining a criminal action is quite detailed. It includes both pretrial procedures and the actual trial.

Pretrial Criminal Procedure

Pretrial criminal procedure consists of several distinct stages, including *arrest, indictment* or *information, arraignment,* and *plea bargaining.*

Arrest   Before the police can arrest a person for the commission of a crime, they usually must obtain an **arrest warrant** based upon a showing of "probable cause." *Probable cause* is defined as the substantial likelihood that the person either committed or is about to commit a crime. If there is no time for the police to obtain a warrant (e.g., if the police arrive during the commission of a crime, when a person is fleeing from the scene of the crime, or when it is likely that evidence will be destroyed), the police may still arrest the suspect. *Warrantless arrests* are also judged by the probable cause standard.

After a person is arrested, he or she is taken to the police station to be "booked." Booking is the administrative proceeding for recording the arrest, fingerprinting, and so on.

Indictment or Information   Accused persons must be formally charged with a crime before they can be brought to trial. This is usually done by the issuance of a *grand jury indictment* or a *magistrate's information* statement.

Evidence of serious crimes, such as murder, is usually presented to a *grand jury.* Most grand juries comprise between 6 and 24 citizens who are charged with evaluating the evidence presented by the government. Grand jurors sit for a fixed period of time, such as one year. If the grand jury determines that there is sufficient evidence to hold the accused for trial, it issues an **indictment**. Note that the grand jury does not determine guilt. If an indictment is issued, the accused will be held for later trial.

For lesser crimes (e.g., burglary, shoplifting, and such), the accused will be brought before a *magistrate* (judge). A magistrate who finds that there is enough evidence to hold the accused for trial will issue an **information**.

The case against the accused is dismissed if neither an indictment nor an information is issued.

Arraignment   If an indictment or information is issued, the accused is brought before a court for an **arraignment** proceeding during which the accused is (1) informed of the charges against him or her and (2) asked to enter a **plea**. The accused may plead *guilty, not*

The magnitude of a crime is proportionate to the magnitude of the injustice which prompts it. Hence, the smallest crimes may be actually the greatest.

Aristotle
The Rhetoric, BK, 1. Ch. XIV

arrest warrant
A document for a person's detainment based upon a showing of probable cause that the person committed the crime.

indictment
The charge of having committed a crime (usually a felony), based on the judgment of a grand jury.

information
The charge of having committed a crime (usually a misdemeanor), based on the judgment of a judge (magistrate).

arraignment
A hearing during which the accused is brought before a court and is (1) informed of the charges against him or her and (2) asked to enter a plea.

guilty, or *nolo contendere*. A plea of *nolo contendere* means that the accused agrees to the imposition of a penalty but does not admit guilt. A *nolo contendere* plea cannot be used as evidence of liability against the accused at a subsequent civil trial. Corporate defendants often enter this plea. The government has the option of accepting a *nolo contendere* plea or requiring the defendant to plead guilty or not guilty.

plea bargain

When the accused admits to a lesser crime than charged. In return, the government agrees to impose a lesser sentence than might have been obtained had the case gone to trial.

Plea Bargaining Sometimes the accused and the government enter into a **plea bargaining agreement**. The government engages in plea bargaining to save costs, avoid the risks of a trial, and prevent further overcrowding of the prisons. This type of arrangement allows the accused to admit to a lesser crime than charged. In return, the government agrees to impose a lesser penalty or sentence than might have been obtained had the case gone to trial.

The Criminal Trial

At a criminal trial, all jurors must *unanimously* agree before the accused is found *guilty* of the crime charged. If even one juror disagrees (i.e., has reasonable doubt) about the guilt of the accused, the accused is *not guilty* of the crime charged. If all of the jurors agree that the accused did not commit the crime, the accused is *innocent* of the crime charged. After trial, the following rules apply:

hung jury

A jury that cannot come to a unanimous decision about the defendant's guilt. The government may choose to retry the case.

- If the defendant is found guilty, he or she may appeal.
- If the defendant is found innocent, the government cannot appeal.
- If the jury cannot come to a unanimous decision about the defendant's guilt, the jury is considered a **hung jury**. The government may choose to retry the case before a new judge and jury.

Contemporary Business Application

MONEY LAUNDERING

The term *money laundering* is used to refer to the process by which criminals convert tainted proceeds into apparently legitimate funds or property. It applies equally to an international wire transfer of hundreds of millions of dollars in drug proceeds and the purchase of an automobile with funds robbed from a bank.

Money laundering is a federal crime. The following activities are among those that were criminalized by the Money Laundering Control Act:

- Knowingly engaging in a *financial transaction* involving the proceeds of some form of specified unlawful activity. Transactions covered include the sale of real property, personal property, intangible assets, and anything of value [18 U.S.C. § 1956].
- Knowingly engaging in a *monetary transaction* by, through, or to a financial institution involving property of a value greater than $10,000, which is derived from specified unlawful activity. Money transaction is defined as a deposit, withdrawal, transfer between accounts, and use of a monetary instrument [18 U.S.C. § 1957].

"Specified unlawful activity" includes narcotics activities and virtually any white-collar crime.

Money laundering statutes have been used to go after entities and persons involved in illegal check-cashing schemes, bribery, insurance fraud, Medicaid fraud, bankruptcy fraud, bank fraud, fraudulent transfer of property, criminal conspiracy, environmental crime, and other types of illegal activities.

Conviction for money laundering carries stiff penalties. Persons can be fined up to $500,000 or twice the value of the property involved, whichever is greater, and sentenced to up to 20 years in federal prison. In addition, violation subjects the defendant to provisions that mandate forfeiture to the government of any property involved in or traceable to the offense [18 U.S.C. §§ 981–982]. Any financial institution convicted of money laundering can have its charter revoked or its insurance of deposit accounts terminated.

To avoid running afoul of these increasingly complex statutes, banks and businesses must develop and implement policies and procedures to detect criminal activity and report money laundering by customers to the federal government.

CRIMES AFFECTING BUSINESS

Many crimes are committed against business property. These crimes often involve the theft, misappropriation, or fraudulent taking of property. Many of the most important crimes against business property are discussed in the following paragraphs.

Robbery

At common law, **robbery** is defined as the taking of personal property from another person by the use of fear or force. For example, if a robber threatens to physically harm a storekeeper unless the victim surrenders the contents of the cash register, it is robbery. If a criminal pickpockets somebody's wallet, it is not robbery because there has been no use of force or fear. Robbery with a deadly weapon is generally considered aggravated robbery (or armed robbery) and carries a harsher penalty.

robbery
Taking personal property from another person by use of fear or force.

Burglary

At common law, **burglary** was defined as "breaking and entering a dwelling at night" with the intent to commit a felony. Modern penal codes have broadened this definition to include daytime thefts and thefts from offices and commercial and other buildings. In addition, the "breaking-in" element has been abandoned by most modern definitions of burglary. Thus, unauthorized entering of a building through an unlocked door is sufficient. Aggravated burglary (or armed burglary) carries stiffer penalties.

burglary
Taking personal property from another's home, office, commercial, or other type of building.

Larceny

At common law, **larceny** is defined as the wrongful and fraudulent taking of another person's personal property. Most personal property—including tangible property, trade secrets, computer programs, and other business property—is subject to larceny. The stealing of automobiles and car stereos, pickpocketing, and such are larceny. Neither the use of force nor the entry of a building is required.

Some states distinguish between grand larceny and petit larceny. This distinction depends on the value of the property taken.

larceny
Taking another's personal property other than from his or her person or building.

Theft

Some states have dropped the distinction among the crimes of robbery, burglary, and larceny. Instead, these states group these crimes under the general crime of **theft**. Most of these states distinguish between grand theft and petit theft. The distinction depends upon the value of the property taken.

Law cannot persuade, where it cannot punish.
Thomas Fuller
Gnomolgia *(1732)*

Receiving Stolen Property

It is a crime for a person to (1) knowingly receive stolen property and (2) intend to deprive the rightful owner of that property. Knowledge and intent can be inferred from the circumstances. The stolen property can be any tangible property (e.g., personal property, money, negotiable instruments, stock certificates, and such).

receiving stolen property
A person (1) knowingly receives stolen property and (2) intends to deprive the rightful owner of that property.

Arson

At common law, **arson** was defined as the malicious or willful burning of the dwelling of another person. Modern penal codes expanded this definition to include the burning of all types of private, commercial, and public buildings. Thus, in most states, an owner who burns his or her own building to collect insurance proceeds can be found liable for arson. If arson is found, the insurance company does not have to pay proceeds of any insurance policy on the burned property.

arson
Willfully or maliciously burning another's building.

Forgery

forgery
Fraudulently making or altering a written document that affects the legal liability of another person.

The crime of **forgery** occurs if a written document is fraudulently made or altered and that change affects the legal liability of another person. Counterfeiting, falsifying public records, and the material altering of legal documents are examples of forgery. One of the most common forms of forgery is the signing of another person's signature to a check or changing the amount of a check. Note that signing another person's signature without intent to defraud is not forgery. For instance, forgery has not been committed if one spouse signs the other spouse's payroll check for deposit in a joint checking or savings account at the bank.

Extortion

extortion
Threat to expose something about another person unless that other person gives money or property. Often referred to as "blackmail."

The crime of **extortion** means the obtaining of property from another, with his or her consent, induced by wrongful use of actual or threatened force, violence, or fear. For example, extortion occurs when a person threatens to expose something about another person unless that other person gives money or property. The truth or falsity of the information is immaterial. Extortion of private persons is commonly referred to as **blackmail**. Extortion of public officials is called **extortion "under color of official right."**

Credit-Card Crimes

At the present time in this country there is more danger that criminals will escape justice than that they will be subjected to tyranny.

J. Holmes
Dissenting Kepner v.
United States *(1904)*

A substantial number of purchases in this country are made with credit cards. This poses a problem if someone steals and uses another person's credit cards. Many states have enacted statutes that make the misappropriation and use of credit cards a separate crime. In other states, credit-card crimes are prosecuted under the forgery statute.

Bad Check Legislation

Many states have enacted *bad check legislation* that makes it a crime for a person to make, draw, or deliver a check at a time when that person knows that there are insufficient funds in the account to cover the amount of the check. Some states require proof that the accused intended to defraud the payee of the check.

Ethical Perspective

WHISTLEBLOWERS SING FOR MILLIONS

The federal government is the largest purchaser of goods and services in the country. As such, it is also the target of substantial fraud by the firms it deals with. If caught, a government contractor who defrauds the government is subject to criminal prosecution. But in addition, the federal government relies on a revamped law that elicits employees of government contractors and others to become modern-day bounty hunters and report anyone who defrauds the government. The law is the **Civil False Claims Act**, commonly known as the **Whistleblower Statute**. This act was originally enacted in 1863 to protect the federal government from corrupt government contractors after the Civil War. It was strengthened in 1986 to provide a penalty of *treble damages* plus up to $10,000 per false claim against the defendant and allows the court to award between 15 and 30 percent of the recov-

ery to the whistleblower, who is now politely called a "relator." These lawsuits are called *qui tam* cases (from the Latin phrase "he who sues as much for the king as for himself").

The procedure for bringing a *qui tam* lawsuit is simple: the relator files the lawsuit, notifies the federal government, and then waits to see if the federal government chooses to intervene in the lawsuit. If the federal government intervenes, it pursues the lawsuit; if not, the relator must pursue the lawsuit alone, which is very costly. The federal government intervenes in only 20 percent of the *qui tam* cases filed, and 95 percent of the recoveries are from these cases. Many cases in which the federal government does not intervene are dropped. There is a strong incentive for a defendant to settle *qui tam* cases that are pursued by the federal government, however. If the defendant loses, it faces the possibility of treble damages, plus a penalty of up to $10,000 per false claim, and a ban on ever doing business with the federal government again.

The greatest number of whistleblower cases have involved hospitals and other medical facilities that have been caught overbilling the federal government under Medicare and other government aid programs. The second greatest number of cases have involved oil and gas companies that have cheated the federal government out of royalty and lease payments due on contracts for drilling on federal land. Other cases have been brought against government contractors who overbill the federal government for other products and services, file false claims to receive government subsidies, and overcharge the government for building and construction contracts. Sometimes a potential relator does not even know he or she has a whistleblower claim. For example, Evelyn Knoob walked into a lawyer's office to file a worker's compensation claim worth $400 per week when she was placed on leave by her employer, Illinois Blue Cross/Blue Shield. After talking to her attorney, she filed a

qui tam case against the Illinois Blues, alleging overbilling of the federal government. Several years later the defendants settled with the federal government for $150 million. Ms. Knoob's share was $29 million.

Proponents of the modern Civil False Claim Act cite that the federal government has recovered over $3 billion from fraudulent government contractors. They also allege that the act deters fraud and saves the federal government over $10 billion per year by making government contractors more honest. Detractors argue that the whistleblower statute generates frivolous lawsuits by disgruntled employees who are taking a shot at the lottery. Currently, over 600 new *qui tam* cases are filed each year.

1. Do you think there is much fraud in government contracting? Does the Civil False Claims Act make government contractors more honest?
2. Do employees face an ethical dilemma when filing a *qui tam* action against their employer? If so, how do you think most employees solve this dilemma?

*W*HITE-COLLAR CRIME

Certain types of crime are prone to be committed by businesspersons. These crimes are often referred to as **white-collar crimes**. These crimes usually involve cunning and deceit rather than physical force. Many of the most important white-collar crimes are discussed in the paragraphs that follow.

white-collar crimes
Crimes usually involving cunning and deceit rather than physical force.

Embezzlement

Unknown at common law, the crime of **embezzlement** is now a statutory crime. Embezzlement is the fraudulent conversion of property by a person to whom that property was entrusted. Typically, embezzlement is committed by an employer's employees, agents, or representatives (e.g., accountants, lawyers, trust officers, and treasurers). Embezzlers often try to cover their tracks by preparing false books, records, or entries.

The key element here is that the stolen property was *entrusted* to the embezzler. This differs from robbery, burglary, and larceny, where property is taken by someone not entrusted with the property. For example, embezzlement has been committed if a bank teller absconds with money that was deposited by depositors. The employer (the bank) entrusted the teller to take deposits from its customers.

embezzlement
The fraudulent conversion of property by a person to whom that property was entrusted.

Criminal Fraud

Obtaining title to property through deception or trickery constitutes the crime of **false pretenses**. This crime is commonly referred to as **criminal fraud** or **deceit**.

criminal fraud
Obtaining title to property through deception or trickery. Also known as *false pretenses* or *deceit*.

Consider This Example Bob Anderson, a stockbroker, promises Mary Greenberg, a prospective investor, that he will use any money she invests to purchase interests in oil wells. Based on this promise, Ms. Greenberg decides to make the investment. Mr. Anderson never intended to invest the money. Instead, he used the money for his personal needs. This is criminal fraud.

mail fraud
The use of mail to defraud another person.

wire fraud
The use of telephone or telegraph to defraud another person.

Mail and Wire Fraud   Federal law prohibits the use of mails or wires (e.g., telegraph or telephone) to defraud another person. These crimes are called **mail fraud**[3] and **wire fraud**,[4] respectively. The government often prosecutes a suspect under these statutes if there is insufficient evidence to prove the real crime that the criminal was attempting to commit or did commit.

E-Commerce & Internet Law

FEDERAL LAW HELPS VICTIMS OF IDENTITY FRAUD

For centuries, some people—for various purposes, mostly financial in nature—have attempted to take the identity of other persons. Today, taking on the identity of another can be extremely lucrative, earning the spoils of another's credit cards, bank accounts, Social Security benefits, and such. The use of new technology—computers and the Internet—have made such "identity fraud" even easier. But the victim of such fraud is left with funds stolen, a dismantled credit history, and thousands of dollars in costs trying to straighten out the mess. Identity fraud is the fastest growing financial fraud in America. Credit reporting firms say identity fraud cases have increased from 10,000 in 1990 to over 500,000 cases per year today.

Consider the case of Mari Frank. Her misfortune started late one night in 1996 when she got a telephone call from the Bank of New York, asking why she had not made the monthly payment on her credit card. There was one hitch: Frank did not have a credit card with the bank. But Frank's double—who looked nothing like her but had taken Frank's name, background, Social Security number, credit history, and even her business cards—did. The imposter had bought $50,000 in clothing and luxury items and a Mustang convertible and had charged them to

Frank's credit. The imposter had used Frank's identity for a year before the fraud was detected. It then took Frank over 500 hours and thousands of dollars in costs to clean up the situation and clear her credit history of the imposter's spending spree. Luckily, Frank was not responsible for more than $50 on her credit-card debts or for any other debt taken out in her name by the imposter. Several banks, however, had to write off the debts incurred by the imposter in Frank's name as bad debts. Identity fraud costs businesses over $1 billion per year.

To combat such fraud, Congress passed the **Identity Theft and Assumption Deterrence Act of 1998**. This act criminalizes identity fraud, making it a federal felony punishable with prison sentences ranging from 3 to 25 years. The act also appoints a federal administrative agency, the Federal Trade Commission (FTC), to help victims restore their credit and erase the impact of the imposter. Law enforcement officials suggest the following steps to protect against identity fraud: never put your Social Security number on any document unless it is legally required, obtain and review copies of your credit report at least twice each year, and use passwords other than maiden names and birthdays on bank accounts and other accounts that require personal identification numbers (PINs).

Bribery

bribery
When one person gives another person money, property, favors, or anything else of value for a favor in return. Often referred to as a payoff or "kickback."

Bribery is one of the most prevalent forms of white-collar crime. A bribe can be money, property, favors, or anything else of value. The crime of commercial bribery prohibits the payment of bribes to private persons and businesses. This type of bribe is often referred to as a **kickback** or **payoff**. Intent is a necessary element of this crime. The offeror of a bribe commits the crime of bribery when the bribe is tendered. The offeree is guilty of the crime of bribery when he or she accepts the bribe. The offeror can be found liable for the crime of bribery even if the person to whom the bribe is offered rejects the bribe.

Consider This Example   Harriet Landers is the purchasing agent for the ABC Corporation and is in charge of purchasing equipment to be used by the corporation. Neal Brown, the sales representative of a company that makes equipment that can be used by the ABC Corporation, offers to pay her a 10 percent kickback if she buys equipment from him. She accepts the bribe and orders the equipment. Both parties are guilty of bribery.

At common law, the crime of bribery was defined as the giving or receiving of anything of value in corrupt payment for an "official act" by a public official. Public officials include legislators, judges, jurors, witnesses at trial, administrative agency personnel, and other government officials. Modern penal codes also make it a crime to bribe public officials. For example, a developer who is constructing an apartment building cannot pay the building inspector to overlook a building code violation.

Business Brief
Bribery is probably the most prevalent form of business crime.

International Perspective

The Foreign Corrupt Practices Act

During the 1970s, several scandals were uncovered where American companies were found to have bribed foreign government officials to obtain lucrative contracts. Congressional investigations discovered that the making of such payments—or bribes—was pervasive in conducting international business. To prevent American companies from engaging in this type of conduct, the U.S. Congress enacted the **Foreign Corrupt Practices Act of 1977 (FCPA)** [15 U.S.C. § 78m]. Congress amended the FCPA as part of the Omnibus Trade and Competitiveness Act of 1988.

The FCPA attacks the problem in two ways. First, it requires firms to keep accurate books and records of all foreign transactions and install internal accounting controls to ensure transactions and payments are authorized. Inadvertent or technical errors in maintaining books and records do not violate the FCPA.

Second, the FCPA makes it illegal for American companies, or their officers, directors, agents, or employees, to bribe a foreign official, a foreign political party official, or a candidate for foreign political office. A bribe is illegal only where it is meant to influence the awarding of new business or the retention of a continuing business activity. Payments to secure ministerial, clerical, or routine government action (such as scheduling inspections, signing customs docu-

ments, unloading and loading of cargo, and the like) do not violate the FCPA.

The FCPA imposes criminal liability only in circumstances where a person knowingly fails to maintain the proper system of accounting, pays the illegal bribe himself, or supplies a payment to a third party or agent knowing that it will be used as a bribe. A firm can be fined up to $2 million and an individual can be fined up to $100,000 and imprisoned for up to five years for violations of the FCPA.

The 1988 amendments created two defenses. One excuses a firm or person charged with bribery under the FCPA if the firm or person can show that the payment was lawful under the written laws of that country. The other allows a defendant to show that a payment was a reasonable and bona fide expenditure related to the furtherance or execution of a contract.

Some people argue that the FCPA is too soft and permits American firms to engage in the payment of bribes internationally that would otherwise be illegal in this country. Others argue that the FCPA is difficult to interpret and apply, and that American companies are placed at a disadvantage in international markets where commercial bribery is commonplace and firms from other countries are not hindered by laws similar to the FCPA.

Racketeer Influenced and Corrupt Organizations Act (RICO)

Organized crime has a pervasive influence on many parts of the American economy. In 1980, Congress enacted the Organized Crime Control Act. The **Racketeer Influenced and Corrupt Organizations Act (RICO)** is part of this act.[5] Originally, RICO was intended to apply only to organized crime. However, the broad language of the RICO statute has been used against nonorganized crime defendants as well. RICO, which provides for both criminal and civil penalties, is one of the most important laws affecting business today.

Racketeer Influenced and Corrupt Organizations Act (RICO)
An act that provides for both criminal and civil penalties for "racketeering."

Business Brief
In 1992, mob boss John Gotti was sentenced to life in prison after being convicted of criminal racketeering and murder charges.

There can be no equal justice where the kind of trial a man gets depends on the amount of money he has.

J. Black
Griffin v. Illinois (1956)

RICO makes it a federal crime to acquire or maintain an interest in, use income from, or conduct or participate in the affairs of an "enterprise" through a "pattern" of "racketeering activity." An "enterprise" is defined as a corporation, a partnership, a sole proprietorship, another business or organization, and the government. *Racketeering activity* consists of a number of specifically enumerated federal and state crimes, including such activities as gambling, arson, robbery, counterfeiting, dealing in narcotics, and such. Business-related crimes, such as bribery, embezzlement, mail fraud, wire fraud, and the like, are also considered racketeering.

To prove a *pattern of racketeering*, at least two predicate acts must be committed by the defendant within a 10-year period. For example, committing two different frauds would be considered a pattern. Individual defendants found criminally liable for RICO violations can be fined up to $25,000 per violation, imprisoned for up to 20 years, or both. In addition, RICO provides for the *forfeiture* of any property or business interests (even interests in a legitimate business) that were gained because of RICO violations. This provision allows the government to recover investments made with monies derived from racketeering activities. The government may also seek civil penalties for RICO violations. These include injunctions, orders of dissolution, reorganization of businesses, and the divestiture of the defendant's interest in an enterprise.

Whether a criminal RICO violation occurred is the issue addressed in the following case.

Russello v. United States
464 U.S. 16, 104 S.Ct. 296, 78 L.Ed.2d 17 (1983)
United States Supreme Court

CASE 7.1

FACTS

Joseph C. Russello was a member of an arson ring that operated in Florida. The group consisted of property owners, arsonists, and insurance adjusters. A member of the group would buy a building, the arsonists would burn it, and the insurance adjusters would help the owner recover inflated insurance awards. Members of the group would share in the proceeds. The ring burned numerous buildings between July 1973 and April 1976. Russello owned the Capital Professional Building in Tampa. He arranged for the ring's arsonists to burn the building, which they did. Russello submitted an inflated claim to the insurance company. Joseph Carter, another member of the ring, was the adjuster on the insurance claim and helped Russello obtain the highest payment possible—$340,043. From the proceeds, Carter was paid $30,000 for his assistance. Russello took the remaining money out of the illegitimate enterprise and invested in other things. The federal government brought criminal RICO charges against Russello. The U.S. district court found Russello guilty and ordered forfeiture of the insurance proceeds. The U.S. court of appeals affirmed. Russello appealed to the U.S. Supreme Court, which granted certiorari.

ISSUE

Are the insurance proceeds obtained by Russello subject to forfeiture under the criminal RICO statute?

IN THE LANGUAGE OF THE COURT

Blackmun, Justice *Before profits of an illegal enterprise are divided, each participant may be said to own an interest in the ill-gotten gains. After distribution, each will have a possessory interest in currency or other items so distributed. We therefore conclude that the language of the statute plainly covers the insurance proceeds petitioner received as a result of his arson activities.*

We note that the RICO statute's definition of the term "enterprise" encompasses both legal entities and illegitimate associations-in-fact. Forfeiture of an interest in an illegitimate association-in-fact ordinarily would be of little use because an association of that kind rarely has identifiable assets; instead, proceeds or profits usually are distributed immediately. Thus, to reach only interests in an enterprise would blunt the effectiveness of the provision in combating illegitimate enterprises, and would mean that whole areas of organized criminal activities would be placed beyond the reach of the statute.

Congress emphasized the need to fashion new remedies to achieve its far-reaching objectives. From all this, the intent to authorize forfeiture of racketeering profits seems obvious.

DECISION AND REMEDY

The U.S. Supreme Court held that the insurance proceeds obtained by Russello were an interest that was gained because of a RICO violation. Affirmed.

INCHOATE CRIMES

In addition to the substantive crimes previously discussed, a person can be held criminally liable for committing an *inchoate crime*. Inchoate crimes include incomplete crimes and crimes committed by nonparticipants. The most important inchoate crimes are discussed in the following paragraphs.

Criminal Conspiracy

A **criminal conspiracy** occurs when two or more persons enter into an *agreement* to commit a crime. To be liable for a criminal conspiracy, an *overt act* must be taken to further the crime. The crime itself does not have to be committed, however.

criminal conspiracy
When two or more persons enter into an agreement to commit a crime and an overt act is taken to further the crime.

Consider This Example   Two securities brokers agree over the telephone to commit a securities fraud. They also obtain a list of potential victims and prepare false financial statements necessary for the fraud. Because they entered into an agreement to commit a crime and took overt action, the brokers are guilty of the crime of criminal conspiracy even if they never carry out the securities fraud. The government usually brings criminal conspiracy charges if (1) the defendants have been thwarted in their efforts to commit the substantive crime or (2) there is insufficient evidence to prove the substantive crime.

Business Brief
The use of computers to commit business crimes is increasing. Businesses must implement safeguards to prevent computer crimes.

Attempt to Commit a Crime

The **attempt to commit a crime** is itself a crime. For example, suppose a person wants to kill his or her neighbor. He shoots at her but misses. The perpetrator is not liable for the crime of murder. He is, however, liable for the crime of attempted murder.

attempt to commit a crime
When a crime is attempted but not completed.

Aiding and Abetting the Commission of a Crime

Sometimes persons assist others in the commission of a crime. The act of **aiding and abetting the commission of a crime** is a crime. This concept, which is very broad, includes rendering support, assistance, or encouragement to the commission of a crime. Harboring a criminal after he or she has committed a crime is considered aiding and abetting.

The court addressed the issue of aiding and abetting in the following case.

aiding and abetting the commission of a crime
Rendering support, assistance, or encouragement to the commission of a crime; harboring a criminal after he or she has committed a crime.

United States v. Cloud
870 F.2d 594 (1989)
United States Court of Appeals, Ninth Circuit

CASE 7.2

FACTS
In 1980, Ronald V. Cloud purchased the Cal-Neva Lodge, a hotel and casino complex located in the Lake Tahoe area near the California-Nevada border, for $10 million. Cloud is a sophisticated 68-year-old entrepreneur who is experienced in buying and selling real estate and has real estate holdings valued at more than $65 million. He also has experience in banking and finance, having been the founder and chairman

(case continues)

of Continental National Bank of Fresno. After two years of mounting operation losses, Cloud closed the Cal-Neva Lodge and actively began seeking a new buyer. In December 1984, Cloud met with Jon Perroton and orally agreed to transfer the lodge to Perroton for approximately $17 million. On January 2, 1985, Perroton met with an executive of Hibernia Bank (Hibernia) to discuss a possible loan to finance the purchase of the lodge. Perroton made multiple false representations and presented false documents to obtain a $20-million loan from Hibernia. In particular, Perroton misrepresented the sale price for the lodge ($27.5 million) and stated that $7.5 million had already been paid to Cloud. An escrow was opened with Transamerica Title Company (Transamerica).

On January 15, 1985, Cloud and his attorney and Perroton met at Transamerica to sign mutual escrow instructions. Cloud reviewed the instructions and noticed that the sale price and down payment figures were incorrectly stated at $27.5 million and $7.5 million, respectively, and that the Hibernia loan was for $20 million, almost $3 million above what he knew to be the true sale price. Cloud signed the escrow instructions. Later, Cloud signed a settlement statement containing the same false figures and signed a grant deed to the property. The sale closed on January 23, 1985, with Hibernia making the $20-million loan to Perroton. Subsequently, when the loan went into default, Continental Insurance Company (Continental) paid Hibernia its loss of $7.5 million on the bank's blanket bond insurance policy. The United States sued Cloud for aiding and abetting a bank fraud in violation of federal law (18 U.S.C. §§ 2 and 1344). The jury convicted Cloud of the crime and ordered him to make restitution of $7.5 million to Continental. Cloud appealed.

ISSUE

Is Cloud guilty of aiding and abetting a bank fraud?

IN THE LANGUAGE OF THE COURT

Hall, Circuit Judge   Aiding and abetting means to assist the perpetrator of a crime. An abettor's criminal intent may be inferred from the attendant facts and circumstances and need not be established by direct evidence.

The evidence in this case established that sometime in December 1984 or early January 1985, Jon Perroton launched a fraudulent scheme to obtain money from Hibernia Bank by means of false representations. The issue before this court is whether a rational trier of fact could conclude on the basis of all the evidence that Cloud at some point knowingly came aboard and participated in Perroton's bank fraud scheme. We conclude that a reasonable jury could have found that Cloud came aboard on January 15, 1985, at the meeting to sign the escrow instructions.

There was no question Cloud knew that the sale price was not $27.5 million, that he had not received $7.5 million outside of escrow, and that on their face the escrow instructions and settlement statement reflected these false figures. There is likewise no doubt that Cloud, who was a sophisticated businessman with extensive experience both in real estate transactions and in banking, knew that the escrow would not have closed and that the Hibernia funds would not have been disbursed if he had not signed the escrow instructions.

DECISION AND REMEDY

The court of appeals held that Cloud was guilty of the crime of aiding and abetting a bank fraud in violation of federal law. Affirmed.

Case Questions

Critical Legal Thinking   Should the law recognize the crime of aiding and abetting? Why or why not?

Ethics   Did Cloud act ethically in this case?

Business Application   What is the moral of this case? Do you think bank fraud of the type in this case happens very frequently?

E-Commerce & Internet Law

COMPUTER CRIMES

Many business transactions are initiated, processed, and completed through the use of computers. Computers may keep a company's financial records; issue its payroll checks; and store its trade secrets, engineering drawings, databases, and other proprietary information. The potential for the misuse of computers is enormous. Federal and state governments have enacted several laws that address computer crimes. The most

important computer crime laws are discussed in the paragraphs that follow.

Counterfeit Access Device and Computer Fraud and Abuse Act of 1984

The **Counterfeit Access Device and Computer Fraud and Abuse Act of 1984**, as amended, makes it a federal crime to access a computer knowingly to obtain (1) restricted federal government information, (2) financial records of financial institutions, and (3) consumer reports of consumer reporting agencies. The act also makes it a crime to use counterfeit or unauthorized access devices, such as cards or code numbers, to obtain things of value or transfer funds or to traffic in such devices [Public Law 98-473, Title II].

Electronic Funds Transfer Act

The **Electronic Funds Transfer Act** regulates the payment and deposit of funds using electronic funds transfers, such as direct deposit of payroll and Social Security checks in financial institutions, transactions using automated teller machines (ATMs), and such. The act makes it a federal crime to use, furnish, sell, or transport a counterfeit, stolen, lost, or fraudulently obtained ATM card, code number, or other device used to conduct electronic funds transfers. The act imposes criminal penalties of up to 10 years' imprisonment and fines up to $10,000 [15 U.S.C. § 1693].

State Laws

Often, larceny statutes cover only the theft of tangible property. Because computer software, programs, and data are intangible property, they are not covered by some existing state criminal statutes. To compensate for this, many states have either modernized existing laws to include computer crime or amended existing penal codes to make certain abuses of computers a criminal offense. Computer trespass, the unauthorized use of computers, tampering with computers, and the unauthorized duplication of computer-related materials are usually forbidden by these acts [See New York Session Laws, 1986, Chapter 514].

Our growing reliance on computers has made us more aware of the risks associated with losing the data stored on them. As a result, it is likely that the safety of the nation's ever-expanding computer networks will be legislated even more in the future.

E-Commerce & Internet Law

THE INFORMATION INFRASTRUCTURE PROTECTION ACT

The Internet and Information Age ushered in a whole new world for education, business, and consumer transactions. But with it followed a new rash of digital crimes. Prosecutors and courts wrestled over how to apply existing laws written in a non-digital age to new Internet-related abuses. In many instances, criminal cases were dismissed because the statutory language of existing criminal laws could not be stretched to reach unauthorized computer breaches.

In 1996, Congress responded by enacting the **Information Infrastructure Protection Act (IIP Act)**. In this new federal law, Congress addressed computer-related crimes as distinct offenses. Previously, the Computer Abuse Act outlawed knowingly damaging federal computers, but this act did not cover non-federal interest computers owned by businesses and individuals. Also, existing criminal acts required that unauthorized access to computer data had to be for the defendant's commercial benefit before it was illegal. The IIP Act cleared up both of these deficiencies in criminal law in the following ways:

- The IIP Act applies to all "protected computers" not only to federal computers. By statutory definition, a protected computer includes any computer which is used in interstate or foreign commerce. Thus, the IIP Act provides protection for any computer attached to the Internet.
- The IIP Act does not require that the defendant accessed a protected computer for commercial benefit. The act makes it clear that simply accessing and obtaining information from a protected computer in excess of one's authorization is unlawful.

The IIP Act makes it a criminal offense for anyone to intentionally access and obtain information from a protected computer without authorization or access of his or her authorization. Thus, persons who transmit a computer virus over the Internet or hackers who trespass into Internet-connected computers may be criminally prosecuted under the IIP Act. Even merely observing data on a protected computer without authorization is sufficient to meet the requirement that the defendant has accessed a protected computer. Criminal penalties for violating the IIP Act include imprisonment for up to 10 years and fines.

The IIP Act gives the federal government a much needed weapon for directly prosecuting cyber-crooks, hackers, and others who enter, steal, destroy, or look at others' computer data without authorization.

Corporate Criminal Liability

Business Brief

Corporations may be held criminally liable for actions of their officers, employees, or agents.

A corporation is a fictitious legal person that is granted legal existence by the state only after certain requirements are met. A corporation cannot act on its own behalf. Instead, it must act through *agents* such as managers, representatives, and employees.

The question of whether a corporation can be held criminally liable has intrigued legal scholars for some time. Originally, under the common law, it was generally held that corporations lacked the criminal mind *(mens rea)* to be held criminally liable. Modern courts, however, are more pragmatic. These courts have held that corporations are criminally liable for the acts of their managers, agents, and employees. In any event, because corporations cannot be put in prison, they are usually sanctioned with fines, loss of a license or franchise, and the like.

Business Brief

Corporate directors, officers, and employees are personally liable for the crimes they commit while acting on behalf of the corporation.

Corporate directors, officers, and employees are individually liable for crimes that they personally commit, whether for personal benefit or on behalf of the corporation. In addition, under certain circumstances a corporate manager can be held criminally liable for the criminal activities of his or her subordinates. To be held criminally liable, the manager must have failed to supervise the subordinate appropriately. This is an evolving area of the law.

Contemporary Business Application

Hughes Aircraft Downed as a Criminal Conspirator

Hughes Aircraft Co., Inc. (Hughes), an aircraft manufacturer, contracted with the U.S. government to manufacture microelectronic circuits, known as "hybrids," which are used as components in weapons defense systems. The contract required Hughes to perform tests on each hybrid. A Hughes's employee, Donald LaRue, was the supervisor responsible for ensuring the accuracy of the hybrid testing process. LaRue falsely reported that all tests had been performed and that each hybrid had passed the test. When LaRue's subordinates called his actions to the attention of LaRue's supervisors, they did nothing about it. Instead, they responded that LaRue's decisions were his own and were not to be questioned. The United States sued Hughes and LaRue, charging criminal conspiracy to defraud the government. At trial, LaRue was acquitted, but Hughes was convicted of criminal conspiracy and fined $3.5 million. Hughes appealed its conviction, asserting that it should not be convicted of criminal conspiracy if its alleged co-conspirator, LaRue, was acquitted.

Should Hughes be acquitted as a matter of law because the same jury that convicted Hughes acquitted its alleged co-conspirator of the charge of criminal conspiracy? No. The court of appeals held that Hughes may be found guilty of criminal conspiracy even though its co-conspirator had been acquitted of the same crime. Affirmed.

The court of appeals, as a matter of law, held that the inconsistency of the jury verdicts of two defendants charged with criminal conspiracy does not mean that the convicted defendant should also be acquitted. The court noted that the jury may have been more lenient with defendant LaRue, an individual, than they were with Hughes, the corporate defendant. Moreover, the court stated that the jury could have found Hughes guilty of the required act of conspiracy based on evidence provided at trial by the other Hughes's employees that were called as witnesses. [*United States v. Hughes Aircraft Company, Inc.*, 20 F.3d 974 (9th Cir. 1994)]

The criminal is to go free because the constable has blundered.

J. Cardozo
People v. Defore (1926)

Constitutional Safeguards

When our Forefathers drafted the U.S. Constitution, they included provisions that protect persons from unreasonable government intrusion and provide safeguards for those accused of crimes. Although these safeguards originally applied only to federal cases, the

Fourteenth Amendment's Due Process Clause made them applicable to state criminal law cases as well. The most important of these constitutional safeguards are discussed in the following paragraphs.

Fourth Amendment Protection Against Unreasonable Searches and Seizures

The *Fourth Amendment* to the U.S. Constitution protects persons and corporations from overzealous investigative activities by the government. It protects the rights of the people from **unreasonable search and seizure** by the government. It permits people to be secure in their persons, houses, papers, and effects.

"Reasonable" search and seizure by the government is lawful. **Search warrants** based on probable cause are necessary in most cases. Such warrants specifically state the place and scope of the authorized search. General searches beyond the specified area are forbidden. *Warrantless searches* are permitted only (1) incident to arrest, (2) where evidence is in "plain view," or (3) where it is likely that evidence will be destroyed. Warrantless searches are also judged by the probable cause standard.

Evidence obtained from an unreasonable search and seizure is considered tainted evidence ("fruit of a tainted tree"). Under the **exclusionary rule**, such evidence generally can be prohibited from introduction at a trial or administrative proceeding against the person searched. However, this evidence is freely admissible against other persons. The U.S. Supreme Court created a *good faith exception* to the exclusionary rule.[6] This exception allows evidence otherwise obtained illegally to be introduced as evidence against the accused if the police officers who conducted the unreasonable search reasonably believed that they were acting pursuant to a lawful search warrant.

Searches of Business Premises Generally, the government does not have the right to search business premises without a search warrant.[7] Certain hazardous and regulated industries—such as sellers of firearms and liquor, coal mines, and the like—are subject to warrantless searches if proper statutory procedures are met. In the following case, the U.S. Supreme Court held that a warrantless search of a business premise was lawful.

unreasonable search and seizure
Any search and seizure by the government that violates the Fourth Amendment.

search warrant
A warrant issued by a court that authorizes the police to search a designated place for specified contraband, articles, items, or documents. The search warrant must be based on probable cause.

exclusionary rule
A rule that says evidence obtained from an unreasonable search and seizure can generally be prohibited from introduction at a trial or administrative proceeding against the person searched.

New York v. Burger
482 U.S. 691, 107 S.Ct. 2636, 96 L.Ed.2d 601 (1987)
United States Supreme Court

CASE 7.3

FACTS
Joseph Burger is the owner of a junkyard in Brooklyn, New York. His business consists, in part, of dismantling automobiles and selling their parts. The state of New York enacted a statute that requires automobile junkyards to keep certain records. The statute authorizes warrantless searches of vehicle dismantlers and automobile junkyards without prior notice. At approximately noon on November 17, 1982, five plainclothes officers of the Auto Crimes Division of the New York City Police Department entered Burger's junkyard to conduct a surprise inspection. Burger did not have either a license to conduct the business or records of the automobiles and vehicle parts on his premises as required by state law.

After conducting an inspection of the premises, the officers determined that Burger was in possession of stolen vehicles and parts. He was arrested and charged with criminal possession of stolen property. Burger moved to suppress the evidence. The New York Supreme Court and appellate division held the search to be constitutional. The New York court of appeals reversed. New York appealed.

ISSUE
Does the warrantless search of an automobile junkyard pursuant to a state statute that authorizes such search constitute an unreasonable search and seizure in violation of the Fourth Amendment to the U.S. Constitution?

(case continues)

IN THE LANGUAGE OF THE COURT

Blackmun, Justice   The Court has long recognized that the Fourth Amendment's prohibition on unreasonable searches and seizures is applicable to commercial premises, as well as to private homes.

An expectation of privacy in commercial premises, however, is different from, and indeed less than, a similar expectation in an individual's home. This expectation is particularly attenuated in commercial property employed in "closely regulated" industries. Because the owner or operator of commercial premises in a closely regulated industry has a reduced expectation of privacy, the warrant and probable cause requirements—which fulfill the traditional Fourth Amendment standard of reasonableness for a government search—have a lessened application in this context. The nature of the regulatory statute reveals that the operation of a junkyard, part of which is devoted to vehicle dismantling, is a closely regulated business in the state of New York. A warrantless inspection of commercial premises may well be reasonable within the meaning of the Fourth Amendment.

This warrantless inspection, however, even in the context of a pervasively regulated business, will be deemed to be reasonable only so long as three criteria are met. First, there must be a "substantial" government interest that informs the regulatory scheme pursuant to which the inspection is made. Second, the warrantless inspections must be necessary to further the regulatory scheme. Finally, the statute's inspection program, in terms of the certainty and regularity of its application, must provide a constitutionally adequate substitute for a warrant.

The New York regulatory scheme satisfies the three criteria necessary to make reasonable warrantless inspections. First, the state has a substantial interest in regulating the vehicle dismantling and automobile junkyard industry because motor vehicle theft has increased in the state of New York and because the problem of theft is associated with this industry. Second, regulation of the vehicle dismantling industry reasonably serves the state's substantial interest in eradicating automobile theft. It is well established that the theft problem can be addressed effectively by controlling the receiver of, or market in, stolen property. Automobile junkyards and vehicle dismantlers provide the major market for stolen vehicles and vehicle parts. Third, the New York law provides a constitutionally adequate substitute for a warrant. The statute informs the operator of a vehicle dismantling business that inspections will be made on a regular basis.

A search conducted pursuant to the New York statute, therefore, clearly falls within the well-established exception to the warrant requirement for administrative inspections of closely regulated businesses.

DECISION AND REMEDY

The U.S. Supreme Court held that the New York statute that authorizes warrantless searches of vehicle dismantling businesses and automobile junkyards does not constitute an unreasonable search in violation of the Fourth Amendment to the U.S. Constitution. The Supreme Court reversed the judgment of the New York court of appeals and remanded the case for further proceedings consistent with its decision.

Case Questions

Critical Legal Thinking   Should the Fourth Amendment's protection against unreasonable searches and seizures apply to businesses? Why or why not?

Ethics   Was it ethical for the defendant to assert the Fourth Amendment's prohibition against unreasonable searches and seizures?

Business Application   Is auto theft a big business? Will the New York law that regulates vehicle dismantling businesses and junkyards help to alleviate this crime?

Fifth Amendment Privilege Against Self-Incrimination

The *Fifth Amendment* to the U.S. Constitution provides that no person "shall be compelled in any criminal case to be a witness against himself." Thus, a person cannot be compelled to give testimony against him or herself, although nontestimonial evidence (e.g., fingerprints, body fluids, and the like) may be required. A person who asserts this right is described as having "taken the Fifth." This protection applies to federal cases and is extended to state and local criminal cases through the Due Process Clause of the Fourteenth Amendment.

The protection against **self-incrimination** applies only to natural persons who are accused of crimes. Therefore, artificial persons (such as corporations and partnerships) cannot raise this protection against incriminating testimony.[8] Thus, business records of corporations and partnerships are not generally protected from disclosure, even if they incriminate individuals who work for the business. However, certain "private papers" of businesspersons (such as personal diaries) are protected from disclosure.

self-incrimination

The Fifth Amendment states that no person shall be compelled in any criminal case to be a witness against him- or herself.

Business Brief

It is improper for a jury to infer guilt from the defendant's exercise of his or her constitutional right to remain silent.

Immunity from Prosecution   On occasion, the government may want to obtain information from a suspect who has asserted his or her Fifth Amendment privilege against self-incrimination. The government can often achieve this by offering the suspect **immunity from prosecution**. Immunity from prosecution means that the government agrees not to use any evidence given by a person granted immunity against that person. Once immunity is granted, the suspect loses the right to assert his or her Fifth Amendment privilege. Grants of immunity are often given when the government wants the suspect to give information that will lead to the prosecution of other more important criminal suspects. Partial grants of immunity are also available. For example, a suspect may be granted immunity from prosecution for a serious crime, but not a lesser crime, in exchange for information. The suspect must agree to a partial grant of immunity.

immunity from prosecution
The government agrees not to use any evidence given by a person granted immunity against that person.

Business Brief
Some persons who are granted immunity are placed in witness protection programs. They are usually given a new identity, relocated, and found a job.

The Attorney-Client Privilege and Other Privileges   To obtain a proper defense, the accused person must be able to tell his or her attorney facts about the case without fear that the attorney will be called as a witness against the accused. The **attorney-client privilege** is protected by the Fifth Amendment. Either the client or the attorney can raise this privilege. For the privilege to apply, the information must be told to the attorney in his or her capacity as an attorney, and not as a friend or neighbor or such.

The following privileges have also been recognized under the Fifth Amendment: (1) *psychiatrist/psychologist-patient privilege*, (2) *priest/minister/rabbi-penitent privilege*, (3) *spouse-spouse privilege*, and (4) *parent-child privilege*. There are some exceptions. For example, a spouse or child who is beaten by a spouse or parent may testify against the accused. An *accountant-client privilege* has not been recognized under the Fifth Amendment. Several states have, however, enacted statutes that create an accountant-client privilege for state law criminal matters.

attorney-client privilege
A rule that says a client can tell his or her lawyer anything about the case without fear that the attorney will be called as a witness against the client.

Business Brief
There is no accountant-client privilege under federal law. Some states have enacted statutes that create an accountant-client privilege for state law criminal matters.

Contemporary Business Application

THE MIRANDA RIGHTS

The Fifth Amendment privilege against self-incrimination is not useful unless a criminal suspect has knowledge of this right. In the landmark case, *Miranda v. Arizona* [384 U.S. 436, 86 S.Ct. 1602 (1966)], the Supreme Court held that criminal suspects must be informed of certain rights before they can be interrogated by the police or other government officials. Generally, any confession obtained from the suspect prior to being read his or her *Miranda* rights can be excluded from evidence. The following rights, which are called the **Miranda rights**, must be read to a criminal suspect:

- You have the right to remain silent.
- Anything you say can and will be used against you.
- You have the right to consult with a lawyer, and to have a lawyer present with you during interrogation.
- If you cannot afford a lawyer, a lawyer will be appointed (free of charge) to represent you. The accused does not have the right to the appointment of a lawyer in criminal cases of a minor nature (such as traffic violations).

Fifth Amendment Protection Against Double Jeopardy

The **double jeopardy clause** of the *Fifth Amendment* protects persons from being tried twice for the same crime. For example, if the state tries a suspect for the crime of murder, and the suspect is found innocent, the state cannot bring another trial against the accused for the same crime. However, if the same criminal act involves several different crimes, the accused may be tried for each of the crimes without violating the double jeopardy

double jeopardy clause
A clause of the Fifth Amendment that protects persons from being tried twice for the same crime.

clause. Suppose the accused kills two people during a robbery. The accused may be tried for two murders and the robbery.

If the same act violates the laws of two or more jurisdictions, each jurisdiction may try the accused. For instance, if an accused kidnaps a person in one state and brings the victim across a state border into another state, the act violates the laws of two states and the federal government. Thus, three jurisdictions can prosecute the accused without violating the double jeopardy clause.

Sixth Amendment Right to a Public Jury Trial

The *Sixth Amendment* guarantees certain rights to criminal defendants. These rights are (1) to be tried by an impartial jury of the state or district in which the accused crime was committed, (2) to confront (cross-examine) the witnesses against the accused, (3) to have the assistance of a lawyer, and (4) to have a speedy trial.[9]

cruel and unusual punishment
A clause of the Eighth Amendment that protects criminal defendants from torture or other abusive punishment.

Eighth Amendment Protection Against Cruel and Unusual Punishment

The *Eighth Amendment* protects criminal defendants from **cruel and unusual punishment**. For example, it prohibits the torture of criminals. However, this clause does not prohibit capital punishment.[10]

Working the Web

e·biz

U.S. Department of Justice You can locate all sorts of Department of Justice information from its home page. You can link to Department of Justice organizations, find press releases, and link to federal documents.

Visit at **www.usdoj.gov**

U.S. Constitution There are many places to find the U.S. Constitution on the Internet. One such place is the Cornell University Web site.

Visit at **www.law.cornell.edu/constitution/constitution.billofrights.html**

National Rifle Association The National Rifle Association is an example of a powerful organization with a large presence on the Internet. From this page you can link to state firearm laws and state legislative updates.

Visit at **www.nra.org**

CYBER EXERCISES

1. From the Department of Justice Web site, find the Civil Rights Division of the Department of Justice. Can you find the report on Commonly Asked Questions about Child Care Centers and the ADA?

2. One of the constitutional amendments of interest to criminal law researchers is Amendment VI. What does that Amendment cover? Using the Cornell University Web site, find a copy of Amendment VI.

3. From the National Rifle Association Web site, find a recent speech transcript.

CASES AND EXERCISES

CRITICAL LEGAL THINKING CASES

7.1. Representatives of hotels, restaurants, hotel and restaurant supply companies, and other businesses located in Portland, Oregon, organized an association to attract conventions to their city. Members were asked to make contributions equal to 1 percent of their sales to finance the association. To aid collections, hotel members, including Hilton Hotels

Corporation (Hilton Hotels), agreed to give preferential treatment to suppliers who paid their assessments and to curtail purchases from those who did not. This agreement violated federal antitrust laws. The United States sued the members of the association, including Hilton Hotels, for the crime of violating federal antitrust laws. Can a corporation be held criminally liable for the acts of its representatives? If so, what criminal penalties can be assessed against the corporation? [*United States v. Hilton Hotels Corp.*, 467 F.2d 1000 (9th Cir. 1973)]

7.2. Acme Markets, Inc. (Acme), is a national retail food chain with approximately 36,000 employees working in 874 retail stores and 16 warehouses. Mr. Park is the president and chief executive officer of the corporation. In April 1970, the federal Food and Drug Administration (FDA) inspected Acme's Philadelphia warehouse and found unsanitary conditions, including rodent infestation. The FDA advised Mr. Park by letter of these conditions and demanded that they be corrected. In 1971, the FDA found that similar conditions existed at the warehouse. It again notified Park to correct the situation. An FDA inspection in March 1972 still showed unsanitary conditions and rodent infestation at the warehouse. Evidence showed that corporate employees did not take appropriate action to correct this situation. The federal Food, Drug, and Cosmetic Act makes individuals, as well as corporations, criminally liable for violations of the act. The United States brought a criminal action against Mr. Park for the violations. Can a corporate officer such as Mr. Park be held criminally liable for actions of his subordinates? [*United States v. Park*, 421 U.S. 658, 95 S.Ct. 658 (1974)]

7.3. In December 1982, Whitehead bought a stereo from his friend, Walter Gibbs, for between $10 and $40. When Whitehead first saw the stereo, it was one of three in Gibbs's home. Whitehead knew that the stereo was new and was worth between $169 and $189. The stereo system, identified as one stolen in late 1982 from the J. C. Penney Warehouse, was found by police officers in Whitehead's bedroom on January 27, 1983. The serial number on the stereo had been scratched out. Is Whitehead guilty of any crime? Explain. [*Whitehead v. State of Georgia*, 313 S.E.2d 775 (Ga.App. 1984)]

7.4. Evidence showed that there was a burglary in which a checkbook belonging to Mary J. Harris, doing business as "The Report Department," and a check encoder machine were stolen. Two of the checks from that checkbook were cashed at the Citizens & Southern National Bank branch office in Riverdale, Georgia, by Joseph Leon Foster, who was accompanied by a woman identified as Angela Foxworth. The bank teller who cashed the checks testified that the same man and woman cashed the checks on two different occasions at her drive-up window at the bank and that on both occasions they were in the same car. Each time the teller wrote the license

tag number of the car on the back of the check. The teller testified that both times the checks and the driver's license used to identify the woman were passed to her by the man driving, and that the man received the money from her. What crime has been committed? [*Foster v. State of Georgia*, 387 S.E.2d 637 (Ga.App. 1989)]

7.5. On February 3, 1987, the victim (Mr. X) went to the premises at 42 Taylor Terrace in New Milford, Connecticut, where his daughter and her husband lived. Lisa Perococo, who was Gregory Erhardt's girlfriend, was at the residence. Mr. X and Perococo were in the bedroom, partially dressed, engaging in sexual activity when Erhardt entered the room and photographed them. He then informed Mr. X that unless he procured $5,000 and placed it in a mailbox at a designated address by 8 P.M. that night, Erhardt would show the photographs to Mr. X's wife. Mr. X proceeded to make telephone arrangements for the procurement and placement of the money according to Erhardt's instructions. If the money were paid, what crime would have been committed? [*State of Connecticut v. Erhardt*, 553 A.2d 188 (Conn.App. 1989)]

7.6. Remi Olu Abod, a Nigerian national, obtained a VISA credit card from a supplier, which bore the name "Norman Skinner." Abod purchased a counterfeit international driving permit bearing the name Norman Skinner at a passport photo shop in California. On June 27, 1984, Abod traveled from Los Angeles, California, to Corpus Christi, Texas. He first used the credit card to obtain $2,400 cash from each of two banks. He next appeared at the jewelry counter at Dillard's Department Store and tried to purchase $2,335 of jewelry with the credit card. When the store employee telephoned the VISA credit authorization center for approval, he was informed that the card was counterfeit. Corpus Christi police were summoned to the store, where they arrested Abod. What crime did Abod commit? [*United States v. Abod*, 770 F.2d 1293 (5th Cir. 1985)]

7.7. In 1978, Miriam Marlowe's husband purchased a life insurance policy on his own life, naming her as the beneficiary. After Marlowe's husband died in a swimming accident in July 1981, she received payment on the policy. Marlowe later met John Walton, a friend of a friend. He convinced her that he had a friend who worked for the State Department and had access to gold in Brazil, and that the gold could be purchased in Brazil for $100 an ounce and sold in the United States for $300 an ounce. Walton convinced Miriam to invest $25,000. Instead of investing the money in gold in Brazil, Walton opened an account at Tracy Collins Bank in the name of Jeffrey McIntyre Roberts and deposited Miriam's money in that account. He later withdrew the money in cash. What crime is Walton guilty of? [*State of Utah v. Roberts*, 711 p.2d 235 (Utah 1985)]

7.8. Marty W. Orr was employed as a deputy treasurer and bookkeeper in the treasurer's office of Washington County, Virginia. She was responsible for computing each day's revenue and depositing funds received on a daily basis. During the course of her work, she took cash totaling several thousand dollars. What crime has she committed? [*Orr v. Commonwealth of Virginia*, 344 S.E.2d 627 (Va.App. 1986)]

7.9. In 1979, the city of Peoria, Illinois, received federal funds from the Department of Housing and Urban Development (HUD) to be used for housing rehabilitation assistance. The city of Peoria designated United Neighborhoods, Inc. (UNI), a corporation, to administer the funds. Arthur Dixon was UNI's executive director and James Lee Hinton was its housing rehabilitation coordinator. In these capacities, they were responsible for contracting with suppliers and tradespeople to provide the necessary goods and services to rehabilitate the houses. Evidence showed that Dixon and Hinton used their positions to extract 10 percent payments back on all contracts they awarded. What crime have they committed? [*Dixon and Hinton v. United States*, 465 U.S. 482, 104 S.Ct. 1172 (1984)]

7.10. Mary G. Smith's MasterCard credit card was in her purse when it was stolen in June 1985. On June 28, 1985, Beulah Houston entered a Ventura store located in Griffith, Indiana, and indicated to the manager of the jewelry department that she wished to purchase a man's watch. After making a selection, Houston handed the manager a MasterCard bearing the name Mary G. Smith. Upon contacting the bank for authorization, the manager was told to hold the card. Houston then left the store and was later arrested. Can Houston be convicted of attempting to commit credit-card fraud? [*Houston v. State of Indiana*, 528 N.E.2d 818 (Ind.App. 1988)]

7.11. Lee Stuart Paulson owns the liquor license for "My House," a bar in San Francisco. The California Department of Alcoholic Beverage Control (Department) is the administrative agency that regulates bars in that state. The California Business and Professions Code, which the Department administers, prohibits "any kind of illegal activity on licensed premises." On February 11, 1988, an anonymous informer tipped the Department that narcotics sales were occurring on the premises of "My House" and that the narcotics were kept in a safe behind the bar on the premises. A special Department investigator entered the bar during its hours of operation, identified himself, and informed Paulson that he was conducting an inspection. The investigator, who did not have a search warrant, opened the safe without seeking Paulson's consent. Twenty-two bundles of cocaine, totaling 5.5 grams, were found in the safe. Paulson was arrested. At his criminal trial, Paulson challenged the lawfulness of the search. Was the warrantless search of the safe a lawful search? [*People v. Paulson*, 216 Cal.App.3d 1480, 265 Cal.Rptr. 579 (Cal.App. 1990)]

7.12. The Center Art Galleries-Hawaii (Center) sells artwork. Approximately 20 percent of its business involves art by Salvador Dali. The federal government, which suspected the Center of fraudulently selling forged Dali artwork, obtained identical search warrants for six locations controlled by the Center. The warrants commanded the executing officer to seize items that were "evidence of violations of federal criminal law." The warrants did not describe the specific crimes suspected and did not stipulate that only items pertaining to the sale of Dali's work could be seized. There was no evidence of any criminal activity unrelated to that artist. Is the search warrant valid? [*Center Art Galleries-Hawaii, Inc. v. United States*, 875 F.2d 747 (9th Cir. 1989)]

7.13. John Doe is the owner of several sole proprietorship businesses. In 1980, during the course of an investigation of corruption in awarding county and municipal contracts, a federal grand jury served several subpoenas on John Doe demanding the production of the following business records: (1) general ledgers and journals, (2) invoices, (3) bank statements and canceled checks, (4) financial statements, (5) telephone company records, (6) safe-deposit box records, and (7) copies of tax returns. John Doe filed a motion in federal court seeking to quash the subpoenas, alleging that producing these business records would violate his Fifth Amendment privilege of not testifying against himself. Do the records have to be disclosed? [*United States v. John Doe*, 465 U.S. 605, 104 S.Ct. 1237 (1984)]

ETHICS CASES

7.14. R. Foster Winans was a reporter for *The Wall Street Journal* from 1981 through 1984 during which time he wrote a column called "Heard on the Street." In the column, Winans discussed the future prospects of companies and their securities. Evidence showed that positive comments would make the company's stock increase in value; negative comments would have the opposite result. Winans systematically leaked the contents of his future "Heard" columns prior to publication to Peter Brant, a stockbroker, in exchange for a share of the profits made by Brant. Upon discovery, Winans was convicted of wire and mail fraud, which are federal crimes. The crimes were committed within the state of New

York. In September 1985, Winans entered into a book publishing contract with St. Martin's Press and in 1988 St. Martin's published Winans's book *Trading Secrets*. The book details Winans's own actions that resulted in his federal conviction for insider trading. New York had previously adopted a "Son of Sam" law. The New York State Crime Victim's Board moved for an order directing St. Martin's to turn over the royalties due Winans, which would be deposited in an escrow account and held for the benefit of and payable to any victims of Winans's crimes. Who legally is entitled to the royalties? Is it ethical for a convicted criminal to make money by selling the media rights to the story about the crime? [*St. Martin's Press v. Zweibel, N.Y. Law Journal*, 2/26/90 (N.Y.Sup.Ct. 1990)]

7.15. John H. Evans, Jr., was an elected member of the Board of Commissioners of DeKalb County, Georgia. During 1986, the Federal Bureau of Investigation (FBI) investigated allegations of public corruption in the Atlanta area. An FBI agent posing as a real estate developer talked on the telephone and met with Evans on a number of occasions. In the conversations, the agent sought Evans's assistance in an effort to rezone a 25-acre tract of land for high-density residential use. The conversations were recorded on audio- or videotape. On July 25, 1986, the agent handed Evans $7,000 cash. Evans took the money. Evans was later indicted for the crime of extortion under color of official right in violation of the federal Hobbs Act [26 U.S.C. § 7206(1)]. He was convicted by a jury. Evans appealed, alleging that he could not be found guilty of extortion unless the government could prove that he had demanded the payment. Is Evans guilty of extortion? Did Evans act ethically in accepting the payment? [*Evans v. United States*, 112 S.Ct. 1881 (1992)]

7.16. In 1979, Leo Shaw, an attorney, entered into a partnership agreement with three other persons to build and operate an office building. From the outset, it was agreed that Shaw's role was to manage the operation of the building. Management of the property was Shaw's contribution to the partnership; the other three partners contributed the necessary capital. In January 1989, the other partners discovered that the loan on the building was in default and that foreclosure proceedings were imminent. Upon investigation, they discovered that Shaw had taken approximately $80,000 from the partnership's checking account. After heated discussions, Shaw repaid $13,000. In May 1989, when no further payment was forthcoming, a partner filed a civil suit against Shaw and notified the police. The state filed a criminal complaint against Shaw on March 15, 1990. On April 3, 1990, Shaw repaid the remaining funds as part of a civil settlement. At his criminal trial in November 1990, Shaw argued that the repayment of the money was a defense to the crime of embezzlement. Did Shaw act ethically in this case? Would your answer be different if he had really only "borrowed" the money and had intended to return it? [*People v. Shaw*, 10 Cal.App.4th 969, 12 Cal.Rptr.2d 665 (Cal.App. 1992)]

CRITICAL LEGAL THINKING WRITING ASSIGNMENT

Read Case A.7 in the Case Appendix [*Schalk v. Texas*]. This case is excerpted from the appellate court opinion. Review and brief the case. In your brief, be sure to answer the following questions.

1. What activities had the defendants engaged in?
2. What crime were the defendants accused of?
3. What was the decision of the appellate court?

NOTES

1. Title 18 of the U.S. Code contains the federal criminal code.
2. Sentencing Reform Act of 1984, 18 U.S.C. § 3551 et. seq. The sentencing guidelines for federal crimes, which were promulgated by the U.S. Sentencing Commission, became effective on November 1, 1987.
3. 18 U.S.C. § 1341.
4. 18 U.S.C. § 1343.
5. 18 U.S.C. §§ 1961–1968.
6. *United States v. Leon*, 468 U.S. 897, 104 S.Ct. 3405, 82 L.Ed.2d 677 (1984).

7. *Marshall v. Barlow's, Inc.*, 436 U.S. 307, 98 S.Ct. 1816, 56 L.Ed.2d 305 (1978).
8. *Bellis v. United States*, 417 U.S. 85, 94 S.Ct. 2179, 40 L.Ed.2d 678 (1974).
9. The Speedy Trial Act requires that a criminal defendant be brought to trial within 70 days after indictment [18 U.S.C. § 3161(c)(1)]. Continuances may be granted by the court to serve the "ends of justice."
10. *Baldwin v. Alabama*, 472 U.S. 372, 105 S.Ct. 2727, 86 L.Ed.2d 300 (1985).

Ethics and Social Responsibility of Business

Ethical considerations can no more be excluded from the administration of justice, which is the end and purpose of all civil laws, than one can exclude the vital air from his room and live.

JOHN F. DILLON *Laws and Jurisprudence of England and America Lecture 1 (1894)*

Chapter Objectives

After studying this chapter, you should be able to

1. Describe ethical fundamentalism.
2. Describe utilitarianism as a moral theory.
3. Describe Kantian ethics.
4. Describe Rawls's social justice theory.
5. Describe ethical relativism.
6. Describe maximizing profits as a theory of social responsibility.
7. Describe the moral minimum theory of social responsibility.
8. Describe the stakeholder interest theory of social responsibility.
9. Describe the corporate citizenship theory of social responsibility.
10. Describe corporate social audits.

Chapter Contents

Businesses organized in the United States are subject to its laws. They are also subject to the laws of other countries in which they operate. In addition, businesspersons owe a duty to act ethically in the conduct of their affairs, and businesses owe a social responsibility not to harm society.

Although much of the law is based on ethical standards, not all ethical standards have been enacted as law. The law establishes a minimum degree of conduct expected by persons and businesses in society. Ethics demands more.

This chapter discusses business ethics and the social responsibility of business.

Ethics precede laws as man precedes society.

Jason Alexander
Philosophy for Investors
(1979)

Law and Ethics

Sometimes the rule of law and the golden rule of **ethics** demand the same response by the person confronted with a problem. For example, federal and state laws make bribery unlawful. Thus, a person violates the law if he or she bribes a judge for a favorable decision in a case. Ethics would also prohibit this conduct.

The law may permit something that would be ethically wrong.

Consider This Example   Occupational safety laws set standards for emissions of dust from toxic chemicals in the workplace. Suppose a company can reduce the emissions below the legal standard by spending additional money. The only benefit from the expenditure would be better employee health. Ethics would require the extra expenditure; the law would not.

Another alternative occurs where the law demands certain conduct but a person's ethical standards are contrary.

Consider This Example   Federal law prohibits employers from hiring certain illegal alien workers. Suppose an employer advertises the availability of a job and receives no responses except from a person who cannot prove he or she is a citizen of this country or does not possess a required visa. The worker and his or her family are destitute. Should the employer hire him or her? The law says no, but ethics says yes (see Exhibit 8.1).

ethics

A set of moral principles or values that governs the conduct of an individual or a group.

Business Brief

What is lawful conduct is not always ethical conduct.

Business Brief

Corruption by government officials and the influence of criminal mafias are the largest impediments to the growth of the economies of several countries. Can such corruption be contained?

Exhibit 8.1   *Law and Ethics*

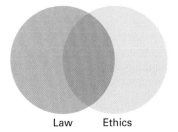

Law   Ethics

Ethical Perspective

Can Company Canned

The Continental Can Company (Continental) manufactured and sold steel cans to food, beverage, and packaging companies. It had more than 50 plants located throughout the United States. In the late 1960s, Continental was the leading producer of metal cans in this

country. Its workers were represented by the United Steel Workers Union.

Beginning in the 1960s, many users began self-manufacturing the cans they needed. In addition, aluminum cans were introduced and took over a large segment

(box continues)

of the beverage can market. By 1980, over 90 percent of the beverage business was in aluminum cans. As a result of self-manufacturing and aluminum cans, the demand for Continental's steel cans declined. Continental was left with obsolete factories and underutilized workers. Continental decided to reduce employment in its steel can business and enter new lines of business.

There was a problem with reducing the number of employees, however. Continental had entered into a collective bargaining agreement with the United Steel Workers Union that required Continental to pay a special pension (the "Magic Number" pension) to workers who were discharged who met stipulated qualifications. A discharged worker qualified for this special pension if he or she had at least 15 years of regular continuous service with Continental and was 50 years of age or older. The pension liability was unfunded, however. Consequently, the monies to pay the pensions would have to be paid out of current income and assets at a cost of more than $100,000 per worker.

Continental's top management devised a secret plan, called the "Bell" system, to reduce its work force while avoiding liability for the Magic Number pensions. Under the system, workers who had already qualified for the pension were not discharged. Instead, the company targeted employees who were close to qualifying.

Continental developed a sophisticated computer program that enabled management to identify which employees to target. These employees were then discharged.

In addition, a "red flag" program was instituted to keep track of laid-off employees to prevent their rehire anywhere in the company because that would resurrect their pension rights. The Bell and red flag systems were kept secret from the affected employees.

In 1983, when the systems came to light, many discharged employees sued Continental for damages. They asserted that Continental violated Section 510 of the federal **Employee Retirement Income Security Act of 1974 (ERISA)** [29 U.S.C. § 1140]. This section provides, "It shall be unlawful for any person to discharge, fine, suspend, expel, discipline, or discriminate against a participant or beneficiary for exercising any right to which he is entitled under the provisions of an employee benefit plan, or for interfering with the attainment of any right to which such participant may become entitled under the plan."

After a lengthy trial, the court held in favor of the plaintiffs. The court stated, "The court has found that Continental violated ERISA and set upon a deliberate course of conduct aimed at depriving employees of eligibility for bargained-for pensions." The court added, "For a corporation of this magnitude to engage in a complex, secret and deliberate scheme to deny its workers bargained-for pension benefits raises questions of corporate morality, ethics and decency which far transcend the factual and legal issues posed in this matter."

Eventually, a settlement was reached and the affected workers received payment of their pension benefits. [*McLendon v. Continental Group, Inc.*, 749 F.Supp. 582 (D.N.J. 1989)].

1. Did the top management of Continental act unethically by instituting the Bell and red flag systems?
2. Did Continental act unethically in defending the lawsuits? Is it ever ethical to defend a lawsuit when the defendant knows that he or she is guilty?

$\mathscr{M}$ORAL THEORIES AND BUSINESS ETHICS

How can ethics be measured? The answer is very personal: What is considered ethical by one person may be considered unethical by another. However, there do seem to be some universal rules about what conduct is ethical and what conduct is not. The following discussion highlights five major theories of ethics.

Ethical Fundamentalism

ethical fundamentalism

When a person looks to an outside source for ethical rules or commands.

Under **ethical fundamentalism**, a person looks to an *outside source* for ethical rules or commands. This may be a book (e.g., the Bible or the Koran) or a person (e.g., Karl Marx). Critics argue that ethical fundamentalism does not permit people to determine right and wrong for themselves. Taken to an extreme, the result could be considered unethical under most other moral theories. For example, a literal interpretation of the maxim "an eye for an eye" would permit retaliation.

Ethical Perspective _____

SEARS'S AUTO REPAIR CENTERS: WHO GOT THE LUBE JOB?

Sears Roebuck & Co. is a venerable retailer at which generations of Americans have shopped for clothes, tools, appliances, and other goods and services. For years, the company billed itself as the place "where Americans shop." Today, Sears's auto repair centers, which generate more than $3 billion in annual sales, have been charged with being the place where Americans get robbed.

Spurred by a 50 percent increase in consumer complaints over a three-year period, several states conducted undercover investigations to determine the legitimacy of those complaints. The New Jersey Division of Consumer Affairs found that all six Sears Auto Centers visited by undercover agents recommended unnecessary repairs. The California Department of Consumer Affairs found that Sears—the largest provider of auto services in the state—had systematically over-charged an average of $223 for repairs and routinely billed for work that was not done. Forty-one other states lodged similar complaints.

The "bait and rip off" scheme worked as follows: Sears would send consumers coupons advertising discounts on brake jobs. When customers came in to redeem their coupons, the sales staff would convince them to authorize additional repairs. Sears also established quotas for repair services that their employees had to meet.

California officials got the company's attention when the state started proceedings to revoke Sears's auto repair license. Sears quickly agreed to settle all lawsuits against it. As part of the settlement, Sears agreed to distribute $50 worth of coupons to almost 1 million customers nationwide who obtained one of five specific repair services from Sears between August 1, 1990, and January 31, 1992. The coupons could be redeemed for merchandise and services at Sears stores. In addition, Sears agreed to pay $3.5 million to cover the costs of various government investigations, to contribute $1.5 million to community colleges to conduct auto mechanic training programs, and to abandon its repair service quotas. The settlement cost Sears $30 million.

In agreeing to the settlement, Sears denied any wrongdoing, simply stating that "mistakes were made." It said that it agreed to the settlement to avoid the burden, expenses, and uncertainty of prolonged litigation.

1. Did Sears act ethically in this case? Should it have admitted culpability?
2. Why do you think Sears chose to settle the cases instead of defending itself in court?
3. Do you think Sears let the "profit motive" overshadow its ethics?

Utilitarianism

Utilitarianism is a moral theory with its origins in the works of Jeremy Bentham (1748–1832) and John Stuart Mill (1806–1873). This moral theory dictates that people must choose the action or follow the rule that provides the *greatest good to society*. This does not mean the greatest good for the greatest number of people. For instance, if one action would increase the good of 25 people one unit each, and an alternative action would increase the good of one person 26 units, the latter action should be taken.

utilitarianism
A moral theory that dictates that people must choose the action or follow the rule that provides the greatest good to society.

Consider This Example   A company is trying to determine whether it should close an unprofitable plant located in a small community. Utilitarianism would require that the benefits to shareholders from closing the plant be compared to the benefits to employees, their families, and others in the community in keeping it open.

Utilitarianism has been criticized because it is difficult to estimate the "good" that will result from different actions, it is hard to apply in an imperfect world, and it treats morality as if it were an impersonal mathematical calculation.

The ultimate justification of the law is to be found, and can only be found, in moral considerations.

Lord MacMillan
Law and Other Things *(1937)*

Ethical Perspective

GENERAL MOTORS SKIPS TOWN

For decades, job-hungry communities have offered tax abatements, low-interest loans, and other financial inducements to lure companies to locate in their community. Some companies take these incentives but then leave town when they run out. Cities are fighting back, and many are bringing lawsuits.

Consider the case of Ypsilanti, Michigan. From 1984 to 1988, Ypsilanti gave General Motors Corporation (GM) $13 million in tax abatements to keep its Willow Run plant, which produced Chevrolet automobiles, in the city. In 1991, GM announced that it was going to close the Willow Run plant and move the work being done there to its Arlington, Texas, plant. The closure meant the loss of thousands of jobs in a city already suffering severe unemployment and financial difficulties.

Ypsilanti sued GM for reneging on its implied promise to stay put in return for the tax breaks. The trial court judge invoked the doctrine of promissory estoppel and enjoined GM from closing its plant in Ypsilanti.

The trial court judge stated, "There would be a gross inequity and patent unfairness if General Motors, having

lulled the people of the Ypsilanti area into giving up millions of tax dollars which they desperately need to educate their children and provide basic governmental services, is allowed to simply decide it will desert 4,500 workers and their families because it thinks it can make these same cars cheaper somewhere else."

The Michigan court of appeals reversed, however. The appeals court held that GM made no promise to stay put in Ypsilanti as a quid pro quo for the tax abatements. The court held that any statements made by GM concerning maintaining continuous employment at the Willow Run plant were merely expressions of hope or expectation, but did not amount to a promise. The court's decision permits GM to transfer production from the Michigan plant to Texas.

Did GM act ethically by attempting to close its plant in Ypsilanti? Would your answer be different if GM were losing money at the plant? [*Charter Township of Ypsilanti, Michigan v. General Motors Corporation*, No. 161245 (Mich. App. 1993)]

Kantian Ethics

Kantian or duty ethics

A moral theory that says that people owe moral duties that are based on universal rules, such as the categorical imperative "Do unto others as you would have them do unto you."

Immanuel Kant (1724–1804) is the best-known proponent of **duty ethics**, or **deontology** (from the Greek word *deon*, meaning duty). Kant believed that people owe moral duties that are based on *universal* rules. For example, keeping a promise to abide by a contract is a moral duty even if that contract turns out to be detrimental to the obligated party. Kant's philosophy is based on the premise that people can use reasoning to reach ethical decisions. His ethical theory would have people behave according to the *categorical imperative* "Do unto others as you would have them do unto you."

Deontology's universal rules are based on two important principles: (1) consistency, that is, all cases are treated alike with no exceptions and (2) reversibility, that is, the actor must abide by the rule he or she uses to judge the morality of someone else's conduct. Thus, if you are going to make an exception for yourself, that exception becomes a universal rule that applies to all others. For instance, if you rationalize that it is all right for you to engage in deceptive practices, it is all right for competitors to do so also. A criticism of Kantian ethics is that it is hard to reach a consensus as to what the universal rules should be.

The following case raised ethical issues.

Zivich v. Mentor Soccer Club, Inc.
696 N.E.2d 201 (1998)
Supreme Court of Ohio

CASE 8.1

FACTS
In May 1993, Pamela Zivich registered her seven-year-old son, Bryan, to play soccer with the Mentor Soccer Club, Inc.

(Club), for the 1993–1994 season. The Club is a nonprofit organization composed primarily of volunteers in the Mentor, Ohio, area who provide children with the opportunity to learn and play soccer. The Club's registration form, which Mrs. Zivich signed, contained the following language:

> *Recognizing the possibility of physical injury associated with soccer and for the Mentor Soccer Club, and the USYSA [United States Youth Soccer Association] accepting the registrant for its soccer programs and activities, I hereby release, discharge and/or otherwise indemnify the Mentor Soccer Club and the USYSA, its affiliated organizations and sponsors, their employees, and associated personnel, including the owners of the fields and facilities utilized by the Soccer Club, against any claim by or on behalf of the registrant as a result of the registrant's participation in the Soccer Club.*

On October 7, 1993, Bryan attended soccer practice with his father, Philip Zivich. During practice, the team participated in an intrasquad scrimmage. After the scrimmage, Bryan jumped onto the soccer goal and was swinging back and forth on it, but the goal was not anchored down. It tipped backward, and Bryan fell. The goal came down on his chest, breaking three of his ribs and his collarbone and severely bruising his lungs. Bryan's parents sued the Club for negligence to recover damages for injuries suffered by Bryan and the loss of consortium for themselves. The Club moved for summary judgment, asserting that the exculpatory agreement signed by Bryan's mother barred the claims. The trial court agreed and granted the Club's summary judgment motion. The court of appeals affirmed. The plaintiffs appealed to the Supreme Court of Ohio.

ISSUE

Did the exculpatory agreement signed by Mrs. Zivich on behalf of her son release the Club from liability for the child's claims and the parents' claims?

IN THE LANGUAGE OF THE COURT

Sweeney, Justice   With respect to adult participants, the general rule is that releases from liability for injuries caused by negligent acts arising in the context of recreational activities are enforceable. Here, however, the exculpatory agreement was executed by a parent on behalf of the minor child.

*   It cannot be disputed that volunteers in community recreational activities serve an important function. Organized recreational activities offer children the opportunity to learn valuable life skills. It is here that many children learn how to work as a team and how to operate within an organizational structure. Children also are given the chance to exercise and develop coordination skills. Due in great part to the assistance of volunteers, nonprofit organizations are able to offer these activities at minimal cost. In fact, the American Youth Soccer Organization pays only nineteen of its four hundred thousand staff members. The Little League pays only seventy of its 2.5 million members. Clearly, without the work of its volunteers, these nonprofit organizations could not exist, and scores of children would be without the benefit and enjoyment of organized sports.*

*   Yet the threat of liability strongly deters many individuals from volunteering for nonprofit organizations. Therefore, faced with the very real threat of a lawsuit, and the potential for substantial damage awards, nonprofit organizations and their volunteers could very well decide that the risks are not worth the effort. Hence, invalidation of exculpatory agreements would reduce the number of activities made possible through the uncompensated services of volunteers and their sponsoring organizations.*

*   Therefore, we conclude that although Bryan, like many children before him, gave up his right to sue for the negligent acts of others, the public as a whole received the benefit of these exculpatory agreements. Because of this agreement, the Club was able to offer affordable recreation and to continue to do so without the risks and overwhelming costs of litigation. Bryan's parents agreed to shoulder the risk. Public policy does not forbid such an agreement. In fact, public policy supports it.*

DECISION AND REMEDY

A parent's signature on an exculpatory agreement on behalf of his or her child releases the other party from liability to the child, the parent who signed the agreement, and the other parent. Affirmed.

Case Questions

Critical Legal Thinking   Do exculpatory agreements serve any valid purpose? Should exculpatory agreements be enforceable?

Ethics   Was it ethical for Mrs. Zivich to sign the exculpatory agreement and then bring this lawsuit?

Business Application   What would have been the consequences if the court had found the exculpatory agreement to be invalid in this case?

Rawls's Social Justice Theory

John Locke (1632–1704) and Jean Jacques Rousseau (1712–1778) proposed a **social contract** theory of morality. Under this theory, each person is presumed to have entered into a social contract with all others in society to obey moral rules that are necessary for people to live in peace and harmony. This implied contract states, "I will keep the rules if everyone else does." These moral rules are then used to solve conflicting interests in society.

The leading proponent of the modern social justice theory is John Rawls, a contemporary philosopher at Harvard University. Under Rawls's *distributive justice theory*, fairness is

Rawls's social contract
A moral theory that says each person is presumed to have entered into a social contract with all others in society to obey moral rules that are necessary for people to live in peace and harmony.

considered the essence of justice. The principles of justice should be chosen by persons who do not yet know their station in society—thus, their "veil of ignorance" would permit the fairest possible principles to be selected. For instance, the principle of equal opportunity would be promulgated by people who would not yet know if they were in a favored class. As a caveat, Rawls also proposes that the least advantaged in society must receive special assistance to allow them to realize their potential.

Rawls's theory of distributive justice is criticized for two reasons. First, establishing the blind "original position" for choosing moral principles is impossible in the real world. Second, many persons in society would choose not to maximize the benefit to the least advantaged persons in society.

Ethical Perspective

TOY SALES NOT CHILD'S PLAY

When a child opens a new toy, there is a 30 percent probability that the toy was purchased at a Toys "R" Us retail store; the company controls that much of the retail toy market in the United States. But Toys "R" Us did not gain this 30 percent market share by being a stuffed animal on a shelf. In fact, the Federal Trade Commission (FTC), the federal government agency empowered to protect consumers, decided that Toys "R" Us needed to be disciplined for its unruly behavior on the playground.

Toys "R" Us, the nation's largest toy retailer, built a reputation for being a low-cost toy seller, but it now faces price competition from warehouse clubs such as Costco and Wal-Mart. Not liking this competition, Toys "R" Us decided to bully its suppliers, the toy manufacturers. Toys "R" Us used its dominance as a toy distributor to extract agreements from toy manufacturers to *boycott*—not sell—toys to warehouse clubs. The manufacturers that were "persuaded" to join the Toys "R" Us—sponsored boycott account for 40 percent of the toys sold in the United States. To police its policy, Toys "R" Us threatened to stop buying from any toy manufacturer that violated this vertical boycott. In addition, the company used its muscle to orchestrate a horizontal boycott agreement among most of these manufacturers to adhere to the restriction on toy sales to warehouse clubs and to "tattle" on one another for any violations.

The FTC investigated and found that Toys "R" Us and its reluctant collaborators unfairly stifled competition in the marketplace. The FTC held that the Toys "R" Us boycott was an unreasonable restraint of trade in violation of the federal Sherman Antitrust Act. They also ruled that the boycott caused harmful effects to consumers and to the warehouse clubs and that there was no legal business justification for this conduct. The FTC issued a *cease and desist order* that barred Toys "R" Us from entering into any agreement with toy manufacturers to limit the supply of toys that can be sold to discount warehouse stores and prohibited Toys "R" Us from attempting to facilitate any agreement among its suppliers regarding the sale of toys to any retailer. [*Federal Trade Commission v. Toys "R" Us*]

1. Did Toys "R" Us act unfairly, or was this just good, clean competition?
2. Did Toys "R" Us misuse its market power?
3. What would be the consequences if Toys "R" Us got away with what it was doing?

Ethical Relativism

ethical relativism

A moral theory that holds that individuals must decide what is ethical based on their own feelings as to what is right or wrong.

Ethical relativism holds that *individuals must decide what is ethical based on their own feelings as to what is right or wrong.* Under this moral theory, if a person meets his or her own moral standard in making a decision, no one can criticize him or her for it. Thus, there are no universal ethical rules to guide a person's conduct. This theory has been criticized because action that is usually thought to be unethical (e.g., committing fraud) would not be unethical if the perpetrator thought it was in fact ethical. Few philosophers advocate ethical relativism as an acceptable moral theory.

Ethical Perspective

SHATTERING THE GLASS CEILING

Females have long been discriminated against in employment. **Title VII of the Civil Rights Act of 1969**, a federal statute, prohibits sex discrimination in employment. Today, a "glass ceiling" may still prevent women from reaching the highest employment positions. The following case demonstrates how blatant this can be.

Ann Hopkins was a senior manager in the Washington, DC, office of Price Waterhouse, a national firm of certified public accountants. In 1982, Hopkins was proposed for partnership in the firm. Of the 88 persons proposed for partnership that year, only one—Hopkins—was a woman. Hopkins was a project leader, worked long hours, met deadlines, and was productive, energetic, and creative. In addition, she had secured a $25-million contract for the firm. No other candidate had a comparable record for securing major contracts for the firm. Evidence did show, however, that Hopkins lacked some interpersonal skills.

All partners of the firm were invited to submit written comments on each candidate. Thirteen partners supported Hopkins's bid for partnership and eight recommended that she be denied partnership. Some of the partners reacted negatively to Hopkins's personality because she was an aggressive woman. One partner described her as "macho," another suggested that she "over-compensated for being a woman," a third advised her to take "a course at charm school," and a fourth objected to her swearing "because it is a lady using foul language."

Price Waterhouse neither offered nor denied her admission to the firm but held her candidacy for reconsideration the following year. The male partner who had the responsibility of telling Hopkins the reasons for the decision told her that she should "walk more femininely, talk more femininely, dress more femininely, wear makeup, have her hair styled, and wear jewelry." When the partners in her office refused to repropose her for partnership the next year, she sued Price Waterhouse for sex discrimination in violation of Title VII. The case went all the way to the U.S. Supreme Court.

The Supreme Court held that Price Waterhouse's actions constituted "sex stereotyping" in violation of Title VII. The Court stated, "We are beyond the day when an employer could evaluate employees by assuming or insisting that they matched the stereotype associated with their group. An employer who objects to aggressiveness in women but whose positions require this trait places women in an intolerable and impermissible Catch-22: out of a job if they behave aggressively and out of a job if they don't. Title VII lifts women out of this bind. We sit not to determine whether Ms. Hopkins is nice, but to decide whether the partners reacted negatively to her personality because she is a woman."

The Supreme Court remanded the case to the district court. On remand, judgment was entered in favor of Ms. Hopkins against Price Waterhouse. The court ordered Price Waterhouse to admit Ms. Hopkins as a partner retroactively effective July 1, 1983, pay her back compensation of $371,175, and pay her costs and attorneys' fees of $422,460. [*Price Waterhouse v. Hopkins*, 490 U.S. 228, 109 S.Ct. 1775 (1989)]

1. Do you think the partners who stereotyped Hopkins acted ethically?
2. Do you think the glass ceiling still exists?

*C*ONCEPT SUMMARY   THEORIES OF ETHICS

Theory	Description
Ethical fundamentalism	Persons look to an outside source (e.g., Bible or Koran) or central figure for ethical guidelines.
Utilitarianism	Persons choose the alternative that would provide the greatest good to society.
Kantian ethics	A set of universal rules establishes ethical duties. The rules are based on reasoning and require (1) consistency in application and (2) reversibility.
Rawls's social justice theory	Moral duties are based on an implied social contract. Fairness is justice. The rules are established from an original position of a "veil of ignorance."
Ethical relativism	Individuals decide what is ethical based on their own feelings as to what is right or wrong.

The Social Responsibility of Business

Business does not operate in a vacuum. Decisions made by businesses have far-reaching effects on society. In the past, many business decisions were made solely on a cost-benefit analysis and how it affected the "bottom line." Such decisions, however, may cause negative externalities for others. For example, the dumping of hazardous wastes from a manufacturing plant into a river affects homeowners, farmers, and others who use the river's waters. Thus, corporations are considered to owe some degree of **social responsibility** for their actions. Four theories of the social responsibility of business are discussed in the following paragraphs.

social responsibility
Duty owed by businesses to act socially responsible in producing and selling goods and services.

White lily on pond, Japan. *Different countries and cultures have different ethical standards. Some acts that are considered unethical in one country may not be thought so in other countries.*

Maximizing Profits

The traditional view of the social responsibility of business is that business should **maximize profits** for shareholders. This view, which dominated business and the law during the nineteenth century, holds that the interests of other constituencies (e.g., employees, suppliers, residents of the communities in which businesses are located) are not important in and of themselves.

maximizing profits
A theory of social responsibility that says a corporation owes a duty to take actions that maximize profits for shareholders.

In the famous case of *Dodge v. Ford Motor Company,*[1] a shareholder sued the car company when Henry Ford introduced a plan to reduce the price of cars so that more people would be put to work and more people could own cars. The shareholders alleged that such a plan would not increase dividends. Mr. Ford testified, "My ambition is to employ still more men, to spread the benefits of this industrial system to the greatest number, to help them build up their lives and their homes." The court sided with the shareholders and stated that

> [Mr. Ford's] testimony creates the impression that he thinks the Ford Motor Company has made too much money, has had too large profits and that, although large profits might still be earned, a sharing of them with the public, by reducing the price of the output of the company, ought to be undertaken.
>
> There should be no confusion of the duties which Mr. Ford conceives that he and the stockholders owe to the general public and the duties which in law he and his codirectors owe to protesting, minority stockholders. A business corporation is organized and carried on primarily for the profit of the stockholders. The powers of the directors are to be employed for that end. The discretion of directors is to be exercised in the choice of means to attain that end, and does not extend to a change in the end itself, to the reduction of profits, or to the nondistribution of profits among stockholders in order to devote them to other purposes.

Public policy: That principle of the law which holds that no subject can lawfully do that which has a tendency to be injurious to the public, or against the public good.

Lord Truro
Egerton v. Brownlow (1853)

Milton Friedman, who won the Nobel Prize in economics when he taught at the University of Chicago, advocated this theory. Friedman asserted that in a free society, "there is one and only one social responsibility of business—to use its resources and engage in activities designed to increase its profits as long as it stays within the rules of the game, which is to say, engages in open and free competition without deception and fraud."[2]

International Perspective

ETHICAL ISSUE IN INTERNATIONAL BUSINESS: PAYMENT OF BRIBES

Universal ethical rules may exist within a country, but they definitely do not exist for the world as a whole. This is because the cultures and laws of countries are different. Thus, what may be unethical in one country may be considered ethical in another. A corporation that operates in many countries—a "transnational company"—is faced with a dilemma: Does it follow the ethical rule of its parent country or its host country?

The Lockheed Corporation (Lockheed), a *Fortune* 500 company that manufactures aircraft, faced this problem. In the 1970s, it manufactured the L-1011, or "TriStar," commercial airliner. It competed with McDonnell Douglas and Boeing, both U.S. corporations, as well as other competitors, to sell the aircraft to airline carriers in the United States and other countries.

In 1975, an investigation revealed that Lockheed had paid more than $12 million to the president of All Nippon Airlines (ANA) and several Japanese politicians and government officials in conjunction with its sale of L-1011s to the airline carrier. A. Carl Kotchian, the chairman of Lockheed, authorized the payments. Congressional hearings on the matter revealed that such payments were common in the aircraft industry.

Mr. Kotchian provided several justifications for his actions. First, he cited the fact that such payments by Lockheed in Japan did not at the time violate any U.S. laws. Second, he testified that the payments were "worthwhile from Lockheed's standpoint" because "they would provide Lockheed workers with jobs, and thus redound to the benefit of their dependents, their communities, and stockholders of the corporation."

Concerning one of the payments, Mr. Kotchian wrote:

> Soon after landing in Japan, I found myself deep in conversation with Toshiharu Okubo, an official of Marubeni, the trading company that was serving as Lockheed's representative and go-between in the already ongoing TriStar negotiations.
>
> Beaming, Okubo reviewed Marubeni's efforts on behalf of TriStar, then gave me the good news that "tomorrow at

> 7:30 A.M. we are seeing Prime Minister Tanaka" about the matter. I was quite impressed with and encouraged by the "power of Marubeni"—power that made it possible to make an appointment with the prime minister only 24 hours after I had asked Marubeni to set up such a meeting. Then came an unexpected development: When we began to discuss in detail how to bring about the sale of TriStar, Okubo suddenly suggested that I make a "pledge" to pay money for a major favor like this. Though the proposal did not appall and outrage me, I was nonetheless quite astonished that the question of money had been brought up so abruptly.
>
> "How much money do we have to pledge?" I asked.
>
> "The going rate when asking for a major favor is usually five hundred million yen."
>
> I was now faced with the problem of whether to make a payment to Japan's highest government office. Sensing my hesitation. Okubo reiterated, "If you wish to be successful in selling the aircraft, you would do well to pledge five hundred million yen."

Lockheed made this payment and similar payments and was successful in selling planes to the Japanese.

The Lockheed case and similar cases led Congress to enact the **Foreign Corrupt Practices Act of 1977** (15 U.S.C. § 78m). This act, as amended, makes it a crime for U.S. companies to bribe a foreign official, a foreign political party official, or a candidate for foreign political office. The payment of a bribe does not violate the act if the payment was lawful under the written laws of the foreign country in which it was paid, however.

1. Did Lockheed act morally in making the payments? Did it violate the ethical principles dominant in the United States? In Japan?
2. Did the fact that U.S. law did not make the payments unlawful at the time they were made justify them?
3. Should economic factors (e.g., jobs) outweigh ethics? Explain.

Moral Minimum

moral minimum
A theory of social responsibility that says a corporation's duty is to make a profit while avoiding harm to others.

Some proponents of corporate social responsibility argue that a corporation's duty is to *make a profit while avoiding causing harm to others.* This theory of social responsibility is called the **moral minimum.** Under this theory, as long as business avoids or corrects the social injury it causes, it has met its duty of social responsibility. For instance, a corporation that pollutes the waters and then compensates those whom it injures has met its moral minimum duty of social responsibility.

The legislative and judicial branches of government have established laws that enforce the moral minimum of social responsibility on corporations. Occupational safety laws establish minimum safety standards for protecting employees from injuries in the workplace. Consumer protection laws establish safety requirements for products and make manufacturers and sellers liable for injuries caused by defective products. Other laws establish similar minimum standards of conduct for business in other areas.

Business Brief
Many people do not buy tuna because the tuna nets also catch dolphins. Is this socially responsible behavior? Should someone care about the tuna?

Stakeholder Interest

stakeholder interest
A theory of social responsibility that says a corporation must consider the effects its actions have on persons other than its stockholders.

Businesses have relationships with all sorts of people other than their stockholders, including employees, suppliers, customers, creditors, and the local community. Under the **stakeholder interest** theory of social responsibility, a corporation must consider the effects its actions have on these *other stakeholders.* For example, a corporation would violate the stakeholder interest theory if it viewed employees solely as a means of maximizing stockholder wealth.

This theory is criticized because it is difficult to harmonize the conflicting interests of stakeholders. For example, in deciding whether to close a plant, certain stakeholders may benefit (e.g., stockholders and creditors) while other stakeholders may not (e.g., current employees and the local community).

Ethical Perspective

JOE CAMEL EXHALES

Since his introduction in 1988, Joe Camel has become a cartoon icon. R.J. Reynolds Tobacco Company splashed the cool camel on billboards, in magazines, and in other media across the country. Joe Camel could be seen riding motorcycles, playing pool, jamming with a jazz band, and hanging out with his female comrade, Josephine Camel. Joe and his buddies were used to promote R.J. Reynolds' Camel cigarettes.

Why would a cigarette company choose a cartoon character to advertise its cigarettes? In December 1991, San Francisco attorney Janet Mangini thought she knew when she read results of three studies that were published by the *Journal of the American Medical Association (JAMA).* These studies concluded that the popularity of Camel cigarettes had increased 66-fold with teen smokers in the three years following the introduction of Joe Camel. Joe Camel was right up there with Mickey Mouse in recognition by children. Mangini concluded that R.J. Reynolds had gone after children and teens to promote cigarette smoking, so she decided to go after Joe Camel.

But how do you successfully sue a monolith like R.J. Reynolds? Mangini enlisted the lawyers at the five-attorney firm of Bushnell, Caplan & Fielding in San Francisco to help brainstorm the attack on R.J. Reynolds. They were aware that traditional personal-injury lawsuits against cigarette companies had not been successful, so they turned to California Business and Professional Code Section 17200 et seq., also known as the Unfair Business Practices Act. This act permits any individual to act as a private attorney general for the state of California and to file a suit against a company to halt a harmful or unfair business practice. Mangini and the small law firm knew they were in over their heads in taking on R.J. Reynolds, so they sought the help of Milberg Weiss, a large law firm in San Diego known for filing shareholder class action lawsuits. Patrick J. Coughlin, a partner at the firm whose father was a smoker who had died of lung cancer, became interested. Milberg Weiss joined the team and agreed to shoulder 80 percent of the work. Mangini became the plaintiff. The law firms filed an unfair business practices lawsuit against R.J. Reynolds to try to eliminate Joe Camel and his cohorts.

R.J. Reynolds's first action was to try to get the case thrown out of court. The company argued that Joe Camel was protected by the Free Speech Clause of the First Amendment of the U.S. Constitution and that the state law claims were preempted by the Federal Cigarette Labeling and Advertising Act, the act that requires warnings on cigarette packages. The trial court threw the case out of court, but the California Supreme Court reinstated the case, stating

> *The targeting of minors is oppressive and unscrupulous, in that it exploits minors by luring them into an unhealthy and potentially life-threatening addiction before they have achieved the maturity necessary to make an informed decision whether to take up smoking despite its health risks.*

R.J. Reynolds appealed to the U.S. Supreme Court, which declined to hear the case. With the courtroom door finally open, the real work began. The plaintiff's attorneys reviewed more than 30 million pages of documents over a five-year period. The evidence showed that R.J. Reynolds's advertising was aimed at the "youth market." Company reports outlined the importance of attracting "presmokers," aged 12 to 24, and stated that "young adult smokers are the only source of replacement smokers." R.J. Reynolds's market research reported: "Less than one-third of smokers start after age 18. Only 5 percent of smokers start after age 24."

Twenty states, the U.S. Surgeon General, the American Lung Association, the American Cancer Society, and the American Heart Association backed Mangini's claim against R.J. Reynolds. Eventually, the parties entered into settlement negotiations. The plaintiff and her lawyers agreed that there was no amount of money they would accept to settle the case; Joe Camel must go! With mounting pressure and facing trial, in July 1997, R.J. Reynolds formally agreed to terminate the Joe Camel campaign across the nation. [*Mangini v. R.J. Reynolds Tobacco Company*]

1. Do you think that the Joe Camel advertising campaign was aimed at children and teenagers?
2. Do you believe that there was a link between the advertising campaign and smoking? If there was no link, do you think that R.J. Reynolds would have spent millions of dollars on the advertising campaign?
3. Should R.J. Reynolds have been permitted to continue the Joe Camel advertising campaign under free-speech rights of the First Amendment of the U.S. Constitution? Why or why not?
4. Do you think Joe Camel will surface again when people who began smoking between 1988 and 1997 sue R.J. Reynolds in the future?

Corporate Citizenship

The **corporate citizenship** theory of social responsibility argues that business has a *responsibility to do good*. That is, business is responsible for helping to solve social problems that it did little, if anything, to cause. For example, under this theory corporations owe a duty to subsidize schools and help educate children.

This theory contends that corporations owe a duty to promote the same social goals as do individual members of society. Proponents of the "do good" theory argue that corporations owe a debt to society to make it a better place and that this duty arises because of the social power bestowed on them. That is, this social power is a gift from society and should be used to good ends.

A major criticism of this theory is that the duty of a corporation to do good cannot be expanded beyond certain limits. There is always some social problem that needs to be addressed, and corporate funds are limited. Further, if this theory were taken to its maximum limit, potential shareholders might be reluctant to invest in corporations.

corporate citizenship
A theory of social responsibility that says a business has a responsibility to do good.

Business Brief
Patagonia, the Ventura, California-based outdoor apparel company, gives the greater of 10 percent of annual pretax profits or 1 percent of sales to environmental causes.

Contemporary Business Application

THE *EXXON VALDEZ*: DID BUSINESS RUN AGROUND ON ENVIRONMENTAL PROTECTION?

On March 12, 1989, the *Exxon Valdez*, a supertanker carrying more than 11 million gallons of oil, left a terminal near Valdez, Alaska. The weather was calm as it moved through Prince William Sound toward the open waters of the Pacific Ocean and its final destination, an oil refinery located along the West

(box continues)

Coast. The ship was under the command of Captain Hazelwood, who was alleged to have been drinking prior to leaving shore. He had a known history of alcohol abuse and had lost his driver's license for drunk driving. At about midnight, Captain Hazelwood left the bridge of the ship for his cabin, instructing third mate Gregory Cousins to steer clear of any ice in the water.

After passing the Busby Island light, Cousins steered the ship too far south until it was almost on Bligh Reef. When he realized the situation, he called for a hard-right rudder—but it was too late to prevent the ship from crashing into a submerged rock at 12 knots and going aground. The hull of the ship ripped open in eight places, sending millions of gallons of oil surging into the water of the sound.

Alyeska is a service company formed by the seven oil companies with North Slope interests that is primarily responsible for responding to such disasters. When Alyeska's ranking executive was called at home within half an hour of the grounding, he dispatched a subordinate to check things out and rolled over and went back to sleep. The plan that Alyeska had previously submitted to the Alaskan government stipulated that it could reach any disaster site with equipment to deal with the problem within five hours. In actuality, one Alyeska barge reached the site 14 hours after the spill. The millions of gallons of oil overwhelmed the handful of oil skimmers that Alyeska had brought. Over the next few days, a 100-square-mile oil slick formed and moved toward the Alaskan shore. Eventually, 1,100 miles of shoreline were soaked by the oil.

Eventually, Exxon mobilized and paid more than 12,000 people for the cleanup effort—many of them local residents who could no longer fish because of the spill. The company bagged the dead animals, birds, and fish that lay strewn on the shore and used booms and skimmers to try to contain the oil spill. They "treated"—the government would not let Exxon use the word *cleaned*—the 1,100 miles of Alaskan

coastline affected by the spill. Roughly 230 otters were saved at a cost of about $40,000 each.

Approximately six months after the spring accident had occurred, Exxon departed Alaska just ahead of the autumn storms, proclaiming that it had met its social responsibility in addressing the disaster. Of the 11-million-gallon sea of petroleum, 2.6 million gallons were recovered and returned to Exxon. The *Exxon Valdez* was refloated, towed away, repaired, and renamed by Exxon.

The final toll of the disaster was 30,000 to 40,000 dead birds, more than 1,000 dead otters, and unknown numbers of dead fish and other wildlife. And the future? Only time will tell the ultimate effect that the oil spill has had on the ecological system of Prince William Sound and the birds, otters, fish, and other wildlife—and humans—who depend on it.

The wreck of the *Exxon Valdez* has been the greatest environmental disaster in American history to date, and the most expensive. Exxon spent over $1.2 billion on cleanup efforts alone, of which $400 million will be reimbursed by insurance companies. (Exxon's net income for 1989 was more than $5.2 billion.) If Exxon expected thanks for its efforts, it got shredded credit cards and lawsuits. Exxon now faces hundreds of civil lawsuits by fishers and others seeking damages caused by the oil spill.

But the biggest hit was yet to come. In June 1994, an Alaskan jury found that Exxon and Mr. Hazelwood had acted recklessly in causing the accident. The jury awarded 15,000 fishers $287 million in compensatory damages and ordered Exxon to pay $5 billion in punitive damages to all plaintiffs in *Exxon Valdez* cases. The jury also assessed $5,000 in punitive damages against Mr. Hazelwood.

1. Who should be assigned the moral responsibility for the *Exxon Valdez* catastrophe?
2. Did Exxon meet its duty of social responsibility in this case?
3. Should corporations adopt and adhere to the *Valdez* Principles? (See Exhibit 8.2)

---

*E*XHIBIT 8.2   *The* Valdez *Principles*

Recently, a group called the Coalition for Environmentally Responsible Economies (CERES), which takes its acronym from the Roman goddess of agriculture, released a set of 10 commitments it calls the **Valdez Principles** *to guide corporations regarding their social responsibility to protect the environment.*

INTRODUCTION By adopting these principles, we publicly affirm our belief that corporations and their shareholders have a direct responsibility for the environment. We believe that corporations must conduct their business as responsible stewards of the environment and seek profits only in a manner that leaves the Earth healthy and safe. We believe that corporations must not compromise the ability of future generations to sustain their needs.

We recognize this to be a long-term commitment to update our practices continually in light of advances in technology and new understandings in health and environmental science. We intend to make consistent, measurable progress in implementing these principles and to apply them wherever we operate throughout the world.

1. **Protection of the Biosphere** We will minimize and strive to eliminate the release of any pollutant that may cause environmental damage to the air, water or earth or its inhabitants. We will safeguard habitats in rivers, lakes, wetlands, coastal zones, and oceans and will minimize contributing to the greenhouse effect, depletion of the ozone layer, acid rain, or smog.

2. **Sustainable Use of Natural Resources** We will make sustainable use of renewable natural resources, such as water, soils, and forests. We will conserve nonrenewable natural resources through efficient use and careful planning. We will protect wildlife habitats, open spaces, and wilderness, while preserving biodiversity.

3. **Reduction and Disposal of Waste** We will minimize the creation of waste, especially hazardous waste, and whenever possible recycle materials. We will dispose of all wastes through safe and responsible methods.

4. **Wise Use of Energy** We will make every effort to use environmentally safe and sustainable energy sources to meet our needs. We will invest in improved energy efficiency and conservation in our operations. We will maximize the energy efficiency of products we produce or sell.

5. **Risk Reduction** We will minimize the environmental, health, and safety risks to our employees and the communities in which we operate by employing safe technologies and operating procedures and by being constantly prepared for emergencies.

6. **Marketing of Safe Products and Services** We will sell products or services that minimize adverse environmental impacts and that are safe as consumers commonly use them. We will inform consumers of the environmental impacts of our products or services.

7. **Damage Compensation** We will take responsibility for any harm we cause to the environment by making every effort to fully restore the environment and to compensate those persons who are adversely affected.

8. **Disclosure** We will disclose to our employees and to the public incidents relating to our operations that cause environmental harm or pose health or safety hazards. We will disclose potential environmental, health or safety hazards posed by our operations, and we will not take any action against employees who report any condition that creates a danger to the environment or poses health and safety hazards.

9. **Environmental Directors and Managers** At least one member of the board of directors will be a person qualified to represent environmental interests. We will commit management resources to implement these principles, including the funding of an office of vice president for environmental affairs or an equivalent executive position, reporting directly to the CEO, to monitor and report upon our implementation efforts.

10. **Assessment and Annual Audit** We will conduct and make public an annual self-evaluation of our progress in implementing these principles and in complying with all applicable laws and regulations throughout our worldwide operations. We will work toward the timely creation of independent environmental audit procedures which we will complete annually and make available to the public.

CONCEPT SUMMARY   THEORIES OF SOCIAL RESPONSIBILITY

Theory	Social Responsibility
Maximizing profits	To maximize profits for stockholders.
Moral minimum	To avoid causing harm and to compensate for harm caused.
Stakeholder interest	To consider the interests of all stakeholders, including stockholders, employees, customers, suppliers, creditors, and local community.
Corporate citizenship	To do good and solve social problems.

Ethical Perspective

The Corporate Social Audit

It has been suggested that corporate audits should be extended to include not only audits of the financial health of a corporation but also of its moral health. Corporations that conduct social audits

Business Brief
Corporations that conduct social audits will be more apt to prevent unethical and illegal conduct by managers, employees, and agents.

will be more apt to prevent unethical and illegal conduct by managers, employees, and agents. The audit would examine how well employees have adhered to the company's code of ethics and how well the corporation has met its duty of social responsibility. Such audits would focus on the corporation's efforts to promote employment opportunities for members of protected classes, worker safety, environmental protection, consumer protection, and the like. Social audits are not easy. First, it may be hard to conceptualize just what is being audited. Second, it may be difficult to measure results. Despite these fac-

tors, more companies are expected to undertake social audits.

Companies should institute the following procedures when conducting a social audit:

- An independent outside firm should be hired to conduct the audit. This will ensure autonomy and objectivity in conducting the audit.
- The company's personnel should cooperate fully with the auditing firm while the audit is being conducted.
- The auditing firm should report its findings directly to the company's board of directors.
- The results of the audit should be reviewed by the board of directors.
- The board of directors should determine how the company can better meet its duty of social responsibility and can use the audit to implement a program to correct any deficiencies it finds.

E-Commerce & Internet Law

An Outlaw in Cyberspace

In "techie" circles, Kevin D. Mitnick became the underground icon of computer hackers. During a decade's reign, Mitnick terrorized the federal government, universities, and such high-tech companies as Sun Microsystems, Novell Corporation, MCI Communications, Digital Equipment Corporation, and others by breaking into their computer systems. Mitnick used his computer skills to penetrate his victims' computer systems to steal secret information and wreak havoc with their software and data.

Mitnick, a self-taught computer user, has a history of computer-related crime. As a 17-year-old, he was placed on probation for stealing computer manuals from a Pacific Bell Telephone switching center in Los Angeles. Mitnick was next accused of breaking into federal government and military computers in the early 1990s. He has also been accused of breaking into the nation's telephone and cellular telephone networks, stealing thousands of data files and trade secrets from corporate targets, obtaining at least 20,000 credit card numbers of some of the country's richest persons, and sabotaging government, university, and private computer systems around the nation. Mitnick was arrested

and convicted of computer crimes, and served time in prison. Upon release from prison, he was put on probation and placed in a medical program to treat his compulsive addiction to computers, which included a court order to not touch a computer or modem. In 1992, Mitnick dropped out of sight and evaded federal law enforcement officials for several years as he continued a life of computer crime.

Mitnick's undoing came when he broke into the computer of Tsutomu Shimomura, a researcher at the San Diego Supercomputer Center. Shimomura, a cyber sleuth who advises the FBI and major companies on computer and Internet security, made it his crusade to catch the hacker who broke into his computer. Shimomura watched electronically as Mitnick invaded other computers across the country, but he could not physically locate Mitnick because he disguised his whereabouts by breaking into telephone company computers and rerouting all his computer calls. Eventually, Shimomura's patient watching paid off as he traced the electronic burglar to Raleigh, North Carolina. Shimomura flew to Raleigh, where he used a cellular-frequency-direction-finding antenna to locate Mitnick's apartment. The FBI was notified and an arrest warrant was obtained from a judge at his home. At 2:00 A.M., February 15, 1995, the FBI arrested Mitnick at his apartment. Mitnick was placed in jail without bail pending the investigation of his case.

Mitnick's computer crimes spree has been estimated to have cost his victims several hundreds of millions of dollars in losses. Mitnick has not been accused of benefiting financially from his deeds. In 1999, Mitnick entered into a plea agreement with federal prosecutors. U.S. District Court judge Mariana Pfaelzer sentenced Kevin Mitnick to 46 months in prison, including time served,

and ordered him to pay $4,125 in restitution to the companies he victimized. The judge called this a token amount but did not order a larger restitution because she believed Mitnick would not be able to pay more. With time served pending trial, Mitnick was released from prison in January 2000. As part of the sentencing, Mitnick cannot use electronic devices, from PCs to cellular telephones, during an additional probationary period following his release from prison. This sentence brings about the close of one of the most publicized computer crime cases in history. Or has it?

e·biz

WWW *Working the Web*

KPMG U.S.—Business Ethics Practice This site aims to provide a place where business people can turn for guidance on ethical problems that threaten their progress as well as the prosperity of their organizations. Are you looking for ways to measure whether your organization is grounded in sound values such as integrity, respect, trust, and fairness? Try this site for an answer.

Visit at **www.us.kpmg.com/ethics**

Net Impact—New Leaders for Better Business Net Impact has established a communications network that facilitates the exchange of ideas, information, and experiences. Do you want to find out about Net Impact's summer internship program, annual conference, career services, or membership information? Check out this site for this and other information.

Visit at **www.srb.org**

Business for Social Responsibility BSR is an organization that believes that member companies can achieve long term success by implementing policies and practices that honor high ethical standards and meet their responsibilities to all who are impacted by their decisions. It publishes a simple, informative guidebook on social responsibility titled *BSR Social Responsibility Starter Kit*. Check out this site to find out what companies are members.

Visit at **www.bsr.org**

Business Ethics Resources on the WWW This site provides information such as corporate and business

association codes of ethics and articles and publications about business ethics. There are also links to other resources.

Visit at **www.ethics.ubc.ca/resources/business.html**

On-Line Journal of Ethics This site is an on-line journal of cutting edge research in the field of business and professional ethics published by the Institute for Business and Professional Ethics at DePaul University.

Visit at **www.depaul.edu/ethics/ojbea.html**

CYBER EXERCISES

1. One part of the KPMG US Business Ethics Practice site is "Business Ethics Resources." One resource is the Markula Center for Applied Ethics at Santa Clara University that publishes an electronic version of *Issues in Ethics* magazine. Who is the editor of *Issues in Ethics*?

e·biz

2. In the "Resource Center" area of Net Impact, find out about internships.

3. Using the Business for Social Responsibility site, find out about the next annual conference.

4. Use the Business Ethics Resources on the WWW site to find the corporate code of ethics for Texas Instruments. When was the Ethics Committee established at Texas Instruments?

5. Randy Richards wrote an article in volume 1, issue 2 of the *On-Line Journal of Ethics* called "Cicero and the Ethics of Honest Business Dealings." Using the *On-Line Journal of Ethics* site, find out where Randy Richards teaches.

CASES AND EXERCISES

ETHICS CASES

8.1. On July 5, 1884, an English yacht sank in a storm off the Cape of Good Hope. Four members of the crew—Dudley, Stephens, Brooks, and Parker—were cast adrift in a small lifeboat 1,600 miles from shore. After three days, they ran out of food and water. On the fourth day they caught a small turtle, on which they fed until the twelfth day. On the eighteenth day, after being without food for a week, Dudley and Stephens proposed that the four sailors draw lots to see who should be killed so that the others could eat his body and live. Brooks refused to draw lots.

Dudley and Stephens then suggested that they kill the boy Parker, who by then was living at the bottom of the boat weak from hunger. Brooks dissented. Dudley and Stephens told Brooks to go to the other end of the boat, which he did. Dudley and Stephens offered a prayer, then slit the boy's throat with a knife. Dudley, Stephens, and Brooks fed on the boy until they were rescued four days later. England sued Dudley and Stephens, charging them with the crime of murder. Did Dudley and Stephens act ethically? What would you have done? Did Brooks act ethically in refusing to participate in the killing but then feeding on the boy? [*The Queen v. Dudley and Stephens*, 14 Q.B.D. 273 (1884)]

8.2. The Johns-Manville Corporation, a profitable company that made a variety of building and other products, was a major producer of asbestos, which was used for insulation in buildings and for a variety of other uses. It has been medically proven that excessive exposure to asbestos causes asbestosis, a fatal lung disease. Thousands of employees of the company and consumers who were exposed to asbestos and contracted this fatal disease sued the company for damages. In 1983, the lawsuits were being filed at the rate of more than 400 per week.

As a response, the company filed for reorganization bankruptcy. It argued that if it did not, an otherwise viable company that provided thousands of jobs and served a useful purpose in this country would be destroyed, and that without the declaration of bankruptcy a few of the plaintiffs who first filed their lawsuits would win awards of hundreds of millions of dollars, leaving nothing for the remainder of the plaintiffs. Under the bankruptcy court's protection, the company was restructured to survive. As part of the release from bankruptcy, the company contributed money to a fund to pay current and future claimants. The fund is not large enough to pay all injured persons the full amount of their claims.

Was it ethical for Johns-Manville to declare bankruptcy? Did it meet its duty of social responsibility in this case? If you were a member of the board of directors of the company, would you have voted to place the company in bankruptcy? Why or why not? [*In re Johns-Manville Corporation*, 36 B.R. 727 (S.D.N.Y. 1984)]

8.3. The A. H. Robbins Company manufactured the Dalkon Shield, an intrauterine device (IUD) used by over 2 million women for contraception during the early 1970s. The device was defectively designed and caused women problems of infection, pelvic inflammatory disease, infertility, and spontaneous abortion, as well as health defects in their children. Thousands of product liability lawsuits were filed against the company by the women and children injured by the Dalkon Shield. The company and its insurers chose to fight these cases aggressively and spent multimillions of dollars in legal fees.

U.S. District Court Judge Miles Lord, who handled many of these cases, called the Dalkon Shield an "instrument of death, mutilation, and disease" and chastised the executives of the company for violating "every ethical precept" of the Hippocratic oath, the medical profession's promise to save lives. Judge Lord stated.

> *Your company in the face of overwhelming evidence denies its guilt and continues its monstrous mischief. You have taken the bottom line as your guiding beacon and the low road as your route. This is corporate irresponsibility at its meanest.*

The company eventually filed for bankruptcy. The U.S. court of appeals censored Judge Lord for being too vocal. Is it ethical for a company to aggressively contest lawsuits that are filed against it even if it knows that it is responsible for the injury?

8.4. The Warner-Lambert Company (Warner-Lambert) has manufactured and distributed Listerine antiseptic mouthwash since 1879. Its formula has never changed. Ever since its introduction, the company has represented Listerine as being beneficial in preventing and curing colds and sore throats. Direct advertising of these claims to consumers began in 1921. In 1971 Warner-Lambert spent $10 million advertising these claims in print media and in television commercials.

In 1972, the Federal Trade Commission (FTC) filed a complaint against Warner-Lambert alleging that the company engaged in false advertising in violation of federal law. Four months of hearings were held before an administrative law judge that produced an evidentiary record of over 4,000 pages of documents from 46 witnesses. In 1975, after examining the evidence, the FTC issued an opinion that held that the company's representations that Listerine prevented and cured colds and sore throats were false. The U.S. court of appeals affirmed.

Did Warner-Lambert act ethically in making its claims for Listerine? What remedy should the court impose on the company? Would making Warner-Lambert cease such advertising be sufficient? [*Warner-Lambert Company v. Federal Trade Commission*, 562 F.2d 749 (1)C. (Cir. 1977)]

8.5. Stanford University is one of the premiere research universities in the country. Stanford has an operating budget of approximately $400 million a year and receives about $175 million a year in direct research funding from the federal government. In addition, the government reimburses the university for certain overhead and indirect costs associated with the research. This amounts to about $85 million a year.

In 1990, a Navy accountant took a close look at Stanford's books and alleged that the university may have overstated overhead and indirect costs associated with research by as much as $200 million during the 1980s. The university provided a house for its president, Donald Kennedy. Some of the expenses charged against overhead for research were (a) $3,000 for a cedar-lined closet at the president's home, (b) $4,000 for the president's 1987 wedding reception, (c) $7,000 in bedsheets and table linens, and (d) $184,000 in depreciation on a yacht donated to Stanford's sailing program. Did the administration of Stanford act ethically in charging these expenditures as overhead against research? What penalty should be assessed?

8.6. In 1977, Reverend Leon H. Sullivan, a Baptist minister from Philadelphia who was also a member of the board of directors of General Motors Corporation, proposed a set of rules to guide American-owned companies doing business in the Republic of South Africa. The Sullivan Principles, as they became known, call for the nonsegregation of races in South Africa. They call for employers to (a) provide equal and fair employment practices for all employees and (b) improve the quality of employees' lives outside the work environment in such areas as housing, schooling, transportation, recreation, and health facilities. The principles also require signatory companies to report regularly and be graded on their conduct in South Africa.

Eventually, the Sullivan Principles were subscribed to by several hundred U.S. corporations with affiliates doing business in South Africa. Concerning the companies that have subscribed to the Sullivan Principles, which of the following theories of social responsibility are they following?

1. Maximizing profits
2. Moral minimum
3. Stakeholder interest
4. Corporate citizenship

To put additional pressure on the government of the Republic of South Africa to end apartheid, in 1987 Reverend Sullivan called for the complete withdrawal of all U.S. companies doing business in or with South Africa. Very few companies agreed to do so. Did companies owe a social duty to withdraw from South Africa?

8.7. In 1974, Kaiser Aluminum & Chemical Corporation (Kaiser) entered into a collective bargaining agreement with the United Steelworkers of America (USWA), a union that represented employees at Kaiser's plants. The agreement contained an affirmative action program to increase the representation of minorities in craft jobs. To enable plants to meet these goals, on-the-job training programs were established to teach unskilled production workers the skills necessary to become craft workers. Assignment to the training program was based on seniority; however, the plan reserved 50 percent of the openings for black employees.

In 1974, 13 craft trainees were selected from Kaiser's Gramercy plant for the training program. Of these, seven were black and six were white. The most senior black selected had less seniority than several white production workers who had applied for the positions but were rejected. Brian Webster, one of the rejected white employees, instituted a class action lawsuit alleging that the affirmative action plan violated Title VII of the Civil Rights Act of 1964, which made it "unlawful to discriminate because of race" in hiring and selecting apprentices for training programs. The U.S. Supreme Court upheld the affirmative action plan in this case. The decision stated,

> *We therefore hold that Title VII's prohibition against racial discrimination does not condemn all private, voluntary, race-conscious affirmative action plans. At the same time, the plan does not unnecessarily trammel the interests of the white employees. Moreover, the plan is a temporary measure; it is not intended to maintain racial balance, but simply to eliminate a manifest racial imbalance.*

Do companies owe a duty of social responsibility to provide affirmative action programs? [*Steelworkers v. Weber*, 443 U.S. 193, 99 S.Ct. 2721, 61 L.Ed.2d 480 (1979)]

8.8. Iroquois Brands, Ltd. (Iroquois), is a Delaware corporation that had $78 million in assets, $141 million in sales, and $6 million in profits in 1984. As part of its business, Iroquois imports pâté de foie gras (goose pâté) from France and sells it in the United States. Iroquois derived only $79,000 in revenues from sales of such pâté. The French producer force-feeds the geese from which the pâté is made. Peter C. Lovenheim, who owns 200 shares of Iroquois common stock, proposed to include a shareholder proposal in Iroquois's annual proxy materials to be sent to shareholders. His proposal criticized the company because the force-feeding caused "undue stress, pain, and suffering" to the geese and requested that shareholders vote to have Iroquois discontinue importing and selling pâté produced by this method.

Iroquois refused to allow the information to be included in its proxy materials. Iroquois asserted that its refusal was based on the fact that Lovenheim's proposal was "not economically significant" and had only "ethical and social" significance. The company reasoned that because corporations are economic entities, only an economic test applied to its activities and it was not subject to an ethical or social responsibility test. Is the company correct, that is, should only an economic test be applied in judging the activities of a corporation? Or should a corporation also be subject to an ethical or social responsibility test? [*Lovenheim v. Iroquois Brands, Ltd.*, 618 F.Supp. 554 (D.C. 1985)]

CRITICAL LEGAL THINKING WRITING ASSIGNMENT

Read Case A.8 in the Case Appendix [*Ramirez v. Plough, Inc.*]. This case is excerpted from the court of appeals opinion. Review and brief the case. In your brief, be sure to answer the following questions.

1. Did Plough, Inc., act ethically in participating in efforts to influence the government to reject mandatory warning labels?

2. Did the company act ethically in voluntarily providing the warning labels? How "voluntary" was its decision?

3. Does a company owe a duty of social responsibility to provide warning labels in foreign languages? If so, under what circumstances?

4. If a causal connection is shown between the use of aspirin and Reye's syndrome, would you find Plough liable for the death of the child? If so, what amount of damages would you award?

NOTES

1. 170 N.W. 668 (Mich. 1919).
2. Milton Friedman. "The Social Responsibility of Business Is to Increase Its Profits," *The New York Times Magazine*, September 13, 1970.

Nature of Traditional and Internet Contracts

The movement of the progressive societies has hitherto been a movement from status to contract.

SIR HENRY MAINE *Ancient Law, Ch. 5*

Chapter Objectives

After studying this chapter, you should be able to

1. Define *contract*.
2. List the elements necessary to form a valid contract.
3. List and describe the sources of contract law.
4. Describe how the Uniform Computer Information Transactions Act applies to Internet contracts.
5. Distinguish between bilateral and unilateral contracts.
6. Describe and distinguish between express and implied-in-fact contracts.
7. Define and distinguish between executed and executory contracts.
8. Describe and distinguish among valid, void, voidable, and unenforceable contracts.
9. Define and describe quasi-contracts.
10. Apply the concept of equity to contracts.

Chapter Contents

Contracts must not be the sports of an idle hour, mere matters of pleasantry and badinage, never intended by the parties to have any serious effect whatever.

*Lord Stowell
Dalrymple v. Dalrymple
(1811)*

legally enforceable contract

If one party fails to perform as promised, the other party can use the court system to enforce the contract and recover damages or other remedy.

Contracts are the basis of many of our daily activities. They provide the means for individuals and businesses to sell and otherwise transfer property, services, and other rights. The purchase of goods, such as books and automobiles, is based on sales contracts; the hiring of employees is based on service contracts; the lease of an apartment is based on a rental contract; the sale of goods and services over the Internet is based on electronic contracts. The list is almost endless. Without enforceable contracts, commerce would collapse.

Contracts are voluntarily entered into by parties. The terms of the contract become *private law* between the parties. One court has stated that "The contract between parties is the law between them and the courts are obliged to give legal effect to such contracts according to the true interests of the parties."[1]

Nevertheless, most contracts are performed without the aid of the court system. This is usually because the parties feel a moral duty to perform as promised. Although some contracts, such as illegal contracts, are not enforceable, most are **legally enforceable.**[2] This means that if a party fails to perform a contract, the other party may call upon the courts to enforce the contract.

This chapter introduces you to the study of traditional and Internet contract law. Such topics as the definition of a contract, requirements for forming a contract, sources of contract law, and the various classifications of contracts are discussed.

DEFINITION OF A CONTRACT

A contract is an agreement that is enforceable by a court of law or equity. A simple and widely recognized definition of a contract is provided by the Restatement (Second) of Contracts: "A contract is a promise or a set of promises for the breach of which the law gives a remedy or the performance of which the law in some way recognizes a duty."[3]

Parties to a Contract

offeror

The party who makes an offer to enter into a contract.

offeree

The party to whom an offer to enter into a contract is made.

Every contract involves at least two parties. The **offeror** is the party who makes an offer to enter into a contract. The **offeree** is the party to whom the offer is made (see Exhibit 9.1). In making an offer, the offeror promises to do—or to refrain from doing—something. The offeree then has the power to create a contract by accepting the offeror's offer. A contract is created if the offer is accepted. No contract is created if the offer is not accepted.

EXHIBIT 9.1   *Parties to a Contract*

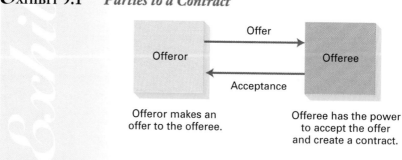

Offeror makes an offer to the offeree.

Offeree has the power to accept the offer and create a contract.

A man must come into a court of equity with clean hands.

*C. B. Eyre
Dering v. Earl of Winchelsea
(1787)*

Elements of a Contract

To be an enforceable contract, the following four basic requirements must be met

1. **Agreement** To have an enforceable contract, there must be an agreement between the parties. This requires an *offer* by the offeror and an *acceptance* of the offer by the offeree. There must be mutual assent by the parties (Chapter 10).

2. **Consideration** The promise must be supported by a bargained-for consideration that is legally sufficient. Gift promises and moral obligations are often not considered supported by valid consideration (Chapter 11).
3. **Contractual Capacity** The parties to a contract must have contractual capacity. Certain parties, such as persons adjudged insane, do not have contractual capacity (Chapter 12).
4. **Lawful Object** The object of the contract must be lawful. Contracts to accomplish illegal objects or contracts that are against public policy are void (Chapter 12).

Defenses to the Enforcement of a Contract

There are two *defenses* that may be raised to the enforcement of contracts. These defenses are as follows.

1. **Genuineness of Assent** The consent of the parties to create a contract must be genuine. If the consent is obtained by duress, undue influence, or fraud, there is no real consent (Chapter 13).
2. **Writing and Form** The law requires that certain contracts be in writing or in a certain form. Failure of these contracts to be in writing or to be in proper form may be raised against the enforcement of the contract (Chapter 14).

Contemporary Business Application

THE EVOLUTION OF THE MODERN LAW OF CONTRACTS

The use of contracts originally developed in ancient times. The common law of contracts developed in England around the fifteenth century. American contract law evolved from the English common law.

At first, the United States adopted a *laissez-faire* approach to the law of contracts. The central theme of this theory was *freedom of contract*. The parties (such as consumers, shopkeepers, farmers, and traders) generally dealt with one another face-to-face, had equal knowledge and bargaining power, and had the opportunity to inspect the goods prior to sale. Contract terms were openly negotiated. There was little, if any, government regulation of the right to contract. This "pure" or **classical law of contracts** produced objective rules, which, in turn, produced certainty and predictability in the enforcement of contracts. It made sense until the Industrial Revolution.

The Industrial Revolution changed many of the underlying assumptions of pure contract law. For example, as large corporations developed and gained control of crucial resources, the traditional balance of parties' bargaining power shifted: Large corporations now had the most power. The chain of distribution for goods also changed because (1) buyers did not have to deal face-to-face with sellers, and (2) there was not always an opportunity to inspect the goods prior to sale.

Eventually, sellers began using *form contracts* that offered their goods to buyers on a take-it-or-leave-it basis. The majority of contracts in this country today are form contracts. Automobile contracts, mortgage contracts, sales contracts for consumer goods, and such are examples of form contracts.

Both federal and state governments enacted statutes intended to protect consumers, creditors, and others from unfair contracts. In addition, the courts began to develop certain common law legal theories that allowed some oppressive or otherwise unjust contracts to be avoided. Today, under this **modern law of contracts**, there is substantial government regulation of the right to contract.

SOURCES OF CONTRACT LAW

There are several sources of contract law in the United States, including the *common law of contracts*, the *Uniform Commercial Code*, and the *Restatement (Second) of Contracts*. The following paragraphs explain these sources in more detail.

The Common Law of Contracts

A major source of contract law is the **common law of contracts**. The common law of contracts developed from early court decisions that became precedent for later decisions. There is a limited federal common law of contracts that applies to contracts made by the

common law of contracts
Contract law developed primarily by state courts.

federal government. The larger and more prevalent body of common law has been developed from state court decisions. Thus, although the general principles remain the same throughout the country, there is some variation from state to state.

The Uniform Commercial Code

Uniform Commercial Code
Comprehensive statutory scheme that includes laws that cover aspects of commercial transactions.

Another major source of contract law is the **Uniform Commercial Code (UCC)**. The UCC, which was first drafted by the National Conference of Commissioners on Uniform State Law in 1952, has been amended several times. Its goal is to create a uniform system of commercial law among the 50 states. The provisions of the UCC normally take precedence over the common law of contracts (Chapters 19–22).

The UCC is divided into nine main articles. Every state has adopted at least part of the UCC.

The Restatement of the Law of Contracts

Restatement of the Law of Contracts
A compilation of model contract law principles drafted by legal scholars. The Restatement is not law.

In 1932, the American Law Institute completed the **Restatement of the Law of Contracts**. The Restatement is a compilation of contract law principles as agreed upon by the drafters. The Restatement, which is currently in its second edition, will be cited in this book as **Restatement (Second) of Contracts**. Note that the Restatement is not law. However, lawyers and judges often refer to it for guidance in contract disputes because of its stature.

E-Commerce & Internet Law

e-biz

THE UNIFORM COMPUTER INFORMATION TRANSACTIONS ACT (UCITA)

The United States and the global economy have witnessed several major economic shifts in the past centuries. In the nineteenth century, agricultural production dominated the economy. In the Agricultural Age, farms dotted local landscapes. Family farmers in Iowa, ranchers in Nebraska, and fishers in Washington sold their products locally as well as to far-away markets such as Chicago, New York, and San Francisco. The common law of contracts was sufficient to handle most of these transactions. At the beginning of the twentieth century, the United States and many major countries of the world moved into the Industrial Age. Manufacturing and the distribution of goods nationally, and eventually internationally, dominated commerce. To handle this goods-oriented economy, Article 2 (Sales) of the Uniform Commercial Code (UCC) was developed. Article 2 prescribes a set of uniform rules for the creation and enforcement of sales of goods contracts. As leasing of goods (e.g., automobiles, equipment) flourished in the later part of the twentieth century, Article 2A (Leases) was added to the UCC to govern the formation and enforcement of lease agreements.

Throughout history, laws have changed to address new commercial situations. The beginning of the twenty-first

century saw its own evolution of commerce and contract law. As we entered the new century, a new economic shift brought the United States and the world into the Information Age. Computer technology and the use of the Internet increased dramatically. By the year 2000, a new form of commerce—**electronic commerce**, or **e-commerce**—was flourishing. All sorts of goods and services are now sold over the Internet. You can purchase automobiles and children's toys, participate in auctions, purchase airline tickets, make hotel reservations, and purchase other goods and services over the Internet. In fact, in the early 2000s, the economic value of computer technology and e-commerce exceeded that of the manufacturing sector of the U.S. economy.

A problem that developed was that the common law of contracts and Articles 2 (Sales) and 2A (Leases) of the UCC did not provide adequate rules for contracting over the Internet and in e-commerce. That is because much of the new cyberspace economy is based on electronic contracts and the licensing of computer information. E-commerce created problems for forming contracts over the Internet, enforcing e-commerce contracts, and providing consumer protection. To address these problems, the National Conference of Commissioners on Uniform

State Laws (a group of lawyers, judges, and legal scholars) drafted the **Uniform Computer Information Transactions Act (UCITA)**.

The UCITA establishes uniform legal rules for the formation and enforcement of electronic contracts and licenses. The UCITA address most of the legal issues that are encountered while conducting e-commerce over the Internet. The UCITA is a model act that does not become law until a state legislature adopts it as a statute for the state. Since its promulgation in July 1999, the UCITA has been adopted in whole or part by many states. Because of the need for uniformity of e-commerce rules, the UCITA is expected to become the basis for the creation and enforcement of cyberspace contracts and licenses. The UCITA is so important that it is covered in Chapter 18 of this book.

CLASSIFICATIONS OF CONTRACTS

There are several types of contracts. Each differs somewhat in formation, enforcement, performance, and discharge. The different types of contracts are discussed in the following paragraphs.

Bilateral and Unilateral Contracts

Contracts are either *bilateral or unilateral*, depending upon what the offeree must do to accept the offeror's offer. The contract is **bilateral** if the offeror's promise is answered with the offeree's promise of acceptance. In other words, a bilateral contract is a "promise for a promise." This exchange of promises creates an enforceable contract. No act of performance is necessary to create a bilateral contract.

A contract is **unilateral** if the offeror's offer can be accepted only by the performance of an act by the offeree. There is no contract until the offeree performs the requested act. An offer to create a unilateral contract cannot be accepted by a promise to perform. It is a "promise for an act."

The language of the offeror's promise must be carefully scrutinized to determine whether it is an offer to create a bilateral or a unilateral contract. If there is any ambiguity as to which it is, it is presumed to be a bilateral contract.

bilateral contract
A contract entered into by way of exchange of promises of the parties; a "promise for a promise."

unilateral contract
A contract in which the offeror's offer can be accepted only by the performance of an act by the offeree; a "promise for an act."

Consider the Following Examples Suppose Mary Douglas, the owner of the Chic Dress Shop, says to Peter Jones, a painter, "If you promise to paint my store by July 1, I will pay you $2,000." Peter promises to do so. A bilateral contract was created at the moment Peter promised to paint the dress shop (a promise for a promise). If Peter fails to paint the store, he can be sued for whatever damages result from his breach of contract. Similarly, Peter can sue Mary if she refuses to pay him after he has performed as promised.

However, if Mary had said, "If you paint my shop by July 1, I will pay you $2,000," the offer would have created a unilateral contract. The offer can be accepted only by the painter's performance of the requested act. If Peter does not paint the shop by July 1, there has been no acceptance and the painter cannot be sued for damages.

Business Brief
Distinguish bilateral from unilateral contracts according to the number of promises involved. Bilateral is "promise for promise." Unilateral is "promise for act."

Incomplete or Partial Performance Problems can arise if the offeror of a unilateral contract attempts to revoke an offer after the offeree has begun performance. Generally, an offer to create a unilateral contract can be revoked by the offeror anytime prior to the offeree's performance of the requested act. However, the offer cannot be revoked if the offeree has begun or has substantially completed performance. Suppose Alan Matthews tells Sherry Levine that he will pay her $5,000 if she finishes the Boston Marathon. Alan cannot revoke the offer once Sherry starts running the marathon.

Entrepreneur and the Law

READY FOR LOVE? NOT BEFORE YOU'VE BEEN NDA'D

You're out on a date and your partner whispers sweet nothings in your ear. What's a guy or girl to do? Quick, whip out a **nondisclosure agreement**—or **NDA** as they are called—and have the other side sign it before responding. That is what many entrepreneurs and techies are doing, having their boyfriends, girlfriends, family members, friends, and others sign NDAs before revealing anything about what they are doing.

NDAs have been around for a long time, and traditionally have been used among lawyers, investment bankers, and others involved in secret takeovers and other large corporate deals. NDAs swear the signatory to secrecy about confidential ideas, trade secrets, and other nonpublic information revealed by the party proffering the NDA. But today many entrepreneurs, particularly those in high-tech industries, are handing out NDAs as fast as business cards. NDAs serve a purpose in that it protects a person who has a great idea (or so they think) and wants to share it with a potential partner, investor, lawyer, or investment banker, but wants an assurance that the recipient of the information will not steal or reveal the information to anyone else.

NDAs are enforceable contracts, so if someone violates it the disclosing party can sue the breaching party for damages. Bill Gates of Microsoft has plumbers and other persons who work on his house sign NDAs. Sabeer Bhatia, the founder of Hotmail, collected more than 400 NDAs in two years before selling his company to Microsoft for $400 million.

Although it may not be hard to get some people to sign NDAs, others balk. Some friends and relatives refuse to sign NDAs thrust on them because they present an aura of distrust. And it is particularly insulting to sign an NDA and then to hear a hairpin idea from the disclosing party. Industry bigwigs—venture capitalists, securities analysts, and successful technology companies—routinely refuse to sign NDAs because they see too many similar ideas and do not want their tongues tied by any single one. NDAs will continue to increase in use, however. So the next time you are at a party and you ask someone what they do, don't be surprised if you are NDA'd!

Express and Implied-in-Fact Contracts

An *actual contract* (as distinguished from a quasi-contract, which is discussed later in this chapter) may be either *express* or *implied-in-fact*.

Express contracts are stated in oral or written words. Examples of such contracts include an oral agreement to purchase a neighbor's bicycle and a written agreement to buy an automobile from a dealership.

Implied-in-fact contracts are implied from the conduct of the parties. Implied-in-fact contracts leave more room for questions. The following elements must be established to create an implied-in-fact contract:

express contract
An agreement that is expressed in written or oral words.

implied-in-fact contract
A contract where agreement between parties has been inferred from their conduct.

1. The plaintiff provided property or services to the defendant.
2. The plaintiff expected to be paid by the defendant for the property or services and did not provide the property or services gratuitously.
3. The defendant was given an opportunity to reject the property or services provided by the plaintiff but failed to do so.

Entrepreneur and the Law

OWNER OF SCRABBLE SPELLED "L-O-S-E-R"

Implied-in-fact contracts are implied from the conduct of the parties. Consider the following case.

Selchow & Richter (S&R) owns the trademark to the famous board game *Scrabble*. Mark Landsberg wrote a book on strategy for winning at Scrabble and contacted S&R to request permission to use the Scrabble trademark. In response, S&R requested a copy of Landsberg's manuscript, which he provided. After prolonged negotiations between the parties regarding the possibility of S&R's publication of the manuscript broke off, S&R brought out its own Scrabble strategy book. No express contract was ever entered into between Landsberg and S&R. Landsberg sued S&R and its subsidiary, Scrabble Crossword Game Players, Inc., for damages for breach of an implied contract.

   Was there an implied-in-fact contract between the parties?

   The district court and appellate court held that an implied-in-fact contract had been formed between the parties and that the contract was breached by the defendants. The court noted that the law allows for recovery for the breach of an implied-in-fact contract when the recipient of a valuable idea accepts and uses the information without paying for it even though he knows that compensation is expected. Here, the court found (1) that Landsberg's disclosure of his manuscript was confidential and for the limited purpose of obtaining approval for the use of the Scrabble mark, and (2) given Landsberg's express intention to exploit his manuscript commercially, the defendants' use of any portion of it was conditioned on payment. Landsberg was awarded $440,300 damages.

Objective Theory of Contracts

The **objective theory of contracts** holds that the intent to enter into an express or implied-in-fact contract is judged by the **reasonable person standard**. Would a hypothetical reasonable person conclude that the parties intended to create a contract after considering (1) the words and conduct of the parties and (2) the surrounding circumstances? For example, no valid contract results from offers that are made in jest, anger, or undue excitement.

   Under the objective theory of contracts, the subjective intent of a party to enter into a contract is irrelevant. The following case illustrates the application of the objective theory of contracts.

objective theory of contracts

A theory that says the intent to contract is judged by the reasonable person standard and not by the subjective intent of the parties.

City of Everett, Washington v. Mitchell
631 P.2d 366 (1981)
Supreme Court of Washington

CASE 9.1

FACTS
Al and Rosemary Mitchell owned a small secondhand store. On August 12, 1978, the Mitchells attended Alexander's Auction, where they frequently shopped to obtain merchandise for their business. While at the auction, they purchased a used safe for $50. They were told by the auctioneer that the inside compartment of the safe was locked and that no key could be found to unlock it. The safe was part of the Sumstad Estate. Several days after the auction, the Mitchells took the safe to a locksmith to have the locked compartment opened. When the locksmith opened the compartment he found $32,207 in cash. The locksmith called the City of Everett Police, who impounded the money. The City of Everett commenced an interpleader action against the Sumstad Estate and the Mitchells. The trial court entered summary judgment in favor of Sumstad Estate. The court of appeals affirmed. The Mitchells appealed.

ISSUE
Was a contract formed between the seller and the buyer of the safe?

IN THE LANGUAGE OF THE COURT
Dolliver, Justice The objective manifestation theory of contracts lays stress on the outward manifestation of assent made by each party to the other. The subjective intention of the parties is irrelevant. A contract is an obligation attached by the mere force of law to certain acts of the parties, usually words, which ordinarily accompany and represent a known intent. If, however, it were proved by twenty bishops that either party, when he used the words intended something else than the usual meaning which the law imposes upon them, he would still be held.

   The Mitchells were aware of the rule of the auction that all sales were final. Furthermore, the auctioneer made no statement reserving rights to any contents of the safe to the Estate. Under these cir-

(case continues)

cumstances, we hold reasonable persons would conclude that the auctioneer manifested an objective intent to sell the safe and its contents and that the parties mutually assented to enter into that sale of the safe and the contents of the locked compartment.

DECISION AND REMEDY

The state supreme court held that under the objective theory of contracts, a contract was formed between the seller and the buyer of the safe. The court reversed the court of appeals grant of summary judgment to the Sumstad Estate and remanded the case to the trial court for entry of judgment in favor of the Mitchells.

Case Questions

Critical Legal Thinking Does the objective theory of contracts work? Is it easy to define a "reasonable person"?

Ethics Did the seller of the safe act ethically in alleging that no contract had been made with the Mitchells?

Business Application What do you think the economic consequences to businesses would be if the courts recognized a subjective theory of contracts?

Quasi-Contracts (Implied-in-Law Contracts)

quasi- or implied-in-law contract

An equitable doctrine whereby a court may award monetary damages to a plaintiff for providing work or services to a defendant even though no actual contract existed. The doctrine is intended to prevent unjust enrichment and unjust detriment.

The equitable doctrine of **quasi-contract**, also called **implied-in-law contract**, allows a court to award monetary damages to a plaintiff for providing work or services to a defendant even though no actual contract existed between the parties. Recovery generally is based on the reasonable value of the services received by the defendant.

This doctrine is intended to prevent *unjust enrichment* and *unjust detriment*. It does not apply where there is an enforceable contract between the parties.

A quasi-contract is imposed where (1) one person confers a benefit on another who retains the benefit and (2) it would be unjust not to require that person to pay for the benefit received. The following case illustrates the doctrine of quasi-contract.

Dines v. Liberty Mutual Insurance Company
548 N.E.2d 1268 (1990)
Appeals Court of Massachusetts

CASE 9.2

FACTS

Roger J. Dines is engaged in the business of towing and storing vehicles. On October 15, 1985, the state police recovered a stolen trailer and ordered it stored at Dines's facility. The rightful owner of the trailer, the Liberty Mutual Insurance Company (Liberty), learned that it was stored at Dines's facility on January 7, 1986, but it did nothing to recover its property. Dines discovered that Liberty owned the trailer on March 11, 1986. On March 14, 1986, Dines gave written notice to Liberty that its trailer was at his storage facility. He enclosed an invoice for storage fees computed at $20 per day. Liberty refused to pay the charges. On March 11, 1987, Liberty sued to replevy the trailer. Dines released the trailer to Liberty on March 18, 1987, but sued Liberty to recover $10,400 in storage fees. The trial court found an implied-in-law contract and awarded Dines $5,000, which represented the value of the trailer. Both parties appealed.

ISSUE

Do the facts and circumstances justify the imposition of an implied-in-law contract?

IN THE LANGUAGE OF THE COURT

Smith, Justice   The judge's finding that a contract implied-in-law or a quasi-contract existed between the parties was not erroneous. It has long been recognized that one who has involuntarily received another's property has the right to recover compensation for the care and expense of keeping and preserving it. The underlying basis for awarding damages in a quasi-contract case is unjust enrichment of one party and unjust detriment to the other party. Here, once the property was recovered by the police, it was stored in a safe facility, preventing vandalism. The defendant Liberty Mutual Insurance Company benefited from the storage of its property.

The defendant's argument that an owner of a vehicle, stored in the circumstances of the present case, does not incur storage costs until receipt of notice of the vehicle's location is not sound. The benefit to the owner starts from the first day of storage. In these circumstances, the amount of the plaintiff's recovery, however, is limited to the fair market value of the stored item. If the plaintiff were allowed to recover more than the fair market value of the trailer, he would then have more than the benefit conferred on the defendant.

DECISION AND REMEDY

The appeals court held that the facts and circumstances of the case justified the imposition of an implied-in-law contract. Affirmed.

Case Questions

Critical Legal Thinking   What public policy underlies the doctrine of implied-in-law contract?

Ethics   When should Liberty have notified Dines that he was holding its property? Was it ethical for Liberty to refuse to pay the storage charges?

Business Application   Should a business be made to pay contract damages when it has not entered into an express contract with the plaintiff?

Formal and Informal Contracts

Formal Contracts   Contracts may be classified as either *formal or informal.* **Formal contracts** are contracts that require a special form or method of creation. The Restatement (Second) of Contracts identifies the following types of formal contracts.[4]

- **Contracts Under Seal**   This type of contract is one to which a seal (usually a wax seal) is attached. Although no state currently requires contracts to be under seal, a few states provide that no consideration is necessary if a contract is made under seal.
- **Recognizances**   In a recognizance, a party acknowledges in court that he or she will pay a specified sum of money if a certain event occurs. A bail bond is an example of a recognizance.
- **Negotiable Instruments**   Negotiable instruments, which include checks, drafts, notes, and certificates of deposit, are special forms of contracts recognized by the UCC. They require a special form and language for their creation and must meet certain requirements for their transfer.
- **Letters of Credit**   A letter of credit is an agreement by the issuer of the letter to pay a sum of money upon the receipt of an invoice and bill of lading. Letters of credit are governed by the UCC.

Informal Contracts   All contracts that do not qualify as formal contracts are called **informal contracts** (or **simple contracts**). The term is a misnomer. Valid informal contracts (e.g., leases, sales contracts, service contracts) are fully enforceable and may be sued upon if breached. They are called informal contracts only because no special form or method is required for their creation.

formal contract
A contract that requires a special form or method of creation.

Business Brief
Originally, only contracts under seal were recognized as valid contracts in England. Around 1600, the common law courts of England began to enforce simple contracts that were not made under seal.

informal contract
A contract that is not formal. Valid informal contracts are fully enforceable and may be sued upon if breached.

A lady looking at a store window on Rodeo Drive in Beverly Hills, California. Businesses offer a variety of goods and services for sale or lease.

valid contract

A contract that meets all of the essential elements to establish a contract; a contract that is enforceable by at least one of the parties.

void contract

A contract that has no legal effect; a nullity.

voidable contract

A contract where one or both parties have the option to avoid their contractual obligations. If a contract is avoided, both parties are released from their contractual obligations.

unenforceable contract

A contract where the essential elements to create a valid contract are met, but there is some legal defense to the enforcement of the contract.

Valid, Void, Voidable, and Unenforceable Contracts

A **valid contract** is one that meets all of the essential elements to establish a contract. In other words, it must (1) consist of an agreement between the parties, (2) be supported by legally sufficient consideration, (3) be between parties with contractual capacity, and (4) accomplish a lawful object. Valid contracts are enforceable by at least one of the parties.

A **void contract** is one that has no legal effect. It is as if no contract had ever been created. For example, a contract to commit a crime is void. If a contract is void, neither party is obligated to perform and neither party can enforce the contract.

A **voidable contract** is one where at least one party has the *option* to avoid his or her contractual obligations. If the contract is avoided, both parties are released from their obligations under the contract. If the party with the option chooses to ratify the contract, both parties must fully perform their obligations. With certain exceptions, contracts may be voided by minors; insane persons; intoxicated persons; persons acting under duress, undue influence, or fraud; and cases involving mutual mistake.

An **unenforceable contract** is one where there is some legal defense to the enforcement of the contract. For example, if a contract is required to be in writing under the Statute of Frauds but is not, the contract is unenforceable. The parties may voluntarily perform a contract that is unenforceable.

E-Commerce & Internet Law

CLICK-WRAP LICENSES

e·biz

In the past, most business and consumer contracts consisted of written agreements signed by both parties. With the advent of the Internet, many on-line contracts no longer fit this traditional mode. Take **click-wrap licenses**, for example. A click-wrap license is a contract used by many software companies to sell their software over the Internet or in physical packages where the software is later installed on a computer. The software company, called the *licensor*, typically displays a series of dialogue boxes on the computer screen that states the terms of the agreement before the software is downloaded or installed by the potential licensee. The terms of a software click-wrap license are typically not negotiable, and the *licensee* (the person who is granted the license) indicates his or her acceptance by clicking on a prompt button on the screen labeled "I accept" or "I agree." Click-wrap licenses contain terms of the agreement, disclaimers of warranties, guarantees for the protection of trademarks and trade secrets, and other provisions that would normally be contained in a paper license. Click-wrap agreements provide a fast, inexpensive, and convenient way for licensors to mass market their software to users without requiring paper contracts or physical signatures.

A question recently presented to the courts is whether click-wrap licenses are enforceable since they lack paper and signatures of traditional contracts. The courts have applied the general principle of the Uniform Commercial Code Article 2 "Sales" that provides that a contract for the sale of goods may be made in any manner sufficient to show agreement, including conduct by both parties that recognize the contract's existence. Courts have also referred to the Restatement (Second) of Contracts § 19, which provides that "manifestation of assent may be made by written or spoken words or by other action." The courts reason by analogy that a party is considered to have manifested her consent to enter into a contract by her physical action of using a mouse to click the "I agree" prompt button for the click-wrap license.

The new **Uniform Computer Information Transactions Act (UCITA)**, which is a proposed model act for conducting e-commerce, specifically provides that a licensee who has the opportunity to review the terms of the license is bound by those terms if the licensee "manifests assent" before or during the party's initial use of or access to the licensor's software [UCITA § 210(a)]. Thus, under the modern e-commerce interpretation of the law of contracts, popular click-wrap licenses are enforceable contracts between software licensors and user licensees.

Executed and Executory Contracts

A completed contract, that is, one that has been fully performed on both sides, is called an **executed contract**. A contract that has not been performed by both sides is called an **executory contract**. Contracts that have been fully performed by one side but not by the other are classified as executory contracts.

executed contract
A contract that has been fully performed on both sides; a completed contract.

Consider These Examples   (1) Suppose Elizabeth Andrews signs a contract to purchase a new Jaguar automobile from Ace Motors. She has not yet paid for the car and Ace Motors has not yet delivered it. This is an executory contract. (2) Assume that the car was paid for, but Ace Motors has not yet delivered the car. Here, the contract is executed by Elizabeth but is executory as to Ace Motors. This is an executory contract. (3) Assume that Ace Motors now delivers the car to Elizabeth. The contract has been fully performed by both parties. It is an executed contract.

executory contract
A contract that has not been fully performed by either or both sides.

CONCEPT SUMMARY   CLASSIFICATIONS OF CONTRACTS

Formation	
	1. **Bilateral contract** A promise for a promise.
	2. **Unilateral contract** A promise for an act.
	3. **Express contract** A contract expressed in oral or written words.
	4. **Implied-in-fact contract** A contract inferred from the conduct of the parties.
	5. **Formal contract** A contract that requires a special form or method of creation.
	6. **Informal contract** A contract that requires no special form or method of creation.
	7. **Quasi-contract** A contract implied by law to prevent unjust enrichment.
Enforceability	
	1. **Valid contract** A contract that meets all of the essential elements to establish a contract.
	2. **Void contract** No contract exists.
	3. **Voidable contract** A party has the option of voiding or enforcing the contract.
	4. **Unenforceable contract** A contract that cannot be enforced because of a legal defense.
Performance	
	1. **Executed contract** A contract that is fully performed on both sides.
	2. **Executory contract** A contract that is not fully performed by one or both parties.

EQUITY

Recall that two separate courts developed in England, a court of law and a chancery court (or court of equity). The equity courts developed a set of maxims based on fairness, equality, moral rights, and natural law that were applied in settling disputes. **Equity** was resorted to when (1) an award of money damages "at law" would not be the proper remedy or (2) fairness required the application of equitable principles. Today, in most states of the United States, the courts of law and equity have been merged into one court. In an action "in equity" the judge decides the equitable issue; there is no right to a jury trial in an equitable action. The doctrine of equity is sometimes applied in contract cases.

equity
A doctrine that permits judges to make decisions based on fairness, equality, moral rights, and natural law.

Ethical Perspective _____

EQUITY TO THE RESCUE

The courts usually interpret a valid contract as a solemn promise to perform. This view of the sanctity of a contract can cause an ethical conflict. Consider the following case.

In 1975, a landlord leased a motel he owned to lessees for a 10-year period. The lessees had an option to extend the lease for an additional 10 years, commencing on March 1, 1985. To do so, they had to give written notice to the landlord on or before December 1, 1984. The lease provided for forfeiture of all furniture, fixtures, and equipment installed by the lessees, free of any liens, upon termination of the lease.

From 1975 to 1985, the lessees devoted most of their assets and a great deal of their energy building up the business. During this time, they transformed a disheveled, unrated motel into a AAA three-star operation. With the landlord's knowledge, the lessees made extensive long-term improvements that greatly increased the value of both the property and the business. The landlord knew that the lessees had obtained long-term financing for the improvements that would extend well beyond the first 10-year term of the lease. The landlord also knew that the only source of income the lessees had to pay for these improvements was the income generated from the motel business. The lessees told the landlord in a conversation that they intended to extend the lease.

The lessees had instructed their accountant to timely exercise the option by December 1, 1984. Despite reminders from the lessees, the accountant failed to give the written notice by December 1, 1984. On December 13, 1984, as soon as they discovered the mistake, the lessees personally delivered written notice of renewal of the option to the landlord, who rejected it as late and instituted a lawsuit for unlawful detainer to evict the lessees.

The trial and appellate courts held in favor of the lessees. They rejected the landlord's argument for the strict adherence to the deadline for giving notice of renewal of the lease. Instead, the courts granted **equitable relief** and permitted the late renewal notice. The court reasoned that "there is only minimal delay in giving notice, the harm to the lessor is slight, and the hardship to the lessee is severe." [*Romasanta v. Mitton*, 234 Cal.Rptr. 729 (Cal.App. 1987)]

1. Did the landlord act ethically in this case?
2. Should the court have applied equity and saved the lessees from their mistake? Or should they have been held to the terms of the lease?

International Perspective _____

THE UNITED NATIONS CONVENTION ON CONTRACTS FOR THE INTERNATIONAL SALE OF GOODS

The United Nations Convention on Contracts for the International Sale of Goods (CISG) came into effect on January 1, 1988, climaxing more than 50 years of negotiations. The CISG supersedes two earlier conventions, the Convention Relative to a Uniform Law on the International Sale of Goods (ULIS) and the Convention Relating to a Uniform Law on the Formation of Contracts for the International Sale of Goods (ULF).

Neither the ULIS nor the ULF was widely adopted because both were drafted without the participation of the Third World or the Eastern bloc. The CISG, on the other hand, is the work of more than 60 countries and several international organizations. Many of its provisions are remarkably similar to the American Uniform Commercial Code, for example. It incorporates rules from all the major legal systems. It has, accordingly, received widespread support from developed, developing, and communist countries. Countries that have adopted it include Argentina, Austria, China, Egypt, Finland, France, Hungary, Italy, Mexico, Sweden, Syria, and the United States. Because the United States has ratified the CISG, Americans engaged in sales overseas need to be aware of the CISG.

The CISG applies to contracts for the international sale of goods. That is, the buyer and seller must have their places of business in different countries. Additionally, either (1) both of the nations must be parties to the convention, or (2) the contract specifies that the CISG controls. The contracting parties may agree to exclude (i.e., opt out of) or modify its application. In the United States, such a provision would be honored.

E-Commerce & Internet Law

Encryption Technology Unlocked for Export

Encryption technology permits a computer user to basically put a lock around its computer information to protect it from being discovered by others. Encryption technology is like a lock on a house: Without the lock in place unwanted persons can easily enter the house and steal its contents; with the lock in place it is more difficult to enter and take the house's contents. Encryption software serves a similar function in that it lets a computer user scramble information so that only those who have the encryption code can enter the database and discover the information.

Software companies in the United States led the development of encryption technology. For years, however, the U.S. government permitted American software companies to sell its encryption software domestically but prohibited the export of the most powerful encryption technology to foreigners. The U.S. government worried that powerful encryption and data-scrambling technology would fall into the hands of criminals and terrorists who would use it to protect their illegal and clandestine activities. Based on this fear, the Clinton Administration issued an executive order that prohibited the export of much of the most powerful encryption technology developed in the United States. These export restrictions remained in effect during most of the 1990s.

In September 1999, after much lobbying by software companies located in the United States, the Clinton Administration changed its export policy to allow the export of the most powerful American-made encryption technology. The export rule was changed because criminals and terrorists could obtain similar data-scrambling technology from software producers in other countries. Therefore the American policy prohibiting the export of encryption technology to foreigners was no longer effective. The Clinton Administration's export controls on encryption technology were lifted for all countries except Iran, Iraq, Syria, Sudan, North Korea, and Cuba, countries that have a history of terrorist activities.

Working the Web

Lawschool.org Do you want to find some free outlines to help you study contracts? Then you might want to check out Lawschool.org. Here you will find course and bar outlines galore.

Visit at **www.lawschool.org**

USALAW USALAW, sponsored by a Florida law firm, has been providing legal information to the Internet for several years. It has many interesting features including articles about contract law.

Visit at **www.usalaw.com**

FindLaw FindLaw is a search engine that will help you find lots of legal information including information on contracts. In it, you can find documents like the Uniform Commercial Code and articles from journals about contract law. Cases, opinions, statutes, codes, law schools, law firms, consultants, experts, government resources, forms, software, law reviews, and legal associations are accessible from this site.

Visit at **www.findlaw.com**

Cornell Law School Legal Information Institute
Cornell Law School Legal Information Institute maintains a site that provides links to federal materials, state materials, and other key Internet sites on contracts.

Visit at **www.law.cornell.edu**

Cyber Exercises

1. Use Lawschool.org to find a contracts outline.

2. Using USALAW, find an article by Morris Silberman called *Avoiding Contract Lawsuits*.

3. Using the FindLaw search engine, find materials on contracts.

4. Using the Cornell Law School Legal Information Institute Web site, find out if your state has adopted the Uniform Commercial Code.

CASES AND EXERCISES

CRITICAL LEGAL THINKING CASES

9.1. On January 23, 1974, G. S. Adams, Jr., vice president of the Washington Bank & Trust Co., met with Bruce Bickham. An agreement was reached whereby Bickham agreed to do his personal and corporate banking business with the bank and the bank agreed to loan Bickham money at 7½ percent interest per annum. Bickham would have 10 years to repay the loans. From January 1974 to September 1976, the bank made several loans to Bickham at 7½ percent interest. In September 1976, Adams resigned from the bank. The bank then notified Bickham that general economic changes made it necessary to charge a higher rate of interest on both outstanding and new loans. Bickham sued the bank for breach of contract. Was the contract a bilateral or a unilateral contract? Does Bickham win? [*Bickham v. Washington Bank & Trust Company*, 515 So.2d 457 (La.App. 1987)]

9.2. From October 1964 through May 1970, Lee Marvin, an actor, lived with Michelle Marvin. They were not married. In May 1970, Lee Marvin compelled Michelle Marvin to leave his household. He continued to support her until November 1971 but thereafter refused to provide further support. During their time together, Lee Marvin earned substantial income and acquired property, including motion-picture rights worth over $1 million. Michelle Marvin brought an action against Lee Marvin, alleging that an implied-in-fact contract existed between them and that she was entitled to half of the property they had acquired while living together. She claimed that she had given up a lucrative career as an entertainer and singer to be a full-time companion, homemaker, housekeeper, and cook. Can an implied-in-fact contract result from conduct of unmarried persons who live together? [*Marvin v. Marvin*, 557 P.2d 106 (Cal. 1976)]

ETHICS CASES

9.3. On Sunday, October 6, 1974, the Lewiston Lodge of Elks sponsored a golf tournament at the Fairlawn Country Club in Poland, Maine. For promotional purposes, Marcel Motors, an automobile dealership, agreed to give any golfer who shot a hole-in-one a new 1974 Dodge Colt. Fliers advertising the tournament were posted in the Elks Club and sent to potential participants. On the day of the tournament, the 1974 Dodge Colt was parked near the clubhouse with one of the posters conspicuously displayed on the vehicle. Alphee Chenard, Jr., who had seen the promotional literature regarding the hole-in-one offer, registered for the tournament and paid the requisite entrance fee. While playing the thirteenth hole of the golf course, and in the presence of the other members of his foursome, Chenard shot a hole-in-one. When Marcel Motors refused to tender the automobile, Chenard sued for breach of contract. Was the contract a bilateral or a unilateral contract? Does Chenard win? Was it ethical for Marcel Motors to refuse to give the automobile to Chenard? [*Chenard v. Marcel Motors*, 387 A.2d 596 (Maine 1978)]

9.4. Loren Vranich, a doctor practicing under the corporate name, Family Health Care, P.C., entered into a written employment contract to hire Dennis Winkel. The contract provided for an annual salary, insurance benefits, and other employment benefits. Another doctor, Dr. Quan, also practiced with Dr. Vranich. About nine months later, when Dr. Quan left the practice, Vranich and Winkel entered into an oral modification of their written contract whereby Winkel was to receive a higher salary and a profit-sharing bonus. During the next year Winkel received the increased salary. However, a disagreement arose, and Winkel sued to recover the profit-sharing bonus. Under Montana law, a written contract can be altered only in writing or by an executed oral agreement. Dr. Vranich argued that the contract could not be enforced because it was not in writing. Does Winkel receive the profit-sharing bonus? Did Dr. Vranich act ethically in raising the defense that the contract was not in writing? [*Winkel v. Family Health Care, P.C.*, 668 P.2d 208 (Mont. 1983)]

CRITICAL LEGAL THINKING WRITING ASSIGNMENT

Read Case A.9 in the Case Appendix [*Mark Realty, Inc. v. Rogness*]. This case is excerpted from the appellate court's opinion. Review and brief the case. In your brief, be sure to answer the following questions.

1. Who is the plaintiff? Who is the defendant?
2. Why did it make a difference if the court found the contract to be unilateral or bilateral? Who would win in each situation?

3. Which party did the appellate court find in favor of? What evidence did the court cite in reaching its conclusion?

4. How might an owner of property protect him- or herself from paying a broker's commission if the owner sold the property him- or herself?

NOTES

1. Rebstock v. Birthright Oil & Gas Co., 406 So.2d 636 (La.App. 1981).
2. Restatement (Second) of Contracts, § 1.
3. *Ibid.*
4. Restatement (Second) of Contracts, § 6.

Agreement

"When I use a word," Humpty Dumpty said, in rather a scornful tone, "it means just what I choose it to mean—neither more nor less."

"The question is," said Alice, "whether you can make words mean so many different things."

"The question is," said Humpty Dumpty, "which is to be master—that's all."

LEWIS CARROLL
Alice's Adventures in Wonderland (1865)

Chapter Objectives

After studying this chapter, you should be able to

1. Define *offer* and *acceptance*.
2. Describe the requirements of an offer.
3. Identify the terms that can be implied in a contract.
4. Describe the special offers of advertisements, rewards, and auctions.
5. Describe on-line auctions.
6. Describe how offers are terminated by action of the parties.
7. Define *counteroffer* and describe its effects.
8. Define *option contract*.
9. Describe how computer shrinkwrap licenses are enforceable.
10. Apply the mailbox rule.

Chapter Contents

Contracts are voluntary agreements between the parties; that is, one party makes an offer that is accepted by the other party. Without *mutual assent*, there is no contract. Assent may be expressly evidenced by the oral or written words of the parties or implied from the conduct of the parties. This chapter discusses offer and acceptance.

A contract is a mutual promise.

William Paley
The Principles of Moral and
Political Philosophy (1784)

AGREEMENT

Agreement is the manifestation by two or more persons of the substance of a contract. It requires an *offer* and an *acceptance*. The process of reaching an agreement usually proceeds as follows: Prior to entering into a contract, the parties may engage in preliminary negotiations about price, time of performance, and such. At some point during these negotiations, one party makes an *offer*. The person who makes the offer is called the **offeror**, and the person to whom the offer is made is called the **offeree**. The offer sets forth the terms under which the offeror is willing to enter into the contract. The offeree has the power to create an agreement by accepting the offer.

agreement
The manifestation by two or more persons of the substance of a contract.

offeror
The party who makes an offer.

offeree
The party to whom an offer has been made.

REQUIREMENTS OF AN OFFER

Section 24 of the Restatement (Second) of Contracts defines an **offer** as: "The manifestation of willingness to enter into a bargain, so made as to justify another person in understanding that his assent to that bargain is invited and will conclude it." The following three elements are required for an offer to be effective.

1. The offeror must *objectively intend* to be bound by the offer.
2. The terms of the offer must be definite or reasonably *certain*.
3. The offer must be *communicated* to the offeree.

offer
The manifestation of willingness to enter into a bargain, so made as to justify another person in understanding that his or her assent to that bargain is invited and will conclude it.

Objective Intent

The intent to enter into a contract is determined using the **objective theory of contracts**, that is, whether a reasonable person viewing the circumstances would conclude that the parties intended to be legally bound. Subjective intent is irrelevant. Therefore, no valid contract results from preliminary negotiations; from offers made in jest, anger, or undue excitement; or from offers that are an expression of opinion.

objective theory of contracts
A theory that says the intent to contract is judged by the reasonable person standard and not by the subjective intent of the parties.

Consider These Examples A question such as "Are you interested in selling your building for $2 million?" is not an offer. It is an invitation to make an offer or an invitation to negotiate. However, the statement "I will buy your building for $2 million" is a valid offer because it indicates the offeror's present intent to contract.

Suppose the owner of company A has lunch with the owner of company B. In the course of their conversation, company A's owner exclaims in frustration, "For $2 I'd sell the whole computer division!" A valid contract cannot result from that offer.

A lawyer who tells his or her client that he or she thinks the lawsuit will result in an award of $100,000 cannot be sued for the difference if the trial jury awards only $50,000. The lawyer's opinion is not an enforceable promise.

If a man will improvidently bind himself up by a voluntary deed, and not reserve a liberty to himself by a power of revocation, this court will not loose the fetters he hath put upon himself, but he must lie down under his own folly.

Lord Nottingham, L.C.
Villers v. Beaumont (1682)

Business Brief
It is always best to expressly state all the essential terms in the contract. This practice will prevent many lawsuits.

Definiteness of Terms

The terms of an offer must be clear enough for the offeree to be able to decide whether to accept or reject the terms of the offer. If the terms are indefinite, the courts cannot enforce the contract or determine an appropriate remedy for its breach.

Generally, an offer (and contract) must contain the following terms: (1) identification of the parties, (2) identification of the subject matter and quantity, (3) consideration to be paid, and (4) time of performance. Complex contracts usually state additional terms.

Implied Terms The common law of contracts required an exact specification of contract terms. If one essential term was omitted, the courts would hold that no contract had been made. This rule was inflexible.

The modern law of contracts is more lenient. The Restatement (Second) of Contracts merely requires that the terms of the offer be *reasonably certain*. Accordingly, the court can supply a missing term if a reasonable term can be implied.[1] The definition of *reasonable* depends on the circumstances. Terms that are supplied in this way are called **implied terms**.

Generally, time of performance can be implied. Price can be implied if there is a market or source from which to determine the price of the item or service (e.g., "blue book" for an automobile price, New York Stock Exchange for a stock price).

The parties or subject matter of the contract usually cannot be implied if an item or service is unique or personal—such as the construction of a house or the performance of a professional sports contract.

implied term

A term in a contract that can reasonably be supplied by the courts.

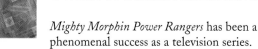

Contemporary Business Application

OWNER OF MIGHTY MORPHIN POWER RANGERS BATTLES LOGO DESIGNER

Mighty Morphin Power Rangers has been a phenomenal success as a television series. The Power Rangers have battled to save the universe from all sorts of diabolical plots and bad guys. They are also featured in a profitable line of toys and garments bearing the Power Rangers' logo. The Power Rangers' name and logo are known to millions of children and their parents worldwide. The claim of ownership of the logo for the Power Rangers ended up in a battle itself, this time in a courtroom.

David Dees is a designer who works as d/b/a David Dees Illustration. Saban Entertainment, Inc. (Saban), which owns the copyright and trademark to Power Ranger figures and the name "Power Ranger," hired Dees as an independent contractor to design a logo for the Power Rangers. The contract signed by the parties was entitled "Work-for-Hire/Independent Contractor Agreement." The contract was drafted by Saban with the help of its attorneys; Dees signed the agreement without the represen-

tation of legal counsel. Dees designed the logo currently used for the Power Rangers and was paid $250 to transfer his copyright ownership in the logo. Subsequently, Dees sued Saban to recover damages for copyright and trademark infringement. Saban defended, arguing that a contract is a contract is a contract, and Dees was bound by the agreement he had signed.

The trial court agreed with Saban, finding that the "Work-for-Hire/Independent Contractor Agreement" was an enforceable contract between the parties and that Dees had transferred his ownership interests in the logo to Saban. Dees appealed. The court of appeals affirmed the judgment for Saban, stating, "The disputed agreement transferred plaintiff's copyright in the Mighty Morphin Power Rangers' logo with as much specificity as the law requires." The court found that a contract is a contract is a contract, at least in this case. Dees's appeal to the U.S. Supreme Court was denied. [*Dees, d/b/a David Dees Illustration v. Saban Entertainment, Inc..* 131 F.3d 146 (1997)]

Communication

An offer cannot be accepted if it is not communicated to the offeree by the offeror or a representative or agent of the offeror. For example, suppose Mr. Jones, the CEO of Ace Corporation, decides to sell a manufacturing division to Baker Corporation and puts the offer in writing. Assume that the offer is on Mr. Jones's desk. Suppose Mr. Griswald, the CFO of Baker Corporation, sees the offer when he visits Mr. Jones and tells Mr. Smith, his CEO about it. The offer is not acceptable by Mr. Smith because Mr. Jones never communicated it to Mr. Smith.

SPECIAL OFFER SITUATIONS

There are several special situations where there is a question whether an offer has been made. Advertisements, rewards, and auctions are examples of such situations.

Advertisements

advertisement

Advertisements for the sale of goods, even at specific prices, generally are treated as *invitations to make an offer*. Catalogs, price lists, quotation sheets, offering circulars, and other sales materials are viewed in the same way. This rule is intended to protect advertiser-sellers from the unwarranted breach of contract suits for nonperformance that would otherwise arise if the seller ran out of the advertised goods.

There is one exception to this rule: An advertisement is considered an offer if it is so definite or specific that it is apparent that the advertiser has the present intent to bind him- or herself to the terms of the advertisement. For example, an automobile dealer's advertisement to sell a "previously owned red 1994 Chrysler LeBaron, serial no. 3210674, $15,000" is an offer. Because the advertisement identifies the exact automobile for sale, the first person to accept the offer owns the automobile.

In the following case, the court had to decide whether an advertisement was a solicitation of an offer or an offer.

> **advertisement**
>
> **A general advertisement is an invitation to make an offer. A specific advertisement is an offer.**

Mesaros v. United States
845 F.2d 1576 (1988)
United States Court of Appeals, Federal Circuit

CASE 10.1

FACTS
In July 1985, the U.S. Congress directed the Secretary of the Treasury to mint and sell a stated number of specially minted commemorative coins to raise funds to restore and renovate the Statue of Liberty. In November and December 1985, the United States Mint mailed advertising materials to persons, including Mary and Anthony C. Mesaros, wife and husband, that described the various types of coins that were to be issued. Payment could be made by check, money order, or credit card. The materials included an order form. Directly above the space provided on this form for the customer's signature was the following: "YES. Please accept my order for the U.S. Liberty Coins I have indicated." On November 26, 1985, Mary Mesaros forwarded to the Mint a credit-card order of $1,675 for certain coins, including the $5 gold coin. All credit-card orders were forwarded by the Mint to Mellon Bank in Pittsburgh, Pennsylvania, for verification. This took a period of time. Meanwhile, cash orders were filled immediately, and orders by check were filled as the checks cleared. The issuance of 500,000 gold coins was exhausted before

Mesaros's credit-card order could be filled. The Mint sent a letter to the Mesaroses notifying them of this fact. The gold coin increased in value by 200 percent within the first few months of 1986. On May 23, 1986, Mary and Anthony C. Mesaros filed a class action lawsuit against the United States seeking in the alternative either damages for breach of contract or a decree of mandamus ordering the United States Mint to deliver the gold coins to the plaintiffs. The district court held for the Mint. The Mesaroses appealed.

ISSUE
Was the United States Mint's advertisement a solicitation of an offer or an offer?

IN THE LANGUAGE OF THE COURT
Skelton, Senior Circuit Judge   The plaintiffs contend that the materials sent to them by the Mint, including the order form, constituted an offer that upon acceptance by the plaintiffs created a binding contract between them and the government whereby the government was bound and obligated to deliver the coins ordered by them. The great weight of authority is against the

(case continues)

plaintiffs. It is well established that materials such as those mailed to prospective customers by the Mint are no more than advertisements or invitations to deal. They are mere notices and solicitations for offers that create no power of acceptance in the recipient.

A basic rule of contracts holds that whether an offer has been made depends on the objective reasonableness of the alleged offeree's belief that the advertisement or solicitation was intended as an offer. Generally, it is considered unreasonable for a person to believe that advertisements and solicitations are offers that bind the advertiser. Otherwise, the advertiser could be bound by an excessive number of contracts requiring delivery of goods far in excess of amounts available. That is particularly true in the instant case where the gold coins were limited to 500,000 by the act of Congress.

We conclude that a thorough reading, construction, and interpretation of the materials sent to the plaintiffs by the Mint makes clear that the contention of the plaintiffs that they reasonably believed the materials were intended as an offer is unreasonable as a matter of law. This is especially true in view of the words "YES, Please accept my order . . ." that were printed on the *credit-card form, which showed that the credit-card order was an offer from the plaintiffs to the Mint to buy the coins, which offer might or might not be accepted by the Mint. Accordingly, the Mint materials were intended solely as solicitations of offers from customers that were subject to acceptance by the Mint before the Mint would be bound by a contract.*

DECISION AND REMEDY

The court of appeals held that the advertising materials sent out by the U.S. Mint was a solicitation to make an offer and not an offer. Therefore, the U.S. Mint wins.

Case Questions

Critical Legal Thinking Should an advertisement be treated as an offer instead of an invitation to make an offer? Why or why not?

Ethics Do you think the Mesaroses acted unethically by suing the U.S. Mint?

Business Application Would it cause any problems for businesses if advertisements were considered offers? Explain.

Rewards

reward

To collect a reward, the offeree must (1) have knowledge of the reward offer prior to completing the requested act and (2) perform the requested act.

An offer to pay a **reward** (e.g., for the return of lost property or for the capture of a criminal) is an offer to form a unilateral contract. To be entitled to collect the reward, the offeree must (1) have knowledge of the reward offer prior to completing the requested act and (2) perform the requested act.

Consider This Example John Anderson accidentally leaves a briefcase containing $500,000 in negotiable bonds on a subway train. He places newspaper ads stating "$5,000 reward for return of briefcase left on a train in Manhattan on January 10, 2000, at approximately 10 A.M. Call 212-555-6789." Helen Smith, who is unaware of the offer, finds the briefcase. She reads the luggage tag containing Mr. Anderson's name, address, and telephone number, and returns the briefcase to him. She is not entitled to the reward money because she did not know about it when she performed the requested act.

Auctions

auction with reserve

Unless expressly stated otherwise, an auction is an auction with reserve; that is, the seller retains the right to refuse the highest bid and withdraw the goods from sale.

auction without reserve

An auction in which the seller expressly gives up his or her right to withdraw the goods from sale and must accept the highest bid.

At an auction, the seller offers goods for sale through an auctioneer. Unless otherwise expressly stated, an auction is considered an **auction with reserve**, that is, it is an invitation to make an offer. The seller retains the right to refuse the highest bid and withdraw the goods from sale. A contract is formed only when the auctioneer strikes the gavel down or indicates acceptance by some other means. The bidder may withdraw his or her bid at any time before the gavel is struck down.

If an auction is expressly announced to be an **auction without reserve**, the participants reverse their roles: The seller is the offeror and the bidders are the offerees. The seller must accept the highest bid and cannot withdraw the goods from sale. If the seller sets a minimum bid, he or she has to sell the item only if the highest bid is equal to or greater than the minimum bid.

CONCEPT SUMMARY   TYPES OF AUCTIONS

Type	Offer
Auction with reserve	No. It is an invitation to make an offer. Because the bidder is the offeror, the seller (the offeree) may refuse to sell the goods. An auction is with reserve unless otherwise stated.
Auction without reserve	Yes. The seller is the offeror and must sell the goods to the highest bidder (the offeree). An auction is without reserve only if it is stipulated as such.

E-Commerce & Internet Law

ON-LINE AUCTIONS

Auctions have been used traditionally to sell horses, antiques, paintings, and other such one-of-a-kind items. A bidder usually had to be physically present at the auction to bid, although some auctions allow telephone bids from prequalified callers. Because of these restrictions, auctions occupied a small portion of the U.S. economy. But no more, thanks to the advent of the Internet.

Led by the giant on-line auction house, eBay, on-line auctions have exploded on the Internet. eBay started as a small on-line auction house that made a market in such consumer collectibles as Pez dispensers, Beanie Babies, and such. After seeing how successful this mode of business was for these items, eBay expanded into a full-service on-line auctioneer. By the year 2000, eBay was offering several million items each day for sale over the Internet. The millions of eBay's cybershoppers are loyal, spending an average of 130 minutes per month at the eBay auction site.

eBay does not own the items it sells. Instead, sellers list the items they want to auction on the eBay site, and buyers bid for the items. The purchase contract is between the cyber seller and the cyber buyer. One of the problems with Internet auctions is that many sellers do not take credit cards, so payment must be made by check or cash. Thus, many transactions takes days, if not weeks, to complete. eBay takes a 6 percent commission on items sold by its on-line auction house. In the beginning of on-line auctions, most of the goods sold were goods that were customarily sold at flea markets, antique stores, and classified advertisements. Today, many businesses have started using eBay auctions to sell their excess inventory or to sell mainstream consumer and business goods. Business sales through on-line auctions now exceed nonbusiness sales.

eBay is now receiving stiff competition from many other on-line auctioneers. The giant e-commerce leader Amazon.com conducts on-line auctions, and many small on-line auction houses specialize in selling jewelry, baseball cards, horses, and other items. eBay itself began offering localized auctions in individual cities for such large items as cars and furniture. Even such traditional auction houses such as Sotheby's, which auctions pricey items such as paintings, jewelry, and antiques, have begun selling through on-line auctions. As proven by the success of eBay and other on-line auctioneers, consumers and businesses have embraced the dynamic pricing and fluid give-and-take of Internet auctions. Auctions, which have been around for most of history, are again giving fixed-priced selling, which has only been around for about 100 years, a run for its money.

e·biz

TERMINATION OF THE OFFER BY ACTION OF THE PARTIES

A valid offer gives the offeree the power to accept the offer and thereby create a contract. This power, however, does not continue indefinitely. An offer can be terminated by the *action of the parties*.

Revocation of the Offer by the Offeror

Under the common law, an offeror may **revoke** (i.e., withdraw) an offer anytime prior to its acceptance by the offeree. Generally, this is so even if the offeror promised to keep the offer open for a longer period of time. The revocation may be (1) communicated to the

revocation
Withdrawal of an offer by the offeror terminates the offer.

offeree by either the offeror or a third party and (2) made by the offeror's express statement (e.g., "I hereby withdraw my offer") or by an act of the offeror that is inconsistent with the offer (e.g., selling the goods to another party). Most states provide that the revocation is not effective until it is actually received by the offeree or the offeree's agent.

Offers made to the public may be revoked by communicating the revocation by the same means used to make the offer. For example, if a reward offer for a lost watch was published in two local newspapers each week for four weeks, notice of revocation must be published in the same newspapers for the same length of time. The revocation is effective against all offerees, even those who saw the reward offer but not the notice of revocation.

Rejection of the Offer by the Offeree

rejection

Express words or conduct by the offeree that rejects an offer. Rejection terminates the offer.

An offer is terminated if the offeree **rejects** it. Any subsequent attempt by the offeree to accept the offer is ineffective and is construed as a new offer that the original offeror (now the offeree) is free to accept or reject. A rejection may be evidenced by the offeree's express words (oral or written) or conduct. Generally, a rejection is not effective until it is actually received by the offeror.

Consider This Example Harriet Jackson, sales manager of IBM Corporation, offers to sell 1,000 computers to Ted Green, purchasing manager of General Motors Corporation, for $250,000. The offer is made on August 1. Mr. Green telephones Ms. Jackson to say that he is not interested. This rejection terminates the offer. If Mr. Green later decides that he wants to purchase the computers, an entirely new contract must be formed.

Counteroffer by the Offeree

counteroffer

A response by an offeree that contains terms and conditions different from or in addition to those of the offer. A counteroffer terminates an offer.

A **counteroffer** by the offeree simultaneously terminates the offeror's offer and creates a new offer. For example, suppose in the prior example Mr. Green says, "I think $250,000 is too high for the computers. I will pay you $200,000." He has made a counteroffer. The original offer is terminated, the counteroffer is a new offer that Ms. Jackson is free to accept or reject. The following case illustrates the effect of counteroffers.

Logan Ranch, Karg Partnership v. Farm Credit Bank of Omaha
472 N.W.2d 704 (1991)
Supreme Court of Nebraska

CASE 10.2

FACTS

Logan Ranch, Karg Partnership (Logan), is a partnership that owned farmland. The Farm Credit Bank of Omaha (FCB) made a loan to Logan and took back a mortgage on the farmland to secure the loan. When Logan ran into financial difficulty in 1984, it deeded the land to FCB in lieu of foreclosure. In 1988, Gene Welsh offered to purchase the land from FCB. Pursuant to the federal Agricultural Credit Act, FCB had to offer the previous owner, Logan, the opportunity to purchase the land first. On March 15, 1988, FCB made an offer to sell the land to Logan for $988,500. The balance of the purchase price (less the deposit) was to be paid when the deed was delivered, and closing was to occur on or before April 15, 1988.

On April 15, 1988, Logan returned FCB's offer, which it had altered by adding the following terms and conditions:

(1) a balance of $150,000 to be paid when the deed is delivered, (2) conditional upon Logan's ability to obtain a loan in the amount of at least $739,650 from NorWest Trust, and (3) the loan to be obtained within 60 days. FCB rejected these terms and made arrangements to sell the land to Welsh. Logan sued for specific performance, alleging that it had accepted FCB's offer. The trial court granted summary judgment to FCB. Logan appealed.

ISSUE

Had Logan accepted FCB's original offer, or had it made a counteroffer?

IN THE LANGUAGE OF THE COURT

Hastings, Chief Justice A definite proposal and an unconditional and absolute acceptance thereof are necessary to establish an express contract. Where the acceptance differs from the offer and is coupled with any condition that varies or adds to the offer, it is not an acceptance; rather, it is a counteroffer.

If the purchase agreement sent by FCB was an offer, the offer was never unconditionally accepted by Logan. Logan did not accept the terms of the offer and in fact added new terms to the offer. The new terms included acceptance conditional upon financing, allowing Logan up to 60 more days to attain financing. The offer was not unconditionally accepted by Logan. The new terms added by Logan were in essence a counteroffer by Logan to FCB. A counteroffer acts as a rejection of the original offer. Logan rejected the offer of FCB to purchase the property; therefore, the remedy of specific performance on the purchase agreement is not available.

If, instead, Logan is requesting specific performance of the purchase agreement as amended by Logan, the remedy of specific performance on this purchase agreement is also not available. The counteroffer made by Logan was never accepted by FCB. Because

there was no acceptance of the counteroffer made by Logan, there is no legally enforceable contract.

DECISION AND REMEDY

The state supreme court held that the additional terms and conditions submitted by Logan constituted a counteroffer. Thus, no contract had been formed between Logan and FCB.

Case Questions

Critical Legal Thinking   Should a counteroffer be considered a rejection of the original offer? Why or why not?

Ethics   Did Logan act ethically in suing FCB in this case?

Business Application   Businesses often engage in protracted negotiations before entering into a contract. Is it sometimes difficult to determine what the terms of an offer are?

Promissory Estoppel

In some cases, the withdrawal of an offer by an offeror may adversely affect an offeree who had changed his or her position in justifiable reliance on the offer. To prevent this type of injustice, the courts have adopted the equitable *doctrine of detrimental reliance*, commonly called **promissory estoppel**.[2]

Consider This Example   ABC Building Corporation is a general contractor that is preparing a bid to construct a new school building for the school district. The company seeks bids from subcontractors to perform portions of the work. Best Plumbing Company, a plumbing subcontractor, submits the lowest bid to ABC Building Corp. to do the plumbing work. ABC incorporates Best Plumbing's bid in its bid to the school district. ABC is awarded the contract to build the school. Best Plumbing attempts to revoke its offer to do the plumbing work, but ABC cannot find another plumbing contractor to do the work at the same low price. In this case, ABC detrimentally relied on Best Plumbing's offer. Best Plumbing would be prevented from withdrawing its offer under the doctrine of promissory estoppel.

promissory estoppel
An equitable doctrine that prevents the withdrawal of an offer by an offeror if it will adversely affect an offeree who has adjusted his or her position in justifiable reliance on the offer.

Entrepreneur and the Law

OPTION CONTRACTS

An offeree can prevent the offeror from revoking his or her offer by paying the offeror compensation to keep the offer open for an agreed-upon period of time. This is called an **option contract**. In other words, the offeror agrees not to sell the property to anyone but the offeree during the option period. The death or incompetency of either party does not terminate an option contract unless it is for the performance of a personal service.

Consider This Example
Anne Mason offers to sell a piece of real estate to Harold Greenberg for $1 million. Mr. Greenberg wants time to make a decision, so he pays Ms. Mason $20,000 to keep her offer open to him for six months. At any time during the option period, Mr. Greenberg may exercise his option and pay Ms. Mason the $1 million purchase price. If he lets the option expire, however, Ms. Mason may keep the $20,000 and sell the property to someone else.

TERMINATION OF THE OFFER BY OPERATION OF LAW

Offers can be terminated by *operation of law* in the following situations.

Destruction of the Subject Matter

Business Brief
Destruction of the subject matter terminates an offer. It does not terminate the contract if the offer has already been accepted, however.

The offer terminates if the subject matter of the offer is destroyed through no fault of either party prior to its acceptance. For example, if a fire destroys an office building that has been listed for sale, the offer automatically terminates.

Death or Incompetency of the Offeror or the Offeree

The death or incompetency of either the offeror or the offeree terminates the offer. Notice of the other party's death or incompetence is not a requirement. Suppose on June 1, Shari Hunter offers to sell her house to Damian Coe for $100,000, providing he decides on or before June 15. Ms. Hunter dies on June 7 before Mr. Coe has made up his mind. Because there is no contract prior to her death, the offer automatically terminates on June 7.

Supervening Illegality

supervening illegality
The enactment of a statute or regulation or court decision that makes the object of an offer illegal. This terminates the offer.

If prior to the acceptance of an offer the object of the offer is made illegal, the offer terminates. This usually occurs when a statute is enacted or a court case is announced that makes the object of the offer illegal. This is called a **supervening illegality**. For example, suppose City Bank offers to loan ABC Corporation $5 million at an 18 percent interest rate. Prior to ABC's acceptance of the offer, the state legislature enacts a statute that sets a usury interest rate of 12 percent. City Bank's offer to ABC Corporation was automatically terminated when the usury statute became effective.

Lapse of Time

Business Brief
An offer terminates when a stated time period expires. If no time is stated, an offer terminates after a reasonable time.

The offer may state that it is effective only until a certain date. Unless otherwise stated, the time period begins to run when the offer is actually received by the offeree and terminates when the stated time period expires. Statements such as "This offer is good for 10 days" and "This offer must be accepted by January 1, 2002" are examples of such notices. If no time is stated in the offer, the offer terminates after a "reasonable time" dictated by the circumstances. Thus, a reasonable time to accept an offer to purchase stock traded on a national stock exchange may be a few moments, but a reasonable time to accept an offer to purchase a house may be a few days. Unless otherwise stated, an offer made face-to-face or during a telephone call usually expires after the conversation.

ACCEPTANCE

acceptance
A manifestation of assent by the offeree to the terms of the offer in a manner invited or required by the offer as measured by the objective theory of contracts.

Acceptance is a manifestation of assent by the offeree to the terms of the offer in a manner invited or required by the offer as measured by the objective theory of contracts.[3] Recall that generally (1) unilateral contracts can be accepted only by the offeree's performance of the required act and (2) a bilateral contract can be accepted by an offeree who promises to perform (or where permitted, by performance of) the requested act.

Who Can Accept the Offer?

Only the offeree has the legal power to accept an offer and create a contract. Third persons do not usually have the power to accept an offer. If an offer is made individually to two or more persons, each has the power to accept the offer. Once an offeree accepts the offer, though, it terminates as to the other offerees. An offer that is made to two or more persons jointly must be accepted jointly.

Unequivocal Acceptance

The offeree's acceptance must be *unequivocal*. The **mirror image rule** requires the offeree to accept the offeror's terms. Generally, a "grumbling acceptance" is a legal acceptance. For example, a response such as "Okay, I'll take the car, but I sure wish you would make me a better deal" creates an enforceable contract. An acceptance is equivocal if certain conditions are added to the acceptance. For example, suppose the offeree had responded, "I accept, but only if you repaint the car red." There is no acceptance in this case.

mirror image rule
States that in order for there to be an acceptance, the offeree must accept the terms as stated in the offer.

Trees Reflected in Water. *The common law of contracts follows the mirror image rule of contracting. A contract is made if the offeree accepts the terms offered by the offeror.*

Silence as Acceptance

Silence usually is not considered acceptance even if the offeror states that it is. This rule is intended to protect offerees from being legally bound to offers because they failed to respond. Nevertheless, silence *does* constitute acceptance in the following situations:

1. The offeree has indicated that silence means assent. (For example, "If you do not hear from me by Friday, ship the order.")
2. The offeree signed an agreement indicating continuing acceptance of delivery until further notification. Book-of-the-month club memberships are examples of such acceptances.
3. Prior dealings between the parties indicate that silence means acceptance. For example, a fish wholesaler who delivers 30 pounds of fish to a restaurant each Friday for several years and is paid for the fish can continue the deliveries with expectation of payment until notified otherwise by the restaurant.
4. The offeree takes the benefit of goods or services provided by the offeror even though he or she (a) has an opportunity to reject the goods or services but fails to do so and (b) knows the offeror expects to be compensated. For example, a homeowner who stands idly by and watches a painter whom he or she has not hired mistakenly paint his or her house owes the painter for the work.

E-Commerce & Internet Law

COMPUTER SHRINKWRAP LICENSES AND CONTRACTS ENFORCEABLE

Although around for centuries, sales of goods through the mail reached new heights with the sale of computer hardware and software through the Internet. One only has to pick up the telephone or log onto the computer to order thousands of dollars of computer hardware and software. Computer hardware usually *(box continues)*

e-biz

arrives via mail or overnight carrier (United Parcel Service) within a few days, whereas software can arrive the same way or downloaded from your computer. Also in the box, or on the computer, is the contract, either a license agreement in the case of most software or a sales contract in the case of most computer equipment. These licenses or contracts contain the terms upon which the licensor or seller is willing to license or sell the goods to the user. The user usually has some stated period of time, often 30 days, to accept or reject the goods based on the license or contract terms. One issue has been presented to the courts by these types of licenses and sales: Are the terms of the previously unseen license or sales contract valid and enforceable? This issue was addressed by the court in the following two cases.

In *ProCD, Incorporated v. Ziedenberg*, ProCD had spent over $10 million to develop a database of names called SelectPhone. ProCD sells this database to both commercial and consumer users who are licensed to use the information in seeking customers. Matthew Zeidenberg purchased a version of SelectPhone for $150 but then offered it for sale over the Internet at a lower price than ProCD charged. ProCD sued Ziedenberg for violating its license agreement, which prohibited the resale of the data. Ziedenberg countered that the license agreement did not apply because it was included in the software box and that he had not had the opportunity to read it before buying the software. The trial court sided with Ziedenberg and held that the "shrinkwrap license"—so called because retail software packages are covered in plastic or cellophane—was not enforceable. ProCD appealed.

In the second case, *Hill v. Gateway 2000, Inc.*, Rich and Enza Hill purchased a Gateway computer by telephoning Gateway and ordering the computer. The computer arrived in a box, and the Hills unpacked the computer and began using it. The Hills failed to read the sales contract that was enclosed in the box. This contract contained an arbitration clause stating that customers had 30 days in which to return the computer; if they did not, they therefore accepted the computer and any complaints thereafter would be settled by arbitration. After more than 30 days, the Hills filed a class action lawsuit against Gateway, alleging that Gateway had engaged in wire fraud and mail fraud and had violated federal racketeering laws. Gateway moved for arbitration, but the Hills argued that the sales contract was unenforceable against them because they had not had the opportunity to read it before they purchased the computer. The trial court agreed with the Hills and allowed their lawsuit against Gateway to proceed. Gateway appealed.

In these two decisions, the court of appeals had to address an issue of first impression: Are licenses and contracts inside software boxes and computer equipment boxes enforceable against the purchaser? In each of these two cases the court answered yes. The court noted that modern commercial transactions would be hindered if such contracts and licenses were not recognized as enforceable. The court found that with the "accept-or-return" nature of these agreements, the purchaser or licensee could read and accept the terms of the offer or could return the goods. Therefore, potential licensees or purchasers had adequate protection against contracts they did not want to accept; they could return the goods and not accept them. The court of appeals held that both Ziedenberg and the Hills were bound by the license and sales contract they received in the boxes from ProCD and Gateway, respectively. [*ProCD, Incorporated v. Ziedenberg*, 86 F.3d 1447 (1996); *Hill v. Gateway 2000, Inc.*, 105 F.3d 1147 (1997)]

Time and Mode of Acceptance

Contract law establishes the following rules concerning the time and mode of acceptance.

Mailbox Rule   Under the common law of contracts, acceptance of a bilateral contract occurs when the offeree *dispatches* the acceptance by an authorized means of communication. This rule is called the **acceptance-upon-dispatch rule** or, more commonly, the **mailbox rule**. Under this rule, the acceptance is effective when it is dispatched even if it is lost in transmission. If an offeree first dispatches a rejection and then sends an acceptance, the mailbox rule does not apply to the acceptance.[4]

The problem of lost acceptances can be minimized by expressly altering the mailbox rule. The offeror can do this by stating in the offer that acceptance is effective only upon actual receipt of the acceptance. In the following case, the court enforced the mailbox rule.

mailbox rule

A rule that states that an acceptance is effective when it is dispatched, even if it is lost in transmission.

e·biz

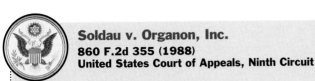

CASE 10.3

Soldau v. Organon, Inc.
860 F.2d 355 (1988)
United States Court of Appeals, Ninth Circuit

FACTS

John Soldau was discharged by his employer, Organon, Inc. (Organon). He received a letter from Organon offering to pay him double the normal severance pay in exchange for a release by Soldau of all claims against Organon regarding the discharge. Soldau signed and dated the release and deposited it in a mailbox outside of a post office. When he returned home, he had received a check from Organon for the increased severance pay. Soldau returned to the post office, persuaded a postal employee to open the mailbox, and retrieved the release. He cashed the severance paycheck and brought this action against Organon, alleging a violation of the federal Age Discrimination in Employment Act. The district court granted summary judgment for Organon. Soldau appealed.

ISSUE

Did Soldau accept the release contract?

IN THE LANGUAGE OF THE COURT

Per Curiam The district court was clearly correct under California law. Under federal as well as California law, Soldau's acceptance was effective when it was mailed. The so-called "mailbox" or "effective when mailed" rule was adopted and followed as federal common law by the Supreme Court prior to Erie R.R. Co. v. Tomkins, *304 U.S. 64 (1938).*

We could not change the rule, and there is no reason to believe the Supreme Court would be inclined to do so. It is almost universally accepted in the common law world. It is enshrined in the Restatement (Second) of Contracts, Section 63(a), and endorsed by the major contract treatises. Commentators are also virtually unanimous in approving the "effective when mailed" rule, pointing to the long history of the rule; its importance in creating certainty for contracting parties; and its essential soundness, on balance, as a means of allocating the risk during the period between the making of the offer and the communication of the acceptance or rejection to the offeror.

DECISION AND REMEDY

The court of appeals applied the "mailbox rule" and found that the acceptance was effective when Soldau first deposited it in the mailbox outside the post office. His later retrieval of the release did not undo his acceptance.

Case Questions

Critical Legal Thinking Should the mailbox rule be changed to place the risk of loss of lost letters on the sender? Or is the present rule the best rule?

Ethics Did Soldau act ethically in this case?

Business Application How can businesses that make offers protect themselves from the risk of loss associated with the mailbox rule?

Proper Dispatch Rule The acceptance must be **properly dispatched**. According to § 66 of the Restatement (Second) of Contracts, the acceptance must be properly addressed, packaged in an appropriate envelope or container, and have prepaid postage or delivery charges. Under common law, if an acceptance is not properly dispatched, it is not effective until it is actually received by the offeror.

Section 67 of the Restatement (Second) of Contracts provides an exception to this rule. Under this exception, an acceptance is effective upon dispatch even if it is sent by an unauthorized means of communication or is improperly dispatched if (1) it is timely sent and (2) the offeror receives the communication within the same time period that a properly transmitted acceptance would have arrived.

Mode of Acceptance Generally, an offeree must accept an offer by an authorized means of communication. The offer can stipulate that acceptance must be by a specified means of communication (e.g., registered mail, telegram). Such stipulation is called **express authorization**. If the offeree uses an unauthorized means of communication to transmit the acceptance, the acceptance is not effective even if it is received by the offeror within the allowed time period because the means of communication was a condition of acceptance.

proper dispatch
An acceptance must be properly addressed, packaged, and posted to fall within the mailbox rule.

express authorization
A stipulation in the offer that says the acceptance must be by a specified means of communication.

implied authorization
Mode of acceptance that is implied from what is customary in similar transactions, usage of trade, or prior dealings between the parties.

Most offers do not expressly specify the means of communication required for acceptance. The common law recognizes certain implied means of communication. **Implied authorization** may be inferred from what is customary in similar transactions, usage of trade, or prior dealings between the parties. Section 30 of the Restatement (Second) of Contracts permits implied authorization "by any medium reasonable in the circumstances."

CONCEPT SUMMARY OFFER AND ACCEPTANCE

Communication by Offeror	Effective When
Offer	Received by offeree
Revocation of offer	Received by offeree
Communication by Offeree	**Effective When**
Rejection of offer	Received by offeror
Counteroffer	Received by offeror
Acceptance of offer	Sent by offeree
Acceptance after previous rejection of offer	Received by offeror

Contemporary Business Application

CONTRACTING BY FAX

Throughout history, contract law, which dates back thousands of years, has struggled to keep pace with inventions that change the way that we communicate—and hence form contracts—with each other. The latest technological challenge to come down the pike is the fax machine, which has quickly become an indispensable means of business communications. Although faxes have revolutionized communications by enabling the instantaneous exchange of written documents between people in distant corners of the world, they have also caused a variety of problems. For example, amidst the flurry of faxes that are sent back and forth during contractual negotiations, it is sometimes difficult to tell exactly if and when the haggling ended and an agreement was reached.

There are several problems that the courts must address concerning faxes as contracts. First, the courts must examine the faxes to determine if an agreement was reached and, if so, the terms of the agreement. Courts examine faxes the same way they examine other documents in determining whether a meeting of the minds was reached. Therefore, it is important for businesses to retain copies of faxes so they can substantiate the contracts they have entered into. Second, to enforce a written contract against a party, his or her signature must appear on the writing. Most court decisions that have addressed the issue have recognized the enforceability of signatures sent by fax. Otherwise, the rules regarding oral contracts apply to faxes.

As faxes are used increasingly to communicate everything from orders for concert tickets to multi-million-dollar orders for equipment, judges and juries will be called upon to read through stacks of faxes to help them decide if disputing parties ever really reached an agreement and, if so, what they really agreed upon.

Working the Web

CataLaw CataLaw is a catalog of catalogs of law on the Internet. It speeds research by arranging all legal and government indexes on the Internet into a single, simple, intuitive metaindex.

Visit at **www.catalaw.com**

LawCrawler The LawCrawler search engine narrows searches to sites with legal information and within specific domains.

Visit at **www.findlaw.com**

Internet Legal Resource Guide The Internet Legal Resource Guide is a categorized index of 3,100 selected Web sites in 238 nations, islands, and territories. In addition, it contains more than 850 locally stored Web pages and files. This site serves as a comprehensive resource of the information available on the Internet concerning law and the legal profession, with emphasis on the United States.

Visit at **www.ilrg.com**

Intralaw Intralaw is a fee-based desktop interface that accesses legal information directly related to a jurisdiction of practice area.

Visit at **www.intralaw.com**

The Law Engine The law engine links to many on-line law sources from a well-organized, single-page format.

Visit at **www.fastsearch.com/law**

CYBER EXERCISES

1–5. Select a recent U.S. Supreme Court case such as *Baker v. GMC*, 522 U.S. 222, 118 S. Ct. 657, 139 L.Ed.2d 580 (1998). Select at least two of the search engines or indexes listed above and try to find the full text of the case.

CASES AND EXERCISES

CRITICAL LEGAL THINKING CASES

10.1. While A. H. and Ida Zehmer, husband and wife, were drinking with W. O. Lucy, Mr. Zehmer made a written offer to sell a 471-acre farm the Zehmers owned to Lucy for $50,000. Zehmer contends that his offer was made in jest and that he only wanted to bluff Lucy into admitting that he did not have $50,000. Instead, Lucy appeared to take the offer seriously, offered $5 to bind the deal, and had Mrs. Zehmer sign it. When the Zehmers refused to perform the contract, Lucy brought this action to compel specific performance of the contract. Is the contract enforceable? [*Lucy v. Zehmer*, 84 S.E.2d 516 (Va.App. 1954)]

10.2. On July 24, 1973, Warren Treece appeared before the Washington State Gambling Commission to testify on an application for a license to distribute punchboards. During his testimony, Treece made the following statement. "I'll put a hundred thousand dollars to anyone to find a crooked board. If they find it, I'll pay it." The next day, Vernon Barnes watched a television news report of the proceeding and heard Treece's statement. He also read a newspaper report of the hearings that quoted Treece's statement. A number of years earlier, while employed as a bartender, Barnes had obtained two fraudulent punchboards. When Barnes presented the two crooked punchboards to Treece and demanded payment of the $100,000, Treece refused to pay. Did Treece's statement form the basis for an enforceable contract? [*Barnes v. Treece*, 549 P.2d 1152 (Wash.App. 1976)]

10.3. Ben Hunt and others operated a farm under the name S.B.H. Farms. Hunt went to McIlroy Bank and Trust and requested a loan to build hog houses, buy livestock, and expand farming operations. The bank agreed to loan S.B.H. Farms $175,000, for which short-term promissory notes were signed by Hunt and the other owners of S.B.H. Farms. At that time, oral discussions were held with the bank officer regarding long-term financing of S.B.H.'s farming operations;

no dollar amount, interest rate, or repayment terms were discussed. When the owners of S.B.H. Farms defaulted on the promissory notes, the bank filed for foreclosure on the farm and other collateral. S.B.H. Farms counterclaimed for $750,000 damages, alleging that the bank breached its oral contract to provide long-term financing. Was there an oral contract for long-term financing? [*Hunt v. McIlroy Bank and Trust*, 616 S.W.2d 759 (Ark.App. 1981)]

10.4. MacDonald Group, Ltd. (MacDonald), is the managing general partner of "Fresno Fashion Square," a regional shopping mall in Fresno, California. The mall has several major anchor tenants and numerous smaller stores and shops, including Edmond's of Fresno, a jeweler. In 1969, Edmond's signed a lease with MacDonald that provided that "there shall not be more than two jewelry stores" located in the mall. In 1978, MacDonald sent Edmond's notice that it intended to expand the mall and lease space to other jewelers. The lease was silent as to the coverage of additional mall space. Edmond's sued MacDonald, arguing that the lease applied to mall additions. Who wins? [*Edmond's of Fresno v. MacDonald Group, Ltd.*, 171 Cal.App.3d 598, 217 Cal.Rptr. 375 (Cal.App. 1985)]

10.5. Howard R. Wright hired John W. Cerdes to construct a home for him at a price of $43,150. The contract was silent regarding the time of completion. Construction was not completed after nine months. At that time, Wright obtained an injunction ordering Cerdes to stop work. Wright hired other contractors to complete the building. Cerdes sued Wright for breach of contract, claiming that he was due the contract price. How long should Cerdes have had to complete the house? [*Cerdes v. Wright*, 408 So.2d 926 (La.App. 1982)]

10.6. On July 31, 1966, Lee Calan Imports, Inc. (Calan Imports) placed an advertisement in the *Chicago Sun-Times* to sell a 1964 Volvo station wagon. Calan Imports had instructed the newspaper to advertise the price of the automobile at $1,795. Instead, through an error of the newspaper and without fault of Calan Imports, the newspaper inserted the price of $1,095 in the advertisement. Christopher D. O'Brien saw the advertisement, visited Calan Imports's showroom and examined the automobile, and stated that he wished to purchase it for the advertised price of $1,095. When Calan Imports refused to sell the automobile at the advertised price, O'Brien brought suit for breach of contract. Did the advertisement constitute a binding offer? [*O'Brien v. Lee Calan Imports, Inc.*, 262 N.E.2d 758 (Ill.App. 1970)]

10.7. Rudy Turilli operated the "Jesse James Museum" at Stanton, Missouri. He contends the man who was shot, killed, and buried as the notorious desperado Jesse James in 1882 was an impostor and that Jesse James lived for many years thereafter under the alias J. Frank Dalton and last lived with Turilli at his museum until the 1950s. On February 27, 1967, Turilli appeared before a nationwide television audience and stated that he would pay $10,000 to anyone who could prove that his statements were wrong. After hearing this offer, Stella James, a relative of Jesse James, produced affidavits of persons related to and acquainted with the Jesse James family constituting evidence that Jesse James was killed as alleged in song and legend on April 3, 1882. When Turilli refused to pay the reward, James sued for breach of contract. Who wins? [*James v. Turilli*, 473 S.W.2d 757 (Mo.App. 1972)]

10.8. ETCO Corporation (ETCO) owned a commercial building located at 1185 Mission Street, San Francisco. On April 22, 1976, ETCO leased commercial premises in the building to Ellen B. Hauer for a period of five years. The lease granted Hauer an option to extend the lease for an additional five years. All the terms and conditions would be the same except the rent, which would be agreed upon "at that time." Hauer gave timely notice to ETCO of her desire to renew the lease. She was paying $955 rent per month at that time. ETCO contended that the new rent should be between $2,500 and $3,000 per month, whereas Hauer contended it should be no more than $1,100 per month. ETCO filed a lawsuit seeking declaratory judgment that the option was unenforceable. Who wins? [*ETCO Corporation v. Hauer*, 161 Cal.App.3d 1154, 208 Cal.Rptr. 118 (Cal.App. 1984)]

10.9. Glende Motor Company (Glende), an automobile dealership that sold new cars, leased premises from certain landlords. In October 1979, fire destroyed part of the leased premises, and Glende restored the leasehold premises. The landlords received payment of insurance proceeds for the fire. Glende sued the landlords to recover the insurance proceeds. On May 7, 1982, 10 days before the trial was to begin, the defendants jointly served on Glende a document entitled "Offer to Compromise Before Trial," which was a settlement offer of $190,000. On May 16, Glende agreed to the amount of the settlement but made it contingent upon the execution of a new lease. On May 17, the defendants notified Glende that they were revoking the settlement offer. Glende thereafter tried to accept the original settlement offer. Has there been a settlement of the lawsuit? [*Glende Motor Company v. Superior Court*, 159 Cal.App.3d 389, 205 Cal.Rptr. 682 (Cal.App. 1984)]

10.10. General Motors Corporation requested bids from contractors to construct a central air-conditioning unit at its

Mesa, Arizona, proving grounds. Burr & Sons Construction Co. (Burr) decided to submit a bid to be the general contractor, and itself requested bids from subcontractors to do some of the work. Corbin-Dykes Electric Company (Corbin-Dykes) submitted a bid to Burr to do the electrical work on the project. Burr incorporated Corbin-Dykes's bid in its own bid to General Motors. When Burr was awarded the General Motors contract, it hired another subcontractor—not Corbin-Dykes—to do the electrical work. Corbin-Dykes sued Burr for breach of contract. Was a contract formed between Corbin-Dykes and Burr? [*Corbin-Dykes Electric Company v. Burr*, 500 P.2d 632 (Ariz.App. 1972)]

10.11. Peter Andrus owned an apartment building that he had insured under a fire insurance policy sold by J.C. Durick Insurance (Durick). Two months prior to the expiration of the policy, Durick notified Andrus that the building should be insured for $48,000 (or 80 percent of the building's value) as required by the insurance company. Andrus replied that (1) he wanted insurance to match the amount of the outstanding mortgage on the building (i.e., $24,000) and (2) if Durick could not sell this insurance, he would go elsewhere. Durick sent a new insurance policy in the face amount of $48,000 with the notation that the policy was automatically accepted unless Andrus notified him to the contrary. Andrus did not reply. However, he did not pay the premiums on the policy. Durick sued Andrus to recover these premiums. Who wins? [*J.C. Durick Insurance v. Andrus*, 424 A.2d 249 (Vt. 1980)]

10.12. William Jenkins and Nathalie Monk owned a building in Sacramento, California. In 1979, they leased the building to Tuneup Masters for five years. The lease provided that Tuneup Masters could extend the lease for an additional five years if it gave written notice of its intention to do so by certified or registered mail at least six months prior to the expiration of the term of the lease, or August 1, 1983.

On July 29, 1983, Larry Selditz, vice president of Tuneup Masters, prepared a letter exercising the option, prepared and sealed an envelope with the letter in it, prepared U.S. Postal Service Form 3800 and affixed the certified mail sticker on the envelope, and had his secretary deliver the envelope to the Postal Service annex located on the ground floor of the office building. Postal personnel occupied the annex only between the hours of 9 and 10 A.M. At the end of each day, between 5 and 5:15 P.M., a postal employee picked up outgoing mail. The letter to the landlords was lost in the mail. The landlords thereafter refused to renew the lease and brought an unlawful detainer action against Tuneup Masters. Was the notice renewing the option effective? [*Jenkins v. Tuneup Masters*, 190 Cal.App.3d 1, 235 Cal.Rptr. 214 (Cal.App. 1987)]

ETHICS CASES

10.13. Kortney Dempsey took a cruise on a ship operated by Norwegian Cruise Line (Norwegian). In general, suits for personal injuries arising out of maritime torts are subject to a three-year statute of limitations. However, Congress permits this period to be reduced to one year by contract. The Norwegian passenger ticket limited the period to one year. Evidence showed that the cruise line ticket contained the notation "Important Notice" in a bright red box at the bottom right-hand corner of each of the first four pages of the ticket. The information in the box stated that certain pages of the ticket contain information that "affect[s] important legal rights." In addition, at the top of page 6 of the ticket, where the terms and conditions begin, it is stated in bold letters: "Passengers are advised to read the terms and conditions of the Passenger Ticket Contract set forth below." The clause at issue, which appears on page 8, clearly provides that suits must be brought within one year of injury.

More than one year after Dempsey had taken the cruise (but within three years), she filed suit against Norwegian seeking damages for an alleged injury suffered while on the cruise. Dempsey asserted that the one-year limitations period had not been reasonably communicated to her. Did Dempsey act ethically in suing when she did? Did Norwegian act ethically in reducing the limitations period to one year? Who wins the lawsuit? [*Dempsey v. Norwegian Cruise Line*, 972 F.2d 998 (9th Cir. 1992)]

10.14. Genaro Munoz owned property that he leased to Goodwest Rubber Corporation (Goodwest) for five years. The lease granted Goodwest the option to buy the property at a fair market value. Goodwest sought to exercise the option to purchase the property and tendered $80,000 to Munoz. When Munoz rejected this offer, Goodwest filed suit seeking specific performance of the option agreement. The court was presented with a single issue for review: Was a price designation of "fair market value" definite enough to support an action for specific performance? Do you think Munoz acted ethically in refusing to honor the option? Who wins? [*Goodwest Rubber Corp. v. Munoz*, 170 C.A.3d 919, 216 Cal.Rptr. 604 (Cal.App. 1985)]

CRITICAL LEGAL THINKING WRITING ASSIGNMENT

Read Case A.10 in the Case Appendix [*Traco, Inc. v. Arrow Glass Co., Inc.*]. This case is excerpted from the appellate court opinion. Review and brief the case. In your brief, be sure to answer the following questions.

1. Who was the plaintiff? Who was the defendant?

2. Was there an express agreement between the parties?

3. What does the doctrine of promissory estoppel provide? Explain.

4. Did the court apply the doctrine of promissory estoppel in this case?

NOTES

1. Restatement (Second) of Contracts, § 204.
2. Section 87(2) of the Restatement (Second) of Contracts states that an offer which the offeror should reasonably expect to induce action or forbearance of a substantial character on the part of the offeree before acceptance and which does induce such action or forbearance is binding as an option contract to the extent necessary to avoid injustice.
3. Restatement (Second) of Contracts, § 50(1).
4. Restatement (Second) of Contracts, § 40.

Consideration

𝒯he law has outgrown its primitive stage of formalism when the precise word was the sovereign talisman, and every slip was fatal. It takes a broader view today. A promise may be lacking, and yet the whole writing may be "instinct with an obligation," imperfectly expressed.

JUSTICE CARDOZO
Wood v. Duff-Gordon, 222 N.Y. 88, 91
(1917)

Chapter Objectives

After studying this chapter, you should be able to

1. Define *consideration*.
2. Define *nominal consideration*.
3. Identify when there is inadequacy of consideration.
4. Define "best efforts" contracts and identify if they are supported by consideration.
5. Describe requirements and output contracts.
6. Analyze whether contracts are lacking in consideration.
7. Define and describe the results of finding illegal consideration.
8. Explain the doctrines of preexisting duty and past consideration.
9. Describe the settlement of claims.
10. Apply the doctrine of promissory estoppel.

Chapter Contents

The concept of *consideration* is firmly embedded in the law of contracts. To be enforceable, a contract must be supported by "consideration," which is broadly defined as something of legal value. Consideration can consist of money, property, the provision of services, the forbearance of a right, or anything else of value. Most contracts that are not supported by consideration are not enforceable. However, the parties may voluntarily perform a contract that is lacking in consideration.

This chapter discusses consideration, promises that lack consideration, and promises that are enforceable without consideration.

CONSIDERATION

consideration
Something of legal value given in exchange for a promise.

Consideration is a necessary element for the existence of a contract. **Consideration** is defined as the thing of value given in exchange for a promise. Consideration can come in many forms. The most common types consist of either a tangible payment (e.g., money or property) or the performance of an act (e.g., providing legal services). Less usual forms of consideration include the forbearance of a legal right (e.g., accepting an out-of-court settlement in exchange for dropping a lawsuit) and noneconomic forms of consideration (e.g., refraining from "drinking, using tobacco, swearing, or playing cards or billiards for money" for a specified time period).[1]

Written contracts are presumed to be supported by consideration. This is a rebuttable presumption that may be overcome by sufficient evidence. A few states provide that contracts made under seal cannot be challenged for lack of consideration.

Consideration consists of two elements: (1) Something of legal value must be given (e.g., either a legal benefit must be received or a legal detriment suffered), and (2) there must be a bargained-for exchange. Each of these is discussed in the paragraphs that follow.

Golden Temple, Kyoto, Japan. International trade is often governed by the laws of nations. The parties can agree as to which country's law will apply by including a choice of law clause in their contract.

Business Brief

The more formal approach to finding consideration has been replaced by a modern definition that considers a contract supported by consideration of either (1) the promisee suffers a legal detriment or (2) the promisor receives a legal benefit.

Legal Value

Something of *legal value* must be given. Under the modern law of contracts, a contract is considered supported by legal value if (1) the promisee suffers a *legal detriment* or (2) the promisor receives a *legal benefit*.

Consider This Example   Suppose the Dallas Cowboys contracts with a tailor to have uniforms made for the team. The tailor completes the uniforms, but the team manager thinks the color is wrong and refuses to allow the team to wear them. Here, there has been no benefit to either the manager or the players. However, the tailor has suffered a legal detriment (time spent making the uniforms). Under the modern rule of contracts, there is sufficiency of consideration and the contract is enforceable.

In the following case, the court had to determine whether a contract was supported by consideration.

Paterek v. Liberty Park of America
465 N.W.2d 342 (1990)
Court of Appeals of Michigan

CASE 11.1

FACTS
Daniel Paterek was a member of an amateur softball team. Before the start of the 1986 softball season, he signed a document entitled "1986 Official Team Roster and Contract" with Liberty Park of America (Liberty), the owner of the softball field where the games were to be played. In the contract, the players acknowledged that softball was a hazardous and dangerous activity and agreed to personally assume all risks of injury. Paterek injured his knee while running to catch a fly ball during one of the games on the field. He sued Liberty for damages, claiming that the field was improperly maintained. Paterek argued that the release agreement was not valid because it was not supported by consideration. The trial court granted Liberty's motion for summary judgment. Paterek appealed.

ISSUE
Were the contract and release agreement supported by adequate consideration?

IN THE LANGUAGE OF THE COURT
Per Curiam   We find no merit in plaintiff's argument that the release was invalid for lack of consideration. Defendant's agreement to allow Daniel Paterek to play softball on its field was adequate consideration because it was (1) a legal detriment, (2) which induced plaintiff's promise to release defendant from liability, and (3) plaintiff's promise to release defendant from liability induced defendant to suffer the detriment.

DECISION AND REMEDY
The appellate court held that the contract and release agreement were supported by consideration and were therefore enforceable. Affirmed.

Case Questions

Critical Legal Thinking   Should contracts be required to be supported by consideration? Why or why not?

Ethics   Was it ethical for Paterek to sign the release agreement and then sue Liberty?

Business Application   Should release agreements be enforced? Do they serve any useful business purpose?

Bargained-for Exchange

To be enforceable, a contract must arise from a **bargained-for exchange**. In most business contracts, the parties engage in such exchanges. The commercial setting in which business contracts are formed leads to this conclusion.

Gift promises, also called **gratuitous promises**, are unenforceable because they lack consideration. To change a gift promise into an enforceable promise, the promisee must offer to do something in exchange—that is, consideration—for the promise.

Consider This Example   Suppose Mrs. Colby promised to give her son $10,000 and then rescinded the promise. The son would have no recourse because it was a gift promise that lacked consideration. However, if Mrs. Colby promised her son $10,000 for getting an

bargained-for exchange
Exchange that parties engage in that leads to an enforceable contract.

gift promise
An unenforceable promise because it lacks consideration.

Business Brief
A "completed gift promise" becomes a true gift, which by definition is irrevocable.

"A" in his business law course and the son performed as required, the contract would be enforceable. A completed gift promise cannot be rescinded for lack of consideration.

In the following case, the court refused to enforce a gift promise.

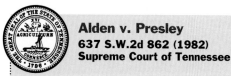

Alden v. Presley
637 S.W.2d 862 (1982)
Supreme Court of Tennessee

CASE 11.2

FACTS
Elvis Presley, a singer of great renown and a man of substantial wealth, became engaged to Ginger Alden. He was generous with the Alden family, paying for landscaping the lawn, installing a swimming pool, and making other gifts. When his fiancé's mother, Jo Laverne Alden, sought to divorce her husband, Presley promised to pay off the remaining mortgage indebtedness on the Alden home, which Mrs. Alden was to receive in the divorce settlement. On August 16, 1977, Presley died suddenly, leaving the mortgage unpaid. When the legal representative of Presley's estate refused to pay the $39,587 mortgage, Mrs. Alden brought an action to enforce Presley's promise. The trial court denied recovery. Mrs. Alden appealed.

ISSUE
Was Presley's promise to pay the mortgage enforceable?

IN THE LANGUAGE OF THE COURT
Fones, Justice   In the instant case, the trial court held decedent did make a promise unsupported by consideration to plaintiff, that no gift was consummated for failure of delivery, that plaintiff suffered no detriment as she "wound up much better

after her association with Elvis A. Presley than if he had never made any promise to Jo Laverne Alden." The court of appeals concurred in the finding that there was no gift for failure to deliver, holding that delivery is not complete unless complete dominion and control of the gift is surrendered by the donor and acquired by the donee.

DECISION AND REMEDY
The state supreme court held that Presley's promise was a gratuitous executory promise that was not supported by consideration. As such, it was unenforceable against Presley's estate. The court dismissed the case and assessed costs against the plaintiff.

Case Questions

Critical Legal Thinking Should gratuitous promises be enforced?

Ethics Was it unethical for the representative of Presley's estate to refuse to complete the gift? Did he have any other choice?

Business Application Does it make a difference if a gift promise is executed or executory? Explain.

Nominal Consideration

Historically, the problem of lack of consideration associated with gift promises was avoided by naming a low dollar amount such as $1 as consideration for the contract. Such consideration is referred to as *nominal consideration*. Nominal consideration is not considered legally sufficient in states that recognize the "shock the conscience of the court" standard for examining the adequacy of consideration (discussed in the following box).

Contemporary Business Application _____

WHEN IS CONSIDERATION INADEQUATE?

The courts usually do not inquire into the **adequacy of consideration**. Generally, parties are free to agree on the consideration they are willing to pay or receive under a contract. This rule is based on the court's reluctance to inquire into the motives of a

party for entering into a contract or to save a party from a "bad deal."

Some states recognize an exception to the general rule that the courts will not examine the sufficiency of consideration. These states permit a party to escape from a contract if the inadequacy of consideration **"shocks the conscience of the court."** This standard, which is applied on a case-by-case basis, considers the value of the item or service contracted for, the amount of consideration paid, the relationship of the parties, and other facts and circumstances of the case.

Consider this fact situation: Mr. and Mrs. James Paul DeLaney were married in January 1953. A few years later they acquired a painting, allegedly the work of Peter Paul Rubens entitled "Hunting of the Caledonian Boar." In 1966, the DeLaneys moved into an apartment building and became friends with Mr. and Mrs. Nicholas T. O'Neill. Mr. DeLaney and Mr. O'Neill became close friends. On August 18, 1970, Mr. DeLaney purportedly sold the Rubens painting to Mr. O'Neill for $10 and "other good and valuable consideration." A written contract embodying the terms of the agreement was prepared and signed by Mr. DeLaney and Mr. O'Neill. Mrs. DeLaney was not informed of the sale. At the time of the sale, Mr. DeLaney told Mr. O'Neill that the painting was worth at least $100,000. The painting, however, remained with DeLaney and was in storage at the time of this lawsuit. In 1974, Mrs. DeLaney instituted a divorce action against Mr. DeLaney. At that time she learned of the purported sale of the painting to O'Neill. In the divorce action, Mrs. DeLaney claimed an interest in the painting as marital property. Mr.

O'Neill instituted this action seeking a declaratory judgment regarding title to the painting.

The trial court held in favor of Mrs. DeLaney and voided the sales contract between Mr. DeLaney and Mr. O'Neill. The appellate court affirmed. The courts held that the consideration paid by Mr. O'Neill for the painting "shocked the conscience of the court" and thereby rendered the transfer void. The appellate court stated: "Plaintiff expressly testified that 'other good and valuable consideration' meant the love and affection plaintiff and James Paul DeLaney had for one another. In Illinois, love and affection do not constitute legal consideration. Thus, the only remaining valid consideration for the transaction was the tender of $10. A purchase price of $10 for such a valuable work of art is so grossly inadequate consideration as to shock the conscience of this court, as it did the trial court's. To find $10 valid consideration for this painting would be to reduce the requirement of consideration to a mere formality. This we will not do."

Critics of this case argue that the parties should be free to contract based upon what they feel is adequate consideration in the circumstances. Proponents of this case argue that courts should be allowed to examine the adequacy of consideration underlying a contract to prevent unfair contracts. [*O'Neill v. DeLaney*, 415 N.E.2d 1260 (Ill.App. 1980)]

Entrepreneur and the Law

LAWYERS FOR INTERNET ENTREPRENEURS

Entrepreneurs have been leaders in developing start-up companies that currently dominate the area of e-commerce and the Internet. Entrepreneur Bill Gates created Microsoft Corporation and is now the richest person in the world. The entrepreneurs who started Netscape, Yahoo, AOL, Amazon.com, and eBay are now multimillionaires. Many new entrepreneurs are hatching the successful Internet and e-commerce businesses of the future in their dorm rooms, juice bars, and chat rooms on the Net. These Internet and e-commerce entrepreneurs are a new breed who think big, move fast, and are willing to take risks.

These new cyberspace entrepreneurs need a new type of lawyer who understands their mindset. These lawyers practice "entrepreneur law" in that they must be able to give competent legal and business advice on a moment's notice. Although having to be careful to protect the interests of their clients, and to give correct legal advice, entrepreneurial lawyers must recognize that e-commerce and Internet businesses must sometimes act faster than traditional businesses.

In such cases, the client may be willing to skip some of the minute details that lawyers would insist on for traditional clients. These "techie-owners" often find "Wall Street" lawyers too slow, too expensive, and too risk adverse. The new entrepreneur lawyer is more to their liking.

There is a growing need for lawyers who know e-commerce and Internet law, have specialized skills in handling transactional law, and know small client management. At the start, entrepreneur lawyers need strong skills in finance law, e-commerce contract law, selecting and drafting business entity formation documents, preparing transactional documents of shipping, drawing licensing agreements, drafting shareholder agreements, drafting employment agreements, and protecting trademarks, service marks, and trade secrets. Eventually, the lawyer would be looking at handling the Internet company's initial public offering (IPO) and debt financing. It is hoped that after the Internet company is successful, it will not trade in its entrepreneur lawyer for the "traditional" lawyer.

e-biz

Special Issues Concerning Consideration in Business Contracts

Generally, the courts tolerate a greater degree of uncertainty in business contracts than in personal contracts under the premise that sophisticated parties know how to protect themselves when negotiating contracts. The following are special types of business contracts that specifically allow a greater degree of uncertainty concerning consideration.

Option-to-Cancel Clauses

Many business contracts contain clauses that allow one or both of the parties to cancel the contract. Such **option-to-cancel clauses** do not render a business contract illusory if a party to the contract has given legal consideration for the right to cancel.

option-to-cancel clause
A clause inserted in many business contracts that allows one or both of the parties to cancel the contract.

Consider This Example   Suppose an employer contracts to hire a personnel manager for three years. The parties sign a written contract that contains an option-to-cancel clause that gives the employer the right to terminate the manager upon a 30-day paid notice. This clause is enforceable because it is supported by consideration (e.g., the notice period).

Best Efforts Contracts

Many business contracts contain a clause that requires one or both of the parties to use their *best efforts* to achieve the objective of the contract. For example, real estate listing contracts often require a real estate broker to use his or her best efforts to find a buyer for the listed real estate. Contracts often require underwriters to use their best efforts to sell securities on behalf of their corporate clients. The courts generally have held that the imposition of the best efforts duty provides sufficient consideration to make a contract enforceable.

Contemporary Business Application

BEST EFFORTS CONTRACT

Ballantine & Sons (Ballantine) was a venerable brewer located in Newark, New Jersey. The company marketed its product in the Northeast.

Although the beer was a local favorite, Ballantine experienced serious financial difficulties in the late 1960s and early 1970s. On March 21, 1972, Falstaff Brewing Corporation (Falstaff), a national brewer, purchased Ballantine for $4 million plus a 50 cents per barrel royalty for each barrel of Ballantine beer sold over the next six years. The contract specified two things: (1) Falstaff must "use its best efforts to promote and maintain a high volume of sales" of Ballantine beer, and (2) the "substantial discontinuance" of the distribution of Ballantine beer would trigger a payment of $1.1 million in liquidated damages to Ballantine for each year remaining of the royalty period.

In April 1975, Paul Kalmanowitz gained control of Falstaff. In an attempt to make Falstaff more profitable, he slashed Ballantine's advertising budget from $1 million to $115,000, closed its distribution depot, and took other measures that decreased sales of Ballantine beer. With 1974 as a base, sales volume of Ballantine beer decreased 63.1 percent by 1977. Falstaff showed substantial financial gain during the same period. Not surprisingly, Ballantine's trustees sued Falstaff on the grounds that it violated the first condition.

The district court held that Falstaff breached its duty to use its best efforts to maintain a high sales volume of Ballantine beer and awarded damages to Ballantine based on volume lost. The court of appeals affirmed this judgment. The court stated that Falstaff's failure to treat Ballantine products evenhandedly with Falstaff's was a breach of the best efforts clause. [*Bloor v. Falstaff Brewing Corporation*, 601 F.2d 609 (2d Cir. 1979)]

Entrepreneur and the Law

THE USE OF OUTPUT AND REQUIREMENTS CONTRACTS IN BUSINESS

Generally, the courts tolerate a greater degree of uncertainty in business contracts than in personal contracts under the premise that sophisticated parties know how to protect themselves when negotiating contracts. The law imposes an obligation of good faith on the performance of the parties to requirements and output contracts.

The following are special types of business contracts that specifically allow a greater degree of uncertainty concerning consideration:

- **Output Contracts** In an **output contract**, the seller agrees to sell all of its production to a single buyer.

Output contracts serve the legitimate business purposes of (1) assuring the seller of a purchaser for all its output and (2) assuring the buyer of a source of supply for the goods it needs.

- **Requirements Contracts** A **requirements contract** is one where a buyer contracts to purchase all of the requirements for an item from one seller. Such contracts serve the legitimate business purposes of (1) assuring the buyer of a uniform source of supply and (2) providing the seller with reduced selling costs.

CONTRACTS LACKING CONSIDERATION

Some contracts seem as though they are supported by consideration even though they are not. The following types of contracts fall into this category.

Illegal Consideration

A contract cannot be supported by a promise to refrain from doing an illegal act because that is **illegal consideration**. Contracts based on illegal consideration are void. For example, statements such as, "I will burn your house down unless you agree to pay me $10,000," cannot become enforceable contracts. Even if the threatened party agrees to make the payment, the contract is unenforceable and void because it is supported by illegal consideration (arson is unlawful).

illegal consideration
A promise to refrain from doing an illegal act. Such a promise will not support a contract.

Illusory Promises

If parties enter into a contract, but one or both of the parties can choose not to perform their contractual obligations, the contract lacks consideration. Such promises, which are known as **illusory promises** (or **illusory contracts**), are unenforceable. For example, a contract that provides that one of the parties only has to perform if he or she chooses to do so is an illusory contract.

illusory promise
A contract into which both parties enter, but one or both of the parties can choose not to perform their contractual obligations. Thus the contract lacks consideration.

Moral Obligations

Promises made out of a sense of *moral obligation* or honor are generally unenforceable on the ground that they lack consideration. In other words, moral consideration is not treated as legal consideration. Contracts based on love and affection and deathbed promises are examples of such promises. A minority of states hold that moral obligations are enforceable.

Business Brief
Promises made out of a sense of moral obligation lack consideration. Such promises are unenforceable in most states.

Preexisting Duty

A promise lacks consideration if a person promises to perform an act or do something he or she is already under an obligation to do. This is called a **preexisting duty**. The promise is unenforceable because no new consideration has been given. For example, many states have adopted statutes that prohibit police officers from accepting rewards for apprehending criminals.

preexisting duty
A promise lacks consideration if a person promises to perform an act or do something he or she is already under an obligation to do.

In the private sector, the preexisting duty rule often arises when one of the parties to an existing contract seeks to change the terms of the contract during the course of its performance. Such midstream changes are unenforceable: The parties have a preexisting duty to perform according to the original terms of the contract.

Sometimes a party to a contract runs into substantial *unforeseen difficulties* while performing his or her contractual duties. If the parties modify their contract to accommodate these unforeseen difficulties, the modification will be enforced even though it is not supported by new consideration.

Consider This Example Suppose a landowner enters into a contract with a contractor who agrees to excavate the hole for the foundation of a major office building. When the excavation is partially completed, toxic wastes are unexpectedly found at the site. Removal of toxic wastes is highly regulated by law and would substantially increase the cost of the excavation. If the landowner agrees to pay the contractor increased compensation to remove the toxic wastes, this modification of the contract is enforceable even though it is unsupported by new consideration.

Past Consideration

past consideration
A prior act or performance. Past consideration (e.g., prior acts) will not support a new contract. New consideration must be given.

In a business setting, problems of **past consideration** often arise when a party to a contract promises to pay additional compensation for work done in the past.

Consider This Example Felipe Chavez, who has worked for the Acme Corporation for 30 years, is retiring. The president of Acme says, "Because you were such a loyal employee, Acme will pay you a bonus of $25,000." The corporation refuses to pay the $25,000. Unfortunately for Mr. Chavez, the contract is unenforceable because it is based on past consideration.

The following case illustrates the past consideration rule.

Dementas v. Estate of Tallas
764 P.2d 628 (1988)
Court of Appeals of Utah

CASE 11.3

FACTS
Jack Tallas emigrated to the United States from Greece in 1914. He lived in Salt Lake City for nearly 70 years, during which time he achieved considerable success in business, primarily as an insurance agent and landlord. Over a period of 14 years, Peter Dementas, a close personal friend of Tallas's, rendered services to Tallas, including picking up his mail, driving him to the grocery store, and assisting with the management of his rental properties. On December 18, 1982, Tallas met with Dementas and dictated a memorandum to him, in Greek, stating that he owed Dementas $50,000 for his help over the years. Tallas indicated in the memorandum that he would change his will to make Dementas an heir for this amount. Tallas signed the document. Tallas died on February 4, 1983, without changing his will to include Dementas as an heir. He left a substantial estate. Dementas filed a claim for $50,000 with Tallas's estate. When the estate denied the claim, Dementas brought this action to enforce the contract. The trial court dismissed Dementas's

claim, stating that his contract with Tallas lacked consideration. Dementas appealed.

ISSUE
Was the contract enforceable?

IN THE LANGUAGE OF THE COURT
Orme, Judge *The burden of proving consideration is on the party seeking to recover on the contract. Even though the testimony showed that Dementas rendered at least some services for Tallas, the subsequent promise by Tallas to pay $50,000 for services already performed by Dementas is not a promise supported by legal consideration. Events which occur prior to the making of the promise and not with the purpose of inducing the promise in exchange are viewed as "past consideration" and are the legal equivalent of no consideration. This is so because the promisor is making his promise because those events occurred, but he is not making his promise in order to get them. There is no bargaining, no saying that if you will do this for me I will do that for you. A benefit conferred or detriment incurred in the past is not adequate consideration for a present bargain.*

This rule can surely work unfair results and has accordingly been criticized. We acknowledge, as have other courts in disregarding contracts for lack of consideration, that appellant will probably remain convinced he should be paid. Nevertheless, he failed to meet his burden of proof, and this court will not find a contract where one has not been proved to exist.

DECISION AND REMEDY

The appellate court held that Tallas's promise to pay Dementas $50,000 was unenforceable because it was based on past consideration. The court cited the rule of contract law that a promise based on a party's past consideration lacks consideration.

Case Questions

Critical Legal Thinking   Should past consideration be considered legal consideration? Why or why not?

Ethics   Did the executor of Tallas's estate act ethically in failing to pay Dementas the money? Do you think the executor's decision is what Tallas would have wanted?

Business Application   Can you think of any situations where a business may be involved in a contract based on past consideration? What is the moral of this case?

CONCEPT SUMMARY   PROMISES LACKING CONSIDERATION

Type of Consideration	Description of Promise
Illegal consideration	Promise to refrain from doing an illegal act.
Illusory promise	Promise where one or both parties can choose not to perform their obligation.
Moral obligation	Promise made out of a sense of moral obligation or honor or love or affection. Some states enforce these types of contracts.
Preexisting duty	Promise based on the preexisting duty of the promisee to perform. The promise is enforceable if (1) the parties rescind the contract and enter into a new contract or (2) there are unforeseen difficulties.
Past consideration	Promise based on the past performance of the promisee.

SETTLEMENT OF CLAIMS

The law promotes the voluntary settlement of disputed claims. Settlement saves judicial resources and serves the interests of the parties entering into the settlement. The most common forms of settlement agreements are discussed in the paragraphs that follow.

In some situations, one of the parties to a contract believes that he or she did not receive what he or she was due. This party may attempt to reach a compromise with the other party (e.g., by paying less consideration than was provided for in the contract). The compromise agreement is called an **accord**. If the accord is performed, it is called the **satisfaction**. This type of settlement is called an **accord and satisfaction** (or a **compromise**). If the accord is not satisfied, the other party can sue to enforce either the accord or the original contract. The issue of whether an accord and satisfaction require additional consideration to be enforceable depends on whether the debt is liquidated or unliquidated.

Consider This Example   Suppose that a contract stipulated that the cost of a computer system that keeps track of inventory, accounts receivable, and so on is $100,000. After it is installed, the computer system does not perform as promised. To settle the dispute, the parties agree that $70,000 is to be paid in full and final payment for the computer. This accord is enforceable even though no new consideration is given because reasonable persons would differ as to the worth of the computer system that actually was installed.

accord

An agreement whereby the parties agree to accept something different in satisfaction of the original contract.

satisfaction

The performance of an accord.

International Perspective

THE SOCIALISTIC LAW SYSTEM

The youngest of the major legal systems is the **Sino–Soviet socialist law system**, which applies to over 30 percent of the people of the world. The Sino–Soviet theory of law is based on the philosophy of Karl Marx, which advocated the eradication of capitalism and the elimination of the private ownership of property. After the creation of the Soviet state following the Russian Revolution of 1917, Lenin replaced the old court system with a system of law meted out by workers, peasants, and the military. This legal nihilism (or absence of law) did not last long, and a formal legal system was restored pursuant to new criminal and civil law codes that promoted the socialist ideal. With its emphasis on codes, the Sino–Soviet legal system is a variant of the civil law.

Because private property in most respects is not permitted under Sino–Soviet law, the legal system comprises mostly of public law. Therefore, property law, contract law, and business organization law (e.g., corporation and partnership law) that are prevalent in common law and civil law countries are not as important in Sino–Soviet law. Sino–Soviet public law preserves the authority of the state over property and the means of production.

As the republics of the now dismantled Soviet Union and Eastern bloc countries adopt free market economies, Sino–Soviet public law is being replaced by laws establishing and protecting private property rights. Today, socialist law forms the basis of the legal systems of Angola, Cambodia, China, Cuba, Ethiopia, Guinea, Guyana, Laos, Libya, Mozambique, North Korea, Somalia, and Vietnam. But even Communist China is promoting capitalism and permitting individual ownership of property. This will require the development of business and property laws and the establishment of a court system to decide commercial and property-related disputes.

*P*ROMISSORY ESTOPPEL

promissory estoppel

An equitable doctrine that prevents the withdrawal of a promise by a promisor if it will adversely affect a promisee who has adjusted his or her position in justifiable reliance on the promise.

The courts have developed the doctrine of **promissory estoppel** (or **detrimental reliance**) to avoid injustice. This is a broad policy-based doctrine. It is used to provide a remedy to a person who has relied on another person's promise, but that person withdraws his or her promise and is not subject to a breach of contract action because one of the two elements discussed in this chapter (i.e., agreement or consideration) is lacking. The doctrine of promissory estoppel *estops* (prevents) the promisor from revoking his or her promise. Therefore, the person who has detrimentally relied on the promise for performance may sue the promisor for performance or other remedy the court feels is fair to award in the circumstances.

For the doctrine of promissory estoppel to be applied, the following elements must be shown:

Now equity is no part of the law, but a moral virtue, which qualifies, moderates, and reforms the rigour, hardness, and edge of the law, and is an universal truth.

Lord Cowper
Dudley v. Dudley (1705)

1. The promisor made a promise.
2. The promisor should have reasonably expected to induce the promisee to rely on the promise.
3. The promisee actually relied on the promise and engaged in an action or forbearance of a right of a definite and substantial nature.
4. Injustice would be caused if the promise were not enforced.

Consider This Example XYZ Construction Co., a general contractor, requests bids from subcontractors for work to be done on a hospital building that XYZ plans to submit a bid to build. Bert Plumbing Co. submits the lowest bid for the plumbing work, and XYZ incorporates Bert's low bid in its own bid for the general contract. In this example, the doctrine of promissory estoppel prevents Bert from withdrawing its bid. If XYZ is awarded the contract to build the hospital, it could enforce Bert's promise to perform.

International Perspective

THE LAW OF THE SEA

For centuries, the oceans were considered "high seas" over which no nation had jurisdiction. In the middle of the nineteenth century, coastal nations began claiming exclusive rights to territorial waters and seabeds that bordered their nations. Nations claimed exclusive rights to seas extending anywhere from 12 to 200 miles from the shoreline. Most of these national laws were enacted to protect fishing rights.

In 1971, the United Nations Conference on the Law of the Sea (LOS Convention) established a 200-mile exclusive economic zone (EEZ) for coastal nations. This Convention grants sovereign rights to coastal nations to explore, exploit, conserve, and manage living resources in their EEZs. It also grants these nations sovereign right over nonliving resources of the seabed and subsoil in the EEZs.

The LOS Convention grants all nations the freedom of navigation and overflight over EEZs as well as the right to lay submarine cables and pipelines. In exercising these rights, nations must comply with the lawful and nondiscriminatory laws of the coastal nation. A coastal nation may permit other nations to fish and use the waters and seabeds of its EEZ, subject to conservation and other laws established by the coastal nation.

The LOS Convention gives coastal nations the right to board and inspect ships, arrest a ship and its crew, and institute legal proceedings against violators. Appeals may be made to the International Tribunal for the Law of the Sea.

In 1983, President Ronald Reagan issued a proclamation that establishes a 200-mile EEZ similar to that established by the LOS Convention. The United States has enacted several statutes that regulate fishing and mineral exploration within the EEZ and the Continental Shelf.

Working the Web

Frequently Used Sites This is one of the most comprehensive sites collecting U.S. federal government information. Subject areas include business and economics, census, Congress, consumer information, copyright, patents, trademarks, crime and justice, education, foreign countries, health and welfare, impeachment, laws and regulations, natural resources, President and executive branch, scientific and technical reports, statistics, Supreme Court, tax forms, travel, and voting and elections. This site is organized by the Federal Documents Task Force of the American Library Association, Government Documents Round Table. Bookmark this site or add to your favorite places.

Visit at **www.library.vanderbilt.edu/central/staff/fdtf.html**

FedStats More than 70 agencies in the U.S. federal government produce statistics of interest to the public. The Federal Interagency Council on Statistical Policy maintains this site to provide easy access to the full range of statistics and information produced by these agencies for public use. Some state, county, and local level data is also available.

Visit at **www.fedstats.gov/**

Commonly Requested Federal Services This site provides one-stop access to federal services. Included are online transactions, information, and forms and publications available for downloading and printing. Do you want to find out if your auto has been recalled, how to get a passport, or how to get a tax form at the last minute? Then, this is the site for you.

Visit at **www.whitehouse.gov/WH/Services/**

CYBER EXERCISES

1. Find a tax form using Frequently Used Sites.

2. Using FedStats, find a profile of your state and county with MapStats.

3. Find out about student aid, fellowships, and grants using Commonly Requested Federal Services.

CASES AND EXERCISES

CRITICAL LEGAL THINKING CASES

11.1. Clyde and Betty Penley were married in 1949. In late 1967, Clyde operated an automotive tire business while Betty owned an interest in a Kentucky Fried Chicken (KFC) franchise. That year, when Betty became ill, she requested that Clyde begin spending additional time at the KFC franchise to ensure its continued operation. Subsequently, Betty agreed that if Clyde would devote full-time to the KFC franchise, they would operate the business as a joint enterprise, share equally in the ownership of its assets, and divide its returns equally. Pursuant to this agreement, Clyde terminated his tire business and devoted his full time to the KFC franchise. On December 31, 1979, Betty abandoned Clyde and denied him any rights in the KFC franchise. Clyde sued to enforce the agreement with Betty. Is the agreement enforceable? [*Penley v. Penley*, 332 S.E.2d 51 (N.C. 1985)]

11.2. On February 4, 1966, Frank Handler, an employee of the *Monroe Evening News*, was delivering newspapers door-to-door. He was accompanied by his younger brother Nicholas and his friend Daniel Higgins, who were both five years old. In return for helping deliver the papers, Frank paid Nicholas and Daniel a dime, a bottle of pop, or candy. While helping deliver the papers, Daniel was struck by a motor vehicle and seriously injured. Daniel filed a claim to recover workers' compensation for his injuries, arguing that he was an employee of the newspaper. Was there a contract between Daniel and the *Monroe Evening News* that was supported by legal consideration? [*Higgins v. Monroe Evening News*, 272 N.W.2d 537 (Mich. 1978)]

11.3. When John W. Frasier died, he left a will that devised certain of his community and separate property to his wife, Lena, and their three children. These devises were more valuable to Lena than just her interest in the community property that she would otherwise have received without the will. The devises to her, however, were conditioned upon the filing of a waiver by Lena of her interest in the community property, and if she failed to file the waiver, she would then receive only her interest in the community property and nothing more. Lena hired her brother, D. L. Carter, an attorney, to represent her. Carter failed to file the waiver on Lena's behalf, thus preventing her from taking under the will. Instead, she received her interest in the community property, which was $19,358 less than she would have received under the will. Carter sent Lena the following letter:

This is to advise and confirm our agreement—that in the event the J. W. Frasier estate case now on appeal is not terminated so that you will receive settlement equal to your share of

the estate as you would have done if your waiver had been filed in the estate in proper time, I will make up any balance to you in payments as suits my convenience and will pay interest on your loss at 6 percent.

The appeal was decided against Lena. When she tried to enforce the contract against Carter, he alleged that the contract was not enforceable because it was not supported by valid consideration. Who wins? [*Frasier v. Carter*, 437 P.2d 32 (ID 1968)]

11.4. Mr. and Mrs. Voight were husband and wife. Mrs. Voight had two sons, Thomas and John Kapsa, from a prior marriage. Mr. and Mrs. Voight carefully kept separate their financial matters and separate property. At one time, Mrs. Voight and her two sons owned certain property together. When the property was sold, Mrs. Voight signed two promissory notes of $13,500 each, one to each son, for money that she owed them. Mrs. Voight died before she paid the amounts due on the notes. Less than four months before he died, Mr. Voight visited John Kapsa and signed two promissory notes promising to pay his stepsons the monies that their mother had not paid them. When Mr. Voight died, Thomas and John Kapsa filed a claim to collect the money due on the notes from Mr. Voight's estate. Will they be successful? [*Estate of Voight v. Kapsa*, 624 P.2d 1022 (NM 1981)]

11.5. A.J. Whitmire and R. Lee Whitmire were brothers. From 1923 to 1929, A. J. lived with his brother and his brother's wife, Lillie Mae. During this period, A. J. performed various services for his brother and sister-in-law. In 1925, R. Lee and Lillie Mae purchased some land. In 1944, in the presence of Lillie Mae, R. Lee told A. J., "When we're gone, this land is yours." A. J. had not done any work for R. Lee or Lillie Mae since 1929, and none was expected or provided in the future. On May 26, 1977, after both R. Lee and Lillie Mae had died, A. J. filed a claim with the estate of Lillie Mae seeking specific performance of the 1944 promise. Does A. J. get the property? [*Whitmire v. Watkins*, 267 So.2d 6 (GA 1980)]

11.6. Robert Chuckrow Construction Company (Chuckrow) was employed as the general contractor to build a Kinney Shoe Store. Chuckrow employed Ralph Gough to perform the carpentry work on the store. The contract with Gough stipulated that he was to provide all labor, materials, tools, equipment, scaffolding, and other items necessary to complete the carpentry work. On May 15, 1965, Gough's employees erected 38 trusses at the job site. The next day, 32 of the trusses fell off the building. The reason for the trusses' falling was unexplained, and evidence showed that it was not due to Chuckrow's fault or a deficiency in the building plans. Chuckrow told Gough that he would pay him to reerect the trusses and continue work. When the job was complete, Chuckrow paid Gough the original contract price but refused to pay him for the additional cost of reerecting the trusses. Gough sued Chuckrow for this expense. Can Gough recover? [*Robert Chuckrow Construction Company v. Gough*, 159 S.E.2d 469 (Ga.App. 1968)]

11.7. In 1972, Marna Balin was involved in two automobile accidents in which she suffered severe injuries. She hired Norman H. Kallen, an attorney, to represent her. Kallen filed lawsuits on behalf of Balin seeking damages for her injuries. Kallen repeatedly urged Balin to settle the lawsuits for $25,000. In late 1974, when she became disappointed with Kallen's representation, she retained another attorney, Samuel P. Delug, and instructed him to obtain her legal files from Kallen. The California Rules of Professional Conduct for attorneys provide that an attorney may not retain a client's files [Rule 2-111 (A)(2)]. However, Kallen refused to release the files until Delug agreed to give Kallen 40 percent of the attorney's fees recovered in the case. The cases were ultimately settled for $810,000, resulting in attorney's fees of $324,000. When Delug refused to pay Kallen 40 percent of these fees, Kallen sued Delug. Was the fee-splitting agreement between Kallen and Delug supported by legal consideration? [*Kallen v. Delug*, 157 Cal.App.3d 940, 203 Cal.Rptr. 879 (Cal.App. 1984)]

11.8. Milton Polinger pledged $210,000 as a charitable subscription to the United Jewish Appeal Federation of Greater Washington, Inc. (UJA). The pledge was not for a specific purpose and was not made in consideration of pledges by others, and UJA borrowed no money against this pledge. The pledge was to the UJA generally and to the Israel Emergency Fund. After paying $76,500 toward the pledge, Polinger died and the Maryland National Bank was appointed representative of the Polinger estate. The UJA filed a claim against the estate for the balance of $133,500. The bank, however, denied the claim, alleging that the promise was unenforceable for lack of consideration. Who wins? [*Maryland National Bank v. United Jewish Appeal Federation of Greater Washington, Inc.*, 407 A.2d 1130 (Md.App. 1979)]

11.9. Nalley's, Inc. (Nalley's), was a major food distributor with its home office in the state of Washington. In 1964,

Jacob Aronowicz and Samuel Duncan approached Nalley's about the possibility of their manufacturing a line of sliced meat products to be distributed by Nalley's. When Nalley's showed considerable interest, Aronowicz and Duncan incorporated as Major Food Products, Inc. (Major). Meetings to discuss the proposal continued at length with Charles Gardiner, a vice president and general manager of Nalley's Los Angeles division. On February 5, 1965, Gardiner delivered a letter to Major agreeing to become the exclusive Los Angeles and Orange County distributor for Major's products, but stated in the letter "that should we determine your product line is not representative or is not compatible with our operation we are free to terminate our agreement within 30 days." Nalley's was to distribute the full production of products produced by Major.

Based on Gardiner's assurances, Major leased a plant, modified the plant to its specifications, purchased and installed equipment, signed contracts to obtain meat to be processed, and hired personnel. Both Aronowicz and Duncan resigned from their positions at other meat processing companies to devote full-time to the project. Financing was completed when Aronowicz and Duncan used their personal fortunes to purchase the stock of Major. Gardiner and other representatives of Nalley's visited Major's plant and expressed satisfaction with the premises. Major obtained the necessary government approvals regarding health standards on June 15, 1965, and immediately achieved full production. Because Nalley's was to pick the finished products up at Major's plant, Nalley's drivers visited Major's plant to acquaint themselves with its operations.

Gardiner sent the final proposal regarding the Nalley's-Major relationship to Nalley's home office for final approval. On June 22, 1965, Nalley's home office in Washington made a decision not to distribute Major's products. Nalley's refused to give any reason to Major for its decision. No final agreement was ever executed between the parties. Immediate efforts by Major to secure other distribution for its products proved unsuccessful. Further, because Major owned no trucks itself and had no sales organization, it could not distribute the products itself. In less than six months, Major had failed and Aronowicz's and Duncan's stock in Major was worthless. Major, Aronowicz, and Duncan sued Nalley's for damages under the doctrine of promissory estoppel. Do they win? [*Aronowicz v. Nalley's. Inc.*, 30 C.A.3d 27, 106 Cal.Rptr. 424 (Cal.App. 1972)]

ETHICS CASES

11.10. Ocean Dunes of Hutchinson Island Development Corporation (Ocean Dunes) was a developer of condominium units. Prior to the construction, Albert and Helen Colangelo

entered into a Purchase Agreement to buy one of the units and paid a deposit to Ocean Dunes. A provision in the Purchase Agreement provided that

If Developer shall default in the performance of its obligations pursuant to this agreement, Purchaser's only remedy shall be to terminate this agreement, whereupon the Deposit shall be refunded to Purchaser and all rights and obligations thereunder shall thereupon become null and void.

The Purchase Agreement provided that if the buyer defaulted, the developer could retain the buyer's deposit or sue the buyer for damages and any other legal or equitable remedy. When Ocean Dunes refused to sell the unit to the Colangelos, they sued, seeking a decree of specific performance to require Ocean Dunes to sell them the unit. Ocean Dunes alleged that the above-quoted provision prevented the plaintiffs from seeking any legal or equitable remedy. Was the defendant's duty under the contract illusory? Was it ethical for Ocean Dunes to place the provision at issue in the contract? [*Ocean Dunes of Hutchinson Island Development Corporation v. Colangelo*, 463 So.2d 437 (Fla.App. 1985)]

11.11. Red Owl Stores, Inc., a Minnesota corporation with its home office at Hopkins, Minnesota, owns and operates grocery supermarkets and grants franchises to franchisees to also operate such stores. Joseph Hoffman, who operated a bakery with his wife in Wautoma, Wisconsin, was interested in obtaining a Red Owl franchise to operate a grocery store in Wisconsin. In November 1959, he contacted a representative of Red Owl and had numerous conversations regarding this proposal. In September 1960, Mr. Lukowitz became Red Owl's representative for the territory comprising Upper Michigan and most of Wisconsin. Hoffman mentioned to Lukowitz that he had $18,000 capital to invest, and Lukowitz assured him that would be sufficient to open a Red Owl franchise.

To gain experience in the grocery store business, and upon the advice of Lukowitz and other Red Owl representatives, Hoffman bought a small grocery store in Wautoma. After three months of operating this store, a Red Owl representative came in and took inventory, checked operations, and found that the store was operating at a profit. Lukowitz advised Hoffman to sell the store to his manager and assured Hoffman

that Red Owl would find a larger store for him elsewhere. Although Hoffman was reluctant to sell at that time because it meant losing the summer tourist business, he sold on the assurance that he would be operating a Red Owl store at a new location by the fall. Again, Lukowitz assured Hoffman that $18,000 was sufficient to open a Red Owl franchise.

By June, Red Owl had selected a site in Chilton, Wisconsin, for the proposed store. On Red Owl's insistence, Hoffman paid $1,000 and obtained an option to purchase the site. Hoffman and his wife rented a house in Chilton. In September, Hoffman met with Lukowitz, who assured him, "Everything is ready to go. Get your money together and we are set." Lukowitz told Hoffman that he must sell his bakery business and building in Wautoma and that this was the only "hitch" in the entire plan. On November 6, 1961, Hoffman sold his bakery building for $10,000, but retained the equipment to be used in the proposed Red Owl store. Hoffman incurred a $2,000 loss on the sale. In September and October, Red Owl prepared various financial projections for the proposed site. On November 22, 1961, Hoffman met with Lukowitz and the credit manager for Red Owl, who demanded that Hoffman have $24,000 of capital to invest in the store. Hoffman contacted his father-in-law, who agreed to provide the additional money. A week later Red Owl sent Hoffman a telegram demanding that he have $26,000 capital to invest. When Hoffman could not raise the additional money, the transaction fell through. Hoffman did not purchase the store site in Chilton and forfeited the $1,000 option payment. The parties had never entered into a final agreement regarding the franchise.

Hoffman sued Red Owl under the doctrine of promissory estoppel, seeking damages for the $1,000 lost on the option payment on the Chilton property, the $2,000 loss on the sale of the bakery in Wautoma, and the lease payments on the house in Chilton. Did the representatives of Red Owl Stores, Inc., act ethically in this case? Should the equitable doctrine of promissory estoppel apply in this case? [*Hoffman v. Red Owl Stores, Inc.*, 133 N.W.2d 267 (Wis. 1965)]

CRITICAL LEGAL THINKING WRITING ASSIGNMENT

Read Case A.11 in the Case Appendix [*Congregation Kadimah Toras-Moshe v. DeLeo*]. This case is excerpted from the court of appeals opinion. Review and brief the case. In your brief, be sure to answer the following questions.

1. What was the plaintiff suing for? Explain.
2. What was the defendant estate's defense?
3. How did the court decide this case?

NOTE

1. *Hamer v. Sidway*, 124 N.Y. 538, 27 N.E. 256 (N.Y. 1891).

Capacity and Legality

An unconscionable contract is one which no man in his senses, not under delusion, would make, on the one hand, and which no fair and honest man would accept on the other.

CHIEF JUSTICE FULLER
Hume v. United States, 132 U.S. 406,
10 S.Ct. 134, 33 L.Ed. 393 (1889)

Chapter Objectives

After studying this chapter, you should be able to

1. Define and describe the infancy doctrine.
2. Identify contracts that may be disaffirmed by minors.
3. Explain a minor's obligation to pay for necessaries of life.
4. Define *legal insanity* and explain how it affects contractual capacity.
5. Define *intoxication* and describe how it affects contractual capacity.
6. Identify illegal contracts that are contrary to statutes.
7. Identify illegal contracts that violate public policy.
8. Describe covenants not to compete and identify when they are lawful.
9. Describe exculpatory clauses and identify when they are lawful.
10. Define *unconscionable contracts* and determine when they are unlawful.

Chapter Contents

Generally, the law presumes that the parties to a contract have the requisite *contractual capacity* to enter into the contract. However, certain persons do not have this capacity. They include minors, insane persons, and intoxicated persons. Both the common law of contracts and many state statutes protect persons who lack contractual capacity from having contracts enforced against them. The party asserting incapacity, his or her guardian, conservator, or other legal representative bears the burden of proof.

An essential element for the formation of a contract is that the object of the contract be lawful. A contract to perform an illegal act is called an *illegal contract*. Illegal contracts are void. That is, they cannot be enforced by either party to the contract. The term *illegal contract* is a misnomer, however, because no contract exists if the object of the contract is illegal. In addition, courts hold that *unconscionable contracts* are unenforceable. An unconscionable contract is one that is so oppressive or manifestly unfair that it would be unjust to enforce it.

Capacity to contract and the lawfulness of contracts are discussed in this chapter.

Minors

minor

A person who has not reached the age of majority.

Minors do not always have the maturity, experience, or sophistication needed to enter into contracts with adults. The common law defines minor as females under the age of 18 and males under the age of 21. In addition, many states have enacted statutes that specify the *age of majority*. The most prevalent age of majority is 18 years of age for both males and females. Any age below the statutory age of majority is called the *period of minority*.

The Infancy Doctrine

infancy doctrine

A doctrine that allows minors to disaffirm (cancel) most contracts they have entered into with adults.

To protect minors, the law recognizes the **infancy doctrine**, which allows minors to *disaffirm* (or *cancel*) most contracts they have entered into with adults. A minor's right to disaffirm a contract is based on public policy. The reasoning is that minors should be protected from unscrupulous behavior of adults.

Under the infancy doctrine, a minor has the option of choosing whether to enforce the contract (i.e., the contract is *voidable* by a minor). The adult party is bound to the minor's decision. If both parties to the contract are minors, both parties have the right to disaffirm the contract.

The twins. *The Infancy Doctrine protects minors by permitting them to disavow (void) certain contracts. These contracts are voidable because only the minor, and not the adult on the other side of the contract, may disavow the contract.*

If performance of the contract favors the minor, the minor will probably enforce the contract. Otherwise, the contract will probably be disaffirmed. However, a minor may not affirm one part of the contract and disaffirm another part.

In most states, the infancy doctrine is an objective standard. If a person's age is below the age of majority, the court will not inquire into his or her knowledge, experience, or sophistication.

Disaffirmance   A minor can expressly **disaffirm** a contract orally, in writing, or by the minor's conduct. No special formalities are required. The contract may be disaffirmed at any time prior to reaching the age of majority plus a "reasonable time." The designation of a reasonable time is determined on a case-by-case basis.

disaffirmance
The act of a minor to rescind a contract under the infancy doctrine. Disaffirmance may be done orally, in writing, or by the minor's conduct.

Duties of Restitution and Restoration

If the minor's contract is executory and neither party has performed, the minor can simply disaffirm the contract. There is nothing to recover because neither party has given the other party anything of value. However, if the parties have exchanged consideration and partially or fully performed the contract at the time the minor disaffirms the contract, the issue becomes one of what consideration or restitution must be made. The following rules apply:

- **Competent Party's Duty of Restitution** If the minor has transferred consideration—money, property, or other valuables—to the competent party before disaffirming the contract, that party must place the minor in status quo. That is, the minor must be restored to the same position he or she was in before the minor entered into the contract. This restoration is usually done by returning the consideration to the minor. If the consideration has been sold or has depreciated in value, the competent party must pay the minor the cash equivalent. This action is called the **competent party's duty of restitution**.
- **Minor's Duty of Restoration** Generally, a minor is obligated only to return the goods or property he or she has received from the adult in the condition it is in at the time of disaffirmance (subject to several exceptions discussed later in this chapter), even if the item has been consumed, lost, or destroyed or has depreciated in value at the time of disaffirmance. This rule is called the **minor's duty of restoration**. It is based on the rationale that if a minor had to place the adult in status quo upon disaffirmance of a contract, there would be no incentive for an adult not to deal with a minor.
- **Minor's Duty of Restitution** Most states provide that the minor must put the adult in status quo upon disaffirmance of the contract if the minor's intentional or grossly negligent conduct caused the loss of value to the adult's property. A few states have enacted statutes that require the minor to make restitution of the reasonable value of the item when disaffirming any contract. This rule is called the **minor's duty of restitution**.

competent party's duty of restitution
If a minor has transferred money, property, or other valuables to the competent party before disaffirming the contract, that party must place the minor in status quo.

minor's duty of restoration
As a general rule a minor is obligated only to return the goods or property he or she has received from the adult in the condition it is in at the time of disaffirmance.

Misrepresentation of Age

On occasion, minors might misrepresent their age to an adult when entering into a contract. Under the common law, such a minor would still have the right to disaffirm the contract. Most states have changed this rule in recognition of its unfairness to adults. These states provide that minors who misrepresent their age must place the adult in status quo if they disaffirm the contract. In other words, a minor who has misrepresented his or her age when entering into a contract owes a duty of restoration and restitution when disaffirming it.

Business Brief
A business should require a customer to prove that he or she is an adult if there is doubt as to age. This practice is extremely important concerning major purchases.

Consider This Example   Sherry McNamara, a minor, misrepresents that she is an adult and enters into a contract to purchase an automobile costing $20,000 from Bruce Ruffino, a competent adult. Mr. Ruffino delivers the automobile after he receives payment in full. The automobile later sustains $7,000 worth of damage in an accident that is not Ms.

Business Brief
Many businesses, such as car dealerships, require a minor's parent or another competent adult to co-sign the contract before they will sell an item to a minor.

ratification
The act of a minor after the minor has reached the age of majority by which he or she accepts a contract entered into when he or she was a minor.

McNamara's fault. To disaffirm the contract, Ms. McNamara must return the damaged automobile plus $7,000 to Mr. Ruffino.

Ratification

If a minor does not disaffirm a contract either during the period of minority or within a reasonable time after reaching the age of majority, the contract is considered ratified (accepted). This means that the minor (who is now an adult) is bound by the contract: The right to disaffirm the contract has been lost. Note that any attempt by a minor to ratify a contract while still a minor can be disaffirmed just as the original contract can be disaffirmed.

The **ratification**, which relates back to the inception of the contract, can be by express oral or written words or implied from the minor's conduct (e.g., after reaching the age of majority the minor remains silent regarding the contract). The following case presents the issue of whether a minor had ratified a contract when he reached the age of majority.

Jones v. Free Flight Sport Aviation, Inc.
623 P.2d 370 (1981)
Supreme Court of Colorado

CASE 12.1

FACTS
On November 17, 1973, William Michael Jones, a 17-year-old minor, signed a contract with Free Flight Sport Aviation, Inc. (Free Flight), for the use of recreational sky-diving facilities. A covenant not to sue and an exculpatory clause exempting Free Flight from liability were included in the contract. On December 28, 1973, Jones attained the age of majority (18 years of age). Ten months later, while on a Free Flight sky-diving operation, the airplane crashed shortly after take-off from Littleton Airport, causing severe personal injuries to Jones. Jones filed suit against Free Flight alleging negligence and willful and wanton misconduct. The trial court granted summary judgment in favor of Free Flight. The Colorado court of appeals affirmed. Jones appealed.

ISSUE
Did Jones ratify the contract?

IN THE LANGUAGE OF THE COURT
Erickson, Justice   As a matter of public policy, the courts have protected minors from improvident and imprudent contractual commitments by declaring that the contract of a minor is voidable at the election of the minor after he attains his majority. A minor may disaffirm a contract made during his minority within a reasonable time after attaining his majority or he may, after becoming of legal age, by acts recognizing the contract, ratify it.

Affirmance is not merely a matter of intent. It may be determined by the actions of a minor who accepts the benefits of a contract after reaching the age of majority, or who is silent or acquiesces in the contract for a considerable length of time. We conclude that the trial court properly determined that Jones ratified the contract, as a matter of law, by accepting the benefits of the contract when he used Free Flight's facilities on October 19, 1974.

DECISION AND REMEDY
The state supreme court held that Jones had ratified his contract with Free Flight by continuing, for 10 months after reaching the age of majority, to perform under the contract. Therefore, the covenant not to sue and the exculpatory clause exempting Free Flight from liability to Jones are enforceable.

Case Questions

Critical Legal Thinking   Should children be allowed to disaffirm a minor's contract after reaching the age of majority? What is a reasonable length of time after reaching the age of majority to permit disaffirmance?

Ethics   Did Jones act ethically by suing Free Flight Sport Aviation in this case?

Business Application   Should the covenant not to sue have been enforced here even though Jones was an adult?

necessaries of life
A minor must pay the reasonable value of food, clothing, shelter, medical care, and other items considered necessary to the maintenance of life.

Necessaries of Life

Minors are obligated to pay for the **necessaries of life** that they contract for. Otherwise, many adults would refuse to sell these items to them. Although there is no standard definition of what is a *necessary of life*, items such as food, clothing, shelter, medical services, and the like are generally understood to fit this category. Goods and services such as automobiles, tools of trade, education, and vocational training have also been found to be necessaries of life in some situations. The minor's age, lifestyle, and status in life influence what is considered necessary. For example, necessaries for a married minor are greater than for an unmarried minor.

The seller's recovery is based on the equitable doctrine of *quasi-contract* rather than on the contract itself. Under this theory, the minor is obligated only to pay the reasonable value of the goods or services received. Reasonable value is determined on a case-by-case basis.

Contemporary Business Application _____

STATUTES THAT MAKE MINORS LIABLE FOR SPECIAL TYPES OF CONTRACTS

The infancy doctrine of the common law of contracts allows minors to disaffirm many contracts they have entered into with adults. Based on public policy, many states have enacted statutes that make certain specified contracts enforceable against minors—that is, minors cannot assert the infancy doctrine against enforcement of these contracts. These usually include contracts for

- Medical, surgical, and pregnancy care
- Psychological counseling
- Health insurance
- Life insurance
- The performance of duties relating to stock and bond transfers, bank accounts, and the like
- Educational loan agreements
- Contracts to support children
- Contracts to enlist in the military
- Artistic, sports, and entertainment contracts that have been entered into with the approval of the court (many of these statutes require that a certain portion of the wages and fees earned by the minor be put in trust until the minor reaches the age of majority)

Parents' Liability for Their Children's Contracts

Generally, parents owe a legal duty to provide food, clothing, shelter, and other necessaries of life for their children. Parents are liable for their children's contracts for necessaries of life that they have not adequately provided.

The parental duty of support terminates if a minor becomes emancipated. **Emancipation** occurs when a minor voluntarily leaves home and lives apart from his or her parents. The courts consider factors such as getting married, setting up a separate household, joining the military service, and the like in determining whether a minor is emancipated. Each situation is examined on its merits.

emancipation
When a minor voluntarily leaves home and lives apart from his or her parents.

Contemporary Business Application _____

A BABE IN THE WOODS?

Many entrepreneurs and businesses that deal with minors say that it is time for a change in the infancy doctrine. They cite that young persons are demanding and assuming more responsibilities in their daily lives. In many respects, they are acting as adults. For instance, they are engaged in businesses, are charged with

the responsibility for committing crimes, are being sued in tort claims for acts of negligence, are subject to military service, and are getting married and raising families. Businesses also argue that minors are using the infancy doctrine as a "sword rather than a shield" to get out of fair contracts.

(box continues)

Businesses are asking courts to reexamine the law pertaining to the contractual rights and duties of minors. Some courts are listening.

Consider the following case. In early April 1987, Joseph Eugene Dodson, then 16 years old, purchased a used 1984 pickup truck from Shrader's Auto Sales in Columbia, Tennessee. He paid $4,900. Shrader testified that Dodson looked 18 or 19 years of age.

Nine months after the purchase, the truck developed a mechanical problem. A mechanic diagnosed the problem as a burnt valve. Dodson did not have the money to make the repairs, so he drove the truck until its engine "blew up" and the truck became inoperable. He parked the truck in the front yard of his parents' home where he lived. While parked there, the truck was struck by a hit-and-run driver. Due to the engine damage and the collision, the truck's value plunged to $500.

Dodson asserted the infancy doctrine and sued to disaffirm the purchase agreement. The trial court permitted Dodson to rescind the contract and ordered Shrader, upon tender and delivery of the truck, to reimburse Dodson his $4,900 purchase price.

On appeal, the Tennessee supreme court reconsidered the fairness of this result. In an effort to balance more fairly the rights of minors against those of innocent merchants, the court adopted a new approach to the infancy doctrine. The court held that a minor's recovery of the full purchase price is subject to a deduction for his "use" of the consideration he received under the contract, or for the "depreciation" or "deterioration" of the consideration in his possession.

The court stated the following rule: "Where the minor has not been overreached in any way, and there has been no undue influence, and the contract is a fair and reasonable one, and the minor has actually paid money on the purchase price, and taken and used the article purchased, that he ought not to be permitted to recover the amount actually paid, without allowing the vendor of the goods reasonable compensation for the use of depreciation, and willful or negligent damage to the article purchased, while in his hands. If there has been any fraud or imposition on the part of the seller or if the contract is unfair, or any unfair advantage has been taken of the minor inducing him to make the purchase, then the rule does not apply."

Based on this new rule, the court remanded the case for a determination of damages.

The basic premise of the infancy doctrine is the same: An infant's contract is voidable and the infant has an absolute right to disaffirm. What has changed is that the minor now owes a duty of restitution—rather than a duty of restoration—under the circumstances outlined by the Tennessee supreme court.

The court noted that this new standard is not a quantum leap in the evolution of the common law, only a practical recognition of the status of minors in our society. The court stated that the new rule will have a better moral influence on minors because the old rule lead to the "corruption of principles and encouraged young people in habits of trickery and dishonesty." The modern trend among states is to adopt this new standard for the infancy doctrine.
[*Dodson v. Shrader's Auto Sales*, 824 S.W.2d 545 (TN 1992)]

MENTALLY INCOMPETENT PERSONS

Insanity vitiates all acts.

Sir John Nicholl
Countess of Portsmouth v.
Earl of Portsmouth *(1828)*

Mental incapacity may arise because of mental illness, brain damage, mental retardation, senility, and the like. The law protects people suffering from substantial mental incapacity from enforcement of contracts against them because such persons may not understand the consequences of their actions in entering into a contract.

To be relieved of his or her duties under a contract, the law requires a person to have been legally insane at the time of entering into the contract. This is called **legal insanity**. Most states use the *objective cognitive "understanding" test* to determine legal insanity. Under this test, the person's mental incapacity must render that person incapable of understanding or comprehending the nature of the transaction. Mere weakness of intellect, slight psychological or emotional problems, or delusions do not constitute legal insanity. The law has developed the following two standards concerning contracts of mentally incompetent persons.

legal insanity

A state of contractual incapacity as determined by law.

Adjudged Insane

adjudged insane

A person who has been adjudged insane by a proper court or administrative agency. A contract entered into by such person is *void*.

In certain cases, a relative, loved one, or other interested party may institute a legal action to have someone declared legally (i.e., adjudged) insane. If, after hearing the evidence at a formal judicial or administrative hearing, the person is **adjudged insane**, the court will make that person a ward of the court and appoint a guardian to act on that person's behalf. If a person has been adjudged insane, any contract entered into by that person is *void*. That is, no contract exists. The court-appointed guardian is the only one who has the legal authority to enter into contracts on behalf of the person.

Insane, but Not Adjudged Insane

If no formal ruling has been made, any contracts entered into by a person who suffers from a mental impairment that makes him or her legally insane are voidable by the insane person. Unless the other party does not have contractual capacity, he or she does not have the option to avoid the contract.

Some people have alternating periods of sanity and insanity. Any contracts made by such a person during a lucid interval are enforceable. Contracts made while the person was not legally sane can be disaffirmed.

A person who has dealt with an insane person must place that insane person in status quo if the contract is either void or voided by the insane person. Most states hold that a party who did not know he or she was dealing with an insane person must be placed in status quo upon avoidance of the contract. Insane persons are liable in *quasi-contract* to pay the reasonable value for necessaries of life they receive.

insane, but not adjudged insane
A person who is insane but has not been adjudged insane by a court or administrative agency. A contract entered into by such a person is generally *voidable*. Some states hold that such a contract is void.

CONCEPT SUMMARY   DISAFFIRMANCE OF CONTRACTS BASED ON LEGAL INSANITY

Type of Legal Insanity	Disaffirmance Rule
Adjudged insane	Contract is void. Neither party can enforce the contract.
Insane, but not adjudged insane	Contract is voidable by the insane person; the competent party cannot void the contract.

INTOXICATED PERSONS

Most states provide that contracts entered into by **intoxicated persons** are voidable by that person. The intoxication may occur because of alcohol or drugs. The contract is not voidable by the other party if that party had contractual capacity.

Under the majority rule, the contract is voidable only if the person was so intoxicated when the contract was entered into that he or she was incapable of understanding or comprehending the nature of the transaction. In most states, this rule holds even if the intoxication was self-induced. Some states only allow the person to disaffirm the contract if the person were forced to become intoxicated or did so unknowingly.

The amount of alcohol or drugs that are necessary to be consumed by a person to be considered legally intoxicated to disaffirm contracts varies from case to case. The factors that are considered include the user's physical characteristics and his or her ability to "hold" intoxicants.

A person who disaffirms a contract based on intoxication generally must be returned to the status quo. In turn, the intoxicated person generally must return the consideration received under the contract to the other party and make restitution that returns the other party to status quo. After becoming sober, an intoxicated person can ratify the contracts he or she entered into while intoxicated. Intoxicated persons are liable in *quasi-contract* to pay the reasonable value for necessaries of life they receive.

intoxicated person
A person who is under contractual incapacity because of ingestion of alcohol or drugs to the point of incompetence.

In the following case, the court permitted a person to disaffirm the contract because she was intoxicated.

Smith v. Williamson
429 So.2d 598 (1983)
Court of Civil Appeals of Alabama

CASE 12.2

FACTS

Carolyn Ann Williamson entered into a contract to sell her house to Mr. and Mrs. Matthews at a time when her house was threatened with foreclosure. Evidence showed that Williamson was an alcoholic. Having read about the threatened foreclosure in the newspaper, attorney Virgil M. Smith appeared at Williamson's home to discuss the matter with her. Williamson told Smith that she expected to receive $17,000 from the sale but had actually received $1,700. On the following day, after drinking a pint of 100-proof vodka, Williamson and her son went to Smith's office, where Smith prepared a lawsuit to have the sale of the house set aside based on Williamson's lack of capacity due to alcoholism. At that time, Smith loaned Williamson $500 and took back a note and mortgage on her house to secure repayment of this amount and his attorney fees. Evidence showed that Smith did not allow Williamson's son to read the mortgage. The sale to Mr. and Mrs. Matthews was set aside. Subsequently, Smith began foreclosure proceedings on Williamson's house to recover attorney's fees and advances. Williamson filed this lawsuit to enjoin the foreclosure. The trial court held that Smith's mortgage was void and permanently enjoined him from foreclosing on it. Smith appealed.

ISSUE

Was Williamson's alcoholism a sufficient mental incapacity to void the mortgage?

IN THE LANGUAGE OF THE COURT

Bradley, Judge   In essence, Smith takes the position that while Ms. Williamson had been drinking on the morning that she executed the mortgage to him, the transaction was still valid because she had sufficient capacity to understand the nature of the act, and it was free from fraud and undue influence.

To accept Smith's position would require us to ignore certain subtle ironies arising from the facts of this appeal and the nature of the fiduciary relationship between attorney and client. The transaction between Ms. Williamson and the Matthewses that was eventually set aside by the Supreme Court on the ground of mental incapacity occurred on October 11, 1978. The record indicates that on that evening Smith appeared unsolicited at Ms. Williamson's home and assured her that he could help her with her legal problem. In overturning the contract and deed to the Matthewses, the Alabama Supreme Court found that Ms. Williamson was incapable of understanding the nature of the transaction and also found that her intoxication, coupled with the gross inadequacy of consideration, supported this result.

The record indicates that Ms. Williamson executed the note and mortgage on her home to Smith on October 12, 1978, the following morning. The record further shows that Ms. Williamson had consumed a pint of 100-proof vodka and that she remained in an agitated state over the sale of her home. To hold that Ms. Williamson was incapable of understanding the nature of the transaction with the Matthewses and then to hold that she was able to comprehend the nature of her dealings with Smith would be to reach illogical results, especially in light of the facts presented at trial.

DECISION AND REMEDY

The appellate court held that Williamson was not bound to the contract and mortgage with attorney Smith because she was mentally incompetent by reason of intoxication at the time she signed the documents. Affirmed.

Case Questions

Critical Legal Thinking   Should the law protect persons who voluntarily become intoxicated from their contracts?

Ethics   Do you think that attorney Smith acted ethically in this case?

Business Application   Do you think many business deals are entered into after the parties have been drinking? Should these deals be allowed to be voided?

ILLEGALITY—CONTRACTS CONTRARY TO STATUTES

Both federal and state legislatures have enacted statutes that prohibit certain types of conduct. For example, penal codes make certain activities crimes, antitrust statutes prohibit certain types of agreements between competitors, and so on. Contracts to perform an activity that is prohibited by statute are illegal contracts.

Usury Laws

State **usury laws** set an upper limit on the annual interest rate that can be charged on certain types of loans. The limits vary from state to state. Lenders who charge a higher rate than the state limit are guilty of usury. The primary purpose of these laws is to protect unsophisticated borrowers from loan sharks and others who charge exorbitant rates of interest.

Most states provide criminal and civil penalties for making usurious loans. Some states require lenders to remit the difference between the interest rate charged on the loan and the usury rate to the borrower. Other states prohibit lenders from collecting any interest on the loan. Still other states provide that a usurious loan is a void contract, permitting the borrower not to have to pay the interest or the principal of the loan to the lender.

Most usury laws exempt certain types of lenders and loan transactions involving legitimate business transactions from the reach of the law. Often, these exemptions include loans made by banks and other financial institutions, loans above a certain dollar amount, loans made to corporations and other businesses, and such.

usury law
A law that sets an upper limit on the interest rate that can be charged on certain types of loans.

Gambling Statutes

All states either prohibit or regulate gambling, wagering, lotteries, and games of chance. States provide various criminal and civil penalties for illegal gambling. There is a distinction between lawful risk-shifting contracts and gambling contracts. For example, if property insurance is purchased on one's own car and the car is destroyed in an accident, the insurance company must pay the claim. This is a lawful risk-shifting contract because the purchaser had an "insurable interest" in the car. However, insurance purchased on a neighbor's car would be considered to be gambling. The purchaser does not have an insurable interest in the car and is betting only on its destruction.

There are many exceptions to wagering laws. For example, many states have enacted statutes that permit games of chance under a certain dollar amount, bingo games, lotteries conducted by religious and charitable organizations, and the like. Many states also permit and regulate horse racing, harness racing, dog racing, and state-operated lotteries.

gambling statutes
Statutes that make certain forms of gambling illegal.

Business Brief
Many states have amended gambling laws to permit state-operated lotteries.

Sabbath Laws

Certain states have enacted laws—called **Sabbath laws, Sunday laws,** or **blue laws**—that prohibit or limit the carrying-on of certain secular activities on Sundays. Except for contracts for the necessaries of life, charitable donations, and such, these laws generally prohibit or invalidate executory contracts that are entered into on Sunday. Many states do not actively enforce these laws. In some states, they have even been found to be unconstitutional.

Sabbath law
A law that prohibits or limits the carrying-on of certain secular activities on Sundays.

Contracts to Commit a Crime

As mentioned previously, contracts to commit criminal acts are void. If the object of a contract became illegal after the contract was entered into because the government enacted a statute that made it unlawful, the parties are discharged from the contract. The contract is not an illegal contract unless the parties agree to go forward and complete it.

Licensing Statutes

All states require members of certain professions and occupations to be licensed by the state in which they practice. Lawyers, doctors, real estate agents, insurance agents, certified public accountants, teachers, contractors, hairdressers, and such are among them. In most instances, a **license** is granted to persons who demonstrate that they have the proper schooling, experience, and moral character required by the relevant statute. Sometimes a written examination is also required.

licensing statute
Statute that requires a person or business to obtain a license from the government prior to engaging in a specified occupation or activity.

Problems arise if an unlicensed person tries to collect payment for services provided to another under a contract. Some statutes expressly provide that unlicensed persons cannot enforce contracts to provide these services. If the statute is silent on the point, enforcement depends on whether it is a *regulatory statute* or a *revenue raising statute*.

regulatory statute
A licensing statute enacted to protect the public.

Regulatory Statutes   Licensing statutes enacted to protect the public are called **regulatory statutes**. Generally, unlicensed persons cannot recover payment for services that a regulatory statute requires a licensed person to provide.

Consider This Example   State law provides that legal services can be provided only by the lawyers who have graduated from law school and passed the appropriate bar exam. Nevertheless, Marie Sweiger, a first-year law student, agrees to draft a will for Randy McCabe for a $150 fee. Because Ms. Sweiger is not licensed to provide legal services, she has violated a regulatory statute. She cannot enforce the contract and recover payment from Mr. McCabe.

revenue raising statute
A licensing statute with the primary purpose of raising revenue for the government.

Revenue Raising Statutes   Licensing statutes enacted to raise money for the government are called **revenue raising statutes**. A person who provides services pursuant to a contract without the appropriate license required by such a statute can enforce the contract and recover payment for services rendered. For example, suppose a state licensing statute requires licensed attorneys to pay an annual $200 license fee without requiring continuing education or other new qualifications. A licensed attorney who forgets to pay the fee can enforce contracts and recover payment for the legal services he or she renders. That is because the statute merely gathers revenue—protection of the public is not a factor.

Contemporary Business Application

AN UNLICENSED CONTRACTOR GETS DUNKED

The doctrine of illegality is designed to protect persons from certain types of contracts deemed unfair, unscrupulous, or unconscionable by society. The doctrine denies violators access to taxpayer-supported courts to enforce their illegal contracts. Should parties sometimes be allowed to enforce their otherwise illegal contract? Consider the following case.

Hydrotech Systems, Ltd. (Hydrotech), is a New York corporation that manufactures and installs patented equipment to simulate ocean waves. Oasis Waterpark (Oasis) is a California corporation that owns and operates a water-oriented amusement park in Palm Springs, California. Wessman Construction Company, Inc. (Wessman), is Oasis's general contractor at the park.

In July 1985, Wessman contracted with Hydrotech to design and construct a 29,000-square foot "surfing pool" at the park using Hydrotech's wave equipment. The total contract price was $850,000. Hydrotech was aware of a California law that requires a contractor to have a California contractor's license to provide construction services in California. The statute stipulates that an unlicensed con-

tractor cannot sue in a California court to recover compensation for work requiring a California contractor's license [California Business and Professional Code § 7031].

Because it was concerned with the licensing problem, Hydrotech wished only to sell and deliver the equipment and to avoid involvement in the design or construction of the pool. Oasis, however, insisted that Hydrotech's unique expertise in design and construction was essential. Oasis induced Hydrotech to provide these services by promising to pay Hydrotech even if the law provided otherwise.

In reliance on these promises, Hydrotech furnished equipment and services in full compliance with the contract. Hydrotech had been paid $740,000 during the course of the contract. When it billed Oasis for the remaining $110,000, Oasis refused to pay. Hydrotech sued Oasis and Wessman for damages in California court for breach of contract and fraud. The defendants moved the court to dismiss the action because Hydrotech did not possess a California contractor's license as required by law.

The California Supreme Court agreed with the defendants and ordered Hydrotech's complaint dismissed. The court found that Hydrotech had violated the licensing statute. The supreme court stated: "The obvious statutory intent is to discourage persons who have failed to comply with the licensing law from offering or providing their unlicensed services for pay. Because of the strength and clarity of this policy, it is well settled that Section 7031 applies despite injustice to the unlicensed contractor." [*Hydrotech Systems, Ltd. v. Oasis Waterpark*, 52 Cal.3d 988, 277 Cal.Rptr. 517 (Cal. 1991)]

ℐLLEGALITY—CONTRACTS CONTRARY TO PUBLIC POLICY

Certain contracts are illegal because they are **contrary to public policy**. Such contracts are void. Although *public policy* eludes a precise definition, the courts have held contracts to be contrary to public policy if they have a negative impact on society or interfere with the public's safety and welfare.

> **contracts contrary to public policy**
> Contracts that have a negative impact on society or interfere with the public's safety and welfare.

Immoral Contracts

Immoral contracts, that is, contracts whose objective is the commission of an act that is considered immoral by society, may be found to be against public policy. For example, a contract that is based on sexual favors has been held an immoral contract void as against public policy. Judges are not free to define morality based on their individual views. Instead, they must look to the practices and beliefs of society when defining immoral conduct.

The following case raises the issue of whether a contract violates public policy and is therefore illegal.

> *The law relating to public policy cannot remain immutable, it must change with the passage of time. The wind of change blows on it.*
>
> L. J. Danckwerts
> Nagle v. Feilden (1966)

Flood v. Fidelity & Guaranty Life Insurance Co.
394 So.2d 1311 (1981)
Court of Appeals of Louisiana

CASE 12.3

FACTS
Ellen and Richard Alvin Flood, who were married in 1965, lived in a house trailer in Louisiana. Richard worked as a maintenance man and Ellen was employed at an insurance agency. Evidence at trial showed that Ellen was unhappy with her marriage. Ellen took out a life insurance policy on the life of her husband and named herself as beneficiary. The policy was issued by Fidelity & Guaranty Life Insurance Co. (Fidelity). In June 1972, Richard became unexpectedly ill. He was taken to the hospital, where his condition improved. After a visit at the hospital from his wife, Richard died. Ellen was criminally charged with the murder of her husband by poisoning. Evidence showed that six medicine bottles at the couple's home, including Tylenol and paregoric bottles, contained arsenic. The court found that Ellen had fed Richard ice cubes laced with arsenic at the hospital. Ellen was tried and convicted of the murder of her husband. Ellen, as beneficiary of Richard's life insurance policy, requested Fidelity to pay her the benefits. Fidelity refused to pay the benefits and returned all premiums paid on the policy. This suit followed. The district court held in favor of Ellen Flood and awarded her the benefits of the life insurance policy. Fidelity appealed.

ISSUE
Was the life insurance policy an illegal contract that is void?

IN THE LANGUAGE OF THE COURT
Lear, Judge   Louisiana follows the majority rule that holds, as a matter of public policy, that a beneficiary named in a life insurance policy is not entitled to the proceeds of the insurance if the beneficiary feloniously kills the insured.

The genesis of this litigation is the escalating criminal action of Ellen Flood, bent on taking the life of her lawful husband. Our courts have previously adjudicated (1) the issue of the cause of death of Richard Flood, (2) the culprit in that death, and (3) the motives for the death. Under the peculiar circumstances of the case, it was unreasonable of the trial court not to consider and to assign great weight to the mountain of evidence tending to prove Mrs. Flood's scheme to defraud both the insurer, Fidelity, and the insured, Mr. Flood. It is clear to us that the entirety of the transaction here reviewed is tainted with the intendment of Ellen Flood to contravene the prohibitory law.

(case continues)

Life insurance policies are procured because life is, indeed, precarious and uncertain. Our law does not and cannot sanction any scheme that has as its purpose the certain infliction of death for, inter alia, financial gain through receipt of the proceeds of life insurance. To sanction this policy in any way would surely shackle the spirit, letter, and life of our laws.

DECISION AND REMEDY

The appellate court held that the life insurance policy that Ellen Flood had taken out on the life of her husband was void based on public policy. Reversed.

Case Questions

Critical Legal Thinking Should Ellen Flood have been allowed to retain the insurance proceeds in this case?

Ethics Did Ellen Flood act unethically in this case? Did she act illegally?

Business Application What would be the economic consequences if persons could recover insurance proceeds for losses caused by their illegal activities (e.g., murder, arson)?

Exculpatory Clauses

exculpatory clause

A contractual provision that relieves one (or both) parties to the contract from tort liability for ordinary negligence.

An **exculpatory clause** is a contractual provision that relieves one (or both) parties to the contract from tort liability. Exculpatory clauses can relieve a party of liability for ordinary negligence. They cannot be used in situations involving willful conduct, intentional torts, fraud, recklessness, or gross negligence. Exculpatory clauses are often found in leases, sales contracts, ticket stubs to sporting events, parking lot tickets, services contracts, and the like. Such clauses do not have to be reciprocal (i.e., one party may be relieved of tort liability while the other party is not).

Generally, the courts do not favor exculpatory clauses unless both parties have equal bargaining power. The courts are willing to permit competent parties of equal bargaining power to establish which of them bears the risk.

Consider This Example Jim Jackson voluntarily enrolled in a parachute jump course and signed a contract containing an exculpatory clause that relieved the parachute center of liability. After receiving proper instructions, he jumped from an airplane. Unfortunately, Jim was injured when he could not steer his parachute toward the target area. He sued the parachute center for damages, but the court enforced the exculpatory clause, reasoning that parachute jumping did not involve an essential service and that there was no decisive advantage in bargaining power between the parties.

Business Brief

Exculpatory clauses are void as against public policy if they either (1) affect the *public interest* or (2) result from the superior bargaining power of the party asserting the clause.

Exculpatory clauses that either affect the *public interest* or result from superior bargaining power are usually found to be void as against public policy. Although the outcome varies with the circumstances of the case, the greater the degree that the party serves the general public, the greater the chance that the exculpatory clause will be struck down as illegal. The courts will consider such factors as the type of activity involved and the relative bargaining power, knowledge, experience, and sophistication of the parties.

In the following case, the court had to decide the legality of an exculpatory clause.

Gardner v. Downtown Porsche Audi
180 Cal.App.3d 713, 225 Cal.Rptr. 757 (1986)
Court of Appeals of California

CASE 12.4

FACTS

In late June 1978, Bruce Gardner took his 1976 Porsche 911 automobile to be repaired at Downtown Porsche Audi (Downtown), located in downtown Los Angeles, California. Evidence showed that Gardner signed Downtown's repair-

order form contract, which contained the following exculpatory clause disclaiming Downtown from liability: "NOT RESPONSIBLE FOR LOSS OR DAMAGE TO CARS OR ARTICLES LEFT IN CARS IN CASE OF FIRE, THEFT OR ANY OTHER CAUSE BEYOND OUR

CONTROL." Someone stole Gardner's Porsche while it was parked at Downtown's repair garage. Gardner sued Downtown for failing to redeliver the car to him. The trial court found in favor of Gardner and awarded him $16,000 plus costs against Downtown. Downtown appealed.

ISSUE

Does the contract involve a "public interest" that would cause the exculpatory clause to be void?

IN THE LANGUAGE OF THE COURT

Johnson, Justice   This case raises an issue common in daily life: May an automobile repair garage avoid liability for its negligence by having car owners sign a waiver form when they leave their cars with the garage? California now follows the modern view of § 485 of the Restatement (Second) of Contracts—"a contract exempting from liability for ordinary negligence is valid where no public interest is involved and no statute expressly prohibits it." An automobile repair garage cannot exempt itself from liability even for ordinary negligence if the services it provides implicate the public interest.

The modern citizen lives—and all too frequently dies—by the automobile. Members of the general public need cars not merely for discretionary recreational purposes but to get to and from their places of employment, to reach the stores where they can purchase the necessities—as well as the frivolities—of life, and the like. An out-of-repair automobile is an unreliable means of transporta-tion. Moreover, it is a dangerous one as well—to pedestrians and other drivers, not just the owner. What is true of modern societies in general is doubly true in Southern California, the capital of the motor vehicle. Indeed it is virtually impossible to exist in the Los Angeles area without a fully operational automobile. Thus, except for the few who can afford to buy a new car every time the ashtrays fill up, people in this area find the automobile repair business a service of great importance and a practical necessity.

We conclude automobile repair contracts affect the "public interest." It follows that clauses that exculpate repair firms for ordinary negligence in handling and securing vehicles under repair are invalid as contrary to public policy.

DECISION AND REMEDY

The appellate court held that the car repair contract involved the public's interest and the exculpatory clause was therefore void. Affirmed.

Case Questions

Critical Legal Thinking   Should exculpatory clauses that involve the public interest be struck down as void as against public policy? Would an exculpatory clause used by a doctor be valid?

Ethics   Did Downtown Porsche Audi act ethically in denying liability in this case?

Business Application   Why do firms use exculpatory clauses?

Entrepreneur and the Law

USING A COVENANT NOT TO COMPETE WITH A SALE OF A BUSINESS

Entrepreneurs and others often buy and sell businesses. The sale of a business includes its "goodwill" or reputation. To protect this goodwill after the sale, the seller often enters into an agreement with the buyer not to engage in a similar business or occupation within a specified geographical area for a specified period of time following the sale. This agreement is called a **covenant not to compete**, or a **noncompete clause**.

Covenants not to compete that are *ancillary* to a legitimate sale of a business or employment contract are lawful if they are reasonable in three aspects: (1) the line of business protected, (2) the geographical area protected, and (3) the duration of the restriction. A covenant that is found to be unreasonable is not enforceable as written. The reasonableness of covenants not to compete are examined on a case-by-case basis. If a covenant not to compete is unreasonable, the courts may either refuse to enforce it or change it so that it is reasonable. Usually, the courts choose the first option.

Consider This Example   Suppose Stacy Rogers is a certified public accountant (CPA) with a lucrative practice in San Diego, California. Her business includes a substantial amount of goodwill. When she sells her practice she agrees not to open another accounting practice in the state of California for a 50-year period. This covenant not to compete is reasonable in the line of business protected but is unreasonable in geographical scope and duration. It will not be enforced by the courts as written. The covenant not to compete would be reasonable and enforceable if it prohibited Ms. Rogers only from practicing as a CPA in the city of San Diego for five years.

A covenant not to compete that is not *ancillary* to a legitimate business transaction is void as against public policy because the noncompete clause is not protecting a

(box continues)

legitimate business interest. For example, a contract where one lawyer paid another lawyer not to open an office nearby would be void as against public policy because it is not ancillary to a legitimate business transaction.

Employment contracts often contain noncompete clauses that prohibit an employee from competing with his or her employer for a certain time period after leaving the employment.

EFFECT OF ILLEGALITY

Because illegal contracts are void, the parties cannot sue for nonperformance. Further, if an illegal contract is executed, the court will generally leave the parties where it finds them.

Exceptions to the General Rule

Business Brief

As a general rule, the courts will refuse to enforce or rescind an illegal contract and will leave the parties where it finds them.

Certain situations are exempt from the general rule of the effect of finding an illegal contract. If an exception applies, the innocent party may use the court system to sue for damages or to recover consideration paid under the illegal contract. Persons who can assert an exception are

- Innocent persons who were justifiably ignorant of the law or fact that made the contract illegal. For example, a person who purchases insurance from an unlicensed insurance company may recover insurance benefits from the unlicensed company.
- Persons who were induced to enter into an illegal contract by fraud, duress, or undue influence. For example, a shop owner who pays $5,000 "protection money" to a mobster so that his or her store will not be burned down by the mobster can recover the $5,000.
- Persons who entered into an illegal contract withdraw before the illegal act is performed. For example, if the president of New Toy Corporation pays $10,000 to an employee of Old Toy Corporation to steal a trade secret from his or her employer, but reconsiders and tells the employee not to do it before he or she has done it, the New Toy Corporation may recover the $10,000.
- Persons who were less at fault than the other party for entering into the illegal contract. At common law, parties to an illegal contract were considered **in pari delicto** (in equal fault). Some states have changed this rule and permit less at fault parties to recover restitution of the consideration they paid under an illegal contract from the more-at-fault parties.

in pari delicto

When both parties are equally at fault in an illegal contract.

In the following case, the court found an illegal contract and left the parties where it found them.

Ryno v. Tyra
752 S.W.2d 148 (1988)
Court of Appeals of Texas

CASE 12.5

FACTS
R. D. Ryno, Jr., owned Bavarian Motors, an automobile dealership in Fort Worth, Texas. On March 5, 1981, Lee Tyra discussed purchasing a 1980 BMW M-1 from Ryno for $125,000. Ryno then suggested a double-or-nothing coin flip, to which Tyra agreed. When Tyra won the coin flip, Ryno said, "It's yours," and handed Tyra the keys and German title to the car. Tyra drove away in the car. This suit ensued as to the ownership of the car. The trial court held in favor of Tyra. Ryno appealed.

ISSUE
Was there an illegal contract? If so, who owns the car?

IN THE LANGUAGE OF THE COURT
Farris, Justice *Ryno complains that the trial court erred in granting Tyra judgment because the judgment enforces a gambling contract. We find there was sufficient evidence to sustain the jury finding that Ryno intended to transfer to Tyra his ownership interest in the BMW at the time he delivered the documents, keys, and possession of the automobile to Tyra. We agree*

with appellant Ryno that his wager with Tyra was unenforceable. The trial court could not have compelled Ryno to honor his wager by delivering the BMW to Tyra. However, Ryno did deliver the BMW to Tyra and the facts incident to that delivery are sufficient to establish a transfer by gift of the BMW from Ryno to Tyra.

DECISION AND REMEDY

Tyra, the patron at the car dealership who won the coin toss, owns the car. The appellate court found that there was an illegal contract and left the parties where it found them—that is, with Tyra in possession of the car. Affirmed.

Case Questions

Critical Legal Thinking Should the court have lent its resources to help Ryno recover the car?

Ethics Did Ryno act ethically in this case?

Business Application What is the moral of this story if you ever win anything in an illegal gambling contract?

UNCONSCIONABLE CONTRACTS

The general rule of freedom of contract holds that if (1) the object of a contract is lawful and (2) the other elements for the formation of a contract are met, the courts will enforce a contract according to its terms. Although it is generally presumed that parties are capable of protecting their own interests when contracting, it is a fact of life that dominant parties sometimes take advantage of weaker parties. As a result, some lawful contracts are so oppressive or manifestly unfair that they are unjust. To prevent the enforcement of such contracts, the courts developed the equitable **doctrine of unconscionability**, which is based on public policy. A contract found to be unconscionable under this doctrine is called an **unconscionable contract**, or a **contract of adhesion**.

The courts are given substantial discretion in determining whether a contract or contract clause is unconscionable. There is no single definition of *unconscionability*. The doctrine may not be used merely to save a contracting party from a bad bargain.

unconscionability
A doctrine under which courts may deny enforcement of unfair or oppressive contracts.

Elements of an Unconscionable Contract

The following elements must be shown to prove that a contract or clause in a contract is unconscionable:

1. The parties possessed severely unequal bargaining power.
2. The dominant party unreasonably used its unequal bargaining power to obtain oppressive or manifestly unfair contract terms.
3. The adhering party had no reasonable alternative.

In other words, the dominant party must *misuse* its greater power to obtain oppressive contract terms from the adhering party, and the adhering party must prove that it could not reasonably refuse to accept those terms. This is often proven by showing that the oppressive terms are contained in standard contracts used industrywide.

Business Brief
Unconscionability is extremely subjective. This doctrine does not change the general rule that parties are free to make a bad bargain. Only *unconscionable* contracts are unenforceable.

Remedies for Unconscionability

If the court finds that a contract or a contract clause is unconscionable, it may (1) refuse to enforce the contract, (2) refuse to enforce the unconscionable clause but enforce the remainder of the contract, or (3) limit the applicability of any unconscionable clause so as to avoid any unconscionable result. The appropriate remedy depends on the facts and circumstances of each case. Note that because unconscionability is a matter of law, the judge may opt to decide the case without a jury trial.

Ethical Perspective _____

SUPERCUTS GIVEN CREWCUT BY THE COURT

Sometimes contracts favor one party over another party. This unbalance often occurs when the strongest party drafts the contract and presents it to the other party on a take-it-or-leave-it basis. Mere unbalanced contracts are not necessarily illegal, but those that overreach and are too lopsided can be found to be unenforceable under the equitable doctrine of **unconscionability**. Consider the following case.

Supercuts, Inc., a Delaware corporation, conducts a national hair care franchise business. The president of Supercuts is David E. Lipson. From January 1993 until March 1994, Supercuts employed William N. Stirlen as its vice president and chief financial officer. Stirlen signed an employment agreement that was prepared by Supercuts. The contract provided for Stirlen to receive an annual salary of $150,000, stock options, a bonus plan, a supplemental retirement plan, and a $10,000 signing bonus. The contract was an at-will employment contract, meaning that Stirlen could be terminated without cause at any time.

Late in 1993 and early in 1994, Stirlen informed Lipson and other corporate officers of various problems and "accounting irregularities" he feared might be in violation of state and federal statutes. Stirlen also expressed concern that the company's decline in profits "was being hidden in the books and from public shareholders." At a meeting in November 1993, Stirlen provided senior managers with accounting statements outlining the accounting irregularities. After Stirlen brought these issues to Supercuts's outside auditors, Lipson allegedly reprimanded Stirlen and accused him of being a "troublemaker." Lipson also told him that if Stirlen did not reverse his position on these issues, he would no longer be considered a "member of the team." At the end of February 1994, Lipson suspended Stirlen from his job; Stirlen was fired the following month.

Stirlen sued Supercuts and Lipson for breach of contract, wrongful termination in violation of public policy, and intentional misrepresentation. The defendants made a motion to the court alleging that the arbitration clause in

Stirlen's employment contract required the dispute to be arbitrated. Stirlen countered that the arbitration clause, and other clauses in Supercuts' contract, were unconscionable and therefore unenforceable. The challenged clauses provided that (1) Stirlen would have to submit to final and binding arbitration of all disputes concerning the contract, but that Supercuts could go to court on most matters if it sued Stirlen, (2) any damages that could be awarded Stirlen could not exceed the actual damages for breach of contract, and (3) any salary or benefits payable to Stirlen would cease pending the outcome of any action between the parties.

Stirlen argued that the employment contract was so one-sided as to be "unconscionable." The court of appeals held that a contract is unconscionable if it "does not fall within the reasonable expectations of the weaker party" or if the contract is "unduly oppressive." Supercuts's attorneys argued that Stirlen was a sophisticated business executive who knew what he was doing when he signed Supercuts' contract.

After weighing all the evidence, the court found that Supercuts's contract was an **unconscionable contract**—a **contract of adhesion**—that was unenforceable. The court found Supercuts' contract to be unconscionable in the following ways: Supercuts reserved the right to sue in court but denied this right to Stirlen; Supercuts limited the damages that Stirlen could recover from them in violation of the law; and state law provided that a party could not require another party to waive the ability to sue for fraud, which Supercuts required Stirlen to do. The court also held that Stirlen could proceed with his lawsuit against Supercuts to recover damages. [*Stirlen v. Supercuts, Inc.*, 52 Cal.App.4th 1519, 60 Cal.Rptr.2d 138 (1997)]

1. Is the doctrine of unconscionability supported by ethical principles? Explain.
2. Did Supercuts act ethically in drafting its employment contract? Should it have been more "fair"?
3. Did Stirlen act ethically by refusing to be a "team member"? What would you have done?

International Perspective _____

COMITY: THE GOLDEN RULE AMONG NATIONS

The **comity principle** is a rule among nations—that each will respect the laws of others. It is not a rule of law, but one of practice. The

courts of the United States resort to the comity principle as a rationale for not applying U.S. law to foreign persons or situations where (1) concurrent jurisdiction exists with a foreign country and (2) foreign law is different from U.S. law. The following case is an example of the application of this doctrine.

Lee Wong, a U.S. citizen and California resident, was a produce grower who wanted to set up farming operations in Mexico. The Mexican Constitution, however, prohibited foreign ownership and control of farming operations. Therefore, Wong contracted with several Mexican citizens to act as "front men" for him to own and operate his farming operations in Mexico. Wong provided the money, and the front men acquired farming property in Mexico.

Wong entered into marketing contracts with a subsidiary of Tenneco, Inc. (Tenneco), a California corporation. Tenneco, with full knowledge of the nature of Wong's interest in the Mexican farming operations, purchased farm products from Wong. After several years, the Mexican government discovered Wong's interest and began threatening the front men with foreclosure and government action for nonpayment of taxes on the farming operation. In January 1975, Tenneco bowed to the demands of the front men and severed its ties with Wong. Tenneco began purchasing the farm produce directly from the front men. Wong sued Tenneco in California court to recover damages for breach of contract. The jury awarded Wong $1,691,422 in damages.

Tenneco argued that its contract with Wong violated Mexican law and therefore the United States should not enforce the contract. The California Supreme Court agreed and refused to enforce the jury's verdict. The court stated

A contract with a view of violating the laws of another country, though not otherwise obnoxious to the law of the forum, will not be enforced. Protection of persons, like Wong, who wrongfully seek to circumvent the substantive laws of one jurisdiction by enlisting the aid of the courts in another violates and offends public policy of both jurisdictions. In the interest of comity, our courts must vigilantly resist such recruitment efforts.

Applying principles of comity, we conclude that Wong's failure to comply with the requirements of Mexican law casts a pall of illegality over all of his business transactions tied to the Mexican farming operation, including the marketing arrangement with Tenneco. California public policy dictates that we leave the parties as we found them.

Adherence to the comity principle demonstrates nations' respect for the laws of other nations. It has been characterized as the golden rule among nations, and it will grow in importance as the number of international transactions increase. [*Wong v. Tenneco, Inc.*, 39 Cal.3d 126, 216 Cal.Rptr. 412 (Cal. 1985)]

Working the Web

LawGuru.com LawGuru is a way to access over 340 legal search engines and tools.

Visit at **www.lawguru.com**

LawRunner LawRunner has advanced query parameters for legal researchers. It offers more than 1,100 advanced query templates to make locating legal information more efficient. It has a superior index of more than 30,000,000 Web pages found on 476,000 servers.

Visit at **www.lawrunner.com**

UNC Legal Research Project LibClient was developed by the University of North Carolina in conjunction with the American Association of Law Libraries. It is a very intelligent search tool for legal researchers.

Visit at **legalresearch.ils.unc.edu**

Yahoo-Law Yahoo-Law is a great index of links to many legal topics such as law schools, lawyer jokes, legal ethics, legal research, and tax.

Visit at **www.yahoo.com/Law**

CYBER EXERCISES

1–5. Select a recent U.S. Court of Appeals case such as *Atkin v. Smith*, 137 F.3d 1169 (1998). Select at least two of the search engines or indexes listed above and try to find the full text of the case.

CASES AND EXERCISES

CRITICAL LEGAL THINKING CASES

12.1. James Halbman, Jr., a minor, entered into a contract to purchase a 1968 Oldsmobile automobile from Michael Lemke. Halbman paid $1,000 cash and agreed to pay $25 per week until the full purchase price was paid. Five weeks later a connecting rod on the vehicle's engine broke, and Halbman took the car to a garage where it was repaired at a cost of $637.40. Halbman refused to pay for the repairs, disaffirmed the contract with Lemke, and notified Lemke where the car was located. When Lemke refused to pick up the car and pay the repair bill, the garage legally satisfied its garageman's lien by removing the vehicle's engine. It then towed the car to Halbman's residence. Halbman notified Lemke to remove the car, but Lemke refused to do so. The car was subsequently vandalized, making it worthless and unsalvageable. Halbman sued to disaffirm the contract and recover the consideration from Lemke. Lemke argued that Halbman must make full restitution. Who is correct? [*Halbman v. Lemke*, 298 N.W.2d 562 (Wis. 1980)]

12.2. Steven M. Kiefer purchased an automobile from Fred Howe Motors, Inc. At the time of the purchase, Kiefer was a minor of 20 years of age, married, the father of a child, and emancipated from his parents. Kiefer then disaffirmed the contract, claiming his rights as a minor. Howe urged that emancipated minors were an exception to this rule and that emancipated minors were legally responsible for their contracts. Can Kiefer disaffirm the contract? [*Kiefer v. Fred Howe Motors, Inc.*, 158 N.W.2d 288 (WI 1968)]

12.3. Charles Edwards Smith, a minor, purchased an automobile from Bobby Floars Toyota (Toyota) on August 15, 1973. Smith executed a security agreement to finance part of the balance due on the purchase price, agreeing to pay off the balance in 30 monthly installments. On September 25, 1973, Smith turned 18, which was the age of majority. Smith made 10 monthly payments after turning 18. He then decided to disaffirm the contract and stopped making the payments. Smith claimed that he may disaffirm the contract entered into when he was a minor. Toyota argued that Smith had ratified the contract since attaining the age of majority. Who is correct? [*Bobby Floars Toyota, Inc. v. Smith*, 269 S.E. 320 (N.C.App. 1980)]

12.4. Bobby I. Rogers, a 19-year-old emancipated minor, had to quit engineering school and go to work to support his wife and expected baby. Rogers contracted with Gastonia Personnel Corporation (Gastonia), an employment agency, agreeing to pay Gastonia a $295 fee if it found him employment. Soon thereafter, Rogers was employed by a company referred to him by Gastonia. Rogers sought to disaffirm the contract to pay Gastonia the $295 fee. Gastonia sued for the fee, claiming that the contract was for necessaries. Who wins? [*Gastonia Personnel Corporation v. Rogers*, 172 S.E.2d 19 (NC 1970)]

12.5. Dwaine Ebsen, an 18-year-old minor, lived with his widowed mother, Violet. After numerous arguments with his mother regarding the people he associated with, Dwaine and his mother agreed that he should move out and support himself. Dwaine took his personal belongings and moved to Orchard, Nebraska. After moving out, Dwaine received no further support from his mother. While living in Orchard, Dwaine was shot and was taken to a hospital for treatment. He remained in the hospital for two weeks. Thereafter, the hospital sought payment from Violet. When she refused to pay, the hospital turned the matter over to Accent Service Company, a collection agency, that brought this action against Violet. Is Violet liable for her son's medical expenses? [*Accent Service Company v. Ebsen*, 306 N.W.2d 575 (NE 1981)]

12.6. Manzelle Johnson, who had been adjudicated insane, executed a quitclaim and warranty deed conveying real estate she owned to her guardian, Obbie Neal. Neal subsequently conveyed the real estate to James R. Beavers by warranty deed. Charles L. Weatherly, Miss Johnson's present guardian, brought this action seeking a decree of the court that title to the real estate be restored to Miss Johnson because of her inability to contract. Should Miss Johnson be allowed to void the contract? [*Beavers v. Weatherly*, 299 S.E.2d 730 (GA 1983)]

12.7. Betty Galloway, an alcoholic, signed a settlement agreement upon her divorce from her husband, Henry Galloway. Henry, in Betty's absence in court, stated that she had lucid intervals from her alcoholism, had been sober for two months, and was lucid when she signed the settlement agreement on September 22, 1978. Betty moved only to vacate the settlement agreement on September 27, 1978, after she had retained present legal counsel. On January 23, 1979,

Betty was declared incompetent to handle her person and her affairs, and a guardian and conservator was appointed. Betty, through her guardian, sued to have the settlement agreement voided. Who wins? [*Galloway v. Galloway*, 281 N.W.2d 804 (ND 1979)]

12.8. In 1972, Jordanos', Inc. (Jordanos') suspected and accused one of its employees, Arthur T. Allen, of theft. The union to which Allen belonged negotiated an oral contract with Jordanos' whereby Allen agreed to accept a permanent layoff if Jordanos' would not report the suspected theft to the state's unemployment agency so that Allen could collect unemployment benefits. Jordanos' agreed. It is a crime for an employer and employee to withhold relevant information from the state's unemployment agency. Jordanos' subsequently reported the suspected theft to the state's unemployment agency, and Allen was denied unemployment benefits. Allen sued Jordanos' for damages for breach of contract. Can Allen recover against Jordanos'? [*Allen v. Jordanos', Inc.*, 52 Cal.App.3d 160, 125 Cal.Rptr. 31 (Cal.App. 1975)]

12.9. James L. Strickland paid an unsolicited $2,500 bribe to Judge Sylvania W. Woods so that the judge would be lenient on a friend of Strickland's who had a case pending before Judge Woods. Paying a bribe to a government official is a crime. Judge Woods reported the incident and turned the money over to the state's attorney general. The state of Maryland indicted Strickland for bribery and sentenced him to four years in prison. Strickland filed a motion to recover the $2,500 from the state. Can Strickland recover the money? [*State of Maryland v. Strickland*, 400 A.2d 451 (Md.App. 1979)]

12.10. The state of Hawaii requires a person who wants to practice architecture to meet certain educational requirements and to pass a written examination before that person is granted a license to practice. After receiving the license, an architect must pay an annual license fee of $15. In 1967, Ben Lee Wilson satisfied the initial requirements and was granted an architecture license. He renewed his license by paying the annual fee up until April 1971, when he failed to pay the annual fee. In February 1972, Wilson contracted with Kealakekua Ranch, Ltd., and Gentry Hawaii (defendants) to provide architectural services for the Kealakekua Ranch Center Project. During the period February 1972 through May 1972, Wilson provided $33,994 of architectural services to the defendants. The defendants refused to pay this fee because Wilson did not have an architectural license. Wilson sued to collect his fees. Who wins? [*Wilson v. Kealakekua Ranch, Ltd., and Gentry Hawaii*, 551 P.2d 525 (HI 1976)]

12.11. American Home Enterprises, Inc. (American Home), was a corporation that made jewelry and drug paraphernalia, such as roach clips and bongs to smoke marijuana and tobacco. Evidence showed that American Home predominantly produced drug paraphernalia and was not engaged significantly in jewelry production. In 1978, Robert Bovard and James T. Ralph contracted to purchase American Home and, as part of the purchase price, executed several promissory notes payable to the sellers. Although at the time of the sale the manufacture of drug paraphernalia was not itself illegal, the possession, use, and transfer of marijuana was illegal. When Bovard and Ralph defaulted on the promissory notes, the sellers sued to enforce the notes. Bovard and Ralph allege that the contract is illegal and unenforceable as against public policy. Who wins? [*Bovard v. American Home Enterprises, Inc.*, 201 Cal.App.3d 832, 247 Cal.Rptr. 340 (Cal.App. 1988)]

12.12. Gerry Morris owned a silk screening and lettering shop in Tucson, Arizona. On April 11, 1974, Morris entered into a contract to sell the business to Alfred and Connie Gann. The contract contained the following covenant not to compete: "Seller agrees not to enter into silk screening or lettering shop business within Tucson and a 100-mile radius of Tucson, a period of ten (10) years from the date of this Agreement and will not compete in any manner whatsoever with buyers, and seller further agrees that he will refer all business contacts to buyers." Morris opened a silk screening and lettering business in competition with the Ganns and in violation of the noncompetition clause. The Ganns brought this action against Morris for breach of contract and to enforce the covenant not to compete. Is the covenant not to compete valid and enforceable in this case? [*Gann v. Morris*, 596 P.2d 43 (Ariz.App. 1979)]

12.13. Grady Perkins owned the Raleigh Institute of Cosmetology (Institute), and Ray Monk and Rovetta Allen were employed as instructors at the Institute. The school trains students to do hairstyling and coloring, cosmetology, and other beauty services. The students receive practical training by providing services to members of the public under the supervision of the instructors. On March 28, 1985, Francis I. Alston went to the Institute to have her hair colored and styled by a student who was under the supervision of Monk and Allen. Before receiving any services, Alston signed a written release form that released the Institute and its employees from liability for their negligence. While coloring Alston's hair, the student negligently used a chemical that caused Alston's hair to fall out. Alston sued the Institute, Perkins, Monk, and Allen for damages. The defendants asserted that the release form signed by Alston barred her suit. Is the exculpatory clause valid? [*Alston v. Monk*, 373 S.E.2d 463 (N.C.App. 1988)]

12.14. Wilbur Spaulding owned and operated the Jacksonville racetrack at the Morgan County Fairgrounds, where automobile races were held. Lawrence P. Koch was a flagman at the raceway. On May 28, 1982, when Koch arrived at the pit shack at the raceway, he was handed a clipboard upon which there was a track release and waiver of liability form that released the racetrack from liability for negligence. Koch signed the form and took up his position as flagman. During the first race, the last car on the track lost control and slid off the end of the track, striking Koch. Koch suffered a broken leg and other injuries and was unable to work for 14 months. Koch sued Spaulding for damages for negligence. Spaulding asserted that the release form signed by Koch barred his suit. Is the exculpatory clause valid against Koch? [*Koch v. Spaulding*, 529 N.E.2d 19 (Ill.App. 1988)]

12.15. Bill Graham, an experienced promoter and producer of musical concerts, entered into a contract with Leon Russell, a rock singer who did business under the corporate name Scissor-Tail, Inc., whereby Graham would promote several concerts for Russell. Russell belonged to the American Federation of Musicians (AFM), a union that represented most big-name musicians. The contract between Graham and Russell was on a standard, preprinted form required to be used by all AFM members. The contract contained an arbitration clause that required any disputes regarding the contract to be heard and decided by the executive board of the AFM. When a monetary dispute arose between Graham and Russell regarding the division of proceeds from the concerts, Graham sued Russell in court. Russell filed a motion to compel arbitration. Graham asserted that the arbitration clause in the AFM contract is unconscionable. Is it? [*Graham v. Scissor-Tail, Inc.*, 28 Cal.App.3d 807, 171 Cal.Rptr. 604 (Cal.App. 1981)]

ETHICS CASES

12.16. Joe Plumlee owned and operated an ambulance company. He alleged that the law firm of Paddock, Loveless, and Roach agreed to pay him an up-front fee and a percentage of the law firm's fees generated from personal-injury case referrals. When the law firm did not pay Plumlee, he sued to recover damages for breach of contract. Texas law prohibits lawyers from sharing fees with laypersons [Tex. Penal Code § 38.12; Supreme Court of Texas]. A disciplinary rule also forbids such activity [State Bar Rules Art. X, § 9]. The law firm asserted that the contract could not be enforced because it would be an illegal contract. Who wins? Did Plumlee act ethically in this case? If the contract existed, did the lawyers act ethically? [*Plumlee v. Paddock, Loveless, and Roach*, 832 S.W.2d 757 (Tex.App. 1992)]

12.17. Richard Zientara was friends with Chester and Bernice Kaszuba. All three were residents of Indiana. Bernice, who was employed in an Illinois tavern where Illinois state lottery tickets were sold, had previously obtained lottery tickets for Zientara because Indiana did not have a state lottery. In early April 1984, Zientara requested that Kaszuba purchase an Illinois lottery ticket for him. He gave Kaszuba the money for the ticket and the numbers 6-15-16-23-24-37. Kaszuba purchased the ticket, but when it turned out to be the winning combination worth $1,696,800 she refused to give the ticket

to Zientara and unsuccessfully tried to collect the money. Zientara filed suit against Kaszuba in Indiana claiming the ticket and proceeds thereof. Was the contract legal? Did Kaszuba act ethically in this case? [*Kaszuba v. Zientara*, 506 N.E.2d 1 (IN 1987)]

12.18. On August 31, 1965, Clifton and Cora Jones, who were welfare recipients, received a visit from a salesman representing You Shop at Home Service, Inc. After a sales presentation, Jones signed a retail installment contract to purchase a home freezer unit for the sale price of $900.00. With the addition of time credit charges, credit life insurance, and credit property insurance, the contract price totaled $1,234.80. The freezer had a maximum retail value of $300.00. Evidence showed that the Joneses were unsophisticated and uneducated concerning contracts.

After paying $619.88, Jones brought an action to rescind the contract. Star Credit Corporation, which had come into possession of the credit contract, counterclaimed for $819.81, the amount remaining on the contract plus charges for missed payments. Is the contract unconscionable in the legal sense? If so, what remedy should be awarded? Was it ethical for the sales representative to prey upon ignorant and unsophisticated consumers? Was it ethical for the Joneses to attempt to get out of the contract they signed? [*Jones v. Star Credit Corp.*, 298 N.Y.S.2d 264 (N.Y.Sup. 1969)]

CRITICAL LEGAL THINKING WRITING ASSIGNMENT

Read Case A.12 in the Case Appendix [*Carnival Leisure Industries, Ltd. v. Aubin*]. This case is excerpted from the court of appeals opinion. Review and brief the case. In your brief, be sure to answer the following questions:

1. What were the plaintiff's contentions on appeal?

2. What law was applied by the court in this case, Bahamian law or Texas law? Why was that law applied?

3. What is the consequence of finding an illegal contract? Apply this rule to the facts of this case.

4. Did Aubin act ethically in avoiding an obligation that he knowingly made? Do you think he would have given back the money if he had won at gambling?

Genuineness of Assent

Freedom of contract begins where equality of bargaining power begins.

OLIVER WENDELL HOLMES, JR.
June 4, 1928

Chapter Objectives

After studying this chapter, you should be able to

1. Explain genuineness of assent.
2. Describe how assent is given to software "click-wrap" licenses.
3. Explain how mutual mistake of fact excuses performance.
4. Describe intentional misrepresentation (fraud).
5. Distinguish between fraud in the inception and fraud in the inducement.
6. Describe fraud by concealment or by silence.
7. Explain innocent misrepresentation.
8. Describe physical duress.
9. Describe economic duress.
10. Define *undue influence*.

Chapter Contents

As discussed in the previous chapters, the elements for the creation of a contract are met if there is an agreement between parties with contractual capacity that is supported by consideration and has a lawful purpose as its object. Because it would be unfair to permit a party to escape from a contract that meets these criteria, most such contracts are enforceable. Some are not. For instance, contracts are unenforceable if parties have actually consented to the contract but their assent is not genuine.

If a party's assent to a contract is not genuine, the courts will permit the innocent party to avoid the contract. **Genuineness of assent** is an issue in the areas of *mistake, misrepresentation, duress,* and *undue influence.* Problems concerning genuineness of assent are discussed in this chapter.

> *Most of the disputes in the world arise from words.*
> Lord Mansfield. C.J.
> Morgan v. Jones *(1773)*

genuineness of assent
The requirement that a party's assent to a contract be genuine.

ASSENT

Voluntary **assent** by the parties is necessary to create an enforceable contract. Assent is determined by the relevant facts surrounding the negotiation and formation of the contract. Assent may be manifested in any manner sufficient to show agreement, including express words or conduct of the parties.

assent
Assent to enter into a contract may be manifested in any manner sufficient to show agreement, including express words or conduct of the parties.

Indonesia. *Styles of contracting vary around the world. In Asia, substantial time is necessary to build a relationship of trust before contract negotiations ensue.*

MISTAKES

A *mistake* occurs where one or both of the parties have an erroneous belief about the subject matter, value, or some other aspect of the contract. Mistakes may be either *unilateral* or *mutual.* The law permits **rescission** of some contracts made in mistake.

rescission
An action to undo the contract.

Muslim Temple. *In the Middle East, the parties usually engage in faster negotiations that involve substantial posturing prior to agreeing on a final price.*

Unilateral Mistakes

unilateral mistake
When only one party is mistaken about a material fact regarding the subject matter of the contract.

Unilateral mistakes occur when only one party is mistaken about a material fact regarding the subject matter of the contract. Generally, the mistaken party will not be permitted to rescind the contract. The contract will be enforced on its terms.

Consider This Example   Suppose Trent Anderson wants to purchase a car from the showroom floor. He looks at several models. Although he decides to purchase a car with a sunroof, he does not tell the salesman about this preference. The model named in the contract he signs does not have this feature, although he believes it does. Mr. Anderson's unilateral mistake will not relieve him of his contractual obligation to purchase the car.

There are three types of situations where the contract may not be enforced:

Words are chameleons, which reflect the color of their environment.

L. Hand. J. Commissioner v. National Carbide Co. (1948)

1. One party makes a unilateral mistake of fact and the other party knew (or should have known) that a mistake was made.
2. A unilateral mistake occurs because of a clerical or mathematical error that is not the result of gross negligence.
3. The mistake is so serious that enforcing the contract would be unconscionable.[1]

In the following case, the court had to decide whether to allow a party out of a contract because of its unilateral mistake.

Wells Fargo Credit Corp. v. Martin
605 So.2d 531 (1992)
District Court of Appeals of Florida

CASE 13.1

FACTS

Wells Fargo Credit Corporation (Wells Fargo) obtained a judgment of foreclosure on a house owned by Mr. and Mrs. Clevenger. The total indebtedness stated in the judgment was $207,141. The foreclosure sale was scheduled for 11:00 A.M. on July 12, 1991, at the west front door of the Hillsborough County Courthouse. Wells Fargo was represented by a paralegal, who had attended more than 1,000 similar sales. Wells Fargo's handwritten instruction sheet informed the paralegal to make one bid at $115,000, the tax-appraised value of the property. Because the first "1" in the number was close to the "$," the paralegal misread the bid instruction as $15,000 and opened the bidding at that amount. Harley Martin, who was attending his first judicial sale, bid $20,000. The county clerk gave ample time for another bid and then announced "$20,000 going once,

$20,000 going twice, sold to Harley...." The paralegal screamed, "Stop, I'm sorry, I made a mistake!" The certificate of sale was issued to Martin. Wells Fargo filed suit to set aside the judicial sale based on its unilateral mistake. The trial court held for Martin. Wells Fargo appealed.

ISSUE

Does Wells Fargo's unilateral mistake constitute grounds for setting aside the judicial sale?

IN THE LANGUAGE OF THE COURT

Altenbernd, Judge *We accept the trial court's conclusion that the amount of the sale was grossly inadequate. This inadequacy, however, occurred due to an avoidable, unilateral mistake by an agent of Wells Fargo. As between Wells Fargo and a good faith purchaser at the judicial sale, the trial court had the discretion to place the risk of this mistake upon Wells Fargo.*

Thus, we affirm the trial court's orders denying relief to Wells Fargo.

We are certain that this result seems harsh to Wells Fargo. Nevertheless, Mr. Martin's bid was accepted when the clerk announced "sold." Without ruling that a unilateral mistake by the complaining party could never justify relief, we hold that the trial court had the discretion under these facts to make Wells Fargo suffer the loss.

DECISION AND REMEDY

The appellate court held that Wells Fargo's unilateral mistake did not entitle it to relief from the judicial sale.

Case Questions

Critical Legal Thinking Should contracts be allowed to be rescinded because of unilateral mistakes? Why or why not?

Ethics Did Wells Fargo act ethically in trying to set aside the judicial sale?

Business Application Do you think mistakes such as that made by Wells Fargo happen very often in business?

Mutual Mistakes

Either party may rescind the contract if there has been a **mutual mistake of a past or existing material fact**.[2] A material fact is one that is important to the subject matter of the contract. An ambiguity in a contract may constitute a mutual mistake of a material fact. An ambiguity occurs where a word or term in the contract is susceptible to more than one logical interpretation. If there has been a mutual mistake, the contract may be rescinded on the ground that no contract has been formed because there has been no "meeting of the minds" between the parties.

In the celebrated case of *Raffles v. Wichelhaus*,[3] which has become better known as the case of the good ship *Peerless*, the parties agreed on a sale of cotton that was to be delivered from Bombay by the ship. However, there were two ships named *Peerless*, and each party, in agreeing to the sale, was referring to a different ship. Because the sailing time of the two ships was materially different, neither party was willing to agree to shipment by the other *Peerless*. The court ruled that there was no binding contract because each party had a different ship in mind when the contract was entered into.

The courts must distinguish between *mutual mistakes of fact* and *mutual mistakes of value*. A **mutual mistake of value** exists if both parties know the object of the contract but are mistaken as to its value. Here, the contract remains enforceable by either party because the identity of the subject matter of the contract is not at issue. If the rule were different, almost all contracts could later be rescinded by the party who got the "worst" of the deal.

mutual mistake of fact
A mistake made by both parties concerning a material fact that is important to the subject matter of the contract.

mutual mistake of value
A mistake that occurs if both parties know the object of the contract, but are mistaken as to its value.

Consider This Example Suppose Eileen Ney cleans her attic and finds a painting of tomato soup cans. She has no use for it, so she offers to sell it to Fred Lee for $100. Fred, who likes the painting, accepts the offer and pays Eileen $100. It is later discovered that the painting is worth $200,000 because it was painted by Andy Warhol. Neither party knew this at the time of contracting. It is a mistake of value. Eileen cannot recover the painting.

The issue of mutual mistake was raised in the following case.

Konic International Corp. v. Spokane Computer Services, Inc.
708 P.2d 932 (1985)
Court of Appeals of Idaho

CASE 13.2

FACTS

David Young, an employee of Spokane Computer Services, Inc. (Spokane Computer), was instructed by his employer to investigate the possibility of purchasing a surge protector, a device that protects computers from damaging surges of electrical current. Although Young's investigation turned up several units priced from $50 to $200, none was appropriate for his employer's needs. Young then contacted Konic International Corporation (Konic) by telephone and was referred to a salesman. The salesman described a unit Young thought would be good, and Young inquired as to the price. The salesman replied, "Fifty-six twenty." The salesman meant $5,620. Young thought he meant $56.20. Young ordered the unit by telephone, and it was shipped and installed in Spokane Computer's office. The error was not discovered until two weeks later when Konic sent Spokane Computer an invoice for $5,620. Spokane Computer decided to return the unit to Konic. Konic sued Spokane Computer for the purchase price of the unit. The trial court held in favor of Spokane Computer. Konic appealed.

ISSUE

Was there a mutual mistake of fact that permitted Spokane Computer to rescind the contract?

IN THE LANGUAGE OF THE COURT

Walters, Chief Judge   Basically what is involved here is a failure of communication between the parties. Both parties attributed different meanings to the same term, "fifty-six twenty." Thus, there was no meeting of the minds of the parties. With a hundredfold difference in the two prices, obviously price was a material term. Because the "fifty-six twenty" designation was a material term expressed in an ambiguous form to which two meanings were obviously applied, we conclude that no contract between the parties was ever formed. The mutual misunderstanding of the parties was so basic and so material that any agreement the parties thought they had reached was merely an illusion.

DECISION AND REMEDY

The appellate court held that there was a mutual mistake of material fact that permitted Spokane Computer to rescind its contract with Konic. The appellate court affirmed the trial court's judgment in favor of Spokane Computer.

Case Questions

Legal Thinking   Should parties be able to rescind a contract because of mutual mistake of fact? Why or why not?

Ethics   Did either party act unethically in this case?

Business Application   Are there any winners or losers when a contract is rescinded based on mutual mistake of fact?

---

misrepresentation
An assertion that is made that is not in accord with the facts.

intentional misrepresentation
Occurs when one person consciously decides to induce another person to rely and act on a misrepresentation. Also called *fraud*.

FRAUDULENT MISREPRESENTATION

A **misrepresentation** occurs when an assertion is made that is not in accord with the facts.[4] An **intentional misrepresentation** occurs when one person consciously decides to induce another person to rely and act on a misrepresentation. Intentional misrepresentation is commonly referred to as **fraudulent misrepresentation**, or **fraud**. When a fraudulent misrepresentation is used to induce another to enter into a contract, the innocent party's assent to the contract is not genuine and the contract is voidable by the innocent party.[5] The innocent party can either rescind the contract and obtain restitution or enforce the contract and sue for contract damages.

Entrepreneur and the Law

DON'T BE TAKEN BY FRAUD

Entrepreneurs and other business persons must be on guard in their commercial dealings not to be taken by fraud. Basically, if it sounds "too good to be true," it is a signal that the situation might be fraudulent. Other frauds are difficult to detect. To prove fraud, the following elements must be shown:

1. The wrongdoer made a false representation of material fact.
2. The wrongdoer intended to deceive the innocent party.
3. The innocent party justifiably relied on the misrepresentation.
4. The innocent party was injured.

Each of these elements is discussed in the following paragraphs.

1. *Material Misrepresentation of Fact* A misrepresentation may occur by words (oral or written) or by the conduct of the party. To be actionable as fraud, the misrepresentation must be of a past or existing *material fact*. This means that the misrepresentation must have been a significant factor in inducing the innocent party to enter into the contract. It does not have to be the sole factor. Statements of opinion or predictions about the future generally do not form the basis for fraud.
2. *Intent to Deceive* To prove fraud, the person making the misrepresentation must have either had knowledge that the representation was false or made it without sufficient knowledge of the truth. This is called **scienter** ("guilty mind"). The misrepresentation must have been made with the intent to deceive the innocent party. Intent can be inferred from the circumstances.
3. *Reliance on the Misrepresentation* A misrepresentation is not actionable unless the innocent party to whom the misrepresentation was directed acted upon it. Further, an innocent party who acts in reliance on the misrepresentation must justify his or her reliance.[5] Justifiable reliance generally is found unless the innocent party knew that the misrepresentation was false or was so extravagant as to be obviously false. For example, reliance on a statement such as "This diamond ring is worth $10,000, but I'll sell it to you for $100" would not be justified.
4. *Injury to the Innocent Party* To recover damages, the innocent party must prove that the fraud caused economic injury. The measure of damages is the difference between the value of the property as represented and the actual value of the property. This measure of damages gives the innocent party the "benefit of the bargain." In the alternative, the buyer can rescind the contract and recover the purchase price.

Types of Fraud

There are various types of fraud. Some of the most common ones follow.

Fraud in the Inception   **Fraud in the inception**, or **fraud in the factum**, occurs if a person is deceived as to the nature of his or her act and does not know what he or she is signing. Such contracts are void rather than just voidable. For example, suppose Heather brings her professor a grade card to sign. The professor signs the front of the grade card. On the back, however, are contract terms that transfer all of the professor's property to Heather. Here there is fraud in the inception. The contract is void.

> **fraud in the inception**
> Occurs if a person is deceived as to the nature of his or her act and does not know what he or she is signing.

Fraud in the Inducement   A great many fraud cases concern **fraud in the inducement**. Here, the innocent party knows what he or she is signing but has been fraudulently induced to enter into the contract. Such contracts are voidable by the innocent party.

> **fraud in the inducement**
> Occurs when the party knows what he or she is signing, but has been fraudulently induced to enter into the contract.

Consider This Example   Suppose Lyle Green tells Candice Young he is forming a partnership to invest in drilling for oil and invites her to invest in this venture. In reality, though, Lyle Green intends to use whatever money he receives for his personal expenses, and he absconds with Ms. Young's $30,000 investment. Here there has been fraud in the inducement. Ms. Young can rescind the contract and recover the money from Lyle Green—if he can be found.

Fraud by Concealment   **Fraud by concealment** occurs when one party takes specific action to conceal a material fact from another party.[6] For example, suppose that ABC Blouses, Inc., contracts to buy a used sewing machine from Wear-Well Shirts, Inc. Wear-Well did not show ABC the repair invoices for the sewing machine even though ABC

> **fraud by concealment**
> Occurs when one party takes specific action to conceal a material fact from another party.

asked to see them. Relying on the fact that the machine was not repaired, ABC bought the machine. If ABC discovers that a significant repair record has been concealed, it can sue Wear-Well for fraud.

Silence as Misrepresentation   Generally, neither party to a contract owes a duty to disclose all the facts to the other party. Ordinarily, such silence is not a misrepresentation unless (1) nondisclosure would cause bodily injury or death, (2) there is a fiduciary relationship (i.e., a relationship of trust and confidence) between the contracting parties, or (3) federal and state statutes require disclosure. The Restatement (Second) of Contracts specifies a broader duty of disclosure: Nondisclosure is a misrepresentation if it would constitute a failure to act in "good faith."[7]

Misrepresentation of Law   Usually, a misrepresentation of law is not actionable as fraud. The innocent party cannot generally rescind the contract. This is because each person to a contract is assumed to know the law that applies to the transaction either through his or her own investigation or by hiring a lawyer. There is one major exception to this rule: The misrepresentation will be allowed as a ground for rescission of the contract if one party to a contract is a professional who should know what the law is and intentionally misrepresents the law to a less sophisticated contracting party.[8]

The following case illustrates fraud by concealment.

Wilson v. Western National Life Insurance Co.
235 Cal.App.3d 981, 1 Cal.Rptr.2d 157 (1991)
California Court of Appeals

CASE 13.3

FACTS
Daniel and Doris Wilson were husband and wife. On August 13, 1985, Daniel fainted from a narcotics overdose and was rushed unconscious to the hospital. Doris accompanied him. Daniel responded to medication used to counteract a narcotics overdose and recovered. The emergency room physician noted that Daniel had probably suffered from a heroin overdose and had multiple puncture sites on his arms.

On October 8, 1985, Gil Cantrell, an agent for Western National Life Insurance Company (Western), met with the Wilsons in their home for the purpose of taking their application for life insurance. Cantrell asked questions and recorded the Wilsons' responses on a written application form. Daniel answered the following questions:

> 13. *In the past 10 years, have you been*   Yes   No
> *treated or joined an organization for*
> *alcoholism or drug addiction?*   X
> *If "Yes," explain on the reverse side.*
>
> 17. *In the past 5 years, have you*   Yes   No
> *consulted or been treated or examined*
> *by any physician or practitioner?*   X

Both of the Wilsons signed the application form and paid the agent the first month's premium. Under insurance law and the application form, the life insurance policy took effect

immediately. Daniel Wilson died from a drug overdose two days later. Western rescinded the policy and rejected Doris Wilson's claim to recover the policy's $50,000 death benefit for Daniel's death, alleging failure to disclose the August 13, 1985, incident. Doris sued to recover the death benefits. The trial court granted summary judgment for Western. Doris appealed.

ISSUE
Was there a concealment of a material fact that justified Western's rescission of the life insurance policy?

IN THE LANGUAGE OF THE COURT
Stone, Presiding Judge   *Plaintiff asserts the court erroneously granted summary judgment because Western failed to prove she or decedent made a misrepresentation in the application. We disagree.*

In her deposition, plaintiff testified neither she nor decedent told Cantrell about decedent's fainting spell or his hospital treatment two months earlier. Thus, there is no question but that they omitted medical information. Knowledge of the true facts by plaintiff and decedent is beyond dispute.

Plaintiff further argues the misrepresentation, if one occurred, was not material. Plaintiff's argument must fail. The trial court properly found the omissions to be material and the evidence supporting its materiality uncontradicted. The trial court had before it evidence from Western that the application would not have been accepted, and decedent would not have been found to be insurable, had he disclosed on the application the episode in August when he became unconscious from a narcotics overdose.

A material misrepresentation or concealment entitles the injured party to rescission. Concealment, whether intentional or unintentional, entitles the injured party to rescind insurance. Western properly rescinded the insurance contract and its obligation to provide coverage terminated as of the date of application.

DECISION AND REMEDY
The appellate court held that there was a concealment by the Wilsons that warranted rescission of the life insurance policy by Western.

Case Questions

Critical Legal Thinking Should a contract be allowed to be rescinded because of an *innocent* misrepresentation? Why or why not?

Ethics Do you think the concealment was intentional or innocent?

Business Application Do you think there is very much insurance fraud in this country? Explain.

Innocent Misrepresentation

An **innocent misrepresentation** occurs when a person makes a statement of fact that he or she honestly and reasonably believes to be true, even though it is not. Innocent misrepresentation is not fraud. If an innocent misrepresentation has been made, the aggrieved party may rescind the contract but may not sue for damages. Often, innocent misrepresentation is treated as a mutual mistake.

innocent misrepresentation
Occurs when a person makes a statement of fact that he or she honestly and reasonably believes to be true, even though it is not.

CONCEPT SUMMARY   TYPES OF MISREPRESENTATION

Type of Misrepresentation	Legal Consequences—Innocent Party May:	
	Sue for Damages	**Rescind Contract**
Fraud in the inception	Yes	Yes
Fraud in the inducement	Yes	Yes
Fraud by concealment	Yes	Yes
Silence as a misrepresentation	Yes	Yes
Misrepresentation of law	Usually no	Usually no
Innocent misrepresentation	No	Yes

International Perspective

UNITED NATIONS CODE OF CONDUCT FOR TRANSNATIONAL CORPORATIONS

Respect for National Sovereignty
Transnational corporations shall respect the national sovereignty of the countries in which they operate and the right of each State to exercise its permanent sovereignty over its natural wealth and resources. Transnational corporations should carry out their activities in conformity with the development policies, objectives and priorities set out by the Governments of the countries in which they operate and work seriously towards making a positive contribution to the achievement of such goals at the national and, as appropriate, the regional level, within the framework of regional integration programmes. Transnational corpora-

(box continues)

tions should cooperate with the Governments of the countries in which they operate with a view to contributing to the development process and should be responsive to requests for consultation in this respect, thereby establishing mutually beneficial relations with these countries.

Adherence to Socio-Cultural Objectives and Values

Transnational corporations should respect the social and cultural objectives, values, and traditions of the countries in which they operate. While economic and technological development is normally accompanied by social change, transnational corporations should avoid practices, products or services which cause detrimental effects on cultural patterns and socio-cultural objectives as determined by Governments. For this purpose, transnational corporations should respond positively to requests for consultations from Governments concerned.

Respect for Human Rights and Fundamental Freedoms

Transnational corporations shall respect human rights and fundamental freedoms in the countries in which they operate. In their social and industrial relations, transnational corporations shall not discriminate on the basis of race, colour, sex, religion, language, social, national and ethnic origin or political or other opinion. Transnational corporations shall conform to government policies designed to extend equality of opportunity and treatment.

Abstention from Corrupt Practices

Transnational corporations shall refrain, in their transactions, from the offering, promising or giving of any payment, gift or other advantage to or for the benefit of a public official as consideration for performing or refraining from the performance of his duties in connection with those transactions.

$\mathcal{D}$URESS

duress

Occurs where one party threatens to do a wrongful act unless the other party enters into a contract.

economic duress

Occurs when one party to a contract refuses to perform his or her contractual duties unless the other party pays an increased price, enters into a second contract with the threatening party, or undertakes a similar action.

Duress occurs where one party threatens to do some wrongful act unless the other party enters into a contract. If a party to a contract has been forced into making the contract, the assent is not voluntary. Such contracts are not enforceable against the innocent party.

The threat to commit physical harm or extortion unless someone enters into a contract constitutes duress. So does a threat to bring (or not drop) a criminal lawsuit. This is so even if the criminal lawsuit is well founded.[9] However, a threat to bring (or not drop) a civil lawsuit does not constitute duress unless such a suit is frivolous or brought in bad faith.

The courts have recognized another type of duress—*economic duress*. **Economic duress** usually occurs when one party to a contract refuses to perform his or her contractual duties unless the other party pays an increased price, enters into a second contract with the threatening party, or the like. The duressed party must prove that he had no alternative but to acquiesce to the other party's threat.

Contemporary Business Application

ECONOMIC DURESS

Economic duress is also called **business compulsion, business duress**, and **economic coercion**. The appropriateness of these terms becomes apparent when the facts of the following case are examined.

Ashton Development, Inc. (Ashton), hired Bob Britton, Inc. (Britton), a general contractor, to build a development for it. Britton signed a contract with a subcontractor, Rich & Whillock, Inc. (R & W), to provide grading and excavation work at the project. The contract stated that "any rock encountered will be considered an extra at current rates"

and expressly excluded blasting work. The contract price was $112,990. In late March 1981, when R & W encountered rock at the project site, a meeting was held between the parties to discuss the problem. Britton directed R & W to go ahead with the rock work and agreed to pay for the additional work. R & W proceeded with the excavation work and rock removal, which included blasting.

On June 17, 1981, after completing all of the required work and receiving $109,363 in payments to date, R & W submitted a final bill to Britton for $72,286. The total bill was $68,659 above the original contract price.

Ashton and Britton refused to pay this amount. R & W told Britton that it would go "broke" if payment was not received. On July 10, 1981, Britton presented R & W with an agreement whereby Britton would pay $25,000 upon the signing of the agreement and another $25,000 on August 10, 1981. When R & W complained of the financial bind it was in, Britton stated: "I have a check for you, and you just take it or leave it, this is all you get. If you don't take this, you have got to sue me." After claiming that it was "blackmail," R & W accepted the $25,000 check. Britton did not pay the other $25,000 until August 20, 1981, after requiring R & W to sign a release of claims form.

In December 1981, R & W sued Ashton and Britton for breach of contract. The defendants argued that the settlement agreement and release signed by R & W prevented it from collecting. The trial and appellate courts held in favor of R & W, finding that Ashton and Britton's tactics amounted to economic duress. In applying the doctrine of economic duress to the case, the court stated: "The underlying concern of the economic duress doctrine is the enforcement in the marketplace of certain minimal standards of business ethics." The court found that Ashton and Britton had acted in bad faith when they refused to pay R & W's final billing and offered instead to pay a compromise amount of $50,000. At the time of their bad faith breach and settlement offer, Ashton and Britton knew that R & W was a new company overextended to creditors and subcontractors and faced with imminent bankruptcy if not paid its final billing. Under these circumstances, the court found that the July 10 agreement and the August 20 release were products of economic duress and were therefore unenforceable. The court ordered Ashton and Britton to pay the balance due on the contract to R & W. [*Rich & Whillock, Inc. v. Ashton Development, Inc.*, 157 Cal.App.3d 1154, 204 Cal.Rptr. 86 (Cal.App. 1984)]

Undue Influence

The courts may permit the rescission of a contract based on the equitable doctrine of **undue influence**. Undue influence occurs when one person (the dominant party) takes advantage of another person's mental, emotional, or physical weakness and unduly persuades that person (the servient party) to enter into a contract. The persuasion by the wrongdoer must overcome the free will of the innocent party. A contract that is entered into because of undue influence is voidable by the innocent party.[10] Wills are often challenged as having been made under undue influence.

The following elements must be shown to prove undue influence:

1. A fiduciary or confidential relationship must have existed between the parties.
2. The dominant party must have unduly used his or her influence to persuade the servient party to enter into a contract.

If there is a confidential relationship between persons—such as lawyer and client, doctor and patient, psychiatrist and patient—any contract made by the servient party that benefits the dominant party is presumed to be entered into under undue influence. This is a rebuttable presumption that can be overcome by proper evidence.

In the following Ethical Perspective, the court applied the doctrine of undue influence and set aside a trust agreement.

undue influence

Occurs where one person takes advantage of another person's mental, emotional, or physical weakness and unduly persuades that person to enter into a contract; the persuasion by the wrong doer must overcome the free will of the innocent party.

Ethical Perspective

The Doctrine of Undue Influence

In 1966, Ralla Klepak, an attorney, met Virgil Robert Woodruff when she represented him in a criminal misdemeanor proceeding. Although their relationship began as attorney and client, it developed into one of friendship. They dined, attended operas, and vacationed together. Prior to his death, Woodruff retained Klepak in her capacity as an attorney to represent his interests in various legal and personal matters.

(box continues)

In October 1973, Woodruff purchased a condominium unit in the John Hancock Building on North Michigan Avenue in Chicago. Klepak represented Woodruff in the purchase of the condominium. At the same time, Klepak represented Woodruff in establishing a land trust that provided that the beneficial interest in the condominium would remain Woodruff's for his life and then pass to Klepak upon his death. The Lake Shore Bank was named as trustee of the trust. Klepak notarized the land trust agreement while they were at a restaurant. Woodruff died on May 29, 1984, at the age of 54. He was a bachelor, had never married, and had no living issue. His only heirs were two maternal aunts and a paternal cousin. Two days after Woodruff's death, Klepak delivered a certified copy of his death certificate to the Lake Shore Bank. Klepak took possession of the condominium shortly after Woodruff's death and has had sole use and possession of the premises since that time. William L. Klaskin, who was named administrator of Woodruff's estate, brought this action to recover the condominium from Klepak. The trial court held in favor of the estate. The appellate court reversed. The estate appealed.

Did Ralla Klepak, as an attorney, rebut the presumption of undue influence that arose from this transaction?

Transactions between attorneys and clients are closely scrutinized. When an attorney engages in a transaction with a client and is benefitted thereby, a presumption arises that the transaction proceeded from undue influence. Once a presumption is raised, the burden shifts to the attorney to come forward with evidence that the transaction was fair, equitable, and just and that the benefit did not proceed from undue influence. Courts require clear and convincing evidence to rebut this presumption.

Some of the factors that the Supreme Court of Illinois deemed persuasive in determining whether the presumption of undue influence has been overcome include a showing by the attorney (1) that he or she made a full and frank disclosure of all relevant information, (2) that adequate consideration was given, and (3) that the client had independent advice before completing the transaction. In this case, the court evaluated the evidence adduced at trial in light of these factors and concluded that Klepak failed to overcome the presumption of undue influence. The court held that Klepak never informed Woodruff of the legal consequences of naming her as beneficiary. The court also concluded that Klepak gave no consideration for being named as beneficiary and never advised Woodruff to seek independent legal advice after learning that she was named as beneficiary.

The state supreme court held that Ralla Klepak did not rebut the presumption of undue influence that arose from the transaction at issue in this case. The court reversed the judgment of the appellate court and affirmed the judgment of the trial court. [*Klaskin v. Klepak*, 534 N.E.2d 971 (Ill. 1989)]

1. Did Ralla Klepak act unethically in this case?
2. Should there be a presumption that transactions between an attorney and a client have been based on undue influence? Do you think there was actual undue influence in this case?

Working the Web

Many business school libraries and law libraries have set up their own Web sites. These sites always contain information links about the school and campus, but can also provide valuable links to legal and business resources. Some even have their library catalogs on-line. The following are some sites to visit:

Harvard Business School Library

library.hbs.edu

Babson College Library

www.babson.edu/library/index.html

Harvard Law School Library

www.law.harvard.edu/library

University of Colorado Law Library

www.colorado.edu/Law/lawlib

University of Denver Law Library

www.law.du.edu/library

1. Find out if the business library at your business school has a Web site. If so, visit the site to see what information you can find there.

2. If your college or university has a law school, find out whether the law library has a Web site. If so, visit the site to see what information you can find there.

3. Visit the Harvard Business School Library Web site. Find a book in the Baker Online Catalog.

4. Check out the research guides at the Babson College Library Web site.

5. Visit the University of Colorado Law Library Web site. Who is that library's director?

CASES AND EXERCISES

CRITICAL LEGAL THINKING CASES

13.1. Mrs. Chaney died in 1985, leaving a house in Annapolis, Maryland. The representative of her estate listed the property for sale with a real estate broker, stating that the property was approximately 15,650 square feet. Drs. Steele and Faust made an offer of $300,000 for the property, which was accepted by the estate. A contract for the sale of the property was signed by all the parties on July 3, 1985. When a subsequent survey (done before the deed was transferred) showed that the property had an area of 22,047 square feet, the estate requested the buyers to pay more money for the property. When the estate refused to transfer the property to the buyers, they sued for specific performance. Can the estate rescind the contract? [*Steele v. Goettee*, 542 A.2d 847 (Md.App. 1988)]

13.2. The County of Contra Costa, California, held a tax sale in which it offered for sale a vacant piece of property located in the city of El Cerrito. Richard J. Schultz, a carpenter, saw the notice of the pending tax sale and was interested in purchasing the lot to build a house. Prior to attending the tax sale, Schultz visited and measured the parcel, examined the neighborhood and found the houses there to be "very nice," and had a title search done that turned up no liens or judgments against the property. Schultz did not, however, check with the city zoning department regarding the zoning of the property.

Schultz attended the tax sale and, after spirited bidding, won with a bid of $9,100 and received a deed to the property. Within one week of the purchase, Schultz discovered that the city's zoning laws prevented building a residence on the lot. In essence, the lot was worthless. Schultz sued to rescind the contract. Can the contract be rescinded? [*Schultz v. County of Contra Costa, California*, 157 Cal.App.3d 242, 203 Cal.Rptr. 760 (Cal.App. 1984)]

13.3. Ron Boskett, a part-time coin dealer, purchased a dime purportedly minted in 1916 at the Denver Mint for nearly $450. The fact that the "D" on the coin signified Denver mintage made the coin rare and valuable. Boskett sold the coin to Beachcomber Coins, Inc. (Beachcomber), a retail coin dealer, for $500. A principal of Beachcomber examined the coin for 15 to 45 minutes prior to its purchase. Soon thereafter, Beachcomber received an offer of $700 for the coin subject to certification of its genuineness by the American Numismatic Society. When this organization labeled the coin counterfeit, Beachcomber sued Boskett to rescind the purchase of the coin. Can Beachcomber rescind the contract? [*Beachcomber Coins, Inc. v. Boskett*, 400 A.2d 78 (NJ 1979)]

13.4. Betty J. Tarrant brought her diamond ring to Verdum H. Monson, a jeweler in Salt Lake City, Utah, for repairs. When Mrs. Tarrant returned to retrieve the ring, Monson could not find it. After several months of looking, Monson could still not find the ring. He offered to replace it with a ring of Mrs. Tarrant's choice. Mrs. Tarrant selected a replacement ring that was worth $450 more than the ring that was lost. Monson agreed with the choice, and Mrs. Tarrant left with the new ring. Six months later Monson found Mrs. Tarrant's ring in a mislabeled envelope in his safe. He offered to exchange rings with Mrs. Tarrant, but she refused unless he agreed to also give her a pair of diamond earrings. Monson refused and brought this suit to rescind the replacement contract. Can the replacement contract be rescinded? [*Tarrant v. Monson*, 619 P.2d 1210 (NV 1980)]

13.5. Robert McClure owned a vehicle salvage and rebuilding business. He listed the business for sale and had a brochure printed that described the business and stated that during 1981 the business grossed $581,117 and netted $142,727. Fred H. Campbell saw the brochure and inquired about buying the business. Campbell hired a CPA to review McClure's business records and tax returns, but the CPA could not reconcile these with the income claimed for the business in the brochure. When Campbell asked McClure about the discrepancy, McClure stated that the business records did—and tax returns did not—accurately reflect the cash flow or profits of the business because it was such a high-cash operation with much of the cash not being reported to the Internal Revenue Service on tax returns. McClure signed a warranty that stated that the true income of the business was as represented in the brochure.

Campbell bought the business based on these representations. However, the business, although operated in substantially the same manner as when owned by McClure, failed to yield a net income similar to that warranted by McClure. Evidence showed that McClure's representations were substantially overstated. Campbell sued McClure for damages for fraud. Who wins? [*Campbell v. McClure*, 182 Cal.App.3d 806, 227 Cal.Rptr. 450 (Cal.App. 1986)]

13.6. James L. "Skip" Deupree, a developer, was building a development of townhouses called Point South in Destin, Florida. All the townhouses in the development were to have individual boat slips. Sam and Louise Butner, husband and wife, bought one of the townhouses. The sales contract between Deupree and the Butners provided that a boat slip would be built and was included in the price of the townhouse. The contract stated that permission from the Florida Department of Natural Resources (DNR) had to be obtained to build the boat slips. It is undisputed that a boat slip adds substantially to the value of the property and that the Butners relied on the fact that the townhouse would have a boat slip.

Prior to the sale of the townhouse to the Butners, the DNR had informed Deupree that it objected to the plan to build the boat slips and that permission to build them would probably not be forthcoming. Deupree did not tell the Butners this information, but instead stated that there would be "no problem" in getting permission from the state to build the boat slips. The Butners purchased the townhouse. When the DNR would not approve the building of the boat slips for the Butners' townhouse, they sued for damages for fraud, Who wins? [*Deupree v. Butner*, 522 So.2d 242 (Ala 1988)]

13.7. W. F. Yost, who owned the Red Barn Barbecue Restaurant (Red Barn), listed it for sale. Richard and Evelyn Ramano of Rieve Enterprises, Inc. (Rieve), were interested in buying the restaurant. After visiting and conducting a visual inspection of the premises, Rieve entered into a contract on January 11, 1982, to purchase the assets and equipment of Red Barn, as well as the five-year lease of, and option to buy, the land and the building. Prior to the sale, the restaurant had been cited for certain health violations that Yost had corrected. In the contract of sale Yost warranted that "the premises will pass all inspections" to conduct the business.

Rieve took possession immediately after the sale on January 11 and operated the business until January 27, when the Board of Health conducted a routine inspection, cited 52 health code violations, and thereupon closed the restaurant. Rieve sued to rescind the purchase agreement. Evidence established that Yost's misrepresentations were innocently made. Can Rieve rescind the contract? [*Yost v. Rieve Enterprises, Inc.*, 461 So.2d 178 (Fla.App. 1984)]

13.8. Judith and Donald Eckstein were married in Maryland on May 25, 1968. They had two daughters. On February 1, 1975, Judith left the marital abode in the parties' jointly owned 1973 Volkswagen van with only the clothes on her back. She did not take the children, who were six and eight years old at the time. She had no funds, and the husband promptly closed the couple's bank account. The wife was unemployed. Shortly after she left, the husband discovered her whereabouts and the location of the van and seized and secreted the van. The husband refused the wife's request to visit or communicate with her children and refused to give her her clothing. He told her that she could see the children and take her clothes only if she signed a separation agreement prepared by his lawyer. The wife contacted Legal Aid, but was advised that she did not qualify for assistance.

On February 10, 1975, the wife was directed to go to her husband's lawyer's office. A copy of a separation agreement was given to her to read. The separation agreement provided that the wife (1) give custody of the children to her husband, (2) deed her interest in their jointly owned house to the husband, (3) assign her interest in a jointly owned new 1975 Chevrolet van to her husband, and (4) waive alimony, support, maintenance, court costs, attorney's fees, and any right to inheritance in her husband's estate. By the agreement, she was to receive $1,100 cash, her clothes, the Volkswagen van, and any furniture she desired. The wife testified that her husband told her over an interoffice phone in the lawyer's office that if she did not sign the separation agreement he would get her for desertion, that she would never see her children again, and that she would get nothing—neither her clothes nor the van—unless she signed the agreement. The wife signed the separation agreement. Immediately thereafter her clothes were surrendered to her, and she was given $1,100 cash and the keys to the Volkswagen van. The husband filed for divorce. The wife filed an answer seeking to rescind the separation agreement. Can she rescind the separation agreement? [*Eckstein v. Eckstein*, 379 A.2d 757 (Md.App. 1978)]

13.9. Conrad Schaneman, Sr., had eight sons and five daughters. He owned an 80-acre farm in the Scotts bluff area of Nebraska. Conrad was born in Russia and could not read or write English. Prior to 1974, all his children had frequent contact with Conrad and helped with his needs. In 1974, his eldest son, Lawrence, advised the other children that he would henceforth manage his father's business affairs. On March 18, 1975, after much urging by Lawrence, Conrad deeded the farm to Lawrence for $23,500. Evidence showed that at the time of the sale the reasonable fair market value of the farm was between $145,000 and $160,000.

At the time of the conveyance, Conrad was over 80 years old, had deteriorated in health, suffered from heart problems and diabetes, had high and uncontrollable blood sugar levels, weighed almost 300 pounds, had difficulty breathing, could not walk more than 15 feet, and had to have a jackhoist lift him in and out of the bathtub. He was for all purposes an invalid, relying on Lawrence for most of his personal needs, transportation, banking, and other business matters. After Conrad died, the conservators of the estate brought this action to cancel the deed transferring the farm to Lawrence. Can the conservators cancel the deed? [*Schaneman v. Schaneman*, 291 N.W.2d 412 (NE 1980)]

13.10. Margaret Delorey was a client of Joseph P. Plonsky, an attorney. In addition, they were friends of long standing. In September 1976, Delorey telephoned Plonsky's office and told him that she wanted him to draft a will for her, naming him as executor and leaving everything she owned to him. Plonsky drafted the will and mailed it to her. She had the will executed and witnessed at a bank and mailed the will back to Plonsky. When Delorey died, Plonsky, as the sole legatee, attempted to take under the will. At the time of her death, Delorey was survived by two nephews, two nieces, two grandnephews, and one grandniece, none of whom were named in the will. Does the doctrine of undue influence apply in this case? [*Matter of Delorey*, 529 N.Y.S.2d 153, 141 A.D.2d 540 (N.Y.App. 1988)]

ETHICS CASES

13.11. The First Baptist Church of Moultrie, Georgia, invited bids for the construction of a music, education, and recreation building. The bids, which were to be opened on May 15, 1986, were to be accompanied by a bid bond of 5 percent of the bid amount. Barber Contracting Company (Barber Contracting) submitted a bid in the amount of $1,860,000. A bid bond in the amount of 5 percent of the bid—$93,000—was issued by The American Insurance Company. The bids were opened by the church on May 15, 1986, as planned, and Barber Contracting's was the lowest bid.

On May 16, 1986, Albert W. Barber, the president of Barber Contracting, informed the church that his company's bid was in error and should have been $143,120 higher. The error was caused in totaling the material costs on Barber Contracting's estimate worksheets. The church had not been provided these worksheets. On May 20, 1986, Barber Contracting sent a letter to the church stating that it was withdrawing its bid. The next day the church sent a construction contract to Barber Contracting containing the original bid amount. When Barber Contracting refused to sign the contract and refused to do the work for the original contract price, the church signed a contract with the second lowest bidder, H & H Construction and Supply Company, Inc., to complete the work for $1,919,272. The church sued Barber Contracting and The American Insurance Company seeking to recover the amount of the bid bond. Who wins? Did Barber act ethically in trying to get out of the contract? Did the church act ethically in trying to enforce Barber's bid? [*First Baptist Church of Moultrie v. Barber Contracting Co.*, 377 S.E.2d 717 (Ga.App. 1989)]

13.12. In 1988, Lockheed Missiles & Space Company, Inc. (Lockheed), sent out a request to potential subcontractors seeking bids for the manufacture of 124 ballast cans for the Trident II nuclear submarines it was building for the U.S. Navy. In February 1989, Lockheed received eight bids, including one from Sulzer Bingham Pumps, Inc. (Sulzer). Sulzer was the lowest bidder at $6,544,055. The next lowest bid was $10,176,670, and the bids ranged up to $17,766,327. Lockheed itself estimated that the job would cost at least $8.5 million. Lockheed's employees were shocked by Sulzer's bid and thought it was surprisingly low.

Lockheed then inspected Sulzer's Portland facility to evaluate Sulzer's technical capabilities. The inspection revealed that Sulzer would have to make many modifications to its existing facility in order to complete the contract.

Lockheed did not reveal its findings to Sulzer. In addition, it never notified Sulzer that its bid was significantly lower than the next lowest bid, and lower than Lockheed's own estimate of the cost of the job as well. Finally, Sulzer was never told that Lockheed suspected the contract could not be completed at the bid price.

In late February 1989, Lockheed accepted Sulzer's bid and Sulzer started work. In November 1989, Sulzer revised its estimate of the cost of the job and asked Lockheed for an additional $2,110,000 in compensation. When Lockheed rejected this request, Sulzer sued Lockheed, asking the court to either increase the price of the contract to $8,645,000 or, alternatively, to rescind its bid. Did Lockheed act ethically in this case by not notifying Sulzer of the suspected mistake? Did Sulzer act ethically by trying to get out of the contract because of its own economic misjudgments? Legally, who wins? [*Sulzer Bingham Pumps, Inc. v. Lockheed Missiles & Space Company, Inc.*, 947 F.2d 1362 (9th Cir. 1991)]

13.13. Mr. Weller, who was in business in Coalinga, California, filed tax returns for 1943, 1944, and 1945 using the cash basis. In 1946, Weller hired Mr. Eyman, a CPA, to prepare his income tax return for 1946. While preparing the 1946 return using the accrual basis, Eyman examined the prior years' returns. Based on Eyman's suggestion, Eyman prepared revised tax returns for the prior years and Weller submitted these to the Internal Revenue Service (IRS), claiming an $1,800 refund. Instead of receiving the refund, however, the IRS assessed Weller $118,000 in unpaid taxes and fines. Eyman told Weller that the proposed assessment was asinine, and it was a simple matter to clean up. Weller contracted with Eyman to do the necessary work for $1,000.

After obtaining several extensions, the IRS notified Weller and Eyman that Monday, September 18, 1950, was the deadline for filing a protest to the proposed assessment. On Saturday, September 16, Eyman called Weller to his office to sign the protest. When Weller got there, Eyman produced a written contract purporting to be a fee arrangement whereby Eyman was to receive $1,000 plus 7½ percent of any monies saved on the assessment. When Weller refused to sign the new fee agreement, Eyman told him that the protest had to be in the mail that afternoon to reach the IRS on Monday and that if it were not filed Weller would be liable for the $118,000 assessment. Weller signed the fee agreement, and the protest was timely filed with the IRS. Weller filed a complaint to have the new fee agreement rescinded. Did Eyman act ethically in this case? Did Weller have any choice but to agree to Eyman's proposal? Who wins? [*Thompson Crane & Trucking Co. v. Eyman*, 267 P.2d 1043, 123 Cal.App.2d 904 (Cal.App. 1954)]

CRITICAL LEGAL THINKING WRITING ASSIGNMENT

Read Case A.13 in the Case Appendix [*Continental Airlines, Inc. v. McDonnell Douglas Corporation*]. This case is excerpted from the appellate court opinion. Review and brief the case. In your brief, be sure to answer the following questions:

1. When did the action commence? When was the decision of the appellate court rendered?

2. Were the statements made by McDonnell Douglas opinions (i.e., puffing) or statements of fact?

3. Were the statements made by McDonnell Douglas material? What evidence supports your conclusion?

4. Did Continental rely on the statements of McDonnell Douglas? What evidence supports your conclusion?

5. Do false representations made recklessly and without regard to the truth constitute fraud?

6. What damages were awarded to Continental?

NOTES

1. Restatement (Second) of Contracts, § 153.
2. Restatement (Second) of Contracts, § 152.
3. 59 Eng. Rep. 375 (1864).
4. Restatement (Second) of Contracts, § 159.
5. Restatement (Second) of Contracts, §§ 163 and 164.
6. Restatement (Second) of Contracts, § 160.
7. Restatement (Second) of Contracts, § 161.
8. Restatement (Second) of Contracts, § 170.
9. Restatement (Second) of Contracts, § 176.
10. Restatement (Second) of Contracts, § 177.

Writing and Contract Form

A verbal contract isn't worth the paper it's written on.

SAMUEL GOLDWYN

Chapter Objectives

After studying this chapter, you should be able to

1. List the contracts that must be in writing under the Statute of Frauds.
2. Explain the effect of noncompliance with the Statute of Frauds.
3. Apply the Statute of Frauds to contracts for the sale of land and the part performance exception to this rule.
4. Apply the Statute of Frauds to contracts that cannot be performed within one year.
5. Define *guaranty contracts* and explain when they must be in writing.
6. Identify when agents' contracts must be in writing.
7. Describe the Statute of Frauds applicable to the sale of goods.
8. Define and apply the doctrine of promissory estoppel.
9. Apply the parol evidence rule.
10. Describe writing requirements for international contracts.

Chapter Contents

To break an oral agreement which is not legally binding is morally wrong.

Talmud.
Bava Metzi'a

Even if the elements necessary for the formation of a contract are met, some contracts are not enforceable unless they meet certain formalities. For example, certain types of contracts must be in writing. Other issues regarding the form of the contract include the form of signature that is required on a written contract, whether a contract can be created by the integration of several documents that could not stand alone as a contract, whether any previous oral or written agreements between the parties on the same subject matter can be given effect, and how contract language should be interpreted by the courts. These issues are discussed in this chapter.

Statute of Frauds—Writing Requirement

In 1677, the English Parliament enacted a statute called "An Act for the Prevention of Frauds and Perjuries." This act required that certain types of contracts had to be in writing and signed by the party against whom enforcement was sought. Today, all states have enacted a **Statute of Frauds** that requires certain types of contracts to be in *writing*. This statute is intended to ensure that the terms of important contracts are not forgotten, misunderstood, or fabricated.

Statute of Frauds
State statute that requires certain types of contracts to be in writing.

Although the statutes vary slightly from state to state, most states require the following types of contracts to be in writing.[1]

- Contracts involving interests in land
- Contracts that by their own terms cannot possibly be performed within one year
- Collateral contracts where a person promises to answer for the debt or duty of another
- Promises made in consideration of marriage
- Contracts for the sale of goods for more than $500
- Real estate agents' contracts
- Agents' contracts where the underlying contract must be in writing
- Promises to write a will
- Contracts to pay debts barred by the statute of limitations or discharged in bankruptcy
- Contracts to pay compensation for services rendered in negotiating the purchase of a business
- Finders fee contracts

Statute of Frauds: That unfortunate statute, the misguided application of which has been the cause of so many frauds.

Bacon, V.C.
Morgan v. Worthington (1878)

Effect of Noncompliance with the Statute of Frauds

Generally, an *executory contract* that is not in writing even though the **Statute of Frauds** requires it to be is unenforceable by either party. (If the contract is valid in all other respects, however, it may be voluntarily performed by the parties.) The Statute of Frauds is usually raised by one party as a defense to the enforcement of the contract by the other party. If an oral contract that should have been in writing under the Statute of Frauds is already executed, neither party can seek to rescind the contract on the ground of noncompliance with the Statute of Frauds.

Business Brief
Although only certain contracts must be in writing under the Statute of Frauds, it is good practice to place other contracts in writing so there is no dispute as to the terms of the contract at a later date.

Entrepreneur and the Law

An Oral Contract isn't Worth the Paper it's Written On

The Statute of Frauds, which requires certain contracts to be in writing before they are enforceable, is designed to prevent fraud. Entrepreneurs and other business persons should know the requirements of the state's Statute of Frauds; otherwise they may find themselves with an unenforceable oral contract. Consider the following case.

Whitman Heffernan Rhein & Co., Inc. (Whitman) is a company that provides financial advice to firms planning acquisitions and mergers. The Griffin Company (Griffin), which is owned primarily by Merv Griffin, was negotiating to purchase Resorts International, Inc. from Donald Trump. Whitman alleged that it entered into an oral contract to provide The Griffin Company with financial and investment advice in connection with the negotiation of the purchase of Resorts International. Once Griffin completed the acquisition of Resorts International from Trump, Whitman requested payment for its services from Griffin. When Griffin did not pay, Whitman sued Griffin to recover payment. Griffin asserted the New York Statute of Frauds in defense, arguing that Whitman's alleged contract to provide services in negotiating the purchase of a business had to be in writing to be enforceable, and because Whitman's complaint alleged that it was an oral contract, it was not enforceable.

The New York court agreed with Griffin and held that the alleged contract was oral and therefore barred by the Statute of Frauds. The court stated:

> New York General Obligations Law § 5-701(a)(10) provides that an agreement is void, unless evidenced by a writing signed by the party to be charged, if the agreement is a contract to pay compensation for services rendered in negotiating the purchase of a business. The term "negotiating" includes assisting in the consummation of the transaction.

The moral of the story for entrepreneurs and other business persons is: Get it in writing! [*Whitman Heffernan Rhein & Co., Inc. v. The Griffin Co.*, 557 N.Y.S.2d 342 (NY 1990)]

Contracts Involving Interests in Land

Any contract that transfers an *ownership interest* in **real property** must be in writing under the Statute of Frauds to be enforceable. Real property includes the land itself, buildings, trees, soil, minerals, timber, plants, crops, fixtures, and things permanently affixed to the land or buildings. Certain personal property that is permanently affixed to the real property—for example, built-in cabinets in a house—are **fixtures** that become part of the real property. Note that contracts to construct buildings or to insure buildings or real property do not have to be in writing under the Statute of Frauds because no ownership interest in the real property is being transferred.

real property
The land itself as well as buildings, trees, soil, minerals, timber, plants, crops, and other things permanently affixed to the land.

fixtures
Personal property that is permanently affixed to the real property, such as built-in cabinets in a house.

Transfer of Other Interests in Real Property

Other contracts that transfer an ownership interest in land must be in writing under the Statute of Frauds. These interests include mortgages, leases, life estates, and most easements.

Mortgages   Borrowers often give a lender an interest in real property as security for the repayment of a loan. This must be done through the use of a written **mortgage** or deed of trust.

mortgage
An interest in real property given to a lender as security for the repayment of a loan.

Consider This Example   Suppose Procter & Gamble Corporation purchases a factory and borrows part of the purchase price from City Bank. City Bank requires that the factory be used as collateral for the loan and takes a mortgage on the factory. Here, the mortgage must be in writing to be enforceable.

Leases   A **lease** is the transfer of the right to use real property for a specified period of time. Most Statutes of Frauds require leases for a term over one year to be in writing. Some states have enacted specific statutes (other than the Statute of Frauds) that address the writing requirements and formalities of lease contracts.

lease
The transfer of the right to use real property for a specified period of time.

Life Estates   On some occasions, a person is given a **life estate** in real property. This means that (1) the person has an interest in the land for his or her lifetime and (2) the interest will be transferred to another party on that person's death. A life estate is an ownership interest in land that must be in writing under the Statute of Frauds.

life estate
An interest in the land for a person's lifetime; upon that person's death, the interest will be transferred to another party.

easement
A right to use someone else's land without owning or leasing it.

Easements   An **easement** is a given or required right to use another person's land without owning or leasing it. Easements may be either express or implied. Express easements must be in writing to be enforceable, whereas implied easements need not be written.

Consider This Example   Suppose Unisys, Inc., buys a piece of real property that is "land locked"; that is, there is no road leading to the property. If the company's neighbor expressly agrees to allow it to use a road across his property to reach the property, their agreement must be in writing to be enforceable. However, if the person who sold Unisys the property had been crossing the neighbor's property for 20 years to get to his property, the implied easement created by the conduct of the parties transfers to Unisys without the neighbor's consent.

Part Performance Exception

part performance
An equitable doctrine that allows the court to order an oral contract for the sale of land or transfer of another interest in real property to be specifically performed if it has been partially performed and performance is necessary to avoid injustice.

If an oral contract for the sale of land or transfer of another interest in real property has been partially performed, it may not be possible to return the parties to their status quo. To solve this problem, the courts have developed the equitable doctrine of **part performance**. This doctrine allows the court to order such an oral contract to be specifically performed if performance is necessary to avoid injustice. Most courts require that the purchaser either pay part of the purchase price and take possession of the property or make valuable improvements on the land for this performance exception to apply.

The following case applies the doctrine of part performance.

Sutton v. Warner
12 Cal.App.4th 415, 15 Cal.Rptr.2d 632 (1993)
California Court of Appeals

CASE 14.1

FACTS
In 1983, Arlene and Donald Warner inherited a one-third interest in a home at 101 Molimo Street in San Francisco. The Warners bought out the other heirs and obtained a $170,000 loan on the property. Donald Warner and Kenneth Sutton were friends. In January 1984, Donald Warner proposed that Sutton and his wife purchase the residence. His proposal included a $15,000 down payment toward the purchase price of $185,000. The Suttons were to pay all mortgage payments and real estate taxes on the property for five years, and at any time during the five-year period they could purchase the house. All this was agreed to orally. The Suttons paid the down payment and cash payments equal to the monthly mortgage ($1,881) to the Warners. They paid the annual property taxes on the house. The Suttons also made improvements to the property. In July 1988, the Warners reneged on the sales/option agreement. At that time the house had risen in value to between $250,000 and $320,000. The Suttons sued for specific performance of the sales agreement. The Warners defended, alleging that the oral promise to sell real estate had to be in writing under the Statute of Frauds and was therefore unen-

forceable. The trial court applied the equitable doctrine of part performance and ordered specific performance. The Warners appealed.

ISSUE
Does the equitable doctrine of part performance take this oral contract for the sale of real property out of the Statute of Frauds?

IN THE LANGUAGE OF THE COURT
Kline, Presiding Judge   *The doctrine of part performance by the purchaser is a well-recognized exception to the Statute of Frauds as applied to contracts for the sale of real property. The question here, then, is whether the continued possession of the property by the Suttons and their other actions are sufficiently related to the option contract to constitute part performance. The trial court responded in the affirmative. After entering the oral agreement, the Suttons made a $15,000 down payment and increased their monthly payments to the Warners from the original monthly rental payment to payments in the precise amount of the variable mortgage payments due under the $170,000 loan. They reimbursed the Warners for property taxes in the sum of $800 every six months.*

Although it was disputed whether the dollar value of improvements made by the Suttons in reliance upon the oral agreement constituted "substantial" improvements, it is undisputed that many of the improvements—such as painting the interior of the house and the installation of a toilet and entry lamp—were done by the Suttons' own labor. The trial court found that these actions were unequivocally related to the purchase agreement.

The actions taken by the Suttons in reliance upon the oral agreement, when considered together with the Warners' admission that there was an oral agreement of some duration, satisfy both elements of the part performance doctrine.

The record supports the trial court's determination that part performance by the Suttons sufficed to remove the bar of the statute.

DECISION AND REMEDY

The appellate court held that the doctrine of part performance applied and that the Statute of Frauds did not prevent the enforcement of the oral contract to sell real estate.

Case Questions

Critical Legal Thinking What purposes are served by the Statute of Frauds? Explain.

Ethics Did the Warners act ethically in this case? Did the Statute of Frauds give them a justifiable reason not to go through with the deal?

Business Application Should important business contracts be reduced to writing? Why or why not?

ONE YEAR RULE

According to the Statute of Frauds, an executory contract that cannot be performed by its own terms within one year of its formation must be in writing.[2] This **one year rule** is intended to prevent disputes about contract terms that may otherwise occur toward the end of a long-term contract. If the performance of the contract is possible within the one year period, the contract may be oral.

Consider These Examples The manager of a Texaco service station orally contracts to hire an auto repairman to work for him for five years. The contract is unenforceable because its terms exceed the one year Statute of Frauds and it is not in writing.

Assume a son-in-law makes an oral promise to support his mother-in-law "for life." The mother-in-law is frail and the son-in-law does not think she will live longer than one year. She does, though. The oral contract is enforceable against the son-in-law because it was possible by the contract's own terms to be completed within one year if the mother-in-law died.

The extension of an oral contract might cause the contract to violate the Statute of Frauds. For example, suppose the owner of a Burger King franchise hires Eugene Daly as a manager for six months. This contract may be oral. Assume that after three months, the owner and manager agree to extend the contract for an additional 11 months. At the time of the extension, the contract would be for 14 months (the three left on the contract plus 11 added by the extension). The modification would have to be in writing because it exceeds the one year Statute of Frauds.

The following case brings up the one year rule.

one year rule
An executory contract that cannot be performed by its own terms within one year of its formation must be in writing.

Business Brief
Employment contracts are often for periods longer than one year. These contracts should be in writing to be enforceable.

Doherty v. Doherty Insurance Agency, Inc.
878 F.2d 540 (1989)
United States Court of Appeals, First Circuit

CASE 14.2

FACTS
In the mid-1930s, Bill and Jim Doherty, who were brothers, founded an insurance and real estate agency in Andover, Massachusetts. The business was successful. In 1955, Bill discovered that he was seriously ill. Concerned that Jim would be left to run the family business alone, Bill and Jim asked another brother, Joseph, if he was interested in joining the family business. Joseph was apprehensive about doing so

(case continues)

because he was superintendent of schools in Easthampton, Connecticut, and was concerned about losing his retirement benefits. Jim (on behalf of the business) orally promised Joe "retirement benefits for his remaining life" equal to his salary at age 65 when he retired. Relying on this promise, Joe quit his job and joined the business. Bill retired on full salary in 1970. Joe retired in 1978 and was paid $2,000 a month in retirement benefits. Jim retired in 1980 on full salary. The business passed on to the next generation, consisting of Jim's and Joe's children. In 1981, a dispute arose, and Joe's children left the business. Jim's children terminated Joe's retirement payments. Joe sued. The defendants argued that the oral lifetime retirement contract was unenforceable under the Statute of Frauds because it ended up being longer than one year. The trial court held in favor of Joe. The defendants appealed.

ISSUE

Does the Statute of Frauds prevent the enforcement of an oral lifetime retirement contract?

IN THE LANGUAGE OF THE COURT

Campbell, Chief Judge   *A contract for a term of years is distinguishable from one for an individual's lifetime. In the case of a contract for a term of years, a party who dies cannot be said to have "performed" the contract. Instead, the contract is one which is subject to "defeasance or cancellation" by the death of the party during the term of the agreement.*

The fact that the present contract provided for retirement benefits and that the instant dispute, arising during Joe's senior years, pertains to the payment of compensation during retirement, does not indicate that the contract could not have been performed within its initial year, had Joe had the misfortune to die then, while still in his 40s. The jury expressly found that in exchange for Joe's promise to join his brothers in Andover and "work with them for the balance of his working days," Jim (on behalf of Insurance) promised that Joe's "compensation would include retirement benefits for his remaining life." If Joe were to have died within the year, he would have completely fulfilled his promise to work "for the balance of his working days" (because his working days would have been over), and Insurance would have fulfilled its promise to compensate him for his remaining life.

This oral agreement falls outside the Statute of Frauds. The oral agreement was enforceable under Massachusetts law.

DECISION AND REMEDY

The appellate court held that the oral contract was enforceable. Affirmed.

Case Questions

Critical Legal Thinking   Should oral lifetime contracts be enforced? Or should they be required to be in writing?

Ethics   Was it ethical for Jim's children to terminate Joe's retirement benefits?

Business Application   Do businesses make many oral promises to employees? Should these contracts be in writing?

*C*OLLATERAL PROMISES

collateral contract

A promise where one person agrees to answer for the debts or duties of another person.

guaranty contract

The contract between the guarantor and the original creditor.

guarantor

The person who agrees to pay the debt if the primary debtor does not.

A **collateral** or **guaranty contract** occurs where one person agrees to answer for the debts or duties of another person. Collateral promises are required to be in writing under the Statute of Frauds.[3]

In a guaranty situation, there are at least three parties and two contracts. (See Exhibit 14.1.) The *first contract*, which is known as the *original* or *primary contract*, is between the debtor and the creditor. It does not have to be in writing (unless another provision of the Statute of Frauds requires it to be). The *second contract*, called the **guaranty contract**, is between the person who agrees to pay the debt if the primary debtor does not (i.e., the **guarantor**) and the original creditor. The guarantor's liability is secondary because it does not arise unless the party primarily liable fails to perform.

Consider This Example   Jay Hoberman, a recent college graduate, offers to purchase a new automobile on credit from a General Motors dealership. Because the purchaser does not have a credit history, the dealer will agree to sell the car only if there is a guarantor. Jay's mother signs the guaranty contract and then becomes responsible for any payments her son fails to make.

EXHIBIT **14.1** *Original and Guaranty Contracts*

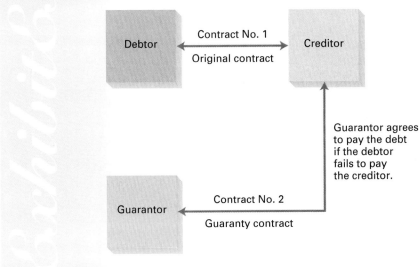

The Main Purpose Exception

If the main purpose of a transaction and an oral collateral contract is to provide pecuniary (i.e., financial) benefit to the guarantor, the collateral contract is treated like an original contract and does not have to be in writing to be enforced.[4] This is called the **main purpose** or **leading object exception** to the Statute of Frauds. The exception is intended to ensure that the primary benefactor of the original contract (i.e., the guarantor) is answerable for the debt or duty.

main purpose or **leading object exception**

If the main purpose of a transaction and an oral collateral contract is to provide pecuniary benefit to the guarantor, the collateral contract does not have to be in writing to be enforced.

Consider This Example Suppose Ethel Brand is president and sole shareholder of Brand Company Corporation, Inc. Assume that (1) the corporation borrows $100,000 from City Bank for working capital and (2) Ethel orally guarantees to repay the loan if the corporation fails to pay it. City Bank can enforce the oral guaranty contract against Ethel if the corporation does not meet its obligation because the main purpose of the loan was to benefit her as the sole shareholder of the corporation.

CONTRACTS FOR THE SALE OF GOODS

Section 201 of the **Uniform Commercial Code (UCC)** is the basic **Statute of Frauds** provision for sales contracts. It requires that contracts for the sale of goods costing *$500 or more* must be in writing to be enforceable.[5] If the contract price of an original sales contract is below $500 and does not have to be in writing under the UCC Statute of Frauds, but a modification of the contract increases the sales price to $500 or more, the *modification* has to be in writing to be enforceable.[6]

UCC Statute of Frauds

Contracts for the sale of goods costing $500 or more must be in writing.

Collateral Promises

Many states require that *agents' contracts* to sell property covered by the Statute of Frauds must be in writing to be enforceable. This requirement is often referred to as the **equal dignity rule**.

equal dignity rule

A rule that says that agents' contracts to sell property covered by the Statute of Frauds must be in writing to be enforceable.

The Uniform Commercial Code (UCC) requires contracts for the sale of goods costing $500 or more, such as these horses, to be in writing.

Consider This Example Suppose Barney Berkowitz hires Cynthia Lamont, a licensed Century-21 real estate agent, to sell his house. Because a contract to sell real estate must be in writing pursuant to the Statute of Frauds, the equal dignity rule requires the agent's contract to be in writing as well. Some state Statutes of Frauds expressly list the agents' contracts that must be in writing.

International Perspective

WRITING REQUIREMENTS FOR INTERNATIONAL CONTRACTS

Traditionally, many countries require certain contracts to be in writing. In the civil law countries, this requirement generally does not apply to commercial transactions. In socialist countries, written contracts usually are required because of the need for certainty both in interpreting and enforcing foreign trade contracts.

Most of the delegates involved in the drafting of the United Nations Convention on Contracts for the International Sale of Goods (CISG) decided that a writing requirement would be inconsistent with modern commercial practice, especially in market economies where speed and informality characterize so many transactions. Some delegates, however, insisted that a writing requirement is important for protecting their country's longtime pattern of making foreign trade contracts.

The result of this disagreement was a compromise. Article 11 of the Convention states: "A contract of sale need not be concluded in or evidenced by writing and is not subject to any other requirement as to form. It may be proved by any means, including witnesses." The CISG's Article 96, however, authorizes a contracting nation that requires written sales contracts to stipulate at the time of ratification that Article 11 (and some other provisions of the Convention) does not apply if any party operates a business in that nation.

promissory estoppel

An equitable doctrine that permits enforcement of oral contracts that should have been in writing. It is applied to avoid injustice.

Promissory Estoppel

The doctrine of **promissory estoppel**, or **equitable estoppel**, is another equitable exception to the strict application of the Statute of Frauds. The Restatement (Second) of Contracts version of promissory estoppel provides that if parties enter into an oral contract that should be in writing under the Statute of Frauds, the oral promise is enforceable against the promisor if these three conditions are met: (1) The promise induces action or forbearance of action by another, (2) the reliance on the oral promise was foreseeable, and (3) injustice can be avoided only by enforcing the oral promise.[7] Where this doctrine applies, the promisor is *estopped* (prevented) from raising the Statute of Frauds as a defense to the enforcement of the oral contract.

Ethical Perspective

GRAPE GROWER STOMPED

Bronco Wine Company (Bronco) crushed grapes and sold them for use in bulk wines. It purchased the grapes it needed from various grape growers. In 1981, Bronco entered into an oral contract with Allied Grape Growers (Allied), a cooperative corporation of many grape growers, to purchase 850 tons of Carnelian grapes for delivery in 1982. Allied had originally contracted to sell these grapes to United Vintners but received special permission to sell the grapes to Bronco instead.

The 1982 grape crop was the largest to date in California history, and there was a glut of foreign wines on the market. Thus, the price of grapes and wines decreased substantially. Bronco accepted and paid for one shipment of Carnelian grapes from Allied but refused to accept the rest. By the time Bronco started to reject the highly perishable goods, it was too late for Allied to resell the grapes to United Vintners or others.

Allied sued for breach of contract, and Bronco alleged the Statute of Frauds as its defense. In essence, Bronco argued that it did not have to perform because the contract was not in writing.

The appellate court applied the doctrine of promissory estoppel and prohibited Bronco from raising the Statute of Frauds against enforcement of its oral promise to buy the grapes from Allied. The court stated: "In California, the doctrine of estoppel is proven where one party suffers an unconscionable injury if the Statute of Frauds is asserted to prevent enforcement of oral contracts. There is substantial evidence that Allied's loss was unconscionable given these facts. The Statute of Frauds should not be used in this instance to defeat the oral agreement reached by the parties in this case." The appellate court affirmed the trial court's verdict awarding damages to Allied. [*Allied Grape Growers v. Bronco Wine Company*, 203 Cal.App.3d 432, 249 Cal.Rptr. 872 (Cal.App. 1988)]

1. Is it ever ethical to raise the Statute of Frauds against the enforcement of an oral contract?
2. Should courts apply the equitable doctrine of estoppel to save contracting parties from the Statute of Frauds?

SUFFICIENCY OF THE WRITING

Both the common law of contracts and the UCC have adopted several rules regarding the legal sufficiency of written contracts. These rules are discussed in the paragraphs that follow.

Formality of the Writing

Many written commercial contracts are long, detailed documents that have been negotiated by the parties and drafted and reviewed by their lawyers. Other written contracts are preprinted forms that are prepared in advance to be used in recurring situations.

However, a written contract does not have to be either drafted by a lawyer or formally typed to be legally binding. Generally, the law only requires a writing containing the essential terms of the parties' agreement. Any writing—including letters, telegrams, invoices, sales receipts, checks, handwritten agreements written on scraps of paper, and such—can be an enforceable contract under this rule.

Counsel Randle Jackson: In the book of nature, my lords, it is written—Lord Ellenborough: Will you have the goodness to mention the page. Sir, if you please.

Lord Campbell
Lives of the Chief Justices
(1857)

Required Signature

The Statute of Frauds and the UCC require the written contract, whatever its form, to be signed *by the party against whom enforcement is sought*. The signature of the person who is enforcing the contract is not necessary. Thus, a written contract may be enforceable against one party but not the other party.

Consider This Example   Suppose Travis McQuire and Holly Berger, who are not merchants, enter into an oral contract whereby Ms. Berger agrees to sell her motor home to Mr. McQuire for $35,000. She sends him a signed letter setting forth the terms of their agreement. The contract can be enforced against Ms. Berger because she signed a written memorandum (i.e., the letter) containing the essential terms of the contract. However, the contract cannot be enforced against Mr. McQuire since he can raise the Statute of Frauds as a defense.

The meaning of words varies according to the circumstances of and concerning which they are used.

Blackburn, J.
Allgood v. Blake (1873)

Generally, the signature may appear anywhere on the writing. In addition, it does not have to be a person's full legal name. The person's last name, first name, nickname, initials, seal, stamp, engraving, or other symbol or mark (e.g., an X) that indicates the person's intent can be binding. The signature may be affixed by an authorized agent.

Contemporary Business Application

WHAT CONSTITUTES A SIGNATURE?

In the past, courts have accepted nicknames, first names, initials, symbols, and X's as proper signatures of a promisor. But what happens if the promisor does not actually sign the document? Can it be enforced? One court said yes. Consider the following facts.

MRLS Construction Corporation (MRLS), which was the construction manager on a building project, hired a subcontractor, Sime Construction Company (Sime), to work on the project. When Parma Tile, Mosaic & Marble Company, Inc. (Parma), refused to deliver tile to Sime unless MRLS guaranteed payment, MRLS sent the following fax to Parma: "MRLS would guarantee payment for goods delivered to the Nehemiah project in the event Sime Construction does not pay within terms."

The name MRLS was printed across the top of the unsigned fax. Parma delivered the tile to Sime and, when Sime failed to pay, billed MRLS in reliance on the purported guarantee. MRLS refused to pay. MRLS argued that there was no enforceable contract because the fax was not signed. Parma sued MRLS.

The court rejected this argument and held that the fax constituted an enforceable guarantee because the printed name MRLS appeared across the top of the fax. The court found that this satisfied the signature requirement of the Statute of Frauds. The court stated, "The Statute of Frauds was not meant to be utilized to evade an obligation intentionally incurred. MRLS should not be permitted to evade its obligation because of the current and extensive use of electronic transmissions in modern business transactions." [*Parma Tile, Mosaic & Marble Company, Inc. v. Estate of Short, New York Law Journal,* December 10, 1992]

Integration of Several Writings

integration
The combination of several writings to form a single contract.

incorporation by reference
When integration is made by express reference in one document that refers to and incorporates another document within it.

Both the common law of contracts and the UCC permit several writings to be **integrated** to form a single written contract. That is, the entire writing does not have to appear in one document to be an enforceable contract.

Integration may be by an *express reference* in one document that refers to and incorporates another document within it. This is called **incorporation by reference**. Thus, what may often look like a simple one-page contract may actually be hundreds of pages long. For example, credit cards often incorporate by express reference such documents as the master agreement between the issuer and cardholders, subsequent amendments to the agreement, and such.

Several documents may be integrated to form a single written contract if they are somehow physically attached to each other to indicate a party's intent to show integration. For example, attaching several documents together by a staple, a paper clip, or some other means may indicate integration. Placing several documents in the same container (e.g., an envelope) may also indicate integration. This is called *implied integration*.

Entrepreneur and the Law

INTERPRETING CONTRACT WORDS AND TERMS

When contracts are at issue in a lawsuit, courts are often called upon to interpret the meaning of certain contract words or terms. The parties to a contract may define the words and terms used in their contract. Many written contracts contain a detailed definitional section—usually called a **glossary**—that defines many of the words and terms used in the contract. In interpreting the contract, the court is assisted by the glossary's definitions. Businesspersons should consider including a glossary of words and terms in their contracts to make interpretation easier and clearer.

If the parties have not defined the words and terms of a contract, the courts apply the following **standards of interpretation**:

- *Ordinary* words are given their usual meaning according to the dictionary.
- *Technical words* are given their technical meaning, unless a different meaning is clearly intended. Testimony from expert witnesses is often necessary to determine the precise meaning of technical words.

- *Specific terms* are presumed to qualify *general terms*. For example, if a provision in a contract refers to the subject matter as "corn," but a later provision refers to the subject matter as "feed corn" for cattle, this specific term qualifies the general term.
- Where a preprinted form contract is used, typed words in a contract prevail over *preprinted words*. *Handwritten words* prevail over both preprinted and typed words.
- If there is an ambiguity in a contract, the ambiguity will be resolved against the party who drafted the contract.
- If both parties are members of the same trade or profession, words will be given their meaning as used in the trade (i.e., *usage of trade*). If the parties do not want trade usage to apply, the contract must indicate that.
- Words will be interpreted to promote the *principal object* of the contract. For example, if a word is subject to two or more definitions, the court will choose the definition that will advance the principal object of the contract.

THE PAROL EVIDENCE RULE

By the time a contract is reduced to writing, the parties usually have engaged in prior or contemporaneous discussions and negotiations or exchanged prior writings. Any oral or written words outside of the *four corners* of the written contract are called **parol evidence**. *Parol* means "word."

The **parol evidence rule** was originally developed by courts as part of the common law of contracts. The UCC has adopted the parol evidence rule as part of the law of sales contracts.[8] The parol evidence rule states that if a written contract is a complete and final statement of the parties' agreement (i.e., a *complete integration*), any prior or contemporaneous oral or written statements that alter, contradict, or are in addition to the terms of the written contract are inadmissible in any court proceeding concerning the contract.[9] In other words, a completely integrated contract is viewed as the best evidence of the terms of the parties' agreement.

parol evidence

Any oral or written words outside the four corners of the written contract.

parol evidence rule

A rule that says if a written contract is a complete and final statement of the parties' agreement, any prior or contemporaneous oral or written statements that alter, contradict, or are in addition to the terms of the written contract are inadmissible in court regarding a dispute over the contract. There are several exceptions to this rule.

Exceptions to the Parol Evidence Rule

There are several major exceptions to the general rule excluding parol evidence. Parol evidence may be admitted in court if it

- Shows that a contract is void or voidable (e.g., evidence that the contract was induced by fraud, misrepresentation, duress, undue influence, or mistake).
- Explains ambiguous language.
- Concerns a *prior course of dealing* or *course of performance* between the parties or a *usage of trade*.[10]
- *Fills in the gaps* in the contract (e.g., if a price term or time of performance term is omitted from a written contract, the court can hear parol evidence to imply the reasonable price or time of performance under the contract).
- Corrects an obvious clerical or typographical error. The court can *reform* the contract to reflect the correction.

merger clause

A clause in a contract that stipulates that it is a complete integration and the exclusive expression of the parties' agreement. Parol evidence may not be introduced to explain, alter, contradict, or add to the terms of the contract.

Merger, or Integration, Clause

The parties to a written contract may include a clause stipulating that the contract is a complete integration and the exclusive expression of their agreement and that parol evidence may not be introduced to explain, alter, contradict, or add to the terms of the contract. This type of clause, called a **merger**, or **integration, clause**, expressly reiterates the parol evidence rule. Merger clauses do not prevent the introduction of parol evidence to prove fraud, misrepresentation, duress, undue influence, or mistake.

Contemporary Business Application

INTEGRATION CLAUSE SUPERSEDES PAROL EVIDENCE

On January 2, 1977, Carl M. Malmstrom applied for a job at Kaiser Aluminum & Chemical Corporation (Kaiser) in its aluminum can division. During the prehiring interviews with Kaiser, Malmstrom questioned his interviewers about the permanency of the position he was offered. Malmstrom testified that at the time he was hired, Mr. Johnson of Kaiser told him "as long as one does a commendable job up to Kaiser's expectations, that you had no fear of being laid off" and that "Kaiser never laid off anyone unless there was due cause obviously of some nature."

On January 13, 1977, Malmstrom was employed by Kaiser. He signed a one-page agreement with the company concerning his employment. Paragraph 1 provided: "Employer employs and shall continue to employ Employee at such compensation and for such a length of time as shall be mutually agreeable to Employer and Employee." Paragraph 6 of the employment contract was an integration clause that provided "This agreement shall supersede all previous agreements by and between Employer and Employee and shall be retroactive to the date on which Employee commenced his employment."

In April 1981, because of a decrease in business, Kaiser began terminating many employees. On January 5, 1982, Malmstrom was told he was terminated as part of the staff reduction. In the two-year period following Malmstrom's layoff, the number of Kaiser employees declined from 27,000 to 18,000. Malmstrom sued Kaiser for breach of alleged oral contracts to provide permanent employment to him. The trial court granted summary judgment for Kaiser. Malmstrom appealed.

Does the parol evidence rule make the evidence concerning the alleged oral contracts inadmissible? The appellate court held that the written employment agreement between Malmstrom and Kaiser was integrated, and evidence of other alleged oral contracts between the parties was inadmissible, under the parol evidence rule.

Paragraph 6 of the contract provided that the agreement "shall supersede all previous agreements by and between Employer and Employee." The court held that the meaning of this paragraph was clear on its face and Malmstrom offered no alternative meaning. Contrary to Malmstrom's assertion, the alleged oral agreement occurred before he signed the written agreement. The scope of the contract covered the term of employment and the compensation of the employee. It is unlikely that there would be two agreements concerning the term of the employment. The court found that the alleged oral agreement was completely inconsistent with the terms of the written contract.

The court held that the contract was a contract for employment terminable at will and that, because the contract was integrated and provided that it superseded all prior agreements, evidence of an implied agreement that contradicts the terms of the written agreement is not admissible. [*Malmstrom v. Kaiser Aluminum & Chemical Corp.*, 187 Cal.App.3d 299, 231 Cal.Rptr. 820 (Cal.App. 1986)]

International Perspective

THE ISLAMIC LAW SYSTEM

Approximately 20 percent of the world's population is Muslim. Islam is the principal religion of Afghanistan, Algeria, Bangladesh, Egypt, Indonesia, Iran, Iraq, Jordan, Kuwait, Libya, Malaysia, Mali, Mauritania, Morocco, Niger, North Yemen, Oman, Pakistan, Qatar, Saudi Arabia, Somalia, South Yemen, Sudan, Syria, Tunisia, Turkey, and the United Arab Emirates. *Islamic law* (or *Shari'a*) is the only law in Saudi Arabia. In other Islamic countries, the *Shari'a* forms the basis of family law but coexists with other laws.

The Islamic law system is derived from the Koran, the Sunnah (decisions and sayings of the Prophet Muhammad), and reasoning by Islamic scholars. By the tenth century A.D., Islamic scholars decided that no further improvement of the divine law could be made, closed the door of *ijtihad* (independent reasoning), and froze the evolution of Islamic law at that point. Islamic law prohibits *riba*, or the making of unearned or unjustified profit. Making a profit from the sale of goods or the provision of services is permitted. The most notable consequence of *riba* is that the payment of interest on loans is forbidden. To circumvent this result, the party with the money is permitted to purchase the item and resell it to the other party at a profit or to advance the money and become a trading partner who shares in the profits of the enterprise.

Today, Islamic law is primarily used in the areas of marriage, divorce, and inheritance and to a limited degree in criminal law. To resolve the tension between *Shari'a* and the practice of modern commercial law, the *Shari'a* is often ignored in commercial transactions.

Working the Web

Do you want to save big money on books? One of the newest trends is bookstores on-line. Often you can save 50 percent or more by buying your books this way. Some great on-line bookstores include:

Amazon

Visit at **www.amazon.com**

Barnes and Noble

Visit at **www.bn.com**

BestBookBuys

Visit at **www.bestbookbuys.com**

Magazine Outlet

Visit at **www.magazineoutlet.com**

CYBER EXERCISES

1. Visit one of the on-line bookstores to buy a book as a gift.

CASES AND EXERCISES

CRITICAL LEGAL THINKING CASES

14.1. In 1976, Fritz Hoffman and Fritz Frey contacted the Sun Valley Company (Company) about purchasing a 1.64-acre piece of property known as the "Ruud Mountain Property," located in Sun Valley, Idaho, from the Company. Mr. Conger, a representative of the Company, was authorized to sell the property, subject to the approval of the executive committee of the Company. On January 21, 1977, Conger reached an agreement on the telephone with Hoffman and Frey whereby they would purchase the property for $90,000, payable at 30 percent down, with the balance to be payable quarterly at an annual interest rate of $9\frac{3}{4}$ percent. The next day Hoffman sent Conger a letter confirming the conversation.

The executive committee of the Company approved the sale. Sun Valley Realty prepared the deed of trust, note, seller's closing statement, and other loan documents. However, before the documents were executed by either side, Sun Valley Company sold all of its assets, including the Ruud Mountain property, to another purchaser. When the new owner refused to sell the Ruud Mountain lot to Hoffman and Frey, they brought this action for specific performance of the oral contract. Who wins? [*Hoffman v. Sun Valley Company*, 628 P.2d 218 (ID 1981)]

14.2. In 1955, Robert Briggs and his wife purchased a home located at 167 Lower Orchard Drive, Levittown, Pennsylvania. They made a $100 down payment and borrowed the balance of $11,600 on a 30-year mortgage. In late 1961, when the Briggs were behind on their mortgage payments, they entered into an oral contract to sell the house to Winfield and Emma Sackett if the Sacketts would pay the three months' arrearages on the loan and agree to make the future payments on the mortgage. Mrs. Briggs and Mrs. Sackett were sisters. The Sacketts paid the arrearages, moved into the house, and have lived there to date. In 1976, Robert Briggs filed an action to void the oral contract as in violation of the Statute of Frauds and evict the Sacketts from the house. Who wins? [*Briggs v. Sackett*, 418 A.2d 586 (Pa.App. 1980)]

14.3. Robert S. Ohanian was vice president of sales for the West Region of Avis Rent a Car System, Inc. (Avis). Officers of Avis testified that Ohanian's performance in the West Region was excellent, and, in a depressed economic period, Ohanian's West Region stood out as the one region that was growing and profitable. In the fall of 1980, when Avis's Northeast Region was doing badly, the president of Avis asked Ohanian to take over that region. Ohanian was reluctant to do so, because he and his family liked living in San Francisco and he had developed a good "team" in the West Region, was secure in his position, and feared the politics of the Northeast Region. Ohanian agreed to the transfer only after the general manager of Avis orally told him "unless you screw up badly, there is no way you are going to get fired—you will never get hurt here in this company." Ohanian did a commendable job in the Northeast Region. Approximately one year later, on July 27, 1982, at the age of 47, Ohanian was fired without cause by Avis. Ohanian sued Avis for breach of the oral lifetime contract. Avis asserted the Statute of Frauds against this claim. Who wins? [*Ohanian v. Avis Rent a Car System, Inc.*, 779 F.2d 101 (2nd Cir. 1985)]

14.4. On May 17, 1979, David Brown met with Stan Steele, a loan officer with the Bank of Idaho (now First Interstate Bank) to discuss borrowing $5,000 from the bank to start a new business. After learning that he did not qualify for the loan on the basis of his own financial strength, Brown told Steele that his former employers, James and Donna West of California, might be willing to guarantee the payment of the loan. On May 18, 1979, Steele talked to Mr. West, who orally stated on the telephone that he would personally guarantee the loan to Brown. Based on this guaranty, the bank loaned Brown $5,000. The bank sent a written guarantee to Mr. and Mrs. West for their signatures, but it was never returned to the bank. When Brown defaulted on the loan, the bank filed suit against the Wests to recover on their guaranty contract. Are the Wests liable? [*First Interstate Bank of Idaho, N.A. v. West*, 693 P.2d 1053 (ID 1984)]

14.5. Six persons, including Benjamin Rosenbloom and Alfred Feiler, were members of the board of directors of the Togs Corporation. A bank agreed to loan the corporation $250,000 if the members of the board would personally guarantee the payment of the loan. Feiler objected to signing the guaranty to the bank because of other pending personal financial negotiations that the contingent liability of the guaranty might adversely affect. Feiler agreed with Rosenbloom and the other board members that if they were held personally liable on the guaranty, he would pay his one-sixth share of that amount to them directly. Rosenbloom and the other members of the board signed the personal guaranty with the bank, and the bank made the loan to the corporation. When the corporation defaulted on the loan, the five guarantors had to pay the loan amount to the bank. When they attempted to collect a one-sixth share from Feiler, he refused to pay, alleging that his oral promise had to be in writing under the Statute of Frauds. Does Feiler have to pay the one-sixth share to the other board members? [*Feiler v. Rosenbloom*, 416 A.2d 1345 (Md.App. 1980)]

14.6. Paul L. McGirr operated an Enco service station in Los Angeles that sold approximately 25,000 to 35,000 gallons of gasoline a month. McGirr telephoned Gulf Oil Corporation (Gulf) regarding an advertisement for dealers. McGirr met with Theodore Marks, an area representative of Gulf, to discuss the possibility of McGirr's operating a Gulf service station. McGirr asked Marks if Gulf had any good, high-producing units available. Marks replied that he had a station at the corner of Figueroa and Avenue 26 that sold about 200,000 gallons of gasoline a month. Marks told McGirr that this station would not be available for about 90 days because Gulf had to terminate the arrangement with the current operator of the station. Marks told McGirr that he could have the Figueroa station only if he also took a "dog" station on Garvey Avenue. Marks agreed to take this station only if he also was assured he would get the Figueroa station. Marks assured him he would. When McGirr asked Marks for this assurance in writing, Marks stated that he did not have to put it in writing because he was the "kingpin in his territory." So they shook hands on the deal.

McGirr terminated his arrangement with Enco and moved to the Garvey Avenue station. He signed a written lease for the Garvey station, which was signed by Max Reed, Gulf's regional sales manager. Under the Statute of Frauds, the lease for a service station must be in writing. Nothing in writing was ever signed by the parties regarding the Figueroa station. A few months later Marks was transferred to a different territory, and Gulf refused to lease the Figueroa station to McGirr. McGirr sued Marks and Gulf for breach of an oral contract. Is Marks or Gulf liable? [*McGirr v. Gulf Oil Corporation*, 41 Cal.App.3d 246, 115 Cal.Rptr. 902 (Cal.App. 1974)]

14.7. Natale and Carmela Castiglia were married in 1919 in Colorado. Carmela had a son from a previous marriage, Christie Lo Greco, who lived with them. Natale and Carmela moved to California where they invested their assets of $4,000 in agricultural property. Christie, then in his early teens, moved with them to California. In 1926, Christie, then 18 years old, decided to leave home and seek an independent living. Natale and Carmela, however, wanted him to stay with them and participate in the family venture. They made an oral promise to Christie that if he stayed home and worked, they would leave their property to him by will. Christie accepted and remained home and worked the family venture. He received only his room and board and spending money. When Christie married, Natale told him that his wife should move in with the family and that Christie need not worry, for he would receive all the property when Natale and Carmela died. Natale and Carmela entered into identical wills leaving their property to Christie when they died. Natale died in the late 1940s. Shortly before his death, without the knowledge of Christie or Carmela, he changed his will and left his share of the property to his grandson, Carmen Monarco. Christie sued to enforce Natale's oral promise. Does the doctrine of promissory estoppel prevent the application of the Statute of Frauds in this case? [*Monarco v. Lo Greco*, 220 P.2d 737, 35 Cal.2d 621 (CA 1950)]

14.8. The Atlantic Wholesale Co., Inc. (Atlantic), which is located in Florence, South Carolina, is in the business of buying and selling gold and silver for customers' accounts. Gary A. Solondz, a New York resident, became a customer of Atlantic in 1979 and thereafter made several purchases through Atlantic. On January 23, 1980, Solondz telephoned Atlantic and received a quotation on silver bullion. Solondz then bought 300 ounces of silver for a total price of $12,978. Atlantic immediately contacted United Precious Metals in Minneapolis and purchased the silver for Solondz. The silver was shipped to Atlantic, who paid for it.

Atlantic placed the silver in its vault while it waited payment from Solondz. When Atlantic telephoned Solondz about payment, he told Atlantic to continue to hold the silver in its vault until he decided whether to sell it. Meanwhile, the price of silver had fallen substantially and continued to fall. When Solondz refused to pay for the silver, Atlantic sold it for $4,650, sustaining a loss of $8,328. When Atlantic sued Solondz to recover this loss, Solondz asserted that the Statute of Frauds prevented enforcement of his oral promise to buy the silver. Does the doctrine of promissory estoppel prevent the application of the Statute of Frauds in this case? [*Atlantic Wholesale Co., Inc. v. Solondz*, 320 S.E.2d 720 (S.C.App. 1984)]

14.9. Irving Levin and Harold Lipton owned the San Diego Clippers Basketball Club, a professional basketball franchise. On December 3, 1980, Levin and Lipton met with Philip Knight to discuss the sale of the Clippers to Knight. After the meeting, they all initialed a three-page handwritten memorandum that Levin had drafted during the meeting. The memorandum outlined the major terms of their discussion, including subject matter, price, and the parties to the agreement. On December 13, 1980, Levin and Lipton forwarded to Knight a letter and proposed sale agreement. Two days later, Knight informed Levin that he had decided not to purchase the Clippers. Levin and Lipton sued Knight for breach of contract. Knight argued in defense that the handwritten memorandum was not enforceable because it did not satisfy the Statute of Frauds. Is he correct? [*Levin v. Knight*, 865 F.2d 1271 (9th Cir. 1989)]

14.10. Anthony Gallo hired an attorney and brought a personal injury action against Frank William Getz. Mr. Getz's insurance company defended the lawsuit. On March 14, 1985, the parties reached a settlement of the case by telephone. On the same day, Gallo's attorney wrote to the insurance company, stating "This is to confirm our telephone conversation of March 14, 1985, wherein the case of Anthony Gallo has been settled for the sum of $33,237.25. Please draw up the paperwork and checks as soon as possible." Gallo's attorney signed the letter. Under California law, a settlement of a legal proceeding must be in writing and signed by the parties. The insurance company prepared a settlement agreement and drafts and mailed them to Gallo's attorney. The drafts, which were made payable to Gallo and his attorney, were endorsed by both of them and cashed. Gallo never signed the settlement agreement. Eight months later, Gallo notified the insurance company that he was not willing to go along with the settlement. Is the settlement agreement enforceable against Gallo? [*Gallo v. Getz*, 205 Cal.App.3d 329, 252 Cal.Rptr. 193 (Cal.App. 1988)]

14.11. William Keeton and Robert Stewart entered into a partnership for the purpose of building a house on Lot 9, Chestnut Hill Estates, in Tuscaloosa, Alabama. Keeton and Stewart borrowed $68,000 from the First National Bank of Tuscaloosa to construct the house. They signed promissory notes evidencing the loans. In addition, they executed a construction loan agreement authorizing the bank to advance loan proceeds from time to time from this account. The loans were secured by mortgages on Lot 9 and other property. In October 1983, Stewart, on behalf of the partnership, opened two checking accounts at the bank under the name RS&K Development Co. The checking account and signature cards authorized Stewart, Keeton, and Robert Rabinette to withdraw funds from the checking accounts. The money borrowed from the bank was deposited in these accounts. In 1984, the bank informed Keeton that the partnership checking accounts were overdrawn and that $34,000 of credit advanced from the construction loan had been depleted. Keeton sued the bank for breach of contract, alleging that he had orally told the bank not to permit any withdrawals from the checking accounts or advances from the construction loan account without his approval. Is the evidence regarding this alleged oral agreement admissible in court? [*Keeton v. First National Bank of Tuscaloosa*, 529 So.2d 963 (AL 1988)]

Ethics Cases

14.12. On March 29, 1979, American Broadcasting Company Merchandising, Inc., a subsidiary of American Broadcasting Company, Inc. (collectively, ABC), entered into a written contract with model Cheryl Tiegs whereby ABC would pay Tiegs $400,000 per year for the right to be the exclusive agent to license the merchandising of goods under her name. When ABC was unsuccessful in attracting licensing arrangements for Tiegs, a representative of ABC contacted Paul Sklar who had previous experience in marketing apparel and licensing labels. Sklar enlisted the help of Mark Blye, and together they introduced ABC and Tiegs to Sears, Roebuck and Company (Sears). This introduction led to an agreement between Sears, ABC, and Tiegs whereby Sears marketed a line of "Cheryl Tiegs" female apparel through Sears department stores and catalog sales. Blye and Sklar sued ABC for a finder's fee for introducing ABC to Sears. Because there was no express written or oral contract between ABC and Blye and Sklar, they alleged that there was an implied-in-fact contract between the parties. Section 5-701(a)(10) of the New York Statute of Frauds requires a finder's fee contract of the type in this case to be in writing. Who wins? Did ABC act ethically in this case? [*Blye v. American Broadcasting Company Merchandising, Inc.*, 476 N.Y.S.2d 874 (N.Y.Sup. 1986)]

14.13. Adolfo Mozzetti, who owned a construction company, orally promised his son, Remo, that if Remo would manage the family business for their mutual benefit and would take care of him for the rest of his life, he would leave the family home to Remo. Section 2714 of the Delaware Code requires contracts for the transfer of land to be in writing. Section 2715 of the Delaware Code requires testamentary transfers of real property to be in writing. Remo performed as requested—he managed the family business and took care of his father until the father died. When the father died, his will devised the family home to his daughter, Lucia M. Shepard. Remo brought this action to enforce his father's oral promise that the home belonged to him. The daughter argued that the will should be upheld. Who wins? Did the daughter act ethically in trying to defeat the father's promise to leave the property to the son? Did the son act ethically in trying to defeat his father's will? [*Shepard v. Mozzetti*, 545 A.2d 621 (DE 1988)]

14.14. In 1968, Jane Fonda, an entertainer and California resident, retained the services of a New York law firm. She entered into an oral agreement with the firm that she would pay 5 percent of her earnings as compensation for the firm's services. Richard Rosenthal, an attorney with the firm, assumed responsibility for most of the firm's activities on behalf of Fonda. In 1971, the law firm dissolved, and in 1972 Rosenthal began to represent Fonda as an independent private practitioner. Rosenthal alleges that in April 1972, he and Fonda entered into an oral contract whereby he agreed to continue performing a variety of services for Fonda and she, in turn, agreed to pay him 10 percent of all gross professional income derived from the projects that were initiated during his tenure. In 1978, Rosenthal and his family moved to California, at Fonda's request, so that he could be closer to her and represent her more efficiently. Fonda discharged Rosenthal approximately two years later, on May 30, 1980. Rosenthal brought this suit against Fonda to recover commissions on projects initiated during his tenure that produced income after his termination. Did Jane Fonda act ethically in this case by raising the Statute of Frauds against enforcement of an oral contract? Who wins? [*Rosenthal v. Fonda*, 862 F.2d 1398 (9th Cir. 1988)]

CRITICAL LEGAL THINKING WRITING ASSIGNMENT

Read Case A.14 in the Case Appendix [*Hampton v. Federal Express Corporation*]. This case is excerpted from the court of appeals opinion. Review and brief the case. In your brief, be sure to answer the following questions.

1. Why was the plaintiff suing the defendant? What amount of damages was the plaintiff suing for?

2. What did the written contract stipulate regarding the recovery of damages? Explain.

3. Was the written contract enforced by the court in this case?

NOTES

1. Restatement (Second) of Contracts, § 110.
2. Restatement (Second) of Contracts, § 130.
3. Restatement (Second) of Contracts, § 112.
4. Restatement (Second) of Contracts, § 116.
5. UCC § 2-201(1).
6. UCC § 2-209(3).
7. Restatement (Second) of Contracts, § 139.
8. UCC § 2-202.
9. Restatement (Second) of Contracts, § 213.
10. UCC §§ 1-205, 2-202, and 2-208.

15

Third-Party Rights and Discharge of Contracts

An honest man's word is as good as his bond.

DON QUIXOTE

Chapter Objectives

After studying this chapter, you should be able to

1. Describe assignment of contracts and what contract rights are assignable.
2. Define *antiassignment* and *approval clauses* and determine their lawfulness.
3. Describe a delegation of duties and explain the liability of the parties to a delegation.
4. Define *intended beneficiary* and describe his or her rights under a contract.
5. Define *incidental beneficiary.*
6. Define *covenant.*
7. Distinguish among conditions precedent, conditions subsequent, and concurrent conditions.
8. Explain when the performance of a contract is excused because of objective impossibility.
9. Define and apply the doctrine of commercial impracticability.
10. Explain how contracts are discharged by operation of law.

Chapter Contents

The parties to a contract are said to be in **privity of contract**. That means that if one party fails to perform as promised, the other party may enforce the contract and sue for breach.

With two exceptions, third parties do not acquire any rights under other people's contracts. The exceptions are (1) *assignees* to whom rights subsequently are transferred and (2) *intended third-party beneficiaries* to whom contracting parties intended to give rights under the contract at the time of contracting.

Contracting parties have a legal obligation to perform the duties specified in their contract. A party's duty of performance may be *discharged* by agreement of the parties, excuse of performance, or operation of law.

This chapter discusses the rights of third parties under a contract, conditions to performance, and ways of discharging the duty of performance.

> **privity of contract**
> The state of two specified parties being in a contract.

ASSIGNMENT OF RIGHTS

In many cases, the parties to a contract can transfer their *rights* under the contract to other parties. The transfer of contractual rights is called an **assignment of rights** or just an **assignment**.

> **assignment**
> The transfer of contractual rights by the obligee to another party.

Form of Assignment

The party who owes the duty of performance is called the *obligor*. The party owed a right under the contract is called the *obligee*. An obligee who transfers the right to receive performance is called an **assignor**. The party to whom the right has been transferred is called the **assignee**. The assignee can assign the right to yet another person (called a *subsequent assignee*, or *subassignee*). Exhibit 15.1 illustrates these relationships.

> **assignor**
> The obligee who transfers the right.

> **assignee**
> The party to whom the right has been transferred.

Exhibit 15.1　*Assignment of a Right*

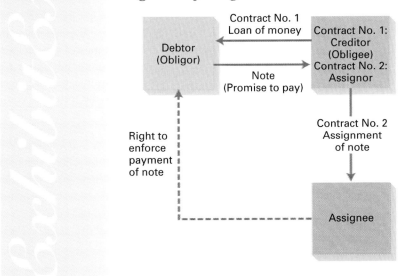

Consider This Example　Suppose the owner of a clothing store purchases $5,000 worth of goods on credit from a manufacturer. Payment is due in 120 days. Assume that the manufacturer needs cash before that period expires, so he or she sells his or her right to collect the money to another party, called a factor, for $4,000. If the store owner is given

Business Brief
The word *assignment* does not have to be used to create an assignment.

proper notice of the assignment, he or she must pay $5,000 to the factor. The manufacturer is the assignor and the factor is the assignee.

Generally, no formalities are required for a valid assignment of rights. Although the assignor often uses the word *assign*, other words or terms, such as *sell, transfer, convey, give*, and the like, are sufficient to indicate an intent to transfer a contract right.

Unless otherwise agreed, an assignor can *partially assign* his or her contract rights. These rights may be assigned to several assignees. For example, suppose Cathy Owens owes Dan Crawford $20,000. He may choose to assign the right to receive $5,000 of this amount to another and still retain the right to receive the remaining $15,000.

Rights That Can and Cannot Be Assigned

In the United States, public policy favors a free flow of commerce. That is why most contract rights are assignable, including sales contracts, contracts for the payment of money, and the like.

The types of contracts that present special problems for assignment are discussed below.

Business Brief
Personal service contracts are generally not assignable.

Personal Service Contracts   Contracts for the provision of personal services are generally not assignable.[1] For example, if an artist contracts to paint someone's portrait, the artist cannot send a different artist to do the painting without the prior approval of the person to be painted. The parties may agree that a personal service contract may be assigned. For example, many professional athletes' contracts contain a clause permitting assignability of the contract.

Assignment of Future Rights   Usually, a person cannot assign a currently nonexistent right that he or she expects to have in the future. For example, suppose a multimillion-airess signs a will leaving all of her property to her grandson. The grandson cannot assign his expected right to receive his inheritance.

Business Brief
Businesses often sell (assign) their accounts receivable to another party called a *factor* for collection. Accounts receivable are usually sold at a discount to reflect risk of noncollection of some accounts.

Contracts Where Assignment Would Materially Alter the Risk   A contract cannot be assigned if the assignment would materially alter the risks or duties of the obligor. Suppose Laura Peters, who has a safe driving record, purchases automobile insurance from an insurance company. She cannot assign her rights to be insured to Earl Jones because the assignment would materially alter the risk and duties of the insurance company.

Assignment of Legal Actions   Legal actions involving *personal rights* cannot be assigned. For example, suppose Donald Matthews is severely injured by Alice Hollyfield in an automobile accident caused by her negligence. Mr. Matthews can sue Ms. Hollyfield to recover damages for his injuries, but he may not assign his right to sue her to another person.

A legal right that arises out of a *breach of contract* may be assigned, however. For example, suppose Andrea borrows $10,000 from the bank. If she defaults on the loan, the bank may assign the legal right to collect the money to a collection agency.

Business Brief
Where there has been an assignment of a right, the assignee "stands in the shoes of the assignor" and is entitled to performance from the obligor.

Effect of an Assignment of Rights

Where there has been a valid assignment of rights, the assignee "stands in the shoes of the assignor." That is, the assignor is entitled to performance from the obligor. The unconditional assignment of a contract right extinguishes all of the assignor's rights, including the right to sue the obligor directly for nonperformance.[2] In the event of nonperformance, the assignee can bring a legal action directly against the obligor.

Consider This Example   Suppose the owner of a paint store owes $5,000 to a paintbrush supplier. Assume that the supplier assigns the right to receive the money and that the store owner is notified of the assignment. If the store owner fails to pay, the assignee can sue him or her to recover payment of the $5,000.

An assignee takes no better rights under the contract than the assignor had. An obligor can assert any defenses he or she had against the assignor or the assignee. For example, an obligor can raise fraud, duress, undue influence, minority, insanity, illegality of the contract, mutual mistake, or payment by worthless check by the assignor against enforcement of the contract by the assignee. The obligor can also raise any personal defenses (e.g., participation in the assignor's fraudulent scheme) he or she may have directly against the assignee.

Notice of Assignment

When an assignor makes an assignment of a right under a contract, the assignee is under a duty to notify the obligor that (1) the assignment has been made and (2) performance must be rendered to the assignee. If the assignee fails to notify the obligor of the assignment, the obligor may continue to render performance to the assignor, who no longer has a right to it. The assignee cannot sue the obligor to recover payment because the obligor has performed according to the original contract. The assignee's only course of action is to sue the assignor for damages.

The result changes if the obligor is notified of the assignment but continues to render performance to the assignor. In such situations, the assignee can sue the obligor and recover payment. The obligor will then have to pay twice—once wrongfully to the assignor and then rightfully to the assignee. The obligor's only recourse is to sue the assignor for damages.

Antiassignment and Approval Clauses

Some contracts contain **antiassignment clauses** that prohibit the assignment of rights under the contract. Such clauses may be used if the obligor does not want to deal with or render performance to an unknown third party. Some contracts contain an **approval clause**. Such clauses require the obligor to approve any assignment. Many states prohibit the obligor from unreasonably withholding approval.

Entrepreneur and the Law

SUCCESSIVE ASSIGNMENTS OF THE SAME RIGHT

An obligee (the party who is owed a performance, money, right, or other thing of value) has the right to assign a contract right or benefit to another party. If the obligee fraudulently or mistakenly makes successive assignments of the same right to a number of assignees, which assignee has the legal right to the assigned right? To answer this question, the following rules are applied:

- **The American rule** (or New York rule) provides that the first assignment *in time* prevails, regardless of notice. Most states follow this rule.
- **The English rule** provides that the first assignee to *give notice* to the obligor (the person who owes the performance, money, duty, or other thing of value) prevails.

- **The possession of tangible token rule** provides that under either the American or English rule if the assignor makes successive assignments of a contract right that is represented by a tangible token, such as a stock certificate or a savings account passbook, the first assignee who receives delivery of the tangible token prevails over subsequent assignees. However, if the first assignee leaves the tangible token with the assignor, the subsequent assignee prevails. This is because the first assignee could have prevented the problem by having demanded delivery of the tangible token. In other words, physical possession of the tangible token is the pivotal issue.

CONCEPT SUMMARY RIGHTS OF SUCCESSIVE ASSIGNEES

Rule	Rights of Assignees
American rule (New York rule)	First assignee in time prevails, regardless of notice.
English rule	First assignee to give notice prevails.
Possession of tangible token rule	First assignee who receives delivery of the tangible token prevails over subsequent assignees.

delegation of duties
A transfer of contractual duties by the obligor to another party for performance.

delegator
The obligor who transferred his or her duty.

delegatee
The party to whom the duty has been transferred.

DELEGATION OF DUTIES

Unless otherwise agreed, the parties to a contract generally can transfer the performance of their *duties* under the contract to other parties. This is called the **delegation of duties**, or just **delegation**.

The obligor who transferred his or her duty is the **delegator**. The party to whom the duty has been transferred is the **delegatee**. The party to whom the duty is owed is the *obligee*. Generally, no special words or formalities are required to create a delegation of duties. Exhibit 15.2 illustrates the parties to a delegation of a duty.

Business Brief
Certain types of duties cannot be delegated for another to perform.

EXHIBIT 15.2 *Delegation of a Duty*

Duties That Can and Cannot Be Delegated

Often, contracts are entered into with companies or firms rather than with individuals. In such cases, the firm may designate any of its qualified employees to perform the contract. For example, if a client retains a firm of lawyers to represent him or her, the firm can delegate the duties under the contract to any qualified member of the firm.

However, if the obligee has a substantial interest in having the obligor perform the acts required by the contract, duties may not be transferred.[3] This includes obligations under the following types of contracts:

1. ***Personal service contracts calling for the exercise of personal skills, discretion, or expertise.*** For example, if Counting Crows are hired to give a concert on campus, Pearl Jam cannot appear in their place.
2. ***Contracts whose performance would materially vary if the obligor's duties were delegated.*** For example, if a person hires an experienced doctor to perform a complex surgery, a recent medical school graduate cannot be substituted in the operating room.

Effect of Delegation of Duties

If the delegation is valid, the delegator remains legally liable for the performance of the contract. If the delegatee does not perform properly, the obligee can sue the obligor-delegator for any resulting damages.

The question of the delegatee's liability to the obligee depends on whether there has been an *assumption of duties* or a *declaration of duties*. Where a delegation of duties contains the term *assumption* or other similar language, there is an **assumption of duties** by the delegatee. The delegatee is liable to the obligee for nonperformance. The obligee can sue either the delegator or the delegatee.

If the delegatee has not assumed the duties under a contract, the delegation of duties is called a **declaration of duties**. Here, the delegatee is not legally liable to the obligee for nonperformance. The obligee's only recourse is to sue the delegator. A delegatee who fails to perform his or her duties is liable to the delegator for damages arising from this failure to perform.

Antidelegation Clauses

The parties to a contract can include an **antidelegation clause** indicating that the duties cannot be delegated. Antidelegation clauses are usually enforced. However, some courts have held that duties that are totally impersonal in nature—such as the payment of money—can be delegated despite such clauses.

assumption of duties
When a delegation of duties contains the term *assumption* or *I assume the duties* or other similar language, the delegatee is legally liable to the obligee for nonperformance.

declaration of duties
If the delegatee has not assumed the duties under a contract, the delegatee is not legally liable to the obligee for nonperformance.

antidelegation clause
A clause that prohibits the delegation of duties under the contract.

Celebration in Taipei, Taiwan. *After World War II, Taiwan, an island of just over 20 million people off the coast of China, developed a successful economy based on the production of textiles and other products. Today its economy is based on the production of computers and other high-technology products.*

An Assignment and Delegation

assignment and delegation
Transfer of both rights and duties under the contract.

An **assignment and delegation** occurs where there is a transfer of both rights and duties under a contract. If the transfer of a contract to a third party contains only language of assignment, the modern view holds that there is a corresponding delegation of the duties of the contract.[4]

THIRD-PARTY BENEFICIARIES

Third parties sometimes claim rights under others' contracts. Such third parties are either *intended* or *incidental beneficiaries*. Each of these designations is discussed here.

Intended Beneficiaries

intended third-party beneficiary
A third party who is not in privity of contract but who has rights under the contract and can enforce the contract against the obligor.

When the parties enter into a contract, they can agree that one of the party's performances should be rendered to or directly benefit a third party called an **intended third-party beneficiary**. An intended third-party beneficiary can enforce the contract against the party who promised to render performance.[5]

The beneficiary may be expressly named in the contract from which he or she is to benefit or may be identified by another means. For example, there is sufficient identification if the testator of a will leaves his estate to "all of my children, equally."

Historically, intended third-party beneficiaries are classified as either *donee* or *creditor* beneficiaries. The Restatement (Second) of Contracts has dropped the distinction between donee and creditor beneficiaries and refers to both collectively as intended beneficiaries.[6] Many states have done the same.

donee beneficiary contract
A contract entered into with the intent to confer a benefit or gift on an intended third party.

Donee Beneficiaries   Where a person enters into a contract with the intent to confer a benefit or gift on an intended third party, the contract is called a **donee beneficiary contract**. A life insurance policy with a named beneficiary is an example of such a contract. The three persons involved in such a contract are

1. The *promisee* (the contracting party who directs that the benefit be conferred on another).
2. The *promisor* (the contracting party who agrees to confer performance for the benefit of the third person).
3. The **donee beneficiary** (the third person on whom the benefit is to be conferred).

donee beneficiary
The third party on whom the benefit is to be conferred.

If the promisor fails to perform the contract, the donee beneficiary can sue the promisor directly.

creditor beneficiary contract
A contract that arises in the following situation: (1) A debtor borrows money, (2) the debtor signs an agreement to pay back the money plus interest, (3) the debtor sells the item to a third party before the loan is paid off, and (4) the third party promises the debtor that he or she will pay the remainder of the loan to the creditor.

Consider This Example   Brian Peterson hires a lawyer to draft his will. He directs the lawyer to leave all of his property to his best friend, Jeffrey Silverman. Assume that (1) Mr. Peterson dies and (2) the lawyer's negligence in drafting the will causes it to be invalid. Consequently, Mr. Peterson's distant relatives receive the property under the state's inheritance statute. Mr. Silverman can sue the lawyer for damages because he was the intended donee beneficiary of the will. (See Exhibit 15.3.)

Creditor Beneficiaries   The second type of intended beneficiary is the creditor beneficiary. A **creditor beneficiary contract** usually arises in the following fact situation:

1. A debtor borrows money from a creditor to purchase some item.
2. The debtor signs an agreement to pay the creditor the amount of the loan plus interest.
3. The debtor sells the item to another party before the loan is paid.
4. The new buyer promises the debtor that he or she will pay the remainder of the loan amount to the creditor.

$\mathscr{E}$XHIBIT **15.3** *Donee Beneficiary Contract*

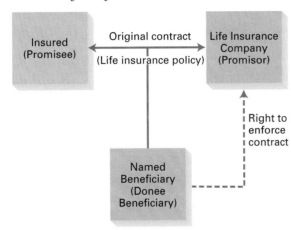

The creditor is the new intended creditor beneficiary to this second contract.[7] The parties to the second contract are the original debtor (the promisee), the new party (the promisor), and the original creditor (the **creditor beneficiary**). (See Exhibit 15.4.)

creditor beneficiary
Original creditor who becomes a beneficiary under the debtor's new contract with another party.

$\mathscr{E}$XHIBIT **15.4** *Creditor Beneficiary Contract*

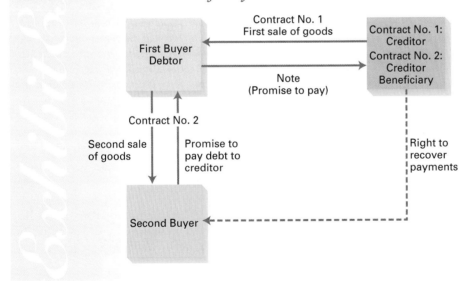

If the promisor fails to perform according to the contract, the creditor beneficiary may either (1) enforce the original contract against the debtor-promisee or (2) enforce the new contract against the promisor. The creditor, however, can collect only once.

Consider This Example   Suppose Hilton Hotels, Inc., obtains a loan from City Bank to refurbish a hotel in Atlanta, Georgia. The parties sign a promissory note requiring the loan to be paid off in equal monthly installments over the next 10 years. Before the loan is paid, Hilton sells the hotel to ABC Hotels, another chain of hotels. ABC Hotels agrees with Hilton to complete the payments due on the City Bank loan. The bank has two options if ABC Hotels fails to pay: It can sue Hilton Hotels, Inc., on the promissory note to recover the unpaid loan amount, or it can use its status as a creditor beneficiary to sue ABC Hotels.

Incidental Beneficiaries

incidental beneficiary

A party who is unintentionally benefited by other people's contract.

In many instances, the parties to a contract unintentionally benefit a third party—called an **incidental beneficiary**—when the contract is performed. An incidental beneficiary has no rights to enforce or sue under other people's contracts. Generally, the public and tax-payers are only incidental beneficiaries to contracts entered into by the government on their behalf. As such, they acquire no rights to enforce government contracts or to sue parties who breach these contracts.

The courts are often asked to decide whether a third party is an intended or an incidental beneficiary, as in the following case.

Bain v. Gillispie
357 N.W.2d 47 (1984)
Court of Appeals of Iowa

CASE 15.1

FACTS

James C. Bain, a college basketball referee, had a contract with the Big 10 Basketball Conference (Big 10) to referee various basketball games. During a game that took place on March 6, 1982, Bain called a foul on a University of Iowa player that permitted free throws by a Purdue University player. That player scored the point that gave Purdue a last-minute victory and eliminated Iowa from the Big 10 championship. Some Iowa fans, including John and Karen Gillispie, asserted that the foul call was clearly in error. The Gillispies operated a novelty store in Iowa City that sold University of Iowa sports memorabilia. They filed a complaint against Bain, alleging that his negligent refereeing constituted a breach of his contract with the Big 10 and destroyed a potential market for their products. The Gillispies sought $175,000 compensatory damages plus exemplary damages. The trial court granted Bain's motion for summary judgment. The Gillispies appealed.

ISSUE

Were the Gillispies intended beneficiaries of the contract between Bain and the Big 10?

IN THE LANGUAGE OF THE COURT

Snell, Presiding Judge   *The trial court found that there was no issue of material fact on the Gillispies' claim that they were beneficiaries under Bain's contract with the Big 10. Because the Gillispies would not be privy to the contract, they must be direct beneficiaries to maintain a cause of action, and not merely incidental beneficiaries.*

A direct beneficiary is either a donee beneficiary or a creditor beneficiary. Gillispies make no claim that they are creditor beneficiaries of Bain, the Big 10 Athletic Conference, or the University of Iowa. The real test is said to be whether the contracting parties intended that a third person should receive a benefit that might be enforced in the courts. It is clear that the purpose of any promise that Bain might have made was not to confer a gift on Gillispies. Likewise, the Big 10 did not owe any duty to the Gillispies such that they would have been donee beneficiaries. If a contract did exist between Bain and the Big 10, Gillispies can be considered nothing more than incidental beneficiaries and as such are unable to maintain a cause of action. Consequently, there is no genuine issue for trial that could result in Gillispies obtaining a judgment under a contract theory of recovery.

DECISION AND REMEDY

The appellate court held that the Gillispies were merely incidental beneficiaries of the contract between Bain and the Big 10. Therefore, they could not maintain their lawsuit for an alleged breach of that contract. Affirmed.

Case Questions

Critical Legal Thinking   Should the law allow incidental beneficiaries to recover damages for the breach of other people's contracts? Why or why not?

Ethics   Did the Gillispies have a legitimate lawsuit in this case?

Business Application   Do third parties have rights under many business contracts? Give some examples.

*P*ROMISES OF PERFORMANCE

In contracts, parties make certain promises to each other. These promises may be classified as *covenants* or *conditions*. The difference between each of these is discussed in the following paragraphs.

Covenants

A **covenant** is an unconditional promise to perform. Nonperformance of a covenant is a breach of contract that gives the other party the right to sue. For example, if Medcliff Corporation borrows $100,000 from a bank and signs a promissory note to repay this amount plus 10 percent interest in one year, this promise is a covenant. That is, it is an unconditional promise to perform.

Conditions of Performance

A conditional promise (or qualified promise) is not as definite as a covenant. The promisor's duty to perform (or not perform) arises only if the **condition** does (or does not) occur.[8] However, it becomes a covenant if the condition is met.

Generally, contractual language such as *if, on condition that, provided that, when, after, as soon as,* and the like indicate a condition. A single contract may contain numerous conditions that trigger or excuse performance. There are three types of conditions: *conditions precedent, conditions subsequent,* and *concurrent conditions.*

Conditions Precedent   If the contract requires the occurrence (or nonoccurrence) of an event *before* a party is obligated to perform a contractual duty, there is a **condition precedent**. The happening (or nonhappening) of the event triggers the contract or duty of performance. If the event does not occur, no duty to perform arises because there is a failure of condition.

Consider This Example   Suppose E.I. duPont offers Joan Andrews a job as an industrial engineer upon her graduation from college. If Ms. Andrews graduates, the condition has been met. If the employer refuses to hire Ms. Andrews at that time, she can sue the employer for breach of contract. However, if Ms. Andrews does not graduate, duPont is not obligated to hire her because there has been a failure of condition.

The following case raises the issue of a condition precedent.

covenant
An unconditional promise to perform.

Business Brief
Nonperformance of a covenant is a breach of contract that gives the other party the right to sue.

condition
A qualification of a promise. There are three types of conditions: *conditions precedent, conditions subsequent,* and *concurrent conditions.*

condition precedent
A condition that requires the occurrence (or nonoccurrence) of an event before a party is obligated to perform a duty under a contract.

Architectural Systems, Inc. v. Gilbane Building Co.
760 F.Supp. 79 (1991)
United States District Court, Maryland

CASE 15.2

FACTS
Carley Capital Group (Carley) was the owner of a project in the city of Baltimore known as "Henderson's Wharf." The project was designed to convert warehouses into residential condominiums. On September 4, 1987, Carley hired Gilbane Building Company (Gilbane) to be the general contractor and construction manager for the project. Gilbane hired Architectural Systems, Inc. (ASI), as the subcontractor to perform drywall and acoustical tile work on the project. The subcontract included the following clause: "It is specifically under-

stood and agreed that the payment to the trade contractor is dependent, as a condition precedent, upon the construction manager receiving contract payments from the owner."

Gilbane received periodic payments from Carley and paid ASI as work progressed. By late 1988, ASI had satisfactorily performed all of its obligations under the subcontract and submitted a final bill of $348,155 to Gilbane. Gilbane did not pay this bill because it had not received payment from Carley. On March 10, 1989, Carley filed for bankruptcy. ASI sued Gilbane seeking payment.

(case continues)

ISSUE
Must Gilbane pay ASI?

IN THE LANGUAGE OF THE COURT
Young, Senior District Judge ASI argues that it did not assume the credit risk simply by the inclusion of the statement "as a condition precedent" in the subcontract. It may not be sound business practice to accept such a business proposal but that is what occurred. The provision unambiguously declares that Gilbane is not obligated to pay ASI until it first received payment by the owner. The cause for the owner's nonpayment is not specifically addressed and could be due to a number of causes, including insolvency.

A provision that makes receipt of payment by the general contractor a condition precedent to its obligation to pay the subcontractor transfers from the general contractor to the subcontractor the credit risk of non-payment by the owner for any reason (at least for any reason other than the general owner's own fault), including insolvency of the owner.

DECISION AND REMEDY
The district court held that Gilbane was not obligated to pay ASI because the condition precedent to this payment—receipt of payment from Carley—had not occurred. The court granted summary judgment to Gilbane.

Case Questions

Critical Legal Thinking What is the difference between a covenant and a condition precedent? Explain.

Ethics Did Gilbane act unethically in not paying ASI? Did ASI act unethically in suing Gilbane?

Business Application If the condition precedent had not been expressly provided in the subcontract, who would have borne the risk of Carley's default?

---

condition precedent based on satisfaction
Clause in a contract that reserves the right to a party to pay for the items or services contracted for only if they meet his or her satisfaction.

Conditions Precedent Based on Satisfaction Some contracts reserve the right to a party to pay for services provided by the other party only if the services meet the first party's "satisfaction." The courts have developed two tests—the *personal satisfaction test* and the *reasonable person test*—to examine whether this special form of condition precedent has been met.

personal satisfaction test
Subjective test that applies to contracts involving personal taste and comfort.

The **personal satisfaction test** is a *subjective* test that applies if the performance involves personal taste and comfort (e.g., contracts for decorating, tailoring, etc.). The only requirement is that the person given the right to reject the contract acts in good faith.

Consider This Example Suppose Gretchen Davidson employs an artist to paint her daughter's portrait. Assume the contract provides that the client does not have to pay for the portrait unless she is satisfied with it. Accordingly, Ms. Davidson may reject the painting if she personally dislikes it, even though a reasonable person would be satisfied with it.

reasonable person test
Objective test that applies to commercial contracts and contracts involving mechanical fitness.

The **reasonable person test** is an *objective* test that is used to judge contracts involving mechanical fitness and most commercial contracts. Most contracts that require the work to meet a third person's satisfaction (e.g., an engineer or architect) are judged by this standard.

Consider This Example Suppose Lillian Vernon, Inc., a large mail-order catalog business, hires someone to install a state-of-the-art computer system that will handle its order entry and record-keeping functions. The system is installed and operates to industry standards. According to the reasonable person test, the company cannot reject the contract as not meeting its satisfaction.

Business Brief
If "time is of the essence" is stated in a contract, it is an express condition; failure to perform by the stated date is a material breach of contract.

Time of Performance as a Condition Precedent Generally, there is a breach of contract if the contract is not performed when due. Nevertheless, if the other party is not jeopardized by the delay, most courts treat the delay as a minor breach and give the non-performing party additional time to perform. Conversely, if the contract expressly provides that "*time is of the essence*" or similar language, performance by the stated time is an express condition. There is a breach of contract if the contracting party does not perform by the stated date.

Conditions Subsequent   A **condition subsequent** exists when a contract provides that the occurrence or nonoccurrence of a specific event automatically excuses the performance of an existing duty to perform. For example, many employment contracts include a clause that permits the employer to terminate the contract if the employee fails a drug test.

Note that the Restatement (Second) of Contracts eliminates the distinction between conditions precedent and conditions subsequent. Both are referred to as "conditions."[9]

Concurrent Conditions   **Concurrent conditions** arise when the parties to a contract must render performance simultaneously. That is, when each party's absolute duty to perform is conditioned on the other party's absolute duty to perform.

Consider This Example   Suppose a contract to purchase goods provides that payment is due upon delivery. In other words, the buyer's duty to pay is conditioned on the seller's duty to deliver the goods, and vice versa. Recovery is available if one party fails to respond to the other party's performance.

Implied Conditions   Any of the previous types of conditions may be further classified as either an express or implied condition. An *express condition* exists if the parties expressly agree on it. An **implied-in-fact condition** is one that can be implied from the circumstances surrounding a contract and the parties' conduct. For example, a contract in which a buyer agrees to purchase grain from a farmer implies that there is proper street access to the delivery site, proper unloading facilities, and the like.

condition subsequent
A condition, if it occurs or doesn't occur, that automatically excuses the performance of an existing contractual duty to perform.

concurrent condition
A condition that exists when the parties to a contract must render performance simultaneously; each party's absolute duty to perform is conditioned on the other party's absolute duty to perform.

implied-in-fact condition
A condition that can be implied from the circumstances surrounding a contract and the parties' conduct.

*C*ONCEPT SUMMARY   TYPES OF CONDITIONS

Type of Condition	Description
Condition precedent	A specified event must occur (or not occur) before a party is obligated to perform contractual duties.
Condition subsequent	The occurrence (or nonoccurrence) of a specified event excuses the performance of an existing contractual duty to perform.
Concurrent condition	The parties to a contract are obligated to render performance simultaneously. Each party's duty to perform is conditioned on the other party's duty to perform.
Implied condition	An implied-in-fact condition is implied from the circumstances surrounding the contract and the parties' conduct.

*E*thical *P*erspective

SATISFACTION CLAUSE: "I DON'T LIKE IT"

Commercial contracts often include "satisfaction clauses" that are designed to ensure that an appropriate quality of performance is received before the promisee is obligated to pay. But how satisfied must the contracting party be before there is an obligation to pay? Consider the following case.

General Motors Corporation hired Baystone Construction, Inc. (Baystone), to build an addition to a Chevrolet plant in Muncie, Indiana. Baystone, in turn, hired Morin Building Products Company (Morin) to supply and erect the aluminum walls for the addition. The contract required that the exterior siding of the walls be of

(box continues)

"aluminum with a mill finish and stucco embossed surface texture to match finish and texture of existing metal siding." The contract also included a satisfaction clause. Morin put up the walls. The exterior siding did not give the impression of having a uniform finish when viewed in bright sunlight from an acute angle and General Motors's representative rejected it. Baystone removed Morin's siding and hired another subcontractor to replace it. General Motors approved the replacement siding. When Baystone refused to pay Morin the $23,000 balance owing on the contract, Morin brought suit against Baystone to recover this amount.

The trial court held in favor of Morin and permitted it to recover the balance from Baystone. The court of appeals affirmed. The court held that the objective reasonable person standard governed the satisfaction clause in this commercial dispute.

The reasonable person standard applies to most contracts involving commercial quality, operative fitness, or mechanical utility that other knowledgeable persons can judge. The court of appeals held that Baystone was not justified in rejecting Morin's work under the reasonable person standard. The court stated: "The building for which the aluminum siding was intended was a factory. Aesthetic considerations were decidedly secondary to considerations of function and cost. The parties probably did not intend to subject Morin's rights to aesthetic whims." [*Morin Building Products Co., Inc. v. Baystone Construction, Inc.*, 717 F.2d 413 (7th Cir. 1983)]

1. Do you think General Motors was justified in rejecting Morin's work in this case?
2. Should the law adopt the personal satisfaction test to judge compliance with satisfaction clauses in all instances? Why or why not?

$\mathscr{D}$ISCHARGE BY AGREEMENT

discharge
The termination of contract obligations.

In many situations, the parties to a contract mutually decide to **discharge** their contractual duties. The different types of mutual agreements are discussed below.

Mutual Rescission

If a contract is wholly or partially executory, the parties can agree to rescind (i.e., cancel) the contract. *Mutual rescission* requires the parties to enter into a second agreement that expressly terminates the first one. Unilateral rescission of the contract by one of the parties without the other party's consent is not effective. Unilateral rescission of a contract constitutes a breach of that contract.

Substituted Contract

The parties to a contract may enter into a new contract that revokes and discharges a prior contract. The new contract is called a *substituted contract*. If one of the parties fails to perform his or her duties under a substituted contract, the nonbreaching party can sue to enforce its terms against the breaching party. The prior contract cannot be enforced against the breaching party because it has been discharged.

Novation

novation
An agreement that substitutes a new party for one of the original contracting parties and relieves the exiting party of liability on the contract.

A **novation agreement** (commonly called **novation**) substitutes a third party for one of the original contracting parties. The new substituted party is obligated to perform the contract. All three parties must agree to the substitution. In a novation, the exiting party is relieved of liability on the contract.

Consider This Example Suppose Kohl's Department Stores enters into a contract with Cannon Mills to purchase 10,000 beach towels. Prior to the time of performance, Kohl's decides not to purchase the towels. The Kohl's buyer is aware that Kmart is looking to purchase beach towels. The buyer introduces the Cannon Mills salesperson to the Kmart buyer. The parties enter into an agreement that substitutes Kmart for Kohl's on the contract. This is a novation. If Kmart fails to perform the contract, Cannon Mills cannot sue Kohl's.

Accord and Satisfaction

The parties to a contract may agree to settle a contract dispute by an **accord and satisfaction**. The agreement whereby the parties agree to accept something different in satisfaction of the original contract is called an *accord*.[10] The performance of an accord is called a *satisfaction*.

An accord does not discharge the original contract. It only suspends it until the accord is performed. Satisfaction of the accord discharges both the original contract and the accord. If an accord is not satisfied when it is due, the aggrieved party may enforce either (1) the accord or (2) the original contract.

> **accord and satisfaction**
> The settlement of a contract dispute. The *accord* is the agreement whereby parties agree to settle a contract dispute by accepting something different than provided in the original contract. *Satisfaction* is the performance of an accord.

DISCHARGE BY EXCUSE

Under certain circumstances, the nonperformance of contractual duties is *excused*—discharged. The different doctrines of excuse are discussed below.

Impossibility of Performance

Impossibility of performance (or **objective impossibility**) occurs if the contract becomes impossible to perform.[11] The impossibility must be *objective impossibility* ("it cannot be done") rather than subjective impossibility ("I cannot do it"). The following types of objective impossibility excuse nonperformance:

> **impossibility of performance**
> Nonperformance that is excused if the contract becomes impossible to perform; must be *objective* impossibility, not subjective.

1. The death or incapacity of the promisor prior to the performance of a personal service contract.[12] For example, if a professional athlete dies prior to or during a contract period, his or her contract with the team is discharged.
2. The destruction of the subject matter of a contract prior to performance.[13] For example, if a building is destroyed by fire, lessees are discharged from further performance unless otherwise provided in the lease.
3. A supervening illegality makes performance of the contract illegal.[14] For example, suppose an art dealer contracts to purchase native art found in a foreign country. If, before the contract is performed, the foreign country enacts a law that forbids the removal of native art from the country, the contract is discharged.

In the following case, the court had to decide whether there was impossibility of performance.

Parker v. Arthur Murray, Inc.
295 N.E.2d 487 (1973)
Appellate Court of Illinois

CASE 15.3

FACTS
In November 1959, Ryland S. Parker, a 37-year-old college-educated bachelor, went to the Arthur Murray Studios (Arthur Murray) in Oak Park, Illinois, to redeem a certificate entitling him to three free dancing lessons. At that time he lived alone in a one-room attic apartment. During the free lessons the instructor told Parker that he had "exceptional potential to be a fine and accomplished dancer." Parker thereupon signed a contract for more lessons. Parker attended lessons regularly and was praised and encouraged by his instructors despite his lack of progress. Contract extensions and new contracts for additional instructional hours were executed, which Parker prepaid. Each written contract contained the bold-type words, "NON-CANCELLABLE CONTRACT." On September 24, 1961, Parker was severely injured in an automobile accident, rendering him incapable of continuing his dancing lessons. At that time he had contracted for a total of 2,734 hours of dance lessons, for which he had prepaid $24,812. When Arthur Murray refused to refund any of the money, Parker

(case continues)

sued to rescind the outstanding contracts. The trial court held in favor of Parker and ordered Arthur Murray to return the prepaid contract payments. Arthur Murray appealed.

ISSUE

Does the doctrine of impossibility excuse Parker's performance of the personal service contracts?

IN THE LANGUAGE OF THE COURT

Stamos, Presiding Justice *Plaintiff was granted rescission on the ground of impossibility of performance. Defendants do not deny that the doctrine of impossibility of performance is generally applicable to the case at bar. Rather they assert that certain contract provisions bring the case within the Restatement's limitation that the doctrine is inapplicable if "the contract indicates a contrary intention." It is contended that such bold-type phrases as "NON-CANCELLABLE CONTRACT," "NON-CANCELLABLE NEGOTIABLE CONTRACT," and "I UNDERSTAND THAT NO REFUNDS WILL BE MADE UNDER THE TERMS OF THIS CONTRACT" manifested the parties' mutual intent to waive their respective rights to invoke the doctrine of impossibility.*

This is a construction that we find unacceptable. Courts engage in the construction and interpretation of contracts with the sole aim of determining the intention of the parties. We need rely on no construction aids to conclude that plaintiff never contemplated that by signing a contract with such terms as "NON-CANCELLABLE" and "NO REFUNDS," he was waiving a remedy expressly recognized by Illinois courts. Although neither party to a contract should be relieved from performance on the ground that good business judgment was lacking, a court will not place upon language a ridiculous construction. We conclude that plaintiff did not waive his right to assert the doctrine of impossibility.

Suffice it to say that overwhelming evidence supported plaintiff's contention that he was incapable of continuing his lessons.

DECISION AND REMEDY

The appellate court held that the doctrine of impossibility of performance excused Parker's performance of the personal service contracts. Affirmed.

Case Questions

Critical Legal Thinking Should the doctrine of impossibility excuse parties from performance of their contracts? Why or why not?

Ethics Did Arthur Murray act ethically in not returning Parker's money?

Business Application Why do you think Arthur Murray fought this case?

Contemporary Business Application

FORCE MAJEURE CLAUSES

The parties may agree in their contract that certain events will excuse nonperformance of the contract. These clauses are called **force majeure clauses**.

Usually force majeure clauses excuse nonperformance caused by natural disasters such as floods, tornadoes, earthquakes, and such. Modern clauses often excuse performance due to labor strikes, shortages of raw materials, and the like.

Commercial Impracticability

commercial impracticability
Nonperformance that is excused if an extreme or unexpected development or expense makes it impractical for the promisor to perform.

Many states recognize the doctrine of **commercial impracticability** as an excuse of nonperformance of contracts. Commercial impracticability excuses performance if an *unforeseeable event* makes it *impractical* for the promisor to perform. This doctrine has not yet been fully developed by the courts. It is examined on a case-by-case basis.

Consider This Example A utility company enters into a contract to purchase uranium for its nuclear-powered generator from a uranium supplier at a fixed price of $1 million per year for five years. Suppose a new uranium cartel is formed worldwide and the supplier must pay $3 million for uranium to supply the utility with each year's supply. In this case, the court would likely allow the supplier to rescind its contract with the utility based on commercial impracticability. Note that it is not impossible for the supplier to supply the uranium.

Frustration of Purpose

The doctrine of **frustration of purpose** excuses the performance of contractual obligations if (1) the object or benefit of the contract is made worthless to a promisor, (2) both parties knew what the purpose was, and (3) the act that frustrated the purpose was reasonably unforeseeable.

frustration of purpose
A doctrine that excuses the performance of contractual obligation if (1) the object or benefit of a contract is made worthless to a promisor, (2) both parties knew what the purpose was, and (3) the act that frustrated the purpose was unforeseeable.

Consider This Example   Suppose Shu-Miao Zhou leases a piece of property from a landowner for $1,000 to watch the Rose Bowl parade on January 1 in Pasadena, California. If the parade is unexpectedly canceled, Ms. Zhou is excused from paying the rental fee. Note that the promisor is not prevented from performing, however. Ms. Zhou could have used the leased land even though there was no parade.

Contemporary Business Application

COMMERCIAL IMPRACTICABILITY: NUTS TO YOU!

Sometimes, unforeseen circumstances make the performance of a contract highly impracticable or very expensive. Modern contract law, including the Uniform Commercial Code (UCC), recognizes the doctrine of commercial impracticability as excusing nonperformance in certain situations. Consider the following case.

In July 1980, Alimenta (U.S.A.), Inc. (Alimenta), entered into a contract with Cargill, Incorporated (Cargill), under which Cargill agreed to deliver to Alimenta shelled, edible peanuts. The peanut crop had been planted in the fields at the time the contract was entered into. Cargill, which had contracts with other buyers as well, expected to make a $3 million profit from its peanut sales.

Unfortunately, there was a severe drought that year, and the crop yield was substantially reduced. This meant that Cargill could deliver to Alimenta only about 65 percent of the promised peanuts. Cargill delivered the same percentage to all of its customers. Alimenta filed suit against Cargill for breach of contract. Cargill asserted that further performance under the contract was excused by the doctrine of commercial impracticability. At trial the jury rendered a verdict for Cargill. Alimenta appealed.

Both the trial court and the court of appeals held that the drought in this case was unforeseen. The evidence showed that the shortage of peanuts in 1980 was unprecedented. In fact, there had been a surplus of domestic peanuts for the preceding 20 years.

The trial court found that it was not impossible for Cargill to fully perform the contract. Cargill could have gone into the market and purchased the peanuts, which were selling at a much higher price than contracted for, and delivered the peanuts to Alimenta. However, Cargill had already suffered a $47 million loss on its peanut contracts without doing this.

The court of appeals affirmed the trial court's ruling in favor of Cargill. The court held that Cargill was excused from further performance by the doctrine of *commercial impracticability*. The court stated that "the focus of impracticability analysis is upon the nature of the agreement and the expectations of the parties and not on whether it is physically possible for the defendant to perform the contract." [*Alimenta (U.S.A.), Inc. v. Cargill, Incorporated*, 861 F.2d 650 (11th Cir. 1988)]

DISCHARGE BY OPERATION OF LAW

Certain legal rules discharge parties from performing contractual duties. These rules are discussed below.

Statutes of Limitations

Every state has a **statute of limitations** that applies to contract actions. Although the time periods vary from state to state, the usual period for bringing a lawsuit based on breach of contract is one to five years. The UCC provides that a cause of action based on breach of a

statute of limitations
Statute that establishes the time period during which a lawsuit must be brought; if the lawsuit is not brought within this period, the injured party loses the right to sue.

sales or lease contract must be brought within four years after the cause of action accrues [UCC 2-725, UCC 2A-506].

Consider This Example   Suppose the Golden Nugget Casino enters into a written contract to purchase slot machines from Kaufman Manufacturing, Inc. Delivery and payment are due on April 30, 1994. The goods are tendered on that date, but Golden Nugget refuses to accept or pay for the goods. There has been a breach of contract. Assume that the statute of limitations for breach of a written contract is four years. Kaufman Manufacturing has until the close of court on April 30, 1998, to sue the Golden Nugget Casino for breach of contract. If no suit is brought by that date, Kaufman Manufacturing loses its right to sue for breach of contract.

Bankruptcy

*'If there's no meaning in it,'
said the King, 'that saves a
world of trouble, you know,
we needn't try to find any.'*

*Lewis Carroll
Alice in Wonderland Ch. 12*

Bankruptcy, which is governed by federal law, is a means of allocating the debtor's nonexempt property to satisfy his or her debts. Debtors may also reorganize in bankruptcy. In most cases, the debtor's assets are insufficient to pay all of the creditors' claims. The debtor receives a *discharge* of the unpaid debts. This means that the debtor is relieved of legal liability to pay the discharged debts.

Alteration of the Contract

If a party to a contract intentionally alters the contract materially, the innocent party may opt either to discharge the contract or to enforce it. The contract may be enforced either on its *original* terms or on the *altered terms*. A material alteration is a change in price, quantity, or some other important term.

International Perspective

LAW OF EXCUSE IN INTERNATIONAL SALES CONTRACTS

The **United Nations Convention Contracts for the International Sale of Goods (CISG)** is a treaty that governs international sales contracts. The CISG applies to private sales contracts between parties whose places of business are in different countries. The United States and many other countries are signatories to the CISG.

International contracts are particularly susceptible to problems of changed circumstances that could occur because of market disruptions such as war, revolution, terrorist activities, blockades, shortages, inflation, and other political and economic forces. The question becomes: Are the unforeseen problems so severe as to excuse a party from performance of its obligations under the international contract?

Article 79 of the CISG addresses the problem of changed circumstances. Article 79 exempts a party from

liability for breach of an international sales contract in cases where a party proves that (1) his or her failure to perform is due to an impediment beyond his or her control and (2) he or she could not reasonably be expected to have taken the impediment into account at the time of the conclusion of the contract or to have avoided it or overcome it or its consequences.

The CISG does not define the term *impediment*. Commentators have suggested that it is similar to the common law's doctrine of commercial impracticability. National courts will eventually define the term *impediment* as they apply Article 79 to particular cases involving changed circumstances affecting international sales contracts.

Article 79 is a default provision. That is, the CISG permits parties to international sales contracts to opt out of the CISG and expressly provide in their contracts the events that will excuse nonperformance.

Working the Web

Internet research guides provide links to Internet resources and suggestions for finding legal information.

The Virtual Chase—A Research Site for Legal Professionals The Virtual Chase provides annotated hot links to resources legal professionals and you might find useful in conducting research on the World Wide Web. The guide is arranged by type of information.

Visit at **www.virtualchase.com**

Legal Research Using the Internet, by Lyonette Louis-Jacques This guide, written by a law librarian at the University of Chicago, explains why the Internet is useful for legal research. It describes some of the major resources available on the Internet for researching U.S. law, comparative law, and international law.

Visit at **www.lib.uchicago.edu/~llou/mpoctalk.html**

Finding Law-Related Internet Resources, by Cindy L. Chick At this site, legal information is divided by subject. Subjects such as company information, government

information, court opinions, and services that rate Web sites can be found here.

Visit at **www.llrx.com/sources.html**

The Compleat Internet Researcher: Advanced Strategies and Techniques Among other things, the *Compleat Internet Researcher* has rules (some intended to be broken) about Internet research and explains the odds about sure bets for Internet Research.

Visit at **www.aallnet.org/products/crab**

CYBER EXERCISES

1. Using the Virtual Chase Web site, find an article called *Internet Skills for Legal Professionals.*

2. Go to Legal Research Using the Internet. Can you find a link on the first page dealing with women and the law?

3. Use Finding Law-Related Internet Resources to link to the Law Engine.

4. What is the origin of The Compleat Internet Researcher?

*C*ASES AND *E*XERCISES

CRITICAL LEGAL THINKING CASES

15.1. Eugene H. Emmick hired L. S. Hamm, an attorney, to draft his will. The will named Robert Lucas and others (Lucas) as beneficiaries. When Emmick died, it was discovered that the will was improperly drafted, violated state law, and was therefore ineffective. Emmick's estate was transferred pursuant to the state's intestate laws. Lucas did not receive the $75,000 he would have otherwise received had the will been valid. Lucas sued Hamm for breach of the Emmick-Hamm contract to recover what he would have received under the will. Who wins? [*Lucas v. Hamm,* 364 P.2d 685, 56 Cal.2d 583, 15 Cal.Rptr. 821 (CA 1961)]

15.2. Abrams and others sponsored a condominium project for a luxury condominium building on Manhattan's East

Side. Abrams contracted with Lehrer/McGovern, Inc. (L/M), and other contracting companies to construct the building. After the building was completed and the individual condominium units sold, certain defects in construction appeared. Monarch Owners Committee, the condominium association, and individual condominium owners sued L/M and the other contracting companies for damages for breach of their contracts with Abrams. Can the condominium association and owners sue L/M and the contracting companies? [*Monarch Owners Committee v. Abrams,* 454 N.Y.S.2d 4 (N.Y.Sup. 1982)]

15.3. Angelo Boussiacos hired Demetrios Sofias, a general contractor, to build a restaurant for him. Boussiacos entered into a loan agreement with the Bank of America (B of A) whereby the bank would provide construction financing to build the restaurant. As is normal with most construction loans, the loan agreement provided that loan funds would be periodically disbursed by the bank to Boussiacos at different stages of construction as requested by Boussiacos. Problems arose in the progress of the construction. When Boussiacos did not pay Sofias for certain work that had been done, Sofias sued B of A for breach of contract to collect payment directly from B of A. Can Sofias maintain the lawsuit against B of A? [*Sofias v. Bank of America*, 172 Cal.App.3d 583, 218 Cal.Rptr. 626 (Cal.App. 1985)]

15.4. David Seeley owned an apartment building located at 15 East 21st Street in the Gramercy Park area of New York. Seeley contracted with Rem Discount Security Products, Inc. (Rem), to install security locks on the front door of the building. On June 7, 1981, when Lori Einhorn was visiting her fiancé at the building, she was accosted on the second-floor landing, dragged to her fiancé's apartment, and raped. Einhorn sued Seeley and Rem for breach of contract, alleging that the front-door lock to the building was negligently installed and could be opened by a firm push, even when the door was locked. Can Einhorn sue Rem for breach of contract? [*Einhorn v. Seeley and Rem Discount Security Products, Inc.*, 525 N.Y.S.2d 212 (N.Y.Sup. 1988)]

15.5. William John Cunningham, a professional basketball player, entered into a contract with Southern Sports Corporation (Southern Sports), which owned the Carolina Cougars, a professional basketball team. The contract provided that Cunningham was to play basketball for the Cougars for a three-year period commencing on October 2, 1971. The contract contained a provision that it could not be assigned to any other professional basketball franchise without Cunningham's approval. Subsequently, Southern Sports sold its assets, including its franchise and Cunningham's contract, to the Munchak Corporation (Munchak). There was no change in the Cougars' location after the purchase. When Cunningham refused to play for the new owners, Munchak sued to enforce Cunningham's contract. Is Cunningham's contract assignable to the new owner? [*Munchak Corporation v. Cunningham*, 457 F.2d 721 (4th Cir. 1972)]

15.6. In 1974, Berlinger Foods Corporation (Berlinger), pursuant to an oral contract, became a distributor for Haagen-Dazs ice cream. Over the next decade both parties flourished as the marketing of high-quality, high-priced ice cream took hold. Berlinger successfully promoted the sale of Haagen-Dazs to supermarket chains and other retailers in the Baltimore-Washington, D.C., area. In 1983, The

Pillsbury Company (Pillsbury) acquired Haagen-Dazs. Pillsbury adhered to the oral distribution agreement and retained Berlinger as a distributor for Haagen-Dazs ice cream. In December 1985, Berlinger entered into a contract and sold its assets to Dreyers, a manufacturer of premium ice cream that competed with Haagen-Dazs. Dreyers ice cream had previously been sold primarily in the western part of the United States. Dreyers attempted to expand its market to the east by choosing to purchase Berlinger as a means to obtain distribution in the Mid-Atlantic region. When Pillsbury learned of the sale, it advised Berlinger that its distributorship for Haagen-Dazs was terminated. Berlinger, who wanted to remain a distributor for Haagen-Dazs, sued Pillsbury for breach of contract, alleging that the oral distribution agreement with Haagen-Dazs and Pillsbury was properly assigned to Dreyers. Who wins? [*Berlinger Foods Corporation v. The Pillsbury Company*, 633 F.Supp. 557 (D.Md. 1986)]

15.7. John Handy Jones paid Richard Sullivan, the chief of police of the Addison, Texas, police department, a $6,400 bribe in exchange for Sullivan's cooperation in allowing Jones and others to bring marijuana by airplane into the Addison airport without police intervention. Sullivan accepted the money, but, rather than perform the requested services, he arrested Jones and turned the money over to the Dallas County District Attorney's Office. The $6,400 was introduced as evidence at Jones's criminal trial, where he was convicted. Subsequent to his conviction, Jones assigned his interest in the money to Melvyn Carson Bruder. The city of Addison brought an action, claiming that the money belonged to the city. Bruder intervened in the suit and claimed that he was entitled to the money because of the assignment from Jones. Who wins? [*Bruder v. State of Texas*, 601 S.W.2d 102 (Tex.App. 1980)]

15.8. Lincoln Plaza Associates owned Lincoln Plaza (1900 Broadway at 64th Street) in New York. Chase Manhattan Bank (Chase) entered into a written lease whereby it leased premises in the building. The lease provided that Chase could not sublease or assign the premises without the landlord's prior approval. After occupying the premises for some time, Chase notified the landlord that it wished to sublease the premises to Bank Leumi, which was the twenty-first largest commercial bank in New York with 20 branches in New York City, assets of more than $3 billion, and a net worth of almost $150 million. The landlord refused to grant approval for the assignment. Chase sued the landlord for breach of contract. Who wins? [*The Chase Manhattan Bank, N.A. v. Lincoln Plaza Associates*, N.Y. Law Journal, Jan. 9, 1989 (N.Y.Sup. 1989)]

15.9. In 1976, the city of Vancouver, Washington, contracted with B & B Contracting Corporation (B & B) to construct a well pump at a city-owned water station. The contract contained the following antiassignment clause: "The Contractor shall not assign this contract or any part thereof, or any moneys due or to become due thereunder." The work was not completed on time, and the city withheld $6,510 as liquidated damages from the contract price. B & B assigned the claim to this money to Portland Electric and Plumbing Company (PEPCo). PEPCo, as the assignee, filed suit against the city of Vancouver alleging that the city breached its contract with B & B by wrongfully refusing to pay $6,510 to B & B. Can PEPCo maintain the lawsuit against the city of Vancouver? [*Portland Electric and Plumbing Company v. City of Vancouver*, 627 P.2d 1350 (Wash.App. 1981)]

15.10. C. W. Milford owned a registered quarterhorse named Hired Chico. In March 1969, Milford sold the horse to Norman Stewart. Recognizing that Hired Chico was a good stud, Milford included the following provision in the written contract that was signed by both parties: "I, C. W. Milford, reserve 2 breedings each year on Hired Chico registration #403692 for the life of this stud horse regardless of whom the horse may be sold to." The agreement was filed with the county court clerk of Shelby County, Texas. Stewart later sold Hired Chico to Sam McKinnie. Prior to purchasing the horse, McKinnie read the Milford-Stewart contract and testified that he understood the terms of the contract. When McKinnie refused to grant Milford the stud services of Hired Chico, Milford sued McKinnie for breach of contract. Who wins? [*McKinnie v. Milford*, 597 S.W.2d 953 (TX 1980)]

15.11. Shumann Investments, Inc. (Shumann), hired Pace Construction Corporation (Pace), a general contractor, to build "Outlet World of Pasco County." In turn, Pace hired OBS Company, Inc. (OBS), a subcontractor, to perform the framing, drywall, insulation, and stucco work on the project. The contract between Pace and OBS stipulated: "Final payment shall not become due unless and until the following conditions precedent to final payment have been satisfied . . . (c) receipt of final payment for subcontractor's work by contractor from owner." When Shumann refused to pay Pace, Pace refused to pay OBS. OBS sued Pace to recover payment. Who wins? [*Pace Construction Corporation v. OBS Company, Inc.*, 531 So.2d 737 (Fla.App. 1988)]

15.12. Indiana Tri-City Plaza Bowl, Inc. (Tri-City), leased a building from Charles H. Glueck for use as a bowling alley. The lease provided that Glueck was to provide adequate paved parking for the building. The lease gave Tri-City the right to approve the plans for the construction and paving of the parking lot. When Glueck submitted paving plans to Tri-City, it rejected the plans and withheld its approval. Tri-City argued that the plans must meet its personal satisfaction before it has to approve them. Evidence showed that the plans were commercially reasonable in the circumstances. A lawsuit was filed between Tri-City and Glueck. Who wins? [*Indiana Tri-City Plaza Bowl, Inc. v. Estate of Glueck*, 422 N.E.2d 670 (Ind.App. 1981)]

15.13. Eugene and Irene Leonard owned a hardware business, including the building and land, in Humboldt, Iowa. The Leonards listed the business and property for sale with Merlyn J. Pollock, a licensed real estate broker. The asking price was $650,000, and Pollock was to receive a flat fee of $50,000 if he found a buyer. Pollock introduced the Leonards to Vincent Kopacek. After substantial negotiations, the Leonards and Kopacek signed a contract for the sale of the hardware store. Thereafter, Mr. Leonard went to Pollock's office and tried to get him to lower his commission. After much discussion, Leonard told Pollock that if he would reduce his fee to $15,000, he would get two other hardware store owners to list their stores for sale with Pollock. Pollock agreed. Subsequently, the Leonards refused to sell their business to Kopacek, who sued and won a decree of specific performance. Can Pollock recover damages from the Leonards, and if so, how much? [*Sergeant, as Trustee for the Estate of Merlyn J. Pollock v. Leonard*, 312 N.W.2d 541 (IA 1981)]

15.14. On July 21, 1981, Magnum Enterprises, Inc. (Magnum), executed an offer and agreement to purchase the Diamond Ring Ranch in Haakon County, South Dakota, from the Armstrong family for $10,800,000. Donald A. Haggar was the real estate broker on the transaction. The offer included a provision for a $500,000 earnest money deposit by a promissory note that was payable as follows: $50,000 due on August 10, 1981, $25,000 due on August 31, 1981, and $200,000 due on September 11, 1981. The closing date of the sale was set for November 2, 1981. The offer also contained a provision for liquidated damages of $500,000 if the buyer did not perform. Magnum paid the original $50,000 into Haggar's client trust account. On August 31, 1981, Magnum agreed to let Berja, a Montana investment group, purchase the ranch. Armstrong agreed to the substitution of Berja as the buyer, and Berja executed an offer and agreement to purchase the ranch on the same terms as Magnum. When Berja failed to close the sale, Haggar, as trustee, brought an action against Magnum to recover on the promissory note. Magnum counterclaimed to recover the $50,000 it paid into Haggar's client trust account. Who wins? [*Haggar v. Olfert*, 387 N.W.2d 45 (S.D. 1986)]

ETHICS CASES

15.15. Pabagold, Inc. (Pabagold), a manufacturer and distributor of suntan lotions, hired Mediasmith, an advertising agency, to develop an advertising campaign for Pabagold's Hawaiian Gold Pabatan suntan lotion. In the contract, Pabagold authorized Mediasmith to enter into agreements with third parties to place Pabagold advertisements for the campaign and to make payments to these third parties for the Pabagold account. Pabagold agreed to pay Mediasmith for its services and to reimburse it for expenses incurred on behalf of Pabagold. The Pabagold-Mediasmith contract provided for arbitration of any dispute arising under the contract.

In April 1981, Mediasmith entered into a contract with Outdoor Services, Inc. (Outdoor Services), an outdoor advertising company, to place Pabagold ads on billboards owned by Outdoor Services. Outdoor Services provided the agreed-upon work and billed Mediasmith $8,545 for its services. Mediasmith requested payment of this amount from Pabagold so it could pay Outdoor Services. When Pabagold refused to pay, Outdoor Services filed a demand for arbitration as provided in the Pabagold-Mediasmith contract. Pabagold defended, asserting that Outdoor Services could not try to recover the money because it was not in privity of contract with Pabagold.

Did Pabagold act ethically in refusing to pay Outdoor Services? From a moral perspective, does it matter that Outdoor Services and Pabagold were not in privity of contract? Who wins? [*Outdoor Services, Inc. v. Pabagold, Inc.,* 185 Cal.App.3d 676, 230 Cal.Rptr. 73 (Cal.App. 1986)]

15.16. Jeffrey Pittman was a licensed real estate broker. In 1987, he contacted Lily Canham, then 85 years old, to purchase a 56-acre parcel of property she owned in San Luis Obispo County, California. After many telephone calls, she agreed to sell the parcel to Pittman for $250,000. Pittman drafted a purchase contract dated November 24, 1987. It provided that "time was of the essence" and that closing of escrow would occur on or before December 24, 1987. The contract also provided that Canham was to deliver a deed to escrow and that Pittman was to place a $24,000 deposit in escrow. The full purchase price was to be paid at the close of escrow. When Canham delivered a signed deed to the escrow two weeks before closing, she was told that the law required it to be notarized. Canham took the deed back to get it notarized but never returned it to the escrow. Pittman never tendered the $24,000 deposit or the remainder of the purchase price. In May 1988, Canham informed Pittman that she had sold the property to other buyers for $600,000. Pittman sued Canham to recover damages for breach of contract. Was the purchase contract enforceable? Did Pittman act ethically in this case? Did Canham act ethically? Did either act more unethically than the other? [*Pittman v. Canham,* 2 Cal.App.4th 556, 3 Cal.Rptr.2d 340 (Cal.App. 1992)]

CRITICAL LEGAL THINKING WRITING ASSIGNMENT

Read Case A.15 in the Case Appendix [*Chase Precast Corp. v. John J. Paonessa Co., Inc.*]. This case is excerpted from the appellate court opinion. Review and brief the case. In your brief, be sure to answer the following questions.

1. Who were the contracting parties and what did their contract provide?

2. Why did the defendant not complete the contract?

3. What does the doctrine of frustration of purpose provide?

4. Did the doctrine of frustration of purpose excuse the defendant's nonperformance?

NOTES

1. Restatement (Second) of Contracts, §§ 311 and 318.
2. Restatement (Second) of Contracts, § 317.
3. Restatement (Second) of Contracts, § 318(2).
4. Restatement (Second) of Contracts, § 328.
5. Restatement (Second) of Contracts, § 302.
6. Restatement (Second) of Contracts, § 302(1)(b).
7. Restatement (Second) of Contracts, § 302(1)(a).
8. The Restatement (Second) of Contracts, § 224, defines a *condition* as "An event, not certain to occur, which must occur, unless

its non-performance is excused, before performance under a contract is due."

9. Restatement (Second) of Contracts, § 224.
10. Restatement (Second) of Contracts, § 281.
11. Restatement (Second) of Contracts, § 261.
12. Restatement (Second) of Contracts, § 262.
13. Restatement (Second) of Contracts, § 263.
14. Restatement (Second) of Contracts, § 264.

Contract Remedies and Torts Associated with Contracts

Contracts must not be sports of an idle hour, mere matters of pleasantry and badinage, never intended by the parties to have any serious effect whatsoever.

LORD STOWELL *Dalrymple v. Dalrymple, 2 Hag.Con. 54, at 105 (1811)*

Chapter Objectives

After studying this chapter, you should be able to

1. Explain how complete performance discharges contractual duties.
2. Identify inferior performance and the material breach of a contract.
3. Describe compensatory, consequential, and nominal damages.
4. Describe liquidated damages and identify when they are a penalty.
5. Explain the duty of mitigation of damages.
6. Describe the remedy of rescission of a contract.
7. Define the equitable remedies of a specific performance, quasi-contract, and injunction.
8. Describe torts associated with contracts.
9. Define *punitive damages*.
10. Describe breach of Internet contracts.

Chapter Contents

There are three levels of performance of a contract: complete, substantial, and inferior. *Complete (or strict) performance* by a party discharges that party's duties under the contract. *Substantial performance* constitutes a minor breach of the contract. *Inferior performance* constitutes a material breach that impairs or destroys the essence of the contract. Various remedies may be obtained by a nonbreaching party if a **breach of contract** occurs—that is, if a contracting party fails to perform an absolute duty owed under a contract.[1]

The most common remedy for a breach of contract is an award of *monetary damages*. This is often called the "law remedy." However, if a monetary award does not provide adequate relief, the court may order any one of several *equitable remedies*, including specific performance, reformation, quasi-contract, and injunction. Equitable remedies are based on the concept of fairness.

In addition, certain torts may arise from the breach or interference with contracts. *Tort damages*—including *punitive damages*—may be available for such violations.

This chapter discusses breach of contracts and the remedies available to the nonbreaching party.

$\mathscr{P}$ERFORMANCE AND BREACH

If a contract duty has not been discharged (i.e., terminated) or excused (i.e., relieved of legal liability), the contracting party owes an absolute duty (i.e., covenant) to perform the duty. As mentioned in the chapter introduction, there are three types of performance of a contract: (1) *complete performance*, (2) *substantial performance* (or minor breach), and (3) *inferior performance* (or material breach). These concepts are discussed in the following paragraphs.

Complete Performance

Most contracts are discharged by the **complete** or **strict performance** of the contracting parties. Complete performance occurs when a party to a contract renders performance exactly as required by the contract. A fully performed contract is called an *executed contract*.

Note that **tender of performance** also discharges a party's contractual obligations. Tender is an unconditional and absolute offer by a contracting party to perform his or her obligations under the contract. For example, suppose Ashley's Dress Shops, Inc., contracts to purchase dresses from a dress manufacturer for $25,000. Ashley's has performed its obligation under the contract once it tenders the $25,000 to the manufacturer. If the manufacturer fails to deliver the dresses, Ashley's can sue it for breach of contract.

Substantial Performance—Minor Breach

Substantial performance occurs when there has been a **minor breach** of contract. In other words, it occurs when a party to a contract renders performance that deviates only slightly from complete performance. The nonbreaching party may (1) convince the breaching party to elevate his or her performance to complete performance, (2) deduct the cost to repair the defect from the contract price and remit the balance to the breaching party, or (3) sue the breaching party to recover the cost to repair the defect if the breaching party has already been paid.

Consider This Example   Suppose Donald Trump contracts with Big Apple Construction Co. to have Big Apple construct an office building for $50 million. The architectural plans call for installation of three-ply windows in the building. Big Apple constructs the

---

breach of contract

If a contracting party fails to perform an absolute duty owed under a contract.

It is a vain thing to imagine a right without a remedy; for want of right and want of remedy are reciprocal.

Holt C.J.
Ashby v. White *(1703)*

---

complete performance

Occurs when a party to a contract renders performance exactly as required by the contract; discharges that party's obligations under the contract.

tender of performance

Tender is an unconditional and absolute offer by a contracting party to perform his or her obligations under the contract.

substantial performance

Performance by a contracting party that deviates only slightly from complete performance.

minor breach

A breach that occurs when a party renders substantial performance of his or her contractual duties.

building exactly to plan except that it installs two-ply windows. There has been substantial performance. It would cost $300,000 to install the correct windows. If Big Apple agrees to replace the windows, its performance is elevated to complete performance, and Trump must remit the entire contract price. However, if Trump has to hire someone else to replace the windows, he may deduct this cost of repair from the contract price and remit the difference to Big Apple.

Inferior Performance: Material Breach

A material breach of a contract occurs when a party renders inferior performance of his or her contractual obligations that impairs or destroys the essence of the contract. There is no clear line between a minor breach and a material breach. A determination is made on a case-by-case basis.

Where there has been a material breach of a contract, the nonbreaching party may *rescind* the contract and seek restitution of any compensation paid under the contract to the breaching party. The nonbreaching party is discharged from any further performance under the contract.[2] Alternatively, the nonbreaching party may treat the contract as being in effect and sue the breaching party to recover *damages*.

Consider This Example   Suppose a university contracts with a general contractor to build a new three-story building with classroom space for 1,000 students. However, the completed building can support the weight of only 500 students because the contractor used inferior materials. The defect cannot be repaired without rebuilding the entire structure. Because this is a material breach, the university may rescind the contract and require removal of the building. The university is discharged of any obligations under the contract and is free to employ another contractor to rebuild the building. Alternatively, the university could accept the building and deduct damages caused by the defect from the contract price.

inferior performance
Occurs when a party fails to perform express or implied contractual obligations that impair or destroy the essence of the contract.

material breach
A breach that occurs when a party renders inferior performance of his or her contractual duties.

*C*ONCEPT SUMMARY   TYPES OF PERFORMANCE

Type of Performance	Legal Consequence
Complete performance	The contract is discharged.
Substantial performance (minor breach)	The nonbreaching party may recover damages caused by the breach.
Inferior performance (material breach)	The nonbreaching party may either (1) rescind the contract and recover restitution or (2) affirm the contract and recover damages.

Anticipatory Breach

Anticipatory breach (or **anticipatory repudiation**) of contract occurs when the contracting party informs the other in advance that he or she will not perform his or her contractual duties when due. This type of material breach can be expressly stated or implied from the conduct of the repudiator. Where there is an anticipatory repudiation, the nonbreaching party's obligations under the contract are discharged immediately. The nonbreaching party also has the right to sue the repudiating party when the anticipatory breach occurs; there is no need to wait until performance is due.[3]

anticipatory breach
A breach that occurs when one contracting party informs the other that he or she will not perform his or her contractual duties when due.

E-Commerce & Internet Law

e·biz

BREACH OF AN INTERNET CONTRACT

A contract is a contract is a contract, even if it is over the Internet. Consider the following case. The Hotmail Corporation (Hotmail) is a Silicon Valley company that provides free e-mail on the Internet. Hotmail's on-line services allow its millions of registered subscribers to exchange e-mail messages over the Internet. The company registered the name "Hotmail" as a federal trademark and obtained the Internet domain name "hotmail.com." Every e-mail sent by a Hotmail subscriber automatically displays Hotmail's domain name and mark. To become a Hotmail subscriber, one must agree to abide by a Service Agreement by clicking an "accept" prompt on the computer screen. This click-wrap contract expressly prohibits subscribers from using Hotmail's services to send unsolicited commercial bulk e-mail, or "spam," or to send obscene or pornographic messages. The transmission of spam is a practice widely condemned by the Internet community.

In the fall of 1997, Hotmail discovered that defendants Van$ Money Pie Inc., ALS Enterprises, Inc., LCGM, Inc., and the Genesis Network, Inc. created Hotmail accounts that were facilitating their sending spam e-mail to Hotmail subscribers. The spam messages advertised pornography and "get-rich-quick" schemes, among other things. Hotmail was inundated with complaints from its subscribers who had received the spam, and faced the loss of customers as well as an overloading of its services from the spam e-mail.

Hotmail sued the defendants in district court for breach of contract and sought a preliminary injunction to enjoin the defendants from sending spam e-mail using Hotmail accounts, domain name, and mark. The district court agreed with Hotmail on its breach of contract claim, stating

The evidence supports a finding that plaintiff Hotmail will likely prevail on its breach of contract claim and that there are at least serious questions going to the merits of this claim in that plaintiff has presented evidence of the following: that defendants obtained a number of Hotmail mailboxes and access to Hotmail's services; that in so doing defendants agreed to abide by Hotmail's Terms of Service which prohibit using a Hotmail account for purposes of sending spam and/or pornography; that defendants breached their contract with Hotmail by using Hotmail's services to facilitate sending spam and/or pornography; that Hotmail complied with the conditions of the contract except those from which its performance was excused; and that if defendants are not enjoined they will continue to create such accounts in violation of the Terms of Service.

The district court enforced the click-wrap contract and held the defendants in breach of Hotmail's Internet contract. The court issued a preliminary injunction prohibiting the defendants from using Hotmail accounts or Hotmail's domain name or mark to send spam. [*Hotmail Corporation v. Van$ Money Pie, Inc.,* 47 U.S.P.Q. 1020 (N.D.Cal. 1998)]

MONETARY DAMAGES

monetary damages
An award of money.

A nonbreaching party may recover **monetary damages** from a breaching party. Monetary damages are available whether the breach was minor or material. Several types of monetary damages may be awarded. These include *compensatory, consequential, liquidated,* and *nominal damages.*

Compensatory Damages

compensatory damages
An award of money intended to compensate a nonbreaching party for the loss of the bargain; they place the nonbreaching party in the same position as if the contract had been fully performed by restoring the "benefit of the bargain."

Compensatory damages are intended to compensate a nonbreaching party for the loss of the bargain. In other words, they place the nonbreaching party in the same position as if the contract had been fully performed by restoring the "benefit of the bargain."

Consider This Example Suppose Lederle Laboratories enters into a written contract to employ a manager for three years at a salary of $6,000 per month. Before work is to start, the manager is informed that he or she will not be needed. This is a material breach of contract. Assume the manager finds another job, but it pays only $5,000 a month. The manager may recover $1,000 per month for 36 months (total $36,000) from Lederle Laboratories as compensatory damages. These damages place the manager in the same situation as if the contract with Lederle had been performed.

The amount of compensatory damages that will be awarded for breach of contract depends on the type of contract involved and which party breached the contract. The award of compensatory damages in some special types of contracts is discussed in the following paragraphs.

Sale of Goods   Compensatory damages for a breach of a sales contract involving goods are governed by the Uniform Commercial Code (UCC). The usual measure of damages for a breach of a sales contract is the difference between the contract price and the market price of the goods at the time and place the goods were to be delivered.[4]

Consider This Example   Suppose (1) Revlon, Inc., contracted to buy a piece of equipment from Greenway Supply Co. for $20,000 and (2) the equipment is not delivered. Revlon then purchases the equipment from another vendor but has to pay $25,000 because the current market price for the equipment has risen. Revlon can recover $5,000—the difference between the market price paid ($25,000) and the contract price ($20,000)—in compensatory damages.

Construction Contracts   A construction contract arises when the owner of real property contracts to have a contractor build a structure or do other construction work. The compensatory damages recoverable for a breach of a construction contract vary with the stage of completion the project is in when the breach occurs.

The contractor may recover the profits he or she would have made on the contract if the owner breaches the construction contract before construction begins.

Consider This Example   Suppose RXZ Corporation contracts to have the Ace Construction Co. build a factory for $1.2 million. It will cost the contractor $800,000 in materials and labor to build the factory. If RXZ Corporation breaches the contract before construction begins, the contractor can recover $400,000 in "lost profit."

The contractor can recover his or her lost profits plus the cost of construction to date if RXZ Corporation decides not to go ahead with the new factory after construction begins. Assume in the prior example that Ace Construction Co. had spent $300,000 on materials and labor before the contract was breached. Here, the contractor can recover $700,000—$400,000 lost profit plus $300,000 expended on materials and labor. If the owner breaches the contract after the project is completed, the contractor can recover the full contract price ($1.2 million).

If the builder breaches a construction contract, either before or during construction, the owner can recover the increased cost above the contract price that he or she has to pay to have the work completed by another contractor. For instance, suppose in the previous example Ace Construction Co. breached the contract by refusing to build the factory. Assume that RXZ Corporation has to pay $1.5 million to have the same factory built by another contractor. RXZ can recover the increased cost of construction ($300,000) from the contractor as compensatory damages.

Employment Contracts   An employee whose employer breaches an employment contract can recover lost wages or salary as compensatory damages. If the employee breaches the contract, the employer can recover the costs to hire a new employee plus any increase in salary paid to the replacement.

The very definition of a good award is that it gives dissatisfaction to both parties.

M. R. Plumer
Goodman v. Sayers (1820)

After joining the World Trade Organization (WTO), China revamped its laws on foreign trade, joint ventures, and foreign investment. China also relaxed its regulation of the legal profession to make the legal industry more competitive and to comply with WTO rules.

Consequential Damages

In addition to compensatory damages, a nonbreaching party sometimes can recover **special** or **consequential damages** from the breaching party. Consequential damages are *foreseeable* damages that arise from circumstances outside the contract. To be liable for consequential damages, the breaching party must know or have reason to know that the breach will cause special damages to the other party.

consequential damages
Foreseeable damages that arise from circumstances outside the contract. To be liable for these damages, the breaching party must know or have reason to know that the breach will cause special damages to the other party.

Consider This Example Suppose Soan-Allen Co., a wholesaler, enters into a contract to purchase 1,000 men's suits for $150 each from the Fabric Manufacturing Co., a manufacturer. Prior to contracting, the wholesaler tells the manufacturer that the suits will be resold to retailers for $225. The manufacturer breaches the contract by failing to manufacture the suits. The wholesaler cannot get the suits manufactured by anyone else in time to meet his contracts. He or she can recover $75,000 of lost profits on the resale contracts (1,000 suits × $75 profit) as consequential damages from the manufacturer because the manufacturer knew of this special damage to Soan-Allen Co. if it breached the contract.

In the following case, the court awarded consequential damages against a breaching party.

Super Valu Stores, Inc. v. Peterson
506 So.2d 317 (1987)
Supreme Court of Alabama

CASE 16.1

FACTS

Super Valu Stores, Inc. (Super Valu), a wholesale operator of supermarkets, developed a new concept for a market called "County Market." The basic concept of the County Market was that it must be the lowest priced store in the marketplace and operate on a high-volume, low-profit margin structure. In 1981, Super Valu purchased a parcel of property in Oxford, Alabama, for the development of a County Market.

It planned to lease the store to an independent retailer to operate. Thomas J. Peterson, who was an executive of Super Valu, applied for the operator's position at the proposed store. In January 1984, Peterson was approved as the retail operator of the proposed Oxford County Market. On February 24, 1984, Peterson retired from Super Valu so that he could operate the new store. When Super Valu failed to construct and lease the store to Peterson, he sued Super Valu for breach of contract. The trial court held in favor of Peterson and awarded him $5 million in lost profits that would have been derived by him from the store. Super Valu appealed.

ISSUE

Are lost profits from an unestablished business recoverable as consequential damages even though it can be argued that they are inherently too speculative and conjectural?

IN THE LANGUAGE OF THE COURT

Maddox, Justice   *Super Valu argues that this Court follows the general rule of damages that anticipated profits of a commercial business are too speculative, remote, and uncertain to permit their recovery. Super Valu argues that the "per se" rule of lost profits should apply to this case. The "per se" rule of lost profits is that anticipated profits of a new or hypothetical business can never be recovered, because they are inherently too speculative and conjectural. Super Valu also contends that Peterson's profit projections constitute remote, speculative, and conjectural evidence.*

We are of the opinion that the jury's award of damages to Peterson is completely consistent with the law of Alabama and with the evidence in this case. Current Alabama law, like the law of other states, authorizes recovery of anticipated profits of an unestablished business, if proved with reasonable certainty. This general rule is applied in most states and is referred to as the "rule of reasonable certainty." This Court's explicit rationale for applying the reasonable certainty rule was its recognition that to disallow damages for loss of reasonably certain future profits would encourage breach of contract with new businesses. The rule in Alabama is that jury verdicts awarding lost profits will be affirmed if the plaintiff provides a basis upon which the jury could, with reasonable certainty, calculate the amount of profits that were lost as a result of defendant's wrongful actions.

The fundamental basis for Peterson's evidence as to damages was Super Valu's own projections of profits, produced in its normal course of business long before this dispute arose. These projections were the product of an intense, exhaustive process involving many different Super Valu personnel. Super Valu's projections resulted from the application of a scientific methodology that for many years had accurately predicted the future performance of stores associated with Super Valu. These projections were also based upon the prior successful performances of the Super Valu business system, of which the Oxford County Market would have become a standardized part. The jury could have found that Super Valu and Peterson relied upon these profit projections in making their initial decision to go forward with the Oxford County Market store.

DECISION AND REMEDY

The state supreme court held that lost profits from an unestablished business can be recovered as consequential damages if they can be determined with reasonable certainty. The court held that such damages were determined with reasonable certainty in this case and affirmed the trial court's judgment.

Case Questions

Critical Legal Thinking   Are lost profits too speculative to be awarded in breach of contract actions?

Ethics   Did Super Valu act ethically by denying liability in this case?

Business Application   If unestablished businesses could not recover lost profits, would there be more or fewer breaches of contract with such businesses?

Liquidated Damages

Under certain circumstances, the parties to a contract may agree in advance to the amount of damages payable upon a breach of contract. These are called **liquidated damages**. To be lawful, the actual damages must be difficult or impracticable to determine, and the liquidated amount must be reasonable in the circumstances.[5] An enforceable liquidated damage clause is an exclusive remedy even if actual damages are later determined to be different.

A liquidated damage clause is considered a *penalty* if actual damages are clearly determinable in advance or the liquidated damages are excessive or unconscionable. If a liquidated damage clause is found to be a penalty, it is unenforceable. The nonbreaching party may then recover actual damages.

In the following case, the court had to decide whether a liquidated damage clause was a penalty.

liquidated damages
If the contract is breached, these are damages to which parties to a contract agree in advance.

Business Brief
Many businesses include liquidated damage clauses in their commercial contracts. This helps to provide certainty, avoid lawsuits, and provide an incentive to enter into contracts.

California and Hawaiian Sugar Co. v. Sun Ship, Inc.
794 F.2d 1433 (1986)
United States Court of Appeals, Ninth Circuit

CASE 16.2

FACTS

The California and Hawaiian Sugar Company (C&H), a California corporation, is an agricultural cooperative owned by 14 sugar plantations in Hawaii. It transports raw sugar to its refinery in Crockett, California. Sugar is a seasonal crop, with about 70 percent of the harvest occurring between April and October. C&H requires reliable seasonal shipping of the raw sugar from Hawaii to California. Sugar stored on the ground or left unharvested suffers a loss of sucrose and goes to waste.

After C&H was notified by its normal shipper that it would be withdrawing its services as of January 1981, C&H commissioned the design of a large hybrid vessel—a tug of a catamaran design consisting of a barge attached to the tug. After substantial negotiations, C&H contracted with Sun Ship, Inc. (Sun Ship), a Pennsylvania corporation, to build the vessel for $25,405,000. The contract, which was signed in the fall of 1979, provided a delivery date of June 30, 1981. The contract also contained a liquidated damage clause calling for a payment of $17,000 per day for each day that the vessel was not delivered to C&H after June 30, 1981. Sun Ship did not complete the vessel until March 16, 1982. The vessel was commissioned in mid-July 1982 and christened the *Moku Pahu*.

During the 1981 season, C&H was able to find other means of shipping the crop from Hawaii to its California refinery. Evidence established that actual damages suffered by C&H because of the nonavailability of the vessel from Sun Ship were $368,000. When Sun Ship refused to pay the liquidated damages, C&H filed suit to require payment of $4,413,000 in liquidated damages under the contract. The district court entered judgment in favor of C&H and awarded the corporation $4,413,000 plus interest. Sun Ship appealed.

ISSUE

Is the liquidated damage clause enforceable, or is it a penalty clause that is not enforceable?

IN THE LANGUAGE OF THE COURT

Noonan, Circuit Judge Contracts are contracts because they contain enforceable promises, and absent some over-riding public policy, those promises are to be enforced. Where each of the parties is content to take the risk of its turning out in a particular way, why should one be released from the contract, if there were no misrepresentation or other want of fair dealing? Promising to pay damages of a fixed amount, the parties normally have a much better sense of what damages can occur. Courts must be reluctant to override their judgment. Where damages are real but difficult to prove, injustice will be done the injured party if the court substitutes the requirements of judicial proof for the parties' own informed agreement as to what is a reasonable measure of damages. The liquidated damage clause here functions in lieu of a court's determination of the consequential damages suffered by C&H.

Proof of this loss is difficult. Whatever the loss, the parties had promised each other that $17,000 per day was a reasonable measure. The court must decline to substitute the requirements of judicial proof for the parties' own conclusion. The Moku Pahu, *if available on June 30, 1981, was a great prize, capable of multiple employments and enlarging the uses of the entire C&H fleet. When sophisticated parties with bargaining parity have agreed what lack of this prize would mean, and it is now difficult to measure what the lack did mean, the court will uphold the parties' bargain.*

DECISION AND REMEDY

The court of appeals held that the liquidated damage clause was not a penalty and was therefore enforceable. Affirmed.

Case Questions

Critical Legal Thinking Should liquidated damage clauses be enforced or should nonbreaching parties be allowed to recover only actual damages caused by the breaching party?

Ethics Did either party act unethically in this case?

Business Application Do you think many businesses use liquidated damage clauses? Can you give some examples?

Nominal Damages

> *Men keep their agreements when it is an advantage to both parties not to break them.*
>
> *Solon (c. 600 b.c.)*

The nonbreaching party can sue the breaching party even if no financial loss resulted from the breach. In this case, the court will award only *nominal damages*. This usually consists of $1 or some other small amount. Cases involving nominal damages are usually brought on "principle."

CONCEPT SUMMARY TYPES OF MONETARY DAMAGES

Type of Damage	Description
Compensatory	Compensates a nonbreaching party for the loss of the bargain. It places the nonbreaching party in the same position as if the contract had been fully performed.
Consequential	Compensates a nonbreaching party for foreseeable special damages. The breaching party must have known or should have known that these damages would result from the breach.
Liquidated	Agreement by the parties in advance that sets the amount of damages recoverable in case of breach. These damages are lawful if they do not cause a penalty.
Nominal	Damages awarded against the breaching party even though the nonbreaching party has suffered no actual damages because of the breach. A small amount (e.g., $1) is usually awarded.

Mitigation of Damages

If a contract has been breached, the law places a duty on the innocent nonbreaching party to take reasonable efforts to **mitigate** (i.e., avoid and reduce) the resulting damages. The extent of mitigation required depends on the type of contract involved. For example, if an employer breaches an employment contract, the employee owes a duty to mitigate damages by trying to find substitute employment. The employee is only required to accept comparable employment. The courts consider such factors as compensation, rank, status, job description, and geographical location in determining the comparability of jobs.

The court had to decide if a job was comparable in the following case.

> **mitigation**
> A nonbreaching party is under a legal duty to avoid or reduce damages caused by a breach of contract.

Parker v. Twentieth Century-Fox Film Corp.
3 Cal.3d 176, 89 Cal.Rptr. 737 (1970)
California Supreme Court

CASE 16.3

FACTS

On August 6, 1965, Twentieth Century-Fox Film Corporation (Fox), a major film production studio, entered into an employment contract with Shirley MacLaine Parker (Parker), an actress. Under the contract, Parker was to play the leading female role in a musical production called *Bloomer Girl*, to be filmed in Los Angeles. In the movie, Parker would be able to use her talents as a dancer as well as an actress. The contract provided that Parker was to be paid guaranteed compensation of $53,571.42 per week for 14 weeks commencing on May 23, 1966, for a total of $750,000. On April 4, 1966, Fox sent Parker a letter notifying her that it was not going to film *Bloomer Girl*. The letter, however, offered Parker the leading female role in a film tentatively entitled *Big Country*, which was to be a dramatic Western to be filmed in Australia. The compensation Fox offered Parker was identical to that offered for *Bloomer Girl*.

Fox gave Parker one week to accept. She did not and the offer expired. Parker sued Fox to recover the guaranteed compensation provided in the *Bloomer Girl* contract. The trial court granted summary judgment to Parker. Fox appealed.

ISSUE

Was the job that Fox offered Parker in *Big Country* comparable employment that Parker was obligated to accept to mitigate damages?

IN THE LANGUAGE OF THE COURT

Burke, Justice The general rule is that the measure of recovery by a wrongfully discharged employee is the amount of salary agreed upon for the period of service, less the amount that the employer affirmatively proves the employee has earned or with reasonable effort might have earned from other employment. However, before projected earnings from other employment

(case continues)

opportunities not sought or accepted by the discharged employee can be applied, in mitigation, the employer must show that the other employment was comparable, or substantially similar, to that of which the employee has been deprived; the employee's rejection of or failure to seek other available employment of a different or inferior kind may not be resorted to in order to mitigate damages.

Applying the foregoing rules to the record in the present case, with all intendments in favor of the party opposing the summary judgment motion—here, defendant Fox—it is clear that the trial court correctly ruled that plaintiff's failure to accept defendant's tendered substitute employment could not be applied in mitigation of damages because the offer of the Big Country lead was of employment both different and inferior, and that no factual dispute was presented on that issue. The mere circumstances that Bloomer Girl was to be a musical review, calling upon plaintiff's talents as a dancer as well as an actress, and was to be produced in the City of Los Angeles, whereas Big Country was a straight dramatic role in a Western-type story taking place in an opal mine in Australia, demonstrates the difference in kind between the two employments: The female lead as a dramatic actress in a Western-style motion picture can by no stretch of imagination be considered the equivalent of or substantially similar to the lead in a song-and-dance production.

DECISION AND REMEDY

The state supreme court held that the job that Fox offered to Parker in *Big Country* was not comparable employment to the role Fox had contracted Parker to play in *Bloomer Girl*. Therefore, Parker did not fail to mitigate damages by refusing to accept such employment. The supreme court affirmed the trial court's summary judgment.

Case Questions

Critical Legal Thinking Should nonbreaching parties be under a duty to mitigate damages caused by the breaching party? Why or why not?

Ethics Did Fox act ethically in this case? Did Parker?

Business Application Who is more likely to be able to mitigate damages when there is a breach of an employment contract: (1) the president of a large corporation, (2) a middle manager, or (3) a bank teller?

RESCISSION AND RESTITUTION

rescission

An action to rescind (undo) the contract. Rescission is available if there has been a material breach of contract, fraud, duress, undue influence, or mistake.

Rescission is an action to *undo* the contract. It is available where there has been a material breach of contract, fraud, duress, undue influence, or mistake. Generally, to rescind a contract, the parties must make **restitution** of the consideration they received under the contract.[6] Restitution consists of returning the goods, property, money, or other consideration received from the other party. If possible, the actual goods or property must be returned. If the goods or property has been consumed or is otherwise unavailable, restitution must be made by conveying a cash equivalent. The rescinding party must give adequate notice of the rescission to the breaching party. *Rescission* and *restitution* restore the parties to the position they occupied prior to the contract.

restitution

Returning of goods or property received from the other party in order to rescind a contract; if the actual goods or property is not available, a cash equivalent must be made.

Consider This Example Suppose Filene's Department Stores contracts to purchase $100,000 of goods from a sweater manufacturer. The store pays $10,000 as a down payment, and the first $20,000 of goods are delivered. The goods are materially defective, and the defect cannot be cured. This is a material breach. Filene's can rescind the contract. The store is entitled to receive its down payment back from the manufacturer, and the manufacturer is entitled to receive the goods back from the store.

Contemporary Business Application

ENFORCEMENT OF REMEDIES: ATTACHMENT AND GARNISHMENT

If a nonbreaching party brings a successful lawsuit against a breaching party to a contract, the court will enter a *judgment* in his or her favor. This judgment must then be collected. If the breaching party refuses to pay the judgment, the court may

• **Issue a writ of attachment.** This writ orders the sheriff to seize property in the possession of the breaching party that he or she owns, and to sell the property at auction to satisfy the judgment. In all states, certain property is exempt from attachment.

- **Issue a writ of garnishment.** This writ orders that wages, bank accounts, or other property of the breaching party that is in the hands of third parties be paid over to the nonbreaching party to satisfy the judgment. Federal and state laws limit the amount of the breaching party's wages or salary that can be garnished.

Ethical Perspective

MUST A WEDDING RING BE RETURNED IF THE ENGAGEMENT IS BROKEN OFF?

When a man and woman are in love, the man often asks the woman to marry him and presents her with an engagement ring. But engagements do not always lead to weddings, and are sometimes broken off by one of the parties. The question then is: Who gets the engagement ring? Does the woman get to keep the ring, or can the man recover it? Consider the following case.

In August 1993, Rodger Lindh (Rodger) proposed marriage to Janis Surman (Janis) and presented her with a diamond ring he purchased for $17,400. She accepted his proposal and ring. Discord developed in their relationship, however, and in March 1994 Rodger called off the engagement. He asked Janis to return the engagement ring, but when she refused Rodger sued her seeking recovery of the ring. The Pennsylvania trial court and appellate court applied a no-fault rule and held that Janis must return the ring to Rodger. Janis appealed to the Pennsylvania Supreme Court.

The Pennsylvania Supreme Court noted that Janis favored the "fault" rule for deciding who gets the ring in a broken engagement case. Under this rule if "she" breaks off the engagement, "he" gets the ring back; if "he" breaks off the engagement, "she" gets to keep the ring. Although noting that some states still follow this rule, the Pennsylvania Supreme Court stated that Pennsylvania would not follow the fault-rule. The court noted that the process of determining who is "wrong" and who is "right" is difficult in modern relationships and that this would require parties to aim bitter and unpleasant accusations at each other.

Instead, the Pennsylvania Supreme Court decided to follow the modern, objective "no fault" rule that holds that an engagement ring must be returned to the donor no matter who breaks off the engagement. The court stated:

> Courts that have applied no-fault principles to engagement ring cases have borrowed from the policies of their respective legislatures that have moved away from the notion of fault in their divorce statutes. We agree with those jurisdictions that have looked towards the development of no-fault divorce law for a principle to decide engagement ring cases, and the inherent weaknesses in any fault-based system lead us to adopt a no-fault approach to resolution of engagement ring disputes. We believe that the benefits from the certainty of our rule outweigh its negatives, and that a strict no-fault approach is less flawed than a fault-based theory.

The Pennsylvania Supreme Court affirmed the judgment of the lower courts awarding the engagement ring to Rodger. [*Lindh v. Surman*, 1999 WL 1073639 (PA 1999)]

EQUITABLE REMEDIES

Equitable remedies are available if there has been a breach of contract that cannot be adequately compensated by a legal remedy. They are also available to prevent unjust enrichment. The most common equitable remedies are *specific performance, reformation, quasi-contract,* and *injunction.*

Specific Performance

An award of **specific performance** orders the breaching party to *perform* the acts promised in the contract. The courts have the discretion to award this remedy if the subject matter of the contract is unique.[7] This remedy is available to enforce land contracts because every piece of real property is considered to be unique. Works of art, antiques, items of sentimental value, rare coins, stamps, heirlooms, and such also fit the requirement for

equitable remedies
Remedies that may be awarded by a judge where there has been a breach of contract and either (1) the legal remedy is not adequate or (2) to prevent unjust enrichment.

specific performance
A remedy that orders the breaching party to perform the acts promised in the contract; usually awarded in cases where the subject matter is unique, such as in contracts involving land, heirlooms, paintings, and the like.

uniqueness. Most other personal property does not. Specific performance of personal service contracts is not granted because the courts would find it difficult or impracticable to supervise or monitor performance of the contract.

Entrepreneur and the Law

HARD DEALING FOR THE HARD ROCK CAFE

In the 1970s, Peter Morton operated a popular restaurant and tourist attraction in England known as the "Hard Rock Cafe." At that time, Milton Okun of the United States inquired about investing in the business. Morton declined Okun's offer but indicated that if he contemplated expanding the business to the United States, he would contact Okun. In December 1981, Morton located a site suitable for a Hard Rock Cafe in Los Angeles, California. Morton contacted Okun and offered him stock in the general partnership. An agreement was executed on March 2, 1982, whereby Okun contributed $100,000 in exchange for a 20 percent interest in the general partnership. Paragraph 9 of the agreement gave Okun the option to participate in future Hard Rock Cafes with the same 20 percent interest.

After raising funds from limited partners, the Hard Rock Cafe opened in the Beverly Center in Los Angeles and was a commercial success. As a result, Morton decided to exploit the San Francisco market. Per their agreement, Morton offered Okun a 20 percent interest, which Okun accepted.

In 1984, while Morton was finalizing plans for operating a Hard Rock Cafe in Chicago, Illinois, Morton and Okun had a disagreement. Morton advised Okun that he planned to exclude Okun from participating in the venture. Okun offered to participate on the terms of their 1982 agreement. Morton rejected that offer and proceeded with the development of restaurants in Houston, Honolulu, and Chicago without offering Okun a general partnership interest in these ventures. Okun sued Morton for breach of contract, seeking an order of specific performance of their 1982 agreement. The trial court held in favor of Okun and ordered specific performance of the contract. Morton appealed.

Can the 1982 agreement between Morton and Okun be specifically performed?

The court of appeals noted that as a whole, the terms of the agreement were sufficient to establish from the outset the ways in which future ventures were to be financed, owned, and operated by the parties. The fundamental structure of all such undertakings was to be based on the 20/80 ratio established for the creation of the L.A. Hard Rock Cafe. The court stated that although the agreement admittedly does not deal in specifics, neither law nor equity requires that every term and condition be set forth in the contract. In light of the fact that neither defendant nor plaintiff could predict with any degree of certainty the success of the Los Angeles operation, it is not surprising that Paragraph 9 was drafted broadly enough to accommodate changing circumstances and unforeseen developments.

Defendant asserts, however, that specific performance should not have been granted because enforcement of the contract will require continuous and protracted judicial supervision. The courts of this state have generally followed this "archaic" rule. This case merely involves the offering of an opportunity to participate in a business venture and the concomitant payment of capital and expenses for that participation.

The court stated, "We are not here concerned with the day-to-day management of any particular Hard Rock Cafe or related enterprises that would require the close and ongoing cooperation of the parties or the court." The defendant retains the discretion under the terms of the judgment to structure each venture as he pleases so long as he maintains the 20/80 ratio and does nothing to interfere with or burden plaintiff's right to participate in the deal. Under these circumstances, the court concluded that the decree of specific performance is not unduly burdensome nor requires inordinate supervision by the trial court.

The appellate court held that the subject matter of the agreement between Morton and Okun was unique and therefore that the agreement can be specifically enforced. [*Okun v. Morton*, 203 Cal.App.3d, 250 Cal.Rptr. 220 (Cal.App. 1988)]

---

reformation

An equitable doctrine that permits the court to rewrite a contract to express the parties' true intentions.

Reformation

Reformation is an equitable doctrine that permits the court to *rewrite* a contract to express the parties' true intentions. For example, suppose that a clerical error is made during the typing of the contract and both parties sign the contract without discovering the error. If a dispute later arises, the court can reform the contract to correct the clerical error to read what the parties originally intended.

Quasi-Contract

A **quasi-contract** (also called **quantum meruit** or an **implied-in-law contract**) is an equitable doctrine that permits the recovery of compensation even though no enforceable contract exists between the parties because of lack of consideration, the Statute of Frauds has run out, or the like. Such contracts are imposed by law to prevent unjust enrichment. Under quasi-contract, a party can recover the reasonable value of the services or materials provided. For example, a physician who stops to render aid to an unconscious victim of an automobile accident may recover the reasonable value of his services from that person.

Injunction

An **injunction** is a court order that *prohibits* a person from doing a certain act. To obtain an injunction, the requesting party must show that he or she will suffer irreparable injury unless the injunction is issued.

Consider This Example   Suppose a professional football team enters into a five-year employment contract with a "superstar" quarterback. The quarterback breaches the contract and enters into a contract to play for a competing team. Here, the first team can seek an injunction to prevent the quarterback from playing for the other team.

> *Every unjust decision is a reproach to the law or the judge who administers it. If the law should be in danger of doing injustice, then equity should be called in to remedy it. Equity was introduced to mitigate the rigour of the law.*
>
> Lord Denning, M.R.
> Re Vandervelt's Trusts (1974)

injunction
A court order that prohibits a person from doing a certain act.

CONCEPT SUMMARY   TYPES OF EQUITABLE REMEDIES

Type of Equitable Remedy	Description
Specific performance	Court orders the breaching party to perform the acts promised in the contract. The subject matter of the contract must be unique.
Reformation	Court rewrites a contract to express the parties' true intentions. Usually used to correct clerical errors.
Quasi-contract	Permits the recovery of damages for breach of an implied-in-law contract where no actual contract exists between the parties. Only the reasonable value of the services or materials may be recovered.
Injunction	Court order that prohibits a party from doing a certain act. Available in contract actions only in limited circumstances.

Ethical Perspective

STATE FARM: NOT SUCH A GOOD NEIGHBOR

Most car drivers purchase automobile insurance to cover themselves from liability for accidents. Many drivers also purchase collision insurance, which means that the insurance covers the cost of repairing an insured's damaged automobile. Collision insurance policies routinely provide that replacement parts be of "like kind and quality" to the original damaged parts. But what if the replacement parts are "after-market" parts, that is, parts manufactured by companies other than the original automobile manufacturer. Do these generic parts qualify as

(box continues)

"like kind and quality?" Many insureds (and their lawyers, of course) did not think so and sued their insurance company, State Farm Mutual Automobile Insurance Company, the largest insurance company in the United States, for breach of contract for including replacement parts in their vehicles without telling them.

The plaintiffs' class-action lawsuit on behalf of all similarly situated insureds of State Farm included all those who had their automobiles repaired by State Farm over the past 10 years. The plaintiffs presented evidence that State Farm required body shops to use replacement parts made by aftermarket manufacturers and not by the automobile's original manufacturer. State Farm said it did this to save costs. For example, a replacement hood for a 1995 Pontiac Grand Am cost $307 from General Motors but only $154 from an after-market manufacturer.

The plaintiffs argued that the replacement parts were inferior to original parts, were less safe and had not been crash-tested, and lowered the value of the automobile. The plaintiffs argued that State Farm forced body shops to use after-market parts to save it money at the expense of the insureds, and therefore that State Farm had breached its contract to provide replacement parts of "like kind and quality." The case went to trial in rural Marion, Illinois. After hearing the evidence, the jurors believed the plaintiffs

and held that State Farm had breached its contract with the insureds. As a remedy, the jury returned a verdict of $456 million against State Farm. In a further blow, the trial court judge held that State Farm had committed consumer fraud and tacked on an additional $730 million in punitive and other damages, bringing the total award to almost $1.2 billion. State Farm has over $75 billion in assets. Each of the 4.7 million affected insureds would receive on average about $275 from State Farm.

State Farm argues that it did nothing wrong and that because of this judgment consumers will be hurt by higher insurance costs. The plaintiffs argue that State Farm merely got caught cheating its insureds and now must pay for its misbehavior. Lawsuits are pending against other automobile insurance companies based on the same issue.

1. Did State Farm act ethically in this case? Do you think it was acting in the best interests of its insureds?
2. Should it have told its insureds that it was ordering body shops to use after-market rather than original replacement parts? Why do you think State Farm did not tell its insureds this fact?
3. Do you think the amount of the award was justified? Why or why not? Should punitive damages have been assessed?

$\mathcal{T}$orts Associated with Contracts

The recovery of breach of contract is usually limited to contract damages. However, a party who can prove a contract-related *tort* may also recover *tort damages*. Tort damages include compensation for personal injury, pain and suffering, emotional distress, and possibly punitive damages. The major torts associated with contracts are (1) *intentional interference with contractual relations* and (2) *breach of the implied covenant of good faith and fair dealing*.

Intentional Interference with Contractual Relations

A party to a contract may sue any third person who intentionally interferes with the contract and causes that party injury. This tort, which is known as the tort of **intentional interference with contractual relations**, usually arises when a third party induces a contracting party to breach the contract with another party. The following elements must be shown:

1. A valid, enforceable contract between the contracting parties.
2. Third-party knowledge of this contract.
3. Third-party inducement to breach the contract.

A third party can contract with the breaching party without becoming liable for this tort if a contracting party has already breached the contract. This is because the third party cannot be held to have induced a preexisting breach.

Contemporary Business Application _____

TEXACO V. PENNZOIL: THE MEANING OF A HANDSHAKE

There is substantial danger of being found liable for tortious conduct and being assessed punitive damages if one intentionally interferes with another's contract. Consider the celebrated case of *Texaco, Inc. v. Pennzoil Company* [729 S.W.2d 768 (Tex.App. 1987)].

The saga began in 1983, when Pennzoil tried to buy up 20 percent of Getty Oil's (Getty) outstanding stock for $100 per share. At that time, about 40 percent of Getty's outstanding stock was owned by the Sarah C. Getty Trust (Trust), 11.8 percent was owned by the J. Paul Getty Museum in Los Angeles (Museum), and the rest was held by other investors.

On January 1, 1984, the head of the Trust met with representatives of Pennzoil. Pennzoil decided to make a play for total control of Getty by offering investors a buyout price of $110 per share. The Trust accepted a resolution approving Pennzoil's offer on January 3, 1984. Two days later, Getty, Pennzoil, the Trust, and the Museum issued a joint press release announcing that the parties had "agreed in principle" to a merger of Getty with Pennzoil. The parties shook hands and hoisted glasses of champagne to toast the deal. No writing had yet been signed by the parties, however.

Forty-eight hours later, the party was over. Texaco, Inc. (Texaco), had been tipped that Getty was for sale. Representatives of Texaco met secretly with some trustees of the Trust and officials from the Museum about how Texaco could structure a takeover of Getty. A written deal was reached whereby Texaco would purchase shares held by the Museum and the Trust for $125 per share and thereby acquire more than 50 percent of Getty's outstanding shares in a $10-billion deal. Texaco completed its takeover of Getty.

Not surprisingly, Pennzoil was not pleased with Texaco's maneuver. On February 8, 1985, Pennzoil filed suit in Texas alleging that Texaco had tortiously interfered with its agreement with Getty. Pennzoil argued its handshake deal with Getty was a contract. It cited a Texas oil industry custom according to which handshakes were gentlemen's agreements that were to be honored. Texaco asserted that the argument wouldn't get Pennzoil to first base because the contract had to be formalized in writing to be enforceable.

Before the trial even began, Texaco accused Pennzoil's lawyer of impropriety for having given a $10,000 campaign contribution to the state court judge who was presiding in the case. Another Texas judge found no reason for the trial court judge to withdraw.

After a hard-fought trial, the jury held that the handshake between the Getty and Pennzoil people did count as a contract and that a definitive written agreement was unnecessary to seal the deal. After finding that such an agreement had indeed been reached, the jury moved on to the question of whether the tactics Texaco used to reach its takeover agreement were tortious. The jury found that Texaco had intentionally interfered with Pennzoil's agreement with Getty.

With the issue of liability resolved, the jury awarded a mind-boggling amount of money: $7.53 billion in actual damages. The jury heaped another $3 billion in punitive damages onto Pennzoil's award. This was the largest judgment in history. Texaco's appeals succeeded in getting the punitive damages reduced to $1 billion. Ultimately, to avoid the judgment, Texaco declared bankruptcy. Texaco emerged from bankruptcy one year later after the parties agreed to settle the entire matter for $3 billion. It is estimated that Pennzoil's lawyer, who had taken the case on contingency, earned a fee of approximately $600 million.

Breach of the Implied Covenant of Good Faith and Fair Dealing

Several states have held that a **covenant of good faith and fair dealing** is implied in certain types of contracts. Under this covenant, the parties to a contract not only are held to the express terms of the contract but also are required to act in "good faith" and deal fairly in all respects in obtaining the objective of the contract. A breach of this implied covenant is a tort for which tort damages are recoverable. This tort, which is sometimes referred to as the **tort of "bad faith,"** is an evolving area of the law.

covenant of good faith and fair dealing

Under this implied covenant, the parties to a contract not only are held to the express terms of the contract but also are required to act in "good faith" and deal fairly in all respects in obtaining the objective of the contract.

Punitive Damages

punitive damages
Damages that are awarded to
punish the defendant, to
deter the defendant from
similar conduct in the future,
and to set an example for
others.

Generally, **punitive damages** are not recoverable for breach of contract. They are recoverable, however, for certain *tortious* conduct that may be associated with the nonperformance of a contract. This includes fraud, intentional conduct, or other egregious conduct. Punitive damages are in addition to actual damages and may be kept by the plaintiff. Punitive damages are awarded to punish the defendant, to deter the defendant from similar conduct in the future, and to set an example for others.

The court found a bad faith tort in the following case and awarded punitive damages.

Gourley v. State Farm Mutual Automobile Insurance Co.
227 Cal.App.3d 1099, 265 Cal.Rptr. 634 (1990)
California Court of Appeals

CASE 16.4

FACTS

In late 1981, Julie Gourley was a passenger in an automobile that was struck by an out-of-control vehicle driven by an uninsured drunk driver. Gourley, who was not wearing a seat belt at the time of the accident, suffered a fractured right shoulder when she struck some portion of her vehicle's interior. Gourley made a claim under the uninsured motorist coverage in her automobile policy with State Farm Mutual Automobile Insurance Company (State Farm). Medical evidence showed that Gourley had some permanent disability and a limited range of motion, suffered residual pain, and might require surgery in the future. She demanded the policy limit of $100,000. In September 1982, State Farm's attorney, Barry Allen, advised Gourley that State Farm would contest the proximate cause of the injuries based upon Gourley's failure to wear her seat belt. Evidence showed that under California law the seat belt issue was not a defense. State Farm offered a settlement of $20,000. Gourley refused it. When Gourley reduced her demand to $60,000, State Farm responded with a counteroffer of $25,000. Because the parties could not reach a settlement, the case went to arbitration. In October 1984, the arbitrator awarded Gourley $88,137, which State Farm promptly paid. Gourley sued State Farm for breach of the implied covenant of good faith and fair dealing in handling the claim and sought actual damages for emotional distress and punitive damages. The jury awarded her $15,765 in actual damages and $1,576,000 in punitive damages. State Farm appealed.

ISSUE

Did State Farm's conduct amount to a bad faith tort for which punitive damages could be awarded?

IN THE LANGUAGE OF THE COURT

Wallin, Justice   There is an implied covenant in every insurance contract that the insurer will do nothing to impair the insured's right to receive the benefit of the contractual bargain— that the insurer will promptly pay to the insured all sums due

under the contract. A major motivation for the purchase of insurance is the peace of mind that claims will be paid promptly. When an insurer unreasonably refuses to pay benefits due, it frustrates that motivation and a cause of action in tort arises. Withholding benefits is unreasonable if it is without proper cause. In determining proper cause, the interests of the insured must be given at least as much consideration as those of the insurer.

The jury could reasonably find "intentional" bad faith. The testimony of the expert witness and the arbitrator's award provided ample basis to conclude State Farm intentionally made settlement offers that it knew were inadequate. Although there was conflicting evidence, Gourley presented substantial evidence that State Farm adopted a "stonewall" or "see-you-in-court" attitude as exhibited by grossly insufficient offers to settle. The evidence was sufficient to support the jury's finding of bad faith. To support an award of punitive damages, the plaintiff must show "oppression, fraud, or malice." There was ample evidence to support an award of punitive damages. While there is always some concern that plaintiffs not receive a windfall as a result of punitive damages, their major purpose remains punishment and deterrence.

DECISION AND REMEDY

The appellate court held that State Farm's actions in not settling the claim under the policy limits by asserting an illegal defense (failure of Gourley to wear a seat belt) constituted bad faith. Affirmed.

Case Questions

Critical Legal Thinking   Should the law recognize the doctrine of bad faith tort? Why or why not?

Ethics   Does an insurer act unethically whenever it refuses to settle a claim under the policy limits? Do you think State Farm acted unethically in this case?

Business Application   What effect will the recognition of bad faith torts associated with contracts have on businesses such as insurance companies? Explain.

International Perspective

THE HINDU LAW SYSTEM

Over 20 percent of the world's population is Hindu. Most live in India, where they make up 80 percent of the population. Others live in Burma, Kenya, Malaysia, Pakistan, Singapore, Tanzania, and Uganda. *Hindu law* is a religious law. As such, individual Hindus apply this law to themselves regardless of their nationality or place of domicile.

Classical Hindu law rests neither on civil codes nor on court decisions, but on the works of private scholars that were passed along for centuries by oral tradition and eventually were recorded in the *smitris* (law books). Hindu law—called *dharmasastra* in Sanskrit, that is, the doctrine of proper behavior—is linked to the divine revelation of Veda (the holy collection of Indian religious songs, prayers, hymns, and sayings written between 2000 and 1000 B.C.). Most Hindu law is concerned with family matters and the law of succession.

After India became a British colony, British judges applied a combination of Hindu law and common law in solving cases. This Anglo–Hindu law, as it was called, was ousted once India gained its independence. In the mid-1950s, India codified Hindu law by enacting the Hindu Marriage Act, the Hindu Minority and Guardianship Act, the Hindu Succession Act, and the Hindu Adoptions and Maintenance Act. Outside of India, Anglo–Hindu law applies in most other countries populated by Hindus.

Working the Web

Heiros Gamos—The Comprehensive Legal Site Heiros Gamos contains links to 12 directories, 200 practice areas, 400 discussion groups, current news (in audio if you have the right computer equipment), and many more research tools.

Visit at **www.hg.org**

Duhaime's Canadian Contract Law Centre This site contains a general summary of the common law and equity principles on contract law in Canada.

Visit at **www.duhaime.org/ca-conl.htm**

Professor Ray August's home page Professor August has written *International Business Law, 2d ed.* and *Public International Law*, both published by Prentice Hall. His home page contains a student guide to international business law and an international law dictionary, as well as general reference materials and other useful links.

Visit at **www.august1.com**

CYBER EXERCISES

1. Using the Hieros Gamos site, can you find a treaty called the Convention on the Law Applicable to Contract Obligations?

2. Using the Hieros Gamos site, find the full text of NAFTA.

3. If your computer system is powerful enough and has sound capabilities, use the Heiros Gamos site to find audio of *Preparing Your Clients to Commence Business Operations in the United States*. Click on the audio icon to hear the tape.

4. Using the Duhaime's Canadian Contract Law Centre site, find information about contracts "under seal."

Cases and Exercises

Critical Legal Thinking Cases

16.1. Louis Haeuser, who owned several small warehouses, contracted with Wallace C. Drennen, Inc. (Drennen), to construct a road to the warehouses. The contract price was $42,324. After Drennen completed the work, some cracks appeared in the road, causing improper drainage. In addition, "bird baths" appeared in the road, which accumulated water. When Haeuser refused to pay, Drennen sued to recover the full contract price. Haeuser filed a cross complaint to recover the cost of repairing the road. Who wins? [*Wallace C. Drennen, Inc. v. Haeuser*, 402 So.2d 771 (La.App. 1979)]

16.2. In September 1976, Muhammad Ali (Ali) successfully defended his heavyweight boxing championship of the world by defeating Ken Norton. Shortly after the fight, Ali held a press conference and, as he had done on several occasions before, announced his retirement from boxing. At that time Ali had beaten every challenger except Duane Bobick, whom he had not yet fought. In November 1976, Madison Square Garden Boxing, Inc. (MSGB), a fight promoter, offered Ali $2.5 million if he would fight Bobick. Ali agreed, stating, "We are back in business again." MSGB and Ali signed a Fighters' Agreement and MSGB paid Ali $125,000 advance payment. The fight was to take place in Madison Square Garden on a date in February 1977. On November 30, 1976, Ali told MSGB that he was retiring from boxing and would not fight Bobick in February. Must MSGB wait until the date performance is due to sue Ali for breach of contract? [*Madison Square Garden Boxing, Inc. v. Muhammad Ali*, 430 F.Supp. 679 (N.D.Ill. 1977)]

16.3. In 1978, Hawaiian Telephone Company (Hawaiian Telephone) entered into a contract with Microform Data Systems, Inc. (Microform), for Microform to provide a computerized assistance system that would handle 15,000 calls per hour with a one-second response time and with a "nonstop" feature to allow automatic recovery from any component failure. The contract called for installation of the host computer no later than mid-February 1979. Microform was not able to meet the initial installation date, and at that time it was determined that Microform was at least nine months away from providing a system that met contract specifications. Hawaiian Telephone canceled the contract and sued Microform for damages. Did Microform materially breach the contract to allow recovery of damages? [*Hawaiian Telephone Co. v. Microform Data Systems, Inc.*, 829 F.2d 919 (9th Cir. 1987)]

16.4. Raquel Welch was a movie actress who appeared in about 30 films between 1965 and 1980. She was considered a sex symbol, and her only serious dramatic role was a Roller Derby queen in *Kansas City Bomber*. About 1980, Michael Phillips and David Ward developed a film package based on the John Steinbeck novella *Cannery Row*. In early 1981, Metro-Goldwyn-Mayer Film Co. (MGM) accepted to produce the project and entered into a contract with Welch to play the leading female character, a prostitute named Suzy. At 40 years old, Welch relished the chance to direct her career toward more serious roles. Welch was to receive $250,000 from MGM, with payment being divided into weekly increments during filming. Filming began on December 1, 1980. On December 22, 1980, MGM fired Welch and replaced her with another actress, Debra Winger. Welch sued MGM to recover the balance of $194,444 that remained unpaid under the contract. Who wins? [*Welch v. Metro-Goldwyn-Mayer Film Co.*, 207 Cal.App.3d 164, 254 Cal.Rptr. 645 (Cal.App. 1989)]

16.5. On August 28, 1979, Ptarmigan Investment Company (Ptarmigan), a partnership, entered into a contract with Gundersons, Inc. (Gundersons), a South Dakota corporation in the business of golf course construction. The contract provided that Gundersons would construct a golf course for Ptarmigan for a contract price of $1,294,129. Gundersons immediately started work and completed about one-third of the work by late November 1979, when bad weather forced cessation of most work. Ptarmigan paid Gundersons for the work to that date. In the spring of 1980, Ptarmigan ran out of funds and was unable to pay for the completion of the golf course. Gundersons sued Ptarmigan and its individual partners to recover the lost profits that it would have made on the remaining two-thirds of the contract. Can Gundersons recover these lost profits as damages? [*Gundersons, Inc. v. Ptarmigan Investment Company*, 678 P.2d 1061 (Colo.App. 1983)]

16.6. In December 1974, H.S. Perlin Company, Inc. (Perlin), and Morse Signal Devices of San Diego (Morse) entered into a contract whereby Morse agreed to provide burglar and fire alarm service to Perlin's coin and stamp store. Perlin paid $50 per month for this service. The contract contained a liquidated damage clause limiting Morse's liability to $250 for any losses incurred by Perlin based on Morse's failure of service. During the evening of August 25, 1980, a burglary occurred at Perlin's store. Before entering the store, the burglars cut a telephone line that ran from the burglar system in Perlin's store to Morse's central location. When the line was cut, a signal indicated the interruption of service at Morse's central station. Inexplicably, Morse took no further steps to investigate the interruption of service at Perlin's store. The burglars stole stamps and coins with a wholesale value of $958,000, and Perlin did not have insurance against this loss. Perlin sued Morse to recover damages. Is the liquidated damage clause enforceable? [*H.S. Perlin Company, Inc. v. Morse Signal Devices of San Diego*, 209 Cal.App.3d 1289, 258 Cal.Rptr. 1 (Cal.App. 1989)]

16.7. United Mechanical Contractors, Inc. (UMC), an employer, agreed to provide a pension plan for its unionized workers. UMC was to make monthly payments into a pension fund administered by the Idaho Plumbers and Pipefitters Health and Welfare Fund (Fund). Payments were due by the fifteenth of the month. The contract between UMC and the Fund contained a liquidated damage clause that provided if payments due from UMC were received later than the twentieth of the month, liquidated damages of 20 percent of the required contribution would be assessed against UMC. In June 1985, the fund received UMC's payment on the twenty-fourth. The Fund sued UMC to recover $9,245.23 in liquidated damages. Is the liquidated damage clause enforceable? [*Idaho Plumbers and Pipefitters Health and Welfare Fund v. United Mechanical Contractors, Inc.*, 875 F.2d 212 (9th Cir. 1989)]

16.8. To boost his career as an actor, John Ericson agreed with Playgirl, Inc. (Playgirl), that it could publish a picture of him posing naked at Lion Country Safari as the centerfold of the January 1974 issue of *Playgirl* magazine without compensation. The magazine was published with Ericson as the centerfold, but no immediate career boost to Ericson resulted from the publication. In April 1974, Playgirl wished to use Ericson's photograph in its annual edition entitled *Best of Playgirl*. Playgirl and Ericson entered into a contract whereby Ericson's picture was to occupy a quarter of the front cover of the annual edition. Due to an editorial mix-up, Ericson's picture did not appear on the cover of the *Best of Playgirl*. Ericson sued Playgirl, seeking damages for breach of contract. How much damages should Ericson recover for Playgirl's breach of contract? [*Ericson v. Playgirl, Inc.*, 73 Cal.App.3d 850, 140 Cal.Rptr. 921 (Cal.App. 1977)]

16.9. Liz Claiborne, Inc. (Claiborne), is a large maker of women's better sportswear in the United States and a well-known name in fashion, with sales of over $1 billion a year. Claiborne distributes its products through 9,000 retail outlets in the United States. Avon Products, Inc. (Avon), is a major producer of fragrances, toiletries, and cosmetics, with annual sales of more than $3 billion a year. Claiborne, who desired to promote its well-known name on perfumes and cosmetics, entered into a joint venture with Avon whereby Claiborne would make available its names, trademarks, and marketing experience, and Avon would engage in the procurement and manufacture of the fragrances, toiletries, and cosmetics. The parties would equally share the financial requirements of the joint venture. In 1986, its first year of operation, the joint venture had sales of more than $16 million. In the second year, sales increased to $26 million, making it one of the fastest-growing fragrance and cosmetic lines in the country. In 1987, Avon sought to "uncouple" the joint venture. Avon thereafter refused to procure and manufacture the line of fragrances and cosmetics for the joint venture. When Claiborne could not obtain the necessary fragrances and cosmetics from any other source for the fall/Christmas season, Claiborne sued Avon for breach of contract, seeking specific performance of the contract by Avon. Is specific performance an appropriate remedy in this case? [*Liz Claiborne, Inc. v. Avon Products, Inc.*, 530 N.Y.S.2d 425, 141 A.D.2d 329 (N.Y.Sup.App. 1988)]

16.10. Wood Dimension, Inc. (Wood), manufactured stereo speakers for resale to other companies. Fisher Corporation (Fisher), a major customer, accounted for 30 to 50 percent of Wood's business. In early 1982, Fisher stopped buying from Wood. To regain Fisher's business, the president of Wood solicited the help of L. Dale Watson, who had known the vice president of Fisher for many years. Wood agreed to pay Watson 5 percent of all Fisher's orders if he succeeded in persuading Fisher to buy at Wood again. They shook hands to seal the agreement. Due to Watson's efforts, Fisher again became a customer of Wood's. In May 1984, Wood terminated Watson's position. Between that time and July 1985, Fisher placed orders of almost $10 million with Wood. Although the oral contract between Wood and Watson was terminable at will, Watson sued Wood to recover commissions on Fisher's orders that were placed after he was discharged. Can Watson recover these damages under the theory of quasi-contract? [*Watson v. Wood Dimension, Inc.*, 209 Cal.App.3d 1359, 257 Cal.Rptr. 816 (Cal.App. 1989)]

16.11. In 1982, Anita Baker, a then-unknown singer, signed a multiyear recording contract with Beverly Glen Music, Inc. (Beverly Glen). Baker recorded a record album for Beverly Glen that was moderately successful. After having some difficulties with Beverly Glen, Baker was offered a considerably more lucrative contract by Warner Communications, Inc. (Warner). Baker accepted the Warner offer and informed Beverly Glen that she would not complete her contract because she had entered into an agreement with Warner.

Beverly Glen sued Baker and Warner and sought an injunction to prevent Baker from performing as a singer for Warner. Is an injunction an appropriate remedy in this case? [*Beverly Glen Music, Inc. v. Warner Communications, Inc.*, 178 Cal.App.3rd 1142, 224 Cal.Rpt. 260 (Cal.App. 1986)]

16.12. In 1963, Pacific Gas and Electric Company (PG & E) entered into a contract with Placer County Water Agency (Agency) to purchase hydroelectric power generated by Agency's Middle Fork American River Project. The contract was not terminable until 2013. As energy prices rose during the 1970s, the contract became extremely valuable to PG & E. The price PG & E paid for energy under the contract was much lower than the cost of energy from other sources. In 1982, Bear Stearns & Company (Bear Stearns), an investment bank and securities underwriting firm, learned of Agency's power contract with PG & E. Bear Stearns offered to assist Agency in an effort to terminate the power contract with PG & E in exchange for a share of Agency's subsequent profits and the right to underwrite any new securities issued by Agency. Bear Stearns also agreed to pay the legal fees incurred by Agency in litigation concerning their attempt to get out of the PG & E contract. Under what legal theory can PG & E sue Bear Stearns? [*Pacific Gas and Electric Company v. Bear Stearns & Company*, 50 Cal.3d 1118, 270 Cal.Rptr. 1 (Cal.App. 1990)]

ETHICS CASES

16.13. The Congress-Kenilworth Corporation (Congress) hired W. E. Erickson Construction, Inc. (Erickson), a general contractor, to construct "Thunder Mountain Rapids," a concrete water slide in Creswood, Illinois. The total cost of the slide was not to exceed $535,000. Construction of the water slide began on April 15, 1981, and the slide was completed on July 3, 1981, the day before the projected opening date. After construction, cracks appeared in the concrete flumes of the slide. The cracks did not interfere with the operation of the slide, but the defects did need to be repaired at a substantial cost. Erickson billed Congress $550,000 for full performance of the contract. At that point, Congress had paid Erickson $150,000. When Congress refused to pay Erickson for full performance, Erickson sued Congress for breach of contract to recover the full contract price. The trial court awarded Erickson $352,000, less the $150,000 already paid by Congress, for a judgment of $202,000. The appellate court affirmed. An appeal was taken. Was there substantial performance? Do you think either party acted unethically in this case? [*W. E. Erickson Construction, Inc. v. Congress-Kenilworth Corp.*, 503 N.E.2d 233 (IL 1986)]

16.14. Walgreen Company (Walgreen) has operated a pharmacy in the Southgate Mall in Milwaukee since 1951, when the mall opened. Its current lease, signed in 1971 and carrying a 30-year term, contains an exclusivity clause in which the landlord, Sara Creek Property Company (Sara Creek), promises not to lease space in the mall to anyone else who wants to operate a pharmacy or a store containing a pharmacy. In 1990, after its anchor tenant went broke, Sara Creek informed Walgreen that it intended to lease the anchor tenant space to Phar-Mor Corporation (Phar-Mor). Phar-Mor, a "deep discount" chain, would occupy 100,000 square feet, of which 12,000 square feet would be occupied by a pharmacy the same size as Walgreen's. The entrances to the two stores would be within a few hundred feet of each other. Walgreen sued Sara Creek for breach of contract and sought a permanent injunction against Sara Creek's leasing the anchor premises to Phar-Mor. Do the facts of this case justify the issuance of a permanent injunction? Did Sara Creek act ethically in not living up to the contract? [*Walgreen Co. v. Sara Creek Property Co.*, 966 F.2d 273 (7th Cir. 1992)]

16.15. Rosina Crisci owned an apartment building in which Mrs. DiMare was a tenant. One day while DiMare was descending a wooden staircase on the outside of the apartment building, she fell through the staircase and was left hanging 15 feet above the ground until she was saved. Crisci had a $10,000 liability insurance policy on the building from the Security Insurance Company of New Haven, Connecticut (Security). DiMare sued Crisci and Security for $400,000 for physical injuries and psychosis suffered from the fall. Prior to trial, DiMare agreed to take $10,000 in settlement of the case. Security refused this settlement offer. DiMare reduced her settlement offer to $9,000, of which Crisci offered to pay $2,500. Security again refused to settle the case. The case proceeded to trial and the jury awarded DiMare and her husband $110,000. Security paid $10,000 pursuant to the insurance contract, and Crisci had to pay the difference. Crisci, a widow of 70 years of age, had to sell her assets, became dependent on her relatives, declined in physical health, and suffered from hysteria and suicide attempts. Crisci sued Security for tort damages for breach of the implied covenant of good faith and fair dealing. Did Security act in bad faith? [*Crisci v. Security Insurance Company of New Haven, Connecticut*, 426 P.2d 173, 66 Cal.App.2d 425, 58 Cal.Rptr. 13 (Cal.App. 1967)]

Critical Legal Thinking Writing Assignment

Read Case A.16 in the Case Appendix [*E. B. Harvey & Company, Inc. v. Protective Systems, Inc.*]. This case is excerpted from the appellate court opinion. Review and brief the case. In your brief, be sure to answer the following questions.

1. What were Protective System's duties under the contract?

2. What amount of damages was Protective Systems liable for under the express terms of the contract?

3. Was Protective Systems negligent in this case?

4. What policy considerations did the court cite in upholding the liquidated damage clause?

Notes

1. Restatement (Second) of Contracts, § 235(2).
2. Restatement (Second) of Contracts, § 241.
3. Restatement (Second) of Contracts, § 253; UCC § 2-610.
4. UCC §§ 2-708 and 2-713.
5. Restatement (Second) of Contracts, § 356(1).
6. Restatement (Second) of Contracts, § 370.
7. Restatement (Second) of Contracts, § 359.

Intellectual Property and Internet Law

In all well-tempered governments there is nothing which should be more jealously maintained than the spirit of obedience to law, more especially in small matters; for transgression creeps in unperceived and at last ruins the state, just as the constant recurrence of small expenses in time eat up a fortune.

ARISTOTLE *Politics, Bk. 5, Ch. 8*
(Jowett trans.)

Chapter Objectives

After studying this chapter, you should be able to

1. Define *unfair competition* and describe the business tort misappropriating trade secrets.
2. Describe the criminal conduct that violates the Economic Espionage Act.
3. Describe how an invention can be patented under federal patent laws and the penalties for patent infringement.
4. Describe how cyber business plans qualify for patent protection.
5. List the writings that can be copyrighted and describe the penalties for copyright infringement.
6. Describe the legal rights that computer and software designers have in their works.
7. Describe the changes made in copyright law by the Digital Millennium Copyright Act and the Sony Bono Copyright Term Extension Act.
8. Define *trademarks* and *service marks*, and describe the penalties for trademark infringement.
9. Describe how the Federal Dilution Act restricts the use of Internet domain names.
10. Describe international protection of intellectual property rights.

Chapter Contents

The American economy is based on a principle of freedom of competition under which persons and businesses compete openly to produce and distribute goods and services. This system gives entrepreneurs the opportunity to start new businesses and ensures that consumers have a range of products and services to choose from. There are limits on how the progress and efficiency engendered by the system are achieved, however.

Reputation and goodwill might be the most important assets a business or individual has. The law protects a business's reputation. A business also has a right to protect its trade secrets. If any of these rights are violated, the injured business or individual can recover damages from the responsible party. A violation of these rights is called *unfair competition*.

In addition, federal law provides certain protections for **intellectual property rights**, such as patents, copyrights, and trademarks. The holders of these rights are given exclusive control over their use. In addition, businesses and individuals may register *domain names* to use on the Internet. Anyone who infringes on these rights may be stopped from doing so and is liable for damages. Computers and computer software are accorded special protection from infringement.

This chapter discusses unfair competition, infringement of intellectual property rights, domain names, and computer law.

> **intellectual property rights**
> **Intellectual property rights, such as patents, copyrights, trademarks, trade secrets, trade names, and domain names are very valuable business assets. Federal and state laws protect intellectual property rights from misappropriation and infringement.**

$\mathscr{U}$NFAIR COMPETITION

In most situations, competitors are free to compete vigorously, even if that means that someone is driven out of business or sustains severe losses. However, competitors may not engage in illegal **unfair competition** or **predatory practices**. The most common forms of unfair competition are discussed in the paragraphs that follow.

> **unfair competition**
> **Competition that violates the law.**

Palming Off

The common law tort of **palming off** is one of the oldest forms of unfair competition. This tort usually occurs when a small company tries to "palm off" its products as those of a larger rival. For example, if a company implied that it was affiliated with International Business Machines (IBM) by selling computers under the IBM label, it would be liable for the business tort of palming off.

> **palming off**
> **Unfair competition that occurs when a company tries to pass off one of its products as that of a rival.**

To prove the tort of palming off, the plaintiff must prove that (1) the defendant used the plaintiff's logo, symbol, mark, and so on, and that (2) there is a likelihood of confusion as to the source of the product. Actual consumer confusion need not be shown. The key element is whether consumers are likely to be confused as to the origin of the copied product. This doctrine is not used often because many products and services are now patented, copyrighted, or trademarked, and the plaintiff can bring an infringement lawsuit under federal law.

Disparagement

Business firms rely on their reputation and the quality of their products and services to attract and keep customers. That is why state unfair competition laws protect businesses from disparaging statements made by competitors or others. A disparaging statement is an untrue statement made by one person or business about the products, services, property, or reputation of another business.

To prove **disparagement**, which is also called **product disparagement, trade libel,** or **slander of title**, the plaintiff must show that the defendant (1) made an untrue statement about the plaintiff's products, services, property, or business reputation, (2) published this untrue statement to a third party, (3) knew the statement was not true, and (4) made the statement maliciously (i.e., with intent to injure the plaintiff).

> **product disparagement**
> **False statements about a competitor's products, services, property, or business reputation.**

Section 43(a) of the Lanham Act A federal statute that prohibits false and misleading advertising is **Section 43(a) of the Lanham Act**.[1] Under this act, private parties may obtain injunctions and recover damages from competitors who make disparaging or false or misleading statements about the plaintiff's products. For example, companies often engage in comparative advertising in which they compare the qualities of their products to those of competitors. Truthful comparative advertising is lawful. However, untruthful comparative advertising constitutes disparagement of product and false and misleading advertising in violation of Section 43(a) of the Lanham Act.

Misappropriation of Trade Secrets

Many businesses are successful because their **trade secrets** set them apart from their competitors. Trade secrets may be product formulas, patterns, designs, compilations of data, customer lists, or other business secrets. Many trade secrets either do not qualify to be— or simply are not—patented, copyrighted, or trademarked. Many states have adopted the **Uniform Trade Secrets Act** to give statutory protection to trade secrets.

State unfair competition laws allow the owner of a trade secret to bring a lawsuit for *misappropriation* against anyone who steals a trade secret. To be actionable, the defendant (often an employee of the owner or a competitor) must have obtained the trade secret through unlawful means such as theft, bribery, or industrial espionage. No tort has occurred if there is no misappropriation. For example, a competitor can lawfully discover a trade secret by performing reverse engineering (i.e., taking apart and examining a rival's product).

The owner of a trade secret is obliged to take all reasonable precautions to prevent those secrets from being discovered by others. Such precautions include fencing in buildings, placing locks on doors, hiring security guards, and the like. If the owner fails to take such actions, the secret is no longer subject to protection under state unfair competition laws.

Generally, a successful plaintiff in a trade secret action can (1) recover the profits made by the offender from the use of the trade secret, (2) recover for damages, and (3) obtain an injunction prohibiting the offender from divulging or using the trade secret.

Contemporary Business Application

THE ECONOMIC ESPIONAGE ACT

Although the stealing of trade secrets exposes the offender to a civil lawsuit by the injured party to recover economic damages, the offender seldom faced criminal charges except under a few state laws. All that changed with the enactment by Congress of the federal **Economic Espionage Act of 1996** [18 U.S.C. 1831–1839]. This act makes it a federal crime to steal another's trade secrets. Previously, no federal statute directly addressed economic espionage and the stealing of trade secrets.

Under the Espionage Act, it is a federal crime for any person to convert a trade secret to his or her benefit or for the benefit of others, knowing or intending that the act would cause injury to the owner of the trade secret. The definition of *trade secret* under the Espionage Act is very broad, and parallels the definition used under the civil laws

of misappropriating a trade secret. Under the Espionage Act, a trade secret includes any economic, business, financial, technical, scientific, or engineering information, including processes, software programs, and codes.

One of the major reasons for the passage of the Espionage Act was to address the ease of stealing trade secrets through computer espionage and using the Internet. For example, hundreds of pages of confidential information can be downloaded onto a small computer diskette, placed in a pocket, and taken from the legal owner. In addition, computer hackers can crack into a company's computers and steal customer lists, databases, formulas, and other trade secrets. The Espionage Act adds a very important weapon to address and penalize computer and Internet espionage.

e·biz

The Espionage Act provides for severe criminal penalties. An organization can be fined up to $5 million per criminal act and $10 million if the criminal act was committed to benefit a foreign government. The act imposes prison terms on individuals of up to 15 years per criminal violation, which can be increased to 25 years per violation if the criminal act was done with the intent to benefit a foreign government. By adding criminal penalties, the Espionage Act adds another weapon to safeguard trade secrets and intellectual property in this country.

INTELLECTUAL PROPERTY

Intellectual property such as inventions, writings, trademarks, and the like, are often a business's most valuable asset. A comprehensive federal statutory scheme protects the following three types of intellectual property: (1) *patents*, (2) *copyrights*, and (3) *trademarks* and other marks. They are discussed in the paragraphs that follow.

intellectual property
Objects such as inventions, writings, trademarks, and so on, which are often a business's most valuable asset.

International Perspective

INTERNATIONAL PROTECTION OF INTELLECTUAL PROPERTY RIGHTS

For centuries, national patent, copyright, and trademark laws defined the rights of inventors, authors, and businesses. These laws offered protection within a country's borders, but not in other countries. Beginning in the late 1800s, countries began entering into treaties and conventions with other countries that provided international protection of intellectual property rights. The major international agreements protecting intellectual property rights are discussed below.

The major convention that provides international protection to patents is the **1883 Convention of the Union of Paris (Paris Convention)**. The Convention's major purpose is to allow the nationals of each member country to file for patents in all other member nations. The Convention does not, however, eliminate the need to file separate patent applications in each member nation in which the applicant desires protection. The Convention gives an applicant who has filed for a patent in one member country 12 months to submit applications in other member countries.

The **Paris Convention** also allows nationals of each member nation to file for trademarks and service marks in all other member nations on an individual, nondiscriminatory basis, even if the applicant does not own the mark in the country of origin. The applicant has six months after his or her original registration to submit applications to other member countries.

The major copyright treaty is the **Berne Convention of 1886**, as revised, to which the United States became a signatory in 1989. The Convention provides for the recognition of a copyright in all member nations. The Convention establishes a minimum copyright term of the life of the author plus 50 years and eliminated the requirement to put a © on copyrighted works.

In 1997, the World Intellectual Property Organization (WIPO), an agency of the United Nations, promulgated two new "**Internet Treaties**". These treaties recognized the importance of new digital technologies and the Internet. The first treaty, the WIPO **Copyright Treaty**, extends copyright protection to computer programs and data compilations and grants copyright holders the exclusive right to make their works available on the Internet as well as by any other wire or wireless means. The second treaty, the WIPO **Phonogram Treaty**, gives performers and producers the exclusive right to broadcast, reproduce, and distribute copies of their performances by any means, including video recording, digital sound, or encryption signal.

e-biz

PATENTS

Pursuant to the express authority granted in the U.S. Constitution,[2] Congress enacted the **Federal Patent Statute of 1952**.[3] This law is intended to provide an incentive for inventors to invent and make their inventions public and to protect patented inventions from infringement. Federal patent law is exclusive; there are no state patent laws. The *United*

Federal Patent Statute of 1952
Federal statute that establishes the requirements for obtaining a patent and protects patented inventions from infringement.

States Court of Appeals for the Federal Circuit in Washington, DC, was created in 1982 to hear patent appeals. The court was established to promote uniformity in patent law.

International Perspective

CHANGES IN PATENT LAW MANDATED BY GATT

In 1994, the **General Agreement on Tariffs and Trade (GATT)** established the **World Trade Organization (WTO)**, an international trade organization of which the United States is a member. GATT's intellectual property provisions, and implementing legislation passed by Congress, made the following important changes in U.S. patent law:

1. Patents are valid for *20 years*, instead of the previous term of 17 years.

2. The patent term begins to run from the date the patent application is *filed* instead of when the patent is issued as was previously the case.

These changes, which became effective June 8, 1995, brought the U.S. patent system in harmony with the majority of other developed nations. The United States still follows the first to invent rule rather than the first to file rule followed by some other countries.

The patent system added the fuel of interest to the fire of genius.

Abraham Lincoln
Lectures on Discoveries,
Inventions, and Improvements
(1859)

Business Brief

According to International Trade Commission estimates, American companies lose $40 billion to $50 billion annually—or 30 to 40 percent of our trade deficit—because their technology and intellectual property are misappropriated by foreign manufacturers.

Patenting an Invention

To be patented, the invention must be *novel, useful,* and *nonobvious.* In addition, only certain subject matters can be patented. Patentable subject matter includes (1) machines, (2) processes, (3) compositions of matter, (4) improvements to existing machines, processes, or compositions of matter, (5) designs for an article of manufacture, (6) asexually reproduced plants, and (7) living material invented by a person.[4] Abstractions and scientific principle cannot be patented unless they are part of the tangible environment. For example, Einstein's Theory of Relativity ($E=MC^2$) cannot be patented.

Patent applicants must file a *patent application* containing a written description of the invention with the **United States Patent and Trademark Office** in Washington, DC. If a patent is granted, the invention is assigned a patent number. Patent holders usually affix the word *Patent* or *Pat.* and the patent number to the patented article. If a patent application is filed but a patent has not yet been issued, the applicant usually places the words *patent pending* on the article. Any party can challenge either the issuance of a patent or the validity of an existing patent.

In the following case, the court had to decide whether the subject matter was patentable.

Lamb-Weston, Inc. v. McCain Foods, Ltd.
78 F.3d 540 (1996)
United States Court of Appeals, Federal Circuit

CASE 17.1

FACTS
Plaintiff Lamb-Weston, Inc., is a food-processing company that sells frozen potato products. The defendant, McCain Foods, Ltd., competes with Lamb-Weston in this industry. Both Lamb-Weston and McCain Foods make partially fried

(parfried) and frozen potato products that are distributed to grocery stores, restaurants, and other users.

In October 1979, Mr. Matsler offered to sell the waffle-slicing machine he had invented to Lamb-Weston, but the company turned it down. In February 1980, Lamb-Weston examined a waffle-fry cutting machine invented by Mr. Jayne. Again Lamb-Weston found the machine unacceptable. Eventually, Lamb-Weston developed its own "waffle fry," a potato slice somewhere in size between a potato chip and a french fry with a waffle shape. In 1983, Lamb-Weston began selling waffle fries under the name "CrissCut." Lamb-Weston filed for a patent on its process for making these frozen potato slices. Its claim in the patent application read:

A parfried potato product, suitable for reconstitution by cooking, comprising: a frozen, sliced potato section having a substantially ellipsoidal shape and a variable thickness, including a peak to peak thickness within the range of about 4/16 to 10/16 inch; the section including opposed first and second sides, each side having longitudinal ridges and grooves therebetween, the ridges and grooves of the first side extending angularly to the ridges and grooves of the second side; the grooves of the first and second sides having a depth sufficient to intersect one another to form a grid of openings in the potato section; the section, before reconstitution, having an oil content of about 6–20 percent, by weight, and a solids content of about 32–40 percent by weight; whereby the product, upon reconstitution by cooking, is characterized by very thin, crisp portions of locally increased oil flavor adjacent the openings, relatively thick portions defined by intersecting ridges having an internal mealy texture and strong potato flavor similar to thick-cut french fried potato strips, and portions of intermediate thickness whose characteristics are similar to french fried shoe string potato strips.

The Patent Board granted the patent to Lamb-Weston. In 1985, McCain Foods began making and selling a competing parfried waffle fry. Lamb-Weston sued McCain Foods for patent infringement. McCain Foods counterclaimed for a declaratory judgment to have Lamb-Weston's patent declared invalid. The district court held that the patent was invalid and unenforceable. Lamb-Weston appealed.

ISSUE

Was Lamb-Weston's patent for the process of making frozen, partially fried lattice-shaped french fries called "waffle fries" a valid patent?

IN THE LANGUAGE OF THE COURT

Per Curiam *The ultimate determination of obviousness is a legal conclusion, resting on factual determinations. Ample prior art suggests a motivation to cook potato products of various shapes using a parfry process. The evidence of prior use and sale of waffle fries and parfried potato products provides sufficient motivation to combine the known waffle-cut shape and the parfry cooking method. This combination renders the '084 patent obvious. The prior art parfried potato products and the knowledge and use of waffle-cut potato products of sufficient thickness and shape suitable for parfrying provided the motivation to combine the waffle-cut shape with the parfry process. The prior art suggests the desirability and the obviousness of such a combination. The claims of the '084 patent are invalid as obvious.*

DECISION AND REMEDY

The court of appeals ruled that the process of making waffle fries was too obvious to be patentable. The court held that Lamb-Weston's patent was invalid. Affirmed.

Case Questions

Critical Legal Thinking What is the purpose of the federal government granting patents? What statutory requirements must be met for a patent to be granted?

Ethics Was there any unethical conduct by any of the parties in this case? Do you think Lamb-Weston knew its waffle fry process was unpatentable?

Business Application What were the financial consequences of the court's decision in this case? Who were the winners and who were the losers?

Contemporary Business Application

THE AMERICAN INVENTORS PROTECTION ACT OF 1999

In 1999, Congress enacted the **American Inventors Protection Act**. This statute, which was a watered-down version of the initial bill that was introduced, still made significant changes in federal patent law. The act reorganized the U.S. Patent and Trademark Office (PTO) and granted the PTO new regulatory powers. The act does the following:

- Establishes "Inventor's Rights" by giving the PTO power to regulate "invention promoters." This part of the statute addresses problems created by unscrupulous invention registration services that took advantage of individual inventors by charging substantial fees for marketing services that generally were unsuccessful. The act provides for penalties and fines for violations of Inventor's Rights.

(box continues)

- Permits an inventor to file a provisional application with the PTO pending the preparation and filing of a final and complete patent application. This part of the law grants "provisional rights" to an inventor for three months pending the filing of a final application.
- Requires the PTO to issue a patent within three years after the filing of a patent application unless the applicant engages in dilatory activities.
- Provides that non-patent holders may challenge a patent as overly broad by requesting a contested

reexamination of the patent application by the PTO. This provides that the reexamination will be within the confines of the PTO; the decision of the PTO can be appealed to the U.S. Court of Appeals for the Federal Circuit in Washington, D.C.

The new act also upgrades the PTO Commissioner to an Assistant Secretary of Commerce with authority to advise the U.S. government on intellectual policy.

Patent Infringement

patent infringement
Unauthorized use of another's patent. A patent holder may recover damages and other remedies against a patent infringer.

Patent holders own exclusive rights to use and exploit their patent. **Patent infringement** occurs when someone makes unauthorized use of another's patent. In a suit for patent infringement, a successful plaintiff can recover (1) money damages equal to a reasonable royalty rate on the sale of the infringed articles, (2) other damages caused by the infringement (such as loss of customers), (3) an order requiring the destruction of the infringing articles, and (4) an injunction preventing the infringer from such action in the future. The court has the discretion to award up to treble damages if the infringement was intentional.

Entrepreneur and the Law

INVENTOR WIPES FORD'S AND CHRYSLER'S WINDSHIELDS CLEAN

In 1967, Robert Kearns, a professor at Wayne State University in Detroit, Michigan, patented his design for the electronic intermittent windshield wiper for automobiles and other vehicles. He peddled his invention around to many automobile manufacturers but never reached a licensing deal with any of them. In 1969, automobile manufacturers began producing cars with Kearns's invention. Virtually all cars sold in the United States today now have these wipers as standard equipment.

Kearns filed patent infringement lawsuits against Ford in 1978 and Chrysler in 1982. He later filed patent infringement cases against virtually all automobile manufacturers. The Ford case went to trial first. Kearns sought $325 million in damages from Ford. Ford alleged that Kearns's patents were not valid because of obviousness and prior art. The jury disagreed with Ford and decided that Kearns's patents were valid. The jury ordered Ford to pay $5.2 million, plus interest. In 1990, Ford settled by paying Kearns $10.2 million and agreeing to drop all appeals. This represented 50¢ per Ford vehicle that used the wiper system.

Kearns sought $468 million in damages from Chrysler. In that case, Kearns fired his lawyers and represented himself. This was at least the fourth law firm hired and fired in the course of Kearns's patent infringement lawsuits. Kearns

won a second victory: In 1991, the jury found that Chrysler had infringed Kearns's patents and awarded him $11.3 million. The court denied Kearns injunctive relief because his 17-year patents had expired years ago. The court of appeals affirmed the judgment and the Supreme Court refused to hear Kearns's appeal. Kearns received over $21 million from Chrysler, which amounted to 90¢ for every vehicle sold by Chrysler with the wiper system.

In 1993 and 1994, courts dismissed Kearns's lawsuits against 23 automobile manufacturers, including General Motors, Porsche, Nissan, Toyota, Honda, and Rolls Royce, among others, because Kearns failed to comply with court orders to disclose documents relevant to the cases. The district court then ordered Kearns to pay his fired lawyers $6.4 million in contingency fees. Thus ended Kearns's over 30-year saga and legal battle with the automobile industry. In an interview Kearns stated, "The patent system is a fraud pure and simple."

1. Did the automobile manufacturers act unethically in these cases? Other than Ford and Chrysler, did the other auto manufacturers get off too easily?
2. Do you think Kearns could have won more money? Explain.

Contemporary Business Application

SAY CHEESE! CAMERA COMPANIES LOSE PATENT INFRINGEMENT CASE

U.S. companies often complain that they spend huge amounts of money on research and development only to find that foreign companies make profits by selling goods that contain the misappropriated technology. The following case demonstrates that the courts may be a good place to begin tackling this problem.

In the early 1970s, researchers at Honeywell, Inc., which is based in Minneapolis, invented autofocus technology for cameras. This technology, which uses computer chips to focus camera lenses automatically, takes over a task previously done manually by photographers. Between 1975 and 1977, Honeywell obtained four patents for the technology, but it left the camera business without ever using the technology. Instead, it tried to market the technology to other manufacturers, most of them in Japan.

The companies Honeywell approached chose not to purchase or license Honeywell's technology. Instead, they developed their own autofocus technology. One such company was Minolta, which introduced the Maxxum camera with autofocus technology in 1985. The Maxxum was a hit with consumers. It sent Minolta into its current position as the leading camera maker in the United States, with annual sales of more than $400 million and 30 percent of the market.

There was only one hitch: Honeywell thought Minolta had infringed on its patented autofocus technology. Honeywell sued Minolta, as well as 14 other camera makers from the Far East, alleging patent infringement.

In 1992, after a four-month trial, a federal jury of nine persons found that Minolta had infringed two of Honeywell's four patents. The jury ordered Minolta to pay Honeywell $96 million in back royalties. Within months, Minolta paid Honeywell $124 million in a settlement in which Honeywell agreed not to seek a ban on the sale of Minolta cameras in the United States. The two patents found to have been infringed expired in late 1992.

Since the jury verdict against Minolta was announced, 14 other camera makers have settled infringement suits with Honeywell. These companies include Canon, Nikon, Pentax, Olympus, Ricoh, Chinon, and Vivitar. The settlements put more than $300 million in Honeywell's coffer.

The Minolta decision and the other settlements should mean that foreign companies will be more apt to license technology from U.S. patent holders legally. Pirating the technology will not be as attractive an option as it once appeared.

Entrepreneur and the Law

PROTECTING A PATENT IS EXPENSIVE BUSINESS

Inventors spend years dreaming up new products and inventions, then file an application with the Patent and Trademark Office and wait to see if their patent is granted. The day the patent is issued is a cause for celebration, or is it? Ask Donald BonAsia. The young entrepreneur invented "forkchops"—two eating utensils with chopsticks on one end and a knife and fork on the other end. He spent two years and $7,500 to receive a patent on his invention.

But his worst fear happened. Other manufacturers began copying his invention and selling them without seeking BonAsia's permission or paying him a royalty fee. BonAsia contacted a patent lawyer and found out the following: The normal cost to pursue a patent infringement case through trial is $1.5 million, and $1 million if it

settles near trial. Attorneys typically want over $100,000 in retainer fees before filing a patent infringement case. BonAsia discovered he had a patent, but not enough money to protect it.

BonAsia's plight is typical for small-time inventors who are under the misconception that a patent gives the holder an exclusive right to make the item. Wrong: What a patent gives the holder is the right to defend the patent and try to stop others from making the patented article. BonAsia learned a valuable lesson: patent law is usually the playing field of big corporations that have deep pockets to protect their patents. It may be that small entrepreneurs have the same legal rights, it is just that as in many areas of the law, justice can only be obtained at a price.

Public Use Doctrine

public use doctrine

A doctrine that says a patent may not be granted if the invention was used by the public for more than one year prior to the filing of the patent application.

Under the **public use doctrine**, a patent may not be granted if the invention was used by the public for more than one year prior to the filing of the patent application. This doctrine forces inventors to file their patent applications at the proper time.

Consider This Example   Suppose Cindy Parsons invents a new invention on January 1. She allows the public to use this invention and does not file a patent application until February of the following year. The inventor has lost the right to patent her invention.

E-Commerce & Internet Law

CYBER BUSINESS PLANS ARE PATENTABLE

Federal patent law recognizes four categories of innovation: (1) machines, (2) articles of manufacture, (3) compositions, and (4) processes. For centuries most patents involved tangible inventions, such as the telephone and the light bulb. But the computer and Internet have changed the traditional view of what can be patented. Consider the case of *State Street Bank & Trust Co. v. Signature Financial Group, Inc.*, 149 F.3d 1368 (Fed.Cir. 1998).

Signature Financial Group, Inc. (Signature), filed for and was granted a patent for a computerized accounting system that determines share prices through a series of mathematical calculations and is then used to manage mutual funds [U.S. Patent No. 5,193,056]. State Street Bank, another financial institution that wanted to offer a similar mutual fund investment program to clients, sued to have Signature's patent declared invalid. Signature defended, arguing that its intangible financial business model was a "process" that was protected under federal patent law. The U.S. Court of Appeals, Federal Circuit, upheld the patent as a "practical application of a mathematical, algorithm, formula, or calculation, because it produces a useful, concrete and tangible result."

Taking the lead from the *State Street* case, many persons and businesses have filed for and received patents for business and financial models that are used over the Internet. Critics contend that Congress did not intend to grant patents for intangible processes when it enacted federal patent law. Business plan patent holders counter that the trend reflects a necessary evolution in patent law and claim that business plan patents are to the Internet Age what machine patents were to the Industrial Age. These proponents argue that critics had the same complaints when chemicals, polymers, and biotech patents were first granted. One thing is certain: The exponential growth in computer and Internet business plan patents will lead to an avalanche of patent litigation.

Copyright Revision Act of 1976

Federal statute that (1) establishes the requirements for obtaining a copyright and (2) protects copyrighted works from infringement.

Berne Convention

An international copyright treaty. The United States and many other nations are signatories to this treaty.

COPYRIGHTS

Congress enacted a federal copyright law pursuant to an express grant of authority in the U.S. Constitution.[5] This law protects the work of authors and other creative persons from the unauthorized use of their copyrighted materials and provides a financial incentive for authors to write, thereby increasing the number of creative works available in society. The **Copyright Revision Act of 1976** governs copyright law.[6] Effective March 1, 1989, the United States became a member of the **Berne Convention**, an international copyright treaty. Federal copyright law is exclusive; there are no state copyright laws.

Photographs, such as this one titled Colorful Dream, *no longer need the © to be placed on it to be copyrighted.*

International Perspective

BERNE CONVENTION ELIMINATES NEED FOR COPYRIGHT NOTICE

In 1989, the United States signed the Berne Convention. This international convention provides the copyright law that is now followed by most countries of the world. The convention made a major change in U.S. copyright law. Prior to 1989, to protect a copyright in a published work in the United States, the copyright holder had to place a copyright notice on the work that contained the following information: (1) the copyright holder's name, (2) a "(c)" or "©" or "Copyright" or "copr.," and (3) the year the material was copyrighted. Under the Berne Convention, however, notice is not required on works entering the public domain on or after March 1, 1989. Although notice is now permissive, it is recommended that notice be placed on copyrighted works to defeat a defendant's claim of innocent infringement.

Registration of Copyrights

Only *tangible writings*—that is, writings that can be physically seen—are subject to copyright registration and protection. The term *writing* has been broadly defined to include books, periodicals, and newspapers; lectures, sermons, and addresses; musical compositions; plays, motion pictures, radio and television productions; maps; works of art, including paintings, drawings, sculpture, jewelry, glassware, tapestry, and lithographs; architectural drawings and models; photographs, including prints, slides, and filmstrips; greeting cards and picture postcards; photoplays, including feature films, cartoons, newsreels, travelogues, and training films; and sound recordings published in the form of tapes, cassettes, compact discs, and phonograph albums.

To be protected under federal copyright law, the work must be the original work of the author. Published and unpublished works may be copyrighted and registered with the **United States Copyright Office** in Washington, DC. Registration is permissive and voluntary and can be effected at any time during the term of the copyright. Registration itself does not create the copyright.

Business Brief
The expression of an idea is copyrightable. The idea itself is not.

The law in respect to literature ought to remain upon the same footing as that which regards the profits of mechanical inventions and chemical discoveries.

William Wordsworth
Letter (1838)

Contemporary Business Application

A MICKEY MOUSE COPYRIGHT LAW

The Founding Fathers decided to provide copyright protection in the U.S. Constitution when they granted Congress authority to secure for "limited times" to authors the exclusive right to their writings. In 1790, copyright law guaranteed 14 years of protection with a 14-year renewal. The period of protection has been extended several times since, and in 1998 stood at the life of the author plus 50 years. A corporation-owned copyright was good for 75 years from the date of publication or 100 years from the date of creation, whichever was shorter.

After the copyright period runs out, the work enters the **public domain**, which means that anyone can publish the work without paying the prior copyright holder. Many small publishers and Internet sites were dedicated to publishing great works—and not-so-great works—once they entered the public domain. These publishers and Internet content providers waited anxiously as such popular works as A. A. Milne's *Winnie the Pooh*, Ernest Hemingway's *Three Stories and Ten Poems*, and the Walt Disney Company's first Mickey Mouse cartoon were set to enter the public domain. Cartoons starring such Disney characters as Donald Duck and Goofy would follow shortly after.

The Walt Disney Company was driven goofy at the prospect of their leading cartoon characters joining the likes of Santa Claus and Uncle Sam (both created by nineteenth century cartoonist Thomas Nast) in the public domain. So the long-arm of Disney went into action, lobbying Congress for a new copyright law that would increase the length of copyright protection for its characters. Disney, joined by the American Society of Composers, Authors, and Publishers, and other publishing and entertainment companies, persuaded Congress to pass the **Sony Bono Copyright Term Extension Act of 1998 (CTEA)**. Although not restoring copyright protection to works already in the public domain, the act added 20 years to existing copyrighted works and works to be copyrighted in the future. The act grants the following copyright terms to the following copyright holders:

- **Individual Copyright Holder.** Life of the author plus 70 years.
- **Corporate Copyright Holder.** Ninety-five years from the year of first publication or 120 years from the year of creation, whichever is shorter.

Opponents of the new copyright law argue that it was passed to fill the pockets of large publishers and entertainment companies and the heirs of famous writers. They also argue that the act is unconstitutional because life of the writer plus 70 years and corporate copyrights of 95 or 120 years exceed the constitutional mandate of "limited time" copyrights. Proponents of the new copyright act argue that corporations such as the Walt Disney Company should be rewarded for spending millions of dollars in creating such cartoon icons as Mickey Mouse. Proponents also assert that the law is good for the country because the United States is the world's leading exporter of intellectual property.

E-Commerce & Internet Law

COPYRIGHTING SOFTWARE

The advent of new technology challenges the ability of laws to protect it. For example, the invention of computers and the writing of software programs caused problems for existing copyright laws. These laws had to be changed to afford protection to software.

In 1980, Congress enacted the **Computer Software Copyright Act,** which amended the Copyright Act of 1976. The 1980 amendments included computer programs in the list of tangible items protected by copyright law. The amendments define *computer program* broadly as "a set of statements or instructions to be used directly or indirectly in a computer in order to bring about a certain result" [17 U.S.C. § 101].

A computer program is written first in programming language, which is called a "source code." It is then translated into another language, called an "object code," which is understood by the computer. In an important decision, *Apple Computer, Inc. v. Franklin Computer Corp.*, 714 F.2d 1240 (3d Cir. 1983), the court held that object codes could be copyrighted.

As with other works, the creator of a copyrightable software program obtains automatic copyright protection. The **Judicial Improvement Act of 1990** authorizes the Register of Copyright to accept and record any document pertaining to computer software, and to issue a **certificate of recordation** to the recorder [P.L. 101–650]. Congress passed the **Semiconductor Chip Protection Act of 1984** to provide greater protection of the hardware components of a computer. This law protects masks that are used to create computer chips. A *mask* is an original layout of software programs that is used to create a semiconductor chip. This act is sometimes referred to as the "Mask Work Act." Notice on the work is optional but when used must contain (1) the words *Mask Work* or the symbol *M* or (M) and (2) the name of the owner [17 U.S.C. §§ 901–914].

Copyright Infringement

Copyright infringement occurs when a party copies a substantial and material part of the plaintiff's copyrighted work without permission. The copying does not have to be either word for word or the entire work. A successful plaintiff can recover (1) the profit made by the infringer from the copyright infringement, (2) damages suffered by the plaintiff, (3) an order requiring the impoundment and destruction of the infringing works, and (4) an injunction preventing the infringer from doing so in the future. The court, in its discretion, can award statutory damages ranging from $200 for innocent infringement up to $100,000 for willful infringement in lieu of actual damages.

The court had to decide whether copyright infringement occurred in the following case.

> **copyright infringement**
> When a party copies a substantial and material part of the plaintiff's copyrighted work without permission. A copyright holder may recover damages and other remedies against the infringer.

Ty, Inc. v. GMA Accessories, Inc.
132 F.3d 1167 (1997)
United States Court of Appeals, Seventh Circuit

CASE 17.2

FACTS
In 1993, Ty, Inc., began selling the "Beanie Babies" line of small stuffed animals and introduced a new stuffed design each month. Beanie Babies became an immensely popular line of toys. Children, teenagers, and even adults collect some or all of the line of stuffed animals. Beanie Babies are copyrighted as "soft sculpture" under federal copyright law. Ty limits the production of individual Beanie Babies, thus creating a secondary market in them. Some Beanie Babies that originally sold for $5 now have a price as high as $2,000. One Beanie Baby produced by Ty was Squealer the pig. Subsequently, GMA Accessories, Inc. (GMA), a competing toy manufacturer, brought out a line of its own small stuffed animals. One of GMA's animals was Preston the pig. GMA's Preston the pig was identical to Ty's Squealer. Ty sued GMA for copyright infringement. The district court granted a preliminary injunction against GMA prohibiting the company from producing Preston. GMA appealed.

ISSUE
Did GMA engage in copyright infringement?

IN THE LANGUAGE OF THE COURT
Posner, Chief Judge   *The two pigs are so nearly identical that if the second is a copy of the first, the second clearly infringes Ty's copyright. But identity is not infringement. The Copyright Act forbids only copying; if independent creation results in an identical work, the creator of that work is free to sell it. The practical basis for this rule is that unlike the case of patents and trademarks, the creator of an expressive work—an author or sculptor or composer—cannot canvass the entire universe of copyrighted works to discover whether his poem or song or, as in this case, "soft sculpture" is identical to some work in which copyright subsists, especially since unpublished, unregistered works are copyrightable. But identity can be powerful evidence of copying. The more a work is both like an already copyrighted work and—for this is equally important—unlike anything that is in the public domain, the less likely it is to be an independent creation.*

The issue of copying can be broken down into two subissues. The first is whether the alleged copier had access to the work that he is claimed to have copied; the second is whether, if so, he used his access to copy. Here it is both. GMA's pig is strikingly similar to Ty's pig but not to anything in the public domain—a real pig,

(case continues)

for example. The parties' bean-bag pigs bear little resemblance to real pigs. Real pigs are not the only pigs in the public domain. But GMA has not pointed to any fictional pig in the public domain that Preston resembles. Preston resembles only Squealer, and resembles him so closely as to warrant an inference that GMA copied Squealer.

DECISION AND REMEDY

The court of appeals held that GMA engaged in copyright infringement and affirmed the district court's grant of the preliminary injunction against GMA.

Case Questions

Critical Legal Thinking Do copyright laws serve any useful purpose? What would the consequences be if copyright laws did not exist?

Ethics Did GMA act unethically in this case? Why do you think GMA fought this case all the way to the court of appeals?

Business Application Did Ty have much to lose if it had not won this case? Explain.

The Fair Use Doctrine

fair use doctrine

A doctrine that permits certain limited use of a copyright by someone other than the copyright holder without the permission of the copyright holder.

The copyright holder's rights in the work are not absolute. The law permits certain limited unauthorized use of copyrighted materials under the **fair use doctrine**. The following uses are protected under this doctrine: (1) quotation of the copyrighted work for review or criticism or in a scholarly or technical work, (2) use in a parody or satire, (3) brief quotation in a news report, (4) reproduction by a teacher or student of a small part of the work to illustrate a lesson, (5) incidental reproduction of a work in a newsreel or broadcast of an event being reported, and (6) reproduction of a work in a legislative or judicial proceeding. The copyright holder cannot recover for copyright infringement where fair use is found.

The U.S. Supreme Court examined the fair use doctrine in the following case.

Campbell v. Acuff-Rose Music, Inc.
510 U.S. 569, 114 S.Ct. 1164 (1994)
United States Supreme Court

CASE 17.3

FACTS

In 1964, Roy Orbison collaborated with another songwriter and wrote a rock ballad called "Oh, Pretty Woman." The song was copyrighted under federal copyright law. Roy Orbison recorded the song, which became a memorable classic from the 1960s. The writers assigned their rights in the song to Acuff-Rose Music, Inc. (Acuff-Rose).

2 Live Crew is a popular rap music group led by Luther R. Campbell. In 1989, Campbell wrote a song called "Pretty Woman" that was a parody of Roy Orbison's original recording. The lyrics of Campbell's version differed from Roy Orbison's version, except for the first line, which was verbatim from the original. 2 Live Crew wrote Acuff-Rose and asked permission to record their rap version of the song and stated that they were willing to pay a fee for the right to do so. When Acuff-Rose refused the permission, 2 Live Crew recorded the song anyway and put it on their rap album "As Clean as They Wanna Be," which sold over 250,000 copies. The rap version of "Pretty Woman" used the same rhythm as the original, although the rap version included additional sounds such as scraper noises, overlays of different keys, and

altered drum beats. The lyrics of the two versions of the song appear on page 333.

Acuff-Rose sued 2 Live Crew and their record company, Luke Skyywalker Records, for copyright infringement. The defendants asserted the affirmative defense of fair use based on parody. The district court found fair use, but the court of appeals reversed. The U.S. Supreme Court agreed to hear the case.

ISSUE

Can commercial parody be fair use?

IN THE LANGUAGE OF THE COURT

Souter, Justice *It is uncontested here that 2 Live Crew's song would be an infringement of Acuff-Rose's rights in "Oh, Pretty Woman," under the Copyright Act of 1976, but for a finding of fair use through parody. Modern dictionaries describe a parody as a "literary or artistic work that imitates the characteristic style of an author or a work for comic effect or ridicule." [American Heritage Dictionary, 1317 (3d ed. 1992)].*

Parody needs to mimic an original to make its point. The words of 2 Live Crew's song copy the original's first line, but then quickly degenerates into a play on words, substituting predictable lyrics with shocking ones that derisively demonstrate how bland and banal the Orbison song seems to them. 2 Live Crew juxtaposes the romantic musings of a man whose fantasy comes true, with degrading taunts, a bawdy demand for sex, and a sigh of relief from paternal responsibility. The later words can be taken as a comment on the naivete of the original of an earlier day, as a rejection of its sentiment that ignores the ugliness of street life and the debasement that it signifies.

It is true, of course, that 2 Live Crew copied the characteristic opening bass riff (or musical phrase) of the original, and true that the words of the first line copy the Orbison lyrics. But if quotation of the opening riff and the first line may be said to go to the "heart" of the original, the heart is also what most readily conjures up the song for parody, and it is the heart at which parody takes aim.

Suffice it to say here that, as to the lyrics, we think that no more was taken than necessary.

DECISION AND REMEDY

The U.S. Supreme Court held that commercial parody can qualify as fair use of another's copyrighted work. The Court reversed the judgment of the court of appeals and remanded the case for further proceedings.

Case Questions

Critical Legal Thinking   Should there be a fair use exception to copyright infringement? What purpose is served by the fair use doctrine?

Ethics   Did 2 Live Crew act ethically in using the "Oh Pretty Woman" song even though the copyright holder denied them permission to do so?

Business Application   Do you think 2 Live Crew's parody version caused any economic loss to the original copyright holder?

ROY ORBISON'S VERSION OF "OH, PRETTY WOMAN"

Pretty Woman, walking down the street,
Pretty Woman, the kind I like to meet,
Pretty Woman, I don't believe you, you're not the truth,
No one could look as good as you
Mercy
Pretty Woman, won't you pardon me,
Pretty Woman, I couldn't help but see,
Pretty Woman, that you look lovely as can be
Are you lonely just like me?
Pretty Woman, stop a while,
Pretty Woman, talk a while,
Pretty Woman give your smile to me
Pretty Woman, yeah, yeah, yeah
Pretty Woman, look my way,
Pretty Woman, say you'll stay with me
'Cause I need you, I'll treat you right
Come to me baby, Be mine tonight
Pretty Woman, don't walk on by,
Pretty Woman, don't make me cry,
Pretty Woman, don't walk away,
Hey, O.K.
If that's the way it must be, O.K.
I guess I'll go on home, it's late
There'll be tomorrow night, but wait!
What do I see
Is she walking back to me?
Yeah, she's walking back to me!
Oh, Pretty Woman.

2 LIVE CREW'S VERSION OF "PRETTY WOMAN"

Pretty woman walkin' down the street
Pretty woman girl you look so sweet
Pretty woman you bring me down to that knee
Pretty woman you make me wanna beg please
Oh, pretty woman
Big hairy woman you need to shave that stuff
Big hairy woman you know I bet it's tough
Big hairy woman all that hair it ain't legit
'Cause you look like 'Cousin It'
Big hairy woman
Bald headed woman girl your hair won't grow
Bald headed woman you got a teeny weeny afro
Bald headed woman you know your hair could look nice
Bald headed woman first you got to roll it with rice
Bald headed woman here, let me get this hunk of biz for ya
Ya know what I'm saying you look better than rice a roni
Oh bald headed woman
Big hairy woman come on in
And don't forget your bald headed friend
Hey pretty woman let the boys
Jump in
Two timin' woman girl you know you ain't right
Two timin' woman you's out with my boy last night
Two timin' woman that takes a load off my mind
Two timin' woman now I know the baby ain't mine
Oh, two timin' woman
Oh pretty woman

Ethical Perspective

KINKO'S K.O.'D BY COPYRIGHT LAW

Kinko's Graphics Corporation (Kinko's) operates approximately 200 stores, or "copy-shops," nationwide. The stores provide photocopying and other services and serve many colleges and universities and millions of students.

Since the mid-1980s, Kinko's has offered a service called "Professor Publishing." Under this program, Kinko's photocopies excerpts from selected materials at the request of college professors for educational use in the classroom. The materials are then bound into packets that contain a cover page printed with Kinko's logo, the name of the course and professor, and a price list. The packets—or "anthologies," as Kinko's calls them—are sold to students at Kinko's stores.

The majority of the materials in the packets are copied from copyrighted books and materials. Many packets contained full chapters from books, and some packets contained up to 100 pages from the same source. In most instances, Kinko's did not obtain permission from the copyright holder to reproduce the materials and did not pay anything to the holder.

Eight major textbook publishing houses brought suit against Kinko's for copyright infringement. The publishers sought an injunction against Kinko's use of their copyrighted materials without permission. They also sought damages. The publishers did not name professors or students as defendants.

Kinko's defense asserted the doctrine of "fair use." Kinko's claimed that the course packets are of tremendous importance to teaching and learning. It argued that an injunction against its educational copying would pose a serious threat to teaching and the welfare of education. The district court responded.

Although Kinko's tried to impress this court with its altruistic motives, the facts show that Kinko's copying had the intended purpose of supplanting the copyright holder's commercial valuable rights. The extent of Kinko's insistence that theirs are educational concerns and not profit-making ones boggles the mind.

The district court held that Kinko's preparation of the packets violated fair use because (1) there was multiple (as opposed to single) copying of materials, (2) a lot of material was copied (rather than of a selected quote or passage), and (3) Kinko's was a commercial enterprise, without nonprofit academic purposes. Therefore, the court held that Kinko's had engaged in infringement of the plaintiff's copyrighted materials.

As a remedy, the court granted the plaintiffs' request for an injunction and assessed damages of $510,000 and attorneys' fees and costs against Kinko's. The court also noted that the nature of Kinko's business meant that the threat of continued infringement remained even after its decision. [*Basic Books, Inc. v. Kinko's Graphics Corporation*, 758 F.Supp. 1522 (S.D.N.Y. 1991)]

1. Did Kinko's act morally in this case?
2. Do you think that the fair use doctrine should have protected Kinko's action?
3. Did the students who purchased the anthologies do anything wrong?

E-Commerce & Internet Law

THE DIGITAL MILLENNIUM COPYRIGHT ACT

The Internet makes it easier for people to illegally copy and distribute copyrighted works. To combat this, software and entertainment companies developed "wrappers" and encryption technology to protect their copyrighted works from unauthorized access. Not to be outdone, software pirates and other Internet users devised ways to crack these wrappers and protection devices. Seeing that they were losing the battle, software companies and the entertainment industry lobbied Congress to enact legislation that made the cracking of their wrappers and selling of technology to do so illegal. In 1998, Congress responded by enacting the **Digital Millennium Copyright Act (DMCA)** [17 U.S.C. 1201], which does the following:

- Prohibits unauthorized *access* to copyrighted digital works by circumventing the wrapper or encryption technology that protects the intellectual property. This "black box" protection prohibits simply accessing the protected information and does not require that the accessed information be misused.

- Prohibits the manufacture and distribution of technologies, products, or services primarily designed for the purpose of circumventing wrappers or encryption protection. Multipurpose devices that can be used in ways other than cracking wrappers or encryption technology can be manufactured and sold without violating the DMCA.

The DMCA changes the traditional fair use doctrine of copyright law. Historically, it has never been a crime to access or make a copy of a copyrighted work; what has been a crime is the misuse of that information. This rule remains valid for the nondigital world of copyrighted works. The DMCA changes this rule for digital protected works, making it illegal to merely access the copyrighted material by breaking through the digital wrapper or encryption technology that protects the work. Thus, a professor who can access and quote a nondigital copyrighted work in a paper he or she is writing pursuant to the fair use doctrine would violate the DMCA by merely accessing a digital work protected by the act.

Congress granted the following exceptions to DMCA liability to

- Software developers to achieve compatibility of their software with the protected work.
- Federal, state, and local law enforcement agencies conducting criminal investigations.
- Parents who are protecting children from pornography or other harmful materials available on the Internet.
- Internet users who are identifying and disabling "cookies" and other identification devices that invade their personal privacy rights.

- Nonprofit libraries, educational institutions, and archives who access a protected work to determine whether to acquire the work.

The DMCA imposes civil and criminal penalties. A successful plaintiff in a civil action can recover actual damages from first-time offenders and treble damages from repeat offenders, costs and attorney's fees, an order for the destruction of illegal products and devices, and an injunction against future violations by the offender. As an alternative to actual damages, a plaintiff can recover statutory damages of not less than $2,500 and up to $25,000 per act of circumvention. The following criminal penalties can be accessed for willful violations committed for "commercial advantage" or "private financial gain": First-time violators can be fined up to $500,000 and imprisoned for up to 5 years; subsequent violators can be fined up to $1 million and imprisoned up to 10 years.

The passage of the DMCA marks a significant victory for the software and entertainment industries, who allege that the new law will allow a huge growth in electronic commerce. Opponents, such as academics, scientists, libraries, and consumers argue that the act restricts access to information that would have previously been available under the fair use doctrine. They also note that the act paves the way for the software and entertainment industries to impose a per-use fee for their works. In the end, the DMCA has elevated the protection of digital copyrighted works above the protection of nondigital copyrighted works.

e·biz

Contemporary Business Application

ARTISTS GRANTED "MORAL RIGHTS" IN CREATIVE WORKS

Today, an artist who produces a painting, sculpture, photograph, or other work of art holds a copyright in the work. Prior to 1990, when the artist sold the work, the buyer usually obtained the copyright unless the artist and buyer contracted otherwise.

Things changed when Congress passed the **Visual Artists Rights Act** in 1990. The act gives artists **moral rights** in their creations that continue even after the sale of the artwork. Although long recognized in European countries, the notion of moral rights is new in this country.

The rights granted to artists under the act include

- The artist is given moral right in his or her work that transcends the sale of the artwork and the transfer of the copyright to it.

- Before an owner of the artist's work can change, modify, or tamper with the artwork, reproduce it in any other medium (e.g., produce prints from a painting), or remove certain artwork (e.g., remove a mural from a building wall), the owner must notify the artist.
- The artist has 90 days after notice to respond to the owner. If the artist and owner do not settle the issue, the artist may file a lawsuit that seeks an injunction to prevent the owner from taking the proposed action.
- If the case goes to litigation, the court must decide whether the artist's moral rights have been violated and whether to grant injunctive relief.
- When purchasing a piece of artwork, the buyer can seek a waiver of moral rights from the artist so that the buyer is not restricted in the future use of the artwork.

E-Commerce & Internet Law

e·biz

THE NET ACT: CRIMINAL COPYRIGHT INFRINGEMENT

A copyright holder owns a valuable right and may sue an infringer in a civil lawsuit to recover damages, injunctions, and other remedies for copyright infringement. In 1997, Congress enacted the **No Electronic Theft Act (NET Act)**, which criminalizes certain copyright infringement as well. The impetus for the passage of this act was the failure of the U.S. government to obtain criminal convictions against copyright infringers under existing, non-Internet specific criminal statutes.

In one notable case, David LaMacchia, a 21-year-old student at the Massachusetts Institute of Technology (MIT), encouraged Internet users to upload computer games and software to a bulletin board, which he then transferred to another bulletin board. LaMacchia then made this software available free to Internet users without compensating the copyright holders. The worldwide traffic generated by the availability of free software attracted the notice of university and federal authorities. The U.S. government sued LaMacchia, asserting a violation of the federal wire fraud statute, but the federal court judge dismissed the case holding that this statute's language did not prohibit LaMacchia's conduct because he did not recognize financial gain. [*United States v. LaMacchia*, 871 F.Supp. 535 (D. Mass. 1994)]

So Congress passed the NET Act to directly criminalize such copyright infringement. The NET Act prohibits any person from willfully infringing a copyright for either the purpose of commercial advantage or financial gain, or by reproduction or distribution even without commercial advantage or financial gain, including by electronic means, where the retail value of the copyrighted work exceeds $1,000. Criminal penalties for violating the act include imprisonment for up to one year and fines of up to $100,000.

The NET Act has closed the "LaMacchia loophole." For example, Jeffery Gerald Levy, a 22-year-old University of Oregon senior, pleaded guilty to criminal copyright infringement in violation of the Net Act because he was caught maintaining a Web site on the university's server where the public could make copies of thousands of software programs, movies, and musical recordings [*United States v. Levy* (D. Or. 1999)]. The NET Act adds a new law for the federal government to criminally attack copyright infringement and curb digital piracy.

TRADEMARKS

Trademark law is intended to (1) protect the owner's investment and goodwill in a **mark** and (2) prevent consumers from being confused as to the origin of goods and services. In 1946, Congress enacted the **Lanham Trademark Act** to provide federal protection to trademarks, service marks, and other marks.[7] Congress passed the **Trademark Law Revision Act of 1988**, which amended trademark law in several respects.[8] The amendments made it easier to register a trademark but harder to maintain it. States may also enact trademark laws.

Registration of Trademarks

Trademarks are registered with the **United States Patent and Trademark Office** in Washington, DC. The original registration of a mark is valid for 10 years and can be renewed for an unlimited number of 10-year periods.[9] The registration of a trademark, which is given nationwide effect, serves as constructive notice that the mark is the registrant's personal property. The registrant is entitled to use the registered trademark symbol ® in connection with a registered trademark or service mark. Use of the symbol is not mandatory. Note that the frequently used notations "TM" and "SM" have no legal significance.

An applicant can register a mark if (1) it was in use in commerce (e.g., actually used in the sale of goods or services) or (2) the applicant verifies a bona fide intention to use the mark in commerce and actually does so within six months of its registration. Failure to do

Lanham Trademark Act (as amended)

Federal statute that (1) establishes the requirements for obtaining a federal mark and (2) protects marks from infringement.

Business Brief

Toys "R" Us has successfully defended its trademarked name against numerous copycats [*Toys "R" Us, Inc. v. Canarsie Kiddie Shop*, 559 F.Supp. 1189 (E.D.N.Y. 1983)] [*Kids "R" Us*]; [*Geoffrey, Inc. v. Douglas S. Stratton*, 951 F.2d 359 (9th Cir. 1991)] [Phones-"R"-Us].

so during this period causes loss of the mark to the registrant. A party other than the registrant can submit an opposition to a proposed registration of a mark or the cancellation of a previously registered mark.

Distinctiveness of a Mark

To qualify for federal protection, a mark must be **distinctive** or have acquired a "**secondary meaning**." For example, marks such as *Acura, Dr. Pepper, Roto Rooter,* and *Apple Computer* are *distinctive*. A term such as *English Leather*, which literally means leather processed in England, has taken on a "secondary meaning" as a trademark for an aftershave lotion. Words that are *descriptive* but have no secondary meaning cannot be trademarked. For example, the word *cola* alone could not be trademarked.

distinctive
A brand name that is unique and fabricated.

"secondary meaning"
When an ordinary term has become a brand name.

Companies can trademark a distinctive mark, symbol, name, word, motto, or device that distinguishes its business from that of its competitors.

Marks That Can Be Trademarked

The following types of **marks** can be trademarked:

- **Trademarks** A **trademark** is a distinctive mark, symbol, name, word, motto, or device that identifies the *goods* of a particular business. For example, the words *Xerox, Coca-Cola,* and *IBM* are trademarks.
- **Service marks** A **service mark** is used to distinguish the *services* of the holder from those of its competitors. The trade names *United Airlines, Marriott Hotels,* and *Weight Watchers* are examples of service marks.
- **Certification marks** A **certification mark** is a mark that is used to certify that goods and services are of a certain quality or originate from particular geographical areas; for example, wines from the "Napa Valley" of California or "Florida" oranges. The owner of the mark is usually a nonprofit corporation that licenses producers that meet certain standards or conditions to use the mark.
- **Collective marks** A **collective mark** is a mark used by cooperatives, associations, and fraternal organizations. "Boy Scouts of America" is an example of a collective mark.

mark
The collective name for trademarks, service marks, certification marks, and collective marks that all can be trademarked.

trademark
A distinctive mark, symbol, name, word, motto, or device that identifies the goods of a particular business.

service mark
A mark that distinguishes the services of the holder from those of its competitors.

Certain marks cannot be registered. They include (1) the flag or coat of arms of the United States, any state, municipality, or foreign nation, (2) marks that are immoral or scandalous, (3) geographical names standing alone (e.g., "South"), (4) surnames standing alone (note that a surname can be registered if it is accompanied by a picture or fanciful name, such as "Smith Brothers' Cough Drops", and (5) any mark that resembles a mark already registered with the federal Patent and Trademark Office.

Contemporary Business Application

COLOR MAY BE TRADEMARKED

The issue of whether color could be trademarked confused the courts of appeals for years: Some said it could, whereas others said it could not. In 1995, the U.S. Supreme Court ended this division and decided the issue in the following case.

Since the 1950s, Qualitex Company has manufactured and sold dry cleaning pads with a special shade of green-gold color. These pads are used on cleaning presses at dry cleaning firms. Qualitex registered the special green-gold color of its pads with the Patent and Trademark Office as a trademark.

In 1989, Jacobson Products, a Qualitex rival, began to sell its own press pads to dry cleaning firms, and it colored these pads a similar green-gold. Qualitex sued Jacobson for trademark infringement. Qualitex won the lawsuit in the district court, but the court of appeals reversed. Qualitex appealed to the U.S. Supreme Court.

The Supreme Court, in a unanimous decision, held that color qualifies for registration as a trademark when it is associated with a particular good where the color has obtained a secondary meaning that identifies a particular brand and manufacturer as its source. The Court held that Qualitex's special green-gold color on its press pads met this requirement and could be registered and protected as a trademark. [*Qualitex Company v. Jacobson Products Company, Inc.*, 115 S.Ct. 1300, 131 L.Ed.2d 248 (1995)]

Trademark Infringement

trademark infringement
Unauthorized use of another's mark. The holder may recover damages and other remedies from the infringer.

The owner of a mark can sue a third party for the unauthorized use of a mark. To succeed in a **trademark infringement** case, the owner must prove that (1) the defendant infringed the plaintiff's mark by using it in an unauthorized manner and (2) such use is likely to cause confusion, mistake, or deception of the public as to the origin of the goods or services. A successful plaintiff can recover (1) the profits made by the infringer by the unauthorized use of the mark, (2) damages caused to the plaintiff's business and reputation, (3) an order requiring the defendant to destroy all goods containing the unauthorized mark, and (4) an injunction preventing the defendant from such infringement in the future. The court has discretion to award up to *treble* damages where intentional infringement is found.

The following case raises a trademark issue.

Ethical Perspective

WAL-MART KNOCKS OFF DESIGNER'S CLOTHES

Fashion designers spend a fortune of money and time in creating unique fashion designs for their clothing. They then produce these clothes and sell them at upscale prices. But what is the designer to do if another manufacturer or retailer copies the original design and sells these "knockoffs" at much lower prices? Sue, that's what! Consider the following case.

Samara Brothers, Inc. (Samara) is a designer and manufacturer of children's clothing. The core of Samara's business is its annual new line of spring and summer children's garments. Wal-Mart Stores, Inc. (Wal-Mart) operates a large chain of budget warehouse stores that sells thousands of items at very low prices. In 1995, Wal-Mart contacted one of its suppliers, Judy-Philippine, Inc. (JPI) about the possibility of making a line of children's clothes just like Samara's successful line. Wal-Mart sent photographs of Samara's children's clothes to JPI (the name "Samara" was readily discernible on the labels of the garments) and directed JPI to produce children's clothes exactly like those in the photographs. JPI produced a line of children's clothes for Wal-Mart that copied the designs, colors, flower patterns, etc. of Samara's clothing. Wal-Mart then sold this line of children's clothing in its stores, making a gross profit of over $1.15 million on these clothes sales during the 1996 selling season.

In June 1996, one of the retailers that purchased Samara's children's clothing complained to Samara that Wal-Mart was selling the knockoff clothes at less than the retailer was paying Samara for its clothes. Samara investigated and discovered Wal-Mart had copied its designs. After sending unsuccessful cease and desist letters to Wal-Mart, Samara sued Wal-Mart, alleging trade dress infringement in violation of the Lanham Act. The U.S. district court held in favor of Samara and awarded damages. Wal-Mart appealed all the way to the U.S. Supreme Court, which granted review.

In a 9-0 decision, the Supreme Court came down on the side of Wal-Mart and held that, in this case, Wal-Mart had not violated the Lanham Act. The Court ruled that Samara's children's clothing had not acquired a "secondary meaning" in the minds of the public—that is, when most people saw Samara's clothing they did not automatically think "that is a Samara design." The Supreme Court established the following legal rule for product design infringement cases under the Lanham Act: If a product design has not acquired a secondary meaning in the minds of the public, it can be knocked off; If a product design has acquired a secondary meaning, then it cannot be knocked off. Thus, designers of nondistintive goods, such as dresses, shoes, jewelry, golf clubs, and other products that have not acquired a secondary meaning, will find look-alikes being sold at discount stores such as Wal-Mart, Target, and Mervyn's.

There are some limitations to copying, however. Under the Supreme Court's *Wal-Mart* decision, goods that have acquired a secondary meaning—such as Ferrari automobile or Apple Computer's iMac computer—are protected from being copied. Goods that are patented, such as Nike's "air" technology in its athletic shoes, cannot be copied because it would constitute patent infringement. And counterfeiting—selling knockoff goods with a fake original manufacturer's trademarked name or logo on them—is illegal trademark infringement. [*Wal-Mart Stores, Inc. v. Samara Brothers, Inc.*, 2000 WL 293238, United States Supreme Court (2000)]

1. Under ethical principles, should Wal-Mart sell knock off goods?
2. What are the economic effects of the U.S. Supreme Court's decision? Who wins? Who losses?

E-Commerce & Internet Law

FEDERAL DILUTION ACT: TRADEMARKS PREEMPT DOMAIN NAMES

One of the most important assets of many businesses is its name. Companies often trademark their name and then spend millions of dollars each year advertising and promoting the quality of the goods and services sold under the name. Coca-Cola, McDonald's, Microsoft, and others are household names that are recognized by millions of consumers. Once the use of the Internet exploded, and goods and services started to be sold over the Internet, many companies sought to conduct business over the Internet using their famous names. When they got there, many found that certain persons had already registered these famous names as domain names (i.e. ".com"). These domain name holders are called *cybersquatters* because they register domain names with the primary purpose of exacting a ransom payment from the trademark owner to buy the domain name from them.

Traditional trademark law was of little help to the trademark owners in many of these cases because to sue for trademark infringement consumers had to be confused as to the source of the goods or services. In many cases the cybersquatters either did not sell any goods or services or sold goods and services different from those sold by the trademark holder, therefore avoiding the consumer confusion requirement of a trademark infringement case.

To combat this situation, owners of trademarks and service marks lobbied Congress for help. Congress responded by enacting the **Federal Dilution Act of 1995**. This act protects famous marks from dilution. The Dilution Act provides that owners of marks have a valuable property right in their marks that should not be eroded, blurred, tarnished, or diluted in any way by another. The Dilution Act does not require consumer confusion before there is a violation of the act. The Federal Dilution Act has three fundamental requirements:

1. The mark must be famous.
2. The use by the other party must be commercial.
3. The use must cause dilution of the distinctive quality of the mark.

In determining the fame of the mark, the court examines such factors as the distinctiveness of the mark, the duration

e-biz

(box continues)

and extent of the use of the mark, the channels of trade it is used in, and such. The second element, the commercial use requirement, is meant to avoid First Amendment free speech concerns. Finally, *dilution* is broadly defined as the lessening of the capacity of a famous mark to identify and distinguish goods and services, regardless of the presence or absence of competition between the owner of the mark and the other party or the likelihood of confusion, mistake, or deception.

The Federal Dilution Act is designed to stop those who attempt to benefit from the time and money spent by a company to develop and promote its famous marks. The act is primarily aimed at unseating cybersquatters who have appropriated famous marks on the Internet. Although most cases brought under the Federal Dilution Act have been domain name cases, the act applies to non-Internet dilution of famous marks as well.

Generic Names

generic name

A term for a mark that has become a common term for a product line or type of service and therefore has lost its trademark protection.

Most companies promote their trademarks and service marks to increase the public's awareness of the availability and quality of their products and services. At some point in time, however, the public may begin to treat the mark as a common name to denote the type of product or service being sold, rather than as the trademark or trade name of an individual seller. A trademark that becomes a common term for a product line or type of service is called a **generic name**. Once that happens, the term loses its protection under federal trademark law because it has become *descriptive* rather than *distinctive* (see Exhibit 17.1).

E-Commerce & Internet Law

AOL'S "YOU'VE GOT MAIL" A GENERIC NAME

America Online, Inc. (AOL), operates the world's largest interactive on-line service. More than 20 million people subscribe to, and are members of, AOL on-line service. For a basic monthly fee, AOL service enables its members to receive computer information, access the Internet, and receive and send e-mail. For nearly a decade, AOL used the terms "You Have Mail" and "You've Got Mail" in connection with its automatic e-mail notification service. When an AOL member starts on-line and has e-mail, the cheerful spoken words "You've Got Mail" are immediately heard. At the same time this voice sounds, a red signal flag is pictured prominently on the member's computer screen above the phrase "You Have Mail." AOL applied for service mark protection for the two phrases "You've Got Mail" and "You Have Mail."

AT&T Corp. (AT&T), a telecommunications company, began offering Internet access to subscribers for a monthly fee that included e-mail services. In December 1998, AT&T added a "You Have Mail!" notification to its e-mail service. AOL sent a letter to AT&T to cease and desist from using "You Have Mail!" When AT&T refused,

AOL sued AT&T in federal district court for unauthorized appropriation and infringement of AOL's common-law service marks "You Have Mail" and "You've Got Mail." AT&T argued that these terms were generic and that AOL had no protectable interest in them.

The district court held as a matter of law that the two phrases were generic and thus were not protected marks. The court stated that a mark is generic when it "identifies a class of product or service, regardless of source." The court found that "You Have Mail" and "You've Got Mail" are common words and phrases that are used for their ordinary meaning. The court stated that the phrases "You Have Mail" and "You've Got Mail" indicate to the public at large what the service is, not where it came from. The court cited evidence that many of AOL's competitors used the term *mail* and *e-mail* when delivering e-mail to their subscribers. The court held that a generic term cannot receive service mark protection. The court granted summary judgment to AT&T and allowed it to use the term "You Have Mail!" when delivering e-mail to its subscribers. [*America Online, Inc. v. AT&T Corp.*, 1999 WL 688152 (E.D.Va. 1999)]

ᏋXHIBIT 17.1   *Reprinted with permission of Xerox Corporation*

Business Brief

Nestlé Company, Inc., lost its trademark on the term "Toll House" for its chocolate chip cookies when a court ruled that the term had become generic because the public had come to associate the name Toll House with chocolate chip cookies in general, not only those sold by Nestlé [*Nestlé Company, Inc. v. Chester's Market, Inc.* 571 F.Supp. 763 (D.Conn. 1983)].

CONCEPT SUMMARY   TYPES OF INTELLECTUAL PROPERTY PROTECTED BY FEDERAL LAW

Type	Subject Matter	Term
Patent	Inventions (e.g., machines; processes; compositions of matter; designs for articles of manufacture; and improvements to existing machines, processes). Invention must be 1. Novel 2. Useful 3. Nonobvious Public use doctrine: Patent will not be granted if the invention was used in public for more than one year prior to the filing of the patent application.	Patents on articles of manufacture and processes: 20 years; design patents: 14 years.
Copyright	Tangible writing (e.g., books, magazines, newspapers, lectures, operas, plays, screenplays, musical compositions, maps, works of art, lithographs, photographs, postcards, greeting cards, motion pictures, newsreels, sound recordings, computer programs, and mask works fixed to semiconductor chips). Writing must be the original work of the author. Fair use doctrine: It permits use of copyrighted material without consent for limited uses (e.g., scholarly work, parody or satire, and brief quotation in news reports).	Individual registrant: life of author plus 70 years. Business registrant: for the shorter of either (1) 120 years from the date of creation or (2) 95 years from the date of publication.
Trademark	Marks (e.g., name, symbol, word, logo, or device). Marks include trademarks, service marks, certification marks, and collective marks. Mark must be distinctive or have acquired a secondary meaning. Generic name: A mark that becomes a common term for a product line or type of service loses its protection under federal trademark law.	Original registration: 10 years. Renewal registration: unlimited number of renewals for 10-year terms.

State Antidilution Statutes

antidilution statutes
State laws that allow persons and companies to register trademarks and service marks.

States recognize common law trademarks. In addition, many states have enacted their own trademark statutes. These state laws, which allow persons and companies to register trademarks and service marks, are often called **antidilution statutes**. They prevent others from infringing on and diluting a registrant's mark. Companies that only do business locally sometimes register under these laws.

Contemporary Business Application

BOOTLEGGING OUTLAWED AGAIN

In the 1920s, *bootlegging* referred to manufacturing, selling, and transporting of alcohol in violation of Prohibition law (Amendment XVIII to the U.S. Constitution). Prohibition ended in 1933 with the adoption of Amendment XXI, but the term *bootlegging* resurrected itself in another context—the unauthorized recording of musical concerts.

In 1995, the United States joined over 130 other countries and became a member of the World Trade Organization (WTO). The WTO member nations adopted the international **Agreement on Trade Related Aspects of Intellectual Property (TRIPs)**, which outlawed unauthorized taping of sounds or images of live musical performances. To enforce this agreement in the United States, the U.S. Congress enacted the following federal antibootlegging statutes:

- **18 U.S.C. 2319A.** Imposes criminal liability for the unauthorized taping of the sounds and images of live musical performances "knowingly and for purposes of commercial advantage or private financial gain." A first offense carries a prison term of up to five years; subse-

quent offenses carry prison terms up to 10 years. The court can order unauthorized recordings to be destroyed.

- **17 U.S.C. 1101.** Imposes civil liability for similar conduct but without the commercial advantage or private financial gain requirement. A successful plaintiff can recover actual damages and any profits made by the defendant, destruction of any unauthorized recordings, and an injunction against any future violations by the defendant.

It is important to note that both recording the sound of the concert and taking photographs of the performance are conduct that is outlawed by these statutes. The lawfulness of the antibootlegging statute has been upheld as a valid exercise of Congress's power under the Commerce Clause of the U.S. Constitution. [*United States v. Moghadam*, 175 F.3d 1269 (11th Cir. 1999)]

International Perspective

ENFORCEMENT OF INTELLECTUAL PROPERTY RIGHTS UNDER TRIPs

Since the late 1800s, many countries have entered into treaties and conventions with each other to protect intellectual property rights such as patents, copyrights, and trademarks. However, if a country was not a party to an international treaty, persons and businesses within that country sometimes freely used patents, copyrights, and trademarks of persons and businesses from other countries without penalty or repercussion. And even if the infringer's country was a party to an international treaty, the infringement charge would be heard by a national court whose judgment was not always satisfactory to the intellectual property holder in the other country. This system of having national courts hear intellectual property disputes continued until 1967.

In 1967, the United Nations established the **World Intellectual Property Organization (WIPO)**. This special agency was created to administer intellectual property treaties and conventions that member nations had signed. Although being of some benefit in deciding intellectual property disputes, the WIPO had no means of enforcing its decisions. Therefore, decisions issued by the WIPO against offending countries were often ignored.

The United States, the largest producer of intellectual property rights in the world, lost billions of dollars annually as its patents, copyrights, and trademarks were "knocked off" by infringers in many countries of the world. The development of digital technologies and the Internet increased the United States' concern of how to rein in infringement of intellectual property rights. When the

United States attended the Uruguay Round of the General Agreement on Tariffs and Trade (GATT) in the early 1990s, it not only argued for reductions of tariffs and trade barriers worldwide, but made the international protection of intellectual property rights a major issue of negotiation. In addition to obtaining an agreement for the reduction of tariffs and trade restrictions, the United States, Japan, and other developed nations secured the passage of the **Agreement on Trade-Related Aspects of Intellectual Property Rights (TRIPs)**. TRIPs, which became effective on January 1, 1995, mandates that member nations comply with international treaties and conventions protecting copyrights in traditional works, computer programs, and digital works, and related intellectual property laws.

In order to remedy the enforcement problems of the WIPO, the United States urged, and obtained agreement, that TRIPs would be administered by the **World Trade Organization (WTO)**. What this means is that if one country believes another country is not enforcing international intellectual property laws, a nation can file a charge with the WTO. The dispute is heard by a WTO panel, with an appeal to the WTO court. The WTO has the authority to enforce its decisions by ordering economic sanctions against infringing member nations that do not comply with its decision. Thus, the United States and other developed nations for the first time have an effective mechanism to pursue disputes against rogue nations who either promote infringement or do not protect intellectual property rights within their borders.

e·biz

Working the Web

e·biz

U.S. Library of Congress The Library of Congress Web site contains a database of copyright records from 1978 to the present.

Visit at **lcweb.loc.gov**

U.S. Patent and Trademark Office The U.S. Patent and Trademark Office has a Web site where you can download forms, order copies, link to legal materials, and find statistical information.

Visit at **www.uspto.gov**

U.S. Federal Communications Commission The U.S. Federal Communications Commission Web site links to economic information, industry statistics, consumer information, and a host of other resources.

Visit at **www.fcc.gov**

U.S. Copyright Office Information about copyright basics, copyright law, copyright forms, copyright records, and other copyright materials can be found at this Web site.

Visit at **www.loc.gov/copyright**

International Trademark Association The International Trademark Association is an association of trademark owners and advisors worldwide. It is dedicated to the support and advancement of trademarks and related intellectual property concepts as essential elements of effective national and international commerce.

Visit at **www.inta.org**

CYBER EXERCISES

1. Using the Library of Congress Web site, find the home page for the U.S. Copyright Office Records.

2. Using the Patent and Trademark Office Web site, find out about jobs at the U.S. Patent and Trademark Office.

3. Use the U.S. Federal Communications Web site to find information about the v-chip.

4. Using the U.S. Copyright Office Web site, find the materials on copyright registration.

5. Using the International Trademark Association Web site, visit the Brand Names Education Foundation.

CASES AND EXERCISES

CRITICAL LEGAL THINKING CASES

17.1. Stiffel Company (Stiffel) designed a pole lamp (a vertical tube that can stand upright between the floor and ceiling of a room with several lamp fixtures along the outside of it). Pole lamps proved to be a decided commercial success. Soon after Stiffel brought them on the market, Sears, Roebuck & Company (Sears) put a substantially identical pole lamp on the market. The Sears's retail price was about the same as Stiffel's wholesale price. Sears used its own name on the lamps it sold. Stiffel sued Sears for unfair competition, alleging that Sears had engaged in the tort of palming off. Is Sears liable for palming off? [*Sears, Roebuck & Co. v. Stiffel Co.*, 376 U.S. 225, 84 S.Ct. 1131, 12 L.Ed.2d 87 (1964)]

17.2. CRA-MAR Video Center, Inc. (CRA-MAR), sells electronic equipment and videocassettes, as does its competitor, Koach's Sales Corporation (Koach's). Both CRA-MAR and Koach's purchased computers from Radio Shack. CRA-MAR used the computer to store customer lists, movie lists, personnel files, and financial records. Because the computer was new to CRA-MAR, Randall Youts, Radio Shack's salesman and programmer, agreed to modify CRA-MAR's programs when needed, including the customer list program. At one point, CRA-MAR decided to send a mailing to everyone on its customer list. The computer was unable to perform the function, so Youts took the disks containing the customer lists to the Radio Shack store to work on the program. Somehow Koach's came into possession of CRA-MAR's customer lists and did advertising mailings to the parties on the lists. When CRA-MAR discovered this fact, it sued Koach's, seeking an injunction against any further use of its customer lists. Is a customer list a trade secret that can be protected from misappropriation? [*Koach's Sales Corp. v. CRA-MAR Video Center, Inc.*, 478 N.E.2d 110 (Ind.App. 1985)]

17.3. Robin Williams, a comedian, did a comedy performance at the Great American Music Hall, a San Francisco nightclub. During the performance he told a joke that contained the following words: "Whoa—White Wine. This is a little wine here. If it's not wine it's been through somebody already. Oh—There are White wines, there are Red wines, but why are there no Black wines like: Rege. It goes with fish, meat, any damn thing it wants to. I like my wine like I like my women, ready to pass out." Audio versions of the performance were distributed by Polygram Records, Inc. (Polygram), and a video version was shown on Home Box Office (HBO). David H. Rege, who sells and distributes assorted varieties of "Rege" brand wines from his San Francisco store, Rege Cellars, sued Williams, Polygram, and HBO for disparagement of his products and business (trade libel). Are the defendants liable for disparagement? [*Polygram Records, Inc. v. Rege*, 170 Cal.App.3d 543, 216 Cal.Rptr. 252 (Cal.App. 1985)]

17.4. In the mid-1960s, the Beatles, a rock group from Liverpool, England, became one of the most famous and successful singing and recording groups in history. The Beatles produced and sold millions of records and albums. Two members of the group, John Lennon and Paul McCartney, wrote most of the music and lyrics for the Beatles. The two other members of the group were George Harrison and Ringo Starr. The Beatles disbanded as a group in the early 1970s and assigned their right to publicity to Apple Corps Limited, a corporation. In the mid-1970s, Steven Leber, David Krebs, and Beatlemania, Ltd., produced a multimedia stage production called *Beatlemania*. Imitators of the Beatles, wearing clothes and haircuts in the style of the Beatles from the 1960s, performed live onstage. During each 90-minute live performance, these imitators sang Beatles songs, with slides, movie clips, and pictures of events from the 1960s being shown on a screen in the background. The New York company of *Beatlemania* alone performed eight concerts a week for over three years. In addition, two national touring companies and a road group performed *Beatlemania* concerts across the country. Millions of people saw *Beatlemania* in 7,000 live performances, which grossed more than $45 million. Apple Corps and the Beatles objected to these performances. Apple Corps brought this action against Leber,

Krebs, and Beatlemania, Ltd., to recover damages. Did the defendants misappropriate the Beatles's (and Apple Corps's) right to publicity? [*Apple Corps Ltd. v. Leber*, No. C 299149 (Cal.Sup.Ct. 1986)]

17.5. When Spiro Agnew resigned as Vice President of the United States, President Richard M. Nixon appointed Gerald R. Ford as Vice President. In 1974, amid growing controversy surrounding the Watergate scandal, President Nixon resigned and Vice President Ford acceded to the presidency. As President, Ford pardoned Nixon for any wrongdoing regarding the Watergate affair and related matters. Ford served as President until he was defeated by Jimmy Carter in the 1976 presidential election. In 1973, Ford entered into a contract with Harper & Row, Publishers, Inc. (Harper & Row), to publish his memoirs in book form. The memoirs were to contain significant unpublished materials concerning the Watergate affair and Ford's personal reflections on that time in history. The publisher instituted security measures to protect the confidentiality of the manuscript. Several weeks before the book was to be released, an unidentified person secretly brought a copy of the manuscript to Victor Navasky, editor of *The Nation*, a weekly political commentary magazine. Navasky, knowing that his possession of the purloined manuscript was not authorized, produced a 2,250-word piece entitled "The Ford Memoirs" and published it in the April 3, 1979, issue of *The Nation*. Verbatim quotes of between 300 and 400 words from Ford's manuscript, including some of the most important parts, appeared in the article. Harper & Row sued the publishers of *The Nation* for copyright infringement. Who wins? [*Harper & Row, Publishers, Inc. v. Nation Enterprises*, 471 U.S. 539, 105 S.Ct. 2218, 85 L.Ed.2d 588 (1985)]

17.6. The Sony Corporation of America (Sony) manufactures videocassette recorders (VCRs) that can be used to videotape programs and films that are shown on television and cable stations. VCRs are used by consumers and others to videotape both copyrighted and uncopyrighted works. The primary use for VCRs is by consumers for "time shifting"— that is, taping a television program for viewing at a more convenient time. Universal City Studios, Inc. (Universal), and Walt Disney Productions (Disney) hold copyrights on a substantial number of motion-picture and audiovisual works that are shown on television and cable stations, which pay them a fee to do so. Some of Universal's and Disney's copyrighted works have been copied by consumers using Sony's VCRs. Universal and Disney sued Sony, seeking an injunction against the sale of VCRs by Sony. Is Sony liable for contributory copyright infringement? [*Sony Corp. of Am. v. Universal City Studios, Inc.*, 464 U.S. 417, 104 S.Ct. 774, 78 L.Ed.2d 574 (1984)]

17.7. Professional Real Estate Investors, Inc., and Kenneth Irwin own and operate La Mancha, a resort hotel in Palm Springs, California. Guests at La Mancha may rent movie videodiscs from the lobby gift shop for a $5 daily fee per disc, which can be charged on the hotel bill. Each guest room is equipped with a large-screen projection television and videodisc player. Guests view the videodisc movies projected on the television screen in their rooms. After learning of these activities, Columbia Pictures, Inc., and six other motion-picture studios (Columbia) who owned copyrights on films rented on videodisc at La Mancha filed suit to prevent La Mancha from renting videodiscs to its guests, alleging copyright infringement. Is La Mancha liable for copyright infringement? [*Columbia Pictures Industries, Inc. v. Professional Real Estate Investors, Inc.*, 866 F.2d 278 (9th Cir. 1989)]

17.8. In the dark days of 1977, when the City of New York teetered on the brink of bankruptcy, on the television screens of America there appeared an image of a top-hatted Broadway showgirl, backed by an advancing phalanx of dancers, chanting: "I-I-I-I-I Love New Yo-o-o-o-o-o-rk." As an ad campaign for an ailing city, it was an unparalleled success. Crucial to the campaign was a brief but exhilarating musical theme written by Steve Karmin called "I Love New York." Elsmere Music, Inc., owned the copyright to the music. The success of the campaign did not go unnoticed. On May 20, 1978, the popular weekly variety program "Saturday Night Live" (SNL) performed a comedy sketch over National Broadcasting Company's network (NBC). In the sketch the cast of SNL, portraying the mayor and members of the chamber of commerce of the biblical city of Sodom, were seen discussing Sodom's poor public image with out-of-towners, and its effect on the tourist trade. In an attempt to recast Sodom's image in a more positive light, a new advertising campaign was revealed, with the highlight of the campaign being a song "I Love Sodom" sung a cappella by a chorus line of SNL regulars to the tune of "I Love New York." Elsmere Music did not see the humor of the sketch and sued NBC for copyright infringement. Who wins? [*Elsmere Music, Inc. v. National Broadcasting Co., Inc.*, 623 F.2d 252 (2d Cir. 1980)]

17.9. Clairol Incorporated manufactures and distributes hair tinting, dyeing, and coloring preparations. In 1956, Clairol embarked on an extensive advertising campaign to promote the sale of its "Miss Clairol" hair-color preparations that included advertisements in national magazines, on outdoor billboards, on radio and television, in mailing pieces, and on point-of-sale display materials to be used by retailers and beauty salons. The advertisements prominently displayed the slogans "Hair Color So Natural Only Her Hairdresser Knows for Sure" and "Does She or Doesn't She?" Clairol registered

these slogans as trademarks. During the next decade Clairol spent more than $22 million for advertising materials resulting in more than a billion separate audio and visual impressions using the slogans. Roux Laboratories, Inc., a manufacturer of hair-coloring products and a competitor of Clairol's, filed an opposition to Clairol's registration of the slogans as trademarks. Do the slogans qualify for trademark protection? [*Roux Laboratories, Inc. v. Clairol, Inc.*, 427 F.2d 823 (Cust.Pat.App. 1970)]

17.10. In 1967, two friends from California designed a sailing surfboard that combined the sports of sailing and surfing. Originally they called it a "sailboard." They filed for and were granted a patent on the sailboard, which was assigned to the company Windsurfing International, Inc. (WSI). In 1968, WSI's Seattle dealer coined the term *windsurfing*. WSI applied for and was granted trademarks for terms using the word *Windsurfer*. Between 1969 and 1976, WSI produced a particular type of board called the Windsurfer. At that time, WSI controlled over 95 percent of the market. In the early years, there was no generic word for the sport or craft. To promote sales, WSI and its employees continually referred to the sport as windsurfing and individual sportspeople as windsurfers. WSI also engaged in an extensive advertising campaign using the terms *windsurfing* to describe the sport and *windsurfer* to describe individual sportspersons. People who participated in the sport, trade magazines, and the general public used the word *windsurfing* to describe the sport. In 1977, WSI started to police the use of its trademarked term. However, it's remained rather futile, as evidence showed that the general public used the terms *windsurfing* and *windsurfer* in a general, common sense to mean the sport and its participants. AMF Incorporated (AMF) seeks cancellation of WSI's trademarks containing the term *Windsurfer*. Should the trademark be canceled? [*AMF Inc. v. Windsurfing Internat'l, Inc.*, 613 F.Supp. (D.C.N.Y. 1985)]

17.11. Since 1972, Mead Data Central, Inc. (Mead), has provided computer-assisted legal research services to lawyers and others under the trademark "LEXIS." LEXIS is based on *lex*, the Latin word for law, and *IS*, for information systems. Through extensive sales and advertising, Mead has made LEXIS a strong mark in the computerized legal research field, particularly among lawyers. However, LEXIS is recognized by only 1 percent of the general population, with almost half of this 1 percent being attorneys. Toyota Motor Corporation has for many years manufactured automobiles, which it markets in the United States through its subsidiary Toyota Motor Sales, U.S.A., Inc. (Toyota). On August 24, 1987, Toyota announced a new line of luxury automobiles to be called LEXUS. Toyota planned on spending almost $20 million for marketing and advertising LEXUS during the first nine months of 1989. Mead filed suit against Toyota, alleging that Toyota's use of the name LEXUS violated New York's antidilution statute and would cause injury to the business reputation of Mead and a dilution of the distinctive quality of the LEXIS mark. Who wins? [*Mead Data Central, Inc. v. Toyota Motor Sales, U.S.A., Inc.*, 875 F.2d 1026 (2d Cir. 1989)]

17.12. The Miller Brewing Company (Miller), a national brewer, produces a reduced-calorie beer called "Miller Lite."

Miller began selling beer under this name in the 1970s and has spent millions of dollars promoting the Miller Lite brand name on television, print, and other forms of advertising. Since July 11, 1980, Falstaff Brewing Corporation (Falstaff) has been brewing and distributing a reduced-calorie beer called "Falstaff Lite." Miller brought suit under the Lanham Trademark Act seeking an injunction to prevent Falstaff from using the term *Lite*. Is the term *Lite* a generic name that does not qualify for trademark protection? [*Miller Brewing Co. v. Falstaff Brewing Corp.*, 655 F.2d 5 (1st Cir. 1981)]

ETHICS CASES

17.13. Integrated Cash Management Services, Inc. (ICM), designs and develops computer software programs and systems for banks and corporate financial departments. ICM's computer programs and systems are not copyrighted, but they are secret. After Alfred Sims Newlin and Behrouz Vafa completed graduate school, they were employed by ICM as computer programmers. They worked at ICM for several years writing computer programs. In March 1987, they left ICM to work for Digital Transactions, Inc. (DTI). Before leaving ICM, however, they copied certain ICM files onto personal diskettes. Within two weeks of starting to work at DTI, they created prototype computer programs that operated in substantially the same manner as comparable ICM programs and were designed to compete directly with ICM's programs. ICM sued Newlin, Vafa, and DTI for misappropriation of trade secrets. Are the defendants liable? Did the defendants act ethically in this case? [*Integrated Cash Management Services, Inc. v. Digital Transactions, Inc.*, 920 F.2d 171 (2d Cir. 1990)]

17.14. John W. Carson (Carson) was the host and star of *The Tonight Show*, a well-known nightly television talk show broadcast by the National Broadcasting Company (NBC) until he retired in 1992. Carson also appears as an entertainer in theaters and nightclubs around the country. From the time that he began hosting *The Tonight Show* in 1962, he had been introduced on the show each night with the phrase "Here's Johnny." The phrase "Here's Johnny" was generally associated with Carson by a substantial segment of the television viewing public. Carson had licensed the use of the phrase to a chain of restaurants, a line of toiletries, and other business ventures. Johnny Carson Apparel, Inc. (Apparel), founded in 1970, manufactures and markets men's clothing to retail stores. Carson, president of Apparel and owner of 20 percent of its stock, had licensed Apparel to use the phrase "Here's Johnny" on labels for clothing and in advertising campaigns. The

phrase had never been registered by Carson or Apparel as a trademark or service mark.

Earl Broxton was the owner and president of Here's Johnny Portable Toilets, Inc. (Toilets), a Michigan corporation that engages in the business of renting and selling "Here's Johnny" portable toilets. Broxton was aware when he formed the corporation that the phrase "Here's Johnny" was the introductory slogan for Carson on *The Tonight Show*. Broxton indicated that he coupled the phrase "Here's Johnny" with a second one, "The World's Foremost Commodian," to make a good play on the phrase. Shortly after Toilets went into business in 1976, Carson and Apparel sued Toilets, seeking an injunction prohibiting the further use of the phrase "Here's Johnny" as a corporate name for or in connection with the sale or rental of its portable toilets. Who wins? Did Broxton act ethically by appropriating the phrase "Here's Johnny" to promote the sale and rental of portable toilets? [*Carson v. Here's Johnny Portable Toilets, Inc.*, 698 F.2d 831 (6th Circ. 1983)]

17.15. Master Distributors, Inc. (MDI), manufactures and sells "Blue Max," a blue leader splicing tape, which is used to attach undeveloped film to a leader cord for photoprocessing through a minilab machine that develops the film and prints the photographs. Leader tape can be created in any color, and MDI dyed its Blue Max tape aquamarine blue. Blue Max is well known and enjoys a reputation as the industry standard. Both distributors and customers often order Blue Max by asking for "the blue tape" or simply for "blue." When MDI learned that Pakor, Inc. (Pakor), was manufacturing and selling a brand of aquamarine blue leader splicing tape, "Pakor Blue," it brought suit for trade infringement. Did Pakor act morally in copying MDI's color for its splicing tape? Why do you think Pakor did this? Was there trademark infringement? [*Master Distributors, Inc. v. Pakor Corp., Inc.*, 956 F.2d219 (8th Cir. 1993)]

Critical Legal Thinking Writing Assignment

Read Case A.17 in the Case Appendix [*Feist Publications, Inc. v. Rural Telephone Service Company, Inc.*]. This case is excerpted from the U.S. Supreme Court opinion. Review and brief the case. In your brief, be sure to answer the following questions.

1. Who was the plaintiff? Who was the defendant?
2. What had the defendant done that caused the plaintiff to sue?
3. What is the issue in this case?
4. What was the decision of the U.S. Supreme Court?

Notes

1. 15 U.S.C. § 1125(a).
2. Article I, Section 8, clause 8 of the U.S. Constitution provides:
   The Congress shall have the power ... To promote the Progress of Science and useful Arts, by securing for limited Times to Authors and Inventors the exclusive Right to their respective Writings and Discoveries.
3. 35 U.S.C. § 10 et seq.
4. *Diamond v. Chakrabarry*, 447 U.S. 303, 100 S.Ct. 2204, 65 L.Ed.2d 144 (1980). The U.S. Supreme Court held that genetically engineered bacterium that was capable of breaking up oil spills was patentable subject matter.
5. Article I, Section 8, clause 8 of the U.S. Constitution.
6. 17 U.S.C. §§ 101 et seq.
7. 15 U.S.C. §§ 1114 et seq.
8. Senate Bill 1883, effective November 16, 1989.
9. Prior to the 1988 amendments, original registration of a mark was valid for 20 years and could be renewed for an unlimited number of 20-year periods.

E-Commerce
and Internet Law

Through the use of chat rooms, any person with a phone line can become a town crier with a voice that resonates farther than it could from any soapbox. Through the use of Web pages, mail exploders, and newsgroups, the same individual can become a pamphleteer.

STEVENS, JUSTICE *Reno v. American Civil Liberties Union, 521 U.S. 844 (1997)*

Chapter Objectives

After studying this chapter, you should be able to

1. Describe the free-speech protection granted to the Internet by the U.S. Supreme Court's opinion *Reno v. American Civil Liberties Union.*
2. Describe the process for obtaining Internet domain names.
3. Describe how the Federal Dilution Act prohibits domain names from diluting or tarnishing famous trademarks.
4. Describe how Internet domain names are being sold for millions of dollars.
5. Define *license* and the parties to a licensing agreement.
6. Describe the Uniform Electronic Transactions Act (UETA).
7. Describe the Uniform Computer Information Transactions Act (UCITA).
8. Define the informational rights protected by the UCITA.
9. Describe how the UCITA provides comprehensive rules for the creation, performance, and enforcement of licensing agreements.
10. Describe how federal law permits the exportation of encryption technology.

Chapter Contents

e-commerce
The sale of goods and services by computer over the Internet.

Business Brief
The use of the Internet and the sale of goods and services through e-commerce has exploded in the United States and worldwide.

Uniform Computer Information Transactions Act (UCITA)
A model act that provides uniform and comprehensive rules for contracts involving computer information transactions and software and information licenses.

Internet
A collection of millions of computers that provide a network of electronic connections between computers.

Our legal system faces no theoretical dilemma but a single continuous problem: how to apply to ever changing conditions the never changing principles of freedom.

Earl Warren
(1955)

In the late 1990s and early 2000s the use of the Internet and the World Wide Web, and the sale of goods and services through **e-commerce**, exploded. Large and small businesses began selling goods and services over the Internet through Web sites and registered domain names. Consumers and businesses can purchase almost any good or service they want over the Internet using such sites as Amazon.com, eBay, eToys, and others. In addition, software and information may be licensed either by physically purchasing the software or information and installing it on a computer or by merely downloading the software or information directly into the computer.

Many legal scholars and lawyers argued that traditional rules of contract law do not adequately meet the needs of Internet transactions and software and information licensing. These concerns led to an effort to create a new contract law for electronic transactions. After much debate, the National Conference of Commissioners on Uniform State Laws developed the **Uniform Electronic Transactions Act (UETA)** and the **Uniform Computer Information Transactions Act (UCITA)**. These model acts provide uniform and comprehensive rules for contracts involving computer information transactions and software and information licenses.

This chapter covers the registration of domain names and the operation of Web businesses and explains how the UETA and UCITA and other laws regulate the creation, transfer, and enforcement of e-commerce and informational rights licensing contracts.

THE INTERNET

The **Internet**, or "Net," is a collection of millions of computers that provide a network of electronic connections between the computers. The Internet was begun in 1969 by the U.S. Department of Defense to create electronic communications for military and national defense purposes. Building on this start, in the 1980s the National Science Foundation, the federal government's main scientific and technical agency, established the Net to facilitate high-speed communications among research centers at academic and research institutions around the world.

Eventually, individuals and businesses began using the Internet for communication of information and data. In 1980 there were fewer than 250 computers hooked to the Internet, growth was rapid in the late 1990s and into the early 2000s, and today there are several hundred million computers connected to the Internet. The Internet's evolution helped usher in the Information Age of today.

E-Commerce & Internet Law

RENO V. AMERICAN CIVIL LIBERTIES UNION

In 1997, the U.S. Supreme Court decided *Reno v. American Civil Liberties Union*, a major case involving free-speech rights over the Internet. In this decision, the Supreme Court recognized the importance and uniqueness of the Internet and World Wide Web and issued an opinion guaranteeing the users of the Internet the highest constitutional free-speech protection. This edited decision, in the language of the Supreme Court, follows.

Reno v. American Civil Liberties Union
521 U.S. 844, 117 S.Ct. 2329 (1997) Supreme Court of the United States

Stevens, Justice

Facts *The Internet is an international network of interconnected computers. The Internet has experienced extraordinary growth. The number of "host" computers—those that store* *information and relay communications—increased from about 300 in 1981 to approximately 9,400,000 by the time of the trial in 1996. Roughly 60% of these hosts are located in the United States. About 40 million people used the Internet at the time of trial, a number that is expected to mushroom to 200 million by 1999. Individuals can obtain access to the Internet from many different sources, generally hosts themselves or entities with a host affiliation. Most colleges and universities provide access for their students and faculty; many corporations provide their employees with access through an office network. Several major national "online services" such as America Online, CompuServe, the Microsoft Network, and Prodigy offer access to their own extensive proprietary networks as well as a link to the much larger resources of the Internet.*

Anyone with access to the Internet may take advantage of a wide variety of communication and information retrieval methods. These methods are constantly evolving and difficult to categorize precisely. But, as presently constituted, those most relevant to this case are electronic mail ("e-mail"), automatic mailing list services ("mail exploders," sometimes referred to as "listservs"), "newsgroups," "chat rooms," and the "World Wide Web." All of these methods can be used to transmit text; most can transmit sound, pictures, and moving video images. Taken together, these tools constitute a unique medium—known to its users as "cyberspace"—located in no particular geographical location but available to anyone, anywhere in the world, with access to the Internet.

The best known category of communication over the Internet is the World Wide Web, which allows users to search for and retrieve information stored in remote computers, as well as, in some cases, to communicate back to designated sites. In concrete terms, the Web consists of a vast number of documents stored in different computers all over the world. Some of these documents are simply files containing information. However, more elaborate documents, commonly known as Web "pages," are also prevalent. Navigating the Web is relatively straightforward. A user may either type the address of a known page or enter one or more keywords into a commercial "search engine" in an effort to locate sites on a subject of interest. Users generally explore a given Web page, or move to another, by clicking a computer "mouse" on one of the page's icons or links. Sexually explicit material on the Internet includes text, pictures, and chat and extends from the modestly titillating to the hardest-core. Some of the communications over the Internet that originate in foreign countries are also sexually explicit.

Statute Being Interpreted *The Telecommunications Act of 1996, Pub.L. 104-104, 110 Stat. 56, was an unusually important legislative enactment. Title V—known as the "Communications Decency Act of 1996" (CDA)—contains*

provisions that were either added in executive committee after Congressional hearings were concluded or as amendments offered during floor debate on the legislation. An amendment offered in the Senate was the source of the two statutory provisions challenged in this case. They are informally described as the "indecent transmission" provision and the "patently offensive display" provision. The first, 47 U.S.C.A. Section 223(a), prohibits the knowing transmission of obscene or indecent messages to any recipient under 18 years of age. The second provision, Section 223(d), prohibits the knowing sending or displaying of patently offensive messages in a manner that is available to a person under 18 years of age.

Lower Court's Opinion *On February 8, 1996, immediately after the President signed the statute, 20 plaintiffs filed suit against the Attorney General of the United States and the Department of Justice challenging the constitutionality of Sections 223(a) and 223(d). A second suit was then filed by 27 additional plaintiffs, the two cases were consolidated, and a three-judge District Court was convened pursuant to Section 561 of the Act. After an evidentiary hearing, that Court entered a preliminary injunction against enforcement of both of the challenged provisions.*

Issue *At issue is the constitutionality of two statutory provisions enacted to protect minors from "indecent" and "patently offensive" communications on the Internet.*

e·biz

U.S. Supreme Court's Reasoning *Each medium of expression may present its own problems. Thus, some of our cases have recognized special justifications for regulation of the broadcast media that are not applicable to other speakers. In these cases, the Court relied on the history of extensive government regulation of the broadcast medium, the scarcity of available frequencies at its inception, and its "invasive" nature. Those factors are not present in cyberspace. Neither before nor after the enactment of the CDA have the vast democratic fora of the Internet been subject to the type of government supervision and regulation that has attended the broadcast industry. Moreover, the Internet is not as "invasive" as radio or television. The District Court specifically found that "communications over the Internet do not invade an individual's home or appear on one's computer screen unbidden. Users seldom encounter content by accident." It also found that "almost all sexually explicit images are preceded by warnings as to the content," and cited testimony that "odds are slim that a user would come across a sexually explicit sight by accident."*

Unlike the conditions that prevailed when Congress first authorized regulation of the broadcast spectrum, the Internet can hardly be considered a "scarce" expressive commodity. It pro-

(box continues)

vides relatively unlimited, low-cost capacity for communication of all kinds. This dynamic, multifaceted category of communication includes not only traditional print and news services, but also audio, video, and still images, as well as interactive, real-time dialogue. Through the use of chat rooms, any person with a phone line can become a town crier with a voice that resonates farther than it could from any soapbox. Through the use of Web pages, mail exploders, and news-groups, the same individual can become a pamphleteer. As the District Court found, "the content on the Internet is as diverse as human thought."

The vagueness of the CDA is a matter of special concern for two reasons. First, the CDA is a content-based regulation of speech. The vagueness of such a regulation raises special First Amendment concerns because of its obvious chilling effect on free speech. Second, the CDA is a criminal statute. In addition to the opprobrium and stigma of a criminal conviction, the CDA threatens violators with penalties including up to two years in prison for each act of violation. The severity of criminal sanctions may well cause speakers to remain silent rather than communicate even arguably unlawful words, ideas, and images. Given the vague contours of the coverage of the statue, it unquestionably silences some speakers whose messages would be entitled to constitutional protection.

Systems have been developed to help parents control the material that may be available on a home computer with Internet access. A system may either limit a computer's access to an approved list of sources that have been identified as containing no adult material, it may block designated inappro-priate sites, or it may attempt to block messages containing identifiable objectionable features. Although parental control software currently can screen for certain suggestive words or for known sexually explicit sites, it cannot now screen for sexually explicit images. Nevertheless, the evidence indicates that a reasonably effective method by which parents can prevent their children from accessing sexually explicit and other material which parents may believe is inappropriate for their children will soon be available.

We are persuaded that the CDA lacks the precision that the First Amendment requires when a statute regulates the content of speech. In order to deny minors access to potentially harmful speech, the CDA effectively suppresses a large amount of speech that adults have a constitutional right to receive and to address to one another. In evaluating the free speech rights of adults, we have made it perfectly clear that "sexual expression which is indecent but not obscene is protected by the First Amendment" [Sable Communications of Cal., Inc. v. FCC, 492 U.S. 115 (1989)]. The Government may not reduce the adult population to only what is fit for children. The CDA, casting a far darker shadow over free speech, threatens to torch a large segment of the Internet community.

Holding *Notwithstanding the legitimacy and importance of the congressional goal of protecting children from harmful materials, we agree with the three-judge District Court that the statute abridges "the freedom of speech" protected by the First Amendment. For the foregoing reasons, the judgment of the district court is affirmed. It is so ordered.*

Electronic Mail

electronic mail (e-mail)
Electronic written communication between individuals and businesses using computers connected to the Internet.

Electronic mail, or **e-mail**, is one of the most widely used applications for communication over the Internet. Using e-mail, individuals and businesses can instantaneously communicate in electronic writing with one another around the world. Each person can have his or her own e-mail address, which identifies the user by a unique address. E-mail will continue to grow in use in the future as it replaces some telephone and paper correspondence and increases new communication between persons.

E-Commerce & Internet Law

E-MAIL CONTRACTS

E-mail has exploded as a means of personal and business communication. In the business environment, e-mail is sometimes the method used to negotiate and agree on contract terms and to send and agree to the final contract. The question presented is whether an e-mail contract is enforceable. Assuming that all of the elements to establish a contract are present, an e-mail contract is valid and enforceable. The main problem in a lawsuit seeking to enforce an e-mail contract is evidence, but this problem, which exists in almost all lawsuits, can be overcome by printing out the e-mail contract and its prior e-mail negotiations, if necessary.

A further issue arises if the contract is required to be in writing by the state Statute of Frauds. Because the parties to an e-mail contract can print a paper version of the electronic contract, this would meet the writing requirement of the Statute of Frauds. The analogy would be that a contract that is printed from the e-mail message is no different from a contract that is printed on the same printer from a word-processing program. Similarly, the use of names, symbols, codes, or other information that identifies the sender and his or her intent to be bound to the terms of the e-mail contract satisfies the signature requirement. The e-mail contract does not have to have a personal signature to be enforceable; electronic signatures have been held to be sufficient. Thus, e-mail contracts meet the writing and signature requirements for enforceable contracts.

E-Commerce & Internet Law

ELECTRONIC COMMUNICATIONS PRIVACY ACT

E-mail, computer data, and other electronic communications are sent daily by millions of people using computers and the Internet. Recognizing how the use of computer and electronic communications raise special issues of privacy, the federal government enacted the **Electronic Communications Privacy Act (ECPA)**. The ECPA makes it a crime to intercept an "electronic communication" at the point of transmission, while in transit, when stored by a router or server, or after receipt by the intended recipient. An electronic communication includes any transfer of signals, writings, images, sounds, data, or intelligence of any nature. The ECPA makes it illegal to access stored e-mail as well as e-mail in transmission.

The ECPA provides that stored electronic communications may be accessed without violating the law by the following:

1. The party or entity providing the electronic communication service. The primary example would be an employer who can access stored e-mail communications of employees using the employer's service.
2. Government and law enforcement entities that are investigating suspected illegal activity. Disclosure would be required only pursuant to a validly issued warrant.

The ECPA provides for criminal penalties. In addition, the ECPA provides that an injured party may sue for civil damages for violations of the act.

The World Wide Web

The **World Wide Web** consists of millions of computers that support a standard set of rules for the exchange of information called Hypertext Transfer Protocol (HTTP). Web-based documents are formatted using common coding languages such as Hypertext Markup Language (HTML) and Java. Businesses and individuals can hook up to the Web by registering with a server such as America Online (AOL) or other servers.

Individuals and businesses can have their own Web sites. A Web site is composed of electronic documents known as Web pages. The Web sites and pages are stored on servers throughout the world. They are viewed by using Web browsing software such as Microsoft Internet Browser and Netscape Navigator. Each Web site has a unique on-line address. Web pages can contain a full range of multimedia content, including text, images, video, sound, and animation. Web pages can include references, called *hyperlinks*, or *links*, to other Web pages or sites.

The Web has made it extremely attractive to conduct commercial activities on-line. New companies, such as Amazon.com and eBay, are e-commerce powerhouses that sell all sorts of goods and services. Existing companies, such as Wal-Mart, Merrill Lynch, and Dell Computers, sell their goods and services on-line as well. E-commerce over the Web will continue to grow dramatically each year.

World Wide Web
An electronic connection of millions of computers that support a standard set of rules for the exchange of information.

Business Brief
E-commerce over the Web has increased dramatically and will continue to grow in the future.

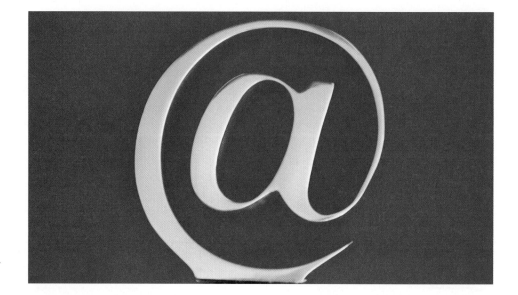

The use of the Internet and the World Wide Web have required courts to apply existing laws to new technologies, as well as spurring the federal Congress and state legislatures to enact new laws to govern modern means of communications and the conduct of electronic business.

International Perspective

e·biz

CHINA OPENS THE INTERNET

In November 1999, China and the United States entered into a historic trade pact that reduced tariffs and other barriers to entry for selling goods and services between the two countries. Prior to this trade pact, China had announced that it would not allow investment by foreign firms in China's Internet markets. In exchange for the United States opening its borders to more Chinese-made goods, China agreed to allow U.S. firms to invest in China's Internet businesses.

Although it agreed to open up its Internet markets, China has placed restrictions on foreign investment in Internet businesses. These restrictions include

- Foreign companies cannot own more than 50 percent of any Internet business in China.
- Foreign companies must obtain a special license from the Chinese government for such investments.
- China will regulate the content of Internet Web sites, including advertisements placed on the Web.

Critics of the pact argue that China could use the licensing procedures and content-approval rules to erect bureaucratic nontariff barriers to entry. Proponents argue that China has an incentive not to enforce the restrictions too harshly because strict enforcement would cause China to lose much needed foreign investment and technological knowledge and to risk retaliatory actions by the United States. Others argue that there are always ways around such restrictions, such as the traditional method of paying the appropriate government officials to get things done. In the borderless world of the Internet, some foreign companies may set up business in countries and areas near China and offer Internet services to China from these locations.

With over 1.2 billion people, China offers a great potential for the growth of the use of the Internet and e-commerce. If foreign companies are allowed up to a 50 percent investment in Internet companies and businesses in China, this is still far better than being shut out of the market altogether.

Internet Domain Names

domain name
A unique name that identifies an individual's or company's Web site.

e·biz

Each Web site is identified by a unique Internet **domain name**. For example, the domain name for the publisher of this book is www.prenhall.com. The four top-level suffixes for domain names are *com* for commercial use, *net* for networks, *org* for organizations, and *edu* for educational institutions.

Domain names can be registered. The first step in registering a domain name is determining whether any other party already owns the name. For this purpose, InterNIC maintains a "Whois" database that contains the domain names that have been registered. The InterNIC Web site is located on-line at internic.net. Domain names can also be registered at Network Solutions, Inc.'s, Web site, which is located on-line at www.network-solutions.com, as well as at other on-line sites. An applicant must complete a registration form, which can be done on-line. It costs $70 to register a domain name for two years, and the fee may be paid by credit card on-line.

Business Brief
Domain names may be registered by filing the appropriate form with the domain name registration service and paying the appropriate fee.

Entrepreneur and the Law

WEB DOMAIN NAMES SOLD FOR MILLIONS

What is a name worth? Plenty! It used to be that a person could make money by trademarking a name before a large company wanted to use the name for a product or service or as a new company name. Once in possession of the trademark, the owner could sell it at a profit if some company wanted it desperately enough. But trying to guess what names would be wanted took some work. In addition, trademark law required the name to be used in commerce. Although trademarking and selling trademark names is still a way to make money, the hottest area for name-selling is registering and selling Internet domain names.

Take the case of the domain name *business.com*. This name, which was originally registered as a domain name for $70, was sold to entrepreneur Marc Ostrofsky for $150,000 in 1996. Many people at the time thought this was an out-rageous sum to pay for a domain name—that is, until Mr. Ostrofsky turned around and resold the name to ECompanies in 1999 for $7,500,000. That was the most ever paid for an Internet domain name. ECompanies thought it was a bargain and plans to use it for its new Web site, where it will offer a form of Internet Yellow Pages.

Other domain names have been sold at high prices too. *Altavista.com* was purchased by Compaq Computer for its Internet search engine. Other domain names sold for high prices include *wine.com* for $3 million, *bingo.com* for $1.1 million, *wallstreet.com* for $1 million, and *drugs.com* for $800,000. As commerce over the Internet increases, and as unregistered memorable names become harder to find, transactions in the sale of domain names are expected to accelerate, with multi-million dollar price tags being paid for the most desirable names—which were originally registered for $70.

E-Commerce & Internet Law

ANTICYBERSQUATTING ACT PASSED BY CONGRESS

When the famous actor Brad Pitt went to register his name as the Internet domain name *bradpitt.com*, he discovered that someone else had already registered this domain name. When he checked the Web site, he was rudely faced with an offer to buy the name for $50,000. When Brad Pitt went to the next level and checked on *bradpitt.net*, he found that it had been taken by a company that was selling Brad Pitt memorabilia. So what's a famous person to do? Rely on Congress to pass a law that helps him or her. And that is exactly what the U.S. Congress did.

In November 1999, the U.S. Congress enacted, and the President signed, the **Anticybersquatting Consumer** **Protection Act**. The act was specifically aimed at cybersquatters who register Internet domain names of famous companies and people and hold them hostage by demanding ransom payments from the famous company or person. In the past, trademark law was of little help, either because the famous person's name was not trademarked or because, even if the name was trademarked, trademark law required distribution of goods or services to find infringement and most cybersquatters did not distribute goods or services but merely sat on the Internet domain name. The new act has two fundamental requirements: 1. The name must be famous. 2. The domain name was registered in bad faith. Thus, the law prohibits the act of

(box continues)

cybersquatting itself if it is done in *bad faith*. Proponents of the act state that the mere act of trying to profit from someone else's name shows the requisite bad faith. In determining bad faith, the law provides that courts may consider the extent that the domain name resembles the holder's name or the famous person's name, whether goods or services are sold under the name, the holder's offer to sell or transfer the name, and whether the holder has acquired multiple Internet domain names of famous companies and persons.

The act provides for the issuance of cease-and-desist orders and injunctions by the court. In addition, the law adds monetary penalties: A plaintiff has the option of seeking statutory damages of between $1,000 and $300,000 in lieu of proving damages. The Anticybersquatting Consumer Protection Act gives owners of trademarks and persons with famous names a new weapon to attack the kidnapping of Internet domain names by cyberpirates. Brad Pitt immediately sued the holders of *bradpitt.com* and *bradpitt.net* for violating the act.

E-Commerce & Internet Law

Domain Name Disputes Set for Arbitration

Under a contract with the United States government, the **Internet Corporation for Assigned Names and Numbers (ICANN)** is responsible for regulating the issuance of domain names on the Internet. ICANN contracted with Network Solutions, a private company, to register domain names. Until June 1999, Network Solutions was the exclusive registrar for all domain names bearing .com, .net, and .org. Since then, other registrars of domain names have been approved by ICANN.

Domain names are sometimes challenged for infringing on trademarks or service marks owned by businesses and individuals. In addition, the passage of the federal Anticybersquatting Consumer Protection Act of 1999 allows owners of famous names to challenge similar domain names that have been registered in bad faith. Civil lawsuits alleging violations of trademark law or the anticybersquatting law may take years to go to trial and cost a fortune to pursue.

In October 1999, ICANN approved an arbitration procedure for challenging cybersquatting. This procedure, called the **Uniform Dispute Resolution Policy (UDRP)**, requires all ICANN-approved registrars of domain names to agree to use this dispute resolution policy as part of their accreditation. The UDRP requires arbitration of domain name disputes. The dispute is heard by an arbitration panel approved by ICANN. ICANN has approved the World

Intellectual Property Organization (WIPO), an agency of the United Nations, as an arbitrator of domain name disputes. ICANN has also approved several private companies, including the National Arbitration Forum and the Disputes.org/eResolution.ca Consortium, to be dispute resolution arbitrators. In a UDRP arbitration hearing, a panel of trademark and intellectual property experts, who usually are scholars, retired judges, or other professionals, hear and decide the dispute. The decision of the arbitration panel can be appealed to the U.S. courts.

In its first ruling under the UDRP, the WIPO held that Michael Bosman, a resident of Redlands, California, had registered the domain name *www.worldwrestlingfederation.com* in bad faith. The World Wrestling Federation (WWF), a promoter of professional wrestling, had long owned the trademark to its name. Bosman, after registering the domain name, contacted the WWF and offered to sell it to the trademark holder. Instead of buying the name, the WWF filed a case with the WIPO. The WIPO arbitrator found that Bosman registered the domain name in bad faith in violation of the law. The arbitrator noted that the domain name was not Bosman's nickname or a name of any family member, and that he had not made any use of the name. The arbitrator concluded that the domain name was identical to the WWF's trademark and that Bosman had no legal rights to the domain name. The arbitrator ordered the domain name transferred to the WWF.

Business Brief
Intellectual property and information rights are valuable assets of individuals and businesses.

*L*icensing of Informational Rights

Intellectual property and informational rights are an extremely important asset of many individuals and companies. Patent, trademark, copyright, trade secret, and other laws protect intellectual property from misappropriation and infringement (see Chapter 17).

The owners of intellectual property and information rights often wish to transfer limited rights in the property or information to parties for specified purposes and limited duration. The agreement that is used to transfer such limited rights is called a **license**, which is defined as [UCITA § 102(a)(40)]

> *License means a contract that authorizes access to, or use, distribution, performance, modification, or reproduction of, information or informational rights, but expressly limits the access or uses authorized or expressly grants fewer than all rights in the information, whether or not the transferee has title to a licensed copy. The term includes an access contract, a lease of a computer program, and a consignment of a copy.*

The parties to a license are the licensor and the licensee. The **licensor** is the party who owns the intellectual property or informational rights and obligates him- or herself to transfer rights in the property or information to the licensee. The **licensee** is the party who is given limited rights in or access to the intellectual property of informational rights [UCITA § 102(a)(41),(42)]. A licensing arrangement is illustrated in Exhibit 18.1.

license
A contract that transfers limited rights in intellectual property and informational rights.

licensor
The owner of intellectual property or informational rights who transfers rights in the property or information to the licensee.

licensee
The party who is given limited rights in or access to intellectual property or informational rights owned by the licensor.

*Ɛ*XHIBIT 18.1   *Licensing Arrangement*

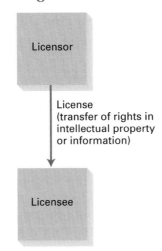

A license grants the contractual rights expressly described in the license and the right to use any informational rights within the licensor's control that are necessary to exercise the expressly described rights [UCITA § 307(a)].

There are times when the national interest is more important than the law.
Henry Kissinger (1976)

Exclusive License   A license can grant the licensee the exclusive rights to use the information. An **exclusive license** means that for the specified duration of the license the licensor will not grant to any other person rights in the same information [UCITA § 307(f)(2)].

exclusive license
A license that grants the licensee exclusive rights to use informational rights for a specified duration.

Licensing Agreement

The licensor and licensee usually enter into a written **licensing agreement** that expressly states the terms of their agreement. Licensing agreements tend to be very detailed and comprehensive contracts. This is primarily because of the nature of the subject matter and the limited uses granted in the intellectual property or informational rights.

licensing agreement
Detailed and comprehensive written agreement between the licensor and licensee that sets for the express terms of their agreement.

E-Commerce & Internet Law

e-biz

SOFTWARE AND INFORMATION ACCESS CONTRACTS

Sometimes instead of transferring a copy of information to a licensee, a software license grants the licensee the right to access information in the possession of the licensor. This type of license is called an **access contract**. Access contracts provide for access by the licensee to the information for an agreed-upon time or number of uses. The licensee's access to the information must be available at times and in a manner that complies with the express terms of the license. If such terms are not stated in the agreement, access by the licensee shall be at times and in a manner that is reasonable for the particular type of contract in light of ordinary standards of the business, trade, or industry.

The licensee's right of access is to information as periodically modified and updated by the licensor. A change in the content of the information is not a breach of contract unless the change conflicts with express terms in the license. An occasional failure to have access available is not a breach of contract if it is either (1) normal in the business, trade, or industry or (2) is caused by scheduled downtime; reasonable periods of failure of equipment, communications, or computer programs; or reasonable needs for maintenance [UCITA § 611].

e-biz

*T*HE UNIFORM COMPUTER INFORMATION TRANSACTIONS ACT (UCITA)

In July 1999, after years of study and debate, the National Conference of Commissioners on Uniform State Laws (a group of lawyers, judges, and legal scholars) issued the **Uniform Computer Information Transactions Act (UCITA)**. This is a model act that establishes a uniform and comprehensive set of rules that regulates the creation, performance, and enforcement of computer information transactions. A **computer information transaction** is an agreement to create, transfer, or license computer information or informational rights [UCITA § 102(a)(11)].

The UCITA does not become law until a state's legislature enacts it as a state statute. States are expected to adopt the UCITA or laws similar to the UCITA as their law for computer transactions and the licensing of informational rights. The UCITA will be used as the basis for discussing contract law affecting computer transactions and licensing of informational rights in this chapter.

Any provisions of the UCITA that are preempted by federal law are unenforceable to the extent of the preemption [UCITA § 105(a)]. Unless displaced by the UCITA, state law and equity principles, including principal and agent law, fraud, duress, mistake, trade secret law, and other state laws, supplement the UCITA [UCITA § 114].

Formation of a Contract

A contract may be formed in any manner that shows agreement, including an offer and acceptance, conduct of both parties, or operation of electronic agents [UCITA § 202(a)].

Offer and Acceptance   An offer to make a contract invites acceptance in any manner and by any medium reasonable under the circumstances. If an offer is received, the offer may be accepted by either promptly promising to ship a copy or shipping a copy of it. If an offer in an electronic message evokes an electronic message accepting the offer, a contract is formed when an electronic acceptance is received [UCITA § 203].

Acceptance with Varying Terms   A party can expressly make an offer conditional on agreement by the other party to all the terms of the offer. Acceptance by the other party of

---

computer informational transaction

An agreement to create, transfer, or license computer information or informational rights.

Business Brief

States are expected to adopt the UCITA or laws similar to the UCITA as their law for computer transactions and the licensing of informational rights.

People say law, but they mean wealth.

Ralph Waldo Emerson (1841)

all the terms creates a contract, but varying the terms in the purported acceptance does not create a contract [UCITA § 205].

If an offer has not been made conditional on acceptance of all the terms, and the party purporting to accept has varied the terms of the offer in his or her acceptance, the following rules apply: If the transaction is between merchants, the proposed additional nonmaterial terms offered by the offeree become part of the contract unless the original offeror gives notice of objection to these terms within a reasonable time after receiving them. If one of the parties is not a merchant, varying the terms of an offer by the offeree is a rejection of the offer and constitutes a counteroffer. Any material alteration of the terms of the offer by the offeree, even between merchants, rejects the offer and no contract is formed [UCITA § 204].

E- Commerce & Internet Law

COUNTEROFFERS INEFFECTUAL AGAINST ELECTRONIC AGENTS

In today's e-commerce, many sellers use electronic agents to sell goods and services. An electronic agent is any telephonic or computer system that has been established by a seller to accept orders. Voice mail and Web page order systems are examples of electronic agents.

In the past, when humans dealt with each other face to face, by telephone, or in writing, their negotiations might have consisted of an exchange of several offers and counteroffers until agreed-upon terms were reached and a contract was formed. Each new counteroffer extinguished the previous offer and became a new viable offer. Most electronic agents do not have the ability to evaluate and accept counteroffers or to make counteroffers. The Uniform Computer Information Transactions Act (UCITA) recognizes this limitation of e-commerce and provides that a contract is formed if an individual takes action that causes the electronic agent to cause performance or promise benefits to the individual. Thus, counteroffers are not effective against electronic agents [UCITA § 206(a)].

Consider This Example

"Birdie" is an electronic ordering system for placing orders for electronic information sold by the Green Company, a producer of computer software and electronic information. Freddie Calloway dials the Green Company's 800 telephone number and orders new software for $1,000 using the Birdie voice mail electronic ordering system. Freddie enters the product code and description, his mailing address and credit card information, and other data needed to complete the transaction, but at the end of the order states "I will accept this software if, after two weeks of use, I am satisfied with the software." Because Freddie has placed the order with an electronic agent, Freddie has ordered the software and his counteroffer is ineffectual.

e·biz

Duration   A contract may specify the duration of the license. If a contract does not specify its duration, the contract is valid for a time that is reasonable in light of the licensed subject matter and the commercial circumstances of the situation [UCITA § 308].

Parol Evidence   If the parties have entered into an electronic or written record of their contract that is intended to be a final expression of their agreement, the terms of that agreement cannot be contradicted by any previous agreement or contemporaneous oral agreement. For interpretation purposes, an electronic or written record may be explained by course of prior performance, course of dealing, or usage of trade [UCITA § 301].

Title to Copy   Title to a copy of the software or electronic information is determined by the license. In many licenses, the licensor reserves title to a copy; in other licenses title to the copy transfers to the licensee. A licensee's right under the license to possess, control, and use a copy is governed by the license [UCITA § 502(a)].

Authenticating the Record

authenticate

Signing the contract or executing an electronic symbol, sound, or message attached to, included in, or linked with the record.

attribution procedure

A procedure using codes, algorithms, identifying words or numbers, encryption, callback, or other acknowledgment to verify an authentication of a record.

e·biz

If a contract requires payment of a contract fee of $5,000 or more, the contract is enforceable against a party only if that party authenticated the record [UCITA § 201(a)]. **Authenticate** means either signing the contract or executing an electronic symbol, sound, or message attached to, included in, or linked with the record [UCITA § 102(a)(6)].

An electronic authentication is attributed to a person if it was the act of that person or his or her electronic agent [UCITA § 213]. Authentication may be proven in any manner, including a showing that a party made use of information or access that could have been available only if he or she engaged in operations that authenticated the record [UCITA § 108]. Authentication may be shown by using an **attribution procedure** to verify the electronic authentication and to detect errors or changes in electronic authentication. This procedure requires the use of codes, algorithms, identifying words or numbers, encryption, callback, or other acknowledgment [UCITA § 102(a)(5)].

Consider This Example   Yuan uses the Internet and places an order to license software for her computer from License.com, Inc., through its electronic Web site ordering system. The Web page order form asks Yuan to type in her name, address, telephone number, credit card information, computer information, and a personal identification number. The electronic agent requests that Yuan verify this information a second time before accepting the order, which Yuan does. Only after doing so does License.com, Inc.'s, electronic agent place the order and send an electronic copy of the software to Yuan's computer, where she installs the new software program. There has been authentication of Yuan's signature and a proper attribution procedure to verify the authentication.

A transaction that is covered by the UCITA is not subject to the Statute of Frauds, which requires contracts to be in writing, or by other state laws [UCITA § 201(f)].

Confirmation Letter   If the parties to a contract are merchants and the contract fee is $5,000 or more, the contract may be enforced even without authentication if one party to the contract sends a record confirming the contract and the other party does not reject the confirmation within 10 days after receiving it [UCITA § 201(d)].

E- Commerce & Internet Law

e·biz

THE UNIFORM ELECTRONIC TRANSACTIONS ACT (UETA)

To avoid impeding the growth of electronic commerce, there is a substantial need for a uniform law that regulates certain aspects of contracting over the Internet. To this end, the National Conference of Commissioners on Uniform State Laws promulgated the **Uniform Electronic Transactions Act (UETA)**. This model act is designed to create uniform laws for electronic records and electronic signatures. The goal of the act is to place electronic records and signatures on the same level as paper contracts and written signatures. Thus, electronic contracts should be as enforceable, as well as avoidable, as paper contracts.

The UETA applies only to transactions between parties who have agreed to conduct their transaction by electronic

means. Whether the parties agree to conduct a transaction by electronic means is determined from the context and surrounding circumstances, including the parties' conduct, customer initiation of Internet communications, and such [UETA § 5].

Once a transaction is determined to be covered by the UETA, the UETA recognizes two main concepts. First, the UETA states that an *electronic record* satisfies the requirement for a contract and also the requirement for writing where the contract is required to be in writing by the Statute of Frauds. Second, the UETA recognizes that an *electronic signature* is a signature that is enforceable equal to a written signature on a paper contract [UETA § 2]. In addition, the UETA specifies that if a law requires a record or signature to be notarized, acknowledged, or made under oath, the requirement is satisfied by an electronic signature of the authorized person, provided all information required in the notarization, acknowledgment, and so forth, is included [UETA § 11].

The UETA supports the increased use of electronic commerce by assuring that electronic records receive legal recognition on a par with paper contracts and that electronic signatures are treated equally to signatures written on paper. The UETA does not displace existing contract law concerning offer and acceptance, consideration, reliance, mistake, fraud, undue influence, duress, duties of care, and other contract requirements or defenses. The UETA does not become law until a state adopts the model act as its own statute. States are expected to adopt the UETA to provide uniformity of law for enforcing electronic records and signatures as contracts.

e·biz

Performance

A party to a licensing agreement owes a duty to perform in a manner that conforms to the contract. Each party owes a duty to tender performance when performance is due. **Tender of performance** occurs when a party who has the ability and willingness to perform offers to complete the performance of his or her duties under the contract [UCITA § 601].

tender of performance
Occurs when a party who has the ability and willingness to perform offers to complete the performance of his or her duties under the contract.

Consider This Example Maria enters into a licensing agreement to license electronic information from DataBase, Inc. DataBase, Inc., notifies Maria that a copy of the electronic information that she has licensed is available for her to download from its Web site; DataBase, Inc., has tendered performance. Maria offers to pay DataBase, Inc., the licensing fee by credit card; Maria has tendered performance.

Delivery of a Copy A software license requires the delivery of software, information, or data from the licensor to the licensee. The parties may designate in their contract the place for the electronic or physical delivery of a copy of the information. If no place is stated in the contract, the place of delivery is the licensor's place of business. Tender of delivery of a copy requires the tendering party to hold a confirming copy of the information at the licensee's disposition and to give the licensee reasonable notice to enable the licensee to obtain access or possession of the copy [UCITA § 606].

The Federal Congress and state legislatures are enacting laws that govern e-commerce and the Internet.

Licensee's Duty to Pay   The time and place of payment owed by the licensee may be specified in the license agreement. If payment is due upon the delivery of the copy of the information, the licensor's tender of delivery of the copy is conditioned on the licensee's tender of payment. If payment is not received from the licensee at that time, the licensor does not have to tender the copy [UCITA § 607].

Risk of Loss of the Copy   When the copy is delivered electronically or is not delivered by a carrier, the risk of loss of the copy passes to the licensee upon its receipt of the copy.

If a copy is delivered from the licensor to the licensee by a carrier, one of two rules apply: (1) If the agreement requires the licensor to deliver the copy to a particular destination, the risk of loss remains with the licensor until the copy is tendered at the designated destination, or (2) if the agreement does not require the licensor to deliver the copy to a particular destination, the risk of loss transfers to the licensee when the licensor delivers the copy to the carrier [UCITA § 614].

e·biz

Acceptance of a Copy   A licensee who has been tendered a copy by the licensor is deemed to have accepted the copy if the licensee (1) signifies that the tender was conforming, (2) acts with respect to the copy in a manner that signifies that the tender was conforming, (3) retains a copy despite its nonconformity, (4) commingles the copy or information with other copies or information, (5) obtains a substantial benefit from the copy that cannot be returned, or (6) acts in a manner inconsistent with the licensor's ownership of the copy [UCITA § 610].

A licensor is not required to provide instruction or other support for the licensee's use of the information or access to the information. If a licensor agrees to provide instruction or other support to the licensee, the licensor shall provide the support in conformity with the express terms of the agreement [UCITA § 612].

Excuse of Performance   The UCITA provides that a party's delay in performance or nonperformance under a license agreement is excused if the performance has been made impracticable. The UCITA stipulates that delay or nonperformance is made **impracticable** by (1) the occurrence of a contingency whose nonoccurrence was a basic assumption on which the contract was made or (2) compliance with any domestic or foreign statute or governmental rule. Where there is a delay or nonperformance excused by impracticability, there is no breach of contract.

Business Brief

The UCITA excuses performance if performance has been rendered *impracticable* by (1) the occurrence of a contingency whose nonoccurrence was a basic assumption on which the contract was made or (2) compliance with any domestic or foreign statute or governmental rule.

A party claiming the excuse of impracticability must reasonably notify the other party that there has been a delay in performance. If an excuse affects only part of the party's capacity to perform, the party claiming the excuse shall allocate performance among its customers in any manner that is fair and reasonable and notify the other party of the quota it is to receive. Whenever a party is notified that there is a delay or nonperformance caused by impracticability, that party may terminate the contract and thereby be discharged from the unperformed portion of the contract [UCITA § 615].

Consider This Example   Zeke, a foreign national and businessperson, enters into a licensing agreement to license certain informational rights from Zendex Corporation, a corporation located in the United States. Zeke is to take possession of the information when it is made available to him on Zendex's Web site, and he will be able to download it to his computer. Prior to the delivery of the informational rights, however, the U.S. Congress enacts a statute restricting the exporting of the type of information that Zeke has contracted to receive. In this instance Zendex's performance is excused because its performance of the contract has been made illegal by government statute.

Unconscionable Contract   A court, as a matter of law, may find that a contract is unconscionable at the time it was made. If a court finds that a contract or term in a contract is unconscionable, the court may refuse to enforce the contract, enforce the remainder of the contract without the unconscionable term, or limit the application of the unconscionable term so as to avoid an unconscionable result [UCITA § 111]. An unconscionable contract is one that the court finds to be so unfair that its enforcement would cause an unjust result. The doctrine of unconscionability is an equity doctrine that is sparingly applied by the courts on a case-by-case basis. It is never used to save a party from a bad deal it has negotiated and is usually used to save consumers, rather than businesses, from unjust contracts.

> *The precepts of the law are these: to live honestly, to injure no one, and to give everyone his due.*
>
> Justinian I Justinian Code, A.D. 533

E-Commerce & Internet Law

CONSUMERS SAVED FROM ELECTRONIC ERRORS

Under the common law of contracts, many parties who make unilateral mistakes while contracting are not relieved of the consequences of their error. The Uniform Computer Information Transactions Act (UCITA), which governs licenses of informational rights, is more lenient. The UCITA provides that consumers are not bound by their unilateral electronic errors if the consumer

1. Promptly upon learning of the error notifies the other party of the error.
2. Does not use or receive any benefit from the information, or make the information or benefit available to a third party.
3. Delivers all copies of the information to the third party or destroys all copies of the information pursuant to reasonable instructions from the other party.
4. Pays all shipping, reshipping, and processing costs of the other party [UCITA § 217].

Section 217 of the UCITA applies only to consumers who make electronic errors in contracting. Electronic errors by nonconsumers are handled under the common law of contracts or Uniform Commercial Code, whichever applies. The UCITA does not relieve a consumer of his or her electronic error if the other party provides a reasonable method to detect and correct or avoid the error. Thus, many sellers establish methods whereby the buyer must verify the information and purchase order a second time before an electronic order is processed. This procedure strips the consumer of the defense of UCITA Section 217.

Consider This Example
Kai, a consumer, intends to order 10 copies of a video game over the Internet from Cybertendo, a video game producer. In fact, Kai makes an error and orders 110 games. The electronic agent maintaining Cybertendo's Web site's ordering process electronically disburses 110 games. The next morning Kai discovers his mistake and immediately e-mails Cybertendo, describing the mistake and offering to return or destroy the copies at his expense. When Kai receives the games, he returns the 110 copies unused. Under the UCITA, Kai has no contract obligation for 110 copies but bears the cost of returning them to Cybertendo or destroying them if Cybertendo instructs him to do so. If Cybertendo's Web site's electronic ordering system had asked Kai to confirm his order of 110 copies of the purchase order, and Kai confirmed the original order of 110 copies, Kai has to pay for the 110 copies, even if his confirmation was in error.

e·biz

Warranties

Certain warranties may attach to a license of informational rights because either the licensor has made express warranties or the law has imposed one or more implied warranties. The law, however, permits some of these warranties to be disclaimed if certain requirements are met.

Warranties of Noninterference and Noninfringement   A licensor of information warrants that no third person holds any claim or interest in the information or claim of

> **Business Brief**
> **A licensor warrants that no third person holds any claim or interest in the information or claim of infringement or misappropriation that would interfere with the licensee's use or enjoyment of the information.**

infringement or misappropriation that would interfere with the licensee's use or enjoyment of the information. The UCITA permits these warranties to be disclaimed by specific language in the license if the language is conspicuous. Language such as "There is no warranty against interference with your enjoyment of the information or against infringement" is sufficient [UCITA § 401].

Consider This Example Antoine licenses a certain database from Data.com, Inc., for three years to use in her business. After using the database for a short time, Antoine receives notice from a court to desist from using the database because the data infringes a copyright held by Information.com, Inc. Here, there has been a breach of the warranty of noninfringement by Data.com, Inc.; Antoine can recover damages from Data.com, Inc., for the breach of this warranty.

express warranty

Any affirmation of fact or promise by the licensor about the quality of its software or information.

Express Warranty Licensors are not required to do so, but they often make express warranties concerning the quality of their software or information. An express warranty is any affirmation of fact or promise by the licensor about the quality of its software or information. An express warranty can result from a description of the information, advertising, samples or models, demonstrations of the final product, and such. It is not necessary that the licensor use the formal words "warranty" or "guaranty" to create an express warranty. An express warranty is not created by the licensor's statements of opinion [UCITA § 402].

Business Brief

The UCITA does not require a licensor to make an express warranty about the quality of its software or information.

Consider This Example Info, Inc., has developed software for the pricing of securities sold on Nasdaq. Info, Inc., warrants that its software is free from defects and will pay $10,000 liquidated damages and replace the software free of charge if the software does not perform correctly within the first year of use. Here, Info, Inc., has made an express warranty about the quality of its information. Financial Times, Inc., a financial services company, licenses the software from Info, Inc., but after three months of use the software fails. Info, Inc., owes Financial Times, Inc., $10,000 and a free replacement copy of the software.

Any language that attempts to disclaim an express warranty is inoperative to the extent it is inconsistent with the express warranty. Many disclaimers of express warranties are held to be invalid, because there is no reason to let a licensor make an express warranty that it can later take away [UCITA § 406(a)].

Implied Warranty of Merchantability of the Computer Program The law implies that a merchant licensor warrants that the computer program is fit for the ordinary purposes for which the computer program is used. This warranty is called **the implied warranty of merchantability of the computer program**. This implied warranty includes a warranty that the copies of the computer program are within the parameters permitted by the licensing agreements, that the computer program has been adequately packaged and labeled, and that the program conforms to any promises or affirmations of fact made on the container or label [UCITA § 403].

implied warranty of merchantability of the computer program

An implied warranty that the copies of the computer program are within the parameters permitted by the licensing agreement, that the computer program has been adequately packaged and labeled, and that the program conforms to any promises or affirmations of fact on the container or label.

Consider This Example Juan licenses a software program from Medi, Inc., to sort data and information from his extensive databases and to run with other software and database programs used in his medical supplies business. The licensing agreement and label on the Medi software program state that the copy of the licensed program has been tested and will run without error. Juan installs the Medi, Inc., software, but every third or fourth time he runs the software it fails to operate properly and shuts down his computer and other programs. There has been a breach of the implied warranty of the merchantability of the computer program because the Medi software does not fall within the parameters of the licensing agreement or affirmation of fact on the label. Juan can recover remedies from Medi, Inc.

The implied warranty of merchantability of the computer program can be disclaimed by the licensor, but only if the language of the disclaimer mentions the word "merchantability" or "quality" or words of similar import. The disclaimer must be conspicuous [UCITA § 406(b)(1)(A)].

Implied Warranty of Informational Content   A merchant that collects, compiles, processes, provides, or transmits informational content warrants to the licensee that there is no inaccuracy in the informational content caused by the merchant's failure to perform with reasonable care. This warranty is called the **implied warranty of informational content** [UCITA § 404].

Consider This Example   Christine licenses a database of historical and current interest rate information from DataMarket, Inc.; the information is updated daily by DataMarket, Inc. Christine uses the information to make extensive bond investments for her clients. Christine uses the information one day to make certain investments. It turns out, however, that DataMarket, Inc., made several accidental errors in inputting the interest-rate data, thus causing an error in Christine's calculations and decisions. Here there has been a breach of the implied warranty of informational content because the licensor, DataMarket, Inc., failed to perform with reasonable care. Christine can seek remedies against DataMarket, Inc.

The implied warranty of informational content can be disclaimed by the licensor, but only if the disclaimer mentions the word "accuracy" or uses words of similar import [UCITA § 406(b)(1)(B)].

Implied Warranty of Fitness for a Particular Purpose   A licensor that has reason to know of any particular purpose for which the computer information is required and knows that the licensee is relying on the licensor's skill or judgment to select or furnish suitable information warrants that the information is fit for the licensee's purpose. This warranty is called the **implied warranty of fitness for the particular purpose**. There is no implied warranty of fitness for a licensee's particular purpose concerning aesthetics, appeal, suitability to taste, or subjective quality of informational content [UCITA § 405].

Consider This Example   Ahmad, who operates a large Internet order-taking and delivery business, contacts IMB, Inc., a large software developer, about licensing software to operate his business. Ahmad tells the IMB representative about the volume of his business and his business needs and informs the IMB representative that he is relying on her to select the software that will meet his business needs. The IMB representative selects certain software for Ahmad, which he installs to run his business. The software, however, is inadequate to handle Ahmad's business needs. Here there has been a breach of the implied warranty of fitness for a particular purpose. Ahmad may pursue remedies against IMB, Inc.

The implied warranty of fitness for a licensee's particular purpose can be disclaimed, but the disclaimer must be in the electronic or written record. The disclaimer must state "There is no warranty that this information, our efforts, or the system will fulfill any of your particular purposes or needs" or words of similar import. The disclaimer must be conspicuous [UCITA § 406(b)(2)].

implied warranty of informational content
An implied warranty that there is no inaccuracy in the informational content caused by the merchant-licensor's failure to perform with reasonable care.

e·biz

implied warranty of fitness for a particular purpose
An implied warranty that information is fit for the licensee's purpose that applies if the licensor (1) knows of any particular purpose for which the computer information is required and (2) knows that the licensee is relying on the licensor's skill or judgment to select or furnish suitable information.

General Disclaimer of Warranties Instead of disclaiming each implied warranty individually, the UCITA permits a licensor to disclaim all implied warranties by expressions like "as is" or "with all faults" or other language that in common understanding calls the licensee's attention to the disclaimer and makes plain there are no implied warranties [UCITA § 406(c)]. All of the implied warranties are also disclaimed by stating "Except for express warranties stated in this contract, if any, this 'information' [or 'computer program'] is provided with all faults, and the entire risk as to satisfactory quality, performance, accuracy, and effort is with the user" or by using words of similar import [UCITA § 406(b)(3)]. General disclaimers must be conspicuous. Implied warranties may also be disclaimed by course of performance, course of dealing, or usage of trade [UCITA § 406(e)].

E-Commerce & Internet Law

ELECTRONIC SELF-HELP

When a licensor licenses its software to a licensee, it expects that the licensee will abide by the terms of the license. This includes protecting the licensor's trade secrets, using the software or information pursuant to the terms of the license, and paying the agreed-upon license fee. Just like normal contracts, however, electronic licenses can be breached by licensees. If such breach occurs, the licensor can resort to remedies provided in the UCITA. Sections 815 and 816 of the UCITA provide that a licensor can resort to electronic self-help if a breach occurs, for example, if the licensee fails to pay the license fee. Such electronic self-help can consist of activating disabling bugs and time bombs that have been embedded in the software or information that will prevent the licensee from further using the software or information.

Section 816 provides that a licensor is entitled to use electronic self-help only if the following requirements are met:

1. The licensee specifically agrees to the inclusion in the license of self-help as a remedy. General assent to the license is not sufficient; there must be a specific self-help option to which the licensee assents.

2. The licensor must give the licensee at least 15 days notice prior to the disabling action. The notice must contain the name and location of the person to whom the licensee can communicate regarding the issue. The notice period allows the licensee to make lawful adjustments to minimize the effects of the licensor's self-help or to seek a judicial remedy to combat the use of the self-help.

3. The licensor may not use self-help if it would cause a breach of the peace, risk personal injury, cause significant damage or injury to information other than the licensee's information, result in injury to the public health or safety, or cause grave harm to national security.

A licensor who violates these provisions and uses self-help improperly is liable for damages. This liability cannot be disclaimed. The UCITA gives licensees the right to obtain an expedited hearing in court if any of the self-help restrictions are violated. Licensors will continue to install and use such self-help devices, subject to the requirements and restrictions of the UCITA.

Breach of License Agreements

The parties to a contract for the licensing of information owe a duty to perform the obligations stated in the contract. If a party fails to perform as required, there is a breach of the contract. Breach of contract by one party to a licensing agreement gives the nonbreaching party certain rights, including recovering damages or other remedies.

Breach of contract occurs if a party fails to perform an obligation owed under the contract in a timely manner, repudiates the contract, exceeds a contractual use term, or otherwise does not comply with an obligation of the contract or one imposed by the UCITA. A breach is material if it amounts to a substantial failure to perform an essential element of the contract, practices of the business or industry, or the expectations of the parties or the breach is likely to cause substantial harm to the nonbreaching party [UCITA § 701].

Licensee's Refusal of Defective Tender   If the licensor tenders a copy that is a material breach of the contract, the nonbreaching party to whom tender is made may either (1) refuse the tender, (2) accept the tender, or (3) accept any commercially reasonable units and refuse the rest. In a mass-market transaction that calls for a single tender of a copy, the licensee may refuse the tender if the tender does not conform to the contract [UCITA § 704].

Licensee's Revocation of Acceptance   If a licensee has accepted tender of a copy where the nonconformity is a material breach, the licensee may later revoke his or her acceptance if (1) acceptance was made because discovery was difficult at the time of tender but was then later discovered or (2) the nonconformity was discovered at the time of tender but the licensor agreed to cure the defect, and the defect has not been reasonably cured. The licensee's revocation of acceptance is not effective until the licensee notifies the licensor of the revocation [UCITA § 707].

If a licensee refuses a tender of a copy or revokes a tender of a nonconforming copy, the licensee must deliver the copy and any copies made of it, all access materials, and documentation to the tendering party or hold them with reasonable care for a reasonable time for disposal at the tendering party's instructions. Upon refusal of tender by the licensee, any use, sale, display, or transfer of a copy of the information is a breach of the contract, and the licensee shall pay the licensor the reasonable value of such use [UCITA § 706].

Adequate Assurance of Performance   Each party to a license agreement expects to receive due performance from the other party. If any reasonable grounds arise prior to the performance date that make one party think that the other party might not deliver performance when due, the aggrieved party may demand adequate assurance of due performance from the other party. Until such assurance is received, the aggrieved party may, if commercially reasonable, suspend performance until assurance is received. Failure to provide assurance within 30 days permits the aggrieved party to repudiate the contract [UCITA § 708].

Anticipatory Repudiation   If a party to a contract repudiates the contract before performance is due, it is called an **anticipatory repudiation** of the contract. Upon an anticipatory repudiation, the nonbreaching party may (1) await performance by the repudiating party for a commercially reasonable time or (2) resort to any remedy available for breach of contract (remedies are discussed in the following section of this chapter). In either case, the nonrepudiating party may suspend its own performance of the obligation under the contract [UCITA § 709].

A repudiating party may retract its repudiation until the date of performance is due unless the nonrepudiating party has either canceled the contract or materially changed its position [UCITA § 710].

Remedies

The UCITA provides certain remedies to an aggrieved party upon the breach of a licensing agreement. A party may not recover more than once for the same loss, and his or her remedy (other than liquidated damages) may not exceed the loss caused by the breach [UCITA § 801]. A nonbreaching party may deduct any damages he or she has suffered because of a breach of contract from any payments he or she still owes under the same contract [UCITA § 810]. The UCITA provides that a cause of action must be

It will be of little avail to the people, that the laws are made by men of their own choice, if the laws be so voluminous that they cannot be read, or so incoherent that they cannot be understood.

Alexander Hamilton
The Federalist Papers *(1788)*

Business Brief
The UCITA provides various remedies that injured parties can obtain against breaching parties.

commenced within one year after the breach was or should have been discovered, but not more than five years after the breach actually occurred [UCITA § 805]. Remedies are discussed in the following paragraphs.

Cancellation   If there has been a material breach of the contract that has not been cured or waived, the aggrieved party may cancel the contract. **Cancellation** is effective when the canceling party notifies the breaching party of the cancellation. Upon cancellation, the breaching party in possession or control of copies, information, documentation, or other materials that are the property of the other party must use commercially reasonable efforts to return them or hold them for disposal on instructions from the other party. All obligations that are executory on both sides at the time of cancellation are discharged [UCITA § 802(a),(b)].

Cancellation of a license by the licensor ends any right of the licensee to use the information, copies, or materials subject to the license [UCITA § 802(c)(3)]. If the licensee cancels the license, the licensee can use the information or copy subject to the license for a limited time after the license has been canceled if the use would avoid or reduce loss [UCITA § 802(c)(4)]. A contract may provide that it cannot be canceled, but such restriction does not limit availability of other remedies [UCITA § 802(d)].

Licensor's Damages   If a licensee breaches a contract, the licensor may sue and recover monetary damages from the licensee caused by the breach, plus any consequential and incidental damages [UCITA § 808].

If the contract provides for a nonexclusive license, the licensor can recover lost profits caused by the licensee's failure to accept or complete performance of the contract. Lost profits is a proper measure of damages in this case because the licensor has effectively unlimited capability to make access available to others so there will be no license to substitute to reduce damages owed by the breaching licensee.

Consider This Example   iSuperSoftware.com licenses a master disk of its software program to Distributors, Inc, to make and distribute 10,000 copies of the software. This is a nonexclusive license and the license fee is $1 million. It costs iSuperSoftware.com $15 to produce the disk. If Distributors, Inc., refuses the disk and breaches the contract, iSuperSoftware.com can recover $1 million less $15 as damages for the profits lost on the transaction.

If a contract is an exclusive license, the damages that the licensor can recover from the breaching licensee depend on whether the licensor found a substitute transaction that mitigates damages. If a substitute transaction is found, for example, the licensor grants the exclusive license to another licensee, the recoverable damages are the difference between the original license fee and the lower license fee paid by the substitute licensee (there are no damages if a higher license fee is paid by the substitute licensee). If no substitute transaction occurs, the licensor can recover the lost profits on the transaction from the breaching licensee.

Consider This Example   Computers.com grants an exclusive license to National Wholesalers, Inc., to distribute its software in the United States. The license fee is to be $10 million, and it costs Computers.com $20 to produce the disk. National Wholesalers, Inc., refuses to accept the disk and breaches the exclusive license. Computers.com signs an exclusive license with Distributors, Inc., to distribute the software in the United States for a license fee of $8.5 million. In this case, Computers.com can recover $1.5 million less $20 as damages from National Wholesalers, Inc., for breaching the license. If, however,

e·biz

---

cancellation

The termination of a contract by a contracting party upon the material breach of the contract by the other party.

---

licensor's damages

If a licensee breaches a contract, the licensor may sue and recover monetary damages from the licensee caused by the breach.

Business Brief

If the contract is a *nonexclusive license*, the licensor can recover lost profits caused by the licensee's failure to accept or complete performance of the contract.

Business Brief

If the contract is an *exclusive license*, the licensor can recover lost profits from the breaching party if no substitute transaction is found; if a substitute transaction is found, the licensor can recover damages measured by the difference between the original license fee and the lower license fee paid by the substitute licensee.

Computers.com could not find a substitute licensor to distribute its software in the United States, Computers.com could recover $10 million less $20 from National Wholesalers, Inc., as damages.

Licensor's Right to Discontinue Access   If a licensee materially breaches the contract, the licensor may discontinue all rights of access of the licensee to the electronic facility provided by the licensor. This ability to quickly terminate access is important for the licensor to avoid on-going liability or continuing to provide benefits to the licensee who has breached the contract. The contract may provide for discontinuing access by the licensor upon the licensee's breach, even if it is not a material breach [UCITA § 813].

Licensor's Right to Possession and to Prevent Use   Upon cancellation of a license, the licensor has the right to have all copies of the licensed information returned by the licensee and to prevent the licensee from continued use of the licensed information. The licensor can do this by itself unless it would cause a breach of the peace or physical damage to the licensee's information or property. In this situation, the licensor must use the judicial process to obtain the information and an injunction against the licensee's further use of the information. These cases are given an expedited hearing in court [UCITA § 815].

Licensor's Right to Cure   Unlike the common law of contracts, the UCITA provides that a licensor may **cure** a breach of a license in certain circumstances. A breach of contract may be cured if (1) the time of performance of the contract has not expired and the licensor makes conforming performance within the time of performance, (2) the time of performance has expired but the licensor had reasonable grounds to believe the performance would be acceptable, then the licensor has a reasonable time to make conforming performance, or (3) the licensor makes a conforming performance before the licensee cancels the contract. In all three situations the licensor must seasonably notify the licensee of its intent to cure [UCITA § 703(a)].

Licensee's Damages   When a licensor breaches a contract, the licensee may sue and recover monetary damages from the licensor. The amount of the damages depends on the facts of the situation. Upon the licensor's breach, the licensee may either (1) cover by purchasing other electronic information from another source and recover the difference between the value of the promised performance from the licensor and the cost of cover or (2) not cover and recover the value of the performance from the licensor. **Cover** means engaging in a commercially reasonable substitute transaction. The licensee may obtain an award of consequential and incidental damages in either case. A licensee cannot obtain excessive or double recovery [UCITA § 809].

Consider These Examples   Auction.com is an Internet company that operates an on-line auction service. Auction.com enters into a contract with MicroHard, Inc., a software producer, for a site license to use MicroHard, Inc.'s, software. Auction.com agrees to pay $500,000 as an initial license fee and $10,000 per month for the license duration of three years. Before Auction.com pays any money under the license, MicroHard, Inc., breaches the contract and does not deliver the software. Auction.com covers by licensing commercially similar software from another software company for the payment of $600,000 initial licensing fee and $11,000 per month for the license duration of three years. Under the facts of this case, Auction.com can recover $100,000 for the increased initial license fee and $36,000 for the increased monthly costs from MicroHard, Inc., for breach of contract.

Business Brief

Upon cancellation of a license, the licensor has the right to have all copies of the licensed information returned by the licensee and to prevent the licensee from continued use of the licensed information.

Business Brief

If a licensee materially breaches the contract, the licensor may discontinue all rights of access of the licensee to the electronic facility provided by the licensor.

e·biz

right to cure

A licensor has the right to cure a contract if (1) the time of performance of the contract has not expired and the licensor makes conforming performance within the time of performance, (2) the licensor had reasonable grounds to believe the performance would be acceptable the licensor has a reasonable time to make conforming performance, and (3) the licensor makes a conforming performance before the licensee cancels the contract.

Business Brief

When a licensor breaches a contract, the licensee may sue and recover monetary damages from the licensor.

cover

The licensee's right to engage in a commercially reasonable substitute transaction after the licensor has breached the contract.

There is far too much law for those who can afford it and far too little for those who cannot.

Derek Bok (1983)

Assume in the prior example that MicroHard, Inc., delivers the software to Auction.com, but one of the promised elements of the licensed information is lacking. The software as contracted for would be worth $500,000, but the software as delivered is worth only $400,000. If Auction.com accepts the software as delivered with the missing information, Auction.com can sue MicroHard, Inc., and recover the value between the proper software and the software as delivered—$100,000 ($500,000 minus $400,000).

Licensee's Right to Continue Use   If the licensor breaches the contract, the licensee may continue to use the information contracted for. If it does so, the licensee is bound to the terms of the contract, must comply with the contracted use restrictions, and must pay the contracted for fees.

specific performance
Judgment of the court ordering a licensor to specifically perform the license by making the contracted-for unique information available to the licensee.

Licensee Can Obtain Specific Performance   The UCITA provides the remedy of **specific performance** if the parties have agreed to this remedy in their contract or if the agreed-upon performance is unique. The test of uniqueness requires the court to examine the total situation that characterizes the contract. Specific performance cannot be ordered for a personal service contract, however. This reflects the principle that an individual cannot be forced to perform a contract against the individual's will [UCITA § 811].

Consider This Example   Nedra enters into a licensing agreement to obtain access to certain informational rights from Info, Inc., for a specified monthly license fee. The data are proprietary to Info, Inc., and are not available from any other vendor. If Info, Inc., breaches the license and refuses to give Nedra access to the information, Nedra can sue and obtain an order of specific performance whereby the court orders Info, Inc., to make the contracted-for information available to Nedra for the duration of the license.

Limitations of Remedies

The UCITA provides that the parties to an agreement may limit the remedies available for breach of the contract. This is done by including contract provisions in the contract. Remedies may be restricted to return of copies and repayment of the licensing fee or limiting the remedy to the repair or replacement of the nonconforming copies. Limitation of remedies in licenses subject to the UCITA are enforceable unless they are unconscionable [UCITA § 803].

In the following case, the court upheld a limitation on remedies clause in a software license.

M.A. Mortenson Company, Inc. v. Timberline Software Corporation
970 P.2d 803 (1999)
Court of Appeals of Washington

CASE 18.1

FACTS
The Timberline Software Corporation (Timberline) produces software programs that are used by contractors to prepare bids to do work on construction projects. The M.A. Mortenson Company (Mortenson), a contractor, had been using Timberline software for some time without any problem. In 1993, Timberline introduced an advanced version of its bidding software program called "Precision." Mortenson, as the licensee, entered into a license agreement with Timberline, the licensor, to license the use of the Precision software. Timberline delivered the software to Mortenson and a Timberline representative installed the software on Mortenson's computer. The software license agreement contained the following terms, which were printed on the outside of the envelope in which the software disks were packaged and on the inside cover of the user's manual, and they also appear on the introductory computer screen each time the software program is executed:

CAREFULLY READ THE FOLLOWING TERMS AND CONDITIONS BEFORE USING THE PROGRAMS. USE OF THE PROGRAMS INDICATES YOUR ACKNOWLEDGEMENT THAT YOU HAVE READ THIS LICENSE, UNDERSTAND IT, AND AGREE TO BE BOUND BY ITS TERMS AND CONDITIONS. IF YOU DO NOT AGREE TO THESE TERMS AND CONDITIONS, PROMPTLY RETURN THE PROGRAMS AND USER MANUALS TO THE PLACE OF PURCHASE AND YOUR PURCHASE PRICE WILL BE REFUNDED. YOU AGREE THAT YOUR USE OF THE PROGRAM ACKNOWLEDGES THAT YOU HAVE READ THIS LICENSE, UNDERSTAND IT, AND AGREE TO BE BOUND BY ITS TERMS AND CONDITIONS.

LIMITATION OF REMEDIES AND LIABILITY NEITHER TIMBERLINE NOR ANYONE ELSE WHO HAS BEEN INVOLVED IN THE CREATION, PRODUCTION OR DELIVERY OF THE PROGRAMS OR USER MANUALS SHALL BE LIABLE TO YOU FOR ANY DAMAGES OF ANY TYPE, INCLUDING BUT NOT LIMITED TO, ANY LOST PROFITS, LOST SAVINGS, LOSS OF ANTICIPATED BENEFITS, OR OTHER INCIDENTAL, OR CONSEQUENTIAL DAMAGES ARISING OUT OF THE USE OR INABILITY TO USE SUCH PROGRAMS, WHETHER ARISING OUT OF CONTRACT, NEGLIGENCE, STRICT TORT, OR UNDER ANY WARRANTY, OR OTHERWISE, EVEN IF TIMBERLINE HAS BEEN ADVISED OF THE POSSIBILITY OF SUCH DAMAGES OR FOR ANY OTHER CLAIM BY ANY OTHER PARTY. TIMBERLINE'S LIABILITY FOR DAMAGES IN NO EVENT SHALL EXCEED THE LICENSE FEE PAID FOR THE RIGHT TO USE THE PROGRAMS.

On December 2, 1993, Mortenson used the Precision software and prepared a bid to do contracting work for the Harborview Hospital project. While preparing the bid, the program aborted at least five times before Mortenson's employees finished the bid. Subsequently, Mortenson claimed that its bid was $2 million under what it should have been had the Precision software program worked correctly. Mortenson sued Timberline to recover consequential damages, arguing that the Precision software calculated an inaccurate bid. Timberline defended, alleging that the limitation of remedies clause in the software license prevented Mortenson's lawsuit. Mortenson countered that the limitations of remedies clause was unconscionable and therefore unenforceable. The trial court granted summary judgment to Timberline and dismissed the lawsuit. Mortenson appealed.

ISSUE

Was the limitation of remedies clause in the Timberline software license unconscionable?

IN THE LANGUAGE OF THE COURT

Webster, Judge Mortenson makes much of the fact that Timberline never mentioned the license agreement or any of its terms during the negotiations. But the negotiations between the parties involved only the number of copies and the price. Timberline's failure to bring up the license terms during price-quantity discussions is hardly surprising. We hold that the terms of the present license agreement are part of the contract as formed between the parties. We find that Mortenson's installation and use of the software manifested its assent to the terms of the license and that it is bound by all terms of that license that are not found to be illegal or unconscionable.

Whether a limitation on consequential damages is unconscionable is a question of law. Considering all the circumstances surrounding the transaction in this case, the limitations clause is not unconscionable. Although Mortenson and Timberline did not specifically negotiate the limitations of remedies clause, this one factor is not conclusive. The introductory screen warned that use of the program was subject to a license. This warning placed Mortenson on notice that use of the software was governed by a license. Mortenson had reasonable opportunity to learn and understand the terms of the agreement. The limitations provision was not hidden in a maze of fine print but appeared in all capital letters. Finally, such limitations provisions are widely used in the computer software industry.

Limitations on consequential damages in commercial transactions are prima facie conscionable. Such clauses are standard in the software industry and do not shock the conscience. Indeed, they are useful in making software affordable. If software developers were prohibited from limiting consequential damages, the significant costs to the industry would be passed on to the consumer. We conclude that the limitations of remedies provision is not unconscionable. Thus, the limitations of remedies clause bars Mortenson's claim for consequential damage.

e·biz

DECISION AND REMEDY

The court of appeals held that the limitation of remedies clause in the software license was conspicuous and not unconscionable and that it therefore prohibited Mortenson's lawsuit to recover consequential damages from Timberline. The court of appeals affirmed the trial court's grant of summary judgment to Timberline that dismissed the case.

Case Questions

Critical Legal Thinking What does the doctrine of unconscionability provide? Does the doctrine serve any useful purpose?

Ethics Did Timberline act ethically when it included a limitation of remedies clause in its software license?

Business Application What would the business consequences be if limitation of remedies clauses in software licenses were all held to be *per se* illegal?

liquidated damages
Damages that are specified in the contract rather than determined by the court.

Liquidation of Damages   The parties to a license may provide that damages for breach of contract may be liquidated. **Liquidated damages** are damages that are specified in the contract rather than determined by the court. The amount of liquidated damages must be reasonable in light of the loss anticipated at the time of contracting or the anticipated difficulties of proving loss in the event of breach. The fixing of unreasonably large liquidated damages is void [UCITA § 804].

Working the Web

e·biz

History of the Internet

The Internet is an international network of computer networks connected via telephone lines, microwave links, and satellite links. The Internet began over 20 years ago as a way for the Department of Defense to communicate about military research. Originally the Internet meant the ARPANET, a modest network started in the late 1960s that connected four research centers—the University of California Los Angeles, the University of California Santa Barbara, Stanford Research Institute, and the University of Utah. About 10 years ago, the military aspects and educational aspects split, although funding remained with the Department of Defense.

Beginning in the mid-1980s, the National Science Foundation became interested in the Internet and decided to provide the technology to many universities. This developed into a loose federation of universities, government agencies, and private organizations concerned with communications and information exchange that are linked together. By the late 1980s, the Internet had crept all over the world, partially due to the proliferation of fiber optic and satellite links.

For the first decade of its existence, computer vendors were not actively involved, nor was advertising. The original National Science Foundation Acceptable Use Policy states that use is restricted to research and educational purposes. Commercial traffic is excluded. By the early 1990s, this changed. Commercial use is now the fastest growing aspect of the Internet. And businesses, law firms, government agencies, law libraries, and others have home pages on the Internet with links to other sites.

How to Evaluate Information on the Internet

How accurate is information found on the Internet? To evaluate this, you need to ask yourself several questions. First, what is the source of the information? This is the first question you need to ask when evaluating *any* information. If the information is published and main-

tained by a major university, a government entity, or a reputable business, it is probably as reliable and accurate as its corresponding print source. If the information is published and maintained by an individual, particularly if it mostly contains links to other information, it is probably reliable also. But if a Web site is a soapbox for a particular point of view, it is probably no more reliable than vanity press print material. Many Web sites are created and maintained by individuals on personal computers and are merely a reflection of that individual's life experiences and prejudices.

The second question you need to ask is whether the information is a form of advertising, such as a business Web page. Such sources are putting their best feet forward. However, because of possible sanctions for false advertising, these sources are quite reliable. If the information comes to you via unsolicited advertising or spamming, consider the probability that the information is the equivalent of junk mail and proceed accordingly. Political information on the Internet is no more accurate than political commercials on TV.

The third question to ask is how the information was added to the database. If you are familiar with computer assisted legal research databases such as LEXIS and WESTLAW, you know that some of the information is loaded onto those databases using scanning technology. Scanning technology has greatly improved, but still can create many typos. If you suspect that, for example, a case has been scanned into the database, it may be wise to check the print source as well (a practice that is equally wise when using LEXIS and WESTLAW).

Finally, determine when the Web site was last updated. Sites that are constantly updated can be very valuable sources of information. However, information that is several years old or contains links to outdated sites is not very valuable.

CYBER EXERCISE

1. Pick several business Web sites of your choice and evaluate the quality of information you find on them.

CASES AND EXERCISES

CRITICAL LEGAL THINKING CASES

18.1. Francis Net, a freshman in college and computer expert, browses Internet Web sites for hours each day. One day she thinks to herself, "I can make money registering domain names and selling them for a fortune." She has recently seen an advertisement for "Classic Coke," a cola drink produced and marketed by the Coca Cola Company. The Coca Cola Company has a famous trademark on the term "Classic Coke" and has spent millions of dollars advertising this brand and making the term famous throughout the United States and the world. Francis goes to the Web site, www.networksolutions.com, an Internet domain name registration service to see if the Internet domain name "classic-coke.com" has been taken. She discovers that it is available, so she immediately registers the Internet domain name "classic-coke.com" for herself and pays the $70 registration fee with her credit card. Coca Cola Company decides to register the Internet domain name "classiccoke.com," but when it checks at Network Solutions, Inc.'s, Web site, it discovers that Francis Net has already registered the Internet domain name. Coca Cola Company contacts Francis, who demands $500,000 for the name. Coca Cola Company sues Francis to prevent Francis from using the Internet domain name "classiccoke.com" and to recover it from her under the federal Anticybersquatting Consumer Protection Act. Who wins?

18.2. Francis Net, a freshman in college and computer expert, browses Internet Web sites for hours each day. One day she thinks to herself, "I can make money registering domain names and selling them for a fortune." She has recently seen advertisements for "Classic Coke," a cola drink produced and marketed by the Coca Cola Company, and for "Pepsi," a cola drink produced and marketed by Pepsi, Inc. The Coca Cola Company has a famous trademark on the term "Classic Coke," and Pepsi, Inc., has a famous trademark on "Pepsi"; both companies have spent millions of dollars advertising their brands and making the terms famous throughout the United States and the world. Francis, realizing that she cannot trade off the famous names "Classic Coke" or "Pepsi," thinks about what terms soda manufacturers might want to use as their domain name. Francis, who has traveled throughout the country, realizes that in some parts of the United States people call soda by the name "pop." Francis goes to the Web site, www.networksolutions.com, an Internet domain name registration service to see if the Internet domain name "pop.com" has been taken. She discovers that it is available, so she immediately registers the Internet domain name

"pop.com" for herself and pays the $70 registration fee with her credit card. Coca Cola Company decides to register the Internet domain name "pop.com," but when it checks at Network Solutions, Inc.'s, Web site, it discovers that Francis Net has already registered the Internet domain name "pop.com." Coca Cola Company contacts Francis, who demands $200,000 for the name. Coca Cola Company sues Francis to prevent Francis from using the Internet domain name "pop.com" and to recover it from her under the federal Anticybersquatting Consumer Protection Act. Who wins?

18.3. The Litle Steel Company is a small steel fabricator that makes steel parts for various metal machine shop clients. When Litle Steel Company receives an order from a client, it must locate and purchase 10 tons of a certain grade of steel to complete the order. The Litle Steel Company sends an e-mail to West Coast Steel Company, a large steel company, inquiring about the availability of 10 tons of the described grade of steel. The West Coast Steel Company replies by e-mail that it has available the required 10 tons of steel and quotes $450 per ton. The Litle Steel Company's purchasing agent replies by e-mail that the Litle Steel Company will purchase the 10 tons of described steel at the quoted price of $450 per ton. The e-mails are signed electronically by the Litle Steel Company's purchasing agent and the selling agent of the West Coast Steel Company. When the steel arrives at the Litle Steel Company's plant, the Litle Steel Company rejects the shipment, claiming the defense of the Statute of Frauds. The West Coast Steel Company sues the Litle Steel Company for damages. Who wins?

18.4. The Minute Steel Company is a small steel fabricator that makes steel parts for various metal machine shop clients. When Minute Steel Company receives an order from a client, it must locate and purchase 10 tons of a certain grade of steel to complete the order. The Minute Steel Company's purchasing agent opens the Internet and goes to a Web site called "steelauction.com." This is a Web site where sellers and buyers of steel can locate one another and make deals. On this Web site, the purchasing agent for Minute Steel Company finds that the East Coast Steel Company, a large steel company, has available the required 10 tons of the described steel at $450 per ton. The Minute Steel Company's agent agrees on-line to purchase the 10 tons of described steel at the quoted price of $450 per ton from East Coast Steel Company. The record and the signatures of both sides agreeing to the transaction are electronic. When the steel arrives at the Minute Steel Company's plant, the Minute Steel Company rejects the shipment, claiming the defense of the Statute of Frauds and invalid signatures. The Uniform Electronic Transactions Act (UETA) applies to the transaction. The East Coast Steel Company sues the Minute Steel Company for damages. Who wins?

18.5.   Einstein Financial Analysts, Inc. (EFA), has developed an electronic database that has recorded the number of plastic pails manufactured and sold in the United States since plastic was first invented. Using this data, and a complicated patented software mathematical formula developed by EFA, a user can predict with 100 percent accuracy (historically) how the stock of each of the companies of the Dow Jones Industrial Average will perform on any given day of the year. William Buffet, an astute billionaire investor, wants to increase his wealth, so he enters into an agreement with EFA whereby he is granted the sole right to use the EFA data (updated daily) and its financial model for the next five years. Buffet pays EFA $100 million for the right to the data and mathematical formula. After using the data and software formula for one week, Buffet discovers that EFA has also transferred the right to use the EFA plastic pail database and software formula to his competitor. Buffet sues EFA. What type of arrangement has EFA and Buffet entered into? Who wins?

18.6.   The Silicon Encryption Company, Inc. (SEC) has developed a very powerful encryption technology that permits a user to establish an encryption code that no person or computer program can figure out. Therefore, the encryption code developed by SEC is impenetrable when it is "wrapped" around electronic data. Imports, Inc., a United States company organized in the state of Florida, contacts SEC about acquiring the encryption technology. SEC conducts a reasonable investigation and due diligence review of Imports, Inc., and finds that the company is an importer of goods from around the world; SEC discovers no adverse information about Imports, Inc. SEC decides to deal with Imports, Inc., and Imports, Inc., pays SEC $10 million for the right to use SEC's encryption technology for five years. After one year, the United States government believes that Imports, Inc., is engaged in smuggling illegal drugs into the United States and has used SEC's encryption technology to protect any data implicating Import, Inc., in the illegal activity. The United States Department of Justice prosecutes Imports, Inc., for the crime of illegal drug smuggling, but the government loses the case because it cannot produce the necessary evidence that is protected by SEC's encryption technology. The U.S. Department of Justice therefore sues SEC for selling its powerful encryption technology to Imports, Inc. Is SEC guilty?

18.7.   An Internet firm called Info.com, Inc., licenses computer software and electronic information over the Internet.

Info.com has a Web site, "info.com," where users can license Info.com software and electronic information. The Web site is operated by an electronic agent; a potential user enters into Info.com's Web site and looks at available software and electronic information that is available from Info.com. Mildred Hayward pulls up the Info.com Web site on her computer screen and decides to order a certain type of Info.com software. Hayward enters the appropriate product code and description; her name, mailing address, and credit card information; and other data needed to complete the order for a three-year license at $300 per month; the electronic agent has Hayward verify all of the information a second time. When Hayward has completed verifying the information, she types at the end of her order, "I accept this electronic software only if after I have used it for two months do I still personally like it." Info.com's electronic agent delivers a copy of the software to Hayward, who downloads the copy of the software onto her computer. Two weeks later Hayward sends the copy of the software back to Info.com stating, "Read our contract: I personally don't like this software, cancel my license." Info.com sues Hayward to recover the license payments for three years. Who wins?

18.8.   David Abacus uses the Internet and places an order to license software for his computer from Inet.License, Inc. (Inet), through Inet's electronic Web site ordering system. Inet's Web page order form asks David to type in his name, mailing address, telephone number, e-mail address, credit card information, computer location information, and personal identification number. Inet's electronic agent requests that David verify the information a second time before it accepts the order, which David does. The license duration is two years at a license fee of $300 per month. Only after receiving the verification of information does Inet's electronic agent place the order and sends an electronic copy of the software to David's computer, where he installs the new software program. David later refuses to pay the license fee due Inet because he claims his electronic signature and information were not authentic. Inet sues David to recover the license fee. Is David's electronic signature enforceable against him?

18.9.   Tiffany Pan, a consumer, intends to order three copies of a financial software program from iSoftware, Inc. Tiffany, using her computer, enters iSoftware's Web site "isoftware.com" and places an order with the electronic agent taking orders for the Web site. The license provides for a duration of three years at $300 per month for each copy of the software program. Tiffany enters the necessary product code and description; her name, mailing address, and credit card information; and other data necessary to place the order. When the electronic order form prompts Tiffany to enter the number of copies of the software program she is ordering,

Tiffany mistakenly types in "30." Isoftware's electronic agent places the order and ships out 30 copies of the software program to Tiffany. When Tiffany receives the 30 copies of the software program, she ships them back to iSoftware with a note stating, "Sorry, there has been a mistake. I only meant to order three copies of the software, not 30." When iSoftware bills Tiffany for the license fees for the 30 copies, Tiffany refuses to pay. Isoftware sues Tiffany to recover the license fees for 30 copies. Who wins?

18.10. Silvia Miofsky licenses a software program from Accura.com, Inc., to sort information from a database to be used in Silvia's financial planning business. The license is for three years and the license fee is $500 per month. The new software program from Accura.com will be used to run in conjunction with other software programs and databases used by Silvia in her business. The licensing agreement between Accura.com and Silvia, as well as the label on the software package, state that the copy of the licensed software program has been tested by Accura.com and will run without error. Silvia installs the copy of Accura.com's software, but every fifth or sixth time the program is run it fails to operate properly and shuts down Silvia's computer and other programs. Silvia sends the software back to Accura.com marked "defective." When Accura.com bills Silvia for the unpaid license fees for the three years of the license, Silvia refuses to pay. Accura.com sues Silvia to recover the license fees under the three-year license. Who wins?

18.11. Harold Harrington operates a large personal financial planning business. He contacts Hardware/Software, Inc., a seller of software programs and electronic information, about licensing a software program from Hardware/Software, Inc. Harold tells the Hardware/Software sales representative about the scope and volume of his business and his business needs and informs the Hardware/Software representative that he is relying on her to select the software that will meet his business needs. The Hardware/Software sales representative selects the software program called "PerFinPlan III" for Harold's business. The license is $500 per month for three years. Harold installs the PerFinPlan III software. The software, however, is inadequate to handle Harold's financial planning requirements of his clients. After one month, Harold notifies the sales representative for Hardware/Software that the PerFinPlan III software does not meet his described business needs. Harold returns the copy of the software to Hardware/Software and demands the return of his one month's license fee. Hardware/Software sues Harold to recover the unpaid license fees for the duration of the license. Who wins?

18.12. Metatag, Inc., is a developer and distributor of software and electronic information rights over the Internet. Metatag produces a software program called "Virtual 4-D Links;" a user of the program merely types in the name of a city and address anywhere in the world and the computer transports the user there and creates a four-dimensional space and a sixth-sense unknown to the world before. The software license is nonexclusive and Metatag licenses its Virtual 4-D Link to millions of users worldwide. Nolan Bates, who has lived alone with his mother too long, licenses the Virtual 4-D Link program for five years at $350 per month license fee. Bates uses the program for two months before his mother discovers why he has had a smile on his face lately. Bates, upon his mother's urging, returns the Virtual 4-D Link software program to Metatag stating that he is canceling the license. Metatag sues Bates to recover the unpaid license fees. Who wins?

ETHICS CASES

18.13. BluePeace.org is a new environmentalist group that has decided that expounding its environmental causes over the Internet is the best and most efficient way to spend its time and money to advance its environmental causes. To draw attention to its Web sites, BluePeace.org comes up with "catchy" Internet domain names. One is "macyswearus.org," another is "exxonvaldezesseals.org," and another is "general-motorscrashesdummies.org." The "macyswearus.org" Web site first shows beautiful women dressed in mink fur coats sold by Macy's Department Stores and then goes into graphic photos of minks being slaughtered and skinned and made into the coats. The "exxonvaldezesseals.org" Web site first shows a beautiful pristine bay in Alaska with the Exxon Valdez oil tanker quietly sailing through the waters and then shows photos of the ship breaking open and spewing forth oil and then seals who are gooed with oil suffocating and dying on the shoreline. The Web site "generalmotorscrashesdummies.org" shows a General Motors automobile involved in normal crash tests with dummies followed by photographs of automobile accident scenes where people and children lay bleeding and dying after an accident involving General Motors automobiles. Macy's Department Stores, the Exxon Oil Company, and the General Motors Corporation sue BluePeace.org for violating the federal Anticybersquatting Consumer Protection Act. Who wins? Has BluePeace.org acted unethically in this case?

18.14. Apricot.com is a major software developer that licenses software to be used over the Internet. One of its programs called "Match" is a search engine that searches personal ads on the Internet and provides a "match" for users for potential dates and possible marriage partners. Norlan Bates subscribes to the Match software program from Apricot.com. The license duration is five years at $200 per month license fee. For each subscriber, Apricot.com produces a separate Web page that shows photos of the subscriber and personal data. Bates places a photo of himself with his mother with the caption, "Male, 30 years old, lives with mother, likes quiet nights at home." Bates licenses the Apricot.com "Match" software and uses it 12 hours each day searching for his Internet match. Bates does not pay Apricot.com the required monthly licensing fees for any of the three months he uses the software. After using the Match software but refusing to pay Apricot.com its licensing fee, Apricot.com activates the disabling bug in the software and disables the Match software on Bates's computer. Apricot.com did this with no warning to Bates. It then sends a letter to Bates stating, "Loser, the license is canceled!" Bates sues Apricot.com for disabling the Match software program. Who wins? Did Bates act ethically? Did Apricot.com act ethically?

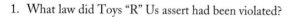

CRITICAL LEGAL THINKING WRITING ASSIGNMENT

e·biz

Read Case A.18 in the Case Appendix [*Toys "R" Us, Inc. v. Abir*]. This case is excerpted from the district court opinion. Review and brief the case. In your brief, be sure to answer the following questions:

1. What law did Toys "R" Us assert had been violated?

2. What elements must be shown to prove that this law has been violated?

3. Did the court find that the law had been violated?

4. Was defendant Abir's conduct ethical?

Formation of Sales and Lease Contracts

Commercial law lies within a narrow compass, and is far purer and freer from defects than any other part of the system.

HENRY PETER BROUGHAM
House of Commons, February 7, 1828

Chapter Objectives

After studying this chapter, you should be able to

1. Define sales contracts governed by Article 2 of the UCC.
2. Define lease contracts governed by Article 2A of the UCC.
3. Apply the basic UCC principles of good faith and reasonableness.
4. Describe the formation of sales and lease contracts.
5. Describe the gap-filling rules of the UCC.
6. Define the UCC's firm offer rule.
7. Describe the UCC's additional terms rule and apply it to solve the "battle of the forms."
8. Define the UCC's written confirmation rule.
9. Describe how sales and lease contracts can be modified.
10. Identify unconscionable sales and lease contracts.

Chapter Contents

goods
Tangible things that are movable at the time of their identification to the contract.

Uniform Commercial Code
Comprehensive statutory scheme that includes laws that cover most aspects of commercial transactions.

Article 2 (Sales)
Article of the UCC that governs sale of goods.

Most tangible items—books, clothing, cars, and such—are considered **goods**. In medieval times, merchants gathered at fairs in Europe to exchange such goods. Over time, certain customs and rules evolved for enforcing contracts and resolving disputes. These customs and rules, which were referred to as the "Law Merchant," were enforced by "fair courts" established by the merchants. Eventually, the customs and rules of the Law Merchant were absorbed into the common law.

Toward the end of the 1800s, England enacted a statute (the Sales of Goods Act) that codified the common law rules of commercial transactions. In the United States, laws governing the sale of goods also developed. In 1906, the **Uniform Sales Act** was promulgated in the United States. This act was enacted in many states. It was quickly outdated, however, as mass production and distribution of goods developed in the twentieth century.

In 1952, the Commissioners on Uniform State Laws promulgated a comprehensive statutory scheme called the **Uniform Commercial Code** (the UCC). The UCC covers most aspects of commercial transactions. Exhibit 17.1 provides an overview of the entire statute. Different states have enacted all or part of the various articles. The UCC is set forth in Appendix B.

Article 2 (Sales) and Article 2A (Leases) of the UCC govern sales contracts and personal property leases. These articles are intended to provide clear, easy-to-apply rules for the formation and performance of sales and lease contracts. The common law of contracts governs if either Article 2 or Article 2A is silent on an issue.

This chapter discusses the formation of sales and lease contracts.

SCOPE OF ARTICLE 2 (SALES)

All states except Louisiana have adopted some version of **Article 2 (Sales)** of the UCC. Article 2 is also applied by federal courts to sales contracts governed by federal law.

Contemporary Business Application _____

THE UNIFORM COMMERCIAL CODE (UCC)

One of the major frustrations of business-persons conducting interstate business is that they are subject to the laws of each of the states in which they operate. To address this problem, in 1949 the National Conference of Commissioners on Uniform State Laws promulgated the **Uniform Commercial Code (UCC)**. The UCC is a **model act** that contains uniform rules that govern commercial transactions. To create this uniformity, individual states needed to enact the UCC as their commercial law statute. In fact, they did, and every state (except Louisiana, which has adopted only parts of the UCC) enacted the UCC as a commercial statute.

The UCC is divided into articles, with each article establishing uniform rules for a particular facet of commerce in this country. The articles of the UCC are

Article 1	General provisions
Article 2	Sales
Article 2A Revised	Leases
Article 3	Negotiable instruments

Article 4	Bank deposits and collections
Article 4A	Wire transfers
Article 5	Letters of credit
Article 6	Bulk transfers
Article 7	Documents of title
Article 8	Investment securities
Article 9	Secured transactions

Each of these articles is discussed in the chapters in this section of this book.

The UCC is continually being revised to reflect changes in modern commercial practices and technology. For example, Article 2A was drafted to govern leases of personal property, and Article 4A was added to regulate the use of wire transfers in the banking system. Articles 3 and 4, which cover the creation and transfer of negotiable instruments and the clearing of checks through the banking system, were substantially amended in 1990. Article 2, which covers the sale of goods, currently is in the initial stages of revision.

What Is a Sale?

Article 2 applies to *transactions in goods* [UCC 2-102]. All states have held that Article 2 applies to the sale of goods. A **sale** consists of the passing of title from a seller to a buyer for a price [UCC 2-106(1)]. For example, the purchase of a book is a sale subject to Article 2. This is so whether the book was paid for by cash, check, credit card, or other form of consideration.

sale
The passing of title from a seller to a buyer for a price.

The Uniform Commercial Code (UCC) provides a set of uniform and comprehensive rules for governing the creation, performance, and enforcement of contracts involving the lease of goods, such as these bicycles.

What Are "Goods"?

Goods are defined as tangible things that are movable at the time of their identification in the contract [UCC 2-105(1)]. Specially manufactured goods and the unborn young of animals are examples of goods.

Money and intangible items, such as stocks, bonds, and patents, are not tangible goods. Therefore, they are not subject to Article 2. Real estate is not subject to Article 2, either, because it is not movable [UCC 2-105(1)]. Minerals, structures, growing crops, and other things that are severable from real estate may be classified as goods subject to Article 2, however. For example, the sale (and removal) of a chandelier in a house is a sale of a good subject to Article 2 because its removal would not materially harm the realty. However, the sale and removal of the furnace would be a sale of real property because its removal would cause material harm [UCC 2-107(2)].

Business Brief
Article 2 applies only to transactions in *goods*. Article 2 does not apply to transactions in intangible items, real estate or service.

Goods Versus Services   Contracts for the provision of services—including legal services, medical services, dental services, and such—are not covered by Article 2. Sometimes, however, a sale involves both the provision of a service and a good in the same transaction. This is referred to as a **mixed sale**. Article 2 applies only to mixed sales if the goods are the predominant part of the transaction. The UCC provides no guidance for deciding cases based on mixed sales. Therefore, the courts decide these issues on a case-by-case basis.

In the following case, the court had to decide whether a sale was of a good or a service.

mixed sale
A sale that involves the provision of a service and a good in the same transaction.

Hector v. Cedars-Sinai Medical Center
180 Cal.App.3d 493, 225 Cal.Rptr. 595 (1986)
California Court of Appeals

CASE 19.1

FACTS

Frances Hector entered Cedars-Sinai Medical Center (Cedars-Sinai), Los Angeles, California, for a surgical operation on her heart. During the operation, a pacemaker was installed in Hector. The pacemaker, which was manufactured by American Technology, Inc., was installed at Cedars-Sinai by Hector's physician, Dr. Eugene Kompaniez. The pacemaker was defective, causing injury to Hector. Hector sued Cedars-Sinai under Article 2 of the UCC for breach of warranty. The trial court held that the sale was primarily a sale of a service and not of goods, and therefore the UCC did not apply. The court granted Cedars-Sinai's motion for summary judgment and dismissed Hector's lawsuit. Hector appealed.

ISSUE

Is the installation of a pacemaker by a hospital a sale of a good subject to Article 2 of the UCC?

IN THE LANGUAGE OF THE COURT

Spencer, Presiding Judge *Plaintiff Hector seeks to extend liability to a hospital that furnishes, in connection with the care and treatment of a patient, a product that proves to have a defect that causes injury to the patient. The theory upon which she seeks to predicate such liability is that the hospital is a "supplier" of such product and, therefore, should be subject to the same standard of liability as any other supplier of articles or products.*

The physician's services depend upon his skill and judgment derived from his specialized training, knowledge, experience, and skill. A doctor diagnosing and treating a patient normally is not selling either a product or insurance. A hospital is not ordinarily engaged in the business of selling any of the products or equipment it uses in providing such services. The essence of the relationship *between a hospital and its patients does not relate essentially to any product or piece of equipment it uses but to the professional services it provides. This principle does not apply where the hospital is engaged in activities not integrally related to its primary function of providing medical services, such as the situation where the hospital operates a gift shop that sells a defective product.*

Testimony indicates that Cedars-Sinai does not routinely stock pacemakers, nor is it in the business of selling, distributing, or testing pacemakers. The treatment provided by Cedars-Sinai in relation to implantation of pacemakers includes pre- and post-operative care, nursing care, a surgical operating room, and technicians. The foregoing declarations indicate Cedars-Sinai is not engaged in the business of distributing pacemakers to the public. As a provider of services rather than a seller of a product, the hospital is not subject to liability for a defective product provided to the patient during the course of his or her treatment.

DECISION AND REMEDY

The court of appeals held that Cedars-Sinai was a provider of medical services and not a seller of goods. Therefore, Cedars-Sinai was not liable for breach of warranty under the UCC because the UCC did not apply. Affirmed.

Case Questions

Critical Legal Thinking Should the UCC be extended to service providers?

Ethics Was it ethical for the hospital to deny liability in this case?

Business Application Could American Technology, Inc., be held liable to the plaintiff in this case? Why do you think the plaintiff sued Cedars-Sinai?

Who Is a Merchant?

Business Brief

UCC Article 2 defines a *merchant* as a person who (1) deals in the goods of the kind involved in the transaction or (2) by his or her occupation holds himself or herself out as having knowledge or skill peculiar to the goods involved in the transaction.

Generally, Article 2 applies to all sales contracts, whether they involve merchants or not. However, Article 2 contains several provisions that either apply only to merchants or impose a greater duty on merchants. UCC 2-104(1) defines a *merchant* as (1) a person who deals in the goods of the kind involved in the transaction or (2) a person who by his or her occupation holds him- or herself out as having knowledge or skill peculiar to the goods involved in the transaction. For example, a sporting goods dealer is a merchant with respect to sporting goods but is not if he or she sells his or her lawn mower to a neighbor. The courts disagree as to whether farmers are merchants within this definition.

SCOPE OF ARTICLE 2A (LEASES)

Personal property leases are a billion-dollar industry. Consumer rentals of automobiles or equipment and commercial leases of such items as aircraft and industrial machinery fall into this category. In the past, these transactions were governed by a combination of common law principles, real estate law, and reference to Article 2. Some of these legal rules and concepts do not quite fit a lease transaction.

Article 2A of the UCC was promulgated in 1987. This article is cited as the **Uniform Commercial Code—Leases** and directly addresses personal property leases [UCC 2A-101]. It establishes a comprehensive, uniform law covering the formation, performance, and default of leases in goods [UCC 2A-102, 2A-103(h)].

Article 2A is similar to Article 2. In fact, many Article 2 provisions were changed to reflect leasing terminology and practices and were carried over to Article 2A. Many states have adopted Article 2A, and many more are expected to do so in the future.

Definition of a Lease

A **lease** is a transfer of the right to the possession and use of the named goods for a set term in return for certain consideration [UCC 2A-103(1)(i)(x)]. The leased goods can be anything from a hand tool leased to an individual for a few hours to a complex line of industrial equipment leased to a multinational corporation for a number of years.

In an ordinary lease, the **lessor** is the person who transfers the right of possession and use of goods under the lease [UCC 2A-103(1)(p)]. The **lessee** is the person who acquires the right to possession and use of goods under a lease [UCC 2A-103(1)(n)].

Special Forms of Leases

Certain provisions of Article 2A apply only to special forms of leases, such as consumer leases and finance leases. A **consumer lease** is one with a value of $25,000 or less between a lessor regularly engaged in the business of leasing or selling and a lessee who leases the goods primarily for a personal, family, or household purpose [UCC 2A-103(1)(e)].

A **finance lease** is a three-party transaction consisting of the lessor, the lessee, and the supplier (or vendor). The lessor does not select, manufacture, or supply the goods. Instead, the lessor acquires title to the goods or the right to their possession and use in connection with the terms of the lease [UCC 2A-103(1)(g)].

Consider This Example   The Dow Chemical Company decides to use robotics to manufacture most of its products. It persuades Ingersoll-Rand to design the robotic equipment that would meet its needs. To finance the purchase of the equipment, Dow Chemical goes to City Bank, which purchases the robotics equipment from Ingersoll-Rand and leases it to Dow Chemical. City Bank is the lessor, Dow Chemical is the lessee, and Ingersoll-Rand is the supplier.

Article 2A (Leases)
Article of the UCC that governs lease of goods.

lease
A transfer of the right to the possession and use of the named goods for a set term in return for certain consideration.

lessor
The person who transfers the right of possession and use of goods under the lease.

lessee
The person who acquires the right to possession and use of goods under a lease.

consumer lease
A lease with a value of $25,000 or less between a lessor regularly engaged in the business of leasing or selling and a lessee who leases the goods primarily for a personal, family, or household purpose.

finance lease
A three-party transaction consisting of the lessor, the lessee, and the supplier.

Ethical Perspective

GOOD FAITH AND REASONABLENESS GOVERN THE PERFORMANCE OF SALES AND LEASE CONTRACTS

Generally, the common law of contracts only obligates the parties to perform according to the terms of their contract. There is no breach of contract unless the parties fail to meet these terms. It is as simple as that.

Recognizing that certain situations may develop that are not expressly provided for in the contract or that strict adherence to the terms of the contract without doing more may not be sufficient to accomplish the contract's objective,

the Uniform Commercial Code (UCC) adopts two broad principles that govern the performance of sales and lease contracts: *good faith* and *reasonableness*.

UCC 1-203 states that "Every contract or duty within this Act imposes an obligation of good faith in its performance or enforcement." Although both parties owe a duty of good faith in the performance of a sales or lease contract, merchants are held to a higher standard of good faith than nonmerchants.

(box continues)

Nonmerchants are held to the subjective standard of honesty in fact whereas merchants are held to the objective standard of fair dealing in the trade [UCC 2-103(1)(b)].

The words *reasonable* and *reasonably* are used throughout the UCC to establish the duties of performance by the parties to sales and lease contracts. For example, unless otherwise specified, the parties must act within a "reasonable" time [UCC 1-204(1)(2)]. Another example is if the seller does not deliver the goods as contracted, the buyer may make "reasonable" purchases to cover (i.e., obtain substitute performance) [UCC 2-712(1)]. The term *commercial reasonableness* is used to establish certain duties of merchants under the UCC. Articles 2 and 2A do not specifically define the terms *reasonable* and *commercial reasonableness*. Instead, these terms are defined by reference to the course of performance or the course of dealing between the parties, usage of trade, and such.

Note that the concepts of good faith and reasonableness extend to the "spirit" of the contract as well as the contract terms. The underlying theory is that the parties are more apt to perform properly if their conduct is to be judged against these principles. This is a major advance in the law of contracts. Some state courts have extended the UCC duties of good faith and reasonableness to common law contracts.

1. Do the UCC concepts of *good faith* and *reasonableness* enhance ethical conduct?
2. Should the concept of *good faith* be implied in every contract? Why or why not?

FORMATION OF SALES AND LEASE CONTRACTS

Like general contracts, the formation of sales and lease contracts requires an *offer*, an *acceptance, consideration*, and so on. The UCC established rules for each of these elements that often differ considerably from common law. Any rules established by Articles 2 and 2A take precedent over the common law of contracts.

Ethical Perspective

UNCONSCIONABLE SALES AND LEASE CONTRACTS

Can a contract term ever be so unfair as to be legally ignored by a party to the contract? After all, law and morality require that contracting parties adhere to the terms of their contract. The UCC's doctrine of **unconscionability** says that if a sales or lease contract (or any clause in it) is unconscionable, the court may either refuse to enforce the contract or limit the application of the unconscionable clause [UCC 2-302, 2A-108]. Consider the following case.

Dynatron, Inc. (Dynatron), executed a lease agreement with Hertz Commercial Leasing Corporation (Hertz) to finance a lease of a Minolta copy machine that was supplied by A-Copy of Glastonbury, Connecticut (A-Copy). The lease agreement, which was prepared by Hertz, designated Dynatron as the lessee and Hertz as the lessor. The vendor was A-Copy. The lease was for a 60-month term, at a monthly rental of $3,720. Paragraph 11 of the lease is a liquidated damage clause that stipulates that in event of default, the lessee is obligated to pay the lessor any arrears of rentals, the entire balance of the rent, the lessor's expenses in retaking possession and removing the equipment, and up to 20 percent of attorneys' fees.

Dynatron claimed that almost immediately following delivery, the machine developed operational problems and that its reproduction qualities were defective. Dynatron wrote letters to Hertz and A-Copy demanding repair or replacement of the machine. The machine was not repaired or replaced. Dynatron made no payments on the lease. Finally, Dynatron requested that Hertz repossess the machine. Dynatron then purchased a Xerox copying machine. After the lapse of about one year, or about February 14, 1978, Hertz picked up the machine. In May 1978, Hertz sold the machine for $500. On August 30, 1980, Hertz sued Dynatron to recover a deficiency judgment.

The court held that the terms and conditions of the finance lease agreement in this case were *unconscionable* and that the provisions of the lease are not enforceable against the lessee in any respect whatsoever. Judgment was therefore entered for Dynatron [*Hertz Commercial Leasing Corporation v. Dynatron, Inc.*, 472 A. 2d 872 (CI 1980)]

1. Was it ethical for Hertz to include the liquidated damage clause in its form contract?
2. Did Dynatron act morally in signing the lease and then trying to get out from under its provisions?

OFFER

A contract for the sale or lease of goods may be made in any manner sufficient to show agreement, including conduct by both parties that recognizes the existence of a contract [UCC 2-204(1), 2A-204(1)]. Under the UCC, an agreement sufficient to constitute a contract for the sale or lease of goods may be found even though the moment of its making is undetermined [UCC 2-204(2), 2A-204(2)].

Open Terms

Sometimes the parties to a sales or lease contract leave open a major term in the contract. The UCC is tolerant of open terms. According to UCC 2-204(3) and 2A-204(3), the contract does not fail for indefiniteness if (1) the parties intended to make a contract and (2) there is a reasonably certain basis for giving an appropriate remedy. In effect, certain *open terms* are permitted to be "read into" a sales or lease contract. These are commonly referred to as **gap-filling rules**.

Some examples of terms that are commonly left open follow.

Open Price Term   If a sales contract does not contain a specific price *(open price term)*, a "reasonable price" is implied at the time of delivery. The contract may provide that a price is to be fixed by a market rate (e.g., a commodities market), as set or recorded by a third person or agency (e.g., a government agency), or by another standard either upon delivery or on a set date. If the agreed-upon standard is unavailable when the price is to be set, a reasonable price is implied at the time of delivery of the goods [UCC 2-305(1)].

A seller or buyer who reserves the right to fix a price must do so in good faith [UCC 2-305(2)]. When one of the parties fails to fix an open price term, the other party may opt either (1) to treat the contract as canceled or (2) to fix a reasonable price for the goods [UCC 2-305(3)].

Open Payment Term   If the parties to a sales contract do not agree on *payment terms*, payment is due at the time and place at which the buyer is to receive the goods. If delivery is authorized and made by way of document of title, payment is due at the time and place at which the buyer is to receive the document of title, regardless of where the goods are to be received [UCC 2-310].

Open Delivery Term   If the parties to a sales contract do not agree to the time, place, and manner of delivery of the goods, the *place for delivery* is the seller's place of business. If the seller does not have a place of business, delivery is to be made at the seller's residence. If identified goods are located at some other place and both parties know of this fact at the time of contracting, that place is the place of delivery [UCC 2-308].

Where goods are to be shipped, but the shipper is not named, the seller is obligated to make the shipping arrangements. Such arrangements must be made in good faith and within limits of commercial reasonableness [UCC 2-311(2)].

Open Time Term   If the parties to the contract do not set a specific *time of performance* for any obligation under the contract, the contract must be performed within a reasonable time. If the sales contract provides for successive performances over an unspecified period of time, the contract is valid for a reasonable time [UCC 2-309].

Open Assortment Term   If the *assortment of goods* to a sales contract is left open, the buyer is given the option of choosing those goods. For example, suppose Macy's contracts to purchase 1,000 dresses from Liz Claiborne, Inc. The contract is silent as to the

gap-filling rule
A rule that says an open term can be "read into" a contract.

Business Brief
In recent years, the leasing of goods has increased dramatically in this country. Lease transactions include consumer leases of automobiles as well as business leasing of equipment such as copying machines, computers, tractors, and the like. In 1987, Article 2A was added to the UCC to address personal property leases. Article 2A establishes uniform rules for the formation and enforcement of personal property leases.

assortment of colors of the dresses. The buyer may pick the assortment of colors for the dresses from the seller's stock. The buyer must make the selection in good faith and within limits set by commercial reasonableness [UCC 2-311(2)].

Contemporary Business Application

UCC Firm Offer Rule Changes the Common Law of Contracts

Recall that the common law of contracts allows the offeror to revoke the offer anytime prior to its acceptance. The only exception allowed by the common law is an *option contract* (i.e., where the offeree paid the offeror consideration to keep the offer open).

The UCC recognizes another exception, which is called the **firm offer rule**. This rule states that a merchant who (1) offers to buy, sell, or lease goods and (2) gives a written and signed assurance on a separate form that the offer will be held open cannot revoke the offer for the time stated or, if no time is stated, for a reasonable time. The maximum amount of time permitted under this rule is three months [UCC 2-205, 2A-205].

Consider This Example   On June 1, a merchant-seller offers to sell a Mercedes-Benz to a buyer for $50,000. The merchant-seller signs a written assurance to keep that offer open until August 30. On July 1, the merchant-seller sells the car to another buyer. On August 21, the original offeree tenders $50,000 for the car. The merchant-seller is liable to the original offeree for breach of contract.

Acceptance

The foundation of justice is good faith.

Cicero.
De Officiis, Bk. 1, Ch. VII

Both the common law and the UCC provide that a contract is created when the offeree (i.e., the buyer or lessee) sends an acceptance to the offeror—not when the offeror receives the acceptance. For example, a contract is made when the acceptance letter is delivered to the post office. The contract remains valid even if the post office loses the letter.

Unless otherwise unambiguously indicated by language or circumstance, an offer to make a sales or lease contract may be *accepted* in any manner and by any reasonable medium of acceptance [UCC 2-206(1)(a), 2A-206(1)]. Applications of this rule are discussed in the following paragraphs.

Methods of Acceptance

The UCC permits acceptance by any reasonable manner or method of communication.

Consider This Example   A seller sends a telegram to a proposed buyer offering to sell the buyer certain goods. The buyer responds by mailing a letter of acceptance to the seller. In most circumstances, mailing the letter of acceptance would be considered reasonable. However, if the goods were extremely perishable or the market for the goods was very volatile, a faster means of acceptance (such as a telegram) might be warranted.

If an order or other offer to buy goods requires prompt or current shipment, the offer is accepted if the seller (1) promptly promises to ship the goods or (2) promptly ships either conforming or nonconforming goods [UCC 2-206(1)(b)]. The shipment of conforming goods signals acceptance of the buyer's offer.

Acceptance of goods occurs after the buyer or lessee has a reasonable opportunity to inspect them and signifies that (1) the goods are conforming, (2) he or she will take or retain the goods in spite of their nonconformity, or (3) he or she fails to reject the goods within a reasonable time after tender or delivery [UCC 2-513(1), 2A-515(1)].

Accommodation Shipment

A shipment of nonconforming goods does not constitute an acceptance if the seller reasonably notifies the buyer that the shipment is offered only as an **accommodation** to the buyer [UCC 2-206(1)(b)]. For example, suppose a buyer offers to purchase 500 red candles from a seller. The seller is temporarily out of red candles and sends the buyer 500 green candles and notifies the buyer that these candles are being sent as an accommodation. The seller has not accepted (or breached) the contract. The accommodation is a counteroffer from the seller to the buyer. The buyer is free either to accept or to reject the counteroffer.

> **accommodation**
> A shipment that is offered to the buyer as a replacement for the original shipment when the original shipment cannot be filled.

Contemporary Business Application

UCC PERMITS ADDITIONAL TERMS IN SALES AND LEASE CONTRACTS

Under common law's **mirror image rule**, the offeree's acceptance must be on the same terms as the offer. The inclusion of additional terms in the acceptance is considered a **counteroffer** rather than an acceptance. Thus, the offeror's original offer is extinguished.

UCC 2-207(1) is more liberal. It permits definite and timely expressions of acceptance or written confirmations to operate as an acceptance even though they contain terms that are additional to or different from the offered terms unless the acceptance is expressly conditional on assent to such terms. This rule differs for merchants and nonmerchants, as discussed below.

One or Both Parties Are Nonmerchants
If one or both parties to the sales contract are nonmerchants, any additional terms are considered **proposed additions** to the contract. The proposed additions do not constitute a counteroffer or extinguish the original offer. If the offeree's proposed additions are accepted by the original offeror, they become part of the contract. If they are not accepted, the sales contract is formed on the basis of the terms of the original offer [UCC 2-207(2)].

Consider This Example A salesperson at a Lexus dealership offers to sell a top-of-the-line coupe to a buyer for $47,000. The buyer replies, "I accept your offer but I would like to have a CD player in the car." The CD player is a proposed addition to the contract. If the salesperson agrees, the contract between the parties consists of the terms of the original offer plus the additional term regarding the CD player. If the salesperson rejects the proposed addition, the sales contract consists of the terms of the original offer because the buyer made a definite expression of acceptance.

Entrepreneur and the Law

WHO WINS THE "BATTLE OF THE FORMS"?

When merchants negotiate sales contracts, they often exchange preprinted forms. These "boilerplate" forms usually contain terms that favor the drafter. Thus, an offeror who sends a standard form contract as an offer to the offeree may receive an acceptance drafted on the offeree's own form contract. This scenario—commonly called the **battle of the forms**—raises important questions: Is there a contract? If so, what are its terms? The UCC provides guidance in answering these questions.

Under UCC 2-207(2), if both parties are merchants, any additional terms contained in an acceptance become part of the sales contract unless (1) the offer expressly limits acceptance to the terms of the offer, (2) the additional terms materially alter the terms of the original contract, or (3) the offeror notifies the offeree that he or she objects to the additional terms within a reasonable time after receiving the offeree's modified acceptance.

The most important point in the battle of the forms is that there is no contract if the additional terms so materially alter the terms of the original offer that the parties cannot agree on the contract. This fact-specific determination is made by the courts on a case-by-case basis.

International Perspective

THE INTERNATIONAL BATTLE OF FORMS

Seller sends an offer to buyer. Buyer responds with an acceptance that modifies some of the terms in the offer. Is there a contract? This scenario—commonly called the "battle of the forms"—occurs when merchants use preprinted forms both to make offers and to send back acceptances. The typed descriptions commonly match up; it is the fine print on the back of the forms that often contains differences.

Under Article 19(3) of the United Nations Convention on Contracts for the International Sale of Goods (CISG), if the inconsistencies are material, the would-be acceptance is a counteroffer. Additions that are not material are considered to be proposals for incorporation into the contract unless the offeror promptly objects.

The CISG rule is closer to the common law's mirror image rule than to the UCC's additional terms rule. This is because the CISG sets out a broad and nonexhaustive list of items that the drafters considered to be material. These are those terms that relate, among other things, to the price, payment, quality, and quantity of the goods; the place and time of delivery; the extent of one party's liability to the other; and the settlement of disputes. Because the list is so extensive, virtually any addition or variation in an acceptance will materially vary the terms of the offer and thus constitute a counteroffer.

The drafters of the CISG hoped that this provision would encourage the parties to negotiate and mutually agree on all the material terms of an international sales contract before they began performing. One can only conclude that it is harder to form a contract under the CISG in a battle-of-forms situation than under the UCC.

*O*THER RULES AFFECTING THE FORMATION OF SALES AND LEASE CONTRACTS

Consideration

The formation of sales and lease contracts requires *consideration*. However, the UCC changes the common law rule that requires the modification of a contract to be supported by new consideration. An agreement modifying a sales or lease contract needs no consideration to be binding [UCC 2-209(1), 2A-208(1)].

Modification of a sales or lease contract must be made in good faith [UCC 1-203]. As in the common law of contracts, modifications are not binding if they are obtained through fraud, duress, extortion, and such.

Statute of Frauds

UCC statute of frauds

A rule that requires all contracts for the sale of goods costing $500 or more and lease contracts involving payments of $1,000 or more to be in writing.

Business Brief

Following are exceptions to the writing requirement of the UCC Statute of Frauds: (1) specially manufactured goods, (2) admissions in pleadings or court, and (3) part acceptance.

The **UCC** includes **Statute of Frauds** provisions that apply to all sales and lease contracts. All contracts for the sale of goods costing $500 or more and lease contracts involving payments of $1,000 or more must be in writing [UCC 2-201(1), 2A-201(1)]. The writing must be sufficient to indicate that a contract has been made between the parties. Except as discussed in the paragraphs that follow, the writing must be signed by the party against whom enforcement is sought or by his or her authorized agent or broker. If a contract falling within these parameters is not written, it is unenforceable.

Consider This Example   A seller orally agrees to sell his or her computer to a buyer for $550. When the buyer tenders the purchase price, the seller asserts the Statute of Frauds and refuses to sell the computer to him or her. The seller is correct. The contract must be in writing to be enforceable because the contract price for the computer exceeds $499.99.

Exceptions to the Statute of Frauds   The three situations in which a sales or lease contract that would otherwise be required to be in writing is enforceable even if it is not in writing are discussed in the following paragraphs [UCC 2-201(3), UCC 2A-201(4)].

1. **Specially Manufactured Goods** Buyers and lessees often order specially manufactured goods. If the contract to purchase or lease such goods is oral, the buyer or lessee may not assert the Statute of Frauds against the enforcement of the contract if (a) the goods are not suitable for sale or lease to others in the ordinary course of the seller's or lessor's business and (b) the seller or lessor has made either a substantial beginning of the manufacture of the goods or commitments for their procurement.

2. **Admissions in Pleadings or Court** If the party against whom enforcement of an oral sales or lease contract is sought admits in pleadings, testimony, or otherwise in court that a contract for the sale or lease of goods was made, the oral contract is enforceable against that party. However, the contract is only enforceable as to the quantity of goods admitted.

3. **Part Acceptance** An oral sales or lease contract that should otherwise be in writing is enforceable to the extent to which the goods have been received and accepted by the buyer or lessee. For example, a lessor orally contracts to lease 100 personal computers to a lessee. The lessee accepts the first 20 computers tendered by the lessor. This is part acceptance. The lessee refuses to take delivery of the remaining 80 computers. Here the lessee must pay for the 20 computers he or she originally received and accepted. The lessee does not have to accept or pay for the remaining 80 computers.

Contemporary Business Application

UCC WRITTEN CONFIRMATION RULE EXCEPTION TO STATUTE OF FRAUDS

If both parties to an oral sales or lease contract are merchants, the Statute of Frauds requirement can be satisfied if (1) one of the parties to an oral agreement sends a written confirmation of the sale or lease to the other within a reasonable time after contracting and (2) the other merchant does not give written notice of an objection to the contract within 10 days after receiving the confirmation. This situation is true even though the party receiving the written confirmation has not signed it. The only stipulations are that the confirmation is sufficient and that the party to whom it is sent has reason to know its contents [UCC 2-201(2)].

Consider This Example
A merchant-seller in Chicago orally contracts by telephone to sell goods to a merchant-buyer in Phoenix for $25,000. Within a reasonable time after contracting, the merchant-seller sends a sufficient written confirmation to the buyer. The buyer, who has reason to know the contents of the confirmation, fails to object to the contents of the confirmation in writing within 10 days after receiving it. The Statute of Frauds has been met and the buyer cannot thereafter raise it against enforcement of the contract.

Ethical Perspective

A CHICKEN FARMER GETS PLUCKED

Sometimes the Statute of Frauds, which was designed to prevent fraud, is used by a party to try to renege on an oral sales contract. Consider the following case.

Perdue Farms, Inc. (Perdue), sells dressed poultry under the brand name "Perdue Roasters." On October 30, 1975, Motts, Inc., of Mississippi (Motts) entered into an oral contract with Perdue to purchase 1,500 boxes of roasters

(box continues)

from Perdue at $0.50 per pound. Motts was to pick the roasters up at Perdue's Maryland plant. Motts entered into a contract to resell the roasters to Dairyland, Inc. Motts sent a confirmation letter to Perdue confirming their oral agreement. Perdue received the confirmation and did not object to it. When Motts's truck arrived at Perdue's Maryland plant to pick up the roasters, Perdue informed Motts's drivers that the roasters would not be loaded unless complete payment was made before delivery. Under previous contracts between the parties, payment was due seven days after delivery. Perdue informed Motts that the roasters would not be sold to Motts on credit. Perdue then sold the roasters directly to Dairyland, Inc.

Motts sued Perdue to recover damages for breach of the sales contract. Perdue denied liability, arguing that the contract had to be in writing because it was over $500. Motts argued that the situation fell under the written confirmation rule exception to the UCC Statute of Frauds.

The district court agreed with Motts. UCC 2-201(2) binds merchants to oral sales contracts if one sends the other a confirmation letter that is not objected to within 10 days after its receipt. Both parties in this case were merchants, and Perdue did not object to Motts's confirmation letter within the 10-day period. The court denied Perdue the Statute of Frauds as a defense, thereby making Motts's confirmation letter enforceable against Perdue. [*Perdue Farms, Inc. v. Motts, Inc., of Mississippi*, 25 UCC Rep.Serv. 9 (1978)]

1. Did Perdue act morally in refusing to perform the sales contract?
2. Is it ever ethical to raise the Statute of Frauds in defense to get out of an oral contract?

When Written Modification Is Required

Oral modification of the contract is not enforceable if the parties agree that any modification of the sales or lease contract must be in a signed writing [UCC 2-209(2), 2A-208(2)]. In the absence of such an agreement, oral modifications to sales and lease contracts are binding if they do not violate the Statute of Frauds.

If the oral modification brings the contract within the Statute of Frauds, it must be in writing to be enforceable.

Consider This Example A lessor and lessee enter into an oral lease contract for the lease of goods at a rent of $950. Subsequently, the contract is modified by raising the rent to $1,150. Because the modified contract rent is more than $1,000, the contract comes under the UCC Statute of Frauds, and the modification must be in writing to be enforceable.

Parol Evidence

parol evidence rule

A rule that says if a written contract is a complete and final statement of the parties agreement, any prior or contemporaneous oral or written statements that alter, contradict, or are in addition to the terms of the written contract are inadmissible in court regarding a dispute over the contract.

The **parol evidence rule** states that when a sales or lease contract is evidenced by a writing that is intended to be a final expression of the parties' agreement or a confirmatory memorandum, the terms of the writing may not be contradicted by evidence of (1) a prior oral or written agreement or (2) a contemporaneous oral agreement (i.e., parol evidence) [UCC 2-202, 2A-202]. The rule is intended to ensure certainty in written sales and lease contracts.

Occasionally, the express terms of a written contract are not clear on their face and must be interpreted. In such cases, reference may be made to certain sources outside the contract. These sources are construed together when they are consistent with each other. If that is unreasonable, they are considered in descending order of priority [UCC 2-208(2), 2A-207(2)].

1. **Course of Performance** The previous conduct of the parties regarding the contract in question.
2. **Course of Dealing** The conduct of the parties in prior transactions and contracts.
3. **Usage of Trade** Any practice or method of dealing that is regularly observed or adhered to in a place, a vocation, a trade, or an industry.

Consider This Example A cattle rancher contracts to purchase corn from a farmer. The farmer delivers feed corn to the rancher. The rancher rejects this corn and demands delivery of corn that is fit for human consumption. Ordinarily, usage of trade would be the first source of interpretation of the word *corn*. If the parties had prior dealings, though, the usage of the term in their prior dealings would become the primary source of interpretation.

*6*ONCEPT SUMMARY COMPARISON OF CONTRACT LAW AND THE LAW OF SALES

Topic	Common Law of Contracts	UCC Law of Sales
Definiteness	Contract must contain all of the material terms of the parties' agreement.	UCC gap-filling rules permit terms to be implied if the parties intended to make a contract [UCC 2-204].
Irrevocable offers	Option contracts.	Option contracts. Firm offers by merchants to keep an offer open are binding up to three months without any consideration [UCC 2-205].
Counteroffers	Acceptance must be a mirror image of the offer. A counteroffer rejects and terminates the offer.	Additional terms of an acceptance become part of the contract if (1) they do not materially alter the terms of the offer and (2) the offeror does not object within a reasonable time after reviewing the acceptance [UCC 2-207].
Statute of Frauds	Writing must be signed by the party against whom enforcement is sought.	Writing may be enforced against a party who has not signed it if (1) both parties are merchants, (2) one party sends a written confirmation of their oral agreement within a reasonable time after contracting, and (3) the other party does not give written notice of objection within 10 days after receiving the confirmation [UCC 2-201].
Modification	Consideration is required.	Consideration is not required [UCC 2-209].

E- Commerce & Internet Law

UNFAIR AND DECEPTIVE ACTS OVER THE INTERNET

Little did Congress know over 80 years ago when it passed the **Federal Trade Commission Act** that Section 5 of the act would be used to prosecute fraud over the Internet. **Section 5** prohibits "unfair and deceptive" acts affecting commerce. The FTC has demonstrated recently that old laws can learn new tricks. Consider the following case.

Powerful search engines have been developed to allow surfers to browse the Internet and connect to Web sites in which they are interested. Certain scammers came up with a scheme where they would entice unwitting surfers to connect to their porn sites and not be able to get out. The scheme worked as follows. The scammers made fake copies of over 25 million popular Web sites such as the *Harvard Business Review, Japanese Friendship Gardens*, and others. Search engines trolling the Web for new pages found these

Web sites and added them to their listings. The scammers added to the faked Web pages an extra bit of coding so that as soon as surfers found the bogus Web page, it rerouted— "page-jacked"—them to the scammer's porn Web site. Once there, the user was "mouse-trapped" at the porn site and efforts to escape led only to new porn pages. The porn site operators made money by selling advertisements, and ad prices were often based on the number of "hits" on the site.

The Federal Trade Commission (FTC), a federal government agency, investigated and sued porn site operators in federal court for violating Section 5 of the FTC Act. The court found that the porn site operators had engaged in unfair and deceptive practices in violation of Section 5 and issued an injunction to shut down the porn sites and ordered the operators not to engage in such conduct in the future.

e·biz

Working the Web

CASES AND EXERCISES

CRITICAL LEGAL THINKING CASES

19.1. Mark Hemphill was a football player at Southern Illinois State University. As a member of the team, Hemphill was furnished with a uniform and helmet. He was injured while playing football for the school. Hemphill claimed that his helmet was defective and contributed to his injuries. Hemphill's attorneys suggested that he sue the university's athletic director, Sayers, and the head football coach, Shultz. The attorneys told Hemphill that he may be able to recover for his injuries based on several provisions of the Uniform Commercial Code. The attorneys specifically suggested that he use the UCC provisions that impose certain obligations upon merchants. Hemphill brought suit against Sayers and Shultz. Does Article 2 apply to this case? [*Hemphill v. Sayers*, 552 F.Supp. 685 (S.D.Ill. 1982)]

19.2. Gulash lived in Shelton, Connecticut. He wanted an above-ground swimming pool installed in his backyard. Gulash contacted Stylarama, Inc. (Stylarama), a company specializing in the sale and construction of pools. The two parties entered into a contract that called for Stylarama to "furnish all labor and materials to construct a Wavecrest brand pool, and furnish and install pool with vinyl liners." The total cost for

materials and labor was $3,690. There was no breakdown of costs between labor and materials. After the pool was installed, its sides began bowing out, the 2″ × 4″ wooden supports for the pool rotted and misaligned, and the entire pool became tilted. Gulash brought suit alleging that Stylarama had violated several provisions of Article 2 of the UCC. Is this transaction one involving "goods," making it subject to Article 2? [*Gulash v. Stylarama*, 364 A.2d 1221 (Conn. 1975)]

19.3. Black Butte Coal Company entered into a contract to supply coal for 20 years to Commonwealth Edison Company (Edison), a utility. The contract called for the two parties to determine each year how much coal was to be delivered during that period. The contract specified a minimum amount of coal that Edison was obligated to buy each year but allowed Edison to purchase less than that amount if the coal could not be used due to environmental reasons. Several years after the contract was signed, Edison's business began to slump, and it was faced with an oversupply of coal. The utility began to reduce the amount of coal it purchased each year. Also, there was an accident at one of Edison's generating plants, which left the plant inoperative for six months. Faced with these problems, the utility ordered less than the minimum amount of coal for the following year. Edison asserted that an "environmental" problem caused it to order less than the minimum amount of coal. The coal company sued Edison. Who wins? [*Black Butte Coal Co. v. Commonwealth Edison Co.*, 852 F.2d 1259 (10th Cir. 1988)]

19.4. Allsopp Sand and Gravel (Allsopp) and Lincoln Sand and Gravel (Lincoln) both were in the business of supplying sand to construction companies. In March 1986, Lincoln's sand dredge became inoperable. To continue in business, Lincoln negotiated a contract with Allsopp to purchase sand over the course of a year. The contract called for the sand to be loaded on Lincoln's trucks during Allsopp's regular operating season (March through November). Loading at other times was to be done by "special arrangement." By November 1986, Lincoln had taken delivery of one-quarter of the sand it had contracted for. At this point, Lincoln requested that several trucks of sand be loaded in December. Allsopp informed Lincoln that it would have to pay extra for this special arrangement. Lincoln refused to pay extra, pointing out that the sand was already stockpiled at Allsopp's facilities. Lincoln also offered to supply an employee to supervise the loading. Negotiations between the parties broke down, and Lincoln informed Allsopp that it did not intend to honor the remainder of the contract. Allsopp sued Lincoln. Is it commercially reasonable for Lincoln to demand delivery of sand during December? [*Allsopp Sand and Gravel v. Lincoln Sand and Gravel*, 525 N.E.2d 1185 (Ill.App. 1988)]

19.5. Jane Wilson leased a Toyota pickup truck from World Omni Leasing, Inc. (Omni). Wilson had experience in business and had signed contracts before. In the past, Wilson had read the contracts before signing them. When signing the contract for the lease of the truck, however, Wilson did not take the opportunity to read the lease. She even signed a statement declaring that she had read and understood the lease. The lease contained a provision that made Wilson responsible for payments on the truck even if the truck was destroyed. Several months after leasing the truck, Wilson was involved in a two-vehicle collision. The pickup truck was destroyed. Omni demanded to be paid for the balance of the lease. Wilson refused, claiming that the lease was unconscionable. Is the lease unconscionable? [*Wilson v. World Omni Leasing, Inc.*, 540 So.2d 713 (AL 1989)]

19.6. St. Charles Cable TV (St. Charles) was building a new cable television system in Louisiana. It contacted Eagle Comtronics, Inc. (Eagle), by phone and began negotiating to buy descrambler units for its cable system. These units would allow St. Charles's customers to receive the programs they had paid for. Although no written contract was ever signed, St.

Charles ordered several thousand descramblers. The descramblers were shipped to St. Charles, along with a sales acknowledgment form. St. Charles made partial payment for the descramblers before discovering that some of the units were defective. Eagle accepted a return of the defective scramblers. St. Charles then attempted to return all the descramblers, asking that they be replaced by a newer model. When Eagle refused to replace all the old descramblers, St. Charles stopped paying Eagle. Eagle sued St. Charles claiming that no valid contract existed between the parties. Is there a valid sales contract? [*St. Charles Cable TV v. Eagle Comtronics, Inc.*, 687 F.Supp. 820 (S.D.N.Y. 1988)]

19.7. Gordon Construction Company (Gordon) was a general contractor in the New York City area. Gordon planned on bidding for the job of constructing two buildings for the Port Authority of New York. In anticipation of its own bid, Gordon sought bids from subcontractors. On April 22, 1963, E. A. Coronis Associates (Coronis), a fabricator of structured steel, sent a signed letter to Gordon. The letter quoted a price for work on the Port Authority project and stated that the price could change, based upon the amount of steel used. The letter contained no information other than the price Coronis would charge for the job. On May 27, Gordon was awarded the Port Authority project. On June 1, Coronis sent Gordon a telegram withdrawing its offer. Gordon replied that it expected Coronis to honor the price quoted in its April 22 letter. When Coronis refused, Gordon sued. Gordon claimed that Coronis was attempting to withdraw a firm offer. Who wins? [*E. A. Coronis Associates v. Gordon Construction Co.*, 216 A.2d 246 (N.J.Super. 1966)]

19.8. Dan Miller was a commercial photographer who had taken a series of photographs that had appeared in *The New York Times*. *Newsweek* magazine wanted to use the photographs. When a *Newsweek* employee named Dwyer phoned Miller, he was told that 72 images were available. Dwyer said that he wanted to inspect the photographs and offered a certain sum of money for each photo *Newsweek* used. The photos were to remain Miller's property. Miller and Dwyer agreed to the price and the date for delivery. *Newsweek* sent a courier to pick up the photographs. Along with the photos, Miller gave the courier a "Delivery Memo" that set out various conditions for the use of the photographs. The memo included a clause that required *Newsweek* to pay $1,500 each if any of the photos were lost or destroyed. After *Newsweek* received the package, it decided it no longer needed Miller's work. When Miller called to have the photos returned, he was told that they all had been lost. Miller demanded that *Newsweek* pay him $1,500 for each of the 72 lost photos. Assuming that the court finds Miller and *Newsweek* to be merchants, are the clauses in the delivery memo part of the sales contract? [*Miller v. Newsweek, Inc.*, 660 F.Supp. 852 (D.Del. 1987)]

19.9. Alvin Cagle was a potato farmer in Alabama who had had several business dealings with the H. C. Schmieding Produce Co. (Schmieding). Several months before harvest, Cagle entered into an oral sales contract with Schmieding. The contract called for Schmieding to pay the market price at harvest time for all the red potatoes that Cagle grew on his 30-acre farm. Schmieding asked that the potatoes be delivered during the normal harvest months. As Cagle began harvesting his red potatoes, he contacted Schmieding to arrange delivery. Schmieding told the farmer that no contract had been formed because the terms of the agreement were too indefinite. Cagle demanded that Schmieding buy his crop. When Schmieding refused, Cagle sued to have the contract enforced. Has a valid

sales contract been formed? [*H. C. Schmieding Produce Co. v. Cagle*, 529 So.2d 243 (AL 1988)]

19.10. Collins was a sales representative of Donzi Marine Corp. (Donzi), a builder of light speedboats. Collins met Wallach, the owner of a retail boat outlet, at a marine trade show. Collins offered him a Donzi dealership, which would include the right to purchase and then market Donzi speedboats. Wallach tendered a check for $50,000 to Collins. Collins accepted the check, but neither party ever signed a written contract. Wallach ordered several boats. Donzi terminated the dealership because it had found another boat dealer willing to pay more for the franchise. Wallach sued Donzi for breach of contract. Is the contract enforceable under the UCC? [*Wallach Marine Corp. v. Donzi Marine Corp.*, 675 F.Supp. 838 (S.D.N.Y. 1987)]

ETHICS CASES

19.11. Kurt Perschke was a grain dealer in Indiana. In September 1972, he phoned Ken Sebasty, the owner of a large wheat farm, and offered to buy 14,000 bushels of wheat for $1.95 a bushel. Sebasty accepted the offer. Perschke said that he could send a truck for the wheat in March 1973. On the day of the phone call, Perschke's office manager sent a memorandum to Sebasty, stating the price and quantity of wheat that had been contracted for. In February 1973, Perschke called Sebasty to arrange for the loading of the wheat. Sebasty stated that no contract had been made. When Perschke brought suit, Sebasty claimed that the contract was unenforceable because of the Statute of Frauds. Was it ethical for Sebasty to raise the Statute of Frauds as a defense? Assuming that both parties are merchants, who wins the suit? [*Sebasty v. Perschke*, 404 N.E.2d 1200 (Ind.App. 1980)]

19.12. In 1974, Alex Abatti was the sole owner of A&M Produce Company (A&M), a small farming company located in California's Imperial Valley. Although Abatti had never grown tomatoes, he decided to do so. He sought the advice of FMC Corporation (FMC), a large diversified manufacturer of farming and other equipment, as to what kind of equipment he would need to process the tomatoes. An FMC representative recommended a certain type of machine, which A&M purchased from FMC pursuant to a form sales contract provided by FMC. Within the fine print, the contract contained one clause that disclaimed any warranty liability by FMC and a second clause that stated that FMC would not be liable for consequential damages if the machine malfunctioned.

A&M paid $10,680 down toward the $32,041 purchase price, and FMC delivered and installed the machine. A&M immediately began experiencing problems with the machine. It did not process the tomatoes quickly enough. Tomatoes began piling up in front of the belt that separated the tomatoes for weight-sizing. Overflow tomatoes had to be sent through the machine at least twice, causing damage to them. Fungus spread through the damaged crop. Because of these problems, the machine had to be continually started and stopped, which significantly reduced processing speed.

A&M tried on several occasions to get additional equipment from FMC, but on each occasion its request was rejected. Because of the problems with the machine, on June 17, 1974, A&M closed its tomato operation. A&M finally stated, "Let's call the whole thing off," and offered to return the machine if FMC would refund A&M's down payment. When FMC rejected this offer and demanded full payment of the balance due A&M sued to recover its down payment and damages. It alleged breach of warranty caused by defect in the machine. In defense, FMC pointed to the fine print of the sales contract, stating that the buyer waived any rights to sue it for breach of warranty or to recover consequential damages from it.

Was it ethical for FMC to include waiver of liability and waiver of consequential damage clauses in its form contract? Did A&M act morally in signing the contract and then trying to get out from under its provisions? Legally, are the waiver clauses so unconscionable as to not be enforced? [*A&M Produce Co. v. FMC Corp.*, 135 Cal.App.3d 473, 186 Cal.Rptr. 114 (Cal.App. 1982)]

CRITICAL LEGAL THINKING WRITING ASSIGNMENT

Read Case A.19 in the Case Appendix [*Cafazzo v. Central Medical Health Services, Inc.*]. This case is excerpted from the Supreme Court of Pennsylvania's opinion. Review and brief the case. In your brief, be sure to answer the following questions.

1. What was the plaintiff suing for? Explain.
2. What issue was presented to the court? Why was this issue important? Explain.
3. How did the court decide this case?

20

Performance of Sales and Lease Contracts

A lawyer without history or literature is a mechanic, a mere working mason; if he possesses some knowledge of these, he may venture to call himself an architect.

SIR WALTER SCOTT
Guy Mannering, Ch. 37 (1815)

Chapter Objectives

After studying this chapter, you should be able to

1. Identify when title to goods passes in shipment and destination contracts.
2. Define shipment and delivery terms.
3. Describe who bears the risk of loss when goods are lost or damaged in shipment.
4. Distinguish between a sale on approval and a sale or return.
5. Describe a sale on consignment.
6. Identify who has an insurable interest in goods.
7. Identify who bears the risk of loss when goods are stolen and resold.
8. Define a good faith purchaser for value.
9. Define a buyer in the ordinary course of business.
10. Explain the rules designed to prevent fraud in bulk transfers of goods.

Chapter Contents

Under the common law, the rights and obligations of the buyer, the seller, and third parties were determined based upon who held technical title to the goods. Article 2 of the UCC establishes precise rules for determining the *passage of title* in sales contracts. Other provisions of Article 2 apply irrespective of title except as otherwise provided [UCC 2-401].

The common law placed the *risk of loss* to goods on the party who had title to the goods. Article 2 rejects this notion and adopts concise rules for risk of loss that are not tied to title. It also gives the parties to the sales contract the right to *insure* the goods against loss if they have an "insurable interest" in the goods. Title, risk of loss, and insurable interest are discussed in this chapter.

IDENTIFICATION

The **identification of goods** is rather simple. It simply means distinguishing the goods named in the contract from the seller's or lessor's other goods. The seller or lessor retains the risk of loss of the goods until he or she identifies them to a sales or lease contract. Further, UCC 2-401(1) and 2-501 prevent title to goods from passing from the seller to the buyer unless the goods are identified to the sales contract. In a lease transaction, title to the leased goods remains with the lessor or a third party. It does not pass to the lessee.

> **identification of goods**
> Distinguishing the goods named in the contract from the seller's or lessor's other goods.

Time and Manner of Identification

Identification of goods can be made at any time and in any manner explicitly agreed to by the parties to the contract. In the absence of such an agreement, the UCC mandates when identification occurs [UCC 2-501(1), 2A-217].

Existing goods are identified when the contract is made and names the specific goods sold or leased. For example, a piece of farm machinery, a car, or a boat is identified when its serial number is listed on the sales or lease contract.

Goods that are part of a larger mass of goods are identified when the specific merchandise is designated. For example, if a food processor contracts to purchase 150 cases of oranges from a farmer who has 1,000 cases of oranges, the buyer's goods are identified when the seller explicitly separates or tags the 150 cases.

Future goods are goods not yet in existence. Unborn animals (such as unborn cattle) are identified when the young are conceived. Crops to be harvested are identified when the crops are planted or otherwise become growing crops. Future goods other than crops and unborn young are identified when the goods are shipped, marked, or otherwise designated by the seller or lessor as the goods to which the contract refers.

> **future goods**
> Goods not yet in existence (ungrown crops, unborn stock animals).

PASSAGE OF TITLE

Once the goods exist and have been identified, title to the goods may be transferred from the seller to the buyer. Article 2 of the UCC establishes precise rules for determining the passage of title in sales contracts. (As mentioned earlier, lessees do not acquire title to the goods they lease.)

Under UCC 2-401(1), **title** to goods passes from the seller to the buyer in any manner and on any conditions explicitly agreed upon by the parties. If the parties do not agree to a specific time, title passes to the buyer when and where the seller's performance with reference to *physical delivery* is completed. This point in time is determined by applying the rules discussed on the next page [UCC 2-401(2)].

> **title**
> Legal, tangible evidence of ownership of goods.

Shipment and Destination Contracts

shipment contract

A contract that requires the seller to ship the goods to the buyer via a common carrier.

A **shipment contract** requires the seller to ship the goods to the buyer via a common carrier. The seller is required to (1) make proper shipping arrangements and (2) deliver the goods into the carrier's hands. Title passes to the buyer at the time and place of shipment [UCC 2-401(2)(a)].

destination contract

A contract that requires the seller to deliver the goods either to the buyer's place of business or to another destination specified in the sales contract.

A **destination contract** requires the seller to deliver the goods either to the buyer's place of business or to another destination specified in the sales contract. Title passes to the buyer when the seller tenders delivery of the goods at the specified destination [UCC 2-401(2)(b)].

Delivery of Goods Without Moving Them

document of title

An actual piece of paper, such as a warehouse receipt or bill of lading, that is required in some transactions of pick up and delivery.

Sometimes a sales contract authorizes the goods to be delivered without requiring the seller to move them. In other words, the buyer might be required to pick up the goods from the seller. In such situations, the time and place of the passage of title depends on whether the seller is to deliver a **document of title** (i.e., a warehouse receipt or bill of lading) to the buyer. If a document of title is required, title passes when and where the seller delivers the document to the buyer [UCC 2-401(3)(a)]. For example, if the goods named in the sales contract are located at a warehouse, title passes when the seller delivers a warehouse receipt representing the goods to the buyer.

If (1) no document of title is needed and (2) the goods are identified at the time of contracting, title passes at the time and place of contracting [UCC 2-401(3)(b)]. For example, if the buyer signs a sales contract to purchase bricks from the seller and the contract stipulates that the buyer will pick up the bricks at the seller's place of business, title passes when the contract is signed by both parties. This is true even if the bricks are not picked up until a later date.

International Perspective

USE OF LETTERS OF CREDIT IN INTERNATIONAL TRADE

The major risks in any business transaction involving the sale of goods are (1) that the seller will not be paid after delivering the goods and (2) that the buyer will not receive the goods after paying for them. These risks are even more acute in international transactions where the buyer and seller may not know each other, the parties are dealing at long distance, and the judicial system of the parties' countries may not have jurisdiction to decide a dispute if one should arise. The irrevocable **letter of credit** has been developed to manage these risks in international sales. The function of a letter of credit is to substitute the credit of a recognized international bank for that of the buyer.

An irrevocable letter of credit works this way. Suppose a buyer in one country and a seller in another country enter into a contract for the sale of goods. The buyer goes to his or her bank and pays the bank a fee to issue a letter of credit in which the bank agrees to pay the amount of the letter (which is the amount of the purchase price of the goods) to the seller's bank if certain conditions are met. These conditions are usually the delivery of documents indicating that the seller has placed the goods in the hands of a shipper. The buyer is called the **account party**, the bank that issues the letter of credit is called the **issuing bank**, and the seller is called the **beneficiary** of the letter of credit.

The issuing bank then forwards the letter of credit to a bank that the seller has designated in his or her country. This bank, which is called the **correspondent** or **confirming bank**, relays the letter of credit to the seller. Now that the seller sees that he or she is guaranteed payment, he or she makes arrangements to ship the goods and receives a

bill of lading from the carrier proving so. The seller then delivers these documents to the confirming bank. The confirming bank will examine the documents and, if it finds them in order, will pay the seller and forward the documents to the issuing bank. By this time, the buyer will usually have paid the amount of the purchase price to the issuing bank (unless an extension of credit has been arranged), and the issuing bank then charges the buyer's account. The issuing bank forwards the bill of lading and other necessary documents to the buyer, who then picks up the goods from the shipper when they arrive.

If the documents (e.g., the bill of lading, proof of insurance) conform to the conditions specified in the letter of credit, the issuing bank must pay the letter of credit. If the account party does not pay the issuing bank, the bank's only recourse is to sue the account party to recover damages.

Article 5 (Letters of Credit) of the Uniform Commercial Code governs letters of credit unless otherwise agreed by the parties. The International Chamber of Commerce has promulgated the **Uniform Customs and Practices for Documentary Credits (UCP)**, which contains rules governing the formation and performance of letters of credit. Although the UCP is neither a treaty nor a legislative enactment, most banks incorporate the terms of the UCP in letters of credit they issue.

*R*ISK OF LOSS—NO BREACH OF SALES CONTRACT

In the case of sales contracts, the common law placed the *risk of loss* of goods on the party who had title to the goods. Article 2 rejects this notion and allows the parties to a sales contract to agree among themselves who will bear the risk of loss if the goods subject to the contract are lost or destroyed. If the parties do not have a specific agreement concerning the assessment of the risk of loss, the UCC mandates who will bear the risk.

Carrier Cases—Movement of Goods

Unless otherwise agreed, goods that are shipped via carrier (e.g., railroad, ship, truck) are considered to be sent pursuant to a *shipment contract* or a *destination contract*. Absent any indication to the contrary, sales contracts are presumed to be shipment contracts rather than destination contracts.

Shipment Contracts   With **shipment contracts**, the risk of loss passes to the buyer when the seller delivers the conforming goods to the carrier. The buyer bears the risk of loss of the goods during transportation [UCC 2-509 (1)(a)].

Shipment contracts are created in two ways. The first requires the use of the term *shipment contract*. The second requires the use of one of the following shipping terms: *F.O.B., F.A.S., C.I.F.,* or *C.&F.*

shipment contract
The buyer bears the risk of loss during transportation.

Destination Contracts   **Destination contracts** require the seller to bear the risk of loss of the goods during their transportation. Thus, with the exception of a no-arrival, no-sale contract, the seller is required to replace any goods lost in transit. The buyer does not have to pay for destroyed goods. The risk of loss does not pass until the goods are tendered to the buyer at the specified destination [UCC 2-509(1)(b)].

Unless otherwise agreed, destination contracts are created in two ways. The first method requires the use of the term *destination contract*. The alternative method requires use of the following shipping terms: *F.O.B. place of destination, ex-ship,* or *no-arrival, no-sale contract.*

destination contract
The seller bears the risk of loss during transportation.

Contemporary Business Application _____

SHIPPING TERMS

F.O.B. (free on board) point of shipment (e.g., F.O.B. Anchorage, Alaska) requires the seller to arrange to ship the goods and put the goods in the carrier's possession. The seller bears the expense and risk of loss until this is done [UCC 2-319 (1) (a)].

F.A.S. (free alongside) or **F.A.S. (vessel) port of shipment** (e.g., *The Gargoyle.* New Orleans) requires the seller to deliver and tender the goods alongside the named vessel or on the dock designated and provided by the buyer. The seller bears the expense and risk of loss until this is done [UCC 2-319 (2)(a)].

C.I.F. (cost, insurance, and freight) and **C. & F. (C.F., cost and freight)** are pricing terms that indicate the cost for which the seller is responsible. These terms require the seller to bear the expense and the risk of loss of loading the goods on the carrier [UCC 2-320 (1) and (3)].

F.O.B. place of destination (e.g., F.O.B. Miami, Florida) requires the seller to bear the expense and risk of loss until the goods are tendered to the buyer at the place of destination [UCC 2-319 (1) (b)].

Ex-ship (from the carrying vessel) requires the seller to bear the expense and risk of loss until the goods are unloaded from the ship at its port of destination [UCC 2-322 (1) and (2) (b)].

No-arrival, no-sale contracts require the seller to bear the expense and risk of loss of the goods during transportation. However, the seller is under no duty to deliver replacement goods to the buyer because there is no contractual stipulation that the goods will arrive at the appointed destination [UCC 2-324 (a) (b)].

International Perspective _____

INTERNATIONAL TRADE TERMS

Sales contracts involving transportation customarily contain abbreviated terms describing the time and place where the buyer is to take delivery. These trade terms, such as F.O.B. and C.I.F., may also define other matters, including the time and place of payment, the price, the time the risk of loss shifts from the seller to the buyer, and the costs of freight and insurance.

The same trade abbreviations are widely used in both domestic and international transactions. Unfortunately, they have different meanings depending on the governing law. In the United States, for example, the Uniform Commercial Code (UCC) defines trade terms for domestic sales. In the United Kingdom, the terms are defined by reference to case law. The United Nations Convention on Contracts for the International Sale of Goods (CISG) also allows parties to incorporate trade terms of their choosing.

The most widely used private trade terms are those published by the International Chamber of Commerce. Called *Incoterms*, they are well known throughout the world. Their use in international sales is encouraged by trade councils, courts, and international lawyers. First published in 1936, the current version is *Incoterms 1990*.

Parties who adopt the *Incoterms*, or any other trade terms, should make sure they express their desire clearly. For example, a contract might refer to F.O.B. *(Incoterms 1990)* or C.I.F. *(U.S. Uniform Commercial Code).* Otherwise, the courts will apply the definitions used in their own jurisdiction. Finally, the parties should be wary about making additions or varying the meaning of any particular term, except to the extent that it is allowed by the rules they adopt or by judicial decision. The courts are as apt to ignore a variation, or hold that the entire term is ineffective, as they are to apply it.

Noncarrier Cases—No Movement of Goods

Sometimes a sales contract stipulates that the buyer is to pick up the goods, either at the seller's place of business or another specified location. This type of arrangement raises a question: Who bears the risk of loss if the goods are destroyed or stolen after the contract date and before the buyer picks the goods up from the seller? The UCC provides two different rules for this situation. One applies to merchant-sellers and the other to nonmerchant-sellers [UCC 2-509(3)].

The law is not a series of calculating machines where definitions and answers come tumbling out when the right levers are pushed.

William O. Douglas
The Dissent. A Safeguard of
Democracy (1948)

Merchant-Seller   If the seller is a merchant, the risk of loss does not pass to the buyer until the goods are received. In other words, a merchant-seller bears the risk of loss between the time of contracting and the time the buyer picks up the goods.

Consider This Example   On June 1, Tyus Motors, a merchant, contracts to sell a new automobile to a consumer. Tyus Motors keeps the car for a few days after contracting to prep it. During this period, the car is destroyed by fire. Under the UCC, Tyus Motors bears the risk of loss because of its merchant status.

Nonmerchant-Seller   Nonmerchant-sellers pass the risk of loss to the buyer upon "tender of delivery" of the goods. Tender of delivery occurs when the seller (1) places or holds the goods available for the buyer to take delivery and (2) notifies the buyer of this fact.

Consider This Example   On June 1, a nonmerchant contracts to sell his or her automobile to his or her next-door neighbor. Delivery of the car is tendered on June 3 and the buyer is notified of this. The buyer tells the seller he or she will pick the car up "in a few days." The car is destroyed by fire before the buyer picks it up. In this situation, the buyer bears the risk of loss because (1) the seller is a nonmerchant and (2) delivery was tendered on June 3. If the car were destroyed on June 2—that is, before delivery was tendered—the seller would bear the risk of loss.

The court had to decide who bore the risk of loss of goods in the following case.

Conway v. Larsen Jewelers, Inc.
429 N.Y.S.2d 378 (1980)
Civil Court of the City of New York, Kings County

CASE 20.1

FACTS
Theresa D. Conway purchased a necklace from Larsen Jewelers, Inc. (Larsen), on a layaway plan. Under this plan, Conway paid a portion of the $450 purchase price and made additional payments from time to time. In return, Larsen retained possession of the necklace. The necklace would be released to Conway after she paid the full purchase price. On the night of May 12, 1979, Larsen was burglarized. Theresa Conway's necklace was among the items that were stolen. At the time of the burglary, Conway had paid $265 toward the purchase price of the necklace. Conway sued Larsen to recover the value of the necklace.

ISSUE
Who should bear the risk of loss of the necklace, Larsen or Theresa Conway?

IN THE LANGUAGE OF THE COURT
Steinberg, Judge   Clearly, the parties never contemplated the occurrence that brings them into court, and there was no specific agreement between them to cover the situation. Thus we must look to the Uniform Commercial Code for guidance. UCC 2-509 is entitled "Risk of Loss in the Absence of Breach." Subsection 3 states, "The risk of loss passes to the buyer on his receipt of the goods, if the seller is a merchant; otherwise the risk passes to buyer on tender of delivery."

(case continues)

Here, Conway never received possession of the necklace. Conway did not have the right to use or possession of the necklace until some time in the future, when the balance of the purchase price was paid. There was no delivery. Defendant Larsen Jewelers is clearly a merchant under UCC 2-104(1). Even had payment been made in full, the risk of loss would remain with defendant until actual receipt by buyer or tender of delivery by seller. The underlying theory is that since a merchant, who is to make physical delivery at his own place of business, has complete control of the goods, he is expected to insure his interest in them.

Having reached a conclusion on the question of liability, we turn to the second question, that of damages. The article in question was a necklace of gold filigree beads, uniformly interspersed with pearls and coral beads. The agreed price was $450, upon which Conway had made payments to the date of theft of $265. The value of the necklace had appreciated substantially between the time the lay-away began, and the time of its theft; and therein lies the principal bone of contention between the parties. Conway asserts that the recovery should be the value of the necklace at the time of its theft. Larsen Jewelers argues that its maxi-

mum liability should be the $265 in payments made by Conway. When the subject matter of a contract is destroyed (or, as in this case, stolen) through no fault of the seller, the contract is deemed avoided [UCC 2-613(a)]. The defendant's only obligation is to return what has already been paid to him. Conway would not be entitled to the market value of the necklace at the time of its theft.

DECISION AND REMEDY

The court held that Larsen was a merchant-seller who bore the risk of loss. The court ordered Larsen Jewelers to refund Conway her $265.

Case Questions

Critical Legal Thinking Should the risk of loss depend on whether the seller is a merchant or not? Explain.

Ethics Was it ethical for Larsen Jewelers to deny liability in this case? Is UCC 2-509 clear on its face?

Business Application How should the seller have protected itself from loss?

---

bailee

A holder of goods who is not a seller or a buyer (e.g., a warehouse).

Goods in the Possession of a Bailee Goods sold by a seller to a buyer are sometimes in the possession of a **bailee** (e.g., a warehouse). If such goods are to be delivered to the buyer without moving them, the risk of loss passes to the buyer when (1) the buyer receives a negotiable document of title (such as a warehouse receipt or bill of lading) covering the goods, (2) the bailee acknowledges the buyer's right to possession of the goods, or (3) the buyer receives a nonnegotiable document of title or other written direction to deliver *and* has a reasonable time to present the document or direction to the bailee and demand the goods. If the bailee refuses to honor the document or direction, the risk of loss remains on the seller [UCC 2-509(2)].

CONDITIONAL SALES

Sellers often entrust possession of goods to buyers on a trial basis. These transactions are classified as *sales on approval* or *sales or returns* [UCC 2-326].

Sale on Approval

sale on approval

A type of sale in which there is no actual sale unless and until the buyer accepts the goods.

In a **sale on approval**, there is no sale unless and until the buyer accepts the goods. A sale on approval occurs when a merchant (e.g., a computer store) allows a customer to take the goods (e.g., a computer) home for a specified period of time (e.g., three days) to see if it fits the customer's needs. The prospective buyer may use the goods to try them out during this time.

Acceptance of the goods occurs if the buyer (1) expressly indicates acceptance, (2) fails to notify the seller of rejection of the goods within the agreed-upon trial period (or, if no time is agreed upon, a reasonable time), or (3) uses the goods inconsistently with the purpose of the trial (e.g., the customer resells the computer to another person).

The goods are not subject to the claims of the buyer's creditors until the buyer accepts them. In a sale on approval, the risk of loss and title to the goods remain with the seller. They do not pass to the buyer until acceptance [UCC 2-327(1)]. The following case demonstrates this risk of loss rule.

Prewitt v. Numismatic Funding Corp.
745 F.2d 1175 (1984)
United States Court of Appeals, Eighth Circuit

CASE 20.2

FACTS

Numismatic Funding Corp. (Numismatic), with its principal place of business in New York, sells rare and collector coins by mail throughout the United States. Frederick R. Prewitt, a resident of St. Louis, Missouri, responded to Numismatic's advertisement in *The Wall Street Journal*. Prewitt received several shipments of coins from Numismatic via the mails. These shipments were "on approval" for 14 days. Numismatic gave no instructions as to the method for returning unwanted coins. Prewitt kept and paid for several coins and returned the others to Numismatic fully insured via Federal Express. On February 10, 1982, Numismatic mailed Prewitt 28 gold and silver coins worth over $60,000 on a 14-day approval. On February 23, 1982, Prewitt returned all of the coins via certified mail and insured them for the maximum allowed, $400. Numismatic never received the coins. Prewitt brought this action seeking a declaratory judgment as to his nonliability. Numismatic filed a counterclaim. The trial court awarded Prewitt a declaratory judgment of nonliability. Numismatic appealed.

ISSUE

Who bears the risk of loss, Prewitt or Numismatic?

IN THE LANGUAGE OF THE COURT

Bright, Circuit Judge   The trial court determined, and the parties do not dispute, that the delivery of coins between seller Numismatic and buyer Prewitt constituted a sale "on approval." Under the provisions of the UCC relating to risk of loss, as adopted in Missouri, the risk of loss remains with the seller.

Appellant Numismatic contends that the parties impliedly agreed to shift the risk of loss to Prewitt. It argues that an agreement by Prewitt to assume the risk of loss arose by implication from the prior course of dealing between the parties in which Prewitt had returned coins fully insured via Federal Express. The trial court found that Numismatic shipped the coins to Prewitt through the U.S. Postal Service and that no instructions on the method of return were ever given by Numismatic. In light of this finding, and the absence of any specific evidence in the record indicating that the parties had agreed upon a method of return, we reject Numismatic's contention that there was an understanding between the parties that Prewitt would return the coins fully insured via Federal Express.

DECISION AND REMEDY

The court of appeals held that the transaction in question was a sale on approval and that under UCC 2-327(1) Numismatic, the owner of the coins, bore the risk of their loss during the return shipment from Prewitt. Affirmed.

Case Questions

Critical Legal Thinking   Do you agree with how the UCC assesses risk of loss in sale on approval transactions?

Ethics   Should Prewitt have fully insured the coins before sending them back to Numismatic?

Business Application   How could Numismatic have protected its interests in this case?

Sale or Return

In a **sale or return** contract, the seller delivers goods to a buyer with the understanding that the buyer may return them if they are not used or resold within a stated period of time (or a reasonable time if no specific time is stated). The sale is considered final if the buyer fails to return the goods within the specified time or reasonable time if no time is specified. The buyer has the option of returning all of the goods or any commercial unit of the goods.

sale or return
A contract that says the seller delivers goods to a buyer with the understanding that the buyer may return them if they are not used or resold within a stated or reasonable period of time.

Consider This Example   Suppose a fashion designer delivers 10 dresses to a fashion boutique on a sale or return basis. The boutique pays $10,000 ($1,000 per dress). If the boutique does not resell the dresses within three months, it may return the unsold garments to the designer. At the end of three months, the boutique has sold four of the dresses. The remaining six dresses may be returned to the designer. The boutique can recover the compensation paid for the returned dresses.

In a sale or return contract, the risk of loss and title to the goods pass to the buyer when the buyer takes possession of the goods. In the previous example, if the dresses were destroyed while they were at the boutique, the boutique's owner would be responsible for paying the designer for them [UCC 2-327(2)]. Goods sold pursuant to a sale or return contract are subject to the claims of the buyer's creditors while the goods are in the buyer's possession.

Consignment

consignment

An arrangement where a seller (the consignor) delivers goods to a buyer (the consignee) for sale.

In a **consignment**, a seller (the *consignor*) delivers goods to a buyer (the *consignee*) to sell. The consignee is paid a fee if he or she sells the goods on behalf of the consignor. A consignment is treated as a sale or return under the UCC. Whether the goods are subject to the claims of the buyer's creditors usually depends on whether the seller filed a financing statement as required by Article 9 of the UCC. If the seller files a financing statement, the goods are subject to the claims of the seller's creditors. If the seller fails to file such statement, the goods are subject to the claims of the buyer's creditors [UCC 2-326(3)].

ℛISK OF LOSS—BREACH OF SALES CONTRACT

The risk of loss rules just discussed apply where there is no breach of contract. Separate risk of loss rules apply to situations involving breach of the sales contract [UCC 2-510].

Seller in Breach

Laws are not masters but servants, and he rules them who obeys them.

Henry Ward Beecher
Proverbs from Plymouth
Pulpit *(1887)*

A seller breaches a sales contract if he or she tenders or delivers nonconforming goods to the buyer. If the goods are so nonconforming that the buyer has the right to reject them, the risk of loss remains on the seller until (1) the defect or nonconformity is cured, or (2) the buyer accepts the nonconforming goods.

Consider This Example A buyer orders 1,000 talking dolls from a seller. The contract is a shipment contract, which normally places the risk of loss during transportation on the buyer. The seller ships nonconforming dolls that cannot talk. The goods are destroyed in transit. The seller bears the risk of loss because he or she breached the contract by shipping nonconforming goods.

Buyer in Breach

Buyers breach a sales contract if they (1) refuse to take delivery of conforming goods, (2) repudiate the contract, or (3) otherwise breach the contract. A buyer who breaches a sales contract before the risk of loss would normally pass to him or her bears the risk of

Cabs, London. Often companies that enter into international contracts designate that the United Nations Convention on Contracts for the International Sale of Goods (CISG) governs the performance of the contract.

loss to any goods identified to the contract. The risk of loss rests on the buyer for only a commercially reasonable time. The buyer is only liable for any loss in excess of insurance recovered by the seller.

Risk of Loss in Lease Contracts

The parties to a lease contract may agree as to who will bear the risk of loss of the goods if they are lost or destroyed. If the parties do not so agree, the UCC supplies the following risk of loss rules:

1. In the case of an ordinary lease, the risk of loss is retained by the lessor. If the lease is a finance lease, the risk of loss passes to the lessee [UCC 2A-219].
2. If a tender of delivery of goods fails to conform to the lease contract, the risk of loss remains with the lessor or supplier until cure or acceptance [UCC 2A-220(1)(a)].

Entrepreneur and the Law

INSURING AGAINST LOSS

To protect against the financial loss that would occur if goods are damaged, destroyed, lost, or stolen, the parties to sales and lease contracts should purchase insurance against such loss. If the goods are then lost or damaged, the insured party receives reimbursement from the insurance company for the loss.

To purchase insurance, a party must have an *insurable interest* in the goods. A seller has an insurable interest in goods as long as he or she retains title or has a security interest in the goods. A lessor retains an insurable interest in the goods during the term of the lease. A buyer or lessee obtains an insurable interest in the goods when they are identified to the sales or lease contract. Both the buyer and seller, or lessee and lessor, can have an insurable

interest in the goods at the same time [UCC 2-501 and 2A-218].

To obtain and maintain proper insurance coverage on goods, a contracting party should

- Determine the value of goods subject to the sales or lease contract.
- Purchase insurance from a reputable insurance company covering the goods subject to the contract.
- Maintain the insurance by paying the premiums when they are due.
- Immediately file the proper claim and supporting documentation with the insurance company if the goods are damaged, destroyed, lost, or stolen.

Sales by Nonowners

Sometimes, people sell goods even though they do not hold valid title to them. The UCC anticipated many of the problems this could cause and established rules concerning the title, if any, that could be transferred to the purchasers.

Void Title and Lease—Stolen Goods

In a case where a buyer purchases goods or a lessee leases goods from a thief who has stolen them, the purchaser does not acquire title to the goods and the lessee does not acquire any leasehold interest in the goods. The real owner can reclaim the goods from the purchaser or lessee [UCC 2-403(1)]. This is called **void title**.

void title
A thief acquires no title to the goods he or she steals, nor does the buyer or lessee of stolen goods.

Consider This Example Suppose someone steals a truckload of Sony television sets that are owned by Sears. The thief resells the televisions to City-Mart, which does not know that the goods were stolen. If Sears finds out where the televisions are, it can reclaim

voidable title

Title that a purchaser has if the goods were obtained by (1) fraud, (2) a check that is later dishonored, or (3) impersonating another person.

good faith purchaser for value

A person to whom good title can be transferred from a person with voidable title. The real owner cannot reclaim goods from a good faith purchaser for value.

good faith subsequent lessee

A person to whom a lease interest can be transferred from a person with voidable title. The real owner cannot reclaim the goods from the subsequent lessee until the lease expires.

buyer in the ordinary course of business

A person who in good faith and without knowledge that the sale violates the ownership or security interests of a third party buys the goods in the ordinary course of business from a person in the business of selling goods of that kind. A buyer in the ordinary course of business takes the goods free of any third-party security interest in the goods.

them. Because the thief had no title in the goods, title was not transferred to City-Mart. City-Mart's only recourse is against the thief—if he or she can be found.

Voidable Title—Sales or Lease of Goods to Good Faith Purchasers for Value

A seller or lessor has **voidable title** to goods if the goods were obtained by fraud, a check that is later dishonored, or impersonating another person. A person with voidable title to goods can transfer good title to a **good faith purchaser for value** or a **good faith subsequent lessee**. A good faith purchaser or lessee for value is someone who pays sufficient consideration or rent for the goods to the person he or she honestly believes has good title to those goods [UCC 2-201(1), 1-201(44)(d)]. The real owner cannot reclaim goods from such a purchaser or lessee [UCC 2-403(1)].

Consider These Examples   Suppose a person buys a Rolex watch from a neighbor for near fair market value. It is later discovered that the seller obtained the watch from a jewelry store with a "bounced check." The jewelry store cannot reclaim the watch because the second purchaser purchased the watch in good faith and for value.

Assume instead that the purchaser bought the watch from a stranger for far less than fair market value. It is later discovered that the seller obtained the watch from a jewelry store by fraud. The jewelry store can reclaim the watch because the second purchaser was not a good faith purchaser for value.

Entrustment Rule

The rule found in UCC 2-403(2) holds that if an owner *entrusts* the possession of his or her goods to a merchant who deals in goods of that kind, the merchant has the power to transfer all rights (including title) in the goods to a **buyer in the ordinary course of business**. The real owner cannot reclaim the goods from this buyer.

Consider This Example   Kim Jones brings her computer into the Computer Store to be repaired. The Computer Store both sells and services computers. Jones leaves (entrusts) her computer at the store until it is repaired. The Computer Store sells her computer to Harold Green. Green, a buyer in the ordinary course of business, acquires title to the computer. Jones cannot reclaim the computer from Green. Her only recourse is against the Computer Store.

The entrustment rule also applies to leases. If a lessor entrusts the possession of his or her goods to a lessee who is a merchant who deals in goods of that kind, the merchant-lessee has the power to transfer all of the lessor's and lessee's rights in the goods to a buyer or sublessee in the ordinary course of business [UCC 2A-305(2)].

Ethical Perspective

CORN FARMERS GET SHUCKED

The entrustment rule is raised in the following case. Robert, David, and Hazel Schluter (Schluters) are grain farmers in Starbuck, Minnesota. They often hired a specific trucker to haul their grain to the public grain elevator, United Farmers Elevator, to whom they would sell their grain. On some occasions, the Schluters would sell their grain to the trucker, who would then resell the grain to the elevator or others. In the case at hand, the Schluters hired the trucker to haul their corn to the elevator. When the trucker got to the elevator, he represented that he owned the corn and sold it to the elevator for $288,000. The trucker absconded with the money.

The Schluters sued the elevator to recover payment for their corn. Who owns the corn, the Schluters or the elevator? The trial court applied the entrustment rule and held that the elevator had title to the corn as a buyer in the ordinary course of business. The appellate court stated:

It is undisputed the trucker had for several years bought and sold grain in the farmers' area, and the elevator had done business with the trucker not only as a hauler of grain belonging to others but also as a seller of grain belonging to himself. Thus, he was known in the area as a buyer and seller. This combination of the trucker's own conduct over time and his reputation in the area are sufficient to qualify him as a merchant of grain under the UCC, since he dealt in goods of the kind or otherwise held himself out as having knowledge or skill as a grain buyer and seller.

Under these facts, the trucker was a "merchant" and the farmers entrusted their grain to him. The undisputed facts show the farmers entrusted their grain to an independent trucker who was also a merchant, thereby empowering him to transfer ownership to the elevator as a buyer in the ordinary course of business. Under the UCC entrustment rule the elevator owned the corn. [*Schluter v. United Farmers Elevator,* 479 N.W.2d 82 (Minn.App. 1992)]

1. Did the trucker act ethically in this case?
2. Do you think the UCC entrustment rule places loss on the right party? Explain.

CONCEPT SUMMARY   PASSAGE OF TITLE IN SALES BY NONOWNER THIRD PARTIES AND SALES OF GOODS SUBJECT TO SECURITY AGREEMENTS

Type of Transaction	Title Possessed by Seller	Innocent Purchaser	Purchaser Acquires Title to Goods
Goods acquired by theft are resold.	Void title.	Good faith purchaser for value.	No. Original owner may reclaim the goods.
Goods acquired by fraud or dishonored check are resold.	Voidable title.	Good faith purchaser for value.	Yes. Purchaser takes free of claim of original owner.
Goods entrusted by owner to merchant who deals in that type of good are resold.	No title.	Buyer in ordinary course of business.	Yes. Purchaser takes free of claim of original owner.
Creditor possesses security interest in goods that are sold.	Good title.	Buyer in ordinary course of business.	Yes. Purchaser takes free of creditor's security interest.

Contemporary Business Application

BULK SALES LAW DUMPED

Article 6 (Bulk Sales) of the UCC establishes rules that were designed to prevent fraud when there is a bulk transfer of goods. A **bulk transfer** occurs when an owner transfers a major part of a business's material, merchandise, inventory, or equipment not in the ordinary course of business. This usually occurs upon the sale of the assets of a business.

If there is a bulk transfer of assets, Article 6 requires that (1) the seller furnish the buyer with a list of all of the creditors of the business, and (2) the buyer notify all of the listed

(box continues)

creditors at least 10 days before taking possession of or paying for the goods, whichever occurs first. The buyer is not responsible for or liable to unlisted creditors [UCC 6-105].

If all of the requirements of Article 6 are met, the buyer receives title to the goods free of all claims of the seller's creditors. If the requirements of Article 6 are not met, the goods in the buyer's possession are subject to the claims of the seller's creditors for six months after the date of possession [UCC 6-111].

In 1988, after much review, the National Conference of Commissioners on Uniform State Laws (NCCUSL) and the American Law Institute (ALI) reported that the regulation of bulk sales was no longer necessary. Consequently, they withdrew their support for Article 6 and encouraged states that had enacted the Article to repeal it.

The report criticized the bulk transfer law for adding costs—without corresponding benefits—to business transactions. The report claimed that it was unfair to impose liability on an innocent buyer because a dishonest seller failed to pay its creditors. The committee then stated that changing laws and economics, as well as improved communications, made it more difficult for merchants to sell their merchandise and abscond with the proceeds. Further, the report noted that modern jurisdictional laws make it easier to obtain and enforce judgments against debtors who have left the state.

Recognizing that some state legislatures may wish to continue to regulate bulk transfers, the committee also promulgated a revised version of Article 6.

Working the Web

e·biz

Zip Codes and Addresses The U.S. Post Office has a database of zip codes and addresses.

Visit at **www.usps.gov/ncsc/**

Ultimate Yellow Pages The Ultimate Yellow Pages is a good place to find a business in another city even if you do not have the address. Check out this site which allows you to search various databases by name, city, and category.

Visit at **www.theultimates.com/yellow/**

BISNIS Online BISNIS Online is the Department of Commerce's Business Information Service for the Newly

Independent States—a one stop shop for doing business in Russia and the other states of the former Soviet Union.

Visit at **www.bisnis.doc.gov**

CYBER EXERCISES

1. Use the USPS site to find your parents' address and zip code.

2. Using BISNIS, find a country report on a country from the former Soviet Union.

3. Use the Ultimate Yellow Pages to find a business in another state.

CASES AND EXERCISES

CRITICAL LEGAL THINKING CASES

20.1. The Big Knob Volunteer Fire Company (Fire Co.) agreed to purchase a fire truck from Hamerly Custom Productions (Hamerly), which was in the business of assembling various component parts into fire trucks. Fire Co. paid Hamerly $10,000 toward the price two days after signing the contract. Two weeks later, it gave Hamerly $38,000 more

toward the total purchase price of $53,000. Hamerly bought an engine chassis for the new fire truck on credit from Lowe and Meyer Garage (Lowe and Meyer). After installing the chassis, Hamerly painted the Big Knob Fire Department's name on the side of the cab. Hamerly never paid for the engine chassis and the truck was repossessed by Lowe and

Meyer. The Fire Co. sought to recover the fire truck from Lowe and Meyer. Although the Fire Co. was the buyer of a fire truck, Lowe and Meyer questioned whether any goods had ever been identified to the contract. Were they? [*Big Knob Volunteer Fire Co. v. Lowe and Meyer Garage*, 487 A.2d 953 (Pa.Super. 1985)]

20.2. On October 18, 1980, New England Yacht Sales (Yacht Sales) sold a yacht to Robert Pease. Pease paid for the yacht in full, and Yacht Sales delivered to him a marine bill of sale. The marine bill of sale stated that Yacht Sales was transferring "all of its right, title, and interest" in the yacht to Pease. The yacht never left the Connecticut shipyard that Yacht Sales rented. During the winter of 1980–1981, Yacht Sales did repair work on the yacht. On May 8, 1981, Yacht Sales delivered the yacht to Pease in Rhode Island. At issue in this case was when the sales tax was due to the state of Connecticut—October 18, 1980, or May 8, 1981. When did the title actually pass? [*New England Yacht Sales v. Commissioner of Revenue Services*, 504 A.2d 506 (CT 1986)]

20.3. John Torniero was employed by Micheals Jewelers, Inc. (Micheals). During the course of his employment Torniero stole pieces of jewelry, including several diamond rings, a sapphire ring, a gold pendant, and several loose diamonds. Over a period of several months, Torniero sold individual pieces of the stolen jewelry to G&W Watch and Jewelry Corporation (G&W). G&W had no knowledge of how Torniero obtained the jewels. Torniero was arrested when Micheals discovered the thefts. After Torniero admitted that he had sold the stolen jewelry to G&W, Micheals attempted to recover it from G&W. G&W claimed title to the jewelry as a good faith purchaser for value. Micheals challenged G&W's claim to title in court. Who wins? [*United States v. Micheals Jewelers, Inc.*, 42 UCC Rep.Serv. 141 (D.C.Conn. 1985)]

20.4. J.A. Coghill owned a 1979 Rolls Royce Corniche, which he sold in 1984 to a man claiming to be Daniel Bellman. Bellman gave Coghill a cashier's check for $94,500. When Coghill tried to cash the check, his bank informed him that the check had been forged. Coghill reported the vehicle as stolen. Early in September 1984, Barry Hyken responded to a newspaper ad listing a 1980 Rolls Royce Corniche for sale. Hyken went to meet the seller of the car, the man who claimed to be Bellman, in a parking lot. When Hyken asked why the car was advertised as a 1980 model when it was in fact a 1979, Bellman replied that it was a newspaper mistake. Hyken agreed to pay $62,000 for the car. When Hyken asked to see Bellman's identification, Bellman provided documents with two different addresses. Bellman explained that he was in the process of moving. Although there seemed to be some

irregularities in the title documents to the car, Hyken took possession anyway. Three weeks later, the Rolls was seized by the police. Hyken sued to get it back. Who wins? [*Landshire Food Service, Inc. v. Coghill*, 709 S.W.2d 509 (Mo.App. 1986)]

20.5. On July 19, 1985, Cherry Creek Dodge, Inc. (Cherry Creek), sold a 1985 Dodge Ramcharger to Executive Leasing of Colorado (Executive Leasing). Executive Leasing, which was in the business of buying and selling cars, paid for the Dodge with a draft. Cherry Creek maintained a security interest in the car until the draft cleared. The same day that Executive Leasing bought the Dodge, it sold the car to Bruce and Peggy Carter. The Carters paid in full for the Dodge with a cashier's check and the vehicle was delivered to them. The Carters had no knowledge of the financial arrangement between Executive Leasing and Cherry Creek. The draft that Executive Leasing gave Cherry Creek was worthless. Cherry Creek attempted to recover the vehicle from the Carters. Who wins? [*Cherry Creek Dodge, Inc. v. Carter*, 733 P.2d 1024 (WY 1987)]

20.6. Fuqua Homes, Inc. (Fuqua), is a manufacturer of prefabricated houses. MMM was a partnership created by two men named Kirk and Underhill. MMM operated as a dealer of prefabricated homes. On seven occasions before the disputed transactions occurred, MMM had ordered homes from Fuqua. In early 1977, MMM was contacted by Kenneth Ryan. Ryan wanted to purchase a 55-foot modular home. MMM called Fuqua and ordered a prefabricated home that met Ryan's specifications. Fuqua delivered the home to MMM and retained a security interest in it until MMM paid the purchase price. MMM installed the house on Ryan's property and collected full payment from Ryan. Kirk and Underhill then disappeared, taking Ryan's money with them. Fuqua was never paid for the prefabricated home it had manufactured. Ryan had no knowledge of the dealings between MMM and Fuqua. Fuqua claimed title to the house based upon its security interest. Who has title to the home? [*Fuqua Homes, Inc. v. Evanston Bldg. & Loan Co.*, 370 N.E.2d 780 (OhioApp. 1977)]

20.7. In June 1973, All America Export-Import Corp. (All America) placed an order for several thousand pounds of yarn with A. M. Knitwear (Knitwear). On June 4, All America sent Knitwear a purchase order. The purchase order stated the terms of the sale, including language that stated that the price was F.O.B. the seller's plant. On Friday, June 22, 1973, a truck hired by All America arrived at Knitwear's plant. On Monday, June 24, Knitwear turned the yarn over to the carrier and notified All America that the goods were now on the truck. The truck left Knitwear's plant and proceeded to a local warehouse. Sometime during the night of June 24, the truck was hijacked and all the yarn was stolen. All America had paid for the yarn by check but stopped payment on it when it learned that the goods had been stolen. Knitwear sued All America, claiming that it must pay for the stolen goods because it bore the risk of loss. Who wins? [*A. M. Knitwear v. All America, Etc.*, 390 N.Y.S.2d 832, 41 N.Y.2d 14 (N.Y.App. 1976)]

20.8. Mitsubishi International Corporation (Mitsubishi) entered into a contract with the Crown Door Company (Crown), which called for Mitsubishi to sell 12 boxcar loads of plywood to Crown. According to the terms of the contract, Mitsubishi would import the wood from Taiwan and deliver it to Crown's plant in Atlanta. Mitsubishi had the wood shipped from Taiwan to Savannah, Georgia. At Savannah, the plywood was loaded onto trains and hauled to Atlanta. When the plywood arrived in Atlanta, it was discovered that the railroad had been negligent in loading the train. The negligent loading had caused the cargo to shift during the trip, and the shifting had caused extensive damage to the wood. Who bore the risk of loss? [*Georgia Port Authority v. Mitsubishi International Corporation*, 274 S.E.2d 699 (Ga.App. 1980)]

20.9. In 1982, Martin Silver ordered two rooms of furniture from Wycombe, Meyer & Co., Inc. (Wycombe), a manufac-

turer and seller of custom-made furniture. On February 23, 1982, Wycombe sent invoices to Silver advising him that the furniture was ready for shipment. Silver tendered payment in full for the goods and asked that one room of furniture be shipped immediately and that the other be held for shipment on a later date. Before any instructions were received as to the second room of furniture, it was destroyed in a fire. Silver and his insurance company attempted to recover the money he paid for the destroyed furniture. Wycombe refused to return the payment, claiming that the risk of loss was upon Silver. Who wins? [*Silver v. Wycombe, Meyer & Co., Inc.*, 477 N.Y.S.2d 288 (N.Y.City Civ.Ct. 1984)]

20.10. On February 7, 1967, Donald Hayward signed a sales contract with Dry Land Marina, Inc. (Dry Land). The contract was for the purchase of a 30-foot Revel Craft Playmate Yacht for $10,000. The contract called for Dry Land to install a number of options on Hayward's yacht and then deliver it to him in April 1967. On March 1, 1967, before taking delivery of the yacht, Hayward signed a security agreement in favor of Dry Land and a promissory note. Several weeks later, a fire swept through Dry Land's showroom. Hayward's yacht was among the goods destroyed in the fire. Who had an insurable interest in the yacht? [*Hayward v. Potsma*, 188 N.W.2d 31 (Mich.App. 1971)]

ETHICS CASES

20.11. In mid-1975, Raceway Auto Auction (Raceway), New York, sold a red two-door 1973 Oldsmobile Toronado automobile to Triangle Auto Sales (Triangle). Triangle paid for the car with a check. Raceway delivered possession of the car to Triangle. Thereafter, Triangle's check "bounced" for insufficient funds. In the meantime, Triangle sold the car to Campus Auto Sales (Campus), Rhode Island, who sold it to Charles Motor Co., Inc. (Charles), Rhode Island, who sold it to Lee Oldsmobile-Cadillac, Inc. (Lee Oldsmobile), Maine, who sold it to Stephanie K. LeBlanc of Augusta, Maine. When Triangle's check bounced, Raceway reported the car as stolen. Four months after she purchased the car, Stephanie was stopped by the Maine police, who seized the car. To maintain good relations with its customer, Lee Oldsmobile paid Raceway $2,000 to obtain the certificate of title to the automobile and then sued Charles to recover. Did Triangle Auto Sales act ethically in this case? Did Charles Motor Co. obtain valid title to the automobile? [*Lee Oldsmobile-Cadillac, Inc. v. Labonte*, 30 UCC Rep.Serv. 74 (RI 1980)]

20.12. In the summer and fall of 1982, Executive Financial Services, Inc. (EFS), purchased three tractors from Tri-

County Farm Company (Tri-County), a John Deere dealership owned by Gene Mohr and James Loyd. The tractors cost $48,000, $19,000, and $38,000, respectively. EFS did not take possession of the tractors but instead left the tractors on Tri-County's lot. EFS leased the tractors to Mohr-Loyd Leasing (Mohr-Loyd), a partnership between Mohr and Loyd, with the understanding and representation by Mohr-Loyd that the tractors would be leased out to farmers. Instead of leasing the tractors, Tri-County sold them to three different farmers. EFS sued and obtained judgment against Tri-County, Mohr-Loyd, and Mohr and Loyd personally for breach of contract. Because that judgment remained unsatisfied, EFS sued the three farmers who bought the tractors to recover the tractors from them. Did Mohr and Loyd act ethically in this case? Who owns the tractors, EFS or the farmers? [*Executive Financial Services, Inc. v. Pagel*, 715 P.2d 381 (KS 1986)]

20.13. On March 11, 1985, Dugdale of Nebraska, Inc. (Dugdale), purchased a 1985 Ford LTD Crown Victoria automobile from Vannier Ford, an automobile dealership. Dugdale traded in a 1984 vehicle and paid cash for the remaining purchase price of the car. On the day that the vehicle was delivered, the president of Vannier Ford told the representative of Dugdale that the title papers to the vehicle had not yet been received, but would be given to him as soon as they were received.

Approximately five days before selling the vehicle to Dugdale, Vannier Ford had pledged it as security for a loan from First State Bank, Gothenburg, Nebraska (First State Bank), and delivered the certificate of title to the bank. This fact was unknown by Dugdale. Vannier Ford did not transmit the proceeds of the sale to First State Bank. After the sale,

Dugdale made numerous inquiries regarding the title papers, and each time was told by Vannier Ford that the papers had not yet arrived. Approximately two months later, after Vannier Ford defaulted on the loan, First State Bank contacted Dugdale and made demand for possession of the vehicle. Dugdale brought suit seeking a declaratory judgment as to its ownership rights. First State Bank filed a counterclaim. Did Vannier Ford act ethically in this case? Who owns title to the vehicle, Dugdale or First State Bank? [*Dugdale of Nebraska Inc. v. First State Bank, Gothenburg, Nebraska*, 420 N.W.2d 273 (NE 1988)]

CRITICAL LEGAL THINKING WRITING ASSIGNMENT

Read Case A.20 in the Case Appendix [*Burnett v. Purtell*]. This case is excerpted from the court of appeals opinion. Review and brief the case. In your brief, be sure to answer the following questions.

1. Who were the plaintiff and defendant? Were they merchants?

2. Describe the sales transaction.

3. Was there tender of delivery of the goods? Why is this issue important to the outcome of the case?

4. Who bore the risk of loss when the goods were destroyed?

Remedies for Breach of Sales and Lease Contracts

Trade and commerce, if they were not made of India rubber, would never manage to bounce over the obstacles which legislators are continually putting in their way.

HENRY D. THOREAU
Resistance to Civil Government (1849)

Chapter Objectives

After studying this chapter, you should be able to

1. Describe the doctrines of good faith and reasonableness that govern the performance of sales and lease contracts.
2. Define *perfect tender rule*.
3. Identify when the buyer or lessee has a right to reject nonconforming goods.
4. Identify when the seller or lessor has a right to cure a nonconforming delivery of goods.
5. Identify when the buyer or lessee has the right to revoke a prior acceptance.
6. List and describe the seller's remedies for the buyer's breach of the sales contract.
7. List and describe the buyer's remedies for the seller's breach of the sales contract.
8. List and describe the lessor's remedies for the lessee's breach of the lease contract.
9. List and describe the lessee's remedies for the lessor's breach of the lease contract.
10. Identify limitations on remedies.

Chapter Contents

Usually, the parties to a sales or lease contract owe a duty to perform the *obligations* specified in their agreement [UCC 2-301, 2A-301]. The seller's or lessor's general obligation is to transfer and deliver the goods to the buyer or lessee. The buyer's or lessee's general obligation is to accept and pay for the goods.

When one party **breaches** the sales or lease contract, the UCC provides the injured party with a variety of *prelitigation* and *litigation* remedies. These remedies are designed to place the injured party in as good a position as if the breaching party's contractual obligations were fully performed [UCC 1-106(1), 2A-401(1)]. The best remedy depends on the circumstances of the particular case.

The performance of obligations and remedies available for breach of sales and lease contracts are discussed in this chapter.

breach
Failure of a party to perform an obligation in a sales or lease contract.

Seller's and Lessor's Obligations

Tender of delivery, or the transfer and delivery of goods to the buyer or lessee in accordance with the sales or lease contract, is the seller's or lessor's basic obligation [UCC 2-301]. Tender of delivery requires the seller or lessor to (1) put and hold *conforming goods* at the buyer's or lessee's disposition and (2) give the buyer or lessee any notification reasonably necessary to enable delivery of the goods. The parties may agree as to the time, place, and manner of delivery. If there is no special agreement, tender must be made at a reasonable hour, and the goods must be kept available for a reasonable period of time. For example, the seller cannot telephone the buyer at 12:01 A.M. and say that he or she has 15 minutes to accept delivery [UCC 2-503(1), 2A-508(1)].

Unless otherwise agreed or the circumstances permit either party to request delivery in lots, the goods named in the contract must be tendered in a single delivery. Payment of a sales contract is due upon tender of delivery unless an extension of credit between the parties has been arranged. If the goods are rightfully delivered in lots, the payment is apportioned for each lot [UCC 2-307]. Payment of rent is due in accordance with the terms of the lease contract.

tender of delivery
The obligation of the seller to transfer and deliver goods to the buyer in accordance with the sales contract.

A proceeding may be perfectly legal and may yet be opposed to sound commercial principles.

Lindley, L.J.
Verner v. General and
Commercial Trust (1894)

Place of Delivery

Many sales and lease contracts state where the goods are to be delivered. Often, the contract will say that the buyer or lessee must pick up the goods from the seller or lessor. If the contract does not expressly state where the delivery will take place, the UCC will stipulate place of delivery on the basis of whether a carrier is involved.

Noncarrier Cases Unless otherwise agreed, the place of delivery is the seller's or lessor's place of business. If the seller or lessor has no place of business, the place of delivery is the seller's or lessor's residence. If the parties have knowledge at the time of contracting that identified goods are located in some other place, that place is the place of delivery. For example, if the parties contract regarding the sale of wheat located in a silo, then the silo is the place of delivery [UCC 2-308].

Sometimes the goods are in the possession of a **bailee** (e.g., a warehouse) and are to be delivered without being moved. In such cases, tender of delivery occurs when the seller either (1) tenders to the buyer a negotiable document of title covering the goods or (2) procures acknowledgment from the bailee of the buyer's right to possession of the goods, or (3) tenders a nonnegotiable document of title or a written direction to the bailee to deliver the goods to a buyer. The seller must deliver all such documents in correct form [UCC 2-503(4) and (5)].

bailee
A holder of goods who is not a seller or a buyer (e.g., a warehouse).

Carrier Cases   Unless the parties have agreed otherwise, if delivery of the goods to the buyer is to be made by carrier, the UCC establishes different rules for shipment contracts and destination contracts. These rules are described below.

Shipment Contracts   Sales contracts that require the seller to send the goods to the buyer but not to a specifically named destination, are called **shipment contracts**. Under such contracts, the seller must do all of the following:

shipment contract
A sales contract that requires the seller to send the goods to the buyer, but not to a specifically named destination.

1. Put the goods in the carrier's possession and contract for the proper and safe transportation of the goods.
2. Obtain and promptly deliver or tender in correct form any documents (a) necessary to enable the buyer to obtain possession of the goods, (b) required by the sales contract, or (c) required by usage of trade.
3. Promptly notify the buyer of the shipment [UCC 2-504].

The buyer may reject the goods if a material delay or loss is caused by the seller's failure to make a proper contract for the shipment of goods or properly notify the buyer of the shipment. For example, if a shipment contract involves perishable goods and the seller fails to ship the goods via a refrigerated carrier, the buyer may rightfully reject the goods if they spoil during transit.

Destination Contracts   A sales contract that requires the seller to deliver the goods to the buyer's place of business or another specified destination is a **destination contract**. Unless otherwise agreed, destination contracts require delivery to be tendered at the buyer's place of business or other location specified in the sales contract. Delivery must be at a reasonable time and in a reasonable manner and with proper notice to the buyer. Appropriate documents of title must be provided by the seller to enable the buyer to obtain the goods from the carrier [UCC 2-503].

destination contract
A sales contract that requires the seller to deliver the goods to the buyer's place of business or another specified destination.

Perfect Tender Rule

The seller or lessor is under a duty to deliver *conforming goods*. If the goods or tender of delivery fails in any respect to conform to the contract, the buyer or lessee may opt to (1) reject the whole shipment, (2) accept the whole shipment, or (3) reject part and accept part of the shipment. This is referred to as the **perfect tender rule** [UCC 2-601, 2A-509].

perfect tender rule
A rule that says if the goods or tender of a delivery fails in any respect to conform to the contract, the buyer may opt to (1) reject the whole shipment, (2) accept the whole shipment, or (3) reject part and accept part of the shipment.

Consider This Example   A sales contract requires the seller to deliver 100 shirts to a buyer. When the buyer inspects the delivered goods, it is discovered that 99 shirts conform to the contract and one shirt does not conform. Pursuant to the perfect tender rule, the buyer may reject the entire shipment. If a buyer accepts nonconforming goods, the buyer may seek remedies against the seller.

Exceptions to the Perfect Tender Rule   The UCC alters the perfect tender rule in the following situations:

Agreement of the Parties The parties to the sales or lease contract may agree to limit the effect of the perfect tender rule. For example, they may decide that (1) only the defective or nonconforming goods may be rejected, (2) the seller or lessor may replace nonconforming goods or repair defects, or (3) the buyer or lessee will accept nonconforming goods with appropriate compensation from the seller or lessor.

Substitution of Carriers The UCC requires the seller to use a commercially reasonable substitute if (1) the agreed-upon manner of delivery fails or (2) the agreed-upon type of carrier becomes unavailable [UCC 2-614(1)].

Consider This Example   A sales contract specifies delivery of goods by MacTrucks, Inc., a common carrier, but a labor strike prevents delivery by this carrier. The seller must use any commercially reasonable substitute (such as another truck line, the rails, or the like). The buyer cannot reject the delivery because there is a substitute carrier. Unless otherwise agreed, the seller bears any increased cost of the substitute performance.

Cure   The UCC gives a seller or lessor who delivers nonconforming goods an opportunity to **cure** the nonconformity. Although the term *cure* is not defined by the UCC, it generally means an opportunity to repair or replace defective or nonconforming goods [UCC 2-508, 2A-513].

A cure may be attempted if the time for performance has not expired and the seller or lessor notifies the buyer or lessee of his or her intention to make a conforming delivery within the contract time. For example, a lessee contracts to lease a BMW 850i automobile from a lessor for delivery July 1. On June 15, the lessor delivers a BMW 740i to the lessee, which the lessee rejects as nonconforming. The lessor has until July 1 to cure the nonconformity by delivering the BMW 850i specified in the contract.

A cure may also be attempted if the seller or lessor had reasonable grounds to believe the delivery would be accepted. The seller or lessor may have a further reasonable time to substitute a conforming tender. For example, a buyer contracts to purchase 100 red dresses from a seller for delivery July 1. On July 1, the seller delivers 100 blue dresses to the buyer. In the past, the buyer has accepted different-colored dresses than those ordered. This time, though, the buyer rejects the blue dresses as nonconforming. The seller has a reasonable time after July 1 to deliver conforming red dresses to the buyer.

In the following case, a seller attempted to cure a defective delivery.

> **cure**
> **An opportunity to repair or replace defective or nonconforming goods.**

> *This is the kind of order which makes the administration of justice stink in the nostrils of commercial men.*
>
> A. L. Smith, L.J.
> Graham v. Sutton,
> Carden & Co. *(1897)*

Joc Oil USA, Inc. v. Consolidated Edison Co. of New York, Inc.
30 UCC Rep.Serv. 426 (1980)
New York Supreme Court, New York County

CASE 21.1

FACTS
Joc Oil USA, Inc. (Joc Oil), contracted to purchase low-sulfur fuel oil from an Italian oil refinery. The Italian refinery issued a certificate to Joc Oil indicating that the sulfur content of the oil was 0.50%. Joc Oil entered into a sales contract to sell the oil to Consolidated Edison Co. of New York, Inc. (Con Ed). Con Ed agreed to pay $17.875 per barrel for oil not to exceed 0.50% sulfur. When the ship delivering the oil arrived, it discharged the oil into three Con Ed storage tanks. On February 20, 1974, a final report issued by Con Ed stated that the sulfur content of the oil was 0.92%. At a meeting that day, Joc Oil offered to reduce the price of the oil by 50 cents to 80 cents per barrel. Con Ed expressed a willingness to accept the oil at $13 per barrel (the market price of oil at that time). Joc Oil then made an offer to cure the defect by substituting a conforming shipment of oil that was already on a ship that was to arrive within two weeks. Con Ed rejected Joc Oil's offer to cure. Joc Oil sued Con Ed for breach of contract.

ISSUE
Did Joc Oil have a right to cure the defect in delivery?

IN THE LANGUAGE OF THE COURT
Egeth, Judge   Uniform Commercial Code, Section 2-508(2), sets forth the seller's right to cure a defective tender thereunder: (1) when the seller has reasonable grounds to believe the tender would be acceptable to the buyer "with or without money allowance," (2) upon reasonable notice to the buyer of the seller's intention to cure, and (3) upon substitution of a conforming tender within a reasonable time.

There is no serious dispute that reasonable notice of an intention to cure the defect in delivery was given to Con Ed by Joc Oil. It was given one day after the February 20, 1974 meeting at which the parties discussed a possible price adjustment. It is equally clear that there can be and there is no serious challenge as to the reasonableness of the notice or as to the time of the tendered curative delivery. At the time the offer was made, the substitute shipment was already on a ship due to arrive one week later. It must be found that the statutory requirement of reasonable notice of an intention to cure a defective delivery with a substitute conforming delivery within a reasonable time has been complied with by Joc Oil.

The actual issue in dispute between these parties, on both the law and the facts, centers upon whether within the contemplation

(case continues)

of the statute, Joc Oil had "reasonable grounds to believe" that the original shipment would be "acceptable" to Con Ed. Moreover, although Joc Oil had no predelivery knowledge of the 0.92% sulfur content disclosed after delivery, it would still have believed that such a shipment would have been acceptable to Con Ed based upon its prior knowledge of Con Ed purchase and use practices during this period of oil scarcity and volatile pricing. This belief was additionally buttressed by Con Ed's expressed willingness during the February 20, 1974 meeting to keep and use the nonconforming 0.92% sulfur oil, if an appropriate price adjustment could be effectuated. Therefore, prior to delivery and at the time Joc Oil made its offer to cure by tendering a new conforming shipment, it had cause to believe that the original shipment would have been accepted by the buyer "with or without money allowance" [UCC 2-508(2)].

DECISION AND REMEDY

The court held that under the circumstances of this case Joc Oil had the right to cure the defect in delivery and that Con Ed breached the contract by refusing to permit this cure. The court entered judgment against Con Ed and awarded Joc Oil $1,385,512 in damages plus interest and the costs of this action.

Case Questions

Critical Legal Thinking   Should the law recognize the right to cure a defective tender of goods? Why or why not?

Ethics   Did Con Ed act ethically in this case? Did Joc Oil?

Business Application   Why do you think Con Ed rejected Joc Oil's offer to cure the defect in delivery? Explain.

Installment Contracts

installment contract

A contract that requires or authorizes goods to be delivered and accepted in separate lots.

An **installment contract** is one that requires or authorizes goods to be delivered and accepted in separate lots. Such contracts must contain a clause that states "each delivery is a separate contract" or equivalent language. An example of an installment contract is one in which a buyer orders 100 shirts, to be delivered in four equal installments of 25 items.

The UCC alters the perfect tender rule with regard to installment contracts. The buyer or lessee may reject the entire contract only if the nonconformity or default with respect to any installment or installments substantially impairs the value of the entire contract. The buyer or lessee may reject any nonconforming installment if the value of the installment is impaired and the defect cannot be cured. Thus, in each case the court must determine whether the nonconforming installment impairs the value of the entire contract or only that installment [UCC 2-612, 2A-501].

Destruction of Goods

Convenience is the basis of mercantile law.

Lord Mansfield
Medcalf v. Hall (1782)

The UCC provides that if goods identified to a sales or lease contract are *totally destroyed* without the fault of either party before the risk of loss passes to the buyer or lessee, the contract is void. Both parties are then excused from performing the contract.

If the goods are only *partially destroyed*, the buyer or lessee may inspect the goods and then choose either to treat the contract as void or to accept the goods. If the buyer or lessee opts to accept the goods, the purchase price or rent will be reduced in compensation for the damage [UCC 2-613, 2A-221].

Consider This Example   A buyer contracts to purchase a sofa from a seller. The seller agrees to deliver the sofa to the buyer's home. The truck delivering the sofa is hit by an automobile and the sofa is totally destroyed. Because the risk of loss has not passed to the buyer, the contract is voided and the buyer does not have to pay for the sofa.

International Perspective

NONCONFORMITY IN INTERNATIONAL SALES CONTRACTS

In the United States, the UCC lets a buyer reject goods if the goods or tender of delivery does not conform to the contract. Once the goods are accepted, however, the buyer may refuse to keep the goods only if they have a substantial nonconformity that impairs their value to the buyer. The UCC rules are not widely copied in other countries, because they are generally perceived as unresponsive to commercial practice and the significant interests of the parties.

Outside the United States, sales laws try to encourage the seller to correct any defects, while cautioning the buyer to be patient in awaiting the seller's performance. For example, under the French Civil Code a contracting party must seek a court order that releases him or her from his or her obligation to perform. In deciding whether to grant the request, the court considers a variety of factors, including the defendant's degree of fault and the seriousness of the breach.

In Germany, if a seller defaults, the buyer is required to give the breaching seller a reasonable time to correct the defect at the seller's expense. This is accompanied by the buyer's declaration that he or she will refuse to accept performance after the expiration of the stated period. This declaration is known as a *Nachfrist* notice.

Many countries have adopted rules similar to these. The avoidance procedure adopted by the United Nations Convention on Contracts for the International Sale of Goods (CISG) is also based on the German rule.

Under the CISG, a buyer is allowed to avoid a contract (1) if the seller commits a fundamental breach or (2) if the seller either rejects the buyer's *Nachfrist* notice or does not perform within the period it specifies. Both the period and the obligation to perform have to be clearly stated.

*B*UYER'S AND LESSEE'S OBLIGATIONS

Once the seller or lessor has properly tendered delivery, the buyer or lessee is obligated to accept and pay for the goods in accordance with the sales or lease contract. If there is no agreement, the provisions of the UCC control.

Right of Inspection

Unless otherwise agreed, the buyer or lessee has the right to inspect goods that are tendered, delivered, or identified to the sales contract prior to accepting or paying for them. If the goods are shipped, the inspection may take place after their arrival. If the inspected goods do not conform to the contract, the buyer or lessee may reject them without paying for them [UCC 2-513(1), 2A-515(1)].

The parties may agree as to the time, place, and manner of inspection. If there is no such agreement, the inspection must occur at a reasonable time, place, and manner. Reasonableness depends on the circumstances of the case, common usage of trade, prior course of dealing between the parties, and such. If the goods conform to the contract, the buyer pays for the inspection. If the goods are rejected for nonconformance, the cost of inspection can be recovered from the seller [UCC 2-513(2)].

Buyers who agree to **C.O.D (cash on delivery)** deliveries are not entitled to inspect the goods before paying for them. In certain sales contracts [e.g., cost, insurance, and freight (or C.I.F.) contracts], payment is due from the buyer upon receipt of documents of title even if the goods have not yet been received. In such cases, the buyer is not entitled to inspect the goods before paying for them [UCC 2-513(3)].

C.O.D. shipment
A type of shipment contract where the buyer agrees to pay the shipper cash upon the delivery of the goods.

Payment

Goods that are accepted must be paid for [UCC 2-607(1)]. Unless the parties agree otherwise, payment is due from a buyer when and where the goods are delivered even if the place of delivery is the same as the place of shipment. Buyers often purchase goods on credit extended by the seller. Unless otherwise agreed by the parties, the credit period begins to run from the time of shipment of the goods [UCC 2-310]. A lessee must pay rent in accordance with the lease contract [UCC 2A-516(1)].

The goods can be paid for in any manner currently acceptable in the ordinary course of business (e.g., check, credit card, or the like) unless the seller demands payment in cash or the contract names a specific form of payment. If the seller requires cash payment, the buyer must be given an extension of time necessary to procure the cash. If the buyer pays by check, payment is conditional on the check being honored (paid) when it is presented to the bank for payment [UCC 2-511].

The buyer needs a hundred eyes, the seller not one.

George Herbert
Jacula Prudentum (1651)

Acceptance

acceptance

Occurs when a buyer or lessee takes any of the following actions after a reasonable opportunity to inspect the goods: The buyer or lessee either (1) signifies to the seller or lessor in words or by conduct that the goods are conforming or that the goods will be taken or retained in spite of their nonconformity or (2) fails to effectively reject the goods within a reasonable time after their delivery or tender by the seller or lessor. Acceptance also occurs if a buyer acts inconsistently with the seller's ownership rights in the goods.

Acceptance occurs when the buyer or lessee takes any of the following actions after a reasonable opportunity to inspect the goods: The buyer or lessee either (1) signifies to the seller or lessor in words or by conduct that the goods are conforming or that the goods will be taken or retained in spite of their nonconformity or (2) fails to effectively reject the goods within a reasonable time after their delivery or tender by the seller or lessor. Acceptance also occurs if a buyer acts inconsistently with the seller's ownership rights in the goods. For example, the buyer resells the goods delivered by the seller [UCC 2-606(1), 2A-515(1)].

Buyers and lessees may only accept delivery of a "commercial unit." A *commercial unit* is a unit of goods that commercial usage deems is a single whole for purpose of sale. Thus, it may be a single article (such as a machine), a set of articles (such as a suite of furniture or an assortment of sizes), a quantity (such as a bale, a gross, or a carload), or any other unit treated in use or in the relevant market as a single whole. Acceptance of a part of any commercial unit is acceptance of the entire unit [UCC 2-606(2), 2A-515(2)].

Revocation of Acceptance

A buyer or lessee who has accepted goods may subsequently revoke his or her acceptance if (1) the goods are nonconforming, (2) the nonconformity substantially impairs the value of the goods to the buyer or lessee, and (3) one of the following factors is shown: (a) The seller's or lessor's promise to reasonably cure the nonconformity is not met, (b) the goods were accepted before the nonconformity was discovered and the nonconformity was difficult to discover, or (c) the goods were accepted before the nonconformity was discovered and the seller or lessor assured the buyer or lessee that the goods were conforming.

Revocation is not effective until the seller or lessor is so notified. In addition, the revocation must occur within a reasonable time after the buyer or lessee discovers or should have discovered the grounds for the revocation. The revocation, which must be of a lot or commercial unit, must occur before there is any substantial change in the condition of the goods (e.g., before perishable goods spoil) [UCC 2-608(1), 2A-517(1)].

In the following case, the court had to decide whether to allow revocation of a sales contract.

Fortin v. Ox-Bow Marina, Inc.
557 N.E.2d 1157 (1990)
Supreme Judicial Court of Massachusetts

CASE 21.2

FACTS
In the spring of 1985, Robert and Marie Fortin ordered a 32-foot Bayliner Conquest powerboat from Ox-Bow Marina, Inc. (Ox-Bow). In May, on the day of closing, the Fortins checked their boat and found that none of the preparation work had been done, none of the special equipment they had ordered had been installed, and several defects needed to be repaired or corrected, including a nonfunctioning hot water pump, a broken pedestal seat, a nonfunctioning flush mechanism in the marine toilet system, and chips in the wood trim. Ox-Bow's representative assured the Fortins that the problems would be corrected if they closed

on the transaction. The Fortins agreed to close. To pay Ox-Bow, they traded in their old boat, paid $6,259 cash, and borrowed $51,500 from Horizon Financial.

In May and June, the Fortins requested Ox-Bow to correct the problems, which Ox-Bow did not do. When the Fortins set out on their maiden voyage on June 22, 1985, they discovered that the depth finder and marine radio did not work, the marine toilets were not functioning properly, and one of the two engines overheated and had to be shut down. Ox-Bow promised to fix these defects but again did not. The Fortins continued to request Ox-Bow to correct all of the defects. Although Ox-Bow always promised to comply, it never did.

Finally, on October 31, 1985, the Fortins notified Ox-Bow that they were revoking their acceptance of the Bayliner and sought a refund of their purchase price, plus damages. The judge ruled that the Fortins had effectively revoked acceptance of the boat and awarded them damages in the amount of $24,364, including sales tax and interest paid on the loan. Ox-Bow appealed.

ISSUE
Was the Fortins' revocation of acceptance effective?

IN THE LANGUAGE OF THE COURT
Lynch, Justice   A buyer may revoke an acceptance providing that he or she can show that the nonconformity in the goods that the buyer has purchased substantially impairs their value to him or her and that he or she revoked acceptance within a reasonable time after the buyer discovers or should have discovered the ground for it.

Ox-Bow's arguments that the plaintiffs failed to prove that the Bayliner's defects substantially impaired its value to them are based primarily on the defendant's own view of the facts. We have reviewed the record and conclude that the judge had evidentiary support for all his findings. The evidence that the starboard engine overheated twice; the bilge pump was defective; there was an array of malfunctioning electrical equipment; and the marine toilet only functioned partially—none of which alone could be characterized as a minor, cosmetic, or insubstantial problem with a powerboat—in concert support a finding of substantial impairment of the boat's value.

We have no difficulty in concluding that the judge's finding of substantial impairment was not clearly erroneous.

Beginning weeks before they accepted the Bayliner, right up through the time of revocation, the Fortins were in frequent contact with Ox-Bow Marina in an effort to have their boat repaired. It would be anomalous, given the UCC's purpose to encourage buyers and sellers to reach reasonable accommodations to minimize losses, to penalize buyers like the Fortins for their patience in giving sellers like Ox-Bow the opportunity to rectify nonconformities before revoking acceptance of the goods.

The findings of fact by the trial judge, not clearly erroneous, support his conclusion that the Fortins' delayed revocation of acceptance of the Bayliner was timely in the circumstances of this case.

DECISION AND REMEDY
The appellate court held that the Fortins' revocation of acceptance was effective. Affirmed.

Case Questions

Critical Legal Thinking   Should a buyer be permitted to revoke his or her acceptance once it has been made? Why or why not?

Ethics   Did Ox-Bow act ethically in this case?

Business Application   Why do you think Ox-Bow acted as it did in this case? Would it have been cheaper to have fixed the boat in the first place?

ASSURANCE OF PERFORMANCE

Each party to a sales or lease contract expects that every other party will perform its contractual obligations. If one party to the contract has reasonable grounds to believe that the other party either will not or cannot perform his or her contractual obligations, an **adequate assurance of due performance** may be demanded in writing. If it is commercially reasonable, the party making the demand may suspend his or her performance until adequate assurance of due performance is received from the other party [UCC 2-609, 2A-401].

> **adequate assurance of due performance**
> A party to a sales or lease contract may demand an adequate assurance of performance from the other party if there is an indication that the contract will be breached by that party.

Consider This Example   A buyer contracts to purchase 1,000 bushels of wheat from a farmer. The contract requires delivery on September 1. In July, the buyer learns that floods have caused substantial crop loss in the area of the seller's farm. The farmer receives the buyer's written demand for adequate assurance on July 15. The farmer fails to give adequate assurance of performance. The buyer may suspend performance and treat the sales contract as repudiated.

ANTICIPATORY REPUDIATION

Occasionally, a party to a sales or lease contract repudiates the contract before his or her performance is due. If the repudiation impairs the value of the contract to the aggrieved party, it is called **anticipatory repudiation**. Mere wavering on performance does not meet the test for anticipatory repudiation.

> **anticipatory repudiation**
> The repudiation of a sales or lease contract by one of the parties prior to the date set for performance.

In addition to the express terms of a contract, the Uniform Commercial Code (UCC) imposes a duty of good faith on the parties to a sales contract, requires merchants to act with commercial reasonableness, and prohibits unconscionable contracts.

If an anticipatory repudiation does occur, the aggrieved party can (1) await performance by the repudiating party for a commercially reasonable time (e.g., until the delivery date or shortly thereafter) or (2) treat the contract as breached at the time of the anticipatory repudiation, which gives the aggrieved party an immediate cause of action. In either case, the aggrieved party may suspend performance of his or her obligations under the contract [UCC 2-610, 2A-402].

An anticipatory repudiation may be retracted before the repudiating party's next performance is due if the aggrieved party has not (1) canceled the contract, (2) materially changed his or her position (e.g., purchased goods from another party), or (3) otherwise indicated that the repudiation is considered final. The retraction may be made by any method that clearly indicates the repudiating party's intent to perform the contract [UCC 2-611, 2A-403].

Entrepreneur and the Law

IS IT BETTER TO FINANCE OR LEASE A VEHICLE?

Most automobiles and other vehicles in this country are not purchased with cash. Instead, the user either finances the purchase by borrowing the money from a lender or leases the vehicle. Twenty years ago, leasing was a seldom-used option of new-car buyers. Today, over 50 percent of luxury automobiles, sport-utility vehicles, and family sedans are leased. Even used cars are now being acquired through leasing.

Analyzing whether it is better to finance the purchase of a vehicle or lease it is a complicated decision. Some of the factors that should be considered in making the decision are:

- Financing usually requires a down payment (e.g., 10 percent), whereas leasing requires little or no down payment.
- Monthly lease payments tend to be lower than finance payments for a similar vehicle.
- Leases tend to be for three to five years. Leasing therefore is relatively trouble-free because the vehicle is driven during the most worry-free period and while it is under warranty.
- Leases establish the number of miles that may be driven during the lease period. Most leases impose a charge of from $.12 to $.16 for each mile over the lease limit.

- The lease contract establishes a residual value for the vehicle at the end of the lease that takes into consideration normal wear and tear. Additional damage caused from unrepaired accidents and so forth reduce the residual value.
- When a vehicle is purchased, the buyer owns the vehicle when the loan is paid. Under a lease, the lessee does not own the vehicle at the end of the lease term, although some leases give the lessee the option of purchasing the vehicle for the amount of the residual value.
- Both finance and lease contracts require the buyer or lessee to maintain collision and damage insurance on the vehicle.

Seller's and Lessor's Remedies

Various remedies are available to sellers and lessors if a buyer or lessee breaches the contract. These remedies are discussed in the paragraphs that follow.

Right to Withhold Delivery

Delivery of the goods may be withheld if the seller or lessor is in possession of them when the buyer or lessee breaches the contract. This remedy is available if the buyer or lessee wrongfully rejects or revokes acceptance of the goods, fails to make a payment when due, or repudiates the contract. If part of the goods under a contract have been delivered when the buyer or lessee materially breaches the contract, the seller or lessor may **withhold delivery** of the remainder of the affected goods [UCC 2-703(a), 2A-523(1)(c)].

A seller or lessor who discovers that the buyer or lessee is insolvent before the goods are delivered may refuse to deliver as promised unless the buyer or lessee pays cash for the goods [UCC 2-702(1), 2A-525(1)]. Under the UCC, a person is *insolvent* when he or she (1) ceases to pay his or her debts in the ordinary course of business, (2) cannot pay his or her debts as they become due, or (3) is insolvent within the meaning of the federal bankruptcy law [UCC 1-201(23)].

withholding delivery
The act of the seller or lessor purposefully refusing to deliver goods to the buyer or lessee upon breach of the sales or lease contract by the buyer or lessee or the insolvency of the buyer or lessee.

Right to Stop Delivery of Goods in Transit

Often, sellers and lessors employ common carriers and other bailees (e.g., warehouses) to hold and deliver goods to buyers and lessees. The goods are considered to be *in transit* while they are in possession of these carriers or bailees. A seller or lessor that learns of the buyer's or lessee's insolvency while the goods are in transit may **stop delivery** of the goods irrespective of the size of the shipment.

Essentially the same remedy is available if the buyer or lessee repudiates the contract, fails to make payment when due, or otherwise gives the seller or lessor some other right to withhold or reclaim the goods. However, in these circumstances the delivery can be stopped only if it constitutes a carload, a truckload, a planeload, or larger express or freight shipment [UCC 2-705(1), 2A-526(1)].

The seller or lessor must give sufficient notice to allow the bailee, by reasonable diligence, to prevent delivery of the goods. After receipt of notice, the bailee must hold and deliver the goods according to the directions of the seller or lessor. The seller or lessor is responsible for all expenses borne by the bailee in stopping the goods [UCC 2-705(3), 2A-526(3)]. Goods may be stopped in transit until the buyer or lessee obtains possession of the goods or the carrier or other bailee acknowledges that it is holding the goods for the buyer or lessee [UCC 2-705(2), 2A-526(2)].

stopping delivery of goods in transit
A seller or lessor may stop delivery of goods in transit if he or she learns of the buyer's or lessee's insolvency or the buyer or lessee repudiates the contract, fails to make payment when due, or gives the seller or lessor some other right to withhold the goods.

Right to Reclaim Goods

reclamation

The right of a seller or lessor to demand the return of goods from the buyer or lessee under specified situations.

In certain situations, a seller or lessor may demand the return of the goods it sold or leased that are already in the possession of the buyer or lessee. In a sales transaction, **reclamation** is permitted in two situations. If the goods are delivered in a credit sale and the seller then discovers that the buyer is insolvent, the seller has 10 days within which to demand that the goods be returned. If the buyer misrepresented his or her solvency in writing within three months before delivery [UCC 2-702(2)] or paid for goods in a cash sale with a check that bounces [UCC 2-507(2)], the seller may reclaim the goods at any time. A lessor may reclaim goods in the possession of the lessee if the lessee is in default on the contract [UCC 2A-525(2)].

To exercise a right of reclamation, the seller or lessor must send the buyer or lessee a written notice demanding return of the goods. The seller or lessor may not use self-help to reclaim the goods if the buyer or lessee refuses to honor his or her demand. Instead, appropriate legal proceedings must be instituted.

Right to Dispose of Goods

disposition of goods

A seller or lessor that is in possession of goods at the time the buyer or lessee breaches or repudiates the contract may in good faith resell, release, or otherwise dispose of the goods in a commercially reasonable manner and recover damages, including incidental damages, from the buyer or lessee.

If the buyer or lessee breaches or repudiates the sales or lease contract before the seller or lessor has delivered the goods, the seller or lessor may resell or re-lease the goods and recover damages from the buyer or lessee [UCC 2-703(d), 2-706(1); UCC 2A-523(1)(e), 2A-527(1)]. This right also arises if the seller or lessor has reacquired the goods after stopping them in transit.

The **disposition of the goods** by the seller or lessor must be made in good faith and in a commercially reasonable manner. The goods may be disposed of as a unit or in parcels in a public or private transaction. The seller or lessor must give the buyer or lessee reasonable notification of his or her intention to dispose of the goods unless the goods threaten to quickly decline in value or are perishable. The party who buys or leases the goods in good faith for value takes the goods free of any rights of the original buyer or lessee [UCC 2-706(5), 2A-527(4)].

The seller or lessor may recover any damages incurred on the disposition of the goods. In the case of a sales contract, damages are defined as the difference between the disposition price and the original contract price. In the case of a lease contract, damages are the difference between the disposition price and the rent the original lessee would have paid.

The profit does not revert to the original buyer or lessee if the seller or lessor disposes of the goods at a higher price than the buyer or lessee contracted to pay. The seller or lessor may also recover any **incidental damages** (i.e., reasonable expenses incurred in stopping delivery, transportation charges, storage charges, sales commissions, and the like [UCC 2-710, 2A-530]) incurred on the disposition of the goods [UCC 2-706(1), 2A-527(2)].

incidental damages

When goods are resold or released, incidental damages are reasonable expenses incurred in stopping delivery, transportation charges, storage charges, sales commissions, and so on.

Consider This Example A buyer contracts to purchase a racehorse for $20,000. When the seller tenders delivery, the buyer refuses to accept the horse or pay for it. The seller, in good faith and in a commercially reasonable manner, resells the horse to a third party for $17,000. Incidental expenses of $500 are incurred on the resale. The seller can recover $3,500 from the original buyer—the $3,000 difference between the resale price and the contract price and $500 for incidental expenses.

Unfinished Goods Sometimes the sales or lease contract is breached or repudiated before the goods are finished. In such cases, the seller or lessor may choose either to (1) cease manufacturing the goods and resell them for scrap or salvage value or (2) complete the manufacture of the goods and resell, re-lease, or otherwise dispose of them to another party [UCC 2-704(2), 2A-524(2)]. The seller or lessor may recover damages from the breaching buyer or lessee.

Right to Recover the Purchase Price or Rent

In certain circumstances, the UCC provides that the seller or lessor may sue the buyer or lessee to recover the purchase price or rent stipulated in the sales or lease contract. This remedy is available in the following situations:

1. The buyer or lessee accepts the goods but fails to pay for them when the price or rent is due.
2. The buyer or lessee breaches the contract after the goods have been identified to the contract and the seller or lessor cannot resell, re-lease, or dispose of them.
3. The goods are damaged or lost after the risk of loss passes to the buyer or lessee [UCC 2-709(1), 2A-529(1)].

To recover the purchase price or rent, the seller or lessor must hold the goods for the buyer or lessee. However, if resale, re-lease, or other disposition of the goods becomes possible prior to the collection of the judgment, the seller or lessor may resell, re-lease, or dispose of them. In such situations, the net proceeds of any disposition must be credited against the judgment [UCC 2-709(2), 2A-529(2)(3)]. The seller or lessor may also recover incidental damages from the buyer or lessee.

recovery of the purchase price or rent
A seller or lessor may recover the contracted-for purchase price or rent from the buyer or lessee if the buyer or lessee (1) fails to pay for accepted goods, (2) breaches the contract and the seller or lessor cannot dispose of the goods, or if (3) the goods are damaged or lost after the risk of loss passes to the buyer or lessee.

Right to Recover Damages for Breach of Contract

If a buyer or lessee repudiates a sales or lease contract or wrongfully rejects tendered goods, the seller or lessor may sue to recover the damages caused by the buyer's or lessee's breach. Generally, the amount of damages is calculated as the difference between the contract price (or rent) and the market price (or rent) of the goods at the time and place the goods were to be delivered to the buyer or lessee, plus incidental damages [UCC 2-708(1), 2A-528(1)].

If the preceding measure of damage will not put the seller or lessor in as good a position as performance of the contract would have, the seller or lessor can seek to recover any *lost profits* that would have resulted from the full performance of the contract, plus an allowance for reasonable overhead and incidental damages [UCC 2-708(2), 2A-528(2)].

recovery of damages
A seller or lessor may recover damages measured as the difference between the contract price (or rent) and the market price (or rent) at the time and place the goods were to be delivered, plus incidental damages, from a buyer or lessee who repudiates the contract or wrongfully rejects tendered goods.

Contemporary Business Application

LOST VOLUME SELLER

Should a seller be permitted to recover the profits it lost on a sale to a defaulting buyer if the seller sold the goods to another buyer? The answer is, it depends. If the seller had only one item or a limited number of items and could produce no more, the seller cannot recover lost profits from the defaulting buyer. This is because the seller made those profits on the sale of the item to the new buyer. If, however, the seller could have produced more of the item, the seller is a "lost volume seller." In this situation, the seller can make the profit from the sale of the item to the new buyer and sue the defaulting buyer to recover the profit it would have made from this sale. Consider the following case.

National Controls, Inc. (NCI), manufactures electronic weighing and measuring devices. Among its products is the model 3221 electronic scale that is designed to interface with cash registers at checkout stands. On March 31, 1981, Commodore Business Machines, Inc. (Commodore), placed an order to purchase 900 scales from NCI, 50 to be delivered in May, 150 in June, 300 in July, and 400 in August. The evidence was undisputed that in 1980 and 1981, NCI's manufacturing plant was operating at approximately 40 percent capacity.

Commodore accepted only the first 50 scales and did not accept or pay for the remaining 850 units. Thereafter, NCI sold all of the 850 units to National Semiconductor.

(box continues)

NCI sued Commodore to recover the profits it lost because Commodore did not purchase the scales. Can NCI recover?

The trial court said it could and awarded NCI the $280,000 in lost profits that it would have made had Commodore performed the sales contract. The court of appeals affirmed.

The courts found that NCI was a lost volume seller with excess capacity to make the electronic scales it sold. The courts held that even though NCI resold the scales it would have sold to Commodore, that sale to the new buyer would have been made regardless of Commodore's breach. Thus, if Commodore had performed, NCI would have realized profits from two sales—one to Commodore, and one to the new buyer. [*National Controls, Inc. v. Commodore Business Machines, Inc.*, 163 Cal.App.3d 622, 209 Cal.Rptr. 636 (Cal.App.1985)]

Right to Cancel the Contract

The seller or lessor may *cancel* a sales or lease contract if the buyer or lessee breaches that contract by rejecting or revoking acceptance of the goods, failing to pay for the goods, or repudiating all or any part of the contract. The **cancellation** may refer only to the affected goods or to the entire contract if the breach is material [UCC 2-703(f), 2A-523(1)(a)].

A seller or lessor who rightfully cancels a sales or lease contract by notifying the buyer or lessee is discharged of any further obligations under that contract. The buyer's or lessee's duties are not discharged, however. The seller or lessor retains the right to seek damages for the breach [UCC 2-106(4), 2A-523(3)].

cancellation

A seller or lessor may cancel a sales or lease contract if the buyer or lessee rejects or revokes acceptance of the goods, fails to pay for the goods, or repudiates the contract in part or in whole.

CONCEPT SUMMARY   SELLER'S AND LESSOR'S REMEDIES

Possession of Goods at Time of Buyer's Breach	Seller's or Lessor's Remedies

Goods in the possession of the seller	1. Withhold delivery of the goods [UCC 2-703(a), 2A-523(1)(c)].
	2. Demand payment in cash if the buyer is insolvent [UCC 2-702(1), 2A-525(1)].
	3. Resell or re-lease the goods and recover the difference between the contract or lease price and the resale or re-lease price [UCC 2-706, 2A-527].
	4. Sue for breach of contract and recover as damages either
	   a. Difference between the market price and the contract price [UCC 2-708(1), 2A-528(1)] or
	   b. Lost profits [UCC 2-708(2), 2A-528(2)].
	5. Cancel the contract [UCC 2-703(f), 2A-523(1)(a)].

Goods in the possession of a carrier or bailee	1. Stop goods in transit [UCC 2-705(1), 2A-526(1)].
	   a. Carload, truckload, planeload, or larger shipment if the buyer is solvent.
	   b. Any size shipment if the buyer is insolvent.

Goods in the possession of the buyer	1. Sue to recover the purchase price or rent [UCC 2-709(1), 2A-529(1)].
	2. Reclaim the goods [UCC 2-507(2), 2A-525(2)].
	   a. Seller delivers goods in cash sale and the buyer's check is dishonored.
	   b. Seller delivers goods in a credit sale and the goods are received by an insolvent buyer.

BUYER'S AND LESSEE'S REMEDIES

The UCC provides a variety of remedies to a buyer or lessee upon the seller's or lessor's breach of a sales or lease contract. These remedies are discussed in the paragraphs that follow.

Right to Reject Nonconforming Goods or Improperly Tendered Goods

If the goods or the seller's or lessor's tender of delivery fails to conform to the sales or lease contract in any way, the buyer or lessee may (1) reject the whole, (2) accept the whole, or (3) accept any commercial unit and reject the rest. If the buyer or lessee chooses to reject the goods, he or she must identify defects that are ascertainable by reasonable inspection. Failure to do so prevents the buyer or lessee from relying on those defects to justify the rejection if the defect could have been cured by a seller or lessor who was notified in a timely manner [UCC 2-601, 2A-509].

Nonconforming or improperly tendered goods must be rejected within a reasonable time after their delivery or tender. The seller or lessor must be notified of the rejection. The buyer or lessee must hold any rightfully rejected goods with reasonable care for a reasonable time [UCC 2-602(2), 2A-512(1)].

If the buyer or lessee is a merchant, and the seller or lessor has no agent or place of business at the market where the goods are rejected, the merchant-buyer or merchant-lessee must follow any reasonable instructions received from the seller or lessor with respect to the rejected goods [UCC 2-603, 2A-511]. If the seller or lessor gives no instructions and the rejected goods are perishable or will quickly decline in value, the buyer or lessee may make reasonable efforts to sell them on the seller's or lessor's behalf [UCC 2-604, 2A-512].

Any buyer or lessee who rightfully rejects goods is entitled to reimbursement from the seller or lessor for reasonable expenses incurred in holding, storing, reselling, shipping, and otherwise caring for the rejected goods.

rejection of nonconforming goods
If the goods or the seller's or lessor's tender of delivery fails to conform to the contract, the buyer or lessee may (1) reject the whole, (2) accept the whole, or (3) accept any commercial unit and reject the rest.

Right to Recover Goods from an Insolvent Seller or Lessor

If the buyer or lessee makes partial or full payment for the goods before they are received and the seller or lessor becomes insolvent within 10 days after receiving the first payment, the buyer or lessee may recover the goods from the seller or lessor. To do so, the buyer or lessee must tender the unpaid portion of the purchase price or rent due under the sales or lease contract. Only conforming goods that are identified to the contract may be recovered [UCC 2-502, 2A-522]. This remedy is often referred to as **capture**.

recovery of goods from an insolvent seller or lessor
A buyer or lessee who has wholly or partially paid for goods before they are received may recover the goods from a seller or lessor who becomes insolvent within 10 days after receiving the first payment; the buyer or lessee must tender the remaining purchase price or rent due under the contract. Also known as *capture*.

Right to Obtain Specific Performance

If the goods are unique, or the remedy at law is inadequate, a buyer or lessee may obtain **specific performance** of the sales or lease contract. A decree of specific performance orders the seller or lessor to perform the contract. Specific performance is usually used to obtain possession of works of art, antiques, rare coins, and other unique items [UCC 2-716(1), 2A-521(1)].

specific performance
A decree of the court that orders a seller or lessor to perform his or her obligations under the contract; usually occurs when the goods in question are unique, such as art or antiques.

Consider This Example A buyer enters into a sales contract to purchase a specific Rembrandt painting from a seller for $10 million. When the buyer tenders payment, the seller refuses to sell the painting to the buyer. The buyer may bring an equity action to obtain a decree of specific performance from the court ordering the seller to sell the painting to the buyer.

Right to Cover

cover

Right of a buyer or lessee to purchase or lease substitute goods if a seller or lessor fails to make delivery of the goods or repudiates the contract, or if the buyer or lessee rightfully rejects the goods or justifiably revokes their acceptance.

The buyer or lessee may **cover** by purchasing or renting substitute goods if the seller or lessor fails to make delivery of the goods or repudiates the contract or the buyer or lessee rightfully rejects the goods or justifiably revokes their acceptance. The buyer's or lessee's cover must be made in good faith and without unreasonable delay. If the exact commodity is not available, the buyer or lessee may purchase or lease any commercially reasonable substitute.

A buyer or lessee who rightfully covers may sue the seller or lessor to recover as damages the difference between the cost of cover and the contract price or rent. The buyer or lessee may also recover incidental and consequential damages, less expenses saved (such as delivery costs) [UCC 2-712, 2A-518]. The UCC does not require a buyer or lessee to cover when a seller or lessor breaches a sales or lease contract. Failure of the buyer or lessee to cover does not bar the buyer from other remedies against the seller.

The issue of cover is addressed in the following case.

Red River Commodities, Inc. v. Eidsness
459 N.W.2d 811 (1990)
Supreme Court of North Dakota

CASE 21.3

FACTS
In early 1988, George Eidsness, a North Dakota farmer, entered into a contract to grow and sell 229,000 pounds of confection sunflowers to Red River Commodities, Inc. (RRC), at a price of 11.25 cents per pound. When Eidsness did not deliver any sunflowers to RRC from his 1988 crop, RRC purchased replacement sunflowers from other sellers at 26 cents per pound. In mid-December 1988, RRC learned that Eidsness was selling sunflowers to a competitor at 22 cents per pound. RRC sued Eidsness to recover damages. The trial court held in favor of RRC and awarded it the difference between the cost of cover at 26 cents per pound and the contract price of 11.25 cents per pound. The award amounted to $3,377.75 (14.75 cents × 229,000). Eidsness appealed.

ISSUE
Can RRC recover as damages the difference between the cost of cover and the original contract price?

IN THE LANGUAGE OF THE COURT
Meschke, Justice An anticipatory repudiation, which will substantially impair the value of the contract, authorizes the aggrieved party to resort to any remedy for breach. We conclude that the trial court reasonably found that RRC was entitled to

damages for Eidsness's breach of the whole of the contract because he failed to deliver any product whatsoever.

The Uniform Commercial Code—Sales authorizes "cover" damages based on the cost of procuring substitute goods. The trial court found that in an attempt to mitigate damages RRC purchased "cover" at $26.00 per hundred weight. Implicitly, this determined that RRC's substitute purchases at 26 cents per pound were reasonable. We conclude that the trial court's finding about RRC's cost of cover was not clearly erroneous.

DECISION AND REMEDY
The appellate court held that RRC properly covered by purchasing replacement goods and was entitled to recover the increased cost of cover from Eidsness.

Case Questions

Critical Legal Thinking Should a buyer be permitted to cover by purchasing replacement goods even if they are more expensive than the contract price? Why or why not?

Ethics Did Eidsness act ethically in this case?

Business Application Does the cover and recovery of damages rule make an innocent buyer whole against the defaulting seller? Explain.

Right to Replevy Goods

A buyer or lessee may *replevy* (recover) goods from a seller or lessor who is wrongfully withholding them. The buyer or lessee must show that he or she was unable to cover or that attempts at cover will be unavailing. Thus, the goods must be scarce, but not unique.

Replevin actions are available only for goods identified to the sales or lease contract [UCC 2-716(3), 2A-521(3)].

replevin
An action by a buyer or lessor to recover scarce goods wrongfully withheld by a seller or lessor.

Consider This Example On January 1, IBM contracts to purchase monitors for computers from a seller for delivery on June 1. IBM intends to attach the monitors to a new computer that will be introduced on June 30. On June 1, the seller refuses to sell the monitors to IBM because it can get a higher price from another buyer. IBM tries to cover but cannot. IBM may successfully replevy the monitors from the seller.

Right to Cancel the Contract

If a seller or lessor fails to deliver conforming goods or repudiates the contract or the buyer or lessee rightfully rejects the goods or justifiably revokes acceptance of the goods, the buyer or lessee may **cancel** the sales or lease contract. The contract may be canceled with respect to the affected goods or, if there is a material breach, the whole contract. A buyer or lessee who rightfully cancels a contract is discharged from any further obligations on the contract and retains his or her rights to other remedies against the seller or lessor [UCC 2-711(1), 2A-508(1)(a)].

cancellation
A buyer or lessee may cancel a sales or lease contract if the seller or lessor fails to deliver conforming goods or repudiates the contract, or the buyer or lessee rightfully rejects the goods or justifiably revokes acceptance of the goods.

Right to Recover Damages for Nondelivery or Repudiation

If a seller or lessor fails to deliver the goods or repudiates the sales or lease contract, the buyer or lessee may recover **damages**. The measure of damages is the difference between the contract price (or original rent) and the market price (or rent) at the time the buyer or lessee learned of the breach. Incidental and consequential damages, less expenses saved, can also be recovered [UCC 2-713, 2A-519].

damages
A buyer or lessee may recover damages from a seller or lessor who fails to deliver the goods or repudiates the contract; damages are measured as the difference between the contract price (or original rent) and the market price (or rent) at the time the buyer or lessee learned of the breach.

Consider This Example Fresh Foods Company contracts to purchase 10,000 bushels of soybeans from Sunshine Farms for $5 per bushel. Delivery is to be on August 1. On August 1 the market price of soybeans is $7 per bushel. Sunshine Farms does not deliver the soybeans. Fresh Foods decides not to cover and to do without the soybeans. Fresh Foods sues Sunshine for market value minus the contract price damages. It can recover $20,000 ($7 market price minus $5 contract price multiplied by 10,000 bushels) plus incidental damages less expenses saved because of Sunshine's breach. Fresh Foods cannot recover consequential damages because it did not attempt to cover.

Right to Recover Damages for Accepted Nonconforming Goods

A buyer or lessee may accept nonconforming goods from a seller or lessor. The acceptance does not prevent the buyer or lessee from suing the seller or lessor to recover as damages any loss resulting from the seller's or lessor's breach. Incidental and consequential damages may also be recovered. The buyer or lessee must notify the seller or lesser of the nonconformity within a reasonable time after the breach was or should have been discovered. Failure to do so bars the buyer or lessee from any recovery. If the buyer or lessee accepts nonconforming goods, he or she may deduct all or any part of the damages resulting from the breach from any part of the purchase price or rent still due under the contract [UCC 2-714(1), 2A-516(1)].

damages for accepted nonconforming goods
A buyer or lessee may accept nonconforming goods and recover the damages caused by the breach from the seller or lessor or deduct the damages from any part of the purchase price or rent still due under the contract.

Consider This Example A retail clothing store contracts to purchase 100 designer dresses for $100 per dress from a seller. The buyer pays for the dresses prior to delivery. After the dresses are delivered, the buyer discovers that 10 of the dresses have a flaw in them. The buyer may accept these nonconforming dresses and sue the seller for reasonable damages resulting from the nonconformity.

CONCEPT SUMMARY BUYER'S AND LESSEE'S REMEDIES

Situation	Buyer's or Lessee's Remedy
Seller or lessor refuses to deliver the goods or delivers nonconforming goods that the buyer or lessee does not want.	1. Reject nonconforming goods [UCC 2-601, 2A-509]. 2. Revoke acceptance of nonconforming goods [UCC 2-608, 2A-517(1)]. 3. Cover [UCC 2-712, 2A-518]. 4. Sue for breach of contract and recover damages [UCC 2-713, 2A-519]. 5. Cancel the contract [UCC 2-711(1), 2A-508(1)(a)].
Seller or lessor tenders nonconforming goods and the buyer or lessee accepts them.	1. Sue for ordinary damages [UCC 2-714(1), 2A-516(1)]. 2. Deduct damages from the unpaid purchase price [UCC 2-714(1), 2A-516(1)].
Seller or lessor refuses to deliver the goods and the buyer or lessee wants them.	1. Sue for specific performance [UCC 2-716(1), 2A-521(1)]. 2. Replevy the goods [UCC 2-716(3), 2A-521(3)]. 3. Recover the goods from an insolvent seller or lessor [UCC 2-502, 2A-522].

STATUTE OF LIMITATIONS

UCC statute of limitations

A rule that provides that an action for breach of any written or oral sales or lease contract must commence within four years after the cause of action accrues. The parties may agree to reduce the limitations period to one year.

The **UCC statute of limitations** provides that an action for breach of any written or oral sales or lease contract must commence within four years after the cause of action accrues. The parties may agree to reduce the limitations period to one year, but they cannot extend it beyond four years.

A cause of action for breach of a sales contract accrues when the breach occurs, regardless of the aggrieved party's lack of knowledge of the breach. In the case of the default of a lease contract, a cause of action accrues either when the default occurs or when it is or should have been discovered by the aggrieved party, whichever is later.

If a warranty explicitly extends to future performance, a cause of action does not accrue until the breach is or should have been discovered.

Consider This Example A buyer purchases a snowmobile at a retailer's April "end of winter" sale. The buyer does not intend to use it until the following winter. In December, when the buyer first uses the snowmobile, it does not work properly. The statute of limitations begins to run in December.

The UCC statute of limitations does not apply if the action concerning the goods is based on a legal theory not provided in the UCC (e.g., strict liability, negligence). In such cases, the appropriate state's statute of limitations governs [UCC 2-725, 2A-506].

AGREEMENTS AFFECTING REMEDIES

The parties to a sales or lease contract may agree on remedies in addition to or in substitution for the remedies provided by the UCC. For example, the parties may limit the buyer's or lessee's remedies to repair and replacement of defective goods or parts or to the return of the goods and repayment (refund) of the purchase price or rent. The remedies agreed upon by the parties are in addition to the remedies provided by the UCC unless the parties expressly provide that they are exclusive. If an exclusive remedy fails of its essential purpose (e.g., there is an exclusive remedy of repair but there are no repair parts available), any remedy may be had as provided in the UCC.

Consequential damages for breach of a sales or lease contract may be limited or excluded unless the limitation or exclusion is *unconscionable*. With respect to consumer goods, a limitation of consequential damages for personal injuries is prima facie unconscionable. It is not unconscionable to limit consequential damages for a commercial loss [UCC 2-719, 2A-503].

The UCC permits parties to a sales or lease contract to establish in advance the damages that will be paid upon a breach of the contract. Such preestablished damages, called **liquidated damages**, substitute for actual damages. In a sales or lease contract, liquidated damages are valid if they are reasonable in light of the anticipated or actual harm caused by the breach, the difficulties of proof of loss, and the inconvenience or nonfeasibility of otherwise obtaining an adequate remedy [UCC 2-718(1), 2A-504].

liquidated damages
Damages that will be paid upon a breach of contract that are established in advance.

Ethical Perspective

SALE OF GOODS WITH A DESIGN DEFECT

Manufacturers can often design products to be safer, but at a cost. The extra money or additional time necessary to do so is usually weighed against the benefits of creating a safer product. These cost–benefit decisions often present ethical dilemmas. Consider the following case.

Shortly after midnight on October 21, 1989, Shannon Moseley, age 17, was returning home after bringing his date to her house. He was driving a 1985 GMC Sierra pickup truck that his parents had bought him for his birthday. The truck was manufactured by General Motors Corporation (GM). As Shannon drove his truck through an intersection, David Ruprecht, a drunk driver, ran a red light and rammed into the driver's side of Shannon's truck. Shannon, whose truck immediately burst into flames, died in the accident.

Ruprecht, who was *judgment-proof* (i.e., did not have money to pay a jury award), served jail time for his offense. Shannon's parents also sued GM for product liability. They alleged that Shannon's pickup had dangerous side-saddle gas tanks mounted on the side of the vehicle outside the frame rail of the truck. Other manufacturers of pickup trucks placed their gas tanks inside the frame so that the vehicles could withstand collisions better. The Moseleys argued that GM's side-saddle gas tank was a design defect that caused Shannon's death.

The Moseleys' attorney, through the introduction of evidence, portrayed 20 years of corporate villainy by GM. This included evidence of clandestine crash testing, the results of which were never disclosed to the public, as well

as document shredding. This evidence was designed to show not only poor product design but also GM's evil intent in keeping dangerous vehicles on the road. The Moseleys' attorney played to the emotions of the jury, portraying GM as an impersonal giant that ignored the danger to human life when designing its pickup trucks.

GM's counsel presented a very technical defense designed to show that the impact of Reprecht's vehicle—and not the design and placement of the fuel tank—killed Shannon instantly.

The star witness against GM was a disgruntled former employee, Ronald E. Elwell. When he had been employed at GM, Elwell was GM's fuel-tank safety expert who testified in cases on behalf of GM. Elwell testified as to the dangers of mounting gas tanks outside the frame rails on the type of pickup truck Shannon had been driving. He also testified as to secret crash tests that GM conducted on its pickup trucks and had not disclosed to the public or to him.

In the first phase of the trial, the jury returned a verdict of $4.24 million for Shannon's life plus $1 for pain and suffering. In the second phase, the jury returned a punitive damage verdict of *$101 million* against GM.

GM appealed, and the appellate court overturned the decision. The case was later settled for an undisclosed sum of money. [*Moseley v. General Motors Corporation.* (1994)]

1. Did GM act ethically in this case?
2. Do you think an award of punitive damages would be justified in this case?

Working the Web

Many publishers, including Prentice Hall, are producing robust Web sites for their business law texts. A number of the Cheeseman texts have such Web sites. Go to **www.prenhall.com/cheeseman** to see all the texts with Web sites. Included are such things as study guides, current events, Internet exercises that include scoring and hints, and other materials.

CYBER EXERCISES

Go to one of the Cheeseman Web sites. The one for this text might be a good choice. Try taking one of the online quizzes.

CASES AND EXERCISES

CRITICAL LEGAL THINKING CASES

21.1. The Jacob Hartz Seed Company, Inc. (Hartz), bought soybeans for use as seed from E. R. Coleman. Coleman certified that the seed had an 80 percent germination rate. Hartz paid for the beans and picked them up from a warehouse in Card, Arkansas. After the seed was transported to Georgia, a sample was submitted for testing to the Georgia Department of Agriculture. When the department reported a germination level of only 67 percent, Coleman requested that the seed be retested. The second set of tests reported a germination rate of 65 percent. Hartz canceled the contract after the second test, and Coleman reclaimed the seed. Hartz sought a refund of the money it paid for the seed, claiming that the soybeans were nonconforming goods. Who wins? [*Jacob Hartz Seed Co., Inc. v. Coleman*, 612 S.W.2d 91 (AR 1981)]

21.2. On December 21, 1982, Connie R. Grady purchased a new Chevrolet Chevette from Al Thompson Chevrolet (Thompson). Grady gave Thompson a down payment on the car and financed the remainder of the purchase price through the General Motors Acceptance Corporation (GMAC). On December 22, 1982, Grady picked up the Chevette. The next day the car broke down and had to be towed back to Thompson. Grady picked up the repaired car on December 24. The car's performance was still unsatisfactory in that the engine was hard to start, the transmission slipped, and the brakes had to be pushed to the floor to function. Grady again returned the Chevette for servicing on January 6, 1983. When she picked the car up that evening, the engine started, but the engine and brake warning lights came on. This pattern of malfunction and repair continued until March 3, 1983. On that day, Grady wrote a letter to Thompson revoking the sale.

Thompson repossessed the Chevette. GMAC sued Grady to recover its money. Grady sued Thompson to recover her down payment. Thompson claimed that Grady's suit is barred because the company was not given adequate opportunity to cure. Who wins? [*General Motors Acceptance Corp. v. Grady*, 2 UCC Rep.Serv.2d 887 (OhioApp. 1985)]

21.3. Roy E. Farrar Produce Co. (Farrar) was a packer and shipper of tomatoes in Rio Arribon County, Mexico. Farrar contacted Wilson, an agent and salesman for International Paper Co. (International), and ordered 21,500 tomato boxes for 64 cents per box. The boxes were each to hold between 20 and 30 pounds of tomatoes for shipping. When the boxes arrived at Farrar's plant, 3,624 of them were immediately used to pack tomatoes. When the boxes were stacked, they began to collapse and crush the tomatoes contained within them. The produce company was forced to repackage the tomatoes and store the unused tomato boxes. Farrar contacted International and informed it that it no longer wanted the boxes because they could not perform as promised. International claimed that Farrar had accepted the packages and must now pay for them. Who wins? [*International Paper Co. v. Farrar*, 700 P.2d 642 (N.M. 1985)]

21.4. Gal-Tex Oil Corporation (Gal-Tex) owned and operated several oil rigs in the Gulf of Mexico. Gal-Tex provided living quarters for its workers on the oil rigs. These facilities included a small hospital ward. When Gal-Tex needed to lease some medical equipment for the hospital on its newest oil rig, it signed a five-year lease with International Medical Company (International). The contract called for International to provide five specific pieces of equipment. Two weeks after the contract was signed, Gal-Tex executives learned that International was insolvent. Gal-Tex's attorneys wrote to International requesting assurance that the lease would be complied with. International never replied to the letter. Forty-five days later, Gal-Tex enters into a new lease for hospital equipment with a different company. Does Gal-Tex still have any obligation under its lease with International?

21.5. Charles C. Campbell was a farmer who farmed some 600 acres in the vicinity of Hanover, Pennsylvania. In May 1973, Campbell entered into a contract with Hostetter Farms, Inc. (Hostetter), a grain dealer with facilities in Hanover. The sales agreement called for Campbell to sell Hostetter 20,000 bushels of No. 2 yellow corn at $1.70 per bushel. Delivery was to be made in October 1973. Unfortunately, the summer of 1973 was an unusually rainy one, and Campbell could not plant part of his crop because of the wet ground. After the corn was planted, part of the crop failed due to the excessive rain. As a result, Campbell delivered only 10,417 bushels. Hostetter sued Campbell for breach of contract. Campbell asserted the defense of commercial impracticability. Who wins? [*Campbell v. Hostetter Farms, Inc.*, 380 A.2d 463 (PA 1977)]

21.6. Ramco Steel, Inc. (Ramco), a steel manufacturer located in Buffalo, New York, made a sales agreement with Murdock Machine & Engineering Company of Utah (Murdock) to sell cold drawn steel to Murdock. The steel was sold to Murdock on credit. The contract called for the steel to be shipped from Ramco's plant in Buffalo to a warehouse in Indiana for reshipment to Murdock at Clearfield, Utah, the final destination. A shipment of steel bars left Ramco's plant on May 22, 1975. Murdock became insolvent on May 13, and Ramco learned of this fact on May 23. On that same day, Ramco stopped delivery of the steel that was being trucked to the warehouse in Indiana. Murdock had bought the steel to fulfill a government contract to build fins and nozzles for missiles. The government claimed that Ramco had no right to stop delivery of the steel. Did Ramco act properly in stopping delivery? [*In re Murdock Machine & Engineering Company of Utah*, 620 F.2d 767 (10th Cir. 1980)]

21.7. Archer Daniels Midland Company (Archer) sold ethanol for use in gasoline. Between April 11 and April 19, 1984, Archer sold 80,000 gallons of ethanol on credit to Charter International Oil Company (Charter). The ethanol was shipped to Charter's facilities in Houston. Charter became insolvent sometime during that period. On April 21, Archer sent a written notice to Charter demanding the return of the ethanol. At the time Charter received the reclamation demand, it had only 12,000 gallons of ethanol remaining at its Houston facility. When Charter refused to return the unused ethanol, Archer sued to recover the ethanol. Who wins? [*Archer Daniels Midland Co. v. Charter International Oil Co.*, 60 B.R. 854 (M.D.Fla. 1986)]

21.8. Meuser Material & Equipment Company (Meuser) was a dealer in construction equipment. On December 13, 1973, Meuser entered into an agreement with Joe McMillan for the sale of a bulldozer to McMillan. The agreement called for Meuser to deliver the bulldozer to McMillan's residence in Greeley, Colorado. McMillan paid Meuser with a check. On December 24, before taking delivery, McMillan stopped payment on the check. Meuser entered into negotiations with McMillan in an attempt to get McMillan to abide by the sales agreement. During this period, Meuser paid for the upkeep of the bulldozer. When it became apparent that further negotiations would be fruitless, Meuser began looking for a new buyer. Fourteen months after the original sale was supposed to have taken place, the bulldozer was resold for less than the original contract price. Meuser sued McMillan to recover the difference between the contract price and the resale price and the cost of upkeep on the bulldozer for 14 months. Who wins? [*McMillan v. Meuser Material & Equipment Co.*, 541 S.W.2d 911 (AR 1976)]

21.9. C. R. Daniels, Inc. (Daniels), entered into a contract for the design and sale of grass catcher bags for lawn mowers to Yazoo Manufacturing Co., Inc. (Yazoo). Daniels contracted to design grass catcher bags that would fit the "S" series mower made by Yazoo. Yazoo provided Daniels with a lawn mower to design the bag. After Yazoo approved the design of the bags, it issued a purchase order for 20,000 bags. Daniels began to ship the bags. After accepting 8,000 bags, Yazoo requested that the shipments stop. Officials of Yazoo told Daniels that they would resume accepting shipments in a few months. Despite several attempts, Daniels could not get Yazoo to accept delivery of the remaining 12,000 bags. Daniels sued Yazoo to recover the purchase price of the grass bags still in their inventory. Who wins? [*C. R. Daniels, Inc. v. Yazoo Mfg. Co., Inc.*, 641 F. Supp. 205 (S.D.Miss. 1986)]

21.10. Saber Energy, Inc. (Saber), entered into a sales contract with Tri-State Petroleum Corporation (Tri-State). The contract called for Saber to sell Tri-State 110,000 barrels of gasoline per month from July to December 1981. Saber was to deliver the gasoline through the colonial pipeline in Pasadena, Texas. The first 110,000 barrels were delivered on time. On August 1, Saber was informed that Tri-State was canceling the contract. Saber sued Tri-State for breach of contract and sought to recover its lost profits as damages. Tri-State admitted its breach but claimed that lost profits was an inappropriate measure of damages. Who wins? [*Tri-State Petroleum Corp. v. Saber Energy, Inc.*, 845 F.2d 575 (5th Cir. 1988)]

21.11. Dr. and Mrs. Sedmak were collectors of Chevrolet Corvettes. In July 1977, the Sedmaks saw an article in *Vette Vues* magazine concerning a new, limited-edition Corvette. The limited edition was designed to commemorate the selection of the Corvette as the official pace car of the Indianapolis 500. Chevrolet was manufacturing only 6,000 of these pace cars. The Sedmaks visited Charlie's Chevrolet, Inc. (Charlie's), a local Chevrolet dealer. Charlie's was to receive only one special-edition car, which the sales manager agreed to sell to the Sedmaks for the sticker price of $15,000. When the Sedmaks went to pick up and pay for the car, they were told that because of the great demand for the special edition, it was going to be auctioned to the highest bidder. The Sedmaks sued the dealership for specific performance. Who wins? [*Sedmak v. Charlie's Chevrolet, Inc.*, 622 S.W.2d 694 (Mo.App. 1981)]

21.12. Kent Nowlin Construction, Inc. (Nowlin), was awarded a contract by the state of New Mexico to pave a number of roads. After Nowlin was awarded the contract, it entered into an agreement with Concrete Sales & Equipment Rental Company, Inc. (C&E). C&E was to supply 20,000 tons of paving material to Nowlin. Nowlin began paving the roads, anticipating C&E's delivery of materials. However, on the delivery date C&E shipped only 2,099 tons of paving materials. Because Nowlin had a deadline to meet, the company contracted with Gallup Sand and Gravel Company (Gallup) for substitute materials. Nowlin sued C&E to recover the difference between the higher price it had to pay Gallup for materials and the contract price C&E had agreed to. C&E claimed that it was not responsible for Nowlin's increased costs. Who wins? [*Concrete Sales & Equipment Rental Co., Inc. v. Kent Nowlin Construction, Inc.*, 746 P.2d 645 (NM 1987)]

21.13. Earl Miller, a well-known sailor and builder of sailboats, operated his own company, Miller Marine, Inc., on Bainbridge Island, Washington. In 1981, Carole Badgley saw an advertisement for a sailboat built by Miller. The advertised sailboat was a lightweight, high-performance racing vessel named *The Bonnie*. Badgley entered into a contract with Miller for the purchase of *The Bonnie* at a price of $135,000. After she took possession of the sailboat, Badgley noticed a steady leak. Badgley had several naval engineers examine the vessel. The engineers attributed the leak to a design defect. Badgley paid $20,000 to have extensive repairs made to stop the leak. She then sued Miller to recover the $20,000. Who wins? [*Miller v. Badgley*, 753 P.2d 530 (Wash.App. 1988)]

ETHICS CASES

21.14. Adrien Miron owned a racehorse named "Red Carpet." On October 19, 1965, Miron offered Red Carpet for sale at an auction called the "Old Glory Horse Sale" sponsored and conducted by Yonkers Raceway, Inc. (Raceway). The horses were offered for sale according to the law of sales of the state of New York. Saul Finkelstein attended the auction as a potential buyer of horses. He was not accompanied by a trainer, a veterinarian, or other horse professional. Finkelstein submitted the highest bid ($32,000) for Red Carpet. The auctioneer (Raceway) delivered possession of Red Carpet to Finkelstein without collecting the purchase price. That afternoon Finkelstein had Red Carpet transported to his barn at Roosevelt Raceway in Westbury, Long Island. The next morning Finkelstein's trainer took Red Carpet out of the stall. The trainer observed some swelling on Red Carpet's left hind leg and saw that Red Carpet favored his left hind leg when he walked. Dr. Bernard F. Brennan, a veterinarian, examined Red Carpet and found its left hind leg swollen, warm, and sensitive. Finkelstein immediately notified the Raceway that Red Carpet was lame and not sound and demanded that Miron take the horse back. Miron refused to take Red Carpet back. Finkelstein refused to pay the purchase price for the horse. Miron sued Finkelstein to recover the purchase price of the horse. Based on the evidence, do you think anyone acted unethically in this case? Who wins? [*Miron v. Finkelstein*, 400 F.2d 112 (2nd Cir. 1968)]

21.15. Ruby and Carmen Ybarra purchased a new double-wide mobile home from Modern Trailer Sales, Inc. (Modern). On March 11, 1974, Modern delivered the mobile home to the Ybarras. A few days after delivery, portions of the floor began to rise and bubble, creating an unsightly and troublesome situation for the Ybarras. The Ybarras complained to Modern about the floor as soon as the defects were discovered. Modern sent repairmen to cure the defective floor on at least three occasions, but each time they were unsuccessful. The Ybarras continued to complain about the defects. The Ybarras continued to rely on Modern's assurances that it was able and willing to repair the floor. After four years of complaints, Ybarras sued to revoke their acceptance of the sales contract. Did the Ybarras properly revoke their acceptance of their sales contract? Did Modern act ethically in this case? Did the Ybarras? [*Ybarras v. Modern Trailer Sales, Inc.*, 609 P.2d 331 (NM 1980)]

CRITICAL LEGAL THINKING WRITING ASSIGNMENT

Read Case A.21 in the Case Appendix [*LNS-Investment Company, Inc. v. Phillips 66 Company*]. This case is excerpted from the district court opinion. Review and brief the case. In your brief be sure to answer the following questions.

1. What did the sales contract provide?

2. Was the contract performed?

3. What is the issue in this case?

4. In whose favor did the court rule?

Warranties

When a manufacturer engages in advertising in order to bring his goods and their quality to the attention of the public and thus to create consumer demand, the representations made constitute an express warranty running directly to a buyer who purchases in reliance thereon. The fact that the sale is consummated with an independent dealer does not obviate the warranty.

JUSTICE FRANCIS
Henningsen v. Bloomfield Motors, Inc.,
161 A.2d 69 (NJ 1960)

Chapter Objectives

After studying this chapter, you should be able to

1. Describe the warranties of good title and no infringements.
2. Identify and describe express warranties.
3. Describe the implied warranty of merchantability.
4. Describe the implied warranty of fitness for human consumption.
5. Describe the implied warranty of fitness for a particular purpose.
6. Identify warranty disclaimers and determine when they are unlawful.
7. Determine the priority of overlapping and inconsistent warranties.
8. Identify the damages recoverable for a breach of warranty.
9. Describe how the Magnuson–Moss Warranty Act affects warranties regarding consumer goods.
10. Describe warranty disclaimers and limitation of liability clauses in software licenses.

Chapter Contents

The doctrine of *caveat emptor*—let the buyer beware—governed the law of sales for centuries. The law finally recognized that greater protection was needed for consumers and other purchasers of goods. Article 2 of the UCC, which has been adopted in whole or in part by all 50 states, establishes certain **warranties** that apply to the sale of goods. Because Article 2 applies only to *sales* transactions, most courts have been reluctant to extend the warranty provisions of Article 2 to lease transactions. To rectify this situation, Article 2A of the UCC was promulgated in 1987. Article 2A establishes warranties that apply to *lease* transactions. Many states have now enacted Article 2A.

Warranties are the buyer's or lessee's assurance that the goods meet certain standards. Warranties, which are based on contract law, may be either expressly stated or implied by law. If the seller or lessor fails to meet a warranty, the buyer or lessee can sue for breach of warranty. Sales and lease warranties are discussed in this chapter.

warranty
A buyer's or lessee's assurance that the goods meet certain standards.

WARRANTIES OF TITLE AND NO INFRINGEMENTS

The UCC imposes the following warranties on sellers and lessors of goods.

Good Title

Unless properly disclaimed, sellers of goods warrant that they have valid title to the goods they are selling and that the transfer of title is rightful [UCC 2-312(1)(a)]. This is called the **warranty of good title**. Persons who transfer goods without proper title breach this warranty.

warranty of good title
Sellers warrant that they have valid title to the goods they are selling and that the transfer of title is rightful.

Consider This Example Ingersoll-Rand owns a heavy-duty crane. A thief steals the crane and sells it to Turner Corp. Turner does not know that the crane is stolen. If Ingersoll-Rand discovers that Turner has the equipment, it can reclaim it. Turner, in turn, can recover against the thief for breach of the warranty of title. This is because the thief impliedly warranted that he or she had good title to the equipment and that the transfer of title to Turner was rightful.

No Security Interests

Under the UCC, sellers of goods automatically warrant that the goods they sell are delivered free from any third-party security interests, liens, or encumbrances that are unknown to the buyer [UCC 2-312(1)(b)]. This is called the **warranty of no security interests**.

warranty of no security interests
Sellers of goods warrant that the goods they sell are delivered free from any third-party security interests, liens, or encumbrances that are unknown to the buyer.

Consider This Example Albert Connors purchases a refrigerator on credit from Trader Horn's, an appliance store. The store takes back a security interest in the refrigerator. Before completely paying off the refrigerator, Connors sells it to a friend for cash. The friend has no knowledge of the store's security interest. After Connors misses several payments, the appliance store repossesses the refrigerator. Connors's friend may recover against him based on his breach of warranty of no security interests in the goods [UCC 2-312(1)(b)].

The warranties of good title and no security interests may be excluded or modified by specific language [UCC 2-312(2)]. For example, specific language such as "seller hereby transfers only those rights, title, and interest as he or she has in the goods" is sufficient to disclaim these warranties. General language such as "as is" or "with all faults" is not specific enough to be a disclaimer to the warranties of good title and no security interests. The special nature of certain sales (e.g., sheriffs' sales) tells the buyer that the seller is not giving title warranties with the sale of the goods.

No Infringements

Unless otherwise agreed, a seller or lessor who is a merchant regularly dealing in goods of the kind sold or leased automatically warrants that the goods are delivered free of any

warranty against infringements

A seller or lessor who is a merchant who regularly deals in goods of the kind sold or leased automatically warrants that the goods are delivered free of any third-party patent, trademark, or copyright claim.

third-party patent, trademark, or copyright claim [UCC 2-312(3), UCC 2A-211(2)]. This is called the **warranty against infringement**.

Consider This Example   Adams & Co., a manufacturer of machines that make shoes, sells a machine to Smith & Franklin, a shoe manufacturer. Subsequently, Alice Jones claims that she has a patent on the machine. Jones proves her patent claim in court. Jones notifies Smith & Franklin that the machine can no longer be used without permission (and, perhaps, the payment of a fee). Smith & Franklin may rescind the contract with Adams & Co. based on the breach of the no infringement warranty.

No Interference

warranty against interference

The lessor warrants that no person holds a claim or interest in the goods that arose from an act or omission of the lessor that will interfere with the lessee's enjoyment of his or her leasehold interest.

When goods are leased, the lessor warrants that no person holds a claim or an interest in the goods that arose from an act or omission of the lessor that will interfere with the lessee's enjoyment of his or her leasehold interest [UCC 2A-211(1)]. This is referred to as the **warranty against interference** or the **warranty of quiet possession**.

Consider This Example   Suppose Occidental Petroleum leases a piece of heavy equipment from Aztec Drilling Co. Aztec later gives a security interest in the equipment to City Bank as collateral for a loan. If Aztec defaults on the loan and City Bank repossesses the equipment, Occidental can recover damages from Aztec for breach of the warranty of no interference.

Warranties of Quality

warranties of quality

Seller's or lessor's assurance to buyer or lessee that the goods meet certain standards of quality. Warranties may be expressed or implied.

Warranties are the buyer's or lessee's assurance that the goods meet certain standards of quality. **Warranties of quality**, which are based on contract law, may be either expressly stated or implied by law. If the goods fail to meet a warranty, the buyer or lessee can sue the seller or lessor for breach of warranty.

Warranties of quality include (1) *express warranties* made by a seller or lessor of a product and (2) *warranties implied by law*, including *implied warranties of merchantability*, *fitness for human consumption*, *fitness for a particular purpose*, *course of dealing*, and *usage of trade*. These warranties are discussed in the following sections.

Express Warranties

express warranty

A warranty that is created when a seller or lessor makes an affirmation that the goods he or she is selling or leasing meet certain standards of quality, description, performance, or condition.

Express warranties, which are the oldest form of warranty, are created when a seller or lessor affirms that the goods he or she is selling or leasing meet certain standards of quality, description, performance, or condition [UCC 2-313(1), UCC 2A-210(1)]. Express warranties can be either written, oral, or inferred from the seller's conduct.

Sellers and lessors are not required to make such warranties. Generally, they are made to entice consumers and others to buy or lease their products. That is why these warranties often are in the form of advertisements, brochures, catalogs, pictures, illustrations, diagrams, blueprints, and so on.

Creating an Express Warranty

Express warranties are created when the seller or lessor indicates that the goods will conform to

Warranties are favored in law, being a part of a man's assurance.

Coke
First Institute

1. All *affirmations of fact or promise* made about them (e.g., statements such as "This car will go 100 miles per hour" or "This house paint will last at least five years").
2. Any *description* of them (e.g., terms such as *Idaho potatoes* and *Michigan cherries*).
3. Any *model* or *sample* of them (e.g., a model oil drilling rig or a sample of wheat taken from a silo).

It is not necessary to use formal words such as *warrant* or *guarantee* to create an express warranty. Express warranties can be made by mistake because the seller or lessor does not have to specifically intend to make the warranty [UCC 2-313(2), UCC 2A-210(2)].

Basis of the Bargain

Buyers and lessees can recover for breach of an express warranty if the warranty was a contributing factor—not necessarily the sole factor—that induced the buyer to purchase the product or the lessee to lease the product. This is known as the *basis of the bargain* [UCC 2-313(1), UCC 2A-210(1)]. The UCC does not define the term *basis of the bargain*, so this test is broadly applied by the courts. Generally, all statements by the seller or lessor prior to or at the time of contracting are presumed to be part of the basis of the bargain unless good reason is shown to the contrary. Postsale statements that modify the contract are part of the basis of the bargain.

Generally a retailer is liable for the express warranties made by manufacturers of goods it sells. Manufacturers are not liable for express warranties made by wholesalers and retailers unless the manufacturer authorizes or ratifies the warranty.

> **Business Brief**
> Sellers and lessors of goods do not have to make express warranties concerning the quality of their goods. They often make such warranties to convince people or businesses to purchase or lease goods from them.

Statements of Opinion

Many express warranties arise during the course of negotiations between the buyer and the seller (or lessor and lessee). The seller's or lessor's *statements of opinion* (i.e., *puffing*) or commendations of the goods do not create an express warranty [UCC 2-313(2)]. Therefore, a used car salesperson's statement that "This is the best used car available in town" does not create an express warranty. However, a statement such as "This car has been driven only 20,000 miles" is an express warranty. It is often difficult to determine whether the seller's statement is an affirmation of fact (which creates an express warranty) or a statement of opinion (which does not create a warranty).

An affirmation of the *value* of goods does not create an express warranty [UCC 2-313(2)]. For example, statements such as "This painting is worth a fortune" or "Others would gladly pay $20,000 for this car" do not create an express warranty.

In the following case, the court had to decide whether an express warranty had been created.

> **Business Brief**
> Sales "puffing" by salespersons usually does not create a warranty; it is merely a statement of opinion.

Daughtrey v. Ashe
413 S.E.2d 336 (1992)
Supreme Court of Virginia

CASE 22.1

FACTS

In October 1985, W. Hayes Daughtrey consulted Sidney Ashe, a jeweler, about the purchase of a diamond bracelet as a Christmas present for his wife. Ashe showed Daughtrey a diamond bracelet that he had for sale for $15,000. When Daughtrey decided to purchase the bracelet, Ashe completed and signed an appraisal form that stated that the diamonds were "H color and v.v.s. quality." (V.v.s. is one of the highest ratings in a quality classification employed by jewelers.) After Daughtrey paid for the bracelet, Ashe put the bracelet and the appraisal form in a box. Daughtrey gave the bracelet to his wife as a Christmas present. In February 1987, when another jeweler looked at the bracelet, Daughtrey discovered that the diamonds were of substantially lower grade than v.v.s. Daughtrey filed a specific performance suit against Ashe to compel him to replace the bracelet with one mounted with v.v.s. diamonds or pay appropriate damages. The trial court denied relief for breach of warranty. Daughtrey appealed.

ISSUE

Was an express warranty made by Ashe regarding the quality of the diamonds in the bracelet?

IN THE LANGUAGE OF THE COURT

Whiting, Justice We consider whether Ashe's statement of the grade of the diamonds was an express warranty. The Ashes contend

(case continues)

that Ashe's statement of the grade of the diamonds is a mere opinion and, thus, cannot qualify as an express warranty.

It is not necessary to the creation of an express warranty that the seller use formal words such as "warrant" or "guarantee" or that he have a specific intention to make a warranty. Here, Ashe did more than give a mere opinion of the value of the goods; he specifically described them as diamonds of "H color and v.v.s. quality." Ashe did not qualify his statement as a mere opinion. And, if one who has superior knowledge makes a statement about the goods sold and does not qualify the statement as his opinion, the statement will be treated as a statement of fact. The trial judge found that the diamonds were of a grade substantially less than v.v.s.

Given these considerations, we conclude that Ashe's description of the goods was more than his opinion; rather, he intended it to be a statement of a fact. Therefore, the court erred in holding that the description was not an express warranty.

DECISION AND REMEDY

The appellate court held that an express warranty had been created. The trial court's decision was reversed and the case was remanded for a determination of appropriate damages to be awarded to Daughtrey.

Case Questions

Critical Legal Thinking What is the remedy when an express warranty has been breached? Is the remedy sufficient?

Ethics Did Ashe act ethically in denying that his statement created an express warranty?

Business Application Do businesses have to make express warranties? Why do businesses make warranties about the quality of their products?

*I*MPLIED WARRANTY OF MERCHANTABILITY

implied warranty of merchantability

Unless properly disclosed, a warranty that is implied that sold or leased goods are fit for the ordinary purpose for which they are sold or leased, and other assurances.

If the seller or lessor of a good is a merchant with respect to goods of that kind, the sales contract contains an **implied warranty of merchantability** unless it is properly disclaimed [UCC 2-314(1), UCC 2A-212(1)]. This requires the following standards to be met:

- **The goods must be fit for the ordinary purposes for which they are used.** For example, a chair must be able to safely perform the function of a chair. Thus, if a normal-sized person sits in a chair that has not been tampered with, and the chair collapses, there has been a breach of the implied warranty of merchantability. If, however, the same person is injured because he or she used the chair as a ladder and it tips over, there is no breach of implied warranty because serving as a ladder is not the ordinary purpose of a chair.
- **The goods must be adequately contained, packaged, and labeled.** Thus, the implied warranty of merchantability applies to the milk bottle as well as to the milk inside the bottle.
- **The goods must be of an even kind, quality, and quantity within each unit.** For example, all of the goods in a carton, package, or box must be consistent.
- **The goods must conform to any promise or affirmation of fact made on the container or label.** For example, the goods can be used safely in accordance with the instructions on the package or label.
- **The quality of the goods must pass without objection in the trade.** That is, other users of the goods would not object to their quality.
- **Fungible goods must meet a fair average or middle range of quality.** For example, to be classified as a certain grade, grain or ore must meet the average range of quality of that grade.

Business Brief

The implied warranty of merchantability does not apply to sales or leases by nonmerchants or casual sales.

Note that the implied warranty of merchantability does not apply to sales or leases by nonmerchants or casual sales. For example, the implied warranty of merchantability applies to the sale of a lawn mower that is sold by a merchant who is in the business of selling lawn mowers. It does not apply when one neighbor sells a lawn mower to another neighbor.

The following case raised the issue of implied warranty of merchantability.

Denny v. Ford Motor Company
639 N.Y.S.2d 250, 87 N.Y.2d 248 (1995)
Court of Appeals of New York

CASE 22.2

FACTS

Nancy Denny purchased a Bronco II, a small utility vehicle that was manufactured by Ford Motor Company. Denny testified that she purchased the Bronco for use on paved city and suburban streets, and not for off-road use. On June 9, 1986, when Denny was driving the vehicle on a paved road, she slammed on the brakes in an effort to avoid a deer that had walked directly into her motor vehicle's path. The Bronco II rolled over and Denny was severely injured. Denny sued Ford Motor Company to recover damages for breach of the implied warranty of merchantability.

Denny alleged that the Bronco II presented a significantly higher risk of occurrence of rollover accidents than did ordinary passenger vehicles. Denny introduced evidence at trial that showed that the Bronco II had a low stability index because of its high center of gravity, narrow tracks, shorter wheel base, and the design of its suspension system. Ford countered that the Bronco II was intended as an off-road vehicle and was not designed to be used as a conventional passenger automobile on paved streets. The trial court found Ford liable and awarded Denny $1.2 million in damages. Ford appealed.

ISSUE

Did Ford Motor Company breach the implied warranty of merchantability?

IN THE LANGUAGE OF THE COURT

Titone, Judge   Plaintiff introduced a Ford marketing manual that predicted many buyers would be attracted to the Bronco II because utility vehicles were suitable to "contemporary lifestyles" and were "considered fashionable" in some suburban areas. According to this manual, the sales presentation of the Bronco II should take into account the vehicle's "suitability for commuting and for suburban and city driving." Additionally, the vehicle's ability to switch between two-wheel and four-wheel drive would "be particularly appealing to women who may be concerned about

driving in snow and ice with their children." Plaintiff testified that the perceived safety benefits of its four-wheel drive capacity was what attracted her to the Bronco II. She was not at all interested in its off-road use.

The law implies a warranty by a manufacturer that places its product on the market that the product is reasonably fit for the ordinary purpose for which it was intended. If it is, in fact, defective and not reasonably fit to be used for its intended purpose, the warranty is breached. Plaintiff's proof focused on the sale of the Bronco II for suburban driving and everyday road travel. Plaintiff also adduced proof that the Bronco II's design characteristics made it unusually susceptible to rollover accidents when used on paved roads. All of this evidence was useful in showing that routine highway and street driving was the "ordinary purpose" for which the Bronco II was sold and that it was not "fit"—or safe—for that purpose. Thus, under the evidence in this case, a rational fact finder could have concluded that the vehicle was not safe for the "ordinary purpose" of daily driving for which it was marketed and sold.

DECISION AND REMEDY

The court of appeals held that Ford had breached the implied warranty of merchantability and upheld the jury award for the plaintiff.

Case Questions

Critical Legal Thinking   Should the law impose an *implied* warranty of merchantability in the sale of goods? What is the public policy underlying this implied warranty?

Ethics   Did Ford act ethically in defending that the Bronco II was sold only as an off-road vehicle? Was this argument persuasive?

Business Application   What are the business implications of this decision? Do you think that utility vehicles such as the Bronco II have a higher rollover danger than normal passenger automobiles?

Contemporary Business Application

LEMON LAWS PROTECT CONSUMERS FROM SOUR DEALS

In the past, consumers who purchased automobiles and other vehicles that developed nagging mechanical problems had to try to convince the dealer or manufacturer to correct the problem. If the problem was not corrected, the consumer's only recourse was to seek redress through costly and time-consuming litigation.

(box continues)

Today, most states have enacted **lemon laws**, which give consumers a new weapon in this battle.

Lemon laws provide a procedure for consumers to follow to correct recurring problems in vehicles. Lemon laws establish an administrative procedure that is less formal than a court proceeding. Most of these laws require that an arbitrator decide the dispute between a consumer and car dealer. Lemon laws stipulate that if the dealer or manufacturer does not correct a recurring defect in a vehicle within a specified number of tries (e.g., four tries) within a specified period of time (e.g., two years), the purchaser can rescind the purchase and recover a full refund of the vehicle's purchase price.

To properly invoke a state's lemon law, a consumer should take the following steps:

- Notify the car dealer immediately of any mechanical or other problems that develop in the vehicle.
- Take the vehicle back to the dealer for the statutory number of times to give the dealer the opportunity to correct the defect.
- File a claim with the appropriate state agency seeking arbitration of the claim if the defect is not corrected during the number of times and time period established by the state's lemon law.
- Attend the arbitration hearing and present evidence to substantiate the claim that the vehicle suffered from a defect that was not corrected by the dealer or manufacturer within the statutorily prescribed period.

*I*MPLIED WARRANTY OF FITNESS FOR HUMAN CONSUMPTION

implied warranty of fitness for human consumption
A warranty that applies to food or drink consumed on or off the premises of restaurants, grocery stores, fast-food outlets, and vending machines.

The common law implied a special warranty—the **implied warranty of fitness for human consumption**—to food products. The UCC incorporates this warranty, which applies to food and drink consumed on or off the premises, within the implied warranty of merchantability. Restaurants, grocery stores, fast-food outlets, and vending machine operators all are subject to this warranty.

Restaurants and other food providers warrant that the food and drink they serve is fit for human consumption. States apply either the foreign substance test or the consumer expectation test in determining whether this implied warranty has been breached.

foreign substance test
A test to determine merchantability based on foreign objects that are found in food.

Foreign Substance Test

Some states apply a **foreign substance test** to determine whether food products are unmerchantable. Under this test, a food product is unmerchantable if a foreign object in that product causes injury to a person. For example, the warranty would be breached if an injury were caused by a nail in a cherry pie. If the same injury was caused by a cherry pit in the pie, the pie would not be unmerchantable.

Consumer Expectation Test

The majority of states have adopted the modern **consumer expectation test** to determine the merchantability of food products. Under this implied warranty, if a person is injured by a chicken bone while eating fried chicken, the injury would not be actionable. However, the warranty would be breached if a person were injured by a chicken bone while eating a chicken salad sandwich. This is because a consumer would expect that the food preparer would have removed all bones from the chicken salad.

The following is a modern implied warranty of fitness for human consumption case.

consumer expectation test
A test to determine merchantability based on what the average consumer would expect to find in food products.

Goodman v. Wendy's Foods, Inc.
1423 S.E.2d 444 (1992)
Supreme Court of North Carolina

CASE 22.3

FACTS

On October 28, 1983, Fred Goodman purchased a double hamburger sandwich with "everything" on it from a Wendy's Old Fashioned Hamburger restaurant (Wendy's). According to Goodman's testimony, about halfway through the sandwich, he bit a hard substance. He found a bone one-and-one-half inches in length, and the width of one-quarter inch at its widest, from which it narrowed to a point. As a result of biting the bone, Goodman broke three teeth. He incurred substantial dental expenses for root canal surgery, temporary and permanent crowns, and tooth extraction. Goodman sued Wendy's to recover damages for breach of the implied warranty of fitness for human consumption. Wendy's argued that the foreign substance test applied and protected it from liability. Goodman alleged that the consumer expectation test applied and that Wendy's was liable. The trial court directed a verdict for Wendy's. Goodman appealed.

ISSUE

Does the foreign substance test or the consumer expectation test apply to a breach of implied warranty of fitness for human consumption case?

IN THE LANGUAGE OF THE COURT

Exum, Judge   We think the modern and better view is that there may be recovery, notwithstanding the injury-causing substance's naturalness to the food, if because of the way in which the food was processed or the nature, size or quantity of the substance, or both, a consumer should not reasonably have anticipated the substance's presence. It is not the fact that a defect is a natural one that is important to this inquiry, but the fact that the ordinary consumer would expect that he might encounter it, and thus he would normally take his own precautions.

Surely it is within the expectation of the consumer to find a bone in a T-bone steak; but just as certainly it is reasonable for a consumer not to expect to find a bone in a package of hamburger meat. A triangular, one-half-inch, inflexible bone shaving is indubitably "inherent" in or "natural" to a cut of beef, but whether it is so "natural" to hamburger as to put a consumer on his guard—whether it "is to be reasonably expected by the consumer"—is, in most cases, a question for the jury.

We thus conclude, as did the Court of Appeals majority, that a jury could reasonably determine the meat to be of such a nature, i.e., hamburger, and the bone in the meat of such a size that a consumer of the meat should not reasonably have anticipated the bone's presence. The Court of Appeals therefore properly reversed directed verdict for Wendy's on plaintiff's implied warranty of merchantability claim.

DECISION AND REMEDY

The state supreme court followed the recent trend and held that the consumer expectation test applied to cases of alleged injuries caused by food products. The supreme court reversed and remanded the case for trial using the consumer expectation test.

Case Questions

Critical Legal Thinking   Which do you think is a better test for determining warranty liability of food sellers, the foreign substance test or the consumer expectation test? Explain.

Ethics   Was it ethical for the defendant to argue against liability in this case?

Business Application   On remand, would you find Wendy's liable? If so, what amount of damages would you award?

IMPLIED WARRANTY OF FITNESS FOR A PARTICULAR PURPOSE

warranty of fitness for a particular purpose

A warranty that arises where a seller or lessor warrants that the goods will meet the buyer's or lessee's expressed needs.

The UCC contains an implied **warranty of fitness for a particular purpose**. This implied warranty is breached if the goods do not meet the buyer's or lessee's expressed needs. The warranty applies to both merchant and nonmerchant sellers and lessors.

The warranty of fitness for a particular purpose is implied at the time of contracting if

1. The seller or lessor has reason to know the particular purpose for which the buyer is purchasing the goods or the lessee is leasing the goods.
2. The seller or lessor makes a statement that the goods will serve this purpose.
3. The buyer or lessee relies on the seller's or lessor's skill and judgment and purchases or leases the goods [UCC 2-315, UCC 2A-213].

Consider This Example   Susan Logan wants to buy lumber to build a house, so she goes to Winter's lumber yard. Logan describes the house she intends to build to Winter. She also tells Winter that she is relying on him to select the right lumber. Winter selects the lumber, and Logan buys it and builds the house. Unfortunately, the house collapses because the lumber was not strong enough to support it. Logan can sue Winter for breach of the implied warranty of fitness for a particular purpose.

The following case raises the issue of implied warranty of fitness for a particular purpose.

Mack Massey Motors, Inc. v. Garnica
814 S.W.2d 167 (1991)
Court of Appeals of Texas

CASE 22.4

FACTS

Felicitas Garnica sought to purchase a vehicle capable of towing a 23-foot Airstream trailer she had on order. She went to Mack Massey Motors, Inc. (Massey Motors), to inquire about purchasing a Jeep Cherokee that was manufactured by Jeep Eagle. After Garnica explained her requirements to the sales manager, he called the Airstream dealer concerning the specifications of the trailer Garnica was purchasing. The sales manager advised Garnica that the Jeep Cherokee could do the job of pulling the trailer. After purchasing the vehicle, Garnica claimed that it did not have sufficient power to pull the trailer. She brought the Jeep Cherokee back to Massey Motors several times for repairs for a slipping transmission. Eventually, she was told to go to another dealer. The drive shaft on the Jeep Cherokee twisted apart at 7,229 miles. Garnica sued Massey Motors and Jeep Eagle for damages, alleging breach of the implied warranty of fitness for a particular purpose. The jury returned a verdict in favor of Garnica. Massey Motors and Jeep Eagle appealed.

ISSUE

Did the defendants make and breach an implied warranty of fitness for a particular purpose?

IN THE LANGUAGE OF THE COURT

Fuller, Justice   In the instant case, the service provided by Massey Motors's sales staff included undertaking the responsibil-

ity of checking with the Airstream dealer and thereafter representing that the Jeep Cherokee, with an automatic transmission, was suitable for pulling the Airstream. Massey Motors's sales manager testified he knew the intended purpose for the Appellee's use of the proposed vehicle and that he undertook to investigate the specifications of the Airstream. After having undertaken the inquiry, he recommended the Jeep Cherokee as being suitable for the purposes Mrs. Garnica was seeking—that of towing the Airstream trailer she had on order.

A claim of warranty of fitness requires that goods serve their particular purpose. The evidence supported the jury determination that the Jeep Cherokee simply was exceeding its towing capacity and that Massey Motors had misrepresented the fact that this was the proper vehicle suitable for towing the Airstream trailer.

The sales manager, after investigating the specifications of the Airstream trailer, then represented to Mrs. Garnica that the Jeep Cherokee was suitable for the purpose intended. In light of Massey Motors's superior knowledge and expertise concerning Mrs. Garnica's inquiry and reliance, the evidence was sufficient to support the jury's finding.

DECISION AND REMEDY

The appellate court held that Massey Motors had made and breached an implied warranty of fitness for a particular purpose, but that Jeep Eagle had not.

Case Questions

Critical Legal Thinking Should the law recognize the implied warranty of fitness for a particular purpose? Or should buyers be held to know their own requirements?

Ethics Did Massey Motors act unethically in this case?

Business Application Do you think damages should have been awarded in this case?

𝒞ONCEPT SUMMARY EXPRESS AND IMPLIED WARRANTIES OF QUALITY

Type of Warranty	How Created	Description
Express warranty	Made by the seller or lessor.	Affirmation that the goods meet certain standards of quality, description, performance, or condition [UCC 2-313(1), UCC 2A-210(1)].
Implied warranty of merchantability	Implied by law if the seller or lessor is a merchant.	Implied that the goods 1. Are fit for the ordinary purposes for which they are used. 2. Are adequately contained, packaged, and labeled. 3. Are of an even kind, quality, and quantity within each unit. 4. Conform to any promise or affirmation of fact made on the container or label. 5. Pass without objection in the trade. 6. Meet a fair average or middle range of quality for fungible goods [UCC 2-314(1), UCC 2A-212(1)].
Implied warranty for fitness for a particular purpose	Implied by law.	Implied that the goods are fit for the purpose for which the buyer or lessee acquires the goods if (1) the seller or lessor has reason to know the particular purpose for which the goods will be used, (2) the seller or lessor makes a statement that the goods will serve that purpose, and (3) the buyer or lessee relies on the statement and buys or leases the goods [UCC 2-315, UCC 2A-213].

𝒲ARRANTY DISCLAIMERS

Subject to other state laws and the Magnuson–Moss Warranty Act (discussed later in this chapter), warranties can be **disclaimed** or limited. The rules for making such disclaimers are

warranty disclaimer
Statements that negate express and implied warranties.

- If an express warranty is made, it can be limited if the disclaimer and the warranty can be reasonably construed with each other. The limitation is inoperative to the extent that such construction is unreasonable [UCC 2-316(1), UCC 2A-214(1)]. For example, if a seller or lessor makes an express warranty in one part of the contract and disclaims the warranty in another part, the courts consider the disclaimer unreasonable and thereby void.
- All implied warranties of quality may be disclaimed by expressions like *as is, with all faults,* or other such language that makes it clear to the buyer that there are no implied warranties [UCC 2-316(3)(a), UCC 2A-214(3)(a)]. This type of disclaimer, which is often included in sales contracts for used products, is effective whether it is oral or written.

- If the preceding language is not used, disclaimers of the *implied warranty of merchantability* must specifically mention the term *merchantability*. The disclaimer may be oral or written [UCC 2-316(2), UCC 2A-214(2)].
- The *implied warranty of fitness for a particular purpose* may be disclaimed in general language without specific use of the term *fitness*. Language such as "There are no warranties that extend beyond the description on the face hereof" is sufficient to disclaim the fitness warranty. The disclaimer must be in writing [UCC 2-316(2), UCC 2A-214(3)].
- When a buyer or lessee either (1) examines the goods (or sample or model) as fully as he or she desires or (2) refuses to examine the goods after the seller or lessor demands him or her to do so, there are no implied warranties with regard to any defects that such an examination would have revealed [UCC 2-316(3)(b), UCC 2A-214(3)(b)]. Examination only includes obvious defects (e.g., a broken car windshield). Latent (nonobvious) defects (e.g., a problem in the transmission of the car) are not expected to be discovered during such an examination. Note that refusal only occurs if the seller or lessor demands the buyer or lessee to examine the goods and the buyer or lessee refuses to do so.

Ethical Perspective

USED CAR DEALER DISSED BY COURT

On December 11, 1992, Charles Forshey did what millions of people in this country have done: He bought a used vehicle from a used car dealership. Forshey brought two older vehicles he owned, traded them in for a value of $3,100, added some cash, and purchased a used 1983 three-quarter-ton Chevrolet Suburban for $5,995 from Carr Chevrolet, Inc., in Oregon. The truck's odometer read 100,608 miles. Forshey bought the vehicle "as is," which means that the dealership disclaimed any warranties of quality.

Shortly after the purchase, Forshey noticed that the Suburban was missing all its emission control equipment. Through library research, he learned that the engine had a distributor coil that did not belong to the year and engine he thought he had bought. He learned later that the 1983 Suburban had a 1981 engine. He also noticed that the vehicle identification number (VIN) was not on the door, transmission, or glove box. On January 14, 1993, Forshey took the vehicle to an environmental agency. He was told that the Suburban did not have the required smog control equipment and that the vehicle could not be brought into compliance because of the two-year age difference with the vehicle and the engine. Forshey conducted his own title search and found that the truck had been previously stolen in California and had been stripped of its parts.

After discovering this information, Forshey tried to return the truck to the dealer and recover his two vehicles and the cash he had paid. The dealer refused, saying that

Forshey had purchased the Suburban "as is." Exasperated, Forshey sued the dealership for fraud.

At trial, evidence proved that the vehicle had a rear-wheel alignment problem; that the driver's door was misaligned, was a different color than the rest of the paint, and had been replaced; that the dashboard came from a different vehicle; that the VIN number had been cut out of the glove box and the door; that the VIN number had been ground off the transmission; that the engine was not the original; that the odometer had been tampered with; and that the truck had been heavily reconditioned.

The dealership denied any knowledge of these facts, but the trial court disagreed, stating "Together with the suspect proof of ownership, the appearance of the truck as a reconstructed vehicle should have alerted the dealership to a possible salvage history." The jury returned a verdict in favor of Forshey and awarded him $11,496 in compensatory damages and $1 million in punitive damages. The trial court judge granted the dealership's motion for remittitur and reduced the punitive damages to $50,000. Both parties appealed.

On appeal, the dealership argued that the "as is" clause saved it from liability. But the court of appeals rejected this argument, stating that an "as is" clause saves a seller from being liable for normal features—that is, the engine fails because of honestly disclosed miles—but does not save a seller who concealed facts from the buyer and who has engaged in fraud. The court of appeals affirmed the trial court's finding of fraud by concealment and stated that the defendant's conduct was "reprehensible" and an "extraordinary egregious violation" of the law. The court of appeals increased the award of punitive damages to $300,000 and awarded the plaintiff $55,468 to cover his attorneys' fees. The court stated that this award would "accomplish the legitimate state interest in punishing the defendant and deterring its future misconduct." [*Forshey v. Carr Chevrolet, Inc.*, 965 P.2d 440 (OR 1998)]

1. How reprehensible was the dealership's conduct? Was this conduct ethical?
2. Was the award of punitive damages sufficient in this case?

Conspicuous Display of Disclaimer

Written disclaimers must be conspicuously displayed to be valid. The courts construe **conspicuous** as noticeable to a reasonable person [UCC 2-316, 2A-214]. Thus, a heading printed in capitals or a typeface that is larger or in a different style than the rest of the body of a sales or lease contract will be considered to be conspicuous. Different-color type is also considered conspicuous.

conspicuous
A requirement that warranty disclaimers be noticeable to the average person.

Unconscionable Disclaimers

As a matter of law, a court may find a warranty disclaimer clause in a sales or lease contract to be **unconscionable**. In such cases, the court may avoid an unconscionable result by (1) refusing to enforce the clause, (2) refusing to enforce the entire contract, or (3) limiting the application of the clause [UCC 2-302(1), UCC 2A-108(1)]. In determining whether warranty disclaimers are unconscionable, the courts generally consider factors such as the sophistication, education, and bargaining power of the parties and whether the sales contract was offered on a take-it-or-leave-it basis.

unconscionable disclaimer
A disclaimer that is so oppressive or manifestly unfair that it will not be enforced by the court.

Ethical Perspective

SHOULD A DISCLAIMER BE SACKED?

Robert and Chuck Curry ran a farming, livestock, and cattle-feeding business as a father-and-son partnership under the business name of Diamond Ring Farms. Their farm was located in Wyoming and was run on a slim profit margin. In fact, the enterprise would not show a profit if they purchased their cattle feed from outside sources, and so they grew their own.

One of the chief pests in that part of the country is the western corn rootworm. To combat the pest, the Currys selected Dyfonate 20-G, an insecticide manufactured by Stauffer Chemical Company (Stauffer). One of the reasons the Currys selected this product was because Stauffer's promotional literature stated that Dyfonate would seep down into the soil and be effective upon reaching the roots of corn plants.

In 1985, all the Currys' corn crops were heavily infested with corn rootworm. As a result, the Currys suffered heavy losses the following winter in their livestock-raising operations.

Was the failure of Dyfonate responsible for the 1985 corn rootworm infestation? It seems so. Evidence showed that normal weather and moisture were present in 1985 and that the Currys followed the proper suggested procedures for applying the insecticide. The conclusion was that the failure of the Dyfonate was the actual cause of the loss of crops on the Currys' farm.

Stauffer argued that it never guaranteed that Dyfonate would prevent corn rootworm. Indeed, it explicitly denied that it would. Each 50-pound sack of Dyfonate contained the following warranty limitation:

WARRANTY LIMITATION

Stauffer warrants that this product conforms to the chemical description on the label and is reasonably fit for the purposes referred to in the directions for use on the label subject to the inherent risks referred to below. Stauffer makes no other express warranties: THERE IS NO IMPLIED WARRANTY OF MERCHANTABILITY and there are

(box continues)

no warranties which extend beyond the description on the label hereof.

The limitation was printed separately from the other written material and bordered by a heavy red rectangle. However, it was printed at the bottom of the sack in type that was approximately one-half the size of the type used to provide other information. If the bag were standing upright, the disclaimer would be very difficult to see.

Stauffer claims that the warranty disclaimer absolves it from liability. The trial and appellate courts disagreed and

found that the disclaimer was not conspicuous and therefore not effective against the Currys. The appellate court upheld a jury verdict awarding damages for breach of express and implied warranties. [*Stauffer Chemical Company v. Curry*, 778 P.2d 1083 (Wyo. 1989)]

1. Is it morally right for a company to hype a product's quality and then disclaim any warranties concerning the product?
2. Why do you think that the disclaimer was made in small type and placed where it was?

E-Commerce & Internet Law

e-biz

WARRANTY DISCLAIMERS IN SOFTWARE LICENSES

Most software companies license their software to users. The software license is a complex contract that contains the terms of the license. Most software licenses contain warranty disclaimer and limitation on liability clauses that limit the licensor's liability if the software malfunctions. Disclaimer of warranty and limitation on liability clauses that are included in a typical software license appear below.

Limited Warranty. Software.com, Inc. warrants that (a) the software will perform substantially in accordance with the accompanying written materials for a period of 90 days from the date of receipt, and (b) any hardware accompanying the software will be free from defects in materials and workmanship under normal use and service for a period of one year from the date of the receipt. Any implied warranties on the software and hardware are limited to 90 days and one (1) year, respectively. Some states do not allow limitations on duration of an implied warranty, so the above limitation may not apply to you.

Customer Remedies. Software.com, Inc.'s entire liability and your exclusive remedy shall be, at Software.com, Inc.'s option, either (a) return of the price paid or (b) repair or replacement of the software or hardware that does not meet Software.com, Inc.'s Limited Warranty and that is returned to Software.com, Inc. with

a copy of your receipt. This Limited Warranty is void if failure of the software or hardware has resulted from accident, abuse, or misapplication. Any replacement software will be warranted for the remainder of the original warranty or 30 days, whichever is longer. These remedies are not available outside the United States of America.

No Other Warranties. Software.com, Inc. disclaims all other warranties, either express or implied, including but not limited to implied warranties of merchantability and fitness for a particular purpose, with respect to the software, the accompanying written materials, and any accompanying hardware. This Limited Warranty gives you specific legal rights. You may have others, which vary from state to state.

No Liability for Consequential Damages. In no event shall Software.com, Inc. or its suppliers be liable for any damages whatsoever (including, without limitation, damages for loss of business profits, business interruption, loss of business information, or other pecuniary loss) arising out of the use of or inability to use this Software.com, Inc. product, even if Software.com, Inc. has been advised of the possibility of such damages. Because some states do not allow the exclusion or limitation of liability for consequential or incidental damages, the above limitation may not apply to you.

OTHER ISSUES CONCERNING WARRANTIES

Overlapping and Inconsistent Warranties

Often, two or more warranties are present in the same sales or lease transaction. For example, a transaction may be subject to the seller's or lessor's express warranties with respect to the goods as well as the implied warranties of merchantability and fitness for a particular purpose. In such cases, the UCC provides that the warranties are cumulative if they are consistent with each other.

If the warranties are inconsistent, however, the intention of the parties determines which warranty is dominant. The following rules apply in determining intent [UCC 2-317, UCC 2A-215]:

1. Express warranties displace inconsistent implied warranties other than implied warranties of fitness for a particular purpose.
2. Exact or technical specifications displace inconsistent models or general language of description.
3. A sample from an existing bulk displaces inconsistent general language of description.

Third-Party Beneficiaries of Warranties

Third parties who are injured in their person or property by products may be able to recover from the sellers and lessors of the product for damages caused by breach of warranty. Generally, the common law of contracts only gives the parties to a contract (i.e., those in **privity of contract**) rights under the contract.

In the landmark case, *Henningsen v. Bloomfield Motors, Inc.*,[1] the court held that lack of privity did not prevent a third-party plaintiff from suing for breach of the implied warranty of merchantability. The UCC continued this evolutionary trend by limiting the doctrine of privity. The UCC gives each state the option of choosing between three alternative provisions for liability to third parties [UCC 2-318, UCC 2A-216].

Disclaimers and limitations of liability are ineffective against third parties. This is because they do not have knowledge of and have not agreed to these terms.

Damages Recoverable for Breach of Warranty

Where there has been a breach of warranty, the buyer or lessee may sue the seller or lessor to recover **compensatory damages**. The amount of recoverable compensatory damages is generally equal to the difference between (1) the value of the goods as warranted and (2) the actual value of the goods accepted at the time and place of acceptance [UCC 2-714(2), UCC 2A-508(4)].

Consider This Example   Suppose a used car salesperson warrants that a used car has been driven only 20,000 miles. If true, that would make the car worth $10,000. The salesperson gives the buyer a "good deal" and sells the car for $8,000. Unfortunately, the car was worth only $4,000 because it was actually driven 100,000 miles. The buyer discovers the breach of warranty and sues the salesperson for damages. The buyer can recover $6,000 ($10,000 warranted value minus $4,000 actual value). The contract price ($8,000) is irrelevant to this computation.

A purchaser or lessee can recover for personal injuries that are caused by a breach of warranty.

Consider This Example   Suppose Frances Gordon purchases new tires for her car and the manufacturer expressly warrants the tires against blowout for 50,000 miles. Suppose one of the tires blows out after being used only 20,000 miles, causing severe injury to Ms. Gordon. She can recover personal injury damages from the manufacturer because of the breach of warranty.

Unless legally excluded, modified, or otherwise limited by the parties, a buyer or lessee may also recover **consequential damages** from the seller or lessor for breach of warranty. The same is true of incidental damages [UCC 2-714(3), UCC 2A-519(4)]. Consequential damages may be limited or excluded unless the limitation is unconscionable. Limitation of consequential damages for personal injury with respect to consumer goods is prima facie unconscionable.

privity of contract
The state of two specified parties being in contract.

Business Brief
In *Henningsen v. Bloomfield Motors, Inc.*, the court held that lack of privity of contract did not prevent a third-party plaintiff from suing for breach of warranty.

compensatory damages
Damages that are generally equal to the difference between the value of the goods as warranted and the actual value of the goods accepted at the time and place of acceptance.

consequential damages
Foreseeable damages that arise from circumstances outside the contract. To be liable for these damages, the breaching party must know or have reason to know that the breach will cause special damages to the other party.

UCC statute of limitations
The UCC provides for a four-year statute of limitations for breach of warranty actions. The parties may agree to reduce this period to not less than one year.

Statute of Limitations

The **UCC** contains a four-year **statute of limitations** that applies to both hidden and obvious defects. The parties may agree to reduce the period of limitation to not less than one year. However, they may not extend it beyond four years. The statute begins to run when the goods are tendered to the buyer or lessee. The only exception is if the warranty extends to the future performance of the goods (such as a "5 years or 50,000 miles" warranty).

Contemporary Business Application

Magnuson-Moss Warranty Act

In 1975, Congress enacted the **Magnuson-Moss Warranty Act** (the Act), which covers written warranties relating to *consumer* products. The Act is administered by the Federal Trade Commission (FTC) [15 U.S.C. § 2301–2312].

Commercial and industrial transactions are not governed by the Act. The Act does not require a seller or lessor to make express written warranties. However, persons who do make such warranties are subject to the provisions of the Act.

Full and Limited Warranties
If the cost of the good is more than $10 and the warrantor chooses to make an express warranty, the Magnuson–Moss Warranty Act requires that the warranty be labeled as either "full" or "limited."

To qualify as a **full warranty**, the warrantor must guarantee free repair or replacement of the defective product. The warrantor must indicate whether there is a time limit on the full warranty (e.g., "full 36-month warranty").

In a **limited warranty**, the warrantor limits the scope of a full warranty in some way (e.g., to return of the purchase price or replacement or such). The fact that the warranty is full or limited must be conspicuously displayed. The disclosures must be in "understandable language."

A consumer may bring a civil action against a defendant for violating the provisions of the Act. A successful plaintiff can recover damages, attorneys' fees, and other costs incurred in bringing the action. The Act authorizes warrantors to establish an informal dispute resolution procedure. The procedure must be conspicuously described in the written warranty. Aggrieved consumers must assert their claims through this procedure before they can take legal action.

Limitation on Disclaiming Implied Warranties
The Act does not create any implied warranties. It does, however, modify the state law of implied warranties in one crucial respect: Sellers or lessors who make express written warranties are forbidden from disclaiming or modifying the implied warranties of merchantability and fitness for a particular purpose. A seller or lessor may set a time limit on implied warranties, but this time limit must correspond to the duration of any express warranty.

Working the Web

FinanceNet FinanceNet is the Internet's home for public financial management. It was established in 1994 to link government financial management administrators and taxpayers worldwide to catalyze continuous improvements in the productivity of government personnel and in the stewardship and accountability for taxpayer resources.

Visit at **www.financenet.gov**

CFOL.com Commercial Finance Online is a really effective business finance search engine. It links capital seekers with capital providers.

Visit at **www.cfol.com**

Wall Street Directory Wall Street Directory is a great way to learn something about trading and investing, do research, shop financial malls, and find free offers.

Visit at **wallstreetdirectory.com**

Cyber Exercises

1. Who established FinanceNet?

2. When was CFOL.com established?

3. Use Wall Street Directory to get a stock quote on a stock you own or are tracking.

CASES AND EXERCISES

CRITICAL LEGAL THINKING CASES

22.1. When James Redmond wanted to purchase an automobile, he spoke to a salesman at Bill Branch Chevrolet, Inc. (Bill Branch). The salesman offered to sell Redmond a blue Chevrolet Caprice for $6,200. The car was to be delivered to Redmond's residence. Redmond gave the salesman $1,000 cash and received a receipt in return. The next day, the salesman delivered the car to Redmond and Redmond paid the remaining amount due. The salesman gave Redmond a printed sales contract that reflected the payments made with no balance due. One month later, Redmond called Bill Branch and asked for the title papers to the car. Redmond was told that the car had been reported stolen prior to the sale and that he could not receive title until he contacted Bill Branch's insurance company. Redmond sued Bill Branch Chevrolet, Inc. Is Bill Branch liable? [*Bill Branch Chevrolet v. Redmond*, 378 So.2d 319 (Fla.App. 1980)]

22.2. On February 4, 1978, Gloria Crandell purchased a used Coronado clothes dryer from Larkin and Jones Appliance Company (Larkin and Jones). The dryer, which was displayed on the sales floor, had a tag affixed to it that described the machine as a "quality reconditioned unit" that was "tag tested" and "guaranteed." In addition to these written statements, a salesman assured Crandell that the dryer carried a 90-day guarantee for "workmanship, parts, and labor." Crandell bought the dryer because of the guarantee and the low price. Two weeks after the machine was delivered, Crandell asked her son to put a blanket in the dryer to dry. Twenty minutes later, she noticed smoke pouring into her bedroom. By the time Crandell reached the laundry room, the machine was engulfed in flames. A defect in the clothes dryer caused the fire. Crandell sued Larkin and Jones for breach of an express warranty. Is there an express warranty? [*Crandell v. Larkin and Jones Appliance Co.*, 334 N.W.2d 31 (SD 1983)]

22.3. The House of Zog manufactures and sells the "Golfing Gizmo," a training device designed to help golfers improve their swing. The device consists of a golf ball attached to one end of a cotton string, the other end of the string being tied to the middle of an elastic cord. The elastic cord is then stretched between two stakes placed in the ground forming a "T" configuration. This allows the ball to return automatically after it has been struck. The "Golfing Gizmo" is sold in a package that states "COMPLETELY SAFE—BALL WILL NOT HIT PLAYER." In 1966, Louise Hauter gave a Golfing Gizmo to her 13-year-old son, Fred, for Christmas. One afternoon, Fred decided to use the device, which had been set up in his front yard. Having used the Gizmo before, Fred felt no apprehension as he took his normal swing at the ball. The last thing he remembers is pain and dizziness. Fred had been hit in the head by the ball and had suffered serious injuries. Fred Hauter sued the House of Zog. Who wins? [*Hauter v. Zogarts*, 13 Cal.3d 104, 120 Cal.Rptr. 681 (CA 1975)]

22.4. Jack Crothers went to Norm's Auto World (Norm's) to buy a used car. Maurice Boyd, a salesman at Norm's, showed Crothers a 1970 Dodge. While running the car's engine, Boyd told Crothers that the Dodge "had a rebuilt carburetor" and "was a good runner." After listening to the sales pitch, Crothers bought the car. As Crothers was driving the Dodge the next day, the car suddenly went out of control and crashed into a tree. Crothers was seriously injured. The cause of the crash was an obvious defect in the Dodge's accelerator linkage. Crothers sued Norm's. Who wins? [*Crothers v. Norm's Auto World*, 384 N.W.2d 562 (Minn.App. 1986)]

22.5. Geraldine Maybank took a trip to New York City to visit her son and her two-year-old grandson. She borrowed her daughter's camera for the trip. Two days before leaving for New York, Maybank purchased a package of G.T.E. Sylvania Blue Dot flash cubes at a Kmart store. Kmart is owned by the S. S. Kresge Company. On the carton of the package were words to the effect that each bulb was safely coated. Upon arriving in New York, Maybank decided to take a picture of her grandson. She opened the carton of flash cubes and put one on the camera. When Maybank pushed down the lever to take a picture, the flash cube exploded. The explosion knocked her glasses off and caused cuts to her left eye. Maybank was hospitalized for eight days. Maybank sued S. S. Kresge Company. Who wins? [*Maybank v. S. S. Kresge Company*, 266 S.E.2d 409 (N.C.App. 1980)]

22.6. Gladys Flippo went to a ladies' clothing store in Baresville, Arkansas, known as Mode O'Day Frock Shops of Hollywood (Mode O'Day). Flippo tried on two pairs of pants that were shown to her by a saleswoman. The first pair proved to be too small. When Flippo put on the second pair, she suddenly felt a burning sensation on her thigh. Flippo immediately removed the pants, shook them, and a spider fell to the ground. An examination of her thigh revealed a reddened area, which grew progressively worse. Flippo was subsequently hospitalized for 30 days. According to her physician, the injury was caused by the bite of a brown recluse spider. Flippo sued Mode O'Day. Is Mode O'Day liable? [*Flippo v. Mode O'Day Frock Shops of Hollywood*, 449 S.W.2d 692 (AR 1970)]

22.7. Tina Keperwes went to a Publix Supermarket (Publix) in Florida and bought a can of Doxsee brand clam chowder. Keperwes opened the can of soup and prepared it at home. While eating the chowder, she bit down on a clam shell and injured one of her molars. Keperwes filed suit against Publix and Doxsee for breach of an implied warranty. In the lawsuit, Keperwes alleged that the clam chowder "was not fit for use as food, but was defective, unwholesome, and unfit for human consumption" and "was in such condition as to be dangerous to life and health." At the trial, Doxsee's general manager testified as to the state-of-the-art methods Doxsee uses in preparing its chowder. Are Publix and Doxsee liable for the injury to Keperwes's tooth? [*Keperwes v. Publix Supermarkets. Inc.*, 534 So.2d 872 (Fla.App. 1988)]

22.8. Dennis Walker is the owner of several pizza parlors in Nebraska that operate under the name of El Fredo Pizza, Inc. (El Fredo). Walker planned on opening a new restaurant in 1973. A business associate suggested that Walker purchase an oven from the Roto-Flex Oven Co. (Roto-Flex). Walker contacted an agent of Roto-Flex and negotiated to buy a new oven. Walker told the agent the particular purpose for which he was buying the oven—to cook pizza—and that he was relying on the agent's skill and judgment in selecting a suitable oven. Based on the agent's suggestions, Walker entered into a contract to purchase a custom-built, Roto-Flex "Pizza Oven Special."

The oven was installed in the new restaurant and problems immediately ensued. The oven failed to bake pizzas properly because of uneven heating. Constant monitoring of the oven was required, and delays occurred in serving customers. Roto-Flex was notified of the problem and attempted to fix the oven. The oven, however, continued to bake pizzas improperly. El Fredo sued Roto-Flex. Is a warranty of fitness for a particular purpose created in this case? [*El Fredo Pizza, Inc. v. Roto-Flex Oven Co.*, 291 N.W.2d 358 (NE 1978)]

22.9. Automatic Sprinkler Corporation of America (Automatic Sprinkler) wished to purchase a dry chemical fire protection system from Ansul Company (Ansul). An Ansul representative gave Automatic Sprinkler a proposal on the company's behalf. The proposal was a document five pages long. Each page included printed information describing the fire extinguisher system. Only the fifth and last page had printing on the back. The information on the back of page 5 contained a limited five-year warranty that covered only the replacement of defective parts. The limited warranty concluded with this statement: "This warranty is in lieu of all other warranties express or implied."

Automatic Sprinkler purchased the system and installed it in a client's building. Several years later, a fire broke out in the building and the Ansul fire extinguisher system failed to discharge. Automatic Sprinkler sued Ansul for a breach of an implied warranty of merchantability. Ansul claimed that all warranties except the limited five-year warranty were disclaimed. Is Ansul's disclaimer enforceable? [*Ins. Co. of North America v. Automatic Sprinkler*, 423 N.E.2d 151 (OH 1981)]

22.10. Cole Energy Development Company (Cole Energy) wanted to lease a gas compressor for use in its business of pumping and selling natural gas and began negotiating with the Ingersoll-Rand Company (Ingersoll-Rand). On December 5, 1983, the two parties entered into a lease agreement for a KOA gas compressor. The lease agreement contained a section labeled "WARRANTIES." Part of the section read:

THERE ARE NO IMPLIED WARRANTIES OF MERCHANTABILITY OR FITNESS FOR A PARTICULAR PURPOSE CONTAINED HEREIN.

The gas compressor that was installed failed to function properly. As a result, Cole Energy lost business. Cole Energy sued Ingersoll-Rand for the breach of an implied warranty of merchantability. Is Ingersoll-Rand liable? [*Cole Energy Development Company v. Ingersoll-Rand Company*, 678 F.Supp. 208 (C.D.Ill, 1988)]

22.11. Edward Cate owned and operated an automotive repair shop. Cate wanted to purchase a set of automotive lifts (i.e., the devices used to elevate vehicles for repair work). In 1984, Cate purchased a set of Rotary Brand lifts, manufactured by Dover Corporation (Dover). The contract for the lifts contained a five-year written warranty covering the repair of all defective parts returned to the factory. The warranty section of the contract, printed in black ink, also contained a separate paragraph stating:

This warranty is exclusive and in lieu of all other warranties express or implied including any implied warranty of merchantability or implied warranty of fitness for a particular purpose.

The entire warranty section was framed by double blue lines, and the word "Warranty" was printed in solid blue letters. After the lifts were installed in Cate's shop, they began to malfunction. Cars would suddenly fall off the lifts. Dover's employees made several unsuccessful repair attempts. Rather than sending the lifts back to the factory, Cate sued Dover for breach of implied warranty of merchantability. Who wins? [*Cate v. Dover Corporation*, 776 S.W.2d 680 (Tex.App. 1989)]

Ethics Cases

22.12. During October 1978, Brian Keith, an actor, attended a boat show in Long Beach, California. At the boat show Keith obtained sales literature on a sailboat called the "Island Trader 41" from a sales representative of James

Buchanan, a seller of sailboats. One sales brochure described the vessel as "a picture of sure-footed seaworthiness." Another brochure called the sailboat "a carefully well-equipped and very seaworthy live-aboard vessel." In November 1978, Keith purchased an Island Trader 41 sailboat from Buchanan for a total purchase price of $75,610. After delivery of the sailboat, a dispute arose in regard to the seaworthiness of the vessel. Keith sued Buchanan for breach of warranty. Buchanan defended, arguing that no warranty had been made. Is it ethical for Buchanan to try to avoid being held accountable for statements of quality about the product that were made in the sales brochures given Keith? Should sales "puffing" be considered to create an express warranty? Why or why not? Who wins this case? [*Keith v. Buchanan*, 173 Cal.App.3d 13, 220 Cal.Rptr. 392 (Cal.App. 1985)]

22.13. The Delano Growers' Cooperative Winery (Delano), a California winery, produced wine in bulk. Supreme Wine Co., Inc. (Supreme), operated a wine-bottling plant in Boston. Since 1968, Supreme purchased finished wine in bulk from Delano and other wine producers, which it then bottled and sold to retailers under the "Supreme" label. Supreme purchased all its sweet wine from Delano, which was delivered to Supreme's bottling plant in tank cars. Supreme then pumped the wine into redwood vats in its building.

In 1973, Supreme began receiving widespread returns of sweet wine from its customers. All of the returned wine was produced by Delano. The wine was producing sediment, was cloudy, and contained a cottony or hairy substance. Supreme complained to Delano, which promised to correct the situation. Delano made other shipments of sweet wine to Supreme, but customers continued to return defective wine to Supreme. Evidence showed that the wine contained *lactobacillus trichodes*, also called "Fresno mold." Over 8,000 cases of wine were spoiled by the Fresno mold. When Supreme refused to pay an invoice of $25,825 for shipment of wine, Delano sued to collect this amount. Supreme filed a counterclaim to recover damages. Is it ethical for the seller to disavow liability in this case?

Who wins? [*Delano Growers' Cooperative Winery v. Supreme Wine Co., Inc.*, 473 N.E.2d 1066 (MA 1985)]

22.14. In July 1976, Peter Troy, president and owner of Troy's Custom Smoking Co., Inc. (Troy's), contacted Peter Bader, president of Swan Island Sheet Metal Works, Inc. (Swan Island), and asked Bader if Swan Island could manufacture two stainless steel gas-burner crab cookers for Troy's. Troy explained to Bader the planned use of the cooker and some of the special needs a crab cooker must satisfy—that is, that crab is cooked by dropping it into boiling water, allowing the water to recover to a rolling boil and boiling the crab for 10 minutes. If the recovery time exceeds 10 minutes, or if the cooker cannot sustain a rolling boil, the crab is immersed too long in hot water and the finished product is unpalatable. Troy and Bader were equally unknowledgeable about gas-burner cookers, but Bader assured Troy that he would hire an expert to assist in manufacturing a crab cooker to meet Troy's needs.

Bader sent Troy a brochure illustrating the type of burner the expert had selected to meet Troy's needs. Troy ordered the cooker, which was delivered to Troy's Beaverton, Oregon, store on November 18, 1976. Within a week or two after delivery, Troy complained to Swan Island concerning the cooker's performance. The cooker cooked too slowly and the pilot light and burner were difficult to light and keep lit. Swan Island attempted but could not correct the defects. Between December 1976 and March 1977 Troy's cooked crab in the Swan Island cooker. Because of the poor performance of the cooker, Troy's ruined a substantial amount of crab and had to obtain cooked crab from another outlet to serve its customers. In March 1977, Troy's notified Swan Island to pick up the crab cooker. Swan Island sued Troy's to recover the purchase price of the cooker. Troy's filed a counterclaim against Swan Island to rescind the contract and recover damages. Did Swan Island breach an implied warranty of fitness for a particular purpose? Is Swan Island acting ethically in denying liability in this case? [*Swan Island Sheet Metal Works, Inc. v. Troy's Custom Smoking Co., Inc.*, 619 P.2d 1326 (Or.App. 1980)]

CRITICAL LEGAL THINKING WRITING ASSIGNMENT

Read Case A.22 in the Case Appendix [*Simpson v. Hatteras Island Gallery Restaurant, Inc.*]. This case is excerpted from the court of appeals opinion. Review and brief the case. In your brief, be sure to answer the following questions.

1. What injury occurred in this case?

2. Who were the defendants?

3. What implied warranty was alleged to have been breached?

4. What test did the court apply in determining whether this warranty was breached?

NOTE

1. 161 A.2d 69 (NJ 1960).

Creation of Negotiable Instruments

The great object of the law is to encourage commerce.

JUDGE CHAMBRE
Beale v. Thompson (1803)

Chapter Objectives

After studying this chapter, you should be able to

1. Distinguish between a negotiable and a nonnegotiable instrument.
2. Describe the functions served by negotiable instruments.
3. Distinguish between orders to pay and promises to pay.
4. Describe a check and identify the parties to a check.
5. Describe a promissory note and identify the parties to the note.
6. Describe a certificate of deposit and identify the parties to the CD.
7. Describe the requirements of permanence and portability of a negotiable instrument.
8. Describe how a negotiable instrument must be signed.
9. Distinguish between instruments payable on demand and payable at a definite time.
10. Distinguish between instruments payable to order and payable to bearer.

Chapter Contents

Negotiable instruments (or **commercial paper**) are important for the conduct of business and personal affairs. In this country, modern commerce could not continue without them. Examples of negotiable instruments include checks (such as the one that may have been used to pay for this book) and promissory notes (such as the one executed by a borrower of money to pay for tuition).

To qualify as a negotiable instrument, the document must meet certain requirements established by Article 3 of the Uniform Commercial Code (UCC). If these requirements are met, a transferee who qualifies as a *holder in due course (HDC)* takes the instrument free of many defenses that can be asserted against the original payee. An instrument that does not meet the requirements of Article 3 is subject to contract law.

This chapter introduces several of the important concepts regarding negotiable instruments and examines the elements that must be met to create them.

REVISED ARTICLE 3 (NEGOTIABLE INSTRUMENTS) OF THE UCC

Although negotiable instruments have been used in commerce since medieval times, the English law courts did not immediately recognize their validity. To compensate for this failure, the merchants developed rules governing their use. These rules, which were enforced by local private merchant courts, became part of what was called the *Law Merchant*. Eventually, in 1882, England enacted the Bills of Exchange Act, which codified the rules of the Law Merchant.

In 1886, the National Conference of Commissioners of Uniform Laws promulgated the **Uniform Negotiable Instruments Law (NIL)** in the United States. By 1920, all of the states had enacted the NIL as law, but the rapid development of commercial paper soon made the law obsolete.

Article 3 (Commercial Paper) of the **Uniform Commercial Code**, which was promulgated in 1952, established rules for the creation of, transfer of, enforcement of, and liability on negotiable instruments. All the states have replaced the NIL with Article 3.

In 1990, the American Law Institute and the National Conference of Commissioners on Uniform State Laws repealed Article 3 and replaced it with **Revised Article 3**. The new article, which is called "Negotiable Instruments" instead of "Commercial Paper," is a

negotiable instrument
A special form of contract that satisfies the requirements established by Article 3 of the UCC. Also called *commercial paper.*

Uniform Negotiable Instruments Law (NIL)
The predecessor of the UCC developed by the National Conference of Commissioners of Uniform Laws; used from 1886 until 1952.

Article 3 of the UCC
A code promulgated in 1952 that established rules for the creation of, transfer of, enforcement of, and liability on negotiable instruments.

Revised Article 3
A comprehensive revising of the UCC law of negotiable instruments, which was released in 1990, that reflects modern commercial practices.

Domestic and international commerce is facilitated by the use of negotiable instruments, such as checks and promissory notes.

comprehensive revision of Article 3. Individual states are currently replacing Article 3 with Revised Article 3. Revised Article 3 forms the basis of the discussion of negotiable instruments in this book.

FUNCTIONS OF NEGOTIABLE INSTRUMENTS

Negotiable instruments serve several functions. These functions are discussed in the following paragraphs.

Substitute for Money

Merchants and consumers often do not carry cash for fear of loss or theft. Further, it would be almost impossible to carry enough cash for large purchases (e.g., a car or a house). Thus, certain forms of negotiable instruments—such as checks—serve as a *substitute for money.*

Credit Device

Some forms of negotiable instruments extend credit from one party to another. For instance, a seller may sell goods to a customer on the customer's promise to pay for the goods at a future time, or a bank may lend money to purchase goods to a buyer who signs a note promising to repay the money. Both these examples represent *extensions of credit.* Without negotiable instruments, the "credit economy" of the United States and other modern industrial countries would not be possible.

One cannot help regretting that where money is concerned it is so much the rule to overlook moral obligations.

Malms, V.C.
Ellis v. Houston (1878)

Recordkeeping Device

Negotiable instruments often serve as a *recordkeeping device.* For example, banks usually return canceled checks to checking account customers each month. These act as a recordkeeping device for the preparation of financial statements, tax returns, and the like.

International Perspective

NEGOTIABLE INSTRUMENTS PAYABLE IN FOREIGN CURRENCY

The UCC expressly provides that an instrument may state that it is payable in foreign money [UCC 3-107]. For example, an instrument "payable in 10,000 yen in Japanese currency" is a negotiable instrument that is governed by Article 3 of the UCC.

Unless the instrument states otherwise, an instrument that is payable in foreign currency can be satisfied by the equivalent in U.S. dollars as determined on the due date. The conversion rate is the current bank-offered spot rate at the place of payment on the due date. The instrument can expressly provide that it is payable only in the stated foreign currency. In this case, the instrument cannot be paid in U.S. dollars.

TYPES OF NEGOTIABLE INSTRUMENTS

instrument
Term that means *negotiable instrument.*

The term **instrument** means negotiable instrument [UCC 3-104(b)]. These terms are often used interchangeably.

Revised Article 3 recognizes four kinds of instruments. They are (1) drafts, (2) checks, (3) promissory notes, and (4) certificates of deposit. Each of these is discussed in the following paragraphs.

Drafts

A **draft**, which is a *three-party instrument*, is an unconditional written order by one party (the **drawer**) that orders a second party (the **drawee**) to pay money to a third party (the **payee**) [UCC 3-104(e)]. The drawee must be obligated to pay the drawer money before the drawer can order the drawee to pay this money to a third party (the payee).

For the drawee to be liable on a draft, the drawee must accept the drawer's written order to pay it. Acceptance is usually shown by the written word *accepted* on the face of the draft along with the drawee's signature and the date. The drawee is called the **acceptor** of the draft because it changes his or her obligation from that of having to pay the drawer to that of having to pay the payee. After the drawee accepts the draft, it is returned to the drawer or the payee. The drawer or the payee, in turn, can freely transfer it as a negotiable instrument to another party.

Consider This Example Mary Owens owes Hector Martinez $1,000. Mr. Martinez writes out a draft that orders Ms. Owens to pay this $1,000 to Cindy Choy. Ms. Owens agrees to this change of obligation and accepts the draft. Mr. Martinez is the drawer, Ms. Owens is the drawee, and Ms. Choy is the payee.

Time and Sight Drafts A draft can be either a time draft or a sight draft. A **time draft** is payable at a designated future date. Language such as "pay on January 1, 2010" or "pay 120 days after date" creates a time draft (see Exhibit 23.1). A **sight draft**, also called a **demand draft**, is payable on sight. Language such as "on demand pay" or "at sight pay" creates a sight draft. A draft can be both a time and a sight draft. Such a draft would provide that it is payable at a stated time *after* sight. This type of draft is created by language such as "payable 90 days after sight."

> **draft**
> **A three-party instrument that is an unconditional written order by one party that orders the second party to pay money to a third party.**

> **drawer of a draft**
> **The party who writes the order for a draft.**

> **drawee of a draft**
> **The party who must pay the money stated in the draft. Also called the *acceptor* of a draft.**

> **payee of a draft**
> **The party who receives the money from a draft.**

> **time draft**
> **A draft payable at a designated future date.**

> **sight draft**
> **A draft payable on sight. Also called a *demand draft*.**

*E*XHIBIT 23.1 *A Time Draft*

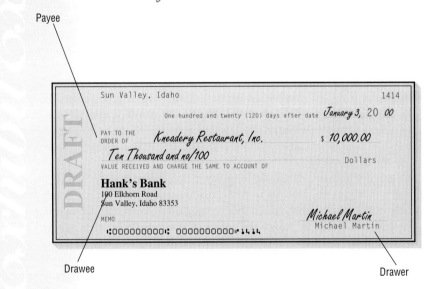

Payee

Drawee

Drawer

Sun Valley, Idaho   1414
One hundred and twenty (120) days after date *January 3*, 20 *00*
PAY TO THE ORDER OF *Kneadery Restaurant, Inc.* $ *10,000.00*
Ten Thousand and no/100   Dollars
VALUE RECEIVED AND CHARGE THE SAME TO ACCOUNT OF
Hank's Bank
100 Elkhorn Road
Sun Valley, Idaho 83353
MEMO
⑆000000000⑆ 0000000000⑈1414
Michael Martin
Michael Martin

A trade acceptance is a sight draft that arises when credit is extended with the sale of goods. In this type of draft, the seller is both the drawer and the payee. The buyer to whom credit is extended is the drawee. Even though only two actual parties are involved, it is considered a three-party instrument because three legal positions are involved.

> **trade acceptance**
> **A sight draft that arises when credit is extended (by a seller to a buyer) with the sale of goods. The seller is both the drawer and the payee, and the buyer is the drawee.**

Checks

A check is a distinct form of draft. It is unique in that it is drawn on a financial institution (the drawee) and is payable on demand [UCC 3-104(f)]. In other words, a check is an order to pay (see Exhibit 23.2). Most businesses and many individuals have checking accounts at financial institutions.

*Ɛ*XHIBIT 23.2   *A Check*

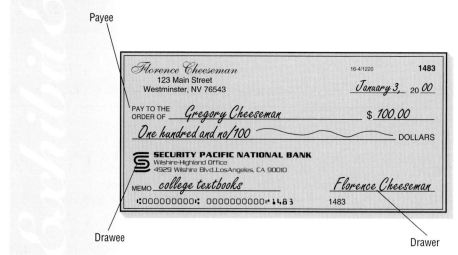

Payee

Drawee

Drawer

> *Florence Cheeseman*
> 123 Main Street
> Westminster, NV 76543
>
> 16-4/1220   **1483**
>
> *January 3,* 20 *00*
>
> PAY TO THE ORDER OF ___ *Gregory Cheeseman* ___ $ *100.00*
>
> *One hundred and no/100* _____ DOLLARS
>
> Ⓢ **SECURITY PACIFIC NATIONAL BANK**
> Wilshire-Highland Office
> 4929 Wilshire Blvd.LosAngeles, CA 90010
>
> MEMO *college textbooks* _____   *Florence Cheeseman*
>
> ⑈000000000⑆ 0000000000‖ 1483   1483

drawer of a check
The customer who has the checking account and writes (draws) the check.

drawee of a check
The financial institution where the drawer has his or her account.

payee of a check
The party to whom the check is written.

Like other drafts, a check is a *three-party instrument*. The customer who has the checking account and writes (draws) the check is the **drawer**; the financial institution upon whom the check is written is the **drawee**; and the party to whom the check is written is the **payee**.

In addition to traditional checks, there are several forms of special checks, including *certified checks*, *cashier's checks*, and *traveler's checks*. These special checks are discussed in Chapter 26.

Promissory Notes

promissory note
A two-party negotiable instrument that is an unconditional written promise by one party to pay money to another party.

A **promissory note** (or **note**) is an unconditional written promise by one party to pay money to another party [UCC 3-104(e)]. It is a *two-party instrument* (see Exhibit 23.3), not an order to pay. Promissory notes usually arise when one party borrows money from another. The note is evidence of (1) the extension of credit and (2) the borrower's promise to repay the debt.

maker of a note
The party who makes the promise to pay (borrower).

payee of a note
The party to whom the promise to pay is made (lender).

The party who makes the promise to pay is the **maker** of the note (i.e., the borrower). The party to whom the promise to pay is made is the **payee** (i.e., the lender). A promissory note is a negotiable instrument that the payee can freely transfer to other parties.

time note
A note payable at a specific time.

demand note
A note payable on demand.

The parties are free to design the terms of the note to fit their needs. For example, notes can be payable at a specific time (**time note**) or on demand (**demand note**). Notes can be made payable to a named payee or to "bearer." They can be payable in a single payment or in installments. The latter are called *installment notes*. Most notes require the borrower to pay interest on the principal.

collateral
Security against repayment of the note that lenders some times require; can be a car, a house, or other property.

Lenders sometimes require the maker of a note to post security for the repayment of the note. This security, called **collateral**, may be in the form of automobiles, houses, securities, or other property. If the maker fails to repay the note when it is due, the lender can foreclose and take the collateral as payment for the note. Notes are often named after the security that underlies the note. For example, notes that are secured by real estate are called *mortgage notes*, and notes that are secured by personal property are called *collateral notes*.

*E*XHIBIT **23.3**   *A Promissory Note*

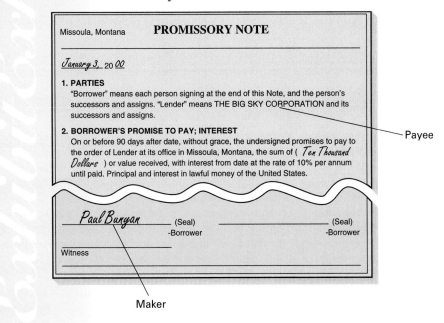

Certificates of Deposit

A **certificate of deposit (CD)** is a special form of note that is created when a depositor deposits money at a financial institution in exchange for the institution's promise to pay back the amount of the deposit plus an agreed-upon rate of interest upon the expiration of a set time period agreed upon by the parties [UCC 3-104(j)].

The financial institution is the borrower (the **maker**) and the depositor is the lender (the **payee**). A CD is a *two-party instrument* (see Exhibit 23.4). Note that a CD is a promise to pay, not an order to pay.

*E*XHIBIT **23.4**   *A Certificate of Deposit*

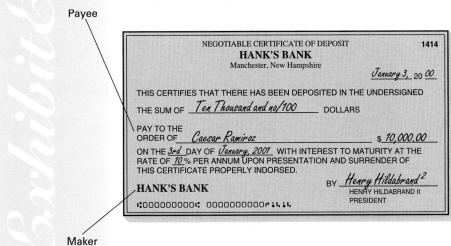

certificate of deposit (CD)
A two-party negotiable instrument that is a special form of note created when a depositor deposits money at a financial institution in exchange for the institution's promise to pay back the amount of the deposit plus an agreed-upon rate of interest upon the expiration of a set time period agreed upon by the parties.

maker of a CD
The bank (borrower).

payee of a CD
The depositor (lender).

Unlike a regular passbook savings account, a CD is a negotiable instrument. CDs under $100,000 are commonly referred to as *small CDs*. CDs of $100,000 or more are usually called *jumbo CDs*.

Contemporary Business Application

PROMISSORY NOTES AS NEGOTIABLE INSTRUMENTS

People and businesses borrow money from banks and other lenders to purchase automobiles, equipment, real estate, and other items. When people or businesses borrow money from lenders, they usually sign **promissory notes** promising to repay the borrowed money, plus interest, according to the terms of the note. The borrower is the **maker** of the note and the lender is the **payee**. The borrower is obligated to make payments (often monthly) until the principal amount borrowed, plus interest, is repaid.

A note that contains an unconditional written promise by one party to pay money to another party qualifies as a promissory note that is subject to the rules of **Revised Article 3** of the Uniform Commercial Code. This means that the promissory note can be negotiated to other parties, who can enforce the note according to its terms against the borrower. In essence, the promissory note can be transferred like money, and its enforcement is subject to only a few defenses (these defenses are discussed in Chapter 25).

CONCEPT SUMMARY TYPES OF NEGOTIABLE INSTRUMENTS

Type of Instrument Orders to Pay	Party	Description of Party
Draft	Drawer	Person who issues the draft.
	Drawee	Person who owes money to the drawer; person who is ordered to pay the draft and accepts the draft.
	Payee	Person to whom the draft is made payable.
Check	Drawer	Owner of a checking account at a financial institution; person who issues the check.
	Drawee	Financial institution where drawer's checking account is located; party who is ordered to pay the check.
	Payee	Person to whom the check is made payable.
Promises to Pay		
Promissory note	Maker	Party who issues the promissory note; this is usually the borrower.
	Payee	Party to whom the promissory note is made payable; this is usually the lender.
Certificate of deposit (CD)	Maker	Financial institution that issues the certificate of deposit.
	Payee	Party to whom the certificate of deposit is made payable; this is usually the depositor.

Business Brief

A negotiable instrument must be in writing; oral promises or orders do not qualify as negotiable instruments. (They are enforceable, however, under ordinary contract law.)

CREATING A NEGOTIABLE INSTRUMENT

According to UCC 3-104(a), a **negotiable instrument** must

- Be in writing.
- Be signed by the maker or drawer.
- Be an unconditional promise or order to pay.

- State a fixed amount of money.
- Not require any undertaking in addition to the payment of money.
- Be payable on demand or at a definite time.
- Be payable to order or to bearer.

These requirements must appear on the *face* of the instrument. If they do not, the instrument does not qualify as negotiable. Each of these requirements is discussed in the paragraphs that follow. A promise or order that conspicuously states that it is not negotiable or is not subject to Article 3 is not a negotiable instrument [UCC 3-104(d)].

A Writing

A negotiable instrument must be (1) in writing and (2) *permanent and portable*. Often, the requisite writing is on a preprinted form, but typewritten, handwritten, or other tangible agreements are also acceptable [UCC 1-201(46)]. In addition, the instrument can be a combination of different kinds of writing. For example, a check is often a preprinted form on which the drawer handwrites the amount of the check, the name of the payee, and the date of the check. Oral promises do not qualify as negotiable instruments because they are not clearly transferable in a manner that will prevent fraud. Tape recordings and videotapes are not negotiable instruments because they are not considered writings.

Most writings on paper meet the **permanency requirement**, although a writing on tissue paper does not because of its impermanence. The courts have held that writings on other objects (e.g., baseballs, shirts, and such) meet this requirement. A promise or order to pay that is written in snow or sand is not permanent—and, therefore, is not a negotiable instrument. However, a photograph of such a writing that was signed by the maker or drawer would qualify as a negotiable instrument. The picture meets the requirement of permanence.

The **portability requirement** is intended to ensure free transfer of the instrument. For example, a promise to pay chiseled in a California redwood tree would not qualify as a negotiable instrument because the tree is not freely transferable in commerce. However, writing the same promise or order to pay on a small block of wood could qualify as a negotiable instrument.

The best practice is to place the written promise or order to pay on traditional paper. This ensures that the permanency and portability requirements are met so that transferees will readily accept the instrument.

Signed by the Maker or the Drawer

A negotiable instrument must be *signed* by the maker if it is a note or certificate of deposit and by the drawer if it is a check or draft. The maker or drawer is not liable on the instrument unless his or her signature appears on it. The signature can be placed on the instrument by the maker or drawer or by an authorized agent [UCC 3-401(a)]. Although the signature of the maker, drawer, or agent can be located anywhere on the face of the negotiable instrument, it is usually placed in the lower right-hand corner.

The UCC broadly defines **signature** as any symbol executed or adopted by a party with a present intent to authenticate a writing [UCC 1-201(39)]. A signature is made by the use of any name, including a trade or assumed name, or by any word or mark used in lieu of a written signature [UCC 3-401(b)]. Thus, the requisite signature can be the maker's or drawer's formal name (Henry Richard Cheeseman), informal name (Hank Cheeseman), initials (HRC), or nickname (The Big Cheese). Any other symbol or device (e.g., an X or a thumbprint) adopted by the signer as his or her signature also qualifies. The signer's intention to use the symbol as his or her signature is controlling. Typed, printed, lithographed, rubber-stamped, or other mechanical means of signing instruments are recognized as valid by the UCC.

permanency requirement
A requirement of negotiable instruments that says they must be in a permanent state, such as written on ordinary paper.

portability requirement
A requirement of negotiable instruments that says they must be able to be easily transported between areas.

signature requirement
A negotiable instrument must be signed by the drawer or maker. Any symbol executed or adopted by a party with a present intent to authenticate a writing qualifies as his or her signature.

Business Brief
Corporations, partnerships, and other forms of businesses must use agents, such as corporate officers and employees, to sign the businesses' negotiable instruments.

Contemporary Business Application

SIGNATURE BY AN AUTHORIZED REPRESENTATIVE

A maker or drawer can appoint an *agent* to sign a negotiable instrument on his or her behalf. For example, corporations and other organizations use agents, usually corporate officers or employees, to sign the corporation's negotiable instruments. Individuals can also appoint agents to sign their negotiable instruments.

A maker or drawer is liable on a negotiable instrument signed by an authorized agent. The agent is not personally liable on the negotiable instrument if his or her signature properly unambiguously discloses (1) his or her agency status and (2) the identity of the maker or drawer [UCC 3-402(b)]. In the case of an organization, the agent's signature is proper if the organization's name is preceded or followed by the name and office of the authorized agent.

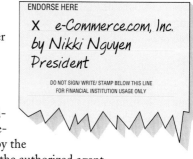

Unconditional Promise or Order to Pay

To be a negotiable instrument under the requirements of UCC 3-104(a), the writing must contain either an **unconditional promise to pay** (note or certificate of deposit) or an **unconditional order to pay** (draft or check). It is the term *unconditional*, which is discussed shortly, that is key.

unconditional promise or order to pay requirement
A negotiable instrument must contain either an *unconditional promise to pay* (note or CD) or an *unconditional order to pay* (draft or check).

Promise or Order   To be negotiable, a **promise to pay** must be an unconditional and affirmative undertaking. The mere acknowledgment of a debt is not sufficient to constitute a negotiable instrument. In other words, an implied promise to pay is not negotiable, but an expressly stated promise to pay is negotiable. For example, the statement "I owe you $100" is merely an I.O.U. It acknowledges a debt, but it does not contain an express promise to repay the money. However, if the I.O.U. uses language such as "I promise to pay" or "the undersigned agrees to pay," a negotiable instrument would be created because the note would contain an affirmative obligation to pay.

promise to pay
A maker's (borrower's) unconditional and affirmative undertaking to repay a debt to a payee (lender).

Certificates of deposit (CDs) are an exception to this rule. CDs do not require an express promise to pay because the bank's acknowledgment of the payee's bank deposit and other terms of the CD clearly indicate the bank's promise to repay the certificate holder. Nevertheless, most CDs contain an express promise to pay.

order for the drawee to pay
A drawer's unconditional order for a drawee to pay a payee.

To be negotiable, a draft or check must contain the drawer's unconditional **order for the drawee to pay** a payee. An order is a direction to pay and must be more than an authorization or request to pay. The language of the order must be precise and contain the word *pay*. For example, the printed word *pay* on a check is a proper order that is sufficient to make the check negotiable. The order can be in a courteous form, such as "please pay" or "kindly pay." A mere request or acknowledgment, such as "I wish you would pay," is not sufficient because it lacks a direction to pay.

An order to pay a draft or check must identify the drawee who is directed to make the payment. The name of the drawee financial institution that is preprinted on a check is sufficient. The order can be directed to one or more parties jointly, such as "to A *and* B," or in the alternative, such as "to A *or* B." The order cannot, however, be in succession, such as "to A, and if she does not pay, then to B."

Unconditional Promise or Order To be negotiable, the promise or order must be **unconditional** [UCC 3-104(a)]. A promise or order that is *conditional* on another promise or event is not negotiable because the risk of the other promise or event not occurring would fall on the person who held the instrument. A conditional promise is subject to normal contract law.

Consider This Example Suppose American Airlines buys a $10-million airplane from Boeing Aircraft. American signs a promissory note that promises to pay Boeing if it is "satisfied" with the airplane. This is a conditional promise. The condition—that American is satisfied with the airplane—destroys the negotiability of the note.

A promise or order is conditional and, therefore, not negotiable if it states (1) an express condition to payment, (2) that the promise or order is subject to or governed by another writing, or (3) that the rights or obligations with respect to the promise or order are stated in another writing. The mere reference to another writing does not make the promise or order conditional [UCC 3-106(a)].

Consider This Example Dow Chemical purchases equipment from Illinois Tool Works and signs a sales contract. Dow Chemical borrows the purchase price from Citibank and executes a promissory note evidencing this debt and promising to repay the borrowed money plus interest. The note contains the following reference: "sales contract—purchase of equipment." This reference does not affect the negotiability of the note. However, the note would not be negotiable if the reference stated, "This note hereby incorporates by this reference the terms of the sales contract between Dow Chemical and Illinois Tool Works of this date."

A promise or order remains unconditional even though it refers to another writing for rights to collateral, prepayment, or acceleration (e.g., "see collateral agreement dated January 15, 2000"). A promise or order may also stipulate that payment is limited to a particular fund or source (e.g., "payable out of the proceeds of the Tower Construction Contract") [UCC 3-106(b)].

Fixed Amount of Money

To be negotiable, an instrument must contain a promise or order to pay a **fixed amount of money** [UCC 3-104(a)]. This phrase can be analyzed as two promises or orders: (1) to pay a *fixed amount* and (2) to pay *in money*.

Fixed Amount The **fixed amount** requirement ensures that the value of the instrument can be determined with certainty. The principal amount of the instrument must appear on the *face* of the instrument.

An instrument does not have to be payable with interest, but, if it is, the amount of interest being charged may be expressed as either a *fixed* or a *variable* rate. The amount or rate of interest may be stated or described in the instrument or may require reference to information not contained in the instrument. If an instrument provides for interest, but the amount of interest cannot be determined from the description, interest is payable at the judgment rate (legal rate) in effect at the place of payment of the instrument [UCC 3-112].

Thus, a note that contains a promise to pay $10,000 in one year at a stated rate of 10 percent interest is a negotiable instrument because the value of the note can be determined at any time. Article 3 expressly provides that variable interest rate notes are negotiable instruments [UCC 3-112(b)]. A note that contains a promise to pay in goods or services is not a negotiable instrument because the value of the note would be difficult to determine at any given time.

unconditional
Promises to pay and orders to pay must be unconditional for them to be negotiable.

Business Brief
A negotiable instrument may refer to another writing for rights as to collateral, prepayment, or acceleration.

fixed amount of money
A negotiable instrument must contain a promise or order to pay a fixed amount of money.

fixed amount
A requirement of a negotiable instrument that ensures that the value of the instrument can be determined with certainty.

money

A "medium of exchange authorized or adopted by a domestic or foreign government" [UCC 1-201(24)].

Payable in Money UCC 3-104(a) provides that the fixed amount must be payable in "money." The UCC defines **money** as a "medium of exchange authorized or adopted by a domestic or foreign government as part of its currency" [UCC 1-201(24)]. For example, an instrument that is "payable in $10,000 U.S. currency" is a negotiable instrument.

Instruments that are fully or partially payable in a medium of exchange other than money are not negotiable. Thus, an instrument that is "payable in $10,000 U.S. gold" is not negotiable. Although the stated amount is a *fixed amount*, it is not payable in a medium of exchange of the U.S. government. Likewise, instruments that are payable in diamonds, commodities, goods, services, stocks, bonds, and such do not qualify as negotiable instruments.

Contemporary Business Application

ARE VARIABLE INTEREST RATE NOTES NEGOTIABLE INSTRUMENTS?

Prior to the mid-1970s, most loans that were made in this country were fixed-rate loans, that is, they bore a stated interest rate (e.g., 8 percent) that did not change during the life of the loan. This type of loan was fine for the lender as long as market interest rates did not change considerably. Since the mid-1970s, however, interest rates have become quite volatile.

To compensate for this volatility, many lending institutions began offering *variable interest rate loans*. These loans tied the interest rate to some set measure, such as a major bank's prime rate (e.g., Citibank's prime) or other well-known rate (e.g., Freddie Mac rate). A huge "secondary market" has developed where these loans are bought and sold.

These loans raised one major question: Are variable interest rate notes negotiable instruments? If they are, they are governed by Article 3 of the UCC, which provides certain protection to the holder against third-party claims and defenses. If they are not, they are ordinary contracts that are not subject to the protection of Article 3.

The drafters of Revised Article 3 solved this dilemma. Prior to the revision of Article 3 in 1990, UCC 3-104(1)(b) stipulated that to be a qualified negotiable instrument, a promise or order to pay must state a "sum certain in money." The key legal issue was whether variable interest rate notes were promises to pay a "sum certain in money." The courts were divided on this issue.

The drafters of Revised Article 3 settled the matter by expressly providing that variable interest rate notes are negotiable instruments. UCC 3-112(b) provides: "Interest may be stated in an instrument as a fixed or variable amount of money or it may be expressed as a fixed or variable rate or rates." UCC 3-112(b) also provides that the amount or rate of interest may be determined by reference to information not contained in the instrument.

This change in Article 3, which recognizes variable interest rate notes as negotiable instruments, reflects modern commercial and banking practices.

Not Require Any Undertaking in Addition to the Payment of Money

To qualify as a negotiable instrument, a promise or order to pay cannot state any other undertaking by the person promising or ordering payment to do any act in addition to the payment of money [UCC 3-104(a)(3)]. For example, if a note required the maker to pay a stated amount of money *and* perform some type of service, it would not be negotiable.

A promise or order may include authorization or power to protect collateral, dispose of collateral, waive any law intended to protect the obligee, and the like.

payable on demand or at a definite time requirement

A negotiable instrument must be payable either *on demand* or *at a definite time.*

Payable on Demand or at a Definite Time

For an instrument to be negotiable, it is necessary to know when the maker, drawee, or acceptor is required to pay it. UCC 3-104(a)(2) requires the instrument to be **payable** either **on demand** or **at a definite time**, as noted on the face of the instrument.

Payable on Demand   Instruments that are payable on demand are called **demand instruments**. Demand instruments are created by (1) language such as "payable on demand," "payable at sight," or "payable on presentment" or (2) silence regarding when payment is due [UCC 3-108(a)].

By definition, checks are payable on demand [UCC 3-104(f)]. Other instruments, such as notes, certificates of deposit, and drafts, can be, but are not always, payable on demand.

demand instrument
An instrument payable on demand.

Payable at a Definite Time   Instruments that are payable at a definite time are called **time instruments**. UCC 3-108(b) and (c) states that an instrument is payable at a definite time if it is payable

1. At a fixed date (e.g., "payable on January 1, 2010").
2. On or before a stated date (e.g., "payable on or before January 1, 2010"). The maker or drawee has the option of paying the note before—but not after—the stated maturity date.
3. At a fixed period after sight (e.g., "payable 60 days after sight"). Drafts often contain this type of language. The holder must formally present this type of instrument for acceptance so that the date of sight can be established.
4. At a time readily ascertainable when the promise or order is issued (e.g., "payable 60 days after January 1, 2000").

time instrument
An instrument payable (1) at a fixed date, (2) on or before a stated date, (3) at a fixed period after sight, or (4) at a time readily ascertainable when the promise or order is issued.

Instruments that are payable upon an uncertain act or event are not negotiable. For example, suppose Sarah Smith's father executes a promissory note stating, "I promise to pay to the order of my daughter, Sarah, $100,000 on the date she marries Bobby Boggs." This note is nonnegotiable because the act and date of marriage are uncertain.

Prepayment, Acceleration, and Extension Clauses   The inclusion of prepayment, acceleration, or extension clauses in an instrument does not affect its negotiability. Such clauses are commonly found in promissory notes. A *prepayment clause* permits the maker to pay the amount due prior to the due date of the instrument. An *acceleration clause* allows the payee or holder to accelerate payment of the principal amount of an instrument, plus accrued interest, upon the happening of an event (e.g., default). An *extension clause* is the opposite of an acceleration clause. It allows the date of maturity of an instrument to be extended to some time in the future.

Entrepreneur and the Law

BE CAREFUL WHETHER NEGOTIABLE INSTRUMENTS ARE PAYABLE TO ORDER OR TO BEARER

Because negotiable instruments are primarily intended to act as a substitute for money, they must be freely transferable to other persons or entities. The UCC requires that negotiable instruments be either **payable to order** or **payable to bearer** [UCC 3-104(a)(1)]. Promises or orders to pay that do not meet this requirement are not negotiable. They may, however, be assignable under contract law.

Order Instruments
An instrument is an **order instrument** if it is payable (1) to the order of an identified person or (2) to an identified person or orders [UCC 3-109(b)]. For example, an instrument that states "payable to the order of IBM" or "payable to IBM or order" is negotiable. It would not be negotiable if it stated either "payable to IBM" or "pay to IBM" because it is not payable to *order*.

(box continues)

An instrument can be payable to the order of the maker, the drawer, the drawee, the payee, two or more payees together, or, alternatively, to an office, an officer by his or her title, a corporation, a partnership, an unincorporated association, a trust, an estate, or another legal entity. A person to whom an instrument is payable may be identified in any way, including by name, identifying number, office, or account number. An instrument is payable to the person intended by the signer of the instrument even if that person is identified in the instrument by a name or other identification that is not that of the intended person [UCC 3-110].

For example, an instrument made "payable to the order of Lovey" is negotiable. The identification of "Lovey" may be determined by evidence. On the other hand, an instrument made "payable to the order of my loved ones" is not negotiable because the payees are not ascertainable with reasonable certainty.

Bearer Instruments

A **bearer instrument** is payable to anyone in physical possession of the instrument who presents it for payment when it is due. The person in possession of the instrument is called the **bearer**. Bearer paper results when the drawer or maker does not make the instrument payable to a specific payee.

An instrument is payable to bearer when any of the following language is used: "payable to the order of bearer," "payable to bearer," "payable to Xerox or bearer," "payable to cash," or "payable to the order of cash." In addition, any other indication that does not purport to designate a specific payee creates bearer paper [UCC 3-109(a)]. For example, an instrument "payable to my dog Fido" creates a bearer instrument.

CONCEPT SUMMARY FORMAL REQUIREMENTS FOR A NEGOTIABLE INSTRUMENT

Requirement	Description
Writing	Writing must be permanent and portable. Oral or implied instruments are nonnegotiable [UCC 3-104(d)].
Signed by maker or drawer	Signature must appear on the face of the instrument. It may be any mark intended by the signer to be his or her signature. Signature may be by an authorized representative [UCC 3-401(a)].
Unconditional promise or order to pay	Instrument must be an unconditional promise or order to pay [UCC 3-104(a)]. Permissible notations listed in UCC 3-106(a) do not affect instrument's negotiability. If payment is conditional on the performance of another agreement, the instrument is nonnegotiable.
Fixed amount of money	Fixed amount: Amount required to discharge the instrument must be on the face of the instrument [UCC 3-104(a)]. Amount may include payment of interest, discount, and costs of collection. Revised Article 3 provides that variable interest rate notes are negotiable instruments. In money: Amount must be payable in U.S. or foreign country's currency. If payment is to be made in goods, services, or nonmonetary items, the instrument is nonnegotiable [UCC 3-104(a)].
Cannot require any undertaking in addition to the payment of money	A promise or order to pay cannot state any other undertaking to do an act in addition to the payment of money [UCC 3-104(a)(3)]. A promise or order may include authorization or power to protect collateral, dispose of collateral, waive any law intended to protect the obligee, and the like.
Payable on demand or at a definite time	Payable on demand: Payable at sight, upon presentation, or when no time for payment is stated [UCC 3-108(a)]. Payable at a definite time: Payable on a definite date, on or before a stated date, at a fixed period after a stated date, or at a fixed period after sight [UCC 3 108(b) and (c)]. Instrument payable only upon the occurrence of an uncertain act or event is nonnegotiable.

| Payable to order or to bearer | Payable to order: Payable to a specific payee [UCC 3-109(b)]. An instrument made payable both to order and to bearer is payable to order unless the bearer's words are handwritten or typewritten. |
| | Payable to bearer: Payable to bearer, order of bearer, cash, a specified person or bearer, or any other indication that does not purport to designate a specific payee [UCC 3-109 (a)]. |

*N*ONNEGOTIABLE CONTRACTS

If a promise or order to pay does not meet one of the previously discussed requirements of negotiability, it is a **nonnegotiable contract**. As such, it is not subject to the provisions of UCC Article 3. However, this does not render the contract either nontransferable or nonenforceable. A nonnegotiable contract can be enforced under normal contract law. If the maker or drawer of a nonnegotiable contract fails to pay it, the holder of the contract can sue the nonperforming party for breach of contract.

In the following case, the court had to decide whether an installment sales contract was a negotiable instrument or an ordinary nonnegotiable contract.

nonnegotiable contract
Fails to meet the requirements of a negotiable instrument and, therefore, is not subject to the provisions of UCC Article 3.

Sunrizon Homes, Inc. v. American Guaranty Investment Corp.
7 U.C.C. Rep.Serv.2d 796 (1988)
Supreme Court of Oklahoma

CASE 23.1

FACTS
In October 1984, Roland and Rebecca Renault purchased a mobile home from Apple Homes (Apple). They borrowed a portion of the purchase price from Apple and signed an installment sales contract promising to repay the loan. The contract contained the words *pay to the seller*. Apple assigned the contract to American Guaranty Investment Corp. (American Guaranty), which paid Apple a check for $39,154. American Guaranty immediately assigned the contract to Continental Federal Savings and Loan Association (Continental) for $40,012. The Renaults were notified of the assignments and made timely payments to Continental. American Guaranty's check was returned for insufficient funds. When Apple's attempt to recover from American Guaranty failed, it sued Continental to recover the payments made by the Renaults and the contract. The trial court found that the installment sales contract signed by the Renaults was a negotiable instrument and that Continental was a holder in due course from whom Apple could not recover. The court granted summary judgment in favor of Continental. The court of appeals affirmed. Apple appealed.

ISSUE
Was the installment sales contract signed by the Renaults a negotiable instrument (a promissory note)?

IN THE LANGUAGE OF THE COURT
Kauger, Justice   The nature of the instrument, that is, negotiable or nonnegotiable, is essential to determine what rights Continental received under its assignment from American Guaranty. If the contract for sale is a negotiable instrument, Continental may qualify as a holder in due course, taking the assignment free of any claim or defense. If the contract for sale is not a negotiable instrument, Continental stands in the shoes of its assignor, American Guaranty, and the instrument is subject to the defense of failure of consideration—the bad check.

Before one may be a holder in due course, the holder must take a negotiable instrument. UCC 2-104 provides that a negotiable instrument must be (1) signed by the maker or drawer, (2) contain an unconditional promise to pay a sum certain in money, and (3) be made payable to order or to bearer. It is undisputed that the sales contract meets the first two requirements of a negotiable instrument. It is signed by the maker or drawer, and it contains an unconditional promise to pay a sum certain in money. Nevertheless, Apple argues that because the contract does not contain the indispensable words of negotiability, "pay to order or to bearer," Continental is not a holder in due course. The installment sales contract states that the buyer promises "to pay the seller" monthly installments for a period of 15 years.

The words "order" or "bearer" place a party on notice that the assignment is negotiable. The general rule in jurisdictions that
(case continues)

have considered this question is that a note payable to a specific person, rather than to order or to bearer, is nonnegotiable. The sales contract fails to meet the criteria of UCC 3-104 that a negotiable instrument be made payable to order or to bearer. Continental is not a holder in due course of a negotiable instrument, and is subject to the defenses of failure of consideration.

DECISION AND REMEDY

The contract signed by the Renaults did not meet the requirements necessary to be a negotiable instrument. Reversed.

Case Questions

Critical Legal Thinking What is the policy underlying the requirement that the words *pay to order* or *pay to bearer* appear on an instrument before it qualifies as a negotiable instrument? Explain.

Ethics Did anyone act unethically in this case?

Business Application What are the economic consequences of buying an instrument that does not contain the words *pay to order* or *pay to bearer*?

WWW Working the Web

e-biz

New York Stock Exchange Check stock quotes, access your personal stock tracker, get the latest on listed companies and IPOs, learn about the investment community, and learn how the NYSE works.

Visit at **www.nyse.com**

U.S. Treasury Department Are you working on your income or other taxes? This is the place to find and download all the forms as well as lots of other information about the Treasury Department.

Visit at **www.ustreas.gov**

American Stock Exchange Get current information about the American Stock Exchange at this Web site.

Visit at **www.amex.com**

NASDAQ Find out what is happening in the NASDAQ stock market.

Visit at **www.nasdaq.com**

CYBER EXERCISES

1. Using the NYSE site, go to the trading floor.

2. Use the U.S. Treasury Department Web site to find and download a tax form.

3. Use the American Stock Exchange to get today's closing statistics from the American Stock Exchange.

4. Find information about the NASD's Year 2000 Program.

CASES AND EXERCISES

CRITICAL LEGAL THINKING CASES

23.1. Marcus Wiley, James Tate, and James Irby were partners engaged in buying and selling used cars under the trade name Wiley, Tate & Irby. Over an extended period of time, the partnership sold a number of automobiles to Billy Houston, a sole proprietor doing business as Houston Auto Sales. In connection with each purchase, Houston executed and delivered to the partnership a negotiable instrument drawn on the Peoples Bank and Trust Company of Tupelo, Mississippi. Upon delivery of each negotiable instrument, the automobiles were delivered to Houston. Each of the instruments involved in these transactions contained a number of variations in text and form. However, each of them was similar in that each was drawn on a bank, signed by their maker, and contained an unconditional promise to pay a sum certain on the demand of the payee. What type of negotiable instrument is involved in these transactions? [*Wiley v. Peoples Bank and Trust Company*, 438 F.2d 513 (5th Cir. 1971)]

23.2. A. A. Cervantes was a cattle rancher in Mississippi who operated under the name Cattle Company. It was Cervantes's practice to pay for all cattle he purchased with a draft. The drawee was Covington County Bank (the Bank), where Cervantes maintained an account. The drafts stated on their face, "Upon acceptance pay to the order of _____." This method worked well until the Bank refused to make payment on the drafts presented by two sellers, Poling and Horney, because Cervantes had become insolvent and would be unable to repay the Bank. The livestock had been delivered to Cervantes's ranch. Poling and Horney claimed that the drafts were demand instruments and sued the Bank to recover the funds. The Bank argued that the language "upon acceptance" made the instruments time drafts, payable at a time when the Bank chose to accept them. Who wins? [*Horney v. Covington County Bank*, 716 F.2d 335 (5th Cir. 1983)]

23.3. Walter J. Kassuba held two certificates of deposit (CDs) issued by Midland National Bank (Midland). The certificates were for $225,000 and $250,000. In August 1973, Kassuba pledged the CDs to First Wisconsin National Bank of Milwaukee (First Wisconsin) as security for repayment of a $990,000 loan. In pledging the CDs, Kassuba signed a form stating that he had transferred to First Wisconsin the CDs and any subsequent replacement, renewal, extension, or reissue of the CDs as security for the repayment of all present and future liabilities. In December 1973, Kassuba filed for bankruptcy. As of the date of the filing, Kassuba was substantially indebted to Midland. On March 12, 1974, Midland set off the amount it was owed against the CDs. First Wisconsin countered that the CDs were rightfully transferred to it as collateral for the $990,000 loan. Can the CDs be transferred in this manner? [*First Wisconsin National Bank of Milwaukee v. Midland National Bank*, 251 N.W.2d 829 (WI 1977)]

23.4. Mullins Enterprises, Inc. (Mullins), was a business operating in the state of Kentucky. To raise capital, Mullins obtained loans from Corbin Deposit Bank & Trust Co. (Corbin Bank). Between 1971 and 1975, Corbin Bank made eight loans to Mullins. Mullins executed a promissory note setting out the amount of the debt, the dates and times of installment payments, and the date of final payment and delivered it to the bank each time a loan was made. The notes were signed by an officer of Mullins. In 1980, a dispute arose between Mullins and Corbin Bank as to the proper interpretation of the language contained in the notes. The bank contended that the notes were demand notes. Mullins claimed that the notes were time instruments. Who wins? [*Corbin Deposit Bank & Trust Co. v. Mullins Enterprises, Inc.*, 34 UCC Rep.Ser. 1201 (Ky App. 1982)]

23.5. On August 17, 1979, Sandra McGuire and her husband entered into a contract to purchase the inventory, equipment, accounts receivable, and name of "Becca's Boutique" from Pascal and Rebecca Tursi. Becca's Boutique was a clothing store that was owned as a sole proprietorship by the Tursis. The McGuires agreed to purchase the store for $75,000, with a down payment of $10,000 and the balance to be paid by October 5, 1979. The promissory note signed by the McGuires read: "For value received, Thomas J. McGuire and Sandra A. McGuire, husband and wife, do promise to pay to the order of Pascal and Rebecca Tursi the sum of $65,000." Is the note an order to pay or a promise to pay? [*PP Inc. v. McGuire*, 509 F.Supp. 1079 (D.N.J. 1981)]

23.6. Mr. Higgins operated a used car dealership in the state of Alabama. In 1978, Higgins purchased a 1977 Chevrolet Corvette for $8,115. He paid for the car with a draft on his account at the First State Bank of Albertville. Soon after, Higgins resold the car to Mr. Holsonback for $8,225. To pay for the car, Holsonback signed a check that was printed on a standard-sized envelope. The reason the check was printed on the envelope is that this practice made it easier to transfer title and other documents from the seller to the buyer. The envelope on which the check was written contained a certificate of title, a mileage statement, and a bill of sale. Does a check printed on an envelope meet the formal requirements to be classified as a negotiable instrument under the UCC? [*Holsonback v. First State Bank of Albertville*, 30 UCC Rep.Serv. 222 (AL 1980)]

23.7. M. S. Horne executed a $100,000 note in favor of R. C. Clark stipulating that it could not be transferred, pledged, or assigned without Horne's consent. Along with the note, Horne signed a letter authorizing Clark to use the note as collateral for a loan. Clark pledged the note as collateral for a $50,000 loan from First State Bank of Gallup (First State). First State telephoned Horne to confirm that Clark could pledge the note and Horne indicated that it was okay. Clark eventually defaulted on the loan. First State attempted to collect on the note, but Horne refused to pay. Does the restriction written on Horne's promissory note cause it to be nonnegotiable despite the letter of authorization? [*First State Bank of Gallup v. Clark and Horne*, 570 P.2d 1144 (NM 1977)]

23.8. In 1982, William H. Bailey, M.D., executed a note payable to California Dreamstreet (Dreamstreet), a joint venture that solicits investments for a cattle breeding operation. Bailey's promissory note read: "Dr. William H. Bailey hereby promises to pay to the order of California Dreamstreet the sum of $329,800." In 1986, Dreamstreet negotiated the note to Cooperatieve Centrale Raiffeisen-Boerenleenbank B.A. (Cooperatieve), a foreign bank. A default occurred and Cooperatieve filed suit against Bailey to recover on the note. Is the note executed by Bailey a negotiable instrument? [*Cooperatieve Centrale Raiffeisen-Boerenleenbank B.A. v. Bailey*, 9 UCC Rep.Serv.2d 145 (C.D.Cal. 1989)]

23.9. In 1972, Holly Hill Acres, Ltd. (Holly Hill), purchased land from Rogers and Blythe. As part of its consideration, Holly Hill gave Rogers and Blythe a promissory note and purchase money mortgage. The note, which was executed on April 28, 1972, read in part: "This note with interest is secured by a mortgage on real estate made by the maker in favor of said payee. The terms of said mortgage are by reference made a part hereof." Rogers and Blythe assigned this note and mortgage to Charter Bank of Gainesville (Charter Bank) as security in order to obtain a loan from the bank. Within a few months, Rogers and Blythe defaulted on their obligation to Charter Bank. Charter Bank sued to recover on Holly Hill's note and mortgage. Does the reference to the mortgage in the note cause it to be nonnegotiable? [*Holly Hill Acres, Ltd. v. Charter Bank of Gainesville*, 314 So.2d 209 (Fla.App. 1975)]

23.10. In July 1977, Stewart P. Blanchard borrowed $50,000 from Progressive Bank & Trust Company (Progressive) to purchase a home. As part of the transaction, Blanchard signed a note secured by a mortgage. The note provided for a 10 percent annual interest rate. Under the terms of the note, payment was "due on demand, if no demand is made, then $600 monthly beginning 8/1/77." Blanchard testified that he believed Progressive could only demand immediate payment if he failed to make the monthly installments. After one year, Blanchard received notice that the rate of interest on the note would rise to 11 percent. Despite the notice, Blanchard continued to make $600 monthly payments. One year later, Progressive notified Blanchard that the interest rate on the loan would be increased to 12.75 percent. Progressive requested that Blanchard sign a form consenting to the interest rate adjustment. When Blanchard refused to sign the form, Progressive demanded immediate payment of the note balance. Progressive sued Blanchard to enforce the terms of the note. Is the note a demand instrument? [*Blanchard v. Progressive Bank & Trust Company*, 413 So.2d 589 (La.App. 1982)]

23.11. Robert and Sandra Evans were stockholders in Traditional Development, Inc. (Traditional), which planned to build townhouses in Arizona. In 1972, the Evanses approached Security Mortgage Company (Security) to obtain financing for the project. Security agreed to make Traditional a $514,000 loan that would be secured by a note. On May 19, 1972, the note was executed, and the Evanses signed as guarantors. The note contained the following language: "The makers and endorsers expressly agree that this note, or any payment thereunder, may be extended from time to time without in any way affecting the liability of the makers and endorsers hereof."

The original maturity date of the note was January 14, 1973, or 245 days after origination. However, the project was delayed so the note's due date was extended to May 13, 1973, an additional 114 days. The guarantors consented to the extension in writing. Several months later, the note was extended to January 15, 1974. When Traditional realized it was unable to complete the project, it assigned its interest in the note to Union Construction Company, Inc. (Union). One final extension of the note was granted, making the maturity date of the loan January 15, 1975. Do the multiple extensions of the note render it nonnegotiable? [*Union Construction Company, Inc. v. Beneficial Standard Mortgage Investors*, 28 UCC Rep.Serv. 711 (Ariz.App. 1980)]

ETHICS CASES

23.12. Broadway Management Corporation (Broadway) owned and operated the American Nursing Center (Center). Conan Briggs had received services from the center and had executed an instrument to pay for these services. The instrument reads in relevant part: "Ninety days after date, I, we, or either of us, promises to pay to the order of _____ $3,498.45." Briggs refused to pay on the note. Broadway claimed that this note is "bearer paper" and as such is payable to the holder. Briggs claimed that the note is "order paper" and is therefore payable only to a named payee. Can Broadway collect on this note as its bearer? [*Broadway Management Corporation v. Briggs*, 332 N.E.2d-131 (Ill.App. 1975)]

23.13. Mike J. Rogers, owner of Arkansas Parts and Equipment Company (Arkansas Parts), invited Paul Mollenhour to be an officer of the business. Rogers wanted Mollenhour to join the business because his strong financial position would allow Rogers to more easily secure operating financing. With Mollenhour's assistance, Arkansas Parts secured financing in 1986. On February 19, 1986, Arkansas

Parts executed a revolving credit note with State First National Bank of Texarkana (State First) in the amount of $150,000. The note was signed as follows:

/s/Mike Rogers
_____
        Mike Rogers, Individually

/s/Dave Mollenhour, V. Pres.
_____
        Dave Mollenhour, Individually

EQUIPMENT CO., INC.
_____

by:/s/Mike Rogers
_____
        Mike Rogers, President

by:/s/Dave Mollenhour, V. Pres.
_____
        Dave Mollenhour, Vice President and Secretary

The note stipulated that the parties were jointly and severally obligated to State First. After Arkansas Parts defaulted on the note, State First sued Arkansas Parts and Rogers and Mollenhour, individually. Mollenhour claimed that he is not liable because his signature indicated his representative capacity. Who wins? [*Mollenhour v. State First National Bank of Texarkana*, 8 UCC Rep.Serv.2d 759 (Ark.App. 1989)]

CRITICAL LEGAL THINKING WRITING ASSIGNMENT

Read Case A.23 in the Case Appendix [*Federal Deposit Insurance Corporation v. Woodside Construction, Inc.*]. This case is excerpted from the court of appeals opinion. Review and brief the case. In your brief, be sure to answer the following questions.

1. Was Galt acting as an agent when he signed the negotiable instrument? If so, who was his principal?

2. What type of negotiable instrument did Galt sign? How did he sign it?

3. Was Galt's signature proper to notify a holder that his signature was made in a representative capacity?

4. Was Galt found personally liable on the negotiable instrument?

24 Transfer of Negotiable Instruments

Small debts are like small shot; they are rattling on every side, and can scarcely be escaped without a wound; great debts are like cannon; of loud noise, but little danger.

SAMUEL JOHNSON
Letter to Joseph Simpson (1759)

Chapter Objectives

After studying this chapter, you should be able to

1. Describe the concept of negotiation.
2. Distinguish between assignment and negotiation of an instrument.
3. Describe how negotiable instruments are indorsed and transferred.
4. Describe how order and bearer paper are negotiated.
5. Explain how order and bearer paper can be converted to the other by indorsement.
6. Distinguish between blank and special indorsements.
7. Distinguish between unqualified and qualified indorsements.
8. Distinguish between nonrestrictive and restrictive indorsements.
9. Define and apply the imposter rule.
10. Define and apply the fictitious payee rule.

Chapter Contents

The concept of *negotiation* is important to the law of negotiable instruments. The primary benefit of a negotiable instrument is that it can be used as a substitute for money. As such, it must be freely transferable to subsequent parties. Technically, a negotiable instrument is negotiated when it is originally issued. However, the term **negotiation** is usually used to describe the transfer of negotiable instruments to subsequent transferees.

After they have been issued, negotiable instruments can be transferred to subsequent parties by *assignment* or by *negotiation*. The rights acquired by subsequent transferees differ according to the method of transfer. The different methods of transferring negotiable instruments are discussed in this chapter.

TRANSFER BY ASSIGNMENT

An **assignment** is the transfer of rights under a contract. It transfers the rights of the transferor (**assignor**) to the transferee (**assignee**). Because normal contract principles apply, the assignee acquires only the rights that the assignor possessed. Thus, any defenses to the enforcement of the contract that could have been raised against the assignor can also be raised against the assignee.

An assignment occurs when a nonnegotiable contract is transferred. In the case of a negotiable instrument, assignment occurs when the instrument is transferred but the transfer fails to qualify as a negotiation under Article 3. In this case, the transferee is an *assignee* rather than a *holder*.

assignment
The transfer of rights under a contract.

assignor
The transferor in an assignment situation.

assignee
The transferee in an assignment situation.

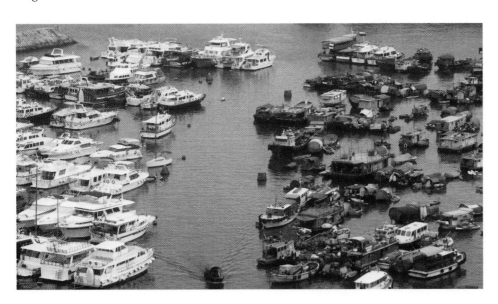

Hong Kong. As a member of the English Commonwealth, Hong Kong became one of the leading financial and commercial centers of the world. In July 1997, Communist China took over capitalist Hong Kong from Great Britain with the policy of "one country, two systems."

TRANSFER BY NEGOTIATION

Negotiation is the transfer of a negotiable instrument by a person other than the issuer. The person to whom the instrument is transferred becomes the *holder* [UCC 3-201(a)]. The **holder** receives at least the rights of the transferor, and may acquire even greater rights than the transferor if he or she qualifies as a *holder in due course (HDC)* [UCC 3-302]. An HDC has greater rights because he or she is not subject to some of the defenses that could otherwise have been raised against the transferor.

The proper method of negotiation depends on whether the instrument is order or bearer paper, as discussed next.

negotiation
Transfer of a negotiable instrument by a person other than the issuer to a person who thereby becomes a *holder*.

holder
What the transferee becomes if a negotiable instrument has been transferred by *negotiation*.

Negotiating Order Paper

order paper

Order paper is negotiated by (1) *delivery* **and (2)** *indorsement.*

An instrument that is payable to a specific payee or indorsed to a specific indorsee is **order paper**. Order paper is negotiated by delivery with the necessary indorsement [UCC 3-201(b)]. Thus, for order paper to be negotiated there must be *delivery* and *indorsement.* (See Exhibit 24.1.)

*E*XHIBIT 24.1   *Negotiation of Order Paper*

Consider This Example   Sam Bennett receives a weekly payroll check from his employer, Ace Plumbing Corporation. Bennett takes the check to a local store, signs the back of the check (indorsement), gives the check to the cashier (delivery), and receives cash for the check. Bennett has *negotiated* the check to the store. There has been delivery and indorsement.

Negotiating Bearer Paper

bearer paper

Bearer paper is negotiated by *delivery* **; indorsement is not necessary.**

An instrument that is not payable to a specific payee or indorsee is **bearer paper**. Bearer paper is negotiated by *delivery*; indorsement is not necessary [UCC 3-201(b)] (see Exhibit 24.2). Substantial risk is associated with the loss or theft of bearer paper.

*E*XHIBIT 24.2   *Negotiation of Bearer Paper*

Consider This Example   Suppose Mary draws a check "pay to cash" and gives it to Peter. There has been a negotiation because Mary delivered a bearer instrument (the check) to Peter. Subsequently, Carmen steals the check from Peter. There has not been a negotiation because the check was not voluntarily delivered. The fact that Carmen physically possesses the check is irrelevant. However, the negotiation is complete if Carmen delivers the check to an innocent third party. That party is a holder and may qualify as an HDC with all the rights in the check [UCC 3-302]. If the holder is an HDC, Peter's only recourse is to recover against Carmen.

Converting Order and Bearer Paper

Instruments can be converted from order paper to bearer paper, and vice versa, many times until the instrument is paid [UCC 3-109(c)]. The deciding factor is the type of indorsement placed on the instrument at the time of each subsequent transfer. (See Exhibit 24.3.)

Business Brief
Negotiable instruments can be converted from order paper to bearer paper, and vice versa, depending on the form of the indorsement.

*E*XHIBIT 24.3   *Converting Order and Bearer Paper*

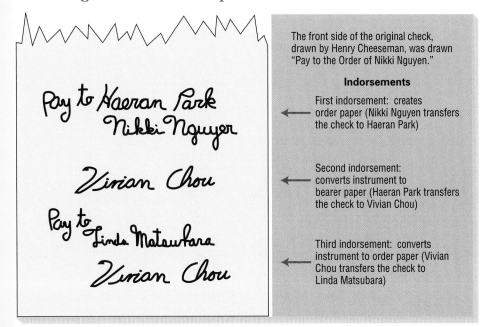

Pay to Haeran Park
Nikki Nguyen

Vivian Chou

Pay to Linda Matsubara

Vivian Chou

The front side of the original check, drawn by Henry Cheeseman, was drawn "Pay to the Order of Nikki Nguyen."

Indorsements

First indorsement: creates order paper (Nikki Nguyen transfers the check to Haeran Park)

Second indorsement: converts instrument to bearer paper (Haeran Park transfers the check to Vivian Chou)

Third indorsement: converts instrument to order paper (Vivian Chou transfers the check to Linda Matsubara)

Consider This Example   Susan draws a check "pay to the order of Dan Jones." The check is order paper because it is made payable to a specific payee. If Dan indorses the back of the check without naming a specific indorsee, the check is converted to bearer paper. If he delivers the check to Constance and she indorses the back of the check "pay to Ferdinand Friendly," the bearer paper is converted to order paper.

*I*NDORSEMENTS

An **indorsement** is the signature of a signer (other than as a maker, a drawer, or an acceptor) that is placed on an instrument to negotiate it to another person. The signature may (1) appear alone, (2) name an individual to whom the instrument is to be paid, or (3) be accompanied by other words [UCC 3-204(2)]. The person who indorses an instrument is called the **indorser**. If the indorsement names a payee, this person is called the **indorsee**.

Consider This Example   Mallory Choy receives a $500 check for her birthday. She can transfer the check to anyone merely by signing her name on the back of the check. Suppose she indorses it "pay to Rob Dewey." Ms. Choy is the indorser; Rob Dewey is the indorsee.

indorsement
The signature (and other directions) written by or on behalf of the holder somewhere on the instrument.

indorser
The person who indorses a negotiable instrument.

indorsee
The person to whom a negotiable instrument is indorsed.

allonge

A separate piece of paper attached to the instrument on which the indorsement is written.

Indorsements are usually placed on the reverse side of the instrument, such as on the back of a check (see Exhibit 24.4). If there is no room on the instrument, the indorsement may be written on a separate piece of paper called an **allonge**. The allonge must be affixed (e.g., stapled or taped) to the instrument [UCC 3-204(a)].

*E*XHIBIT 24.4 *Proper Placement of an Indorsement*

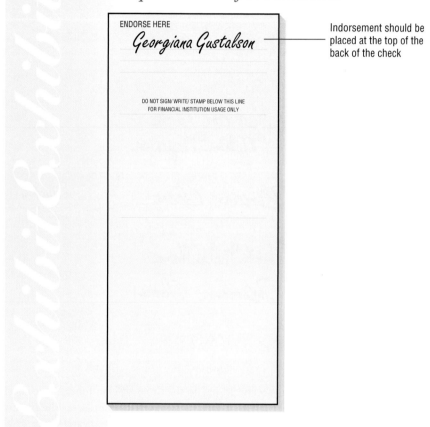

ENDORSE HERE
Georgiana Gustalson

DO NOT SIGN/ WRITE/ STAMP BELOW THIS LINE
FOR FINANCIAL INSTITUTION USAGE ONLY

Indorsement should be placed at the top of the back of the check

Indorsements are required to negotiate order paper. Indorsements are not required to negotiate bearer paper [UCC 3-201(b)]. However, for identification purposes and to impose liability on the transferor, the transferee often requires the transferor to indorse the bearer paper at negotiation.

Contemporary Business Application

THE $19-MILLION STAPLING ERROR

Empire of America Federal Savings Bank (Empire) may have been the victim of one of the most costly clerical errors in history. The story began in the mid-1980s, when Madison Partnerships, an invest-

ment firm, offered tax-advantaged real estate partnerships for sale to the public. Investors in the partnership were required to sign promissory notes made payable to one of three banks. Eventually, these notes wound up in the hands of Empire, which purchased them for $19 million from the original banks.

About 18 months after the investors joined the partnerships, they learned that an infamous swindler and a convicted embezzler were principals in Madison Partnerships. They also discovered that much of the property they had invested in had already been lost through foreclosures.

The investors immediately sued Madison Partnerships, the three originator banks, the brokerage firms, and Empire. The plaintiffs alleged that the defendants had fraudulently induced them to invest in the partnerships. Although the plaintiffs did not allege that Empire had participated in the fraudulent scheme, they argued that the notes should be rescinded because they were procured by means of fraud.

Empire argued that it was not susceptible to the plaintiffs' personal defense of *fraud in the inducement* because it was a holder in due course. The plaintiffs countered that the bank was not immune because the notes were not indorsed and negotiated in strict compliance with the terms of the Uniform Commercial Code (UCC). Their argument centered upon the particular manner in which the two-page documents had been drawn up and signed over to Empire by the originator banks. The first page of the note listed the originator bank (the bank that held the notes before Empire) and set forth the terms of the note. The second page contained only the indorsement by an authorized representative of the originator bank. However, the indorsement page (the *allonge*) was not stapled or otherwise attached to the note—it was merely inserted within a fold in the first page. This was a violation of the UCC, which expressly required that an indorsement page be "affixed" to the note itself. The plaintiffs argued that this was enough to deny Empire holder in due course status.

The court of appeals agreed with the plaintiffs and held that there had not been a proper negotiation of the notes to Empire. Therefore, Empire was not an HDC, and the plaintiffs could assert the other defendants' fraud against enforcement of the notes by Empire.

This ruling stands as an unmistakable warning about the perils of not strictly complying with UCC rules. [*Adams v. Madison Realty & Development*, 853 F.2d 163 (3d Cir. 1988)]

*T*YPES OF INDORSEMENTS

Every indorsement is

1. Blank or special.
2. Unqualified or qualified.
3. Nonrestrictive or restrictive.

These different types of indorsements are discussed in the following paragraphs.

Blank and Special Indorsements

Blank Indorsements   A **blank indorsement** does not specify a particular indorsee. It may consist of a mere signature [UCC 3-205(b)]. For example, suppose Harold Green draws a check "pay to the order of Victoria Rudd" and delivers the check to Victoria. Victoria indorses the check in blank by writing her signature on the back of the check (see Exhibit 24.5).

blank indorsement
An indorsement that does not specify a particular indorsee. It creates *bearer paper*.

*E*XHIBIT 24.5   *A Blank Indorsement*

ENDORSE HERE

Frederick Richards

DO NOT SIGN/ WRITE/ STAMP BELOW THIS LINE
FOR FINANCIAL INSTITUTION USAGE ONLY

Order paper that is indorsed in blank becomes *bearer paper*. As mentioned earlier, bearer paper can be negotiated by delivery; indorsement is not required. So, if Victoria Rudd loses the check she indorsed in blank and Mary Smith finds it, Mary Smith can deliver it to another person without indorsing it. Thus, the lost check can be presented for payment or negotiated to another holder.

special indorsement

An indorsement that contains the signature of the indorser and specifies the person (indorsee) to whom the indorser intends the instrument to be payable. Creates *order paper*.

Special Indorsements   A **special indorsement** contains the signature of the indorser and specifies the person (indorsee) to whom the indorser intends the instrument to be payable [UCC 3-205(a)]. Words of negotiation (e.g., *pay to the order of . . .*) are not required for a special indorsement. Words such as *pay Emily Ingman* are sufficient to form a special indorsement. For example, a special indorsement would be created if Betsy McKenny indorsed her check and then wrote "pay to Dan Jones" above her signature (see Exhibit 24.6). The check is negotiated when Betsy gives it to Dan. A special indorsement creates *order paper*. As mentioned earlier, order paper is negotiated by indorsement and delivery.

*E*XHIBIT 24.6   *A Special Indorsement*

```
ENDORSE HERE

Pay to Tom Blanford
Cri Cri Eastin


DO NOT SIGN/ WRITE/ STAMP BELOW THIS LINE
FOR FINANCIAL INSTITUTION USAGE ONLY
```

To prevent the risk of loss from theft, a special indorsement (which creates order paper) is preferred over a blank indorsement (which creates bearer paper). A holder can convert a blank indorsement into a special indorsement by writing any contract consistent with the character of the indorsement over the signature of the indorser in blank [UCC 3-205(c)]. Words such as *pay to John Jones* written above the indorser's signature are enough to convert bearer paper to order paper.

Unqualified and Qualified Indorsements

unqualified indorsement

An indorsement whereby the indorser promises to pay the holder or any subsequent indorser the amount of the instrument if the maker, drawer, or acceptor defaults on it.

Unqualified Indorsements   Generally, an indorsement is a promise by the indorser to pay the holder or any subsequent indorser the amount of the instrument if the maker, drawer, or acceptor defaults on it. This is called an **unqualified indorsement**. Unless otherwise agreed, the order and liability of the indorsers is presumed to be the order in which they indorse the instrument [UCC 3-415(a)].

unqualified indorser

An indorser who signs an *unqualified indorsement* to an instrument.

Consider This Example   Cindy draws a check payable to the order of John. John (indorser) indorses the check and negotiates it to Steve (indorsee). When Steve presents the check for payment, there are insufficient funds in Cindy's account to pay the check. John, as an **unqualified indorser**, is liable on the check. John can recover from Cindy.

In the following case, the court held that an indorser was liable on a promissory note because of her unqualified indorsement.

Alves v. Baldaia
470 N.E.2d 459 (1984)
Court of Appeals of Ohio

CASE 24.1

FACTS
In January 1973, Keith R. Alves loaned $15,000 to Beatrice and William Baldaia. The Baldaias signed a promissory note payable to the order of Keith's wife, Joyce Ann Alves, who was the Baldaias' daughter. In February, Keith and Joyce (now Joyce Schaller) were divorced. As part of the settlement agreement, Joyce agreed to transfer her rights in the note to Keith. The separation agreement provided: "Wife agrees to assign to Husband any and all rights, title, and interest she may have in a certain note, executed by her parents, dated January 3, 1973, on or before the date of the final hearing." Joyce signed the promissory note, "Pay to the Order of Keith R. Alves, /s/ Joyce Ann Alves," and delivered the note to Keith.

Sometime later, Keith sought to collect payment on the note from the makers of the note, the Baldaias. They defaulted and refused to pay the note. Keith notified his former wife, Joyce Schaller, that the makers had dishonored the note. Keith sued the Baldaias as makers and his ex-wife Joyce as an indorser to recover payment on the note. The court entered judgment for Keith Alves. Joyce Schaller appealed.

ISSUE
Did Joyce Schaller place an unqualified indorsement on the note and is therefore secondarily liable on it as an indorser?

IN THE LANGUAGE OF THE COURT
Handwork, Judge   As the trial court stated, "The legal effect of the signature is an indorsement regardless of the subjective intention of the signer." Schaller cannot be relieved of her liability as an indorser merely because she previously or contemporaneously executed a collateral separation agreement, intending to "assign" to Alves "any and all right, title, and interest" in the promissory

note. Had Schaller wished only to "assign" the note, as she uses the term, she should have delivered the instrument to Alves without signing it. Then, the instrument would not have been technically negotiated, and he would not have acquired the rights of a holder. As matters stood, the promissory note here contained the words: "Pay to the order of Keith R. Alves," below which Schaller signed her name. This constituted a special indorsement by the payee, and formal negotiation of the instrument occurred on its delivery to Alves. Schaller's signature on the promissory note is, therefore, conclusively presumed to be (and operates as) an indorsement.

Thus, when Schaller signed the promissory note, she contracted to pay the instrument, according to its tenor, to the holder thereof if the maker dishonored the note at maturity. If Schaller had desired to pass title to the note (i.e., to formally negotiate it), without creating any potential contract liability for herself, she had but to qualify her indorsement with the language "without recourse." However, not having done so, she acquired the full contractual liability of an indorser and was thereby obligated to pay the instrument following dishonor by the makers.

DECISION AND REMEDY
The court of appeals held that Joyce Schaller's signature on the promissory note operated as an unqualified indorsement. As such, she is secondarily liable on the note to plaintiff Keith Alves. Affirmed.

Case Questions
Critical Legal Thinking   Should indorsers be held secondarily liable on negotiable instruments when the makers (acceptors or drawers) default? Why or why not?

Ethics   Did anyone act unethically in this case?

Business Application   What is the economic lesson of this case?

Qualified Indorsements   The UCC permits **qualified indorsements**, that is, indorsements that disclaim or limit liability on the instrument. A **qualified indorser** does not guarantee payment of the instrument if the maker, drawer, or acceptor defaults on it. A qualified indorsement is created by placing a notation such as *without recourse* or other similar language that disclaims liability as part of the indorsement [UCC 3-415(b)]. A qualified indorsement protects only the indorser who wrote it on the instrument. Subsequent indorsers must also place a qualified indorsement on the instrument to be protected from liability. An instrument containing a qualified indorsement can be further negotiated.

Qualified indorsements are often used by persons signing instruments in a representative capacity. For example, suppose an insurance company that is paying a claim makes out a check payable to the order of the attorney representing the payee. The attorney can indorse the check to his or her client (the payee) with the notation "without recourse."

qualified indorsement
An indorsement that includes the notation "without recourse" or similar language that disclaims liability of the indorser.

qualified indorser
An indorser who signs a *qualified indorsement* to an instrument.

forged indorsement
The forged signature of a payee or holder on a negotiable instrument.

The notation ensures that the attorney is not liable as an indorser if the insurance company fails to pay the check.

A qualified indorsement can be either a special qualified indorsement or a blank qualified indorsement. A *special qualified indorsement* creates order paper that can be negotiated by indorsement and delivery (see Exhibit 24.7). A *blank qualified indorsement* creates bearer paper that can be further negotiated by delivery without further indorsement (see Exhibit 24.8).

*ℰ*XHIBIT 24.7 *A Special Qualified Indorsement*

*ℰ*XHIBIT 24.8 *A Blank Qualified Indorsement*

Nonrestrictive and Restrictive Indorsements

nonrestrictive indorsement
An indorsement that has no instructions or conditions attached to the payment of the funds.

Nonrestrictive Indorsements Most indorsements are **nonrestrictive**. Nonrestrictive indorsements do not have any instructions or conditions attached to the payment of the funds. For example, the indorsement is nonrestrictive if the indorsee merely signs his or her signature to the back of an instrument or includes a notation to pay a specific indorsee ("pay to Sam Smith").

restrictive indorsement
An indorsement that contains some sort of instruction from the indorser.

Restrictive Indorsements Occasionally, an indorser includes some form of instruction in an indorsement. This is called a **restrictive indorsement**. A restrictive indorsement restricts the indorsee's rights in some manner. An indorsement that purports to prohibit further negotiation of an instrument does not destroy the negotiability of the instrument. For example, a check that is indorsed "pay to Sarah Stein only" can still be negotiated to other transferees. Because of its ineffectiveness, this type of restrictive indorsement is seldom used.

UCC 3-206 recognizes the following types of restrictive indorsements:

- **Conditional Indorsement** An indorser can condition the guarantee of payment of an instrument dependent on the happening or nonhappening of a specified event. For example, Vincent White, a holder of a check, indorses the check "pay to John Jones if he completes construction of my house by January 1, 2003." This is a valid conditional indorsement. Neither Jones nor any subsequent holder can require Vincent White to pay this check until this condition is met.
- **Indorsement for Deposit or Collection** An indorser can indorse an instrument so as to make the indorsee his collecting agent. This is often done when an indorser deposits a check or other instrument for collection at a bank. Words such as *for collection, for deposit only, pay any bank,* and the like, create this type of indorsement. Banks use this type of indorsement in the collection process.
- **Indorsement in Trust** An indorsement can state that it is for the benefit or use of the indorser or another person. For example, checks are often indorsed to attorneys, executors of estates, real estate agents, and other fiduciaries in their representative capacity for the benefit of clients, heirs, or others. These are called *trust indorsements* or *agency indorsements* (see Exhibit 24.9). The indorser is not personally liable on the instrument if there is a proper trust or agency indorsement.

An indorsee who does not comply with the instructions of a restrictive indorsement is liable to the indorser for all losses that occur because of such noncompliance.

*Ɛ*XHIBIT 24.9   *A Trust Indorsement*

ENDORSE HERE

Pay to Lana Cheeseman in trust for Gregory Cheeseman, Jr. and Nikki Cheeseman

Gregory Cheeseman, Sr.

DO NOT SIGN/ WRITE/ STAMP BELOW THIS LINE
FOR FINANCIAL INSTITUTION USAGE ONLY

Consider This Example   Suppose a check is drawn "payable to Ann Spencer, Attorney, in trust for Joseph Watkins." If Ms. Spencer indorses the check to an automobile dealer in payment for a car that she purchases personally, the automobile dealer (indorsee) has not followed the instructions of the restrictive indorsement. He is liable to Joseph Watkins for any losses that arise because of his noncompliance with the restrictive indorsement.

*O*THER ISSUES CONCERNING INDORSEMENTS

Misspelled or Wrong Name

Where the name of a payee or indorsee is misspelled on a negotiable instrument, the payee or indorsee can indorse the instrument in the misspelled name, the correct name, or both. For example, if Susan Worth receives a check payable to "Susan Wirth," she can indorse the check "Susan Wirth" or "Susan Worth" or both. A person paying or taking the instrument for value or collection may require signature in both the misspelled and the correct name [UCC 3-204(d)].

Entrepreneur and the Law

MULTIPLE PAYEES OR INDORSEES

Drawers, makers, and indorsers often make checks, promissory notes, and other negotiable instruments payable to two or more payees or indorsees. The question then arises: Can the instrument be negotiated by the signature of one payee or indorsee, or are all of their signatures required to negotiate the instrument?

UCC 3-110(d) of Revised Article 3 and cases that have interpreted that section establish the following rules:

- If an instrument is *payable jointly* using the word "and" (e.g., pay to Shou-Yi Kang and Min-Wer Chen), both

persons' indorsement is necessary to negotiate the instrument.

- If the instrument is *payable in the alternative* using the word "or" (e.g., pay to Shou-Yi Kang or Min-Wer Chen), either person's indorsement alone is sufficient to negotiate the instrument.
- If a *virgule*—a slash mark—is used, courts have held that the instrument is payable in the alternative. Thus, if a virgule is used (e.g., pay to Shou-Yi Kang/Min-Wer Chen), either person may individually indorse and negotiate the instrument [*Mumma v. Rainer National Bank*, 808 P.2d 767 (Wash.App. 1991)].

*C*ONCEPT SUMMARY   TYPES OF INDORSEMENTS

Type of Indorsement	Description
Blank	Does not specify a particular indorsee (e.g., /s/ Mary Jones). This indorsement creates bearer paper.
Special	Specifies the person to whom the indorser intends the instrument to be payable (e.g., "Pay to the order of John Smith" /s/ Mary Jones). This indorsement creates order paper. [If it is not payable to order (e.g., "Pay to John Smith" /s/ Mary Jones), it can be converted to order paper (e.g., "Pay to the order of Fred Roe" /s/ John Smith).]
Unqualified	Does not disclaim or limit liability. The indorsee is liable on the instrument if it is not paid by the maker, acceptor, or drawer.
Qualified	Disclaims or limits the liability of the indorsee. There are two types: 1. Special qualified indorsement (e.g., "Pay to the order of John Smith, without recourse" /s/ Mary Jones). 2. Blank qualified indorsement (e.g., "Without recourse" /s/ Mary Jones).
Nonrestrictive	No instructions or conditions attached to the payment of funds (e.g., "Pay to John Smith or order" /s/ Mary Jones).
Restrictive	Conditions or instructions restrict the indorsee's rights. There are four types: 1. Conditional indorsement (e.g., "Pay to John Smith if he completes construction of my garage by June 1, 1996" /s/ Mary Jones). 2. Indorsement prohibiting further indorsement (e.g., "Pay to John Smith only" /s/ Mary Jones). 3. Indorsement for deposit or collection (e.g., "For deposit only" /s/ Mary Jones). 4. Indorsement in trust (e.g., "Pay to John Smith, trustee" /s/ Mary Jones).

Forged Indorsements

Article 3 establishes certain rules for assessing liability when a negotiable instrument has been paid over a **forged document**. With few exceptions, unauthorized indorsements are wholly inoperative as that of the person whose name is signed [UCC 3-401(a)]. Where an indorsement on an instrument has been forged or is unauthorized, the general rule is that the loss falls on the party who first takes the forged instrument after the forgery.

forged indorsement
The forged signature of a payee or holder on a negotiable instrument.

Consider This Example   Suppose Andy draws a check payable to the order of Mallory. Leslie steals the check from Mallory, forges Mallory's indorsement, and cashes the check at the Liquor Store. The Liquor Store is liable. Andy, the drawer, is not. The Liquor Store can recover from Leslie, the forger (if she can be found).

There are two exceptions to this rule where a drawer or maker bears the loss where an indorsement is forged. The rules governing these circumstances—the *imposter rule* and the *fictitious payee rule*—are discussed in the paragraphs that follow.

The Imposter Rule

For purposes of the imposter rule, an **imposter** is one who impersonates a payee and induces the maker or drawer to issue an instrument in the payee's name and to give the instrument to the imposter. If the imposter forges the indorsement of the named payee, the drawer or maker is liable on the instrument to any person who, in good faith, pays the instrument or takes it for value or for collection [UCC 3-404(a)]. This is called the **imposter rule**.

imposter
A person who impersonates a payee and induces a maker or drawer to issue an instrument in the payee's name and to give it to the imposter.

imposter rule
A rule that says if an imposter forges the indorsement of the named payee, the drawer or maker is liable on the instrument and bears the loss.

Consider This Example   Suppose Fred purchases goods by telephone from Cynthia. Fred has never met Cynthia. Beverly goes to Fred and pretends to be Cynthia. Fred draws a check payable to the order of Cynthia and gives the check to Beverly, believing her to be Cynthia. Beverly forges Cynthia's indorsement and cashes the check at the Liquor Store. Under the imposter rule, Fred is liable. The Liquor Store is not. This is because Fred was in the best position to have prevented the forged indorsement.

The imposter rule does not apply if the wrongdoer poses as the agent of the drawer or maker. For instance, suppose in the prior example that Beverly lied to Fred and said that she was Cynthia's agent. Believing this, Fred draws the check payable to the order of Cynthia and gives it to Beverly. Beverly forges Cynthia's indorsement and cashes the check at the Liquor Store. Here, the Liquor Store is liable because the imposter rule does not apply. The Liquor Store may recover from Beverly, if she can be found.

In the following case, the court applied the imposter rule.

Cornwell Quality Tool Co. v. Centran Bank
532 N.E.2d 772 (1987)
Court of Appeals of Ohio

CASE 24.2

FACTS

Linda Zelnar embezzled $57,000 from Akron Novelty Company while she was employed there as a bookkeeper. Her defalcation was discovered, and she was discharged on April 6, 1984. On April 30, 1984, Zelnar was employed as an accounts payable clerk at Cornwell Quality Tool Company (Cornwell). She filed an employee application listing Akron

Novelty as her previous employer, but Cornwell did not make any inquiry about this employment. Zelnar's duties at Cornwell included the preparation of checks to pay the company's creditors. Cornwell regularly did business with Model Industries, Inc., of Chicago. When mailing more than one check to a creditor, it was Cornwell's practice to make the first check in the group payable to the full name of the payee

(case continues)

(e.g., Model Industries, Inc., of Chicago) and the remaining checks payable to an abbreviated name (e.g., "Model"). The first check would be inserted in the window of the envelope, and the remaining checks would be placed behind this check.

Zelnar opened an account at Centran Bank in the name of Linda R. Zelnar, d.b.a. "Model." Over a three-month period, she prepared six checks payable to "Model," which were drawn on Cornwell's account at First National Bank. She presented the checks to her superiors at Cornwell for proper signatures and then took the checks, indorsed them "For Deposit Only, Model," and deposited them in her account at Centran. First National debited Cornwell's account when the checks were presented for payment. The checks exceeded $50,000. When Cornwell discovered the embezzlement, it sued Centran Bank, alleging that it had failed to exercise ordinary care in establishing Zelnar's account and collecting the "Model" checks. The trial court applied the imposter rule and found Cornwell liable on the checks. The court granted summary judgment to the bank. Cornwell appealed.

ISSUE

Does the imposter rule prevent Cornwell from recovering from Centran Bank?

IN THE LANGUAGE OF THE COURT

Capioppo, Judge Application of the imposter rule deems a forgery effective to pass good title to a negotiable instrument. The rule is an exception to the strict liability imposed on a bank that pays on a forged instrument. The loss is shifted to the drawer because the responsibility for the payment can be attributed more to the drawer's actions than to the bank's failure to obtain a proper indorsement.

The policy behind this rule is explained in Official Comment 4: The principle followed is that the loss should fall upon the employer as a risk of his business enterprise rather than upon the subsequent holder or drawee. The reasons are that the employer is normally in a better position to prevent such forgeries by reasonable care in the selection or supervision of his employees, or, if he is not, is at least in a better position to cover the loss by fidelity insurance, and that the cost of such insurance is properly an expense of his business rather than of the business of the holder or drawee.

To receive protection of this rule, Centran has to meet both prongs of the imposter rule: (1) that Linda Zelnar supplied the name of the payee, "Model," to her employer, Cornwell, and (2) that Linda Zelnar intended the payee, "Model," to have no interest in the checks. Linda Zelnar freely admitted that, at the time she presented the checks to her superiors for their signatures, she never intended the true payee, Model Industries, Inc., of Chicago, to have any interest in the checks.

DECISION AND REMEDY

The court of appeals held that the imposter rule made Cornwell, the drawer, liable on the checks. Affirmed.

Case Questions

Critical Legal Thinking Should the law recognize the imposter rule? Or should holders and drawee/payor/collecting banks always be held liable for forged documents?

Ethics Did Ms. Zelnar act ethically in this case? Did Cornwell act ethically in suing the bank?

Business Application As an employer, what is the moral of this case?

The Fictitious Payee Rule

fictitious payee rule

A rule that says the drawer or maker is liable on a forged or unauthorized indorsement of a fictitious payee.

A drawer or maker is liable on a forged or unauthorized indorsement under the **fictitious payee rule**. This rule applies when a person signing as or on behalf of a drawer or maker intends the named payee to have no interest in the instrument or the person identified as the payee is a fictitious person [UCC 3-404(b)].

Consider This Example Marcia is the treasurer of the Weld Corporation. As treasurer, Marcia makes out and signs the payroll checks for the company. Marcia draws a payroll check to the order of her neighbor Harold Green, who does not work for the company. Marcia does not intend for Harold to receive this money. She indorses Harold's name on the check and names herself as the indorsee. She cashes the check at the Liquor Store. Under the fictitious payee rule, Weld Corporation is liable because it was in a better position to have prevented the fraud.

The fictitious payee rule also applies if an agent or employee of the drawer or maker supplies the drawer or maker with the name of the fictitious payee [UCC 3-405(c)].

Consider This Example   Elizabeth is an accountant for the Baldridge Corporation. She is responsible for drawing up a list of employees who are to receive payroll checks. The treasurer of Baldridge Corporation actually signs the checks. Elizabeth places the name "Annabelle Armstrong" (a fictitious person) on the list. Baldridge Corporation issues a payroll check to this fictitious person. Elizabeth indorses the instrument "Annabelle Armstrong" and names herself as indorsee. She cashes the check at the Liquor Store. Under the fictitious payee rule, Baldridge Corporation is liable. The Liquor Store is not.

Ethical Perspective

THE FICTITIOUS PAYEE: SHOULD THE EMPLOYER ALWAYS BEAR THE LOSS?

In the summer of 1981, John Efler, a section manager of Prudential-Bache's dividend department, launched an embezzlement scheme that successfully escaped his employer's notice for nearly two years and netted him a cool $18.9-million profit.

The scheme worked like this: On a regular basis, Efler would order the issuance of Prudential-Bache dividend checks, which were drawn on the firm's account with Banker's Trust Company and made payable to phony companies with names like those of some of Prudential-Bache's real corporate clients. Because Efler's department was responsible for making dividend payments to customers, Efler was able to create a trail of false records that gave his coworkers the impression that Prudential-Bache procedures were followed and that the checks were requisitioned by one person and approved by another. In reality, Efler both requested and approved the checks.

Once a check was issued, Lawrence Artese, a friend of Efler's, would deposit it in an account that had been opened in the name of the phony corporations named on the Prudential-Bache check at Citibank. Artese had paid $165,000 in bribes to two Citibank employees. In exchange, the bank employees set up checking accounts without proper records and with fake corporate officers. Additionally, they did not file transaction reports to the Internal Revenue Service. (Such reports are required for

cash withdrawals in excess of $10,000.) This enabled Artese to deposit phony checks and leave with a valise full of cash on a nearly daily basis. During one five-month period, for example, Artese deposited $3.7 million in checks at Citibank and withdrew an equal amount in cash.

Eventually, after a tip was received, a Prudential-Bache audit uncovered Efler's scheme.

In an attempt to recover the laundered funds, Prudential-Bache brought an action against Citibank in a New York State court. The suit involved a variety of civil claims, including conversion and commercial bad faith. Citibank responded by asserting that the action should be dismissed under the fictitious payee rule. That UCC rule passes the burden of the loss to the employer when an employee issues checks to nonexistent (i.e., fictitious) parties.

The New York Court of Appeals, which is the highest court of the state, held that the fictitious payee rule applied to the fact situation. Therefore, under New York's UCC, the loss occasioned by Prudential-Bache's employee's wrongdoing should fall upon it, rather than upon the depository bank, Citibank. [*Prudential-Bache Securities, Inc. v. Citibank, N.A.*, 539 N.Y.S.2d 699 (N.Y. 1989)]

1. Did Efler act ethically in this case? Did he act illegally?
2. Was it morally right for Prudential-Bache to try to shift liability for its employee's defalcations to Citibank?

Working the Web

Chambers of Commerce Directory Here you can find information on chambers of commerce anywhere in the world.

Visit at **clickcity.com**

Companies Online At this site, you can search for companies by name, city, and ticker symbol.

Visit at **www.companiesonline.com**

(box continues)

Doing Business Guides A group of law firms called Lex Mundi has written guides to doing business in many jurisdictions. Some are even available on audio if you have the right computer equipment.

Visit at **www.hg.org/guides.html**

CYBER EXERCISES

1. Using the Chambers of Commerce Directory, find the chamber of commerce in your city.

2. Find a company in your city using Companies Online.

3. Is there a Doing Business Guide for Sweden?

CASES AND EXERCISES

CRITICAL LEGAL THINKING CASES

24.1. Samuel C. Mazilly wrote a personal check that was drawn on Calcasieu-Marine National Bank of Lake Charles, Inc. (CMN Bank). The check was made payable to the order of Lee St. Mary and was delivered to him. St. Mary indorsed the check in blank and delivered it to Leland H. Coltharp, Sr., in payment for some livestock. Coltharp accepted the check and took it to the City Savings Bank & Trust Company (City Savings) to deposit it. He indorsed the check as follows: "Pay to the order of City Savings Bank & Trust Company, DeRidder, Louisiana." City Savings accepted the check and forwarded it to CMN Bank for payment. The check never arrived at CMN Bank. Some unknown person stole the check while it was in transit and presented it directly to CMN Bank for payment. The teller at CMN Bank cashed the check without indorsement of the person who presented it. At the time CMN Bank accepts the check, is it order or bearer paper? [*Coltharp v. Calcasieu-Marine National Bank of Lake Charles, Inc.*, 199 So.2d 568 (La.App. 1967)]

24.2. Charles Pribus owed $126,500 to Ford and Mary Williams (Williams). At Pribus's request, his mother, Helen Pribus, executed a promissory note for $126,500 in favor of the Williams. Within a few months, the Williams bought Philip L. Bush's option to purchase an apartment complex in Texas. As partial payment for the option, Williams gave Bush the promissory note they had received from Helen Pribus. A letter, which was signed by Williams, was stapled to the note. It read: "For valuable consideration, the undersigned do hereby assign the attached note to Philip L. Bush." There was sufficient space on the note itself to write an indorsement and the words contained in the letter. When Bush went to collect on the note, Helen Pribus refused to pay. Bush sued Pribus to enforce the note. Is the note properly indorsed? [*Pribus v. Bush*, 31 UCC Rep.Serv. 599 (Cal.App. 1981)]

24.3. Wilson was the office manager of Palmer & Ray Dental Supply of Abilene, Inc. (Dental Supply). Each workday, James

Frank Ray, the president of Dental Supply, would take the checks received from customers and place them on Wilson's desk. Wilson was authorized to (1) indorse these checks through the use of a rubber stamp reading "Palmer & Ray Dental Supply, Inc. of Abilene, Box 2894, 3110 B.N. 1st, Abilene, Texas 79603" and (2) deposit the indorsed checks into the company's account at the First National Bank of Abilene (First National Bank). After several years of working at Dental Supply, Wilson began to embezzle money from the company. Her scheme involved indorsing the checks made payable to Dental Supply with the rubber stamp and drawing cash on them instead of making a deposit. The bank cashed these checks without requiring any further indorsement. Is the bank liable? [*Palmer & Ray Dental Supply of Abilene, Inc. v. First National Bank of Abilene*, 477 S.W.2d 954 (Tex.App. 1972)]

24.4. Charles R. Joy was the bankruptcy receiver for the Quantum Developments Company. In this capacity, he had the authority to handle any funds received by the newly bankrupt corporation. On March 21, 1973, the American Fidelity Fire Insurance Company (American Fidelity) was ordered by the District Court of the Virgin Islands to deliver a check in the amount of $84,858 to the court. This represented an amount of money owed by American Fidelity to Quantum. Joy was contacted after the check was delivered to the court. He went to the courthouse and picked up the check, which had been made payable to his order. Before Joy left the courthouse, he indorsed the check as follows: "For deposit in Quantum Acct. Quantum Bankruptcy. Charles R. Joy." What type of indorsement is this and what effect does it have? [*American Fidelity Fire Insurance Company v. Joy*, 17 UCC Rep.Serv. 454 (D.V.I. 1975)]

24.5. William Gabovitch agreed to purchase $17,210.50 worth of Scotch malt whiskey from a distillery in Scotland. Gabovitch was to forward payment for the whiskey, which would then be delivered to a bonded warehouse in Scotland.

As partial payment for the liquor, Gabovitch sent four checks to the distillery, made payable to "Scotch Whiskey, Inc." These checks were drawn on Gabovitch's account with the Coolidge Bank & Trust Company (Coolidge Bank). The distillery received the checks and indorsed them as follows: "Scotch Whiskey, Inc." When the checks were presented to Coolidge Bank for payment, the bank paid them and debited Gabovitch's account. Gabovitch never received the Scotch whiskey. Instead, Scotch Whiskey, Inc., shipped another liquor it produced to the warehouse in Scotland. When Gabovitch learned of the improper shipment, he sued Coolidge Bank to recover on the checks it paid to Scotch Whiskey, Inc. Who wins? [*Gabovitch v. Coolidge Bank & Trust Company*, 29 UCC Rep.Serv. 1313 (Ma.App. 1980)]

24.6. Murray Walter, Inc. (Walter, Inc.), was the general contractor for the construction of a waste treatment plant in New Hampshire. Walter, Inc., contracted with H. Johnson Electric, Inc. (Johnson Electric), to install the electrical system in the treatment plant. Johnson Electric purchased its supplies for the project from General Electric Supply (G.E. Supply). On May 1, 1980, Walter, Inc., issued a check payable to "Johnson Electric and G.E. Supply" in the amount of $54,900 drawn on its account at Marine Midland Bank (Marine Midland). Walter, Inc., made the check payable to both the subcontractor and its material supplier to be certain that the supplier was paid by Johnson Electric. Despite this precautionary measure, Johnson Electric negotiated the check without G.E. Supply's indorsement, and the check was paid by Marine Midland. Johnson Electric never paid G.E. Supply. G.E. Supply then demanded payment from Walter, Inc. When Walter, Inc., learned that Marine Midland paid the check without G.E. Supply's indorsement, it demanded to be reimbursed. When Marine Midland refused, Walter, Inc., sued Marine Midland to recover for the check. Is Johnson Electric's indorsement sufficient to legally negotiate the check to Marine Midland? [*Murray Walter, Inc. v. Marine Midland Bank*, 39 UCC Rep.Serv. 972 (N.Y.Sup.Ct. 1984)]

ETHICS CASES

24.7. Llobell was the president of Klem Ventures, Ltd. (Klem Ventures). Klem Ventures owed P.J. Panzeca, Inc. (Panzeca), a total of $47,000 for labor and materials used in a construction project. On February 1, 1972, Llobell, acting in his capacity as president, executed two notes to pay the debt owed by Klem Ventures to Panzeca. One of the notes was in the amount of $18,000 and was payable 30 days from the date of making; the other note was for $29,000 and was payable 60 days from the date of making. Llobell signed both notes on the reverse side. His signature was the only thing written on the back of the notes. When Panzeca presented the notes for payment, they were both dishonored. On September 20, 1974, Panzeca sued Llobell, claiming that he was personally liable for the amount of the notes. Llobell argued he was not personally liable because he signed the notes as an agent for the corporation. Did Llobell act ethically in denying personal liability? Who wins? [*P.J. Panzeca, Inc. v. Llobell*, 19 UCC Rep.Serv. 564 (N.Y.Sup.Ct. 1976)]

24.8. Samuel K. Yucht was an attorney practicing law in the state of New Jersey. Yucht specialized in personal injury cases. Over the course of a year, Yucht submitted numerous claims on behalf of his clients against the Allstate Insurance Company (Allstate). In each case, Yucht informed Allstate that his client was willing to settle the claim and submitted a signed release. All of the signatures on the releases were forged by Yucht. When Allstate issued settlement checks made payable to the client and Yucht as their attorney, Yucht again forged his clients' indorsements. He added his own indorsement and then deposited the checks into his personal account. Yucht never informed his clients of the settlements he had made on their behalf or of the money he had received in their names. Did Yucht act ethically in this case? Is Allstate liable for the losses caused by Yucht's actions under the imposter rule? [*Clients' Security Fund of the Bar of New Jersey v. Allstate Insurance Company*, 5 UCC Rep.Serv. 2d 127 (N.J.Sup.Ct. 1987)]

CRITICAL LEGAL THINKING WRITING ASSIGNMENT

Read Case A.24 in the Case Appendix [*Dynalectron Corporation v. Equitable Trust Company*]. This case is excerpted from the court of appeals opinion. Review and brief the case. In your brief, be sure to answer the following questions.

1. Who was the plaintiff? Who was the defendant?
2. What was the issue presented to the court?
3. How did the court decide this issue?

25

Holder in Due Course and Defenses

If one wants to know the real value of money, he needs but to borrow some from his friends.

CONFUCIUS *Analects, c. 500 B.C.*

Chapter Objectives

After studying this chapter you should be able to

1. Define *holder* and *holder in due course*.
2. Identify and apply the requirements for becoming a holder in due course.
3. Describe the signature liability of makers, drawers, drawees, and accommodation parties.
4. Distinguish between primary and secondary liability on negotiable instruments.
5. List the transfer warranties and describe the liability of parties for breaching them.
6. List the presentment warranties and describe the liability of parties for breaching them.
7. Identify real defenses that can be asserted against a holder in due course.
8. Identify personal defenses that cannot be asserted against a holder in due course.
9. Describe how liability on a negotiable instrument is discharged.
10. Describe the Federal Trade Commission rule that prohibits the holder in due course rule in consumer transactions.

Chapter Contents

If payment is not made on a negotiable instrument when it is due, the holder can use the court system to enforce the instrument. Various parties, including both signers and non-signers, may be liable on it. Some parties are *primarily liable* on the instrument, whereas others are *secondarily liable*. Accommodation parties (i.e., guarantors) can also be held liable.

Recall that the primary purpose of commercial paper is to act as a substitute for money. For this to occur, the holder of a negotiable instrument must qualify as a *holder in due course (HDC)*. Commercial paper held by an HDC is virtually as good as money because HDCs take an instrument free of all claims and most defenses that can be asserted by other parties.

This chapter discusses the liability of parties on negotiable instruments, the requirements that must be met to qualify as an HDC, the defenses that can be raised against the imposition of liability, and the discharge of liability.

A negotiable bill or note is a courier without luggage.

Gibson, C.J.
Overton v. Tyler *(1846)*

Holder Versus Holder in Due Course

Two of the most important concepts of the law of negotiable instruments are that of a *holder* and a *holder in due course*. A **holder** is a person in possession of an instrument that is payable to bearer or an identified person who is in possession of an instrument payable to that person [UCC 1-201(20)]. The holder of a negotiable instrument has the same rights as an assignee of an ordinary nonnegotiable contract. That is, the holder is subject to all of the claims and defenses that can be asserted against the transferor.

The concept of holder in due course is unique to the area of negotiable instruments. A **holder in due course (HDC)** is a holder who takes an instrument for value, in good faith, and without notice that it is defective or is overdue. An HDC takes a negotiable instrument free of all claims and most defenses that can be asserted against the transferor of the instrument. Only *real defenses*—and not *personal defenses*—may be asserted against an HDC. (Defenses are discussed later in this chapter.) Thus, an HDC can acquire greater rights than those of the transferor.

The difference between the concepts of holder and holder in due course is illustrated by the following example. John purchases an automobile from Shannen. At the time of sale, Shannen tells John that the car has had only one previous owner and has been driven

holder

A person who is in possession of a negotiable instrument that is drawn, issued, or indorsed to him or his order, to bearer, or in blank.

holder in due course (HDC)

A holder who takes a negotiable instrument for value, in good faith, and without notice that it is defective or is overdue.

The Federal Trade Commission (FTC), a federal administrative agency, has adopted a rule that eliminates the holder in due course status with regards to consumer credit transactions, such as the purchase of this automobile on credit by a consumer.

only 20,000 miles. John, relying on these statements, purchases the car. He pays 10 percent down and signs a promissory note to pay the remainder of the purchase price, with interest, in 12 equal monthly installments. Shannen transfers the note to Patricia. Then John discovers the car has actually had four previous owners and had been driven 100,000 miles. If Patricia were a *holder* (but not an HDC) of the note, John could assert Shannen's fraudulent representations against enforcement of the note by Patricia. John could rescind the note and refuse to pay Patricia. Patricia's only recourse would be against Shannen.

If Patricia qualified as an *HDC*, however, the result would be different. John could not assert Shannen's fraudulent conduct against enforcement of the note by Patricia. This is because this type of fraud is a personal defense that cannot be raised against an HDC. Therefore, Patricia could enforce the note against John. John's only recourse would be against Shannen, if she could be found.

*R*EQUIREMENTS FOR HDC STATUS

To qualify as an HDC, the transferee must meet the requirements established by the UCC: The person must be the *holder* of a negotiable instrument that was taken (1) for value, (2) in good faith, (3) without notice that it is overdue, dishonored, or encumbered in any way, and (4) without any apparent evidence of forgery, alterations, or irregularity [UCC 3-302]. These requirements are discussed in the paragraphs that follow. Exhibit 25.1 illustrates the holder in due course doctrine.

*E*XHIBIT 25.1   *Holder in Due Course*

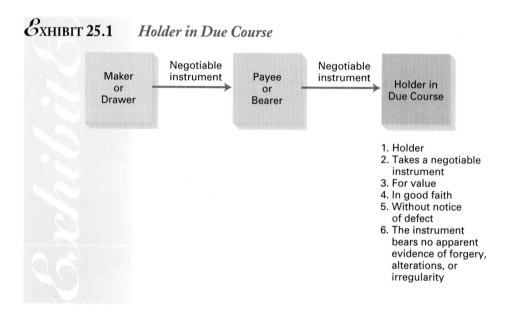

Taking for Value

The holder must have *given value* for the negotiable instrument to qualify as an HDC [UCC 3-302(a)(2)(i)]. For example, suppose Ted draws a check "payable to the order of Mary Smith" and delivers the check to Mary. Mary indorses it and gives it as a gift to her daughter. Mary's daughter cannot qualify as an HDC because she has not given value for it. The purchaser of a limited interest in a negotiable instrument is an HDC only to the extent of the interest purchased.

Under the UCC, value has been given if the holder [UCC 3-303]

1. Performs the agreed-upon promise.
2. Acquires a security interest or lien on the instrument.
3. Takes the instrument in payment of or as security for an antecedent claim.
4. Gives a negotiable instrument as payment.
5. Gives an irrevocable obligation as payment.

If a person promises to perform but has not yet done so, no value has been given and he or she is not an HDC.

Consider This Example   Karen executes a note payable to Fred for $3,000 for goods she has purchased from him. Fred transfers the note to Amy for her promise to pay the note in 90 days. Before Amy pays for the note, Karen discovers that the goods she purchased from Fred are defective. Karen can raise this defect against enforcement of the note by Amy because no value has yet been given for the note. If Amy had already paid for the note, she would qualify as an HDC, and Karen could not raise the issue of defect against enforcement of the note by Amy.

Taking in Good Faith

A holder must take the instrument in **good faith** to qualify as an HDC [UCC 3-302(a)(2)(ii)]. Good faith means honesty in fact in the conduct or transaction concerned [UCC 1-201(19)]. Honesty in fact is a subjective test that examines the holder's actual belief. A holder's subjective belief can be inferred from the circumstances.

Consider This Example   If a sophisticated holder acquires an instrument from a stranger under suspicious circumstances and at a deep discount, it could be inferred that the holder did not take the instrument in good faith. However, a naive person who acquired the same instrument at the same discount may be found to have acted in good faith and thereby to have qualified as an HDC. Each case must be reviewed separately.

Note that the good faith test applies only to the holder. It does not apply to the transferor of the instrument. For example, suppose a thief steals a negotiable instrument and transfers it to Harry. Harry does not know that the instrument is stolen. Harry meets the good faith test and qualifies as an HDC.

Taking Without Notice of Defect

Except as allowed under the shelter principle (discussed later in this chapter), a person cannot qualify as an HDC if he or she has *notice* that the instrument is defective in any of the following ways [UCC 3-302(a)(2)]:

- It is overdue.
- It has been dishonored.
- It contains an unauthorized signature or has been altered.
- There is a claim to it by another person.
- There is a defense against it.

Overdue Instruments   If a **time instrument** is not paid on its expressed due date, it becomes overdue the next day. The fact that an instrument has not been paid when due indicates that there is some defect to its payment.

Consider This Example   Suppose that a promissory note is due June 15, 1998. To qualify as an HDC, a purchaser must acquire the note before midnight of June 15, 1998. A purchaser who acquires the note on June 16 or later is a holder but not an HDC. Often, a debt is payable in installments or in a series of notes. If a maker misses an installment pay-

---

Business Brief

If a holder of a negotiable instrument qualifies as a *holder in due course (HDC)*, the HDC takes the instrument free of all claims and most defenses that can be asserted by other parties. In other words, the instrument is almost as good as cash.

good faith

Honesty in fact in the conduct or transaction concerned. This is a subjective test.

taking in good faith requirement

A holder must take the instrument in *good faith* to qualify as an HDC.

taking without notice of defect requirement

A person cannot qualify as an HDC if he or she has notice that the instrument is defective in certain ways.

time instrument

An instrument that specifies a definite date for payment of the instrument.

ment or fails to pay one note in a series of notes, the purchaser of the instrument is on notice that it is overdue [UCC 3-304(b)].

demand instrument

An instrument payable on demand.

A **demand instrument** is payable on demand. A purchaser cannot be an HDC if the instrument is acquired either (1) after demand or (2) at an unreasonable length of time after its issue. A "reasonable time" for presenting a check for payment is presumed to be 90 days. Business practices and the circumstances of the case determine a reasonable time for the payment of other demand instruments [UCC 3-304(a)].

dishonored

Occurs when an instrument has been presented for payment and payment has been refused.

Dishonored Instruments   An instrument is **dishonored** when it is presented for payment and payment is refused. A holder who takes the instrument with notice of its dishonor cannot qualify as an HDC. For example, a person who takes a check that has been marked by the payor bank "payment refused—insufficient funds" cannot qualify as an HDC.

red light doctrine

A doctrine that says a holder cannot qualify as an HDC if he or she has notice of an unauthorized signature or an alteration of the instrument, or any adverse claim against or defense to its payment.

Red Light Doctrine   A holder cannot qualify as an HDC if he or she has notice that the instrument contains an unauthorized signature or has been altered or that there is any adverse claim against or defense to its payment. This is commonly referred to as the **red light doctrine**.

Notice of a defect is given when the holder has (1) actual knowledge of the defect, (2) received a notice or notification of the defect, or (3) reason to know from the facts and circumstances that the defect exists [UCC 1-201(25)]. The filing of a public notice does not of itself constitute notice unless the person actually reads the public notice [UCC 3-302(b)].

no evidence of forgery, alterations, or irregularity requirement

A holder cannot become an HDC to an instrument that is apparently forged or altered or is otherwise so irregular or incomplete as to call into question its authenticity.

No Evidence of Forgery, Alterations, or Irregularity

A holder does not qualify as an HDC if at the time the instrument was issued or negotiated to the holder it bore apparent evidence of forgery or alteration or was otherwise so irregular or incomplete as to call into question its authenticity [UCC 3-302(a)(1)].

Clever and undetectable forgeries and alterations are not classified as obvious irregularities. Determining whether a forgery or alteration is apparent and whether the instrument is so irregular or incomplete that its authenticity should be questioned are issues of fact that must be decided on a case-by-case basis.

Payee as an HDC

Payees generally do not meet the requirements for being an HDC because they know about any claims or defenses against the instrument. However, in a few situations, a payee who does not have such knowledge would qualify as an HDC.

Consider This Example   Suppose Kate purchases an automobile from Jake for $5,000. Jake owes Sherry Smith $5,000 from another transaction. Jake has Kate make out the $5,000 check for the automobile "payable to the order of Sherry Smith." Jake gives the check to Sherry. The car Jake sold to Kate is defective, and she wants to rescind the purchase. Sherry (payee), who did not have notice of the defect in the car, is an HDC. As such, Sherry can enforce the check against Kate. Kate's only recourse is to recover from Jake.

Contemporary Business Application _____

ACQUIRING HDC STATUS UNDER THE SHELTER PRINCIPLE

A holder who does qualify as a holder in due course in his or her own right becomes a holder in due course if he or she acquires the instrument through a holder in due course. This is called the **shelter principle**.

Consider This Example

Jason buys a used car from Debbie. He pays 10 percent down and signs a negotiable promissory note promising to pay Debbie the remainder of the purchase price with interest in 36 equal monthly installments. At the time of sale, Debbie materially misrepresented the mileage of the automobile. Later, Debbie negotiates the note to Eric, who has no notice of the misrepresentation. Eric, a holder in due course, negotiates the note to Jaime. Assume Jaime does not qualify as an HDC in her own right. She becomes an HDC, however, because she acquired the note through an HDC (Eric). Jaime can enforce the note against Jason.

To qualify as an HDC under the shelter principle, the following rules apply:

- The holder does not have to qualify as an HDC in his or her own right.
- The holder must acquire the instrument from an HDC or be able to trace his or her title back to an HDC.
- The holder must not have been a party to a fraud or illegality affecting the instrument.
- The holder cannot have notice of a defense or claim against the payment of the instrument.

SIGNATURE LIABILITY OF PARTIES

A person cannot be held *contractually liable* on a negotiable instrument unless his or her signature appears on it [UCC 3-401(a)]. Therefore, this type of liability is often referred to as **signature liability** or **contract liability**. The signatures on a negotiable instrument identify those who are obligated to pay it. If it is unclear who the signer is, parol evidence can identify the signer. This liability does not attach to bearer paper since no indorsement is needed.

Signers of instruments sign in many different capacities, including makers of notes and certificates of deposit, drawers of drafts and checks, drawees who certify or accept checks and drafts, indorsers who indorse an instrument, agents who sign on behalf of others, and accommodation parties.

The location of the signature on the instrument generally determines the signer's capacity. For example, a signature in the lower right-hand corner of a check indicates that the signer is the drawer of the check, and a signature in the lower right-hand corner of a promissory note indicates the signer is the maker of the note. The signature of the drawee named in a draft on the face of the draft or other location on the draft indicates that the signer is an acceptor of the draft. Most indorsements appear on the back or reverse side of an instrument. Unless the instrument clearly indicates that such a signature is made in some other capacity, it is presumed to be that of the indorser.

Every party that signs a negotiable instrument (except a qualified indorser and agents that properly sign the instrument) is either *primarily* or *secondarily* liable on the instrument. The following discussion outlines the particular liability of signers.

Signature Defined

The **signature** on a negotiable instrument can be any name, word, or mark used in lieu of a written signature [UCC 3-401(b)]. In other words, a signature is any symbol that is (1) handwritten, typed, printed, stamped, or made in almost any other manner and (2) executed or adopted by a party to authenticate a writing [UCC 1-201(39)]. This rule permits trade names and other assumed names to be used as signatures on negotiable instruments.

The unauthorized signature of a person on an instrument is ineffective as that person's signature. It is effective as the signature of the unauthorized signer in favor of an HDC, however. For example, a person who forges a signature on a check may be held liable to an HDC. An unauthorized signature may be ratified [UCC 3-403(a)].

Agent's Signature

A person may either sign a negotiable instrument him- or herself or authorize a representative to sign the instrument on his or her behalf [UCC 3-401(a)]. The representative is the **agent** and the represented person is the **principal**. The authority of an agent to sign an instrument is established under general agency law. No special form of appointment is necessary.

signature liability

A person cannot be held contractually liable on a negotiable instrument unless his or her signature appears on the instrument. Also called *contract liability*.

signer

A person signing an instrument who acts in the capacity of (1) a maker of notes and certificates of deposit, (2) a drawer of drafts and checks, (3) a drawee who certifies or accepts checks and drafts, (4) an indorser who indorses an instrument, (5) an agent who signs on behalf of others, or (6) an accommodation party.

signature

Any name, word, or mark used in lieu of a written signature; any symbol that is (1) handwritten, typed, printed, stamped, or made in almost any other manner and (2) executed or adopted by a party to authenticate a writing.

agent

A person who has been authorized to sign a negotiable instrument on behalf of another person.

principal

A person who authorizes an agent to sign a negotiable instrument on his or her behalf.

Authorized Signature If an authorized agent signs an instrument by signing either the name of the principal or the agent's own name, the principal is bound by the signature to the same extent that the principal would be bound if the signature were made on a simple contract. It does not matter whether the principal is identified in the instrument [UCC 3-402(2)].

For example, the following signatures of Anderson, the agent for Puttkammer, on a negotiable instrument would bind Puttkammer on the instrument:

1. Puttkammer, by Anderson, agent.
2. Puttkammer.
3. Puttkammer, Anderson.
4. Anderson.

Whether an authorized agent is personally liable on an instrument he or she signs on behalf of a principal depends on information disclosed in the signature. If the signature shows unambiguously that it is made on behalf of a principal who is identified in the instrument, the agent is not liable on the instrument [UCC 3-402(b)(1)]. The signature in Number 1 in the list above ("Puttkammer, by Anderson, agent") satisfies this requirement.

Unless the agent can prove that the original parties did not intend him or her to be liable on the instrument, if the authorized agent's signature does not show unambiguously that the signature was made in a representative capacity, the agent is liable (1) to an HDC who took the instrument without notice that the agent was not intended to be liable on the instrument and (2) to any person other than an HDC [UCC 3-402(b)(2)].

Number 3 ("Puttkammer, Anderson") and Number 4 ("Anderson") in the previous list place the agent at risk of personal liability to an HDC that does not have notice that the agent was not intended to be liable on the instrument. To avoid liability to a non-HDC in signatures Number 3 ("Puttkammer, Anderson") and Number 4 ("Anderson") in the previous list, the agent would have to prove that the third-party non-HDC did not intend to hold the agent liable on the instrument.

There is one exception to these rules. If an agent signs his or her name as the drawer of a check without indicating the agent's representative status and the check is payable from the account of the principal who is identified on the check, the agent is not liable on the check [UCC 3-402(c)].

Unauthorized Signature An **unauthorized signature** is a signature made by a *purported agent* without authority from the purported principal. Such a signature arises if (1) a person signs a negotiable instrument on behalf of a person for whom he or she is not an agent or (2) an authorized agent exceeds the scope of his or her authority. An unauthorized signature by a purported agent does not act as the signature of the purported principal. The purported agent is liable to any person who in good faith pays the instrument or takes it for value [UCC 3-403(a)]. The purported principal is liable if he or she *ratifies* the unauthorized signature [UCC 3-403(a)].

Consider This Example A purported agent signs a contract and promissory note to purchase a building for a purported principal. Suppose that the purported principal likes the deal and accepts it. He or she has ratified the transaction and is liable on the note.

𝒫RIMARY LIABILITY

Makers of promissory notes and certificates of deposit have **primary liability** for the instrument. Upon signing a promissory note, the maker unconditionally promises to pay the amount stipulated in the note when it is due. Makers are absolutely liable to pay the instrument, subject only to certain real defenses. The holder need not take any action to give rise to this obligation. Generally, the maker is obligated to pay the note according to its original terms. If the note was incomplete when it was issued, the maker is obligated to pay the note as completed as long as he or she authorized the terms as they were filled in [UCC 3-412].

A draft or a check is an order from a drawer to a drawee to pay the instrument to a payee (or other holder) according to its terms. No party is primarily liable when the draft or check is issued because such instruments are merely an order to pay. Thus, a drawee who refuses to pay a draft or a check is not liable to the payee or holder. If there has been a wrongful dishonor of the instrument, the drawee may be liable to the drawer for certain damages.

On occasion, a drawee is requested to accept a draft or check. Acceptance of a draft occurs when the drawee writes the word *accepted* across the face of the draft. The *acceptor*—that is, the drawee—is primarily liable on the instrument. A check, which is a special form of draft, is accepted when it is certified by a bank. The bank's certification discharges the drawer and all prior indorsers from liability on the check. Note that the bank may choose to refuse to certify the check without liability. The issuer of a cashier's check is also primarily liable on the instrument [UCC 3-411].

In the following case, the court held that a comaker was primarily liable on a promissory note.

Business Brief
The following parties are *primarily liable* on negotiable instruments: (1) *makers* of promissory notes and certificates of deposit and (2) *acceptors* of drafts and checks.

Grand Island Production Credit Assn. v. Humphrey
388 N.E.2d 807 (1986)
Supreme Court of Nebraska

CASE 25.1

FACTS
The Grand Island Production Credit Association (Grand Island) is a federally chartered credit union. On November 25, 1980, Carl M. and Beulah C. Humphrey, husband and wife, entered into a loan arrangement with Grand Island for a $50,000 line of credit. Mr. and Mrs. Humphrey signed a line of credit promissory note that provided in part: "As long as the Borrower is not in default, the Association will lend to the Borrower, and the Borrower may borrow and repay and reborrow at any time from date of said 'Line of Credit' Promissory Note in accordance with the terms thereof and prior to maturity thereof, up to an aggregate maximum amount of principal at any one time outstanding of $50,000."

Mr. Humphrey borrowed money against the line of credit to purchase cattle. In January 1981, Mrs. Humphrey went to Grand Island's office and told the loan officer that she had left Mr. Humphrey and filed for a divorce. She told the loan officer not to advance any more money to Mr. Humphrey for cattle purchases. The bank did loan additional money to Mr. Humphrey in accordance with the credit agreement. When the Humphreys failed to pay the outstanding balance on the line of credit, Grand Island sued Mr. and Mrs. Humphrey to recover the unpaid balance of $13,936.71. A default judgment was entered against Mr. Humphrey. The district court held Mrs. Humphrey not liable for the full outstanding balance. Grand Island appealed.

ISSUE
Was Mrs. Humphrey a comaker of the line of credit promissory note and, therefore, primarily liable for the outstanding principal balance of the note, plus interest?

IN THE LANGUAGE OF THE COURT
Krivosha, Chief Justice There is no question that unless the conversation that Mrs. Humphrey had with the Grand Island loan officer in January of 1981 relieved her of her obligation to pay Grand Island, she is equally indebted to Grand Island for the full amount of the debt. We believe Mrs. Humphrey was not so relieved. Had Grand Island refused to advance the funds previously committed, it very well could have been held liable to Mr. Humphrey.

Under the provisions of Neb. UCC § 3-413(1), the maker of a note engages that he or she will pay the instrument according to its tenor at the time of his or her engagement. Mrs. Humphrey admits that she signed the promissory note and the supplemental agreement. Consequently, as a comaker of the note, she is jointly and severally liable for the obligations of the note. If Mrs. Humphrey was to be relieved of this obligation, it was a matter that she needed to arrange and take up with her husband in the divorce action. No such arrangement could, however, be binding
(case continues)

upon Grand Island, which entered into this transaction in reliance upon the promise of both Mr. Humphrey and Mrs. Humphrey that they would be liable and would pay the amounts so advanced. The fact of the pending divorce was irrelevant.

DECISION AND REMEDY

The state supreme court held that Mrs. Humphrey was a comaker on the line of credit promissory note and was therefore primarily liable to Grand Island in the amount of $13,936.71, plus interest. Reversed.

Case Questions

Critical Legal Thinking   Should family problems, such as the separation and divorce action in this case, take precedence over the commercial law rules of the UCC? Why or why not?

Ethics   Was it ethical for Mrs. Humphrey to deny liability on the promissory note in this case?

Business Application   What would have been the economic effects if the district court's decision had been upheld in this case?

SECONDARY LIABILITY

secondary liability
Liability on a negotiable instrument that is imposed on a party only when the party primarily liable on the instrument defaults and fails to pay the instrument when due.

Drawers of checks and drafts and *unqualified indorsers* of negotiable instruments have **secondary liability** on the instrument. This liability is similar to that of a guarantor of a simple contract. It arises when the party primarily liable on the instrument defaults and fails to pay the instrument when due.

Liability of Drawers

If an unaccepted draft or check is dishonored by the drawee or acceptor, the *drawer* is obliged to pay it according to its terms either when it is issued or, if incomplete when issued, as properly completed [UCC 3-414(a)].

Business Brief
The following parties are *secondarily liable* on negotiable instruments: (1) *drawers* on unaccepted drafts and checks and (2) *unqualified indorsers*.

Consider This Example   Elliot draws a check on City Bank "payable to the order of Phyllis Jones." When Phyllis presents the check for payment, City Bank refuses to pay it. Phyllis can collect the amount of the check from Elliot. This is because Elliot—the drawer—is secondarily liable on the check when it is dishonored.

Liability of Unqualified Indorsers

Unqualified indorsers have *secondary liability* on negotiable instruments. In other words, they must pay any dishonored instrument to the holder or to any subsequent indorser according to its terms, when issued or properly completed. Unless otherwise agreed, indorsers are liable to each other in the order in which they indorsed the instrument [UCC 3-415(a)].

Consider This Example   Dara borrows $10,000 from Todd and signs a promissory note promising to pay Todd this amount plus interest in one year. Todd indorses the note and negotiates it to Frank. Frank indorses the note and negotiates it to Linda. Dara refuses to pay the note when it is presented for payment by Linda. Because Frank became secondarily liable on the note when he indorsed it to Linda, he must pay the note to her. He can then require Todd to pay the note because Todd (as payee) became secondarily liable on the note when he indorsed it to Frank. Todd can then enforce the note against Dara. Linda could have skipped over Frank and required the payee, Todd, to pay the note. In this instance, Frank would have been relieved of any further liability because he indorsed the instrument after the payee.

indorsers' liability
Unqualified indorsers are secondarily liable on negotiable instruments they indorse; *qualified indorsers* disclaim liability and are not secondarily liable on instruments they indorse.

Liability of Qualified Indorsers

Qualified indorsers (i.e., indorsers who indorse instruments "without recourse" or similar language that disclaims liability) are not secondarily liable on the instrument. This is because they have expressly disclaimed liability [UCC 3-415(b)]. The drawer can disclaim all liability on a draft (but not a check) by drawing the instrument "without recourse." In this instance, the drawer becomes a qualified drawer [UCC 3-414(e)]. However, many payees will not accept a draft or check that has been drawn without recourse.

Requirements for Imposing Secondary Liability

Parties are secondarily liable on a negotiable instrument only if the following requirements are met.

1. **The Instrument Is Properly Presented for Payment** *Presentment* is a demand for acceptance or payment of an instrument made upon the maker, the acceptor, the drawee, or other payor by or on behalf of the holder. Presentment may be made by any commercially reasonable means, including oral, written, or electronic communication. Presentment is effective when it is received by the person to whom presentment is made [UCC 3-501].

2. **The Instrument Is Dishonored** An instrument is dishonored when acceptance or payment of the instrument is refused or cannot be obtained from the party required to accept or pay the instrument within the prescribed time after presentment is duly made [UCC 3-502].

3. **Timely Notice of the Dishonor Is Given to the Person to be Held Secondarily Liable on the Instrument** A secondarily liable party cannot be compelled to accept or pay the instrument unless proper notice of dishonor has been given. Notice may be given by any commercially reasonable means. The notice must reasonably identify the instrument and indicate that it has been dishonored. Return of an instrument given to a bank for collection is sufficient notice of dishonor. Banks must give notice of dishonor before midnight of the next banking day following the day the presentment is made. Others must give notice of dishonor within 30 days following the day on which the person receives notice of dishonor [UCC 3-503].

presentment
A demand for acceptance or payment of an instrument made upon the maker, the acceptor, the drawee, or other payor by or on behalf of the holder.

In the following case, the court held that an indorser was not secondarily liable on a check because he had not received proper notice of dishonor.

Clements v. Central Bank of Georgia
29 U.C.C. Rep.Serv. 1536 (1980)
Court of Appeals of Georgia

CASE 25.2

FACTS
On September 19, 1978, Mr. Ridley drew a check on a Tennessee bank made payable to the order of Mr. Clements. On September 25, 1978, Clements indorsed the check and negotiated it to Continental Equity Corporation (Continental). Continental indorsed the check and deposited it in the Central Bank of Georgia (Central Bank) for collection. Central Bank sent the check to the Tennessee bank for payment. On September 29, 1978, the branch manager of the Tennessee bank informed Central Bank by telephone that Ridley's check was "no good" because of insufficient funds. Central Bank authorized the Tennessee bank to hold the check. During October, Central Bank made several unsuccessful attempts to collect the check from Ridley. On October 21, 1978, Central Bank requested the Tennessee bank to return the check. On November 3, Central Bank received the check, and on that date it sent written notice to Clements that Ridley's check had been dishonored. Central Bank sued Clements (the indorser) to recover on the check. The court granted summary judgment to Central Bank. Clements appeals.

ISSUE
Did Central Bank give timely notice of dishonor of the check to Clements, the indorser, in order to hold Clements secondarily liable on Ridley's check?

IN THE LANGUAGE OF THE COURT
Birdsong, Judge   *Every indorser engages that upon dishonor and any necessary notice of dishonor and protest he will pay the instrument according to its tenor at the time of his indorsement to the holder. Unless excused, notice of any dishonor is necessary to charge any indorser. Central Bank contends the notice of dishonor to Clements on November 3 was timely because it was given within the midnight deadline after Central Bank received the dishonored check from the Tennessee bank, also on November 3. We cannot agree. Article 3 of the Commercial Code is quite clear that notice of dishonor of an instrument must be given in order to charge any secondary party with liability thereon within specific time limits of dishonor. The principal question becomes: When was the check dishonored?*

    The clear application of the Code to this case is that, assuming the check was presented on September 29, the check that was

(case continues)

refused payment on September 29 was by law dishonored by the Tennessee bank by September 30, and that although the holder, Central Bank, could in good faith attempt to obtain acceptance for an additional business day, without dishonor and without discharging the indorser, after October 1 the indorser was discharged unless necessary notice had been given. Central Bank was without authority from the indorser to continue representing the check, and therefore had no legal authority to do so without discharging the indorser in the meantime.

The notice of dishonor to the indorser Clements on November 3 came too late as a matter of law. The delay in notice of dishonor to the indorser was not due to circumstances beyond Central Bank's control, but was due simply to the bank's failure to give it once the bank itself had notice of the dishonor and was under obligation to take action.

DECISION AND REMEDY

The court of appeals held that Central Bank did not give timely notice to the indorser, Clements. Therefore, he is not secondarily liable on the check he indorsed. Reversed.

Case Questions

Critical Legal Thinking Should indorsers be held secondarily liable on a negotiable instrument that is drawn or made by another party? Why or why not?

Ethics Was it ethical for Central Bank to try to hold the indorser Clements liable on the check?

Business Application Who bore the loss of the uncollected check in this case?

ACCOMMODATION PARTY

accommodation party

A party who signs an instrument and lends his or her name (and credit) to another party to the instrument.

The party who signs the instrument for the purpose of lending his or her name (and credit) to another party to that instrument is the **accommodation party**. The accommodation party, who may sign the instrument as maker, drawer, acceptor, or indorser, is obliged to pay the instrument in the capacity in which he or she signs [UCC 3-419(a) and (b)].

An accommodation party who pays an instrument can recover reimbursement from the accommodated party and enforce the instrument against him or her [UCC 3-419(e)].

Guarantee of Payment

guaranteeing payment

A form of accommodation where the accommodation party guarantees *payment* of a negotiable instrument; the accommodation party is *primarily liable* on the instrument.

The accommodation party may sign an instrument guaranteeing either *payment* or *collection*. An accommodation party who signs an instrument **guaranteeing payment** is *primarily liable* on the instrument. That is, the debtor can seek payment on the instrument directly from the accommodation maker without first seeking payment from the maker.

Consider This Example Sonny, a college student, wants to purchase an automobile on credit from ABC Motors. He does not have a sufficient income or credit history to justify the extension of credit to him alone. Sonny asks his mother to *cosign* the note to ABC Motors, which she does. Mother is an *accommodation maker* and is *primarily liable* on the note.

Guarantee of Collection

guaranteeing collection

A form of accommodation where the accommodation indorser guarantees *collection* of a negotiable instrument; the accommodation indorser is *secondarily liable* on the instrument.

An accommodation party may sign an instrument **guaranteeing collection** rather than payment of an instrument. In this situation, the *accommodation indorser* is only *secondarily liable* on the instrument. To reserve this type of liability, the signature of the accommodation party must be accompanied by words indicating that he or she is guaranteeing collection rather than payment of the obligation.

An accommodation party that guarantees collection is obligated to pay the instrument only if (1) execution of judgment against the other party has been returned unsatisfied, (2) the other party is insolvent or in an insolvency proceeding, (3) the other party cannot be served with process, or (4) it is otherwise apparent that payment cannot be obtained from the other party [UCC 3-419(d)].

CONCEPT SUMMARY   LIABILITY OF ACCOMMODATION MAKERS AND ACCOMMODATION INDORSERS COMPARED

Accommodation Party	Contract Liability
Accommodation maker	Primarily liable on the instrument
Accommodation indorser	Secondarily liable on the instrument

Entrepreneur and the Law

WHY BE SO ACCOMMODATING?

An accommodation party is one who signs a negotiable instrument in any capacity for the purpose of lending his or her name to it. The accommodation party does not have to receive any consideration for signing the instrument and may be bound to pay it even though the accommodation was made gratuitously [UCC 3-419(b)]. Consider the following case.

Michael and Marilu Burke were married in September 1971. Shortly after the marriage, Michael formed a partnership with his cousin to operate an automobile dealership. In 1973, Michael decided to buy his cousin out of the dealership. Michael's father agreed to loan Michael $25,000 for this purpose. However, Michael's father refused to make the loan unless Marilu cosigned the promissory note. Michael's father prepared the promissory note for $25,000 plus interest, and took the note to the home of Michael and Marilu, where they both signed it. Michael's father paid Michael a $25,000 check. The check was payable to Michael Burke only. Marilu did not receive any of the proceeds herself. Sometime after the note was executed, Michael and Marilu separated. Michael defaulted on the note. Michael's father sued Marilu to recover the amount of the loan. Marilu tried to avoid liability by asserting that the note was unenforceable against her because she received no consideration for signing it.

The trial and appellate courts held that Marilu was an accommodation party and was therefore liable on Michael's note to his father. Marilu was required to pay Michael's father $31,167. The appellate court held that separate consideration is not required to establish primary liability as an accommodation maker. The court stated, "As is true with suretyship in general, the accommodating party is bound by the consideration moving to the primary obligator and the obligation of the accommodation maker need not be supported by separate or additional consideration." [*Burke v. Burke*, 412 N.E.2d 204 (Ill.App. 1980)]

WARRANTY LIABILITY OF PARTIES

In addition to signature liability, transferors can be held liable for breaching certain **implied warranties** when negotiating instruments. Warranty liability is imposed whether or not the transferor signed the instrument. Note that *transferors* make implied warranties; they are not made when the negotiable instrument is originally issued.

There are two types of implied warranties: *transfer warranties* and *presentment warranties*. Transfer and presentment warranties shift the risk of loss to the party who was in the best position to prevent the loss. This is usually the party who dealt face-to-face with the wrongdoer. Both of these implied warranties are discussed in the paragraphs that follow.

implied warranties

The law *implies* certain warranties on transferors of negotiable instruments. There are two types of implied warranties: transfer and presentment.

Transfer Warranties

Any passage of an instrument other than its issuance and presentment for payment is considered a **transfer**. Any person who transfers a negotiable instrument for consideration

transfer

Any passage of an instrument other than its issuance and presentment for payment.

transfer warranties

Any of the following five implied warranties: (1) The transferor has good title to the instrument or is authorized to obtain payment or acceptance on behalf of one who does have good title, (2) all signatures are genuine or authorized, (3) the instrument has not been materially altered, (4) no defenses of any party are good against the transferor, and (5) the transferor has no knowledge of any insolvency proceeding against the maker, acceptor, or drawer of an unaccepted instrument.

makes the following five **transfer warranties** to the transferee. If the transfer is by indorsement, the transferor also makes these warranties to any subsequent transferee [UCC 3-416(a)]:

1. The transferor has good title to the instrument or is authorized to obtain payment or acceptance on behalf of one who does have good title.
2. All signatures are genuine or authorized.
3. The instrument has not been materially altered.
4. No defenses of any party are good against the transferor.
5. The transferor has no knowledge of any insolvency proceeding against the maker, acceptor, or drawer of an unaccepted instrument.

Transfer warranties cannot be disclaimed with respect to checks, but they can be disclaimed with respect to other instruments. An indorsement that states "without recourse" disclaims the transfer warranties [UCC 3-416(c)].

A transferee who took the instrument in good faith may recover damages for breach of transfer warranty from the warrantor equal to the loss suffered. The amount recovered cannot exceed the amount of the instrument plus expenses and interest [UCC 3-416(b)].

Consider This Example Jill issues a $1,000 note to Adam. Adam cleverly raises the note to $10,000 and negotiates the note to Nick. Nick indorses the note and negotiates it to Matthew. When Matthew presents the note to Jill for payment, she has to pay only the original amount of the note—$1,000. Matthew can collect the remainder of the note ($9,000) from Nick based on a breach of the transfer warranty. If Nick is lucky, he can recover the $9,000 from Adam.

Presentment Warranties

presentment warranties

Any person who presents a draft or check for payment or acceptance makes the following three presentment warranties to a drawee or acceptor who pays or accepts the instrument in good faith: (1) The presenter has good title to the instrument or is authorized to obtain payment or acceptance of the person who has good title, (2) the instrument has not been materially altered, and (3) the presenter has no knowledge that the signature of the maker or drawer is unauthorized.

Any person who presents a draft or check for payment or acceptance makes the following **presentment warranties** to a drawee or acceptor who pays or accepts the instrument in good faith [UCC 3-417(a)]:

1. The presenter has good title to the instrument or is authorized to obtain payment or acceptance of the person who has good title.
2. The instrument has not been materially altered.
3. The presenter has no knowledge that the signature of the maker or drawer is unauthorized.

A drawee who pays an instrument may recover damages for breach of presentment warranty from the warrantor. The amount that can be recovered is limited to the amount paid by the drawee less the amount the drawee received or is entitled to receive from the drawer because of the payment, plus expenses and interest [UCC 3-417(b)].

Consider This Example Suppose Maureen draws a $1,000 check on City Bank "payable to the order of Paul." Paul cleverly raises the check to $10,000 and indorses and negotiates the check to Neal. Neal presents the check for payment to City Bank. As the presenter of the check, Neal makes the presentment warranties of UCC 3-417(a) to City Bank. City Bank pays the check as altered ($10,000) and debits Maureen's account. When Maureen discovers the alteration, she demands that the bank recredit her account, which the bank does. City Bank can recover against the presenter (Neal) based on breach of the presentment warranty that the instrument was not altered when it was presented. Neal can recover against the wrongdoer (Paul) based on breach of the transfer warranty that the instrument was not altered.

DEFENSES

The creation of negotiable instruments may give rise to a defense against its payment. Many of these defenses arise from the underlying transaction. There are two general types of defenses: *real* and *personal*. A **holder in due course** (or a holder through an HDC) takes the instrument free from personal defenses but not from real defenses. Real and personal defenses can be raised against a normal holder of a negotiable instrument. Both of these types of defenses are discussed in the sections that follow.

holder in due course (HDC)
A holder of a negotiable instrument who takes an instrument free of all claims and personal defenses but not real defenses.

REAL DEFENSES

Real (or universal) **defenses** can be raised against both holders and HDCs [UCC 3-305(b)]. If a real defense is proven, the holder or HDC cannot recover on the instrument. Real defenses are discussed in the following paragraphs.

real defense
A defense that can be raised against both holders and HDCs.

Minority

Infancy, or *minority*, is a real defense to a negotiable instrument to the extent that it is a defense to a simple contract [UCC 3-305(a)(1)(i)]. In most states, a minor who does not misrepresent his or her age can disaffirm contracts, including negotiable instruments. Usually, minors must pay the reasonable value for necessaries of life.

Extreme Duress

Ordinary duress is a personal defense (discussed later in this chapter). **Extreme duress** is a real defense against the enforcement of a negotiable instrument by a holder or an HDC [UCC 3-305(a)(1)(ii)]. Extreme duress usually requires some form of force or violence (e.g., a promissory note signed at gunpoint).

extreme duress
Extreme duress, but not ordinary duress, is a real defense against enforcement of a negotiable instrument.

Mental Incapacity

Adjudicated mental incompetence is a real defense that can be raised against holders and HDCs [UCC 3-305(a)(1)(ii)]. Such a person cannot issue a negotiable instrument; the instrument is void from its inception. Nonadjudicated mental incompetence, which usually is only a personal defense, is discussed later.

Illegality

If an instrument arises out of an illegal transaction, the *illegality* is a real defense if the law declares the instrument void [UCC 3-305(a)(1)(ii)].

Bad money drives out good money.
  Sir Thomas Gresham (1560)

Consider This Example Assume that a state's law declares gambling to be illegal and gambling contracts to be void. Gordon wins $1,000 from Jerry in an illegal poker game. He signs a promissory note promising to pay Gordon this amount plus interest in 30 days. Gordon negotiates this note to Dawn, an HDC. When Dawn presents the note to Jerry for payment, Jerry can raise the real defense of illegality against the enforcement of the note. Dawn's recourse is against Gordon.

If the law makes an illegal contract voidable instead of void, it is only a personal defense. This is discussed later in this chapter.

Discharge in Bankruptcy

Bankruptcy law is intended to relieve debtors of burdensome debts, including obligations to pay negotiable instruments. Thus, **discharge in bankruptcy** is a real defense

discharge in bankruptcy
A real defense against the enforcement of a negotiable instrument; bankruptcy law is intended to relieve debtors of burdensome debts, including negotiable instruments.

against the enforcement of a negotiable instrument by a holder or an HDC [UCC 3-305(a)(1)(iv)].

Consider This Example Hunt borrows $10,000 from Amy and signs a note promising to pay Amy this amount plus interest in one year. Amy negotiates the note to Richard, an HDC. Before the note is due, Hunt declares bankruptcy and receives a discharge of his unpaid debts. Richard cannot thereafter enforce the note against Hunt, but he can recover against Amy.

Fraud in the Inception

fraud in the inception
A real defense against the enforcement of a negotiable instrument; a person has been deceived into signing a negotiable instrument thinking that it is something else.

Fraud in the inception (also called **fraud in the factum** or **fraud in the execution**) is a real defense against the enforcement of a negotiable instrument by a holder or an HDC [UCC 3-305(a)(1)(iii)]. It occurs when a person is deceived into signing a negotiable instrument thinking that it is something else.

Consider This Example Suppose Sam, a door-to-door salesman, convinces Lance, an illiterate consumer, to sign a document purported to be an agreement to use a set of books on a 90-day trial basis. In actuality, the document is a promissory note in which Lance has agreed to pay $1,000 for the books. Sam negotiates the note to Stephanie, an HDC. Lance can raise the real defense of fraud in the inception against the enforcement of the note by Stephanie. Stephanie, in turn, can recover from Sam.

A person is under a duty to use reasonable efforts to ascertain what he or she is signing. The court inquires into a person's age, experience, education, and other factors before allowing fraud in the inception to be asserted as a real defense to defeat an HDC. Fraud in the inducement (discussed in this chapter) is only a personal defense.

Business Brief
Distinguishing between *fraud in the inception* (real defense) and *fraud in the inducement* (personal defense) can be difficult.

Forgery

forgery
A real defense against the enforcement of a negotiable instrument; the unauthorized signature of a maker, drawer, or indorser.

Another real defense to the payment of a negotiable instrument is *forgery*. The unauthorized signature of a maker, a drawer, or an indorser is wholly inoperative as that of the person whose name is signed unless that person either ratifies it or is precluded from denying it. In the latter case, a person can be estopped from raising the defense of forgery if his or her negligence substantially contributes to the forgery. A forged signature operates as the signature of the forger. Thus, the forger is liable on the instrument [UCC 3-403(a)].

Material Alteration

An instrument that has been fraudulently and materially *altered* cannot be enforced by an ordinary holder. Material alteration consists of adding to or removing any part of a signed instrument, making changes in the number of relations of the parties, or the unauthorized completion of an incomplete instrument.

Under the UCC rule that (words control figures) correcting the figure on a check to correspond to the written amount on the check is not a material alteration [UCC 3-118(c)]. If an alteration is not material, the instrument can be enforced by any holder in the original amount for which the drawer wrote the check [UCC 3-407(b)].

material alteration
A partial defense against enforcement of a negotiable instrument by an HDC. An HDC can enforce an altered instrument in the original amount for which the drawer wrote the check.

Material alteration of a negotiable instrument is only a partial defense against an HDC. Subsequent holders in due course can enforce any instrument, including an altered instrument, according to its original terms if the alteration is not apparent. An obvious change puts the holder on notice of the alteration and disqualifies him or her as an HDC [UCC 3-407(c)].

PERSONAL DEFENSES

Although **personal defenses** cannot be raised against an HDC, they can be raised against enforcement of a negotiable instrument by an ordinary holder. Personal defenses are discussed in the paragraphs that follow.

Breach of Contract

Breach of contract is one of the most common defenses raised by a party to a negotiable instrument. This is a personal defense that is effective only against an ordinary holder.

Consider These Examples   When Brian purchases a used car on credit from Karen, he signs a note promising to pay Karen the $10,000 purchase price plus interest in 36 equal monthly installments. The sales agreement warrants that the car is in perfect working condition. A month later the car's engine fails; the cost of repair is $3,000. Brian, the maker of the note, can raise breach of warranty as a defense against enforcement of the note by Karen.

The outcome would be different if Karen negotiated the promissory note to Max (an HDC) immediately after the car was sold to Brian. Max would be an HDC and Brian could not raise the breach of warranty defense against him. Max could enforce the note against Brian. Brian's only recourse would be to seek recovery for breach of warranty from Karen.

Fraud in the Inducement

Fraud in the inducement occurs when a wrongdoer makes a false statement (i.e., a misrepresentation) to another person to lead that person to enter into a contract with the wrongdoer. Negotiable instruments often arise out of such transactions. Fraud in the inducement is a personal defense that is not effective against HDCs. It is effective against ordinary holders, however.

Consider These Examples   Morton represents to investors that he will accept funds to drill for oil and that the investors will share in the profits from the oil wells. However, he plans to use these funds himself. Relying on Morton's statements, Mimi draws a $50,000 check payable to him. Morton absconds with the funds. Because Morton is an ordinary holder, Mimi can raise the personal defense of fraud in the inducement and recover the funds from Morton. If she stops payment on the check before Morton receives payment, the check will not be paid.

If Morton had negotiated the check to Tim, an HDC, Tim could enforce the check against Mimi. Because personal defenses are not effective against Tim (an HDC), Mimi's only recourse is to recover against the wrongdoer (Morton), if he can be found.

Other Personal Defenses

The following personal defenses can be raised against enforcement of a negotiable instrument by an ordinary holder:

1. Mental illness that makes a contract voidable instead of void (usually a nonadjudicated mental illness).
2. Illegality of a contract that makes the contract voidable instead of void.
3. Ordinary duress or undue influence [UCC 3-305(a)(1)(ii)].
4. Discharge of an instrument by payment or cancellation [UCC 3-602 and 3-604].

personal defense
A defense that can be raised against enforcement of a negotiable instrument by an ordinary holder but not against an HDC.

Business Brief
Personal defenses cannot be raised against an HDC.

Business Brief
Breach of the underlying contract cannot be raised as a defense against enforcement of a negotiable instrument by an HDC.

fraud in the inducement
A personal defense against the enforcement of a negotiable instrument; a wrongdoer makes a false statement to another person to lead that person to enter into a contract with the wrongdoer.

*C*ONCEPT SUMMARY REAL AND PERSONAL DEFENSES

Defense	Effect
Real Defenses	Real defenses can be raised against a holder in due course.
1. Minority	
2. Extreme duress	
3. Mental incapacity	
4. Illegality	
5. Discharge in bankruptcy	
6. Fraud in the inception	
7. Forgery	
8. Material alteration	
Personal Defenses	Personal defenses cannot be raised against a holder in due course.
1. Breach of contract	
2. Fraud in the inducement	
3. Mental illness that makes a contract voidable instead of void (usually a nonadjudicated mental illness)	
4. Illegality of a contract that makes the contract voidable instead of void	
5. Ordinary duress or undue influence [UCC 3-305(a)(1)(ii)]	
6. Discharge of an instrument by payment or cancellation [UCC 3-602 and 3-604]	

*C*ontemporary *B*usiness *A*pplication

THE FTC ELIMINATES HDC STATUS WITH RESPECT TO CONSUMER CREDIT TRANSACTIONS

In certain situations, the HDC rule can cause a hardship for the consumer. To illustrate, Greg, a consumer, purchases a stereo on credit from Lou's Stereo. He signs a note promising to pay the purchase price plus interest to Lou's Stereo in 12 equal monthly installments. Lou's Stereo immediately negotiates the note at a discount to City Bank for cash. City Bank is an HDC. The stereo is defective. Greg would like to stop paying on it, but the HDC rule prevents him from asserting any personal defenses against City Bank. Under the UCC, Greg's only recourse is to sue Lou's Stereo. However, this is often an unsatisfactory result because Greg has no leverage against Lou's Stereo and bringing a court action is expensive and time-consuming.

To correct this harsh result, the Federal Trade Commission (FTC) has adopted a rule that eliminates HDC status with regard to negotiable instruments arising out of certain *consumer* credit transactions [16 C.F.R. 433.2 (1987)]. This federal law takes precedence over state UCCs.

The rule equates the HDC of a consumer credit contract with the assignee of a simple contract. Thus, sellers of goods and services are prevented from separating the consumer's duty to pay the credit and the seller's duty to perform. This subjects the HDC of a consumer credit instrument to *all* of the defenses and claims of the consumer. In the prior example, Greg can raise the defect in the stereo as a defense against enforcement of the promissory note by City Bank, an HDC.

The FTC rule applies to consumer credit transactions in which (1) the buyer signs a sales contract that includes a promissory note, (2) the buyer signs an installment sales contract that contains a waiver of defenses clause, and (3) the seller arranges consumer financing with a third-party lender. Note that payment for goods and services with a check is not covered by this rule because it is not a credit transaction.

The FTC rule requires that the following clause be included in bold type in covered consumer credit sales and installment contracts:

NOTICE. ANY HOLDER OF THIS CONSUMER CREDIT CONTRACT IS SUBJECT TO ALL CLAIMS AND DEFENSES WHICH THE DEBTOR COULD ASSERT AGAINST THE SELLER OF THE GOODS OR SERVICES OBTAINED PURSUANT HERETO OR WITH THE PROCEEDS HEREOF. RECOVERY HEREUNDER BY THE DEBTOR

SHALL NOT EXCEED AMOUNTS PAID BY THE DEBTOR HEREUNDER.

A consumer creditor may assert the FTC rule to prevent enforcement of a note that arose from a covered transaction. The FTC can impose a fine of $10,000 for each violation.

Ethical Perspective

MAKER OF PROMISSORY NOTE LIABLE TO HDC

Promissory notes usually arise out of an underlying transaction. That is, a party will sign a promissory note to finance the purchase of goods or services from a seller. In normal contract situations, if there is a problem with the underlying transaction, such as breach of contract or fraud in the inducement by the seller, the buyer can discontinue payments and raise these issues as defenses against the seller's attempt to enforce the contract. This is not so if the note is a negotiable instrument that has been transferred to a holder in due course (HDC). Consider the following case.

In 1983, Leonard Smith was a 22-year-old college senior who was selected in the first round of the National Football League (NFL) draft. He hired an agent, BP&M Sports, Inc. (BP&M), to act as his investment advisor. On BP&M's advice, Smith invested in a cattle-breeding tax-sheltered operation operated by California Dreamstreet (Dreamstreet). Smith signed a promissory note agreeing to pay $490,500 over the next five years. Dreamstreet negotiated the promissory note to Rabobank, a Dutch bank. After paying only $40,336, Smith discovered that Dreamstreet had operated a sham transaction and the sought-after tax

benefits would not be forthcoming. When Smith refused to pay the remaining payments on the note, Rabobank sued to enforce the note against Smith.

Smith countered by asserting that BP&M and Dreamstreet had engaged in fraud in obtaining his signature on the note. The court held that any fraud perpetrated on Smith was fraud in the inducement and that Smith knew what he was signing when he signed the promissory note. Because fraud in the inducement is a personal defense and not a real defense, it cannot be raised against an HDC. The FTC rule excepting consumer credit transactions from the HDC rule did not save Smith because this was not a consumer transaction. The court ordered Smith to pay Rabobank $727,422, representing unpaid principal of $450,163 and interest of $277,259 (at the annual default rate of 10 percent), plus attorneys' fees. [*DH Cattle Holdings Company v. Smith*, 607 N.Y.S.2d 227 (N.Y.App. 1994)]

1. Did Smith act ethically in trying to get out of paying the amount of the promissory note?
2. Do you think the court reached the proper result in this case? Explain.

DISCHARGE

The UCC specifies when and how certain parties are **discharged** (relieved) from liability on negotiable instruments. Generally, all parties to a negotiable instrument are discharged from liability if (1) the party primarily liable on the instrument *pays it in full* to the holder of the instrument or (2) a drawee in good faith pays an unaccepted draft or check in full to the holder. When a party other than a primary obligor (e.g., an indorser) pays a negotiable instrument, that party and all subsequent parties to the instrument are discharged from liability [UCC 3-602].

The holder of a negotiable instrument can discharge the liability of any party to the instrument by *cancellation* [UCC 3-604]. Cancellation can be accomplished by (1) any manner apparent on the face of the instrument or the indorsement (e.g., writing

discharge
Actions or events that relieve certain parties from liability on negotiable instruments. There are three methods of discharge: (1) payment of the instrument, (2) cancellation, and (3) impairment of the right of recourse.

"canceled" on the instrument) or (2) destroying or mutilating a negotiable instrument with the intent of eliminating the obligation.

Intentionally striking out the signature of an indorser cancels that party's liability on the instrument and the liability of all subsequent indorsers. Prior indorsers are not discharged from liability. The instrument is not canceled if it is destroyed or mutilated by accident or by an unauthorized third party. The holder can bring suit to enforce the destroyed or mutilated instrument.

impairment of right of recourse
Certain parties (holders, indorsers, accommodation parties) are discharged from liability on an instrument if the holder (1) releases an obligor from liability or (2) surrenders collateral without the consent of the parties who would benefit by it.

A party to a negotiable instrument sometimes posts collateral as security for the payment of the obligation. Other parties (e.g., holders, indorsers, accommodation parties, etc.) look to the credit standing of the party primarily liable on the instrument, the collateral (if any) that is posted, and the liability of secondary parties for the payment of the instrument when it is due. A holder owes a duty not to impair the rights of others when seeking recourse against the liable parties or the collateral. Thus, a holder who either (1) *releases an obligor* from liability or (2) *surrenders the collateral* without the consent of the parties who would benefit thereby discharges those parties from their obligation on the instrument [UCC 3-605(e)]. This is called **impairment of the right of recourse**.

$\mathcal{W}$orking the Web

American Bar Association, Business Law Section Find out all about the Business Law Section of the ABA by visiting its Web site.

Visit at **www.abannet.org/buslaw/home.html**

e-biz

World Wide Legal Information Association Find out all about law in the United States, Canada, Australia, New Zealand, and the United Kingdom. There is a dictionary and other features as well.

Visit at **www.wwlia.org/wwlia.htm**

U.S. Federal Trade Commission The U.S. Federal Trade Commission has a Web site full of trade information.

Visit at **www.ftc.gov**

U.S. International Trade Commission This quasi-judicial agency provides objective trade expertise to both the legislative and executive branches of government, determines the impact of imports on U.S. agencies, and directs actions against unfair trade practices.

Visit at **www.usitc.gov**

CYBER EXERCISES

1. From the ABA Business Law Section Web site, navigate to the Women's Business Law Network.

2. Who is the webmaster of the World Wide Legal Information Association?

3. Using the U.S. Federal Trade Commission site, find the regional office closest to you.

4. Using the U.S. International Trade Commission Web site, find U.S. trade statistics.

$\mathcal{C}$ASES AND $\mathcal{E}$XERCISES

CRITICAL LEGAL THINKING CASES

25.1. On May 8, 1974, Royal Insurance Company, Ltd. (Royal), issued a draft in the amount of $12,000 payable through the Morgan Guaranty Trust Company (Morgan Guaranty). The draft was made payable to Gary E. Terrell in settlement of a claim on an insurance policy for fire damage to premises located at 3031 North 11th Street, Kansas City,

Kansas. On May 9, the attorney for Mr. and Mrs. Louis Wexler notified Royal that his clients had an insurable interest in the damaged property. As a result, Royal immediately stopped payment on the draft. On the same day, the draft was indorsed by Gary E. Terrell and deposited in his account at the UAW-CIO Local #31 Federal Credit Union (Federal). Over the next two days, Terrell withdrew $9,000 from this account. Immediately upon receiving the draft, Federal indorsed it and forwarded it to Morgan Guaranty for payment. The draft was returned to Federal on May 14 with the notation "payment stopped." When Royal refused to pay Federal the amount of the draft, Federal sued. The basis of the suit was whether Federal was a holder in due course. Who wins? [*UAW-CIO Local #31 Federal Credit Union v. Royal Insurance Company, Ltd.*, 594 S.W.2d 276 (MO 1980)]

25.2. On September 30, 1976, Betty Ellis and her then-husband W. G. Ellis executed and delivered to the Standard Finance Company, Ltd. (Standard), a promissory note in the amount of $2,800. After receiving the note, Standard issued a check to the couple for $2,800. The check was made payable to "W. G. Ellis and Betty Ellis." The check was cashed after both parties indorsed it. Shortly thereafter, the Ellises were divorced. Mrs. Ellis claims that (1) she never saw or used the money and (2) Standard understood that all of the money went to her ex-husband. W. G. Ellis was declared bankrupt. When the note became due in 1980, Betty Ellis refused to pay it. Standard sued her, seeking payment as a holder in due course. She claimed that Standard is not a holder in due course in regard to her because she never received consideration for the note and, therefore, Standard did not take the note for value. Who wins? [*Standard Finance Company, Ltd. v. Ellis*, 657 P.2d 1056 (HawaiiApp. 1983)]

25.3. In 1974, William and Eugene Slough executed two notes payable to the order of Quality Mark, Inc. (Quality Mark). The notes were made in payment of the debts of a partnership in which the Sloughs were involved. The aggregate amount of the notes was $42,150. They were due on or before January 1, 1986. On the day the instruments were executed, Quality Mark assigned them for consideration to Philip Baer, Jr. In 1975, Baer sold the notes at discount to the Southtowne Company (Southtowne). One year later, Southtowne resold the notes to Edward Rettig. By this time, the notes had been discounted to the point that Rettig paid only $5,000 for them. However, Southtowne assured Rettig that the notes had not yet been dishonored. Shortly after Rettig's purchase, the Sloughs announced that they had already defaulted on the notes. Rettig sued all the prior indorsers. Southtowne claimed that the Sloughs had no defenses against Rettig because he was a holder in due course. The Sloughs claim that because the notes had been dis-

counted to less than 50 percent of their value, Rettig must have taken them with notice of their dishonor. Who wins? [*Rettig v. Slough*, No. 5-82-7, Slip Op. (OhioApp. 1984)]

25.4. John Wade was employed by Mike Fazzari. Fazzari was an immigrant who was unable to speak or read English. In December 1957, Wade prepared a promissory note in the amount of $400, payable at the Glen National Bank, Watkins Glen, New York. Wade took the note to Fazzari and told him that the document was a statement of wages earned by Wade during the course of his employment. Fazzari signed the instrument after Wade told him it was necessary for income tax purposes. Fazzari was not in debt to Wade and there was no consideration given for the note. On April 10, 1958, the note was presented to the First National Bank of Odessa by Wellington Doane, a customer of the bank and an indorsee of the payee, Wade. Doane indorsed the check in blank and accepted a $400 cashier's check in exchange for the note. Fazzari and Glen National Bank refused payment of the note. Can the First National Bank of Odessa enforce payment of the note as a holder in due course? [*First National Bank of Odessa v. Fazzari*, 179 N.E.2d 493 (N.Y.App. 1961)]

25.5. J. H. Thompson went to the Central Motor Company (Central), an automobile dealership, to purchase a car. With the assistance of Central's sales manager, Ed Boles, Thompson selected a 1966 Imperial automobile. Boles drew up a loan agreement that stipulated 35 monthly installments of $125 and a final installment of $5,265. Under this agreement, Thompson would be charged an annual interest rate of 8 percent. Boles assured Thompson that when the $5,265 installment became due, he would be allowed to sign a second note to cover that amount. Thompson was told that the interest rate on this second note would also be 8 percent. With this assurance, Thompson signed the original loan agreement and note and made all the payments except the final one. When Thompson went to Central to sign the second note he was told that the interest rate on the second installment note would be 12 percent—not 8 percent. Thompson refused to sign the second note or make the balloon payment of the original note. Instead, he returned the car. Central was able to sell the car, but sued Thompson to recover a deficiency judgment. Who wins? [*Central Motor Company v. J. H. Thompson*, 465 S.W.2d 405 (Tex.App. 1971)]

25.6. Warren and Kristina Mahaffey were approached by a salesman from the Five Star Solar Screens Company (Five Star). The salesman offered to install insulation in their home at a cost of $5,289. After being told that the insulation would reduce their heating bills by 50 percent, the Mahaffeys agreed to the purchase. To pay for the work, the Mahaffeys executed a note promising to pay the purchase price with interest in installments. The note, which was secured by a deed of trust on the Mahaffeys' home, contained the following language: "Notice: Any holder of this consumer credit contract is subject to all claims and defenses which the debtor could assert against the seller of goods or services obtained pursuant hereto or with the proceeds thereof." Several days after Five Star finished working at the Mahaffeys' home, it sold the installment note to Mortgage Finance Corporation (Mortgage Finance).

There were major defects in the way the insulation was installed in the Mahaffey home. Large holes were left in the walls, and heater blankets and roof fans were never delivered as called for by the purchase contract. Because of these defects, the Mahaffeys refused to make the payments due on the note. Mortgage Finance instituted foreclosure proceedings to collect the money owed. Can the Mahaffeys successfully assert the defense of breach of contract against the enforcement of the note by Mortgage Finance? [*Mahaffey v. Investor's National Security Company*, 747 P.2d 890 (NV 1987)]

25.7. David M. Cox was a distributor of tools manufactured and sold by Matco Tools Corporation (Matco). Cox purchased tools from Matco pursuant to a credit line that he repaid as the tools were sold. The credit line was secured by Cox's Matco tool inventory. To expedite payment on Cox's line of credit, Matco decided to authorize Cox to deposit any customer checks that were made payable to "Matco Tools" or "Matco" into Cox's own account. Matco's controller sent Cox's bank, Pontiac State Bank (Pontiac), a letter stating that Cox was authorized to make such deposits. Several years later, some Matco tools were stolen from Cox's inventory. The Travelers Indemnity Company (Travelers), which insured Cox against such a loss, sent Cox a settlement check in the amount of $24,960. The check was made payable to "David M. Cox and Matco Tool Co." Cox indorsed the check and deposited it in his account at Pontiac. Pontiac forwarded the check through the banking system for payment by the drawee bank. Cox never paid Matco for the stolen tools. Matco sued Pontiac for accepting the check without the proper indorsements. Is Pontiac liable? [*Matco Tools Corporation v. Pontiac State Bank*, 41 UCC Rep.Serv. 883 (E.D.Mich. 1985)]

25.8. John Waddell Construction Company (Waddell) maintained a checking account at the Longview Bank & Trust Company (Longview Bank). Waddell drafted a check from this account made payable to two payees, Engineered Metal Works (Metal Works) and E. G. Smith Construction (Smith Construction). The check was sent to Metal Works, which promptly indorsed the check and presented it to the First National Bank of Azle (Bank of Azle) for payment. The Bank of Azle accepted the check with only Metal Works's indorsement and credited Metal Works's account. The Bank of Azle subsequently presented the check to Longview Bank

through the Federal Reserve System. Longview Bank accepted and paid the check. When Waddell received the check along with its monthly checking statements from Longview Bank, a company employee noticed the missing endorsement and notified Longview Bank. Longview Bank returned the check to the Bank of Azle, and the Bank of Azle's account was debited the amount of the check at the Federal Reserve. Did the Bank of Azle breach its warranty of good title? [*Longview Bank & Trust Company v. First National Bank of Azle*, 750 S.W.2d 297 (Tex.App. 1988)]

25.9. In March 1977, James Wright met with Jones, the president of The Community Bank (Community Bank), to request a loan of $7,500. Because Wright was already obligated on several existing loans, he was informed that his request would have to be reviewed by the bank's loan committee. Jones suggested that this delay could be avoided if the loan were made to Mrs. Wright. Wright asked his wife to go to the bank and "indorse" a note for him. Mrs. Wright went to the bank and spoke to Jones. Although she claims that Jones told her that she was merely indorsing the note, the language of the note clearly indicated that she would be liable in the case of default. Mrs. Wright signed the instrument in its lower right-hand corner. Wright did not sign the instrument. The $7,500 was deposited directly into Wright's business account. The Wrights were subsequently separated. Following the separation, Mrs. Wright received notice that she was in default on the note. The notice indicated that she was solely obligated to repay the instrument. Is Mrs. Wright obligated to repay the note? [*The Community Bank v. Wright*, 267 S.E.2d 159 (Va. 1980)]

25.10. John Valenti contracted with American Oil Company (Amoco), the licensor of Amoco service stations, to lease a service station and become a dealer of Amoco products. The documents that made up the lease agreement included a promissory note and guaranty. Because Valenti had no established credit history, Amoco required that his father be a cosigner. Both Valentis signed the lease and note. After about one year, the younger Valenti abandoned the operation. Amoco sued both Valentis to recover on the note and guaranty. The suit against the son was dropped when Amoco learned that he had no assets from which to satisfy a judgment. The father claimed that Amoco could not go after him because it was not suing his son. Who wins? [*American Oil Company v. Valenti*, 28 UCC Rep.Serv. 118 (Conn.Sup. 1979)]

25.11. The Georgia Farm Bureau Mutual Insurance Company (Georgia Farm Bureau) issued a check payable to the order of Willie Mincey, Jr., and MIC for $658. Without indorsing the check, MIC forwarded it to Mincey for his indorsement. Mincey indorsed the check and attempted to cash it at the First National Bank of Allentown (First National). First National would not accept the check because Mincey was not a customer of the bank. Mincey returned to the bank later that day with his uncle, Montgomery, who was a customer of the bank. First National accepted the check after Montgomery added his indorsement to Mincey's. First National forwarded the check to the drawee bank, which dishonored it because it did not bear MIC's indorsement. First National sued Montgomery for the amount of the check as an accommodation indorser. Who wins? [*First National Bank of Allentown v. Montgomery*, 27 Rep.Serv. 164 (Pa.Com. 1979)]

25.12. John Smith was the corporate secretary for Carriage House Mobile Homes, Inc. (Carriage House). Beginning on November 9, 1973, Smith signed a series of checks totaling $13,900 made payable to Danube Carpet Mills (Danube). The checks were in payment for carpeting ordered by Carriage House. Each check was signed in the following manner: "Carriage House Mobile Homes, Inc., General Account, By: /s/ John Smith." When Danube presented the checks for payment to the drawee bank, the First State Bank of Phil Campbell, Alabama, payment was refused. The reason

for the refusal was that the checks were drawn against uncollected funds. The holder of these checks, Southeastern Financial Corporation, sued Smith and Carriage House to recover the $13,900. Who is liable on the checks? [*Southeastern Financial Corporation v. Smith*, 397 F.Supp. 649 (N.D.Ala. 1975)]

25.13. Richard G. Lee was the president of Village Homes, Inc. (Village Homes), which had several outstanding loans from Farmers & Merchants National Bank of Hattan, North Dakota (Farmers Bank), that were in default. Lee and Farmers Bank worked out an arrangement to consolidate the delinquent loans and replace them with a new loan. The new loan would be secured by a promissory note. The parties drafted a note in the amount of $85,000 with a 17 percent annual interest rate. Lee signed the note without indicating that he was signing as an agent of Village Homes. The name "Village Homes, Inc." did not appear on the note. Six months after the note was signed, Village Homes defaulted on it. Farmers Bank sued Lee, seeking to hold him personally liable for the note. Who wins? [*Farmers & Merchants National Bank of Hattan, North Dakota v. Lee*, 333 N.W.2d 792 (N.D. 1983)]

ETHICS CASES

25.14. Anthony and Dolores Angelini entered into a contract with Lustro Aluminum Products, Inc. (Lustro). Under the contract, Lustro agreed to replace exterior veneer on the Angelini home with Gold Bond Plasticrylic avocado siding. The cash price for the job was $3,600 and the installment plan price was $5,363.40. The Angelinis chose to pay on the installment plan and signed a promissory note as security. The note's language provided that it would not mature until 60 days after a certificate of completion was signed. Ten days after the note was executed Lustro assigned it for consideration to General Investment Corporation (General), an experienced home improvement lender. General was aware that Lustro (1) was nearly insolvent at the time of the assignment and (2) had engaged in questionable business practices in the past. Lustro never completed the installation of siding at the Angelini home. General demanded payment of the note from the Angelinis as a holder in due course. Did General act morally in this case? Who wins? [*General Investment Corporation v. Angelini*, 278 A.2d 193 (NJ 1971)]

25.15. Marvin Ornstein resides in Pipersville, Pennsylvania. After submitting credit applications, he received a $10,000 line of credit from both the MGM Grand Hotel and Caesar's Palace, in Las Vegas, Nevada. In April 1977, Ornstein traveled to Las Vegas on a gambling junket and borrowed $5,000 at Caesar's Palace. In June 1977, he went to the MGM Grand Hotel and borrowed $10,000. In each instance, the borrowed money was advanced in the form of gambling chips, in exchange for which Ornstein executed counterchecks (i.e., markers) evidencing the debt. Ornstein did not repay the borrowed money. In November 1978, the casinos assigned their claims against Ornstein to National Recovery Systems (NRS), a New York corporation that is a credit and collection agency for casinos. Did Ornstein act ethically in not repaying his gambling markers? Does the fact that the notes arose from a gambling debt make them illegal and, if so, is this illegality a real defense that can be asserted against enforcement of the notes by an HDC? [*National Recovery Systems v. Ornstein*, 541 F.Supp. 1131 (E.D.Pa. 1982)]

25.16. In 1976, Gerald Tinker purchased for investment purposes a used 1972 Jaguar from De Maria Porsche Audi, Inc. (De Maria). De Maria represented to Tinker, prior to making the sale, that the automobile was in good operating condition, was powered by its original engine, and had never been involved in a major collision. Tinker relied on these representations and executed a retail installment contract and note with De Maria. The contract and note contained the

FTC-required notice. De Maria assigned the contract and note to Central Bank of Miami (Central Bank), which provided floor financing for De Maria.

Tinker had problems with the automobile immediately after its purchase. The car operated poorly and Tinker soon discovered that it was not powered by its original engine, had previously been involved in a major collision, and was determined to be a total loss by its previous owner's insurance company. The title held by the owner preceding De Maria stated that it was a "parts car." The title obtained by Tinker from De Maria did not contain this disclaimer. When De Maria failed to replace or successfully repair the automobile after it became totally inoperable, Tinker ceased making payments on the note and sued De Maria and Central Bank for fraud. Central Bank counterclaimed for the amount due on the note. Is it ethical for a third-party lender to assert its HDC status to collect on a note when the seller has engaged in fraud or other misconduct? Does the FTC rule prevent Central Bank from being a holder in due course? [*Tinker v. De Maria Porsche Audi, Inc.*, 459 So.2d 487 (Fla.App. 1984)]

CRITICAL LEGAL THINKING WRITING ASSIGNMENT

Read Case A.25 in the Case Appendix [*Kedzie & 103rd Currency Exchange, Inc. v. Hodge*]. This case is excerpted from the appellate court opinion. Review and brief the case. In your brief, be sure to answer the following questions.

1. Who was the drawer of the check? Who was the payee of the check?

2. What firm cashed the check? Did it qualify as a holder in due course (HDC)?

3. What defense did the defendant assert?

4. Was the defense effective against enforcement of the negotiable instrument?

Checks and Wire Transfers

B̲ankers have no right to establish a customary law among themselves, at the expense of other men.

JUSTICE FOSTER Hankey v. Trotman,
1 Black. W. 1 (1746)

Chapter Objectives

After studying this chapter, you should be able to

1. Describe the system of processing and collecting checks through the banking system.
2. Describe the difference among certified, cashier's, and traveler's checks.
3. Define *stale* and *postdated checks*.
4. Identify when a bank engages in a wrongful dishonor of a check.
5. Describe the liability of parties when a signature or indorsement on a check is forged.
6. Describe the liability of parties when a check has been altered.
7. Describe the requirements of the Expedited Funds Availability Act.
8. Explain a bank's midnight deadline for determining whether to dishonor a check.
9. Describe electronic fund transfer systems.
10. Define *wire transfer* and describe the main provisions of Article 4A of the Uniform Commercial Code (UCC).

Chapter Contents

Money speaks sense in a language all nations understand.
Aphra Behn
(1640–1689) The Rover

Checks are the most common form of negotiable instrument used in this country. More than 70 billion checks are written annually. Checks act both as a substitute for money and as a recordkeeping device, but they do not serve a credit function. In addition, trillions of dollars are transferred each day by *wire transfer* between businesses and banks. This chapter discusses the various forms of checks, the procedure for paying and collecting checks through the banking system, the duties and liabilities of banks and other parties in the collection process, and electronic fund transfers.

THE BANK–CUSTOMER RELATIONSHIP

creditor–debtor relationship

Created when a customer deposits money into the bank; the customer is the creditor and the bank is the debtor.

When a customer makes a deposit into a bank, a **creditor–debtor relationship** is formed. The customer is the creditor and the bank is the debtor. In effect, the customer is loaning money to the bank.

A *principal–agent relationship* is created if (1) the deposit is a check that the bank must collect for the customer or (2) the customer writes a check against his or her account. The customer is the principal and the bank is the agent. The bank is obligated to follow the customer's order to collect or pay the check. The rights and duties of a bank and a checking account and wire transfer customer are contractual. The signature card and other bank documents signed by the customer form the basis of the contract.

Contemporary Business Application

FEDERAL CURRENCY REPORTING LAW

Federal currency reporting laws require financial institutions and other entities (e.g., retailers, car and boat dealers, antique dealers, jewelers, travel agencies, real estate brokers, and other businesses) to file a **Currency Transaction Report (CTR)** with the Internal Revenue Service (IRS) reporting:

- The receipt in a single transaction or a series of related transactions of cash in an amount greater than $10,000. "Cash" is not limited to currency, but includes cashier's checks, bank drafts, traveler's checks, and money orders (but not ordinary checks) [26 U.S.C. § 60501].

- Suspected criminal activity by bank customers involving a financial transaction of $1,000 or more in funds [12 C.F.R. § 21.11(b)(3)].

The law also stipulates that it is a crime to structure or assist in structuring any transaction for the purpose of evading these reporting requirements [31 U.S.C. § 5324]. Financial institutions and entities may be fined for negligent violations of the currency reporting requirements. A $50,000 fine may be levied for a pattern of negligent violations. Willful failure to file reports may subject the violator to civil money penalties, charges of aiding and abetting the criminal activity, and prosecution for violating the money laundering statutes.

Article 3 of the UCC

Sets forth the requirements for finding a negotiable instrument, including checks.

Revised Article 3

A revision of Article 3 promulgated in 1990.

Article 4 of the UCC

Establishes the rules and principles that regulate bank deposit and collection procedures.

THE UNIFORM COMMERCIAL CODE AND BANKING

Various articles of the Uniform Commercial Code (UCC) establish rules for creating, collecting, and enforcing checks and wire transfers. These articles are

- **Article 3 (Negotiable Instruments)** establishes the requirements for finding a negotiable instrument. Because a check is a negotiable instrument, the provisions of Article 3 apply. **Revised Article 3** was promulgated in 1990. The provisions of Revised Article 3 will serve as the basis of the discussion of Article 3 in this chapter.
- **Article 4 of the UCC (Bank Deposits and Collections)** establishes the rules and principles that regulate bank deposit and collection procedures for checking accounts offered by

commercial banks, NOW accounts (negotiable orders of withdrawal), and other checklike accounts offered by savings and loan associations, savings banks, credit unions, and other financial institutions. Article 4 controls if the provisions of Article 3 and 4 conflict [UCC 4-102(a)]. Article 4 was substantially amended in 1990. The amended Article 4 will serve as the basis of the discussion of Article 4 in this chapter.

- **Article 4A (Funds Transfers)** establishes rules that regulate the creation and collection of and liability for wire transfers. Article 4A was added to the UCC in 1989.

Article 4A of the UCC
Article added to the UCC in 1989 that establishes rules regulating the creation and collection of and liability for wire transfers.

The financing of international trade is made easier by the fast same-day use of commercial wire transfers. Trillions of dollars are transferred each day between banks and businesses in different countries to pay for the sale of goods and services.

ORDINARY CHECKS

Most adults and businesses have at least one checking account at a bank. A customer opens a checking account by going to the bank, completing the necessary forms (including a *signature card*), and making a deposit to the account. The bank issues checks to the customer. The customer then uses the checks to purchase goods and services.

Parties to a Check

UCC 3-104(f) defines a **check** as an order by the drawer to the drawee bank to pay a specified sum of money from the drawer's checking account to the named payee (or holder). There are three parties to an ordinary check:

1. The **drawer** The customer who maintains the checking account and writes (draws) checks against the account.
2. The **drawee** (or payor bank) The bank on which the check is drawn.
3. The **payee** The party to whom the check is written.

Consider This Example The Kneadery Restaurant has a checking account at Mountain Bank. The Kneadery writes a check for $1,500 from this account to Sun Valley Bakery to pay for food supplies. The Kneadery Restaurant is the drawer, Mountain Bank is the drawee, and Sun Valley Bakery is the payee.

Indorsement of a Check

The payee is a *holder* of the check. As such, the payee has the right either (1) to demand payment of the check or (2) to **indorse** the check to another party by signing the back of the check. This latter action is called **indorsement** of a check. The payee is the **indorser**,

check
An order by the drawer to the drawee bank to pay a specified sum of money from the drawer's checking account to the named payee (or holder).

drawer of a check
The checking account holder and writer of the check.

drawee of a check
The bank where the drawer has his or her account.

payee of a check
The party to whom the check is written.

indorsement of a check
Occurs when a payee indorses a check to another party by signing the back of the check.

indorser
The payee who indorses a check to another party.

indorsee
The party to whom a check is indorsed.

and the person to whom the check is indorsed is the **indorsee**. The indorsee in turn becomes a holder who can either demand payment of the check or indorse it to yet another party. Any subsequent holder can demand payment of the check or further transfer the check [UCC 3-204(a)].

Consider This Example Referring to the previous example, the Sun Valley Bakery may either present the Kneadery Restaurant's check to Mountain Bank for payment, or it can indorse the check to another party. Assume that Sun Valley Bakery indorses the check to the Flour Company in payment for flour. Sun Valley Bakery is the indorser and the Flour Company is the indorsee. The Flour Company may either present the check for payment or indorse it to another party.

E-Commerce & Internet Law

e·biz

ELECTRONIC FUND TRANSFER SYSTEMS

Computers and electronic technology have made it possible for banks to offer electronic payment and collection systems to bank customers. This technology is collectively referred to as **electronic fund transfer systems (EFTS)**. EFTS are supported by contracts among and between customers, banks, private clearinghouses, and other third parties. The most common forms of EFTS are discussed in the following paragraphs.

Automated Teller Machines

An **automated teller machine (ATM)** is an electronic machine that is located either on a bank's premises or at some other convenient location, such as a shopping center or supermarket. These devices are connected on-line to the bank's computers. Bank customers are issued a secret personal identification number (PIN) to access their bank accounts through ATMs.

ATMs are commonly used when the bank is not open. They are also being used as an alternative means of conducting banking when the bank is open. They are used to withdraw cash from bank accounts, cash checks, make deposits to checking or savings accounts, and make payments owed to the bank.

Point-of-Sale Terminals

Many banks issue *debit cards* to customers. Debit cards replace checks in that customers can use them to make purchases. No credit is extended. Instead, the customer's bank account is immediately debited for the amount of the purchase.

Debit cards can be used only if the merchant has a **point-of-sale (POS) terminal** at the checkout counter.

These terminals are connected on-line to the bank's computers. To make a purchase, the customer inserts the debit card into the terminal for the amount of the purchase. If there are sufficient funds in the customer's account, the transaction will debit the customer's account and credit the merchant's account for the amount of the purchase. If there are insufficient funds in the customer's account, the purchase is rejected unless the customer has overdraft protection. Some POS terminals allow for the extension of credit in the transaction. Gasoline station POS terminals are one example.

Direct Deposits and Withdrawals

Many banks provide the service of paying recurring payments and crediting recurring deposits on behalf of customers. Commonly, payments are for utilities, insurance premiums, mortgage payments, and the like. Social Security checks, wages, and dividend and interest checks are examples of recurring deposits. To provide this service, the customer's bank and the payee's bank must belong to the same clearinghouse.

Pay-by-Internet

Many banks permit customers to pay bills from their bank accounts by use of personal computer by using the Internet. To do so, the customer must enter his or her PIN and account number, the amount of the bill to be paid, and the account number of the payee to whom the funds are to be transferred. Internet banking is expected to increase dramatically in the future.

SPECIAL TYPES OF CHECKS

If a payee fears that there may be insufficient funds in the drawer's account to pay the check when it is presented for payment or that the drawer has stopped payment of the check, the payee may be unwilling to accept an ordinary check from the drawer. However, the payee probably would be willing to accept a **bank check**, that is, a *certified check, a cashier's check*, or a *traveler's check*. This is because these types of checks are usually considered "as good as cash" because the bank is solely or primarily liable for payment. These forms of checks are discussed in the following paragraphs.

Certified Checks

When a bank **certifies** a check, it agrees in advance to (1) accept the check when it is presented for payment and (2) pay the check out of funds set aside from the customer's account and either placed in a special certified check account or held in the customer's account. Certified checks do not become stale. Thus, they are payable at any time from the date they were issued.

The check is certified when the bank writes or stamps the word *certified* across the face of an ordinary check. The certification should also contain the date and the amount being certified and the name and title of the person at the bank who certifies the check (see Exhibit 26.1). Note that the bank is not obligated to certify a check. The bank's refusal to do so is not a dishonor of the check [UCC 3-409(d)].

bank check

A certified check, a cashier's check, or a traveler's check; the payment for which the bank is solely or primarily liable.

certified check

A type of check where a bank agrees in advance *(certifies)* to accept the check when it is presented for payment.

process of certification

The accepting bank writes or stamps the word *certified* on the ordinary check of an account holder and sets aside funds from that account to pay the check.

EXHIBIT 26.1   *A Certified Check*

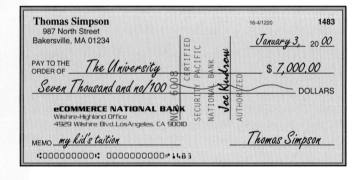

Liability on a Certified Check   Either the drawer or the payee (or holder) can present the check to the drawee bank for certification. If the drawee bank certifies the check, the drawer is discharged from liability on the check, regardless of who obtained the certification [UCC 3-414(c)]. The holder must recover from the certifying bank, which can be held liable for the amount of the check, expenses, and loss of interest resulting from nonpayment. If the bank refuses to pay after receiving notice of particular circumstances giving rise to such damages, it can also be held liable for consequential damages [UCC 3-411].

Problems may arise if a certified check was *altered*. If the alteration occurred before the check was certified, the certifying bank is liable for the certified amount. If the check was altered after certification, the bank is liable for only the certified amount, not the raised amount. The drawer cannot stop payment on a certified check. Because certification constitutes acceptance of the check, the certifying bank can revoke its certification only in limited circumstances [UCC 3-413].

Business Brief

The drawer is discharged from liability if the drawee bank certifies a check.

Cashier's Checks

cashier's check

A check issued by a bank where the customer has paid the bank the amount of the check and a fee. The bank guarantees the payment of the check.

A person can purchase a **cashier's check** from a bank by paying the bank the amount of the check plus a fee for issuing the check. Usually, a specific payee is named. The purchaser does not have to have a checking account at the bank. The check is a noncancellable negotiable instrument upon issue.

A cashier's check is a two-party check for which (1) the issuing bank serves as both the drawer and the drawee and (2) the holder serves as payee [UCC 3-104(g)]. The bank, which has been paid for the check, guarantees its payment. When the check is presented for payment, the bank debits its own account [UCC 3-412]. (See Exhibit 26.2.)

Exhibit 26.2   *A Cashier's Check*

eCOMMERCE NATIONAL BANK 10341504   16-4/1220
Bank Check Accounting Services
Brea, California 92621-6398   OFFICE
                                           NUMBER
                                           142   DATE: August 16, 2000

PAY TO THE
ORDER OF   * * * * * * * * * * HELEN PITTS * * * * * * * * * * $ 1,000.00

        EXACTLY 1,000 AND 00   DOLLARS
($100,000 AND OVER REQUIRES TWO SIGNATURES)
                             CASHIER'S CHECK

Dg Lotten
AUTHORIZED SIGNATURE   AUTHORIZED SIGNATURE
⑈10341504⑈ ⑆1220000043⑆928⑈917016⑈

An obligated bank that wrongfully refuses to pay a cashier's check is liable to the person asserting the right to enforce the check for expenses and loss of interest resulting from nonpayment and consequential damages [UCC 3-411].

Traveler's Checks

Business Brief

Many businesses require payment by certified or cashier's checks because these are "as good as cash." By doing so, businesses avoid the problem of being paid by normal checks that may "bounce."

traveler's check

A form of check sold by banks and other issuers. They are issued without a named payee. The purchaser fills in the payee's name when he or she uses the check to purchase goods or services.

Traveler's checks derive their name from the fact that travelers often purchase them to use as a safe substitute for cash while on vacations or other trips. They may be issued by banks or by companies other than banks (e.g., American Express). A traveler's check is a two-party instrument drawn by the bank upon itself, where the issuing bank serves as both the drawer and the drawee.

Traveler's checks may be purchased in many denominations. Unlike cashier's checks, traveler's checks are issued without a named payee (see Exhibit 26.3). The checks have

Exhibit 26.3   *A Traveler's Check*

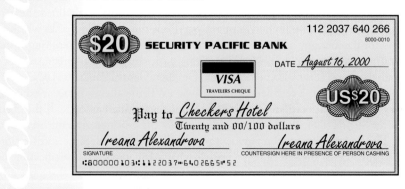

$20 SECURITY PACIFIC BANK   112 2037 640 266
                                           8000-0010
         VISA   DATE August 16, 2000
         TRAVELERS CHEQUE   US$20

    Pay to Checkers Hotel
         Twenty and 00/100 dollars
    Ireana Alexandrova   Ireana Alexandrova
    SIGNATURE   COUNTERSIGN HERE IN PRESENCE OF PERSON CASHING
    ⑆800000103⑆112037⑈640266⑈52

two signature blanks. The purchaser signs one blank when the traveler's checks are issued and enters the payee's name and signs the second blank when he or she uses the check to purchase goods or services. The traveler's check is not a negotiable instrument until it is signed the second time [UCC 3-104(i)].

Purchasers of traveler's checks do not have to have a checking account at the issuing bank. The purchaser pays the bank the amount of the checks to be issued. When a traveler's check is presented for payment, the bank debits its own account. Most banks charge a fee for this service, but some banks merely earn interest on the "float" while the checks are not written. If a traveler's check is stolen or lost prior to its use, the purchaser can stop payment on the check. Payment cannot be stopped once the check has been negotiated.

> **Business Brief**
> Traveler's checks are used in place of cash when people are on vacation or business trips. Credit cards are replacing the use of traveler's checks.

E-Commerce & Internet Law

BANK DEBIT CARDS

The computer has made it much easier and faster for banks and their customers to conduct banking transactions. For example, bank customers can now use **debit cards** to pay for goods and services. When a bank customer uses a debit card to pay, the money is immediately deducted electronically from his or her bank account. There is no extension of credit as there is when a credit card is used; using a debit card is like writing an electronic check.

Congress enacted the **Electronic Fund Transfer Act** [15 U.S.C. §§ 1693 et seq.] to regulate consumer electronic fund transfers. The Federal Reserve Board, which is empowered to enforce the provisions of the act, adopted **Regulation E** to further interpret it. Regulation E has the force of law. The Electronic Fund Transfer Act and Regulation E establish the following consumer rights:

1. **Unsolicited cards** A bank can send unsolicited EFTS debit cards to a consumer only if the cards are not valid for use. Unsolicited cards can be validated for use by a consumer's specific request.
2. **Lost or stolen debit cards** Debit cards are sometimes lost or stolen. If a customer notifies the issuer bank within two days of learning that his or her debit card has been lost or stolen, the customer is liable for only $50 for unauthorized use. If a customer does not notify the bank within this two-day period, the customer's lia-

bility increases to $500. If the customer fails to notify the bank within 60 days after an unauthorized use appears on the customer's bank statement, the customer can be held liable for more than $500. Federal law allows states to impose a lesser liability on customers for lost or stolen debit cards.

3. **Evidence of transaction** Other than for a telephone transaction, a bank must provide a customer with a written receipt of a transaction made through a computer terminal. This receipt is prima facie evidence of the transaction.
4. **Bank statements** A bank must provide a monthly statement to an electronic funds transfer customer at the end of the month that the customer conducts a transaction. Otherwise, a quarterly statement must be provided to the customer. The statement must include the date and amount of the transfer, the name of the retailer, the location or identification of the terminal, and the fees charged for the transaction. Bank statements must also contain the address and telephone number where inquiries or errors can be reported.

Banks are required to disclose the foregoing information to their customers. A bank is liable for wrongful dishonor when it fails to pay an electronic fund transfer when there are sufficient funds in the customer's account to do so.

e·biz

HONORING CHECKS

When a customer opens a checking account at a bank, the customer impliedly agrees to keep sufficient funds in the account to pay any checks written against it. Thus, when the drawee bank receives a properly drawn and payable check, the bank is under a duty to **honor** the check and charge (debit) the drawer's account the amount of the check [UCC 4-401(a)].

> **honor**
> Payment of a drawer's properly drawn check by the drawee bank.

Stale Checks

stale check

A check that has been out-standing for more than six months.

Occasionally, payees or other holders in possession of a check fail to present the check immediately to the payor bank for payment. A check that has been outstanding for more than six months is considered **stale**, and the bank is under no obligation to pay it. A bank that pays a stale check in good faith may charge the drawer's account [UCC 4-404].

Incomplete Checks

Business Brief

A bank may pay an incomplete check as completed by the payee as long as it acts in good faith and without notice that the completion was improper.

Drawers sometimes write checks that omit certain information, such as the amount of the check or the payee's name, either on purpose or by mistake. In such cases, the payee or any holder can complete the check, and the payor bank that in good faith makes payment on the completed check can charge the customer's account the amount of the completed check unless it has notice that the completion was improper [UCC 3-407(c) and 4-401(d)(2)]. The UCC places the risk of loss of an incomplete item on the drawer.

Consider This Example Suppose Richard, who owes Sarah $500, draws a check payable to Sarah on City Bank. Richard signs the check but leaves the amount blank. Sarah fraudulently fills in "$1,000" and presents the check to City Bank, which pays it. City Bank can charge Richard's account $1,000. Richard's only recourse is to sue Sarah. However, if Richard telephoned the bank to tell them that he owed Sarah only $500, City Bank would be liable for paying any greater amount to Sarah.

Death or Incompetence of a Drawer

Business Brief

As a practical matter, banks usually freeze a checking account upon learning of the death of a customer.

Checks may be paid against the accounts of deceased customers or customers who have been adjudicated incompetent until the bank has actual knowledge of such condition and has reasonable opportunity to act on the information. In the case of a deceased customer, the bank may pay or certify checks drawn on the deceased customer's account on or prior to the date of death for 10 days after the date of death. This rule applies unless a person claiming an interest in the account, such as an heir or a taxing authority, orders the bank to stop payment. A bank that pays a check of a deceased or incompetent customer when it should not have is liable for the amount improperly paid [UCC 4-405].

Contemporary Business Application

REQUIREMENTS FOR POSTDATING CHECKS

Prior to a recent revision of Article 4 of the UCC, all a drawer had to do to **postdate** a check was to write the check and date it a date in the future. The bank was then obligated not to pay the check until this later date, and if it did pay the check sooner it was liable for any damages caused to the drawer.

In 1990, Article 4 was amended to make it more difficult to postdate a check. Under new UCC 4-401(c), to require a bank to abide by a postdated check, the drawer must take the following steps:

- The drawer must postdate the check to some date in the future.
- The drawer must give *separate written notice* to the bank describing the check with reasonable certainty and notifying the bank not to pay the check until the date on the check.

If these steps are taken and the bank pays the check before its date, the bank is liable to the drawer for any losses resulting from its act.

Stop-Payment Orders

A **stop-payment order** is an order by a drawer of a check to the payor bank not to pay or certify a check. Only the drawer can order a stop-payment. Payees, holders, and indorsers cannot. The bank must be given a reasonable opportunity to act on a stop-payment order. The order is ineffectual if the bank has already accepted or certified the check. If the signature of more than one person is required to draw on an account, any of these persons may stop payment on the account. The stop-payment order can be given orally or in writing. An *oral order* is binding on the bank for only 14 calendar days, unless confirmed in writing during this time. A **written order** is effective for six months and can be renewed in writing for additional six-month periods [UCC 4-403].

If the payor bank fails to honor a valid stop-payment order, it must recredit the customer's account. The bank is subrogated to the rights of the drawer. In addition, the bank is liable only for the actual damages suffered by the drawer, who must prove the fact and amount of loss resulting from the payment of a check on which a stop-payment order was issued.

Consider This Example Suppose Karen buys a car from Silvio. She pays for the car by drawing a $10,000 check on City Bank payable to the order of Silvio. Karen thinks the car is defective and stops payment on the check. If City Bank mistakenly pays Silvio over the stop-payment order, it is liable and must recredit Karen's account. However, if it is determined that the car is not defective, City Bank does not have to recredit Karen's account. This is because Karen has suffered no actual loss—she owed Silvio for the car.

Overdrafts

If the drawer does not have enough money in his or her account when a properly payable check is presented for payment, the payor bank can either (1) dishonor the check or (2) honor the check and create an overdraft in the drawer's account [UCC 4-401(a)]. The bank notifies the drawer of the dishonor and returns the check to the holder marked "insufficient funds." The holder often resubmits the check to the bank, hoping that the drawer has deposited more money into the account and the check will clear. If the check does not clear, the holder's recourse is against the drawee of the check.

If the bank chooses to pay the check even though there are insufficient funds in the drawer's account, it can later charge the drawer's account for the amount of the **overdraft** [UCC 4-401(a)]. This is because there is an implied promise that the drawer will reimburse the bank for paying checks the drawer orders the bank to pay. If the drawer does not fulfill this commitment, the bank can sue him or her to recover payment for the overdrafts and overdraft fees. A bank cannot charge interest on the amount of the overdraft without the drawer's permission. Therefore, many banks offer optional overdraft protection to their customers.

Wrongful Dishonor

If the bank does not honor a check when there are sufficient funds in a drawer's account to pay a properly payable check, it is liable for **wrongful dishonor**. The payor bank is liable to the drawer for damages proximately caused by the wrongful dishonor as well as for consequential damages, damages caused by criminal prosecution, and such. A payee or holder cannot sue the bank for damages caused by the wrongful dishonor of a drawer's check. Their only recourse is to sue the drawer to recover the amount of the check [UCC 4-402].

stop-payment order
An order by a drawer of a check to the payor bank not to pay or certify a check.

Business Brief
An oral stop-payment order is binding on the bank for only 14 days unless confirmed in writing during the 14-day period.

written order
A stop-payment order that is good for six months after the date it is written.

Business Brief
When a check is dishonored because of insufficient funds, it is said to have "bounced" (i.e., like a rubber check).

overdraft
The amount of money a drawer owes a bank after it has paid a check despite insufficient funds in the drawer's account.

wrongful dishonor
Occurs when there are sufficient funds in a drawer's account to pay a properly payable check, but the bank does not pay the check.

International Perspective

HIDING MONEY IN OFFSHORE BANKS

Little did Christopher Columbus know in 1503 when he sailed past the Cayman Islands in the Caribbean that these tiny islands would become a bastion of international finance in the late twentieth and early twenty-first century. These tiny islands of 35,000 people host about 600 banks with over $500 million in deposits. Why is so much money being hoarded there? The answer is: Bank secrecy laws.

Every nation has banking laws, but all banking laws are not equal. What the Cayman Islands banking law provides is confidentiality. In most instances, no party other than the depositor has the right to know the identity of the depositor, account number, or amount in the account. In fact, most accounts are held in the name of trusts instead of the depositor's actual name. This bank secrecy law has attracted many persons—and in some instances crooks—to park their ill-gotten gains in a Cayman Islands bank. Often the bank is usually no more than a lawyer's office.

Switzerland was once the primary location for depositing money that did not want to be found. After some pressure from the United States and other countries, however, Switzerland entered into memorandums of understanding agreeing to cooperate with criminal investigations by these countries and to help uncover money deposited in Switzerland made through securities frauds and other crimes. Therefore, Switzerland has lost some of its luster as an international money hideout.

So Switzerland has been replaced by other places offering even more secret bank secrecy laws. The Cayman Islands is now the "Switzerland of the Caribbean." There are several other bank secrecy hideouts around the world, including the Bahamas in the Caribbean, the country of Liechtenstein in Europe, the Isle of Jersey off of Great Britain, and the micro-island of Niue in the South Pacific. These tiny countries and islands follow the adage: "Write a good law and they will come."

*F*ORGED SIGNATURES AND ALTERED CHECKS

The love of money is the root of all evil.

Bible
I Timothy 6:10

Major problems associated with checks are that (1) certain signatures are sometimes forged and (2) the check itself may have been altered prior to presentment for payment. The UCC rules that apply to these situations are discussed in the following paragraphs. These rules apply to all types of negotiable instruments but are particularly important concerning checks.

Forged Signature of the Drawer

When a check is presented to the payor bank for payment, the bank is under a duty to verify the drawer's signature. This is usually done by matching the signature on the signature card on file at the bank to the signature on the check.

forged instrument
A check with a forged drawer's signature on it.

A check with a *forged drawer's signature* is called a **forged instrument**. A forged signature is wholly inoperative as the signature of the drawer. The check is not "properly payable" because it does not contain an order of the drawer. The payor bank cannot charge the customer's account if it pays a check over the forged signature. If the bank has charged the customer's account, it must recredit the account and the forged check must be dishonored [UCC 3-401].

Business Brief
The ultimate loss for the payment of a check over the *forged signature of the drawer* usually falls on the bank that paid the check. The payor bank may recover from the forger, if he or she can be found.

The bank can recover only from the party who presented the check to it for payment if that party had knowledge that the signature of the drawer on the check was unauthorized [UCC 3-417(a)(3)]. The forger is liable on the check because the forged signature acts as the forger's signature [UCC 3-403(a)]. Although the payor bank can sue the forger, the forger usually cannot be found or is judgment-proof.

Business Brief
A payor bank that has paid a check over the forged signature of a drawer can recover only from (1) prior transferors who had knowledge that the signature of the drawer was unauthorized or (2) the forger.

Consider This Example Suppose Gregory has a checking account at Country Bank. Lana steals a check, completes it, and forges Gregory's signature. She indorses it to Mike, who knows that Gregory's signature has been forged. Mike indorses it to Barbara, who is innocent and does not know of the forgery. She presents it to Country Bank, the payor bank, which pays the check. Country Bank may recover from the original forger, Lana, and from Mike, who knew of the forgery. It cannot recover from Barbara because she did not have knowledge of the forgery.

Altered Checks

Sometimes, a check is altered before it is presented for payment. This is an unauthorized change in the check that modifies the legal obligation of a party [UCC 3-407(a)]. The payor bank can dishonor an **altered check** if it discovers the alteration.

If the payor bank pays the altered check, it can charge the drawer's account for the **original tenor** of the check but not the altered amount [UCC 3-407(c) and UCC 4-401(d)(1)].

If the payor bank has paid the altered amount, it can recover the difference between the altered amount and the original tenor from the party who presented the altered check for payment. This is because the presenter of the check for payment and each prior transferor *warrant* that the check has not been altered [UCC 3-417(a)(2)]. This is called the **presentment warranty**. If there has been an alteration, each party in the chain of collection can recover from the preceding transferor based on a breach of this warranty. The ultimate loss usually falls on the party that first paid the altered check because that party was in the best position to identify the alteration. The forger is liable for the altered amount—if he or she can be found and is not judgment-proof.

Consider This Example   Father draws a $100 check on City Bank made payable to his daughter. The daughter alters the check to read "$1,000" and cashes the check at the liquor store. The liquor store presents the check for payment to City Bank. City Bank pays the check. Father is liable only for the original tenor of the check ($100), and City Bank can charge the father's account this amount. City Bank is liable for the $900 difference, but it can recover this amount from the liquor store for breach of presentment warranty. The liquor store can seek to recover the $900 from the daughter.

If the same wrongdoer engages in a *series of forgeries* or *alterations* on the same account, the customer must report that to the payor bank within a reasonable period of time, not exceeding 30 calendar days from the date that the bank statement was made available to the customer [UCC 4-406(d)(2)]. The customer's failure to do so discharges the bank from liability on all similar forged or altered checks after this date and prior to notification.

The drawer's failure to report a forged or altered check to the bank within *one year* of receiving the bank statement and canceled checks containing it relieves the bank of any liability for paying the instrument [UCC 4-406(e)]. Thus, the payor bank is not required after this time to recredit the customer's account for the amount of the forged or altered check even if the customer later discovers the forgery or alteration.

𝒯HE COLLECTION PROCESS

A bank is under a duty to accept deposits into a customer's account. This includes collecting checks that are drawn on other banks and made payable or indorsed to the depositor. The collection process, which may involve several banks, is governed by **Article 4** of the **UCC**.

When a payee or holder receives a check, he or she can either go to the drawer's bank (the **payor bank**) and present the check for payment in cash or—as is more common—deposit the check into a bank account at his or her own bank, called the **depository bank**. (The depository bank may also serve as the payor bank if both parties have accounts at the same bank.)

---

altered check
A check that has been altered without authorization that modifies the legal obligation of a party.

original tenor
The original amount for which the drawer wrote the check.

Business Brief
If the payor bank pays the altered check, it can charge the drawer's account the *original tenor* of the check but not the altered amount.

presentment warranty
Each prior transferor warrants that the check has not been altered.

Business Brief
A checking account customer owes a duty to examine bank statements promptly and with reasonable care to determine if any payment was made because of alteration of a check or forged signature of the customer.

payor bank
The bank where the drawer has a checking account and on which the check is drawn.

depository bank
The bank where the payee or holder has an account.

*E*XHIBIT 26.4 *The Check Collection Process*

The depository bank must present the check to the **payor bank** for collection. At this point in the process, the Federal Reserve System (discussed next) and other banks may be used in the collection of a check. The depository bank and these other banks are called **collecting banks**. Banks in the collection process that are not the depository or payor bank are called **intermediary banks**. A bank can have more than one role during the collection process [UCC 4-105]. The collection process is illustrated in Exhibit 26.4.

collecting bank

The depository bank and other banks in the collection process (other than the payor bank).

intermediary bank

A bank in the collection process that is not the depository or payor bank.

Federal Reserve System

A system of 12 regional Federal Reserve banks that assist banks in the collection of checks.

The Federal Reserve System

The **Federal Reserve System**, which consists of 12 regional Federal Reserve banks located in different geographical areas of the country, assists banks in the collection of checks. Rather than send a check directly to another bank for collection, member banks may submit paid checks to the Federal Reserve banks for collection.

Most banks in this country have accounts at the regional Federal Reserve banks. This is usually done by electronic presentment (i.e., by computer). The Federal Reserve banks debit and credit the accounts of these banks daily to reflect the collection and payment of checks. Banks pay the Federal Reserve banks a fee for this service. In large urban areas, private clearinghouses may provide a similar service [UCC 4-110 and 4-213(a)].

Deferred Posting

deferred posting rule

A rule that allows banks to fix an afternoon hour of 2:00 P.M. or later as a cutoff hour for the purpose of processing items.

The **deferred posting rule** applies to all banks in the collection process. This rule allows banks to fix an afternoon hour of 2:00 P.M. or later as a cutoff hour for the purpose of processing checks. Any check or deposit of money received after this cutoff hour is treated as received on the next banking day [UCC 4-108]. Saturdays, Sundays, and holidays are not *banking days* unless the bank is open to the public for carrying on substantially all banking functions [UCC 4-104(a)(3)].

Provisional Credits

provisional credit

Occurs when a collecting bank gives credit to a check in the collection process prior to its final settlement. Provisional credits may be reversed if the check does not "clear."

When a customer deposits a check into a checking account for collection, the depository bank does not have to pay the customer the amount of the check until the check "clears"—that is, until final settlement occurs. The depository bank may **provisionally credit** the customer's account. Each bank in the collection process provisionally credits the account of the prior transferor [UCC 4-201(a)]. If the check is dishonored by the payor bank (e.g., insufficient funds, a stop-payment order, or closed account), the check is returned to the payee or holder, and the provisional credits are reversed. The collecting bank must either return the check to the prior transferor or notify that party within a reasonable time that provisional credit is being revoked. If the collecting bank fails to do this, it is liable for any losses caused by its delay [UCC 4-214].

Depository banks often allow their customers to withdraw the funds prior to final settlement. If the bank later learns that the check was dishonored, it can debit the customer's account for the amount withdrawn. If this is not possible (e.g., the payee or holder does not have sufficient funds in his or her account or has closed the account), the depository bank can sue the customer to recover the funds.

Final Settlement

A check is finally paid when the payor bank (1) pays the check in cash, (2) settles for the check without having a right to revoke the settlement, or (3) fails to dishonor the check within certain statutory time periods. These time periods are discussed in the following paragraphs.

When a check is finally settled, the provisional credits along the chain of collecting banks "firm up" and become **final settlements** [UCC 4-215(a)].

"On Us" Checks   If the drawer and the payee or holder have accounts at the *same* bank, the depository bank is also the payor bank. The check is called an **"on us" item** when it is presented for payment by the payee or holder. In this case, the bank has until the opening for business on the second banking day following the receipt of the check to dishonor it. If it fails to do so, the check is considered paid. The payee or holder can withdraw the funds at this time [UCC 4-215(e)(2)].

Consider This Example   Christine and Jim both have checking accounts at Country Bank. On Tuesday morning, Christine deposits a $1,000 check from Jim into her account. Country Bank issues a provisional credit to Christine's account for this amount. On Thursday morning when the bank opens for business, the check is considered honored.

"On Them" Checks   If the drawer and the payee or holder have accounts at *different* banks, the payor and depository bank are not the same bank. In this case, the check is called an **"on them" item**.

Each bank in the collection process, including the payor bank, but excepting the collecting bank, must take proper action on the check prior to its "midnight deadline". The **midnight deadline** is the midnight of the next banking day following the banking day on which the bank received an "on them" check for collection [UCC 4-104(a)(10)]. Collecting banks are permitted to act within a reasonably longer time, but the bank then has the burden of establishing the timeliness of its action [UCC 4-202(b)].

This deadline is of particular importance to the payor bank: If the payor bank does not dishonor a check by its midnight deadline, the bank is *accountable* (liable) for the face amount of the check. It does not matter whether the check is properly payable or not [UCC 4-302(a)].

Consider This Example   If on Wednesday morning a payor bank receives an on them check drawn on an account at the bank, it has until midnight of the next banking day, Thursday, to dishonor the check. If it does not, the check is considered paid by the bank. This deadline does not apply to on us checks, which clear when the bank opens on the second business day following receipt of the checks (unless they are dishonored).

final settlement
Occurs when the payor bank (1) pays the check in cash, (2) settles for the check without having a right to revoke the settlement, or (3) fails to dishonor the check within certain statutory time periods.

"on us" item
A check that is presented for payment where the depository bank is also the payor bank. That is, the drawer and payee or holder have accounts at the same bank.

"on them" item
A check presented for payment by the payee or holder where the depository bank and the payor bank are not the *same* bank.

midnight deadline
The midnight of the next banking day following the banking day on which the bank received the on them check for collection.

Instead of depositing an on them check for collection, a depositor can physically present the check for payment at the payor bank. This is called **presentment across the counter**. In this case, the payor bank has until the end of that banking day to dishonor the check. If it fails to do so, it must pay the check [UCC 4-301(a)].

Deposit of Money   A deposit of money to an account becomes available for withdrawal at the opening of the next banking day following the deposit [UCC 4-215(a)].

The "Four Legals" That Prevent Payment of a Check

Sometimes the payor bank will receive some form of notice that affects the payment of a check that has been presented for collection and is in the process of being *posted*. The following types of notices or actions—known as the **four legals**—effectively prevent payment of the check:

1. Receipt of a notice affecting the account, such as a notice of the customer's death, adjudgment of incompetence, or bankruptcy.
2. Receipt of service of a court order or other legal process that "freezes" the customer's account, such as a writ of garnishment.
3. Receipt of a stop-payment order from the drawer.
4. The payor bank's exercise of its right of setoff against the customer's account.

If one of these four legals is received before the payor bank has finished its process of posting, the check cannot be paid contrary to the legal notice or action. However, the account is not affected if the check was paid or the process of posting was completed before the notice was received. The **process of posting** is considered completed when (1) the responsible bank officer has made a decision to pay the check, and (2) the proper book entry has been made to charge the drawer's account the amount of the check.

Failure to Examine Bank Statements in a Timely Manner

Ordinarily, banks send their checking account customers monthly statements of account. The canceled checks usually accompany the statement, although banks are not required to send them. If the canceled checks are not sent to the customer, the statement of account must provide sufficient information to allow the customer to identify the checks paid (e.g., check number, amount, date of payment) [UCC 4-406(a)]. In addition, if the checks are not returned to the customer, the bank must retain either the original checks or legible copies for seven years. A customer may request the check or a copy of it during this period [UCC 4-406(b)].

The customer owes a duty to examine the statements (and canceled checks, if received) promptly and with reasonable care to determine if any payment was not authorized because of alteration of a check or a forged signature. The customer must promptly notify the bank of unauthorized payments [UCC 4-406(c)]. The customer is liable if the payor bank suffers a loss because of the customer's failure to perform these duties [UCC 4-406(d)(1)].

Liability of Collecting Banks for Their Own Negligence

The collecting bank owes a **duty to use ordinary care** in presenting and sending a check for collection, sending notices of dishonor, and taking other actions in the collection process. Failure to do so constitutes *negligence*. A collecting bank that takes proper action on a check prior to its midnight deadline is deemed to have exercised ordinary care. A bank is liable only for losses caused by its own negligence [UCC 4-202].

Contemporary Business Application

MISSING THE "MIDNIGHT DEADLINE"—A BANK TURNS INTO A PUMPKIN

In processing checks for collection, each bank in the collection process must take proper action on the check prior to its "**midnight deadline**." The midnight deadline is the midnight of the next banking day following the banking day in which the bank received an "on them" item—that is, a check drawn on another bank—for collection. What happens if a bank misses its midnight deadline and the check bounces? The following case answers this question.

Robert Dean Financial (RDF), a mortgage broker, and George I. Benny, one of its clients, used Chicago Title Insurance Company (Title Company) as the escrow agent to close certain real estate transactions in which they were engaged. RDF and Benny wrote checks totaling $17 million drawn on their account at the San Mateo, California, branch office of California Canadian Bank. The checks were payable to the Title Company as payee.

The Title Company deposited the checks from RDF and Benny at its bank, the Bank of San Francisco, for collection. This bank forwarded them to Crocker Bank, which in turn forwarded them to the San Francisco home office of California Canadian Bank for presentment. The next day,

the home office of California Canadian Bank sent the checks to its San Mateo branch office for payment. The San Mateo branch dishonored the checks because there were no funds in the drawer's account to pay the checks. The checks left the San Mateo branch by courier for California Canadian Bank's in-house data-processing and computer center prior to the midnight deadline, but the checks were not delivered back to Crocker Bank until the next day—which was after the midnight deadline.

Unfortunately, RDF and Benny were engaged in a massive check fraud operation, and as a result either the Title Company or California Canadian Bank would end up bearing the loss. Litigation ensued between these two parties. The court held that California Canadian Bank should bear the loss because it failed to return the dishonored checks to Crocker Bank before the midnight deadline prescribed by the UCC. With interest, the judgment against California Canadian Bank totaled $25 million. That is a high price to pay for being one day late in returning bounced checks! [*Chicago Title Insurance Company v. California Canadian Bank*, 1 Cal.App. 4th 798, 2 Cal.Rptr.2d 422 (Cal.App. 1992)]

E-Commerce & Internet Law

COMMERCIAL WIRE TRANSFERS

Commercial or **wholesale wire transfers** are often used to transfer payments between businesses and financial institutions. Trillions of dollars per day are transferred over the two principal wire payment systems—the **Federal Reserve wire transfer network (Fedwire)** and the **New York Clearing House Interbank Payments System (CHIPS)**. A wire transfer often involves a large amount of money (multimillion-dollar transactions are commonplace). The benefits of using wire transfers are their speed—most transfers are completed in the same day—and low cost. Banks sometimes require a customer to pay for a fund transfer in advance. On other occasions, however, a bank will extend credit to a customer and pay the fund transfer. The customer is liable to pay the bank for any properly paid fund transfer.

Article 4A—Fund Transfers of the UCC, which was promulgated in 1989, governs wholesale wire transfers. Most states have adopted this article. Where adopted, Article 4A governs the rights and obligations between parties to a fund transfer unless they have entered into a contrary agreement. Article 4A applies only to *commercial* electronic fund transfers; consumer electronic fund transfers subject to the Electronic Fund Transfer Act are not subject to Article 4A.

Fund transfers are not complex transactions. For example, suppose Diebold Corporation wants to pay Bethlehem Steel for supplies it purchased. Instead of delivering a negotiable instrument such as a check to Bethlehem, Diebold instructs its bank to wire the funds to Bethlehem's bank with instructions to credit Bethlehem's account. Diebold's

e-biz

(box continues)

order is called a *payment order*. Diebold is the *originator* of the wire transfer and Bethlehem is the *beneficiary*. Diebold's bank is called the *originator's bank* and Bethlehem's bank is called the *beneficiary's bank*. In more complex transactions, there may be one or more additional banks known as *intermediary banks* between the originator's bank and the beneficiary's bank [UCC 4A-103(a)].

If a receiving bank mistakenly pays a greater amount to the beneficiary than ordered, the originator is liable for only the amount he or she instructed to be paid. The receiving bank that erred has the burden of recovering any overpayment from the beneficiary [UCC 4A-303(a)]. If a wrong beneficiary is paid, the originator is not obliged to pay his or her payment order. The bank that issued the erroneous

payment order has the burden of recovering the payment from the improper beneficiary [UCC 4A-303(c)].

Banks and customers usually establish security procedures (e.g., codes, identifying numbers, or words) to prevent unauthorized electronic payment orders. To protect the bank from liability for unauthorized payment orders, the security procedure must be commercially reasonable. If the bank verifies the authenticity of a payment order by complying with such a security procedure and pays the order, the customer is bound to pay the order even if it was not authorized [UCC 4A-202]. The customer is not liable if it can prove that the unauthorized order was not initiated by an employee or other agent or by a person who obtained that information from a source controlled by the customer [UCC 4A-203].

Working the Web

Internet Banking and Financial Index Here is a site where you can find out about careers in banking, national banks, international banks, mortgage banks, bank technology, and other resources.

Visit at **www.ddsi.com/banking**

World Bank Find out all about the World Bank Group at their Web site.

Visit at **www.worldbank.org**

Organization for Economic Development The Organization for Economic Development maintains a Web site full of useful information.

Visit at **www.oecd.org**

Bank of Canada Everything you ever wanted to know about the Bank of Canada is available at its Web site.

Visit at **www.bank-banque-canada.ca/english**

CYBER EXERCISES

1. Using the Internet Banking and Financial Index, find out about banking jobs.

2. Using the World Bank Web site, find the date of the next annual Conference on Development Economics.

3. From the OECD Web site, find and print the summary of a free document called "Electronic Commerce Opportunities and Challenges for Government (The *Sacher Report*)".

4. Is information on the Bank of Canada Web site available in English?

*C*ASES AND *E*XERCISES

CRITICAL LEGAL THINKING CASES

26.1. In October 1978 Dr. Graham Wood purchased a cashier's check in the amount of $6,000 from Central Bank of the South (Bank). The check was made payable to Ken

Walker and delivered to him. In September 1979, the Bank's branch manager informed Wood that the cashier's check was still outstanding. Wood subsequently signed a form requesting that payment be stopped and a replacement check issued. He also agreed to indemnify Bank for any damages resulting from the issuance of the replacement check, which was issued to Wood. In April 1980, Walker deposited the original cashier's check in his bank, which was paid by Bank. Bank requested that Wood repay the bank $6,000. When he refused, Bank sued Wood to recover this amount. Who wins? [*Wood v. Central Bank of the South*, 435 So.2d 1287 (Ala.App. 1982)]

26.2. Louise Kalbe maintained a checking account at the Pulaski State Bank (Bank) in Wisconsin. In December 1981, Kalbe made out a check of $7,260 payable to cash. Thereafter, she misplaced it but did not report the missing check to Bank or stop payment on it. In January 1982, some unknown person presented the check to a Florida bank for payment. The Florida bank paid the check and sent it to Bank for collection. Bank paid the check even though it created a $6,542.12 overdraft in Kalbe's account and requested that Kalbe pay it this amount. When she refused, Bank sued Kalbe to collect the overdraft. Who wins? [*Pulaski State Bank v. Kalbe*, 364 N.W.2d 162 (Wis.App. 1985)]

26.3. Larry J. Goodwin and his wife maintained a checking and savings account at City National Bank of Fort Smith (Bank). Bank also had a customer named Larry K. Goodwin. In November 1985, two loans of Larry K. Goodwin were in default. Bank mistakenly took money from Larry J. Goodwin's checking account to pay the loans. On Saturday, November 30, 1985, the Goodwins received written notice that four of their checks, which were written to merchants, had been dishonored for insufficient funds. When the Goodwins investigated, they discovered their checking account balance was zero and Bank had placed their savings account on hold. After being informed of the error, Bank promised to send letters of apology to the four merchants and to correct the error. However, Bank subsequently "bounced" several other checks of the Goodwins. Eventually, Bank notified all of the parties of its error. On January 14, 1986, the Goodwins closed their accounts at Bank and were paid the correct balances due. They sued Bank for consequential and punitive damages for wrongful dishonor. Who wins? [*City National Bank of Fort Smith v. Goodwin*, 783 S.W.2d 335 (AR 1990)]

26.4. On June 30, 1972, Charles Ragusa & Son (Ragusa), a partnership consisting of Charles and Michael Ragusa, issued a check in the amount of $5,000 payable to Southern Masonry, Inc. (Southern). The check was drawn on Community State Bank (Bank). Several days later, Southern informed Ragusa that the check had been lost. Ragusa issued a replacement check for the same amount and sent it to Southern, which cashed it. At the same time, Ragusa gave a verbal stop payment to Bank regarding the original check. In July 1975, the original check was deposited by Southern into its account at the Bank of New Orleans. When the check was presented to Bank, it paid it and charged $5,000 against Ragusa's account. The partnership was not made aware of this transaction until August 4, 1975, when it received its monthly bank statement, Ragusa demanded that Bank recredit its account $5,000. When Bank refused to do so, Ragusa sued. Who wins? [*Charles Ragusa & Son v, Community State Bank*, 360 So.2d 231 (La.App. 1978)]

26.5. David Siegel maintained a checking account with the New England Merchants National Bank (Bank). On September 14, 1973, Siegel drew and delivered a $20,000 check dated November 14, 1973, payable to Peter Peters. Peters immediately deposited the check in his own bank, which forwarded it for collection. On September 17, 1973, Bank paid the check and charged it against Siegel's account. Siegel discovered that the check had been paid when another of his checks was returned for insufficient funds. Siegel informed Bank that the check to Peters was postdated November 14 and requested that Bank return the $20,000 to his account. When Bank refused, Siegel sued for wrongful debit of his account. Must Bank recredit Siegel's account? [*Siegel v. New England Merchants National Bank*, 437 N.E.2d 218 (Mass.Sup. 1982)]

26.6. Dynamite Enterprises, Inc. (Dynamite), a corporation doing business in Florida, maintained a checking account at Eagle National Bank of Miami (Bank). Sometime in 1985, Dynamite drew a check on this account payable to one of its business associates. Before the check had been cashed or deposited, Dynamite issued a written stop-payment order to Bank. Bank informed Dynamite that it would not place a stop-payment order on the check because there were insufficient funds in the account to pay the check. Several weeks later the check was presented to Bank for payment. By this time, sufficient funds had been deposited in the account to pay the check. Bank paid the check and charged Dynamite's account. When Dynamite learned that the check had been paid, it requested Bank to recredit its account. When Bank refused, Dynamite sued to recover the amount of the check. Who wins? [*Dynamite Enterprises, Inc. v. Eagle National Bank of Miami*, 517 So.2d 112 (Fla.App. 1987)]

26.7. Mr. Gennone maintained a checking account at Peoples National Bank & Trust Co. of Pennsylvania (Bank). In June 1965, Gennone noticed that he was not receiving his bank statements and canceled checks. When Gennone contacted Bank, he was informed that the statements had been mailed to him. Bank agreed to hold future statements so that he could pick them up in person. Gennone picked up the statements, but did not reconcile the balance of the account. As a result, it was not until March 1967 that he discovered that beginning in January 1966 his wife had forged his signature on 25 checks. Gennone requested Bank to reimburse him for the amount of these checks. When Bank refused, Gennone sued Bank to recover. Who wins? [*Gennone v. Peoples National Bank & Trust Co.*, 9 UCC Rep.Serv. 707 (PA 1971)]

26.8. Dr. Robert L. Pracht received a check in the amount of $6,571.25 from Northwest Feedyards in payment for three loads of corn. The check was drawn on a checking account at Oklahoma State Bank (Bank). Pracht also maintained an account at Bank. On Friday, January 17, 1975, Pracht indorsed the check and gave it to an associate to deposit to Pracht's account at Bank. When the associate arrived at Bank around 3:00 P.M., he discovered that Bank's doors were locked. After gaining the attention of a Bank employee, the associate was allowed into Bank, where he gave the check and deposit slip to a teller. Because Bank's computer had shut down at 3:00 P.M., the teller put the check aside. The associate testified that several Bank employees were working at their desks as he left Bank. Bank was not open on Saturday or Sunday. On Monday, January 20, 1975, Bank dishonored the check due to insufficient funds. Pracht sued to recover the amount of the check from

Bank. Who wins? [*Pracht v. Oklahoma State Bank*, 26 UCC Rep.Serv. 141 (OK 1979)]

26.9. On November 28, 1978, States Steamship Company (States Steamship) drew a check for $35,948 on its checking account at Crocker National Bank (Crocker). The check was made payable to Nautilus Leasing Services, Inc. (Nautilus). Nautilus deposited the check in its account at Chartered Bank of London, which forwarded the check to Crocker for collection. The check was received at Crocker's processing center at 8:00 A.M. on Friday, December 1, 1978.

At the time the check was presented for payment, States Steamship was indebted to Crocker for loans in the amount of $2 million. These loans were payable on demand. During the latter part of 1978, States Steamship was in severe financial difficulty and was conducting merger negotiations with another steamship company. On the morning of Monday, December 4, 1978, Crocker learned that these merger negotiations had broken down and demanded immediate payment of the $2 million. Crocker then seized the $1,726,032 in States Steamship's checking account at the bank. This action left States Steamship's account with a zero balance. States Steamship's check to Nautilus, as well as other checks that had been presented for payment, were returned unpaid. Nautilus sued Crocker to recover the amount of the check. Who wins? [*Nautilus Leasing Services, Inc. v. Crocker National Bank*, 195 Ca.Rptr. 478 (Cal.App. 1983)]

ETHICS CASES

26.10. In 1982, Actors Equity, a union that represents 37,000 stage actors and actresses, sought to hire a new comptroller. A man named Nicholas Scotti applied for the position and submitted an extensive resume showing that he was currently employed by Paris Maintenance Co. as its comptroller. Scotti also stated that he had held various financial positions with the Equitable Life Assurance Society and the Investors Funding Corporation. Officers of Actors Equity interviewed Scotti and offered him the job. No attempt was made to verify Scotti's background or prior employment history.

Actors Equity maintained a checking account at the Bank of New York. During the first six months as comptroller, Scotti forged the signature of the appropriate company employee on four Actors Equity checks totaling $100,000. The checks were made payable to N. Piscotti and were cashed by Scotti and paid by the Bank of New York. The forged signatures were of professional quality. After Scotti resigned as comptroller, the forgeries were discovered. Subsequent investigation revealed that Scotti's real name was Piscotti, the information on his resume was false, and he had an extensive

criminal record. Actors Equity sued the drawee bank to recover the $100,000. Did Scotti act ethically in this case? Should Actors Equity have sued the bank to recover on the forged checks? Who wins? [*Fireman's Fund Insurance Co. v. The Bank of New York*, 539 N.Y.S.2d 339 (N.Y.Sup. 1989)]

26.11. Golden Gulf, Inc. (Golden Gulf), opened a checking account at AmSouth Bank, N.A. (AmSouth). On August 27, 1988, Golden Gulf entered into a subscription agreement wherein Albert M. Rossini agreed to pay $250,000 for stock in the company. Rossini tendered a check drawn on the Mark Twain Bank in Kansas City, Missouri, to Golden Gulf for that amount. Golden Gulf deposited the check in its checking account at AmSouth on August 30, 1988. On September 2, 1988, Golden Gulf contacted AmSouth and asked if the funds were "available." AmSouth said the funds were available for use. Golden Gulf requested AmSouth to wire transfer the funds to it in New York for use in that state. AmSouth complied with the request. On September 7, 1988, AmSouth received notice from the Mark Twain Bank that Rossini's check would not be paid due to insufficient funds. On September 8, 1988, AmSouth notified Golden Gulf that the check had been dishonored. AmSouth revoked the credit it had given to Golden Gulf's account, resulting in an overdraft of $248,965.69.

AmSouth sued to recover this amount. Did Golden Gulf act ethically in this case? Did AmSouth extend a provisional or final settlement to Golden Gulf's account? [*Golden Gulf, Inc. v. AmSouth Bank, N.A.*, 565 So.2d 114 (AL 1990)]

CRITICAL LEGAL THINKING WRITING ASSIGNMENT

Read Case A.26 in the Case Appendix [*First American Bank and Trust v. Rishoi*]. This case is excerpted from the court of appeals opinion. Review and brief the case. In your brief, be sure to answer the following questions.

1. Who was the plaintiff? Who was the defendant?

2. What type of negotiable instrument was at issue in this case?

3. Was the issuer's dishonor of the negotiable instrument proper or wrongful?

Credit and Suretyship

Creditors have better memories than debtors.

BENJAMIN FRANKLIN
Poor Richard's Almanack (1758)

Chapter Objectives

After studying this chapter, you should be able to

1. Distinguish between unsecured and secured credit.
2. Define *mortgages* and *deeds of trust*.
3. Describe the effects of not complying with recording statutes.
4. Describe the process of foreclosure.
5. Define *deficiency judgment* and describe the effects of an antideficiency statute.
6. Explain lender liability.
7. Describe material person's liens.
8. Define and distinguish between surety and guaranty arrangements.
9. Define *attachment, execution*, and *garnishment*.
10. Describe a composition agreement and assignment for the benefit of creditors.

Chapter Contents

The American economy is a credit economy. Consumers borrow money to make major purchases (e.g., homes, automobiles, and appliances) and use credit cards (e.g., VISA or MasterCard) to purchase goods and services at restaurants, clothing stores, and the like. Businesses use credit to purchase equipment, supplies, and other goods and services. In a credit transaction, the borrower is the **debtor** and the lender is the **creditor**.

In the past, debtors who did not pay their debts promptly were treated harshly. Some countries sentenced defaulting debtors to "debtor's prisons", and others compelled the debtor to involuntary servitude to the creditor until the debt had been worked off. Today, in the United States, federal and state consumer protection laws exist to protect debtors from abusive and unfair conduct by creditors.

This chapter discusses the rights of creditors and debtors under these laws and the resolution of credit disputes.

debtor
The borrower in a credit transaction.

creditor
The lender in a credit transaction.

Business Brief
The United States is a credit economy. Businesses and individuals use credit to purchase many goods and services.

*T*YPES OF CREDIT

Credit may be extended on either an *unsecured* or *secured* basis. The following paragraphs discuss these types of credit.

Unsecured Credit

Unsecured credit does not require any security (collateral) to protect the payment of the debt. Instead, the creditor relies on the debtor's promise to repay the principal (plus any interest) when it is due. If the debtor fails to make the payments, the creditor may bring legal action and obtain a judgment against him or her. If the debtor is *judgment-proof* (i.e., has little or no property or no income that can be garnished), the creditor may never collect.

unsecured credit
Credit that does not require any security (collateral) to protect the payment of the debt.

Many consumer purchases are made with credit cards. This creates a debtor-creditor relationship between the consumer-borrower and the issuer of the credit card.

Secured Credit

To minimize the risk associated with extending unsecured credit, a creditor may require a security interest in the debtor's property (collateral). The collateral secures payment of the loan. This is called **secured credit**. Security interests may be taken in real, personal, intangible, and other property.

secured credit
Credit that requires security (collateral) to secure payment of the loan.

deficiency judgment
Judgment of a court that permits a secured lender to recover other property or income from a defaulting debtor if the collateral is insufficient to repay the unpaid loan.

If the debtor fails to make the payments when due, the collateral may be repossessed to recover the outstanding amount. Generally, if the sale of the collateral is insufficient to repay the amount of the loan (plus any interest), the creditor may bring a lawsuit against the debtor to recover a **deficiency judgment** for the difference. Some states prohibit or limit deficiency judgments with respect to certain types of loans.

Contemporary Business Application

KLONDIKE BAR'S UNSECURED CLAIM MELTS

Generally, a creditor would rather be a secured creditor than an unsecured creditor because of the extra protection and priority status the secured position gives the creditor. The following case shows why.

Sunstate Dairy & Food Products Co. (Sunstate) distributed dairy products in Florida. It had the following two debts among its other debts:

1. On November 19, 1990, Sunstate borrowed money from Barclays Business Credit, Inc. (Barclays), and signed a security agreement granting Barclays a continuing security interest in and lien upon substantially all of Sunstate's personal property, including all of Sunstate's inventory, equipment, accounts receivable, and general intangibles then existing or thereafter acquired. Barclays perfected its security interest by filing a financing statement with the proper state government authorities.

2. On February 14, 1992, Sunstate purchased $49,512 of Klondike ice cream bars from Isaly Klondike Company

(Klondike) on credit. Klondike did not take a security interest in the ice cream bars.

On February 19, 1992, Sunstate filed for bankruptcy. At that time, Sunstate owed Barclays $10,050,766, and $47,731 of unpaid-for Klondike bars remained in Sunstate's possession. Barclays and Klondike fought over the Klondike bars. Klondike filed a motion with the court seeking to reclaim the Klondike bars. Barclays sought to enforce its security agreement and recover the Klondike bars.

The court sided with Barclays because it was a secured creditor with a perfected security interest. The court found that Klondike, as an unsecured creditor, had no legal right to reclaim the Klondike bars. Klondike was merely one of many unsecured general creditors that would receive but pennies on the dollar in Sunstate's bankruptcy. Klondike learned a costly lesson: It is better to be a secured creditor than an unsecured creditor. [*In the Matter of Sunstate Dairy & Food Products Co.*, 145 Bankr. 341, 19 U.C.C. Rep.Serv.2d 113 (Bk.M.D. Fla.)]

personal property
Property that consists of tangible property such as automobiles, furniture, and jewelry as well as intangible property such as securities, patents, and copyrights.

SECURITY INTERESTS IN PERSONAL PROPERTY

Personal property consists of tangible property such as automobiles, furniture, and jewelry as well as intangible property such as securities, patents, and copyrights. The law provides for various types of security interests and liens in personal property by sellers of goods and providers of service.

Service Providers' Liens

common law lien
A lien given to artisans, laborers, innkeepers, common carriers, and other service providers on personal property of customers to secure reasonable payment for services rendered.

The common law gives artisans, laborers, innkeepers, common carriers, and other service providers liens on the personal property of customers to secure reasonable payment for labor or services rendered with the customer's consent. Such liens, which apply only as long as the lienholder holds the goods subject to the lien, are called **common law liens** or **possessory liens**. The lien terminates if the lienholder voluntarily releases the property to the debtor or a third party.

Consider This Example Suppose John takes his car into Hillary's Auto Repair Service (Hillary) to be fixed. Hillary completes the repairs, which cost $500. Hillary is given a common law lien in John's car for this amount (assuming it is reasonable) until John pays for the repairs. If no payment is received after a reasonable time, Hillary may foreclose and sell the car, retain the costs of repair (plus other costs regarding the sale), and remit the surplus to John. No lien would attach if the repairs were made without John's consent.

Statutory liens officially recognize the liens of artisans, innkeepers, common carriers, laborers, and other service providers. They are often the same as common law liens, except that they have been codified by statute.

The statutes that regulate these liens usually establish procedures allowing for the foreclosure of the lien and the sale of the secured property. Most states have enacted **Article 7** of the **Uniform Commercial Code (UCC)**, which provides a detailed statutory scheme for the creation, perfection, and foreclosure on common carriers' and warehouse operators' liens. Generally, the lienholder must send a foreclosure notice to the owner of the property before it can be foreclosed on and sold. Some state laws give the property owner the right to *redeem* the property prior to sale by paying the amount owed plus other reasonable costs incurred by the lienholder.

Many lien statutes permit the lienholder to record the lien by filing it in the appropriate public office (e.g., the county recorder's office). This is constructive notice to the world of the lienholder's rights in the property. Also, a recorded lien remains in effect even if the lienholder releases the property to the debtor or a third party.

statutory lien
A lien that codifies by statute a service provider's common law lien.

Article 7 of the UCC
An article of the Uniform Commercial Code that provides a detailed statutory scheme for the creation, perfection, and foreclosure on common carriers' and warehouse operators' liens.

Foreclosure of a Lien

Lienholders must follow the statutory procedures established by state law before the debtor's property can be sold to satisfy the debt. Most states require the lienholder to (1) notify the debtor of the proposed foreclosure and (2) advertise the proposed sale (usually by publishing a notice of the sale in a newspaper of general circulation serving the immediate area). Many statutes also establish a procedure for sale that includes the time of sale, who can bid, and the like. If no such procedure exists, the lienholder must bring a lawsuit and obtain a judgment against the debtor before foreclosing. Once the judgment is obtained, the lienholder can have the sheriff seize the property and sell it at a judicial sale.

In the following case, the court found that a statutory lien for unpaid services had priority over another lien in the same personal property.

Security Pacific Bank and Trust Company of Norman, Oklahoma v. Reiginger
610 P.2d 1222 (1980)
Supreme Court of Oklahoma

CASE 27.1

FACTS
Hacienda Hernandez, Inc. (Hernandez), a corporation, operates several Mexican food restaurants in Oklahoma. On December 22, 1976, Hernandez entered into a lease agreement to rent a storage locker at the Norman Self Storage Warehouse (Warehouse). Rent was payable on a monthly basis. Hernandez placed certain articles and equipment in the storage locker that were subject to a security interest held by Security Pacific Bank and Trust Company of Norman (Security Pacific), a bank that had loaned money to Hernandez originally to purchase the articles and equipment. At the time the loans were made, Security Pacific filed the required financing statements with the Oklahoma county clerk giving public notice of its security interests in the articles and equipment.

After Hernandez failed to pay rent for the months of February and March 1977, Warehouse mailed a certified letter to Hernandez requesting the overdue payment. No response or payment was received. A second notice was sent on March 29, 1977, informing Hernandez that if the rent was not paid by April 4, 1977, the articles inside the storage locker would be sold for the overdue rent. Again, no payment was received. The property was sold on April 14, 1977, for $79.50 pursuant to Oklahoma's statutory lien statute.

(case continues)

Security Pacific filed suit against Warehouse seeking damages. The trial court granted summary judgment in favor of Warehouse. Security Pacific appealed.

ISSUE

Does a sale of goods pursuant to a statutory lien on personal property for services have priority over a perfected security interest?

IN THE LANGUAGE OF THE COURT

Hodges, Justice   Pursuant to 12A O.S. 1971, Section 9–310, a person who furnishes goods or services to another may have a lien upon the goods in his possession. A statutory lien has priority over a prior reported security interest unless the statute expressly provides that the statutory lien does not have priority. Title 42 O.S. 1971, Section 92, does not mention whether the liens created thereunder have priority over security interests. However, it has been held that possessory liens created pursuant to this section have priority over secured parties. This rule has been followed in Oklahoma, and in other jurisdictions.

The lessee and the secured creditors assert that the lessor had a duty to discover if the property in the storage locker was subject to a perfected security interest by checking the records in the office of the Oklahoma County Clerk, where the financing statements were filed in Oklahoma County as required by the Uniform Commercial Code. It was admitted that no records were checked before the property was sold. The failure of the lessor to inspect these records did not prejudice the lessee or the secured creditors.

DECISION AND REMEDY

The court held that Norman Self Storage Warehouse's statutory lien had priority over Security Pacific's previously perfected security interest. Affirmed.

Case Questions

Critical Legal Thinking   Should a warehouses' statutory lien take precedence over a prior perfected security interest?

Ethics   Did any party act unethically in this case?

Business Application   Is a bank guaranteed that it will be able to foreclose on a security interest in goods?

Entrepreneur and the Law

ARTISAN'S AND MECHANIC'S LIEN

If a worker in the ordinary course of business works on or provides materials to another person with respect to goods, most states have statutes that grant an **artisan's** or **mechanic's lien** on the goods until the work or materials are paid for. For example, if an owner takes his or her car into an automobile service department or body shop for repairs, the mechanic who repairs the car has an *automatic lien* on the car in the amount of the services and materials provided to repair the car. If the car owner refuses or fails to pay the bill, the mechanic can sell the car to pay off the lien.

The following rules apply to artisan's and mechanic's liens:

- The owner of an automobile or other good authorizes an artisan or mechanic to repair the good.

- The artisan or mechanic does the work and provides the materials as requested.
- The owner does not pay for the services rendered and materials provided.
- The artisan or mechanic gives the required notices and sells the automobile or other good pursuant to the requirements of the relevant state statute.
- If the sale proceeds exceed the amount of the artisan's or mechanic's lien, the balance is paid to other lien-holders in the goods, and then to the owner.
- Artisan's and mechanic's liens are given priority over any existing lien on the goods. Artisan's and mechanic's liens are therefore called **super-priority liens**.

SECURITY INTERESTS IN REAL PROPERTY

Owners of real estate can create security interests in their property. This occurs if the owner borrows money from a lender and pledges real estate as security for the repayment of the loan. Security interests in real estate are discussed in the following paragraphs.

℮XHIBIT 27.1   *Parties to a Mortgage*

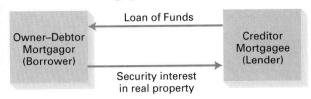

Mortgages

A person who owns a piece of real property has an ownership interest in that property. This interest is generally described in a writing known as a *deed*. A property owner who borrows money from a creditor may use this interest as collateral for repayment of the loan. This type of collateral arrangement, known as a **mortgage**, is a *two-party instrument*. The *owner-debtor* is the **mortgagor**, and the *creditor* is the **mortgagee**. The parties to a mortgage are illustrated in Exhibit 27.1.

Consider This Example   Suppose General Electric purchases a manufacturing plant for $10 million, pays $2 million cash as a down payment, and borrows the remaining $8 million from City Bank. To secure the loan, City Bank requires General Electric to give it a mortgage on the plant. If General Electric defaults on the loan, the bank may take action under state law to foreclose on the property.

Notes and Deeds of Trust

Some state laws provide for the use of a *deed of trust* and *note* in place of a mortgage. The **note** is the instrument that evidences the borrower's debt to the lender; the **deed of trust** is the instrument that gives the creditor a security interest in the debtor's property that is pledged as collateral.

    A deed of trust is a *three-party instrument*. Under it, legal title to the real property is placed with a **trustee** (usually a trust corporation) until the amount borrowed has been paid. The *owner-debtor* is called the **trustor**. Although legal title is vested in the trustee, the trustor has full legal rights to possession of the real property. The *creditor* is called the **beneficiary**. Exhibit 27.2 illustrates the relationship between the parties.

mortgage
A collateral arrangement where a property owner borrows money from a creditor who uses a deed as collateral for repayment of the loan.

mortgagor
The owner-debtor in a mortgage transaction.

mortgagee
The creditor in a mortgage transaction.

note
An instrument that evidences the borrower's debt to the lender.

deed of trust
An instrument that gives the creditor a security interest in the debtor's property that is pledged as collateral.

trustee
The holder of legal title of the real property in a deed of trust and note transaction.

trustor
The owner-debtor in a deed of trust and note transaction.

beneficiary
The creditor in a deed of trust and note transaction.

℮XHIBIT 27.2   *Parties to a Note and Deed of Trust*

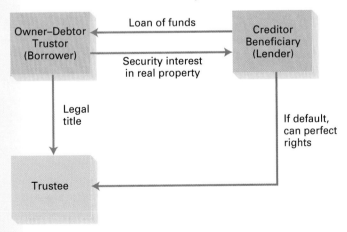

Recording Statutes

Most states have enacted **recording statutes** that require the mortgage or deed of trust to be recorded in the county recorder's office of the county in which the real property is located. This record gives potential lenders or purchasers of real property the ability to determine whether there are any existing liens (mortgages) on the property.

The nonrecordation of a mortgage or deed of trust does not affect either the legality of the instrument between the mortgagor and the mortgagee or the rights and obligations of the parties. In other words, the mortgagor is obligated to pay the amount of the mortgage according to the terms of the mortgage even if the document is not recorded. However, an improperly recorded document is not effective against either (1) subsequent purchasers of the real property or (2) other mortgagees or lienholders who have no notice of the prior mortgages.

Consider This Example   Suppose Debbie Brown purchases a house for $100,000. She borrows $75,000 from Country Bank and gives the bank a mortgage on the house for this amount. Country Bank fails to record the mortgage. Brown contracts to sell the house to Edward Johnson. He reviews the recordings and finds no mortgage against the property. Johnson pays $125,000 cash to Brown for the house. Brown defaults on her loan from Country Bank. In this case, Country Bank cannot foreclose because it failed to record the mortgage. Johnson owns the house free of Country Bank's mortgage. The bank's only recourse is to sue Brown to recover the amount of the loan (if she can be found).

In the following case, the court had to determine the priority of mortgages on the same property.

Bank of South Palm Beaches v. Stockton, Whatley, Davin & Company
473 So.2d 1358 (1985)
District Court of Appeals of Florida

CASE 27.2

FACTS
In 1980, Stockton, Whatley, Davin & Company (SWD) loaned $448,200 to Castle Builders Construction Company (Castle Builders). This loan was secured by a promptly recorded mortgage on two parcels of land. Thereafter, several additional creditors, including the Bank of South Palm Beaches (Bank), lent Castle Builders various sums that were secured by duly recorded mortgages on the same two parcels of land. The Bank's secured note from Castle Builders was in the amount of $77,500. Eventually, Castle Builders fell behind in its payments on the loan from SWD and asked SWD for additional loan funds in the amount of $150,000. SWD was willing to advance the additional money but only on the condition that the other creditors agreed to subordinate their security interests to SWD's new loans. The other creditors agreed to do so, and subordination agreements were duly executed and recorded. Apparently through an oversight of SWD, however, it never procured a subordination agreement from the Bank. SWD advanced the

$150,000 to Castle Builders, with most of the proceeds being applied to pay the amount owed to SWD on the initial loan. The deed of trust was modified to show that increase in the loan and was properly recorded. Castle Builders defaulted on the SWD loans, and SWD initiated foreclosure proceedings. The Bank was brought into the action. The trial court held that SWD had first lien priority regarding its entire loan to Castle Builders. The Bank appealed.

ISSUE
Did the modification loan from SWD have lien priority over the loans from Bank?

IN THE LANGUAGE OF THE COURT
Hurley, Judge   *This is an appeal from a final judgment determining the lien priority of competing mortgages and claims in a foreclosure action. In an apparent attempt to reach the fairest result, the trial court disregarded the "first in time" maxim and ruled that appellee's interest was superior to that of appellant bank, notwithstanding the fact that the bank's interest was*

recorded first. The well-established rule governing priority of lien interests is "the first in time is the first in right." If notice—actual or constructive—has been given, the priority of a mortgage will be determined by priority in time. The very act of recording a mortgage in compliance with the Florida recording statute constitutes constructive notice to all subsequent mortgagees.

It is not disputed that the bank's mortgage securing the $77,500 note from Castle Builders was recorded in compliance with the Florida recording statute and before SWD either recorded or entered into the modification agreement with Castle Builders. SWD therefore had constructive knowledge of the bank's prior interest, and the priority in time rule governs. Consequently, the bank's mortgage securing the $77,500 note had lien priority over all funds advanced to Castle Builders pursuant to the mortgage modification agreement.

DECISION AND REMEDY

The court held that Bank's mortgage had priority because it was recorded prior to SWD's second loan to Castle Builders. Reversed.

Case Questions

Critical Legal Thinking Should the "first in time to record" rule control the priority of competing liens? Would any other rule work?

Ethics Did SWD act ethically in arguing its second note took priority over the Bank's previously recorded note?

Business Application What is a subordination agreement? What are the economic consequences of a creditor agreeing to subordinate its loan to another loan?

Foreclosure

If a mortgagor defaults on a mortgage, the mortgagee can declare the entire debt due and payable immediately. This right can be enforced through a procedure called **foreclosure**.

All states permit *foreclosure sales*. Under this method, the debtor's default may trigger a legal court action for foreclosure. Any party having an interest in the property—including owners of the property and other mortgagees or lienholders—must be named as a defendant. If the mortgagee's case is successful, the court will issue a judgment that orders the real property to be sold at a judicial sale. The procedures for a foreclosure action and sale are mandated by state statute. Any surplus must be paid to the mortgagor.

Most states permit foreclosure by *power of sale*, although this must be expressly conferred in the mortgage or deed of trust. Under a power of sale, the procedure for that sale is contained in the mortgage or deed of trust itself. No court action is necessary. Some states have enacted statutes that establish the procedure for conducting the sale. Such a sale must be by auction for the highest price obtainable. Any surplus must be paid to the mortgagor.

foreclosure

Legal procedure by which a secured creditor causes the judicial sale of the secured real estate to pay a defaulted loan.

Deficiency Judgments

Some states permit the mortgagee to bring a separate legal action to recover a deficiency from the mortgagor. If the mortgagee is successful, the court will award a *deficiency judgment* that entitles the mortgagee to recover the amount of the judgment from the mortgagor's property.

Several states have enacted statutes that prohibit deficiency judgments regarding certain types of mortgages, such as those on residential property. These statutes are called **antideficiency statutes**.

Consider This Example Kaye buys a house in San Francisco, puts $100,000 down, and borrows $300,000 of the purchase price from a bank, which takes a deed of trust on the property to secure the loan. Suppose that Kaye defaults and when the bank forecloses on the property, it is worth only $240,000. The bank cannot recover the $60,000 deficiency from Kaye because California has an antideficiency statute.

antideficiency statute

A statute that prohibits deficiency judgments regarding certain types of mortgages, such as those on residential property.

Right of Redemption

The common law and many state statutes give the mortgagor the right to redeem real property after default and before foreclosure. This right, which is called the **right of redemption**, requires the mortgagor to pay the full amount of the debt—that is, principal, interest, and other costs—incurred by the mortgagee because of the mortgagor's default. Redemption of a partial interest is not permitted. Upon redemption, the mortgagor receives title to the property free and clear of the mortgage debt.

Some states only allow the mortgagor to redeem real property for a specified period (usually six months or one year) after foreclosure. This is called the *statutory period of redemption*. If this right exists, the deed to the real property is not delivered to the purchaser at the foreclosure sale until after the statutory period of redemption has expired.

Most state laws provide that any party in interest—such as second mortgage holder or another lienholder—may redeem the property during the redemption period.

Land Sales Contracts

Most states permit the transfer and sale of real property pursuant to **land sales contracts**. Here, the owner of real property agrees to sell the property to a purchaser, who agrees to pay the purchase price to the owner-seller over an agreed-upon period of time. Often, making such a loan is referred to as "carrying the paper."

Land sales contracts are often used to sell undeveloped property, farms, and the like. Under such contracts, the seller retains title to the property until the purchaser pays the purchase price (plus interest). During the period of the contract, the purchaser (1) has the legal right to possession and use of the property and (2) is responsible for the payment of insurance, taxes, and such.

If the purchaser defaults, the seller may declare a forfeiture and retake possession of the property. Many states provide a statutory procedure that must be followed to foreclose on a land sales contract. These procedures are often simpler, less time-consuming, and less expensive than foreclosure on a mortgage or deed of trust. Many states give the debtor the right to redeem the real property within a specified statutory period.

Contemporary Business Application

LENDER LIABILITY

Lenders, in certain circumstances, have liability exposure in making loans to borrowers. A lender is, of course, liable to a borrower if he, she, or it breaches the loan agreement or engages in fraud. Liability may also be imposed on lenders by statutes enacted by federal and state governments. This is particularly true with regard to environmental laws. Consider the following case.

The Swainsboro Print Works (SPW) owned and operated a cloth-printing facility in Georgia. In 1976, it entered into a factoring agreement with Fleet Factors Corporation (Fleet) in which Fleet agreed to advance funds to SPW against assignment of SPW's accounts receivable. As collateral, Fleet obtained a security interest in SPW's textile facility and all its equipment, inventory, and fixtures. In August 1979, SPW filed for bankruptcy. The factoring agreement between SPW and Fleet continued, but Fleet became involved with SPW's financial and management decisions to protect its security interest.

Fleet's involvement with SPW, according to the government, increased substantially after SPW ceased printing operations at the facility on February 27, 1981, and began to wind down its affairs. Fleet required SPW to seek its approval before shipping its goods to customers, established the price for excess inventory, dictated when and to whom the finished goods should be shipped, determined when employees should be laid off, supervised the activity of the office administrator at the site, received and processed SPW's employment and tax forms, controlled access to the facility, and contracted to dispose of the fixtures and equipment at SPW.

In early 1981, Fleet ceased advancing funds to SPW because SPW's debts exceeded the value of its accounts receivable. After SPW was adjudicated bankrupt, Fleet foreclosed on its security interest in some of SPW's inventory and equipment and had these items sold at auction.

On January 20, 1984, the federal Environmental Protection Agency (EPA) inspected the SPW facility and found 700 55-gallon drums containing toxic chemicals and 45 truckloads of material containing asbestos. The EPA incurred costs of approximately $400,000 in cleaning up the hazardous waste at the facility. Under the federal Superfund Law, the government can recover environmental cleanup costs from any party who owns or operates a facility at which hazardous wastes are disposed. The government sued Fleet to recover the cleanup costs. The district court denied Fleet's motion for summary judgment. Fleet appealed.

Superfund excludes from the definition of owner or operator any person who, without participating in the management of a facility, holds indicia of ownership primarily to protect his or her security interest in the facility. Fleet had the burden of establishing its entitlement to this exemption. The court of appeals held that Fleet had failed to qualify for this exemption. The court stated

> There is no dispute that Fleet held an indicia of ownership in the facility through its deed of trust to SPW, and that this interest was held primarily to protect its security interest in the facility. The critical issue is whether Fleet participated in management sufficiently to incur liability under the statute.
>
> Fleet's involvement in the financial management of the facility was pervasive, if not complete. Furthermore, the government's allegations indicate that Fleet was also involved in the operational management of the facility. Either of these allegations is sufficient as a matter of law to impose Superfund liability on a secured creditor.

The court of appeals held that the district court properly denied Fleet's motion for summary judgment. Because there remained disputed issues of material fact, the court remanded for further proceedings. [*United States v. Fleet Factors Corporation*, 901 F.2d 1550 (11th Cir. 1990)]

Material Person's Liens

Owners of real property often hire contractors and laborers (e.g., painters, plumbers, roofers, bricklayers, furnace installers, and the like) to make improvements to that property. The contractors and laborers expend the time to provide their services as well as money to provide the materials for the improvements. Their investments are protected by state statutes that permit them to file a **material person's lien** (sometimes called a mechanic's lien) against the improved real property.

When a lien is properly filed, the real property to which the improvements have been made becomes security for the payment of these services and materials. In essence, the lienholder has the equivalent of a mortgage on the property. If the owner defaults, the lienholder may foreclose on the lien, sell the property, and satisfy the debt plus interest and costs out of the proceeds of the sale. Any surplus must be paid to the owner-debtor.

Generally, the lien must be foreclosed on during a specific period of time (commonly six months to two years) from the date the lien is filed. Material person's liens are usually subject to the debtor's right of redemption.

material person's lien
A contractor's and laborer's lien that makes the real property to which improvements are being made become security for the payment of the services and materials for those improvements.

Procedure for Obtaining a Material Person's Lien Although the procedures for obtaining a material person's lien vary from state to state, the following requirements generally must be met:

1. The lienholder must file a *notice of lien* with the county recorder's office in the county in which the real property subject to the lien is located.
2. The notice must state the amount of the claim, the name of the claimant, the name of the owner of the real property, and a description of the real property.
3. The notice must be filed within a specified time period (commonly 30 to 120 days) after the services have been performed or materials delivered.
4. Notice of the lien must be given to the owner of the real property.

Lien Release If the contractor, laborer, or material person has been paid, the property owner should obtain a *release of lien* (also called **lien release**), which is an affidavit attesting to receipt of the payment. The release of lien should be signed by all subcontractors, laborers, and material persons who have contributed services or materials to the project. The release can be used to defeat a lienholder's attempt to obtain payment.

Consider This Example   Suppose Travis Company, which owns an undeveloped piece of property, hires Mason Corporation, a general contractor, to build a warehouse on the lot. Mason builds the warehouse and hires Rouse Company, a roofer, as a subcontractor to put the roof on the house. When the warehouse is complete, Travis pays Mason the full contract price for the warehouse but fails to obtain a release of lien. Mason does not pay Rouse. Rouse files a material person's lien against the warehouse and demands payment from Travis. Here, Travis must pay Rouse for the roofing work. If he does not, Rouse may foreclose on the warehouse, have it sold, and satisfy the debt out of the proceeds of the sale. Travis's only recourse is to sue Mason. Travis ends up paying twice for the roofing work.

E-Commerce & Internet Law

LAWYER'S LEGAL DUTY TO SURF THE NET

Sometimes an injured party has a valid complaint upon which to base a lawsuit but has waited too long to do so. In such a case, the defendant asserts that the relevant statute of limitations has not been met and that the case should be thrown out of court. In lawsuits based on fraud, the statute of limitations does not start to run until the defendant should have been on notice—**inquiry notice**—that he or she has been defrauded. Often there is a battle between the plaintiff and defendant about when this inquiry notice day occurred. Consider the following case.

In July 1991, Whirlpool Financial Corporation (Whirlpool) made a $10 million loan to GN Holdings, Inc. (GN), to help GN acquire another company, Cross Country Healthcare Personnel, Inc., which provided temporary nurses and other health care professionals to hospitals across the United States. GN executed a promissory note agreeing to pay Whirlpool the borrowed money at a 15.5 percent annual interest rate (payable in quarterly installments) with a balloon payment of the principal in 1998. To secure the financing, GN prepared a private placement memorandum that provided financial data, narrative information, and projections about future performance. Whirlpool relied on this information when making the loan to GN.

As happens in many new ventures, the projections painted a much rosier picture than what actually unfolded. In the years 1991 through 1993, net sales were 32 to 48 percent lower than projected, operating profit was 50 to 73 percent lower than projected, pretax profit was 95 to 257 percent lower than projected, and net income was

104 to 283 percent lower than projected. GN defaulted on the interest payment due on April 1, 1994. In July 1994, Whirlpool filed suit against GN for securities fraud, three years after having made the loan to GN. GN asserted even assuming that it committed fraud, that the one-year statute of limitations in federal securities law barred Whirlpool's lawsuit. Whirlpool contended that the one-year period did not begin to run until an inquiry date sometime after July 1993. The federal district court agreed with the defendants and dismissed the lawsuit. The court of appeals affirmed.

The court of appeals analyzed Whirlpool's contention that GN had information that it concealed from Whirlpool, causing the inquiry date to be extended. First, the court dismissed Whirlpool's claim that GN failed to disclose legislation that could affect the provision of temporary medical care personnel. The court stated that Whirlpool could have easily discovered this public information itself. Second, the court ruled against Whirlpool's claim that GN did not disclose economic trends in the temporary nursing care industry. The court noted that with reasonable diligence, which included using the Internet, Whirlpool could have easily discovered the industry trends it alleged GN concealed from it. The court admonished Whirlpool for failing to investigate GN's claims, particularly with the availability of new technology like the Internet to conduct a "due diligence" investigation. The court of appeals held that Whirlpool had not shown any reason to extend the statute of limitations beyond the date that the loan was made and held that Whirlpool's claim was time-barred by the statute of limitations. [*Whirlpool Financial Corporation v. GN Holdings, Inc.,* 67 F.3d 605 (1995)]

SURETY AND GUARANTY ARRANGEMENTS

Sometimes a creditor refuses to extend credit to a debtor unless a third person agrees to become liable on the debt. The third person's credit becomes the security for the credit extended to the debtor. This relationship may be either a *surety* or *guaranty* arrangement. Each of these arrangements is discussed in the following paragraphs.

Surety Arrangement

In a strict **surety arrangement**, a third person—known as the *surety* or *codebtor*—promises to be liable for the payment of another person's debt. A person who acts as a surety is commonly called an *accommodation* party.

> **surety arrangement**
> An arrangement where a third party promises to be *primarily liable* with the borrower for the payment of the borrower's debt.

Along with the principal debtor, the surety is *primarily liable* for paying the principal debtor's debt when it is due. The principal debtor does not have to be in default on the debt, and the creditor does not have to have exhausted all its remedies against the principal debtor before seeking payment from the surety.

Guaranty Arrangement

In a **guaranty arrangement**, a third person (the *guarantor*) agrees to pay the debt of the principal debtor if the debtor defaults and does not pay the debt when it is due. In this type of arrangement, the guarantor is *secondarily liable* on the debt. In other words, the guarantor is obligated to pay the debt only if the principal debtor defaults and the creditor has attempted unsuccessfully to collect the debt from the debtor.

> **guaranty arrangement**
> An arrangement where a third party promises to be *secondarily liable* for the payment of another's debt.

CONCEPT SUMMARY LIABILITY OF SURETIES AND GUARANTORS COMPARED

Type of Arrangement	Party	Liability
Surety contract	Surety	Primarily liable. The surety is a codebtor who is liable to pay the debt when it is due.
Guaranty contract	Guarantor	Secondarily liable. The guarantor is liable to pay the debt if the debtor defaults and does not pay the debt when it is due.

Defenses of a Surety or Guarantor

Generally, the defenses the principal debtor has against the creditor may also be asserted by a surety or guarantor. For example, if credit has been extended for the purchase of a piece of machinery that proves to be defective, the debtor and surety both can assert the defect as a defense to liability. The defenses of fraudulent inducement to enter into the surety or guaranty agreement and duress may also be cited as personal defenses to liability. The surety or guarantor cannot assert the debtor's incapacity (i.e., minority or insanity) or bankruptcy as a defense against liability. However, the surety's or guarantor's own incapacity or bankruptcy may be asserted.

> **Business Brief**
> Many businesses will not sell goods and services to minors or persons with a bad credit history unless a competent adult cosigns or guarantees payment.

Right of Subrogation

When a surety or guarantor pays a debt owed to a creditor by a debtor, the surety or guarantor acquires all of the creditor's rights against the debtor. This is called the **right of subrogation**. For example, suppose Taymour borrows $100,000 from City Bank, and Sabrina guarantees the payment of the debt. Taymour defaults and City Bank collects the

> **right of subrogation**
> The right that says the surety or guarantor acquires all of the creditor's rights against the debtor when a surety or guarantor pays a debt owed to a creditor by a debtor.

$100,000 from Sabrina. Under her right of subrogation, Sabrina acquires City Bank's right to collect the $100,000. She may bring a legal action to recover this amount from Taymour.

COLLECTION REMEDIES

When a debt is past due, the creditor may bring a legal action against the debtor. If the creditor is successful, the court will award a **judgment** against the debtor. The judgment will state that the debtor owes the creditor a specific sum of money. The amount usually consists of principal and interest past due on the debt, other costs resulting from the debtor's default, and court costs. A creditor's remedies are discussed in the following paragraphs.

Attachment

attachment

Seizure by the creditors of property in the debtor's possession to collect on a debt while their lawsuit is pending.

Many states allow a creditor to **attach** (or seize) the debtor's property to collect on a debt while their lawsuit is pending. This is a *prejudgment* remedy. To obtain a *writ of attachment* the creditor must follow the strict procedures of state law. This generally involves posting a bond with the court. The bond, which assures the debtor of recovery if the creditor loses his or her lawsuit, must cover court costs, the debtor's costs for the loss of use of the property, and the value of the attached property.

The debtor must be given notice and a hearing prior to the seizure of the property. The creditor must file an affidavit with the court (1) stating that the debtor is in default on the payment of a debt owed the creditor, (2) naming the statutory ground under which attachment is sought, and (3) giving evidence that the debtor is attempting to transfer the property prior to trial.

Once the court issues a writ of attachment, the sheriff may seize and hold the subject property pending the outcome of the creditor's lawsuit. If the lawsuit is successful, the seized property is sold to satisfy the judgment and costs of sale. Any surplus is paid to the debtor.

Execution

execution

Postjudgment seizure and sale of the debtor's property to satisfy a creditor's judgment against the debtor.

Execution is a *postjudgment* remedy. A *writ of execution* is a court order directing the sheriff to seize the debtor's property and authorizing a judicial sale of that property. The proceeds are used to pay the creditor the amount of the final judgment. Any surplus must be paid to the debtor.

Most states provide that certain real and personal property is exempt from attachment or execution. For example, many states provide a *homestead exemption*, which permits the debtor to retain his or her residence either in its entirety or up to a certain dollar amount. Exempt personal property usually includes furniture (up to a certain dollar amount), clothing, pets and livestock, vehicles (up to a certain dollar amount), tools of trade, and such.

Garnishment

garnishment

A postjudgment remedy that is directed against property of the debtor that is in the possession of third person.

Garnishment is another *postjudgment* remedy. Garnishment is directed against property of the debtor that is in the possession of third persons. To avail oneself of this remedy, the creditor (also known as the *garnishor*) must go to court to seek a *writ of garnishment*. The third person is called the *garnishee*. Common garnishees are employers who possess wages due a debtor, banks in possession of funds belonging to the debtor, and other third parties in the possession of property of the debtor.

To protect debtors from abusive and excessive garnishment actions by creditors, Congress enacted Title III of the Consumer Credit Protection Act.[1] This law allows debtors who are subject to a writ of garnishment to retain the greater of (1) 75 percent of their weekly disposable earnings (after taxes) or (2) an amount equal to 30 hours of work paid at federal minimum wage. State law limitations on garnishment control if they are more stringent than federal law.

CONCEPT SUMMARY — CREDITOR'S PREJUDGMENT AND POSTJUDGMENT REMEDIES

Remedy	Available	Description
Attachment	Prejudgment	Court order that permits the seizure of the debtor's property while the lawsuit is pending. Creditor must follow the procedures of state law, give the debtor notice, and post a bond with the court.
Execution	Postjudgment	Court order that permits the seizure of the debtor's property that is in the possession of the debtor. Certain property is exempt from levy (e.g., homestead exemption).
Garnishment	Postjudgment	Court order that permits the seizure of the debtor's property in the possession of third parties. Subject to the limitations of the Consumer Credit Protection Act and applicable state law.

Composition of Creditor's Agreements

If a debtor is overextended and owes several creditors money, the creditors can enter into an agreement with the debtor whereby they agree to accept payment of a sum less than the debt as full satisfaction of the debtor's debts. This type of arrangement is called a **composition of creditor's agreements** or a **composition agreement**. Not all of the creditors must assent. Creditors who do not assent may proceed to collect or settle their claims in their own way. If the debtor fails to perform a composition agreement, the creditors may elect to enforce either the composition or the original debt.

composition agreement
An agreement that a debtor and several creditors enter into; if the debtor is overextended and owes several creditors money, the creditors agree to accept payment of a sum less than the debt as full satisfaction of the debtor's debts.

Assignment for the Benefit of Creditors

Many states provide for an **assignment for the benefit of creditors**. This assignment allows debtors voluntarily to assign title to their property to a trustee or an assignee for the benefit of their creditors. The creditors have the choice of accepting or rejecting this tender of assets. Creditors who accept the tender are paid on a pro rata basis with the proceeds from the sale of the assets. If a creditor rejects the offer, the creditor may proceed with a legal action against any of the debtor's remaining nonexempt assets.

assignment for the benefit of creditors
An assignment that allows debtors to voluntarily assign title to their property to a trustee or an assignee for the benefit of their creditors.

International Perspective

AVAILABILITY OF INTERNATIONAL CREDIT

Commercial banks offer some financing of international and export operations. National governments and international organizations provide credit for international investments as well. Nevertheless, businesses often find it extremely difficult to obtain credit to finance international operations. This is because international ventures and transactions are perceived as riskier than domestic transactions. Third World countries also

(box continues)

have a hard time obtaining credit to develop their economies.

The **International Bank for Reconstruction and Development**, commonly called the **World Bank**, is a United Nations agency that finances development projects in member nations. The World Bank is primarily funded by developed nations. Projects include the building of dams, roads, power plants, and other infrastructures. In addition, the World Bank engages in direct investment in private enterprises through a combination of loans and equity investments.

Nations have also created and capitalized regional development banks that extend loans and offer loan guarantees to assist the economic development in member nations. These include the African Development Bank, the Asian Development Bank, the Arab Fund for Economic and Social Development, the Caribbean

Development Bank, the European Investment Bank, and the Inter-American Development Bank (comprised of Latin American countries).

National governments often extend credit to private businesses to stimulate export sales. For example, the **Export-Import Bank (Eximbank)** supports U.S. companies engaged in exporting by loaning overseas buyers funds at below-market rates of interest to purchase U.S.-made goods. The Eximbank also provides loan guarantees and insurance to foreign buyers of U.S. products. Credits have been extended for the purchase of agricultural products, heavy machinery, airplanes, and such. The Eximbank often works closely with commercial banks in structuring credit to foreign buyers.

As international trade continues to develop and become more important to the United States and other countries, credit will become more available to finance international investment and trade.

Working the Web

e·biz

FannieMae FannieMae is the world's largest source of home mortgage funds. This Web site contains links to listings of FannieMae owned properties for sale.

> Visit at **www.fanniemae.com**

Restatement of Suretyship and Guaranty The American Law Institute comprehensively sets forth and analyzes the doctrines, principles, and policies of suretyship law in the Restatement of the Law Third, Suretyship and Guaranty.

> Visit at **www.ali.org/ali/Surety.htm**

InfoUSA From this site, produced by American Business Information, Inc., you can find many businesses and

order in-depth company profiles. You can also look up businesses and people using the American Yellow Pages and American Directory Assistance.

> Visit at **www.abii.com**

CYBER EXERCISES

1. From the FannieMae Web site, find out if there are any FannieMae-owned homes in your city that are available for sale.

2. How many tentative drafts of the Restatement of Suretyship and Guaranty are there?

3. Using InfoUSA, find a business in your city.

*C*ASES AND *E*XERCISES

CRITICAL LEGAL THINKING CASES

27.1. On April 25, 1985, Ozark Financial Services (Ozark) loaned money to Lonnie and Patsy Turner to purchase a tractor truck unit. The Turners signed a security agreement giving Ozark a security interest in the tractor truck. Ozark properly filed a financing statement giving public notice of its security interest. In June 1985, the Turners took the truck to Pete &

Sons Garage, Inc. (Pete & Sons), for repairs. When the Turners arrived to pick up the truck, they could not pay for the repairs. Pete & Sons returned the truck to the Turners upon their verbal agreement that if they did not pay for the repairs, they would return the truck to Pete & Sons. The Turners did not pay Pete & Sons for the repair services and defaulted on the loan payments due Ozark. Ozark brought this action to recover the truck under its security agreement. Pete & Sons asserts that it has a common law artisan's lien on the truck for the unpaid repair services that it claims takes priority over Ozark's security interest. Who wins? [*Ozark Financial Services v. Turner*, 735 S.W.2d 374 (Mo.App. 1987)]

27.2. On November 8, 1983, Philip and Rosemary Coman entered into a contract to sell the real property known as 9 Woodland Drive, Crete, Illinois, to Robert Talbot for $120,000. On November 15, 1983, Talbot applied for a $96,000 loan from Pathway Financial (Pathway). Without telling Pathway, Talbot also obtained a $24,000 loan from Skidmore, Owings & Merrill (Skidmore), the seller's employer. At the closing on December 13, 1983, Pathway issued a check to the Comans, and Talbot gave his $96,000 note and mortgage to Pathway. Talbot paid the remainder of the purchase price—$24,000—in cash. Some of the cash was given to him as a gift from his parents. On December 15, 1983, Talbot, without giving notice to Pathway, executed a $24,000 note and trust deed to Skidmore. Skidmore filed its trust deed with the Will County recorder's office on December 27, 1983. Pathway filed the deed from the Comans to Talbot and its mortgage from Talbot with the Will County recorder's office later in the day on December 27, 1983. When Talbot defaulted on the loans, both Pathway and Skidmore filed foreclosure actions that were consolidated. Which lien has priority? [*Skidmore, Owings & Merrill v. Pathway Financial*, 527 N.E.2d 1033 (Ill.App. 1988)]

27.3. Ironwood Exploration, Inc. (Ironwood), owned a lease on oil and gas property located in Duchesne County, Utah. Ironwood contracted to have Lantz Drilling and Exploration Company, Inc. (Lantz), drill an oil well on the property. Thereafter, Lantz rented equipment from Graco Fishing and Rental Tools, Inc. (Graco), for use in drilling the well. Graco billed Lantz for these rentals, but Lantz did not pay. Graco filed a notice of a material person lien on the well in the amount of $19,766. Ironwood, which had paid Lantz, refused to pay Graco. Graco sued to foreclose on its material person lien. Who wins? [*Graco Fishing and Rental Tools, Inc. v. Ironwood Exploration, Inc.*, 766 P.2d 1074 (UT 1988)]

27.4. On October 13, 1972, Atlantic Ocean Kampgrounds, Inc. (Atlantic), borrowed $60,000 from Camden National

Bank (Camden National) and executed a note and mortgage on property located in Camden, Maine, securing that amount. Maine permits strict foreclosure. Atlantic defaulted on the loan, and commenced strict foreclosure proceedings pursuant to state law. After the one-year period of redemption, Camden National sold the property to a third party in an amount in excess of the mortgage and costs of the foreclosure proceeding. Atlantic sued to recover the surplus from Camden National. Who wins? [*Atlantic Ocean Kampgrounds, Inc. v. Camden National Bank*, 473 A.2d 884 (ME 1984)]

27.5. Elmer and Arletta Hans, husband and wife, owned a parcel of real property in Illinois. On April 26, 1986, they borrowed $100,000 from First Illinois National Bank (First Illinois) and executed a note and mortgage to First Illinois making the real estate security for the loan. The security agreement authorized First Illinois to take possession of the property upon the occurrence of a default and required the Hanses to execute a quitclaim deed in favor of First Illinois. The state of Illinois recognizes the doctrine of equitable redemption. When the Hanses defaulted on the loan, First Illinois filed this lawsuit, seeking an order requiring the Hanses to execute immediately a quitclaim deed to the property. Must the Hanses execute the quitclaim deed before the foreclosure sale? [*First Illinois National Bank v. Hans*, 493 N.E.2d 1171 (Ill.App. 1986)]

27.6. Kenneth B. and Marilyn M. Knox owned a parcel of real estate in Nebraska. N Double C, Inc. (N Double C), a corporation, entered into a contract with the Knoxes whereby they would construct a restaurant on the site, and N Double C would lease the property for a 15-year term. The lease called for a monthly payment of $5,437 as rent due on the first day of each month during the lease. David O. Carlson, Walter Nickel, and William W. Cook, Jr., the sole shareholders of N Double C, signed personal guarantees that stated that:

> In case of default by lessee, David O. Carlson, Walter Nickel, and William W. Cook, Jr., the sole shareholders of N Double C, Inc., will guarantee the monthly payments as heretofore set out until the property herein described is re-leased or up to a term of thirty-six (36) months, whichever is sooner.

The Knoxes constructed the restaurant that N Double C occupied in November 1981. N Double C paid its monthly rent through November 1985, when it defaulted and vacated the premises. When the Knoxes' good faith attempt to relet the property proved unsuccessful, they sued N Double C, Carlson, Nickel, and Cook for the unpaid rent. Are the individual defendants liable? [*Knox v. Cook*, 446 N.W.2d 1 (NE 1989)]

27.7. On December 27, 1979, Vincent Crudele sold real property located in Dade County, Florida, to Don Waters.

Waters signed a note and mortgage in favor of Crudele for a portion of the purchase price, but the mortgage was not recorded. On January 25, 1982, in an attempt to satisfy its judgment, Accent Realty of Jacksonville, Inc. (Accent Realty), delivered a writ of execution to the sheriff of Dade County to execute on all property owned by Waters. On March 19, 1982, Crudele instituted a foreclosure action against Waters. On May 4, 1982, in settlement of the foreclosure action, Waters quitclaimed (deeded) his interest in the property back to Crudele, and Waters and Crudele canceled their original agreement. Can Accent Realty execute on the property? [*Accent Realty of Jacksonville, Inc. v. Crudele*, 496 So.2d 158 (Fla.App. 1986)]

27.8. Gilbert and Alicia Loera received various medical services from St. Luke's Medical Center in Iowa (St. Luke's) during the 1970s. When the Loeras failed to pay for some of their services, St. Luke's obtained two separate court judgments against them, one for hospital services through 1979 and the other for hospital services through 1978. The state of Iowa has enacted a statute that limits garnishment of a person's wages to $250 by a single creditor per calendar year. During 1980, St. Luke's garnished Gilbert's employer, Iowa Beef Packers, Inc., on six separate occasions concerning the first judgment. After withholding a total of $250 from Gilbert's wages pursuant to these garnishments, the employer refused to withhold any additional amount. Later in 1980, St. Luke's served the employer with a notice of garnishment on the second judgment. The employer refused to comply with the garnishment. Can St. Luke's garnish any more of Gilbert's wages? [*St. Luke's Medical Center v. Loera*, 319 N.W.2d 254 (IA 1982)]

27.9. David Moxley extended credit to Mooney-Kiefer-Stewart Co., Inc. (MKS), and MKS executed three promissory notes agreeing to pay Moxley back in equal annual installments of principal and interest. The Henry B. Gilpin Company (Gilpin) unconditionally guaranteed payment of the notes in the event MKS defaulted on them. In the event of default, Moxley could elect to accelerate the entire remaining amounts on the notes plus interest. MKS suffered financial difficulty and defaulted on the payment due in July 1979.

To avoid declaring bankruptcy, MKS suggested to its creditors that they enter into a composition agreement whereby they would be paid 60 percent of the face amount of their underlying claims over a certain period of time. On July 11, 1979, all of MKS's creditors, including Moxley, accepted the offer and executed the composition agreement. On August 10, 1979, MKS rescinded the agreement in favor of a new composition agreement that extended the time of payment. All of MKS's creditors accepted the new composition agreement except Moxley, who sued MKS and Gilpin to recover the original debt owed by MKS plus interest. Who wins? [*The Henry B. Gilpin Company v. Moxley*, 434 N.E.2d 914 (Ind.App. 1982)]

27.10. In December 1982, Everything New, Inc. (Everything), voluntarily filed an assignment for the benefit of creditors under New York law. Everything's creditors approved the assignment. Albert Lyons was named assignee. Title to Everything's property was assigned to the trustee, who acted on behalf of the creditors. The assignee learned of a bank account of Everything's at Marine Midland Bank (Marine Midland). However, before the assignee could obtain these funds, Century Factors, which had obtained a judgment against Everything two days after the assignment for the benefit of creditors, served an executory lien on Marine Midland and obtained the $2,027 in Everything's account. The assignee sued to recover the money from Century Factors. Who wins? [*Century Factors v. Everything New, Inc.*, 468 N.Y.S.2d 987 (N.Y.City CivilCt. 1983)]

ETHICS CASES

27.11. On February 26, 1982, Jessie Lynch became seriously ill and needed medical attention. Her sister, Ethel Sales, took her to the Forsyth County Memorial Hospital (Forsyth CMH), in North Carolina for treatment. Lynch was admitted for hospitalization. Sales signed Lynch's admission form, which included the following section:

> The undersigned, in consideration of hospital services being rendered or to be rendered by Forsyth County Memorial Hospital Authority, Inc., in Winston-Salem, N.C., to the above patient, does hereby guarantee payment to Forsyth County Hospital Authority, Inc., on demand all charges for said services and incidentals incurred on behalf of such patient.

Lynch received the care and services rendered by Forsyth CMH until her discharge over 30 days later. The total bill during her hospitalization amounted to $7,977. When Lynch refused to pay the bill, Forsyth CMH instituted an action against Lynch and Sales to recover the unpaid amount. Is Sales liable? Did Sales act ethically in denying liability? Did she have a choice when she signed the contract? [*Forsyth County Memorial Hospital Authority, Inc. v. Lynch*, 346 S.E.2d 212 (N.C.App. 1986)]

27.12. On August 2, 1982, Sally Fitch obtained a loan from Buffalo Federal Savings and Loan Association (Buffalo Federal). She signed a promissory note for $130,000 with interest at 17 percent. The loan was secured with a real estate mortgage on property owned by Fitch located in Johnson County, Wyoming. Wyoming does not have an antideficiency statute. By October 22, 1986, Fitch was in default on the note. When she was unable to pay the loan to current status, Buffalo Federal sent her a notice of foreclosure. After publication of proper public notice, the sheriff conducted the sale as advertised on the steps of the Johnson County Courthouse. The property sold for a high bid of $66,000. Buffalo Federal applied the $66,000 to the $150,209 balance on the note and sued Fitch to recover a judgment for the deficiency of $84,209. Who wins? Do antideficiency statutes serve any social purpose? [*Fitch v. Buffalo Federal Savings and Loan Association*, 751 P.2d 1309 (WY 1988)]

CRITICAL LEGAL THINKING WRITING ASSIGNMENT

Read Case A.27 in the Case Appendix [*General Motors Acceptance Corporation v. Daniels*]. This case is excerpted from the court of appeals opinion. Review and brief the case. In your brief, be sure to answer the following questions.

1. What is the difference between a surety and a guarantor?
2. Why did this difference matter in this case?
3. Which was the defendant found to be, a surety or a guarantor?

NOTE

1. 15 U.S.C. §§ 1601 et seq.

28 Secured Transactions

Debtors are liars.

GEORGE HERBERT
Jacula Prudentum (1651)

Chapter Objectives

After studying this chapter, you should be able to

1. Describe the scope of Article 9 of the UCC.
2. Define a securing interest in personal property.
3. Describe how a security interest in personal property is created.
4. Describe the perfection of a security interest by filing a financing statement.
5. Describe the perfection of a security interest by taking possession of the collateral.
6. Define *purchase money security interest*.
7. Define *floating lien*.
8. Explain the priority of claims of competing security interests.
9. Describe the rights of a buyer in the ordinary course of business.
10. List the remedies available to secured creditors upon default by a debtor.

Chapter Contents

Many items of personal property are purchased with credit rather than cash. This is true for both consumers and businesses. Because lenders are reluctant to loan large sums of money simply on the borrower's promise to repay, many of them take a *security interest* either in the item purchased or some other personal property of the debtor. The property in which the security interest is taken is called *collateral*. When a creditor extends credit to a debtor and takes a security interest in some property of the debtor, it is called a **secured transaction**. If the debtor defaults and does not repay the loan, generally the secured party can foreclose and recover the collateral.

Article 9 of the UCC governs secured transactions in personal property. Article 9 has been adopted in one form or another by all states except Louisiana. Although there may be some variance among states, most of the basics of Article 9 are the same. This chapter discusses the rules of Article 9.

$\mathscr{A}$RTICLE 9 OF THE UCC—SECURITY INTERESTS IN PERSONAL PROPERTY

Basic Terminology

Several terms are used consistently in secured transactions. The UCC defines them as follows:

- **Debtor** The party who owes payment or other performance of the secured obligation. This definition includes sellers of accounts or chattel paper. If the debtor does not own the collateral, the term *debtor* means the owner of the collateral or the obligor of the obligation, depending on the context [UCC 9-105(1)(d)].

- **Secured Party** A seller, lender, or other party in whose favor there is a security interest, including a party to whom accounts or chattel paper has been sold [UCC 9-105(1)(m)].

- **Security Interest** An interest in personal property or fixtures that secures payment or performance of an obligation [UCC 1-201(37)].

- **Security Agreement** The agreement between the debtor and the secured party that creates or provides for a security interest [UCC 9-105(1)(l)].

- **Collateral** The property subject to a security interest, including accounts and chattel paper that have been sold [UCC 9-105(1)(c)].

Secured Transactions

Exhibit 28.1 illustrates a *two-party secured transaction*. This occurs, for example, where a seller sells goods to a buyer on credit and retains a security interest in the goods.

$\mathscr{E}$XHIBIT 28.1   *Two-Party Secured Transaction*

A *three-party secured transaction* is illustrated in Exhibit 28.2. This type of situation occurs where a seller sells goods to a buyer who has obtained financing from a third-party lender (e.g., bank) who takes a security interest in the goods sold.

---

secured transaction
A transaction that is created when a creditor makes a loan to a debtor in exchange for the debtor's pledge of personal property as security.

Article 9 of the UCC
An article of the Uniform Commercial Code that governs secured transactions in personal property.

By no means run in debt.
George Herbert
The Temple *1633*

collateral
The property that is subject to the security interest.

Exhibit 28.2   *Three-Party Secured Transaction*

CREATING A SECURITY INTEREST IN PERSONAL PROPERTY

A secured party must meet the requirements discussed below to have an enforceable secured interest in collateral.

Written Security Agreement

security agreement

The agreement between the debtor and the secured party that creates or provides for a security interest.

Unless the creditor has possession of the collateral, there must be a written security agreement. To be valid, a written **security agreement** must (1) clearly describe the collateral so that it can be readily identified, (2) contain the debtor's promise to repay the creditor, including terms of repayment (e.g., the interest rate, time of payment), (3) set forth the creditor's rights upon the debtor's default, and (4) be signed by the debtor [UCC 9-203(1)].

personal property

Property that consists of goods (such as automobiles, furniture, and jewelry), securities, patents, copyrights, instruments, chattel paper, documents of title, and accounts.

Consider This Example   Suppose Ashley borrows $1,000 from Chris and gives Chris her gold ring as security for the loan. This agreement does not have to be in writing because the creditor is in possession of the collateral. This oral security agreement is enforceable. However, if Ashley retained possession of the ring, a written security interest describing the collateral (the ring) and signed by Ashley would be required.

Value Given to the Debtor

The secured party must give value to the debtor. *Value* is defined as any consideration sufficient to support a simple contract [UCC 1-201(44)]. Normally, a creditor gives value by extending credit to the debtor to buy newly purchased goods. However, value can also be given as security for or in total or partial satisfaction of preexisting claims. There is no security agreement if the debtor does not owe a debt to the creditor.

Debtor Has Rights in Collateral

Debt is the Prolific Mother of folly and of crime.

Benjamin Disreli
Henrietta Temple *(1837)*

The debtor must have a current or future legal right in or the right to possession of the collateral. For example, a debtor may give a creditor a security interest in goods currently owned or in the possession of the debtor or in goods to be later acquired by the debtor. A debtor who does not have ownership or possessory rights to property cannot give a security interest in that property.

If these requirements are met, the rights of the secured party *attach* to the collateral. **Attachment** means that the creditor has an enforceable security interest against the debtor and can satisfy the debt out of the designated collateral (subject to priority rules discussed later in this chapter) [UCC 9-203(2)].

In the following case, the court found that a security agreement had been created.

attachment
The creditor has an enforceable security interest against the debtor and can satisfy the debt out of the designated collateral.

In re Ziluck
139 Bankr. 44, 17 U.C.C. Rep.Serv.2d 950 (1992)
United States District Court, Southern District of Florida

CASE 28.1

FACTS
Radio Shack is a retailer of computers and other consumer electronic goods. On March 28, 1989, David S. Ziluck applied for a Radio Shack credit card by signing the front of the application form below the following language: "I have read the Radio Shack Credit Account and Security Agreement. I agree to the terms of the Agreement." Paragraph 12 on the reverse side of the application form stated: "SECURITY INTEREST. We retain a security interest under the Uniform Commercial Code in all merchandise charged to your account." There was no signature line on this side of the application form. Radio Shack issued Ziluck a credit card, and Ziluck used the card to purchase several items from Radio Shack. On December 21, 1990, Ziluck filed for bankruptcy. Radio Shack filed an application with the bankruptcy court to enforce its security agreement and recover the goods from Ziluck. The bankruptcy court denied the motion, finding that a security agreement was not created because Ziluck did not sign the reverse side of the application form and because the collateral was insufficiently described. Radio Shack appealed.

ISSUE
Was a security agreement created between Ziluck and Radio Shack?

IN THE LANGUAGE OF THE COURT
Gonzalez, Judge   *The Court finds that Ziluck did in fact sign the security agreement. Ziluck signed the front of the credit card application on a line provided. The Court believes that Ziluck's signature on the front of the credit card application was sufficient to comply with the UCC. The bankruptcy court's contrary finding was in error.*

The Court also finds that the bankruptcy court erred in finding that the description of the collateral in the security agreement was insufficient. Florida Statute § 679.110 provides that "any description of personal property is sufficient whether or not it is specific if it reasonably identifies what is described." The Court believes that the language in paragraph 12 of the security agreement, "We retain a security interest under the Uniform Commercial Code in all merchandise charged to your account," reasonably identifies the property subject to the security interest— namely any property purchased with the subject credit card.

DECISION AND REMEDY
The district court held that a security agreement had been created. It vacated the order of the bankruptcy court and remanded the case for entry of an order in Radio Shack's favor.

Case Questions

Critical Legal Thinking   Should a legal contract be required to be signed at the end of the document? Why or why not?

Ethics   Did anyone act unethically in this case?

Business Application   Why do sellers take a security interest in goods sold on credit? Explain.

Contemporary Business Application

PERSONAL PROPERTY SUBJECT TO A SECURITY AGREEMENT

A security interest may be given in various types of **personal property**, including

- **Goods**, including (1) **consumer goods** bought or used primarily for personal, family, or household purposes, (2) **equipment** bought or used primarily for business, (3) **farm products**, including crops, livestock, and supplies, used or produced in farming operations, (4) **inventory** held for sale or lease, including work in progress and materials, and (5) **fixtures** affixed to real estate so as to become part thereof.

(box continues)

- **Instruments**, such as checks, notes, stocks, bonds, and other investment securities.
- **Chattel paper** (i.e., a writing or writings that evidence both a monetary obligation and a security interest), such as a conditional sales contract.
- **Documents of title**, including bills of lading, warehouse receipts, and such.
- **Accounts** (i.e., any right of payment not evidenced by an instrument or chattel paper), such as accounts receivable.

- **General intangibles**, such as patents, copyrights, money, franchises, royalties, and the like.

Article 9 does not apply to transactions involving real estate mortgages, landlord's liens, artisan's or mechanic's liens, liens on wages, judicial liens, and the like [UCC 9-104]. These types of liens are usually covered by other laws. Further, certain security interests governed by federal statutes are exempt from Article 9. For example, security interests in airplanes are subject to the provisions of the Federal Aviation Act.

*P*ERFECTING A SECURITY INTEREST

perfection of a security interest
Establishes the right of a secured creditor against other creditors who claim an interest in the collateral.

The concept of **perfection of a security interest** establishes the right of a secured creditor against other creditors who claim an interest in the collateral. Perfection is a legal process. The three main methods of perfecting a security interest under the UCC are discussed in the following paragraphs.

Perfection by Filing a Financing Statement

financing statement
A document filed by a secured creditor with the appropriate government office that constructively notifies the world of his or her security interest in personal property.

Often, the creditor's physical possession of the collateral is impractical because it would deprive the debtor of use of that collateral (e.g., farm equipment, industrial machinery, and consumer goods); other times it is simply impossible (e.g., accounts receivable). Filing a **financing statement** in the appropriate government office is the most common method of perfecting a creditor's security interest in such collateral. The person who files the financing statement should request the filing officer to note the file number, date, and hour of filing on his or her copy of the document [UCC 9-402(1)]. A financing statement covering fixtures is called a *fixture filing*.

Financing statements are available for review by the public. They are *constructive notice* to the world that the creditor claims an interest in the property. Financing statements are effective for five years from the date of filing. A *continuation statement* may be filed up to six months prior to the expiration of the financing statement's five-year term. Such statements are effective for a new five-year term. Succeeding continuation statements may be filed [UCC 9-403(2) and (3)].

Business Brief
It is good practice for a creditor who plans on taking a security interest in personal property to check whether any previous financing statements have been filed concerning the property and, if not, to properly file a financing statement covering his or her interest in the property.

To be enforceable, the financing statement must contain (1) the debtor's name and mailing address, (2) the name and address of the secured party from whom information concerning the security interest can be obtained, and (3) a statement (preferably exactly as shown in the security agreement) indicating the types, or describing the items, of collateral. The secured party can file the security agreement as a financing statement [UCC 9-402(1)].

State law specifies where the financing statement must be filed. The UCC provides that a state may choose either the secretary of state, the county clerk in the county of the debtor's residence, or, if the debtor is not a resident of the state, in the county where the goods are kept or other county office or both. Most states require financing statements covering farm equipment, farm products, accounts, and consumer goods to be filed with the county clerk [UCC 9-401].

In the following case, the court found there was a defective filing of the financing statement.

In re Greenbelt Cooperative, Inc.
124 Bankr. 465, 14 U.C.C. Rep.Serv.2d 920 (1991)
United States Bankruptcy Court, Maryland

CASE 28.2

FACTS

Greenbelt Cooperative, Inc. (Greenbelt), was a consumer-owned cooperative engaged in the retail furniture business. It engaged in the business under the trade name SCAN, and it was well known among consumers by that name. On May 4, 1987, Greenbelt executed an Equipment Lease and Security Agreement with Raymond Leasing Corporation (Raymond) to lease forklifts and other items. At the conclusion of the lease term, Greenbelt could purchase the equipment for $1. On July 6, 1987, Raymond filed a financing statement covering the equipment in the proper state government office. Raymond listed "SCAN Furniture" as the debtor on the financing statement. On December 4, 1988, Greenbelt filed for bankruptcy. The bankruptcy trustee made a motion to avoid Raymond's claimed security interest in the equipment.

ISSUE

Did Raymond properly identify the debtor on the financing statement?

IN THE LANGUAGE OF THE COURT

Derby, Judge This court concludes a Maryland court would apply a rule which requires, for it to be effective, that a financing statement be filed either under the legal name of the debtor or under a name which is substantially similar to the legal name of the debtor, so that it would not mislead a reasonably diligent creditor searching the financing records. A creditor should only be required to search under the legal name of a debtor to obtain notice of a security interest or to be put on notice to inquire further. Such a rule follows the weight of authority, it makes commercial sense, it promotes uniformity, and it is sufficiently flexible to accommodate minor errors and oversights which are not misleading.

A filing under SCAN would not be found by those looking for security interests in the assets of Greenbelt Cooperative, Inc. Consequently, Raymond's financing statement was not sufficient to perfect its security interest in Debtor's assets against the claims of others.

DECISION AND REMEDY

The bankruptcy court held that Raymond failed to identify the actual debtor in its financing statement. The court voided Raymond's lien on the equipment.

Case Questions

Critical Legal Thinking Should creditors searching financing records be required to search for financing statements filed under the debtor's trade names as well as its legal name?

Ethics Did the bankruptcy trustee act ethically in avoiding the secured creditor's security interest?

Business Application Was the filing of the financing statement under the wrong name an error that could have easily been prevented?

Perfection by Possession of Collateral

If the creditor has *physical possession* of the collateral, no financing statement has to be filed. The rationale behind this rule is that if someone other than the debtor is in possession of the property, a potential creditor is on notice that another may claim an interest in the debtor's property. A secured creditor who holds the debtor's property as collateral must use reasonable care in its custody and preservation [UCC 9-207].

Consider This Example Suppose Alan borrows $3,000 from Karen and gives his motorcycle to her as security for the loan. Another creditor obtains a judgment against Alan. This creditor cannot recover the motorcycle from Karen. Even though Karen has not filed a financing statement, her security interest in the motorcycle is perfected because she has possession of the motorcycle.

Generally, a security interest in money and most negotiable instruments can be perfected only by taking possession of the collateral. A security interest in negotiable documents is temporarily perfected for 21 days without filing a financing statement or taking possession of the documents or instruments [UCC 9-304(4) and (5)].

perfection by possession of the collateral

If a secured creditor has physical possession of the collateral, no financing statement has to be filed; the creditor's possession is sufficient to put other potential creditors on notice of his or her secured interest in the property.

We are either debtors or creditors before we have had time to look around.

Johann Wolfgang von Goethe
Elective Affinities Bk. II *(1808)*

Perfection by a Purchase Money Security Interest in Consumer Goods

Sellers and lenders often extend credit to consumers to purchase consumer goods. *Consumer goods* include furniture, television sets, stereos, home appliances, and other goods used primarily for personal, family, or household purposes.

A creditor who extends credit to a consumer to purchase a consumer good under a written security agreement obtains a **purchase money security interest** in the goods. This automatically perfects the creditor's security interest at the time of the sale. The creditor does not have to file a financing statement or take possession of the goods to perfect his or her security interest. This is called *perfection by attachment* or the *automatic perfection rule.*

> **purchase money security interest**
>
> An interest a creditor automatically obtains when he or she extends credit to a *consumer* to purchase consumer goods.

Consider This Example Marcia buys a $3,000 large-screen TV for her home on credit extended by the seller, Circuit City. Circuit City requires Marcia to sign a security agreement. Circuit City has a purchase money security interest in the TV that is automatically perfected at the time of the credit sale. Now suppose Marcia borrowed the money from Country Bank to buy the TV for cash from Circuit City. If the bank required Marcia to sign a security agreement, its security interest in the TV is automatically perfected at the time Marcia buys the TV from Circuit City.

Two types of consumer goods are excepted from this rule. Financing statements must be filed to perfect a security interest in *motor vehicles* and *fixtures.* [UCC 9-302(1)(d)].

CONCEPT SUMMARY
METHODS FOR PERFECTING A SECURITY INTEREST

Perfection Method	How Created
Financing statement	Creditor files a financing statement with the appropriate government office.
Possession of collateral	Creditor obtains physical possession of the collateral.
Purchase money security interest	Creditor extends credit to a debtor to purchase consumer goods and obtains a security interest in the goods.

The Floating-Lien Concept

A security agreement may provide that the security interest attaches to property that was not originally in the possession of the debtor when the agreement was executed. This is usually referred to as a **floating lien**. A floating lien can attach to the types of property discussed below.

> **floating lien**
>
> A security interest in property that was not in the possession of the debtor when the security agreement was executed; this includes *after-acquired property, sale proceeds,* and *future advances.*

After-Acquired Property Many security agreements contain a clause that gives the secured party a security interest in **after-acquired property** of the debtor. After-acquired property is property that the debtor acquires after the security agreement is executed [UCC 9-204(1)].

> **after-acquired property**
>
> Property that the debtor acquires after the security agreement is executed.

Consider This Example Manufacturing Corp. borrows $100,000 from First Bank and gives the bank a security interest in both its current and after-acquired inventory. If Manufacturing Corp. defaults on its loan to First Bank, the bank can claim any available original inventory as well as enough after-acquired inventory to satisfy its secured claim.

Sale Proceeds   Unless otherwise stated in the security agreement, if a debtor sells, exchanges, or disposes of collateral subject to such an agreement, the secured party automatically has the right to receive the **proceeds** of the sale, exchange, or disposition [UCC 9-203(3) and 9-306].

sale proceeds
The resulting assets from the sale, exchange, or disposal of collateral subject to a security agreement.

Consider This Example   Zip, Inc., is a retail automobile dealer. To finance its inventory of new automobiles, Zip borrows money from First Bank and gives the bank a security interest in the inventory. Zip sells an automobile subject to the security agreement to Phyllis, who signs an installment sales contract agreeing to pay Zip for the car in 24 equal monthly installments. If Zip defaults on its payment to First Bank, the bank is entitled to receive the remaining payments from Phyllis.

Future Advances   Often, debtors establish a continuing or revolving *line of credit* at a bank. Certain personal property of the debtor is designated as collateral for future loans from the line of credit. A maximum limit that the debtor may borrow is set, but the debtor can draw against the line of credit at any time. Any **future advances** made against the line of credit are subject to the security interest in the collateral. A new security agreement does not have to be executed each time a future advance is taken against the line of credit [UCC 9-204(3)].

future advances
Personal property of the debtor that is designated as collateral for future loans from a line of credit.

Contemporary Business Application _____

PERFECTION OF SECURITY INTERESTS IN AUTOMOBILES

Automobiles, like many other forms of personal property, are easily movable from state to state. Under the UCC, a secured party who has properly perfected a security interest has either (1) four months after the collateral is moved to another state or (2) the period of time remaining under the perfection in the original state, whichever expires first, to perfect his or her security interest in the property in the new state. Any subsequent perfected security interest in the new state prevails if the secured party does not comply with this rule [UCC 9-103(1)(d) and 9-103(3)(e)].

Most states have enacted **state vehicle licensing statutes** that require security interests in motor vehicles to be noted on **certificates of title** to motor vehicles. In most states, these statutes take precedence over the UCC. If a security interest is not noted on a vehicle's certificate of title, and the buyer does not have knowledge of the defect in title, the buyer is permitted to rely on the ownership and registration certificates without any further inquiry—that is, without having to search for UCC financing statements.

Information Requests and Certificate of Filing

The debtor may request information from the secured creditor about the status of the indebtedness at any time. The debtor is entitled to one statement every six months without charge; the secured party may charge up to $10 for each additional statement. The request must be in the form of a signed writing that indicates (1) what the debtor believes to be the aggregate indebtedness as of a specific date or (2) the identity of the collateral securing the indebtedness. The debtor may request the secured party to approve or correct the statement and return it. The secured party must send a written reply within two weeks of receipt of the request. Failure to do so makes the secured party liable for any resulting loss to the debtor [UCC 9-208].

Any person may request a filing officer to issue a **certificate of filing** showing (1) whether any presently effective financing statements naming a particular debtor are on

certificate of filing
A document that shows (1) whether any presently effective financing statement naming a particular debtor is on file, (2) the date and hour of any such filing, and (3) the names and addresses of the secured parties.

file, (2) the date and hour of any such filing, and (3) the names and addresses of the secured parties. The filing officer may charge a fee for this service. Such requests are usually made by persons contemplating extending credit to the debtor [UCC 9-407(2)].

Assignment, Amendment, and Release

statement of assignment

A document that is filed when a secured party assigns all or part of his or her rights under a financing statement.

A secured party may assign all or part of his or her rights under a financing statement. This is done when the secured party of record files a signed **statement of assignment** in the place where the original financing statement was filed. The statement of assignment must contain the name of the secured party of record, the name of the debtor, the file number, the date of the filing of the financing statement, the name of the assignee, and a description of the collateral [UCC 9-405(2)].

A financing statement may be *amended* by filing a writing signed by both the debtor and the secured party [UCC 9-402(4)]. A secured party of record may *release* all or any part of any collateral described in a filed financing statement. A release ends the secured party's security interest in the collateral named in the release [UCC 9-406].

Contemporary Business Application

REVISED ARTICLE 9 SECURED TRANSACTIONS

In 1999, the National Conference of Commissioners on Uniform State Laws (Commissioners) promulgated **Revised Article 9 Secured Transactions** of the Uniform Commercial Code (UCC). Revised Article 9, which is the result of almost a decade of study by the Commissioners, is designed to supercede Article 9 of the UCC. Revised Article 9

- Provides that collateral for secured transactions can include deposit accounts at banks and other financial institutions, promissory notes, permits, franchises, licenses, letters of credit, and payment intangibles where the principal obligation is monetary.
- Clarifies the law and expressly brings agricultural liens within the scope of Article 9.
- Changes the place to file for perfection purposes to the jurisdiction where the debtor is located. For a "registered organization" such as a corporation or limited

liability company (LLC), that location is the state under whose laws the debtor-organization is organized (e.g., a corporation's state of incorporation). For Article 9 purposes, an individual debtor is located at his or her principal residence.

- Allows persons other than the debtor to file a financing statement or any given record as long as the debtor authorizes the filing.

Revised Article 9 is a comprehensive proposed statute that incorporates most of the principles and concepts of the law of Article 9, and it also updates and clarifies many of these principles. The Commissioners recommend that Revised Article 9 be adopted by states to replace existing Article 9. It is expected that states will begin to enact Revised Article 9 as a state statute, either in whole or part, to replace Article 9.

PRIORITY OF CLAIMS

Often, two or more creditors claim an interest in the same collateral or property. The priority of the claims is determined according to (1) whether the claim is unsecured or secured and (2) the time at which secured claims were attached or were perfected.

UCC Rules for Determining Priority

priority

The order in which conflicting claims of creditors in the same collateral are solved.

The UCC establishes the following set of rules for determining **priority** among *conflicting claims* of creditors [UCC 9-301(1)(a), 9-312(5), and 9-315(2)]:

1. **Secured Versus Unsecured Claims** A creditor who has the only secured interest in the debtor's collateral has priority over unsecured interests.

2. **Competing Unperfected Secured Claims** If two or more secured parties claim an interest in the same collateral, but neither has a perfected claim, the first to attach has priority.
3. **Perfected Versus Unperfected Claims** If two or more secured parties claim an interest in the same collateral, but only one has perfected his or her security interest, the perfected security interest has priority.
4. **Competing Perfected Secured Claims** If two or more secured parties have perfected security interests in the same collateral, the first to perfect (e.g., by filing a financing statement or taking possession of the collateral) has priority.
5. **Perfected Secured Claims in Fungible, Commingled Goods** If a security interest in goods is perfected but the goods are later commingled with other goods in which there are perfected security interests and the goods become part of a product or mass and lose their identity, the security interests rank equally according to the ratio that the cost of goods to which each interest originally attached bears to the cost of the total product or mass.

Creditor: One of a tribe of savages dwelling beyond the Financial Straits and dreaded for their desolating excursions.

Ambrose Bierce
The Devil's Dictionary *(1911)*

Exceptions to the Perfection-Priority Rule

Perfection does not always protect a secured party from third-party claims. As discussed in the paragraphs that follow, the UCC recognizes several exceptions to the *perfection-priority rule*.

Purchase Money Security Interest—Inventory as Collateral   Under certain circumstances, a perfected *purchase money security interest* prevails over perfected nonpurchase money security interests in after-acquired property. The order of perfection is irrelevant. If the collateral is inventory, the perfected purchase money security interest prevails if the purchase money secured party gives written notice of the perfection to the perfected nonpurchase money secured party before the debtor receives possession of the inventory [UCC 9-312(3)].

Consider This Example   Toy Shops, Inc., a retailer, borrows money from First Bank for working capital. In return, First Bank gets a security interest in all of Toy Shops's current and after-acquired inventory. First Bank perfects its security interest by filing a financing statement. Later, Toy Shops purchases new inventory on credit from Mattel, a toy manufacturer. Mattel perfects its purchase money security interest by filing a financing statement and notifies First Bank of this fact prior to delivery of the new inventory. Toy Shops defaults on its loans. Mattel's lien has priority.

Business Brief
Perfection does not always protect a secured party from third-party claims. Exceptions include (1) purchase money security interests involving inventory, (2) purchase money security interests involving goods other than inventory, (3) buyers in the ordinary course of business, (4) secondhand consumer goods, and (5) artisan's and mechanic's liens.

Businesses often purchase goods on credit from suppliers. A supplier often takes a security interest in personal property to secure the loan, such as the inventory in this store.

*Debt. A rope to your foot,
cocklebars in your hair, and
a clothespin on your tongue.*

Frank McKinney Hubbard
The Roycroft Dictionary
(1923)

Purchase Money Security Interest—Noninventory as Collateral   If the collateral is something other than inventory, the perfected purchase money security interest would prevail over a perfected nonpurchase money security interest in after-acquired property if it was perfected before or within 10 days after the debtor receives possession of the collateral [UCC 9-312(4)].

Consider This Example   On September 1, Matco, a manufacturer, borrows money for working capital from First Bank and gives First Bank a security interest in its current and after-acquired equipment. First Bank perfects its security interest by filing a financing statement. On September 20, Matco purchases a new piece of equipment on credit from Allegheny Industries (Allegheny), an equipment manufacturer. On September 30, Allegheny perfects its purchase money security interest by filing a financing statement. Matco defaults on its loans. Here, Allegheny's perfected purchase money security interest prevails because the lien was perfected within 10 days after the debtor received the collateral. If Allegheny had waited until October 1 to perfect its purchase money security interest, First Bank would have prevailed.

buyer in the ordinary course of business
A person who in good faith and even with knowledge of another's ownership or security interest in goods buys the goods in the ordinary course of business from person in the business of selling goods of that kind [UCC 1-201(9)].

Buyers in the Ordinary Course of Business   A **buyer in the ordinary course of business** who purchases goods from a merchant takes the goods free of any perfected or unperfected security interest in the merchant's inventory even if the buyer knows of the existence of the security interest. This rule is necessary because buyers would be reluctant to purchase goods if the merchant's creditors could recover the goods if the merchant defaults on loans owed to secured creditors [UCC 9-307(1)].

Consider This Example   Suppose Central Car Sales, Inc. (Central), a new car dealership, finances all of its inventory of new automobiles at First Bank. First Bank takes a security interest in Central's inventory of cars and perfects this security interest. Kim, a buyer in the ordinary course of business, purchases a car from Central for cash. The car cannot be recovered from Kim even if Central defaults on its payments to First Bank.

Secondhand Consumer Goods   Buyers of secondhand consumer goods take the goods free of security interest if they do not have actual or constructive knowledge about the security interest, and they give value and buy the goods for personal, family, or household purposes. The filing of a financing statement by a creditor provides constructive notice of the security interest [UCC 9-307(2)].

Consider This Example   Suppose Jeff purchases a microwave oven on credit from Stearns, Inc., a retailer, to be used for household purposes. Pursuant to a security agreement, Stearns acquires an automatically perfected purchase money security interest in the oven. Suppose Stearns does not file a financing statement. Jeff sells the microwave oven to his neighbor, Anne, for cash. Jeff defaults on his loan payments to Stearns. Stearns cannot recover the microwave oven from Anne. Note, however, that Stearns could recover the oven from Anne if it had filed a financing statement prior to the sale to Anne.

Entrepreneur and the Law

SUPER-PRIORITY LIENS

If a worker in the ordinary course of business furnishes services or materials to someone with respect to goods and receives a lien on the goods by statute or rule of law, this **artisan's** or **mechanic's lien** prevails over all other security interests in the goods unless a statutory lien provides otherwise.

Thus, such liens are often called *super-priority liens* [UCC 9-310].

Consider This Example   Suppose Janice borrows money from First Bank to purchase an automobile. First Bank has a purchase money security interest in the car and files a financing statement. The automobile is involved in an acci- dent and Janice takes the car to Joe's Repair Shop (Joe's) to be repaired. Joe's retains a mechanic's lien in the car for the amount of the repair work. When the repair work is com- pleted, Janice refuses to pay. She also defaults on her pay- ments to First Bank. If the car is sold to satisfy the liens, the mechanic's lien is paid in full from the proceeds before First Bank is paid anything.

Secured Creditor's Remedies

Article 9 defines the rights, duties, and remedies of the secured party and the debtor in the event of **default**. The term *default* is not defined. Instead, the parties are free to define it in their security agreement. Failure to make scheduled payments when due, bankruptcy of the debtor, breach of the warranty of ownership as to the collateral, and other such events are commonly defined in the security agreement as default [UCC 9-501(1)].

Upon default by the debtor, the secured party may reduce his or her claim to judgment, foreclose, or otherwise enforce his or her security interest by any available judicial proce- dure [UCC 9-501 (1)]. The UCC provides the secured party with the remedies discussed in the following paragraphs.

Taking Possession of the Collateral

Most secured parties seek to cure a default by *taking possession of the collateral*. This is usu- ally done by **repossessing** the goods from the defaulting debtor. After repossessing the goods, the secured party can either (1) retain the collateral or (2) sell or otherwise dispose of it and satisfy the debt from the proceeds of the sale or disposition. There is one caveat: The secured party must act in *good faith*, with *commercial reasonableness,* and with *reason- able care* to preserve the collateral in his or her possession [UCC 9-503].

Consider This Example   Western Drilling, Inc., purchases a piece of oil-drilling equip- ment on credit from Haliburton, Inc. Haliburton files a financing statement covering its security interest in the equipment. If Western Drilling fails to make the required pay- ments, Haliburton can foreclose on its lien and repossess the equipment.

Retention of Collateral   A secured creditor who repossesses collateral may propose to retain the collateral in satisfaction of the debtor's obligation. Notice of the proposal must be sent to the debtor unless he or she has signed a written statement renouncing this right. In the case of consumer goods, no other notice need be given. Otherwise, notice of the proposal must be sent to any other secured party who has given written notice of a claim of interest in the collateral.

A secured creditor may not retain the collateral (and must dispose of the collateral) in the following two situations:

1. **Written Objection** The secured party receives a written objection to the proposal from a per- son entitled to receive notice within 21 days after the notice was sent [UCC 9-505(2)].
2. **Consumer Goods** The debt involves consumer goods and the debtor has paid 60 percent of the cash price or loan. In this case, the secured creditor must dispose of the goods within 90 days after taking possession of them. A consumer may renounce his or her rights under this section [UCC 9-505(1)].

A secured creditor may retain the collateral as satisfaction of the debtor's obligation if neither of the preceding two situations prevents this action.

default
Failure to make scheduled payments when due, bank- ruptcy of the debtor, breach of the warranty of ownership as to the collateral, and other events defined by the parties to constitute default.

Business Brief
The parties usually specify in their security agreement the acts that constitute default.

repossession
A right granted to a secured creditor to take possession of the collateral upon default by the debtor.

disposition of collateral

If a secured creditor repossesses collateral upon a debtor's default, he or she may sell, lease, or otherwise dispose of it in a commercially reasonable manner.

Disposition of Collateral   A secured party who chooses not to retain the collateral may *sell, lease*, or *otherwise dispose* of it in its then condition or following any commercially reasonable preparation or processing. Disposition of the collateral may be by public or private proceedings. The method, manner, time, place and terms of the disposition must be *commercially reasonable*.

The secured party must notify the debtor in writing about the time and place of any public or private sale or any other intended disposition of the collateral unless the debtor has signed a statement renouncing or modifying his or her rights to receive such notice. In the case of consumer goods, no other notification need be sent. In other cases, the secured party must send notice to any other secured party from whom the secured party has received written notice of a claim of an interest in the collateral. Notice of the sale or disposition is not required if the collateral is perishable, is threatening to decline steadily in value, or is a type customarily sold on a recognized market [UCC 9-504(3)].

Disposition discharges the security interest under which it is made as well as any subordinate security interests or liens [UCC 9-504(4)].

Proceeds from Disposition   The *proceeds* from a sale, lease, or other disposition of the collateral must be applied in the following order:

1. Reasonable expenses of retaking, holding, and preparing the collateral for sale, lease or other disposition are paid first. Attorney's fees and legal expenses may be paid if provided for in the security agreement and not prohibited by law.
2. Satisfaction of the balance of the indebtedness owed by the debtor to the secured party is next made.
3. Satisfaction of subordinate (junior) security interests whose written notifications of demand have been received before distribution of the proceeds is completed is paid third. The secured party may require subordinate security interests to furnish reasonable proof of his or her interest [UCC 9-504(1)].
4. The debtor is entitled to receive any surplus that remains [UCC 9-504(2)].

deficiency judgment

A judgment that allows a secured creditor to successfully bring a separate legal action to recover a deficiency from the debtor. Entitles the secured creditor to recover the amount of the judgment from the debtor's other property.

Deficiency Judgment   Unless otherwise agreed, if the proceeds from the disposition of the collateral are not sufficient to satisfy the debt to the secured party, the debtor is personally liable to the secured party for the deficiency. The secured party may bring an action to recover a **deficiency judgment** against the debtor. If the underlying transaction was a sale of accounts or chattel paper, the debtor is liable for any deficiency only if the security agreement so provides [UCC 9-504(2)].

right of redemption

A right granted to a defaulting debtor or other secured creditor to recover the collateral from a secured creditor before he or she contracts to dispose of it or exercises his or her right to retain the collateral. Requires the redeeming party to pay the full amount of the debt and expenses caused by the debtor's default.

Consider This Example   Sean borrows $15,000 from First Bank to purchase a new automobile. He signs a security agreement giving First Bank a purchase money security interest in the automobile. Sean defaults after making payments that reduce the debt to $13,250. First Bank repossesses the automobile and sells it at a public auction for $11,000. The selling expenses and sales commission are $1,250. This is deducted from the proceeds. The remaining $9,750 is applied to the $13,250 balance of the debt. Sean remains personally liable to First Bank for the $3,500 deficiency.

Redemption Rights   The debtor or another secured party may **redeem** the collateral before the priority lienholder has disposed of it, entered into a contract to dispose of it, or discharged the debtor's obligation by exercising a right to retain the collateral. The **right of redemption** may be accomplished by payment of all obligations secured by the collateral, all expenses reasonably incurred by the secured party in retaking and holding the collateral, and any attorneys' fees and legal expenses provided for in the security agreement and not prohibited by law [UCC 9-506].

Relinquishing the Security Interest and Proceeding to Judgment on the Underlying Debt

Instead of repossessing the collateral, the secured creditor may relinquish his or her security interest in the collateral and proceed to **judgment against the debtor** to recover the underlying debt. This course of action is rarely chosen unless the value of the collateral has been reduced below the amount of the secured interest and the debtor has other assets from which to satisfy the debt [UCC 9-501(1)].

Consider This Example Suppose Jack borrows $100,000 from First Bank to purchase a piece of equipment, and First Bank perfects its security interest in the equipment for this amount. Jack defaults on the loan. If the equipment has gone down in value to $60,000 at the time of default, but Jack has other personal assets to satisfy the debt, it may be in the bank's best interest to relinquish its security interest and proceed to judgment on the underlying debt.

The secured party is not required to elect one of the remedies. Instead, if one remedy is unsuccessful, the secured party can move on to the next. If the collateral is documents, the secured party may proceed either as to the documents or as to the goods covered thereby [UCC 9-501(1)].

judgment on the underlying debt

A right granted to a secured creditor to relinquish his or her security interest in the collateral and sue a default debtor to recover the amount of the underlying debt.

Words pay no debts.
Troilus and Cressida. *Act III*

Security Agreements Covering Real and Personal Property

If a security agreement covers both real property and personal property (i.e., fixtures), the secured party may either (1) proceed against the personal property under Article 9 or (2) proceed as to both properties in accordance with the rights and remedies provided for real property under state law. If the latter course is chosen, the provisions of Article 9 do not apply [UCC 9-501(4)].

Ethical Perspective

THE REPO MAN

If a debtor defaults on a loan, the law permits a secured creditor to use self-help to take physical possession of the goods pledged as collateral. Self-help is allowed as long as it does not cause a *breach of the peace*. This means that the use of force, threats of force, fraud, and violence are prohibited [UCC 9-503]. Many secured parties hire repossession companies to repossess automobiles, equipment, and other secured property. Was there a breach of peace in the following case?

C. W. Rutherford (C. W.) purchased a 1974 Cadillac automobile from Big Three Motors, Inc. (Big Three Motors). Big Three Motors extended credit to C. W. In exchange, C. W. signed a security agreement giving Big Three Motors a security interest in the Cadillac to secure the loan. C. W. defaulted by failing to make several scheduled payments for the automobile.

Christine Rutherford (Christine), C. W.'s common-law wife, testified at trial as follows: While she was driving the Cadillac on Interstate 65 in Mobile County, Alabama, Fred E. Roan (Roan) and another Big Three Motors employee, who were driving in a truck, forced Christine to pull her car off the road. They parked the truck to block Christine's access back onto the Interstate. After Christine and Roan exchanged words, Roan got into the Cadillac and rode with her to the Big Three Motors dealership. After arriving at the dealership, Christine locked the car, took the keys, and went into the office. When Christine left the office, she discovered that someone had taken the Cadillac from the spot where she had parked it. An employee of Big Three Motors informed her that the car had been put "in storage" because C. W. owed payments.

(box continues)

C. W. and Christine sued Big Three Motors for damages. The jury found that Big Three Motors's actions constituted a breach of the peace in violation of the UCC. Therefore, its repossession of the Cadillac automobile was a wrongful possession. The jury returned a verdict in favor of C. W. for $10,000 punitive damages and in favor of Christine for $15,000 punitive damages. The state supreme court agreed, stating that the jury could reasonably conclude from the evidence that "Big Three Motors used force, trickery, and fraud in the repossession" of the Cadillac. [*Big Three Motors, Inc. v. Rutherford*, 432 So.2d 483 (AL 1983)]

1. Did the employees of Big Three Motors act ethically?
2. Should secured creditors be allowed to use self-help to repossess goods from defaulting debtors?
3. Is the breach of the peace standard easy to apply?

TERMINATION OF A SECURED INTEREST

termination statement
A document filed by the secured party that ends a secured interest because the debt has been paid.

Once a secured *consumer debt* is paid, the secured party must file a **termination statement** with each filing officer with whom the financing statement was filed. The termination statement must be filed within one month after the debt is paid or 10 days after receipt of the debtor's written demand, whichever occurs first. In all other cases, the secured party must either file a termination statement with each filing officer with whom the financing statement has been filed or send the termination statement to the debtor within 10 days of receipt of a written demand by the debtor. If the affected secured party fails to file or send the termination statement as required, he or she is liable to the debtor for $100. In addition, the secured party is liable for any other losses caused to the debtor [UCC 9-404(1)].

E-Commerce & Internet Law

e-biz

REVISED ARTICLE 9 RECOGNIZES E-COMMERCE

Revised Article 9, which was promulgated in 1999 as a model act to replace Article 9 Secured Transactions, recognizes many aspects of e-commerce and the digital world. Some of the modern e-commerce features of Revised Article 9 are

- Filing of financing statements and other records with the secretary of state, county recorder's office, or other filing office may be made electronically as well as in writing.
- To facilitate electronic filings, the debtor's signature or other authorized signature does not have to appear on the financing statement or other electronic record.
- Electronic chattel paper, which is a record consisting of information stored in an electronic medium (i.e., not written), can be collateral of Article 9 purposes. Perfection of a security interest in electronic chattel paper may be by filing.
- The seller of software is given a purchase money security interest (PMSI) in its software that has priority over other secured interests. For example, if software with a PMSI is placed on the licensee's computer system that is subject to a security interest itself, the software PMSI takes precedence over the security interest in the computer hardware.

Revised Article 9 reflects the drafters' concern for upgrading commercial law to recognize the increased use of digital information and e-commerce.

Working the Web

Lender Liability Law Page This page, presented by an attorney for a large bank, provides accurate and authoritative information about lender liability as well as to links to case law and other Internet legal resources.

Visit at **www.america.net/~jerryb/index.html**

National Credit Union Administration This independent federal agency supervises and insures federal credit unions and insures state credit unions. It is entirely funded by credit unions and receives no tax dollars.

Visit at **www.ncua.gov**

Consumer Credit Protection Act This statute governs most aspects of consumer credit.

Visit at **www.4law.cornell.edu/uscode/15/1605.text.html**

CYBER EXERCISES

1. From the Lender Liability Law Page, find an overview of lender liability theories.

2. Can you find out information on your area credit union(s) using the NCUA site?

3. What section of the Consumer Credit Protection Act governs finance charges?

*C*ASES AND *E*XERCISES

CRITICAL LEGAL THINKING CASES

28.1. In 1984, C&H Trucking, Inc. (C&H), borrowed $19,747.56 from S&D Petroleum Company, Inc. (S&D). S&D hired Clifton M. Tamsett to prepare a security agreement naming C&H as the debtor and giving S&D a security interest in a 1984 Mack truck. The security agreement prepared by Tamsett declared that the collateral also secured any other indebtedness or liability of the debtor to the secured party direct or indirect, absolute or contingent, due or to become due, now existing or hereafter arising, including all future advances or loans which may be made at the option of the secured party.

Tamsett failed to file a financing statement or the executed agreement with the appropriate government office. C&H subsequently paid off the original debt, and S&D continued to extend new credit to C&H. In March 1986, when C&H owed S&D over $17,000, S&D learned that (1) C&H was insolvent, (2) the Mack truck had been sold, and (3) Tamsett failed to file the security agreement. Does S&D have a security interest in the Mack truck? Is Tamsett liable to S&D? [*S&D Petroleum Company, Inc. v. Tamsett*, 534 N.Y.S.2d 800 (N.Y.Sup.Ct.App. 1988)]

28.2. On July 15, 1980, World Wide Tracers, Inc. (World Wide), sold certain of its assets and properties, including equipment, furniture, uniforms, accounts receivable, and contract rights, to Metropolitan Protection, Inc. (Metropolitan). To secure payment of the purchase price, Metropolitan executed a security agreement and financing statement in favor of World Wide. The agreement, which stated that "all of the property listed on Exhibit A (equipment, furniture, and fixtures) together with any property of the debtor acquired after July 15, 1980" was collateral, was filed with the Minnesota secretary of state on July 16, 1980.

In February 1982, State Bank (Bank) loaned money to Metropolitan, which executed a security agreement and financing statement in favor of Bank. Bank filed the financing statement with the Minnesota secretary of state's office on March 3, 1982. The financing statement contained the following language describing the collateral:

> *All accounts receivable and contract rights owned or hereafter acquired. All equipment now owned and hereafter acquired, including but not limited to, office furniture and uniforms.*

When Metropolitan defaulted on its agreement with World Wide in the fall of 1982, World Wide brought suit asserting its alleged security interest in Metropolitan's accounts receivable. Bank filed a counterclaim, asserting its perfected security interest in Metropolitan's accounts receivable. Who wins? [*World Wide Tracers, Inc. v. Metropolitan Protection, Inc.*, 384 N.W.2d 442 (MN 1986)]

28.3. On March 17, 1973, Joseph H. Jones and others (Debtors) borrowed money from Columbus Junction State Bank (Bank) and executed a security agreement in favor of Bank. On March 29, 1973, Bank perfected its security interest by filing financing statements covering "equipment, farm products, crops, livestock, supplies, contract rights, and all accounts and proceeds thereof" with the Iowa secretary of state. On January 28, 1978, Bank filed a continuation statement with the Iowa secretary of state. On February 10, 1983, Bank filed a second continuation statement with the Iowa secretary of state. On January 31, 1986, Debtors filed for Chapter 7 (liquidation) bankruptcy. The bankruptcy collected $10,073 from the sale of Debtors' 1985 crops and an undetermined amount of soybeans harvested in 1986 on farmland owned by Debtors. The bankruptcy trustee claims the funds and soybeans on behalf of the bankruptcy estate. Bank claimed the funds and soybeans as a perfected secured creditor. Who wins? [*In re Jones*, 79 B.R. 839 (Bk.N.D. Iowa 1987)]

28.4. In March 1982, the First National Bank of Chicago (Bank) loaned more than $6 million to J. Catton Farms, Inc. (Catton), a huge farming operation. The loan was secured by "receivables, accounts, inventory, equipment, and fixtures and the proceeds and products thereof" and "all accounts, contract rights including, without limitation, all rights under installment sales contracts and lease rights with respect to rental lands, instruments, documents, chattel paper, and general intangibles in which the debtor has or hereafter acquires any right." To perfect its security interest, Bank filed the security agreement in the appropriate state or county recording office in every state Catton's farms were located.

In March 1983, Catton signed a payment in kind (PIK) contract with the U.S. Department of Agriculture whereby it agreed not to plant specific crops (corn) and would receive payment in kind after the growing season. On April 30, 1983, Catton filed for Chapter 11 (reorganization) bankruptcy. Catton assigned its right to receive the payment in kind to Cargill, a large grain elevator company, in exchange for over $200,000 cash. The payment in kind was made to Cargill under the assignment. The corn received by Cargill was estimated to be worth $334,666. Bank filed a motion with the bankruptcy court to enforce its security interest against the payment in kind. Does Bank have a security interest in the payment in kind? [*J. Catton Farms, Inc. v. First National Bank of Chicago*, 779 F.2d 1242 (7th Cir. 1985)]

28.5. Valley Bank has a general security interest in "all equipment" of a debtor known as Curtis Press. Rockwell International Credit Corporation (Rockwell) has a purchase money security interest in a particular item of equipment acquired by the debtor. Both security interests were duly perfected in Idaho. Generally, the purchase money security interest held by Rockwell has priority over the general security interest held by Valley Bank (Bank). A controversy arose after Press moved the equipment to Wyoming and then defaulted on the obligations owed to both Rockwell and Bank. UCC 9-103, which has been adopted by both Idaho and Wyoming, provides that the perfection of a security interest follows the collateral into a foreign jurisdiction for a period of four months or the expiration of the perfection period, whichever is less.

Neither Rockwell nor Bank reperfected their security interest in the equipment within the time requirement. Eventually, Bank located the equipment in Wyoming and reperfected its security interest by taking possession of the collateral. Rockwell then belatedly reperfected its security interest by filing a continuation statement with the Wyoming secretary of state. Rockwell brought this action to recover the equipment from Bank, alleging that its purchase money security interest has priority over Bank's general security interest. Who wins? [*Rockwell International Credit Corporation v. Valley Bank*, 707 P.2d 517 (IdahoApp. 1985)]

28.6. Clyde and Marlys Trees, owners of the Wine Shop, Inc. (Wine Shop), borrowed money from the American Heritage Bank & Trust Company (Bank). They personally and on behalf of the corporation executed a promissory note, security agreement, and financing statement to Bank. Bank properly filed a security agreement and financing statement naming Wine Shop's inventory, stock-in-trade, furniture, fixtures, and equipment "now owned or hereafter to be acquired" as collateral. The Trees also borrowed money from a junior lienholder, whose promissory note was secured by the same collateral. Wine Shop subsequently defaulted on both notes. Without informing Bank, the junior lienholder took over the assets of Wine Shop and transferred them to a corporation, O.&E., Inc. Fearing that its security interest would not be adequately protected, Bank filed a motion to enforce its security interest. Can Bank enforce its security interest even though the collateral was transferred to another party? [*American Heritage Bank & Trust Company v. O.&E., Inc.*, 576 P.2d 566 (Colo.App. 1978)]

28.7. On October 8, 1980, Paul High purchased various items of personal property and livestock from William and Marilyn McGowen. To secure the purchase price, High granted the McGowens a security interest in the personal property and livestock. On December 18, 1980, High borrowed $86,695 from Nebraska State Bank (Bank) and signed a promissory note granting Bank a security interest in all his farm products, including but not limited to all of his livestock. On December 20, 1980, Bank perfected its security agreement by filing a financing statement with the county clerk in Dakota County, Nebraska. The McGowens perfected their security interest by filing a financing statement and security agreement with the county clerk on April 28, 1981. In 1984, High defaulted on the obligations owed to the McGowens and Bank. Whose security interest has priority? [*McGowen v. Nebraska State Bank*, 427 N.W.2d 772 (NE 1988)]

28.8. In 1974, Prior Brothers, Inc. (PBI), began financing its farming operations through the Bank of California, N.A. (Bank). Bank's loans were secured by PBI's equipment and after-acquired property. On March 22, 1974, Bank filed a financing statement perfecting its security interest. On April 8, 1976, PBI contacted the International Harvester dealership in Sunnyside, Washington, about the purchase of a new tractor. A retail installment contract for a model 1066 International Harvester tractor was executed. PBI took delivery of the tractor "on approval," agreeing that if it decided to purchase the tractor, it would inform the dealership of its intention and send a $6,000 down payment. On April 22, 1976, the dealership received a $6,000 check. The dealership filed a financing statement concerning the tractor on April 27, 1976. Later, when PBI went into receivership, the dealership filed a complaint asking the court to declare that its purchase money security interest in the tractor had priority over Bank's security interest. Does it? [*In the Matter of Prior Brothers, Inc.*, 632 P.2d 522 (Wash.App. 1981)]

28.9. In 1973, Sandwich State Bank (Sandwich) made general farm loans to David Klotz and Hinckley Grain Company (Klotz). The loan was secured by the assets of Klotz's farm and after-acquired property. Sandwich filed a financing statement with the Kane County recorder to perfect its security interest. Sandwich filed the necessary continuation statements so its security interest remained in effect up to and during the time of trial. On February 3, 1984, DeKalb Bank (DeKalb) loaned Klotz funds for the particular purpose of purchasing certain cattle. DeKalb filed a financing statement on February 3, 1984, to perfect its security interest in the cattle. The cattle in question were all purchased using funds loaned to Klotz by DeKalb. When Klotz defaulted on its loan to DeKalb, DeKalb sued to enforce its security interest and to recover possession of the cattle. Does DeKalb's security interest have priority over Sandwich's security interest? [*DeKalb Bank v. Klotz*, 502 N.E.2d 1256 (Ill.App. 1987)]

28.10. Heritage Ford Lincoln Mercury, Inc. (Heritage), was in the business of selling new cars. In April 1978, Heritage entered into an agreement with Ford Motor Credit Company (Ford) whereby Ford extended a continuing line of credit to Heritage to purchase vehicles. Heritage granted Ford a purchase money security interest in all motor vehicles it owned and thereafter acquired and in all proceeds from the sale of such motor vehicles. Ford filed its financing statement with the secretary of state of Kansas on May 11, 1978. When the dealership experienced financial trouble, two Heritage officers decided to double-finance certain new cars by issuing dealer papers to themselves and obtaining financing for two new cars from First National Bank and Trust Company of El Dorado (Bank). The loan proceeds were deposited in the dealership's account to help its financial difficulties. The cars were available for sale. When the dealership closed its doors and turned over the car inventory to Ford, Bank alleged that it had priority over Ford because Heritage officers were buyers in the ordinary course of business. Who wins? [*First National Bank and Trust Company of El Dorado v. Ford Motor Credit Company*, 646 P.2d 1057 (KS 1982)]

28.11. Kent Cobado sold Gerald Hilliman and John Szata a herd of cattle. To secure payment of the purchase price, Hilliman and Szata granted Cobado a security interest in 66 cows and one bull. Cobado protested when he learned that Hilliman and Szata had culled a number of cattle from the herd. Hilliman and Szata gave Cobado 37 replacement cows as additional security. Cobado filed a financing statement with the office of the county clerk.

Cobado continued to be disturbed by Hilliman and Szata's continuing practice of culling cattle from the herd. Suddenly, without any prior warning, Cobado, aided by two men, arrived at Hilliman and Szata's premises. Szata was advised of Cobado's intention to repossess the collateral. Szata replied that all of the payments had been made on time. Cobado restated his intent. The county sheriff arrived before the cattle could be loaded onto Cobado's trucks. The sheriff warned Cobado that he would be arrested if he left with the cattle. Cobado ignored the warning, loaded the cattle onto the trucks, and left with the cattle. Is Cobado's repossession of the cattle proper under Article 9 of the UCC? [*Hilliman v. Cobado*, 499 N.Y.S.2d 610 (N.Y.Sup.Ct. 1986)]

28.12. Murphy Oldsmobile, Inc., (Murphy), operated an automobile dealership that sold new and used automobiles. General Motors Acceptance Corporation (GMAC) loaned funds to Murphy to finance the purchase of new automobiles as inventory. The loan was secured by a duly perfected security agreement in all existing and after-acquired inventory and the proceeds therefrom. Section 9-306 of the New York UCC provides that a security interest in collateral continues in "identifiable proceeds." During the first week of May 1980, Murphy received checks and drafts from the sale of the secured inventory in the amount of $97,888, which it deposited in a general business checking account at Norstar Bank, N.A. (Bank).

During that week, Murphy defaulted on certain loans it had received from Bank. Bank exercised its right of setoff and seized the funds on deposit in Murphy's checking account.

GMAC sued to enforce its security claim against these funds. Who wins? [*General Motors Acceptance Corporation v. Norstar Bank, N.A.*, 532 N.Y.S.2d 685 (N.Y.Sup.Ct. 1988)]

ETHICS CASES

28.13. On February 25, 1975, Harder & Sons, Inc. (Harder), an International Harvester dealership in Ionia, Michigan, sold a used International Harvester model 1066 diesel tractor to Terry Blaser on an installment contract. Although the contract listed Blaser's address as Ionia County, Blaser informed Harder at the time of purchase that he was going to work and live in Barry County. Blaser took delivery of the tractor at his Ionia County address on February 28, 1975. On the same day, Harder filed a financing statement, which was executed by Blaser with the installment contract, in Barry County. The state of Michigan UCC requires an Article 9 financing statement to be filed in the debtor's county of residence. The contract and security agreement were immediately assigned to International Harvester Credit Corporation (International Harvester).

Blaser subsequently moved to Barry County for about three months, then to Ionia County for a few months, then to Kent County for three weeks, and then to Muskegon County, where he sold the tractor to Jay and Dale Vos. At the time of sale, Blaser informed the Vos brothers that he owned the tractor. He did not tell them that it was subject to a lien. The Vos brothers went to First Michigan Bank & Trust Company (Bank) to obtain a loan to help purchase the tractor. When Bank checked the records of Ionia County and found that no financing statement was filed against the tractor, it made a $7,000 loan to the Vos brothers to purchase the tractor. Bank filed a financing statement on the tractor. On May 19, 1977, International Harvester filed suit to recover the tractor from the Vos brothers on the grounds that it had a prior perfected security interest. Did Blaser act ethically in this case? Who wins? [*International Harvester Credit Corporation v. Vos*, 290 N.W.2d 401 (Mich.App. 1980)]

CRITICAL LEGAL THINKING WRITING ASSIGNMENT

Read Case A.28 in the Case Appendix [*Davenport v. Chrysler Credit Corporation*]. This case is excerpted from the court of appeals opinion. Review and brief the case. In your brief, be sure to answer the following questions.

1. Who was the plaintiff? Who was the defendant?
2. Was there a default in the repayment of the loan? What actions did the creditor take to recover the security?
3. Was there a "breach of the peace" in the repossession of the vehicle?
4. What damages did the court award? How were they calculated?

Bankruptcy and Reorganization

A trifling debt makes a man your debtor, a large one makes him your enemy.

SENECA *Epistulae Morales ad Lucilium, 63–65*

Chapter Objectives

After studying this chapter, you should be able to

1. Describe the procedure for filing for bankruptcy.
2. Define *fresh start* and the discharge of unpaid debts.
3. Describe a Chapter 7 liquidation bankruptcy.
4. Define an automatic stay in bankruptcy.
5. Identify voidable transfers and preferential payments.
6. List the order of priority for paying creditors in a Chapter 7 bankruptcy.
7. Define secured and unsecured creditors' rights in bankruptcy.
8. Describe how a business is reorganized in a Chapter 11 bankruptcy.
9. Define *executory contract* and explain how it can be avoided in bankruptcy.
10. Describe a Chapter 13 consumer debt adjustment bankruptcy.

Chapter Contents

The extension of credit from creditors to debtors in commercial and personal transactions is important to the viability of the American and world economies. On occasion, however, borrowers become overextended and are unable to meet their debt obligations.

Years ago in Britain and Europe, persons who could not meet their debts were sentenced to debtors' prisons or indentured to their creditor until the debt was "worked off." To avoid such harsh results, many countries adopted bankruptcy laws that were intended to achieve a better balance between debtors' rights and creditors' rights.

The founders of our country thought the plight of debtors was so important that they included a provision in the U.S. Constitution giving Congress the authority to establish uniform bankruptcy laws. The goal of federal bankruptcy law is to give debtors a "fresh start" by relieving them from legal responsibility for past debts. This chapter discusses federal bankruptcy law, which is the exclusive law that governs throughout this country.

Overview of Federal Bankruptcy Law

Business Brief
Bankruptcy law is *federal* law. There are no state bankruptcy laws.

Article I, section 8, clause 4 of the U.S. Constitution provides that "The Congress shall have the power . . . to establish . . . uniform laws on the subject of bankruptcies throughout the United States." Federal bankruptcy law establishes procedures for filing for bankruptcy, resolving creditors' claims, and protecting debtors' rights. Bankruptcy law is exclusively federal law; there are no state bankruptcy laws.

The Bankruptcy Code

Business Brief
Under the old Bankruptcy Act, a debtor in bankruptcy was called a *bankrupt*. Under the Bankruptcy Reform Act of 1978, a debtor in bankruptcy is called a *debtor*.

Congress enacted the original **Bankruptcy Act** in 1878. It was amended in 1938 by the **Chandler Act**, and that law was completely revised by the **Bankruptcy Reform Act of 1978**.[1] The 1978 act, which became effective on October 1, 1979, substantially changed—and eased—the requirements for filing bankruptcy.

Several years later, Congress enacted the **Bankruptcy Amendments and Federal Judgeship Act of 1984**,[2] which made bankruptcy courts part of the federal district court system and attached a bankruptcy court to each district court. Bankruptcy judges are appointed by the President for 14-year terms. Other provisions of the 1984 amendments remedied abuses and misuses of bankruptcy and clarified procedures for filing bankruptcy. The Bankruptcy Reform Act of 1978, as amended, is referred to as the **Bankruptcy Code**.

Bankruptcy Code
The name given to the Bankruptcy Reform Act of 1978, as amended.

Jurisdiction of the Bankruptcy Courts

core proceedings
Proceedings that bankruptcy judges decide that have to do with creditor claims, deciding preferences, confirming plans of reorganization, and so on.

Bankruptcy judges decide **core proceedings** (e.g., allowing creditor claims, deciding preferences, confirming plans of reorganization) regarding bankruptcy cases. **Noncore proceedings** concerning the debtor (e.g., decisions on personal injury, divorce, and other civil proceedings) are resolved in federal or state court. The jurisdiction of the bankruptcy courts became effective on July 10, 1984.

Types of Bankruptcy

The Bankruptcy Code is divided into chapters. Chapters 1, 3, and 5 include definitional provisions and provisions for the administration of bankruptcy proceedings. They apply to all forms of bankruptcy. The most common forms of bankruptcy are provided by the following chapters: Chapter 7 (liquidation), Chapter 11 (reorganization), and Chapter 13 (consumer debt adjustment). The remaining chapters of the Bankruptcy Code govern the bankruptcies of municipalities, stockbrokers, and railroads.

The "Fresh Start"

The primary purpose of federal bankruptcy law is to discharge the debtor from burdensome debts. The law gives debtors a **fresh start** by freeing them from legal responsibility for past debts by (1) protecting debtors from abusive activities by creditors in collecting debts, (2) preventing certain creditors from obtaining an unfair advantage over other creditors, (3) protecting creditors from actions of the debtor that would diminish the value of the bankruptcy estate, (4) providing for the speedy, efficient, and equitable distribution of the debtor's nonexempt property to claim holders, and (5) preserving existing business relations.

fresh start
The goal of federal bankruptcy law: to discharge the debtor from burdensome debts and allow him or her to begin again.

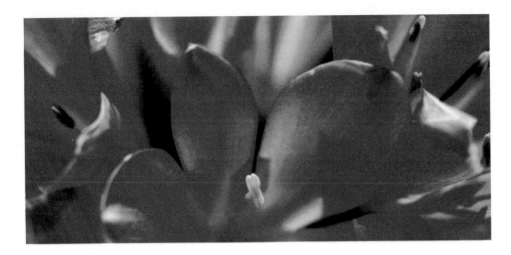

Federal bankruptcy law provides a method for individuals and businesses to discharge all or a portion of their debt and obtain a "fresh start" free of certain of their debts.

CHAPTER 7 LIQUIDATION BANKRUPTCY

Chapter 7 liquidation bankruptcy (also called **straight bankruptcy**) is the most familiar form of bankruptcy. In this type of proceeding, the debtor's nonexempt property is sold for cash, the cash is distributed to the creditors, and any unpaid debts are **discharged**. Any person, including individuals, partnerships, and corporations, may be debtors in a Chapter 7 proceeding. Certain businesses, including banks, savings and loan associations, credit unions, insurance companies, and railroads, are prohibited from filing bankruptcy under Chapter 7.

Chapter 7 liquidation bankruptcy
The most familiar form of bankruptcy; the debtor's nonexempt property is sold for cash, the cash is distributed to the creditors, and any unpaid debts are discharged.

Bankruptcy Procedure

The filing and maintenance of a Chapter 7 case must follow certain procedures. The following paragraphs outline the major steps in the liquidation process.

Business Brief
Approximately 1.5 million personal bankruptcies are filed under Chapter 7 each year.

Filing a Petition   A Chapter 7 bankruptcy is commenced when a **petition** is filed with the bankruptcy court. The petition may be filed by either the debtor (voluntary) or one or more creditors (involuntary).

Voluntary petitions only have to state that the debtor has debts; insolvency (i.e., that debts exceed assets) need not be declared. The petition must include the following schedules: (1) a list of secured and unsecured creditors, including their addresses and the amount of debt owed to each, (2) a list of all property owned by the debtor, including property claimed to be exempt by the debtor, (3) a statement of the financial affairs of the

petition
A document filed with the bankruptcy court that sets the bankruptcy proceedings into motion.

voluntary petition
A petition filed by the debtor; states that the debtor has debts.

debtor, and (4) a list of the debtor's current income and expenses. The petition must be signed and sworn to under oath. Married couples may file a joint petition.

An **involuntary petition** can be filed against any debtors who can file a voluntary petition under Chapter 7 except farmers, ranchers, and nonprofit organizations. An involuntary petition must allege that the debtor is not paying his or her debts as they become due. If the debtor has more than 12 creditors, the petition must be signed by at least three of them. If there are 12 or fewer creditors, any creditor can sign the petition. The creditor or creditors who sign the petition must have valid unsecured claims of at least $10,000 (in the aggregate).

Order for Relief

The filing of either a voluntary petition or an unchallenged involuntary petition constitutes an **order for relief**. If the debtor challenges an involuntary petition, a trial will be held to determine whether an order for relief should be granted. If the order is granted, the case is accepted for further bankruptcy proceedings. In the case of an involuntary petition, the debtor must file the same schedules filed by voluntary debtors.

Meeting of the Creditors

Within a reasonable time (not less than 10 days nor more than 30 days) after the court grants an order for relief, the court must call a **meeting of the creditors** (also called the **first meeting of the creditors**). The judge cannot attend this meeting. The debtor, however, must appear and submit to questioning by creditors. Creditors may ask questions regarding the debtor's financial affairs, disposition of property prior to bankruptcy, possible concealment of assets, and such. The debtor may have an attorney present at this meeting.

Appointment of a Trustee

A trustee must be appointed in a Chapter 7 proceeding. An interim trustee is appointed by the court when an order for relief is entered. A **permanent trustee** is elected at the first meeting of the creditors. Trustees, who are often lawyers or accountants, are entitled to receive reasonable compensation for their services and reimbursement for expenses. Once appointed, the trustee becomes the legal representative of the bankrupt debtor's estate. Generally, the trustee must

- Take immediate possession of the debtor's property.
- Separate secured and unsecured property.
- Set aside exempt property.
- Investigate the debtor's financial affairs.
- Employ disinterested professionals (e.g., attorneys, accountants, and appraisers) to assist in the administration of the estate.
- Examine proof of claims.
- Defend, bring, and maintain lawsuits on behalf of the estate.
- Invest the property of the estate.
- Sell or otherwise dispose of property of the estate.
- Distribute the proceeds of the estate.
- Make reports to the court, creditors, and debtor regarding the administration of the estate.

Proof of Claims

Unsecured creditors must file a **proof of claim** stating the amount of their claims against the debtor. The form for the statement is provided by the court. The proof of claim must be "timely filed," which generally means within six months of the first meeting of the creditors. Secured creditors are not required to file proof of claim. A secured creditor whose claim exceeds the value of the collateral, however, may submit a proof of claim and become an unsecured claimant as to the difference.

---

involuntary petition
A petition filed by creditors of the debtor; alleges that the debtor is not paying his or her debts as they become due.

order for relief
The filing of either a voluntary petition, an unchallenged involuntary petition, or a grant of an order after a trial of a challenged involuntary petition.

meeting of the creditors
A meeting of the creditors in a bankruptcy case that must occur not less than 10 days nor more than 30 days after the court grants an order for relief.

permanent trustee
A legal representative of the bankruptcy debtor's estate, usually an accountant or lawyer; elected at the first meeting of the creditors.

Business Brief
Beginning April 1, 1998, the dollar amount stated in the Bankruptcy Code will be adjusted every three years based on changes in the Consumer Price Index.

proof of claim
A document required to be filed by unsecured creditors that states the amount of their claim against the debtor.

The claim must be allowed by the court before a creditor is permitted to participate in the bankruptcy estate. Any party of interest may object to a claim. If an objection to a claim is raised, the court will hold a hearing to determine the validity and amount of the claim.

Automatic Stay

The filing of a voluntary or involuntary petition automatically stays—that is, suspends—certain action by creditors against the debtor or the debtor's property.[3] This is called an **automatic stay**. The stay, which applies to collection efforts of both secured and unsecured creditors, is designed to prevent a scramble for the debtor's assets in a variety of court proceedings. The following creditor actions are stayed:

1. Instituting or maintaining legal actions to collect prepetition debts.
2. Enforcing judgments obtained against the debtor.
3. Obtaining, perfecting, or enforcing liens against property of the debtor.
4. Attempting to set off debts owed by the creditor to the debtor against the creditor's claims in bankruptcy.
5. Nonjudicial collection efforts, such as self-help activities (e.g., repossession of a car).

The court also has the authority to issue injunctions preventing creditor activity not covered by the automatic stay provision. Actions to recover alimony and child support are not stayed in bankruptcy. The automatic stay does not preclude collection efforts by creditors against codebtors and guarantors of the bankrupt debtor's debts, except (1) in a Chapter 13 bankruptcy (discussed later in this chapter) or (2) if the codebtor is also in bankruptcy.

Relief from Stay   A secured creditor may petition the court for a **relief from stay**, which usually occurs in situations involving depreciating assets where the secured property is not adequately protected during the bankruptcy proceeding. The court may opt to provide adequate protection rather than granting relief from stay. In such cases, the court may (1) order cash payments equal to the amount of the depreciation, (2) grant an additional or replacement lien, or (3) grant an "indubitable equivalent" (e.g., a guarantee from a solvent party).

PROPERTY OF THE BANKRUPTCY ESTATE

The **bankruptcy estate** is created upon the commencement of a Chapter 7 proceeding. It includes all the debtor's legal and equitable interests in real, personal, tangible, and intangible property, wherever located, that exist when the petition is filed. The debtor's separate and community property are included in the estate.

Property acquired after the petition does not become part of the bankruptcy estate. The only exceptions are gifts, inheritances, life insurance proceeds, and property from divorce settlements that the debtor is entitled to receive within 180 days after the petition is filed. Earnings from property of the estate—such as rents, dividends, and interest payments—are property of the estate.

Exempt Property

Because the Bankruptcy Code is not designed to make the debtor a pauper, certain property is exempt from the bankruptcy estate. The debtor may retain **exempt property**.

The Bankruptcy Code establishes a *federal* exemption scheme (see Exhibit 29.1).

---

automatic stay
The result of the filing of a voluntary or involuntary petition; the suspension of certain actions by creditors against the debtor or the debtor's property.

Business Brief
The importance of the automatic stay in bankruptcy should not be underestimated. For example, in *Pennzoil v. Texaco*, Texaco filed a voluntary petition in bankruptcy to stay any attempt by Pennzoil to perfect its $10 billion judgment against Texaco.

relief from stay
May be granted in situations involving depreciating assets where the secured property is not adequately protected during the bankruptcy proceeding; asked for by a secured creditor.

bankruptcy estate
An estate created upon the commencement of a Chapter 7 proceeding that includes all the debtor's legal and equitable interests in real, personal, tangible, and intangible property, wherever located, that exist when the petition is filed, minus exempt property.

exempt property
Property that may be retained by the debtor pursuant to federal or state law; debtor's property that does not become part of the bankruptcy estate.

*ℰ*XHIBIT 29.1   *Federal Exemptions from the Bankruptcy Estate*

1. Interest up to $15,000 in equity in property used as a residence and burial plots. This is called the homestead exemption.
2. Interest up to $2,400 in one motor vehicle.
3. Interest up to $400 per item in household goods and furnishings, wearing apparel, appliances, books, animals, crops, or musical instruments, up to an aggregate value of $8,000 for all items.
4. Interest in jewelry up to $1,000 that is held for personal use.
5. Interest in any property the debtor chooses (including cash) up to $800, plus up to $7,500 of any unused portion of the $15,000 homestead exemption.
6. Interest up to $1,500 in value in implements, tools, or professional books used in the debtor's trade.
7. Any unmatured life insurance policy owned by the debtor (other than a credit life insurance contract) and up to $8,000 of any accrued dividends, interest, or cash surrender value of any unmatured life insurance policy.
8. Professionally prescribed health aids.
9. Many government benefits regardless of value, including Social Security benefits, unemployment compensation, veteran's benefits, disability benefits, and public assistance benefits.
10. Certain rights to receive income, including alimony and support payments, pension benefits, profit sharing, and annuity payments, but only to the extent reasonably necessary to support the debtor or his or her dependents.
11. Interests in wrongful death benefits, life insurance proceeds, and personal injury awards (up to $15,000) to the extent reasonably necessary to support the debtor or his or her dependents, and crime victim compensation awards without limit.

State Law Exemptions   The Bankruptcy Code also permits states to enact their own exemptions. States that do so may (1) give debtors the option of choosing between federal and state exemptions or (2) require debtors to follow state law.[4] The exemptions available under state law are often quite liberal. For example, homestead exemptions are often higher under state law than under the federal exemption scheme. Many states require the debtor to file a **Declaration of Homestead** prior to bankruptcy. This document is usually filed in the county recorder's office in the county in which the property is located.

If the debtor's equity in property (above liens and mortgages) exceeds the exemption limits, the trustee may liquidate the property to realize the excess value for the bankruptcy estate.

Consider This Example   Assume that the debtor owns a home worth $100,000 that is subject to a $60,000 mortgage. The trustee may sell the home, pay off the mortgage, pay the debtor $15,000 (applying the federal exemption), and use the remaining proceeds ($25,000) for distribution to the debtor's creditors.

In the following case, the court found that an asset was exempt from the debtor's bankruptcy estate.

Business Brief
States that provide liberal exemptions (e.g., California, Florida, Texas) are called "debtors' havens."

Neither a borrower nor a lender be: For loan oft loses both itself and friend. And borrowing dulls the edge of husbandry.

William Shakespeare
Hamlet. 1.13 (1600)

In re Witwer
148 Bankr. 930 (1992)
United States Bankruptcy Court, Central District of California

CASE 29.1

FACTS
Dr. James J. Witwer is the sole stockholder, sole employee, and president of James J. Witwer, M.D., Inc., a California corporation under which he practices medicine. He is also the sole beneficiary of the corporation's retirement plan, which was established in 1970. On October 21, 1991, Witwer filed a voluntary petition for relief under Chapter 7 (liquidation). At the time, the value of the assets in his

retirement plan was $1.8 million. California law exempted retirement plans from a debtor's bankruptcy estate. When Witwer claimed that his retirement plan was exempt from the bankruptcy estate, several creditors filed objections.

ISSUE

Is Witwer's retirement plan exempt from the bankruptcy estate?

IN THE LANGUAGE OF THE COURT

Wilson, Bankruptcy Judge   The Debtor's Plan may be entirely exempt if the Plan was designed and used for retirement purposes. It cannot be said that this Debtor attempted to hide otherwise ineligible assets from bankruptcy administration nor can it be said that this Debtor's transactions were not in furtherance of legitimate long-term retirement purposes. As the Debtor's Plan was designed and used for retirement purposes, the Plan may be entirely exempt.

Regardless of the inequities that may result from a debtor's use of the California exemption scheme, this Court is constrained by the plain meaning of the statutes in the context of this case.

Allowing the Debtor to retain over $1.8 million in retirement benefits in bankruptcy while being discharged from debts legitimately owed to creditors seems fundamentally unfair. The remedy is for the state legislature to promote creditor objectives rather than for courts to restrict the meaning of an unambiguous state exemption statute.

DECISION AND REMEDY

The bankruptcy court held that Witwer's retirement plan is fully exempt from his bankruptcy estate.

Case Questions

Critical Legal Thinking   Do you think bankruptcy law was intended to reach the result in this case?

Ethics   Was it ethical for the debtor to declare bankruptcy and wipe out his unsecured creditors while retaining $1.8 million in his retirement account?

Business Application   Should businesspeople establish and fund retirement programs?

Contemporary Business Application

HOMESTEAD EXEMPTIONS: MORE THAN JUST A LOG CABIN

When the term *homestead* is used, many people think of the Wild West, wide-open prairies, and a pioneer's log cabin built with sweat and tears. Long ago, many states enacted laws that protected a debtor's homestead from greedy creditors.

Today, a debtor's homestead may be a condo in a luxury apartment building or a multimillion-dollar split-level home. Depending upon state law, at least a portion of the equity in a debtor's homestead may still be protected from creditors if the owner declares bankruptcy. For example, New York exempts $20,000 of equity in a married couple's home from the bankruptcy estate ($10,000 for a single debtor). California exempts $55,000 for a married couple and $35,000 for a single debtor. These exemptions look generous compared to most states except Florida and Texas.

The Florida constitution and statutes give a homestead exemption from bankruptcy without dollar limit. The homestead is 160 acres outside a municipality and one-half acre inside a municipality.

The Texas homestead exemption is even bigger. Texas has an urban homestead of one acre and a rural homestead of up to 200 acres, without any dollar limit.

Florida and Texas are known as "debtor's havens" because of their generous homestead exemptions from bankruptcy. In fact, relocating to these states has become attractive to people in financial difficulty, who take what money they have and place it beyond the reach of their creditors in homesteads in these states before declaring bankruptcy. How long a person must reside in the state before declaring bankruptcy is an open question. It is just one factor in deciding whether the debtor has engaged in a bankruptcy fraud that makes the debtor's debts nondischargeable. So far, few bankruptcies have been undone under such a charge.

Proponents of homestead exemptions argue that they are needed to provide a debtor with a fresh start and a roof over his or her head. Critics argue that debtors are using homestead exemptions to run roughshod over creditors.

Voidable Transfers

The Bankruptcy Code prevents debtors from making unusual payments or transfers of property on the eve of bankruptcy that would unfairly benefit the debtor or some creditors at the expense of others. The following paragraphs discuss the transfers that may be avoided by the bankruptcy court.

voidable transfer
An unusual payment or transfer of property by the debtor on the eve of bankruptcy that would unfairly benefit the debtor or some creditors at the expense of other creditors. Such transfer may be avoided by the bankruptcy court.

Preferential Transfers within 90 Days before Bankruptcy A **preferential transfer** occurs when (1) a debtor transfers property to a creditor within 90 days before the filing of a petition in bankruptcy, (2) the transfer is made for an antecedent (preexisting) debt, and (3) the creditor would receive more from the transfer than it would from Chapter 7 liquidation. The Bankruptcy Code presumes that the debtor is insolvent during this 90-day period.

preferential transfer
Occurs when (1) a debtor transfers property to a creditor within 90 days before the filing of a petition in bankruptcy, (2) the transfer is made for a preexisting debt, and (3) the creditor would receive more from the transfer than it would from Chapter 7 liquidation.

Consider This Example Assume six months prior to filing bankruptcy that the debtor purchases $10,000 of equipment on credit from a supplier. Within 90 days of filing the petition, the debtor still owes the money to this creditor, which is not due for 120 days. The debtor pays the creditor the $7,000 before filing the petition. In a Chapter 7 liquidation proceeding, the creditor would have received $1,000. This payment is a voidable preference because it was made within 90 days of filing the petition, was made to pay an antecedent debt, and gives the creditor more than he or she would receive in liquidation.

There are exceptions to the 90-day rule. They include (1) transfers for current consideration (e.g., equipment purchased for cash within 90 days of the petition), (2) credit payments made in the ordinary course of the debtor's business (e.g., supplies purchased on credit and paid for within the normal payment term of 30 days after purchase), and (3) payment of up to $600 by a consumer-debtor to a creditor within 90 days of the petition.

Business Brief
Sometimes prior to declaring bankruptcy, debtors transfer property to others as gifts or for less than fair market value, perhaps with a promise that the property will be returned to the debtor after the bankruptcy is over. This is *bankruptcy fraud*.

Preferential Liens Debtors sometimes attempt to favor certain unsecured creditors on the eve of bankruptcy by giving them a secured interest in property. This type of interest is called a **preferential lien**. Preferential liens occur when (1) the debtor gives the creditor a secured interest in property within 90 days of the petition, (2) the secured interest is given for an antecedent debt, and (3) the creditor would receive more because of this lien than it would as an unsecured creditor in liquidation.

preferential lien
Occurs when (1) a debtor gives an unsecured creditor a secured interest in property within 90 days before the filing of a petition in bankruptcy, (2) the transfer is made for a preexisting debt, and (3) the creditor would receive more because of this lien than it would as an unsecured creditor.

Preferential Transfers to Insiders The Bankruptcy Code provides that preferential transfers and liens made to "insiders" within one year of the filing of the petition in bankruptcy may be avoided by the court. **Insiders** are defined as relatives, partners, partnerships, officers and directors of a corporation, corporations, and others who have a relationship with the debtor. To avoid a transfer to an insider within the one-year period (other than the first 90 days prior to the petition), the trustee must prove that the debtor was insolvent at the time of the transfer.

preferential transfer to an insider
A transfer of property by an insolvent debtor to an "insider" within one year before the filing of a petition in bankruptcy.

Fraudulent Transfers Section 548 of the Bankruptcy Code gives the court the power to avoid **fraudulent transfers** of property that occur within one year of the filing of the petition in bankruptcy. Any transfer of property by the debtor made with actual intent to "hinder, delay, or defraud" creditors is considered a voidable fraudulent transfer. The debtor's actual intent must be proved, although it may be inferred from the circumstances. For example, a transfer of property by an insolvent debtor for substantially less than fair market value would be voidable as a fraudulent transfer. In addition, Section 544(b) of the Bankruptcy Code gives the trustee the power to avoid fraudulent transfers made in violation of state fraudulent conveyances acts. Because these acts usually contain a longer statute of limitations (e.g., six years), a court can void any fraudulent transfer made during this period.

fraudulent transfer
Occurs when (1) a debtor transfers property to a third person within one year before the filing of a petition in bankruptcy and (2) the transfer was made by the debtor with an intent to hinder, delay, or defraud creditors.

If a transfer is voided, a bona fide good faith purchaser must receive the value he or she paid for the property. Thus, if an insolvent debtor sold property worth $50,000 to a bona fide purchaser for $30,000 within the one-year period and the court rescinds the transfer, the trustee must return the $30,000 to the bona fide purchaser.

Ethical Perspective

BANKRUPTCY FRAUD: VOIDABLE TRANSFERS

Often, a debtor who knows in advance that he or she is heading for bankruptcy will try to get assets out of his or her possession. That way, when bankruptcy comes, the only things left are the debts.

Sometimes the assets are transferred to relatives and friends with a promise to give them back once the bankruptcy is over. Other times, they are transferred to businesses or entities in which the debtor has a secret interest. Debtors usually rationalize these transfers on the grounds that it does not matter if "faceless" creditors—such as banks and trade creditors—lose out. But are these transfers unethical or illegal? Or both? Consider the following case.

Blair and Marie Woodfield and Parley and Deanna Pearce (Debtors), as partners, operated two "Wendy's Famous Hamburger" restaurants in Washington and Oregon pursuant to a franchise from Wendy's International, Inc. On March 10, 1989, Debtors filed their petitions for bankruptcy under Chapter 7.

Within 10 days prior to filing for bankruptcy, Debtors had formed a new corporation called Quality Foods, Inc. (QFI), in which they each held a 50 percent interest. They then transferred the franchise operating rights, equipment, fixtures, inventory, and restaurant supplies of the two restaurants to QFI. In addition, Woodfield transferred $10,000 cash and Pearce $6,954 cash to QFI within this 10-day period.

Prior to their bankruptcy filings, Debtors somehow ascertained that Wade Bettis, Jr. would be their trustee in bankruptcy. They discussed all the foregoing transactions with him prior to filing bankruptcy. At the creditors' meeting on April 25, 1989, Bettis certified that the Debtors had no assets and had abandoned the assets of the two Wendy's franchises. A creditor, Emmett Valley Associates (EVA), objected. Nevertheless, the bankruptcy court approved the abandonment, and the district court affirmed.

The court of appeals, however, asked, "Where's the beef?" The court stated: "The transaction here carried many badges of fraud. The relationship between the Debtors and QFI could not have been closer; the Debtors created and operated the transferee corporation. The transfer was admittedly made in anticipation of the bankruptcy filing. The partnership was admittedly in poor financial condition at the time, having defaulted on several obligations. Substantially all of the partnership's property relating to the Wendy's franchises was transferred, leaving nothing to satisfy any judgments." The court of appeals held that Debtors transferred property with the intent to hinder, delay, and defraud their creditors. Because of this fraud, the court denied the Debtors' discharge. [*In Re Woodfield*, 978 F.2d 516 (9th Cir. 1992)]

1. Did the Debtors act unethically in this case? Did they act illegally?
2. Did the trustee act unethically?
3. Do you think many debtors engage in insider and fraudulent transfers prior to declaring bankruptcy?

*D*ISTRIBUTION OF PROPERTY AND DISCHARGE

Priority of Distribution

Under Chapter 7, the nonexempt property of the bankruptcy estate must be distributed to the debtor's secured and unsecured creditors. The statutory priority of distribution is discussed in the following paragraphs.

Secured Creditors   A secured creditor's claim to the debtor's property has priority over the claims of unsecured creditors. The secured creditor may (1) accept the collateral in full

distribution of property
Nonexempt property of the bankruptcy estate must be distributed to the debtor's secured and unsecured creditors pursuant to the statutory priority established by the Bankruptcy Code.

satisfaction of the debt, (2) foreclose on the collateral and use the proceeds to pay the debt, or (3) allow the trustee to retain the collateral, dispose of it at sale, and remit the proceeds of the sale to him or her.

If the value of the collateral exceeds the secured interest, the excess becomes available to satisfy the claims of the debtor's unsecured creditors. Before the excess funds are released, however, the secured creditor is allowed to deduct reasonable fees and costs resulting from the default. If the value of the collateral is less than the secured interest, the secured creditor becomes an unsecured creditor to the difference.

Unsecured Creditors The Bankruptcy Code stipulates that unsecured claims are to be satisfied out of the bankruptcy estate in the order of their statutory priority.[5] The statutory priority of an unsecured claim is

1. Fees and expenses of administrating the estate, including court costs, trustee fees, attorneys' fees, appraisal fees, and other costs of administration.
2. In an involuntary bankruptcy, secured claims of "gap" creditors who sold goods or services on credit to the debtor in the ordinary course of the debtor's business between the date of the filing of the petition and the date of the appointment of the trustee or issuance of the order for relief (whichever occurred first).
3. Unsecured claims for wages, salary, or commissions earned by the debtor's employees within 90 days immediately preceding the filing of the petition, up to $4,000 per employee; any claim exceeding $4,000 is treated as a claim of a general unsecured creditor (item 9 below).
4. Unsecured claims for contributions to employee benefit plans based on services performed within 180 days immediately preceding the filing of the petition, up to $4,000 per employee.
5. Farm producers and fishermen against debtors who operate grain storage facilities or fish produce storage or processing facilities, up to $4,000 per claim.
6. Unsecured claims for cash deposited by a consumer with the debtor prior to the filing of the petition in connection with either the purchase, lease, or rental of property or the purchase of services that were not delivered or provided by the debtor, up to $1,800 per claim.
7. Debts owed for child support, paternity, alimony, and spousal support.
8. Certain tax obligations owed by the debtor to federal, state, and local governmental units.
9. Claims of general unsecured creditors.
10. If there is any balance remaining after the allowed claims of the creditors are satisfied, it is returned to the debtor.

Each class must be paid in full before any lower class is paid anything. If a class cannot be paid in full, the claims of that class are paid pro rata (proportionately).

Discharge

After the property is distributed to satisfy the allowed claims, the remaining unpaid claims are **discharged** (i.e., the debtor is no longer legally responsible for them). Only individuals may be granted a discharge. Discharge is not available to partnerships and corporations. These entities must liquidate under state law before or upon completion of the Chapter 7 proceeding. A debtor can be granted a discharge in a Chapter 7 proceeding only once every six years.

Consider This Example Maryjane files for Chapter 7 bankruptcy. At the time of filing, she has many unsecured creditors. Nordstrom's Department Store is one of them. She owes Nordstrom's $3,000. The bankruptcy estate has only enough assets to pay

---

Business Brief
Secured creditors are made whole in a Chapter 7 bankruptcy if the value of the collateral equals or exceeds the amount of their security interest.

Business Brief
Generally, unsecured creditors often receive little if anything in a Chapter 7 bankruptcy.

I will pay you some, and, as most debtors do, promise you infinitely.

*William Shakespeare
Henry IV, Pt. II (1597)*

discharge
The termination of the legal duty of a debtor to pay debts that remain unpaid upon the completion of a bankruptcy proceeding.

It is the policy of the law that the debtor be just before he be generous.

*Finch, J.
Hearn 45 St. Corp. v. Jano
(1940)*

unsecured creditors 10 cents on the dollar. Nordstrom's receives $300; the remaining $2,700 is discharged. Nordstrom's cannot thereafter collect this money and will write it off as a bad debt.

E- Commerce & Internet Law

e-biz

BANKRUPT COMPANY HOLDS DIGITAL GARAGE SALE

When a company files for bankruptcy under Chapter 7 of the Bankruptcy Code, it must liquidate its assets and terminate its existence. In the past, the trustee for a bankrupt company would often advertise and hold a traditional auction to sell the remaining inventory, fixtures, and other assets of the company. The auction would be held by an auction company at the bankrupt company's property, at the auction company, or at some other physical site. This was usually the best method for obtaining the best price for the sale items. There were several problems, however. First, advertising was by mail and print media, which is very costly and limited. Second, the number of persons who showed up in person or bid by telephone at the auction was often quite small.

When Atlantic Rancher, a company that specialized in selling high-end outdoor clothing, filed for Chapter 7 bankruptcy in 1999, it did something very different: It held an on-line auction over the Internet to get rid of its assets. On-line auctions had already proven tremendously successful in consumer-to-consumer transactions. For example, eBay started and grew as the Internet's largest auction portal. It was followed by Priceline.com, uBid, Amazon.com, and other Internet companies offering on-line auctions. On-line auctions are less expensive, reach a greater number of interested parties, and assure competitive bidding.

Atlantic Rancher successfully completed its Internet auction and liquidated its assets. The use of cyberspace auctions by bankrupt companies provides an extremely effective way of liquidating assets quickly and ensuring the highest price possible. Internet auctions are being used by more companies who file and liquidate under Chapter 7 of the Bankruptcy Code. Atlantic Rancher used a Web site to announce its Internet liquidation.

Nondischargeable Debts

The following debts are not dischargeable in a Chapter 7 proceeding:

- Claims for taxes accrued within three years prior to the filing of the petition in bankruptcy.
- Certain fines and penalties payable to federal, state, and local governmental units.
- Claims based on the debtor's liability for causing willful or malicious injury to a person or property.
- Claims arising from the fraud, larceny, or embezzlement by the debtor while acting in a fiduciary capacity.
- Alimony, maintenance, and child support.
- Unscheduled claims.
- Claims based on the consumer-debtor's purchase of luxury goods of more than $1,000 from a single creditor within 60 days of the order for relief.
- Cash advances in excess of $1,000 obtained by a consumer-debtor by use of a revolving line of credit or credit card within 60 days of the order for relief.
- Judgments and consent decrees against the debtor for liability incurred as a result of the debtor's operation of a motor vehicle while legally intoxicated.

Business Brief
Not all debts are dischargeable in bankruptcy.

Beggars can never be bankrupts.

Thomas Fuller
Gnomologia *(1732)*

Creditors who have nondischargeable claims against the debtor may participate in the distribution of the bankruptcy estate. The nondischarged balance may be pursued by the creditor against the debtor after bankruptcy.

In the following case, the court had to decide whether a debt was dischargeable.

Kawaauhau v. Geiger
118 S. Ct. 974 (1998)
Supreme Court of the United States

CASE 29.2

FACTS
Margaret Kawaauhau sought treatment from Dr. Paul Geiger for a foot injury. Geiger examined Kawaauhau and admitted her to the hospital to attend to the risks of infection. Although Geiger knew that intravenous penicillin would have been the more effective treatment, he prescribed oral penicillin, explaining that he thought that his patient wished to minimize the cost of her treatment. Geiger then departed on a business trip, leaving Kawaauhau in the care of other physicians. When Geiger returned, he discontinued all antibiotics because he believed that the infection had subsided. Kawaauhau's condition deteriorated over the next few days, requiring the amputation of her right leg below the knee. Kawaauhau and her husband sued Geiger for medical malpractice. The jury found Geiger liable and awarded the Kawaauhaus $355,000 in damages. Geiger, who carried no malpractice insurance, filed for bankruptcy in an attempt to discharge the judgment. The bankruptcy court denied discharge and the district court agreed. The court of appeals reversed and allowed discharge, and the Kawaauhaus appealed to the U.S. Supreme Court.

ISSUE
Is a debt arising from a medical malpractice judgment that is attributable to negligent or reckless conduct dischargeable in bankruptcy?

IN THE LANGUAGE OF THE COURT
Ginsburg, Justice   Section 523(a)(6) of the Bankruptcy Code provides that a debt "for willful and malicious injury by the debtor to another" is not dischargeable. The question before us is whether a debt arising from a medical malpractice judgment, attributable to negligent or reckless conduct, falls within this statutory exception. We hold that it does not and that the debt is dischargeable. Had Congress meant to exempt debts resulting from unintentionally inflicted injuries, it might have selected an additional word or words, i.e., "reckless" or "negligent," to modify "injury."

The Kawaauhaus maintain that, as a policy matter, malpractice judgments should be excepted from discharge, at least when the debtor acted recklessly or carried no malpractice insurance. Congress, of course, may so decide. But unless and until Congress makes such a decision, we must follow the current direction § 523(a)(6) provides.

DECISION AND REMEDY
The U.S. Supreme Court ruled that a medical malpractice judgment based on negligent or reckless conduct—and not intentional conduct—is dischargeable in bankruptcy. Affirmed.

Case Questions

Critical Legal Thinking   What public policy is promoted by denying discharge for "willful" injurious conduct? Do you think Geiger's conduct would have been willful?

Ethics   Was it ethical for Geiger to avoid liability to the Kawaauhaus by declaring bankruptcy?

Business Application   What purpose is served by allowing individuals and businesses to declare bankruptcy? What are the business implications of bankruptcy laws?

Contemporary Business Application

REAFFIRMATION AGREEMENTS

Creditors often attempt to persuade a debtor to agree to pay an unsatisfied debt that is dischargeable in bankruptcy. A debtor may voluntarily choose to enter into a **reaffirmation agreement**, which is a formal agreement that sets out the terms of repayment. Before signing a reaffirmation agreement, the debtor needs to decide if there is an important reason to do so, such as the continuation of a valuable relationship with the creditor.

To prevent abuses, the Bankruptcy Code stipulates that the following requirements must be met before a reaffirmation agreement is legally enforceable:

- The reaffirmation agreement must be made before the debtor is granted a discharge.
- The agreement must be filed with the court.
- If the debtor is not represented by an attorney, court approval of the agreement is necessary.
- The debtor may rescind the agreement at any time prior to discharge or within 60 days after filing the agreement with the court, whichever is later. This right of rescission must be conspicuously stated in the reaffirmation agreement.

Acts That Bar Discharge

Any party of interest may file an objection to the discharge of a debt. The court will then hold a hearing. Discharge of the unsatisfied debts will be denied if the debtor

- Made false representations about his or her financial position when he or she obtained an extension of credit.
- Transferred, concealed, or removed property from the estate with the intent to hinder, delay, or defraud creditors.
- Falsified, destroyed, or concealed records of his or her financial condition.
- Failed to account for any assets.
- Failed to submit to questioning at the meeting of the creditors (unless excused).

> **Business Brief**
> Certain acts by the debtor may bar discharge.

If the discharge is obtained through the fraud of the debtor, a party of interest may bring a motion to have the bankruptcy revoked. The bankruptcy court may revoke a discharge within one year after it was granted.

Contemporary Business Application

DISCHARGE OF STUDENT LOANS

In the past, many students who borrowed a lot of money in student loans sought to avoid paying back their loans by filing a voluntary petition for bankruptcy immediately on leaving college. Section 523(a)(8) of the Bankruptcy Code was enacted to prevent this practice. For any bankruptcy case commenced after October 7, 1998, Section 523(a)(8)(A) mandates that student loans can only be discharged in bankruptcy if nondis-charge would cause an "undue hardship" to the debtor and his or her dependents [Higher Education Amendments of 1998, P. L. 105-244]. Undue hardship is construed very strictly and would include not being able to pay for food or shelter for the debtor or the debtor's family.

Cosigners (e.g., parents who guarantee their child's student loan) must also meet the heightened undue hardship test to discharge their obligation.

CHAPTER 11 REORGANIZATION BANKRUPTCY

Chapter 11 of the Bankruptcy Code provides a method for reorganizing the debtor's financial affairs under the supervision of the Bankruptcy Court.[6] Its goal is to reorganize the debtor with a new capital structure so that it will emerge from bankruptcy as a viable concern. This option, which is referred to as **reorganization bankruptcy**, is often in the best interests of the debtor and its creditors.

> **Chapter 11**
> A bankruptcy method that allows reorganization of the debtor's financial affairs under the supervision of the Bankruptcy Court.

Reorganization Proceeding

Chapter 11 is available to individuals, partnerships, corporations, nonincorporated associations, and railroads. It is not available to banks, savings and loan associations, credit unions, insurance companies, stockbrokers, or commodities brokers. The majority of Chapter 11 proceedings are filed by corporations.

A Chapter 11 petition may be filed voluntarily by the debtor or involuntarily by its creditors. The principles discussed earlier under Chapter 7 regarding the filing of petitions, the first meeting of creditors, the entry of the order for relief, automatic stay, and relief from stay also apply to Chapter 11 proceedings.

> **Business Brief**
> Chapter 11 is used primarily by businesses to reorganize their finances under the protection of the bankruptcy court. The debtor usually emerges from bankruptcy a "leaner" business, having restructured and discharged some of its debts.

Debtor-in-Possession

debtor-in-possession
A debtor who is left in place to operate the business during the reorganization proceeding.

In most Chapter 11 cases, the debtor is left in place to operate the business during the reorganization proceeding. In such cases, the debtor is called a **debtor-in-possession**. The court may appoint a trustee to operate the debtor's business only upon a showing of cause, such as fraud, dishonesty, or gross mismanagement by the debtor or its management. Even if a trustee is not appointed, however, the court may appoint an examiner to investigate the debtor's financial affairs.

The debtor-in-possession (or the trustee if one is appointed) has the same powers and duties as a trustee in a Chapter 7 proceeding. In addition, the debtor-in-possession (or trustee) is empowered to operate the debtor's business during the bankruptcy proceeding. This power includes authority to enter into contracts, purchase supplies, incur debts, and so on. Some suppliers will accept only cash for their goods or services during this time, whereas others will extend credit. Credit extended by postpetition unsecured creditors in the ordinary course of business is given automatic priority as an administrative expense in bankruptcy. Further, upon notice and hearing, the court may create a secured interest by granting a postpetition unsecured creditor a lien on the debtor-in-possession's property.

Business Brief
Approximately 25,000 U.S. companies file for Chapter 11 protection each year.

Creditors' Committees

creditor's committee
The creditors holding the seven largest unsecured claims are usually appointed to the creditors' committee. Representatives of the committee appear at Bankruptcy Court hearings, participate in the negotiation of a plan of reorganization, assert objections to proposed plans, and so on.

Once an order for relief is granted, the court will appoint a **creditors' committee** composed of representatives of the class of unsecured claims. Generally, the creditors holding the seven largest claims are appointed to the committee. The court may also appoint a committee of secured creditors and a committee of equity holders. Committee members owe a fiduciary duty to represent the interest of the class. Committees may appear at Bankruptcy Court hearings, participate in the negotiation of a plan of reorganization, assert objections to proposed plans, and the like.

Entrepreneur and the Law _____

SMALL BUSINESS BANKRUPTCY

Large firms, such as Macy's, Continental Airlines, and Dow Corning have reorganized under Chapter 11 of the Bankruptcy Code. These large firms have resources to hire lawyers, investment bankers, and other professionals to assist them in the time-consuming and expensive Chapter 11 reorganization process. Smaller firms often do not have the resources or the luxury of the time necessary to use a Chapter 11 proceeding, however.

To address this problem, Congress enacted the **Bankruptcy Reform Act of 1994**, which amended Chapter 11. **Section 217** of this act permits businesses with total debts of less than $2 million to elect a "fast-track" for processing its Chapter 11 case. This procedure makes creditors' committees optional and sets up deadlines aimed at concluding the Chapter 11 case within 160 days of the bankruptcy filing. Section 217 "small business bankruptcy" provides an efficient and cost-saving method for smaller firms to seek bankruptcy protection and reorganize as a going concern using Chapter 11 of the Bankruptcy Code.

PLAN OF REORGANIZATION

plan of reorganization
A plan that sets forth a proposed new capital structure for the debtor to have when it emerges from reorganization bankruptcy. The debtor has the exclusive right to file the first plan of reorganization; any party of interest may file a plan thereafter.

The debtor has the exclusive right to file a **plan of reorganization** with the Bankruptcy Court within the first 120 days after the date of the order for relief. The debtor also has the right to obtain creditor approval of the plan within the first 180 days after the date of the order. After that, any party of interest (i.e., a trustee, a creditor, or an equity holder) may propose a plan. The court has discretion to extend the 120- and 180-day periods in complex cases.

The plan of reorganization sets forth the debtor's proposed new capital structure. In a Chapter 11 proceeding, creditors have claims and equity holders have interests. The plan must designate the different classes of claims and interests. The reorganization plan may propose altering the rights of creditors and equity holders. For example, it might require claims and interests to be reduced, the conversion of unsecured creditors to equity holders, the sale of assets, or the like.

Disclosure Statement

The debtor must supply the creditors and equity holders with a **disclosure statement** that contains adequate information about the proposed plan of reorganization. The court must approve the disclosure statement before it is distributed.

Executory Contracts

Under the Bankruptcy Code, the debtor-in-possession (or trustee) is given the authority to assume or reject **executory contracts** (i.e., contracts that are not fully performed by both sides). In general, unfavorable executory contracts will be rejected and favorable executory contracts will be assumed. For example, a debtor-in-possession may reject an unfavorable lease. Court approval is necessary to reject an executory contract. Executory contracts may also be rejected in Chapter 7 and Chapter 13 proceedings.

Rejection of Collective Bargaining Agreements   Companies that file for Chapter 11 reorganization sometimes argue that agreements with labor unions that still have years to run are executory contracts that may be rejected in bankruptcy. The U.S. Supreme Court has upheld the right of companies to reject union contracts in bankruptcy.[7] The court held that rejection was permitted if necessary for the successful rehabilitation of the debtor.

Subsequently, labor unions lobbied Congress for a change in the law. Congress responded by enacting Section 1113 of the 1984 amendments to the Bankruptcy Code. Section 1113 established the following multistep process that must be followed before a collective bargaining agreement may be rejected or modified:

1. The debtor must make a proposal to the union regarding the modification of the agreement.
2. The debtor must meet with the union to discuss the proposal.
3. The court must hold a hearing if the union refuses to accept the proposal.

If these requirements are met, the court may order the modification or rejection of the labor agreement if (1) such rejection or modification is necessary to the reorganization, (2) the debtor acted in good faith, and (3) the balance of equities favor rejection or modification of the collective bargaining agreement.

Confirmation of a Plan of Reorganization

A plan of reorganization must be **confirmed** by the court before it becomes effective. The plan may be confirmed by either (1) the acceptance method or (2) the "cram down" method. These two methods are discussed in the paragraphs that follow. If more than one plan is proposed, the court may confirm only one plan.

Confirmation by the Acceptance Method

Classes of creditors and interests must be given the opportunity to vote to accept or reject the plan before the court considers its confirmation. Under **Section 1129(a)**—that is, the **acceptance method**—the court must confirm a plan of reorganization if the following tests are met:

1. The plan must be in the best interests of each class of claims and interests as indicated by either (a) a unanimous vote of acceptance by the members of the class or (b) the property

Business Brief
In a Chapter 11 proceeding, creditors have *claims* and equity holders have *interests*.

disclosure statement
A statement that must contain adequate information about the proposed plan of reorganization that is supplied to the creditors and equity holders.

executory contract
A contract that has not been fully performed. With court approval, executory contracts may be rejected by a debtor in bankruptcy.

Business Brief
Chapter 11 reorganization bankruptcy permits a debtor to assume or reject executory contracts, such as leases for office space, and sales and purchase contracts.

Business Brief
A collective bargaining agreement may be rejected or modified as an executory contract if (1) it is necessary to the reorganization, (2) the debtor acted in good faith, and (3) the balance of the equities favors rejection or modification of the agreement.

confirmation
The bankruptcy court's approval of a plan of reorganization.

acceptance method
The bankruptcy court must approve a plan of reorganization if (1) the plan is in the *best interests* of each class of claims and interests, (2) the plan is *feasible*, (3) at least one class of claims *votes to accept* the plan, and (4) each class of claims and interests is *nonimpaired*.

received by the class members under the plan is worth at least as much as they would receive upon liquidation.

2. The plan must be feasible. That is, the debtor must have a good probability of surviving as a going concern. The court examines the debtor's estimated earnings and expenses as proposed by the plan before making this determination.

3. At least one class of claims must vote to accept the plan. A plan is deemed accepted by a class of claims if at least one-half the number of creditors who vote to accept the plan and the accepting creditors represent two-thirds the dollar amount of allowed claims who vote.

4. Each class of claims and interests is nonimpaired. A class is nonimpaired if (a) its legal, equitable, and contractual rights are unaltered by the plan, or (b) the class votes to accept the plan. A class of claims accepts the plan if one-half the number who vote accept the plan and they represent two-thirds the dollar amount of allowed claims that vote accept the plan. A class of interests accepts a plan if at least two-thirds of the amount of interests that vote accept the plan.

A plan of reorganization cannot discriminate unfairly against members of a class. For example, no member of any class can receive more than any other member of that class. No class of claims or interests may be paid more than the full amount of its claim.

Confirmation by the Cram Down Method

If a dissenting class of claims is impaired, the plan of reorganization cannot be confirmed using the acceptance method. The court can, however, force an impaired class to participate in a plan of reorganization under the **cram down method** of **Section 1129(b)**. As discussed below, to be crammed down, the plan must be fair and equitable to the impaired class.

Secured Creditors A plan is fair and equitable to an impaired class of secured creditors if the reorganization allows the class to (1) retain its lien on the collateral (whether the property is retained by the debtor or transferred to another party), (2) place a lien on the proceeds from the sale of the collateral, or (3) receive an "indubitable equivalent," such as a lien on other property.

Unsecured Creditors A reorganization plan is fair and equitable to an impaired class of unsecured creditors if (1) that class is paid cash or property that has a discounted present value equal to the allowed amount of the claim or (2) no class below it receives anything in the plan (the **absolute priority rule**).[8]

Consider This Example Assume that in a Chapter 11 case there is a class of secured creditors, a class of unsecured creditors, and a class of equity holders. The secured creditors vote to accept the plan. The unsecured creditors, who are impaired because they are given only 10 percent of their claim, vote to reject the plan. Nevertheless, the plan can be crammed down on the unsecured class under the absolute priority rule if the plan does not give the equity holders anything.

Equity Holders A plan is fair and equitable to an impaired class of equity holders if that class is paid the greater of (1) the fixed liquidation preference (if any), (2) the fixed redemption preference (if any), or (3) the discounted present value of their equity interest. Alternatively, the absolute priority rule can be applied to an impaired equity class if no class below it receives anything.

Business Brief
Creditors and equity holders are given the opportunity to vote on the confirmation of a plan of reorganization.

cram down method
A method of confirmation of a plan of reorganization where the court forces an impaired class to participate in the plan of reorganization.

Business Brief
The term *cram down* derives from the notion that the plan of reorganization is being "crammed down the throats" of the impaired dissenting class.

absolute priority rule
A rule that says a reorganization plan is fair and equitable to an impaired class of unsecured creditors or equity holders if no class below it receives anything in the plan.

Discharge

Upon confirmation of a plan of reorganization, the debtor is granted a **discharge** of all claims not included in the plan. The plan is binding on all parties once it is confirmed.

discharge
Creditors' claims that are not included in a Chapter 11 reorganization are discharged.

Entrepreneur and the Law

PLANET HOLLYWOOD PLUNGES TO EARTH

When Planet Hollywood International, Inc., opened its first "Planet Hollywood" restaurant in Beverly Hills, it looked like the stars would shine on the company. Entrepreneur-celebrities such as Bruce Willis, Demi Moore, Sylvester Stallone, and Arnold Schwarzenegger—who combined owned about 20 percent of the company's stock—showed up along with a virtual "Who's Who" list of Hollywood for the grand opening. Other major shareholders of Planet Hollywood were Saudi Arabian Prince Alwaleed bin Talal, Singapore billionaire Ong Beng Seng, and cofounder and CEO Robert Earl. Planet Hollywood, a theme restaurant, featured movie memorabilia hanging from the walls and ceiling.

Planet Hollywood enjoyed great early success as a leader in the "eatertainment" industry and went on an expansion spree, opening 48 company-owned restaurants. Planet Hollywood also franchised an additional 32 restaurants worldwide, including outlets in Hong Kong, Rome, and Moscow. The company gave movie stars stock and stock options in exchange for showing up at Planet Hollywood openings. In 1996, the company went public—that is, sold stock to public shareholders—at $18 per share. The price climbed to $32 per share the first day of trading, its highest price ever.

Eventually Planet Hollywood's star crashed, however. Other theme restaurants opened, causing an increase in competition in this niche market. Planet Hollywood restaurants were successful in drawing in first-timers to its outlets, but had trouble luring them back for repeat business. And high prices and a perception of mediocre food stalled sales as well. Profits plunged until the company was bleeding with red ink and could no longer pay interest payments on its crushing debt. Planet Hollywood's share price fell until August 18, 1999, when it reached $.75 per share. On that date the company publicly announced it would seek protection under Chapter 11 of the Bankruptcy Code to financially reorganize itself.

After negotiating with its creditors, Planet Hollywood filed a prepackaged Chapter 11 bankruptcy filing. In a *prepackaged filing*, the creditors and investors have already negotiated and agreed on the terms of the reorganization when the bankruptcy petition is filed. Planet Hollywood's agreed-upon restructuring plan called for the following:

- There was a dramatic 75 percent reduction of the number of restaurants. The company continues to operate its most successful outlets, such as those in Beverly Hills, Las Vegas, and at Disney World in Orlando but closed many other outlets. The company used the executory contract provision of the Bankruptcy Code to get out of high-cost leases and other contracts at money-losing locations.
- The debt-holders of $250 million in subordinated notes agreed to cancel their debt and the back-interest owed them by Planet Hollywood in exchange for $47.5 million in cash, $60 million of new notes, and new common stock representing 30 percent of the equity in the new Planet Hollywood.
- Equity holders, including the celebrities and public shareholders alike, were wiped out, that is, their shares were worth nothing in the reorganization. They received warrants to purchase shares in Planet Hollywood in the future at a predetermined price that would not be reached unless Planet Hollywood was successful as a reorganized going concern.
- An investor group led by Prince Alwaleed bin Talal, Ong Beng Seng, and Robert Earl's trust for his children invested $30 million in exchange for 70 percent equity ownership in the new reorganized Planet Hollywood.

The new Planet Hollywood revised its menu and added new merchandise (25 percent of its revenue comes from the sale of T-shirts) with the hope of revitalizing its lost luster. Only time will tell whether Planet Hollywood has staying power or will become a vanishing star.

International Perspective

REORGANIZATION UNDER BRITISH BANKRUPTCY LAW

Many of our country's forefathers were debtors fleeing the harsh laws of Britain and European countries where debtors were often sent to debtors' prisons or were required to work off the debt owed to creditors. When this country was founded, the right to declare bankruptcy was considered just as important as the right to free speech, and both rights were included in the U.S. Constitution.

Even today, U.S. bankruptcy law treats debtors more leniently than the bankruptcy laws of other countries. Consider the case of bankruptcy reorganization laws in Britain versus those of the United States.

In 1987, Britain enacted a new bankruptcy law for handling the reorganization of bankrupt companies. The law banishes lawyers from the reorganization process and puts it in the hands of specially licensed accountants. When a firm files for reorganization bankruptcy in Britain, an administrative order is issued. The order permits the credi-

tors of the troubled company to appoint a team of bankruptcy accountants to handle the company's reorganization.

British law assumes that the company's misfortune is not a result of bad luck but is based on mismanagement by the company's officers and directors. Consequently, the bankruptcy accountants are empowered to remove the firm's existing management and take over control of its operations. The accountants then orchestrate the reorganization and sale of the company's assets.

Many U.S. bankruptcy lawyers allege that British bankruptcy law tramples too hard on debtors' rights. They argue that British law thwarts the fresh start theory underlying American bankruptcy law. Proponents of the British system argue that it is faster, cheaper, and more efficient than a bankruptcy reorganization under Chapter 11 of the U.S. Bankruptcy Code. They assert that the British system does not coddle debtors and make lawyers rich, as the U.S. bankruptcy system does.

*C*HAPTER 13 CONSUMER DEBT ADJUSTMENT

Chapter 13
A rehabilitation form of bankruptcy that permits the courts to supervise the debtor's plan for the payment of unpaid debts by installments.

Business Brief
A Chapter 13 proceeding can be initiated only by the voluntary filing of a petition by the debtor. Creditors cannot file an involuntary petition to place a debtor in Chapter 13 bankruptcy.

Chapter 13, which is called a **consumer debt adjustment**, is a rehabilitation form of bankruptcy for natural persons. Chapter 13 permits the courts to supervise the debtor's plan for the payment of unpaid debts by installments.

The debtor has several advantages under Chapter 13. They include avoidance of the stigma of Chapter 7 liquidation, retention of more property than is exempt under Chapter 7, and less expense and less complication than a Chapter 7 proceeding. The creditors have advantages, too. They may recover a greater percentage of the debts owed them than they would under a Chapter 7 proceeding.

Filing the Petition

A Chapter 13 proceeding can be initiated only by the voluntary filing of a petition by a debtor who alleges that he or she is (1) insolvent or (2) unable to pay his or her debts when they become due. The petition must state that the debtor desires to effect an extension or composition of debts, or both. An **extension** provides for a longer period of time for the debtor to pay his or her debts. A **composition** provides for a reduction of debts.

Only individuals (including sole proprietors) with regular income who owe individually (or with their spouse) noncontingent, liquidated, unsecured debts of less than $250,000 and secured debts of less than $750,000 may file such a petition. The key is the debtor's regular income, which may be from any source, including wages, salary, commissions, income from investments, Social Security, pension income, or public assistance. The amount of the debtor's assets is irrelevant. Most Chapter 13 petitions are filed by homeowners who want to protect nonexempt equity in their residences.

When (or shortly after) the petition is filed, the debtor must file a list of creditors, assets, and liabilities with the court. The court then schedules a meeting of creditors. The debtor must appear at this meeting. Creditors may submit proof of claims, which will be allowed or disallowed by the court. No creditor committees are appointed, but the court must appoint a trustee upon confirmation of the plan.

Automatic Stay

The filing of a Chapter 13 petition automatically stays (1) liquidation bankruptcy proceedings, (2) judicial and nonjudicial actions by creditors to collect prepetition debts from the debtor, and (3) collection activities against codebtors and guarantors of consumer debts. The automatic stay continues until the Chapter 13 plan is completed or dismissed. The stay does not apply to business debts.

The Plan of Payment

The debtor's plan of payment must be filed within 15 days of filing the petition. The debtor must file information about his or her finances, including a budget of estimated income and expenses during the period of the plan. The plan period cannot exceed three years unless the court approves a longer period (of up to five years). During the plan period, the debtor retains possession of his or her property, may acquire new property and incur debts, and so on.

The debtor must begin making the planned installment payments to the trustee within 30 days after the plan is filed. These interim payments must continue until the plan is confirmed or denied. If the plan is denied, the trustee must return the interim payments to the debtor less any administrative costs. If the plan is confirmed, the debtor must continue making payments to the trustee. The trustee is responsible for remitting these payments to the creditors. The trustee is paid 10 percent of the debts paid under the plan.

A Chapter 13 plan may be modified if the debtor's circumstances materially change. For example, if the debtor's income subsequently decreases, the court may decrease the debtor's payments under the plan. Request for the modification of a plan may be made by the debtor, the trustee, or a creditor. If an interested party objects to the modification, the court must hold a hearing to determine whether it should be approved.

Confirmation of the Plan

The plan may modify the rights of unsecured creditors and some secured creditors. Any objections they have may be voiced at the confirmation hearing held by the court. The plan must (1) be proposed in good faith, (2) pass the feasibility test (e.g., the debtor must be able to make the proposed payments), and (3) be in the best interests of the creditors (i.e., the present value of the payments must equal or exceed the amount that the creditors would receive in a Chapter 7 liquidation proceeding).

Secured Creditors   The plan must be submitted to the secured creditors for acceptance. The plan will be confirmed if the secured creditors unanimously accept it. If a secured creditor does not accept the plan, the court may still confirm the plan if (1) it permits the secured creditor to retain its lien and the value of the plan's distribution to the creditor is more than its secured interest or (2) the debtor surrenders the property securing the claim to the secured creditor.

Unsecured Creditors   Although a vote of unsecured creditors is not required for confirmation of a Chapter 13 plan, their objection to the plan can delay or defeat confirmation. The court cannot confirm the plan unless (1) it proposes to pay the objecting

Business Brief
A Chapter 13 is a form of reorganization bankruptcy. The debtor must file a proposed *plan of payment* on how the debts are to be rescheduled.

Debt rolls a man over and over, binding him hand and foot, and letting him hang upon the fatal mesh until the long-legged interest devours him.

Henry Ward Beecher
Proverbs from Plymouth
Pulpit *(1887)*

I am ashamed to owe debts I cannot pay but I am not ashamed of being classed with those to whose rank I belong.

Sir Walter Scott
Journal, *February 16, 1826*

discharge

A discharge is granted to a debtor in a Chapter 13 consumer debt adjustment bankruptcy only after all the payments under the plan are completed by the debtor.

hardship discharge

A discharge granted if (1) the debtor fails to complete the payments due to unforeseeable circumstances, (2) the unsecured creditors have been paid as much as they would have been paid in a Chapter 7 liquidation proceeding, and (3) it is not practical to modify the plan.

unsecured creditor the present value of his or her claim or (2) the debtor agrees to commit all his or her disposable income during the plan period to pay his or her creditors. (Disposable income is all income not necessary to maintain the debtor and his or her dependents.)

Consider This Example   Suppose a debtor earns $1,800 per month, of which $1,200 is reasonably necessary to support the debtor and his or her family. If the $400 per month disposable income is committed to pay prepetition debts, the court may confirm the plan even if the debts of the unsecured creditors are substantially modified or liquidated.

Discharge

The court will grant an order **discharging** the debtor from all unpaid debts covered by the plan after all the payments required under the plan are completed. All debts are dischargeable under Chapter 13 except alimony and child support and priority debts such as trustee fees. Dischargeable debts include student loans, fraudulently incurred debts, and debts arising from malicious or willful injury from drunken driving. Thus, a Chapter 13 discharge may be more beneficial to a debtor than a Chapter 7 liquidation discharge. A discharge can be revoked within one year if it was obtained by fraud. There is a timebar to filing a petition for Chapter 13 proceeding. Thus, a debtor may file successive petitions for Chapter 13 bankruptcy.

Hardship Discharge   Even if the debtor does not complete the payments called for in the plan, the court may grant the debtor a **hardship discharge**. Such a discharge will be granted if (1) the debtor fails to complete the payments due to unforeseeable circumstances (e.g., the debtor loses his or her job through no fault of his or her own), (2) the unsecured creditors have been paid as much as they would have been paid in a Chapter 7 liquidation proceeding, and (3) it is not practical to modify the plan.

Entrepreneur and the Law

CHAPTER 12 FAMILY FARMER BANKRUPTCY

In the 1980s, farms across the country experienced financial difficulty as farm prices and real estate values fell. Many farmers who found it difficult to meet their financial obligations and faced bankruptcy lobbied Congress for help. In 1986, Congress responded and added **Chapter 12** to the Bankruptcy Code. Chapter 12 gives "family farmers"—defined as farmers whose total debt does not exceed $1.5 million and are at least 80 percent farm related—a special form of bankruptcy protection.

Chapter 12 is a reorganization provision that allows family farmers to reorganize financially. Upon filing, an automatic stay goes in place against creditors' actions against the family farmer. The farmer-debtor must file a plan of reorganization within 90 days of the order for relief. Creditors cannot vote on the plan of reorganization.

The major provision of Chapter 12 allows family farmers to have mortgage loans rewritten to the fair market value of the property in cases where the value of the farm land has decreased below the value of the loan. For example, assume a farm is worth $1,000,000 at the time a family farmer borrows $800,000 from Rural Bank, which takes back a mortgage on the farm for this amount. After several years the farmer suffers financial difficulty and files Chapter 12 bankruptcy. At the time of the bankruptcy filing, the farm land is only worth $500,000. Under Chapter 12, the mortgage is reduced to $500,000 under the plan of reorganization.

Chapter 12 allows family farmers to file for a special type of reorganization bankruptcy that gives them added protections not available under Chapter 11 of the Bankruptcy Code.

Working the Web

Bankruptcy Online Information for Bankruptcy Online comes from Federal Filings Business News, a leading provider of bankruptcy news covering major Chapter 11 bankruptcy cases in the United States.

Visit at **www.fedfil.com/bankruptcy**

Bankruptcy Statistics Bankruptcy Statistics are compiled by the American Bankruptcy Institute.

Visit at **www.abiworld.org**

Legal Resources—Bankruptcy This Web site compiles materials on bankruptcy, taxes, credit repair, and other related subjects.

Visit at **www.legalresource.com**

Bankruptcy Alternatives This Web site, compiled by an attorney, gives detailed information about alternatives to bankruptcy.

Visit at **www.berkshire.net/mkb**

CYBER EXERCISES

1. Using Bankruptcy Online, find and visit the pages on Status of Major Bankruptcies.

2. Using the Bankruptcy Statistics Web site, find out how many business filings there were in 1990.

3. Using the Legal Resources—Bankruptcy Web site, find a do-it-yourself bankruptcy kit.

4. Using the Bankruptcy Alternatives Web site, find a document on who to pay when you can't pay everyone.

CASES AND EXERCISES

CRITICAL LEGAL THINKING CASES

29.1. In March 1988, Daniel E. Beren, John M. Elliot, and Edward F. Mannino formed Walnut Street Four, a general partnership, to purchase and renovate an office building in Harrisburg, Pennsylvania. They borrowed more than $200,000 from Hamilton Bank to purchase the building and begin renovation. Disagreements among the partners arose when the renovation costs exceeded their estimates. When Beren was unable to obtain assistance from Elliot and Mannino regarding obtaining additional financing, the partnership quit paying its debts. Beren filed an involuntary petition to place the partnership into Chapter 7 bankruptcy. The other partners objected to the bankruptcy filing. At the time of the filing, the partnership owed debts of more than $380,000 and had approximately $550 in the partnership bank account. Should the petition for involuntary bankruptcy be granted? [*In re Walnut Street Four*, 106 B.R. 56 (Bk.M.D.Pa. 1989)]

29.2. In 1983, Bill K. and Marilyn E. Hargis, husband and wife, filed a Chapter 11 bankruptcy proceeding. In 1984, more than 120 days after the bankruptcy petition was filed,

Bill died. His life was insured for $700,000. His wife was the beneficiary of the policy. The bankruptcy trustee moved to recover the $700,000 as property of the bankruptcy estate. Who gets the insurance proceeds? [*In re Matter of Hargis*, 887 F.2d 77 (5th Cir. 1989)]

29.3. In 1985, James F. Kost filed a voluntary petition for relief under Chapter 11 of the Bankruptcy Code. First Interstate Bank of Greybull (First Interstate) held a first mortgage on the debtor's residence near Basin, Wyoming. Appraisals and other evidence showed that the house was worth $116,000. The debt owed to First Interstate was almost $103,000 and was increasing at the rate of $32.46 per day. The debtor had only an 11.5 percent equity cushion in the property. Further evidence showed that the (1) Greybull/Basin area was suffering from tough economic times, (2) there were more than 90 homes available for sale in the area, (3) the real estate market in the area was declining, (4) the condition of the house was seriously deteriorating and the debtor was not financially able to make the necessary improvements, and (5) the insurance on the property had lapsed. First Interstate moved for a relief from stay so that it could foreclose on the property and sell it. Should the motion be granted? [*In re James F. Kost*, 102 B.R. 829 (Bk.D.Wyo. 1989)]

29.4. In November 1974, Peter and Geraldine Tabala (Debtors), husband and wife, purchased a house in Clarkstown, New York. In November 1976, they purchased a Carvel ice cream business for $70,000 with a loan obtained from People's National Bank. In addition, the Carvel Corporation extended trade credit to Debtors. On October 23, 1978, Debtors conveyed their residence to their three daughters, ages 9, 19, and 20, for no consideration. Debtors continued to reside in the house and to pay maintenance expenses and real estate taxes due on the property. On the date of the transfer Debtors owed obligations in excess of $100,000. On March 28, 1980, Debtors filed a petition for Chapter 7 bankruptcy. The bankruptcy trustee moved to set aside Debtors' conveyance of their home to their daughters as a fraudulent transfer. Who wins? [*In re Tabala*, 11 B.R. 405 (Bk.S.D.N.Y. 1981)]

29.5. Air Florida System, Inc. (Air Florida), an airline company, filed a voluntary petition to reorganize under Chapter 11 of the Bankruptcy Code. Within 90 days prior to the commencement of the case, Air Florida paid $13,575 to Compania Panamena de Aviacion, S.A. (COPA), in payment of an antecedent debt. This payment enabled COPA to receive more than it would have received if Air Florida were liquidated under Chapter 7. Is the payment to COPA an avoidable preferential transfer? [*In re Jet Florida System, Inc., f/k/a Air Florida System, Inc.*, 105 B.R. 137 (Bk.S.D.Fla. 1989)]

29.6. On October 15, 1980, The Record Company, Inc. (The Record Company), entered into a purchase agreement to buy certain retail record stores from Bummbusiness, Inc. (Bummbusiness). All assets and inventory were included in the deal. The Record Company agreed to pay Bummbusiness $20,000 and to pay the $380,000 of trade debt owed by the stores. In exchange, Bummbusiness agreed not to compete with the new buyer for two years within a 15-mile radius of the stores and to use its best efforts to obtain an extension of the due dates for the trade debt. The Record Company began operating the stores but shortly thereafter filed a petition for Chapter 11 bankruptcy. At the time of the bankruptcy filing (1) The Record Company owed Bummbusiness $10,000 and owed the trade debt of $380,000, and (2) Bummbusiness was obligated not to compete with The Record Company. Can The Record Company reject the purchase agreement? [*In re The Record Company*, 8 B.R. 57 (Bk.S.D.Ind. 1981)]

29.7. Richard P. Friese (Debtor) filed a voluntary petition for Chapter 11 bankruptcy. In May 1989, Debtor filed a plan of reorganization that divided his creditors into three classes. The first class, administrative creditors, were to be paid in full. The second class, unsecured creditors, were to receive 50 percent on their claims. The IRS was the third class. It was to receive $20,000 on confirmation and the balance in future payments. No creditors voted to accept the plan. The unsecured creditors are impaired because their legal, equitable, and contractual rights are being altered. Can the bankruptcy court confirm Debtor's plan of reorganization? [*In re Friese*, 103 B.R. 90 (Bk.S.D.N.Y. 1989)]

29.8. Manuel Guadalupe (Debtor) was a tool and die machinist who was employed at Elco Industries for more than five years. He accumulated more than $19,000 in unsecured debt, including deficiencies owed after secured creditors repossessed a van (leaving a deficiency of $1,066) and a car (leaving a deficiency of $3,130). Shortly after the second automobile was repossessed, Debtor borrowed approximately $19,000 from the Elco Credit Union to purchase a 1988 four-wheel-drive Chevrolet Blazer. The $472 monthly payment was to be taken directly from Debtor's earnings.

On February 28, 1989, Debtor filed a voluntary petition for Chapter 13 consumer debt adjustment. The schedule listed total secured debts of $22,132, which included the debt for the Blazer, furniture, and a camcorder. Total unsecured debt was $19,575, which included $2,160 owed to General Finance Corporation (General). Debtor's budget projected that $700 per month would be left over for funding the Chapter 13 plan after his monthly expenses were deducted from his $25,000 gross income. Secured creditors were to be paid in full; unsecured creditors would receive 10 percent of their claims. General objected to the plan. Should Debtor's Chapter 13 plan be confirmed? [*In re Guadalupe*, 106 B.R. 155 (Bk.N.D.Ill. 1989)]

29.9. Donald Wayne Doyle (Debtor) obtained a guaranteed student loan to enroll in a school for training truck drivers. Due to his impending divorce, Debtor never attended the program. The first monthly installment of approximately $50 to pay the student loan became due on September 1, 1988. On September 16, 1988, Debtor filed a voluntary petition for Chapter 7 bankruptcy.

Debtor is a 29-year-old man who earns approximately $1,000 per month at an hourly wage of $7.70 as a truck driver, a job that he had held for 10 years. Debtor resided on a farm where he performed work in lieu of paying rent for his quarters. Debtor was paying monthly payments of $89 on a bank loan for his former wife's vehicle, $200 for his truck, $40 for health insurance, $28 for car insurance, $120 for gasoline and vehicular maintenance, $400 for groceries and meals, and $25 for telephone charges. In addition, a state court had ordered Debtor to pay $300 per month to support his children, ages four and five. Debtor's parents were assisting him by buying him $130 of groceries per month. Should Debtor's student loan be discharged in bankruptcy? [*In re Doyle*, 106 B.R. 272 (Bk.N.D.Ala. 1989)]

29.10. On December 17, 1986, ZZZZ Best Co., Inc. (Debtor), borrowed $7 million from Union Bank. On July 8, 1987, Debtor filed a voluntary petition under Chapter 7 (liquidation). During the preceding 90-day period, Debtor made two interest payments on its loan to Union Bank totaling $100,000. The trustee of Debtor's estate filed a complaint against Union Bank to recover those interest payments as preferential transfers made within 90 days of the bankruptcy filing. Can payments on long-term debt qualify as payments within the ordinary course of business exception to the 90-day preference rule? [*Union Bank v. Wolas*, 112 S.Ct.2d 527 (1991)]

ETHICS CASES

29.11. Scott Greig Keebler (Debtor) became indebted and his debts exceeded his assets. The Internal Revenue Service (IRS) had levied his wages for nonpayment of taxes. Debtor was healthy and capable of earning a substantial income. Evidence showed that Debtor did not try his best to pay his debts, lived an affluent lifestyle, and determined not to pay his principal creditors. Debtor voluntarily quit his job and filed a voluntary petition for Chapter 7 bankruptcy. The petition stated that he was unemployed. Shortly after filing for bankruptcy, the petitioner resumed work. Should Debtor's Chapter 7 case be dismissed because he filed the petition in bad faith? [*In re Scott Greig Keebler*, 106 B.R. 662 (Bk.D.Hawaii 1989)]

29.12. On February 3, 1983, Douglas G. and Aleta Brantz (Debtor), husband and wife, borrowed $40,000 from Meritor Financial Services, Inc. (Meritor), and signed a promissory note evidencing the debt. The proceeds of the loan were used in a business operated by Douglas.

After a portion of the debt had been paid, the business began to fail and the Brantzes defaulted on the loan. Debtors made several attempts to cure the default but failed. On August 11, 1988, Meritor filed a collection action and obtained a judgment lien against Debtors' residence.

On August 16, 1988, a $40,000 mortgage on Debtors' home in favor of Aleta's parents, Philip and Sondra Schley, was recorded. The mortgage was dated February 1, 1988. On May 25, 1989, Debtors filed a voluntary petition for bankruptcy. The parties stipulated that Debtors' home was worth $65,000 and was subject to unvoidable mortgages of $38,000. The Schleys asserted their mortgage of $40,000 preceded Meritor's judicial lien of $28,441. Debtors also claimed an exemption of $15,800 in the premises. Who wins? Was Debtors' behavior unethical? [*In re Brantz* 106 B.R. 62 (Bk.E.D.Pa. 1989)]

29.13. On September 20, 1985, Jane Gnidovec, David Towell, and Robert Dawson (Plaintiffs) obtained a judgment in state court against Alwan Brothers Co., Inc., and Alwan Brothers Partnership and its general partners (jointly Alwans) for $110,059 compensatory damages and $750,000 punitive damages. When the judgment was upheld on appeal, Alwans filed a voluntary petition for Chapter 11 bankruptcy. Is the judgment for compensatory damages and punitive damages dischargeable in bankruptcy? Is it ethical to seek to discharge judgments in bankruptcy? [*In re Alwan Brothers Co., Inc.*, 105 B.R. 886 (Bk.C.D.Ill. 1989)]

CRITICAL LEGAL THINKING WRITING ASSIGNMENT

Read Case A.29 in the Case Appendix [*Dewsnup v. Timm*]. This case is excerpted from the U.S. Supreme Court opinion. Review and brief the case. In your brief, be sure to answer the following questions.

1. Who was the debtor? Who was the creditor? What was the collateral for the secured loan?

2. What amount did the debtor owe on the loan when he filed for bankruptcy? What was the value of the collateral at this time?

3. Succinctly state the issue that was presented to the U.S. Supreme Court.

4. How did the Supreme Court decide this issue? Explain.

NOTES

1. 11 U.S.C. §§ 101-1330.
2. P.L. 98-353.
3. 11 U.S.C. § 362(a).
4. The following states require debtors to take state law exemptions: Alabama, Alaska, Arizona, Arkansas, California, Colorado, Delaware, Florida, Georgia, Idaho, Illinois, Indiana, Iowa, Kansas, Kentucky, Louisiana, Maine, Maryland, Missouri, Montana, Nebraska, Nevada, New Hampshire, New York, North Carolina, North Dakota, Oklahoma, Oregon, South Carolina, South Dakota, Tennessee, Utah, Virginia, West Virginia, and Wyoming.
5. 11 U.S.C. § 507.
6. 11 U.S.C. §§ 1101-1174.
7. *National Labor Relations Board v. Bildisco and Bildisco*, 465 U.S. 513, 104 S.Ct. 1188 (1984).
8. The absolute priority rule was announced in *Consolidated Rock Products Co v. Du Bois*, 312 U.S. 510, 61 S.Ct. 675 (1941). The doctrine was codified in the Bankruptcy Reform Act of 1978.

Agency Formation and Termination

30

$\mathcal{L}$et every eye negotiate for itself, and trust no agent.

WILLIAM SHAKESPEARE
Much Ado About Nothing (1598)

Chapter Objectives

After studying this chapter, you should be able to

1. Define *agency.*
2. Identify and define a principal-independent contractor relationship.
3. Describe when a principal is liable for actions of independent contractors.
4. Describe how express and implied agencies are created.
5. Define *apparent agency.*
6. Describe how an agency is terminated by the acts of the parties.
7. Describe how an agency is terminated by operation of law.
8. Identify who should be notified when an agency is terminated.
9. Identify a wrongful termination of an agency contract.
10. Define *irrevocable agency.*

Chapter Contents

agency law

The large body of common law that governs agency; a mixture of contract law and tort law.

principal

The party who employs another person to act on his or her behalf.

agent

The party who agrees to act on behalf of another.

agency

The principal-agent relationship; the fiduciary relationship "which results from the manifestation of consent by one person to another that the other shall act in his behalf and subject to his control, and consent by the other so to act."

If businesspeople conducted all of their business personally, the scope of their activities would be severely curtailed. In fact, commercial activity in this country would collapse. Partnerships would not be able to operate, corporations could not act through managers and employees, and sole proprietorships would not be able to hire employees.

The use of agents solves this problem. The party who employs another person to act on his or her behalf is called the *principal*. The party who agrees to act on behalf of another is called the *agent*. The principal-agent relationship is commonly referred to as an *agency*. Agency is governed by a large body of common law, known as **agency law**.

THE NATURE OF AGENCY

Agency relationships are formed by the mutual consent of a principal and an agent. Section 1(1) of the Restatement (Second) of Agency defines an *agency* as a *fiduciary relationship* "which results from the manifestation of consent by one person to another that the other shall act in his behalf and subject to his control, and consent by the other so to act." The *Restatement (Second) of Agency* is the reference source of the rules of agency. A party who employs another person to act on his or her behalf is called a **principal**. A party who agrees to act on behalf of another is called an **agent**. The principal-agent relationship is commonly referred to as an **agency**. This relationship is depicted in Exhibit 30.1.

EXHIBIT 30.1   The Principal-Agent Relationship

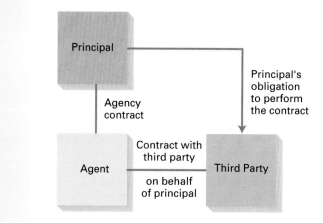

There are numerous examples of agency relationships. They include a salesperson who sells goods for a store, an executive who works for a corporation, a partner who acts on behalf of a partnership, an attorney who is hired to represent a client, a real estate broker who is employed to sell a house, and so on.

Persons Who Can Initiate an Agency Relationship

Any person who has the capacity to contract can appoint an agent to act on his or her behalf. Generally, persons who lack **contractual capacity**, such as insane persons and minors, cannot appoint an agent. However, the court can appoint a legal guardian or other representative to handle the affairs of insane persons, minors, and others who lack capacity to contract. With approval of the courts, these representatives can enter into enforceable contracts on behalf of the persons they represent.

Almost anyone, including someone who lacks the capacity to contract, can act as an agent for another person. For example, an adult principal can employ a child to convey a contract

Business Brief

Businesses such as corporations and partnerships can act only through agents.

offer to a third person. The agent's lack of contractual capacity is immaterial because the third party is entering into a contract with the identified principal, not the agent.

Agency Relationship Must Have Legal Purpose

An agency can be created only to accomplish a *lawful purpose*. Agency contracts that are created for illegal purposes or that are against public policy are void and unenforceable. For example, a principal cannot hire an agent to kill another person.

Some agency relationships are prohibited by law. For example, (1) unlicensed agents cannot be hired to perform the duties of certain licensed professionals (e.g., doctors and lawyers), (2) agents cannot be employed to vote in public elections or serve a criminal sentence, and (3) certain personal service contracts, such as those entered into by a professional sports personality or movie star, cannot be executed by an agent without the consent of the party with whom the principal contracted.

International Perspective

STRATEGIC ALLIANCE IN FOREIGN COUNTRIES

A **strategic alliance** is an agreement between two or more businesses from different countries to accomplish a specific purpose or function. For example, an agreement between an American automobile company and a Japanese automobile company to jointly produce an automobile to be sold in the United States is a joint venture. A joint venture may also be between a corporation and a foreign government.

Joint ventures are often entered into if it is (1) commercially efficient to do so (e.g., neither party has sufficient capital or expertise to accomplish the objective alone) or (2) required by law (e.g., some countries prohibit a foreign company from owning more than 49 percent of a business that operates in the country).

KINDS OF EMPLOYMENT RELATIONSHIPS

There are generally three kinds of **employment relationships**: (1) employer–employee relationships, (2) principal–agent relationships, and (3) principal–independent contractor relationships. These relationships are discussed in the following paragraphs.

employment relationships
**(1) Employer-employee,
(2) principal-agent, and
(3) principal-independent
contractor.**

Employer–Employee Relationship

This type of relationship results when an employer (*the master*) hires an employee (*the servant*) to perform some form of physical service. For example, a welder on General Motors Corporation's assembly line is employed in a master–servant relationship because he or she performs a physical task. The term *master–servant* is anachronistic and is generally not used today. Instead, the relationship is usually referred to as an **employer–employee relationship**.

The term *employee* has no separate legal significance in the law of agency. An employee is not an agent unless he or she is empowered to enter into contracts on the principal employer's behalf. Thus, the welder in the previous example cannot enter into contracts on behalf of the General Motors Corporation (unless he or she is given authority to do so).

**employer–employee
relationship**
**A relationship that results
when an employer hires an
employee to perform some
form of physical service.**

Principal–Agent Relationship

A **principal–agent relationship** is formed when an employer hires an employee and gives that employee authority to act and enter into contracts on his or her behalf. The extent of this authority is governed by an express agreement between the parties and implied from the circumstances of the agency.

Employees in an agency relationship have authority to enter into contracts that are within their scope of employment. For example, the president of a corporation usually has

principal–agent relationship
**An employer hires an
employee and gives that
employee authority to act and
enter into contracts on his or
her behalf.**

the authority to enter into major contracts on the corporation's behalf, but a supervisor on the corporation's assembly line may have the authority to purchase only the supplies necessary to keep the line running.

Principal–Independent Contractor Relationship

Principals often employ outsiders—that is, persons and businesses who are not employees—to perform certain tasks on their behalf. These persons and businesses are called **independent contractors**. Doctors, dentists, consultants, stockbrokers, architects, certified public accountants, real estate brokers, and plumbers are examples of other types of professions and trades that commonly act as independent contractors. An independent contractor who is a professional, such as a lawyer, is called a *professional agent*.

A principal can authorize an independent contractor to enter into contracts. Principals are bound by the authorized contracts of their independent contractors. For example, if a client authorizes an attorney to settle a case within a certain dollar amount and the attorney does so, the settlement agreement is binding.

Independent Contractor Defined   Section 2 of the *Restatement (Second) of Agency* defines an **independent contractor** as "A person who contracts with another to do something for him who is not controlled by the other nor subject to the other's right to control with respect to his physical conduct in the performance of the undertaking."

Independent contractors usually work for a number of clients, have their own offices, hire employees, and control the performance of their work. Merely labeling someone an "independent contractor" is not enough. The crucial factor in determining whether someone is an employee or an independent contractor is the *degree of control* that the employer has over the agent. Critical factors in determining independent contractor status include

- Whether the worker is engaged in a distinct occupation or an independently established business.
- The length of time the agent has been employed by the principal.
- The amount of time that the agent works for the principal.
- Whether the principal supplies the tools and equipment used in the work.
- The method of payment, whether by time or by the job.
- The degree of skill necessary to complete the task.
- Whether the worker hires employees to assist him or her.
- Whether the employer has the right to control the manner and means of accomplishing the desired result.

If an examination of these factors shows that the principal asserts little control, the person is an independent contractor. Substantial control indicates an employer–employee relationship.

Individuals and businesses often employ independent contractors, such as this transportation company, to conduct their affairs or business. Generally, the principal is not liable for the torts of an independent contractor.

In the following case, the court applied these factors in order to determine whether an injured worker was an employee or an independent contractor.

Torres v. Reardon
3 Cal.App.4th 831, 5 Cal.Rptr.2d 52 (1992)
California Court of Appeals

CASE 30.1

FACTS
Jose Torres was a self-employed gardener, doing business under the name Jose Torres Gardening Service. From 1984 until June 1988, Torres performed weekly general gardening services at several homes in Torrance, California, including the home of Michael and Ona Reardon (Reardons). In June 1988, the Reardons employed Torres to trim a 70-foot-tall tree located in their front yard. At 11:00 A.M., on the morning of June 20, 1988, Torres arrived at the Reardons' home with one helper. The Reardons were not at home. David Boice, Reardons' next-door neighbor, cautioned Torres to take care in cutting a large branch 25 feet from the ground that overhung the roof of Boice's house.

When Torres was ready to cut the branch, Boice came outside to hold a rope that was tied to the branch, with the intention of pulling the branch away from his house as it fell. Torres positioned himself on the branch next to the trunk and began to cut at a point just beyond where he was standing. According to Torres, Boice pulled on the rope when Torres was not expecting a pull. As a result, Torres's chain saw "kicked back," and Torres fell from the tree, landing on his back. Torres was rendered a paraplegic as a result of his fall.

Torres sued the Reardons to recover for his injuries, alleging that he was their employee and therefore could recover from them for failing to provide him with workers' compensation insurance. The Reardons countered this argument by saying that Torres was an independent contractor to whom they were not liable. The trial court agreed with the Reardons and granted their motion for summary judgment. Torres appealed.

ISSUE
Was Torres an employee or an independent contractor?

IN THE LANGUAGE OF THE COURT
Croskey, Judge Here, uncontradicted evidence, largely furnished by Torres's own testimony in his deposition, established that under the foregoing criteria, Torres was engaged as an independent contractor in all services that he performed for the Reardons. First, it was established by undisputed testimony that the Reardons engaged Torres to produce the result of trimming their tree to a certain size. The means by which the result

was to be produced were not discussed and were not part of the agreement. In addition, uncontradicted evidence established that: (1) Torres performed services for the Reardons, including both general gardening services and the special project of trimming the Reardons' tree, in the course of his independently established business, Jose Torres Gardening Service, a business in which he customarily engaged; (2) it appears that Torres supplied the equipment he used in the job; (3) Torres was not hired by the day or hour, but contracted with the Reardons to produce the specified result of trimming the tree for the specified price of $350, a price quoted by Torres and accepted by the Reardons; (4) the work that Torres contracted to perform was not work ordinarily done in the course of the Reardons' business, but was maintenance work done on their home; (5) Torres had a substantial investment in his gardening business, including a truck and equipment; (6) Torres had employees who assisted him both in his general gardening business and in the tree-trimming project.

The question of whether one engaged to perform services for another is an employee or an independent contractor is ordinarily a question of fact. However, if only one inference may be drawn from all the facts, the question is one of law. From the foregoing facts, only one inference is possible. The evidence establishes as a matter of law that Torres was not an employee of the Reardons, but was an independent contractor at the time he was injured.

DECISION AND REMEDY
The court of appeals held that Torres was an independent contractor and that the Reardons were not liable to him. Affirmed.

Case Questions

Critical Legal Thinking Suppose that Torres had negligently cut the branch and it had fallen on Boice and injured him. Could Boice have recovered damages from the Reardons? Explain.

Ethics Did Torres act ethically in suing the Reardons? Why do you think he did so?

Business Application Can businesses reduce their liability exposure by hiring more independent contractors and fewer employees to do jobs?

CONCEPT SUMMARY   KINDS OF EMPLOYMENT RELATIONSHIPS

Type of Relationship	Description
Employer–employee	The employer has the right to control the physical conduct of the employee.
Principal-agent	The agent has authority to act on behalf of the principal as authorized by the principal and implied from the agency. An employee is often the agent of his employer.
Principal independent contractor	The principal has no control over the details of the independent contractor's conduct. An independent contractor is usually not an agent of the principal.

Ethical Perspective

PRINCIPAL BITTEN BY INDEPENDENT CONTRACTOR'S TORT

Certain duties may not be delegated. For example, railroads owe a duty to maintain safe railroad crossings. They cannot escape this liability by assigning the task to an independent contractor. Consider the following case.

Yvonne Sanchez borrowed money from MBank El Paso (MBank) to purchase an automobile. She gave MBank a security interest in the vehicle to secure the loan. When Sanchez defaulted on the loan, MBank hired El Paso Recovery Service, an independent contractor, to repossess the automobile. The two men who were dispatched to Sanchez's house found the car parked in the driveway, and hooked it to a tow truck. Sanchez demanded that they cease their efforts and leave the premises, but the men nonetheless continued with the repossession. Before the men could tow the automobile into the street, Sanchez jumped into the car, locked the doors, and refused to leave. The men towed the car at a high rate of speed to the repossession yard. They parked the car in the fenced repossession yard, with Sanchez inside, and padlocked the gate. Sanchez was left in the repossession lot with a Doberman Pinscher guard dog loose in the yard. Later, she was rescued by the police. The law prohibits the repossession of a vehicle if a breach of peace would occur. Sanchez filed suit against MBank, alleg-

ing that it was liable for the tortious conduct of El Paso Recovery Service. The trial court granted summary judgment to MBank, but the court of appeals reversed. MBank appealed.

Is the repossession of a vehicle an inherently dangerous activity in which a secured creditor remains liable for the physical harm resulting from the repossessor's tortious conduct?

The Supreme Court of Texas held that MBank, the principal, was liable for the tortious conduct of El Paso Recovery Service, an independent contractor. The court held that the act of repossessing an automobile from a defaulting debtor is an inherently dangerous activity and a nondelegable duty. The court concluded that El Paso Recovery Service had breached the peace in repossessing the car from Sanchez and caused her physical and emotional harm. The court held that MBank, the principal, could not escape liability by hiring an independent contractor to do this task. The court found MBank liable to Sanchez.

1. Did the independent contractor act responsibly in this case?
2. Should the principal bank have been held liable in this case? Why or why not?

FORMATION OF THE AGENCY RELATIONSHIP

An agency and the resulting authority of an agent can arise in any of these four ways: (1) *express agency*, (2) *implied agency*, (3) *apparent agency*, and (4) *agency by ratification*. Each of these types of agencies is discussed in the sections that follow.

Express Agency

express agency

An agency that occurs when a principal and an agent expressly agree to enter into an agency agreement with each other.

Express agency is the most common form of agency. It occurs when a principal and an agent expressly agree to enter into an agency agreement with each other. Express agency contracts can be either oral or written unless the Statute of Frauds stipulates that they must be written. For example, in most states a real estate broker's contract to sell real estate must be in writing.

A principal and an agent can enter into an **exclusive agency contract**. Under this type of contract, the principal cannot employ any agent other than the exclusive agent. If the principal does so, the exclusive agent can recover damages from the principal. If an agency is not an exclusive agency, the principal can employ more than one agent to try to accomplish a stated purpose. When multiple agents are employed, the agencies with all of the agents terminate when any one of the agents accomplishes the stated purpose.

In an express agency, the agent has the authority to contract or otherwise act on the principal's behalf as expressly stated in the agency agreement. In addition, the agent may also possess certain implied or apparent authority to act on the principal's behalf (as discussed later in this chapter).

Power of Attorney   A **power of attorney** is one of the most formal types of express agency agreements. It is often used to give an agent the power to sign legal documents, such as deeds to real estate, on behalf of the principal. There are two kinds of powers of attorney: *general*, which confers broad powers on the agent to act in any matters on the principal's behalf, and *special*, which limits the agent to those acts specifically enumerated in an agreement. The agent is called an *attorney-in-fact* even though he or she does not have to be a lawyer. Powers of attorney must be written. In addition, they usually must be notarized. A sample general power of attorney is shown in Exhibit 30.2.

Implied Agency

In many situations, a principal and an agent do not expressly create an agency. Instead, the agency is implied from the conduct of the parties. This type of agency is referred to as **implied agency**. The extent of the agent's authority is determined from the facts and circumstances. Implied authority can be conferred by either industry custom, prior dealing between the parties, the agent's position, the acts deemed necessary to carry out the agent's duties, or other factors the court deems relevant. Implied authority cannot conflict with express authority or with stated limitations on express authority.

Incidental Authority   Often, even where there is an express agency agreement, it does not provide enough details to cover all contingencies that may arise in the future regarding the performance of the agency. In this case, the agent possesses certain implied authority to act. This is sometimes referred to as **incidental authority**.

Emergency Powers   Certain emergency situations may arise in the course of an agency. If the agent cannot contact the principal for instructions, the agent has implied *emergency powers* to take all actions reasonably necessary to protect the principal's property and rights.

Apparent Agency

Apparent agency (or agency by estoppel) arises when a principal creates the appearance of an agency that in actuality does not exist. Where an apparent agency is established, the principal is estopped from denying the agency relationship and is bound to contracts entered into by the apparent agent while acting within the scope of the apparent agency. Note that it is the principal's actions—not the agent's—that create an apparent agency.

Consider This Example   Suppose Georgia-Pacific, Inc., interviews Albert Iorio for a sales representative position. Albert, accompanied by Jane Franklin, the national sales manager, visits retail stores located in the open sales territory. While visiting one store, Jane tells the store manager, "I wish I had more sales reps like Albert." Nevertheless, Albert is not

exclusive agency contract
A contract a principal and an agent enter into that says the principal cannot employ any agent other than the exclusive agent.

power of attorney
An express agency agreement that is often used to give an agent the power to sign legal documents on behalf of the principal.

implied agency
An agency that occurs when a principal and an agent do not expressly create an agency, but it is inferred from the conduct of the parties.

incidental authority
Implied power that an agent has where the terms of the express agency agreement do not cover the contingency that has arisen.

apparent agency
Agency that arises when a principal creates the appearance of an agency that in actuality does not exist.

Business Brief
Where an apparent agency is established, the principal is *estopped* from denying the agency relationship.

EXHIBIT 30.2   *A Sample General Power of Attorney*

Power of Attorney

Know All Men by These Presents: That _____

_____

the undersigned (jointly and severally, if more than one) hereby make, constitute and appoint _____

_____

My true and lawful Attorney for me and in my name, place and stead and for my use and benefit:

(a)   To ask, demand, sue for, recover, collect and receive each and every sum of money, debt, account, legacy, bequest, interest, dividend, annuity and demand (which now is or hereafter shall become due, owing or payable) belonging to or claimed by me, and to use and take any lawful means for the recovery thereof by legal process or otherwise, and to execute and deliver a satisfaction or release therefor, together with the right and power to compromise or compound any claim or demand;

(b)   To exercise any or all of the following powers as to real property, any interest therein and/or any building thereon: To contract for, purchase, receive and take possession thereof and of evidence of title thereto; to lease the same for any term or purpose, including leases for business, residence, and oil and/or mineral development; to sell, exchange, grant or convey the same with or without warranty; and to mortgage, transfer in trust, or otherwise encumber or hypothecate the same to secure payment of a negotiable or non-negotiable note or performance of any obligation or agreement;

(c)   To exercise any or all of the following powers as to all kinds of personal property and goods, wares and merchandise, chosen in action and other property in possession or in action: To contract for, buy, sell, exchange, transfer and in any legal manner deal in and with the same and to mortgage, transfer in trust, or otherwise encumber or hypothecate the same to secure payment of a negotiable or non-negotiable note or performance of any obligation or agreement;

(d)   To borrow money and to execute and deliver negotiable or non-negotiable notes therefor with or without security, and to loan money and receive negotiable or non-negotiable notes therefor with such security as said Attorney shall deem proper;

(e)   To create, amend, supplement and terminate any trust and to instruct and advise the trustee of any trust wherein I am or may be trustor or beneficiary; to represent and vote stock, exercise stock rights, accept and deal with any dividend, distribution or bonus, join in any corporate financing reorganization, merger, liquidation, consolidation or other action and the extension, compromise, conversion, adjustment, enforcement or foreclosure, singly or in conjunction with others of any corporate stock, bond, note, debenture or other security; to compound, compromise, adjust, settle and satisfy any obligation, secured or unsecured, owing by or to me and to give or accept any property and/or money whether or not equal to or less in value than the amount owning in payment, settlement or satisfaction thereof;

(f)   To transact business of any kind or class and as my act and deed to sign, execute, acknowledge and deliver any deed, lease, assignment of lease covenant, indenture, indemnity, agreement, mortgage, deed of trust, assignment of mortgage or of the beneficial interest under deed of trust, extension or renewal of any obligation, subordination or waiver of priority, hypothecation, bottomry, charter-party, bill of lading, bill of sale, bill, bond, note, whether negotiable or non-negotiable, receipt, evidence of debt, full or partial release or satisfaction of mortgage, judgment and other debt, request for partial or full reconveyance of deed of trust and such other instruments in writing of any kind or class as may be necessary or proper in the premises.

Giving and Granting unto my said Attorney full power and authority to do and perform all and every act and thing whatsoever, requisite, necessary or appropriate to be done in and about the premises as fully to all intents, and purposes as I might or could do if personally present, hereby ratifying all that my said Attorney shall lawfully do or cause to be done by virtue of these presents. The powers and authority hereby conferred upon my said Attorney shall be applicable to all real and personal property or interests therein now owned or hereafter required by me and whenever situate.

My said Attorney is empowered hereby to determine in said Attorney's sole discretion the time when, purpose for and manner in which any power herein conferred upon said Attorney shall be exercised, and the conditions, provisions and covenants of any instrument or document which may be executed by said Attorney pursuant hereto and in the acquisition or disposition of real or personal property, my said Attorney shall have exclusive power to fix the terms thereof for cash, credit and/or property, and if on credit with or without security.

The undersigned, if a married person, hereby further authorizes and empowers my said Attorney, as my duly authorized agent, to join in my behalf, in the execution of any instrument by which any community real property or any interest therein, now owned or hereafter acquired by my spouse and myself, or either of us, is sold, leased, encumbered, or conveyed.

When the context to requires, the masculine gender includes the feminine and/or neuter, and the singular number includes the plural.

Witness my hand this _____ **day of** _____ ,20 _____.

STATE OF CALIFORNIA   } SS
COUNTY OF

On _____ before me, the undersigned,   _____

a Notary Public in and for said State personally appeared _____   _____

_____   _____

_____   _____

_____ personally known   _____

to me (or proved to me on the basis of satisfactory evidence) to be the   _____

person _____ whose name _____

subscribed to the within instrument and acknowledge that _____   _____

_____ executed the same.

WITNESS my hand and official seal.

Signature _____

_____
        Name (Typed or Printed)   (This area for official seal)

hired. If Albert later enters into contracts with the store on behalf of Georgia-Pacific and Jane has not controverted the impression of Albert she left with the store manager, the company will be bound to the contract.

Contemporary Business Application

A SIGN OF THE TIMES: APPARENT AGENCY IN FRANCHISING

Franchising has become a major form of conducting business in the United States. In a franchise agreement, one company (called the **franchisor**) licenses another company (called the **franchisee**) to use its trade name, trademarks and service marks, and trade secrets. Many fast-food restaurants, gasoline stations, motels and hotels, and other businesses are operated in this fashion.

The franchisor and franchisee are independently owned businesses. A principal–agent relationship usually is not created by the franchise. If no express or implied agency is created, the franchisor would not normally be civilly liable for the tortious conduct (e.g., negligence) of the franchisee. Liability could be imposed on the franchisor, however, if an apparent agency is shown. Consider the following case.

The Howard Johnson Company (HJ) operates a chain of hotels, motels, and restaurants across the United States. Approximately 75 percent of the HJ motor lodges are owned and operated by franchisees that are licensed by HJ to do business under the "Howard Johnson" trade name and trademarks. The rest are company-owned.

Orlando Executive Park, Inc. (OEP), is a corporate franchisee that owns and operates an HJ motor lodge franchise in Orlando, Florida. The motor lodge is part of a large complex known as "Howard Johnson's Plaza" located off Interstate 4. The motor lodge contains approximately 300 guest rooms in six separate buildings.

P.D.R. (name withheld by the court), a 35-year-old married woman and mother of a small child, worked as a supervisor for a restaurant chain. Her work occasionally required her to travel and stay overnight in Orlando. On October 22, 1975, P.D.R. stopped to stay at the HJ motor lodge in Orlando. At approximately 9:30 P.M., P.D.R. registered for her previously reserved room at the lodge. The registration form did not inform her that the hotel was an HJ franchisee. P.D.R. parked her car in the motor lodge parking lot and proceeded with her suitcase to her ground-floor room in Building A, which was located directly behind the registration office. P.D.R. then went back to her car to get some papers. After obtaining the papers from her car, P.D.R. returned to Building A. As she proceeded down an interior hallway of the building toward her room, she was accosted by a man she had previously seen standing behind the registration office. The man struck her in the

throat and neck and choked her until she became semiconscious. When P.D.R. fell to the floor, her assailant sat on top of her and stripped her of her jewelry. He then dragged her down the hallway and beneath a secluded stairway where he brutally beat her. The assailant then disappeared into the night and has never been identified.

P.D.R. suffered serious physical and psychological injury, including memory loss, mental confusion, and an inability to tolerate and communicate with people. She lost her job within one year of the assault. P.D.R. suffers permanent injury that requires expensive, long-term medical and psychiatric treatment. P.D.R brought a tort action against OEP and HJ and sought actual and punitive damages against both of them.

The jury had little trouble finding that OEP had breached its duty of care and was liable. Evidence showed that other criminal activity had occurred previously on the premises, but that OEP failed to warn guests, including P.D.R., of the danger. In fact, OEP management actively discouraged criminal investigations by the sheriff's deputies, thus minimizing any deterrent effect they may have had. Further evidence showed that the dark and secluded stairwell area where P.D.R. was dragged was a security hazard that should have been boarded up or better lit.

The jury also found HJ liable to P.D.R. under the doctrine of apparent agency. The appellate court stated: "While OEP might not be HJ's agent for all purposes, the signs, national advertising, uniformity of building design and color schemes allow the public to assume that this and other similar motor lodges are under the same ownership. An HJ official testified that it was the HJ marketing strategy to appear as a 'chain that sells a product across the nation.'" The court continued, "There was sufficient evidence for the jury to reasonably conclude that HJ represented to the traveling public that it could expect a particular level of service at a Howard Johnson Motor Lodge. The uniformity of signs, design and color schemes easily leads the public to believe that each motor lodge is under common ownership or conforms to common standards, and the jury could find they are intended to do so." The appellate court upheld an award of $750,000 compensatory damages against OEP and HJ jointly. [*Orlando Executive Park, Inc. v. P.D.R.*, 402 So.2d 442 (Fla.App. 1981)]

Agency by Ratification

Agency by ratification occurs when (1) a person misrepresents him- or herself as another's agent when in fact he or she is not and (2) the purported principal ratifies (accepts) the unauthorized act. In such cases, the principal is bound to perform and the agent is relieved of any liability for misrepresentation.

Consider This Example   Bill Levine sees a house for sale and thinks his friend Sherry Maxwell would want it. Bill Levine enters into a contract to purchase the house from the seller and signs the contract "Bill Levine, agent for Sherry Maxwell." Because Bill is not Sherry Maxwell's agent, she is not bound to the contract. However, if Sherry agrees to purchase the house, there is an agency by ratification. The ratification "relates back" to the moment Bill Levine entered into the contract. Upon ratification of the contract, Sherry Maxwell is obligated to purchase the house.

CONCEPT SUMMARY   FORMATION OF AGENCY RELATIONSHIPS

Type of Agency	Definition	Enforcement of the Contract
Express	Authority is expressly given to the agent by the principal.	Principal and third party are bound to the contract.
Implied	Authority is implied from the conduct of the parties, custom and usage of trade, or act incidental to carrying out the agent's duties.	Principal and third party acts are bound to the contract.
Apparent	Authority created when the principal leads a third party into believing that the agent has authority.	Principal and third party are bound to the contract.
By ratification	Acts of the agent committed outside the scope of his authority.	Principal and third party are not bound to the contract unless the principal ratifies the contract.

International Perspective

INTERNATIONAL LICENSING

A company that owns a valuable property right or expertise—such as a patent or other form of technology—may wish to distribute it or products that contain it in foreign countries without selling it. A method for doing so is the **license**. In licensing, one party (the *licensor*) sells the right to use its patent or other technology in another country to another company (the *licensee*). The licensor and licensee are independent entities. The licensee is usually granted an exclusive right to sell the technology or product in a specified territory (e.g., a countrywide license). The licensee usually pays royalties or other fees to the licensor.

Consider This Example   The Walt Disney Company, which is a United States company, often grants licenses to businesses in other countries to put Mickey Mouse, Mulan, and its other trademarked characters on clothing, toys, and other items sold in other countries. The Walt Disney Company is the licensor and the foreign company is the licensee. Many Internet companies license software and other intellectual property in conducting international e-commerce.

If licensing is used, the exporter (1) does not have to sell its valuable property right, (2) is not subject to the tort or contract liability of the licensee, (3) often avoids any restrictions against foreign entry into a country, (4) does not have to make a substantial investment in foreign country operations, and (5) can control the use of its property right through specific contract provisions (e.g., grant only a limited-time license, impose quality control standards).

TERMINATION OF AN AGENCY

An agency can be terminated by the acts of the parties or by operation of law, as discussed below.

Termination of an Agency by Acts of the Parties

The parties to an agency contract can terminate an agency contract by agreement or by their actions. The four methods of **termination** of an agency relationship **by acts of the parties** follow.

Mutual Agreement As with any contract, the parties to an agency contract can mutually agree to terminate their agreement. By doing so, the parties relieve each other of any further rights, duties, obligations, or powers provided for in the agency contract. Either party can propose the termination of an agency contract.

Lapse of Time Agency contracts are often written for a specific period of time. The agency terminates when the specified time period elapses. Suppose, for example, that the principal and agent enter into an agency contract "beginning January 1, 2000, and ending December 31, 2003." The agency automatically terminates on December 31, 2003. If the agency contract does not set forth a specific termination date, the agency terminates after a reasonable time has elapsed. The courts often look to the custom of an industry in determining the reasonable time for the termination of the agency.

Purpose Achieved A principal can employ an agent for the time it takes to accomplish a certain task, purpose, or result. Such agencies automatically terminate once they are completed. For example, suppose a principal employs a licensed real estate broker to sell his or her house. The agency terminates when the house is sold and the principal pays the broker the agreed-upon compensation.

Occurrence of a Specified Event An agency contract can specify that the agency exists until a specified event occurs. The agency terminates when the specified event happens. For example, if a principal employs an agent to take care of his or her dog until he or she returns from a trip, the agency terminates when the principal returns from the trip.

> **termination by acts of the parties**
> An agency may be terminated by the following acts of the parties: (1) mutual agreement, (2) lapse of time, (3) purpose achieved, or (4) occurrence of a specified event.

Termination of an Agency by Operation of Law

Agency contracts can be terminated by **operation of law** as well as by agreement. The six methods of terminating an agency relationship by operation of law are discussed below.

Death The death of either the principal or the agent terminates the agency relationship. This rule is based on the old legal principle that because a dead person cannot act, no one can act for him or her. Note that the agency terminates even if one party is unaware of the other party's death. An agent's actions that take place after the principal's death do not bind the principal's estate.

Insanity The insanity of either the principal or the agent generally terminates the agency relationship. A few states have modified this rule to provide that a contract entered into by an agent on behalf of an insane principal is enforceable if (1) the insane person has not been adjudged insane, (2) the third party does not have knowledge of the principal's insanity at the time of contracting, and (3) the enforcement of the contract will prevent injustice.

> **termination by operation of law**
> An agency is terminated by operation of law if there is (1) death of the principal or the agent, (2) insanity of the principal or the agent, (3) bankruptcy of the principal, (4) impossibility of performance, (5) change in circumstances, or (6) war between the principal's and the agent's countries.

Bankruptcy The agency relationship is terminated if the principal is declared bankrupt. Bankruptcy requires the filing of a petition for bankruptcy under federal bankruptcy law. The principal's financial difficulties without bankruptcy does not terminate an agency relationship. The agent's bankruptcy usually does not terminate an agency unless the agent's credit standing is important to the agency relationship.

Impossibility The agency relationship terminates if a situation arises that makes its fulfillment impossible. The following circumstances can lead to termination on this ground:

- **The Loss or Destruction of the Subject Matter of the Agency** For example, assume that a principal employs an agent to sell his or her horse, but the horse dies before it is sold. The agency relationship terminates at the moment the horse dies.
- **The Loss of a Required Qualification** For example, suppose a principal employs a licensed real estate agent to sell his or her house and the real estate agent's license is revoked. The agency terminates at the moment the license is revoked.
- **A Change in the Law** For example, suppose that a principal employs an agent to trap alligators. If a law is passed that makes trapping alligators illegal, the agency contract terminates when the law becomes effective.

Changed Circumstances An agency terminates when there is an unusual change in circumstances that would lead the agent to believe that the principal's original instructions should no longer be valid. For example, a principal employs a licensed real estate agent to sell a farm for $100,000. The agent thereafter learns that oil has been discovered on the property that makes it worth $1 million. The agency terminates because of this change in circumstances.

War The outbreak of a war between the principal's country and the agent's country terminates the agency relationship between the parties. Such an occurrence usually makes the performance of the agency contract impossible.

Entrepreneur and the Law

CERTAIN NOTIFICATION REQUIRED AT THE TERMINATION OF AN AGENCY

If the agency is terminated by agreement between the parties, the principal is under a duty to give certain third parties notification of the termination. Unless otherwise required, the notice can be from the principal or some other source (e.g., the agent). If an agency terminates by operation of law, there is no duty to notify third parties about the termination, however.

The termination of an agency extinguishes an agent's actual authority to act on the principal's behalf. However, if the principal fails to give the proper notice of termination to a third party, the agent still has apparent authority to bind the principal to contracts with these third parties. If this happens, the contract is enforceable against the principal. The principal's only recourse is against the agent to recover damages caused by these unauthorized contracts.

The following notification requirements must be met:

- **Parties Who Dealt with the Agent** Direct notice of termination must be given to all persons with whom the agent dealt. Although the notice may be either written or oral, it is better practice to give written notice.
- **Parties Who Have Knowledge of the Agency** The principal must give direct or constructive notice to any third party who has knowledge of the agency but with whom the agent has not dealt. **Direct notice** often is in the form of a letter. **Constructive notice** usually consists of placing a notice of the termination of the agency in a newspaper serving the relevant community. This notice is effective even against persons who do not see it.

- **Parties Who Have No Knowledge of the Agency**
  Generally, a principal is not obligated to give notice of termination to strangers who have no knowledge of the agency. However, a principal who has given the agent written authority to act but fails to recover the writing upon termination of the agency may be liable to strangers who later rely on this writing and deal with the agent. The laws of most states provide that this liability can be avoided by giving constructive notice (e.g., newspaper announcement) of the termination of the agency.

Wrongful Termination of an Agency Contract

Generally, agency contracts that do not specify a definite time for their termination can be terminated at will by either the principal or the agent without liability to the other party. When a principal terminates an agency contract, it is called a *revocation of authority*. When an agent terminates an agency, it is called a *renunciation of authority*.

Unless an agency is irrevocable (discussed later in this chapter), both the principal and the agent have an individual *power* to unilaterally terminate any agency contract. Note that having the power to terminate an agency agreement is not the same as having the *right* to terminate it. The *unilateral termination* of an agency contract may be wrongful. If the principal's or the agent's termination of an agency contract breaches the contract, the other party can sue for damages for **wrongful termination**.

wrongful termination
The termination of an agency contract in violation of the terms of the agency contract. The nonbreaching party may recover damages from the breaching party.

Business Brief
The distinction between the *power* and the *right* to terminate an agency is critical. Be certain it is clear.

Consider This Example   A principal employs a licensed real estate agent to sell his or her house. The agency contract gives the agent an exclusive listing for three months. After one month, the principal unilaterally terminates the agency. The principal has the power to do so and the agent can no longer act on behalf of the principal. However, because the principal did not have the right to terminate the contract, the agent can sue him or her and recover damages (i.e., lost commission) for wrongful termination.

In the following case, the court had to decide whether an agent's actions violated the agency contract.

Wil-Helm Agency v. Lynn
618 S.W.2d 748 (1981)
Court of Appeals of Tennessee

CASE 30.2

FACTS
In 1966, Loretta Lynn, a famous country singer, entered into a performance agency contract with the Wil-Helm Agency (Wil-Helm). Wil-Helm was a partnership composed of four Wilburn brothers—Teddy, Doyle, Leslie, and Lester. Wil-Helm represented performers and entertainers. It conducted public relations, negotiated contracts, obtained work, and otherwise provided advice and services to clients. Teddy Wilburn was primarily responsible for the Loretta Lynn account. In about 1967, Doyle Wilburn began to drink alcohol excessively, becoming extremely abusive and boorish when he was drinking or drunk. This conduct caused Teddy Wilburn to leave the Wil-Helm Agency in 1971. With Teddy gone, Doyle took it upon himself to be more closely involved with Lynn and her work. Doyle was drunk on several occasions while acting as Lynn's agent. Some of the more glaring instances of misconduct were (1) insulting the producer of *The Johnny Carson Show* while there to close a deal for Lynn to appear on that show, (2) drunkenness on the part of Doyle Wilburn while on the stage acting as master of ceremonies, (3) actually disturbing Loretta during performances, (4) drunken vomiting on the dinner table at a postperformance party given for patrons, promoters, disc jockeys and their wives, and (5) being drunk on practically

(case continues)

every road trip, interfering with Loretta's need for rest on the bus, ignoring instructions of airline personnel while on flights, and generally being an obnoxious drunk in the presence of people upon whom the success of the artist depended.

In April 1971, Lynn notified the Wil-Helm Agency that it had breached the performance contract and that she would no longer be held to the contract. The Wil-Helm Agency sent Lynn a bill for $178,566 for services rendered. When Lynn refused to pay this amount, Wil-Helm brought an action against Lynn for breach of contract. Lynn filed a cross-complaint against Wil-Helm, alleging that Wil-Helm breached the contract and owed her damages caused by the breach. The trial court held that Lynn owed Wil-Helm $178,566, that the Wil-Helm Agency breached the performance contract and caused Lynn $178,566 in damages, and that Wil-Helm's breach terminated the contract, thus releasing Lynn from any further performance under the contract. Wil-Helm Agency appealed.

ISSUE
Did the agent's conduct breach the performance agency contract?

IN THE LANGUAGE OF THE COURT
Matherne, Judge   We agree with the chancellor that the conduct of Doyle Wilburn as the representative of the agency was entirely inconsistent with the duty owed the artist under the contract. The agreement is a bilateral contract wherein each party was obligated to the other to render certain performances, the carrying out of which by each party was essential to the real-ization of benefits under the contract. Each party to the contract was under an implied obligation to restrain from doing any act that would delay or prevent the other party's performance of the contract.

There is ample material evidence that the Wil-Helm Agency, by the conduct of its representative Doyle Wilburn, committed a substantial breach of its contract with Loretta Lynn. The chancellor is affirmed in this respect. We accept the figure of $178,566.72 as the amount due Wil-Helm Agency under the contract up until the date of termination with allowances for dates already booked to November 1971. We agree with the chancellor that the damages suffered by the artist more than offset those amounts claimed by the agency for its part performance of the contract.

DECISION AND REMEDY
The appellate court held that the agent's conduct breached the performance contract, giving Loretta Lynn the right to terminate the agency contract. Affirmed.

Case Questions

Critical Legal Thinking   Should a party to an agency contract always have the *power* to terminate the contract? Should the party also always be given the *right* to do so?

Ethics   Did Doyle Wilburn act ethically in this case? Did Loretta Lynn act ethically in this case by terminating the agency contract?

Business Application   Do you think the result reached by the court in this case was fair to the parties? Explain.

Irrevocable Agency

agency coupled with an interest

A special type of agency relationship that is created for the agent's benefit; irrevocable by the principal.

An **agency coupled with an interest** is a special type of agency relationship that is created for the agent's benefit. This type of agency is *irrevocable* by the principal (e.g., the principal cannot terminate it). An agency coupled with an interest is commonly used in security agreements to secure loans.

Consider This Example   Heidi Norville owns a piece of real estate. She goes to Wells Fargo Bank to obtain a loan on the property. The bank makes the loan but requires her to sign a security agreement (e.g., a mortgage) pledging the property as collateral for the loan. The security agreement contains a clause that appoints the bank as Norville's agent and permits the bank to sell the property and recover the amount of the loan from the sale proceeds if she defaults on her payments. This agency is irrevocable by Norville, the principal.

An agency coupled with an interest is not terminated by the death or incapacity of either the principal or the agent. It terminates only when the agent's obligations are performed. However, the parties can expressly agree that an agency coupled with an interest is terminated.

Working the Web

U.S. Small Business Administration This site is a one stop shop for information about Small Business Administration programs and services.

Visit at **www.sbaonline.sba.gov**

Restatement of the Law of Agency The Restatement of the Law Second, Agency deals with the relations between principal and agent, principal and third person, and agent and third person. It was developed by the American Law Institute.

Visit at **www.ali.org/ali/Agency.htm**

The Group.net This Web site contains lots of valuable information dealing with the federal Fair Labor Standards Act.

Visit at **www.the group.net**

CYBER EXERCISES

1. Check out the Internet Business Cards on the Small Business Administration site.

2. Is a Third Restatement of the Law of Agency currently under development?

3. Using the Group.net Web site, find an article on the definition of an employee.

CASES AND EXERCISES

CRITICAL LEGAL THINKING CASES

30.1. Renaldo, Inc., d.b.a. Baker Street, owns and operates a nightclub in Georgia. On the evening in question, plaintiff Ginn became "silly drunk" at the nightclub and was asked by several patrons and the manager to leave the premises. The police were called and Ginn left the premises. When Ginn realized that his jacket was still in the nightclub, he attempted to reenter the premises. He was met at the door by the manager, who refused him admittance. When Ginn persisted, an unidentified patron, without the approval of the manager, pushed Ginn, who lost his balance and fell backward. To break his fall, Ginn put his hand against the door jamb. The unidentified patron slammed the door on Ginn's hand and held it shut for several minutes. Ginn, who suffered severe injuries to his right hand, sued the nightclub for damages. Is the unidentified patron an agent of the nightclub? [*Ginn v. Renaldo, Inc.*, 359 S.E.2d 390 (Ga.App. 1987)]

30.2. Sexton was the general partner of a limited partnership known as the Birmingham/Crabapple Properties, Ltd. (Birmingham/Crabapple), which was formed to acquire interests in certain tracts of land. Sexton was also associated with an unrelated company, Barton & Ludwig, Inc. (Barton & Ludwig). When Shivers invested in Birmingham/Crabapple, Sexton represented that he was acting on behalf of Barton & Ludwig, thanked him for "placing your confidence in Barton/Ludwig, Inc., with your investment," and welcomed him into the "Barton/Ludwig family." Barton & Ludwig neither signed a partnership agreement nor indicated to Shivers that Sexton was its agent. When the partnership ran into financial difficulties, Shivers sued Barton & Ludwig for damages. Is Barton & Ludwig liable? [*Shivers v. Sexton*, 296 S.E.2d 749 (Ga.App. 1983)]

30.3. The Butler Telephone Company, Inc. (Butler), contracted with the Sandidge Construction Company (Sandidge) to lay 18 miles of telephone cable in a rural area. In the contract, Butler reserved the right to inspect the work for compliance with the terms of the contract. Butler did not control how Sandidge performed the work. Johnnie Carl Pugh, an employee of Sandidge, was killed on the job when the sides of an excavation in which he was working caved in on top of him. Evidence disclosed that the excavation was not properly shored or sloped and that it violated general safety standards. Pugh's parents and estate brought a wrongful death action against Butler. Is Butler liable? [*Pugh v. Butler Telephone Company, Inc.*, 512 So.2d 1317 (AL 1987)]

30.4. Mercedes Connolly and her husband purchased airline tickets and a tour package for a tour to South Africa from Judy Samuelson, a travel agent doing business as International

Tours of Manhattan. Samuelson sold tickets for a variety of airline companies and tour operators, including African Adventurers that was the tour operator for the Connollys' tour. Mercedes injured her left ankle and foot on September 27, 1984, while the tour group was on a walking tour to see hippopotami in a river at a game reserve. Mercedes fell while trying to cross a 6-inch-deep stream. She sued Samuelson for damages. Is Samuelson liable? [*Connolly v. Samuelson*, 671 F.Supp. 1312 (D.Kan. 1987)]

30.5. In 1968, as a result of marital problems, Howard R. Bankerd "left for the west" and Virginia Bankerd, his wife, continued to reside in their jointly owned home. Before his departure, Howard executed a power of attorney to Arthur V. King, which authorized King to "convey, grant, bargain, and/or sell" Howard's interest in the property. For the ensuing decade, Howard lived in various locations in Nevada, Colorado, and Washington but rarely contacted King. Howard made no payments on the mortgage, for taxes, or for maintenance or upkeep of the home.

In September 1977, Virginia, who was nearing retirement, requested King to exercise his power of attorney and transfer Howard's interest in the home to her. King's attempts to locate Howard were unsuccessful. He believed that Howard, who would then be 69 years of age, might be dead. King gifted Howard's interest in the property to Virginia, who sold the property for $62,500. In 1981, Howard returned and filed suit against King, alleging breach of trust and fiduciary duty. Is King liable? [*King v. Bankerd*, 492 A.2d 608 (MD 1988)]

30.6. Tom and Judith Sullivan owned real property on which they obtained a loan from the Federal Land Bank of Omaha (FLB). The property secured the loan. The Sullivans defaulted on the loan, and the FLB brought an action to foreclose on the mortgage. The FLB's lawyer wrote a letter to the Sullivans outlining a settlement offer. A copy of the letter was sent to FLB's regional office located in Yankton, South Dakota. The regional office did not notify the attorney that he did not have the authority to offer the settlement without its permission. When the Sullivans accepted the settlement offer, FLB's regional office refused to approve the deal. The Sullivans sued to enforce it. Does the attorney for FLB have authority to settle the case? [*Federal Land Bank of Omaha v. Sullivan*, 430 N.W.2d 700 (SD 1988)]

30.7. Robert Bolus was engaged in various businesses in which he sold and repaired trucks. In 1976, he decided to build a truck repair facility in Bartonsville, Pennsylvania. Bolus contacted United Penn Bank (Bank) to obtain financing for the project and was referred to Emmanuel Ziobro, an assistant vice president. Ziobro orally agreed that Bank would provide funding for the project. He did not tell Bolus that he only had express authority to make loans up to $10,000. After extending $210,000 in loans to Bolus, Bank refused to provide further financing. When Bolus defaulted on the loan, Bank pressed judgment against Bolus. Bank sought to recover Bolus's assets in payment for the loan. Bolus sued Bank for damages for breach of contract. Who wins? [*Bolus v. United Penn Bank*, 525 A.2d 1215 (Pa.Super. 1987)]

30.8. Both Gene Mohr and James Loyd own 50 percent of Tri-County Farm Equipment Company (Tri-County). Tri-County has its depository bank account at First National Bank of Olathe, Kansas. Loyd also personally owns an oil business known as Earthworm Energy (Earthworm), which has its bank account at the State Bank of Stanley (State Bank). Neither Mohr nor Tri County has any ownership interest in Earthworm. Mohr did not indicate to State Bank that Loyd had any authority to personally sign checks on behalf of Tri County. In 1982, Loyd took eight checks that were payable to Tri-County and indorsed and deposited them into Earthworm's account at State Bank. Mohr brought an action for conversion against State Bank to recover the amount of the checks. State Bank argued in defense that Loyd had apparent authority to deposit the checks in his personal business account. Does Loyd possess apparent authority? [*Mohr v. State Bank of Stanley*, 734 P.2d 1071 (KS 1987)]

30.9. After Francis Pusateri retired, he met with Gilbert J. Johnson, a stockbroker with E.F. Hutton & Co., Inc. (E.F. Hutton), and informed Johnson that he wished to invest in tax-free bonds and money market accounts. Pusateri opened an investment account with E.F. Hutton and checked the box stating his objective was "tax-free income and moderate growth." During the course of a year, Johnson churned Pusateri's account to make commissions and invested Pusateri's funds in volatile securities and options. Johnson kept telling Pusateri that his account was making money, and the monthly statement from E.F. Hutton did not indicate otherwise. The manager at E.F. Hutton was aware of Johnson's activities but did nothing to prevent them. When Johnson left E.F. Hutton, Pusateri's account—which had been called the "laughingstock" of the office—had shrunk from $196,000 to $96,880. Pusateri sued E.F. Hutton for damages. Is E.F. Hutton liable? [*Pusateri v. E.F. Hutton & Co., Inc.*, 225 C.R. 526 (Cal.App. 1986)]

30.10. Boettcher DTC Building Joint Venture (Boettcher) owns an office building in which it leases space to tenants. Harmon Wilfred, an independent leasing agent, contacted Boettcher on behalf of Landmark Associates (Landmark), which was interested in leasing office space in the Boettcher building. Wilfred represented Boettcher as a special agent in the transaction. In January 1983, Landmark executed a 68-month lease with Boettcher. Boettcher paid Wilfred a commission. Shortly thereafter, Landmark began negotiating with Boettcher for additional lease space. Landmark also contacted Wilfred to inquire about the availability of lease space in other buildings. When Wilfred found Landmark lease space in another office building, Landmark vacated its premises at the Boettcher building and defaulted on its lease agreement. Boettcher sued Wilfred for damages, alleging that Wilfred violated his fiduciary duty to Boettcher. Who wins? [*Boettcher DTC Building Joint Venture v. Wilfred*, 762 P.2d 788 (Colo.App. 1988)]

30.11. Elizabeth Krempasky, who was 82 years old, owned a house worth $24,000 and four certificates of deposit (CDs) worth $5,000 each. In her will, Krempasky devised her estate to her niece, Lydia Vrablova Wanamaker. Krempasky died on June 8, 1979, while a patient at a hospital. Wanamaker, who was appointed executrix of the decedent's estate, could not find the CDs. Upon further inquiry, she discovered that the name of Anna A. Parana, an acquaintance of Krempasky's, had been added to the CDs on the day of the decedent's death. Evidence showed that (1) Parana prepared the forms necessary to authorize the bank to add her name to the CDs, (2) the decedent signed the forms on the day of her death sometime before dying at 2:45 P.M., and (3) Parana presented the authorization forms to the bank sometime between 3:00 P.M. and 4:00 P.M. on the same day. A transfer of CDs to joint tenancy is not effective until the bank officially makes the transfer on its records, which it did because it did not have notice of Krempasky's death. Wanamaker, as executrix of the decedent's estate, filed a petition requesting that the CDs be ordered returned to the decedent's estate. Who wins? [*In re Krempasky*, 501 A.2d 618 (Pa.Super. 1985)]

ETHICS CASES

30.12. The Hagues, husband and wife, owned a 160-acre tract that they decided to sell. On March 19, 1976, they entered into a listing agreement with Harvey C. Hilgendorf, a licensed real estate broker, which gave Hilgendorf the exclusive right to sell the property for a period of 12 months. The Hagues agreed to pay Hilgendorf a commission of 6 percent of the accepted sale price if a bona fide buyer was found during the listing period.

By letter of August 13, 1976, the Hagues terminated the listing agreement with Hilgendorf. Hilgendorf did not acquiesce to the Hagues' termination, however. On September 30, 1976, Hilgendorf presented an offer to the Hagues from a buyer willing to purchase the property at the full listing price. The Hagues ignored the offer and sold the property to another buyer. Hilgendorf sued the Hagues for breach of the agency agreement. Did the Hagues act ethically in this case? Who wins the lawsuit? [*Hilgendorf v. Hague*, 293 N.W.2d 272 (IA 1980)]

CRITICAL LEGAL THINKING WRITING ASSIGNMENT

Read Case A.30 in the Case Appendix [*Penthouse International, Ltd. v. Barnes*]. This case is excerpted from the court of appeals opinion. Review and brief the case. In your brief, be sure to answer the following questions.

1. Who were the defendants? What was their working relationship?

2. Describe the accident that occurred.

3. What issue was presented to the court? How did the court decide this issue?

31

Liability of Principals and Agents

The law, wherein, as in a magic mirror, we see reflected not only our lives, but the lives of all men that have been! When I think on this majestic theme, my eyes dazzle.

OLIVER WENDELL HOLMES, JR.
To the Suffolk Bar Association (1885)

Chapter Objectives

After studying this chapter, you should be able to

1. Describe the agent's duties to the principal.
2. Classify and define the agent's breaches of loyalty to the principal.
3. Name and describe the principal's duties to the agent.
4. Describe the principal's and the agent's liability on third-party contracts.
5. Describe the agent's liability for his own torts.
6. Describe the principal's liability for the misrepresentations of the agent.
7. Explain the doctrine of *respondeat superior*.
8. Identify and describe the principal's liability for the negligent conduct of an agent.
9. Describe the principal's liability for the intentional torts of the agent.
10. Describe the principal's liability for torts of an independent contractor.

Chapter Contents

Principals employ agents to expand their ability to act. Principals and agents owe certain duties to each other and are liable to each other for breaching these duties. When acting for the principal, an agent often enters into contracts and otherwise deals with third parties. Agency law has established certain rules that make principals and agents liable to third persons for their acts or inaction. This chapter focuses on the liability of principals and agents to each other and to third parties.

AGENT'S DUTIES

An agent owes certain duties to the principal. These duties may be either set forth in the agency agreement or implied by law. Generally, agents owe the principal the duties of (1) performance, (2) notification, (3) loyalty, (4) obedience, and (5) accountability. Each of these duties is discussed in the sections that follow.

Duty of Performance

An agent who enters into a contract with a principal has two distinct obligations: (1) performing the lawful duties expressed in the contract and (2) meeting the standards of reasonable care, skill, and diligence implicit in all contracts. Collectively, these duties are referred to as the agent's **duty of performance**.

Normally, an agent is required to render the same standard of care, skill, and diligence that a fictitious reasonable agent in the same occupation would render in the same locality and under the same circumstances. For instance, a general medical practitioner in a rural area would be held to the standard of a reasonable general practitioner in rural areas. In some professions, such as accounting, a national standard of performance, called generally accepted accounting standards, is imposed. If an agent holds him- or herself as possessing higher-than-customary skills, the agent will be held to this higher standard of performance. For example, a lawyer who claims to be a specialist in securities law will be held to a reasonable specialist-in-securities-law standard.

An agent who does not perform his or her express duties or fails to use the standard degree of care, skill, or diligence is liable to the principal for breach of contract. An agent who has negligently (or intentionally) failed to perform properly is also liable in tort.

duty of performance

An agent's duty to a principal that includes (1) performing the lawful duties expressed in the contract and (2) meeting the standards of reasonable care, skill, and diligence implicit in all contracts.

CONCEPT SUMMARY   TORT LIABILITY OF PRINCIPALS AND AGENTS TO THIRD PARTIES

Agent's Conduct	Agent Liable	Principal Liable
Misrepresentation	Yes	The principal is liable for the intentional and innocent misrepresentations made by an agent acting within the scope of her authority.
Negligence	Yes	The principal is liable under the doctrine of *respondeat superior* if the agent's negligent act was committed within the scope of his employment.
Intentional tort	Yes	Motivation test: The principal is liable if the agent's motivation in committing the intentional tort was to promote the principal's business.
	Yes	Work-related test: The principal is liable if the agent committed the intentional tort within work-related time and space.

Duty of Notification

In the course of an agency, the agent usually learns information that is important to the principal. This information may come from third parties or other sources. The agent's duty to notify the principal of such information is called the **duty of notification**. The agent is liable to the principal for any injuries resulting from a breach of this duty.

duty of notification

An agent's duty to notify the principal of information he or she learns from a third party or other source that is important to the principal.

Imputed Knowledge   Most information learned by an agent in the course of the agency is *imputed* to the principal. This means that the principal is assumed to know what the agent knows. This is so whether the agent actually does tell the principal the relevant information.

Duty of Loyalty

Because the agency relationship is based on trust and confidence, an agent owes the principal a **duty of loyalty** in all agency-related matters. Thus, an agent owes a fiduciary duty not to act adversely to the interests of the principal. If this duty is breached, the agent is liable to the principal. The most common types of breaches of loyalty by an agent are discussed below.

duty of loyalty

A duty an agent owes the principal not to act adversely to the interests of the principal.

Dual Agency   An agent cannot meet a duty of loyalty to two parties with conflicting interests. *Dual agency* occurs when an agent acts for two or more different principals in the same transaction. This practice is generally prohibited unless all of the parties involved in the transaction agree to it. If an agent acts as an undisclosed dual agent, he or she must forfeit all compensation received in the transaction.

Some agents, such as middlemen and finders, are not considered dual agents. This is because they bring only interested parties together; they do not take part in any negotiations.

usurp an opportunity

When an agent appropriates an opportunity for him- or herself by failing to let the principal know about it.

Usurping an Opportunity   An agent cannot **usurp an opportunity** that belongs to the principal. For example, a third-party offer to an agent must be conveyed to the principal. The agent cannot appropriate the opportunity for him- or herself unless the principal rejects it after due consideration. Opportunities to purchase real estate, businesses, products, ideas, and other property are subject to this rule.

Self-Dealing   Agents are generally prohibited from undisclosed *self-dealing* with the principal. For example, a real estate agent who is employed to purchase real estate for a principal cannot secretly sell his or her own property in the transaction. However, the deal is lawful if the principal agrees to buy the property after the agent discloses his or her ownership.

Misuse of Confidential Information   In the course of an agency, the agent often acquires confidential information about the principal's affairs (e.g., business plans, technological innovations, customer lists, trade secrets, and such). The agent is under a legal duty not to disclose or misuse such information either during or after the course of the agency. There is no prohibition against using general information, knowledge, or experience acquired during the course of the agency.

Competing with the Principal   Agents are prohibited from competing with the principal during the course of an agency unless the principal agrees. The reason for this rule is that an agent cannot meet his or her duty of loyalty when personal interests conflict with the principal's interests. If the parties have not entered into an enforceable covenant not to compete, an agent is free to compete with the principal once the agency has ended.

Ethical Perspective

DOUBLE AGENT

Wartime "double agents" have been the subject of numerous novels and movies. Most of these stories end with one side or the other (or both) finding out this secret, and the double agent suffering the consequences of his or her double-dealing. The law of agency treats dual agents with the same disdain. Instead of bloodshed, though, agency law hits the double agent in the pocketbook. Consider the following case.

Del Rayo Properties (Del Rayo) hired L. Byron Culver & Associates (Culver), a real estate brokerage firm, to find suitable real estate for acquisition by Del Rayo. Culver became aware of approximately 33.5 acres of land owned by Jaoudi Industrial & Trading Corporation (Jaoudi) located in Rancho Santa Fe, California. Culver obtained approval from Del Rayo to enter into negotiations on Del Rayo's behalf to acquire Jaoudi's property.

On February 8, 1985, Culver telephoned Joseph Jaoudi, president of the company, and inquired if the 33.5-acre property in Rancho Santa Fe was for sale. Jaoudi indicated that it was. Culver asked whether it could list the property, and Jaoudi agreed to give Culver a one-time listing for that particular property. Jaoudi and Culver agreed on a 3 percent commission.

On February 13, 1985, Culver presented Jaoudi with a written offer from Del Rayo to purchase the property for $1,750,000. When Jaoudi inquired whether Culver and Del Rayo were associated in any way, Culver denied any association. Jaoudi agreed to the deal.

Prior to the closing of escrow on March 13, 1985, Jaoudi instructed the escrow not to pay the commission to Culver. Escrow closed and Culver did not receive the commission. Culver sued Jaoudi to recover the commission. Jaoudi defended by arguing that Culver was an undisclosed dual agent who did not deserve to collect the commission because of his double-dealing.

The court held that a real estate agent must refrain from dual representation in a sales transaction unless he obtains the consent of both principals after full disclosure. This Culver did not do. The trial and appellate courts denied Culver recovery of the $52,500 commission. The appellate court stated, "The fact that Jaoudi Industrial received a financial benefit from Culver's efforts is of no consequence on the issue of no recovery for failure to disclose a dual agency. A bar to recovery is a matter of public policy." [*L. Byron Culver & Associates v. Jaoudi Industrial & Trading Corporation*, 1 Cal. App. 4th 300, 1 Cal.Rptr.2d 680 (Cal.App. 1991)]

1. Did Culver act ethically in this case?
2. What policy underlies the rule against undisclosed dual agents?
3. Did Jaoudi act ethically in refusing to pay the commission? Should Jaoudi benefit financially from Culver's secret conduct?

Duty of Obedience

Both gratuitous agents and agents for hire have a duty to obey the lawful instructions of the principal during the performance of the agency. This is called the **duty of obedience**.

If the principal's instructions are unclear or confusing, the agent is required to inquire and seek clearer directions from the principal. If this is not possible, the agent owes a duty to act in good faith and in a reasonable manner based on the circumstances. In emergency situations where the principal cannot be consulted, the agent can deviate from the principal's instructions and take whatever actions are reasonable to protect the principal's property. In the absence of instructions, the agent may use his or her own best judgment in acting on the principal's behalf.

The agent owes no duty to obey the principal's instructions to engage in crimes, torts, or unethical conduct. If the agent does so, he or she will be personally liable (as is the principal). For example, a sales representative can ignore the principal's instructions to misrepresent the quality of the principal's goods.

duty of obedience

A duty that agents have to obey the lawful instructions of the principal during the performance of the agency.

Duty of Accountability

Unless otherwise agreed, an agent owes a duty to maintain an accurate accounting of all transactions undertaken on the principal's behalf. This **duty of accountability (duty to account)** includes keeping records of all property and money received and expended during the course of the agency. A principal has a right to demand an accounting from the agent at any time, and the agent owes a legal duty to make the accounting. This duty also requires the agent to (1) maintain a separate account for the principal and (2) use the principal's property in an authorized manner.

Any property, money, or other benefit received by the agent in the course of the agency belongs to the principal. For example, all secret profits received by the agent are the property of the principal. If an agent breaches the agency contract, the principal can sue the agent to recover damages caused by the breach. The court can impose a *constructive trust* on any secret profits on property purchased with secret profits for the benefit of the principal.

𝒞ONCEPT SUMMARY   AGENT'S DUTIES TO THE PRINCIPAL

Name of Duty	Duty
Duty of performance	To perform the lawful duties expressed in the agency contract and to use reasonable care, skill, and diligence in the performance of these duties.
Duty of notification	To notify the principal of any information that is important to the agency. Knowledge possessed by the agent concerning the agency is imputed to the principal.
Duty of loyalty	Not to act adversely to the interests of the principal. Breaches of this duty include acting as an unauthorized dual agent, usurping the principal's opportunity, unauthorized self-dealing with the principal, misusing confidential information, and unauthorized competition with the principal.
Duty of obedience	To obey the lawful instructions of the principal. The agent owes no duty to engage in crimes, torts, or unethical conduct on the principal's behalf.
Duty of accountability	To maintain accurate records of all transactions taken on the principal's behalf and not to commingle personal money or property with that of the principal.

𝒫RINCIPAL'S DUTIES

The principal owes certain duties to the agent. These duties, which can be expressed in the agency contract or implied by law, include (1) the duty of compensation, (2) the duties of reimbursement and indemnification, (3) the duty of cooperation, and (4) the duty to provide safe working conditions.

Duty of Compensation

A principal owes a **duty to compensate** an agent for services provided. Usually, the agency contract (whether written or oral) specifies the compensation to be paid. The principal must pay this amount either upon the completion of the agency or at some other mutually agreeable time.

If there is no agreement as to the amount of compensation, the law implies a promise that the principal will pay the agent the customary fee paid in the industry. If the compensation cannot be established by custom, the principal owes a duty to pay the reasonable value of the agent's services.

There is no duty to compensate a gratuitous agent. However, gratuitous agents who agree to provide their services free of charge may be paid voluntarily.

Certain types of agents traditionally perform their services on a *contingency fee* basis. Under this type of arrangement, the principal owes a duty to pay the agent the agreed-upon contingency fee only if the agency is completed. Real estate brokers, finders, lawyers, and salespersons often work on this basis.

Basketball players and other professional sports figures usually hire sports agents to represent them in negotiations with owners of the professional teams they are interested in playing for. Professional sports stars also use sports agents to negotiate endorsement contracts with sporting goods companies and other advertisers.

Duties of Reimbursement and Indemnification

In carrying out the agency, an agent may spend his or her own money on the principal's behalf. Unless otherwise agreed, the principal owes a **duty to reimburse** the agent for all such expenses if they were (1) authorized by the principal, (2) within the scope of the agency, and (3) necessary to discharge the agent's duties in carrying out the agency. For example, a principal must reimburse an agent for authorized business trips taken on the principal's behalf.

A principal also owes a **duty to indemnify** the agent for any losses the agent suffers because of the principal. This duty usually arises where an agent is held liable for the principal's misconduct. For example, suppose an agent enters into an authorized contract with a third party on the principal's behalf, the principal fails to perform on the contract, and the third party recovers a judgment against the agent. The agent can recover indemnification of this amount from the principal.

Duty of Cooperation

Unless otherwise agreed, the principal owes a **duty to cooperate** with and assist the agent in the performance of the agent's duties and the accomplishment of the agency. For example, unless otherwise agreed, a principal who employs a real estate agent to sell his or her house owes a duty to allow the agent to show the house to prospective purchasers during reasonable hours.

duty of reimbursement
A duty that a principal owes to repay money to the agent if the agent spent his or her own money during the agency on the principal's behalf.

duty to indemnify
A duty that a principal owes to protect the agent for losses the agent suffered during the agency because of the principal's misconduct.

duty to cooperate
A duty that a principal owes to cooperate with and assist the agent in the performance of the agent's duties and the accomplishment of the agency.

duty to provide safe working conditions
A duty that a principal owes to provide safe premises, equipment, and other working conditions; also includes inspection by the principal.

Duty to Provide Safe Working Conditions

The principal owes a **duty to provide safe working conditions** to its agents. Federal and state statutes establish many safety standards for the workplace. These include safe premises, equipment, and other working conditions. The principal also owes a duty to inspect for unsafe working conditions, to warn agents of dangerous conditions, and to repair and remedy unsafe conditions. Agents can sue principals for violating these duties.

CONCEPT SUMMARY   PRINCIPAL'S DUTIES TO THE AGENT

Name of Duty	Duty
Duty of compensation	To pay the agent the agreed-upon compensation for services, but if there is no agreement, to pay compensation customarily paid in the industry; if there is no such custom, to pay reasonable compensation. Agents sometimes perform services on a contingency fee basis. Gratuitous agents need not be paid.
Duties of reimbursement and indemnification	To reimburse the agent for all expenses incurred as authorized by the principal and within the scope of the agency or expenses necessary to discharge the agent's duties. The principal must also indemnify the agent for any losses (e.g., judgments) the agent suffers because of the principal.
Duty of cooperation	To cooperate with and assist the agent in the performance of the agent's duties and the accomplishment of the agency.
Duty to provide safe working conditions	To provide safe working conditions for agents and to repair and remedy unsafe working conditions.

CONTRACT LIABILITY TO THIRD PARTIES

A principal who authorizes an agent to enter into a contract with a third party is liable on the contract. Thus, the third party can enforce the contract and recover damages if the principal fails to perform it.

The agent can also be held liable on the contract in certain circumstances. Imposition of such liability depends upon whether the agency is classified as (1) *fully disclosed*, (2) *partially disclosed*, or (3) *undisclosed*.

Fully Disclosed Agency

fully disclosed agency
An agency that results if the third party entering into the contract knows (1) that the agent is acting as an agent for a principal and (2) the actual identity of the principal.

A **fully disclosed agency** results if the third party entering into the contract knows (1) that the agent is acting as an agent for a principal and (2) the actual identity of the principal.[1] The third party has the requisite knowledge if the principal's identity is disclosed to the third party by either the agent or some other source.

In a fully disclosed agency, the contract is between the principal and the third party. Thus, the principal, who is called a *fully disclosed principal*, is liable on the contract. The agent, however, is not liable on the contract because the third party relied on the principal's credit and reputation when the contract was made. An agent is liable on the contract if he or she guarantees that the principal will perform the contract.

Partially Disclosed Agency

partially disclosed agency
An agency that occurs if the agent discloses his or her agency status but does not reveal the principal's identity and the third party does not know the principal's identity from another source.

A **partially disclosed agency** occurs if the agent discloses his or her agency status but does not reveal the principal's identity and the third party does not know the principal's identity from another source. The nondisclosure may be because (1) the principal instructs the agent not to disclose his or her identity to the third party or (2) the agent forgets to tell the third party the principal's identity. In this kind of agency, the principal is called a *partially disclosed principal*.

In a partially disclosed agency, both the principal and the agent are liable on third-party contracts.[2] This is because the third party must rely on the agent's reputation, integrity, and credit because the principal is unidentified. If the agent is made to pay the contract, the agent can sue the principal for indemnification. The third party and the agent can agree to relieve the agent's liability.

Undisclosed Agency

An **undisclosed agency** occurs when the third party is unaware of either the existence of an agency or the principal's identity. The principal is called an *undisclosed principal*. Undisclosed agencies are lawful. They are often used when the principal feels that the terms of the contract would be changed if his or her identity were known. For example, a wealthy person may use an undisclosed agency to purchase property if he or she thinks that the seller would raise the price of the property if his or her identity were revealed.

In an undisclosed agency, both the principal and the agent are liable on the contract with the third party. This is because the agent, by not divulging that he or she is acting as an agent, becomes a principal to the contract. The third party relies on the reputation and credit of the agent in entering into the contract. If the principal fails to perform the contract, the third party can recover against the principal or the agent. If the agent is made to pay the contract, he or she can recover indemnification from the principal.

In the following case, the court was presented with the issue of whether an agent was liable on a contract.

undisclosed agency
An agency that occurs when the third party is unaware of either (1) the existence of an agency or (2) the principal's identity.

Agency Relationship

You'll See Seafoods, Inc. v. Gravois
520 So.2d 461 (1988)
Court of Appeals of Louisiana

CASE 31.1

FACTS
In 1978, James Gravois purchased a restaurant and named it "The Captain's Raft." The restaurant was actually owned by Computer Tax Services of La., Inc., a corporation owned by Gravois. Gravois did not inform the managers, employees, or suppliers that the restaurant was owned by a corporation. Further, the menus were printed with the name "The Captain's Raft" with no indication it was a corporate entity. Supplies purchased by the restaurant were paid for by checks signed by Gravois with no indication of his agency capacity. You'll See Seafoods, Inc. (You'll See), supplied fresh seafood to the restaurant and was paid for the merchandise by checks signed by Gravois. On February 28, 1984, You'll See filed suit against Gravois d.b.a. The Captain's Raft to recover unpaid invoices. Gravois responded by saying that he was merely acting as an agent for a corporate principal. The corporation was in bankruptcy.

ISSUE
Was Gravois liable on the debt owed You'll See Seafoods, Inc.?

IN THE LANGUAGE OF THE COURT
Kliebert, Judge   *Under Louisiana law, an agent is liable to those with whom he contracts on behalf of his principal when he has bound himself personally by entering into an agreement without disclosing the identity of his principal, and the agent has the burden of proving he disclosed his capacity and the identity of his principal if he wishes to escape personal liability. Express notice of the agent's status and the principal's identity is not required if the facts and circumstances indicate that a third party should have known or was put on notice of the principal-agent relationship.*

Pretermitting the question of whether Gravois established corporate ownership of the restaurant, after review of the record before us we discern no clear error in the trial court's factual finding that You'll See was unaware an agency relationship existed

(case continues)

between Gravois and the corporation. *Although Gravois contends he was under no obligation to disclose his corporate capacity because he neither placed the orders nor accepted from You'll See, he does not deny that he spoke on occasion with the president/representative of You'll See and signed all checks issued against the You'll See account without indicating he was acting in a corporate capacity. As Gravois failed to disclose the alleged agency relationship, he is individually liable for all debts incurred.*

DECISION AND REMEDY

The appellate court held that Gravois was an agent for an undisclosed corporate principal and, therefore, was liable for the debts owed to You'll See Seafoods, Inc.

Case Questions

Critical Legal Thinking   Should agents for undisclosed principals be held personally liable on contracts? Why or why not?

Ethics   Did Gravois act ethically in arguing that the debts owed to You'll See belonged to the corporation and not to himself individually?

Business Application   Why do you think Gravois wanted the debts to be placed in the corporation? Why do you think You'll See did not want the debts placed in the corporation?

Agent Exceeding the Scope of Authority

implied warranty of authority

An agent who enters into a contract on behalf of another party impliedly warrants that he or she has the authority to do so.

An agent who enters into a contract on behalf of another party impliedly warrants that he or she has the authority to do so. This is called the agent's **implied warranty of authority**. If the agent lacks or exceeds the scope of his or her authority, the principal is not liable on the contract unless the principal *ratifies* it. The agent, however, is liable to the third party for breaching the implied warranty of authority. To recover, the third party must show (1) reliance on the agent's representation and (2) ignorance of the agent's lack of status.

Consider This Example   Suppose Sam, Sara, Satchel, Samantha, and Simone form a rock band called SSSSSex. SSSSSex is just a voluntary association without any legal status. Sam enters into a contract with Rocky's Musical Instruments (Rocky's) to purchase instruments and equipment for the band on credit and signs the contract, "Sam, for SSSSSex." When SSSSSex fails to pay the debt, Rocky's can sue Sam and recover. Sam must pay the debt because he breached his implied warranty of authority when he acted as an agent for a *nonexistent principal*; that is, the purported principal was not a legal entity upon which liability could be imposed.

Entrepreneur and the Law

SIGNING PROPERLY AS AN AGENT

The agent's signature on a contract entered into on the principal's behalf is important. It can establish the agent's status and therefore his or her liability. For instance, in a fully disclosed agency the agent's signature must clearly indicate that he or she is acting as an agent for a specifically identified principal. Examples of proper signature include "Allison Adams, agent for Peter Perceival," "Peter Perceival, by Allison Adams, agent," and "Peter Perceival, by Allison Adams."

An agent who is authorized to sign a contract for a fully disclosed principal but fails to properly do so can be held personally liable on the contract. For example, in the prior example a partially disclosed agency would be created if the contract was signed "Allison Adams, agent." If Adams merely signed the contract "Allison Adams," the agency would be an undisclosed agency. In both these instances the agent is liable on the contract.

CONCEPT SUMMARY   CONTRACT LIABILITY OF PRINCIPALS AND AGENTS TO THIRD PARTIES

Type of Agency	Principal Liable	Agent Liable
Fully disclosed	Yes	No, unless the agent (1) acts as a principal or (2) guarantees the performance of the contract.
Partially disclosed	Yes	Yes, unless the third party relieves the agent's liability.
Undisclosed	Yes	Yes.
Nonexistent	No, unless the principal ratifies the contract	Yes, the agent is liable for breaching the implied warranty of authority.

TORT LIABILITY TO THIRD PARTIES

The principal and the agent are both personally liable for their own tortious conduct. A principal is also liable for the tortious conduct of an agent who is acting within the scope of his or her authority. On the other hand, an agent is liable for the tortious conduct of a principal only if he or she directly or indirectly participates in or aids and abets the principal's conduct.

The courts have applied a broad and flexible standard in interpreting *scope of authority* in the context of employment. Although other factors may also be considered, the courts rely on the following factors to determine whether an agent's conduct occurred within the scope of his or her employment:

- Was the act specifically requested or authorized by the principal?
- Was it the kind of act that the agent was employed to perform?
- Did the act occur substantially within the time period of employment authorized by the principal?
- Did the act occur substantially within the location of employment authorized by the principal?
- Was the agent advancing the principal's purpose when the act occurred?

Where liability is found, *tort remedies* are available to the injured party. These remedies include recovery for medical expenses, lost wages, pain and suffering, emotional distress, and, in some cases, punitive damages. As discussed in the following sections, the three main sources of tort liability for principals and agents are misrepresentation, negligence, and intentional torts.

An agent's scope of authority was at issue in the following case.

Edgewater Motels, Inc. v. Gatzke and Walgreen Co.
277 N.W.2d 11 (1979)
Supreme Court of Minnesota

CASE 31.2

FACTS

Arlen Gatzke (Gatzke) was a district manager for the Walgreen Company (Walgreen). In August 1979, Gatzke was sent to Duluth, Minnesota, to supervise the opening of a new Walgreen store. In Duluth, Gatzke stayed at the Edgewater Motel (Edgewater). While in Duluth, Gatzke was "on call" 24 hours a day to other Walgreen stores located

in his territory. About midnight on the evening of August 23, 1979, Gatzke, after working 17 hours that day, went with several other Walgreen employees to a restaurant and bar to drink. Within one hour's time, Gatzke had consumed three "doubles" and one single brandy Manhattan. About 1:30 A.M., he went back to the Edgewater Motel and filled out his expense report. Soon thereafter a fire broke out in Gatzke's

(case continues)

motel room. Gatzke escaped, but the fire spread and caused extensive damage to the motel. Evidence showed that Gatzke smoked two packs of cigarettes a day. An expert fire reconstruction witness testified that the fire started from a lit cigarette in or next to the wastepaper basket in Gatzke's room. Edgewater Motels, Inc., sued Gatzke and Walgreen. The parties stipulated that the damage to the Edgewater Motel was $330,360. The jury returned a verdict against defendants Gatzke and Walgreen. The court granted Walgreen's posttrial motion for judgment notwithstanding the verdict. Plaintiff Edgewater and defendant Gatzke appealed.

ISSUE
Was Gatzke's act of smoking within his "scope of employment" making his principal, the Walgreen Company, vicariously liable for his negligence?

IN THE LANGUAGE OF THE COURT
Scott, Justice The question of whether smoking can be within an employee's scope of employment is a close one, but after careful consideration of the issue we are persuaded by the reasoning of the courts that hold that smoking can be an act within an employee's scope of employment. It seems only logical to conclude that an employee does not abandon his employment as a matter of law while temporarily acting for his personal comfort when such activities involve only slight deviations from work that are reasonable under the circumstances. We hold that an employer can be held vicariously liable for his employee's negligent smoking of a cigarette if he was otherwise acting in the scope of his employment at the time of the negligent act.

The record contains a reasonable basis from which a jury could find that Gatzke was involved in serving his employer's interests at the time he was at the bar. Gatzke testified that, while at the

Bellows, he discussed the operation of the newly opened Walgreen's store with other Walgreen employees. But more important, even assuming that Gatzke was outside the scope of his employment while he was at the bar, there is evidence from which a jury could reasonably find that Gatzke resumed his employment activities after he returned to his motel room and filled out his expense account.

Additionally, the record indicates that Gatzke was an executive type of employee who had no set working hours. He considered himself a 24-hour-a-day man; his room at the Edgewater Motel was his "office away from home." It was therefore also reasonable for the jury to determine that the filling out of his expense account was done within authorized time and space limits of his employment. In light of the above, we hold it was reasonable for the jury to find that Gatzke was acting within the scope of his employment when he completed his expense account.

DECISION AND REMEDY
The state supreme court held that Gatzke's negligent act of smoking was within the scope of his employment while acting as an employee of the Walgreen Company. The supreme court reinstated the jury's verdict awarding damages to plaintiff Edgewater Motels, Inc.

Case Questions

Critical Legal Thinking Should smoking cigarettes be held to be within an employee's "scope of employment"? Why or why not?

Ethics Do employers owe a duty to police the personal habits of their employees?

Business Application Because of the dangers of smoking, would employers be justified in hiring only nonsmokers as employees?

*M*ISREPRESENTATION

intentional misrepresentation

Occurs when an agent makes an untrue statement that he or she knows is not true. Also known as *fraud* or *deceit*.

innocent misrepresentation

Occurs when an agent makes an untrue statement that he or she honestly and reasonably believes to be true.

Intentional misrepresentations are also known as **fraud** or **deceit**. They occur when an agent makes untrue statements that he or she knows are not true. An **innocent misrepresentation** occurs when an agent negligently makes a misrepresentation to a third party.

A principal is liable for the intentional and innocent misrepresentations made by an agent acting within the scope of his or her employment. The third party can either (1) rescind the contract with the principal and recover any consideration paid or (2) affirm the contract and recover damages.

Consider This Example Assume that (1) a car salesman is employed to sell the principal's car and (2) the principal tells the agent that the car was repaired after it was involved in a major accident. If the agent intentionally tells the buyer that the car was never involved in an accident, the agent has made an intentional misrepresentation. Both the principal and the agent are liable for this misrepresentation.

NEGLIGENCE

Principals are liable for the negligent conduct of agents acting within the scope of their employment. This liability is based on the common law doctrine of ***respondeat superior*** ("let the master answer"), which, in turn, is based on the legal theory of *vicarious liability* (liability without fault). In other words, the principal is liable because of his or her employment contract with the negligent agent, not because the principal was personally at fault.

This doctrine rests on the principle that if someone (i.e., the principal) expects to derive certain benefits from acting through others (i.e., an agent), that person should also bear the liability for injuries caused to third persons by the negligent conduct of an agent who is acting within the scope of his or her employment.

respondeat superior
A rule that says an employer is liable for the tortious conduct of its employees or agents while they are acting within the scope of its authority.

Frolic and Detour

Agents sometimes do things during the course of their employment to further their own interests rather than the principal's. For example, an agent might take a detour to run a personal errand while on assignment for the principal. This is commonly referred to as a **frolic and detour**. Negligence actions stemming from frolic and detour are examined on a case-by-case basis. Agents are always personally liable for their tortious conduct in such situations. Principals are generally relieved of liability if the agent's frolic and detour is substantial. However, if the deviation is minor, the principal is liable for the injuries caused by the agent's tortious conduct.

frolic and detour
When an agent does something during the course of his or her employment to further his or her own interests rather than the principal's.

Consider These Examples   James Jones, salesperson, stops home for lunch while on an assignment for his principal. While leaving his home, the agent hits and injures a pedestrian with his automobile. The principal is liable if the agent's home was not too far out-of-the-way from the agent's assignment. However, the principal would not be liable if an agent who is supposed to be on assignment to Los Angeles flies to San Francisco to meet a friend and is involved in an accident. The facts and circumstances of each case will determine its outcome.

The "Coming and Going" Rule

Under the common law, a principal generally is not liable for injuries caused by its agents and employees while they are on their way to or from work. This so-called "**coming and going**" **rule** applies even if the principal supplies the agent's automobile or other transportation or pays for his or her gasoline, repairs, and other automobile operating expenses. This rule is quite logical. Because principals do not control where their agents and employees live, they should not be held liable for tortious conduct of agents on their way to and from work.

"coming and going" rule
A rule that says a principal is generally not liable for injuries caused by its agents and employees while they are on their way to or from work.

Dual-Purpose Mission

Sometimes, principals request that agents run errands or conduct other acts on their behalf while the agent or employee is on personal business. In this case, the agent is on a **dual-purpose mission**. That is, he or she is acting partly for him- or herself and partly for the principal. Most jurisdictions hold both the principal and the agent liable if the agent injures someone while on such a mission.

dual-purpose mission
An errand or other act that a principal requests of an agent while the agent is on his or her own personal business.

Consider This Example   Suppose a principal asks an employee to drop a package off at a client's office on the employee's way home. If the employee negligently injures a pedestrian while on this dual-purpose mission, the principal is liable to the pedestrian.

In the following case, the court found that an employee was not acting within the scope of her employment when negligence caused injuries to a third person.

Sussman v. Florida East Coast Properties, Inc.
557 So.2d 74 (1990)
District Court of Appeals of Florida

CASE 31.3

FACTS
Elizabeth Paraiso, a fitness instructor at a health spa owned by Florida East Coast Properties, Inc. (Properties), received a telephone call from a fellow employee asking her to stop off at a supermarket on the way to work and pick up a birthday cake for another employee's birthday party. Paraiso departed for work earlier than usual and deviated five blocks from her normal route to purchase the cake. Paraiso lost control of the car when she reached over to prevent the cake from falling off the seat. The car left the road and struck William Sussman as he sat on a bench waiting for a bus. Sussman sued Properties to recover damages for his injuries. The trial court granted summary judgment to Properties. Sussman appealed.

ISSUE
Was Paraiso acting within the scope of her employment when she struck Sussman with her car?

IN THE LANGUAGE OF THE COURT
Ferguson, Judge   The conduct of an employee is within the scope of his employment, for the purpose of determining the employer's vicarious liability to third persons injured by the employee, only if (1) the conduct is of the kind the employee is hired to perform, (2) the conduct occurs substantially within the time and space limits authorized or required by the work to be performed, and (3) the conduct is activated at least in part by a purpose to serve the master.

The employee detoured on her way to work to stop at a supermarket, where she purchased a cake for a fellow employee's birthday celebration. Although she was enroute to her place of employment when she struck and injured a pedestrian with her personal vehicle, she was outside the scope of the employer's business as a matter of law. The employee's deposition testimony supports the finding that the purchase of the cake was outside the scope of duties the employee was employed to perform. Mrs. Paraiso testified

> *We were friends, like aerobics teachers and fitness instructors, and we just decided to give him a cake because it was his birthday. I didn't do it because it was my boss. I didn't do it because my boss said so.*

DECISION AND REMEDY
The court held that Properties was not liable to Sussman. Affirmed.

Case Questions

Critical Legal Thinking   What is the policy underlying the coming and going rule? Do you agree with this rule?

Ethics   Do you think the employer should have been held liable in this case?

Business Application   Should an employer be concerned about how "accident prone" a person is before the employer hires that person as an employee?

INTENTIONAL TORTS

intentional tort

Occurs when a person has intentionally committed a wrong against (1) another person or his or her character or (2) another person's property.

Intentional torts include such acts as assault, battery, false imprisonment, and other intentional conduct that cause injury to another person. A principal is not liable for the intentional torts of agents and employees that are committed outside the principal's scope of business. For example, if an employee attends a sporting event after working hours and gets into a fight with another spectator at the event, the employer is not liable.

However, a principal is liable under the doctrine of vicarious liability for intentional torts of agents and employees committed within their scope of employment. The courts generally apply one of the following two tests discussed below in determining whether an agent's intentional torts were committed within the agent's scope of employment.

The Motivation Test

Under the **motivation test**, if the agent's motivation in committing the intentional tort is to promote the principal's business, the principal is liable for any injury caused by the tort. However, if the agent's motivation in committing the intentional tort was personal, the principal is not liable even if the tort took place during business hours or on business premises. For example, a principal is not liable if his agent was motivated by jealousy to beat up someone on the job who dated her boyfriend.

The Work-Related Test

Some jurisdictions have rejected the motivation test as too narrow. These jurisdictions apply the **work-related test** instead. Under this test, if an agent commits an intentional tort within a work-related time or space—for example, during working hours or on the principal's premises—the principal is liable for any injuries caused by the agent's intentional torts. Under this test, the agent's motivation is immaterial.

In the following case, the court applied the work-related test in determining whether an employer was liable for its agent's intentional tort.

> **motivation test**
> A test to determine the liability of the principal; if the agent's motivation in committing the intentional tort is to promote the principal's business, then the principal is liable for an injury caused by the tort.

> **work-related test**
> A test to determine the liability of a principal; if an agent commits an intentional tort within a work-related time or space, the principal is liable for any injury caused by the agent's intentional tort.

Desert Cab Inc. v. Marino
823 P.2d 898 (1992)
Supreme Court of Nevada

CASE 31.4

FACTS

On October 6, 1986, Maria Marino, a cab driver with Yellow-Checkered Cab Company (Yellow Cab), and James Edwards, a cab driver with Desert Cab Inc. (Desert Cab), parked their cabs at the taxicab stand at the Sundance Hotel and Casino in Las Vegas to await fares. Marino's cab occupied the first position in the line and Edwards occupied the third. As Marino stood alongside her cab conversing with the driver of another taxi, Edwards began verbally harassing her from inside his cab. When Marino approached Edwards to inquire as to the reason for the harassment, a verbal argument ensued. Edwards jumped from his cab, grabbed Marino by her neck and shoulders, began choking her, and threw her in front of his taxicab. A bystander pulled Edwards off Marino and escorted her back to her cab. Marino sustained injuries that rendered her unable to work for a time. Edwards was convicted of misdemeanor assault and battery. Marino brought a personal injury action against Desert Cab. The jury found Desert Cab liable and awarded Marino $65,000. Desert Cab appealed.

ISSUE

Is Desert Cab liable for the intentional tort of its employee?

IN THE LANGUAGE OF THE COURT

Per Curiam The district court admitted into evidence the judgment of Edwards' misdemeanor assault and battery convic-

tion. The court found this evidence to conclusively prove Edwards' civil liability to Marino. Edwards' judgment of conviction provides conclusive evidence of his civil liability to Marino.

A finding that Edwards committed a wrongful act by attacking Marino is a prerequisite to imposing liability upon Desert Cab. In order to find Desert Cab liable, Marino still had to establish that Desert Cab was "responsible" for Edwards' conduct. Desert Cab could be found "responsible" only if Marino proved that the attack arose out of the course and scope of Edwards' employment with Desert Cab. We affirm the judgment of the district court.

DECISION AND REMEDY

The appellate court held that Desert Cab was liable for the intentional tort committed by its employee.

Case Questions

Critical Legal Thinking Should employers be held liable for the intentional torts of their employees?

Ethics Did Desert Cab act ethically in denying liability?

Business Application Should employers give prospective employees psychological examinations to determine if they have any dangerous propensities?

L IABILITY FOR I NDEPENDENT C ONTRACTOR'S T ORTS

A principal is generally not liable for the torts of its independent contractors. Independent contractors are personally liable for their own torts. The rationale behind this rule is that principals do not control the means by which the results are accomplished. Nevertheless, there are several exceptions to this rule:

- **Special Risks** Principals cannot avoid strict liability for dangerous activities assigned to independent contractors. For example, the use of explosives, clearing land by fire, crop dusting, and such involve special risks that are shared by the principal.
- **Negligence in the Selection of an Independent Contractor** A principal who hires an unqualified or knowingly dangerous person as an independent contractor is liable if that person injures someone while on the job.

In the following case, the court addressed the issue of the liability of a principal for the tortious conduct of an independent contractor.

A. Teichert & Son, Inc. v. The Superior Court of Sacramento County, California
179 Cal.App.3d 657, 225 Cal.Rptr. 10 (1986)
Court of Appeals of California

CASE 31.5

FACTS
A. Teichert & Son, Inc. (Teichert), owned and operated a plant located just off State Highway 16 (Jackson Road) in Sacramento County, California. Teichert hired Jewell W. Farmer, an independent contractor, to haul a truckload of asphalt from another site to Teichert's plant on Jackson Road. On September 15, 1985, Farmer was hauling the asphalt for Teichert in a dump truck. Robert Gumpert, a minor, was riding a bicycle westbound along the shoulder of Jackson Road in front of Teichert's plant. As the dump truck driven by Farmer turned left from the eastbound lane of Jackson Road into Teichert's plant, it collided with Gumpert's bicycle. Gumpert was killed in the accident. John Gumpert, Robert's father, brought this wrongful death action against defendants Farmer and Teichert. Teichert asserted that it was not liable for the tortious conduct of the independent contractor, Farmer. The trial court denied Teichert's motion for summary judgment. Teichert appealed.

ISSUE
Were there any "special risks" involved in this case that would make the principal (A. Teichert & Son, Inc.) vicariously liable for the tortious conduct of the independent contractor (Jewell W. Farmer)?

IN THE LANGUAGE OF THE COURT
Puglia, Presiding Judge   A special or peculiar risk is a risk that is peculiar to the work to be done and arises out of its character or

the place where it is to be done, and against which a reasonable person would recognize the necessity of taking special precautions. It is something other than the ordinary and customary dangers that may arise in the course of the work or of normal human activity.

Plaintiff Gumpert has failed to identify any special risk inherent in the work in which Farmer was engaged, apart from the ordinary risk that he would not use due care in the driving of his dump truck. There was no direct relationship between the particular work performed by Farmer, that is, hauling a truckload of asphalt, and the accident. The incident could have occurred just as easily if Farmer were driving a standard passenger vehicle or an "18-wheeler." Nor did the frequency of truck traffic into Teichert's plant create a special risk. The collision between decedent and Farmer's truck would have happened in the same way regardless of whether that truck was the first or the hundredth to enter the facility on that day.

Farmer's negligence, if any, entailed nothing more than ordinary failure to exercise due care in the operation of a motor vehicle. This is not sufficient to invoke the "special risks" exception to the rule of nonliability of a principal for the negligence of an independent contractor.

DECISION AND REMEDY
The appellate court held as a matter of law that there was no special risk involved in this case that would make the

principal, A. Teichert & Son, Inc., liable for the negligent act (tort) of Farmer, the independent contractor.

Case Questions

Critical Legal Thinking   Should principals be allowed to avoid tort liability by hiring independent contractors, rather than employees, to act on their behalf? Explain.

Ethics   Was it ethical for the plaintiff to sue A. Teichert & Son, Inc., in this case? For Teichert to deny liability?

Business Application   Do you think many businesses hire independent contractors (rather than employees) to do work so as to avoid tort liability?

Working the Web

U.S. Department of Labor   The U.S. Department of Labor has a Web site full of employment information.

Visit at **www.dol.gov**

Employment Standards Administration   The Employment Standards Administration Web site contains information and links to information about labor standards.

Visit at **www.dol.gov/dol/esa/**

The Minimum Wage   Everything you ever wanted to know about the minimum wage is available at this site.

Visit   at   **www.dol.gov/dol/esa/public/minwage/main.htm**

CYBER EXERCISES

1. Find information about Welfare to Work on the U.S. Department of Labor Web site.

2. Find the Family and Medical Leave Act on the Employment Standards Administration Web site.

3. Can you find a chart of minimum wage increases?

*C*ASES AND *E*XERCISES

CRITICAL LEGAL THINKING CASES

31.1.   Norman R. Barton and his wife decided to vacation in Florida in November 1984. In March 1984, they contacted Wonderful World of Travel, Inc. (Wonderful World), a travel agency licensed by the state of Ohio, to make the arrangements. They requested a room with a view of the ocean, a kitchenette so they would be saved the expense of dining out, free parking, and a free spa. In August, with the Bartons' approval, Wonderful World made reservations at the Beau Rivage motel in Bal Harbour, Florida. It did not confirm the reservations prior to the Bartons' departure in November. When the Bartons arrived at the motel, they found it closed, chained, and guarded. The only other hotel or motel in the area was a Sheraton, which was almost triple the room cost of the Beau Rivage. The Sheraton overlooked the ocean, but it did not have a kitchenette, free parking, or free spa privileges. The Bartons stayed at the Sheraton. They sued Wonderful World upon their return. Is Wonderful World liable for the increased costs incurred by the Bartons? [*Barton v. Wonderful World of Travel, Inc.*, 502 N.E.2d 715 (Ohio Mun. 1986)]

31.2.   On March 31, 1981, Iota Management Corporation (Iota) entered into a contract to purchase the Bel Air West Motor Hotel in the city of St. Louis from Boulevard Investment Company (Boulevard). The agreement contained the following warranty: "Seller has no actual notice of any substantial defect in the structure of the Hotel or in any of its plumbing, heating, air-conditioning, electrical, or utility systems."

When the buyer inspected the premises, no leaks in the pipes were visible. Iota purchased the hotel for $2 million. When Iota removed some of the walls and ceilings during remodeling, it found evidence of prior repairs to leaking pipes and ducts, as well as devices for catching water (e.g., milk cartons, cookie sheets, and buckets). The estimate to repair these leaks was $500,000. Evidence at trial showed that Cecil Lillibridge, who was Boulevard's maintenance supervisor from 1975 until the sale of the hotel in 1981, had actual knowledge of these problems and had repaired some of the pipes. Iota sued Boulevard to rescind the contract. Is Boulevard liable? [*Iota Management Corporation v. Boulevard Investment Company*, 731 S.W.2d 399 (Mo.App. 1987)]

31.3. Chemical Bank (Chemical) is the primary bank for Washington Steel Corporation (Washington Steel). As an agent for Washington Steel, Chemical expressly and impliedly promised that it would advance the best interests and welfare of Washington Steel. During the course of the agency, Washington Steel provided Chemical with comprehensive and confidential financial information, other data, and future business plans.

At some point during the agency, TW Corporation (TW) and others approached Chemical to request a loan of $7 million to make a hostile tender offer for the stock of Washington Steel. Chemical agreed and became an agent for TW. Management at Chemical did not disclose its adverse relationship with TW to Washington Steel, did not request Washington Steel's permission to act as an agent for TW, and directed employees of the bank to conceal Chemical's involvement with TW from Washington Steel. After TW commenced its public tender offer, Washington Steel filed suit seeking to obtain an injunction against Chemical and TW. Who wins? [*Washington Steel Corporation v. TW Corporation*, 465 F.Supp. 1100 (W.D.Pa. 1979)]

31.4. Peter Shields was the president and a member of the board of directors of Production Finishing Corporation (Production Finishing) from 1974 through August 1981. The company provided steel polishing services. It did most, if not all, of the polishing work in the Detroit area except for that of the Ford Motor Company (Ford). (Ford did its own polishing.) Shields discussed this matter with Ford on behalf of Production Finishing on a number of occasions. When Shields learned that Ford was discontinuing its polishing operation, he incorporated Flat Rock Metal and submitted a confidential proposal to Ford that provided that he would buy Ford's equipment and provide polishing services to Ford. It was not until he resigned from Production Finishing that he informed the board of directors that he was pursuing the Ford business himself. Production Finishing sued Shields. Did Shields breach his fiduciary duty of loyalty to Production

Finishing? [*Production Finishing Corporation v. Shields*, 405 N.W.2d 171 (Mich.App. 1987)]

31.5. Leroy Behlman and 18 other football fans from Connecticut and New York decided to attend Super Bowl XII in New Orleans. They entered into contracts with Octagon Travel Center, Inc. (Octagon), a tour operator, and paid $399 each for transportation, lodging, and a ticket to Super Bowl XII. They purchased the tour package through Universal Travel Agency, Inc. (Universal), a travel agency that acts as a broker for a number of airline companies and tour operators. The individual contracts, however, were between the football fans and Octagon. When they arrived in New Orleans, no tickets to Super Bowl XII were forthcoming. Upon returning, they sued Universal for breach of contract. Is Universal liable? [*Behlman v. Universal Travel Agency, Inc.*, 496 A.2d 962 (Conn.App. 1985)]

31.6. In May 1978, Sebastian International, Inc. (Sebastian), entered into a five-year lease for a building in Chadsworth, California. In September 1980, with the consent of the master lessors, Sebastian sublet the building to West Valley Grinding, Inc. (West Valley). In conjunction with the execution of the sublease, the corporate officers of West Valley, including Kenneth E. Peck, each signed a guaranty of lease personally ensuring the payment of West Valley's rental obligations. The guaranty contract referred to Peck in his individual capacity; however, on the signature line he was identified as "Kenneth Peck, Vice President." In May 1981, West Valley went out of business, leaving 24 months remaining on the sublease. After unsuccessful attempts to secure another sublease, Sebastian surrendered the leasehold back to the master lessors and brought suit against Peck to recover the unpaid rent. Peck argues he is not personally liable because his signature was that of an agent for a disclosed principal and not that of a principal himself. Who wins? [*Sebastian International, Inc. v. Peck*, 195 C.A.3d 803, 240 C.R. 911 (Cal.App. 1987)]

31.7. G. Elvin Grinder of Marbury, Maryland, was a building contractor who, prior to May 1, 1973, did business as an individual and traded as "Grinder Construction." Grinder maintained an open account, on his individual credit, with Bryans Road Building & Supply Co., Inc. (Bryans). Grinder would purchase materials and supplies from Bryans on credit and later pay the invoices. On May 1, 1973, Elvin Grinder Construction, Inc., a Maryland corporation, was formed with Grinder personally owning 52 percent of the stock of the corporation. Grinder did not inform Bryans that he had incorporated and continued to purchase supplies on credit from Bryans under the name "Grinder Construction." In May 1978, after certain invoices were not paid by Grinder, Bryans sued Grinder personally to recover. Grinder asserted that the debts were owed by the corporation. Bryans amended its complaint to include the corporation as a defendant. Who is liable to Bryans? [*Grinder v. Bryans Road Building & Supply Co., Inc.*, 432 A.2d 453 (Md.App. 1981)]

31.8. In the spring of 1974, certain residents of Harrisville, Utah, organized the Golden Spike Little League for the youngsters of the town. This was an unincorporated association. David Anderson and several other organizers contracted with Smith & Edwards, a sporting goods store, that agreed to give them favorable prices on merchandise. During the course of the summer, parents went into Smith & Edwards and picked up uniforms and equipment for their children and other Little Leaguers. At the end of the summer, Smith & Edwards sent them a bill for $3,900. Fund-raising activities produced only $149, and the organizers refused to pay the difference. Smith & Edwards sued Anderson and the other organizers for the unpaid balance. Are the organizers personally liable for the debt? [*Smith & Edwards v. Anderson*, 557 P.2d 132 (Utah 1978)]

31.9. On April 16, 1982, Ray Johnson and his eight-year-old son David were waiting for a "walk" sign before crossing a street in downtown Salt Lake City. A truck owned by Newspaper Agency Corporation (NAC) and operated by its employee, Donald Rogers, crossed the intersection and jumped the curb, killing David and injuring Ray. Before reporting for work on the evening of the accident, Rogers had consumed approximately seven mixed drinks containing vodka and had chugalugged a 27-ounce drink containing two minibottles of tequila. His blood alcohol content after the accident was .18 percent.

Evidence showed that the use of alcohol and marijuana was widespread at NAC and that the company made no effort to curtail such use. Evidence further showed that NAC vehicles were returned with beer cans in them and that on one occasion a NAC supervisor who observed drivers smoking marijuana told the drivers to "do it on the road." Ray Johnson sued Rogers and NAC for the wrongful death of his child, David, and physical injury to Ray. Is NAC liable? [*Johnson v. Rogers*, 763 P.2d 771 (Utah 1988)]

31.10. Intrastate Radiotelephone, Inc. (Intrastate), is a public utility that supplies radiotelephone utility service to the general public for radiotelephones, pocket pagers, and beepers. Robert Kranhold, an employee of Intrastate, was authorized to use his personal vehicle on company business. On the morning of March 9, 1976, as Kranhold was driving his vehicle to Intrastate's main office, he negligently struck a motorcycle being driven by Michael S. Largey, causing severe and permanent injuries to Largey. The accident occurred at the intersection where Intrastate's main office is located. Evidence showed that Kranhold acted as a consultant to Intrastate, worked both in and out of Intrastate's offices, had no set hours of work, often attended meetings at Intrastate's offices, and went to Intrastate's offices to pick things up or drop things off. Largey sued Intrastate for damages. Is Intrastate liable? [*Largey v. Intrastate Radiotelephone, Inc.*, 136 C.A.3d 660, 186 C.R. 520 (Cal.App. 1982)]

31.11. In 1979, Donnie Joe Jackson hired Ted Green to do some remodeling work on his house. Jackson never paid Green for his work and a dispute arose as to how much was owed to Green. Jackson worked at the Higgenbotham-Bartlett Lumber Company, a lumberyard where Green often purchased lumber and supplies. During the course of the following year when Green went to the lumber yard to do business, Green was verbally accosted by Jackson on at least three separate occasions. Each time, Green left the lumberyard. On May 21, 1980, Green, accompanied by his son, made two trips to the facility. On the first trip, Jackson and Green had a verbal altercation. On the second trip, Jackson hit Green, knocking him unconscious and causing injuries. Green sued Jackson's employer for damages. Is the lumber company liable for the intentional tort of its agent? [*Green v. Jackson*, 674 S.W.2d 395 (Tex.App. 1984)]

ETHICS CASES

31.12. William Venezio, a real estate broker, conducted his business under the trade name "King Realty" and had properly filed the required name certificate in the Schenectady county clerk's office. On May 19, 1984, King Realty entered into a contract to purchase property located in the town of Rotterdam, Schenectady County, from Ermino Bianchi. Venezio signed the end of the contract "King Realty for Customer." On May 23, 1984, King Realty entered into a contract to sell the property to Mario Attanasio. However, Bianchi refused to sell the property to King Realty, alleging that because the original contract failed to adequately identify the purchaser, there was not a binding contract. Venezio, d.b.a. King Realty, brought this action for specific performance against Bianchi. Was it ethical for Bianchi to try to back out of the contract? Can King Realty, as an agent for a partially disclosed principal, enforce the contract against Bianchi? [*Venezio v. Bianchi*, 508 N.Y.S.2d 349 (N.Y.App. 1986)]

31.13. The National Biscuit Company (Nabisco) is a corporation that produces and distributes cookies and other food products to grocery stores and other outlets across the nation. In October 1968, Nabisco hired Ronnell Lynch as a cookie salesman-trainee. On March 1, 1969, Lynch was assigned his own sales territory. Lynch's duties involved making sales calls, taking orders, and making sure that shelves of stores in his territory were stocked with Nabisco products. During the period March 1 to May 1, 1969, Nabisco received numerous complaints from store owners in Lynch's territory that Lynch was overly aggressive and was taking shelf space for Nabisco products that was reserved for competing brands.

On May 1, 1969, Lynch visited a grocery store that was managed by Jerome Lange. Lynch was there to place previously delivered merchandise on the store's shelves. An argument developed between Lynch and Lange. Lynch became very angry and started swearing. Lange told Lynch to stop swearing or leave the store, because children were present. Lynch became uncontrollably angry and went behind the counter and dared Lange to fight. When Lange refused to fight, Lynch proceeded to viciously assault and batter Lange, causing severe injuries. When Lange sued Nabisco, Nabisco denied liability. Was it ethical for Nabisco to deny liability in this case? Do you think the prior complaints against Lynch had any effect on the decision reached in this case? Is Nabisco liable for the intentional tort (assault and battery) of its employee, Ronnell Lynch? [*Lange v. National Biscuit Company*, 211 N.W.2d 783 (Minn. 1983)]

CRITICAL LEGAL THINKING WRITING ASSIGNMENT

Read Case A.31 in the Case Appendix [*District of Columbia v. Howell*]. This case is excerpted from the court of appeals opinion. Review and brief the case. In your brief, be sure to answer the following questions.

1. Was A. Louis Jagoe hired by the District of Columbia as an employee or as an independent contractor?

2. Describe the accident that occurred. Who was injured?

3. Normally, an employer is not liable for the tortious conduct of an independent contractor it has hired. Describe the "special risks" exception to this rule.

4. What damages were awarded to the plaintiff?

NOTES

1. Restatement (Second) of Agency, § 4.
2. Restatement (Second) of Agency, § 321.

Law for Entrepreneurs

*𝒞ommerce never really flourishes so much, as when it is delivered
from the guardianship of legislators and ministers.*

WILLIAM GODWIN *Enquiry
Concerning Political Justice (1798)*

Chapter Objectives

After studying this chapter, you should be able to

1. Describe the role of entrepreneurs in starting and operating businesses.
2. List and describe the forms of conducting domestic business.
3. Describe sole proprietorships and the liability of sole proprietors.
4. Distinguish between general and limited partnerships.
5. Describe limited liability partnerships.
6. Describe limited liability companies.
7. Describe corporations.
8. Describe the taxation of the major forms of conducting business.
9. Describe the use of agents, representatives, and distributors in conducting international business.
10. Explain the difference between using a branch and a subsidiary to conduct international business.

Chapter Contents

entrepreneur

A person who forms and operates a new business either by him- or herself or with others.

It is the privilege of a trader in a free country, in all matters not contrary to law, to regulate his own mode of carrying it on according to his own discretion and choice.

B. Alderson
Hilton v. Eckersly *(1855)*

An **entrepreneur** is a person who forms and operates a new business. An entrepreneur may start the business by him- or herself or cofound the business with others. Most businesses started by entrepreneurs are small, although some grow into substantial organizations. For example, Bill Gates started Microsoft Corporation, which grew into the giant software and Internet company. Michael Dell started Dell Computers as a mail-order business; it has become a leader in computer sales. Entrepreneurs in this country and around the world create new businesses daily that hire employees, provide new products and services, and make economies of countries grow.

Entrepreneurs who want to conduct domestic or international business must decide whether the business should operate as one of the major forms of business organization—sole proprietorship, general partnership, limited partnership, corporation, and limited liability company—or under some other available legal business form (e.g., franchise, joint venture). The selection depends on many factors, including the ease and cost of formation, the capital requirements of the business, the flexibility of management decisions, the extent of personal liability, tax considerations, and the like.

This chapter discusses the major forms for conducting domestic and international business. It also discusses in detail the use of sole proprietorships in conducting business.

*E*NTREPRENEURIAL FORMS OF CONDUCTING BUSINESS

Entrepreneurs contemplating starting a business have many options when choosing the legal form in which to conduct the business. Each of these forms of business has advantages and disadvantages for the entrepreneur. The primary characteristics of the major types of business organizations are briefly outlined in the paragraphs that follow. Each of these forms of business is discussed in more detail in the chapters that follow.

Sole Proprietorship

sole proprietorship

A noncorporate business that is owned by one person.

A **sole proprietorship** is a noncorporate business that is owned by one person. That person is called a *sole proprietor*. No formalities need be followed to create a sole proprietorship. A sole proprietorship is not a separate taxpaying entity for federal income tax purposes, and a sole proprietor need not even file an informational return with the Internal Revenue Service (IRS). Income and losses are reported on his or her personal income tax return. The sole proprietor is personally liable for the debts and obligations of the business.

General Partnership

general partnership

A voluntary association of two or more persons for the carrying on of a business as co-owners for profit.

A **general partnership** (also called an **ordinary partnership** or **partnership**) is a voluntary association of two or more persons for the carrying on of a business as co-owners for profit. Partners of a general partnership are called either *general partners* or *partners*. No formalities need be followed to create a general partnership. A general partnership is not a separate taxpaying entity for federal tax purposes. The partnership's income and losses "flow through" to the personal income tax returns of the partners. A general partnership must file an informational return with the IRS. Partners are personally liable for the debts and obligations of the partnership.

Limited Partnership

limited partnership

A special form of partnership that has both limited and general partners.

A **limited partnership** is a special form of partnership that has both limited and general partners. The *limited partners* contribute capital to the business in return for a share of its profits (and losses). They are only liable for the debts and obligations of the limited partnership to the extent of their capital contributions; that is, they are not personally liable beyond their capital contribution. The *general partners* have unlimited personal liability for the debts and obligations of the limited partnership. Every limited partnership must have at least one general partner.

Limited partnerships are created according to statutory requirements. They are not separate taxpaying entities for federal income tax purposes. Although they must file an informational return with the IRS, the income and losses from the limited partnership are reported on the personal income tax returns of the partners.

Limited Liability Partnership (LLP)

Many states have recently enacted legislation that permits the formation of a **limited liability partnership (LLP)**. In an LLP, there does not have to be a general partner. Instead, all partners are limited partners who are not personally liable for the obligations of the partnership. The limited partners may participate in management, however. An LLP is taxed as a partnership. Most LLPs are formed by professionals, such as accountants and lawyers.

limited liability partnership (LLP)
A type of partnership that has only limited partners.

Limited Liability Company (LLC)

In recent years, a majority of states have authorized a form of business called a **limited liability company (LLC)**. An LLC may be formed by two or more persons according to statutory requirements. This form of business combines the most favorable attributes of both partnerships and corporations. Owners of an LLC (called *members*) are not personally liable for the obligations of the LLC. Yet, an LLC is taxed as a partnership.

limited liability company (LLC)
A hybrid form of business that has the attributes of both partnerships and corporations.

Restaurant, Sault Ste. Marie, Michigan.
Entrepreneurs have many choices of legal forms for conducting their businesses, such as this restaurant.

Corporation

A **corporation** is a fictitious legal entity that (1) is created according to statutory requirements and (2) is a separate taxpaying entity for federal income tax purposes. The corporation must file a federal income tax return with the IRS and pay the amount of taxes owed on corporate income. Any dividends paid by the corporation are personally taxable to the

corporation
A fictitious legal entity that (1) is created according to statutory requirements and (2) is a separate taxpaying entity for federal income tax purposes.

shareholders. That is why corporations are said to be subject to *double taxation*—once at the corporate level and again at the shareholder level.

Corporations are owned by *shareholders*, whose ownership interests are evidenced by *stock certificates*. Generally, shareholders are not personally liable for the debts and obligations of the corporation except to the extent of their capital contributions. Therefore, shareholders are said to have *limited liability*.

close corporation
A corporation owned by one or a few shareholders.

public corporation
A corporation that has many shareholders and whose securities are traded on national stock exchanges.

There are several types of for-profit corporations. They range from **close corporations**, owned by one or a few shareholders, to large **public corporations**, which have thousands of shareholders and whose securities are traded on national stock exchanges, to *professional corporations*, formed by lawyers, doctors, and such.

Certain small corporations can elect to be *S Corporations*, which are corporations that are taxed as partnerships. Corporations that do not or cannot elect to be S Corporations are *C Corporations*, which must pay federal income taxes at the corporate level. If dividends are paid to shareholders, they must report these on their individual income tax returns.

Nonprofit corporations can be formed to operate charitable institutions, colleges, and universities.

CONCEPT SUMMARY   FEDERAL INCOME TAX LIABILITY OF BUSINESS ORGANIZATIONS

Type of Business	Taxpaying Entity	Federal Income Tax Form to Be Filed
Sole proprietorship	No	No separate form. Income and expenses of the business reported on the sole proprietor's individual income tax return.
General partnership	No	Informational form must be filed by the partnership. Each partner's share of the income or loss from the partnership reported on his or her individual income tax return.
Limited partnership	No	Informational form must be filed by the partnership. Each partner's share of the income or loss from the partnership reported on his or her individual income tax return.
Limited liability company (LLC)	No	Informational form must be filed by the limited liability company. Each member's share of the income or loss from the company is reported on his or her individual income tax return.
Limited liability partnership (LLP)	No	Informational return must be filed by the limited liability partnership. Each member's share of the income or loss from the partnership is reported on his or her individual income tax return.
S Corporation	No	An S Corporation must file an informational form. Each shareholder's share of the income or loss from the corporation is reported on his or her individual income tax return.
C Corporation	Yes	A C Corporation must file a separate corporate return and pay the tax owed on corporate income. If the corporation pays dividends, the shareholders must report the dividend income on their separate returns and pay tax on the dividends received.

Entrepreneur and the Law

THE ENTREPRENEURIAL SPIRIT: THE CREATION OF AMAZON.COM

In 1994, Jeff Bezos, the son of a Cuban immigrant to the United States, had made it big. After graduating from Princeton University, he had gone on to Wall Street where he worked for a hedge fund. But Bezos saw an even greater opportunity: on-line commerce. So he quit his job, jumped in the car with his wife, MacKenzie, and headed west. While she drove, he typed on his laptop computer. Bezos drew up a list of 20 products that he figured he could sell on-line but then narrowed it to two—books and music. Bezos settled on books for two reasons. First, there are more to sell (about 1.3 million books in print versus 300,000 music titles). Second, the Goliath's of publishing seemed less imposing than the six record companies that dominated music; there were thousands of bookstores, the largest being Barnes & Noble with 12 percent of the industry's $25 billion annual sales.

After checking out Colorado and Oregon, Bezos and his wife settled in Seattle, Washington. They rented a house, hired four employees, and started Amazon.com out of their garage. Bezos and his family incorporated the business, sold some stock to friends and other investors, and kept the rest of the stock for themselves. Bezos took a traditional business—bookselling—on-line. He reasoned that books were fungible—everyone sold the same product—and that a portion of a traditional bookseller's cost represented the real estate on which the store sat. So Bezos lined up a distribution center in Oregon and began taking orders in cyberspace. Amazon.com sold its first book in July 1995.

Amazon.com became a success, at least at selling books. However, it was not a success at making a profit, losing money for years. But Bezos's business plan called for building a client base and making "Amazon.com" a readily recognized e-commerce name. He accomplished these goals, attracting a client base of over 10 million loyal book-buying customers and getting the Amazon.com brand name to be recognized by over one-quarter of Americans. Like most start-ups, Amazon.com needed more seed money. Undeterred by the company's unprofitability, the venture capitalist firm Kleiner Perkins Caufield & Byer put up $10 million for preferred stock, which represented a 15 percent stake in Amazon.com.

Following on the heels of its book-selling success, Amazon.com began selling other products over the Internet, including CDs, videos, gifts, greeting cards, and thousands of other items. Amazon.com entered the world of on-line auctions; linked with other companies selling pet supplies, drugstore goods, and more; and agreed to pay fees of 4 to 8 percent to other Web site owners who linked a purchaser to Amazon.com. Purchasers pay Amazon.com by credit card, submitted over the telephone or the Web, and the transaction is guarded by encryption. Amazon.com offers one-click ordering, which lets buyers store credit cards and addresses after their first purchase.

After several years of operation and quick growth, Amazon.com needed more money to reach its goals. In May 1997, Amazon.com went public, raising over $40 million by selling stock for $18 per share. The price of Amazon.com doubled on the first day of trading and reached $200 per share over the next year before retreating. Bezos became a billionaire before the age of 34. Bezos and his family own about 40 percent of Amazon.com. In the span of less than five years, Bezos had taken his business plan and created the largest, most recognized e-commerce company in the world. This entrepreneur's dream became reality. But when asked if he fears Barnes & Noble's entry into on-line bookselling, Bezos replied that he feared "two guys or girls in a garage" more because they represented the most dangerous of competitors—entrepreneurs.

e·biz

Franchise

Franchising is one of the most important forms of business operation in the United States today. Many fast-food restaurants, gasoline stations, hotels and motels, copy centers, real estate brokerage offices, and so on are operated as franchises. In a **franchise**, the owner of a trademark, a trade secret, a patent, or a product (the *franchisor*) licenses another party (the *franchisee*) to sell products or services under the franchisor's name. The franchisee pays a fee to the franchisor (often a royalty) in exchange for such services as design, marketing, and advertising. The franchisor and franchisee are separate legal entities.

franchise

The owner of a trademark, a trade secret, a patent, or a product licenses another party to sell products or services under the franchisor's name.

Joint Venture

A **joint venture** is a voluntary association of two or more parties (natural persons, partnerships, corporations, or other legal entities) to conduct a *single* or *isolated project* with a limited duration. The parties to a joint venture are called *joint adventurers*. In most respects (including federal income tax purposes, personal liability for the venture's debts and obligations, right to an accounting, and such), joint ventures are governed by partnership law.

Consider This Example   Suppose that Urban Realty, Inc., and Tri-County Development, Inc., own adjacent pieces of real property. Although the individual properties are too small for the development of a shopping center, together they are well suited for that purpose. Assume that Urban Realty and Tri-County enter into an agreement to sell their properties jointly to the highest bidder and to divide the proceeds in proportion to the size of their properties. Their agreement is a joint venture because their association will end when the properties are sold.

Joint Venture Corporation   Corporation law applies if the joint venture is a corporation. For example, suppose two oil companies form a corporation called Antarctica Drilling, Inc., whose sole purpose is to drill for oil in Antarctica. Suppose both oil companies are shareholders in the new corporation. A *joint venture corporation* has been formed.

Syndicate or Investment Group

A group of individuals who join together to finance a project or transaction is called a **syndicate** or an **investment group**. Syndicates are often formed to finance real estate developments, to sell new issues of securities, and so on. A syndicate in a noncorporate form is treated as a joint venture. A syndicate in a corporate form is treated as a joint venture corporation.

Business Trust

A **trust** is established when a person (*trustor*) transfers title to property to another person (*trustee*) to be managed for the benefit of specifically named persons (*beneficiaries*). The trustee is under a duty to manage and invest trust funds and property and to distribute profits to the beneficiaries. Trusts are commonly used to transfer property from one generation to another generation to avoid certain inheritance and other taxes.

In a business context, trusts are sometimes used to conduct commercial enterprises. *Business trusts* resemble a corporation in the following ways: (1) The beneficiaries are not personally liable for the debts and obligations of the trust, and (2) the death or bankruptcy of a beneficiary does not terminate the trust. The trustee's personal liability extends to the contracts of the trust (unless the contracting party agrees to look to the trust estate for satisfaction) and to any torts committed by him- or herself or his or her employees while acting on behalf of the trust. Businesses that pool their assets in a trust are issued *trust certificates*.

Cooperative

Businesses often voluntarily join together to create a **cooperative** that provides services to its members. For example, farmers may form a cooperative to provide grain storage facilities, sellers may form a cooperative to market their goods jointly, and consumers may form a cooperative to obtain price advantages from volume purchasing. The profits of a cooperative are distributed to the members on an agreed-upon basis. Unincorporated cooperatives are subject to partnership law, and incorporated cooperatives are subject to corporation law.

Entrepreneur and the Law

VA LINUX IPO SOARS

The exponential growth of the use of computers, the Internet, and the World Wide Web has changed the way people live and businesses work. The Information Age has also created tremendous opportunities for inventors and entrepreneurs to reap the rewards of their intellectual property and informational rights and for investors who believe in them to prosper as well. Take the case of VA Linux, for example.

In 1994, VA Linux began to build computers around the Linux operating system, a free operating system for computers that was designed to compete with Microsoft's dominant operating system. VA Linux was started by engineers and others associated with Stanford University. VA Linux sells what are essentially generic personal computers to compete with the ones sold by PC titan Dell Computer and others that are based on the Microsoft operating system. In 1999, Microsoft had a monopoly of 90 percent of the market for operating systems, with the Linux system and others controlling the rest of the market.

In December 1999, VA Linux decided to "go public" by issuing shares of stock to the public in an **initial public offering (IPO)**. By the time VA Linux decided to go public, many investors were betting that the Linux operating system was a serious contender to Microsoft and that companies building their future around this system were good investments. But no one quite knew how deep this commitment was until December 9, 1999, when VA Linux went public at the initial offering price of $30 per share. By the time the dust settled on its opening day, investors had bid VA Linux to $239 per share, over a 700 percent jump in price for the day. The stock of the president of VA Linux, Larry M. Augustine, was worth over $1.5 billion by the end of the day, and VA Linux's total capitalization reached about $10 billion.

The success of VA Linux follows on the heels of many Internet and Web stocks that had issued IPOs earlier, including Yahoo!, Amazon.com, and Red Hat. What future IPOs bring is anyone's guess.

e·biz

International Perspective

CONDUCTING INTERNATIONAL BUSINESS USING AGENTS, REPRESENTATIVES, AND DISTRIBUTORS

A corporation organized in one country may wish to conduct business in other countries. To do so, it has a variety of choices available to it depending upon the extent of involvement and market penetration desired, the amount of capital to be invested, the legal and cultural restrictions of the foreign country, and so on. Several major forms of conducting business in a foreign country are by direct selling or by using sales agents, representatives, or distributors.

Direct Export and Import Sales The simplest form of conducting international business is to engage in **direct export** or **import** sale. For example, if Haliburton Corporation wishes to sell equipment overseas, it can merely enter into a contract with a company in a foreign country that wishes to buy the equipment. Haliburton Corporation is the **exporter** and the firm in the foreign country is the **importer**. If a U.S. company buys goods

from a firm in a foreign country, the roles are reversed. The main benefits of conducting international business this way are that (1) it is inexpensive and (2) it usually involves just entering into contracts.

Sales Agents, Representatives, and Distributorships
Companies wishing to do business in a foreign country often appoint a local agent or representative to represent them in that country. A **sales representative** may solicit and take orders for his or her foreign employer but does not have the authority to bind the company contractually. A **sales agent**, on the other hand, may enter into contracts on his or her foreign employer's behalf. The scope of a sales agent's or representative's authority should be explicitly stated in the employment agreement. Sales agents and representatives do not take title to the goods. They are usually paid commissions for business that they generate.

(box continues)

Another commonly used form for engaging in international sales is through a **foreign distributor**. Often, the distributor is a local firm that is separate and independent from the exporter. Distributors are usually given an exclusive territory (e.g., a country or portion of a country). A distributor takes title to the goods and makes a profit on the resale of the goods in the foreign country. A foreign distributor generally is used when a company wants a greater presence in a foreign market than is possible through a sales agent or representative.

Sole Proprietorship

sole proprietorship

A form of business where the owner is actually the business; the business is not a separate legal entity.

Many small businesses—and a few large ones—operate as sole proprietorships. In a **sole proprietorship**, the owner is actually the business. There is no separate legal entity. Sole proprietorships are the most common form of business organization in the United States.

There are several major advantages to operating a business as a sole proprietorship. They include the following:

1. The ease and low cost of formation.
2. The owner's right to make all management decisions concerning the business, including those involving hiring and firing employees.
3. The sole proprietor owns all of the business and has the right to receive all of the business's profits.
4. A sole proprietorship can be easily transferred or sold if and when the owner desires to do so; no other approval (such as from partners or shareholders) is necessary.

Business Brief

A major detriment of operating a business as a sole proprietorship is that the owner is personally liable for the debts of the business.

There are important disadvantages to this business form, too. They are that (1) the sole proprietor's access to capital is limited to personal funds plus any loans he or she can obtain, and (2) the sole proprietor is legally responsible for the contracts and torts committed by him- or herself and his or her employees in the course of employment.

Creation of Sole Proprietorship

The creation of a sole proprietorship is simple. There are no formalities. No federal or state government approval is required; some local governments require all businesses, including sole proprietorships, to obtain a license to do business within the city. If no other form of business organization is chosen, the business is a sole proprietorship by default.

Entrepreneur and the Law

d.b.a.—"Doing Business As"

A sole proprietorship can operate under the name of the sole proprietor or a *trade name*. For example, the author of this book can operate a sole proprietorship under the name "Henry R. Cheeseman" or under a trade name such as "The Big Cheese." Operating under a trade name is commonly designated as a **d.b.a. (doing business as)** (e.g., Henry R. Cheeseman, doing business as "The Big Cheese.")

Most states require all businesses that operate under a trade name to file a **fictitious business name statement** (or **certificate of trade name**) with the appropriate government agency. The statement must contain the name and address of the applicant, the trade name, and the address of the business. Most states also require notice of the trade name to be published in a newspaper of general circulation serving the area in which the applicant does business.

These requirements are intended to disclose the real owner's name to the public. Noncompliance can result in a fine. Some states prohibit violators from maintaining lawsuits in the state's courts. A sample fictitious business name statement is shown in Exhibit 32.1.

*ℰ*XHIBIT 32.1　　*Sample Fictitious Business Name Statement*

Return To:	PUBLISH IN:

Name:　　Thomas Simpson, Esq.
Address:　100 Broadway, Suite 1250
City:　　 Glendale, CA 91210
Telephone #　(818) 500-0511
Cust. Ref. #　53247

COUNTY CLERK S FILING STAMP

☒ First Filing　　　☐ Renewal Filing
　　　　Current Registration No.

FICTITIOUS BUSINESS NAME STATEMENT

THE FOLLOWING PERSON(S) IS (ARE) DOING BUSINESS AS:

1 Fictitious Business Name(s)
　　The Big Cheese

2 Street address & Principal place of Business in California　　　　　　Zip Code
　　1000 Exposition Boulevard　　　　Los Angeles　　　California　　90089

3 Full name of Registrant　　　　　　(if corporation - incorporated in what state)
　　Henry R. Cheeseman

Residence Address	City	State	Zip Code
575 Barrington Ave.	Los Angeles	California	90049

Full Name of Registrant　　　　　　(if corporation - incorporated in what state)

Residence Address	City	State	Zip Code

Full name of Registrant　　　　　　(if corporation - incorporated in what state)

Residence Address	City	State	Zip Code

Full name of Registrant　　　　　　(if corporation - incorporated in what state)

Residence Address	City	State	Zip Code

4 This Business is　　　(X) an Individual　　( ) a general partnership　　( ) joint venture　　　( ) a business trust
conducted by:　　　　( ) co-partners　　　 ( ) husband and wife　　 ( ) a corporation　　( ) a limited partnership
(check one only)　 ( ) an unincorporated association other than a partnership　　( ) other (*please specify*) _____

5 The registrant commenced to transact business under the fictitious business name or names listed above on _____

6

a. Signed:

Henry R. Cheeseman (signature)
SIGNATURE　　　　　　Henry R. Cheeseman
　　　　　　　　　　TYPE OR PRINT NAME

_____
SIGNATURE　　　　　　TYPE OR PRINT NAME

_____
SIGNATURE　　　　　　TYPE OR PRINT NAME

b. If Registrant a corporation sign below:

_____
CORPORATION NAME

_____
SIGNATURE & TITLE

_____
TYPE OR PRINT NAME

This statement was filed with the County Clerk of ___ Los Angeles ___ County on date indicated by file stamp above.

NOTICE THIS FICTITIOUS NAME STATEMENT EXPIRES FIVE YEARS FROM THE DATE IT WAS FILED IN THE OFFICE OF THE COUNTY CLERK. A NEW FICTITIOUS BUSINESS NAME STATEMENT MUST BE FILED BEFORE THAT TIME. THE FILING OF THIS STATEMENT DOES NOT OF ITSELF AUTHORIZE THE USE IN THIS STATE OF A FICTITIOUS BUSINESS NAME IN VIOLATION OF THE RIGHTS OF ANOTHER UNDER FEDERAL, STATE, OR COMMON LAW (SEE SECTION 14400 ET SEQ., BUSINESS AND PROFESSIONS CODE).

I HEREBY CERTIFY THAT THIS COPY IS A CORRECT COPY OF THE ORIGINAL STATEMENT ON FILE IN MY OFFICE.

Helen Pitts
COUNTY CLERK

Deborah Cantrell　　　DEPUTY
BY _____

FILE NO. ___ 081646 ___

Personal Liability of Sole Proprietors

Business Brief
Sole proprietorships are the most common form of business organization in the United States.

The sole proprietor bears the entire risk of loss of the business; that is, the owner will lose his or her entire capital contribution if the business fails. In addition, the sole proprietor has *unlimited personal liability*. Therefore, creditors may recover claims against the business from the sole proprietor's personal assets (e.g., home, automobile, and bank accounts).

Consider This Example   Suppose Ken Smith opens a clothing store called The Rap Shop and operates it as a sole proprietorship. Smith files the proper statement and publishes the necessary notice of the use of the trade name. He contributes $25,000 of his personal funds to the business and borrows $100,000 in the name of the business from a bank. Assume that after several months Smith closes the business because it was unsuccessful. At the time it is closed, the business has no assets, owes the bank $100,000, and owes rent, trade credit, and other debts of $25,000. Here, Smith is personally liable to pay the bank and all of the debts from his personal assets.

Entrepreneur and the Law

SOLE PROPRIETORSHIP AND SOLE PROPRIETOR ARE ONE AND THE SAME

The law holds that a sole proprietorship is not a distinct legal entity. Instead, the sole proprietorship and the sole proprietor are one and the same. The following case demonstrates this principle. James Schuster was a sole proprietor doing business as (d/b/a) "Diversity Heating and Plumbing." Diversity Heating was in the business of selling, installing, and servicing heating and plumbing systems. George Vernon and others (Vernon) owned a building that needed a new boiler. In November 1989, Vernon hired Diversity Heating to install a new boiler in the building. Diversity Heating installed the boiler and gave a warranty that the boiler would not crack for 10 years. On October 20, 1993, James Schuster died. On that date, James's son, Jerry Schuster, inherited his father's business and thereafter ran the business as a sole proprietorship under the d/b/a "Diversity Heating and Plumbing." In February 1994, the boiler installed in Vernon's building broke and could not be repaired. Vernon demanded that Jerry Schuster honor the warranty and replace the boiler. When Jerry Schuster refused to do so, Vernon had the boiler replaced at the cost of $8,203 and sued Jerry Schuster to recover this amount for breach of warranty. The trial court dismissed Vernon's complaint, but the appellate court reinstated the case. Jerry Schuster appealed to the Supreme Court of Illinois. The issue presented to the supreme court was, Is Jerry Schuster liable for the warranty made by his father?

The supreme court held that Jerry Schuster was not liable for the warranty made by his father. The court stated

Common identity of ownership is lacking when one sole proprietorship succeeds another. It is well settled that a sole

proprietorship has no legal identity separate from that of the individual who owns it. The sole proprietor may do business under a fictitious name if he or she chooses. However, doing business under another name does not create an entity distinct from the person operating the business. The individual who does business as a sole proprietor under one or several names remains one person, personally liable for all his or her obligations. There is generally no continuity of existence because on the death of the sole proprietor, the sole proprietorship obviously ends.

In this case, therefore, it must be remembered that "Diversity Heating" has no legal existence. Diversity Heating was only a pseudonym for James Schuster. Once he died, Diversity Heating ceased to exist. Now, Diversity Heating is only a pseudonym for the defendant, Jerry Schuster. Once sole proprietor James Schuster died, he could not be the same sole proprietor as defendant Jerry Schuster, who became a sole proprietor after his father's death. James Schuster and Jerry Schuster, one succeeding the other, cannot be the same entity. Even though defendant Jerry Schuster inherited Diversity Heating from his father, defendant would not have continued his father's sole proprietorship, but rather would have started a new sole proprietorship.

This case demonstrates the legal principle that a sole proprietorship has no legal status separate from its owner. The sole proprietorship and sole proprietor are one and the same. In this case, Vernon should have made a claim against the estate of James Schuster, the sole proprietor who made the warranty, and not against Jerry Schuster. [*Vernon v. Schuster, d/b/a Diversity Heating and Plumbing*, 688 N.E.2d 1172 (IL 1997)]

International Perspective

CONDUCTING INTERNATIONAL BUSINESS THROUGH A BRANCH OFFICE OR A SUBSIDIARY CORPORATION

A corporation that wants to conduct business in a foreign country has the choice of conducting the business through a branch office or a subsidiary corporation. There are different costs, efficiencies, rules, and liability exposure associated with each of these forms of conducting international business.

Branch Office

A company can enter a foreign market by establishing a **branch** in the foreign country. Branches are often used where a corporation wants to enter a foreign market in a substantial way but wants to retain exclusive control over the operation. For example, an American manufacturing company can establish a presence in a foreign country by building a plant there. A branch is not a separate corporation or legal entity (see Exhibit 32.2). It is merely an extension of the corporate owner and is wholly owned by the home corporation.

There are detriments to this form of operation. For instance, it is expensive (because the owner must build or lease plant or office premises), and it exposes the owner to tort and contract liability in the foreign country and to foreign laws.

Subsidiary Corporation

A business can enter a foreign market by establishing a separate corporation to conduct business in a foreign country.

Such a corporation, which is called a **subsidiary**, must be formed pursuant to the laws of the country in which it is to be located. The **parent corporation** usually owns all or a majority of the subsidiary corporation. The parent corporation and the subsidiary corporation are separate legal entities that are individually capitalized (see Exhibit 32.3).

A foreign subsidiary is usually used where the parent corporation wants to establish a substantial presence in a foreign country. The benefit of using a subsidiary corporation over a branch is that it isolates the parent corporation from the tort and contract liability of the subsidiary corporation (and vice versa), unless the foreign country's laws provide otherwise. On the other hand, establishing and operating a subsidiary corporation in a foreign country is often expensive and complicated. Also, it exposes the subsidiary corporation to the laws of the foreign country.

Consider These Examples

Ford Motor Company, Inc., a United States corporation organized in the state of Delaware, opens a branch office in India to sell its automobiles there. If an employee at the branch office in India negligently injures an Indian citizen in India while on a test drive, Ford Motor Company, Inc., in the United States is wholly liable for the injured person's damages. Suppose instead that Ford

---

EXHIBIT 32.2   *Conducting International Business Using a Branch Office*

Corporation A
(in Country A)

No limited liability shield—
Corporation A in Country A is liable
for the tort and contract liabilities
of its branch office in Country B.

Branch Office
(in Country B)

The branch office
is not a separate
legal entity.

*Ɛ*XHIBIT **32.3** *Conducting International Business Using a Subsidiary Corporation*

Corporation A
(in Country A)

Limited liability shield—Corporation A in Country A is not liable for the tort and contract liabilities of its subsidiary corporation in Country B except up to its capital contribution in Corporation B.

Corporation B
(in Country B)

Corporation B is a separate legal entity.

Motor Company, Inc., forms a subsidiary corporation called Ford.India Corporation in India pursuant to Indian law. Ford Motor, Inc., is the parent corporation and shareholder of Ford.India Corporation; Ford.India Corporation is the subsidiary corporation. If an employee of Ford.India Corporation negligently injures an Indian citizen in India while on a test drive, only Ford.India Corporation is liable; Ford Motor Company, Inc., in the United States is not liable other than it may lose its capital contribution in Ford.India Corporation if the judgment is large.

Ɛntrepreneur and the *ℒaw*

AOL ACQUIRES TIME-WARNER IN MEGAMERGER

In 1989, entrepreneur Steve Case introduced a nationwide service called America Online (AOL) that provided Internet access to subscribers. In 1990, this upstart company was in desperate need of cash and offered to sell 11 percent ownership to media giant Time Warner for $5 million. Time Warner rejected the offer. Ten years later AOL made a second offer to Time Warner, this time to buy Time Warner for $180 billion in AOL stock. Time Warner accepted the offer. Although the agreement is called a merger, there is no doubt as to who the buyer is: AOL, the new-kid-on-the-block and member of the high-tech community, is buying the venerable media company Time Warner. The trading symbol for the new company, tellingly, is AOL. When announced in January 2000, the AOL-Time Warner merger was the largest in history.

AOL had only become a public company seven years prior to the merger when it sold stock to the public at $11. Since that time, its stock had increased 35,000 percent in value. At the time of the merger announcement, AOL was worth more than 2.5 times more than Time Warner on the stock market. With no historical reference for valuing Net companies, AOL and Time Warner negotiated a trade that valued AOL 1.5 times more than Time Warner. This gave a premium of 70 percent to each Time Warner stockholder over the then current stock price per share. After the merger, the AOL stockholders would own 55 percent of the $350 billion merged company. The Time Warner part of the merger, with over 82,000 employees, would provide 80 percent of the profits compared to AOL, with its 12,000 employees.

The merger marries content with the Internet. Time Warner is a media conglomerate that owns Warner Bros.

Studios, New Line Cinema, and Castle Rock film companies; Warner Bros. and HBO television companies, Time Warner Cable, TNT, TBS, and CNN cable companies; Warner and Elektra music labels; 33 magazines including *Time*, *People*, and *Sports Illustrated*; and Warner Bros. and Little Brown book publishers. AOL, on the other hand, is a high-tech Internet company that owns America Online Internet service, AOL sites, MapQuest, MovieFone, CompuServe, Netscape, part of DIRECTV, deals with regional bells for providing DSL service, and strategic alliances with other Internet companies. The merger also combines customer databases. AOL has 25 million Internet subscribers, while Time Warner has 28 million magazine subscribers, 35 million HBO subscribers, and 75 million households that have the TBS and TNT television channels. The merger provides substantial synergies for delivering media content over the Internet and providing opportu-

nities for cross-marketing of products and services to customers.

Before the merger, Time Warner made forays into becoming an Internet company by internal expansion, but failed. It realized it couldn't get there unless it bought an Internet company, but with large debt and a low stock price it did not have the currency to buy a large Internet company. AOL, on the other hand, had currency to buy in the form of its Net-inflated stock value. So the old-line media giant, with content and wires, sold to the upstart, with a connection to the Internet and the future. The result is a new kind of conglomerate in the digital economy. The merger validates both the Internet and the value of content. The AOL-Time Warner merger may be the first of many that combine entertainment and high-technology, but probably no other merger can match the size and scope of this landmark deal.

WWW *Working the Web*

International Business Resources on the WWW This site is produced by Michigan State University Center for International Business Education and Research. It contains lots of valuable international trade information.

Visit at **ciber.bus.msu.edu/busres.htm**

The Trade Zone The Trade Zone is provided by the reference section of the Global Trade Center.

Visit at **www.tradezone.com/trdzone.htm**

International Small Business Consortium This site is a good source of knowledge, products, and services for those interested in small business.

Visit at **www.isbc.com**

CYBER EXERCISES

1. Using International Business Resources on the WWW, find international trade leads.
2. Check out Global Roulette in the Trade Zone.
3. Using the ISBC site, find tips for doing business using the Internet.

*C*ASES AND *E*XERCISES

CRITICAL LEGAL THINKING CASES

32.1. Tokyo's Boeki Ltd. (Boeki Japan) is a Japanese corporation that manufactures and exports steel products. Boeki Japan owns all of the 200 shares of stock of Tokyo Boeki (U.S.A.), Inc. (Boeki USA), a separately incorporated entity under the laws of New York. Boeki USA acts as a sales agent for Boeki Japan and

arranges sales in the United States of steel products manufactured by Boeki Japan. Boeki USA keeps its own, separate books, but sends copies of certain financial and sales reports, major contracts, corporate minutes, and litigation reports to Boeki Japan. The members of the board of directors of the two corporations overlap. The administrative staff and other supervisory personnel of Boeki USA have primarily been former employees of Boeki Japan. The letterhead of Boeki Japan lists Boeki USA's New York office as an "Overseas Office" of Boeki Japan.

Boeki USA ordered a shipment of steel pipe from Boeki Japan that was to be shipped from Wakayama, Japan, to Newark, New Jersey. Boeki USA intended to resell the pipe to a customer in the United States. Boeki Japan arranged to have the steel shipped by Zim Israel Navigation Company, Ltd. (Zim).

When the pipe arrived in Newark, it was found to be damaged. Boeki USA sued Zim in U.S. district court in New York for damages. Zim filed a third-party complaint against Boeki Japan and served Boeki USA with the complaint. Boeki Japan made a special appearance, alleging that the court did not have jurisdiction over it because it was not present in New York. What form of business is Boeki USA in relation to Boeki Japan? Does the court have jurisdiction over Boeki Japan? [*Tokyo Boeki (U.S.A.), Inc. v. SS Navarino*, 324 F.Supp. 361 (S.D.N.Y. 1971)]

ETHICS CASES

32.2. Chase Manhattan Bank (Chase) operated a branch office in Saigon, South Vietnam, from 1966 until April 24, 1975. Among its depositors were 10 corporations (including Vishipco Line), owned principally by Tran Dinh Truong and Nguyen Thi Cham. The corporations had on deposit some 163,971,597 Vietnamese piasters, and Cham held a certificate of deposit from Chase for the sum of 200,000 Vietnamese piasters. Chase's operations in Saigon came to an end at noon on April 24, 1975, after Chase officials in New York determined that Saigon would soon fall to the communists. After closing the branch without having given any notice to depositors, the local Chase officials balanced the day's books, shut the vaults and the building itself, and delivered keys and financial records needed to operate the branch to personnel at the French Embassy in Saigon. Saigon fell on April 30, and on May 1 the new government confiscated the assets of all banks in the country.

Tran Dinh Truong and Nguyen Thi Cham fled South Vietnam just prior to the communist takeover. After arriving in the United States, Truong and Cham demanded that Chase repay the piaster deposits made in Saigon, but Chase refused to do so. Truong, acting under his powers of attorney, subsequently brought this suit on behalf of the 10 corporations seeking recovery from Chase of the dollar value of the piaster deposits held by its Saigon branch at the time it was closed. Cham sued for the value of her certificate of deposit. Was it ethical for Chase to deny liability? Who wins? [*Vishipco Line v. Chase Manhattan Bank, N.A.*, 660 F.2d 854 (2nd Cir. 1981)]

CRITICAL LEGAL THINKING WRITING ASSIGNMENT

Read Case A.32 in the Case Appendix [*Bulova Watch Company, Inc. v. K. Hattori & Co., Ltd.*]. This case is excerpted from the district court's opinion. Review and brief the case. In your brief, be sure to answer the following questions.

1. Where was K. Hattori & Co., Ltd. (Hattori), incorporated? Describe the arrangement whereby it sold its products in the United States.

2. Where was the Bulova Watch Company, Inc. (Bulova), incorporated? Why did Bulova sue Hattori?

3. What issue was presented to the court? How did the court decide this issue?

General Partnerships

One of the most fruitful sources of ruin to men of the world is the recklessness or want of principle of partners, and it is one of the perils to which every man exposes himself who enters into partnership with another.

MALINS, V.C. Mackay v. Douglas,
14 Eq. 106 at 118 (1872)

Chapter Objectives

After studying this chapter, you should be able to

1. Define *general partnership* and describe how general partnerships are formed.
2. List and explain the rights and duties among partners.
3. Describe the partners' right to participation in the management of the partnership.
4. Describe the right to share in the partnership's profits and losses.
5. Define *duty of loyalty* among partners and identify violations of this duty.
6. Explain the duty of care owed by a partner.
7. Explain the contract and tort liability of partners.
8. Describe the liability of incoming and outgoing partners.
9. Describe how a partnership is dissolved and terminated.
10. Explain how partners may continue a dissolved partnership.

Chapter Contents

General, or ordinary, partnerships have been recognized since ancient times. The English common law of partnerships governed early U.S. partnerships. The individual states expanded the body of partnership law.

The formation of a partnership creates certain rights and duties among partners and with third parties. These rights and duties are established in the partnership agreement, the Uniform Partnership Act (UPA), and other laws (e.g., contract law, tort law, and agency law). Partners and third parties may bring legal action to enforce their rights or to recover damages for breach of duties. This chapter discusses the formation of general partnerships, the rights and duties of partners among themselves, the contract and tort liability of the partnership and partners to third persons, and the termination of general partnerships.

The partner of my partner is not my partner.

Legal Maxim

$\mathcal{U}$NIFORM PARTNERSHIP ACT (UPA)

Uniform Partnership Act (UPA)

Model act that codifies partnership law. Most states have adopted the UPA in whole or in part.

In 1914, the National Conference of Commissioners on Uniform State Laws (a group of lawyers, judges, and legal scholars) promulgated the **Uniform Partnership Act (UPA)**, which codified partnership law. Its goal was to establish consistent partnership law that was uniform throughout the United States. The UPA has been adopted in whole or in part by 48 states, the District of Columbia, Guam, and the Virgin Islands. Georgia and Louisiana have not adopted the UPA. These states enacted their own partnership statutes.

The UPA covers most problems that arise in the formation, operation, and dissolution of ordinary partnerships. Other rules of law or equity govern if there is not an applicable provision of the UPA [UPA § 5]. Because it is so important, the UPA will form the basis of the study of general partnerships in this chapter.

$\mathcal{D}$EFINITION OF A GENERAL PARTNERSHIP

entity theory

A theory that holds that partnerships are separate legal entities that can hold title to personal and real property, transact business in the partnership name, sue in the partnership name, and the like.

The UPA adopted the **entity theory** of partnerships, which considers partnerships as separate legal entities. As such, partnerships can hold title to personal and real property, transact business in the partnership name, sue in the partnership name, and the like. *General partners*, or *partners*, are personally liable for the debts and obligations of the partnership (see Exhibit 33.1).

Requirements for a General Partnership

general partnership

An association of two or more persons to carry on as co-owners of a business for profit [UPA § 6(1)].

A business must meet four criteria to qualify as a **general partnership** under the UPA [UPA § 6(1)]. It must be (1) an association of two or more persons (2) carrying on a business (3) as co-owners (4) for profit. Each of these elements is discussed below.

Association of Two or More Persons   Partnerships are voluntary associations of two or more persons [UPA § 18(g)]. All partners must agree to the participation of each copartner. A person cannot be forced to be a partner or to accept another person as a partner. The UPA definition of person includes natural persons, partnerships (including limited partnerships), corporations, and other associations [UPA § 2].

Business Brief

A partnership is a *voluntary* association. A person cannot be forced to be a partner or to accept another person as a partner.

Carrying on a Business   The mere co-ownership of property by joint tenancy, tenancy in common, tenancy by the entireties, joint property, community property, or part ownership does not itself establish a partnership [UPA § 7(2)]. A business—trade, occupation, or profession—must be carried on [UPA § 2]. Generally, this means a series of transactions

Exhibit **33.1** *General Partnership*

Partners of general partnerships owe one another a duty of care in conducting partnership business. Partners of general partnerships have unlimited personal liability for the debts and obligations of the partnership.

carried on over a period of time. Single or isolated transactions usually do not qualify as a partnership.

Co-ownership of the Business Co-ownership of a business is essential to create a partnership. The most important factors in determining co-ownership are whether the parties share the business's profits and share management responsibility.

Receipt of a share of business profits is prima facie evidence of a partnership because nonpartners usually are not given the right to share in the business's profits. No inference of the existence of a partnership is drawn if profits are received in payment of (1) a debt owed to a creditor in installments or otherwise, (2) wages owed to an employee, (3) rent owed to a landlord, (4) an annuity owed to a widow, a widower, or a representative of a deceased partner, (5) interest owed on a loan, or (6) consideration for the sale of goodwill of a business [UPA § 7]. An agreement to share losses of a business is strong evidence of a partnership.

The right to participate in the management of a business is important evidence for determining the existence of a partnership, but it is not conclusive evidence because the right to participate in management is sometimes given to employees, creditors, and others. It is compelling evidence of the existence of a partnership if a person is given the right to share in profits, losses, and management of a business.

Profit Motive The organization or venture must have a profit motive to qualify as a partnership even though the business does not actually have to make a profit. Nonprofit organizations, such as charitable or fraternal organizations, cannot be organized as partnerships because they do not meet this requirement.

In the following case, the court had to decide whether a partnership had been created.

Vohland v. Sweet
435 N.E.2d 860 (1982)
Court of Appeals of Indiana

CASE 33.1

FACTS
Norman E. Sweet began working for Charles Vohland as an hourly employee at a garden nursery owned by Vohland in 1956, when he was a youngster. Upon completion of military service (from 1958 to 1960), Sweet resumed his former employment. In 1963, Charles Vohland retired and his son Paul Vohland (Vohland) commenced what became known as Vohland's Nursery, the business of which was landscape gardening. Vohland purchased the interests of his brothers and sisters in the nursery. At that time, Sweet's status changed: He was to receive a 20 percent share of the net profit of the business after all expenses were paid, including labor, supplies, plants, and other expenses. Sweet contributed no capital to the enterprise. The compensation was paid on an irregular basis—every several weeks Vohland and Sweet would sit down, compute the income received and expenses paid, and Sweet would be issued a check for 20 percent of the balance. No Social Security or income taxes were withheld from Sweet's checks.

Vohland and Sweet did not enter into a written agreement. No partnership income tax returns were filed by the business. Sweet's tax returns declared that he was a self-employed salesman. He paid self-employment Social Security taxes. Vohland handled all of the finances and books of the nursery and borrowed money from the bank solely in his own name for business purposes. Vohland made most of the sales for the business. Sweet managed the physical aspects of the nursery, supervised the care of the nursing stock, and oversaw

the performance of the contracts for customers. Sweet testified that in the early 1970s, Vohland told him that:

> He was going to take me in and that I wouldn't have to punch a time clock anymore, that I would be on a commission basis and that I would be—have more of an interest in the business if I had an interest in the business. He referred to it as a "piece of the action."

Vohland denied making this statement. Sweet brought this action for dissolution of the alleged partnership and for an accounting. He sought payment for 20 percent of the business's inventory. The trial court held in favor of Sweet and awarded him $58,733. Vohland appealed.

ISSUE
Did Vohland and Sweet enter into a partnership?

IN THE LANGUAGE OF THE COURT
Neal, Judge   We note that both parties referred to the 20% as "commissions." To us the term "commission," unless defined, does not mean the same thing as a share of the net profits. However, this term, when used by landscape gardeners and not lawyers, should not be restricted to its technical definition. "Commission" was used to refer to Sweet's share of the profits, and the receipt of a share of the profits is prima facie evidence of a partnership.

Though evidence is conflicting, there is evidence that the payments were not wages, but a share of the profit of a partnership. It can readily be inferred from the evidence most favorable to support the judgment that the parties intended a community of interest in any increment in the value of the capital and in the profit. Absence of contribution to capital is not controlling, and contribution of labor and skill will suffice. There is evidence from which it can be inferred that the parties intended to do the things that amount to the formation of a partnership, regardless of how they may later characterize the relationship.

DECISION AND REMEDY

The court of appeals held that partnership had been created between Vohland and Sweet. Affirmed.

Case Questions

Critical Legal Thinking   Do you think a partnership was formed in this case? Should all partnership agreements be required to be in writing?

Ethics   Do you think either party acted unethically in this case?

Business Application   What are the economic consequences of founding a partnership?

FORMATION OF GENERAL PARTNERSHIPS

A general partnership may be formed with little or no formality. The following paragraphs discuss the formation of general partnerships.

Creation of a General Partnership

A general partnership may be created by words, either verbal or written. Such partnerships are called **express partnerships**. Partnerships can also be implied from the conduct of the parties. This is called an **implied partnership**.

In most states, a general partnership does not have to file its partnership agreement (if any) or any other document with the secretary of state's office or other government agency. A few states require general partnerships to file **certificates of partnership** with an appropriate government agency.

Partnership Capital   Money and property contributed by partners for the permanent use of the partnership are called **partnership capital**. Such property cannot be withdrawn from the partnership prior to dissolution unless all of the partners consent to the withdrawal.

The partners can make loans of property or money to the partnership. Partners who do so become creditors of the partnership. Loans and the value of services provided to a partnership are not included in the partnership capital.

Partnership Name   An ordinary partnership can operate under the names of any one or more of the partners or under a fictitious business name. If the partnership operates under a fictitious name, it must file a fictitious business name statement with the appropriate government agency and publish a notice of the name in a newspaper of general circulation where the partnership does business. The name selected by a partnership cannot indicate that it is a corporation (e.g., it cannot contain the term *Inc.*) and cannot be similar to the name used by any existing business entity.

Duration of Partnership   The duration of a partnership can be for a fixed term (e.g., five years) or until a particular undertaking is accomplished (e.g., until a real estate development is completed). A partnership with a fixed duration is called a **partnership for a term**. A partnership with no fixed duration is called a **partnership at will**.

The Partnership Agreement

Although a partnership may be oral or implied from the parties' conduct, it is good practice for partners to put their partnership agreement in writing. A written document is important evidence of the terms of agreement, particularly if a dispute arises among the partners.

---

express partnership
General partnership created by words, either verbal or written.

implied partnership
General partnership implied from the conduct of the parties.

certificate of partnership
A document that a partnership must file with the appropriate state government agency in some states to acknowledge that the partnership exists.

partnership capital
Money and property contributed by partners for the permanent use of the partnership.

Business Brief
Partnerships often operate under a fictitious business name. Those that do must file a fictitious business name statement with the appropriate government agency.

partnership for a term
A partnership with a fixed duration.

partnership at will
A partnership with no fixed duration.

Written Partnership Agreement A written partnership agreement is called a **partnership agreement** or **articles of partnership**. The partners can agree to almost any term in their partnership agreement, except terms that are illegal. The articles of partnership can be short and simple or long and complex. In all events, however, the partnership agreement should contain the following information:

- The firm name
- The names and addresses of the partners
- The principal office of the partnership
- The nature and scope of the partnership business
- The duration of the partnership
- The capital contributions of each partner
- The division of profits and losses among the partners
- The salaries, if any, to be paid to partners
- The duties of the partners regarding the management of the partnership
- Limitations, if any, on the authority of partners to bind the partnership
- Provisions for the admission and withdrawal of partners from the firm and the terms, conditions, and notices required for withdrawal
- Provisions for continuing the partnership upon the withdrawal of a partner, death of a partner, or other dissolution of the partnership
- Any other provisions deemed relevant by the partners

If the agreement fails to provide for an essential term or contingency, the provisions of the UPA control. Thus, the UPA acts as a gap-filling device to the partners' agreement.

Partnership by Estoppel

A **partnership by estoppel** arises when a person who is not a partner either makes a representation or consents to a partner's representation that he or she is a partner. The nonpartner (or *ostensible partner*) is liable to any person who reasonably relied on the representation when deciding to extend credit to the partnership. The nonpartner has the same liability as an actual partner. Both the nonpartner and the partner who consents to the representation are *estopped*—forbidden—from denying liability [UPA § 16]. If all of the partners of a partnership consent to the representation, the credit contract becomes an obligation of the partnership.

Consider This Example Suppose Dean, Sunny, and Bob form a partnership to operate a men's clothing store. One day Dean's daughter Gail, who has just graduated from college, accompanies Dean on partnership business. On a visit to Threads, Inc., a clothing supplier to the partnership, Dean introduces Gail as the "new partner." Although she is not really a partner, Gail enters into a contract with Threads, Inc., to purchase $100,000 of Madras cloth (on credit) on behalf of the partnership. Dean remains silent while Gail signs the contract. Neither the partnership nor the other partners are liable on the contract. The partnership by estoppel is between Dean and Gail, who are personally liable for the contract.

𝒫ROPERTY RIGHTS OF THE PARTNERSHIP AND THE PARTNERS

There is an important distinction between property owned by the partnership and individual partners' property rights in the partnership.

Partnership Property

All property originally brought into the partnership on account of the partnership is **partnership property**. Unless otherwise stated in the partnership agreement, property that is subsequently acquired by purchase or otherwise on account of the partnership or with partnership funds is also partnership property. This is true even if title is retained by the individual partners [UPA § 8].

The partnership agreement should indicate which property originally contributed by partners is partnership property. It is good practice to keep a written record of all partnership property that is subsequently contributed, used, or acquired by the partnership.

Title to real property owned in the partnership name can be conveyed only in that name [UPA § 8(3)]. Any partner can execute the conveyance of title in the partnership name [UPA § 10(1)]. If title to partnership property is held in the name of one or more partners rather than in the partnership name, title to the property can be transferred only by a conveyance signed by these partners.

Specific partnership property is subject to attachment or execution by creditors of the partnership.

Partners' Rights in Partnership Property

A partner is a co-owner with the other partners of the specific partnership property as a *tenant in partnership* [UPA § 25(1)]. This is a special legal status that exists only in a partnership. Upon the death of a partner, the deceased partner's right in specific partnership property vests in the remaining partner or partners—it does not pass to his or her heirs or next of kin. This is called the **right of survivorship**. Upon the death of the last surviving partner, the rights in specific partnership property vest in the deceased partner's legal representative [UPA § 25(2)C]. The *value* of the deceased partner's interest in the partnership passes to his or her beneficiaries or heirs upon his or her death, however.

right of survivorship
Rule that states that a deceased partner's right in specific partnership property vests with the remaining partners upon his or her death.

Consider This Example   Jamie, Harold, Shou-Ju, and Jesus form a general partnership to operate a new restaurant. After their first restaurant is successful, they expand until the partnership owns 100 restaurants. At that time Jamie dies. None of the partnership assets transfer to Jamie's heirs; for example, they do not get 25 of the restaurants. Instead, under the right of survivorship, they inherit Jamie's ownership interest, and his heirs now have the right to receive Jamie's one-quarter of the partnership's profits each year.

Assignment of a Partnership Interest

A **partner's interest** in a partnership is his or her share of the profits and surplus of the partnership; this is the partner's personal property [UPA § 26]. A partner may voluntarily *assign* his or her partnership interest to a third party. The assignment can be full or partial. The assignee does not become a partner of the partnership or acquire any management or information rights. The assigning partner remains a partner with all rights and duties of a partner.

partner's interest
A partner's share of profits and surplus of the partnership.

The assignment of a partnership interest merely entitles the assignee to receive the profits to which the assigning partner is entitled. When the partnership is dissolved, the assignee is entitled to receive the rights on liquidation to which the assigning partner is entitled [UPA § 27].

Judgment Creditors

If the creditor of an individual partner obtains a judgment against the partner, the creditor becomes a *judgment creditor*. To satisfy the debt, a judgment creditor can ask the court to issue a **charging order** against the debtor–partner's partnership interest. A charging order, which is a form of judicial lien, entitles the judgment creditor to be paid from the debtor–partner's partnership profits. The partnership or any other partner can redeem the interest charged by paying the judgment creditor the amount due on the judgment [UPA § 28].

charging order
A document that the court issues against the debtor–partner's partnership interest in order to satisfy a debt.

Judgment creditors do not become partners and are not entitled to participate in the management of the partnership. The debtor–partner against whom the charging order is issued remains a partner with all of the rights and duties of a partner.

Business Brief
A judgment creditor does not become a partner in the partnership.

RIGHTS AMONG PARTNERS

When partners enter into a general partnership, the law provides that the partners have certain rights. The extent of these rights is discussed in the following paragraphs.

Right to Participate in Management

management

Unless otherwise agreed, each partner has a right to participate in the management of the partnership and has an equal vote on partnership matters.

In the absence of an agreement to the contrary, all partners have equal rights in the **management** and conduct of the partnership business [UPA § 18(e)]. In other words, each partner has one vote regardless of the proportional size of his or her capital contribution or share in the partnership's profits. Under the UPA, a simple majority decides most ordinary partnership matters [UPA § 18(h)]. If the vote is tied, the action being voted on is considered to be defeated. The following issues require the unanimous consent of the partners:

1. Assignment of partnership property for the benefit of creditors
2. Disposal of the goodwill of the business
3. Actions that would make it impossible to carry on the ordinary business of the partnership
4. Submission of a partnership claim or liability to arbitration [UPA § 9(3)]
5. Admission of a new partner to the partnership [UPA § 18(g)]
6. Actions in contravention of the partnership agreement [UPA § 18(h)]
7. Actions that are not apparently for the carrying on of the business of the partnership in the usual way or that change the nature of the business [UPA § 9(2)]

The partners may agree to modify the majority and unanimous consent rules just discussed. The partners may delegate management responsibility to a committee of partners or to a managing partner. The partnership agreement can also create classes of partners with unequal voting powers.

Entrepreneur and the Law

PARTNERS' RIGHTS TO SHARE IN PROFITS

Unless otherwise agreed, the UPA mandates that a partner has the right to an equal share in the partnership's profits and losses [UPA § 18(a)]. Partnership agreements often provide that profits and losses are to be allocated in proportion to the partners' capital contributions. The right to share in the profits of the partnership is considered to be the right to share in the earnings from the investment of capital.

For example, suppose LeAnn Pearson and Mark Butler form a partnership. Pearson contributes $75,000 capital and Butler contributes $25,000 capital. They do not have an agreement as to how profits or losses are to be shared. Assume the partnership makes $100,000 in profits. Under the UPA, Pearson and Butler share the profits equally— $50,000 each.

Where a partnership agreement provides for the sharing of profits but is silent as to how losses are to be shared, losses are shared in the same proportion as profits. The reverse is not true, however. If a partnership agreement provides for the sharing of losses but is silent as to how profits are to be shared, profits are shared equally.

Expressly providing how profits and losses are to be shared by partners can increase the benefits to partners. For example, partners with high incomes from other sources can benefit most from the losses generated by a partnership.

Right to an Accounting

action for an accounting

A formal judicial proceeding in which the court is authorized to (1) review the partnership and the partners' transactions and (2) award each partner his or her share of the partnership assets.

Partners are not permitted to sue the partnership or other partners at law. Instead, they are given the right to bring an **action for an accounting** against other partners. An accounting is a formal judicial proceeding in which the court is authorized to (1) review the partnership and the partners' transactions and (2) award each partner his or her share of the partnership assets [UPA § 24]. This results in a money judgment for or against partners according to the balance struck.

Other Rights of Partners

Right to Compensation Unless otherwise agreed, the UPA provides that no partner is entitled to remuneration for his or her performance in the partnership's business [UPA § 18(f)]. Under this rule, partners are not entitled to receive either a salary for providing services to the partnership, even if the services provided are disproportionate to the services provided by other partners, or rents for personal property used by the partnership. However, the agreement may specifically state that a particular partner is to receive such remuneration.

Under the UPA, it is implied that partners will devote full time and service to the partnership. This, unless otherwise agreed, income earned by partners from providing services elsewhere belongs to the partnership [UPA § 21].

Business Brief
A partner is not entitled to compensation for services provided to the partnership unless the partnership agreement so provides.

Right of Indemnification Partners sometimes incur personal travel, business, and other expenses on behalf of the partnership. A partner is entitled to **indemnification** (i.e., reimbursement) for such expenditures if they are reasonably incurred in the ordinary and proper conduct of the business and for the preservation of partnership property [UPA § 18(b)].

indemnification
Right of a partner to be reimbursed for expenditures incurred on behalf of the partnership.

Right to Return of Advances A partner who makes an *advance* (loan) to the partnership becomes a creditor of the partnership. The partner is entitled to repayment of the loan, but this right is subordinated to the claims of creditors who are not partners [UPA § 40(b)]. The partner is also entitled to receive interest from the date of the advance [UPA § 18(c)].

Right to Return of Capital Upon termination of a partnership, the partners are entitled to have their capital contributions returned to them [UPA § 18(a)]. However, this right is subordinated to the rights of creditors, who must be paid their claims first [UPA § 40(b)]. Unless otherwise agreed, no interest is paid on a partner's capital contribution [UPA § 18(d)].

Right to Information Every partner has the right to demand true and full information from any partner of all things affecting the partnership [UPA § 20]. The corollary to this rule is that each partner has a duty to provide such information upon the receipt of a reasonable demand. The personal representative (lawyer or accountant) of a partner or deceased partner has the same rights and duties in this regard as the party represented.

The partnership books (financial records, tax records, and such) must be kept at the partnership's principal place of business unless all of the partners consent to their removal [UPA § 19]. The partners have an absolute right to inspect and copy these records.

Business Brief
The partners of a general partnership have an absolute right to inspect and copy the partnership's books and records.

DUTIES AMONG PARTNERS

Partners owe certain duties to the partnership and the other partners. These duties include (1) a duty of loyalty, (2) a duty of obedience, (3) a duty of care, and (4) a duty to inform. Each of these is discussed in the sections that follow.

Duty of Loyalty

Partners are in a *fiduciary relationship* with one another. As such, they owe each other a **duty of loyalty**. This duty is imposed by law and cannot be waived. If there is a conflict between partnership interests and personal interests, the partner must choose the interest of the partnership.

duty of loyalty
A duty that a partner owes not to act adversely to the interests of the partnership.

Examples of the Breach of the Duty of Loyalty Some basic forms of breach of loyalty involve

1. *Self-Dealing* Self-dealing occurs when a partner deals personally with the partnership, such as buying or selling goods or property to the partnership. Such actions are permitted only if full disclosure is made and consent of the other partners is obtained. For example, suppose a partnership in which Dan is a partner is looking for a piece of property on which to build a new store. Dan owns a desirable piece of property. To sell the property to the partnership, Dan must first disclose his ownership interest and receive his partners' consent.

2. *Usurping a Partnership Opportunity* A partner who is offered an opportunity on behalf of the partnership cannot take the opportunity for him- or herself. In other words, if a third party offers an opportunity to a partner in his or her partnership status (e.g., the opportunity to purchase a business), the partner cannot take the opportunity for him- or herself before offering it to the partnership. If the partnership rejects the opportunity, the partner is free to pursue it if it does not violate any other duty he or she owes to the partnership.

3. *Competing with the Partnership* A partner may not compete with the partnership without the permission of the other partners. For example, a partner in a partnership that operates an automobile dealership cannot open a competing automobile dealership without his or her co-partners' permission.

4. *Secret Profits* Partners may not make secret profits from partnership business. For example, a partner may not keep a kickback from a supplier.

5. *Breach of Confidentiality* Partners owe a duty to keep partnership information (e.g., trade secrets, customer lists, and the like) confidential.

6. *Misuse of Property* Partners owe a duty not to use partnership property for personal use.

A partner who breaches the duty of loyalty must disgorge any profits made from the breach to the partnership. In addition, the partner is liable for any damages caused by the breach.

Business Brief

Partners breach their duty of loyalty if they:

1. Self-deal with the partnership without permission
2. Usurp a partnership opportunity
3. Compete with the partnership without permission
4. Make secret profits from partnership business
5. Disclose confidential partnership information
6. Misuse partnership property
7. Make other breaches of their fiduciary duty

Ethical Perspective

PARTNER DISLOYALTY

Partnership law firmly establishes that partners owe a duty of loyalty to one another. This legal and ethical rule is firmly and consistently supported by precedent. Does this duty, however, extend to a partner who quits the partnership, and if so, for how long? Consider the following case.

In 1969, Ted Leff, who had been a real estate developer for 30 years, became aware that the U.S. government was soliciting bids for the construction of an Internal Revenue Service (IRS) center to be located in Fresno, California. Once built, the federal government would lease the center back from the owner. Subsequently, Leff, Henry Sender, William Gunter, and some associates of Gunter orally agreed to form a joint venture partnership to bid on the IRS center. Thereafter, Leff kept the other partners fully informed about building sites, engineering data, labor mar-

ket statistics, water and utility availability, and the like. The partners focused on building the IRS center on property known as the Pilobos site, which was owned by a third party. Leff and Sender prepared a final bid for the site and sent it to Gunter.

In March 1970, Gunter and his associates withdrew from the partnership. On April 10, 1970, Leff and Sender submitted a bid to the government concerning the Pilobos site. The job, however, was awarded to Russell & Associates, who had submitted a lower bid to build the IRS center at the Pilobos site.

Later, Leff learned that Gunter and his associates were secretly part of Russell & Associates. Leff sued his former partners for breach of fiduciary duty and sought damages from them. Gunter and the others defended, arguing that they were merely engaging in fair competition with a former partner after termination of the partnership.

The trial court held that the defendants had violated their fiduciary duty to their partner, Leff, by taking the partnership opportunity for themselves. The court awarded Leff $416,666 in damages. The court of appeals affirmed and added interest to the judgment. [*Leff v. Gunter*, 33 Cal.3d 508, 658 P.2d 740 (Cal. 1983)]

1. Does a partner's duty of loyalty end when the partnership is terminated?
2. Did Gunter act ethically in this case?

Duty of Obedience

The **duty of obedience** requires the partners to adhere to the provisions of the partnership agreement and the decisions of the partnership. A partner who breaches this duty is liable to the partnership for any damages caused by the breach.

duty of obedience
A duty that partners must adhere to the provisions of the partnership agreement and the decisions of the partnership.

Consider This Example Jodie, Bart, and Denise form a partnership to develop real property. Their partnership agreement specifies that acts of the partners are limited to those necessary to accomplish the partnership's purpose. Suppose Bart, acting alone, loses $100,000 of partnership funds in commodities trading. Bart is personally liable to the partnership for the lost funds because he breached the partnership agreement.

Duty of Care

A partner must use reasonable care and skill in transacting partnership business. The **duty of care** calls for the partners to use the same level of care and skill that a reasonable business manager in the same position would use in the same circumstances. Breach of the duty of care is **negligence**. A partner is liable to the partnership for any damages caused by his or her negligence. The partners are not liable for honest errors in judgment.

duty of care
The obligation partners owe to use the same level of care and skill that a reasonable person in the same position would use in the same circumstances. A breach of the duty of care is *negligence*.

Consider This Example Suppose Tina, Eric, and Brian form a partnership to sell automobiles. Tina, who is responsible for ordering inventory, orders large, expensive cars. Assume that a war breaks out in the Middle East that interrupts the supply of oil to the United States. The demand for large cars drops substantially, and the partnership cannot sell its inventory. Tina is not liable because the duty of care was not breached. The situation might have been different if the war had broken out before the order was placed.

Duty to Inform

Partners owe a **duty to inform** their co-partners of all information they possess that is relevant to the affairs of the partnership [UPA § 20]. Even if a partner fails to do so, the other partners are imputed with knowledge of all notices concerning any matters relating to partnership affairs. Knowledge is also imputed regarding information acquired in the role of partner that affects the partnership and should have been communicated to the other partners [UPA § 12].

duty to inform
A duty a partner owes to inform his or her co-partners of all information he or she possesses that is relevant to the affairs of the partnership.

Consider This Example Suppose Ted and Diane are partners. Ted knows that a piece of property owned by the partnership contains dangerous toxic wastes but fails to inform Diane of this fact. Even though Diane does not have actual knowledge of this fact, it is imputed to her.

LIABILITY TO THIRD PARTIES

Partners must deal with third parties in conducting partnership business. This often includes entering into contracts with third parties on behalf of the partnership. It also includes agents or representatives of the partnership who injures a third party while conducting partnership business. Contract and tort liability of partnerships and their partners is discussed in the following paragraphs.

Contract Liability of Partnerships and Partners

Business Brief
General partners are *personally liable* for contract liability of their partnership.

As a legal entity, a partnership must act through its agents, that is, its partners. Contracts entered into with suppliers, customers, lenders, or others on the partnership's behalf are binding on the partnership if the partner who enters into the contract had any of the following kinds of authority:

- **Express Authority** Express authority can be stated orally or in writing. It may be set forth in the partnership agreement, a collateral agreement of the partners, or a decision of the partners [UPA § 18(h)].
- **Implied Authority** Implied authority is deduced from the partnership's business, the express powers of the partners, the customs of the industry, and such [UPA § 9(1)]. It includes the power to purchase equipment, hire and fire employees, open a checking account at a bank, issue negotiable instruments (e.g., checks), make deposits of cash and other consideration, enter into contracts necessary to conduct the partnership business, borrow money for the operation of the business, sign promissory notes on behalf of the partnership, pledge partnership assets as security for loans, make representations and warranties, and take other action reasonably necessary for the conduct of partnership business [UPA § 11].
- **Apparent Authority** Apparent authority arises when a partner's implied authority has been restricted by agreement among the partners but a third party who deals with the partnership has not been informed of this fact. The partnership is not bound to a contract entered into by a third party who has received proper notification [UPA §§ 9(1) and 9(4)].

In some instances, the partners may decide to *ratify* an unauthorized contract. If they do, the ratification binds the partnership to the contract from the time of its execution.

joint liability
Partners are *jointly liable* for contracts and debts of the partnership. This means that a plaintiff must name the partnership and all of the partners as defendants in a lawsuit.

Joint Contract Liability of Partners   Under the UPA, partners are **jointly liable** for the contracts and debts of the partnership [UPA § 15(b)]. This means that a third party that sues to recover on a partnership contract or debt must name all of the partners in the lawsuit. If such a lawsuit is successful, the plaintiff can collect the entire amount of the judgment against any or all of the partners. If the third party's suit does not name all of the partners, the judgment cannot be collected against any of the partners or the partnership assets. Similarly, releasing any partner from the lawsuit releases them all.

A partner who is made to pay more than his or her proportionate share of contract liability may seek **indemnification** from the partnership and from those partners who have not paid their share of the loss.

In the following case, the court found partners jointly liable on a partnership contract.

Edward A. Kemmler Memorial Foundation v. Mitchell
584 N.E.2d 695 (1992)
Supreme Court of Ohio

CASE 33.2

FACTS
Clifford W. Davis and Dr. William D. Mitchell formed a general partnership to purchase and operate rental properties for investment purposes. The partnership purchased a parcel of real property from the Edward A. Kemmler Memorial Foundation (Foundation) on credit. Davis signed a $150,000 promissory note to the Foundation as

"Cliff W. Davis, Partner." Prior to executing the note, Davis and Mitchell entered into an agreement that provided that only Davis, and not Mitchell, would be personally liable on the note to the Foundation. They did not inform the Foundation of this side agreement, however. When the partnership defaulted on the note, the Foundation sued the partnership and both partners to recover on the note. Mitchell asserted in defense that the side agreement with Davis relieved him of personal liability. The trial court found Davis and Mitchell jointly liable. The appellate court reversed, excusing Mitchell from liability. The Foundation appealed.

ISSUE

Are both partners, Davis and Mitchell, jointly liable on the note?

IN THE LANGUAGE OF THE COURT

Brown, Justice   *Every partner is an agent of the partnership for the purpose of its business, and the act of every partner, including the execution in the partnership name of any instrument, for apparently carrying on in the usual way the business of the partnership of which he is a member binds the partnership, unless the partner so acting has in fact no authority to act for the partnership in the particular matter, and the person with whom he is dealing has knowledge of the fact that he has no such authority.*

Thus, if a promissory note is executed in the name of the partnership, the partnership is bound, unless a contradictory agreement between the partners is known to the parties with whom they are dealing. The trial court found that the Foundation had no knowledge of the agreement between Davis and Mitchell regarding Mitchell's liability for the note.

DECISION AND REMEDY

The Supreme Court of Ohio held that both partners were jointly liable on the note. Reversed.

Case Questions

Critical Legal Thinking   What is joint liability? Should one general partner be liable to pay a judgment against the partnership?

Ethics   Should Davis and Mitchell have notified the Foundation of their side agreement?

Business Application   Is it financially dangerous to be a partner in a general partnership? Explain.

Tort Liability of Partnerships and Partners

While acting on partnership business, a partner or an employee of the partnership may commit a *tort* that causes injury to a third person. This tort could be caused by a negligent act, a breach of trust (such as embezzlement from a customer's account), a breach of fiduciary duty, defamation, fraud, or other intentional tort.

The partnership is liable if the tortious act of a partner or an employee or agent of the partnership is committed while the person is acting within the ordinary course of partnership business or with the authority of his or her co-partners [UPA §§ 13 and 14].

Business Brief

General partners are *personally liable* for tort liability of their partnership.

Joint and Several Tort Liability of Partners

Under the UPA, partners are **jointly and severally liable** for torts and breaches of trust [UPA § 15(a)]. This is so even if a partner did not participate in the commission of the act. This type of liability permits a third party to sue one or more of the partners *separately*. Judgment can be collected only against the partners who are sued. The partnership and partners who are made to pay tort liability may seek indemnification from the partner who committed the wrongful act. A release of one partner does not discharge the liability of other partners.

Consider This Example   Suppose Nicole, Jim, and Maureen form a partnership. Assume that Jim, while on partnership business, causes an automobile accident that injures Kurt, a pedestrian. Kurt suffers $100,000 in injuries. Kurt, at his option, can sue Nicole, Jim, or Maureen separately, any two of them, or all of them.

A judgment against one partner does not extinguish the liability of the other partners. For example, if Kurt could recover only $25,000 from Nicole, he can later sue Jim or Maureen to recover the remaining $75,000. The decision of the first action is

joint and several liability

Partners are *jointly and severally liable* for tort liability of the partnership. This means that the plaintiff can sue one or more of the partners separately. If successful, the plaintiff can recover the entire amount of the judgment from any or all of the defendant-partners.

usually conclusive as to liability. Thus, if in the first action against one partner the court found the partnership not liable, the third party cannot bring another action against other partners.

Contemporary Business Application

JOINT AND SEVERAL LIABILITY OF GENERAL PARTNERS

The court applied the doctrine of joint and several liability in the following situation. Jose Pena and Joseph Antenucci were both medical doctors who were partners in a medical practice. Both doctors treated Elaine Zuckerman during her pregnancy. Her son, Daniel Zuckerman, was born with severe physical problems. Elaine, as Daniel's mother and natural guardian, brought this medical malpractice suit against both doctors. The jury found that Pena was guilty of medical malpractice but that Antenucci was not. The amount of the verdict totaled $4 million. The trial court entered judgment against Pena but not against Antenucci. The plaintiffs have made a posttrial motion for judgment against both defendants.

Is Antenucci jointly and severally liable for the medical malpractice of his partner, Pena? The court said yes.

The court noted that a partnership is liable for the tortious act of a partner, and a partner is jointly and severally liable for tortious acts chargeable to the partnership. When a tort is committed by the partnership, the wrong is imputable to all of the partners jointly and severally, and an action may be brought against all or any of them in their individual capacities or against the partnership as an entity. Therefore, even though the jury found that defendant Antenucci was not guilty of malpractice in his treatment of the patient, but that defendant Pena, his partner, *was* guilty of malpractice in his treatment of the patient, they were then both jointly and severally liable for the malpractice committed by defendant Pena by operation of law. [*Zuckerman v. Antenucci*, 478 N.Y.S.2d 578 (N.Y. 1984)]

Wrongful Dissolution A partner has the *power* to withdraw and dissolve the partnership at any time, but he or she may not have the *right* to do so. For example, a partner who withdraws from a partnership before the expiration of the term stated in the partnership agreement does not have the right to do so. The partner's action causes a **wrongful dissolution** of the partnership. The partner is liable for damages caused by the wrongful dissolution of the partnership.

wrongful dissolution
When a partner withdraws from a partnership without having the right to do so at that time.

CONCEPT SUMMARY PERSONAL LIABILITY OF GENERAL PARTNERS

Issue	Joint Liability	Joint and Several Liability
Type of lawsuit	Contract action.	Tort action.
Defendants	Plaintiff must name all partners as defendants.	Plaintiff can sue partners individually.
Recovery	If successful, the plaintiff can recover the judgment against all or any of the defendants.	If successful, the plaintiff can recover the judgment against all or any of the named defendants.
Indemnification	Partner who pays judgment can recover contribution from other partners for their share of the judgment.	Partner who pays judgment can recover contribution from other partners for their share of the judgment.

Liability of Incoming Partners

A new partner who is admitted to the partnership is liable for the existing debts and obligations *(antecedent debts)* of the partnership only to the extent of his or her capital contribution [UPA § 17]. The new partner is personally liable for debts and obligations incurred by the partnership after becoming a partner.

Consider This Example   Mitchell, Kyle, and Sun-Sook form a general partnership to operate an Internet company. Three years later, the partners vote to accept Angela as a new partner, who contributes $50,000 capital. At the time Angela became a partner, the partnership had $500,000 in debts. After Angela becomes a partner, the partnership borrows $1 million from Urban Bank. A few months later the partnership goes bankrupt, still owing the $500,000 it did when Angela became partner and the $1 million bank loan after she became partner. Angela's capital contribution of $50,000 will go to pay part of the $500,000 debt when she became partner; she is not personally liable for the unpaid portion of this debt. Angela is personally liable (as are each of her partners) for the $1 million loan still owed Urban Bank.

International Perspective

PARTNERSHIPS OUTSIDE THE UNITED STATES

The English forms of business organizations are essentially the same as those in the United States. Partnership law, in particular, is virtually identical. Thus, in both countries (and in countries following the English model), a partnership is an association of two or more persons carrying on a business with the intent to make a profit.

In the civil law countries, including France and Germany, every form of business organization, including a partnership, is a "company" (*société* in French, *Gesellschaft* in German). A French partnership, because it is a company, is considered as having separate legal or juridical personality independent from its partners and thus can own property or sue or be sued in its own name. At the election of the partners, it can also opt to be treated as a separate tax entity and pay taxes as if it were a corporation. In Germany, by comparison, a partnership does not have a separate juridical personality. Therefore, even though a German partnership is a company, it is the partners who own the property, and the partners must sue or be sued.

Although partnerships are categorized as companies in both France and Germany, they remain associations of persons who have full individual liability for the actions of their company. Similarly, because they are associations, they must have two or more partners.

Partnerships are supposed to generate profits for the partners. In Germany, however, the partnership agreement may include a "Leonine clause." Such clauses can exclude a particular partner from sharing in either the profits or losses of the company. In France a Leonine clause is void.

A specialized form of partnership, the limited partnership, is recognized in the civil law countries. At least one partner must be a general partner (with personal unlimited liability) and one must be a limited partner. Limited partners have limited liability of the kind that investors in stock companies have. They may invest only cash or property in France, but in Germany services may be fixed and recognized as a contribution. In both countries persons can be either general or limited partners, but they cannot be both. In France, limited partners can participate in the internal administration of the partnership. In Germany, they can participate in internal administration and be given broad powers to deal with third parties on behalf of the partnership.

Germany recognizes another type of partnership, known as the silent partnership. This is a secret relationship between the partners that is unknown to third parties. The active partner conducts the business in his or her name alone, never mentioning the silent partner. So long as the silent partner's participation is not disclosed, the silent partner's risk is limited to the amount he or she invested. Silent partnerships are useful business forms for investment in Germany because the interest paid to the silent partner is treated as interest on a loan and is therefore tax deductible as a business expense from the earnings of the active partner. In France, where partnerships are regarded as separate legal entities, a silent partnership is not recognized as a separate entity and, therefore, is not governed by partnership law.

TERMINATION OF PARTNERSHIPS

General partnerships are dissolved and terminated in three stages: (1) dissolution, (2) winding-up, and (3) termination. The **dissolution** of a partnership is "the change in the relation of the partners caused by any partner ceasing to be associated in the carrying on of the business" [UPA § 29].

Dissolution by Act of the Partners

A partnership is dissolved by the following acts of the partners [UPA § 31(1)]:

1. **Termination of a stated time or purpose** A partnership that is formed for a specific time (e.g. 10 years) or purpose (e.g., the completion of a real estate development) dissolves automatically upon the expiration of the time or the accomplishment of the objective.
2. **Withdrawal of a partner** Any partner of a **partnership at will** (i.e., one without a stated time or purpose) may rightfully withdraw and dissolve the partnership at any time.
3. **Expulsion of a partner** If the partnership agreement provides that partners can be expelled upon the happening of certain events, then expulsion of a partner in accordance with the provision dissolves the partnership.
4. **Admission of a partner** The admission of a new partner to an existing partnership dissolves the partnership. The new partnership is comprised of the continuing partners and the newly admitted partners.
5. **Mutual agreement of the partners** All of the partners of an ordinary partnership may at any time mutually agree to dissolve the partnership.

Wrongful Dissolution

A partner has the *power* to withdraw and dissolve the partnership at any time, but he or she may not have the *right* to do so. For example, a partner who withdraws from a partnership before the expiration of the term stated in the partnership agreement does not have the right to do so. The partner's action causes a **wrongful dissolution** of the partnership. The partner is liable for damages caused by the wrongful dissolution of the partnership.

dissolution

"The change in the relation of the partners caused by any partner ceasing to be associated in the carrying on of the business" [UPA § 29].

A judge should not stand in judgment over a person whom he likes or dislikes.

Talmud (A.D. 1st–6th cent.). Rabbinical writings

wrongful dissolution

When a partner withdraws from a partnership without having the right to do so at that time.

Entrepreneur and the Law

CONTINUATION OF A PARTNERSHIP AFTER DISSOLUTION

The surviving or remaining partners are given the right to continue the partnership after dissolution. It is good practice for the partners of a partnership to enter into a *continuation agreement* that expressly sets forth the events that allow for continuation of the partnership, the amount to be paid outgoing partners, and other details.

When a partnership is continued, the old partnership is dissolved and a new partnership is created. The new partnership is composed of the remaining partners and any new partners admitted to the partnership. The creditors of the old partnership become creditors of the new partnership and have equal status with the creditors of the new partnership [UPA § 41].

The dissolution of a partnership does not of itself discharge the liability of outgoing partners for existing partnership debts and obligations. An outgoing partner can be relieved of liability if the outgoing partner, the continuing partners, and the creditor enter into a **novation agreement** that expressly relieves the outgoing partner from liability [UPA § 36].

Dissolution by Operation of Law

A partnership is dissolved by *operation of law* upon the happening of any of the following events:

1. **Death of Any Partner** A partnership dissolves automatically when a partner dies [UPA § 31(4)]. This is because the liability of the other partners is affected by the partner's death. Even

if the partnership agreement allows the remaining partners to continue the partnership, a new partnership is created.

2. **Bankruptcy of Any Partner or the Partnership** The liquidation bankruptcy of either a partner or the partnership dissolves the partnership [UPA § 31(5)]. The bankruptcy of a partner affects that partner's ability to meet his or her obligations and liabilities, including partnership liabilities. The partnership does not dissolve if a partner becomes insolvent.

3. **Illegality** Any event that makes it unlawful for the business of the partnership to be carried on, or for the partners to carry it on, dissolves the partnership [UPA § 31(3)].

Dissolution by Judicial Decree

A partnership may be dissolved by a **judicial decree of dissolution**. To obtain such a decree, an application or petition must be filed by either a partner or an assignee of a partnership interest with the appropriate state court. The circumstances must indicate that dissolution is an equitable solution. Some of the more common reasons that result in the issuance of a judicial decree of dissolution are [UPA § 32(1)]:

1. A partner is adjudicated insane or is shown to be of unsound mind.
2. A partner becomes incapable of performing his or her partnership duties. For example, a partner is involved in an accident or becomes ill.
3. A partner is guilty of improper conduct that either prejudices his or her ability to perform partnership business (e.g., a partner commits fraud on the other partners) or willfully and persistently breaches the partnership agreement (e.g., enters into unauthorized contracts).
4. The partnership can be carried on only at a loss.

judicial decree of dissolution
Order of the court that dissolves a partnership. An application or petition must be filed by a partner or an assignee of a partnership interest with the appropriate state court; the court will issue a judicial decree of dissolution if warranted by the circumstances.

₢ONCEPT SUMMARY   WAYS THAT A PARTNERSHIP CAN BE DISSOLVED

Dissolution by acts of the partners	1. Termination at a stated time or upon the accomplishment of the stated purpose of the partnership. 2. Withdrawal of a partner. 3. Expulsion of a partner. 4. Addition of a partner. 5. Mutual agreement of the partners.
Dissolution by operation of law	1. Death of any partner. 2. Bankruptcy of any partner or the partnership. 3. Illegality.
Dissolution by judicial decree	1. Partner is adjudicated insane. 2. Partner is incapable of performing his or her partnership duties. 3. Partner is guilty of improper conduct (e.g., breach of fiduciary duty) that prejudices his or her ability to perform partnership business or persistently breaches the partnership agreement. 4. The partnership can be carried on only at a loss.

Notice of Dissolution

The dissolution of a partnership terminates the partners' actual authority to enter into contracts or otherwise act on behalf of the partnership [UPA § 33]. Notice of dissolution must be given to all partners. If a partner who has not received notice of dissolution enters into a contract on behalf of the partnership in the course of partnership business, the contract is binding on all of the partners.

Business Brief

If a partnership is dissolved other than by operation of law, notice of the dissolution must be given to certain third parties. Partners may be liable for debts and obligations incurred on behalf of the partnership after the dissolution if the required notice is not given.

Notice of dissolution must be given to certain third parties if the partnership is dissolved other than by operation of law. The degree of notice depends on the relationship of the third person with the partnership [UPA § 35]:

1. Third parties who have actually dealt with the partnership must be given *actual notice* (verbal or written) of dissolution or have acquired knowledge of the dissolution from another source.
2. Third parties who have not dealt with the partnership but have knowledge of it must be given either actual or *constructive notice* of dissolution. Constructive notice consists of publishing a notice of dissolution in a newspaper of general circulation serving the area where the business of the partnership was regularly conducted.
3. Third parties who have not dealt with the partnership and do not have knowledge of it do not have to be given notice.

If proper notice is not given to a required third party after the dissolution of a partnership, and a partner enters into a contract with the third party, liability may arise on the grounds of *apparent authority.*

Notification of the dissolution of a partnership was not given to a creditor in the following case.

Contemporary Business Application _____

CONSEQUENCES OF FAILING TO GIVE NOTICE OF PARTNERSHIP DISSOLUTION

In 1974, Emil Heimos, Jr., and Milton D. Lawrence were engaged in a general partnership known as H&G Equipment Co. (H&G). H&G borrowed money from the Lemay Bank & Trust Co. (Lemay Bank) for partnership purposes. On July 26, 1974, Heimos and his wife executed a personal guaranty whereby they guaranteed payment of any existing or future debts of the partnership to Lemay Bank. At some point in 1975, Heimos and Lawrence dissolved their partnership by mutual agreement. However, neither of them notified Lemay Bank of this fact. On May 17, 1977, Lawrence executed a demand note for $21,800 purportedly on behalf of H&G to Lemay Bank. Three more notes were subsequently executed by Lawrence on behalf of H&G to Lemay Bank, the last one on December 2, 1979. When the last note became due and was not paid, Lemay Bank sued Heimos to recover the debt.

Is Heimos liable to Lemay Bank on the notes? The court of appeals held that Heimos was still liable on the notes because Lemay Bank had not been given notice of the dissolution of the partnership. The court stated that such notice must be given directly or delivered through some channels that the law recognizes as legitimate means of communication. The court found that the evidence did not support a finding that notice of dissolution was brought home to Lemay Bank before 1979. Lemay Bank expressly denied receiving such notice, and Heimos, in his communications with Lemay Bank, never gave any direct notice of dissolution. [*Lemay Bank & Trust Co. v. Lawrence*, 710 S.W.2d 318 (Mo.App. 1986)]

Winding-Up

winding-up

Process of liquidating the partnership's assets and distributing the proceeds to satisfy claims against the partnership.

Unless the partnership is continued, the **winding-up** of the partnership follows its dissolution. The process of winding-up consists of the liquidation (sale) of partnership assets and the distribution of the proceeds to satisfy claims against the partnership.

Usually, the surviving or remaining partners have the right to wind up the partnership. A bankrupt partner cannot participate in the winding-up of a partnership. If a surviving partner performs the winding-up, he or she is entitled to reasonable compensation for his or her services [UPA § 18(f)]. If a partner proves fraud, embezzlement, gross mismanagement, or other breach of fiduciary duty by other partners, that partner can ask the court to wind up the affairs of the partnership. If the court grants the request, a receiver will be appointed to wind up the partnership's affairs.

Distribution of Assets

After the partnership assets have been liquidated and reduced to cash, the proceeds are distributed to satisfy claims against the partnership. The debts are satisfied in the following order: (1) creditors (except partners who are creditors), (2) creditor-partners, (3) capital contributions, and (4) profits [UPA § 40(b)]. The partners can agree to change the priority of **distribution of assets** among themselves. In certain circumstances, they can also choose to take a distribution in kind rather than cash. If the partnership cannot satisfy its creditors' claims, the partners are personally liable for the partnership's debts and obligations [UPA §§ 40(d) and (f)].

distribution of assets
Upon the winding-up of a dissolved partnership, the assets of the partnership are distributed in the following order [UPA § 40(b)]:
1. Creditors (except partners who are creditors)
2. Creditor-partners
3. Capital contributions
4. Profits

Termination

After the proceeds are distributed, the partnership automatically *terminates*. Termination ends the legal existence of the partnership [UPA § 30].

Working the Web

'Lectric Law Library This site is hard to describe. Developed by the University of Nevada and highly acclaimed as a "wonder of the Web," this site is a must visit for legal researchers. Take a tour of this virtual law library, and you will wish all Web sites were this much fun.

Visit at **www.lectlaw.com**

U.S. Business Advisor This site is a one-stop electronic link to government information, services, and transactions for business.

Visit at **www.business.gov**

Idea Café—The Small Business Channel This site provides a fun approach to serious business. Here is a place to find out about financing a business, creating good relationships with customers, and more.

Visit at **www.ideacafe.com**

Cyber Exercises

1. Visit the Business Law Lounge of the 'Lectric Law Library. Find a document called *"Limited Liability Companies: A Summary."*

2. Visit the Reference Room of the Lectric Law Library. Find and read an article called *"Limited Liability Partnerships and Limited Liability Limited Partnerships."* Who is the author?

3. Using the U.S. Small Business Advisor, find out how to address and package your mail.

e-biz

Cases and Exercises

Critical Legal Thinking Cases

33.1. In early 1986, Thomas Smithson, a housebuilder and small-scale property developer, decided that a certain tract of undeveloped land in Franklin, Tennessee, would be extremely attractive for development into a subdivision. Smithson contacted the owner of the property, Monsanto Chemical Company (Monsanto), and was told that the company would sell the property at the "right price."

Smithson did not have the funds with which to embark

unassisted in the endeavor, so he contacted Frank White, a co-owner of the Andrews Realty Company, and two agents of the firm, Dennis Devrow and Temple Ennis. Smithson showed them a sketch map with the proposed layout of the lots, roads, and so forth. Smithson testified that they all orally agreed to develop the property together, and in lieu of a financial investment, Smithson would oversee the engineering of the property. Subsequently, H. R. Morgan was brought into the deal to provide additional financing.

Smithson later discovered that White had contacted Monsanto directly. When challenged about this, White assured Smithson that he was still "part of the deal" but refused to put the agreement in writing. White, Devrow, Ennis, and Morgan purchased the property from Monsanto. They then sold it to H.A.H. Associates, a corporation, for a $184,000 profit. When they refused to pay Smithson, he sued to recover an equal share of the profits. Is a partnership formed between Smithson and the defendants? [*Smithson v. White*, 1988 W.I. 42645 (Tenn.App. 1988)]

33.2. Richard Filip owned Trans Texas Properties (Trans Texas). Tracy Peoples was an employee of the company. To obtain credit to advertise in the *Austin American-Statesman* newspaper, which was owned by Cox Enterprises, Inc. (Cox), Peoples completed a credit application that listed Jack Elliot as a partner in Trans Texas. Evidence showed that Elliot did not own an interest in Trans Texas and did not consent to or authorize Peoples to make this representation to Cox. Cox made no effort to verify the accuracy of the representation and extended credit to Trans Texas. When Trans Texas defaulted on payments owed Cox, Cox sued both Filip and Elliot to recover the debt. Is Elliot liable? [*Cox Enterprises, Inc. v. Filip and Elliot*, 538 S.W.2d 836 (Tex.App. 1976)]

33.3. Virgil Welch leased the feed concession at the Ruidoso, New Mexico, race track. Sam Dunn guaranteed the $65,000 note securing the lease. While Welch operated the business, Dunn had the sole right to maintain records, inventory controls, and accounts receivable. They opened a joint checking account in the name of "Ruidoso Downs Feed Concession."

Welch entered into a contract with Anderson Hay and Grain Co. (Anderson) to purchase feed for the concession. Anderson extended credit to the business on the strength of Dunn's financial responsibility. Someone stated in the presence of an Anderson representative and Dunn that Welch and Dunn were partners; Dunn did not state otherwise. When payments to Anderson became past due, it would call Dunn on the telephone and Dunn would send a check. When the account became substantially overdue, Anderson sued Welch and Dunn to recover the debt. Dunn answered, claiming that he was not a partner in Ruidoso Downs Feed Concession. Is Dunn liable on the debt owed Anderson? [*Anderson Hay and Grain Co. v. Dunn*, 467 P.2d 5 (N.M. 1970)]

33.4. In 1976, Leonard Sumter, Sr., entered into a partnership agreement with his son, Michael T. Sumter, to conduct a plumbing business in Shreveport, Louisiana, under the name "Sumter Plumbing Company." On June 18, 1976, the father, on behalf of the partnership, executed a credit application with Thermal Supply of Louisiana, Inc. (Thermal), for an open account to purchase supplies on credit. From that date until the spring of 1978, the Sumters purchased plumbing supplies from Thermal on credit and paid their bills without fail. Both partners and one employee signed for supplies at Thermal. In May 1980, the partnership was dissolved, and all outstanding debts to Thermal were paid in full. The Sumters did not, however, notify Thermal that the partnership had been dissolved.

A year later, the son decided to reenter the plumbing business. He used the name previously used by the former partnership, listed the same post office address for billing purposes, and hired the employee of the former partnership who signed for supplies at Thermal. The father decided not to become involved in this venture. The son began purchasing supplies on credit from Thermal on the open credit account of the former partnership. Thermal was not informed that he was operating a new business. When the son defaulted on payments to Thermal, it sued the original partnership to recover the debt. Is the father liable for these debts? [*Thermal Supply of Louisiana, Inc. v. Sumter*, 452 So.2d 312 (La.App. 1984)]

33.5. In 1970, R. D. Summerville and Howard Dunn formed a partnership to engage in drilling operations. The partnership agreement did not contain a provision regarding how partnership profits were to be divided. During the course of the partnership, Dunn took $39,986 more in partnership draws against the firm's profits than Summerville. When an action was brought for dissolution of the partnership and an accounting, Summerville sought a money judgment to recover the difference in partnership draws. Who wins? [*Dunn v. Summerville*, 669 S.W. 2d 319 (Tex. 1984)]

33.6. In 1976, a partnership was formed to own and manage a medical office building. The partnership agreement did not provide that the general partners would be paid compensation for services provided in the furtherance of partnership business. One partner, Sidney Newman, devoted substantial time to managing the building, including leasing space, collecting rents, designing and drawing plans for medical suites as they were leased, dealing with tenants' complaints and requests, and performing other management duties. Over the objection of another partner, Penny Broffman, the partnership paid Newman $100,000 for his services during a one-year period.

Broffman sued to recover this compensation. Who wins? [*Broffman v. Newman*, 213 Cal.App.3d 252, 261 Cal.Rptr. 532 (Cal.App. 1989)]

33.7. Melvin K. Grosberg and Sheldon Goldman were partners in the development, construction, and operation of Chatham Fox Hills Shopping Center. Grosberg supplied the necessary cash resources and Goldman provided management services. Goldman's responsibilities included supervising the construction of the shopping center, soliciting tenants and negotiating commercial leases, and receiving all incoming checks (representing rent and other payments) and depositing them into a partnership account at a bank. Grosberg authorized Goldman to indorse and deposit checks and withdraw funds from the partnership account. Subsequently, Goldman diverted funds from the partnership account for his own personal use. When Grosberg discovered this fact, he sued the bank seeking to recover the diverted funds. Who wins? [*Grosberg v. Michigan National Bank—Oakland, N.A.*, 362 N.W.2d 715 (Mich. 1984)]

33.8. Edgar and Selwyn Husted, attorneys, formed Husted and Husted, a law partnership. Herman McCloud, who was the executor of his mother's estate, hired them as attorneys for the estate. When taxes were due on the estate, Edgar told McCloud to make a check for $18,000 payable to the Husted and Husted trust account and that he would pay the Internal Revenue Service from this account. There was no Husted and Husted trust account. Instead, Edgar deposited the check into his own personal account and converted the funds to his own personal use. When Edgar's misconduct was uncovered, McCloud sued the law firm for conversion of estate funds. Is the partnership liable for Edgar's actions? [*Husted v. McCloud*, 436 N.E.2d 341 (Ind.App. 1982)]

33.9. Thomas McGrath was a partner in the law firm of Torbenson, Thatcher, McGrath, Treadwell & Schoonmaker.

At approximately 4:30 P.M. on February 11, 1980, McGrath went to a restaurant-cocktail establishment in Kirkland, Washington. From that time until about 11:00 P.M. he imbibed a considerable amount of alcohol while socializing and discussing personal and firm-related business. After 11 o'clock, McGrath did not discuss firm business but continued to socialize and drink until approximately 1:45 A.M., when he and Frederick Hayes, another bar patron, exchanged words. Shortly thereafter, the two encountered each other outside and after another exchange, McGrath shot Hayes. Hayes sued McGrath and the law firm for damages. Who is liable? [*Hayes v. Torbenson, Thatcher, McGrath, Treadwell & Schoonmaker*, 749 P.2d 178 (Wash.App. 1988)]

33.10. On December 1, 1976, Drs. Rudolph J. Bourgeois, Armand A. Jacques, Raymond A. Schwarz, Felix G. Rabito, Frank J. Rabito, Anthony F. Rabito, and Frank P. Incaprera entered into a partnership to conduct business as the Medical Center of East New Orleans (Medical Center). The partnership agreement designated Frank J. Rabito as the managing partner with the authority to sign leases and other contracts, and to otherwise manage the partnership. The partnership agreement contained a right of first refusal that required any partner who wished to sell his interest in the partnership to first offer it for sale to the other partners.

On May 24, 1985, the managing partner sent a letter to the other partners informing them of his desire to sell his partnership interest and offering them the right of first refusal. In the letter, he stated that he had received an offer from Hospital Properties, Inc. (Hospital Properties), to purchase his partnership interest, including his right under the partnership agreement to manage the partnership. The $2 million offer from Hospital Properties included a premium for the management right. What rights can Hospital Properties acquire from Rabito? [*Bourgeois v. Medical Center of East New Orleans*, 482 So.2d 795 (La.App. 1986)]

ETHICS CASES

33.11. Harriet Hankin, Samuel Hankin, Moe Henry Hankin, Perch P. Hankin, and Pauline Shanken, and their spouses, for many years operated a family partnership composed of vast real estate holdings. Some of the properties included restaurants, industrial buildings, shopping centers, golf courses, a motel chain, and hundreds of acres of developable ground, estimated to be worth $72 million in 1977. In that year, because of family disagreement and discontent, the Hankin family agreed to dissolve the partnership. When they could not agree on how to liquidate the partnership assets, in August 1977, Harriet and Samuel (collectively called Harriet) initiated this equity action.

Based on assurances from Moe and Perch that they would sell the partnership assets as quickly as possible and at the highest possible price, the court appointed them as liquidators of the partnership during the winding-up period. Based on similar assurances, the court again appointed them liquidators for the partnership in 1979. But by 1981, only enough property had been sold to retire the debt of the partnership. Evidence showed that Moe and Perch had not aggressively marketed the remaining properties and that Moe wished to purchase some of the properties for himself at a substantial discount from their estimated value. Six years and three appeals to the superior court later, Harriet brought this action seeking the appointment of a receiver to liquidate the remaining partnership assets.

Did the winding-up partners breach their fiduciary duties? Should the court appoint a receiver to liquidate the remaining partnership assets? Did Moe Henry Hankin act ethically in this case? [*Hankin v. Hankin*, 493 A.2d 675 (Pa. 1985)]

33.12. John Gilroy, an established commercial photographer in Kalamazoo, Michigan, had a small contractual clientele of schools for which he provided student portrait photographs. In 1974, Robert Conway joined Gilroy's established business and they formed a partnership called "Skylight Studios." Both partners solicited schools with success, and gross sales, which were $40,000 in 1974, increased every year and amounted to over $200,000 in 1980.

On June 1, 1981, Conway notified Gilroy that the partnership was dissolved. Gilroy discovered that Conway had closed up the partnership's place of business and opened up his own business, had purchased equipment and supplies in preparation for opening his own business and charged them to the partnership, had taken with him the partnership's employees and most of its equipment, had personally taken over business of some customers by telling them the partnership was being dissolved, and withdrew partnership funds for personal use. Gilroy sued Conway for an accounting, alleging that Conway had converted partnership assets. Did Conway act ethically in this case? Who wins? [*Gilroy v. Conway*, 391 N.W.2d 419 (Mich.App. 1986)]

CRITICAL LEGAL THINKING WRITING ASSIGNMENT

Read Case A.33 in the Case Appendix [*Catalina Mortgage Company, Inc. v. Monier*]. This case is excerpted from the Supreme Court of Arizona's opinion. Review and brief the case. In your brief, be sure to answer the following questions.

1. Who was the plaintiff? Who were the defendants?

2. What business arrangement were the defendants engaged in? How did this lead to the lawsuit?

3. What is joint and several liability?

4. Did the court impose joint and several liability in this case?

Limited Partnerships and Limited Liability Partnerships

There are a great many of us who will adhere to that ancient principle that we prefer to be governed by the power of laws, and not by the power of men.

WOODROW WILSON *Speech,*
September 25, 1912

Chapter Objectives

After studying this chapter, you should be able to

1. Define *limited partnership*.
2. Distinguish between limited and general partners.
3. Describe the process for forming a limited partnership.
4. Identify when a limited partnership is defectively formed.
5. Define *foreign limited partnership*.
6. Define *master limited partnership*.
7. Identify and describe the liability of general and limited partners.
8. Define *limited liability partnership (LLP)*.
9. Describe the limited liability of partners of an LLP.
10. Describe the process of dissolution and winding-up of limited partnerships.

Chapter Contents

limited partnership

A type of partnership that has two types of partners: (1) general partners and (2) limited partners.

General partnerships are not suitable for all partnership arrangements. Limited partnerships offer a compromise. **Limited partnerships** have two types of partners: (1) *general partners*, who invest capital, manage the business, and are personally liable for partnership debts, and (2) *limited partners*, who invest capital but do not participate in management and are not personally liable for partnership debts beyond their capital contribution. Limited partnerships are used for such business ventures as investing in real estate, drilling oil and gas wells, investing in movie productions, and the like.

limited liability partnership (LLP)

A type of partnership that has no general partner. All partners have limited liability.

Limited liability partnerships (LLPs) are a new form of partnership entity that provides limited liability to all of its partners. There is no general partner in an LLP. LLPs are used mainly by professionals such as accountants and lawyers.

This chapter discusses the formation, operation, and dissolution of limited partnerships and limited liability partnerships.

𝒯HE REVISED UNIFORM LIMITED PARTNERSHIP ACT (RULPA)

Limited partnerships are statutory creations that have been used since the Middle Ages. Today, all states have enacted statutes that provide for the creation of limited partnerships. In most states, these partnerships are called **limited partnerships** or **special partnerships**. Louisiana calls them *partnerships in commendam*.

limited partnership

A special form of partnership that has both limited and general partners.

In 1916 the National Conference of Commissioners on Uniform State Laws, a group composed of lawyers, judges, and legal scholars, promulgated the **Uniform Limited Partnership Act (ULPA)**. The ULPA contained a uniform set of provisions for the formation, operation, and dissolution of limited partnerships. Most states originally enacted this law.

Revised Uniform Limited Partnership Act (RULPA)

A 1976 revision of the ULPA that provides a more modern comprehensive law for the formation, operation, and dissolution of limited partnerships.

In 1976, the National Conference on Uniform State Laws promulgated the **Revised Uniform Limited Partnership Act (RULPA)**, which provides a more modern comprehensive law for the formation, operation, and dissolution of limited partnerships. A majority of states have now adopted the RULPA, which supersedes the ULPA in the states that have adopted it. The RULPA provides the basic foundation for the discussion of limited partnership law in the following materials.

Many businesses, such as these windmills near Palm Springs, California, are operated as limited partnerships.

DEFINITION OF A LIMITED PARTNERSHIP

Limited partnerships have two types of partners: (1) **general partners**, who invest capital, manage the business, and are personally liable for partnership debts, and (2) **limited partners**, who invest capital but do not participate in management and are not personally liable for partnership debts beyond their capital contribution (see Exhibit 34.1).

A limited partnership must have at least one general partner and one limited partner [RULPA § 101(7)]. There are no restrictions on the number of general or limited partners allowed in a limited partnership. Any person may be a general or limited partner. This includes natural persons, partnerships, limited partnerships, trusts, estates, associations, and corporations [RULPA § 101(11)]. A person may be both a general and limited partner in the same limited partnership [RULPA § 404].

general partners

Partners in a limited partnership who invest capital, manage the business, and are personally liable for partnership debts.

limited partners

Partners in a limited partnership who invest capital but do not participate in management and are not personally liable for partnership debts beyond their capital contributions.

EXHIBIT 34.1   *Limited Partnership*

A Corporation as the Sole General Partner

The RULPA permits a corporation to be the sole *general partner* of a limited partnership [RULPA § 101(11)]. Where this is permissible, it affects the liability of the limited partnership. This is because the limited partners are liable only to the extent of their capital contributions, and the corporation acting as general partner is liable only to the extent of its assets. The following case demonstrates this concept.

Business Brief

A corporation may be the sole general partner of a limited partnership. Shareholders of corporations are liable only up to their capital contributions.

Frigidaire Sales Corp. v. Union Properties, Inc.
562 P.2d 344 (1977)
Supreme Court of Washington

CASE 34.1

FACTS

Commercial Investors (Commercial) is a limited partnership that was properly formed under the laws of the state of Washington. The limited partners were Leonard Mannon and Raleigh Baxter. There was one general partner, Union Properties, Inc. (Union Properties), a corporation whose shares were owned by Mannon and Baxter. They were also the officers and directors of Union Properties. Thus, through Union Properties, Mannon and Baxter exercised day-to-day control and management of Commercial. Commercial entered into a contract to purchase certain goods on credit from the Frigidaire Sales Corporation (Frigidaire). When Commercial defaulted on the loan, Frigidaire sued Union Properties, Mannon, and Baxter to recover on the debt. The trial court entered judgment for Frigidaire against the general partner Union Properties, but held that Mannon and Baxter were not liable because they were limited partners. Frigidaire appealed.

ISSUE

Are Mannon and Baxter liable on the debt owed by Commercial to Frigidaire?

IN THE LANGUAGE OF THE COURT

Hamilton, Associate Justice We first note that petitioner Frigidaire does not contend that respondents Mannon and Baxter acted improperly by setting up the limited partnership with a corporation as the sole general partner. Limited partnerships are a statutory form of business organization, and parties creating a limited partnership must follow the statutory requirements. In Washington, parties may form a limited partnership with a corporation as the sole general partner. Petitioner's sole contention is that respondents should incur general liability for the limited partnership's obligations because they exercised the day-to-day control and management of Commercial. Respondents, on the other hand, argue that Commercial was controlled by Union Properties, a separate legal entity, and not by respondents in their individual capacities.

There can be no doubt that respondents, in fact, controlled the corporation. However, they did so only in their capacities as agents for their principal, the corporate general partner. Although the corporation was a separate entity, it could act only through its board of directors, officers, and agents. Frigidaire entered into the contract with Commercial. Mannon and Baxter signed the contract in their capacities as president and secretary-treasurer of Union Properties, the general partner of Commercial. In the eyes of the law, it was Union Properties, as a separate corporate entity, that entered into the contract with Frigidaire and controlled the limited partnership.

If Frigidaire had not wished to rely on the solvency of Union Properties as the only general partner, it could have insisted that respondents personally guarantee contractual performance. Because Frigidaire entered into the contract knowing that Union Properties was the only party with general liability, and because in the eyes of the law it was Union Properties, a separate entity, that controlled the limited partnership, there is no reason for us to find that respondents incurred general liability for their acts done as officers of the corporate general partner.

DECISION AND REMEDY

The Supreme Court of Washington held that Mannon and Baxter, limited partners of Commercial, are not personally liable for the debt to Frigidaire.

Case Questions

Critical Legal Thinking Should a corporation be permitted to be the sole general partner of a limited partnership? Why or why not?

Ethics Did Frigidaire act ethically in suing Mannon and Baxter?

Business Application Why do you think Mannon and Baxter formed Union Properties, Inc., as the sole general partner of their limited partnership?

ℱORMATION OF LIMITED PARTNERSHIPS

The creation of a limited partnership is formal and requires public disclosure. The entity must comply with the statutory requirements of the RULPA or other state statute.

Certificate of Limited Partnership

certificate of limited partnership
A document that two or more persons must execute and sign that makes the limited partnership legal and binding.

Under the RULPA, two or more persons must execute and sign a **certificate of limited partnership** [RULPA §§ 201 and 206]. The certificate must contain the following information [RULPA § 201(a)]:

1. Name of the limited partnership
2. General character of the business

3. Address of the principal place of business, and the name and address of the agent to receive service of legal process
4. Name and business address of each general and limited partner
5. The latest date upon which the limited partnership is to dissolve
6. Amount of cash, property, or services (and description of property or services) contributed by each partner and any contributions of cash, property, or services promised to be made in the future
7. Any other matters the general partners determine to include

The certificate of limited partnership must be filed with the secretary of state of the appropriate state and, if required by state law, with the county recorder in the county or counties in which the limited partnership carries on business. The limited partnership is formed when the certificate of limited partnership is filed [RULPA § 210(b)].

Amendments to the Certificate of Limited Partnership A limited partnership must keep its certificate of limited partnership current by filing necessary **certificates of amendment** at the same offices where the certificate of limited partnership is filed [RULPA § 202(a)]. Such amendments are filed to apprise creditors and others of current information regarding the limited partnership and its partners. The certificate of amendment must be filed within 30 days of the occurrence of the following events:

1. A change in a partner's capital contribution
2. The admission of a new partner
3. The withdrawal of a partner
4. The continuation of the business after a judicial decision dissolving the limited partnership after the withdrawal of the last general partner

Exhibit 34.2 contains a sample certificate of limited partnership.

Capital Contributions

Under the RULPA, the capital contribution of general and limited partners may be in cash, property, services rendered, or a promissory note or other obligation to contribute cash or property or to perform services [RULPA § 501]. A partner or creditor of the limited partnership may bring a lawsuit to enforce a partner's promise to make a contribution [RULPA § 502(a)].

Name of the Limited Partnership

The firm name of a limited partnership may not include the surname of a limited partner unless (1) it is also the surname of a general partner or (2) the business was carried on under that name before the admission of the limited partner [RULPA § 102(2)]. A limited partner who knowingly permits his or her name to be used in violation of this provision becomes liable as a general partner to any creditors who extend credit to the partnership without actual knowledge of his or her true status [RULPA § 303(d)].

Other restrictions on the name of a limited partnership are that (1) the name cannot be the same as or deceptively similar to the names of corporations or other limited partnerships, (2) states can designate words that cannot be used in limited partnership names, and (3) the name must contain without abbreviation the words *limited partnership* [RULPA § 102].

Limited Partnership Agreements

Although not required by law, the partners of a limited partnership often draft and execute a **limited partnership agreement** (also called the **articles of limited partnership**) that sets forth the rights and duties of the general and limited partners; the terms and conditions regarding the operation, termination, and dissolution of the partnership; and so on. Where there is no such agreement, the certificate of limited partnership serves as the articles of limited partnership.

Exhibit 34.3 contains a sample limited partnership agreement.

---

certificate of amendment
A document that keeps the certificate of limited partnership current.

Business Brief
It is good practice to have a written limited partnership agreement that sets forth in detail the rights and duties of both general and limited partners. This will reduce later disputes and lawsuits.

limited partnership agreement
A document that sets forth the rights and duties of the general and limited partners; the terms and conditions regarding the operation, termination, and dissolution of the partnership; and so on.

*E*XHIBIT 34.2 *Copy of a Sample Certificate of Limited Partnership*

State of California
March Fong Eu
Secretary of State

CERTIFICATE OF LIMITED PARTNERSHIP

1. NAME OF LIMITED PARTNERSHIP

The Wilshire Investment Company, a California Limited Partnership

2. STREET ADDRESS OF PRINCIPAL EXECUTIVE OFFICE	CITY AND STATE	ZIP CODE
4000 Wilshire Boulevard	Los Angeles, California	90010

3. STREET ADDRESS OF CALIFORNIA OFFICE IF EXECUTIVE OFFICE IS IN ANOTHER STATE	CITY	ZIP CODE
	CA	

4. COMPLETE IF LIMITED PARTNERSHIP WAS FORMED PRIOR TO JULY 1, 1984 AND IS IN EXISTENCE ON DATE THIS CERTIFICATE IS EXECUTED.

THE ORIGINAL LIMITED PARTNERSHIP CERTIFICATE WAS RECORDED ON _____ 19_____ WITH THE

RECORDER OF _____ COUNTY. FILE OR RECORDATION NUMBER _____

5. NAMES AND ADDRESSES OF ALL GENERAL PARTNERS: (CONTINUE ON SECOND PAGE, IF NECESSARY)

A. NAME:	John Weston	C. NAME:	Susan Martinez
ADDRESS:	500 Ocean Boulevard	ADDRESS:	800 Palm Drive
CITY: Los Angeles STATE: CA ZIP CODE: 90405		CITY: Miami STATE: FL ZIP CODE: 33125	
B. NAME:	Wai Chan	D. NAME:	
ADDRESS:	700 Apple Road	ADDRESS:	
CITY: Seattle STATE: WA ZIP CODE: 98109		CITY: STATE: ZIP CODE:	

6. NAME AND ADDRESS OF AGENT FOR SERVICE OF PROCESS:

NAME: Frederick Friendly, Esq.

ADDRESS: 2500 Century Park East   CITY: Los Angeles   STATE: CA   ZIP CODE: 90067

7. ANY OTHER MATTERS TO BE INCLUDED IN THIS CERTIFICATE MAY BE NOTED ON SEPARATE PAGES AND BY REFERENCE HEREIN ARE A PART OF THIS CERTIFICATE.	8. INDICATE THE **NUMBER** OF GENERAL PARTNERS SIGNATURES REQUIRED FOR FILING CERTIFICATES OF AMENDMENT, DISSOLUTION, CONTINUATION AND CANCELLATION.
NUMBER OF PAGES ATTACHED: 3	NUMBER OF GENERAL PARTNER(S) SIGNATURE(S) IS/ARE: 3
	(PLEASE INDICATE NUMBER ONLY)

9. IT IS HEREBY DECLARED THAT I AM (WE ARE) THE PERSON(S) WHO EXECUTED THIS CERTIFICATE OF LIMITED PARTNERSHIP WHICH EXECUTION IS MY (OUR) ACT AND DEED. (SEE INSTRUCTIONS)

THIS SPACE FOR FILING OFFICER USE

SIGNATURE *John Weston*	SIGNATURE *Susan Martinez*
General Partner 1/2/00	General Partner 1/2/00
POSITION OR TITLE DATE	POSITION OR TITLE DATE
SIGNATURE *Wai Chan*	SIGNATURE
General Partner 1/2/00	
POSITION OR TITLE DATE	POSITION OR TITLE DATE

10. RETURN ACKNOWLEDGEMENT TO:

NAME   Frederick Friendly, Esq.
ADDRESS 2500 Century Park East
CITY   Los Angeles
STATE   California
ZIP CODE 90067

ƐXHIBIT 34.3 *Sample Limited Partnership Agreement*

LIMITED PARTNERSHIP AGREEMENT

1. **Introduction.** This agreement of Limited Partnership dated January 2, 2000 by and between John Weston, Wai Chan, and Susan Martinez (General Partners) and Shari Berkowitz, Raymond Wong, and Harold Johnson (Limited Partners).

The General Partners and Limited Partners agree to form a Limited Partnership (Partnership) pursuant to the provisions of the California Revised Limited Partnership Act on the terms and conditions hereinafter set forth.

2. **Name of Partnership.** The name of the Partnership shall be "The Wilshire Investment Company, a California Limited Partnership." The business of the Partnership shall be conducted in that name.

3. **Principal Place of Business.** The principal office of the Partnership shall be at 4000 Wilshire Boulevard, Los Angeles, California 90010 or at such other place within California as may be determined from time to time by the General Partners.

4. **Purpose of the Partnership.** The Partnership shall be engaged in the business of buying, selling, and developing commercial and industrial real estate and such activities as are related or incidental thereto.

5. **Agent for Service of Process.** The name of the agent for service of process is Frederick Friendly, whose address is 2500 Century Park East, Suite 600, Los Angeles, California 90067.

6. **Term of Partnership.** The term of the Partnership shall commence on the date on which the Partnership's Certificate of Limited Partnership is filed by the Secretary of State of California and shall continue until it terminates in accordance with the provisions of this Agreement.

7. **Certificate of Limited Partnership.** The General Partners shall immediately execute a Certificate of Limited Partnership and cause that Certificate to be filed in the office of the secretary of state of California. The General Partners shall also record a certified copy of the Certificate in the office of the county recorder of every county in which the Partnership owns real property.

8. **Members of the Partnership.**

(a) The names and addresses of each original General Partner is as follows:

Name	Address
John Weston	500 Ocean Boulevard, Los Angeles, California
Wai Chan	700 Apple Road, Seattle, Washington
Susan Martinez	800 Palm Drive, Miami, Florida

(b) The names and addresses of each original Limited Partner is as follows:

Name	Address
Shari Berkowitz	700 Apple Street, New York, New York
Raymond Wong	900 Flower Avenue, San Francisco, California
Harold Johnson	300 Oil Field Road, Houston, Texas

9. **General Partners' Capital Contributions.** The General Partners shall make the following contributions to the Partnership's capital no later than January 2, 2000.

Cash

John Weston	$60,000

Property

Wai Chan	$30,000
Susan Martinez	$30,000

No interest will be paid on any balances in the General Partners' capital accounts.

10. **Limited Partners' Capital Contributions.** The Limited Partners shall make the following contributions to the Partnership's capital no later than January 2, 2000.

Cash

Shari Berkowitz	$100,000
Raymond Wong	$ 50,000
Harold Johnson	$ 50,000

No interest will be paid on any balances in the Limited Partners' capital accounts.

11. **Additional Capital Contributions from Limited Partners.** The General Partners may call for additional cash contributions to the Partnership's capital from the Limited Partners. The aggregate of all additional capital contributions made by the Limited Partners pursuant to this Paragraph shall not exceed 100 percent of the original capital contributions made by them pursuant to Paragraph 10 of this Agreement. Notice of the call shall be made by registered mail, return receipt requested, and shall be deemed made when posted. The Limited Partners's additional capital contribution must be made no later than 60 days following the call.

12. **Division of Profits.** Each Partner shall receive the following share of the net profits of the Partnership:

Partner	Percent
General Partners:	
John Weston	30%
Wai Chan	15%
Susan Martinez	15%
Limited Partners:	
Shari Berkowitz	20%
Raymond Wong	10%
Harold Johnson	10%

(continued)

Exhibit **34.3**   *Continued*

13.   Sharing of Losses.   Each Partner shall bear a share of the losses of the Partnership equal to the share of the profits to which he is entitled. The share of the losses of each Partner shall be charged against his contribution to the capital of the Partnership.

The Limited Partners will not be liable for any Partnership debts or losses beyond the amounts to be contributed to them pursuant to Paragraphs 10 and 11 of this Agreement.

After giving effect to the share of losses chargeable against the capital contributions of Limited Partners, the remaining Partnership losses shall be borne by the General Partners in the same proportions in which, between themselves, they are to share profits.

14.   Management of Partnership.   The General Partners shall have the sole and exclusive control of the Limited Partnership.

The General Partners shall have an equal voice in the management of the Partnership, and each shall devote his or her full time to the conduct of the Partnership's business.

The General Partners shall have the power and authority to take such action from time to time as they may deem to be necessary, appropriate, or convenient in connection with the management and conduct of the business and affairs of the Partnership, including, without limitation, the power to

(a)   Acquire property, including real and personal property.
(b)   Dispose of Partnership property.
(c)   Borrow or lend money.
(d)   Make, deliver, or accept commercial paper.
(e)   Pledge, mortgage, encumber, or grant a security interest in the Partnership properties as security for repayment of loans.
(f)   Take any and all other action permitted by law that is customary in or reasonably related to the conduct of the Partnership business or affairs.

15.   Limited Partners Not to Manage Business.   The Limited Partners will not manage the business of the Partnership or assist in its management.

16.   Partnership Books and Records.   The Partnership books of account will be kept in accordance with generally accepted accounting principles. The books and supporting records will be maintained at the Partnership's principal office and will be examined by the Partnership's certified public accountants at least annually. The Partnership's fiscal year shall start on January 1 and close on December 31.

17.   General Partner's Salaries.   The General Partners shall each receive a salary of $60,000 per annum, payable in monthly installments, as compensation for managing the Partnership. No increases shall be made in the General Partners' salaries without the written consent of a majority of the Limited Partners.

18.   Admission of New General Partners.   No new General Partners will be admitted to the Partnership without the written consent of all the General Partners and Limited Partners as to both his or her admission and the terms on which the new General Partner is admitted.

19.   Admission of New Limited Partners.   No new Limited Partners will be admitted to the Partnership without the written consent of all the General Partners and Limited Partners as to both his or her admission and the terms on which the new Limited Partner is admitted.

20.   No Sale or Assignment of, or Granting Lien on Partnership Interest by General Partner.   Without the written consent of all the General Partners and Limited Partners, no General Partner shall assign, mortgage, or give a security interest in his or her Partnership interest.

21.   Right of Limited Partner to Assign Partnership Interest or Substitute New Limited Partner.   Upon 30 days' written notice to the General Partners, a Limited Partner can assign his or her interest in the Partnership's profits to a third party. Such assignment shall not constitute a substitution of the third party as a new Limited Partner in the place of the assignor. A Limited Partner may substitute a third party in his or her place as a new Limited Partner only with the consent in writing of all the General Partners and Limited Partners.

22.   Effect of Death, Disability, or Retirement of a General Partner.   The death, retirement, or permanent disability of a General Partner (the withdrawing General Partner) that makes it impossible for him or her to carry out his or her duties under this Agreement shall terminate the Partnership.

If a General Partner survives, the remaining General Partners may continue the Partnership business and may purchase the interest of the withdrawing General Partner in the assets and goodwill of the Partnership. The remaining General Partners have the option, exercisable by them at any time within 30 days after the date on which the withdrawing General Partner ceases to be a General Partner, to purchase the withdrawing General Partner's interest by paying to the person legally entitled thereto the value of that interest as shown on the last regular accounting of the Partnership preceding the date on which the General Partner ceased to be a General Partner, together with the full unwithdrawn portion of the withdrawing General Partner's distributive share of any net profits earned by the Partnership between the date of that accounting and the date on which the withdrawing General Partner ceased to be a General Partner of the Partnership.

23.   Duties of Remaining Purchasing General Partners.   Upon the purchase of a withdrawing General Partner's interest, the remaining General Partners shall assume all obligations of the Partnership and shall hold the withdrawing General Partner, the personal representative and estate of the withdrawing General Partner, and the property of the withdrawing General Partner free and harmless from all liability for those obligations.

The remaining General Partners shall immediately amend the Certificate of Limited Partnership and shall file such amendment with the office of the Secretary of State, and shall cause to be prepared, filed, served, and published all other notices required by law to protect the withdrawing General Partner or the personal representative and estate of the withdrawing General Partner from all liability for the future obligations of the Partnership business.

24.   Effect of Death of Limited Partner or Substitution of Limited Partner.   The death of a Limited Partner or the substitution of a new Limited Partner for a Limited Partner shall not affect the continuity of the Partnership of the conduct of its business.

25.   Voluntary Dissolution.   A General Partner may terminate the Partnership at any time upon 120 days written notice to each Limited Partner. Upon termination of the Partnership, it shall be liquidated in accordance with Paragraph 26 of this Agreement.

26.   Liquidation of Partnership.   If the Partnership is liquidated, its assets, including its goodwill and name, shall be sold in the manner designed to produce the greatest return. The proceeds of the liquidation shall be distributed in the following order:

(a)   To creditors of the Partnership including Partners who are creditors to the extent permitted by law, in satisfaction of liabilities of the Partnership
(b)   To Partners in payment of the balances in their income accounts
(c)   To Partners in payment of the balances in their capital accounts
(d)   To Partners in payment of the remainder of the proceeds

(continued)

*E*XHIBIT 34.3   *Continued*

27. **Certificate of Dissolution.** Upon dissolution of the Partnership, the General Partners shall execute and file in the office of the secretary of state a Certificate of Dissolution. If dissolution occurs after a sole General Partner ceases to be a General Partner, the Limited Partners conducting the winding up of the Partnership's affairs shall file the Certificate of Dissolution.

28. **Entire Agreement.** This Agreement contains the entire understanding among the Partners and supersedes any prior written or oral agreements between them respecting the subject matter contained herein. There are no representations, agreements, arrangements, or understandings, oral or written, between and among the Partners relating to the subject matter of this Agreement that are not fully expressed herein.

29. **Controlling Law.** This Agreement shall be interpreted under the law of the State of California. Further, each Partner consents to the jurisdiction of the courts of the State of California.

30. **Service of Notices.** Service of notice upon the Partnership will be made by registered or certified mail, return receipt requested, addressed to the Partnership's principal place of business.
    Service of notice upon any or all Partners will be made by registered or certified mail, return receipt requested, addressed to the addresses given in this Agreement or such other addresses as a Partner may from time to time give to the Partnership.

31. **Severability.** If any provisions of this Agreement shall be declared by a court of competent jurisdiction to be invalid, void, or unenforceable, the remaining provisions shall continue in full force and effect.

32. **Arbitration of Disputes.** Any controversy concerning this Agreement will be settled by arbitration according to the rules of the American Arbitration Association, and judgment upon the award may be entered and enforced in any court.

_____   _____
General Partner   Limited Partner

_____   _____
General Partner   Limited Partner

Defective Formation

Defective formation occurs when (1) a certificate of limited partnership is not properly filed, (2) there are defects in a certificate that is filed, or (3) some other statutory requirement for the creation of a limited partnership is not met. However, the limited partnership is deemed to have been properly formed if there has been "substantial compliance in good faith" with the statutory requirements [RULPA § 201(b)].

Note that a defect in compliance does not affect the rights between the partners. Even if the court finds that a limited partnership has not been created, the rights and duties of the partners are determined from the defective certificate of limited partnership and the limited partnership agreement.

Persons Erroneously Believing Themselves to Be Limited Partners   If there is a substantial defect in the creation of a limited partnership, persons who thought they were limited partners can find themselves liable as general partners. Such persons who erroneously but in good faith believe they have become limited partners can escape liability as general partners by either (1) causing the appropriate certificate of limited partnership (or certificate of amendment) to be filed or (2) withdrawing from any future equity participation in the enterprise and causing a certificate showing this withdrawal to be filed. Nevertheless, the limited partner remains liable to any third party who transacts business with the enterprise before either certificate is filed if the third person believed in good faith that the partner was a general partner at the time of the transaction [RULPA § 304].

defective formation

Occurs when (1) a certificate of limited partnership is not properly filed, (2) there are defects in a certificate that is filed, or (3) some other statutory requirement for the creation of a limited partnership is not met.

Business Brief

A limited partner may be held liable as a general partner if the limited partnership is defectively formed.

Foreign Limited Partnerships

domestic limited partnership
A limited partnership in the state in which it was formed.

A limited partnership is a **domestic limited partnership** in the state in which it is organized. It is a **foreign limited partnership** in all other states. Under the RULPA, the law of the state in which the entity is organized governs its organization, its internal affairs, and the liability of its limited partners [RULPA § 901].

foreign limited partnership
A limited partnership in all other states than the one in which it was formed.

Registration of Foreign Limited Partnerships   Before transacting business in a foreign state, the foreign limited partnership must file an application for registration with the secretary of state. If the application conforms with law, a **certificate of registration** permitting the foreign limited partnership to transact business will be issued [RULPA § 902].

certificate of registration
A document permitting a foreign limited partnership to transact business in a foreign state.

Once registered, a foreign limited partnership may use the courts of the foreign state to enforce contracts and other rights. Failure to register neither impairs the validity of any act or contract of the unregistered foreign limited partnership nor prevents it from defending itself in any proceeding in the courts of the foreign state. However, unregistered foreign limited partnerships may not initiate litigation in the foreign jurisdiction. The limited partner's status is not affected by whether the limited partnership is registered or unregistered. For example, if a foreign limited partnership has failed to register in a foreign state and causes an injury to someone in that state, the limited partners are not personally liable [RULPA § 907].

Contemporary Business Application _____

MASTER LIMITED PARTNERSHIPS

One of the major drawbacks for investors who are limited partners in a limited partnership is that their investment usually is not liquid because there is no readily available market for buying and selling limited partnership interests. The introduction of **master limited partnerships (MLPs)** is changing this situation.

An MLP is a limited partnership whose limited partnership interests are traded on organized securities exchanges such as the New York Stock Exchange. Often, MLPs are created by corporations that transfer certain corporate assets (such as real estate) to an MLP and then sell limited partnership interests to the public. The corporation usually remains as the general partner. Some MLPs are formed to make original investments.

There are tax benefits to owning a limited partnership interest in an MLP rather than corporate stock. MLPs pay no income tax—partnership income and losses flow directly onto the individual partner's income tax return. Profit and other distributions of MLPs also avoid the double taxation of corporate dividends.

The use of master limited partnerships is expected to increase in the future.

LIABILITY OF GENERAL AND LIMITED PARTNERS

The *general partners* of a limited partnership have *unlimited personal liability* for the debts and obligations of the limited partnership. This liability extends to debts that cannot be satisfied with the existing capital of the limited partnership. Generally, *limited partners* are liable only for the debts and obligations of the limited partnership up to their *capital contributions*.

Business Brief
General partners of a limited partnership have unlimited liability for debts and obligations of the partnership. Limited partners are liable only up to their capital contributions.

Limited Partners' Participation in Management

As a trade-off for limited liability, limited partners give up their right to participate in the control and management of the limited partnership. This means, in part, that limited partners have no right to bind the partnership to contracts or other obligations. Under the RULPA, a limited partner is liable as a general partner if his or her participation in the control of the business is substantially the same as that of a general partner, but the limited partner is liable only to persons who reasonably believe him or her to be a general partner [RULPA § 303(a)].

Permissible Activities of Limited Partners

The RULPA clarifies the types of activities that a limited partner may engage in without losing his or her limited liability. These activities include [RULPA §§ 303(b) and (c)]:

1. Being an agent, an employee, or a contractor of the limited partnership or a general partner
2. Being a consultant or advisor to a general partner regarding the limited partnership
3. Acting as a surety for the limited partnership
4. Approving or disapproving an amendment to the limited partnership agreement
5. Voting on the following partnership matters:
   a. The dissolution and winding-up of the limited partnership
   b. The sale, transfer, exchange, lease, or mortgage of substantially all of the assets of the limited partnership
   c. The incurrence of indebtedness by the limited partnership other than in the ordinary course of business
   d. A change in the nature of the business of the limited partnership
   e. The removal of a general partner

The limited liability status of limited partners was challenged in the following case.

Business Brief

As a trade-off for limited liability, limited partners give up their right to participate in the control and management of the limited partnership. If a limited partner participates in forbidden activities, he or she can become liable as a general partner.

Business Brief

A limited partner can engage only in certain activities on behalf of the limited partnership.

Entrepreneur and the Law

LIMITED PARTNER LIABLE ON PERSONAL GUARANTEE

Many small businesses, including limited partnerships attempt to borrow money from banks or obtain an extension of credit from suppliers. Often these lenders require owners of small businesses to personally guarantee the loan to the business; otherwise the extensions of credit will not be made. Consider the following case.

Linnane Magnavox Home Entertainment Center (Linnane Magnavox) was a limited partnership that was organized under the laws of Kansas. Paul T. Linnane was the sole general partner, and Richard Gale Stover was the limited partner. Stover was the silent partner who provided the capital for the partnership. Stover took no part in the day-to-day management or control of the partnership, employment or discharge of employees, the purchase or sale of inventory, or any other incident of partnership business. In November 1977, Linnane Magnavox entered into a contract with General Electric Credit Corporation (GE Credit) whereby GE Credit would provide financing to the partnership. GE Credit refused to grant credit to the undercapitalized partnership unless Stover signed as the guarantor of the credit. It was not until Stover furnished his personal financial statements to GE Credit and personally signed the credit agreement as a guarantor that it extended credit to the partnership. When Linnane Magnavox defaulted on the debt and Paul Linnane was adjudicated bankrupt, GE Credit sued Stover to recover on the debt.

The trial court held in favor of GE Credit. Stover appealed. Is Richard Gale Stover, the limited partner, personally liable for Linnane Magnavox's debt to GE Credit?

The court of appeals held that defendant Stover was liable to pay the debts of Linnane Magnavox to GE Credit. The court stated:

> The question for decision was whether, for the purpose of the extension of credit to Linnane Magnavox, Stover put his personal assets at stake and GE Credit was therefore induced to extend its credit to the partnership. The evidence before the trial court was that GE Credit would not have extended credit to Linnane Magnavox had not Stover signed the credit agreement. It was a stipulated fact that prior to the execution of the credit agreement, GE Credit requested, and Stover furnished, his personal financial statement. In terms of partnership principle, the question is that of holding out: whether the Stover signature induced GE Credit to extend credit on reliance that Stover would be personally bound on those obligations. Stover had every reason to know that his unqualified signature on the documents would bind his personal credit as that of the general partner.

The court held the limited partner Stover to his word. [*General Electric Credit Corporation v. Stover*, 708 S.W.2d 355 (Missouri 1986)]

𝒞ONCEPT SUMMARY   LIABILITY OF LIMITED PARTNERS

General rule	Limited partners are not individually liable for the obligations or conduct of the partnership beyond the amount of their capital contribution.
Exceptions to the general rule	Limited partners are individually liable for the debts, obligations, and tortious acts of the partnership in three situations:

Exceptions to the general rule:

1. **Defective Formation** There has not been substantial compliance in good faith with the statutory requirements to create a limited partnership.
   Exception: Persons who erroneously believed themselves to be limited partners either (1) caused the appropriate certificate of limited partnership or amendment thereto to be filed or (2) withdrew from any future equity participation in the profits of the partnership and caused a certificate of withdrawal to be filed.
2. **Participation in Management** The limited partner participated in the management and control of the partnership.
   Exception: The limited partner was properly employed by the partnership as a manager or executive.
3. **Personal Guarantee** The limited partner signed an enforceable personal guarantee that guarantees the performance of the limited partnership.

Partners' Rights

The rights, powers, duties, and responsibilities of the partners in a limited partnership are specified in the articles of limited partnership or the certificate of limited partnership, the state's limited partnership statute, and the common law. The general partners of a limited partnership have the same rights, duties, and powers as partners in a general partnership [RULPA § 403].

Share of Profits and Losses   The limited partnership agreement may specify how profits and losses from the limited partnership are to be allocated among the general and limited partners. If there is no such agreement, the RULPA provides that profits and losses from a limited partnership are shared on the basis of the value of the partner's capital contribution [RULPA § 503]. A limited partner is not liable for losses beyond his or her capital contribution.

Consider These Examples   Suppose there are four general partners, each of whom contributes $50,000 in capital to the limited partnership, and four limited partners, each of whom contributes $200,000 capital. The total amount of contributed capital is $1 million. The limited partnership agreement does not stipulate how profits and losses are to be allocated. Assume that the limited partnership makes $3 million in profits. Under the RULPA, each general partner would receive $150,000 profit, while each limited partner would receive $600,000.

Suppose instead that the limited partnership loses $3 million. Under the RULPA, each limited partner would suffer a loss of $200,000 (up to their capital contribution), while each general partner would suffer a personal loss of $500,000 (after their capital of $50,000 each is used to pay the debt).

Right to Information   Upon reasonable demand, each limited partner has the right to obtain from the general partners true and full information regarding the state of the business, the financial condition of the limited partnership, and so on [RULPA

§ 305]. In addition, the limited partnership must keep the following records at its principal office:

1. A copy of the certificate of limited partnership and all amendments thereto.
2. A list of the full name and business address of each partner.
3. Copies of effective written limited partnership agreements.
4. Copies of federal, state, and local income tax returns.
5. Copies of financial statements of the limited partnership for the three most recent years.

Voting Rights

It is good practice to establish voting rights in the limited partnership agreement or certificate of limited partnership. The limited partnership agreement can stipulate which transactions must be approved by which partners (i.e., general, limited, or both) [RULPA §§ 302 and 405]. General and limited partners may be given unequal voting rights.

Admission and Withdrawal of Partners

The makeup of the partners of a limited partnership often changes. The *admission of new partners* and the *withdrawal of existing partners* are discussed in the following paragraphs.

Admission of New Partners   Once a limited partnership has been formed, a new limited partner can be added only upon the written consent of all partners unless the limited partnership agreement provides otherwise. New general partners can be admitted only with the specific written consent of each partner [RULPA § 401]. The limited partnership agreement cannot waive the right of partners to approve the admission of new general partners. The admission is effective when an amendment of the certificate of limited partnership reflecting that fact is filed [RULPA § 301].

Withdrawal of Partners   Under the RULPA, a limited partner can withdraw from a limited partnership only (1) at a time stated in the certificate of limited partnership, (2) upon the happening of an event stated in the certificate, or, (3) if no time or event is stated in the certificate, upon six months' prior notice to each general partner [RULPA § 603].

A general partner may withdraw from a limited partnership at any time by giving written notice to the other partners. If the withdrawal violates the limited partnership agreement, the withdrawing partner is liable to the limited partnership for damages caused by the withdrawal. These damages may be offset against the amount owed to the withdrawing partner by the limited partnership [RULPA § 602].

All withdrawing partners are entitled to receive any distribution (including a return of capital) to which they are due under the limited partnership agreement. The withdrawing partners are also entitled to receive, within a reasonable time after withdrawal, the fair value of their interest in the limited partnership as of the date of withdrawal [RULPA § 604]. This amount is limited by the amount that the partnership assets exceed partnership liabilities [RULPA § 607].

*D*ISSOLUTION AND WINDING-UP

A limited partnership may be dissolved and its affairs wound up just like an ordinary partnership. The RULPA establishes rules for the dissolution and winding-up of limited partnerships. Upon the dissolution and the commencement of winding-up a limited partnership, a *certificate of cancellation* must be filed by the limited partnership with the secretary of state of the state in which the limited partnership is organized [RULPA § 203].

Causes of Dissolution

Under the RULPA, the following four events cause the dissolution of a limited partnership [RULPA § 801]:

1. The end of the life of the limited partnership as specified in the certificate of limited partnership, that is, at the end of a set time period or the completion of a project.
2. The written consent of all general and limited partners.
3. The withdrawal of a general partner. Withdrawal includes the retirement, death, bankruptcy, adjudged insanity, or removal of a general partner or the assignment by a general partner of his or her partnership interest. If a corporation or partnership is a general partner, the dissolution of the corporation or partnership is considered withdrawal.
4. The entry of a **decree of judicial dissolution**, which may be granted to a partner whenever it is *not reasonably practical* to carry on the business in conformity with the limited partnership agreement [RULPA § 802] (e.g., if the general partners are deadlocked over important decisions affecting the limited partnership).

decree of judicial dissolution

A decree of dissolution that is granted to a partner whenever it is not reasonably practical to carry on the business in conformity with the limited partnership agreement.

A limited partnership is not dissolved upon the withdrawal of a general partner if (1) the certificate of limited partnership permits the business to be carried on by the remaining general partner or partners or (2) within 90 days of the withdrawal all partners agree in writing to continue the business (and select a general partner or partners, if necessary) [RULPA § 801].

Winding-Up

A limited partnership must *wind up* its affairs upon dissolution. Unless otherwise provided in the limited partnership agreement, the partnership's affairs may be wound up by the general partners who have not acted wrongfully or, if there are none, the limited partners. Any partner may petition the court to wind up the affairs of a limited partnership [RULPA § 803]. A partner who winds up the affairs of a limited partnership has the same rights, powers, and duties as a partner winding up an ordinary partnership.

Distribution of Assets After the assets of the limited partnership have been liquidated, the proceeds must be distributed. The RULPA provides the following order of distribution of partnership assets upon the winding-up of a limited partnership [RULPA § 804]:

1. *Creditors* of the limited partnership, including partners who are creditors (except for liabilities for distributions)
2. *Partners* with respect to
   a. Unpaid distributions
   b. Capital contributions
   c. The remainder of the proceeds

The partners may provide in the limited partnership agreement for a different distribution among the partners, but the creditors must retain their first priority.

LIMITED LIABILITY PARTNERSHIPS (LLPs)

limited liability partnership (LLP)

A special form of partnership where all partners are limited partners and there are no general partners.

Many states have enacted legislation to permit the creation of **limited liability partnerships (LLPs)**. In an LLP, there does not have to be a general partner who is personally liable for the debts and obligations of the partnership. Instead, *all* partners are limited partners who stand to lose only their capital contribution should the partnership fail. None of the partners is personally liable for the debts and obligations of the partnership beyond his or her capital contribution (see Exhibit 34.4).

LLPs enjoy the "flow-through" tax benefit of other types of partnerships, that is, there is no tax paid at the partnership level and all profits and losses are reported on the individual partners' income tax returns.

*Ɛ*XHIBIT **34.4**   *Limited Liability Partnership (LLP)*

Articles of Partnership

LLPs must be created formally by filing *articles of partnership* with the secretary of state of the state in which the LLP is organized. This is a public document. The LLP is a **domestic LLP** in the state in which it is organized. The limited liability partnership law of the state governs the operation of the LLP. An LLP may do business in other states, however. To do so, the LLP must register as a **foreign LLP** in any state in which it wants to conduct business.

Liability Insurance Required

In most states limited liability partnership law restricts the use of LLPs to certain types of professionals, such as accountants and lawyers. Many state laws require LLPs to carry a minimum of $1 million of liability insurance that covers negligence, wrongful acts, and misconduct by partners or employees of the LLP. This requirement guarantees that injured third parties will have compensation to recover for their injuries and is a quid pro quo for permitting partners of LLPs to have limited liability.

Business Brief
Limited liability partnerships (LLPs) are mainly used by professionals, such as accountants and lawyers.

Contemporary Business Application

ACCOUNTING FIRMS OPERATE AS LLPS

Prior to the advent of the limited liability partnership (LLP) form of doing business, accounting firms operated as general partnerships. As such, the general partners were personally liable for the debts and obligations of the general partnership. In large accounting firms, this personal liability was rarely imposed. This was because the general partnership usually carried sufficient liability insurance to cover most awards to third-party plaintiffs in negligence tort actions. Creditors usually extended credit to the large accounting firms based on the

(box continues)

reputation of the firms and the fact that these large accounting firms had sufficient capital in the partnership to meet most loan obligations.

Beginning in the early 1980s, large accounting firms were hit with many large court judgments. These cases were brought in conjunction with the failure of large savings banks and commercial banks and the failure of other large firms that accountants had audited. Many of these firms failed because of fraud by their major owners and officers. The shareholders and creditors of these failed companies sued the auditors, alleging that the auditors had been negligent in not catching the fraud. Many juries agreed and awarded large sums against the accounting firms. Sometimes the accounting firm's liability insurance was not enough to cover the judgment, thus imposing personal liability on partners. General partners in accounting firms became worried that the inability of the profession to shield itself from such liability jeopardized the profession.

In response, in the 1990s state legislatures created a new form of business, the limited liability partnership (LLP). This entity was particularly created for accountants, lawyers, and other professionals to offer their services under an umbrella of limited liability. The partners of an LLP have limited liability up to their capital contribution; the partners do not have personal liability for the debts and liabilities of the LLP, however.

Once LLPs were permitted by law, all of the Big Five accounting firms changed their status from general partnerships to LLPs. The signs and letterhead of the Big Five accounting firms prominently announce that the accounting firm is an "LLP." Many accounting firms other than the Big Five have also changed over to LLP status, as have many law firms. The LLP form of business has changed how accountants, lawyers, and other professionals offer their services.

Working the Web

e·biz

Business-Related Hate Sites on the Internet

Many of America's biggest brand names have been targeted by so-called "hate sites" on the Internet. Customers who have had bad experiences with companies or people who dislike a company's policies have started Internet sites to lash out at companies. What have companies done to protect themselves?

- Some have bought the URLs for their name followed by the word "sucks.com" or preceded by "I hate."
- Some have apologized to the creator of the hate site.

- Some have created Web sites telling their side of the story.
- Some have sued hate-site creators.

So far, despite some sites' invective and outlandish claims, courts have upheld their creators' First Amendment rights.

CYBER EXERCISES

1. Visit some of the "hate" sites on the Internet such as: www.ihatemicrosoft.com or www.ihateford.com to see what kinds of information they contain.

*C*ASES AND *E*XERCISES

CRITICAL LEGAL THINKING CASES

34.1. Pat McGowan, Val Somers, and Brent Robertson were general partners of Vermont Place, a limited partnership formed on January 20, 1984, for the purpose of constructing duplexes on an undeveloped tract of land in Fort Smith, Arkansas. The general partners appointed McGowan and his company, Advance Development Corporation (Advance), to develop the project, including contracting with materialmen, mechanics, and other suppliers. None of the limited partners took part in the management or control of the partnership.

On September 3, 1984, Somers and Robertson discovered that McGowan had not been paying the suppliers. They removed McGowan from the partnership and took over the project. The suppliers sued the partnership to recover the money owed them. The partnership assets were not sufficient to pay all of their claims. Who is liable to the suppliers? [*National Lumber Company v. Advance Development Corporation*, 732 S.W.2d 840 (AR 1987)]

34.2. Union Station Associates of New London (USANL) is a limited partnership formed under the laws of Connecticut. Allen M. Schultz, Anderson Nolter Associates, and the Lepton Trust were limited partners. The limited partners did not take part in the management of the partnership. The National Railroad Passenger Association (NRPA) entered into an agreement to lease part of a railroad facility from USANL. NRPA sued USANL for allegedly breaching the lease and also named the limited partners as defendants. Are the limited partners liable? [*National Railroad Passenger Association v. Union Station Associates of New London*, 643 F.Supp. 192 (D.D.C. 1986)]

34.3. 8 Brookwood Fund (Brookwood) is a limited partnership that was formed to invest in securities. The original certificate of limited partnership, which was filed with the Westchester County, New York, clerk on April 24, 1987, listed Kenneth Stein as the general partner and Barbara Stein as the limited partner. Between May and August 1987, additional investors joined Brookwood as limited partners. However, no certificate amending the original certificate was filed to reflect the newly admitted limited partners. The newly added partners conducted themselves at all times as limited partners.

The partnership purchased securities on margin (i.e., it borrowed a percentage of the purchase price of the securities) from the securities firms of Sloate, Weisman, Murray & Co., Inc. (Sloate), and Bear Stearns & Co., Inc. (Bear Stearns). On October 19, 1987, the stock market crashed, causing many of the securities that Brookwood purchased to go down in value. The securities firms made margin calls on Brookwood to pay more money to cover the losses. When the margin calls were not met, Sloate and Bear Stearns immediately initiated arbitration proceedings to recover the balance of $1,849,183 allegedly due after Brookwood's accounts were liquidated. On October 28, 1987, Brookwood filed a certificate amending the original certificate of limited partnership to reflect the recently added limited partners.

Upon receiving the notice of arbitration, the recently added limited partners renounced their interest in the profits of the limited partnership. Can these limited partners be held individually liable for the partnership debts owed to Sloate and Bear Stearns? [*8 Brookwood Fund v. Bear Stearns & Co., Inc.*, 539 N.Y.S.2d 411 (N.Y.A.D.2dDept. 1989)]

34.4. Virginia Partners, Ltd. (Virginia Partners), a limited partnership organized under the laws of Florida, conducted business in Kentucky but failed to register as a foreign limited partnership as required by Kentucky law. On August 2, 1980, Robert Day was tortiously injured in Garrard County, Kentucky, by a negligent act of Virginia Partners. At the time of the accident, Day was a bystander observing acid being injected into an abandoned oil well by Virginia Partners. The injury occurred when a polyvinyl chloride (PVC) valve failed, causing a hose to rupture from its fitting and spray nitric acid on Day, severely injuring him. Day sued Virginia Partners and its limited partners to recover damages. Are the limited partners liable? [*Virginia Partners, Ltd. v. Day*, 738 S.W.2d 837 (Ky.App. 1987)]

34.5. Raugust-Mathwig, Inc., a corporation, was the sole general partner of a limited partnership. Calvin Raugust was the major shareholder of this corporation. The three limited partners were (1) Cal-Lee Trust, (2) W. J. Mathwig, Inc., and (3) W. J. Mathwig, Inc., and Associates. All three of the limited partners were valid corporate entities. Although the limited partnership agreement was never executed and a certificate of limited partnership was not filed with the state, the parties opened a bank account and began conducting business.

On May 9, 1973, John Molander, an architect, entered into an agreement with the limited partnership to design a condominium complex and professional office building to be located in Spokane, Washington. The contract was signed on behalf of the limited partnership by its corporate general partner. Molander provided substantial architectural services to the partnership, but neither project was completed because of a lack of financing. Molander sued the limited partnership, its corporate general partner, the corporate limited partners, and Calvin Raugust individually to recover payments allegedly due him. Whom can Molander recover against? [*Molander v. Raugust-Mathwig, Inc.*, 722 P.2d 103 (Wash.App. 1986)]

34.6. The Courts of the Phoenix was a limited partnership that owned a building that housed several racquetball and handball courts. William Reich was its general partner. Charter Oaks Fire Insurance Company (Charter Oaks) issued a fire insurance policy that insured the building. In May 1980, a fire caused extensive damage to the building. When the Chicago fire department found evidence of arson, Charter Oaks denied the partnership's $1.7 million-plus insurance claim. It reasoned that Reich either set the fire or had arranged to have it set in order to liquidate a failing investment. Can the limited partnership recover on the fire insurance policy? [*Courts of the Phoenix v. Charter Oaks Fire Insurance Company*, 560 F.Supp. 858 (N.D.Ill. 1983)]

34.7. The Aztec Petroleum Corporation (Aztec) was the general partner of a limited partnership. The partnership agreement provided that it could be amended by a vote of 70 percent of the limited partnership units. Over 70 percent of these units voted to amend the partnership agreement to provide that a vote of 70 percent of the limited partnership units could remove the general partner and replace it with another general partner. Prior to this amendment, there was no provision for the removal and substitution of a general partner. Texas law requires unanimous approval of new partners unless the partnership agreement provides otherwise.

When a vote was held, over 70 percent of the limited partnership units voted to remove Aztec as the general partner and replace it with the MHM Company. Aztec challenged its removal. Who wins? [*Aztec Petroleum Corporation v. MHM Company*, 703 S.W.2d 290 (Tex.App. 1986)]

34.8. When the Chrysler Credit Corporation (Chrysler Credit) extended credit to Metro Dodge, Inc. (Metro Dodge), Donald P. Peterson signed an agreement guaranteeing to pay the debt if Metro Dodge did not pay. When Metro Dodge failed to pay, Chrysler Credit sued Peterson on the guarantee and obtained a judgment of $350,000 against him. After beginning collection efforts, Chrysler Credit learned through discovery that Peterson owned four limited partnership units in Cedar Riverside Properties, a limited partnership. Can Chrysler Credit charge Peterson's limited partnership interests? [*Chrysler Credit Corporation v. Peterson*, 342 N.W.2d 170 (Minn.App. 1984)]

ETHICS CASES

34.9. Robert K. Powers and Lee M. Solomon were among other limited partners of the Cosmopolitan Chinook Hotel (Cosmopolitan), a limited partnership. On October 25, 1972, Cosmopolitan entered into a contract to lease and purchase neon signs from Dwinell's Central Neon (Dwinell's). The contract identified Cosmopolitan as a "partnership" and was signed on behalf of the partnership, "R. Powers, President." At the time the contract was entered into, Cosmopolitan had taken no steps to file its certificate of limited partnership with the state as required by limited partnership law. The certificate was not filed with the state until several months after the contract was signed. When Cosmopolitan defaulted on payments due under the contract, Dwinell's sued Cosmopolitan and its general and limited partners. Did the limited partners act ethically in denying liability on the contract? Are the limited partners liable? [*Dwinell's Central Neon v. Cosmopolitan Chinook Hotel*, 587 P.2d 191 (Wash.App. 1978)]

34.10. The Second Montclair Company was a limited partnership organized under the laws of Alabama to develop an office building in Birmingham called Montclair II. Joseph Cox, Sr., and F&S were general partners, each owning a one-third interest in the limited partnership. Eleven limited partners owned equal shares of the remaining one-third interest. Cox was president of Cox Realty and Development Company (Cox Realty), which had its offices in Montclair II. Cox Realty managed Montclair II under a written agreement with the limited partnership. Evidence showed that Cox used assets of the limited partnership for personal use. F&S sued Cox, seeking dissolution and liquidation of the limited partnership and damages. Did Cox act ethically in this case? Should the limited partnership be dissolved? Should damages be awarded? [*Cox v. F&S*, 489 So.2d 516 (AL 1986)]

CRITICAL LEGAL THINKING WRITING ASSIGNMENT

Read Case A.34 in the Case Appendix [*Commonwealth of Pennsylvania v. McKelvey and Bradley*]. This case is excerpted from the Supreme Court of Pennsylvania's opinion. Review and brief the case. In your brief, be sure to answer the following questions.

1. Who was the plaintiff? On whose property did the plaintiff place a lien?
2. What did defendant Bradley argue in defense against the lien?
3. Was defendant Bradley successful in his defense?

Limited Liability Companies

Justice is the end of government. It is the end of civil society. It ever has been, and ever will be pursued, until it be obtained, or until liberty be lost in the pursuit.

JAMES MADISON *The Federalist No. 51*
(1788)

Chapter Objectives

After studying this chapter, you should be able to

1. Define *limited liability company (LLC)*.
2. Describe the process of organizing an LLC.
3. Explain the differences between an S corporation and an LLC.
4. Describe the limited liability shield provided by an LLC.
5. Describe how an LLC can be taxed as a partnership.
6. Define *foreign limited liability company*.
7. Describe the contents of an LLC's operating agreement.
8. Compare a member-managed LLC to a manager-managed LLC.
9. Determine when members and managers owe fiduciary duties of loyalty and care to the LLC.
10. Explain the equivalent forms of business to the LLC that are used in foreign countries.

Chapter Contents

In recent years, a majority of states have approved a new form of business entity called a **limited liability company (LLC)**. An LLC is an unincorporated business entity that combines the most favorable attributes of general partnerships, limited partnerships, and corporations. An LLC may elect to be taxed as a partnership, the owners can manage the business, and the owners have limited liability. Many entrepreneurs who begin new businesses choose the LLC as their legal form for conducting business. The formation and operation of LLCs are discussed in this chapter.

limited liability company (LLC)

An unincorporated business entity that combines the most favorable attributes of general partnerships, limited partnerships, and corporations.

$\mathscr{T}$HE UNIFORM LIMITED LIABILITY COMPANY ACT

In 1995, the National Conference of Commissioners on Uniform State Laws (a group of lawyers, judges, and legal scholars) issued the **Uniform Limited Liability Company Act (ULLCA)**. The ULLCA codifies limited liability company law. Its goal is to establish comprehensive LLC law that is uniform throughout the United States. The ULLCA covers most problems that arise in the formation, operation, and termination of LLCs. The ULLCA is not law unless a state adopts it as its LLC statute. Many states have adopted all or part of the ULLCA as their limited liability company law. Because it is so important, the ULLCA will form the basis of the study of limited liability companies in this chapter.

The Uniform Limited Liability Company Act (ULLCA)

A model act that provides comprehensive and uniform laws for the formation, operation, and dissolution of LLCs.

Business Brief

An LLC combines the tax benefits of a partnership with the limited personal liability attribute of a corporation.

$\mathscr{N}$ATURE OF THE LIMITED LIABILITY COMPANY

Limited liability companies are creatures of state law, not federal law. Limited liability companies can only be created pursuant to the laws of the state in which the LLC is being organized. These statutes, commonly referred to as **limited liability company codes**, regulate the formation, operation, and dissolution of LLCs. The state legislature may amend

limited liability company codes

State statutes that regulate the formation, operation, and dissolution of LLCs.

$\mathscr{E}$XHIBIT 35.1   *Limited Liability Company (LLC)*

its LLC statute at any time. The courts interpret state LLC statutes to decide LLC and member disputes.

The LLC as a Legal Person

A limited liability company is a separate **legal entity** (or legal person) distinct from its members [ULLCA § 201]. Limited liability companies are treated as artificial persons who can sue or be sued, enter into and enforce contracts, hold title to and transfer property, and be found civilly and criminally liable for violations of law.

Members' Limited Liability

The owners of LLCs are usually called **members**. The general rule is that members are not personally liable to third parties for the debts, obligations, and liabilities of an LLC beyond their capital contribution. Members are said to have **limited liability** (see Exhibit 35.1). The debts, obligations, and liabilities of an LLC, whether arising from contracts, torts, or otherwise, are solely those of the LLC [ULLCA § 303(a)].

Consider This Example Jasmin, Shan-Yi, and Vanessa form an LLC and each contributes $25,000 in capital. The LLC operates for a period of time during which it borrows money from banks and purchases goods on credit from suppliers. After some time, the LLC experiences financial difficulty and goes out of business. If the LLC fails with $500,000 in debts, each of the members will lose her capital contribution of $25,000 but will not be personally liable for the rest of the unpaid debts of the LLC.

In the following case, the court addressed the issue of the limited liability of a member of an LLC.

---

legal entity

An LLC is a separate legal entity—an *artificial person*—that can own property, sue and be sued, enter into and enforce contracts, and such.

member

An owner of an LLC.

limited liability

Members are liable for the LLC's debts, obligations, and liabilities only to the extent of their capital contributions.

Page v. Roscoe, LLC
497 S.E.2nd 422 (1998)
Court of Appeals of North Carolina

CASE 35.1

FACTS

Dale C. Bone was a member of Roscoe, LLC, a limited liability company organized under the laws of North Carolina. In August 1994, Roscoe, LLC, purchased two acres of land near the town of Apex, North Carolina. In January 1995, Apex approved Roscoe, LLC's, plan to construct and operate a propane gas bulk storage and distribution facility on the land. This use was permitted under Apex's zoning ordinance. In April 1995, Daylene Page and other homeowners in the area sued Roscoe, LLC, and Dale C. Bone, alleging that the gas storage facility, if constructed, would constitute a nuisance. In December 1995, after the trial court denied the plaintiffs' motion to obtain a preliminary injunction against construction of the facility, the plaintiffs dismissed the lawsuit. Subsequently, Bone sued the plaintiffs for sanctions to recover the attorneys fees that he spent in defending against the plaintiffs' lawsuit. The trial court ordered the plaintiffs to pay Bone's attorney's fees. The plaintiffs appealed.

ISSUE

Were the sanctions warranted against the plaintiffs for naming an individual member of a limited liability company in the lawsuit they brought against the LLC?

IN THE LANGUAGE OF THE COURT

Walker, Judge We do find that the allegations against Bone individually are not well-grounded in law. N.C.Gen.Stat. § 57C-3-30 (1993) provides in pertinent part:

(a) A person who is a member or manager, or both, of a limited liability company is not liable for the obligations of a limited liability company solely by reason of being a member or manager or both, and does not become so by participating, in whatever capacity, in the management or control of the business.

(b) A member of a limited liability company is not a proper party to proceedings by or against a limited liability company.

The record sustains the trial court's conclusion that no acts by Bone, individually, were properly alleged. Therefore, under the above statute, it was improper to name an individual member of

(case continues)

a limited liability company as a party defendant without any evidence to support it. As such, the naming of Bone as an individual defendant was not well-grounded in law.

DECISION AND REMEDY

The court of appeals held that Bone, as a member of Roscoe, LLC, was not liable as a matter of law for the acts of the LLC and was therefore improperly named as a defendant in the lawsuit filed by the plaintiffs. The plaintiffs were held liable for sanctions and were required to pay Bone's attorney's fees that he expended in defending against the plaintiffs' lawsuit.

Case Questions

Critical Legal Thinking   Should members of a limited liability company be released from personal liability for the debts and obligations incurred by the LLC?

Ethics   Did the plaintiff homeowners act ethically in naming Bone as a defendant? Why do you think they named Bone as a defendant?

Business Application   Is this case good precedent for business persons wishing to conduct business as an LLC?

Personal Guarantees   A member is personally liable for the debts of an LLC only if he or she agrees to be in either the articles of organization or other writing, or if he or she personally guarantees the repayment of the LLC's debts [ULLCA § 303(c)].

Business Brief

A member is personally liable if he or she personally guarantees repayment of the debts of the LLC.

Consider This Example   Patricia, Arnold, and Emory form a new LLC. When they go to a bank to have the LLC borrow money from the bank, the bank refuses to make the loan to such a new LLC unless the members personally guaranty the loan. To obtain the loan, Patricia, Arnold, and Emory sign personal guarantees with the bank agreeing to repay the loan if the LLC does not. In this case, if the LLC fails to repay the loan, the bank may enforce the personal guarantees and recover the amount of the loan from the members.

In the following case, the court enforced a personal guaranty against a manager of a limited liability company.

Creative Resource Management, Inc. v. Soskin
1998 WL 813420 (1998)
Court of Appeals of Tennessee

CASE 35.2

FACTS

Nashville Pro Hockey, LLC, was a limited liability company organized under the laws of Tennessee. The LLC owned and operated the Nashville Nighthawks, a minor league professional hockey team. On September 4, 1996, Nashville Pro Hockey, LLC, contracted with Creative Resource Management, Inc. (CRM), whereby CRM, for fees and other consideration, would provide employee leasing services to Nashville Pro Hockey, LLC. The contract was signed by Barry Soskin, the president of Nashville Pro Hockey, LLC. A paragraph in the contract provided

> *By affixing my hand and seal to this agreement, I personally guarantee any and all payments payable as represented and outlined in this agreement.*

Nashville Pro Hockey, LLC, failed, owing CRM $29,626. CRM sued Nashville Pro Hockey, LLC, and Barry Soskin to recover the unpaid compensation. Soskin defended, alleging that his signature on the contract was in his representative capacity only and not in his individual capacity as a guarantor. The trial court agreed and granted summary judgment to Soskin. CRM appealed.

ISSUE

Did Soskin's signature on the contract constitute a personal guarantee for the payment of the debt of Nashville Pro Hockey, LLC, to CRM?

IN THE LANGUAGE OF THE COURT

Cain, Judge   *The well settled precedent in Tennessee suggests that a corporate officer's signature preceded by a corporation's name and followed by a designation of the signer's corporate capacity is evidence that the signer was acting as an agent of the corporation rather than individually.*

This rule, however, must yield where the language of the contract compels a different conclusion. The language of the contract involved in the case at bar distinguishes this case from the general rule. This case concerns a contract which contains personal guarantee language in the body of the contract.

The words "I personally guarantee any and all payments payable as represented and outlined in this agreement" reflect indisputably a guarantee by someone. Soskin insists that he signed only as a representative of the limited liability company. CRM insists that his signature imposes personal liability upon him. The stark fact is that the words "I personally guarantee" are meaningless if applied to Nashville Pro Hockey, LLC and not to Barry Soskin individually.

Since the words "I personally guarantee" cannot refer to Nashville Pro Hockey, LLC and retain any meaning at all in the context of this agreement, they must of necessity reflect the personal guarantee of Barry Soskin.

DECISION AND REMEDY

The court of appeals held that Soskin was a guarantor and that he was liable to repay the money owed to CRM by Nashville Pro Hockey, LLC. The court of appeals reversed the judgment of the trial court and granted summary judgment to CRM.

Case Questions

Critical Legal Thinking   In this case a contracting party, CRM, was able to break the limited liability shield of an LLC and have a manager of the LLC personally guarantee its contract with the LLC. Are tort victims of negligent conduct of an LLC's employees and agents granted the same benefit?

Ethics   Did Soskin act ethically in arguing that he was not liable on the contract? Was the language of the contract clear?

Business Application   What purpose do personal guarantees serve in business transactions?

Contemporary Business Application

"CHECK-THE-BOX" REGULATIONS FOR PARTNERSHIP TAXATION OF LLCS

A limited liability company (LLC) is an unincorporated business entity formed under state law. Because an LLC is neither a partnership nor a corporation, a question arises as to how it should be taxed for federal income tax purposes. Under the Internal Revenue Code, a partnership is not taxed at the entity level, but its income or losses "flow through" to the partners' individual income tax returns. This avoids double taxation. On the other hand, corporations are generally taxed once at the entity level and then again if it pays dividends to shareholders, who must pay tax on these dividends when they file their personal income tax returns. Thus, there is double taxation.

In most cases, an LLC would prefer to be taxed as a partnership than as a corporation. When the first LLC was formed under Wyoming law, the Internal Revenue Service (IRS) issued a Revenue Ruling that classified the LLC as a partnership for federal income tax purposes. After this initial ruling, the IRS issued regulations that provided that an LLC could be taxed as a partnership if it gave up two of the following corporate attributes: (1) associates, (2) objective to carry on the business for a profit, (3) centralized management, (4) limited liability, (5) continuity of life, and (6) free transferability of interests. To obtain partnership taxation, in most instances LLCs gave up continuity of life by stating a term for the LLC (e.g., 50 years) and free transferability of interests by agreeing to buy-and-sell agreements and other restrictions on the sale or transfer of their ownership interests.

This method of obtaining partnership taxation was used by LLCs until 1997. Effective January 1, 1997, the IRS adopted **"Check-the-Box" Regulations** that made it easier for LLCs to be taxed as partnerships. These regulations provide that a business entity falls into one of the following categories:

1. ***Per se* Corporations**   These are defined as corporations incorporated under state law and are taxed as corporations for federal income tax purposes.
2. **Eligible Entities**   These are defined as entities other than *per se* corporations. Eligible entities include unincorporated businesses with two or more owners, such as LLCs, LLPs, limited partnerships, and general partnerships. An eligible entity is taxed as a partnership unless it elects to be taxed as a corporation.
3. **Single-Owner Entity**   A single-owner entity is taxed as a sole proprietorship unless the owner elects to be taxed as a corporation.

The Check-the-Box Regulations have default rules that provide that eligible entities, such as an LLC, are treated as partnerships with flow-through taxation unless an election is made to be taxed as a corporation. This election is made by filing Form 8832 with the IRS and must be signed by all owners or a manager who is given authority to sign such an election. The Check-the-Box Regulations make it easier for LLCs to obtain partnership taxation status for federal income tax purposes. Most states automatically apply the federal classification rules for state income tax purposes, although a few do not.

ORGANIZING PROCEDURES

Limited liability companies are creatures of statute. As such, certain formalities must be taken and statutory requirements met to form an LLC.

Lawful Purpose

An LLC may be organized for any lawful purpose [ULLCA § 112(a)]. Most LLCs are organized to operate businesses, real estate developments, and such. LLCs cannot conduct business in certain regulated industries, such as banking and insurance, unless they meet special requirements and obtain required licenses. LLCs cannot operate the practice of certain professionals, such as accountants, lawyers, and doctors. Most states allow such professionals to operate as a limited liability partnership (discussed in Chapter 34).

Selecting a State for Organization

Business Brief

Most LLCs are organized under the laws of the state in which it will conduct most of its business.

An LLC can be organized in only one state even though it can conduct business in all other states. When choosing a state for organization, the members should consider the LLC codes of the states under consideration. For sake of convenience, most LLCs, particularly smaller ones, choose the state in which the LLC will be doing most of its business as the state of organization.

Selecting an LLC's Name

When starting a new LLC, the organizers must choose a name for the entity. To ensure that the name selected meets the state's LLC code and is not already being used by another business, the organizers should take the following steps:

Business Brief

The name of an LLC must contain the words "limited liability company" or "limited company" or the abbreviation "L.L.C.," "LLC," "L.C.," or "LC." "Limited" may be abbreviated as "Ltd.," and "company" may be abbreviated as "Co."

- Make sure that the name chosen contains the words "limited liability company" or "limited company" or the abbreviation "L.L.C.," "LLC," "L.C.," or "LC." "Limited" may be abbreviated as "Ltd.," and "company" may be abbreviated as "Co." [ULLCA § 105(a)]
- Determine whether the name selected is federally trademarked by another company or business and is therefore unavailable for use. Trademark lawyers and specialized firms will conduct trademark searches for a fee.
- Determine whether the chosen name is similar to other nontrademarked names used by other businesses and is therefore unavailable for use. Lawyers and specialized firms will conduct such searches for a fee.
- When the LLC name selected is determined to be available, reserve the name by filing an application with the secretary of state of the state of organization. The name may be reserved for a nonrenewable period (e.g., 120 days). During this time, the organizers should complete the process of organization [ULLCA § 106].

Entrepreneur and the Law

WHY OPERATE A BUSINESS AS A LIMITED LIABILITY COMPANY (LLC)?

Why should an LLC be used instead of an S Corporation or a partnership? S Corporations and partnerships are subject to many restrictions and adverse consequences that do not exist with an LLC. Some differences are

- S Corporations cannot have shareholders other than estates, certain trusts, and individuals (who cannot be nonresident aliens). S Corporations can have no more than 75 shareholders and one class of stock and may not own more than 80 percent of another corporation. LLCs have no such restrictions.
- In a general partnership, the partners are personally liable for the obligations of the partnership. Members of LLCs have limited liability.

- Limited partnerships must have at least one general partner who is personally liable for the obligations of the partnership (although this partner can be a corporation). Limited partners are precluded from participating in the management of the business. An LLC provides limited liability to all members, even though they participate in management of the business.

Filing the Articles of Organization

Under the ULLCA, an LLC may be organized by one or more persons. Some states require at least two members to organize an LLC. In states where an LLC may be organized by only one member, sole proprietors can obtain the benefit of the limited liability shield of an LLC.

An LLC is formed by delivering **articles of organization** to the office of the secretary of state of the state of organization for filing. If the articles are in proper form, the secretary of state will file the articles. The existence of an LLC begins when the articles of organization are filed. The filing of the articles of organization by the secretary of state is conclusive proof that the organizers have satisfied all conditions necessary to create the LLC [ULLCA § 202].

Under the ULLCA the articles of organization of an LLC must set forth [ULLCA § 203}

1. The name of the LLC
2. The address of the LLC's initial office
3. The name and address of the initial agent for service of process
4. The name and address of each organizer
5. Whether the LLC is a term LLC and, if so, the term specified
6. Whether the LLC is to be a manager-managed LLC, and, if so, the name and address of each manager
7. Whether one or more of the members of the LLC are to be personally liable for the LLC's debts and obligations

The articles of organization may set forth provisions from the members' operating agreement and any other matter not inconsistent with law. A sample articles of organization is set forth in Exhibit 35.2. The articles of organization may be amended at any time by filing *articles of amendment* with the secretary of state [ULLCA § 204]. Any person may request the secretary of state to furnish a *certificate of existence* for an LLC [ULLCA § 208].

Anyone who suffers loss because of any false statement made in the articles of organization or amendments thereto may recover damages from the person who signed the document and knew that the statement was false [ULLCA § 209].

Duration

An LLC is an at-will LLC unless it is designated as a **term LLC** and the duration of the term is specified in the articles of organization [ULLCA § 203(a)(5)]. The duration of a term LLC may be specified in any manner that sets forth a specific and final date for the dissolution of the LLC. Mere specification of a particular undertaking is not valid unless it is accompanied by a longer fixed period. An **at-will LLC** has no specified term.

Consider These Examples   Periods specified as "50 years from the date of filing of the articles of organization" or "the period ending January 1, 2050" are valid to create a term LLC. The designation "Until the building is completed" does not create a term LLC, but the designation "January 1, 2010 or until the building is completed, whichever occurs first" does create a term LLC.

---

articles of organization
The formal documents that must be filed at the secretary of state's office of the state of organization of an LLC to form the LLC.

Business Brief
The filing of the articles of organization by the secretary of state is conclusive proof that an LLC has been created.

Business Brief
The articles of organization must contain required statutory information and may contain information from the members' operating agreement and any other matters not inconsistent with law.

Laws too gentle are seldom obeyed; too severe, seldom executed.

Benjamin Franklin
Poor Richard's Almanack
(1756)

term LLC
An LLC that has a specified term of duration.

at-will LLC
An LLC that has no specified term of duration.

*Ɛ*XHIBIT 35.2 *Sample Articles of Organization*

**ARTICLES OF ORGANIZATION
FOR FLORIDA LIMITED LIABILITY COMPANY**

ARTICLE I - NAME

The name of the Limited Liability Company is
iCitrusSystems.com

ARTICLE II - ADDRESS

The mailing address and street address of the principal office of the Limited Liability
Company is

3000 Dade Boulevard
Suite 200
Miami Beach, Florida 33139

ARTICLE III - DURATION

The period of duration for the Limited Liability Company shall be
50 years

ARTICLE IV - MANAGEMENT

The Limited Liability Company is to be managed by a manager and the name and
address of such manager is

Susan Escobar
1000 Collins Avenue
Miami Beach, Florida 33141

_____

Thomas Blandford

_____

Quan Trang

Capital Contribution

A member's capital contribution to an LLC may be in the form of money, personal property, real property, other tangible property, intangible property (e.g., a patent), services performed, contracts for services to be performed, promissory notes, or other agreements to contribute cash or property [ULLCA § 401].

A member's obligation to contribute capital is not excused by the member's death, disability, or other inability to perform. If a member cannot make the required contribution of property or services, he or she is obligated to contribute money equal to the value of the promised contribution. The LLC or any creditor who extended credit to the LLC in reliance on the promised contribution may enforce the promised obligation [ULLCA § 402].

Agent for Service of Process

An LLC must designate an agent in the state of organization to receive service of process, notices, and demands if the LLC is sued or involved in an administrative proceeding [ULLCA § 108(b)]. This agent is often the LLC's lawyer, although other persons may

Business Brief

A member's capital contribution may be money, tangible or intangible property, services performed or promised to be performed, promissory notes, or other agreements to contribute cash or property.

act as an agent for service of process. An LLC must notify the secretary of state if there is a change of the agent or if the agent's address changes [ULLCA § 109].

Certificate of Interest

An LLC's operating agreement may provide that a member's ownership interest may be evidenced by a **certificate of interest** issued by the LLC [ULLCA § 501(c)]. The certificate of interest acts the same as a stock certificate issued by a corporation.

certificate of interest
Document that evidences a member's ownership interest in an LLC.

Contemporary Business Application

DREAMWORKS SKG, LLC: SCRIPT FOR A MOVIE COMPANY

In 1995, Steven Spielberg, Jeffrey Katzenberg, and David Geffen formed **DreamWorks SKG**, which is a major movie and recording production company. Spielberg's fame and money came from directing such films as *E. T.*, Katzenberg was a leading executive at Disney, and Geffen built and sold Geffen Records. These multimillionaire multimedia giants combined their talents to form a formidable entertainment company.

Interestingly, DreamWorks was hatched as a Delaware limited liability company, or LLC. The organizers chose an LLC because it is taxed as a partnership and the profits (or losses) flow directly to the owners, but like a corporation, the owners are protected from personal liability beyond their capital contributions.

DreamWorks issued several classes of stock, or interests. The three principals put up $100 million ($33.3 million each) for **"SKG" stock**, which grants the principals 100 percent voting control and 67 percent of the firm's profits. In addition, each principal has a seven-year employment contract that pays them $1 million annually, plus other fringe benefits and perquisites on terms that are customary for similarly situated executives in the entertainment industry.

DreamWorks raised the other $900 million of its $1 billion capital from other investors, who received a third of future profits. The other investors were issued the following classes of stock:

Class	Investment
A	Outside investors. Class A stock was sold to big investors with over $20 million to invest. Microsoft's cofounder, Paul Allen, has purchased $500 million of Class A stock. Class A investors got seats on the board of directors.
S	Outside investors. Class S stock was issued for smallish, "strategic" investments with other companies for cross-marketing purposes.
E	Employees. Employees were granted the right to participate in an employee stock purchase plan.

Conversion of an Existing Business to an LLC

Many LLCs are formed by entrepreneurs to start new businesses. In addition, many existing businesses may want to convert to an LLC to obtain its tax benefits and limited liability shield. General partnerships, limited partnerships, and corporations may be converted to an LLC if the following requirements are met [ULLCA § 902]:

1. An **agreement of conversion** is drafted that sets forth the terms of the conversion.
2. The terms of the conversion are approved by all of the parties or by the number or percentage of owners required for conversion.
3. Articles of organization of the LLC are filed with the secretary of state. The articles must state that the LLC was previously another form of business and the prior business's name.

The conversion takes effect when the articles of organization are filed with the secretary of state or at any later date specified in the articles of organization. When the conversion takes effect, all property owned by the prior business vests in the LLC, and all debts, obligations, and liabilities of the prior business become those of the LLC [ULLCA § 903].

agreement of conversion
Document that states the terms for converting an existing business to an LLC.

Business Brief
Some existing businesses, such as general partnerships, limited partnerships, and corporations, may want to convert to an LLC. The law permits such conversions.

A general partner who becomes a member of an LLC as a result of a conversion remains personally liable for the obligations incurred by the partnership before the conversion takes effect [ULLCA § 902(g)]. A limited partner of a converted limited partnership only has limited liability for the obligations incurred by the limited partnership prior to conversion. After the conversion, the prior general partners and limited partners become members of the LLC with limited liability for any new obligations incurred by the LLC [ULLCA § 902(h)].

Consider This Example   Benjamin, Esther, and Stacy are general partners of a general partnership. The partners vote to convert to an LLC, sign an agreement of conversion, and file the articles of organization with the secretary of state to create the LLC. At the time of conversion, the partnership owed $300,000 to Rural Bank. After converting to an LLC, the LLC borrows $500,000 from City Bank. If the LLC later fails while still owing these bank loans, Benjamin, Esther, and Stacy are personally liable for the $300,000 owed to Rural Bank but are not personally liable for the LLC's $500,000 loan from City Bank. Only the LLC is liable to City Bank.

domestic LLC
An LLC in the state in which it is organized.

foreign LLC
An LLC in any state other than the one in which it is organized.

alien LLC
An LLC that is organized in another country.

certificate of authority
Formal document that must be issued by the secretary of state of a state before a foreign LLC may conduct business in that state.

FOREIGN LIMITED LIABILITY COMPANY

An LLC organized in one state may conduct business in another state. The LLC is called a **domestic limited liability company** in its state of organization. An LLC is called a **foreign limited liability company** in all other states in which it conducts business. To conduct business in another state, an LLC must obtain a **certificate of authority** from the secretary of state of that state to conduct business there. This requires that the foreign LLC file an application with the secretary of state of the state in which it wants to conduct business [ULLCA § 1002]. For example, if an LLC is organized in Florida and conducts business in Nebraska, it is a domestic LLC in Florida and a foreign LLC in Nebraska.

An **alien limited liability company** is an LLC organized in a foreign country and doing business in the United States. In most states, alien LLCs are treated as foreign LLCs.

Great Britain and many European countries offered forms of limited liability businesses long before the United States developed the limited liability company (LLC).

International Perspective

LIMITED LIABILITY COMPANIES IN FOREIGN COUNTRIES

The use of the limited liability company (LLC) as a form of conducting business in the United States is of recent origin. In 1977 Wyoming was the first state in the United States to enact legislation creating an LLC as a legal form for conducting business. This new form of business received little attention until the early 1990s when several more states enacted legislation to allow the creation of LLCs. The evolution of LLCs then grew at blinding speed, with all states having enacted LLC statutes by 1998. Most LLC laws are quite similar, although some differences do exist between these state statutes.

The United States did not invent the LLC as a form of business, however. An LLC form of business has been used in different countries of the world for a long time. The **limitada**, a form of business used in Latin America, has many similarities to the LLC. Limitadas have been used in Argentina, Brazil, Mexico, and other Latin American countries for a century. These entities share the features of limited liability of owners and centralized management with the LLC. In creating its LLC law, the state of Florida noted that its LLC law was necessary to provide a form of business similar to Latin limitadas, with which Central and South American investors were familiar.

On the European continent, an equivalent form of business to the LLC has existed for centuries. In Spain it was called the **sociedad de responsibilidades limitada**. Modern continental LLCs provide for limited liability of owners and centralized management. Germany was one of the latest European countries to add the LLC as a form of business—one century ago. In England, an antecedent to the LLC called the **stock company** was developed around 1555. These companies, while technically partnerships, had limited liability of owners, free transferability of ownership interests, and centralized management similar to modern LLCs.

In the United States, the LLC has rapidly become the business of choice for nonpublicly traded business. Although the use of LLCs by entrepreneurs and other business owners has received much attention in this country, it must not be forgotten that the LLC is not a United States' invention but is an international form of business that has been in use in other countries of the world for centuries.

*O*PERATING A LIMITED LIABILITY COMPANY

The ULLCA specifies certain rights, duties, and rules for conducting the affairs of an LLC. The operation of an LLC is discussed in the following paragraphs.

Powers of an LLC

An LLC has the same powers as an individual to do all things necessary or convenient to carry on its business or affairs. These include the power to own and transfer personal property; sell, lease, and mortgage real property; make contracts and guarantees; borrow and lend money; issue notes and bonds; sue and be sued; and take other actions to conduct the affairs and business of the LLC [ULLCA § 112].

Operating Agreement

Members of an LLC may enter into an **operating agreement** that regulates the affairs of the company and the conduct of its business and governs relations among the members, managers, and company [ULLCA § 103(a)]. The operating agreement may be amended by the approval of all members unless otherwise provided in the agreement. The operating agreement and amendments may be oral but are usually written. Sample provisions from an operating agreement appear in Exhibit 35.3.

Business Brief
The two governing documents of an LLC are the (1) articles of organization and (2) operating agreement.

Morality cannot be legislated, but behavior can be regulated. Judicial decrees may not change the heart, but they can restrain the heartless.

Martin Luther King, Jr.
Strength to Love (1963)

operating agreement
An agreement entered into among members that governs the affairs and business of the LLC and the relations among members, managers, and the LLC.

Exhibit 35.3 *Sample Provisions from an LLC Operating Agreement*

Management

1. **Management by Managers** The management of the Company's business shall be vested in Managers designated by the Members. The Members hereby designate each of Nikki Nguyen, Frederick Richards, and Sylvia Maiorescu to be the initial Managers of the Company.

2. **Powers of Managers** The property, business, and affairs of the Company will be managed, and the conduct of its business will be controlled by, the Managers. The Managers shall have all of the rights, powers, and obligations as provided in the Limited Liability Company Act and as otherwise provided by law. The Managers shall have the following powers and the Managers are authorized on behalf of the Company to do or cause to be done the following:

   (i) To supervise with respect to the property, business, and affairs of the Company and hire, on behalf of the Company, such professionals or other experts as may be necessary or desirable in connection therewith.

   (ii) To determine, in their sole judgment, the amount, manner of payment, and date of any Distributions to be made to the Members hereunder.

   (iii) To make any and all filings on behalf of the Company and its Members as they shall deem necessary, including, without limitation, filings of articles or certificates with the Secretary of State and the filing of such documents, forms, and requests for exemption as may be required pursuant to federal and state securities laws.

   (iv) To make such filings with governmental and other authorities and to take any and all other actions as may be necessary to maintain the limited liability of the Members of the Company.

   (v) To establish and maintain bank accounts, including savings accounts and demand deposit accounts, and cash management accounts.

   (vi) To do generally all things in connection with any of the foregoing, generally manage, oversee, and administer the property, business, and affairs of the Company and execute all documents on behalf of the Company in connection therewith and sign or accept all checks, notes, and drafts on the Company's behalf and, except as expressly restricted herein, pay as Company expenses all costs or expenses connected with the operation or management of the Company.

3. **Managers as Agents** The Managers shall be agents of the Company for the purpose of transacting its business, and the acts of the Managers, including the execution in the name of the Company of any instrument, for apparently carrying on in the usual way the business of the Company shall bind the Company, unless (1) the Manager acting has in fact no authority to act for the Company in the particular matter and (2) the Person with whom such Manager is dealing has knowledge of the fact that such Manager has no such authority. No Member, solely by reason of being a Member, shall be an agent of the Company for the purpose of transacting its business except to the extent that authority has been expressly delegated to such Member in writing by the Managers or by the provisions in this Operating Agreement. An act of a Member or the Managers that is not apparently for the carrying on of the business of the Company in the usual way shall not bind the Company unless authorized in fact by the Company in the particular matter. No act of a Member, a Manager or other agent of the Company in contravention of a restriction on authority shall bind the Company to Persons having knowledge of such restriction.

4. **Duties of Managers** Each Manager shall perform his or her duties in good faith and with that degree of care that an ordinarily prudent person in a like position would use under similar circumstances. In performing their duties, each Manager shall be entitled to rely on information, opinions, reports, or statements, including financial statements and other financial data, in each case prepared or presented by: (1) one or more agents or employees of the Company or (2) counsel, accountants or other Persons as to matters that such Manager believes to be within such Person's professional or expert competence, provided such Manager has no knowledge concerning the matter in question that would cause such reliance to be unwarranted. A Person who so performs his or her duties in accordance with this Section shall have no liability by reason of being or having been a Manager of the Company.

5. **Qualification of Managers** A Manager may, but need not, be a Member of the Company.

6. **Term of Managers** Each Manager shall hold office and have the terms and responsibilities accorded to him or her by this Operating Agreement until resignation or removal by the Members.

7. **Election of Managers** Each initial Manager shall hold office until the earlier of the first annual meeting of the Company or until resignation or removal by the Members. The Members shall thereafter vote to elect or designate any subsequent Managers of the Company. Any Manager of the Company may be removed or replaced with or without cause by a vote of a Majority in Interest of the Members entitled to vote thereon.

8. **Action by Managers** The Managers shall manage the Company by the affirmative vote of a majority of the Managers. Any action required or permitted to be taken by the Managers may be taken without a vote if all of the Managers consent thereto in writing and such writing is filed with the records of the Company. The Managers may participate in a meeting by means of conference telephone or similar communications equipment by means of which all persons participating in the meeting hear each other. Such participation shall constitute presence in person at such meeting.

*E*XHIBIT 35.3   *Continued*

9. **Resignation of Managers** A Manager may resign at any time by giving written notice to the Company. However, if such resignation violates any provision contained in this Operating Agreement or the provision of any contractual agreement between such Manager and the Company, the Company may recover from such Manager damages for such breach as provided in this Operating Agreement or by contract or law. The election of a Manager shall not of itself create contract rights in favor of any such party.

10. **Vacancies** Vacancies occurring among the Managers shall be filled by the vote of a Majority in Interest of the Members entitled to vote thereon. Any Manager chosen to fill a vacancy shall serve the unexpired term of his or her predecessor.

11. **Fees and Compensation** The Company may pay the Managers, or any accountants, agents, attorneys, consultants or advisors to the Company, compensation, and fees in compensation for services rendered to the Company. Any such fees shall be treated as expenses of the Company and shall not be deemed to constitute Distributions to the recipient of any Profit, Loss or capital of the Company.

12. **Reimbursement** The Company shall reimburse the Managers for all ordinary and necessary out-of-pocket expenses incurred by them on behalf of the Company. Such reimbursement shall be treated as an expense of the Company that shall be deducted in computing the Net Cash Flow and shall not be deemed to constitute a distributive share of Profits or a Distribution or return of capital to the Managers, and such reimbursement shall be made out of the assets of the Company. The Managers' sole determination of which expenses may be reimbursed and the amount thereof shall be conclusive.

13. **Indemnification** To the fullest extent permitted by law, the Company shall indemnify and hold harmless each Manager from and against any and all losses, claims, damages, liabilities, or expenses of whatever nature, as incurred, arising out of or relating to the fact that such party was or is a Manager of the Company. Notwithstanding the foregoing, no indemnification may be made to or on behalf of a Manager if a judgment or other final adjudication adverse to such Manager establishes (1) that his or her acts were committed in bad faith or were the result of active and deliberate dishonesty and were material to the cause of action so adjudicated or (2) that he or she personally gained in fact a financial profit or other advantage to which he or she was not legally entitled.

14. **Interested Managers** No contract or other transaction between the Company and one or more of the Managers or between the Company and any other limited liability company or other business entity in which one or more of the Managers are managers, directors, or officers or have a substantial financial interest, shall be either void or voidable for this reason alone or by reason alone that such Manager or Managers were present at the meeting of Managers which approved such contract or transaction or that his or her or their votes were counted for such purposes, (i) if the material facts as to such Manager's interest in such contract or transaction and as to any such common managership, directorship, officership, or financial interest are disclosed in good faith or known to the other Managers, and the Managers approve such contract or transaction by a vote sufficient for such purpose without counting the vote of such interested Manager or, if the votes of the disinterested Managers are insufficient to constitute an act of the Managers by unanimous vote of the disinterested Managers or (ii) if the material facts as to such Manager's interest in such contract or transaction and as to any such common managership, directorship, officership, or financial interest are disclosed in good faith or known to the Members entitled to vote thereon, and such contract or transaction is approved by the vote of such Members.

Liability of the LLC

An LLC is liable for any loss or injury caused to anyone as a result of a wrongful act or omission by a member, manager, agent, or employee of the LLC who commits the wrongful act while acting within the ordinary course of business of the LLC or with authority of the LLC [ULLCA § 302].

Consider This Example   Sable, Silvia, and Samantha form the SSS, LLC, to own and operate a business. Each member contributes $10,000 capital. While on LLC business, Sable drives her automobile and accidently hits and injures Damon. Damon can recover damages for his injuries from Sable personally because she committed the negligent act. Damon can also recover damages from the SSS, LLC, because Sable was acting within the scope of the ordinary business of the LLC when the accident occurred. Silvia and Samantha have limited liability only up to their capital contribution in the SSS, LLC.

Managers of LLCs are not personally liable for the debts, obligations, and liabilities of the LLC they manage [ULLCA § 303(a)].

Business Brief

An LLC is liable for any loss or injury caused to anyone as a result of a wrongful act or omission by a member, manager, agent, or employee of the LLC who commits the wrongful act while acting within the ordinary course of business of the LLC or with authority of the LLC.

Consider This Example   An LLC that does real estate development hires Sarah Goldstein, a nonmember, to be its president. While acting within the scope of her LLC authority, Sarah signs a loan agreement whereby the LLC borrows $1,000,000 from a bank to complete the construction of an office building. If the LLC subsequently suffers financial difficulty and defaults on the bank loan, Sarah is not personally responsible for the loan. The LLC is liable for the loan, but Sarah is not because she is the manager of the LLC.

The failure of an LLC to observe the usual company formalities is not ground for imposing personal liability on the members of the LLC [ULLCA § 303(b)]. For example, if the LLC does not keep minutes of the company's meetings, the members do not become personally liable for the LLC's debts.

Member-Managed and Manager-Managed LLCs

An LLC can be either a **member-managed LLC** or a **manager-managed LLC**. An LLC is a member-managed LLC unless it is designated as a manager-managed LLC in its articles of organization [ULLCA § 203(a)(6)].

The designation of an LLC as a member-managed LLC or manager-managed LLC is important in determining who has authority to bind the LLC to contracts. In a member-managed LLC, all members have agency authority to bind the LLC to contracts. On the other hand, in a manager-managed LLC, only the designated managers have authority to bind the LLC to contracts; nonmanager members do not have such authority. An LLC is only bound to contracts that are in the ordinary course of business or that the LLC has authorized [ULLCA § 301].

Management of an LLC

In a member-managed LLC, each member has equal rights in the management of the business of the LLC, irrespective of the size of his or her capital contribution. Any matter relating to the business of the LLC is decided by a majority vote of the members [ULLCA § 404(a)].

Consider This Example   Allison, Jaeson, Stacy, Lan-Wei, and Ivy form NorthWest.com LLC. Allison contributes $100,000 capital and the other four members each contributes $25,000 capital. When deciding whether or not to add another line of products to the business, Stacy, Lan-Wei, and Ivy vote to add the line, and Allison and Jaeson vote against it. The line of new products is added to the LLC's business because three members voted yes while two members voted no. It does not matter that the two members who voted no contributed $125,000 in capital collectively versus $75,000 in capital contributed by the three members who voted yes.

In a manager-managed LLC, the members and nonmembers who are designated managers control the management of the LLC. The members who are not managers have no rights to manage the LLC unless otherwise provided in the operating agreement. A manager must be appointed by a vote of a majority of the members; managers may also be removed by a vote of the majority of the members [ULLCA § 404(b)(3)]. In a manager-managed LLC, each manager has equal rights in the management and conduct of the company's business. Any matter relating to the business of the LLC may be exclusively decided by the managers by a majority vote of the managers [ULLCA § 403(b)].

Certain actions cannot be delegated to managers but must be voted on by all members of the LLC. These include (1) amending the articles of organization, (2) amending the operating agreement, (3) admitting new members, (4) consenting to dissolve the LLC, (5) consenting to merge the LLC with another entity, and (6) selling, leasing, or disposing of all or substantially all of the LLC's property [ULLCA § 404(c)].

A member or manager may appoint a proxy to vote or otherwise act for him or her by signing an appropriate proxy card [ULLCA § 404(e)].

There shall be one law for the native and for the stranger who sojourns among you.

Moses
Exodus 12:49

---

member-managed LLC
An LLC that has not designated that it is a manager-managed LLC in its articles of organization.

manager-managed LLC
An LLC that has designated in its articles of organization that it is a manager-managed LLC.

Business Brief

In a member-managed LLC, all members can bind the LLC to authorized contracts. In a manager-managed LLC, only the managers can bind the LLC to authorized contracts.

Business Brief

In a member-managed LLC, each member has an equal right in the management of the LLC. A majority vote of the members controls.

Business Brief

In a manager-managed LLC, the managers control the management of the LLC; nonmanager members have no rights to manage the LLC except as provided in the operating agreement or for issues that are nondelegable by law.

Restrictions on Contracting Authority

Members' and managers' authority to bind the LLC to contracts may be restricted in either the articles of organization or the operating agreement. Restrictions on authority of members or managers to bind the LLC to contracts do not affect the apparent authority of members or managers to bind the LLC to third parties who do not have notice of the restriction. Restrictions in the articles of organization that are filed with the secretary of state are public and therefore considered proper notice; restrictions in an operating agreement do not give proper notice unless the third party is directly notified of the restriction.

Consider This Example   Mario, Tran, and Susan form the Hampton LLC. The operating agreement among the members states that Susan does not have power to bind the LLC to contracts. This restriction does not appear in the LLC's articles of organization. Susan signs a lease on behalf of the LLC with the Xerox Corporation to lease a Xerox copier for the LLC. Xerox is not made aware of the restriction on Susan's authority contained in the operating agreement. In this case, the LLC is bound to the lease with Xerox.

> **Business Brief**
> Restrictions on members' and managers' authority to bind the LLC to contracts in the articles of organization are effective against third parties; restrictions on contract authority contained in the operating agreement are only effective against parties who are given notice of the restriction.

Entrepreneur and the Law

DIVIDING AN LLC'S PROFITS AND LOSSES

Unless otherwise agreed, the ULLCA mandates that a member has the right to an equal share in the LLC's profits [ULLCA § 405(a)]. This is a default rule that the members can override by agreement and is usually a provision in their operating agreement. For example, in many instances the members may not want the profits of the LLC to be shared equally. This would normally occur if the capital contributions of the members were unequal. If the members want the profits divided in the same proportion as their capital contributions, this should be specified in the operating agreement.

Consider This Example   Lilly and Harrison form an LLC. Lilly contributes $75,000 capital and Harrison contributes $25,000 capital. They do not have an agreement as to how profits are to be shared. If the LLC makes $100,000 in profits, under the ULLCA Lilly and Harrison will share the profits equally—$50,000 each. To avoid this outcome, Lilly and Harrison should agree in their operating agreement how they want the profits to be divided.

Losses from an LLC are shared equally unless otherwise agreed. Sometimes members will not want to divide losses equally and maybe not even in the same way as their capital contributions. If the LLC has chosen to be taxed as a partnership, the losses from an LLC flow to the members' individual income tax returns. Losses from an LLC can sometimes be offset against members' gains from other sources. Therefore, the members may want to agree to divide the losses so that the members who can use them to offset other income will receive a greater share of the losses.

Profits and losses from an LLC do not have to be distributed in the same proportion. For example, a member who has the right to a 10 percent share of profits may be given the right to receive 25 percent of the LLC's losses.

Compensation and Reimbursement

A nonmanager member is not entitled to remuneration for services performed for the LLC (except for winding up the business of the LLC). Managers of an LLC, whether they are members or not, are paid compensation and benefits as specified in their employment agreements with the LLC [ULLCA § 403(d)].

An LLC is obligated to reimburse members and managers for payments made on behalf of the LLC (e.g., business expenses) and to indemnify members and managers for liabilities incurred in the ordinary course of LLC business or in the preservation of the LLC's business or property [ULLCA § 403(a)].

Right to Information

An LLC must give members and their agents access to its records at the LLC's principal office or other reasonable location. This includes the opportunity to inspect any records during ordinary business hours. A member has the right upon written demand to obtain a copy of the LLC's written operating agreement [ULLCA § 408].

Member Lawsuits

direct lawsuit

A lawsuit that a member can bring against an LLC to enforce his or her personal rights as a member.

A member of an LLC may bring a **direct lawsuit** against his or her LLC for any legal or equitable relief, with or without an accounting. Direct lawsuits are brought to enforce the member's rights under the articles of organization, operating agreement, the state's LLC code, and other federal, state, or local laws [ULLCA § 410]. Typically, direct lawsuits are often brought to enforce a member's right to vote, inspect the books and records of the LLC, and compel the dissolution of the LLC. If a member is successful in a direct lawsuit against his or her LLC, any award of damages belongs to the member.

derivative action

A lawsuit that a member may bring against an offending third party on behalf of his or her LLC when the LLC fails to bring the lawsuit or a request of the LLC to do so is excused.

If an LLC is harmed by a third party, the members or managers have the authority to bring an action on behalf of the LLC against the offending party to recover damages or other relief. If the member or manager having the authority to bring the lawsuit against a third party refuses to do so, or an effort to cause the members or managers to bring the lawsuit is unlikely to succeed, any member has the right to bring the lawsuit against the third party on behalf of the LLC. This is called a **derivative action** or **derivative lawsuit** [ULLCA § 101]. In a derivative action, the complaint must set forth the effort that the plaintiff-member took to secure initiation of the lawsuit by the LLC or the reasons for not making such effort [ULLCA § 1103].

If a derivative action is successful, the court may award the plaintiff-member reasonable expenses, including attorney's fees. The remainder of the award belongs to the LLC [ULLCA § 1104].

It is the spirit and not the form of law that keeps justice alive.

Earl Warren The Law and the Future (1955)

Consider This Example Tai-Chi is one of the 20 members who own Japan Import, LLC, an LLC organized in New York. Tai-Chi has reasonable grounds to believe that Nora and Bradford, two of the four member-managers of the LLC, have jointly embezzled funds from the LLC. Tai-Chi can bring a derivative action on behalf of the LLC against Nora and Bradford to recover the embezzled funds. Under the facts of this case, Tai-Chi would be excused from making a demand on the member-managers to bring the lawsuit because Nora and Bradford would not be likely to bring a lawsuit against themselves. Tai-Chi's complaint must state this reason.

Members' Distributional Interest

distributional interest

A member's ownership interest in an LLC that entitles the member to receive distributions of money and property from the LLC.

A member's ownership interest in an LLC is called a **distributional interest**. A member's distributional interest in an LLC is personal property and may be transferred in whole or part [ULLCA § 501(b)]. Generally, a transfer of an interest in an LLC does not entitle the transferee to become a member of the LLC or to exercise any right of a member. A transfer entitles the transferee to receive only distributions from the LLC to which the transferor would have been entitled [ULLCA § 502].

Business Brief

A transferee of a distributional interest in an LLC receives the right to receive profit and other distributions of the LLC.

Consider This Example Cleveland, Heather, and Archibald are members of the Boston Tea Party, LLC; each owns a one-third interest in the LLC and the members agree to divide the distributions of the LLC equally in one-third portions. Cleveland sells his one-third interest to Theodore. The LLC makes $99,999 in profits. Theodore is entitled to receive one-third of the distributions ($33,333). Theodore is not a member of the LLC, however.

A transferee of a distributional interest becomes a member of the LLC if it is so provided in the operating agreement or if all the other members of the LLC consent [ULLCA § 503(a)]. A transferee who transfers his or her distributional interest is not released from liability for the debts, obligations, and liabilities of the LLC [ULLCA § 503(c)].

A member has no property interest in the property of the LLC, however. Therefore, a member has no transferable interest in the property of the LLC [ULLCA § 501(a)].

Consider This Example Everett, Jae Moon, and Harvey each own a one-third interest in the New York Construction, LLC. The LLC owns 20 pieces of heavy construction equipment valued at $10 million. Jae Moon transfers her one-third interest to Vinnie. Vinnie receives Jae Moon's one-third interest in the distributions of profits of the LLC; Vinnie does not receive a one-third ownership interest in the individual pieces of construction equipment, however.

Judgment Creditor's Charging Order

If a creditor of an individual member of an LLC obtains a judgment against a member, the creditor becomes a judgment creditor. To satisfy the debt, a judgment creditor can ask the court to issue a **charging order** against the debtor-member's LLC distributional interest. A charging order, which is a form of a judicial lien, entitles the judgment creditor to be paid out of the debtor-member's LLC profits and distributions. Judgment creditors do not become members and are not entitled to participate in the management of the LLC. The debtor-member against whom the charging order is issued remains a member of the LLC with all of the rights and duties of a member.

The LLC or any member can redeem the interest subject to the charging order by paying the judgment creditor the amount due on the judgment [ULLCA § 504].

charging order
Order of the court mandating that an LLC pay a debtor-member's distributional interest to a judgment creditor.

𝓕IDUCIARY DUTIES OF LOYALTY AND CARE OWED TO LLC

A member of a member-managed LLC and a manager of a manager-managed LLC owe two fiduciary duties to the LLC: (1) a duty of loyalty and (2) a duty of care [ULLCA § 409(a) and § 409(h)(2)]. These duties are discussed in the following paragraphs.

Business Brief
Members of member-managed LLCs and managers of manager-managed LLCs owe fiduciary duties of loyalty and care to the LLC.

Duty of Loyalty Owed to LLC

A member of a member-managed LLC and a manager of a manager-managed LLC owe the **duty of loyalty** to the LLC. This means that these parties must act honestly in their dealings with the LLC. The duty of loyalty includes the duty not to usurp the LLC's opportunities, make secret profits, secretly deal with the LLC, secretly compete with the LLC, or represent any interest adverse to that of the LLC [ULLCA § 409(b)]. For example, making secret kickbacks on the purchase of goods by the LLC and transacting business with the LLC without first disclosing this position and obtaining approval from the LLC to do so are breaches of the duty of loyalty.

duty of loyalty
A duty owed by a member of a member-managed LLC and a manager of a manager-managed LLC to be honest in his or her dealings with the LLC and to not act adversely to the interests of the LLC.

Consider This Example Viola is a member of the member-managed Auction.com, LLC. The LLC is in the business of operating on-line auctions over the Internet. The owner of Dolls & Toys.com., LLC, a company that conducts on-line auctions over the Internet to sell Beanie Babies, Pokémon cards, and such, approaches Viola to inquire whether Auction.com would be interested in purchasing Dolls & Toys.com. Instead of disclosing this opportunity to her LLC, Viola pays the asking price and personally purchases Dolls & Toys.com. In this case, Viola has breached her duty of loyalty to Auction.com by usurping (stealing) an LLC opportunity. To legally purchase Dolls & Toys.com, Viola would have first had to offer the opportunity to Auction.com and give it a reasonable time

Business Brief
Breaches of the duty of loyalty by a covered member or manager include (1) usurping an LLC opportunity, (2) making secret profits, (3) secretly dealing with the LLC, (4) secretly competing with the LLC, and (5) representing any interest adverse to that of the LLC.

to accept or reject the offer. Only if the offer is rejected by Auction.com, or a reasonable time passed and Auction.com has not acted, is Viola free to purchase Dolls & Toys.com.

In the following case, the court found a member-manager of an LLC to have breached his fiduciary duty of loyalty.

Advanced Orthopedics, LLC v. Moon
656 So.2d 1103 (1995)
Court of Appeal of Louisiana

CASE 35.3

FACTS

In November 1992, Bryon Heath and John Moon organized a limited liability company called "Advanced Orthopedics, L.L.C." (Advanced) under Louisiana law. The articles of organization were filed with the Louisiana State Secretary of State's office, which issued a certificate of organization establishing the LLC. Advanced, under the management of Heath and Moon, provided prosthetic and orthotic services to the community. By June 1993, Moon and Heath were having difficulties managing Advanced together. While at Advanced, Moon took steps to set up a competing business. By November 1993, Moon opened his own prosthetic and orthotic services business. He thereafter resigned from Advanced.

Advanced filed a petition for permanent injunction and damages against Moon, alleging that Moon violated his fiduciary duty of loyalty to Advanced by setting up his competing business while still a member-manager of Advanced. The trial court granted a preliminary injunction in favor of Advanced, enjoining Moon from soliciting any of Advanced's patients or using any of Advanced's records. The court rejected Moon's defense that Advanced was not a legally formed limited liability company because he allegedly did not have the subjective intent to form an LLC. Moon appealed.

ISSUE

Was a limited liability company formed by Heath and Moon, thereby justifying the trial court's finding that Moon had violated his fiduciary duty of loyalty to Advanced Orthopedics, L.L.C.?

IN THE LANGUAGE OF THE COURT

Gothard, Judge   In Moon's first assignment of error, he argues that he did not have the subjective intent to form an L.L.C. with

Heath. During the year that Moon participated in the management of Advanced, he never questioned its viability as an L.L.C. He testified in his deposition that he reviewed informational materials regarding LLCs prior to Advanced's inception and that he knew that he and Heath were operating their business as an L.L.C. Advanced clearly provided enough evidence to the trial court to support its argument that an L.L.C. was formed and operating.

On appeal, Moon argues that he did not adequately understand the concept of an L.L.C. Attaining a certain level of understanding regarding LLCs is not a prerequisite to the formation of and participation in one. After a thorough review of the record, we cannot find any support for Moon's assertion that somehow he did not have the subjective intent to form an L.L.C. with Heath.

DECISION AND REMEDY

The court of appeal held that Heath and Moon had formed a limited liability company and upheld the trial court's finding that Moon had violated his fiduciary duty of loyalty to the LLC. The court of appeal affirmed the decision of the trial court.

Case Questions

Critical Legal Thinking   Should the law impose fiduciary duties of loyalty and care on member-managers and managers of LLCs? Why or why not?

Ethics   Do you think Moon acted ethically in denying that an LLC had been formed?

Business Application   What are the economic implications if a member-manager or manager competes with his or her LLC? Should this practice be illegal?

---

duty of care

A duty owed by a member of a member-managed LLC and a manager of a manager-managed LLC to not engage in (1) a known violation of law, (2) intentional conduct, (3) reckless conduct, or (4) grossly negligent conduct that injures the LLC.

Limited Duty of Care Owed to LLC

A member of a member-managed LLC and a manager of a manager-managed LLC owe a **duty of care** to the LLC not to engage in (1) a known violation of law, (2) intentional conduct, (3) reckless conduct, or (4) grossly negligent conduct that injures the LLC. This is a *limited duty of care* because it does not include ordinary negligence. Thus, if a covered member or manager commits an ordinarily negligent act that is not grossly negligent, he or she is not liable to the LLC.

An LLC is liable to third parties injured by a member of a member-managed LLC or manager of a manager-managed LLC who is acting on LLC business whether the injury was caused by a known violation of law, intentional or reckless conduct, or gross or ordinary negligence. A member or manager is also personally liable for injuries caused to third parties by his or her ordinary negligence.

Consider This Example   Charlene is a member of a member-managed LLC. While engaging in LLC business, Charlene is driving an automobile and accidently hits Zubin, a pedestrian, and severely injures him. Under agency theory, Zubin sues the LLC and recovers $1 million in damages. If the court determines that Charlene was ordinarily negligent when she caused the accident—for example, she was driving the speed limit and did not see Zubin because the sun was in her eyes—she will not be liable to the LLC for any losses caused to the LLC by her negligence. If instead the court determines that Charlene was driving 65 mph in a 35 mph zone and thus was grossly negligent, Charlene is liable to the LLC for the $1 million it was ordered to pay Zubin.

Business Brief
A member or manager of an LLC is not liable to the LLC for injuries caused to the LLC by his or her ordinary negligence. The ordinarily negligent member or manager, and the LLC on whose behalf the member or manager was acting when the negligent act occurred, are liable to the injured third party.

Duty of Good Faith and Fair Dealing Owed to LLC

The ULLCA imposes an obligation of **good faith and fair dealing** on a member of a member-managed LLC in discharging his or her duties to the LLC and its other members [ULLCA § 409(d)]. Under this duty, the members of a member-managed LLC not only are held to the express terms of the LLC's articles of organization and operating agreement but are also required to act in "good faith" and deal fairly in all respects in achieving the objectives of the LLC.

Business Brief
Members of a member-managed LLC owe a duty of good faith and fair dealing when discharging his or her LLC duties.

Consider This Example   Edward, Elvira, and Estonia are members of Book Publishers, LLC, a member-managed LLC. The business, which is 20 years old, was originally formed to engage in hardcover book publishing. The business converted to an LLC seven years ago with the stated purpose of engaging in book publishing. Today, Elvira sees an opportunity for on-line publishing over the Internet and would like to do this herself. However, under the doctrine of good faith and fair dealing, Elvira should take her idea for electronic on-line publishing to Edward and Estonia to see if they want to consider having Book Publishers, LLC, engage in this business. This is so even though the original business of the LLC is hardcover book publishing.

No Fiduciary Duty Owed by a Nonmanager-Member

A member of a manager-managed LLC who is not a manager owes no fiduciary duty of loyalty or care, or duty of good faith and fair dealing, to the LLC or its other members [ULLCA § 409(h)(1)]. Basically, a nonmanager member of a manager-managed LLC is treated equally to a shareholder in a corporation.

Consider This Example   Felicia is a member of a 30-person manager-managed LLC that is engaged in buying, developing, and selling real estate. Felicia is not a manager of the LLC but is just a member-owner. If a third party approaches Felicia with the opportunity to purchase a large and valuable piece of real estate that is ripe for development, and the price is below fair market value, Felicia owes no duty to offer the opportunity to the LLC. She may purchase the piece of real estate for herself without violating any duty to the LLC.

Business Brief
A nonmanager member of a manager-managed LLC owes no fiduciary duties of loyalty, care, or good faith and fair dealing to the LLC or its members.

*D*ISSOLUTION AND WINDING UP

The ULLCA gives a member of an LLC the power to disassociate him- or herself from the LLC. This could cause the dissolution of the LLC. Other events specified in the ULLCA also may cause the dissolution of an LLC.

Member's Disassociation from an LLC

If the operating agreement does not provide otherwise, a member has the *power* to withdraw from both an at-will LLC and a term LLC by express will [ULLCA § 602(a)]. Although a member has the power to withdraw from both an at-will LLC and a term LLC, the effects of the withdrawal are remarkably different.

The disassociation of a member from a term LLC before the expiration of the specified term is wrongful. The disassociation of a member from an at-will LLC is not wrongful unless the power to withdraw is eliminated in the operating agreement [ULLCA § 602(b)]. A member who wrongfully disassociates him- or herself from an LLC is liable to the LLC and to the other members for any damages caused by his or her **wrongful disassociation** [ULLCA § 602(c)].

A member's disassociation from an LLC terminates that member's right to participate in the management of the LLC, act as an agent of the LLC, or conduct the LLC's business [ULLCA § 603(b)(3)]. Disassociation also terminates the disassociating member's duties of loyalty and care to the LLC [ULLCA § 603(b)(3)].

If a member disassociates from an at-will LLC without causing a wrongful disassociation, the LLC must purchase the disassociated member's **distributional interest** [ULLCA § 701(a)(1)]. The price and terms of a distributional interest may be fixed in the operating agreement [ULLCA § 701(c)]. If the price is not agreed to in the operating agreement, the LLC must pay the fair market value of the distributional interest. The LLC must make an offer to the disassociating member within 30 days after the distributional interest is vested. If the parties do not reach an agreement within another 90 days, the member can bring an action to have the court determine the fair market value of his or her distributional interest [ULLCA § 701(e)].

If a member disassociates him- or herself from a term LLC, the LLC must only purchase the disassociating member's distributional interest on the expiration of the specified term of the LLC [ULLCA § 701(a)(2)]. Any damages caused by wrongful withdrawal must be offset against the purchase price [ULLCA § 701(f)].

Consider This Example   Wendy, Juanita, and Gabriella form an LLC to develop and produce a new documentary film. The term of the LLC is three years. Each member contributes $100,000 capital and agrees, as member-managers, to work full-time on the production of the film. After one year, Gabriella decides to quit and disassociates herself from the LLC. Several things happen: First, Gabriella has the *power* to disassociate from the LLC and may do so; thus, she is no longer a member of the LLC. Second, Gabriella does not have the *right* to disassociate from the LLC prior to the expiration of the LLC's term; so Gabriella is liable for any damages caused by her wrongful disassociation from the LLC. Third, Gabriella is not due any payment for her distributional interest until the end of the LLC's term, and any damages caused by her wrongful disassociation may be deducted from her distributional interest at that time.

Notice of Disassociation

For two years after a member disassociates him- or herself from an LLC that continues in business, the disassociating member has apparent authority to bind the LLC to contracts in the ordinary course of business except to parties who either (1) know of the disassociation or (2) are given notice of the disassociation [ULLCA § 703].

An LLC can give *constructive notice* of a member's disassociation by filing a **statement of disassociation** with the secretary of state stating the name of the LLC and the name of the member disassociated from the LLC [ULLCA § 704]. This notice is effective against any person who later deals with the disassociated member, whether the person was aware of the notice or not.

Consider This Example   William, Jesse, and Sandy are members of a member-managed LLC that operates an automobile dealership. Jesse disassociates from the LLC. The LLC fails to file a statement of disassociation with the secretary of state. Although Jesse has no express agency authority to bind the LLC to contracts because she is no longer a member of the LLC, Jesse has apparent authority to bind the LLC to contracts in the ordinary course of business for two years after the disassociation or until the LLC files a statement of disassociation with the secretary of state.

Dissolution of an LLC

An LLC is dissolved upon the occurrence of any of the following events:

1. An event specified in the operating agreement.
2. The consent of the percentage or number of members specified in the operating agreement.
3. The occurrence of an event that makes it unlawful for all or substantially all of the business of the LLC to be continued [ULLCA § 801].
4. A member applies to a court to have the LLC dissolved by judicial decree. To obtain a judicial decree, the applicant member must prove either it is impracticable to carry on the LLC's business or the economic purpose of the LLC is likely to be unreasonably frustrated [ULLCA § 801(4)].
5. The secretary of state commences a proceeding to dissolve an LLC administratively if the LLC does not pay required taxes or fees or fails to deliver an annual report to the secretary of state within 60 days after it is due [ULLCA § 809]. An LLC that is administratively dissolved continues in existence but may only carry on business necessary to wind up and liquidate its business and affairs [ULLCA § 810].

Continuation of an LLC

At the expiration of the term of a term LLC, some of its members may want to continue the LLC. At the expiration of its term, a term LLC can be continued in two situations. First, the members of the LLC may vote prior to the expiration date to continue the LLC for an additional specified term. This requires the unanimous vote of all of the members and the filing of an amendment to the articles of organization with the secretary of state stating this fact. Second, absent the unanimous vote to continue the term LLC, the LLC may be continued as an at-will LLC by a simple majority vote of the members of the LLC [ULLCA § 411(b)].

Winding Up an LLC's Business

If the LLC is not continued, an LLC is wound up. **Winding-up** an LLC is the process of preserving and selling the assets of the LLC and distributing the money and property to creditors and members.

After dissolution, any member who has not wrongfully disassociated from the LLC may participate in the winding up of the LLC's business. A member winding up the LLC's business may preserve the LLC's business and property as a going concern for a reasonable time, dispose of and transfer LLC property, discharge the LLC's debt, settle and close the business, and distribute the assets of the LLC [ULLCA § 803].

The assets of the LLC must be applied to first pay off the creditors; thereafter the surplus amount is distributed to the members in equal shares unless the operating agreement provides otherwise [ULLCA § 806]. It is good practice for members to specify in the operating agreement how distributions will be made to members.

After dissolution and winding up, an LLC may terminate its existence by filing **articles of termination** with the secretary of state. The existence of the LLC is terminated upon the filing of the articles of termination by the secretary of state or upon a later effective date specified in the articles of termination [ULLCA § 805].

winding-up

The process of preserving and selling the assets of the LLC and distributing the money and property to creditors and members.

Business Brief

When winding up and distributing the assets of an LLC, creditors are paid first; thereafter surplus amounts are distributed to members in equal amounts unless the operating agreement provides otherwise.

articles of termination

Document that is filed with the secretary of state that terminates the LLC as of the date of filing or upon a later effective date specified in the document.

Working the Web

e-biz

LLC-USA This Web site is a good resource for people interested in limited liability companies.

Visit at **www.llc-usa.com**

Wall Street Research Net Want to find out information about a company or get a company's current stock quote? Then, this is the site for you.

Visit at **www.wsrn.com/home/companyResearch.html**

Web100 Big Business on the Web This site links you to the top 100 companies on the World Wide Web.

Visit at **www.metamoney.com/framed/indexMain.html**

CYBER EXERCISES

1. Find the Resources page of the LLC-USA site. Print out and read the materials on *Limited Liability Company History*.

2. Using Wall Street Research Net, find a current stock quote for your favorite company.

3. From the Web100, what publishing companies are in the top 100?

CASES AND EXERCISES

CRITICAL LEGAL THINKING CASES

35.1. Harold, Jasmine, Caesar, and Yuan form "Microhard.com, LLC," a limited liability company, to sell computer hardware and software over the Internet. Microhard.com, LLC, hires Heather, a recent graduate of the University of Chicago and a brilliant software designer, as an employee. Heather's job is to design and develop software that will execute a computer command when the computer user thinks of the next command he or she wants to execute on the computer. Using Heather's research, Microhard.com, LLC, develops the "Third Eye" software program that does this. Microhard.com, LLC, sends Heather to the annual Comdex Computer Show in Las Vegas, Nevada, to unveil this revolutionary software. Heather goes to Las Vegas and while there rents an automobile to get from the hotel to the computer show and to meet interested buyers at different locations in Las Vegas. While Heather is driving from her hotel to the site of the Comdex Computer Show, she negligently causes an accident where she runs over Harold Singer, a pedestrian. Singer, who suffers severe personal injuries, sues Microhard.com, LLC; Heather; Harold; Jasmine; Caesar; and Yuan to recover monetary damages for his injuries. Who is liable?

35.2. Albert, Lin, and Rafael want to form a limited liability company called "iToys.com, LLC," to sell toys over the

Internet. They hire Laura, a licensed practicing attorney, to do the legal work to prepare and file the articles of organization to create the LLC. Laura drafts the articles of organization and other required legal documents and has Albert, Lin, and Rafael come to her office where they sign the documents. Laura tells the owners that she will file the articles of organization with the secretary of state that afternoon. Relying on this statement, the next day Albert, Lin, and Rafael obtain a bank loan for $500,000 from Business Bank in the name of the LLC. Laura, who became busy doing other things, forgets to file the articles of organization for iToys.com, LLC, with the secretary of state. One year later iToys.com goes bankrupt still owing the $500,000 to Business Bank. Business Bank sues iToys.com, LLC; Albert; Lin; and Rafael to recover the amount of the unpaid loan. Who is liable to Business Bank?

35.3. Isabel, Koshi, and Winchester each contribute $50,000 capital and form a limited liability company called "Fusion Restaurant, LLC," which operates an up-scale restaurant serving "fusion" cuisine combining foods from cultures around the world. Fusion Restaurant, LLC, as a business, borrows $1 million from Melon Bank for operating capital. Isabel, Koshi, and Winchester are so busy cooking, serving, and running the restaurant that they forget to hold members' meetings, keep minute books, or otherwise observe any usual company formalities for the entire first year of business. After this one year of hard work, Fusion Restaurant, LLC, suffers financial difficulties and defaults on the $1 million bank loan from Melon Bank. Melon Bank sues Fusion Restaurant, LLC; Isabel; Koshi; and Winchester to recover the unpaid bank loan. Who is liable?

35.4. Tran, Donald, and Elvira form a limited liability company called "Real Estate Developers, LLC." Each of the three owners contributes $50,000 capital to the LLC, and the LLC then purchases a 400-acre parcel of vacant land 75 miles from Chicago, Illinois. Real Estate Developers, LLC, wants to build a tract of homes on the site. The owners of Real Estate Developers, LLC, go to City Bank and ask to borrow $100 million to complete the development and construction of the homes. City Bank agrees to make the loan to Real Estate Developers, LLC, but only if Donald agrees to personally guarantee the LLC's loan and give security for the loan by pledging his 12-story penthouse in Manhattan, worth $100 million, as collateral for the loan. Donald agrees and signs the personal guarantee that pledges his penthouse as collateral for the loan; City Bank makes the $100 million loan to the LLC. Real Estate Developers, LLC, makes regular interest payments on the loan for one year and then defaults on the loan with $100 million still owed to City Bank. At the time of default, Real Estate Developers, LLC's, only asset is the 400-acre parcel of land that is still worth $150,000. City Bank sues Real Estate Developers, LLC, Tran; Donald; and Elvira to recover the amount of the unpaid loan. Who is liable to City Bank?

35.5. Gregory and Carol are general partners of a general partnership called "Wash Me." The general partnership owns and operates a chain of car washes in Memphis, Tennessee. The general partnership owes $65,000 to Middle Bank for a loan it took out in 1998 to start the business. In the year 2000, due to the tax consequences and limited liability shield offered by limited liability companies, Gregory and Carol convert their general partnership to a limited liability company called "Wash Me, LLC." At the time of conversion, $65,000 is still owed to Middle Bank on the partnership's loan. After conversion, Wash Me, LLC, borrows $100,000 from Commercial Bank to expand its business. After operating the LLC for one year, the business fails with $65,000 still owed to Middle Bank and $100,000 still owed to Commercial Bank. Middle Bank and Commercial Bank sue Wash Me, LLC; Gregory; and Carol to recover for the unpaid bank loans. Who is liable?

35.6. Jennifer, Martin, and Edsel form a limited liability company called the "Big Apple, LLC," to operate a bar in New York City. Jennifer, Martin, and Edsel are member-managers of the LLC. One of Jennifer's jobs as a member-manager is to drive the LLC's truck and pick up certain items of supply for the bar each Wednesday. On the way back to the bar one Wednesday after picking up the supplies for that week, Jennifer negligently runs over a pedestrian, Tilly Tourismo, on a street in Times Square. Tilly is severely injured and sues Big Apple, LLC; Jennifer; Martin; and Edsel to recover monetary damages for her injuries. Who is liable?

35.7. Maria, Richard, and Dakota form a limited liability company called "Ummmmm, LLC," to operate a spa in Santa Fe, New Mexico. Each member contributes $100,000 in capital to start the LLC. Ummmmm, LLC, is a member-managed LLC. Maria enters into a contract on behalf of the LLC where she contracts to have a new hot tub installed at the spa by Hot Tubs, Inc., for $80,000. Hot Tubs, Inc., installs the hot tub and sends a bill for $80,000 to Ummmmm, LLC. When Ummmmm, LLC, fails to pay the bill, Hot Tub, Inc., sues Ummmmm, LLC, to recover the unpaid $80,000. Is Ummmmm, LLC, liable?

35.8. Juan, Min-Yi, and Chelsea form "Unlimited, LLC," a limited liability company that operates a chain of women's retail clothing stores that sell eclectic women's clothing. The company is a manager-managed LLC, and Min-Yi has been designated in the articles of organization filed with the secretary of state as the manager of Unlimited, LLC. Min-Yi sees a store location on Rodeo Drive in Beverly Hills, California, that she thinks would be an excellent location for an Unlimited store. Min-Yi enters into a five-year lease on behalf of Unlimited, LLC, with Landlord, Inc., the owner of the store building, to lease the store at $100,000 rent per year. While visiting Chicago, Chelsea sees a store location on North Michigan Avenue in Chicago that she thinks is a perfect location for an Unlimited store. Chelsea enters into a five-year lease on behalf of Unlimited, LLC, with Real Estate, Inc., the owner of the store building, to lease the store location at $100,000 rent per year. Is Unlimited, LLC, bound to either of these leases?

35.9. Donna, Arnold, Jose, and Won-Suk form a limited liability company called "Millennium Foods, LLC," to operate an organic foods grocery store in Portland, Oregon. Donna and Arnold each contribute $25,000 capital, Jose contributes $50,000, and Won-Suk contributes $100,000. The LLC's articles of organization are silent as to how profits and losses of the LLC are to be divided. The organic foods grocery store is an immediate success and Millennium Foods, LLC, makes $200,000 profit the first year. Jose and Won-Suk want the profits distributed based on the amount of the members' capital contribution. Arnold and Donna think the profits should be distributed equally. Who is correct?

35.10. Daniel is one of five members of the "Blue Note, LLC," a limited liability company that operates a jazz club in New Orleans, Louisiana. The LLC's operating agreement provides that Daniel has the right to receive 20 percent of the LLC's profits. Daniel also owns another business as a sole proprietorship and has taken out a $100,000 loan from River Bank to operate this other business. Daniel defaults on his loan from River Bank, and River Bank sues Daniel and obtains a charging order against Daniel's ownership interest in Blue Note, LLC. What rights does River Bank have with regards to Blue Note, LLC, and Daniel's interest in Blue Note, LLC?

35.11. Ally is a member and a manager of the manager-managed limited liability company called "Movers & You, LLC," a moving company. Movers & You, LLC's, main business is moving large corporations from old office space to new office space in other buildings. After Ally has been a member-manager of Movers & You, LLC, for several years, she decides to join her friend Lana and form another LLC called "Lana & Me, LLC." This new LLC provides moving services that move large corporations from old office space to new office space. Ally becomes a member-manager of Lana & Me, LLC, while retaining her member-manager position at Movers & You, LLC. Ally does not disclose her new position at Lana & Me, LLC, to the other members or managers of Movers & You, LLC. Several years later the other members

of Movers & You, LLC, discover Ally's other ownership and management position at Lana & Me, LLC. Movers & You, LLC, sues Ally to recover damages for her working for Lana & Me, LLC. Is Ally liable?

35.12. Jonathan is a member of a member-managed limited liability company called "Custom Homes, LLC." Custom Homes, LLC, is hired by an owner of a piece of vacant land located on Hilton Head Island, South Carolina, to build a new custom home on the site. Custom Homes, LLC, begins work on the house. Jonathan is responsible for making sure that flashing warning lights are placed in front of the house while it is being constructed to mark open holes in the ground and other dangerous conditions. One night Jonathan leaves from work and forgets to place a flashing warning light marking a hole in front of the house that the LLC is building. That night, Candy, a neighbor who lives in one of the houses in the housing tract where the new house is being built, takes her dog for a walk. As Candy is walking by the unmarked area in front of the new house, she falls into the hole and is severely injured. Candy sues Custom Homes, LLC, to recover damages for her injuries. The jury finds that Jonathan had been ordinarily negligent when he failed to place the flashing warning lights to mark the hole that Candy fell in, and awards Candy $1 million for her injuries. Custom Homes, LLC, pays Candy the $1 million and then sues Jonathan to recover the $1 million. Is Jonathan liable?

ETHICS CASES

35.13. Angela, Yoko, Cherise, and Serena want to start a new business that designs and manufactures toys for children. At a meeting where the owners want to decide what type of legal form to use to operate the business, Cherise states

> *We should use a limited liability company to operate our business because this form of business provides us, the owners, with a limited liability shield, which means that if the business gets sued and loses, we the owners are not personally liable to the injured party except up to our capital contribution in the business.*

The others agree and form a limited liability company called Fuzzy Toys, LLC, to conduct the member-managed business. Each of the four owners contributes $50,000 as their capital contribution to the LLC. Fuzzy Toys, LLC, purchases $800,000 of liability insurance from Allied Insurance Company and starts business. Fuzzy Toys, LLC, designs and produces "Heidi," a new toy doll and female action figure. The new toy doll is an instant success and Fuzzy Toys, LLC, produces and sells millions of these female action figures. After a few months, however, the LLC starts getting complaints that

one of the parts of the female action figure is breaking off quite regularly and some children are swallowing the part. The concerned member-managers of Fuzzy Toys, LLC, issue an immediate recall of the female action figure, but before all of the dolls are returned for a refund, Catherine, a seven-year old child, swallows the toy's part and is severely injured. Catherine, through her mother, sues Fuzzy Toys, LLC, Allied Insurance Company, Angela, Yoko, Cherise, and Serena to recover damages for product liability. At the time of suit, Fuzzy Toys, LLC, has $200,000 of assets. The jury awards Catherine $10 million for her injuries. Who is liable to Catherine and for how much? How much does Catherine recover? Did Angela, Yoko, Cherise, and Serena act ethically in using an LLC as a form of conducting their toy business? Explain.

35.14. Christopher, Melony, Xie, and Ruth form "iNet.com, LLC," a limited liability company. The four members are all Ph.D. scientists who have been working together in a backyard garage to develop a hand-held wireless device that will let you receive and send e-mail, surf the Internet, type word processing that will be printed on any printer in the world, view cable television stations, and keep track of anyone you want anywhere in the world and let you zoom in on the person being tracked without that person knowing you are doing so. This new device, called "Eros," costs only $29.00 but makes the owners $25.00 profit per unit sold. The owners agree that they will buy a manufacturing plant and start producing the unit in six months. Melony, who owns a one-quarter interest in iNet.com, LLC, decides she wants "more of the action" and soon, so she secretly sells the plans and drawings for the new Eros unit to a competitor for $100 million. The competitor comes out with the exact same device, called Zeus, in one month and beats iNet.com, LLC, to the market. The LLC, iNet.com, LLC, which later finds out about Melony's action, suffers damages of $100 million because of Melony's action. Is Melony liable to iNet.com, LLC? Explain. Did Melony act ethically in this case?

CRITICAL LEGAL THINKING WRITING ASSIGNMENT

Read Case A.35 in the Case Appendix [*Water, Waste, and Land, Inc. v. Preferred Income Investors, L.L.C.*]. This case is excerpted from the appellate court opinion. Review and brief the case. In your brief, be sure to answer the following questions:

1. What was the liability of the disclosed agent and the undisclosed agent for the LLC's contracts?

2. Did the notice provision of LLC law change the law of agency in this case?

36

Franchises and Licensing

It has been uniformly laid down in this Court, as far back as we can remember, that good faith is the basis of all mercantile transactions.

BULLER, J. Salomons v. Nissen (1788)

Chapter Objectives

After studying this chapter, you should be able to

1. Define *franchise* and identify the parties to a franchise arrangement.
2. List and describe the various forms of franchises.
3. Describe the disclosures required by state and federal disclosure rules.
4. Describe the rights and duties of the parties to a franchise agreement.
5. Describe various forms of franchise fees.
6. Explain how a franchisor licenses its trademarks, service marks, and trade secrets to franchisees.
7. Identify the contract liability of franchisors and franchisees.
8. Identify the tort liability of franchisors and franchisees.
9. Describe the remedies available for the wrongful termination of a franchise.
10. Describe international franchising.

Chapter Contents

Franchising is an important method for distributing goods and services to the public. Originally pioneered by the automobile and soft drink industries, franchising today is used in many other forms of business. The 700,000-plus franchise outlets in the United States account for over 25 percent of retail sales and about 15 percent of the gross domestic product (GDP).

This chapter discusses the creation of a franchise, the rights and duties of the parties to a franchise, and the termination of a franchise arrangement.

FRANCHISES

A **franchise** is established when one party (the **franchisor** or **licensor**) licenses another party (the **franchisee** or **licensee**) to use the franchisor's trade name, trade marks, commercial symbols, patents, copyrights, and other property in the distribution and selling of goods and services. Generally, the franchisor and the franchisee are established as separate corporations. The term *franchise* refers to both the agreement between the parties and the franchise outlet.

There are several advantages to franchising, including (1) the franchisor can reach lucrative new markets, (2) the franchisee has access to the franchisor's knowledge and resources while running an independent business, and (3) consumers are assured of uniform product quality.

A typical franchise arrangement is illustrated in Exhibit 36.1.

EXHIBIT 36.1 *Parties to a Typical Franchise Arrangement*

Franchisor (Licensor)

Grant of franchise and license to use trademarks, service marks, and trade secrets

Franchisee (Licensee)

TYPES OF FRANCHISES

There are several forms of franchises. They are discussed in the following paragraphs.

Distributorship Franchises

A **distributorship franchise** occurs when a franchisor manufactures a product and licenses a retail dealer to distribute the product to the public. For example, the Ford Motor Company manufactures automobiles and franchises independently owned automobile dealers (franchisees) to sell them to the public.

processing plant franchise
The franchisor provides a secret formula or process to the franchisee, and the franchisee manufactures the product and distributes it to retail dealers.

Processing Plant Franchises

A **processing plant franchise** results when a franchisor provides a secret formula or the like to the franchisee and the franchisee then manufactures the product at its own location and distributes it to retail dealers. For example, the Coca-Cola Corporation, which owns the secret formulas for making Coca-Cola and other soft drinks, licenses regional bottling companies to manufacture and distribute soft drinks under "Coca-Cola" and other brand names.

chain-style franchise
The franchisor licenses the franchisee to make and sell its products or distribute services to the public from a retail outlet serving an exclusive territory.

Chain-Style Franchises

If a franchisor licenses the franchisee to make and sell its products or services to the public from a retail outlet serving an exclusive geographical territory, it is called a **chain-style franchise**. Most fast-food franchises use this form. For example, the Pizza Hut Corporation licenses independently owned restaurant franchises to make and sell pizzas to the public under the "Pizza Hut" name.

International Perspective

STARBUCKS INVADES TAIWAN

Starbucks Coffee has been a tremendous success in the United States. Beginning with a single outlet in Seattle, Washington, the company has expanded Starbucks Coffee shops across the country. Now even some of the smaller cities in America have a Starbucks Coffee shop. The company expanded in the United States through company-owned stores; that is, Starbucks has not granted franchises in the United States. When Starbucks wanted to enter overseas markets, however, it realized it could not expand solely

Exhibit 36.2 *Example of an Area Franchise*

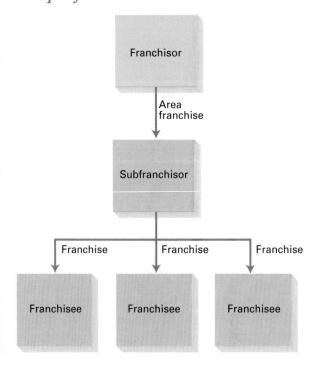

through company-owned outlets. This was because (1) government restrictions in some countries prohibit 100 percent ownership of a business by a foreign investor and (2) the company lacked the business expertise and cultural knowledge necessary to enter many foreign markets. To enter foreign markets, Starbucks turned to franchising.

Consider Starbuck's entry into Taiwan, for example. Taiwan is an Asian island with over 20 million people. It has a very successful business climate, and its per capita income is one of the highest in Asia. So the market seemed ripe for entry by Starbucks. After substantial research and investigation, Starbucks decided it would grant an **area franchise** to a local Taiwanese company to develop Starbucks outlets in Taiwan. In an area franchise, the franchisor grants the franchisee a franchise for an agreed-upon geographical area. In this case, Starbucks granted the Taiwanese company an area franchise for Taiwan. The Taiwanese company could then determine where to locate Starbucks outlets in Taiwan. The Taiwanese company paid Starbucks several million dollars for the area franchise.

Oftentimes, an area franchisee is granted the authority to negotiate and sell franchises in the designated area on behalf of the franchisor. In this arrangement, the franchisee is also called the subfranchisor (see Exhibit 36.2).

Franchising and the use of area franchises allow major U.S. companies, and companies around the world, to enter foreign markets more easily, efficiently, and economically than expanding to many foreign countries through company-owned outlets.

DISCLOSURE PROTECTION

In the past, certain franchisors made material misrepresentations and omissions of facts to potential franchisees concerning the financial future of their franchises. Since then, the **Federal Trade Commission (FTC)** and many states have enacted laws that promote full disclosure to prospective franchisees.

Federal Trade Commission (FTC)

Federal government agency empowered to enforce federal franchising rules.

State Disclosure Laws

Prior to the 1970s, franchising was not highly regulated by either state or federal governments. In 1971, California enacted its *Franchise Investment Law*,[1] which requires franchisors to register and deliver disclosure documents to prospective franchisees. Since then, many other states have enacted franchise disclosure statutes. For a while, franchisors struggled to comply with the various state statutes. Finally, in the mid-1970s, the state franchise administrators developed a uniform disclosure document called the **Uniform Franchise Offering Circular (UFOC)**.

The UFOC and state laws require the franchisor to make specific presale disclosures to prospective franchisees. Information that must be disclosed includes a description of the franchisor's business, balance sheets and income statements of the franchisor for the preceding three years, material terms of the franchise agreement, any restrictions on the franchisee's territory, grounds for termination of the franchise, and other relevant information.

Uniform Franchise Offering Circular (UFOC)

A uniform disclosure document that requires the franchisor to make specific presale disclosures to prospective franchisees.

FTC's Franchise Rule

In 1979, the **FTC franchise rule** became law. The FTC rule requires franchisors to make full presale disclosure nationwide to prospective franchisees.[2] The FTC does not require the registration of the disclosure document prior to its use. The UFOC satisfies both state regulations and the FTC. If a franchisor violates FTC disclosure rules, the wrongdoer is subject to an injunction against further franchise sales, civil fines of up to $10,000 per violation, and an FTC civil action on behalf of injured franchisees to recover damages from the franchisor that were caused by the violation.

FTC franchise rule

A rule set out by the FTC that requires franchisors to make full presale disclosures to prospective franchisees.

Entrepreneur and the Law

REQUIRED DISCLOSURES BY FRANCHISORS

Many potential franchisees are entrepreneurs who want to own and operate their own business. Franchisors, on the other hand, are looking for potential franchisees to whom to sell their franchises. In the past, there has been some fraud by franchisors and failure to disclose important information to prospective franchisees. To remedy this situation, the Federal Trade Commission (FTC) has adopted the following rules.

First, if a franchisor makes sales or earnings projections for a potential franchise location that is based on the actual sales, income, or profit figures of an existing franchise, the franchisor must disclose

- The number and percentage of its actual franchises that have obtained such results; and
- A cautionary statement in at least 12-point boldface type that reads, "**Caution: Some outlets have sold (or earned) this amount. There is no assurance you'll do as well. If you rely upon our figures, you must accept the risk of not doing so well.**"

Second, if a franchisor makes sales or earnings projections based on hypothetical examples, the franchisor must disclose

- The assumptions underlying the estimates;
- The number and percentage of actual franchises that have obtained such results; and

- A cautionary statement in at least 12-point boldface print that reads, "**Caution: These figures are only estimates of what we think you may earn. There is no assurance you'll do as well. If you rely upon our figures, you must accept the risk of not doing so well.**"

Third, the FTC requires that the following statement appear in at least 12-point boldface type on the cover of a franchisor's required disclosure statement to prospective franchisees:

To protect you, we've required your franchisor to give you this information.

We haven't checked it, and don't know if it's correct. It should help you make up your mind. Study it carefully. While it includes some information about your contract, don't rely on it alone to understand your contract. Read all of your contract carefully. Buying a franchise is a complicated investment. Take your time to decide. If possible, show your contract and this information to an adviser, like a lawyer or an accountant. If you find anything you think may be wrong or anything important that's been left out, you should let us know about it. It may be against the law. There may also be laws on franchising in your state. Ask your state agencies about them.

The FTC hopes that the required disclosures by franchisors will protect prospective entrepreneur-franchisees from fraud and from acting on insufficient information.

THE FRANCHISE AGREEMENT

franchise agreement

An agreement that the franchisor and the franchisee enter into that sets forth the terms and conditions of the franchise.

Business Brief

The public expects each franchisee of a franchisor to sell products or services of a similar quality. If one franchisee sells products or services of a lesser quality, it reflects on the entire franchise. Therefore, a franchisor should set exacting quality control standards in the franchise agreement.

A prospective franchisee must apply to the franchisor for a franchise. The application often includes detailed information about the applicant's previous employment, financial and educational history, credit status, and so on. If an applicant is approved, the parties enter into a **franchise agreement** that sets forth the terms and conditions of the franchise. Although some states permit oral franchise agreements, most have enacted a Statute of Frauds that requires franchise agreements to be in writing. To prevent unjust enrichment, the courts will occasionally enforce oral franchise agreements that violate the Statute of Frauds.

Common Terms of a Franchise Agreement

Franchise agreements do not usually have much room for negotiation. Generally, the agreement is a standard form contract prepared by the franchisor. Franchise agreements cover the following topics:

1. **Quality Control Standards** The franchisor's most important assets are its name and reputation. The quality control standards set out in the franchise agreement—such as the

The major growth in franchising opportunities for U.S. franchisors such as McDonald's, in the future is in international markets.

franchisor's right to make periodic inspections of the franchisee's premises and operations—are intended to protect these assets. Failure to meet the proper standards can result in loss of the franchise.

2. **Training Requirements** Franchisees and their personnel usually are required to attend training programs either on-site or at the franchisor's training facilities.
3. **Covenant not to Compete** Covenants not to compete prohibit franchisees from competing with the franchisor during a specific time and in a specified area after the termination of the franchise. Unreasonable (overextensive) covenants not to compete are void.
4. **Arbitration Clause** Most franchise agreements contain an arbitration clause that provides that any claim or controversy arising from the franchise agreement or an alleged breach thereof is subject to arbitration. The U.S. Supreme Court has held such clauses to be enforceable.[3]
5. **Other Terms and Conditions** Capital requirements: restrictions on the use of the franchisor's trade name, trademarks, and logo; standards of operation; duration of the franchise; record-keeping requirements; sign requirements; hours of operation; prohibition as to the sale or assignment of the franchise; conditions for the termination of the franchise; and other specific terms pertinent to the operation of the franchise and the protection of the parties' rights are included in the agreement.

Franchise Fees

Franchise fees payable by the franchisee are usually stipulated in the franchise agreement. The franchisor may require the franchisee to pay any or all of the following fees:

1. **Initial License Fee** A lump-sum payment for the privilege of being granted a franchise.
2. **Royalty Fee** A fee for the continued use of the franchisor's trade name, property, and assistance that is often computed as a percentage of the franchisee's gross sales.
3. **Assessment Fee** A fee for such things as advertising and promotional campaigns and administrative costs, billed either as a flat monthly or annual fee or as a percentage of gross sales.
4. **Lease Fees** Payment for any land or equipment leased from the franchisor, billed either as a flat monthly or annual fee or as a percentage of gross sales or other agreed-upon amount.
5. **Cost of Supplies** Payment for supplies purchased from the franchisor.

Sample provisions from a franchise agreement are set forth in Exhibit 36.3.

Business Brief
A franchisee should be careful to understand the fees he or she is responsible for paying to the franchisor pursuant to the franchise agreement.

*E*XHIBIT **36.3** *Sample Provisions from a Franchise Agreement*

FRANCHISE AGREEMENT

Agreement, this 2nd day of January, 2000, between ALASKA PANCAKE HOUSE, INC., an Alaska corporation located in Anchorage, Alaska (hereinafter called the Company) and PANCAKE SYRUP COMPANY, INC., a Michigan corporation located in Detroit, Michigan (hereinafter called the Franchisee), for one KLONDIKE PANCAKE HOUSE restaurant to be located in the City of Mackinac Island, Michigan.

RECITALS

A. The Company is the owner of proprietary and other rights and interests in various service marks, trademarks, and trade names used in its business including the trade name and service mark "KLONDIKE PANCAKE HOUSE."

B. The Company operates and enfranchises others to operate restaurants under the trade name and service mark "KLONDIKE PANCAKE HOUSE" using certain recipes, formulas, food preparation procedures, business methods, business forms, and business policies it has developed. The Company has also developed a body of knowledge pertaining to the establishment and operation of restaurants. The Franchisee acknowledges that he does not presently know these recipes, formulas, food preparation procedures, business methods, or business policies, nor does the Franchisee have these business forms or access to the Company's body of knowledge.

C. The Franchisee intends to enter the restaurant business and desires access to the Company's recipes, formulas, food preparation procedures, business methods, business forms, business policies, and body of knowledge pertaining to the operation of a restaurant. In addition, the Franchisee desires access to information pertaining to new developments and techniques in the Company's restaurant business.

D. The Franchisee desires to participate in the use of the Company's rights in its service marks and trademarks in connection with the operation of one restaurant to be located at a site approved by the Company and the Franchisee.

E. The Franchisee understands that information received from the Company or from any of its officers, employees, agents, or franchisees is confidential and has been developed with a great deal of effort and expense. The Franchisee acknowledges that the information is being made available to him so that he may more effectively establish and operate a restaurant.

F. The Company has granted, and will continue to grant others, access to its recipes, formulas, food preparation procedures, business methods, business forms, business policies, and body of knowledge pertaining to the operation of restaurants and information pertaining to new developments and techniques in its business.

G. The Company has and will continue to license others to use its service marks and trademarks in connection with the operation of restaurants at Company-approved locations.

H. The Franchise Fee and Royalty constitute the sole consideration to the Company for the use by the Franchisee of its body of knowledge, systems, and trademark rights.

I. The Franchisee acknowledges that he received the Company's franchise offering prospectus at or prior to the first personal meeting with a Company representative and at least ten (10) business days prior to the signing of this Agreement and that he has been given the opportunity to clarify provisions he did not understand and to consult with an attorney or other professional advisor. Franchisee represents he understands and agrees to be bound by the terms, conditions, and obligations of this Agreement.

J. The Franchisee acknowledges that he understands that the success of the business to be operated by him under this Agreement depends primarily upon his efforts and that neither the Company nor any of its agents or representatives have made any oral, written, or visual representations or projections of actual or potential sales, earnings, or net or gross profits. Franchisee understands that the restaurant operated under this Agreement may lose money or fail.

AGREEMENT

Acknowledging the above recitals, the parties hereto agree as follows:

1. Upon execution of this Agreement, the Franchisee shall pay to the Company a Franchise Fee of $30,000 that shall not be refunded in any event.

2. The Franchisee shall also pay to the Company, weekly, a Royalty equal to eight (8%) percent of the gross sales from each restaurant that he operates throughout the term of this Agreement. "Gross sales" means all sales or revenues derived from the Franchisee's location exclusive of sales taxes.

3. The Company hereby grants to the Franchisee:

a. Access to the Company's recipes, formulas, food preparation procedures, business methods, business forms, business policies, and body of knowledge pertaining to the operation of a restaurant.

b. Access to information pertaining to new developments and techniques in the Company's restaurant business.

c. License to use of the Company's rights in and to its service marks and trademarks in connection with the operation of one restaurant to be located at a site approved by the Company and the Franchisee.

4. The Company agrees to:

a. Provide a training program for the operator of restaurants using the Company's recipes, formulas, food preparation procedures, business methods, business forms, and business policies. The Franchisee shall pay all transportation, lodging, and other expenses incurred in attending the program. The Franchisee must attend the training program before opening his restaurant.

b. Provide a Company Representative that the Franchisee may call upon for consultation concerning the operation of his business.

c. Provide the Franchise with a program of assistance that shall include periodic consultations with a Company Representative, publish a periodical advising of new developments and techniques in the Company's restaurant business, and grant access to Company personnel for consultations concerning the operation of his business.

5. The Franchisee agrees to:

a. Begin operation of a restaurant within 365 days. The restaurant will be at a location found by the Franchisee and approved by the Company. The Company or one of its designees will lease the premises and sublet them to the Franchisee at cost. The Franchisee will then construct and equip his unit in accordance with Company specifications contained in the Operating Manual. Upon written request from the Franchisee, the Company will grant a 180-day extension that is effective immediately upon receipt of the request. Under certain circumstances, and at the sole discretion of the Company, the Company may grant additional time in which to open the business. In all instances, the location of each unit must be approved by the Company and the Franchisee. If the restaurant is not operating within 365 days, or within any approved extensions, this Agreement will automatically expire.

b. Operate his business in compliance with applicable laws and governmental regulations. The Franchisee will obtain at his expense, and keep in force, any permits, licenses, or other consents required for the leasing, construction, or operation of his business. In addition, the Franchisee shall operate his restaurant in accordance with the Company's Operation Manual, which may be amended from time to time as a result of experience, changes in the law, or changes in the marketplace. The Franchisee shall refrain from conducting any business or selling any products other than those approved by the Company at the approved location.

c. Be responsible for all costs of operating his unit, including but not limited to, advertising, taxes, insurance, food products, labor, and utilities. Insurance shall include, but not be limited to, comprehensive liability insurance including products liability coverage in the minimum amount of $1,000,000. The Franchisee shall keep these policies in force for the mutual benefit of the parties. In addition, the Franchisee shall save the Company harm from any claim of any type that arises in connection with the operation of his business.

Breach of the Franchise Agreement

A lawful franchise agreement is an enforceable contract. Each party owes a duty to adhere to and perform under the terms of the franchise agreement. If the agreement is breached, the aggrieved party can sue the breaching party for rescission of the agreement, restitution, and damages.

Business Brief

If the franchise agreement is breached, the aggrieved party can sue the breaching party for rescission of the agreement, restitution, and damages.

Ethical Perspective

HÄAGEN-DAZS ICE CREAM FRANCHISE MELTS

Franchise agreements are detailed documents that are carefully drafted to spell out the rights and duties of the parties. A franchisee must be careful to read and understand the terms of the agreement, as the following case demonstrates.

In the late 1950s, Reuben Mattus developed a "super premium" ice cream and named it "Häagen-Dazs" to give the product a Scandinavian flair. Mattus began selling Häagen-Dazs ice cream in prepackaged pints to small stores and delicatessens in the New York metropolitan area. During the 1970s, sales of the product were expanded into some grocery stores and other retail outlets.

In 1976, Mattus's daughter, Doris Mattus-Hurley, opened the first "Häagen-Dazs Shoppe" in Brooklyn Heights, New York. After this shop prospered, Mattus-Hurley began franchising other shops to independent franchisees throughout the country. Häagen-Dazs ice cream is manufactured, distributed, and franchised through a variety of corporate entities (collectively referred to as Häagen-Dazs). The franchise agreement, which has been the same since 1978, grants a limited license to the franchisee to operate a single shop under the Häagen-Dazs trademark at a specific location for a specified term ranging from 5 to 12 years. The franchisee agrees to purchase all its ice cream from the franchisor at prices set by Häagen-Dazs.

In 1983, the Pillsbury Company (Pillsbury), a diversified international food and restaurant company headquartered in Minneapolis, Minnesota, purchased the Häagen-Dazs Company, including its franchise operations. The franchise agreements were assigned to Pillsbury as part of the sale. Pillsbury decided that it could maximize sales of Häagen-Dazs ice cream by expanding sales through methods of distribution that did not involve franchisees. Pillsbury substantially increased sales of Häagen-Dazs products to national grocery store chains, convenience stores like 7-Eleven, and other retail outlets.

This change severely harmed sales at existing franchises. Franchisees located in many states sued Pillsbury, alleging breach of the franchise agreement. Plaintiffs claimed that the defendant breached the franchise agreement by distributing Häagen-Dazs ice cream through nonfranchised outlets that were not "upscale" and by mass distribution of prepackaged pints that competed with franchise outlet sales.

The district court held that the express terms of the franchise agreement had not been violated. The franchise agreement expressly reserved the right of the franchisor to distribute Häagen-Dazs products "through not only Häagen-Dazs Shoppes, but through any other distribution method, which may from time to time be established." The court held that this language gave Pillsbury the right to aggressively distribute prepackaged pints of Häagen-Dazs ice cream through nonfranchise outlets even though that distribution adversely affected retail sales by franchisees. The district court granted Pillsbury's motion for summary judgment. [*Carlock v. Pillsbury Company*, 719 F.Supp. 791 (D.Minn. 1989)]

1. Even though the express terms of the franchise agreement allowed Pillsbury to distribute Häagen-Dazs ice cream through nonfranchise outlets, do you think Pillsbury acted ethically in doing so?
2. Should a covenant of good faith and fair dealing be implied in franchise agreements? Why or why not?

TRADEMARK LAW, TRADE SECRETS, AND FRANCHISING

A franchisor's ability to maintain the public's perception of the quality of the goods and services associated with its trade name, **trademarks**, and **service marks** is the essence of its success. The size of the advertising budgets of many franchisors supports this view.

trademarks and service marks

A distinctive mark, symbol, name, word, motto, or device that identifies the goods or services of a particular franchisor.

Trademarks

Lanham Trademark Act

An act enacted in 1946 that provides for the registration of trademarks and service marks with the federal Patent and Trademark Office in Washington, DC.

The **Lanham Trademark Act**, which was enacted in 1946, provides for the registration of trademarks and service marks with the federal **Patent and Trademark Office** in Washington, DC. Most franchisors license the use of their trade names, trademarks, and service marks and prohibit their franchisees from misusing these marks.

Trademark Infringement   Anyone who uses a mark without authorization may be sued for *trademark infringement*. The trademark holder can seek to recover damages and obtain an injunction prohibiting further unauthorized use of the mark.

In the following case, the court found that the defendant franchisee had infringed a franchisor's trademark.

Baskin-Robbins Ice Cream Co. v. D&L Ice Cream Co., Inc.

576 F.Supp. 1055 (1983)
United States District Court, Eastern District, New York

CASE 36.1

FACTS

The Baskin-Robbins Ice Cream Co. (Baskin-Robbins) is a franchisor that has established a system of more than 2,700 franchise ice cream retail stores nationwide. The franchisees agree to purchase ice cream in bulk only from Baskin-Robbins or an authorized Baskin-Robbins source, to sell only Baskin-Robbins ice cream under the "Baskin-Robbins" trademarks, and to keep specific business hours. Franchisees agree to pay ice cream invoices to Baskin-Robbins when due. If ice cream invoices are not paid within seven days of delivery of the ice cream, payment by certified check is required. If such check is not received, prepayment in cash is then required. If Baskin-Robbins must institute a lawsuit for a breach of the franchise agreement, the franchisee is required to pay all costs incurred by Baskin-Robbins if it is successful in the lawsuit.

In 1978, Baskin-Robbins entered into a standard franchise agreement with D&L Ice Cream Co., Inc. (D&L), granting it a franchise to operate a retail ice cream store in Brooklyn, New York. During the course of the franchise, D&L consistently failed to maintain proper business hours and failed to satisfy ice cream invoices when due. Baskin-Robbins properly invoked its right to require payment by certified check. When such payment was not received, Baskin-Robbins required prepayment in cash for ice cream deliveries. D&L then purchased bulk ice cream from other manufacturers and sold it in its store bearing the Baskin-Robbins trademarks. Upon discovering this fact, Baskin-Robbins sent a notice of termination to D&L. D&L ignored the notice and continued to operate the Baskin-Robbins store and sell other brands of ice cream in cups and containers bearing the Baskin-Robbins trademarks. Baskin-Robbins sued D&L for trademark infringement.

ISSUE

Did D&L infringe the Baskin-Robbins trademarks?

IN THE LANGUAGE OF THE COURT

McLaughlin, District Judge Section 32 of the Lanham Trademark Act imposes liability for trademark infringement on any person who uses a counterfeit, copy, or colorable imitation of a registered trademark in connection with the advertising, distribution, and/or sale of goods. The sale by a licensee of unauthorized products, that is, products outside the scope of the license, is likely to confuse the public into believing that such products are in fact manufactured or authorized by the trademark owner. Thus, such conduct constitutes trademark infringement.

In this case, the sale by D&L of ice cream other than Baskin-Robbins ice cream was outside the scope of the trademark license/franchise agreement. The sale of such alternate ice cream in a retail store prominently displaying Baskin-Robbins signs and in cups bearing the Baskin-Robbins trademarks was likely to result in confusion, mistake, and deception of the purchasing public. As such, D&L's activities during the course of its franchise agreements constituted an infringement of plaintiff's federally registered trademarks. As a result of such acts of trademark infringement and additional breaches of the franchise agreement, D&L's franchises were validly terminated for cause on August 13, 1983.

DECISION AND REMEDY

The district court held that D&L had engaged in trademark infringement. The court held that Baskin-Robbins was entitled to a permanent injunction, to outstanding monies owed by D&L, to all profits made by D&L as a result of the trademark infringement, and to full costs and attorneys' fees incurred in connection with this litigation.

Case Questions

Critical Legal Thinking   Should a franchisor's trademarks and service marks be protected by law? Why or why not?

Ethics   Did the franchisee act ethically in this case?

Business Application   Why was Baskin-Robbins so concerned about D&L's activities? Explain.

Misappropriation of Trade Secrets

Trade secrets are ideas that make a franchise successful but that do not qualify for trademark, patent, or copyright protection. Most state laws protect trade secrets.

The misappropriation of a trade secret is called *unfair competition*. The holder of the trade secret can sue the offending party for damages and obtain an injunction to prohibit further unauthorized use of the trade secret.

trade secrets
Ideas that make a franchise successful but that do not qualify for trademark, patent, or copyright protection.

CONTRACT AND TORT LIABILITY OF FRANCHISORS AND FRANCHISEES

Franchisors and franchisees are liable for their own *contracts*. The same is true of *tort liability*. For example, if a person is injured by a franchisee's negligence, the franchisee is liable.

In the following case, the court held that a franchisor was directly liable to the plaintiffs.

Business Brief
Franchisors and franchisees are liable for their own contracts and torts.

Martin v. McDonald's Corporation
572 N.E.2d 1073 (1991)
Appellate Court of Illinois

CASE 36.2

FACTS

McDonald's Corporation (McDonald's) is a franchisor that licenses franchisees to operate fastfood restaurants and to use McDonald's trademarks and service marks. One such franchise, which was located in Oak Forest, Illinois, was owned and operated by McDonald's Restaurants of Illinois, the franchisee.

Recognizing the threat of armed robbery at its franchises, especially in the time period immediately after closing, McDonald's established an entire corporate division to deal with security problems at franchises. McDonald's prepared a manual for restaurant security operations and required its franchisees to adhere to these procedures.

Jim Carlson was McDonald's regional security manager for the area in which the Oak Forest franchise was located. Carlson visited the Oak Forest franchise on October 31, 1979, to inform the manager of security procedures. He specifically mentioned these rules: (1) No one should throw garbage out the backdoor after dark, and (2) trash and grease were to be taken out the side glass door at least one hour prior to closing. During his inspection, Carlson noted that the locks had to be changed at the restaurant and an alarm system needed to be installed for the backdoor. Carlson never followed up to determine whether these security measures had been taken.

On the evening of November 29, 1979, a six-woman crew, all teenagers, was working to clean up and close the Oak Forest restaurant. Laura Martin, Therese Dudek, and Maureen Kincaid were members of that crew. A person later identified as Peter Logan appeared at the back of the restaurant with a gun. He ordered the crew to open the safe and get him the money and then ordered them into the refrigerator. In the course of moving the crew into the refrigerator, Logan shot and killed Martin, and assaulted Dudek and Kincaid. Dudek and Kincaid suffered severe emotional distress from the assault.

(case continues)

Evidence showed that Logan had entered the restaurant through the backdoor. Trial testimony proved that the work crew used the backdoor exclusively, both before and after dark, and emptied garbage and grease through the backdoor all day and all night. In addition, there was evidence that the latch on the backdoor did not work properly. Evidence also showed that the crew had not been instructed about the use of the backdoor after dark and had never received copies of McDonald's security manual, and that the required warning about not using the backdoor after dark had not been posted at the restaurant.

Martin's parents, Dudek, and Kincaid sued McDonald's to recover damages for negligence. The trial court awarded damages of $1,003,445 to the Martins for the wrongful death of their daughter, and awarded $125,000 each to Dudek and Kincaid. McDonald's appealed.

ISSUE

Is McDonald's liable for negligence?

IN THE LANGUAGE OF THE COURT

McNulty, Judge The trial court correctly determined that McDonald's Corporation had a duty to protect plaintiffs Laura Martin, Maureen Kincaid, and Therese Dudek from harm. Although it did not specifically state that such duty was "assumed," there is ample support in case law and the facts of this case to support a determination that McDonald's Corporation voluntarily assumed a duty to provide security to plaintiffs and protect them from harm.

Once McDonald's Corporation assumed the duty to provide security and protection to plaintiffs, it had the obligation to perform this duty with due care and competence, and any failure to do so would lead to a finding of breach of duty. Accordingly, there was ample evidence for the jury to determine that McDonald's had breached its assumed duty to plaintiffs.

DECISION AND REMEDY

The appellate court held that McDonald's was negligent for not following up and making sure that the security deficiencies it had found at the Oak Forest franchise had been corrected. Affirmed.

Case Questions

Critical Legal Thinking Should businesses be held liable for criminal actions of others? Why or why not?

Ethics Should McDonald's have denied liability in this case?

Business Application What is the benefit to a franchisor to establish and require its franchisees to adhere to security rules? Is there any potential detriment? Explain.

Business Brief

If properly organized and operated as a separate business, a franchisee is not the agent of the franchisor, and the franchisor is not liable for the franchisee's contracts or torts.

Independent Contractor Status

If properly organized and operated, the franchisor and franchisee are separate legal entities. Therefore, the franchisor deals with the franchisee as an *independent contractor*. Because there is no agency relationship, neither party is liable for the contracts or torts of the other.

In the following case, the court applied the independent contractor rule and held that the franchisor was not liable for the tortious conduct of a franchisee.

Cislaw v. Southland Corp.
4 Cal.App.4th 1384, 6 Cal.Rptr.2d 386 (1992)
Court of Appeals of California

CASE 36.3

FACTS

The Southland Corporation (Southland) owns the "7-Eleven" trademark and licenses franchisees to operate convenience stores using this trademark. Each franchise is independently owned and operated. The franchise agreement stipulates that the franchisee is an independent contractor who is authorized to make all inventory, employment, and operational decisions for the franchise.

Timothy Cislaw, 17 years old, died of respiratory failure on May 10, 1984. His parents filed a wrongful death action against the franchisee and Southland, alleging that Timothy's death resulted from his consumption of Djarum Specials (clove cigarettes) sold at a Costa Mesa, California, 7-Eleven franchise store. The Costa Mesa 7-Eleven was franchised to Charles Trujillo and Patricia Colwell-Trujillo. After answering the complaint, Southland moved for summary judgment, arguing that it was not liable for the alleged tortious conduct of its franchisee because the franchisee was an independent contractor. The plaintiffs alleged that the franchisee was Southland's agent, and therefore Southland was liable for its agent's alleged negligence of selling the clove cigarettes to their son. The trial court granted Southland's motion. The Cislaws appealed.

ISSUE
Was the Costa Mesa franchisee an agent of Southland?

IN THE LANGUAGE OF THE COURT
Sonenshine, Associate Justice   In this field of franchise agreements, the question of whether the franchisee is an independent contractor or an agent is ordinarily one of fact, depending on whether the franchisor exercises complete or substantial control over the franchisee.

Colwell-Trujillo said that, as provided under the franchise agreement, she exercised "full and complete control over" the store's employees and "any and all labor relations," including "hiring, firing, disciplining, compensation and work schedules." She attested, "I could purchase whatever inventory I chose and from whomever I wanted and I did so." She decided how much of any particular item to order, how frequently to order it, and what to charge for it. Colwell-Trujillo stated, "Southland had no control over my decision to sell or not sell clove cigarettes at the store. It was my sole decision to sell clove cigarettes. I alone set the prices. In no way did Southland ever advertise, promote or merchandise the clove cigarettes sold in my store."

The agreement recites that the franchisees are independent contractors, and two provisions give the Trujillos the right to make all inventory, employment and operational decisions. The Cislaws were not entitled to proceed to trial.

DECISION AND REMEDY
The court of appeals held that the Costa Mesa 7-Eleven franchisee was not an agent of Southland, but was an independent contractor. Affirmed.

Case Questions

Critical Legal Thinking   Should franchisors be automatically held liable for the tortious conduct of their franchisees? Why or why not?

Ethics   Did the Cislaws act ethically in suing Southland?

Business Application   How careful must a franchisor be to retain enough control to protect the quality of the goods and services sold by its franchisees, but not to retain too much control so as to become liable for the actions of its franchisees?

Agency Status

If the franchisee is the *actual* or *apparent agent* of the franchisor, the franchisor is responsible for the torts and contracts the franchisee committed or entered into within the scope of the agency. **Apparent agency** is created when a franchisor leads a third person into believing that the franchisee is its agent. For example, a franchisor and franchisee who use the same trade name and trademarks and make no effort to inform the public of their separate legal status may find themselves in such a situation. However, mere use of the same name does not automatically make the franchisor liable for the franchisee's actions.

In the following case, the court found that a franchisee was the apparent agent of the franchisor, thereby making the franchisor liable for the tortious conduct of the franchisee.

> **apparent agency**
> Agency that arises when a franchisor creates the appearance that a franchisee is its agent when in fact an actual agency does not exist.

Holiday Inns, Inc. v. Shelburne
576 So.2d 322 (1991)
District Court of Appeals of Florida

CASE 36.4

FACTS
Holiday Inns, Inc. (Holiday Inns), is a franchisor that licenses franchisees to operate hotels using its trademarks and service marks. Holiday Inns licensed Hospitality Venture to operate a franchised hotel in Fort Pierce, Florida. The Rodeo Bar, which had a reputation as the "hottest bar in town," was located in the hotel.

The Fort Pierce Holiday Inn and Rodeo Bar did not have sufficient parking, so security guards posted in the Holiday Inn parking lot required Rodeo Bar patrons to park in vacant lots that surrounded the hotel but that were not owned by the hotel. The main duty of the guards was to keep the parking lot open for hotel guests. Two unarmed security guards were on duty on the night in question. One guard was drinking on the job, and the other was an untrained temporary fill-in.

The record disclosed that although the Rodeo Bar had a capacity of 240 people, the bar regularly admitted 270 to 300 people with 50 to 75 people waiting outside. Fights occurred all the time in the bar and the parking lots, and often there were three or four fights a night. Police reports involving 58 offenses, including several weapons charges and battery and

(case continues)

assault charges, had been filed during the previous 18 months.

On the night in question, the two groups involved in the altercation did not leave the Rodeo Bar until closing time. According to the record, these individuals exchanged remarks as they moved toward their respective vehicles in the vacant parking lots adjacent to the Holiday Inn. Ultimately, a fight erupted. The evidence shows that during the course of physical combat, Mr. Carter shot David Rice, Scott Turner, and Robert Shelburne. Rice died from his injuries.

Rice's heirs, Turner, and Shelburne sued the franchisee, Hospitality Venture, and the franchisor, Holiday Inns, for damages. The trial court found Hospitality Venture negligent for not providing sufficient security to prevent the foreseeable incident that took the life of Rice, and injured Turner and Shelburne. The court also found that Hospitality Venture was the apparent agent of Holiday Inns, and therefore Holiday Inns was vicariously liable for its franchisee's tortious conduct. Turner was awarded $3,825,000 for his injuries, Shelburne received $1 million, and Rice's interests were awarded $1 million. Hospitality Venture and Holiday Inns appealed.

ISSUE

Are the franchisee and the franchisor liable?

IN THE LANGUAGE OF THE COURT

Hersey, Chief Judge *There was testimony that Holiday Inns, Inc. gave Hospitality Venture, the franchisee, use of the Holiday Inns, Inc. logo and made the franchisee part of the corporation's reservation system. In fact, Holiday Inns, Inc.'s standard sign was displayed in front of the Fort Pierce Holiday Inn in order to draw customers through name recognition. Clearly, this evidence shows that Holiday Inns, Inc. represented to the public that this particular hotel was a part of the national chain of Holiday Inns and that it could find a certain level of service and safety at its hotel and bar.*

Clearly, on the question of reliance, the jury had a right to conclude that appellees believed exactly what Holiday Inns, Inc. wanted them to believe—that the Fort Pierce Holiday Inn and its Rodeo Bar were part of Holiday Inns' system. For these reasons, the evidence supported the jury's finding that Hospitality Venture was the apparent agent of Holiday Inns, Inc. and was acting within the scope of its apparent authority.

DECISION AND REMEDY

The court of appeals held that the franchisee was negligent, and that the franchisee was the apparent agent of the franchisor. Affirmed.

Case Questions

Critical Legal Thinking What does the doctrine of apparent agency provide? How does it differ from actual agency?

Ethics Did Hospitality Venture act ethically in denying liability? Did Holiday Inns act ethically in denying liability?

Business Application Why do you think the plaintiffs included Holiday Inns as a defendant in their lawsuit? Do you think the damages that were awarded were warranted?

Entrepreneur and the Law

LICENSING: POKÉMON INVADES THE UNITED STATES

In the 1990s, the Japanese company Nintendo's animated Pokémon creatures were a huge hit in Japan. In this role-playing game, children manipulate Pokémon characters with different stated strengths and weaknesses in a variant of the rock, paper, scissors game. The several hundred cute, gender-neutral characters, with such names as Pikachu, Piyo Piyo, Dalki, and Dragon Ball, show up in TV cartoons and Nintendo video games and on playing cards, book bags, and thousands of other items. Japanese children are crazy about acquiring the next Pokémon character. When one new character was introduced at the Nintendo Science World Fair in Japan, over 100,000 kids lined up to get the new character.

But would American children buy into the oddly animated creatures and their interactive games? Nintendo Co. had doubts and did not want to take the exporting risk directly. Up stepped Alfred Kahn and Thomas Kenney, both prior toy company executives, who formed 4Kids Entertainment, Inc., a U.S. company. They approached Nintendo about bringing the Pokémon games and characters to the United States through the concept of licensing. In 1997, after much negotiation, Nintendo agreed to 4Kids to be its licensing agent in the U.S.

4Kids went looking for their first television deal, but the major TV networks turned them down. Not to be deterred, 4Kids syndicated the TV series themselves, dubbed episodes in English, and gave them free to TV stations in exchange for a percentage of advertising revenue. Within four months, Pokémon was the top-rated syndicated kids program in the United States. After this TV success, Nintendo released the first Pokémon video games in the

U.S., followed by trading cards, comic books, home videos, and compact disks. 4Kids have signed over 100 licensing deals for Pokémon, including Hasbro toy company as its master toy licensee and Time-Warner for the Pokémon TV series. The first Pokémon movie, *Mewtwo Strikes Back*, was released in 1999 in the United States and was a huge hit. The Pokémon craze reached a fever pitch in the United States as it had in Japan.

The Pokémon invasion of the United States has reaped a plethora of royalties for Nintendo and its local entrepreneurs. Neither Nintendo or 4Kids will disclose their licensing arrangement or royalty fees. But retailers usually pay a licensing fee between 5 to 15 percent of their retail sales, and 4Kids, as the licensing agent, typically earns commissions from 20 to 50 percent of that royalty. With Pokémon sales exceeding $1 billion in the United States, 4Kids can have earned up to $75 million, making its owners multimillionaires. Nintendo claims that it needs licensing agents such as 4Kids to enter a foreign market because of the expertise they bring in finding hot companies in the foreign country to produce and market T-shirts, school supplies, athletic shoes, and the thousands of other items its Pokémon characters now appear on in the United States. Licensing agents, such as 4Kids, take the ball and run with it, sometimes very successfully.

$\mathcal{T}$ERMINATION OF FRANCHISES

The franchise agreement usually contains provisions that permit the franchisor to terminate the franchise if certain events occur. The franchisor's right to terminate a franchise has been the source of litigation.

Termination "For Cause"

Most franchise agreements permit franchisors to terminate the franchise "for cause." For example, the continued failure of a franchisee to meet legitimate quality control standards would be deemed just cause.

Unreasonably strict application of a just cause termination clause constitutes wrongful termination. A single failure to meet a quality control standard, for example, is not cause for termination.

In the following case, the court held that a franchisor had properly terminated a franchisee.

> **Business Brief**
>
> A franchisor can terminate a franchise agreement for "just cause" (e.g., nonpayment of franchise fees by the franchisee or continued failure to meet quality control standards).

Dunkin' Donuts of America, Inc. v. Middletown Donut Corp.
495 A.2d 66 (1985)
Supreme Court of New Jersey

CASE 36.5

FACTS
Dunkin' Donuts of America, Inc. (Dunkin' Donuts), is a franchisor that has licensed hundreds of franchised doughnut shops throughout the country. Gerald Smothergill, through two corporations, entered into franchise and lease agreements with Dunkin' Donuts to operate Dunkin' Donuts franchise stores in Middletown and West Long Branch, New Jersey. Smothergill paid about $115,000 for the two franchises. Under each franchise agreement, Smothergill was required to keep accurate sales records, pay a basic franchise fee of 4.9 percent of gross sales, and pay an advertising fee of 2 percent of gross sales. The lease agreements were conditioned on Smothergill's remaining a franchisee in good standing under the franchise agreements.

In August 1978, Dunkin' Donuts notified Smothergill that his franchise agreements were being terminated due to his intentional underreporting of gross sales. The termination notice provided an opportunity for Smothergill to cure the breach by making prompt payment of the amounts due. Smothergill made no attempt to cure and refused to abandon his Dunkin' Donuts stores. Dunkin' Donuts sued to enforce its claimed right of termination and to collect damages. The trial court permitted Dunkin'

(case continues)

Donuts to terminate the franchise agreements. The appellate court affirmed. Smothergill appealed.

ISSUE

Was the franchise agreement properly terminated "for cause" by Dunkin' Donuts?

IN THE LANGUAGE OF THE COURT

Clifford, Justice   *At the conclusion of the trial, the trial court found as fact that Smothergill had been guilty of substantial, intentional, and long-continued underreporting of gross sales at both of his Dunkin' Donuts stores. The court determined that Smothergill had failed to keep the financial records that were required under the franchise agreements and that the failure to keep records was not the result of carelessness or incompetence. Rather, Smothergill's delinquency in recordkeeping was part of a deliberate effort to underreport sales, which in turn would result in the underpayment of franchise fees, underpayment of advertising fund fees, underpayment of rental override charges, and evasion of federal and state taxes. In short, the trial court found as fact that Smothergill was "guilty of unconscionable cheating."*

Here the franchisee deserves to have the full weight of the legal remedies fall upon him. He has been found guilty of unconscionable cheating. Dunkin' Donuts, as franchisor of a sizable network of New Jersey franchises, has a real and legitimate interest in maintaining the integrity of its system. Other Dunkin' Donuts franchisees also have an interest in promoting honest reporting because a percentage of their reported gross sales are pooled in a common advertising fund that benefits all. To the extent that a franchisee such as Smothergill underreports gross sales, he cheats not only the franchisor but all other franchisees as well. Upon signing the Dunkin' Donuts franchise agreement, both franchisor and franchisee were aware of the rules of the game. Those rules seem fair. A franchisee who gets caught with his hand in the proverbial cookie jar (or doughnut box, as the case may be) must suffer the known consequences.

DECISION AND REMEDY

The state supreme court held that Smothergill intentionally breached the franchise agreements and that Dunkin' Donuts had properly terminated Smothergill as a franchisee.

Case Questions

Critical Legal Thinking   Should franchisors be permitted to terminate franchisees "at will"? Or is the rule that they can only terminate franchisees "for cause" a better rule? Explain.

Ethics   Did Smothergill act ethically in this case?

Business Application   Do you think many franchisees "cheat" when franchise royalty fees are based on sales?

Wrongful Termination

Termination at will clauses in franchise agreements are generally held to be void on the grounds that they are unconscionable. The rationale for this position is that the franchisee has spent time, money, and effort developing the franchise.

wrongful termination
Termination of a franchise without just cause.

If a franchise is terminated without just cause, the franchisee can sue the franchisor for **wrongful termination**. The franchisee can then recover damages caused by the unlawful termination and recover the franchise.

Petroleum Marketing Practices Act

Gasoline stations are among the oldest franchises in the United States. The **Petroleum Marketing Practices Act**, enacted in 1979, prohibits oil company franchisors from terminating gasoline station franchises without just cause.[4]

It is when merchants dispute about their own rules that they invoke the law.

Brett, J.
Robinson v. Mollen (1875)

Automobile Dealers Day in Court Act

Automobile company franchisors are prohibited from terminating automobile dealer franchises without just cause. The **Automobile Dealers Day in Court Act** was enacted to ensure that this does not happen.[5]

International Perspective

INTERNATIONAL FRANCHISING

Franchising as a form of business is well established in the United States. Sometimes it seems that certain types of franchises (e.g., gasoline stations) have saturated the market. The international market presently offers the greatest opportunity for U.S. franchisors to expand their businesses. Many U.S. franchisors view international expansion as their number one priority. However, in addition to providing lucrative new markets, international franchising also poses difficulties and risks.

The expansion into other countries through franchising means that U.S. franchisors can expand internationally without the huge capital investments that would be required if they tried to penetrate these markets with company-owned stores or branches. In addition, a foreign franchisee will know things about the cultural and business traditions of the foreign country that the franchisor will not. Consequently, the franchisee will be better able to serve the consumers and customers in the particular market.

Utilizing this foreign expertise probably means that U.S. franchisors will grant area franchises in many foreign countries. The U.S. franchisor will rely on the area franchisee to locate, investigate, and approve individual franchisees.

Foreign franchising is not without its difficulties, however. For example, the host country's laws may differ from U.S. laws. This will have to be taken into consideration in drafting the franchise agreement and operating the franchise. Foreign cultures may also require different advertising, marketing, and promotional approaches. In addition, the franchisor may be subjecting itself to government regulation in the host country. A regional group like the European Community (EC) may possibly become involved. Finally, different dispute settlement procedures may be in place that will have to be used if there is a dispute between the U.S. franchisor and the foreign franchisee.

To aid the development of U.S. franchising abroad, the federal *Agency for International Development (USAID)* guarantees loans to U.S. franchisors' area licensees and franchisees in developing countries. The foreign franchisee would seek financing from its own bank, but the USAID would back 50 percent of the loan through a guarantee. Franchisors must apply and be approved to participate in the program.

In addition to U.S. franchisors' expanding to other countries, foreign franchisors also view the United States as a potential market. This will provide an opportunity for U.S. entrepreneurs to become franchisees for foreign franchisors. As a result, in the future, U.S. consumers will be able to purchase foreign goods and services from franchises located in this country.

Working the Web

The Franchise Handbook: On-Line This Web site contains articles on franchising, lists of worldwide franchise associations, and a directory of business opportunities.

Visit at **www.franchise1.com**

FranNet FranNet is the world's largest network of franchise consultants. It contains a large research library.

Visit at **www.frannet.com**

International Franchise Association At the International Franchise Association site, you can search by company name, category, investment range, and location.

It serves as a resource center for current and prospective franchisees and franchisors.

Visit at **www.franchise.org**

CYBER EXERCISES

1. Using *The Franchise Handbook: On-Line*, find an article called "The Franchisor's Duty of Care."

2. Using FranNet, find and read an article in the research library called "Checklist for Franchises."

3. Find a franchise opportunity in your area using the International Franchise Association site.

CASES AND EXERCISES

CRITICAL LEGAL THINKING CASES

36.1. H&R Block, Inc. (H&R Block), is a franchisor that licenses franchisees to provide tax preparation services to customers under the "H&R Block" service mark. In 1975, June McCart was granted an H&R Block franchise at 900 Main Street, Rochester, New York. From 1972 to 1979, her husband, Robert, was involved in the operation of an H&R Block franchise in Rensselaer, New York. After that, he assisted June in the operation of her H&R Block franchise. All of the McCarts' income during the time in question came from the H&R Block franchises.

The H&R Block franchise agreement that June signed contained a provision whereby she agreed not to compete (1) in the business of tax preparation (2) within 250 miles of the franchise (3) for a period of two years after the termination of the franchise. Robert did not sign the Rochester franchise agreement. On December 31, 1981, June wrote a letter to H&R Block giving notice she was terminating the franchise. Shortly thereafter, the McCarts sent a letter to people who had been clients of the Rochester H&R Block office informing them that June was leaving H&R Block and that Robert was opening a tax preparation service and June would assist him. H&R Block granted a new franchise in Rochester to another franchisee. It sued the McCarts to enforce the covenant not to compete. Who wins? [*McCart v. H&R Block, Inc.*, 470 N.E.2d 756 (Ind.App. 1984)]

36.2. Libby-Broadway Drive-In, Inc. (Libby), is a corporation licensed by the McDonald's System, Inc. (McDonald's) to operate a McDonald's fast-food franchise restaurant. Libby was granted a license to operate a McDonald's store in Cleveland, Ohio, and was granted an exclusive territory in which McDonald's could not grant another franchise. The area was described as "bound on the north by the south side of Miles Avenue, on the west and south side by Turney Road, on the east by Warrensville Center Road." In December 1976, McDonald's granted a franchise to another franchisee to operate a McDonald's restaurant on the west side of Turney Road. Libby sued McDonald's, alleging a breach of the franchise agreement. Is McDonald's liable? [*Libby-Broadway Drive-In, Inc. v. McDonald's System, Inc.*, 391 N.E.2d 1 (Ill.App. 1979)]

36.3. My Pie International, Inc, (My Pie), an Illinois corporation, is a franchisor that licenses franchisees to open pie shops under its trademark name. My Pie has licensed 13 restaurants throughout the country, including one owned by Dowmont, Inc. (Dowmont), in Glen Ellyn, Illinois. The Illinois Franchise Disclosure Act requires a franchisor that desires to issue franchises in the state to register with the state, or qualify for an exemption from registration, and to make certain disclosures to prospective franchisees. My Pie granted the license to Dowmont without registering with the state of Illinois, or qualifying for an exemption from registration, and without making the required disclosures to Dowmont. Dowmont operated its restaurant as a "My Pie" franchise between July 1976 and May 1980, and since then has operated it under the name "Arnold's." Dowmont paid franchise royalty fees to My Pie prior to May 1980. My Pie sued Dowmont for breach of the franchise agreement and to recover royalties it claimed were due from Dowmont. Dowmont filed a counterclaim seeking to rescind the franchise agreement and recover the royalties it had paid to My Pie. Who wins? [*My Pie International, Inc. v. Dowmont, Inc.*, 687 F.2d 919 (7th Cir. 1982)]

36.4. Georgia Girl Fashions, Inc. (Georgia Girl), is a franchisor that licenses franchisees to operate women's retail clothing stores under the "Georgia Girl" trademark. Georgia Girl granted a franchise to a franchisee to operate a store on South Cobb Drive in Smyrna, Georgia. Georgia Girl did not supervise or control the day-to-day operations of the franchisee. Melanie McMullan entered the store to exchange a blouse she had previously purchased at the store. When she found nothing that she wished to exchange the blouse for, she began to leave the store. At that time, she was physically restrained and accused of shoplifting the blouse. McMullan was taken to the local jail where she was held until her claim of prior purchase could be verified. The store then dropped the charges against her and she was released from jail. McMullan filed an action against the store owner and Georgia Girl to recover damages for false imprisonment. Is Georgia Girl liable? [*McMullan v. Georgia Girl Fashions, Inc.*, 348 S.E.2d 748 (Ga.App. 1988)]

36.5. The Seven-Up Company (Seven-Up) is a franchisor that licenses local bottling companies to manufacture, bottle, and distribute soft drinks using the "7 Up" trademark. The Brooks Bottling Company (Brooks) is a Seven-Up franchisee that bottles and sells 7 Up soft drinks to stores in Michigan. Under the franchise agreement, the franchisee is required to purchase the 7 Up syrup from Seven-Up, but it can purchase its bottles, cartons, and other supplies from independent suppliers if Seven-Up approves the design of these articles.

Brooks used cartons designed and manufactured by Olinkraft, Inc., using a design that Seven-Up had approved. Sharon Proos Kosters, a customer at Meijers Thrifty Acre Store in Holland, Michigan, removed a cardboard carton containing six bottles of 7 Up from a grocery store shelf, put it under her arm, and walked toward the checkout counter. As she did so, a bottle slipped out of the carton, fell on the floor, and exploded, causing a piece of glass to strike Kosters in her eye as she looked down; she was blinded in that eye. Evidence showed that the 7 Up carton was designed to be held from the top and was made without a strip on the side of the carton that would prevent a bottle from slipping out if held underneath. Kosters sued Seven-Up to recover damages for her injuries. Is Seven-Up liable? [*Kosters v. Seven-Up Company*, 595 F.2d 347 (6th Cir. 1979)]

36.6. KFC Corporation (KFC) is the franchisor of "Kentucky Fried Chicken" restaurants. Franchisees must purchase equipment and supplies from manufacturers approved in writing by KFC. Equipment includes cookers, fryers, ovens, and the like; supplies include carry-out boxes, napkins, towelettes, and plastic eating utensils known as "sporks." These products are not trade secrets. KFC may not "unreasonably withhold" approval of any suppliers who apply and whose goods are tested and found to meet KFC's quality control standards. The 10 manufacturers who went through KFC's approval process were approved. KFC also sells supplies to franchisees in competition with these independent suppliers. All supplies, whether produced by KFC or the independent suppliers, must contain "Kentucky Fried Chicken" trademarks.

Upon formation in 1972, Diversified Container Corporation (Diversified) began manufacturing and selling supplies to Kentucky Fried Chicken franchisees without applying for or receiving KFC's approval. All of the items sold by Diversified contained Kentucky Fried Chicken trademarks. Diversified represented to franchisees that its products met "all standards" of KFC and that it sold "approved supplies." Diversified even affixed Kentucky Fried Chicken trademarks to the shipping boxes in which it delivered supplies to franchisees. Evidence showed that Diversified's products did not meet the quality control standards set by KFC. KFC sued Diversified for trademark infringement. Who wins? [*Kentucky Fried Chicken Corporation v. Diversified Container Corporation*, 549 F.2d 368 (5th Cir. 1977)]

36.7. Ramada Inns, Inc. (Ramada Inns), is a franchisor that licenses franchisees to operate motor hotels using the "Ramada Inns" trademarks and service marks. In August 1977, the Gadsden Motel Company (Gadsden), a partnership, purchased a motel in Attalla, Alabama, and entered into a franchise agreement with Ramada Inns to operate it as a Ramada Inns motor hotel. In 1982, the motel began receiving poor ratings from Ramada Inns's inspectors, and Gadsden fell behind on its monthly franchise fee payments. Despite proddings from Ramada Inns, the motel never met Ramada Inns's operational standards again. On November 17, 1983, Ramada Inns properly terminated the franchise agreement, citing quality deficiencies and Gadsden's failure to pay past-due franchise fees. The termination notice directed Gadsden to remove any materials or signs identifying the motel as a Ramada Inns. Gadsden continued using Ramada Inns's signage, trademarks, and service marks inside and outside the motel. In September 1984, Ramada Inns sued Gadsden for trademark infringement. Who wins? [*Ramada Inns, Inc. v. Gadsden Motel Company*, 804 F.2d 1562 (11th Cir.)]

36.8. In 1976, Amoco Oil Company (Amoco) purchased the land in question and constructed a two-bay gasoline station at a total cost of $125,000. The property was then leased to Robert F. Burns, who operated an Amoco franchise gasoline station. The franchise was maintained through a series of written one-year leases. The leases provided for automatic renewal unless either party gave written notice of cancellation prior to the end of the current term. On June 8, 1977, Amoco gave Burns written notice of nonrenewal and directed Burns to vacate the premises effective September 10, 1977. Evidence showed that the gasoline station had been suffering a steadily decreasing sales volume and that the station was an unprofitable location for Amoco. Evidence further showed that no reasonable steps could be taken to increase the sales volume at the site to make it profitable. Amoco planned on discontinuing the sale of gasoline at the site and selling the property. Burns sued Amoco for wrongful termination. Who wins? [*Amoco Oil Company v. Burns*, 437 A.2d 381 (PA 1981)]

36.9. Kawasaki Motors Corporation (Kawasaki), a Japanese corporation, manufactures motorcycles that it distributes in the United States through its subsidiary, Kawasaki Motors Corporation, U.S.A. (Kawasaki USA). Kawasaki USA is a franchisor that grants franchises to dealerships to sell Kawasaki motorcycles. In 1971, Kawasaki USA granted the Kawasaki Shop of Aurora, Inc. (Dealer), a franchise to sell Kawasaki motorcycles in Aurora, Illinois. The franchise changed locations twice. Both moves were within the five-mile exclusive territory granted Dealer in the franchise agreement.

Dealer did not obtain Kawasaki USA's written approval for either move as required by the franchise agreement. Kawasaki USA acquiesced to the first move but not to the second. At the second new location, Dealer also operated Honda and Suzuki motorcycle franchises and was negotiating to operate a Yamaha franchise. The Kawasaki franchise agreement expressly permitted multiline dealerships.

Kawasaki USA objected to the second move, asserting that Dealer had not received written approval for the move as required by the franchise agreement. However, evidence showed that the real reason Kawasaki objected to the move was because it did not want its motorcycles to be sold at the same location as other manufacturers' motorcycles. Kawasaki terminated Dealer's franchise. Dealer sued Kawasaki USA for wrongful termination. Who wins? [*Kawasaki Shop of Aurora, Inc. v. Kawasaki Motors Corporation*, U.S.A., 544 N.E.2d 457 (Ill.App. 1989)]

ETHICS CASES

36.10. The Southland Corporation (Southland) owned the "7-Eleven" trademark and licensed franchisees throughout the country to operate 7-Eleven stores. The franchise agreement provides for fees to be paid to Southland by each franchisee based on a percentage of gross profits. In return, franchisees receive a lease of premises, a license to use the 7-Eleven trademark and trade secrets, advertising, merchandise, and bookkeeping assistance. Vallerie Campbell purchased an existing 7-Eleven store in Fontana, California, and became a Southland franchisee. The franchise was designated #13974 by Southland. As part of the purchase, she applied to the state of California for transfer of the beer and wine license from the prior owner. Southland also executed the application. California approved the transfer and issued the license to "Campbell Vallerie Southland #13974."

On September 9, 1978, an employee of Campbell's store sold beer to Jesse Lewis Cope, a minor who was allegedly intoxicated at the time. After drinking the beer, Cope drove his vehicle and struck another vehicle. Two occupants of the other vehicle, Denise Wickham and Tyrone Crosby, were severely injured, and a third occupant, Cedrick Johnson, was killed. Johnson (by his parents), Wickham, and Crosby sued Southland—but not Campbell—to recover damages. Is Southland legally liable for the tortious acts of its franchisee? Is it morally responsible? [*Wickham v. The Southland Corporation*, 168 Cal.App.3d 49, 213 Cal.Rptr. 825 (Cal.App. 1985)]

36.11. KFC Corporation (KFC), with its principal place of business in Louisville, Kentucky, is the franchisor of "Kentucky Fried Chicken" restaurants. KFC's registered trademarks and service marks include "Kentucky Fried Chicken," "It's Finger Lickin' Good," the portrait of Colonel Harlan Sanders, and others. KFC grants a license to its franchisees to use these marks in connection with the preparation and sale of "Original Recipe Kentucky Fried Chicken." Original Recipe Kentucky Fried Chicken, which is sold only by KFC franchisees, is prepared by a special cooking process featuring the use of a secret recipe seasoning known as "KFC Seasoning." This blend of seasoning was developed by KFC's founder Colonel Harlan Sanders. As a condition of each franchise agreement, KFC requires that its franchisees use only KFC Seasoning in connection with the preparation and sale of Kentucky Fried Chicken.

KFC Seasoning is a trade secret. To make the seasoning, KFC has entered into contracts with two spice blenders, the John W. Sexton Co., Inc. (Sexton), and Strange Co. (Strange). Each of these companies blends approximately one-half of the spices of KFC Seasoning: neither has knowledge of the complete formulation of KFC Seasoning, and both entered into secrecy agreements to maintain the confidentiality of their formulation. After the seasoning is blended by Sexton and Strange, it is mixed together and sold directly to all KFC franchisees. KFC does not receive a royalty or other economic benefit from the sale of KFC Seasoning. KFC's relationship with Sexton and Strange has existed for more than 25 years; no other companies are licensed to blend KFC Seasoning.

Marion-Kay Company, Inc. (Marion-Kay), is a spice blender engaged in the manufacture of chicken seasoning known as "Marion-Kay Seasoning." In 1977, KFC learned that Marion-Kay was supplying some KFC franchisees with Marion-Kay Seasoning and demanded it cease this practice. When Marion-Kay refused, KFC sued it for interference with contractual relations. Who wins? Is KFC justified in preventing Marion-Kay from selling its seasoning? Is Marion-Kay acting morally in selling seasoning to KFC franchisees? [*KFC Corporation v. Marion-Kay Company, Inc.*, 620 F.Supp. 1160 (S.D.Ind. 1985)]

CRITICAL LEGAL THINKING WRITING ASSIGNMENT

Read Case A.36 in the Case Appendix [*Little v. Howard Johnson Company*]. This case is excerpted from the court of appeals opinion. Review and brief the case. In your brief, be sure to answer the following questions:

1. Describe how the plaintiff was injured. Whom did she sue?

2. Was Howard Johnson Company directly liable for the plaintiff's injuries? Explain.

3. Was the franchisee an actual agent of Howard Johnson Company?

4. Did Howard Johnson's actions create an apparent agency between it and the franchisee?

NOTES

1. Cal. Corp. Code §§ 31000-31019.
2. 16 C.F.R. Part 436.
3. *Southland Corporation v. Keating*, 465 U.S. 1, 104 S.Ct. 852 (1985).
4. 15 U.S.C. §§ 1221 et seq.
5. 15 U.S.C. §§ 2801 et seq.

Corporate Formation and Financing

A corporation is an artificial being, invisible, intangible, and existing only in the contemplation of law. Being the mere creature of the law, it possesses only those properties which the charter of its creation confers upon it, either expressly, or as incidental to its very existence. These are such as are supposed best calculated to effect the object for which it was created. Among the most important are immortality, and, if the expression may be allowed, individuality; properties by which a perpetual succession of many persons are considered as the same, and may act as a single individual.

JOHN MARSHALL Chief Justice, U.S. Supreme Court
Dartmouth College v. Woodward,
4 Wheaton 518, 636 (1819)

Chapter Objectives

After studying this chapter, you should be able to

1. Define *corporation* and list the major characteristics of a corporation.
2. Describe the process of forming a corporation.
3. Distinguish between publicly held and closely held corporations.
4. Distinguish among domestic, foreign, and alien corporations.
5. Identify when promoters are liable on preincorporation contracts.
6. Define *S Corporation* and describe its tax benefits.
7. Define *common stock* and distinguish among authorized, issued, treasury, and outstanding shares.
8. Describe the preferences associated with preferred stock.
9. Describe the rights of debenture holders and bondholders.
10. Describe multinational corporations.

Chapter Contents

Corporations are the most dominant form of business organization in the United States, generating over 85 percent of the country's gross business receipts. Corporations range in size from one owner to thousands of owners. Owners of corporations are called *shareholders*.

Corporations were first formed in medieval Europe. Great Britain granted charters to certain trading companies from the 1500s to the 1700s. The English law of corporations applied in most of the colonies until 1776. After the War of Independence, the states of the United States developed their own corporation law.

Originally, corporate charters were individually granted by state legislatures. In the late 1700s, however, the states began enacting *general corporation statutes* that permitted corporations to be formed without the separate approval of the legislature. Today, most corporations are formed pursuant to general corporation laws of the states.

The formation and financing of corporations is discussed in this chapter.

NATURE OF THE CORPORATION

Corporations can only be created pursuant to the laws of the state of incorporation. These statutes—commonly referred to as **corporations codes**—regulate the formation, operation, and dissolution of corporations. The state legislature may amend its corporate statute at any time. Such changes may require the corporation's articles of incorporation to be amended.

The courts interpret state corporation statutes to decide individual corporate and shareholder disputes. As a result, a body of common law has evolved concerning corporate and shareholder rights and obligations.

The Corporation as a Legal "Person"

A corporation is a separate *legal entity* (or *legal person*) for most purposes. Corporations are treated, in effect, as artificial persons created by the state that can sue or be sued in their own names, enter into and enforce contracts, hold title to and transfer property, and be found civilly and criminally liable for violations of law. Because corporations cannot be put in prison, the normal criminal penalty is the assessment of a fine, loss of a license, or other sanction.

Characteristics of Corporations

Corporations have the following unique characteristics:

Limited Liability of Shareholders As separate legal entities, corporations are liable for their own contracts and debts. Generally, the shareholders have only **limited liability**. That is, they are liable only to the extent of their capital contributions.

Free Transferability of Shares Corporate shares are freely transferable by the shareholder by sale, assignment, pledge, or gift unless they are issued pursuant to certain exemptions from securities registration. Shareholders may agree among themselves on restrictions on the transfer of shares. National securities markets, such as the New York Stock Exchange, the American Stock Exchange, and NASDAQ, have been developed for the organized sale of securities.

Perpetual Existence Corporations exist in perpetuity unless a specific duration is stated in the corporation's articles of incorporation. The existence of a corporation can be voluntarily terminated by the shareholders. Corporations may be involuntarily terminated by the corporation's creditors if an involuntary petition for bankruptcy against the corporation is granted. The death, insanity, or bankruptcy of a shareholder, a director, or an officer of the corporation does not affect its existence.

corporation
A fictitious legal entity that is created according to statutory requirements.

corporations codes
State statutes that regulate the formation, operation, and dissolution of corporations.

Business Brief
A corporation is a separate legal entity—an *artificial person*—that can own property, sue and be sued, enter into contracts, and such.

limited liability
Shareholders are liable for the corporation's debts and obligations only to the extent of their capital contributions.

Centralized Management   The *board of directors* makes policy decisions concerning the operation of the corporation. The members of the board of directors are elected by the shareholders. The directors, in turn, appoint corporate *officers* to run the corporation's day-to-day operations. Together, the directors and the officers form the corporate "management."

The doctrine of limited liability of shareholders was imposed by the court in the following case.

Joslyn Manufacturing Co. v. T. L. James & Co., Inc.
893 F.2d 80 (1990)
United States Court of Appeals, Fifth Circuit

CASE 37.1

FACTS
The Lincoln Creosoting Company, Inc. (Lincoln), was a Louisiana corporation that was incorporated in 1935. The company operated a wood-treating and creosoting plant on its property. Although the company had a treatment plant, creosoting chemicals dripped into an open pit and were washed away by rain to surrounding land areas and waterways. From 1935 until 1950, Lincoln was 60 percent owned by T. L. James & Company, Inc. (James & Co.). Lincoln maintained separate books and records; held regularly scheduled shareholders' and directors' meetings; owned its own property and equipment; maintained its own employees, payroll, insurance, pension plan, and workers' compensation program; and filed its own tax returns. Thus, Lincoln, the subsidiary corporation, was run separately from its parent corporation, James & Co.

In 1950, Lincoln was sold to Joslyn Manufacturing Company (Joslyn), which in turn sold the plant in 1969. Since that time, the property has passed through six separate owners, the last of which subdivided the property. The current owners of the property and adjacent property owners brought suit under the Comprehensive Environmental Response, Compensation, and Liability Act (CERCLA), a federal environmental statute, to recover damages from Joslyn's and Lincoln's other prior owners for environmental cleanup costs. Joslyn's, which was ordered to clean up the contaminated site, sued James & Co. to recover costs of the cleanup. James & Co. asserted in defense that it was merely a shareholder of Lincoln and was protected by the limited liability doctrine. The district court granted James & Co.'s motion for summary judgment. Joslyn appealed.

ISSUE
Is James & Co. liable for the environmental pollution caused by Lincoln?

IN THE LANGUAGE OF THE COURT
Gee, Circuit Judge   *The district court granted James & Co.'s motion for summary judgment, concluding that Congress, in* enacting CERCLA, did not intend an exception to the general rule in corporation law of limited liability. CERCLA Section 107(a)(2) makes liable: (2) any person who at the time of disposal of any hazardous substance owned or operated any facility at which such hazardous substances were disposed of [42 U.S.C. § 9607(a)(2)].

Joslyn urges this court to read CERCLA's definition of "owner or operator" liberally and broadly to reach parent corporations whose subsidiaries are found liable under the statute.

Significantly, CERCLA does not define "owners" or "operators" as including the parent company of offending wholly owned subsidiaries. Nor does the legislative history indicate that Congress intended to alter so substantially a basic tenet of corporation law. Joslyn asks this court to rewrite the language of the Act significantly and hold parents directly liable for their subsidiaries' activities. To do so would dramatically alter traditional concepts of corporation law. Any bold rewriting of corporation law in this area is best left to Congress. Appellants have pointed this court to little in the legislative history of CERCLA to indicate that Congress intended to make such a significant change in corporation law principles.

DECISION AND REMEDY
The court of appeals held that the corporate doctrine of limited liability shielded James & Co. from liability for the environmental pollution caused by Lincoln.

Case Questions

Critical Legal Thinking   Should parent corporations be held liable for the acts of subsidiary corporations? Or should they be accorded limited liability like other shareholders?

Ethics   Is it ethical for a shareholder to hide behind the shield of limited liability?

Business Application   Should Congress eliminate the concept of limited liability for shareholders of corporations that have caused environmental pollution?

REVISED MODEL BUSINESS CORPORATION ACT (RMBCA)

The Committee on Corporate Laws of the American Bar Association (the Committee) first drafted the **Model Business Corporation Act (MBCA)** in 1950. The model act was intended to provide a uniform law regulating the formation, operation, and termination of corporations.

In 1984, the Committee completely revised the MBCA and issued the **Revised Model Business Corporation Act (RMBCA)**. Certain provisions of the RMBCA have been amended since 1984. The RMBCA arranged the provisions of the act more logically, revised the language of the act to be more consistent, and made substantial changes in the provisions of the model act. Many states have adopted all or part of the RMBCA. The RMBCA will serve as the basis for the discussion of corporations law in this book.

There is no general federal corporations law governing the formation and operation of private corporations. Many federal laws regulate the operation of private corporations, however. These include federal securities laws, labor laws, antitrust laws, consumer protection laws, environmental protection laws, bankruptcy laws, and the like. These federal statutes are discussed in separate chapters of this book.

Model Business Corporation Act (MBCA)

A model act drafted in 1950 that was intended to provide a uniform law for regulation of corporations.

Revised Model Business Corporation Act (RMBCA)

A revision of the MBCA in 1984 that arranged the provisions of the act more logically, revised the language to be more consistent, and made substantial changes in the provisions.

E-Commerce & Internet Law

INTERNET ALLIANCES IN CHINA

By the year 2005, China will have the largest number of Internet users in the world. Leading Internet companies in the United States have eyed this market for its tremendous growth potential. But China prohibits complete ownership of Internet companies in China by foreigners. In addition, the legendary Chinese "connections" method of conducting business places another hurdle in the way of foreign companies wishing to do business there. So what is the main way to tap into this Internet market? Strategic alliances.

A major strategic alliance by U.S. companies in China was their tie-in and investment in China.com. China.com is a Chinese-language Web portal backed by investments by U.S. companies America Online (AOL), Sun Microsystems, and Bay Networks. China.com became China's largest Internet company when it raised over $84 million in an initial public offering in July 1999. Intel Corp., another major U.S. company, has aligned itself with Sohu.com, a Chinese Internet company located in Beijing. CMGI Inc., a U.S. Internet holding company, has joined with Pacific Century Cyber-Works (PCCW), a Hong Kong company, to sell Web content and e-commerce services to the exploding Chinese Internet market from its base in Hong Kong.

Although the Chinese government has permitted these strategic alliances, it has stated that it will not allow foreign companies to own Internet service providers (ISPs) in China. Some U.S. companies have set up ISPs in countries and areas near China, which will be able to serve the Chinese market. The Information Industries Minister of China has announced that China will control the content of materials delivered via the Internet in China. Analysts predict that this will be hard to do given the global nature of the Internet.

Based on the communist government's rules in China and a culture that favors business connections, U.S. Internet companies will continue to enter the Chinese Internet market through strategic alliances with Chinese Internet firms. These strategic alliances bring together the expertise of all parties, bring China fully into the information age, and provide Internet users in China the most affordable options.

e-biz

*C*LASSIFICATIONS OF CORPORATIONS

Corporations are classified based on their locations, purpose, or owners. The various classifications of corporations are discussed in the following paragraphs.

Profit and Nonprofit Corporations

profit corporation

A corporation created to conduct a business for profit that can distribute profits to shareholders in the form of dividends.

Private corporations may be classified as either for profit or nonprofit. **Profit corporations** are created to conduct a business for profit and can distribute profits to shareholders in the form of dividends. Most private corporations fit this definition.

Nonprofit corporations are formed for charitable, educational, religious, or scientific purposes. Although nonprofit corporations may make a profit, they are prohibited by law from distributing this profit to their members, directors, or officers. About a dozen states have enacted the **Model Nonprofit Corporations Act** that governs the formation, operation, and termination of nonprofit corporations. All other states have their own individual statutes that govern the formation, operation, and dissolution of such corporations.

nonprofit corporation

A corporation that is formed to operate charitable institutions, colleges, universities, and other not-for-profit entities.

Public and Private Corporations

public corporation

A corporation formed to meet a specific governmental or political purpose.

Government-owned (or **public**) **corporations** are formed to meet a specific governmental or political purpose. For example, most cities and towns are formed as corporations, as are most water, school, sewage, and park districts. Local government corporations are often called *municipal corporations.*

Private corporations are formed to conduct privately owned business. They are owned by private parties, not by the government. Most corporations fall into this category.

private corporation

A corporation formed to conduct privately owned business.

Publicly Held and Closely Held Corporations

publicly held corporation

A corporation that has many shareholders and whose securities are often traded on national stock exchanges.

Publicly held corporations have many shareholders. Often, they are large corporations with hundreds or thousands of shareholders whose shares are traded on organized securities markets. IBM Corporation and General Motors Corporation are examples of publicly held corporations. The shareholders rarely participate in the management of such corporations.

Japan. Multinational corporations have grown to immense size and power in recent years. For example, the Mitsubishi Group of Japan operates subsidiary corporations in many nations of the world.

A closely held (or **close**) **corporation** is one whose shares are owned by few shareholders who are often family members, relatives, or friends. Frequently, the shareholders are involved in the management of the corporation. The shareholders sometimes enter into buy-and-sell agreements that prevent outsiders from becoming shareholders.

closely held corporation
A corporation owned by one or a few shareholders.

Professional Corporations

Professional corporations are formed by professionals such as lawyers, accountants, physicians, and dentists. The abbreviations *P.C.* (professional corporation), *P.A.* (professional association), and *S.C.* (service corporation) often identify professional corporations. Shareholders of professional corporations are often called *members*. Generally, only licensed professionals may become members.

All states permit the incorporation of professional corporations, although some states allow only designated types of professionals to incorporate. Professional corporations have normal corporate attributes and are formed like other corporations.

Members of the corporation are not usually liable for the torts committed by its agents or employees. Some states impose liability on members for the malpractice of other members of the corporation.

professional corporation
A corporation formed by lawyers, doctors, or other professionals.

Ethical Perspective

PROFESSIONALS DODGE CORPORATE LIABILITY

Professionals may form corporations to limit their liability. Consider the following case.

Three lawyers, Howard R. Cohen, Richard L. Stracher, and Paul J. Bloom, formed a professional corporation to engage in the practice of law. The three men were the sole shareholders, directors, and officers of the corporation. The corporation entered into an agreement to lease office space from We're Associates Company (We're Associates) in a building in Lake Success, New York. The lease was executed on behalf of the corporation "by Paul J. Bloom, Vice President." We're Associates sued the corporation and its three shareholders to recover $9,000 allegedly due and owing under the lease.

The trial court dismissed the plaintiff's case, and the appellate court affirmed. The appellate court noted that prior to 1970, attorneys, physicians, and other professionals in New York were barred from joining with other members of their respective professions in organizing corporations for the purpose of rendering professional services. In that year, however, with the enactment of Article 15 of the Business Corporation Law, New York joined other states in affording the privilege of incorporation to professionals.

In holding that the three lawyers who formed the professional corporation were not personally liable to We're Associates on the corporation's lease, the appellate court stated

It is well established that in the absence of some constitutional, statutory, or charter provision, the shareholders of a corporation are not liable for its contractual obligations and that parties having business dealings with a corporation must look to the corporation itself and not the shareholders for payment of their claims. Indeed, this insulation from individual liability for corporate obligations is one of the fundamental purposes of operating through corporate form. . . . The members of professional corporations are to enjoy the same benefits of limited liability afforded to shareholders of any other form of corporation.

The court concluded

Any analysis of the possible ethical considerations or moral obligations of attorneys in this situation is a separate matter and does not bear upon the

(box continues)

substantive legal issue of the scope of liability under the statute.

[*We're Associates Company v. Cohen, Stracher & Bloom, P.C.*, 478 N.Y.S.2d 670 (N.Y.App. 1984)]

1. Did the attorneys act ethically in not paying the lease payments themselves?
2. How could We're Associates have protected itself in this case?

Domestic, Foreign, and Alien Corporations

domestic corporation
A corporation in the state in which it was formed.

A corporation is a **domestic corporation** in the state in which it is incorporated. It is a **foreign corporation** in all other states and jurisdictions. For example, suppose a corporation is incorporated in Texas and does business in Montana. The corporation is a domestic corporation in Texas and a foreign corporation in Montana.

foreign corporation
A corporation in any state or jurisdiction other than the one in which it was formed.

A state can require a foreign corporation to *qualify* to conduct intrastate commerce within the state. Where a foreign corporation is required to qualify to do intrastate commerce in a state, it must obtain a *certificate of authority* from the state [RMBCA § 15.01(a)]. This requires the foreign corporation to file certain information with the secretary of state, pay the required fees, and appoint a registered agent for service of process.

Conduct that usually constitutes "doing business" includes maintaining an office to conduct intrastate business, selling personal property in intrastate business, entering into contracts involving intrastate commerce, using real estate for general corporate purposes, and the like. Activities that are generally *not* considered doing business within the state include maintaining, defending, or settling a lawsuit or an administrative proceeding; maintaining bank accounts; effectuating sales through independent contractors; soliciting orders through the mail; securing or collecting debts; transacting any business in interstate commerce; and the like [RMBCA § 15.01(b) and (c)].

Conducting intrastate business in a state in which it is not qualified subjects the corporation to fines. In addition, the corporation cannot bring a lawsuit in the state, although it can defend itself against lawsuits and administrative proceedings brought by others [RMBCA § 15.02].

alien corporation
A corporation that is incorporated in another country.

An **alien corporation** is a corporation that is incorporated in another country. In most instances, alien corporations are treated as foreign corporations.

*C*ONCEPT SUMMARY   TYPES OF CORPORATIONS

Type of Corporation	Description
Domestic	A corporation is a domestic corporation in the state in which it is incorporated.
Foreign	A corporation is a foreign corporation in states other than the one in which it is incorporated.
Alien	A corporation is an alien corporation in the United States if it is incorporated in another country.

promoter
A person or persons who organize and start the corporation, negotiate and enter into contracts in advance of its formation, find the initial investors to finance the corporation, and so forth.

*P*ROMOTERS' ACTIVITIES

The **promoter** is the person or persons who organize and start the corporation, negotiate and enter into contracts in advance of its formation, find the initial investors to finance the corporation, and so on. As discussed shortly, these activities may subject the promoter to personal liability.

Promoters' Liability

Promoters often enter into contracts on behalf of the corporation prior to its actual incorporation. **Promoters' contracts** include leases, sales contracts, contracts to purchase property, employment contracts, and the like. If the corporation never comes into existence, the promoters have joint personal liability on the contract unless the third party specifically exempts them from such liability.

If the corporation is formed, it becomes liable on a promoter's contract only if it agrees to become bound to the contract. This requires a resolution of the board of directors to be bound by the promoter's contract.

The promoter remains liable on the contract unless the parties enter into a novation [RMBCA § 2.04]. A *novation* is a three-party agreement whereby the corporation agrees to assume the contract liability of the promoter with the consent of the third party. After a novation, the corporation is solely liable on the promoter's contract.

In the following case, the court found a promoter liable on a promoter's contract.

promoters' contracts
A collective term for such things as leases, sales contracts, contracts to purchase property, and employment contracts entered into by promoters on behalf of the proposed corporation prior to its actual incorporation.

Coopers & Lybrand v. Fox
758 P.2d 68 (1988)
Colorado Court of Appeals

CASE 37.2

FACTS
On November 3, 1981, Garry J. Fox met with a representative of Coopers & Lybrand (Coopers), a national accounting firm. Fox informed Coopers that he was acting on behalf of a corporation he was in the process of forming, G. Fox and Partners, Inc., and requested a tax opinion and other accounting services for the corporation. Coopers accepted the engagement with the knowledge that the corporation was not yet in existence. The corporation was incorporated on December 4, 1981. Coopers completed its work by mid-December and billed the corporation and Fox $10,827 for services rendered. When neither Fox nor the corporation paid the bill, Coopers sued Fox as a promoter to recover the debt. The trial court held in favor of Fox. Coopers appealed.

ISSUE
Is Fox liable on the Coopers & Lybrand contract as a promoter?

IN THE LANGUAGE OF THE COURT
Kelly, Chief Judge   As a preliminary matter, we reject Fox's argument that he was acting only as an agent for the future corporation. One cannot act as the agent of a nonexistent principal. On the contrary, the uncontroverted facts place Fox squarely within the definition of a promoter. Coopers asserts that the trial court erred in finding that Fox was under no obligation to pay Coopers' fee in the absence of an agreement that he would be personally liable. We agree. As a general rule, promoters are personally liable for the contracts they make, though made on behalf of a corporation to be formed.

The well-recognized exception to the general rule of promoter liability is that if the contracting party knows the corporation is not in existence but nevertheless agrees to look solely to the corporation and not to the promoter for payment, then the promoter incurs no personal liability. Release of the promoter depends on the intent of the parties. As the proponent of an alleged agreement to release the promoter from liability, the promoter has the burden of proving the release agreement. Fox seeks to bring himself within the exception to the general rule of promoter liability. However, as the proponent of the exception, he must bear the burden of proving the existence of the alleged agreement releasing him from liability. The trial court found no agreement regarding Fox's liability. Thus, Fox failed to sustain his burden of proof, and the trial court erred in granting judgment in his favor.

DECISION AND REMEDY
The court of appeals held that Fox was liable, as a matter of law, under the doctrine of promoter liability. Reversed.

Case Questions

Critical Legal Thinking   Should promoters be held liable on their contracts even if the corporation is subsequently formed and accepts the contract as its own?

Ethics   Did Fox act ethically in this case?

Business Application   To avoid promoters' liability, when should contracts on behalf of a proposed corporation be executed?

*In*corporation Procedures

Business Brief
Corporations are creatures of statute: They can be formed only if certain statutory formalities are followed.

Corporations are creatures of statute. Thus, the organizers of the corporation must comply with the state's incorporation statute to form a corporation. Although relatively similar, the procedure for *incorporating* a corporation varies somewhat from state to state. The procedure for incorporating a corporation is discussed in the following paragraphs.

Selecting a State for Incorporation

Business Brief
Over half of the corporations listed on the New York Stock Exchange are incorporated in Delaware because of its laws that favor management.

A corporation can be incorporated in only one state even though it can do business in all other states in which it qualifies to do business. In choosing a state for incorporation, the incorporators, directors, and/or shareholders must consider the corporations law of the states under consideration.

For the sake of convenience, most corporations (particularly small ones) choose the state in which the corporation will be doing most of its business as the state for incorporation. Large corporations generally opt to incorporate in the state with the laws that are most favorable to the corporation's internal operations (e.g., Delaware).

Incorporators

incorporator
The person or persons, partnerships, or corporations that are responsible for incorporation of a corporation.

One or more persons, partnerships, domestic or foreign corporations, or other associations may act as an **incorporator** of a corporation [RMBCA § 2.01]. The incorporator's primary duty is to sign the articles of incorporation. Incorporators often become shareholders, directors, or officers of the corporation.

Articles of Incorporation

articles of incorporation
The basic governing documents of the corporation. These documents must be filed with the secretary of state of the state of incorporation.

The **articles of incorporation** (or **corporate charter**) are the basic governing documents of the corporation. They must be drafted and filed with, and approved by, the state before the corporation can be officially incorporated. Under the RMBCA, the articles of incorporation must include [RMBCA § 2.02(a)]

1. The name of the corporation
2. The number of shares the corporation is authorized to issue
3. The address of the corporation's initial registered office and the name of the initial registered agent
4. The name and address of each incorporator

The articles of incorporation may also include provisions concerning (1) the period of duration (which may be perpetual), (2) the purpose or purposes for which the corporation is organized, (3) limitation or regulation of the powers of the corporation, (4) regulation of the affairs of the corporation, or (5) any provision that would otherwise be contained in the corporation's bylaws.

Exhibit 37.1 illustrates sample articles of incorporation.

The corporation is, and must be, the creature of the state, into its nostrils the state must breathe the breath of a fictitious life for otherwise it would be no animated body but individualistic dust.

Frederic Wm. Maitland
Introduction to Gierke,
Political Theories of the
Middle Ages

Amending the Articles of Incorporation The articles of incorporation can be amended to contain any provision that could have been lawfully included in the original document [RMBCA § 10.01]. Such an amendment must show that (1) the board of directors adopted a *resolution* recommending the amendment and (2) the shareholders voted to approve the amendment [RMBCA § 10.03]. The board of directors of a

EXHIBIT 37.1   *Sample Articles of Incorporation*

ARTICLES OF INCORPORATION
OF
THE BIG CHEESE CORPORATION

ONE: The name of this corporation is:

THE BIG CHEESE CORPORATION

TWO: The purpose of this corporation is to engage in any lawful act or activity for which a corporation may be organized under the General Corporation Law of California other than the banking business, the trust company business, or the practice of a profession permitted to be incorporated by the California Corporations Code.

THREE: The name and address in this state of the corporation's initial agent for service of process is:

Nikki Nguyen, Esq.
1000 Main Street
Suite 800
Los Angeles, California 90010

FOUR: This corporation is authorized to issue only one class of shares which shall be designated common stock. The total number of shares it is authorized to issue is 1,000,000 shares.

FIVE: The names and addresses of the persons who are appointed to act as the initial directors of this corporation are:

Shou-Yi Kang	100 Maple Street Los Angeles, California 90005
Frederick Richards	200 Spruce Road Los Angeles, California 90006
Jessie Qian	300 Palm Drive Los Angeles, California 90007
Richard Eastin	400 Willow Lane Los Angeles, California 90008

SIX: The liability of the directors of the corporation from monetary damages shall be eliminated to the fullest extent possible under California law.

SEVEN: The corporation is authorized to provide indemnification of agents (as defined in Section 317 of the Corporations Code) for breach of duty to the corporation and its stockholders through bylaw provisions or through agreements with the agents, or both, in excess of the indemnification otherwise permitted by Section 317 of the Corporations Code, subject to the limits on such excess indemnification set forth in Section 204 of the Corporations Code.

IN WITNESS WHEREOF, the undersigned, being all the persons named above as the initial directors, have executed these Articles of Incorporation.

Dated: January 1, 2000

corporation may approve an amendment to the articles of incorporation without shareholder approval if the amendment does not affect rights attached to shares [RMBCA § 10.02]. After the amendment is approved by the shareholders, the corporation must file *articles of amendment* with the secretary of state [RMBCA § 10.06].

Entrepreneur and the Law

e·biz

SELECTING A CORPORATE NAME

When starting a new corporation, the organizers must choose a name for the entity. To ensure that the name selected is not already being used by another business, the organizers should take the following steps [RMBCA § 4.01]:

- Choose a name (and alternative names) for the corporation. The name must contain the words *corporation, company, incorporated,* or *limited* or an abbreviation of one of these words (i.e., *Corp., Co., Inc.,* or *Ltd.*).
- Make sure that the name chosen does not contain any word or phrase that indicates or implies that the corporation is organized for any purpose other than those stated in the articles of incorporation. For example, a corporate name cannot contain the word *Bank* if it is not authorized to conduct the business of banking.

- Determine whether the name selected is federally trademarked by another company and is therefore unavailable for use. Trademark lawyers and specialized firms will conduct trademark searches for a fee.
- Determine whether the chosen name is similar to other nontrademarked names and is therefore unavailable for use. Lawyers and specialized firms will conduct such searches for a fee.
- Determine whether the name selected is available as a domain name on the Internet. If the domain name is already owned by another person or business, the new corporation cannot use this domain name to conduct e-commerce over the Internet. Therefore, it is advisable to select another corporate name.

Purpose

general-purpose clause
A clause often included in the articles of incorporation that authorizes the corporation to engage in any activity permitted corporations by law.

A corporation can be formed for "any lawful purpose." Many corporations include a **general-purpose clause** in their articles of incorporation. Such a clause allows the corporation to engage in any activity permitted corporations by law. Corporations may choose to limit the purpose or purposes of the corporation by including a *limited-purpose clause* in the articles of incorporation [RMBCA § 3.01]. For example, a corporation may be organized "to engage in the business of real estate development."

Registered Agent

registered agent
A person or corporation that is empowered to accept service of process on behalf of the corporation.

The articles of incorporation must identify a **registered office** with a designated **registered agent** (either an individual or a corporation) in the state of incorporation [RMBCA § 5.01]. The registered office does not have to be the same as the corporation's place of business. A statement of change must be filed with the secretary of state of the state of incorporation if either the registered office or the registered agent is changed.

The registered agent is empowered to accept service of process on behalf of the corporation. For example, if someone were suing the corporation, the complaint and summons would be served on the registered agent. If no registered agent is named or the registered agent cannot be found at the registered office with reasonable diligence, service may be made by mail or alternative means [RMBCA § 5.04].

Corporate Bylaws

bylaws
A detailed set of rules adopted by the board of directors after the corporation is incorporated that contains provisions for managing the business and the affairs of the corporation.

In addition to the articles of incorporation, corporations are governed by their **bylaws**. Either the incorporators or initial directors can adopt the bylaws of the corporation. The bylaws are much more detailed than are the articles of incorporation. Bylaws may contain any provisions for managing the business and affairs of the corporation that are not inconsistent with law or the articles of incorporation [RMBCA § 2.06]. They do not have to be filed with any government official. The bylaws are binding on the directors, officers, and shareholders of the corporation.

The bylaws govern the internal management structure of the corporation. Typically, they specify the time and place of the annual shareholders' meeting, how special meetings of shareholders are called, the time and place of annual and monthly board of directors' meetings, how special meetings of the board of directors are called, the notice required for meetings, the quorum necessary to hold a shareholders' or board of directors' meeting, the required vote necessary to enact a corporate matter, the corporate officers and their duties, the committees of the board of directors and their duties, where the records of the corporation are to be kept, directors' and shareholders' inspection rights of corporate records, the procedure for transferring shares of the corporation, and such. Sample provisions of corporate bylaws are set forth in Exhibit 37.2.

The board of directors has the authority to amend the bylaws unless the articles of incorporation reserve that right for the shareholders. The shareholders of the corporation

Business Brief
The bylaws, which are much more detailed than the articles of incorporation, regulate the internal management structure of the corporation.

Exhibit 37.2 *Sample Provisions from Corporate Bylaws*

BYLAWS
of
THE BIG CHEESE CORPORATION

ARTICLE I   Offices

Section 1. Principal Executive Office. The corporation's principal executive office shall be fixed and located at such place as the Board of Directors (herein called the Board) shall determine. The Board is granted full power and authority to change said principal executive office from one location to another.

Section 2. Other Offices. Branch or subordinate offices may be established at any time by the Board at any place or places.

ARTICLE II   Shareholders

Section 1. Annual Meetings. The annual meetings of shareholders shall be held on such date and at such time as may be fixed by the Board. At such meetings, directors shall be elected and any other proper business may be transacted.

Section 2. Special Meetings. Special meetings of the shareholders may be called at any time by the Board, the Chairman of the Board, the President, or by the holders of shares entitled to cast not less than ten percent of the votes at such meeting. Upon request in writing to the Chairman of the Board, the President, any Vice President or the Secretary by any person (other than the Board) entitled to call a special meeting of shareholders, the officer forthwith shall cause notice to be given to the shareholders entitled to vote that a meeting will be held at a time requested by the person or persons calling the meeting, not less than thirty-five nor more than sixty days after the receipt of the request. If the notice is not given within twenty days after receipt of the request, the persons entitled to call the meeting may give the notice.

Section 3. Quorum. A majority of the shares entitled to vote, represented in person or by proxy, shall constitute a quorum at any meeting of shareholders. If a quorum is present, the affirmative vote of a majority of the shares represented and voting at the meeting (which shares voting affirmatively also constitute at least a majority of the required quorum) shall be the act of the shareholders, unless the vote of a greater number or voting by classes is required by law or by the Articles, except as provided in the following sentence. The shareholders present at a duly called or held meeting at which a quorum is present may continue to do business until adjournment, notwithstanding the withdrawal of enough shareholders to leave less than a quorum, if any action taken (other than adjournment) is approved by at least a majority of the shares required to constitute a quorum.

ARTICLE III   Directors

Section 1. Election and term of office. The directors shall be elected at each annual meeting of the shareholders, but if any such annual meeting is not held or the directors are not elected thereat, the directors may be elected at any special meeting of shareholders held for that purpose. Each director shall hold office until the next annual meeting and until a successor has been elected and qualified.

Section 2. Quorum. A majority of the authorized number of directors constitutes a quorum of the Board for the transaction of business. Every act or decision done or made by a majority of the directors present at a meeting duly held at which a quorum is present shall be regarded as the act of the Board, unless a greater number be required by law or by the Articles. A meeting at which a quorum is initially present may continue to transact business notwithstanding the withdrawal of directors, if any action taken is approved by at least a majority of the required quorum for such meeting.

Section 3. Participation in Meetings by Conference Telephone. Members of the Board may participate in a meeting through use of conference telephone or similar communications equipment, so long as all members participating in such meeting can hear one another.

Section 4. Action Without Meeting. Any action required or permitted to be taken by the Board may be taken without a meeting if all members of the board shall individually or collectively consent in writing to such action. Such consent or consents shall have the same effect as a unanimous vote of the Board and shall be filed with the minutes of the proceedings of the Board.

EXHIBIT 37.3 *Sample Corporate Resolutions from an Organizational Meeting*

MINUTES OF FIRST MEETING
OF
BOARD OF DIRECTORS
OF
THE BIG CHEESE CORPORATION
January 1, 2000
10:00 A.M.

The Directors of said corporation held their first meeting on the above date and at the above time pursuant to required notice.

The following Directors, constituting a quorum of the Board of Directors, were present at such meeting:

Shou-Yi Kang
Frederick Richards
Jessie Quian
Richard Eastin

Upon motion duly made and seconded, Show-Yi was unanimously elected Chairman of the meeting and Frederick Richards was unanimously elected Secretary of the meeting.

1. Articles of Incorporation and Agent for Service of Process

The Chairman stated that the Articles of Incorporation of the Corporation were filed in the office of the California Secretary of State. The Chairman presented to the meeting a certified copy of the Articles of Incorporation. The Secretary was directed to insert the copy in the Minute Book. Upon motion duly made and seconded, the following resolution was unanimously adopted:

RESOLVED, that the agent named as the initial agent for service of process in the Articles of Incorporation of this corporation is hereby confirmed as this corporation's agent for the purpose of service of process.

2. Bylaws

The matter of adopting Bylaws for the regulation of the affairs of the corporation was next considered. The Secretary presented to the meeting a form of Bylaws, which was considered and discussed. Upon motion duly made and seconded, the following recitals and resolutions were unanimously adopted:

WHEREAS, there has been presented to the directors a form of Bylaws for the regulation of the affairs of this corporation; and

WHEREAS, it is deemed to be in the best interests of this corporation that said Bylaws be adopted by this Board of Directors as the Bylaws of this corporation;

NOW, THEREFORE, BE IT RESOLVED, that Bylaws in the form presented to this meeting are adopted and approved as the Bylaws of this corporation until amended or repealed in accordance with applicable law.

RESOLVED FURTHER, that the Secretary of this corporation is authorized and directed to execute a certificate of the adoption of said Bylaws and to enter said Bylaws as so certified in the Minute Book of this corporation, and to see that a copy of said Bylaws is kept at the principal executive or business office of this corporation in California.

3. Corporate Seal

The secretary presented for approval a proposed seal of the corporation. Upon motion duly made and seconded, the following resolution was unanimously adopted:

RESOLVED, that a corporate seal is adopted as the seal of this corporation in the form of two concentric circles, with the name of this corporation between the two circles and the state and date of incorporation within the inner circle.

4. Stock Certificate

The Secretary presented a proposed form of stock certificate for use by the corporation. Upon motion duly made and seconded, the following resolution was unanimously adopted:

RESOLVED, that the form of stock certificate presented to this meeting is approved and adopted as the stock certificate of this corporation.

The secretary was instructed to insert a sample copy of the stock certificate in the Minute Book immediately following these minutes.

5. Election of officers

The Chairman announced that it would be in order to elect officers of the corporation. After discussion and upon motion duly made and seconded, the following resolution was unanimously adopted:

RESOLVED, that the following persons are unanimously elected to the offices indicated opposite their names

Title	Name
Chief Executive Officer	Shou-Yi Kang
President	Frederick Richards
Secretary and Vice President	Jessie Quian
Treasurer	Richard Eastin

There being no further business to come before the meeting, on motion duly made, seconded and unanimously carried, the meeting was adjourned.

have the absolute right to amend the bylaws even though the bylaws may also be amended by the board of directors [RMBCA § 10.20].

Organizational Meeting

An **organizational meeting** of the initial directors of the corporation must be held after the articles of incorporation are filed. At this meeting, the directors must adopt the bylaws, elect corporate officers, and transact such other business as may come before the meeting [RMBCA § 2.05]. The last category includes such matters as accepting share subscriptions, approving the form of the stock certificate, authorizing the issuance of the shares, ratifying or adopting promoters' contracts, authorizing the reimbursement of promoters' expenses, selecting a bank, choosing an auditor, forming committees of the board of directors, fixing the salaries of officers, hiring employees, authorizing the filing of applications for government licenses to transact the business of the corporation, and empowering corporate officers to enter into contracts on behalf of the corporation. Exhibit 37.3 contains sample corporate resolutions from an organizational meeting of a corporation.

Corporate Seal

Most corporations adopt a **corporate seal** [RMBCA § 3.02(2)]. Generally, the seal is a design that contains the name of the corporation and the date of incorporation. It is imprinted by the corporate secretary on certain legal documents (e.g., real estate deeds and the like) that are signed by corporate officers or directors. The seal is usually affixed by a metal stamp.

> **corporate seal**
> A design containing the name of the corporation and the date of incorporation that is imprinted by the corporate secretary using a metal stamp on certain legal documents.

Corporate Status

The RMBCA provides that corporate existence begins when the articles of incorporation are filed. The secretary of state's filing of the articles of incorporation is *conclusive proof* that the incorporators satisfied all conditions of incorporation. After that, only the state can bring a proceeding to cancel or revoke the incorporation or involuntarily dissolve the corporation. Third parties cannot thereafter challenge the existence of the corporation or raise it as a defense against the corporation [RMBCA § 2.03]. The corollary to this rule is: Failure to file articles of incorporation is conclusive proof of the nonexistence of the corporation.

> **Business Brief**
> The filing of the articles of incorporation is *conclusive proof* that a corporation exists. After that, only the state can challenge the status of the corporation; third parties cannot.

Entrepreneur and the Law

S CORPORATIONS

Corporations are separate legal entities. As such, they generally must pay corporate income taxes to federal and state governments. If a corporation distributes its profits to shareholders in the form of dividends, shareholders must pay personal income tax on the dividends. This *double taxation* of corporations is one of the major disadvantages of doing business in the corporate form. Some corporations and their shareholders can avoid double taxation by electing to be an S Corporation.

In 1982, Congress enacted the **Subchapter S Revision Act**. The act divided all corporations into two groups:

S Corporations, which are those that elect to be taxed under Subchapter S, and **C Corporations**, which are all other corporations [26 U.S.C. §§ 6242 et seq.].

If a corporation elects to be taxed as an S Corporation, it pays no federal income tax at the corporate level. As in a partnership, the corporation's income or loss flows to the shareholders' individual income tax returns. Thus, this election is particularly advantageous if (1) the corporation is expected to have losses that can be offset against other income of the shareholders or (2) the corporation is expected to make profits and the shareholders' income tax

(box continues)

brackets are lower than the corporation's. Profits are taxed to the shareholders even if the income is not distributed. The shares retain other attributes of the corporate form, including limited liability.

Corporations that meet the following criteria can elect to be taxed as S Corporations:

1. The corporation must be a domestic corporation.
2. The corporation cannot be a member of an affiliated group.
3. The corporation can have no more than 75 shareholders.
4. Shareholders must be individuals, estates, or certain trusts. Corporations and partnerships cannot be shareholders.

5. Shareholders must be citizens or residents of the United States. Nonresident aliens cannot be shareholders.
6. The corporation cannot have more than one class of stock. Shareholders do not have to have equal voting rights.
7. No more than 20 percent of the corporation's income can be from passive investment income.

An S Corporation election is made by filing a Form 2553 with the Internal Revenue Service (IRS). The election can be rescinded by shareholders who collectively own at least a majority of the shares of the corporation. However, if the election is rescinded, another S Corporation election cannot be made for five years.

FINANCING THE CORPORATION WITH EQUITY SECURITIES

A corporation needs to finance the operation of its business. The most common way to do this is by selling equity securities and debt securities. **Equity securities** (or **stocks**) represent ownership rights in the corporation. Equity securities can be *common stock* and *preferred stock*. These are discussed in the following paragraphs.

equity securities

Representation of ownership rights to the corporation. Also called *stocks*.

Common Stock

Common stock is an equity security that represents the residual value of the corporation. Common stock has no preferences. That is, creditors and preferred shareholders must receive their required interest and dividend payments before common shareholders receive anything. Common stock does not have a fixed maturity date. If the corporation is liquidated, the creditors and preferred shareholders are paid the value of their interests first, and the common shareholders are paid the value of their interests (if any) last. Corporations may issue different classes of common stock [RMBCA § 6.01(a) and (b)].

common stock

A type of equity security that represents the *residual* value of the corporation.

Persons who own common stock are called **common stockholders**. A common stockholder's investment in the corporation is represented by a **common stock certificate**. Common shareholders have the right to elect directors and to vote on mergers and other important matters. In return for their investment, common shareholders receive *dividends* declared by the board of directors.

common stockholder

A person who owns common stock.

A sample share of common stock is shown in Exhibit 37.4.

common stock certificate

A document that represents the common shareholder's investment in the corporation.

Par Value and No Par Shares Common shares are sometimes categorized as either par or no par. *Par value* is a value assigned to common shares by the corporation, usually in the articles of incorporation, which sets the lowest price at which the shares may be issued by the corporation. It does not affect the market value of the shares. Most shares that are issued by corporations are *no par shares*. No par shares are not assigned a par value. The RMBCA has eliminated the concept of par value.

preferred stock

A type of equity security that is given certain preferences and rights over common stock

Preferred Stock

Preferred stock is an equity security that is given certain *preferences and rights over common stock* [RMBCA § 6.01(c)]. The owners of preferred stock are called **preferred stockholders**. Preferred stockholders are issued a **preferred stock certificate** to evidence their ownership interest in the corporation.

preferred stockholder

A person who owns preferred stock.

preferred stock certificate

A document that represents a shareholder's investment in preferred stock in the corporation.

EXHIBIT **37.4** *Sample Stock Certificate*

INCORPORATED UNDER THE LAWS OF THE STATE OF DELAWARE

SPINNER, INC.

The Corporation is authorized to issue 100,000 Common Shares Par Value $5.00 Each

This Certifies that _____ JEAN RICHLAND _____ is the owner of _____ TEN THOUSAND (10,000) _____ fully paid and non-assessable Shares of the above Corporation transferable only on the books of the Corporation by the holder hereof in person or by duly authorized Attorney upon surrender of this Certificate properly endorsed.

In Witness Whereof, the said Corporation has caused this Certificate to be signed by its duly authorized officers and to be sealed with the Seal of the Corporation. Dated _____

SECRETARY-TREASURER PRESIDENT

Preferred stock can be issued in classes or series. One class of preferred stock can be given preferences over another class of preferred stock. Like common shareholders, preferred shareholders have limited liability. Preferred shareholders generally are not given the right to vote for the election of directors or such. However, they are often given the right to vote if there is a merger or if the corporation has not made the required dividend payments for a certain period of time (e.g., three years).

Preferences Preferences of preferred stock must be set forth in the articles of incorporation. Preferred stock may have any or all of the following preferences or rights.

- *Dividend Preference* A **dividend preference** is the right to receive a *fixed dividend* at set periods during the year (e.g., quarterly). The dividend rate is usually a set percentage of the initial offering price.

Consider This Example Suppose a stockholder purchases $10,000 of a preferred stock that pays an 8 percent dividend annually. The stockholder has the right to receive $800 each year as a dividend on the preferred stock.

- *Liquidation Preference* The right to be paid before common stockholders if the corporation is dissolved and liquidated is called a **liquidation preference**. A liquidation preference is normally a stated dollar amount.

Business Brief
Preferred stock is given certain *preferences* and its value is based on these preferences.

dividend preference
The right to receive a fixed dividend at stipulated periods during the year (e.g., quarterly).

liquidation preference
The right to be paid a stated dollar amount if the corporation is dissolved and liquidated.

Consider This Example A corporation issues a preferred stock that has a liquidation preference of $200. This means that if the corporation is dissolved and liquidated, the holder of each preferred share will receive at least $200 before the common shareholders receive anything. Note that because the corporation must pay its creditors first, there may be insufficient funds to pay this preference.

cumulative preferred stock
Stock that provides any missed dividend payments must be paid in the future to the preferred shareholders before the common shareholders can receive any dividends.

- *Cumulative Dividend Right* Corporations must pay a preferred dividend if they have the earnings to do so. **Cumulative preferred stock** provides that any missed dividend payments must be paid in the future to the preferred shareholders before the common shareholders can receive any dividends. The amount of unpaid cumulative dividends is called dividend *arrearages*. Usually, arrearages can be accumulated for only a limited period of time (such as three years). If the preferred stock is **noncumulative**, there is no right of accumulation. In other words, the corporation does not have to pay any missed dividends.

participating preferred stock
Stock that allows the stockholder to participate in the profits of the corporation along with the common stockholders.

- *Right To Participate In Profits* **Participating preferred stock** allows the stockholder to participate in the profits of the corporation along with the common stockholders. Participation is in addition to the fixed dividend paid on preferred stock. The terms of participation vary widely. Usually, the common stockholders must be paid a certain amount of dividends before participation is allowed. **Nonparticipating preferred stock** does not have a right to participate in the profits of the corporation beyond its fixed dividend rate. Most preferred stock falls into this category.

convertible preferred stock
Stock that permits the stockholders to convert their shares into common stock.

- *Conversion Right* **Convertible preferred stock** permits the stockholders to convert their shares into common stock. The terms and exchange rate of the conversion are established when the shares are issued. The holders of the convertible preferred stock usually exercise this option if the corporation's common stock increases significantly in value. Preferred stock without a conversion feature is called **nonconvertible preferred stock**. Nonconvertible stock is more common.

The preceding list of preferences and rights is not exhaustive [RMBCA § 6.01(d)]. Corporations may establish other preferences and rights for preferred stock.

redeemable preferred stock
Stock that permits the corporation to buy back the preferred stock at some future date.

Redeemable Preferred Stock **Redeemable preferred stock** (or **callable preferred stock**) permits the corporation to redeem (i.e., buy back) the preferred stock at some future date. The terms of the redemption are established when the shares are issued. Corporations usually redeem the shares when the current interest rate falls below the dividend rate of the preferred shares. Preferred stock that is not redeemable is called **nonredeemable preferred stock**. Nonredeemable stock is more common.

Authorized, Issued, and Outstanding Shares

authorized shares
The number of shares provided for in the articles of incorporation.

The number of shares provided for in the articles of incorporation is called **authorized shares** [RMBCA § 6.01]. The shareholders may vote to amend the articles of incorporation to increase this amount. Authorized shares that have been sold by the corporation are called **issued shares**. Not all authorized shares have to be issued at the same time. Authorized shares that have not been issued are called *unissued shares*. The board of directors can vote to issue unissued shares at any time without shareholder approval.

issued shares
Shares that have been sold by the corporation.

treasury shares
Shares of stock repurchased by the company itself.

A corporation is permitted to repurchase its own shares [RMBCA § 6.31]. Repurchased shares are commonly called **treasury shares**. Treasury shares cannot be voted by the corporation and dividends are not paid on these shares. Treasury shares can be reissued by the corporation. The shares that are in shareholder hands, whether originally issued or reissued treasury shares, are called **outstanding shares**. Only outstanding shares have the right to vote [RMBCA § 6.03].

outstanding shares
Shares of stock that are in shareholder hands.

CONCEPT SUMMARY   TYPES OF SHARES

Type of Share	Description
Authorized	Shares authorized in the corporation's articles of incorporation.
Issued	Shares sold by the corporation.
Treasury	Shares repurchased by the corporation. They do not have the right to vote.
Outstanding	Issued shares minus treasury shares. These shares have the right to vote.

Consideration to Be Paid for Shares

The RMBCA allows shares to be issued in exchange for any benefit to the corporation, including cash, tangible property, intangible property, promissory notes, services performed, contracts for services to be performed, or other securities of the corporation. In the absence of fraud, the judgment of the board of directors or shareholders as to the value of consideration received for shares is conclusive [RMBCA § 6.21(b) and (c)].

Business Brief

Shares of a corporation may be sold in exchange for any property or benefit to the corporation as determined by the board of directors.

Stock Options and Stock Warrants

A corporation can grant stock options (options) and stock warrants (warrants) that permit parties to purchase common or preferred shares at a certain price for a set time [RMBCA § 6.24].

Corporations commonly grant **stock options** to top-level managers. They are non-transferable. A stock option gives the recipient the right to purchase shares of the corporation from the corporation at a stated price (called the *striking price*) for a specified period of time (called the *option period*). If the profitability of the corporation and the market value of its securities increase during the option period, the holder of the option is likely to *exercise the option*, that is, purchase the shares subject to the option.

A **stock warrant** is a stock option that is evidenced by a certificate. Warrants are commonly issued in conjunction with other securities. A warrant holder can exercise the warrant and purchase the common stock at the strike price anytime during the warrant period. Warrants can be transferable or nontransferable.

stock option

A nontransferable right to purchase shares of the corporation from the corporation at a stated price for a specified period of time.

stock warrant

A stock option that is evidenced by a certificate. Warrants can be transferable or nontransferable.

FINANCING THE CORPORATION WITH DEBT SECURITIES

A corporation often raises funds by issuing debt securities [RMBCA § 3.02(7)]. **Debt securities** (also called **fixed income securities**) establish a debtor–creditor relationship in which the corporation borrows money from the investor to whom the debt security is issued. The corporation promises to pay interest on the amount borrowed and to repay the principal at some stated maturity date in the future. The corporation is the *debtor* and the holder is the *creditor*. There are three classifications of debt securities: debentures, bonds, and notes.

A **debenture** is a *long-term* (often 30 years or more), *unsecured* debt instrument that is based on the corporation's general credit standing. If the corporation encounters financial difficulty, unsecured debenture holders are treated as general creditors of the corporation (i.e., they are paid only after the secured creditors' claims are met).

debt securities

Securities that establish a debtor–creditor relationship in which the corporation borrows money from the investor to whom the debt security is issued.

debenture

A long-term unsecured debt instrument that is based on the corporation's general credit standing.

bond
A long-term debt security that is secured by some form of collateral.

note
A debt security with a maturity of five years or less.

indenture agreement
A contract between the corporation and the holder that contains the terms of a debt security.

A **bond** is a *long-term* debt security that is *secured* by some form of *collateral* (e.g., real estate, personal property, and such). Thus, bonds are the same as debentures except that they are secured. Secured bondholders can foreclose on the collateral in the event of non-payment of interest, principal, or other specified events.

A **note** is a debt security with a maturity of five years or less. Notes can be either unsecured or secured. They usually do not contain a conversion feature. They are sometimes made redeemable.

Indenture Agreement

The terms of a debt security are commonly contained in a contract between the corporation and the holder known as an **indenture agreement** (or simply an **indenture**). The indenture generally contains the maturity date of the debt security, the required interest payment, the collateral (if any), conversion rights into common or preferred stock, call provisions, any restrictions on the corporation's right to incur other indebtedness, the rights of holders upon default, and such. It also establishes the rights and duties of the indenture trustee. Generally, a trustee is appointed to represent the interest of the debt security holders. Bank trust departments often serve in this capacity.

CORPORATE POWERS

A corporation has the same basic rights to perform acts and enter into contracts as a physical person [RMBCA § 3.02]. The express and implied powers of a corporation are discussed in the following paragraphs.

Express Powers

express powers
Powers given to a corporation by (1) the U.S. Constitution, (2) state constitutions, (3) federal statutes, (4) state statutes, (5) articles of incorporation, (6) bylaws, and (7) resolutions of the board of directors.

A corporation's **express powers** are found in (1) the U.S. Constitution, (2) state constitutions, (3) federal statutes, (4) state statutes, (5) articles of incorporation, (6) bylaws, and (7) resolutions of the board of directors. Corporation statutes normally state the express powers granted to the corporation.

Generally, a corporation has the power to purchase, own, lease, sell, mortgage, or otherwise deal in real and personal property; make contracts; lend money; borrow money; incur liabilities; issue notes, bonds, and other obligations; invest and reinvest funds; sue and be sued in its corporate name; make donations for the public welfare or for charitable, scientific, or educational purposes; and the like. RMBCA § 3.02 provides a list of express corporate powers.

Corporations formed under general incorporation laws cannot engage in certain businesses, such as banking, insurance, or operating public utilities. Corporations must obtain a corporate charter under special incorporation statutes and receive approval of special government administrative agencies before engaging in these businesses.

Implied Powers

implied powers
Powers beyond express powers that allow a corporation to accomplish its corporate purpose.

Neither the governing laws nor the corporate documents can anticipate every act necessary for a corporation to carry on its business. **Implied powers** allow the corporation to exceed its express powers in order to accomplish its corporate purpose. For instance, a corporation has the implied power to open a bank account, reimburse its employees for expenses, engage in advertising, purchase insurance, and the like.

Ultra Vires *Acts*

An act by a corporation that is beyond its express or implied powers is called an ***ultra vires act***. The following remedies are available if an *ultra vires* act is committed:

1. Shareholders can sue for an injunction to prevent the corporation from engaging in the act.
2. The corporation (or the shareholders on behalf of the corporation) can sue the officers or directors who caused the act for damages.
3. The attorney general of the state of incorporation can bring an action to enjoin the act or to dissolve the corporation [RMBCA § 3.04].

ultra vires act
An act by a corporation that is beyond its express or implied powers.

Business Brief
Today, the doctrine of *ultra vires* has lost significance because most corporations select general-purpose clauses (making very few acts *ultra vires*).

International Perspective

ORGANIZATION AND OPERATION OF THE MULTINATIONAL CORPORATION

In the past, the size, power, and range of activities of corporations were limited. This changed at the beginning of the twentieth century, when corporations won the right to own stock in each other. National corporate networks soon followed. Eventually, parent corporations, mostly American, expanded these networks overseas by setting up subsidiary corporations under the laws of other countries. These international networks (or multinational enterprises) are made up of companies of different nationalities that constitute a single economic unit connected by shareholding, managerial control, or contractual agreement. The simplest international operating structure is one that subcontracts with independent firms in the host country to carry out sales or purchases. "National multinational" firms that establish wholly owned branches and subsidiaries overseas are somewhat more complex. "International multinational" firms are even more complicated. They are made up of two or more parents from different countries that co-own operating businesses in two or more countries.

The Ford Motor Company is an example of a national multinational firm. Organized in the United States at the beginning of the 20th century, Ford has always viewed the entire world as its market. The company's policy is for the American parent to own and control all of its overseas subsidiaries. Ford's 10 European subsidiaries are all owned entirely by the American parent. The Mitsubishi Group is another example of this organizational format. It is actually made up of several Japanese companies that use joint directors' meetings to coordinate their activities in Japan and overseas.

The Royal Dutch/Shell Group is an example of an international multinational corporation. In 1907, the Dutch and British parents each formed a wholly owned holding company in their respective countries. Each then transferred the ownership of the operating subsidiary to the holding company and exchanged shares in the holding companies. The Dutch parent held 60 percent of each holding company, and the British parent held 40 percent. In addition, the management and operation of the two companies were organized to function as a single economic unit. Unilever, Dunlop Pirelli, and VFW/Fokker also operate under an international multinational umbrella.

There is a special type of international multinational: a publicly owned transnational enterprise. One example is Air Afrique, which was created by several West African countries through the use of a treaty granting each government a voice in the company's operation.

*D*ISSOLUTION AND TERMINATION OF CORPORATIONS

The life of a corporation may be terminated voluntarily or involuntarily. The methods for dissolving and terminating corporations are discussed in the following paragraphs.

Voluntary Dissolution

A corporation can be **voluntarily dissolved**. If the corporation has not commenced business or issued any shares, it may be dissolved by a vote of the majority of the incorporators or initial directors [RMBCA § 14.01]. After that, the corporation can be voluntarily dissolved if the board of directors recommends dissolution and a majority of shares entitled

voluntary dissolution
A corporation that has begun business or issued shares can be dissolved upon recommendation of the board of directors and a majority vote of the shares entitled to vote.

to vote (or a greater number if required by the articles of incorporation or bylaws) votes for dissolution as well [RMBCA § 14.02].

For a voluntary dissolution to be effective, **articles of dissolution** must be filed with the secretary of state of the state of incorporation. A corporation is dissolved upon the effective date of the articles of dissolution [RMBCA § 14.03].

Administrative Dissolution

administrative dissolution

Involuntary dissolution of a corporation that is ordered by the secretary of state if the corporation has failed to comply with certain procedures required by law.

The secretary of state can obtain **administrative dissolution** of a corporation if (1) it failed to file an annual report, (2) it failed for 60 days to maintain a registered agent in the state, (3) it failed, for 60 days after a change of its registered agent, to file a statement of such change with the secretary of state, (4) it did not pay its franchise fee, or (5) the period of duration stated in the corporation's articles of incorporation has expired [RMBCA § 14.20].

Administrative dissolution is simple. If the corporation does not cure the default within 60 days of being notified of it, the secretary of state issues a *certificate of dissolution* that dissolves the corporation [RMBCA § 14.21].

Judicial Dissolution

judicial dissolution

Occurs when a corporation is dissolved by a court proceeding instituted by shareholders, creditors, or the state. Permitted only for certain reasons.

A corporation can be involuntarily dissolved by a judicial proceeding. **Judicial dissolution** can be instituted by shareholders, creditors, or the state for any reason listed in the following paragraphs. If a court judicially dissolves a corporation, it enters a *decree of dissolution* that specifies the date of dissolution [RMBCA § 14.33]. The courts are often reluctant to dissolve a corporation by judicial decree.

Dissolution by the State   The attorney general of the state of incorporation can obtain judicial dissolution of a corporation if the corporation (1) procured its articles of incorporation through fraud or (2) exceeded or abused the authority conferred upon it by law [RMBCA § 14.30(1)].

Dissolution by Creditors   Corporate creditors can obtain a judicial dissolution of an insolvent corporation if (1) the creditor's claim was reduced to judgment and the execution of the judgment has been returned unsatisfied, or (2) the corporation admitted in writing that the creditor's claim is due and owing [RMBCA § 14.30(3)].

Entrepreneur and the Law

JUDICIAL DISSOLUTION OF A CLOSELY HELD CORPORATION

Shareholders and directors of smaller closely held corporations sometimes disagree about management and policy decisions concerning the operation of the business. What happens if there is a deadlock as to the direction the corporation should take, or if damage is being caused to corporate assets? Most corporation statutes solve this problem by providing that a shareholder can go to court and seek judicial dissolution of a corporation if

• The directors are deadlocked in the management of corporate affairs, the shareholders are unable to break

the deadlock, and irreparable injury is being suffered by or threatened to the corporation.
• The shareholders are deadlocked in voting power and have failed for at least two consecutive annual meetings to elect directors whose terms have expired.
• The acts of the directors or those in control of the corporation are illegal, oppressive, or fraudulent.
• The corporate assets are being misapplied or wasted [RMBCA § 14.30(2)].

Winding-Up, Liquidation, and Termination

A dissolved corporation continues its corporate existence but may not carry on any business except as required to **wind up and liquidate** its business and affairs [RMBCA § 14.05].

In a voluntary dissolution, the liquidation is usually carried out by the board of directors. If (1) the dissolution is involuntary or (2) the dissolution is voluntary but the directors refuse to carry out the liquidation, a court-appointed receiver carries out the winding-up and liquidation of the corporation [RMBCA § 14.32].

Termination occurs only after the winding-up of the corporation's affairs, the liquidation of its assets, and the distribution of the proceeds to the claimants. The liquidated assets are paid to claimants according to the following priority: (1) expenses of liquidation and creditors according to their respective liens and contract rights, (2) preferred shareholders according to their liquidation preferences and contract rights, and (3) common shareholders.

The dissolution of a corporation does not impair any rights or remedies available against the corporation or its directors, or officers, or shareholders for any right or claim existing or incurred prior to dissolution.

winding-up and liquidation
The process by which a dissolved corporation's assets are collected, liquidated, and distributed to creditors, shareholders, and other claimants.

termination
The ending of a corporation that occurs only after the winding-up of the corporation's affairs, the liquidation of its assets, and the distribution of the proceeds to the claimants.

Working the Web

Many large corporations have well developed Web sites. Here are some good examples:

Information corporation: Microsoft.

Visit at **www.microsoft.com**

Manufacturing corporation: Hewlett Packard.

Visit at **www.hp.com**

Service corporation: Federal Express.

Visit at **www.fedex.com**

International corporation: Mercedes Benz.

Visit at **www.mercedes-benz.com**

Publishing corporation: Prentice Hall (business law site).

Visit at **www.prenhall.com/phblaw**

e·biz

CYBER EXERCISES

1–5. Visit all of these large corporations. Notice the different techniques used in developing the Web sites. See what kind of information each site has.

CASES AND EXERCISES

CRITICAL LEGAL THINKING CASES

37.1. Jeffrey Sammak was the owner of a contracting business known as Senaco. In the early part of 1980, Sammak decided to enter the coal reprocessing business. In April 1980, Sammak attended the "Coal Show" in Chicago, Illinois, at which he met representatives of the Deister Co., Inc, (Deister). Deister was incorporated under the laws of Pennsylvania. Sammak began negotiating with Deister to purchase equipment to be used in his coal reprocessing business. Deister sent Sammak literature guaranteeing a certain level of performance for the equipment. On April 3, 1981, Sammak purchased the equipment. After the equipment was installed, Sammak became dissatisfied with its performance. Sammak believes that Deister breached an express warranty and wants to sue. Can a suit be brought against a corporation such as Deister? [*Blackwood Coal v. Deister Co., Inc.*, 626 F.Supp. 727 (E.D.Pa. 1985)]

37.2. Joseph M. Billy was an employee of the USM Corporation (USM). USM is a publicly held corporation. On October 21, 1976, Billy was at work when a 4,600-pound ram from a vertical boring mill broke loose and crushed him to death. Billy's widow brought suit against USM alleging that the accident was caused by certain defects in the manufacture and design of the vertical boring mill and in the two moving parts directly involved in the accident, a metal lifting arm and the 4,600-pound ram. If Mrs. Billy's suit is successful, can the shareholders of USM be held personally liable for any judgment against USM? [*Billy v. Consolidated Mach. Tool. Corp.*, 412 N.E.2d 934, 51 N.Y.2d 152 (N.Y.App. 1980)]

37.3. William O'Donnel and Vincent Marino worked together as executives of a shipping container repair company known as Marine Trailers. Marine Trailers's largest customer was American Export Lines (American Export). When American Export became unhappy with the owners of Marine Trailers, it let O'Donnel and Marino know that if they formed their own company, American Exports would give them its business. O'Donnel and Marino decided to take American Export's suggestion and bought the majority of shares of a publicly traded corporation known as Marine Repair Services, Inc. (Repair Services). O'Donnel and Marino operated Repair Services as a container repair company at the Port of New York. The company prospered, expanding to five other states and overseas. O'Donnel and Marino's initial $12,000 investment paid off. Ten years after buying the company, both men were earning over $150,000 a year in salary alone. What type of corporation is Repair Services? [*O'Donnel v. Marine Repair Services, Inc.*, 530 F.Supp. 1199 (S.D.N.Y. 1982)]

37.4. Hutchinson Baseball Enterprises, Inc. (Hutchinson, Inc.), was incorporated under the laws of Kansas on August 31, 1980. Among the purposes of the corporation, according to its bylaws, are to "promote, advance, and sponsor baseball, which shall include Little League and Amateur baseball, in the Hutchinson, Kansas, area." The corporation is involved in a number of activities, including the leasing of a field for American Legion teams, furnishing instructors as coaches for Little League teams, conducting a Little League camp, and the leasing of a baseball field to a local junior college for a nominal fee. Hutchinson, Inc., raises money through ticket sales to amateur baseball games, concessions, and contributions. Any profits are used to improve the playing fields. Profits are never distributed to the corporation's directors or members. What type of corporation is Hutchinson, Inc.? [*Hutchinson Baseball Enterprises, Inc. v. Commissioner of Internal Revenue*, 696 F.2d 757 (10th Cir. 1982)]

37.5. In November 1979, Elmer Balvik and Thomas Sylvester formed a partnership, named Weldon Electric, for the purpose of engaging in the electrical contracting business. Balvik contributed $8,000 and a vehicle worth $2,000 and Sylvester contributed $25,000 to the partnership's assets. The parties operated the business as a partnership until 1984, when they decided to incorporate. Stock was issued to Balvik and Sylvester in proportion to their partnership ownership interests, with Sylvester receiving 70 percent and Balvik 30 percent of the stock. Balvik and his wife and Sylvester and his wife were the four directors of the corporation. Sylvester was elected president of the corporation. Balvik was vice president. The corporation's bylaws stated that "sales of shares of stock by any shareholder shall be as set forth in a 'Buy Sell Agreement' entered into by the shareholders." What type of corporation is Weldon Electric? [*Balvik v. Sylvester*, 411 N.W.2d 383 (N.D. 1987)]

37.6. Leo V. Mysels was the president of Florida Fashions of Interior Design, Inc. (Florida Fashions). Florida Fashions, which was a Pennsylvania corporation, had never registered to do business in the state of Florida. In 1973, while acting in the capacity of a salesman for the corporation, Mysels took an order for goods from Francis E. Barry. The transaction took place in Florida. Barry paid Florida Fashions for the goods ordered. When Florida Fashions failed to perform its obligations under the sales agreement, Barry brought suit in Florida. What type of corporation was Florida Fashions in regards to the state of Pennsylvania and to the state of Florida? Can Florida Fashions defend itself in a lawsuit? [*Mysels v. Barry*, 332 So.2d 38 (Fla.App. 1976)]

37.7. Lippman, Inc. (Lippman), a wholly owned subsidiary of Litton Systems, Inc., was incorporated on September 11, 1973, under the laws of the state of Wisconsin. As a subsidiary, Lippman seldom transacted business under its own name. On October 4, 1976, organizers filed articles of incorporation with the secretary of state of Wisconsin to form a corporation called Lippman-Milwaukee, Inc. (Lippman-Milwaukee). Lippman and the proposed Lippman-Milwaukee were two separate entities with different businesses and different owners. After the secretary of state granted a certificate of incorporation to Lippman-Milwaukee, Lippman sued to prevent Lippman-Milwaukee from using the name. Lippman claimed that the name of the new corporation was too similar and could cause confusion. Who wins? [*Litton Systems, Inc. v. Lippman-Milwaukee, Inc.*, 481 F.Supp. 788 (E.D.Wis. 1979)]

37.8. On December 27, 1972, the Homes Corporation (Home), a closely held corporation whose sole stockholders were Jerry and Beverly Ann Allen, purchased 10 acres of real estate near Kahaluu on the island of Oahu, Hawaii. Homes made a down payment of $50,000. It was the Allens' intention to obtain approval for a planned unit development (PUD) from the city and county of Honolulu and then develop the property with some 60 condominium townhouses. To further this project, the Allens sought an outside investor. Herbert Handley, a real estate developer from Texas, decided to join the Allens' project. The two parties entered an agreement whereby a new Hawaiian corporation would be formed to build the condominiums, with Handley owning 51 percent of the corporation's stock and the Allens the remaining 49 percent. The two parties began extensive planning and design of the project. They also took out a $69,500 loan from the Bank of Hawaii. After a year had gone by, Handley informed the Allens that he was no longer able to advance funds to the project. Soon thereafter, the city and county denied their PUD zoning application. The new corporation was never formed. Who is liable for the failed condominium project's contractual obligations? [*Handley v. Ching*, 627 P.2d 1132 (HawaiiApp. 1981)]

37.9. Martin Stern, Jr., was an architect who worked in Nevada. In January 1969, Nathan Jacobson asked Stern to draw plans for Jacobson's new hotel/casino, the Kings Castle at Lake Tahoe. Stern agreed to take on the project and immediately began preliminary work. At this time, Stern dealt directly with Jacobson, who referred to the project as "my hotel." In February 1969, Stern wrote to Jacobson detailing, among other things, the architect's services and fee. Stern's plans were subsequently discussed by the two men and Stern's fee was set at $250,000. On May 9, 1969, Jacobson formed Lake Enterprises, Inc. (Lake Enterprises), a Nevada corporation of which Jacobson was the sole shareholder and president. Lake Enterprises was formed for the purpose of owning the new casino. During this period, Stern was paid monthly by checks drawn on an account belonging to another corporation controlled by Jacobson. Stern never agreed to a contract with any of these corporations and always dealt exclusively with Jacobson. When Stern was not paid the full amount of his architectural fee, he sued Jacobson to recover. Jacobson claims that he is not personally liable for any of Stern's fee because a novation has taken place. Who wins? [*Jacobson v. Stern*, 605 P.2d 198 (NV 1980)]

37.10. On June 24, 1970, Commonwealth Edison Co. (Commonwealth Edison), through its underwriters, sold 1 million shares of preferred stock at an offering price of $100 per share. Commonwealth Edison wanted to issue the stock with a dividend rate of 9.26 percent, but its major underwriter, First Boston Corporation (First Boston), advised that a rate of 9.44 percent should be paid. According to First Boston, a shortage of investment funds existed and a higher dividend rate was necessary for a successful stock issue. Commonwealth Edison's management was never happy with the high dividend rate being paid on this preferred stock. On April 2, 1971, Commonwealth Edison's vice chairman was quoted in the report of the annual meeting of the corporation as saying "we were disappointed in the 9.44 percent dividend rate on the preferred stock we sold last August, but we expect to refinance it when market conditions make it feasible." On March 20, 1972, Commonwealth Edison, pursuant to the terms under which the stock was sold, bought back the 1 million shares of preferred stock at a price of $110 per share. What type of preferred stock is this? [*The Franklin Life Insurance Company v. Commonwealth Edison Company*, 451 F.Supp. 602 (S.D.Ill. 1978)]

37.11. United Financial Corporation of California (United Financial) was incorporated in the state of Delaware on May 8, 1959. United Financial owned the majority of a California savings and loan association as well as three insurance agencies. In 1960, the original investors in United Financial decided to capitalize on an increase in investor interest in savings and loans. In June 1960, the first public offering of United Financial stock was made. The stock was sold as a unit, with 60,000 units being offered. Each unit consisted of two shares of United Financial stock and one $100, 5 percent interest-bearing debenture bond. This initial offering was a success. It provided $7.2 million to the corporation, of which $6.2 million was distributed as a return of capital to the original investors. What is the difference between the stock offered for sale by United Financial and the debenture bonds? [*Jones v. H. F. Ahmanson & Company*, 1 Cal.3d 93, 81 Cal.Rptr. 592 (Cal. 1969)]

ETHICS CASES

37.12. John A. Goodman was a real estate salesman in the state of Washington. In 1979, Goodman sold an apartment building that needed extensive renovation to Darden, Doman & Stafford Associates (DDS), a general partnership. Goodman represented that he personally had experience in renovation work. During the course of negotiations on a renovation contract, Goodman informed the managing partner of DDS that he would be forming a corporation to do the work.

A contract was executed in August 1979 between DDS and "Building Design and Development (In Formation), John A. Goodman, President." The contract required the renovation work to be completed by October 15. Goodman immediately subcontracted the work, but the renovation was not completed on time. DDS also found that the work that was completed was of poor quality. Goodman did not file the articles of incorporation for his new corporation until November 1. The partners of DDS sued Goodman to hold him liable for the renovation contracts. Goodman denied personal liability. Was it morally correct for Goodman to deny liability? Is Goodman personally liable? [*Goodman v. Darden, Doman & Stafford Associates*, 670 P.2d 648 (WA 1983)]

37.13. In 1983, pursuant to a public offering, Knoll International, Inc. (Knoll), issued debentures to investors. The debentures bore interest at $8\frac{1}{8}$ percent, matured in 30 years, and were subordinated, convertible into common stock at the rate of each $19.20 of principal amount for one share of common stock, and redeemable. Section 8.08 of the indenture agreement provided that no debenture holder could sue unless the holders of 35 percent of the debentures requested the trustee to sue. The indenture also gave the trustee the authority to amend the indenture agreement.

Knoll was controlled through a series of subsidiaries by Knoll International Holdings, Inc. (Holdings), which, in turn, was controlled by Marshall S. Cogan. On January 22, 1987, Knoll merged into Holdings and paid its common shareholders $12 cash per share. Knoll and the indenture trustee executed a supplemental indenture that provided that each debenture holder would receive $12 cash for each $19.20 principal amount of debentures. Simons, a debenture holder who did not own 35 percent of the debentures, brought this suit against Knoll and Cogan. Does Knoll International, Inc., or Cogan owe a fiduciary duty to the debenture holders? Is Cogan breaching an ethical duty to the debenture holders? [*Simons v. Cogan*, 542 A.2d 785 (Del.Ch. 1987)]

CRITICAL LEGAL THINKING WRITING ASSIGNMENT

Read Case A.37 in the Case Appendix [*Johnson v. Dodgen*]. This case is excerpted from the state supreme court's opinion. Review and brief the case. In your brief, be sure to answer the following questions.

1. Who were the plaintiffs? Who were the defendants?

2. Describe the contract alleged to have been breached in this case.

3. Was the contract signed by a corporation?

4. Did the court find the individual defendant liable on the contract?

Directors, Officers, and Shareholders

Corporation, n. An ingenious device for obtaining individual profit without individual responsibility.

AMBROSE BIERCE
The Devil's Dictionary (1911)

Chapter Objectives

After studying this chapter, you should be able to

1. Describe the function of shareholders, directors, and officers in managing the affairs of a corporation.
2. Describe how shareholders' and directors' meetings are called and conducted.
3. Distinguish between straight and cumulative voting for directors.
4. Explain the directors' authority to pay dividends.
5. Describe the agency authority of officers to enter into contracts on behalf of a corporation.
6. Distinguish how the management of close corporations differs from that of publicly held corporations.
7. Describe a director's and officer's duty of care and the business judgment rule.
8. Describe a director's and officer's duty of loyalty and how this duty is breached.
9. Describe directors' and officers' liability insurance and corporate indemnification.
10. Define the piercing of the corporate veil or alter ego doctrine.

Chapter Contents

Shareholders, directors, and officers have different rights in managing the corporation. The shareholders elect the directors and vote on other important issues affecting the corporation. The directors are responsible for making policy decisions and employing officers. The officers are responsible for the corporation's day-to-day operations.

As a legal entity, a corporation can be held liable for the acts of its directors and officers and for authorized contracts entered into on its behalf. The directors and officers of a corporation have certain rights and owe certain duties to the corporation and its shareholders. A director or officer who breaches any of these duties can be held personally liable to the corporation, to its shareholders, or to third parties. Insurance is available against certain of these losses. Except in a few circumstances, shareholders do not owe a fiduciary duty to other shareholders or the corporation.

This chapter discusses the rights, duties, and liability of corporate shareholders, directors, and officers.

RIGHTS OF SHAREHOLDERS

A corporation's shareholders own the corporation. Nevertheless, they are not agents of the corporation (i.e., they cannot bind the corporation to any contracts), and the only management duties they have is the right to vote on matters such as the election of directors and the approval of fundamental changes in the corporation.

Shareholders' Meetings

Business Brief
Shareholders are not agents of the corporation. They cannot bind the corporation to contracts.

annual shareholders' meeting
Meeting of the shareholders of a corporation that must be held annually by the corporation to elect directors and to vote on other matters.

Annual shareholders' meetings are held to elect directors, choose an independent auditor, or take other actions. The meeting must be held at the time fixed in the bylaws [RMBCA § 7.01]. If the meeting is not held within either 15 months of the last annual meeting or 6 months after the end of the corporation's fiscal year, whichever is earlier, a shareholder may petition the court to order the meeting held [RMBCA § 7.03].

special shareholders' meetings
Meetings of shareholders that may be called to consider and vote on important or emergency issues, such as a proposed merger or amending the articles of incorporation.

Special shareholders' meetings may be called by the board of directors, the holders of at least 10 percent of the voting shares of the corporation, or any other person authorized to do so by the articles of incorporation or bylaws (e.g., the president) [RMBCA § 7.02]. Special meetings may be held to consider important or emergency issues, such as a merger or consolidation of the corporation with one or more other corporations, the removal of directors, amending the articles of incorporation, or dissolution of the corporation.

Any act that can be taken at a shareholders' meeting can be taken without a meeting if all of the corporate shareholders sign a written consent approving the action [RMBCA § 7.04].

Notice of Meetings   The corporation is required to give the shareholders written *notice* of the place, day, and time of annual and special meetings. If the meeting is a special meeting, the purpose of the meeting must also be stated. Only matters stated in the notice of a special meeting can be considered at the meeting. The notice, which must be given not less than 10 days or more than 50 days before the date of the meeting, may be given in person or by mail [RMBCA § 7.05]. If the required notice is not given or is defective, any action taken at the meeting is void.

Proxies

proxy
The written document that a shareholder signs authorizing another person to vote his or her shares at the shareholders' meetings in the event of the shareholder's absence.

Shareholders do not have to attend the shareholders' meeting to vote. Shareholders may vote by **proxy**; that is, they can appoint another person (the proxy) as their agent to vote at the shareholders' meeting. The proxy may be directed exactly how to vote the shares or may be authorized to vote the shares at his or her discretion. Proxies must be in writing. The written document itself is called the **proxy** (or **proxy card**). Unless otherwise stated, a proxy is valid for 11 months [RMBCA § 7.22].

Voting Requirements

At least one class of shares of the corporation must have voting rights. The RMBCA permits corporations to grant more than one vote per share to some classes of stock and less than one vote per share to others [RMBCA § 6.01].

Only those shareholders who own stock as of a set date may vote at a shareholders' meeting. This date, which is called the **record date**, is set forth in the corporate bylaws. The record date may not be more than 70 days before the shareholders' meeting [RMBCA § 7.07].

The corporation must prepare a *shareholders' list* that contains the names and addresses of the shareholders as of the record date and the class and number of shares owned by each shareholder. This list must be available for inspection at the corporation's main office [RMBCA § 7.20].

record date
A date specified in the corporate bylaws that determines whether a shareholder may vote at a shareholders' meeting.

Quorum   Unless otherwise provided in the articles of incorporation, if a majority of shares entitled to vote are represented at the meeting in person or by proxy, there is a **quorum** to hold the meeting. Once a quorum is present, the withdrawal of shares does not affect the quorum of the meeting [RMBCA § 7.25(a) and (b)].

quorum
The required number of shares that must be represented in person or by proxy to hold a shareholders' meeting. The RMBCA establishes a majority of outstanding shares as a quorum.

Vote Required for Elections Other than for Directors   The affirmative vote of the majority of the voting shares represented at a shareholders' meeting constitutes an act of the shareholders for actions other than for the election of directors [RMBCA § 7.25(c)].

Consider This Example   Suppose there are 20,000 shares outstanding of a corporation. Assume that a shareholders' meeting is duly called to amend the articles of incorporation and that 10,001 shares are represented at the meeting. A quorum is present because a majority of the shares entitled to vote are represented. Suppose that 5,001 shares are voted in favor of the amendment. The amendment passes. In this example, just over 25 percent of the shares of the corporation bound the other shareholders to the action taken at the shareholders' meeting.

It appears to me that the atmosphere of the temple of Justice is polluted by the presence of such things as companies.

*James, L.J.
Wilson v. Church (1879)*

Voting Methods for Electing Directors   The election of directors by shareholders may be by one of the following two methods:

- **Straight (Noncumulative) Voting**   Unless otherwise stated in the corporation's articles of incorporation, voting for the election of directors is by the **straight voting** method. This voting method is quite simple: Each shareholder votes the number of shares he or she owns on candidates for each of the positions open for election. Thus, a majority shareholder can elect the entire board of directors.

straight voting
Each shareholder votes the number of shares he or she owns on candidates for each of the positions open.

Consider This Example   Assume that a corporation has 10,000 outstanding shares. Erin Caldwell owns 5,100 shares (or 51 percent) and Michael Rhodes owns 4,900 shares (49 percent). Suppose that three directors of the corporation are to be elected. Caldwell casts 5,100 votes each for her chosen candidates. Rhodes votes 4,900 shares for each of his chosen candidates, who are different from those favored by Caldwell. Each of the three candidates whom Caldwell voted for wins with 5,100 votes.

- **Cumulative Voting**   The articles of incorporation may provide for **cumulative voting** for the election of directors. Under this method, a shareholder can accumulate all of his or her votes and vote them all for one candidate or split them among several candidates. This means that each shareholder is entitled to multiply the number of shares he or she owns by the number of directors to be elected and cast the product for a single candidate or distribute the product among two or more candidates [RMBCA § 7.28]. Cumulative voting gives a minority shareholder a better opportunity to elect someone to the board of directors.

cumulative voting
A shareholder can accumulate all of his or her votes and vote them all for one candidate or split them among several candidates.

Consider This Example Suppose Lisa Monroe owns 1,000 shares. Assume that four directors are to be elected to the board. Under cumulative voting, Monroe can multiply the number of shares she owns by the number of directors to be elected. She can take the resulting number of votes (4,000) and cast them all for one candidate or split them. Examples of cumulative voting are set forth in Exhibit 38.1.

Exhibit 38.1 Examples of Cumulative Voting

Formula for Cumulative Voting. A shareholder can use the following formula to determine whether or not he or she owns a sufficient number of shares to elect a director to the board of directors using cumulative voting:

$$\frac{S \times T}{D + 1} + 1 = X$$

where X is the number of shares needed by a shareholder to elect a director to the board, S is the number of shares that actually vote at the shareholders' meeting, T is the number of directors the shareholder wants to elect, and D is the number of directors to be elected at the shareholders' meeting.

Example 1 Suppose there are 9,000 outstanding shares of a corporation. Shareholder 1 owns 1,000 shares, shareholder 2 owns 4,000 shares, and shareholder 3 owns 4,000 shares. Assume nine directors are to be elected to the board of directors. All the shares are voted. Under cumulative voting, does shareholder 1 have enough votes to elect a director to the board? The answer is yes:

$$\frac{9,000 \times 1}{9 + 1} + 1 = 901$$

Example 2 If a board of directors is divided into classes and elected by staggered elections, the ability of a minority shareholder to elect a director to the board is diminished. Suppose in Example 1 that the corporation staggered the election of the board of directors so that three directors are elected each year to serve three-year terms. How many shares would a shareholder have to own to elect a director to the board?

$$\frac{9,000 \times 1}{3 + 1} + 1 = 2,251$$

Because of the staggered election of the board of directors, shareholder 1 (who owns 1,000 shares) would not be able to elect a director to the board without the assistance of another shareholder.

Supramajority Voting Requirement The articles of incorporation or the bylaws of a corporation can require a greater than majority of shares to constitute a quorum or the vote of the shareholders [RMBCA § 7.27]. This is called a **supramajority voting requirement** (or **supermajority**). Such votes are often required to approve mergers, consolidation, the sale of substantially all of the assets of the corporation, and such. To add a supramajority voting requirement, the amendment must be adopted by the number of shares of the proposed increase. For example, to increase a majority voting requirement to an 80 percent supramajority voting requirement would require an 80 percent affirmative vote.

supramajority voting requirement

A requirement that a greater than majority of shares constitutes a quorum of the vote of the shareholders.

Voting Agreements

Sometimes shareholders agree in advance as to how their shares will be voted. The two major forms of shareholder agreements are discussed in the following paragraphs.

Voting Trusts   A **voting trust** is an arrangement whereby shareholders transfer their stock certificates to a trustee. Legal title to these shares is held in the name of the trustee. In exchange, *voting trust certificates* are issued to the shareholders. The trustee of the voting trust is empowered to vote the shares held by the trust. The trust may either specify how the trustee is to vote the shares or authorize the trustee to vote the shares at his or her discretion. The members of the trust retain all other incidents of ownership of the stock.

A voting trust agreement must be in writing and cannot exceed 10 years. It must be filed with the corporation and is open to inspection by shareholders of the corporation [RMBCA § 7.30].

voting trust
The shareholders transfer their stock certificates to a trustee who is empowered to vote the shares.

Shareholder Voting Agreements   Two or more shareholders may enter into an agreement that stipulates how they will vote their shares for the election of directors or other matters that require shareholder vote. These **voting agreements** are not limited in duration and do not have to be filed with the corporation. They are specifically enforceable [RMBCA § 7.31]. Shareholder voting agreements can be either revocable or irrevocable [RMBCA § 7.22(d)].

shareholder voting agreements
Agreement between two or more shareholders agreeing on how they will vote their shares.

Right to Transfer Shares

Subject to certain restrictions, shareholders have the right to transfer their shares. The transfer of securities is governed by **Article 8 of the Uniform Commercial Code (UCC)**. Most states have adopted all or part of Article 8. Usually, shares are transferred by indorsement and delivery of the shares to the new owner.

If a stock certificate has been lost, stolen, or destroyed, the corporation is required to issue a *replacement certificate* if the shareholder posts an indemnity bond to protect the corporation from loss for issuing the replacement certificate. If a lost or stolen certificate reappears in the hands of a bona fide purchaser, that certificate must be registered by the corporation. The corporation can recover on the indemnity bond.

Article 8 of the UCC
The article of the UCC that governs transfer of securities.

Transfer Restrictions

Shareholders may enter into agreements with one another to prevent unwanted persons from becoming owners of the corporation [RMBCA § 6.27]. The following are the two most common forms of agreements.

right of first refusal agreement
An agreement that requires the selling shareholder to offer his or her shares for sale to the other parties to the agreement before selling them to anyone else.

- **Right of First Refusal** A **right of first refusal** is an **agreement** entered into by shareholders whereby they grant each other the right of first refusal to purchase shares they are going to sell. A selling shareholder must offer his or her shares for sale to the other parties to the agreement before selling them to anyone else. If the shareholders do not exercise their right of first refusal, the selling shareholder is free to sell his or her shares to another party. A right of first refusal may be granted to the corporation as well.
- **Buy-and-Sell Agreement** A **buy-and-sell agreement** is one entered into by shareholders that requires selling shareholders to sell their shares to the other shareholders or to the corporation at the price specified in the agreement. The price of the shares is normally determined by a formula that considers, among other factors, the profitability of the corporation. The purchase of shares of a deceased shareholder pursuant to a buy-and-sell agreement is often funded by the purchase of life insurance.

buy-and-sell agreement
An agreement that requires selling shareholders to sell their shares to the other shareholders or to the corporation at the price specified in the agreement.

Preemptive Rights

preemptive rights

Rights that give existing shareholders the option of subscribing to new shares being issued in proportion to their current ownership interest.

The articles of incorporation can grant shareholders preemptive rights. **Preemptive rights** give existing shareholders the option of subscribing to new shares being issued by the corporation in proportion to their current ownership interest [RMBCA § 6.30]. Such a purchase can prevent a shareholder's interest in the corporation from being *diluted*. Shareholders are given a reasonable period of time (such as 30 days) to exercise their preemptive rights. If the shareholders do not exercise their preemptive rights during this time, the shares can then be sold to anyone.

Consider This Example Suppose that the ABC Corporation has 10,000 outstanding shares and that Linda Norton owns 1,000 shares (10 percent). Assume that the corporation plans to raise more capital by issuing another 10,000 shares of stock. With preemptive rights, Norton must be offered the option to purchase 1,000 of the 10,000 new shares before they are offered to the public. If she does not purchase them, her ownership in the corporation will be diluted from 10 percent to 5 percent.

Right to Receive Information and Inspect Books and Records

annual financial statement

A statement provided to the shareholders that contains a balance sheet, an income statement, and a statement of changes in shareholder equity.

Shareholders have the right to be informed about the affairs of the corporation. A corporation must furnish its shareholders with an **annual financial statement** containing a balance sheet, an income statement, and a statement of changes in shareholder equity [RMBCA § 16.20].

right of inspection

A right that shareholders have to inspect the books and records of the corporation.

Shareholders have an absolute **right to inspect** the shareholders' list, the articles of incorporation, the bylaws, and the minutes of shareholders' meetings held within the past three years. To inspect accounting and tax records, minutes of board of directors' and committee meetings, and minutes of shareholders' meetings held more than three years in the past, a shareholder must demonstrate a "proper purpose" [RMBCA § 16.02]. Proper purposes include deciding how to vote in a shareholder election, identifying fellow shareholders to communicate with them regarding corporate matters, investigating the existence of corporate mismanagement or improper action, and the like. A shareholder can employ an agent, such as a lawyer, an accountant, or a business manager, to inspect the books and records of the corporation on his or her behalf [RMBCA § 16.03].

Direct Lawsuits

direct lawsuit

A lawsuit that a shareholder can bring against the corporation to enforce his or her personal rights as a shareholder.

A shareholder can bring **direct lawsuits** against the corporation for many reasons, including to (1) enforce the right to vote, (2) enforce preemptive rights, (3) compel payment of declared but unpaid dividends, (4) inspect the books and records of the corporation, (5) enjoin the corporation from committing an *ultra vires* act, and (6) compel dissolution of the corporation. If a shareholder is successful in a direct action against the corporation, the award belongs to that shareholder.

Derivative Lawsuits

derivative lawsuit

A lawsuit a shareholder brings against an offending party on behalf of the corporation when the corporation fails to bring the lawsuit.

If a corporation is harmed by someone, the directors of the corporation have the authority to bring an action on behalf of the corporation against the offending party to recover damages or other relief. If the corporation fails to bring the lawsuit, shareholders have the right to bring the lawsuit on behalf of the corporation. This is called a **derivative action** or **derivative lawsuit** [RMBCA § 7.40].

A shareholder can bring a derivative action if he or she (1) was a shareholder of the corporation at the time of the act complained of, (2) fairly and adequately represents the interests of the corporation [RMBCA § 7.41], and (3) made a written demand upon the corporation to take suitable actions, and the corporation either rejected the demand or 90 days have passed from the date of the demand [RMBCA § 7.42].

A derivative lawsuit will be dismissed by the court if either a majority of independent directors or a panel of independent persons appointed by the court determines that the lawsuit is not in the best interests of the corporation. This decision must be reached in good faith and only after conducting a reasonable inquiry [RMBCA § 7.44].

If a shareholder derivative action is successful, any award goes into the corporate treasury. The plaintiff-shareholder is entitled to recover payment for reasonable expenses, including attorneys' fees, incurred in bringing and maintaining the derivative action [RMBCA § 7.46]. Any settlement of a derivative action requires court approval [RMBCA § 7.45].

The right to bring a derivative lawsuit was the issue in the following case.

Kamen v. Kemper Financial Services, Inc.
111 S.Ct. 1711 (1991)
United States Supreme Court

CASE 38.1

FACTS
Jill S. Kamen is a shareholder of Cash Equivalent Fund, Inc. (Fund), a mutual fund that employs Kemper Financial Services, Inc. (Kemper), as its investment advisor. Kamen brought a derivative lawsuit on behalf of Fund against Kemper, alleging that Kemper violated fiduciary duties owed to Fund as imposed by the Investment Company Act of 1940 (Act), a federal statute. Kamen did not make a demand on Fund's board of directors to sue Kemper any earlier. She alleged that it would have been futile to do so because the directors were acting in a conspiracy with Kemper. The Act was silent as to the rule concerning derivative actions under the Act. The trial court granted Kemper's motion to dismiss the lawsuit. The court of appeals adopted a "universal demand rule" as part of the federal common law and affirmed. This rule requires a shareholder always to make a demand on the directors of a corporation before bringing a derivative lawsuit. Kamen appealed to the U.S. Supreme Court.

ISSUE
Should federal law adopt the universal demand rule for bringing derivative actions?

IN THE LANGUAGE OF THE COURT
Marshall, Justice   The presumption that state law should be incorporated into federal common law is particularly strong in areas in which private parties have entered legal relationships with the expectation that their rights and obligations would be governed by state law standards. Corporation law is one such area. Corporations are creatures of state law, state law which is the font of corporate directors' powers. Consequently, we conclude that gaps in federal statutes bearing on the allocation of governing power within the corporation should be filled with state law.

The purpose of requiring a precomplaint demand is to protect the directors' prerogative to take over the litigation or to oppose it. Thus, the demand requirement implements the basic principle of corporate governance that the decisions of a corporation—including the decision to initiate litigation—should be made by the board of directors or the majority of shareholders. To the extent that a jurisdiction recognizes the futility exception to demand, the jurisdiction places a limit upon the directors' usual power to control the initiation of corporate litigation. Demand typically is deemed to be futile when a majority of the directors have participated in or approved the alleged wrongdoing. Superimposing a rule of universal demand over the corporate doctrine of these States would clearly upset the balance that they have struck between the power of the individual shareholder and the power of the directors to control corporate litigation.

DECISION AND REMEDY
The U.S. Supreme Court refused to adopt the universal demand rule as federal common law but instead held that federal law should follow the appropriate state law concerning demands in derivative lawsuits if a federal statute is silent as to this issue. Reversed.

Case Questions

Critical Legal Thinking   Which do you think is the better rule: (1) the universal demand rule or (2) the futility exception rule? Why?

Ethics   Should Kamen have given the directors of Fund the opportunity to have sued Kemper before she did?

Business Application   Do derivative lawsuits serve any legitimate purposes? Explain.

RIGHTS OF DIRECTORS

board of directors
A panel of decision makers, the members of which are elected by the shareholders.

The **board of directors** of a corporation is responsible for formulating the *policy decisions* affecting the management, supervision, and control of the operation of the corporation [RMBCA § 8.01]. Such policy decisions include deciding the business or businesses in which the corporation should be engaged, selecting and removing the top officers of the corporation, determining the capital structure of the corporation, declaring dividends, and the like.

Business Brief
The directors of a corporation are responsible for formulating the *policy* decisions affecting the corporation.

The board may initiate certain actions that require shareholders' approval. These actions are initiated when the board of directors adopts a *resolution* that approves a transaction and recommends that it be submitted to the shareholders for a vote. Examples of such transactions include mergers, sale of substantially all of the corporation's assets outside the course of ordinary business operations, amending the articles of incorporation, and the voluntary dissolution of the corporation.

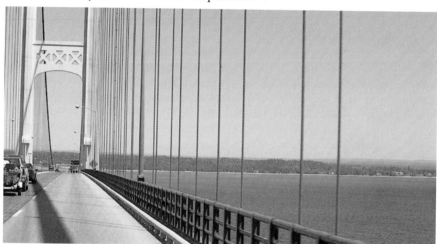

Members of the board of directors of nonprofit corporations are held to a lesser standard of liability for actions taken on behalf of the corporation than are members of the board of directors of for-profit corporations.

Selecting Directors

Boards of directors are typically composed of inside and outside directors. An **inside director** is a person who is also an officer of the corporation. For example, the president of the corporation often sits as a director of the corporation.

inside director
A member of the board of directors who is also an officer of the corporation.

An **outside director** is a person who sits on the board of directors of a corporation but is not an officer of that corporation. Outside directors are often officers and directors of other corporations, bankers, lawyers, professors, and others. Outside directors are often selected for their business knowledge and expertise.

outside director
A member of the board of directors who is not an officer of the corporation.

There are no special qualifications that a person must meet to be elected a director of a corporation. A director need not be a resident of the state of incorporation or a shareholder of the corporation. The articles of incorporation or bylaws may prescribe qualifications for directors, however [RMBCA § 8.02].

Number of Directors   A board of directors can consist of one or more individuals. The number of initial directors is fixed by the articles of incorporation. This number can be amended in the articles of incorporation or the bylaws. The articles of incorporation or bylaws can establish a variable range for the size of the board of directors. The exact number of directors within the range may be changed from time to time by the board of directors or the shareholders [RMBCA § 8.03].

Term of Office

The term of a director's office expires at the next annual shareholders' meeting following his or her election unless terms are staggered [RMBCA § 8.05]. The RMBCA allows boards of directors that consist of nine or more members to be divided into two or three classes (each class to be as nearly equal in number as possible) that are elected to serve *staggered terms* of two or three years [RMBCA § 8.06]. The specifics of such an arrangement must be outlined in the articles of incorporation.

Business Brief
The terms of office of directors may be *staggered* so that only a portion of the board of directors is up for election each year.

Consider This Example   Suppose a board of directors consists of nine directors. The board can be divided into three classes of three directors each, each class to be elected to serve a three-year term. Only three directors of the nine-member board would come up for election each year. This nine-member board could also have been divided into two classes of five and four directors, each class to be elected to two-year terms.

Vacancies and Removal of Directors   Vacancies on the board of directors can occur because of death, illness, the resignation of a director before the expiration of his or her term, or an increase in the number of positions on the board. Such vacancies can be filled by the shareholders or the remaining directors [RMBCA § 8.10].

Any director—or the entire board of directors—can be removed from office by a vote of the holders of a majority of the shares entitled to vote at the election. The articles of incorporation provide that directors can be removed only for cause, however [RMBCA § 8.08(a)]. Cause might be for defalcation, breach of the duty of loyalty, gross mismanagement, and such.

The director is really a watch-dog, and the watch-dog has no right, without the knowledge of his master, to take a sop from a possible wolf.

L. J. Bowen
Re The North Australian
Territory Co. Ltd. (1891)

Meetings of the Board of Directors

The directors can act only as a board. They cannot act individually on the corporation's behalf. Every director has the right to participate in any meeting of the board of directors. Each director has one vote. Directors cannot vote by proxy.

Regular meetings of the board of directors are held at the times and places established in the bylaws. Such meetings can be held without notice. The board can call **special meetings** as provided in the bylaws [RMBCA § 8.20(a)]. They are usually convened for such reasons as issuing new shares, considering proposals to merge with other corporations, adopting maneuvers to defend against hostile takeover attempts, and the like. The directors must be given at least two days' notice of special meetings unless such notice is waived by the director [RMBCA §§ 8.22 and 8.23].

The board of directors may act without a meeting if all of the directors sign written consents that set forth the actions taken. Such consent has the effect of a unanimous vote [RMBCA § 8.21]. The RMBCA permits meetings of the board to be held via conference calls [RMBCA § 8.20(b)].

regular meeting
A meeting held by the board of directors at the time and place established in the by-laws.

special meeting
A meeting convened by the board of directors to discuss new shares, merger proposals, hostile takeover attempts, and so forth.

Business Brief
To reflect modern technology the RMBCA permits board of directors meetings to be held via conference call.

Quorum and Voting Requirement   A simple majority of the number of directors established in the articles of incorporation or bylaws usually constitutes a **quorum** for transacting business. However, the articles of incorporation and the bylaws may increase this number. If a quorum is present, the approval or disapproval of a majority of the quorum binds the entire board. The articles of incorporation or the bylaws can require a greater than majority of directors to constitute a quorum or the vote of the board [RMBCA § 8.24].

quorum
The number of directors necessary to hold a board of directors' meeting or transact business of the board.

Contemporary Business Application _____

COMMITTEES OF THE BOARD OF DIRECTORS

In the current complex business world, the demands on directors have increased. To help handle this increased workload, boards of directors have turned to creating committees of their members to handle specific duties. Board members with special expertise or interests are appointed to the various committees.

Unless the articles of incorporation or bylaws provide otherwise, the board of directors may create committees of the board and delegate certain powers to those committees [RMBCA § 8.25]. All members of these committees must be directors. An act of a committee pursuant to delegated authority is the act of the board of directors.

Committees commonly appointed by the board of directors include

- **Executive Committee** Has authority to (1) act on certain matters on behalf of the board during the interim period between board meetings and (2) conduct preliminary investigations of proposals on behalf of the full board. Most members of the committee are inside directors because it is easier for them to meet to address corporate matters.

- **Audit Committee** Recommends independent public accountants and supervises the audit of the financial records of the corporation by the accountants.
- **Nominating Committee** Nominates the management slate of directors to be submitted for shareholder vote.
- **Compensation Committee** Approves management compensation, including salaries, bonuses, stock option plans, fringe benefits, and such.
- **Investment Committee** Is responsible for investing and reinvesting the funds of the corporation.
- **Litigation Committee** Reviews and decides whether to pursue requests by shareholders for the corporation to sue persons who have allegedly harmed the corporation.

The following powers cannot be delegated to committees but must be exercised by the board itself: (1) declaring dividends, (2) initiating actions that require shareholders' approval, (3) appointing members to fill vacancies on the board, (4) amending the bylaws, (5) approving a plan of merger that does not require shareholder approval (short-form merger), and (6) authorizing the issuance of shares.

Compensation of Directors

Originally, it was considered an honor to serve as a director. No payment was involved. Today, directors often are paid an annual retainer and an attendance fee for each meeting attended. Unless otherwise provided in the articles of incorporation, the directors are permitted to fix their own compensation [RMBCA § 8.11].

Right of Inspection

dividend
Distribution of profits of the corporation to shareholders.

Corporate directors are required to have access to the corporation's books and records, facilities and premises, as well as any other information affecting the operation of the corporation. This right of inspection is absolute. It cannot be limited by the articles of incorporation, the bylaws, or board resolution.

Directors' Authority to Pay Dividends

Business Brief
Dividends are not automatically paid to shareholders; they are paid at the discretion of the board of directors.

For-profit corporations operate to make a profit. The objective of the shareholders is to share in those profits, either through capital appreciation, the receipt of dividends, or both. **Dividends** are paid at the discretion of the board of directors [RMBCA § 6.40]. The directors are responsible for determining when, where, how, and how much will be paid in dividends. This authority cannot be delegated to a committee of the board of directors or to officers of the corporation.

record date
A date that determines whether a shareholder receives payment of a declared dividend.

When a corporation declares a dividend, it sets a date, usually a few weeks prior to the actual payment that is called the **record date**. Persons who are shareholders on that date are entitled to receive the dividend even if they sell their shares before the payment date.

Once declared, a cash or property dividend cannot be revoked. Shareholders can sue at law to recover declared but unpaid dividends.

The board of directors may opt to retain the profits in the corporation to be used for corporate purposes rather than pay them as dividends. Profits retained by the corporation are called **retained earnings.**

Legal Restrictions on the Payment of Dividends   The law imposes certain restrictions on the payment of dividends to common shareholders. Under the RMBCA, a dividend cannot be paid if (1) the corporation would not be able to pay its debts as they became due in the usual course of business, or (2) the corporation's total assets would be less than its total liabilities, and these would be insufficient funds to pay liquidation preferences to preferred shareholders if the corporation were terminated [RMBCA § 6.40(c)].

Directors who vote for or assent to an illegal dividend or distribution are jointly and severally liable to the corporation for that amount [RMBCA § 8.33].

Stock Dividends   Corporations may use additional shares of stock as a dividend. **Stock dividends** are not a distribution of corporate assets. They are paid in proportion to the existing ownership interests of shareholders, so they do not increase a shareholder's proportionate ownership interest.

Consider This Example   Suppose Betty owns 1,000 shares (10 percent) of the 10,000 outstanding shares of the ABC Corporation. If the ABC Corporation declares a stock dividend of 20 percent, Betty will receive a stock dividend of 200 shares. She now owns 1,200 shares—or 10 percent—of a total of 12,000 outstanding shares.

> **retained earnings**
> Profits retained by the corporation and not paid out as dividends.

> **Business Brief**
> There are certain legal restrictions on the payment of dividends if the corporation is experiencing financial difficulties.

> **stock dividend**
> Additional shares of stock paid as a dividend.

Ethical Perspective

STATES ENACT CONSTITUENCY STATUTES

Under the traditional *business judgment rule,* directors of a corporation owe a *fiduciary duty* to act on an informed basis, with reasonable care, and in good faith. Historically, this duty has been rigidly and exclusively owed to the corporation and its shareholders and to no others. Under this classical theory of the corporation, the rights of other constituents—such as employees, bondholders and creditors, suppliers and customers—exist by contract, period.

This view prevailed during the 1980s, when leveraged buyouts and the greed of corporate raiders caused the demise of many venerable companies, dislodged workers, destroyed pension rights, and ruined many local economies. In response, more than 30 states have enacted **constituency statutes** that allow directors to consider constituents other than shareholders when making decisions.

For example, Minnesota adopted the following statute:

In discharging the duties of the position of director, a director may, in considering the best interests of the corporation, consider the interests of the corporation's employees, *customers, suppliers, and creditors, the economy of the state and nation, community and societal considerations, and the long-term as well as short-term interests of the corporation and its shareholders, including the possibility that these interests may be best served by the continued independence of the corporation. [Minn. Stat. § 302A.251(5)]*

Most constituency statutes are permissive, not mandatory. That is, directors may take into account nonstockholder interests but are not required to do so.

Constituency statutes recognize the complex nature of the modern corporation and the modern view that shareholders are not the only "owners" of corporations. These statutes acknowledge the rights of a variety of participants, including lenders, employees, managers, suppliers, distributors, customers, and the local communities in which corporations are located.

1. Why did state legislatures enact constituency statutes?
2. Do constituency statutes make corporate boards of directors more socially responsible?

Rights of Officers

The board of directors has the authority to appoint the **officers** of the corporation. The officers are elected by the board of directors at such time and by such manner as prescribed in the corporation's bylaws. The directors can delegate certain management authority to the officers of the corporation.

At minimum, most corporations have the following officers: (1) a president, (2) one or more vice presidents, (3) a secretary, and (4) a treasurer. The bylaws or the board of directors can authorize duly appointed officers the power to appoint assistant officers. The same individual may simultaneously hold more than one office in the corporation [RMBCA § 8.40]. The duties of each officer are specified in the bylaws of the corporation.

Agency Authority of Officers

Officers and agents of the corporation have such authority as may be provided in the bylaws of the corporation or as determined by resolution of the board of directors [RMBCA § 8.41]. As agents, the authority of officers to bind a corporation to contracts is derived from express authority, implied authority, and apparent authority.

Ratification of Unauthorized Actions A corporation can **ratify** an unauthorized act of a corporate officer or agent. For example, suppose an officer acts outside the scope of his or her employment and enters into a contract with a third person. If the corporation accepts the benefits of the contract, it has ratified the contract and is bound by it. The ratification relates back to the moment the unauthorized act was performed. Officers are liable on an unauthorized contract if the corporation does not ratify it.

Removal of Officers

Unless an employment contract provides otherwise, any officer of a corporation may be removed by the board of directors. The board only has to determine that the best interests of the corporation will be served by such removal [RMBCA § 8.43(b)]. Officers who are removed in violation of an employment contract can sue the corporation for damages.

Concept Summary MANAGEMENT OF A CORPORATION

Management Group	Function
Shareholders	Owners of the corporation. They vote on the directors and other major actions to be taken by the corporation.
Board of directors	Responsible for making policy decisions and employing the major officers for the corporation. They also make recommendations regarding actions to be taken by the shareholders.
Officers	Responsible for the day-to-day operation of the corporation. Includes acting as agents for the corporation, hiring other officers and employees, and the like.

Entrepreneur and the Law

MANAGING CLOSE CORPORATIONS

Many of the formal rules in state corporation statutes are designed to govern the management of large publicly held corporations. These rules may not be relevant for regulating the management of **close corporations**, that is, corporations formed by entrepreneurs with few shareholders who often work for the corporation and manage its day-to-day operations.

To correct this problem, a **Model Statutory Close Corporation Supplement (Supplement)** has been added to the RMBCA. Only corporations with 50 or fewer shareholders may elect statutory close corporation (SCC) status. To choose this status, the following requirements must be met:

1. Two thirds of the shares of each class of shares of the corporation must approve the election [Supp. § 3(b)].
2. The articles of incorporation must contain a statement that the corporation is a statutory close corporation [Supp. § 3(a)].
3. The share certificates must conspicuously state that the shares have been issued by a statutory close corporation [Supp. § 10].

The Supplement permits SCCs to dispense with some of the formalities of operating a corporation. For example, if all of the shareholders approve, an SCC may operate without a board of directors, and the articles of incorporation contain a statement to that effect [Supp. § 21]. The powers and affairs of the corporation are then managed by the shareholders. An SCC need not adopt bylaws if the provisions required by law to be contained in bylaws are contained in the articles of incorporation or a shareholders' agreement [Supp. § 22]. An SCC need not hold annual shareholders' meetings unless one or more shareholders demand in writing that such meetings be held [Supp. § 23]. The shareholders may enter into a shareholders' agreement about how the corporation will be managed [Supp. § 20(a)]. In effect, the shareholders can treat the corporation as a partnership for governance purposes [Supp. § 20(b)(3)].

Selecting statutory close corporation status does not affect the limited liability of shareholders [Supp. § 25].

The Supplement contains a mandatory right of first refusal. A shareholder of an SCC who desires to transfer his or her shares must first offer them to the corporation on the same terms that a third party is willing to pay for them [Supp. § 12]. If the corporation does not purchase the shares, other holders of the same class of shares may purchase them on the offered terms [Supp. § 11]. Only after the shares have been rejected by the corporation and other shareholders can they be sold to nonshareholders. The articles of incorporation of an SCC may include a provision requiring the corporation to purchase a deceased shareholder's shares [Supp. § 14].

The articles of incorporation of an SCC may authorize one or more shareholders to dissolve the corporation at will or upon the occurrence of a specified event or contingency [Supp. § 33]. Judicial dissolution may be ordered by a court if there is an unbreakable deadlock in the management of the corporation; the directors have acted in an illegal, oppressive, or fraudulent manner; or other such statutory grounds [Supp. § 40].

LIABILITY OF CORPORATE DIRECTORS AND OFFICERS

A corporation's directors and officers owe the **fiduciary duties** of trust and confidence to the corporation and its shareholders. More specifically, they owe the (1) *duty of obedience*, (2) *duty of care*, and (3) *duty of loyalty*. Each of these is discussed in detail in the paragraphs that follow.

Duty of Obedience

The directors and officers of a corporation must act within the authority conferred upon them by the state corporation statute, the articles of incorporation, the corporate bylaws, and the resolutions adopted by the board of directors. This duty is called the **duty of obedience**. Directors and officers who either intentionally or negligently act outside their authority are personally liable for any resultant damages caused to the corporation or its shareholders.

fiduciary duty
Duty of loyalty, honesty, integrity, trust, and confidence owed by directors and officers to their corporate employers.

duty of obedience
A duty that directors and officers of a corporation have to act within the authority conferred upon them by the state corporation statute, the articles of incorporation, the corporate bylaws, and the resolutions adopted by the board of directors.

Consider This Example   Suppose the articles of incorporation authorize the corporation to invest in real estate only. If a corporate officer invests corporate funds in the commodities markets, the officer is liable to the corporation for any losses suffered.

Contemporary Business Application

INDEMNIFICATION AND D&O INSURANCE PROTECTION FOR CORPORATE DIRECTORS AND OFFICERS

Directors and officers of corporations are sometimes personally named in lawsuits that involve actions they have taken on behalf of the corporation. Such lawsuits often are brought by disgruntled shareholders or third parties who claim they have suffered damages because of the director's or officer's negligence or other conduct.

Directors and officers can protect themselves against personal liability by making sure the corporation does the following:

- Purchases **directors' and officers' liability insurance (D&O insurance)**. Corporations can purchase D&O insurance from private insurance companies by paying an annual premium for the insurance. The insurance company is required to defend a corporate director or officer who has been sued in his or her corporate capacity. The insurance company is also required, sub-

ject to the terms of the insurance coverage, to pay the litigation costs incurred in defending the lawsuit (e.g., attorneys' fees and court costs) and any judgments or settlement costs. Most D&O policies contain deductible clauses and maximum coverage limits [RMBCA § 8.57].

- Provides **indemnification**. Corporations may provide that directors and officers who are sued in their corporate capacities will be **indemnified** by the corporation for the costs of the litigation as well as any judgments or settlements stemming from the lawsuit. Indemnification means that the corporation—and not the director or officer personally—pays these costs. The RMBCA provides that a court may order indemnification if a director or officer is found to be fairly and reasonably entitled to such indemnification [RMBCA § 8.54 and 8.56(1)].

Duty of Care

duty of care
A duty that corporate directors and officers have to use care and diligence when acting on behalf of the corporation.

The **duty of care** requires corporate directors and officers to use *care and diligence* when acting on behalf of the corporation. To meet this duty, the directors and officers must discharge their duties (1) in good faith, (2) with the care that an *ordinary prudent person* in a like position would use under similar circumstances, and (3) in a manner he or she reasonably believes to be in the best interests of the corporation [RMBCA §§ 8.30(a) and 8.42(a)].

A director or officer who breaches this duty of care is personally liable to the corporation and its shareholders for any damages caused by the breach. Such breaches, which are normally caused by **negligence**, often involve a director's or officer's failure to (1) make a reasonable investigation of a corporate matter, (2) attend board meetings on a regular basis, (3) properly supervise a subordinate who causes a loss to the corporation through embezzlement and such, or (4) keep adequately informed about corporate affairs. Breaches are examined by the courts on a case-by-case basis.

negligence
Failure of a corporate director or officer to exercise the duty of care while conducting the corporation's business.

business judgment rule
A rule that says directors and officers are not liable to the corporation or its shareholders for honest mistakes of judgment.

Business Judgment Rule   The determination of whether a corporate director or officer has met his or her duty of care is measured as of the time the decision is made—the benefit of hindsight is not a factor. Therefore, the directors and officers are not liable to the corporation or its shareholders for honest mistakes of judgment. This is called the **business judgment rule**.

Consider This Example Suppose after conducting considerable research and investigation, the directors of a major automobile company decide to produce a large and expensive automobile. When the car is introduced to the public for sale, few of the automobiles are sold because of the public's interest in buying smaller, less expensive automobiles. Because this was an honest mistake of judgment on the part of corporate management, their judgment is shielded by the business judgment rule.

The court had to decide whether directors were protected by the business judgment rule in the following case.

Business Brief

Were it not for the protection afforded by the business judgment rule, many high-risk but socially desirable endeavors might not be undertaken.

Smith v. Van Gorkom
488 A.2d 858 (1985)
Supreme Court of Delaware

CASE 38.2

FACTS

Trans Union Corporation (Trans Union) was a publicly traded, diversified holding company that was incorporated in Delaware. Its principal earnings were generated by its railcar leasing business. Jerome W. Van Gorkom was a Trans Union officer for more than 24 years, its chief executive officer for more than 17 years, and the chairman of the board of directors for 2 years. Van Gorkom, a lawyer and certified public accountant, owned 75,000 shares of Trans Union. He was approaching 65 years of age and mandatory retirement. Trans Union's board of directors was composed of 10 members—five inside directors and five outside directors.

In September 1980, Van Gorkom decided to meet with Jay A. Pritzker, a well-known corporate takeover specialist and a social acquaintance of Van Gorkom's, to discuss the possible sale of Trans Union to Pritzker. Van Gorkom met Pritzker at Pritzker's home on Saturday, September 13, 1980. He did so without consulting Trans Union's board of directors. At this meeting, Van Gorkom proposed a sale of Trans Union to Pritzker at a price of $55 per share. The stock was trading at about $38 in the market. On Monday, September 15, Pritzker notified Van Gorkom that he was interested in the $55 cash-out merger proposal. Van Gorkom, along with two inside directors, privately met with Pritzker on September 16 and 17. After meeting with Van Gorkom on Thursday, September 18, Pritzker notified his attorney to begin drafting the merger documents.

On Friday, September 19, Van Gorkom called a special meeting of Trans Union's board of directors for the following day. The board members were not told the purpose of the meeting. At the meeting, Van Gorkom disclosed the Pritzker offer and described its terms in a 20-minute presentation. Neither the merger agreement nor a written summary of the terms of the agreement was furnished to the directors. No valuation study as to the value of Trans Union was prepared for the meeting. After two hours, the board voted in favor of the cash-out merger with Pritzker's company at $55

per share for Trans Union's stock. The board also voted not to solicit other offers. The merger agreement was executed by Van Gorkom during the evening of September 20 at a formal social event he hosted for the opening of the Chicago Lyric Opera's season. Neither he nor any other director read the agreement prior to its signing and delivery to Pritzker.

Trans Union's board of directors recommended the merger be approved by its shareholders and distributed proxy materials to the shareholders stating that the $55 per share price for their stock was fair. In the meantime, Trans Union's board of directors took steps to dissuade two other possible suitors who showed an interest in purchasing Trans Union. On February 10, 1981, 69.9 percent of the shares of Trans Union stock was voted in favor of the merger. The merger was consummated. Alden Smith and other Trans Union shareholders sued Van Gorkom and the other directors for damages. The plaintiffs alleged that the defendants were negligent in their conduct in selling Trans Union to Pritzker. The Delaware Court of Chancery held in favor of the defendants. The plaintiffs appealed.

ISSUE

Did Trans Union's directors breach their duty of care?

IN THE LANGUAGE OF THE COURT

Horsey, Justice In the specific context of a proposed merger of domestic corporations, a director has a duty, along with his fellow directors, to act in an informed and deliberate manner in determining whether to approve an agreement of merger before submitting the proposal to the stockholders. Certainly in the merger context, a director may not abdicate that duty by leaving to the shareholders alone the decision to approve or disapprove the agreement. Only an agreement of merger satisfying these requirements may be submitted to the shareholders. It is against these standards that the conduct of the directors of Trans Union must be tested, as a matter of law and as a matter of fact, regarding their exercise of an informed business judgment in voting to approve the Pritzker merger approval.

(box continues)

The issue of whether the directors reached an informed decision to sell the company on September 20, 1980 must be determined only upon the basis of the information then reasonably available to the directors and relevant to their decision to accept the Pritzker merger proposal. On the record before us, we must conclude that the board of directors did not reach an informed business judgment on September 20, 1980 in voting to sell the company for $55 per share pursuant to the Pritzker cash-out merger proposal. Our reasons, in summary, are as follows:

The directors (1) did not adequately inform themselves as to Van Gorkom's role in forcing the sale of the company and in establishing the per share purchase price; (2) they were uninformed as to the intrinsic value of the company; and (3) given these circumstances, at a minimum, they were grossly negligent in approving the sale of the company upon two hours' consideration, without prior notice, and without the exigency of a crisis or emergency.

Without any documents before them concerning the proposed transaction, the members of the board were required to rely entirely upon Van Gorkom's 20-minute oral presentation of the proposal. No written summary of the terms of the merger was presented; the directors were given no documentation to support the adequacy of $55 price per share for sale of the company; and the board had before it nothing more than Van Gorkom's statement of his understanding of the substance of an agreement that he admittedly had never read, or that any member of the board

had ever seen. Thus, the record compels the conclusion that on September 20 the board lacked valuation information to reach an informed business judgment as to the fairness of $55 per share for sale of the company. We conclude that Trans Union's board was grossly negligent in that it failed to act with informed reasonable deliberation in agreeing to the Pritzker merger proposal on September 20, 1980.

DECISION AND REMEDY

The Supreme Court of Delaware held that the defendant directors had breached their duty of care. The supreme court remanded the case to the court of chancery to conduct an evidentiary hearing to determine the fair value of the shares represented by the plaintiffs' class. If that value is higher than $55 per share, the difference shall be awarded to the plaintiffs as damages. Reversed and remanded.

Case Questions

Critical Legal Thinking What does the business judgment rule provide? Is this a good rule? Explain.

Ethics Do you think that Van Gorkom and the other directors had the shareholders' best interests in mind? Were the plaintiff-shareholders being greedy?

Business Application Is there any liability exposure for sitting on a board of directors?

Contemporary Business Application

DID DISNEY'S BOARD OF DIRECTORS ACT GOOFY?

The business judgment rule was designed to protect corporate officers and directors from being second-guessed by judges and juries for making business decisions they thought were in the best interests of the corporation. How far, however, does the business judgment rule go in protecting board members who make a goofy decision? Consider the following case.

In 1995, Michael D. Eisner was the chairman of the board and chief executive officer of the Walt Disney Company (Disney). In September 1995, in a move to make Disney even more "Hollywood" and more into the digital age, Eisner recruited and hired his friend Michael S. Ovitz to serve as Disney's president. At the time, Ovitz was head of Creative Artists Agency (CAA), a firm of talent agents, and was notably the "most powerful man in Hollywood." To entice Ovitz away from CAA, Disney's board of directors unanimously approved a five-year employment contract

with Ovitz. All parties signed. Ovitz was appointed president and was nominated and elected to Disney's board.

The employment contract provided for Ovitz to receive an annual salary of $1 million, a discretionary bonus determined by the board, and options to purchase (at a discount price) and exercise one million shares of Disney's common stock each year for five years. The contract contained a severance package that included the following provisions: (1) that Disney could terminate Ovitz for "good cause"—which was defined as gross negligence or malfeasance in the execution of his duties—without liability and (2) that if Disney terminated Ovitz without good cause or if Ovitz resigned from Disney with the consent of the board, he would get his remaining salary payments and three million of his options on Disney stock would immediately vest upon his separation from the company. At the time of signing the severance package, no Disney board member bothered to quantify the benefits Ovitz would receive if his employment was terminated before the expiration of the five-year term.

Ovitz began his term as Disney's president amid media hype, but the glamour only lasted about as long as a first-run movie. Within a year, Ovitz was unhappy with his role at Disney and the Disney board of directors did not think Ovitz's employment was working out very well. Ovitz began looking for alternative employment. In September 1996, he sent a letter to Eisner stating his desire to leave Disney. On December 11, 1996, only 14 months after Ovitz joined Disney, Eisner consented to Ovitz's request for a nonfault termination. The next day Disney's board agreed, and Ovitz left Disney. His severance pay package—which included salary, bonus, and three million stock options—was worth $140 million!

Several Disney shareholders brought a derivative lawsuit against the Disney board of directors alleging that they had breached their fiduciary duty to the shareholders by giving away the kingdom. The shareholders argued that the Disney board should have terminated Ovitz for "good cause" instead of agreeing to the nonfault termination and

severance pay package. The Disney directors defended, arguing that the business judgment rule protected their largess. Because Disney is incorporated in Delaware, Delaware's chancery court was given the opportunity to write the ending to this script.

The Delaware court, known to favor management over shareholders—why else are so many companies organized there?—decided in favor of the Disney board and dismissed the lawsuit. The judge stated:

> The Board made a business decision to grant Ovitz a Non-Fault Termination. Plaintiffs may disagree with the Board's judgment as to how this matter should have been handled. But where, as here, there is no reasonable doubt as to the disinterest of or absence of fraud by the Board, mere disagreement cannot serve as grounds for imposing liability based on alleged breaches of fiduciary duty and waste.

The Delaware judge decided this case in favor of Disney's board of directors and then quickly exclaimed, "I'm Going to Disneyland!" [*In re The Walt Disney Company Derivative Litigation*, 1998 WL 731587 (Del.Ch. 1998)]

Reliance on Others

Corporate directors and officers usually are unable to investigate personally every corporate matter brought to their attention. Under the RMBCA, directors and officers are entitled to rely on information, opinions, reports, or statements, including financial statements and other financial data, prepared or presented by [RMBCA §§ 8.30(b) and 8.42(b)]:

- Officers and employees of the corporation whom the director believes are reliable and competent in the matter presented.
- Lawyers, public accountants, and other professionals as to any matters that the director reasonably believes to be within their professional or expert competence.
- A committee of the board of directors upon which the director does not serve as to matters within the committee's designated authority and which committee the director reasonably believes to merit confidence.

A director is not liable if such information is false, misleading, or otherwise unreliable unless he or she has knowledge that would cause such reliance to be unwarranted [RMBCA §§ 8.30(c) and 8.42(c)]. The degree of an officer's reliance on such sources is more limited than that given to directors because they are more familiar with corporate operations.

Business Brief

A corporate director or officer who breaches his or her duty of care is liable to the corporation and its shareholders for any damages caused by the breach.

Business Brief

Corporate directors and officers may rely on information and reports prepared by competent and reliable officers and employees, lawyers, accountants, other professionals, and committees of the board of directors.

Dissent to Directors' Action

On some occasions, individual directors may oppose the action taken by the majority of the board of directors. To avoid liability for such action, the dissenting director must either resign from the board or register his or her **dissent**. Dissent may be registered by (1) entering it in the minutes of the meeting, (2) filing a written dissent with the secretary before the adjournment of the meeting, or (3) forwarding a written dissent by registered mail to the secretary immediately following the adjournment of the meeting [RMBCA § 8.24(d)]. A dissenting director who has not attended the meeting must follow the latter course of action to register his or her dissent.

dissension

When an individual director opposes the action taken by the majority of the board of directors.

Ethical Perspective

SHOULD DIRECTORS BE LEFT OFF THE HOOK?

In the past, being made a member of a board of directors of a corporation was considered to be an honor. Many persons outside the company, such as lawyers, doctors, businesspeople, professors, and others, were asked to sit on boards because of their knowledge, expertise, or contacts. Meetings were held once a month and usually did not take a lot of time, and votes were often just a formality to "rubber stamp" management's preordained decisions.

In the 1980s, all this changed. The primary cause was the explosion of lawsuits against boards of directors by disgruntled shareholders, bondholders, and others. Under the law, directors are personally liable for their intentional or negligent conduct that causes harm to others. Most of these lawsuits alleged that directors were negligent in one regard or another, and juries often agreed.

Large and mid-sized corporations usually purchased directors' and officers' liability insurance—D&O insurance—that paid any judgments. Many small corporations could not afford to carry such insurance. When D&O carriers were hit with increasing payouts, they did what any good businessperson would do: raised the premiums, increased the deductibles, and reduced the activities covered by the insurance. These changes created a so-called insurance crisis. Many corporations' coverage was severely reduced or they were forced to go "bare" and not carry D&O insurance because of the high expense.

Inside directors—that is, directors who are also executives of the corporation—remained on boards because of their vested interests, and their liability as officers would remain anyway. But "outside directors"—that is, the directors from outside the company—began fleeing from corporations and refusing to accept nominations to boards of directors. The honor of sitting on a board of directors

became a liability, and all their personal assets—house, investments, and bank accounts—were at risk.

In response to this situation, in 1985 the Delaware legislature enacted a statute that provided that an outside director of a Delaware corporation could not be held liable for ordinary negligence. Thus, this statute overrode the common law of negligence as it applied to outside directors. The law was hailed as a landmark, and many major corporations who were not already incorporated in Delaware abandoned their current states of incorporation and reincorporated there.

Since then many other states have enacted similar statutes. The Revised Model Business Corporation Act contains a similar provision [RMBCA § 2.02(b)(4)]. The main features of these statutes are that they

- Apply to outside directors but not to inside directors.
- Relieve liability for ordinary negligence but not for intentional conduct, recklessness, or gross negligence.
- Do not apply to violations of federal and state securities laws.

Proponents of these laws assert that they are necessary to attract the most qualified individuals to sit on corporate boards of directors. Critics argue that the laws are merely a scam whereby fat-cat directors are favorably treated and relieved of liability for their negligent conduct when no one else in society (e.g., motorists, entrepreneurs) is given the same privilege.

1. Should "outside" directors be relieved of ordinary negligence liability? Why or why not?
2. Do you think outside directors will act more or less carefully because of RMBCA § 2.02(b)(4)?

Duty of Loyalty

duty of loyalty

A duty that directors and officers have not to act adversely to the interests of the corporation and to subordinate their personal interests to those of the corporation and its shareholders.

The **duty of loyalty** requires directors and officers to subordinate their personal interests to those of the corporation and its shareholders. Justice Benjamin Cardozo defined this duty of loyalty as follows:

[A corporate director or officer] owes loyalty and allegiance to the corporation—a loyalty that is undivided and an allegiance that is influenced by no consideration other than the welfare of the corporation. Any adverse interest of a director [or officer] will be subjected to a scrutiny rigid and uncompromising. He may not profit at the expense of his corporation and in conflict with its rights; he may not for personal gain divert unto himself the opportunities that in equity and fairness belong to the corporation.

Many forms of conduct permissible in a workaday world for those acting at arm's length are forbidden to those bound by fiduciary ties. Not honesty alone, but the punctilio of an honor the most sensitive, is then the standard of behavior. As to this there has developed a tradition that is unbending and inveterate.[1]

If a director or officer breaches his or her duty of loyalty and makes a secret profit on a transaction, the corporation can sue the director or officer to recover the secret profit. Some of the most common breaches of the duty of loyalty are discussed in the following paragraphs.

Usurping a Corporate Opportunity

Directors and officers may not personally usurp (steal) a corporate opportunity for themselves. **Usurping a corporate opportunity** constitutes a violation of a director's or officer's duty of loyalty. If usurping is proven, the corporation can (1) acquire the opportunity from the director or officer and (2) recover any profits made by the director or officer.

The following elements must be shown to prove usurping:

1. The opportunity was presented to the director or officer in his or her corporate capacity.
2. The opportunity is related to or connected with the corporation's current or proposed business.
3. The corporation has the financial ability to take advantage of the opportunity.
4. The corporate officer or director took the corporate opportunity for him- or herself.

However, the director or officer is free personally to take advantage of a corporate opportunity if it was fully disclosed and presented to the corporation and the corporation rejected it.

usurping a corporate opportunity
A director or officer steals a corporate opportunity for him- or herself.

Self-Dealing

Under the RMBCA, a contract or transaction with a corporate director or officer is voidable by the corporation if it is unfair to the corporation [RMBCA § 8.31]. Contracts of a corporation to purchase property from, sell property to, or make loans to corporate directors or officers where the directors or officers have not disclosed their interest in the transaction are often voided under this standard. Contracts or transactions with corporate directors or officers are enforceable if their interest in the transaction has been disclosed to the corporation and the disinterested directors or the shareholders have approved the transaction.

self-dealing
If the directors or officers engage in purchasing, selling, or leasing of property with the corporation, the contract must be fair to the corporation; otherwise, it is voidable by the corporation. The contract or transaction is enforceable if it has been fully disclosed and approved.

Competing with the Corporation

Directors and officers cannot engage in activities that *compete* with the corporation unless full disclosure is made and a majority of the disinterested directors or shareholders approve the activity. The corporation can recover any profits made by nonapproved competition and any other damages caused to the corporation.

Disgorgement of Secret Profits

If a director or officer breaches his or her duty of loyalty and makes a secret profit on a transaction, the corporation can sue the director or officer to recover the secret profit. If the corporation does not do so, any shareholder can bring a derivative action and recover the secret profit on behalf of the corporation.

Consider This Example   Suppose Maxine Chambers is the purchasing agent for the Roebolt Corporation. Her duties require her to negotiate and execute contracts to purchase office supplies and equipment for the corporation. Assume Bruce Nevel, a computer salesperson, pays Chambers a $10,000 kickback to purchase typewriters needed by the Roebolt Corporation. The Roebolt Corporation can sue and recover the $10,000 secret profit from Chambers.

*C*ONCEPT SUMMARY   FIDUCIARY DUTIES OF CORPORATION DIRECTORS AND OFFICERS

Duty	Description	Violation
Duty of obedience	Duty to act within the authority conferred by law and the corporation.	Acts outside of corporate officer's or director's authority.
Duty of care	Duty to use care and diligence when acting on behalf of the corporation. This duty is discharged if an officer or director acts 1. In good faith. 2. With the care that an ordinary prudent person in a like position would use under similar circumstances. 3. In a manner he or she reasonably believes to be in the best interests of the corporation.	Acts of negligence and mismanagement. Such acts include failure to 1. Make a reasonable investigation of a corporate matter. 2. Attend board meetings on a regular basis. 3. Properly supervise a subordinate who causes a loss to the corporation. 4. Keep adequately informed about corporate matters. 5. Take other actions necessary to discharge duties.
Duty of loyalty	Duty to subordinate personal interests to those of the corporation and its shareholders.	Acts of disloyalty. Such acts include unauthorized 1. Self-dealing with the corporation. 2. Usurping of a corporate opportunity. 3. Competing with the corporation. 4. Making a secret profit that belongs to the corporation.

Liability for Crimes

Corporate directors, officers, employees, and agents are personally liable for the crimes they commit while acting on behalf of the corporation. Criminal law sanctions include fines and imprisonment.

Under the law of agency, a corporation is liable for the crimes committed by its directors, officers, employees, or agents while acting within the scope of their employment. Because a corporation cannot be placed in prison, the criminal penalty imposed on a corporation usually is the assessment of a monetary fine or the loss of some legal privilege (such as a license).

*C*ontemporary *B*usiness *A*pplication

ARE BONDHOLDERS OWED A FIDUCIARY DUTY?

In 1986, Steven Pittelman purchased a 25-year 8¼ percent convertible subordinated debenture issued by American Medical International, Inc. (AMI), for $1,000. In 1989, AMI was acquired in a leveraged buyout by IMA Acquisition Corporation (IMA). To complete the purchase of 86 percent of the stock of AMI, IMA borrowed $2.4 billion from banks and through the issue of high-yield junk bonds. IMA paid interest rates from 16.75 percent to 24 percent on this debt.

Following the leveraged buyout, IMA caused the merger of AMI and IMA. After the merger, IMA's $2.4-billion debt became AMI's obligation. The merged company had to sell off important assets to help pay some of the bank loans. Pittelman's low-interest-yielding debenture became a "junk bond," and it sank in value. Pittelman sued the directors of AMI to recover this lost value as damages. He alleged in a class action that the directors had breached a fiduciary duty of honesty and loyalty that they owed to him and to the other 8¼ percent debenture holders. The trial court granted the defendant's motion for summary judgment. Pittelman appealed.

Do directors of a corporation owe a fiduciary duty to debenture holders? The court of appeals held that directors of a corporation do not owe a fiduciary duty to debenture holders.

The court of appeals stated

> It appears to us that California shares Delaware's view that a bondholder is not owed any special fiduciary duty by either the corporation or the corporation's directors. In making his argument that fiduciary duties admittedly owed to shareholders should now be extended to a corporation's bondholders, plaintiff overlooks the fundamental conflict which exists between these two investing groups in the corporate family. The potential for conflict exists because bondholders have prior but fixed claims on a firm's assets, while shareholders have limited liability for the firm's debts and unlimited claims on a firm's assets. As the debt to equity ratio increases, the probability and magnitude of these conflicts increase. Where, as in this case, there is an increase in corporate debt, there is a significant change in the debt to equity ratio which is obviously unfavorable to bondholders. Thus, we have here a maximization of the potential for conflict between the interest of shareholders and bondholders. In such circumstances, the directors would be hard pressed to discharge a fiduciary duty to both groups.

He continued

> A bondholder, even of a convertible debenture, is simply a creditor of the corporation. He is not entitled to any special protections which he has failed to negotiate for himself at the time of the purchase of the bond. It is not enough to argue, as does plaintiff, that the marketplace has become more dangerous. Absent fraud, or other similar misconduct, the courts have no brief to interfere in an established business relationship. If we begin here, where does it end? Would not all creditors, however minor or unsecured, be entitled to the same judicial oversight to ensure that a corporation's subsequent business conduct did not damage its credit rating or potential to ultimately make a timely discharge of the outstanding debt? This is a slippery slope which we see no need to test. The issue raised by plaintiff is one which must be addressed at the time of the extension of credit and provided for in the indenture contract, not later when subsequent events may prove the error of the investor's original evaluation of the risk. A bondholder is a creditor whose remedies are necessarily limited to an action for breach of the indenture agreement. Admittedly, no such breach has occurred here, nor has one even been threatened." [*Pittelman v. Pearce*, 6 Cal.App.4th 1436, 8 Cal.Rptr.2d 359 (Cal.App. 1992)]

*L*IABILITY OF SHAREHOLDERS

Shareholders of a corporation generally have **limited liability** (i.e., they are liable for the debts and obligations of the corporation only to the extent of their capital contribution). However, shareholders can be found personally liable if (1) the corporate entity is disregarded or (2) a controlling shareholder breaches a fiduciary duty to minority shareholders.

limited liability
Liability that shareholders have only to the extent of their capital contribution. Shareholders are generally not personally liable for debts and obligations of the corporation.

Disregard of the Corporate Entity

If a shareholder or shareholders dominate a corporation and use it for improper purposes, a court of equity can *disregard the corporate entity* and hold the shareholders of a corporation personally liable for the corporation's debts and obligations. This doctrine is commonly referred to as **piercing the corporate veil**. It is often resorted to by unpaid creditors who are trying to collect from shareholders a debt owed by the corporation.

Courts will pierce the corporate veil if (1) the corporation has been formed without sufficient capital (i.e., *thin capitalization*) or (2) separateness has not been maintained between the corporation and its shareholders (e.g., commingling of personal and corporate assets, failure to hold required shareholders' meetings, failure to maintain corporate records and books). The courts examine this doctrine on a case-by-case basis.

The piercing the corporate veil doctrine was raised in the following case.

piercing the corporate veil
A doctrine that says if a shareholder dominates a corporation and uses it for improper purposes, a court of equity can disregard the corporate entity and hold the shareholder personally liable for the corporation's debts and obligations.

Kinney Shoe Corp. v. Polan
939 F.2d 209 (1991)
United States Court of Appeals, Fourth Circuit

CASE 38.3

FACTS

In 1984, Lincoln M. Polan formed Industrial Realty Company (Industrial), a West Virginia corporation. Polan was the sole shareholder of Industrial. Although a certificate of incorporation was issued, no organizational meeting was held and no officers were elected. Industrial issued no stock certificates because nothing was ever paid in to the corporation. Other corporate formalities were not observed. Polan, on behalf of Industrial, signed a lease to sublease commercial space in a building controlled by Kinney Shoe Corporation (Kinney). The first rental payment to Kinney was made out of Polan's personal funds, and no further payments were made on the lease. Kinney filed suit against Industrial and obtained a judgment of $66,400 for unpaid rent. When the amount was unpaid by Industrial, Kinney sued Polan individually and sought to pierce the corporate veil to collect from Polan. The district court held for Polan. Kinney appealed.

ISSUE

Is Polan personally liable for Industrial's debts?

IN THE LANGUAGE OF THE COURT

Chapman, Senior Circuit Judge   Kinney seeks to pierce the corporate veil of Industrial so as to hold Polan personally liable on the sublease debt. The Supreme Court of Appeals of West Virginia has set forth a two prong test to be used in determining whether to pierce a corporate veil in a breach of contract case. This test raises two issues: first, is the unity of interest and ownership such that the separate personalities of the corporation and
the individual shareholder no longer exist; and second, would an equitable result occur if the acts are treated as those of the corporation alone.

The district court found that the two prong test had been satisfied. The court concluded that Polan's failure to carry out the corporate formalities with respect to Industrial, coupled with Industrial's gross undercapitalization, resulted in damage to Kinney. We agree. It is undisputed that Industrial was not adequately capitalized. Actually, it had no paid in capital. Polan had put nothing into this corporation, and it did not observe any corporate formalities. Polan was obviously trying to limit his liability by setting up a paper curtain constructed of nothing more than Industrial's certificate of incorporation. These facts present the classic scenario for an action to pierce the corporate veil so as to reach the responsible party and produce an equitable result.

DECISION AND REMEDY

The court of appeals pierced the corporate veil and held Polan personally liable on Industrial's debt to Kinney. Reversed.

Case Questions

Critical Legal Thinking   Is the doctrine of piercing the corporate veil needed? Should parties like Kinney bear the risk of dealing with corporations like Industrial?

Ethics   Is it ethical for persons to form corporations to avoid personal liability? Should this be allowed?

Business Application   What is the risk if corporate formalities are not observed? Explain.

Controlling Shareholders' Breach of Fiduciary Duty

Shareholders usually do not owe a fiduciary duty to their fellow shareholders. However, many courts have held that a *controlling shareholder* does owe a fiduciary duty to minority shareholders. A controlling shareholder is one who owns a sufficient number of shares to control the corporation effectively. This may or may not be majority ownership.

The courts have held that controlling shareholders breach their fiduciary duty to minority shareholders if they

- Sell assets of the corporation that cause an unusual loss to the minority shareholders.
- Sell corporate assets to themselves at less than fair market value.
- Sell controlling interest in the corporation to someone who they know intends to loot the corporation, and does.
- Take other action that oppresses the minority shareholders.

This is a developing area of the law. The courts examine each case on its particular facts.

International Perspective

IMPORT AND EXPORT RESTRICTIONS STILL EXIST

Countries of the world impose many restrictions on international trade. They consist of laws restricting imports into a country and exports out of a country. Trade restrictions are imposed for a variety of reasons, including protecting local jobs, national security, and domestically made products and services from foreign competition.

Import Restrictions All countries, including the United States, impose restrictions on the importation of certain products or services from some countries. The most common forms of import controls are:

- **Import Quotas** These either prohibit entirely or restrict the numerical amount of designated goods or services that may be imported.
- **Tariffs** These are taxes or duties charged on imported goods or services. Tariffs make imported goods or services more expensive to buy.
- **Nontariff Restrictions** These are requirements that imported goods or services meet certain manufacturing requirements or standards, receive government approval before they are allowed to be imported into the country, or go through time-consuming customs procedures.

The United States has entered into the **North American Free Trade Agreement (NAFTA)** with Canada and Mexico, which is a regional trade treaty that reduces or eliminates many of the tariffs and other trade barriers between these countries. Many other countries of the world have entered into regional trade pacts that reduce tariffs and other import restriction among the member countries. The United States is also a member of the **World Trade Organization (WTO)**, an international convention among over 130 countries to reduce tariffs and other restrictions on international trade. Despite all these trade agreements, most countries still maintain import restrictions on certain types of goods or services or imports from certain countries. Import barriers will continue to be reduced in the future as countries negotiate additional trade agreements.

Export Restrictions Although countries usually promote exports, most place restrictions on certain exports. Under the **Export Administration Act of 1979,** as amended [50 U.S.C. §§ 2402 et seq.], the President of the United States may prevent or restrict the export of goods, commodities, and technology that involves (1) national security, (2) foreign policy, (3) nuclear proliferation, or (4) scarce commodities. The U.S. Department of Commerce maintains a list of the goods, commodities, and technology that are subject to export controls. Other countries restrict exports for similar reasons. Cultural property (e.g., artifacts, art) is often subject to export restrictions.

Working the Web

One of the easiest ways to start surfing the Internet is to subscribe to an Internet service provider. Internet service providers (ISPs) will enable you to have an e-mail address and access via modem to the Internet. Some ISPs also maintain databases of information that are included with a subscription. Most ISPs charge between $15 and $25 per month for this service. Most large ISPs will give you some free hours to try their services. Some even have deals where you can get a free computer if you sign up for 2-3 years of service. Some Internet service providers include:

America Online

Visit at **www.aol.com**

e-biz

e·biz

Compuserve

Visit at **www.compuserve.com**

Prodigy

Visit at **www.prodigy.com**

Local Internet providers

Many areas have a number of local ISPs

1–4. Visit all of the major ISPs. How many free hours can you get from each to try out their services?

5. Check out local ISPs. Find out if they are cheaper than the big services. Find out what services they provide.

CASES AND EXERCISES

CRITICAL LEGAL THINKING CASES

38.1. Ocilla Industries, Inc. (Ocilla), owned 40 percent of the stock of Direct Action Marketing, Inc. (Direct Action). Direct Action was a New York corporation that specialized in the marketing of products through billing inserts. In 1985, Ocilla helped place Howard Katz and Joseph Esposito on Direct Action's five-member board of directors. A dispute between Ocilla and the two directors caused Ocilla to claim that Katz and Esposito wanted excess remuneration in exchange for leaving the board at the end of their terms. As a result, no shareholders' meeting was held between September 19, 1986, and January 27, 1988. Under the Model Business Corporations Act, can Ocilla compel Direct Action to hold the meeting earlier? [*Ocilla Industries, Inc. v. Katz*, 677 F.Supp. 1291 (E.D.N.Y. 1987)]

38.2. Jack C. Schoenholtz was a shareholder and member of the board of directors of Rye Psychiatric Hospital Center, Inc. (Rye Hospital). The hospital was incorporated in 1973. By 1977, a split had developed among the board of directors concerning the operation of the facility. Three directors stood on one side of the dispute and three directors on the other. In an attempt to break the deadlock, Schoenholtz, who owned over 10 percent of the corporation's voting stock, asked the corporation's secretary to call a special meeting of the shareholders. In response, the secretary sent a notice to the shareholders stating that a special meeting of the shareholders would be held on November 12, 1982, "for the purpose of electing directors." The meeting was held as scheduled. Some stockholders brought suit claiming that the special shareholders' meeting was not called properly. Who wins? [*Rye Psychiatric Hospital Center, Inc. v. Schoenholtz*, 476 N.Y.S.2d 339 (A.D. 2 Dept. 1984)]

38.3. George Gibbons, William Smith, and Gerald Zollar were all shareholders in GRG Operating, Inc. (GRG). On May 13, 1983, Zollar contributed $1,000 of his own funds so that the corporation could begin to do business. In exchange for this contribution, Gibbons and Smith both granted Zollar the right to vote their shares of GRG stock. They gave Zollar a signed form that stated that "Gibbons and Smith, for a period of 10 years from the date hereof, appoint Zollar as their proxy. This proxy is solely intended to be an irrevocable proxy." A year after the agreement was signed, Gibbons and Smith wanted to revoke their proxies. Can they? [*Zollar v. Smith*, 710 S.W.2d 155 (Tex. App. 1986)]

38.4. Bookstop, Inc. (Bookstop), was founded in 1982 by Gary Hoover. The corporation met with early and marked success. By 1985, it was one of the largest retail booksellers in Texas and had expanded into California. To finance this rapid growth, Hoover sought outside investors. In 1985, Hoover agreed to sell 18 percent of Bookstop's common stock to H. E. Butt Grocery Company (HEB). As part of the sale of stock, the parties agreed that each had the right to place two nominees on Bookstop's board of directors. For several years, the parties abided by the terms of the agreement. A dispute then arose between Bookstop's shareholders. Can the shareholders' agreement be enforced? [*Crown Books Corporation v. Bookstop, Inc.*, 1990 WL 26166 (Del.Ch. 1990)]

38.5. Stater Brothers Markets (Stater Brothers), a chain of supermarkets located throughout southern California, was a wholly owned subsidiary of Petrolane, Inc. (Petrolane). The company's top executives and an outside investor named Lisa Garrett purchased the chain in a leveraged buyout in March

1983. The executives, known collectively as the La Cadena group, bought 51 percent of Stater Brother's stock; Garrett owned the other 49 percent. In an effort to preserve the continuity of harmonious management, Garrett and the La Cadena group entered into a stockholders' agreement effective March 22, 1983. The agreement prohibited the sale of any Stater Brothers stock without the consent of the other stockholders. Absent such consent, the nonselling stockholders were given the right of first refusal to meet the terms of the proposed sale and be substituted for the outside investor. Is this agreement valid? [*Garrett v. Brown*, 511 A.2d 1044 (Del. Supreme 1986)]

38.6. On July 20, 1983, Helmsman Management Services, Inc. (Helmsman), became a 25 percent stockholder of A&S Consultants, Inc. (A&S), a Delaware corporation. Helmsman paid $50,000 for its interest in A&S. At the time of the stock purchase, Helmsman was also a customer of A&S, paying the company for the use of a computer software program. Since 1983, Helmsman verified A&S's billings by a periodic review of certain of A&S's books and records. In January 1986, Helmsman conducted a review of A&S's records over a six-day period. The review showed that A&S had never paid any dividends on the stock held by Helmsman and that Helmsman had never received notice of A&S's stockholder meetings. Suspecting that A&S was being mismanaged, Helmsman sent a letter to A&S asking to inspect all A&S's records. The letter stated several purposes for the inspection, including to (1) determine the reasons for nonpayment of dividends and (2) gain information to be used in determining how to vote in stockholders' elections. Under the Model Business Corporations Act, should Helmsman's request be honored? [*Helmsman Management Services, Inc. v. A&S Consultants, Inc.*, 525 A.2d 160 (Del.Ch. 1987)]

38.7. Dick Gregory was the chairman of the board of directors of Correction Connection, Inc. (CCI). CCI's bylaws permit special meetings of the board of directors if each board member is given notice of the meeting and informed of the business to be conducted at the meeting. On September 27, 1988, a notice of a special meeting of the board of directors was sent to each director, including Gregory. The notice specified the meeting date of September 30, 1988, and the agenda for the meeting, which included a plan to acquire additional capital. The meeting began as planned on September 30 and reconvened on October 4, October 6, and October 7. Gregory did not attend any of the meetings. In Gregory's absence, the board voted to issue certain authorized but unissued shares of the corporation's stock. Gregory objected to this decision and brought an action to prevent the stock from being issued. Who wins? [*Gregory v. Depte*, 1989 WL 67329 (E.D.Pa. 1989)]

38.8. Gay's Super Markets, Inc. (Super Markets) was a corporation formed under the laws of the state of Maine. Hannaford Bros. Company held 51 percent of the corporation's common stock. Lawrence F. Gay and his brother Carrol were both minority shareholders in Super Markets. Lawrence Gay was also the manager of the corporation's store at Machias, Maine. On July 5, 1971, he was dismissed from his job. At the January 1972 meeting of Super Markets's board of directors, a decision was made not to declare a stock dividend for 1971. The directors cited expected losses from increased competition and the expense of opening a new store as reasons for not paying a dividend. Lawrence Gay claims that the reason for not paying a dividend was to force him to sell his shares in Super Markets. Lawrence sued to force the corporation to declare a dividend. Who wins? [*Gay v. Gay's Super Markets, Inc.*, 343 A.2d 577 (Maine Sup. 1975)]

38.9. Edward Hellenbrand ran a comedy club known as the Comedy Cottage in Rosemont. Illinois. The business was incorporated, with Hellenbrand and his wife as the corporation's sole shareholders. The corporation leased the premises in which the club was located. In 1978, Hellenbrand hired Jay Berk as general manager of the club. In 1980, Berk was made vice president of the corporation and given 10 percent of its stock. Hellenbrand experienced health problems and moved to Nevada, leaving Berk to manage the daily affairs of the business. In June 1984, the ownership of the building where the Comedy Cottage was located changed hands. Shortly thereafter, the club's lease on the premises expired. Hellenbrand instructed Berk to negotiate a new lease. Berk arranged a month-to-month lease but had the lease agreement drawn up in his name instead of that of the corporation. When Hellenbrand learned of Berk's move, he fired him. Berk continued to lease the building in his own name and opened his own club there, known as the Comedy Company, Inc. Hellenbrand sued Berk for an injunction to prevent Berk from leasing the building. Who wins? [*Comedy Cottage, Inc. v. Berk*, 495 N.E.2d 1006 (Ill. App. 1986)]

38.10. Lawrence Gaffney was the president and general manager of Ideal Tape Company (Ideal). Ideal, which was a subsidiary of Chelsea Industries, Inc. (Chelsea), was engaged in the business of manufacturing pressure-sensitive tape. In 1975, Gaffney recruited three other Ideal executives to join him in starting a tape manufacturing business. The four men remained at Ideal for the two years it took them to plan the new enterprise. During this time, they used their positions at Ideal to travel around the country to gather business ideas, recruit potential customers, and purchase equipment for their business. At no time did they reveal to Chelsea their intention to open a competing business. In November 1977, the new business was incorporated as Action Manufacturing Company

(Action). When executives at Chelsea discovered the existence of the new venture, Gaffney and the others resigned from Chelsea. Chelsea sued them for damages. Who wins? [*Chelsea Industries, Inc. v. Gaffney*, 449 N.E.2d 320 (Mass.Sup. 1983)]

38.11. William G. Young was a director of Pool Builders Supply, Inc. (Pool Builders). Pool Builders experienced financial difficulties and was forced to file for bankruptcy. Eddie Lawson was appointed the receiver for the creditors of the corporation. Lawson believed that Young had mismanaged the corporation. Lawson filed a suit against Young and Pool Builders, alleging that Young had used Pool Builders personally to obtain money, goods, and property from creditors on the credit of the corporation. Lawson's suit also alleged that Young attempted to convert corporate assets for his own use. Young defended the suit for himself and the corporation. At trial, the judge found insufficient evidence to support Lawson's charges, and the suit was dismissed. Young now seeks to have Pool Builders pay the legal fees he incurred while defending the suit. Can Young recover this money from the corporation? [*Lawson v. Young*, 486 N.E.2d 1177 (Ohio App. 1984)]

38.12. In 1948, four brothers—Monnie, Mechel, Merko, and Sam Dotlich—formed a partnership to run a heavy equipment rental business. By 1957, the company had been incorporated as Dotlich Brothers, Inc. Each brother owned 25 percent of the corporation's stock, and each served on the board of directors. In 1951, the business acquired a 56-acre tract of land in Speedway, Indiana. This land was held in the name of Monnie Dotlich. Each of the brothers was aware of this arrangement. By 1976, the corporation had purchased six other pieces of property, all of which were held in Monnie's name. Sam Dotlich was not informed that Monnie was the record owner of these other properties. In 1976, Sam discovered this irregularity and requested that the board of directors take action to remedy the situation. When the board refused to do so, Sam initiated a lawsuit on behalf of the corporation. Can Sam bring this lawsuit? [*Dotlich v. Dotlich*, 475 N.E.2d 331 (Ind. App. 1985)]

38.13. M. R. Watters was the majority shareholder of several closely held corporations, including Wildhorn Ranch, Inc. (Wildhorn). All these businesses were run out of Watter's home in Rocky Ford, Colorado. Wildhorn operated a resort called the Wildhorn Ranch Resort in Teller County, Colorado. Although Watters claimed that the ranch was owned by the corporation, the deed for the property listed Watters as the owner. Watters paid little attention to corporate formalities, holding corporate meetings at his house, never taking minutes of these meetings, and paying the debts of one corporation with the assets of another. During August 1986, two guests of Wildhorn Ranch Resort drowned while operating a paddleboat at the ranch. The family of the deceased guests sued for damages. Can Watters be held personally liable? [*Geringer v. Wildhorn Ranch, Inc.*, 760 F.Supp. 1442 (D.Colo. 1988)]

38.14. Robert Orchard and Arthur Covelli owned seven McDonald's franchises in Erie, Pennsylvania. Each individual franchise was owned by a separate corporation. Orchard owned a 27 percent interest in each of these corporations, and Covelli owned 73 percent. Although Orchard and Covelli worked together harmoniously for many years, they eventually became dissatisfied with the relationship. In 1977, they unsuccessfully attempted to have Covelli buy out Orchard's stock. Covelli became angry with Orchard and had him terminated from his position as vice president of the corporations. Six months later, Covelli removed Orchard from the corporations' boards of directors and replaced him with his own son. Covelli also allowed three of the corporations' franchise agreements with McDonald's to lapse and then resigned them in his own name. Throughout this period, Orchard received no dividends or other compensation from the corporations. Orchard sued Covelli for damages. Who wins? [*Orchard v. Covelli*, 590 F.Supp. 1548 (W.D.Pa. 1984)]

ETHICS CASES

38.15. Alfred S. Johnson, Incorporated (Corporation), was incorporated in 1955 by Alfred S. Johnson, who owned 70 shares of the corporation. Two employees of the corporation, James DeBaun and Walter Stephens, owned 20 and 10 shares, respectively. When Johnson died in 1965, his will created a testamentary trust in which his 70 shares were placed. Johnson's will named First Western Bank and Trust Company (Bank) trustee for the trust. Several years later, Bank decided to sell the 70 shares but did not tell anyone associated with Corporation of its decision. An appraisal was obtained that valued the corporation at $326,000 as a going concern.

On May 27, 1968, Raymond J. Mattison submitted an offer to purchase the 70 shares for $250,000, payable in $50,000 in securities of companies Mattison owned and the $200,000 balance over a five-year period. Bank obtained a Dun & Bradstreet report that showed several outstanding tax liens against Mattison. Bank accepted Mattison's explanation that they were not his fault. At the time, Mattison owned Bank a judgment for fraud. Bank was also aware that

Mattison owned unpaid debts and that several entities in which he was involved were insolvent. Bank did not investigate these matters. If it had, the public records of Los Angeles County would have revealed 38 unsatisfied judgments against Mattison and his entities totaling $330,886, 54 pending lawsuits claiming damages of $373,588, and 18 tax liens aggregating $20,327. Bank agreed to sell the 70 shares to Mattison and accepted the assets of Corporation as security for the repayment of the $200,000 balance. As part of the transaction, Bank required Mattison to agree to have Corporation give its banking business to Bank.

At the time of sale, Corporation was a successful going business with a bright future. It had cash of $76,000 and other liquid assets of over $120,000. Its net worth was about $220,000. Corporation was profitable, and its trend of earnings indicated a pattern of growth. Mattison immediately implemented a systematic scheme to loot Corporation. He (1) diverted $73,000 in corporate cash to himself and a shell company he owned, (2) caused Corporation to assign all its assets, including accounts receivable, to the shell company, (3) diverted all corporate mail to a post office box and extracted incoming checks to Corporation, (4) refused to pay corporate creditors on time or at all, (5) issued payroll checks without sufficient corporate funds, and (6) removed Corporation's books and records. On June 20, 1969, hopelessly insolvent, Corporation shut down operations and was placed in receivership. At that time, its debts exceeded its assets by over $200,000. DeBaun's and Stephens's shares were worthless. They sued Bank for damages, alleging that Bank, as the majority shareholder of Corporation, breached its fiduciary duty to the minority shareholders.

Did Bank have knowledge of the dangerous situation in which it placed Corporation? Did Bank, as the controlling shareholder of Corporation, breach its fiduciary duty to the minority shareholders? [*DeBaun v. First Western Bank and Trust Co.*, 46 Cal.App.3d 791, 120 Cal.Rptr. 354 (Cal. App. 1975)]

38.16. Jon-T Chemicals, Inc. (Chemicals), was an Oklahoma corporation engaged in the fertilizer and chemicals business. John H. Thomas was its majority shareholder and its president and board chairman. In April 1971, Chemicals incorporated Jon-T Farms, Inc. (Farms), as a wholly owned subsidiary to engage in the farming and land-leasing business. Chemicals invested $10,000 to establish Farms. All the directors and officers of Farms were directors and officers of Chemicals, and Thomas was its president and board chairman. In addition, Farms used offices, computers, and accountants of Chemicals without paying a fee, and Chemicals paid the salary of Farms' only employee. Chemicals made regular informal advances to pay Farms' expenses. These payments reached $7.5 million by January 1975.

Thomas and Farms engaged in a scheme whereby they submitted fraudulent applications for agricultural subsidies from the federal government under the Uplands Cotton Program. As a result of these applications, the Commodity Credit Corporation, a government agency, paid over $2.5 million in subsidies to Thomas and Farms. After discovering the fraud, the federal government obtained criminal convictions against Thomas and Farms. In a separate civil action, the federal government obtained a $4.7 million judgment against Thomas and Farms, finding them jointly and severally liable for the tort of fraud. Farms declared bankruptcy, and Thomas was unable to pay the judgment. Because Thomas and Farms were insolvent, the federal government sued Chemicals to recover the judgment. Was Farms the alter ego of Chemicals, permitting the United States to pierce the corporate veil and recover the judgment from Chemicals? Did Thomas act ethically in this case? [*United States of America v. Jon-T Chemicals, Inc.*, 768 F.2d 868 (5th Cir. 1985)]

CRITICAL LEGAL THINKING WRITING ASSIGNMENT

Read Case A.38 is the Case Appendix [*United States v. WRW Corporation*]. This case is excerpted from the court of appeals opinion. Review and brief the case. In your brief, be sure to answer the following questions.

1. Who was the plaintiff? What was it suing for?
2. Who were the defendants?
3. Explain the doctrine of piercing the corporate veil.
4. Did the court find the defendants personally liable?

NOTE

1. *Meinhard v. Salmon*, 164 N.E.2d 545, 546 (N.Y.App. 1928).

39

Mergers and Hostile Takeovers of Corporations

To supervise wisely the great corporations is well; but to look backward to the days when business was polite pillage and regard our great business concerns as piratical institutions carrying letters of marque and reprisal is a grave error born in the minds of little men. When these little men legislate they set the brakes going uphill.

ELBERT HUBBARD (1856–1915)
Notebook, p. 16

Chapter Objectives

After studying this chapter, you should be able to

1. Describe the process for soliciting proxies from shareholders.
2. Define *proxy contests*.
3. Identify when a shareholder can include a proposal in proxy materials.
4. Distinguish between a merger and a consolidation.
5. Describe the process for approving a merger or share exchange.
6. Describe dissenting shareholder appraisal rights.
7. Define *tender offer*.
8. Describe poison pills, white knight mergers, greenmail, and other defensive maneuvers to prevent a hostile takeover.
9. Apply the business judgment rule in examining the lawfulness of defensive strategies.
10. Analyze the lawfulness of state antitakeover statutes.

Chapter Contents

During the course of its existence, a corporation may go through certain *fundamental changes*. A corporation must seek shareholder approval for many changes. This requires the solicitation of votes or proxies from shareholders. Persons who want to take over the management of a corporation often conduct proxy contests to try to win over shareholder votes.

Corporations often engage in acquisitions of other corporations or businesses. This may occur by friendly merger or consolidation or by hostile tender offer. In defense, a corporation may erect certain barriers or impediments to a hostile takeover.

This chapter discusses fundamental changes to a corporation, including the solicitation of proxies, mergers and consolidations, hostile tender offers, and defensive strategies of corporations.

Solicitation of Proxies

Corporate shareholders have the right to vote on the election of directors, mergers, charter amendments, and the like. They can exercise their power to vote either in person or by proxy [RMBCA § 7.22]. Voting by proxy is common in large corporations with thousands of shareholders located across the country and the world.

A proxy is a written document (often called a **proxy card**) completed and signed by the shareholder and sent to the corporation. The proxy authorizes another person—the proxy holder—to vote the shares at the shareholders' meeting as directed by the shareholder. The proxy holder is often a director or officer of the corporation.

Federal Proxy Rules

Section 14(a) of the Securities Exchange Act of 1934 gives the Securities and Exchange Commission (SEC) the authority to regulate the solicitation of proxies.[1] The federal proxy rules promote full disclosure. In other words, management or any other party soliciting proxies from shareholders must prepare a **proxy statement** that fully describes (1) the matter for which the proxy is being solicited, (2) who is soliciting the proxy, and (3) any other pertinent information.

A copy of the proxy, the proxy statement, and all other solicitation material must be filed with the SEC at least 10 days before the materials are sent to the shareholders. If the SEC requires additional disclosures, the solicitation can be held up until these disclosures are made.

Antifraud Provision

Section 14(a) of the Securities Exchange Act of 1934 prohibits material misrepresentations or omissions of a material fact in the proxy materials. Known false statements of facts, reasons, opinions, or beliefs in proxy solicitation materials are actionable. Violations of this rule can result in civil and criminal actions by the SEC and the Justice Department, respectively. The courts have implied a private cause of action under this provision. Thus, shareholders who are injured by a material misrepresentation or omission in proxy materials can sue the wrongdoer and recover damages. The court can also order a new election if a violation is found.

Proxy Contests

Shareholders sometimes oppose the actions taken by the incumbent directors and management. These shareholders may challenge the incumbent management in a **proxy contest** in which both sides solicit proxies from the other shareholders. The side that receives the greatest number of votes wins the proxy contest. Such contests are usually held with regard to the election of directors.

Management must either (1) provide a list of shareholders to the dissenting group or (2) mail the proxy solicitation materials of the challenging group to the shareholders.

The usual trade and commerce is cheating all round by consent.

Thomas Fuller Gnomologia (1732)

proxy card

A written document signed by a shareholder that authorizes another person to vote the shareholder's shares.

Section 14(a)

Provision of the Securities Exchange Act of 1934 that gives the SEC the authority to regulate the solicitation of proxies.

proxy statement

A document that fully describes (1) the matter for which the proxy is being solicited, (2) who is soliciting the proxy, and (3) any other pertinent information.

Business Brief

Section 14(a) of the 1934 act prohibits misrepresentations or omissions of a material fact in proxy materials. The SEC, U.S. Justice Department, or shareholders who are injured by the misrepresentation or omission may sue the wrongdoer.

proxy contest

When opposing factions of shareholders and managers solicit proxies from other shareholders, the side that receives the greatest number of votes wins the proxy contest.

Reimbursement of Expenses

In a proxy contest, both sides usually spend considerable amounts of money on legal expenses, media campaigns, mailers, telephone solicitations, and the like. If a proxy contest involves an issue of policy, the corporation must reimburse the incumbent management for its expenses whether it wins or loses the proxy contest. The expenses of the dissenting group are reimbursed only if it wins the proxy contest. If the proxy contest concerns a personal matter, neither side may recover its expenses from the corporation.

Contemporary Business Application

THE SEC'S PROXY RULES

Critics argued for a long time that the SEC's proxy rules did not require sufficient or clear enough disclosures for shareholders to make informed decisions. Finally, in 1992, after three years of study, the SEC adopted new proxy rules. The new rules were designed to allow shareholders to communicate more easily with each other and to give them additional information about management and its compensation.

Prior to the adoption of the 1992 rules, any shareholder who wished to communicate with 10 or more fellow shareholders faced the daunting and expensive task of filing proxy solicitation materials with the SEC. This tended to thwart shareholder communication and insulate management from shareholder criticism. The 1992 rules exempt from these requirements oral and written communications to shareholders from any shareholder who is not seeking proxy voting authority. For instance, shareholders can now ask each other how the corporation should be run or suggest changes. They have to register with the SEC only if they decide to solicit proxies.

Shareholders who own more than $5 million of the company's securities are not covered by this rule. They must still register any written communication to shareholders with the SEC.

Another 1992 rule change requires companies seeking proxies to "unbundle" the propositions set for shareholder

vote so that the shareholders can vote on each separate issue. The old proxy rules allowed companies to bundle the propositions and present them as one package for a single shareholder vote. This tactic prevented shareholders from considering the merits of individual propositions. The 1992 rules also require all companies to include performance charts in their annual reports. These charts must compare the company's stock performance to that of a general index of companies, such as the Standard and Poor's 500, and companies in its peer group index (e.g., retailers).

Finally, the 1992 rules broadened the disclosure requirements concerning executive compensation. The 1992 rules mandate that companies provide tables in their annual reports that succinctly summarize executive compensation for the chief executive officer and its four other most highly compensated executives for the past three years. The tables must disclose salary, stock options, stock appreciation rights, and long-term incentive plans of these executives, including the value of each item. This is the change that generated the most attention.

Proponents of these rule changes assert that shareholders will now get the information they need to make informed decisions. Some argue for disclosure of even more information to shareholders. Some company management, particularly the most highly compensated executives, dislike the new rules.

Ethical Perspective

SHAREHOLDER RESOLUTIONS: DO THEY PROMOTE SOCIAL RESPONSIBILITY OF BUSINESS?

Shareholders have become more active in corporate governance, as witnessed by the hundreds of shareholder resolutions that are filed each year for vote at annual shareholder meetings.

During the 1980s, apartheid in South Africa was the primary issue of shareholder issues. Prompted by such proposals and the publicity they generated, many U.S. companies left South Africa. The world pressure worked, and

South Africa ended apartheid. Free elections were held and new leaders were elected. U.S. and other corporations from around the world have returned to do business in South Africa.

In the 1990s, the fastest growth was in shareholder resolutions urging more corporate sensitivity to the environment. The biggest corporate target in this area has been Exxon Corporation, whose March 1989 *Valdez* oil spill fouled the Alaska coastline. Other environmental issues that have appeared as shareholder resolutions address global warming of the ozone layer, overcutting of the rain forests in Brazil, and saving the spotted owl in the Northwest. Shareholder resolutions promoting environmental concerns are expected to continue to increase in the future.

Several new themes have emerged as well. Ever since the Securities and Exchange Commission (SEC), which oversees what resolutions can be included in proxy statements, reversed an earlier position and has now held that cigarette smoking is an area in which shareholders are entitled to vote, resolutions opposing tobacco products are appearing in proxy statements. These resolutions urge cigarette manufacturers, such as Philip Morris Company and American Brands, to quit producing cigarettes and media companies to quit advertising them. Such resolutions are expected to increase in the future.

Other recent shareholder resolutions deal with proposals to prohibit animal testing by companies, place a moratorium on nuclear weapons and a ban on the use of nuclear power, and dismantle antitakeover devices.

Most shareholder resolutions have a slim chance of being enacted because large-scale investors usually support management. They can, however, cause a corporation to change the way it does business. For example, to avoid the adverse publicity such issues can create, some corporations voluntarily adopt the changes contained in shareholder proposals. Others negotiate settlements with the sponsors of resolutions to get the measures off the agenda before the annual shareholders meetings.

Furthermore, shareholder resolutions are no longer just the bailiwick of individual or eccentric shareholders. Many state, municipal, and private pension funds now advocate socially responsible investing. These funds, which own billions of dollars of stock in American companies, are flexing their muscles and sponsoring shareholder resolutions to protect the environment, promote ethics, and curtail the greed of corporate managers.

1. Do you think shareholder proposals cause companies to act more socially responsible? Explain.
2. Should investors be socially conscious when making investments? Why or why not?

MERGERS AND ACQUISITIONS

Corporations may agree to friendly acquisitions or combinations of one another. This may be by merger, consolidation, share exchange, or sale of assets. Each of these types of combinations is discussed in the following paragraphs.

Mergers

A **merger** occurs when one corporation is absorbed into another corporation and ceases to exist. The corporation that continues to exist is called the *surviving corporation*. The other is called the *merged corporation* [RMBCA § 11.01]. The surviving corporation gains all the rights, privileges, powers, duties, obligations, and liabilities of the merged corporation. Title to property owned by the merged corporation transfers to the surviving corporation without formality or deeds. The shareholders of the merged corporation receive stock or securities of the surviving corporation or other consideration as provided in the plan of merger.

Suppose, for example, that Corporation A and Corporation B merge and it is agreed that Corporation A will absorb Corporation B. Corporation A is the surviving corporation. Corporation B is the merged corporation. A symbolic representation of this merger is A + B = A (see Exhibit 39.1).

Business Brief
Mergers, consolidations, share exchanges, and sale of assets are *friendly* in nature. That is, both corporations have agreed to the combination of corporations or acquisition of assets.

merger
Occurs when one corporation is absorbed into another corporation and ceases to exist.

Business Brief
In 1995, Chase Manhattan Bank and Chemical Bank merged. Chase Manhattan Bank was the surviving name in this $10-billion merger.

*E*XHIBIT 39.1   *Example of a Merger*

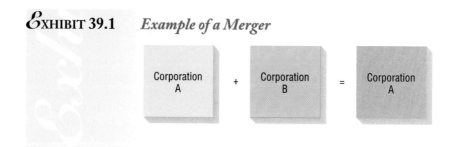

Consolidations

consolidation

Occurs when two or more corporations combine to form an entirely new corporation.

A **consolidation** occurs when two or more corporations combine to form an entirely new corporation (i.e., there is no surviving corporation). The new corporation is called the *consolidated corporation*, and the articles of incorporation of the new corporation replace the articles of incorporation of the component corporations.

Consider This Example   Corporation A and Corporation B consolidate to form a new organization called Corporation C. A symbolic representation of this combination is A + B = C (see Exhibit 39.2).

*E*XHIBIT 39.2   *Example of a Consolidation*

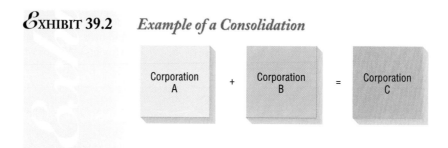

The new corporation accedes to all the rights, privileges, powers, duties, obligations, and liabilities of the constituent corporations. Title to property owned by the component corporations transfers to the new corporation without any formality. The shareholders receive stock or other securities in the consolidated corporation or other agreed-upon consideration.

Today, consolidations are not used very often because it is generally advantageous for one of the corporations to survive. The Revised Model Business Corporation Act (RMBCA) has deleted all references to consolidations.

Share Exchanges

share exchange

When one corporation acquires all the shares of another corporation and both corporations retain their separate legal existence.

One corporation can also acquire all the shares of another corporation through a **share exchange**. In a share exchange, both corporations retain their separate legal existence. After the exchange, one corporation (*parent corporation*) owns all of the shares of the other corporation (*subsidiary corporation*) [RMBCA § 11.02]. (See Exhibit 39.3.) Such exchanges are often used to create holding company arrangements (e.g., bank or insurance holding companies).

Exhibit 39.3 *Example of a Share Exchange*

Consider This Example Suppose Corporation H is a bank holding company that wishes to acquire First Bank. Assume that Corporation H offers to exchange its shares for those of First Bank and that First Bank's shareholders approve of the transaction. After the share exchange, Corporation H is the parent corporation, and First Bank is the wholly owned subsidiary of Corporation H.

Required Approvals for a Merger

An ordinary merger or share exchange requires (1) the recommendation of the board of directors of each corporation and (2) an affirmative vote of the majority of shares of each corporation that is entitled to vote [RMBCA § 11.03]. The articles of incorporation or corporate bylaws can require the approval of a *supramajority*, such as 80 percent of the voting shares.

The approval of the surviving corporation's shareholders is not required if the merger or share exchange increases the number of voting shares of the surviving corporation by 20 percent or less [RMBCA § 11.03(g)].

The approved *articles of merger or share exchange* must be filed with the secretary of state. The state normally issues a *certificate of merger or share exchange* to the surviving corporation after all the formalities are met and the requisite fees are paid [RMBCA § 11.05].

If one corporation (called the *parent corporation*) owns 90 percent or more of the outstanding stock of another corporation (known as the *subsidiary corporation*), a **short-form merger** procedure may be followed to merge the two corporations. The short-form merger procedure is simpler than an ordinary merger because neither the approval of the shareholders of either corporation nor the approval of the board of directors of the subsidiary corporation is needed. All that is required is the approval of the board of directors of the parent corporation [RMBCA § 11.04].

Sale or Lease of Assets

A corporation may sell, lease, or otherwise dispose of all or substantially all of its property in other than the usual and regular course of business. Such a sale or lease transaction requires (1) the recommendation of the board of directors and (2) an affirmative vote of the majority of the shares of the selling or leasing corporation that is entitled to vote (unless a greater vote is required) [RMBCA § 12.02]. This rule prevents the board of directors from selling all or most of the assets of the corporation without shareholder approval.

Business Brief

An ordinary merger or share exchange requires (1) the recommendation of the board of directors of each corporation and (2) an affirmative vote of the majority of shares of each corporation that is entitled to vote.

short-form merger

A merger between a parent corporation and a subsidiary corporation that does not require the vote of the shareholders of either corporation or the board of directors of the subsidiary corporation.

Business Brief

Approval of the selling or leasing corporation's shareholders is required for the sale, lease, or disposition of all or substantially all of a corporation's property not in the usual and regular course of business.

E-Commerce & Internet Law

THE TELECOMMUNICATIONS MEGAMERGER: MCI + SPRINT

e-biz

Move over AT&T. AT&T, the world's largest telecommunications company, has a new challenger—WorldCom—which is the combination of MCI WorldCom and Sprint Corp. In October 1999, the two companies announced their proposed merger, which is the largest corporate merger in history, with MCI paying $115 billion in stock to Sprint shareholders. The merger will create the second largest telecommunications company next to AT&T. The new company's stated goal is to unseat AT&T as the largest company.

The MCI and Sprint merger is synergistic. MCI provides a broad base of telecom services, including long-distance, cable, and Internet access. Sprint, on the other hand, is a leader in wireless communications, an area that MCI wanted desperately to be in. The new WorldCom can offer a bundle of telecom services to both businesses and consumers. The vision of the new company is to assemble an unsurpassed digital network of telecommunications services. WorldCom has pinned its hopes on several technologies. The first is providing high-speed digital lines to business and residential users. Another is expanding wireless technology that gives WorldCom a direct link to customers. And finally, the company is banking on the explosion of broadband technology, called MMDS (for Multichannel Multipoint Distribution Technology). The merged MCI and Sprint have combined to increase technology offerings to customers while saving costs.

The Federal Communications Commission (FCC), a federal administrative agency, must approve all telecommunications mergers, including the MCI Sprint megadeal. After the merger, two companies—AT&T and WorldCom—control 85 percent of the long-distance telephone market in the United States. WorldCom itself controls over 24 percent of the consumer long-distance market, 50 percent of the wholesale telephone market (hawking telephone usage to resellers), and 45 percent of the U.S. access points to the Internet. The FCC's usual approach is to require such large merging companies to shed some of their businesses as part of the approval process.

The colossal MCI and Sprint merger is only the largest of hundreds of combinations of telecommunications, computer software, and Internet companies. MCI itself was an outgrowth of over 60 mergers prior to the Sprint deal. The trend toward technology mergers will continue in the future as the lines between all types of telephone, computer, Internet, and other high-tech industries blur.

DISSENTING SHAREHOLDER APPRAISAL RIGHTS

dissenting shareholder appraisal rights

Shareholders who object to a proposed merger, share exchange, or sale or lease of all or substantially all of the property of a corporation have a right to have their shares valued by the court and receive cash payment of this value from the corporation.

Specific shareholders sometimes object to a proposed ordinary or short-form merger, share exchange, or sale or lease of all or substantially all of the property of the corporation, even though the transaction received the required approvals. Objecting shareholders are provided a statutory right to dissent and obtain payment of the fair value of their shares [RMBCA § 13.02]. This is referred to as a **dissenting shareholder appraisal right** (or **appraisal right**). Shareholders have no other recourse unless the transaction is unlawful or fraudulent.

The corporation must notify shareholders of the existence of their appraisal rights before the transaction can be voted on [RMBCA § 13.20]. To obtain appraisal rights, a dissenting shareholder must (1) deliver written notice of his or her intent to demand payment of his or her shares to the corporation before the vote is taken and (2) not vote his or her shares in favor of the proposed action [RMBCA § 13.21]. The shareholder must deposit his or her share certificates with the corporation [RMBCA § 13.23]. Shareholders who fail to comply with these statutory procedures lose their appraisal rights.

As soon as the proposed action is taken, the corporation must pay each dissenting shareholder the amount the corporation estimates to be the fair value of his or her shares, plus accrued interest [RMBCA § 13.25]. If the dissenter is dissatisfied, the corporation must petition the court to determine the fair value of the shares [RMBCA § 13.30].

After a hearing, the court will issue an order declaring the fair value of the shares. Appraisers may be appointed to help in determining this value. Court costs and appraisal fees usually are paid by the corporation. However, the court can assess these costs against the dissenters if they acted arbitrarily, vexatiously, or in bad faith [RMBCA § 13.31].

The court had to determine the appraisal value of a company's shares in the following case.

Business Brief

The court must determine the "fair value" of the shares of dissenting shareholders. Courts usually use appraisers to assist in determining this value.

In the Matter of the Appraisal of Shell Oil Company

607 A.2d 1213 (1992)
Supreme Court of Delaware

CASE 39.1

FACTS

Royal Dutch Petroleum Company (Royal Dutch), a large natural resource conglomerate, owned 94.6 percent of the stock of Shell Oil Company (Shell). The remaining shares of Shell were held by minority, public shareholders. On June 7, 1985, Royal Dutch effectuated a short-form merger with Shell and offered $60 cash per share for the outstanding shares of Shell it did not own. After the merger was complete, 1,005,001 shares had not accepted the offer and qualified for appraisal rights. The Delaware Chancery Court conducted an appraisal hearing. The parties offered extensive evidence through expert witnesses. These experts gave the following estimated per share value for Shell's shares:

Valuation Method	Shell's Expert	Shareholders' Expert
Liquidation value	$57	$100
Comparative value	$60	$106
Market value	$43–$45	$92–$143

Liquidation value was the estimated value if Shell were dissolved and its assets sold. Comparative value was an estimate based on a price reflected by prices in similar transactions in the oil and gas industry. Market value was an estimated price that Shell shares would sell for without the effect of merger speculation.

The chancery court determined that the fair value was $71.20 per share. It further held that the shareholders were entitled to 10 percent interest on that amount from the date of the merger to the date of payment. Both parties appealed.

ISSUE

What price should Shell be required to pay its minority shareholders who demanded appraisal rights?

IN THE LANGUAGE OF THE COURT

Walsh, Justice After reviewing the valuation evidence in its effort to fix the fair value of Shell stock on the date of the merger, the Court of Chancery expressed some dissatisfaction with the lack of objectivity in the presentations. The court noted that it was "obvious that the dynamics of this litigation and the economic interest of the parties contributed to the wide differences in the expert opinions." The appraisal quest at the Court of Chancery level admits of a broad latitude.

At the appellate level, when this Court reviews a Court of Chancery determination, we impart a "high level of deference" to that court's findings. Recognizing that the Court of Chancery, over time, has developed an expertise in cases of this type, we will accept the court's findings if supported by the record and the product of an orderly and logical deductive process. Valuation is an art rather than a science. So too is the weighing of evidence in the appraisal process. More than anything else, this emphasizes the broad discretion which the Court of Chancery must have in fixing values. The Vice Chancellor's conclusions are amply supported by the record and the product of an orderly and logical deductive process. We therefore decline to disturb them.

DECISION AND REMEDY

The Supreme Court of Delaware affirmed the award.

Case Questions

Critical Legal Thinking Should the law provide dissenting shareholder appraisal rights? Why or why not?

Ethics Do you think expert witnesses act objectively?

Business Application Is there a temptation for a company to "low-ball" the cash-out price offered to shareholders in a merger? Explain.

*T*ENDER OFFERS

tender offer

An offer that an acquirer makes directly to a target corporation's shareholders in an effort to acquire the target corporation.

target corporation

The corporation that is proposed to be acquired in a tender offer situation.

tender offeror

The party that makes a tender offer.

Recall that a merger, a consolidation, a share exchange, and a sale of assets all require the approval of the board of directors of the corporation whose assets or shares are to be acquired. If the board of directors of the target corporation does not agree to the merger or acquisition, the acquiring corporation can make a **tender offer** for the shares directly to the shareholders of the **target corporation**. The shareholders each make an individual decision about whether to sell their shares to the **tender offeror** (see Exhibit 39.4). Such offers are often referred to as *hostile tender offers*.

The tender offeror's board of directors must approve the offer, although the shareholders do not have to approve. The offer can be made for all or a portion of the shares of the target corporation.

In a tender offer, the tendering corporation and the target corporation retain their separate legal status. A successful tender offer is sometimes followed, however, by a merger of the two corporations.

*E*XHIBIT 39.4   *Illustration of a Tender Offer*

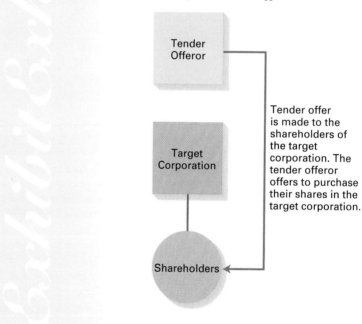

The Williams Act

Prior to 1968, tender offers were not federally regulated. However, securities that were issued in conjunction with such offers had to be registered with the SEC or qualify for an exemption from registration. Tender offers made with cash were not subject to any federal disclosure requirements.

In 1968, Congress enacted the **Williams Act** as an amendment to the Securities Exchange Act of 1934.[2] This act specifically regulates all tender offers, whether they are made with securities, cash, or other consideration, and establishes certain disclosure requirements and antifraud provisions.

Williams Act

An amendment to the Securities Exchange Act of 1934 made in 1968 that specifically regulates all tender offers.

Contemporary Business Application

LEVERAGED BUYOUTS

A raider or other party making a tender offer usually does not have the hundreds of millions or billions of dollars necessary to purchase the stock from the shareholders of the target corporation. Instead, a raider relies heavily on the fact that the money can be raised from creditors (e.g., banks). Many tender offers are not possible without such loans. Because of the use of borrowed money, these acquisitions are called **leveraged buyouts** or **LBOs**.

A typical LBO works as follows. The raider identifies a potential target and then contacts a large commercial bank and an investment banker. The commercial bank, for a large fee, agrees to supply some of the funds necessary to make the initial acquisition. The bank will be paid off at a later date, after the acquisition is successful. The funds to pay back the bank usually come from the raider selling off some of the assets of the target corporation. These bank loans are often referred to as *bridge loans*.

Most of the rest of the purchase price comes from money raised by the investment banker by selling **junk bonds** of the acquiring firm to investors. Junk bonds are nothing more than risky bonds that pay a higher rate of interest than normal corporate bonds. Generally, the buyers are banks, savings and loan associations, pension funds, investment pools, and wealthy individuals. The investment banker is paid a huge fee by the raider for raising this money.

With the money in hand—or at least the pledge that the money will be there when it is needed—the raider commences its hostile tender offer for the shares of the target corporation. When the desired number of shares are tendered, the tender offer is closed using the money borrowed from the bank and raised through the sale of junk bonds. The raider's investment in the tender offer usually amounts to 5 percent or 10 percent of the total.

After the tender offer is completed, the tender offeror—which is usually a shell corporation that is saddled with huge debts (i.e., the bank loans and junk bonds)—merges with the target corporation. The target corporation has all of the assets (e.g., brand names) and income. The resulting entity is a highly leveraged corporation. Its capital structure consists of a low amount of equity and huge amounts of debt.

The raider usually has to sell off some of the assets to pay the bank loans, fees, and other expenses of the takeover. Some LBOs are successful, but others run into problems because the income from the remaining assets is not sufficient to pay the interest on the junk bonds.

Tender Offer Rules

The Williams Act does not require the tender offeror to notify either the management of the target company or the SEC until the offer is made.[3] Detailed information regarding the terms, conditions, and other information concerning the tender offer must be disclosed at that time.

Tender offers are governed by the following rules:

1. The offer cannot be closed before 20 business days after the commencement of the tender offer.
2. The offer must be extended for 10 business days if the tender offeror increases the number of shares that it will take or the price that it will pay for the shares.
3. The **fair price rule** stipulates that any increase in price paid for shares tendered must be offered to all shareholders, even those who have previously tendered their shares.
4. The **pro rata rule** holds that the shares must be purchased on a pro rata basis if too many shares are tendered.

A shareholder who tenders his or her shares has the absolute right to withdraw them at any time prior to the closing of the tender offer. The dissenting shareholder appraisal rights are not available.

fair price rule

A rule that says any increase in price paid for shares tendered must be offered to all shareholders, even those who have previously tendered their shares.

pro rata rule

A rule that says shares must be purchased on a pro rata basis if too many shares are tendered.

Antifraud Provision

Section 14(e)

A provision of the Williams Act that prohibits fraudulent, deceptive, and manipulative practices in connection with a tender offer.

Section 14(e) of the Williams Act prohibits fraudulent, deceptive, and manipulative practices in connection with a tender offer.[4] Violations of this section may result in civil charges brought by the SEC or criminal charges brought by the Justice Department. The courts have implied a private civil cause of action under Section 14(e). Therefore, a shareholder who has been injured by a violation of Section 14(e) can sue the wrongdoer for damages.

Ethical Perspective

GOLDEN PARACHUTES: WHEN IS THE LANDING TOO CUSHY?

The term *golden parachute* has been coined to describe the large severance payments received by top executives when they leave their employ at a corporation. They are called "golden" because of their lucrative nature. They are called "parachutes" because they are "pulled" when an executive leaves or is fired from a company that has been taken over.

Golden parachutes—formally called change-in-control severance agreement plans—are long-term employment contracts. They usually provide that all cash payments and stock options due under the contract become due and payable immediately upon the occurrence of the trigger—the takeover of the company.

For example, a company enters into a three-year employment contract with its president and agrees to pay a $1-million salary annually and grant options to purchase 10,000 shares of the company stock at $10 per share. The contract includes a golden parachute clause in the event of a takeover. Suppose the company is taken over in a $15-per-share tender offer. The president can "pull" his or her parachute and demand $3 million in salary as well as making $1.5-million profit by exercising his stock options.

Two benefits of golden parachutes are often cited. First, they are necessary to lure talented executives and keep them from looking for other positions when a takeover of the company is pending. Second, they act as an antitakeover device, thus protecting the company from

hostile takeovers. Both of these reasons have been challenged as a coverup for the real reason for golden parachutes: top executives' greed.

Golden parachutes are often criticized by lower-level managers and rank-and-file workers who complain that management can walk away in comfort after a takeover, whereas they are left hanging out to dry. To address these concerns, some companies have added "silver parachutes" to protect lower-level managers and "tin parachutes" to protect wage-earning workers in case of a takeover. As the names indicate, the compensation paid under these plans is much lower than that paid under golden parachutes.

In the past, the SEC has held that golden parachutes need only be approved by a company's outside directors, rather than by a vote of the shareholders. In a recent decision involving a proposed golden parachute to be installed by Transamerica Corporation, the SEC changed its position and ruled that the company must submit the plan for shareholder vote. This decision sends a signal that golden parachutes will receive closer scrutiny in the future than they have in the past.

1. Do you think top executives' compensation is too high? Explain.
2. Are golden parachutes a legitimate compensation scheme? Or are they an egregious example of management greed?

Fighting a Tender Offer

The incumbent management of many targets of hostile tender offers does not want the corporation taken over by the tender offeror. Therefore, it engages in varied activities to impede and defeat the tender offer.

Hostile takeovers are usually not welcomed by the target company. Companies that are possible targets of hostile takeovers often implement antitakeover strategies and tactics, such as adopting "poison pills," to try to thwart any possible takeover.

Defensive Strategies and Tactics

Some of the strategies and tactics used by incumbent management in defending against hostile tender offers are described as follows:

1. **Persuasion of Shareholders** Media campaigns are organized to convince shareholders that the tender offer is not in their best interests.
2. **Delaying Lawsuits** Lawsuits are filed alleging that the tender offer violates securities laws, antitrust laws, or other laws. The time gained by this tactic gives management the opportunity to erect or implement other defensive maneuvers.
3. **Selling a Crown Jewel** Such assets as profitable divisions or real estate that are particularly attractive to outside interests are sold. This tactic makes the target corporation less attractive to the tender offeror.
4. **Adopting a Poison Pill** Poison pills are defensive strategies that are built into the target corporation's articles of incorporation, corporate bylaws, or contracts and leases. For example, contracts and leases may provide that they will expire if the ownership of the corporation changes hands. These tactics make the target corporation more expensive to the tender offeror.
5. **White Knight Merger** White knight mergers are mergers with friendly parties, that is, parties that promise to leave the target corporation and/or its management intact.
6. **Pac-Man (or Reverse) Tender Offer** The target corporation makes a tender offer on the tender offeror. Thus, the target corporation tries to purchase the tender offeror.
7. **Issuing Additional Stock** Placing additional stock on the market increases the number of outstanding shares that the tender offeror must purchase in order to gain control of the target corporation.
8. **Creating an Employee Stock Ownership Plan (ESOP)** A company creates an ESOP and places a certain percentage of the corporation's securities (e.g., 15 percent) in it. The ESOP is then expected to vote the shares it owns against the potential acquirer in a proxy contest or tender offer because the beneficiaries (i.e., the employees) have a vested interest in keeping the company intact.

Business Brief
Target corporations initiate and implement a variety of defensive maneuvers and tactics to defend against unwanted hostile tender offers.

crown jewel
A valuable asset of the target corporation's that the tender offeror particularly wants to acquire in the tender offer.

pac-man tender offer
Occurs when a corporation that is the target of a tender offer makes a *reverse tender offer* for the stock of the tender offeror.

9. **Flip-Over and Flip-In Rights Plans** These plans provide that existing shareholders of the target corporation may convert their shares for a greater amount (e.g., twice the value) of shares of the acquiring corporation (*flip-over rights plan*) or debt securities of the target company (*flip-in rights plan*). Rights plans are triggered if the acquiring firm acquires a certain percentage (e.g., 20 percent) of the shares of the target corporation. They make it more expensive for the acquiring firm to take over the target corporation.

10. **Greenmail and Standstill Agreements** Most tender offerors purchase a block of stock in the target corporation before making an offer. Occasionally, the tender offeror will agree to give up its tender offer and agree not to purchase any further shares if the target corporation agrees to buy back the stock at a premium over fair market value. This payment is called **greenmail**. The agreement of the tender offeror to abandon its tender offer and not purchase any additional stock is called a *standstill agreement*.

greenmail

The purchase by a target corporation of its stock from an actual or perceived tender offeror at a premium.

There are many other strategies and tactics that target companies initiate and implement in defending against a tender offer.

Contemporary Business Application

TIME-WARNER-PARAMOUNT: JUST SAY NO!

Time, Inc. (Time), is a publishing company that publishes *People, Money, Sports Illustrated*, and other magazines and newspapers; it owns cable television and pay television channels. Warner Communications, Inc. (Warner), is a communications company that produces and sells movies, television programs, and records, and owns cable stations. In 1989, after years of negotiations, Time and Warner agreed to a merger. Based on the agreed-upon ratio of exchange, Time shareholders were to receive $120 in stock of the new Time/Warner for each share of Time stock they owned. The shareholders meetings to vote on the merger were set.

Paramount Communications, Inc. (Paramount), is a film production and distribution company. For years, it had been looking for an acquisition in the publishing and communications industry. Two weeks before the Time shareholders were to vote on the planned merger with Warner, Paramount announced a hostile tender offer for Time's shares at $175 per share.

Time, which was obviously going to lose the shareholder vote, canceled the proposed merger with Warner and made a friendly tender offer to acquire 50 percent of Warner's stock for $70 per share. This acquisition would make Time too big for Paramount to take over. In addition, the vote of Time shareholders would not be required.

Time had other defensive maneuvers in place as well. These plans consisted of flip-over and flip-in rights plans that would permit Time shareholders to exchange their Time shares for approximately twice the value of the tender offeror's securities if the poison pills were removed by Time's management before the tender offer was completed.

Paramount sued Time, alleging that Time management's refusal to dismantle the poison pills and put Time on the block violated their fiduciary duty. In defense, Time argued that the merger of Time and Warner was in the best interests of Time shareholders over the long run. In other words, the long-term benefits of the combination of Time and Warner and their cultures would create synergism that would pay off in the future; Paramount's tender offer offered only one-time short-term profits.

The Delaware court, applying the business judgment rule, sided with Time. The court held that the projected long-term benefits to Time shareholders justified Time management's refusal to dismantle the poison pills. The court stated: "The corporation law does not operate on the theory that directors are obligated to follow the wishes of a majority of shares. In fact, directors, not shareholders, are charged with the duty to manage the firm." Thus, incumbent management of a target corporation can "just say no" to a tender offer as long as it can show that it is acting in the long-term interests of the shareholders. [*Paramount Communications, Inc. v. Time, Inc.*, 571 A.2d 1140 (Del. 1990)]

Business Judgment Rule

The board of directors of a corporation owe a **fiduciary duty** to the corporation and its shareholders. This duty, which requires the board to act carefully and honestly, is truly tested when a tender offer is made for the stock of the company. That is because shareholders and others then ask whether the board's initiation and implementation or defensive measures were taken in the best interests of the shareholders or to protect the board's own interests and jobs.

The legality of defensive strategies is examined using the **business judgment rule**. This rule protects the decisions of a board of directors that acts on an informed basis, in good faith, and in the honest belief that the action taken was in the best interests of the corporation and its shareholders.[5] In the context of a tender offer, the defensive measures chosen by the board must be reasonable in relation to the threat posed.[6]

fiduciary duty
The duty the directors of a corporation owe to act carefully and honestly when acting on behalf of the corporation.

business judgment rule
A rule that protects the decisions of the board of directors, who act on an informed basis, in good faith, and in the honest belief that the action taken was in the best interests of the corporation and its shareholders.

Contemporary Business Application

THE SAGA OF PARAMOUNT-VIACOM-QVC

In the past, the Delaware courts generally sided with the management of target companies in suits involving hostile raids. In most of these cases, the Delaware courts upheld defensive maneuvers taken by target companies to fend off unwanted suitors. This long line of cases ended with a recent Delaware court decision concerning the takeover of Paramount Communications, Inc.

It all started on September 12, 1993, when Viacom, Inc. (Viacom), and Paramount Communications, Inc. (Paramount), announced a friendly merger agreement. Basically, Viacom and its chairman and largest shareholder, billionaire Sumner Redstone, were taking over Paramount. Viacom controlled national cable networks, including Showtime and The Movie Channel. Paramount's holdings included Paramount Pictures, the Simon & Schuster publishing house, Madison Square Garden, the New York Knicks basketball team, and the New York Rangers hockey team. Both sides touted the synergism of the marriage of these two companies into a media colossus.

There was only one hitch to this merger: Five days later QVC Network, Inc. (QVC), a rival cable operator led by Barry Diller, made a $90 per share hostile bid for Paramount that topped Viacom's offer. QVC owned the Home Shopping Network. Paramount's board of directors, which was dominated by its chairman, Martin Davis, did not want to be taken over by QVC. Paramount's board adopted the following antitakeover strategies:

1. A **no-shop provision** whereby the Paramount board guaranteed Viacom that it would not investigate QVC's offer or meet with QVC.

2. A **lockup option** that granted Viacom (but not QVC) the right to buy 23.7 million shares of Paramount at $69.14 each if a bidder other than Viacom bought Paramount. (This would cost a competing bidder almost $400 million.)

3. An agreement to drop certain **poison pill** defenses as to Viacom but not as to QVC. (Thus, Viacom could pursue its acquisition of Paramount, but QVC could not.)

QVC sued Paramount in Delaware Chancery Court, alleging that these tactics violated the Paramount board of directors' fiduciary duties to the corporation and its shareholders. To many observers' surprise, the Delaware court agreed with QVC. The court ruled that the "no-shop" provision was unlawful, stating that Paramount directors "had a duty to continue their search for the best value available to shareholders." The court also invalidated the "lockup option" stock purchase plan as being an illegal transfer of corporate wealth to Viacom at the expense of Paramount shareholders.

The chancery court held that the poison pills Paramount had erected must be dismantled for QVC (and any other bidder) as they had been for Viacom. The court also ordered that Paramount be put on the block and auctioned to the highest bidder. The Delaware Supreme Court affirmed this decision.

Both sides lined up their lawyers, investment banks, and commercial banks, as well as enlisting other companies, to assist them in the bidding process. Most significantly, Viacom merged with Blockbuster Entertainment, a national video rental chain, in making its bid. On February 15, 1994, after escalating bids by both sides, the five-month

(box continues)

saga ended when Viacom won the right to buy Paramount with a $10-billion-plus bid.

When it was all over, Sumner Redstone of Viacom toasted: "Here's to us that won." Barry Diller of QVC tersely concluded: "They won. We lost. Next." Only time will tell who the real winners and losers are in the Paramount takeover battle. The price of Viacom's stock plummeted on the news of the merger. Redstone has to cope with an unwieldy conglomerate comprised of Viacom, Paramount, and Blockbuster, where the group's combined debt of $10 billion must now be serviced. QVC walks away virtually debt-free and having forced Viacom to pay $2 billion more than its original friendly merger offer for Paramount. QVC will look for other multimedia companies with which to combine. Martin Davis of Paramount walked away from the deal $117 million richer.

State Antitakeover Statutes

state antitakeover statutes
Statutes enacted by state legislatures that protect corporations incorporated in or doing business in the state from hostile takeovers.

Many states have enacted **antitakeover statutes** that are aimed at protecting corporations that are either incorporated in or do business within the state from hostile takeovers. Many of these state statutes have been challenged as being unconstitutional because they violate the Williams Act and the Commerce and Supremacy clauses of the U.S. Constitution.

In the following case, the U.S. Supreme Court held that a state antitakeover law was constitutional.

CTS Corp. v. Dynamics Corp.
481 U.S. 69, 107 S.Ct. 1637 (1987)
United States Supreme Court

CASE 39.2

FACTS
On March 4, 1986, Indiana enacted the Control Share Acquisitions Chapter (Act). The Act covers corporations that (1) are incorporated in Indiana and have at least 100 shareholders, (2) have their primary place of business or substantial assets in Indiana, and (3) have either 10 percent of their shareholders in Indiana or 10 percent of their shares owned by Indiana residents. The Act provides that if any entity acquires 20 percent or more of the voting shares of a covered corporation, the acquirer loses voting rights to these shares unless a majority of the disinterested shareholders of the acquired corporation vote to restore such voting rights. The acquirer can request that such vote be held within 50 days after its acquisition. If the shareholders do not restore the voting rights, the target corporation may redeem the shares from the acquirer at fair market value, but it is not required to do so.

On March 10, 1986, Dynamics Corporation of America (Dynamics), a Delaware corporation, announced a tender offer for 1 million shares of CTS Corporation (CTS), an Indiana corporation covered by the act. The purchase of these shares would have brought Dynamics's voting interest in CTS to 27.5 percent. Dynamics sued in federal court, alleging that Indiana's Control Share Acquisitions Chapter was unconstitutional. The federal district court held for Dynamics. The court of appeals affirmed. CTS appealed.

ISSUE
Does the Indiana Control Share Acquisitions Chapter conflict with the Williams Act or violate the Commerce Clause of the U.S. Constitution by unduly burdening interstate commerce?

IN THE LANGUAGE OF THE COURT
Powell, Justice   The first question in this case is whether the Williams Act preempts the Indiana Act. As we have stated frequently, absent an explicit indication by Congress of an intent to preempt state law, a state statute is preempted only where compliance with both federal and state regulations is a physical impossibility or where the state law stands as an obstacle to the accomplishment and execution of the full purposes and objectives of Congress. Because it is entirely possible for entities to comply with both the Williams and the Indiana acts, the state statute can be preempted only if it frustrates the purposes of the federal law.

The statute now before the court protects the independent shareholder against both of the contending parties. Thus, the act furthers a basic purpose of the Williams Act, placing investors on an equal footing with the takeover bidder. The Indiana Act operates on the assumption, implicit in the Williams Act, that independent shareholders faced with tender offers often are at a disadvantage. By allowing such shareholders to vote as a group, the act protects them from the coercive aspects of some tender offers. If, for example, shareholders believe that a successful tender offer will be followed by a purchase of nontendering shares at a depressed price [in a second tier merger], individual shareholders may tender their shares—even if they doubt the tender offer is in the corporation's best interest—to protect themselves from being forced to sell their shares at a depressed price. In such a situation under the Indiana Act, the shareholders as a group, acting in the corporation's best interest, could reject the offer although individual shareholders might be inclined to accept it. The desire of the Indiana legislature to protect shareholders of Indiana corporations from this type of coercive offer does not conflict with the Williams Act. Rather, it furthers the federal policy of investor protection.

DECISION AND REMEDY

The U.S. Supreme Court held that the Indiana Control Share Acquisitions Chapter neither conflicted with the Williams Act nor violated the Commerce Clause of the U.S. Constitution. Reversed.

Case Questions

Critical Legal Thinking Should states be permitted to adopt antitakeover statutes? Why or why not? Whom do you think these statutes actually protect?

Ethics Is it ethical for a target corporation's management to assert a state antitakeover statute?

Business Application What are the economic effects of a state antitakeover statute?

International Perspective

THE EXON-FLORIO LAW: REGULATING FOREIGN ACQUISITIONS OF U.S. BUSINESSES

Until 1988, foreign investors had virtually the same rights to acquire businesses located in the United States as domestic investors. However, the **Exon-Florio Law** of 1988 [50 U.S.C. 2170], as amended by the **Byrd-Exon amendment** of 1992 [P.L. 102–484, Sec. 837], mandates the President of the United States to suspend, prohibit, or dismantle the acquisition of U.S. businesses by foreign investors if there is credible evidence that the foreign investor might take action that threatens to impair the "national security."

Exon-Florio is administered through the **Committee on Foreign Investment in the United States (CFIUS)**, an interagency committee that is chaired by the U.S. Treasury Department. The provisions apply to mergers, acquisitions, takeovers, stock purchases, asset purchases, joint ventures, and proxy contests that would result in foreign control of U.S. businesses engaged in interstate commerce in the United States. The U.S. business could be a corporation, a partnership, a sole proprietorship, or another business. The size of the U.S. operation is irrelevant.

Exon-Florio and the regulations adopted thereunder do not define the term *national security*. The Treasury Department has interpreted the term broadly to include not only defense contractors but also other businesses. The following factors must be considered in conducting a national security analysis of a proposed foreign U.S. investment:

1. The domestic production needed for defense requirements for national security.

2. The potential effect of a transaction on the international technological leadership of the United States in areas affecting national security.

3. The potential effect of a transaction on sales of military goods to any country that is identified as supporting terrorism.

The term *control* includes any investment exceeding 10 percent ownership in a U.S. business by a foreign investor. The Exon-Florio provision does not apply to "greenfield" investments by foreigners—that is, start-ups of new businesses.

When a foreign investor proposes to acquire an interest in a U.S. business, it may voluntarily notify CFIUS of its intention. CFIUS must commence its investigation within 30 days after receipt of written notification of the transaction. The investigation must be completed within 45 days after receipt of such notice, and the President must announce a decision to take no action no later than 15 days after completion of the investigation. If the President finds a threat to the national security, the acquisition may be prohibited. If the foreign investor chooses not to notify CFIUS and completes the acquisition, it remains indefinitely subject to divestment if the President subsequently determines that the acquisition threatens the national security. The President's decision is not subject to judicial review.

Proponents of Exon-Florio argue that the law is needed to protect U.S. interests in vital industries. Critics allege that the law could discourage foreign investment in the United States.

Working the Web

e-biz

Law firm Web sites vary in form and content. Some are a simple page listing the specialties of the firm and a link to the firm's e-mail address. Others are more developed and elaborate. Some contain general legal information and links to other sources of information. Here are some law firm Web sites that have won numerous awards.

Brobeck, Phleger & Harrison This site directs new visitors to a virtual "receptionist" where they will find general information about the firm and a breakdown of what is available through the site.

Visit at **www.brobeck.com**

Satterlee, Stephens, Burke & Burke This site has pages devoted to immigration and cyberlaw. It contains attractive graphics and is easy to use.

Visit at **www.ssbb.com**

Procopio, Cory, Hargreaves & Savitch This Web site looks like a law firm with content organized in different rooms.

Visit at **www.procopio.com**

KuesterLaw This is one of the most comprehensive collections of technology resources on the Web, with original materials as well as links to other sites, all in an easy to navigate format.

Visit at **www.kuesterlaw.com**

The Tax Prophet This site combines snappy graphics with an abundance of content and a bit of humor to create one of the most popular legal sites on the Internet.

Visit at **www.taxprophet.com**

CYBER EXERCISES

1. On the Brobeck, Phleger & Harrison site, visit the Business Litigation Practice Area. Where does Kenneth J. King practice?

2. Where is the principal office of Satterlee, Stephens, Burke & Burke?

3. From the Procopio Web site, go to the law library. Browse the materials on corporate law.

4. What is the specialty of Jeffrey Kuester's firm?

5. In what newspaper does the Tax Prophet's columns appear?

*C*ASES AND *E*XERCISES

CRITICAL LEGAL THINKING CASES

39.1. Western Maryland Company (Western) was a timbering and mining concern. A substantial portion of its stock was owned by CSX Minerals (CSX), its parent corporation. The remaining shares were owned by several minority shareholders, including Sanford E. Lockspeiser. Western's stock was not publicly traded. In 1983, the board of directors of Western voted to merge the company with CSX. Western distributed a proxy statement to the minority shareholders that stated that CSX would vote for the merger and recommended approval of the merger by the other shareholders. The proxy materials disclosed Western's natural resource holdings in terms of acreage of minerals and timber. It also stated real property values as carried on the company's books, that is, a book value of $17.04 per share. It included an opinion of the First Boston Corporation, an investment banking firm, that the merger was fair to shareholders; First Boston did not undertake an independent evaluation of Western's physical assets. Lockspeiser sued, alleging that the proxy materials were misleading because they did not state tonnage of Western's coal reserves, timber holdings in board feet, and actual value of Western's assets. Did Lockspeiser state a claim for relief? [*Lockspeiser v. Western Maryland Company*, 768 F.2d 558 (4th Cir. 1985)]

39.2. The Medfield Corporation (Medfield) is a publicly held corporation engaged in operating hospitals and other health-care facilities. Medfield established March 1, 1974, as the date for its annual shareholders' meeting, at which time the board of directors would be elected. In its proxy statement, management proposed the incumbent slate of directors. A group known as the Medfield Shareholders Committee (Committee) nominated a rival slate of candidates and also solicited proxies. Medfield sent proxy solicitation material to shareholders that

1. Failed to disclose that Medfield had been overpaid more than $1.8 million by Blue Cross and this amount was due and owing Blue Cross.
2. Failed to disclose that Medicare funds were being withheld because of Medfield's nonpayment.
3. Failed to adequately disclose self-dealing by one of the directors with Medfield who owned part of a laboratory used by Medfield.
4. Failed to disclose that Medfield was attempting to sell two nursing homes.
5. Impugned the character, integrity, and personal reputation of one of the rival candidates by stating that he had previously been found liable for patent infringement when, in fact, the case had been reversed on appeal.

At the annual meeting, the incumbent slate of directors received 50 percent of the votes cast, against 44 percent of the insurgent slate of directors. The Gladwins, who own voting stock, sued to have the election overturned. Who wins? [*Gladwin v. Medfield Corporation*, 540 F.2d 1266 (5th Cir. 1976)]

39.3. The Fairchild Engine and Airplane Corporation (Fairchild) is a privately held corporation whose management proposed the incumbent slate of directors for election at its annual shareholders' meeting. An insurgent slate of directors challenged the incumbents for election to the board. After the solicitation of proxies and a hard-fought proxy contest, the insurgent slate of directors was elected. Evidence showed the proxy contest was waged over matters of corporate policy and for personal reasons. The old board of directors had spent $134,000 out of corporate funds to wage the proxy contest. The insurgents had spent $127,000 of their personal funds in their successful proxy contest and sought reimbursement from Fairchild for this amount. The payment of these expenses was ratified by a 16-to-1 majority vote of the stockholders. Mr. Rosenfeld, an attorney who owned 25 of the 2,300,000 outstanding shares of the corporation, filed an action to recover the amounts already paid by the corporation and to prevent any further payments of these expenses. Who wins? [*Rosenfeld v. Fairchild Engine and Airplane Corporation*, 128 N.E.2d 291 (N.Y.App. 1955)]

39.4. The Medical Committee for Human Rights (Committee) is a nonprofit corporation organized to advance concerns for human life. Committee received a gift of shares of Dow Chemical (Dow) stock. Dow manufactured napalm, a chemical defoliant that was used during the Vietnam conflict. Committee objected to the sale of napalm by Dow primarily because of its concerns for human life. Committee owned sufficient shares for a long enough time to propose a shareholders' resolution as long as it met the other requirements to propose such a resolution. Committee proposed that the following resolution be included in the proxy materials circulated by management for the 1969 annual shareholders' meeting:

> RESOLVED, *that the shareholders of the Dow Chemical Company request that the Board of Directors, in accordance with the law, consider the advisability of adopting a resolution setting forth an amendment to the composite certificate of incorporation of the Dow Chemical Company that the company shall not make napalm.*

Dow's management refused to include the requested resolution in its proxy materials. Committee sued, alleging that its resolution met the requirements to be included in the proxy materials. Who wins? [*Medical Committee for Human Rights v. Securities and Exchange Commission*, 432 F.2d 659 (D.C.Cir. 1970)]

39.5. During the last six months of 1980, the board of directors of Plant Industries, Inc. (Plant), under the guidance of Robert B. Bregman, the chief executive officer of the corporation, embarked on a course of action that resulted in the sale of several unprofitable subsidiaries. Bregman then engaged in a course of action to sell Plant National (Quebec) Ltd., a subsidiary that constituted Plant's entire Canadian operations. This was a profitable subsidiary that comprised over 50 percent of Plant's assets, sales, and profits. Do Plant's shareholders have to be accorded voting and appraisal rights regarding the sale of this subsidiary? [*Katz v. Bregman*, 431 A.2d 1274 (Del.Ch. 1981)]

39.6. Over a period of several years, the Curtiss-Wright Corporation (Curtiss-Wright) purchased 65 percent of the stock of Dorr-Oliver Incorporated (Dorr-Oliver). In early 1979, Curtiss-Wright's board of directors decided that a merger with Dorr-Oliver would be beneficial to Curtiss-Wright. The board voted to approve a merger of the two companies and to pay $23 per share to the stockholders of Dorr-Oliver. The Dorr-Oliver board and 80 percent of Dorr-Oliver's shareholders approved the merger. The merger became effective on May 31, 1979. John Bershad, a minority shareholder of Dorr-Oliver, voted against the merger, but thereafter tendered his 100 shares and received payment of $2,300. Bershad subsequently sued, alleging that the $23 per share paid to Dorr-Oliver shareholders was grossly inadequate. Can Bershad obtain minority shareholder appraisal rights? [*Bershad v. Curtiss-Wright Corporation*, 535 A.2d 840 (DE 1987)]

39.7. On October 30, 1981, Mobil Corporation (Mobil) made a tender offer to purchase up to 40 million outstanding common shares of stock in Marathon Oil Company (Marathon) for $85 per share in cash. It further stated its intentions to follow the purchase with a merger of the two companies. Mobil was primarily interested in acquiring Marathon's oil and mineral interests in certain properties, including the Yates Field. Marathon directors immediately held a board meeting and determined to find a white knight. Negotiations developed between Marathon and United States Steel Corporation (U.S. Steel). On November 18, 1981, Marathon and U.S. Steel entered into an agreement whereby U.S. Steel would make a tender offer for 30 million common shares of Marathon stock at $125 per share, to be followed by a merger of the two companies.

The Marathon-U.S. Steel agreement was subject to the following two conditions: (1) U.S. Steel was given an irrevocable option to purchase 10 million authorized but unissued shares of Marathon common stock for $90 per share (or 17 percent of Marathon's outstanding shares), and (2) U.S. Steel was given an option to purchase Marathon's interest in oil and mineral rights in Yates Field for $2.8 billion (Yates Field option). The latter option could be exercised only if U.S. Steel's offer did not succeed and if a third party gained control of Marathon. Evidence showed that Marathon's interest in the Yates Field was worth up to $3.6 billion. Marathon did not give Mobil either of these two options. Mobil sued, alleging that these two options violated Section 14(e) of the Williams Act. Who wins? [*Mobil Corporation v. Marathon Oil Company*, 669 F.2d 366 (6th Cir. 1981)]

39.8. The Fruehauf Corporation (Fruehauf) is engaged in the manufacture of large trucks and industrial vehicles. The Edelman group (Edelman) made a cash tender offer for the shares of Fruehauf for $48.50 per share. The stock sold in the low $20-per-share range a few months earlier. Fruehauf's management decided to make a competing management-led leveraged buyout (MBO) tender offer for the company in conjunction with Merrill Lynch. The MBO would be funded using $375 million borrowed from Merrill Lynch, $375 million borrowed from Manufacturers Hanover Bank, and $100 million contributed by Fruehauf. Total equity contribution to the new company under the MBO would be only $25 million: $10 million to $15 million from management and the rest from Merrill Lynch. In return for their equity contributions, management would receive between 40 and 60 percent of the new company.

Fruehauf's management agreed to pay $30 million to Merrill Lynch for brokerage fees that Merrill Lynch could keep even if the deal did not go through. Management also agreed to a no-shop clause whereby they agreed not to seek a better deal with another bidder. Incumbent management received better information about the goings-on. They also gave themselves golden parachutes that would raise the money for management's equity position in the new company.

Edelman informed Fruehauf's management that it could top their bid, but Fruehauf's management did not give them the opportunity to present their offer. Management's offer was accepted. Edelman sued, seeking an injunction. Did Fruehauf's management violate the business judgment rule? [*Edelman v. Fruehauf Corporation*, 798 F.2d 882 (6th Cir. 1986)]

39.9. Household International. Inc. (Household), is a diversified holding company with its principal subsidiaries engaged in financial services, transportation, and merchandising. On August 14, 1984, the board of directors of Household adopted a 48-page "Rights Plan" by a 14-to-2 vote. Basically, the plan provides that Household common stockholders are entitled to the issuance of one irrevocable right per common share if any party acquires 20 percent of Household's shares. The right permits Household shareholders to purchase $200 of the common stock of the tender offeror for $100. In essence, this forces any party interested in taking over Household to negotiate with Household's directors. Dyson-Kissner-Moran Corporation (DKM), which was interested in taking over Household, filed suit alleging that this flip-over rights plan violated the business judgment rule. Who wins? [*Moran v. Household International, Inc.*, 500 Ad.2d 1346 (DE 1985)]

39.10. The state of Illinois enacted a statute that protects certain defined "target companies" from unwanted takeovers. The protection extends to (1) corporations of which shareholders located in Illinois own 10 percent of a class of equity securities and (2) corporations that are incorporated in Illinois or have their principal place of business in the state. Tender offers for protected companies must be registered with the Illinois secretary of state 20 days before the proposed tender offer is made. The secretary may call a hearing at any time during the 20-day waiting period. The statute does not provide a deadline for when the hearing must be completed. The secretary may deny the tender offer if he finds that it is inequitable.

Chicago Rivet and Machine Co. (Chicago Rivet) is a publicly held Illinois corporation that is covered by the Illinois antitakeover statute. On July 19, 1979, MITE Corporation (MITE), a Delaware corporation, made a cash tender offer for all of the outstanding shares of Chicago Rivet. MITE did not comply with the Illinois Act and brought suit challenging the lawfulness of the state law. Is the Illinois antitakeover statute lawful? [*Edgar, Secretary of State of Illinois v. MITE Corporation*, 457 U.S. 624, 102 S.Ct. 2629 (1982)]

39.11. The state of Wisconsin enacted an antitakeover statute that protects corporations that are incorporated in Wisconsin and have their headquarters, substantial operations, or 10 percent of their shares or shareholders in the state. The statute prevents any party that acquires a 10 percent interest in a covered corporation from engaging in a business combination (e.g., merger) with the covered corporation for three years unless approval of the management is obtained in advance of the combination. Wisconsin firms cannot opt out of the law. This statute effectively eliminates hostile leveraged buyouts because buyers must rely on the assets and income of the target company to help pay off the debt incurred in effectuating the takeover.

Universal Foods (Universal) is a Wisconsin corporation covered by the statute. On December 1, 1988, Amanda Acquisition Corporation (Amanda) commenced a cash tender offer for up to 75 percent of the stock of Universal. Universal asserted the Wisconsin law. Is Wisconsin's antitakeover statute lawful? [*Amanda Acquisition Corporation v. Universal Foods*, 877 F.2d 496 (7th Cir. 1989), cert. denied 110 S.Ct. 367 (1989)]

ETHICS CASES

39.12. MCA, Inc. (MCA), a corporate holding company, owned 92 percent of the stock of Universal Pictures Company (Universal) and 100 percent of the stock of Universal City Studios, Inc. (Universal City). On March 25, 1966, these two subsidiaries merged pursuant to Delaware's short-form merger statute. The minority shareholders of Universal were offered $75 per share for their shares. Francis I. Du Pont & Company and other minority shareholders (Plaintiffs) rejected the offer and then perfected their dissenting shareholder appraisal rights. On March 29, 1973, the appraiser filed a final report in which he found the value of Universal stock to be $91.47 per share. Both parties filed exceptions to this report.

The parties' ultimate disagreement is, of course, over the value of the stock. Plaintiffs submit that the true value is $131.89 per share; defendant says it is $52.36. The computations are as follows:

Plaintiffs

Value Factor	Value	Weight	Result
Earnings	$129.12	70%	$90.38
Market	144.36	20	28.87
Assets	126.46	10	12.64
	Value per share		$131.89

Defendants

Value Factor	Value	Weight	Result
Earnings	$51.93	70%	$36.35
Dividends	41.66	20	8.33
Assets	76.77	10	7.68
	Value per share		$52.36

Appraiser

Value Factor	Value	Weight	Result
Earnings	$92.89	80%	$74.31
Assets	85.82	20	17.16
	Value per share		$91.47

Defendant takes exception to the appraiser's failure to find that, in the years prior to merger, the industry was declining and that Universal was ranked near its bottom. And it argues that Universal was in the business of producing and distributing feature motion pictures for theatrical exhibition. It contends that such business, generally, was in a severe decline at the time of merger and that Universal, in particular, was in a vulnerable position because it had failed to diversify, its feature films were of low commercial quality, and, unlike other motion picture companies, substantially all of its film library had already been committed to distributors for television exhibition. In short, defendant pictures Universal as a weak "wasting asset" corporation in a sick industry with poor prospects for revival.

The stockholders see a different company. They say that Universal's business was indeed the production and distribution of feature films, but not merely for theatrical exhibition. They argue that there was a dramatic increase in the television market for such feature films at the time of the merger. This new market, they contend, gave great new value to a fully amortized film library and significantly enhanced the value of Universal's current and future productions. They equate the television market to the acquisition of a new and highly profitable business whose earnings potential was just beginning to be realized at the time of the merger. Finally, say plaintiffs, the theatrical market itself was recovering in 1966. Thus, they paint the portrait of a well-situated corporation in a rejuvenated industry.

Did the parties act ethically in arriving at their proposed value of the company? What is the value of the minority shareholders' shares of Universal Pictures Company? [*Francis I. Du Pont & Company v. Universal City Studios, Inc.*, 312 A.2d 344 (Del.Ch. 1973)]

39.13. Realist, Inc. (Realist), is a Delaware corporation that has its principal place of business in Wisconsin. In March 1988, Royal Business Group, Inc. (Royal), a New Hampshire corporation, acquired 8 percent of the outstanding voting stock of Realist. Royal sent a series of letters to Realist declaring its intention to acquire all of Realist's outstanding shares at an above-market premium. Realist repulsed Royal's overtures. Unbeknownst to Royal, Realist began negotiations to acquire Ammann Laser Technik AG (Ammann), a Swiss-based company.

Royal instituted a proxy contest and nominated two candidates for the two Realist directorships to be filed at Realist's

June 6, 1989, annual shareholders' meeting. Realist and Royal both submitted proxy statements to Realist's shareholders.

The insurgent Royal nominees prevailed. On June 30, 1989, Realist announced that it had acquired Ammann. This acquisition made Realist much less attractive as a takeover target. Royal immediately withdrew its offer to acquire Realist and sued Realist to recover the $350,000 it had spent in connection with the proxy contest. Royal alleged that Realist had engaged in fraud in violation of Section 14(a) of the Securities Exchange Act of 1934 by failing to disclose its secret negotiations with Ammann in its proxy materials. The basis of Royal's complaint was that if Realist had disclosed that it intended to acquire Ammann, Royal would not have engaged in the costly proxy contest. Is Realist liable to Royal? Did Realist act unethically in seeking to acquire Ammann to thwart Royal's takeover attempt? [*Royal Business Group, Inc. v. Realist, Inc.*, 933 F.2d 1056 (1st Cir. 1991)]

······

CRITICAL LEGAL THINKING WRITING ASSIGNMENT

Read Case A.39 in the Case Appendix [*Neal v. Alabama By-Products Corporation*]. This case is excerpted from the court of chancery's opinion. Review and brief the case. In your brief, be sure to answer the following questions:

1. What are dissenting shareholder appraisal rights?

2. What type of transaction occurred that triggered these rights in this case?

3. What value were the dissenting shareholders offered in the original transaction? What value is being offered by the corporation in the court proceeding? What value are the dissenting shareholders seeking in the court proceeding?

4. What amount did the court determine to be the fair value of the shares?

······

NOTES

1. 15 U.S.C. 78n(a).
2. 15 U.S.C. 78n(d) and (e).
3. Section 13(d) of the Securities Exchange Act of 1934 requires that any party which acquires 5 percent or more of any equity security of a company registered with the SEC must report the acquisition to the SEC and disclose its intentions regarding the acquisition. This is public information.

4. 15 U.S.C. 78n(e).
5. *Smith v. Van Gorkum*, 488 A.2d 858 (Del. 1985).
6. *Unocal Corporation v. Mesa Petroleum Company*, 493 A.2d 946 (Del. 1985).

Securities Regulation and Investor Protection

Fraud is infinite in variety; sometimes it is audacious and unblushing; sometimes it pays a sort of homage to virtue, and then it is modest and retiring; it would be honesty itself, if it could only afford it.

LORD MACNAGHTEN
Reddaway v. Banham (1896)

Chapter Objectives

After studying this chapter, you should be able to

1. Define a security for purposes of federal and state securities laws.
2. Describe how securities are registered with the Securities and Exchange Commission.
3. Describe the requirements for qualifying for private placement, intrastate, and small offering exemptions from registration.
4. Describe how to conduct an initial public offering over the Internet.
5. Describe how the Small Corporate Offering Registrations form (SCOR) permits small companies to make public offerings of securities.
6. Define insider trading that violates Section 10(b) of the Securities Exchange Act of 1934.
7. Describe the liability of tippers and tippees for insider trading.
8. Describe the criminal liability and penalties for violating federal securities laws.
9. Describe short-swing profits that violate Section 16(b) of the Securities Exchange Act of 1934.
10. Describe commodities trading and apply the antifraud provision of the Commodity Exchange Act.

Chapter Contents

Prior to the 1920s and 1930s, the securities and commodities markets in this country were not regulated by the federal government. Securities and commodities were sold to investors with little, if any, disclosure. Fraud in these transactions was common.

Following the stock market crash of 1929, Congress enacted a series of statutes designed to regulate securities and commodities markets. The *Securities Act of 1933* requires disclosure by companies and others who wish to issue securities to the public. The *Securities Exchange Act of 1934* was enacted to prevent fraud in the subsequent trading of securities, including insider trading.

These federal and state statutes are designed to (1) require disclosure of information to investors and (2) prevent fraud. This chapter discusses federal and state securities laws and regulations that provide investor protection.

THE SECURITIES AND EXCHANGE COMMISSION (SEC)

The Securities Exchange Act of 1934 created the **Securities and Exchange Commission (SEC)** and empowered it to administer federal securities laws. The SEC is an administrative agency composed of five members who are appointed by the President. The major responsibilities of the SEC are

1. Adopting rules (also called regulations) that further the purpose of the federal securities statutes. These rules have the force of law.
2. Investigating alleged securities violations and bringing enforcement actions against suspected violators. This may include a recommendation of criminal prosecution. Criminal prosecutions of violations of federal securities laws are brought by the U.S. Department of Justice.
3. Regulating the activities of securities brokers and advisors. This includes registering brokers and advisors and taking enforcement action against those who violate securities laws.

*D*EFINITION OF A SECURITY

A **security** must exist before securities laws apply. Securities are defined as:

1. Interests or instruments that are commonly known as securities (e.g., common stock, preferred stock, bonds, debentures, and warrants).
2. Interests or instruments that are expressly mentioned in securities acts (e.g., preorganization subscription agreements; interests in oil, gas, and mineral rights; and deposit receipts for foreign securities).
3. *Investment contracts*, that is, any contract whereby an investor invests money or other consideration in a common enterprise and expects to make a profit off the significant efforts of others. Limited partnership interests, pyramid sales schemes, and investments in farm animals accompanied by care agreements have been found to be securities under this test, which is known as the *Howey test*.[1]

In the following case, the court found an investment to be a security subject to federal securities laws.

Margin notes

Business Brief
Federal law did not regulate the securities markets until after the stock market crash of 1929. Securities laws are designed to help prevent a similar crash today.

Securities and Exchange Commission (SEC)
Federal administrative agency that is empowered to administer federal securities laws. The SEC can adopt rules and regulations to interpret and implement federal securities laws.

security
(1) An interest or instrument that is common stock, preferred stock, a bond, a debenture, or a warrant, (2) an interest or instrument that is expressly mentioned in securities acts, and (3) an investment contract.

Hocking v. Dubois
839 F.2d 560 (1988)
United States Court of Appeals, Ninth Circuit

CASE 40.1

FACTS
Gerald Hocking visited Hawaii and became interested in buying a condominium there as an investment. Maylee Dubois, who was a licensed real estate broker in Hawaii, agreed to help Hocking find a suitable unit. Dubois found a condominium unit owned by Tovik and Yaacov Liberman that was for sale. The unit was located in a resort complex developed by Aetna Life Insurance Company (Aetna) and managed by the Hotel Corporation of the Pacific (HCP). Aetna and HCP offered purchasers of condominium units in

the project to participate in a rental pool agreement. The Libermans had not participated in the pool. Hocking purchased the unit from the Libermans and entered into a rental pool agreement with HCP. Hocking subsequently filed suit against Dubois, alleging violations of federal securities laws. The trial court granted summary judgment in favor of the defendant. Hocking appealed.

ISSUE
Was the offer of a condominium unit with an option to participate in a rental pool agreement a "security" under federal securities laws?

IN THE LANGUAGE OF THE COURT
Reinhart, Circuit Judge   Generally, simple transactions in real estate, without more, do not satisfy the Howey criteria. When a purchaser is motivated exclusively by a desire to occupy or develop the land personally, no security is involved. Real estate transactions may involve an offer of securities when an investor is offered both an interest in real estate and a collateral expectation of profits. However, drawing the line between the offering of land sales contracts and investment contracts has not been easy. We find that under the three Howey criteria an offer of a condominium with a rental pool agreement constitutes an offer of an investment contract.

1. *Investment of money* Defendants do not dispute that the condominium purchase satisfied *Howey*'s first requirement. Hocking invested money in the condominium.
2. *Common enterprise* It is readily apparent that a rental pool agreement for condominiums is a common enterprise. Each investor buys one share—a condominium—in a common venture that pools the rents

from all of the units. The success of each participant's individual investment clearly depends on the entire rental pool agreement's success.

3. *Expectation of profits produced by others' efforts* With respect to the third prong of *Howey*, that is, the expectation of profits produced by the efforts of others, we conclude that this requisite is met whenever a condominium is sold with a rental pool agreement option. Where a rental pool is made available in the course of the offering, what is really being sold to the purchaser is an investment contract whereby profits are expected to be produced if at all, through the efforts of a party other than the purchaser-owner. The purchase of a condominium with a rental pool agreement option thus meets the third *Howey* requisite that there be an expectation of profits based upon the entrepreneurial or managerial efforts of others.

DECISION AND REMEDY
The court of appeals held that the transaction constituted an offer of a security, and that Hocking could sue Dubois for alleged violations of federal securities laws. Reversed and remanded.

Case Questions

Critical Legal Thinking   What is an investment contract? Why did Congress leave the definition of a *security* flexible?

Ethics   Did Dubois act unethically in denying liability under federal securities laws?

Business Application   Why did the plaintiff allege the transaction involved a security? Explain.

$\mathcal{T}$HE SECURITIES ACT OF 1933—REGISTRATION OF SECURITIES

The **Securities Act of 1933** primarily regulates the issuance of securities by a corporation, a general or limited partnership, an unincorporated association, or an individual. Unless a security or transaction qualifies for an exemption, Section 5 of the Securities Act of 1933 requires securities offered to the public through the use of the mails or any facility of interstate commerce to be *registered* with the SEC by means of a registration statement and an accompanying prospectus.

Registration Statement

A covered issuer must file a written **registration statement** with the SEC. The issuer's lawyer normally prepares the statement with the help of the issuer's management, accountants, and underwriters.

A registration statement must contain descriptions of (1) the securities being offered for sale, (2) the registrant's business, (3) the management of the registrant, including compensation, stock options and benefits, and material transactions with the registrant, (4) pending litigation, (5) how the proceeds from the offering will be used, (6) government

Securities Act of 1933
A federal statute that primarily regulates the issuance of securities by corporations, partnerships, associations, and individuals.

Business Brief
Section 5 of the Securities Act of 1933 requires an issuer to register securities with the SEC before they can be sold to the public.

registration statement
Document that an issuer of securities files with the SEC that contains required information about the issuer, the securities to be issued, and other relevant information.

regulation, (7) the degree of competition in the industry, and (8) any special risk factors. In addition, the registration statement must be accompanied by financial statements as certified by certified public accountants.

Registration statements usually become effective 20 business days after they are filed unless the SEC requires additional information to be disclosed. A new 20-day period begins each time the registration statement is amended. At the registrant's request, the SEC may "accelerate" the *effective date* (i.e., not require the registrant to wait 20 days after the last amendment is filed).

The SEC does not pass upon the merits of the securities offered. It decides only whether the issuer has met the disclosure requirements.

Prospectus

The **prospectus** is a written disclosure document that must be submitted to the SEC along with the registration statement. Much of the information included in the prospectus can be found in the registration statement. The prospectus is used as a selling tool by the issuer. It is provided to prospective investors to enable them to evaluate the financial risk of the investment.

A prospectus must contain the following language in capital letters and boldface (usually red) type:

THESE SECURITIES HAVE NOT BEEN APPROVED OR DISAPPROVED BY THE SECURITIES AND EXCHANGE COMMISSION OR ANY STATE SECURITIES COMMISSION NOR HAS THE SECURITIES AND EXCHANGE COMMISSION OR ANY STATE SECURITIES COMMISSION PASSED UPON THE ACCURACY OR ADEQUACY OF THIS PROSPECTUS. ANY REPRESENTATION TO THE CONTRARY IS A CRIMINAL OFFENSE.

Limitations on Activities During the Registration Process

Section 5 of the Securities Act of 1933 limits the types of activities that an issuer, an underwriter, and a dealer may engage in during the registration process. These limitations are divided into three time periods: (1) the prefiling period, (2) the waiting period, and (3) the posteffective period.

The Prefiling Period The **prefiling period** begins when the issuer first contemplates issuing the securities and ends when the registration statement is filed. During this time, the issuer cannot either sell or offer to sell the securities. The issuer also cannot *condition the market* for the upcoming securities offering. This rule makes it illegal for an issuer to engage in a public relations campaign (e.g., newspaper and magazine articles and advertisements) that touts the prospects of the company and the planned securities issue. However, sending annual reports to shareholders and making public announcements of factual matters (such as the settlement of a strike) are permissible because they are considered normal corporate disclosures.

The Waiting Period The **waiting period** begins when the registration statement is filed with the SEC and continues until the registration statement is declared effective.

The issuer is encouraged to condition the market during this time. Thus, the issuer may (1) make oral offers to sell (including face-to-face and telephone conversations), (2) distribute a *preliminary prospectus* (usually called a red herring), which contains most of the information to be contained in the final prospectus except for price, (3) distribute a *summary prospectus*, which is a summary of the important terms contained in the prospectus, and (4) publish *tombstone ads* in newspapers and other publications. Unapproved writings (which are considered illegal offers to sell) as well as actual sales are prohibited during the waiting period.

E-Commerce & Internet Law

INTERNET COMPANY GOES PUBLIC

Many Internet companies have gone public, making billionaires of many of their founders. Some of the biggest-named companies in the Internet business—Microsoft Corp., Yahoo!, Netscape, eBay, and Amazon.com—have issued stock through initial public offerings (IPOs). Other Internet-related companies will continue to "go public." The cover of the prospectus of one such Internet company's IPO appears below.

8,320,000 Shares

eToys Inc.

Common Stock

This is an initial public offering of shares of common stock of eToys Inc. All of the 8,320,000 shares of common stock are being sold by eToys.

Prior to this offering, there has been no public market for the common stock. The common stock has been approved for quotation on the Nasdaq National Market under the symbol "ETYS".

See "Risk Factors" beginning on page 8 to read about factors you should consider before buying shares of the common stock.

Neither the Securities and Exchange Commission nor any other regulatory body has approved or disapproved of these securities or passed upon the accuracy or adequacy of this prospectus. Any representation to the contrary is a criminal offense.

	Per Share	Total
Initial public offering price	$20.00	$166,400,000
Underwriting discount	$ 1.35	$ 11,232,000
Proceeds, before expenses, to eToys	$18.65	$155,168,000

In connection with this offering, the underwriters have reserved up to 1,365,000 shares of common stock being sold by eToys for sale at the initial public offering price to directors, officers, employees and friends of eToys.

The underwriters may, under specific circumstances, purchase up to an additional 1,248,000 shares from eToys at the initial public offering price, less the underwriting discount.

Goldman, Sachs & Co.

BancBoston Robertson Stephens

Donaldson, Lufkin & Jenrette

Merrill Lynch & Co.

Prospectus dated May 19, 1999.

e-biz

posteffective period

The period of time that begins when the registration statement becomes effective and runs until the issuer either sells all of the offered securities or withdraws them from sale.

final prospectus

A final version of the prospectus that must be delivered by the issuer to the investor prior to or at the time of confirming a sale or sending a security to a purchaser.

Regulation A

A regulation that permits the issuer to sell securities pursuant to a simplified registration process.

The Posteffective Period The **posteffective period** begins when the registration statement becomes effective and runs until the issuer either sells all of the offered securities or withdraws them from sale. Thus, the issuer and its underwriter and dealers may close the offers received prior to the effective date and solicit new offers and sales.

Prior to or at the time of confirming a sale or sending a security to a purchaser, the issuer (or its representative) must deliver a **final prospectus** (also called **a statutory prospectus**) to the investor. Failure to do so is a violation of Section 5. Tombstone ads are often used during this period.

If an issuer violates any of the prohibitions on activities during these periods, the investor may rescind his or her purchase. If an underwriter or dealer violates any of these prohibitions, the SEC may issue sanctions, including the suspension of securities licenses.

Regulation A Offerings

Regulation A permits an issuer to sell up to $5 million of securities during a 12-month period pursuant to a simplified registration process. Such offerings may have an unlimited number of purchasers who do not have to be sophisticated investors.

This regulation also stipulates that offerings exceeding $100,000 must file an *offering statement* with the SEC. The offering statement requires less disclosure than does a registration statement and is less costly to prepare. Investors must be provided an offering circular prior to the purchase of securities. There are no resale restrictions on the securities.

Contemporary Business Application

SECURITIES OFFERINGS MUST BE WRITTEN IN PLAIN ENGLISH

Nonlawyers have always been frustrated by the legalese used by lawyers in contracts, court documents, and regulatory disclosures. No greater place has arcane legal language shown up than in prospectuses offering securities for sale to the public. These documents, which are supposed to provide relevant information to potential investors before they invest in company stock and securities, are usually barely skimmed, let alone read, by potential investors.

The Securities and Exchange Commission (SEC) decided to change this practice in 1998, when it adopted a "plain English" rule for securities offerings. Under this new rule, issuers of securities must use plain English language on the cover page, in the summary, and in the risk factor sections of their prospectuses. Issuers must now use

- Active voice
- Short sentences
- "Everyday" words
- Bullet lists for complex information
- No legal jargon or highly technical terms
- No multiple negatives

The plain English rule will require a major cultural change by issuers, underwriters, and securities lawyers who are used to using long, complicated, and confusing language. The SEC has stated that it will not be the "grammar police," but will instead focus on the clarity of disclosures to potential investors by issuers. The SEC hopes that its new rule will encourage issuers to use plain English throughout the entire prospectus. [Rule 421 (d) of Regulation C].

SECURITIES EXEMPT FROM REGISTRATION

Business Brief

Certain *securities* do not have to be registered with the SEC.

Certain *securities* are exempt from registration. Once a security is exempt, it is exempt forever. It does not matter how many times the security is transferred. Exempt securities include

1. Securities issued by any government in the United States (e.g., municipal bonds issued by city governments)
2. Short-term notes and drafts that have a maturity date that does not exceed nine months (e.g., commercial paper issued by corporations)

3. Securities issued by nonprofit issuers, such as religious institutions, charitable institutions, and colleges and universities
4. Securities of financial institutions (e.g., banks and savings associations) that are regulated by the appropriate banking authorities
5. Securities issued by common carriers (e.g., railroads and trucking companies) that are regulated by the Interstate Commerce Commission (ICC)
6. Insurance and annuity contracts issued by insurance companies
7. Stock dividends and stock splits
8. Securities issued in a corporate reorganization where one security is exchanged for another security

E-Commerce & Internet Law

SELLING INITIAL PUBLIC OFFERINGS (IPOs) OVER THE INTERNET

In the past, if a small company wanted to raise capital by selling stock, it faced the daunting and expensive task of trying to find potential investors, paying for the printing of securities, offering circulars, paying mailing costs, and such. The burgeoning Internet provides a new opportunity for small companies to inexpensively reach millions of prospective investors to try to raise capital. Companies can now establish Web sites and post the necessary information about the securities offering; a click of an interested party's mouse lawfully delivers the offering circular and other relevant information to the potential investor.

In 1995, Spring Street Brewery marked the dawn of the electronic securities offering with its IPO over the Internet. Spring Street, a microbrewery that produced premium beer, raised $1.6 million from Internet investors. Spring Street established a home page on the Web that allowed potential investors using the Internet to examine and download the offering circular and other offering documents. Since Spring Street's success, other companies have also made Internet stock offerings. Most of these have consisted of small offerings like that of Spring Street.

The Securities and Exchange Commission (SEC) has expressed a desire to encourage small companies to use the Internet to raise capital. The SEC has announced that securities disclosure and antifraud laws apply to Internet IPOs, however. Cyberspace offers a new means of capital formation for small companies at a fraction of the cost of traditional methods of selling stock. The SEC monitors these sales to require full disclosure and prevent fraud.

e-biz

TRANSACTIONS EXEMPT FROM REGISTRATION

Certain *transactions* in securities are exempt from registration. Exempt transactions are subject to the antifraud provisions of the federal securities laws. Therefore, the issuer must provide investors with adequate information—including annual reports, quarterly reports, proxy statements, financial statements, and so on—even though a registration statement is not required. The exempt transactions are discussed in the paragraphs that follow.

> **Business Brief**
>
> If a business plans to issue nonexempt securities, it must either (1) register the securities with the SEC or (2) qualify for an exemption from registration.

Nonissuers

Nonissuers, such as average investors, do not have to file a registration statement prior to reselling securities they have purchased. This is because the Securities Act of 1933 exempts securities transactions not made by an issuer, an underwriter, or a dealer from registration.[2] For example, an investor who owns shares of IBM can resell these shares to another at any time without having to register with the SEC.

Intrastate Offerings

intrastate offering exemption

An exemption from registration that permits local businesses to raise capital from local investors to be used in the local economy without the need to register with the SEC.

The purpose of the **intrastate offerings exemption** is to permit local businesses to raise capital from local investors to be used in the local economy without the need to register with the SEC.[3] There is no limit on the dollar amount of capital that can be raised pursuant to an intrastate offering exemption. An issuer can qualify for this exemption in only one state.

Three requirements must be met to qualify for this exemption[4]:

1. The issuer must be a resident of the state for which the exemption is claimed. A corporation is a resident of the state in which it is incorporated.
2. The issuer must be doing business in that state. This requires that 80 percent of the issuer's assets are located in the state, 80 percent of its gross revenues are derived from the state, its principal office is located in the state, and 80 percent of the proceeds of the offering will be used in the state.
3. The purchasers of the securities all must be residents of that state.

Private Placements

An issue of securities that does not involve a public offering is exempt from the registration requirement.[5] This exemption—known as the **private placement exemption**—allows issuers to raise capital from an unlimited number of accredited investors without having to register the offering with the SEC.[6] There is no dollar limit on the amount of securities that can be sold pursuant to this exemption.

private placement exemption

An exemption from registration that permits issuers to raise capital from an unlimited number of accredited investors and no more than 35 nonaccredited investors without having to register the offering with the SEC.

An *accredited investor* may be[7]

1. Any natural person (including spouse) who has a net worth of at least $1 million
2. Any natural person who has had an annual income of at least $200,000 for the previous two years and reasonably expects to make $200,000 income in the current year
3. Any corporation, partnership, or business trust with total assets in excess of $5 million
4. Insiders of the issuers, such as executive officers and directors of corporate issuers and general partners of partnership issuers
5. Certain institutional investors, such as registered investment companies, pension plans, colleges and universities, and the like

Business Brief

Up to 35 nonaccredited investors may purchase securities pursuant to a private placement exemption. They must be sophisticated investors through their own experience and education or through representatives.

No more than 35 *nonaccredited investors* may purchase securities pursuant to a private placement exemption. Nonaccredited investors must be sophisticated investors, however, either through their own experience and education or through representatives (such as accountants, lawyers, and business managers). General selling efforts, such as advertising to the public, are not permitted.

Small Offerings

Securities offerings that do not exceed a certain dollar amount are exempt from registration.[8] Rule 504 exempts the sale of securities not exceeding $1 million during a 12-month period from registration. The securities may be sold to an unlimited number of accredited and unaccredited investors, but general selling efforts to the public are not permitted. This is called the **small offering exemption**.

small offering exemption

For the sale of securities not exceeding $1 million during a 12-month period.

Resale Restrictions

Certain *resale restrictions* are placed on securities issued pursuant to exemptions from registration. These restrictions are discussed in the following paragraphs.

restricted securities

Securities that were issued for investment purposes pursuant to the intrastate, private placement, or small offering exemption.

Restricted Securities   Securities sold pursuant to the intrastate, private placement, or small offering exemptions are called **restricted securities** because they cannot be resold for a limited period of time after their initial issue. The following restrictions apply:

- **Rule 147** stipulates that securities sold pursuant to an intrastate offering exemption cannot be sold to nonresidents for a period of nine months.

- **Rule 144** provides that securities sold pursuant to the private placement or small offering exemption must be held for one year from the date when the securities are last sold by the issuer. After that time, investors may sell the greater of (1) 1 percent of the outstanding securities of the issuer or (2) the average weekly volume of trading in the securities (i.e., the four-week moving average) in any three-month period. Information about the issuer must be available to the public. Generally, all restrictions are lifted after two years.

Preventing Transfer of Restricted Securities   To protect the nontransferability of restricted shares, the issuer must

1. Require the investors to sign an *affidavit* stating that they are buying the securities for investment, acknowledging that they are purchasing restricted securities, and promising not to transfer the shares in violation of the restriction.
2. Place a *legend* on the stock certificate describing the restriction.
3. Notify the *transfer agent* not to record a transfer of the securities that would violate the restriction.

If the issuer has taken these precautions, it will not lose its exemption from registration even if isolated transfers of stock occur in violation of the restricted periods. If these precautions are not taken, the issuer may lose its exemption from registration. In that event, it has sold unregistered securities in violation of Section 5, permitting all purchasers to rescind their purchases of the securities.

> **Business Brief**
> The issuer must take certain actions to ensure that restricted securities are not sold in violation of the restrictions imposed by Rules 144 and 147.

Rule 144A

To establish a more liquid and efficient secondary market in unregistered securities, the SEC adopted Rule 144A in 1990. This rule permits "qualified institutional investors"—defined as institutions that own and invest at least $100 million in securities—to buy unregistered securities without being subject to the holding periods of Rule 144. This rule is designed to create an institutional market in unregistered securities as well as to permit foreign issuers to raise capital in this country from sophisticated investors without making registration process disclosures.

> **Business Brief**
> To increase the liquidity of the registered securities, the SEC adopted Rule 144A in 1990 that permits "qualified institutional investors" to buy unregistered securities without being subject to the holding periods of Rule 144.

Integration of Exempt Offerings

Separate offerings that qualify for individual exemptions from registration will be **integrated** if they are really part of one large offering. This larger offering must then be examined to see if it qualifies for an exemption from registration. In deciding whether to integrate offerings, the SEC and the courts examine whether the offerings (1) are part of a single plan of financing, (2) involve the issuance of the same class of securities, (3) are made about the same time, (4) receive the same consideration, and (5) are made for the same general purpose.

Safe harbor rules protect securities offerings made more than six months before or after the current offering from being integrated with the present offering.[9] This creates a 12-month period outside of which none of the securities offering will be integrated with the current offering.

> **integration of offerings**
> When separate offerings that might otherwise qualify for individual exemptions are combined if they are really part of one large offering.

Consider This Example   On January 1, the ABC Corporation issued $4 million of common stock for cash to 25 accredited and 15 sophisticated but nonaccredited investors, some of whom are located out of state. The proceeds are to be used for working capital. This offering qualifies for the private placement exemption.

On April 1 of the same year, ABC Corporation issued another $4 million of common stock for cash to 25 accredited and 25 sophisticated but nonaccredited investors, some of whom are located out of state. The proceeds are to be used for working capital. Again, this individual offering qualifies for the private placement exemption.

These offerings must be integrated because they occur within six months of each other, they are the same security, the consideration is the same, and the proceeds from both

> **Business Brief**
> If offerings are integrated and the combined offering does not qualify for an exemption, the issuer has illegally sold unregistered securities. This subjects the issuer to certain civil fines and criminal penalties. In addition, purchasers may *rescind* their purchases and recover the price they paid.

offerings are used for the same purpose. The integrated offering does not qualify for an exemption from registration. There are 40 nonaccredited investors, too many to qualify for the private placement exemption. The integrated offering does not qualify for the intrastate exemption (there are out-of-state investors) or for the Rule 504 small offering exemption (the securities issued exceed $1 million). As a remedy, the investors can rescind their purchases because there has been a violation of Section 5 of the 1933 act.

Entrepreneur and the Law

SCOR SIMPLIFIES STOCK OFFERINGS BY SMALL COMPANIES

Like large corporations, small businesses often need to raise capital and must find public investors to buy their company's stock. Unlike large corporations, however, small businesses often do not have the money or resources to hire the lawyers, investment bankers, CPAs, and other professionals or to pay the printing and other costs associated with an initial public offering (IPO). Also, these small businesses often cannot find enough qualified investors or meet other requirements necessary to qualify for a private placement or other exemptions from registration. And in most cases, the small business only needs to raise a small amount of capital through a public offering.

In 1992, after years of investigation, the Securities and Exchange Commission (SEC) amended its regulations to facilitate capital raising by small businesses. As part of this small business initiative, the SEC amended Regulation A by adopting the **Small Corporate Offering Registration Form (SCOR)**. The SCOR form—**Form U-7**—is a question-and-answer disclosure form that small businesses can complete and file with the SEC if they plan on raising $1 million or less from the public issue of securities. An issuer must answer the questions on Form U-7, which then becomes the offering circular that must be given to prospective investors.

Form U-7 simplifies and demystifies the registration process. The questions are so clearly and specifically drawn that they can be answered by the issuer without the help of an expensive securities lawyer. The SCOR questions require the issuer to develop a business plan that states specific company goals and how it plans to reach them. An overriding concern of SCOR is uniformity. Form U-7 is designed to replace the myriad of forms previously required by state laws for securities offerings that are exempt from complete SEC registration requirements, but it must comply with state securities laws. Many states have elected to allow SCOR Form U-7 to replace their disclosure requirements. SCOR is limited to domestic businesses and cannot be used by partnerships, foreign corporations, or companies involved in petroleum exploration or mining. The SCOR offering cannot exceed $1 million and the offering price of the common stock or its equivalent may not be less than $5.00 per share. SCOR offerings are a welcomed addition for entrepreneur-owners who want to raise money through a small public offering.

*L*IABILITY PROVISIONS OF THE SECURITIES ACT OF 1933

Violations of the Securities Act of 1933 may result in various penalties and remedies against the perpetrator. These penalties and remedies are discussed in the following paragraphs.

Criminal Liability

Section 24
A provision of the Securities Act of 1933 that imposes criminal liability on any person who willfully violates the 1933 act or the rules or regulations adopted thereunder.

Section 24 of the 1933 act imposes *criminal liability* on any person who *willfully* violates either the act or the rules and regulations adopted thereunder.[10] The maximum penalty is five years' imprisonment. Criminal actions are brought by the Justice Department.

SEC Actions

The SEC may (1) issue a *consent order* whereby a defendant agrees not to violate securities laws in the future but does not admit to violating securities laws in the past, (2) bring an action in federal district court to obtain an *injunction*, or (3) request the court to grant ancillary relief, such as *disgorgement of profits* by the defendant.

Private Actions

Private parties who have been injured by violations of the 1933 act have recourse against the violator, as discussed in the following paragraphs.

Section 12   **Section 12** of the 1933 act imposes *civil liability* on any person who violates the provisions of Section 5 of the act. Violations include selling securities pursuant to an unwarranted exemption and making misrepresentations concerning the offer or sale of securities. The purchaser's remedy for a violation of Section 12 is either to rescind the purchase or to sue for damages.

Section 11   **Section 11** of the 1933 act provides for civil liability for damages when a registration statement on its effective date misstates or omits a material fact. Liability under Section 11 is imposed on those who (1) intentionally defraud investors or (2) are negligent in not discovering the fraud. Thus, the issuer, certain corporate officers (chief executive officer, chief financial officer, chief accounting officer), directors, signers of the registration statement, underwriters, and experts (accountants who certify financial statements and lawyers who issue legal opinions that are included in a registration statement) may be liable.

All defendants except the issuer may assert a **due diligence defense** against the imposition of Section 11 liability. If this defense is proven, the defendant is not liable. To establish a due diligence defense, the defendant must prove that after reasonable investigation, he or she had reasonable grounds to believe and did believe that, at the time the registration statement became effective, the statements contained therein were true and that there was no omission of material facts.

The following is a classic case where the court imposed civil liability on defendants who failed to prove their due diligence defense.

Section 12

A provision of the Securities Act of 1933 that imposes civil liability on any person who violates the provisions of Section 5 of the act.

Section 11

A provision of the Securities Act of 1933 that imposes civil liability on persons who intentionally defraud investors by making misrepresentations or omissions of material facts in the registration statement or who are negligent for not discovering the fraud.

due diligence defense

A defense to a Section 11 action that, if proven, makes the defendant not liable.

Escott v. BarChris Construction Corp.
283 F.Supp. 643 (1968)
United States District Court, Southern District of New York

CASE 40.2

FACTS
In 1961, BarChris Construction Corp. (BarChris), a company primarily engaged in the construction and sale of bowling alleys, was in need of additional financing. To raise working capital, BarChris decided to issue debentures to investors. A registration statement, including a prospectus, was filed with the SEC on March 30, 1961. After two amendments, the registration statement became effective May 16, 1961. Peat, Marwick, Mitchell & Co. (Peat, Marwick) audited the financial statements of the company that were included in the registration statement and prospectus. The debentures were sold by May 24, 1961. Investors were provided a final prospectus concerning the debentures. Unbeknown to the investors, however, the registration statement and prospectus contained the following material misrepresentations and omissions of material fact:

1. Current assets on the 1960 balance sheet were overstated by $609,689 (15 percent).

2. Contingent liabilities of April 30, 1961, were understated by $618,853 (42 percent).

3. Sales for the quarter ending March 31, 1961, were overstated by $519,810 (32 percent).

4. Gross profits for the quarter ending March 31, 1961, were overstated by $230,755 (92 percent).

5. Backlog of orders as of March 31, 1961, was overstated by $4,490,000 (186 percent).

6. Loans to officers of BarChris of $386,615 were not disclosed.

7. Customer delinquencies and BarChris's potential liability thereto of $1,350,000 were not disclosed.

8. The use of the proceeds of the debentures to pay old debts was not disclosed.

In 1962, BarChris was failing financially, and on October 29, 1962, it filed a petition for protection to be reorganized under federal bankruptcy law. On November 1, 1962, BarChris defaulted on interest payments due to be paid on

(case continues)

the debentures to investors. Barry Escott and other purchasers of the debentures brought this civil action against executive officers, directors, and the outside accountants of BarChris. The plaintiffs alleged that the defendants had violated Section 11 of the Securities Act of 1933 by submitting misrepresentations and omissions of material facts in the registration statement filed with the SEC.

ISSUE

Are the defendants liable for violating Section 11 or have they proved their due diligence defense?

IN THE LANGUAGE OF THE COURT

McLean, District Judge   I turn now to the question of whether defendants have proved their due diligence defenses. The position of each defendant will be separately considered.

Russo Russo was, to all intents and purposes, the chief executive officer of BarChris. He was a member of the executive committee. He was familiar with all aspects of the business. He was thoroughly aware of BarChris's stringent financial condition in May 1961. In short, Russo knew all the relevant facts. He could not have believed that there were no untrue statements or material omissions in the prospectus. Russo has no due diligence defenses.

Vitolo and Pugliese They were the founders of the business. Vitolo was president and Pugliese was vice president. Vitolo and Pugliese each are men of limited education. It is not hard to believe that for them the prospectus was difficult reading, if indeed they read it at all. But whether it was or not is irrelevant. The liability of a director who signs a registration statement does not depend upon whether or not he read it or, if he did, whether or not he understood what he was reading. And in any case, there is nothing to show that they made any investigation of anything that they may not have known about or understood. They have not proved their due diligence defenses.

Trilling Trilling was BarChris's controller. He signed the registration statement in that capacity, although he was not a director. He was a comparatively minor figure in BarChris. He was not considered an executive officer. Trilling may well have been unaware of several of the inaccuracies in the prospectus. But he must have known of some of them. As a financial officer, he was familiar with BarChris's finances and with its books of account. Trilling did not sustain the burden of proving his due diligence defenses.

Auslander Auslander was an "outside" director, that is, one who was not an officer of BarChris. He was chairman of the board of Valley Stream National Bank in Valley Stream, Long Island. In February 1961 Vitolo asked him to become a director of BarChris. Vitolo gave him an enthusiastic account of BarChris's progress and prospects. As an inducement, Vitolo said that when BarChris received the proceeds of a forthcoming issue of securities, it would deposit $1 million in Auslander's bank. Auslander was elected a director on April 17, 1961. The registration statement in its original form had already been filed, of course, without his

signature. On May 10, 1961, he signed a signature page for the first amendment to the registration statement that was filed with the SEC on May 11, 1961. This was a separate sheet without any document attached. Auslander did not know that it was a signature page for a registration statement. He vaguely understood that it was something "for the SEC." Auslander never saw a copy of the registration statement in its final form. Section 11 imposes liability upon a director no matter how new he is. Auslander has not established his due diligence defenses.

Peat, Marwick Peat, Marwick's work was in general charge of a member of the firm, Cummings, and more immediately in charge of Peat, Marwick's manager, Logan. Most of the actual work was performed by a senior accountant, Berardi, who has junior assistants, one of whom was Kennedy. Berardi was then about 30 years old. He was not yet a CPA. He had had no previous experience with the bowling industry. This was his first job as a senior accountant. He could hardly have been given a more difficult assignment.

First and foremost is Berardi's failure to discover that Capital Lanes had not been sold. This error affected both the sales figure and the liability side of the balance sheet. Berardi erred in computing the contingent liabilities. Berardi did not make a reasonable investigation in this instance. The purpose of reviewing events subsequent to the date of a certified balance sheet (referred to as an S-1 review when made with reference to a registration statement) is to ascertain whether any material change has occurred in the company's financial position that should be disclosed in order to prevent the balance sheet figures from being misleading. The scope of such a review, under generally accepted auditing standards, is limited. It does not amount to a complete audit. Berardi made the S-1 review in May 1961. He devoted a little over two days to it, a total of 20½ hours. He did not discover any of the errors or omissions pertaining to the state of affairs in 1961, all of which were material. Apparently the only BarChris officer with whom Berardi communicated was Trilling. He could not recall making any inquiries of Russo, Vitolo, or Pugliese. In conducting the S-1 review, Berardi did not examine any important financial records other than the trial balance. As to minutes, he read only the board of directors' minutes of BarChris. He did not read such minutes as there were of the executive committee. He did not know that there was an executive committee. He did not read the minutes of any subsidiary. He asked questions, he got answers that he considered satisfactory, and he did nothing to verify them.

Berardi had no conception of how tight the cash position was. He did not discover that BarChris was holding up checks in substantial amounts because there was no money in the bank to cover them. He did not know of the officers' loans. Since he never read the prospectus, he was not even aware that there had ever been any problem about loans. There had been a material change for the worse in BarChris's financial position. That change was sufficiently serious so that the failure to disclose it made the 1960 figures misleading. Berardi did not discover it. As far as results were concerned, his S-1 review was useless.

Accountants should not be held to a standard higher than that recognized in their profession. Berardi's review did not come up to that standard. He did not take some of the steps that Peat, Marwick's written program prescribed. He did not spend an adequate amount of time on a task of this magnitude. Most important of all, he was too easily satisfied with glib answers to his inquiries. There were enough danger signals to require some further investigation on his part. Generally accepted accounting standards required such further investigation under these circumstances. It is not always sufficient merely to ask questions. Here, again, the burden of proof is on Peat, Marwick. That burden has not been satisfied. Peat, Marwick has not established its due diligence defense.

DECISION AND REMEDY
The district court held that the defendants had failed to prove their due diligence defenses.

Case Questions

Critical Legal Thinking   Should defendants in a Section 11 lawsuit be permitted to prove a due diligence defense to the imposition of liability? Or should liability be strictly imposed?

Ethics   Who do you think committed the fraud in this case? Did any of the other defendants act unethically?

Business Application   Who do you think bore the burden of paying the judgment in this case?

Entrepreneur and the Law

TWO NEW IPO BILLIONAIRES MADE ON THE SAME DAY

On October 19, 1999, the *Forbes* 400 richest people in the world list had two new members, both the recipients of paper money made when their respective companies went public. The first was Martha Stewart, the "Miss Manners" of the late 1990s and early 2000s, who has propelled herself centerstage into America's conscience as the guru of good taste. The one-time stockbroker, turned catering business owner, turned magazine editor, started her empire by writing the 1982 best-selling book *Entertaining*. She then wrote books on gracious living, cooking, hosting parties, and gardening and created a media empire that includes radio and television shows and a syndicated newspaper column. She has nurtured a superbrand name that now appears on K-Mart towels, bedspreads, paints, garden tools, and almost anything used in and around the house. Her company, **Martha Stewart Living Omnimedia,** went public at $18 per share, and on the first day of trading rose to $52 before closing the day at $35. This initial public offering (IPO) of $1.2 billion propelled Stewart into the wealthy elite. Stewart is now one of the richest women in the world.

The second IPO billionaire of the day was Vince McMahon, who took his company, the **World Wrestling Federation (WWF),** public. The WWF is a company that promotes professional wrestling matches, arranges TV coverage of its fights, and sells wrestling memorabilia. McMahon is a third-generation owner of the company. The wrestlers do not own the WWF but merely contract with the WWF to provide their services. Because you have to tell the truth to the SEC and the investing public, WWF's registration statement filed with the SEC and its prospectus given to investors admitted that professional wrestling is basically entertainment and not truly a sport. The documents also disclosed that there were several substantial lawsuits pending against the company and that it faces competition from World Championship Wrestling (WCW), a company backed by Time Warner. The WWF went public at $16, rose to $34 on the first day of trading, before closing the day at $25. After the IPO, McMahon was worth over $1 billion.

Martha Stewart and Vince McMahon are new entrepreneur-billionaires. Will the public investors who bought their companies' stock recognize similar gains, or have they been made-up by Stewart and put in a head lock by McMahon? Only time will tell.

$\mathscr{T}$HE SECURITIES EXCHANGE ACT OF 1934— TRADING IN SECURITIES

Unlike the Securities Act of 1933, which regulates the original issuance of securities, the **Securities Exchange Act of 1934** primarily regulates subsequent trading. (1) It provides for the registration of certain companies with the SEC; continuous filing of periodic reports by these companies to the SEC; and the regulation of securities exchanges, brokers, and dealers. (2) It contains provisions that assess civil and criminal liability on violators of the 1934 act and rules and regulations adopted thereunder.

Securities exchange act of 1934
A federal statute that primarily regulates the trading in securities.

Continuous Reporting Requirements

The Securities Exchange Act of 1934 requires issuers (1) with assets of more than $5 million and at least 500 shareholders, (2) whose equity securities are traded on a national securities exchange or (3) who have made a registered offering under the Securities Act of 1933, to file periodic reports with the SEC. These issuers, called *reporting companies*, must file an annual report *(Form 10-K)*, quarterly reports *(Form 10-Q)*, and monthly reports within 10 days of the end of the month in which a material event (such as a merger) occurs *(Form 8-K)*. These reports may be sent to the SEC on computer tapes or disks.

Section 10(b) and Rule 10b-5

Section 10(b) is one of the most important sections in the entire 1934 act. It prohibits the use of manipulative and deceptive devices in contravention of the rules and regulations prescribed by the SEC.

Pursuant to its rule-making authority, the SEC has adopted **Rule 10b-5**, which provides that:

> *It shall be unlawful for any person, directly or indirectly, by use of any means or instrumentality of interstate commerce or of the mails, or of any facility of any national securities exchange,*
> a. *to employ any device, scheme, or artifice to defraud,*
> b. *to make any untrue statement of a material fact or to omit to state a material fact necessary in order to make the statements made, in light of the circumstances under which they were made, not misleading, or*
> c. *to engage in any act, practice, or course of business that operates or would operate as a fraud or deceit upon any person, in connection with the purchase or sale of any security.*

Rule 10b-5 is not restricted to purchases and sales of securities of reporting companies.[11] All transfers of securities, whether made on a stock exchange, in the over-the-counter market, in a private sale, or in connection with a merger, are subject to this rule.[12] The U.S. Supreme Court has held that only conduct involving **scienter** (intentional conduct) violates Section 10(b) and Rule 10b-5. Negligent conduct is not a violation.[13]

Section 10(b) and Rule 10b-5 require reliance by the injured party on the misstatement. However, many sales and purchases of securities occur in open market transactions (e.g., over stock exchanges) where there is no direct communication between the buyer and the seller.

Section 10(b)
A provision of the Securities Exchange Act of 1934 that prohibits the use of manipulative and deceptive devices in the purchase or sale of securities in contravention of the rules and regulations prescribed by the SEC.

Rule 10b-5
A rule adopted by the SEC to clarify the reach of Section 10(b) against deceptive and fraudulent activities in the purchase and sale of securities.

scienter
Means intentional conduct. Scienter is required for there to be a violation of Section 10(b) and Rule 10b-5.

Contemporary Business Application

SECURITIES INVESTOR PROTECTION CORPORATION (SIPC)

Millions of investors use securities brokerage firms to buy, sell, and hold their securities in "street name." What happens if a securities firm that holds these securities fails? The securities are insured by the **Securities Investor Protection Corporation (SIPC)**, a private insurance company that is funded by annual assessments paid by securities firms.

Some vital statistics and information that investors should know about the SIPC insurance are

- The SIPC provides insurance coverage of up to $500,000 per customer.

- Of the $500,000 coverage, only $100,000 of cash is covered per customer.
- Unlike deposit insurance for savings and checking accounts at banks, the SIPC is not backed by the full faith and credit of the U.S. government.
- The SIPC currently has under $1 billion in its coffers and an additional $500-million line of credit with banks it can draw on. This is sufficient to cover the failure of many small brokerage firms but is inadequate to cover the failure of large brokerage firms.

𝒥NSIDER TRADING

One of the most important purposes of Section 10(b) and Rule 10b-5 is to prevent **insider trading**. Insider trading occurs when a company employee or company advisor uses material nonpublic information to make a profit by trading in the securities of the company. This practice is considered illegal because it allows insiders to take advantage of the investing public.

In the **Matter of Cady, Roberts & Co.,**[14] the SEC announced that the duty of an insider who possesses material nonpublic information is to either (1) abstain from trading in the securities of the company or (2) disclose the information to the person on the other side of the transaction before the insider purchases the securities from or sells the securities to him or her.

> **insider trading**
>
> **When an insider makes a profit by personally purchasing shares of the corporation prior to public release of favorable information or by selling shares of the corporation prior to the public disclosure of unfavorable information.**

Insiders

For purposes of Section 10(b) and Rule 10b-5, *insiders* are defined as (1) officers, directors, and employees at all levels of the company, (2) lawyers, accountants, consultants, and other agents and representatives who are hired by the company on a temporary and nonemployee status to provide services or work to the company, and (3) others who owe a fiduciary duty to the company.

Following are classical and nonclassical cases of insider trading.

Securities and Exchange Commission v. Texas Gulf Sulphur Co.
401 F.2d 833 (1968)
United States Court of Appeals, Second Circuit

CASE 40.3

FACTS

Texas Gulf Sulphur Co. (TGS) had for several years conducted aerial geophysical surveys in eastern Canada. On November 12, 1963, TGS drilled an exploratory hole—Kidd 55—near Timmins, Ontario. Assay reports showed that the core from this drilling proved to be remarkably high in copper, zinc, and silver. Because TGS did not own the mineral rights to properties surrounding the drill site, TGS kept the discovery secret, camouflaged the drill site, and diverted drilling efforts to another site. This allowed TGS to engage in extensive land acquisition around Kidd 55.

Eventually, rumors of a rich mineral strike began circulating. On Saturday, April 11, 1964, *The New York Times* and the *New York Herald-Tribune* published unauthorized reports of TGS drilling efforts in Canada and its rich mineral strike. On Sunday, April 12, officers of TGS met with a public relations consultant and drafted a press release that was issued that afternoon. The press release appeared in morning newspapers of general circulation on Monday, April 13. It read in pertinent part:

> *The work done to date has not been sufficient to reach definite conclusions and any statement as to size and grade of ore would be premature and possibly misleading. When we have progressed to the point where reasonable and logical conclusions can*

be made, TGS will issue a definite statement to its stockholders and to the public in order to clarify the Timmins project.

The rumors persisted. On April 16, 1964, at 10:00 A.M., TGS held a press conference for the financial media. At this conference, which lasted about 10 minutes, TGS disclosed the richness of the Timmins's mineral strike and that the strike would run to at least 25 million tons of ore. In early November 1963, TGS stock was trading at $173 per share. On April 15, 1964, the stock closed at $298. Several officers, directors, and other employees of TGS who had knowledge of the mineral strike at Timmins traded in the stock of TGS during the period November 12, 1963, to April 16, 1964. By May 15, 1964, the stock was selling at $58¼.

The SEC brought this action against David M. Crawford and Francis G. Coates, two TGS executives who possessed the nonpublic information about the ore strike and who traded in TGS securities. The SEC sought to rescind their stock purchases. The district court found Crawford liable for insider trading but dismissed the complaint against Coates. Appeals were taken from this judgment.

ISSUE

Are Crawford and Coates liable for trading on material inside information in violation of Section 10(b) and Rule 10b-5?

(case continues)

In The Language of The Court

Waterman, Circuit Judge The insiders here were not trading on an equal footing with the outside investors. They alone were in a position to evaluate the probability and magnitude of what seemed from the outset to be a major ore strike.

Crawford. Crawford telephoned his orders to his Chicago broker about midnight on April 15 and again at 8:30 in the morning of April 16 with instructions to buy at the opening of the Midwest Stock Exchange that morning. The trial court's finding that "he sought to, and did, 'beat the news,'" is well documented by the record. Before insiders may act upon material information, such information must have been effectively disclosed in a manner sufficient to ensure its availability to the investing public. Particularly here, where a formal announcement to the entire financial news media had been promised in a prior official release known to the media, all insider activity must await dissemination of the promised official announcement.

Coates. Coates was absolved by the court below because his telephone order was placed shortly before 10:20 A.M. on April 16, which was after the announcement had been made even though the news could not be considered already a matter of public information. This result seems to have been predicated upon a misinterpretation of dicta in Cody Roberts, where the SEC instructed insiders to "keep out of the market until the established procedures for public release of the information are carried out instead of hastening to execute transactions in advance of, and in frustration of, the objectives of the release." The reading of a news release, which prompted Coates into action, is merely the first step in the process of dissemination required for compliance with the regulatory objective of providing all investors with an equal opportunity to make informed investment judgments. Assuming that the contents of the official release could instantaneously be acted upon, at the minimum Coates should have waited until the news could reasonably have been expected to appear over the media of widest circulation, the Dow Jones broad tape, rather than hastening to ensure an advantage to himself and his broker son-in-law.

Decision and Remedy

The court of appeals held that both executives, Crawford and Coates, had engaged in illegal insider trading.

Case Questions

Critical Legal Thinking Should insider trading be illegal? Why or why not?

Ethics Did Crawford and Coates act ethically in this case?

Business Application How can businesses protect against their employees engaging in insider trading? Explain.

United States v. O'Hagan
1997 WL 345229 (1997)
United States Supreme Court

CASE 40.4

Facts

James O'Hagan was a partner in the law firm of Dorsey & Whitney in Minneapolis, Minnesota. In July 1988, Grand Metropolitan PLC (Grand Met), a company based in London, England, hired Dorsey & Whitney to represent it in a secret tender offer for the stock of the Pillsbury Company, headquartered in Minneapolis. On August 18, 1988, O'Hagan began purchasing call options for Pillsbury stock. Each call option gave O'Hagan the right to purchase 100 shares of Pillsbury stock at a specified price. O'Hagan continued to purchase call options in August and September and became the largest holder of call options for Pillsbury stock. In September, O'Hagan also purchased 5,000 shares of Pillsbury common stock at $39 per share. These purchases were all made while Grand Met's proposed tender offer for Pillsbury remained secret to the public. When Grand Met publicly announced its tender offer in October, 1988, Pillsbury stock increased to nearly $60 per share. O'Hagan sold his Pillsbury call options and common stock, making a profit of more than $4.3 million.

The Securities and Exchange Commission (SEC) investigated, and the Justice Department charged O'Hagan with criminally violating Section 10(b) and Rule 10b-5. Because this was not a case of classical insider trading because O'Hagan did not trade in the stock of his law firm's client, Grand Met, the government alleged that O'Hagan was liable under the "misappropriation theory" for trading in Pillsbury stock by engaging in deceptive conduct by misappropriating the secret information about Grand Met's tender offer from his employer, Dorsey & Whitney, and from its client, Grand Met. The district court found O'Hagan guilty and sentenced him to 41 months in prison. The Eighth Circuit Court of Appeals reversed, finding that liability under Section 10(b) and Rule 10b-5 cannot be based on the misappropriation theory. The government appealed to the U.S. Supreme Court.

Issue

Can a defendant be criminally convicted of violating Section 10(b) and Rule 10b-5 based on the misappropriation theory?

In The Language of The Court

Ginsburg, Associate Judge Under the "traditional" or "classical theory" of insider trading liability, Section 10(b) and Rule 10b-5 are violated when a corporate insider *trades in the securities of* his *corporation on the basis of material, nonpublic information. Trading on such information qualifies as a "deceptive device" under Section 10(b) because a relationship of trust and confidence exists between the shareholders of a corporation and those insiders who have obtained confidential information by reason of their position with that corporation.*

The "misappropriation theory" holds that a person commits fraud "in connection with" a securities transaction, and thereby violates Section 10(b) and Rule 10b-5, when he misappropriates confidential information for securities trading purposes, in breach of a duty owed to the source of the information. Under this theory, a fiduciary's undisclosed, self-serving use of a principal's information to purchase or sell securities, in breach of a duty of loyalty and confidentiality, defrauds the principal of the exclusive use of that information.

The two theories are complementary, each addressing efforts to capitalize on nonpublic information through the purchase or sale of securities. The classical theory targets a corporate insider's breach of duty to shareholders with whom the insider transacts; the misappropriation theory outlaws trading on the basis of non-public information by a corporate "outsider" in breach of a duty owed not to a trading party, but to the source of the information.

The misappropriation theory comports with Section 10(b)'s language, which requires deception "in connection with the purchase or sale of any security," not deception of an identifiable pur-chaser or seller. In sum, considering the inhibiting impact on market participation of trading on misappropriated information, and the congressional purposes underlying Section 10(b), it makes scant sense to hold a lawyer like O'Hagan a Section 10(b) viola-tor if he works for a law firm representing the target of a tender offer, but not if he works for a law firm representing the bidder. The text of the statute requires no such result. The misappropria-tion at issue here was properly made the subject of a Section 10(b) charge because it meets the statutory requirement that there be "deceptive" conduct "in connection with" securities transactions.

DECISION AND REMEDY

The Supreme Court held that a defendant can be criminally convicted of violating Section 10(b) and Rule 10b-5 under the misappropriation theory.

Case Questions

Critical Legal Thinking Should the misappropriation theory be recognized as a basis for criminal liability under Section 10(b) and Rule 10b-5? Do you agree with the Supreme Court's decision?

Ethics If the Supreme Court had upheld the Eighth Circuit's decision, would ethics alone be enough to prevent persons like O'Hagan from trading on secret information?

Business Application Will the securities markets be more or less honest because of the Supreme Court's ruling?

Tipper-Tippee Liability

A person who discloses material nonpublic information to another person is called a **tip-per**. The person who receives such information is known as the **tippee**. The tippee is liable for acting on material information that he or she knew or should have known was not public. The tipper is liable for the profits made by the tippee. If the tippee tips other persons, both the tippee (who is now a tipper) and the original tipper are liable for the profits made by these remote tippees. The remote tippees are liable for their own trades if they knew or should have known that they possessed material inside information.

tipper
A person who discloses mate-rial nonpublic information to another person.

tippee
The person who receives material nonpublic informa-tion from a tipper.

Prior to the enactment of the Securities Act of 1933 and the Securities Exchange Act of 1934, many "stool pigeons" were defrauded by securities schemes. Today there may still be fraud in the purchase and sale of securities, but these federal laws permit the government and the victims of these frauds to sue and recover criminal and civil remedies, respectively.

LIABILITY PROVISIONS OF THE SECURITIES EXCHANGE ACT OF 1934

The civil and criminal penalties that may be assessed for violations of the Securities Exchange Act of 1934 are discussed in the following paragraphs.

Criminal Liability

Section 32

A provision of the Securities Exchange Act of 1934 that imposes criminal liability on any person who willfully violates the 1934 act or the rules or regulations adopted thereunder.

Section 32 of the Securities Exchange Act of 1934 makes it a criminal offense to violate willfully the provisions of the act or the rules and regulations adopted thereunder.[15] Upon conviction, a natural person may be fined up to $1 million, imprisoned for up to 10 years, or both. A person cannot be imprisoned unless he or she had knowledge of the rule or regulation violated, however. A corporation or other entity may be fined up to $2.5 million for violating Section 32.

SEC Actions

The SEC may investigate suspected violations of the Securities Exchange Act of 1934 and the rules and regulations adopted thereunder. The SEC may enter into *consent orders* with defendants, seek *injunctions* in federal district court, or seek court orders requiring defendants to *disgorge* illegally gained profits.

Insider Trading Sanctions Act of 1984

A federal statute that permits the SEC to obtain a civil penalty of up to three times the illegal benefits received from insider trading.

In 1984, Congress enacted the **Insider Trading Sanctions Act**.[16] which permits the SEC to obtain a *civil penalty* of up to three times the illegal profits gained or losses avoided on insider trading. The fine is payable to the U.S. Treasury.

Private Actions

Although Section 10(b) and Rule 10b-5 do not expressly provide for a private right of action, courts have implied such a right. Generally, a private plaintiff may seek rescission of the securities contract or recover damages (e.g., disgorgements of the illegal profits by the defendants).

Ethical Perspective

e-biz

ON-LINE "FREE" STOCK SCAM DELETED BY SEC

Do free stock for Internet users sound too good to be true? The Securities and Exchange Commission (SEC), the government agency charged with enforcing federal securities laws, thought so and has launched a crackdown on this recent Internet craze. The scam works as follows: For agreeing to buy certain products or services or for merely agreeing to give some personal information about oneself, the Internet operator gives "free" stock in the company to the buyer or the provider of information. The Internet user is lured into this deal by promises of receiving stock that has value and will become more valuable in the future. These offers are usually made through Internet chat rooms or e-mail messages.

Federal securities laws, which prohibit fraud in the sale or purchase of securities, apply to Internet sales of securities. The SEC applied these antifraud provisions and has sued many Internet companies for "free" stock fraud. The SEC determined that the person receiving the stock paid something of value, such as buying products or services or by providing valuable personal information that the stock scam operator uses or sells.

One company the SEC brought charges against was Web Works Marketing.com. The company offered shares of its stock to Internet users who registered on its Web site or signed up for long-distance telecommunications services. Investors were told that the shares had a value of $38 and could appreciate to $200 when the company went public and that the company had more than 10,000 customers. In fact, the company had 35 customers, no contract with a long-distance provider, and had taken no steps toward a public offering. The company settled the charges with the SEC. The SEC has targeted many more so-called "free stock" companies for running fraudulent Internet scams.

Short-Swing Profits

Section 16(a) of the 1934 act defines any person who is an executive officer, a director, or a 10 percent shareholder of an equity security of a reporting company as a *statutory insider* for Section 16 purposes. Statutory insiders must file reports with the SEC disclosing their ownership and trading in the company's securities.[17] These reports must be filed within 10 days after the end of the month in which the trade occurs.

Section 16(b)

Section 16(b) requires that any profits made by a statutory insider on transactions involving so-called *short-swing profits*—that is, trades involving equity securities occurring within six months of each other—belong to the corporation.[18] The corporation may bring a legal action to recover these profits. Involuntary transactions, such as forced redemption of securities by the corporation or an exchange of securities in a bankruptcy proceeding, are exempt. Section 16(b) is a strict liability provision. Generally, no defenses are recognized. Neither intent nor the possession of inside information need be shown.

Consider This Example Rosanne is the president of a corporation and a statutory insider who does not possess any inside information. On February 1, she purchases 1,000 shares of her employer's stock at $10 per share. On June 1, she sells the stock for $14 per share. The corporation can recover the $4,000 profit because the trades occurred within six months of each other. Rosanne would have to wait until after August 1 to sell the securities.

SEC Rules

In 1991, the SEC adopted new rules concerning Section 16.[19] This was the first major change in the rules in 57 years. These rules

- Clarify the definition of *officer* to include only executive officers who perform policy-making functions. This would include the president, the chief executive officer, the vice presidents in charge of business units or divisions, the principal financial officer, the principal accounting officer, and the like. Officers who run day-to-day operations but are not responsible for policy decisions are not included.
- Create a new *Form 5* report that must be filed by all insiders within 45 days of the end of the company's calendar year.
- Relieve insiders of liability for transactions that occur within six months before becoming an insider. For example, if a noninsider buys shares of his or her company January 15, becomes an insider March 15, and sells the shares May 15, the January 15 purchase is not matched against the May 15 sale.
- Continue the rule that insiders are liable for transactions that occur within six months of the last transaction engaged in while an insider. For example, if an insider buys shares in his or her company April 30 and leaves the company May 15, this purchase must be matched against any sale of the company's shares that occurs on or before October 30.
- Treat derivative securities (e.g., stock options, warrants) as follows: The acquisition or disposition of a derivative security is a Section 16 event; the exercise of the derivative security is a nonevent for Section 16 purposes. For example, suppose a company issues a stock option to its president May 15, who exercises the option June 15 and sells the shares on December 1. There is no violation of Section 16.
- Require companies to disclose delinquent filings of Section 16 forms in their proxy statements.

Section 16(a)

A section of the Securities Exchange Act of 1934 that defines any person who is an executive officer, a director, or a 10 percent shareholder of an equity security of a reporting company as a *statutory insider* for Section 16 purposes.

Section 16(b)

A section of the Securities Exchange Act of 1934 that requires that any profits made by a statutory insider on transactions involving *short-swing profits* belong to the corporation.

Business Brief

In 1991, the SEC issued rules that clarify the persons and transactions subject to Section 16's short-swing profit rule.

CONCEPT SUMMARY   SECTION 10(B) AND SECTION 16(B) COMPARED

Element	Section 10(b) and Rule 10b-5	Section 16(b)
Covered securities	All securities.	Securities required to be registered with the SEC under the 1934 act.
Inside information	Defendant made a misrepresentation or traded on inside (or perhaps misappropriated) information.	Short-swing profits recoverable whether or not they are attributable to misappropriation or inside information.
Recovery	Belongs to the injured purchaser or seller.	Belongs to the corporation.

International Perspective

ENFORCEMENT OF INTERNATIONAL SECURITIES LAWS

The United States is not the only country in the world that outlaws insider trading and securities fraud. For example, Britain has outlawed insider dealing in securities for years. In 1993, the British government even implemented new legislation to strengthen its insider trading laws. The French insider trading law makes it illegal for a person to trade on nonpublic information received by reason of his or her position or profession. The European Community (EC) has directed all member countries to adopt laws against insider trading. Japan has an insider trading law that is rarely enforced.

Many persons who engage in illegal insider trading in the United States often do so using businesses or "fronts" located in other countries. In addition, these traders often deposit their ill-gotten gains in secret bank accounts located in off-shore bank havens. Can U.S. authorities obtain documents and evidence, as well as information about the location of bank accounts, from other countries? The answer is yes, in many situations.

In 1990, Congress enacted the **International Securities Enforcement Cooperation Act** [P.L. 101-550, 104 Stat. 2713]. The act authorizes the SEC to cooperate with foreign securities authorities, to provide records to foreign securities authorities, and to sanction securities professionals in this country who violate foreign securities laws.

The SEC has entered in **memoranda of understandings**, or **MOUs**, with several foreign governments or authorities. As a general rule, the MOUs provide that the SEC and its foreign counterparts will cooperate in the enforcement of each country's securities laws. Thus, the SEC can obtain evidence about the location of bank accounts and other information concerning persons suspected of violating U.S. securities laws from foreign authorities. Currently, the SEC has entered into MOUs with Argentina, Brazil, Canada, France, Great Britain, Italy, Japan, the Netherlands, and Switzerland.

As securities trading becomes more international, it is going to become easier for investors and others to engage in insider trading and securities fraud across national boundaries. The United States and other countries will have to cooperate in finding, prosecuting, and penalizing perpetrators of securities frauds.

OTHER FEDERAL SECURITIES LAWS

Securities Enforcement Remedies and Penny Stock Reform Act of 1990

Securities Enforcement Remedies and Penny Stock Reform Act of 1990
A federal statute that gives the SEC greater enforcement powers and increases and expands the remedies available for securities violations.

The **Securities Enforcement Remedies and Penny Stock Reform Act of 1990**[20] added new weapons to the SEC's enforcement powers. Namely, it authorizes

- **Cease-and-Desist Orders** After holding an appropriate administrative proceeding, the SEC may order a *cease-and-desist order* against any person who is violating, has violated, or is about to violate any provision of federal securities laws to cease and desist from committing such violation. The act authorizes the SEC to issue a *temporary cease-and-desist order* prior to completion of the proceeding if it determines that the alleged violation is likely to result in substantial dissipation or conversion of assets, significant harm to investors or the public interest, or losses to the **Securities Investor Protection Corporation (SIPC)**.

- **Civil Money Penalties** The SEC may bring an action in federal court seeking *civil money penalties* against any person or entity for violating federal securities laws, SEC rules or regulations, and SEC cease-and-desist orders. The court may assess penalties as the greater of (1) the defendant's pecuniary gain obtained as a result of the violation or (2) any one of the following three tiers of fines, as the circumstances warrant:
  - *Tier 1*: $5,000 for a natural person or $50,000 for any other person.
  - *Tier 2*: $50,000 for a natural person or $250,000 for any other person.
  - *Tier 3*: $100,000 for a natural person or $500,000 for any other person.
- **Penny Stock Reform** In the past, there has been significant fraud in the sale of penny stocks. **Penny stocks** are low-priced stocks (i.e., stocks that are sold for a few cents to a few dollars). The act requires the SEC to adopt rules to require securities brokers and dealers to provide specific information to investors concerning stock prices and the inherent risk of the penny stock market. This enhanced disclosure should help prevent some penny stock fraud.

Market Reform Act of 1990

The **Market Reform Act of 1990**[21] establishes a number of measures to enhance financial market stability. It authorizes the SEC to promulgate rules to proscribe manipulative practices related to market price levels and trading practices during periods of extraordinary market volatility. Under this authority, the SEC sets limits on program trading (i.e., computer-driven trading strategies). The act also authorizes the SEC to take emergency action (e.g., suspend trading) to ensure fair and orderly markets during periods of market stress.

Market Reform Act of 1990
A federal statute that authorizes the SEC to regulate trading practices during periods of extraordinary market volatility.

Racketeer Influenced and Corrupt Organizations Act

The **Racketeer Influenced and Corrupt Organizations Act (RICO)** makes it a federal crime to engage in a pattern of racketeering activity.[22] Because securities fraud falls under the definition of racketeering activity, the government often brings a RICO allegation in conjunction with a securities fraud allegation.

In addition, persons injured by a RICO violation can bring a private civil action against the violator and recover treble (triple) damages but only if the defendant has been criminally convicted in connection with the securities fraud.[23] A third-party independent contractor (e.g., an outside accountant) must have participated in the operation or management of the enterprise to be liable for civil RICO.[24]

Racketeer Influenced and Corrupt Organizations Act (RICO)
A federal statute that provides for both criminal and civil penalties.

Private Securities Litigation Reform Act of 1995

Sometimes companies include forward-looking statements about future economic plans and projections of financial data in prospectuses and other documents filed with the SEC and provided to investors. The **Private Securities Litigation Reform Act of 1995** provides a *safe harbor* from liability for companies that make such statements if they are accompanied by meaningful cautionary statements that identify risk factors that could cause actual results to differ from those in the statement.

Private Securities Litigation Reform Act of 1995
Provides a safe harbor from liability for companies that make forward-looking statements that are accompanied by meaningful cautionary statements of risk factors.

STATE SECURITIES LAWS

Most states have enacted securities laws. These laws, which are often called *blue-sky laws*, generally require the registration of certain securities and provide exemptions from registration. They also contain broad antifraud provisions.

The **Uniform Securities Act** has been adopted by many states. This act is drafted to coordinate state securities laws with federal securities laws.

Business Brief
State securities laws presumably originated to protect investors from foolishly buying a piece of the blue sky.

Contemporary Business Application

COMMODITIES REGULATION

Commodities include grains (e.g., wheat, soybeans, oats), animals (e.g., cattle, hogs), animal products (e.g., pork bellies), foods (e.g., sugar, coffee), metals (e.g., gold, silver), and oil. A *commodities futures contract* is an agreement to buy or sell a specific amount and type of commodity at some future date at a price established at the time of contracting. For example, a futures contract may be to sell 5,000 bushels of oats on July 31 at $2.87 per bushel. Standardized terms are established for futures contracts (e.g., quantity and quality of the commodity, time and place of delivery). Thus, each similar contract is *fungible*. This makes the contracts liquid; that is, they can be bought and sold on the commodities exchanges just as stocks and bonds are bought and sold on securities exchanges. Farmers, ranchers, food processors, milling companies, mineral producers, oil companies, and investors often buy and sell futures contracts.

Commodities exchanges have been established at different locations across the country where commodity futures contracts can be bought and sold by food producers, farmers, and speculators. The major commodity exchanges are

- The Chicago Board of Trade (CBOT)
- The Chicago Mercantile Exchange (CME)
- The Commodity Exchange of New York (COMEX)
- Kansas City Board of Trade (KBOT)

- New York Coffee, Sugar, & Cocoa Exchange (NYCSCE)
- New York Cotton Exchange (NYCTN)
- New York Mercantile Exchange (NYME)
- New York Futures Exchange (NYF)

The **Commodity Exchange Act (CEA)** was enacted by Congress in 1936 to regulate the trading of commodity futures contracts. The **Commodity Futures Trading Commission Act**, which was enacted in 1974, significantly amended the prior act [7 U.S.C. §§ 1-17a]. **Section 4b** of the **CEA** prohibits fraudulent conduct in connection with any order or contract of sale of any commodity for future delivery.

The 1974 amendments created the **Commodity Futures Trading Commission (CFTC)** to administer and enforce the CEA. The CFTC is a federal administrative agency consisting of five members appointed by the President. The CFTC has the authority to regulate trading in commodities futures contracts. It has the power to adopt regulations, conduct investigations, bring administrative proceedings against suspected violators, issue cease-and-desist orders and injunctions, and impose civil fines. Suspected criminal violations can be referred to the Justice Department for criminal action.

WWW *Working the Web*

U.S. Securities and Exchange Commission This large government Web site links you to many securities materials.

   Visit at **www.sec.gov/**

Securities Act of 1933 This searchable copy of the Act is maintained by the University of Cincinnati.

   Visit at **www.law.uc.edu/CCL/33Act**

Securities Act of 1934 This searchable copy of the Act is maintained by the University of Cincinnati.

   Visit at **www.law.uc.edu/CCL/34Act**

Securities Law Home Page This site is an on-line guide to securities law.

   Visit at **www.seclaw.com**

CYBER EXERCISES

1. If you have a complaint or question about your investments, you might want to contact the U.S. Securities and Exchange Commission, Office of Investor Education and Assistance. What is its e-mail address?

2. What subject does Section 4 of the Securities Act of 1933 cover?

3. What commission does the Securities Act of 1934 establish?

4. Using the Securities Law Home Page, read the current issue of *Securities Law Letter*.

*C*ASES AND *E*XERCISES

CRITICAL LEGAL THINKING CASES

40.1. Dare To Be Great, Inc. (Dare), was a Florida corporation wholly owned by Glenn W. Turner Enterprises, Inc. (Turner). Dare offered self-improvement courses aimed at improving self-motivation and sales ability. In return for an investment of money, the purchaser received certain tapes, records, and written materials. In addition, depending on the level of involvement, the purchaser had the opportunity to help sell Dare courses to others and to receive part of the purchase price as a commission. There were four different levels of involvement.

The task of salespersons was to bring prospective purchasers to "Adventure Meetings." The meetings, which were conducted by Dare people and not the salespersons, were conducted in a preordained format that included great enthusiasm, cheering and chanting, exuberant handshaking, standing on chairs, and shouting. Dare people and the salespersons dressed in modern, expensive clothes, displayed large sums of cash, drove new and expensive automobiles, and engaged in "hard-sell" tactics to induce prospects to sign their name and part with their money. In actuality, few Dare purchasers ever attained the wealth promised. The tape recordings and materials distributed by Dare were worthless. Is this sales scheme a "security" that should have been registered with the SEC? [*Securities and Exchange Commission v. Glenn W. Turner Enterprises, Inc.*, 474 F.2d 476 (9th Cir. 1973)]

40.2. The Farmers' Cooperative of Arkansas and Oklahoma (Co-Op) was an agricultural cooperative that had approximately 23,000 members. To raise money to support its general business operations, Co-Op sold promissory notes (notes) to investors that were payable upon demand. Co-Op offered the notes to both members and nonmembers, advertised the notes as an "investment program," and offered an interest rate higher than that available on savings accounts at financial institutions. More than 1,600 people purchased notes worth a total of $10 million. Subsequently, Co-Op filed for bankruptcy. A class of holders of the notes filed suit against Ernst & Young, a national firm of certified public accountants that had audited Co-Op's financial statements, alleging that Ernst & Young had violated Section 10(b) of the Securities Exchange Act of 1934. Are the notes issued by Co-Op "securities"? [*Reves v. Ernst & Young*, 495 U.S. 56, 110 S.Ct. 945 (1990)]

40.3. The McDonald Investment Company (McDonald) was a corporation organized and incorporated in the state of Minnesota. The principal and only place of business from which the company conducted operations was located in Rush City, Minnesota. Over 80 percent of the company's assets were located in, and over 80 percent of its income was derived from, Minnesota. On January 18, 1972, McDonald sold securities to Minnesota residents only. The proceeds from the sale were used entirely to make loans and other investments in real estate and other assets located outside the state of Minnesota. The company did not file a registration statement with the SEC. Does this offering qualify for an intrastate offering exemption from registration? [*Securities and Exchange Commission v. McDonald Investment Company*, 343 F.Supp. 343 (D. Minn. 1972)]

40.4. Lomasney & Co. (Lomasney) was a securities broker-dealer and principal underwriter for securities to be issued by Continental Travel, Inc. (Continental). Mr. Diskin was an investor who was interested in purchasing some Continental securities when they were issued. The following activities occurred with respect to the registration and sale of Continental's securities:

August 28, 1968	Continental filed a registration statement with the SEC.
September 17, 1968	Lomasney sent a letter to Diskin that stated: "This letter will assure you that we will commit to you the sale at the public offering price when, as and if issued, 5,000 shares of Continental Travel, Inc."
February 11, 1969	Continental's registration statement became effective.
February 12, 1969	Lomasney sent a letter to Diskin confirming the sale; the letter did not include a final Continental prospectus.
February 28, 1969	On or just before this date, Lomasney sent Diskin a final prospectus; on this date, Diskin paid for the Continental stock.

Subsequently, Continental suffered financial difficulties and Diskin's investment in Continental decreased substantially in value. On November 19, 1969, Diskin demanded rescission of his Continental stock purchase. Are there any violations of securities laws that would permit Diskin to rescind his stock purchase? [*Diskin v. Lomasney & Co.*, 452 F.2d 871 (2d Cir. 1971)]

40.5. Continental Enterprises, Inc. (Continental), had 2,510,000 shares of stock issued and outstanding. Louis E. Wolfson and members of his immediate family and associates owned in excess of 40 percent of those shares. The balance was in the hands of approximately 5,000 outside shareholders. Wolfson was Continental's largest shareholder and the guiding spirit of the corporation who gave direction to and controlled the company's officers. Between August 1, 1960, and January 31, 1962, without public disclosure, Wolfson and his family and associates sold 55 percent of their stock through six brokerage houses. Wolfson and his family and associates did not file a registration statement with the SEC with respect to these sales. Do the securities sales by Wolfson and his family and associates qualify for an exemption for registration as a sale "not by an issuer, underwriter, or dealer"? [*United States v. Wolfson*, 405 F.2d 779 (2d Cir. 1968)]

40.6. Chiarella worked as a "markup man" in the New York composing room of Pandick Press, a financial printer. Among the documents that Chiarella handled were five secret announcements of corporate takeovers. The tender offerors had hired Pandick Press to print the offers, which would later be made public when the tender offers were made to the shareholders of the target corporations. When the documents were delivered to Pandick Press, the identities of the acquiring and target corporations were concealed by blank spaces or false names. The true names would not be sent to Pandick Press until the night of the final printing.

Chiarella was able to deduce the names of the target companies before the final printing. Without disclosing this knowledge, he purchased stock in the target companies and sold the shares immediately after the takeover attempts were made public. Chiarella realized a gain of $30,000 in the course of 14 months. The federal government indicted Chiarella for criminal violations of Section 10(b) of the Securities Exchange Act of 1934. Is Chiarella guilty? [*Chiarella v. United States*, 445 U.S. 222, 100 S.Ct. 1108 (1980)]

40.7. Leslie Neadeau was the president of T.O.N.M. Oil & Gas Exploration Corporation (TONM). Charles Lazzaro was a registered securities broker employed by Bateman Eichler, Hill Richards, Inc. (Bateman Eichler). The stock of TONM was traded in the over-the-counter market. Lazzaro made statements to potential investors that he had "inside information" about TONM, including that (1) vast amounts of gold had been discovered in Surinam and that TONM had options on thousands of acres in the gold-producing regions of Surinam, (2) the discovery was "not publicly known, but would be subsequently announced", and (3) when this information was made public, TONM stock, which was then selling from $1.50 to $3.00 per share, would increase to $10.00 to $15.00 within a short period of time and might increase to $100.00 per share within a year.

The potential investors contacted Neadeau at TONM, who confirmed that the information was not public knowledge. In reliance on Lazzaro's and Neadeau's statements, the investors purchased TONM stock. The so-called "inside information" turned out to be false, and the shares declined substantially below the purchase price. The investors sued Lazzaro, Bateman Eichler, Neadeau, and TONM, alleging violations of Section 10(b) of the Securities Exchange Act of 1934. The defendants asserted that the plaintiffs' complaint should be dismissed because they participated in the fraud. Who wins? [*Bateman Eichler, Hill Richards, Inc. v. Berner*, 472 U.S. 299, 105 S.Ct. 2622 (1985)]

40.8. Donald C. Hoodes was the chief executive officer of the Sullair Corporation (Sullair). As an officer of the corporation, he was regularly granted stock options to purchase stock of the company at a discount. On July 20, 1982, Hoodes sold 6,000 shares of Sullair common stock for $38,350. On July 31, 1982, Sullair terminated Hoodes as an officer of the corporation. On August 20, 1982, Hoodes exercised options to purchase 6,000 shares of Sullair stock that cost him $3.01 per share ($18,060); at the time, they were trading at $4.50 per share ($27,000). Hoodes did not possess material nonpublic information about Sullair when he sold or purchased the securities of the company. The corporation brought suit against Hoodes to recover the profits Hoodes made on these trades. Who wins? [*Sullair Corporation v. Hoodes*, 672 F.Supp. 337 (N.D.Ill. 1987)]

ETHICS CASES

40.9. Stephen Murphy owned Intertie, a California company that was involved in financing and managing cable television stations. Murphy was both an officer of the corporation and chairman of the board of directors. Intertie would buy a cable television station, make a small cash down payment, and finance the remainder of the purchase price. It would then create a limited partnership and sell the cable station to the partnership for a cash down payment and a promissory note in favor of Intertie. Finally, Intertie would lease the station back from the partnership. Intertie purchased more than 30 stations and created an equal number of limited partnerships, from which it received more than $7.5 million from approximately 400 investors.

Evidence showed that most of the limited partnerships were not self-supporting but that this fact was not disclosed to investors. Intertie commingled partnership funds, taking funds generated from the sale of new partnership offerings to meet debt service obligations of previously sold cable systems; Intertie also used funds from limited partnerships that were formed but that never acquired cable systems. Intertie did not keep any records regarding the qualifications of investors to purchase the securities and also refused to make its financial statements available to investors.

Intertie suffered severe financial difficulties and eventually filed for bankruptcy. The limited partners suffered substantial losses. Did each of the limited partnership offerings alone qualify for the private placement exemption from registration?

Should the 30 limited partnership offerings be integrated? [*Securities and Exchange Commission v. Murphy*, 626 F.2d 633 (9th Cir. 1980)].

40.10. In January and February 1986, Mrs. Weill was a patient of Dr. Robert Howard Willis, a psychiatrist. During the course of their sessions, Mrs. Weill disclosed that her husband, Sanford I. Weill, a wealthy businessman, had developed an interest in becoming the chief executive officer of BankAmerica Corporation. She also disclosed that Mr. Weill was secretly negotiating with representatives of BankAmerica and that he had secured a commitment from Shearson Loeb Rhodes, an investment banking firm, to invest $1 billion in BankAmerica if he was successful in his negotiations. None of this information was public knowledge.

From approximately January 14, 1986, until February 6, 1986, Dr. Willis purchased 13,000 shares of BankAmerica common stock for himself and his children at prices ranging from $12⅛ to $14¾ per share. On February 20, 1986, BankAmerica disclosed Mr. Weill's proposal. The price of BankAmerica's stock went up on the news. On February 21, 1986, Dr. Willis sold all of the BankAmerica shares at $15⅜ per share, making a total profit of $27,475. The United States brought criminal charges against Dr. Willis for insider trading in violation of Section 10(b). Who wins? Did Willis act ethically? [*United States v. Willis*, 737 F.Supp. 269 (S.D.N.Y. 1990)]

CRITICAL LEGAL THINKING WRITING ASSIGNMENT

Read Case A.40 in the Case Appendix [*Lampf, Pleva, Lipkind, Prupis & Petigrow v. Gilbertson*]. This case is excerpted from the U.S. Supreme Court opinion. Review and brief the case. In your brief, be sure to answer the following questions:

1. Were the limited partnership interests "securities"?

2. What statute did the plaintiffs allege that the defendants had violated?

3. Succinctly state the issue presented to the U.S. Supreme Court.

4. How did the U.S. Supreme Court decide this issue?

Notes

1. *Securities and Exchange Commission v. W. J. Howey Co.*, 328 U.S. 293, 66 S.Ct. 1100 (1946).
2. Securities Act of 1933, § 4(1).
3. Securities Act of 1933, § 3(a)(11).
4. SEC Rule 147.
5. Securities Act of 1933, § 4(2).
6. SEC Rule 506.
7. SEC Rule 501.
8. Securities Act of 1933, § 3(b).
9. SEC Rules 502(a) and 147(b)(2).
10. 15 U.S.C. § 77x.
11. Litigation instituted pursuant to § 10(b) and Rule 10b-5 must be commenced within one year after the discovery of the violation and within three years after such violation [*Lampf, Pleva, Lipkind, Prupis & Petigrow v. Gilbertson*, 111 S.Ct. 2773 (1991)].
12. The U.S. Supreme Court has held that the sale of a business is a sale of securities that is subject to Section 10(b). See *Gould v. Ruefenacht*, 471 U.S. 701, 105 S.Ct. 2308 (1985) (where 50 percent of a business was sold) and *Landreth Timber Co. v. Landreth*, 471 U.S. 681, 105 S.Ct. 2297 (1985) (where 100 percent of a business was sold).
13. *Ernst & Ernst v. Hochfelder*, 425 U.S. 185, 96 S.Ct. 1375 (1976).
14. 40 SEC 907 (1961).
15. 15 U.S.C. § 78 ff.
16. P.L. 98-376.
17. 15 U.S.C. § 78l.
18. 15 U.S.C. § 78p(b).
19. Ownership Reports and Trading by Officers, Directors and Principal Security Holders, Exchange Act Release No. 28869.
20. P.L. 101-429, 104 Stat. 931 (1990).
21. P.L. 101-432, 104 Stat. 963 (1990).
22. 18 U.S.C. §§ 1961 to 1968.
23. Private Securities Litigation Reform Act of 1995.
24. *Reves v. Ernst & Young*, 113 S.Ct. 1163 (1993).

Employment and Worker Protection Laws

It is difficult to imagine any grounds, other than our own personal economic predilections, for saying that the contract of employment is any the less an appropriate subject of legislation than are scores of others, in dealing with which this Court has held that legislatures may curtail individual freedom in the public interest.

STONE, J. Dissenting Opinion,
Morehead v. New York (1936) 298 U.S. 587, 56 S.Ct. 918

Chapter Objectives

After studying this chapter, you should be able to

1. Define *employment at-will doctrine.*
2. Explain the public policy exception to the employment at-will doctrine.
3. Explain how state workers' compensation programs work and describe the benefits available.
4. Describe employer's duty to provide safe working conditions under the Occupational Safety and Health Act.
5. Describe the minimum wage and overtime pay rules of the Fair Labor Standards Act.
6. Describe the protections afforded employees from drug and polygraph testing in the workplace.
7. Explain the rules governing private pensions under the Employment Retirement Income Security Act.
8. Describe how the Immigration Reform and Control Act affects employers and employees.
9. List the benefits provided by unemployment compensation and Social Security laws.
10. Describe the rights guaranteed by the Family and Medical Leave Act.

Chapter Contents

Before the Industrial Revolution, the doctrine of *laissez-faire* governed the employment relationship in this country. Generally, this meant that employment was subject to the common law of contracts and agency law. In most instances, the employee and employer had somewhat equal bargaining power.

After the country became industrialized in the late 1800s, the employment relationship changed dramatically. For one thing, employees no longer had equal bargaining power with large corporate employers. For another, the use of child labor, unsafe working conditions, long hours, and low pay caused concern. The result was both federal and state legislation to protect workers' rights. Today, employment law is a mixture of contract law, agency law, and government regulation.

This chapter discusses employment contracts and the exceptions to the employment at-will doctrine. It also discusses workers' compensation statutes, minimum wage and overtime pay laws, occupational safety statutes, pension laws, immigration laws, unemployment laws, Social Security, and other employee protection laws.

EMPLOYMENT AT WILL

Employees who are offered express employment contracts for a definite term cannot be discharged in violation of the contract. Employment contracts that cannot be performed within one year must be in writing under most state Statute of Frauds laws. Most employees, however, do not have employment contracts. They are considered **at-will employees**.

at-will employees
Employees who do not have employment contracts.

Under common law, an at-will employee could be discharged by an employer at any time for any reason. This laissez-faire doctrine gave the employer great flexibility in responding to its changing needs. It also caused unfair results for some employees. Today, there are many statutory, contract, public policy, and tort exceptions to the at-will doctrine. These exceptions are discussed in the following paragraphs. An employee who has been **wrongfully discharged** can sue his or her employer for damages and other remedies (reinstatement, back pay, and such).

wrongful discharge
The discharge of an employee in violation of a statute, an employment contract, or public policy, or tortiously. As a result, the employee can recover damages and other remedies.

Statutory Exceptions

Federal and state statutes that restrict the employment at-will doctrine include federal labor laws that prohibit employers from discharging employee-members of labor unions in violation of labor laws or collective bargaining agreements. Title VII and other federal and state antidiscrimination laws that prohibit employers from engaging in race, sex, religious, age, handicap, or other forms of discrimination are other examples of such laws.

Contract Exceptions

implied-in-fact contract
A contract where agreement between parties has been inferred because of their conduct.

The courts have held that an **implied-in-fact contract** can be created between an employer and an employee. Implied-in-fact contracts develop from the conduct of the parties. For example, a company bulletin, handbook, or personnel policy might mention that employees who do their jobs properly will not be discharged. This can be construed as an implied promise that an employee can only be discharged for good cause. Thus, the employer's ability to discharge an employee at will is removed. An employee who is discharged in violation of an implied-in-fact contract can sue the employer for breach of contract.

Public Policy Exception

public policy exception
An exception to the employment at-will doctrine that states an employee cannot be discharged if such discharge violates the public policy of the jurisdiction.

The most used common law exception to the employment at-will doctrine is the **public policy exception**. This rule states that an employee cannot be discharged if such discharge violates the public policy of the jurisdiction. Discharging an employee for serving as a juror, refusing to do an act in violation of the law (e.g., refusing to engage in dumping of toxic wastes in violation of environmental protection laws), refusing to engage in illegal research (e.g., research that violates patent laws or animal protection laws), refusing to distribute defective products, and the like has been held to violate public policy.

Tort Exceptions

Wrongful discharge actions can be based on several tort theories. In certain instances, an employee can sue an employer for (1) fraud, (2) intentional infliction of emotional distress, or (3) defamation of character. A few states permit employees to sue their employers for breach of the implied covenant of good faith and fair dealing. Most states do not recognize this doctrine in employment situations. If an employee is successful in a tort action, punitive damages may be recovered.

In the following case, the court held that an employee had been wrongfully discharged.

Toussaint v. Blue Cross and Blue Shield of Michigan
292 N.W.2d 880 (1980)
Supreme Court of Michigan

CASE 41.1

FACTS
Charles Toussaint sought the assistance of an employment agency to obtain suitable employment, and in early 1967 the agency referred him to Blue Cross and Blue Shield of Michigan (Blue Cross). After several interviews, Toussaint was hired by Blue Cross on May 1, 1967, as an assistant to the company treasurer. The parties did not sign a written contract, and his employment was for an indefinite term. Toussaint testified that when he inquired about job security, he was told that he would be with the company "as long as I did my job." Blue Cross gave Toussaint a 260-page employment policy manual that promised "to treat employees leaving Blue Cross on a fair and consistent manner and to release employees for just cause only."

In early 1971, Toussaint was assigned the duty of administering the company's car program. On May 7, 1972, the company's treasurer notified Toussaint that his employment with the company was terminated. This decision was reviewed and upheld by the company's president and chairman of the board of trustees. On November 20, 1972, Toussaint filed a complaint against Blue Cross alleging wrongful termination of his employment contract. The jury returned a verdict in favor of Toussaint, awarding him $72,835. The court of appeals reversed. Toussaint appealed.

ISSUE
Was there an enforceable agreement to terminate Toussaint's employment only for good cause?

IN THE LANGUAGE OF THE COURT
Levin, Justice *We see no reason why an employment contract that does not have a definite term—the term is "indefinite"—cannot legally provide job security. When a prospective employee inquires about job security and the employer agrees that the employee shall be employed as long as he does the job, a fair construction is that the employer has agreed to give up his right to discharge at will with-*

out assigning cause and may discharge only for good or just cause. The result is that the employee, if discharged without good or just cause, may maintain an action for wrongful discharge.

While an employer need not establish personnel policies or practices, where an employer chooses to establish such policies and practices and makes them known to its employees, the employment relationship is presumably enhanced. The employer secures an orderly, cooperative, and loyal work force, and the employee the peace of mind associated with job security and the conviction that he will be treated fairly. It is enough that the employer chooses, presumably in its own interest, to create an environment in which the employee believes that, whatever the personnel policies and practices, they are established and official, purport to be fair, and are applied consistently and uniformly to each employee. The employer has then created a situation "instinct with an obligation."

If there is in effect a policy to dismiss for cause only, the employer may not depart from that policy at whim simply because he was under no obligation to institute the policy in the first place. Having announced the policy, presumably with a view to obtaining the benefit of improved employee attitudes and behavior and improved quality of the work force, the employer may not treat its promise as illusory.

DECISION AND REMEDY
The state supreme court reversed the judgment of the court of appeals in favor of Blue Cross and remanded the case to the trial court with instructions to reinstate the verdict in favor of Toussaint.

Case Questions

Critical Legal Thinking   Should employers only be permitted to discharge employees for good cause? Why or why not?

Ethics   Did Blue Cross act ethically in this case?

Business Application   What are the economic consequences of this decision to employers? To employees?

*W*orkers' Compensation Acts

Many types of employment are dangerous, and each year many workers are injured on the job. At common law, employees who were injured on the job could sue their employer for negligence. This time-consuming process placed the employee at odds with his or her employer. In addition, there was no guarantee that the employee would win the case. Ultimately, many injured workers—or the heirs of deceased workers—were left uncompensated.

workers' compensation acts were enacted in response to the unfairness of that result. These acts create an administrative procedure for workers to receive compensation for injuries that occur on the job. First, the injured worker files a claim with the appropriate state government agency (often called the workers' compensation board or commission). Next, that entity determines the legitimacy of the claim.

If a worker disagrees with the agency's findings, he or she may appeal the decision through the state court system. Workers' compensation benefits are paid according to preset limits established by statute or regulation. The amounts that are recoverable vary from state to state.

Employment-Related Injury

To be compensable under workers' compensation, the claimant must prove that the injury arose out of and in the course of his or her employment. An accident that occurs while an employee is actively working is clearly within the scope of this rule. For example, accidents that occur at a company cafeteria or while on a business lunch for an employer are covered. Accidents that happen while the employee is at an off-premises restaurant during his or her personal lunch hour are not covered, however. Many workers' compensation acts include stress as a compensable work-related injury.

Exclusive Remedy

Workers' compensation is an *exclusive remedy*. Thus, workers cannot sue their employers in court for damages. There is one exception to this rule: If an employer intentionally injures a worker, the worker can collect workers' compensation benefits and sue the employer. Workers' compensation acts do not bar injured workers from suing responsible third parties to recover damages.

In the following case, the court had to decide whether an accident was work related.

> **workers' compensation acts**
> Acts that compensate workers and their families if workers are injured in connection with their jobs.
>
> **Business Brief**
> Depending on the state, employers are required either to pay for workers' compensation insurance or to self-insure by making payments into a contingency fund. This is a substantial expense for business.
>
> **Business Brief**
> Generally, workers' compensation is an *exclusive remedy* for an injured employee. It precludes the injured employee from suing the employer for other damages or remedies. An exception occurs when an employer intentionally injures an employee.

Smith v. Workers' Compensation Appeals Board
191 Cal.App.3d 154, 236 Cal.Rptr. 248 (1987)
Court of Appeals of California

CASE 41.2

FACTS
Ronald Wayne Smith was employed by Modesto High School as a temporary math instructor. In addition, he coached the girls' baseball and basketball teams. The contract under which he was employed stated that he "may be required to devote a reasonable amount of time to other duties" in addition to instructional duties. The teachers in the school system were evaluated once a year regarding both instructional duties and noninstructional duties, including "sponsorship or the supervision of out-of-classroom student activities."

The high school's math club holds an annual end-of-year outing. For the 1983–1984 school year, a picnic was scheduled for June 7, 1984, at the Modesto Reservoir. The students invited their math teachers, including Smith, to attend. The food was paid for by math club members' dues. Smith attended the picnic with his wife and three children. One of the students brought along a windsurfer. Smith watched the students as they used it before and after the picnic. When Smith tried it himself, he fell and was seriously injured. He died shortly thereafter. Mrs. Smith filed a claim for workers' compensation benefits, which was objected to by the employer. The workers' compensation judge denied benefits. The Workers' Compensation Appeals Board affirmed. Mrs. Smith appealed.

ISSUE

Was Smith engaged in employment-related activities when the accident occurred?

IN THE LANGUAGE OF THE COURT

Ballantyne, Associate Justice   In the instant case, decedent was a temporary instructor at Modesto High. As such, he was more vulnerable to pressure or suggestion that he participate in extracurricular activities to better his chances of being rehired. The math club was an official school club. Notices of meetings to plan the picnic appeared in the school bulletin. The picnic was not an impromptu and informal gathering. Students were required to submit permission slips to the school. The food for the event was paid for out of the math club funds. The school was more than minimally involved in the picnic. Teachers were encouraged to involve themselves in extracurricular activities of the school, thus conferring the benefit of better teacher-student relationships. More importantly, teachers were evaluated on whether they shared equally in the sponsorship or the supervision of out-of-classroom student activities, and decedent had been commended for his participation in this area. We are persuaded to conclude that the employee's heir should be compensated.

Respondent argues that if this court finds that decedent's attendance at the picnic was required by his employment, then his activities in using the windsurfer were outside the course and scope of his employment. An injury is deemed to have arisen out of one's employment if there is an incidental or causal connection between the employment and the accident. Because attendance at the picnic was an implied requirement of decedent's employment, his accident that resulted from his engaging in the recreational activities that were part and parcel of the picnic's "entertainment" is causally connected to his employment.

DECISION AND REMEDY

The court of appeals held that decedent's accident was causally connected to his employment for purposes of awarding workers' compensation benefits to his heirs. Reversed and remanded.

Case Questions

Critical Legal Thinking   Should workers' compensation benefits be awarded only for accidents that occur at the job site? Why or why not?

Ethics   Did the employer act ethically in objecting to the payment of benefits in this case?

Business Application   How costly is workers' compensation for business? Do you think that many fraudulent workers' compensation claims are filed?

Contemporary Business Application

EMPLOYEE POLYGRAPH PROTECTION ACT

In the past, some employers used polygraph (lie detector) tests to screen job applicants and employees. To correct abuses in this practice and to protect workers' privacy, Congress enacted the **Employee Polygraph Protection Act of 1988** [29 U.S.C. §§ 2001–2009]. The act prohibits most private employers from using polygraph tests. Federal and state governments are not covered by the act. Polygraph tests may also be used by

- Employers in matters dealing with the national defense (e.g., certain defense contractors).
- Security services that hire employees who protect the public health and safety (e.g., guards at electric power plants).
- Drug manufacturers and distributors that hire employees that will have access to the drugs.

- Employers that are investigating incidents of theft, embezzlement, espionage, and the like by current employees. The employer must have a reasonable suspicion that the employee was involved in the incident.

The act requires private employers that are permitted to use polygraph testing to follow certain procedures, including giving notice to the person to be tested, using licensed examiners, and prohibiting certain questions (e.g., those relating to the religion or sexual behavior of the subject).

The act is administered by the Department of Labor, which has the authority to adopt regulations to enforce the act. It can assess civil penalties up to $10,000 and can seek injunctive and legal relief against violators. Employees and job applicants are given a private right of action to sue under the act.

*O*ccupational Safety and Health Act

In 1970, Congress enacted the **Occupational Safety and Health Act**[1] to promote safety in the workplace. Virtually all private employers are within the scope of the act, but federal, state, and local governments are exempt. Industries regulated by other federal safety legislation are also exempt.[2] The act established the **Occupational Safety and Health Administration (OSHA)**, a federal administrative agency within the Department of Labor. It also imposes recordkeeping and reporting requirements on employers and requires them to post notices in the workplace informing employees of their rights under the act.

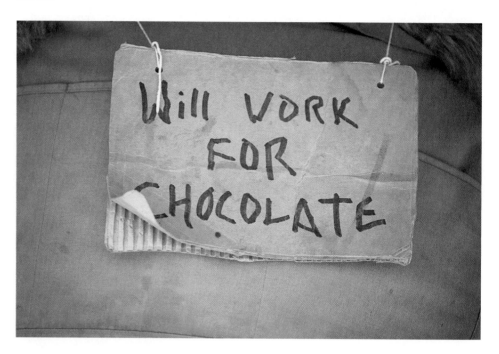

The federal Occupational Safety and Health Act requires employers to provide safe working conditions. Workers' compensation acts require employers to carry workers' compensation insurance to compensate workers who are injured on the job.

Specific and General Duty Standards

OSHA is empowered to administer the act and adopt rules and regulations to interpret and enforce it. OSHA has adopted thousands of regulations to enforce the safety standards established by the act. These include the following:

- **Specific Duty Standards** Many of the OSHA standards address safety problems of a **specific duty** nature. For example, OSHA standards establish safety requirements for equipment (e.g., safety guards), set maximum exposure levels to hazardous chemicals, regulate the location of machinery, establish safety procedures for employees, and the like.

- **General Duty Standards** The act imposes a **general duty** on an employer to provide a work environment "free from recognized hazards[3] that are causing or are likely to cause death or serious physical harm to his employees." This is so even if no specific regulation applies to the situation.

OSHA is empowered to inspect places of employment for health hazards and safety violations. If a violation is found, OSHA can issue a *written citation* that requires the employer to abate or correct the situation. Contested citations are reviewed by the Occupational Safety and Health Review Commission. Its decision is appealable to the federal circuit court of appeals. Employers who violate the act, OSHA rules and regulations, or OSHA citations are subject to both civil and criminal penalties.

Ethical Perspective

ROOFING COMPANY TARRED BY OSHA

Corbesco, Inc. (Corbesco), an industrial roofing and siding installation company, was hired to put metal roofing and siding over the skeletal structure of five aircraft hangars at Chennault Air Base in Louisiana. In April 1987, Corbesco assigned three of its employees to work on the partially completed flat roof of Hangar B, a large single-story building measuring 60 feet high, 374 feet wide, and 574 feet long. On April 2, 1987, one of the workers, Roger Matthew, who was on his knees installing insulation on the roof, lost his balance and fell 60 feet to the concrete below. He was killed by the fall. The next day, an OSHA compliance officer cited Corbesco for failing to install a safety net under the work site. The officer cited a general industry standard that provides that safety nets should be provided when workers are more than 25 feet above the ground [25 C.F.R. § 1926.105(a)]. The Department of Labor affirmed the citation and assessed a $50 penalty against Corbesco. Corbesco appealed.

Did Corbesco violate the OSHA general industry regulation that required employers to install safety nets below employees working more than 25 feet above the ground?

The court of appeals noted the OSHA rule that stated if a workplace is more than 25 feet above the ground, an employer must furnish some form of fall protection. The language of Section 1926.105(a) gave Corbesco knowledge of this general duty. However, the essence of Corbesco's claim is that it believed that it was complying with the regulation. Corbesco was required to furnish its worker with a safety net only if none of the following safety devices was being used: "Ladders, scaffolds, catch platforms, temporary floors, safety lines, or safety belts." Corbesco argues that the flat roof on which the employees were working served as a "temporary floor" and that the language of the standard is not specific enough to notify it otherwise.

The court held that Corbesco had constructive notice that it was required to install safety nets under its crew while they were working on the edge of a flat roof some 60 feet above a concrete floor. The commission frequently has said that a flat roof cannot serve as a temporary floor if workers must operate along the perimeter of such a roof because it does not provide fall protection; either a safety net or one of the alternate safety devices listed in Section 1926.105(a) must be used. A reasonable construction company in Corbesco's position would have known about these interpretations of this standard.

The court of appeals held that Corbesco violated 25 C.F.R. Section 1926.105(a) by not providing a safety net below its employees who were working more than 60 feet above the ground. [*Corbesco, Inc. v. Dole, Secretary of Labor,* 926 F.2d 422 (5th Cir. 1991)]

1. Did Corbesco act ethically in arguing that the flat roof created a temporary floor that relieved it of the duty to install a safety net under it?
2. Why are occupational safety laws enacted? Would just letting employees sue their employers for injuries caused by unsafe working conditions accomplish the same result? Explain.

*F*AIR LABOR STANDARDS ACT

In 1938, Congress enacted the **Fair Labor Standards Act (FLSA)** to protect workers.[4] The FLSA applies to private employers and employees engaged in the production of goods for interstate commerce. The main provisions of the FLSA are discussed in the following paragraphs.

Fair Labor Standards Act (FLSA)

A federal act enacted in 1938 to protect workers; prohibits child labor and establishes minimum wage and overtime pay requirements.

Child Labor

The FLSA forbids the use of oppressive child labor and makes it unlawful to ship goods produced by businesses that use oppressive child labor. The Department of Labor has adopted the following regulations that define lawful child labor: (1) Children under the age of 14 cannot work except as newspaper deliverers, (2) children ages 14 and 15 may work limited hours in nonhazardous jobs approved by the Department of Labor (e.g., restaurants and gasoline stations), and (3) children ages 16 and 17 may work unlimited hours in nonhazardous jobs. The Department of Labor determines which occupations are hazardous (e.g., mining, roofing, and working with explosives). Children who work in agricultural employment and child actors and performers are exempt from these restrictions. Persons age 18 and older may work at any job whether it is hazardous or not.

Entrepreneur and the Law

MINIMUM WAGE AND OVERTIME PAY REQUIREMENTS

The FLSA establishes minimum wage and overtime pay requirements for workers. Managerial, administrative, and professional employees are exempt from the act's wage and hour provisions. As outlined below, the FLSA requires employers to pay covered workers at least the minimum wage for their regular work hours. Overtime pay is also mandated.

- **Minimum wage** The minimum wage is set by Congress and can be changed. Currently, it is set at $5.15 per hour. The Department of Labor permits employers to pay less than the minimum wage to students and apprentices. An employer may reduce minimum wages by an amount equal to the reasonable cost of food and lodging provided to employees.
- **Overtime pay** Under the FLSA, an employer cannot require nonexempt employees to work more than 40 hours per week unless they are paid one-and-a-half times their regular pay for each hour worked in excess of 40 hours. Each week is treated separately. For example, if an employee works 50 hours one week and 30 hours the next, the employer owes the employee 10 hours of overtime pay.

Ethical Perspective

MICROSOFT VIOLATES EMPLOYMENT LAW

Microsoft Corporation is the world's largest provider of computer operating systems, software programs, and Internet browsers. The company has grown into a monopoly and made one of its founders, Bill Gates, the richest person in the world. But the company has been caught nickel-and-diming some of its workers out of their stock option benefits. It all started with an Internal Revenue Service (IRS) investigation. Here is the story.

Microsoft is headquartered in the state of Washington. In addition to having regular employees, Microsoft used the services of other workers who are classified as *independent contractors* (called *freelancers*) and temporary agency employees (called *temps*). Most of these special employees worked fulltime for Microsoft doing jobs that were identical to jobs performed by Microsoft's regular employees. Microsoft paid the special employees by check as outside workers. In 1990, the IRS conducted an employment tax examination and determined that Microsoft had misclassified these special workers as independent contractors and that the workers in these positions should be reclassified as "employees" for federal tax purposes.

The IRS used the following factors to reach the conclusion that the special workers were Microsoft employees rather than independent contractors:

- The party that has the right to control the manner and means by which the service or product is produced
- The skill required
- The source of the instrumentalities and tools
- The location of the work
- The duration of the relationship between the parties
- The extent of the hiring party's discretion over when and how long to work
- The hiring party's role in hiring and paying assistants
- Whether the work is part of the regular business of the hiring party

The IRS applied these factors to both the freelancers and temps who worked at Microsoft and found both to be employees of Microsoft. But that was not the end of the story. Plaintiff Donna Vizcaino and other freelancers sued Microsoft in a class action lawsuit alleging that they were denied employment benefits, especially employee stock options, that were paid to regular employees. Microsoft contributed 3 percent of an employee's salary to the stock option plan. The court of appeals agreed with the plaintiffs, citing the Internal Revenue Code that requires such stock option plans to be available to all employees. Thus, Microsoft's attempt to define certain full time employees as freelancers and temps was rebuffed by the courts [*Vizcaino v. United States District Court for the Western District of Washington*, 173 F.3d 713 (9th Cir. 1999)].

1. Why did Microsoft use freelancers and temps instead of regular employees?
2. Do you think Microsoft knew that it was running afoul of the law when it did not pay its freelancers and temps regular job benefits?
3. Did Microsoft act ethically in this case? Why or why not?

EMPLOYEE RETIREMENT INCOME SECURITY ACT (ERISA)

Employers are not required to establish pension plans for their employees. If they do, however, they are subject to the recordkeeping, disclosure, and other requirements of the **Employee Retirement Income Security Act (ERISA)**.[5] ERISA is a complex act designed to prevent fraud and other abuses associated with private pension funds. Federal, state, and local government pension funds are exempt from its coverage. ERISA is administered by the Department of Labor and the Internal Revenue Service (IRS).

Among other things, ERISA requires pension plans to be in writing and to name a pension fund manager. The plan manager owes a fiduciary duty to act as a "prudent person" in managing the fund and investing its assets. No more than 10 percent of a pension fund's assets can be invested in the securities of the sponsoring employer.

Vesting occurs when an employee has a nonforfeitable right to receive pension benefits. First, ERISA provides for immediate vesting of each employee's own contributions to the plan. Second, it requires employers' contributions to be either (1) completely forfeitable for a set period of up to five years and totally vested after that (*cliff vesting*) or (2) gradually vested over a seven-year period and completely vested after that time.

Employee Retirement Income Security Act (ERISA)
A federal act designed to prevent fraud and other abuses associated with private pension funds.

CONSOLIDATED OMNIBUS BUDGET RECONCILIATION ACT (COBRA)

The **Consolidated Omnibus Budget Reconciliation Act of 1985 (COBRA)**[6] provides that an employee of a private employer or the employee's beneficiaries must be offered the opportunity to continue his or her group health insurance after the dismissal or death of the employee or the loss of coverage due to certain qualifying events defined in the law. The employer must notify covered employees and their beneficiaries of their rights under COBRA. To continue coverage, a person must pay the required group rate premium. Government employees are subject to parallel provisions found in the Public Health Service Act.

Consolidated Omnibus Budget Reconciliation Act (COBRA)
Federal law that permits employees and their beneficiaries to continue their group health insurance after an employee's employment has ended.

International Perspective

NIKE CLEANS UP ITS ACT IN VIETNAM

Nike produces basketball, running, and other athletic shoes that it sells in the United States and worldwide. Nike, with over 40 percent of the athletic shoe market, has basketball great Michael Jordan as its pitchman. The majority of Nike's shoes are produced by subcontractors located in some of the poorest countries of the world. In 1997, Nike faced a public relations and ethical nightmare: It was being charged with selling shoes made by slave and child laborers who worked in horrid conditions.

(box continues)

In Vietnam, where Nike has 12 percent of its shoes manufactured, subcontractors worked employees eight hours per day, six days per week, and paid them as little as $40 per month in wages. These workers, who were mostly women in their 20s, worked under terrible conditions. They were subject to hot and noisy working conditions, exposed to toxic chemicals and fumes, and were mistreated by the managers. Workers were hit for not working fast enough or for talking, were made to run in stifling heat or lick the factory floor if they did not do what the managers told them to do, and were subject to sexual harassment. These conditions were brought to light not by Nike but by humanitarian organizations. After first vehemently denying the allegations, Nike backed down and agreed to improve the working conditions at its subcontractors in Vietnam.

Nike took the following steps:

- Required many managers at the subcontractors to be fired for their abusive conduct.

- Reduced toxic petroleum-based compounds used in making Nike shoes.
- Banned its subcontractors from paying below Vietnam's minimum wage of $45 per month.
- Installed Nike managers in the subcontractor's plants to monitor working conditions.
- Opened the manufacturing plants to outside inspectors.

Nike states that it has taken the necessary steps to prohibit and prevent abuses by its subcontractors in Vietnam and that its decision to have its shoes made in Vietnam is an economic one. Critics contend that Nike is outsourcing the production of its shoes to workers in poor countries that do not have the same worker protections as provided in the United States. They cite the fact that Michael Jordan's payment of $25 million from Nike exceeds the wages of all 35,000 persons who work for Nike's subcontractors in Vietnam.

𝒥MMIGRATION REFORM AND CONTROL ACT (IRCA)

Immigration Reform and Control Act of 1986 (IRCA)

A federal statute that makes it unlawful for employers to hire illegal immigrants.

INS Form I-9

A form that must be filled out by all U.S. employers for each employee; states that the employer has inspected the employee's legal qualifications to work.

The **Immigration Reform and Control Act of 1986 (IRCA)** is administered by the U.S. Immigration and Naturalization Service (INS).[7] The act makes it unlawful for employers to hire illegal immigrants. As of June 1, 1987, all U.S. employers must complete **INS Form I-9** for each employee. The form attests that the employer has inspected documents of the employee and has determined that he or she is either a U.S. citizen or is otherwise qualified to work in the country (e.g., has a proper work visa). Employers must maintain records and post notices in the workplace of the contents of the law. Violators are subject to both civil and criminal penalties.

In the following case, the court upheld the imposition of fines against an employer for violating the act.

Furr's/Bishop's Cafeterias, L.P. v. U.S. Immigration and Naturalization Service

976 F.2d 1366 (1992)
United States Court of Appeals, Tenth Circuit

CASE 41.3

FACTS

Furr's/Bishop's Cafeterias, L.P. (Furr's) owns and operates more than 150 cafeterias and restaurants located throughout the mid-western United States. Furr's divides its cafeterias into regions. Regional directors have authority to terminate nonmanagement employees at cafeterias located in their regions. The general manager of each cafeteria is responsible for hiring between 40 and 80 employees for the day-to-day operation of the cafeteria. In August 1988, Furr's was ordered to pay a $5,100 penalty for violating the Immigration Reform and Control Act of 1986 (IRCA) concerning the hiring of

undocumented aliens at its Kansas City, Kansas, cafeteria. The penalty was imposed under the first-time offender provision of the act. In the instant case, Furr's was ordered to pay a $12,000 fine for hiring two undocumented aliens in its Olathe, Kansas, cafeteria. The fine was imposed as a second-time offender because both cafeterias are located in the same region. Furr's challenged the assessment of the fine as a repeat offender, arguing that each cafeteria should be considered as a separate employer. The Immigration and Naturalization Service (INS) held that each region should be considered as an employer. Furr's appealed.

ISSUE

Was it lawful for the INS to impose a fine on Furr's as a repeat violator of the Immigration Reform and Control Act of 1986?

IN THE LANGUAGE OF THE COURT

Logan, Circuit Judge *Furr's argues that the food industry will quit hiring individuals who look foreign for fear of liability. They want a looser standard, treating the subdivisions as separate entities if they do their own hiring and recruitment; they say Congress surely did not intend to discourage parent corporations from having general hiring policies. These are arguments that should be addressed to Congress.*

We thus turn to the application of the statute to the facts before us. The INS followed a fact-based inquiry, considering Furr's corporate structure and the degree of autonomy under which its subsidiaries operate. It found that the general employment policies dictated by Furr's central office through the "Field Management Manual," coupled with the specific guidelines relating to compliance with the IRCA, the retained power to terminate unauthorized employees and to discipline managers of individual cafeterias for IRCA violations, and Furr's conduct of company-wide education workshops, demonstrated that Furr's "exercised a significant degree of 'control' over hiring procedures by the individual cafeterias." These findings are not clearly erroneous.*

DECISION AND REMEDY

The court of appeals held that the INS had acted properly when it considered each region of Furr's cafeteria chain to be an employer under the IRCA. Affirmed.

Case Questions

Critical Legal Thinking Should the government impose a duty on employers to determine if workers are undocumented aliens? Is this too great a burden to impose on employers?

Ethics Is it ethical for employers to hire undocumented aliens as employees? Is it ethical for undocumented aliens to enter this country seeking employment?

Business Application Why do employers hire undocumented aliens? Do you think cases like this one will stop this practice?

$\mathcal{U}$NEMPLOYMENT COMPENSATION

In 1935, Congress established an unemployment compensation program to assist workers who were temporarily unemployed. Under the **Federal Unemployment Tax Act (FUTA)**[8] and state laws enacted to implement the program, employers are required to pay unemployment contributions (taxes). The tax rate and unemployment wage level are subject to change. Employees do not pay unemployment taxes.

State governments administer unemployment compensation programs under general guidelines set by the federal government. Each state establishes its own eligibility requirements and the amount and duration of the benefits. To collect benefits, applicants must be able and available for work and seeking employment. Workers who have been let go because of bad conduct (e.g., illegal activity, drug use on the job) or who voluntarily quit work without just cause are not eligible to receive benefits.

Federal Unemployment Tax Act (FUTA)

A federal act that requires employers to pay unemployment taxes; unemployment compensation is paid to workers who are temporarily unemployed.

$\mathcal{S}$OCIAL SECURITY

In 1935, Congress established the federal **Social Security** system to provide limited retirement and death benefits to certain employees and their dependents. The Social Security system is administered by the Social Security Administration. The program has expanded greatly since it was first enacted. Today, it provides benefits to approximately 9 out of every 10 workers.[9]

Social Security benefits include (1) retirement benefits, (2) survivors' benefits to family members of deceased workers, (3) disability benefits, and (4) medical and hospitalization benefits (Medicare).

Under the **Federal Insurance Contributions Act (FICA)**,[10] employees and employers must make contributions (pay taxes) into the Social Security fund. The employer must

Social Security

Federal system that provides limited retirement and death benefits to covered employees and their dependents.

Federal Insurance Contributions Act (FICA)

A federal act that says employees and employers must make contributions into the Social Security fund.

pay a matching amount. Social Security does not operate like a savings account. Instead, current contributions are used to fund current claims. The employer is responsible for deducting employees' portions from their wages and remitting the entire payment to the Internal Revenue Service.

Self-Employment Contributions Act
A federal act that says self-employed persons must pay Social Security taxes equal to the combined employer–employee amount.

Under the **Self-Employment Contributions Act**,[11] self-employed individuals must pay Social Security, too. The amount of taxes self-employed individuals must pay is equal to the combined employer–employee amount.

Failure to submit Social Security taxes subjects the violator to interest payments, penalties, and possible criminal liability. Social Security taxes may be changed by act of Congress.

Contemporary Business Application

FAMILY AND MEDICAL LEAVE ACT OF 1993

In February 1993, Congress enacted the **Family and Medical Leave Act**. The act guarantees workers unpaid time off from work for medical emergencies. The act, which applies to companies with 50 or more workers as well as federal, state, and local governments, covers about half of the nation's workforce. To be covered by the act, an employee must have worked for the employer for at least one year and have performed more than 1,250 hours of service during the previous 12-month period.

Covered employers are required to provide up to 12 weeks of unpaid leave during any 12-month period due to the

1. Birth of, and care for, a son or daughter
2. Placement of a child for adoption or in foster care
3. Serious health condition that makes the employee unable to perform his or her duties

4. Care for a spouse, child, or parent with a serious health problem

Leave because of the birth of a child or the placement of a child for adoption or foster care cannot be taken intermittently unless the employer agrees. Other leaves may be taken on an intermittent basis. The employer may require medical proof of claimed serious health conditions.

An eligible employee who takes leave must, upon returning to work, be restored to either the same or an equivalent position with equivalent employment benefits and pay. The restored employee is not entitled to the accrual of seniority during the leave period, however. A covered employer may deny restoration to a salaried employee who is among the highest-paid 10 percent of that employer's employees if the denial is necessary to prevent "substantial and grievous economic injury" to the employer's operations.

Working the Web

e-biz

AFL-CIO The mission of the AFL-CIO is to improve the lives of working families and to bring economic justice to the workplace. Find out all about unions on this useful Web site.

Visit at **www.aflcio.org**

Bureau of Labor Statistics Keeping statistics is one of the things our government does best. Here you will find statistics on employment, unemployment, prices, living conditions, and more.

Visit at **stats.bls.gov**

United States National Labor Relations Board The NLRB is an independent federal agency created in 1935 to enforce the National Labor Relations Act. It conducts secret-ballot elections to determine whether employees want union representation, and it investigates unfair labor practices by employers and unions.

Visit at **www.nlrb.gov**

CYBER EXERCISES

1. From the AFL-CIO Web site, find the Equal Pay Web site. How much will the pay gap cost women?

2. From the BLS page, find and print the table called "Economy at a Glance."

3. Find out where the local NLRB office nearest you is located.

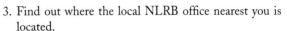

CASES AND EXERCISES

CRITICAL LEGAL THINKING CASES

41.1. Ralph Mundy was employed by Household Finance Corporation (HFC) in 1953. Over the years, he received regular salary increases and promotions. In 1974, he was promoted to an area manager for the company. In 1986, the Hawthorne, California, branch was one of several HFC branches under his supervision. Mundy's employment at HFC was governed by a written agreement signed in 1954 that provided "employment hereunder may be terminated at will by either party without advance notice." The agreement also stated that it could not be modified except by a writing signed by both parties. The agreement has never been modified.

On June 20, 1986, HFC discovered that the branch manager of its Hawthorne, California, office had been manipulating payments and diverting funds for his personal use. Because of the seriousness of the situation, HFC terminated some supervisory employees responsible for the Hawthorne branch—including Mundy—for failing to uncover the defalcation earlier. Mundy sued HFC for breach of the implied covenant of good faith and fair dealing. Who wins? [*Mundy v. Household Finance Corporation*, 885 F.2d 542 (9th Cir. 1989)]

41.2. The Hyatt Corporation (Hyatt) operates the Hyatt Regency Hotel in Milwaukee, Wisconsin. In May 1980, Hyatt employed Annunzio Ferraro, a former boxer, as a security guard at its Milwaukee hotel. The written employment agreement signed by Ferraro stated, "I agree that my employment may be terminated by this Company at any time without liability for wages or salary except such as may have been earned at the date of such termination." Ferraro was given the Hyatt employee handbook at that time. A paragraph in the 48-page handbook stated: "In order for Hyatt to maintain

a desirable level of employee conduct and productivity, Hyatt policies must be enforced. Hyatt policy requires that employees not be dismissed or laid off without just cause."

Ferraro was reprimanded on several occasions for using excessive force and abusive conduct toward guests and female employees. On February 25, 1981, Thomas Koelsch was attempting to visit a guest at the hotel and parked in the hotel employees' parking lot. When Ferraro told Koelsch to leave, and Koelsch did not, a shouting match developed and Ferraro grabbed Koelsch and attempted to force him back into his car. Hyatt discharged Ferraro on March 18, 1981, because of these incidents. Ferraro sued Hyatt to recover damages for wrongful discharge. Is Ferraro an at-will employee? Who wins? [*Ferraro v. Hyatt Corporation*, 368 N.W.2d 666 (WI. 1985)]

41.3. Ray Palmateer worked for International Harvester Company (IH) for 16 years. He had risen from a unionized job at an hourly rate to a managerial position on a fixed salary. Palmateer was an at-will employee. Palmateer supplied information to local law enforcement authorities that an IH employee was involved in a violation of the Illinois Criminal Code and agreed to assist in the investigation and testify at trial against the employee if called by the prosecuting attorney. Shortly thereafter, Palmateer was discharged by IH. He sued IH to recover damages for retaliatory discharge. Does his complaint state a cause of action for retaliatory discharge? [*Palmateer v. International Harvester Company*, 421 N.E.2d 876 (IL. 1981)]

41.4. In 1983, Ely Group, Inc. (Ely), a clothing manufacturer, borrowed $11 million from Citicorp Industrial Credit, Inc. (Citicorp). In return, Citicorp took a security interest in

Ely's clothing inventory to secure the loan. About one year later, Ely began experiencing financial difficulties. On February 19, 1985, Ely ceased all operations, closed its plant, and defaulted on $9.5 million still owed Citicorp. At that time, Ely had also defaulted on its payroll for the pay periods ending January 27 and February 19, 1985. Citicorp foreclosed on Ely's clothing inventory and planned to transport it in interstate commerce for future disposition. The secretary of labor brought an action to enjoin the shipment of the goods as "hot cargo" in violation of the Fair Labor Standards Act. Who wins? [*Citicorp Industrial Credit, Inc. v. Brock, Secretary of Labor*, 483 U.S. 27, 107 S.Ct. 2694 (1987)]

41.5. John B. Wilson was employed by the city of Modesto, California, as a police officer. He is a member of the special emergency reaction team (SERT), a tactical unit of the city's police department that is trained and equipped to handle highly dangerous criminal situations. Membership in SERT is voluntary for police officers. No additional pay or benefits are involved. To be a member of SERT, each officer is required to pass physical tests four times a year. One such test requires members to run two miles in 17 minutes. Other tests call for a minimum number of push-ups, pull-ups, and sit-ups. Officers who do not belong to SERT are not required to undergo these physical tests. On June 27, 1984, Wilson completed his patrol shift, changed clothes, and drove to the Modesto Junior College track. While running there, he injured his left ankle. Wilson filed a claim for workers' compensation benefits, which was contested by his employer. Who wins? [*Wilson v. Workers' Compensation Appeals Board*, 196 Cal.App.3d 302, 239 Cal.Rptr. 719 (Cal.App. 1987)]

41.6. Joseph Albanese was employed as a working foreman by Atlantic Steel Company, Inc., for approximately 20 years prior to 1970. His duties included the supervision of plant employees. In 1967, the business was sold to a new owner. In 1969, after the employees voted to unionize, friction developed between Albanese and the workers. Part of the problem was caused by management's decision to eliminate overtime work, which required Albanese to go out into the shop and prod the workers to expedite the work.

Additional problems resulted from the activities of Albanese's direct supervisor, the plant manager. On one occasion in 1968, the manager informed Albanese that the company practice of distributing Thanksgiving turkeys was to be discontinued. In 1969, the manager told Albanese that the company did not intend to give the workers a Christmas bonus. The plant manager also informed Albanese that he did not intend to pay overtime wages to any worker. On each occasion, after Albanese relayed the information to the workers, the plant manager reversed his own decision.

After the last incident, Albanese became distressed and developed chest pains and nausea. When the chest pains became sharper, he went home to bed. Albanese has not worked since. He has experienced continuing pain, sweatiness, shortness of breath, headaches, and depression. Albanese filed a claim for workers' compensation based on stress. The employer contested the claim. Who wins? [*Albanese's Case*, 389 N.E.2d 83 (MA. 1979)]

41.7. Getty Oil Company (Getty) operates a separation facility where it gathers gas and oil from wells and transmits them to an outgoing pipeline under high pressure. Getty engineers designed and produced a pressure vessel, called a fluid booster, that was to be installed to increase pressure in the system. Robinson, a Getty engineer, was instructed to install the vessel. Robinson picked the vessel up from the welding shop without having it tested. After he completed the installation, the pressure valve was put into operation. When the pressure increased from 300 to 930 pounds per square inch, an explosion occurred. Robinson died from the explosion, and another Getty employee was seriously injured. The secretary of labor issued a citation against Getty for violating the general duty provision for worker safety contained in the Occupational Safety and Health Act. Getty challenged the citation. Who wins? [*Getty Oil Company v. Occupational Safety and Health Review Commission*, 530 F.2d 143 (5th Cir. 1976)]

41.8. United Artists is a Maryland corporation doing business in the state of Texas. United Pension Fund (Plan) is a defined-contribution employee pension benefit plan sponsored by United Artists for its employees. Each employee has his or her own individual pension account, but Plan's assets are pooled for investment purposes. Plan is administered by a board of trustees. During the period 1977 through 1986, seven of the trustees used Plan to make a series of loans to themselves. The trustees did not (1) require the borrowers to submit written applications for the subject loans, (2) assess the prospective borrowers' ability to repay the loans, (3) specify a period in which the loans were to be repaid, or (4) call the loans when they remained unpaid. The trustees also charged less than fair market value interest rates for the loans. The secretary of labor sued the trustees, alleging that they breached their fiduciary duty in violation of ERISA. Who wins? [*McLaughlin v. Rowley*, 698 F.Supp. 1333 (N.D.Tex. 1988)]

41.9. Air traffic controllers are federal government employees who are responsible for directing commercial and private air traffic in this country. They are subject to regulation by the secretary of transportation (Secretary). Secretary adopted a regulation that provides for postaccident urinalysis drug testing of air traffic controllers responsible for the airspace in which an airplane accident has occurred. The National Air Traffic Controllers Association, MEBA/NNU, AFL-CIO, sued, alleging that such drug testing was an unreasonable search and seizure in violation of the Fourth Amendment to the U.S. Constitution. Who wins? [*National Air Traffic Controllers Assn., MEBA/NNU, AFL-CIO v. Burnley*, 700 F.Supp. 1043 (N.D.Cal. 1988)]

41.10. Devon Overstreet, who worked as a bus driver for the Chicago Transit Authority (CTA) for over six years, took a sick leave from January 30 to March 15, 1985. Because she had been on sick leave for more than seven days, CTA required her to take a medical examination. The blood and urine analysis indicated the presence of cocaine. A second test confirmed this finding. On March 20, 1985, CTA suspended her and placed her in the Employee's Assistance Program for Substance Abuse for not less than 30 days, with a chance of reassignment to a nonoperating job if she successfully completed the program. The program is an alternative to discharge and is available at the election of the employee. Overstreet filed for unemployment compensation benefits. CTA contested her claim. Who wins? [*Overstreet v. Illinois Department of Employment Security*, 522 N.E.2d 185 (Ill.App. 1988)]

ETHICS CASES

41.11. Jeffrey Glockzin was an employee of Nordyne, Inc. (Nordyne), which manufactured air-conditioning units. Sometimes Glockzin worked as an assembly line tester. The job consisted of attaching one of two wire leads with bare metal alligator-type clips leading from the testing equipment to each side of the air-conditioning unit. When the tester turned on a toggle switch, the air-conditioning unit was energized. Once a determination was made that the air-conditioning unit was working properly, the toggle switch would be turned off and the wire leads removed. On April 20, 1988, while testing an air-conditioning unit, Glockzin grabbed both alligator clips at the same time. He had failed to turn off the toggle switch, however. Glockzin received a 240-volt electric shock, causing his death. His heirs sued Nordyne for wrongful death and sought to recover damages for an intentional tort. Nordyne made a motion for summary judgment, alleging that workers' compensation benefits were the exclusive remedy for Glockzin's death. Does the "intentional tort" exception to the rule that workers' compensation is the exclusive remedy for a worker's injury apply in this case? Did Nordyne's management violate its ethical duty by not providing safer testing equipment? [*Glockzin v. Nordyne, Inc.*, 815 F.Supp. 1050 (N.D.Mich. 1992)]

41.12. Whirlpool Corporation (Whirlpool) operates a manufacturing plant in Marion, Ohio, for the production of household appliances. Overhead conveyors transport appliance components throughout the plant. To protect employees from objects that occasionally fall from the conveyors, Whirlpool installed a horizontal wiremesh guard screen approximately 20 feet above the plant floor. The mesh screen is welded to angle-iron frames suspended from the building's structural steel skeleton.

Maintenance employees spend several hours each week removing objects from the screen, replacing paper spread on the screen to catch grease drippings from the materials on the conveyors, and performing occasional maintenance work on the conveyors. To perform these duties, maintenance employees usually are able to stand on the iron frames, but sometimes they find it necessary to step onto the wire-mesh screen itself. Several employees have fallen partly through the screen. On June 28, 1974, a maintenance employee fell to his death through the guard screen.

On July 7, 1974, two maintenance employees, Virgil Deemer and Thomas Cornwell, met with the plant supervisor to voice their concern about the safety of the screen. Unsatisfied with the supervisor's response, on July 9 they met with the plant safety director and voiced similar concerns. When they asked him for the name, address, and telephone number of the local OSHA office, he told them they "had better stop and think about" what they were doing. The safety director then furnished them with the requested information, and later that day one of the men contacted the regional OSHA office and discussed the guard screen.

The next day, Deemer and Cornwell reported for the night shift at 10:45 P.M. Their foreman directed the two men to perform their usual maintenance duties on a section of the screen. Claiming that the screen was unsafe, they refused to carry out the directive. The foreman sent them to the personnel office, where they were ordered to punch out without working or being paid for the remaining six hours of the shift. The two men subsequently received written reprimands, which were placed in their employment files.

The secretary of labor filed suit, alleging that Whirlpool's actions constituted discrimination against the two men in violation of the Occupational Safety and Health Act. Did Whirlpool act ethically in this case? Can employees engage in self-help under certain circumstances under OSHA regulations? [*Whirlpool Corporation v. Marshall, Secretary of Labor*, 445 U.S. 1, 100 S.Ct. 883 (1980)]

CRITICAL LEGAL THINKING WRITING ASSIGNMENT

Read Case A.41 in the Case Appendix [*Snyder v. Michael's Stores, Inc.*]. This case is excerpted from the court of appeals opinion. Review and brief the case. In your brief, be sure to answer the following questions.

1. Who is the plaintiff and how was the plaintiff injured?
2. What defense did the defendant raise against the imposition of liability?
3. What did the court hold?

NOTES

1. For example, the Railway Safety Act and the Coal Mine Safety Act regulate workplace safety of railway workers and coal miners, respectively.
2. 29 U.S.C. § 651–678.
3. 29 U.S.C. § 654(a)(1).
4. 29 U.S.C. §§ 201 et seq.
5. 29 U.S.C. §§ 1001 et seq.
6. Internal Revenue Code § 4980B(f), 26 U.S.C. § 1161(a).
7. 29 U.S.C. § 1802.
8. 26 U.S.C. §§ 3301–3311.
9. Some federal, state, and local government employees who are covered by comparable legislation are not subject to the Social Security Act.
10. 26 U.S.C. §§ 3101–3126.
11. 26 U.S.C. §§ 1401–1403.

Equal Opportunity in Employment

*What people have always sought is equality of rights before the law.
For rights that were not open to all equally would not be rights.*

CICERO (106–43 B.C.)
De officiis, Bk. II, Ch. XII

Chapter Objectives

After studying this chapter, you should be able to

1. Describe the scope of coverage of Title VII of the Civil Rights Act of 1964.
2. Identify race, color, and national origin discrimination that violates Title VII.
3. Identify sex discrimination—including sexual harassment—that violates Title VII.
4. Describe the accommodations that employers must make to avoid religious discrimination in violation of Title VII.
5. Describe the protections afforded by the Equal Pay Act of 1963.
6. Describe the business necessity and bona fide occupational qualification defenses.
7. Describe the scope of coverage of the Age Discrimination in Employment Act.
8. Describe the protections afforded by the Americans with Disabilities Act of 1990.
9. Define and apply the doctrine of affirmative action.
10. List and describe the remedies for violations of equal employment opportunity laws.

Chapter Contents

At common law, employers could terminate an employee at any time and for whatever reason. In this same vein, employers were free to hire and promote anyone they chose without violating the law. This often created unreasonable hardship on employees and erected employment barriers to certain minority classes.

Starting in the 1960s, Congress began enacting a comprehensive set of federal laws that eliminated major forms of employment discrimination. These laws, which were passed to guarantee **equal employment opportunity** to all employees and job applicants, have been broadly interpreted by the federal courts, particularly the U.S. Supreme Court. States have also enacted antidiscrimination laws.

This chapter discusses federal and state equal opportunity in employment laws.

Equal Employment Opportunity Commission (EEOC)

The **Equal Employment Opportunity Commission (EEOC)** is the federal agency responsible for enforcing most federal antidiscrimination laws. The members of the EEOC are appointed by the President. The EEOC is empowered to conduct investigations, interpret the statutes, encourage conciliation between employees and employers, and bring suit to enforce the law. The EEOC can also seek injunctive relief.

Title VII of the Civil Rights Act of 1964

After substantial debate, Congress enacted the **Civil Rights Act of 1964. Title VII** of the Civil Rights Act of 1964 (entitled the **Fair Employment Practices Act**) was intended to eliminate job discrimination based on the following *protected classes*: (1) *race*, (2) *color*, (3) *religion*, (4) *sex*, or (5) *national origin*.[1] As amended by the **Equal Employment Opportunity Act of 1972**, Section 703(a)(2) of Title VII provides in pertinent part that

> *It shall be an unlawful employment practice for an employer*
> *(1) to fail or refuse to hire or to discharge any individual, or otherwise to discriminate against any individual with respect to his compensation, terms, conditions, or privileges of employment, because of such individual's race, color, religion, sex, or national origin; or*
> *(2) to limit, segregate, or classify his employees or applicants for employment in any way which would deprive or tend to deprive any individual of employment opportunities or otherwise adversely affect his status as an employee, because of such individual's race, color, religion, sex, or national origin.*

Scope of Coverage of Title VII

Title VII applies to (1) employers with 15 or more employees, (2) all employment agencies, (3) labor unions with 15 or more members, (4) state and local governments and their agencies, and (5) most federal government employment. Indian tribes and tax-exempt private clubs are expressly excluded from coverage.

Title VII prohibits discrimination in hiring, decisions regarding promotion or demotion, payment of compensation and fringe benefits, availability of job training and apprenticeship opportunities, referral systems for employment, decisions regarding dismissal, work rules, and any other "*term, condition, or privilege*" of employment. Any employee of covered employers, including undocumented aliens,[2] may bring actions for employment discrimination under Title VII.

---

equal opportunity in employment

The right of all employees and job applicants (1) to be treated without discrimination and (2) to be able to sue employers if they are discriminated against.

Equal Employment Opportunity Commission (EEOC)

The federal administrative agency responsible for enforcing most federal antidiscrimination laws.

Title VII of the Civil Rights Act of 1964 (Fair Employment Practices Act)

Intended to eliminate job discrimination based on five protected classes: *race, color, religion, sex,* or *national origin.*

Business Brief

As originally proposed, sex discrimination was not included in Title VII. The amendment (Equal Employment Opportunity Act), designed to kill the entire legislation, backfired when the Civil Rights Act of 1964 passed.

Business Brief

Title VII applies to any term, condition, or privilege of employment including but not limited to hiring, firing, promotion, and payment of fringe benefits decisions.

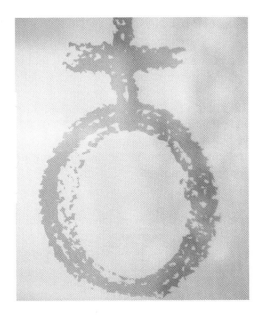

The federal government has enacted a series of statutes that guarantee equal opportunity in employment. For example, Title VII of the Civil Rights Act of 1964 prohibits discrimination in employment based on sex.

Forms of Title VII Actions

Title VII prohibits the following forms of employment discrimination based on any of the five prohibited factors listed previously.

Disparate Treatment Discrimination Disparate treatment discrimination occurs when an employer treats a specific *individual* less favorably than others because of that person's race, color, national origin, sex, or religion. In such situations, the complainant must prove that (1) he or she belongs to a Title VII protected class, (2) he or she applied for and was qualified for the employment position, (3) he or she was rejected despite this, and (4) the employer kept the position open and sought applicants from persons with the complainant's qualifications.[3]

disparate treatment discrimination
Occurs when an employer discriminates against a specific *individual* because of his or her race, color, national origin, sex, or religion.

Disparate Impact Discrimination Disparate impact discrimination occurs when an employer discriminates against an entire protected *class*. Many disparate impact cases are brought as class action lawsuits. Often, this type of discrimination is proven through statistical data about the employer's employment practices. The plaintiff must demonstrate a *causal link* between the challenged practice and the statistical imbalance. Showing a statistical disparity between the percentage of protected class employees versus the percentage of the population that the protected class makes within the surrounding community is not enough, by itself, to prove discrimination.

Disparate impact discrimination occurs when an employer adopts a work rule that is neutral on its face but is shown to cause an adverse impact on a protected class.

disparate impact discrimination
Occurs when an employer discriminates against an entire protected *class*. An example would be where a facially neutral employment practice or rule causes an adverse impact on a protected class.

Procedure for Bringing a Title VII Action

To bring an action under Title VII, a private complainant must first file a complaint with the EEOC.[4] The EEOC is given the opportunity to sue the employer on the complainant's behalf. If the EEOC chooses not to bring suit, it will issue a *right to sue letter* to the complainant. This gives the complainant the right to sue the employer.

Remedies for Violations of Title VII

A successful plaintiff in a Title VII action can recover up to two years' back pay and reasonable attorneys' fees. In cases involving malice or reckless indifference to federally protected rights, the aggrieved party can recover compensatory and punitive damages. The statute caps the amounts that are recoverable on the basis of the size of the employer: (1) 15 to 100 employees, $50,000, (2) 101 to 200 employees, $100,000, (3) 201 to 500 employees, $200,000, and (4) more than 500 employees, $300,000.

The courts also have broad authority to grant equitable remedies. For instance, the courts can order reinstatement, grant fictional seniority, or issue injunctions to compel the hiring or promotion of protected minorities.

Race, Color, and National Origin Discrimination

Title VII of the Civil Rights Act of 1964 was primarily enacted to prohibit employment discrimination based on *race, color,* and *national origin*. Race refers to broad categories such as Black, Caucasian, Asian, and Native American. *Color* refers to the color of a person's skin. *National origin* refers to the country of a person's ancestors or cultural characteristics.

The following cases demonstrate race and national origin discrimination.

> *Racial discrimination in any form and in any degree has no justifiable part whatever in our democratic way of life, it is unattractive in any setting but it is utterly revolting among a free people who have embraced the principles set forth in the Constitution of the United States.*
>
> Murphy, J. dissenting
> Korematsu v. U.S. (1944)

> *Rights matter most when they are claimed by unpopular minorities.*
>
> Michael Kirby, J.
> Sydney Morning Herald
> November 30, 1985

National Association for the Advancement of Colored People, Newark Branch v. Town of Harrison, New Jersey
907 F.2d 1408 (1990)
United States Court of Appeals, Third Circuit

CASE 42.1

FACTS

The town of Harrison, New Jersey (Harrison), followed a policy of hiring only town residents as town employees for as long as any townspeople could remember. In 1978, New Jersey adopted an Act Concerning Residency Requirements for Municipal and County Employees that permitted towns, cities, and counties in the state to require that their employees be bona fide residents of the local government unit. Pursuant to this statute, Harrison adopted Ordinance 747, which stipulated that "all officers and employees of the Town shall, as a condition of employment, be bona fide residents of the Town."

Although Harrison is a small industrial community located in Hudson County, New Jersey, it is clearly aligned with Essex County to the west and is considered an extension of the city of Newark, which it abuts. Adjacent counties are within an easy commute of Harrison. Only 0.2 percent of Harrison's population is Black. None of the 51 police officers, 55 firefighters, or 80 nonuniformed employees of the town are Black. Several Blacks who were members of the National Association for the Advancement of Colored People, Newark Branch (NAACP) applied for employment with Harrison but were rejected because they did not meet the residency requirement. The NAACP sued Harrison for employment discrimination.

ISSUE

Does the residency requirement of the town of Harrison violate Title VII of the Civil Rights Act of 1964?

IN THE LANGUAGE OF THE COURT

Debevoise, District Judge   The geographical area from which Harrison draws employees includes its own county of Hudson as well as Bergen, Essex, and Union counties. These four counties have a total civilian labor force of 1,353,555 of which 214,747 are black. By reason of the geographical location and the flow of transportation facilities, Harrison could reasonably be viewed as functionally a component of the city of Newark and a part of Essex County. Newark's population is approximately 60% black. Essex County's civilian labor force totals 391,612, of which 130,397 (or 33.3%) are black. It would be hard to conclude that among the very substantial number of black workers in the four-county labor market there are not large numbers of persons qualified to serve as police officers, firefighters, clerk typists, and laborers.

There is substantial additional evidence demonstrating the availability of qualified black employees. Private employers in Harrison, an industrial town, hire large numbers of people in a wide variety of jobs. Of the persons employed by private industry, 819 or 22.1% are black. Since so few black persons live in Harrison, most of these persons must have commuted from *elsewhere in the labor market that serves Harrison. This evidence alone requires the conclusion that there is a material disparity between the pool of qualified applicants for each and every Harrison position and the actual makeup of persons holding those jobs.*

I find that the evidence also compels the conclusion that the residency requirements are the cause of at least a substantial part of the disparity. For all practical purposes, Harrison has no black residents. Thus, to limit employment or applications for employment to residents effectively excludes black persons from employment by the municipality. There is strong evidence that, if the residency requirement were removed, qualified black persons would seek positions with Harrison's municipal government. Thus, Harrison's facially neutral residency requirements have been shown to have a disproportionate impact upon black persons.

DECISION AND REMEDY

The district court held that the plaintiffs had established that the ordinance constituted disparate impact race discrimination in violation of Title VII of the Civil Rights Act of 1964. The court issued an injunction against enforcement of the ordinance.

Case Questions

Critical Legal Thinking   Would the same residency requirement rule cause disparate impact discrimination if it were adopted by New York City or Los Angeles?

Ethics   Did the town of Harrison act ethically when it adopted the residency requirements?

Business Application   Could a private business impose a residency requirement on its employees?

Rivera v. Baccarat, Inc.
10 F. Supp.2d 318 (1998)
United States District Court, S.D. New York

CASE 42.2

FACTS

Irma Rivera is an Hispanic woman who was born in Puerto Rico. In September 1984, she began working for Baccarat, Inc. (Baccarat), a distributor of fine crystal, as a sales representative in its retail store in Manhattan. Rivera was the top sales representative at the Baccarat store from 1992 through 1994. J. D. Watts, the store's manager, stated that Rivera was "one of the best salespeople I have encountered in my 15 years in quality tabletop and gift retailing."

In October 1994, Jean Luc Negre became the new president of Baccarat, with ultimate authority for personnel decisions. Sometime later, Negre angrily told Rivera that he did not like her attitude and that he did not want her to speak Spanish on the job. On July 14, 1995, Dennis Russell, the chief financial officer of Baccarat, notified Rivera that Negre had made a decision to terminate her. Rivera pressed Russell to tell her why she was being fired. According to Rivera, he replied, "Irma, he doesn't want Hispanics." Ivette Brigantty, another Hispanic sales representative, was also terminated by Negre. The non-Hispanic salesperson was retained by the store. Rivera sued Baccarat for national origin discrimination in violation of Title VII of the Civil Rights Act. The jury found Bacarrat liable. Baccarat appealed.

ISSUE

Did Baccarat engage in unlawful national origin discrimination?

IN THE LANGUAGE OF THE COURT

Francis, United States Magistrate   *Under Equal Employment Opportunity Commission regulations, national origin discrimination includes the denial of employment opportunity because an individual has the linguistic characteristics of a national origin group. Accent and national origin are obviously inextricably intertwined in many cases. Thus, unless an employee's accent materially interferes with her job performance, it cannot legally be the basis for an adverse employment action.*

In this case, Ms. Rivera testified that during her one face-to-face meeting with Mr. Negre, he specifically stated that he did not like her accent. While Baccarat characterizes this as a single stray remark insufficient to support a finding of discriminatory intent, its probative value, if credited, is substantial. It is a statement by the president of the company who himself made the decision to terminate Ms. Rivera. It is no less probative of bias than if a supervisor says to an employee shortly before firing her, "I don't like the color of your skin." Mr. Negre's criticism of Ms. Rivera's accent, his statement that he did not want Hispanic sales employees, and the fact that two Hispanic sales representatives were discharged while the non-Hispanic salesperson was retained all buttress the jury's finding of liability.

An employer who discriminates on the basis of national origin acts illegally even if he is not biased against everyone whose national origin differs from his. Title VII forbids both selective discrimination and general xenophobia. Thus, the jury could have

(case continues)

found that Baccarat's hiring pattern reflected discrimination against Hispanics even if not against other ethnic groups.

DECISION AND REMEDY

The district court held that Baccarat had engaged in national origin discrimination in violation of Title VII. The court awarded Ms. Rivera $104,373 in damages, attorney's fees of $102,437, and prejudgment interest.

Case Questions

Critical Legal Thinking   Why did Congress include national origin discrimination under Title VII? How does it differ from race discrimination?

Ethics   Did the president of Baccarat act ethically in this case?

Business Application   Do you think national origin discrimination is very prevalent in business?

---

sex discrimination

Discrimination against a person solely because of his or her gender.

Pregnancy Discrimination Act

Amendment to Title VII that forbids employment discrimination because of "pregnancy, childbirth, or related medical conditions."

Sex Discrimination

Although the prohibition against **sex discrimination** applies equally to men and women, the overwhelming majority of Title VII sex discrimination cases are brought by women. The old airline practice of ignoring the marital status of male flight attendants but hiring only single female flight attendants is an example of such discrimination.

In 1978, the **Pregnancy Discrimination Act** was enacted as an amendment to Title VII.[5] This amendment forbids employment discrimination because of "pregnancy, childbirth, or related medical conditions." Thus, a work rule that prohibits the hiring of pregnant women violates Title VII.

In the following case, the court found sex discrimination in violation of Title VII.

Barbano v. Madison County

922 F.2d 139 (1990)
United States Court of Appeals, Second Circuit

CASE 42.3

FACTS

In February 1980, the position of director of the Madison County Veterans Service Agency became vacant. The Madison County Board of Supervisors (Board) appointed a committee of five men to hold interviews. Maureen E. Barbano applied for the position and was interviewed by the committee. Upon entering the interview, Barbano heard someone say, "Oh, another woman." When the interview began, Donald Greene, a committee member, said he would not consider "some woman" for the position. He then asked Barbano personal questions about her plans on having a family and whether her husband would object to her transporting male veterans. When Barbano said the questions were irrelevant and discriminatory, Greene replied that the questions were relevant because he did not want to hire a woman who would get pregnant and quit. Another committee member said the questions were relevant. No committee member said they were not relevant or asked Barbano any substantive questions.

The committee interviewed several other candidates and found them all (including Barbano) to be qualified for the position. Ultimately, the Board acted on the committee's recommendation and hired a male candidate.

Barbano sued Madison County for sex discrimination in violation of Title VII. The district court held in favor of Barbano and awarded her $55,000 in back pay, prejudgment interest, and attorneys' fees. Madison County appealed.

ISSUE

Did the defendant engage in sex discrimination in violation of Title VII?

IN THE LANGUAGE OF THE COURT

Feinberg, Circuit Judge   *There is little doubt that Greene's statements during the interview were discriminatory. He said he would not consider "some woman" for the position. His questioning Barbano about whether she would get pregnant and quit was also discriminatory, since it was unrelated to a bona fide occupational qualification. Similarly, Greene's questions about whether Barbano's husband would mind if she had to "run around the country with men," and that he would not want his wife to do it, were discriminatory.*

Moreover, the import of Greene's discriminatory questions was substantial, since apart from one question about her qualifications, none of the interviewers asked Barbano about other areas that allegedly formed the basis for selecting a candidate. Thus, Greene's questioning constituted virtually the entire interview.

Given the discriminatory tenor of the interview, and the acquiescence of the other Committee members to Greene's line of questioning, it follows that the trial court judge could find that those present at the interview, and not merely Greene, discriminated against Barbano. The record before us supports the district court's finding that the Board discriminated in making the hiring decision.

DECISION AND REMEDY

The court of appeals held that the defendant Madison County had engaged in sex discrimination in violation of Title VII. The court affirmed the award of damages to plaintiff Barbano.

Case Questions

Critical Legal Thinking   Why are questions concerning family obligations made illegal by Title VII?

Ethics   Was Greene's conduct morally reprehensible?

Business Application   What actions should employers take to make sure their interviewers and other personnel understand Title VII and other antidiscrimination laws?

Sexual Harassment

In the modern work environment, coworkers sometimes become sexually interested or involved with each other voluntarily. On other occasions, though, a coworker's sexual advances are not welcome.

Refusing to hire or promote someone unless he or she has sex with the manager or supervisor is sex discrimination that violates Title VII. Other forms of conduct, such as lewd remarks, touching, intimidation, posting pinups, and other verbal or physical conduct of a sexual nature, constitute **sexual harassment** and violate Title VII.[6]

To determine what conduct creates a hostile work environment, the Supreme Court stated:

> *We can say that whether an environment is "hostile" or "abusive" can be determined only by looking at all the circumstances. These may include the frequency of the discriminatory conduct; its severity; whether it is physically threatening or humiliating, or a mere offensive utterance; and whether it unreasonably interferes with an employee's work performance.[7]*

In the following case, the Supreme Court decided that the challenged conduct created a hostile work environment.

sexual harassment

Lewd remarks, touching, intimidation, posting pinups, and other verbal or physical conduct of a sexual nature that occur on the job.

Harris v. Forklift Systems, Inc.
114 S.Ct. 367 (1993)
United States Supreme Court

CASE 42.4

FACTS

Teresa Harris worked as a manager at Forklift Systems, Inc. (Forklift), an equipment rental company, from April 1985 until October 1987. Charles Hardy was Forklift's president. Throughout Harris's time at Forklift, Hardy often insulted her because of her gender and made her the target of unwanted sexual innuendos. Hardy told Harris on several occasions, in the presence of other employees, "You're a woman, what do you know" and "We need a man as the rental manager"; at least once, he told her she was "a dumb ass woman." Again in front of others, he suggested that the two of them "go to the Holiday Inn to negotiate Harris's raise." Hardy occasionally asked Harris and other female employees to get coins from his front pants pocket. He threw objects on the ground in front of Harris and other women and asked them to pick the objects up. He made sexual innuendos about Harris's and other women's clothing.

In mid-August 1987, Harris complained to Hardy about his conduct. Hardy said he was surprised that Harris was offended, claimed he was only joking, and apologized. He also promised he would stop, and based on this assurance Harris stayed on the job. But in early September, Hardy began anew: While Harris was arranging a deal with one of Forklift's customers, he asked her, again in front of other employees, "What did you do, promise the guy . . . some

(case continues)

[sex] Saturday night?" On October 1, Harris collected her paycheck and quit.

Harris then sued Forklift, claiming that Hardy's conduct had created an abusive work environment for her because of her gender. The district court held that because Harris had not suffered severe psychological injury, she could not recover. The court of appeals affirmed. Harris appealed to the U.S. Supreme Court.

ISSUE
Must conduct, to be actionable as abusive work environment harassment, seriously affect the victim's psychological well-being?

IN THE LANGUAGE OF THE COURT
O'Connor, Justice   When the workplace is permeated with discriminatory intimidation, ridicule, and insult, that is sufficiently severe or pervasive to alter the conditions of the victim's employment and create an abusive working environment, Title VII is violated.

A discriminatorily abusive work environment, even one that does not seriously affect employees' psychological well-being, can and often will detract from employees' job performance, discourage employees from remaining on the job, or keep them from advancing in their careers. Moreover, even without regard to these tan-

gible effects, the very fact that the discriminatory conduct was so severe or pervasive that it created a work environment abusive to employees because of their race, gender, religion, or national origin offends Title VII's broad rule of workplace equality.

Certainly Title VII bars conduct that would seriously affect a reasonable person's psychological well-being, but the statute is not limited to such conduct. So long as the environment would reasonably be perceived, and is perceived, as hostile or abusive, there is no need for it also to be psychologically injurious.

DECISION AND REMEDY
The Supreme Court held that Title VII does not require a victim to prove that the challenged conduct seriously affected her psychological well-being. The case was remanded to the district court for trial.

Case Questions

Critical Legal Thinking   Should an employer be held liable for sexual harassment committed by one of its employees?

Ethics   What penalty should be assessed against Hardy for his conduct?

Business Application   How can businesses eliminate sexual harassment on the job?

Contemporary Business Application

THE REASONABLE WOMAN STANDARD

In most cases, the courts use a "reasonable person" standard to determine whether certain conduct violates the norms of society. This traditional standard was used in sexual harassment cases until recently, when several courts held that it was inappropriate. A "reasonable woman" standard was adopted in its place. The following case illustrates how this new standard works.

Kerry Ellison worked as a revenue agent for the Internal Revenue Service. A male coworker, whose desk was 20 feet from Ellison's, wrote her detailed love letters. When Ellison complained, the male employee was transferred to another location for six months, but then he was transferred back. He again wrote love letters to Ellison. The IRS did not take any further action to transfer the male employee elsewhere. Ellison filed a Title VII action against her employer, claiming sexual harassment. The district court granted the defendant's motion for summary judgment.

The court of appeals reversed and remanded the case. In doing so, the court articulated the **reasonable woman standard** for examining sexual harassment cases brought by females. The court stated

We believe that in evaluating the severity and pervasiveness of sexual harassment, we should focus on the perspective of the victim. If we only examined whether a reasonable person would engage in allegedly harassing conduct, we would run the risk of reinforcing the prevailing level of discrimination. Harassers could continue to harass merely because a particular discriminatory practice was common, and victims of harassment would have no remedy.

We therefore prefer to analyze harassment from the victim's perspective. Conduct that many men consider unobjectionable may offend many women.

We hold that a female plaintiff states a prima facie case of hostile environment sexual harassment when she alleges conduct which a reasonable woman would consider sufficiently severe or pervasive to alter the conditions of employment and create an abusive working environment.

More courts are expected to adopt the reasonable woman standard in analyzing sexual harassment hostile work discrimination cases. [*Ellison v. Brady, Secretary of the Treasury*, 924 F.2d 872 (9th Cir. 1991)]

*E*XHIBIT 42.1 *Policies against Sexual Harassment*

Many businesses have taken steps to prevent sexual harassment in the workplace. For example, some businesses have explicitly adopted policies (see below) forbidding sexual harassment, implemented procedures for reporting incidents of sexual harassment, and conducted training programs to sensitize managers and employees about the issue.

Statement of Prohibited Conduct

The management of Company considers the following conduct to illustrate some of the conduct that violates Company's Sexual Harassment Policy:

A. Physical assaults of a sexual nature, such as
   1. Rape, sexual battery, molestation, or attempts to commit these assaults.
   2. Intentional physical conduct that is sexual in nature, such as touching, pinching, patting, grabbing, brushing against another employee's body, or poking another employee's body.

B. Unwanted sexual advances, propositions or other sexual comments, such as
   1. Sexually oriented gestures, noises, remarks, jokes, or comments about a person's sexuality or sexual experience directed at or made in the presence of any employee who indicates or has indicated in any way that such conduct is unwelcome in his or her presence.
   2. Preferential treatment or promises of preferential treatment to an employee for submitting to sexual conduct, including soliciting or attempting to solicit any employee to engage in sexual activity for compensation or reward.
   3. Subjecting, or threats of subjecting, an employee to unwelcome sexual attention or conduct or intentionally making performance of the employee's job more difficult because of the employee's sex.

C. Sexual or discriminatory displays or publications anywhere in Company's workplace by Company employees, such as
   1. Displaying pictures, posters, calendars, graffiti, objects, promotional materials, reading materials, or other materials that are sexually suggestive, sexually demeaning, or pornographic, or bringing into Company's work environment or possessing any such material to read, display, or view at work.

      A picture will be presumed to be sexually suggestive if it depicts a person of either sex who is not fully clothed or in clothes that are not suited to or ordinarily accepted for the accomplishment of routine work in and around the workplace and who is posed for the obvious purpose of displaying or drawing attention to private portions of his or her body.
   2. Reading or otherwise publicizing in the work environment materials that are in any way sexually revealing, sexually suggestive, sexually demeaning, or pornographic.
   3. Displaying signs or other materials purporting to segregate an employee by sex in any area of the workplace (other than restrooms and similar semi-private lockers/changing rooms).

E-Commerce & Internet Law

E-MAIL'S ROLE IN HOSTILE WORK ENVIRONMENT LAWSUITS

The use of e-mail in business has dramatically increased efficiency and information sharing among employees. Managers and workers alike can communicate with each other, send documents, and keep each other apprised of business developments. In many organizations, e-mail has replaced the telephone as the most used method of communication and has eliminated the need for many meetings. This is a boon for business. But the downside is that e-mail has increased the exposure of businesses to sexual and racial harassment lawsuits. For example, the largest settlement regarding a sexual harassment case arose from e-mail. In 1995, Chevron

(box continues)

Corporation paid $2.2 million to settle sexual harassment charges brought by female employees for offensive e-mail messages sent by male coworkers, including one about "25 Reasons Beer Is Better Than Women." The employees had signed a complaint letter about the e-mail harassment, but the company had ignored the complaint.

E-mail often sets the social tone of an office and has been permitted to be slightly ribald. At some point, however, e-mail conduct becomes impermissible and crosses the line to actionable sexual or racial harassment. The standard of whether e-mail creates an illegal hostile work environment is the same as that for measuring harassment in any other context: The offensive conduct must be severe and cannot consist of isolated or trivial remarks and incidents. And, as in other harassment cases, an employer may raise the defense that requires two elements: (1) the employer exercised reasonable care to prevent and correct the behavior and (2) the plaintiff employee unreasonably failed to take advantage of any preventive or corrective opportunities provided by the employer or to avoid the harm.

E-mail differs from many other incidents of harassment because it is subtle and insidious. Unlike paper pin-up calendars in plain view, an employer does not readily see

e-mail messages. Obscenity pulled off the Internet or scanned into a computer can be sent as a clipping to an e-mail message. Because e-mail is hidden, to detect offensive messages, employers must take affirmative action to review e-mail messages on its network. Courts have generally held that an employee does not have an expectation of privacy of e-mail. Stored e-mail is the property of the employer, which may review it freely. Employers can also use software to scan and filter e-mail messages that contain any of a predefined list of objectionable words or phrases or certain "to" or "from" headers. Employers can also use software programs to scan graphics and block X-rated pictures.

E-mail has not only increased the possibility of there being sexual or racial harassment on the job, but it has also become the smoking gun that undermines a company's attempt to defend such cases. Therefore, employers must adopt policies pertaining to the use of e-mail by its employees and make their employees aware that certain e-mail messages constitute sexual or racial harassment and violate the law. Employers should make periodic inspections and audits of stored e-mail to ensure that employees are complying with the company's antiharassment policies.

Business Brief
Title VII prohibits same-sex employment discrimination.

Same-Sex Discrimination   The U.S. Supreme Court has held that same-sex sexual harassment is actionable under Title VII.[8] State and local laws often also prohibit this form of discrimination.

Contemporary Business Application

EMPLOYERS MAY PROVE AN AFFIRMATIVE DEFENSE IN SOME SEXUAL HARASSMENT CASES

The law of sexual harassment has been evolving since the U.S. Supreme Court first recognized it as a violation of Title VII in *Meritor Savings Bank, FSB v. Vinson*, 477 U.S. 57, 106 S.Ct. 2399 (1986). During the 1997 term, the Supreme Court, in two parallel decisions, again established important rules for sexual harassment cases brought under Title VII.

In *Faragher v. City of Boca Raton*, Beth Ann Faragher worked as a parttime ocean lifeguard for the City of Boca Raton, Florida. Bill Terry and David Silverman were her immediate supervisors. Faragher proved that the men created a sexually hostile atmosphere by repeatedly touching her body, including her buttocks, without her consent; making lewd comments about her body; asking her to have sex; pantomiming oral sex; and making crude and demeaning comments about females in general. Although the city

had a policy against sexual harassment, it had never disseminated it to the lifeguards or supervisors. Faragher did not complain to higher management, but resigned and sued the city for sexual harassment. The trial court held for Faragher, but the court of appeals reversed. Faragher appealed to the Supreme Court.

In *Burlington Industries, Inc. v. Ellerth*, Kimberly Ellerth worked as a salesperson for Burlington. She alleged that she was subjected to the following sexual harassment by her supervisor, Ted Slovik: He made comments about her breasts, told her she was not "loose enough"; touched her body without her consent; once stated, when she called for information "I don't have time for you right now, Kim, unless you want to tell me what you are wearing"; and made other offensive remarks and gestures. Ellerth did not inform anyone of this conduct, even though Burlington had a policy against sexual harassment. Ellerth quit and sued Burlington for sexual harassment. The trial court entered summary judgment for Burlington, but the court of appeals reversed. Burlington appealed to the Supreme Court.

In the past, the circuit courts of appeal were divided as to whether an employer was strictly liable for the sexual harassment of its supervisors. In *Faragher* and *Burlington Industries*, the Supreme Court issued opinions that reject automatic or strict liability. Instead, the Supreme Court ordered trial and appellate courts to examine the evidence in sexual harassment cases using a preponderance of the evidence standard under the following rules.

The Supreme Court stated that an employer is vicariously liable to a victimized employee for a hostile work environment created by a supervisor with immediate or successively higher authority over the employee. The Court announced, however, that an employer may raise an *affirmative defense* against liability or damages by proving the following two elements:

1. The employer exercised reasonable care to prevent and correct promptly any sexual-harassing behavior
2. The plaintiff employee unreasonably failed to take advantage of any preventive or corrective opportunities provided by the employer or to otherwise avoid harm

The defendant employer has the burden of proving this affirmative defense. Courts should consider the following factors in determining whether such defense has been proven: (1) did the employer have an antiharassing policy, (2) did the employer have a complaint mechanism in place, (3) were employees informed of the antiharassment policy and complaint procedure, and (4) other factors the court deems relevant.

The Supreme Court held that this newly established defense could only be asserted by employers where the harassing conduct created a "hostile work environment" absent any *tangible* employment action affecting the victimized employee. For example, if the complaining employee had been fired, demoted, or reassigned to an undesirable position, this action would constitute a "tangible employment action" that would prevent the employer from raising an affirmative defense.

In applying these rules to these two cases, the Supreme Court held that the City of Boca Raton had failed to exercise reasonable care to prevent or correct the discrimination and therefore could not avail itself to an affirmative defense. The Court reversed in favor of Beth Ann Faragher. In *Burlington Industries*, the Court remanded the case to the trial court for the employer to have an opportunity to assert and prove an affirmative defense.

Now that the U.S. Supreme Court has announced these decisions, it will be the job of lower federal courts to apply the "reasonable" tests of the newly announced affirmative defense to specific-fact cases. [*Faragher v. City of Boca Raton*, 118 S.Ct. 2275 (1998); *Burlington Industries, Inc. v. Ellerth*, 118 S.Ct. 2257 (1998)]

Religious Discrimination

Title VII prohibits employment discrimination based on a person's religion. Religions include traditional religions, other religions that recognize a supreme being, and religions based on ethical or spiritual tenets. Many **religious discrimination** cases involve a conflict between an employer's work rule and an employee's religious beliefs (e.g., when an employee is required to work on his or her religious holiday).

The right of an employee to practice his or her religion is not absolute. Under Title VII, an employer is under a duty to *reasonably accommodate* the religious observances, practices, or beliefs of its employees if it does not cause an *undue hardship* on the employer. The courts must apply these general standards to specific fact situations. In making their decisions, the courts must consider such factors as the size of the employer, the importance of the employee's position, and the availability of alternative workers.

Title VII expressly permits religious organizations to give preference in employment to individuals of a particular religion. For example, if a person applies for a job with a religious organization but does not subscribe to its religious tenets, the organization may refuse to hire that person.

religious discrimination
Discrimination against a person solely because of his or her religion or religious practices.

Business Brief
Employers owe a duty to *reasonably* accommodate an employee's religious practices, observances, or beliefs if it does not cause *undue hardship* to the employer.

*D*EFENSES TO A TITLE VII ACTION

Title VII and case law recognize the following defenses to a charge of discrimination under Title VII.

Merit

Employers can select or promote employees based on *merit*. Merit decisions are often based on work, educational experience, and professionally developed ability tests. To be lawful under Title VII, the requirement must be job related. For example, requiring a person to pass a typing test to be hired as a typist would be lawful. Requiring a person to pass a college-level English composition test to be employed as a maintenance worker would violate Title VII.

Seniority

Many employers maintain *seniority* systems that reward long-term employees. Higher wages, fringe benefits, and other preferential treatment (e.g., choice of working hours and vacation schedule) are examples of such rewards. Seniority systems provide an incentive for employees to stay with the company. Such systems are lawful if they are not the result of intentional discrimination.

Bona Fide Occupational Qualification (BFOQ)

Discrimination based on protected classes (other than race or color) is permitted if it is shown to be a **bona fide occupational qualification (BFOQ)**. To be legal, a BFOQ must be both *job related* and a *business necessity*. For example, allowing only women to be locker room attendants in a women's gym is a valid BFOQ, but prohibiting males from being managers or instructors at the same gym would not be a BFOQ. As the following case shows, BFOQ exceptions are narrowly interpreted by the courts.

International Union, United Automobile, Aerospace and Agricultural Implement Workers of America, UAW v. Johnson Controls, Inc.
499 U.S. 187, 111 S.Ct. 1196 (1991)
United States Supreme Court

CASE 42.5

FACTS

Johnson Controls, Inc. (Johnson Controls), manufactures batteries. Lead is the primary ingredient in the manufacturing process. Exposure to lead entails health risks, including risk of harm to any fetus carried by a female employee. To protect unborn children from such risk, Johnson Controls adopted an employment rule that prevented pregnant women and women of childbearing age from working at jobs involving lead exposure. Only women who were sterilized or could prove they could not have children were not affected by the rule. Consequently, most female employees were relegated to lower-paying clerical jobs at the company. Several female employees filed a class action suit challenging Johnson Controls's fetal-protection policy as sex discrimination in violation of Title VII. The district court held that the policy was justified as a bona fide occupational qualification (BFOQ) and granted summary judgment to Johnson Controls. The court of appeals affirmed. The plaintiffs appealed to the U.S. Supreme Court.

ISSUE

Is Johnson Controls's fetal-protection policy a BFOQ?

IN THE LANGUAGE OF THE COURT

Blackmun, Justice *The bias in Johnson Controls' policy is obvious. Fertile men, but not fertile women, are given a choice as to whether they wish to risk their reproductive health for a particular job. Johnson Controls' fetal-protection policy explicitly discriminates against women on the basis of their sex. The policy excludes women with childbearing capacity from lead-exposed jobs and so creates a facial classification based on gender.*

The bona fide occupational qualification's (BFOQ) defense is written narrowly, and this Court has read it narrowly. We have no difficulty concluding that Johnson Controls cannot establish a BFOQ. Fertile women, as far as appears in the record, participate in the manufacture of batteries as efficiently as anyone else. Johnson Controls' professed moral and ethical concerns about the welfare of the next generation do not suffice to establish a BFOQ of female sterility. Decisions about the welfare of future children must be left to the parents who conceive, bear, support, and raise them rather than to the employers who hire those parents. Congress has mandated this choice through Title VII, as amended by the Pregnancy Discrimination Act (PDA). Johnson Controls has attempted to exclude women because of their reproductive capacity. Title VII and the PDA simply do not allow a woman's dismissal because of her failure to submit to sterilization.

A word about tort liability and the increased cost of fertile women in the workplace is perhaps necessary. According to Johnson Controls, the company complies with the lead standard developed by the Occupational Health and Safety Administration (OSHA) and warns its female employees about the damaging effects of lead. Without negligence, it would be difficult for a court to find liability on the part of the employer. If, under general tort principles, Title VII bans sex-specific fetal-protection policies, the employer fully informs the woman of the risk, and the employer has not acted negligently, the basis for holding an employer liable seems remote at best.

DECISION AND REMEDY

The U.S. Supreme Court held that Johnson Controls's fetal-protection policy was not a BFOQ. Instead, it was sex discrimination in violation of Title VII. Reversed and remanded.

Case Questions

Critical Legal Thinking Should any BFOQ exceptions to Title VII actions be permitted? Why or why not?

Ethics Should Johnson Controls's moral and ethical concerns about the welfare of the next generation justify its actions?

Business Application Does Johnson Controls have any tort liability to children who are born injured by exposure to lead? How can Johnson Controls limit such liability?

---

*C*ONCEPT SUMMARY — TITLE VII OF THE CIVIL RIGHTS ACT OF 1964

Covered Employers and Employment Decisions	1. **Employers** Employers with 15 or more employees for 20 weeks in the current or preceding year, all employment agencies, labor unions with 15 or more members, state and local governments, and most federal agencies. 2. **Employment Decisions** Decisions regarding hiring; promotion; demotion; payment of salaries, wages, and fringe benefits; dismissal; job training and apprenticeships; work rules; or any other *term, condition,* or *privilege* of employment. Decision to admit a partner to a partnership is also covered.
Protected Classes	1. **Race** Broad class of individuals with common characteristics (e.g., Black, Caucasian, Asian, Native American). 2. **Color** Color of a person's skin (e.g., light-skinned person, dark-skinned person). 3. **National Origin** A person's country of origin or national heritage (e.g., Italian, Hispanic). 4. **Sex** A person's sex, whether male or female. Includes sexual harassment and discrimination against females who are pregnant. 5. **Religion** A person's religious beliefs. An employer has a duty to reasonably accommodate an employee's religious beliefs if it does not cause an undue hardship on the employer.
Types of Discrimination	1. **Disparate Treatment Discrimination** Discrimination against a specific individual because that person belongs to a protected class. 2. **Disparate Impact Discrimination** Discrimination that occurs where a neutral-looking employment rule causes discrimination against a protected class.
Defenses	1. **Merit** Job-related experience, education, or unbiased employment test. 2. **Seniority** Length of time an employee has been employed by the employer. Intentional discrimination based on seniority is unlawful. 3. **Bona Fide Occupational Qualification (BFOQ)** Discrimination based on sex, religion, or national origin is permitted if it is a valid BFOQ for the position. Qualification based on race or color is not a permissible BFOQ.
Remedies	1. The court may order the payment of two years' back pay, issue an injunction awarding reinstatement, grant fictional seniority, or order some other equitable remedy.

International Perspective

Iɴᴛᴇʀɴᴀᴛɪᴏɴᴀʟ Rᴇᴀᴄʜ ᴏғ U.S. Aɴᴛɪᴅɪsᴄʀɪᴍɪɴᴀᴛɪᴏɴ Lᴀᴡs

Does Title VII extend beyond the territorial reach of the United States? The **Civil Rights Act of 1991** stipulates that it does. The 1991 act expressly protects *U.S. citizens*—but not foreign nationals—employed in a foreign country by U.S.-controlled employers. Foreign operations not controlled by U.S. employers are not covered.

An employer of a U.S. citizen abroad is subject to claims under Title VII in the following two situations:

1. An employer that is incorporated in the United States and operates a branch office in a foreign country is liable for Title VII violations against U.S. citizens that occur in its foreign operation.
2. If a U.S. parent corporation owns a foreign corporation that is incorporated in another country, the foreign-controlled subsidiary is subject to Title VII because the 1991 act expressly states that discriminatory practices of "controlled foreign corporations" are presumed to be acts engaged in by the parent corporation.

The 1991 act contains an express exception that protects employers from conflicting foreign laws. If required conduct under Title VII would cause the employer to violate the law of a foreign nation (e.g., foreign law does not permit the employment of female workers), compliance with Title VII is excused.

The 1991 act also extends its international reach to the Americans with Disabilities Act (ADA) and the Age Discrimination in Employment Act (ADEA). Both of these acts are discussed later in this chapter.

*E*QUAL Pᴀʏ Aᴄᴛ ᴏғ 1963

Equal Pay Act of 1963

Protects both sexes from pay discrimination based on sex; extends to jobs that require equal skill, equal effort, equal responsibility, and similar working conditions.

Discrimination often takes the form of different pay scales for men and women performing the same job. The **Equal Pay Act of 1963** protects both sexes from pay discrimination based on sex.[9] This act covers all levels of private sector employees and state and local government employees. Federal workers are not covered, however.

The act prohibits disparity in pay for jobs that require *equal skill* (i.e., equal experience), *equal effort* (i.e., mental and physical exertion), *equal responsibility* (i.e., equal supervision and accountability), or *similar working conditions* (i.e., dangers of injury, exposure to the elements, and the like). To make this determination, the courts examine the actual requirements of jobs to determine whether they are equal and similar. If two jobs are determined to be equal and similar, an employer cannot pay disparate wages to members of different sexes.

Employees can bring a private cause of action against an employer for violating the act. Back pay and liquidated damages are recoverable. In addition, the employer must increase the wages of the discriminated-against employee to eliminate the unlawful disparity of wages. The wages of other employees may not be lowered.

Criteria That Justify a Differential in Wages

The Equal Pay Act expressly provides four criteria that justify a differential in wages. These defenses include payment systems that are based on

Business Brief

The Equal Pay Act expressly provides four criteria that justify a differential in wages. The employer bears the burden of proving these defenses.

- **Seniority**
- **Merit** (as long as there is some identifiable measurement standard)
- **Quantity or quality of product** (commission, piecework, or quality-control-based payment systems are permitted)
- **"Any factor other than sex"** (including shift differentials, i.e., night versus day shifts, and such)

The employer bears the burden of proving these defenses. An employer asserted the "any factor other than sex" defense in the following case.

Glenn v. General Motors Corporation
841 F.2d 567 (1988)
United States Court of Appeals, Eleventh Circuit

CASE 42.6

FACTS

Sheila Ann Glenn, Patricia Johns, and Robbie Nugent, three female employees of General Motors Corporation (GM), sued their employer for violation of the Equal Pay Act. The three females worked in the tools stores department of GM as "Follow Ups." A Follow Up basically ensures that adequate tools are on hand in GM plants to keep the plants running. From 1975 through 1985, the three women were paid less than all their male comparators in the same position, and the most highly paid of the three earned less than the lowest-paid man. When hired, all three women received lower starting salaries than men hired at the same time. The trial court held in favor of the three women and awarded damages against GM. GM appealed.

ISSUE

Did GM violate the Equal Pay Act?

IN THE LANGUAGE OF THE COURT

Johnson, Circuit Judge Once the appellees established a prima facie case, the burden shifted to GM to prove that the difference in pay was justified by one of the four exceptions in the Equal Pay Act: (1) a seniority system, (2) a merit system, (3) a system that measures earnings by quantity or quality of production,

(4) a differential based on any factor other than sex. GM seeks to justify the pay disparity on the fourth ground—a factor other than sex.

GM seeks to defend the pay disparity as a result of the market force theory. This court and the Supreme Court have long rejected the market force theory as a "factor other than sex." The argument that supply and demand dictates that women may be paid less is exactly the kind of evil that the Equal Pay Act was designed to eliminate and has been rejected. The market force theory that a woman will work for less than a man is not a valid consideration under the Equal Pay Act.

DECISION AND REMEDY

The court of appeals held that General Motors Corporation had violated the Equal Pay Act and affirmed the award of damages to the plaintiffs.

Case Questions

Critical Legal Thinking   Do you think the Equal Pay Act was necessary to eliminate pay disparities between men and women?

Ethics   Was it ethical for GM to pay women less than men for the same job?

Business Application   What does the market force theory provide? Does it make economic sense?

*A*GE DISCRIMINATION IN EMPLOYMENT ACT OF 1967

In the past, some employers discriminated against employees and prospective employees based on their age. For example, employers often refused to hire older workers. The **Age Discrimination in Employment Act (ADEA)**, which prohibits certain *age discrimination* practices, was enacted in 1967.[10]

The ADEA covers nonfederal employers with at least 20 employees, labor unions with at least 25 members, and all employment agencies. State and local government employees except those in policy-making positions are covered, as well as employees of certain sectors of the federal government.

The ADEA prohibits age discrimination in all employment decisions, including hiring, promotions, payment of compensation, and other terms and conditions of employment. The **Older Workers Benefit Protection Act (OWBPA)** amended the ADEA to prohibit age discrimination with regard to employee benefits.[11] Employers cannot use employment advertisements that discriminate against applicants covered by ADEA.

The same defenses that are available in a Title VII action are also available in an ADEA action.

Age Discrimination in Employment Act (ADEA) of 1967
Prohibits age discrimination practices against employees who are 40 and older.

Older Workers Benefit Protection Act (OWBPA)
Prohibits age discrimination in employee benefits.

Protected Age Categories

Originally, ADEA prohibited employment discrimination against persons between the ages of 40 and 65. In 1978, its coverage was extended to persons up to the age of 70. Further amendments completely eliminated an age ceiling, so ADEA now applies to employees who are 40 and older.[12] As a result, covered employers cannot establish mandatory retirement ages for their employees.

Because persons under 40 are not protected by ADEA, an employer can maintain an employment policy of hiring only workers who are 40 years of age or older without violating the ADEA. However, the employer could not maintain an employment practice whereby it hired only persons 50 years of age and older because it would discriminate against persons aged 40 to 49.

The ADEA is administered by the EEOC. Private plaintiffs can also sue under ADEA. A successful plaintiff in an ADEA action can recover back wages, attorneys' fees, and equitable relief, including hiring, reinstatement, and promotion. Where a violation of ADEA is found, the employer must raise the wages of the discriminated-against employee. It cannot lower the wages of other employees.

Ethical Perspective

"YOU'RE OVERQUALIFIED FOR THE JOB!"

On October 20, 1982, Preview Subscription Television, Inc. (Preview), a subsidiary of Time Incorporated (Time), hired Thomas Taggart as a print production manager for Preview's magazine *Guide*. Taggart was 58 years old at the time and had more than 30 years' experience in the printing industry. In May 1983, Time notified Preview employees that Preview would be dissolved and, though not guaranteed a job, the employees were told they would receive special consideration for other positions at Time. Time sent weekly job bulletins to former Preview employees, including Taggart.

Taggart applied for 32 positions in various divisions at Time and its subsidiaries, including *Sports Illustrated, People Magazine, Life, Money,* and *Discover* magazines. Although Taggart interviewed for many of these openings, he was not offered employment. Time explained this by saying that Taggart was overqualified for many of the positions. Taggart contends that Time hired less qualified, younger applicants for many of the positions for which he was rejected. Taggart sued Time for age discrimination in violation of the Age Discrimination in Employment Act (ADEA). The district court granted Time's motion for summary judgment. Taggart appealed.

The court of appeals held that an employer's proffered reason for not hiring an applicant for a position because he was overqualified is a circumstance from which a reasonable juror could infer discriminatory animus.

The court noted that Taggart was over 40 years old and belonged to the protected age group. The fact that Taggart was found overqualified for some of the jobs he applied for at Time supported his allegation that he was capable of performing the jobs. Further, Time hired persons younger than he for those jobs. Thus, Taggart established a prima facie case of age discrimination. The court of appeals reversed and remanded the case. Why do businesses tend to want to hire younger workers rather than older ones? [*Taggart v. Time Incorporated*, 924 F.2d 43 (2d Cir. 1991)]

1. Did Time Incorporated act ethically in adopting the "you are overqualified" reason for not hiring Mr. Taggart?
2. Do you think older workers have a harder time finding employment than younger persons and therefore need the protection of the ADEA? Should younger persons be covered by the ADEA, too?

REHABILITATION ACT OF 1973

The **Rehabilitation Act of 1973** forbids discrimination in employment against handicapped persons by an employer who receives federal contracts or assistance (i.e., *federal contractors*).[13] Covered employers include defense contractors, state and local government employers, and certain federal government agencies. Federal contractors must include a clause in their contracts that obliges them to abide by the provisions of the Rehabilitation Act and regulations adopted thereunder.

The Rehabilitation Act prohibits employers from discriminating against handicapped individuals who can perform at the minimum level of productivity expected of a nonhandicapped person after *reasonable accommodation* is made for the handicap. For example, an employer would have to reasonably accommodate someone in a wheelchair who can otherwise perform the job. There is not a violation of the act if an employer refuses to hire or promote a handicapped person who cannot perform the job.

The Labor Department administers the act in most situations. The courts have recognized a private cause of action under the Rehabilitation Act. Private plaintiffs can recover damages resulting from violations of the act.

Rehabilitation Act of 1973
Prohibits discrimination against handicapped persons by an employer who receives federal contracts or assistance.

AMERICANS WITH DISABILITIES ACT OF 1990

The **Americans with Disabilities Act (ADA)**, which was signed into law on July 26, 1990,[14] is the most comprehensive piece of civil rights legislation since the Civil Rights Act of 1964. The ADA imposes obligations on employers and providers of public transportation, telecommunications, and public accommodations to accommodate individuals with disabilities.

Americans with Disabilities Act (ADA) of 1990
Imposes obligations on employers and providers of public transportation, telecommunications, and public accommodations to accommodate individuals with disabilities.

Title I of the ADA

Title I of the ADA prohibits employment discrimination against qualified individuals with disabilities in regard to job application procedures, hiring, compensation, training, promotion, and termination. Title I, which became effective July 26, 1992, covers employers with 25 or more employees for two years after the effective date and those with 15 or more employees thereafter. The United States, corporations wholly owned by the United States, and bona fide tax-exempt private membership clubs are exempt from Title I coverage.

Title I requires an employer to make reasonable accommodations to individuals with disabilities that do not cause undue hardship to the employer. *Reasonable accommodations* may include making facilities readily accessible to individuals with disabilities, providing part-time or modified work schedules, acquiring equipment or devices, modifying examination and training materials, and providing qualified readers or interpreters.

Employers are not obligated to provide accommodations that would impose an *undue burden*. This means actions that would require significant difficulty or expense. Factors such as the nature and cost of accommodation, the overall financial resources of the employer, and the employer's type of operation are considered by the EEOC and the courts. Obviously, what may be a significant difficulty or expense for a small employer may not be an undue hardship for a large employer.

Business Brief
Title I of the ADA requires an employer to make *reasonable accommodations* to employees with disabilities that do not cause *undue hardship* to the employer.

Qualified Individual with a Disability

A **qualified individual with a disability** is a person who, with or without reasonable accommodation, can perform the essential functions of the job that person desires or holds. A disabled person is someone who (1) has a physical or mental impairment that substantially limits one or more of his or her major life activities, (2) has a record of such

qualified individual with a disability
A person who (1) has a physical or mental impairment that substantially limits one or more of his or her major life activities, (2) has a record of such impairment, or (3) is regarded as having such impairment.

impairment, or (3) is regarded as having such impairment. Mental retardation, paraplegia, schizophrenia, cerebral palsy, epilepsy, diabetes, muscular dystrophy, multiple sclerosis, cancer, infection with HIV (human immunodeficiency virus), and visual, speech, and hearing impairments are covered under the ADA. A current user of illegal drugs or an alcoholic who uses alcohol or is under the influence of alcohol at the workplace is not covered. However, recovering alcoholics and former users of illegal drugs are protected.

> *By what justice can an association of citizens be held together when there is no equality among the citizens?*
>
> Cicero
> De Re Publica De Legibus J
> XXXII. 49

Title I limits an employer's ability to inquire into or test for an applicant's disabilities. Title I forbids an employer from asking a job applicant about the existence, nature, and severity of a disability. An employer may, however, inquire about the applicant's ability to perform job-related functions. Preemployment medical examinations are forbidden before a job offer. Once a job offer has been made, an employer may require a medical examination and may condition the offer on the examination results as long as all entering employees are subject to such an examination. The information must be kept confidential.

Procedure and Remedies

Title I, which is administered by the EEOC, borrows much of its procedural framework from Title VII of the Civil Rights Act of 1964. An aggrieved individual must first file a charge with the EEOC, which may take action against the employer or permit the individual to pursue a private cause of action.

Relief can take the form of an injunction, hiring or reinstatement (with back pay), payment of attorneys' fees, and recovery of compensatory and punitive damages (subject to the same caps as Title VII damages).

In the following case, the U.S. Supreme Court addressed the issue of what is a disability for purposes of the ADA.

Sutton v. United Air Lines, Inc.
119 S.Ct. 2139 (1999)
Supreme Court of the United States

CASE 42.7

FACTS
In 1992, Karen Sutton and Kimberly Hinton (petitioners), twin sisters, applied to United Air Lines, Inc., for employment as commercial airline pilots. They met United's education and experience requirements and the Federal Aviation Administration (FAA) certification qualifications. Both of the petitioners have severe myopia, with uncorrected visual acuity of 20/200 or worse and 20/400 or worse. Each of the petitioners has vision that is 20/20 or better with the use of corrective lens. Without corrective lens, neither of the petitioners can see to conduct activities such as driving a vehicle, watching television, or shopping in public stores, but with corrective lens both function identically to persons without similar impairment. United rejected the petitioners' employment applications because they did not meet United's minimum visual requirement of uncorrected visual acuity of 20/100 or better. Petitioners filed a charge of disability discrimination against United for allegedly violating the Americans with Disabilities Act (ADA). The district court dismissed petitioners' complaint and the circuit court of

appeals affirmed. Petitioners appealed to the U.S. Supreme Court, which granted review.

ISSUE
Are the petitioners disabled within the meaning of the ADA?

IN THE LANGUAGE OF THE COURT
O'Connor, Justice   With respect to the disability definition, our decision turns on whether disability is to be determined with or without reference to corrective measures. Petitioners maintain that whether an impairment is substantially limiting should be determined without regard to corrective measures. United, in turn, maintains that an impairment does not substantially limit a major life activity if it is corrected. We conclude that United is correct. Looking at the ADA as a whole, it is apparent that if a person is taking measures to correct for, or mitigate, a physical or mental impairment, the effects of those measures—both positive and negative—must be taken into account when judging whether that person is "substantially limited" in a major life activity and thus "disabled" under the ADA.

The ADA defines a "disability" as "a physical or mental impairment that substantially limits one or more of the major life activities" of an individual. A person whose physical or mental impairment is corrected by medication or other measures does not have an impairment that presently substantially limits a major life activity. To be sure, a person whose physical or mental impairment is corrected by mitigating measures still has an impairment, but if the impairment is corrected it does not substantially limit a major life activity.

Congress found that "some 43,000,000 Americans have one or more physical or mental disabilities, and this number is increasing as the population as a whole is growing older." This figure is inconsistent with the definition of disability pressed by petitioners. Indeed, the number of people with vision impairments alone is 100 million. And there were approximately 50 million people with high blood pressure. Had Congress intended to include all persons with corrected physical limitations among those covered by the ADA, it undoubtedly would have cited this much higher number of disabled persons in its findings. That it did not is evidence that the ADA's coverage is restricted to only those whose impairments are not mitigated by corrective measures.

DECISION AND REMEDY

The U.S. Supreme Court held that *disability* under the Americans with Disabilities Act (ADA) does not include persons with corrected conditions, such as petitioners corrected vision. The Supreme Court concluded that the petitioners' complaint was properly dismissed. Affirmed.

Case Questions

Critical Legal Thinking   Does the Americans with Disabilities Act promote an important social policy? Do you think a federal law was needed to effectuate this policy?

Ethics   Did United act ethically in this case? What reasons underlie its decision not to hire the petitioners?

Business Application   What is the business implication of the U.S. Supreme Court's decision? What would have been the economic implications for business if the Supreme Court would have held in the petitioners' favor?

CIVIL RIGHTS ACT OF 1866

The **Civil Rights Act of 1866** was enacted after the Civil War. *Section 1981* of this act states that all persons "have the same right . . . to make and enforce contracts ... as is enjoyed by white persons."[15] Employment decisions are covered because the employment relation is contractual. Most employers other than the federal government are subject to this act.

Section 1981 expressly prohibits racial discrimination; it has also been held to forbid discrimination based on national origin. Although most racial and national origin employment discrimination cases are brought under Title VII, there are two reasons that a complainant would bring the action under Section 1981: (1) A private plaintiff can bring an action without going through the procedural requirements of Title VII, and (2) there is no limitations period on the recovery of back pay and no cap on the recovery of compensatory or punitive damages.

Civil Rights Act of 1866
An act enacted after the Civil War that says all persons "have the same right . . . to make and enforce contracts . . . as is enjoyed by white persons"; it prohibits racial and national origin employment discrimination.

CIVIL RIGHTS ACT OF 1991

After a two-year battle, Congress enacted the **Civil Rights Act of 1991** [P.L. 102-166]. This act overturned all or a portion of eight U.S. Supreme Court decisions that had limited the rights of plaintiffs to bring suits under federal antidiscrimination laws, particularly Title VII of the Civil Rights Act of 1964.

The Civil Rights Act of 1991 amended Title VII of the Civil Rights Act of 1964, the Americans with Disabilities Act, Section 1981 of the Civil Rights Act of 1866, and other federal equal opportunity in employment laws in several significant ways. For example, it increased the damages available for intentional employment discrimination, made it easier for plaintiffs to prove disparate impact discrimination, and made it more difficult for employers to prove a business necessity defense to a charge of unlawful discrimination.

The Civil Rights Act of 1991 provides that the plaintiff will prevail in a Title VII action if he or she can prove that a prohibited factor (e.g., race or sex) was a "motivating factor" for the employer's adverse decision. The employer's ability to prove that it would have taken the same action regardless of the prohibited factor has no impact on this result; the plaintiff still wins.

Entrepreneur and the Law

SMALL BUSINESSES EXEMPT FROM FEDERAL EQUAL OPPORTUNITY IN EMPLOYMENT LAWS

In passing federal equal opportunity in employment laws, Congress exempted small businesses from the reach of many of these laws. In several of these statutes, Congress set a threshold number of employees that an employer must have to be covered by each act. Some of the threshold requirements are

• **Title VII** Employers with 15 or more employees.

• **Age Discrimination in Employment Act** Employers with 20 or more employees.
• **Americans with Disabilities Act of 1990** Employers with 15 or more employees.

The rationale behind these exemptions is that it may be too costly for small employers to comply with the laws and face lawsuits that could arise thereunder. These employers should make every effort to comply with these laws, however.

AFFIRMATIVE ACTION

affirmative action

Policy that provides that certain job preferences will be given to minority or other protected class applicants when an employer makes an employment decision.

Employers often adopt **affirmative action plans** that provide that certain job preferences will be given to minority or other protected class applicants when an employer makes an employment decision. Such plans can be voluntarily adopted by employers, undertaken to settle a discrimination action, or ordered by the courts. Employee approval is not required.

Affirmative action plans are often controversial. Proponents of such plans argue that the plans are necessary to address imbalances in the workforce and to remedy past discrimination against protected classes. Opponents argue that affirmative action plans actually cause **reverse discrimination,** work hardship on innocent employees, and cause the employment of less qualified individuals.

reverse discrimination

Discrimination against a group that is usually thought of as a majority.

The Civil Rights Act of 1991 prohibits the practice of "race norming" and other practices that are used to alter or adjust test scores on the basis of race. It does not affect how an employer uses accurately reported test scores or require that test scores be used at all in making employment decisions, however.

Contemporary Business Application

AFFIRMATIVE ACTION NARROWED

Affirmative action was dealt a severe blow when, in April 1995, the U.S. Supreme Court refused to hear appeals in two cases that gave victories to white men in reverse discrimination lawsuits. These decisions show a willingness by the courts to apply the

Equal Protection Clause of the U.S. Constitution and equal opportunity in employment laws to protect white employees as well as minorities from discrimination.

The first case involved an affirmative action plan implemented by the city of Birmingham, Alabama, to ensure the promotion of black firefighters. The case began over 20 years ago when black firefighters sued the city for discrimination because it had only a few black firefighters and none in supervisory positions. After a heated lawsuit, in 1981 the city agreed to promote white and black firefighters to the rank of lieutenant on a 1-to-1 basis until the number of blacks equaled the 28 percent of the surrounding county's workforce that was black. The target was reached in 1989, but the city continued this quota system.

In 1989, several white firefighters challenged the city's affirmative action plan. The white firefighters lost in federal district court, but the court of appeals reversed, finding that the city's affirmative action plan violated the Equal Protection Clause of the Constitution and Title VII. The court of appeals denounced the city's plan as outright racial balancing, stating, "We can imagine nothing less conducive to eliminating the vestiges of past discrimination than a government separating its employees into two categories, black and nonblack, and allocating a rigid, inflexible number of promotions to each group, year in and year out."

The second case was brought by Frederick Claus, a white engineer with a bachelor's degree in electrical engineering who had worked 29 years for his employer, Duquesne Light Co. Claus, along with four other whites

and one black, sought promotion for an open managerial job. The black employee did not have a bachelor's degree or the required seven years' experience for the position. When the company applied its affirmative action plan and chose the black employee for the position, Claus sued under Title VII, claiming that he was a victim of racial discrimination. The jury agreed and awarded him $25,000 in compensatory damages and $400,000 in punitive damages. The court of appeals upheld the verdict.

Without comment, the U.S. Supreme Court turned down appeals in both cases [*Arrington v. Wilks*, 115 S.Ct. 1695 (1995); *Duquesne Light Co. v. Claus*, 115 S.Ct. 1700 (1995)].

What is left of affirmative action? For one thing, affirmative action was not held to be per se illegal in either case. Instead, the courts of appeal held that an affirmative action plan, to be legal, must be "narrowly tailored" to achieve some "compelling interest." In these two cases, the courts found that the affirmative action plans were not narrowly tailored but were blatant quotas that were unlawful. Government and private employers must now tailor their affirmative action programs narrowly or face reverse discrimination lawsuits by passed-over nonminority employees.

STATE AND LOCAL GOVERNMENT ANTIDISCRIMINATION LAWS

Many state and local governments have adopted laws that prevent discrimination in employment. These laws usually include classes protected by federal equal opportunity laws, as well as classes of persons not protected by federal laws, such as homosexuals and other minority groups.

International Perspective

JAPAN ADOPTS AN EQUAL OPPORTUNITY IN EMPLOYMENT LAW

Prior to April 1, 1999, job openings in Japan were restricted by gender; that is, jobs could be reserved for men only without violating the law. Classified advertisements in major Japanese newspapers typically listed "men only" jobs, which were executive positions and high-paying blue collar jobs. "Women only" listings tended to be for nurses, secretaries, food-service employees, and other low-paying jobs. Japanese women hold only 10 percent of professional positions, as compared to 45 percent in the United States. Only 8 out of every

1,000 factory workers in Japan are women, compared to 160 per 1,000 in the United States. In addition to gender-based discrimination, sexual harassment against females in the workplace was usually ignored.

All this changed with Japan's enactment of the **Equal Employment Opportunity and Labor Standard Law** in 1999. The new statute grants equal opportunity rights to females in being hired for jobs and promoted to higher positions. The law bans the use of gender-specific advertising, so the "men only" and "women only" job listings have

(box continues)

disappeared. Women may now compete equally, under the law, for jobs and promotions. The new law also makes other gender-based discrimination illegal. For example, prior to the new law, women were banned from working after 10:00 P.M. or putting in more than six hours of overtime per week. Both of these restrictions have been removed, allowing females to earn higher wages from working night shifts and overtime. Women are still forbidden from holding positions involving heavy lifting or those involving certain chemicals.

The Equal Opportunity Law prohibits sexual harassment in the workplace. Prior to the passage of the new law, sexual harassment—known in Japan as *seku hara*—was difficult to sue for. Previously, companies could veto any sexual harassment complaint brought against them, which helped explain why fewer than a dozen cases were even ruled on during the 1990s. Under the new law, a woman can file a complaint with the Labor Ministry, a government administrative agency empowered to investigate such charges. So companies are now advising male managers to remove X-rated calendars from offices and to not pressure female employees to accompany them to karaoke, dancing, or other endeavors.

Proponents of the Equal Opportunity Law hail it as a victory for women's rights in Japan, a male-dominated culture. They assert that the law will open up executive positions and high-paying factory jobs that were previously barred to women. Critics contend that the new law amounts to little more than a cosmetic make-over and that companies will continue to enforce the opaque ceiling that has kept females from obtaining the better jobs in the Japanese economy.

Working the Web

e·biz

U.S. Equal Employment Opportunity Commission The mission of the EEOC is to promote equal opportunity employment by enforcing the federal civil rights employment laws through administrative and judicial actions, education, and technical assistance.

Visit at **www.eeoc.gov**

Americans with Disabilities Act Document Center This site contains the statute itself, regulations, technical sheets, and other assistance documents.

Visit at **janweb.icdi.wvu.edu/kinder**

National Mediation Board The National Mediation Board is an independent U.S. government agency estab-lished by the 1934 Amendments to the Railway Labor Act. Its principal role is to foster harmonious labor-management relations in the rail and air transport industries, thereby minimizing disruptions to the flow of interstate commerce.

Visit at **www.nmb.gov**

CYBER EXERCISES

1. Find out how to file a charge with the EEOC.

2. Who created the Americans with Disabilities Act Document Center?

3. From the NMB site, click on *Mediation* to find out more about this agency.

*C*ASES AND *E*XERCISES

CRITICAL LEGAL THINKING CASES

42.1. For years, certain state laws prevented females from working at night. Therefore, Corning Glass Works (Corning) employed male workers for night inspection jobs and female workers for day inspection jobs. Males working the night shift were paid higher wages than were females who worked the day shift. When the law changed and Corning began hiring females for night shift jobs, it instituted a "red circle" wage rate that permitted previously hired male night shift workers to continue to receive higher wages than newly hired night shift workers. Does this violate the Equal Pay Act? [*Corning Glass Works v. Brennan, Secretary of Labor*, 417 U.S. 188, 94 S.Ct. 2223 (1974)]

42.2. Winnie Teal is an African-American employee of the Department of Income Maintenance of the state of Connecticut. The first step to being promoted to a supervisor position is to attain a passing score on a written test. When the written test was administered, 54 percent of the African-American candidates passed and 68 percent of the white candidates passed. Teal, who failed the examination, filed a disparate impact Title VII action alleging that the test was biased against African-Americans. To reach a nondiscriminatory bottom-line result, the employer promoted 22.9 percent of the African-American candidates who passed the test but only 13.5 percent of the white candidates who passed. Teal was not promoted because she did not pass the test. Is this result a defense to Teal's Title VII action? [*Connecticut v. Teal*, 457 U.S. 440, 102 S.Ct. 2525 (1982)]

42.3. The city of Los Angeles Department of Water and Power maintains a pension plan for its employees that is funded by both employer and employee contributions. The plan pays men and women retirees pensions with the same monthly benefits. However, because statistically women on average live several years longer than men, female employees are required to make monthly contributions to the pension fund that are 14.84 percent higher than the contributions required of male employees. Because employee contributions are withheld from paychecks, a female employee takes home less pay than a male employee earning the same salary. Does this practice violate Title VII? [*City of Los Angeles Department of Water and Power v. Manhart*, 435 U.S. 702, 98 S.Ct. 1370 (1978)]

42.4. Shirley Huddleston became the first female sales representative of Roger Dean Chevrolet, Inc. (RDC), in West Palm Beach, Florida. Shortly after she began working at RDC, Philip Geraci, a fellow sales representative, and other male employees began making derogatory comments to and about her, expelled gas in her presence, called her a bitch and a whore, and such. Many of these remarks were made in front of customers. The sales manager of RDC participated in the harassment. On several occasions, Huddleston complained about this conduct to RDC's general manager. Is Title VII violated? [*Huddleston v. Roger Dean Chevrolet, Inc.*, 845 F.2d 900 (11th Cir. 1988)]

42.5. The Newport News Shipbuilding and Dry Dock Company (Newport) provides hospitalization and medical-surgical coverage to its employees and dependents of employees. Under the plan, all covered males, including employees and spouses of female employees, were treated alike for pur-

poses of hospitalization coverage. All covered females, including employees and spouses of male employees, were treated alike except for one major exception: Female employees were provided full hospital coverage for pregnancy whereas female spouses of male employees were provided limited hospital coverage for pregnancy. Does this practice violate Title VII? [*Newport News Shipbuilding and Dry Dock Company v. EEOC*, 462 U.S. 669, 103 S.Ct. 2622 (1983)]

42.6. The Federal Bureau of Investigation (FBI) engaged in a pattern and practice of discrimination against Hispanic FBI agents. Job assignments and promotions were areas that were especially affected. Bernardo M. Perez, an Hispanic, brought this Title VII action against the FBI. Did the FBI violate Title VII? [*Perez v. Federal Bureau of Investigation*, 714 F.Supp. 1414 (W.D.Texas 1989)]

42.7. Walker, a clerk typist with the Internal Revenue Service (IRS), is a light-skinned African-American. Her supervisor is a dark-skinned African-American. Walker filed an action alleging that she was terminated by her supervisor in violation of Title VII. Does she have a cause of action under Title VII? [*Walker v. Internal Revenue Service*, 713 F.Supp. 403 (N.D.Ga. 1989)]

42.8. Trans World Airlines (TWA), an airline, operates a large maintenance and overhaul base for its airplanes at Kansas City, Missouri. Because of its essential role, the stores department at the base must operate 24 hours per day, 365 days per year. The employees at the base are represented by the International Association of Machinists and Aerospace Workers (Union). TWA and Union entered into a collective bargaining agreement that includes a seniority system for the assignment of jobs and shifts.

Larry Hardison was hired by TWA to work as a clerk in the stores department. Soon after beginning work, Hardison joined the Worldwide Church of God, which does not allow its members to work from sunset on Friday until sunset on Saturday and on certain religious holidays. Hardison, who had the second lowest seniority within the stores department, did not have enough seniority to observe his Sabbath regularly. When Hardison asked for special consideration, TWA offered to allow him to take his Sabbath off if he could switch shifts with another employee-union member. None of the other employees would do so. TWA refused Hardison's request for a four-day workweek because it would have to either hire and train a part-time worker to work on Saturdays or incur the cost of paying overtime to an existing full-time worker on Saturdays. Hardison sued TWA for religious discrimination in violation of Title VII. Do TWA's actions violate Title VII? [*Trans World Airlines v. Hardison*, 432 U.S. 63, 97 S.Ct. 2264 (1977)]

42.9. At the age of 60, Manuel Fragante emigrated from the Philippines to Hawaii. In response to a newspaper ad, Fragante applied for an entry-level civil service clerk job with the city of Honolulu's Division of Motor Vehicles and Licensing. The job required constant oral communication with the public either at the information counter or on the telephone. Fragante scored the highest of 731 test takers on a written examination that tested word usage, grammar, and spelling. As part of the application process, two civil service employees who were familiar with the demands of the position interviewed Fragante. They testified that his accent made it difficult to understand him. Fragante was not hired for the position, which was filled by another applicant. Fragante sued, alleging national origin discrimination in violation of Title VII. Who wins? [*Fragante v. City and County of Honolulu*, 888 F.2d 591 (9th Cir. 1989)]

42.10. Walker Boyd Fite was an employee of First Tennessee Production Credit Association (First Tennessee) for 19 years. He had attained the position of vice president-credit. During the course of his employment, he never received an unsatisfactory review. On December 26, 1983, at the age of 57, Fite was hospitalized with a kidney stone. On January 5, 1984, while Fite was recovering at home, an officer of First Tennessee called to inform him that he had been retired as of December 31, 1983. A few days later, Fite received a letter stating that he had been retired because of poor job performance. Fite sued First Tennessee for age discrimination. Who wins? [*Fite v. First Tennessee Production Credit Association*, 861 F.2d 884 (6th Cir. 1989)]

42.11. Woolworth Davis, Salvatore D'Elia, and Herbert Sims, Jr., applied for various jobs with the city of Philadelphia. The city of Philadelphia receives federal government assistance. When Davis reported for a medical examination, scars revealed that he had previously injected illegal drugs intravenously. D'Elia, a former narcotics addict, was enrolled in a methadone program. Sims was a former user of morphine and heroin during his two-year tour of duty with the armed forces. Although the three applicants were rehabilitated and otherwise qualified for the positions, the city of Philadelphia refused to hire them because of their past drug use. The three applicants sued the city of Philadelphia, alleging a violation of the Rehabilitation Act of 1973. Are the three applicants protected by the act? [*Davis v. Bucher*, 451 F.Supp. 791 (E.D.Pa. 1978)]

42.12. In 1974, the Kaiser Aluminum & Chemical Corp. (Kaiser) and the United Steelworkers of America (Union) entered into a collective bargaining agreement covering the terms and conditions of employment at 15 Kaiser plants. The agreement included an affirmative action plan designed to eliminate racial imbalances in Kaiser's almost exclusively white craft workforce. The plan reserved 50 percent of the openings in craft training programs to African-Americans until the percentage of African-American craftworkers equaled the percentage of African-Americans in the local labor force. Trainees were selected on the basis of seniority.

During the plan's first year of operation, seven African-American and six white craft trainees were selected for the program. The most senior African-American trainee had less seniority than many white workers whose bids for admission to the program were rejected. Weber, one of the rejected white workers, instituted this class action against Kaiser and Union, alleging that the affirmative action plan violated Title VII. Who wins? [*United Steelworkers of America, AFL-CIO-CLC v. Weber*, 443 U.S. 193, 99 S.Ct. 2721 (1979)]

42.13. Rita Machakos, a white female, worked for the Civil Rights Division (CRD) of the Department of Justice. During her employment, she was denied promotion to certain paralegal positions. In each instance, the individual selected was an African-American female. Evidence showed that the CRD maintained an institutional and systematic discrimination policy that favored minority employees over white employees. Machakos sued CRD for race discrimination under Title VII. Who wins? [*Machakos v. Attorney General of the United States*, 859 F.2d 1487 (D.C.Cir. 1988)]

Ethics Cases

42.14. Dianne Rawlinson, 22 years old, is a college graduate whose major course of study was correctional psychology. After graduation, she applied for a position as a correctional counselor (prison guard) with the Alabama Board of Corrections (Board). Her application was rejected because she failed to meet the minimum 120-pound weight requirement of an Alabama statute that also established a height minimum of 5 feet 2 inches. In addition, Board adopted Administrative Regulation 204, which established gender criteria for assigning correctional counselors to maximum-security prisons for "contact positions." These are correctional counselor positions that require continual close physical proximity to inmates. Under this rule, Rawlinson did not qualify for contact positions with male prisoners in Alabama maximum-security prisons. Rawlinson brought a class action lawsuit against Dothard, who was the director of the Department of Public

Safety of Alabama. Does either the height-weight requirement or the contact position rule constitute a bona fide occupational qualification that justifies the sexual discrimination in this case? Does society owe a duty of social responsibility to protect women from dangerous job positions? Or is this "romantic paternalism"? [*Dothard, Director, Department of Public Safety of Alabama v. Rawlinson*, 433 U.S. 321, 97 S.Ct. 2720 (1977)]

CRITICAL LEGAL THINKING WRITING ASSIGNMENT

Read Case A.42 in the Case Appendix [*Robinson v. Jacksonville Shipyards, Inc.*]. This case is excerpted from the district court opinion. Review and brief the case. In your brief, be sure to answer the following questions:

1. Who is the plaintiff? Who is the defendant?
2. What is sexual harassment?
3. Did the court find sexual harassment in this case?
4. What remedy did the court order?

NOTES

1. 42 U.S.C. §§ 2000e et seq. Other portions of the Civil Rights Act of 1964 prohibit discrimination in housing, education, and other facets of life.
2. *Equal Employment Opportunity Commission v. Tortilleria "La Mejor,"* 758 F.Supp. 585 (E.D.Cal 1991).
3. *McDonnell Douglas v. Green*, 411 U.S. 792, 93 S.Ct. 1817 (1973).
4. In some states, the complaint must be filed with the appropriate state agency rather than the EEOC.
5. 42 U.S.C. § 2000e(K).
6. *Meritor Savings Bank v. Vinson*, 477 U.S. 57, 106 S.Ct. 2399 (1986).
7. *Harris v. Forklift Systems, Inc.*, 114 S.Ct. 367 (1993).
8. *Omcale v. Sundowner Offshore Services, Incorporated*, 118 S.Ct. 998 (1998).
9. 29 U.S.C. § 206(d).
10. 29 U.S.C. §§ 621-634.
11. P.L. 101-433.
12. 29 U.S.C. § 626. Age Discrimination in Employment Amendments of 1986, P.L. 99-592.
13. 29 U.S.C. §§ 701 et seq.
14. P.L. 101-136, 104 Stat. 327, 42 U.S.C. §§ 1201 et seq.
15. 42 U.S.C. § 1981.

Labor Relations Law

*Strong responsible unions are essential to industrial fair play.
Without them the labor bargain is wholly one-sided.*

LOUIS D. BRANDEIS (1935)

Chapter Objectives

After studying this chapter, you should be able to

1. Describe how a union is organized.
2. Explain the consequences of an employer's illegal interference with a union election.
3. Describe the process of collective bargaining.
4. Describe the rights granted by the Plant Closing Act.
5. Distinguish between union and agency shops.
6. Explain state right-to-work laws.
7. Describe employees' right to strike.
8. Describe an illegal strike.
9. Describe the process of picketing.
10. Define *illegal secondary boycott*.

Chapter Contents

Until the mid-1880s, the American economy was composed primarily of farmers and self-employed individuals. It was only after the Civil War that the United States started to become industrialized. In the 1880s, few laws protected workers against employment abuses. The workers began to organize unions in an attempt to gain bargaining strength. Unlike unions in many European countries, unions in the United States did not form their own political party.

The **American Federation of Labor (AFL)** was formed in 1886 under the leadership of Samuel Gompers. Only skilled craft workers such as silversmiths and artisans were allowed to belong. Semiskilled and unskilled workers could not become members. In 1935, after an unsuccessful attempt to take over the AFL, John L. Lewis formed the **Congress of Industrial Organizations (CIO)**. The CIO permitted semiskilled and unskilled workers to become members. In 1955, the AFL and CIO combined to form the **AFL-CIO**. Individual unions (such as the United Auto Workers and United Steel Workers) may choose to belong to the AFL-CIO. Not all unions opt to join.

Today, approximately 12 percent of private-sector wage and salary workers belong to labor unions. Many government employees also belong to unions. This chapter discusses the federal and state labor laws regulating employment.

*F*EDERAL LABOR LAW

In the early 1900s, members of the labor movement lobbied Congress to pass laws to protect their rights to organize and bargain with management. During the Great Depression of the 1930s, several statutes were enacted giving workers certain rights and protections. Several other statutes have been added since then. The major federal statutes in this area are

- **Norris-LaGuardia Act** Enacted in 1932,[1] this act stipulates that it is legal for employees to organize. Thus, it removes the federal courts' power to enjoin peaceful union activity. In response, the courts often ignored the act or found union "violence" to escape their provisions.
- **National Labor Relations Act** This act, also known as the Wagner Act or the NLRA, was enacted in 1935.[2] The NLRA establishes the right of employees to form, join, and assist labor organizations; to bargain collectively with employers; and to engage in concerted activity to promote these rights. The act places an affirmative duty on employers to bargain and deal in good faith with unions. This act is the heart of American labor law.
- **Labor-Management Relations Act** Industrywide strikes occurred in the rail, maritime, coal, lumber, oil, automobile, and textile industries between 1945 and 1947. As a result, public sympathy for unions waned. In 1947, Congress enacted the Labor-Management Relations Act (the Taft-Hartley Act),[3] which amended the Wagner Act. This act (1) expands the activities that labor unions can engage in, (2) gives employers the right to engage in free-speech efforts against unions prior to a union election, and (3) gives the President the right to seek an injunction (for up to 80 days) against a strike that would create a national emergency.
- **Labor-Management Reporting and Disclosure Act** After discovering substantial corruption in labor unions, Congress enacted the Labor-Management Reporting and Disclosure Act of 1959 (the Landrum-Griffin Act).[4] This act regulates internal union affairs and establishes the rights of union members. Specifics of this act include (1) a requirement for regularly scheduled elections for union officials by secret ballot, (2) a prohibition against ex-convicts and communists from holding union office, and (3) a rule that makes union officials accountable for union funds and property.
- **Railway Labor Act** The Railway Labor Act of 1926, as amended in 1934, covers employees of railroad and airline carriers.[5] This act permits self-organization of employees, prohibits interference with this right, and provides for the adjustment of grievances.

Business Brief
Unions in the United States have not formed their own political party as they have in many other countries.

Management and union may be likened to that serpent of the fables who on one body had two heads that fighting with poisoned fangs, killed themselves.

Peter Drucker
The New Society (1951)

Business Brief
Labor law in the United States is primarily governed by these federal statutes.

Business Brief
The right of workers to form, join, and assist labor unions is a statutorily protected right in the United States.

National Labor Relations Board (NLRB)

National Labor Relations Board (NLRB)
A federal administrative agency that oversees union elections, prevents employers and unions from engaging in illegal and unfair labor practices, and enforces and interprets certain federal labor laws.

The National Labor Relations Act created the **National Labor Relations Board (NLRB)**. The NLRB is an administrative body comprised of five members appointed by the President and approved by the Senate. The NLRB oversees union elections, prevents employers and unions from engaging in illegal and unfair labor practices, and enforces and interprets certain federal labor laws. The decisions of the NLRB are enforceable in court.

In the United States, federal labor laws protect the rights of workers to form and join unions and to engage in lawful strikes and picketing.

*O*RGANIZING A UNION

Section 7 of the NLRA
A law that gives employees the right to join together and form a union.

Section 7 of the NLRA gives employees the right to join together and form a union.[6] The process of organizing a union is discussed in the paragraphs that follow.

Appropriate Bargaining Unit

appropriate bargaining unit
The group that a union seeks to represent.

Before a union can petition for an election as a bargaining agent, the group that it is seeking to represent must be defined. This is called the **appropriate bargaining unit**. This group can be the employees of a single company or plant, a group within a single company (e.g., maintenance workers at all of a company's plants), or an entire industry (e.g., nurses at all hospitals in the country).[7]

Business Brief
An employer may not sponsor or control a union.

Managers and professional employees may not belong to unions formed by employees whom they manage. Security guards may not join unions that represent other employees, but they may form their own union. *Company unions* sponsored or controlled by an employer are illegal.

Petition for an Election

If it can be shown that at least 30 percent of the employees in the bargaining unit are interested in joining or forming a union, the NLRB can be petitioned to investigate and set an election date. The NLRB will ask to see petitions or authorization cards signed by at least 30 percent of the targeted employees before it holds a hearing on the matter. The NLRB will not permit an election to be held if

1. A union election was held within the past 12 months by any union, even if the union was not elected.
2. The employees of the appropriate bargaining unit already are represented by a union and have a valid collective bargaining agreement with the employer. In such cases, a new election cannot be held for the duration of the agreement or three years (whichever is shorter).

A petition for an election may be withdrawn at any time. A new petition cannot be filed for six months, however.

Types of Union Elections

Most union elections are contested by the employer. The NLRB is required to supervise all *contested elections*. A simple majority vote (over 50 percent) wins the election. For example, if 51 of 100 employees vote for the union, the union is certified as the bargaining agent for all 100 employees. If management does not contest the election, a *consent election* may be held without NLRB supervision.

If employees no longer want to be represented by a union, a *decertification election* will be held. Such elections must be supervised by the NLRB.

Union Solicitation on Company Property

If union solicitation is being conducted by fellow employees, an employer may restrict solicitation activities to the employees' free time (e.g., coffee breaks, lunch hours, and before and after work). The activities may also be limited to nonworking areas such as the cafeteria, restroom, or parking lot. Off-duty employees may be barred from union solicitation on company premises, and nonemployees (e.g., union management) may be prohibited from soliciting on behalf of the union anywhere on company property.

An exception to this rule applies if the location of the business and the living quarters of the employees place the employees beyond the reach of reasonable union efforts to communicate with them. This so-called *inaccessibility exception* applies to logging camps, mining towns, company towns, and the like. Employers may dismiss employees who violate these rules.

In the following case, the U.S. Supreme Court addressed the issue of whether an employer had to allow nonemployee union organizers on its property.

> **Business Brief**
>
> **An employer may restrict union solicitation activities by employees to nonworking areas during employees' free time (e.g., coffee breaks, lunch hours, and before and after work).**

Lechmere, Inc. v. National Labor Relations Board
112 S.Ct. 841 (1992)
United States Supreme Court

CASE 43.1

FACTS

Lechmere, Inc. (Lechmere), owns and operates a retail store in the Lechmere Shopping Plaza in Newington, Connecticut. Thirteen smaller stores are located between Lechmere's store and the parking lot, which is owned by Lechmere. In June 1987, the United Food and Commercial Workers Union, AFL-CIO (Union), attempted to organize Lechmere's 200 employees, none of whom belonged to a union. After a full-page advertise-

ment in a local newspaper drew little response, nonemployee Union organizers entered Lechmere's parking lot and began placing handbills on windshields of cars parked in the employee section of the parking lot. Lechmere's manager informed the organizers that Lechmere prohibited solicitation or handbill distribution of any kind on the property and asked them to leave. They did so, and Lechmere personnel removed the handbills. Union organizers renewed their handbill effort in the parking lot on

(case continues)

several subsequent occasions, but each time they were asked to leave and the handbills were removed. Union filed a grievance with the National Labor Relations Board (NLRB). The NLRB ruled in favor of Union and ordered Lechmere to allow handbill distribution in the parking lot. The court of appeals affirmed. Lechmere appealed to the U.S. Supreme Court.

ISSUE

May a store owner prohibit nonemployee union organizers from distributing leaflets in a shopping mall parking lot owned by the store?

IN THE LANGUAGE OF THE COURT

Thomas, Justice   In practice, nonemployee organizational trespassing had generally been prohibited except where "unique obstacles" prevented nontrespassory methods of communication with the employees. The inaccessibility exception is a narrow one. It does not apply wherever nontrespassory access to employees may be cumbersome or less-than-ideally effective, but only where the location of a plant and the living quarters of the employees place the employees beyond the reach of reasonable union efforts to communicate with them.

The NLRB's conclusion in this case that the union had no reasonable means short of trespass to make Lechmere's employees aware of its organizational efforts is based on a misunderstanding of the limited scope of this exception. Because the employees do not reside on Lechmere's property, they are presumptively not "beyond the reach" of the union's message. Although the employees live in a large metropolitan area (Greater Hartford), that fact does not in itself render them "inaccessible." Their accessibility is suggested by the union's success in contacting a substantial percentage of them directly, via

mailings, phone calls, and home visits. Such direct contact, of course, is not a necessary element of "reasonably effective" communication; signs or advertising also may suffice. In this case, the union tried advertising in local newspapers. Whatever the merits of that conclusion, other alternative means of communication were readily available. Thus, signs (displayed, for example, from the public grassy strip adjoining Lechmere's parking lot) would have informed the employees about the union's organizational efforts. Access to employees, not success in winning them over, is the critical issue. Because the union in this case failed to establish the existence of any "unique obstacles" that frustrated access to Lechmere's employees, the NLRB erred in concluding that Lechmere committed an unfair labor practice by barring the nonemployee organizers from its property.

DECISION AND REMEDY

The U.S. Supreme Court held that under the facts of this case, Lechmere could prohibit nonemployee Union organizers from distributing leaflets to employees in the store's parking lot. Reversed.

Case Questions

Critical Legal Thinking   Should property rights take precedence over a union's right to organize employees?

Ethics   Is it ethical for an employer to deny union organizers access to company property to conduct their organization efforts? Is it ethical for union organizers to demand this as a right?

Business Application   What implications does this case have for business? Is this a pro- or antibusiness decision?

Illegal Interference with an Election

Section 8(a) of the NLRA
A law that makes it an *unfair labor practice* for an employer to interfere with, coerce, or restrain employees from exercising their statutory right to form and join unions.

Section 8(b) of the NLRA
A law that prohibits unions from engaging in unfair labor practices that interfere with a union election.

Section 8(a) of the NLRA makes it an *unfair labor practice* for an employer to interfere with, coerce, or restrain employees from exercising their statutory right to form and join unions. Threats of loss of benefits for joining the union, statements such as "I'll close this plant if a union comes in here," and the like are considered unfair labor practices. An employer may not form a company union.

Section 8(b) of the NLRA prohibits unions from engaging in unfair labor practices that interfere with a union election. Coercion, physical threats, and such are considered unfair labor practices. Where an unfair labor practice has been found, the NLRB (or the courts) may issue a cease-and-desist order or an injunction to restrain unfair labor practices, and set aside an election and order a new election.

In the following case, the Supreme Court found that an employer had engaged in an unfair labor practice and ordered a new election.

National Labor Relations Board v. Exchange Parts Co.
375 U.S. 405, 84 S.Ct. 457 (1964)
United States Supreme Court

CASE 43.2

FACTS

Exchange Parts Co. (Exchange Parts) is engaged in the business of rebuilding automobile parts in Fort Worth, Texas. Prior to November 1959, its employees were not represented by a union. On November 9, 1959, the International Brotherhood of Boilermakers, Iron Shipbuilders, Blacksmiths, Forgers and Helpers, AFL-CIO (Union), advised Exchange Parts that it was going to conduct a campaign to organize the workers at the plant. After obtaining sufficient support from members of the appropriate bargaining unit, Union petitioned the NLRB to set an election date. After completing its investigation on February 19, 1960, the NLRB issued an order setting March 18, 1960, as the election date. On February 25, 1960, Exchange Parts held a dinner for its employees at which management announced a new company benefit allowing employees to have an extra holiday (their birthday). On March 4, Exchange Parts sent a letter to its employees that announced new increased wages for overtime pay and an extended vacation plan for employees. Union subsequently lost the election. Union filed a complaint with the NLRB, which held in favor of Union and ordered a new election. The court of appeals reversed. The NLRB appealed to the U.S. Supreme Court.

ISSUE

Is it an unfair labor practice for an employer to confer new economic benefits on its employees on the eve of a union election?

IN THE LANGUAGE OF THE COURT

Harlan, Justice *The broad purpose of Section 8(a) is to establish the right of employees to organize for mutual aid without employer interference. We have no doubt that it prohibits not only intrusive*

threats but also conduct immediately favorable to employees that is undertaken with the express purpose of impinging upon their freedom of choice for or against unionization and is reasonably calculated to have that effect. The danger inherent in well-timed increases in benefits is the suggestion of a "fist inside a velvet glove." Employees are not likely to miss the inference that the source of benefits now conferred is also the source from which future benefits must flow and which may dry up if it is not obliged.

We cannot agree with the court of appeals that enforcement of the NLRB's order will have the ironic result of discouraging benefits for labor. The beneficence of an employer is likely to be ephemeral if prompted by a threat of unionization that is subsequently removed. Insulating the right of collective organization from calculated goodwill of this sort deprives employees of little that has lasting value.

DECISION AND REMEDY

The U.S. Supreme Court held that an employer's conferral of benefits on employees on the eve of a union election, which are designed to affect the outcome of that election, is an unfair labor practice. Reversed.

Case Questions

Critical Legal Thinking Should a company be prohibited from taking away (or giving) economic benefits in its fight with a union?

Ethics Was it ethical for the employer in this case to increase employee benefits on the eve of the union election?

Business Application Do you think the employer's conduct in this case constituted a "fist in a velvet glove"? Were the benefits conferred in this case likely to be ephemeral?

COLLECTIVE BARGAINING

Once a union has been elected, the employer and the union discuss the terms of employment of union members and try to negotiate a contract that embodies these terms. The act of negotiating is called **collective bargaining**, and the resulting contract is called a **collective bargaining agreement**. The employer and the union must negotiate with each other in good faith. For example, this would prohibit making take-it-or-leave-it proposals.

Subjects of Collective Bargaining

Wages, hours, and other terms and conditions of employment are *compulsory subjects* of collective bargaining. These include fringe benefits, health benefits, retirement plans, work assignments, safety rules, and the like. *Illegal subjects* (e.g., closed shops and discrimination) may not be negotiated.

collective bargaining
The act of negotiating contract terms between an employer and the members of a union.

collective bargaining agreement
The resulting contract from a collective bargaining procedure.

Subjects that are not compulsory or illegal are *permissive subjects* of collective bargaining. These include such issues as the size and composition of the supervisory force, location of plants, and corporate reorganizations. These subjects may be bargained for if the company and union agree to do so.

The following case presents the issue of whether an employer's decision to close a business unit is a compulsory subject of collective bargaining.

First National Maintenance Corp. v. National Labor Relations Board
452 U.S. 666, 101 S.Ct. 2573 (1981)
United States Supreme Court

CASE 43.3

FACTS

The First National Maintenance Corp. (First Maintenance) is engaged in the business of providing cleaning, maintenance, and related services to commercial buildings in the New York City area. It contracts with and hires personnel separately for each customer, and it does not transfer employees between locations. On March 31, 1977, a majority of the employees of First Maintenance selected the National Union of Hospital and Health Care Employees, Retail, Wholesale and Department Store Union, AFL-CIO (Union), to represent them as their bargaining agent.

One of First Maintenance's customers was the Greenpark Care Center (Greenpark) in Brooklyn. First Maintenance became aware that it was losing money at Greenpark, but Greenpark would not agree to an increase in the fee charged for First Maintenance's services. On July 6, 1977, First Maintenance discontinued its contract with Greenpark and dismissed its employees who had been working there. Union filed an unfair labor practice charge with the National Labor Relations Board. The NLRB ordered First Maintenance to bargain with Union about its decision to terminate the Greenpark contract. The court of appeals enforced the NLRB's order. First Maintenance appealed to the U.S. Supreme Court.

ISSUE

Is closing a part of a business operation a mandatory subject of collective bargaining?

IN THE LANGUAGE OF THE COURT

Blackmun, Justice   Although parties are free to bargain about any legal subject, Congress has limited the mandate or duty to bargain on matters of "wages, hours, and other terms and conditions of employment." Congress deliberately left the words "wages, hours, and other terms and conditions of employment" without further definition, for it did not intend to deprive the NLRB of the power further to define those terms in light of specific industrial practices. Nonetheless, in establishing what issues must be submitted to the process of bargaining, Congress had no expectation that the elected union representative would become an equal

partner in the running of the business enterprise in which the union's members are employed.

Some management decisions, such as the choice of advertising and promotion, product type and design, and financing arrangements, have only an indirect and attenuated impact on the employment relationship. Other management decisions, such as layoffs and recalls, production quotas, and work rules, are almost exclusively an aspect of the relationship between employer and employee. The present case concerns a third type of management decision, one that had a direct impact on employment, since jobs were inexorably eliminated by the termination, but had as its focus only the economic profitability of the contract with Greenpark, a concern under these facts wholly apart from the employment relationship. This decision, involving a change in the scope and direction of the enterprise, is akin to the decision whether to be in business at all.

There is an important difference between permitted bargaining and mandated bargaining. Labeling this type of decision mandatory could afford a union with a powerful tool for achieving delay, a power that might be used to thwart management's intentions in a manner unrelated to any feasible solution the union might propose. The decision to halt work at this specific location represented a significant change in First Maintenance's operations, a change not unlike opening a new line of business or going out of business entirely.

DECISION AND REMEDY

The Supreme Court held that an employer's decision to close a business unit is not part of the terms and conditions over which Congress mandated bargaining. Reversed and remanded.

Case Questions

Critical Legal Thinking   Do you think the closing of part of a company's operations should be a mandatory subject of collective bargaining? Why or why not?

Ethics   Does a company owe a duty not to discontinue non-profitable operations because it would cause employees to lose their jobs?

Business Application   What would have been the economic consequences if the Court had decided the case the other way?

Contemporary Business Application _____

PLANT CLOSING ACT

Often, a company would choose to close a plant without giving its employees prior notice of the closing. To remedy this situation, on August 4, 1988, Congress enacted the **Worker Adjustment and Retraining Notification Act**, also called the **Plant Closing Act** or **WARN Act** [P.L. 100-379, 102 Stat. 840]. The act, which covers employers with 100 or more employees, requires employers to give their employees 60 days' notice before engaging in certain plant closings or layoffs.

If the employees are represented by a union, the notice must be given to the union; if they are not, the notice must be given to the employees individually.

The actions covered by the act are

1. **Plant Closings** A permanent or temporary shutdown of a single site that results in a loss of employment of 50 or more employees during any 30-day period.

2. **Mass Layoffs** A reduction of 33 percent of the employees or at least 50 employees during any 30-day period.

An employer is exempted from having to give such notice if

1. The closing or layoff is caused by business circumstances that were not reasonably foreseeable as of the time that the notice would have been required.
2. The business was actively seeking capital or business that, if obtained, would have avoided or postponed the shutdown and the employer in good faith believed that giving notice would have precluded it from obtaining the needed capital or business.

UNION SECURITY AGREEMENTS

To obtain the greatest power possible, elected unions sometimes try to install a *union security agreement*. The two types of security agreements are

- **Union Shop** Under a **union shop** agreement, an employee must join the union within a certain number of days (e.g., 30 days) after being hired. Employees who do not join must be discharged by the employer upon notice from the union. Union members pay union dues to the union. Union shops are lawful.
- **Agency Shop** Under an **agency shop** agreement, employees do not have to become union members, but they do have to pay an agency fee (an amount equal to union dues) to the union. Agency shops are lawful.

union shop
An establishment where an employee must join the union within a certain number of days after being hired.

agency shop
An establishment where an employee does not have to join the union, but must pay a fee equal to the union dues.

Upon proper notification by the union, union and agency shop employers are required to (1) deduct union dues and agency fees from employees' wages and (2) forward these dues to the union. This is called a *check-off provision*.

Illegal Closed Shops

An establishment where union membership is a condition of employment is called a *closed shop*. This requires an applicant to belong to the union before the employer can consider hiring him or her. The Taft-Hartley Act made closed shops illegal because they put conditions on the employer's right to select its employees.

Business Brief
A closed shop that requires union membership as a condition of employment is illegal.

Consider This Example Suppose the United Workers of America (Union) and an employer agree that a worker must belong to Union before he or she will be considered for employment by an employer. This is an illegal closed shop because belonging to Union is a condition of employment—that is, the employer cannot consider hiring qualified persons who are not Union members.

Contemporary Business Application _____

State Right-to-Work Laws

In 1947, Congress amended the Taft-Hartley Act by enacting Section 14(b), which provides: "Nothing in this Act shall be construed as authorizing the execution or application of agreements requiring membership in a labor organization as a condition of employment in any State or Territory in which such execution or application is prohibited by State or Territorial Law." In other words, states can enact **right-to-work laws**—either by constitutional amendment or statute—that outlaw union and agency shops.

If a state enacts a right-to-work law, individual employees cannot be forced to join a union or pay union dues and fees even though a union has been elected by other employees. Right-to-work laws are often enacted by states to attract new businesses to a nonunion and low-wage environment. Unions vehemently oppose the enactment of right-to-work laws because they substantially erode union power.

Today, the following 21 states have enacted right-to-work laws:

Alabama	Nevada
Arizona	North Carolina
Arkansas	North Dakota
Florida	South Carolina
Georgia	South Dakota
Idaho	Tennessee
Iowa	Texas
Kansas	Utah
Louisiana	Virginia
Mississippi	Wyoming
Nebraska	

The remedies for violation of right-to-work laws vary from state to state but usually include damages to persons injured by the violation, injunctive relief, and often criminal penalties.

Strikes and Picketing

strike

A cessation of work by union members in order to obtain economic benefits.

The NLRA gives union management the right to recommend that the union call a **strike** if a collective bargaining agreement cannot be reached. A strike is a cessation of work by union members to obtain economic benefits. Before there can be a strike, though, a majority vote of the union's members must agree to the action.

Crossover and Replacement Workers

crossover worker

A person who does not honor a strike by either (1) choosing not to strike or (2) returning to work after joining the strikers for a time.

Individual members of a union do not have to honor a strike. They may (1) choose not to strike or (2) return to work after joining the strikers for a time. Employees who choose either of these options are known as **crossover workers.**

replacement worker

A worker who is hired either on a temporary or on a permanent basis to take the place of a striking worker.

Once a strike begins, the employer may continue operations by using management personnel and hiring **replacement workers** to take the place of the striking employees. Replacement workers can be hired either on a temporary or on a permanent status. If replacement workers are given permanent status, they do not have to be dismissed when the strike is over.

Ethical Perspective _____

Work or Featherbedding?

Unions often oppose change that would cause members to lose their jobs. Union workers steadfastly defend their right to preserve their jobs. Others argue that unions sometimes use their economic muscle to preserve jobs that are no longer necessary, an action called "featherbedding." Featherbedding impedes technological progress and raises the cost of goods and services to consumers. Consider these views in the following case.

Longshoremen are employed by steamship and stevedoring companies to load and unload cargo into and out of oceangoing vessels at the pier. Cargo arriving at the pier on trucks or railroad cars is transferred piece by piece from the truck or railroad car to the ship by the longshoremen. The longshoremen check the cargo, sort it, place it on pallets, move it by forklift to the side of the ship, and lift it by means of a sling or hook into the ship's hold. The process is reversed for cargo taken off ships. The longshoremen are represented by a union, the International Longshoremen's Association, AFL-CIO (ILA).

The introduction of "containerization" revolutionized the transportation of cargo. Containers are large metal boxes that are designed to fit onto trucks and railroad cars and can be removed and placed on ships without unloading and loading their contents. When a ship reaches its destination, the containers are loaded onto trucks or railroad cars for transport to their destination. Containerization eliminates most of the work traditionally performed by longshoremen.

After a prolonged strike, ILA and the steamship and stevedoring companies reached an agreement whereby 80 percent of the containers could pass over the pier intact and be loaded onto the ships. The remaining 20 percent of the containers must be unloaded and reloaded by longshoremen even if this work is unnecessary. This agreement was called the Rules on Containers (Rules). Several transportation companies brought suit challenging the legality of Rules under federal labor law. The National Labor Relations Board (NLRB) held Rules to be unlawful. The court of appeals reversed. NLRB appealed to the U.S. Supreme Court.

The Supreme Court sided with ILA and upheld Rules. The Court concluded that Congress, in enacting federal labor law, had no thought of prohibiting labor agreements directed to work preservation. In essence, that is the purpose of a union. The Supreme Court stated:

> *The question is not whether the Rules represent the most rational or efficient response to innovation, but whether they are a legally permissible effort to preserve jobs. We have often noted that a basic premise of the labor laws is that collective discussions backed by the parties' economic weapons will result in decisions that are better for both management and labor and for society as a whole. The Rules represent a negotiated compromise of a volatile problem bearing directly on the well-being of our national economy.*

Not all the justices agreed, however. A dissenting opinion stated

> *As illustrated by this very case, absent restrictions unions are free to exercise their considerable power, through concerted action, to manipulate the allocation of resources in our economy—even to the point where in the name of 'work preservation' a union could literally halt technological advance. The Court engages in nothing but a shell game.* [National Labor Relations Board v. International Longshoremen's Association, AFL-CIO, *473 U.S. 61, 105 S.Ct. 3045 (1985)]*

1. Is it ethical for members of a union to strike to preserve jobs that are no longer needed?
2. Should work preservation be considered a legitimate goal of federal labor policy? Why or why not?
3. Will the decision of the Supreme Court increase or decrease the cost of goods and services to consumers? Explain.

Illegal Strikes

Several types of strikes have been held to be illegal and are not protected by federal labor law. Illegal strikes are:

- **Violent Strikes** Striking employees cause substantial damage to property of the employer or a third party. Courts usually tolerate a certain amount of isolated violence before finding that the entire strike is illegal.
- **Sit-Down Strikes** Striking employees continue to occupy the employer's premises. Such strikes are illegal because they deny the employer's statutory right to continue its operations during the strike.
- **Partial or Intermittent Strikes** Employees strike part of the day or workweek and work the other part. This type of strike is illegal because it interferes with the employer's right to operate its facilities at full operation.
- **Wildcat Strikes** Individual union members go out on strike without proper authorization from the union. The courts have recognized that a wildcat strike becomes lawful if it is quickly ratified by the union.
- **Strikes during the 60-day Cooling-Off Period** Strikes begin during the mandatory 60-day cooling-off period. This time is designed to give the employer and the union time to negotiate

No private business monopoly, producer organization or cartel wields the market (and physical) power or commands the discipline over its members which many unions have achieved.

Gottfried Haberler
Economic Growth and
Stability *(1974)*

cooling-off period
Requires a union to give an employer at least 60 days' notice before a strike can commence.

a settlement of the union grievances and avoid a strike. Any strike without a proper 60-day notice is illegal.

- **Strikes in Violation of a No-Strike Clause** Strikes take place in violation of a negotiated no-strike clause, under which an employer gives economic benefits to the union and, in exchange, the union agrees that no strike will be called for a set time.

Illegal strikers may be discharged by the employer with no rights to reinstatement.

Employer Lockout

employer lockout

Act of the employer to prevent employees from entering the work premises when the employer reasonably anticipates a strike.

If an employer reasonably anticipates a strike by some of its employees, it may prevent those employees from entering the plant or premises. The same tactic may be used if collective bargaining negotiations have reached an impasse or if there has been a threat of damage to the employer's plant or equipment. This is called an **employer lockout**.

Picketing

picketing

The action of strikers walking in front of the employer's premises carrying signs announcing their strike.

Striking union members often engage in **picketing** in support of their strike. Picketing usually takes the form of the striking employees and union representatives walking in front of the employer's premises carrying signs announcing their strike. It is used to put pressure on an employer to settle a strike. The right to picket is implied from the NLRA.

Picketing is lawful unless it (1) is accompanied by violence, (2) obstructs customers from entering the employer's place of business, (3) prevents nonstriking employees from entering the employer's premises, or (4) prevents pickups and deliveries at the employer's place of business. An employer may seek an injunction against unlawful picketing.

Ethical Perspective

LABOR UNION VIOLENCE PUNISHED

The primary purpose of a union is to organize employees so that they will have greater bargaining power in negotiating wages and other terms of employment with their employers. If an agreement with an employer is not reached, the union may call a strike of its members and set up picket lines at the employer's place of business to try to bring added pressure on the employer to settle. But when does pressure cross over the ethical line? Consider the following case.

Peter Vargas and Kenneth Henderson owned Chino Farms Market, a grocery store. The employees at the market belonged to the Retail Clerk's Union Local 1428. When the existing collective bargaining agreement expired, the parties began negotiations for a new contract. After several months, the negotiations reached an impasse and the union workers went out on strike. Vargas, Henderson, and workers they hired tried to operate the store.

On the first night of the strike, Henderson voiced concern about the employees' welfare to the union's local agent, who replied, "We don't care about the people. We're going to break you." The union hired professional picketers to join the striking workers on the picket line.

During the course of the picketing, which lasted approximately one year, the picketers

- Blocked the entrances to the store.
- Blocked the driveways leading to the store's parking lot.
- Swore at and threatened customers.
- Scattered nails and carpet tacks over the parking lot.
- Broke windows of delivery trucks trying to make deliveries to the store.
- Spray-painted delivery trucks.
- Painted graffiti on the exterior walls at the store.

- Pushed the store's shopping carts into the street.
- Threw eggs and other food at the store.
- Threw water balloons at customers.
- Placed horse manure in front of the store to offend customers.
- Physically attacked workers at the store and destroyed their vehicles.

The owners of the store obtained court injunctions ordering the picketers from engaging in such conduct. When presented with the injunctions, the picketers tore them up. Customers who complained about the picketers' activities simply stopped shopping at the market. The market was driven out of business.

Vargas and Henderson sued the union for the tort of intentional interference with business relations. The jury found that the striking workers had engaged in illegal activities while picketing the market and that these activities had been condoned by the union. The jury awarded Chino Farms Market $2,602,765 in compensatory damages and $2,602,765 in punitive damages against the union. The court of appeals affirmed the judgment. [*Vargas v. Retail Clerk's Union Local 1428*, 212 Cal.App.2d 287, 260 Cal.Rptr. 650 (Cal.App. 1989)]

1. Were the picketers' activities morally reprehensible?
2. Why did the picketers engage in violent and dangerous activities during their strike?
3. Was the award of damages, particularly punitive damages, warranted in this case?

Secondary Boycott Picketing

Unions sometimes try to bring pressure against an employer by picketing his or her suppliers or customers. Such **secondary boycott picketing** is lawful only if it is *product picketing* (i.e., if the picketing is against the primary employer's product). The picketing is illegal if it is directed against the neutral employer instead of the struck employer's product.

secondary boycott picketing
A type of picketing where unions try to bring pressure against an employer by picketing his or her suppliers or customers.

Consider This Example Suppose the apple pickers' union in the state of Washington goes on strike against its primary employers, the apple growers. Picketing the apple orchards may do little to draw attention of the strike to the public. Therefore, members of the apple pickers union may picket grocery stores in metropolitan areas that sell Washington apples. If the signs the picketers carry ask shoppers at the grocery stores not to buy Washington apples, the secondary boycott is lawful. However, it is unlawful if the signs ask customers not to shop at the grocery stores.

ℐNTERNAL UNION AFFAIRS

Unions may adopt *internal union rules* to regulate the operation of the union, acquire and maintain union membership, and the like. The undemocratic manner in which many unions were formulating these rules prompted Congress to enact **Title I of the Landrum-Griffin Act**. Title I, which is often referred to as **labor's "bill of rights,"** gives each union member equal rights and privileges to nominate candidates for union office, vote in elections, and participate in membership meetings. It further guarantees union members the right of free speech and assembly, provides for due process (notice and hearing), and permits union members to initiate judicial or administrative action.

Title I of the Landrum-Griffin Act
Referred to as labor's "bill of rights"; it gives each union member equal rights and privileges to nominate candidates for union office, vote in elections, and participate in membership meetings.

A union may discipline members for participating in certain activities, including (1) walking off the job in a nonsanctioned strike, (2) working for wages below union scale, (3) spying for an employer, and (4) engaging in any other unauthorized activity that has an adverse economic impact on the union. A union may not punish a union member for participating in a civic duty, such as testifying in court against the union.

International Perspective

MEXICAN LABOR LAWS

Labor and employment in Mexico are subject to the **Federal Labor Law of Mexico**, which is administered by the **Labor Board of Conciliation and Arbitration**. Because this law promotes unionized labor, labor unions are easy to form. Most collective bargaining agreements are unlimited in duration, although the terms of the agreements are usually revised biannually. Under Mexican law, if there is a strike, the plant will shut down. This will force the parties to settle the strike.

The Mexican government publishes a biannual list of required salaries by occupation. Manual laborers must be paid weekly, whereas other employees must be paid in pay periods not exceeding 15 days. Employees receive an overtime bonus of 25 percent of their wages for working on Sunday. Employees are also paid a bonus equivalent to at least 15 days' pay as a Christmas bonus. Under the law, employers must include workers in profit-sharing programs that distribute 8 percent of earnings, before taxes, to the workers.

Employees who pass a 30-day trial period may not be dismissed for lack of qualification for the job. After one year, employees can be dismissed only for statutory reasons. An employee who is unjustly dismissed is entitled to recover three months' severance pay plus 20 days' salary for each year of employment.

Another Mexican law establishes a social security system. Both the employer and employee must contribute to this system. Employers must pay fees for workers' compensation, disability, old age, unemployment, death, and maternity leave benefits. In addition, employers are required to contribute an amount equivalent to 5 percent of their employees' wages to the national housing fund, 1 percent to day-care facilities, 1 percent to public education, and 1 percent to payroll taxes.

Although the foregoing employment benefits may seem generous, in reality they are not. There are several reasons for this. First, the cost of a minimum-wage employee in Mexico, including wages, benefits, and taxes, is less than $1 per hour. Second, Mexican labor laws have not been stringently enforced by the government. Many U.S. companies have moved manufacturing plants to Mexico to take advantage of the low wage rates there.

 Working the Web

U.S. Department of Labor The Department of Labor has a great Web site including America's Job Bank which draws together thousands of computer jobs and resumes.

Visit at **www.dol.gov**

Bureau of International Labor Affairs Find out all about international labor issues at this Web site.

Visit at **www.dol.gov/dol/ilab**

Occupational Safety and Health Administration OSHA protects workers from the harmful effects of many things, such as hazardous waste. It targets dangerous job sites.

Visit at **www.osha.gov**

CYBER EXERCISES

1. Using the DOL Web site, visit America's Job Bank.

2. From the Bureau of International Labor Affairs page, browse through the report titled *By the Sweat & Toil of Children: Consumer Labels and Child Labor.*

3. From the OSHA home page, find out about ergonomics.

CASES AND EXERCISES

CRITICAL LEGAL THINKING CASES

43.1. In July 1965, the Teamsters Union (Teamsters) began a campaign to organize the employees at a Sinclair Company (Sinclair) plant. When the president of Sinclair learned of the Teamsters's drive, he talked with all of his employees and emphasized the results of a long 1952 strike that he claimed "almost put our company out of business" and expressed worry that the employees were forgetting the "lessons of the past." He emphasized that Sinclair was on "thin ice" financially, that the Teamsters's "only weapon is to strike," and that a strike "could lead to the closing of the plant" because Sinclair had manufacturing facilities elsewhere. He also noted that because of the employees' ages and the limited usefulness of their skills, they might not be able to find reemployment if they lost their jobs. Finally, he sent literature to the employees stating that "the Teamsters Union is a strike happy outfit" and that they were under "hoodlum control," and included a cartoon showing the preparation of a grave for Sinclair and other headstones containing the names of other plants allegedly victimized by unions. The Teamsters lost the election 7 to 6 and then filed an unfair labor practice charge with the NLRB. Did Sinclair violate labor law? [*N.L.R.B. v. Gissel Packing Co.*, 395 U.S. 575, 89 S.Ct. 1918 (1969)]

43.2. Mobile Oil Corporation (Mobile) has its headquarters in Beaumont, Texas. It operates a fleet of eight oceangoing tankers that transport its petroleum products from Texas to ports on the East Coast. A typical trip on a tanker from Beaumont to New York takes about five days. No more than 10 percent to 20 percent of the seamen's work time is spent in Texas. The 300 or so seamen who are employed to work on the tankers belong to the Oil, Chemical & Atomic Workers International Union, AFL-CIO (Union), which has an agency shop agreement with Mobile. The state of Texas enacts a right-to-work law. Mobile sues Union, claiming that the agency shop agreement is unenforceable because it violates the Texas right-to-work law. Who wins? [*Oil, Chemical & Atomic Workers International Union, AFL-CIO v. Mobile Oil Corp.*, 426 U.S. 407, 96 S.Ct. 2140 (1976)]

43.3. The employees of the Johnson-Bateman Co. (Company) are represented by a union (Union). The parties have had collective bargaining agreements for almost 20 years, with the current agreement being for the period August 1, 1986–July 31, 1989. On December 1, 1986, Company posted the following notice: "Attention all employees: As of

December 1, 1986, any injuries requiring treatment will now be accompanied by a drug/alcohol test."

The drug- and alcohol-testing policy was implemented without consulting with Union. Union filed a complaint with the NLRB alleging that Company could not unilaterally adopt and implement this policy without first bargaining with Union. Did Company have to bargain with Union before adopting this rule? [*Johnson-Bateman Company*, 295 N.L.R.B. 26 (1989)]

43.4. Arrow Automotive Industries, Inc. (Arrow), is engaged in the remanufacture and distribution of automobile and truck parts. All of its operating plants produce identical product lines. Arrow is now planning to open a new facility in Santa Maria, California.

The employees at the Arrow plant in Hudson, Massachusetts, are represented by the United Automobile, Aerospace, and Agricultural Implement Workers of America (Union). The Hudson plant has a history of unprofitable operations. Union called a strike when the existing collective bargaining agreement expired and a new agreement could not be reached. After several months, the board of directors of Arrow voted to close the striking plant. The closing gave Arrow a 24 percent increase in gross profits and freed capital and equipment for the new Santa Maria plant. In addition, the existing customers of the Hudson plant could be serviced by the Spartanburg plant, which was currently being underutilized. Union filed an unfair labor practice claim with the NLRB. Does Arrow have to bargain with Union over the decision to close a plant? What would have to be done if the Plant Closing Act applied to this situation? [*Arrow Automotive Industries, Inc. v. N.L.R.B.*, 853 F.2d 223 (4th Cir. 1989)]

43.5. The Frouge Corporation (Frouge) was the general contractor on a housing project in Philadelphia. The carpenter employees of Frouge were represented by the Carpenters' International Union (Union). Traditional jobs of carpenters included taking blank wooden doors and mortising them for doorknobs, routing them for hinges, and beveling them to fit between the door jambs. Union had entered into a collective bargaining agreement with Frouge that provided that no member of Union would handle any doors that had been fitted prior to being furnished to the job site. The housing project called for 3,600 doors. Frouge contracted for the purchase of premachined doors that were already mortised, routed, and beveled. When Union ordered its members not to hang the prefabricated doors, the National Woodwork Manufacturers Association filed an unfair labor practice charge against Union with the NLRB. Is Union's refusal to hang prefabricated doors lawful? [*National Woodwork Manufacturers Association v. N.L.R.B.*, 386 U.S. 612, 87 S.Ct. 1250 (1967)]

43.6. In September 1966, the employees of the Shop Rite Foods, Inc. (Shop Rite), warehouse in Lubbock, Texas, elected the United Packinghouse, Food and Allied Workers (Union) as its bargaining agent. Negotiations for a collective bargaining agreement began in late November 1966. In February and March 1967, when an agreement had not yet been reached, Shop Rite found excessive amounts of damage to merchandise in its warehouse and concluded that it was being intentionally caused by dissident employees as a pressure tactic to secure concessions from Shop Rite. Shop Rite notified the Union representative that employees caught doing such acts would be terminated; the Union representative in turn notified the employees.

On March 31, 1967, a Shop Rite manager observed an employee in the flour section—where he had no business being—making quick motions with his hands. The manager found several bags of flour that had been cut. The employee was immediately fired. Another employee (fellow Union member) led about 30 other employees in an immediate walkout. The company discharged these employees and refused to rehire them. The employees filed a grievance with the NLRB. Can they get their jobs back? [*N.L.R.B. v. Shop Rite Foods, Inc.*, 430 F.2d 786 (5th Cir. 1970)]

43.7. The American Ship Building Company (American) operates a shipyard in Chicago, Illinois, where it repairs Great Lakes ships during the winter months when freezing on the Great Lakes renders shipping impossible. The workers at the shipyard are represented by several unions. On May 1, 1961, the unions notified American of their intention to seek modification of the current collective bargaining agreement when it expired on August 1, 1961. On five previous occasions, agreements had been preceded by strikes (including illegal strikes) that were called just after the ships had arrived in the shipyard for repairs so that the unions increased their leverage in negotiations with the company.

Based on this prior history, American displayed anxiety as to the unions' strike plans and possible work stoppage. On August 1, 1961, after extended negotiations, American and the unions reached an impasse in their collective bargaining. In response, American decided to lay off most of the workers at the shipyard. It sent them the following notice: "Because of the labor dispute which has been unresolved since August 1, 1961, you are laid off until further notice." The unions filed unfair labor practice charges with the NLRB. Are American's actions legal? [*American Ship Building Company v. N.L.R.B.*, 380 U.S. 300, 85 S.Ct. 955 (1965)]

43.8. The union (Union) member-employees of the Erie Resistor Company (Company) struck Company over the terms of a new collective bargaining agreement that was being negotiated between Company and Union. Company continued production operations during the strike by hiring new hires and crossover union members who were persuaded to abandon the strike and come back to work. Company promised all replacement workers superseniority. This would take the form of adding 20 years to the length of a worker's actual service for the purpose of future layoffs and recalls. Many union members accepted the offer. Union filed an unfair labor practice charge with the NLRB. Is Company's offer of the superseniority lawful? [*N.L.R.B. v. Erie Resistor Co.*, 373 U.S. 221, 83 S.Ct. 1139 (1963)]

43.9. Safeco Title Insurance Company (Safeco) is a major insurance company that underwrites title insurance for real estate in the state of Washington. Five local title companies act as insurance brokers that exclusively sell Safeco insurance. In 1972, Local 1001 of the Retail Store Employees Union, AFL-CIO (Union), was elected as the bargaining agent for certain Safeco employees. When negotiations between Safeco and Union reached an impasse, the employees went on strike. Union did not confine its picketing to Safeco's office in Seattle but also picketed each of the five local title companies. The pickets carried signs declaring that Safeco had no contract with Union and distributed handbills asking consumers to support the strike by canceling their Safeco insurance policies. The local title companies filed a complaint with the NLRB. Is the picketing of the neutral title insurance companies lawful? [*N.L.R.B. v. Retail Store Employees Union, Local 1001, Retail Clerks International Association, AFL-CIO*, 447 U.S. 607, 100 S.Ct. 2372 (1980)]

Ethics Cases

43.10. On April 23, 1971, the International Association of Machinists and Aerospace Workers, AFL-CIO (Union), began soliciting the employees of Whitcraft Houseboat Division, North American Rockwell Corp. (Whitcraft), to organize a union. On April 26, 27, and 28, Whitcraft management dispersed congregating groups of employees. During these three days, production was down almost 50 percent. On April 28, Whitcraft adopted the following no-solicitation rule and mailed a copy to each employee and posted it around the workplace:

> *As you well know working time is for work. No one will be allowed to solicit or distribute literature during our working time, that is, when he or she should be working. Anyone doing so and neglecting his work or interfering with the work of another employee will be subject to discharge.*

On April 30, a manager of Whitcraft found that two employees of the company were engaged in union solicitation during working hours in a working area. Whitcraft discharged them for violating the no-solicitation rule. Is their discharge lawful? Did Whitcraft act ethically in discharging the employees? [*Whitcraft Houseboat Division, North American Rockwell Corporation v. International Association of Machinists and Aerospace Workers*, AFL-CIO, 195 N.L.R.B. 1046 (1972)]

43.11. Most local musicians belong to the American Federation of Musicians (Union), which represents over 200,000 members in the United States. Union is divided into separate local unions (Locals) that represent the members from a certain geographical area. Gamble Enterprises, Inc. (Gamble), owns and operates the Palace Theater in Akron, Ohio, which stages the performances of local and traveling musicians. Union adopted the following rule: "Traveling members cannot, without the consent of a Local, play any presentation performance unless a local house orchestra is also employed."

This meant that the theater owner might have to pay two bands or orchestras. Gamble's refusal to abide by this rule caused Union to block the appearances of traveling bands and orchestras. Gamble filed an unfair labor practice charge with the NLRB. Is the Union rule lawful? [*N.L.R.B. v. Gamble Enterprises, Inc.*, 345 U.S. 117, 73 S.Ct. 560 (1953)]

CRITICAL LEGAL THINKING WRITING ASSIGNMENT

Read Case A.43 in the Case Appendix [*Wiljef Transportation, Inc. v. National Labor Relations Board*]. This case is excerpted from the court of appeals opinion. Review and brief the case. In your brief, be sure to answer the following questions:

1. Who was the plaintiff? Who was the defendant?
2. What did the defendant do that caused the plaintiff to file this action?
3. What is an unfair labor practice?
4. Did the court find an unfair labor practice in this case?

NOTES

1. 29 U.S.C. §§ 101–110 and 113–115.
2. 29 U.S.C. §§ 151 et seq.
3. 29 U.S.C. §§ 141 et seq.
4. 29 U.S.C. §§ 153 and 158–164.
5. 45 U.S.C. §§ 151–162 and 181–188.
6. Section 7 provides that employees shall have the right to self-organization; to form, join, or assist labor organizations; to bargain collectively through representatives of their own choosing; and to engage in other concerted activities for the purpose of collective bargaining or other mutual aid protection.
7. *American Hospital Assn. v. National Labor Relations Board*, 111 S.Ct. 1539 (1991).

Liability of Accountants

In our complex society the accountant's certificate and the lawyer's opinion can be instruments for inflicting pecuniary loss more potent than the chisel or the crowbar.

JUSTICE BLACKMUN Dissenting Opinion,
Ernst & Ernst v. Hochfelder, 425 U.S. 185 (1976)

Chapter Objectives

After studying this chapter, you should be able to

1. Define *audit* and describe the different types of auditor's opinions.
2. Describe an accountant's liability to his or her client for breach of contract and fraud.
3. Define *accountant malpractice*.
4. Describe an accountant's liability to third parties under the *Ultramares* doctrine.
5. Describe an accountant's liability to third parties under the *Restatement (Second) of Torts* and foreseeability standard.
6. Describe an accountant's civil liability under federal securities laws.
7. Describe an accountant's criminal liability under federal securities laws and other laws.
8. Identify when the accountant-client privilege applies.
9. Define *accountants' work papers*.
10. Identify the liability of other professionals.

Chapter Contents

Although accountants provide a wide variety of services to corporations and other businesses, their primary functions are (1) auditing financial statements and (2) rendering opinions about those audits. Accountants also prepare unaudited financial statements for clients, render tax advice, prepare tax forms, and provide consulting and other services to clients.

Audits generate the majority of litigation against accountants. Lawsuits against accountants are based on the common law (e.g., breach of contract, misrepresentation, and negligence) or on violation of certain statutes (particularly federal securities laws). Accountants can be held liable both to clients and to third parties. This chapter examines the legal liability of accountants and other professionals.

Accountants are sometimes faced with an ethical dilemma when they uncover improper activities of their clients while they are conducting audits. As independent auditors, their duty is to objectively verify and report their findings.

PUBLIC ACCOUNTANTS AND CERTIFIED PUBLIC ACCOUNTANTS

The term *accountant* applies to persons who perform a variety of services, including bookkeepers, tax preparers, and so on. The term **certified public accountant (CPA)** applies to accountants who meet certain educational requirements, pass the CPA examination, and have a certain number of years of audit experience. A person who is not certified is generally referred to as a *public accountant*.

certified public accountant (CPA)

An accountant who has met certain educational requirements, has passed the CPA examination, and has had a certain number of years of audit experience.

GENERALLY ACCEPTED ACCOUNTING STANDARDS

Certified public accountants must comply with two uniform standards of professional conduct. They are (1) **generally accepted accounting principles (GAAPs)**, which are standards for the preparation and presentation of financial statements,[1] and (2) **generally accepted auditing standards (GAASs)**, which specify the methods and procedures that must be used to conduct audits.[2]

generally accepted accounting principles (GAAPs)

Standards for the preparation and presentation of financial statements.

generally accepted auditing standards (GAASs)
Standards for the methods and procedures that must be used to conduct audits.

audit
The verification of a company's books and records pursuant to federal securities laws, state laws, and stock exchange rules that must be performed by an independent CPA.

Audits

Audits may be defined as the verification of a company's books and records. Pursuant to federal securities laws, state laws, and stock exchange rules, the audit must be performed by an independent CPA. The CPA must review the financial records, check their accuracy, and otherwise investigate the financial position of the company.

The auditor must also (1) conduct a sampling of inventory to verify the figures contained in the client's financial statements and (2) verify information from third parties (contracts, bank accounts, real estate, accounts receivable, etc.). An accountant's failure to follow GAASs when conducting audits constitutes negligence.

Contemporary Business Application

AUDITOR'S OPINIONS

After the audit is complete, the auditor must render an **opinion** about how fairly the financial statements present the company's financial position, result of operations, and change in financial position. The auditor's opinion may be unqualified, qualified, or adverse. Alternatively, the auditor may offer a disclaimer of opinion. Most auditors give unqualified opinions. The various types of opinions are

- **Unqualified Opinion** Represents the auditor's finding that the company's financial statements fairly present the company's financial position, the results of its operations, and the changes in its financial position for the period under audit, in conformity with consistently applied generally accepted accounting principles. This is the most favorable opinion an auditor can give.
- **Qualified Opinion** States that the financial statements are fairly presented except for (or subject to) a departure from generally accepted accounting principles, a change in accounting principles, or a material uncertainty. The exception, departure, or uncertainty is noted in the auditor's opinion.

- **Adverse Opinion** Determines that the financial statements do not fairly represent the company's financial position, results of operations, or changes in financial position in conformity with generally accepted accounting principles. This type of opinion is usually issued when the auditor determines that the company has materially misstated certain items on its financial statements.
- **Disclaimer of Opinion** Expresses the auditor's inability to draw a conclusion as to the accuracy of the company's financial records. This opinion is generally issued when the auditor lacks sufficient information about the financial records to issue an overall opinion.

The issuance of other than an *unqualified opinion* can have substantial adverse effects on the company audited. For example, it may not be able to sell its securities to the public, merge with another company, or obtain loans from banks. The Securities and Exchange Commission (SEC) has warned publicly held companies against "shopping" for a favorable opinion.

COMMON LAW LIABILITY OF ACCOUNTANTS TO THEIR CLIENTS

Accountants are employed by their clients to perform certain accounting services. Under the *common law*, accountants may be found liable to the clients who hire them under several legal theories, including breach of contract, fraud, and negligence.

Breach of Contract

The terms of an **engagement** are specified when an accountant and a client enter into a contract. An accountant who fails to perform may be sued for damages caused by the *breach of contract*. Generally, the courts consider damages to be the expenses the client incurs in securing another accountant to perform the needed services as well as any fines or penalties incurred by the client for missed deadlines, lost opportunities, and such.

> **engagement**
> A formal entrance into a contract between a client and an accountant.

Fraud

Where an accountant has been found liable for actual or constructive fraud, the client may recover any damages proximately caused by that fraud. Punitive damages may be awarded in cases of actual fraud. *Actual fraud* is defined as intentional misrepresentation or omission of a material fact that is relied on by the client and causes the client damage. Such cases are rare. *Constructive fraud* occurs when the accountant acts with "reckless disregard" for the truth or the consequence of his or her actions. This type of fraud is sometimes categorized as "gross negligence."

Negligence

Accountants owe a duty to use *reasonable care, knowledge, skill*, and *judgment* when providing auditing and other accounting services to a client. In other words, an accountant's actions are measured against those of a "reasonable accountant" in similar circumstances. The development of GAAPs, GAASs, and other uniform accounting standards have generally made this a national standard.

An accountant who fails to meet this standard may be sued for **negligence** (also called **accountant malpractice**). To illustrate, an accountant who does not comply with GAASs when conducting an audit and thereby fails to uncover a fraud or embezzlement by an employee of the company being audited can be sued for damages arising from this negligence. If the audit turns up a suspicious transaction or entry, the accountant is under a duty to investigate it and to inform the client of the results of the investigation.

> **accountant malpractice**
> Occurs when the accountant breaches the duty of reasonable care, knowledge, skill, and judgment that he or she owes to a client when providing auditing and other accounting services to the client.

Violations of GAAPs or GAASs are prima facie evidence of negligence, although compliance does not automatically relieve the accountant of such liability. Accountants can also be held liable for their negligence in preparing unaudited financial statements.

In the following case, the court held accountants liable to their client for malpractice.

Greenstein, Logan & Company v. Burgess Marketing, Inc.

744 S.W.2d 170 (1987)
Court of Appeals of Texas

CASE 44.1

FACTS

Burgess Marketing, Inc. (Burgess Marketing), whose principal owner is Jack Burgess, sells gasoline and other fuels in central Texas through convenience stores it owns or leases. Greenstein, Logan & Company (Greenstein, Logan), certified public accountants (CPAs), had performed Burgess Marketing's annual audit from 1970 through 1985. From September 1982 until July 1985, Burgess Marketing's controller underaccrued and underpaid the company's federal excise tax. Greenstein, Logan failed to discover these errors during its 1984 and 1985 audits. Evidence showed that

Greenstein, Logan had not complied with generally accepted auditing standards in conducting these audits.

In September 1985, Burgess Marketing fired Greenstein, Logan and employed Patillo, Brown & Hill (Patillo, Brown) as its accountants. Patillo, Brown's investigation revealed that Burgess Marketing owed approximately $1,177,000 in delinquent excise taxes on March 31, 1985, and not $137,473 as shown on the 1985 audited financial statements prepared by Greenstein, Logan. Instead of a net profit and a positive net worth, as shown on these statements, Burgess Marketing actually had been operating at a substantial monthly deficit,

(box continues)

was bankrupt, and had a negative net worth of $1.7 million. At the time of trial, the company's total liability for federal excise taxes, including interest and penalties, was approximately $2.7 million. The Internal Revenue Service (IRS) levied a tax lien for this amount against Burgess Marketing's assets and against Burgess individually. Burgess and Burgess Marketing sued Greenstein, Logan and six of its partners for accounting malpractice. The jury found the defendants liable for accountant malpractice and awarded $3.5 million in damages to the plaintiffs. The defendants appealed.

ISSUE

Is Greenstein, Logan liable to Burgess Marketing for accounting malpractice?

IN THE LANGUAGE OF THE COURT

Thomas, Justice Certified public accountants are liable for the damages proximately caused by their negligence just like other skilled professions. Accordingly, they owe their clients a duty to exercise the degree of care, skill, and competence that reasonably competent members of their profession would exercise under similar circumstances. An accountant usually discharges the duty owed to his client by complying with recognized industry standards, such as the generally accepted auditing standards, when performing an audit.

Stanley Scott, a professor of accounting at Southern Methodist University, reviewed Burgess Marketing's ledgers, journals and financial statements, as well as Greenstein, Logan's audit work

papers, for fiscal years 1983 through 1985, and explained to the jury in detail how Greenstein, Logan had departed from the GAASs during the 1984 and 1985 audits. He described their work on the two audits as such a "flagrant, violent violation of the generally accepted auditing standards" that he felt compelled to testify against them. Dr. Bill Thomas, the head of Baylor University's accounting department, agreed that Greenstein, Logan had not complied with the GAASs while performing the two audits. Dr. Thomas was Greenstein, Logan's own accounting expert. Scott and Thomas both said that the tax delinquency would have been easily discovered during the audits if Greenstein, Logan had only adhered to the GAASs. The evidence from these experts was both legally and factually sufficient to support the finding that the failure to perform the audits in accordance with GAASs was negligence.

DECISION AND REMEDY

The court affirmed the jury's finding of accounting malpractice by Greenstein, Logan and its partners.

Case Questions

Critical Legal Thinking Should accountants be held liable to their clients for negligence?

Ethics Did Greenstein, Logan act ethically in this case?

Business Application Should accountants purchase malpractice insurance? Why or why not?

NEGLIGENCE LIABILITY OF ACCOUNTANTS TO THIRD PARTIES

Many lawsuits against accountants fall into this category. The plaintiffs are third parties (e.g., shareholders and bondholders, trade creditors, or banks) who relied on information supplied by the auditor. There are three major rules of liability that a state may adopt in determining whether an accountant is liable in negligence to third parties: (1) the *Ultramares* doctrine, (2) Section 552 of the *Restatement (Second) of Torts*, and (3) the foreseeability standard. Each of these rules is discussed in the paragraphs that follow.

The Ultramares Doctrine

The landmark case that initially defined the liability of accountants to third parties was *Ultramares Corp. v. Touche.*[3] In that case, Touche Niven & Co. (Touche), a national firm of certified public accountants, was employed by Fred Stern & Co. (Stern) to conduct an audit of the company's financial statements. Touche was negligent in conducting the audit and did not uncover over $700,000 of accounts receivable that were based on fictitious sales and other suspicious activities. Touche rendered an unqualified opinion and provided 32 copies of the audited financial statements to Stern. Stern gave one copy to Ultramares Corporation (Ultramares). Ultramares made a loan to Stern on the basis of the information contained in the audited statements. When Stern failed to repay the loan, Ultramares brought a negligence action against Touche.

In his now-famous opinion, Judge Cardozo held that an accountant could not be held liable for negligence unless the plaintiff was in either *privity of contract* or a *privity-like relationship* with the accountant. Judge Cardozo wrote

> *If liability for negligence exists, a thoughtless slip or blunder, the failure to detect a theft or forgery beneath the cover of deceptive entries may expose accountants to a liability in an indeterminate amount for an indeterminate time to an indeterminate class. The hazards of a business conducted on these terms are so extreme as to enkindle doubt whether a flaw may not exist in the implication of a duty that exposes to these consequences.*

For this purpose, a relationship would occur where a client employed an accountant to prepare financial statements to be used by a third party for a specific purpose. For example, if (1) a client employs an accountant to prepare audited financial statements to be used by the client to secure a bank loan and (2) the accountant is made aware of this special purpose, the accountant is liable for any damages incurred by the bank because of a negligently prepared report. The **Ultramares doctrine** remains the majority rule for accountants' liability in this country.

In the following case, the court reaffirmed the *Ultramares* doctrine and held accountants not liable to third-party plaintiffs.

ultramares doctrine

A rule that an accountant is liable only for negligence to third parties who are in *privity of contract* or a *privity-like relationship* with the accountant. Provides the narrowest standard for holding accountants liable to third parties for negligence.

Credit Alliance Corporation v. Arthur Andersen & Co.
493 N.Y.S.2d 435 (1985)
Court of Appeals of New York

CASE 44.2

FACTS
L. B. Smith, Inc., of Virginia (Smith) was a Virginia corporation engaged in the business of selling, leasing, and servicing heavy construction equipment. It was a capital-intensive business that regularly required debt financing. Arthur Andersen & Co. (Andersen), a large national accounting firm of certified public accountants, was employed to audit Smith's financial statements. Andersen audited Smith's financial statements for the years ending 1977 through 1979. During this period of time, Andersen issued unqualified opinions concerning Smith's financial statements. Without Andersen's knowledge, Smith gave copies of its audited financial statements to Credit Alliance Corporation (Credit Alliance). Credit Alliance, in reliance on these financial statements, extended over $15 million of credit to Smith to finance the purchase of capital equipment through installment sales and leasing arrangements.

The audited financial statements overstated Smith's assets, net worth, and general financial position. In performing the audits, Andersen was negligent and failed to conduct investigations in accordance with generally accepted auditing standards. Because of this negligence, Andersen failed to discover Smith's precarious financial condition. In 1980, Smith filed a petition for bankruptcy. Smith defaulted on obligations owed Credit Alliance in an amount exceeding $8.8 million. In August 1981, plaintiff Credit Alliance brought this action against Andersen for negligence. The

trial court denied Andersen's motion to dismiss. The appellate division affirmed. Andersen appealed.

ISSUE
Should the state of New York continue to follow the *Ultramares* doctrine? Or should New York adopt a broader standard for holding accountants liable to third parties for negligence?

IN THE LANGUAGE OF THE COURT
Jasen, Judge Upon examination of Ultramares, *certain criteria may be gleaned. Before accountants may be held liable in negligence to noncontractual parties who rely to their detriment on inaccurate financial reports, certain prerequisites must be satisfied: (1) the accountants must have been aware that the financial reports were to be used for a particular purpose or purposes, (2) in the furtherance of which a known party or parties was intended to rely, and (3) there must have been some conduct on the part of the accountants linking them to that party or parties, which evinces the accountants' understanding of that party or parties' reliance. While these criteria permit some flexibility in the application of the doctrine of privity to accountants' liability, they do not represent a departure from the principles articulated in* Ultramares, *but, rather, they are intended to preserve the wisdom and policy set forth therein.*

In the appeal we decide today, application of the foregoing principles presents little difficulty. The facts as alleged by plaintiffs fail to demonstrate the existence of a relationship between the parties sufficiently approaching privity. While the allegations in

(case continues)

the complaint state that Smith sought to induce plaintiffs to extend credit, no claim is made that Andersen was being employed to prepare the reports with that particular purpose in mind. Moreover, there is no allegation that Andersen had any direct dealings with plaintiffs, had specifically agreed with Smith to prepare the report for plaintiffs' use or according to plaintiffs' requirements, or had specifically agreed with Smith to provide plaintiffs with a copy or actually did so. Indeed, there is simply no allegation of any word or action on the part of Andersen directed to plaintiffs or anything contained in Andersen's retainer agreement with Smith that provided the necessary link between them.

DECISION AND REMEDY

The court of appeals held that the state of New York should continue to follow the *Ultramares* doctrine in examining the liability of accountants to third parties for negligence. The court reversed the lower court's decision and dismissed Credit Alliance's cause of action for negligence against defendant Andersen.

Case Questions

Critical Legal Thinking   Do you agree with the *Ultramares* doctrine? Or should a different standard for assessing accountants' liability be used?

Ethics   Should an accountant's ethical duty parallel the *Ultramares* doctrine?

Business Application   Do you think accountants favor the *Ultramares* doctrine of liability to third parties?

Section 552 of the Restatement (Second) of Torts

Section 552 of the Restatement (Second) of Torts

A rule that an accountant is liable only for negligence to third parties who are *members of a limited class of intended users* of the client's financial statements. Provides a broader standard for holding accountants liable to third parties for negligence than the *Ultramares* doctrine.

Section 552 of the Restatement (Second) of Torts provides a broader standard for holding accountants liable to third parties for negligence than the *Ultramares* doctrine. Under the Restatement standard, an accountant is liable for his or her negligence to any member of *a limited class of intended users* for whose benefit the accountant has been employed to prepare the client's financial statements or to whom the accountant knows the client will supply copies of the financial statements. In other words, the accountant does not have to know the specific name of the third party. Many states have adopted this standard.

Consider This Example   Suppose a client employs an accountant to prepare financial statements to be used to obtain investors for the company. The accountant is negligent in preparing these statements and overstates the company's earnings. If the company provides copies of the financial statements to potential investors, the accountant may be held liable to any investor who relies on the information in the financial statements, purchases securities in the company, and is injured thereby. This is so even though the accountant does not know the identity of these investors when the financial statements are prepared.

In the following case, the court held that accountants were not liable to third-party plaintiffs under the Restatement standard.

Industrial Loan Thrift Guaranty Corporation of Iowa v. Reese & Company, P.C.
422 N.W.2d 178 (1988)
Supreme Court of Iowa

CASE 44.3

FACTS

First Security Acceptance Corporation (First Security) was an industrial loan company organized under the laws of the state of Iowa. Reese & Company, P.C., which was owned by Bill M. Reese, C.P.A., was First Security's auditor. Reese prepared audited financial statements for First Security for the accounting years ending September 30, 1974 through 1981. Reese knew that the statements were being filed by First Security with the Iowa state auditor as required by law. In 1981, the Industrial Loan Thrift Guaranty Corporation (Guaranty Corporation) was established by the state of Iowa to insure depository-type accounts at industrial loan corporations that qualified for membership. First Security applied for membership and submitted its financial statements to support its application. After examining the financial reports, Guaranty Corporation made a decision to admit First Security as a member. Reese, however, did not know that the financial statements he prepared would be submitted by First Security to Guaranty Corporation.

In 1982, First Security became insolvent, and Guaranty Corporation had to pay the investors who lost money on thrift certificates issued by First Security. Guaranty Corporation sued Reese & Co., P.C. and Reese to recover damages for accounting malpractice, alleging that First Security's audited financial statements overstated the financial health of the company. The trial court granted Reese's motion for summary judgment. Guaranty Corporation appealed.

ISSUE

Is Reese liable for accounting malpractice under Section 552 of the Restatement (Second) of Torts?

IN THE LANGUAGE OF THE COURT

Larson, Justice   We believe the position announced in Section 552 may be accepted to the extent that it extends the right to recover for negligence to persons whose benefit and guidance the accountant knows the information is intended, especially when the party to be benefited is identified before the statement or report is submitted by the accountant. Further refinement in the rule is provided by the comment h to Section 552, which states, in part:

> *Under this Section, it is not necessary that the maker should have any particular person in mind as the intended, or even the probable, recipient of the information. In other words, it is not required that the person who is to become the plaintiff be identified or known to the defendant as an individual when the information is supplied. It is enough that the maker of the representation intends to reach and influence either a particular person or persons, known to him, or a group or class of persons, distinct from the much larger class who might reasonably be expected sooner or later to have access to the information and foreseeably to take some action in reliance upon it.*

In the present case, the plaintiff Guaranty Corporation suggests that it would fall within the coverage of such a rule—when the reports were filed with the auditor, it should have been foreseen by Reese that another agency such as the Guaranty Corporation would use them. We do not agree. The end and aim of the report in the present case could be said to be an assistance to First Security in the internal management of its affairs and to allow it to comply with Iowa law by filing copies with the state auditor. It cannot reasonably be said, however, that the end and aim of the report was to allow use by filing with an entity such as the Guaranty Corporation. Under these circumstances, it would not be reasonable to assume that other parties beyond First Security and the auditor would be intended users of the information.

DECISION AND REMEDY

The state supreme court held that Guaranty Corporation was not within the class of parties identifiable by Reese at the time the audits were made, or a member of the class intended by Reese to be a user under the Restatement rule. The court affirmed the dismissal of the plaintiff's action.

Case Questions

Critical Legal Thinking   Do you think the Restatement rule is better than the *Ultramares* doctrine in assessing accountants' liability to third parties?

Ethics   Did the accountant act ethically in denying liability in this case?

Business Application   Are accountants often sued as "deep pockets"? Explain.

The Foreseeability Standard

A few states have adopted a broad rule known as the **foreseeability standard** for holding accountants liable to third parties for negligence. Under this standard, an accountant is liable to any foreseeable user of the client's financial statements. The accountant's liability does not depend on his or her knowledge of the identity of either the user or the intended class of users.

foreseeability standard
A rule that an accountant is liable for negligence to third parties who are *foreseeable users* of the client's financial statements. Provides the broadest standard for holding accountants liable to third parties for negligence.

Consider This Example   Suppose a corporation makes a tender offer for the shares of a target corporation whose financial statements have been audited by a CPA. If the CPA negligently prepared the financial statements and the tender offeror relied on them to purchase the target corporation, the accountant is liable for injuries suffered by the tender offeror.

CONCEPT SUMMARY   ACCOUNTANTS' NEGLIGENCE LIABILITY TO THIRD PARTIES

Legal Theory	To Whom Liable
Ultramares doctrine	Any person in privity of contract or a privity-like relationship with the accountant.
Section 552 of the Restatement (Second) of Torts	Any member of a limited class of intended users for whose benefit the accountant has been employed to prepare the client's financial statements or who the accountant knows will be supplied copies of the client's financial statements.
Foreseeability standard	Any foreseeable user of the client's financial statements.

Contemporary Business Application

ACCOUNTANTS' NEGLIGENCE LIABILITY TO THIRD PARTIES

Accountants owe a duty to use **reasonable care, knowledge, skill, and judgment** when providing auditing and other accounting services to a client. In other words, an accountant's actions are measured against those of a *reasonable accountant* in similar circumstances. The development of **generally accepted accounting principles (GAAPs)** and **generally accepted auditing standards (GAASs)** has generally made this a national standard. An accountant who fails to meet this standard may be sued for negligence (also called *accountant malpractice*).

Clients may sue their own accountants for malpractice. Third parties, such as shareholders or creditors of the audited company, may be able to sue accountants if state law permits it. There are three major rules of liability that a state may adopt in determining whether an accountant is liable in negligence to *third parties*:

- **The Ultramares Doctrine** provides that an accountant is not liable for negligence to third parties unless the plaintiff was either in *privity of contract* or a *privity-like relationship* with the accountant [*Ultramares Corp. v. Touche*, 174 N.E. 441 (N.Y. App. 1931)]. Privity of contract would occur if a client employed an accountant to prepare financial statements to be used by an identified third party for a specific purpose that the accountant was made aware of (e.g., to secure a bank loan from a specific bank).

- **Section 552 of the Restatement (Second) of Torts** is a broader standard than the *Ultramares* doctrine. It provides that an accountant is liable for his or her negligence to any member of a *limited class of intended users*, including the client for whose benefit he or she has prepared the financial statements, and those to whom he or she knows copies will be distributed. The accountant does not have to know the specific identity of the third party.

- **The foreseeability standard**, which is the broadest standard for finding accountants' liability to third parties, has been adopted by a few states. Under this standard, an accountant is liable to any *foreseeable user* of the client's financial statements. The accountant's liability does not depend on his or her knowledge of the identity of either the user or the intended class of users. This standard is the traditional means for assessing tort liability in nonaccounting contexts. Thus, other than under this standard, accountants are provided more limited liability than most other professionals.

OTHER COMMON LAW DOCTRINES THAT IMPOSE LIABILITY ON ACCOUNTANTS TO THIRD PARTIES

Breach of Contract

privity of contract
The state of two specified parties being in a contract.

Third parties usually cannot sue accountants for breach of contract because the third parties are merely incidental beneficiaries who do not acquire any rights under the accountant–client contract. That is, they are not in **privity of contract** with the accountants.

Consider This Example   An accountant contracts to perform an audit for Kim Manufacturing Company (Kim) but then fails to do so. A supplier to Kim cannot sue the accountant. This is because the supplier is not in privity of contract with the accountant.

Fraud

If an accountant engages in *actual* or *constructive fraud*, a third party who relies on the accountant's fraud and is injured thereby may bring a tort action against the accountant to recover damages.

Consider This Example   Salvo Retailers, Inc. (Salvo), applies for a bank loan, but the bank requires audited financial statements of the company before making the loan. Salvo hires a CPA to do the audit, and the CPA falsifies the financial position of the company. The bank extends the loan to Salvo, which is not repaid. The bank can recover its losses from the CPA who committed fraud.

Ethical Perspective

ACCOUNTANTS REQUIRED TO REPORT CLIENT'S ILLEGAL ACTIVITIES

In the course of conducting an audit of a client company's financial statements, an accountant could uncover information about the client's illegal activities. The ethical dilemma faced by accountants was whether to report this conduct to the Securities and Exchange Commission (SEC), the Justice Department, or other governmental authority. In 1995, Congress added **Section 10A** to the Securities Exchange Act of 1994, which removed this dilemma.

Section 10A imposes duties on auditors to detect and report illegal acts committed by their clients. Auditors must apply "procedures designed to provide reasonable assurance of detecting illegal acts that would have a direct and material effect on the financial statement accounts" of the client. Under Section 10A, an *illegal act* is defined as an "act or omission that violates any law, or any rule or regulation having the force of law."

Section 10A imposes the following reporting requirements on accountants:

1. Unless an illegal act is "clearly inconsequential," the auditor must inform the client's management and audit committee of the illegal act.

2. If management fails to take timely and appropriate remedial action, the auditor must report the illegal act to the client's full board of directors if (a) the illegal act will have a material effect on the client's financial statements and (b) the auditor expects to issue a nonstandard audit report or intends to resign from the audit engagement.

3. Once the auditor reports the illegal act to the board of directors, the board of directors must inform the Securities and Exchange Commission (SEC) of the auditor's conclusion within one business day; if the client fails to do so, the auditor must notify the SEC on the next business day.

Auditors cannot be held liable to private parties, including clients, for statements made in their *Section 10A reports*.

1. Should accountants report illegal activities of their clients without the law requiring them to do so?
2. Should accountants report unethical conduct of clients that does not arise to illegal conduct? Why or why not?

STATUTORY LIABILITY OF ACCOUNTANTS

Accountants can be held liable for violating various federal and state statutes, most importantly federal securities laws. This section examines the civil liability of accountants under these statutes.

The Securities Act of 1933

Accountants are employed to prepare and certify financial statements that are included in the registration statements filed with the SEC and the prospectuses given to potential investors. Accountants are considered *experts*, and the financial statements they prepare are considered an *expertised portion* of the registration statement.[4]

Section 11(a)

A section of the Securities Act of 1933 that imposes civil liability on accountants and others for (1) making misstatements or omissions of material facts in a registration statement or (2) failing to find such misstatements or omissions.

Section 11(a)   **Section 11(a)** of the Securities Act of 1933 imposes civil liability on accountants and others for (1) making misstatements or omissions of material facts in a registration statement or (2) failing to find such misstatements or omissions. Accountants can be held liable for fraud or negligence under Section 11(a) if the financial statements they prepare for the registration statement and prospectus contain such errors. Accountants can, however, assert a *due diligence defense* to liability.

Consider This Example   While conducting an audit, the accountants fail to detect a fraud in the financial statements. The accountants' unqualified opinion is included in the registration statement and prospectus for the offering. An investor purchases the securities and suffers a loss when the fraud is uncovered. The investor can sue the makers of the misrepresentations for fraud and the accountants for negligence.

The plaintiff may recover the difference between the price he or she paid for the security and the value of the security at the time of the lawsuit (or at the time the security was sold if it was sold prior to the lawsuit). The plaintiff does not have to prove that he or she relied on the misstatement or omission. Privity of contract is irrelevant.

Contemporary Business Application

PRIVATE SECURITIES LITIGATION REFORM ACT OF 1995

In response to intense lobbying by the accounting profession, high-tech firms, and other business groups, Congress enacted the **Private Securities Litigation Reform Act of 1995**. This act changed the liability of accountants and other securities professionals in the following ways:

- The act imposes new pleading and procedural requirements that make it more difficult for plaintiffs to bring class action securities lawsuits.
- The act replaces *joint and several liability* of defendants (one party of several at-fault parties could be made to pay all of a judgment) with **proportionate liability**. This new rule limits a defendant's liability to its *proportionate* degree of fault. It therefore relieves accountants from being the "deep pocket" defendant except up to their degree of fault. The only exception to this rule—where joint and several

liability is still imposed—is if the defendant acted knowingly.

For example, suppose plaintiffs are the victims of a securities fraud perpetrated by a firm and they suffer $1 million in damages. If the accountants for the firm are found to be 25 percent liable, the accountants are only required to pay their proportionate share in damages—$250,000. If the accountants knowingly participated in the fraud, they would be jointly and severally liable for the entire $1 million in damages, however.

The new rules established by the Private Securities Litigation Reform Act of 1995 should curtail litigation against accountants and other securities professionals. The rules do, however, impose new detection and reporting requirements on auditors.

The Securities Exchange Act of 1934

Section 10(b) and Rule 10b-5   **Section 10(b)** of the Securities Exchange Act of 1934 prohibits any manipulative or deceptive practice in connection with the purchase or sale of any security. Rule 10b-5 makes it unlawful for any person, by the use or means or instrumentality of interstate commerce, to employ any device or artifice to defraud; to make misstatements or omissions of material fact; or to engage in any act, practice, or course of conduct that would operate as a fraud or deceit upon any person in connection with the purchase or sale of any security.

The scope of these antifraud provisions is quite broad, and the courts have implied a civil private cause of action. Thus, plaintiffs injured by a violation of these provisions can sue the offending party for monetary damages. Only purchasers and sellers of securities can sue under Section 10(b) and Rule 10b-5. Privity of contract is irrelevant.

Accountants are often defendants in Section 10(b) and Rule 10b-5 actions. The U.S. Supreme Court has decided that only intentional conduct and recklessness of accountants and others, but not ordinary negligence, violates Section 10(b) and Rule 10b-5.[5]

Section 18(a)   **Section 18(a)** of the Securities Exchange Act of 1934 imposes civil liability on any person who makes false or misleading statements in any application, report, or document filed with the SEC. Because accountants often file reports and other documents with the SEC on behalf of clients, they can be found liable for violating this section.

Like Section 10(b), Section 18(a) requires a showing of fraud or reckless conduct on the part of the defendant. Thus, the plaintiffs in a Section 18(a) action must prove that they relied on the misleading statement and that it affected the price of the security. Negligence is not actionable.

There are two ways an accountant or other defendant can defeat the imposition of liability under Section 18(a). First, the defendant can show that he or she acted in *good faith*. Second, he or she can show that the plaintiff had knowledge of the false or misleading statement when the securities were purchased or sold.

Section 10(b)

A section of the Securities Exchange Act of 1934 that prohibits any manipulative or deceptive practice in connection with the purchase or sale of any security.

Section 18(a)

A section of the Securities Exchange Act of 1934 that imposes civil liability on any person who makes false or misleading statements in any application, report, or document filed with the SEC.

Contemporary Business Application

CENTRAL BANK ELIMINATES AIDING AND ABETTING LIABILITY

Accountants are often the target defendant in a Section 10(b) and Rule 10b-5 securities fraud lawsuit. This is often because the perpetrators of the fraud cannot be found or are judgment-proof, that is, they do not have sufficient assets to pay a judgment against them. Accountants, particularly the "Big Six" accounting firms, have money themselves as well as liability insurance. Because accountants usually do not directly perpetrate the fraud, plaintiffs often sue auditors alleging that they *aided and abetted* the securities violation.

Aiding and abetting is a very difficult concept to define or apply. However, if a plaintiff's lawyers could convince a jury that the accountants had aided and abetted a Section 10(b) and Rule 10b-5 securities violation, the accountants would be found civilly liable and would have to pay damages.

The issue of whether any defendant could be held liable for aiding and abetting a Section 10(b) and Rule 10b-5 violation was addressed by the U.S. Supreme Court in the *Central Bank of Denver, N.A. v. First Interstate Bank of Denver, N.A.* case (*Central Bank*). In that case, the Supreme Court held in a 5–4 decision that defendants could not be held liable for aiding and abetting under Section 10(b) and Rule 10b-5. The Court noted that Congress did not expressly provide such a cause of action in Section 10(b)

(box continues)

and that the U.S. Supreme Court would not imply such a cause of action.

Although *Central Bank* did not involve accountants as defendants, the implication of this decision is important for accountants. After *Central Bank*, accountants can no longer be sued for aiding and abetting a Section 10(b) and Rule 10b-5 securities violation.

However, accountants can still be held liable for direct violations of Section 10(b) and Rule 10b-5 caused by their *intentional* or *reckless* conduct. To win, a plaintiff must show that the auditor made a material misstatement or omission of fact. For example, direct liability would be imposed if the auditor knowingly or recklessly certified false financial statements.

[*Central Bank of Denver, N.A. v. First Interstate Bank of Denver, N.A.*, 114 S.Ct. 1439 (1994)]

CRIMINAL LIABILITY OF ACCOUNTANTS AND OTHER PROFESSIONALS

Accountants and other professionals can be held *criminally liable* for violating certain federal and state securities laws and for other law violations. For example, criminal liability exists for violations of the Securities Act of 1933, the Securities Exchange Act of 1934, the Racketeer Influenced and Corrupt Organizations Act, the Internal Revenue Code, federal mail and wire fraud statutes, and many state securities laws.

Criminal Violations of the Securities Act of 1933

Section 24

A section of the Securities Act of 1933 that makes it a criminal offense for any person to (1) willfully make any untrue statement of material fact in a registration statement filed with the SEC, (2) omit any material fact necessary to ensure that the statements made in the registration statement are not misleading, or (3) willfully violate any other provision of the Securities Act of 1933 or rule or regulation adopted thereunder.

Section 24 of the Securities Act of 1933 makes it a criminal offense for any person to (1) willfully make any untrue statement of material fact in a registration statement filed with the SEC, (2) omit any material fact necessary to ensure that the statements made in the registration statement are not misleading, or (3) willfully violate any other provision of the Securities Act of 1933 or rule or regulation adopted thereunder. Because accountants prepare the financial reports included in the registration statements, they are subject to criminal liability for violating this section. Penalties for a violation of this statute include fines of up to $10,000, imprisonment for up to five years, or both.[6]

Criminal Violations of the Securities Exchange Act of 1934

Section 32(a)

A section of the Securities Exchange Act of 1934 that makes it a criminal offense for any person willfully and knowingly to make or cause to be made any false or misleading statement in any application, report, or other document required to be filed with the SEC pursuant to the Securities Exchange Act of 1934 or any rule or regulation adopted thereunder.

Section 32(a) of the Securities Exchange Act of 1934 makes it a criminal offense for any person willfully and knowingly to make or cause to be made any false or misleading statement in any application, report, or other document required to be filed with the SEC pursuant to the Securities Exchange Act of 1934 or any rule or regulation adopted thereunder. Because accountants often file reports and documents with the SEC on behalf of clients, they are subject to this rule. Insider trading also falls within the parameters of this section.

Upon conviction under Section 32(a), an individual may be fined up to $1 million, imprisoned for up to 10 years, or both. A corporation or other entity may be fined up to $2.5 million. A person cannot be imprisoned under Section 32(a) unless he or she had knowledge of the rule or regulation violated.[7]

If the SEC finds evidence of fraud or other willful violation of federal securities laws, or other federal law (such as mail and wire fraud statutes), the matter may be referred to the U.S. Department of Justice with a recommendation that the suspected offending party be criminally prosecuted. The Department of Justice determines whether actual criminal charges will be brought. State attorney generals prosecute criminal violations of state securities laws and other state statutes.

Racketeer Influenced and Corrupt Organizations Act

Accountants and other professionals can be named as defendants in lawsuits that assert violations of the **Racketeer Influenced and Corrupt Organizations Act (RICO)**.[8] Because securities fraud falls under the definition of racketeering activity, the government often brings a RICO allegation in conjunction with a securities fraud allegation.

In addition, persons injured by a RICO violation can bring a private civil action against the violator and recover treble (triple) damages, but only if the defendant has been criminally convicted in connection with the securities fraud.[9] A third-party independent contractor (e.g., an outside accountant) must have participated in the operation or management of the enterprise to be liable for civil RICO.[10]

> **Racketeer Influenced and Corrupt Organizations Act (RICO)**
> An act that provides for both criminal and civil penalties for securities fraud.

Criminal Liability Regarding Tax Preparation

The **1976 Tax Reform Act** imposes criminal liability on accountants and others who prepare federal tax returns.[11] The act specifically imposes the following penalties: (1) a $500 fine for the willful understatement of a client's tax liability, (2) a $100 fine for the negligent understatement of the tax liability, and (3) a $500 fine for wrongfully indorsing a client's tax refund check. Accountants who have violated these provisions can be enjoined from further federal income tax practice.

> **1976 Tax Reform Act**
> An act that imposes criminal liability on accountants and others who prepare federal tax returns if they (1) willfully understate a client's tax liability, (2) negligently understate the tax liability, or (3) wrongfully indorse a client's tax refund check.

State Securities Laws and the Uniform Securities Act

Most states have enacted securities laws that are often patterned after federal securities laws. State securities laws provide for a variety of civil and criminal penalties for violations of these laws. Many states have enacted all or part of the **Uniform Securities Act**. *Section 101* of this act makes it a criminal offense for accountants and others to willfully falsify financial statements and other reports.

> **Uniform Securities Act**
> An act that has been adopted by many states; it was drafted to coordinate state securities laws with federal securities laws.

Contemporary Business Application

ACCOUNTANT–CLIENT PRIVILEGE?

The common law has long recognized an attorney–client privilege that protects communications between a client and his or her lawyer from discovery in a lawsuit. In other words, lawyers cannot testify against their own clients. The rationale for this rule is that if an attorney could be called to testify against a client, the client might choose to withhold information from the attorney. This might prevent the attorney from preparing the best defense.

Although a similar situation occurs when accountants are supplied with information and documents by their clients, the U.S. Supreme Court has found that there is no corresponding accountant–client privilege under federal law. [*Couch v. U.S.*, 409 U.S. 322, 93 S.Ct. 611 (1973)]. Thus, an accountant could be called as a witness in cases involving federal securities laws, federal mail or wire fraud, or federal RICO. Nevertheless, approximately 20 states have enacted special statutes that create an **accountant–client privilege**. An accountant cannot be called as a witness against a client in a court action in a state where these statutes are in effect. Federal courts do not recognize these laws, however.

Accountants' Work Papers

Accountants often generate substantial internal *work papers* as they perform their services. These papers often include plans for conducting audits, work assignments, notes regarding the collection of data, evidence as to the testing of accounts, notes concerning the client's internal controls, notes reconciling the accountant's report and the client's records, research, comments, memorabilia, explanations, opinions, information regarding the affairs of the client, and so on.

> **Business Brief**
> The accountant–client privilege is a law enacted in approximately 20 states that says an accountant cannot be called as a witness against a client in a court action in that state; federal courts do not recognize this law.

work product immunity

A state statute that says an accountant's work papers cannot be used in a court action in that state; federal courts do not recognize this statute.

The federal courts allow discovery of these papers. Some state statutes provide **work product immunity** for accountants. Working papers generated by lawyers (e.g., legal research, notes on legal strategy, opinions, and trial preparation prepared on behalf of a client) are not discoverable in a lawsuit involving the client.

Ownership of Work Papers

Because accountants who do work for clients are independent contractors, the internal work papers they generate belong to them. However, the accountant does owe the client some rights and duties regarding these papers, including (1) the right to review them upon reasonable notice, (2) the duty to transfer the papers upon the client's request, and (3) the duty not to transfer the papers without the client's permission. This is so even if there is a fee dispute between the accountant and the client.

In the following case, the U.S. Supreme Court held that accountants' work papers had to be disclosed pursuant to an IRS administrative subpoena.

United States v. Arthur Young & Co.
465 U.S. 805, 104 S.Ct. 1495 (1984)
United States Supreme Court

CASE 44.4

FACTS

Arthur Young & Co. (Young) is a national firm of certified public accountants. The Amerada Hess Corp. (Amerada) employed Young to audit its financial statements, including an evaluation of Amerada's reserves for contingent liabilities. During the course of the audit, Young generated certain work papers, memoranda, and documents (work papers) relating to the evaluation of Amerada's contingent liabilities.

In 1975, the Internal Revenue Service (IRS) began a routine audit of Amerada's corporate income tax liability for the tax years 1972 through 1974. When the audit revealed that Amerada had made questionable payments from a "special disbursement account," the IRS instituted a criminal investigation of Amerada's tax returns. In that process, the IRS issued an administrative summons to Young that required Young to make its tax accrual work papers generated during the audit of Amerada available to the IRS. Amerada instructed Young not to comply with the IRS summons. The IRS brought this action against Young to obtain the tax accrual work papers. Amerada intervened in the lawsuit. The district court ruled in favor of the IRS. The court of appeals reversed. The IRS appealed.

ISSUE

Is there a federal accountant–client privilege that protects work papers in the possession of independent accountants from discovery by the IRS?

IN THE LANGUAGE OF THE COURT

Burger, Chief Justice   Our complex and comprehensive system of federal taxation, relying as it does upon self-assessment and reporting, demands that all taxpayers be forthright in the disclosure of relevant information to the taxing authorities. Without such disclosure, and the concomitant power of the government to compel disclosure, our national tax burden would not be fairly and equitably distributed. In order to encourage effective tax investigations, Congress has endowed the IRS with expansive information-gathering authority; the IRS administrative summons is the centerpiece of that congressional design.

We do not find persuasive the argument that a work product immunity for accountants' tax accrual work papers is a fitting analogue to the attorney work product doctrine. The attorney work product doctrine was founded upon the private attorney's role as the client's confidential advisor and advocate, a loyal representative whose duty it is to present the client's case in the most favorable possible light.

An independent certified accountant performs a different role. By certifying the public reports that collectively depict a corporation's financial status, the independent auditor assumes a public responsibility transcending any employment relationship with the client. The independent public accountant performing this special function owes ultimate allegiance to the corporation's creditors and stockholders, as well as to the investing public. This "public watchdog" function demands that the accountant maintain total independence from the client at all times and requires complete fidelity to the public trust. To insulate from disclosure a certified public accountant's interpretations of the client's financial statements would be to ignore the significance of the accountant's role as a disinterested analyst charged with public obligations. Thus, the independent auditor's obligation to serve the public interest assures that the integrity of the securities markets will be preserved, without the need for a work product immunity for accountants' tax accrual work papers.

DECISION AND REMEDY

The Supreme Court held that the work product of accountants is not privileged from disclosure and must be disclosed pursuant to a validly issued IRS administrative summons. The Court reversed the judgment of the court of appeals.

Case Questions

Critical Legal Thinking Do you think that there should be an accountant–client privilege like there is an attorney–client privilege? Why or why not?

Ethics Did Amerada act ethically when it instructed Young not to disclose its work product to the IRS?

Business Application Is it more dangerous for a company to tell information to its accountant than to its lawyer?

LAWSUITS BY ACCOUNTANTS

An accountant can be the plaintiff in a lawsuit. For example, if a client (1) does not perform under the terms of a contract, (2) fails to pay the accountant for services provided, (3) otherwise breaches the contract, or (4) commits fraud, the accountant can bring an action against the client to recover damages.

LIABILITY OF PROFESSIONALS OTHER THAN ACCOUNTANTS

Certain professionals, such as lawyers, investment bankers, consultants, and appraisers, are hired to provide services to businesses. These professionals can be held liable to their clients for breach of contract, negligence, or fraud in the performance of their services. Professionals can also be held liable to third parties for their fraudulent or negligent conduct. Most states apply the foreseeability standard in finding professionals liable to third parties for their negligent conduct.

Working the Web

American Bar Association The American Bar Association maintains a Web site, ABANetwork, as a service to its members and the Internet community. It has news about legal issues, ABA entities, ABA meetings, and technology. Here you can buy books and other publications, join a discussion group, or link to other legal sites.

Visit at **www.abanet.org**

Academy of Legal Studies in Business The Academy of Legal Studies in Business is the leading national organization for college and university business law teachers. Here you can find information about regional and national meetings, job placement, and the *Journal of Legal Studies Education*.

Visit at **www.alsb.org**

American Institute of Certified Public Accountants AICPA has more than 330,000 members and is the national professional association for CPAs in the United States. You can find out all about accreditation

e·biz

of specialized practice areas in accounting. On-line publications include the AICPA code of conduct.

Visit at **www.aicpa.org**

CYBER EXERCISES

1. Visit ABANet and see what it has to offer. Then click on *Lawmart*. What kind of Internet services are advertised in this area?

2. Visit the Academy of Legal Studies in Business home page. Find information about the next annual meeting.

3. Using the AICPA site, find out about CPA societies and boards of accountancy in your state.

*C*ASES AND *E*XERCISES

CRITICAL LEGAL THINKING CASES

44.1. Accountants perform three basic types of financial analysis: (1) the compilation, which is essentially the gathering of financial information, (2) a review, which results in the issuance of a review report, and (3) an audit, which is conducted in accordance with generally accepted accounting standards. Louisiana enacted the Public Accountancy Law, which provides that only certified public accountants (CPAs) may conduct reviews and audits. The Accountants' Association of Louisiana, whose members include non-CPAs, sued, alleging that the Louisiana law was unconstitutional as a violation of the Freedom of Speech Clause of the U.S. Constitution. Is the Louisiana law constitutional? [*Accountants' Association of Louisiana v. State of Louisiana*, 553 So.2d 1251 (La.App. 1988)]

44.2. Jacob S. Eisenberg, who was licensed to practice as a certified public accountant (CPA) by the state of New York, conducted his practice as J. S. Eisenberg & Company. On February 15, 1978, he issued a financial statement with regard to Eaton Factors, Inc. (Eaton). The unqualified opinion indicated that Eaton had a net worth of $477,680 for the calendar year, when in fact Eaton's liabilities exceeded its assets by a substantial sum. In August 1978, Eaton filed a petition for bankruptcy. At the time Eisenberg conducted the audit, he had loans outstanding to Eaton on which he was receiving payments. In addition, his wife had $85,000 of debentures in Eaton, and his wife, son, and daughter also possessed other substantial interests in Eaton. Further, Eisenberg received commissions on investments his clients made in Eaton. The New York Commissioner of Education brought a proceeding against Eisenberg to revoke his license. Should Eisenberg's CPA license be revoked? [*Eisenberg v. State of New York Education Department*, 510 N.Y.S.2d 207 (N.Y. 1986)]

44.3. Stephens Industries, Inc. (Stephens), agreed to purchase the stock of Colorado Rent-A-Car, Inc. (Rent-A-Car), subject to an audit of the car rental company by Haskins and Sells (Haskins & Sells), a national accounting and CPA firm. When Haskins & Sells conducted the audit, it found that the accounts receivable records were so poorly maintained that the figures could not be reconciled. Haskins & Sells issued a qualified opinion that clearly stated that the accounts receivable had not been audited. The purchase agreement between Stephens and Rent-A-Car stated that the accounts receivable had not been adjusted to reflect uncollectibility. Stephens later sued Haskins & Sells regarding the audit of accounts receivable. Does the qualified opinion protect the accountants from liability? [*Stephens Industries, Inc. v. Haskins and Sells*, 438 F.2d 357 (10th Cir. 1971)]

44.4. Michael H. Clott was chairman and chief executive officer of First American Mortgage Company, Inc. (FAMCO), which originated loans and sold them to investors, including E. F. Hutton Mortgage Corp. (Hutton). FAMCO employed Ernst & Whinney, a national CPA firm, to conduct audits of its financial statements for the 1984 fiscal year. Hutton received a copy of the financial statements with an unqualified certification by Ernst & Whinney. From January 1984 through June 1985, Hutton bought more than $100 million of loans from FAMCO. As a result of massive fraudulent activity by Clott, which was undetected by Ernst & Whinney during its audit, many of the loans purchased by Hutton proved to be worthless. Ernst & Whinney had no knowledge of Clott's activities. Hutton's own negligence contributed to most of the losses it suffered. Hutton sued Ernst & Whinney for fraud and negligence. Is Ernst & Whinney liable? [*E. F. Hutton Mortgage Corporation v. Pappas*, 690 F.Supp. 1465 (D.Md. 1988)]

44.5. Guarente-Harrington Associates was a limited partnership formed for the purpose of investing in securities. There were two general partners and 40 limited partners. The partnership agreement provided that no partner may withdraw any part of his or her interest in the partnership except at the end of the fiscal year and with not less than 30 days' prior notice. Arthur Andersen & Co. (Arthur Andersen), a national CPA firm, was hired to audit the books of the limited partnership. In certifying the financial statements of the partnership and preparing its tax returns, Arthur Andersen failed to report that the general partners had withdrawn $2 million of their $2.6 million capital investment at times other than at the end of the fiscal year and without proper notice. The partnership suffered losses because of this lack of capital. Shelby White, a limited partner, sued Arthur Andersen for accounting malpractice. Is Arthur Andersen liable under the *Ultramares* doctrine? [*White v. Guarente*, 372 N.E.2d 315 (N.Y.Ct.App. 1977)]

44.6. Giant Stores Corporation (Giant) hired Touche Ross & Co. (Touche), a national CPA firm, to conduct audits of the company's financial statements for years ending 1971 and 1972. Touche gave an unqualified opinion for both years. Touche was unaware of any specific use of the audited statements by Giant. In May 1972, after receiving copies of these audited financial statements from Giant, Harry and Barry Rosenblum (Rosenblums) sold their retail catalog showroom business to Giant in exchange for 80,000 shares of Giant stock.

In 1973, a major fraud was uncovered at Giant that caused its bankruptcy. Because of the bankruptcy, the stock that the Rosenblums received became worthless. In conducting the 1971 and 1972 audits, Touche had failed to uncover that Giant did not own certain assets that appeared on its financial statements and that Giant had omitted substantial amounts of accounts payable from its records. The Rosenblums sued Touche for accounting malpractice. Is Touche liable for accounting malpractice under any of the three negligence theories discussed in this chapter? [*Rosenblum v. Adler*, 461 A.2d 138 (N.J. 1983)]

44.7. Texscan Corporation (Texscan) was a corporation located in Phoenix, Arizona. The company was audited by Coopers & Lybrand (Coopers), a national CPA firm that prepared audited financial statements for the company. The Lindner Fund, Inc., and the Lindner Dividend Fund, Inc. (Lindner Funds), are mutual funds that invest in securities of companies. After receiving and reviewing the audited financial statements of Texscan, Lindner Funds purchased securities in the company. Thereafter, Texscan suffered financial difficulties, and Lindner Funds suffered substantial losses on its investment. Lindner Funds sued Coopers, alleging that

Coopers was negligent in conducting the audit and preparing Texscan's financial statements. Can Coopers be held liable to Lindner Funds for accounting malpractice under the *Ultramares* doctrine, Section 552 of the *Restatement (Second) of Torts*, or the foreseeability standard? [*Lindner Fund v. Abney*, 770 S.W.2d 437 (Mo.App. 1989)]

44.8. The Firestone Group, Ltd. (Firestone), a company engaged in real estate development, entered into a contract to sell nursing homes it owned to a buyer. The buyer paid a $30,000 deposit to Firestone and promised to pay the remainder of the $28-million purchase price in the future. The profit on the sale, if consummated, would have been $2 million.

To raise capital, Firestone planned on issuing $7.5 million of securities to investors. Firestone hired Laventhol, Krekstein, Horwath & Horwath (Laventhol), a national CPA firm, to audit the company for the fiscal year ending 1969. When Laventhol proposed to record the profit from the sale of the nursing homes as unrealized gross profit, Firestone threatened to withdraw its account from Laventhol. Thereafter, Laventhol decided to recognize $235,000 as profit and to record the balance of $1,795,000 as "deferred gross profit." This was done even though, during the course of the audit, Laventhol learned that there was no corporate resolution approving the sale, the sale transaction was not recorded in the minutes of the corporation, and the buyer had a net worth of only $10,000. Laventhol also failed to verify the enforceability of the contracts.

Gerald M. Herzfeld and other investors received copies of the audited financial statements and invested in the securities issued by Firestone. Later, when the buyer did not purchase the nursing homes, Firestone declared bankruptcy. Herzfeld and the other investors lost most of their investment. Herzfeld sued Laventhol for securities fraud in violation of Section 10(b) of the Securities Exchange Act of 1934. Is Laventhol liable? [*Herzfeld v. Laventhol, Krekstein, Horwath & Horwath*, 540 F.2d 27 (2d Cir. 1976)]

44.9. From 1980 through 1985, Chaple, an accountant licensed by the state of Georgia, provided accounting services to Roberts and several corporations in which Roberts was an officer and shareholder (collectively called Roberts). During this period, Roberts provided Chaple with confidential information with the expectation that this information would not be disclosed to third parties. Georgia statutes provide for an accountant-client privilege. When the IRS began investigating Roberts, Chaple voluntarily, and without being subject to a subpoena, released some of this confidential information about Roberts to the IRS. Roberts sued Chaple, seeking an injunction to prevent further disclosure, requesting return of all information in Chaple's possession, and seeking monetary damages. Who wins? [*Roberts v. Chaple*, 369 S.E.2d 482 (Ga.App. 1988)]

Ethics Cases

44.10. In 1968, the archdiocese of Miami established a health and welfare plan to provide medical coverage for its employees. In 1969, the archdiocese purchased a stop-loss insurance policy from Lloyd's of London (Lloyd's), which provided insurance against losses that exceeded the basic coverage of the plan. The archdiocese employed Coopers & Lybrand (Coopers), a national firm of CPAs, to audit the health plan every year from 1969 through 1981.

The audit program required Coopers to obtain a copy of the current stop-loss policy and record any changes. After 1971, Coopers neither obtained a copy of the policy nor verified the existence of the Lloyd's insurance. Nevertheless, Coopers repeatedly represented to the trustees of the archdiocese that the Lloyd's insurance policy was in effect, when in fact it had been canceled. During this period of time, Dennis McGee, an employee of the archdiocese, had embezzled funds that were to be used to pay premiums on the Lloyd's policy. The archdiocese sued Coopers for accounting malpractice and sought to recover the funds stolen by McGee. Did Coopers act ethically in this case? Is Coopers liable? [*Coopers &*

Lybrand v. Trustees of the Archdiocese of Miami, 536 So.2d 278 (Fla.App. 1989)]

44.11. In 1960, Milton Mende purchased the Star Midas Mining Co., Inc., for $6,500. This Nevada corporation was a shell corporation with no assets. Mende changed the name of the corporation to American Equities Corporation (American Equities) and hired Bernard Howard to prepare certain accounting reports so that the company could issue securities to the public. In preparing the financial accounts, Howard (1) made no examination of American Equities's books, (2) falsely included an asset of over $700,000 on the books, which was a dormant mining company that had been through insolvency proceedings, (3) included companies in the profit and loss statement that Howard knew American Equities did not own, and (4) recklessly stated as facts things of which he was ignorant. The United States sued Howard for criminal conspiracy in violation of federal securities laws. Is Howard criminally liable? [*United States v. Howard*, 328 F.2d 854 (2d Cir. 1964)]

Critical Legal Thinking Writing Assignment

Read Case A.44 in the Case Appendix [*United States v. Natelli*]. This case is excerpted from the court of appeals opinion. Review and brief the case. In your brief, be sure to answer the following questions:

1. Who were the defendants in this case?
2. What charges were brought against them? Were they civil or criminal charges?
3. Were the defendants found guilty?

Notes

1. GAAPs are official standards promulgated by the Financial Accounting Standards Board (FASB). GAAPs also include unofficial pronouncements, interpretations, research studies, textbooks, and the like.
2. GAASs are issued by the Auditing Standards Committee of the American Institute of Certified Public Accountants (AICPA).
3. 174 N.E. 441 (N.Y.App. 1931).
4. Other experts include appraisers, engineers, architects, lawyers, and other professionals who prepare opinions and reports that are included in registration statements.
5. *Ernst & Ernst v. Hochfelder*, 425 U.S. 185, 96 S.Ct. 1375 (1976).
6. 15 U.S.C. § 77x.
7. 15 U.S.C. § 78 ff.
8. 18 U.S.C. §§ 1961–1968.
9. Private Securities Litigation Reform Act of 1995.
10. *Reves v. Ernst & Young*, 113 S.Ct. 1163 (1993).
11. 26 U.S.C. §§ 7206(1) and (2).

Administrative Law and Government Regulation

Good government is an empire of laws.

JOHN ADAMS Thoughts on Government (1776)

Chapter Objectives

After studying this chapter, you should be able to

1. Describe government regulation.
2. Distinguish between regulation and a compensable "taking" of property by the government.
3. Define and describe the functions of administrative agencies.
4. Describe the major provisions of the Administrative Procedure Act.
5. Explain the difference among substantive rules, interpretive rules, and statements of policy.
6. Analyze the lawfulness of administrative agency searches.
7. Describe the process for administrative agency adjudication of disputes.
8. Explain the procedure for judicial review of administrative agency decisions.
9. Describe the Freedom of Information Act.
10. Describe the Government in the Sunshine Act.

Chapter Contents

administrative agencies
Agencies that the legislative and executive branches of federal and state governments establish.

Congress and the executive branch of government have created over 100 federal **administrative agencies**. These agencies are intended to provide resources and expertise in dealing with complex commercial organizations and businesses. Additionally, state governments have created many state administrative agencies. Thousands of *rules and regulations* regarding business operations have been adopted and enforced by federal and state administrative agencies.

Since the 1960s, the number of administrative agencies, and the regulations they produce, have increased substantially. Because of their importance, administrative agencies are informally referred to as the *fourth branch of government*. (In reality, they only have the powers delegated from the actual branches of government.) The federal government's ability to create administrative agencies is implied in the U.S. Constitution.

Business Brief
Businesses spend billions of dollars each year complying with administrative agency rules and regulations.

G<small>OVERNMENT</small> R<small>EGULATION</small>

The government's recordkeeping and reporting requirements form a large part of administrative law. Other government regulations concern proper business purpose and conduct, entry restrictions into an industry, government rate setting, and the like.

Proponents of government regulation argue that it is needed to protect consumers and others from unethical and deceptive business practices. Opponents say that the time and compliance and enforcement costs outweigh the benefits of regulation. The debate rages on, but one fact is certain: Government regulation will continue to affect business operations.

Business Brief
Businesses are subject to *general government regulation* that applies to many businesses and industries collectively (e.g., antidiscrimination laws).

Title III of the Americans With Disabilities Act of 1990 requires buildings to be accessible to disabled persons.

General Government Regulation

Business Brief
Many industries are subject to specific regulation that regulates companies in that industry (e.g., banking, television, railroads).

Most government regulation applies to many businesses and industries collectively. For example, the National Labor Relations Board (NLRB) is empowered to regulate the formation and operation of labor unions in most industries, the Occupational Health and Safety Administration (OSHA) is authorized to formulate and enact safety and health standards for the workplace, the Consumer Product Safety Commission (CPSC) is empowered to establish mandatory safety standards for products sold in this country, and the Securities and Exchange Commission (SEC) is authorized to enforce federal securities laws that apply to issuers and persons who trade in securities.

Regulated Industries

Congress and the executive branch created some administrative agencies to monitor certain industries. For example, the Federal Communications Commission (FCC) regulates the operation of television and radio stations, the Interstate Commerce Commission (ICC) regulates railroads, the Federal Aviation Administration (FAA) regulates commercial airlines, and the Office of the Comptroller of the Currency (OCC) regulates national banks. Although a detailed discussion of these agencies and the laws they administer is beyond the scope of this book, it is important to know that they exist.

The agricultural population, says Cato, produces the bravest men, the most valiant soldiers, and a class of citizens the least given of all to evil designs.

Gaius Plinius Secundus (A.D. 23–79) Natural History, Bk. I, dedication

Entrepreneur and the Law

U.S. DEPARTMENT OF AGRICULTURE ADMINISTERS FARMING LAWS

In May 1862, Congress created the **U.S. Department of Agriculture (USDA)** to administer the country's farm-oriented programs. The USDA, which is headed by the secretary of agriculture, a cabinet-level post, is composed of several administrative agencies and programs. Other federal administrative agencies (such as the Veterans Administration and the Environmental Protection Agency) and state administrative agencies also have an impact on farming operations. The USDA may affect farmers through (1) rule making, (2) adjudication proceedings, and (3) reparation proceedings that decide disputes between private parties (discussed later).

Agency proceedings are governed by the **Administrative Procedures Act** [5 U.S.C. §§ 55 et seq.] and USDA general rules of practice [7 C.F.R. §§ 1.130 et seq.]. These generally call for proper notice and hearing before any action is taken. After the administrative proceeding is final and all administrative remedies have been exhausted, an affected party can seek judicial review of the decision in the appropriate federal court of appeals unless such an appeal is precluded by statute.

The federal statutes administered by the U.S. Department of Agriculture include the following:

- Agricultural Marketing Agreement Act
- Animal Quarantine Act
- Animal Welfare Act
- Archaeological Resources Protection Act
- Beef Research and Information Act
- Cotton Research and Promotion Act
- Egg Products Inspection Act
- Egg Research and Consumer Information Act
- Endangered Species Act
- Federal Land Policy and Management Act
- Federal Meat Inspection Act
- Federal Seed Act
- Horse Protection Act
- Meat Inspection Act
- Packers and Stockyards Act
- Perishable Agricultural Commodities Act
- Potato Research and Promotion Act
- Poultry Production Inspection Act
- Poultry Products Protection Act
- Swine Health Protection Act
- United States Cotton Standards Act
- United States Grain Standards Act
- United States Warehouse Act
- Virus-Serum-Toxin Act
- Wheat and Wheat Foods Research and Nutrition Education Act

GOVERNMENT REGULATION VERSUS COMPENSABLE "TAKING" OF PROPERTY

The government may use its power of **eminent domain** to acquire private property for public purposes. However, the Due Process Clause of the U.S. Constitution (and state constitutions where applicable) requires the government to allow the owner to make a case for keeping the property. The **Just Compensation Clause** of the Constitution mandates that the government must compensate the property owner (and possibly others, such as lessees) when it exercises the power of eminent domain. Anyone who is not

eminent domain

Power of the government to acquire private property for public purposes.

Just Compensation Clause

Clause in the U.S. Constitution that mandates that the government must compensate owners and lessees for property taken under the power of eminent domain.

satisfied with the compensation offered by the government can bring an action to have the court determine the compensation to be paid. Often, the government's action is not considered a "taking" even if it causes economic losses to property owners and others.

Consider This Example Assume that ITT acquired a large piece of property with the intention of erecting a commercial building at some future time. Now suppose the government wants to build a new highway that passes through property owned by ITT. The government can use its power of eminent domain to acquire the property. There has been a "taking," so the government must pay ITT just compensation. Suppose, instead, that the government enacts a zoning law that affects ITT's property by restricting building in the area to single-family housing. Although ITT would suffer a substantial economic loss, the zoning law, nevertheless, would probably not constitute a "taking" that required the payment of compensation.

In the following case, the U.S. Supreme Court held that a government regulation was not a "taking."

Penn Central Transportation Company v. City of New York
438 U.S. 104, 98 S.Ct. 2646 (1978)
United States Supreme Court

CASE 45.1

FACTS
In 1965, the city of New York adopted the Landmark Preservation Law to encourage and require the preservation of buildings and areas with historic and aesthetic importance. The law was adopted to promote civic pride in the beauty and noble accomplishments of the past; protect and enhance the city's attractions to tourists and visitors; and enhance the pleasure, welfare, and quality of life of people. The primary responsibility of administering the law is vested in the Landmark Preservation Commission (Commission). Once a structure is designated a "landmark" by Commission, no modification or change to the exterior of the building or site can be made without the permission of Commission.

On August 2, 1967, Commission designated the Grand Central Terminal (Terminal) as a landmark building and the city block it occupies as a landmark site. Terminal, which is owned by the Penn Central Transportation Company (Penn Central) is one of New York City's most famous buildings. Opened in 1913, this eight-story structure is a magnificent example of the French Beaux Arts style. Penn Central opposed the designation of Terminal as a landmark, but to no avail.

In January 1968, Penn Central filed an application with Commission to construct a 55-story office building in the airspace above the existing facade of Terminal. Commission denied Penn Central's application. Commission stated

We have no fixed rule against making additions to designated buildings—it all depends on how they are done. But to balance a 55-story office tower above a flamboyant Beaux Arts

facade seems nothing more than an aesthetic joke. Quite simply, the tower would overwhelm the Terminal by its sheer mass.

Penn Central filed suit in New York Supreme Court. The trial court held in favor of Penn Central and granted an injunction and declaratory relief. The appellate division reversed. The court of appeals affirmed. Penn Central appealed.

ISSUE
Does New York City's Landmark Preservation Law effectuate a taking of Penn Central's property without just compensation in violation of the Fifth and Fourteenth amendments to the U.S. Constitution?

IN THE LANGUAGE OF THE COURT
Brennan, Justice In contending that the New York City law has "taken" their property in violation of the Fifth and Fourteenth Amendments, appellants make a series of arguments. They first observe that the airspace above the Terminal is a valuable property interest. They urge that the Landmark law has deprived them of any gainful use of their air rights above the Terminal. The submission that appellants may establish a taking simply by showing that they have been denied the ability to exploit a property interest that they heretofore had believed was available for development is quite simply untenable.

Second, appellants, focusing on the character and impact of the New York City law, argue that it effects a taking because its operation has significantly diminished the value of the Terminal site. Stated boldly, appellants' position appears to be that the only means of ensuring that selected owners are not singled out to endure financial hardship for no reason is to hold that any restriction imposed on individual landmarks pursuant to the New York City scheme is a taking requiring the payment of just compensation. Agreement with this argument would, of course, invalidate not just the New York City law, but all comparable landmark legislation in the nation. We find no merit in it.

It is, of course, true that the Landmark law has a more severe impact on some landowners than others, but that in itself does not mean that the law effects a "taking." Legislation designed to promote the general welfare commonly burdens some more than others. In any event, appellants' repeated suggestions that they are solely burdened and unbenefited is factually inaccurate. This contention overlooks the fact that the New York City law applies to vast numbers of structures in the city in addition to the Terminal—all the structures contained in the 31 historic districts and over 400 individual landmarks, many of which are close to the Terminal.

DECISION AND REMEDY

The U.S. Supreme Court held that the application of New York City's Landmark Preservation Law is a permissible government regulation that does not effectuate a taking of Penn Central's property under the Fifth and Fourteenth amendments to the U.S. Constitution.

Case Questions

Critical Legal Thinking   Does the government owe a duty of social responsibility to protect historic buildings and districts from destruction? Or should the market be permitted to determine the highest value and best use for property?

Ethics   Did Penn Central act ethically in trying to construct a 55-story building above Terminal?

Business Application   Does government regulation help or hurt business? Explain.

ADMINISTRATIVE AGENCIES

Administrative agencies are generally established with the goal of creating a body of professionals who are experts in a particular field. These experts have delegated authority to regulate an individual industry or a specific area of commerce.

Administrative agencies are created by federal, state, and local governments. They range from large, complex federal agencies, such as the Department of Health and Human Resources, to local zoning boards. Many administrative agencies are given the authority to adopt **rules and regulations** that enforce and interpret statutory law (the rule-making power of administrative agencies is discussed later in this chapter).

rules and regulations
Adopted by administrative agencies to interpret the statutes that they are authorized to enforce.

Federal Administrative Agencies

The most pervasive government regulations have developed from the statutes enforced by and the rules and regulations adopted by **federal administrative agencies**. The majority of federal administrative agencies—including the Justice Department, the Department of Housing and Urban Development, the Labor Department, the Transportation Department, and the Commerce Department—are part of the executive branch of government.

Congress has established many federal administrative agencies. These agencies are independent of the executive branch and have broad regulatory powers over key areas of the national economy. Many of these independent agencies are discussed separately in this book.

federal administrative agencies
Administrative agencies that are part of the executive or legislative branch of government.

State Administrative Agencies

All states have created administrative agencies to enforce and interpret state law. For example, most states have a corporations department to enforce state corporations law, a banking department to regulate the operation of banks, fish and game departments, and workers' compensation boards. **State administrative agencies** also have a profound effect on business. Local governments and municipalities create administrative agencies, such as zoning commissions, to administer local law.

state administrative agencies
Administrative agencies that states create to enforce and interpret state law.

*A*DMINISTRATIVE LAW

Administrative law is a combination of substantive and procedural law. Each federal administrative agency is empowered to administer a particular statute or statutes. For example, the Securities and Exchange Commission (SEC) is authorized to enforce the Securities Act of 1933, the Securities Exchange Act of 1934, and other federal statutes dealing with securities markets. These statutes are the *substantive law* that is enforced by the agency.

Administrative Procedure Act

Administrative Procedure Act (APA)

An act that establishes certain administrative procedures that federal administrative agencies must follow in conducting their affairs.

In 1946, Congress enacted the **Administrative Procedure Act (APA)**.[1] This act establishes certain administrative procedures that federal administrative agencies must follow in conducting their affairs. For example, the APA establishes notice and hearing requirements, rules for conducting agency adjudicative actions, and procedures for rule making. Most states have enacted administrative procedural acts that govern state administrative agencies.

*D*ELEGATION OF POWERS

delegation doctrine

A doctrine that says when an administrative agency is created, it is delegated certain powers; the agency can only use those legislative, judicial, and executive powers that are delegated to it.

Because the U.S. Constitution does not stipulate that administrative agencies are a separate branch of the government, they must be created by the legislative or executive branch. When an administrative agency is created, it is delegated certain powers. The agency has only the legislative, judicial, and executive powers that are delegated to it. This is called the **delegation doctrine**.

Thus, an agency can adopt a rule or regulation (a legislative function), prosecute a violation of the statute or rule (an executive function), and adjudicate the dispute (a judicial function). The courts have generally upheld this combined power of administrative agencies as being constitutional. If an administrative agency acts outside the scope of its delegated powers, it is an unconstitutional act.

*I*nternational *P*erspective

WHAT DOES "MADE IN AMERICA" MEAN?

Many goods contain the label "Made in America." But what does this label really mean? In 1998, the Federal Trade Commission (FTC), the administrative agency charged with protecting consumers from deception, issued new standards that define *"Made in America."* The new standards try to balance domestic origin claims and the global marketplace.

The 1998 FTC guidelines require goods that are "substantially made" in the United States to bear the "Made in America" label. This new test rejects the "wholly domestic" 100 percent standard. Instead, the FTC states that a marketer may claim the "Made in America" label if either of the following "safe harbor" rules are met:

1. At least 75 percent of the total cost of manufacturing the product are U.S. manufacturing costs.
2. The final product was last "substantially transformed" in

the United States. This rule requires that the manufacturing process results in a new and different article of commerce having a name, character, and use different than what existed prior to processing. For example, using foreign steel to make a new automobile qualifies, but adding a tail light to an already-made automobile would not.

The FTC guidelines also permit marketers to make qualified U.S. origin claims even where their products would not meet the unqualified "Made in America" label. For example, a product assembled in the United States but made primarily with foreign parts could be labeled "Made in USA of foreign parts."

The new labeling law is designed to protect consumers from false "Made in USA" claims. The FTC is empowered to seek sanctions against violators and to turn over fraudulent cases to the Justice Department for criminal prosecution.

*L*EGISLATIVE POWERS OF ADMINISTRATIVE AGENCIES

Administrative agencies usually are delegated certain *legislative powers*. These include rule-making and licensing powers, as discussed in the following paragraphs and boxes.

Substantive Rule Making

Many federal statutes expressly authorize an administrative agency to issue **substantive rules**. A substantive regulation is much like a statute: It has the force of law and must be adhered to by covered persons and businesses. Violators may be held civilly or criminally liable, depending on the rule. All substantive rules are subject to judicial review.

A federal administrative agency that proposes to adopt a substantive rule must follow procedures set forth in the APA.[2] This means the agency must do the following:

1. Publish a general notice of the proposed rule making in the *Federal Register*. The notice must include
   a. The time, place, and nature of the rule-making proceeding.
   b. The legal authority pursuant to which the rule is proposed.
   c. The terms or substance of the proposed rule or a description of the subject and issues involved.
2. Give interested persons an opportunity to participate in the rule-making process. This may involve oral hearings.
3. Review all written and oral comments. Then the agency announces its *final rule making* in the matter. This procedure is often referred to as *notice-and-comment rule making*, or *informal rule making*.
4. Require, in some instances, *formal rule making*. Here, the agency must conduct a trial-like hearing at which the parties may present evidence, engage in cross-examination, present rebuttal evidence, and such.[3]

substantive rules
Government regulation that has the force of law and must be adhered to by covered persons and businesses.

Interpretive Rule Making

Administrative agencies can issue so-called **interpretive rules** that interpret existing statutory language. Such rules do not establish new laws. Neither public notice nor public participation is required.

interpretive rules
Rules issued by administrative agencies that interpret existing statutory language.

Statements of Policy

Statements of policy may be issued by administrative agencies. These statements announce a proposed course of action that an agency intends to follow in the future. Such statements do not have the force of law. Again, public notice and participation are not required.

statement of policy
A statement issued by administrative agencies announcing a proposed course of action that an agency intends to follow in the future.

*C*ontemporary *B*usiness *A*pplication

LICENSING POWERS OF ADMINISTRATIVE AGENCIES

Statutes often require the issuance of a government *license* before a person can enter certain types of industries (e.g., the operation of banks, television and radio stations, and commercial airlines) or professions (e.g., doctors, lawyers, dentists, certified public accountants, and contractors). Most administrative agencies have the power to determine whether to grant licenses to applicants.

Applicants must usually submit detailed applications to the appropriate administrative agency. In addition, the agency usually accepts written comments from interested parties and holds hearings on the matter. The administrative agency's decision is subject to judicial review. However, the courts generally defer to the expertise of administrative agencies in licensing matters.

Executive Powers of Administrative Agencies

Administrative agencies are usually granted **executive powers**, such as the investigation and prosecution of possible violations of statutes, administrative rules, and administrative orders. To perform these functions successfully, the agency must often obtain information from the persons and businesses under investigation as well as from other sources. If the required information is not supplied voluntarily, the agency may issue an administrative subpoena to search the business premises. However, as discussed shortly, these powers are subject to certain constitutional constraints.

executive powers
Powers that administrative agencies are granted, such as the investigation and prosecution of possible violations of statutes, administrative rules, and administrative orders.

Administrative Subpoena

An **administrative subpoena** is an order that directs the subject of the subpoena to disclose the requested information. Judicial enforcement may be sought if the party does not comply with the subpoena and the agency can prove that it has reasonable grounds to believe that the information sought will prove a violation of the law. "Fishing expeditions" are prohibited. If a party ignores a judicial order to enforce an administrative subpoena, the party may be held in contempt of court.

administrative subpoena
An order that directs the subject of the subpoena to disclose the requested information.

Administrative Searches

Sometimes a physical inspection of the business premises is crucial to the investigation. Most inspections by administrative agencies are considered "searches" that are subject to the Fourth Amendment of the U.S. Constitution. The Fourth Amendment protects persons (including businesses) from ***unreasonable search and seizures***.

Searches by administrative agencies are generally considered to be reasonable within the meaning of the Fourth Amendment if

unreasonable search and seizure
Any search and seizure by the government that violates the Fourth Amendment.

- The party voluntarily agrees to the search.
- The search is conducted pursuant to a validly issued *search warrant*.
- A warrantless search is conducted in an emergency situation.
- The business is part of a special industry where warrantless searches are automatically considered valid (such as liquor or firearm sales).
- The business is part of a hazardous industry and a statute expressly provides for nonarbitrary warrantless searches (such as coal mines).

Evidence from an unreasonable search and seizure ("tainted evidence") may be inadmissible in court, depending on the circumstances of the case.

In the following case, the U.S. Supreme Court had to decide whether aerial photography of a business by an administrative agency violated the Fourth Amendment.

Dow Chemical Company v. United States
476 U.S. 227, 106 S.Ct. 1819 (1986)
United States Supreme Court

CASE 45.2

FACTS
Since the 1890s, Dow Chemical Company (Dow) has manufactured chemicals at a facility in Midland, Michigan. Its complex covers 2,000 acres and contains a number of chemical-processing plants. Many of these are "open-air" plants, with reactor equipment, loading and storage facilities, motors, transfer lines, and piping conduits located in the open areas between the buildings. Dow has undertaken elaborate precautions to secure the facility from unwelcome intrusion: An eight-foot-high chain-link fence completely surrounds the facility, security personnel guard the plant and monitor it by closed-circuit television, unauthorized entry into the facility triggers alarm systems, motion detectors indicate movement of persons within restricted areas, and the use of camera equipment by anyone other than authorized Dow personnel is prohibited. Dow considers its entire facility a trade secret.

The Environmental Protection Agency (EPA) is a federal administrative agency empowered to administer and enforce the federal Clean Air Act. In 1978, Dow denied an EPA request to conduct an on-site inspection of the Midland facility. EPA did not seek an administrative search warrant. Instead, EPA employed a commercial aerial photographer to take photographs of the facility from altitudes of 12,000, 3,000, and 1,200 feet. Using a standard floor-mounted, precision aerial-mapping camera, this firm took approximately 75 color photographs of various parts of the plant. When the photographs taken from 1,200 feet were enlarged, it was possible to discern equipment, pipes, and power lines as small as one-half inch in diameter. Several weeks later, after Dow learned about the EPA-authorized flight from independent sources, it filed suit against EPA. The district court held in favor of Dow and issued an injunction against the EPA's use of the photographs. The court of appeals reversed. Dow appealed.

ISSUE

Did EPA's aerial photography of Dow's plant constitute an unreasonable search in violation of the Fourth Amendment to the U.S. Constitution?

IN THE LANGUAGE OF THE COURT

Burger, Chief Justice   *We turn to Dow's contention that taking aerial photographs constituted a search without warrant, thereby violating Dow's rights under the Fourth Amendment. Plainly a business establishment or an industrial or commercial facility enjoys certain protections under the Fourth Amendment. Dow plainly has a reasonable, legitimate, and objective expectation of privacy within the interior of its covered buildings, and it is equally clear that expectation is one society is prepared to observe. Dow's inner manufacturing areas are elaborately secured to ensure they are not open or exposed to the public from the ground. Any actual physical entry by EPA into any enclosed area would raise significantly different questions, because the businessman, like the occupant of a residence, has a constitutional right to go about his business free from unreasonable official entries upon his private commercial property.*

The issue raised by Dow's claim of search and seizure, however, concerns aerial observation of a 2,000-acre outdoor manu- *facturing facility without physical entry. The intimate activities associated with family privacy and the home and its curtilage simply do not reach the outdoor areas or spaces between structures and buildings of a manufacturing plant. The government has greater latitude to conduct warrantless inspections of commercial property because the expectation of privacy that the owner enjoys in such property differs significantly from the sanctity accorded an individual's home. We emphasized that unlike a homeowner's interest in his dwelling, the interest of the owner of commercial property is not one in being free from any inspections. And with regard to regulatory inspections, we have held that what is observable by the public is observable without warrant, by the government inspector as well.*

Here, EPA was not employing some unique sensory device that, for example, could penetrate the walls of buildings and record conversations in Dow's plants, offices, or laboratories, but rather a conventional, albeit precise, commercial camera commonly used in map making. It may well be, as the government concedes, that the surveillance of private property by using highly sophisticated surveillance equipment not generally available to the public, such as satellite technology, might be constitutionally proscribed absent warrant. But the photographs here are not so revealing of intimate details as to raise constitutional concerns. Although they undoubtedly give EPA more detailed information than naked-eye views, they remain limited to an outline of the facility's buildings and equipment. The mere fact that human vision is enhanced somewhat, at least to the degree here, does not give rise to constitutional problems.

DECISION AND REMEDY

The Supreme Court held that the taking of photographs of an industrial plant complex from navigable airspace is not a search prohibited by the Fourth Amendment. Affirmed.

Case Questions

Critical Legal Thinking   Should the government be given greater latitude to conduct warrantless searches of business property than personal homes? Why or why not?

Ethics   Did EPA act ethically in this case?

Business Application   Could Dow have in any way protected itself from the search conducted in this case?

𝒥UDICIAL POWERS OF ADMINISTRATIVE AGENCIES

Many administrative agencies have the judicial authority to adjudicate cases through an administrative proceeding. Such a proceeding is initiated when an agency serves a complaint on a party the agency believes has violated a statute or administrative rule or order. The person on whom the complaint is served is called the *respondent*.

In adjudicating cases, an administrative agency must comply with the Due Process Clause of the U.S. Constitution (and state constitution where applicable). **Procedural due**

procedural due process
Due process that requires the respondent to be given (1) proper and timely notice of the allegations or charges against him or her and (2) an opportunity to present evidence on the matter.

substantive due process

Due process that requires that the statute or rule that the respondent is charged with violating be clearly stated.

process requires the respondent to be given (1) proper and timely notice of the allegations or charges against him or her and (2) an opportunity to present evidence on the matter. **Substantive due process** requires that the statute or rule that the respondent is charged with violating be clearly stated.

Procedures for Administrative Adjudication

Administrative law judges (ALJs) preside over administrative proceedings. They decide questions of law and fact concerning the case. There is no jury. The ALJ is an employee of the administrative agency.

administrative law judge (ALJ)

A judge, presiding over administrative proceedings, who decides questions of law and fact concerning the case.

Both the administrative agency and the respondent may be represented by counsel. Witnesses may be examined and cross-examined, evidence may be introduced, objections may be made, and such. Agency rules allow a more liberal introduction of evidence than do court rules.

order

Decision issued by an administrative law judge.

The ALJ's decision is issued in the form of an **order**. The order must state the reasons for the ALJ's decision. The order becomes final if it is not appealed. An appeal consists of a review by the agency. The agency review can result in new findings of fact and law.[4] Further appeal can be made to the appropriate federal court (in federal agency actions) or state court (in state agency actions). Judicial review of agency actions is discussed later in this chapter.

*C*ONCEPT SUMMARY   POWERS OF ADMINISTRATIVE AGENCIES

Power	Description of Power
Legislative Powers	
1. Substantive rule making	To adopt rules that advance the purpose of the statutes that the agency is empowered to enforce. These rules have the force of law. Public notice and participation are required.
2. Interpretive rule making	To adopt rules that interpret statutory language. These rules do not establish new laws. Neither public notice nor participation is required.
3. Statements of policy	To announce a proposed course of action the agency plans to take in the future. These statements do not have the force of law. Public participation and notice are not required.
4. Licensing	To grant licenses to applicants (e.g., television station licenses, bank charters) and to suspend or revoke licenses.
Executive Powers	To prosecute violations of statutes and administrative rules and orders. This includes the power to investigate suspected violations, issue administrative subpoenas, and conduct administrative searches.
Judicial Powers	To adjudicate cases through an administrative proceeding. This includes the power to issue a complaint, hold a hearing by an administrative law judge (ALJ), and issue an order deciding the case and assessing remedies.

*J*UDICIAL REVIEW OF ADMINISTRATIVE AGENCY ACTIONS

Many federal statutes expressly provide for judicial review of administrative agency actions. Where an enabling statute does not provide for review, the Administrative Procedure Act (APA) authorizes judicial review of federal administrative agency actions.[5] The party appealing the decision of an administrative agency is called the **petitioner**.

petitioner

The party appealing the decision of an administrative agency.

Decisions of federal administrative agencies are appealed to the appropriate federal court (see Exhibit 45.1). Decisions of state administrative agencies may be appealed to the

*&*XHIBIT **45.1** *Appeal of a Federal Administrative Agency Rule, Order, or Decision*

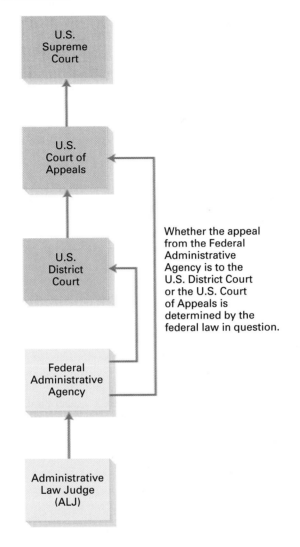

proper state court. A court may order the agency to prepare a detailed writing of the reasons for its decision.[6]

Conditions for Judicial Review

The following conditions must be satisfied before a petitioner can appeal an action of an administrative agency to a reviewing court:

1. The case must be *ripe for review*. For example, a petitioner cannot seek review of an administrative agency's rule, order, policy, or other action unless it specifically applies to the petitioner.
2. The petitioner must have *exhausted all administrative remedies*. For example, a petitioner cannot seek judicial review of a decision of an ALJ if an appeal to the full commission is available.
3. The decision of the administrative agency must be final before judicial review can be sought. (This is called the **final order rule**.) This rule is intended to prevent the disruption of an agency

Business Brief

A party must have exhausted all his or her administrative remedies within the appropriate administrative agency before he or she can seek judicial review of the agency's decision.

final order rule

A rule that says the decision of an administrative agency must be final before judicial review can be sought.

proceeding. For example, an accused party in an administrative agency proceeding cannot appeal to the courts until the agency issues its final ruling in the matter.

The courts may suspend the final order rule if the petitioner would suffer "irreparable injury" or "economic hardship" if he or she had to wait until a final order was issued. This exception is narrowly construed by the courts.

Contemporary Business Application

STANDARDS OF JUDICIAL REVIEW OF ADMINISTRATIVE AGENCY DECISIONS

Depending on the circumstances, different *standards of judicial review* apply to questions of law and questions of fact. The agency's decision can be overturned if it does not meet the appropriate standard of review.

Questions of Law

If the administrative agency has decided a question of law—such as the interpretation of statutory language—the reviewing court is free to substitute its own judgment for that of the administrative agency.

Questions of Fact

Questions of fact are not easily overturned. The reviewing court usually defers to the agency's fact-finding. The APA specifies three different standards of review for fact-finding by administrative agencies:

1. The *arbitrary, capricious abuse of process test.* This standard generally is applied to informal decisions such as rule making or licensing [5 U.S.C. § 706]. It is rarely used to reverse a discretionary fact-finding decision.
2. The *substantial evidence test.* This standard, which is used to review formal decision making [5 U.S.C. § 706(2)(E)], requires the court to examine the entire record to see whether the agency's decision was supported by substantial evidence. If the court finds that it was, the agency's decision will stand.
3. The *unwarranted by the facts test* (or the *de novo standard of review*). This test, which is rarely used, requires the reviewing court to try the case as if it had not been previously heard [5 U.S.C. § 706(2)(F)]. This type of review is available if the agency's fact-finding procedure was inadequate or if new issues arise on appeal.

Immunity of Agency Employees

Federal administrative agency employees are immune from lawsuits for personal liability regarding the actions and decisions they make while performing their agency duties. This places administrative agency employees on a par with judges, legislators, and others involved in the judicial process who are accorded similar immunity.

Consider This Example Suppose a group of persons wishes to form a new national bank. Under the law, a national bank cannot be formed without the approval of the comptroller of the currency (Comptroller), a federal government official. Assume that the Comptroller does not approve the formation of the bank. The applicants may appeal the Comptroller's decision to the proper court, but they may not sue the Comptroller personally for denying their application.

The immunity of agency employees is not absolute. For example, an agency employee who intentionally injures someone while performing agency business is subject to personal liability.

$\mathscr{P}$UBLIC DISCLOSURE OF AGENCY ACTIONS

Public concern over possible secrecy of administrative agency actions led Congress to enact several statutes that (1) promote public disclosure of federal administrative agency actions and (2) protect parties from overobtrusive agency actions. These statutes are discussed in the paragraphs that follow.

The Freedom of Information Act

The **Freedom of Information Act**[7] was enacted to give the public access to most documents in the possession of federal administrative agencies. For purposes of privacy, the following documents are exempt from disclosure: (1) documents classified by the President to be in the interests of national security, (2) documents that are statutorily prohibited from disclosure, (3) records whose disclosure would interfere with law enforcement proceedings, (4) documents describing agency personnel practices, (5) intra- and interagency memoranda, (6) medical, personnel, and similar files, (7) documents containing trade secrets or other confidential or privileged information, (8) documents pertaining to the operation of financial institutions, and (9) geological and geophysical data and maps.

The Freedom of Information Act requires federal administrative agencies to publish agency procedures, rules, regulations, interpretations, and other such information in the *Federal Register*. The act also requires agencies to publish quarterly indexes of certain documents. In addition, the act specifies time limits for agencies to respond to requests for information, sets limits on copying charges, and provides for disciplinary action against agency employees who refuse to honor proper requests for information.

Decisions by federal administrative agencies not to publicly disclose documents requested under the act are subject to judicial review in the proper U.S. district court. The court may award attorneys' fees to a successful petitioner.

Freedom of Information Act
An act that was enacted to give the public access to documents in the possession of federal administrative agencies. There are many exceptions to disclosure.

The Government in the Sunshine Act

The **Government in the Sunshine Act**[8] was enacted to open certain federal administrative agency meetings to the public. Only federal administrative agencies that are headed by two or more persons appointed by the President are subject to this act.

There are some exceptions to this rule. These include meetings (1) about things that are exempt from disclosure under the Freedom of Information Act (see prior section), (2) where a person is accused of a crime, (3) concerning an agency's issuance of a subpoena, (4) where attendance of the public would significantly frustrate the implementation of a proposed agency action, and (5) concerning day-to-day operations. Decisions by federal administrative agencies to close a meeting to the public are subject to judicial review in the proper U.S. district court.

Government in the Sunshine Act
An act that was enacted to open certain federal administrative agency meetings to the public.

The Equal Access to Justice Act

Congress enacted the **Equal Access to Justice Act**[9] to protect persons from harassment by federal administrative agencies. Under this act, a private party who is the subject of an unjustified federal administrative agency action can sue to recover attorneys' fees and other costs. The courts have generally held that the agency's conduct must be extremely outrageous before an award will be made under the act. A number of states have similar statutes.

Equal Access to Justice Act
An act that was enacted to protect persons from harassment by federal administrative agencies.

Privacy Act
An act stipulating that federal administrative agencies can maintain only information about an individual that is relevant and necessary to accomplish a legitimate agency purpose.

Privacy Act

The federal **Privacy Act**[10] concerns individual privacy. It stipulates that federal administrative agencies can maintain only information about an individual that is relevant and necessary to accomplish a legitimate agency purpose. The act affords individuals the right to have access to agency records concerning themselves and to correct these records. Many states have enacted similar privacy acts.

CONCEPT SUMMARY   PUBLIC DISCLOSURE OF AGENCY ACTIONS AND PROTECTION OF INDIVIDUAL RIGHTS

Act	Provision of the Act
Freedom of Information Act	Requires that documents of federal administrative agencies be open to the public; there are certain exemptions from this requirement. Also requires agencies to publish their proceedings, rules, regulations, and other information in the *Federal Register*.
Government in the Sunshine Act	Requires that meetings of federal administrative agencies be open to the public; there are certain exemptions from this requirement.
Equal Access to Justice Act	Gives a private party who was subject to an unjustified federal administrative agency action the right to sue and recover attorneys' fees and costs.
Privacy Act	Requires that federal administrative agencies maintain only information about an individual that is relevant and necessary to accomplish a legitimate agency purpose. Also gives individuals access to these records and a right to correct the records.

 Working the Web

ABA Administrative Procedure Database This site links to uses of the Internet in federal agency decision making.

Visit at **www.law.fsu.edu/library/admin/admin2. html**

Regulation.org This site is all about federal regulations. Do you want to know what a regulation is, why it matters, where to find a particular rule, or what horror stories and outrages there are involving federal regulations? This site is one stop shopping.

Visit at **www.regulation.org**

Administrative Law and Regulatory Practice The Administrative Law Section of the American Bar

Association helps its members and you stay abreast of recent developments in state and federal administrative law.

Visit at **www.abanet.org/adminlaw/home.html**

CYBER EXERCISES

1. From the ABA Administrative Procedure Database site, can you link to the U.S. Nuclear Regulatory Commission?

2. From Regulation.org, find out about hot new federal rules.

3. How many seasonal meetings does the Administrative Law Section of the ABA have?

e-biz

*C*ASES AND *E*XERCISES

CRITICAL LEGAL THINKING CASES

45.1. The Federal Deposit Insurance Corporation (FDIC) insures the deposit accounts of banks up to $100,000. Federal law [12 U.S.C. § 1818(g)] permits FDIC to suspend from office any officer of a federally insured bank who is criminally indicted if that person's continued service poses a threat to the interest of the bank's depositors or threatens to impair public confidence in the bank. The statute entitles suspended bank officers to a hearing before FDIC within 30 days of a written request and to a final decision within 60 days of the hearing. At the administrative hearing, the officer may submit written material or, at the discretion of FDIC, oral testimony.

FDIC suspended James E. Mallen, the president and director of Farmers State Bank in Kanawha, Iowa, upon his indictment for conspiracy to commit mail fraud and for making false statements in violation of federal law. FDIC issued an order suspending Mallen as president and director. A hearing was scheduled to occur within 19 days after his written request. FDIC did not permit oral testimony in this case. Mallen sued, alleging that FDIC's refusal to allow oral testimony at the administrative hearing violated the Due Process Clause to the U.S. Constitution. Is Section 1818(g) constitutional? [*Federal Deposit Insurance Corporation v. Mallen*, 486 U.S. 230, 108 S.Ct. 1780 (1988)]

45.2. The Food and Drug Administration (FDA), a federal administrative agency, is charged with enforcing the Food, Drug, and Cosmetics Act. This statute mandates that FDA limit the amount of "poisonous or deleterious substances" in food. Pursuant to this authority, FDA established certain "action levels" of unavoidable contaminants, such as aflatoxins, in food. Food producers that sell products that are contaminated above the set action level are subject to enforcement proceedings initiated by FDA. In announcing these action levels, FDA did not comply with the notice and comment procedure required for the adoption of a substantive or legislative rule. FDA argues that the "action levels" are merely interpretive rules or statements of policy that do not require notice and comment. The Community Nutrition Institute, a consortium of consumer public interest groups, sued to require FDA to follow the notice and comment procedure. Who wins? [*Community Nutrition Institute v. Young*, 818 F.2d 943 (D.C. Cir. 1987)]

45.3. The Federal Communications Commission (FCC) is a federal administrative agency that is empowered to enforce the Communications Act of 1934. This act, as amended, gives FCC power to regulate broadcasting of radio and television.

The act provides that "broadcasting shall not be deemed a common carrier." In *United States v. Midwest Video Corporation* [406 U.S. 649, 92 S.Ct. 1860 (1972)], the U.S. Supreme Court held that FCC also has the power to regulate cable television.

In May 1976, FCC promulgated rules requiring cable television operators that have 3,500 or more subscribers to (1) develop a 20-channel capacity, (2) make four channels available for use by public, educational, local, governmental, and leased-access users (with one channel assigned to each), (3) make equipment available for those utilizing these public-access channels, and (4) limit the fees cable operators could charge for their services. Do these rules exceed the statutory authority of FCC? [*Federal Communications Commission v. Midwest Video Corporation*, 440 U.S. 689, 99 S.Ct. 1435 (1979)]

45.4. George Carlin, a satiric humorist, recorded a 12-minute monologue "Filthy Words." He began by referring to his thoughts about "the words you couldn't say on the public airwaves" and then proceeded to list those words, repeating them over and over again in a variety of colloquialisms. At about 2 o'clock in the afternoon, a New York radio station owned by Pacifica Foundation (Pacifica) broadcast Carlin's "Filthy Words" monologue. A father who heard the broadcast while driving with his young son filed a complaint with the Federal Communications Commission (FCC), a federal administrative agency charged with regulating broadcasting. The federal Communications Act forbids the use of "any obscene, indecent, or profane language by means of radio communications." Therefore, FCC issued an order granting the complaint and informing Pacifica that the order would be considered in future licensing decisions involving Pacifica. Is the FCC regulation legal? [*Federal Communications Commission v. Pacifica Foundation*, 438 U.S. 726, 98 S.Ct. 3026 (1978)]

45.5. The Interstate Commerce Commission (ICC) is a federal administrative agency empowered to regulate motor carriers involved in interstate commerce. Trucking companies must apply to ICC and obtain a license before they can offer trucking services on a route. The Interstate Commerce Act empowers ICC to grant an application for a license if it finds that (1) the applicant is fit, willing, and able to properly perform the service proposed and (2) the service proposed is or will be required by the present or future "public convenience or necessity."

Thirteen motor carriers applied to offer trucking services between points in the Southwest and Southeast. After reviewing the applications and extensive written evidence (including the testimony of over 900 witnesses), ICC granted licenses to three of the applicants. Arkansas-Best Freight System, Inc., a rejected applicant, brought an action seeking to annul ICC's order. Should ICC's grant of the licenses be overturned on appeal? [*Bowman Transportation, Inc. v. Arkansas-Best Freight System, Inc.*, 419 U.S. 281, 95 S.Ct. 438 (1974)]

45.6. Under Tennessee law, the local planning commission must approve the plot of a proposed subdivision before the plot is recorded. In 1973, a land developer applied to the Williamson County Regional Planning Commission (Commission) for approval of a preliminary plot of a subdivision. The tract was to be developed in accordance with the requirements of the county's zoning ordinance for "cluster" residential areas. In 1977, before the project was built, the county's zoning ordinance was changed so as to reduce the allowable density of dwelling units in such areas. Commission decided that the land developer's tract would be governed by the new ordinance. Instead of seeking a variance from Commission, the developer brought an action in federal court alleging that there had been a compensable "taking" of his property under the Fifth Amendment to the U.S. Constitution. The developer did not seek compensation through the procedures that the state of Tennessee provided for doing so. Can the land developer sustain its lawsuit against Commission? [*Williamson County Regional Planning Commission v. Hamilton Bank of Johnson County*, 473 U.S. 172, 105 S.Ct. 3108 (1985)]

45.7. Arthur N. Economou and Co. (Economou) was registered as a commodities futures commissions merchant with the Department of Agriculture (Department), a federal administrative agency. In 1970, following an audit, Department issued an administrative complaint alleging that Economou violated rules prescribed by Department. A hearing was held at which the hearing examiner recommended sustaining the complaint. The secretary of agriculture (Secretary) affirmed the decision. On appeal, the court of appeals vacated Secretary's order. Economou then filed a civil suit against Earl Butz, the secretary of agriculture, the hearing examiner, the Agriculture Department attorney who prosecuted the enforcement proceeding, and several of the auditors who had investigated the matter. Economou sought to recover monetary damages from these individual defendants. Can the defendants be held liable? [*Butz v. Economou*, 438 U.S. 478, 98 S.Ct. 2894 (1978)]

ETHICS CASES

45.8. The Federal Mine Safety and Health Act of 1977 requires the secretary of labor to develop detailed mandatory health and safety standards to govern the operation of the nation's mines. The act provides that federal mine inspectors are to inspect underground mines at least four times a year and surface mines at least twice a year to ensure compliance with these standards and to make the following inspections to determine whether previously discovered violations have been corrected. The act also grants mine inspectors "a right of entry to, upon or through any coal or other mine" and states that "no advance notice of an inspection shall be provided to any person."

In July 1978, a federal mine inspector attempted to inspect quarries owned by Waukesha Lime and Stone Company (Waukesha) to determine whether all 25 safety and health violations uncovered during a prior inspection had been corrected. Douglas Dewey, Waukesha's president, refused to allow the inspector to inspect the premises without first obtaining a search warrant. Are the warrantless searches of stone quarries authorized by the Mine Safety and Health Act constitutional? Did Dewey act ethically in refusing to allow the inspections? [*Donovan, Secretary of Labor v. Dewey*, 452 U.S. 594, 101 S.Ct. 2534 (1981)]

45.9. A statute of the state of Wisconsin forbids the practice of medicine without a license granted by the Examining Board (Board), a state administrative agency composed of practicing physicians. The statute specifically prohibits certain acts of professional misconduct. Board may investigate alleged violations, issue charges against a licensee, hold hearings, and rule on the matter. Board also has the authority to warn and reprimand violators, suspend or revoke their licenses, and institute criminal actions.

Dr. Larkin was a physician licensed to practice medicine in the state of Wisconsin. On June 20, 1973, Board sent a notice to Larkin that it would hold a hearing to determine whether he had engaged in prohibited acts. Larkin was represented by counsel at the hearing. Evidence was introduced and witnesses gave testimony at the hearing. Board found Larkin guilty and temporarily suspended his license to practice medicine. Larkin then filed suit, alleging that it was an unconstitutional violation of due process to permit an administrative agency to adjudicate a charge that it had investigated and brought. Is there a violation of due process? Did Larkin act ethically in challenging the authority of the administrative agency? [*Withrow v. Larkin*, 421 U.S. 35, 95 S.Ct. 145 (1975)]

CRITICAL LEGAL THINKING WRITING ASSIGNMENT

Read Case A.45 in the Case Appendix [*Lorretto v. Teleprompter Manhattan CATV Corp.*]. This case is excerpted from the U.S. Supreme Court's opinion. Review and brief the case. In your brief, be sure to answer the following questions:

1. What did the New York law provide?
2. What was the landlord/owner's argument?
3. How did the Supreme Court decide the case?

NOTES

1. 5 U.S.C. §§ 551 et seq.
2. 5 U.S.C. § 553.
3. 5 U.S.C. § 556.
4. 5 U.S.C. § 557(b).
5. 5 U.S.C. § 702 states: A person suffering a legal wrong because of a federal agency action, or adversely affected or aggrieved by agency action within the meaning of a relevant statute, is entitled to judicial review thereof.
6. *Camp v. Pitts*, 411 U.S. 138, 93 S.Ct. 1241 (1973).
7. 5 U.S.C. § 552.
8. 5 U.S.C. § 552(b).
9. 5 U.S.C. § 504.
10. 5 U.S.C. § 552(a).

46 Consumer Protection

I should regret to find that the law was powerless to enforce the most elementary principles of commercial morality.

LORD HERSCHELL
Reddaway v. Banham (1896), A.C. 199, at p. 209.

Chapter Objectives

After studying this chapter, you should be able to

1. List the responsibilities of the federal Food and Drug Administration.
2. Describe government regulation of food and food additives.
3. Describe government regulation of drugs, cosmetics, and medicinal devices.
4. Explain the scope of the federal Food and Drug Administration's food labeling regulations.
5. Explain the coverage of consumer product safety acts.
6. Describe the scope of federal laws to childproof containers and packages.
7. Identify unfair and deceptive practices that violate Section 5 of the Federal Trade Commission Act.
8. Describe the coverage of consumer credit protection statutes.
9. List and describe protections afforded credit-card users.
10. Identify conduct prohibited by the Equal Credit Opportunity Act.

Chapter Contents

Originally, sales transactions in this country were guided by the principle of *caveat emptor* ("let the buyer beware"). Today, consumers may bring civil lawsuits against manufacturers and sellers of defective products and services. These lawsuits are based on a variety of legal theories, including breach of warranty, negligence, and strict liability. The time and cost of bringing a lawsuit may be prohibitive, however, particularly if the damages are minimal (such as loss of the sales price).

To promote product safety and prohibit abusive, unfair, and deceptive selling practices, federal and state governments have enacted a variety of statutes that regulate the behavior of businesses that deal with consumers. These laws, which are collectively referred to as **consumer protection laws**, are discussed in this chapter.

𝒯HE FDA's ADMINISTRATION OF THE FEDERAL FOOD, DRUG, AND COSMETIC ACT

The first federal statute regulating the wholesomeness of food and drug products was enacted in 1906. A much more comprehensive act—the federal **Food, Drug, and Cosmetic Act (FDCA)**[1]—was enacted in 1938. This act, as amended, provides the basis for the regulation of much of the testing, manufacture, distribution, and sale of foods, drugs, cosmetics, and medicinal products and devices in the United States.

The act is administered by the **Food and Drug Administration (FDA)**. The FDA can seek search warrants and conduct inspections; obtain orders for the seizure, recall, and condemnation of products; seek injunctions; and seek criminal penalties against willful violations. The U.S. Department of Justice has the authority to bring lawsuits to enforce the FDCA.

caveat emptor
"Let the buyer beware," the traditional guideline of sales transactions.

consumer protection laws
Federal and state statutes and regulations that promote product safety and prohibit abusive, unfair, and deceptive business practices.

Food, Drug, and Cosmetic Act (FDCA)
A federal statute enacted in 1938 that provides the basis for the regulation of much of the testing, manufacture, distribution, and sale of foods, drugs, cosmetics, and medicinal products.

Food and Drug Administration (FDA)
Federal administrative agency that administers and enforces the federal Food, Drug, and Cosmetic Act (FDCA) and other federal consumer protection laws.

The shipment, distribution, and sale of adulterated food, and the false mislabeling of food, is prohibited by the Federal Food, Drug, and Cosmetic Act.

Required FDA Approval

Before certain food additives, drugs, and medicinal devices can be sold to the public, they must receive FDA approval. An applicant must submit an application to the FDA that contains relevant information about the safety and uses of the product. The FDA, after considering the evidence, will either approve or deny the application. The FDA can sue and obtain a seizure order and injunction against further sales of unapproved items.

Regulation of Food

The federal government has enacted a comprehensive scheme of statutes that regulates the manufacture, processing, distribution, and sale of food. These laws are intended to (1) ensure the wholesomeness of food, (2) encourage accuracy in labeling and packaging, and (3) prevent injury to health.

Meat and poultry to be consumed by humans are subject to inspection by the **U.S. Department of Agriculture**, which provides official grading standards. The Department of Agriculture also administers the **Agricultural Marketing Act of 1946**,[2] the **Poultry Inspection Act of 1957**,[3] the **Wholesome Meat Act of 1967**,[4] and the **Egg Products Inspection Act of 1970**.[5]

U.S. Department of Agriculture

A federal agency empowered to inspect and grade meat and poultry consumed by humans.

Business Brief

In 1995, the federal Food and Drug Administration (FDA) issued new regulations that establish safety standards for seafood and shellfish. The FDA is authorized to conduct inspections of seafood processors to ensure compliance with these new regulations.

Adulterated Food The FDCA prohibits the shipment, distribution, or sale of *adulterated food*. Food is deemed adulterated if it consists in whole or in part of any "filthy, putrid, or decomposed substance" or if it is otherwise "unfit for food." Note that food does not have to be entirely pure to be distributed or sold—it only has to be unadulterated.

Business Brief

The FDA prohibits the shipment, distribution, or sale of *adulterated* food and the *false and misleading labeling* of food.

Misbranded Food The FDCA also prohibits *false and misleading labeling* of food products. In addition, it mandates affirmative disclosure of information on food labels, including the name of the food, the name and place of the manufacturer, and a statement of ingredients. A manufacturer may be held liable for deceptive labeling or packaging.

Contemporary Business Application

A HIDDEN SOURCE OF PROTEIN IN PEANUT BUTTER

So you take a big bite of a peanut butter sandwich and savor the taste. It has been processed by a food manufacturer and inspected by the federal government, so you think that it is pure peanut butter. Not necessarily. Under federal FDA guidelines, peanut butter may contain up to 30 insect fragments per 3½ ounces and still be considered "safe" for human consumption.

The FDA has set ceilings, or "action levels," for certain contaminants, or "defects," as the FDA likes to call them, for various foods. Several of these action levels are

Golden raisins—35 fly eggs per 8 ounces
Popcorn—two rodent hairs per pound
Shelled peanuts—20 insects per 100 pounds
Canned mushrooms—20 maggots per 3½ ounces
Tomato juice—10 fly eggs per 3½ ounces

The FDA can mount inspections and raids to enforce its action levels. If it finds that the federal tolerance system has been violated, it can seize the offending food and destroy it at the owner's expense. For example, in the Great Peanut Raid of 1991, the FDA seized 8.5 million pounds of peanuts shipped to the United States from foreign countries. The FDA found these peanuts contained illegal levels of contamination and sent them back to their home countries.

The courts have upheld the presence of some contamination in food as lawful under the federal Food, Drug, and Cosmetic Act. For example, in one case the court found that 28 insect parts in nine pounds of butter did not violate the act. The court stated, "Few foods contain no natural or unavoidable defects. Even with modern technology, all defects in foods cannot be eliminated." [*United States v. Capital City Foods, Inc.*, 345 F.Supp. 277 (N.D. 1972)]

International Perspective

UNITED NATIONS BIOSAFETY PROTOCOL FOR GENETICALLY ALTERED FOODS

Many food processors in the United States and across the world genetically modify some foods by adding genes from other organisms to help crops grow faster or ward off pests. In the past, food processors did not notify consumers that they were purchasing genetically modified agricultural products. Although the companies insist that genetically altered foods are safe, consumers and many countries began to demand that such foods be clearly labeled so that buyers could decide for themselves. When most large food processors balked at this idea, the consumers went to their lawmakers.

The most concerned countries in the world regarding this issue were in Europe. Led by Germany, many European countries wanted to require genetically engineered food products to be labeled as such and be transported separately from non-altered agricultural products. Some European countries wanted genetically altered foods to be banned completely. The United States, a major exporter of agricultural products and the leader in the development of biotech foods, argued that these countries were using this issue to erect trade barriers to keep U.S. produced food products out of their countries in violation of international trade treaties and conventions administered by the World Trade Organization (WTO) that had reduced or eliminated many international trade restrictions.

In January 2000, a compromise was reached when 138 countries, including the United States, agreed to the United Nations-sponsored **Biosafety Protocol**. After much negotiation, the countries agreed that all genetically engineered foods would be clearly labeled with the phrase "May contain living modified organisms." This allows consumers to decide on their own whether to purchase such altered food products. In addition, the boxes and containers in which such goods are shipped must also be clearly marked as containing genetically altered food products. This compromise assures that new biosafety labeling rules will coexist with the free trade agreements of the WTO.

Regulation of Drugs

The FDCA gives the FDA the authority to regulate the testing, manufacture, distribution, and sale of drugs. The **Drug Amendment to the FDCA**,[6] enacted in 1962, gives the FDA broad powers to license new drugs in the United States. After a new drug application is filed, the FDA holds a hearing and investigates the merits of the application. This process can take many years. The FDA may withdraw approval of any previously licensed drug.

This law requires all users of prescription and nonprescription drugs to receive proper directions for use (including the method and duration of use) and adequate warnings about any related side effects. The manufacture, distribution, or sale of adulterated or misbranded drugs is prohibited.

Regulation of Cosmetics

The FDA's definition of cosmetics includes substances and preparations for cleansing, altering the appearance of, and promoting the attractiveness of a person. For example, eye shadow and other facial makeup are cosmetics subject to FDA regulation. Ordinary household soap is expressly exempted from this definition.

The FDA has issued regulations that require cosmetics to be labeled, to disclose ingredients, and to contain warnings if they are carcinogenic (cancer causing) or otherwise dangerous to a person's health. The manufacture, distribution, or sale of adulterated or misbranded cosmetics is prohibited. The FDA may remove from commerce cosmetics that contain unsubstantiated claims of preserving youth, increasing virility, growing hair, and such.

Drug Amendment to the FDCA

An amendment enacted in 1962 that gives the FDA broad powers to license new drugs in the United States.

Business Brief

The FDA may speed up the process for experimental drugs that hold promise in treating incurable diseases (e.g., AIDS).

Business Brief

The federal Public Health Cigarette Smoking Act of 1985 requires cigarette manufacturers to place certain warnings on cigarette packages. Do you think these warnings adequately warn consumers of the dangers of cigarette smoking?

Regulation of Medicinal Devices

Medicinal Device Amendment to the FDCA

An amendment enacted in 1976 that gives the FDA authority to regulate medicinal devices and equipment.

In 1976, Congress enacted the **Medicinal Device Amendment to the FDCA**.[7] This amendment gives the FDA authority to regulate medicinal devices, such as heart pacemakers, kidney dialysis machines, defibrillators, surgical equipment, and other diagnostic, therapeutic, and health devices. The mislabeling of such devices is prohibited. The FDA is empowered to remove "quack" devices from the market.

Contemporary Business Application

SOMETIMES VIAGRA STIRS THE HEART TOO QUICKLY

The anti-impotency drug Viagra, introduced in 1997, was heralded as the most important drug to hit the market since the birth control pill. Viagra is prescribed by doctors to male patients who cannot have or have trouble getting erections and helps such men have intercourse. It became wildly successful and is now used by millions of men worldwide. In the United States, the Food and Drug Administration (FDA) approved the drug for use by the general public. A black market for Viagra has developed in countries where the drug has not been given government approval. Pfizer, the manufacturer of the drug, is receiving a financial bounty from its now-famous drug.

It seems that Viagra not only gets men's hearts stirring again, but it may also cause their hearts to explode, literally. After hundreds of deaths of men taking the drug were reported, the FDA investigated and found that men with certain health predispositions may be at risk of death if they take Viagra. Therefore, the FDA now requires Viagra labels to warn individuals with the following conditions to be careful when taking the drug:

- Men who have had a heart attack or an irregular heartbeat in the past six months
- Men who have a history of cardiac failure or coronary artery disease that caused angina
- Men who have significant high or low blood pressure

Viagra causes visual disturbance—particularly the ability to distinguish between blue and green—in about 3 percent of the men who use it. And Viagra sometimes works too well, causing priapism, or painful erections that last up to four hours. Doctors and consumers must also be warned against these conditions.

Pfizer asserts that its explosively popular drug was not the culprit in the reported deaths, but that the drug was taken by men with health problems who should have not used the drug. By requiring the new warnings, the FDA wants men with the noted risk factors to first ask, "Is sex a good idea for me?" before taking Viagra.

*O*THER ACTS ADMINISTERED BY THE FDA

In addition to the FDCA, the FDA administers the following statutes and amendments to the FDCA:

Business Brief

In many FDA actions, the proceeding is brought against the product.

- **Pesticide Amendment of 1954**[8] Authorizes the FDA to establish tolerances for pesticides used on agricultural products.
- **Food Additives Amendment of 1958**[9] Requires FDA approval of new food ingredients or articles that come in contact with food, such as wrapping and packaging materials.
- **Color Additives Amendment of 1960**[10] Requires FDA approval of color additives used in foods, drugs, and cosmetics.
- **Animal Drug Amendment of 1968**[11] Requires FDA approval of any new animal drug or additive to animal food.

- **Biologies Act of 1902**[12] Gives the FDA power to regulate biological products, including vaccines, blood, blood components and derivatives, and allergenic products.
- **Section 361 of the Public Health Service Act**[13] Gives the FDA power to regulate and set standards for sanitation at food service establishments (including colleges and universities) and on interstate carriers (e.g., airlines and railroads).
- **Section 354 of the Public Health Service Act**[14] and the **Radiation for Health and Safety Act of 1968**.[15] Empower the FDA to regulate the manufacture, distribution, and use of X-ray machines, microwave ovens, ultrasound equipment, and other products that are capable of emitting radiation.

Things are seldom what they seem.

Skim milk masquerades as cream.

Highlows pass as patent leathers.

Jackdaws strut in peacock's feathers.

William S. Gilbert
H.M.S. Pinafore, *Act*

Ethical Perspective

LESS BALONEY ON THE SHELVES

For much of its existence, the federal FDA has been a paper tiger that was led by wine-and-dine-with-the-industry regulators. In April 1991, the FDA shocked the food industry by having U.S. marshals seize 24,000 half-gallon cartons of "Citrus Hill Fresh Choice" orange juice, which is made by mammoth food processor Procter & Gamble (P&G). After trying for a year to get P&G to remove the word *fresh* from the carton—the product is made from concentrate and is pasteurized—the FDA finally got tough. P&G gave in after two days and agreed to remove the word *fresh* from its Citrus Hill products.

Next on the FDA's hit list were Best Foods, which markets "Mazola Corn Oil"; Great Foods of America, makers of "HeartBeat Canola Oil"; and again P&G, manufacturer of "Crisco Corn Oil." These companies had prominently advertised their cooking oils as having "no cholesterol," and some even added cute little hearts to the labels. Although the claim was literally true (these oils do not contain cholesterol), they are in fact 100% fat—which is not especially good for the heart. The FDA felt that these companies were hoodwinking the public and ordered the companies to take the "no cholesterol" labels off their vegetable oils.

In late 1990, Congress passed a sweeping truth-in-labeling law called the **Nutrition Labeling and Education Act**. The statute requires food manufacturers and processors to provide more nutritional information on virtually all foods and bars them from making scientifically unsubstantiated health claims.

The new law requires the more than 20,000 food labels found on grocery store shelves to disclose the number of calories derived from fat and the amount of dietary fiber, saturated fat, cholesterol, and a variety of other substances. The law applies to packaged foods as well as fruit, vegetables, and raw seafood. Meat, poultry, and egg products, which are regulated by the Department of Agriculture, are exempt from the act, as are restaurant food and prepared dishes sold in supermarkets or delicatessens.

In December 1992, the FDA announced final regulations to implement the act. The regulations require food processors to provide uniform information about serving sizes and nutrients on labels of the food products they sell and establish standard definitions for *light, low fat, natural*, and other terms routinely bandied about by food processors.

With the new law on the books and a tough new stand, the FDA is coming out of its corner with its gloves on. The American consumer can only come out a winner.

1. Did Procter & Gamble act ethically when it used the word *"fresh"* on its orange juice cartons? Why do you think it did this?
2. Do you think labeling laws serve a useful purpose? Explain.

REGULATION OF PRODUCT SAFETY

To promote product safety, the federal government has enacted several statutes that directly regulate the manufacture and distribution of consumer products.[16] These acts are discussed in the paragraphs that follow.

Consumer Product Safety Act

Consumer Product Safety Act (CPSA)

A federal statute that regulates potentially dangerous consumer products and created the Consumer Product Safety Commission.

In 1972, Congress enacted the **Consumer Product Safety Act (CPSA)**[17] and created the **Consumer Product Safety Commission (CPSC)**. The CPSC is an independent federal regulatory agency empowered to (1) adopt rules and regulations to interpret and enforce the CPSA, (2) conduct research on the safety of consumer products, and (3) collect data regarding injuries caused by consumer products. Certain consumer products, including motor vehicles, boats, aircraft, and firearms, are regulated by other government agencies.

Consumer Product Safety Commission (CPSC)

An independent federal regulatory agency empowered to (1) adopt rules and regulations to interpret and enforce the Consumer Product Safety Act, (2) conduct research on safety, and (3) collect data regarding injuries.

Because the CPSC regulates potentially dangerous consumer products, it issues product safety standards for consumer products that pose an unreasonable risk of injury. If a consumer product is found to be imminently hazardous—that is, its use can cause an unreasonable risk of death or serious injury or illness—the manufacturer can be required to recall, repair, or replace the product or take other corrective action. Alternatively, the CPSC can seek injunctions, bring actions to seize hazardous consumer products, seek civil penalties for knowing violations of the act or of CPSA rules, and seek criminal penalties for knowing and willful violations of the act or of CPSC rules. A private party can sue for an injunction to prevent violations of the act or of CPSC rules and regulations.

Fair Packaging and Labeling Act

Fair Packaging and Labeling Act

A federal statute that requires the labels on consumer goods to identify the product; the manufacturer, processor, or packager of the product and its address; the net quantity of the contents of the package; and the quantity of each serving.

The **Fair Packaging and Labeling Act**[18] requires the labels on consumer goods to identify the product; the manufacturer, processor, or packager of the product and its address; the net quantity of the contents of the package; and the quantity of each serving if the number of servings is stated. The label must use simple and clear language that a consumer can understand. This act is administered by the Federal Trade Commission (FTC) and the Department of Health and Human Services.

Poison Prevention Packaging Act

Many children suffer serious injury or death when they open household products and inhale, ingest, or otherwise mishandle dangerous products. The **Poison Prevention Packaging Act**[19] is intended to avoid this problem by requiring manufacturers to provide "childproof" containers and packages for all household products.

Magnuson-Moss Warranty Act

Magnuson-Moss Warranty Act

A federal statute enacted in 1975 intended to (1) prevent deceptive warranties, (2) require disclosures by warrantors who make certain written warranties, and (3) restrict the warrantor's ability to disclaim or modify certain warranties.

The **Magnuson-Moss Warranty Act**[20] was enacted in 1975. It requires all sellers who make written warranties regarding consumer products costing more than $15 to state the warranty in simple and clear language and to display the warranty conspicuously. Any limitations on the duration of the warranty or on consequential or consumer remedies must be disclosed.

Other Consumer Product Safety Acts

The CPSC also enforces other consumer product safety acts. They include

- The **Flammable Fabrics Act**,[21] which sets safety standards for flammable fabrics and materials used in clothing.
- The **Child Protection and Toy Safety Act**,[22] which sets safety standards for the manufacture of toys.
- The **Refrigerator Safety Act**,[23] which sets safety standards for refrigerators.

The FTC enforces, or helps to enforce, the **Wool Products Labeling Act**,[24] the **Fur Products Labeling Act**,[25] the **Textile Products Identification Act**,[26] and the **Hobby Protection Act**.[27]

Ethical Perspective

SHOULD ALL-TERRAIN VEHICLES BE GROUNDED?

All-terrain vehicles (ATVs) are three- and four-wheeled motorized vehicles generally characterized by large low-pressure tires, a relatively high center of gravity, a seat designed to be straddled by the operator, and handlebars for steering. They are sold by a variety of manufacturers.

ATVs are intended for off-road, recreational use over rough roads and various nonpaved terrain. The ATV industry's television and print advertising promotes ATVs as "family fun vehicles" that pose little danger to their operators. The truth is that ATVs are extremely dangerous, particularly when operated by inexperienced youthful riders. The danger of death or serious injury associated with the operation of ATVs has received wide public attention. Both the Senate and the House of Representatives have held hearings concerning the dangers of ATVs.

In December 1986, after receiving substantial public comment, the CPSC filed an emergency action in federal district court against the manufacturers of ATVs. The CPSC formally referred the matter to the U.S. Department of Justice to seek a judicial declaration that ATVs present an "imminent and unreasonable risk of death, serious illness, and severe personal injury."

The case never made it to trial, however. The CPSC and the defendant ATV manufacturers entered into a settlement whereby the defendants signed a consent decree in which they agreed to discontinue the "family fun" advertising of ATVs, provide warnings of their danger, publish manuals for their safe operation, provide training to ATV buyers, and set age-limit restrictions for the sale and use of certain ATV models. The CPSC agreed to the settlement because it was designed to alert consumers and reduce the hazards of using ATVs.

Several consumer groups thought that the CPSC had sold out and sought to intervene in the action to compel it to get tougher. Some consumer groups wanted an outright ban on the sale of ATVs in this country. The court of appeals rejected the interveners' arguments and upheld the consent decree. The court held that the settlement reached between the CPSC and the ATV industry was "fair, adequate, reasonable, and in the general public interest." The court stated, "No decree designed to protect consumers has ever gone this far in meeting such a massive national consumer problem." [*United States v. American Honda Motor Co., Inc.*, 143 F.R.D. 1 (D.D.C. 1992)]

1. Do you think that the CPSC acted in the public's best interest by entering into the consent decree with the ATV industry?
2. Should the government just "butt out" and let consumers assume the risk of dangerous activities in which they want to participate?

*U*NFAIR AND DECEPTIVE PRACTICES

Sellers sometimes engage in unfair, deceptive, or abusive sales techniques. If these practices result in fraud, an injured consumer can bring a civil action to recover damages. Such actions are not always brought, though, because it is difficult, costly, and time-consuming to prove fraud. Therefore, the federal government has enacted statutes to regulate sellers' behavior.

Section 5 of the Federal Trade Commission Act

The **Federal Trade Commission Act (FTC Act)** was enacted in 1914.[28] The **Federal Trade Commission (FTC)** was created the following year. The FTC is empowered to enforce the FTC Act as well as other federal consumer protection statutes.

Section 5 of the FTC Act, as amended, prohibits *unfair and deceptive practices*. It has been used extensively to regulate business conduct. This section gives the FTC the authority to bring an administrative proceeding to attack a deceptive or unfair practice. If, after a public administrative hearing, the FTC finds a violation of Section 5, it may order a cease-and-desist order, an affirmative disclosure to consumers, corrective advertising, or the like. The FTC may sue in state or federal court to obtain compensation on behalf of consumers. The decision of the FTC may be appealed to federal court.

Federal Trade Commission (FTC)
Federal administrative agency empowered to enforce the Federal Trade Commission Act and other federal consumer protection statutes.

Section 5 of the FTC Act
Prohibits *unfair and deceptive practices*.

False and Deceptive Advertising

Like a gun that fires at the muzzle and kicks over at the breach, a cheating transaction hurts the cheater as much as the man cheated.

Henry Ward Beecher
Proverbs from Plymouth
Pulpit *(1887)*

Advertising is false and deceptive under Section 5 if it (1) contains misinformation or omits important information that is likely to mislead a "reasonable consumer" or (2) makes an unsubstantiated claim (e.g., "This product is 33 percent better than our competitor's"). Proof of actual deception is not required. Statements of opinion and "sales talk" (e.g., "This is a great car") do not constitute deceptive advertising.

In the following case, the court held that the defendant company had engaged in false and deceptive advertising in violation of Section 5 of the FTC Act.

Federal Trade Commission v. Colgate-Palmolive Co.
380 U.S. 374, 85 S.Ct. 1035 (1965)
United States Supreme Court

CASE 46.1

FACTS

The Colgate-Palmolive Co. (Colgate) manufactures and sells a shaving cream called "Rapid Shave." Colgate hired Ted Bates & Company (Bates), an advertising agency, to prepare television commercials designed to show that Rapid Shave could shave the toughest beards. With Colgate's consent, Bates prepared a television commercial that included the sandpaper test. The announcer informed the audience, "To prove Rapid Shave's super-moisturizing power, we put it right from the can onto this tough, dry sandpaper. And off in a stroke."

While the announcer was speaking, Rapid Shave was applied to a substance that appeared to be sandpaper, and immediately a razor was shown shaving the substance clean. Evidence showed that the substance resembling sandpaper was in fact a simulated prop or "mock-up" made of Plexiglas to which sand had been glued. The Federal Trade Commission (FTC) issued a complaint against Colgate and Bates, alleging a violation of Section 5 of the Federal Trade Commission Act. The FTC held against the defendants. The court of appeals reversed. The FTC appealed to the U.S. Supreme Court.

ISSUE

Did the defendants engage in false and deceptive advertising in violation of Section 5 of the Federal Trade Commission Act?

IN THE LANGUAGE OF THE COURT

Warren, Chief Justice   We agree with the FTC that the undisclosed use of Plexiglas in the present commercial was a material deceptive practice. Respondents claim that it will be impractical to inform the viewing public that it is not seeing an actual test, experiment or demonstration, but we think it inconceivable that the ingenious advertising world will be unable, if it so desires, to conform to the FTC's insistence that the public be not misinformed.

If, however, it becomes impossible or impracticable to show simulated demonstrations on television in a truthful manner, this indicates that television is not a medium that lends itself to this type of commercial, not that the commercial must survive at all

costs. Similarly unpersuasive is respondents' objection that the FTC's decision discriminates against sellers whose product claims cannot be verified on television without the use of simulations. All methods of advertising do not equally favor every seller. If the inherent limitations of a method do not permit its use in the way a seller desires, the seller cannot by material misrepresentation compensate for those limitations.

The court of appeals could find no difference between the Rapid Shave commercial and a commercial which extolled the goodness of ice cream while giving viewers a picture of a scoop of mashed potatoes appearing to be ice cream. We do not understand this difficulty. In the ice cream case the mashed potato prop is not being used for additional proof of the product claim, while the purpose of the Rapid Shave commercial is to give the viewer objective proof of the claims made. If in the ice cream hypothetical the focus of the commercial becomes the undisclosed potato prop and the viewer is invited, explicitly or by implication, to see for himself the truth of the claims about the ice cream's rich texture and full color, and perhaps compared to a rival product, then the commercial has become similar to the one now before us. Clearly, however, a commercial which depicts happy actors delightedly eating ice cream that is in fact mashed potatoes or drinking a product appearing to be coffee but which is in fact some other substance is not covered by the present order.

DECISION AND REMEDY

The U.S. Supreme Court held that Colgate and Bates had engaged in false and deceptive advertising. Reversed and remanded.

Case Questions

Critical Legal Thinking   Does the government owe a duty to protect consumers from false and misleading business practices?

Ethics   Did Colgate and Bates act ethically in this case? Do you think the viewing public believed the commercial?

Business Application   Do you think Colgate needed "some fencing in"?

Bait and Switch

The **bait and switch** is another type of deceptive advertising under Section 5. It occurs when a seller advertises the availability of a low-cost discounted item (the "bait") to attract customers to its store. Once the customers are in the store, however, the seller pressures them to purchase more expensive merchandise (the "switch").

It is often difficult to determine when a seller has engaged in this practice. The FTC states that a bait and switch occurs if the seller refuses to show consumers the advertised merchandise, discourages employees from selling the advertised merchandise, or fails to have adequate quantities of the merchandise available.[29]

bait and switch
A type of deceptive advertising that occurs when a seller advertises the availability of a low-cost discounted item but then pressures the buyer into purchasing more expensive merchandise.

Door-to-Door Sales

Some salespersons sell merchandise and services door-to-door. In some situations, these salespersons use aggressive sales tactics to overcome a consumer's resistance to the sale. To protect consumers from ill-advised decisions, many states have enacted laws that give the consumer a certain number of days to rescind (cancel) a door-to-door sales contract. The usual period is three days.[30] The consumer must send a required notice of cancellation to the seller. An FTC regulation requires the salesperson to permit cancellation of the contract within the stipulated time.

Business Brief
Many states have enacted statutes that permit consumers to rescind contracts made at home with door-to-door sales representatives within a three-day period after signing the contract.

Unsolicited Merchandise

The **Postal Reorganization Act**[31] makes the mailing of unsolicited merchandise an unfair trade practice. The act permits persons who receive unsolicited merchandise through the mail to retain, use, discard, or otherwise dispose of the merchandise without incurring any obligation to pay for it or return it. Unsolicited mailings by charitable organizations and mailings made by mistake are excepted from this rule.

Postal Reorganization Act
An act that makes the mailing of unsolicited merchandise an unfair trade practice.

Contemporary Business Application

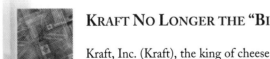

KRAFT NO LONGER THE "BIG CHEESE"

Kraft, Inc. (Kraft), the king of cheese producers in the United States, makes and sells Singles American Pasteurized Process Cheese slices (Singles) that can be used on sandwiches and for other purposes. When Kraft's dominant position in this market began to be eroded by imitation cheese slices made from vegetable oil and other products, Kraft designed a new advertising campaign to tout the health benefits of its Singles. In its campaign, Kraft advertised that (1) a slice of its Singles contained the same amount of calcium as five ounces of milk and (2) its Singles contained more calcium than most imitation slices.

The Federal Trade Commission (FTC) filed charges against Kraft claiming that neither of these statements was true. The FTC found that although Kraft uses five ounces of milk in making each Kraft Single, about one-third of the calcium contained in the milk is lost during processing. The FTC also found that most imitation slices sold in the United States contain the same amount of calcium as a Kraft Single. The FTC held that Kraft's advertisements constituted unfair and deceptive advertising in violation of Section 5 of the Federal Trade Commission Act because they were likely to mislead consumers. The FTC ordered Kraft to cease and desist from making these misrepresentations. The court of appeals upheld the FTC's order. [*Kraft, Inc. v. Federal Trade Commission*, 970 F.2d 311 (7th Cir. 1992)]

Federal Consumer-Debtor Protection Laws

Creditors have been known to engage in various abusive, deceptive, and unfair practices when dealing with consumer-debtors. To protect consumer-debtors from such practices, the federal government has enacted a comprehensive scheme of laws concerning the extension and collection of credit. These laws are discussed in the following sections.

Truth-in-Lending Act

In 1968, Congress enacted the **Truth-in-Lending Act (TILA)** as part of the Consumer Credit Protection Act (CCPA).[32] The TILA, as amended, requires creditors to make certain disclosures to debtors in consumer transactions that do not exceed $25,000 (e.g., retail installment sales, automobile loans) and real estate loans of any amount on the debtor's principal dwelling.

The TILA covers only creditors who regularly (1) extend credit for goods or services to consumers or (2) arrange such credit in the ordinary course of their business. Consumer credit is defined as credit extended to natural persons for personal, family, or household purposes.

Regulation Z

The TILA is administered by the Federal Reserve Board, which has authority to adopt regulations to enforce and interpret the act. **Regulation Z**, which sets forth detailed rules for compliance with the TILA, was adopted under this authority.[33] The uniform disclosures required by the TILA and Regulation Z are intended to help consumers shop for the best credit terms.

The TILA and Regulation Z require the following information to be disclosed by the creditor to the consumer-debtor:

- Cash price of the product or service
- Down payment and trade-in allowance
- Unpaid cash price
- Finance charge, including interest, points, and other fees paid for the extension of credit
- Annual percentage rate of the finance charges *(APR)*
- Charges not included in the finance charge (such as appraisal fees)
- Total dollar amount financed
- Date the finance charge begins to accrue
- Number, amounts, and due dates of payments
- A description of any security interest
- Penalties to be assessed for delinquent payments and late charges
- Prepayment penalties
- Comparative costs of credit (optional)

Right of Rescission and Other Remedies

Consumer-debtors who have used their principal dwelling as security for an extension of credit have the right to **rescind** the credit within three business days after the date the credit transaction was entered or the date the creditor provided the consumer with a required notice of the right to rescind the contract (whichever is later). The creditor has 20 days after rescission to refund any monies paid by the consumer-debtor. The creditor must notify consumer-debtors of their right of rescission. If a creditor fails to provide this notice, the borrower has three years from the date of the loan to rescind the credit agreement. The right of rescission is particularly aimed at abusive home improvement loans that use the borrower's home as security for the contract. Willful violations of the TILA and Regulation Z can result in criminal penalties.

Consumer Leasing Act

Consumers often opt to lease consumer products such as automobiles and large appliances rather than purchase them. As originally enacted, the TILA applied only to certain forms of leases. The **Consumer Leasing Act (CLA)** extended the TILA's coverage to lease terms in consumer leases.[34]

The CLA applies to lessors who engage in leasing or arranging leases for consumer goods in the ordinary course of their business. The lease period must exceed four months. The total lease obligation cannot exceed $25,000. Casual leases (such as leases between consumers) and leases of real property (such as a lease on an apartment) are not subject to the CLA. Creditors who violate the CLA are subject to the same civil and criminal penalties as those provided in the TILA.

> **Consumer Leasing Act (CLA)**
> An amendment to the TILA that extends the TILA's coverage to lease terms in consumer leases.

Fair Credit and Charge Card Disclosure Act of 1988

The **Fair Credit and Charge Card Disclosure Act of 1988**[35] amended the TILA to require disclosure of certain credit terms on credit- and charge-card solicitations and applications.

The regulations adopted under the act require that any direct written solicitation to a consumer display, in tabular form, the following information: (1) the APR, (2) any annual membership fee, (3) any minimum or fixed finance charge, (4) any transaction charge for use of the card for purchases, and (5) a statement that charges are due when the periodic statement is received by the debtor. This information must be orally disclosed in a telephone solicitation. Applications made available to the public (such as in magazines or on counters) must display the information or contain a toll-free number and mailing address where this information can be obtained.

> **Fair Credit and Charge Card Disclosure Act of 1988**
> An amendment to the TILA that requires disclosure of certain credit terms on credit- and charge-card solicitations and applications.

E-Commerce & Internet Law

TELEPHONE CONSUMER PROTECTION ACT

In recent years, telemarketing has become a popular means for advertisers and telemarketers to reach greater numbers of potential consumers. However, many consumers resented receiving these unsolicited calls. In response, Congress enacted the **Telephone Consumer Protection Act of 1991** to address certain telemarketing abuses.

One provision of the act restricts the use of automated devices that dial up to hundreds and thousands of phone numbers an hour and play a prerecorded sales pitch. The act makes it unlawful for phone calls to be initiated by using a prerecorded voice to deliver a message without the prior written consent of the called party. Congress justified the restriction by finding that such calls invaded the privacy of the receiver, cluttered up answering machines, and did

not disconnect if the receiver hung up. Under the act, a prerecorded message can be used only if a live person introduces the call and receives the consumer's permission to play the message. The act exempts calls initiated for emergency purposes, calls made to businesses, and calls made by nonprofit organizations. Personal calls are not covered by the act at all.

The trade association representing telemarketer operators challenged the law, claiming that it violated their First Amendment free-speech rights. The court of appeals upheld the law as a valid time, place, and manner restriction on commercial speech. The court reasoned that the law left open ample alternative channels for the communication of information [*Moser v. Federal Communications Commission*, 46 F.3d 970 (9th Cir. 1995)].

e-biz

Credit-Card Rules

Many consumer purchases are made with *credit cards*. Cardholders are liable to pay for authorized purchases even if they exceed the established dollar limit of the credit card. The TILA regulates the issuance and use of credit cards in the following ways:

- **Unsolicited Credit Cards** Issuers (e.g., VISA, MasterCard) are not prohibited from sending an *unsolicited credit card*. However, the TILA stipulates the addressee is not liable for any charges made on an unsolicited card that is lost or stolen prior to its acceptance by the addressee. Acceptance of the card makes the addressee liable for authorized charges made with it.

- **Faulty Products** A consumer who unknowingly purchases a faulty product with a credit card may withhold payments to the credit-card issuer until the dispute over the defect is resolved. The cardholder may notify the issuer about the defect immediately or wait until receipt of the billing statement. If the consumer and the seller cannot resolve the dispute (e.g., by replacing or repairing the defective product), the credit-card issuer is under a duty to intervene. If the dispute cannot be settled, a legal action may be necessary to resolve the dispute.
- **Lost or Stolen Credit Cards** Sometimes credit cards are lost by or stolen from the cardholder. The TILA limits the cardholder's liability to $50 per card for unauthorized charges made on the card before the issuer is notified that the card is missing.[36] There is no liability if the issuer is notified before the missing card is used.

To contract new debts is not the way to pay old ones.

George Washington
Letter to James Welch (1799)

Consider This Example   Suppose Karen loses her VISA credit card. Before Karen realizes she has lost the card, Michael finds it and charges $750 of goods. When Karen discovers the card is missing, she notifies VISA. Karen is liable for only $50 of the $750 of unauthorized charges. If Karen had notified VISA prior to the charges being made on her card, she would not have been liable for the $50.

ℰQUAL CREDIT OPPORTUNITY ACT

The **Equal Credit Opportunity Act (ECOA)** was enacted in 1975.[37] As originally enacted, the ECOA prohibited discrimination in the extension of credit based on sex or marital status. Its primary goal was to eliminate discrimination against females in credit extension. In 1976, the ECOA was amended to prohibit discrimination in the extension of credit based on race, color, national origin, religion, age, or receipt of income from public assistance programs.

The ECOA applies to all creditors who extend or arrange credit in the ordinary course of their business, including banks, savings and loan associations, automobile dealers, real estate brokers, credit-card issuers, and the like.

Prohibited Conduct

Under the ECOA, a creditor may not ask a credit applicant's race, color, national origin, religion, or age. The applicant's marital status cannot be questioned unless the applicant is relying on his or her spouse's income to establish the credit. In addition, creditors may not ask applicants about plans for childbearing or birth control practices or use the childbearing age of an applicant as a negative factor in making a credit decision.

The only acceptable reasons for a creditor to ask an applicant about any topics listed in the antidiscrimination guidelines named previously are (1) statistical monitoring required by the government and (2) courtesy (e.g., whether the applicant wishes to be addressed as "Miss," "Mrs.," or "Ms."). Answers to courtesy questions must be optional.

Notification of Adverse Action

The creditor must notify the applicant within 30 days regarding the action taken on a credit application. If the creditor takes an **adverse action** (i.e., denies, revokes, or changes the credit terms), the creditor must provide the applicant with a statement containing the specific reasons for the action. A general statement that the applicant does not meet the creditor's "credit standards" is not sufficient.

If a creditor violates the ECOA, the consumer may bring a civil action against the creditor and recover actual damages (including emotional distress and embarrassment). A private plaintiff or the government can obtain injunctive relief. States may adopt equal credit opportunity acts that are more protective than the ECOA.

adverse action
A denial or revocation of credit or a change in the credit terms offered.

Contemporary Business Application

FEDERAL STATUTE OUTLAWS JUNK FAXES

A provision of the Federal **Telephone Consumer Protection Act of 1991** bans unsolicited faxes that contain advertisements. The law was passed to protect owners of fax machines from receiving "junk faxes" for which they were required to pay as the receiver. Unsolicited private and political faxes are exempt from the law. The law gives anyone who gets an unsolicited fax the right to recover $500 in damages from the sender.

This federal law was challenged by a junk advertiser as being an unconstitutional infringement on its First Amendment free-speech rights. The court of appeals upheld the law, finding no free-speech violation. The court stated, "The ban is evenhanded, in that it applies to commercial solicitation by any organization, be it a multinational corporation or the Girl Scouts." [*Destination Ventures Ltd. v. Federal Communications Commission*, 46 F.3d 54 (9th Cir 1995)]

CREDIT REPORTING, BILLING, AND COLLECTION LAWS

Congress has enacted statutes that regulate the reporting and billing of credit accounts, as well as the collection of debts. These statutes are discussed in the following paragraphs.

Fair Credit Reporting Act

In 1970, Congress enacted the **Fair Credit Reporting Act (FCRA)** as Title VI of the TILA.[38] This act protects consumers who are subjects of a **credit report** by setting out guidelines for consumer reporting agencies, that is, credit bureaus that compile and sell credit reports for a fee.

The FCRA provides that a consumer reporting agency may provide consumer credit reports to users for only the following purposes: (1) decisions regarding the extension of credit, (2) underwriting insurance, (3) employment evaluation, (4) other legitimate business purposes, (5) pursuant to a court order, (6) granting of a government license, and (7) upon written permission of the subject of the credit report. Reasonable precautions must be taken to prevent unauthorized uses of credit reports.

The consumer may request the following information at any time: (1) the nature and substance of all of the information in the consumer's credit file (except medical information), (2) the sources of this information (except sources used solely for investigative reports), and (3) the names of recipients of a credit report within the past six months, or 10 months if it was used for employment purposes.

Fair Credit Reporting Act (FCRA)
An amendment to the TILA that protects customers who are subjects of a credit report by setting out guidelines for credit bureaus.

credit report
Information about a person's credit history that can be secured from a credit bureau.

He begs of them that borrowed of him.

James Kelly
Scottish Proverbs (1721)

Correction of Errors Consumer reporting agencies are required to maintain reasonable procedures to ensure the accuracy of their information. If a consumer challenges the accuracy of pertinent information contained in the credit file, the agency may be compelled to reinvestigate. Any information that is shown to be incorrect or that cannot be verified must be deleted from the consumer's credit file.

If the agency cannot find an error despite the consumer's complaint, the consumer may file a 100-word written statement of his or her version of the disputed information. This statement becomes a permanent part of the consumer's credit record. Any subsequent credit report must note the disputed item and be accompanied by the consumer's statement.

obsolete information

Information that is no longer accurate because of time or circumstances.

Obsolete Information Consumer reporting agencies are under a duty to keep credit reports up to date and to delete **obsolete information**. The FCRA expressly states that (1) bankruptcies that occurred more than 14 years prior to the date of the report and (2) any other information (e.g., lawsuits, judgments, tax liens, accounts placed for collection, accounts written off as bad debts, records of arrests, indictments, or convictions of a crime) that is over seven years old are obsolete and cannot be reported.

If a consumer reporting agency or user violates the FCRA, the injured consumer may bring a civil action against the violator and recover actual damages, court costs, and attorneys' fees. Punitive damages can be recovered if the violation was willful. The FCRA also provides for criminal penalties.

Fair Credit Billing Act

Fair Credit Billing Act (FCBA)

An amendment to the TILA that regulates credit billing.

Creditors usually send bills to consumer-debtors regarding payment of their accounts. In 1974, Congress enacted the **Fair Credit Billing Act (FCBA)** as an amendment to the TILA to regulate credit billing.[39] Creditors must advise consumer-debtors of their rights and responsibilities under the FCBA.

Billing Errors A consumer-debtor who receives a billing statement that he or she believes is in error must notify the creditor in writing of the alleged error within 60 days. The consumer must include enough information for the creditor to identify the account and item in question. The creditor must notify the consumer within 30 days that it has received the consumer's notice.

The creditor must then investigate the alleged error and the consumer must be notified of the result of the investigation within two billing cycles or 90 days (whichever is less). If an error is found, it must be corrected. If the creditor concludes that the billing statement is correct, it must provide the debtor with documentation to substantiate its findings.

Business Brief

A creditor is under a legal obligation to correct billing errors made on consumer-debtor accounts.

The creditor must wait 10 days before taking any action to collect the disputed item (plus interest) or making any adverse credit report on the consumer-debtor. If the consumer-debtor still disputes the creditor's decision, the consumer may bring a legal action against the creditor.

Fair Debt Collection Practices Act

Fair Debt Collection Practices Act (FDCPA)

An act enacted in 1977 that protects consumer-debtors from abusive, deceptive, and unfair practices used by debt collectors.

In 1977, Congress enacted the **Fair Debt Collection Practices Act (FDCPA)**.[40] This act protects consumer-debtors from abusive, deceptive, and unfair practices used by debt collectors. A **debt collector** is defined by the FDCPA as a collection agent who collects debts for other parties. A creditor that collects its own debts is not subject to the act. The FDCPA applies only where a debt is sought to be collected by a debt collector from a consumer-debtor.

debt collector

An agent who collects debts for other parties.

The FDCPA expressly prohibits debt collectors from using certain practices. They are (1) harassing, abusive, or intimidating tactics (e.g., threats of violence and obscene or abusive language), (2) false or misleading misrepresentations (e.g., posing as a police officer or attorney), and (3) unfair or unconscionable practices (e.g., threatening the debtor with imprisonment).

Prohibited Contact   The FDCPA limits the contact that a debt collector may have with third persons other than the debtor's spouse or parents. Such contacts are strictly limited. Unless the court has given its approval, third parties can be consulted only for the purpose of locating the debtor. They can be contacted only once. The debt collector may not inform the third person that the consumer owes a debt that is in the process of collection.

In some circumstances, the debt collector may not contact the debtor. These situations include the following:

1. At any inconvenient time. The FDCPA provides that convenient hours are between 8:00 A.M. and 9:00 P.M. unless this time is otherwise inconvenient for the debtor (e.g., the debtor works a night shift and sleeps during the day).
2. At inconvenient places, such as at a place of worship or social events.
3. At the debtor's place of employment if the employer objects to such contact.
4. If the debtor is represented by an attorney.
5. If the debtor gives a written notice to the debt collector that he or she refuses to pay the debt or does not want the debt collector to contact him or her again.

A debtor may bring a civil action against a debt collector for intentionally violating the FDCPA. The FTC may seek cease-and-desist orders against debt collectors.

> **Business Brief**
> **The Fair Debt Collection Practices Act prohibits certain contact by the creditor with third parties and the debtor.**

Contemporary Business Application

FDA CANNOT REGULATE TOBACCO AS A DRUG

The Federal Food and Drug Administration (FDA) is empowered by the Food, Drug, and Cosmetics Act (FDCA) to regulate "drugs" and "devices." In 1996, the FDA asserted jurisdiction to regulate tobacco products, concluding that nicotine in tobacco is a "drug" and that cigarettes and smokeless tobacco are "devices" that deliver nicotine to the body. The FDA was immediately sued by the tobacco manufacturers for overstepping its jurisdiction. The case proceeded to the U.S. Supreme Court. In a widely-watched case, the Supreme Court, in a 5-4 decision, ruled that tobacco was not a drug under the FDCA, therefore, the FDA could not regulate it. The Court noted that Congress already specifically regulates tobacco products through warning laws, no advertising on television or radio laws, and no sale of tobacco products to minors laws, therefore, no new regulation was warranted. [*Food and Drug Administration v. Brown & Williamson Tobacco Corporation,* 2000 WL 289576, United States Supreme Court (2000)]

International Perspective

CONSUMER PROTECTION LAWS IN MEXICO

In the decades following World War II, Mexico developed both an industrial base that created jobs in manufacturing and in service industries and a large consumer base. The ever-growing consumer population gave rise to increased consumer complaints of faulty products, consumer fraud, false advertising, and unfair business practices.

Prior to 1975, the traditional civil remedies provided by mercantile codes in Mexico provided little protection for Mexican consumers because they favored merchants and service providers. In addition, legal cases brought in the civil court system were slow, procedurally complicated, and costly.

In 1975, the Mexican Federal Congress enacted the **Federal Consumer Protection Act (FCPA)** [D.O. Dec. 22, 1975 (Mex.)]. The FCPA was modeled after several U.S. consumer protection statutes. The fact that most consumer transactions are codified and regulated in Mexico in a single statute is a clear advantage for Mexican consumers. The provisions of the FCPA are granted the highest legal rank in Mexico, second only to constitutional precepts.

The FCPA contains the following legal rules designed to protect consumers:

(box continues)

- The legal relationship between the merchant and the consumer is based on the "principle of truthfulness." This includes advertising, labeling, instructions, and warnings.
- Consumer contracts must be drafted in precise and clear language.
- Warranties of any goods and services are legally enforceable.
- Public authorities have the power to establish maximum interest rates and total expenses associated with consumer credit. Total disclosure is required in consumer credit transactions.
- Consumers have the legal right to modify, through judicial means, clauses included in adhesion or unconscionable contracts.
- Federal authorities have the power to regulate offers, advertising, and conduct of sales by businesses selling goods or services to consumers.
- Consumer protection rules contained in the FCPA may not be legally renounced.

The FCPA also created agencies to enforce its rules. For example, it created the **Federal Attorney General for Consumer Affairs**, an independent agency of the Mexican government that is empowered to represent the interests of consumers in proceedings before federal administrative agencies and federal courts.

The **Consumer Affairs Office** is empowered to settle disputes between suppliers and consumers as a *compositeur amiable*. A consumer may file a complaint with this office, which then acts as a conciliator or arbitrator to try to settle the dispute. Most consumer disputes are settled using the conciliation and arbitration method of the Consumer Affairs Office, even though the parties have the option of using traditional judicial avenues.

The **National Consumer Institute** educates the Mexican population concerning their rights and obligations as consumers. The work of the Institute has established a "consumer protection consciousness" among Mexican consumers and merchants selling goods and services in Mexico.

Working the Web

e-biz

Internet FDA The Food and Drug Administration has a Web site that can link you to all sorts of information on foods, human and animal drugs, cosmetics, medical devices, research, and more.

Visit at **www.fda.gov**

Central Notice-Class Actions The movie *A Class Action* has focused attention on what a class action is and how one can possibly recover money by joining in a class action lawsuit. Many class actions involve consumer products. This site even offers automatic e-mail notification of new class action postings.

Visit at **www.notice.com/classactions**

Consumer Product Safety Commission The mandate of the Consumer Product Safety Commission is "to protect the public against unreasonable risks of injuries and deaths associated with consumer products." You can find out about unsafe products and recalls from this site.

Visit at **www.cpsc.gov**

Federal Trade Commission—Bureau of Consumer Protection This bureau's mandate is to protect consumers against unfair, deceptive, or fraudulent practices. It enforces a variety of consumer protection laws as well as trade regulation rules.

Visit at **www.ftc.gov/bcp/bcp.htm**

CYBER EXERCISES

1. From the FDA site, find and print out information on children and tobacco.

2. Using the Class Action Web site, can you find out about tobacco litigation class actions?

3. From the CPSC site, find out how to report an unsafe product.

4. How many divisions are there in the Bureau of Consumer Protection?

CASES AND EXERCISES

CRITICAL LEGAL THINKING CASES

46.1. Barry Engel owned and operated the Gel Spice Co., Inc. (Gel Spice), which specialized in the importation and packaging of various food spices for resale. All of the spices Gel Spice imported were unloaded at a pier in New York City and taken to a warehouse on McDonald Avenue. Storage and repackaging of the spices took place in the warehouse. Between July 1976 and January 1979, the McDonald Avenue warehouse was inspected four times by investigators from the Food and Drug Administration (FDA). The investigators found live rats in bags of basil leaves, rodent droppings in boxes of chili peppers, and mammalian urine in bags of sesame seeds. The investigators produced additional evidence that showed that spices packaged and sold from the warehouse contained insects, rodent excreta pellets, rodent hair, and rodent urine. The FDA brought criminal charges against Engel and Gel Spice. Are they guilty? [*United States v. Gel Spice Co., Inc.*, 601 F.Supp. 1205 (E.D.N.Y. 1984)]

46.2. Coco Rico, Inc., manufactures a coconut concentrate called "Coco Rico" for use as an ingredient in soft drinks. The concentrate that is sold to beverage bottlers in Puerto Rico contains potassium nitrate, which is added for the purpose of developing and fixing a desirable color and flavor. Puerto Rico is subject to U.S. federal laws, including those administered by the Food and Drug Administration (FDA). The FDA has not approved the use of potassium nitrate as a food additive in soft drinks. The FDA learned of the use of the Coco Rico concentrate in soft drinks and, on March 10, 1982, obtained a warrant from a federal district court to search the premises of a Puerto Rican bottler. On March 24, 1982, government investigators discovered three lots of soft drinks containing Coco Rico on the premises of the bottler and seized them pursuant to the warrant. Coco Rico, Inc., sued to reclaim the soft drinks. Who wins? [*United States v. An Article of Food*, 752 F.2d 11 (1st Cir. 1985)]

46.3. Dey Laboratories, Inc. (Dey), is a drug manufacturer operating in the state of Texas. In 1983, Dey scientists created an inhalant known as ASI. The only active ingredient in ASI is atropine sulfate. The inhalant is sold to physicians, who then prescribe the medication for patients suffering from asthma, bronchitis, and other pulmonary diseases. In May 1983, Dey filed a new drug application with the Food and Drug Administration (FDA). By September 1983, Dey was advised that its application would not be approved. In spite of the lack of FDA approval, Dey began marketing ASI in

November 1983. On August 25, 1985, the United States filed a complaint for forfeiture of all ASI manufactured by Dey. The inhalant was seized and Dey sued to have the FDA's seizure declared illegal. Who wins? [*United States v. Atropine Sulfate 1.0 Mg. (Article of Drug)*, 843 F.2d 860 (5th Cir. 1988)]

46.4. FBNH Enterprises, Inc. (FBNH), is a distributor of a product known as "French Bronze Tablets." The purpose of the tablets is to allow a person to achieve an even tan without exposure to the sun. When ingested, the tablets impart color to the skin through the use of various ingredients, one of which is canthaxanthin, a coloring agent. Canthaxanthin has not been approved for use by the Food and Drug Administration (FDA) as a coloring additive. The FDA became aware that FBNH was marketing the tablets and that each contains 30 milligrams of canthaxanthin. On June 16, 1988, the FDA filed a lawsuit seeking the forfeiture and condemnation of eight cases of the tablets in the possession of FBNH. FBNH challenged the government's right to seize the tablets. Who wins? [*United States v. Eight Unlabeled Cases of an Article of Cosmetic*, 888 F.2d 945 (2d Cir. 1989)]

46.5. General Medical Company (General Medical) manufactures and markets a product known as the "drionic" antiperspirant device. The device is designed as a substitute for chemical antiperspirants or for the extensive medical treatment of those who suffer from greatly increased perspiration. The device consists of a housing for two wool felt pads and a battery. The pads are soaked in ordinary tap water and then placed against the treated area, typically the hands, feet, and underarms. An electrical current is passed through the pads and the area of skin between the pads for about 20 minutes. Ions (atoms carrying an electrical charge) are thereby transmitted across the skin. General Medical claims this process works in controlling perspiration in the treated area. The FDA seeks to regulate the device. Does it have authority to do so? [*General Medical Company v. United States Food and Drug Administration*, 770 F.2d 214 (D.C. Cir. 1985)]

46.6. In June 1980, Joseph Wahba had a prescription filled at Zuckerman's Pharmacy (Zuckerman's) in Brooklyn, New York. The prescription was for Lomotil, a drug used to counteract stomach disorders. The pharmacy dispensed 30 tablets in a small, plastic container unequipped with a "childproof"

cap. Joseph took the medicine home, where it was discovered by Wahba's two-year-old son, Mark. Mark opened the container and ingested approximately 20 pills before Mark's mother saw him and stopped him. She rushed him to a hospital but, despite the efforts of the doctors, Mark lapsed into a coma and died. The Wahbas sued H&N Prescription Center, Inc., the company that owns Zuckerman's, for damages. Who wins? [*Wahba v. H&N Prescription Center, Inc.*, 539 F.Supp. 352 (E.D.N.Y. 1982)]

46.7.   In June 1979, Elizabeth Valentine purchased a home in Philadelphia, Pennsylvania. In October 1979, she applied for and received a $4,500 home loan from Salmon Building and Loan Association (Salmon) for the purpose of paneling the cellar walls and redecorating the house. Salmon took a security interest in the house as collateral for the loan. Although Valentine was given a disclosure document by Salmon, nowhere on the document were "finance charges" disclosed. The document did notify Valentine that Salmon had a security interest in the house. In May 1982, Valentine sued Salmon (which had since merged with Influential Savings and Loan Association) to rescind the loan. Who wins? [*Valentine v. Influential Savings and Loan Association*, 572 F.Supp. 36 (E.D.Pa. 1983)]

46.8.   In April 1986, Joyce Givens entered into a rental agreement with Rent-A-Center, Inc. (Rent-A-Center), whereby she rented a bar and entertainment center. The agreement provided that she must pay in advance to keep the furniture for periods of one week or one month. Givens could terminate the agreement at any time by making arrangements for the furniture's return. Givens made payments between April and August of 1986. After that, she failed to make any further payments but continued to possess the property. When Rent-A-Center became aware that Givens had moved and taken the furniture with her, in violation of the rental agreement, it filed a criminal complaint against her. On January 9, 1988, Givens agreed to return the furniture and Rent-A-Center dropped the charges. After Rent-A-Center recovered the furniture, Givens sued the company, claiming that the agreement she had signed violated the Consumer Leasing Act. Who wins? [*Givens v. Rent-A-Center, Inc.*, 720 F.Supp. 160 (S.D.Ala. 1988)]

46.9.   Oscar S. Gray had been an American Express cardholder since 1964. In 1980, Gray used his card to purchase airline tickets costing $9,312. American Express agreed that Gray could pay for the tickets in 12 equal monthly installments. In January and February of 1981, Gray made substantial prepayments of $3,500 and $1,156, respectively. When his March bill arrived, Gray was surprised because American Express had converted the deferred payment plan to a cur-

rently due charge, making the entire amount for the tickets due and payable. Gray paid the normal monthly charge under the deferred payment plan and informed American Express by letter dated April 22, 1981, of its error. In the letter, Gray identified himself, his card number, and the nature of the error. Gray did not learn of any adverse action by American Express until almost one year later, on the night of his and his wife's anniversary. When he offered his American Express card to pay for their wedding anniversary dinner, the restaurant informed Gray that American Express had canceled his account and had instructed the restaurant to destroy the card. Gray sued American Express. Did American Express violate the Fair Credit Billing Act? [*Gray v. American Express Company*, 743 F.2d 10 (D.C. Cir. 1984)]

46.10.   The San Antonio Retail Merchants Association (SARMA) is a business engaged in selling computerized credit reports. In November 1974, William Daniel Thompson, Jr. (Jr.), opened a credit account with Gordon's Jewelers (Gordon's) in San Antonio, listing his Social Security number as 457-68-5778. Jr. subsequently ran up a delinquent account of $77.25 at Gordon's that was subsequently charged off as a bad debt. Gordon's reported the bad debt to SARMA, which placed the information and a derogatory credit rating in Jr.'s file No. 5867114.

In early 1978, William Douglas Thompson III (III) applied for credit with Gulf Oil and Wards. He listed his Social Security number as 407-86-4065. On February 9, 1978, a worker in the credit department at Gulf accepted file No. 5867114 from SARMA as the credit history of III. Thereafter, SARMA combined the credit reports of the two men. III was denied credit by both Gulf and Wards on the basis of this erroneous information. It was not until June 1979 that III learned of the mistake. After straightening out the facts with Gordon's, III requested SARMA to correct the error. SARMA took no action on III's complaint for four months. III sued SARMA for violating the Fair Credit Reporting Act. Who wins? [*Thompson v. San Antonio Retail Merchants Association*, 682 F.2d 509 (5th Cir. 1982)]

46.11.   Stanley M. Juras was a student at Montana State University (MSU) from 1972 to 1976. During his years at MSU, Juras took out several student loans from the school under the National Direct Student Loan program. By the time Juras left MSU, he owed the school over $5,000. Juras defaulted on these loans and MSU assigned the debt to Aman Collection Services, Inc. (Aman), for purposes of collection. Aman obtained a judgment against Juras in a Montana state court for $5,015 on the debt and $1,920 in interest and attorneys' fees. Juras, who now lived in California, still refused to pay these amounts. On May 5, 1982, a vice president of Aman, Mr. Gloss, telephoned Juras twice in California before

8:00 A.M. Pacific Standard Time. Gloss told Juras that if he did not pay the debt, he would not receive a college transcript. Juras sued Aman, claiming that the telephone calls violated the Fair Debt Collection Practices Act. Gloss testified at trial that he made the calls before 8:00 A.M. because he had forgotten the difference in time zones between California and Aman's offices in South Dakota. Who wins? [*Juras v. Aman Collection Services, Inc.*, 829 F.2d 739 (9th Cir. 1987)]

ETHICS CASES

46.12.   Charles of the Ritz Distributing Corporation (Ritz) is a New York corporation engaged in the sale and distribution of a product called "Rejuvenescence Cream." The extensive advertising campaign that accompanied the sale of the cream placed emphasis upon the supposed rejuvenating powers of the product. The ads claimed that the cream would bring to the user's "skin quickly the clear radiance" and "the petal-like quality and texture of youth." Another advertisement claimed that the product would "restore natural moisture necessary for a live, healthy skin" with the result that "Your face need not know drought years." The Federal Trade Commission (FTC) learned of the ads and asked several experts to investigate the claimed benefits of the Rejuvenescence cream. The experts reported to the FTC that it is impossible for an external application of cosmetics to overcome skin conditions that result from physiological changes occurring with the passage of time. The FTC issued a cease-and-desist order with regard to the advertising. Ritz appealed the FTC's decision to a federal court. Did Ritz act ethically in making its advertising claims? Who wins? [*Charles of the Ritz Distributing Corp. v. FTC*, 143 F.2d 676 (2d Cir. 1944)]

46.13.   Leon A. Tashof operated a store known as the New York Jewelry Company. The store was located in an area that serves low-income consumers, many of whom have low-paying jobs and have no bank or charge accounts. About 85 percent of the store's sales are made on credit. The store advertised eyeglasses "from $7.50 complete," including "lenses, frames and case." Tashof advertised this sale extensively on radio and in newspapers. Evidence showed that of the 1,400 pairs of eyeglasses sold by the store, fewer than 10 were sold for $7.50; the rest were more expensive glasses. The Federal Trade Commission sued Tashof for engaging in "bait and switch" marketing. Was Tashof's conduct ethical? Who wins? [*Tashof v. Federal Trade Commission*, 437 F.2d 707 (D.C. Cir. 1970)]

CRITICAL LEGAL THINKING WRITING ASSIGNMENT

Read Case A.46 in the Case Appendix [*X-Tra Art, Inc. v. Consumer Product Safety Commission*]. This case is excerpted from the district court opinion. Review and brief the case. In your brief, be sure to answer the following questions:

1. Who were the plaintiffs? Who was the defendant?
2. What product was being sold by the plaintiffs?
3. What act was alleged to have been violated by the plaintiffs?
4. In whose favor did the district court decide the case?

NOTES

1. 21 U.S.C. § 301.
2. 7 U.S.C. § 1621.
3. 21 U.S.C. § 451.
4. 21 U.S.C. § 601.
5. 21 U.S.C. § 1031.
6. 21 U.S.C. § 321.
7. 21 U.S.C. §§ 360(c) et seq.
8. 21 U.S.C. § 346(a).
9. 21 U.S.C. § 348.
10. 21 U.S.C. § 376(a).
11. 21 U.S.C. § 360(b).
12. 21 U.S.C. § 357.
13. 42 U.S.C. § 264.
14. 42 U.S.C. § 263(b).
15. 42 U.S.C. § 263.
16. A consumer who is injured by a defective product can bring a civil action to recover damages for his or her injuries. Product liability is discussed in Chapter 6.
17. 15 U.S.C. § 2051.
18. 15 U.S.C. §§ 1451 et seq.
19. 15 U.S.C. § 1471.
20. 15 U.S.C. §§ 2301 et seq.
21. 15 U.S.C. § 1191.
22. 15 U.S.C. § 1262(e).

23. 15 U.S.C. § 1211.
24. 15 U.S.C. § 68.
25. 15 U.S.C. § 69.
26. 15 U.S.C. § 70.
27. 15 U.S.C. § 2101.
28. 15 U.S.C. §§ 41–51.
29. *Guide on Bait Advertising*, 16 C.F.R. 238 (1968).
30. See California Civil Code § 1689.6 and N.Y. Personal Property Law § 425.
31. 39 U.S.C. § 3009.
32. 15 U.S.C. §§ 1601 et seq.
33. 12 C.F.R. 226.
34. 15 U.S.C. §§ 1667 et seq.
35. 15 U.S.C. § 1637.
36. 15 U.S.C. § 1643.
37. 15 U.S.C. § 1691.
38. 15 U.S.C. §§ 1681 et seq.
39. 15 U.S.C. § 1681.
40. 15 U.S.C. § 1692.

Environmental Protection

Those who hike the Appalachian Trail into Sunfish Pond, New Jersey, and camp or sleep there, or run the Allagash in Maine, or climb the Guadalupes in West Texas, or who canoe and portage the Quentico Superior in Minnesota, certainly should have standing to defend those natural wonders before courts or agencies, though they live 3,000 miles away. Then there will be assurances that all of the forms of life will stand before the court—the pileated woodpecker as well as the coyote and bear, the lemmings as well as the trout in the streams. Those inarticulate members of the ecological group cannot speak. But those people who have so frequented the place as to know its values and wonders will be able to speak for the entire ecological community.

JUSTICE DOUGLAS, DISSENTING OPINION *Sierra Club v. Morton, Secretary of the Interior 31 L.Ed.2d 636 (1972)*

Chapter Objectives

After studying this chapter, you should be able to

1. Describe an environmental impact statement and identify when one is needed.
2. Describe the national ambient air quality standards required by the Clean Air Act.
3. Describe the effluent water standards required by the Clean Water Act.
4. Describe the pollution control technologies that must be installed to prevent air and water pollution.
5. Explain how environmental laws regulate the use of toxic substances.
6. Explain how environmental laws regulate the storage, transport, and disposal of hazardous wastes.
7. Describe the government's authority to recover the cost of cleaning up hazardous waste sites from responsible parties.
8. Describe how the Endangered Species Act protects endangered and threatened species and their habitats.
9. Describe how the Noise Control Act regulates noise pollution.
10. Describe the scope of state environmental protection laws.

Chapter Contents

Business Brief
Although pollution in many forms has been around for centuries, only in recent times have federal and state governments enacted laws prohibiting or limiting many forms of pollution and requiring their cleanup.

In producing and consuming products, businesses and consumers generate air pollution, water pollution, and hazardous and toxic wastes that cause harm to the environment and to human health. Although environmental protection has been a concern since medieval England enacted laws regulating the burning of soft coal, pollution has now reached alarming rates in this country and the world.

This chapter is concerned with how the federal and state governments are trying to contain the levels of pollution and to clean up hazardous waste sites in this country. It examines the scope and impact of the major environmental protection laws applicable to businesses and individuals.

ENVIRONMENTAL PROTECTION

Business Brief
Common law proved ineffectual to regulate and prevent pollution. Therefore federal and state governments enacted environmental protection statutes to control pollution and penalize violators of these statutes.

Under the common law, both individuals and the government could bring a civil suit against the offending party. Individuals could bring a private civil suit based on *private nuisance* to recover damages from the polluting party. The injured party could also sue for an injunction to prevent further pollution by the offending party. The government could bring a lawsuit against a polluter based on the common law theory of *public nuisance*. By the 1950s and 1960s, federal and state governments realized that this approach was not enough to contain the problems caused by pollution and began enacting legislation to protect the environment.

In the 1970s, the federal government began enacting statutes to protect our nation's air and water from pollution. Federal legislation was also enacted to regulate hazardous wastes and to protect wildlife. In many instances, states enacted their own environmental laws that now coexist with federal law as long as they do not directly conflict with the federal law or unduly burden interstate commerce. These laws provide both civil and criminal penalties. The development of such a vast body of law in such a short period of time is unprecedented in U.S. history. Environmental protection is one of the most important, and costly, issues facing business and society today.

Greenpeace is an international organization that engages in activism to protect animals, fish, birds, and the environment. Greenpeace members often use physically combative tactics to block hunters from killing seals.

THE ENVIRONMENTAL PROTECTION AGENCY

In 1970, Congress created the **Environmental Protection Agency (EPA)** to coordinate the implementation and enforcement of the federal environmental protection laws. The EPA has broad rule-making powers to adopt regulations to advance the laws that it is empowered to administer. The agency also has adjudicative powers to hold hearings, make decisions, and order remedies for violations of federal environmental laws. In addition, the EPA can initiate judicial proceedings in court against suspected violators of federal environmental laws.

Environmental Protection Agency (EPA)

An administrative agency created by Congress in 1970 to coordinate the implementation and enforcement of the federal environmental protection laws.

NATIONAL ENVIRONMENTAL POLICY ACT

The **National Environmental Policy Act (NEPA)**[1] which was enacted in 1969, became effective on January 1, 1970. The **Council on Environmental Quality** was created under this act. The NEPA mandates that the federal government consider the "adverse impact" of proposed legislation, rule making, or other federal government action on the environment before the action is implemented.

National Environmental Policy Act (NEPA)

A federal statute enacted in 1969 that mandates that the federal government consider the adverse impact a federal government action would have on the environment before the action is implemented.

Environmental Impact Statement

The NEPA and rules adopted thereunder require that an **environmental impact statement (EIS)** must be prepared for all proposed legislation or major federal action that significantly affects the quality of the human environment. The purpose of the EIS is to provide enough information about the environment to enable the federal government to determine the feasibility of the project. The EIS is also used as evidence in court whenever a federal action is challenged as violating the NEPA or other federal environmental protection laws. Examples of actions that require an EIS include proposals to build a new federally funded highway, to license nuclear plants, and the like.

The EIS must (1) describe the affected environment, (2) describe the impact of the proposed federal action on the environment, (3) identify and discuss alternatives to the proposed action, (4) list the resources that will be committed to the action, and (5) contain a cost-benefit analysis of the proposed action and alternative actions. Expert professionals, such as engineers, geologists, and accountants, may be consulted during the preparation of the EIS.

Once an EIS is prepared, it is subject to public review. The public has 30 days in which to submit comments to the EPA. After the comments have been received and reviewed, the EPA will issue an order that states whether the proposed federal action may proceed. Decisions of the EPA are appealable to the appropriate U.S. court of appeals.

The NEPA does not apply to action by state or local governments or private parties. Most states and many local governments have enacted laws that require an environmental impact statement to be prepared regarding proposed state and local government action as well as private development.

environmental impact statement (EIS)

A document that must be prepared for all proposed legislation or major federal action that significantly affects the quality of the human environment.

AIR POLLUTION

One of the major problems facing this country is **air pollution**. Prior to the advent of the internal combustion engine, most air pollution consisted of smoke from factories and homes. Today, most air pollution is invisible and odorless. The air pollution is caused by both mobile sources (such as automobiles) and stationary sources (such as public utilities, manufacturing facilities, and households).

air pollution

Pollution caused by factories, homes, vehicles, and the like that affects the air.

Clean Air Act

The federal government's first legislation concerning air pollution came in 1955 when it authorized funds for air pollution research. The **Clean Air Act** was enacted in 1963 to assist states in dealing with air pollution.[2] The act was amended in 1970 and 1977 and, most recently, by the **Clean Air Act Amendments of 1990**.[3] The Clean Air Act, as amended, provides comprehensive regulation of air quality in this country.

National Ambient Air Quality Standards

The Clean Air Act directs the EPA to establish **national ambient air quality standards (NAAQS)** for certain pollutants. These standards are set at two different levels: primary (to protect human beings) and secondary (to protect vegetation, matter, climate, visibility, and economic values). Specific standards have been established for carbon monoxide, nitrogen oxide, sulfur oxide, ozone, lead, and particulate matter.

Although the EPA establishes air quality standards, the states are responsible for their enforcement. The federal government has the right to enforce these air pollution standards if the states fail to do so. Each state is required to prepare a *state implementation plan (SIP)* that sets out how the state plans to meet the federal standards. The EPA has divided each state into *air quality control regions (AQCRs)*. Each region is monitored to ensure compliance.

Nonattainment Areas   Regions that do not meet the air quality standards are designated **nonattainment areas**. Nonattainment areas are classified into one of five categories—(1) marginal, (2) moderate, (3) serious, (4) severe, and (5) extreme—based on the degree to which they exceed the ozone standard. Deadlines are established for areas to meet the attainment level. States must submit compliance plans that (1) identify major sources of air pollution and require them to install pollution control equipment, (2) institute permit systems for new stationary sources, and (3) implement inspection programs to monitor mobile sources. States that fail to develop or implement an approved plan are subject to the following sanctions: (1) loss of federal highway funds and (2) limitations on new sources of emissions (e.g., the EPA can prohibit the construction of a new pollution-causing industrial plant in the nonattainment area).

Stationary Sources of Air Pollution

Substantial amounts of air pollution are emitted by **stationary sources** (e.g., industrial plants, oil refineries, public utilities). The Clean Air Act requires states to identify major stationary sources and develop plans to reduce air pollution from these sources. Stationary sources are required to install pollution control equipment according to the following two standards:

1. **Reasonably Available Control Technology (RACT)** States usually require existing stationary sources to install pollution control equipment that meets this standard. Such factors as cost of the equipment and severity of the pollution are considered.
2. **Best Available Control Technology (BACT)** The Clean Air Act requires new, large stationary sources to install pollution control equipment that meet this standard. States can also require existing stationary sources to meet this standard. The EPA issues guidelines as to the best available technology.

Mobile Sources of Air Pollution

Automobile and other vehicle emissions are one of the major sources of air pollution in this country. In an effort to control emissions from these **mobile sources**, the Clean Air Act requires air pollution controls to be installed on motor vehicles. Emission standards have been set for automobiles, trucks, buses, motorcycles, and airplanes. (The Federal Aviation Administration is responsible for enforcing pollution standards for airplanes.)

Clean Air Act
A federal statute enacted in 1963 to assist states in dealing with air pollution.

Clean Air Act Amendments of 1990
Amendments that provide comprehensive regulation of air quality in the United States.

national ambient air quality standards (NAAQS)
Standards for certain pollutants set by the EPA that protect (1) human beings (primary) and (2) vegetation, matter, climate, visibility, and economic values (secondary).

nonattainment areas
Regions that do not meet air quality standards.

stationary sources
Sources of air pollution such as industrial plants, oil refineries, and public utilities.

mobile sources
Sources of air pollution such as automobiles, trucks, buses, motorcycles, and airplanes.

The manufacture of automobiles is regulated to ensure compliance with EPA emission standards. The Clean Air Act requires new automobiles and light-duty trucks to meet air quality control standards. The EPA can require automobile manufacturers to recall and repair or replace pollution control equipment that does not meet these requirements.

In addition, the Clean Air Act authorizes the EPA to regulate air pollution caused by fuel and fuel additives. The sale, use, and transport of leaded fuel or fuel containing leaded additives are prohibited for highway use after 1995, and the production of engines that use leaded fuel was prohibited after model year 1992.

Contemporary Business Application

SMOG SWAPPING

Businesses have long thought that the enforcement of environmental laws was too burdensome and cumbersome, whereas environmentalists argue that current laws have not brought about sufficient reductions in pollution. Today, the "command and control" environmental regulation—the amount of pollution a plant can produce—is giving way to a market-based trading scheme. It is hoped that the new scheme will reduce pollution without unduly burdening businesses.

The **Clean Air Act Amendments of 1990** include a new program that allows companies to trade sulfur dioxide emissions (which are responsible for acid rain). Under this plan, companies still face strict quotas for reducing such emissions, but they are free to satisfy their limits by buying pollution credits from other companies.

Here's how it works: Company A uses all of its 2,000-pound limit, and it wants to add equipment that would increase the amount of emissions it produces. Company B also has a 2,000-pound limit, but it uses only 1,500 pounds. Company A can buy pollution credits from Company B. The credits are deducted in pounds of pollution allowed per day. For every 1.2 pounds of pollution eliminated by the selling company, the program allows the creation of only one pound of pollution by the buying company. This system is designed to reduce overall pollution. Trades cannot happen until the EPA certifies the pollution credits for sale.

The Southern California Air Quality Management District (AQMD), where the air pollution levels exceed federal health standards more than 180 days each year, has also adopted an extensive market-based trading program. The program covers the three pollutants most responsible for smog: sulfur oxide, nitrogen oxide, and reactive organic gas.

There is even a movement at the United Nations to create an international market for trading emission credits for carbon dioxide. Carbon dioxide is the main cause of global warming.

Markets are developing for the trading of pollution credits. For example, the Chicago Board of Trade will offer futures contracts on pollution credits. Manufacturers, refiners, utilities, and speculators would buy and sell pollution credits on these markets. Companies that buy credits can lock in pollution rights for the future.

Businesses argue that the market-based trading of pollution credits will work to reduce pollution in this country. They feel that trading is the best way to solve social and environmental problems at the least cost to society. Critics, most notably environmental groups, contend that the system will be hard to monitor. They also assert that it is immoral to allow companies to buy and sell the right to pollute the environment.

Toxic Air Pollutants

Section 112 of the Clean Air Act requires the EPA to identify **toxic air pollutants** that cause serious illness or death to humans.[4] So far, more than 180 chemicals have been listed as toxic, including asbestos, mercury, vinyl chloride, benzene, beryllium, and radionuclides.

The act requires the EPA to establish standards for these chemicals and requires stationary sources to install *maximum achievable control technology (MACT)* to control

toxic air pollutants
Air pollutants that cause serious illness or death to humans.

emissions of toxic substances. MACT for existing sources is less stringent than it is for new sources. EPA standards for toxic substances are set without regard to economic or technological feasibility.

Contemporary Business Application _____

INDOOR AIR POLLUTION: A FRONTIER FOR ENVIRONMENTAL LITIGATION

Most people who live or work in our country's urban centers have grown to accept air pollution as an unavoidable peril of modern life. What many of these people don't realize, however, is that they should not breathe a sigh of relief upon entering their offices or homes. According to officials of the EPA, the air inside some buildings may be 100 times more polluted than outside air.

Indoor air pollution, or "**sick building syndrome**," has two primary causes. In an effort to reduce dependence on foreign oil, many recently constructed office buildings were overly insulated and built with sealed windows and no outside air ducts. As a result, absolutely no fresh air enters many workplaces. This absence of fresh air can cause headaches, fatigue, and dizziness among workers.

The other chief cause of sick building syndrome, which is believed to affect up to one-third of U.S. office buildings, is hazardous chemicals and construction materials. In the office, these include everything from asbestos to noxious fumes emitted from copy machines, carbonless paper, and cleaning fluids. In the home, radon, an odorless gas that is emitted from the natural breakdown of uranium in soil, poses a particularly widespread danger. Four million to 10 million homes in the United States have radon levels in excess of EPA guidelines. Radon gas damages and may destroy lung tissue. It is estimated that radon causes 20,000 deaths each year.

Indoor air pollution has placed businesses between a rock and a hard place. Employer inactivity in the face of this danger will surely result in higher health-care bills for employee illnesses as doctors increasingly attribute a wide range of symptoms to sick building syndrome. Indoor air pollution also adversely affects worker productivity and morale and increases absenteeism. On the other hand, the costs of eliminating these conditions can be colossal.

Experts predict that sick building syndrome is likely to spawn a flood of litigation, and that a wide range of parties will be sued. Manufacturers, employers, home sellers, builders, engineers, and architects will increasingly be forced to defend themselves against tort and breach of contract actions filed by homeowners, employees, and others affected by indoor air pollution. Federal and state governments may also be dragged into court to pay for defects in their buildings and to defend their regulatory standards. Insurance companies will undoubtedly be drawn into costly lawsuits stemming from indoor air pollution.

Presently, the government has not adopted any regulations governing indoor air quality.

WATER POLLUTION

water pollution
Pollution of lakes, rivers, oceans, and other bodies of water.

Water pollution affects human health, recreation, agriculture, and business. Pollution of waterways by industry and humans has caused severe ecological and environmental problems, including water sources that are unsafe for drinking water, fish, birds, and animals.

The federal government has enacted a comprehensive scheme of statutes and regulations to prevent and control water pollution. The first regulation dates back to the **River and Harbor Act**, which was enacted in 1886. This act, as codified in 1899, established a permit system for the discharge of refuse, wastes, and sewage into the nation's navigable waterways. This permit system was replaced in 1972 by the *National Pollutant Discharge Elimination System (NPDES)*, which requires any person who proposes to discharge pollution into the water to obtain a permit from the EPA. The EPA can deny or set restrictions on such permits.

River and Harbor Act
A federal statute enacted in 1886 that established a permit system for the discharge of refuse, wastes, and sewage into U.S. navigable waterways.

Clean Water Act

In 1948, Congress enacted the **Federal Water Pollution Control Act (FWPCA)** to regulate water pollution. This act was amended several times before it was updated by the Clean Water Act of 1972, the Clean Water Act of 1977, and the Water Quality Act of 1987. The FWPCA, as amended, is simply referred to as the **Clean Water Act**.[5] This act is administered by the EPA.

Pursuant to the Clean Water Act, the EPA has established water quality standards that define which bodies of water can be used for public drinking water, recreation (such as swimming), propagation of fish and wildlife, and agricultural and industrial uses.

States are primarily responsible for enforcing the provisions of the Clean Water Act and EPA regulations adopted thereunder. If a state fails to do so, the federal government may enforce the act.

Point Sources of Water Pollution

The Clean Water Act authorizes the EPA to establish water pollution control standards for **point sources** of water pollution (i.e., mines, manufacturing plants, paper mills, electric utility plants, municipal sewage plants, and other stationary sources of water pollution). Point sources must install pollution control equipment according to the following two standards:

1. **Best Practical Control Technology (BPCT)** Existing point sources are required to immediately install pollution control equipment that meets this standard. Such factors as the severity of the pollution, time necessary to install the equipment, and the cost of the pollution control equipment are considered.
2. **Best Available Control Technology (BACT)** This refers to the most effective pollution control equipment available. New point sources are required to meet this standard, regardless of cost. The EPA has established timetables for existing point sources to install BACT equipment.

The EPA issues guidelines as to the best available technologies. Dischargers of pollutants are required to keep records, maintain monitoring equipment, and keep samples of discharges.

In the following case, the court found numerous violations of the Clean Water Act.

> **Federal Water Pollution Control Act (FWPCA)**
> A federal statute enacted in 1948 that regulates water pollution.
>
> **Clean Water Act**
> The final version of the FWPCA.
>
> **point sources**
> Sources of water pollution such as paper mills, manufacturing plants, electric utility plants, and sewage plants.

Natural Resources Defense Council, Inc. v. Texaco Refining and Marketing, Inc.
800 F.Supp. 1 (1992)
United States District Court, Delaware

CASE 47.1

FACTS
Texaco Refining and Marketing, Inc. (Texaco), owns and operates an oil refinery on the banks of the Delaware River. The refinery processes approximately 150,000 barrels of crude oil per day and draws an average of about 300 million gallons of water per day from the Delaware River for use in the refinery process. Some of the water comes into contact with raw materials or the products produced by the refinery and absorbs contaminants. This water is routed through the refinery's treatment plant before being discharged into the river. Some pollutants remain in the processed water, however.

Pursuant to the Clean Water Act, the government issued a permit to Texaco authorizing the refinery to discharge limited quantities of various pollutants into the Delaware River. The permit specified parameters on each pollutant and required Texaco to sample each parameter at set intervals, using specified testing methods. The results of the tests were to be reported monthly.

The Natural Resources Defense Council, Inc. (NRDC), an environmental organization, brought a citizens' suit against Texaco under the Clean Water Act. The suit alleged violations of the permit. The NRDC sought the imposition

(case continues)

of a civil fine on Texaco (the Clean Water Act provides for fines up to $25,000 per day) and a permanent injunction against future violations of the permit. The district court found Texaco liable for 365 violations during the period March 1983 through February 1991. This amounted to 3,360 days of violations.

ISSUE

What penalty should be assessed against Texaco for its violations of the Clean Water Act?

IN THE LANGUAGE OF THE COURT

Roth, Circuit Judge *We must determine what civil penalties are appropriate in light of the violations committed by Texaco. Our calculations give us a total of 3360 violations days for which a fine will be imposed. We find that these violations were fairly serious in terms of their size, duration, and frequency. The seriousness of these violations is also linked to the extent to which they threatened harm to the River's ecosystem.*

We reject Texaco's contention that no penalty is appropriate. At trial there was evidence that Texaco made no attempt to understand the impact of its discharges on the waters of Delaware and/or the United States. The fact that Texaco has ignored its responsibility to monitor the impact of its violations argues in favor of imposition of a heavier fine. Texaco has not demonstrated that a large penalty would have an adverse impact on the company. In light of the factual findings, the amount of the fine

for each violation day will be $500, multiplied by the 3360 days of violation. This results in a total fine to be imposed of $1,680,000.

We find that, given the plaintiffs' success in this court, the danger of irreparable harm and the inadequacy of legal remedies, and the public interest in protection of the nation's waters, these factors all weigh in favor of granting the plaintiffs' request for injunctive relief. Texaco is hereby enjoined from further violations of the 1989 permit and is directed to comply with its investigatory, reporting, and monitoring provisions.

DECISION AND REMEDY

The district court ordered Texaco to pay a $1,680,000 fine into the U.S. Treasury and issued an injunction permanently enjoining Texaco from further violations of the discharge permit.

Case Questions

Critical Legal Thinking Should companies be allowed to discharge any pollutants into the nation's waterways? Why or why not?

Ethics Were Texaco's actions socially responsible in letting the violations continue for such a long period of time?

Business Application Was the amount of the fine imposed on Texaco sufficient? Or should a greater monetary fine have been imposed by the court?

Thermal Pollution

thermal pollution
Heated water or material discharged into waterways that upsets the ecological balance and decreases the oxygen content.

The Clean Water Act expressly forbids **thermal pollution** because the discharge of heated waters or materials into the nation's waterways may upset the ecological balance, decrease the oxygen content of water, and harm fish, birds, and animals that use the waterways.[6] Sources of thermal pollution (such as electric utility companies and manufacturing plants) are subject to the provisions of the Clean Water Act and regulations adopted by the EPA.

Wetlands

wetlands
Areas that are inundated or saturated by surface water or ground water that support vegetation typically adapted for life in such conditions.

Wetlands are defined as areas that are inundated or saturated by surface water or ground water that support vegetation typically adapted for life in saturated soil conditions. Wetlands include swamps, marshes, bogs, and similar areas that support birds, animals, and vegetative life. The Clean Water Act forbids the filling or dredging of wetlands unless a permit has been obtained from the **Army Corps of Engineers (Corps)**. The Corps is empowered to adopt regulations and conduct administrative proceedings to enforce the act.

Safe Drinking Water Act

Safe Drinking Water Act
A federal statute enacted in 1974 and amended in 1986 that authorizes the EPA to establish national primary drinking water standards.

The **Safe Drinking Water Act**,[7] which was enacted in 1974 and amended in 1986, authorizes the EPA to establish national primary drinking water standards (minimum quality of water for human consumption). The act also prohibits the dumping of wastes into wells used for drinking water. The states are primarily responsible for enforcing the act. If a state fails to do so, the federal government can enforce the act.

ILLEGAL DUMPING OF POLLUTANTS

Environmental laws establish methods and procedures for treating and disposing of contaminated wastes. Persons and businesses sometimes intentionally violate environmental laws by secretly dumping polluted materials into the environment. Consider the following case.

Mark Irby was plant manager of a waste-water treatment plant. The record shows that Irby ordered employees of the plant to bypass the treatment system after hours and to discharge approximately 500,000 gallons of raw untreated sewage and partially treated sludge sewage at least twice a week for two years into the Reedy River. The court found that these discharges caused environmental damage. Irby was charged with criminal violation of the Clean Water Act. The jury convicted him of six criminal violations of the act, and the district court sentenced him to

the maximum allowable jail sentence (33 months). Irby challenged his sentence.

The court of appeals held that Irby exercised decision-making authority in directing the employees of the waste-water treatment plant to discharge the untreated sewage into the Reedy River. The court also held that the offense resulted in an ongoing, continuous, and repetitive discharge of pollutants into the environment, thus justifying the imposition of the 33 months of jail time. The court stated, "There was absolutely no acceptance of responsibility in this case. No remorse whatsoever was shown by Irby." [*United States v. Irby*, 944 F.2d 902 (4th Cir. 1991)]

1. Did Irby act ethically in this case?
2. What is the incentive for businesses and organizations to avoid environmental laws?

Ocean Dumping

The **Marine Protection, Research, and Sanctuaries Act**,[8] enacted in 1972, extended environmental protection to the oceans. It (1) requires a permit for dumping wastes and other foreign materials into ocean waters and (2) establishes marine sanctuaries in ocean waters as far seaward as the edge of the Continental Shelf and in the Great Lakes and their connecting waters.

Marine Protection, Research, and Sanctuaries Act

A federal statute enacted in 1972 that extends environmental protection to the oceans.

Oil Spills

The Clean Water Act authorizes the U.S. government to clean up oil spills and spills of other hazardous substances in ocean waters within 12 miles of the shore and on the Continental Shelf and to recover the cleanup costs from responsible parties.

THE OIL POLLUTION ACT

In March 1989, the *Exxon Valdez*, an oil supertanker, ran aground in Prince William Sound in Alaska, spilling millions of gallons of oil into the water. Exxon and the oil industry were not prepared to respond to this emergency. The first cleanup barge did not reach the site until 14 hours after the oil spill. The response was totally inadequate, and the oil eventually contaminated 1,100 miles of shoreline. Tens of thousands of dead animals and birds lay strewn on the shore, and there were unknown numbers of dead fish.

Two factors—the devastation caused by the *Exxon Valdez* catastrophe and the oil industry's illpreparedness to address oil spills—caused Congress to enact the **Oil Pollution Act of 1990 (OPA)**. This act, which is administered by the U.S. Coast Guard, requires the oil industry to adopt procedures that can more readily respond to oil spills.

The OPA contains strict requirements for constructing oil tankers. It requires new ships to have double hulls and phases out single-hull tankers between 1995 to 2010. Barges must be double-hulled by 2015. The tanker industry

(box continues)

is upset over the double-hull requirement and is seeking a less-expensive means to ensure protection in case of a mishap.

The OPA also requires each tanker owner–operator to establish an oil pollution cleanup contingency plan. The Coast Guard has issued regulations for emergency response plans by tankers operating in U.S. waters. Under the OPA and Coast Guard regulations, tanker owner–operators must have enough personnel and equipment to handle a "worst case" spill of an entire cargo in "adverse" weather conditions. They will also have to contract with an oil-spill response company. In response, 20 major oil companies funded the creation of the Marine Spill Response

Corporation. Other response firms are also being set up by other oil companies.

The Coast Guard must issue a certificate to a tanker owner–operator before oil may be brought to the United States. To obtain the certificate, the tanker owner–operator must prove that it is fully insured to cover any liability that may occur from an oil spill.

It is hoped that the emergency response procedures mandated by the OPA will not be needed. But at least this time the mechanism will be in place to respond more quickly and adequately to such a spill so that an environmental catastrophe the size of that caused by the *Exxon Valdez* will never occur again.

Toxic Substances

toxic substances

Chemicals used for agricultural, industrial, and mining uses that cause injury to humans, birds, animals, fish, and vegetation.

The use of chemicals for agricultural, industrial, and mining uses has greatly increased productivity in this country. Unfortunately, many of these chemicals contain **toxic substances** that cause cancer, birth defects, and other health-related problems in human beings, as well as injury or death to birds, animals, fish, and vegetation. Because of these dangers, the federal government has enacted legislation to regulate the use of toxic substances. Two of these statutes are discussed in the following paragraphs.

Insecticide, Fungicide, and Rodenticide Act

Insecticide, Fungicide, and Rodenticide Act

A federal statute that requires pesticides, herbicides, fungicides, and rodenticides to be registered with the EPA; the EPA may deny, suspend, or cancel registration.

Farmers and ranchers use chemical pesticides, herbicides, fungicides, and rodenticides to kill insects, pests, and weeds. Evidence shows that the use of some of these chemicals on food, and their residual accumulation in soil, poses health hazards. In 1947, Congress enacted the **Insecticide, Fungicide, and Rodenticide Act**, which gave the federal government authority to regulate pesticides and related chemicals. This act, which was substantially amended in 1972,[9] is administered by the EPA.

Under the act, pesticides must be registered with the EPA before they can be sold. The EPA may deny registration, certify either general or restricted use, or set limits on the amount of chemical residue permitted on crops sold for human or animal consumption. The EPA has authority to register and inspect pesticide manufacturing facilities.

The EPA may suspend the registration of a registered pesticide that it finds poses an imminent danger or emergency. If the EPA finds that the use of a registered pesticide poses environmental risks (but not imminent danger), it may initiate a proceeding to cancel the registration of the pesticide. After reviewing the evidence, the EPA may cancel a registration if it finds use of the pesticide would cause unreasonably adverse effects on the environment.

Toxic Substances Control Act

Toxic Substances Control Act

A federal statute enacted in 1976 that requires manufacturers and processors to test new chemicals to determine their effect on human health and the environment before the EPA will allow them to be marketed.

Many chemical compounds that are used in the manufacture of plastics and products are toxic (e.g., PCBs and asbestos). Hundreds of new chemicals and chemical compounds that may be toxic are discovered each year. In 1976, Congress enacted the **Toxic Substances Control Act**[10] and gave the EPA authority to administer the act.

The act requires manufacturers and processors to test new chemicals to determine the effect on human health and the environment and to report the results to the EPA before they can be marketed. The EPA may limit or prohibit the manufacture and sale of toxic substances, or remove them from commerce, if it finds that they pose an imminent hazard or an unreasonable risk of injury to human health or the environment. The EPA also requires special labeling of toxic substances.

International Perspective

TRANSBORDER POLLUTION

Countries can adopt laws to govern, prevent, and clean up pollution occurring within their own borders. However, in some instances, another country is the source of the pollution. This is called **transborder pollution**.

Whether the affected country has any recourse against the polluting country depends on whether the two countries have entered into a treaty concerning such an occurrence, and whether the polluting country wants to abide by the provisions of the treaty. For example, the United States and Canada have entered into several treaties that coordinate their efforts to control transborder pollution. The two countries have agreed to regulate transborder air pollution (particularly acid rain) and water pollution. The United States is also currently negotiating with Mexico for Mexico to strengthen its environmental laws. Criticism has been leveled at many large U.S. companies that have set up manufacturing plants in Mexico to avoid the stringent environmental laws in the United States.

One of the most important international environmental issues focuses on the rain forests in Brazil and other South American countries. The rain forests are being clear-cut at an alarming rate. Environmental activists are trying to save the rain forests, but to no avail. It is difficult for countries like the United States and those of Western Europe, who have cut down over 90 percent of their own forests, to try to convince Brazil and its neighbors not to cut down the rain forests.

In June 1992, an **Earth Summit** was held in Rio de Janeiro, Brazil. Most countries sent representatives to this conference. The countries at the summit signed the Rio Declaration, which directs signatory nations to enact effective environmental legislation. In addition, two treaties emerged from the summit, the Climate Change Control Convention (CCCC) and the Convention on Biological Diversity (CBD). The focus of the CCCC is the stabilization of the greenhouse gas concentration in the atmosphere that is causing a hole in the ozone layer. The CBD is directed at ensuring that patents and inventions do not harm the environment.

It is obvious that environmental problems are not confined to individual countries. International cooperation is necessary to protect the environment and prevent global pollution.

*H*AZARDOUS WASTE

Wastes, which often contain hazardous substances that can harm the environment or pose a danger to human health, are generated by agriculture, mining, industry, other businesses, and households. Wastes consist of garbage, sewage, industrial discharges, old equipment, and such. The mishandling and disposal of **hazardous wastes** can cause air, water, and **land pollution**.

Prior to the mid-1970s, the disposal of solid wastes was generally regarded as a problem for local governments. However, discovery of thousands of dump sites and landfills containing hazardous wastes (such as the Love Canal in New York) caused concern at the federal level. To prevent future problems, and to assist in cleaning up past problems, Congress enacted the statutes discussed in the following paragraphs to deal with hazardous wastes.

Resource Conservation and Recovery Act

In 1976, Congress enacted the **Resource Conservation and Recovery Act (RCRA)**,[11] which regulates the disposal of new hazardous wastes. This act, which has been amended several times, authorizes the EPA to regulate facilities that generate, treat, store, transport, and dispose of "hazardous" wastes. States have primary responsibility for implementing the standards established by the act and EPA regulations. If states fail to act, the EPA can enforce the act.

The act defines hazardous waste as a solid waste that may cause or significantly contribute to an increase in mortality or serious illness or pose a hazard to human health or

hazardous waste
Solid waste that may cause or significantly contribute to an increase in mortality or serious illness or pose a hazard to human health or the environment if improperly managed.

land pollution
Pollution of the land that is generally caused by hazardous waste being disposed of in an improper manner.

Resource Conservation and Recovery Act (RCRA)
A federal statute that authorizes the EPA to regulate facilities that generate, treat, store, transport, and dispose of hazardous wastes.

the environment if improperly managed. The EPA has designated substances that are toxic, radioactive, or corrosive or that ignite as hazardous and can add to the list of hazardous wastes as needed.

Pursuant to its authority under the act, the EPA has implemented a "cradle to grave" tracking system and regulation of hazardous substances. Under the act, anyone who generates, treats, stores, or transports hazardous wastes must obtain a government permit to do so. It also establishes standards and procedures for the safe treatment, storage, disposal, and transportation of hazardous wastes. Under the act, the EPA is authorized to regulate underground storage facilities, such as underground gasoline tanks.

COMPREHENSIVE ENVIRONMENTAL RESPONSE, COMPENSATION, AND LIABILITY ACT (SUPERFUND)

<div class="sidebar">

Comprehensive Environmental Response, Compensation, and Liability Act (CERCLA)

A federal statute enacted in 1980 and amended in 1986 that gives the federal government a mandate to deal with hazardous wastes that have been spilled, stored, or abandoned; commonly called *Superfund.*

Business Brief

The EPA has identified more than 25,000 sites where hazardous wastes have been disposed of, stored, spilled, or abandoned that require cleanup. The EPA has ranked these sites by severity of the risk.

Business Brief

The Superfund imposes *strict liability* on businesses and other property owners to clean up contaminated property. This will cost businesses billions of dollars each year.

right to know provision

A provision in Superfund that requires businesses to (1) disclose the presence of certain listed chemicals to the community, (2) annually disclose emissions of chemical substances released into the environment, and (3) immediately notify the government of spills, accidents, and other emergencies involving hazardous substances.

</div>

In 1980, Congress enacted the **Comprehensive Environmental Response, Compensation, and Liability Act (CERCLA),**[12] which is commonly called "Superfund." The act, which was significantly amended in 1986, is administered by the EPA. The act gave the federal government a mandate to deal with hazardous wastes that have been spilled, stored, or abandoned.

Designated Hazardous Waste Sites

The Superfund requires the EPA to (1) identify sites in the United States where hazardous wastes had been disposed, stored, abandoned, or spilled and (2) rank these sites regarding the severity of the risk. More than 25,000 sites have been identified. The EPA considers such factors as the types of hazardous waste, the toxicity of the wastes, the types of pollution (air, water, land, or other pollution) caused by the wastes, the number of people potentially affected by the risk, and other factors when it ranks the sites. The hazardous waste sites with the highest ranking are put on a National Priority List. The sites on this list receive first consideration for cleanup. Before the cleanup can begin, though, engineering and scientific studies are conducted to determine the best method for cleaning up the waste site. The EPA has the authority to clean up hazardous priority or nonpriority sites quickly to prevent fire, explosion, contamination of drinking water, or other imminent danger.

The Superfund provides for the creation of a fund to finance the cleanup of hazardous waste sites (hence the name *Superfund*). The fund is financed through taxes on chemicals, feedstocks, motor fuels, and other products that contain hazardous substances.

Liability for Cleanup of Superfund Sites

The EPA can order a responsible party to clean up a hazardous waste site. If that party fails to do so, the EPA can clean up the site and recover the cost of the cleanup. The Superfund imposes strict liability, that is, liability without fault. The EPA can recover the cost of the cleanup from (1) the generator who deposited the wastes, (2) the transporter of the wastes to the site, (3) the owner of the site at the time of the disposal, and (4) the current owner and operator of the site.[13] Liability is *joint and several*; that is, a person who is responsible for only a fraction of the hazardous waste may be liable for all the cleanup costs. The Superfund permits states and private parties who clean up hazardous waste sites to seek reimbursement from the fund.

The Superfund contains a **right to know provision** that requires businesses to (1) disclose the presence of certain listed chemicals to the community, (2) annually disclose emissions of chemical substances released into the environment, and (3) immediately notify the government of spills, accidents, and other emergencies involving hazardous substances.

Entrepreneur and the Law

SUPERFUND LAW CLEANS CAR WASH OWNER

Jim Wilson nearly forgot that he once owned a car wash in Sherman Oaks, California, 30 years ago until he received a bill in the mail from the Environmental Protection Agency (EPA) for $142,500. The bill was his share of the $600-million cost of cleaning up a toxic waste site in Monterey Park, some 20 miles from the site of his prior car wash. The EPA had designated the Monterey Park location, which had been a waste disposal site, as a "Superfund site" and was now sending bills to about 700 prior users to recover money to clean up the site. By designating a Superfund site, the EPA is responsible by law to clean up the site and seek compensation from "polluters" to pay for the cleanup costs.

What was Jim Wilson's sin? He had sent soapy nontoxic carwash water to the Monterey Park dump site in the 1960s. Wilson correctly argues that what he did was legal under existing laws when he did it. The Superfund law, however, was drafted to apply retroactively; that is, a party can be held liable for violating the law for actions it took before the Superfund law was enacted by Congress. Although the retroactive application of the law has been challenged, the federal courts have held that the Superfund law does not violate the Due Process Clause of the U.S. Constitution.

Superfund is a tort law that imposes *strict liability*, or liability without fault, and *joint and several liability*, which means that each individual defendant is legally liable for the entire cleanup cost no matter how small that defendant's pollution was relative to all the pollution at the site. Thus, under these two legal principles, any defendant could be held liable for the entire cleanup cost of an EPA Superfund site without being found to be at fault. Superfund law also allows liable private parties to sue to recover from other polluters for their share of the cleanup costs. Thus, if a party should decide to ignore the EPA's bill, it can be sued by other polluters.

If a party settles with the EPA by paying the bill sent to it, it generally is not liable beyond this amount. If a party does not pay the bill, it risks lawsuits from the EPA and other polluters and could be assessed liability much greater than the billed amount. Persons who receive EPA Superfund bills claim that this law is unfair because the EPA has a hammer that forces them to pay. In addition, if a party decides to fight the bill, it could pay hundreds of thousands of dollars in legal fees with little probability of winning.

Wilson and others like him claim that they have been steamcleaned by the EPA. The EPA claims that Wilson owes a duty to clean the EPA Superfund site as well as he did cars.

NUCLEAR WASTE

Nuclear-powered fuel plants create radioactive wastes that maintain a high level of *radioactivity*. Radioactivity can cause injury and death to humans and other life and can also cause severe damage to the environment. Accidents, human error, faulty construction, and such, all can be causes of **radiation pollution**.

Regulation of nuclear energy in this country is primarily placed with the following two federal agencies:

1. **Nuclear Regulatory Commission** The **Nuclear Regulatory Commission (NRC)**, which was created by Congress in 1977, licenses the construction and opening of commercial nuclear power plants. It continually monitors the operation of nuclear power plants and may close a plant if safety violations are found.
2. **EPA** The EPA is empowered to set standards for radioactivity in the environment and to regulate the disposal of radioactive waste. The EPA also regulates thermal pollution from nuclear power plants and emissions from uranium mines and mills.

Currently, nuclear wastes are stored on an interim basis at the power plants that generated the wastes or other temporary sites. The **Nuclear Waste Policy Act of 1982**[14] mandates that the federal government select and develop a permanent site for the disposal of nuclear wastes.

radiation pollution
Emissions from radioactive wastes that can cause injury and death to humans and other life and can cause severe damage to the environment.

Nuclear Regulatory Commission (NRC)
Federal agency that licenses the construction and opening of commercial nuclear power plants.

Nuclear Waste Policy Act of 1982
A federal statute that says the federal government must select and develop a permanent site for the disposal of nuclear waste.

*P*reservation of Wildlife

Many species of animals are endangered or threatened with extinction. The reduction of certain species of wildlife may be caused by environmental pollution, real estate development, or hunting.

Endangered Species Act

Endangered Species Act

A federal statute enacted in 1973 that protects "endangered" and "threatened" species of animals.

All animals are equal, but some animals are more equal than others.

George Orwell
Animal Farm (1945)

The **Endangered Species Act** was enacted in 1973.[15] The act, as amended, protects "endangered" and "threatened" species of animals. The secretary of the interior is empowered to declare a form of wildlife "endangered" or "threatened." The act requires the EPA and the Department of Commerce to designate "critical habitats" for each endangered and threatened species. Real estate and other development in these areas is prohibited or severely limited. The secretary of commerce is empowered to enforce the provisions of the act as to marine species.

In addition, the Endangered Species Act, which applies to both government and private persons, prohibits the "taking" of any endangered species. Taking is defined as an act intended to "harass, harm, pursue, hunt, shoot, wound, kill, trap, capture, or collect" an endangered animal.

Other Federal Laws That Protect Wildlife

Numerous other federal laws protect wildlife. These include (1) the Migratory Bird Treaty Act, (2) the Bald Eagle Protection Act, (3) the Wild Free-Roaming Horses and Burros Act, (4) the Marine Mammal Protection Act, (5) the Migratory Bird Conservation Act, (6) the Fishery Conservation and Management Act, (7) the Fish and Wildlife Coordination Act, and (8) the National Wildlife Refuge System. Many states have enacted statutes that protect and preserve wildlife.

In the following case, the U.S. Supreme Court enjoined the operation of a dam to save an endangered species of fish.

Tennessee Valley Authority v. Hill, Secretary of the Interior
437 U.S. 153, 98 S.Ct. 2279 (1978)
United States Supreme Court

CASE 47.2

FACTS

The Tennessee Valley Authority (TVA) is a wholly owned public corporation of the United States that operates a series of dams, reservoirs, and water projects that provide electric power, irrigation, and flood control to areas in several southern states. In 1967, with appropriations from Congress, the TVA began construction of the Tellico Dam on the Little Tennessee River. When completed, the dam would impound water covering 16,500 acres, thereby converting the river's shallow, fast-flowing waters into a deep reservoir over 30 miles in length. Construction of the dam continued until 1977, when it was completed.

In 1973, a University of Tennessee ichthyologist found a previously unknown species of perch called the Percina (Imostoma) Tansai—or "snail darter"—in the Little Tennessee River. After further investigation, it was determined that approximately 10,000 to 15,000 of these 3-inch, tannish-colored fish existed in the river's waters that would be flooded by the operation of the Tellico Dam. The snail darter was not found anywhere else in the world. It feeds exclusively on snails and requires substantial oxygen, both supplied by the fast-moving waters of the Little Tennessee River. The impounding of the water behind the Tellico Dam would destroy the snail darter's food and oxygen supplies, thus causing its extinction. Evidence was introduced showing that the TVA could not, at that time, successfully transplant the snail darter to any other habitat.

Also in 1973, Congress enacted the Endangered Species Act (Act). The Act authorizes the secretary of the interior (Secretary) to declare species of animal life "endangered" and to identify the "critical habitat" of these creatures. When a species or its habitat is so listed, Section 7 of the Act mandates that the Secretary take such action as is necessary to ensure that actions of the federal government do not jeopardize the continued existence of such endangered species. The Secretary declared the snail darter an endangered species and the area that would be affected by the dam its critical habitat.

Congress continued to appropriate funds for the construction of the dam, which was completed at a cost of over $100 million. In 1976, a regional association of biological scientists, a Tennessee conservation group, and several individuals filed an action seeking to enjoin the TVA from closing the gates of the dam and impounding the water in the reservoir on the grounds that those actions would violate Section 7 of the Act by causing the extinction of the snail darter. The district court held in favor of the TVA. The court of appeals reversed and remanded with instructions to the district court to issue a permanent injunction halting the operation of the Tellico Dam. The TVA appealed to the U.S. Supreme Court.

ISSUE

Would the TVA be in violation of the Endangered Species Act if it operated the Tellico Dam?

IN THE LANGUAGE OF THE COURT

Burger, Chief Justice   It may seem curious to some that the survival of a relatively small number of 3-inch fish among all the countless millions of species extant would require the permanent halting of a virtually completed dam for which Congress has expended more than $100 million. We conclude, however, that the explicit provisions of the Endangered Species Act required precisely this result.

One would be hard pressed to find a statutory provision whose terms were any plainer than those in Section 7 of the Endangered Species Act. Its very words affirmatively command all federal agencies to ensure that actions authorized, funded, or carried out by them do not jeopardize the continued existence of an endangered species or result in the destruction or modification of habitat of such species. This language admits no exception. Nonetheless, petitioner TVA urges that the Act cannot reasonably be inter-

preted as applying to a federal project that was well under way when Congress passed the Endangered Species Act of 1973. To sustain that position, however, we would be forced to ignore the ordinary meaning of plain language.

Examination of the language, history, and structure of the legislation under review here indicates beyond doubt that Congress intended endangered species to be afforded the highest of priorities. As it was passed, the Endangered Species Act of 1973 represented the most comprehensive legislation for the preservation of endangered species ever enacted by any nation. Virtually all dealings with endangered species, including taking, possession, transportation, and sale, were prohibited. Section 7 of the Act, which of course is relied upon by respondents in this case, provides a particularly good gauge of congressional intent.

DECISION AND REMEDY

The Supreme Court held that the Endangered Species Act prohibited the impoundment of the Little Tennessee River by the Tellico Dam. Affirmed.

NOTE

Eventually, after substantial research and investigation, it was determined that the snail darter could live in another habitat that was found for it. After the snail darter was removed, at government expense, to this new location, the TVA was permitted to close the gates of the Tellico Dam and begin its operation.

Case Questions

Critical Legal Thinking   Should the law protect endangered species? Why or why not?

Ethics   Did the TVA act ethically in this case by completing construction of the dam?

Business Application   Do you think the cost of constructing the Tellico Dam ($100 million) should have been considered by the Court in reaching its decision?

$\mathcal{N}$OISE POLLUTION

Unwanted sound affects almost every member of society on a daily basis. The sources of **noise pollution** include airplanes, manufacturing plants, motor vehicles, construction equipment, gardeners, radios, toys, automobile alarms, and such. Noise pollution causes hearing loss, loss of sleep, depression, and other emotional and psychological symptoms and injuries.

noise pollution

Unwanted sound from planes, manufacturing plants, motor vehicles, construction equipment, stereos, and the like.

Noise Control Act

The **Noise Control Act**,[16] enacted in 1972, authorizes the EPA to establish noise standards for products sold in the United States. The EPA, jointly with the Federal Aviation Administration (FAA), establishes noise limitations on new aircraft. The EPA, jointly with the Department of Transportation, regulates noise emissions from trucks, railroads,

Noise Control Act

A federal statute enacted in 1972 that authorizes the EPA to establish noise standards for products sold in the United States.

and interstate carriers. Other federal agencies also regulate noise pollution. For example, the Occupational Safety and Health Administration (OSHA) regulates noise levels in the workplace.

The **Quiet Communities Act**[17] authorizes the federal government to provide financial and technical assistance to state and local governments in controlling noise pollution. The act, which was enacted in 1978, is administered by the EPA.

Ethical Perspective

DISCLOSING ENVIRONMENTAL LIABILITIES TO SHAREHOLDERS

In the past, most corporations did not disclose environmental liabilities in the financial statements given to shareholders and others. As of 1992, the Securities and Exchange Commission (SEC) adopted rules requiring companies to report their environmental liabilities in their financial statements. The SEC and the EPA share information concerning corporations' compliance with environmental laws. Failure to disclose environmental liabilities under the new rules subjects violators to civil and criminal penalties.

In developing a program to access and report environmental liabilities, companies should take the following steps:

- Designate a senior officer to be responsible for the environmental disclosure process. This environmental officer should report directly to the president and the board of directors.
- Create a committee of the board of directors to oversee the environmental compliance and disclosure process of the company.

- Retain outside environmental consultants, if feasible, to assist in the data gathering, evaluation, and disclosure process. This will lead to a more objective assessment of environmental liabilities.
- Review the company's environmental exposure and make a list of the important environmental problems facing the company.
- Decide which environmental problems are "material" and must be disclosed under SEC rules. Decide whether additional information should be disclosed.
- Document what the company is doing to rectify its environmental problems. Also document why the company thought it was doing the right thing in taking the action it took.
- Prepare the environmental disclosure report as required by the SEC and include the relevant information from this report in the financial statements of the company.
- Monitor new developments and reassess whether additional disclosures have to be periodically made to the SEC, EPA, shareholders, and others.

STATE ENVIRONMENTAL PROTECTION LAWS

Business Brief

States are entitled to set pollution standards that are stricter than federal requirements.

Many state and local governments have enacted statutes and ordinances to protect the environment. For example, most states require that an EIS or report be prepared for any proposed state action. In addition, under their police power to protect the "health, safety, and welfare" of their residents, many states require private industry to prepare EISs for proposed developments.

Some states have enacted special environmental statutes to protect unique areas within their boundaries. For example, Florida has enacted laws to protect the Everglades, and California has enacted laws to protect its Pacific Ocean coastline. State environmental protection law must be consulted by businesses before engaging in major developments.

Working the Web

Environmental Protection Agency The mission of the U.S. Environmental Protection Agency is to "protect human health and to safeguard the environment." Here, you can find out about projects and programs, researchers and scientists, children's health, and more.

Visit at **www.epa.gov**

Environmental Health Information Service This Web site is sponsored by the National Institute of Health and the National Toxicology Program. It contains publications, features, and databases dealing with health issues.

Visit at **ehis.niehs.nih.gov**

Practicing Attorney's Home Page—Environmental Law Although this is a California-based home page, this site has hundreds of links to environmental law sources.

Visit at **www.legalethics.com/pa/enviro/environ. htm**

WWW Virtual Library—Environment The Virtual Library is a collection of different subject-based "libraries" of Internet links. It was developed to keep track and organize Web pages. Each virtual library is divided by subject.

Visit at **earthsystems.org/Environment.html**

CYBER EXERCISES

1. Using the Environmental Protection Agency Web site, find out whether the EPA sponsors programs for Indian tribes.

2. Does the EHIS database have any information on rodents?

3. Using the Practicing Attorneys Home Page— Environmental Law, find out what CANCERLIT is.

4. Can you find information on the biosphere using the WWW Virtual Library—Environment?

CASES AND EXERCISES

CRITICAL LEGAL THINKING CASES

47.1. The U.S. Forest Service is responsible for managing the country's national forests for recreational and other purposes. This includes issuing special use permits to private companies to operate ski areas on federal lands. Sandy Butte is a 6,000-foot mountain located in the Okanogan National Forest in Okanogan County, Washington. Sandy Butte, like the Methow Valley it overlooks, is a pristine, unspoiled, sparsely populated area located within the North Cascades National Park. Large populations of mule deer and other animals exist in the park.

In 1978, Methow Recreation, Inc. (MRI), applied to the Forest Service for a special use permit to develop and operate its proposed Early Winters Ski Resort on Sandy Butte and a 1,165-acre parcel of private land it had acquired adjacent to the National Forest. The proposed development would make use of approximately 3,900 acres of Sandy Butte to provide up to 16 ski

lifts capable of accommodating 10,500 skiers at one time. Is an environmental impact statement required? [*Robertson v. Methow Valley Citizens Council*, 490 U.S. 332, 109 S.Ct. 1835 (1989)]

47.2. Pursuant to the Clean Air Act, the state of New Mexico divided its territory into eight air quality control regions, one of which consisted of the city of Albuquerque and parts of three counties (AQCR 2). AQCR 2 was a nonattainment area for purposes of carbon monoxide (CO). The act requires states to prepare and submit a state implementation plan (SIP) showing how it will attain compliance and have the plan approved by the EPA. As part of the plan, the state must implement a vehicle emission control inspection and maintenance program (I/M program). New Mexico filed an SIP but failed to implement an enforceable I/M program. The EPA engaged in formal, public rule making, disapproved New

Mexico's SIP, and imposed sanctions by cutting off certain federal funds that New Mexico would have otherwise received. New Mexico challenged the EPA's action. Who wins? [*New Mexico Environmental Improvement Division v. Thomas, Administrator, U.S. Environmental Protection Agency,* 789 F.2d 825 (10th Cir. 1986)]

47.3. Pilot Petroleum Associates, Inc., and various affiliated companies (Pilot) distribute gasoline to retail gasoline stations in the state of New York. Pilot owns some of these stations and leases them out to individual operators who are under contract to purchase gasoline from Pilot. At various times during 1984, the EPA took samples of gasoline from five different service stations to which Pilot had sold unleaded gasoline. These samples showed that Pilot had delivered "unleaded gasoline that contained amounts of lead in excess of that permitted by the Clean Air Act and EPA regulations." The United States brought criminal charges against Pilot for violating the act and EPA regulations and sought fines from Pilot. Who wins? [*United States v. Pilot Petroleum Associates, Inc.,* 712 F.Supp. 1077 (E.D.N.Y. 1989)]

47.4. Placer mining is a method used to mine for gold in streambeds of Alaska. The miner removes soil, mud, and clay from the streambed, places it in an on-site sluice box, and separates the gold from the other matter by forcing water through the paydirt. The water in the sluice box is discharged into the stream, causing aesthetic and water quality impacts on the water both in the immediate vicinity and downstream. Toxic metals, including arsenic, cadmium, lead, zinc, and copper, are found in higher concentrations in streams where mining occurs than in nonmining streams.

In 1988, after public notice and comment, the EPA issued rules that require placer miners to use the best practical control technology (BPCT) to control discharges of nontoxic pollutants and the best available control technology (BACT) to control discharges of toxic pollutants. The BACT standard requires miners to construct settling ponds and recycle water through these ponds before discharging the water into the streambed. This method requires substantial expenditure. The Alaska Miners Association challenged the EPA's rule making. Who wins? [*Rybachek v. U.S. Environmental Protection Agency,* 904 F.2d 1276 (9th Cir. 1990)]

47.5. Leslie Salt Company (Leslie) owns a 153-acre tract of undeveloped land south of San Francisco. The property abuts the San Francisco National Wildlife Refuge and lies approximately one-quarter mile from Newark Slough, a tidal arm of the San Francisco Bay. Originally, the property was pastureland. The first change occurred in the early 1900s when Leslie's predecessors constructed facilities to manufacture salt on the property. They excavated pits and created large, shallow watertight basins on the property. Salt production on the property was stopped in 1959. The construction of a sewer line and public roads on and around the property created ditches and culverts on the property. Newark Slough is connected to the property by these culverts, and tidewaters reach the property. Water accumulates in the ponds, ditches, and culverts, providing wetland vegetation to wildlife and migratory birds. Fish live in the ponds on the property. In 1985, Leslie started to dig a ditch to drain the property and began construction to block the culvert that connected the property to the Newark Slough. The Army Corps of Engineers issued a cease-and-desist order against Leslie. Leslie challenged the order. Who wins? [*Leslie Salt Co. v. United States,* 896 F.2d 354 (9th Cir.)]

47.6. The Reserve Mining Company (Reserve) owns and operates a mine in Minnesota that is located on the shores of Lake Superior and produces hazardous waste. In 1947, Reserve obtained a permit from the state of Minnesota to dump its wastes into Lake Superior. The permit prohibited discharges that would "result in any clouding or discoloration of the water outside the specific discharge zone" or "result in any material adverse effects on public water supplies." Reserve discharged its wastes into Lake Superior for years, until they reached 67,000 tons per day in the early 1970s. Evidence showed that the discharges caused discoloration of surface waters outside the zone of discharge and contained carcinogens that adversely affected public water supplies. The United States sued Reserve for engaging in unlawful water pollution. Who wins? [*United States v. Reserve Mining Co.,* 8 Envir. Rep. Cases 1978 (D.Minn. 1976)]

47.7. DDT is a pesticide that is sprayed by farmers on cotton, soybean, peanut, and other crops to control insects and pests. Evidence showed that DDT is an uncontrollable, durable chemical that persists in the aquatic and terrestrial environments. Given its insolubility in water and its propensity to be stored in tissue, it collects in the food chain and is passed up to higher forms of aquatic and terrestrial life. Evidence also shows that DDT can persist in soil for many years and that it will move along with eroding soil. DDT has been found in remote areas and in ocean species, such as whales, far from any known area of application. DDT kills and injures birds, fish, and animals and affects their reproductive capabilities. DDT also poses a threat to human life because it is carcinogenic. The EPA brought a proceeding to cancel all registrations of DDT products and uses. Thirty-one registrants challenged the proposed cancellation. Who wins? [*Consolidated DDT Hearings,* 37 Fed.Reg. 13,369 (EPA 1972)]

47.8. During the U.S. involvement in the Vietnam conflict, the U.S. military used a herbicide called "Agent Orange." It was sprayed from airplanes to defoliate the jungles of Vietnam. People on the ground, including U.S. soldiers, were exposed to the spray. Agent Orange contains dioxin, a poison that causes cancer and other health problems. After returning home from Vietnam, often years later, veterans who had been exposed to Agent Orange began contracting cancer, suffering skin problems, and having children with birth defects. The veterans brought a class action lawsuit against Monsanto Company, Dow Chemical Company, and several other chemical companies that manufactured the Agent Orange used in Vietnam. This action, which would have been the largest, and probably the longest, private toxic injury action in history, was set to go to trial in May 1984 when the defendants offered to establish a $180-million trust fund for the plaintiffs. The settlement would provide each veteran who was exposed to Agent Orange with approximately $2,000 in damages. Should the veterans accept the settlement? [*Agent Orange Settlement* (E.D.N.Y. 1984)]

47.9. Douglas Hoflin was the director of the Public Works Department (Department) for Ocean Shores, Washington. From 1975 to 1982, Department purchased 3,500 gallons of paint for road maintenance. As painting jobs were finished, the 55-gallon drums that had contained the paint were returned to Department's yard. Paint contains hazardous substances such as lead. When 14 of the drums were discovered to still contain unused paint, Hoflin instructed employees to haul the paint drums to the city's sewage treatment plant and bury them. The employees took the drums, dug a hole on the grounds of the treatment plant, and dumped the drums in. Some of the drums were rusted and leaking. The hole was not deep enough, so the employees crushed the drums with a front-end loader to make them fit. The refuge was then covered with sand. Almost two years later, one of the city's employees reported the incident to state authorities, who referred the matter to the EPA. Investigation showed that the paint had contaminated the soil. The United States brought criminal charges against Hoflin for aiding and abetting the illegal dumping of hazardous waste. Who wins? [*United States v. Hoflin*, 880 F.2d 1033 (9th Cir. 1989)]

47.10. Metropolitan Edison Company (Metropolitan) owns and operates two nuclear-fueled power plants at Three Mile Island near Harrisburg, Pennsylvania. Both power plants were licensed by the Nuclear Regulatory Commission (NRC) after extensive proceedings and investigations, including the preparation of the required environmental impact statements. On March 28, 1979, when one of the power plants was shut down for refueling, the other plant suffered a serious accident that damaged the reactor. The governor of Pennsylvania recommended an evacuation of all pregnant women and small children, and many area resi-

dents did leave their homes for several days. As it turned out, no dangerous radiation was released.

People Against Nuclear Energy (PANE), an association of area residents who opposed further operation of either nuclear power plant at Three Mile Island, sued to enjoin the plants from reopening. They argued that the reopening of the plants would cause severe psychological health damage to persons living in the vicinity and serious damage to the stability and cohesiveness of the community. Are these reasons sufficient to prevent the reopening of the nuclear power plants? [*Metropolitan Edison Co. v. People Against Nuclear Energy*, 460 U.S. 766, 103 S.Ct. 1556 (1983)]

47.11. The red-cockaded woodpecker is a small bird that lives almost exclusively in the old pine forests throughout the southern United States. Its survival depends upon a very specialized habitat of pine trees that are at least 30, if not 60, years old in which they build their nests and forage for insects. The population of this bird decreased substantially between 1978 and 1987 as pine forests were destroyed by clear-cutting. The secretary of the interior has named the red-cockaded woodpecker an endangered species.

The Forest Service, which is under the authority of the secretary of agriculture, manages federal forests and is charged with duties to provide recreation, protect wildlife, and provide timber. To accomplish the charge of providing timber, the Forest Service leases national forest lands to private companies for lumbering. When the Forest Service proposed to lease several national forests in Texas, where the red-cockaded woodpecker lives, to private companies for lumbering, the Sierra Club sued. The Sierra Club sought to enjoin the Forest Service from leasing these national forests for lumbering. Who wins? [*Sierra Club v. Lyng, Secretary of Agriculture*, 694 F.Supp. 1260 (E.D.Tex. 1990)]

47.12. The state of Michigan owns approximately 57,000 acres of land that comprises the Pigeon River County State Forest (Forest) in southwestern Michigan. On June 12, 1977, Shell Oil Company (Shell) applied to the Michigan Department of Natural Resources (DNR) for a permit to drill 10 exploratory oil wells in Forest. Roads had to be constructed to reach the proposed drill sites. Evidence showed that the only sizable elk herd east of the Mississippi River annually used Forest as their habitat and returned to this range every year to breed. Experts testified that elk avoid roads, even when there is no traffic, and that the construction of the roads and wells would destroy the elk's habitat. Michigan law prohibits activities that adversely impact natural resources. The West Michigan Environmental Action Council sued DNR, seeking to enjoin DNR from granting the drilling permits to Shell. Who wins? [*West Michigan Environmental Action Council, Inc. v. Natural Resource Commission*, 275 N.W.2d 538 (Mich. 1979)]

ETHICS CASES

47.13. Samuel Gratz was president of Lannett Company (Lannett), which owned Astrochem, Inc. (Astrochem), a subsidiary of Lannett located in Branchburg, New Jersey. When Astrochem ceased operations in March 1986, barrels of chemicals no longer required for any Astrochem manufacturing process were left on the premises. The town of Branchburg and the landlord of the Astrochem building sent letters to Gratz stating that the chemicals left at Astrochem were hazardous and had to be removed immediately. The New Jersey Department of Environmental Protection issued two notices of violations for storage of hazardous waste and storage of hazardous waste in poor containers. Gratz solicited bids for the disposal of the waste but did not hire any of the bidders to dispose of the chemicals.

Instead, Gratz ordered that the barrels containing the chemicals be brought from the Astrochem site to Lannett's property and stored there. Eventually, Gratz ordered Lannett employees to dispose of the Astrochem chemicals by pouring them down a storm drain.

The U.S. government brought an indictment against Gratz for illegally transporting, storing, and disposing of hazardous wastes. Gratz was convicted of these violations. He appealed to the district court for a judgment of acquittal on all counts, claiming that he did not have the requisite knowledge that he was dealing with hazardous wastes. Did Gratz have the requisite knowledge that he was transporting, storing, and disposing of hazardous wastes? Did he act ethically in this case? [*United States v. Gratz*, 1993 WL 19733 (E.D.Pa. 1993)]

47.14. Riverside Bayview Homes, Inc. (Riverside), owns 80 acres of low-lying marshland (wetlands) near the shores of Lake St. Clair in Macomb County, Michigan. In 1976, Riverside began to place fill materials on its property as part of its preparations for construction of a housing development. Riverside did not obtain a permit from the Army Corps of Engineers (Corps). Upon discovery of Riverside's activities, Corps sued, seeking to enjoin Riverside from discharging a pollutant (fill) onto wetlands. Is the property subject to Corps permit system? Did Riverside act ethically in this case? [*United States v. Riverside Bayview Homes, Inc.*, 474 U.S. 121, 106 S.Ct. 455 (1985)]

CRITICAL LEGAL THINKING WRITING ASSIGNMENT

Read Case A.47 in the Case Appendix [*FMC Corp. v. United States Department of Commerce*]. This case is excerpted from the district court opinion. Review and brief the case. In your brief, be sure to answer the following questions:

1. Who was the plaintiff? Who was the defendant?

2. What statute is being applied in this case? What does the statute provide?

3. Succinctly state the issue the court has to decide.

4. What was the district court decision?

NOTES

1. 42 U.S.C. §§ 4321 et seq.
2. 42 U.S.C. §§ 7401 et seq.
3. P.L. 101–549 (1990).
4. 42 U.S.C. § 7412(b).
5. 33 U.S.C. §§ 1251 et seq.
6. 33 U.S.C. § 1254(t).
7. 21 U.S.C. § 349; 42 U.S.C. §§ 201 and 300F et seq.
8. 16 U.S.C. §§ 1431 et seq.; 33 U.S.C. §§ 1407 et seq.
9. 7 U.S.C. §§ 135 et seq.
10. 15 U.S.C. §§ 2601 et seq.
11. 42 U.S.C. § 6901 et seq.
12. 42 U.S.C. § 9601 et seq.
13. 42 U.S.C. § 9607.
14. 42 U.S.C. §§ 10101 et seq.
15. 16 U.S.C. §§ 1531 et seq.
16. 42 U.S.C. § 4901.
17. 42 U.S.C. § 4913.

Antitrust Law

While competition cannot be created by statutory enactment, it can in large measure be revived by changing the laws and forbidding the practices that killed it, and by enacting laws that will give it heart and occasion again. We can arrest and prevent monopoly.

WOODROW WILSON
Speech, August 7, 1912

Chapter Objectives

After studying this chapter, you should be able to

1. List and describe federal antitrust laws.
2. Describe the civil and criminal penalties for violating antitrust laws.
3. Apply the rule of reason and the per se rule to identify unreasonable restraints of trade.
4. Describe the horizontal and vertical restraints of trade that violate Section 1 of the Sherman Act.
5. Identify acts of monopolization that violate Section 2 of the Sherman Act.
6. Describe the defenses to a charge of monopolization.
7. Explain how the lawfulness of mergers is examined under Section 7 of the Clayton Act.
8. Define *price discrimination*.
9. Determine when the "meeting the competition" exception to price discrimination applies.
10. Apply Section 5 of the Federal Trade Commission Act to antitrust cases.

Chapter Contents

The American economic system was built on the theory of freedom of competition. After the Civil War, however, the American economy changed from a rural and agricultural economy to an industrialized and urban one. Many large industrial trusts were formed during this period. These arrangements resulted in a series of monopolies in basic industries such as oil and gas, sugar, cotton, and whiskey.

Because the common law could not deal effectively with these monopolies, Congress enacted a comprehensive system of **antitrust laws** to limit anticompetitive behavior. Almost all industries, businesses, and professions operating in the United States were affected. Although many states have also enacted antitrust laws, most actions in this area are brought under federal law.

This chapter discusses federal and state antitrust laws.

Overview of Federal Antitrust Laws

The **Sherman Act**, enacted in 1890, made certain restraints of trade and monopolistic acts illegal. Both the **Clayton Act** and the **Federal Trade Commission Act** (FTC Act) were enacted in 1914. The Clayton Act regulates mergers and prohibits certain exclusive dealing arrangements. The FTC Act prohibits unfair methods of competition. The **Robinson-Patman Act**, which prohibits price discrimination, was enacted in 1930.

Antitrust Enforcement

The federal antitrust statutes are broadly drafted to reflect the government's enforcement policy and to allow it to respond to economic, business, and technological changes. Each administration that occupies the White House adopts an enforcement policy for antitrust laws. From the 1940s through the 1970s, antitrust enforcement was quite stringent. During the 1980s, government enforcement of antitrust laws was more relaxed. During the 1990s, antitrust enforcement increased.

Antitrust Penalties

Federal antitrust laws provide for both government and private lawsuits.

Government Actions

The federal government is authorized to bring actions to enforce federal antitrust laws. Government enforcement of the federal antitrust law is divided between the Antitrust Division of the Justice Department and the Bureau of Competition of the Federal Trade Commission (FTC).

The Sherman Act is the only major antitrust act with *criminal* sanctions. Intent is the prerequisite for criminal liability under this act. Penalties for individuals include fines of up to $350,000 per violation and up to three years in prison; corporations may be fined up to $10 million per violation.[1]

The government may seek *civil* damages, including treble damages, for violations of antitrust laws.[2] Broad remedial powers allow the courts to order a number of civil remedies, including orders for divestiture of assets, cancellation of contracts, liquidation of businesses, licensing of patents, and such. Private parties cannot intervene in public antitrust actions brought by the government.

Private Actions

Section 4 of the **Clayton Act** permits any person who suffers antitrust injury in his or her "business or property" to bring a *private civil action* against the offender.[3] Consumers who have to pay higher prices because of an antitrust violation have recourse under this

---

The notion that a business is clothed with a public interest and has been devoted to the public use is little more than a fiction intended to beautify what is disagreeable to the sufferers.

Holmes, J.
Tyson & Bro-United Theatre Ticket Offices v. Banton
(1927)

Business Brief
Each administration that occupies the White House adopts an enforcement policy for antitrust laws.

Business Brief
The Sherman Act is the only major federal antitrust act that provides for *criminal* penalties.

Business Brief
Businesses or individuals who are found to violate federal antitrust laws may be assessed *treble* (triple) damages in a private civil lawsuit by any person who suffers injury in his or her business or property because of the violation.

provision.[4] To recover damages, plaintiffs must prove that they suffered *antitrust injuries* caused by the prohibited act. The courts have required that consumers must have dealt *directly* with the alleged violators to have standing to sue; indirect injury resulting from higher prices being "passed on" is insufficient.

Successful plaintiffs may recover **treble damages** (i.e., triple the amount of the damages), plus reasonable costs and attorneys' fees. Damages may be calculated as lost profits, an increase in the cost of doing business, or a decrease in the value of tangible or intangible property caused by the antitrust violation. This rule applies to all violations of the Sherman Act, the Clayton Act, and the Robinson-Patman Act. Only actual damages—not treble damages—may be recovered for violations of the FTC Act.

A private plaintiff has four years from the date on which an antitrust injury occurred to bring a private civil treble damage action. Only damages incurred during this four-year period are recoverable. This statute is *tolled* (i.e., does not run) during a suit by the government.

Effect of a Government Judgment

A government judgment against a defendant for an antitrust violation may be used as prima facie evidence of liability in a private civil treble damage action. Antitrust defendants often opt to settle government-brought antitrust actions by entering a plea of *nolo contendere* in a criminal action or a *consent decree* in a government civil action. These pleas usually subject the defendant to penalty without an admission of guilt or liability.

Section 16 of the **Clayton Act** permits the government or a private plaintiff to obtain an injunction against anticompetitive behavior that violates antitrust laws.[5] Only the FTC may obtain an injunction under the FTC Act.

Business Brief
Many defendants settle government-brought antitrust lawsuits by entering pleas of *nolo contendere* in criminal actions and *consent decree* in civil actions. These pleas cannot be used as evidence in a subsequent private civil action.

$\mathcal{S}$ECTION 1 OF THE SHERMAN ACT—RESTRAINTS OF TRADE

The Sherman Act has been called the "Magna Carta of free enterprise."[6] Section 1, which is discussed in the following paragraphs, outlaws certain restraints of trade.

Koi fish, Japan. *Federal antitrust laws were enacted to promote competitive behavior and to prevent unreasonable restraints of trade.*

Restraints of Trade

Section 1 of the **Sherman Act** is intended to prohibit certain concerted anticompetitive activities. It provides that

> *Every contract, combination in the form of trust or otherwise, or conspiracy, in restraint of trade or commerce among the several states, or with foreign nations, is hereby declared to be illegal. Every person who shall make any contract or engage in any combination or conspiracy hereby declared to be illegal shall be deemed guilty of a felony*[7]

In other words, Section 1 outlaws *contracts, combinations,* and *conspiracies* in restraint of trade. Thus, it applies to unlawful conduct by *two or more parties.* The agreement may be written, oral, or inferred from the conduct of the parties. The two tests the U.S. Supreme Court has developed for determining the lawfulness of a restraint—the *rule of reason* and the *per se rule*—are discussed in the paragraphs that follow.

Rule of Reason   If Section 1 were read literally, it would prohibit almost all contracts. In the landmark case, *Standard Oil Company of New Jersey v. United States,*[8] the Supreme Court adopted the **rule of reason** standard for analyzing Section 1 cases. This rule holds that only *unreasonable restraints of trade* violate Section 1 of the Sherman Act. Reasonable restraints are lawful. The courts examine the following factors in applying the rule of reason:

- The pro- and anticompetitive effects of the challenged restraint
- The competitive structure of the industry
- The firm's market share and power
- The history and duration of the restraint
- Other relevant factors

Per Se Rule   The Supreme Court adopted a **per se rule** that is applicable to those restraints of trade considered inherently anticompetitive. No balancing of pro- and anticompetitive effects is necessary in such cases: The restraint is automatically in violation of Section 1 of the Sherman Act. Once a restraint is characterized as a per se violation, no defenses or justifications for the restraint will save it, and no further evidence need be considered. Restraints that are not characterized as per se violations are examined under the rule of reason.

*H*ORIZONTAL RESTRAINTS OF TRADE

A **horizontal restraint of trade** occurs when two or more competitors at the *same level of distribution* enter into a contract, combination, or conspiracy to restrain trade (see Exhibit 48.1). Many horizontal restraints fall under the per se rule; others are examined under the rule of reason. The most common forms of horizontal restraint are discussed in the following paragraphs.

*E*XHIBIT **48.1**   *Horizontal Restraint of Trade*

Price-Fixing

Horizontal **price-fixing** occurs where the competitors in the same line of business agree to set the price of goods or services they sell. Price-fixing is defined as raising, depressing, fixing, pegging, or stabilizing the price of a commodity or service. Illegal price-fixing includes setting minimum or maximum prices or fixing the quantity of a product or service to be produced or provided. Although most price-fixing agreements occur between sellers, an agreement among buyers to set the price they will pay for goods or services is also price-fixing. The plaintiff bears the burden of proving a price-fixing agreement.

Price-fixing is a *per se violation* of Section 1 of the Sherman Act. No defenses or justifications of any kind—such as "the price-fixing helps consumers or protects competitors from ruinous competition"—can prevent the per se rule from applying.

The following case illustrates price-fixing.

price-fixing
Occurs where competitors in the same line of business agree to set the price of the goods or services they sell; raising, depressing, fixing, pegging, or stabilizing the price of a commodity or service.

Federal Trade Commission v. Superior Court Trial Lawyers Association
493 U.S. 411, 110 S.Ct. 768 (1990)
United States Supreme Court

CASE 48.1

FACTS
In the District of Columbia (District), public defenders—who are full-time employees of the government—represent indigent defendants in serious felony criminal prosecutions. Lawyers in private practice are appointed to represent indigent defendants in less serious felony and misdemeanor cases. These private attorneys are paid pursuant to District's Criminal Justice Act (CJA), which in 1982 provided for fees of $30 per hour for court time and $20 per hour for out-of-court time. Most appointments went to approximately 100 lawyers called "CJA regulars," who handled more than 25,000 cases in 1982. These lawyers derived almost all of their income from representing indigents.

The CJA regulars belonged to the Superior Court Trial Lawyers Association (SCTLA), which was a professional organization and not a labor union. Beginning in 1982, SCTLA unsuccessfully tried to persuade District to increase CJA rates. In August 1983, about 100 CJA lawyers resolved not to accept any new cases after September 6, 1983, if legislation providing for an increase in fees was not passed by that date. When the legislation was not enacted, on September 6 most CJA regulars refused to accept new assignments. As anticipated, their action had a severe impact on District's criminal justice system. Within 10 days, District's criminal justice system was on the brink of collapse.

On September 19, 1983, District offered to increase the fees paid to CJA lawyers to $45 per hour for out-of-court time and $55 for in-court time. On September 19, CJA lawyers accepted the offer and, on September 20, District enacted legislation to increase CJA fees. The Federal Trade Commission (FTC) filed a complaint against SCTLA, alleging that SCTLA's actions restrained trade in violation of federal antitrust law. FTC held against SCTLA. The court of appeals vacated the FTC order. The U.S. Supreme Court agreed to hear FTC's appeal.

ISSUE
Did the actions of SCTLA constitute price-fixing and a per se violation of Section 1 of the Sherman Act?

IN THE LANGUAGE OF THE COURT
Stevens, Justice Prior to the boycott CJA lawyers were in competition with one another, each deciding independently whether and how often to offer to provide services to the District at CJA rates. The agreement among the CJA lawyers was designed to obtain higher prices for their services and was implemented by a concerted refusal to serve an important customer in the market for legal services and, indeed, the only customer in the market for the particular services that CJA regulars offered. This constriction of supply is the essence of price-fixing, whether it be accomplished by agreeing upon a price, which will decrease the quantity demanded, or by agreeing upon an output, which will increase the price offered. The horizontal arrangement among these competitors was unquestionably a "naked restraint" on price and output.

The social justifications preferred for respondents' restraint of trade thus do not make it any less unlawful. The statutory policy underlying the Sherman Act precludes inquiry into the question whether competition is good or bad. No matter how altruistic the motives of respondents may have been, it is undisputed that their immediate objective was to increase the price that they would be paid for their services.

(case continues)

The per se rules are, of course, the product of judicial interpretations of the Sherman Act, but the rules nevertheless have the same force and effect as any other statutory commands. The per se rules also reflect a long-standing judgment that the prohibited practices by their nature have a substantial potential for impact on competition. In part, the justification for these per se rules is rooted in administrative convenience.

DECISION AND REMEDY

The U.S. Supreme Court held that SCTLA lawyers' horizontal agreement to fix prices was a per se violation of Section 1 of the Sherman Act. Reversed and remanded.

Case Questions

Critical Legal Thinking   Do you think that per se rules are necessary? Or should the courts be required to examine fully the pro- and anticompetitive effects of an activity to determine whether it violates Section 1 of the Sherman Act?

Ethics   Do you think CJA lawyers were acting "altruistically"? Did District act ethically by keeping CJA rates low and refusing to increase them?

Business Application   Should professionals be subject to antitrust laws? Why or why not?

Division of Markets

division of markets

When competitors agree that each will serve only a designated portion of the market.

Competitors that agree that each will serve only a designated portion of the market are engaging in a **division of markets** (or **market sharing**), which is a *per se violation* of Section 1 of the Sherman Act. Each market segment is considered a small monopoly served only by its designated "owner." Horizontal market-sharing arrangements include division by geographical territory, customers, and products.

In the following case, the Supreme Court examined an agreement to see if it constituted a division of markets.

Palmer v. BRG of Georgia, Inc.
498 U.S. 46, 111 S.Ct. 401 (1990)
United States Supreme Court

CASE 48.2

FACTS

Harcourt Brace Jovanovich Legal and Professional Publications (HBJ) is the nation's largest provider of bar review materials and lecture services. In 1976, HBJ began offering a Georgia bar review course in direct competition with BRG of Georgia, Inc. (BRG), the only other main provider of bar review services in the state. In 1980, HBJ and BRG entered into an agreement whereby BRG was granted an exclusive license to market HBJ bar review materials in Georgia in exchange for paying HBJ $100 per student enrolled by BRG in the course. HBJ agreed not to compete with BRG in Georgia, and BRG agreed not to compete with HBJ outside of Georgia. Immediately after the 1980 agreement, the price of BRG's course was increased from $150 to $400. Jay Palmer and other law school graduates who took the BRG bar review course in preparation for the 1985 Georgia bar exam sued BRG and HBJ, alleging a violation of Section 1 of the Sherman Act. The district court held in favor of the defendants. The court of appeals affirmed. The Supreme Court agreed to hear the plaintiffs' appeal.

ISSUE

Did the BRG-HBJ agreement constitute a division of markets and a per se violation of Section 1 of the Sherman Act?

IN THE LANGUAGE OF THE COURT

Per Curiam   *The revenue-sharing formula in the 1980 agreement between BRG and HBJ, coupled with the price increase that took place immediately after the parties agreed to cease competing with each other in 1980, indicates that this agreement was formed for the purpose and with the effect of raising the price of the bar review course. It was, therefore, plainly incorrect for the district court to enter summary judgment in respondents' favor. Moreover, it is equally clear that the district court and the court of appeals erred when they assumed that an allocation of markets or submarkets by competitors is not unlawful unless the market in which the two previously competed is divided between them.*

Here, HBJ and BRG had previously competed in the Georgia market; under their allocation agreement, BRG received that market, while HBJ received the remainder of the United States. Each agreed not to compete in the other's territories. Such agreements are anticompetitive regardless of whether the parties split a market within which both do business or whether they merely reserve one market for one and another for the other. Thus, the 1980 agreement between HBJ and BRG was unlawful on its face.

DECISION AND REMEDY

The U.S. Supreme Court held that the 1980 agreement between BRG and HBJ constituted a division of markets and as such was a per se violation of Section 1 of the Sherman Act. Reversed and remanded.

Case Questions

Critical Legal Thinking Should the division of markets be considered a per se violation of Section 1 of the Sherman Act? Or should the rule of reason apply?

Ethics Did BRG and HBJ act ethically in this case? Should the defendants, as bar review providers, have been aware of the antitrust law that prohibits division of markets?

Business Application Why do you think BRG and HBJ entered into the 1980 agreement?

Group Boycotts

A **group boycott** (or **refusal to deal**) occurs when two or more competitors at one level of distribution agree not to deal with others at a different level of distribution. For example, a boycott would occur if a group of television manufacturers agreed not to sell their products to certain discount retailers (see Exhibit 48.2). A boycott would also occur if a group of rental car companies agreed not to purchase Chrysler automobiles for their fleets (see Exhibit 48.3).

group boycott

When two or more competitors at one level of distribution agree not to deal with others at another level of distribution.

*𝓔*XHIBIT **48.2** *Group Boycott by Sellers*

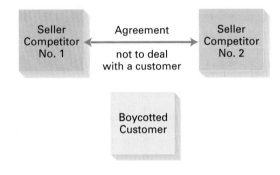

AGREEMENT NOT TO DEAL WITH A CUSTOMER

Seller Competitor No. 1 ← Agreement not to deal with a customer → Seller Competitor No. 2

Boycotted Customer

*𝓔*XHIBIT **48.3** *Group Boycott by Purchasers*

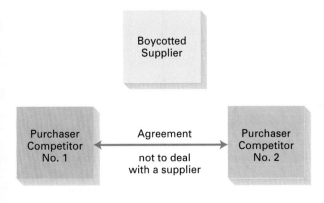

AGREEMENT NOT TO DEAL WITH A SUPPLIER

Boycotted Supplier

Purchaser Competitor No. 1 ← Agreement not to deal with a supplier → Purchaser Competitor No. 2

People of the same trade seldom meet together, even for merriment and diversion, but that the conversation ends in a conspiracy against the public, or in some contrivance to raise prices.

Adam Smith
The Wealth of Nations *(1776)*

Although in the past the U.S. Supreme Court has held that group boycotts were per se illegal, recent Supreme Court decisions have held that only certain group boycotts are per se illegal. Others are to be examined under the rule of reason. Nevertheless, most group boycotts are found to be illegal.

Other Horizontal Agreements

Some agreements entered into by competitors at the same level of distribution—including trade association activities and rules, exchanging nonprice information, participating in joint ventures, and the like—are examined using the *rule of reason*. Reasonable restraints are lawful; unreasonable restraints violate Section 1 of the Sherman Act.

Ethical Perspective

THE JUSTICE DEPARTMENT FLUNKS THE IVY LEAGUE SCHOOLS

Many college students think that tuition is too high and financial aid too low. After conducting an investigation, the U.S. Justice Department thought so, too. It brought an action against the eight Ivy League schools (Brown, Columbia, Cornell, Dartmouth, Harvard, Princeton, the University of Pennsylvania, and Yale) and the Massachusetts Institute of Technology (M.I.T.). The Justice Department alleged that these schools had conspired and engaged in a horizontal restraint of trade in violation of Section 1 of the Sherman Act. The facts of the case are as follows.

For years, the administrators of the Ivy League schools met annually to trade information about applicants seeking scholarships. They then agreed to offer scholarships to the students they thought would attend their schools. Scholarships were not offered to those less likely to attend. The schools defended this practice as preventing "overlap"—that is, certain students getting scholarship offers from many schools and other applicants receiving no scholarship offers. The schools figured this would save administrative costs as well as best serve the interests of the students.

The Justice Department did not think so. It felt that this trading of information and agreements to offer scholarships only to specified students constituted price-fixing by explicitly fixing the amount of scholarship money applicants were paid to attend school. The Justice Department lawyers pointed to what they learned in Economics 101 and asserted that this collegiate cartel was no different from any other cartel—it denied customers (students) the right to "comparison shop" just as they would for other services.

After weathering bad publicity, the eight Ivy League schools agreed to settle the case with the Justice Department. Under the terms of the consent decree, the schools agreed to no longer share financial aid information or discuss future tuition levels or faculty salaries with other schools. M.I.T. chose to fight the case in court and lost. The court found M.I.T. guilty of price-fixing and enjoined the challenged practices. [*U.S. v. Brown University*, 5 F.3d 658 (3d Cir 1993)]

1. Do you think the schools acted ethically in this case?
2. Did their "overlap" argument justify their actions?

---

vertical restraint of trade
A restraint of trade that occurs when two or more parties on *different levels of distribution* enter into a contract, combination, or conspiracy to restrain trade.

resale price maintenance
A per se violation of Section 1 of the Sherman Act; occurs when a party at one level of distribution enters into an agreement with a party at another level to adhere to a price schedule that either sets or stabilizes prices.

*V*ERTICAL RESTRAINTS OF TRADE

A **vertical restraint of trade** occurs when two or more parties on *different levels of distribution* enter into a contract, combination, or conspiracy to restrain trade (see Exhibit 48.4). The Supreme Court has applied both the per se rule and the rule of reason in determining the legality of vertical restraints of trade under Section 1 of the Sherman Act. The most common forms of vertical restraint are discussed in the following paragraphs.

Resale Price Maintenance

Resale price maintenance (or **vertical price-fixing**) is a *per se violation* of Section 1 of the Sherman Act. It occurs when a party at one level of distribution enters into an agreement with a party at another level to adhere to a price schedule that either sets or stabilizes prices. For example, a computer manufacturer that sells its computers only to retailers that agree to resell them at the prices set by the manufacturer is engaging in this illegal practice.

Exhibit 48.4   *Vertical Restraint of Trade*

In the following case, the Supreme Court had to decide whether the setting of a maximum resale price was a per se violation of Section 1 of the Sherman Act.

State Oil Company v. Khan
118 S.Ct. 275 (1997)
United States Supreme Court

CASE 48.3

FACTS
Barkat U. Khan and his corporation entered into an agreement with State Oil Company to lease and operate a gas station and convenience store owned by State Oil. The agreement provided that Khan would obtain his station's gasoline supply from State Oil. The agreement also provided that Khan could charge any price for the gasoline he sold to the station's customers, but if the price charged was higher than State Oil's "suggested retail price," the excess was to be rebated to State Oil. Khan could also choose to sell gasoline for less than State Oil's suggested retail price. After operating the station under these terms for about one year, Khan lost the station back to State Oil for falling behind in lease payments. Khan sued State Oil, alleging that the maximum resale price required by State Oil was a per se violation of Section 1 of the Sherman Act. The district court entered summary judgment for State Oil. The court of appeals reversed and held that the maximum resale price set by State Oil was a per se violation of Section 1. The court of appeals cited a previous U.S. Supreme Court Case—*Albrecht v. Herald Co.*, 390 U.S. 145 (1968)—that held that the setting of maximum resale prices also was a per se violation of Section 1. State Oil appealed to the U.S. Supreme Court.

ISSUE
Is the establishment of a maximum resale price by a supplier a per se violation of Section 1 of the Sherman Act?

IN THE LANGUAGE OF THE COURT
O'Connor, Justice   Although the Sherman Act, by its terms, prohibits every agreement "in restraint of trade," this Court has long recognized that Congress intended to outlaw only unreasonable restraints. As a consequence, most antitrust claims are analyzed under a rule of reason, according to which the finder of fact must decide whether the questioned practice imposes an unreasonable restraint on competition, taking into account a variety of factors, including specific information about the relevant business, its condition before and after the restraint was imposed, and the restraint's history, nature, and effect. Some types of restraints, however, have such predictable and pernicious anticompetitive effect, and such limited potential for procompetitive benefit, that they are deemed unlawful per se.

We find it difficult to maintain that vertically-imposed maximum prices could harm consumers or competition to the extent necessary to justify their per se invalidation. Albrecht reflected the Court's fear that maximum price fixing could be used to disguise arrangements to fix minimum prices, which remain illegal per se.

(case continues)

Although we have acknowledged the possibility that maximum pricing might mask minimum pricing, we believe that such conduct can be appropriately recognized and punished under the rule of reason. Indeed, both courts and antitrust scholars noted that Albrecht's *rule may actually harm consumers and manufacturers. After reconsidering* Albrecht's *rationale and the substantial criticism the decision has received, we conclude that there is insufficient economic justification for per se invalidation of vertical maximum price fixing.*

In overruling Albrecht, *we of course do not hold that all vertical maximum price fixing is per se lawful. Instead, vertical maximum price fixing, like the majority of commercial arrangements subject to the antitrust laws, should be evaluated under the rule of reason. In our view, rule-of-reason analysis will effectively identify those situations in which vertical maximum price fixing amounts to anticompetitive conduct.*

DECISION AND REMEDY

The U.S. Supreme Court reversed Albrecht. The Supreme Court held that the setting of a maximum resale price is not a per se violation of Section 1 of the Sherman Act. The Court remanded the case for trial using the rule of reason standard.

Case Questions

Critical Thinking   How often do you think the U.S. Supreme Court reverses itself? Do you think it should have done so in this case?

Ethics   Was the State Oil contract that set a maximum resale price in this case lawful under the rule of reason standard?

Business Application   How will this decision affect suppliers and the retailers they sell to? Explain.

Nonprice Vertical Restraints

nonprice vertical restraints
Restraints of trade that are unlawful under Section 1 of the Sherman Act if their anticompetitive effects outweigh their procompetitive effects.

The legality of **nonprice vertical restraints** of trade under Section 1 of the Sherman Act is examined using the rule of reason.[9] Nonprice restraints are unlawful under this analysis if their anticompetitive effects outweigh their procompetitive effects. Nonprice vertical restraints include situations where a manufacturer assigns exclusive territories to retail dealers or limits the number of dealers that may be located in a certain territory.

Entrepreneur and the Law

HOW TRADE ASSOCIATION MEMBERS CAN AVOID ANTITRUST LIABILITY

Trade associations are organizations that are formed by industry members to promote the industry, provide education to members, formulate rules for self-regulation of the industry, and conduct lobbying and other activities.

Trade associations usually hold annual and other meetings that industry members attend. To avoid antitrust problems, attendees should avoid sharing and discussing certain information with each other. Here are some activities to avoid:

- Do not discuss or exchange price information about current or future sales to customers.
- Do not agree to share or split customers or geographical areas.
- Do not agree to operate only during agreed-upon hours.

DEFENSES TO SECTION 1 OF THE SHERMAN ACT

The courts have recognized several defenses to alleged violations of Section 1 of the Sherman Act. These defenses are discussed below.

Unilateral Refusal to Deal

unilateral refusal to deal
A unilateral choice by one party not to deal with another party. This does not violate Section 1 of the Sherman Act because there is no concerted action.

The U.S. Supreme Court has held that a firm can unilaterally choose not to deal with another party without being liable under Section 1 of the Sherman Act. A **unilateral refusal to deal** is not a violation of Section 1 because there is no concerted action with others. This rule was announced in *United States v. Colgate & Co.*, and is therefore often referred to as the "**Colgate doctrine**."[10]

Conscious Parallelism

If two or more firms act the same but no concerted action is shown, there is no violation of Section 1 of the Sherman Act. This doctrine is often referred to as **conscious parallelism**. For example, if two competing manufacturers of a similar product both separately reach an independent decision not to deal with a retailer, there is no violation of Section 1 of the Sherman Act. The key is that each of the manufacturers acted on its own.

Noerr *Doctrine*

The *Noerr* **doctrine** holds that two or more persons may petition the executive, legislative, or judicial branch of the government or administrative agencies to enact laws or to take other action without violating the antitrust laws. The rationale behind this doctrine is that the right to petition the government has precedence because it is guaranteed by the Bill of Rights.[11] For example, General Motors and Ford could collectively petition Congress to pass a law that would limit the import of foreign automobiles into this country.

There is an exception to this doctrine. Under the *"sham" exception*, petitioners are not protected if their petition or lawsuit is baseless—that is, if a reasonable petitioner or litigant could not realistically expect to succeed on its merits. If the protection of the *Noerr* doctrine is lost, an antitrust action may be maintained against those parties who had asserted its protection.

$\int$ECTION 2 OF THE SHERMAN ACT—MONOPOLIZATION

By definition, monopolies have the ability to affect the price of goods and services. **Section 2** of the **Sherman Act** was enacted in response to widespread concern about the power generated by this type of anticompetitive activity.

Monopolization

Section 2 of the Sherman Act prohibits the act of monopolization. It provides that

> *Every person who shall monopolize, or attempt to monopolize, or combine or conspire with any other person or persons, to monopolize any part of the trade or commerce among the several States, or with foreign nations, shall be deemed guilty of a felony.*[12]

Proving that a defendant is in violation of Section 2 means proving that the defendant (1) possesses monopoly power in the relative market and (2) is engaged in a willful act of monopolization to acquire or maintain the power. Each of these elements is discussed in the following paragraphs.

Relevant Market Identifying the **relevant market** for a Section 2 action requires defining the relevant product or service market and geographical market. The definition of the relevant market often determines whether the defendant has monopoly power. Consequently, this determination is often litigated.

The **relevant product or service market** generally includes substitute products or services that are reasonably interchangeable with the defendant's products or services. Defendants often try to make their market share seem smaller by arguing for a broad definition of the product or service market. Plaintiffs, on the other hand, usually argue for a narrow definition.

The **relevant geographical market** usually is defined as the area in which the defendant and its competitors sell the product or service. This may be a national, regional, state, or local area, depending on the circumstances.

---

conscious parallelism

If two or more firms act the same but no concerted action is shown, there is no violation of Section 1 of the Sherman Act.

Noerr **doctrine**

Two or more persons may petition the executive, legislative, or judicial branch of the government or administrative agencies to enact laws or take other action without violating the antitrust laws.

Section 2 of the Sherman Act

Prohibits the act of monopolization and attempts or conspiracies to monopolize trade.

Business Brief

Note carefully that, in contrast to Section 1, which requires *concerted action*, Section 2 may apply to individual behavior.

relevant product or service market

A relevant market that includes substitute products or services that are reasonably interchangeable with the defendant's products or services.

relevant geographical market

A relevant market that is defined as the area in which the defendant and its competitors sell the product or service.

monopoly power

The power to control prices or exclude competition measured by the market share the defendant possesses in the relevant market.

act of monopolizing

A required act for there to be a violation of Section 2 of the Sherman Act. Possession of monopoly power without such act does not violate Section 2.

A monopoly granted either to an individual or to a trading company has the same effect as a secret in trade or manufactures. The monopolists, by keeping the market constantly understocked, by never fully supplying the effectual demand, sell their commodities much above the natural price, and raise their emoluments greatly above their natural rate.

Adam Smith
The Wealth of Nations (1776)

Monopoly Power   For an antitrust action to be sustained, the defendant must possess **monopoly power** in the relevant market. Monopoly power is defined by the courts to be the power to control prices or exclude competition. The courts generally apply the following guidelines: Market share above 70 percent is monopoly power; market share under 20 percent is not monopoly power. Otherwise, the courts generally prefer to examine the facts and circumstances of each case before making this determination.

Willful Act of Monopolizing   Section 2 outlaws the **act of monopolizing**, not monopolies. Any act that otherwise violates any other antitrust law (such as illegal restraints of trade in violation of Section 1 of the Sherman Act) is an act of monopolization that violates Section 2. When coupled with monopoly power, certain otherwise lawful acts have been held to constitute an act of monopolization. For example, *predatory pricing*—that is, pricing below average or marginal cost—that is intended to drive out competition has been held to violate Section 2.[13]

Defenses to Monopolization

Only two narrow defenses to a charge of monopolizing have been recognized: (1) innocent acquisition (e.g., acquisition because of a *superior business acumen*, skill, foresight, or industry) and (2) *natural monopoly* (e.g., a small market that can support only one competitor, such as a small-town newspaper). If a monopoly that fits into one of these categories exercises its power in a predatory or exclusionary way, the defense is lost.

Attempts and Conspiracies to Monopolize

Firms that *attempt* or *conspire* to monopolize a relevant market may be found liable under Section 2 of the Sherman Act. A single firm may be found liable for monopolizing or attempting to monopolize. Two or more firms may be found liable for conspiring to monopolize.

E-Commerce & Internet Law

e-biz

U.S. V. MICROSOFT CORPORATION

Not since the days of John D. Rockefeller and the Standard Oil trust has the power of one man's company transfixed so many people as Bill Gates' Microsoft Corporation. In less than 25 years, Microsoft has grown from a start-up company into the world's largest software company, whose products touch the lives of virtually everyone who uses a personal computer. Microsoft dominates the software market with its Windows operating system, which is used in most of the world's personal computers.

One market that Microsoft did not dominate was the rapidly growing Internet web browser market. Netscape developed its Navigator Internet web browser and by 1994, controlled over 80 percent of the market. This posed a serious threat to Microsoft because not only was Navigator extremely popular, bypassing Microsoft's operating system altogether. Microsoft called a meeting with Netscape to offer a "special relationship" that meant that Navigator would be absorbed into Microsoft Windows. Netscape refused.

Microsoft began a campaign to defeat Netscape. Microsoft developed its own browser called *Explorer* and attached it to its Windows operating system for free. Microsoft warned Apple, a manufacturer of personal computers, that it would cancel Microsoft's all-important Office software unless Apple used Explorer; Apple capitulated and made Explorer its web browser. Microsoft muscled AOL into offering Explorer in return for a small placement on the Windows desktop if it would not offer Netscape anywhere on its on-line service. AOL agreed. Microsoft gave Compaq, a maker of personal computers, a lower price for Windows in return for placing a Microsoft icon for the Explorer web browser on Compaq's computers. And when Intel developed technology that would set its own software standards in competition with Microsoft's Windows, Microsoft threatened to cut support for Intel PCs. Intel promptly stopped work on its new technology.

After investigating, the United States and 19 states sued Microsoft in a civil antitrust case. After a nine-month trial and four months of failed settlement negotiations, U.S. District Court Judge Thomas Penfield Jackson decided the case, finding that (1) Microsoft used predatory and anticompetitive conduct to illegally maintain its monopoly in the Windows operating system in violation of Section 2 of the Sherman Act, (2) Microsoft illegally

attempted to monopolize the market for Internet browsing software in violation of Section 2 of the Sherman Act, and (3) Microsoft illegally bundled its web browser Explorer with its successful Windows operating system, thus engaging in a tying arrangement in violation of Section 1 of the Sherman Act.

Microsoft appealed the decision. The appeal is expected to take years. In the meantime, Microsoft must defend over 100 civil class-action antitrust lawsuits brought against it by competitors and consumers. [*United States v. Microsoft Corporation,* (D.D.C., April 3, 2000)]

e·biz

CONCEPT SUMMARY   THE SHERMAN ACT

Section	Description
1	Prohibits contracts, combinations, and conspiracies in restraint of trade. To violate Section 1, the restraint must be found to be unreasonable under either of two tests: 1. Rule of reason 2. Per se rule Requires the concerted action of two or more parties.
2	Prohibits the act of monopolizing and attempts or conspiracies to monopolize. Can be violated by the conduct of one firm.

SECTION 7 OF THE CLAYTON ACT—MERGERS

In the late 1800s and early 1900s, *mergers* led to increased concentration of wealth in the hands of a few wealthy individuals and large corporations. **Section 7 of the Clayton Act** gave the federal government the power to check anticompetitive mergers. Originally, it applied only to stock mergers. The **Celler-Kefauver Act**, which was enacted in 1950, widened Section 7's scope to include asset acquisitions.[14] Today, Section 7 applies to all methods of external expansion, including technical mergers, consolidations, purchases of assets, subsidiary operations, joint ventures, and other combinations.

Section 7 of the Clayton Act
This section, as amended, provides that it is unlawful for a person or business to acquire the stock or assets of another "where in any line of commerce or in any activity affecting commerce in any section of the country, the effect of such acquisition may be substantially to lessen competition, or to tend to create a monopoly."

Elements of a Section 7 Action

Section 7 of the Clayton Act provides that it is unlawful for a person or business to acquire stock or assets of another "where in any line of commerce or in any activity affecting commerce in any section of the country, the effect of such acquisition may be substantially to lessen competition, or to tend to create a monopoly." In considering whether a merger is lawful, the courts must examine the elements discussed below.

Line of Commerce   Determining the **line of commerce** that will be affected by the merger involves defining the relevant *product or service market*. Traditionally, the courts have done this by applying the functional interchangeability test. Under this test, the relevant line of commerce includes products or services that consumers use as substitutes. If two products are substitutes for each other, they are considered as part of the same line of commerce. Suppose a price increase for regular coffee causes consumers to switch to Sanka (decaffeinated coffee). The two products are part of the same line of commerce because they are interchangeable.

line of commerce
Includes products or services that consumers use as substitutes. If an increase in the price of one product or service leads consumers to purchase another product or service, the two products are substitutes for each other.

Section of the Country   Defining the relevant **section of the country** consists of determining the relevant *geographical market*. The courts traditionally identify this market as the geographical area that will feel the direct and immediate effects of the merger. It may be a local, state, or regional market, the entire country, or some other geographical area. For example, Anheuser-Busch and the Miller Brewing Company sell beer nationally, whereas a local brewery, like Anchor Steam, sells beer only in the western states. If Anheuser-Busch and the Miller Brewing Company plan to merge, the relevant section of the country is the nation; if Anheuser-Busch intends to acquire a local brewery that sells beer in the West, the relevant section of the country is the western states.

Probability of a Substantial Lessening of Competition   Once the relevant product or service and geographical market have been defined, the court must determine whether the merger or acquisition is **likely to substantially lessen competition or create a monopoly**. If the court feels that the merger is likely to do either, it may prevent the merger. Section 7 tries to prevent potentially anticompetitive mergers before they occur. It deals in probabilities; an actual showing of the lessening of competition is not required.

In applying Section 7, mergers are generally classified as one of the following: *horizontal merger, vertical merger, market extension merger*, or *conglomerate merger*. Each of these is discussed in the paragraphs that follow.

Horizontal Mergers

A **horizontal merger** is a merger between two or more companies that compete in the same business and geographical market. The merger of two grocery store chains that serve the same geographical market fits this definition. Such mergers are subjected to strict review under Section 7 because they clearly result in an increase in concentration in the relevant market. For example, if General Motors Corporation and Ford Motor Company tried to merge, this horizontal merger would clearly violate Section 7.

In the landmark case *United States v. Philadelphia National Bank*,[15] the U.S. Supreme Court adopted the *presumptive illegality test* for determining the lawfulness of horizontal mergers. This test finds horizontal mergers presumptively illegal under Section 7 if (1) the merged firm would have a 30 percent or more market share in the relevant market and (2) the merger would cause an increase in concentration of 33 percent or more in the relevant market. This presumption is rebuttable—that is, the defendants may overcome it by introducing evidence that shows that the merger does not violate Section 7.

This test is not the only criterion for evaluating the lawfulness of a merger. The court must also examine factors such as the trend toward concentration in the relevant market, the past history of the firms involved, the aggressiveness of the merged firms, the economic efficiency of the proposed merger, and consumer welfare.

Vertical Mergers

A **vertical merger** is a merger that integrates the operations of a supplier and a customer. For example, if Prentice Hall, Inc., a textbook publisher, acquired a paper mill, it would be a **backward vertical merger**. If a book publisher, such as Doubleday, acquired a retail bookstore chain, such as B. Dalton Bookstores, it would be a **forward vertical merger**. In examining the legality of vertical mergers, the courts usually consider such factors as the past history of the firms, the trend toward concentration in the industries involved, the barriers to entry, the economic efficiencies of the merger, and the elimination of potential competition caused by the merger.

Vertical mergers do not create an increase in market share because the merging firms serve different markets. They may, however, cause anticompetitive effects such as *foreclosing* competitors from either selling goods or services to or buying them from the merged firm.

---

section of the country
A division of the country that is based on the relevant geographical market; the geographical area that will feel the direct and immediate effects of the merger.

probability of a substantial lessening of competition
If there is a probability that a merger will substantially lessen competition or create a monopoly, the court may prevent the merger under Section 7 of the Clayton Act.

horizontal merger
A merger between two or more companies that compete in the same business and geographical market.

vertical merger
A merger that integrates the operations of a supplier and a customer.

backward vertical merger
A vertical merger in which the customer acquires the supplier.

forward vertical merger
A vertical merger in which the supplier acquires the customer.

Consider This Example Assume a furniture manufacturer acquires a chain of retail furniture stores. The merger is unlawful if it is likely that the merged firm will not buy furniture from other manufacturers or sell furniture to other retailers.

Market Extension Mergers

A **market extension merger** is a merger between two companies in similar fields whose sales do not overlap. The merger may expand the acquiring firm's geographical or product market. For example, a merger between two regional brewers that do not sell beer in the same geographical area is called a *geographical market extension merger*. A merger between sellers of similar products, such as a soft drink manufacturer and an orange juice producer, is called a *product market extension merger*. The legality of market extension mergers is examined under Section 7 of the Clayton Act. They are treated like conglomerate mergers.

> **market extension merger**
> A merger between two companies in similar fields whose sales do not overlap.

Conglomerate Mergers

Conglomerate mergers are mergers that do not fit into any other category. That is, they are mergers between firms in totally unrelated businesses. If an oil company like Exxon merged with a clothing retailer like Neiman-Marcus, the result would be a conglomerate merger. Section 7 examines the lawfulness of such mergers under the *unfair advantage theory*, the *potential competition theory*, and the *potential reciprocity theory*, which are discussed in the paragraphs that follow.

> **conglomerate merger**
> A merger that does not fit into any other category; a merger between firms in totally unrelated businesses.

Unfair Advantage Theory The **unfair advantage theory** holds that a merger may not give the acquiring firm an unfair advantage over its competitors in finance, marketing, or expertise. This rule is intended to prevent wealthy companies from overwhelming the competition in a given market.

> **unfair advantage theory**
> A theory that holds that a merger may not give the acquiring firm an unfair advantage over its competitors in finance, marketing, or expertise.

Potential Competition Theory The **potential competition** (or **waiting-in-the-wings**) **theory** reasons that the real or implied threat of increased competition keeps businesses more competitive. A merger that would eliminate this perception can be enjoined under Section 7. For example, if IBM were perceived as a potential entrant to the fax machine business de novo, it could not merge with a large manufacturer of such machines.

> **potential competition theory**
> A theory that reasons that the real or implied threat of increased competition keeps businesses more competitive. A merger that would eliminate this perception can be enjoined under Section 7.

Potential Reciprocity Theory A merger may be enjoined if **potential reciprocity** can be shown between the merged firms and other firms. For example, suppose The New York Times Company (Company) purchases paper supplies from Hammermill, a paper manufacturer. Hammermill, in turn, purchases the raw materials for its paper from Northwest Logging Company (Northwest). Assume Company proposes to merge with Northwest. In this merger, the potential danger is that Company can threaten not to purchase its paper supplies from Hammermill unless Hammermill agrees to purchase all its logs from Northwest. The potential reciprocity theory is illustrated in Exhibit 48.5.

> **potential reciprocity theory**
> A theory that says if Company A, which supplies materials to Company B, merges with Company C (which in turn gets its supplies from Company B), the newly merged company can coerce Company B into dealing exclusively with it.

Premerger Notification

In 1976, premerger notification rules were enacted pursuant to the **Hart-Scott-Rodino Antitrust Improvement Act**.[16] These rules require certain firms to notify the FTC and the Justice Department of any proposed merger. This gives those agencies time to investigate and challenge any mergers they deem anticompetitive. If the merger is reportable, the parties must file the notification form and wait 30 days. If within the waiting period the government sues, the suit is entitled to expedited treatment in the courts.

> **Hart-Scott-Rodino Antitrust Improvement Act**
> Requires certain firms to notify the FTC and the Justice Department in advance of a proposed merger. Unless the government challenges the proposed merger within 30 days, the merger may proceed.

EXHIBIT 48.5 *Potential Reciprocity Theory*

Defenses to Section 7 Actions

The Supreme Court has recognized two defenses to a Section 7 action. These defenses can be raised even if the merger would otherwise violate Section 7. The defenses are

- **The Failing Company Doctrine** According to this defense, a competitor may merge with a failing company if (1) there is no other reasonable alternative for the failing company, (2) no other purchaser is available, and (3) the assets of the failing company would completely disappear from the market if the anticompetitive merger were not allowed to go through.
- **The Small Company Doctrine** The courts have permitted two or more small companies to merge without liability under Section 7 if the merger allows them to compete more effectively with a large company.

SECTION 3 OF THE CLAYTON ACT—TYING ARRANGEMENTS

Section 3 of the Clayton Act
Prohibits tying arrangements involving sales and leases of goods.

tying arrangement
A restraint of trade where a seller refuses to sell one product to a customer unless the customer agrees to purchase a second product from the seller.

Section 1 of the Sherman Act
Prohibits tying arrangements involving goods, services, intangible property, and real property.

Section 3 of the Clayton Act prohibits tying arrangements involving sales and leases of goods (tangible personal property).[17] **Tying arrangements** are vertical trade restraints that involve the seller's refusal to sell a product (the *tying* item) to a customer unless the customer purchases a second product (the *tied* item). **Section 1 of the Sherman Act** (restraints of trade) forbids tying arrangements involving goods, services, intangible property, and real property.

The defendant must be shown to have had sufficient economic power in the tying product market to restrain competition in the tied product market. Suppose, for example, that a manufacturer makes one patented product and one unpatented product. A tie-in arrangement occurs if the manufacturer refuses to sell the patented product to a buyer unless the buyer also purchases the unpatented product.

A tying arrangement is lawful if there is some justifiable reason for it. For example, the protection of quality control coupled with a trade secret may save a tie-in arrangement.

Consider This Example Coca-Cola Company owns the right to the formula for the syrup to make "Coca-Cola," which is a trade secret. Suppose Coca-Cola requires its distributors to purchase the syrup to make "Coca-Cola" from it. The tying product is the Coca-Cola franchise distributorship, and the tied product is the syrup. Here, the tying arrangement is lawful because a trade secret is involved and quality control must be preserved.

Contemporary Business Application

KODAK'S COPIER MACHINE REPLACEMENT PARTS JAMMED

Tying arrangements require that there be two products—the *tying* product and the *tied* product. A defendant who proves that the products are not separate cannot be held liable for a tying arrangement. Consider the following case.

Eastman Kodak Company (Kodak) manufactures and sells complex high-volume photocopier machines and micrographics equipment, such as microfilmers, scanners, microfilm viewers, and data-processing peripherals. Kodak equipment is unique because its equipment and parts are not compatible with other manufacturers' equipment and parts, and vice versa.

Kodak provides replacement parts and service for its machines. After the initial warranty period, Kodak provides service either through annual service contracts (which include all necessary parts) or on a per-call basis. Kodak manufactures some of the parts itself; the rest are made to order for Kodak by independent original equipment manufacturers (OEMs). Beginning in the early 1980s, independent service organizations (ISOs) began repairing and servicing Kodak equipment at prices substantially lower than Kodak's. ISOs purchased parts from Kodak and OEMs. Kodak customers sometimes purchased parts from Kodak but hired ISOs to do the actual repairs. Some customers found that the ISO service was of higher quality.

In 1985 and 1986, Kodak implemented a policy to limit ISO access to Kodak parts. Kodak also implemented a policy of selling replacement parts only to owners of Kodak equipment who used Kodak to service and repair their machines. Through these policies, Kodak intended to make it difficult for ISOs to sell service for Kodak machines. It succeeded. Many ISOs were forced out of business, and others lost substantial revenue.

In 1987, many ISOs sued Kodak, alleging that Kodak had unlawfully tied the sale of service for Kodak machines to the sale of parts, in violation of Section 1 of the Sherman Act. Kodak moved for summary judgment, alleging that parts and service were only one item—repair. The district court granted Kodak's motion, but the court of appeals reversed. The U.S. Supreme Court granted certiorari.

The Supreme Court held that the sale of replacement parts and the provision of services to install these parts and repair Kodak machines could be found to be two separate and distinct markets that would support a charge of unlawful tying. The Court found that there was sufficient evidence of a tie between service and parts to deny Kodak's motion for summary judgment. The Court held that the ISOs were entitled to a trial on their claim against Kodak and remanded the case for this trial. [*Eastman Kodak Company v. Image Technical Services, Inc.*, 112 S.Ct. 2072 (1992)]

SECTION 2 OF THE CLAYTON ACT—PRICE DISCRIMINATION

Businesses in the American economy survive by selling their goods and services at prices that allow them to make a profit. Sellers often offer favorable terms to their preferred customers. **Price discrimination** occurs if the seller does this without just cause. The rules regarding this type of unlawful trade practice are found in **Section 2** of the **Clayton Act**, which is commonly referred to as the **Robinson-Patman Act**. *De minimis* price discrimination is not actionable under the act.

price discrimination
Charging different prices to different customers for the same product without any justification.

Robinson-Patman Act
Section 2 of the Clayton Act is commonly referred to by this name.

Price Discrimination

Section 2(a) of the **Robinson-Patman Act** contains the following basic prohibition against price discrimination in the sale of goods:[18]

> It shall be unlawful for any person engaged in commerce, either directly or indirectly, to discriminate in price between different purchases of commodities of like grade and quality, where either or any of the purchases involved in such discrimination are in commerce, where the effect of such discrimination may be substantially to lessen competition or tend to create a monopoly in any line of commerce, or to injure, destroy, or prevent competition with any person who either grants or knowingly receives the benefit of such discrimination, or with customers of either of them.

This section does not apply to the sale of services, real estate, intangible property, securities, leases, consignments, or gifts. Mixed sales (i.e., those involving both services and commodities) are controlled by the dominant nature of the transaction.

Elements of Price Discrimination

To prove a violation of Section 2(a), the following **elements of price discrimination** must be shown:

- **Sales to Two or More Purchasers** To violate Section 2(a), the price discrimination must involve sales to at least two different purchasers at approximately the same time. It is legal to make two or more sales of the same product to the same purchaser at different prices. The Robinson-Patman Act requires that the discrimination occur "in commerce."
- **Commodities of Like Grade and Quality** A Section 2(a) violation must involve goods of "like grade and quality." To avoid this rule, sellers sometimes try to differentiate identical or similar products by using brand names. Nevertheless, as one court stated, "Four Roses under any other name would still swill the same."[19]
- **Injury** To recover damages, the plaintiff must have suffered actual injury because of the price discrimination. The injured party may be the purchaser who did not receive the favored price (*primary line injury*), that party's customers to whom the lower price could not be passed along (*secondary line injury*), and so on down the line (*tertiary line injury*).

A plaintiff who has not suffered injury because of the price discrimination cannot recover. For example, assume that a wholesaler sells cheaper Michelin tires to General Motors than to Ford Motor Company. If Ford could have purchased comparable Michelin tires elsewhere at the lower price, it cannot recover.

Indirect Price Discrimination

Because direct forms of price discrimination are readily apparent, sellers of goods have devised sophisticated ways to provide discriminatory prices to favored customers. Favorable credit terms, freight charges, and such are examples of **indirect price discrimination** that violate the Robinson-Patman Act.

Defenses to Section 2(a) Actions

The Robinson-Patman Act establishes three statutory defenses to Section 2(a) liability: (1) cost justification, (2) changing conditions, and (3) meeting the competition. These defenses are discussed in the following paragraphs.

Cost Justification Section 2(a) provides that a seller's price discrimination is not unlawful if the price differential is due to "differences in the cost of manufacture, sale, or delivery" of the product. This is called the **cost-justification defense**. For example, quantity or volume discounts are lawful to the extent they are supported by cost savings. Sellers may classify buyers into various broad groups and compute an average cost of selling to the group. The seller may then charge members of different groups different prices without being liable for price discrimination. The seller bears the burden of proving this defense.

Consider This Example   If the Proctor & Gamble Company can prove that bulk shipping rates make it less costly to deliver 10,000 boxes of Tide than lesser quantities, it may charge purchasers accordingly. However, Proctor & Gamble may not simply lower its price per box because the buyer is a good customer.

Changing Conditions   Price discrimination is not unlawful if it is in response to "changing conditions in the market for or the marketability of the goods." For example, the price of goods can be lowered to subsequent purchasers to reflect the deterioration of perishable goods (e.g., fish), obsolescence of seasonable goods (e.g., winter coats sold in the spring), a distress sale pursuant to court order, or discontinuance of a business. This is called the **changing conditions defense**.

Meeting the Competition   The **meeting the competition defense** to price discrimination is stipulated in **Section 2(b)** of the **Robinson-Patman Act**.[20] This defense holds that a seller may lawfully engage in price discrimination to meet a competitor's price. For example, assume Rockport sells its "ProWalker" shoe nationally at $100 per pair, while the Great Lakes Shoe Co. (Great Lakes), which produces and sells a comparable walking shoe, sells its product only in Michigan and Wisconsin. If Great Lakes sells its walking shoes at $75 per pair, Rockport can do the same. Rockport does not have to reduce the price of the shoe in the other 48 states. The seller can only meet, not beat, the competitor's price, however.

Discriminatory Fees, Payments, and Services

Congress was aware that sellers might try to circumvent the Section 2(a) price discrimination prohibitions by paying false fees or providing extra payments or services to favored buyers. The following limitations have been placed on these activities by the Robinson-Patman Act.

False Brokerage Fees and Other Compensation   **Section 2(c)** of the **Robinson-Patman Act** makes it illegal for a seller to pay a buyer or for a buyer to receive any commission, brokerage fee, compensation, allowance, or discount except for services actually rendered in connection with the sale and purchase of the goods.[21] For example, a seller may not pay a buyer a kickback for purchasing goods from him. A violation of Section 2(c) is a per se violation. Once a false discriminatory payment is found, no defenses or justifications for the payment are recognized.

Discriminatory Payments for Services   **Section 2(d)** of the **Robinson-Patman Act** prohibits sellers from making discriminatory payments for advertising, promotional, or other services furnished by the buyer unless these payments are available to other buyers on proportionately equivalent terms.[22] For example, a seller may not pay preferred buyers for providing repair services, display cases, shelf space, demonstration services, and such without making these payments available to other buyers. The payments may be adjusted to reflect the size of the buyer (e.g., the seller does not have to pay a Mom & Pop store and a large department store the same fee).

Providing Discriminatory Services   **Section 2(e)** of the **Robinson-Patman Act** makes it illegal for sellers to provide promotional and other services in a discriminatory way. Such services must be made available to all buyers on proportionately equal terms.[23] As an example, Calvin Klein can legally pay a representative to demonstrate Obsession perfume on a daily basis at Macy's department store in New York City, and making this service available to lesser department stores on a weekly or monthly basis and not available at all to small rural stores.

Section 2(f) of the
Robinson-Patman Act
Makes it illegal for a buyer to
knowingly induce or receive a
discriminatory price prohibited by Section 2(a).

Buyer Inducement of Price Discrimination

Section 2(f) of the **Robinson-Patman Act** makes it illegal for a buyer to knowingly induce or receive a discriminatory price prohibited by Section 2(a).[24] This knowledge can be inferred from the circumstances. Buyers cannot be held liable under this section for inducing discriminatory payments or services that violate Section 2(d) or 2(e).

SECTION 5 OF THE FEDERAL TRADE COMMISSION ACT— UNFAIR METHODS OF COMPETITION

Section 5 of the Federal
Trade Commission Act
Prohibits unfair methods of
competition and unfair and
deceptive acts or practices.

In 1914, Congress enacted the **Federal Trade Commission Act** (FTC Act) and created the **Federal Trade Commission (FTC). Section 5** of the **FTC Act** prohibits *unfair methods of competition and unfair or deceptive acts or practices* in or affecting commerce.[25] Section 5, which is broader than the other antitrust laws, covers conduct that (1) violates any provision of the Sherman Act or the Clayton Act (2) violates the "spirit" of those acts, (3) fills the gaps of those acts, and (4) offends public policy, or is immoral, oppressive, unscrupulous, or unethical, or causes substantial injury to competitors or consumers.

The FTC is exclusively empowered to enforce the FTC Act. It can issue interpretative rules, general statements of policy, trade regulation rules, and guidelines that define unfair or deceptive practices, and conduct investigations of suspected antitrust violations. It can also issue cease-and-desist orders against violators. These orders are appealable to federal court. The FTC Act provides for a private civil cause of action for injured parties. Treble damages are not available.

EXEMPTIONS FROM ANTITRUST LAWS

Certain industries and businesses are exempt from federal antitrust laws. The three categories of exemptions—*statutory, implied,* and *state action*—are discussed in the paragraphs that follow.

Statutory Exemptions

statutory exemptions
Exemptions from antitrust
laws that are expressly provided in statutes enacted by
Congress.

Certain statutes expressly exempt some forms of business and other activities from the reach of antitrust laws. **Statutory exemptions** include labor unions,[26] agricultural cooperatives,[27] export activities of American companies,[28] and insurance business that is regulated by a state.[29] Other statutes exempt railroad, utility, shipping, and securities industries from most of the reach of antitrust laws.

Implied Exemptions

implied exemptions
Exemptions from antitrust
laws that are implied by the
federal courts.

The federal courts have implied several exemptions from antitrust laws. Examples of **implied exemptions** include professional baseball[30] (but not other professional sports) and airlines.[31] The airline exemption was granted on the ground that railroads and other forms of transportation were expressly exempt. The Supreme Court has held that professionals, such as lawyers, do not qualify for an implied exemption from antitrust laws.[32] The Supreme Court strictly construes implied exemptions from antitrust laws.

State Action Exemptions

state action exemptions
Business activities that are
mandated by state law are
exempt from federal antitrust
laws.

The U.S. Supreme Court has held that economic regulations mandated by state law are exempt from federal antitrust laws. The **state action exemption** extends to businesses that must comply with these regulations.

Consider This Example States may set the rates that public utilities (e.g., gas, electric, and cable television companies) may charge their customers. The states that set these rates and the companies that must abide by them are not liable for price-fixing in violation of federal antitrust law.

Contemporary Business Application _____

BASEBALL'S GRAND SLAM AGAINST ANTITRUST LAWS

It was 1922. Babe Ruth was slamming home runs as the New York Yankees of the American League won the World Series of baseball. But that year the most important home run in baseball was hit at the U.S. Supreme Court. The opposing team—the U.S. government—struck out. Here is the story.

The American League and the National League were the dominant professional baseball leagues of the day, with such teams as the New York Giants, Boston Red Sox, and Chicago Cubs drawing millions of fans in various metropolitan markets throughout the country. Seeing these leagues' success, an upstart league called the Federal League began fielding teams in competing and other metropolitan markets.

To eliminate this competition, the National League induced some of the Federal League clubs to leave the league and purchased other Federal League teams. The lone remaining Federal League team sued the National League, alleging that it conspired to wreck the Federal League in violation of federal antitrust laws. The trial court agreed with the plaintiff, but the appeals court and the Supreme Court did not.

The Supreme Court justices held that the "national pastime" was exempt from antitrust laws because there was no interstate commerce involved in the National League's activities. Because of the finding of no interstate commerce, federal antitrust laws did not apply and the merit of the case was never decided.

Under the modern broad definition of "interstate commerce," the 1922 decision seems clearly wrong. Other sports have not been accorded a similar exemption from antitrust laws. Attempts to statutorily remove baseball's antitrust exemption during the baseball strike of 1995 failed in Congress. [*Federal Baseball Club of Baltimore, Inc. v. National League of Professional Baseball Clubs*, 259 U.S. 200, 42 S. Ct. 465, 66 L.Ed. 898 (1922)]

STATE ANTITRUST LAWS

Most states have enacted antitrust statutes. These statutes are usually patterned after the federal antitrust statutes. They often contain the same language as well. State antitrust laws are used to attack anticompetitive activity that occurs in intrastate commerce. When federal antitrust laws are laxly applied, plaintiffs often bring lawsuits under state antitrust laws.[33]

International Perspective _____

JAPANESE *KEIRETSUS* IGNORE ANTITRUST LAWS

The United States has the most stringent antitrust laws in the world, enforces them most diligently, and assesses the greatest penalties for their violation. U.S. antitrust laws have been used to break up monopolies and cartels in many industries, including oil, steel, and telecommunications, to name but a few. These laws have also prevented U.S. companies from growing larger through mergers. Many critics argue that the stringent enforcement of antitrust laws has placed U.S. companies at a disadvantage in the international marketplace

(box continues)

where they have to compete against larger foreign firms from countries where antitrust laws do not exist or are not enforced.

Take the case of Japan. In the past 40 or 50 years, Japan has gone from a war-ravaged country to an economic superpower. Much of this success has to do with the cozy relationship between Japan's federal government and the *keiretsu* (industrial groupings). *Keiretsu* cartels are considered a key factor behind the country's economic success.

After World War II, American-style antitrust laws were enacted in Japan; since then, though, they have been virtually ignored. The Japan Fair Trade Commission (JFTC), which is empowered to enforce antitrust laws, is more interested in promoting *keiretsus* than checking them. For example, the JFTC has filed only one antitrust criminal complaint in the past 17 years.

Japan's industry and commerce are rife with cartels—247 were legally permitted as of 1992. These cartels blatantly engage in anticompetitive conduct. Price-fixing permeates the beer, cosmetics, over-the-counter drug,

and construction industries, among others. The cartels are politically entrenched because they are the largest contributors to campaigns of Japanese politicians. They use their political muscle to lobby against the passage of laws that would curtail their monopolistic positions.

This protectionist attitude has helped Japanese *keiretsus* become giants that have a substantial advantage in the international marketplace. This has come at the expense of Japanese consumers, however, who have to pay higher than competitive prices for goods and services sold by these cartels. This helps Japanese cartels compete abroad.

As Japanese consumers became more vocal, and as pressure increased from other countries—particularly the United States—the JFTC issued tougher guidelines for the enforcement of antitrust laws. But, if history is any indicator, these moves are probably little more than window dressing, and *keiretsus* will retain their monopolistic positions with little interference from the Japanese government.

Working the Web

e-biz

Federal Trade Commission The FTC works for consumer protection and a competitive marketplace. One of its missions is antitrust enforcement.

Visit at **www.ftc.gov**

Freedom of Information Act, Antitrust Division The FOIA Antitrust Division is charged with the general enforcement, by civil and criminal proceedings, of federal antitrust laws and other laws relating to the protection of competition and the prohibition of monopolization and restraints of trade.

Visit at **www.usdoj.gov/atr/foia.html**

American Bar Association, Section of Antitrust Law Members of this section stay up to date on pertinent antitrust developments including those involving merg-

ers and acquisitions, joint ventures, distribution and franchising arrangements, pricing practices, collaboration among competitors, class actions, and refusal to deal.

Visit at **www.abanet.org/antitrust/home.html**

CYBER EXERCISES

1. Find out where the regional office of the FTC nearest you is located.

2. Visit the Electronic Reading Room at the FOIA Web site.

3. Click on "About the Section" on the ABA Antitrust Section Web site. What two publications do section members receive each year?

CASES AND EXERCISES

CRITICAL LEGAL THINKING CASES

48.1. The Maricopa County Medical Society (Society) is a professional association that represents doctors of medicine, osteopathy, and podiatry in Maricopa County, Arizona. Society formed the Maricopa Foundation for Medical Care (Foundation), a nonprofit Arizona corporation. Approximately 1,750 doctors, who represent 70 percent of the practitioners in the county, belong to Foundation. Foundation acts as an insurance administrator between its member doctors and insurance companies that pay patients' medical bills.

Foundation established a maximum fee schedule for various medical services. The member doctors agreed to abide by this fee schedule when providing services to patients. The state of Arizona brought this action against Society, Foundation, and its members, alleging price-fixing in violation of Section 1 of the Sherman Act. Who wins? [*Arizona v. Maricopa County Medical Society*, 457 U.S. 332, 102 S.Ct. 2466 (1982)]

48.2. Topco Associates, Inc. (Topco), was founded in the 1940s by a group of small, local grocery store chains to act as a buying cooperative for the member stores. In this capacity, Topco procures and distributes more than 1,000 different food and related items to its members. Topco does not itself own any manufacturing or processing facilities, and the items it procures are shipped directly from the manufacturer or packer to Topco members. Topco members agree to sell only Topco brand products within an exclusive territory. The United States sued Topco and its members, alleging a violation of Section 1 of the Sherman Act. Who wins? [*United States v. Topco Associates, Inc.*, 405 U.S. 596, 92 S.Ct. 1126 (1972)]

48.3. Mercedes-Benz of North America, Inc. (MBNA), is the exclusive franchisor of Mercedes-Benz dealerships in the United States. MBNA's franchise agreements require each dealer to establish a customer service department for the repair of Mercedes-Benz automobiles and for dealers to purchase Mercedes-Benz replacement parts from MBNA. At least eight independent wholesale distributors, including Metrix Warehouse, Inc. (Metrix), sell replacement parts for Mercedes-Benz automobiles. Because they are precluded from selling parts to Mercedes-Benz dealers, these parts distributors sell their replacement parts to independent garages that specialize in the repair of Mercedes-Benz automobiles. Evidence showed that Metrix sold replacement parts for Mercedes-Benz automobiles of equal quality and at a lower price than those sold by MBNA. Metrix sued MBNA, alleging a violation of Section 1 of the Sherman Act. Who wins? [*Metrix Warehouse, Inc. v. Mercedes-Benz of North America, Inc.*, 828 F.2d 1033 (4th Cir. 1987)]

48.4. The Crest Theatre is a movie theater that is located in a neighborhood shopping center in a suburb six miles from downtown Baltimore, Maryland. The owner of the Crest Theatre, Theater Enterprises, Inc., has repeatedly sought to obtain first-run feature films from Paramount Film Distribution Corporation (Paramount) and other film distributors. Each film distributor has independently rejected the request, stating that they restrict "first-run" movies to theaters located in downtown Baltimore. Each cited the same reasons: First-runs are normally granted to the largest theaters, profits are higher from showing films in downtown theaters, the drawing area around the Crest Theatre was less than one-tenth that of the downtown theaters, and the downtown theaters offered greater opportunities for widespread advertisements and exploitation of newly released feature films. There was no evidence of an agreement among the film distributors to restrict the showing of feature films at the Crest Theatre. Evidence showed that each film distributor made an independent decision to show their first-run films in theaters located in downtown Baltimore. Crest Theatre sued Paramount and the other film distributors, alleging a violation of Section 1 of the Sherman Act. Who wins? [*Theatre Enterprises, Inc. v. Paramount Film Distribution Corporation*, 346 U.S. 537, 74 S.Ct. 257 (1954)]

48.5. The Union Oil Company (Union Oil) is a major oil company that operates a nationwide network of franchised service station dealers who sell Union Oil gasoline and other products throughout the United States. The franchise dealers lease their stations from Union Oil; they also sign a franchise agreement to purchase gasoline and other products on assignment from Union Oil. Both the lease and the franchise agreement are one-year contracts that may be canceled by Union Oil if a dealer does not adhere to the contract. The franchise agreement provided that all dealers shall adhere to the retail price of gasoline as set by Union Oil. The retail price set by Union Oil for gasoline during the period in question was 29.9 cents per gallon. Simpson, a franchised dealer, violated this provision in the franchise agreement and sold gasoline at 27.9

cents per gallon to meet competitive prices. Because of this, Union Oil canceled Simpson's lease and franchise agreement. Simpson sued Union Oil, alleging a violation of Section 1 of the Sherman Act. Who wins? [*Simpson v. Union Oil Company*, 377 U.S. 13, 84 S.Ct. 1051 (1964)]

48.6. GTE Sylvania, Inc. (Sylvania), manufactured and sold television sets to independent or company-owned distributors, which in turn resold the sets to a large and diverse group of retailers. Prompted by a decline in its market share, Sylvania instituted a franchise program whereby it phased out its wholesale distribution and began to sell its televisions directly to a smaller and select group of franchised retail dealers. A franchise did not constitute an exclusive territory, and Sylvania retained sole discretion to increase the number of retailers in an area.

In the spring of 1965, Sylvania decided to franchise another outlet in San Francisco that was approximately one mile from a Sylvania retail outlet operated by Continental TV, Inc. (Continental). Continental protested the location of the new outlet, but to no avail. Continental then proposed to open a new Sylvania store in Sacramento, but Sylvania denied the franchise because it believed the Sacramento area was adequately served. In the face of this denial, Continental advised Sylvania that it was in the process of moving Sylvania merchandise from its warehouse to a new retail location in Sacramento. Shortly thereafter, Sylvania terminated Continental's San Francisco franchise. Continental sued Sylvania, alleging that Sylvania had engaged in unreasonable restraint of trade in violation of Section 1 of the Sherman Act. Does the per se rule or the rule of reason apply? [*Continental TV, Inc. v. GTE Sylvania, Inc.*, 433 U.S. 36, 97 S.Ct. 2549 (1977)]

48.7. The International Business Machine Corporation (IBM) manufactures entire computer systems, including mainframes and peripherals, and provides software and support services to customers. IBM both sells and leases computers. Greyhound Computer Corporation, Inc. (Greyhound), is a computer-leasing company that buys older computers from IBM and then leases them to businesses. This makes Greyhound both a customer and a competitor of IBM. Prior to 1963, IBM sold its second-generation equipment at a 10 percent discount per year up to a maximum of 75 percent. Thus, equipment on the market for several years could be purchased at a substantial discount from its original cost.

IBM's market share of this leasing market was 82.5 percent. The portion of the leasing market not controlled by IBM was dispersed among many companies, including Greyhound. IBM officials became concerned that the balance between sales and leases was turned too heavily toward sales and that the rapid increase in leasing companies occurred

because of their ability to purchase second generation computers from IBM at a substantial discount. In 1963, IBM reduced the annual discount to 5 percent per year with a maximum of 35 percent. In 1964, the discount was changed to 12 percent after the first year with no further discounts. Greyhound sued IBM, alleging IBM engaged in monopolization in violation of Section 2 of the Sherman Act. Who wins? [*Greyhound Computer Corporation, Inc. v. International Business Machine Corporation*, 559 F.2d 488 (9th Cir. 1977)]

48.8. In the 1970s, the Eastman Kodak Company (Kodak) was the dominant and preeminent manufacturer and distributor of cameras and film in the United States. In 1972, Kodak introduced a new Instamatic camera called the "110 camera" and a new film called "Kodacolor III" to be used in the cameras. Kodak engineers invented the camera and film with their own ingenuity. Kodak invested substantial money in inventing the new camera and film and held the many patents necessary to develop the 110 system. The camera and film were superior to any others on the market and were an instant success. With the introduction of the new camera and film, Kodak obtained a monopoly position in the amateur photography market.

Berkey Photo, Inc. (Berkey), was a small photography company that competed with Kodak. Berkey's attempt to develop and sell its own version of the 110 camera failed. Berkey then brought an antitrust action against Kodak, alleging that Kodak's introduction of the 110 camera and Kodacolor III film was an attempt to monopolize the camera market in violation of Section 2 of the Sherman Act. Who wins? [*Berkey Photo, Inc. v. Eastman Kodak Company*, 603 F.2d 263 (2d Cir. 1979)]

48.9. The Lipton Tea Co. (Lipton) is the second largest producer of herbal teas, controlling 32 percent of the national market. Lipton announced that it would acquire Celestial Seasonings, the largest U.S. producer of herbal teas, controlling 52 percent of the national market. R. C. Bigelow, Inc. (Bigelow), the third largest producer of herbal teas with 13 percent of the national market, brought this action, alleging that the merger would violate Section 7 of the Clayton Act and seeking an injunction against the merger. What type of merger is proposed? What is the relevant market? Should the merger be enjoined? [*R. C. Bigelow, Inc. v. Unilever, N.V.*, 867 F.2d 102 (2d Cir. 1989)]

48.10. The G. R. Kinney Company, Inc. (Kinney), was the largest independent chain of family-owned shoe stores in the nation. It had assets of $18 million and sold more than 8 million pairs of shoes annually through its 350 retail outlets. Kinney announced that it would merge with the Brown Shoe Company, Inc. (Brown Shoes), which was the fourth largest manufacturer of shoes in the country with assets of more than

$72 million and which sold more than 25 million pairs of shoes annually. The United States brought this action, alleging a violation of Section 7 of the Clayton Act and seeking a preliminary injunction against the merger. What type of merger would this be? What is the relevant market? Does the merger violate Section 7? [*Brown Shoe Company, Inc. v. United States*, 370 U.S. 294, 82 S.Ct. 1502 (1962)]

48.11. Consolidated Foods Corporation (Consolidated), which owns a network of wholesale and retail food stores, purchases a substantial amount of products from food processors that use dehydrated onion and garlic in their products. Consolidated acquired Gentry, Inc. (Gentry), a manufacturer of dehydrated onion and garlic that controlled 32 percent of the market for these products and, with its chief competitor, accounted for 90 percent of total industry sales. Two small competitors accounted for the other 10 percent of sales. Evidence showed that after the acquisition, Consolidated required firms from which it purchased food products to purchase the dehydrated onion and garlic they needed from Gentry. The FTC sued Consolidated, alleging that Consolidated violated Section 7 of the Clayton Act by its acquisition of Gentry. Who wins? [*Federal Trade Commission v. Consolidated Foods Corporation*, 380 U.S. 592, 85 S.Ct. 1220 (1965)]

48.12. The Brunswick Corporation (Brunswick) was the second largest manufacturer of bowling equipment in the United States. In the late 1950s, the bowling industry expanded rapidly. Brunswick's sales of lanes, automatic pinsetters, and ancillary equipment to bowling alley operators rose accordingly. Because the equipment required a major capital expenditure by bowling center operators, Brunswick extended credit for all of the purchase price except a cash down payment, taking a security interest in the equipment.

Brunswick's sales dropped in the early 1960s, when the bowling industry went into a sharp decline. In addition, many of the bowling center operators defaulted on their loans. By the end of 1964, Brunswick was in financial difficulty. It met with limited success when it foreclosed on its security interests and attempted to lease or sell the repossessed equipment and bowling centers. To avoid complete loss, Brunswick started running those that would provide a positive cash flow. This made Brunswick the largest operator of bowling centers in the country, with over five times as many bowling centers as its next largest competitor. Because the bowling industry was so deconcentrated, however, Brunswick controlled less than 2 percent of the bowling centers in the country.

Pueblo Bowl-O-Mat, Inc. (Pueblo Bowl), operated three bowling centers in markets where Brunswick had repossessed bowling centers and began operating them. Pueblo Bowl sued Brunswick, alleging that Brunswick had violated Section 7 of the Clayton Act. Pueblo Bowl alleged that it suffered injury in the form of lost profits that it would have made had Brunswick allowed the bowling centers to go bankrupt, and requested treble damages. Is Brunswick liable? [*Brunswick Corporation v. Pueblo Bowl-O-Mat, Inc.*, 429 U.S. 477, 97 S.Ct. 690 (1977)]

48.13. Corn Products Refining Company (Corn Products) manufactures corn syrup or glucose at two plants, one located in Chicago, Illinois, and the other at Kansas City, Missouri. Glucose is a principal ingredient of low-priced candy. Corn Products sells glucose at the same retail price to all purchasers but charges separately for freight charges. Instead of charging actual freight charges, Corn Products charges every purchaser the freight that it would have cost if the glucose was shipped from Chicago, even if the glucose is shipped from its Kansas City plant. This "base point pricing" system created a favored price zone for Chicago-based purchasers. This put them in a better position to compete for business. The FTC sued Corn Products, alleging that it engaged in price discrimination in violation of Section 2(a) of the Robinson-Patman Act. Did it? [*Corn Products Refining Company v. Federal Trade Commission*, 324 U.S. 726, 65 S.Ct. 961 (1945)]

48.14. The Morton Salt Company (Morton Salt) manufactures and sells table salt in interstate commerce. Morton Salt manufactures several different brands of table salt and sells them directly to (1) wholesalers, which in turn resell to retail stores, and (2) large retailers. Morton Salt sells its finest brand of table salt, "Blue Label," based on the following standard quantity discount system, which is available to all customers:

	Price per case
Less than carload purchase	$1.60
Carload purchases	1.50
5,000-case purchases	1.40
50,000-case purchases	1.35

The standard quantity discount pricing schedule was not based on actual costs incurred by Morton Salt in serving its customers; instead, it was designed to give large purchasers an incentive to purchase salt from Morton Salt. Evidence showed that only five large retail chains ever bought Blue Label salt in sufficient quantities to qualify for the $1.35-per-case price. Evidence also showed that small retailers that could not qualify for any discount had to pay wholesalers higher prices for salt than the large retailers were selling the salt for at retail to their customers. The FTC sued Morton Salt, alleging that it violated Section 2(a) of the Robinson-Patman Act. Is Morton Salt's quantity discount pricing system justified? [*Federal Trade Commission v. Morton Salt Company*, 334 U.S. 37, 68 S.Ct. 822 (1948)]

48.15. Texaco, Inc. (Texaco), is one of the nation's largest petroleum companies. It sells its products through approximately 30,000 franchised service stations, which constitute about 16 percent of all service stations in the United States. Nearly 40 percent of the Texaco dealers lease their stations from Texaco. This is typically a one-year lease that may be terminated (1) at the end of any year upon proper notice or (2) at any time if, in Texaco's judgment, any lease provisions relating to the use and appearance of the station are not fulfilled. The franchise agreement under which the dealers receive their supply of gasoline and other petroleum products also is a one-year agreement and is terminable upon 30 days' notice.

Texaco entered into an agreement with the Goodrich Tire Company (Goodrich) whereby Texaco agreed to promote the sale of Goodrich tires, batteries, and accessories (TBA) through its franchised dealers. The agreement provided that Goodrich would pay Texaco a 10 percent commission on all TBA purchases by Texaco dealers. During the five-year period 1952 to 1956, Texaco received commissions of $22 million.

Although Texaco dealers were not forced to carry TBA, Texaco strongly recommended that they carry the line. In addition, the Texaco representatives who were responsible for recommending the renewal of dealer franchise and lease agreements were told to promote Goodrich products. Texaco also received regular reports on the amount of TBA purchased by its dealers. The FTC brought an action that alleged that Texaco violated Section 5 of the FTC Act. Who wins? [*Federal Trade Commission v. Texaco, Inc.*, 393 U.S. 223, 89 S.Ct. 429 (1968)]

ETHICS CASES

48.16. E.I. du Pont de Nemours & Co. (du Pont) is a manufacturer of chemicals, paints, finishes, fabrics, and other products. General Motors Corporation (General Motors) is a major manufacturer of automobiles. During the period 1917 through 1919, du Pont purchased 23 percent of the stock of General Motors. Du Pont became a major supplier of finishes and fabrics to General Motors.

Du Pont's commanding position as a General Motors supplier was not achieved until shortly after its purchase of a sizable bloc of General Motors stock in 1917. Du Pont's interest in buying into General Motors was stimulated by John J. Raskob, du Pont's treasurer, and Pierre S. du Pont, du Pont's president, who acquired personal holdings of General Motors stock in 1914. General Motors was organized six years earlier by William C. Durant to acquire previously independent automobile-manufacturing companies—Buick, Cadillac, Oakland, and Oldsmobile. Durant later brought in Chevrolet. Chevrolet was organized by him when he was temporarily out of power, during 1910 to 1915, and a bankers' group controlled General Motors. In 1915, when Durant and the bankers deadlocked on the choice of a board of directors, they resolved the deadlock by an agreement under which Pierre S. du Pont was named chairman of the General Motors board, and Pierre S. du Pont, Raskob, and two nominees of Mr. du Pont were named neutral directors. By 1916, Durant settled his differences with the bankers and resumed the presidency and his controlling position in General Motors. He prevailed upon Pierre S. du Pont and Raskob to continue their interest in General Motors's affairs, which both did as members of the finance committee, working closely with Durant in matters of finances and operations and plans for future expansion.

Raskob foresaw the success of the automobile industry and the opportunity for great profit in a substantial purchase of General Motors stock. On December 19, 1917, Raskob submitted a treasurer's report to the du Pont finance committee recommending a purchase of General Motors stock in the amount of $25,000,000. That report makes clear that more than just a profitable investment was contemplated. A major consideration was that an expanding General Motors would provide a substantial market needed by the burgeoning du Pont organization. Raskob's summary of reasons in support of the purchase includes this statement: "Our interest in the General Motors Company will undoubtedly secure for us the entire Fabrikoid, Pyralin (celluloid), paint and varnish business of those companies, which is a substantial factor."

General Motors is the colossus of the giant automobile industry. It accounts annually for upward of two-fifths of the total sales of automotive vehicles in the nation. Expressed in percentages, du Pont supplied 67 percent of General Motors's requirements for finishes in 1946 and 68 percent in 1947. In fabrics, du Pont supplied 52.3 percent of requirements in 1946 and 38.5 percent in 1947. Because General Motors accounts for almost one-half of the automobile industry's annual sales, its requirements for automotive finishes and fabrics must represent approximately one-half of the relevant market for these materials.

In 1949, the United States brought this antitrust action against du Pont, alleging violation of Section 7 of the Clayton Act and seeking the divestiture of du Pont's ownership of stock in General Motors. Does du Pont's ownership of 23 percent of the stock of General Motors constitute a vertical merger that gives du Pont illegal preferences over competitors in the sale of finishes and fabrics to General Motors in violation of Section 7 of the Clayton Act? Did du Pont act ethically in this case? [*United States v. E.I. du Pont de Nemours & Co.*, 353 U.S. 586, 77 S.Ct. 872 (1957)]

48.17. Falls City Industries, Inc. (Falls City), is a regional brewer located in Nebraska. It sells its "Falls City" brand beer in 13 states, including Indiana and Kentucky. In Indiana, Falls City sells its beer to Vanco Beverage, Inc. (Vanco), a beer wholesaler located in Vanderburgh County. In Kentucky, Falls City sells its beer to wholesalers located in Henderson County. The two counties are directly across from each other and are separated only by the Indiana-Kentucky state line. A four-lane interstate highway connects the two counties. When other brewers raised their wholesale prices in Indiana, Falls City also raised its prices. Falls City also raised its wholesale prices in Kentucky, but less than its prices were raised in Indiana. Vanco brought this treble damage action against Falls City, alleging that Falls City had engaged in price discrimination in violation of Section 2(a) of the Robinson-Patman Act by raising prices less in Kentucky than in Indiana. Does meeting the competition defense protect Falls City from liability for price discrimination? Did Falls City act unethically in this case? [*Falls City Industries, Inc. v. Vanco Beverage, Inc.*, 460 U.S. 428, 103 S.Ct. 1282 (1983)]

CRITICAL LEGAL THINKING WRITING ASSIGNMENT

Read Case A.48 in the Case Appendix [*Texaco Inc. v. Hasbrouck, dba Rick's Texaco*]. This case is excerpted from the U.S. Supreme Court opinion. Review and brief the case. In your brief, be sure to answer the following questions:

1. Who were the plaintiffs? Who was the defendant?

2. Describe the activities that the defendant engaged in that the plaintiffs alleged were unlawful.

3. What law did the plaintiffs assert was violated? What does this law prohibit?

4. Did the U.S. Supreme Court find a violation? Explain the reasoning the Supreme Court used in reaching its decision.

NOTES

1. Antitrust Amendments Act of 1990, P.L. 101–588.
2. Antitrust Amendments Act of 1990, P.L. 101–588.
3. 15 U.S.C. § 15.
4. *Reiter v. Sonotone Corporation*, 442 U.S. 330, 99 S.Ct. 2326 (1979).
5. 15 U.S.C. § 26.
6. Justice Marshall, *United States v. Topco Associates, Inc.*, 405 U.S. 596, 92 S.Ct. 1126 (1972).
7. 15 U.S.C. § 1.
8. 221 U.S. 1, 31 S.Ct. 502 (1911). The Court found that Rockefeller's oil trust violated the Sherman Act and ordered the trust broken up into 30 separate companies.
9. *Continental T.V., Inc. v. GTE Sylvania, Inc.*, 433 U.S. 36, 97 S.Ct. 2549 (1977), reversing *United States v. Arnold Schwinn & Co.*, 388 U.S. 365, 87 S.Ct. 1856 (1969).
10. 250 U.S. 300, 39 S.Ct. 465 (1919).
11. This doctrine is the result of two U.S. Supreme Court decisions: *Eastern R.R. President's Conference v. Noerr Motor Freight, Inc.*, 365 U.S. 127, 81 S.Ct. 523 (1961), and *United Mine Workers v. Pennington*, 381 U.S. 657, 85 S.Ct. 1585 (1965).
12. 15 U.S.C. § 2.
13. *William Inglis & Sons Baking Company v. ITT Continental Baking Company, Inc.*, 668 F.2d 1014 (9th Cir. 1982).
14. 15 U.S.C. § 18.
15. 374 U.S. 321, 83 S.Ct. 1715 (1963).
16. 15 U.S.C. § 18(a).
17. 15 U.S.C. § 14.
18. 15 U.S.C. § 13(a).
19. *Hartley & Parker, Inc. v. Florida Beverage Corp.*, 307 F.2d 916, 923 (5th Cir. 1952).
20. 15 U.S.C. § 13(b).
21. 15 U.S.C. § 13(c).
22. 15 U.S.C. § 13(d).
23. 15 U.S.C. § 13(e).
24. 15 U.S.C. § 13(f).
25. 15 U.S.C. § 45.
26. Section 6 of the Clayton Act, 15 U.S.C. § 17; the Norris-LaGuardia Act of 1932, 29 U.S.C. §§ 101–115; and the National Labor Relations Act of 1935, 29 U.S.C. §§ 141 et seq. Labor unions that conspire or combine with nonlabor groups to accomplish a goal prohibited by federal antitrust law lose their exemption.
27. Capper-Volstrand Act of 1922, 7 U.S.C. § 291; Cooperative Marketing Act of 1926, 15 U.S.C. § 521.
28. Webb-Pomerene Act, 15 U.S.C. §§ 61–65.
29. McCarran-Ferguson Act of 1945, 15 U.S.C. §§ 1011–1015.
30. *Flood v. Kuhn*, 407 U.S. 258, 92 S.Ct. 2099 (1972).
31. *Community Communications Co., Inc. v. City of Boulder*, 455 U.S. 40, 102 S.Ct. 835 (1982).
32. *Goldfarb v. Virginia State Bar*, 421 U.S. 773, 95 S.Ct. 2004 (1975).
33. For example, see *California v. ARC America Corporation*, 490 U.S. 93, 109 S.Ct. 1661 (1989).

Personal Property and Bailments

Property and law are born and must die together.

JEREMY BENTHAM
Principles of the Civil Code, 1 Works 309

Chapter Objectives

After studying this chapter, you should be able to

1. Define *personal property*.
2. Describe the methods for acquiring ownership in personal property.
3. Explain how ownership rights are transferred by *inter vivos gift* and *gift causa mortis*.
4. Describe and apply rules regarding ownership rights in mislaid, lost, or abandoned property.
5. Define *ordinary bailments*.
6. List and describe the elements for creating a bailment.
7. List and describe the rights and duties of bailees and bailors.
8. Explain the liability of bailees for lost, damaged, or destroyed goods in ordinary bailment situations.
9. Explain the liability of bailees in special bailment situations.
10. Describe the use of documents of title.

Chapter Contents

Private ownership of property forms the foundation of our economic system. As such, a comprehensive body of law has been developed to protect property rights. The law protects the rights of property owners to use, sell, dispose of, control, and prevent others from trespassing on their rights.

Property in this country is expressly provided protection in the U.S. Constitution. The Fifth Amendment provides, "No person shall be . . . deprived of life, liberty, or property, without due process of law; nor shall private property be taken for public use, without just compensation." The Fourteenth Amendment provides, "No State shall . . . deprive any person of life, liberty, or property, without due process of law." These rights are not absolute. The government can acquire private property for public use (e.g., for highways and parks) as long as it pays just compensation for the property.

The first part of this chapter discusses the two kinds of personal property, methods of acquiring ownership in personal property and property rights in mislaid, lost, and abandoned property. The second part of this chapter discusses bailments—situations where possession of (but not title to) personal property is delivered to another party for transfer, safekeeping, or other purpose.

> *Property is the most ambiguous of categories. It covers a multitude of rights which have nothing in common except that they are exercised by persons and enforced by the state.*
>
> R. H. Tawney
> The Acquisitive Society.
> *Ch. V (1921)*

𝒯HE NATURE OF PERSONAL PROPERTY

There are two kinds of property: real property and personal property. **Real property** includes land and property that is permanently attached to it. For example, minerals, crops, timber, and buildings that are attached to land are generally considered real property. **Personal property** (sometimes referred to as *goods* or *chattels*) consists of everything that is not real property. Real property can become personal property if it is removed from the land. For example, a tree that is part of a forest is real property; a tree that is cut down is personal property.

Personal property that is permanently affixed to land or buildings is called a *fixture*. Such property, which includes things like heating systems and storm windows, is categorized as real property. Unless otherwise agreed, fixtures remain with a building when it is sold. Personal property (e.g., furniture, pictures, and other easily portable household items) may be removed by the seller prior to sale.

real property

The land itself as well as buildings, trees, soil, minerals, timber, plants, and other things permanently affixed to the land.

personal property

Property that consists of tangible property, such as automobiles, furniture, and jewelry, and intangible property, such as securities, patents, and copyrights.

Personal property is tangible property. Even flowers that can be removed from real property are an example of personal property.

tangible property
All real property, and physically defined personal property such as goods, animals, and minerals.

intangible property
Rights that cannot be reduced to physical form, such as stock certificates, CDs, bonds, and copyrights.

Personal property can be either tangible or intangible. **Tangible property** includes physically defined property such as goods, animals, and minerals. **Intangible property** represents rights that cannot be reduced to physical form, such as stock certificates, certificates of deposit, bonds, and copyrights.

Real and personal property may be owned by one person or by more than one person. If property is owned concurrently by two or more persons, there is *concurrent ownership*.

ACQUIRING OWNERSHIP IN PERSONAL PROPERTY

Personal property may be acquired or transferred with a minimum of formality. Commerce would be severely curtailed if the transfers of such items were difficult. The methods for acquiring ownership in personal property are discussed below.

By Possession

taking possession
A method of acquiring ownership of unowned personal property.

A person can acquire ownership in unowned personal property by **taking possession** of it or capturing it. The most notable unowned objects are things in their natural state. For example, people who obtain the proper fishing license acquire ownership of all the fish they catch. This type of property acquisition was important when this country was being developed. In today's urbanized society, however, there are few unowned objects, and this method of acquiring ownership in personal property has become less important.

By Purchase or Production

purchasing property
The most common method of acquiring title to personal property.

The most common method of acquiring title to personal property is by **purchasing the property** from its owner. For example, Urban Concrete Corp. (Urban Concrete) owns a large piece of equipment. City Builders, Inc. (City Builders), purchases the equipment from Urban Concrete for $50,000. Urban Concrete signs over the title to the equipment to City Builders. City Builders is now the owner of the equipment.

Production is another common method of acquiring ownership in personal property. Thus, a manufacturer who purchases raw materials and produces a finished product owns that product.

Ethical Perspective _____

WHAT'S MINE IS MINE AND WHAT'S YOURS IS MINE

The Beech Aircraft Corporation (Beech) and Lowell and Aileen Anderson owned adjacent property in Kansas. The Stalmaker gas reserve, which had long ago been drilled and depleted of natural gas, underlies both properties.

Beech purchased natural gas for its own use and for sale. Ground storage of natural gas is almost impossible because it is not economically feasible to build containers large enough to hold the gas, so Beech began storing gas in the Stalmaker reserve. It purchased large quantities of natural gas from interstate pipelines and injected it through wells into the reservoir. There was only one problem: The nat-

ural gas flowed into the reservoir and came to rest under both Beech's and the Andersons' property. Beech did not obtain a lease, license, or permit from the Andersons to store the gas under their property.

Avanti Petroleum (Avanti) held an oil and gas lease on the Anderson farm. When it discovered that the natural gas was under the property, it began drilling and extracting the natural gas with full knowledge that Beech had placed it there. A lawsuit between Beech and Avanti ensued. Beech argued that it owned the gas because it had paid for it. Avanti argued that because the gas migrated to its lease field, it could rightfully extract it.

The Kansas supreme court decided the case in favor of Avanti. The court stated

> As far as natural gas is concerned, Kansas has long recognized the law of capture, holding that natural gas in the ground is part of the real estate until it is actually produced and severed. At that point, it becomes personalty. The courts have also recognized the nature of oil and gas as being fugitive and migratory, having the power and tendency to escape without the volition of its owner. The courts have analogized oil and gas to wild animals or animals ferae naturale. The ownership of birds and wild animals becomes vested in the person capturing or reducing them to possession. However, when restored to their natural wild and free state, the dominion and individual proprietorship of any person over them is at an end, and they resume their status as common property.

Thus, legally Beech had lost its ownership interest in the natural gas when it flowed under the Andersons' farm. Avanti could drill for the natural gas that Beech had already paid for. [*Anderson v. Beech Aircraft Corp.*, 699 P.2d 1023 (Kan. 1985)]

1. Did Avanti act ethically when it drilled for and removed the natural gas it knew had been paid for and stored in the underground reserve by Beech?
2. Should Beech have requested and received permission from the Andersons before storing the natural gas beneath the Andersons' property? Did it get what it deserved?

By Gift

A **gift** is a voluntary transfer of property without consideration. The lack of consideration is what distinguishes a gift from a purchase. The person making a gift is called the **donor**. The person who receives the gift is called the **donee**. There are three elements of a valid gift: *donative intent*, *delivery*, and *acceptance*:

1. **Donative Intent** For a gift to be effective, the donor must have intended to make a gift. *Donative intent* can be inferred from the circumstances or language used by the donor. The courts also consider such factors as the relationship of the parties, the size of the gift, the mental capacity of the donor, and so on.
2. **Delivery** Delivery must occur for there to be a valid gift. Although *physical delivery* is the usual method of transferring personal property, it is sometimes impracticable. In such circumstances, *constructive delivery* (or *symbolic delivery*) is sufficient. For example, if the property being gifted is kept in a safe-deposit box, physically giving the key to the donee is enough to signal the gift. Most intangible property is transferred by writing conveyance (e.g., conveying a stock certificate represents a transfer of ownership in a corporation).
3. **Acceptance** *Acceptance* usually is not a problem because most donees readily accept gifts. In fact, the courts presume acceptance unless there is proof that the gift was refused. Nevertheless, a person cannot be forced to accept an unwanted gift.

Gifts *Inter Vivos* and Gifts *Causa Mortis* A gift made during a person's lifetime that is an irrevocable present transfer of ownership is an ***inter vivos* gift**. A **gift *causa mortis*** is a gift that is made in contemplation of death. A gift *causa mortis* is established when (1) the donor makes a gift in anticipation of approaching death from some existing sickness or peril, and (2) the donor dies from such sickness or peril without having revoked the gift. Gifts *causa mortis* can be revoked by the donor up until the time he or she dies. A gift *causa mortis* takes precedent over a prior conflicting will.

Consider This Example Suppose Sandy is a patient in the hospital. She is to have a major operation from which she may not recover. Prior to going into surgery, Sandy removes her diamond ring and gives it to her friend Pamela, stating, "In the event of my death, I want you to have this." This is a gift *causa mortis*. If Sandy dies as a result of the operation, the gift is effective—Pamela owns the ring. If Sandy lives, the requisite condition for the gift (her death) has not occurred. Therefore, the gift is not effective, and Sandy can recover the ring from Pamela.

gift
A voluntary transfer of title to property without payment of consideration by the donee. To be a valid gift, the following three elements must be shown: (1) *donative intent*, (2) *delivery*, and (3) *acceptance*.

donor
A person who gives a gift.

donee
A person who receives a gift.

***inter vivos* gift**
A gift made during a person's lifetime that is an irrevocable present transfer of ownership.

gift *causa mortis*
A gift that is made in contemplation of death.

In the following case, the court had to determine whether a gift of a valuable painting had been made.

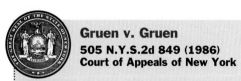

Gruen v. Gruen
505 N.Y.S.2d 849 (1986)
Court of Appeals of New York

CASE 49.1

FACTS

Victor Gruen was a successful architect. In 1959, Victor purchased a painting entitled *Schloss Kammer am Attersee II* by a noted Austrian modernist, Gustav Klimt; he paid $8,000 for the painting. In 1963, Victor wrote a letter to his son Michael, then an undergraduate student at Harvard University, giving the painting to Michael but reserving a life estate in the painting. The letter stated:

> *Dear Michael:*
> *The 21st birthday, being an important event in life, should be celebrated accordingly. I therefore wish to give you as a present the oil painting by Gustav Klimt, of Schloss Kammer which now hangs in the New York living room.*
> *Happy birthday again.*
> *Love,*
> */s/Victor*

As Victor retained a life interest in the painting, Michael never took possession of the painting. Victor died on February 14, 1980. The painting was appraised at $2.5 million. When Michael requested the painting from his stepmother, Kemija Gruen, she refused to turn it over to him. Michael sued to recover the painting. The trial court held in favor of the stepmother. The appellate division reversed. The stepmother appealed.

ISSUE

Did Victor Gruen make a valid *inter vivos* gift of the Klimt painting to his son Michael?

IN THE LANGUAGE OF THE COURT

Simons, Judge   An inter vivos *gift requires that the donor intends to make an irrevocable present transfer of ownership. Defendant contends that the trial court was correct in finding that Victor did not intend to transfer any present interest in the painting to plaintiff in 1963 but only expressed an intention that*

plaintiff was to get the painting upon his death. The evidence is all but conclusive, however, that Victor intended to transfer ownership of the painting to plaintiff in 1963 but to retain a life estate in it and that he did, therefore, effectively transfer a remainder interest in the painting to plaintiff at that time. The letters unambiguously establish that Victor Gruen intended to make a present gift of title to the painting at that time.

In order to have a valid inter vivos *gift, there must be a delivery of the gift, either by a physical delivery of the subject of the gift or a constructive or symbolic delivery such as by an instrument of gift, sufficient to divest the donor of dominion and control over the property. Defendant contends that when a tangible piece of personal property such as a painting is the subject of a gift, physical delivery of the painting itself is the best form of delivery and should be required. Defendant's statement of the rule as applied may be generally true, but it ignores the fact that what Victor Gruen gave plaintiff was not all rights to the Klimt painting, but only title to it with no right of possession until his death. Under these circumstances, it would be illogical for the law to require the donor to part with possession of the painting when that is exactly what he intends to retain.*

DECISION AND REMEDY

The appellate court held that Victor Gruen had made a valid *inter vivos* gift of the Klimt painting to his son Michael. The court affirmed the judgment of the appellate division in favor of Michael Gruen.

Case Questions

Critical Legal Thinking   Should donors who make *inter vivos* gifts be required to relinquish physical possession of the property to the donee?

Ethics   Did the stepmother act ethically in refusing to turn the painting over to Michael?

Uniform Gift to Minors Act and Revised Uniform Gift to Minors Act

Acts that establish procedures for adults to make gifts of money and securities to minors.

Uniform Gift to Minors Acts   All states have adopted in whole or in part the **Uniform Gift to Minors Act** or the **Revised Uniform Gift to Minors Act**. These laws establish procedures for adults to make irrevocable gifts of money and securities to minors. Gifts of money can be made by depositing the money in an account with a financial institution with the donor or another trustee (such as another adult or the bank) as custodian for the minor. Gifts of securities can be made by registering the securities in the name of a trustee as custodian for the minor. The laws give custodians broad discretionary powers to invest the money or securities for the benefit of the minor.

By Will or Inheritance

Title to personal property frequently is acquired by **will or inheritance**. If the person who dies has a valid will, the property is distributed to the *beneficiaries*, pursuant to the provisions of that will. Otherwise, the property is distributed to the *heirs* as provided in the relevant state's inheritance statute.

will or inheritance
A way to acquire title to property that is a result of another's death.

By Accession

Accession occurs when the value of personal property increases because it is added to or improved by natural or manufactured means. Accession that occurs naturally belongs to the owner (e.g., a colt that is born to a mare belongs to the mare's owner). If accession occurs by manufactured means and the owner consents to the improvement, the owner acquires title to the improvement but must pay the improver for labor and services. For example, a business owner who contracts to have an addition built onto his or her factory owns the new structure but must pay the contract price to the improver.

accession
Occurs when the value of personal property increases because it is added to or improved by natural or manufactured means.

Wrongful Improvement   If the improvement was made wrongfully, the owner acquires title to the improved property and does not have to pay the improver for the value of the improvements. For instance, suppose a thief steals the car and puts a new engine in it. The owner is entitled to recover the car as improved without having to pay the thief for the improvements.

Mistaken Improvement   If the improvement was mistakenly made by the improver, the courts generally follow these rules:

1. If the improvements can be easily separated from the original article, the improver must remove the improvements and pay any damages caused by such removal. For example, a builder who puts the wrong door on a house must replace that door with the correct door at his own cost.
2. If the improvements cannot be removed, the owner owns title to the improved property and does not have to pay the improver for the improvements. For example, if a builder misreads blueprints and extends an addition to a building too far, the building owner is entitled to keep the improvement at no extra cost. In some cases, if the improvements are substantial and cannot be removed, the court can permit the improver to acquire title to the personal property by paying the owner the value of the original article.

Only a ghost can exist without material property.

Ayn Rand
Atlas Shrugged *(1957)*

By Confusion

Confusion occurs if two or more persons commingle fungible goods (i.e., goods that are exactly alike, such as the same grade of oil, grains, or cattle). Title to goods can be acquired by confusion. It does not matter whether the goods were commingled by agreement or by accident. Each of the owners thereafter owns a percentage of the commingled goods equal to his or her percentage contribution to the total. The goods are considered to be acquired by confusion because no one knows what exact good he or she owns because the goods are commingled. An owner may withdraw his or her share at any time unless agreed otherwise. If goods are wrongfully or intentionally commingled without permission, the innocent party acquires title to them.

confusion
Occurs if two or more persons commingle fungible goods; title is then acquired by confusion.

Consider This Example   If three farmers agree to store the same amount of grade B winter wheat in a silo, each of them owns one-third. When the grain is sold, the profits are divided into three parts; if the silo burns to the ground, each suffers one-third of the loss.

By Divorce

> Laws are always useful to persons of property, and hurtful to those who have none.
>
> Jean-Jacques Rousseau
> Du Contrat Social *(1761)*

When a marriage is dissolved by a divorce, the parties obtain certain rights in the property of the marital estate. Often, a settlement of property rights is reached. If not, the court must decide the property rights of the spouses. In the following case, the court decided the spouses' ownership rights to personal property upon divorce.

Giha v. Giha
609 A.2d 945 (1992)
Supreme Court of Rhode Island

CASE 49.2

FACTS

On October 7, 1987, Nagib Giha (Husband) filed a complaint for divorce from Nelly Giha (Wife) on the grounds of irreconcilable differences. On May 20, 1988, the parties reached an agreement for the disposition of their property that provided they would divide equally the net proceeds from the sale of their marital assets. They had to wait a statutory waiting period before the divorce was final. On December 25, 1988, Husband learned that he had won $2.4 million in the Massachusetts Megabucks state lottery. Husband kept this fact secret. After the waiting period was over, the family court entered its final judgment severing the parties' marriage on April 27, 1989. Husband claimed his lottery prize on October 6, 1989. In December 1990, after learning of the lottery winnings, Wife sued to recover the lottery prize. She alleged that the lottery prize was a marital asset because her Husband had won it before their divorce was final. The trial court dismissed her complaint. Wife appealed.

ISSUE

Was the $2.4-million lottery prize personal property of the marital estate?

IN THE LANGUAGE OF THE COURT

Fay, Chief Justice We have established that the parties to a divorce action remain as husband and wife until the entry of the final decree of divorce. In the present case the husband won the lottery prize four months before the Family Court entered its final judgment. The parties remained as husband and wife until the entry of the final judgment in 1989. Because the parties' marriage remained in effect throughout the waiting period, so did the property rights each spouse had in the property acquired by the other spouse during that period. Therefore, since the husband won the $2.4 million lottery prize during the existence of the parties' marriage, we conclude that the prize is a marital asset and is subject to the equitable-distribution statute. We conclude that the parties to a divorce action have a continuing duty to provide information about changes in their financial condition until the entry of a final judgment of divorce.*

DECISION AND REMEDY

The appellate court held that the parties remained as husband and wife until the entry of final judgment of divorce in April 1989. Therefore, the lottery prize was a marital asset. Reversed and remanded.

Case Questions

Critical Legal Thinking   Should a spouse's lottery winnings be considered separate property? Why or why not?

Ethics   Did Husband act ethically in this case?

MISLAID, LOST, AND ABANDONED PROPERTY

Often, people find another person's personal property. Ownership rights to the property differ depending on whether the property is *mislaid*, *lost*, or *abandoned*. The following paragraphs discuss these legal rules.

Mislaid Property

mislaid property

When an owner voluntarily places property somewhere and then inadvertently forgets it.

Property is **mislaid** when its owner voluntarily places the property somewhere and then inadvertently forgets it. It is likely that the owner will return for the property upon realizing that it was misplaced.

The owner of the premises where the property is mislaid is entitled to take possession of the property against all except the rightful owner. This right is superior to the rights of the person who finds it. Such possession does not involve a change of title. Instead, the owner of the premises becomes an involuntary bailee of the property (bailments are discussed later in this chapter) and owes a duty to take reasonable care of the property until it is reclaimed by the owner.

Lost Property

Property is considered **lost** when its owner negligently, carelessly, or inadvertently leaves it somewhere. The finder obtains title to such property against the whole world except the true owner. The lost property must be returned to its rightful owner whether the finder discovers the loser's identity or the loser finds him or her. A finder who refuses to return the property is liable for the tort of conversion and the crime of larceny. Many states require the finder to conduct a reasonable search (e.g., place advertisements in newspapers) to find the rightful owner.

lost property
When a property owner leaves property somewhere because of negligence, carelessness, or inadvertence.

Consider This Example   If a commuter finds a diamond ring on the floor of a subway station in New York City, the ring is considered lost property. The commuter can claim title to the ring against the whole world except the true owner. If the true owner discovers that the commuter has her ring, she may recover it from the commuter.

Estray Statutes   Most states have enacted **estray statutes** that permit a finder of *mislaid* or *lost* property to clear title to the property if

1. The finder reports the found property to the appropriate government agency and then turns over possession of the property to this agency,
2. Either the finder or the government agency posts notices and publishes advertisements describing the lost property, and
3. A specified time (usually a year or a number of years) has passed without the rightful owner's reclaiming the property.

estray statutes
Statutes that permit a finder of mislaid or lost property to clear title to the property if (1) the finder reports the found property to the appropriate government agency and turns over possession of the property to this agency, (2) either the finder or the government agency posts notices and publishes advertisements describing the lost property, and (3) a specified amount of time has passed without the rightful owner's reclaiming the property.

Many state estray statutes provide that the government receive a portion of the value of the property. Some statutes provide that title cannot be acquired in found property that is the result of illegal activity. For example, title has been denied to finders of property and money deemed to have been used for illegal drug purchases. The court applied an estray statute in the following case.

Willsmore v. Township of Oceola, Michigan
308 N.W.2d 796 (1981)
Court of Appeals of Michigan

CASE 49.3

FACTS
While hunting on unposted and unoccupied property in Oceola Township, Michigan, Duane Willsmore noticed an area with branches arranged in a crisscross pattern. When he kicked aside the branches and sod, he found a watertight suitcase in a freshly dug hole. Willsmore informed the Michigan state police of his find. A state trooper and Willsmore together pried open the suitcase and discovered $383,840 in cash. The state police took custody of the money, which was deposited in an interest-bearing account. Michigan's "Lost Goods Act" provides that the finder and the township in which the property was found must share the value of the property if the finder publishes required notices and the true owner does not claim the property within one year.

Willsmore published the required notices and brought a declaratory judgment action seeking a determination of the ownership of the money. Thomas Powell, the owner of the land on which the suitcase was found, claimed he was the owner of the suitcase. After Powell incorrectly named the amount of money in the suitcase, he asserted his Fifth Amendment right not to testify at his deposition and at trial. The trial court awarded the money equally to Willsmore and the Township of Oceola. Powell appealed.

ISSUE
Who is the owner of the lost suitcase and its contents?

IN THE LANGUAGE OF THE COURT
Corsiglia, Judge   It is a universally accepted fundamental principle of property law that the true owner, assuming he presented himself within the one-year statute of limitations of the Lost Goods Act, would be entitled to the money before any other party in this case. However, true ownership must be established to the satisfaction of

(box continues)

the court. Voluntarily, and perhaps wisely, claimant Powell did not present himself at trial. At Powell's deposition, virtually the only answer he would give was the bald assertion that he was the true owner of the money. When asked the sum of money in the suitcase, his answer was incorrect. When faced with questions about how he obtained the money and hid it, claimant Powell had the right to assert his constitutional privilege to remain silent. However, the court not only had the right, but also the duty, to conclude from such silence that claimant Powell did not carry his burden of proof. Claimant Powell's claim as true owner fails as a matter of law.

This court finds that the Lost Goods Act is applicable to this property. The Lost Goods Act encourages the goals that this court considers important in such cases. It provides certainty of title to property by eventually vesting clear title after a set period of time. It encourages honesty in finders by providing penalties for not turning in property in accord with its provisions and providing incentives for compliance. The act provides notice to potential true owners and publication to seek them out. It provides for registration of the find in a central location where an owner could locate the goods with ease. The Lost Goods Act provides for appraisal of the goods. There is

a reasonable time limit before title to goods is cut off from the former owner or holder. The public obtains a portion of the benefit of a find through receipt of one-half of the value by the township. The finder receives an award for his honesty by receiving one-half of the value of the property plus costs. We conclude that the statute is in effect a "finder's statute." The provisions of the act are an eminently reasonable solution to a troublesome problem.

DECISION AND REMEDY

The appellate court held that Willsmore and the Township of Oceola were the owners of the suitcase and its contents. The appellate court affirmed the judgment of the trial court and ordered that Willsmore and the township both receive one-half the proceeds of the find after Willsmore's costs were deducted.

Case Questions

Critical Legal Thinking   Do estray statutes serve a useful social purpose? Should the government get half of the find?

Ethics   If you had found the suitcase, would you have turned it in to the government?

---

abandoned property

Property that an owner has discarded with the intent to relinquish his or her rights in it, or mislaid or lost property that the owner has given up any further attempts to locate.

Abandoned Property

Property is classified as **abandoned** if (1) an owner discards the property with the intent to relinquish his or her rights in it or (2) an owner of mislaid or lost property gives up any further attempts to locate it. Anyone who finds abandoned property acquires title to it. The title is good against the whole world, including the original owner. For example, property left at a garbage dump is abandoned property. It belongs to the first person who claims it.

Entrepreneur and the Law

WHO OWNS THE TREASURE TROVE ON THE SS CENTRAL AMERICA?

On Saturday, September 12, 1857, the *SS Central America*, a luxurious steamship that made frequent trips between New York and Panama, lost a desperate three-day battle to keep itself afloat. It sank 169 miles off the coast of South Carolina. The ship carried 587 passengers, many of whom were returning from California, where they had recovered gold from newly discovered mines. Only 166 passengers survived. Insurance companies paid claims for the $1.2 million (1857 value) of gold coins and bricks that sank with the ship.

For nearly 130 years, the *SS Central America* lay peacefully in the icy waters off the East Coast. While many dreamed of finding the ship and its cargo, which is estimated to be worth up to $1 billion in today's market, no one knew exactly where to look.

In 1981, Thomas G. Thompson, an Ohio-based scientist and entrepreneur, organized an expedition called the

Columbus-America Discovery Group to recover the sunken ship by submerging a 5,000-pound robot, with a video camera attached to its arm, into the water. Finally, in 1987, the robot found what Thompson had been tirelessly searching for—the *SS Central America* and its undisturbed cargo of thousands of rare gold coins and even rarer gold bars.

When the jubilant Thompson and crew returned to port, they were greeted by more than just well-wishers. Representatives of several insurance companies immediately claimed that some of the *SS Central America's* loot belonged to them as compensation for the claims they had paid 130 years earlier.

Thompson's group sought to vindicate its exclusive right to the *SS Central America* and her cargo by filing an action in federal court. The U.S. court of appeals applied the maritime **Law of Salvage**. Under the doctrine, original owners retain ownership interest, although the salvager is entitled to a very liberal salvage award.

The district court determined that the salvager was entitled to 90 percent of the gold coins and other treasure trove found on the *SS Central America*. In affirming this award, the court of appeals stated

In addition to surveying more than 1,400 square miles of ocean bottom, an area the size of Rhode Island, hundreds of runs were made to recheck objects and to photograph them. The salvors spent 487 days at sea working shifts of 12 hours each. Personnel logged some 411,295 hours of labor from 1985 through 1992,

at a cost for labor of $8,421,733. This figure does not record the fact that Thompson had been doing research since the early 1970s. A considerable amount of equipment was specially designed, manufactured, and assembled for the project. The salvors had assembled experts in the various fields of science, archaeology, history, maritime, marketing, and publicity, to advise and assist in the use, care, and preservation of the shipwreck site. It is apparent that Columbus-America's effort was monumental. [*Columbus–America Discovery Group v. Atlantic Mutual Insurance Company*, 56 F.2d 556 (4th Cir. 1995)]

CONCEPT SUMMARY   RULES REGARDING OWNERSHIP RIGHTS IN MISLAID, LOST, AND ABANDONED PROPERTY

Common Law Rules

Type of Property	Ownership Rights
Mislaid property	The owner of the premises where property is mislaid is entitled to possession but does not acquire title. He or she holds the property as an involuntary bailee until the owner reclaims it.
Lost property	The finder acquires title to the property against the whole world except the true owner; the owner may reclaim his or her property from the finder.
Abandoned property	The finder acquires title to the property, even against its original owner.

Estray Statutes

Many states have enacted estray statutes that give a **finder** of mislaid or lost property clear title to the property if certain requirements are met, including (1) reporting the find to an appropriate government agency, (2) advertising the lost property, and (3) the owner not claiming the property within a stated time period (e.g., one year). The finder acquires title to the property and is thereafter not required to return the property if the rightful owner appears to claim it.

BAILMENTS

A **bailment** occurs when the owner of personal property delivers his or her property to another person to be held, stored, or delivered, or for some other purpose. In a bailment, the owner of the property is the **bailor** and the party to whom the property is delivered for safekeeping, storage, or delivery (e.g., warehouse or common carrier) is the **bailee** (see Exhibit 49.1). Almost everyone has been involved in a bailment transaction.

bailment
A transaction where an owner transfers his or her personal property to another to be held, stored, delivered, or for some other purpose. Title to the property does not transfer.

bailor
The owner of property in a bailment.

bailee
A holder of goods who is not a seller or a buyer (e.g., a warehouse or common carrier).

EXHIBIT 49.1   *Parties to a Bailment*

A bailment is different from a sale or a gift because title to the goods does not transfer to the bailee. Instead, the bailee must follow the bailor's directions concerning the goods. For example, suppose Hudson Corp. is relocating offices and hires American Van Lines to move its office furniture and equipment to the new location. American Van Lines (the bailee) must follow Hudson's (the bailor) instructions regarding delivery. The law of bailments establishes the rights, duties, and liabilities of parties to a bailment.

Elements Necessary to Create a Bailment

Three **elements** are necessary to create a bailment: *personal property, delivery of possession,* and a *bailment agreement*:

1. **Personal Property** Only *personal property* can be bailed. The property can be *tangible* (e.g., automobiles, jewelry, and animals) or *intangible* (e.g., stocks, bonds, and promissory notes).
2. **Delivery of Possession** Delivery of possession involves two elements: (1) The bailee has exclusive control over the personal property, and (2) the bailee must knowingly accept the personal property. For example, no bailment is created if a patron goes into a restaurant and hangs his or her coat on an unattended coatrack. This is because other patrons have access to the coat. However, bailment is created if the patron checked his or her coat with a checkroom attendant because the restaurant has assumed exclusive control over the coat. If valuable property was left in the pocket of the coat, there would be no bailment of that property because the checkroom attendant did not knowingly accept it.

Most bailments are created by *physical delivery*. For example, Great Lakes Shipping, Inc., delivers a vessel to Marina Repairs, Inc., for repairs. *Constructive delivery* can create bailment, too. For example, there has been constructive delivery of an automobile if the owner gives someone the keys and registration to his car.

3. **Bailment Agreement** The creation of a bailment does not require any formality. A bailment may be either express or implied. Most *express bailments* can be either written or oral. However, under the Statute of Frauds, a bailment must be in writing if it is for more than one year. An example of an *implied bailment* is the finding and safeguarding of lost property.

Bailments generally expire at a specified time or when a certain purpose is accomplished. **A bailment for a fixed term** terminates at the end of the term, or sooner by mutual consent of the parties. A party who terminates a bailment in breach of the bailment agreement is liable to the innocent party for damages resulting from the breach. Bailments without a fixed term are called **bailments at will**. A bailment at will can be terminated at any time by either party. Gratuitous bailees or bailors can generally be permitted to terminate a fixed-term bailment prior to expiration of the term.

Upon termination of the bailment, the bailee is legally obligated to do as the bailor directs with the property. Unless otherwise agreed, the bailee is obligated to return the identical goods bailed. Where commingled *fungible goods* are involved (e.g., grain), identically equivalent goods may be returned by the bailee.

In the following case, the court had to determine whether or not a bailment had been created.

elements of a bailment
The following three elements are necessary to create a bailment: (1) personal property, (2) delivery of possession, and (3) a bailment agreement.

bailment for a fixed term
A bailment that terminates at the end of the term, or sooner by mutual consent of the parties.

bailment at will
A bailment without a fixed term; can be terminated at any time by either party.

Magliocco v. American Locker Co., Inc.
239 Cal.Rptr. 497 (1987)
Court of Appeals of California

CASE 49.4

FACTS

Richard George Whitehurst told Salvatore Magliocco that he could buy gold that had been smuggled out of Vietnam by American soldiers who now sought to sell it. Magliocco agreed to purchase the gold for $409,000. To pay for it, Magliocco placed $409,000 in cash in a locked briefcase, which was then placed in a suitcase provided by Whitehurst that had a combination lock. Both men knew the combination. They then went to the Richmond, California, Greyhound bus station, where Magliocco placed the suitcase in a coin-operated locker owned and operated by American Locker Company, Inc. (American Locker). Magliocco kept the key.

Shortly thereafter, a Whitehurst accomplice told an employee of the Greyhound station that he had lost the key to his locker. The employee opened the locker with a master key. When the man opened the combination lock to the briefcase, the employee released the suitcase to him. When Whitehurst did not contact Magliocco as planned to permit him to inspect the gold, Magliocco discovered the locker was empty. Magliocco sued Greyhound Lines, Inc., and American Locker Company, Inc., for damages. The jury found a bailment and held in favor of Magliocco. The defendants appealed.

ISSUE
Was a bailment created between Magliocco and Greyhound and American Locker?

IN THE LANGUAGE OF THE COURT
Chanell, Associate Justice *American Locker contends that the trial court should not have instructed the jury on bailment, because it was not a bailee of Magliocco's suitcase. The locker company argues that a necessary element of bailment—that possession of the stored goods is given to the bailee—cannot be established in a case involving use of a coin-operated locker.*

A bailment is generally defined as the delivery of a thing to another for some special object or purpose, on a contract, express or implied, to conform to the objects or purposes of the delivery. The question is whether use of a coin-operated locker constitutes a common law bailment is one of first impression in California. Other states considering this question have held that one who stores items in a coin-operated locker does not create a common law bailment. These cases hold that no bailment exists because the user who retains a key to the locker never relinquishes primary physical control of the items stored, even if the person making the lockers available has a master key.

We are persuaded that, as a matter of law, under the facts of this case using a coin-operated locker did not create a common law bailment under California law. Therefore, the trial court erred in instructing the jury that a bailment could have been created.

DECISION AND REMEDY
The court of appeals held that a bailment was not created when Magliocco used the coin-operated locker at the Richmond Greyhound bus station. The court reversed the trial court's judgment and ordered Magliocco to pay all costs of the appeal.

Case Questions

Critical Legal Thinking Do you think the assessment of the loss fell on the proper party? Why or why not?

Ethics Did Magliocco act ethically in suing Greyhound and American Locker? Whose fault was it that the money was stolen?

Business Application What would be the impact on coin-operated locker businesses if the jury's verdict were allowed to stand?

ORDINARY BAILMENTS

There are three classifications of **ordinary bailments**. The difference among these categories is the degree of care owed by the bailee in protecting the bailed property. The three types of ordinary bailments are *bailments for the sole benefit of the bailor, bailments for the sole benefit of the bailee*, and *mutual benefit bailments*. Each of these is discussed in the following paragraphs.

> **ordinary bailments**
> (1) Bailments for the sole benefit of the bailor, (2) bailments for the sole benefit of the bailee, and (3) bailments for the mutual benefit of the bailor and bailee.

Bailments for the Sole Benefit of the Bailor

Bailments for the sole benefit of the bailor are *gratuitous bailments* that benefit only the bailor. They arise when the bailee is requested to care for the bailor's property as a favor. The bailee owes only a **duty of slight care** to protect the bailed property—that is, he or she owes a duty not to be grossly negligent in caring for the bailed goods.

> **bailment for the sole benefit of the bailor**
> A gratuitous bailment that benefits only the bailor. The bailee owes only a *duty of slight care* to protect the bailed property.

Consider This Example The Watkins are going on vacation and ask their neighbors, the Smiths, to feed their dog, which is allowed to run free. The Smiths diligently feed the dog, but the dog runs away and does not return. The Smiths are not liable for the loss of the dog.

An *involuntary bailment* arises when someone finds lost or misplaced property. An involuntary bailee owes a duty of slight care to protect the bailed property.

> **duty of slight care**
> A duty not to be grossly negligent in caring for something in one's possession.

Bailments for the Sole Benefit of the Bailee

bailment for sole benefit of the bailee

A gratuitous bailment that benefits only the bailee. The bailee owes a *duty of great care* to protect the bailed property.

Bailments for the sole benefit of the bailee are *gratuitous bailments* that solely benefit the bailee. They generally arise when a bailee requests to use the bailor's property for personal reasons. In this situation, the bailee owes a **duty of great care** (or **utmost care**) to protect the bailed property—that is, he or she owes a duty not to be slightly negligent in caring for the bailed goods.

duty of utmost care

A duty of care that goes beyond ordinary care.

Consider This Example Suppose Mitch borrows Courtney's lawn mower (free of charge) to mow his own lawn. Mitch is the bailee and Courtney is the bailor. This bailment is for the sole benefit of the bailee. Suppose Mitch, while mowing his lawn, leaves the lawn mower in his front yard while he goes into his house to answer the telephone. While he is gone, the lawn mower is stolen. Here, Mitch will be held liable to Courtney for the loss of the lawn mower. This is because Mitch breached his duty of great care to protect the lawn mower.

Bailments for the Mutual Benefit of the Bailor and the Bailee

mutual benefit bailment

A bailment for the mutual benefit of the bailor and bailee. The bailee owes a *duty of reasonable care* to protect the bailed property.

Mutual benefit bailments are bailments that *benefit both parties*. The bailee owes a **duty of reasonable care** (or **ordinary care**) to protect the bailed goods. This means that the bailee is liable for any goods that are lost, damaged, or destroyed because of his or her negligence. The law presumes that if bailed property is lost, damaged, destroyed, or stolen while in the possession of the bailee, it is because of lack of proper care by the bailee; the bailee may rebut this presumption by the introduction of appropriate evidence. Commercial bailments, where the bailor pays the bailee compensation to store, hold, or transport bailed goods, fall into this category.

duty of reasonable care

The duty that a reasonable bailee in like circumstances would owe to protect the bailed property.

Consider This Example Suppose ABC Garment Co. delivers goods to Lowell, Inc., a commercial warehouseman, for storage. A fee is charged for this service. ABC Garment Co. receives the benefit of having its goods stored, and Lowell, Inc., receives the benefit of being paid compensation for storing the goods. In this example, Lowell, Inc. (the bailee), owes a duty of ordinary care to protect the goods.

Some states have eliminated the above categories of ordinary bailments, ruling that all bailees owe a duty of reasonable care regardless of whether or not they benefit from the bailment.

*C*ONCEPT SUMMARY   ORDINARY BAILEE'S DUTY OF CARE

Type of Bailment	Duty of Care Owed by Bailee	Bailee Liable to Bailor for
For the sole benefit of the bailor	Slight	Gross negligence
For the sole benefit of the bailee	Great	Slight negligence
For the mutual benefit of the bailor and bailee	Ordinary	Ordinary negligence

*R*IGHTS AND DUTIES OF BAILEES AND BAILORS

The bailee and bailor have certain rights and owe certain duties to each other. These rights and duties are discussed in the following sections.

Bailee's Rights

During the term of a bailment, the bailee has the right to exclusive possession of the bailed property. This right is temporary, however, because the property must be returned when the bailment is terminated. If a fixed-term mutual benefit bailment is terminated by the bailor prior to the expiration of its term, the bailee can recover damages for the breach of the bailment contract. Generally, a bailor or bailee can terminate a gratuitous bailment at any time without liability.

In some bailments, the bailee has the right to use the bailed property. This right is determined from the terms of the bailment contract and the facts and circumstances surrounding the bailment. For example, suppose a farmer leases a farm tractor for the summer months. During the course of the bailment, the farmer may use the tractor to plow his or her fields.

In a mutual benefit bailment, the bailee has a right to be compensated for work done or services provided to the bailor. The amount of compensation is usually stated in the bailment contract. If no specific amount is stated, reasonable compensation is presumed. Bailees usually obtain a **possessory lien** (also called an **artisan's lien**) on the bailed property for compensation owed by the bailor. If the bailor refuses to or cannot fulfill this commitment, most states permit the bailee to foreclose on the lien, sell the bailed property at a judicial sale, and recover the amount of compensation due from the sale proceeds. Any excess proceeds must be returned to the bailor.

Gratuitous bailees are not entitled to compensation for services provided. However, they are entitled to reimbursement for all costs and expenses rendered in protecting the bailed property.

Bailor's Duties

Many of the bailor's duties complement the bailee's rights. The bailor owes the duty to pay the agreed-upon compensation to the bailee and to not interfere with the bailee's possessory interest during the term of the bailment.

One of the bailor's primary duties is to notify the bailee of any defects in the bailed property that could cause injury to the bailee or others. The extent of this duty depends on the type of bailment. In a bailment for the sole benefit of the bailee, the bailor must notify the bailee of any known defects in the bailed property. In a bailment for the mutual benefit of both parties, the bailor must notify the bailee of any known defects or defects that could have been discovered through reasonable inspection.

A bailor who fails to fulfill these duties is liable for damages caused by the defects. In addition, bailors can be held liable for breach of any express or implied warranties they make about the bailed property.

bailee's rights

Depending on the type of bailment, bailees may have the right to (1) exclusive possession of the bailed property, (2) use of the bailed property, or (3) compensation for work done or services provided.

possessory lien

Lien obtained by a bailee on bailed property for the compensation owed by the bailor to the bailee.

The right of property enables an industrious man to reap where he has sown.

Anonymous

Entrepreneur and the Law

PARKING LOTS: WHO IS LIABLE IF YOUR CAR IS STOLEN?

Who is liable when a car is stolen while parked in a commercial lot or garage? The answer to this question depends upon whether the parking lot is considered to be a bailee of an automobile or merely a lessor of parking space.

It is clear that parking lots and garages are bailees of automobiles once they assume control and possession of the automobile. Thus, if a valet parking attendant parks the car and keeps the keys, it is relatively certain that a court will recognize the existence of a bailment and hold the garage liable if the vehicle is stolen. Disclaimers to the contrary (either on the ticket or posted at the parking lot) are usually held to be ineffective.

On the other hand, if the owner of a car parks his or her own car in a parking lot and takes the keys, this is considered a lease. The general rule in this case is that the "landlord"—the parking lot—is not responsible for the safety of the car.

Special Bailees

Special (or **extraordinary**) **bailees** include common carriers, warehouse companies, and innkeepers. Special bailees must follow most of the rules applicable to ordinary bailees. In addition, they are subject to special liability rules contained in **Article 7** of the **Uniform Commercial Code (UCC)**.

Common Carriers

Common carriers offer transportation services to the general public. Commercial airlines, railroads, public trucking companies, public pipeline companies, and such are common carriers. Many common carriers are regulated by the government.

The delivery of goods to a common carrier creates a mutual benefit bailment. The person shipping the goods is the **shipper** or **consignor.** (the bailor). The transportation company is called the **common carrier** (the bailee). The person to whom the goods are to be delivered is called the **consignee**.

Common carriers are held to a *duty of strict liability.*[1] This means that if the goods are lost, damaged, destroyed, or stolen, the common carrier is liable even if it was not at fault for the loss. Common carriers are not liable for the loss, damage, or destruction of goods caused by (1) an act of God (e.g., a tornado), (2) an act of a public enemy (e.g., terrorist activity), (3) an order of the government (e.g., statutes, court decisions, and government regulations), (4) an act of the shipper (e.g., improper packaging), or (5) the inherent nature of the goods (e.g., perishability).

Common carriers can limit their liability to a stated dollar amount by expressly stating that in the bailment agreement. Federal law requires common carriers that take advantage of such limitation to offer shippers the opportunity to pay a premium and declare a higher value for the goods.[2]

Warehouse Companies

A **warehouseman** (or **warehouse company**) is a bailee engaged in the business of storing property for compensation.[3] Warehousemen are subject to the rights, duties, and liabilities of an ordinary bailee. As such, they owe a *duty of reasonable care* to protect the bailed property in their possession from harm or loss.[4] Warehousemen are liable only for loss or damage to the bailed property caused by their own negligence. They are not liable for loss or damage caused to bailed goods by another person's negligence or conduct.

Warehousemen can limit the dollar amount of their liability if they offer the bailor the opportunity to increase the liability limit for the payment of an additional charge.[5] Warehouse companies are subject to a comprehensive set of federal and state statutes that governs the operation of warehouse facilities.

Innkeepers

An **innkeeper** is the owner of a facility that provides lodging to the public for compensation (e.g., a hotel or motel). Under the common law, innkeepers are held to a *strict liability standard* regarding loss caused to the personal property of transient guests. Permanent lodgers are not subject to this rule.

Almost all states have enacted statutes that *limit the liability* of innkeepers. Most of these **innkeepers statutes** allow innkeepers to avoid liability for loss caused to guests' property if (1) a safe is provided in which the guests' valuable property may be kept and (2) the guests are aware of the safe's availability. Most state laws also allow innkeepers to limit the dollar amount of their liability by notifying their guests of this limit (e.g., by posting a notice on each guest room door). This limitation on liability does not apply if the loss is caused by an innkeeper's negligence.

special bailees
Include common carriers, warehouse companies, and innkeepers.

Article 7 of the UCC
An article of the Uniform Commercial Code that provides a detailed statutory scheme for the creation, perfection, and foreclosure on common carriers' and warehouse operators' liens.

consignor
The person shipping the goods (the bailor).

common carrier
A firm (the bailee) that offers transportation services to the general public. Owes a *duty of strict liability* to the bailor.

consignee
The person to whom the bailed goods are to be delivered.

warehouse company
A bailee engaged in the business of storing property for compensation. Owes a *duty of reasonable care* to protect the bailed property.

innkeeper
The owner of a facility that provides lodging to the public for compensation (e.g., a hotel or motel).

innkeepers statutes
State statutes that limit an innkeeper's common law liability. An innkeeper can avoid liability for loss caused to a guest's property if (1) a safe is provided in which the guest's valuable property may be kept and (2) the guest is notified of this fact.

Contemporary Business Application

LOSS OF PROPERTY LAWSUIT LODGED AGAINST INNKEEPER

Marvin J. Frockt, a traveling jewelry salesman, checked into a Comfort Inn (Inn) in North Carolina owned by Max H. Goodloe and others. Frockt had in his possession a jewelry sample case that contained approximately $150,000 worth of gems and jewels. Frockt requested that the desk clerk place the case in the safe provided by Inn, stating that the case was "very valuable." The clerk did not give Frockt a receipt for the case.

North Carolina law states that innkeepers have a duty to safely keep up to $500 worth of money, jewelry, or other valuables for any guest who requests such a service. The innkeeper is required to give the guest a receipt that plainly states this limitation on liability. Innkeepers have no liability for valuables that are not given to them for safekeeping. In addition, the statute requires the following:

Every innkeeper shall keep posted in every room of his house occupied by guests, and in the office, a printed copy of this Article and of all regulations relating to the conduct of guests. This Chapter shall not apply to innkeepers, or their guests, where the innkeeper fails to keep such notices posted. [N.C.Gen.Stat. § 72]

Inn had not posted the required notice. When Frockt called for his case the next day, it could not be located and was never recovered. Frockt sued the owners of Inn for damages. Is Inn's liability limited to $500?

The defendants urged that N.C.Gen.Stat. Section 72 held Inn harmless for loss or damage to plaintiff above the statutory amount of $500. The court noted that the defendants' argument would be persuasive absent two facts: (1) no receipt was given to the plaintiff by Inn—that notified him of Section 72 and (2) the evidence is uncontradicted that Inn did not display in the office a copy of Section 72.

In holding that Inn's liability for the lost case was not limited to $500, the court stated

The consequences of failing to post notice as required by Section 72-6 are clear: rather than benefiting from the protection afforded by the statute, the innkeeper must look to the common law to define its duties and liabilities. The common law rule in North Carolina is that the innkeeper is strictly liable for the loss of a guest's property, except in a few rare instances, such as where such loss is occasioned by the guest's own negligence. Had the Inn wished to alleviate the draconian effect of the common law rule, it had only to follow the dictates of the statute by posting the notice required therein. This it did not do; consequently, it will not be heard to complain that the rule is untenable.

CONCEPT SUMMARY   SPECIAL BAILEES' DUTY OF CARE

Type of Bailee	Liability	Limitation on Liability
Common carrier	Strictly liable except for 1. Act of God 2. Act of a public enemy 3. Order of the government 4. Act of the shipper 5. Inherent nature of the goods	May limit the dollar amount of liability by offering the bailor the right to declare a higher value for the bailed goods for an additional charge.
Warehouse company	Ordinary negligence	May limit the dollar amount of liability by offering the bailor the right to declare a higher value for the bailed goods for an additional charge.
Innkeeper	Strictly liable	State statutes may limit the liability of an innkeeper for others' negligence.

*D*OCUMENTS OF TITLE

Goods that are stored or shipped are often represented by a **document of title** issued by the bailee. The document of title generally (1) serves as a receipt for the goods, (2) establishes the terms of the contract between the parties, and (3) evidences title to the goods. It is evidence that the holder of the document is entitled to receive, hold, and dispose of the document and the goods that it covers.[6] Warehouse receipts and bills of lading, which are discussed in the following paragraphs, are the major forms of documents of title. **Article 7** of the **UCC** governs documents of title.

Warehouse Receipts

A **warehouse receipt** is a written document issued by a person who is engaged in the business of storing goods for hire, such as a warehouse company or a storage company.[7] The receipt is often a preprinted form drafted by the warehouseman. Warehouse receipts need not be in any particular form,[8] although the following terms should be included:

1. The location of the warehouse where the goods are stored
2. The date of issue
3. The consecutive number of the receipt
4. Whether the goods are to be delivered to the bearer of the receipt or to a specified person of his or her order
5. The rate of storage and handling charges
6. A description of the goods or of the packages containing them
7. The signature of the warehouseman or his or her authorized agent
8. Whether the warehouseman is the owner of the goods solely, jointly, or in common with others
9. A statement of the amount of advances made and liabilities incurred for which the warehouseman claims a lien or security interest
10. Any other term that is not contrary to the warehouseman's duty of care, duty to deliver the goods, or provisions of the Uniform Commercial Code[9]

If the warehouse receipt specifies an expiration date, the warehouseman may notify the person on whose account the goods are held to pay the charges due and remove the goods at the end of the term. If no specific time is stated in the receipt, the warehouseman must give the bailor at least 30 days' notice to pay the charges due and remove the goods.[10] A shorter notice period is permitted if the goods are about to deteriorate or are hazardous to persons, other property, or the warehouse.[11]

Warehouse Company's Lien As is the case with other bailees, warehousemen have a *lien* on the goods in their possession for necessary expenses incurred in storing and handling the goods.[12] If the charges are not paid, the warehousemen may sell the goods at a public or private auction and apply the proceeds to pay the charges.[13] Any excess proceeds must be held for the persons who had the right to demand delivery of the goods.[14] The UCC establishes procedures for enforcing a warehouseman's lien.[15]

Bills of Lading

A **bill of lading** is a document of title that is issued by a carrier when goods are received for transportation. Bills of lading are issued by common carriers, contract carriers, freight forwarders, and other persons engaged in the business of transporting goods for hire.[16]

A **through bill of lading** provides that connecting carriers may be used to transport the goods to their destination. The original carrier that issued the bill of lading is liable for any damage or loss to the goods caused by the connecting carrier.[17] However, the original carrier is entitled to reimbursement from the connecting carrier for any damages and expenses caused by the connecting carrier.[18] The connecting carrier is liable only for damages or losses to the goods caused while the goods are in its possession.[19]

through bill of lading
A bill of lading that provides that connecting carriers may be used to transport the goods to their destination.

Carrier's Lien A carrier has a lien on the goods in its possession covered by a bill of lading for necessary charges and expenses.[20] If the charges are not paid, the carrier can sell the goods at public or private sale and apply the proceeds to pay the charges.[21] Any excess proceeds must be held for the person who had the right to demand delivery of the goods.[22] The UCC establishes procedures for enforcing a carrier's lien.[23] A purchaser in good faith of goods sold to enforce a warehouseman's lien or a carrier's lien takes the goods free of any rights of persons against whom the lien was valid.[24]

Lost, Stolen, or Destroyed Documents of Title

If a document of title has been lost, stolen, or destroyed, the claimant may petition the court to order the delivery of the goods or the issuance of a substitute document. A carrier or warehouseman may comply with the order without liability to any person. If the document is negotiable, the claimant must post security with the court to indemnify any person who may suffer a loss because of the missing document.[25]

A carrier or warehouseman that delivers goods to a person claiming them under a missing document of title without a court order is liable to any person injured thereby.

International Perspective

WHEN AIRLINES LOSE LUGGAGE

Every day airlines are bailees for hundreds of thousands of pieces of luggage that are checked by domestic and international travelers. As bailees, the common law would impose liability on airlines for the full value of any luggage lost or damaged by their negligence.

However, two statutes protect the airlines from the harsh results of the common law of bailments. Under the first statute, the **Civil Aeronautics Act of 1938** [49 U.S.C. § 646], which applies to domestic flights, airlines can limit their liability for passengers' lost or damaged property to a specific dollar amount per pound or per item by filing tariffs with the Civil Aeronautics Board (CAB). The current tariff is $1,250 per piece of luggage.

The only way for passengers to beat the limitations of liability is to declare that the value of their property exceeds the tariffs and then pay a fee for additional coverage.

The second statute is the **Warsaw Convention** [49 U.S.C. § 1502], which was concluded in 1929. This statute limits recovery for luggage that is lost or damaged on international flights. Passengers can purchase additional coverage upon check-in.

Undoubtedly, passengers who fail to declare the excess value of their luggage will lose money if their luggage is lost. However, the limitations of liability contained in both the Civil Aeronautics Act and the Warsaw Convention are widely viewed as necessary protection for airlines.

There are many kinds of personal property. Listed below are some Web sites that will help you protect your personal property.

Internet commerce

National Telecommunications and Information Administration This Department of Commerce agency is responsible for domestic and international telecommunications and information policy issues as well as being the President's principle advisor on these issues.

Visit at **www.ntia.doc.gov**

Internet Legal Issues All sorts of Internet legal issues, including property rights, are discussed on this site.

Visit at **www.faegre.com**

Keeping your property in divorce

Divorce Online Divorce Online provides free articles and information on the financial, legal, psychological, real estate, and other aspects of divorce.

Visit at **www.divorceonline.com**

Your dog

Nolo Press Nolo Press is a self-help law center that publishes a lot of books about law for lay people. It is a great source of lawyer jokes, too.

Visit at **www.nolo.com**

(And to find out all about dogs, check out the American Kennel Club Web page at www.akc.org)

CYBER EXERCISES

1. Where is the laboratory of the National Telecommunications and Information Administration, the Institute for Telecommunications Sciences, located?

2. From the Internet Legal Issues site, find an article called "Current Issues in Cyberspace."

3. From Divorce Online, find an article about choosing a matrimonial lawyer.

4. From the Nolo Press Web page, check out all the do-it-yourself legal software.

CASES AND EXERCISES

CRITICAL LEGAL THINKING CASES

49.1. NYT Cable TV is a division of The New York Times Company (NYT) that operates a cable television station in Camden County, New Jersey. NYT has erected a 250-foot-high cable antenna tower on real property to distribute its broadcast signals. The structure is attached to a large concrete foundation in the ground and consists of a large vertical, triangular steel superstructure connected by steel crossbars and circular metal ties. The Camden County Board of Taxation assessed a real property tax on the property, including the cable television tower. NYT opposed the tax, alleging that the cable television tower was personal property—not real property—which was exempt from the real property tax. Who

wins? [*NYT Cable TV v. Borough of Audubon, New Jersey*, 553 A.2d 1368 (N.J.Sup. 1989)]

49.2. On June 6, 1983, Mack's Used Cars & Parts, Inc. (Mack's), sold a 1975 GMC one-ton truck with a 1979 Atlas wrecker assembly attached thereto to Jack W. Weaver on credit. At the time of the purchase, the wrecker assembly was bolted to the frame of the truck, and its hydraulic boom operated off the transmission of the truck. To protect its credit extension to Weaver, Mack's took a security interest in the vehicle and perfected its interest by a notation on the truck's title. Mack's filed a financing statement with the Tennessee secretary of state covering the vehicle. Weaver subsequently sold the vehicle to McCall, who removed the wrecker assembly from the truck and sold the wrecker assembly to the Tennessee Truck & Equipment Co. (Tennessee Truck). When the original extension of credit was not paid, Mack's brought this action to repossess the vehicle and also to repossess the wrecker assembly from Tennessee Truck. Who wins? [*Mack's Used Cars & Parts, Inc. v. Tennessee Truck & Equipment Co.*, 694 S.W.2d 323 (Tenn.App. 1985)]

49.3. Olga V. Watson lived in an apartment building that was managed by Edward P. McCarton. During 1980, Watson's health started to deteriorate, and she eventually began to call on McCarton for assistance in her daily affairs. By 1982, Watson's health had deteriorated to the point where she could no longer take care of herself. McCarton arranged for her to move into his apartment. Except for a brief stay in a nursing home, Watson lived in McCarton's apartment until her death. During her stay, she met many of McCarton's relatives. On July 26, 1981, two days before her death, Watson stated that she realized she was dying and asked McCarton to write down her wishes for the disposition of her assets. She directed that McCarton receive her stocks and bonds worth $235,000 and that McCarton's relatives receive her bank accounts worth $354,000. The stock certificates, bonds, and bank statements were located in a dresser in the McCarton apartment. Later, it was discovered that Watson had prepared a will several years earlier in which she left one-half of her estate to her sister and the other half to a nephew. Evidence showed that once, when Watson received a letter from the nephew demanding his inheritance, she stated, "He won't get a dime from me." The will was admitted to probate. Which prevails, Watson's gift letter or the old will? [*McCarton v. Estate of Watson*, 693 P.2d 192 (Wash.App. 1984)]

49.4. Between 1972 and 1984, Theodore Alexander Buder's father made substantial cash gifts to his minor grandchildren. Theodore Buder and his wife (Sartore) divorced during this period. The cash gifts, typically in the form of checks made directly payable to the children, were given to Buder with the understanding that he would safeguard the money and invest it on behalf of the children. Buder invested various amounts of the children's money in "blue-chip" stocks traded over the New York and American stock exchanges. In 1974, he began investing substantial sums of the children's money in speculative penny stocks. The stocks were purchased in Buder's name as custodian for the children as required by the Uniform Gift to Minors Act (UGMA). At one point, almost half of the children's money was invested in penny stocks. All of the penny stocks except one suffered substantial losses. Buder's ex-wife, Sartore, sued him, alleging he breached his fiduciary

duty owed to the children under the UGMA. She sought to recover the funds lost by Buder's investment of the children's fund in penny stocks. Who wins? [*Buder v. Sartore*. 774 P.2d 1383 (Colo. 1989)]

49.5. In June 1983, Danny Lee Smith and his brother, Jeffrey Allen Smith (collectively, Smiths), found a 16-foot fiberglass boat lying beside the roadway in Mobile County, Alabama. Seeing two sheriff's deputies, they stopped them to discuss the boat. Over Smiths' objections, the deputies impounded the boat. Smiths made it clear that, if the true owner of the boat was not found, they wanted the boat. The true owner did not claim the boat. Mobile County claimed the boat and wanted to auction it off to raise money for county recreational programs. Smiths claimed the boat as finders. Alabama did not have an estray statute that applied to the situation. Who gets the boat? [*Smith v. Sheriff Purvis*, 474 So.2d 1131 (Ala.App. 1985)]

49.6. Late in 1975, police officers of the city of Miami, Florida, responded to reports of a shooting at the apartment of Carlos Fuentes. Fuentes had been shot in the neck and shoulder and, shortly after police arrived, was removed to a hospital. In an ensuing search of the apartment, the police found assorted drug paraphernalia, a gun, and cash in the amount of $58,591. The property was seized, taken to the police station, and placed in custody. About nine days later, the police learned that Fuentes had been discharged from the hospital. All efforts by police to locate Fuentes and his girlfriend, a co-occupant of Fuentes's apartment, were unsuccessful. Neither Fuentes nor his girlfriend ever came forward to claim any of the items taken by the police from their apartment. About four years later, in 1979, James W. Green and Walter J. Vogel, the owners of the apartment building in which Fuentes was a tenant, sued the city of Miami to recover the cash found in Fuentes's apartment. The state of Florida intervened in the case, also claiming an interest in the money. Who wins? [*State of Florida v. Green*, 456 So.2d 1309 (Fla.App. 1984)]

49.7. On February 4, 1976, James D. Merritt leased a storage locker from Nationwide Warehouse Co., Ltd. (Nationwide), and agreed to pay $16 per month for leasing the locker. Merritt placed various items in the leased premises but never informed Nationwide as to the nature or quantity of articles stored therein. Merritt was free to store or remove whatever he wished without consultation with, permission from, or notice to Nationwide. Merritt locked the leased premises with his own lock and key. Nationwide was not furnished with a key. Subsequently, certain personal property belonging to Merritt disappeared from the storage space.

Merritt sued Nationwide to recover damages of $5,275. Was a bailment created between Merritt and Nationwide? [*Merritt v. Nationwide Warehouse Co., Ltd.*, 605 S.W.2d 250 (Tenn.App. 1980)]

49.8. On May 14, 1980, Clarence Williams brought his wife's fur coat to Debonair Cleaners (Debonair) for cleaning and storage. The clerk told him that Debonair was experienced in such matters and that the charge would be 3 percent of the stated value of the coat. Williams stated that the coat was worth $13,000 and the clerk gave Williams a claim check and informed Williams that the total fee for storage would be $390, to be paid when the coat was retrieved. That evening, Williams related the substance of his conversation with the clerk to his wife, Armicia, and gave her the claim check. Approximately eight months later, Armicia went to Debonair to retrieve her coat. She presented the claim check to the clerk who, after searching the premises for the coat, told her that it could not be located. Williams was informed that the coat had probably been stolen during a break-in and burglary. Williams sued Debonair to recover the value of the coat. Who wins? [*Mahallati v. Williams*, 479 A.2d 300 (D.C.App. 1984)]

49.9. Marsha Hamilton and Andrea Morris were guests at a dinner party attended by approximately 25 people. The party began about 7:00 P.M. and ended at approximately 1:00 A.M. Alcoholic beverages were served throughout the evening. At approximately 11:30 P.M., while working in the kitchen, Hamilton removed her watch and placed it on the counter. About midnight, Hamilton left the kitchen and went outside. After about 15 minutes, she became ill and fled to the bathroom. Shortly after Hamilton left the kitchen, Morris saw the watch on the counter and, fearing for its safety, picked it up and carried it in her hand as she looked for Hamilton. When Hamilton came out of the bathroom, she and her fiancé left the party. Morris was unable to find Hamilton and cannot recall precisely what she did with the watch. She testified that she either gave it to Hamilton's fiancé or put it somewhere in the host's house for safekeeping. Hamilton's fiancé testified that Morris did not give him the watch. The next day, Hamilton discovered that she did not have her watch but, in a search of the host's home, the watch was not recovered. Hamilton sued Morris for damages. Who wins? [*Morris v. Hamilton*, 302 S.E.2d 51 (Va. 1983)]

49.10. Allright, Inc. (Allright), is a parking lot operator in Houston, Texas. On January 18, 1980, Kirkland Strauder drove his 1978 Buick Regal automobile to a Houston Allright parking lot, placed it in a row of cars to be parked by the attendant, handed the attendant his keys, and was given a receipt by the attendant. When Strauder returned two hours later to reclaim his car, it could not be found. Strauder reported the car stolen. Allright could not explain the loss of the car, which was found one-and-one-half weeks later, wrecked and stripped. Strauder sued Allright for damages. Who wins? [*Allright, Inc. v. Strauder*, 679 S.W.2d 31 (Tex.App. 1984)]

49.11. Alan Brotman and Prem Sahai were the owners and managers of the Brotman Investment Corporation (Corporation), which was engaged in the business of selling rare coins. In August 1980, Leonard Fazio purchased silver coins worth $4,998 from Corporation. The coins were to be put into Corporation's vault for safekeeping. It was understood that Fazio could demand the return of the coins at any time. In November 1980, Fazio unsuccessfully demanded that his coins be returned. Evidence showed that the coins never made it into the vault and that the coins had been converted for one of the cobailee's own use. Fazio sued Brotman and Sahai for damages. Who wins? [*Fazio v. Brotman and Sahai*, 371 N.W.2d 842 (IowaApp. 1985)]

49.12. Vernon Pittman Van Lines (Pittman) is a warehouse company that stores goods for a fee. On May 31, 1977, Trudy Royster hired Pittman to store some of her furniture and household goods. Royster paid Pittman a monthly fee for such services. When Royster decided to remove a few items from storage on September 9, 1979, she found her furniture and cartons in a state of disarray. Several pieces of furniture were substantially damaged, including broken legs, scratches, and so on. Pittman did not produce any evidence showing how the furniture was damaged. Royster sued Pittman to recover damages. Who wins? [*Royster v. Pittman*, 691 S.W.2d 305 (Mo.App. 1985)]

49.13. On January 23, 1982, Joseph Conboy, his wife, and a group of friends convened in Manhattan, New York, for a party at Studio 54, a discotheque where patrons dance to recorded music played on high-fidelity sound equipment. The Conboy party checked their coats, 14 in all, with the coatroom attendant. After paying a 75-cent charge per coat, they received seven check stubs. A small sign in the coatroom stated, "Liability for lost property in this coat/checkroom is limited to $100 per loss of misplaced article." Conboy testified that he did not notice it when he checked his coat, and that the coatroom attendant did not call his attention to the sign. At the end of the evening, Conboy and the other guests of the party attempted to reclaim their coats. Conboy's one-month-old $1,350 leather coat was missing. Conboy sued Studio 54 for damages. Is the disclaimer of liability enforceable? [*Conboy v. Studio 54, Inc.*, 449 N.Y.S.2d 391 (N.Y. 1982)]

ETHICS CASES

49.14. Dr. Arthur M. Edwards died, leaving a will disposing of his property. He left the villa-type condominium in which he lived, its "contents," and $10,000 to his stepson, Ronald W. Souders. Edwards left the residual of his estate to other named legatees. In administrating the estate, certain stock certificates, passbook savings accounts, and other bank statements were found in Edwards's condominium. Souders claimed that these items belonged to him because they were "contents" of the condominium. The other legatees opposed Souders's claim, alleging that the disputed property was intangible property and not part of the contents of the condominium. The value of the property was as follows: condominium, $138,000; furniture in condominium, $4,000; stocks, $377,000; and passbook and other bank accounts, $124,000. Who is entitled to the stocks and bank accounts? Do you think Souders acted ethically in this case? [*Souders v. Johnson*, 501 So.2d 745 (Fla.App. 1987)]

49.15. Darryl Kulwin was employed by Nova Stylings, Inc. (Nova), as a jewelry salesman. In that capacity, he traveled throughout the country carrying with him jewelry owned and manufactured by Nova to show to prospective buyers. Kulwin was visiting Panoria Ruston, who was a guest registered with the Red Roof Inn (Inn) in Overland Park, Kansas. Ruston and Kulwin met at the Inn and later made plans to leave to go to dinner. Kulwin asked Ruston to make arrangements with the desk clerk to leave his sample case in the office of Inn while they went out to dinner. Ruston asked the clerk if she could leave the bag in the manager's office of Inn and the clerk agreed. Ruston advised the clerk

that the contents of the case were valuable but did not describe the contents of the bag. Kansas Statute Section 36-402(b) provides

> *No hotel or motel keeper in this state shall be liable for the loss of, or damage to, merchandise for sale or samples belonging to a guest, lodger or boarder unless the guest, lodger or boarder upon entering the hotel or motel, shall give notice of having merchandise for sale or samples in his possession, together with an itemized list of such property, to the hotel or motel keeper, or his authorized agent or clerk in the registration office of the hotel or motel office.*
>
> *No hotel or motel keeper shall be liable for any loss of such property designated in this subsection (b), after notice an itemized statement having been given and delivered as aforesaid, in an amount in excess of two hundred fifty dollars ($250), unless such hotel or motel keeper, by specific agreement in writing, individually, or by an authorized agent or clerk in charge of the registration office of the hotel or motel, shall voluntarily assume liability for a larger amount with reference to such property. The hotel or motel keeper shall not be compelled to receive such guests, lodgers or boarders with merchandise for sale or samples.*

Inn posted the proper notice of the provisions of this act in all of the guests' rooms, including that of Ruston. An unidentified person obtained access to the manager's office and removed the case from the office. Nova sued Red Roof Inns, Inc., for the alleged value of the jewelry—$650,000. Is Red Roof Inns, Inc., liable? Did either party act unethically in this case? [*Nova Stylings v. Red Roof Inns, Inc.*, 747 P.2d 107 (Kan. 1987)]

CRITICAL LEGAL THINKING WRITING ASSIGNMENT

Read Case A.49 in the Case Appendix [*Michigan Mutual Insurance Co. v. Marriot Corporation*]. This case is excerpted from the district court's opinion. Review and brief the case. In your brief, be sure to answer the following questions:

1. Who is the plaintiff and who is the defendant?
2. What elements must be proven to establish a bailment?
3. Was a bailment found in this case? Why or why not?

NOTES

1. UCC § 7-301(1).
2. UCC § 7-309(2).
3. UCC § 7-102(1)(h).
4. UCC §§ 7-204(1) and 7-403(1).
5. UCC § 7-204(2).
6. UCC § 1-201(15).
7. UCC § 1-201(45).
8. UCC § 7-202(1).
9. UCC § 7-202(3).
10. UCC § 7-206(1).

11. UCC §§ 7-206(2) and (3).
12. UCC § 7-209(1).
13. UCC § 7-209(1).
14. UCC §§ 7-206(5) and 7-210(6).
15. UCC § 7-210.
16. UCC § 1-201(6).
17. UCC § 7-302(1).
18. UCC § 7-302(3).

19. UCC § 7-302(2).
20. UCC § 7-307(1).
21. UCC § 7-308(1).
22. UCC § 7-308(5).
23. UCC §§ 7-308(1), 7-308(7), and 7-210(2).
24. UCC §§ 7-210(5) and 7-308(4).
25. UCC § 7-601(1).

Real Property

*W*ithout that sense of security which property gives, the land would
still be uncultivated.

FRANCOIS QUESNAY (1694-1774)
Maximes, IV

Chapter Objectives

After studying this chapter, you should be able to

1. List and describe the different types of real property.
2. Describe ownership interests in surface, subsurface, and air rights.
3. Distinguish between fee simple absolute and fee simple defeasible.
4. Describe life estates.
5. Describe the future interests of reversion and remainder.
6. Identify the different types of joint tenancy.
7. Distinguish between separate property and community property.
8. Describe how title to real property is acquired by adverse possession.
9. Describe recording statutes.
10. Distinguish between easements appurtenant and easements in gross.

Chapter Contents

Property and ownership rights in **real property** play an important part in this country's society and economy. Individuals and families own or rent houses, farmers and ranchers own farmland and ranches, and businesses own or lease commercial and office buildings. In addition, real property includes some items of personal property (called *fixtures*) that are affixed to real property, minerals found underneath the soil, vegetation and plants growing on real property, and, to a certain extent, air rights above real property.

The concept of real property is concerned with the *legal rights* to the property rather than the physical attributes of the tangible land. Originally, this area of the law was based on the English common law. Since then, a complex body of *real property law* that protects each party's legal rights in the real property has evolved. This chapter covers the nature, ownership, and transfer of property.

Nature of Real Property

Property is usually classified as either real or personal property. **Real property** is immovable or attached to immovable land or buildings, whereas personal property is movable. The various types of real property are discussed in the paragraphs that follow.

real property

The land itself as well as buildings, trees, soil, minerals, timber, plants, and other things permanently affixed to the land.

Land and Buildings

Land is the most common form of real property. A landowner usually purchases the *surface rights* to the land—that is, the right to occupy the land. The owner may use, enjoy, and develop the property as he or she sees fit, subject to any applicable government regulation.

Buildings constructed on land, such as houses, apartment buildings, manufacturing plants, and office buildings, are real property. Such things as radio towers, bridges, and the like are usually considered real property as well.

land

The most common form of real property; includes the land and buildings and other structures permanently attached to the land.

building

A structure constructed on land.

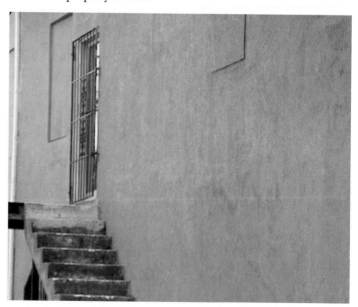

The most valuable asset of many families is their home.

Subsurface Rights

The owner of land possesses **subsurface rights** (or **mineral rights**) to the earth located beneath the surface of the land. These rights can be very valuable. For example, gold, uranium, oil, or natural gas may lie beneath the surface of land. Theoretically, mineral rights extend to the center of the earth. In reality, mines and oil wells usually extend only several miles into the earth. Subsurface rights may be sold separately from surface rights.

subsurface rights

Rights to the earth located beneath the surface of the land.

Plant Life and Vegetation

Plant life and vegetation growing on the surface of land are considered real property. This includes both natural plant life (e.g., trees) and cultivated plant life (e.g., crops). When land is sold, any plant life growing on the land is included unless the parties agree otherwise. Plant life that is severed from the land is considered personal property.

plant life and vegetation
Real property that is growing in or on the surface of the land.

Fixtures

Certain personal property is so closely associated with real property that it becomes part of the realty. Such items are called **fixtures**. For example, kitchen cabinets, carpeting, and doorknobs are fixtures, but throw rugs and furniture are personal property.

Unless otherwise provided, if a building is sold, the fixtures are included in the sale. If the sale agreement is silent as to whether an item is a fixture, the courts make their determination on the basis of whether the item can be removed without causing substantial damage to the realty. In the following case, the court held that personal property had become a fixture.

fixtures
Goods that are affixed to real estate so as to become part thereof.

Ford v. Venard
340 N.W.2d 270 (1983)
Supreme Court of Iowa

CASE 50.1

FACTS
In 1978, Norman Van Sickle moved a double-wide mobile home to a plot of land in Silver City, Iowa. He had the real estate landscaped, a foundation poured, concrete blocks set, and steel girders aligned on the blocks. After the hitches and wheels were removed, the mobile home was set on the foundation by a crane. A roof was placed over the entire building and the exterior was joined together with siding. Van Sickle paid the owner of the property, Luelia Jedlicka, $500 as down payment for the purchase of the land. Evidence showed that the mobile home could not be removed from the land without extensive damage. Henry Edsel Ford purchased the property from Jedlicka. William E. Venard, a creditor of Van Sickle, tried to obtain ownership of the mobile home to satisfy a judgment against Van Sickle. A lawsuit later developed in which the issue arose as to whether the mobile home was personal or real property.

ISSUE
Is the mobile home a fixture?

IN THE LANGUAGE OF THE COURT
Harris, Justice The question is whether the mobile home was a fixture included under the terms of the land contract. We think it plainly was. Under our common law rule personal property becomes a fixture when (1) it is actually annexed to the realty or to something appurtenant thereto, (2) it is put to the same use as the realty with which it is connected, and (3) the party making

the annexation intends to make a permanent accession to the freehold. The intention of the party annexing the improvement is the paramount factor in determining whether the improvement is a fixture.

The home passes this test. The home's tongues and wheels have been removed, it was set on a foundation and girders, it has been extensively remodeled into a single unit, and its removal would be expensive and damaging. The home was used as a homestead, which is the use for which the realty had been appropriated. A building that cannot be removed without destruction of a substantial part of its value becomes almost unavoidably an integral part of the real estate. We are convinced the home became attached to the land. It could not be removed from its present location except in the sense that any permanent home could be. We hold that it has become an integral part of the real estate.

DECISION AND REMEDY
The supreme court held that the mobile home was a fixture and, as such, was part of the real property. Affirmed.

Case Questions

Critical Legal Thinking   Should the law recognize the doctrine of fixtures? Why or why not?

Ethics   Was it ethical for a party to argue that the mobile home was personal property?

Business Application   What are the economic consequences of finding that personal property has become a fixture?

Contemporary Business Application

Air Rights: Value in the Heavens

Common law provided that the owners of real property owned that property from the center of the earth to the heavens. This rule has been eroded by modern legal restrictions such as land use control laws, environmental protection laws, and air navigation requirements. Even today, however, the owners of land may sell or lease air space parcels above their land.

An **air space parcel** is a three-dimensional cube of air above the surface of the earth. Air space parcels are valuable property rights, particularly in densely populated metropolitan areas where building property is scarce. For example, many developments have been built in air space parcels in New York City. The most notable are Madison Square Garden and Two Penn Plaza, which were built in air space parcels above Penn Station. More developments are expected to be built in air space parcels in the future.

*E*STATES IN LAND

estate

Ownership rights in real property; the bundle of legal rights that the owner has to possess, use, and enjoy the property.

A person's ownership rights in real property are called an **estate in land** (or **estate**). An estate is defined as the bundle of *legal rights* that the owner has to possess, use, and enjoy the property. The type of estate that an owner possesses is determined from the deed, will, lease, or other document that transferred the ownership rights to him or her.

*F*REEHOLD ESTATES

freehold estate

An estate where the owner has a present possessory interest in the real property.

A **freehold estate** is one where the owner has a *present possessory interest* in the real property; that is, the owner may use and enjoy the property as he or she sees fit, subject to any applicable government regulation or private restraint. The two types of freehold estates are *estates in fee* and *life estates*.

Estates in Fee

fee simple absolute

A type of ownership of real property that grants the owner the fullest bundle of legal rights that a person can hold in real property.

A **fee simple absolute** (or **fee simple**) is the highest form of ownership of real property because it grants the owner the fullest bundle of legal rights that a person can hold in real property. It is the type of ownership most people connect with "owning" real property. It is also the most common form of real estate ownership in the United States. A fee simple owner has the right to exclusively possess and use his or her property to the extent that the owner has not transferred any interest in the property (e.g., by lease). If a person owns real property in fee simple, his or her ownership

- Is infinite in duration (fee).
- Has no limitation on inheritability (simple).
- Does not end upon the happening of any event (absolute).

fee simple defeasible

A type of ownership of real property that grants the owner all the incidents of a fee simple absolute except that it may be taken away if a specified condition occurs or does not occur.

A **fee simple defeasible** (or **qualified fee**) grants the owner all the incidents of a fee simple absolute except that it may be taken away if a specified *condition* occurs or does not occur. For example, a conveyance of property to a church "as long as the land is used as a church or for church purposes" creates a qualified fee. The church has all of the rights of a fee simple absolute owner except that its ownership rights are terminated if the property is no longer used for church purposes.

Life Estates

A **life estate** is an interest in real property that lasts for the life of a specified person, usually the grantee. For example, a conveyance of real property "to Anna for her life" creates a life estate. A life estate may also be measured by the life of a third party (e.g., "to Anna for the life of Benjamin"). This is called an ***estate pour autre vie***. A life estate may be defeasible (e.g., "to John for his life but only if he continues to occupy this residence"). Upon the death of named person, the life estate terminates and the property reverts to the grantor or the grantor's estate or other designated person.

A life tenant is treated as the owner of the property during the duration of the life estate. He or she has the right to possess and use the property except to the extent that it would cause permanent *waste* of the property. A life tenant may sell, transfer, or mortgage his or her estate in the land. The mortgage, however, cannot exceed the duration of the life estate. A life tenant is obligated to keep the property in repair and to pay property taxes.

life estate
An interest in the land for a person's lifetime; upon that person's death, the interest will be transferred to another party.

estate pour autre vie
A life estate measured in the life of a third party.

CONCEPT SUMMARY FREEHOLD ESTATES

Estate	Description
Fee simple absolute	Highest form of ownership of real property. Ownership (1) is infinite in duration, (2) has no limitation on inheritability, and (3) does not end upon the occurrence or nonoccurrence of an event.
Fee simple defeasible	Grants owner all of the incidents of a fee simple absolute except that it may be taken away if a specified condition occurs or does not occur.
Life estate	Interest in property that lasts for the life of a specified person. A life estate terminates upon the death of the named person and reverts back to the grantor or his or her estate or other designated person.

FUTURE INTERESTS

A person may be given the right to possess property in the *future* rather than in the present. This right is called a **future interest**. The two forms of future interests are *reversion* and *remainder*.

Reversion

A **reversion** is a right of possession that returns to the *grantor* after the expiration of a limited or contingent estate. Reversions do not have to be expressly stated because they arise automatically by law. For example, if a grantor conveys property "to M. R. Harrington for life," the grantor has retained a reversion in the property. That is, when Harrington dies, the property reverts to the grantor or, if he or she is not living, then to his or her estate.

future interest
The interest that the grantor retains for him- or herself or a third party.

reversion
A right of possession that returns to the grantor after the expiration of a limited or contingent estate.

Remainder

If the right of possession returns to a *third party* upon the expiration of a limited or contingent estate, it is called a **remainder**. The person who is entitled to the future interest is called a **remainderman**. For example, a conveyance of property "to Joe for life, remainder to Meredith" is a vested remainder—the only contingency to Meredith's possessory interest is Joe's death.

remainder
If the right of possession returns to a third party upon the expiration of a limited or contingent estate.

CONCEPT SUMMARY FUTURE INTERESTS

Future Interest	Description
Reversion	Right to possession of real property returns to the grantor after the expiration of a limited or contingent estate.
Remainder	Right to possession of real property goes to a third person upon the expiration of a limited or contingent estate.

CONCURRENT OWNERSHIP

co-ownership

When two or more persons own a piece of real property. Also called *concurrent ownership*.

Two or more persons may own a piece of real property. This is called **co-ownership** or **concurrent ownership**. The following forms of co-ownership are recognized: *joint tenancy, tenancy in common, tenancy by the entirety, community property, condominium,* and *cooperative*.

Joint Tenancy

joint tenancy

A form of co-ownership that includes the right of survivorship.

The most distinguishing feature of a **joint tenancy** is the co-owners' *right of survivorship*. This means that upon the death of one of the co-owners (or *joint tenants*), the deceased person's interest in the property automatically passes to the surviving joint tenants. Any contrary provision in the deceased's will is ineffective.

Consider This Example Jones, one of four people who own a piece of property in joint tenancy, executes a will leaving all of his property to a university. Jones dies. The surviving joint tenants—not the university—acquire his interest in the piece of property.

To create a joint tenancy, words that clearly show a person's intent to create a joint tenancy must be used. Language such as "Marsha Leest and James Leest, as joint tenants" is usually sufficient. Some states specify that particular language must be used. Each joint tenant has a right to sell or transfer his or her interest in the property, but such conveyance terminates the joint tenancy. The parties then become tenants in common.

Tenancy in Common

tenancy in common

A form of co-ownership where the interest of a surviving tenant in common passes to the deceased tenant's estate and not to the co-tenants.

In a **tenancy in common**, the interests of a surviving *tenant in common* pass to the deceased tenant's estate and not to the co-tenants.

Consider This Example Lopez, who is one of four tenants in common who own a piece of property, has a will that leaves all of his property to his granddaughter. When Lopez dies, the granddaughter receives his interest in the tenancy in common, and the granddaughter becomes a tenant in common with three other owners.

A tenancy in common may be created by express words, such as "Don Hull and Rob Dewey, as tenants in common." There is a presumption that co-ownership of real property is a tenancy in common unless another intent is clearly indicated. For example, the words "to Sandra Steiner and Joe Heider, as co-owners" create a tenancy in common and not a joint tenancy. Unless otherwise agreed, a tenant in common can sell, give, devise, or otherwise transfer his or her interest in the property without the consent of the other co-owners.

Tenancy by the Entirety

Tenancy by the entirety is a form of co-ownership of real property that can be used only by married couples. This type of tenancy must be created by express words, such as "Harold Jones and Maude Jones, husband and wife, as tenants by the entireties." A surviving spouse has the right of survivorship.

Tenancy by the entirety is distinguished from a joint tenancy because neither spouse may sell or transfer his or her interest in the property without the other spouse's consent. A divorce terminates the tenancy because the marriage has ceased. The tenancy is then transformed into a tenancy in common. Only about half of the states recognize a tenancy by the entirety.

In the following case, the court had to decide how to split the proceeds from the sale of real property owned by co-owners.

tenancy by the entirety
A form of co-ownership of real property that can be used only by married couples.

Cunningham v. Hastings
556 N.E.2d 12 (1990)
Court of Appeals of Indiana

CASE 50.2

FACTS
On August 30, 1984, Warren R. Hastings and Joan L. Cunningham, who were unmarried, purchased a house together. Hastings paid a $45,000 down payment toward the purchase price out of his own funds. The deed referred to Hastings and Cunningham as "joint tenants with the right of survivorship." Hastings and Cunningham occupied the property jointly. After their relationship ended, Hastings took sole possession of the property. Cunningham filed a complaint seeking partition of the real estate. Based on its determination that the property could not be split, the trial court ordered it to be sold. The trial court further ordered that $45,000 of the sale proceeds be paid to Hastings to reimburse him for his down payment, and the remainder of the proceeds be divided equally between Hastings and Cunningham. Cunningham appealed, alleging that Hastings should not have been given credit for the down payment.

ISSUE
Is Cunningham entitled to an equal share of the proceeds of the sale of the real estate?

IN THE LANGUAGE OF THE COURT
Baker, Judge   The parties do not dispute that the unequivocal language of the deed created a joint tenancy in the real estate. When a joint tenancy is created, each tenant acquires an equal right to share in the enjoyment of the land during their lives. A joint tenancy relationship confers equivalent legal rights on the tenants that are fixed and vested at the time the joint tenancy is created. The determination of the parties' interests in the present case is simple. There are only two parties involved in the joint tenancy. Once a joint tenancy relationship is found to exist

between two people in a partition action, it is axiomatic that each person owns a one-half interest.

Based on this reasoning, we find that the trial court erred in allowing Hastings a $45,000 credit for the purchase price he paid. Regardless of who provided the money to purchase the land, the creation of a joint tenancy relationship entitles each party to an equal share of the proceeds of the sale upon partition. Equitable adjustments to cotenants' equal shares are allowed when the cotenants hold the property as tenants in common, not when they hold as joint tenants. The deed in the case before us unequivocally states that the parties held the property as joint tenants, not as tenants in common. The equitable adjustment of their equal shares, therefore, was improper.

DECISION AND REMEDY
The court of appeals held that Cunningham was entitled to an equal share of the proceeds of the sale because she and Hastings owned the property as joint tenants. The court ordered that the entire proceeds of the sale be divided equally between Cunningham and Hastings.

Case Questions

Critical Legal Thinking   Should the law recognize so many different forms of ownership of real property? Do you think most people understand the legal consequences of taking title in the various forms?

Ethics   Did Cunningham act ethically in demanding one-half the value of the down payment even though she did not contribute to it?

Business Application   Could Hastings have protected the $45,000 he paid for the down payment? If so, how could he have done it?

Contemporary Business Application

COMMUNITY PROPERTY

Nine states—Arizona, California, Idaho, Louisiana, Nevada, New Mexico, Texas, Washington, and Wisconsin—recognize a form of co-ownership known as **community property**. This method of co-ownership applies only to married couples. It is based on the notion that a husband and wife should share equally in the fruits of the marital partnership. Under these laws, each spouse owns an equal one-half share of the income of both spouses and the assets acquired during the marriage regardless of who earns the income. Property that is acquired through gift or inheritance either before or during marriage remains separate property.

When a spouse dies, the surviving spouse automatically receives one-half the community property. The other half passes to the heirs of the deceased spouse as directed by will or by state intestate statute if there is no will. For example, a husband and wife have community property assets of $1.5 million and the wife dies with a will. The husband automatically has a right to receive $750,000 of the community property. The remaining $750,000 passes as directed by the wife's will. Any separate property owned by the wife, such as jewelry she inherited, also passes in accordance with her will. Her husband has no vested interest in that property.

During the marriage, neither spouse can sell, transfer, or gift community property without the consent of the other spouse. Upon a divorce, each spouse has a right to one-half of the community property.

The location of the real property determines whether community property law applies. For example, if a married couple who lives in a noncommunity property state purchases real property located in a community property state, community property laws apply to that property.

CONCEPT SUMMARY CONCURRENT OWNERSHIP

Form of Ownership	Right of Survivorship	Tenant May Unilaterally Transfer His or Her Interest
Joint tenancy	Yes, deceased tenant's interest automatically passes to co-tenants.	Yes, tenant may transfer his or her interest without the consent of cotenants. Transfer severs joint tenancy.
Tenancy in common	No, deceased tenant's interest passes to his or her estate.	Yes, tenant may transfer his or her interest without the consent of cotenants. Transfer does not sever tenancy in common.
Tenancy by the entirety	Yes, deceased tenant's interest automatically passes to his or her spouse.	No, neither spouse may transfer his or her interest without the other spouse's consent.
Community property	Yes, when a spouse dies the surviving spouse automatically receives one-half of the community property. The other half passes to the heirs of the deceased spouse as directed by a valid will or by state intestate statute if there is no will.	No, neither spouse may transfer his or her interest without the other spouse's consent.

Condominium

Condominiums are a common form of ownership in multiple-dwelling buildings. Purchasers of a condominium (1) have title to their individual units and (2) own the common areas (e.g., hallways, elevators, parking areas, and recreational facilities) as tenants in common with the other owners. Owners may sell or mortgage their units without the permission of the other owners. Owners are assessed monthly fees for the maintenance of common areas. In addition to dwelling units, the condominium form of ownership is offered for office buildings, boat docks, and such.

Cooperative

A **cooperative** is a form of co-ownership of a multiple-dwelling building where a corporation owns the building and the residents own shares in the corporation. Each cooperative owner then leases a unit in the building from the corporation under a renewable, long-term, proprietary lease. Individual residents may not secure loans with the units they occupy. The corporation may borrow money on a blanket mortgage, and each shareholder is jointly and severally liable on the loan. Usually, cooperative owners may not sell their shares or sublease their units without the approval of the other owners.

TRANSFER OF OWNERSHIP OF REAL PROPERTY

Ownership of real property may be transferred from one person to another. Title to real property may be transferred by sale; tax sale; gift, will, or inheritance; and adverse possession. The different methods of transfer provide different degrees of protection to the transferee.

Sale of Real Estate

A **sale** or **conveyance** is the most common method for transferring ownership rights in real property. An owner may offer his or her real estate for sale either by him- or herself or by using a real estate broker. Once a buyer has been located and the parties have negotiated the terms of the sale, a *real estate sales contract* is executed by the parties. The Statute of Frauds in most states requires this contract to be in writing.

The seller delivers a deed to the buyer and the buyer pays the purchase price at the **closing** or **settlement**. Unless otherwise agreed, it is implied that the seller is conveying fee simple absolute title to the buyer. If either party fails to perform, the other party may sue for breach of contract and obtain either monetary damages or specific performance.

Tax Sale

If an owner of real property fails to pay property taxes, the government may obtain a **lien** on the property for the amount of the taxes. If the taxes remain unpaid for a statutory period of time, the government may sell the property at a **tax sale** to satisfy the lien. Any excess proceeds are paid to the taxpayer. The buyer receives title to the property.

Many states provide a **period of redemption** after a tax sale during which the taxpayer may redeem the property by paying the unpaid taxes and penalties. In these states, the buyer at a tax sale does not receive title to the property until the period of redemption has passed.

Gift, Will, or Inheritance

Ownership of real property may be transferred by **gift**. The gift is made when the deed to the property is delivered by the donor to the donee or to a third party to hold for the donee. No consideration is necessary. For example, suppose a grandfather wants to give his farm to his granddaughter. To do so, he only has to execute a deed and give the deed to her or to someone to hold for her, such as her parents.

will or inheritance

If a person dies with a will, his or her property is distributed to the beneficiaries as designated in the will. If a person dies without a will, his or her property is distributed to the heirs as stipulated in the state's intestate statute.

Real property may also be transferred by **will or inheritance**. For example, a person may leave a piece of real estate to his or her best friend by will when he or she dies. This does not require the transfer of a deed during the testator's lifetime. A deed will be issued to the beneficiary when the will is probated. If a person dies without a valid will, his or her property is distributed to the heirs pursuant to the applicable state intestate statute.

Entrepreneur and the Law

WHAT A PERSON SHOULD DO WHEN BUYING REAL ESTATE

The most important purchase most people make in their lives is when they buy a place to live or other real estate. A potential homebuyer should spend sufficient time to investigate and analyze this decision. When purchasing a home, a buyer should

- Employ a reputable real estate broker who will represent the buyer's interests in the transaction. This broker should be someone other than the listing broker hired by the seller. The buyer's broker usually splits the real estate sales commission with the listing broker. The commission is usually paid by the seller from the sales proceeds from the house.
- Request that the seller fully disclose all defects in the property. If the seller refuses to do so, it would probably be wise not to purchase the property. Some states require by law that such disclosure be made by the seller to potential buyers.
- Have the offer agreement prepared by an attorney or the real estate broker if the potential buyer decides to make an offer to purchase the house. Review the offer to make sure it is correct before signing it.
- Make sure the offer contains any necessary contingencies. For example, if the buyer needs bank financing, he or she should make the offer contingent on being approved for such financing at reasonable terms.
- Make the offer contingent on a full inspection and approval of the house. The potential buyer should hire the necessary professionals, such as a general contractor, to examine the house. It is better to spend money

in advance to locate any problems than to purchase the house and discover the defects at a later date.

- Hire a surveyor to conduct a survey to determine the true location of the lot lines and size of the property. Surveys sometimes reveal that a neighboring property owner may be encroaching on the seller's property (e.g., fence line). These problems have to be dealt with on a case-by-case basis.
- Either (1) purchase title insurance if available or (2) hire a lawyer to conduct a title search of the property. The purchase of title insurance is recommended because it warrants that the buyer has "clear title" to the property and, if this is not true, the insurance company will pay the buyer any damages suffered by the buyer.
- Make the offer contingent on an environmental report if there is any concern that there may be environmental pollution on the property. The buyer should employ a reputable and licensed environmental engineer to conduct the proper inspection of the property and prepare the report. If any environmental problems are discovered, it may be best not to purchase the property, because some federal and state environmental laws place cleaning costs on the owner of the property even if that owner did not cause the pollution.
- Either (1) hire a lawyer to represent the buyer at the closing of the transaction or (2) hire an independent escrow service to handle the closing of the transaction, depending on the law of the state.

adverse possession

When a person who wrongfully possesses someone else's real property obtains title to that property if certain statutory requirements are met.

Adverse Possession

In most states, a person who wrongfully possesses someone else's real property obtains title to that property if certain statutory requirements are met. This is called **adverse possession**. Property owned by federal and state governments are not subject to adverse possession.

Under this doctrine, the transfer of the property is involuntary and does not require the delivery of a deed. To obtain title under adverse possession, the wrongful possession must be

- **For a Statutorily Prescribed Period of Time** In most states, this period is between 10 and 20 years.
- **Open, Visible, and Notorious** The adverse possessor must occupy the property so as to put the owner on notice of the possession.
- **Actual and Exclusive** The adverse possessor must physically occupy the premises. The planting of crops, grazing of animals, or building of a structure on the land constitutes physical occupancy.
- **Continuous and Peaceful** The occupancy must be continuous and uninterrupted for the required statutory period. Any break in normal occupancy terminates the adverse possession. This means that the adverse possessor may leave the property to go to work, to the store, on a vacation, and such. The adverse possessor cannot take the property by force from an owner.
- **Hostile and Adverse** The possessor must occupy the property without the express or implied permission of the owner. Thus, a lessee cannot claim title to property under adverse possession.

If the elements of adverse possession are met, the adverse possessor acquires clear title to the land. However, title is acquired only as to the property actually possessed and occupied during the statutory period, and not the entire tract. For example, an adverse possessor who occupies one acre of a 200,000-acre ranch for the statutory period of time acquires title only to the one acre.

> **Business Brief**
> Owners of property should check their property every so many years to determine if anyone is attempting to acquire title by adverse possession. If anyone is found to be doing so, the owner should take appropriate action to prevent the adverse possession.

Ethical Perspective

MODERN-DAY SQUATTERS

Many parts of this country, particularly the West, were settled by "squatters" who came, staked a claim to open property, farmed or ranched the property, and acquired title to it from the government. The federal government encouraged such activity by holding "land rushes" that awarded title to the first person who staked a claim to the designated lands.

Although the days of the Wild West are past, many states today recognize modern-day squatters' rights under the doctrine of adverse possession. Consider the following case.

Edward and Mary Shaughnessey purchased a 16-acre tract in St. Louis county in 1954. Subsequently, they subdivided 12 acres into 18 lots offered for sale and retained possession of the remaining 4-acre tract. In 1967, Charles and Elaine Witt purchased lot 12, which is adjacent to the 4-acre tract. The Witts constructed and moved into a house on their lot. In 1968, they cleared an area of land that ran the length of their property and extended 40 feet onto the 4-acre tract. The Witts constructed a pool and a deck, planted a garden, made a playground for their children, set up a dog run, and built a fence along the edge of the property line, which included the now-disputed property. Neither the Witts nor the Shaughnesseys realized that the Witts had encroached on the Shaughnesseys' property.

In February 1988, the Shaughnesseys sold the 4-acre tract to Thomas and Rosanne Miller. When a survey showed the encroachment, the Millers demanded that the Witts remove the pool and cease using the property. When the Witts refused to do so, the Millers sued to *quiet title*. The Witts defended, arguing that they had obtained title to the disputed property by adverse possession.

The court of appeals agreed with the Witts. The court held that the Witts had proven the necessary elements for adverse possession under state law. The Witts' occupation of the land was open and notorious, actual and exclusive, hostile and adverse, continuous and peaceful, and had been for over the statutory period of 10 years. The court issued an order quieting title to the disputed property in the Witts' favor. [*Witt v. Miller*, 845 S.W.2d 665 (Mo.App. 1993)].

1. Did the Millers act ethically in trying to eject people who had occupied the land for 20 years?
2. Did the Witts act ethically in claiming title to someone else's land? Should they be allowed to benefit from their own mistake?
3. What should owners of property do to protect themselves from adverse possession claims? Explain.

deed
A writing that describes a person's ownership interest in a piece of real property.

grantor
The party who transfers an ownership interest in real property.

grantee
The party to whom an interest in real property is transferred.

recording statute
A state statute that requires the mortgage or deed of trust to be recorded in the county recorder's office of the county in which the real property is located.

Business Brief
Anyone interested in purchasing property or lending on the property should check the county recorder's records of the county in which the real property is located to determine if the grantor or borrower actually owns the property and whether any other parties have an interest in the property.

quiet title action
An action brought by a party seeking an order of the court declaring who has title to disputed property. The court "quiets title" by its decision.

Deeds and Recording Statutes

Deeds

Deeds are used to convey real property by sale or gift. The seller or donor is called the **grantor**. The buyer or recipient is called the **grantee**. A deed may be used to transfer a fee simple absolute interest in real property or any lesser estate (e.g., life estate).

State laws recognize different types of deeds that provide differing degrees of protection to grantees. A **warranty deed** contains the greatest number of warranties and provides the most protection to grantees. A **quitclaim deed** provides the least amount of protection because the grantor conveys only whatever interest he or she has in the property.

Recording Statutes

Every state has a **recording statute** that provides that copies of deeds and other documents concerning interests in real property (e.g., mortgages, liens, easements) may be filed in a government office where they become public records open to viewing by the public. Recording statutes are intended to prevent fraud and to establish certainty in the ownership and transfer of property. Instruments are usually filed in the *county recorder's office* of the county in which the property is located. A fee is charged to record an instrument.

Persons interested in purchasing the property or lending on the property should check these records to determine if the grantor or borrower actually owns the property and whether any other parties (e.g., lienholders, mortgagees, easement holders) have an interest in the property. The recordation of a deed is not required to pass title from the grantor to the grantee. Recording the deed gives *constructive notice* to the world of the owner's interest in the property.

A party who is concerned about his or her ownership rights in a parcel of real property can bring a **quiet title action** to have a court determine the extent of those rights. Public notice of the hearing must be given so that anyone claiming an interest in the property may appear and be heard. After the hearing, the judge declares who has title to the property—that is, the court "quiets title" by its decision.

In the following case, the court had to decide whether a recording statute had been properly complied with.

The Howard Savings Bank v. Brunson
582 A.2d 1305 (1990)
Superior Court of New Jersey

CASE 50.3

FACTS

In January 1986, Burl Brunson purchased a parcel of real property in Newark, New Jersey. The deed for the property was properly recorded and indexed by the county recorder on January 24, 1986. In March 1986, Brunson borrowed $50,000 from The Howard Savings Bank (Howard), secured by a mortgage that was properly recorded on May 1, 1986. The county recorder did not list the mortgage in its index for recorded documents, however. On October 6, 1987, Brunson executed and delivered

a deed for the property to Jesus and Celeste Ijalba, which deed was properly recorded and indexed on November 4, 1987. On October 6, 1987, the Ijalbas borrowed money from Chrysler First Financial Services Corporation (Chrysler), secured by a mortgage on the property that was properly recorded and indexed on November 4, 1987. On February 9, 1988, Howard's mortgage from two years earlier was finally indexed by the county recorder. On May 19, 1988, Howard brought a foreclosure action on the property for default on its loan and claimed that its mortgage had priority over Ijalbas' deed and Chrysler's mortgage. The defendants argued that Howard's mortgage did not have priority because it was not indexed, and therefore when they conducted their title search, Howard's mortgage did not appear in the index. Both parties filed motions for summary judgment.

ISSUE

Was Howard's mortgage on the property properly recorded so as to give notice of its existence to subsequent parties?

IN THE LANGUAGE OF THE COURT

Margolis, Justice   An historical study of the Recording Act, as well as an analysis of the cases interpreting it, leads to the conclusion that it was designed to compel the recording of instruments affecting title, for the ultimate purpose of permitting purchasers to rely upon the record title and to purchase and hold title to lands within this state with confidence.

Clearly, the fundamental purpose of the Recording Act is to provide notice to subsequent parties in interest and the protection of purchasers and encumbrancers of real property against undisclosed titles and liens.

A rule prohibiting title searchers from depending upon the alphabetical index would unduly hinder the commercial transactions in the State: lengthy title searches would cost more and would cause unreasonably long closings; potential purchasers, mortgagors and lenders would hesitate to be involved in commercial transactions where they could not be confident that a reasonable search of the record would reveal prior interests or where they feared being held liable for a clerk's misindexing error; and the cost of title insurance would increase.

Obviously, one effect of finding a duty in the mortgagee to see that his instrument is properly indexed will be that the mortgagee will be required to conduct "run down" searches or to employ some other similar mechanism for ensuring that his interest is properly indexed. Yet such a practice is seen as making good business sense anyway. Furthermore, placing the burden upon the mortgagee to ensure that the requisite notice has been given is not out of step with the equitable maxim that where a loss must be borne by one of two innocent parties, equity will impose the loss on the party whose first act would have prevented the loss.

DECISION AND REMEDY

The court held that Howard's mortgage was not properly recorded as to give the necessary notice to subsequent parties because it was not indexed. The court granted the defendant's motion for summary judgment.

Case Questions

Critical Legal Thinking   What are the purposes of having recording and indexing statutes?

Ethics   Did any party act unethically in this case?

Business Application   Howard and Chrysler were both innocent parties in this case. Do you think the law placed the risk of loss on the right party in this case? Explain.

Marketable Title

A grantor has the obligation to transfer **marketable title** or **good title** to the grantee. Marketable title means that the title is free from any encumbrances, defects in title, or other defects that are not disclosed but would affect the value of the property. The three most common ways of ensuring marketable title are discussed in the following paragraphs.

good title
Title that is free from any encumbrances or other defects that are not disclosed but would affect the value of the property.

Attorney's Opinion   An attorney examines an *abstract of title* (i.e., a chronological history of the chain of title and encumbrances affecting the property) and renders an opinion concerning the status of the title. The attorney may be sued for any losses caused by his or her negligence in rendering the opinion.

Torrens System   The Torrens system is a method of determining title to real property in a judicial proceeding at which everyone claiming an interest in the property may appear and be heard. After the evidence is heard, the court issues a *certificate of title* to the person who is determined to be the rightful owner.

Business Brief
Grantees should purchase title insurance on real property they acquire. The title insurer must reimburse the insured for any losses caused by undiscovered defects in title.

Title Insurance   The best way for a grantee to be sure that he or she has obtained marketable title is to purchase *title insurance* from an insurance company. The title insurer must reimburse the insured for any losses caused by undiscovered defects in the title. Each time a property is transferred, a new title insurance policy must be obtained.

*N*ONPOSSESSORY INTERESTS

A person may own a **nonpossessory interest** in another's real estate. The three non-possessory interests—*easements, licenses,* and *profits*—are discussed in the following paragraphs.

Easements

nonpossessory interest

When a person holds an interest in another person's property without actually owning any part of the property.

An **easement** is an interest in land that gives the holder the right to make limited use of another's property without taking anything from it.

Easements may be *expressly* created by *grant* (where an owner gives another party an easement across his or her property) or *reservation* (where an owner sells land he or she owns but reserves an easement on the land). They also may be *implied* by (1) *implication*, where an owner subdivides a piece of property with a well, path, road, or other beneficial appurtenant that serves the entire parcel, or by (2) *necessity*, for example, "landlocked" property has an implied easement across surrounding property to enter and exit the land-locked property. Easements can also be created by *prescription*, that is, adverse possession.

easement

A given or required right to make limited use of someone else's land without owning or leasing it.

Typical easements include common driveways, party walls, rights-of-ways, and such. There are two types of easements: *easements appurtenant* and *easements in gross*.

Easements Appurtenant An **easement appurtenant** is created when the owner of one piece of land is given an easement over an adjacent piece of land. The land over which the easement is granted is called the *servient estate*. The land that benefits from the easement is called the *dominant estate*. *Adjacent land* is defined as two estates that are in proximity to each other but do not necessarily abut each other. An appurtenant easement runs with the land. For example, if an owner sells the servient estate, the new owner acquires the benefit of the easement. If an owner sells the dominant estate, the buyer purchases the property subject to the easement.

easement appurtenant

A situation created when the owner of one piece of land is given an easement over an adjacent piece of land.

Easements in Gross An **easement in gross** authorizes a person who does not own adjacent land to use another's land. An easement in gross is a personal right because it does not depend on the easement holder owning adjacent land. Thus, there is no dominant estate. Examples of easements in gross include those granted to run power, telephone, and cable television lines across an owner's property. Commercial easements in gross are transferable, but ordinary, noncommercial easements in gross are not. For example, the fact that a farmer grants a hunter the right to hunt pheasant on his or her farm does not mean that other hunters are permitted to hunt on the farmer's property.

easement in gross

An easement that authorizes a person who does not own adjacent land the right to use another's land.

The right of property has not made poverty, but it has powerfully contributed to make wealth.

J. R. McCulloch
(1789-1864) Principles of
Political Economy

Responsibility for Maintenance and Repair The easement holder owes a duty to maintain and repair the easement. The owner of the estate can use the property as long as it does not interfere with the easement. For example, if a piece of property is subject to an easement for an underground pipeline, the owner of the property could graze cattle or plant crops on the land above the easement, subject to the easement holder's right to repair the pipeline.

Licenses

license

Grants a person the right to enter upon another's property for a specified and usually short period of time.

A **license** grants a person the right to enter upon another's property for a specified and usually short period of time. The person granting the license is called the *licensor*; the person receiving the license is called the *licensee*. For example, a common license is a ticket to a movie theater or sporting event that grants the holder the right to enter the premises for the performance. A license does not transfer any interest in the property. A license is a personal privilege that may be revoked by the licensor at any time.

Profits

A **profit a'pendre** (or **profit**) gives the holder the right to remove something from another's real property. Profits usually involve the right to remove gravel, minerals, grain, or timber from another's property. A *profit appurtenant* grants the owner of one piece of land the right to go onto another's adjacent land and remove things from it. A *profit in gross* authorizes someone who does not own adjacent land the right to go onto another's property and remove things from it.

profit
Grants a person the right to remove something from another's real property.

CONCEPT SUMMARY   NONPOSSESSORY INTERESTS

Nonpossessory Interest	Description
Easement appurtenant	Easement over a servient estate that benefits a dominant estate. The easement runs with the land.
Easement in gross	Easement that grants a person a right to use another's land. It is a personal right that does not run with the land.
License	Grants a person the right to enter upon another's real property for a specified event or time (e.g., for a concert).
Profit	Grants the holder the right to remove something from another's real property (e.g., timber, grain).

International Perspective

SORTING OUT REAL PROPERTY OWNERSHIP RIGHTS IN THE FORMER EAST GERMANY

When the Berlin Wall tumbled in 1989, it allowed for the reunification of East and West Germany into one country. The event was heralded as a triumph for democracy because it meant the return of capitalism and private property rights to East Germany. Only one major question remained: Who owns the real property in the former East Germany?

Germany was under the influence and rule of the Nazi Party from 1933 until May 1945, when Germany surrendered to the Allies after World War II. During that time, the Nazis appropriated private property from owners. After the war, Germany was divided between West Germany, which was allied with Europe and the United States, and East Germany, which was under the Soviet Union's control. The city of Berlin, which was located in East Germany, was also divided in half. The Berlin Wall was erected to prevent East Berliners from defecting to the West through West Berlin. From 1945 to 1949, the Soviets appropriated private property in East Germany. In 1949,

the East German government was created. Until 1989, East Germany was a communist state that owned the property of the country.

In 1990, after the reunification of Germany, the German government enacted the **Vermogensgesetz (Statute for the Regulation of Open Property Questions)** and the **Anmeldeverordnung (Regulation on the Filing of Claims)**. Together, the statute and the regulations created a procedure for filing and proving claims to property expropriated by the Nazis before and during World War II, by the Soviets between 1945 and 1949, and by the East German government from 1949 to 1989.

The German property claims law set December 31, 1992, as the final date for the filing of claims for the return of real property. Claimants had to file an application that specified the location, kind, and extent of the property; original ownership; and chain of inheritance. After examining the claims, the German authorities make decisions and award ownership rights. This process will take many years.

(box continues)

In the meantime, the German government enacted a new law that requires a permit for the sale or transfer of real property situated in the former East Germany. The permit will not be issued if a claim for the return of the property has been filed. A claimant can also apply for an injunction in the civil court to prevent the transfer of property until the merits of the claim have been decided.

One provision in the German claims law favors Jewish claimants. There is a presumption in the law that any property sold between January 1933 and May 1945 is considered to be sold under duress, unless the buyer can prove other-

wise. This is because during that time period, Nazi officials forced Jews to transfer their property for little or no consideration under threat of harm or death.

Resolving the property claims in the former East Germany will not be an easy task. Any other governments in other socialist or communist countries that change to a democratic, capitalist system will face similar problems. For example, real property rights in the former Union of Soviet Socialist Republics (USSR) and many East European countries probably will be determined using a procedure similar to that used in Germany.

Working the Web

U.S. Department of Housing and Urban Development
HUD has a Web site full of information about housing.

Visit at **www.hud.gov**

American Bar Association Section of Real Property, Probate, and Trust Law
This section of the ABA publishes its own magazines as well as linking to other real property sites.

Visit at **www.abanet.org/rppt/home.html**

Federal Fair Housing Act
A searchable copy of this Act is maintained by Cornell University.

Visit at **www.law.cornell.edu/uscode/42/ch45.html**

Legal Online
Legal Online is the first Internet periodical for lawyers. It contains many useful articles about real property.

Visit at **www.legalonline.com**

CYBER EXERCISES

1. From the HUD Web site, find information for first time home buyers.

2. From the ABA Section of Real Property, Probate, and Trust Law site, find out about *Probate and Property Magazine*.

3. In what title of the U.S. Code will you find the Federal Fair Housing Act?

4. Using Legal Online, find out who wrote an article titled "A Real Estate Lawyer's Guide to the Internet."

CASES AND EXERCISES

CRITICAL LEGAL THINKING CASES

50.1. In 1883, Isaac McIlwee owned 100 acres of land in Valley Township, Guernsey County, Ohio. In that year, he sold the property to Akron & Cambridge Coal Co. (Akron & Cambridge) in fee simple but reserved in fee simple "the surface of all said lands" to himself. Over the years, the interests in the land were transferred to many different parties. As of 1981, the

Mid-Ohio Coal Company owned the rights originally transferred to Akron & Cambridge, and Peter and Irene Minnich owned the rights reserved by Isaac McIlwee in 1883. The Minniches claim they possess subsurface rights to the property except for coal rights. Who wins? [*Minnich v. Guernsey Savings and Loan Company*, 521 N.E.2d 489 (OhioApp. 1987)]

50.2. Larry M. and Betty E. Divine were granted a judgment of divorce on September 9, 1987. The judgment awarded their house to Betty. After the judgment was entered but before he left the premises, Larry removed six circuit breakers, three phone jacks, one front door lock, curtain rods, a yard gate, five 16-foot steel stock gates, bathroom towel racks, and a toilet tissue holder. Larry was charged with contempt of court for violating the divorce judgment. Is he guilty? [*Divine v. Divine*, 769 S.W.2d 847 (Mo.App. 1989)]

50.3. Baudilio Bowles died testate. His will devised to his sister, Julianita B. Vigil, "one half of any income, rents, or profits from any real property located in Bull Creek or Colonias, New Mexico." The will contained another clause that left to his children "My interest in any real property owned by me at the time of my death, located in Bull Creek and/or Colonias, San Miguel County." The property referred to in both devises is the same property. Julianita died before the will was probated. Her heirs claim a one-half ownership interest in the real property. Bowles's children assert that they own all of his property. Who wins? [*In the Matter of the Estate of Bowles*, 764 P.2d 510 (N.M.App. 1988)]

50.4. In 1941, W. E. and Jennie Hutton conveyed land they owned to the Trustees of Schools of District Number One of the Town of Allison, Illinois, by warranty deed "to be used for school purpose only; otherwise to revert to Grantor." The school district built a school on the site, commonly known as Hutton School. The Huttons conveyed the adjoining farmland and their reversionary interest in the school site to the Jacqmains, who in turn conveyed their interest to Herbert and Betty Mahrenholz (Mahrenholz) in 1959. The 1.5-acre site sits in the middle of Mahrenholz's farmland. In May 1973, the school district discontinued holding regular classes at Hutton School. Instead, it used the school building to warehouse and store miscellaneous school equipment, supplies, unused desks, and the like. In 1974, Mahrenholz filed suit to quiet title to the school property in themselves. Who wins? [*Mahrenholz v. County Board of School, Trustees of Lawrence County*, 544 N.E.2d 128 (Ill.App. 1989)]

50.5. Verna M. Chappell owned a piece of real property. On June 16, 1965, Chappell transferred the property to herself and her niece Bertha M. Stewart as joint tenants. When Chappell died in 1981, Chappell's gross estate was set at $28,321, which included the value of the house. Claims, debts, and charges against the estate totaled $19,451, which included a $14,040 claim by Lorna M. Rembe for services provided as conservator. The probate assets available to pay the claims and debts came to only $1,571 if the real property

went to Stewart as the joint tenant. Rembe sued, alleging that the value of the real property should be used to pay off Chappell's debts and claims. Who wins? [*Rembe v. Stewart*, 387 N.W.2d 313 (Iowa 1986)]

50.6. Charles Jetter Eichman and his wife, Cora Paton Eichman, were married on August 12, 1965. In 1968, they purchased a house in Tallahassee, Florida, taking title in their joint names as husband and wife, thus creating a tenancy by the entireties. In 1971, they separated, and Cora moved to Vancouver, Canada. Charles continued to live in the marital home in Florida. In January 1975, Cora filed a petition for divorce. On March 31, 1975, Charles struck Cora on the head with a pipe, causing injuries that rendered her incapable of managing herself or her affairs and bringing to an end the divorce proceeding. A guardian was appointed for her. Charles was convicted of attempted murder and was sentenced to prison for 10 years. Cora's guardian filed an action seeking to partition the marital property located in Florida. Charles answered, alleging that an estate by the entirety is not subject to partition as long as the parties remain married. Who wins? [*Eichman v. Paton*, 393 So.2d 655 (Fla.App. 1981)]

50.7. Daniel T. Yu and his wife, Bernice, owned a house and two lots as community property. On January 15, 1985, Yu entered into an agreement with Arch, Ltd. (Arch), whereby he agreed to exchange these properties for two office buildings owned by Arch. Yu signed the agreement, but his wife did not. At the date set for closing, Arch performed its obligations under the agreement, executed all documents, and was prepared to transfer title to its properties to Yu. Yu, however, refused to perform his obligations under the agreement. Evidence showed that the office buildings had decreased in value from $800,000 to $700,000 from the date of the agreement to the date set for closing. Arch sued Yu to recover damages for breach of contract. Who wins? [*Arch, Ltd. v. Yu*, 766 P.2d 911 (N.M. 1988)]

50.8. John L. Yutterman died in 1953 and left one piece of property, located in Fort Smith, Arkansas, to his two sons and two daughters. Each child received approximately one-fourth of the property in fee simple. A 40-foot driveway divided the property. Concerning the driveway, Yutterman's will provided as follows: "Further, a specific condition of this will and of these devises is that the forty (40) foot driveway from Free Ferry Road, three hundred (300) feet Northward, shall be kept open for the common use of the devisees in this will." In 1982, one of the daughters wanted to sell her property to a third party. If the third party purchases the property, will he or she have an easement to use the driveway? [*Merriman v. Yutterman*, 723 S.W.2d 823 (Ark. 1987)]

50.9. In 1973, Joseph and Helen Naab purchased a tract of land in a subdivision of Williamstown, West Virginia. At the time of purchase, there was both a house and a small concrete garage on the property. Evidence showed that the garage had been erected sometime prior to 1952 by one of the Naabs' predecessors in title. In 1975, Roger and Cynthia Nolan purchased a lot contiguous to that owned by the Naabs. The following year, the Nolans had their property surveyed. The survey indicated that one corner of the Naabs' garage encroached 1.22 feet onto the Nolans' property, and the other corner encroached 0.91 foot over the property line. The Nolans requested that the Naabs remove the garage from their property. When the Naabs refused, this lawsuit ensued. Who wins? [*Naab v. Nolan*, 327 S.E.2d 151 (W.Va. 1985)]

ETHICS CASES

50.10. On October 13, 1972, Johnnie H. Hill and his wife, Clara Mae, entered into an installment sales contract with Pinelawn Memorial Park, Inc. (Pinelawn), to purchase a mausoleum crypt, making it clear they wanted to buy Crypt "D" that faced eastward toward Kinston. The Hills paid a $1,035 down payment and continued to make $33.02 monthly payments. On February 13, 1974, William C. Shackelford and his wife, Jennie L., entered into an agreement with Pinelawn to purchase Crypt D. They paid a $1,406 down payment and two annual installments of $912.

The Hills were first put on notice of the second contract when they visited Pinelawn in February 1977 and saw the Shackelford name on Crypt D. The Hills then tendered full payment to Pinelawn for Crypt D. On April 25, 1977, the Hills sued Pinelawn and the Shackelfords. They demanded specific performance of the contract and the deed to Crypt D. Upon being served with summons, the Shackelfords discovered that they had no deed to the crypt and demanded one from Pinelawn. Pinelawn delivered them a deed dated August 18, 1977, which the Shackelfords recorded in the county register on September 9, 1977. Who owns Crypt D? Did Pinelawn act ethically in this case? [*Hill v. Pinelawn Memorial Park, Inc.*, 282 S.E.2d 779 (N.C. 1981)]

50.11. On March 19, 1971, Victor and Phyllis Garber (Garber) acquired a piece of real property by warranty deed. The deed was recorded on December 30, 1971. The property consisted of 80 acres that was enclosed by a fence that had been in place for over 50 years. The enclosed area was used to graze cattle and produce hay. Subsequently, William and Herbert Doenz (Doenz) acquired a piece of real property adjacent to Garber's. In March 1981, Doenz employed a surveyor to locate the land's boundaries. As a result of the survey, it was discovered that the shared fence was 20 to 30 feet inside the deed line on Doenz's property. The amount of property between the old fence and the deed line was 3.01 acres. In September 1981, Doenz removed the old fence and constructed a new fence along the deed line. Garber brought suit to quiet title. Did Doenz act ethically in removing the fence? Did Garber act ethically in claiming title to property that originally belonged with the adjacent property? Did Garber acquire title to property between the fence and the deed line through adverse possession? [*Doenz v. Garber*, 665 P.2d 932 (Wy. 1983)]

CRITICAL LEGAL THINKING WRITING ASSIGNMENT

Read Case A.50 in the Case Appendix [*Walker v. Quillen*]. This case is excerpted from the Supreme Court of Delaware's opinion. Review and brief the case. In your brief, be sure to answer the following questions.

1. Who were the plaintiffs (appellees)? Who was the defendant (appellant)?

2. Describe the tract of land owned by the plaintiffs and defendant.

3. What was the issue in this case? How did the court decide this issue?

Landlord–Tenant Relationships

*P*roperty has its duties as well as its rights.

BENJAMIN DISRAELI
Sybil (1845), Bk. II, Ch. XI

Chapter Objectives

After studying this chapter, you should be able to

1. Identify and describe the various types of tenancy.
2. List and describe landlords' duties under a lease.
3. List and describe tenants' duties under a lease.
4. Describe how the fair housing and disabilities acts regulate real estate.
5. Describe the tort liability of landlords and tenants.
6. Describe how a lease can be terminated.
7. Describe how restrictive covenants restrict the use of land.
8. Define *private* and *public nuisances.*
9. Describe how zoning laws regulate the use of land.
10. Describe how the government acquires property through eminent domain.

Chapter Contents

landlord–tenant relationship
A relationship created when the owner of a freehold estate (landlord) transfers a right to exclusively and temporarily possess the owner's property to another (tenant).

nonfreehold estate
An estate in which the tenant has a right to possession of the property but not title to the property.

leasehold
A tenant's interest in the property.

landlord
The owner who transfers the leasehold.

tenant
The party to whom the leasehold is transferred.

lease
A transfer of the right to the possession and use of the real property for a set term in return for certain consideration; the rental agreement between a landlord and a tenant.

Landlord–tenant relationships are very common in the United States because (1) over half of the population rent their homes and (2) many businesses lease office space, stores, manufacturing facilities, and other commercial property. The parties to the relationship have certain legal rights and duties that are governed by a mixture of real estate and contract law.

Although the United States has the most advanced private property system in the world, the ownership and possession of real estate is not free of government regulation. Pursuant to constitutional authority, federal, state, and local governments have enacted myriad laws that regulate ownership, possession, and use of real property. These laws—which are collectively referred to as *land use control*—include zoning laws, building codes, antidiscrimination laws, and the like.

This chapter discusses these topics.

Landlord–Tenant Relationship

A landlord–tenant relationship is created when the owner of a freehold estate (i.e., an estate in fee or a life estate) transfers a right to exclusively and temporarily possess the owner's property. The tenant receives a **nonfreehold estate** in the property—that is, the tenant has a right to possession of the property but not title to the property.

The tenant's interest in the property is called a **leasehold estate**, or **leasehold**. The owner who transfers the leasehold estate is called the **landlord**, or **lessor**. The party to whom the leasehold estate is transferred is called the **tenant**, or **lessee**.

The Lease

The rental agreement between the landlord and the tenant is called the **lease**. Leases can generally be either oral or written except that most statutes of frauds require written leases for periods of time longer than one year. The lease must contain the essential terms of the parties' agreement. The lease is often a form contract that is prepared by the landlord and presented to the tenant. This is particularly true of residential leases. Other leases are negotiated between the parties. For example, Bank of America's lease of a branch office would be negotiated with the owner of the building.

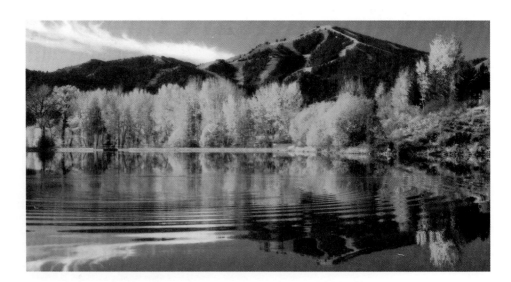

Sometimes the government leases land to private operators, such as this ski mountain in Sun Valley, Idaho.

Types of Tenancy

There are four types of *tenancies*: (1) *tenancy for years*, (2) *periodic tenancy*, (3) *tenancy at will*, and (4) *tenancy at sufferance*. Each is described in the following paragraphs.

Tenancy for Years

A **tenancy for years** is created when the landlord and the tenant agree on a specific duration for the lease. Any lease for a stated period—no matter how long or short—is called a tenancy for years. Examples of such arrangements include office space leased in a high-rise office building on a 30-year lease and a cabin leased for the summer.

A tenancy for years terminates automatically, without notice, upon the expiration of the stated term. Sometimes, such leases contain renewal or extension clauses. If a tenant dies during the lease term, the lease is personal property that transfers to his or her heirs.

tenancy for years
A tenancy created when the landlord and the tenant agree on a specific duration for the lease.

Periodic Tenancy

A **periodic tenancy** is created when a lease specifies intervals at which payments are due but does not specify how long the lease is for. A lease that states, "Rent is due on the first day of the month" establishes a periodic tenancy. Many such leases are created by implication.

A periodic tenancy may be terminated by either party at the end of any payment interval, but adequate notice of the termination must be given. At common law, the notice period equaled the length of the payment period. That is, a month-to-month tenancy requires a one-month notice of termination. Most states have enacted statutes that set forth the required notice periods for termination of periodic tenancies. If a tenant dies during a periodic tenancy, the lease transfers to his or her heirs for the remainder of the current payment interval.

periodic tenancy
A tenancy created when a lease specifies intervals at which payments are due but does not specify how long the lease is for.

Tenancy at Will

A lease that may be terminated at any time by either party is a **tenancy at will**. A tenancy at will may be created expressly (e.g., "to tenant as long as landlord wishes") but is more likely to be created by implication.

At common law, a tenancy at will could be terminated by either party without advance notice—that is, notice of termination ended the lease the moment it was given. Most states have enacted statutes requiring minimum advance notice for the termination of a tenancy at will. The death of either party terminates a tenancy at will.

tenancy at will
A lease that may be terminated at any time by either party.

Tenancy at Sufferance

A **tenancy at sufferance** is created when a tenant retains possession of property after the expiration of another tenancy or a life estate without the owner's consent. That is, the owner suffers the *wrongful possession* of his or her property by the holdover tenant. This is not really a true tenancy but merely the possession of property without right. Technically, a tenant at sufferance is a trespasser.

A tenant at sufferance is liable for the payment of rent during the period of sufferance. Most states require an owner to go through certain legal proceedings, called *eviction proceedings* or *unlawful detainer actions*, to evict a holdover tenant. A few states allow owners to use self-help to evict a holdover tenant if force is not used.

tenancy at sufferance
A tenancy created when a tenant retains possession of property after the expiration of another tenancy or a life estate without the owner's consent.

CONCEPT SUMMARY TYPES OF TENANCIES

Type of Tenancy	Description
Tenancy for years	Continues for the duration of the lease and then terminates automatically without notice. It does not terminate by the death of either party.
Periodic tenancy	Continues from payment interval to payment interval. It may be terminated by either party with adequate notice. It does not terminate upon the death of either party.
Tenancy at will	Continues at the will of the parties and may be terminated by either party at any time with adequate notice. It terminates upon the death of either party.
Tenancy at sufferance	Arises when a tenant wrongfully occupies real property after the expiration of another tenancy or life estate. It continues until the owner either evicts the tenant or holds him or her over for another term. It terminates upon the death of the tenant.

Ethical Perspective

LAWS PROHIBIT DISCRIMINATION IN THE SALE AND RENTAL OF REAL PROPERTY

Federal and state governments have enacted statutes that prohibit discrimination in the sale and rental of real property. The **Civil Rights Act** prohibits racial discrimination in all transfer of real property, including housing and commercial and industrial property [42 U.S.C. §§ 1971 et seq.]. The act prohibits private and public discrimination and permits lawsuits to recover damages and obtain injunctions against offending conduct.

The **Fair Housing Act** makes it unlawful for a party to refuse to rent or sell a dwelling to any person because of his or her race, color, national origin, sex, or religion [42 U.S.C. §§ 360 et seq.]. The act also prohibits discrimination by real estate brokers, mortgage lenders, and advertisers concerning the sale or rental of real property. The law does not apply to the following leases: (1) a person who owns a building of four or fewer units and occupies one of the units and leases the others and (2) a person who leases a single-family dwelling and does not own more than three single-family dwellings. To qualify for either exemption, the lessor cannot use a real estate broker or advertise in a discriminating manner.

Many states and local communities have also enacted statutes and ordinances that prohibit discrimination in the sale or lease of real property. These laws usually prohibit discrimination based on race, color, national origin, sex, or religion but also often prohibit discrimination based on other protected classes such as age, sexual preference, and persons receiving government assistance.

1. Do you think laws prohibiting discrimination in the sale and rental of real property are necessary? Explain.
2. What public purposes are served by these laws?

LANDLORD'S DUTY TO DELIVER POSSESSION OF THE LEASED PREMISES

The duties a landlord owes a tenant are either expressly provided in the lease, set forth in statute, or implied by law. The landlord's duties are discussed in the following paragraphs.

Duty to Deliver Possession

possession

A lease grants the tenant *exclusive possession* of the leased premises for the term of the lease or until the tenant defaults on the obligations under the lease.

A lease grants the tenant **exclusive possession** of the leased premises until (1) the term of the lease expires or (2) the tenant defaults on the obligations under the lease. The landlord is obligated to deliver possession of the leased premises to the tenant on the date the lease term begins. A landlord may not enter leased premises unless the right is specifically reserved in the lease.

Duty Not to Interfere with the Tenant's Right to Quiet Enjoyment

The law implies a **covenant of quiet enjoyment** in all leases. Under this covenant, the landlord may not interfere with the tenant's quiet and peaceful possession, use, and enjoyment of the leased premises. The covenant is breached if the landlord, or anyone acting with the landlord's consent, interferes with the tenant's use and enjoyment of the property. This is called **wrongful** or **unlawful eviction**. It may occur if the landlord *actually evicts* the tenant by physically preventing him or her from possessing or using the leased premises or if the landlord *constructively evicts* the tenant by causing the leased premises to become unfit for its intended use (e.g., by failing to provide electricity). If the landlord refuses to cure the defect after a reasonable time, a tenant who has been constructively evicted may (1) sue for damages and possession of the premises or (2) treat the lease as terminated, vacate the premises, and cease paying rent. The landlord is not responsible for wrongful acts of third persons that were done without his or her authorization.

covenant of quiet enjoyment
A covenant that says a landlord may not interfere with the tenant's quiet, use, and peaceful possession, use, and enjoyment of the leased premises.

wrongful eviction
A violation of the covenant of quiet enjoyment. Also called unlawful eviction.

Contemporary Business Application

TITLE III OF THE AMERICANS WITH DISABILITIES ACT

On July 26, 1990, the **Americans with Disabilities Act (ADA)** was signed into law [42 U.S.C. §§ 1201 et seq.]. Most of the provisions of the ADA became effective on January 26, 1992. The ADA is a broad civil rights statute that prohibits discrimination against disabled individuals in employment, public services, public accommodations and services, and telecommunications. **Title III** of the ADA prohibits discrimination on the basis of disability in places of public accommodation operated by private entities. The attorney general of the United States is empowered to issue regulations that interpret and enforce the ADA.

Title III of the ADA applies to public accommodations and commercial facilities such as motels, hotels, restaurants, theaters, recreation facilities, colleges and universities, department stores, retail stores, and office buildings. It does not generally apply to residential facilities (single- and multifamily housing).

Title III requires facilities that are covered by the law to be designed, constructed, and altered in compliance with specific accessibility requirements established by regulations issued pursuant to the ADA. In 1991, the attorney general issued final regulations that contain minimum guidelines to make covered facilities accessible to disabled individuals. This includes constructing ramps to accommodate wheelchairs, installing railings next to steps, placing signs written in Braille in elevators and at elevator call buttons, and so on. If both the ADA and state law apply, the more stringent rule must be followed.

New construction must be built in such a manner as to be readily accessible to and usable by disabled individuals. Any alterations made to existing buildings must be made so that the altered portions of the building are readily accessible to disabled individuals to the maximum extent feasible. With respect to existing buildings, architectural barriers must be removed if such removal is readily achievable. In determining when an action is readily achievable, the factors to be considered include the nature and cost of the action, the financial resources of the facility, and the type of operations of the facility.

The ADA provides for both private right of action and enforcement by the attorney general. Individuals may seek injunctive relief and monetary damages, while the attorney general may seek equitable relief and civil fines up to $50,000 for the first violation and $100,000 for any subsequent violation.

Proponents of Title III of the ADA argue that the law is necessary to make public accommodations and commercial facilities accommodate the needs of the disabled. They point out that voluntary efforts to make these accommodations were too few and too late. Critics argue that the ADA creates a quagmire of regulations that are difficult to understand and that will cost landowners billions of dollars to comply with.

Building owners, managers, architects, and others involved in the design, construction, ownership, and management of public accommodations and commercial buildings must be knowledgeable about, and comply with, the provisions of Title III of the ADA.

LANDLORD'S DUTY TO MAINTAIN THE LEASED PREMISES

At common law, the doctrine of *caveat lessee*—"lessee beware"—applied to leases. The landlord made no warranties about the quality of leased property and had no duty to repair it. The tenant took the property "as is." Modern real estate law, however, imposes certain statutory and judicially implied duties on landlords to repair and maintain leased premises.

Building Codes

building codes

State and local statutes that impose specific standards on property owners to maintain and repair leased premises.

States and local municipalities have enacted statutes called **building** or **housing codes** that impose specific standards on property owners to maintain and repair leased premises. They often provide certain minimum standards regarding heat, water, lights, and other services. Depending on the statute, violators may be subject to fines by the government, loss of their claim for rent, and imprisonment for serious violations.

Implied Warranty of Habitability

implied warranty of habitability

A warranty that provides that the leased premises must be fit, safe, and suitable for ordinary residential use.

The courts of many jurisdictions hold that an **implied warranty of habitability** applies to residential leases for their duration. This warranty provides that the leased premises must be fit, safe, and suitable for ordinary residential use. For example, unchecked rodent infestation, leaking roofs, and unworkable bathroom facilities have been held to breach the implied warranty of habitability. On the other hand, a small crack in the wall or some paint peeling from a door does not breach this warranty.

If the landlord's failure to maintain or repair the leased premises affects the tenant's use or enjoyment of the premises, state statutes and judicial decisions provide various remedies. Generally, the tenant may (1) withhold from his or her rent the amount by which the defect reduced the value of the premises to him or her, (2) repair the defect and deduct the cost of repairs from the rent due for the leased premises, (3) cancel the lease if the failure to repair constitutes constructive eviction, or (4) sue for damages for the amount the landlord's failure to repair the defect reduced the value of the leasehold.

In the following case, the court found a breach of the implied warranty of habitability.

Solow v. Wellner
569 N.Y.Supp.2d 882 (1991)
Civil Court of the City of New York

CASE 51.1

FACTS
The defendants are approximately 80 tenants of a 300-unit luxury apartment building on the upper East Side of Manhattan. The monthly rents in the all-glass-enclosed building, which won several architectural awards, ranged from $1,064 to $5,379. The landlord brought a summary proceeding against the tenants to recover rent when they engaged in a rent strike in protest against what they viewed as deteriorating conditions and services. Among other things, the evidence showed that during the period in question (May 1982–May 1988), the elevator system made tenants and their guests wait interminable lengths of time, the elevators skipped floors and opened on the wrong floors, a stench emanated from garbage stored near the garage and mice appeared in that area, fixtures were missing in public areas, water seeped into mailboxes, the air conditioning in the lobby was inoperative, and air conditioners in individual units leaked. The defendant-tenants sought abatement of rent for breach of the implied warranty of habitability.

ISSUE
Did the landlord breach the implied warranty of habitability?

IN THE LANGUAGE OF THE COURT
York, Judge   In determining whether the warranty of fitness has been breached, this jurisdiction has adopted the "reasonable

expectation" test. This means that the premises are to be maintained in accordance with the reasonable expectations of the tenant. Certain amenities not necessarily life threatening, but consistent with the nature of the bargain—air conditioning would be an example—fall under the protection of this branch of the warranty. Predictability and reliability of services is another factor.

In applying this branch of the warranty to this case, we start with the obvious expectations of this uniquely designed all-glass-enclosed building on Manhattan's fashionable upper East Side. Add to this the comparatively high rents exacted for these apartments and one would have to assume that the expectations of the tenants encompassed more than the minimal amenities. While the warranty certainly entitled them to freedom from conditions threatening their life, health and safety, their higher rents justified increased expectations of a well-run, impeccably clean building of consistent and reliable services. These expectations were reasonably enhanced by the brochure they received, which was also incorporated into the lease, with its promises of security, air conditioning in the public areas and panoramic views. The promises

and expectations fell far short of the reality. The warranty in the public areas was breached.

DECISION AND REMEDY
The court held that the landlord had breached the implied warranty of habitability. The court abated the rent of each of the tenants individually, in total allowing the landlord to recover only 22 percent of the amount he sued for. The court ordered the landlord to pay the tenants' attorneys' fees.

Case Questions

Critical Legal Thinking Should the law recognize the implied warranty of habitability? Why or why not?

Ethics Did the landlord act ethically in not correcting the defects in the building? Did the tenants act ethically in engaging in a rent strike?

Business Application Was the remedy the court ordered appropriate in this case?

TENANT'S DUTIES

A tenant owes the landlord the duties agreed to in the lease and any duties imposed by law. The tenant's duties are discussed in the following paragraphs.

Duty Not to Use Leased Premises for Illegal or Nonstipulated Purposes

A tenant may use the leased property for any lawful purposes permitted by the lease. Leases often stipulate that the leased premises can be used only for specific purposes. If the tenant uses the leased premises for unlawful purposes (e.g., operating an illegal gambling casino) or nonstipulated purposes (e.g., operating a restaurant in a residence), the landlord may terminate the lease, evict the tenant, and sue for damages.

Duty Not to Commit Waste

A tenant is under a duty not to commit **waste** to the leasehold. Waste occurs when the tenant causes substantial and permanent damage to the leased premises that decreases the value of the property and the landlord's reversionary interest in it. Waste does not include ordinary wear and tear. For example, it would be waste if the floor of the premises buckled because a tenant permitted heavy equipment to be placed on the premises. It would not be waste if the paint chipped from the walls because of the passage of time. The landlord can recover damages from the tenant for waste.

waste
Occurs when a tenant causes substantial and permanent damage to the leased premises that decreases the value of the property and the landlord's reversionary interest in it.

Duty Not to Disturb Other Tenants

A tenant owes a duty not to disturb the use and enjoyment of the leased premises by other tenants in the same building. For example, a tenant in an apartment building breaches this duty if he or she disturbs the sleep of other tenants by playing loud music throughout the night. A landlord may evict the tenant who interferes with the quiet enjoyment of other tenants.

Entrepreneur and the Law _____

DUTY TO PAY RENT

A commercial or residential tenant owes a duty to pay the agreed-upon amount of **rent** for the leased premises to the landlord at the agreed-upon time and terms. Generally, rent is payable in advance (e.g., on the first day of the month for use that month), although the lease may provide for other times and methods for payment. Reasonable late charges may be assessed on rent that is overdue. In a **gross lease** the tenant pays a gross sum to the landlord. The landlord is responsible for paying the property taxes and assessments on the property.

Several of the most common commercial rental arrangements are

- **Net Lease** The tenant is responsible for paying rent and property taxes.
- **Double Net Lease** The tenant is responsible for paying rent, property taxes, and utilities.
- **Net, Net, Net Lease (or Triple Net Lease)** The tenant is responsible for paying rent, property taxes, utilities, and insurance.

Upon nonpayment of rent, the landlord is entitled to recover possession of the leased premises from the tenant. This may require the landlord to *evict* the tenant. Most states provide a summary procedure called **unlawful detainer action** that a landlord can institute to evict a tenant. The landlord may also sue to recover the unpaid rent from the tenant. The more modern rule requires the landlord to make reasonable efforts to *mitigate damages* (i.e., to make reasonable efforts to re-lease the premises).

Tenants often are required to pay a *security deposit* to the landlord. In residential leases, the amount generally is equivalent to one month's rent. The landlord may apply the security deposit against unpaid rent or use it to cover the cost of repairing damages caused by the tenant to the leased premises. Any remaining security must be repaid to the tenant within 14 days after the lease is terminated. Some states require landlords to hold the security deposits in a separate trust account and to pay interest on the deposits.

TORT LIABILITY OF LANDLORDS AND TENANTS

Under the common law, a landlord was not liable for injuries caused on leased premises. This rule was based on the notion that the landlord had relinquished control and possession of the property to the tenant. Court decisions and statutes have eroded this no-liability rule. Now, landlords owe a *duty of reasonable care* to tenants and third parties not to negligently cause them injury. This duty is based on the foreseeability standard of ordinary negligence actions.

A tenant owes a *duty of reasonable care* to persons who enter upon the leased premises. If a tenant's negligence causes injury to a third person, the tenant is liable in tort for any damages sustained by the injured person. For example, a tenant who leaves a skateboard on the steps is liable for the injuries caused to a visitor who trips on it.

premises liability
The liability of landlords and tenants to persons injured on their premises.

The liability of landlords and tenants to persons injured on their premises is called **premises liability**. The following case illustrates premises liability.

Feld v. Merriam
461 A.2d 225 (1983)
Superior Court of Pennsylvania

CASE 51.2

FACTS

Cedarbrook is a complex of approximately 1,000 apartment units located on a 36-acre tract of land in Cheltenham, Pennsylvania, owned by John W. Merriam. Vehicles can enter the grounds through two entrances, each of which is staffed by security guards. Automobiles park in garages located beneath each apartment building. The parking facility under Building No. 1 had spaces for 160 cars. Access to the garages could be gained through two open entrances. The garages were not well lit. Between 1970 and 1975, the crime rate in Cedarbrook had risen. During the three-month period preceding the criminal incident at issue in this case, 21 separate incidents of criminal activity, including robberies, burglaries at apartments, car thefts, and an assault on a tenant, were reported.

On June 27, 1975, at approximately 9:00 P.M., Samuel and Peggy Feld, tenants in Building No. 1, drove into the Cedarbrook complex and parked their car in the garage. After getting out of their car, they walked toward the pedestrian exit. Suddenly, three armed men emerged from behind a parked car, accosted them, and robbed them at gunpoint. They then raped Mrs. Feld. Following the incident, Mrs. Feld began psychotherapy to help alleviate her severe emotional distress. Her psychiatrist testified that she would never recover from the emotional trauma of the event. Following the incident, Mr. Feld was constantly in a fearful, nervous, and agitated state. At the time of trial, he was still unable to discuss the details of the criminal episode with anyone. Although the Felds' marriage deteriorated, they remained together out of compassion for each other.

Mr. and Mrs. Feld sued Cedarbrook for damages. The jury returned a verdict that awarded $2 million compensatory damages to Mrs. Feld, $1 million compensatory damages to Mr. Feld, and $1.5 million punitive damages to each of them. Cedarbrook appealed.

ISSUE

Is Cedarbrook liable for the criminal attack on the Felds?

IN THE LANGUAGE OF THE COURT

Cirillo, Judge   This court believes that imposing a duty on the landlord to provide adequate security for his tenants is in keeping with the current trends in landlord-tenant law in this commonwealth. Therefore, while we do not consider a landlord to be an insurer of his tenants, we hold that in all areas of the leasehold, particularly in the areas under his control, the landlord is under a duty to provide adequate security to protect his tenants from the foreseeable criminal actions of third persons.

It is important to note, however, that the conduct of the landlord must be evaluated in light of all the facts of a particular case.

Therefore, the custom among landlords of buildings of the same class plays a significant role in determining the reasonableness of a landlord's actions. In order to establish a prima facie case of negligence against a landlord for his failure to provide adequate security, a plaintiff must present evidence showing that the landlord had notice of criminal activity that posed risk of harm to his tenants, that he had the means to take precautions to protect the tenant against this risk of harm, and that his failure to do so was the proximate cause of the tenant's injuries.

Cedarbrook contends that since it did not have prior notice of sexual assaults occurring on the Cedarbrook grounds, it cannot be held liable under the facts of the instant case. We disagree. In the instant case, sufficient evidence was presented to show that Cedarbrook was aware of criminal activity on the Cedarbrook grounds. From this evidence, the jury could have concluded that Cedarbrook had sufficient notice that criminal conduct by third parties was likely to endanger the safety of its tenants. Cedarbrook also asserts that insufficient evidence was presented regarding security measures taken at other apartment complexes of the same class as Cedarbrook. We disagree. Two experts testified that the security provided by Cedarbrook did not conform to the accepted standard in buildings of the same class. From this evidence the jury could have logically concluded that Cedarbrook acted unreasonably in failing to implement a more effective security plan.

DECISION AND REMEDY

The appellate court affirmed the judgment except for the punitive damages awarded to Mr. Feld, which it reduced to $750,000.

Case Questions

Critical Legal Thinking   Should a landlord be held liable for the criminal activities of third parties? Why or why not?

Ethics   Did the landlord act ethically in not providing better security? Did the tenants act ethically in suing the landlord for the criminal actions of third parties?

Business Application   Do you think the damage awards were excessive in this case? Were punitive damages warranted?

*T*RANSFERRING RIGHTS TO LEASED PROPERTY

Landlords may sell, gift, devise, or otherwise transfer their interests in the leased property. For example, a landlord can sell the right to receive rents, sell his or her reversionary interest, or do both. If complete title is transferred, the property is subject to the existing lease. The new landlord cannot alter the terms of the lease (e.g., raise the rent) during the term of the lease unless the lease so provides.

The tenant's right to transfer possession of the leased premises to another depends on the terms of the lease. Many leases permit the lessee to assign or sublease his or her rights in the property.

Assignment of the Lease

assignment

A transfer by a tenant of his or her rights under a lease to another.

assignor

The party who transfers the rights.

assignee

The party to whom rights have been transferred.

If a tenant transfers all of his or her interests under a lease, it is an **assignment**. The original tenant is the **assignor** and the new tenant is the **assignee**. Under an assignment, the assignee acquires all of the rights that the assignor had under the lease. The assignee is also obligated to perform the duties that the assignor had under the lease. That is, the assignee must pay the rent and perform other covenants contained in the original lease. The assignor remains responsible for his or her obligations under the lease unless specifically released from doing so by the landlord. If the landlord recovers from the assignor, the assignor has a course of action to recover from the assignee.

Sublease

sublease

When a tenant transfers only some of his or her rights under the lease.

sublessor

The original tenant in a sublease situation.

sublessee

The new tenant in a sublease situation.

If a tenant transfers only some of his or her rights under the lease, it is a **sublease**. The original tenant is the **sublessor** and the new tenant is the **sublessee**. The sublessor is not released from his or her obligations under the lease unless specifically released by the landlord. Subleases differ from assignments in important ways. In a sublease, no legal relationship is formed between the landlord and the sublessee. Therefore, the sublessee does not acquire the rights under the original lease. For example, a sublessee would not acquire the sublessor's option to renew a lease. Further, the landlord cannot sue the sublessee to recover rent payments or enforce duties under the original lease.

In most cases, tenants cannot assign or sublease their leases without the landlord's consent. This right protects the landlord from the transfer of the leasehold to someone who might damage the property or not have the financial resources to pay the rent. Most states, either by statute or judicial decision, hold that the owner's consent cannot be unreasonably withheld.

Contemporary Business Application

RENT CONTROL

Many local communities across the country have enacted **rent control ordinances** that stipulate the amount of rent a landlord can charge for residential housing. Most of these ordinances fix the rent at a specific amount and provide for minor annual increases. Although many communities, such as Santa Monica, California, have adopted rent control ordinances, New York City has the most famous rent control ordinance.

Landlords, of course, oppose rent control, arguing that the government, by enacting rent control, takes property from them (i.e., the higher rents they could charge absent rent control laws). The Fifth Amendment's "taking" clause generally requires just compensation be paid to an owner whose property is taken by the government. Landlords have challenged rent control ordinances as violating the "taking" clause. The U.S. Supreme Court visited this issue in *Yee v. City of Escondido, California*, 112 S.Ct. 1522 (1992).

In that case, the city of Escondido adopted a rent control ordinance that rolled back the rent of "pads" in mobile home parks to 1986 levels. The ordinance prohibits rent increases without the approval of the city council. The owners of many mobile home parks affected by the ordinance sued the city, alleging that the law constituted an uncompensated "taking" in violation of the U.S. Constitution. The trial court, the court of appeals, and the U.S. Supreme Court held otherwise and upheld the rent control ordinance.

Critics argued that rent control ordinances are merely a "regulatory tax" that transfers wealth from landowners to tenants. They also pointed out that tenants of Manhattan's posh upper East Side, or of Santa Monica, California, hardly deserve to be protected by rent controls. Proponents of rent control say that it is necessary to create affordable housing, particularly in high-rent urban areas. They assert that rent control serves a legitimate government purpose. Whatever the arguments, the Supreme Court has given a green light to local communities to adopt rent control ordinances.

LAND USE CONTROL

Generally, the ownership of property entitles the owner to use his or her property as the owner wishes. However, such use is subject to limitations imposed by either *private agreement* or *government regulation*. These limitations, collectively referred to as **land use control** or **land use regulation**, are discussed in the following sections.

land use control
The collective term for the laws that regulate the possession, ownership, and use of real property.

PRIVATE REGULATION OF LAND USE

Private control of the use of land is based on two major principles: *private nuisance* and *restrictive covenants*. Each of these is discussed in the paragraphs that follow.

Private Nuisance

In today's society, the enjoyment and use of a parcel of real property is usually affected by the use of adjoining or nearby property. A landowner or tenant who is injured may bring a **private nuisance** action for damages and for injunctive relief to stop the nuisance. There is no set definition of nuisance, and each case depends on the specific facts of the situation.

private nuisance
A nuisance that affects or disturbs one or a few people.

To determine whether conduct constitutes a nuisance, the courts examine such factors as the importance of the use, the extent and duration of the use, the reasonableness of the use in the area, the loss caused if the use is abated, and such. In addition, use can be considered a nuisance even though it was in existence in the neighborhood before the complaining neighbor purchased or occupied his or her property.

Restrictive Covenants

A **restrictive covenant** is a private agreement between landowners that restricts the use of their land. Restrictive covenants, commonly called *building restrictions* or *CC&Rs (covenants, conditions, and restrictions)*, are often used by residential developments and condominium buildings to establish uniform rules for all occupants. A sample set of restrictive covenants is set forth in Exhibit 51.1.

restrictive covenant
A private agreement between landowners that restricts the use of their land.

Business Brief
In *Shelley v. Kraemer*, the U.S. Supreme Court struck down restrictive covenants in deeds that prohibited minorities from owning residential property in certain neighborhoods.

Lawful restrictive covenants may be enforced in private lawsuits. For example, if several lot owners have agreed not to build houses over one story high to preserve views, any lot holder can sue another lot owner to enforce this covenant against the building of a two-story house. Restrictive covenants that discriminate based on race, national origin, sex, age, religion, or other protected class are illegal and void.

Good fences make good neighbors.
Robert Frost
"Mending Wall" (1914)

PUBLIC REGULATION OF LAND USE

In the United States, the ownership and use of private property is subject to government land use control. These laws and regulations limit how land can be used and give the government the right to take private property for government use. The various forms of government regulation of land use are discussed in the paragraphs that follow.

Public Nuisance

A **public nuisance** occurs when one's use of his or her real property harms members of the public, whether they are landowners or tenants or others. For example, excessive noise or pollution caused by a manufacturing plant would cause harm to anyone in the area, such as workers, consumers, or visitors. Public nuisances tend to affect a broader class of persons than do private nuisances. The government may bring an action to seek the assessment of fines, criminal penalties, and an injunction to stop the offending use.

public nuisance
A nuisance that affects or disturbs the public in general.

Exhibit 51.1 *Sample Restrictive Covenants*

Declaration of Covenants, Conditions and Restrictions

Pine Shores Country Club Association, Inc.

Declarant, the Great Lakes Development Company, a Michigan corporation, is the owner of certain real property located in the City of Evergreen Shores. County of Mackinac, State of Michigan. The Real Property consists of residential condominium units, clubhouse, together with private streets, entry ways, landscaped common areas, lakes, maintenance facilities, swimming pools and certain other recreational facilities, including a golf course consisting of eighteen holes, driving range, ten tennis courts, and a tennis clubhouse.

Together with the purchase of a condominium, each condominium purchaser, in addition to receiving a separate interest in a "Unit," will receive an undivided interest in the "Common Area"; a non-exclusive easement appurtenant for ingress, egress, use and enjoyment over, upon and in The Pine Shores Country Club, subject to certain conditions more fully set forth hereinafter; and a proprietary club membership which will entitle such Owner to use the facilities of The Pine Shores Country Club subject to all of the terms and conditions hereof.

Use Restrictions

The use of the Project and each Condominium therein shall be restricted in accordance with the following provisions:

1. **Residential Use**. None of the Units shall be used except for residential purposes.
2. **Commercial Use**. No industry, business, trade, occupation or profession of any kind, whether commercial, religious, educational or otherwise, shall be conducted, maintained or permitted on any part of the Project.
3. **Signs**. No sign or other advertising device of any character (including but not limited to "For Rent" or "For Lease" signs) shall be erected, maintained or displayed to the public view on any portion of the Project except one sign for each Condominium, of not more than eighteen inches by twenty-four inches, advertising such Condominium for sale or lease.
4. **Lawful Use**. No noxious, offensive, or unlawful activity shall be carried on, in or upon any Condominium or any part of the Project, nor shall anything be done thereon which may be, or may become, an annoyance or offensive to the neighborhood, or which shall in any way interfere with the quiet enjoyment of each Owner of his respective Condominium.
5. **Temporary Structures**. No structure of a temporary character, trailer, basement, tent, shack, garage, barn, or other out-building shall be erected, maintained or used within the Project. No trailer, camper, recreational vehicle, boat or similar equipment shall be permitted to remain within the Project unless placed or maintained within an enclosed garage.
6. **Motorcycles and Mopeds**. No motorcycles, mopeds or other motorized vehicles having less than four wheels may be kept, operated or permitted on or in any part of the Project.
7. **Animals**. No animals, fowl, reptiles, livestock or poultry of any kind shall be raised, bred, or kept on or in any part of the Project, except that dogs, cats or other household pets may be kept on or within the Condominiums, provided they are not kept, bred or maintained for any commercial purpose.

Zoning

zoning ordinances

Local laws that are adopted by municipalities and local governments to regulate land use within their boundaries. Zoning ordinances are adopted and enforced to protect the health, safety, morals, and general welfare of the community.

Pursuant to their constitutional *police power*, state and local governments may enact laws to protect the public health, safety, morals, and general welfare of the community. Pursuant to this power, most counties and municipalities have enacted **zoning ordinances** to regulate land use. For example, zoning ordinances prohibiting the location of adult bookstores near residential areas have been held to be valid to protect public morals. Zoning is the primary form of land use regulation in this country.

Zoning ordinances generally (1) establish use districts within the municipality (i.e., areas are generally designated residential, commercial, or industrial), (2) restrict the height, size, and location of buildings on a building site, and (3) establish aesthetic requirements or limitations for the exterior of buildings.

A **zoning commission** usually formulates zoning ordinances, conducts public hearings, and makes recommendations to the city council, who must vote to enact an ordinance. Once enacted, the zoning ordinance commission enforces the zoning ordinance. If landowners believe that a zoning ordinance is illegal or that it has been applied unlawfully to them or their property, they may institute a court proceeding seeking judicial review of the ordinance or its application.

Variances   An owner who wishes to use his or her property for a use different from that permitted under a current zoning ordinance may seek relief from the ordinance by obtaining a **variance**. To obtain a variance, the landowner must prove that the ordinance causes an undue hardship by preventing him or her from making a reasonable return on the land as zoned. Variances are usually difficult to obtain.

Nonconforming Uses   Zoning laws act prospectively; that is, uses and buildings that already exist in the zoned area are permitted to continue even though they do not fit within new zoning ordinances. Such uses are called **nonconforming uses**. For example, if a new zoning ordinance is enacted making an area a residential zone, an existing funeral parlor is a nonconforming use.

The following case is concerned with the lawfulness of a zoning ordinance.

zoning commission
A local administrative body that formulates zoning ordinances, conducts public hearings, and makes recommendations to the city council.

variance
An exception that permits a type of building or use in an area that would not otherwise be allowed by a zoning ordinance.

nonconforming uses
Uses and buildings that already exist in the zoned area that are permitted to continue even though they do not fit within new zoning ordinances.

Guinnane v. San Francisco City Planning Commission
209 Cal.App.3d 732, 257 Cal.Rptr. 742
California Court of Appeals

CASE 51.3

FACTS
In 1979, Roy Guinnane purchased four vacant lots located on Edgehill Way in San Francisco. In July 1980, the city of San Francisco designated an area, including Guinnane's property, as "Edgehill Woods." In 1982, the city adopted a resolution to exercise its discretionary review power over proposed development in the Edgehill Woods area. Guinnane filed an application for a building permit to construct a four-story, 6,000-square-foot house with five bedrooms, five baths, and parking for two cars on one of his lots. Although the proposed building met the specifications of other zoning laws and building codes, the San Francisco Planning Commission disapproved the application because the proposed structure was "not in character" with other homes in the neighborhood. The board of permit appeals agreed. Guinnane appealed.

ISSUE
Is the aesthetic zoning by the city of San Francisco lawful?

IN THE LANGUAGE OF THE COURT
Racanelli, Judge *The basic standard guiding the Planning Commission in discharging its function is the promotion of the "public health, safety, peace, morals, comfort, convenience, and general welfare." In particular, the Commission is directed to "protect the character and stability of residential areas." Under the Municipal Code, any city department may exercise its discretion*

in deciding whether to approve any application; and in doing so, it may consider the effect of the proposed project upon the surrounding properties.

We conclude that both the Planning Commission and the Board of Permit Appeals are authorized to exercise independent discretionary review of a building permit application, the final authority being reposed in the board. Further, we conclude that such review is not confined to a determination whether the applicant has complied with the city's zoning ordinances and building codes.

DECISION AND REMEDY
The court of appeals held that San Francisco's aesthetic zoning ordinance was lawful. The court found that the ordinance was enacted pursuant to the city's police power to protect its residents' health, safety, and welfare. The appellate court affirmed the trial court's judgment.

Case Questions

Critical Legal Thinking   Should a city be given zoning authority over the aesthetics of an area? Why or why not?

Ethics   Is it ethical for a property owner to build a structure that does not comport with the character of the area?

Business Application   Are businesses helped or harmed by zoning ordinances?

Contemporary Business Application _____

REGULATORY "TAKING"

Federal, state, and local governments may take private property for public use. Under the Fifth Amendment of the U.S. Constitution, the government must pay "just compensation" to the owner of the land taken. For example, if the government is building a highway, it can use its power of **eminent domain** (also called **condemnation**) to forcibly buy the property upon which to build the highway. *Physical taking* of land usually generates few legal problems (except what value to place on the land, and this can be decided in a court).

Suppose a person owns land upon which he or she intends to build four-story apartment buildings. If the local zoning board adopts a zoning ordinance that restricts buildings in the area to two stories, the property decreases in value. Has there been a "taking"? The answer is No. The regulation serves a legitimate social function (e.g., reduces congestion, preserves views, etc.) and still leaves the landowner with a viable option—to build two-story apartment buildings.

But what if the *regulatory taking* is total? Is there a *compensable taking*? Consider the following situation. In 1986, David H. Lucas paid $975,000 for two residential lots on the Isle of Palms in Charleston County, South Carolina, on which he intended to build single-family homes. Single-family houses had already been built on adjacent lots. In 1988, the South Carolina legislature enacted the Beachfront Management Act. This act encompassed Lucas's property. The act flatly prohibited any construction of occupable improvements on "coastal land," which included Lucas's two lots.

Lucas promptly filed suit in South Carolina court, contending that the act's construction ban effected a "taking" of his property without payment of just compensation in violation of the Fifth Amendment. The trial court agreed, finding that the regulation rendered Lucas's lots valueless. The court ordered South Carolina to pay Lucas $1,232,387 as just compensation for the lots. The supreme court of the state reversed, and the U.S. Supreme Court agreed to hear Lucas's appeal.

In a majority opinion, the U.S. Supreme Court held that the South Carolina law constituted a compensable "regulatory taking" of Lucas's property in violation of the U.S. Constitution. The Supreme Court stated, "The Fifth Amendment is violated when land use regulation does not substantially advance legitimate state interests or denies an owner economically viable use of his land." The Supreme Court found that there was a "total taking" of Lucas's property in this case. It reversed the judgment of the state supreme court and remanded the case for proceedings consistent with its opinion.

The *Lucas* decision affords some comfort to landowners because it implies that the government cannot strip them of *all* economically viable uses of their property without paying compensation for doing so. It does not, however, protect landowners from government regulation that causes only a partial loss of the value of their land. [*Lucas v. South Carolina Coastal Council*, 112 S.Ct. 2886 (1992)]

Working the Web ....

TenantNews This site contains lots of information about tenants.

Visit at **tenant.net/tenantnews**

e-biz

Bad Landlords (Renter's Rights and Complaints) Find all about bad landlords at this entertaining site. Resources and complaints by state are included.

Visit at **members.tripod.com/BadLandlords**

Landlord–Tenant Law: An Overview Cornell Law School's Legal Information Institute maintains this site. It links to both federal and state materials.

Visit at **www.law.cornell.edu/topics/landlord_tenant. html**

TenantNet TenantNet is the on-line resource for residential tenants. Although it focuses on New York, information from other areas is also available.

Visit at **www.tenant.net/**

CYBER EXERCISES

1. Use TenantNews to find the current rent guidelines for New York.

2. Can you find any bad landlords in your state?

3. Using Landlord–Tenant Law, find recent U.S. Supreme Court decisions dealing with this issue.

4. Is information for your state available on TenantNet?

CASES AND EXERCISES

CRITICAL LEGAL THINKING CASES

51.1. Community Management Corporation (Landlord) entered into a rental agreement with Bowman (Tenant) to lease an apartment to Tenant on a month-to-month tenancy commencing on October 1, 1981. The agreement required Tenant to give 30 days' notice before vacating the premises. The agreement also required a security deposit of $215, which would be forfeited if Tenant vacated the apartment prior to the end of a month. On September 21, 1982, Tenant informed Landlord that he was vacating the apartment as of September 30, 1982. Because Landlord had only a 9-day notice, Landlord was unable to release the apartment for the month of October 1982. Landlord retained the security deposit to cover rent for October. Tenant sued to recover the security deposit. Who wins? [*Bowman v. Community Management Corp.*, 469 N.E.2d 1038 (OhioApp. 1984)]

51.2. In 1984, T&W Building Company (Landlord) entered into a five-year lease agreement with Merrillville Sport & Fitness, Inc. (Tenant), to lease space in a building to be used as a sports and fitness center. The lease provided that Landlord was to keep the heating and cooling plant "in good order, repair, and condition" and was to commence required repairs as soon as reasonably practicable after receiving written notice of problems. Tenant complained of several problems throughout the first year of its tenancy. First, the heating system did not work properly, causing the premises to be extremely cold, particularly in the winter months. Second, there was no water on many occasions. Third, there was only one plug installed on the premises. Landlord failed to rectify the problems. As a result, Tenant lost members. It gave notice and vacated the premises in February 1985. Tenant and Landlord ended up in a lawsuit regarding the lease. Who wins? [*T&W Building Co. v. Merrillville Sport & Fitness, Inc.*, 529 N.E.2d 865 (Ind.App. 1988)]

51.3. Sharon Love entered into a written lease agreement with Monarch Apartments (Monarch) for apartment #4 at 441 Winfield in Topeka, Kansas. Shortly after moving in, she experienced serious problems with termites. Her walls swelled, clouds of dirt came out, and when she checked on her children one night, she saw termites flying around the room. She complained to Monarch, which arranged for the apartment to be fumigated. When the termite problem persisted, Monarch moved Love and her children to apartment #2. Upon moving in, Love noticed that roaches crawled over the walls, ceilings, and floors of the apartment. She complained, and Monarch called an exterminator, who sprayed the apartment. When the roach problem persisted, Love vacated the premises. Is Love lawfully terminating the lease? [*Love v. Monarch Apartments*, 771 P.2d 79 (Kan.App. 1989)]

51.4. Susan Nylen, Elizabeth Lewis, and Julie Reed, students at Indiana University, signed a Rental Agreement as cosigners to lease an apartment from Park Doral Apartments. The rental term was from August 26, 1986, until August 19, 1987, at a monthly rental of $420. The tenants paid a security deposit of $420, constituting prepayment of rent for the last month of the lease term. At the end of the fall semester, Reed moved out of the apartment and, in February 1987, she refused to pay any further rent. Nylen and Lewis remained in possession of the apartment, paying only two-thirds of the total rent due for the month of February. Nylen and Lewis made a payment of $280 for the rent due in March. They vacated the apartment on March 13, 1987. The landlord, who was unable to release the apartment during the lease term, sued Reed, Nylen, and Lewis for the unpaid rent. Who wins? [*Nylen v. Park Doral Apartments*, 535 N.E.2d 178 (Ind.App. 1989)]

51.5. William Long, d.b.a. Hoosier Homes, owned an apartment building in Indianapolis, Indiana. He rented a second-story apartment to Marvin Tardy. On August 20, 1984, Almedia McLayea visited Tardy with her one-month-old nephew, Garfield Dawson. As McLayea was leaving the apartment, she walked down the stairway carrying Dawson in an infant seat. As she came down four steps to a landing, which led to a flight of 10 stairs, she caught her heel on a stair, slipped, and fell forward. There was no handrail along the stairway (as required by law) by which she could break her fall. Instead, her shoulder struck a window at the landing, the window broke, the rotted screen behind it collapsed, and Dawson fell through the opening to the ground below. He sustained permanent injuries, including brain damage. Dawson (through his mother) sued the landlord to recover damages for negligence. Who wins? [*Dawson v. Long*, 546 N.E.2d 1265 (Ind.App. 1989)]

51.6. In October 1986, Luis and Barbara Chavez leased a house they owned in Arizona to Michael and Terry Diaz. The lease provided that no pets were to be kept on the premises without prior written approval of the landlords. The Diazes, without the landlords' consent or knowledge, kept a pit bull and another dog, which was half pit bull and half rottweiler, at the leased premises. On October 17, 1986, the Diazes' two dogs escaped from the backyard and attacked and injured Josephine Gibbons. Gibbons sued the landlords for damages. Are the landlords liable? Would the tenants be liable? [*Gibbons v. Chavez*, 770 P.2d 377 (Ariz.App. 1988)]

51.7. In December 1972, the Millers owned 80 acres of land in Madison County, Illinois. In January 1973, the Millers sold 8.06 acres to the Statlers. There existed an artificial lake that was primarily on the Millers' property but that also extended to the Statlers' property. The Statlers renovated a house on their property; added several rooms, a garage, and a deck; and landscaped the property. While the Millers and Statlers were neighbors, their children shared and enjoyed the lake for fishing, swimming, and other recreational activities.

In June 1975, Catalano purchased the Millers' property. He began raising livestock on the property. After the Statlers refused to sell their property to Catalano, he erected a barbed wire fence across the lake along the property line that prevented the Statlers from using the lake. He later constructed a rock barrier in the lake, which caused the property in front of the Statlers' home to become a mudhole. Catalano deposited debris—old commodes with plastic flowers in them, used tires, bathtubs, rusted barrels, torn upholstered furniture, and broken machinery—along the property line in clear view of the Statlers' home. He played loud music all night long and shone bright lights on the Statlers' property at various times

during the night. Windows in the Statlers' home were broken by bullets shot onto their property. Catalano placed shooting trophies on the property line that featured men aiming rifles and placed the trophies so that the rifles were aimed at the Statlers' home. The Statlers sued to enjoin Catalano's actions as a nuisance and sought compensatory and punitive damages. Who wins? [*Statler v. Catalano*, 521 N.E.2d 565 (Ill.App. 1988)]

51.8. The city of Ladue is one of the finer suburban residential areas of metropolitan St. Louis. The homes in the city are considerably more expensive than are those in surrounding areas and consist of homes of traditional design such as colonial, French provincial, and English. The city set up an architectural board to approve plans for buildings that "conform to certain minimum architectural standards of appearance and conformity with surrounding structures, and that unsightly, grotesque, and unsuitable structures, detrimental to the stability of value and the welfare of surrounding property, structures, and residents, and to the general welfare and happiness of the community, be avoided."

The owner of a lot in the city submitted a plan to build a house of ultramodern design. It was a pyramid-shaped house, with a flat top and triangular-shaped windows and doors. Although the house plans met other city zoning ordinances and building codes, the architectural board rejected the owner's petition for a building permit based on aesthetic reasons. The owner sued the city. Who wins? [*State of Missouri v. Berkeley*, 458 S.W.2d 305 (Mo. 1970)]

51.9. The town of Hempstead, New Hampshire, enacted a zoning ordinance "in order to retain the beauty and countrified atmosphere of the town, and to promote health, safety, morals, order, convenience, peace, prosperity, and general welfare of its inhabitants." To preserve abutting property owners' views and light, the ordinance limits the homes in the town to one-and-one-half stories. In violation of the ordinance, John M. Alexander built a shell of a second story and a new roof on his house. After the town ordered him to halt construction and denied him permission to occupy the second floor, he applied for a variance. Should the variance be granted? [*Alexander v. Town of Hempstead*, 525 A.2d 276 (N.H. 1987)]

ETHICS CASES

51.10. Moe and Joe Rappaport (Tenants) leased space in a shopping mall owned by Bermuda Avenue Shopping Center Associates, L.P. (Landlord), to use as an indoor golf arcade. The lease was signed in May 1987, and Tenants were given possession of the leased premises on July 23, 1987. Tenants

were not told by Landlord of the extensive renovations planned for the mall. From July 23 until August 18, the golf arcade was busy and earned a net profit. On August 18, the renovation of the mall began in front of the arcade. According to Tenants, their store sign was taken down, there were debris and dust in front of the store, the sidewalks and parking spaces in front of the store were taken away, and their business "died." Tenants closed their arcade on September 30 and sued Landlord for damages. Landlord counterclaimed, seeking to recover lost rental income. Did Landlord act ethically in not explaining the extent of the planned renovations to Tenants? Did Tenants act ethically in terminating the lease? Were Tenants constructively evicted from the leased premise? [*Bermuda Avenue Shopping Center Associates, L.P. v. Rappaport*, 565 So.2d 805 (Fla.App. 1990)]

51.11. The Middleton Tract consists of approximately 560 acres of land located in the Santa Cruz Mountains in San Mateo County, California. The land, which was once owned by William H. Middleton, has been subdivided into 80 parcels of various shapes and sizes that are owned by various parties. The original deeds of conveyance from Middleton to purchasers contained certain restrictive covenants. One covenant limits use of the land exclusively for "residential purposes." Most of the land consists of thickly wooded forest with redwood and Douglas fir trees. The Holmeses, who own parcels totaling 144 acres, propose to engage in commercial logging activities on their land. The plaintiffs, who own other parcels in the tract, sued the Holmeses, seeking an injunction against such commercial activities. Who wins? [*Greater Middleton Assn. v. Holmes Lumber Co.*, 222 Cal.App.3d 980, 271 Cal.Rptr. 917 (Cal.App. 1990)]

CRITICAL LEGAL THINKING WRITING ASSIGNMENT

Read Case A.51 in the Case Appendix [*Nollan v. California Coastal Commission*]. This case is excerpted from the U.S. Supreme Court opinion. Review and brief the case. In your brief, be sure to answer the following questions:

1. What did the California Coastal Commission do to try to obtain the easement across Nollans' property?

2. In whose favor did the following courts rule?

   a. Superior court

   b. Court of appeals

   c. U.S. Supreme Court

3. What is a "taking"? If a "taking" is found, what must the government do?

4. Succinctly state the issue that was presented to the U.S. Supreme Court in this case.

5. Could the state of California have acquired the easement across Nollan's property under its power of eminent domain?

52 Insurance

The underwriter knows nothing and the man who comes to him to ask him to insure knows everything.

SCRUTTON, L.J. *Rozanes v. Bowen, 32 Ll.L.Rep. 98 (1928)*

Chapter Objectives

After studying this chapter, you should be able to

1. Describe the parties to an insurance contract.
2. Define *insurable interest.*
3. List and describe the various types of life, health, and disability insurance.
4. Identify the risks covered by a standard fire insurance policy and a homeowners policy.
5. Describe uninsured motorist coverage.
6. Explain no-fault insurance.
7. List and describe special forms of business insurance.
8. Define *umbrella insurance policy.*
9. Describe an insurance company's duty to defend its insured.
10. Describe the defenses that must be raised by an insurer.

Chapter Contents

Insurance is a means for persons and businesses to protect themselves against the risk of loss. A business may purchase life insurance on key executives, fire insurance to cover its buildings, workers' compensation insurance to pay for injuries suffered by employees, and liability insurance to pay for damages caused to consumers by defective products. Individuals may purchase life insurance on loved ones, automobile insurance, homeowners insurance, and the like. Insurance is crucial to personal, business, and estate planning. This chapter covers the formation of an insurance contract, types of insurance, defenses of insurance companies to liability, and other topics of insurance law.

insurance

A means for persons and businesses to protect themselves against the risk of loss.

REGULATION OF THE INSURANCE INDUSTRY

Based on the Commerce Clause of the U.S. Constitution, the federal government could exclusively or heavily regulate the business of insurance. However, the **McCarran-Ferguson Act**, enacted in 1945, gave the regulation of insurance to the states and exempted insurance companies from the federal antitrust laws.[1] Accordingly, each state has enacted statutes that regulate the operation of domestic insurance companies and out-of-state insurance companies that wish to do business in that state. State regulation covers the incorporation, licensing, supervision, and liquidation of insurance companies and the licensing and supervision of insurance agents and brokers.

THE INSURANCE CONTRACT

Insurance is defined as a contract whereby one undertakes to indemnify another against loss, damage, or liability arising from a contingent or unknown event.[2] It is a means of transferring and distributing risk of loss. The risk of loss is pooled (i.e., spread) among all of the parties (or **insureds**) who pay premiums to a particular insurance company. The insurance company—also called the **insurer** or **underwriter**—is then obligated to pay insurance proceeds to those members of the pool who experience a loss.

insured

The party who pays a premium to a particular insurance company for insurance coverage.

The insurance contract is called a **policy**. The money paid to the insurance company is called a **premium**. Premiums are based upon an estimate of the number of parties within the pool who will suffer the risks insured against. The estimate is based on past experience. The premium must include an amount to cover the insurance company's costs of administration and return a profit to the company.

insurer

The insurance company that underwrites the insurance coverage.

Insurance policies are often sold by insurance agents or brokers. An *insurance agent* usually works exclusively for one insurance company and is an agent of that company. An *insurance broker* is an independent contractor who usually represents a number of insurance companies. The broker is the agent of the insured. Some insurance is sold directly by the insurer to the insured (e.g., by direct mail).

policy

The insurance contract.

premium

The money paid to the insurance company.

Mandatory Provisions

Often, state statutes mandate that specific language be included in different types of insurance contracts. These statutes concern coverage for certain losses and how limitations on coverage must be stated in the contract, and the like. Any provisions that are omitted from the contract even though they are required by statute or regulation to be included will be implied.

When an Insurance Contract Becomes Effective

Generally, the applicant (the offeror) files an application for insurance with the insurance company (the offeree). The insurance company can (1) accept the application, (2) reject the application, or (3) offer different terms of insurance to the applicant. In the last case, the insurance company has made a counteroffer. Insurance contracts are governed by the law of contracts. Most policies are prepared on standardized forms. Some states even make that a requirement.

The date that the coverage is effective is important. If the coverage is effective, the insurer is obligated to pay the insurance proceeds; if it is not, the applicant bears the risk of loss. The following rules apply:

1. An applicant who applies for insurance from an insurance company's agent is usually covered from the moment he or she submits the application and pays the first premium. Although this rule applies even if the agreement is oral, most agents issue a written binder indicating the terms of the policy.
2. An applicant who applies for property or liability insurance from an insurance broker is usually not covered until the broker obtains the insurance.
3. In the case of life insurance, the policy can be made expressly contingent upon the passing of a physical exam. If the applicant has paid the first premium but dies before the exam, the applicant's estate can recover the insurance proceeds only if it can show that the applicant would have passed the physical examination.
4. Insurance that is sold by a vending machine (e.g., flight insurance sold at airports) is effective when the applicant receives the receipt from the machine.

Modification of Insurance Contracts

If both the insurer and the insured agree, an insurance contract may be modified. This is usually done either by adding an **endorsement** to the policy or by the execution of a document called a *rider*. Endorsements and riders control over both conflicting provisions and previously issued endorsements or riders.

Insurable Interest

A person must have an **insurable interest** in anything he or she insures. If there is no insurable interest, the contract is treated as a wager and cannot be enforced. This rule is based upon two public policy reasons: (1) Insurance is a means of shifting an existing risk to an insurer and not a means to make a profit off the misfortune of others, and (2) there would be moral risk that someone might be tempted to murder or destroy property that he or she had insured and had no insurable interest in.

Insurable Interest in Life In the case of life insurance, a person must have a close family relationship or an economic benefit from the continued life of another to have an insurable interest in that person's life. Thus, spouses, parents and children, and sisters and brothers may insure each other's lives. Other, more remote relationships (e.g., aunts, uncles, cousins) require additional proof of an economic interest (e.g., proof of support).

An insurable interest may also be based on a business relationship. For example, a creditor may insure the life of a debtor, but only to the amount owed. The insurable interest must exist when the policy is issued, but need not exist at the time of death.

A person may insure his or her own life and name anyone as the *beneficiary*. The beneficiary does not have to have an insurable interest in the insured's life. For example, a person could take out an insurance policy on his or her life and name a charity as the policy's beneficiary.

Insurable Interest in Property Anyone who would suffer a pecuniary (monetary) loss from the destruction of real or personal property has an insurable interest in that property. Ownership obviously creates an insurable interest. In addition, mortgagees, lienholders, and tenants have an insurable interest in property. Partners may insure partnership property, and shareholders can insure corporate property. However, a person could not insure his or her neighbor's automobile unless he or she received some benefit from it (e.g., carpool to work). The insurable interest in property must exist at the time of loss.

Few of us can pass one of these familiar roadside markers without thinking about the pain and suffering of the occupants of the vehicle, let alone their surviving loved ones.

Deductible Clauses and Exclusions from Coverage

In certain circumstances, an insured will not be offered complete coverage by an insurer. This is because of *deductible clauses* and *exclusions from coverage* that are expressly stated in insurance policies. These are discussed in the following paragraphs.

Deductible Clauses Many insurance policies contain **deductible clauses**, which provide that insurance proceeds are payable only after the insured has paid a certain amount of the damage or loss. Typical deductibles for automotive collision insurance are $100, $250, or $500. Suppose that an insured has a $20,000 automobile collision policy with a $500 deductible and his or her car suffers $4,000 damages in an accident. The insured must pay the first $500; the insurer will pay the remaining $3,500.

deductible clause

Clause in an insurance policy that provides that insurance proceeds are payable only after the insured has paid a certain amount of the loss.

Exclusions from Coverage Most insurance policies include certain **exclusions** from coverage. For example, standard fire insurance policies often exclude coverage for damage caused by the storage of explosives or flammable liquids unless a special premium is paid for this coverage. An insurance policy should be read carefully to determine the extent of coverage.

In the following case, the court imposed a duty on the insurance company and its agent to point out important exclusions in the insurance policy to insureds.

exclusion

Part of an insurance policy that says what it will *not* cover under certain circumstances.

Aetna Casualty and Surety Co. v. Velasco
194 Cal.App.3d 1377, 240 Cal.Rptr. 290 (1987)
California Court of Appeals

CASE 52.1

FACTS
In 1982, Joe A. Velasco purchased the Monte Vista Alta Dena Dairy (Dairy), a "drive-in" convenience store and gasoline station that sold food items, sundries, alcoholic beverages, and automotive products. At the time of the purchase, Dairy was insured by Aetna Casualty and Surety Co. (Aetna). The policy was purchased through Visna Insurance Associates, an insur-

ance brokerage located next door to Dairy. After Velasco was assured that the policy covered all risks associated with the business, he decided to continue the Aetna policy.

On October 2, 1982, an 18-year-old minor bought some beer at Dairy. The minor allegedly drank the beer, became intoxicated, and drove his car across the center line of a highway, seriously injuring a motorcycle driver and killing

(case continues)

his passenger. The driver and the heirs of the passenger sued Dairy for damages.

When Velasco forwarded the complaint to Aetna, Aetna responded that Velasco was not covered because of an exclusion on page 11 of the insurance policy, which stated that insurance coverage did not apply to bodily injury or property damage caused by the insured's selling of alcoholic beverages to minors. Velasco sued Aetna, alleging that the insurance company and its agents owed a duty to point out important exclusions to coverage. The trial court granted summary judgment in favor of Aetna. Velasco appealed.

ISSUE
Do insurance companies and their agents owe a duty to point out important exclusions that eliminate protection an insured could reasonably expect to be part of the policy?

IN THE LANGUAGE OF THE COURT
Johnson, Associate Justice   The exclusion was buried in a lengthy form contract—23 printed pages. In the instant case, most pages of the insurance contract contain 700 to 1,100 printed words—the equivalent of three or four double-spaced typed pages each. It would require the average reader at least two hours to read a document of this length and complexity with any measure of comprehension. The insurance company argued the exclusion was effective, even if it disappointed the insured's reasonable expectations about coverage under the policy, because it was "conspicuous, plain, and clear" to anyone who read the entire policy. However, California Supreme Court decisions impose a duty on insurance companies to call to the insured's attention any exclusions that might eliminate coverage the insured could reasonably expect to be part of his policy.

Here, the insurance company does not even allege Visna Insurance Associates brought the liquor liability exclusion to the attention of Velasco. The only evidence in the record before the

trial judge was to the effect the agent failed to mention any exclusions to Velasco and indeed assured him the policy fully covered him in the operation of his new business. The uncontroverted evidence demonstrates the insurance company's agent was located next door to the insured's business. Indeed the agency's employee shopped in this store. It defies reason to believe they were unaware the insured was selling alcoholic beverages at this establishment. The sale of alcoholic beverages, in turn, involves a special exposure to liability—the possibility the insured will sell beer or wine to a minor who then causes an accident. Yet knowing of this special exposure to liability, the insurance company's agents sold the insured a policy that failed to protect him against this special risk without mentioning the exclusion was contained in the policy.

DECISION AND REMEDY
The court of appeals held that insurance companies and their agents owe a duty to point out important exclusions. The court reversed the trial court's judgment in favor of Aetna and remanded the case to the trial court with directions to enter summary judgment in favor of Velasco.

Case Questions

Critical Legal Thinking   Should insurance companies be required by law to draft "plain English" contracts? Should they be required to summarize the exclusions from coverage on the cover page of the policy?

Ethics   Do insurance companies act ethically in placing exclusions to coverage in their policies? Do they act ethically by doing so in "fine print" contracts?

Business Application   What consequences will this decision have for insurance companies? For the insureds?

ℒIFE INSURANCE

Life insurance is really "death insurance" because the insurer is normally obligated to pay a specified sum of money upon the death of the insured. Some life insurance policies provide for the payment of all or a portion of the proceeds to the insured before death if he or she is suffering from a terminal illness. This allows the insured to pay for medical and other costs associated with the illness. The most common forms of life insurance are described in Exhibit 52.1.

Parties to a Life Insurance Contract

There are four parties to a life insurance contract:

1. The *insurance company* issues the policy.
2. The *owner* of the policy is the person who contracts with the insurance company and pays the premiums.
3. The *insured* is the person whose life is insured.
4. The **beneficiary** is the person who is to receive the insurance proceeds when the insured dies.

℮XHIBIT 52.1   *Kinds of Life Insurance*

Whole Life Insurance Whole life insurance (also called ordinary life or straight life) provides coverage during the entire life of the insured. Premiums are paid during the life of the insured or until the insured reaches a certain age. Whole life insurance involves an element of savings. That is, premiums are set to cover both the death benefit and an additional amount for investment by the insurance company. This builds up a cash surrender value that may be borrowed against by the insured. Premiums for such insurance tend to be high.

Limited-Payment Life Insurance Limited-payment life insurance premiums are paid for a fixed number of years (e.g., 10 years) even though coverage is provided during the entire life of the insured. This form of insurance also has cash surrender value. Premiums are higher than whole life insurance. Insurance companies have introduced single-premium life insurance where the insured pays the entire premium in a lump-sum payment.

Term Life Insurance Term life insurance is issued for a limited period of time (e.g., five years) with premiums payable and coverage effective only during this term. Because term life insurance involves no savings feature, there is no cash surrender value. Because term life is "pure" insurance, premiums are less than for whole life or limited-payment life insurance. Term life policies usually provide for renewal or conversion to other forms of life insurance.

Universal Life Insurance Universal life insurance combines features of both term and whole life insurance. The premium payment—called a contribution—is divided between the purchase of term insurance and an amount invested by the insurance company. The cash value grows at a variable interest rate rather than at a fixed interest rate.

Endorsement and Annuity Contracts Endorsement and annuity contracts are forms of retirement and life insurance contracts. An endorsement contract is an agreement by an insurance company to pay an agreed-upon lump sum of money either to the insured when he or she reaches a certain age or to his or her beneficiary if he or she dies before the age. An annuity contract is an agreement by an insurance company to pay periodic payments (e.g., monthly) to the insured once he or she reaches a certain age.

Often, the owner and the insured are the same person. For example, an owner may take out an insurance policy on his or her own life. The owner and beneficiary may also be the same person. As another example, a son may take out an insurance policy on his father's life and name himself as the beneficiary. In this case, the father is the insured and the son is both the beneficiary and the owner of the policy. The owner of the policy has the power to name the beneficiary of the insurance proceeds. Most life insurance contracts permit the owner to change beneficiaries. If no beneficiary is named, the proceeds go to the insured's estate.

℮ntrepreneur and the ℒaw

BUSINESS OWNERS PURCHASE KEY-PERSON LIFE INSURANCE

Small businesses, such as partnerships, limited liability companies, and close corporations, often purchase key-person life insurance on the owners of the business. The company pays the premiums for the life insurance policies. The life insurance is usually used to fund buy–sell agreements among the owners of the business. Thus, if an insured owner dies, the insurance proceeds are paid to the deceased's beneficiaries. The deceased's interest in the company then reverts to either the other owners or the business, according to the terms of the buy–sell agreement.

(box continues)

The following steps should be followed when purchasing key-person life insurance:

- The owners must agree upon the dollar value of their ownership interests in the business.
- The owners must execute a buy–sell agreement among themselves and the company specifying how a deceased owner's interest will be purchased by the other owners or the company upon his or her death.
- The company should purchase key-person life insurance from a reputable insurance company in an amount necessary to fund the buy–sell agreement.
- The company must pay the premiums for the key-person life insurance policies when due.
- When an owner-insured dies, the other owners and the company must file the claim with the insurance company and take all other steps necessary to ensure that the deceased's beneficiaries are paid the amount specified in the buy–sell agreement in a timely fashion.

Double Indemnity and Exclusions from Coverage

double indemnity clause

A clause that stipulates that the insurer will pay double the amount of the policy if death is caused by accident.

Many life insurance contracts contain a **double indemnity clause** that stipulates that the insurer will pay double the amount of the policy if death is caused by accident. A small additional premium is charged for this protection.

Many life insurance policies exclude liability for death caused by military action, executions by government, or accidents of private aircraft. Most life insurance policies also exclude liability for death caused by suicide during the first year or so of the policy.

Contemporary Business Application

DO LIFE INSURANCE COMPANIES HAVE TO PAY FOR SUICIDE?

In 1982, Farmers New World Life Insurance Co. (Farmers) issued two $100,000 life insurance policies on Lawrence Malcom's life. His wife, Pamela Malcom, and Medmetric Corporation were the beneficiaries. Each policy contained a suicide provision that stated, "Suicide, whether sane or insane, will not be a risk assumed during the first two policy years. In such a case we will refund the premiums paid." In May 1984, within two years after the policies were issued, Lawrence committed suicide. The beneficiaries filed claims with Farmers seeking each policy's $100,000 benefit. When Farmers refused to pay the benefits and refunded the premiums, the beneficiaries sued Farmers for breach of the insurance contract. They argued that the suicide provision should not be enforced because it was not plain and clear and conspicuous. The trial court granted Farmers's motion for summary judgment. The beneficiaries appealed.

Is Farmers liable on the two life insurance policies? The court of appeals held that the policies' suicide provision was conspicuous, bold, clear, and unambiguous and was therefore enforceable.

The court noted that to be conspicuous, an exclusion must be positioned in a place and printed in a form that will attract the reader's attention. The suicide provision was located on the policy's third page—the first operative page after the cover page and the alphabetical guide—and preceded by the bold-faced capitalized word "SUICIDE." The suicide provision contained only 27 words and was clearly separated from its neighboring provisions by several blank lines and blank spaces. None of those words was beyond the working vocabulary of laypersons. The provision was neither submerged in "a sea of print" nor "inserted incidentally in a paragraph dealing with promised benefits." The suicide provision clearly and conspicuously conveyed its message in understandable language.

If the suicide in this case had occurred two years or more after the policy had been issued, the insurance would have to pay this claim. [*Malcom v. Farmers New World Life Insurance Co.*, 4 Cal.App.4th 296, 5 Cal.Rptr.2d 584 (Cal.App. 1992)]

HEALTH AND DISABILITY INSURANCE

Persons can purchase insurance that insures their health. *Health and disability* insurance are discussed in the following paragraphs.

Health Insurance

A person who is injured or sick may have to have medical treatment, surgery, or hospital care. **Health insurance** may be purchased to help cover the costs of such medical care. Health insurance usually covers only a portion of the costs of medical care. Many insurance companies also offer dental insurance.

health insurance
Purchased to help cover the costs of medical treatment, surgery, or hospital care.

Disability Insurance

A person who is injured or becomes sick may not be able to continue gainful employment. **Disability insurance**, which provides a monthly income to an insured who is disabled and cannot work, may be purchased to protect the insured against such an eventuality. The monthly benefits are usually based on the degree of disability.

disability insurance
Insurance that provides a monthly income to an insured who is disabled and cannot work.

FIRE AND HOMEOWNERS INSURANCE

Two major forms of insurance are available for residences: (1) *a standard fire insurance policy* and (2) a *homeowners policy*. Such insurance is often required on real property that is mortgaged. Renters may also purchase insurance policies. These types of policies are discussed in the paragraphs that follow.

Standard Fire Insurance Policy

A standard fire insurance policy protects real and personal property against loss resulting from fire and certain related perils. Most state statutes require the use of the **New York standard fire insurance form** as the standard fire insurance policy. This standard policy protects the homeowner from loss caused by fire, lightning, smoke, and water damage. The coverage of a standard policy can be enlarged by adding *riders* or *endorsements* to the policy. Riders are often added to cover damage caused by windstorms, rainstorms, hail, explosions, theft, and liability. Additional coverage requires the payment of increased premiums. Most policies exclude coverage for loss caused by enemy attack, civil war, revolution, landslides, and floods. In the case of property located in a designated flood area, a separate flood insurance policy is required.

New York standard fire insurance form
A standard fire insurance policy that protects the homeowner from loss caused by fire, lightning, smoke, and water damage.

Within a reasonable time after the fire or other insured peril occurs, an insured must file a *proof of loss* with the insurer. Most modern fire insurance policies provide **replacement cost insurance**. That is, the insurance will pay the cost to replace the damaged or destroyed property up to the policy limits (and subject to coinsurance, as discussed shortly). The insurer has the right to either pay the insured for the loss or pay to have the property restored or replaced. If the insured and the insurer cannot agree on the value of the loss, most insurance policies require the dispute to be settled by arbitration.

replacement cost insurance
Insurance that pays the cost to replace the damaged or destroyed property up to the policy limits.

Coinsurance Clause   Most fires result in only a partial loss of the property. Therefore, many property owners insure their property for less than its full value. To provide an incentive for owners to insure their property for close to its full value, many fire insurance policies contain a *coinsurance clause* that permits an owner who insures his or her property to a certain percent of its value (e.g., 80 percent) to recover up to the face value of the policy. An owner who insures the property for less than the stated percentage must bear a proportionate share of the loss.

Homeowners Policy

homeowners policy

A comprehensive insurance policy that includes coverage for the risks covered by a fire insurance policy as well as personal liability insurance.

A **homeowners policy** is a comprehensive insurance policy that includes coverage for the risks covered by a fire insurance policy as well as personal liability insurance. Thus, a property owner who buys a homeowners policy does not need a separate fire insurance policy.

A homeowners policy covers (1) the dwelling, (2) any appurtenant structures (e.g., garage and storage building), and (3) personal property (e.g., furniture and clothing). A homeowners policy also provides protection for losses caused by theft, whether the items are taken from the home or workplace or taken while traveling.

personal articles floater

An addition to the homeowners policy that covers specific valuable items.

Personal Articles Floater   An insured may wish to obtain insurance for specific valuable items (e.g., jewelry, works of art, and furs). This is accomplished by adding a **personal articles floater** or **personal effects floater** to the homeowners policy. The insured must submit a list of the items he or she wants covered, along with a statement of the value of each item, to the insurance company. The insurance company will charge an increased premium based on the articles insured. A personal articles floater provides coverage for loss or damage to the articles while traveling.

Liability Coverage   A homeowners policy provides comprehensive *personal liability insurance* for the insured and members of his or her family. The insurer must pay property damage, personal injuries, and medical expenses arising from the following situations:

- Persons injured on the insured's property (e.g., a guest slips on the sidewalk)
- Persons injured by the insured or members of the insured's immediate family away from the insured's property (e.g., while golfing)
- Property damaged by the insured or members of the immediate family (e.g., the insured's daughter hits a baseball through a neighbor's window)

residence contents broad form

Insurance that renters purchase to cover loss or damage to their possessions.

Renters Insurance

Renters may purchase insurance to cover loss or damage to their possessions. This policy, called the **residence contents broad form**, covers the renters' possessions against the same perils as a homeowners broad form policy and personal liability coverage.

E-Commerce & Internet Law

e-biz

INSURANCE OFFERED TO COVER INTERNET FRAUD

In the past, a person could pose as another person to commit financial and commercial fraud, but it usually required the crook to obtain fake IDs, copies of bank passbooks, and other documents. Today, with the use of computers and the Internet, financial fraud is much easier and quicker for criminals to pull off. Called *identity fraud*, a perpetrator obtains personal information about the victim using the computer and the Internet. The perpetrator can wreak havoc by electronically impersonating the victim to remove money from bank accounts, purchase goods and services using the victim's credit cards, transfer assets from the victim's securities accounts, and the like. Electronic identity fraud is escalating throughout the country and the world. On average, a crook runs up

over $30,000 of purchases and removed assets before the victim discovers the fraud.

Once the fraud is discovered and stopped, this does not end the victim's plight. The victim is usually not liable beyond $50 on each credit card, and the banks must make good on the money it paid out over fraudulent signatures. However, the victim must take the time and spend the money to restore the bad credit trail left in his or her name. This can take months, and sometimes years, to correct and cost thousands of dollars in legal and other expenses.

Several insurance companies, including Travelers Property Casualty Corp., now offer identity fraud insurance. Any person who has a homeowner's or tenant's insurance policy with the insurance company may purchase identity fraud insurance for an additional premium of around $25 per year. This new coverage pays the expenses a victim incurs in clearing his or her name and correcting financial records after being victimized by identity fraud.

Costs that will be reimbursed include attorney's fees, telephone and certified mailing charges, loan reapplication fees, and lost wages for time taken off from work to deal with the consequences of the fraud. Most identity fraud policies limit recovery to $15,000 to $20,000.

e-biz

*A*UTOMOBILE INSURANCE

Several types of automobile insurance policies include both property and liability insurance. Many states require proof of automobile insurance before license plates are issued. The basic types of automobile insurance policies are discussed in the paragraphs that follow.

Collision Insurance

An owner of an automobile may purchase **collision insurance** that insures his or her car against risk of loss or damage. This form of property insurance pays for damages caused if the car is struck by another car. The coverage is in effect whether the insured's car is moving or standing still. For example, if another motorist hits the insured's automobile while it is parked on the street, collision insurance would pay for the damages. Usually the premium is less if the policy has a deductible.

collision insurance
Insurance that a car owner purchases to insure his or her car against risk of loss or damage.

Comprehensive Insurance

Comprehensive insurance is a form of property insurance that insures an automobile from loss or damage from causes other than collision, namely, fire, theft, explosion, windstorm, hail, falling objects, earthquakes, floods, hurricanes, vandalism, and riot. Many insureds purchase both collision and comprehensive insurance when they insure their automobiles against damage.

comprehensive insurance
A form of property insurance that insures an automobile from loss or damage from causes other than collision.

Liability Insurance

Automobile **liability insurance** covers damages that the insured causes to third parties, including both bodily injury and property damage. The limits of liability insurance are usually stated in three numbers, such as 200/500/50. This limits the insurer's obligation to pay insurance proceeds arising from one accident to $200,000 for bodily injury to one person, $500,000 for total bodily injury to all persons injured, and $50,000 for property damage. States often require insureds to carry minimum liability insurance specified by statute.

liability insurance
Automobile insurance that covers damages that the insured causes to third parties.

A basic automobile liability policy protects the insured when driving his or her own automobile. The owner, however, may wish to expand coverage by adding (1) an *omnibus* or *other-driver clause*, which protects the owner when someone else drives the car with his or her permission, and (2) a *D.O.C. (drive-other coverage)*, which protects the insured while driving other automobiles (e.g., rental cars). Some omnibus clauses extend coverage to third parties who drive automobiles with the permission from a person to whom the owner gave permission to drive the car. Additional premiums are charged for these coverages.

Medical Payment Coverage

An owner can obtain a *medical payment coverage* policy that covers medical expenses incurred by him- or herself, other authorized drivers of the car, and passengers in the car who are injured in an automobile accident. Coverage includes payments for reasonable medical, surgical, and hospital services.

Uninsured Motorist Coverage

uninsured motorist coverage

Automobile insurance that provides coverage to the driver and passengers who are injured by an uninsured motorist or hit-and-run driver.

Usually, people injured in an automobile accident look to the insurer of the party at fault to recover for their personal injury. But what if the person who is at fault has no insurance? An owner of an automobile may purchase **uninsured motorist coverage** that provides coverage to the driver and passengers who are injured by an uninsured motorist or a hit-and-run driver. Certain states require uninsured motorist coverage to be included in automobile insurance policies.

Contemporary Business Application

NO-FAULT AUTOMOBILE INSURANCE

Until fairly recently, most automobile insurance coverage in this country was based on the principle of "fault," whereby a party injured in an accident relied on the insurance of the at-fault party to pay for his or her injuries. This system led to substantial litigation, but many accident victims were unable to recover because the at-fault party had either inadequate insurance or no insurance at all.

To remedy this problem, over half of the states have enacted legislation that mandates **no-fault insurance** for automobile accidents. Under this system, a driver's insurance company pays for any injuries he or she suffered in an accident, no matter who caused the accident.

Most no-fault statutes stipulate that claimants may not sue to recover damages from the party who caused the accident unless the injured party suffered serious injury (e.g., dismemberment or disfigurement) or

death. If the insured recovers the total amount from the at-fault party, he or she must reimburse his or her own insurer for insurance proceeds paid pursuant to the no-fault policy.

No-fault insurance policies provide coverage for medical expenses and lost wages. Pain and suffering are not always covered. No-fault insurance usually covers the insured, members of the insured's immediate family, authorized drivers of the automobile, and passengers.

No-fault insurance reduces litigation costs, lessens the time for an injured person to be compensated for his or her injuries, and assures the insureds that coverage is available if they are injured in an automobile accident. There is also evidence that no-fault insurance reduces the overall cost of automobile insurance. The trend of the law is to replace at-fault systems of automobile insurance with no-fault insurance.

Entrepreneur and the Law

BUSINESS INSURANCE

Businesses purchase insurance to cover myriad risks, including property and liability insurance on buildings, automobile insurance, key-person life insurance, and risks uniquely applicable to businesses. These types of insurance include

- **Business Interruption Insurance** When a business is severely damaged or destroyed by fire or some other peril, it usually takes time to repair or reconstruct the damaged property. During this time, the business is losing money. A business can purchase a **business interruption insurance** policy that will reimburse it for any revenues lost during that period.

- **Workers' Compensation Insurance** Employees are sometimes injured while working within the scope of their employment. All states have enacted legislation that compensates employees for such injuries. Employers may purchase *workers' compensation insurance* to cover this risk. Many states require companies to purchase this form of insurance.

- **Fidelity Insurance** An employer can purchase **fidelity insurance** to protect against the dishonesty and defalcation of employees. For example, a bank can purchase fidelity insurance to protect against losses caused by the embezzlement of bank employees.

- **Directors' and Officers' Liability Insurance** Most large and medium corporations carry **directors' and officers' liability insurance (D&O insurance)** to protect directors and officers from liability for the actions they take on behalf of the corporation. Smaller companies tend to forgo this type of insurance because of the expense involved.

- **Product Liability Insurance** Manufacturers and sellers of products can be held liable for injuries caused by defective products. These businesses may purchase *product liability insurance* specifically to insure against this risk.

OTHER TYPES OF INSURANCE

In addition to the types of insurance already discussed in this chapter, many other types of insurance may be purchased. Some of these are discussed in the following paragraphs.

Professional Malpractice Insurance

Professionals—such as attorneys, accountants, physicians, dentists, architects, and engineers—are liable for injuries resulting from their negligence in practicing their professions. These professionals can purchase *professional malpractice insurance* to insure against liability. Premiums for malpractice insurance are often quite high.

Title Insurance

Owners of real property may purchase **title insurance** to insure that they have clear title to the property. Mortgagees and other lienholders can purchase title insurance on property on which they have a lien.

Title insurance protects against defects in title and liens or encumbrances that are not disclosed on the title insurance policy. An owner or mortgagee pays only one premium for title insurance, usually at closing. Each new owner or mortgagee who wants this coverage must purchase a new title insurance policy. Mortgagees sometimes require a debtor to purchase such a policy as a prerequisite for making a loan.

title insurance
Insurance that owners of real property purchase to insure that they have clear title to the property.

Credit Insurance

Mortgages and other lienholders sometimes purchase *credit insurance* on debtors who owe them money. Likewise, debtors often purchase credit insurance to pay the debts they are unable to pay because of some peril. Credit insurance usually consists of *credit life insurance* and *credit disability insurance*.

Marine Insurance

Owners of vessels may purchase **marine insurance** to insure against loss or damage to the vessel and its cargo caused by perils at sea. Marine insurance is often comprehensive, covering property damage to the vessel or its cargo and liability insurance. Shippers may purchase marine insurance to cover the risk of loss to their goods during shipment. Marine insurance policies sometimes distinguish between *inland marine insurance* (for inland waters) and *ocean marine insurance* (for perils on the ocean).

marine insurance
Insurance that owners of vessels purchase to insure against loss or damage to the vessel and its cargo caused by perils at sea.

Group Insurance

Instead of covering a single insured, insurance is often sold under **group insurance plans**. For example, all the employees of a single employer (e.g., a corporation) may be covered under a group plan. If the premium is paid entirely by the employer, it is a *noncontributory plan*; if the premium is paid in whole or in part by the employee, it is a *contributory plan*. Life, health, dental, and disability insurance is frequently offered in group plans. Premiums for group insurance tend to be lower than for individual insurance.

group insurance plan
An insurance plan that is sold to all the members of a single group, often all the employees of one employer.

Entrepreneur and the Law

UMBRELLA INSURANCE POLICY

Liability coverage under most insurance policies is usually limited to a certain dollar amount. Insureds who want to increase their liability coverage can purchase an **umbrella policy**. Coverage under an umbrella policy usually is at least $1 million and often reaches $5 million. An umbrella policy pays only if the basic policy limits have been exceeded. An insurer will issue an umbrella policy only if a stipulated minimum amount of basic coverage has been purchased by the insured.

Consider This Example

Suppose an insured purchases automobile liability insurance that pays up to $500,000 per accident and an umbrella policy with an additional $3 million of coverage. If the insured's negligence causes an automobile accident in which injuries to other persons total $2 million, the basic automobile policy will pay the first $500,000 and the umbrella policy will pay the remaining $1.5 million.

PERFORMANCE OF INSURANCE CONTRACTS

The parties to an insurance contract are obligated to perform the duties imposed by the contract. The duties of the insured and the insurer are discussed in the paragraphs that follow.

Insured's Duties

Duty to Pay Premiums   The insured must pay the agreed-upon premiums to the insurer for the insurance coverage he or she purchased. Premiums are regulated by state law. If an insured fails to pay the required premiums, the insurer may cancel the policy.

Many insurance policies provide a **grace period** during which an insured may pay an overdue premium. Some states require such an antilapse clause to be included in the policy. The insurer may not cancel the policy during the grace period. Typical grace periods are 30 to 31 days.

grace period

A period of time after the actual expiration date of a payment but during which the insured can still pay an overdue premium without penalty.

Duty to Notify Insurer   An insured is under a duty to give prompt notice to the insurer after the occurrence of an insured event. The insured must file a written claim called a *proof of loss* with the insurer. Many insurance contracts require that such notice be given within a stated period of time (e.g., 60 days). The courts have held that the insured may give notice within a reasonable time even if the policy requires "immediate" notice. Failure to comply with a notification requirement may relieve an insurer from liability. Unreasonable notification requirements are construed against the insurer and may be held to be void.

Duty to Cooperate   An insured is under a *duty to cooperate* with the insurer in investigating claims made against the insurer. This includes providing details to the insurer regarding the occurrence of an insured event, making available documents and other evidence relative to the claim, and assisting the insurer in the defense of any lawsuit (e.g., appearing as a witness at depositions and at trial). Failure of an insured to cooperate may relieve the insurer from liability.

Insurer's Duties

Duty to Defend The insurer has a *duty to defend* against any suit brought against the insured that involves a claim within the coverage of the policy. This means that the insurer must provide and pay for the lawyers and court costs necessary to defend the lawsuit. This duty arises even if the insurer believes the case is without merit. An insurer that wrongfully refuses to defend a lawsuit against one of its insureds is liable for damages, including the cost of any judgment or settlement, attorneys' fees, and litigation costs.

Duty to Pay Insurance Proceeds The insurer's primary duty under a contract of insurance is to pay legitimate claims up to the policy limits. This includes a duty to investigate claims and make reasonable efforts to settle disputed claims. Insurers that do not pay legitimate claims are liable for breach of contract. They may also be liable for tort damages.

> **Business Brief**
> An insurance company owes a duty to defend an insured against a lawsuit. This includes expenses for a lawyer, court costs, deposition fees, and so forth. The cost of defending against a lawsuit is often quite high.

𝒟EFENSES OF THE INSURER

An insurer may be able to raise certain defenses to the imposition of liability. The most common defenses are discussed in the following paragraphs.

Misrepresentation and Concealment

Insurance companies may require applicants to disclose certain information to help them determine whether they will insure the risk and to calculate the premium. The insurer may avoid liability on the policy (1) if its decision is based on a material misrepresentation on the part of the applicant or (2) if the applicant concealed material information from the insurer. This rule applies whether the misrepresentation was intentional or unintentional.

Many states have enacted **incontestability clauses** that prevent insurers from contesting statements made by insureds in applications for insurance after the passage of a stipulated number of years (the typical length of time is two to five years). An incontestability clause was at issue in the following case.

> **incontestability clause**
> A clause that prevents insurers from contesting statements made by insureds in applications for insurance after the passage of a stipulated number of years.

Amex Life Assurance Company v. Slome Capital Corp.
60 Cal.Rptr.2d 898 (1977)
Supreme Court of California

CASE 52.2

FACTS
In January 1991, Jose Morales applied for a life insurance policy from Amex Life Assurance Company (Amex). Morales knew he was HIV (human immunodeficiency virus) positive, but he lied on the application form and denied having AIDS (acquired immune deficiency syndrome). As part of the application process, Amex required Morales to have a medical examination. In March 1991, a paramedic working for Amex met a man claiming to be Morales and took blood and urine samples from him. On his application, Morales had listed his height as 5 feet 6 inches and his weight as 147 pounds. The examiner registered the man taking the exami-

nation as 5 feet 10 inches tall, weighing 172 pounds, and appearing to be "older than the stated age." The blood samples tested HIV negative. Amex issued Morales a life insurance policy on May 1, 1991; the policy included a two-year incontestability clause as required by state law. All premiums were paid. Morales sold the policy to Slome Capital Corporation (Slome), a viatical company that purchased life insurance policies at a discount from AIDS carriers before their death.

On June 11, 1993, Morales died of AIDS-related causes. When Slome presented Morales's policy to Amex for payment, Amex refused to pay, alleging that Morales had

(case continues)

1088

XIII PROPERTY

engaged in fraud and had had an imposter take his physical examination for him. The trial court denied Amex's summary judgment motion. The court of appeals held that the incontestability clause prevented Amex from denying coverage. Amex appealed.

ISSUE

Does the two-year incontestability clause prevent Amex from raising the insured's fraud as a reason not to pay the life insurance proceeds?

IN THE LANGUAGE OF THE COURT

Chin, Justice   Incontestability clauses have been used by the insurance industry for over one hundred years to encourage persons to purchase life insurance. Today, these clauses are required by statute in most states because without them, insurers were apt to deny benefits on the grounds of a pre-existing condition years after a policy had been issued. This left beneficiaries, particularly those in life insurance settings, in the untenable position of having to do battle with powerful insurance carriers. Incontestability clauses are designed to require the insurer to investigate and act with reasonable promptness if it wishes to deny liability on the ground of false representation or warranty by the insured.

Amex argues it insured, if anyone, the person who appeared for the medical examination, not Morales, and that to the extent the policy purported to insure Morales, it was void from the beginning. But imposter fraud is similar to other frauds the

incontestability clause covers. Rejecting the imposter defense under these facts furthers the policy behind incontestability clauses. When the named insured applies for the policy, and the premiums are faithfully paid for over two years, the beneficiaries should be assured they will receive the expected benefits, and not a lawsuit, upon the insured's death. The incontestability clause requires the insurer to investigate fraud before it issues the policy or within two years afterwards. The insurer may not accept the premiums for two years and investigate a possible defense only after the beneficiaries file a claim. Here, with minimal effort, Amex could have discovered the fraud at the outset, as it did finally from information available before it issued the policy.

DECISION AND REMEDY

The California Supreme Court held that the incontestability clause prevented Amex from denying coverage. The court ordered Amex to pay the proceeds of Morales's life insurance policy to Slome.

Case Questions

Critical Legal Thinking   Should the law contain incontestability clauses? What public policy is served by these clauses?

Ethics   Did Morales act ethically in this case? Should unethical conduct be rewarded?

Business Application   Who pays the cost of insurance fraud?

Breach of Warranty

warranty

A representation of the insured that is expressly incorporated in the insurance contract.

A **warranty** is a representation of the insured that is expressly incorporated in the insurance contract:

- An **affirmative warranty** is a statement asserting that certain facts are true (e.g., there are no environmental problems currently existing as to the property the insured is insuring).
- A **promissory warranty** stipulates that facts will continue to be true throughout the duration of the policy (e.g., the insured will not store flammable products in the insured building). An insurer may avoid liability caused by a breach of warranty.

In the following case, the court had to decide whether the insured made a misrepresentation on his application for insurance.

Peckman v. Mutual Life Insurance Company of New York
509 N.Y.S.2d 336 (1986)
New York Supreme Court, Appellate Division

CASE 52.3

FACTS

Alan L. Peckman filed an application with the Mutual Life Insurance Company of New York (MONY) for life insurance in the face amount of $100,000 with double indemnity coverage for accidental death. On the application, Peckman indicated that for the previous six years he had

been self-employed in the occupation of "marketing." MONY issued the policy, which named Peckman's mother as beneficiary.

On August 5, 1981, within the contestability period of the policy, Peckman's body was found in a steamer trunk with a gunshot wound to the head. Peckman's mother filed a claim with MONY for the insurance proceeds from his life insurance policy.

MONY denied the claim, asserting that Peckman falsely misrepresented his occupation and fraudulently concealed that he was a drug dealer. The company introduced police evidence showing that Peckman had been involved in the distribution of drugs for several years. Articles in newspapers stated that Peckman ran a million-dollar marijuana distribution ring.

Peckman's mother sued MONY to recover the insurance proceeds. The trial court granted summary judgment in favor of Peckman's mother and awarded her the double indemnity insurance benefits. MONY appealed.

ISSUE

Did the decedent misrepresent his employment on the life insurance application?

IN THE LANGUAGE OF THE COURT

Memorandum Decision   In the instant case the applicant did not misrepresent his occupation. Webster's dictionary defines marketing as "the act or business of buying or selling in the market."

This definition clearly encompasses the applicant's alleged pursuit of drug dealing.

DECISION AND REMEDY

The appellate court held that the insured had not misrepresented his employment on the life insurance application. The appellate court affirmed the trial court's judgment and award of double indemnity life insurance proceeds to the plaintiff-beneficiary.

Case Questions

Critical Legal Thinking   Should insurance companies be permitted to group persons into "risk categories" and charge higher premiums to members of the higher risk categories (e.g., smokers, teen-age drivers)?

Ethics   Do you think the insured acted ethically in disclosing his occupation as marketing?

Business Application   Do you think an insurance company would issue a life insurance policy if it knew the applicant was a drug dealer?

SUBROGATION

If an insurance company pays a claim to an insured for liability or property damage caused by a third party, the insurer succeeds to the right of the insured to recover from the third party. This is called **subrogation**.

Consider This Example   Suppose (1) an insured has automobile insurance from the Hartford Insurance Company and (2) a third party caused an accident in which the insured's car was damaged and the insured was injured. Hartford pays for the insured's medical expenses and for the car repairs. Hartford is then subrogated to the insured's claim against the third party and may sue the third party (and his or her insurer) to recover. Subrogation does not apply to life insurance policies. An insurer has no right to subrogation against its own insured.

subrogation

If an insurance company pays a claim to an insured for liability or property damage caused by a third party, the insurer succeeds to the right of the insured to recover from the third party.

International Perspective

LLOYD'S OF LONDON

International businesses are often faced with risks that are not a primary concern for domestic businesses. These risks include such things as damage to businesses from military conflict, loss of assets from expropriation by foreign governments, and losses when currency becomes inconvertible. Many domestic insurance companies will not write insurance against such

risks. **Lloyd's of London** is one insurer that is famous for insuring unique international risks. The company, which is based in London, England, has been insuring international business risks for over 300 years.

Lloyd's is organized differently from most insurance companies in that it is really an insurance syndicator. That is, it originates insurance business and then seeks a pool of

(box continues)

investors to guarantee payment if the risk occurs. A separate partnership of investors is arranged to insure individual risks. For example, if a business wants to insure against the risk of loss to an oil tanker traveling in international waters, Lloyd's would seek investors for that insurance pool. If enough investors agreed to guarantee payment if the risk occurred, Lloyd's would write the policy.

The investors are called "Names." To become a Name, an investor must pledge all of his or her assets to pay any losses incurred for the risk he or she has agreed to guarantee. As one Brit put it, "down to their last pair of cufflinks." For years, a Name was almost guaranteed an annual return of about 10 percent on the investment without ever having to put up any cash. The affluent grew even more wealthy just by being a Name.

In the late 1980s and early 1990s, things started to go sour. Lloyd's underwriters had failed to charge sufficient premiums to cover many insured risks. With more strife in the world and major natural disasters, insurance payouts soared. The losses wiped out the personal assets of hundreds of wealthy families whose liability as Names was unlimited. Because of the losses, the number of Names dropped from about 32,000 in 1988 to about 20,000 in 1993.

In 1993, Lloyd's of London restructured. It laid off about 20 percent of its staff, courted new Names, including corporations with limited liability, and instituted more cautious underwriting standards. International risk is still difficult to insure, but as long as Lloyd's of London is around, there will be a place to purchase such insurance—at a premium.

Working the Web

e·biz

Business Insurance This magazine has a Web site with all kinds of information about business insurance.

Visit at **www.businessinsurance.com**

Federal Deposit Insurance Corporation Everything you ever wanted to know about the Federal Deposit Insurance Corporation is available through its Web site.

Visit at **www.fdic.gov**

Insure.com—The Consumer Insurance Guide All kinds of insurance including annuities, auto, business, health, home, and life insurance are discussed. In addition there is an insurance company guide, a complaint finder, and a lawsuit library.

Visit at **www.insure.com**

CYBER EXERCISES

1. Check out Cyberbeat, articles on insurance related technical applications and industry issues, on the Business Insurance Web site.

2. Find the directory of the Federal Deposit Insurance Corporation.

3. Using Insure.com, find out about insurance in your state.

CASES AND EXERCISES

CRITICAL LEGAL THINKING CASES

52.1. Richard Usher's home was protected by a homeowners policy issued by National American Insurance Company of California (National American) that included personal liability insurance. A provision in the policy read: "Personal liability and coverage do not apply to bodily injury or property damage arising out of the ownership, maintenance, use, loading, or unloading of a motor vehicle owned or operated by, or rented or loaned to any insured."

On August 24, 1984, Usher parked a Chevrolet van he owned in his driveway. He left the van's side door open while he loaded the van in preparation for a camping trip. While Usher was inside his house, several children, including two-year-old Graham Coburn, began playing near the van. One of the children climbed into the driver's seat and moved the shift lever from "park" to "reverse." The van rolled backward, crushing Coburn and killing him. Coburn's parents sued Usher for negligence. Is this accident covered by Usher's homeowners policy? [*National American Insurance Company of California v. Coburn*, 209 Cal.App.3d 914, 257 Cal.Rptr. 591 (Cal.App. 1989)]

52.2. On May 23, 1981, William Fryman was killed in a motorcycle accident. At the time of the accident, Fryman had a blood alcohol level of .2 and was operating his motorcycle at an excessive rate of speed. Fryman was survived by two young daughters. At the time of the accident, Fryman was covered by a group life insurance policy issued by the Pilot Life Insurance Company (Pilot Life) through Fryman's employer. The policy provided $10,000 in basic life insurance coverage and twice that amount if death was caused by "external, violent, and accidental means." Fryman's heirs filed a claim for double indemnity. Pilot Life rejected the claim, asserting that the estate is only entitled to payment of $10,000 because Fryman contributed to his own death. Who wins? [*Fryman v. Pilot Life Insurance Company*, 704 S.W.2d 205 (KY 1986)]

52.3. Jowenna Surber owned a 1979 Mercedes-Benz automobile that she insured through an insurance broker, Mid-Century Insurance Company (Mid-Century). Mid-Century secured a policy for Surber with the Farmers Insurance Company (Farmers) on May 23, 1986. Surber gave permission to her friend, Bruce Martin, to use the car. Martin held a valid California driver's license. Surber did not receive any compensation for allowing Martin to use the car. While driving the car, Martin was involved in a collision with another vehicle driven by Loretta Haynes, who suffered severe injuries. Martin admitted that his negligence was the cause of the accident. Surber's policy stipulates that the policy covers "you or any family member or any person using your insured car." Is Farmers liable to Haynes? [*Mid-Century Insurance Company v. Haynes*, 218 Cal.App.3d 737, 267 Cal.Rptr. 248 (Cal.App. 1990)]

52.4. Antonio Munoz and Jacinto Segura won some money from two unidentified men in a craps game in a Los Angeles park. When Munoz and Segura left the park in Segura's car, the two men followed them in another car. They chased Segura's car for several miles and then pulled beside it on a freeway. The men in the other car fired several gunshots at Segura's car, killing Munoz. At the time he was killed, Munoz had an automobile insurance policy issued by Nationwide Mutual Insurance Company (Nationwide). A provision in the policy covered damages from "an accident arising out of the use of an uninsured vehicle." Munoz's widow and child filed a claim with Nationwide to recover for Munoz's death. Nationwide rejected the claim. Who wins? [*Nationwide Mutual Insurance Company v. Munoz*, 245 Cal.Rptr. 324 (Cal.App. 1988)]

52.5. In 1977, Donald Barker, a wealthy Oregon resident, went to the law firm of Winokur, Schoenberg, Maier, Hamerman & Knudson to have his estate planned. An attorney at the firm repeatedly told Barker that he could convey half of his $20-million estate to his wife tax-free under Oregon's marital deduction. Barker had his will drawn based upon the law firm's advice. It was not until after Barker died, on January 5, 1980, that Barker's family learned that Oregon does not recognize the marital deduction. As a result, the will's beneficiaries were subject to significant estate taxes. The beneficiaries sued the law firm for negligence and the case was settled for $2 million. At the time Barker was being advised by the law firm, it had a professional malpractice insurance policy with the Travelers Insurance Company (Travelers) that covered "all sums which the insured shall become legally obligated to pay as damages because of any act or omission of the insured arising out of the performance of professional services for others in the insured's capacity as a lawyer." The policy expired on January 1, 1979. Is Travelers liable for the $2-million settlement? [*Travelers Insurance Company v. National Union Fire Insurance Company of Pittsburgh*, 207 Cal.App.3d 1390, 255 Cal.Rptr. 727 (Cal.App. 1989)]

52.6. The Mutual Life Insurance Company of New York (Mutual Life) issued a $100,000 life insurance policy on the life of 65-year-old Alex Brecher that became effective on December 22, 1977. In consideration for the policy, Brecher agreed to pay an annual insurance premium of $7,830 in 12 monthly installments. On July 14, 1983, Brecher made a written request and authorization to have the insurance company withdraw the premiums directly from his checking account at Citibank. However, the insurance company's first attempt to collect the premium from Brecher's account on July 15, 1983, was returned unpaid. Mutual Life and Brecher were informed that one of Brecher's creditors had placed a restraining order on the bank account. On July 29, 1983, Mutual Life sent Brecher a returned check notice that advised him that the July withdrawal had been dishonored by his bank and that to keep the policy in force, both the July and August premiums totaling $1,358 would have to be paid before August 28. Brecher sent a check for this amount, which was received by Mutual Life on August 26. The check was drawn on the Citibank account, however. When Mutual Life tried to cash the check, Citibank returned it unpaid, marked "refer to maker." Brecher died on September 18, 1983. His widow, the beneficiary of the life insurance policy, filed a claim to recover $100,000 from Mutual Life. When Mutual Life refused to pay, the widow sued. Who wins? [*Brecher v. Mutual Life Insurance Company of New York*, 501 N.Y.S.2d 879 (N.Y.App. 1986)]

52.7. When Michael A. Jaffe, a child psychiatrist practicing in California, was accused of Medi-Cal fraud and theft, he requested that his malpractice insurer, Cranford Insurance Company (Cranford), provide his criminal defense. Cranford refused to defend Jaffe, citing the terms of Jaffe's malpractice insurance policy. The policy describes the insured risk as "psychiatrist's professional liability in respect of insured's practice of psychiatry." Another clause of the policy states that Cranford "agrees to pay such damages as may be awarded in respect of professional services rendered by Jaffe, or which should have been rendered by him, resulting from any claims or suits based solely upon malpractice, error, or mistake."

After Cranford refused to defend him, Jaffe hired his own criminal defense lawyer. The case went to trial and Jaffe was found innocent of all charges. After his acquittal, Jaffe demanded that Cranford reimburse him for the expenses incurred during trial. When Cranford refused this request, Jaffe sued. Who wins? [*Jaffe v. Cranford Insurance Company*, 168 Cal.App.3d 930, 214 Cal.Rptr. 567 (Cal.App. 1985)]

52.8. In February 1983, Judith Isenhart purchased a 1983 Dodge station wagon. At the time of the purchase, she contacted Ed Carpenter, an agent of the National Automobile and Casualty Insurance Company (National) and told him she was interested in obtaining "full coverage" for the car. The policy that Carpenter provided to Judith provided coverage for bodily injury and property damage, medical costs, and collision damage. The policy specifically exempted coverage for accidents involving "non-owned automobiles." In July 1984, Judith's 16-year-old son Matt purchased a 1969 Volkswagen. Insurance for this car was obtained from Allstate Insurance Company (Allstate). Two months after buying the car, Matt had an accident in which a passenger in the Volkswagen, Thea Stewart, was severely injured. Stewart sued Matt and Judith. Allstate agreed to defend the suit up to the limits of its policy. When National was contacted regarding the accident, the company refused to defend Judith in the suit and denied coverage based on the policy's exclusion. Must National defend Judith? [*National Automobile and Casualty Insurance Company v. Stewart*, 223 Cal.App.3d 452, 272 Cal.Rptr. 625 (Cal.App. 1990)]

52.9. M&M Restaurant, Inc. (M&M), operated a restaurant in the state of New York. M&M purchased fire insurance for the restaurant from St. Paul Surplus Lines Insurance Company (St. Paul). On July 10, 1984, a fire caused major damage to the restaurant. An investigation of the fire by the local police department led to the filing of criminal charges against the owners of M&M. Among the findings of the investigation was that M&M had willfully concealed factual information and misled St. Paul in obtaining the insurance. On May 25, 1989, the owners of M&M were convicted of two counts of insurance fraud in the first degree, two counts of grand larceny, and falsifying business records in the first degree. At the time of the fire, M&M submitted a claim against St. Paul for losses sustained by the restaurant in the fire. St. Paul refused to pay the claim. Who wins? [*M&M Restaurant, Inc. v. St. Paul Surplus Lines Insurance Company, N.Y. Law Journal*, June 18, 1990, p. 29 (N.Y.Sup. 1990)]

52.10. In 1977, Home Indemnity Company (Home Indemnity) agreed to insure the Liberty Savings Association (Liberty), a savings and loan association, for losses that Liberty might incur through the dishonest or fraudulent acts of its employees. In August 1983, Liberty filed a proof of loss with Home Indemnity alleging losses of $579,922. The claim was based on the conversion of $98,372 by Richard Doty, the former president and managing officer of Liberty, and related loan losses. The loan losses were the result of four loans approved by Doty and made to his friends and relatives. The loans were unsecured, and none of the borrowers filed financial statements to qualify for the loans. None of the loans was repaid. Home Indemnity paid Liberty for the losses and received a general assignment of Liberty's right to recover against Doty and the borrowers. Home Indemnity then sued Liberty's board of directors, claiming they were negligent in their supervision of Doty. Who wins? [*Home Indemnity Company v. Shaffer*, 860 F.2d 186 (6th Cir. 1988)]

ETHICS CASES

52.11. In 1983, Lewis Coe bought a $500,000 life insurance policy from Farmers New World Life Insurance Company (Farmers) from its authorized agent, Hannify. The policy, which was payable in monthly installments, contained a clause allowing for the insurance to remain in effect for a 31-day grace period if the insured failed to pay a premium by the due date. In February 1984, Coe informed Hannify that he wanted to cancel the policy. Farmers sent Coe a cancellation form that he signed and returned on or about March 1, 1984. At the time Farmers received the written cancellation notice,

Coe had paid the monthly premium for February, covering the period ending March 10, 1984. Coe died on April 8. His widow sued Farmers for the policy proceeds claiming that Coe died during the 31-day grace period provided by the policy. Farmers claimed the policy had been canceled and the grace period did not apply. Who wins? Did either party act unethically in this case? [*Coe v. Farmers New World Life Insurance Company*, 209 Cal.App.3d 600, 257 Cal.Rptr. 411 (Cal.App. 1989)]

52.12. A federal regulation adopted pursuant to the Resource Conservation and Discovery Act on January 12, 1981, required certain manufacturers to insure against pollution hazards. Early in September 1981, Advanced Micro Devices, Inc. (AMD), a company covered by the regulation, purchased the required insurance from Great American Surplus Lines Insurance Company (Great American). Before issuing the policy, Great American asked AMD to disclose any preexisting conditions that could give rise to a claim retroactive to August 27, 1981. AMD warranted that no preexisting conditions existed as of that date. AMD made this statement despite the existence of a company memorandum written by AMD's environmental supervisor, Mike Gingrass. The memo, dated July 21, 1981, warned that toxic waste was escaping from an underground steel tank in AMD's acid neutralization system "C." Gingrass warned the company that AMD was "far from being in compliance" with environmental laws. Great American issued the insurance policy. In 1982, AMD was ordered by the government to clean up the toxic contaminants surrounding the steel tank in system "C." The total cost of the cleanup was $1.5 million. AMD filed a claim for this amount with Great American, which refused to pay. AMD sued. Who wins? [*Advanced Micro Devices, Inc. v. Great American Surplus Lines Insurance Company*, 199 Cal.App.3d 791, 245 Cal.Rptr. 4 (Cal.App. 1988)]

CRITICAL LEGAL THINKING WRITING ASSIGNMENT

Read Case A.52 in the Case Appendix [*Saritejdiam, Inc. v. Excess Insurance Company, Ltd.*]. This case is excerpted from the court of appeals opinion. Review and brief the case. In your brief, be sure to answer the following questions:

1. Was the "close personal custody and control" provision in the insurance policy plain and clear?

2. Summarize the factual details of the case.

3. What public policy is served by the exclusion of coverage in this case?

4. Do you think that the insurance policy met the reasonable expectations of the insured?

NOTES

1. 15 U.S.C. §§ 1011–1015.
2. California Insurance Code § 22.

53

Wills, Trusts, and Estates

When you have told someone you have left him a legacy, the only decent thing to do is to die at once.

SAMUEL BUTLER (1835–1902)

Chapter Objectives

After studying this chapter, you should be able to

1. List and describe the requirements for making a valid will.
2. Describe how a will can be revoked.
3. Describe a holographic will.
4. Define *ademption* and *abatement*.
5. Describe how property is distributed if a husband and wife die simultaneously.
6. Describe the effect of entering into a mutual will.
7. Identify how property is distributed under intestacy statutes if a person dies without a will.
8. Describe the process of probate.
9. Describe a living will.
10. Define *trust* and identify the parties to a trust.

Chapter Contents

Wills and trusts are a means of transferring property. Wills transfer property upon a person's death. A person who dies without a will is said to have died *intestate*. In this case, the deceased's property is distributed to relatives according to state statute. The property escheats (goes) to the state if there are no relatives. Trusts are used to transfer property that is to be held and managed for the benefit of another person. Trusts are created during one's lifetime, but they may be worded to become effective upon the trustor's death. This chapter discusses wills and trusts.

The power of making a will is an instrument placed in the hands of individuals for the prevention of private calamity.

Jerry Bentham
Principles of the Civil Code
(1748)

WILLS

A **will** is a declaration of how a person wants his or her property to be distributed upon his or her death. It is a *testamentary* deposition of property. The person who makes the will is called the **testator** or **testatrix**.[1] The persons designated in the will to receive the testator's property are called **beneficiaries**.

will
A declaration of how a person wants his or her property distributed upon death.

Requirements for Making a Will

Every state has a **Statute of Wills** that establishes the requirements for making a valid will in that state. These requirements are

- **Testamentary Capacity** The testator must have been of legal age and "sound mind" when the will was made. The courts determine testamentary capacity on a case-by-case basis. The legal age for executing a will is set by state statute.
- **Writing** Wills must be in writing to be valid (except for dying declarations that are discussed later in this chapter). The writing may be formal or informal. Although most wills are typewritten, they can be handwritten (see the discussion of holographic wills). The writing may be on legal paper, other paper, scratch paper, envelopes, napkins, or the like. A will may incorporate other documents by reference.
- **Testator's Signature** Wills must be signed.

Most jurisdictions require the testator's signature to appear at the end of the will. This is to prevent fraud that could occur if someone added provisions to the will below the testator's signature. Generally, courts have held that initials ("R.K.H."), a nickname ("Buffy"), title ("mother"), or even an "X" is a valid signature on a will if it can be proven that the testator intended it to be his or her signature.

testator
The person who makes a will.

beneficiary
A person or organization designated in the will that receives all or a portion of the testator's property at the time of the testator's death.

Statute of Wills
A state statute that establishes the requirements for making a valid will.

Attestation by Witnesses

Wills must be **attested** to by mentally competent witnesses. Although state law varies, most states require two or three witnesses. The witnesses do not have to reside in the jurisdiction in which the testator is domiciled. Most jurisdictions stipulate that interested parties (e.g., a beneficiary under the will or the testator's attorney) cannot be witnesses. If an interested party has attested to a will, state law either voids any clauses that benefit such person or voids the entire will.

Witnesses usually sign the will following the signature of the testator. This is called the *attestation clause*. Most jurisdictions require that each witness attest to the will in the presence of the other witnesses.

A will that meets the requirements of the Statute of Wills is called a *formal will*. A sample will is shown in Exhibit 53.1.

attestation
The action of a will being witnessed by two or three objective and competent people.

Changing a Will

A will cannot be amended by merely striking out existing provisions and adding new ones. **Codicils** are the legal way to change an existing will. A codicil is a separate document that must be executed with the same formalities as a will. In addition, it must incorporate by reference the will it is amending. The codicil and the will are then read as one instrument.

codicil
A separate document that must be executed to amend a will. It must be executed with the same formalities as a will.

EXHIBIT 53.1 *A Sample Will*

Last Will and Testament of Florence Winthorpe Blueblood

I, FLORENCE WINTHORPE BLUEBLOOD, presently residing at Boston, County of Suffolk, Massachusetts, being of sound and disposing mind and memory, hereby make, publish, and declare this to be my Last Will and Testament.

FIRST. I hereby revoke any and all Wills and Codicils previously made by me.

SECOND. I direct that my just debts and funeral expenses be paid out of my Estate as soon as practicable after my death.

THIRD. I am presently married to Theodore Hannah Blueblood III.

FOURTH. I hereby nominate and appoint my husband as the Personal Representative of this my Last Will and Testament. If he is unable to serve as Personal Representative, then I nominate and appoint Mildred Yardly Winthorpe as Personal Representative of this my Last Will and Testament. I direct that no bond or other security be required to be posted by my Personal Representative.

FIFTH. I hereby nominate and appoint my husband as Guardian of the person and property of my minor children. In the event that he is unable to serve as Guardian, then I nominate and appoint Mildred Yardly Winthorpe Guardian of the person and property of my minor children. I direct that no bond or other security be required to be posted by any Guardian herein.

SIXTH. I give my Personal Representative authority to exercise all the powers, rights, duties, and immunities conferred upon fiduciaries under law with full power to sell, mortgage, lease, invest, or reinvest all or any part of my Estate on such terms as he or she deems best.

SEVENTH. I hereby give, devise, and bequeath my entire estate to my husband, except for the following specific bequests:

I give my wedding ring to my daughter, Hillary Smythe Blueblood.

I give my baseball card collection to my son, Theodore Hannah Blueblood IV.

In the event that either my above-named daughter or son predeceases me, then and in that event, I give, devise, and bequeath my deceased daughter's or son's bequest to my husband.

EIGHTH. In the event that my husband shall predecease me, then and in that event, I give, devise and bequeath my entire estate, with the exception of the bequests in paragraph SEVENTH, to my beloved children or grandchildren surviving me, per stirpes.

NINTH. In the event I am not survived by my husband or any children or grandchildren, then and in that event, I give, devise, and bequeath my entire estate to Harvard University.

IN WITNESS WHEREOF, I, Florence Winthorpe Blueblood, the Testatrix, sign my name to this Last Will and Testament this 3rd day of January, 2000.

Florence Winthorpe Blueblood
(Signature)

Signed, sealed, published and declared by the above-named Testatrix, as and for her Last Will and Testament, in the presence of us, who at her request, in her presence, and in the presence of one another, have hereunto subscribed our names as attesting witnesses, the day and year last written above.

Witness	Address
Norm Peterson	100 Beacon Hill Rd Boston, Massachusetts
Clifford Claven	200 Minute Man Drive Boston, Massachusetts
Rebecca Howe	300 Charles River Place Boston, Massachusetts

Revoking a Will

A will may be **revoked** by acts of the testator. A will is revoked if the testator intentionally burns, tears, obliterates, or otherwise destroys it. A properly executed *subsequent will* revokes a prior will if it specifically states that it is the testator's intention to do so. If the second will does not expressly revoke the prior will, the wills are read together. If any will provisions are inconsistent, the provision in the second will controls.

Wills can be revoked by operation of law. For example, divorce or annulment revokes disposition of property to the former spouse under the will. The remainder of the will is valid. The birth of a child after a will has been executed does not revoke the will but does entitle the child to receive his or her share of the parents' estate as determined by state statute.

revocation
Termination of a will.

Business Brief
A will cannot be amended or changed by striking out existing provisions and adding new ones onto the will itself.

SPECIAL TYPES OF WILLS

The law recognizes several types of wills that do not meet all of the requirements discussed above. The special types of wills admitted by the courts include

- **Holographic Wills** Holographic wills are entirely handwritten and signed by the testator. The writing may be in ink, pencil, crayon, or some other writing instrument. Many states recognize the validity of such wills even though they are not witnessed.
- **Noncupative Wills** Noncupative wills are oral wills made before witnesses. Such wills are usually valid only if they are made during the testator's last illness. They are sometimes called *deathbed wills* or *dying declarations*.

In the following case, the court found that a holographic will was not made.

holographic will
Will that is entirely handwritten and signed by the testator.

noncupative will
Oral will that is made before a witness during the testator's last illness.

In the Matter of the Estate of Reed
672 P.2d 829 (1983)
Supreme Court of Wyoming

CASE 53.1

FACTS
Robert G. Reed died on March 2, 1982. On April 23, 1982, the court appointed coadministrators of Reed's estate, finding that he died intestate. On October 29, 1982, Margaret F. Buckley filed a petition for probate of a will, alleging that a tape recording found by the police in Reed's home was a valid will of the deceased. The tape recording was found in a sealed envelope on which Reed had written "To be played in the event of my death." The trial court refused to admit the tape recording into probate. Buckley appealed.

ISSUE
Is a tape-recorded statement a holographic will that can be admitted into probate?

IN THE LANGUAGE OF THE COURT
Brown, Justice   Before a will may be admitted to probate it must comport to the state's statutory scheme. Appellant must

demonstrate that the recorded statement offered as a will complies with Wyoming statutes governing wills. The Wyoming Probate Code provides

> *Section 2-6-112. Except as provided in the next section, all wills to be valid shall be in writing, or typewritten, witnessed by two competent witnesses and signed by the testator.*
>
> *Section 2-6-113. A will which does not comply is valid as a holographic will, whether or not witnessed, if it is entirely in the handwriting of the testator and signed by the hand of the testator himself.*

Appellant contends that the tape recording should be admitted to probate as a form of holographic will. Appellant reasons that in this age of advanced electronics and circuitry the tape recorder should be a method of "writing" that conforms with the holographic will statute. The Wyoming statutes are clear and unambiguous in their description of a holographic will. A holographic will must be entirely in the handwriting of the decedent. Handwriting is not an ambiguous word, nor is the word entirely. We are not aware of any definition of

(case continues)

handwriting that includes voice print, nor do we know of any authority that has held that handwriting includes voice prints. It seems to be stating the obvious that a voice print is not writing; therefore, the requirement that a holographic will be "entirely in the handwriting of the testator" has not been met in this case.

DECISION AND REMEDY

The state supreme court held that a tape recording does not meet the requirements for a holographic will under the Wyoming statute. Affirmed.

Case Questions

Critical Legal Thinking   Should tape recordings be admitted into probate? Why or why not?

Ethics   Did Buckley act ethically in trying to probate the tape recording as a will?

Business Application   What were the economic consequences of this decision?

Types of Testamentary Gifts

devise
A gift of real estate by will.

bequest
A gift of personal property by will. Also known as a legacy.

specific gift
Gift of a specifically named piece of property.

general gift
Gift that does not identify the specific property from which the gift is to be made.

residuary gift
Gift of the estate left after the debts, taxes, and specific and general gifts have been paid.

ademption
A principle that says if a testator leaves a specific devise of property to a beneficiary, but the property is no longer in the estate when the testator dies, the beneficiary receives nothing.

abatement
If the property the testator leaves is not sufficient to satisfy all the beneficiaries named in a will and there are both general and residuary bequests, the residuary bequest is abated first (i.e., paid last).

In a will, a gift of real estate by will is called a **devise**. A gift of personal property by will is called a **bequest** or **legacy**. Gifts in wills can be *specific, general,* or *residuary*:

- **Specific Gifts** Specific gifts are of specifically named pieces of property, such as a ring, a boat, or a piece of real estate.
- **General Gifts** General gifts do not identify the specific property from which the gift is to be made, such as a cash amount that can come from any source in the decedent's estate.
- **Residuary Gifts** Residuary gifts are established by a *residuary clause* in the will. Such a clause might state that "I give my daughter the rest, remainder, and residual of my estate." This means that any portion of the estate left after the debts, taxes, and specific and general gifts have been paid belongs to the decedent's daughter.

A person who inherits property under a will or intestacy statute takes the property subject to all of the outstanding claims against it (e.g., liens, mortgages). A person can *renounce* an inheritance and often does where the liens or mortgages against the property exceed the value of the property.

Ademption and Abatement

If a testator leaves a specific gift of property to a beneficiary, but the property is no longer in the estate of the testator when he or she dies, the beneficiary receives nothing. This is called the doctrine of **ademption**.

If the testator's estate is not large enough to pay all of the devises and bequests, the doctrine of **abatement** applies. The doctrine works as follows:

- If a will provides for both general and residuary gifts, the residuary gifts are abated first (i.e., paid last). For example, suppose a testator executes a will when he owns $500,000 of property that leaves (1) $100,000 to the Red Cross, (2) $100,000 to a university, and (3) the residue to his niece. Suppose that when the testator dies, his estate is worth only $225,000. Here, the Red Cross and the university both receive $100,000 and the niece receives $25,000.
- If a will provides only for general gifts, the reductions are proportionate. For example, suppose a testator's will leaves $75,000 to two beneficiaries, but the estate is only $100,000. Each beneficiary would receive $50,000.

In the following case, the court held that a specific bequest failed because of ademption.

Opperman v. Anderson
782 S.W.2d 8 (1989)
Court of Appeals of Texas

FACTS

On September 26, 1983, Ethel M. Ramchissel executed a will that made the following bequests: (1) one-half of the stock she owned in Pabst Brewing Company (Pabst) to Mary Lee Anderson, (2) all of the stock she owned in Houston Natural Gas Corporation (Houston Natural Gas) to Ethel Baker and others (Baker), and (3) the residue and remainder of her estate to Boysville, Inc. In response to an offer by G. Heilman Brewing Company to purchase Pabst, Ramchissel sold all of her stock. She placed the proceeds in a separate bank account to which no other funds have been added. Pursuant to a merger agreement between Internorth, Inc., and Houston Natural Gas, Ramchissel converted her shares to cash. The proceeds were placed in another bank account, to which no other funds have been added. When Ramchissel died on April 4, 1987, her will was admitted into probate. The probate court awarded the money in the two bank accounts to Anderson and Baker, respectively. This appeal ensued.

ISSUE

Were the bequests to Anderson and Baker specific bequests that were adeemed when the stock was sold?

IN THE LANGUAGE OF THE COURT

Biery, Judge   Ademption is the doctrine by which a specific bequest becomes inoperative because of the disappearance of its subject matter from a testator's estate during his lifetime. A specific bequest is one comprised of specific articles of the testator's estate distinguished from all others of the same kind. Because ademption applies only to specific bequests, courts must make a preliminary determination of whether a bequest is specific or general. The intention of the testator must be ascertained at the time the will was executed and from the four corners of the will. We conclude that Ramchissel clearly intended the gifts of stock at issue be specific bequests subject to ademption. We find that ademption occurred when specific shares of stock described were sold prior to the testatrix's death.

DECISION AND REMEDY

The court of appeals held that the bequests of stock at issue in this case were specific bequests that were adeemed when the stock was converted to cash. Therefore, the cash proceeds of these stock sales pass pursuant to the residuary clause of Ramchissel's will.

Case Questions

Critical Legal Thinking   Should the doctrine of ademption be recognized by law? What other solution would there be?

Ethics   Do you think the result reached in this case was fair or what Ramchissel intended?

Business Application   Explain the difference between ademption and abatement.

PER STIRPES AND PER CAPITA DISTRIBUTION

A testator's will may state that property is to be left to his or her **lineal descendants** (children, grandchildren, great-grandchildren, etc.) either *per stirpes* or *per capita*. The difference between these two methods is as follows:

- **Per Stirpes**   In per stirpes, the lineal descendants inherit by representation of their parent; that is, they split what their deceased parent would have received. If their parent is not deceased, they receive nothing.
- **Per Capita**   In per capita, the lineal descendants equally share the property of the estate without regard to degree of relationship to the testator. That is, children of the testator share equally with grandchildren, great-grandchildren, and so forth.

Consider This Example   Suppose Anne dies without a surviving spouse, and she had three children—Bart, Beth, and Bruce. Bart, who survives his mother, has no children. Beth has one child, Carla, and they both survive Anne. Bruce, who predeceased his mother, had two children, Clayton and Cathy; and Cathy, who predeceased Anne, had two children, Deborah and Dominic, both of whom survive Anne.

lineal descendants
Children, grandchildren, great-grandchildren, and so on of the testator.

per stirpes
A distribution of the estate that makes grandchildren and great-grandchildren of the deceased inherit by representation of their parent.

per capita
A distribution of the estate that makes each grandchild and great-grandchild of the deceased inherit equally with the children of the deceased.

*E*XHIBIT **53.2** *Per Stirpes Distribution*

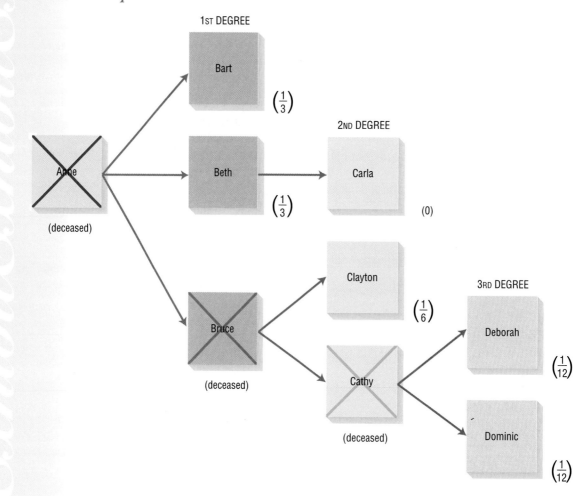

1ST DEGREE

Bart
$\left(\frac{1}{3}\right)$

2ND DEGREE

Beth
$\left(\frac{1}{3}\right)$

Carla
(0)

Anne
(deceased)

Clayton
$\left(\frac{1}{6}\right)$

3RD DEGREE

Bruce
(deceased)

Deborah
$\left(\frac{1}{12}\right)$

Cathy
(deceased)

Dominic
$\left(\frac{1}{12}\right)$

Disinherit: the prankish action of the ghosts in cutting the pockets out of trousers.

Frank McKinney Hubbard
The Roycroft Dictionary
(1923)

If Anne leaves her estate to her lineal descendants *per stirpes*, Bart and Beth each get one-third, Carla receives nothing because Beth is alive, Clayton gets one-sixth, and Deborah and Dominic both get one-twelfth. (See Exhibit 53.2.)

On the other hand, if Anne leaves her estate to her lineal descendants *per capita*, all of the surviving issue—Bart, Beth, Carla, Clayton, Deborah, and Dominic—share equally in the estate. That is, they each get one-sixth of Anne's estate. (See Exhibit 53.3.)

E- Commerce & Internet Law _____

VIDEOTAPED AND ELECTRONIC WILLS

Many acrimonious will contests involve written wills. The contestors allege such things as mental incapacity of the testator at the time the will was made, undue influence, fraud, or duress. Although the written will speaks for itself, the mental capacity of the testator and the voluntariness of his or her actions cannot be determined from the writing alone.

If a challenge to the validity of a will has merit, it, of course, should be resolved. However, some will contests are based on unfounded allegations. After all, the testator is not there to defend his or her testamentary wishes.

To prevent unwarranted will contests, a testator can use a videotaped or electronically recorded will to supplement a written will. Videotaping a will that can withstand challenges by disgruntled relatives and alleged heirs involves a certain amount of planning.

The following procedures should be followed. A written will should be prepared to comply with the state's Statute of Wills. The video session should not begin until after the testator has become familiar with the document. The video should begin with the testator reciting the will verbatim. Next, the lawyer should ask the testator questions to demonstrate the testator's sound mind and understanding of the implications of his or her actions. The execution cer-

emony—the signing of the will by the testator and the attestation by the witnesses—should be the last segment on the film. The videotape should then be stored in a safe place.

With the testator's actions crystallized on videotape, a judge or jury will be able to determine the testator's mental capacity at the time the will was made and the voluntariness of his or her testamentary gifts. In addition, fraudulent competing wills will crumble in the face of such proof.

In the future, it is likely that videotaped wills will become invaluable evidential tools. Whether such wills alone without a writing will be recognized as testamentary instruments will depend on the development of state laws.

e·biz

$\mathcal{E}$XHIBIT 53.3   *Per Capita Distribution*

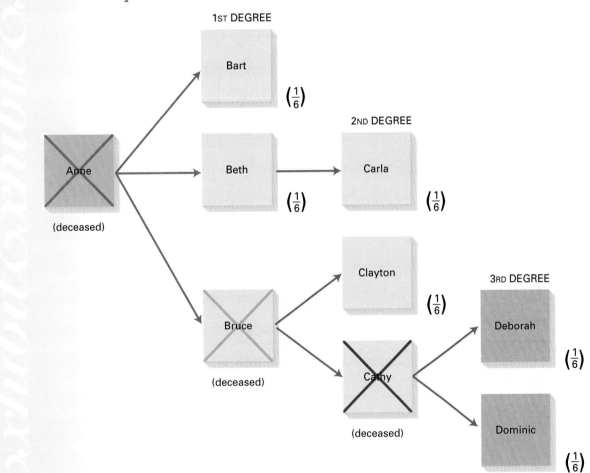

SPECIAL ISSUES CONCERNING WILLS

Simultaneous Deaths

Sometimes, people who would inherit property from each other die simultaneously. If it is impossible to determine who died first, the question becomes one of inheritance. The **Uniform Simultaneous Death Act** provides that each deceased person's property is distributed as though he or she survived.

Uniform Simultaneous Death Act
An act that provides that if people who would inherit property from each other die simultaneously, each person's property is distributed as though he or she survived.

Consider This Example Suppose a husband and wife make wills that leave their entire estate to each other. Assume that the husband and wife are killed simultaneously in an airplane crash. Here, the husband's property would go to his relatives and the wife's property would go to her relatives.

Joint and Mutual Wills

joint will
A will that is executed by two or more testators.

If two or more testators execute the same instrument as their will, the document is called a **joint will**. A joint will may be held invalid as to one testator but not the others.

mutual wills
Occur where two or more testators execute separate wills that leave their property to each other on the condition that the survivor leave the remaining property on his or her death as agreed by the testators.

Mutual or **reciprocal wills** arise where two or more testators execute separate wills that make testamentary dispositions of their property to each other on the condition that the survivor leave the remaining property on his or her death as agreed by the testators. The wills are usually separate instruments with reciprocal terms. Because of their contractual nature, mutual wills cannot be unilaterally revoked after one of the parties has died.

The enforcement of a mutual will was at issue in the following case.

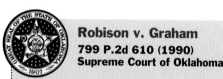

Robison v. Graham
799 P.2d 610 (1990)
Supreme Court of Oklahoma

CASE 53.3

FACTS

Mary Kay Graham (Mary) and William Clyde Graham (Clyde) were married in 1942. On March 3, 1973, Mary and Clyde executed a mutual and joint will in which they left all of each other's property to the survivor, with the survivor agreeing to leave half of the remaining property to Kathryn Robison and the other half in trust to William Lee Robison. Mary and Clyde agreed not to revoke, alter, or amend the will except by mutual written consent.

The will was not revoked prior to Mary's death on April 15, 1979. In May 1981, Clyde married Stella E. Berry (Stella), at which time he placed his property in joint tenancy with Stella and executed a new will. The new will revoked his prior one and, other than a specific devise, designated Stella as the beneficiary of the remainder of his estate. The marriage lasted until Clyde's death in 1985. Stella introduced the new will to probate. The beneficiaries of the mutual will sued, alleging breach of the mutual will. The trial court held in favor of the original beneficiaries. The court of appeals reversed. The original beneficiaries appealed.

ISSUE

Is the mutual will enforceable?

IN THE LANGUAGE OF THE COURT

Lavender, Justice *An oral or written contract to make a will may be enforced in Oklahoma. This is especially true where the joint will is probated and the survivor accepts the benefits. In the present case, proof of a mutually binding contract to devise property was within the four corners of the will executed by Clyde and Mary. The language clearly expresses the intent of Clyde and Mary to make a binding and irrevocable contract concerning the disposition of their property. Clyde offered Mary's will for probate and took the estate subject to its terms. Significantly, Clyde's share was greater than what he would have received had he not taken under the will.*

The specific agreement of the parties to the mutual will, that the survivor agreed not to revoke, alter, or amend the will, carried with it an implicit agreement by the survivor to see to it that the testamentary intent expressed in the mutual will be carried out and to make no disposition of the estate property inconsistent with that intent. It is undisputed that the property that was the subject of the contractual will was intact at Clyde's death even though the legal title was in his surviving spouse, Stella. Clyde breached this contractual will by revoking it and executing subsequent wills.

DECISION AND REMEDY

The state supreme court held that Clyde breached the mutual will that he had made with Mary. The supreme court vacated the judgment of the court of appeals and imposed a constructive trust on Clyde's estate in favor of the beneficiaries of the mutual will.

Case Questions

Critical Legal Thinking Should mutual wills be enforced? Why or why not?

Ethics Did Clyde act ethically in what he did?

Business Application Why are mutual wills made? Explain.

Undue Influence

A will may be found to be invalid if it was made as a result of **undue influence** on the testator. Undue influence can be inferred from the facts and circumstances surrounding the making of the will. For example, if an 85-year-old woman leaves all of her property to the lawyer who drafted her will and ignores her blood relatives, the court is likely to presume undue influence.

Undue influence is difficult to prove by direct evidence, but it may be proved by circumstantial evidence. The elements that courts examine to find the presence of undue influence include

- The benefactor and beneficiary are involved in a relationship of confidence and trust.
- The will contains substantial benefit to the beneficiary.
- The beneficiary caused or assisted in effecting execution of the will.
- There was an opportunity to exert influence.
- The will contains an unnatural disposition of the testator's property.
- The bequests constitute a change from a former will.
- The testator was highly susceptible to the undue influence.

undue influence

Occurs where one person takes advantage of another person's mental, emotional, or physical weakness and unduly persuades that person to make a will; the persuasion by the wrongdoer must overcome the free will of the testator.

Business Brief

Undue influence is very difficult to prove. It may be inferred from the facts and circumstances surrounding the making of a will.

Ethical Perspective

MURDER, SHE WROTE

Most states, by statute or court decision, provide that a person who murders another person cannot inherit the victim's property. This rule, often called the **murder disqualification doctrine**, is based on the public policy that a person should not benefit from his or her wrong-doing. Consider the following case.

Walter A. Gibbs resided with his mother until 1963, when he hired Delores Christenson to help care for her. He married Delores in 1964. The couple were divorced in 1973. Gibbs married Delores's twin sister, Darlene Wahl. That marriage ended in divorce in 1980.

During the winter of 1988–1989, Delores, Darlene, and Darlene's new husband, Jerry Phillips, who were all living together, experienced difficult times due to lack of money. Delores contacted Gibbs, who was over 80 years old at the time, at the nursing home where he resided and offered to

move back into his house and care for him. In February 1989, Delores, Darlene, and Jerry moved Gibbs to his house and moved in with him. The group lived together as a "family" for about one year.

Gibbs had a will that named his first cousin, Bernice Boettner, as sole beneficiary. In January 1990, Delores located an attorney who drafted a new will for Gibbs, and she procured two witnesses for the will's execution. The will disinherited Gibbs's relations and left his entire estate, worth about $175,000, to Delores. Gibbs executed the will on January 5, 1990.

On January 8, 1990, Darlene and Jerry discussed killing Gibbs to "activate the will." A few weeks later, Darlene suggested in the presence of Jerry and Delores that they hasten Gibbs's death by mixing sleeping pills and nitroglycerin in his tea. At one time, when Darlene suggested

(box continues)

smothering Gibbs with a pillow, Delores went to the bedroom, returned with a pillow, and handed it to Jerry, who held it over Darlene's face to see if she could breathe. On the morning of April 1, 1990, Darlene got a pillow from her bedroom and gave it to Jerry. Delores sat at the kitchen table approximately 17 feet from Gibbs's bed. Darlene held Gibbs's arms while Jerry smothered him. After Jerry removed the pillow, Delores went over and embraced Jerry.

In January 1991, Delores, Darlene, and Jerry were indicted on charges of murder, conspiracy to commit murder, and aiding and abetting murder. Jerry pleaded guilty to conspiracy to commit second-degree murder. Darlene was convicted of murder and sentenced to life in prison. Delores was acquitted of all charges.

Delores offered Gibbs's will for probate. Boettner filed a petition to revoke the probate of Gibbs's will and an application to disqualify Delores as the beneficiary as a willful slayer of Gibbs. Delores argued in defense that she should

be allowed to inherit Gibbs's estate because she had not been criminally convicted.

The trial court held that Delores qualified as a willful slayer under the murder disqualification statute even though she had not been convicted at her criminal trial. The state supreme court affirmed. The supreme court stated,

"We are not dealing with criminal responsibility, but with a civil statute which disqualifies a person who procures the death of a testator from reaping the benefits of that death. Moreover, the evidence indicated Delores interjected herself into the conspiracy by voluntarily procuring a pillow to assist Jerry and Darlene in practicing to smother Gibbs. In summation, Delores's claim she was just an innocent bystander and not an accomplice is without merit."

Gibbs's prior will, which left his estate to Boettner, is subject to probate. [*In the Matter of the Estate of Walter A. Gibbs*, 490 N.W.2d 504 (S.D. 1992)]

Entrepreneur and the Law

INTESTATE SUCCESSION

Entrepreneurs often accumulate a sizeable estate. They therefore should have a proper will that designates who receives his or her business and other property when he or she dies. If an entrepreneur or other person dies without a will, or his or her will fails for some legal reason, the property is distributed to his or her relatives pursuant to the state's **intestacy statute**.

Relatives who receive property under these statutes are called **heirs**. Although intestacy statutes differ from state to state, the general rule is that the deceased's real property is distributed according to the intestacy statute of the state where the real property is located, and the deceased's personal property is distributed according to the intestacy statute of the state where the deceased had his or her permanent residence.

Intestacy statutes usually leave the deceased's property to his or her heirs in this order: spouse, children, lineal heirs (e.g., grandchildren, parents, brothers and sisters), collateral heirs (e.g., aunts, uncles, nieces, nephews), and other next of kin (e.g., cousins). If the deceased has no surviving relatives, the deceased's property **escheats** (goes) to the state. In-laws do not inherit under most intestacy statutes. If a child dies before his or her parents, the child's spouse does not receive the inheritance.

To avoid the distribution of an estate as provided in an intestacy statute, a person should have a properly written, signed, and witnessed will that distributes the estate property as the testator wishes.

CONCEPT SUMMARY   COMPARISON OF DYING WITH AND WITHOUT A VALID WILL

Situation	Parties Who Receive Deceased's Property
Deceased dies with a valid will	Beneficiaries named in the will.
Deceased dies without a valid will	Heirs set forth in the applicable intestacy statute. If there are no heirs, the deceased's property escheats to the state.

PROBATE

When a person dies, his or her property must be collected, debts and taxes paid, and the remainder of the estate distributed to the beneficiaries of the will or the heirs under the state intestacy statute. This process is called **settlement of the estate** or **probate**. The process and procedures for settling an estate are governed by state statute. A specialized state court, called the **probate court**, usually supervises the administration and settlement of an estate.

A *personal representative* must be appointed to administer the estate during its settlement phase. If the testator's will names the personal representative, that person is called an *executor* or *executrix*.[2] If no one is named or if the decedent dies intestate, the court will appoint an *administrator* or *administratrix*.[3] Usually, this party is a relative of the deceased or a bank. An attorney is usually appointed to help administer the estate and to complete the probate.

settlement of the estate

The process of a deceased's property being collected, debts and taxes being paid, and the remainder of the estate being distributed.

probate court

A specialized state court that supervises the administration and settlement of an estate.

An individual should have a properly executed and witnessed will that designates the individuals and organizations that are to receive the testator's property upon his or her death. If an individual dies without a will, the deceased person's property is distributed to his or her relatives pursuant to the state's intestacy statute.

The Uniform Probate Code

The **Uniform Probate Code (UPC)** was promulgated to establish uniform rules for the creation of wills, the administration of estates, and the resolution of conflicts in settling estates. These rules provide a speedy, efficient, and less expensive method for settling estates than many existing state laws. Only about one-third of the states have adopted all or part of the UPC.

Uniform Probate Code (UPC)

A model law promulgated to establish uniform rules for the creation of wills, the administration of estates, and the resolution of conflicts in settling estates.

Contemporary Business Application

THE RIGHT TO DIE AND LIVING WILLS

Technological breakthroughs have greatly increased the life span of human beings. This same technology, however, permits life to be sustained long after a person is "brain dead." Some people say they have a right to refuse such treatment. Others argue that human life must be preserved at all costs. The U.S. Supreme Court was called upon to decide the **right to die** issue in the case of Nancy Cruzan.

In 1983, an automobile accident left Cruzan, a 25-year-old Missouri woman, in an irreversible coma. Four years

(box continues)

later, Cruzan's parents petitioned a state court judge to permit the hospital to withdraw the artificial feeding tube that had been keeping Cruzan alive. The judge agreed. However, Missouri's attorney general intervened and asked an appellate court to reverse the lower court's decision. The appellate court sided with the attorney general. The appellate court held that the family had not proven with certainty that Cruzan herself would have wanted the treatment stopped.

In reviewing the Missouri court's decision, eight of the nine justices of the U.S. Supreme Court acknowledged that the right to refuse medical treatment is a personal liberty protected by the U.S. Constitution. However, the Court also recognized that the states have an interest in preserving life. This interest can be expressed through a requirement for clear and convincing proof that the patient did not want to be sustained by artificial means. The Missouri attorney general then withdrew from the case, and a Missouri judge finally permitted the family to have Cruzan's tubes withdrawn. She died shortly afterward.

The clear message of the Supreme Court's opinion is that people who do not want their lives prolonged indefinitely by artificial means should sign a **living will** that stipulates their wishes before catastrophe strikes and they become unable to express it themselves because of an illness or an accident (see Exhibit 53.4). The living will could state which life-saving measures they do and do not want. Alternatively, they could state that they want any such treatments withdrawn if doctors determine that there is no hope of a meaningful recovery. The living will provides clear and convincing proof of a patient's wishes with respect to medical treatment.

Although the Supreme Court's opinion seems to sanction the general use of living wills, there is widespread disparity among states on this issue. For example, several states have yet to enact legislation authorizing the use of living wills. Additionally, there is no consistency among the states that have passed living will laws. For example, some states permit living wills to be activated only when death is at hand. Other state statutes complicate the issue by specifying types of treatment, such as artificial feeding tubes, that cannot be withdrawn, no matter what the patient's living will says.

People realize that what happened to the Cruzans could happen to them—at any age, in any place, without warning. For the over 80 percent of the American adult population who support the right to die, the *Cruzan* case gives the ability, through the use of a living will, to control such decisions. [*Cruzan v. Director, Missouri Department of Health*, 497 U.S. 261, 110 S.Ct. 2841 (1990)]

𝒯RUSTS

trust

A legal arrangement established when one person transfers title to property to another person to be held and used for the benefit of a third person.

settlor or trustor

Person who creates a trust.

trustee

Person who holds legal title to the trust corpus and manages the trust for the benefit of the beneficiary or beneficiaries.

beneficiary

Person for whose benefit a trust is created.

trust corpus

The property held in trust.

A **trust** is a legal arrangement under which one person (the **settlor**, **trustor**, or **transferor**) delivers and transfers legal title to property to another person (the **trustee**) to be held and used for the benefit of a third person (the **beneficiary**). The property held in trust is called the **trust corpus** or **trust res**. The trustee has *legal title* to the trust corpus, and the beneficiary has *equitable title*. Unlike wills, trusts are not public documents, so property can be transferred in privacy. Exhibit 53.5 shows the parties to a trust.

Trusts often provide that any trust income is to be paid to a person called the *income beneficiary*. The person to receive the trust corpus upon the termination of the trust is called the *remainderman*. The income beneficiary and the remainderman can be the same person or different persons. The designated beneficiary can be any identifiable person, animal (such as a pet), charitable organization, or other institution or cause that the settlor chooses. An entire class of persons—for example, "my grandchildren"—can be named.

A trust can allow the trustee to invade (use) the trust corpus for certain purposes that can be specifically named (e.g., "for the beneficiary's college education"). The trust agreement usually specifies how the receipts and expenses of the trust are to be divided between the income beneficiary and the remainderman.

Generally, the trustee has broad management powers over the trust property. This means that the trustee can invest the trust property to preserve its capital and make it productive. The trustee must follow any restrictions on investments contained in the trust agreement or state statute.

EXHIBIT 53.4   *A Sample Living Will and Health Care Proxy*

Living Will and Health Care Proxy

I. Living Will Including Statement Concerning Right to Die

Death is as much a reality as birth, growth, maturity and old age—it is the one certainty of life. If the time comes when I, John Doe, can no longer take part in decisions for my own future, let this statement stand as an expression of my wishes and directions to my Health Care Agent and others while I am still of sound mind. I intend, without otherwise limiting the absolute authority granted to my Health Care Agent in this instrument, that this instrument be binding upon my Health Care Agent.

If the situation should arise in which there is no reasonable expectation of my recovery from extreme physical or mental disability, including, but not limited to, a circumstance where there is no reasonable expectation that I will recover consciousness, commonly referred to as "brain dead," I direct that I be allowed to die and not be kept alive by medications, artificial means, including but not limited to artificial nutrition and hydration, or "heroic measures." Without limiting the generality of the foregoing, I hereby consent in such situation to an order not to attempt cardiopulmonary resuscitation. I do, however, ask that medication be mercifully administered to me to alleviate suffering even though this may shorten my remaining life and retard my consciousness.

II. Health Care Proxy

I hereby appoint my spouse, Jane Doe, to be my health care agent to make any and all health care decisions in accordance with my wishes and instructions as stated above and as otherwise known to her. In the event the person I appoint above is unable, unwilling or unavailable to act as my Health Care Agent, I hereby appoint my twin brother, Jack Doe, as my health care agent.

This health care proxy shall take effect in the event that I become unable to make my own health care decisions. I hereby revoke any prior health care proxy given by me to the extent it purports to confer the authority herein granted. I understand that, unless I revoke it, this health care proxy will remain in effect indefinitely.

Although I do not know today the exact circumstances that will exist if and when my Health Care Agent is called upon to make a decision or decisions on my behalf, I have selected my Health Care Agent with the confidence that such person understands my feelings in these matters and will make the decision I will want made considering the circumstances as they exist at the time. It is my intention, therefore, that the decision of my Health Care Agent be taken as a final and binding decision of mine, and will be the conclusive interpretation of the wishes I have made known in this document.

III. Waiver and Indemnity

To the extent permitted by law, I, for myself and for my heirs, executors, legal representatives and assigns, hereby release and discharge and agree to indemnify and hold harmless my Health Care Agent from and against any claim or liability whatsoever resulting from or arising out of my Health Care Agent's reliance on my wishes and directions as expressed herein. To induce any third party to act hereunder, I hereby agree that any third party receiving a duly executed copy or facsimile of this instrument may act hereunder, and that revocation or termination by me hereof shall be ineffective as to such third party unless and until actual notice or knowledge of such revocation shall have been received by such third party, and, to the extent permitted by law, I, for myself and for my heirs, executors, legal representatives and assigns, hereby release and discharge and agree to indemnify and hold harmless any such third party from and against any claims or liability whatsoever that may arise against such third party by reason of such third party having relied on the provisions of this instrument.

I understand the full import of this directive and I am emotionally and mentally competent to make this directive.

Signed _____ *John Doe* _____

The declarant has been personally known to me and I believe him or her to be of sound mind.

Witness _____ *Fred Friendly* _____

Witness _____ *Ollie Occupant* _____

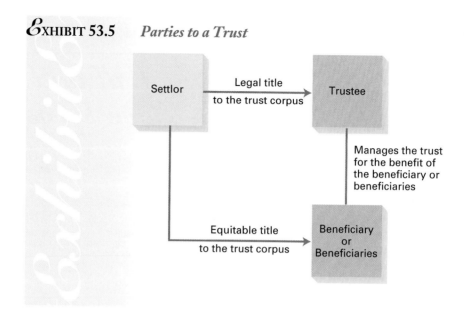

Exhibit 53.5   *Parties to a Trust*

Types of Trusts

Trusts may be either *express* or *implied*. There are also several special types of trusts. Express, implied, and special types of trusts are discussed in the following paragraphs.

express trust
A trust created voluntarily by the settlor.

Express Trusts   **Express trusts** are voluntarily created by the settlor. They usually are written. The written agreement is called a *trust instrument* or *trust agreement*.

Express trusts fall into two categories. The first, **inter vivos trusts** or **living trusts**, are created while the settlor is alive. The settlor transfers legal title of property to a named trustee to hold, administer, and manage for the benefit of named beneficiaries. The second, **testamentary trusts**, are created by will. In other words, the trust comes into existence when the settlor dies. If the will that establishes the trust is found to be invalid, the trust is also invalid.

inter vivos trust
A trust that is created while the settlor is alive.

testamentary trust
A trust created by will: the trust comes into existence when the settlor dies.

Implied Trusts   **Implied trusts** are trusts that are imposed by law or by conduct of the parties. Such trusts are divided into two categories: *constructive trusts* and *resulting trusts*.

A **constructive trust** is an equitable trust that is imposed by law to avoid fraud, unjust enrichment, and injustice. In constructive trust arrangements, the holder of the actual title to property (i.e., the trustee) holds the property in trust for its rightful owner.

implied trust
A trust that is implied by law or from the conduct of the parties.

constructive trust
An equitable trust that is imposed by law to avoid fraud, unjust enrichment, and injustice.

resulting trust
A trust that is created by the conduct of the parties.

Consider This Example   Suppose Thad and Kaye are partners. Assume Kaye embezzles partnership funds and uses the stolen funds to purchase a piece of real estate. In this case, the court can impose a constructive trust under which Kaye (who holds actual title to the land) is considered a trustee who is holding the property in trust for Thad, its rightful owner.

A **resulting trust** is created by the conduct of the parties.

Consider This Example   Henry is purchasing a piece of real estate but cannot attend the closing. He asks his brother, Gregory, to attend the closing and take title to the property until he can return. In this case, Gregory holds the title to the property as trustee for Henry until he returns.

A constructive trust is the formula through which the conscience of equity finds expression.

Cardozo, J.
Beatty v. Guggenheim
Exploration Co. (1919)

Special Types of Trusts

Trusts may be created for special purposes. Three types of special trusts that are fairly common are

1. **Charitable trusts** Created for the benefit of a segment of society or society in general. A trust that is created for the construction and maintenance of a public park is an example of a charitable trust.
2. **Spendthrift trusts** Designed to prevent a beneficiary's personal creditors from reaching his or her trust interest. All control over the trust is removed from the beneficiary. Personal creditors still can go after trust income that is paid to the beneficiary, however.
3. **Totten trusts** Created when a person deposits money in a bank account in his or her own name and holds it as a trustee for the benefit of another person. A totten trust is a tentative trust because (a) the trustee can add or withdraw funds from the account and (b) the trust can be revoked at any time prior to his or her death or prior to completing delivery of the funds to the beneficiary.

Termination of a Trust

A trust is irrevocable unless the settlor reserves the right to revoke it. Most trusts fall into the first category.

Usually, a trust either contains a specific termination date or provides that it will terminate upon the happening of an event (e.g., when the remainderman reaches a certain age). Upon termination, the trust corpus is distributed as provided in the trust agreement.

WWW *Working the Web*

Uniform Probate Code Cornell University maintains the Uniform Probate Code Web site.

Visit at **www.law.cornell.edu/uniform/probate.html**

Social Security On-line The Social Security System has a Web site that gives you lots of information about retirement and other social security benefits.

Visit at **www.ssa.gov**

Free Advice This Web site has lots of general information on legal issues. It is not a substitute for consulting an attorney if you need one.

Visit at **freeadvice.com**

CYBER EXERCISES

1. Has your state adopted the Uniform Probate Code? If so, has it adopted it in its entirety or in part?

2. Using Social Security On-line, find out how to request your Personal Earnings and Benefit Estimate Statement.

3. Can you find Free Advice about gift tax law?

e-biz

CASES AND EXERCISES

CRITICAL LEGAL THINKING CASES

53.1. On or about June 10, 1959, Martha Jansa executed a will naming her two sons as executors of her will and leaving all of her property to them. The will was properly signed and attested to by witnesses. Thereafter, Martha died. When Martha's safe deposit box at a bank was opened, the original of this will was discovered along with two other instruments that were dated after the will. One was a handwritten document that left her home to her grandson, with the remainder of her estate to her two sons; this document was not signed. The second document was a typed version of the handwritten one; this document was signed by Martha but was not attested to by witnesses. Which of the three documents should be admitted to probate? [*In the Matter of the Estate of Jansa*, 670 S.W.2d 767 (Tex.App. 1984)]

53.2. Everett Clark was never married and lived with his sister. On March 18, 1987, Clark met with William Wham, an attorney, to discuss the preparation of a will. Clark was to return the following day to execute his will but was hospitalized that evening with a perforated ulcer. He underwent surgery on March 19. Subsequent to the surgery, and until the time of his death, he was in intensive care and unable to communicate verbally.

On March 23, Clark's cousin John Bailey retrieved the will prepared by Wham and took it to attorney Frank Walker to have him finalize it. Walker testified that he took the will to the hospital on March 25. Immediately prior to the execution of the will, he asked Clark a few questions. Walker testified that Clark knew what he was doing. Dorothy Smith, an attesting witness, testified that Clark could not talk, but answered her questions by nodding yes or no. She asked Clark "if he knew me and if he knew we were all there and he shook his head yes." She testified that he also shook his head yes to the questions "Is this your will and testament?", "Is John Bailey your cousin?", and "Do you want to leave everything to John Bailey?" She testified further that "I believed the man knew what was going on." The second attesting witness, Vera Mae Horton, testified she believed Clark to be of sound mind and memory at the time the will was executed. Clark signed the will with an "X." On March 26, Clark passed into a coma and died. Bailey introduced the will into probate, but another relative of Clark's challenged it. Is the will valid? [*Bailey v. Bailey*, 561 N.E.2d 367 (III.App. 1990)]

53.3. Martha L. Woods and Henry R. Woods, who lived in Georgia, were married on February 21, 1987. Both of them had been previously married, and their respective spouses had died. They had each accumulated separate estates. Prior to departing on an automobile trip to Wichita, Kansas, they executed an instrument entitled "Agreement" dated March 27, 1987. It stated, "It is agreed that in the event of an accident or disaster which would result in the death of one of us, the surviving party is to retain ownership in the other's real and personal property until the time of his or her death." On April 5, 1987, they returned safely from their trip and did not subsequently execute another will. Henry died on June 11, 1988, as a result of a disease. Should the March 27, 1987, agreement be admitted into probate? [*Woods v. Woods*, 379 S.E.2d 291 (GA 1990)]

53.4. In October 1973, Mr. and Mrs. Pate executed separate wills that followed a common plan in disposing of their respective estates. Each will provided for the establishment of trusts with a life estate to their son Billy and, upon his death, the estate was to be distributed "in equal shares per stirpes to my natural born grandchildren."

Mr. and Mrs. Pate had two sons, Billy and Wallace. Billy's first marriage ended in divorce without children. Billy's second marriage also ended in divorce without children, although his second wife had a daughter by her previous marriage. Billy married again, and to date no children have been born to his 32-year-old wife. Wallace first married in 1952. Of that marriage, five children were born, each before the time that the Pates made their wills. After that marriage ended in divorce, Wallace married his present wife. There are no children of the second marriage, but there are stepchildren by Wallace's second wife. One of Wallace's daughters has two children by her marriage.

Mr. Pate died on November 9, 1979, leaving an estate of $1.6 million. Mrs. Pate died on October 21, 1983, leaving an estate of $6.7 million. Who inherits the estate? [*Pate v. Ford*, 360 S.E.2d 145 (S.C.App. 1987)]

53.5. On December 29, 1986, Cecila Fisher died, leaving as her sole survivor her husband William Fisher, Sr. In her will, she provided a number of specific devises. She directed that the remainder of her estate be placed in trust. The trust provided that the trustee pay $350 per month of the trust income to Mr. Fisher and, upon his death, that the trust principal be paid to the Maine Children's Home for Little Wanderers. Does Mr. Fisher have to take under his wife's will or can he obtain a different amount from her estate? [*Estate of Fisher,* 545 A.2d 1266 (Maine 1988)]

53.6. Mrs. Mildred D. Potter executed a will that provided that her residence in Pompano Beach, Florida, was to go to her daughter and an equivalent amount of cash to her son upon her death. Evidence showed that Mrs. Potter's intent was to treat the daughter and son equally in the distribution of her estate. When she died, her will was admitted into probate. At the time, she still possessed her home in Pompano Beach. Unfortunately, there were insufficient assets to pay Mrs. Potter's son the equivalent amount of cash. Can the son share in the value of the house so that his inheritance is equal to his sister's? [*In re Estate of Potter,* 469 So.2d 957 (Fla.App. 1985)]

53.7. Hazel Chapman Kidik executed a will that provided "I give, devise, and bequeath to Wilhelmina K. Chapman my house at 7 Winsteria Road, West Yarmouth, Massachusetts and the contents therein if she should survive me." The will provided for several other specific devises and stipulates the residue of the estate should be divided equally between her niece Cynthia, her nephew Douglas, and Douglas's former wife, Wilhelmina. In the summer of 1986, Kidik sold her house in Yarmouth and received back a mortgage deed securing a $65,000 promissory note from the buyer. Kidik died in September 1986. Kidik's will was admitted into probate. Does Wilhelmina have the right to receive the $65,000 note? [*Chapman v. Chapman,* 577 A.2d 775 (Maine 1990)]

53.8. In 1981, during his first marriage to Miriam Talbot, Robert Mirkil Talbot executed a will in multiple originals that bequeathed his entire estate to Miriam, or if she should predecease him, to his friend J. Barker Killgore. After his first wife's death, Robert married Lois McClen Mills. After consulting a Louisiana intestacy chart, the Talbots determined that if Robert died, Lois would receive Robert's entire estate because he had no descendants, surviving parents, or siblings. However, Lois did have descendants. Lois wanted to leave Robert a portion of her estate. So one day in 1987, Robert and his new wife went to an attorney to execute the new wife's will. While there, the attorney took Robert aside and showed him his prior will that made Killgore the contingent beneficiary. The attorney asked Robert if he wanted to leave his estate to his new wife, and Robert answered "yes." Robert then tore the old will in half in the attorney's presence. After leaving the attorney's office, Robert and Lois went shopping for furnishings for their new house. That night, Robert became short of breath and was taken to a hospital, where he died. Killgore retrieved a multiple original of Robert's 1981 will and petitioned to have it probated. Lois opposed the petition. Who wins? [*Succession of Talbot,* 530 So.2d 1132 (LA 1988)]

53.9. Nineteen days before his death on August 26, 1972, Leo Heil of Reno, Nevada, executed a holographic will consisting of five paragraphs. The first paragraph directed that his debts and his last illness and funeral expenses be paid. The second paragraph appointed James Bargas to serve as executor of the estate. The third paragraph stipulated that none of his relatives, whom he named, should share in his estate. The fourth paragraph gave $20,000 to James Bargas. The final paragraph directed that the residue of his estate be "given to the state of Nevada for the preservation of the wild horses in Nevada." When Heil died, the residue of his estate was $226,637 cash. When his holographic will was admitted to probate, his heirs challenged it. Who wins? [*In re Estate of Heil,* 210 Cal.App.3d 1507, 259 Cal.Rptr. 28 (Cal.App. 1989)]

53.10. On September 22, 1979, Mr. and Mrs. Campbell were out in a small boat on Hyatt Lake near Ashland, Oregon. The boat capsized near the middle of the lake sometime in the afternoon. No one saw the capsizing or either of the Campbells in the water. The deputy sheriff was called to the lake about 5 o'clock after the Campbells' boat was found. Numerous people searched the shoreline and lake, but the Campbells were not located by nightfall. The body of Mrs. Campbell was found the next morning. The body of Mr. Campbell was found on September 26, 1979. The pathologists who conducted the autopsies testified that both Mr. and Mrs. Campbell died of drowning, but could not determine the exact time of death. Both parties died intestate. Mr. Campbell was survived by three sisters and a brother, and Mrs. Campbell was survived by a daughter and son from a prior marriage. Who inherits the Campbells' property? [*In the Matter of the Estate of Campbell,* 641 P.2d 610 (Or.App. 1982)]

53.11. Dr. Duncan R. Danforth, a 75-year-old man of substantial means, married 21-year-old Loretta Ollison on Wednesday, August 13, 1980. Immediately following the ceremony, the newlyweds went to a lawyer's office where Danforth executed a newly prepared will naming Ollison a principal beneficiary of his estate. On Sunday, August 17, 1980, Danforth was murdered by Michael Stith, Ollison's lover, after two ex-convicts employed by Stith and Ollison to kill Danforth reneged on their promise to kill him. In a criminal trial, Ollison was convicted of conspiracy to commit murder and was sentenced to 10 years in prison. Can Ollison recover under the will or take her elective share of the estate under the state's intestate statute? [*In re the Estate of Danforth,* 705 S.W.2d 609 (Mo.App. 1986)]

ETHICS CASES

53.12. In 1967, Homer and Edna Jones, husband and wife, executed a joint will that provided "We will and give to our survivor, whether it be Homer Jones or Edna Jones, all property and estate of which the first of us that dies may be seized and possessed. If we should both die in a common catastrophe, or upon the death of our survivor, we will and give all property and estate then remaining to our children, Leonida Jones Eschman, daughter, Sylvia Marie Jones, daughter, and Grady V. Jones, son, share and share alike."

Homer died in 1975, and Edna Jones received his entire estate under the 1967 will. In 1977, Edna executed a new will that left a substantially larger portion of the estate to her daughter, Sylvia Marie Jones, than to the other two children. Edna Jones died in 1982. Edna's daughter introduced the 1977 will for probate. The other two children introduced the 1967 will for probate. Did Edna act ethically in this case? Who wins? [*Jones v. Jones*, 718 S.W.2d 416 (Tex.App. 1986)]

53.13. Wilmer Breeden, an active socialist, was a very wealthy individual. When he died, his will designated the bulk of his estate to be placed in the Breeden-Schmidt Foundation. This testamentary trust was to be administered by the trustees named in Breeden's will, and the funds of the foundation were to be distributed "to persons, entities and causes advancing the principles of socialism and those causes related to socialism. This shall include, but not be limited to, subsidizing publications, establishing and conducting reading rooms, supporting radio, television and the newspaper media and candidates for public office." Breeden's nephew and niece petitioned the court to have the trust provision declared invalid and the estate residue given to them as intestate heirs. Did the language in Breeden's will create a valid testamentary charitable trust? Did the nephew and niece act ethically in this case? [*In re Estate of Breeden*, 208 Cal.App.3d 981, 256 Cal.Rptr. 813 (Cal.App. 1989)]

CRITICAL LEGAL THINKING WRITING ASSIGNMENT

Read Case A.53 in the Case Appendix [*In re Estate of Vallerius*]. This case is excerpted from the appellate court's opinion. Review and brief the case. In your brief, be sure to answer the following questions:

1. Who was to inherit Adella Vallerius's property when she died?

2. What criminal acts did Douglas and Craig White commit?

3. Who is Renie White? Whose property did she inherit and why?

4. Who was to inherit Renie White's property when she died?

5. Were Douglas or Craig White permitted to inherit either Adella's or Renie's property when they died?

NOTES

1. Some states use the term *testator* regardless of the gender of the person making the will.
2. Some states use the term *executor* regardless of the gender of the named person.

3. Some states use the term *administrator* regardless of the gender of the appointee.

Case Appendix

CASE A.1

Anheuser-Busch, Incorporated v. Schmoke,
Mayor of Baltimore City, 63 F.3d 1305 (1995)
United States Court of Appeals, Fourth Circuit
Niemeyer, Circuit Judge

In January 1994, Baltimore exercised the authority granted it by the State and enacted Ordinance 288 prohibiting the outdoor advertising of alcoholic beverages in certain locations in Baltimore City. It also includes an exception permitting such advertising in certain commercially and industrially zoned areas of the City. By its terms, the ordinance was to become effective February 5, 1994. Before enacting the ordinance, the Baltimore City Council conducted public hearings, receiving testimony and previously conducted studies detailing the adverse effects on minors of alcohol consumption and the correlation between underage drinking and the advertising of alcoholic beverages.

The City Council found that alcoholic beverages are the second most heavily advertised products in America (after cigarettes), and that outdoor billboards are a "unique and distinguishable" medium of advertising which subjects the public to involuntary and unavoidable forms of solicitation. The City Council noted that children are exposed to the advertising of alcoholic beverages "simply by walking to school or playing in their neighborhood" and that children's "attitudes favorable to alcohol are significantly related to their exposure to alcohol advertisements." Attempting to tailor its ban, the City Council allowed advertising of alcoholic beverages in commercial and industrial areas, stating that it was "narrowly focus[ing] its efforts on those advertisements which most directly affect minors where they live, attend school, attend church and engage in recreational activities."

On January 14, 1994, several weeks before the ordinance was to become effective, Anheuser-Busch, Inc., filed suit in federal court, facially challenging the constitutionality of the ordinance under the First Amendment. Anheuser-Busch is the nation's largest brewer of beers and malt beverages, producing approximately 15 different brands, including Budweiser, Michelob, and Busch. It advertises in all media, including outdoor billboards and displays. In addition to contending that there is no correlation between alcoholic beverage advertising and underage drinking, Anheuser-Busch asserts that the purpose of its advertising is "to solidify brand loyalty and increase market share by shifting adult beer drinkers from other brands to the advertised brand of beer."

Following a hearing, the district court issued an opinion upholding the constitutionality of the ordinance. *Anheuser-Busch, Inc. v. Mayor and City Council,* 855 F.Supp. 811 (D.Md.1994). The court held the ordinance constitutional after concluding that it "directly advances the City's asserted interest in promoting the welfare and temperance of minors" and is "narrowly tailored" to that end.

On appeal, Anheuser-Busch argues that the ordinance is unconstitutional on its face because (1) it does not directly and materially advance the government's interest in promoting temperance of minors and (2) it is not narrowly tailored to serve that purpose. They also argue that, as applied, the ordinance would impermissibly restrict their noncommercial speech.

We find that it was reasonable for the Baltimore City Council to have concluded that Ordinance 288's regulation of the outdoor advertising of alcoholic beverages directly and materially advances Baltimore's interest in promoting the welfare and temperance of minors. The City Council found that outdoor advertising is a unique and distinct medium which subjects the public to involuntary and unavoidable solicitation, and that children, simply by walking to school or playing in their neighborhood, are exposed daily to this advertising. The City Council pointed to its legislative finding that the majority of research studies show a definite correlation between alcoholic beverage advertising and underage drinking.

We simply do not believe that the liquor industry spends a billion dollars a year on advertising solely to acquire an added market share at the expense of competitors. We hold, as a matter of law, that prohibitions against the advertising of alcoholic beverages are reasonably related to reducing the sale and consumption of those beverages and their attendant problems. The entire economy of the industries that bring these challenges is based on the belief that advertising increases sales.

It is readily acknowledged that limitations on outdoor advertising of alcoholic beverages designed to protect minors also reduce the opportunities for adults to receive advertised information. And adults, who constitute a majority of the population, are not the object of the government's legislation. But it also appears that no less restrictive means may be available to advance the government's interest. Anheuser-Busch argues that Baltimore could just as effectively advance its goal of promoting the welfare and temperance of minors by increasing enforcement of existing laws prohibiting sales to, and possession of alcoholic beverages by, minors, or by implementing and encouraging educational programs on the dangers of alcohol. These approaches might indeed prove beneficial in reducing underage drinking, but they do not provide an alternative to the approach selected by the City of curbing the enticement to consume alcoholic beverages. In the face of a problem as significant as that which the City seeks to address, the City must be given some reasonable latitude.

The problem of underage drinking is a most serious one that contributes significantly to a variety of social problems. Baltimore was faced with statistics showing that fully one-half of all deaths of minors were alcohol-related, and 40 to 50 percent of juveniles who drowned or had diving accidents had consumed alcohol immediately prior to the incident. The City Council found that alcohol is overwhelmingly and consistently the most widely used "drug" at all adolescent age levels. It pointed to data which showed that over half of all twelfth graders, 40 percent of tenth graders, and over a quarter of eighth graders reported that they consumed alcohol within the past 30 days. Widespread underage drinking was also found to be a major factor in crime. One-third of all juvenile males arrested said they had consumed alcohol within the previous 72 hours, and nearly 40 percent of all youths in adult correctional facilities reported drinking alcohol before committing their crime.

Through outdoor advertising, children are involuntarily and unavoidably confronted daily with the advertised message. Billboards are "seen without the exercise of choice or volition," and viewers have the message "thrust upon them by all the arts and devices that skill can produce." The City argues that the only means to address this problem is to ban such advertising in locations where children generally walk and play. Such a ban still permits adults to receive advertising messages and information from signs in commercial areas of the City and through the numerous other media to which adults are constantly exposed.

In summary, Baltimore City's regulation of stationary outdoor "advertising that advertises alcoholic beverages" in certain locations directly and materially advances a substantial governmental interest in promoting the welfare and temperance of minors who are involuntarily and unavoidably exposed to such advertisements. While the means selected of limiting the location of such outdoor advertising is not a perfect "fit" with the governmental objective, it nevertheless falls well within the range tolerated by the First Amendment for the regulation of commercial speech.

For the reasons stated, we affirm the judgment of the district court, upholding Baltimore City Ordinance 288 against a facial constitutional challenge under the First Amendment. AFFIRMED.

CASE A.2
Gnazzo v. G.D. Searle & Co., 973 F.2d 136 (1992)
U.S. Court of Appeals for the Second Circuit
Pierce, Circuit Judge

On November 11, 1974, Gnazzo had a CU-7 intrauterine device (IUD) inserted in her uterus for contraceptive purposes. The IUD was developed, marketed and sold by G.D. Searle & Co. (Searle). When Gnazzo's deposition was taken, she stated that her doctor had informed her that "the insertion would hurt, but not for long," and that she "would have uncomfortable and probably painful periods for the first three to four months." On October 11, 1975, Gnazzo found it necessary to return to her physician due to excessive pain and cramping. During this visit she was informed by her doctor that he thought she had Pelvic Inflammatory Disease (PID). She recalled that he stated that the infection was possibly caused by venereal disease or the use of the IUD. The PID was treated with antibiotics and cleared up shortly thereafter. Less than one year later, Gnazzo was again treated for an IUD-associated infection. This infection was also treated with antibiotics. Gnazzo continued using the IUD until it was finally removed in December of 1977.

Following a laparoscopy in March of 1989, Gnazzo was informed by a fertility specialist that she was infertile because of PID-induced adhesions resulting from her prior IUD use. Subsequent to this determination, and at the request of her then-attorneys, Gnazzo completed a questionnaire dated May 11, 1989. In response to the following question, "when and why did you first suspect that your IUD had caused you any harm?," Gnazzo responded "sometime in 1981" and explained: "I was married in April 1981 so I stopped using birth control so I could get pregnant—nothing ever happened (of course) then I started hearing and reading about how damaging IUD's could be. I figured that was the problem, however, my marriage started to crumble so I never pursued the issue."

On May 4, 1990, Gnazzo initiated the underlying action against Searle. In an amended complaint, she alleged that she had suffered injuries as a result of her use of the IUD developed by Searle. Searle moved for summary judgment on the ground that Gnazzo's claim was time-barred by Connecticut's three-year statute of limitations for product liability actions. Searle argued, inter alia, that Gnazzo knew in 1981 that she had suffered harm caused by her IUD. Gnazzo contended that her cause of action against Searle accrued only when she learned from the fertility specialist that the IUD had caused her PID and subsequent infertility.

In a ruling dated September 18, 1991, the district court granted Searle's motion for summary judgment on the ground that Gnazzo's claim was time-barred by the applicable statute of limitations. In reaching this result, the court determined that Connecticut law provided no support for Gnazzo's contention that she should not have been expected to file her action until she was told of her infertility and the IUD's causal connection. This appeal followed.

On appeal, Gnazzo contends that the district court improperly granted Searle's motion for summary judgment because a genuine issue of material fact exists as to when she discovered, or reasonably should have discovered, her injuries and their causal connection to the defendant's alleged wrongful conduct. Summary judgment is appropriate when there is no genuine issue as to any material fact and the moving party is entitled to judgment as a matter of law. We consider the record in the light most favorable to the non-movant. However, the non-movant "may not rest upon the mere allegations of denials of her pleading, but must set forth specific facts showing that there is a genuine issue for trial."

Under Connecticut law, a product liability claim must be brought within "three years from the date when the injury is first sustained or discovered or in the exercise of reasonable care should have been discovered." In Connecticut, a cause of action accrues when a plaintiff suffers actionable harm. Actionable harm occurs when the plaintiff discovers or should discover, through the exercise of reasonable care, that he or she has been injured and that the defendant's conduct caused such injury.

Gnazzo contends that "the mere occurrence of a pelvic infection or difficulty in becoming pregnant does not necessarily result in notice to the plaintiff of a cause of action." Thus, she maintains that her cause of action did not accrue until 1989 when the fertility specialist informed her both that she was infertile and that this condition resulted from her previous use of the IUD.

Under Connecticut law, however, "the statute of limitations begins to run when the plaintiff discovers some form of actionable harm, not the fullest manifestation thereof. Therefore, as Gnazzo's responses to the questionnaire indicate, she suspected "sometime in 1981" that the IUD had caused her harm because she had been experiencing trouble becoming pregnant and had "started hearing and reading about how damaging IUD's could be and had figured that was the problem." Thus, by her own admission, Gnazzo had recognized, or should have recognized, the critical link between her injury and the defendant's causal connection to it. In other words she had "discovered or should have discovered through the exercise of reasonable care, that she had been injured and that Searle's conduct caused such injury." However, as Gnazzo acknowledged in the questionnaire, she did not pursue the "issue" at the time because of her marital problems. Thus, even when viewed in the light most favorable to Gnazzo, the non-moving party, we are constrained to find that she knew by 1981 that she had "some form of actionable harm." Consequently, by the time she commenced her action in 1990, Gnazzo was time-barred by the Connecticut statute of limitations.

Since we have determined that Gnazzo's cause of action commenced in 1981, we need not address Searle's additional contention that Gnazzo's awareness in 1975 of her PID and her purported knowledge of its causal connection to the IUD commenced the running of the Connecticut statute of limitations at that time.

We are sympathetic to Gnazzo's situation and mindful that the unavoidable result we reach in this case is harsh. Nevertheless, we are equally aware that "it is within the Connecticut General Assembly's constitutional authority to decide when claims for injury are to be brought. Where a plaintiff has failed to comply with this requirement, a court may not entertain the suit." The judgment of the district court is affirmed.

CASE A.3
Lee v. Weisman, 120 L.Ed. 2d 467, 112 S.Ct. 2649 (1992)
United States Supreme Court
Kennedy, Justice (joined by Blackmun, Stevens, O'Conner, and Souter)

Deborah Weisman graduated from Nathan Bishop Middle School, a public school in Providence, at a formal ceremony in June 1989. She was about 14 years old. For many years it has been the policy of the Providence School committee and the Superintendent of Schools to permit principals to invite members of the clergy to give invocations and benedictions at middle school and high school graduations. Many, but not all, of the principals elected to include prayers as part of the graduation ceremonies. Acting for himself and his daughter, Deborah's father, Daniel Weisman, objected to any prayers at Deborah's middle school graduation, but to no avail. The school principal, petitioner Robert E. Lee, invited a rabbi to deliver prayers at

the graduation exercises for Deborah's class. Rabbi Leslie Gutterman, of the Temple Beth El in Providence, accepted.

It has been the custom of Providence school officials to provide invited clergy with a pamphlet entitled "Guidelines for Civic Occasions," prepared by the National Conference of Christians and Jews. The Guidelines recommended that public prayers at nonsectarian civic ceremonies be composed with "inclusiveness and sensitivity," though they acknowledge that "prayer of any kind may be inappropriate on some civic occasions." The principal gave Rabbi Gutterman the pamphlet before the graduation and advised him the invocation and benediction should be nonsectarian.

Deborah's graduation was held on the premises of Nathan Bishop Middle School on June 29, 1989. Four days before the ceremony, Daniel Weisman, in his individual capacity as a Providence taxpayer and as next friend of Deborah, sought a temporary restraining order in the United States District Court for the District of Rhode Island to prohibit school officials from including an invocation or benediction in the graduation ceremony. The court denied the motion for lack of adequate time to consider it. Deborah and her family attended the graduation, where the prayers were recited. In July 1989, Daniel Weisman filed an amended complaint seeking a permanent injunction barring petitioners, various officials of the Providence public schools, from inviting the clergy to deliver invocations and benedictions at future graduations.

The case was submitted on stipulated facts. The District Court held that petitioners' practice of including invocations and benedictions in public school graduations violated the Establishment Clause of the First Amendment, and it enjoined petitioners from continuing the practice. The court applied the three-part Establishment Clause test. Under that test, to satisfy the Establishment Clause a governmental practice must (1) reflect a clearly secular purpose, (2) have a primary effect that neither advances nor inhibits religion, and (3) avoid excessive government entanglement with religion. On appeal, the United States Court of Appeals for the First Circuit affirmed.

These dominant facts mark and control the confines of our decision: State officials direct the performance of a formal religious exercise at promotional and graduation ceremonies for secondary schools. Even for those students who object to the religious exercise, their attendance and participation in the state-sponsored religious activity are in a fair and real sense obligatory, though the school district does not require attendance as a condition for receipt of the diploma.

The controlling precedents as they relate to prayer and religious exercise in primary and secondary public schools compel the holding here that the policy of the city of Providence is an unconstitutional one. It is beyond dispute that, at a minimum, the Constitution guarantees that government may not coerce anyone to support or participate in religion or its exercise, or otherwise act in a way which "establishes a state religion or religious faith, or tends to do so."

We are asked to recognize the existence of a practice of nonsectarian prayer within the embrace of what is known as the

Judeo-Christian tradition, prayer which is more acceptable than one which, for example, makes explicit references to the God of Israel, or to Jesus Christ, or to a patron saint. If common ground can be defined which permits once conflicting faiths to express the shared conviction that there is an ethic and a morality which transcend human invention, the sense of community and purpose sought by all decent societies might be advanced. But though the First Amendment does not allow the government to stifle prayers which aspire to these ends, neither does it permit the government to undertake that task for itself.

The sole question presented is whether a religious exercise may be conducted at a graduation ceremony in circumstances where, as we have found, young graduates who object are induced to conform. No holding by this Court suggests that a school can persuade or compel a student to participate in a religious exercise. That is being done here, and it is forbidden by the Establishment Clause of the First Amendment.

For the reasons we have stated, the judgment of the Court of Appeals is affirmed.

Scalia, Justice (joined by Rehnquist, White, and Thomas) dissenting, expressed the view that (1) the establishment of religion clause should not have been interpreted so as to invalidate a long-standing American tradition of nonsectarian prayer at public school graduations, (2) graduation invocations and benedictions involve no psychological coercion of students to participate in religious exercises, (3) the only coercion that is forbidden by the establishment of religion clause is that which is backed by a threat of penalty, and (4) the middle school principal did not direct or control the content of the prayers in question, and thus there was no pervasive government involvement with religious activity.

CASE A.4

Ohg v. Kolodny
NY County, Supreme Court,
1st Jud. Dept., IA Part II (1992)
Baer, Justice

Plaintiff is an auction house dealing in works of art. Defendant is an art dealer. His gallery has purchased fine art from the plaintiff over the years, presumably with happier results than in this case. In 1988, defendant received, in New York, a catalogue sent by plaintiff that described works of art that would be put up for auction by plaintiff. Among these, defendant says, was "a bronze sculpture produced by Hiliare Germain Edgar Degas before 1900," to wit, the "Dancer Gazing." Plaintiff phoned defendant in New York during the auction and solicited a bid for the "Dancer." Without ever having set eyes on the right foot or any other part of the sculpture, plaintiff offered a bid of DM 220,000 and triumphed. Defendant was never told the identity of the consignor of the Degas. Defendant wired to plaintiff the purchase price and a commission.

The "Dancer" arrived shortly thereafter in New York, where she immediately did a pirouette and departed for London. Defendant wished to let no grass grow under either of his feet; he would put the Degas up for resale at Christie's and would, he

was confident, earn a great deal of not bronze, but sterling. Eagle eyes at Christie's surveyed the work. Defendant was told, to his horror, that Christie's suspected that the statue was ersatz, in a word, a fake. Defendant contacted Herr Hanstein and advised that his heart was heavy and his wallet, he was afraid, too light. Defendant sought a refund.

Defendant allegedly secured the agreement of plaintiff that the "Dancer" would be given the once or twice over by the world's foremost expert of Degas Bronzes, whose determination would be binding. The statue was brought to New York, where the expert, like many another world's foremost experts, resides. His conclusion unfortunately was that the work was not genuine.

A German court decided in favor of plaintiff, rejecting defendant's contention that he was entitled to an offset for the purchase price of the pseudo-Degas. The court held that plaintiff had disclaimed any warranty as to the authenticity of the "Dancer"; that since the job of an auction house is to sell as commission agent many items owned by others, the authenticity of which the auctioneer cannot readily confirm, disclaimers do not violate the law; and that defendant in his letter on the Riopelle had disavowed any offset.

After plaintiff launched its Blitzkrieg here in New York, defendant responded with a lawsuit of his own. Defendant seeks to recover the purchase price of the ill-fated Degas. Defendant, relying inter alia upon Article 15 of the New York Arts and Cultural Affairs Law (the "Art Law"), contends that plaintiff is liable for having provided inaccurate information about the Degas and that the German judgment contravenes New York public policy, as a consequence of which its enforcement in favor of plaintiff is verboten. The argument, while creative and well presented, must fail.

CPLR Sec. 5304(b)(4) provides that a monetary judgment of a foreign country need not be recognized by New York if the cause of action on which the judgment is based "is repugnant to the public policy of this state." Normally, the judgment of a foreign nation will be given effect. Differences between the laws of New York and those of the many sovereign nations of the world are likely to arise often, but such differences alone cannot constitute a violation of public policy. As Judge Cardozo said, "We are not so provincial as to say that every solution of a problem is wrong because we deal with it otherwise at home." Were we New Yorkers to be overly provincial, we might well inspire foreign nations to reject enforcement of New York judgments, precisely the opposite of the purpose Article 53 was created to achieve and an outcome particularly undesirable as the economy of this country grows everyday more intertwined with those of other nations.

The German court applied German law in this case. This is not unreasonable since the auction occurred in Germany and defendant placed his bid during a telephone call with the auction house in Germany. In addition, plaintiff's conditions of sale stated that legal relations between plaintiff and the bidder would be governed by German law. Defendant appeared in the German action, defended, and lost. There is, of course, no claim that German law and procedures are unfair and unworthy of respect here.

The Germans are less Bismarcian than defendant contends. German law, as exemplified by the decision of the Cologne court in this case, is not indifferent to the general sale of fakes by art merchants. The court relied upon the warranty exclusion that formed a condition of sale.

Enforcement of the German judgment would not undermine the public interest, public confidence in the law or security for individual rights, nor violate fundamental notions of what is decent and fair. The German judgment is enforceable.

Case A.5

Braun v. Soldier of Fortune Magazine, Inc.
968 F.2d 1110 (1992)
United States Court of Appeals for the Eleventh Circuit
Anderson, Circuit Judge

In January 1985, Michael Savage submitted a personal service advertisement to Soldier of Fortune (SOF). After several conversations between Savage and SOF's advertising manager, Joan Steel, the following advertisement ran in the June 1985 through March 1986 issues of SOF:

GUN FOR HIRE: 37-year-old professional mercenary desires jobs. Vietnam Veteran. Discrete [sic] and very private. Body guard, courier, and other special skills. All jobs considered. Phone (615) 436-9785 (days) or (615) 436-4335 (nights), or write: Rt. 2, Box 682 Village Loop Road, Gatlinburg, TN 37738.

Savage testified that, when he placed the ad, he had no intention of obtaining anything but legitimate jobs. Nonetheless, Savage stated that the overwhelming majority of the 30 to 40 phone calls a week he received in response to his ad sought his participation in criminal activity such as murder, assault, and kidnapping. The ad also generated at least one legitimate job as a bodyguard, which Savage accepted.

In late 1984 or early 1985, Bruce Gastwirth began seeking to murder his business partner, Richard Braun. Gastwirth enlisted the aid of another business associate, John Horton Moore, and together they arranged for at least three attempts on Braun's life, all of which were unsuccessful. Responding to Savage's SOF ad, Gastwirth and Moore contacted him in August 1985 to discuss plans to murder Braun. On August 26, 1985, Savage, Moore, and another individual, Sean Trevor Doutre, went to Braun's suburban Atlanta home. As Braun and his sixteen-year-old son Michael were driving down the driveway, Doutre stepped in front of Braun's car and fired several shots into the car with a MAC 11 automatic pistol. The shots hit Michael in the thigh and wounded Braun as well. Braun managed to roll out of the car, but Doutre walked over to Braun and killed him by firing two more shots into the back of his head as Braun lay on the ground.

On March 31, 1988, appellees Michael and Ian Braun filed this diversity action against appellants in the United States District Court for the Middle District of Alabama, seeking damages for the wrongful death of their father. Michael Braun also filed a separate action seeking recovery for the personal injuries he received at the time of his father's death. The district court consolidated these related matters.

Trial began on December 3, 1990. Appellees contended that, under Georgia law, SOF was liable for their injuries because SOF negligently published a personal service advertisement that created an unreasonable risk of the solicitation and commission of violent criminal activity, including murder. To show that SOF knew of the likelihood that criminal activity would result from placing an ad like Savage's, appellees introduced evidence of newspaper and magazine articles published prior to Braun's murder which described links between SOF and personal service ads and a number of criminal convictions including murder, kidnapping, assault, extortion, and attempts thereof. Appellees also presented evidence that, prior to SOF's acceptance of Savage's ad, law enforcement officials had contacted SOF staffers on two separate occasions in connection with investigations of crimes.

In his trial testimony, SOF president Robert K. Brown denied having any knowledge of criminal activity associated with SOF's personal service ads at any time prior to Braun's murder in August 1985. Both Jim Graves, a former managing editor of SOF, and Joan Steel, the advertising manager who accepted Savage's advertisement, similarly testified that they were not aware of other crimes connected with SOF ads prior to running Savage's ad. Steel further testified that she had understood the term "Gun for Hire" in Savage's ad to refer to a "bodyguard or protection service-type thing," rather than to any illegal activity.

The jury returned a verdict in favor of appellee and awarded compensatory damages on the wrongful death claim in the amount of $2,000,000. The jury also awarded appellee Michael Braun $375,000 in compensatory damages and $10,000,000 in punitive damages for his personal injury claim.

To prevail in an action for negligence in Georgia, a party must establish the following elements:

(1) A legal duty to conform to a standard of conduct raised by the law for the protection of others against unreasonable risks of harm, (2) a breach of this standard, (3) a legally attributable causal connection between the conduct and the resulting injury, and (4) some loss or damage flowing to the plaintiff's legally protected interest as a result of the alleged breach of the legal duty. To the extent that SOF denies that a publisher owes any duty to the public when it publishes personal service ads, its position is clearly inconsistent with Georgia law. We believe, however, that the crux of SOF's argument is not that it had no duty to the public, but that, as a matter of law, there is a risk to the public when a publisher prints an "unreasonable" advertisement only if the ad openly solicits criminal activity.

SOF further argues that imposing liability on publishers for the advertisements they print indirectly threatens core, non-commercial speech to which the Constitution accords its full protection. Supreme Court cases discussing the limitations the First Amendment places on state defamation law indicate that there is no constitutional infirmity in Georgia law holding publishers liable under a negligence standard with respect to the commercial advertisements they print. Past Supreme Court decisions indicate, however, that the negligence standard that the First Amendment permits is a "modified" negligence standard. The Court's decisions suggest that Georgia law may impose tort liability on publishers for injury caused by the advertisements they print only if the ad on its face, without the need to investigate, makes it apparent that there is a substantial danger of harm to the public.

We conclude that the First Amendment permits a state to impose upon a publisher liability for compensatory damages for negligently publishing a commercial advertisement where the ad on its face, and without the need for investigation, makes it apparent that there is a substantial danger of harm to the public. The absence of a duty requiring publishers to investigate the advertisements they print and the requirement that the substance of the ad itself must warn the publisher of a substantial danger of harm to the public guarantee that the burden placed on publishers will not impermissibly chill protected commercial speech.

Our review of the language of Savage's ad persuades us that SOF had a legal duty to refrain from publishing it. Savage's advertisement (1) emphasized the term "Gun for Hire," (2) described Savage as a "professional mercenary," (3) stressed Savage's willingness to keep his assignments confidential and "very private," (4) listed legitimate jobs involving the use of a gun-bodyguard and courier-followed by a reference to Savage's "other special skills," and (5) concluded by stating that Savage would consider "all jobs." The ad's combination of sinister terms makes it apparent that there was a substantial danger of harm to the public. The ad expressly solicits all jobs requiring the use of a gun. When the list of legitimate jobs—i.e., bodyguard and courier—is followed by "other special skills" and "all jobs considered," the implication is clear that the advertiser would consider illegal jobs. We agree with the district court that "the language of this advertisement is such that, even though couched in terms not explicitly offering criminal services, the publisher could recognize the offer of criminal activity as readily as its readers obviously did." We find that the jury had ample grounds for finding that SOF's publication of Savage's ad was the proximate cause of Braun's injuries.

For the foregoing reasons, we AFFIRM the district court's judgment.

CASE A.6
Johnson v. Chicago Pneumatic Tool Co.
607 So. 2d 615 (1992)
Court of Appeals of Louisiana
Crain, Judge

This is a products liability action in which William H. Johnson was injured in the course of his employment when a pipejack was accidentally propelled toward Johnson striking him in the back pinning him between the edge of a large diameter pipe which he was grinding and the pipejack. A pipejack is a large mechanical device which is inserted into large pipes which are in the process of being joined together. The pipejack applies pressure forcing the joints into an evenly rounded shape which can then be welded together. The movement of the pipejack was controlled by an air winch manufactured by Chicago Pneumatic Tool Company (Chicago Pneumatic) which had been utilized and incorporated by McDermott, Inc., Johnson's employer, into

a system dedicated to the fitting or joining of large diameter pipe. The accident occurred at the McDermott shipyard when a coemployee either tossed or laid a fifty gallon drum on the ground near the winch in the area where Johnson was working. The drum rolled and toppled over onto the winch throttle pushing the throttle downward which in turn activated the winch and caused the pipejack to move toward Johnson.

Johnson instituted this action against Chicago Pneumatic as manufacturer of the winch, alleging that the winch as designed and manufactured was unreasonably dangerous to normal use. McDermott intervened in this action. After trial on the merits, the jury rendered a special verdict in favor of defendant.

It is uncontroverted that at the time of the accident Johnson was working with his back to the pipejack and the winch; the winch was not being manually operated; and no one was standing at or adjacent to the winch controls. The clutch lever had previously been welded down by McDermott and as a result the clutch remained permanently engaged. Of the other winch controls, the throttle was set in the neutral position and neither the brake nor the safety lock was engaged.

In order to prevail in a products liability action a plaintiff must prove that his damage was a result of a condition of the product which made the product unreasonably dangerous to normal use. The "normal use" of a product encompasses all intended or foreseeable uses and misuses of the product. A manufacturer is obliged to adequately warn the user of any danger inherent in the normal use of the product which is not within the knowledge of or obvious to the normal user. The manufacturer is also required to anticipate the environment in which the product will be used and to notify the user of the potential risks arising from foreseeable use or misuse in the foreseeable environment.

The finding of the jury that the winch was not employed in normal use at the time of the accident is a factual determination which should not be set aside unless clearly wrong. A review of the record reveals that McDermott modified the winch by permanently engaging the clutch; that this modification permanently removed one of the safety and control features designed for its safe and proper operation; the disengagement of the clutch without the engagement of the additional safety features would have prevented the accident; the basic safety mechanisms of the winch were not utilized; the winch was installed backwards thereby requiring the operator to stand away from the controls; and the employees/operators were uninformed regarding familiarity with the controls and proper operation of the winch. After careful review of the record we conclude that the jury's determination in this matter is not manifestly erroneous.

AFFIRMED.

CASE A.7
Schalk v. Texas, 823 S.W.2d 633 (1991)
Court of Criminal Appeals of Texas
Miller, Judge

Appellants Schalk and Leonard are former employees of Texas Instruments (hereafter TI). Both men have doctoral degrees and specialized in the area of speech research at TI. Schalk resigned his position with TI in April 1983 to join a newly developed company, Voice Control Systems (hereafter VCS). In February 1985, Leonard resigned from TI and joined VCS. Several TI employees eventually joined the ranks of VCS. Speech research was the main thrust of the research and development performed by VCS. In fact, VCS was a competitor of TI in this field. In April 1985 Sam Kuzbary, then employed with VCS and a former TI employee, noticed some information which he believed to be proprietary to TI stored in the memory of the computer he was using at VCS. Kuzbary contacted TI and agreed to serve as an "informant" for them.

He then searched the premises of VCS and photographed materials which he recognized from his employment with TI. A TI internal investigation revealed that a few hours prior to Schalk's and Leonard's departures from TI, each appellant, utilizing TI computers, copied the entire contents of the directories respectively assigned to them. This information included computer programs which TI claimed to be its trade secrets. Officials of TI then contacted the Dallas District Attorney's office. A search of the premises of VCS resulted in the seizure of computer tapes containing the alleged TI trade secret programs from appellants' offices. Appellants were arrested.

We granted review to consider, first, whether the evidence was sufficient to establish that the computer programs named in the indictments were trade secrets, and second, to determine whether the items listed in the search warrant were sufficiently described so as to preclude a general exploratory search.

Having determined that computer programs are proper subjects for trade secret litigation under Texas civil and criminal law, we now look to the case *sub judice* to determine whether the programs which appellants copied and took with them to VCS are trade secrets as defined by §31.05 of the Penal Code.

§31.05 Theft of trade secrets:

(a) For the purposes of this section:

(4) "Trade secret" means the whole or any part of any scientific or technical information, design, process, procedure, formula, or improvement that has value and that the owner has taken measures to prevent from becoming available to persons other than those selected by the owner to have access for limited purposes.

Appellants claimed on appeal that the programs did not meet the statutory trade secrets criteria because they alleged their former employer TI failed to take "measures to prevent [the information] from becoming available to persons other than those selected by the owner." We note, as did the court of appeals, that the statute sets no standards for degree of sufficiency of the "measures" taken. Specifically, appellants pointed to considerable disclosure of speech research information, citing the "academic environment" of the laboratory in which they worked as encouraging the sharing of information, rather than maintaining secrecy. Appellants also claimed that TI policy favored protection of its research and development efforts through the patent process, as opposed to trade secret designation. Further, appellants allege that the programs that are the subject of the instant

case were not listed in the TI register of trade secrets and that TI was lax in implementing its standard procedures with regard to notifying employees of trade secrets within the company. The precise issue before us in the case *sub judice* is one of the first impression in Texas, to wit: what constitutes requisite "measures" to protect trade secret status?

We now determine whether the information disclosed with TI's permission or encouragement, such as published articles, seminar papers, speeches given at public meetings, information provided to government agencies, etc., was so extensive as to destroy any trade secret status that may have existed regarding the computer software which is the subject of the instant indictments. It is axiomatic that the core element of a trade secret must be that it remain a secret. However, absolute secrecy is not required.

A trade secret can exist in a combination of characteristics and components, each of which, by itself, is in the public domain, but the unified process and operation of which, in unique combination, affords a competitive advantage and is a protectable secret. We find based on the record in this case that the limited disclosure made by TI in regard to the speech research lab activities merely described the application and configuration of the certain elements of the software but did not reveal the actual composition of the programs. The measures used by TI to secure its premises to prevent unauthorized personnel from admission to or exposure to its proprietary research data were reasonable under the circumstances.

We need not decide today whether any one of the preventive measures listed, standing alone, is factually sufficient to support trade secret status. We do find that the combination of employment agreements, strict plant security, restricted computer access, the non-authorization of disclosure of the subject programs and the general non-disclosure of those programs by TI and its employees served to support trade secret status of the computer programs that are the subject of the instant indictments. Appellants neither requested nor received permission to copy the files containing these programs. The unauthorized copying of the article representing a trade secret constitutes an offense under V.T.C.A. Penal Code §31.05(b)(2).

Therefore we affirm the court of appeals' ruling that the subject programs are trade secrets.

CASE A.8

Ramirez v. Plough, Inc.
15 Cal. App. 4th 1110, 12 Cal. Rptr. 2d 423 (1992)
Court of Appeal of California
Thaxter, Judge

Jorge Ramirez, a minor, by his guardian ad litem Rosa Rivera, appeals from a summary judgment in favor of Plough, Inc. Appellant sued Plough alleging negligence, product liability, and fraud. The action sought damages for injuries sustained in March of 1986 when Jorge, who was then four months old, contracted Reye's Syndrome after ingesting St. Joseph Aspirin for Children (SJAC). Plough marketed and distributed SJAC.

Reye's Syndrome is a serious disease of unknown cause characterized by severe vomiting, lethargy, or irritability which may progress to delirium or coma. The disease generally strikes children or teenagers who are recovering from a mild respiratory tract infection, influenza, chicken pox, or other viral illnesses. The mortality rate of the disease is high, and permanent brain damage occurs in many cases. As a result of contracting Reye's Syndrome, appellant suffered catastrophic injuries including quadriplegia, blindness, and profound mental retardation.

In the early 1980's, there was significant scientific debate concerning the cause of Reye's syndrome. Several state studies suggested a statistical association between the ingestion of aspirin and the disease. In December 1982, the federal government acknowledged the debate. After considering the state studies and their critics, the federal government rejected a proposal which would require a warning label and instead, undertook an independent study. Apparently, Plough participated in efforts to influence government officials and agencies to reject the label proposal which Plough considered premature.

In December 1985, the Food and Drug Administration (FDA) requested that aspirin manufacturers voluntarily place a label on aspirin products warning consumers of the possible association between aspirin and Reye's Syndrome. Plough voluntarily complied and began including a warning and insert in SJAC packaging. On June 5, 1986, the Reye's Syndrome warning became mandatory.

In March 1986, SJAC labeling bore the following warning: "Warning: Reye's Syndrome is a rare but serious disease which can follow flu or chicken pox in children and teenagers. While the cause of Reye's Syndrome is unknown, some reports claim aspirin may increase the risk of developing this disease. Consult a doctor before use in children or teenagers with flu or chicken pox." In addition, the SJAC package insert included the following statement: "The symptoms of Reye's Syndrome can include persistent vomiting, sleepiness and lethargy, violent headaches, unusual behavior, including disorientation, combativeness, and delirium. If any of these symptoms occur, especially following chicken pox or flu, call your doctor immediately, even if your child has not taken any medication. Reye's Syndrome is Serious, so Early Detection and Treatment are Vital."

Rosa Rivera purchased SJAC on March 12, 1986, and administered it to appellant who was suffering from what appeared to be a cold or upper respiratory infection. She gave appellant the aspirin without reading the directions or warnings appearing on the SJAC packaging. The packaging was in English and Ms. Rivera can speak and understand only Spanish. She did not seek to have the directions or warnings translated from English to Spanish, even though members of her household spoke English.

The trial court granted Plough's motion for summary judgment on the grounds that "there is no duty to warn in a foreign language and there is no causal relationship between plaintiff's injury and defendant's activities."

It is undisputed SJAC was marketed and intended for the treatment of minor aches and pains associated with colds, flu, and minor viral illnesses. The SJAC box promised "fast, effective relief of fever and minor aches and pains of colds." Both parties accept the premise that Plough had a duty to warn consumers that the intended use of SJAC after a viral infection or chicken pox could lead to Reye's Syndrome, an illness with serious, possibly fatal, consequences. In March 1986, federal regulations requiring a Reye's Syndrome warning had been promulgated and were final, although not yet effective. The FDA had previously solicited voluntary labeling. In response to the request for voluntary labeling, Plough started packaging SJAC with explicit warnings of the risks of Reye's Syndrome. The scientific community had already confirmed and documented the relationship between Reye's Syndrome and the use of aspirin after a viral illness. There is no doubt Plough had a duty to warn of the Reye's Syndrome risk.

The question thus is whether the warning given only in English was adequate under the circumstances. Respondent argues that as a matter of law it has no duty to place foreign-language warnings on products manufactured to be sold in the United States and that holding manufacturers liable for failing to do so would violate public policy.

While the constitutional, statutory, regulatory, and judicial authorities relied on by respondent may reflect a public policy recognizing the status of English as an official language, nothing compels the conclusion that a manufacturer of a dangerous or defective product is immunized from liability when an English-only warning does not adequately inform non-English literate persons likely to use the product.

Plough's evidence showed that over 148 foreign languages are spoken in the United States and over 23 million Americans speak a language other than English in their homes. That evidence plainly does not prove that Plough used reasonable care in giving an English-only warning. Plough, then, resorts to arguing that the burden on manufacturers and society of requiring additional warnings is so "staggering" that the courts should preclude liability as a matter of law. We are not persuaded.

Certainly the burden and costs of giving foreign-language warnings is one factor for consideration in determining whether a manufacturer acted reasonably in using only English. The importance of that factor may vary from case to case depending upon other circumstances, such as the nature of the product, marketing efforts directed to segments of the population unlikely to be English-literate, and the actual and relative size of the consumer market which could reasonably be expected to speak or read only a certain foreign language. Plough presented no evidence from which we can gauge the extent of the burden under the facts of this case.

Ramirez submitted evidence that Plough knew Hispanics were an important part of the market for SJAC and that Hispanics often maintain their first language rather than learn English. SJAC was advertised in the Spanish media, both radio and television. That evidence raises material questions of fact concerning the foreseeability of purchase by a Hispanic not literate in English and the reasonableness of not giving a Spanish-language warning. If Plough has evidence conclusively showing that it would have been unreasonable to give its label warning in Spanish because of the burden, it did not present that evidence below.

Given the triable issues of material fact, if we accepted Plough's arguments in this case in effect we would be holding that failure to warn in a foreign language is not negligence, regardless of the circumstances. Such a sweeping grant of immunity should come from the legislative branch of government, not the judicial. In deciding that Plough did not establish its right to judgment as a matter of law, we do not hold that manufacturers are required to warn in languages other than English simply because it may be foreseeable that nonEnglish literate persons are likely to use their products. Our decision merely recognizes that under some circumstances the standard of due care may require such warning.

Because the evidence shows triable issues of material fact and because Plough did not establish its immunity from liability as a matter of law, its motion for summary judgment should have been denied.

$\mathcal{C}$ASE A.9
Mark Realty, Inc. v. Rogness 418 So.2d 373 (1982)
District Court of Appeal of Florida
Cowart, Judge

Tilman A. Rogness, owner, entered into four separate agreements with Mark Realty, Inc., a real estate broker. They were entitled "exclusive right of sale" and gave the broker, for a stated period of time, the exclusive right to sell the property for a certain stated price and on certain terms. The broker sued on the four agreements for brokerage commissions, alleging that during the time provided in the agreements the owner had conveyed the four properties. The owner's answer alleged affirmative defenses to the effect that the owner had "canceled, revoked and terminated" the brokerage agreements before the properties were sold and that the broker had never performed under the agreements.

The trial judge construed the brokerage agreements to constitute mere offers to enter into unilateral contracts under which the broker would be entitled to a commission only if he performed by "finding a purchaser of the above property." If the documents in question are merely offers limited to acceptance by performance only, the trial judge's analysis and conclusion would be correct.

We cannot agree that the documents were only offers for a unilateral contract. The documents illustrate what has been termed "the usual practice" in the making of bargains. One party indicates what he will do and what he requires in exchange and the other then agrees. These documents, when first executed by the owner and tendered to the broker, constituted offers which, when accepted by the broker by his execution, constituted contracts. The contract is bilateral because it contains mutual promises made in exchange for each other by each of the two contracting parties.

The most common recurring brokerage transaction is one in which the owner employs a broker to find a purchaser able and willing to buy, on terms stated in advance by the owner, and in which the owner promises to pay a specific commission for the service. Such a transaction as this is an offer by the owner of a unilateral contract, an offered promise to pay by the owner, creating in the broker a power of accepting the offer by actual rendition of the requested services. The only contemplated contract between the owner and broker is a unilateral contract—a promise to pay a commission for services rendered. Such an offer of a promise to pay a commission for services rendered is revocable by the owner by notice before the broker has rendered any part of the requested service. On the other hand, the transaction between the owner and the broker can be a bilateral contract. An owner who puts his land in the hands of a broker for sale usually clearly promises to pay a commission but the broker rarely promises in return that he will produce a purchaser, although he often promises, expressly or impliedly, that he will make certain efforts to do so. If the parties have thus made mutual promises, the transaction no longer has the status of an unaccepted offer—there is an existing bilateral contract and neither party has a power of revocation. During the term of such a contract the owner may withdraw any power the owner has given the broker to contract with a third party in the owner's name, but this is not a revocation of the contract between the owner and the broker and normally such action constitutes a breach of the brokerage contract.

In this case, the broker promised to inspect the property, to list the property with a multiple listing service, to advertise the property in the local newspaper or other media, to furnish information to inquiring cooperating brokers and prospective purchasers, to show the property, to make efforts to find a purchaser, to "make an earnest and continued effort to sell," and to direct the concentrated efforts of his organization in bringing about a sale.

In the instant case, the contract clearly provided that the brokerage commission would be paid "whether the purchaser be secured by you or me, or by any other person." Thus the contract granted the broker an exclusive right of sale and the trial court erred in construing the agreement as an offer of a unilateral contract revocable at will at any time prior to performance.

The final judgment is reversed.

$\mathcal{C}$ASE A.10
Traco, Inc. v. Arrow Glass Co., Inc.
814 S.W. 2d 186 (1991)
Court of Appeals of Texas
Chapa, Justice

This is a construction dispute stemming from a quotation given by Traco, Inc., a Three Rivers Aluminum Company, a material supplier of pre-engineered aluminum and glass sliding doors and windows, to Arrow Glass Company, Inc., a subcontractor, in connection with the USAA Towers project in San Antonio, Texas. Arrow initially brought suit against Traco on the theories of promissory, estoppel and negligence for Traco's failure to supply aluminum and glass sliding doors at the quoted price. After a bench trial, the trial court held for Arrow solely under the theory of promissory estoppel and awarded Arrow judgment against Traco for damages in the amount of $75,843.38, plus attorneys' fees and prejudgment interest.

The facts of this case reflect that on or about October 9, 1986, construction bids were due for the USAA Towers, a $49,000,000 retirement housing project located near Fort Sam Houston, Texas. There were numerous suppliers, subcontractors and general contractors bidding to obtain work on this project including the appellant, Traco, and the appellee, Arrow.

On bid day, a representative for Arrow received a telephone call from Dale Ferrar of Traco. Mr. Ferrar told Bill Morris, the general manager of Arrow Glass, that Traco was a very large window and sliding glass aluminum door manufacturer in Pennsylvania. Mr. Ferrar offered its A-2 aluminum and glass sliding doors, as an alternate product substitution, to Arrow, which was bidding that portion of the project. However, after some discussion of the required specifications, the parties realized that Traco's doors would have to be modified in order to comply with the project specifications. Arrow declined to use Traco's bid and, instead, submitted its original bid, using a different supplier of doors. At approximately noon on bid day, Mr. Ferrar phoned Mr. Morris, quoting a new price for the doors which included a modification of the frame depth which, supposedly, enabled the doors to comply with the specifications. At this time, Mr. Morris informed Mr. Ferrar that his bid was low and asked him to recheck his figures. Mr. Ferrar explained that because of Traco's size and the fact that it could manufacture its products under one roof, Traco could sell the project for that amount. Mr. Ferrar also indicated that Traco was seeking a high profile project to represent Traco in the San Antonio area.

After receiving these assurances, Mr. Morris told Mr. Ferrar that he was going to use Traco's bid. Mr. Morris then phoned the contractors to whom he had originally submitted his bid, and deducted $100,000 in reliance upon Traco's bid. Mr. Morris later told Mr. Ferrar that he had received favorable responses from three or four general contractors, and that it appeared Arrow would get the project. Mr. Morris advised Mr. Ferrar that if Arrow obtained the project, then Traco would be awarded the contract on the doors.

The oral quote by Trico was followed with a written bid confirmation on the next day, which reflected the product that would be supplied and the price agreed upon by the parties. The confirmation also included the 1-¼″ frame extended at a cost of $27,860, which, allegedly, brought the doors into compliance with the project specifications.

Sometime in November, long after Mr. Morris had relied upon Mr. Ferrar's representations in submitting his bid, Mr. Morris began hearing rumors that there was a problem with the doors. Mr. Morris contacted Mr. Ferrar, who admitted that there was a problem with the doors meeting the architect's wind load deflection requirement in the specifications. Shortly after learning of this problem, Mr. Morris received a second quote from Traco, wherein Traco offered its A-3 doors, which were a more expensive, heavy grade commercial door that met the deflection requirement, for a price of $304,300. After receiving this bid, Morris objected to the price and demanded that Traco deliver doors meeting the project specifications at the original price quoted. Traco refused and when it became obvious that Arrow would not be able to use Traco's product, Mr. Morris contracted with another supplier who had bid on the project.

The record clearly reflects the following: that it was Traco that initially contacted Arrow and offered to do a certain specific act, i.e., supply the sliding doors required; that Mr. Ferrar phoned Mr. Morris on several occasions and discussed, among other things, the fact that the doors which Traco wished to bid would not comply with the specifications without some modification; and, that Mr. Ferrar assured Mr. Morris that the doors could be modified to comply with the specifications. Thus, under the present facts, Traco's bid gave Arrow "a right to expect or claim the performance of some particular thing"; specifically, Traco's bid constituted a promise to supply sliding doors meeting the project specifications at a specified price.

Appellant initially argues that the trial court erred in rendering judgment for Arrow because Traco's bid was revocable and properly withdrawn thirty days after it was made. Appellant primarily relies upon the argument that its sliding doors are goods as defined by the Texas Business and Commerce Code. Nevertheless, appellant's arguments ignore the appellee's basic contention and legal theory under which this suit was brought. Appellee sought relief under the equitable doctrine of promissory estoppel, on the premise that appellant's promises, by way of its *oral* bid, caused appellee to substantially rely to its detriment. The appellee relied to its detriment when it reduced its bid based on a telephone conversation with the appellant, prior to the time appellant's confirmation letter was sent or received. We must now resolve whether the equitable theory of promissory estoppel applies to bid construction cases and, if so, whether this doctrine applies under the specific facts of this case. While no Texas case has previously applied the theory of promissory estoppel in a bid construction case, other jurisdictions have consistently applied this doctrine under similar facts, recognizing the necessity for equity in view of the lack of other remedies.

The Texas Supreme Court, in emphasizing that the underlying function of the theory of promissory estoppel is to promote equity, has stated that: "The vital principle is that he who by his language or conduct leads another to do what he would not otherwise have done, shall not subject such person to loss or injury by disappointing the expectations, upon which he acted. This remedy is always so applied as to promote the ends of justice." Clearly promissory estoppel is "a rule of equity" applied to prevent injustice. As is true in most, if not all, bid construction cases, the present situation does not involve a contract. Therefore, were we to hold that promissory estoppel does not exist in bid construction cases, this would necessarily mean that, notwithstanding any language or conduct by the subcontractor which leads the general contractor to do that which he would not otherwise have done and, thereby, incur loss or injury, the general contractor would be denied all relief. This proposition is untenable and conflicts with the underlying premise of promissory estoppel.

Section 90 of the STATEMENT (SECOND) OF CONTRACTS (1981) states the principle of promissory estoppel as follows: "A promise which the promisor should reasonably expect to induce action or forbearance on the part of the promisee or a third person and which does induce such action or forbearance is binding if injustice can be avoided only by enforcement of the promise." Accordingly, the requirements of promissory estoppel are: "(1) a promise, (2) foreseeability of reliance thereon by the promisor, and (3) substantial reliance by the promisee to his detriment." In order to invoke the doctrine of estoppel, all the necessary elements of estoppel must be present and the failure to establish even one of these elements is fatal to the claimant's cause of action.

Appellant insists, however, that because Traco was not an approved manufacturer and bid its doors as an alternate, that by its nature, Traco's bid was conditional and, therefore, promissory estoppel cannot lie. We fail to see how a bid for a specific door at a specific price, which was submitted in response to solicitations that detailed project specifications, is contingent, or somehow not final, merely because the wrong door was bid upon. The appellant's failure to receive the architect's approval was not due to new specifications but was caused by the appellant's failure to regard those specifications originally required when the appellant offered its doors. Appellant's point is rejected.

Notwithstanding the existence of this promise, the appellant argues that appellee could not have justifiably and reasonably relied upon appellant's bid because: Traco was not an approved manufacturer and bid its A-2 doors as an alternate and, further, Traco's bid was lower than the other suppliers who bid upon the contract.

Because of the withdrawal of Traco's bid, Arrow was compelled to seek another supplier of doors at a much greater cost; clearly, this constituted an injustice to the appellee. Additionally, appellee's reliance upon appellant's bid was reasonable in view of the appellant's attempts to modify its doors, and Mr. Ferrar's assurances that the doors, as modified, would meet the project specifications.

We hold that the controlling findings of fact support the promissory estoppel theory.

The judgment is affirmed.

CASE A.11

Congregation Kadimah Toras-Moshe v. DeLeo
540 N.E.2d 691 (1989)
Supreme Judicial Court of Massachusetts
Liacos, Chief Justice

Congregation Kadimah Toras-Moshe (Congregation), an Orthodox Jewish synagogue, commenced this action in the Superior Court to compel the administrator of an estate (estate) to fulfill the oral promise of the decedent to give the Congregation $25,000. The Superior Court transferred the case to the Boston Municipal Court, which rendered summary judgment for the estate. The case was then transferred back to the Superior Court, which also rendered summary judgment for the

estate and dismissed the Congregation's complaint. We granted the Congregation's application for direct appellate review. We now affirm. The facts are not contested. The decedent suffered a prolonged illness, throughout which he was visited by the Congregation's spiritual leader, Rabbi Abraham Halbfinger. During four or five of these visits, and in the presence of witnesses, the decedent made an oral promise to give the Congregation $25,000. The Congregation planned to use the $25,000 to transform a storage room in the synagogue into a library named after the decedent. The oral promise was never reduced to writing. The decedent died intestate in September, 1985. He had no children, but was survived by his wife. The Congregation asserts that the decedent's oral promise is an enforceable contract under our case law, because the promise is allegedly supported either by consideration and bargain, or by reliance. The Superior Court judge determined that "this was an oral gratuitous pledge, with no indication as to how the money should be used, or what [the Congregation] was required to do if anything in return for this promise." There was no legal benefit to the promisor nor detriment to the promisee, and thus no consideration. Moral obligation is not legal obligation. Furthermore, there is no evidence in the record that the Congregation's plans to name a library after the decedent induced him to make or to renew his promise. As to the lack of reliance, the judge stated that the Congregation's "allocation of $25,000 in its budget, for the purpose of renovating a storage room, is insufficient to find reliance or an enforceable obligation." We agree. The inclusion of the promised $25,000 in the budget, by itself, merely reduced to writing the Congregation's expectation that it would have additional funds. A hope or expectation, even though well founded, is not equivalent to either legal detriment or reliance.

We are of the opinion that in this case there is no injustice in declining decedent's promise. The promise to the Congregation is entirely unsupported by consideration or reliance. To enforce such a promise would be against public policy.

Judgment affirmed.

CASE A.12

Carnival Leisure Industries, Ltd. v. Aubin
938 F.2d 624 (1991)
United States Court of Appeals, Fifth Circuit
Garwood, Circuit Judge

During a January 1987 visit to the Bahamas, George J. Aubin, a Texas resident, visited Cable Beach Hotel and Casino (the Casino), which was owned and operated by Carnival Leisure Industries, Ltd. (Carnival Leisure). While gambling at the Casino, Aubin received markers or chips from the Casino and the Casino received drafts drawn on Aubin's bank accounts in Texas. Aubin spent all of the markers provided on gambling, although he could also have spent them on food, beverages, souvenirs, or lodging at the Casino. Aubin ultimately gambled and lost $25,000, leaving the Casino with the same amount in bank drafts.

Carnival Leisure was unable to cash the bank drafts because Aubin had subsequently directed his bank to stop payment.

Carnival Leisure sued Aubin in the United States District Court for the Southern District of Texas to enforce the debt. The district court granted Carnival Leisure's motion for summary judgment against Aubin in the amount of $25,000 and attorney's fees and costs. Carnival Leisure claimed that the debt was enforceable under Texas law because public policy had changed and now favored enforcement of gambling debts. The district court agreed. Aubin raises on appeal only the issue of whether public policy in Texas continues to prevent the enforcement of gambling debts.

Carnival Leisure claims, however, that since 1973 the public policy of Texas toward gambling and the legality of gambling debts has changed. Although gambling is generally proscribed in Texas, there has been an exception for the "social" gambler since 1973. The Texas legislature enacted the Bingo Enabling Act in 1981, the Texas Racing Act in 1986, and the Charitable Raffle Enabling Act in 1989. Provisions were added to the Texas Penal Code excepting these three activities from its general proscription against gambling.

The enactment of statutes legalizing some forms of gambling admittedly evidences some dissipation or narrowing of public disapproval of gambling. However, such statutes hardly introduce a judicially cognizable change in public policy with respect to gambling generally. The social gambling permitted is confined to private places where no one receives any benefit other than his personal winnings and all participants are subject to the same risks, a categorically vastly different kind of activity from the sort involved here. The racing, bingo, and raffling exceptions are narrow, strictly regulated exceptions to a broad public policy in Texas against most forms of gambling. Further, the kind of gambling engaged in here is not of the sort permitted by any of these exceptions.

Even if gambling legislation in Texas were evidence sufficient to warrant judicial notice of a shift in public policy with respect to legalized gambling, such a shift would not be inconsistent with a continued public policy disfavoring gambling on credit. Although Aubin could have used the loaned markers for non-gambling purposes at the Casino, it is undisputed that they were in fact used exclusively for gambling. Aubin's gambling debt therefore fits squarely within the terms of the public policy of Texas prohibiting enforcement of gambling debts owed to gambling participants incurred for the purpose of gambling.

We hold that the public policy in Texas against gambling on credit prevents enforcement of a debt incurred for the purpose of gambling and provided by a participant in the gambling activity. The district court's grant of summary judgment in favor of Carnival Leisure is accordingly reversed and this case is remanded to the district court for further proceedings consistent with this opinion.

$\mathcal{C}$ASE A.13
Continental Airlines, Inc. v. McDonnell Douglas Corporation
216 Cal.App.3d 388, 264 Cal.Rptr. 779 (1990)
Court of Appeals of California
Hoffman, Associate Justice

This action was commenced by plaintiff and respondent Continental Airlines (Continental) in Los Angeles Superior Court on December 3, 1979, and alleged, against defendant and appellant McDonnell Douglas Corporation (Douglas), causes of action for deceit. On January 30, 1986, the jury returned verdicts in favor of Continental for $17 million on its claims for fraud by misrepresentation and fraud by nondisclosure of known facts. The judgment was granted. This appeal is from that judgment. We affirm the judgment as modified.

On March 1, 1978, a Continental DC-10 aircraft, which had been delivered to Continental by Douglas in 1972, was in its takeoff roll at Los Angeles International Airport when two tires burst on the left landing gear. The captain elected to try to stop the plane, but it ran off the end of the runway at 8 miles per hour. The landing gear broke through the tarmac, burrowed into the ground, and was ripped from the wing, making a 3.7 foot hole which allowed fuel to pour from the wing fuel tanks. The plane was severely damaged by the resulting fire and rendered unrepairable.

Douglas had approached Continental in 1968 to sell Continental DC-10 aircraft. Douglas used a series of briefings and sales brochures in its sales campaign. The sales brochure given to Continental consisted of hundreds of pages of technical information drafted by Douglas' engineers, and reviewed by its top management, for the express purpose of explaining the DC-10 design and a "Detail Type Specification" to potential aircraft purchasers. That Specification, as its name implies, described the technical details of the DC-10. The Douglas briefings covered the landing gear and wing design, as did many of its brochures. Continental personnel used the brochures to write portions of Continental's "Tri-Jet Evaluation," a comparison between the DC-10 and Lockheed's L-1011, which became a basis for Continental's decision to purchase the DC-10. When Continental decided to purchase the DC-10, instead of the L-1011 aircraft, it finalized a Purchase Agreement with Douglas which incorporated by reference the Detail Specification for the DC-10.

The brochures contained statements that "the fuel tank will not rupture under crash load conditions"; that the landing gear "are designed for wipe-off without rupturing the wing fuel tank"; that "the support structure is designed to a higher strength than the gear to prevent fuel tank rupture due to an accidental landing gear overload"; that the DC-10 "is designed and tested for crash-worthiness"; that the "landing gear will be tested" to demonstrate the fail safe integrity and wipe-off characteristics of the gear design; and that "good reliability" for the DC-10 landing gear could be predicted with an "unusually high degree of confidence" because of its close similarity to the successful design on the DC-8 and DC-9 aircraft.

Douglas argues that "the Uniform Commercial Code and cases interpreting it have recognized that general promotional observations of this type are merely expressions of opinion that are not actionable as fraudulent statements. The alleged false representations in the subject brochures were not statements of "opinion or mere puffing." They were, in essence, representations that the DC-10 was a safe aircraft. Promises of safety are not statements of opinion—they are representations of fact.

Douglas contends in its opening brief that there was no substantial evidence that its pre-contract representations were *mater-*

ial or that Continental reasonably *relied* on them in deciding to purchase the DC-10. The materiality of the representations can hardly be questioned. Any airline shopping for aircraft to service its customers naturally searches for planes that are safe. Where representations have been made in regard to a material matter and action has been taken, in the absence of evidence showing the contrary, reliance on the representations will be presumed. Here, both materiality and reliance are demonstrated by the fact that Continental evaluated the DC-10 breakaway design in its "Tri-Jet Evaluation," which compared the DC-10 with the L-1011 for the purpose of deciding which aircraft to purchase. Douglas was the only possible source for the information; there was no way Continental could independently investigate or analyze the adequacy of that design. The foregoing provides more than substantial evidence that Continental *relied* on Douglas' representations regarding landing gear breakaway in choosing to purchase the DC-10 and that those representations were *material.*

False representations made recklessly and without regard for their truth in order to induce action by another are equivalent of misrepresentations uttered. Therefore, there is substantial evidence of the requisite intent for intentional fraud. For the forgoing reasons we conclude the evidence supports the jury's findings of liability for fraud. The judgment is modified to reflect an award of prejudgment interest in the amount of $9,549,750. As so modified, the judgment is affirmed.

CASE A.14

Hampton v. Federal Express Corporation
917 F.2d 1119 (1990)
United States Court of Appeals, Eighth Circuit
Re, Chief Judge

In March, 1988, Carl Gerome Hampton, a 13-year-old cancer patient at Children's Memorial Hospital in Omaha, Nebraska, was awaiting a bone marrow transplant. A transplant operation was scheduled at the University of Iowa Hospital in Iowa City, Iowa, where five potential bone marrow donors had been found. On March 21, 1988, in order to match Carl with the most suitable donor, five samples of Carl's blood were sent by the shipper, the Children's Memorial Hospital in Omaha, to Dr. Nancy Goeken, at the Veterans Administration Medical Center in Iowa City. The shipper, the Children's Memorial Hospital, entered into a contract with the carrier, Federal Express, for the transport of the blood samples.

In a paragraph entitled "Damages or Loss," the contract of carriage, set forth in the airbill, stated: "We are liable for no more than $100 per package in the event of physical loss or damage, unless you fill in a higher Declared Value to the left and document higher actual loss in the event of a claim. We charge 30 cents for each additional $100 of declared value up to the maximum shown in our Service Guide." The reverse side of the airbill contains several paragraphs, entitled "Limitations On Our Liability," which state that: "Our liability for loss or damage to your package is limited to your actual damages or $100,

whichever is less, unless you pay for and declare a higher authorized value." It is not disputed that the blood samples were never received by Dr. Goeken, that Carl Hampton, the infant cancer patient, never obtained a bone marrow transplant, and that he died on May 19, 1988. Alleging causes of action for personal injury, wrongful death, and loss of services, Carl Jerry Hampton, individually and on behalf of his deceased son, Carl Gerome Hampton, filed suit in the United States District Court for the Western District of Missouri, seeking $3,081,000 in damages. The district court granted Federal Express' motion for partial summary judgment, and entered judgment in favor of Hampton for $100. Hampton appeals from judgment of the district court.

We have held that, under federal common law, " a common carrier may not exempt itself from liability for its negligence; however, a carrier may limit its liability." *Hopper Furs, Inc. v. Emery Air Freight Corp.,* 749 F.2d 1261, 1264 (8th Cir. 1984).

In this case, the contract entered into by the shipper, the Children's Memorial Hospital, with the carrier, Federal Express, clearly limited the liability of the carrier to $100, and provided the shipper with an opportunity to declare a higher value. Furthermore, it is not disputed that the shipper never declared a higher value for the blood samples. Hence, the liability of the carrier would be limited to $100. Clearly, Federal Express had no knowledge of Hampton, and did not know that the package contained blood samples. It is equally clear that the shipper, Children's Memorial Hospital, did not declare a value higher than $100 for the package. Under these circumstances, Federal Express could not reasonably foresee any injury to Hampton, or the nature and extent of the injury.

Since, on the facts presented, the nature and extent of damages suffered by plaintiff Hampton were not reasonably foreseeable to the carrier, Federal Express, we affirm the judgment of the district court granting Federal Express' motion for partial summary judgment.

CASE A.15

Chase Precast Corporation v. John J. Paonessa Co., Inc.
409 Mass. 371, 566 N.E. 2d 603 (1991)
Supreme Judicial Court of Massachusetts
Lynch, Justice

This appeal raises the question whether the doctrine of frustration of purpose may be a defense in a breach of contract action in Massachusetts, and, if so, whether it excuses the defendant John J. Paonessa Company, Inc. (Paonessa) from performance.

The claim of the plaintiff, Chase Precast Corporation (Chase), arises from the cancellation of its contracts with Paonessa to supply median barriers in a highway construction project of the Commonwealth. Chase brought an action to recover its anticipated profit on the amount of the media barriers called for by its supply contracts with Paonessa but not produced. Paonessa brought a cross action against the Commonwealth for indemnification in the event it should be held liable to Chase. After a jury-waived trial, a Superior Court judge ruled for

Paonessa on the basis of impossibility of performance. Chase and Paonessa cross appealed. The Appeals Court affirmed, noting that the doctrine of frustration of purpose more accurately described the basis of the trial judge's decision than the doctrine of impossibility. We agree. We allowed Chase's application for further appellate review and we now affirm.

The pertinent facts are as follows. In 1982, the Commonwealth, through the Department of Public Works (department), entered into two contracts with Paonessa for resurfacing and improvements to two stretches of Route 128. Part of each contract called for replacing a grass median strip between the north and southbound lanes with concrete resurfacing and precast concrete median barriers. Paonessa entered into two contracts with Chase under which Chase was to supply, in the aggregate, 25,800 linear feet of concrete median barriers according to the specifications of the department for highway construction. The quantity and type of barriers to be supplied were specified in two purchase orders prepared by Chase.

The highway reconstruction began in the Spring of 1983. By late May, the department was receiving protests from angry residents who objected to use of the concrete barriers and removal of the grass median strip. Paonessa and Chase became aware of the protest around June 1. On June 6, a group of about 100 citizens filed an action in the Superior Court to stop installation of the concrete barriers and other aspects of the work. On June 7, anticipating modification by the department, Paonessa notified Chase by letter to stop producing concrete barriers for the projects. Chase did so upon receipt of letter the following day. On June 17, the department and the citizen's group entered into a settlement which provided, in part, that no additional concrete median barriers would be installed. On June 23, the department deleted the permanent concrete median barriers item from its contracts with Paonessa.

Before stopping production on June 8, Chase had produced approximately one-half of the concrete median barriers called for by its contracts with Paonessa, and had delivered most of them to the construction sites. Paonessa paid Chase for all that it had produced, at the contract price. Chase suffered no out-of-pocket expense as a result of cancellation of the remaining portion of barriers.

This court has long recognized and applied the doctrine of impossibility as a defense to an action of breach of contract. Under that doctrine, "where from the nature of the contract it appears that the parties must from the beginning have contemplated the continued existence of some particular specified thing as the foundation of what was to be done, then, in the absence of any warranty that the thing shall exist ... the parties shall be excused ... when[cb] performance becomes impossible from the accidental perishing of the thing without the fault of either party."

On the other hand, although we have referred to the doctrine of frustration of purpose in a few decisions, we have never clearly defined it. Other jurisdictions have explained the doctrine as follows: when an event neither anticipated nor caused by either party, the risk of which was not allocated by the contract, destroys the object or purpose of the contract, thus destroying

the value of performance, the parties are excused from further performance.

In *Mishara Construction Co.*, we called frustration of purpose a "companion rule" to the doctrine of impossibility. Both doctrines concern the effect of supervening circumstances upon the rights and duties of the parties. The difference lies in the effect of the supervening event. Another definition of frustration of purpose is found in the Restatement (Second) of Contracts §265 (1981). "Where, after a contract is made, a party's principal purpose is substantially frustrated without his fault by the occurrence of an event the nonoccurrence of which was a basic assumption on which the contract was made, his remaining duties to render performance are discharged, unless the language or the circumstances indicate the contrary."

Paonessa bore no responsibility for the department's elimination of the median barriers from the projects. Therefore, whether it can rely on the defense of frustration turns on whether elimination of the barriers was a risk allocated by the contracts to Paonessa. The question is, given the commercial circumstances in which the parties dealt: "Was the contingency which developed one which the parties could reasonably be thought to have foreseen as a real possibility which could affect performance? Was it one of that variety of risks which the parties were tacitly assigning to the promisor by their failure to provide for it explicitly? If it was, performance will be required. If it could not be considered, performance is excused."

The record supports the conclusion that Chase was aware of the department's power to decrease quantities of contract items. The Judge found that Chase had been a supplier of median barriers to the department in the past. The provision giving the department the power to eliminate items or portions thereof was standard in its contracts. The Judge's finding that all parties were well aware that lost profits were not an element of damage in either of the public works projects in issue further supports the conclusion that Chase was aware of the department's power to decrease quantities, since the term prohibiting claims for anticipated profit is part of the same sentence in the standard provision as that allowing the engineer to eliminate items or portions of work. In this case, even if the parties were aware generally of the department's power to eliminate contract items, the judge could reasonably have concluded that they did not contemplate the cancellation for a major portion of the project of such a widely used item as concrete median barriers, and did not allocate the risk of such cancellations.

Judgment affirmed.

CASE A.16

E.B. Harvey & Company, Inc. v. Protective Systems, Inc.
1989 Tenn. App. Lexis 105 (1989)
Court of Appeals of Tennessee
Sanders, Presiding Judge

The plaintiff-appellant, E.B. Harvey Company, Inc. (Harvey), is engaged in the manufacture and wholesale of fine jewelry in Chattanooga. It has been engaged in this business for about 10 years. It maintains an inventory in excess of $1 million of gold, silver, precious stones, pearls, and other such materials related to the manufacture of jewelry. A considerable amount of its jewelry is on consignment and, by the very nature of its business, it requires a great deal of insurance. However, the insurance companies will not write the insurance unless it maintains an Underwriters Laboratories (U.L.)-approved AA burglary protection alarm system. The defendant-appellee, Protective Systems, Inc. (Protective), is one of two companies in Hamilton County which furnishes and maintains a U.L.-approved AA burglar protection system. In June, 1981, Harvey entered into a three year contract with Protective to install and maintain a burglar protection system. The contract provided:

It is agreed that Protective is not an insurer and that the payments hereinbefore named are based solely upon the value of the services herein described and it is not the intention of the parties that Protective assume responsibility for any losses occasioned by malfeasance or misfeasance in the performance of the services under this contract or for any loss or damage sustained through burglary, theft, robbery, fire or other cause or any liability on the part of Protective by virtue of this Agreement or because of the relation hereby established.

If there shall at any time be or arise any liability on the part of Protective, by virtue of this Agreement or because of the relation hereby established, whether due to the negligence of Protective or otherwise, such liability is and shall be limited to a sum total in amount to the rental service charge hereunder for a period of service not to exceed six months, which sum shall be paid and received as liquidated damages.

The burglary and hold-up system provided to Harvey operated by means of Grade AA telephone lines between the central monitoring station of Protective and Harvey's premises. Said telephone lines were at all times owned and maintained by the South Central Bell Telephone Company. On July 22, 1984, at 11:14 P.M., an outage condition was indicated on the E.B. Harvey & Company account. For a period of two weeks prior to this date, Protective's computer had been registering an inordinate number of outage signals which had all been traced back to problems in telephone company equipment. For this reason, on July 22, 1984, Protective's president, Pendell Meyers, notified the telephone company of this condition and reported a potential problem to the police department but did not contact a representative of Harvey to notify them of the outage condition.

The phone company was unable to locate the exact nature of the problem despite several telephone conversations with Meyers. The Chattanooga Police Department patrolled the premises surrounding the Harvey's place of business twice that evening but did not note any unusual activity. The following morning when an employee of Harvey reported to work, it was discovered that a burglary had in fact taken place. Some $200,000 worth of jewelry and inventory was stolen. Harvey sued Protective for damages resulting from the burglary. It alleged that Protective was guilty of negligence for its failure to notify Harvey or its employees of the outage which appeared on the burglary monitoring equipment.

Protective, for answer, denied the allegations of Harvey's complaint and, as an affirmative defense, alleged the contract between the parties with its exculpatory and limitation of liability provisions was enforceable and binding upon Harvey. After hearing testimony, the trial court held the extent of Harvey's recovery against Protective would be 650% as liquidated damages. A final judgment was entered and Harvey has appealed.

There is nothing in public policy to render inoperative or nugatory the contractual limitations contained in the agreement. Limitations against liability for negligence or breach of contract have generally been upheld in this state in the absence of fraud or overreaching. Limitations such as those contained in the present contract have generally been deemed reasonable and have been sustained in actions against the providers of burglary and fire alarm systems. Such clauses do not ordinarily protect against liability for fraud or intentional misrepresentation.

We concur with the trial court. The issues are found in favor of the appellees. The judgment of the trial court is affirmed. The cost of this appeal is taxed to the appellant and the case is remanded to the trial court for collection of cost.

*C*ASE A.17

Feist Publications, Inc. v. Rural Telephone Service Co., Inc.
499 U.S. 340, 111 S.Ct. 1282, 113 L.Ed.2d 358 (1991)
United States Supreme Court
O'Connor, Justice

Rural Telephone Service Company is a certified public utility that provides telephone service to several communities in northwest Kansas. It is subject to a state regulation that requires all telephone companies operating in Kansas to issue annually an updated telephone directory. Accordingly, as a condition of its monopoly franchise, Rural publishes a typical telephone directory, consisting of white pages and yellow pages. The white pages list in alphabetical order the names of Rural's subscribers, together with their towns and telephone numbers. The yellow pages list Rural's business subscribers alphabetically by category and feature classified advertisements of various sizes. Rural distributes its directory free of charge to its subscribers, but earns revenue by selling yellow pages advertisements.

Feist Publications, Inc., is a publishing company that specializes in area-wide telephone directories. Unlike a typical directory, which covers only a particular calling area, Feist's area-wide directories cover a much larger geographical range, reducing the need to call directory assistance or consult multiple directories. The Feist directory that is the subject of this litigation covers 11 different telephone service areas in 15 counties and contains 46,878 white pages listings—compared to Rural's approximately 7,700 listings.

Of the 11 telephone companies, only Rural refused to license its listings to Feist. Rural's refusal created a problem for Feist, as omitting these listings would have left a gaping hole in its area-wide directory, rendering it less attractive to potential yellow pages advertisers. Unable to license Rural's white pages listings, Feist used them without Rural's consent.

Rural sued for copyright infringement in the District Court for the District of Kansas taking the position that Feist, in compiling its own directory, could not use the information contained in Rural's white pages. The District Court granted summary judgment to Rural, explaining that "courts have consistently held that telephone directories are copyrightable" and citing a string of lower court decisions. In an unpublished opinion, the Court of Appeals for the Tenth Circuit affirmed "for substantially the reasons given by the district court."

This case concerns the interaction of two well-established propositions. The first is that facts are not copyrightable; the other, that compilations of facts generally are. The key to resolving the tension lies in understanding why facts are not copyrightable. The *sine qua non* of copyright is originality. To qualify for copyright protection, a work must be original to the author. Original, as the term is used in copyright, means only that the work was independently created by the author (as opposed to copied from other works), and that it possesses at least some minimal degree of creativity.

Originality is a constitutional requirement. The source of Congress' power to enact copyright laws is Article 1, §8. C1. 8, of the Constitution, which authorizes Congress to "secure for limited Times to Authors . . . the exclusive Right to their respective Writings." It is this bedrock principle of copyright that mandates the law's seemingly disparate treatment of facts and factual compilations. No one may claim originality as to facts. This is because facts do not owe their origin to an act of authorship. The distinction is one between creation and discovery: the first person to find and report a particular fact has not created the fact; he or she has merely discovered its existence.

If the selection and arrangement of facts are original, these elements of the work are eligible for copyright protection. No matter how original the format, however, the facts themselves do not become original through association.

There is no doubt that Feist took from the white pages of Rural's directory a substantial amount of factual information. At a minimum, Feist copied the names, towns, and telephone numbers of 1,309 of Rural's subscribers. Not all copying, however, is copyright infringement, two elements must be proven: (1) ownership of a valid copyright, and (2) copying of constituent elements of the work that are original. The first element is not at issue here: Feist appears to concede that Rural's directory, considered as a whole, is subject to a valid copyright because it contains some foreword text, as well as original material in its yellow pages advertisements.

The question is whether Rural has proven the second element. In other words, did Feist, by taking 1,309 names, towns, and telephone numbers from Rural's white pages, copy anything that was "original" to Rural? Certainly, the raw data does not satisfy the originality requirement. Rural may have been the first to discover and report the names, towns, and telephone numbers of its subscribers, but this data does not "owe its origin" to Rural. The question that remains is whether Rural selected, coordinated, or arranged these copyrightable facts in an original way. The selection, coordination, and arrangement of Rural's white

pages do not satisfy the minimum constitutional standards for copyright protection. Rural's selection of listings could not be more obvious: it publishes the most basic information—name, town, and telephone number—about each person who applies to it for telephone service. This is "selection" of a sort, but it lacks the modicum of creativity necessary to transform mere selection into copyrightable expression. Rural extended sufficient effort to make the white pages directory useful, but insufficient creativity to make it original.

The judgment of the Court of Appeals is *Reversed.*

CASE A.18

Toys "R" Us, Inc. v. Abir
1999 WL 61817 (1999)
United States District Court, S.D. New York
Koeltl, Judge

In 1997, plaintiff Toys "R" Us, Inc. filed an action alleging violations of federal law related to trademark dilution against the defendants, Eli Abir and Website Management, who had registered the name *Toysareus.com* as their Internet domain name. The plaintiffs alleged that this domain name diluted the plaintiff's mark TOYS "R" US. In November 1997, this Court issued a temporary restraining order enjoining the defendants from "using or inducing others to use the names or marks or any colorable imitation of Plaintiff's TOYS "R" US, KIDS "R" US, BABIES "R" US and/or the family of "R" US marks" pending a decision on the plaintiff's motion for a preliminary injunction.

In December 1997, this Court heard argument on the motion for a preliminary injunction. At that time the plaintiffs alleged that the defendants had also registered the domain name *Kidsareus.com*. This Court then issued a preliminary injunction enjoining the defendants from, among other things, using or inducing others to use any colorable imitation of the family of "R" US marks pending final judgment. On August 27, 1998, this Court granted the plaintiff's motion for summary judgment on the trademark dilution claims. The following day, this Court issued a separate Judgment and Order permanently enjoining the defendants from further infringement of the family of "R" US marks and ordering the transfer of the *Toysareus.com* and *Kidsareus.com* Internet domain names to the plaintiff.

In addition, this Court held that because the defendants' conduct in this case was willful, intentional, deliberate, and in bad faith, the plaintiff is entitled to recover attorneys' fees and costs. In order to determine what constitutes "reasonable" attorneys' fees, the starting point is the "lodestar amount," which is the number of hours reasonably expended on the litigation multiplied by a reasonable hourly rate for attorneys and paralegals.

In determining a reasonable hourly rate, courts consider, inter alia, the size and experience of the firm. In this case, Darby & Darby is a well-known New York firm which specializes in intellectual property; the rates charged for its attorneys are comparable to other specialized intellectual property firms in the New York City legal market. The plaintiff's counsel swore in her declaration in support of this application that care was taken to enhance efficiency by assigning, at any one time, only one partner, one mid- to senior-level associate, one to two junior associates, and one to two legal assistants to the prosecution of this case. Having carefully reviewed the itemized request for disbursements, the Court finds them neither unnecessary nor excessive for a case of this duration and complexity. The plaintiff is also entitled to costs, as well as those reasonable out-of-pocket expenses incurred by the attorneys and which are normally charged fee-paying clients.

Defendant Eli Abir, who is the owner of defendant Website Management, does not argue that the award requested by the plaintiffs is excessive. Instead, he argues that due to his business and personal circumstances he has limited financial resources and would be unable to pay more than a "symbolic" amount in attorneys' fees. However, nothing in the record in this case justifies a financially-based reduction in the award of attorneys' fees and costs. For the reasons stated above, the plaintiff's motion for attorneys' fees and costs is granted in the amount of $55,162.76. SO ORDERED.

CASE A.19

Cafazzo v. Central Medical Health Services, Inc.
668 A.2d 521 (1995)
Supreme Court of Pennsylvania
Montemuro, Justice

In 1986, appellant Albert Cafazzo underwent surgery for implantation of a mandibular prosthesis. In 1992, some time after it was discovered that this device was defective, a complaint was filed against Dr. Norman Stern, the physician who performed the surgery and the hospital where the operation took place, claiming that "all defendants sell, provide or use certain prosthetic devices," and that they should be held strictly liable as having "provided, sold or otherwise placed in the stream of commerce products manufactured by Vitek, Inc., known as Proplast TMJ Implants." The complaint alleged that the prosthesis was defectively designed, unsafe for its intended use, and lacked any warning necessary in order to ensure safety.

Section 402A of the Restatement (Second) of Torts, provides in relevant part as follows:

(1) One who sells any product in a defective condition unreasonably dangerous to the user or consumer or to his property is subject to liability for physical harm thereby caused to the ultimate user or consumer, or to his property, if:

(a) the seller is engaged in the business of selling such a product, and

(b) it is expected to and does reach the consumer without substantial change in the condition in which it is sold.

The thrust of the inquiry is not on whether a separate consideration is charged for the physical material used in the exercise of medical skill, but what service is performed to restore or maintain the patient's health. The determinative question becomes not what is being charged, but what is being done. The provision of medical services is regarded as qualitatively different from the sale of products.

This distinction is made clearer by the fact that case law also supports the application of 402A where what has been provided is not medical service or products connected with diagnosis and treatment, but rather materials related to mechanical or administrative functions. See Thomas v. St. Joseph Hospital, 618 S.W.2d 791 (Tex. Civ. App. 1981) (hospital held strictly liable where hospital gown ignited when lighted match fell on it).

It must be noted that the "seller" need not be engaged solely in the business of selling products such as the defective one to be held strictly liable. An example supporting this proposition appears in comment f of the Restatement (Second) of Torts, §402A and concerns the owner of a motion picture theater who offers edibles such as popcorn and candy for sale to movie patrons. The analogue to the instant case is valid in one respect only: both the candy and the TMJ implant are ancillary to the primary activity, viewing a film or undergoing surgery respectively. However, beyond that any comparison is specious. A movie audience is free to purchase or not any food items on offer, and regardless of which option is exercised the primary activity is unaffected. On the other hand, while the implant was incidental to the surgical procedure here, it was a necessary adjunct to the treatment administered, as were the scalpel used to make the incision, and any other material objects involved in performing the operation, all of which fulfill a particular role in provision of medical service, the primary activity.

When one enters the hospital as a patient, he goes there, not to buy medicines or pills, not to purchase bandages or iodine or serum or blood, but to obtain a course of treatment in the hope of being cured of what ails him. We find, consistent with the decisions cited above which distinguish medical services from merchandising, that appellees are not sellers, providers, suppliers or distributors of products such as to activate 402A.

CASE A.20

Burnett v. Purtell
1992 Ohio App. Lexis 3467 (1992)
Court of Appeals of Ohio
Ford, Presiding Judge

Appellees agreed to purchase a mobile home with shed from appellant. On Saturday, March 3, 1990, appellees paid appellant $6,500 and in return were given the certificate of title to the mobile home as well as a key to the mobile home, but no keys to the shed. At the same time the certificate of title was transferred, the following items remained in the mobile home: the washer and dryer, mattress and box springs, two chairs, items in the refrigerator, and the entire contents of the shed. These items were to be retained by appellant and removed by appellant. To facilitate removal, the estate retained one key to the mobile home and the only keys to the shed.

On Sunday, March 4, 1990, the mobile home was destroyed by fire through the fault of neither party. At the time of the fire, appellant still had a key to the mobile home, as well as the keys to the shed and she had not removed the content of the mobile home nor the shed. The contents of the shed were not destroyed and have now been removed by appellant. The referee determined that the risk of loss remained with appellant because there was no tender of delivery. Appellant objected to the conclusion of law, but the trial court overruled the objection and entered judgment in favor of appellee. First, the appellant argues that because the certificate of title was transferred, appellees were given a key to the mobile home and the full purchase price was paid by appellees, that the risk of loss had shifted from appellant to appellees. The risk of loss passes to the buyer on his receipt of the goods if the seller is a merchant: otherwise the risk passes to the buyer on tender of delivery.

Analyzing the foregoing elements it is clear that, as the trial court stated, appellant did not tender delivery. The parties agreed that appellees would purchase the mobile home and shed from appellant. The contents of both the shed and the mobile home were to be retained by appellant and removed by appellant. At the time of the fire, appellant had not removed the items that she was required to remove from either the mobile home or the shed. Additionally, all keys to the mobile home were not surrendered and none of the keys to the shed were relinquished. Under this scenario, appellant did not tender conforming goods free of items belonging to her which remained in the trailer, nor did she put the mobile home at appellee's disposition without being fettered with the items previously enumerated. Accordingly, the trial court was correct in determining that appellant did not tender delivery within the meaning of the statute, and consequently the risk of loss remained with her. The trial court was correct in determining that appellant did not tender delivery in a manner sufficient to shift the risk of loss to appellees. Therefore, when it ordered appellant to return appellee's purchase money, it effectually mandated that the contract was "avoided."

Based on the foregoing, the judgment of the trial court is affirmed.

CASE A.21

LNS Investment Company, Inc. v. Phillips 66 Co.
731 F. Supp. 1484 (1990). United States District Court
O'Connor, Chief Judge

Plaintiff is the successor to a company known as CompuBlend Corporation ("CBC"), which blended, labeled, and packaged quart plastic bottles of motor oil for, among others, defendant Phillips 66 Company. On July 29, 1986, W. Peter Buhlinger, defendant's manager of lubricants ("Buhlinger"), wrote a letter to Dan Tutcher, plaintiff's vice-president of operations ("Tutcher"), which read as follows: This will confirm our verbal agreement wherein Phillips will purchase additional quantities of plastic bottles from CBC during 1986. CBC, in an effort to increase their packaging capacity has committed to purchase several additional molds to blow the Phillips plastic one-quart container. In order to amortize the cost of the additional equipments Phillips has agreed to take delivery of a maximum of 4,000,000 bottles to be made available by December 31, 1986. This agreement includes the production available now and to be supplemented by the additional equipment. Should CBC not be

able to produce the full 4,000,000 quarts by December 31, 1986, this agreement shall be considered satisfied. Phillips' desire is to receive as many bottles packaged with Phillips motor oil in 1986 from CBC as possible.

Plaintiff experienced numerous problems in maintaining even its pre-contract capacity. Moreover, the quality of goods plaintiff was able to deliver was frequently unacceptable to defendant. Laughlin reiterated defendant's dissatisfaction with plaintiff's products by letter dated October 15, 1986. Discussing bottles tendered by plaintiff, Laughlin stated that, "we definitely do not want bottles on the shelf of the quality submitted." On December 16, 1986, Buhlinger wrote that defendant would not renew any commitments to purchase goods from plaintiff after March 31, 1987, due to plaintiff's poor performance under the July 29 agreement. Plaintiff filed this suit on May 12, 1987, alleging, inter alia, that defendant breached the July 29 agreement by failing to purchase plaintiff's full output of plastic bottles through December 31, 1986.

Plaintiff's failure to provide either the quantity or quality of goods contemplated by the July 29 agreement entitled defendant to suspend its performance. Section 84-2-609 of the Code states as follows: Right to adequate assurance of performance. (1) A contract for sale imposes an obligation on each party that the other's expectation of receiving due performance will not be impaired. When reasonable grounds for insecurity arise with respect to the performance of either party the other may in writing demand adequate assurance of due performance and until he receives such assurance may if commercially reasonable suspend any performance for which he has not already received the agreed return.

It was incumbent upon plaintiff to provide adequate assurance of its future performance to defendant. Plaintiff failed to provide defendant with adequate assurance of its future performance. Official UCC Comment 4 states that what constitutes "adequate" assurance of due performance is subject to the same test of factual conditions as what constitutes "reasonable grounds for insecurity." For example, where the buyer can make use of a defective delivery, a mere promise by a seller of good repute that he is giving the matter his attention and that the defect will not be repeated, is normally sufficient. Under the same circumstances, however, a similar statement by a known corner-cutter might well be considered insufficient without the posting of a guaranty or, if so demanded by the buyer, a speedy replacement of the delivery involved. By the same token where a delivery has defects, even though easily curable, which interfere with easy use by the buyer, no verbal assurance can be deemed adequate which is not accomplished by replacement, repair, money-allowance, or other commercially reasonable cure.

Plaintiff's continual excuses for failing to perform, unaccompanied by corresponding remedial action, cannot be deemed adequate assurance under the Code. Accordingly, defendant was entitled to suspend its own performance of the contract by refusing to place orders with plaintiff and/or canceling unfilled orders already placed, thirty days after either or both the September 18, 1986, and October 15, 1986, letters. In view of this conclusion, defendant did not breach the contract by suspending performance in December, 1986, and judgment will be entered in its favor.

Judgment for defendant.

CASE A.22

Simpson v. Hatteras Island Gallery Restaurant, Inc.
427 S.E.2d 131 (1993)
Court of Appeals of North Carolina
Wynn, Judge

This appeal arises from a personal injury and wrongful death action brought by the plaintiff, Barbara Simpson, originally against the defendant and third-party plaintiff, Hatteras Island Gallery Restaurant, Inc. (hereinafter Restaurant), for the death of her husband, Dr. William Simpson. Dr. Simpson's death was determined to be the result of scombroid fish poisoning, which results from elevated levels of histamine in the scombroid fish family, allegedly incurred from his eating tuna at the Restaurant.

The evidence presented at trial, viewed in a light most favorable to the non-movants, tended to show the following: Dr. Simpson was an active individual with no physical health problems that would prevent him from engaging in physical activity. Both Dr. Simpson and Mr. James Havens ate tuna at the Restaurant on the night of Dr. Simpson's death. Prior to dinner, Dr. Simpson had exhibited no signs of illness or stomach problems. Upon returning from dinner, Dr. Simpson was very flushed and began experiencing shortness of breath, a rapid pulse, vomiting and diarrhea. Mr. Havens also became ill, his face, neck and ears were extremely flushed, his pulse was rapid, he became nauseated, and his ileostomy bag began to fill rapidly, an indication of diarrhea. Medical testimony indicated that Dr. Simpson died as a result of scombroid fish poisoning, the most striking characteristic of such poisoning being red or flushed coloring. The report of the autopsy on Dr. Simpson's body concluded that signs of other causes of death, such as a heart attack, blood clots, or acute bleeding into the brain were nonexistent and no explanation other than scombroid fish poisoning could be found for Dr. Simpson's death. There was also testimony that the histamine level in tuna immediately after it is caught is not above one milligram per 100 grams of fish tissue, and a level of ten milligrams or more of histamine per 100 grams of fish is an indication that the fish has been temperature abused and mishandled. The Restaurant purchased the tuna in question from Etheridge, receiving it in sealed plastic cryovak bags, and placed it in the freezer without breaking the seals. In preparing the tuna to be served, the employees of the Restaurant followed proper procedures, washing their hands and cleaning their knives in bleach before and after cutting the tuna into steaks. All refrigeration units in the Restaurant were in proper working condition. The tuna had been received by the Restaurant from Etheridge in the form of four loins. After Dr. Simpson's death, there were three loins remaining in the refrigeration units at the Restaurant, and tests indicated the histamine levels to be 4.16 milligrams, 7.96 milligrams, and 13.73 milligrams per 100 grams of fish.

Mrs. Simpson filed her complaint against the Restaurant on 29 September 1989, claiming causes of action in negligence and breach of warranty of merchantability. The Restaurant subsequently filed a third-party complaint for indemnity against the Willie R. Etheridge Seafood Co., Inc. (hereinafter Etheridge) as the supplier of the tuna served to Dr. Simpson, and Mrs. Simpson was permitted to amend her complaint to file a direct action against Etheridge. At trial, after the close of all the evidence, Etheridge moved for a directed verdict, which motion was denied. The jury then returned a verdict indicating that both Etheridge and the Restaurant had breached an implied warranty of merchantability in their respective sales of the tuna. Because of the breach of warranty, the jury found that Mrs. Simpson was entitled to recover damages in the amount of $400,000.

The sale of food or drink constitutes a sale of goods, and a warranty of merchantability is implied in all contracts for the sale of goods. The important issue in determining the defective nature of a food product is whether an ordinary consumer would expect the defect to be present and, thus, take precautions to avoid injury from that defect.

We therefore find that the evidence viewed in a light most favorable to the non-moving parties warranted its submission to the jury, and further that the evidence was sufficient to uphold the jury verdict that Etheridge breached an implied warranty of merchantability when it sold the tuna to the Restaurant.

CASE A.23

Federal Deposit Insurance Corporation v.
Woodside Construction, Inc., 979 F.2d 172 (1992)
United States Court of Appeals for the Ninth Circuit
Hug, Circuit Judge

This case arose when Donald Galt signed a deed of trust note twice and signed a contract of guaranty twice. The FDIC claims that Galt is liable for $912,000, first because he signed the note as an indorser or, alternatively, because he signed the contract of guaranty as a guarantor. Galt claims that all of his signatures were in a representative capacity and that he did not sign individually as an indorser or as a guarantor. The FDIC maintains that one of the signatures on the note and one of the signatures on the contract of guaranty were signed in Galt's individual capacity, making him liable as an indorser on the note or, alternatively, as a guarantor on the contract of guaranty. The district court granted summary judgment for Galt on both the endorsement issue and the guaranty issue.

Galt obtained a loan from Alaska Mutual Bank for $912,000 on behalf of Woodside Construction of which he was an officer. The loan was evidenced by a promissory note, a deed of trust, a loan agreement, and a contract of guaranty. The signatures appeared on the note as follows:

(signature of Galt)
Woodside Construction, Inc.
signature(s)
(signature of Galt)
Donald A. Galt, President

The contract of guaranty appears on the form as follows:

Woodside Construction, Inc.
(signature of Galt)
by Donald A. Galt
Title Vice President
by (signature of Galt)
Title
Guarantors:
Guarantor
Donald A. Galt

As can be seen, the note bore Galt's signature below the name of the corporation, on the line designating his representative capacity as president. It also bore Galt's signature above the name of the corporation with no representative capacity designated.

The contract of guaranty bore Galt's signature below the name of the corporation, on the line designating his representative capacity, and then bore his signature on a line where no representative capacity was indicated. He did not sign on the line designated for his signature as guarantor.

Alaska National Bank merged with two other banks and became Alliance Bank, which retained this Woodside obligation. The loan was declared to be in default, and Alliance Bank instituted this action in state court. Alliance Bank was closed by the Alaska Department of Commerce and Economic Development, and the FDIC was appointed receiver. This Woodside obligation was sold by FDIC, as receiver, to FDIC in its corporate capacity. The FDIC then removed this case to federal court. The district court entered summary judgment for the FDIC against Woodside Construction on the note but entered summary judgment for Galt against the FDIC. The FDIC appeals the judgment rendered for Galt.

The manner in which Galt signed the promissory note bound him as an indorser in his individual capacity. He signed the note under the corporate name with the designation of his representative capacity. He also signed the note above the corporate name with no designation of any representative capacity. It is this latter signature that creates Galt's liability.

UCC Sec. 3-403(2) provides:

An authorized representative who signs his own name to an instrument:

(a) is personally obligated if the instrument neither names the person represented nor shows that the representative signed in a representative capacity;

(b) except as otherwise established between the immediate parties, is personally obligated if the Instrument names the person represented but does not show that the representative signed in a representative capacity, or if the instrument does not name the person represented but does show that the representative signed in a representative capacity.

Here, the first signature above the principal designation fails to indicate the representative capacity, and the second signature above the representative capacity fails to indicate the principal. Because the FDIC is the holder of the note here, parol evidence of intent is inadmissible, and Galt is personally liable.

The FDIC argues that Galt is liable for attorneys' fees. The note makes the indorser liable for the costs of collection, including attorneys' fees. Because we hold that Galt is the indorser, he is liable for attorneys' fees.

The judgment is REVERSED.

CASE A.24

Dynalectron Corporation v. Equitable Trust Company
35 U.C.C.Rep.Serv. 1548 (1983)
United States Court of Appeals, Fourth Circuit
Bryan, Senior Circuit Judge

H.A.S. Construction Company (H.A.S.) employed Shrader Professional Communications, Inc. (Shrader), to perform electrical work at a hotel in Arlington, Virginia. Shrader then contracted with Dynacom, a subsidiary of Dynalectron Corp., to install audio equipment at the hotel. Shrader requested that H.A.S. make payments by check to "Shrader, Inc./Dynacom." From March until June 1979, H.A.S. drew three checks on Equitable Trust Co. (Equitable) payable to "Shrader, Inc./ Dynacom." Shrader indorsed the checks and deposited them in its account at Union First National Bank of Washington (Union). Union presented the checks to Equitable, who paid the checks. Shrader failed to pay Dynacom any of the proceeds from the checks. Shrader failed to pay Dynacom any of the proceeds from the checks. Dynalectron sued Equitable to recover on the checks. The district court granted Equitable's motion for summary judgment. Dynalectron appeals.

Commercial transactions in Maryland are governed by that state's version of the Uniform Commercial Code. Where a check contains more than one payee, Section 3-116 governs:

> *An instrument payable to the order of two or more persons*
> *(a) If in the alternative is payable to any one of them and may be negotiated, discharged or enforced by any of them who has possession of it.*
> *(b) If not in the alternative is payable to all of them and may be negotiated, discharged or enforced only by all of them.*

According to the official comment to this section, instruments made payable to "A or B" or instruments made payable to A and/or B are payable in the alternative. Either payee may negotiated the instrument. If a check or other instrument is payable to "A and B," both payees must indorse.

Other jurisdictions have considered situations under the UCC where the names of the payees on an instrument are separated by a virgule ("/"). On the present facts, the Federal District Court concluded that the check was payable in the alternative and thus only one indorsement was necessary. In reaching its decision, the court acknowledged that a virgule is used to separate alternatives. The Georgia Court of Appeals adopted an identical standard for the function of a virgule.* Here, the court declared that the symbol connotes the disjunctive or the alternative.

We hold that the use of a virgule ("/") on a negotiable instrument to separate the names of two payees is payable in the alternative. The defendant, Equitable Trust Co., properly paid the checks on the indorsement of Shrader, Inc. The judgment of the district court is *affirmed*.

CASE A.25

Kedzie & 103rd Currency Exchange, Inc. v. Hodge
601 N.E.2d 803 (Ill. App. I Dist. [1921])
Appellate Court of Illinois
Linn, Justice

Plaintiff, Kedzie & 103rd Street Currency Exchange, Inc., cashed a check for defendant Fred Fentress (who is not a party to this appeal). Defendant Beula M. Hodge, drawer of the check, notified her bank to stop payment on the check when Fentress, engaged to perform plumbing services, did not appear at her home to begin work. As a holder in due course, plaintiff sought damages from Hodge. The trial court, however, granted Hodge's motion to dismiss based on the defense of illegality.

Plaintiff states the issue as whether a holder in due course of a check takes the check free from the defense of illegality where the drawer of the check issued it as a partial advance payment for plumbing services to be rendered, but the payee was not licensed as a plumber.

Background

Plaintiff, an Illinois corporation doing business as a currency exchange, filed suit after the $500 check it had cashed for Fentress was returned marked "payment stopped." Hodge had made out the check to "Fred Fentress—A-OK Plumbing" as partial payment, in advance, for plumbing services at her residence. When he failed to appear on the date work was to begin, Hodge directed her bank to stop payment on the check. Fentress, in the meantime, cashed the check at plaintiff currency exchange, indorsing the back as "Fred Fentress A-OK Plumbing Sole Owner." Plaintiff obtained a default judgment against Fentress.

Hodge filed a motion to dismiss the action as to her, asserting the defense of illegality. She had discovered that Fentress was not a licensed plumber listed with either the State or Chicago. Under An Act in Relation to the Licensing and Regulation of Plumbers (Plumber's Licensing Act), plumbers must obtain a license before practicing their trade. A violation of the Act is a Class B misdemeanor for the first offense. According to Hodge, the plumbing contract was illegal and void; therefore, plaintiff took the check subject to the illegality defense. The trial court agreed and entered judgment in favor of Hodge.

Opinion

Under the Uniform Commercial Code (UCC), commercial instruments including checks are meant to be freely negotiable, and to that end a holder in due course will take the instrument free from "all defenses of any party to the instrument with whom the holder has not dealt except such incapacity, or duress, or illegality of the transaction, as renders the obligation of the party a nullity."

Comment 6 to UCC Sec. 3-305 explains that the question of illegality is a matter of state law and if under the law governing the contract the effect of the illegality is to make the obligation entirely null and void, the defense is good.

The dispositive issue before us, therefore, is whether under Illinois law the contract between Hodge and the plumber was null and void. If so, the defense of illegality was properly asserted and applied in this case. If the underlying obligation was merely voidable, however, the defense fails.

The Illinois legislature, by adopting Sec. 3-305 of the UCC, has expressly declared that illegality is an available defense against a holder in due course, as long as the effect of the illegality is to render the obligation sued upon null and void.

Illinois courts should not apply the illegality defense against holders in due course unless the illegal transaction is of the type that wholly nullifies the contract and thereby renders the instrument subject to the illegality defense.

In this state, the legislature has passed extensive legislation relating to the licensing of many trades and professions, recognizing that the regulation of these professions is essential to the public health, safety and welfare. In furtherance of the legislative goals of providing standards and protecting the public health, the Plumber's Licensing Act provides that one who attempts to practice plumbing without a license may suffer substantial penalties, including criminal prosecution and fines. By judicial construction, the unlicensed plumber also forfeits his right to compensation for illegal services rendered. The contract in question is not void unless the Plumber's Licensing Act or other legislation expressly declares it to be.

As a matter of policy, plaintiff argues that it is unfair to expect a currency exchange to police the negotiable instruments it receives to ferret out possible illegalities in the underlying contracts. While the argument is reasonable enough, the same could be made for all of the defenses which defeat the rights of holders in due course. The currency exchange does not have a way to ascertain if a check has been drafted under duress, if it represents a gambling debt, or if it is the check of one without legal capacity to be bound. The so-called "real" defenses are nonetheless valid and cut off the rights of the innocent holder of the instrument to obtain recourse against makers or endorsers of the instrument in question. Currency exchanges are in the business of cashing checks and undertake the attendant risks.

We conclude that the illegality defense asserted in this case is of the type to render the obligation a nullity under Sec. 3-305 of the Code. Therefore, we affirm the trial court's dismissal of the action against Hodge, as maker of the check.

Affirmed.

CASE A.26

First American Bank and Trust v. Rishoi 553 So.2d 1387
(Fla. App. 5 Dist. 1990)
District Court of Appeals of Florida
Daniel, Chief Judge

First American Bank and Trust appeals a summary judgment in favor of William M. Rishoi as receiver for Clara Lamstein and the business she operated under the name of Interamerican Business Consultants and Associates, Inc.

In Crosby v. Lewis, the Crosbys had purchased $180,000 in cashier's checks, payable to Lamstein, from various banks and financial institutions. The checks were all delivered to Lamstein as investments. Lamstein's business was later closed down by the State on the ground that it was an illegal "ponzi" or pyramiding scheme. The assets of the business were placed in the control of Rishoi as receiver. Eighty thousand dollars of the cashier's checks from the Crosbys had been cashed and deposited by Lamstein prior to the receivership. However, one hundred thousand dollars in cashier's checks remained uncashed in Lamstein's possession. The Crosbys requested that the banks not pay the cashier's checks. The banks issued stop payment orders on the outstanding cashier's checks and subsequently dishonored the checks when presented by the receiver for payment.

Although the issuing banks were not parties to that action, this court stated:

The banks which issued the cashier's checks are primarily liable to the receiver, and by refusing to honor the checks, they have prima facie violated the duties imposed on them.

Rishoi thereafter instituted suit against First American Bank and Trust claiming that the bank had improperly refused to honor the cashier's checks. The court below concluded that the bank had no right to stop payment on the cashier's checks and entered summary judgment in favor of Rishoi.

On appeal, the bank argues that Rishoi is not a holder in due course and therefore it was justified in refusing to honor the cashier's checks. The bank acknowledges that a cashier's check presented by a holder in due course may not be countermanded after issue. It also acknowledges that cashier's checks are treated as the next best thing to cash in the business community. On public policy grounds, however, the bank urges that it should be able to assist its customers by stopping payment on a cashier's check which has been obtained from a customer by a criminal act.

In Warren Finance, Inc. v. Barnett Bank of Jacksonville, N.A., 552 So.2d 194 (Fla. 1989), the Florida Supreme Court recently held that, in accordance with common commercial practice and the use of a cashier's check as a cash substitute, any defenses which a bank may assert to avoid payment must be narrowly limited. The court concluded that, upon presentment for payment by a holder, a bank may only assert its real and personal defenses in order to refuse payment on a cashier's check issued by the bank. The bank may not, however, rely on a third party's defenses to refuse payment. The only inquiry a bank may make on presentment of a cashier's check is whether the payee or indorsee is in fact a legitimate holder, that is, whether the cashier's check is being presented by a thief or one who simply found a lost check, or whether the check has been materially altered. The court concluded that this approach maintains the validity and use of cashier's checks yet acknowledges the valid concerns of banks.

In the present case, the receiver was a legitimate holder and the bank had no real or personal defenses to assert against his claim for payment. Thus, the bank wrongfully dishonored its own obligation and is liable for payment. Accordingly, the trial court properly entered summary judgment in favor of the receiver.

AFFIRMED.

CASE A.27

General Motors Acceptance Corporation v. Daniels
492 A.2d 1306 (1985)
Cole, Judge

In June 1981, John Daniels agreed to purchase a used automobile from Lindsay Cadillac Company (Lindsay Cadillac). Because John had a poor credit rating, his brother, Seymoure, agreed to cosign the installment sales contract. On June 23, 1981, Seymoure accompanied John to Lindsay Cadillac. John signed the contract on the line designated "Buyer." Seymoure signed the contract on the line designated the contract to General Motors Acceptance Corporation (GMAC), a company engaged in the business of financing automobiles. In May 1982, GMAC declared the contract in default. GMAC did not immediately notify Seymoure of the default or that physical damage insurance on the car had lapsed. After attempting to locate the automobile for several months, GMAC brought this action against the Daniel brothers in Maryland court. Because service of process was never effected upon John, the case proceeded to trial against only Seymoure. The trial court held in favor of Seymoure. The appellate court affirmed. GMAC appeals.

Maryland law has consistently maintained a distinction between a contract of suretyship and a contract of guaranty. A review of the distinguishing characteristics of these contracts provides a useful predicate to the resolution to the issue presented in this case.

Suretyship

A contract of suretyship is a tripartite agreement among a principal obligor, his obligee, and a surety. This contract is a direct and original undertaking under which the surety is primarily or jointly liable with the principal obligor, and therefore is responsible at once if the principal obligor fails to perform. A surety is usually bound with his principal by the same instrument, executed at the same time, and on the same consideration. Ultimate liability rests upon the principal obligor rather than the surety, but the obligee has remedy against both. With respect to notice of default, the surety is ordinarily held to know every default of his principal because he is under a duty to make inquiry and ascertain whether the principal obligor is discharging the obligation resting on him. It is generally not necessary for the creditor to notify the surety of the fact that the principal debtor is in default on his promise. It is the duty of the surety to the creditor to see that the debt is paid. Consequently, the surety is ordinarily liable without notice.

Guaranty

A contract of guaranty, similar to a contract of suretyship, is an accessory contract. Despite this similarity, a contract of guaranty has several distinguishing characteristics. First, this particular contract is collateral to and independent of the principal contract that is guaranteed and, as a result, the guarantor is not a party to the principal obligation. A guarantor is therefore secondarily liable to the creditor on his contract, and his promise to answer for the debt, default, or miscarriage of another becomes absolute upon default of the principal debtor and the satisfaction of the conditions precedent to liability. Second, the original contract of the principal is not the guarantor's contract, and the guarantor is not bound to take notice of its nonperformance. Rather, the guarantor insures the ability or solvency of the principal. In sum, the guarantor promises to perform if the principal does not. By contrast, a surety promises to do the same thing that the principal undertakes.

Case Sub Justice

With the distinctions between a contract of suretyship and contract of guaranty in mind, we turn to the case sub justice. Our review of the evidence in this case convinces us that the trial court erred in finding that Seymoure was a guarantor rather than a surety with respect to the installment sales contract. In our judgment the indicia for determining whether a contract is one for suretyship or one for guaranty all point to the existence of a suretyship agreement.

Initially, we note that because the contractual language is clear and unambiguous on its face, we confine our review to the contract itself. Seymoure agreed to purchase the subject automobile by affixing his signature to the installment sales contract on the line designated "Co-buyer." The contract clearly stated that all buyers agreed to be jointly and severally liable for the purchase of that vehicle. Therefore, under the objective law of contracts, a reasonable person knew or should have known that he was subjecting himself to primary liability for the purchase of the automobile. In short, although uncompensated sureties are favorites of the law, Seymoure's careless indifference does not insulate him from primary liability on that agreement.

Seymoure executed the same contract as his brother, thereby making himself a party to the original contract. There is no evidence that Seymoure executed an agreement collateral to and independent of this contract. This fact, standing alone, ordinarily negates the existence of a guaranty. Both Seymoure and John signed the contract at the same time. Although not dispositive, this fact tends to establish the existence of a contract of suretyship rather than a contract of guaranty. Finally, on the facts of this case, it is immaterial that the contract did not expressly designate Seymoure as a "surety." Whether a party has entered into a contract of suretyship or guaranty is to be determined by the substance of the agreement and not by its nomenclature.

We hold that Seymoure signed a contract of suretyship and thus agreed to be primarily and jointly liable with his brother John for the purchase of the automobile. GMAC was therefore not required to notify Seymoure promptly of the default in payments or to proceed against John in the first instance. Accordingly, for the reasons stated earlier, we *reverse*.

Case A.28

Davenport v. Chrysler Credit Corporation
818 S.W. 2d 23 (1991)
Court of Appeals of Tennessee. Koch, Judge

Larry and Debbie Davenport purchased a new 1987 Chrysler LeBaron from Gary Mathews Motors on October 28, 1987. They obtained financing through Chrysler Credit Corporation (Chrysler Credit) and signed a retail installment contract requiring them to make the first of sixty monthly payments on or before December 8, 1987.

The automobile developed mechanical problems before the Davenports could drive it off the dealer's lot. Even before their first payment was due, the Davenports had returned the automobile to the dealer seven times for repair. They were extremely dissatisfied and, after consulting a lawyer, decided to withhold their monthly payments until the matter was resolved.

Chrysler Credit sent the Davenports a standard delinquency notice when their first payment was ten days late. The Davenports did not respond to the notice, and on December 23, 1987, Chrysler Credit telephoned the Davenports to request payment. Mrs. Davenport recounted the problems with the automobile and told Chrysler Credit that she would consult her lawyer and "would let them know about the payment." After consulting the dealer, Chrysler Credit informed Mrs. Davenport that it would repossess the automobile if she did not make the payment.

Employees of American Lender Service arrived at the Davenports' home on the evening of January 14, 1988. They informed the Davenports that they were "two payments in default" and requested the automobile. The Davenports insisted that they were not in default and, after a telephone call to their lawyer, refused to turn over the automobile until Chrysler Credit obtained the "proper paperwork." The American Lender Service employees left without the car.

Before leaving for work the next morning, Mr. Davenport parked the automobile in their enclosed garage and chained its rear end to a post using a logging chain and two padlocks. He also closed the canvas flaps covering the entrance to the garage and secured the flaps with cinder blocks. When the Davenports returned from work, they discovered that someone had entered the garage, cut one of the padlocks, and removed the automobile.

American Lender Service informed Chrysler Credit on January 18, 1988 that it had repossessed the automobile. On the same day, Chrysler Credit notified the Davenports that they could redeem the car before it was offered for sale. The Davenports never responded to the notice. Instead of selling the automobile immediately, Chrysler Credit held it for more than a year because of the Davenports' allegations that the automobile was defective. In July, 1989, Chrysler Credit informed the Davenports that the automobile had been sold and requested payment of the $6,774.00 deficiency. The proof supports the trial court's conclusion that Chrysler Credit had a legal right to initiate repossession procedures.

The Davenports' dissatisfaction with their automobile did not provide them with a basis to unilaterally refuse to honor their payment obligations in the retail installment contract. At the time the repossession took place, the Davenports had not requested rescission of the contract, attempted to revoke their acceptance of the automobile, pursued their remedies under the "lemon law," or taken any other formal steps to resolve their dispute with the dealer concerning the automobile. The Davenports' conduct gave Chrysler Credit an adequate basis to consider the loan to be in default and to decide to protect its collateral by repossessing the automobile.

The Tennessee General Assembly preserved the secured parties' self-help remedies when it enacted the Uniform Commercial Code in 1963. It also preserved the requirement that repossessions must be accomplished without a breach of the peace. The term "breach of the peace" is a generic term that includes all violations or potential violations of the public peace and order. We can find no support for limiting "breach of the peace" to criminal context.

Secured parties may repossess their collateral at a reasonable time and in a reasonable manner. Self-help procedures such as repossession are the product of a careful balancing of the interests of secured parties and debtors. Chrysler Credit and American Lender Service do not dispute that they obtained the automobile by entering a closed garage and by cutting a lock on a chain that would have prevented them from removing the automobile. The Davenports are only entitled to recover their damages stemming directly from the manner in which American Lender Service repossessed their automobile.

We reverse the trial court's judgment dismissing the Davenports' complaint.

CASE A.29

Dewsnup v. Timm, 116 L.Ed. 2d 903, 112 S.Ct. 773 (1992)
Supreme Court of the United States
Blackmun, Justice

We are confronted in this case with an issue concerning §506(d) of the Bankruptcy Code. May a debtor "strip down" a creditor's lien on real property to the value of the collateral, as judicially determined, when that value is less than the amount of the claim secured by the lien?

On June 1, 1978, respondents loaned $119,000 to petitioner Aletha Dewsnup and her husband, T. LaMar Dewsnup, since deceased. The loan was accompanied by a Deed of Trust granting a lien on two parcels of Utah farmland owned by the Dewsnups. Petitioner defaulted the following year. Under the terms of the Deed of Trust, respondents at that point could have proceeded against the real property collateral by accelerating the maturity of the loan, issuing a notice of default, and selling the land at a public foreclosure sale to satisfy the debt.

Respondents did issue a notice of default in 1981. Before the foreclosure sale took place, however, petitioner sought reorganization under Chapter 11 of the Bankruptcy Code. That bankruptcy petition was dismissed, as was a subsequent Chapter 11 petition. In June 1984, petitioner filed a petition seeking liquidation under Chapter 7 of the Code. Because of the pendency of these bankruptcy proceedings, respondents were not able to proceed to the foreclosure sale.

Petitioner-debtor takes the position that §506(a) and §506(d) are complementary and to be read together. Because, under §506(a), a claim is secured only to the extent of the judicially determined value of the real property on which the lien is fixed, a debtor can void a lien on the property pursuant to §506(d) to the extent the claim is no longer secured and thus is not "an allowed secured claim." In other words §506(a) bifurcates classes of claims allowed under §502 into secured claims and unsecured

claims; any portion of an allowed claim deemed to be unsecured under §506(a) is not an "allowed secured claim" within the lien-voiding scope of §506(d). Petitioner argues that there is no exception for unsecured property abandoned by the trustee.

We conclude that respondents' alternative position, espoused also by the United States, although not without its difficulty, generally is the best of the several approaches. Therefore, we hold that §506(d) does not allow petitioner to "strip down" respondents' lien, because respondents' claim is secured by a lien and has been fully allowed pursuant to §502.

The practical effect of petitioner's argument is to freeze the creditor's secured interest at the judicially determined valuation. By this approach, the creditor would lose the benefit of any increase in the value of the property by the time of the foreclosure sale. The increase would accrue to the benefit of the debtor, a result some of the parties describe as a "windfall."

We think, however, that the creditor's lien stays with the real property until the foreclosure. That is what was bargained for by the mortgagor and the mortgagee. Any increase over the judicially determined valuation during bankruptcy rightly accrues to the benefit of the creditor, not to the benefit of the debtor and not to the benefit of other unsecured creditors whose claims have been allowed and who had nothing to do with the mortgagor-mortgagee bargain.

No provision of the pre-Code statute permitted involuntary reduction of the amount of a creditor's lien for any reason other than payment on the debt.

The judgment of the Court of Appeals is affirmed.

CASE A.30

Penthouse International, Ltd. v. Barnes 792 F.2d 943 (1986)
United States Court of Appeals, Ninth Circuit
Boochever, Circuit Judge

Priscilla Barnes is a newscaster for a television station in Los Angeles, California. In 1975, Barnes was a hostess at a club in Hollywood, California. She was approached by Jeff Dunas, a free-lance photographer who sold photographs to *Penthouse*, a magazine that publishes photographs of females. Dunas asked Barnes about posing for a photography session, with the possibility of selling the photographs to *Penthouse*. Dunas was paid by *Penthouse* as an independent contractor. Dunas did not have an office at Penthouse. *Penthouse* provided Dunas with the title "Penthouse Staff Photographer" and included his name on the magazine's masthead. Barnes agreed to be photographed by Dunas but wanted her photographs accompanied by a pseudonym. Dunas agreed. Before the photo session began, Barnes signed the *Penthouse* standard model "Release, Authorization, and Agreement" (the contract).

Dunas added the handwritten term "AKA" ("also known as") on the contract to indicate that Barnes's photographs would be published under a pseudonym. Barnes read and signed the contract. Dunas took photographs of Barnes and submitted them to *Penthouse*. Barnes appeared as the centerfold in the March 1976 issue of *Penthouse* under a pseudonym. In the fall of 1983, after the *National Enquirer* and *People* magazine published a rumor that Barnes was Penthouse's 1976 centerfold, *Penthouse* decided to republish Barnes's photographs using her real name. Before doing so, *Penthouse* submitted the contract to the district court for a declaratory judgment that it had the right to publish the photographs using Barnes's name. Barnes filed an answer and counterclaim for an injunction, alleging that the contract prohibited *Penthouse* from doing so. The district court found for Barnes and issued an injunction against *Penthouse*. *Penthouse* appealed.

Under California law, questions regarding the existence of agency are questions of fact that we review for clear error. California Civil Code Section 2316 defines actual authority as "such as a principal intentionally confers upon the agent, or intentionally, or by want of ordinary care, allows the agent to believe himself to possess." At issue is whether Dunas contracted to act on behalf of *Penthouse*.

Penthouse instructed photographers "to get a signed model release and not to alter the release in any way, without our permission." However, *Penthouse* carried Dunas's name on its masthead, gave him blank *Penthouse* contracts, may have given him business cards, and had him present contracts to models. Thus, although the record conflicts as to whether Dunas was an actual agent of *Penthouse*, on review, we cannot find that the district court clearly erred in finding Dunas to be a *Penthouse* agent.

Having found that the district court did not err in characterizing Dunas as an agent, we next turn to whether Dunas was acting within the scope of his authority by modifying the contract. Barnes does not contend nor is there evidence that Dunas possessed express actual authority to modify the contract. Dunas, however, had implied actual authority. Implied actual authority requires that (1) Dunas believe he was authorized to modify the contract based on *Penthouse* conduct known to him or (2) such a belief was reasonable.

Circumstantial evidence exists that Dunas placed "AKA" on other contracts with no objection from *Penthouse*. In June 1974, a year and a half before Barnes posed, contracts prepared by Dunas had "AKA" on them. Further, *Penthouse* internal memoranda reflect an understanding among *Penthouse* employees that "AKA" added to a contract meant that *Penthouse* was to associate a fictitious name with a woman's photograph. The evidence thus indicates that Dunas reasonably believed he was authorized to add "AKA" and modify the contract to require that only a fictitious name be used.

We conclude that the district court did not clearly err in finding that Dunas was a *Penthouse* agent acting with implied actual authority when he modified the Barnes's contract with the term "AKA." The district court's injunction ordering *Penthouse* not to publish Barnes's nude photographs with her name is *affirmed*.

*C*ASE A.31
District of Columbia v. Howell, 607 A.2d 501
(D.C. Pap. 1992)
District of Columbia Court of Appeals
Farrell, Associate Judge

The Murch School Summer Discovery Program was designed to provide hands-on education for gifted and talented eight- and nine-year-old children. The program originated in 1985 when Mrs. Gill, the Murch School principal, attended a reception at Mount Vernon College arranged by Greg Butta, a Ph.D. candidate at The American University, to advertise the success of a summer program he had conducted at Mount Vernon. The program interested Mrs. Gill, and after several discussions, Butta sent her a formal proposal for conducting a similar program at the Murch School. Gill proposed changes to the proposal, then solicited and received approval for the program from the Assistant Superintendent for the District of Columbia Public Schools.

Butta hired the staff for the summer program, including some of the instructors who had taught in the Mount Vernon program. Mrs. Gill, however, reviewed all of the instructors' resumes, had veto authority over their hiring, and interviewed most of the staff, including A. Louis Jagoe, before the hiring was made final. Jagoe, who was hired to teach chemistry to the eight- and nine-year-olds in the program, held a master's degree in chemistry and was a Ph.D. candidate at The American University. Before the first general staff meeting, he told Butta that as part of the class he would do a luminescence experiment and a "cold-pack" experiment and wanted to make sparklers with the children. Jagoe and Butta discussed the safety of the sparkler experiment only in regard to the location where the children would be allowed to light the sparklers.

On August 1, 1985, a staff meeting was held at which Gill, Butta, and all instructors and counselors were present. Each instructor gave a brief talk about what he or she intended to do in class. Several instructors testified that Jagoe told the group, including Mrs. Gill, that he planned to make sparklers as one of the chemistry experiments. Gill, who was in and out of the meeting, did not remember hearing Jagoe discuss the experiment, although notes she took at the meeting reflect that she heard him discuss the luminescence and cold pack experiments and asked him questions about these. Gill spoke and emphasized the "hands-on" nature of the program and her hopes for its success.

One child attending the program was nine-year-old Dedrick Howell, whose parents enrolled him after receiving the school brochure in the mail. The accident occurred on August 12, 1985. At the beginning of the chemistry class, Jagoe distributed his "recipe" for sparklers to the children and also wrote it on the black board. Along with other chemical ingredients, the recipe called for the use of potassium perchlorate as the oxidizing agent. Potassium perchlorate was described at trial as an extremely unstable and highly volatile chemical often used to make rocket fuel. Commercially made sparklers are not made with potassium perchlorate.

The children scooped the chemicals, including the potassium perchlorate, out of jars and, using pestles, ground up the mixture in mortars. While they were combining the chemicals, Jagoe ignited three different chemical mixtures at the front of the room with a butane lighter. Butta was present for one of the ignitions when he entered the room to drop off metal hangers for use in the experiment. Mrs. Gill also entered the room at one point, and saw the children working at tables wearing goggles or glasses. She also saw Jagoe at the front of the room lighting the chemicals with a fire extinguisher on the table next to him.

The children continued to grind the material while a counselor, Rebecca Seashore, distributed pieces of metal hangers to be dipped into the mixture at a later time. Dedrick Howell was specifically told not to dip the hanger into the material until instructed to do so. Moments later the chemicals exploded in front of Dedrick. The chemicals burned at 5000 degrees Fahrenheit, and Dedrick was burned over 25% of his body including his hands, arms, and chest, and face.

An employer generally is not liable for injuries to third parties caused by an independent contractor over whom (or over whose work) the employer has reserved no control. There are exceptions to the rule, however, one of which is that one who employs an independent contractor to do work involving a special danger to others which the employer knows or has reason to know to be inherent in or normal to the work, or which he contemplates or has reason to contemplate when making the contract, is subject to liability for physical harm caused to such others by the contractor's failure to take reasonable precautions against such danger.

It is sufficient that work of any kind involves a risk, recognizable in advance, of physical harm to others which is inherent in the work itself, or normally to be expected in the ordinary course of the usual or prescribed way of doing it, or that the employer has special reason to contemplate such a risk *under the particular circumstances under which the work is to be done.*

The sparkler experiment combined flammable, combustible chemicals, open flames, and children; for that very reason, presumably, the children had been equipped with goggles. Though sparklers are explosives of a lesser order, conducting controlled explosions is a textbook example of an inherently dangerous activity. It was not unreasonable for the jury to conclude that the manufacture of sparklers by nine-year-old children was an inherently dangerous activity.

Therefore, the jury was well within its authority in finding that Jagoe was an independent contractor performing inherently dangerous work of which the District had actual or constructive knowledge.

The judgment is affirmed as to liability and as to the award of $8 million in damages both for pain and suffering and for past medical expenses.

CASE A.32
Bulova Watch Company, Inc. v. K. Hattori & Co., Ltd.
508 F..Supp. 1322 (1981)
United States District Court, Eastern District of New York
Weinstein, Chief Judge

Bulova Watch Company, Inc. (Bulova), is a New York corporation with its principal place of business in Flushing, New York. It manufactures and sells watches, and has the largest direct sales marketing system in the watch business. K. Hattori & Co., Ltd. (Hattori), is a company incorporated under the laws of Japan, with its principal offices in Tokyo. It owns all the stock of Seiko Corporation of America (SCA). SCA in turn owns all the stock of three New York corporations: Seiko Time Corp.,

Pulsar Time, Inc., and SPD Precision, Inc. Hattori has watches produced in Japan and then sells them to its three American subsidiaries under the Seiko and other brand names. The American subsidiaries have no manufacturing or research facilities but merely act as sales and marketing conduits for Hattori-made watches. Hattori's annual sales are in excess of $1 billion, with over one-half coming from sales of watches in the United States. Hattori was informed of all activities undertaken by its American subsidiaries that had a substantial impact on the American market. Many of Hattori's directors and executives either currently or previously served in similar positions with its American subsidiaries.

In 1978, Seiko Time acquired the "Pulsar" trademark and decided to market a new line of watches under that name. The executives and directors of Hattori were involved in the decision making. To accomplish this, a direct sales network had to be put quickly into place. Seiko Time hired Bulova's director of marketing to head up its Pulsar operation. Between July and December 1978, three regional sales managers and three other senior executives left Bulova to join Seiko Time. In December 1978, four Bulova sales representatives left to join Seiko Time and SPD. In 1979, numerous other Bulova sales representatives were hired by Pulsar Time.

Bulova sued Hattori in a state law tort action, alleging that Hattori had engaged in unfair competition, disparagement, and a conspiracy with its subsidiaries to raid Bulova's marketing staff in order to misappropriate Bulova's trade secrets. Under New York law, a foreign corporation must have been doing or transacting business in the state to be subject to court jurisdiction there. Hattori filed a motion to dismiss the complaint for lack of personal jurisdiction. To any layman it would seem absurd that our courts could not obtain jurisdiction over a billion-dollar multinational which is exploiting the critical New York and American markets to keep its home production going at a huge volume and profit. This perception must have a bearing on our evaluation of fairness. The law ignores the common sense of a situation at the peril of becoming irrelevant as an institution.

New York law confers personal jurisdiction over unlicensed foreign corporations that are "doing business" in New York. A court cannot simply isolate each contact of the defendant with New York and say that each such contact does not constitute the doing of business. Rather it must look to the "cumulative significance" of all activities of a foreign corporation within the state in order to determine whether the corporation is doing business within the state for jurisdictional purposes. The parent-subsidiary relationship has not in itself been treated as sufficient to establish personal jurisdiction over the foreign parent. The factors to be weighed include the significance of the New York business to the defendant's overall activities.

The definition of "doing business" has been variously stated, but the common denominator is that the corporation is operating within the state not occasionally or casually, but with a fair measure of permanence and continuity. It is no longer a matter of doubt that a foreign corporation can do business in New York through its employees or through independent agents. Equally settled is the concept that a corporation may be amenable to New York personal jurisdiction when the systematic activities of a subsidiary in this state may fairly be attributed to the parent. A line of cases establishes the rule that a foreign corporation does business in New York if its affiliated company is in effect a local department separately incorporated or it acts as agent by doing all business which the principal could do were it here by its own officials.

When Cardozo enunciated the standard for doing business in New York, there would have been little need to consider how, or whether, a foreign-based multinational enterprise would be found to be doing business in New York. For one thing, the term "multinational firm," so common in today's parlance, was first used only in about 1960. For another, it was not until after World War II that the phenomenon of the multinational enterprise, as we now know it, became a major factor in the world scene. The vehicles of modern international economic growth were and are the multinational enterprises. Their size is often awesome: The annual sales of General Motors exceeded the gross national products of Switzerland, Pakistan, or South Africa. Aside from their magnitude, today's multinationals are unique in the way vast investments in myriad locations are made to serve the interests of a single organization. Such an organization has the resources and scope to plan and to utilize worldwide markets and resources.

Nevertheless, the means by which the multinational exercises control over its far-flung elements vary. Choice among the various corporate modes of entering a market, e.g., by means of licensing arrangement, joint venture, minority-, majority- or-wholly-owned subsidiary, has very significant implications for the control exercised by the parent. The decision of marketing-oriented firms to choose wholly-owned subsidiaries means that they can exercise more control over their foreign operation in subtle, indirect ways as well as directly.

Another criterion that will determine the "corporate intimacy" joining a parent and its subsidiary is the type and range of products being sold. While Hattori manufactures a number of products, the overwhelming concern of its American marketing operation is with its timepieces—constituting 90% of its total production by value. Thus sales subsidiaries tend to be under especially close control where a company produces a limited number of products.

A crucial factor in the degree of control over the subsidiary is the age of the subsidiary and the extent to which the subsidiary has been able to develop independently of its parent. An important question in assessing presence for jurisdictional purposes is whether a multinational has reached a state in its evolution when it can be said that its sales and marketing subsidiaries truly have a "life of their own." Hattori, like many Japanese export-based multinationals, remains in large part a monocentric organization so far as involves the United States.

While sales and marketing subsidiaries generally are more likely to be controlled by the parent and less likely to develop lives of their own than those involved in manufacturing, Japanese

subsidiaries in particular may be singularly responsive to the wishes of their parent companies. In Japan subsidiaries are commonly referred to as kogaisha (child company) in relation to oya-gaisha (parent). The use of the words "parent" and "child" suggests the existence of a familial relationship of control and dependency. Thus, quite apart from the matter of one-hundred-percent stock ownership, a Japanese parent may expect to exert control over any of its child companies.

The sense of hierarchy is apparently to be found in typical employee-employer relations as well. An inferior in Japanese social organization is conditioned to attribute authority to the wishes of his superior. The subordinate is extremely conscious of his standing in the group. The Japanese corporate employer reinforces the loyalty of its employees by the "implicit guarantee of lifetime security"; this ensures not only his technical and professional loyalty, but more important, his emotional tie to the firm. Under the *shukko* system, an employee may be assigned to another employer or to a subsidiary. While on external assignment the employee keeps his security in, and identity with, his original employer.

The defendant places great stock in the formal separation of Hattori from its 100% directly-owned subsidiary and its 100% indirectly-owned subsidiaries. Plaintiff, on the other hand, points to the complete stock ownership by the parent and additionally draws our attention to the interchange and overlap of directors and officers between parent and subsidiaries. Real rather than formal relationships must be considered. What is involved here is a series of relatively young sales and marketing subsidiaries abroad, whose purpose is to market a single product—timepieces. There is no manufacturing or product research done by any of these subsidiaries. They do not seem to have developed third-country trade except for the purpose of selling Hattori's Japanese-manufactured goods. The use of the wholly-owned subsidiary form here reflects the desire for "unambiguous control" over sales and marketing subsidiaries to ensure uniform quality and promotion of the product sold.

In this case, it is obvious that if the subsidiaries were not in New York and Hattori sought to enter the American market, it would have to do so directly. This market is simply too important to the parent's welfare to use independent and uncontrolled sales agents and distributors as it does in some countries where sales are relatively small. There are undoubtedly special reasons Hattori has chosen to operate in this country by means of incorporated subsidiaries. But these subsidiaries almost by definition are doing for their parent what their parent would otherwise have to do on its own. The question to ask is not whether the American subsidiaries can formally accept orders for their parent, but rather whether, in the truest sense, the subsidiaries' presence substitutes for the presence of the parent. The role of Hattori's New York subsidiaries is substantial. The significance of those subsidiaries in Hattori's "organizational life" is enormous. The New York subsidiaries are the means by which Hattori has established and seeks to maintain its base in the country that is its single largest export market. The subsidiaries do for the parent everything that the parent would have to do if it were here directly. Hattori and its American subsidiaries do maintain some independence—about as much as the egg and vegetables in a western omelette. Just as, from a culinary point of view, we focus on the ultimate omelette and not its ingredients, so, too, from a jurisdictional standpoint, it is the integrated international operation of Hattori affecting activities in New York that is the primary focus of our concern. Large and sophisticated as it may be, Hattori is very much the hub of a wheel with many spokes. It is appropriate, therefore, to look to the center of the wheel in Japan when the spokes violate substantive rights in other countries.

Our holding that the activities of Hattori's subsidiaries allow the court to take jurisdiction of Hattori is buttressed by the fact that the cause of action alleged here is integrally related to the doing of business by Hattori within the state. A court might well find substantial unfairness here were it to drag a foreign parent into court to defend itself against actions completely unrelated to the subsidiary corporation's purposive activities on behalf of its parent. The holding in this case is simply that while a subsidiary establishes and expands a parent's market position, then, so long as that activity is being conducted, and with respect to those activities furthering the parent's end, the parent is doing business in New York. This is particularly true as to activities directly related to primary steps taken to ensure a place for its subsidiaries, as where action is taken to raid an established competitor's personnel in penetrating the American market.

The court holds that Hattori is subject to the jurisdiction of a United States court under New York law. While litigation in a foreign jurisdiction is a burdensome inconvenience for any company, in the appropriate case, were defendant's activities abroad, either directly or through an agent, become as widespread and energetic as the activities in New York conducted by defendants, it would be unfair as well as paradoxical if the parent could transfer to its subsidiaries benefits without shouldering the corresponding burdens. *So ordered.*

CASE A.33

Catalina Mortgage Co., Inc. v. Monier, 166 Ariz. 71, 800 P.2d 574 (1990). Supreme Court of Arizona
Feldman, Vice Chief Judge

In 1984, Michael Monier and Talon Financial Corporation (Talon) formed the Coronado Partnership (Coronado). Monier and Talon were general partners; other individuals and entities were limited partners in the venture.

Shortly after its formation, Coronado purchased an office and warehouse complex in Tucson. In 1986, the partnership refinanced this property with a loan from Catalina Mortgage Company (Catalina). Talon's president, Roger Howard, executed a promissory note in the amount of $675,000 on behalf of Coronado. In mid-1987, Talon withdrew as a general partner, leaving Monier as the sole general partner in Coronado. The

promissory note matured and $687,935.39 plus interest is now due and owing. Coronado filed for protection pursuant to Chapter 11 of the Bankruptcy Code.

In January 1989, Catalina filed a complaint against Monier in United States District Court, seeking judgment for the amount due on the promissory note plus interest, costs, and attorney's fees. Catalina alleged that Monier was jointly and severally liable with the partnership entity for the debt. Monier answered, contending, among other things, that because the note was an obligation of the partnership, the partnership assets had to be exhausted before the creditor sought recovery from an individual general partner.

Discussion

If a partnership's debt is contractual in nature, common law requires creditors to resort to and exhaust partnership assets before reaching the partners' individual assets. At common law, a partner is only jointly liable for the partnership's contractual debts, though partners are jointly and severally liable for tort obligations.

As adopted in most states, the Uniform Partnership Act (UPA) preserves this common law rule. The Arizona version of the UPA, however, provides that all partners are liable jointly and severally for everything chargeable to the partnership, and for all other debts and obligations of the partnership; but any partner may enter into a separate obligation to perform a partnership contract.

Catalina maintains that because the statute imposes joint and several liability on all partners, it may proceed against Monier without exhausting partnership assets. Catalina distinguishes cases from other jurisdictions that have considered the issue on the grounds that the applicable law imposed only joint liability as opposed to joint and several liability, that some states specifically provide by statute that partnership assets must be exhausted prior to imposing liability on individual partners for contractual obligations, and that the bankruptcy courts in some instances have misconstrued the state law involved.

Several liability is separate and distinct from liability of another to the extent that an independent action may be brought without joinder of others. The individual liability associated with partners that are jointly liable is not separate and distinct from the liability of all the partners jointly. Rather, that individual liability arises only after it has been shown that the partnership assets are inadequate. No direct cause of action may be maintained against the individual partners until the above condition is met. Several liability, on the other hand, imposes no such conditions precedent before one can be held individually liable.

Conclusion

We hold, therefore, that the scheme imposed by Arizona statutes is simply that a general partner is jointly and severally liable for partnership debts. The partner may be sued severally and his assets reached even though the partnership or other partners are not sued and their assets not applied to the debt. Under Arizona law a creditor may obtain a judgment against an individual general partner on a partnership debt and may reach the partner's assets prior to exhausting partnership assets.

CASE A.34
Commonwealth of Pennsylvania v. McKelvey and Bradley
587 A.2d 693 (1991)
Supreme Court of Pennsylvania
Larsen, Justice

Appellant Peter Bradley is a school teacher who was requested by Patrick McKelvey to provide the financial backing for a retail bicycle business. The two men entered into a limited partnership agreement, and appellant provided an $18,000.00 loan to the business. As a limited partner, appellant took no part in the operation or management of the bicycle shop. McKelvey, as general partner, handled all of the purchases, sales and financial aspects of the business. Identifying himself as the partnership's "principal" partner (we interpret this as meaning the partnership's general partner), McKelvey filed an application for sales, use and hotel occupancy license with the Department of Revenue of the Commonwealth of Pennsylvania, and designated appellant as a limited partner in the business, which was known as "Different Spokes."

On October 10, 1985, appellee, Commonwealth of Pennsylvania, Department of Revenue for the Bureau of Accounts Settlement, mailed a notice of Sales and Use tax assessment to the business address of Different Spokes for a series of tax periods beginning July 1, 1983, and ending June 30, 1985, in the amount of $17,636.86. The total assessment amounted to $27,974.21 with penalties and interest. No challenge was made to this assessment nor was the assessment paid. In April of 1986, appellee issued liens in the amount of $27,974.21 against the business and its general and limited partners. Appellant, who had not been individually notified of the assessment by the appellee, did not discover the lien that had been filed against properties he owned until he was conducting a title search several months thereafter during a routine application for a mortgage. Appellant promptly filed a Petition to Strike Tax Lien in the Court of Common Pleas of Delaware County.

Appellant's petition to strike tax lien was denied.

Appellant filed an appeal to Commonwealth Court which affirmed, holding that the notice of tax assessment sent to the limited partnership was sufficient to support the lien entered against appellant as a limited partner.

We granted appellant's petition for allowance of appeal, and we now reverse.

The trial court erred in holding by that the personal assets of a limited partner can be liened to satisfy the debt of a limited partnership.

Section 521 of the Uniform Limited Partnership Act which was in effect at the time of the events giving rise to this litigation provided as follows: "A limited partner shall not become liable as a general partner unless, in addition to the exercise of his rights and powers as a limited partner, he takes part in the control of the business."

Appellant was a limited partner and did not take part in the control or management of Different Spokes.

Accordingly, we reverse the decision of the Commonwealth Court, and we remand to the Court of Common Pleas of Delaware County for the entry of an order granting appellant's petition to strike tax lien.

CASE A.35
Water, Waste & Land , Inc., dba Westec v. Lanham
955 P.2d 997(1998)
Supreme Court of Colorado
Scott, Justice

Water, Waste, & Land, Inc., the petitioner, is a land development and engineering company doing business under the name "Westec." At the time of the events in this case, Donald Lanham and Larry Clark were managers and also members of Preferred Income Investors, LLC. (Company or P.I.I.). The Company is a limited liability company organized under the Colorado Limited Liability Company Act.

In March 1995, Clark contacted Westec about the possibility of hiring Westec to perform engineering work in connection with a development project, which involved the construction of a fast-food restaurant known as Taco Cabana. In the course of preliminary discussions, Clark gave his business card to representatives of Westec. The business card included Lanham's address, which was also the address listed as the Company's principal office and place of business in its articles of organization filed with the secretary of state. While the Company's name was not on the business card, the letters "P.I.I." appeared above the address on the card. However, there was no indication as to what the acronym meant or that P.I.I. was a limited liability company.

After further negotiations, an oral agreement was reached concerning Westec's involvement with the Company's restaurant project.

Although Westec never received a signed contract, in mid-August it did receive verbal authorization from Clark to begin work. Westec completed the engineering work and sent a bill for $9,183.40 to Lanham. No payments were made on the bill. Westec filed a claim against Clark and Lanham individually as well as against the Company. At trial, the Company admitted liability for the amount claimed by Westec.

Under the common law of agency, an agent is liable on a contract entered on behalf of a principal if the principal is not fully disclosed. In other words, an agent who negotiates a contract with a third party can be sued for any breach of the contract unless the agent discloses both the fact that he or she is acting on behalf of a principal and the identity of the principal. Westec did not know Clark was acting as an agent for the Company or that the letters "P.I.I." stood for "Preferred Income Investors," a limited liability company registered under Colorado law. Clark and Lanham failed to disclose the existence as well as the identity of the limited liability company they represented.

Section 7-80-208 of the Colorado Limited Liability Company Act (1997) states:

The fact that the articles of organization are on file in the office of the secretary of state is notice that the limited liability company is a limited liability company and is notice of all other facts set forth therein which are required to be set forth in the articles of organization.

In order to relieve Lanham of liability, this provision would have to be read to establish a conclusive presumption that a third party who deals with the agent of a limited liability company always has constructive notice of the existence of the agent's principal. We are not persuaded that the statute can bear such an interpretation.

Such a construction exaggerates the plain meaning of the language in the statute. This broad interpretation would be an invitation to fraud, because it would leave the agent of a limited liability company free to mislead third parties into the belief that the agent would bear personal financial responsibility under any contract, when in fact, recovery would be limited to the assets of a limited liability company not known to the third party at the time the contract was made. This construction would open the door to sharp practices and outright fraud. We may presume that in adopting section 7-80-208, the General Assembly did not intend to create a safe harbor for deceit.

In sum, then, section 7-80-208 places third parties on constructive notice that a fully identified company—that is, identified by a name such as "Preferred Income Investors, LLC," or the like—is a limited liability company provided that its articles of organization have been filed with the secretary of state. Section 7-80-208 is of little force, however, in determining whether a limited liability company's agent is personally liable on the theory that the agent has failed to disclose the identity of the company.

If Clark or Lanham had told Westec's representatives that they were acting on behalf of an entity known as "Preferred Income Investors, LLC" the failure to disclose the fact that the entity was a limited liability company would be irrelevant by virtue of the statute, which provides that the articles of organization operate as constructive notice of the company's limited liability form. Lanham and Clark did not identify Preferred Income Investors, LLC, as the principal in the transaction. The "missing link" between the limited disclosure made by Clark and the protection of the notice statute was the failure to state that "P.I.I.," the Company, stood for "Preferred Income Investors, LLC."

We see no legal basis to excuse the agents of the LLC from liability and therefore we reverse the judgment of the district court that found them not liable.

CASE A.36

Little v. Howard Johnson Co., 183 Mich. App. 675
455 N.W. 2d 390 (1990)
Court of Appeals of Michigan
MacKenzie, Judge

Plaintiff Joy Little was injured on January 23, 1982, when she slipped on a walkway which allegedly had not been adequately cleared of ice and snow. The walkway was located on property on which a restaurant business was being operated as a franchise of defendant, Howard Johnson Company. Plaintiff filed suit alleging liability for her injuries. In district court Howard Johnson moved for summary disposition. The circuit court denied defendant's subsequent motion for summary disposition and the case proceeded to mediation. When it mediated at less than $10,000, the case was removed to district court for lack of circuit court jurisdiction. The district court found no factual dispute and ruled as a matter of law that defendant was neither directly nor vicariously liable for plaintiff's injuries and, accordingly, granted the motion. The circuit court reversed without elaboration.

Little posited three theories under which she claimed Howard Johnson as a franchisor may be held liable for the injuries she sustained at the franchisee's restaurant: (1) direct liability as a possessor of the land, (2) vicarious liability based on agency principles, and (3) liability based on an apparent agency theory.

1. Direct Liability

The general rule in Michigan is that invitors are liable for known dangerous conditions of property and for dangerous conditions which might be discovered with reasonable care. However, an invitor's direct liability requires the presence of both possession and control over the land.

Little contends that defendant should be deemed a "possessor" of the land as a result of the rights of control it retained in its franchise agreement with the restaurant's franchisee. We disagree. The franchise agreement merely provides that the franchisee "at all times will maintain the interior and exterior of the building's and surrounding premises in a clean, orderly, and sanitary condition satisfactory to Howard Johnson." In short, there is no issue of fact that defendant was a possessor of the premises who could be held directly liable for plaintiff's injuries.

2. Vicarious Liability

Generally, a principal is responsible for the negligence of its agent. In Michigan, the test for a principal-agent relationship is whether the principal has the right to control the agent. The threshold question here is what constitutes "control" sufficient to deem a franchisee to be an agent of a franchisor. Howard Johnson argues that a franchisor must have the right to control the day-to-day operations of a franchisee in order to establish an agency relationship. Little, on the other hand, maintains that an agency relationship is created where the franchisor retains the right to set standards regarding the products and services offered by the franchisee, the right to regulate such items as the furnishings and advertising used by the franchisee, and the right to inspect for conformance with the agreement. We agree with defendant.

This Court has repeatedly held that in order to establish vicarious liability in such actions, the landowner must have retained some control and direction over the actual day-to-day work. It is not enough that the owner retained mere contractual control, the right to make safety inspections, or general oversight. The franchise agreement in this case primarily insured the uniformity and standardization of products and services offered by a Howard Johnson restaurant. These obligations do not affect the control of daily operations.

3. Apparent Agency

Howard Johnson argues that the district court properly concluded that no genuine issue of fact existed regarding its liability under an agency theory. We agree. Here, Little has failed to offer any documentary evidence that she was harmed as a result of relying on the perceived fact that the franchise was an agent of Howard Johnson. No evidence was presented which indicated that plaintiff justifiably expected that the walkway would be free of ice and snow because she believed that Howard Johnson operated the restaurant. Reversed.

CASE A.37

Johnson v. Dodgen, 451 N.W. 2d. 168 (1990)
Supreme Court of Iowa
Lavorato, Justice

This breach of contract action is the aftermath of a bank failure caused by the embezzlement of $16.7 million by Des Moines stockbroker Gary Lewellyn. In 1967 Joe W. Dodgen agreed to buy controlling interest in the First National Bank of Humboldt under a stock purchase agreement (agreement) calling for monthly payments. Ben P. and Adeline G. St. John, the sellers, died shortly thereafter. Two trusts were then established to receive payments under the agreement.

Dodgen assigned the agreement to his company, Humboldt Realty Insurance Co., Inc. (Humboldt Realty), which was not in existence at the time the agreement was executed, underwent several name changes until it became known as Iowa Growthland Financial Corporation. After the bank was closed in 1982, Iowa Growthland continued to make payments under the agreement until 1984.

The trusts then sued Dodgen and Iowa Growthland for the payments that were in arrears. Dodgen and Iowa Growthland filed an answer in which they raised failure of consideration as an affirmative defense. Simply put, they were claiming that the consideration for the agreement failed when the bank went out of existence. In addition, Dodgen asserted that he was not personally liable because he signed the agreement as an agent for Humboldt Realty. In its counterclaim, Iowa Growthland sought damages on the theory of unjust enrichment for payments it made after the bank was closed. The case was tried to a jury. By way of answers to special verdict forms, the jury found that the trustees were not entitled to recover for breach of contract, that Dodgen was indeed acting as an agent when he signed the agreement, and that Iowa Growthland was not entitled to damages for its claim of unjust enrichment.

The district court granted new trial on all the issues. Dodgen and Iowa Growthland appealed; the trustees crossappealed.

We reverse and remand with directions to enter judgment in favor of the trustees pursuant to Iowa Rule of Appellate Procedure 26.

I. Failure of Consideration

Dodgen and Iowa Growthland contend that the continued existence of the bank was the essence or root of the agreement—the thing Dodgen really bargained for. They argue that when the bank was closed the consideration for Dodgen's promise to pay failed. This failure of consideration, they assert, excused any future performance on their part. There is a difference between lack of consideration and failure of consideration. A lack of consideration means no contract is ever formed. In contrast, a failure of consideration means the contract is valid when formed but becomes unenforceable because the performance bargained for has not been rendered. In our view the potential failure of any business that is being sold is always a risk in the contemplation of the parties. If the buyer wants protection against the risk, the simple solution is to hedge against it in the agreement. That was not done here. Consequently, Dodgen assumed that risk.

What Dodgen bargained for was control of the bank through the stock he purchased; he got it and had it for fifteen years. The fact that his investment later turned out worthless does not, in our view, constitute failure of consideration.

A. Essence of the Agreement

Under the agreement here, Dodgen agreed to purchase from St. John 506 shares of capital stock of the bank. The 506 shares represented 50.6% of the issued and outstanding stock of the bank. By this purchase, Dodgen was acquiring controlling interest in the bank.

B. The Executory Nature of the Agreement

This issue is inextricably intertwined with the essence of the agreement issue. Dodgen and Iowa Growthland contend that the agreement was still executory when the bank was closed because the trustees had physical possession of the stock. While the trustees are still able to turn over the stock, Dodgen and Iowa Growthland argue such a gesture would be meaningless because the asset that the stock represents is nonexistent. So, they argue, there was a failure of consideration when the bank was closed.

Here we think the parties intended title to the stock to pass to Dodgen once the stock was registered in his name. At this point several things had occurred. Dodgen had made the down payment called for in the agreement and began exercising control of the bank. Likewise, St. John had substantially performed his part of the agreement. Only two promises remained unperformed: Dodgen's full payment of the purchase price and St. John's delivery of physical possession of the stock.

In these circumstances, we think there was a constructive delivery of the stock to Dodgen. Although the collateral provision of the agreement denied Dodgen physical possession of the stock, it did give him the right to such possession upon full payment. The provision also gave him rights of ownership in all other respects. Risk of loss passed with this constructive delivery. The decline in the stock's value gave Dodgen no greater right to avoid his obligation to pay than an enhanced value would have given St. John an excuse for not delivering the stock.

C. Inability to Pledge the Stock as Security

It is true that under the agreement Dodgen could not borrow against the stock. Dodgen and Iowa Growthland assert this constraint as further evidence that consideration for the agreement failed. The short answer to this argument is that Dodgen should not be allowed to take advantage of a provision he agreed to.

II. Unjust Enrichment

We have already determined that there was not, as a matter of law, a failure of consideration. In view of our holding on the failure of consideration issue, we think the district court should have sustained the trustees' motion for directed verdict on the unjust enrichment counterclaim.

III. Agency

The trustees moved for a directed verdict against Dodgen personally because the record showed he signed the agreement. Dodgen resisted the motion, contending there was enough evidence in the record to generate a jury question on his agency defense. The only evidence on this point was Dodgen's testimony. Dodgen testified that when he signed the agreement St. John agreed that Humboldt Realty—Iowa Growthland's predecessor—would be the responsible party. The district court overruled the motion. The jury then determined that Dodgen was acting as an agent for Humboldt Realty when he signed the agreement. For reasons that follow we think the district court should have sustained the motion for directed verdict.

At the time Dodgen and St. John signed the agreement, Humboldt Realty was not in existence. Ordinarily in these circumstances Dodgen would be personally liable. The law is clear that an agent who purports to act on behalf of a nonexistent principal is liable as a party to the agreement. The rationale for the rule is simply that in such circumstances there is no agency. This situation frequently happens when a corporate promoter enters into contracts before the corporation is actually incorporated. There is, however, an exception to this rule. If the other contracting party knows that the principal does not exist and looks to the principal alone for responsibility, the promoter is relieved of personal liability.

Here the pivotal question is whether St. John agreed to look to Humboldt Realty alone for payment. We think reasonable minds would conclude from this record that he did not. We have substantial evidence that establishes Dodgen was acting in his personal capacity. First, as the district court ruled, the language of the agreement is unequivocal on this point. For example, the opening paragraph states that "This agreement made and entered into by and between B. P. St. John and Joe W. Dodgen said B. P. St. John being hereafter referred to as the seller and the said Joe W. Dodgen being hereafter referred to as the buyer." Moreover, Dodgen ostensibly signed the agreement in his individual capacity.

Second, St. John and Dodgen were, at the time of the agreement, very knowledgeable in financial and legal matters. It is inconceivable to us that St. John would turn over valuable assets and look solely to a nonexistent corporation for payment. It is also equally inconceivable to us that Dodgen would fail to insist on express language in the agreement that would relieve him of personal liability. Simply put, we think reasonable minds would conclude that the absence of such language meant that St. John was looking to Dodgen for payment, and Dodgen knew it.

Last, in 1982 Dodgen acknowledged his personal liability. In a letter to one of the trustees—a letter we previously mentioned—Dodgen said:

You are also correct in that the contract between me and Ben and Adeline St. John is a personal obligation even though it was later assigned to First Investors Services, Inc.

This damaging admission coupled with the other evidence leads us to conclude that the district court should have sustained the motion for directed verdict on the agency issue.

IV. Disposition

We reverse the posttrial ruling of the district court. We remand the case to the district court with directions to enter judgment in favor of the trustees for $160,976.26—the delinquent amount at the time of trial—together with interest and costs.

CASE A.38

United States v. WRW Corporation, 986 F.2d 138 (1993)
United States Court of Appeals for the Sixth Circuit
Peck, Judge

In 1985, civil penalties totaling $90,350 were assessed against WRW Corporation (WRW), a Kentucky corporation, for serious violations of safety standards under the Federal Mine Safety and Health Act (the Act) which resulted in the deaths of two miners. Following the imposition of civil penalties, WRW liquidated its assets and went out of business.

Three individual defendants, who were the sole shareholders, officers, and directors of WRW, were later indicted and convicted for willful violations of mandatory health and safety standards under the Act. Roger Richardson, Noah Woolum, and William Woolum each served prison sentences and paid criminal fines. After his release from prison, Roger Richardson filed for bankruptcy under Chapter 7 of the Bankruptcy Code.

The United States (the Government) brought this action in May of 1988 against WRW and Roger Richardson, Noah Woolum, and William Woolum to recover the civil penalties previously imposed against WRW. The district court denied the individual defendants' motion to dismiss and granted summary judgment to the Government piercing the corporate veil under state law and holding the individual defendants liable for the civil penalties assessed against WRW. For the reasons discussed herein, we affirm.

Piercing the Corporate Veil

Having determined that the imposition of a $90,350 sanction upon the defendants does not violate principles of double jeopardy, we turn to the defendants' argument that the district court erred in holding the individual defendants liable for the penalty by piercing the corporate veil of WRW under Kentucky law.

The district court held that it was appropriate to pierce WRW's corporate veil under either an equity theory or an alter ego theory, both of which are recognized under Kentucky law. Under either theory, the following factors must be considered when determining whether to pierce the corporate veil: (1) undercapitalization; (2) a failure to observe the formalities of corporate existence; (3) non-payment or overpayment of dividends; (4) a siphoning off of funds by dominant shareholders; and (5) the majority shareholders having guaranteed corporate liabilities in their individual capacities.

The court first found that WRW was undercapitalized because it was incorporated with only $3,000 of capital, which the record indicates was insufficient to pay normal expenses associated with the operation of a coal mine. The district court next found that WRW failed to observe corporate formalities, noting that no bylaws were produced by the defendants, and all corporate actions taken by the individual defendants were without corporation authorization. Finally, although WRW never distributed any dividends to the individual defendants, and there was no evidence that the individual defendants siphoned off corporate funds, these factors alone do not mitigate against piercing the corporate veil in this case because WRW was never sufficiently capitalized and operated at a loss during its two years of active existence.

In addition to holding that the equities of this case support piercing the corporate veil, the district court held that the corporate veil should be pierced under the "alter ego" theory, because WRW and the defendants did not have separate personalities. In light of the lack of observance of corporate formalities or distinction between the individual defendants and the corporation, we agree with the district court's conclusion that "there was a complete merger of ownership and control of WRW with the individual Defendants."

The specific factual findings made by the district court amply support piercing the corporate veil of WRW and holding the individual defendants liable for the penalty assessed against the corporate entity. For all of the foregoing reasons, the judgment of the district court is AFFIRMED.

*C*ASE A.39

Neal v. Alabama By-Products Corporation
No. 8282, 1990. Del. Ch. Lexis 127 (1990)
Court of Chancery of Delaware
Chandler, Vice Chancellor

Alabama By-Products Corporation (ABC) is a Delaware corporation engaged during the 1970s and 1980s (and for many years before that), primarily in three lines of business. It mined coal on a cost plus basis for Alabama Power Company (a major utility in Alabama); it mined coal for its own account from surface and underground mines that it owned, and it manufactured and sold foundry coke from a plant in Birmingham called the Tarrant plant. To a certain extent ABC was also engaged in the development and sale of timber and forestry products on lands it owned.

ABC's two classes of stock traded in the over the-counter market and were not listed on an exchange. Trading history in the stock was sporadic, but shows that the average bid price between 1977 and 1984 ranged from $47 to $75 per share. Class A stock had voting rights, while class B stock did not. At all times relevant to this lawsuit, there were about 757,300 class A shares and 1,000,000 class B shares authorized, issued, and outstanding.

Drummond, an Alabama Corporation, is also engaged in the mining and sale of coal in the state of Alabama. In 1977 it became interested in acquiring ABC. Between September 1977 and February 1978 Drummond acquired, in privately negotiated transactions, about 75,800 class A shares of ABC stock and 188,167 class B shares. Drummond also obtained a controlling interest in Alabama Chemical Products Company (ACPC), a holding company which at the time held 476,420 class A shares of ABC stock (about 63% of those outstanding). Drummond paid the equivalent of $110 per share of ABC stock in these transactions. The book value of ABC's common stock on December 31, 1977, was $55.47 per share. Drummond eventually caused the liquidation of ACPC, with the resulting distribution of the ABC class A stock to Drummond and other ACPC stockholders.

Drummond reconstituted ABC's board of directors in December 1977, replacing five of the nine ABC directors with Drummond designees. At all relevant times for purposes of this litigation, a majority of ABC's directors were also directors or executive officers of Drummond. Around the time that it gained control of ABC's board, Drummond created an executive committee consisting of Gary Neal Drummond, E.A. Drummond and the then current president of ABC. The executive committee had authority to act on behalf of ABC's board of directors. From its controller position, Drummond caused ABC to lease some of its coal reserves to Drummond. Drummond also purchased ABC mined coal and resold it in certain markets.

In late December 1977 Drummond presented a merger proposal to ABC's board, proposing the acquisition of all outstanding shares not owned by Drummond. This proposal was later withdrawn. Three years later, in 1981, Drummond discussed with Goldman, Sachs, and Company (Goldman Sachs), its investment banker, the possibility of acquiring the remaining equity in ABC. Goldman Sachs recommended at the time that Drummond propose a cash merger at a minimum price of $85 per share. Nevertheless, Drummond decided not to pursue the acquisition at that time.

On March 17, 1983, Drummond again proposed a merger to ABC's board of directors, a proposal by which each share of ABC not owned by Drummond would have been converted into the right to receive $65 in cash and ABC would have become a wholly-owned subsidiary of Drummond. A special committee of ABC's board of directors (consisting of three ABC directors who were not directors or executive officers of Drummond) recommended the retention of the firm of Kidder, Peabody and Company, Inc. (Kidder Peabody), to evaluate the 1983 merger proposal and to determine whether it was fair from a financial point of view to unaffiliated ABC shareholders. Kidder Peabody's report, submitted in September 1983, concluded that Drummond's $65 cash merger offer was not fair from a financial point of view to unaffiliated ABC shareholders. Drummond's 1983 proposal was later withdrawn.

Drummond acquired additional shares of ABC class A and class B stock in 1984 for $54.40 and $55 per share respectively. Although it was provided, in connection with the 1984 acquisitions, that additional payments would be made by Drummond if its board of directors formally approved a tender offer for shares or a merger with ABC within stipulated time limits, no tender offer or merger proposal was made during the time limits.

In December 1984 Drummond made a tender offer for any and all outstanding shares of class A and class B common stock of ABC at $75 per share. Neither Drummond nor ABC sought a fairness opinion from an independent investment banker or financial adviser with respect to the tender offer. Nor was a committee of outside ABC directors appointed to review or comment upon the fairness of the proposed transaction. ABC's board decided it would take no position with respect to the fairness of the tender offer price, leaving the ultimate determination to the judgment of the individual shareholder.

As a result of the tender offer, Drummond became the holder of more than 90% of ABC's outstanding and issued shares. Then, on August 13, 1985, Drummond effected a short-form merger under Delaware law, pursuant to which the minority shareholders were cashed out at $75.60 per share. This amount was determined by adopting the 1984 tender offer price ($75) and adding a 60 cent quarterly dividend that had been missed in 1985.

Following the August 13, 1985 merger, certain minority shareholders perfected their appraisal rights pursuant to §262 of Title 8 of the Delaware Code. These minority shareholders own approximately 50,000 class A shares and 75,000 class B shares. Neal characterizes this proceeding as a two-pronged action in which separate claims for appraisal and for unfair dealing have been joined. Drummond, as successor to ABC, is the only necessary and appropriate defendant, say petitioners, as to both the unfair dealing claim and the appraisal claim.

Neal argues they have avoided the risk of double recovery by limiting the relief requested for the unfair dealing claim to (1) costs of the proceeding, (2) reasonable attorneys fees and disbursements, and (3) expert witness fees incurred by petitioners as part of the appraisals action.

Neal also accuses Drummond of post-merger unfair dealing, complaining that Drummond's defense of the $75.60 merger price is based on contrived liabilities and transparent efforts to ascribe negative values to certain ABC assets, all of which were not disclosed to shareholders at the time of the merger. These allegedly manipulative tactics, added to the unfair dealing associated with the notice of merger and merger price, form the basis for petitioners' unfair dealing claim and, they insist, warrant an award of litigation costs.

Neal challenges the fairness of the merger price, noting that it was fixed unilaterally by Drummond without the benefit of independent expert opinion as to its fairness. They also point out that no committee, special or otherwise, was appointed to review the fairness of the merger proposal, that the merger notice to stockholders failed to disclose certain allegedly material financial information, causing stockholders to make decisions with regard to accepting the merger price or seeking appraisal on the basis of very limited information about the assets and prospects of ABC.

Neal contends that ABC's fair value was $193.40 per share on August 13, 1985. That conclusion rests upon the testimony of their valuation expert, Mr. Kenneth McGraw, based on an analysis performed by Benchmark Valuation Consultants, a division of the accounting firm Peat Marwick Maine & Co. (Benchmark), which in turn was based in part on an analysis and valuation of ABC's coal reserves and coal mining operations by Dames & Moore, a firm with expertise in geologic, mining, and natural resource engineering.

McGraw testified that Benchmark valued ABC using three alternative methods: historical earnings, net asset value, and discounted cash flow. By the historical earnings approach, Benchmark arrived at a value of $166 per share of ABC stock. The net asset methodology resulted in a value of $205 per share. The discounted cash flow approach resulted in a valuation of $225 per share. Benchmark then applied a weighted average, assigning the greatest weight (40%) to the historical earnings and net asset value approaches and the lowest weight (20%) to the discounted cash flow methodology, to arrive at a valuation based on all three valuation methodologies, of $193.40 per share.

Respondents assert that the merger price was fair. The merger price, in fact, was extremely generous, because respondents contend that ABC's statutory fair value is only $64 per share, more than $11 less than Drummond paid in the merger. Respondents' valuation is based upon the testimony of their expert trial witnesses, Arnold Spangler, a general partner at Lazard Freres & Co. (Lazard) and Robert Wilken of Paul Weir Company (Weir) who estimated the company's coal reserves.

Lazard's valuation appears to have been based on a hybrid discounted cash flow and net asset methodology. The analysis was designed to predict the value of future cash flows from ABC's continuing operations, including ABC owned mines, power company mines, and the Tarrant coke plant over a 13 year period from 1985 through 1997. This period corresponded to either the life of a variety of ABC's long-term contracts or to the exhaustion of its coal reserves, leaving only its Tarrant coke operation viable in 1997. Lazard arrived at a net after tax cash flow that ABC's continuing operations were expected to generate from 1985 to 1997, to which Lazard applied a multiple of five against the 1997 projected net cash flow (the terminal value) arriving at a value for ABC's activities following the terminal year.

The contrasting opinions regarding ABC's value in August 1985 demonstrate how differently petitioners and respondents view the business prospect and asset valuations of ABC. These starkly contrasting views have been presented to the Court through expert witnesses who have relied on complex business valuation methodologies. Although Benchmark relied on three different methodologies, there has been remarkably little disagreement over the illegitimacy of the valuation techniques used by the parties in this case. Dispute has been over the assumptions on which the methodologies have been based as well as the underlying information supplied to the experts. With expert opinions arrayed on each side of widely divergent arguments about the worth of certain assets, or the scope of certain liabilities, the Court is forced to pick and choose among the competing contentions, in search of a reasonable, and fair, value. That is this Court's mandate: determine the fair value of the stock of ABC on August 13, 1985.

Both sides have relied on a discounted future returns model and a net asset model, with petitioners' expert also using a historical earnings analysis. Other valuation approaches, with equivalent theoretical legitimacy, could have been used. But I am satisfied that respondents discounted future cash flow methodology is the appropriate valuation model in this case, especially since it was also used by petitioners' expert.

The more difficult task is to move beyond the analytical framework in order to test the underlying assumptions about ABC that the experts poured into the valuation models. This is the heart of the matter, for, as one commentator has noted, methods of valuation, including a discounted cash flow analysis, are only as good as the inputs to the model. A valuation methodology can produce a correct answer for any type of input. So the relevant question is not how correct the resulting answer is, but how correct was the input or datum that produced the answer? Accordingly this Court must view the assumptions and underlying factual premises for the valuation methodology actually used by both respondents and petitioners. Not every assumption need be scrutinized, however, for the parties have managed to agree, despite their best efforts, on certain assumptions and facts. Serious disputes exist in about eight different areas. The four principal areas of disagreement concern the value of ABC's coal reserves, the value of ABC's investment in the VP-5 mine in Virginia, the amount of ABC's excess working capital and, finally, the EME report on the purported environmental liability at ABC's Tarrant coke plant. The Court is satisfied that respondents discounted future cash flow methodology is the appropriate valuation model in this case, especially since it was also used by petitioner's expert.

The fair value of the petitioners' shares subject to the Court's appraisal was $180.67 per share on August 13, 1985. Petitioners shall be entitled to simple interest upon that amount at a rate of 12-½ percent, payable from the date of the merger to the date of payment. The costs of this proceeding, other than expert witness costs and attorneys' fees, shall be assessed against the surviving corporation.

An Order consistent with this Memorandum Opinion has been entered.

Case A.40

Lampf, Pleva, Lipkind, Prupis & Petigrow v. Gilbertson
111 S.CT. 2773, 115 L.ED.2D 321 (1991)
United States Supreme Court

Blackmun, Justice

The controversy arises from the sale of seven Connecticut limited partnerships formed for the purpose of purchasing and leasing computer hardware and software. Petitioner Lampf, Pleva, Lipkind, Prupis & Petigrow is a West Orange, New Jersey, law firm that aided in organizing the partnerships and that provided additional legal services, including the preparation of opinion letters addressing the tax consequences of investing in the partnerships. The several plaintiff-respondents purchased units in one or more of the partnerships during the years 1979 through 1981 with the expectation of realizing federal income tax benefits therefrom.

The partnerships failed, due in part to the technological obsolescence of their wares. In late 1982 and early 1983, Gilbertson, et al., received notice that the United States Internal Revenue Service was investigating the partnerships. The IRS subsequently disallowed the claimed tax benefits because of overvaluation of partnership assets and lack of profit motive. On November 3, 1986, and June 4, 1987, Gilbertson, et al., filed their respective complaints in the United States District Court for the District of Oregon, naming as defendant's petitioner and others involved in the preparation of offering memoranda for the partnerships. The complaints alleged that plaintiff-respondents were induced to invest in the partnerships by misrepresentations in the offering memoranda, in violation of, among other things, § 10(b) of the 1934 Securities Exchange Act and Rule 10b-5. The claimed misrepresentations were said to include assurances that the investments would entitle the purchasers to substantial tax benefits; that the leasing of the hardware and software packages would generate a profit; that the software was readily marketable; and that certain equipment appraisals were accurate and reasonable. Gilbertson, et al., asserted that they became aware of the alleged misrepresentations only in 1985 following the disallowance by the IRS of the tax benefits claimed.

After consolidating the actions for discovery and pretrial proceedings, the District Court granted summary judgment for the defendants on the ground that the complaints were not timely filed. The Court of Appeals for the Ninth Circuit reversed and remanded the cases. In view of the divergence of opinion among the Circuits regarding the proper limitations period for Rule 10b-5 claims, we granted certiorari to address this important issue.

It is the usual rule that when Congress has failed to provide a statute of limitations for a federal cause of action, a court "borrows" or "absorbs" the local time limitation most analogous to the case at hand. This practice, derived from the Rules of Decision Act, has enjoyed sufficient longevity that we may assume that, in enacting remedial legislation, Congress ordinarily "intends by its silence that we borrow state law." The rule, however, is not without exception.

First, the court must determine whether a uniform statute of limitations is to be selected. Where a federal cause of action tends in practice to "encompass numerous and diverse topics and subtopics," such that a single state limitations period may not be consistently applied within a jurisdiction, we have concluded that the federal interests in predictability and judicial economy counsel the adoption of one source, or class of sources, for borrowing purposes.

Second, assuming a uniform limitations period is appropriate, the court must decide whether this period should be derived from a state or federal source. In making this judgment, the court should accord particular weight to the geographic character of the claim.

Finally, even where geographic considerations counsel federal borrowing, the aforementioned presumption of state borrowing that requires that a court determine that an analogous federal source truly affords a "closer fit" with the cause of action at issue than does any available state-law source. Although considerations pertinent to this determination will necessarily vary depending upon the federal cause of action and the available state and federal analogues, such factors as commonality of purpose and similarity of elements will be relevant.

We conclude that where, as here, the claim asserted is one implied under a statute that also contains an express cause of action with its own time limitation, a court should look first to the statute of origin to ascertain the proper limitations period. In the present litigation, there can be no doubt that the contemporaneously enacted express remedial provisions represent "a federal statute of limitations actually designed to accommodate a balance of interests very similar to that at stake here—a statute that is, in fact, an analogy to the present lawsuit more apt than any of the suggested state-law parallels." The 1934 Act contained a number of express causes of action, each with an explicit limitations period. With only one more restrictive exception, each of these includes some variation of a 1-year period after discovery combined with a 3-year period of repose. In adopting the 1934 Act, the 73rd Congress also amended the limitations provision of the 1933 Act, adopting the 1-and-3-year structure for each cause of action contained therein. We therefore conclude that we must reject the Commission's contention that the 5-year period contained in § 20A, added to the 1934 Act in 1988, is more appropriate for § 10(b) actions than is the 1-and-3-year structure in the Act's original remedial provisions.

Litigation instituted pursuant to § 10(b) and Rule 10b-5 therefore must be commenced within one year after the discovery of the facts constituting the violation and within three years after such violation. As there is no dispute that the earliest of plaintiff-respondents' complaints was filed more than three years after petitioner's alleged misrepresentations, Gilbertson et al., claims were untimely.

The judgment of the Court of Appeals is reversed.

CASE A.41
Snyder v. Michael's Stores, Inc.
California Court of Appeal
Varabedian, Judge

Appellant Naomi Snyder (Naomi) was employed by respondent Michael's Stores, Inc., during part of 1993 in its Modesto retail store. Respondent Dennis Cusimano was the manager of the store. Throughout her employment, Naomi was pregnant with appellant Mikayla Snyder (Mikayla), born in January of 1994. During the time of Naomi's employment, respondents permitted a buffing machine, powered by propane gas, to be used in the store without adequate ventilation and monitoring. Respondents had been informed, received complaints from employees of Michael's, and knew, or should have known that a toxic level of carbon monoxide gas was accumulating in the store during the use of the buffer.

In the afternoon of October 2, 1993, such a buildup of carbon monoxide gas occurred, causing 21 customers and employees to

fall ill and be conveyed to hospitals. Naomi was among those made ill. Naomi was diagnosed as suffering from carbon monoxide poisoning. On this and other occasions when Naomi worked for respondent Michael's, Mikayla—in utero—was exposed to toxic levels of carbon monoxide. Carbon monoxide binds to hemoglobin and reduces the capacity of blood to transport oxygen, and poisons a variety of intracellular mechanisms for the transport of oxygen further impairing cellular respiration. The deprivation of adequate oxygen to Mikayla legally caused permanent damage to her brain and other parts of the nervous system and body. As a result, Mikayla suffers from cerebral palsy, seizure disorder, abnormal motor function and other conditions.

Appellants filed their complaint in September 1994. They filed a second amended complaint in January 1995. That complaint, as it relates to the present respondents, states a first cause of action for negligent injury to Mikayla. Respondents demurred to the second amended complaint, alleging that the workers' compensation "exclusive remedy" rule bars the causes of action alleged in the complaint. The trial court granted the demurrer because plaintiffs' exclusive remedy is workers' compensation. Appellants timely appeal the amended judgment of dismissal.

As a general matter, California and the overwhelming majority of American jurisdictions permit an action in tort for prenatal injuries to a child. The applicable rules reflect an implied "bargain" between employee and employer. The workers' compensation plan imposes reciprocal concessions upon employer and employee alike, withdrawing from each certain rights and defenses available at common law; the employer assumes liability without fault, receiving relief from some elements of damage available at common law; the employee gains relatively unconditional protection for impairment of his earning capacity, surrendering his common law right to elements of damages unrelated to earning capacity. If an injury meets the "conditions of compensation"—in essence, if the injury is work-related—the workers' compensation system provides the exclusive remedy for such injury.

Courts have extended the exclusivity rule beyond injury to the employee personally, and in addition have limited to the workers' compensation system all persons injured as a derivative result of the employee's injury. Thus, in California and the majority of jurisdictions, family members' claims for loss of consortium, loss of support, and infliction of emotional distress (e.g., as a result of seeing the employee injured) are barred except as they may be compensated under the workers' compensation laws.

The exclusivity rule applies in derivative injury cases even though the workers' compensation scheme to which the victim is consigned does not actually compensate the type of injury the victim has suffered.

Nevertheless, there are limits to the exclusivity rule, limits that permit the employee's spouse or child to sue in tort where the dependent suffers a direct injury due to the negligence of the employer, as opposed to an injury consequent to the employee's injury.

In the majority of jurisdictions deciding the issue, a child has been permitted to sue in tort when the negligence of the employer of the child's mother has directly resulted in injury to the child while in utero. The workers' compensation bargain is limited, however, to the consequences of injuries to the employee. When the spouse or child of an employee is directly injured by the employer's negligence, and not as a further consequence of injury to the employee, we have noted above that California and most other jurisdictions permit the nonemployee victim to sue under general principles of tort law.

The complaint in the present case does not allege any disabling injury to Naomi. Rather, it alleges direct injury to Mikayla as a result of the employer's negligent contamination of the air inside its store. As such, the complaint states a cause of action that is not barred by the Workers' Compensation Act. The judgment of dismissal is reversed and the matter is remanded to the trial court for an order overruling respondents' general demurrer.

CASE A.42
Robinson v. Jacksonville Shipyards, Inc.
760 F. Supp. 1486 (1991)
United States District Court
Melton, District Judge

Plaintiff Lois Robinson ("Robinson") is a female employee of Jacksonville Shipyards, Inc. ("JSI"). She has been a welder since September 1977. Robinson is one of a very small number of female skilled craftworkers employed by JSI. Between 1977 and the present, Robinson was promoted from third-class welder to second-class welder and from second-class welder to her present position as a first-class welder.

JSI is a Florida corporation that runs several shipyards engaged in the business of ship repair, including the Commercial Yard and the Mayport Yard. As a federal contractor, JSI has affirmative action and non-discrimination obligations. Defendant Arnold McIlwain ("McIlwain") held the office of President of JSI from the time Robinson was hired by the company through the time of the trial of this case.

In addition to a welding department, JSI's other craft departments include shipfitting, sheetmetal, electrical, transportation, shipping, and receiving (including toolroom), carpenter, boilermaker, inside machine, outside machine, rigging, quality assurance, and pipe. Employees in these craft departments may be assigned to work at either the Mayport Yard, situated at the Mayport Naval Station, or the Commercial Yard, situated at a riverfront site in downtown Jacksonville and sometimes referred to as the downtown yard. Robinson's job assignments at JSI have required her to work at both the Commercial Yard and the Mayport yard. Ship repair work is a dangerous profession; JSI acknowledges the need to "provide a working environment that is safe and healthful."

JSI is, in the words of its employees, "a boys club" and "more or less a man's world." Women craftworkers are an extreme rarity. The company's EEO-1 reports from 1980 to 1987 typically show that women form less than 5 percent of the skilled crafts.

Pictures of nude and partially nude women appear throughout the JSI work place in the form of magazines, plaques on the wall, photographs torn from magazines and affixed to the wall or attached to calendars supplied by advertising tool supply companies ("vendors' advertising calendars"). JSI has never distributed nor tolerated the distribution of a calendar or calendars with pictures of nude or partially nude men. Management employees from the very top down condoned these displays; often they had their own pictures.

Robinson credibly testified to the extensive, pervasive posting of pictures depicting nude women, partially nude women or sexual conduct and to the occurrence of other forms of harassing behavior perpetrated by her male coworkers and supervisors. Her testimony covered the full term of her employment, from 1977 to 1988.

Reported incidents included the following:

(1) pictures in the fab shop area, in January 1985, including one of a woman wearing black tights, the top pulled down to expose her breasts to view, and one of a nude woman in an outdoor setting apparently playing with a piece of cloth between her legs.

(2) a picture of a nude woman left on the tool box where Robinson returned her tools in the summer of 1986. The photograph depicted the woman's legs spread apart, knees bent up toward her chest, exposing her breasts and genitals. Several men were present and laughed at Robinson when she appeared upset by the picture.

(3) a drawing on a heater control box, approximately one foot square, of a nude woman with fluid coming from her genital area, in 1987, at the Commercial Yard.

(4) a dart board with a drawing of a woman's breast with her nipple as the bull's eye, in 1987 or 1988, at the Commercial Yard.

Robinson also testified about comments of a sexual nature she recalled hearing at JSI from coworkers. In some instances these comments were made while she also was in the presence of the pictures of nude or partially nude women. Among the remarks Robinson recalled are, "Hey pussycat, come here and give me a whiff," "The more you lick it, the harder it gets," "I'd like to get in bed with that," "I'd like to have some of that," "Black women taste like sardines," "It doesn't hurt women to have sex right after childbirth," etc. Defendants have admitted that pictures of nude or partially nude women have been posted in the shipfitters' trailer at the Mayport Yard during Robinson's employment at JSI.

Based on the foregoing, the Court finds that sexually harassing behavior occurred throughout the JSI working environment with both frequency and intensity over the relevant time period. Robinson did not welcome such behavior.

In April 1987, during the pendency of this lawsuit, JSI adopted a new sexual harassment policy. It was instituted unilaterally, without consulting or bargaining with the union. The official policy statement, signed by Vice-President for Operations Larry Brown, endorses the following policy:

(1) It is illegal and a violation of Jacksonville Shipyards, Inc., Policy for any employee, male or female, to sexually harass another employee by:

a. making unwelcomed sexual advances or request for sexual favors or other verbal or physical conduct of a sexual nature, a condition of an employee's continued employment, or

b. making submission to or rejection of such conduct the basis for employment decisions affecting the employee, or

c. creating an intimidating, hostile, or offensive working environment by such conduct.

(2) Any employee who believes he or she has been the subject of sexual harassment, should report the alleged act immediately to John Stewart Ext. 3716 in our Industrial Relations Department. An investigation of all complaints will be undertaken immediately. Any supervisor, agent or other employee who has been found by the Company to have sexually harassed another employee will be subject to appropriate sanctions, depending on the circumstances, from a warning in his or her file up to and including termination.

The 1987 policy had little or no impact on the sexually hostile work environment at JSI. Employees and supervisors lacked knowledge and training in the scope of those acts that might constitute sexual harassment.

The Court finds that the policies and procedures at JSI for responding to complaints of sexual harassment are inadequate. The company has done an inadequate job of communicating with employees and supervisors regarding the nature and scope of sexually harassing behavior. This failure is compounded by a pattern of unsympathetic response to complaints by employees who perceive that they are victims of harassment. This pattern includes an unwillingness to believe the accusations, an unwillingness to take prompt and stern remedial action against admitted harassers, and an express condonation of behavior that is and encourages sexually harassing conduct (such as the posting of pictures of nude and partially nude women). In some instances, the process of registering a complaint about sexual harassment became a second episode of harassment.

Ordered and Adjudged

That defendant Jacksonville Shipyards, Inc., is hereby enjoined to cease and desist from the maintenance of a work environment that is hostile to women because of their sex and to remedy the hostile work environment through the implementation, forthwith, of the Sexual Harassment Policy, which consists of the "Statement of Policy," "Statement of Prohibited Conduct," "Schedule of Penalties for Misconduct," "Procedures for Making, Investigating and Resolving Sexual Harassment and Retaliation Complaints," and "Procedures and Rules for Education and Training."

Jacksonville Shipyards, Inc. Sexual Harassment Policy
Statement of Policy

Title VII of the Civil Rights Act of 1964 prohibits employment discrimination on the basis of race, color, sex, age, or national origin. Sexual harassment is included among the prohibitions.

Sexual harassment, according to the federal Equal Employment Opportunity Commission (EEOC), consists of unwelcome sexual advances, requests for sexual favors or other

verbal or physical acts of a sexual or sex-based nature where (1) submission to such conduct is made either explicitly or implicitly a term or condition of an individual's employment; (2) an employment decision is based on an individual's acceptance or rejection of such conduct; or (3) such conduct interferes with an individual's work performance or creates an intimidating, hostile or offensive working environment.

Case A.43
Wiljef Transportation, Inc. v. NLRB, 946 F.2d 1308 (1991)
United States Court of Appeals for the Seventh Circuit
Cudahy, Circuit Judge

This case presents an interesting question concerning the balance between an employer's right of expression and its employees' right of association. Approximately two months before a vote on unionization, the employer, Wiljef Transportation, Inc. (Wiljef), read to its employees a corporate bylaw which states:

Section 2—Corporate Dissolution. Wiljef Transportation, Inc. hereby expresses as matter of corporate policy that operations will cease and the corporation will be dissolved in the event of unionization of its employees. As hereby authorized by the Board of Directors, this by-law may be announced to the employees of Wiljef Transportation, Inc. at any time deemed appropriate by the Board.

The by-law was adopted in 1979, and the announcement occurred in 1988. In the ensuing union representation election, the employees rejected unionization. The issue in this case is whether the announcement of the by-law constituted a "permitted prediction" of plant closure or a "proscribed threat." The NLRB held that the announcement was a threat in violation of Section 8(a)(1) of the National Labor Relations Act (NLRA), and Wiljef appealed to this court.

An employer's right to communicate its views to its employees is firmly established in the First Amendment and is recognized in Section 8(c) of the NLRA, which provides that "the expressing of any views, argument, or opinion shall not constitute or be evidence of an unfair labor practice if such expression contains no threat of reprisal or force or promise of benefit." On the other hand, the exceptions to the freedom of expression recognized in Section 8(c) reflect the right of employees to associate free of coercion by the employer. Section 8(a)(1) of the NLRA codifies that right by declaring that it is an unfair labor practice to interfere with, restrain or coerce employees exercising their right to organize in unions. The difficulty in cases attempting to relate these two rights is in determining when speech becomes essentially coercive rather than factually informative or predictive so as to fall outside the protection of the First Amendment and violate the NLRA. The real issue, however, remains credibility and bona fides. A by-law purporting to be a management decision to close a business in the event of unionization is not protected expression unless objective factors demonstrate that it is really controlling on the question of closure. This holding preserves the balance between free expression and the right to organize.

Absent some persuasive evidence of other measures indicating that Wiljef intends to implement the corporate policy described in the by-law, the announcement of the by-law to the employees is coercive and in violation of the NLRA. Objective evidence to lend credibility to the by-law need not be based on economics and need not necessarily indicate circumstances beyond the employer's control.

Analytically the line is clear. To predict a consequence that will occur no matter how well disposed the company is toward unions is not to threaten retaliation; to predict a consequence that will occur because the company wants to punish workers for voting for the union—a consequence desired and freely chosen by a company rather than compelled by economic forces over which it has no control—is.

In light of our conclusion that Wiljef used the by-law in an attempt to coerce its employees and that no objective evidence indicated an intent to implement the by-law, the relief granted by the NLRB is proper. The petition for review is denied, and the order of the NLRB requiring Wiljef to expunge the by-law, cease further coercive activity, and post a notice to employees indicating that it had violated the law and will cease such violations is enforced.

CASE A.44

United States v. Natelli, 527 F.2d 311 (1975)
United States Court of Appeals, Second Circuit

Gurfein, Circuit Judge

Anthony M. Natelli and Joseph Scansaroli appeal from judgments of conviction entered in the United States District Court for the Southern District of New York on December 27, 1974 after a four-week trial before the Hon. Harold R. Tyler and a jury. Judge Tyler imposed a one-year sentence and a $10,000 fine upon Natelli, suspending all but 60 days of imprisonment, and a one-year sentence and a $2,500 fine upon Scansaroli, suspending all but 10 days of the imprisonment.

Both appellants are certified public accountants. Natelli was the partner in charge of the Washington, D.C. office of Peat, Marwick, Mitchell & Co. ("Peat"), a large independent firm of auditors, and the engagement partner with respect to Peat's audit engagement for National Student Marketing Corporation ("Marketing"). Scansaroli was an employee of Peat, assigned as audit supervisor on that engagement.

Count Two of the indictment charged that, in violation of Section 32(a) of the Securities Exchange Act of 1934, four of Marketing's officers and the appellants, as independent auditors, "wilfully and knowingly made and caused to be made false and misleading statements with respect to material facts" in a proxy statement for Marketing dated September 27, 1969 and filed with the Securities and Exchange Commission (SEC) in accordance with Section 14 of the 1934 Act.

The proxy statement was issued by Marketing in connection with a special meeting of its stockholders to consider *inter alia* a charter amendment increasing its authorized capital stock and

the merger of six companies, including Interstate National Corporation ("Interstate") into Marketing.

Marketing was formed in 1966 by Cortes W. Randell. It provided to major corporate accounts a diversified range of advertising, promotional and marketing services designed to reach the youth market.

In late September or early October 1968 (after the close of the fiscal year), Randell and Bernard Kurek, Marketing's Comptroller, met with both appellants and discussed the method of accounting that Marketing had been using with respect to fixed-fee programs. In the fixed-fee program, Marketing would develop overall marketing programs for the client to reach the youth market by utilizing a combination of the mailings, posters and other advertising services offered by Marketing.

The difficulty immediately encountered was that the client "commitments" had not been booked during the fiscal year, and were not in writing. The Marketing stock which had initially been sold at $6 per share was selling in the market by September 1968 for $80, an increase of $74 in five months. A refusal to book the oral "commitments" would have resulted in Marketing's showing a large loss for the fiscal year—according to Kurek's computations, a loss of $232,000.

Pursuant to Randell's urging, Scansaroli did not seek any written verifications. He accepted a schedule prepared by Kurek which showed about $1.7 million in purported "commitments."

On the basis of the above, Natelli decided not only to recognize income on a percentage-of-completion basis, but to permit adjustment to be made on the books after the close of the fiscal year in the amount of $1.7 million for such "unbilled accounts receivable." This adjustment turned the loss for the year into a handsome profit of $388,031, showing an apparent doubling of the profit of the prior year.

After the 1968 audit had been given a full certificate by the auditors on November 14, 1968, things began to happen with respect to the $1.7 million of "sales" that had been recorded as income after fiscal year end. Within five months of publication of the annual report, by May 1969, Marketing had written off over $1 million of the $1.7 million in "sales" which the auditors had permitted to be booked.

Appellants were asked to design the write-off. . . . Instead of reducing 1968 earnings commensurately, however, no such reduction was made. Appellants were informed by tax accountants in Peat's employ that a certain deferred tax item should be reversed, resulting in a tax credit that happened to be approximately the same amount as the profit to be written off. Scansaroli "netted" this extraordinary item (the tax credit) with an unrelated ordinary item (the write-off of sales and profits). By this procedure he helped to conceal on the books the actual write-off of profits, further using the device of rounding off the tax item to make it conform exactly to the write-off. The effect of the netting procedure was to bury the retroactive adjustment which should have shown a material decrease in earnings for the fiscal year ended August 31, 1968.

The Proxy Statement

As part of the proxy statement, appellants set about to draft a footnote purporting to reconcile the Company's prior reported net sales and earnings from the 1968 report with restated amounts resulting from pooled companies reflected retroactively. The earnings summary in the proxy statement included companies acquired after fiscal 1968 and their pooled earnings. The footnote was the only place in the proxy statement which would have permitted an interested investor to see what Marketing's performance had been in its preceding fiscal year 1968, as retroactively adjusted, separate from the earnings and sales of the companies it had acquired in fiscal 1969.

At Natelli's direction, Scansaroli subtracted the written-off Marketing sales from the 1968 sales figures for the seven later acquired pooled companies without showing any retroactive adjustment for Marketing's own fiscal 1968 figures. There was no disclosure in the footnote that over $1 million of previously reported 1968 sales of Marketing had been written off. All narrative disclosure in the footnote was stricken by Natelli. This was a violation of Accounting Principles Board Opinion Number 9, which requires disclosure of prior adjustments which affect the net income of prior periods.

The proxy statement also required an unaudited statement of nine months' earnings through May 31, 1969. This was prepared by the Company, with the assistance of Peat on the same percentage of completion basis as in the 1968 audited statement. A commitment from Pontiac Division of General Motors amounting to $1,200,000 was produced two months after the end of the fiscal period. It was dated April 28, 1969.

The proxy statement was to be printed at the Pandick Press in New York on August 15, 1969. At about 3 A.M. on that day, Natelli informed Randell that the "sale" to the Pontiac Division for more than $1 million could not be treated as a valid commitment because the letter from Pontiac was not a legally binding obligation. Randell responded at once that he had a "commitment from Eastern Airlines" in a somewhat comparable amount attributable to the nine months fiscal period (which had ended more than two months earlier). Kelly, a salesman for Marketing, arrived at the printing plant several hours later with a commitment letter from Eastern Airlines, dated August 14, 1969, purporting to confirm an $820,000 commitment ostensibly entered into on May 14, just before the end of the nine-month fiscal period of September 1, 1968 through May 31, 1969. When the proxy statement was printed in final form the Pontiac "sale" had been deleted, but the Eastern "commitment" had been inserted in its place.

The proxy statement was filed with the SEC on September 30, 1969.

Natelli—Sufficiency of Evidence

It is hard to probe the intent of a defendant. Circumstantial evidence, particularly with proof of motive, where available, is often sufficient to convince a reasonable man of criminal intent beyond a reasonable doubt. When we deal with a defendant who is a professional accountant, it is even harder, at times, to distinguish between simple errors of judgment and errors made with sufficient criminal intent to support a conviction, especially when there is no financial gain to the accountant other than his legitimate fee.

The original action of Natelli in permitting the booking of unbilled sales after the close of the fiscal period in an amount sufficient to convert a loss into a profit was contrary to sound accounting practice, . . . When the uncollectability, and indeed, the nonexistence of these large receivables was established in 1969, the revelation stood to cause Natelli severe criticism and possible liability. He had a motive, therefore, intentionally to conceal the write-offs that had to be made.

Whether or not the deferred tax item was properly converted to a tax credit, the jury had a right to infer that "netting" the extraordinary item against ordinary earnings on the books in a special journal entry was, in the circumstances , motivated by a desire to conceal.

Honesty should have impelled appellants to disclose in the footnote which annotated their own audited statement for fiscal 1968 that substantial write-offs had been taken, after year end, to reflect a loss for the year. A simple desire to right the wrong that had been perpetrated on the stockholders and others by the false audited financial statement should have dictated that course. The failure to make open disclosure could hardly have been inadvertent, or a jury at least could so find, for appellants were themselves involved in determining the write-offs and their accounting treatment. The concealment of the retroactive adjustments to Marketing's 1968 year revenues and earnings could properly have been found to have been intentional for the very purpose of hiding earlier errors. There was evidence that Natelli himself changed the footnote to its final form.

The Eastern contract was a matter for deep suspicion because it was substituted so rapidly for the Pontiac contract to which Natelli had objected, and which had, itself, been produced after the end of the fiscal period, though dated earlier. It was still another unbilled commitment produced by Marketing long after the close of the fiscal period. Its spectacular appearance, as Natelli himself noted at the time, made its replacement of the Pontiac contract "weird." The Eastern "commitment" was not only in substitution for the challenged Pontiac "commitment" but strangely close enough in amount to leave the projected earnings figures for the proxy statement relatively intact. Nevertheless, it was booked as if more than $500,000 of it had already been earned. Natelli contends that he had no duty to verify the Eastern "commitment" because the earnings statement within which it was included was "unaudited."

This raises the issue of the duty of the CPA in relation to an unaudited financial statement contained within a proxy statement where the figures are reviewed and to some extent supplied by the auditors. It is common ground that the auditors were "associated" with the statement and were required to object to anything they actually "knew" to be materially false. We reject the argument of insufficiency of evidence as to Natelli, who could have pointed out the error of his previous certification and deliberately failed to do so. . . .

Scansaroli—Sufficiency of Evidence

There is some merit to Scansaroli's point that he was simply carrying out the judgments of his superior Natelli. The defense of obedience to higher authority has always been troublesome. There is no sure yardstick to measure criminal responsibility except by measurement of the degree of awareness on the part of a defendant that he is participating in a criminal act, in the absence of physical coercion such as a soldier might face. Here the motivation to conceal undermines Scansaroli's argument that he was merely implementing Natelli's instructions, at least with respect to concealment of matters that were within his own ken.

We think the jury could properly have found him guilty on the specification relating to the footnote.

With respect to the major item, the Eastern commitment, we think Scansaroli stands in a position different from that of Natelli. . . . Since in the hierarchy of the accounting firm it was not his responsibility to decide whether to book the Eastern contract, his mere adjustment of the figures to reflect it under orders was not a matter for his discretion. He cannot be held to have acted in reckless disregard of the facts.

We have considered the other arguments raised by appellants and find them without merit.

CASE A.45

Loretto v. Teleprompter Manhattan CATV Corp.
458 U.S. 419 (1982)
United States Supreme Court
Marshall, Justice

New York law provides that a landlord must permit a cable television company to install its cable facilities upon his property. N.Y. Exec. Law § 828 (1) (McKinney Supp. 1982). In this case, the cable installation occupied portions of appellant's roof and the side of her building.

The New York Court of Appeals ruled that this appropriation does not amount to a taking. The Court of Appeals ruled that the law serves a legitimate police power purpose—eliminating landlord fees and conditions that inhibit the development of CATV, which has important educational and community benefits. Rejecting the argument that a physical occupation authorized by government is necessarily a taking, the court stated that the regulation does not have an excessive economic impact upon appellant when measured against her aggregate property rights, and that it does not interfere with any reasonable investment-backed expectations. Accordingly, the court held that Section 828 does not work a taking of appellant's property. We conclude that a permanent physical occupation authorized by government is a taking without regard to the public interests that it may serve.

In *United States v. Pewee Coal Co.*, the Court unanimously held that the Government's seizure and direction of operation of a coal mine to prevent a national strike of coal miners constituted a taking. The plurality had little difficulty concluding that because there had been an "actual taking of possession and control," the taking was as clear as if the Government held full title

and ownership. . . . In *United States v. Central Eureka Mining Co.*, by contrast, the Court found no taking where the Government had issued a war-time order requiring nonessential gold mines to cease operations for the purpose of conserving equipment and manpower for use in mines more essential to the war effort. The Court reasoned that "the Government did not occupy, use, or in any manner take physical possession of the gold mines or the equipment connected with them."

The historical rule that a permanent physical occupation of another's property is a taking has more than tradition to commend it. Such an appropriation is perhaps the most serious form of invasion of an owner's property interests. To borrow a metaphor, *cf. Andrus v. Allard*, the government does not simply take a single "strand" from the "bundle" of property rights: it chops through the bundle, taking a slice of every strand.

This Court has consistently affirmed that States have broad power to regulate housing conditions in general and the landlord-tenant relationship in particular without paying compensation for all economic injuries that such regulation entails. In none of these cases, however, did the government authorize the permanent occupation of the landlord's property by a third party. Consequently, our holding today in no way alters the analysis governing the State's power to require landlords to comply with building codes and provide utility connections, mailboxes, smoke detectors, fire extinguishers, and the like in the common area of a building. So long as these regulations do not require the landlord to suffer the physical occupation of a portion of his building by a third party, they will be analyzed under the multi-factor inquiry general possessory governmental activity.

Our holding today is very narrow. We affirm the traditional rule that a permanent physical occupation of property is a taking. In such a case, the property owner entertains an historically-rooted expectation of compensation, and the character of the invasion is qualitatively more intrusive than perhaps any other category of property regulation.

The issue of the amount of compensation that is due, on which we express no opinion, is a matter for the state courts to consider on remand. The judgment of the New York Court of Appeals is reversed and the case is *remanded* for further proceedings not inconsistent with this opinion.

CASE A.46

X-TRA Art, Inc. v. Consumer Product Safety Commission
1991 W.L. 405183 (N.D. Cal.) (1991)
United States District Court
Patel, District Judge

X-TRA Art, Inc. produces Rainbow Foam Paint (Rainbow) a shaving cream-like paint designed for use by children ages three years and up. In December 1990, Consumers Union, a nonprofit organization, published an article in the children's magazine, "Zillions," which indicated that Rainbow was an unsafe toy because it could catch fire. Plaintiffs demanded a retraction. Irwin Landau, Consumers Union editorial director, initially sent a letter apologizing for the article and indicating that Consumers

Union had made a mistake and would publish a retraction. On December 31, 1990, Landau sent plaintiffs another letter indicating that Consumers Union had conducted additional tests on Rainbow, believed the paint to be in violation of the Federal Hazardous Substances Act (FHSA), and had reported it to the Consumer Product Safety Commission (CPSC). Tests conducted by the CPSC indicated that the Rainbow container, when held upright horizontally, and especially upside down, and exposed to a flame at times produced a flame or flashback (a flame extending back to the dispenser).

On January 17, 1991, Lee Baxter of the CPSC sent plaintiffs a Letter of Advice informing plaintiffs that the CPSC had found Rainbow to be a banned hazardous substance under the FHSA because it was flammable. Baxter requested that X-TRA Art cease distribution and sale of the product and reformulate it. The letter provided plaintiffs with an opportunity to submit opposing views and warned plaintiffs of potential criminal liability if X-TRA Art continued to distribute Rainbow. A copy of the letter was sent to the California Department of Health Services, which subsequently recommended to the California Department of Education that Rainbow not be purchased for use in California public schools.

Plaintiffs sent two letters to the CPSC outlining the objections to the Letter of Advice. The CPSC responded in a letter dated March 18, 1991, which addressed plaintiffs' objections and threatened civil penalties if X-TRA Art did not cease distribution of Rainbow.

As a result of the CPSC findings, on April 26, 1991, the United States Attorney for the Connecticut district secured a warrant authorizing the seizure of Rainbow stored at Early Learning Centre, a toy distribution warehouse in Milford, Connecticut. The warrant was executed on April 29 and the Early Learning Centre instructed its outlets to cease sale of the product. The U.S. Attorney issued a press release detailing the seizure action and CPSC findings regarding Rainbow. Plaintiffs have moved for a preliminary injunction to prevent any further government action against Rainbow.

X-TRA Art bring this action to enjoin the CPSC from taking any action to remove Rainbow Foam Paint from the market pursuant to the Federal Hazardous Substances Act. Plaintiffs argue that: (1) the CPSC has failed to follow statutorily mandated procedural requirements in declaring Rainbow a banned hazardous substance pursuant to the FHSA; (2) the CPSC used invalid and improper testing methods in determining that Rainbow is flammable; (3) the CPSC violated provisions of the Consumer Product Safety Act, governing public disclosure of findings concerning safety hazards posed by products; (4) the CPSC cannot establish that substantial injury or illness can be caused as a proximate result of any customary or reasonably foreseeable use of Rainbow, as required by the FHSA; and (5) plaintiffs' rights to due process and equal protection have been violated.

Following an evidentiary hearing on May 7, 1991, the court ordered the government to desist from taking any action against *Rainbow* for ten days and further ordered the parties to file addi-

tional briefing on the matter. Having reviewed the parties papers and held an additional hearing, the court DENIES plaintiffs' motion for a preliminary injunction.

The CPSC argues that under FHSA a product intended for use by children is automatically banned if the CPSC determines said product to be a hazardous substance. Plaintiffs, citing to other provisions of the FHSA, contend that a children's product such as Rainbow may not be banned without notice, comment, and a public hearing. The plain language of the FHSA supports the CPSC's position.

In 1966 Congress amended the FHSLA to authorize the banning of hazardous toys, children's articles and household goods; "Labeling" was deleted from the title of the FHSLA and the Federal Hazardous Substance Act was created. The legislative history of the 1966 amendments makes it clear that, while the banning of hazardous household substances was to occur only after a public hearing, Congress intended that the Secretary (Commission) have the power to ban hazardous toys and children's articles without regulation. There is no question that plaintiffs were provided with notice of the agency action, given the Letter of Advice and the correspondence between plaintiffs and the CPSC which followed. Moreover, in early 1990 the CPSC determined that foam-like string streamers designed for children and dispensed from self-pressurized containers were flammable and therefore were banned hazardous substances. The manufacturer voluntarily recalled their products and reformulated them with a nonflammable propellant. The agency action against the string streamer products appears to have been well publicized. In light of the similarity between the string streamer products and Rainbow Foam Paint, it is surprising to hear plaintiffs argue that they were caught completely off-guard by the agency action challenged in this case.

The court concludes that X-TRA Art raised serious legal issues with regard to the procedures utilized by the CPSC in declaring Rainbow Foam Paint a "banned hazardous substance" and that plaintiffs are unlikely to prevail on the merits of the issue. This being the case, plaintiffs' motion for a preliminary injunction is DENIED.

CASE A.47

FMC Corp. v. U.S. Department of Commerce
786 F. Supp. 471 (E.D. Pa. 1992)
United States District Court
Newcomer, District Judge

This action is brought pursuant to the Comprehensive Environmental Response, Compensation and Liability Act of 1980, as amended ("CERCLA"), and the Declaratory Judgment Act. Plaintiff FMC Corporation ("FMC") owned and operated, from 1963 to 1976, the Avtex site in Front Royal, Virginia, ("the Facility"), a site which has been listed on the National Priorities List since 1986. FMC seeks indemnification from the defendants for some portion of its present and future response costs of response in performing removal actions and other response actions at the Facility. FMC bases its claim on the United States

Government ("Government") activities during the period of January 1942 through 1945 relating to the operation of a rayon manufacturing facility at the Avtex site, and contends that these activities render the Government liable as an "owner," "operator," and/or "arranger" under section 107 of CERCLA.

During World War II, after the bombing of Pearl Harbor and the Japanese conquest of Asia, the United States suffered a loss of 90% of its crude rubber supply. An urgent need arose for natural rubber substitute to be used in manufacturing airplane tires, jeep tires, and other war related items. The best rubber substitute available was high tenacity rayon tire cord. The Facility was one of the major producers of high tenacity rayon yarn, which was twisted and woven into high tenacity rayon tire cord. FMC presented evidence at trial showing that during the World War II period, the Government participated in managing and controlling the Facility, which was then owned by American Viscose Corporation ("American Viscose"), requiring the Facility to manufacture increasing quantities of high tenacity rayon yarn, which involved the treatment of hazardous materials, and necessitated the disposal of hazardous materials. FMC also presented evidence showing that the Government owned "facilities" and equipment at the plant used in the treatment and disposal of hazardous materials.

The evidence included the following:

(1) During World War II, the Government took over numerous plants which, for a multitude of reasons, failed to meet production requirements, including a plant producing high tenacity rayon yarn. Beginning no later than 1943, the rayon tire cord program received constant attention from the highest officials of the War Production Board (WPB), as well as top officials of the War Department and other Government departments and agencies.

(2) Once the WPB determined that there was a need for substantial expansion of the production capabilities at the Facility, Government personnel were assigned to facilitate and expedite construction. The rayon tire cord program, in general, and the implementation of the program at the Facility, in particular, required and received far more involvement, participation, and control by the Government than the vast majority of the production programs implemented during World War II.

(3) The disposal or treatment of hazardous substance is inherent in the production of high tenacity rayon yarn. The Government was familiar with the Facility's process for producing high tenacity rayon yarn. The Government knew or should have known that the disposal or treatment of hazardous substances was inherent in the manufacture of high tenacity rayon yarn and that its production requirements caused a significant increase in the amount of hazardous substances generated and disposed of at the Facility.

The District Court concluded that the United States, through the actions and authority of the WPB and other departments, agencies, and instrumentalities of the United States Government, "operated" the Facility, from approximately January 1942 to at least November 1945, as defined by section 101(20) of CERCLA. During the period the Government operated the Facility, wastes containing "hazardous substances," as defined by section 101(14) of CERCLA, and as identified in 40 C.F.R. Part 302, Table 302.4 (1990), were "disposed of" at the Facility.

There has been a "release or threatened release" of hazardous substances from facilities which were owned by the United States. Such release or threatened release of hazardous substances has caused and will continue to cause FMC to incur "necessary costs of response" within the meaning of Section 107 of CERCLA, including without limitation the costs which FMC has incurred and will incur in monitoring, assessing, and evaluating the release or threatened release of hazardous substances and performing removal and/or remedial activities and taking other actions required or requested by the EPA, as well as attorneys' fees and expenses associated with this lawsuit.

Liability of an owner or operator of a facility as defined by §107(a) for the cost of removal "is strict and joint and several." The United States Government as owner is responsible for costs resulting from responses to the release of hazardous substances.

And it is so ordered.

CASE A.48

Texaco, Inc. v. Hasbrouck dba Rick's Texaco, 496 U.S. 543 110 S.Ct. 2535, 110 L.Ed.2d 492 (1990)
United States Supreme Court
Stevens, Justice

Petitioner (Texaco) sold gasoline directly to respondents and several other retailers in Spokane, Washington, at its retail tank wagon prices (RTW) while it granted substantial discounts to two distributors. During the period between 1972 and 1981, the stations supplied by the two distributors increased their sales volume dramatically, while respondents' sales suffered a corresponding decline. Respondents filed an action against Texaco under the Robinson-Patman Amendment to the Clayton Act (Act), alleging that the distributor discounts violated Section 2(a) of the Act. Respondents recovered treble damages, and the Court of Appeals for the Ninth Circuit affirmed the judgment. We granted certiorari, to consider Texaco's contention that legitimate functional discounts do not violate the Act because a seller is not responsible for its customers' independent resale pricing decisions. While we agree with the basic thrust of Texaco's argument, we conclude that in this case it is foreclosed by the facts of record.

Respondents are 12 independent Texaco retailers. They displayed the Texaco trademark, accepted Texaco credit cards, and bought their gasoline products directly from Texaco. Texaco delivered the gasoline to respondents' stations. The retail gasoline market in Spokane was highly competitive throughout the damages period, which ran from 1972 to 1981. Stations marketing the nationally advertised Texaco gasoline competed with other major brands as well as with stations featuring independent brands. Moreover, although discounted prices at a nearby Texaco station would have the most obvious impact on a respondent's trade, the cross-city traffic patterns and relatively small size of Spokane produced a city-wide competitive market. Texaco's throughput sales in the Spokane market declined from a monthly volume of 569,269 gallons in 1970 to 389,557 gallons in 1975. Texaco's independent retailers' share of the market for Texaco gas declined from 76 percent to 49 percent. Seven of the respondents' stations were out of business by the end of 1978.

The respondents tried unsuccessfully to increase their ability to compete with lower priced stations. Some tried converting from full service to self-service stations. Two of the respondents sought to buy their own tank trucks and haul their gasoline from Texaco's supply point, but Texaco vetoed that proposal.

While the independent retailers struggled, two Spokane gasoline distributors supplied by Texaco prospered. Gull Oil Company (Gull) had its headquarters in Seattle and distributed petroleum products in four western states under its own name. In Spokane it purchased its gas from Texaco at prices that ranged from six to four cents below Texaco's RTW price. Gull resold that product under its own name; the fact that it was being supplied by Texaco was not known by either the public or the respondents. In Spokane, Gull supplied about 15 stations; some were "consignment stations" and some were "commission stations." In both situations Gull retained title to the gasoline until it was pumped into a motorist's tank. In the consignment stations, the station operator set the retail prices, but in the commission stations Gull set the prices and paid the operator a commission. Its policy was to price its gasoline at a penny less than the prevailing price for major brands. Gull employed two truck drivers in Spokane who picked up product at Texaco's bulk plant and delivered it to the Gull Stations. It also employed one supervisor in Spokane. Apart from its trucks and investment in retail facilities, Gull apparently owned no assets in that market. At least with respect to the commission stations, Gull is fairly characterized as a retailer of gasoline throughout the relevant period.

The Dompier Oil Company (Dompier) started business in 1954 selling Quaker State Motor Oil. In 1960 it became a full line distributor of Texaco products, and by the mid-1970's its sales of gasoline represented over three-quarters of its business. Dompier purchased Texaco gasoline at prices of 3.95 cents to 3.65 cents below the RTW price. Dompier thus paid a higher price than Gull, but Dompier, unlike Gull, resold its gas under the Texaco brand names. It supplied about eight to ten Spokane retail stations. In the period prior to October 1974, two of those stations were owned by the president of Dompier but the others were independently operated. In the early 1970's, Texaco representative encouraged Dompier to enter the retail business directly, and in 1974 and 1975 it acquired four stations. Dompier's president estimated at trial that the share of its total gasoline sales made at retail during the middle 1970's was "probably 84 to 90 percent."

Like Gull, Dompier picked up Texaco's product at the Texaco bulk plant and delivered directly to retail outlets. Unlike Gull, Dompier owned a bulk storage facility, but it was seldom used because its capacity was less than that of many retail stations. Again, unlike Gull, Dompier received from Texaco the equivalent of the common carrier rate for delivering the gasoline product to the retail outlets. Thus, in addition to its discount from the RTW price, Dompier made a profit on its hauling function.

The stations supplied by Dompier regularly sold at retail at lower prices than respondents. Even before Dompier directly entered the retail business in 1974, its customers were selling to consumers at prices barely above the RTW price. Dompier's sales volume increased continuously and substantially throughout the relevant period. Between 1970 and 1975 its monthly sales volume increased from 155,152 gallons to 462,956 gallons; this represented an increase from 20.7 percent to almost 50 percent of Texaco's sales in Spokane.

There was ample evidence that Texaco executives were well aware of Dompier's dramatic growth and believed that it was attributable to "the magnitude of the distributor discount and the hauling allowance." In response to complaints from individual respondents about Dompier's aggressive pricing, however, Texaco representatives professed that they couldn't understand it.

Respondents filed suit against Texaco in July 1976. After a four week trial, the jury awarded damages measured by the difference between the RTW price and the price paid by Dompier. As we subsequently decided in *J. Truett Payne Co. v. Chrysler Motors Corp.*, this measure of damages was improper. Accordingly, although it rejected Texaco's defenses on the issue of liability, the Court of Appeals for the Ninth Circuit remanded the case for a new trial.

At the second trial, Texaco contended that the special prices to Gull and Dompier were justified by cost savings, were the product of a good faith attempt to meet competition, and were lawful "functional discounts." The District Court withheld the cost justification defense from the jury because it was not supported by the evidence other defenses. It awarded respondents actual damages of $449,900. The jury apparently credited the testimony of respondents' expert witness who had estimated what the respondents' profits would have been if they had paid the same prices as the four stations owned by Dompier.

In Texaco's motion for judgment notwithstanding the verdict, it claimed as a matter of law that its functional discounts did not adversely affect competition within the meaning of the Act because any injury to respondents was attributable to decisions made independently by Dompier. The District Court denied the motion. In an opinion supplementing its oral ruling denying Texaco's motion for a directed verdict, the Court assumed, arguendo, that Dompier was entitled to a functional discount, even on the gas that was sold at retail, but nevertheless concluded that the "presumed legality of functional discounts" had been rebutted by evidence that the amount of the discounts to Gull and Dompier was not reasonably related to the cost of any function that they performed.

The Court of Appeals affirmed. It reasoned: "As the Supreme Court long ago made clear, and recently reaffirmed, there may be a Robinson-Patman violation even if the favored and disfavored buyers do not compete, so long as the customers of the favored buyer compete with the disfavored buyer or its customers. Despite the fact that Dompier and Gull, at least in their capacities as wholesalers, did not compete directly with Hasbrouck, a Section 2(a) violation may occur if (1) the discount they received was not cost-based and (2) all or a portion of it was passed on by them to customers of theirs who competed with Hasbrouck. "Hasbrouck presented ample evidence to demonstrate that the services performed by Gull and Dompier were insubstantial and did not justify the functional discount."

The Court of Appeals concluded its analysis by observing: "To hold that price discrimination between a wholesaler and a retailer could never violate the Robinson-Patman Act would leave immune from antitrust scrutiny a discriminatory pricing procedure that can effectively serve to harm competition. We think such a result would be contrary to the objectives of the Robinson-Patman Act."

In order to establish a violation of the Act, respondent had the burden of proving four facts: (1) that Texaco's sales to Gull and Dompier were made in interstate commerce; (2) that the gasoline sold to them was of the same grade and quality as that sold to respondents; (3) that Texaco discriminated in price as between Gull and Dompier on the one hand and respondents on the other; and (4) that the discrimination had a prohibited effect on competition. Moreover, for each respondent to recover damages, he had the burden of proving the extent of his actual injuries.

The first two elements of respondents' case are not disputed in this Court, and we do not understand Texaco to be challenging the sufficiency of respondents' proof of damages. Texaco does argue, however, that although it charged different prices, it did not "discriminate in price" within the meaning of the Act, and that, at least to the extent that Gull and Dompier acted as wholesalers, the price differentials did not injure competition. We consider the two arguments separately.

A supplier need not satisfy the rigorous requirements of the cost justification defense in order to prove that a particular functional discount is reasonable and accordingly did not cause any substantial lessening of competition between a wholesaler's customers and the supplier's direct customers. The record in this case, however, adequately supports the finding that Texaco violated the Act.

The proof established that Texaco's lower prices to Gull and Dompier were discriminatory throughout the entire nine-year period; that at least Gull, and apparently Dompier as well, was selling at retail during that entire period; that the discounts substantially affected competition throughout the entire market; and that they injured each of the respondents. There is no doubt that respondents proof of a continuing violation of the Act throughout the nine year period was sufficient.

The judgment is affirmed.

CASE A.49

Michigan Mutual Insurance Co. v. Marriott Corporation
1992 WL 82498 N.D.III. (1992)
United States District Court, N.D. Illinois
Rovner, District Judge

During the period from October 15 through October 22, 1988, Jack Sonneveldt, president of Sonneveldt, Inc., was a paying guest at the O'Hare Marriott Hotel in Chicago, Illinois. He and his party arrived at the hotel in the company's 1984 Probe Prevost forty-foot, customized coach. Sonneveldt unsuccessfully attempted

to park the Prevost coach in the hotel's valet parking area. At the request of hotel officials, he moved the Prevost coach to the hotel's general parking lot across the street, in front of the hotel.

Sometime during the evening of October 22, 1988 or the next morning, the Prevost coach was stolen from the Marriott parking lot. Sonneveldt, Inc.'s insurer, Michigan Mutual, paid the company $265,000 in full settlement of the resulting claim. As subrogee of Sonneveldt, Inc., Michigan Mutual brought the instant suit. Michigan Mutual asserts liability under a theory of bailment.

Illinois law requires a plaintiff to establish the following in order to make out a prima facie claim of bailment: (1) an agreement, express or implied, to take possession of the plaintiff's property; (2) delivery and acceptance of the property (in good condition) into the exclusive possession and control of the bailee; and (3) failure to return the property or re-delivery in a damaged state. The bailment claim fails because the complaint does not sufficiently allege that Marriott ever accepted delivery and possession, either actual or constructive, of the Prevost coach.

The Illinois Supreme Court considered delivery and acceptance in the parking lot context in Wall v. Airport Parking Co. of Chicago, 41 Ill.2d 506, 244 N.E.2d 190 (1969). The parking lot at issue in Wall was lighted, paved, and marked into parking spaces. Motorists entered through an unattended electronic gate where they received a ticket noting the time of their arrival. Motorists also retained the keys to their vehicles and locked them at their own discretion. An attendant was observed only while paying at check-out. Plaintiff's car was stolen while it was parked in this lot, and he sued under a theory of bailment.

Ruling that these facts showed neither delivery nor acceptance, the court affirmed the lower courts' holdings that no bailment had been established.

Michigan Mutual's pleadings do not inferentially suggest that Marriott exercised even the most remote control over the Prevost coach. The complaint indicates that the Sonneveldt driver drove the Prevost coach into the lot and parked the vehicle himself. Nowhere does it suggest that Marriott was left with a set of keys to the coach, or that the hotel otherwise accepted or obtained actual control over the vehicle. Without the keys, Marriott had neither partial nor complete control over the Prevost coach.

Failure to allege some degree of control over the Prevost coach by Marriott necessitates the conclusion that no delivery or acceptance took place. Insofar as Illinois law requires proof of delivery and acceptance in order to establish a prima facie claim of bailment, Michigan Mutual's complaint fails as a matter of law. Consequently, the defendant's motion for judgment on the pleadings is granted.

CASE A.50

Walker v. Quillen
622 A.2d 1097 (1993)
Supreme Court of Delaware
Moore, Justice

Pursuant to Supreme Court Rule 25(a), appellees, Elizabeth Star Ayres and Clara Louise Quillen, have moved to affirm a judgment of the Court of Chancery granting an implied easement in favor of appellees' servient estate, as against the dominant estate of appellant, Irvin C. Walker ("Walker"). The appellees contend that sufficient evidence supports the findings of the Court of Chancery and that there was no abuse of discretion in granting the implied easement. We agree and affirm.

The appellees own in fee simple absolute a tract of land in Sussex County known as "Bluff Point." The tract is surrounded on three sides by Rehoboth Bay and is landlocked on the fourth side by Walker's land. At one time, the two tracts in question were held by a common owner. In 1878, Bluff Point was sold in fee simple absolute apart from the other holdings, thereby landlocking the parcel. A narrow dirt road, which traverses Walker's land, connects Bluff Point to a public road, and is its only means of access.

Under the doctrine of implied easement or easement by necessity the Court of Chancery found that the appellees were entitled to cross over a portion of Walker's land for access to Bluff Point. The court also found that water access, even if a reasonable substitute for land access, was not feasible because of the shallowness of the water surrounding Bluff Point. There is ample evidence in the record to support the finding that the two tracts originated from the unified holdings of one owner, and that an implied easement was created by the severance which landlocked Bluff Point. The record also sufficiently supports the finding that navigable access to Bluff Point was not feasible. NOW, THEREFORE, IT IS ORDERED that the judgment of the Court of Chancery be, and the same hereby is, AFFIRMED.

CASE A.51

**Nollan v. California Coastal Commission 483 U.S. 825
107 S.Ct. 3141, 97 L.Ed.2d 677 (1987)**
United States Supreme Court
Scalia, Justice

James and Marilyn Nollan own a beachfront lot in Ventura County, California. A quarter-mile north of their property is Faria County Park, an Oceanside public park with a public beach and recreation area. Another public beach area, known locally as "the Cove," lies 1,800 feet south of their lot. The Nollans originally leased their property with an option to buy. The building on the lot was a small bungalow, totaling 504 square feet, which for a time they rented to summer vacationers. After years of rental use, however, the building had fallen into disrepair, and could no longer be rented out.

The Nollans' option to purchase was conditioned on their promise to demolish the bungalow and replace it. In order to do so, they were required to obtain a coastal development permit from the California Coastal Commission. On February 25, 1982, they submitted a permit application to the Commission in which they proposed to demolish the existing structure and replace it with a three-bedroom house in keeping with the rest of the neighborhood.

The Nollans were informed that the Commission staff had recommended that the permit be granted subject to the condition that they allow the public an easement to pass across a portion of their property. This would make it easier for the public to get to Faria County Park and the Cove. The Nollans protested imposition of the condition, but the Commission overruled their objections and granted the permit subject to their recordation of a deed restriction granting the easement.

The Nollans filed a petition for a writ of administrative mandamus with the superior court. The superior court granted the writ of mandamus and directed that the permit condition be struck. The Commission appealed to the California court of appeal. While that appeal was pending, the Nollans satisfied the condition on their option to purchase by tearing down the bungalow and building the new house, and bought the property. They did not notify the Commission that they were taking that action. The court of appeal reversed the superior court. It ruled that the Nollans' "taking" claim failed because, although the condition diminished the value of the Nollans' lot, it did not deprive them of all reasonable use of their property. The Nollans appealed to this Court, raising only the constitutional "taking" question.

Had California simply required the Nollans to make an easement across their beachfront available to the public on a permanent basis in order to increase public access to the beach, rather than conditioning their permit to rebuild their house on their agreeing to do so, we have no doubt there would have been a taking. To say that the appropriation of a public easement across a landowner's premises does not constitute the taking of a property interest but rather (as Justice Brennan contends) "a mere restriction on its use," is to use words in a manner that deprives them of all their ordinary meaning. Indeed, one of the principal uses of the eminent domain power is to assure that the government be able to require conveyance of just such interests, so long as it pays for them. We have repeatedly held that, as to property reserved by its owner for private use, "the right to exclude others is one of the most essential sticks in the bundle of rights that are commonly characterized as property."

We have long recognized that land-use regulation does not effect a taking if it "substantially advances legitimate state interests" and does not "deny an owner economically viable use of his land." Whatever may be the outer limits of legitimate state interests in the takings and land-use context, this is not one of them. The building restriction is not a valid regulation of land use, but an out-and-out plan of extortion. We therefore find that the Commission's imposition of the permit condition cannot be treated as an exercise of its land-use power. To obtain easements of access to private property the State must proceed through its eminent domain power.

The permit condition is simply an expression of the Commission's belief that the public interest will be served by a continuous strip of publicly accessible beach along the coast.

The Commission may well be right that it is a good idea, but that does not establish that the Nollans (and other coastal residents) alone can be compelled to contribute to its realization. Rather, California is free to advance its comprehensive program if it wishes, by using its power of eminent domain for this "public purpose," but if it wants an easement across the Nollan's property, it must pay for it. Reversed.

CASE A.52

Saritejdiam, Inc. v. Excess Insurance Co., 971 F.2d 910 (1992)
United States Court of Appeals for the Second Circuit
Oakes, Chief Judge

Saritejdiam, Inc. (Saritejdiam) is a New York corporation involved in the wholesaling of diamonds and other precious and semi-precious stones and jewelry. In June 1988, Excess Insurance Company, Ltd., et al., (the Underwriters), a group of London-based insurance companies, issued an insurance policy to Saritejdiam. The policy is called a Jeweler's Block Policy and it insures against all risks of physical loss or damage to insured interests, unless specifically excluded by the policy. This appeal requires us to analyze whether Saritejdiam satisfied a clause in the policy requiring that insured interests remain in the "close personal custody and control" of the insured or its agent while in transit.

On May 13, 1989, Mr. Robert Danilin, an independent contractor/salesman for Saritejdiam, lost a package of loose diamonds valued by Saritejdiam at $267,514.30. On that day, Danilin, his wife, and stepson, were in Tuxedo, New York visiting a town house they had just purchased there. At approximately 5:50 p.m., the Danilins arrived at the Orange Top Diner on Route 17 in Tuxedo for dinner. Danilin brought a camera bag into the diner containing two stiff, black, diamond wallets (one of which held Saritejdiam's diamonds), his checkbook, and credit cards. The three were seated at a table. Robert placed the camera bag on top of an empty chair to his left. During dinner, he touched the camera bag to make sure it was still on the chair. When they finished eating, Danilin paid the check with cash out of his pants pocket. The three then left the diner, got into their car, and headed for a golf driving range. When the Danilins reached their destination, they discovered that the camera bag containing the diamond wallet was not in the car. They sped back to the diner. The camera bag, however, was no longer on the chair where it had been previously placed.

Connie Grievas, the daughter of the proprietors of the Orange Top Diner, apparently witnessed the events that transpired after Danilin paid his bill. Grievas was eleven years old at the time. She told Danilin's stepson and, later on, investigators for the Underwriters, that she went to clear Danilin's table after he paid his check. She noticed that a bag with a handle was left behind. Grievas then went to tell her Mother that a customer had left a bag behind. Before she reached her mother, she saw two other customers, a man and a woman, take the bag and walk out. She described the man who picked up the bag as white, approximately forty years old, with shoulder-length black curly hair, standing 5'7", and wearing dark sunglasses. She described the woman as having blonde, waistlength hair.

On the same day, Saritejdiam reported the loss to the Underwriters. On June 3, 1989, after investigating the claim, the Underwriters refused to cover the lost diamonds. The

Underwriters claimed that Saritejdiam had not complied with the Personal Conveyance Clause of the insurance policy. The clause provides: This policy only covers the insured interest in transit when in the close personal custody and control of the Assured and/or Assured's representative and/or agent at all times whilst in transit subject to hotel/motel clause, excluding all losses due to infidelity. (Emphasis added). The denial letter states that "the results of our investigation have revealed that there is no evidence that the theft took place whilst your property was in the close personal custody and control of your salesman, Robert Danilin."

We must decide whether the loss of the diamonds at the Orange Top Diner occurred while they were in the "close personal custody and control" of Danilin, Saritejdiam's salesman/independent contractor. If so, Saritejdiam satisfied the requirements of the Personal Conveyance Clause in the policy, and the Underwriters must cover the loss. The issue traditionally arises in disputes over the rights of the finder against those of the owner of the real property on which the disputed personal property was found. The common law generally distinguished between "lost" and "mislaid" property. Property is mislaid when the owner purposely parts with possession of the property, but then unintentionally leaves it behind. We believe that under New York common law the camera bag containing Saritejdiam's diamond wallets would be classified as mislaid property. Saritejdiam's salesman purposely placed the camera bag on the adjacent chair at his table in the Orange Top Diner. He then walked away from the table and forgot to pick up the camera bag. This is a paradigmatic example of mislaid property under New York's common law definition of the term. Accordingly, we believe a New York court would hold that a person simply cannot maintain "close personal custody and control" over mislaid property.

For the foregoing reasons, we reverse the order of the district court granting summary judgment for Saritejdiam and enter summary judgment for the Underwriters.

CASE A.53

In re Estate of Vallerius, 629 N.E.2d 1185 (1994)
Appellate Court of Illinois
Lewis, Presiding Justice

On December 22, 1987, Douglas White murdered his grandmother, Adella G. Vallerius. On the same day, at the same time, and in the same house, Douglas' brother, Craig White, murdered his grandmother's friend, Carroll Pieper. Douglas was convicted of Mrs. Vallerius' murder. Craig entered a negotiated plea of guilty to, and was convicted of, the murder of Carroll Pieper. Craig testified for the State in Douglas' murder trial as part of his negotiated guilty plea.

Mrs. Vallerius died testate, naming Douglas and Craig as her sole beneficiaries. Mrs. Vallerius' only heir was her daughter, Renie White, Douglas and Craig's mother. On January 11, 1988, Mrs. Vallerius' will was admitted to probate. In compliance with the terms of the will, Douglas White and Dennis Johnson were appointed legal representatives of Mrs. Vallerius' estate. About 2-½ months after Mrs. Vallerius was murdered, on March 7, 1988, Renie White died, intestate, of natural causes. She left as her only heirs her two sons, Douglas and Craig.

On March 12, 1990, the appellees, Peter M. Vallerius, Glenna F. Giacoletto, Lawrence Joe Davis, Helen L. Vallerius, Gail Kadavi, Iione V. Henry, Janis Murray, Terrie L. Illies, and Duffy Joe Vallerius, filed a petition to intervene and to consolidate the estates of Mrs. Vallerius and Renie White and an "Objection to Distribution" in the estate of Mrs. Vallerius, wherein they alleged that "Douglas Keith White and Craig Steven White, having intentionally and unjustifiably caused the death of Adella G. Vallerius, cannot lawfully receive any property, benefit or other interest" by reason of her death, through the estate of Mrs. Vallerius or through the estate of Renie White.

After an evidentiary hearing on the appellees' objection to distribution, the court entered an order granting the appellees' request. The trial court found that the issue in the case was whether Douglas and Craig could receive any property or interest by reason of the death of Mrs. Vallerius, whether through her estate or the estate of Renie White. The court determined that, under both statute and common law, the public policy of Illinois has long been to prevent wrongdoers from profiting from intentionally committed wrongful acts. The court further found that the petitioner-objectors (appellees herein) had sustained their burden of proof, by clear and convincing evidence, that Douglas and Craig intentionally caused the death of their grandmother, Mrs. Vallerius.

Appellants argue that the law does not preclude a murderer from inheriting property from a person other than the victim. The obvious intent of the law is that persons like Douglas and Craig White must not profit from their brutal murder of their grandmother. The fact that there is an intervening estate should not expurgate the wrong of the murderer.

The appellants argue that Craig cannot be held accountable for Douglas' murder of Mrs. Vallerius, since Craig did not actually swing the sledgehammer that killed Mrs. Vallerius but only killed Carroll Pieper after Douglas killed Mrs. Vallerius. Appellants argue that even though Craig "may have borne criminal responsibility for the actions of Douglas White under the criminal accountability statute," Craig cannot be denied his right of inheritance from his mother.

Craig White cannot be permitted to receive any benefit by reason of the death of Mrs. Vallerius, whether through her estate directly or indirectly through the estate of her daughter, Renie White. If we were to allow Craig White to receive any property, benefit, or interest from the estate of Renie White, our decision would directly contravene the state's unambiguous mandate that he not receive any property by reason of his grandmother's death in any capacity or by any circumstance.

Glossary

abandoned property Property that an owner has discarded with the intent to relinquish his or her rights in it, or mislaid or lost property that the owner has given up any further attempts to locate. [990]

abatement If the property the testator leaves is not sufficient to satisfy all the beneficiaries named in a will and there are both general and residuary bequests, the residuary bequest is abated first (i.e., paid last). [1064]

absolute priority rule A rule that says a reorganization plan is fair and equitable to an impaired class of unsecured creditors or equity holders if no class below it receives anything in the plan. [578]

acceptance A manifestation of assent by the offeree to the terms of the offer in a manner invited or required by the offer as measured by the objective theory of contracts. [202] Occurs when a buyer or lessee take any of the following actions after a reasonable opportunity to inspect the goods: The buyer or lessee either (1) signifies to the seller or lessor in words or by conduct that the goods are conforming or that the goods will be taken or retained in spite of their nonconformity or (2) fails to effectively reject the goods within a reasonable time after their delivery or tender by the seller or lessor. Acceptance also occurs if a buyer acts inconsistently with the seller's ownership rights in the goods. [416]

acceptance method The bankruptcy court must approve a plan of reorganization if (1) the plan is in the *best interests* of each class of claims and interests, (2) the plan is *feasible,* (3) at least one class of claims *votes to accept* the plan, and (4) each class of claims and interests is *non-impaired.* [577]

accession Occurs when the value of personal property increases because it is added to or improved by natural or manufactured means. [987]

accommodation A shipment that is offered to the buyer as a replacement for the original shipment cannot be filled. [385]

accommodation party A party who signs an instrument and lends his or her name (and credit) to another party to the instrument. [494]

accord An agreement whereby the parties agree to accept something different in satisfaction of the original contract. [219]

accord and satisfaction The settlement of a contract dispute. The *accord* is the agreement whereby parties agree to settle a contract dispute by accepting something different than provided in the original contract. *Satisfaction* is the performance of an accord. [291]

accountant malpractice Occurs when the accountant breaches the duty of reasonable care, knowledge, skill, and judgment that he or she owes to a client when providing auditing and other accounting services to the client. [881]

action for an accounting A formal judicial proceeding in which the court is authorized to (1) review the partnership and the partners transactions and (2) award each partner his or her share of the partnership assets. [644]

act of monopolizing A required act for there to be a violation of Section 2 of the Sherman Act. Possession of monopoly power without such act does not violate Section 2. [966]

act of state doctrine States that judges of one country cannot question the validity of an act committed by another country within that other country's borders. It is based on the principle that a country has absolute authority over what transpires within its own territory. [82]

actus reus "Guilty act"—the actual performance of the criminal act. [139]

ademption A principle that says if a testator leaves a specific devise of property to a beneficiary, but the property is no longer in the estate when the testator dies, the beneficiary receives nothing. [1064]

adequate assurance of due performance A party to a sales or lease contract may demand an adequate assurance of performance from the other party if there is an indication that the contract will be breached by that party. [417]

adjudged insane A person who has been adjudged insane by a proper court or administrative agency. A contract entered into by such person is *void.* [230]

administrative agencies Agencies that the legislative and executive branches of federal and state governments establish. [898]

administrative dissolution Involuntary dissolution of a corporation that is ordered by the secretary of state if the corporation has failed to comply with certain procedures required by law. [742]

administrative law judge (ALJ) A judge, presiding over administrative proceedings, who decides questions of law and fact concerning the case. [906]

Administrative Procedure Act (APA) An act that establishes certain administrative procedures that federal administrative agencies must follow in conducting their affairs. [902]

administrative subpoena An order that directs the subject of the subpoena to disclose the requested information. [904]

adverse action A denial or revocation of credit or a change in the credit terms offered. [927]

adverse possession When a person who wrongfully possesses someone else's real property obtains title to that property if certain statutory requirements are met. [1014]

advertisement A general advertisement is an invitation to make an offer. A specific advertisement is an offer. [197]

affirmative action Policy that provides that certain job preferences will be given to minority or other protected class applicants when an employer makes an employment decision. [856]

after-acquired property Property that the debtor acquires after the security agreement is executed. [550]

Age Discrimination in Employment Act (ADEA) of 1967 Prohibits age discrimination practices against employees who are 40 and older. [851]

agency The principal-agent relationship: the fiduciary relationship "which results from the manifestation of consent by one person to another that the other shall act in his behalf and subject to his control, and consent by the other so to act." [588]

agency by ratification An agency that occurs when (1) a person misrepresents him- or herself as another's agent when in fact he or she is not and (2) the purported principal ratifies the unauthorized act. [596]

agency coupled with an interest A special type of agency relationship that is created for the agent's benefit; irrevocable by the principal. [600]

agency law The large body of common law that governs agency; a mixture of contract law and tort law. [588]

agency shop An establishment where an employee does not have to join the union, but must pay a fee equal to the union dues. [869]

agent A person who has been authorized to sign a negotiable instrument on behalf of another person. [489]

agent The party who agrees to act on behalf of another. [588]

agreement The manifestation by two or more persons of the substance of a contract. [195]

agreement of conversion Document that states the terms for converting an existing business to an LLC. [685]

aiding and abetting the commission of a crime Rendering support, assistance, or encouragement to the commission of a crime; harboring a criminal after he or she has committed a crime. [149]

air pollution Pollution caused by factories, homes, vehicles, and the like that affects the air. [937]

alien corporation A corporation that is incorporated in another country. [728]

alien LLC An LLC that is organized in another country. [686]

allonge A separate piece of paper attached to the instrument on which the indorsement is written. [472]

altered check A check that has been altered without authorization that modifies the legal obligation of a party. [517]

alternative dispute resolution (ADR) Methods of resolving disputes other than litigation. [38]

Americans with Disabilities Act (ADA) of 1990 Imposes obligations on employers and providers of public transportation, telecommunications, and public accommodations to accommodate individuals with disabilities. [853]

annual financial statement A statement provided to the shareholders that contains a balance sheet, an income statement, and statement of changes in shareholder equity. [752]

annual shareholders' meeting Meeting of the shareholders of a corporation that must be held annually by the corporation to elect directors and to vote on other matters. [748]

answer The defendant's written response to the plaintiff's complaint that is filed with the court and served on the plaintiff. [29]

antiassignment clause A clause that prohibits the assignment of rights under the contract. [281]

anticipatory breach A breach that occurs when one contracting party informs the other that he or she will not perform his or her contractual duties when due. [301]

anticipatory repudiation The repudiation of a sales or lease contract by one of the parties prior to the date set for performance. [417]

antideficiency statute A statute that prohibits deficiency judgments regarding certain types of mortgages, such as those on residential property. [533]

antidelegation clause A clause that prohibits the delegation of duties under the contract. [283]

antidilution statutes State laws that allow persons and companies to register trademarks and service marks. [342]

antitrust laws A series of laws enacted to limit anticompetitive behavior in almost all industries, businesses, and professions operating in the United States. [956]

apparent agency Agency that arises when a franchisor creates the appearance that a franchisee is its agent when in fact an actual agency does not exist. [713] Agency that arises when a principal creates the appearance of an agency that in actuality does not exist. [593]

appeal The act of asking an appellate court to overturn a decision after the trial court's final judgment has been entered. [37]

appellant The appealing party in an appeal. Also known as *petitioner*. [37]

appellate body A panel of seven justices selected from WTO member nations that hear and decide appeals from decisions by the dispute settlement body. [78]

appellee The responding party in an appeal. Also known as *respondent*. [37]

appropriate bargaining unit The group that a union seeks to represent. [864]

approval clause A clause that permits the assignment of the contract only upon receipt of an obligor's approval. [281]

arbitration A form of ADR in which the parties choose an impartial third party to hear and decide the dispute. [38, 85]

arbitration clause A clause contained in many international contracts that stipulates that any dispute between the parties concerning the performance of the contract will be submitted to an arbitrator or arbitration panel for resolution. [38, 85]

arraignment A hearing during which the accused is brought before a court and is (1) informed of the charges against him or her and (2) asked to enter a plea. [141]

arrest warrant A document for a person's detainment based upon a showing of probable cause that the person committed the crime. [141]

arson Willfully or maliciously burning another's building. [143]

articles of incorporation The basic governing documents of the corporation. These documents must be filed with the secretary of state of the state of incorporation. [730]

articles of organization The formal documents that must be filed at the secretary of state's office of the state of organization of an LLC to form the LLC. [683]

articles of termination Document that is filed with the secretary of state that terminates the LLC as of the date of filing or upon a later effective date specified in the document. [697]

Article 2 (Sales) Article of the UCC that governs sale of goods. [378]

Article 2A (Leases) Article of the UCC that governs lease of goods. [381]

Article 3 of the UCC A code promulgated in 1952 that established rules for the creation of, transfer of, enforcement of, and liability on negotiable instruments. [451] Sets forth the requirements for finding a negotiable instrument, including checks. [508]

Article 4 of the UCC Establishes the rules and principles that regulate bank deposit and collection procedures. [508]

Article 4A of the UCC Article added to the UCC in 1989 that establishes rules regulating the creation and collection of and liability for wire transfers. [509]

Article 7 of the UCC An article of the Uniform Commercial Code that provides a detailed statutory scheme for the creation, perfection, and foreclosure on common carriers' and warehouse operators' liens. [529, 996] Article of the Uniform Commercial Code that governs documents of title. [998]

Article 8 of the UCC The article of the UCC that governs transfer of securities. [751]

Article 9 of the UCC An article of the Uniform Commercial Code that governs secured transactions in personal property. [545]

assault (1) The threat of immediate harm or offensive contact or (2) any action that arouses reasonable apprehension of imminent harm. Actual physical contact is unnecessary. [91]

assent Assent to enter into a contract may be manifested in any manner sufficient to show agreement, including express words or conduct of the parties. [247]

assignee The party to whom the right has been transferred. [279, 469, 1032]

assignment The transfer of rights under a contract. [469]

assignment The transfer of contractual rights by the obligee to another

party. [279] A transfer by a tenant of his or her rights under a lease to another. [1032]

assignment and delegation Transfer of both rights and duties under the contract. [284]

assignment for the benefit of creditors An assignment that allows debtors to voluntarily assign title to their property to a trustee or an assignee for the benefit of their creditors. [539]

assignor The obligee who transfers the right. [279, 1032] The transferor in an assignment situation. [469]

assumption of duties When a delegation of duties contains the term *assumption* or *I assume the duties* or other similar language, the delegatee is legally liable to the obligee for nonperformance. [283]

assumption of the risk A defense a defendant can use against a plaintiff who knowingly and voluntarily enters into or participates in a risky activity that results in injury. [107] A defense in which the defendant must prove that (1) the plaintiff knew and appreciated the risk and (2) the plaintiff voluntarily assumed the risk. [129]

attachment Seizure by the creditors of property in the debtor's possession to collect on a debt while their lawsuit is pending. [538] The creditor has an enforceable security interest against the debtor and can satisfy the debt out of the designated collateral. [547]

attempt to commit a crime When a crime is attempted but not completed. [149]

attestation The action of a will being witnessed by two or three objective and competent people. [1061]

attorney-client privilege A rule that says a client can tell his or her lawyer anything about the case without fear that the attorney will be called as a witness against the client. [155]

attribution procedure A procedure using codes, algorithms, identifying words or numbers, encryption, callback, or other acknowledgment to verify an authentication of a record. [360]

at-will employees Employees who do not have employment contracts. [822]

at-will LLC An LLC that has no specified term of duration. [683]

auction with reserve Unless expressly stated otherwise, an auction is an auction with reserve; that is, the seller retains the right to refuse the highest bid and withdraw the goods from sale. [198]

auction without reserve An auction in which the seller expressly gives up his or her right to withdraw the goods from sale and must accept the highest bid. [198]

audit The verification of a company's books and records pursuant to federal securities laws, state laws, and stock exchange rules that must be performed by an independent CPA. [880]

authenticate Signing the contract or executing an electronic symbol, sound, or message attached to, included in, or linked with the record. [360]

authorized shares The number of shares provided for in the articles of incorporation. [738]

automatic stay The result of the filing of a voluntary or involuntary petition; the suspension of certain actions by creditors against the debtor or the debtor's property. [567]

backward vertical merger A vertical merger in which the customer acquires the supplier. [968]

bailee A holder of goods who is not a seller or a buyer (e.g., a warehouse). [400]

bailee A holder of goods who is not a seller or a buyer (e.g., a warehouse). [411]

bailee's rights Depending on the type of bailment, bailees may have the right to (1) exclusive possession of the bailed property, (2) use of the bailed property, or (3) compensation for work done or services provided. [995]

bailment A transaction where an owner transfers his or her personal property to another to be held, stored, delivered, or for some other purpose. Title to the property does not transfer. [991]

bailment at will A bailment without a fixed term; can be terminated at any time by either party. [992]

bailment for a fixed term A bailment that terminates at the end of the term, or sooner by mutual consent of the parties. [992]

bailment for sole benefit of the bailee A gratuitous bailment that benefits only the bailee. The bailee owes a *duty of great care* to protect the bailed property. [994]

bailment for the sole benefit of the bailor A gratuitous bailment that benefits only the bailor. The bailee owes only a *duty of slight care* to protect the bailed property. [993]

bailor The owner of property in a bailment. [991]

bait and switch A type of deceptive advertising that occurs when a seller advertises the availability of a low-cost discounted item but then pressures the buyer into purchasing more expensive merchandise. [723]

bank check A certified check, a cashier's check, or a traveler's check; the payment for which the bank is solely or primarily liable. [511]

Bankruptcy Code The name given to the Bankruptcy Reform Act of 1978, as amended. [564]

bankruptcy estate An estate created upon the commencement of a Chapter 7 proceeding that includes all the debtor's legal and equitable interests in real, personal, tangible, and intangible property, wherever located, that exist when the petition is filed, minus exempt property. [567]

bargained-for exchange Exchange that parties engage in that leads to an enforceable contract. [213]

battery Unauthorized and harmful or offensive physical contact with another person. Direct physical contact is not necessary. [91]

bearer paper Bearer paper is negotiated by *delivery;* indorsement is not necessary. [470]

beneficiary A person or organization designated in the will that receives all or a portion of the testator's property at the time of the testator's death. [1061]

beneficiary The person who is to receive the life insurance proceeds when the insured dies. [1044]

beneficiary The creditor in a deed of trust and note transaction. [531] Person for whose benefit a trust is created. [1072]

Berne Convention An international copyright treaty. The United States and many other nations are signatories to this treaty. [328]

bequest A gift of personal property by will. Also known as a legacy. [1064]

bilateral contract A contract entered into by way of exchange of promises of the parties; a "promise for a promise." [183]

bill of lading A document of title that is issued by a carrier when goods are received for transportation. [998]

blank indorsement An indorsement that does not specify a particular indorsee. It creates *bearer paper.* [473]

board of directors A panel of decision makers, the members of which are elected by the shareholders. [754]

bona fide occupational qualification (BFOQ) Employment discrimination based on a protected class (other than race or color) is lawful if it is *job related* and a *business necessity.* This exception is narrowly interpreted by the courts. [848]

bond A long-term debt security that is secured by some form of collateral. [740]

breach Failure of a party to perform an obligation in a sales or lease contract. [411]

breach of contract If a contracting party fails to perform an absolute duty owed under a contract. [300]

breach of the duty of care A failure to exercise care or to act as a reasonable person would act. [99]

bribery When one person gives another person money, property, favors, or anything else of value for a favor in return. Often referred to as a payoff or "kickback." [146]

building A structure constructed on land. [1006]

building codes State and local statutes that impose specific standards on property owners to maintain and repair leased premises. [1028]

burden of proof The plaintiff bears the burden of proving the allegations made in his complaint. [36]

burglary Taking personal property from another's home, office, commercial, or other type of building. [143]

business judgment rule A rule that protects the decisions of the board of directors, who act on an informed basis, in good faith, and in the honest belief that the action taken was in the best interests of the corporation and its shareholders. [760, 787]

buy-and-sell agreement An agreement that requires selling shareholders to sell their shares to the other shareholders or to the corporation at the price specified in the agreement. [751]

buyer in the ordinary course of business A person who in good faith and without knowledge that the sale violates the ownership or security interests of a third party buys the goods in the ordinary course of business from a person in the business of selling goods of that kind [UCC 1-201(9)]. A buyer in the ordinary course of business takes the goods free of any third-party security interest in the goods. [404, 554]

bylaws A detailed set of rules adopted by the board of directors after the corporation is incorporated that contains provisions for managing the business and the affairs of the corporation. [732]

cancellation A buyer or lessee may cancel a sales or lease contract if the seller or lessor fails to deliver conforming goods or repudiates the contract, or the buyer or lessee rightfully rejects the goods or justifiably revokes acceptance of the goods. [368, 425] A seller or lessor may cancel a sales or lease contract if the buyer or lessee rejects or revokes acceptance of the goods, fails to pay for the goods, or repudiates the contract in part or in whole. [422]

case brief A summary of each of the following items of a case:
1. Case name and citation
2. Key facts
3. Issue presented
4. Holding of the court
5. Court's reasoning. [12]

cashier's check A check issued by a bank where the customer has paid the bank the amount of the check and a fee. The bank guarantees the payment of the check. [512]

causation A person who commits a negligent act is not liable unless his or her act was the cause of the plaintiff's injuries. The two types of causation that must be proven are (1) *causation in fact (actual cause)* and (2) *proximate cause (legal cause).* [101]

causation in fact or actual cause The actual cause of negligence. A person who commits a negligent act is not liable unless causation in fact can be proven. [101]

caveat emptor "Let the buyer beware," the traditional guideline of sales transactions. [915]

certificate of amendment A document that keeps the certificate of limited partnership current. [663]

certificate of authority Formal document that must be issued by the secretary of state of a state before a foreign LLC may conduct business in that state. [686]

certificate of deposit (CD) A two-party negotiable instrument that is a special form of note created when a depositor deposits money at a financial institution in exchange for the institution's promise to pay back the amount of the deposit plus an agreed-upon rate of interest upon the expiration of a set time period agreed upon by the parties. [455]

certificate of filing A document that shows (1) whether any presently effective financing statement naming a particular debtor is on file, (2) the date and hour of any such filing, and (3) the names and addresses of the secured parties. [551]

certificate of interest Document that evidences a member's ownership interest in an LLC. [685]

certificate of limited partnership A document that two or more persons must execute and sign that makes the limited partnership legal and binding. [662]

certificate of partnership A document that a partnership must file with the appropriate state government agency in some states to acknowledge that the partnership exists. [641]

certificate of registration A document permitting a foreign limited partnership to transact business in a foreign state. [668]

certified check A type of check where a bank agrees in advance (*certifies*) to accept the check when it is presented for payment. [511]

certified public accountant (CPA) An accountant who has met certain educational requirements, has passed the CPA examination, and has had a certain number of years of audit experience. [879]

chain of distribution All manufacturers, distributors, wholesalers, retailers, lessors, and subcomponent manufacturers involved in a transaction. [119]

chain-style franchise The franchisor licenses the franchisee to make and sell its products or distribute services to the public from a retail outlet serving an exclusive territory. [704]

changing conditions defense A price discrimination defense that claims prices were lowered in response to changing conditions in the market for or the marketability of the goods. [973]

Chapter 7 liquidation bankruptcy The most familiar form of bankruptcy; the debtor's nonexempt property is sold for cash, the cash is distributed to the creditors, and any unpaid debts are discharged. [565]

Chapter 11 A bankruptcy method that allows reorganization of the debtor's financial affairs under the supervision of the Bankruptcy Court. [575]

Chapter 13 A rehabilitation form of bankruptcy that permits the courts to supervise the debtor's plan for the payment of unpaid debts by installments. [580]

charging order A document that the court issues against the debtor-partner's partnership interest in order to satisfy a debt. [643] Order of the court mandating that an LLC pay a debtor-member's distributional interest to a judgment creditor. [693]

check An order by the drawer to the drawee bank to pay a specified sum of money from the drawer's checking account to the named payee (or holder). [509]

choice of forum clause Clause in an international contract that designates which nation's court has jurisdiction to hear a case arising out of the contract. Also known as a *forum-selection clause.* [81]

choice of law clause Clause in an international contract that designates which nation's laws will be applied in deciding a dispute. [81]

Civil Rights Act of 1866 An act enacted after the Civil War that says all persons "have the same right . . . to make and enforce contracts . . . as is enjoyed by white persons"; it prohibits racial and national origin employment discrimination. [855]

Clean Air Act A federal statute enacted in 1963 to assist states in dealing with air pollution. [938]

Clean Air Act Amendments of 1990 Amendments that provide comprehensive regulation of air quality in the United States. [938]

Clean Water Act The final version of the FWPCA. [941]

close corporation A corporation owned by one or a few shareholders. [626]

closely held corporation A corporation owned by one or a few shareholders. [727]

closing The finalization of a real estate sales transaction that passes title to the property from the seller to the buyer. [1013]

closing arguments Statements made by the attorneys to the jury at the end of the trial to try to convince the jury to render a verdict for their client. [36]

codicil A separate document that must be executed to amend a will. It must be executed with the same formalities as a will. [1061]

C.O.D. shipment A type of shipment contract where the buyer agrees to pay the shipper cash upon the delivery of the goods. [415]

collateral The property that is subject to the security interest. [545] Security against repayment of the note that lenders sometimes require; can be a car, a house, or other property. [454]

collateral contract A promise where one person agrees to answer for the debts or duties of another person. [266]

collecting bank The depository bank and other banks in the collection process (other than the payor bank). [518]

collective bargaining The act of negotiating contract terms between an employer and the members of a union. [867]

collective bargaining agreement The resulting contract from a collective bargaining procedure. [867]

collision insurance Insurance that a car owner purchases to insure his or her car against risk of loss or damage. [1049]

"coming and going" rule A rule that says a principal is generally not liable for injuries caused by its agents and employees while they are on their way to or from work. [615]

Commerce Clause A clause of the U.S. Constitution that grants Congress the power "to regulate commerce with foreign nations, and among the several states, and with Indian tribes." [50, 67]

commercial impracticability Nonperformance that is excused if an extreme or unexpected development or expense makes it impractical for the promisor to perform. [292]

commercial speech Speech used by businesses, such as advertising. It is subject to time, place, and manner restrictions. [54]

common carrier A firm (the bailee) that offer transportation services to the general public. Owes a *duty of strict liability* to the bailor. [996]

common law Developed by judges who issued their opinions when deciding a case. The principles announced in these cases became precedent for later judges deciding similar cases. [7]

common law lien A lien given to artisans, laborers, innkeepers, common carriers, and other service providers on personnel property of customers to secure reasonable payment for services rendered. [528]

common law of contracts Contract law developed primarily by state courts. [181]

common stock A type of equity security that represents the *residual* value of the corporation. [736]

common stock certificate A document that represents the common shareholder's investment in the corporation. [736]

common stockholder A person who owns common stock. [736]

comparative negligence A doctrine that applies to strict liability actions that says a plaintiff who is contributorily negligent for his or her injuries is responsible for a proportional share of the damages. [108, 131]

compensatory damages An award of money intended to compensate a non-breaching party for the loss of the bargain; they place the nonbreaching party in the same position as if the contract had been fully performed by restoring the "benefit of the bargain." [302] Damages that are generally equal to the difference between the value of the goods as war-

ranted and the actual value of the goods accepted at the time and place of acceptance. [445]

competent party's duty of restitution If a minor has transferred money, property, or other valuables to the competent party before disaffirming the contract, that party must place the minor in status quo. [227]

complaint The document the plaintiff files with the court and serves on the defendant to initiate a lawsuit. [29]

complete performance Occurs when a party to a contract renders performance exactly as required by the contract; discharges that party's obligations under the contract. [300]

composition agreement An agreement that a debtor and several creditors enter into: if the debtor is overextended and owes several creditors money, the creditors agree to accept payment of a sum less than the debt as full satisfaction of the debtor's debts. [539]

Comprehensive Environmental Response, Compensation, and Liability Act (CERCLA) A federal statue enacted in 1980 and amended in 1986 that gives the federal government a mandate to deal with hazardous wastes that have been spilled, stored, or abandoned; commonly called *Superfund*. [946]

comprehensive insurance A form of property insurance that insures an automobile from loss or damage from causes other than collision. [1049]

computer informational transaction An agreement to create, transfer, or license computer information or informational rights. [358]

conciliation A form of mediation in which the parties choose an *interested* third party to act as the mediator. [40]

concurrent condition A condition that exists when the parties to a contract must render performance simultaneously; each party's absolute duty to perform is conditioned on the other party's absolute duty to perform. [289]

concurrent jurisdiction Jurisdiction shared by two or more courts. [25]

condition A qualification of a promise. There are three types of conditions: *con-*

ditions precedent, conditions subsequent, and *concurrent conditions.* [287]

condition precedent A condition that requires the occurrence (or nonoccurrence) of an event before a party is obligated to perform a duty under a contract. [287]

condition precedent based on satisfaction Clause in a contract that reserves the right to a party to pay for the items or services contracted for only if they meet his or her satisfaction. [288]

condition subsequent A condition, if it occurs or doesn't occur, that automatically excuses the performance of an existing contractual duty to perform. [289]

condominium A common form of ownership in a multiple-dwelling building where the purchaser has title to the individual unit and owns the common areas as a tenant in common with the other condominium owners. [1013]

confirmation The bankruptcy court's approval of a plan of reorganization. [577]

confusion Occurs if two or more persons commingle fungible goods; title is then acquired by confusion. [987]

conglomerate merger A merger that does not fit into any other category; a merger between firms in totally unrelated businesses. [969]

conscious parallelism If two or more firms act the same but no concerted action is shown, there is no violation of Section 1 of the Sherman Act. [965]

consequential damages Foreseeable damages that arise from circumstances outside the contract. To be liable for these damages, the breaching party must know or have reason to know that the breach will cause special damages to the other party. [304, 445]

consideration Something of legal value given in exchange for a promise. [212]

consignee The person to whom the bailed goods are to be delivered. [996]

consignor The person shipping the goods (the bailor). [996]

consignment An arrangement where a seller (the consignor) delivers goods to a buyer (the consignee) for sale. [402]

Consolidated Omnibus Budget Reconciliation Act (COBRA) Federal law that permits employees and their beneficiaries to continue their group health insurance after an employee's employment has ended. [829]

consolidation The act of a court to combine two or more separate lawsuits into one lawsuit. [30] Occurs when two or more corporations combine to form an entirely new corporation. [778]

conspicuous A requirement that warranty disclaimers be noticeable to the average person. [443]

Constitution of the United States of America The supreme law of the United States. [9]

constructive trust An equitable trust that is imposed by law to avoid fraud, unjust enrichment, and injustice. [1074]

consumer expectation test A test to determine merchantability based on what the average consumer would expect to find in food products. [439]

consumer lease A lease with a value of $25,000 or less between a lessor regularly engaged in the business of leasing or selling and a lessee who leases the goods primarily for a personal, family, or household purpose. [381]

Consumer Leasing Act (CLA) An amendment to the TILA that extends the TILA's coverage to lease terms in consumer leases. [925]

Consumer Product Safety Act (CPSA) A federal statute that regulates potentially dangerous consumer products and created the Consumer Product Safety Commission. [920]

Consumer Product Safety Commission (CPSC) An independent federal regulatory agency empowered to (1) adopt rules and regulations to interpret and enforce the Consumer Product Safety Act, (2) conduct research on safety, and (3) collect data regarding injuries. [920]

consumer protection laws Federal and state statutes and regulations that promote product safety and prohibit abusive, unfair, and deceptive business practices. [915]

contracts contrary to public policy Contracts that have a negative impact on society or interfere with the public's safety and welfare. [235]

contributory negligence A doctrine that says a plaintiff who is partially at fault for his or her own injury cannot

recover against the negligent defendant. [108] A defense that says a person who is injured by a defective product but has been negligent and has contributed to his or her own injuries cannot recover from the defendant. [130]

convention Treaty that is sponsored by an international organization. [68]

conversion of personal property A tort that deprives a true owner of the use and enjoyment of his or her personal property by taking over such property and exercising ownership rights over it. [98]

convertible preferred stock Stock that permits the stockholders to convert their shares into common stock. [738]

cooling-off period Requires a union to give an employer at least 60 days' notice before a strike can commence. [871]

cooperative A voluntary joining together of businesses that provides services to its members. [628] A form of co-ownership of a multiple-dwelling building where a corporation owns the building and the residents own shares in the corporation. [1013]

co-ownership When two or more persons own a piece of real property. Also called *concurrent ownership.* [1010]

copyright infringement When a party copies a substantial and material part of the plaintiff's copyrighted work without permission. A copyright holder may recover damages and other remedies against the infringer. [331]

Copyright Revision Act of 1976 Federal statute that (1) establishes the requirements for obtaining a copyright and (2) protects copyrighted works from infringement. [328]

core proceedings Proceedings that bankruptcy judges decide that have to do with creditor claims, deciding preferences, confirming plans of reorganization, and so on. [564]

corporate citizenship A theory of social responsibility that says a business has a responsibility to do good. [171]

corporate seal A design containing the name of the corporation and the date of incorporation that is imprinted by the corporate secretary using a metal stamp on certain legal documents. [735]

corporation A fictitious legal entity that (1) is created according to statutory requirements and (2) is a separate taxpaying entity for federal income tax purposes. [625] A fictitious legal entity that is created according to statutory requirements. [723]

corporations codes State statutes that regulate the formation, operation, and dissolution of corporations. [723]

cost justification defense A defense in a Section 2(a) action that provides that a seller's price discrimination is not unlawful if the price differential is due to "differences in the cost of manufacture, sale, or delivery" of the product. [972]

counteroffer A response by an offeree that contains terms and conditions different from or in addition to those of the offer. A counteroffer terminates an offer. [200]

Court of Appeals for the Federal Circuit A court of appeals in Washington, DC, that has special appellate jurisdiction to review the decisions of the Claims Court, the Patent and Trademark Office, and the Court of International Trade. [22]

Court of Chancery Court that granted relief based on fairness. Also called *equity court.* [8]

covenant An unconditional promise to perform. [287]

covenant of good faith and fair dealing Under this implied covenant, the parties to a contract not only are held to the express terms of the contract but also are required to act in "good faith" and deal fairly in all respects in obtaining the objective of the contract. [313]

covenant of quiet enjoyment A covenant that says a land lord may not interfere with the tenant's quiet and peaceful possession, use, and enjoyment of the leased premises. [1027]

cover The licensee's right to engage in a commercially reasonable substitute transaction after the licensor has breached the contract. [369] Right of a buyer or lessee to purchase or lease substitute goods if a seller or lessor fails to make delivery of the goods or repudiates the contract, or if the buyer or lessee rightfully rejects the goods or justifiably revokes their acceptance. [424]

cram down method   A method of confirmation of a plan of reorganization where the court forces an impaired class to participate in the plan of reorganization. [578]

crashworthiness doctrine   A doctrine that says automobile manufacturers are under a duty to design automobiles so they take into account the possibility of harm from a person's body striking something inside the automobile in the case of a car accident. [124]

credit report   Information about a person's credit history that can be secured from a credit bureau. [927]

creditor   The lender in a credit transaction. [527]

creditor beneficiary   Original creditor who becomes a beneficiary under the debtor's new contract with another party. [285]

creditor beneficiary contract   A contract that arises in the following situation: (1) A debtor borrows money, (2) the debtor signs an agreement to pay back the money plus interest, (3) the debtor sells the item to a third party before the loan is paid off, and (4) the third party promises the debtor that he or she will pay the remainder of the loan to the creditor. [284]

creditor–debtor relationship   Created when a customer deposits money into the bank; the customer is the creditor and the bank is the debtor. [508]

creditor's committee   The creditors holding the seven largest unsecured claims are usually appointed to the creditors' committee. Representatives of the committee appear at Bankruptcy Court hearings, participate in the negotiation of a plan of reorganization, assert objections to proposed plans, and so on. [576]

crime   A crime is a violation of a statute for which the government imposes a punishment. [138]

criminal conspiracy   When two or more persons enter into an agreement to commit a crime and an overt act is taken to further the crime. [149]

criminal fraud   Obtaining title to property through deception or trickery. Also known as *false pretenses* or *deceit*. [145]

critical legal thinking   The process of specifying the issue presented by a case, identifying the key facts in the case and applicable law, and then applying the law to the facts to come to a conclusion that answers the issue presented. [11]

cross-complaint   Filed by the defendant against the plaintiff to seek damages or some other remedy. [30]

crossover worker   A person who does not honor a strike by either (1) choosing not to strike or (2) returning to work after joining the strikers for a time. [870]

crown jewel   A valuable asset of the target corporation's that the tender offeror particularly wants to acquire in the tender offer. [785]

cure   An opportunity to repair or replace defective or nonconforming goods. [413]

cruel and unusual punishment   A clause of the Eighth Amendment that protects criminal defendants from torture or other abusive punishment. [156]

cumulative preferred stock   Stock that provides any missed dividend payments must be paid in the future to the preferred shareholders before the common shareholders can receive any dividends. [738]

cumulative voting   A shareholder can accumulate all of his or her votes and vote them all for one candidate or split them among several candidates. [749]

custom   The second source of international law, created through consistent, recurring practices between two or more nations over a period of time that have become recognized as binding. [71]

damages for accepted nonconforming goods   A buyer or lessee may accept nonconforming goods and recover the damages caused by the breach from the seller or lessor or deduct the damages from any part of the purchase price or rent still due under the contract. [425]

"danger invites rescue" doctrine   Doctrine that provides that a rescuer who is injured while going to someone's rescue can sue the person who caused the dangerous situation. [105]

debenture   A long-term unsecured debt instrument that is based on the corporation's general credit standing. [739]

debt collector   An agent who collects debts for other parties. [728]

debt securities   Securities that establish a debtor-creditor relationship in which the corporation borrows money from the investor to whom the debt security is issued. [739]

debtor   The borrower in a credit transaction. [527]

debtor-in-possession   A debtor who is left in place to operate the business during the reorganization proceeding. [576]

declaration of duties   If the delegatee has not assumed the duties under a contract, the delegatee is not legally liable to the obligee for nonperformance. [283]

decree of judicial dissolution   A decree of dissolution that is granted to a partner whenever it is not reasonably practical to carry on the business in conformity with the limited partnership agreement. [672]

deductible clause   Clause in an insurance policy that provides that insurance proceeds are payable only after the insured has paid a certain amount of the loss. [1043]

deed   A writing that describes a person's ownership interest in a piece of real property. [1016]

deed of trust   An instrument that gives the creditor a security interest in the debtor's property that is pledged as collateral. [531]

defamation of character   False statement(s) made by one person about another. In court, the plaintiff must prove that (1) the defendant made an untrue statement of fact about the plaintiff and (2) the statement was intentionally or accidentally published to a third party. [92]

default   Failure to make scheduled payments when due, bankruptcy of the debtor, breach of the warranty of ownership as to the collateral, and other events defined by the parties to constitute default. [555]

defect   Something wrong, inadequate, or improper in manufacture, design, packaging, warning, or safety measures of a product. [121]

defect in design   A defect that occurs when a product is improperly designed. [122]

defect in manufacture A defect that occurs when the manufacturer fails to (1) properly assemble a product, (2) properly test a product, or (3) adequately check the quality of the product. [122]

defect in packaging A defect that occurs when a product has been placed in packaging that is insufficiently tamper-proof. [125]

defective formation Occurs when (1) a certificate of limited partnership is not properly filed, (2) there are defects in a certificate that is filed, or (3) some other statutory requirement for the creation of a limited partnership is not met. [667]

defendant's case Process by which the defendant (1), rebuts the plaintiff's evidence, (2) proves affirmative defenses, and (3) proves allegations made in a cross-complaint. [36]

deferred posting rule A rule that allows banks to fix an afternoon hour of 2:00 P.M. or later as a cutoff hour for the purpose of processing items. [518]

deficiency judgment A judgment that allows a secured creditor to successfully bring a separate legal action to recover a deficiency from the debtor. Entitles the secured creditor to recover the amount of the judgment from the debtor's other property. [556]

deficiency judgment Judgment of a court that permits a secured lender to recover other property or income from a defaulting debtor if the collateral is insufficient to repay the unpaid loan. [528]

delegatee The party to whom the duty has been transferred. [282]

delegation doctrine A doctrine that says when an administrative agency is created, it is delegated certain powers; the agency can only use those legislative, judicial, and executive powers that are delegated to it. [902]

delegation of duties A transfer of contractual duties by the obligor to another party for performance. [282]

delegator The obligor who transferred his or her duty. [282]

demand instrument An instrument payable on demand. [461]

demand note A note payable on demand. [454]

deponent Party who gives his or her deposition. [32]

deposition Oral testimony given by a party or witness prior to trial. The testimony is given under oath and is transcribed. [32]

depository bank The bank where the payee or holder has an account. [517]

derivative action A lawsuit that a member may bring against an offending third party on behalf of his or her LLC when the LLC fails to bring the lawsuit or a request of the LLC to do so is excused. [692]

derivative lawsuit A lawsuit a shareholder brings against an offending party on behalf of the corporation when the corporation fails to bring the lawsuit. [752]

destination contract A contract that requires the seller to deliver the goods either to the buyer's place of business or to another destination specified in the sales contract. [396, 412]

devise A gift of real estate by will. [1064]

direct lawsuit A lawsuit that a member can bring against an LLC to enforce his or her personal rights as a member. [692] A lawsuit that a shareholder can bring against the corporation to enforce his or her personal rights as a shareholder. [752]

disability insurance Insurance that provides a monthly income to an insured who is disabled and cannot work. [1047]

disaffirmance The act of a minor to rescind a contract under the infancy doctrine. Disaffirmance may be done orally, in writing, or by the minor's conduct. [227]

discharge The termination of contract obligations. [290] Actions or events that relieve certain parties from liability on negotiable instruments. There are three methods of discharge: (1) payment of the instrument, (2) cancellation, and (3) impairment of the right of recourse. [501] The termination of the legal duty of a debtor to pay debts that remain unpaid upon the completion of a bankruptcy proceeding. [572] A discharge is granted to a debtor in a Chapter 13 consumer debt adjustment bankruptcy only

after all the payments under the plan are completed by the debtor. [582] Creditors' claims that are not included in a Chapter 11 reorganization are discharged. [579]

discharge in bankruptcy A real defense against the enforcement of a negotiable instrument; bankruptcy law is intended to relieve debtors of burdensome debts, including negotiable instruments. [497]

disclosure statement A statement that must contain adequate information about the proposed plan of reorganization that is supplied to the creditors and equity holders. [577]

discovery A legal process during which both parties engage in various activities to discover facts of the case from the other party and witnesses prior to trial. [32]

dishonored Occurs when an instrument has been presented for payment and payment has been refused. [488]

disparate impact discrimination Occurs when an employer discriminates against an entire protected *class*. An example would be where a facially neutral employment practice or rule causes an adverse impact on a protected class. [839]

disparate treatment discrimination Occurs when an employer discriminates against a specific *individual* because of his or her race, color, national origin, sex, or religion. [839]

disposition of collateral If a secured creditor repossesses collateral upon a debtor's default, he or she may sell, lease, or otherwise dispose of it in a commercially reasonable manner. [556]

disposition of goods A seller or lessor that is in possession of goods at the time the buyer or lessee breaches or repudiates the contract may in good faith resell, release, or otherwise dispose of the goods in a commercially reasonable manner and recover damages, including incidental damages, from the buyer or lessee. [420]

dispute settlement body A board comprising of one representative from each WTO member nation that reviews panel reports. [78]

dissension When an individual director opposes the action taken by the majority of the board of directors. [763]

dissenting shareholder appraisal rights Shareholders who object to a proposed merger, share exchange, or sale or lease of all or substantially all of the property of a corporation have a right to have their shares valued by the court and receive cash payment of this value from the corporation. [780]

dissolution "The change in the relation of the partners caused by any partner ceasing to be associated in the carrying on of the business" [UPA § 29]. [652]

distinctive A brand name that is unique and fabricated. [337]

distributional interest A member's ownership interest in an LLC that entitles the member to receive distributions of money and property from the LLC. [692]

distributional interest The ownership interest that a member has in an LLC. [696]

distribution of assets Upon the winding-up of a dissolved partnership, the assets of the partnership are distributed in the following order [UPA § 40 (b)]:
1. Creditors (except partners who are creditors)
2. Creditor-partners
3. Capital contributions
4. Profits [655]

distribution of property *Nonexempt property* of the bankruptcy estate must be distributed to the debtor's secured and unsecured creditors pursuant to the statutory priority established by the Bankruptcy Code. [571]

distributorship franchise The franchisor manufactures a product and licenses a retail franchisee to distribute the product to the public. [703]

diversity of citizenship A case between (1) citizens of different states, (2) a citizen of a state and a citizen or subject of a foreign country, and (3) a citizen of a state and a foreign country where a foreign country is the plaintiff. [25]

dividend Distribution of profits of the corporation to shareholders. [756]

dividend preference The right to receive a fixed dividend at stipulated periods during the year (e.g., quarterly). [737]

division of markets When competitors agree that each will serve only a designated portion of the market. [960]

doctrine of sovereign immunity States that countries are granted immunity from suits in courts of other countries. [83]

doctrine of strict liability in tort A tort doctrine that makes manufacturers, distributors, wholesalers, retailers, and others in the chain of distribution of a defective product liable for the damages caused by the defect *irrespective of fault*. [118]

document of title An actual piece of paper, such as a warehouse receipt or bill of lading, that is required in some transactions of pick up and delivery. [396] A negotiable instrument developed to represent the interests of the different parties in a transaction that uses storage or transportation between the parties. [998]

domain name A unique name that identifies an individual's or company's Web site. [354]

domestic corporation A corporation in the state in which it was formed. [728]

domestic limited partnership A limited partnership in the state in which it was formed. [668]

domestic LLC An LLC in the state in which it is organized. [686]

donee A person who receives a gift. [985]

donee beneficiary The third party on whom the benefit is to be conferred. [284]

donee beneficiary contract A contract entered into with the intent to confer a benefit or gift on an intended third party. [284]

donor A person who gives a gift. [985]

double indemnity clause A clause that stipulates that the insurer will pay double the amount of the policy if death is caused by accident. [1046]

double jeopardy clause A clause of the Fifth Amendment that protects persons from being tried twice for the same crime. [155]

draft A three-party instrument that is an unconditional written order by one party that orders the second party to pay money to a third party. [453]

Dram Shop Act Statute that makes taverns and bartenders liable for injuries caused to or by patrons who are served too much alcohol. [105]

drawee of a check The bank where the drawer has his or her account. [509]

drawee of a draft The party who must pay the money stated in the draft. Also called the *acceptor* of a draft. [453]

drawer of a check The customers who has the checking account and writes (draws) the check. [454, 509]

drawer of a draft The party who writes the order for a draft. [453]

Drug Amendment to the FDCA An amendment enacted in 1962 that gives the FDA broad powers to license new drugs in the United States. [917]

dual-purpose mission An errand or other act that a principal requests of an agent while the agent is on his or her own personal business. [615]

due diligence defense A defense to a Section II action that, if proven, makes the defendant not liable. [805]

Due Process Clause A clause that provides that no person shall be deprived of "life, liberty, or property" without due process of the law. [59]

duress Occurs where one party threatens to do a wrongful act unless the other party enters into a contract. [254]

duty not to willfully or wantonly injure The duty an owner owes a trespasser to prevent intentional injury or harm to the trespasser when the trespasser is on his or her premises. [106]

duty of accountability A duty that an agent owes to maintain an accurate accounting of all transactions undertaken on the principal's behalf. [608]

duty of care The obligation we all owe each other not to cause any unreasonable harm or risk of harm. [99] A breach of the duty of care is *negligence*. [647] A duty owed by a member of a member-managed LLC and a manager of a manager-managed LLC to not engage in (1) a known violation of law, (2) intentional conduct, (3) reckless conduct, or (4) grossly negligent conduct that injures the LLC. [694] A duty that corporate directors and officers have to use care and diligence when acting on behalf of the corporation. [760]

duty of compensation A duty that a principal owes to pay an agreed-upon amount to the agent either upon the completion of the agency or at some other mutually agreeable time. [608]

duty of loyalty A duty that directors and officers have not to act adversely to the interests of the corporation and to subordinate their personal interests to those of the corporation and its shareholders. [69, 606, 764] A duty that a partner owes not to act adversely to the interests of the partnership. [645]

duty of notification An agent's duty to notify the principal of information he or she learns from a third party or other source that is important to the principal. [606]

duty of obedience A duty that agents have to obey the lawful instructions of the principal during the performance of the agency. [607] A duty that partners must adhere to the provisions of the partnership agreement and the decisions of the partnership. [647] A duty that directors and officers of a corporation have to act within the authority conferred upon them by the state corporation statute, the articles of incorporation, the corporate bylaws, and the resolutions adopted by the board of directors. [759]

duty of ordinary care The duty an owner owes an invitee or a licensee to prevent injury or harm when the invitee or licensee steps on the owner's premises. [106] Collecting banks are required to exercise ordinary care in presenting and sending checks for collection. [520]

duty of performance An agent's duty to a principal that includes (1) performing the lawful duties expressed in the contract and (2) meeting the standards of reasonable care, skill, and diligence implicit in all contracts. [605]

duty of reasonable care The duty that a reasonable bailee in like circumstances would owe to protect the bailed property. [994]

duty of reimbursement A duty that a principal owes to repay money to the agent if the agent spent his or her own money during the agency on the principal's behalf. [609]

duty of slight care A duty not to be grossly negligent in caring for something in one's possession. [993]

duty of utmost care A duty of care that goes beyond ordinary care. [994]

duty to cooperate A duty that a principal owes to cooperate with and assist the agent in the performance of the agent's duties and the accomplishment of the agency. [609]

duty to indemnify A duty that a principal owes to protect the agent for losses the agent suffered during the agency because of the principal's misconduct. [609]

duty to inform A duty a partner owes to inform his or her copartners of all information he or she possesses that is relevant to the affairs of the partnership. [647]

duty to provide safe working conditions A duty that a principal owes to provide safe premises, equipment, and other working conditions; also includes inspection by the principal. [610]

duty of utmost care A duty of care that goes beyond ordinary care that says common carriers and innkeepers have a responsibility to provide security to their passengers or guests. [105]

easement A right to use someone else's land without owning or leasing it. [264, 1018]

easement appurtenant A situation created when the owner of one piece of land is given an easement over an adjacent piece of land. [1018]

easement in gross An easement that authorizes a person who does not own adjacent land the right to use another's land. [1018]

e-commerce The sale of goods and services by computer over the Internet. [350]

economic duress Occurs when one party to a contract refuses to perform his or her contractual duties unless the other party pays an increased price, enters into a second contract with the threatening party, or undertakes a similar action. [254]

electronic mail (e-mail) Electronic written communication between individuals and businesses using computers connected to the Internet. [352]

elements of a bailment The following three elements are necessary to create a bailment: (1) personal property, (2)

delivery of possession, and (3) a bailment agreement. [992]

elements of price discrimination To prove a violation of Section 2(a), the following elements must be shown: (1) The defendant sold commodities of like grade and quality, (2) to two or more purchasers at different prices at approximately the same time, and (3) the plaintiff suffered injury because of the price discrimination. [972]

emancipation When a minor voluntarily leaves home and lives apart from his or her parents. [229]

embezzlement The fraudulent conversion of property by a person to whom that property was entrusted. [145]

eminent domain Power of the government to acquire private property for public purposes. [899]

Employee Retirement Income Security Act (ERISA) A federal act designed to prevent fraud and other abuses associated with private pension funds. [829]

employer–employee relationship A relationship that results when an employer hires an employee to perform some form of physical service. [589]

employer lockout Act of the employer to prevent employees from entering the work premises when the employer reasonably anticipates a strike. [872]

employment relationships (1) Employer-employee, (2) principal-agent, and (3) principal-independent contractor. [589]

enabling use The licensor's duty to grant permissions, make copies of software or electonic information available, tender all materials and access codes, and to take all steps necessary to enable the licensee to use the information. [361]

Endangered Species Act A federal statute enacted in 1973 that protects "endangered" and "threatened" species of animals. [948]

endorsement An addition to an insurance policy that modifies it. [1042]

engagement A formal entrance into a contract between a client and an accountant. [881]

entity theory A theory that holds that partnerships are separate legal entities that can hold title to personal and real property, transact business in the partnership name, sue in the partnership name, and the like. [638]

entrepreneur　A person who forms and operates a new business either by himself or herself or with others. [624]

enumerated powers　Certain powers delegated to the federal government by the states. [47]

environmental impact statement (EIS)　A document that must be prepared for all proposed legislation or major federal action that significantly affects the quality of the human environment. [937]

Environmental Protection Agency (EPA)　An administrative agency created by Congress in 1970 to coordinate the implementation and enforcement of the federal environmental protection laws. [937]

Equal Access to Justice Act　An act that was enacted to protect persons from harassment by federal administrative agencies. [909]

Equal Credit Opportunity Act (ECOA)　A federal statute that prohibits discrimination in the extension of credit based on sex, marital status, race, color, national origin, religion, age, or receipt of income from public assistance programs. [926]

equal dignity rule　A rule that says that agents contracts to sell property covered by the Statute of Frauds must be in writing to be enforceable. [267]

Equal Employment Opportunity Commission (EEOC)　The federal administrative agency responsible for enforcing most federal antidiscrimination laws. [838]

equal opportunity in employment　The right of all employees and job applicants (1) to be treated without discrimination and (2) to be able to sue employers if they are discriminated against. [838]

Equal Pay Act of 1963　Protects both sexes from pay discrimination based on sex; extends to jobs that require equal skill, equal effort, equal responsibility, and similar working conditions. [850]

Equal Protection Clause　A clause that provides that a state cannot "deny to any person within its jurisdiction the equal protection of the laws." [57]

equitable remedies　Remedies that may be awarded by a judge where there has been a breach of contract and either (1) the

legal remedy is not adequate or (2) to prevent unjust enrichment. [309]

equity　A doctrine that permits judges to make decisions based on fairness, equality, moral rights, and natural law. [189]

equity securities　Representation of ownership rights to the corporation. Also called *stocks*. [736]

Establishment Clause　A clause to the First Amendment that prohibits the government from either establishing a state religion or promoting one religion over another. [56]

estate　Ownership rights in real property; the bundle of legal rights that the owner has to possess, use, and enjoy the property. [1008]

estate pour autre vie　A life estate measured in the life of a third party. [1009]

estray statutes　Statutes that permit a finder of mislaid or lost property to clear title to the property if (1) the finder reports the found property to the appropriate government agency and turns over possession of the property to this agency, (2) either the finder or the government agency posts notices and publishes advertisements describing the lost property, and (3) a specified amount of time has passed without the rightful owner's reclaiming the property. [989]

ethical fundamentalism　When a person looks to an outside source for ethical rules or commands. [162]

ethical relativism　A moral theory that holds that individuals must decide what is ethical based on their own feelings as to what is right or wrong. [166]

ethics　A set of moral principles or values that governs the conduct of an individual or a group. [161]

European Court of Justice　The judicial branch of the European Community located in Luxembourg. It has jurisdiction to enforce European Community law. [80]

European Union (Common Market)　Comprises many countries of Western Europe; created to promote peace and security plus economic, social, and cultural development. [75]

exclusion　Part of an insurance policy that says what it will *not* cover under certain circumstances. [1043]

exclusionary rule　A rule that says evidence obtained from an unreasonable search and seizure can generally be prohibited from introduction at a trial or administrative proceeding against the person searched. [153]

exclusive agency contract　A contract a principal and an agent enter into that says the principal cannot employ any agent other than the exclusive agent. [593]

exclusive jurisdiction　Jurisdiction held by only one court. [25]

exclusive license　A license that grants the licensee exclusive rights to use informational rights for a specified duration. [357]

exculpatory clause　A contractual provision that relieves one (or both) parties to the contract from tort liability for ordinary negligence. [236]

executed contract　A contract that has been fully performed on both sides; a completed contract. [189]

execution　Postjudgment seizure and sale of the debtor's property to satisfy a creditor's judgment against the debtor. [538]

executive branch　The part of the government that consists of the President and Vice President. [48]

executive order　An order issued by a member of the executive branch of the government. [10]

executive powers　Powers that administrative agencies are granted, such as the investigation and prosecution of possible violations of statutes, administrative rules, and administrative orders. [904]

executory contract　A contract that has not been fully performed by either or both sides. [189] With court approval, executory contracts may be rejected by a debtor in bankruptcy. [577]

exempt property　Property that may be retained by the debtor pursuant to federal or state law; debtor's property that does not become part of the bankruptcy estate. [567]

express agency　An agency that occurs when a principal and an agent expressly agree to enter into an agency agreement with each other. [592]

express authorization　A stipulation in the offer that says the acceptance must be by a specified means of communication. [205]

express contract An agreement that is expressed in written or oral words. [184]

express partnership General partnership created by words, either verbal or written. [641]

express powers Powers given to a corporation by (1) the U.S. Constitution, (2) state constitutions, (3) federal statutes, (4) state statutes, (5) articles of incorporation, (6) bylaws, and (7) resolutions of the board of directors. [748]

express trust A trust created voluntarily by the settlor. [1074]

express warranty Any affirmation of fact or promise by the licensor about the quality of its software or information. [364] A warranty that is created when a seller or lessor makes an affirmation that the goods he or she is selling or leasing meet certain standards of quality, description, performance, or condition. [434]

extortion Threat to expose something about another person unless that other person gives money or property. Often referred to as "blackmail." [144]

extradition Sending a person back to a country for criminal prosecution. [86]

extreme duress Extreme duress, but not ordinary duress, is a real defense against enforcement of a negotiable instrument. [497]

failure to warn A defect that occurs when a manufacturer does not place a warning on the packaging of products that could cause injury if the danger is unknown. [126]

Fair Credit and Charge Card Disclosure Act of 1988 An amendment to the TILA that requires disclosure of certain credit terms on credit- and charge-card solicitations and applications. [925]

Fair Credit Billing Act (FCBA) An amendment to the TILA that regulates credit billing. [928]

Fair Credit Reporting Act (FCRA) An amendment to the TILA that protects customers who are subjects of a credit report by setting out guidelines for credit bureaus. [927]

Fair Debt Collection Practices Act (FDCPA) An act enacted in 1977 that protects consumer-debtors from abusive,

deceptive, and unfair practices used by debt collectors. [928]

Fair Labor Standards Act (FLSA) A federal act enacted in 1938 to protect workers; prohibits child labor and establishes minimum wage and overtime pay requirements. [827]

Fair Packaging and Labeling Act A federal statute that requires the labels on consumer goods to identify the product; the manufacturer, processor, or packager of the product and its address; the net quantity of the contents of the package; and the quantity of each serving. [920]

fair price rule A rule that says any increase in price paid for shares tendered must be offered to all shareholders, even those who have previously tendered their shares. [783]

fair use doctrine A doctrine that permits certain limited use of a copyright by someone other than the copyright holder without the permission of the copyright holder. [332]

false imprisonment The intentional confinement or restraint of another person without authority or justification and without that person's consent. [91]

federal administrative agencies Administrative agencies that are part of the executive or legislative branch of government. [901]

Federal Insurance Contributions Act (FICA) A federal act that says employees and employers must make contributions into the Social Security fund. [831]

Federal Patent Statute of 1952 Federal statute that establishes the requirements for obtaining a patent and protects patented inventions from infringement. [323]

federal question A case arising under the U.S. Constitution. treaties. or federal statutes and regulations. [25]

Federal Reserve System A system of 12 regional Federal Reserve banks that assist banks in the collection of checks. [518]

Federal Trade Commission (FTC) Federal administrative agency empowered to enforce the Federal Trade Commission Act and other federal consumer protection statutes. [705, 921]

Federal Unemployment Tax Act (FUTA) A federal act that requires

employers to pay unemployment taxes; unemployment compensation is paid to workers who are temporarily unemployed. [831]

Federal Water Pollution Control Act (FWPCA) A federal statute enacted in 1948 that regulates water pollution. [941]

federalism The U.S. form of government; the federal government and the 50 state government share powers. [47]

fee simple absolute A type of ownership of real property that grants the owner the fullest bundle of legal rights that a person can hold in real property. [1008]

fee simple defeasible A type of ownership of real property that grants the owner all the incidents of a fee simple absolute except that it may be taken away if a specified condition occurs or does not occur. [1008]

felony The most serious type of crime; inherently evil crime. Most crimes against the person and some business-related crimes are felonies. [138]

fictitious payee rule A rule that says the drawer or maker is liable on a forged or unauthorized indorsement of a fictitious payee. [480]

fiduciary duty The duty the directors of a corporation owe to act carefully and honestly when acting on behalf of the corporation. [787]

fiduciary duty Duty of loyalty, honesty, integrity, trust, and confidence owed by directors and officers to their corporate employers. [759]

final order rule A rule that says the decision of an administrative agency must be final before judicial review can be sought. [907]

final prospectus A final version of the prospectus that must be delivered by the issuer to the investor prior to or at the time of confirming a sale or sending a security to a purchaser. [800]

final settlement Occurs when the payor bank (1) pays the check in cash, (2) settles for the check without having a right to revoke the settlement, or (3) fails to dishonor the check within certain statutory time periods. [519]

finance lease A three-party transaction consisting of the lessor, the lessee, and the supplier. [381]

financing statement A document filed by a secured creditor with the appropriate government office that constructively notifies the world of his or her security interest in personal property. [548]

fixed amount A requirement of a negotiable instrument that ensures that the value of the instrument can be determined with certainty. [459]

fixed amount of money A negotiable instrument must contain a promise or order to pay a fixed amount of money. [459]

fixtures Goods that are affixed to real estate so as to become part thereof. [1007]

fixtures Personal property that is permanently affixed to the real property, such as built-in cabinets in a house. [263]

floating lien A security interest in property that was not in the possession of the debtor when the security agreement was executed; this includes *after-acquired property, sale proceeds,* and *future advances.* [550]

Food and Drug Administration (FDA) Federal administrative agency that administers and enforces the federal Food, Drug, and Cosmetic Act (FDCA) and other federal consumer protection laws. [915]

Food, Drug, and Cosmetic Act (FDCA) A federal statute enacted in 1938 that provides the basis for the regulation of much of the testing, manufacture, distribution, and sale of foods, drugs, cosmetics, and medicinal products. [915]

foreclosure Legal procedure by which a secured creditor causes the judicial sale of the secured real estate to pay a defaulted loan. [533]

foreign corporation A corporation in any state or jurisdiction other than the one in which it was formed. [728]

foreign limited partnership A limited partnership in all other states than the one in which it was formed. [668]

foreign LLC An LLC in any state other than the one in which it is organized. [686]

Foreign Sovereign Immunities Act Exclusively governs suits against foreign nations that are brought in federal or state courts in the United States; codifies the principle of *qualified* or *restricted immunity.* [83]

foreign substance test A test to determine merchantability based on foreign objects that are found in food. [438]

foreseeability standard A rule that an accountant is liable for negligence to third parties who are *foreseeable users* of the client's financial statements. Provides the broadest standard for holding accountants liable to third parties for negligence. [885]

forged indorsement The forged signature of a payee or holder on a negotiable instrument. [475, 479]

forged instrument A check with a forged drawer's signature on it. [516]

forgery Fraudulently making or altering a written document that affects the legal liability of another person. [144] A real defense against the enforcement of a negotiable instrument; the unauthorized signature of a maker, drawer, or indorser. [498]

formal contract A contract that requires a special form or method of creation. [187]

forum-selection clause Contract provision that designates a certain court to hear any dispute concerning nonperformance of the contract. [27]

forward vertical merger A vertical merger in which the supplier acquires the customer. [968]

four legals Four notices or actions that prevent the payment of a check if they are received by the payor bank before it has finished its process of posting the check for payment. [520]

Fourteenth Amendment Amendment that was added to the U.S. Constitution in 1868. It contains the Due Process, Equal Protection, and Privileges and Immunities clauses. [57]

franchise The owner of a trademark, a trade secret, a patent, or a product licenses another party to sell products or services under the franchisor's name. [627] Established when one party licenses another party to use the franchisor's trade name, trademarks, commercial symbols, patents, copyrights, and other property in the distribution and selling of goods and services. [703]

franchise agreement An agreement that the franchisor and the franchisee enter into that sets forth the terms and conditions of the franchise. [706]

franchisee The party who is licensed by the franchisor in a franchise situation. [703]

franchisor The party who does the licensing in a franchise situation. [703]

fraud by concealment Occurs when one party takes specific action to conceal a material fact from another party. [251]

fraud in the inception A real defense against the enforcement of a negotiable instrument; a person has been deceived into signing a negotiable instrument thinking that it is something else. [251, 498]

fraud in the inducement A personal defense against the enforcement of a negotiable instrument; a wrongdoer makes a false statement to another person to lead that person to enter into a contract with the wrongdoer. [251, 499]

fraudulent transfer Occurs when (1) a debtor transfers property to a third person within one year before the filing of a petition in bankruptcy and (2) the transfer was made by the debtor with an intent to hinder, delay, or defraud creditors. [570]

Free Exercise Clause A clause to the First Amendment that prohibits the government from interfering with the free exercise of religion in the United States. [57]

Freedom of Information Act An act that was enacted to give the public access to documents in the possession of federal administrative agencies. There are many exceptions to disclosure. [909]

freedom of speech The right to engage in oral, written, and symbolic speech protected by the First Amendment. [54]

freehold estate An estate where the owner has a present possessory interest in the real property. [1008]

fresh start The goal of federal bankruptcy law: to discharge the debtor from burdensome debts and allow him or her to begin again. [565]

frolic and detour When an agent does something during the course of his or her employment to further his or her own interests rather than the principal's. [615]

frustration of purpose A doctrine that excuses the performance of contractual obligation if (1) the object or benefit of a contract is made worthless to a promisor, (2) both parties knew what the purpose was, and (3) the act that frustrated the purpose was unforeseeable. [293]

FTC franchise rule A rule set out by the FTC that requires franchisors to make full presale disclosures to prospective franchisees. [705]

fully disclosed agency An agency that results if the third party entering into the contract knows (1) that the agent is acting as an agent for a principal and (2) the actual identity of the principal. [610]

future advances Personal property of the debtor that is designated as collateral for future loans from a line of credit. [551]

future goods Goods not yet in existence (ungrown crops, unborn stock animals). [395]

future interest The interest that the grantor retains for him- or herself or a third party. [1009]

gambling statutes Statutes that make certain forms of gambling illegal. [233]

gap-filling rule A rule that says an open term can be "read into" a contract. [383]

garnishment A postjudgment remedy that is directed against property of the debtor that is in the possession of third persons. [538]

general duty A duty that an employer has to provide a work environment "free from recognized hazards that are causing or are likely to cause death or serious physical harm to his employees." [826]

general gift Gift that does not identify the specific property from which the gift is to be made. [1064]

general-jurisdiction trial court A court that hears cases of a general nature that are not within the jurisdiction of limited-jurisdiction trial courts. Testimony and evidence at trial are recorded and stored for future reference. [19]

general partners Partners in a limited partnership who invest capital, manage the business, and are personally liable for partnership debts. [661]

general partnership An association of two or more persons to carry on as co-owners of a business for profit [UPA § 6(1)]. [624, 638]

general principles of law The third source of international law, consisting of principles of law recognized by civilized nations. These are principles of law that are common to the national law of the parties to the dispute. [71]

generally accepted accounting principles (GAAPs) Standards for the preparation and presentation of financial statements. Standards for the methods and procedures that must be used to conduct audits. [879–880]

generally known dangers A defense that acknowledges that certain products are inherently dangerous and are known to the general population to be so. [128]

general-purpose clause A clause often included in the articles of incorporation that authorizes the corporation to engage in any activity permitted corporations by law. [732]

generic name A term for a mark that has become a common term for a product line or type of service and therefore has lost its trademark protection. [340]

genuineness of assent The requirement that a party's assent to a contract be genuine. [247]

gift A voluntary transfer of title to property without payment of consideration by the donee. To be a valid gift, the following three elements must be shown: (1) *donative intent*, (2) *delivery*, and (3) *acceptance*. [985] A transfer of property from one person to another without exchange of money. [1013]

gift *causa mortis* A gift that is made in contemplation of death. [985]

gift promise An unenforceable promise because it lacks consideration. [213]

good faith Honesty in fact in the conduct or transaction concerned. This is a subjective test. [487]

good faith purchaser for value A person to whom good title can be transferred from a person with voidable title. The real owner cannot reclaim goods from a good faith purchaser for value. [404]

good faith subsequent lessee A person to whom a lease interest can be transferred from a person with voidable title. The real owner cannot reclaim the goods from the subsequent lessee until the lease expires. [404]

Good Samaritan law Statute that relieves medical professionals from liability for ordinary negligence when they stop and render aid to victims in emergency situations. [104]

good title Title that is free from any encumbrances or other defects that are not disclosed but would affect the value of the property. [1017]

goods Tangible things that are movable at the time of their identification to the contract. [378]

government contractor defense A defense that says a contractor who was provided specifications by the government is not liable for any defect in the product that occurs as a result of those specifications. [129]

Government in the Sunshine Act An act that was enacted to open certain federal administrative agency meetings to the public. [909]

grace period A period of time after the actual expiration date of a payment but during which the insured can still pay an overdue premium without penalty. [1052]

grantee The party to whom an interest in real property is transferred. [1016]

grantor The party who transfers an ownership interest in real property. [1016]

greenmail The purchase by a target corporation of its stock from an actual or perceived tender offeror at a premium. [786]

group boycott When two or more competitors at one level of distribution agree not to deal with others at another level of distribution. [961]

group insurance plan An insurance plan that is sold to all the members of a single group, often all the employees of one employer. [1051]

guaranteeing collection A form of accommodation where the accommodation indorser guarantees *collection* of a negotiable instrument; the accommodation indorser is *secondarily liable* on the instrument. [494]

guaranteeing payment A form of accommodation where the accommodation party guarantees *payment* of a negotiable instrument; the accommodation party is *primarily liable* on the instrument. [494]

guarantor The person who agrees to pay the debt if the primary debtor does not. [266]

guaranty arrangement An arrangement where a third party promises to be *secondarily liable* for the payment of another's debt. [537]

guaranty contract The contract between the guarantor and the original creditor. [266]

guest statute Statute that provides that if a driver of a vehicle voluntarily and without compensation gives a ride to another person, the driver is not liable to the passenger for injuries caused by the driver's ordinary negligence. [105]

hardship discharge A discharge granted if (1) the debtor fails to complete the payments due to unforeseeable circumstances, (2) the unsecured creditors have been paid as much as they would have been paid in a Chapter 7 liquidation proceeding, and (3) it is not practical to modify the plan. [582]

Hart-Scott-Rodino Antitrust Improvement Act Requires certain firms to notify the FTC and the Justice Department in advance of a proposed merger. Unless the government challenges the proposed merger within 30 days, the merger may proceed. [969]

hazardous waste Solid waste that may cause or significantly contribute to an increase in mortality or serious illness or pose a hazard to human health or the environment if improperly managed. [945]

health insurance Purchased to help cover the costs of medical treatment, surgery, or hospital care. [1047]

holder What the transferee becomes if a negotiable instrument has been transferred by *negotiation*. [469] A person who is in possession of a negotiable instrument that is drawn, issued, or indorsed to him or his order, to bearer, or in blank. [485]

holder in due course (HDC) A holder who takes a negotiable instrument for value, in good faith, and without notice that it is defective or is overdue. [485] A holder of a negotiable instrument who takes an instrument free of all claims and personal defenses but not real defenses. [497]

holographic will Will that is entirely handwritten and signed by the testator. [1063]

homeowners policy A comprehensive insurance policy that includes coverage for the risks covered by a fire insurance policy as well as personal liability insurance. [1048]

honor Payment of a drawer's properly drawn check by the drawee bank. [513]

horizontal merger A merger between two or more companies that compete in the same business and geographical market. [968]

horizontal restraint of trade A restraint of trade that occurs when two or more competitors at the *same level of distribution* enter into a contract, combination, or conspiracy to restrain trade. [958]

hung jury A jury that cannot come to a unanimous decision about the defendant's guilt. The government may choose to retry the case. [142]

identification of goods Distinguishing the goods named in the contract from the seller's or lessor's other goods. [395]

illegal consideration A promise to refrain from doing an illegal act. Such a promise will not support a contract. [217]

illusory promise A contract into which both parties enter, but one or both of the parties can choose not to perform their contractual obligations. Thus the contract lacks consideration. [217]

Immigration Reform and Control Act of 1986 (IRCA) A federal statute that makes it unlawful for employers to hire illegal immigrants. [830]

immunity from prosecution The government agrees not to use any evidence given by a person granted immunity against that person. [155]

impairment of right of recourse Certain parties (holders, indorsers, accommodation parties) are discharged from liability on an instrument if the holder (1) releases an obligor from liability or (2) surrenders collateral without the consent of the parties who would benefit by it. [502]

implied agency An agency that occurs when a principal and an agent do not expressly create an agency, but it is

inferred from the conduct of the parties. [593]

implied authorization Mode of acceptance that is implied from what is customary in similar transactions, usage of trade, or prior dealings between the parties. [206]

implied exemptions Exemptions from antitrust laws that are implied by the federal courts. [974]

implied-in-fact condition A condition that can be implied from the circumstances surrounding a contract and the parties' conduct. [289]

implied-in-fact contract A contract where agreement between parties has been inferred from their conduct. [184]

implied partnership General partnership implied from the conduct of the parties. [641]

implied powers Powers beyond express powers that allow a corporation to accomplish its corporate purpose. [740]

implied term A term in a contract that can reasonably be supplied by the courts. [196]

implied trust A trust that is implied by law or from the conduct of the parties. [1074]

implied warranties The law *implies* certain warranties on transferors of negotiable instruments. There are two types of implied warranties: transfer and presentment. [495]

implied warranty of authority An agent who enters into a contract on behalf of another party impliedly warrants that he or she has the authority to do so. [612]

implied warranty of fitness for human consumption A warranty that applies to food or drink consumed on or off the premises of restaurants, grocery stores, fastfood outlets, and vending machines. [438]

implied warranty of fitness for a particular purpose An implied warranty that information is fit for the licensee's purpose that applies if the licensor (1) knows of any particular purpose for which the computer information is required and (2) knows that the licensee is relying on the licensor's skill or judgment to select of furnish suitable information. [365]

implied warranty of habitability A warranty that provides that the leased premises must be fit, safe, and suitable for ordinary residential use. [1028]

implied warranty of informational content An implied warranty that there is no inaccuracy in the informational content caused by the merchant-licensor's failure to perform with reasonable care. [365]

implied warranty of merchantability of the computer program An implied warranty that the copies of the computer program are within the parameters permitted by the licensing agreement, that the computer program has been adequately packaged and labeled, and that the program conforms to any promises or affirmations of fact on the container or label. [364]

implied warranty of merchantability Unless properly disclosed a warranty that is implied that sold or leased goods are fit for the ordinary purpose for which they are sold or leased, and other assurances. [436]

impossibility of performance Nonperformance that is excused if the contract becomes impossible to perform; must be *objective* impossibility, not subjective. [291]

imposter A person who impersonates a payee and induces a maker or drawer to issue an instrument in the payee's name and to give it to the imposter. [479]

imposter rule A rule that says if an imposter forges the indorsement of the named payee, the drawer or maker is liable on the instrument and bears the loss. [479]

incidental authority Implied power that an agent has where the terms of the express agency agreement do not cover the contingency that has arisen. [593]

incidental beneficiary A party who is unintentionally benefited by other people's contract. [286]

incidental damages When goods are resold or released, incidental damages are reasonable expenses incurred in stopping delivery, transportation charges, storage charges, sales commissions, and so on. [420]

incontestability clause A clause that prevents insurers from contesting statements made by insureds in applications

for insurance after the passage of a stipulated number of years. [1053]

incorporation by reference When integration is made by express reference in one document that refers to and incorporates another document within it. [270]

incorporation doctrine A doctrine that says that most fundamental guarantees contained in the Bill of Rights are applicable to state and local government action. [54]

incorporator The person or persons, partnerships, or corporations that are responsible for incorporation of a corporation. [730]

indemnification Right of a partner to be reimbursed for expenditures incurred on behalf of the partnership. [645]

indenture agreement A contract between the corporation and the holder that contains the terms of a debt security. [740]

independent contractor "A person who contracts with another to do something for him who is not controlled by the other nor subject to the other's right to control with respect to his physical conduct in the performance of the undertaking" *Restatement (Second) of Agency.* [590]

indictment The charge of having committed a crime (usually a felony), based on the judgment of a grand jury. [141]

indirect price discrimination A form of price discrimination (e.g., favorable credit terms) that is less readily apparent than direct forms of price discrimination. [972]

indorsee The person to whom a negotiable instrument is indorsed. [471] The party to whom a check is indorsed. [510]

indorsement The signature (and other directions) written by or on behalf of the holder somewhere on the instrument. [471]

indorsement of a check Occurs when a payee indorses a check to another party by signing the back of the check. [509]

indorser The person who indorses a negotiable instrument. [471, 509]

indorsers' liability *Unqualified indorsers* are secondarily liable on negotiable instruments they indorse: *qualified indorsers* disclaim liability and are not secondarily liable on instruments they indorse. [492]

infancy doctrine A doctrine that allows minors to disaffirm (cancel) most contracts they have entered into with adults. [226]

inferior performance Occurs when a party fails to perform express or implied contractual obligations that impair or destroy the essence of the contract. [301]

informal contract A contract that is not formal. Valid informal contracts are fully enforceable and may be sued upon if breached. [187]

information The charge of having committed a crime (usually a misdemeanor), based on the judgment of a judge (magistrate). [141]

injunction A court order that prohibits a person from doing a certain act. [311]

injury The plaintiff must suffer personal injury or damage to his or her property in order to recover monetary damages for the defendant's negligence. [100]

innkeeper The owner of a facility that provides lodging to the public for compensation (e.g., a hotel or motel). [996]

innkeepers statutes State statutes that limit an innkeeper's common law liability. An innkeeper can avoid liability for loss caused to a guest's property if (1) a safe is provided in which the guest's valuable property may be kept and (2) the guest is notified of this fact. [996]

innocent misrepresentation Occurs when an agent makes an untrue statement that he or she honestly and reasonably believes to be true. [253] Occurs when a person makes a statement of fact that he or she honestly and reasonably believes to be true, even though it is not. [614]

in pari delicto When both parties are equally at fault in an illegal contract. [238]

in personam jurisdiction Jurisdiction over the parties to a lawsuit. [27]

in rem jurisdiction Jurisdiction to hear a case because of jurisdiction over the property of the lawsuit. [27]

insane, but not adjudged insane A person who is insane but has not been adjudged insane by a court or administrative agency. A contract entered into by such person is generally *voidable.*

Some states hold that such a contract is void. [231]

Insecticide, Fungicide, and Rodenticide Act   A federal statute that requires pesticides, herbicides, fungicides, and rodenticides to be registered with the EPA; the EPA may deny, suspend, or cancel registration. [944]

INS Form I-9   A form that must be filled out by all U.S. employers for each employee; states that the employers has inspected the employee's legal qualifications to work. [830]

inside director   A member of the board of directors who is also an officer of the corporation. [754]

insider trading   When an insider makes a profit by personally purchasing shares of the corporation prior to public release of favorable information or by selling shares of the corporation prior to the public disclosure of unfavorable information. [809]

Insider Trading Sanctions Act of 1984   A federal statute that permits the SEC to obtain a civil penalty of up to three times the illegal benefits received from insider trading. [812]

installment contract   A contract that requires or authorizes goods to be delivered and accepted in separate lots. [414]

instrument   Term that means *negotiable instrument*. [452]

insurable interest   A person who purchases insurance must have a personal interest in the insured item or person. [1042]

insurance   A means for persons and businesses to protect themselves against the risk of loss. [1041]

insured   The party who pays a premium to a particular insurance company for insurance coverage. [1041]

insurer   The insurance company that underwrites the insurance coverage. [1041]

intangible property   Rights that cannot be reduced to physical form, such as stock certificates, CDs, bonds, and copyrights. [984]

integration   The combination of several writings to form a single contract. [270]

integration of offerings   When separate offerings that might otherwise qualify for individual exemptions are combined if they are really part of one large offering. [803]

intellectual property   Objects such as inventions, writings, trademarks, and so on, which are often a business's most valuable asset. [323]

intellectual property rights   Intellectual property rights, such as patents, copyrights, trademarks, trade secrets, trade names, and domain names are very valuable business assets. Federal and state laws protect intellectual property rights from misappropriation and infringement. [321]

intended third-party beneficiary   A third party who is not in privity of contract but who has rights under the contract and can enforce the contract against the obligor. [284]

intentional infliction of emotional distress   A tort that says a person whose extreme and outrageous conduct intentionally or recklessly causes severe emotional distress to another person is liable for that emotional distress. Also known as the *tort of outrage*. [96]

intentional interference with contractual relations   A tort that arises when a third party induces a contracting party to breach the contract with another party. [312]

intentional misrepresentation   Occurs when an agent makes an untrue statement that he or she knows is not true. Also known as *fraud* or *deceit*. [109, 117, 250, 614]

intentional tort   A category of torts that requires that the defendant possessed the intent to do the act that caused the plaintiff's injuries. [91] Occurs when a person has intentionally committed a wrong against (1) another person or his or her character, or (2) another person's property. [616]

intermediary bank   A bank in the collection process that is not the depository or payor bank. [518]

intermediate appellate court   An intermediate court that hears appeals from trial courts. [19]

intermediate scrutiny test   Test that is applied to classifications based on protected classes other than race (e.g., *sex* or *age*). [57]

International Court of Justice   The judicial branch of the United Nations that is located in The Hague, the Netherlands. Also called the *World Court*. [80]

international law   Law that governs affairs between nations and that regulates transactions between individuals and businesses of different countries. [67]

Internet   A collection of millions of computers that provide a network of electronic connections between computers. [350]

interpretive rules   Rules issued by administrative agencies that interpret existing statutory language. [903]

interrogatories   Written questions submitted by one party to another party. The questions must be answered in writing within a stipulated time. [33]

interstate commerce   Commerce that moves between states or that affects commerce between states. [51]

intervention   The act of others to join as parties to an existing lawsuit. [30]

inter vivos **gift**   A gift made during a person's lifetime that is an irrevocable present transfer of ownership. [985]

inter vivos **trust**   A trust that is created while the settlor is alive. [1074]

intoxicated person   A person who is under contractual incapacity because of ingestion of alcohol or drugs to the point of incompetence. [231]

intrastate offering exemption   An exemption from registration that permits local businesses to raise capital from local investors to be used in the local economy without the need to register with the SEC. [802]

invasion of the right to privacy   A tort that constitutes the violation of a person's right to live his or her life without being subjected to unwarranted and undesired publicity. [94]

involuntary petition   A petition filed by creditors of the debtor; alleges that the debtor is not paying his or her debts as they become due. [566]

issued shares   Shares that have been sold by the corporation. [738]

joint and several liability   Partners are *jointly and severally liable* for tort liability of the partnership. This means that the plaintiff can sue one or more of the partners separately. If successful, the plaintiff can recover the entire amount of the judgment from any or all of the defendant-partners. [649]

joint liability Partners are *jointly liable* for contracts and debts of the partnership. This means that a plaintiff must name the partnership and all of the partners as defendants in a lawsuit. [648]

joint tenancy A form of co-ownership that includes the right of survivorship. [1010]

joint venture A voluntary association of two or more parties (natural persons, partnerships, corporations, or other legal entities) to conduct a single or isolated project with a limited duration. [628]

joint will A will that is executed by two or more testators. [1068]

judgment The official decision of the court. [36]

judgment notwithstanding the verdict (j.n.o.v.) In a civil case, the judge may overturn the jury's verdict if he or she finds bias or jury misconduct. [36]

judgment on the underlying debt A right granted to a secured creditor to relinquish his or her security interest in the collateral and sue a defaulting debtor to recover the amount of the underlying debt. [557]

judicial branch The part of the government that consists of the Supreme Court and other federal courts. [48]

judicial decision A decision about an individual lawsuit issued by federal and state courts. [10]

judicial decisions and teachings The fourth source of international law, consisting of judicial decisions and writings of the most qualified legal scholars of the various nations involved in the dispute. [71]

judicial decree of dissolution Order of the court that dissolves a partnership. An application or petition must be filed by a partner or an assignee or a partnership interest with the appropriate state court; the court will issue a judicial decree of dissolution if warranted by the circumstances. [653]

judicial dissolution Occurs when a corporation is dissolved by a court proceeding instituted by shareholders, creditors,

or the state. Permitted only for certain reasons. [742]

jurisdiction The authority of a court to hear a case. [26]

jurisprudence The philosophy or science of law. [5]

jury deliberation Process by which the jury retires to the jury room and deliberates its findings. [36]

jury instructions Instructions given by the judge to the jury that informs them of the law to be applied in the case. [36]

Just Compensation Clause Clause in the U.S. Constitution that mandates that the government must compensate owners and lessees for property taken under the power of eminent domain. [900]

Kantian or duty ethics A moral theory that says that people owe moral duties that are based on universal rules, such as the categorical imperative "Do unto others as you would have them do unto you." [164]

land The most common form of real property; includes the land and buildings and other structures permanently attached to the land. [1006]

landlord The owner who transfers the leasehold. [1024]

landlord-tenant relationship A relationship created when the owner of a freehold estate (landlord) transfers a right to exclusively and temporarily posses the owner's property to another (tenant). [1024]

land pollution Pollution of the land that is generally caused by hazardous waste being disposed of in an improper manner. [945]

land sales contract Arrangement where the owner of real property agrees to sell the property to a purchaser, who agrees to pay the purchase price to the owner-seller over an agreed-upon period of time. [534]

land use control The collective term for the laws that regulate the possession, ownership, and use of real property. [1033]

Lanham Trademark Act An act enacted in 1946 that provides for the registration of trademarks and service marks with the federal Patent and

Trademark Office in Washington, D.C. [710]

Lanham Trademark Act (as amended) Federal statute that (1) establishes the requirements for obtaining a federal mark and (2) protects marks from infringement. [336]

larceny Taking another's personal property other than from his or her person or building. [143]

law That which must be obeyed and followed by citizens subject to sanctions or legal consequences; a body of rules of action or conduct prescribed by controlling authority, and having binding legal force. [2]

law court A court that developed and administered a uniform set of laws decreed by the kings and queens after William the Conqueror; legal procedure was emphasized over merits at this time. [8]

lease A transfer of the right to the possession and use of the real property for a set term in return for certain consideration; the rental agreement between a landlord and a tenant. [263, 381, 1024]

leasehold A tenant's interest in the property. [1024]

legal entity An LLC is a separate legal entity—an *artificial person*—that can own property, sue and be sued, enter into and enforce contracts, and such. [679]

legal insanity A state of contractual incapacity as determined by law. [230]

legally enforceable contract If one party fails to perform as promised, the other party can use the court system to enforce the contract and recover damages or other remedy. [180]

legislative branch The part of the government that consists of Congress (the Senate and the House of Representatives). [47]

lessee The person who acquires the right to possession and use of goods under a lease. [381]

lessor The person who transfers the right of possession and use of goods under the lease. [381]

liability insurance Automobile insurance that covers damages that the insured causes to third parties. [1049]

license A contract that transfers limited rights in intellectual property and

informational rights. [357] Grants a person the right to enter upon another's property for a specified and usually short period of time. [1018]

licensee The party who is given limited rights in or access to intellectual property and informational rights owned by the licensor. [357]

licensing agreement Detailed and comprehensive written agreement between the licensor and licensee that sets for the express terms of their agreement. [357]

licensing statute Statute that requires a person or business to obtain a license from the government prior to engaging in a specified occupation or activity. [233]

licensor The owner of intellectual property or informational rights who transfers rights in the property or information to the licensee. [357]

licensor's damages If a licensee breaches a contract, the licensor may sue and recover monetary damages from the licensee caused by the breach. [368]

life estate An interest in the land for a person's lifetime; upon that person's death, the interest will be transferred to another party. [263, 1009]

life insurance A form of insurance where the insurer is obligated to pay a specific sum of money upon the death of the insured. [1044]

limited-jurisdiction trial court A court that hears matters of a specialized or limited nature. [19]

limited liability Members are liable for the LLC's debts, obligations, and liabilities only to the extent of their capital contributions. [679] Shareholders are liable for the corporation's debts and obligations only to the extent of their capital contributions. [732] Liability that shareholders have only to the extent of their capital contribution. Shareholders are generally not personally liable for debts and obligations of the corporation. [767]

limited liability company (LLC) A hybrid form of business that has the attributes of both partnerships and corporations. [625] An unincorporated business entity that combines the most

favorable attributes of general partnerships, limited partnerships, and corporations. [678]

limited liability company codes State statutes that regulate the formation, operation, and dissolution of LLCs. [678]

limited liability partnership (LLP) A type of partnership that has only limited partners. [625] All partners have limited liability. [660, 672]

limited partners Partners in a limited partnership who invest capital but do not participate in management and are not personally liable for partnership debts beyond their capital contributions. [661]

limited partnership A type of partnership that has two types of partners: (1) general partners and (2) limited partners. [620, 624, 660]

limited partnership agreement A document that sets forth the rights and duties of the general and limited partners; the terms and conditions regarding the operation, termination, and dissolution of the partnership; and so on. [663]

lineal descendants Children, grandchildren, great-grandchildren, and so on of the testator. [1065]

line of commerce Includes products or services that consumers use as substitutes. If an increase in the price of one product or service leads consumers to purchase another product or service, the two products are substitutes for each other. [967]

liquidated damages Damages that are specified in the contract rather than determined by the court. [372] Damages that will be paid upon a breach of contract that are established in advance. [427] If the contract is breached these are damages to which parties to a contract agree in advance. [305]

liquidation preference The right to be paid a stated dollar amount if the corporation is dissolved and liquidated. [737]

litigation The process of bringing, maintaining, and defending a lawsuit. [29]

long-arm statute A statute that extends a state's jurisdiction to nonresidents who were not served a summons within the state. [27]

lost property When a property owner leaves property somewhere because of negligence, carelessness, or inadvertence. [989]

Magnuson-Moss Warranty Act A federal statute enacted in 1975 intended to (1) prevent deceptive warranties, (2) require disclosures by warrantors who make certain written warranties, and (3) restrict the warrantor's ability to disclaim or modify certain warranties. [920]

mailbox rule A rule that states that an acceptance is effective when it is dispatched, even if it is lost in transmission. [204]

mail fraud The use of mail to defraud another person. [146]

main purpose or **leading object exception** If the main purpose of a transaction and an oral collateral contract is to provide pecuniary benefit to the guarantor, the collateral contract does not have to be in writing to be enforced. [267]

maker of a CD The bank (borrower). [455]

maker of a note The party who makes the promise to pay (borrower). [455]

manager-managed LLC An LLC that has designated in its articles of organization that it is a manager-managed LLC. [690]

marine insurance Insurance that owners of vessels purchase to insure against loss or damage to the vessel and its cargo caused by perils at sea. [1051]

Marine Protection, Research, and Sanctuaries Act A federal statute enacted in 1972 that extends environmental protection to the oceans. [943]

mark The collective name for trademarks, service marks, certification marks, and collective marks that all can be trademarked. [337]

market extension merger A merger between two companies in similar fields whose sales do not overlap. [969]

Market Reform Act of 1990 A federal statute that authorizes the SEC to regulate trading practices during periods of extraordinary market volatility. [815]

material alteration A partial defense against enforcement of a negotiable instrument by an HDC. An HDC can enforce an altered instrument in the original amount for which the drawer wrote the check. [498]

material breach A breach that occurs when a party renders inferior performance of his or her contractual duties. [301]

material person's lien A contractor's and laborer's lien that makes the real property to which improvements are being made become security for the payment of the services and materials for those improvements. [535]

maximizing profits A theory of social responsibility that says a corporation owes a duty to take actions that maximize profits for shareholders. [168]

mediation A form of ADR in which the parties choose a *neutral* third party to act as the mediator of the dispute. [39]

Medicinal Device Amendment to the FDCA An amendment enacted in 1976 that gives the FDA authority to regulate medicinal devices and equipment. [918]

meeting of the creditors A meeting of the creditors in a bankruptcy case that must occur not less than 10 days nor more than 30 days after the court grants an order for relief. [566]

meeting the competition defense A defense provided in Section 2(b) that says a seller may lawfully engage in price discrimination to meet a competitor's price. [973]

member An owner of an LLC. [679]

member-managed LLC An LLC that has not designated that it is a manager-managed LLC in its articles of organization. [690]

mens rea "Evil intent"—the possession of the requisite state of mind to commit a prohibited act. [139]

Merchant Court The separate set of courts established to administer the "law of merchants." [8]

merchant protection statutes Statutes that allow merchants to stop, detain, and investigate suspected shoplifters without being held liable for false imprisonment if (1) there are reasonable grounds for the suspicion, (2) suspects are detained for only a reasonable time, and (3) investigations are conducted in a reasonable manner. [92]

merger Occurs when one corporation is absorbed into another corporation and ceases to exist. [777]

merger clause A clause in a contract that stipulates that it is a complete integration and the exclusive expression of the parties' agreement. Parol evidence may not be introduced to explain, alter, contradict, or add to the terms of the contract. [272]

midnight deadline The midnight of the next banking day following the banking day on which the bank received the on them check for collection. [519]

minor A person who has not reached the age of majority. [226]

minor breach A breach that occurs when a party renders substantial performance of his or her contractual duties. [300]

minor's duty of restoration As a general rule a minor is obligated only to return the goods or property he or she has received from the adult in the condition it is in at the time of disaffirmance. [227]

mirror image rule States that in order for there to be an acceptance, the offeree must accept the terms as stated in the offer. [203]

misdemeanor A less serious crime; not inherently evil but prohibited by society. Many crimes against property are misdemeanors. [139]

mislaid property When an owner voluntarily places property somewhere and then inadvertently forgets it. [988]

misrepresentation An assertion that is made that is not in accord with the facts. [250]

misuse A defense that relieves a seller of product liability if the user *abnormally* misused the product. Products must be designed to protect against *foreseeable* misuse. [129]

mitigation A nonbreaching party is under a legal duty to avoid or reduce damages caused by a breach of contract. [307]

mixed sale A sale that involves the provision of a service and a good in the same transaction. [379]

mobile sources Sources of air pollution such as automobiles, trucks, buses, motorcycles, and airplanes. [938]

Model Business Corporation Act (MBCA) A model act drafted in 1950 that was intended to provide a uniform law for regulation of corporations. [725]

monetary damages An award of money. [302]

money A "medium of exchange authorized or adopted by a domestic or foreign government" [UCC 1-201 (24)]. [460]

monopoly power The power to control prices or exclude competition measured by the market share the defendant possesses in the relevant market. [966]

moral minimum A theory of social responsibility that says a corporation's duty is to make a profit while avoiding harm to others. [170]

mortgage An interest in real property given to a lender as security for the payment of a loan. [263] A collateral arrangement where a property owner borrows money from a creditor who uses a deed as collateral for repayment of the loan. [531]

mortgagee The creditor in a mortgage transaction. [531]

mortgagor The owner-debtor in a mortgage transaction. [531]

motion for judgment on the pleadings Motion that alleges that if all the facts presented in the pleadings are taken as true, the party making the motion would win the lawsuit when the proper law is applied to these asserted facts. [34]

motion for summary judgment Motion that asserts that there are no factual disputes to be decided by the jury; if so, the judge can apply the proper law to the undisputed facts and decide the case without a jury. These motions are supported by affidavits, documents, and deposition testimony. [34]

motivation test A test to determine the liability of the principal; if the agent's motivation in committing the intentional tort is to promote the principal's business, then the principal is liable for any injury caused by the tort. [617]

mutual benefit bailment A bailment for the mutual benefit of the bailor and bailee. The bailee owes a *duty of reasonable care* to protect the bailed property. [994]

mutual mistake of fact   A mistake made by both parties concerning a material fact that is important to the subject matter of the contract. [249]

mutual mistake of value   A mistake that occurs if both parties know the object of the contract, but are mistaken as to its value. [249]

mutual wills   Occur where two or more testators execute separate wills that leave their property to each other on the condition that the survivor leave the remaining property on his or her death as agreed by the testators. [1068]

national ambient air quality standards (NAAQS)   Standards for certain pollutants set by the EPA that protect (1) human beings (primary) and (2) vegetation, matter, climate, visibility, and economic values (secondary). [938]

national courts   The courts of individual nations. [80]

National Environmental Policy Act (NEPA)   A federal statute enacted in 1969 that mandates that the federal government consider the adverse impact a federal government action would have on the environment before the action is implemented. [937]

National Labor Relations Board (NLRB)   A federal administrative agency that oversees union elections, prevents employers and unions from engaging in illegal and unfair labor practices, and enforces and interprets certain federal labor laws. [864]

necessaries of life   A minor must pay the reasonable value of food, clothing, shelter, medical care, and other items considered necessary to the maintenance of life. [228]

negligence   A tort related to defective products where the defendant has breached a duty of due care and caused harm to the plaintiff. [117] Failure of a corporate director or officer to exercise the duty of care while conducting the corporation's business. [760]

negligence per se   Tort where the violation of a statute or ordinance constitutes the breach of the duty of care. [103]

negligent infliction of emotional distress   A tort that permits a person to recover for emotional distress caused by the defendant's negligent conduct. [102]

negotiable instrument   A special form of contract that satisfies the requirements established by Article 3 of the UCC. Also called *commercial paper*. [451]

negotiation   Transfer of a negotiable instrument by a person other than the issuer to a person who thereby becomes a *holder*. [469]

New York standard fire insurance form   A standard fire insurance policy that protects the homeowner from loss caused by fire, lightning, smoke, and water damage. [1047]

Noerr **doctrine**   Two or more persons may petition the executive, legislative, or judicial branch of the government or administrative agencies to enact laws or take other action without violating the antitrust laws. [965]

no evidence of forgery, alterations, or irregularity requirement   A holder cannot become an HDC to an instrument that is apparently forged or altered or is otherwise so irregular or incomplete as to call into question its authenticity. [488]

Noise Control Act   A federal statute enacted in 1972 that authorizes the EPA to establish noise standards for products sold in the United States. [949]

noise pollution   Unwanted sound from planes, manufacturing plants, motor vehicles, construction equipment, stereos, and the like. [949]

nonattainment areas   Regions that do not meet air quality standards. [938]

nonconforming uses   Uses and building that already exist in the zoned area that are permitted to continue even though they do not fit within new zoning ordinances. [1035]

noncupative will   Oral will that is made before a witness during the testator's last illness. [1063]

nonfreehold estate   An estate in which the tenant has a right to possession of the property but not title to the property. [1024]

nonnegotiable contract   Fails to meet the requirements of a negotiable instrument and, therefore, is not subject to the provisions of UCC Article 3. [463]

nonpossessory interest   When a person holds an interest in another person's property without actually owning any part of the property. [1018]

nonprice vertical restraints   Restraints of trade that are unlawful under Section 1 of the Sherman Act if their anticompetitive effects outweigh their procompetitive effects. [964]

nonprofit corporation   A corporation that is formed to operate charitable institutions, colleges, universities, and other not-for-profit entities. [726]

nonrestrictive indorsement   An indorsement that has no instructions or conditions attached to the payment of the funds. [476]

note   An instrument that evidences the borrower's debt to the lender. [531] A debt security with a maturity of five years or less. [740]

novation   An agreement that substitutes a new party for one of the original contracting parties and relieves the exiting party of liability on the contract. [290]

Nuclear Regulatory Commission (NRC)   Federal agency that licenses the construction and opening of commercial nuclear power plants. [947]

Nuclear Waste Policy Act of 1982   A federal statute that says the federal government must select and develop a permanent site for the disposal of nuclear waste. [947]

objective theory of contracts   A theory that says the intent to contract is judged by the reasonable person standard and not by the subjective intent of the parties. [185]

obscene speech   Speech that (1) appeals to the prurient interest, (2) depicts sexual conduct in a patently offensive way, and (3) lacks serious literary, artistic, political, or scientific value. [55]

obsolete information   Information that is no longer accurate because of time or circumstances. [928]

Occupational Safety and Health Act   A federal act enacted in 1970 that promotes safety in the workplace. [826]

Occupational Safety and Health Administration (OSHA)   A federal administrative agency that administers and enforces the Occupational Safety and Health Act. [826]

offensive speech Speech that is offensive to many members of society. It is subject to time, place, and manner restrictions. [54]

offer The manifestation of willingness to enter into a bargain, so made as to justify another person in understanding that his or her assent to that bargain is invited and will conclude it. [195]

offeree The party to whom an offer to enter into a contract is made. [180, 195]

offeror The party who makes an offer. [195]

offeror The party who makes an offer to enter into a contract. [180]

officers Employees of the corporation who are appointed by the board of directors to manage the day-to-day operations of the corporation. [758]

Older Workers Benefit Protection Act (OWBPA) Prohibits age discrimination in employee benefits. [851]

one year rule An executory contract that cannot be performed by its own terms within one year of its formation must be in writing. [265]

"on them" item A check presented for payment by the payee or holder where the depository bank and the payor bank are not the *same* bank. [519]

"on us" item A check that is presented for payment where the depository bank is also the payor bank. That is, the drawer and payee or holder have accounts at the same bank. [519]

opening statements Statements made by the attorneys to the jury in which they summarize the factual and legal issues of the case. [35]

operating agreement An agreement entered into among members that governs the affairs and business of the LLC and the relations among members, managers, and the LLC. [687]

option-to-cancel clause A clause inserted in many business contracts that allows one or both of the parties to cancel the contract. [216]

order Decision issued by an administrative law judge. [906]

order for the drawee to pay A drawer's unconditional order for a drawee to pay a payee. [458]

order for relief The filing of either a voluntary petition, an unchallenged involuntary petition, or a grant of an order after a trial of a challenged involuntary petition. [566]

order paper Order paper is negotiated by (1) *delivery* and (2) *indorsement*. [470]

ordinances Laws enacted by local government bodies such as cities and municipalities, counties, school districts, and water districts. [10]

ordinary bailments (1) Bailments for the sole benefit of the bailor, (2) bailments for the sole benefit of the bailee, and (3) bailments for the mutual benefit of the bailor and bailee. [993]

original tenor The original amount for which the drawer wrote the check. [517]

outside director A member of the board of directors who is not an officer of the corporation. [754]

outstanding shares Shares of stock that are in shareholder hands. [738]

overdraft The amount of money a drawer owes a bank after it has paid a check despite insufficient funds in the drawer's account. [515]

pac-man tender offer Occurs when a corporation that is the target of a tender offer makes a *reverse tender offer* for the stock of the tender offeror. [785]

palming off Unfair competition that occurs when a company tries to pass off one of its products as that of a rival. [321]

panel A panel of three WTO judges that hears trade disputes between member nations and issues a "panel report." [77]

parol evidence Any oral or written words outside the four corners of the written contract. [271]

parol evidence rule A rule that says if a written contract is a complete and final statement of the parties' agreement, any prior or contemporaneous oral or written statements that alter, contradict, or are in addition to the terms of the written contract are inadmissible in court regarding a dispute over the contract. There are several exceptions to this rule. [271]

partially disclosed agency An agency that occurs if the agent discloses his or her agency status but does not reveal the principal's identity and the third party

does not know the principal's identity from another source. [610]

participating preferred stock Stock that allows the stockholder to participate in the profits of the corporation along with the common stockholders. [738]

partner's interest A partner's share of profits and surplus of the partnership. [643]

partnership agreement A written partnership agreement that the partners sign. Also called *articles of partnership*. [642]

partnership at will A partnership with no fixed duration. [641]

partnership by estoppel When a person who is not a partner either makes a representation or consents to a partner's representation that he or she is a partner. [642]

partnership capital Money and property contributed by partners for the permanent use of the partnership. [641]

partnership for a term A partnership with a fixed duration. [641]

partnership property Property that is originally brought into the partnership on account of the partnership and property that is subsequently acquired by purchase or otherwise on account of the partnership or with partnership funds. [642]

part performance An equitable doctrine that allows the court to order an oral contract for the sale of land or transfer of another interest in real property to be specifically performed if it has been partially performed and performance is necessary to avoid injustice. [264]

past consideration A prior act or performance. Past consideration (e.g., prior acts) will not support a new contract. New consideration must be given. [218]

patent infringement Unauthorized use of another's patent. A patent holder may recover damages and other remedies against a patent infringer. [326]

payable on demand or at a definite time requirement A negotiable instrument must be payable either *on demand* or *at a definite time*. [460]

payee of a CD The depositor (lender). [455]

payee of a check The party to whom the check is written. [454]

payee of a draft   The party who receives the money from a draft. [453]

payee of a note   The party to whom the promise to pay is made (lender). [454]

payor bank   The bank where the drawer has a checking account and on which the check is drawn. [517]

penal codes   A collection of criminal statutes. [138]

per capita   A distribution of the estate that makes each grandchild and great-grandchild of the deceased inherit equally with the children of the deceased. [1065]

perfection by possession of the collateral   If a secured creditor has physical possession of the collateral, no financing statement has to be filed; the creditor's possession is sufficient to put other potential creditors on notice of his or her secured interest in the property. [549]

perfection of a security interest   Establishes the right of a secured creditor against other creditors who claim an interest in the collateral. [548]

perfect tender rule   A rule that says if the goods or tender of a delivery fails in any respect to conform to the contract, the buyer may opt to (1) reject the whole shipment, (2) accept the whole shipment, or (3) reject part and accept part of the shipment. [412]

periodic tenancy   A tenancy created when a lease specifies intervals at which payments are due but does not specify how long the lease is for. [1025]

permanency requirement   A requirement of negotiable instruments that says they must be in a permanent state, such as written on ordinary paper. [457]

permanent trustee   A legal representative of the bankruptcy debtor's estate, usually an accountant or lawyer, elected at the first meeting of the creditors. [566]

per se rule   A rule that is applicable to those restraints of trade considered inherently anticompetitive. Once this determination is made, the court will not permit any defenses or justifications to save it. [958]

personal articles floater   An addition to the home-owners policy that covers specific valuable items. [1048]

personal defense   A defense that can be raised against enforcement of a nego-

tiable instrument by an ordinary holder but not against an HDC. [499]

personal property   Property that consists of tangible property such as automobiles, furniture, and jewelry as well as intangible property such as securities, patents, and copyrights. [528, 546]

personal satisfaction test   Subjective test that applies to contracts involving personal taste and comfort. [288]

per stirpes   A distribution of the estate that makes grandchildren and great-grandchildren of the deceased inherit by representation of their parent. [1065]

petition   A document filed with the bankruptcy court that sets the bankruptcy proceedings into motion. [565]

petition for certiorari   A petition asking the Supreme Court to hear one's case. [24]

petitioner   The party appealing the decision of an administrative agency. [906]

physical or mental examination   A court may order another party to submit to a physical or mental examination prior to trial. [33]

picketing   The action of strikers walking in front of the employer's premises carrying signs announcing their strike. [872]

piercing the corporate veil   A doctrine that says if a shareholder dominates a corporation and uses it for improper purposes, a court of equity can disregard the corporate entity and hold the shareholder personally liable for the corporation's debts and obligations. [767]

plaintiff   The party who files the complaint. [29]

plaintiff's case   Process by which the plaintiff introduces evidence to prove the allegations contained in his or her complaint. [36]

plan of reorganization   A plan that sets forth a proposed new capital structure for the debtor to have when it emerges from reorganization bankruptcy. The debtor has the exclusive right to file the first plan of reorganization; any party of interest may file a plan thereafter. [576]

plant life and vegetation   Real property that is growing in or on the surface of the land. [1007]

plea bargain   When the accused admits to a lesser crime than charged. In return,

the government agrees to impose a lesser sentence than might have been obtained had the case gone to trial. [142]

pleadings   The paperwork that is filed with the court to initiate and respond to a lawsuit. [29]

point sources   Sources of water pollution such as paper mills, manufacturing plants, electric utility plants, and sewage plants. [941]

police power   The power of states to regulate private and business activity within their borders. [52]

policy   The insurance contract. [1041]

portability requirement   A requirement of negotiable instruments that says they must be able to be easily transported between areas. [457]

possession   A lease grants the tenant *exclusive possession* of the leased premises for the term of the lease or until the tenant defaults on the obligations under the lease. [1026]

possessory lien   Lien obtained by a bailee on bailed property for the compensation owed by the bailor to the bailee. [995]

Postal Reorganization Act   An act that makes the mailing of unsolicited merchandise an unfair trade practice. [923]

posteffective period   The period of time that begins when the registration statement becomes effective and runs until the issuer either sells all of the offered securities or withdraws them from sale. [800]

potential competition theory   A theory that reasons that the real or implied threat of increased competition keeps businesses more competitive. A merger that would eliminate this perception can be enjoined under Section 7. [969]

potential reciprocity theory   A theory that says if Company A, which supplies materials to Company B, merges with Company C (which in turn gets its supplies from Company B), the newly merged company can coerce Company B into dealing exclusively with it. [969]

power of attorney   An express agency agreement that is often used to give an agent the power to sign legal documents on behalf of the principal. [593]

precedent   A rule of law established in a court decision. Lower courts must follow the precedent established by higher courts. [10]

preemption doctrine The concept that federal law takes precedent over state or local law. [18]

preemptive rights Rights that give existing shareholders the option of subscribing to new shares being issued in proportion to their current ownership interest. [752]

preexisting duty A promise lacks consideration if a person promises to perform an act or do something he or she is already under an obligation to do. [217]

preferential lien Occurs when (1) a debtor gives an unsecured creditor a secured interest in property within 90 days before the filing of a petition in bankruptcy, (2) the transfer is made for a preexisting debt, and (3) the creditor would receive more because of this lien than it would as an unsecured creditor. [570]

preferential transfer Occurs when (1) a debtor transfers property to a creditor within 90 days before the filing of a petition in bankruptcy, (2) the transfer is made for a preexisting debt, and (3) the creditor would receive more from the transfer than it would from Chapter 7 liquidation. [570]

preferential transfer to an insider A transfer of property by an insolvent debtor to an "insider" within one year before the filing of a petition in bankruptcy. [570]

preferred stock A type of equity security that is given certain preferences and rights over common stock. [736]

preferred stock certificate A document that represents a shareholder's investment in preferred stock in the corporation. [736]

preferred stockholder A person who owns preferred stock. [736]

prefiling period A period of time that begins when the issuer first contemplates issuing the securities and ends when the registration statement is filed. The issuer may not *condition* the market during this period. [798]

Pregnancy Discrimination Act Amendment to Title VII that forbids employment discrimination because of

"pregnancy, childbirth, or related medical conditions." [842]

premises liability The liability of landlords and tenants to persons injured on their premises. [1030]

premium The money paid to the insurance company. [1041]

presentment A demand for acceptance or payment of an instrument made upon the maker, the acceptor, the drawee, or other payor by or on behalf of the holder. [493]

presentment across the counter When a depositor physically presents the check for payment at the payor bank instead of depositing an on them check for collection. [520]

presentment warranty Each prior transferor warrants that the check has not been altered. [517]

presentment warranties Any person who presents a draft or check for payment or acceptance makes the following three presentment warranties to a drawee or acceptor who pays or accepts the instrument in good faith: (1) The presenter has good title to the instrument or is authorized to obtain payment or acceptance of the person who has good title, (2) the instrument has not been materially altered, and (3) the presenter has no knowledge that the signature of the maker or drawer is unauthorized. [496]

pretrial hearing A hearing before the trial in order to facilitate the settlement of a case. Also called a *settlement conference*. [35]

pretrial motion A motion a party can make to try to dispose of all or part of a lawsuit prior to trial. [34]

price discrimination Charging different prices to different customers for the same product without any justification. [971]

price-fixing Occurs where competitors in the same line of business agree to set the price of the goods or services they sell; raising, depressing, fixing, pegging, or stabilizing the price of a commodity or service. [959]

primary liability Absolute liability Absolute liability to pay a negotiable instrument, subject to certain *real* defenses. [490]

principal A person who authorizes an agent to sign a negotiable instrument on his or her behalf. [489, 588]

principal–agent relationship An employer hires an employee and gives that employee authority to act and enter into contracts on his or her behalf. [589]

principal–independent contractor relationship A relationship that results when a person or business that is not an employee is employed by a principal to perform a certain task on his behalf. [590]

principle of comity Courtesies between countries based on respect, goodwill, and civility rather than law. [72]

priority The order in which conflicting claims of creditors in the same collateral are solved. [552]

Privacy Act An act stipulating that federal administrative agencies can maintain only information about an individual that is relevant and necessary to accomplish a legitimate agency purpose. [910]

private corporation A corporation formed to conduct privately owned business. [726]

private nuisance A nuisance that affects or disturbs one or a few people. [1033]

private placement exemption An exemption from registration that permits issuers to raise capital from an unlimited number of accredited investors and no more than 35 nonaccredited investors without having to register the offering with the SEC. [802]

Private Securities Litigation Reform Act of 1995 Provides a safe harbor from liability for companies that make forward-looking statements that are accompanied by meaningful cautionary statements of risk factors. [815]

Privileges and Immunities Clause A clause that prohibits states from enacting laws that unduly discriminate in favor of their residents. [61]

privity of contract The state of two specified parties being in contract. [279]

probability of a substantial lessening of competition If there is a probability that a merger will substantially lessen competition or create a monopoly, the court may prevent the merger under Section 7 of the Clayton Act. [968]

probate court   A specialized state court that supervises the administration and settlement of an estate. [1071]

procedural due process   Requires that the government must give a person proper notice and hearing of the legal action before that person is deprived of his or her life, liberty, or property. [59] Due process that requires the respondent to be given (1) proper and timely notice of the allegations or charges against him or her and (2) an opportunity to present evidence on the matter. [905]

process of certification   The accepting bank writes or stamps the word *certified* on the ordinary check of an account holder and sets aside funds from that account to pay the check. [511]

processing plant franchise   The franchisor provides a secret formula or process to the franchisee, and the franchisee manufactures the product and distributes it to retail dealers. [704]

product disparagement   False statements about a competitor's products, services, property, or business reputation. [321]

production of documents   Request by one party to another party to produce all documents relevant to the case prior to trial. [33]

products liability   The liability of manufacturers, sellers, and others for the injuries caused by defective products. [117]

professional corporation   A corporation formed by lawyers, doctors, or other professionals. [727]

professional malpractice   The liability of a professional who breaches his or her duty of ordinary care. [102]

profit   Grants a person the right to remove something from another's real property. [1019]

profit corporation   A corporation created to conduct a business for profit that can distribute profits to shareholders in the form of dividends. [726]

promise to pay   A maker's (borrower's) unconditional and affirmative undertaking to repay a debt to a payee (lender). [458]

promissory estoppel   An equitable doctrine that prevents the withdrawal of an offer by an offeror of it will adversely affect an offeree who has adjusted his or her position in justifiable reliance on the offer. [201, 220] An equitable doctrine that permits enforcement of oral contracts that should have been in writing. It is applied to avoid injustice. [268]

promissory note   A two-party negotiable instrument that is an unconditional written promise by one party to pay money to another party. [454]

promoter   A person or persons who organize and start the corporation, negotiate and enter into contracts in advance of its formation, find the initial investors to finance the corporation, and so forth. [728]

promoters' contracts   A collective term for such things as leases, sales contracts, contracts to purchase property, and employment contracts entered into by promoters on behalf of the proposed corporation prior to its actual incorporation. [729]

proof of claim   A document required to be filed by unsecured creditors that states the amount of their claim against the debtor. [566]

proper dispatch   An acceptance must be properly addressed, packaged, and posted to fall within the mailbox rule. [205]

pro rata rule   A rule that says shares must be purchased on a pro rata basis if too many shares are tendered. [783]

prospectus   A written disclosure document that must be submitted to the SEC along with the registration statement and given to prospective purchasers of the securities. [798]

provisional credit   Occurs when a collecting bank gives credit to a check in the collection process prior to its final settlement. Provisional credits may be reversed if the check does not "clear." [518]

proximate cause or legal cause   A point along a chain of events caused by a negligent party after which this party is no longer legally responsible for the consequences of his or her actions. [101]

proxy   The written document that a shareholder signs authorizing another person to vote his or her shares at the shareholders' meetings in the event of the shareholder's absence. [748]

proxy card   A written document signed by a shareholder that authorizes another person to vote the shareholder's shares. [775]

proxy contest   When opposing factions of shareholders and managers solicit proxies from other shareholders, the side that receives the greatest number of votes wins the proxy contest. [775]

proxy statement   A document that fully describes (1) the matter for which the proxy is being solicited, (2) who is soliciting the proxy, and (3) any other pertinent information. [775]

public corporation   A corporation that has many shareholders and whose securities are traded on national stock exchanges. [626] A corporation formed to meet a specific governmental or political purpose. [726]

public nuisance   A nuisance that affects or disturbs the public in general. [1033]

public policy exception   An exception to the employment at-will doctrine that states an employee cannot be discharged if such discharge violates the public policy of the jurisdiction. [822]

public use doctrine   A doctrine that says a patent may not be granted if the invention was used by the public for more than one year prior to the filing of the patent application. [328]

publicly held corporation   A corporation that has many shareholders and whose securities are often traded on national stock exchanges. [726]

punitive damages   Damages that are awarded to punish the defendant, to deter the defendant from similar conduct in the future, and to set an example for others. [314]

purchase money security interest   An interest a creditor automatically obtains when he or she extends credit to a *consumer* to purchase consumer goods. [550]

purchasing property   The most common method of acquiring title to personal property. [984]

qualified individual with a disability   A person who (1) has a physical or mental impairment that substantially limits one or more of his or her major life activities, (2) has a record of such impairment, or (3) is regarded as having such impairment. [853]

qualified indorsement An indorsement that includes the notation "without recourse" or similar language that disclaims liability of the indorser. [475]

qualified indorser An indorser who signs a *qualified indorsement* to an instrument. [475]

quasi in rem jurisdiction Jurisdiction allowed a plaintiff who obtains a judgment in one state to try to collect the judgment by attaching property of the defendant located in another state. [27]

quasi- or implied-in-law contract An equitable doctrine whereby a court may award monetary damages to a plaintiff for providing work or services to a defendant even though no actual contract existed. The doctrine is intended to prevent unjust enrichment and unjust detriment. [186]

quiet title action An action brought by a party seeking an order of the court declaring who has title to disputed property. The court "quiets title" by its decision. [1016]

quorum The required number of shares that must be represented in person or by proxy to hold a shareholders' meeting. The RMBCA establishes a majority of outstanding shares as a quorum. [749]

quorum The number of directors necessary to hold a board of directors' meeting or transact business of the board. [755]

Racketeer Influenced and Corrupt Organizations Act (RICO) Federal statute that authorizes civil lawsuits against defendants for engaging in a pattern of racketeering activities. [109, 147, 815] An act that provides for both criminal and civil penalties for securities fraud. [891]

radiation pollution Emissions from radioactive wastes that can cause injury and death to humans and other life and can cause severe damage to the environment. [947]

ratification The act of a minor after the minor has reached the age of majority by which he or she accepts a contract

entered into when he or she was a minor. [228] The acceptance by a corporation of an unauthorized act of a corporate officer or agent. [758]

rational basis test Test that is applied to classifications not involving a suspect or protected class. [58]

Rawls's social contract A moral theory that says each person is presumed to have entered into a social contract with all others in society to obey moral rules that are necessary for people to live in peace and harmony. [165]

real defense A defense that can be raised against both holders and HDCs. [497]

real property The land itself as well as buildings, trees, soil, minerals, timber, plants, and other things permanently affixed to the land. [263, 983]

reasonable person test Objective test that applies to commercial contracts and contracts involving mechanical fitness. [288]

receiving stolen property A person (1) knowingly receives stolen property and (2) intends to deprive the rightful owner of that property. [143]

reclamation The right of a seller or lessor to demand the return of goods from the buyer or lessee under specified situations. [420]

record date A date specified in the corporate bylaws that determines whether a shareholder may vote at a shareholders' meeting. [749] A date that determines whether a shareholder receives payment of a declared dividend. [756]

recording statute A statute that requires the mortgage or deed of trust to be recorded in the county recorder's office of the county in which the real property is located. [532, 1016]

recovery of damages A seller or lessor may recover damages measured as the difference between the contract price (or rent) and the market price (or rent) at the time and place the goods were to be delivered, plus incidental damages, from a buyer or lessee who repudiates the contract or wrongfully rejects tendered goods. [421]

recovery of goods from an insolvent seller or lessor A buyer or lessee who

has wholly or partially paid for goods before they are received may recover the goods from a seller or lessor who becomes insolvent within 10 days after receiving the first payment; the buyer or lessee must tender the remaining purchase price or rent due under the contract. Also known as *capture*. [423]

recovery of the purchase price or rent A seller or lessor may recover the contracted-for-purchase price or rent from the buyer or lessee if the buyer or lessee (1) fails to pay for accepted goods, (2) breaches the contract and the seller or lessor cannot dispose of the goods, or if (3) the goods are damaged or lost after the risk of loss passes to the buyer or lessee. [421]

redeemable preferred stock Stock that permits the corporation to buy back the preferred stock at some future date. [738]

red light doctrine A doctrine that says a holder cannot qualify as an HDC if he or she has notice of an unauthorized signature or an alteration of the instrument, or any adverse claim against or defense to its payment. [488]

reformation An equitable doctrine that permits the court to rewrite a contract to express the parties' true intentions. [310]

registered agent A person or corporation that is empowered to accept service of process on behalf of the corporation. [732]

registration statement Document that an issuer of securities files with the SEC that contains required information about the issuer, the securities to be issued, and other relevant information. [797]

regular meeting A meeting held by the board of directors at the time and place established in the bylaws. [755]

Regulation A A regulation that permits the issuer to sell securities pursuant to a simplified registration process. [800]

Regulation Z An amendment to the TILA that sets forth detailed rules for compliance with the TILA. [924]

regulatory statute A licensing statute enacted to protect the public. [234]

Rehabilitation Act of 1973 Prohibits discrimination against handicapped persons by an employer who receives federal contracts or assistance. [853]

rejection   Express words or conduct by the offeree that rejects an offer. Rejection terminates the offer. [200]

rejection of nonconforming goods   If the goods or the seller's or lessor's tender of delivery fails to conform to the contract, the buyer or lessee may (1) reject the whole, (2) accept the whole, or (3) accept any commercial unit and reject the rest. [423]

relevant geographical market   A relevant market that is defined as the area in which the defendant and its competitors sell the product or service. [965]

relevant product or service market   A relevant market that includes substitute products or services that are reasonably interchangeable with the defendant's products or services. [965]

relief from stay   May be granted in situations involving depreciating assets where the secured property is not adequately protected during the bankruptcy proceeding; asked for by a secured creditor. [567]

religious discrimination Discrimination against a person solely because of his or her religion or religious practices. [847]

remainder   If the right of possession returns to a third party upon the expiration of a limited or contingent estate. [1009]

replacement cost insurance   Insurance that pays the cost to replace the damaged or destroyed property up to the policy limits. [1047]

replacement worker   A worker who is hired either on a temporary or on a permanent basis to take the place of a striking worker. [870]

replevin   An action by a buyer or lessor to recover scarce goods wrongfully withheld by a seller or lessor. [425]

reply   Filed by the original plaintiff to answer the defendant's cross-complaint. [30]

repossession   A right granted to a secured creditor to take possession of the collateral upon default by the debtor. [555]

rescission   An action to undo the contract. [247, 942] Rescission is available if there has been a material breach of con-

tract, fraud, duress, undue influence, or mistake. [308]

residuary gift   Gift of the estate left after the debts, taxes, and specific and general gifts have been paid. [1064]

res ipsa loquitur   Tort where the presumption of negligence arises because (1) the defendant was in exclusive control of the situation and (2) the plaintiff would not have suffered injury but for someone's negligence. The burden switches to the defendant(s) to prove they were not negligent. [104]

resale price maintenance   A per se violation of Section 1 of the Sherman Act; occurs when a party at one level of distribution enters into an agreement with a party at another level to adhere to a price schedule that either sets or stabilizes prices. [962]

residence contents broad form Insurance that renters purchase to cover loss or damage to their possessions. [1048]

Resource Conservation and Recovery Act (RCRA)   A federal statute that authorizes the EPA to regulate facilities that generate, treat, store, transport, and dispose of hazardous wastes. [945]

respondeat superior   A rule that says an employer is liable for the tortious conduct of its employees or agents while they are acting within the scope of its authority. [615]

Restatement of the Law of Contracts A compilation of model contract law principles drafted by legal scholars. The Restatement is not law. [182]

restitution   Returning of goods or property received from the other party in order to rescind a contract; if the actual goods or property is not available, a cash equivalent must be made. [308]

restricted securities   Securities that were issued for investment purposes pursuant to the intrastate, private placement, or small offering exemption. [802]

restrictive covenant   A private agreement between landowners that restricts the use of their land. [1033]

restrictive indorsement   An indorsement that contains some sort of instruction from the indorser. [476]

resulting trust   A trust that is created by the conduct of the parties. [1074]

retained earnings   Profits retained by the corporation and not paid out as dividends. [757]

revenue raising statute   A licensing statute with the primary purpose of raising revenue for the government. [234]

reverse discrimination Discrimination against a group that is usually thought of as a majority. [856]

reversion   A right of possession that returns to the grantor after the expiration of a limited or contingent estate. [1009]

Revised Article 3   A comprehensive revising of the UCC law of negotiable instruments, which was released in 1990, that reflects modern commercial practices. [451, 508]

Revised Model Business Corporation Act (RMBCA)   A revision of the MBCA in 1984 that arranged the provisions of the act more logically, revised the language to be more consistent, and made substantial changes in the provisions. [725]

Revised Uniform Limited Partnership Act (RULPA)   A 1976 revision of the ULPA that provides a more modern comprehensive law for the formation, operation, and dissolution of limited partnerships. [660]

revocation   Withdrawal of an offer by the offeror terminates the offer. [199] Termination of a will. [1063]

reward   To collect a reward, the offeree must (1) have knowledge of the reward offer prior to completing the requested act and (2) perform the requested act. [198]

right of first refusal agreement   An agreement that requires the selling shareholder to offer his or her shares for sale to the other parties to the agreement before selling them to anyone else. [751]

right of inspection   A right that shareholders have to inspect the books and records of the corporation. [752]

right of redemption   A right that says the mortgagor has the right to redeem real property after default and before foreclosure. Requires the mortgagor to pay the full amount of the debt incurred by the mortgagee because of the mortgagor's default. [534] A right granted to a defaulting debtor or other secured creditor to recover the collateral from a secured creditor before he or she contracts to dispose of it or exercises his or her right to retain the collateral. Requires the redeeming party to pay the full amount of the debt and expenses caused by the debtor's default. [556]

right of subrogation The right that says the surety or guarantor acquires all of the creditor's rights against the debtor when a surety or guarantor pays a debt owed to a creditor by a debtor. [537]

right of survivorship Rule that states that a deceased partner's right in specific partnership property vests with the remaining partners upon his or her death. [643]

right to cure A licensor has the right to cure a contract if (1) the time of performance of the contract has not expired and the licensor makes conforming performance within the time of performance; (2) the licensor had reasonable grounds to believe the performance would be acceptable the licensor has a reasonable time to make conforming performance; and (3) the licensor makes a conforming performance before the licensee cancels the contract. [369]

right to know provision A provision in Superfund that requires businesses to (1) disclose the presence of certain listed chemicals to the community, (2) annually disclose emissions of chemical substances released into the environment, and (3) immediately notify the government of spills, accidents, and other emergencies involving hazardous substances. [946]

River and Harbor Act A federal statute enacted in 1886 that established a permit system for the discharge of refuse, wastes, and sewage into U.S. navigable waterways. [940]

robbery Taking personal property from another person by use of fear or force. [143]

Robinson-Patman Act Section 2 of the Clayton Act is commonly referred to by this name. [971]

rule of reason A rule that holds that only unreasonable restraints of trade violate Section 1 of the Sherman Act. The court must examine the pro- and anti-

competitive effects of the challenged restraint. [958]

Rule 10b-5 A rule adopted by the SEC to clarify the reach of Section 10 (b) against deceptive and fraudulent activities in the purchase and sale of securities. [808]

rules and regulations Adopted by administrative agencies to interpret the statutes that they are authorized to enforce. [901]

Sabbath law A law that prohibits or limits the carrying-on of certain secular activities on Sundays. [233]

Safe Drinking Water Act A federal statute enacted in 1974 and amended in 1986 that authorizes the EPA to establish national primary drinking water standards. [942]

sale The passing of title from a seller to a buyer for a price. [379] Also called a *conveyance.* [1013]

sale on approval A type of sale in which there is no actual sale unless and until the buyer accepts the goods. [400]

sale or return A contract that says the seller delivers goods to a buyer with the understanding that the buyer may return them if they are not used or resold within a stated or reasonable period of time. [401]

sale proceeds The resulting assets from the sale, exchange, or disposal of collateral subject to a security agreement. [551]

satisfaction The performance of an accord. [219]

scienter Means intentional conduct. Scienter is required for there to be a violation of Section 10 (b) and Rule 10b-5. [808]

search warrant A warrant issued by a court that authorizes the police to search a designated place for specified contraband, articles, items, or documents. The search warrant must be based on probable cause. [153]

secondary boycott picketing A type of picketing where unions try to bring pressure against an employer by picketing his or her suppliers or customers. [873]

secondary liability Liability on a negotiable instrument that is imposed on a party only when the party primarily liable

on the instrument defaults and fails to pay the instrument when due. [492]

secondary meaning When an ordinary term has become a brand name. [337]

Section 1 of the Sherman Act Prohibits *contracts, combinations, and conspiracies* in restraint of trade. [958] Prohibits tying arrangements involving goods, services, intangible property, and real property. [970]

Section 2 of the Sherman Act Prohibits the act of monopolization and attempts or conspiracies to monopolize trade. [965]

Section 2(a) of the Robinson-Patman Act Prohibits direct and indirect price discrimination by sellers of a commodity of a like grade and quality where the effect of such discrimination may be to substantially lessen competition or to tend to create a monopoly in any line of commerce. [972]

Section 2(b) of the Robinson-Patman Act A defense that provides that a seller may lawfully engage in price discrimination to meet a competitor's price. [973]

Section 2(c) of the Robinson-Patman Act Prohibits the payment of brokerage fees and other compensation by the seller to a buyer except for actual services rendered. [973]

Section 2(d) of the Robinson-Patman Act Prohibits payments by sellers to buyers for advertising, promotional, or other services unless such payments are available to other buyers on proportionately equivalent terms. [973]

Section 2(e) of the Robinson-Patman Act Requires sellers to provide promotional and other services to all buyers in a nondiscriminatory way and on proportionately equal terms. [973]

Section 2(f) of the Robinson-Patman Act Makes it illegal for a buyer to knowingly induce or receive a discriminatory price prohibited by Section 2(a). [974]

Section 3 of the Clayton Act Prohibits tying arrangements involving sales and leases of goods. [970]

Section 5 of the FTC Act Prohibits *unfair and deceptive practices.* [921] Prohibits unfair methods of competition and unfair and deceptive acts or practices. [974]

Section 7 of the Clayton Act This section, as amended, provides that it is unlawful for a person or business to acquire the stock or assets of another "where in any line of commerce or in any activity affecting commerce in any section of the country, the effect of such acquisition may be substantially to lessen competition, or to tend to create a monopoly." [967]

Section 7 of the NLRA A law that gives employees the right to join together and form a union. [864]

Section 8(a) of the NLRA A law that makes it an *unfair labor practice* for an employer to interfere with, coerce, or restrain employees from exercising their statutory right to form and join unions. [866]

Section 8(b) of the NLRA A law that prohibits unions from engaging in unfair labor practices that interfere with a union election. [866]

Section 10(b) A provision of the Securities Exchange Act of 1934 that prohibits the use of manipulative and deceptive devices in the purchase or sale of securities in contravention of the rules and regulations prescribed by the SEC. [808]

Section 10(b) A section of the Securities Exchange Act of 1934 that prohibits any manipulative or deceptive practice in connection with the purchase or sale of any security. [889]

Section 11 A provision of the Securities Act of 1993 that imposes civil liability on persons who intentionally defraud investors by making misrepresentations or omissions of material facts in the registration. Statement or who are negligent for not discovering the fraud. [805]

Section 11(a) A section of the Securities Act of 1933 that imposes civil liability on accountants and others for (1) making misstatements or omissions of material facts in a registration statement or (2) failing to find such misstatements or omissions. [888]

Section 12 A provision of the Securities Act of 1933 that imposes civil

liability on any person who violates the provisions of Section 5 of the act. [805]

Section 14(a) Provisions of the Securities Exchange Act of 1934 that gives the SEC the authority to regulate the solicitation of proxies. [775]

Section 14(e) A provision of the Williams Act that prohibits fraudulent, deceptive, and manipulative practices in connection with a tender offer. [784]

Section 16(b) A section of the Securities Exchange Act of 1934 that requires that any profits made by a statutory insider on transactions involving *short-swing profits* belong to the corporation. [813]

Section 18(a) A section of the Securities Exchange Act of 1934 that imposes civil liability on any person who makes false or misleading statements in any application, report, or document filed with the SEC. [889]

Section 24 A provision of the Securities Act of 1933 that imposes criminal liability on any person who willfully violates the 1933 act or the rules or regulations adopted thereunder. [804] A section of the Securities Act of 1933 that makes it a criminal offense for any person to (1) willfully make any untrue statement of material fact in a registration statement filed with the SEC, (2) omit any material fact necessary to ensure that the statements made in the registration statement are not misleading, or (3) willfully violate any other provision of the Securities Act of 1933 or rule or regulation adopted thereunder. [890]

Section 32 A provision of the Securities Exchange Act of 1934 that imposes criminal liability on any person who willfully violates the 1934 act or the rules or regulations adopted thereunder. [812]

Section 32(a) A section of the Securities Exchange Act of 1934 that makes it a criminal offense for any person willfully and knowingly to make or cause to be made any false or misleading statement in any application, report, or other document required to be filed with the SEC pursuant to the Securities Exchange Act of 1934 or any rule or regulation adopted thereunder. [890]

Section 552 of the Restatement (Second) of Torts A rule that an accountant is liable only for negligence to third parties who are *members of a limited class of intended users* of the client's financial statements. Provides a broader standard for holding accountants liable to third parties for negligence than the *Ultramares* doctrine. [884]

secured credit Credit that requires security (collateral) to secure payment of the loan. [527]

secured transaction A transaction that is created when a creditor makes a loan to a debtor in exchange for the debtor's pledge of personal property as security. [545]

Securities Act of 1933 A federal statute that primarily regulates the issuance of securities by corporations, partnerships, associations, and individuals. [797]

Securities and Exchange Commission (SEC) Federal administrative agency that is empowered to administer federal securities laws. The SEC can adopt rules and regulations to interpret and implement federal securities laws. [796]

Securities Enforcement Remedies and Penny Stock Reform Act of 1990 A federal statute that gives the SEC greater enforcement powers and increases and expands the remedies available for securities violations. [814]

Securities Exchange Act of 1934 A federal statute that primarily regulates the trading in securities. [807]

Security (1) An interest or instrument that is common stock, a preferred stock, a bond, a debenture, or a warrant, (2) an interest or instrument that is expressly mentioned in securities acts, and (3) an investment contract. [796]

security agreement The agreement between the debtor and the secured party that creates or provides for a security interest. [546]

self-dealing If the directors or officers engage in purchasing, selling, or leasing of property with the corporation, the contract must be fair to the corporation; otherwise, it is voidable by the corporation. The contract or transaction is enforceable if it has been fully disclosed and approved. [765]

Self-Employment Contributions Act
A federal act that says self-employed persons must pay Social Security taxes equal to the combined employer-employee amount. [832]

self-incrimination The Fifth Amendment states that no person shall be compelled in any criminal case to be a witness against him- or herself. [154]

service mark A mark that distinguishes the services of the holder from those of its competitors. [337]

service of process A summons is served on the defendant to obtain personal jurisdiction over him or her. [27]

settlement of the estate The process of a deceased's property being collected, debts and taxes being paid, and the remainder of the estate being distributed. [1071]

settlor or trustor Person who creates a trust. [1072]

sex discrimination Discrimination against a person solely because of his or her gender. [842]

sexual harassment Lewd remarks, touching, intimidation, posting pinups, and other verbal or physical conduct of a sexual nature that occur on the job. [843]

share exchange When one corporation acquires all the shares of another corporation while both corporations retain their separate legal existence. [778]

shareholder voting agreements
Agreement between two or more shareholders agreeing on how they will vote their shares. [751]

shipment contract A sales contract that requires the seller to send the goods to the buyer, but not to a specifically named destination. [412]

shipment contract The buyer bears the risk of loss during transportation. [397]

shipment contract A contract that requires the seller to ship the goods to the buyer via a common carrier. [396]

short-form merger A merger between a parent corporation and a subsidiary corporation that does not require the vote of the shareholders of either corporation or the board of directors of the subsidiary corporation. [779]

sight draft A draft payable on sight. Also called a *demand draft.* [453]

signature Any name, word, or mark used in lieu of a written signature; any symbol that is (1) handwritten, typed, printed, stamped, or made in almost any other manner and (2) executed or adopted by a party to authenticate a writing. [489]

signature liability A person cannot be held contractually liable on a negotiable instrument unless his or her signature appears on the instrument. Also called *contract liability.* [489]

signature requirement A negotiable instrument must be signed by the drawer or maker. Any symbol executed or adopted by a party with a present intent to authenticate a writing qualifies as his or her signature. [457]

signer A person signing an instrument who acts in the capacity of (1) a maker of notes and certificates of deposit, (2) a drawer of drafts and checks, (3) a drawee who certifies or accepts checks and drafts, (4) an indorser who indorses an instrument, (5) an agent who signs on behalf of others, or (6) an accommodation party. [489]

small claims court A court that hears civil cases involving small dollar amounts. [19]

small offering exemption For the sale of securities not exceeding $1 million during a 12-month period. [802]

social host liability Rule that provides that social hosts are liable for injuries caused by guests who become intoxicated at a social function. States vary as to whether they have this rule in effect. [105]

social responsibility Duty owed by businesses to act socially responsible in producing and selling goods and services. [168]

sole proprietorship A form of business where the owner is actually the business; the business is not a separate legal entity. [624, 630]

sources of international law Those things that international tribunals rely on in settling international disputes. [68]

special bailees Include common carriers, warehouse companies, and innkeepers. [996]

special federal courts Federal courts that hear matters of specialized or limited jurisdiction. [21]

special indorsement An indorsement that contains the signature of the indorser and specifies the person (indorsee) to whom the indorser intends the instrument to be payable. Creates *order paper.* [474]

special meeting A meeting convened by the board of directors to discuss new shares, merger proposals, hostile takeover attempts, and so forth. [755]

special shareholders' meetings
Meetings of shareholders that may be called to consider and vote on important or emergency issues, such as a proposed merger or amending the articles of incorporation. [748]

specific duty An OSHA standard that addresses a safety problem of a specific duty nature (e.g., requirement for a safety guard on a particular type of equipment). [826]

specific gift Gift of a specifically named piece of property. [1064]

specific performance A remedy that orders the breaching party to perform the acts promised in the contract; usually awarded in cases where the subject matter is unique, such as in contracts involving land, heirlooms, paintings, and the like. [309, 370] A decree of the court that orders a seller or lessor to perform his or her obligations under the contract; usually occurs when the goods in question are unique, such as art or antiques. [423]

stakeholder interest A theory of social responsibility that says a corporation must consider the effects its actions have on persons other than its stockholders. [170]

stale check A check that has been outstanding for more than six months. [514]

standing to sue The plaintiff must have some stake in the outcome of the lawsuit. [26]

stare decisis Latin: "to stand by the decision." Adherence to precedent. [10]

state action exemptions Business activities that are mandated by state law are exempt from federal antitrust laws. [974]

state administrative agencies Administrative agencies that states create to enforce and interpret state law. [901]

state antitakeover statutes Statutes enacted by state legislatures that protect corporations incorporated in or doing business in the state from hostile takeovers. [788]

statement of assignment A document that is filed when a secured party assigns all or part of his or her rights under a financing statement. [552]

statement of disassociation A document filed with the secretary of state that gives constructive notice that a member has disassociated from an LLC. [696]

statement of policy A statement issued by administrative agencies announcing a proposed course of action that an agency intends to follow in the future. [903]

state supreme court The highest court in a state court system; it hears appeals from intermediate state courts and certain trial courts. [20]

stationary sources Sources of air pollution such as industrial plants, oil refineries, and public utilities. [938]

statute Written law enacted by the legislative branch of the federal and state governments that establishes certain courses of conduct that must be adhered to by covered parties. [9]

Statute of Frauds State statute that requires certain types of contracts to be in writing. [262]

statute of limitations Statute that establishes the time period during which a lawsuit must be brought; if the lawsuit is not brought within this period, the injured party loses the right to sue. [31, 129, 293]

statute of repose A statute that limits the seller's liability to a certain number of years from the date when the product was first sold. [129]

Statute of Wills A state statute that establishes the requirements for making a valid will. [1061]

statutory exemptions Exemptions from antitrust laws that are expressly provided in statutes enacted by Congress. [974]

statutory lien A lien that codifies by statute a service provider's common law lien. [529]

stock dividend Additional shares of stock paid as a dividend. [757]

stock option A nontransferable right to purchase shares of the corporation from the corporation at a stated price for a specified period of time. [739]

stock warrant A stock option that is evidenced by a certificate. Warrants can be transferable or nontransferable. [739]

stop payment order An order by a drawer of a check to the payor bank not to pay or certify a check. [515]

stopping delivery of goods in transit A seller or lessor may stop delivery of goods in transit if he or she learns of the buyer's or lessee's insolvency or the buyer or lessee repudiates the contract, fails to make payment when due, or gives the seller or lessor some other right to withhold the goods. [419]

straight voting Each shareholder votes the number of shares he or she owns on candidates for each of the positions open. [749]

strict liability Liability without fault. [109]

strict or absolute liability Standard for imposing criminal liability without a finding of *mens rea* (intent). [140]

strict scrutiny test Test that is applied to classifications based on *race*. [57]

strike A cessation of work by union members in order to obtain economic benefits. [870]

subject matter jurisdiction Jurisdiction over the subject matter of a lawsuit. [27]

sublease When a tenant transfers only some of his or her rights under the lease. [1032]

sublessee The new tenant in a sublease situation. [1032]

sublessor The original tenant in a sublease situation. [1032]

subrogation If an insurance company pays a claim to an insured for liability or property damage caused by a third party, the insurer succeeds to the right of the insured to recover from the third party. [1055]

substantial performance Performance by a contracting party that deviates only slightly from complete performance. [300]

substantive due process Requires that government statutes ordinances, regulations, on other laws be clear on their face and not overly in scope. [59] Due process that requires that the statute or rule that the respondent is charged with violating be clearly stated. [906]

substantive rules Government regulation that has the force of law and must be adhered to by covered persons and businesses. [903]

subsurface rights Rights to the earth located beneath the surface of the land. [1006]

summons A court order directing the defendant to appear in court and answer the complaint. [29]

superseding event A defendant is not liable for injuries caused by a superseding or intervening event for which he or she is not responsible. [106]

supervening event An alteration or modification of a product by a party in the chain of distribution that absolves all prior sellers from strict liability. [128]

supervening illegality The enactment of a statute or regulation or court decision that makes the object of an offer illegal. This terminates the offer. [202]

supramajority voting requirement A requirement that a greater than majority of shares constitutes a quorum or the vote of the shareholders. [750]

Supremacy Clause A clause of the U.S. Constitution that establishes that the federal Constitution, treaties, federal laws, and federal regulations are the supreme law of the land. [48]

surety arrangement An arrangement where a third party promises to be *primarily liable* with the borrower for the payment of the borrower's debt. [537]

syndicate A group of individuals who join together to finance a project or transaction. [628]

taking for value requirement A holder must *give value* for the negotiable instrument to qualify as an HDC. [486]

taking in good faith requirement A holder must take the instrument in *good faith* to qualify as an HDC. [487]

taking possession A method of acquiring ownership of unowned personal property. [984]

taking without notice of defect requirement A person cannot qualify as an HDC if he or she has notice that the instrument is defective in certain ways. [487]

tangible property All real property, and physically defined personal property such as goods, animals, and minerals. [984]

target corporation The corporation that is proposed to be acquired in a tender offer situation. [782]

1976 Tax Reform Act An act that imposes criminal liability on accountants and others who prepare federal tax returns if they (1) will fully understate a client's tax liability, (2) negligently understate the tax liability, or (3) wrongfully indorse a client's tax refund check. [891]

tax sale A method of transferring property ownership that involves a lien on property for unpaid property taxes. If the lien remains unpaid after a certain amount of time, a tax sale is held to satisfy the lien. [1013]

tenancy at sufferance A tenancy created when a tenant retains possession of property after the expiration of another tenancy or a life estate without the owner's consent. [1025]

tenancy at will A lease that may be terminated at any time by either party. [1025]

tenancy by the entirety A form of co-ownership of real property that can be used only by married couples. [1011]

tenancy for years A tenancy created when the landlord and the tenant agree on a specific duration for the lease. [1025]

tenancy in common A form of co-ownership where the interest of a surviving tenant in common passes to the deceased tenant's estate and not to the co-tenants. [1010]

tenant The party to whom the lease hold is transferred. [1024]

tender of delivery The obligation of the seller to transfer and deliver goods to the buyer in accordance with the sales contract. [411]

tender offer An offer that an acquirer makes directly to a target corporation's shareholders in an effort to acquire the target corporation. [782]

tender offeror The party that makes a tender offer. [782]

tender of performance Tender is an unconditional and absolute offer by a contracting party to perform his or her obligations under the contract. [300, 361]

termination The ending of a corporation that occurs only after the winding-up of the corporation's affairs, the liquidation of its assets, and the distribution of the proceeds to the claimants. [743]

termination by acts of the parties An agency may be terminated by the following acts of the parties: (1) mutual agreement, (2) lapse of time, (3) purpose achieved, or (4) occurrence of a specified event. [597]

termination by operation of law An agency is terminated by operation of law if there is (1) death of the principal or the agent, (2) insanity of the principal or the agent, (3) bankruptcy of the principal, (4) impossibility of performance, (5) change in circumstances, or (6) war between the principal's and the agent's countries. [597]

termination statement A document filed by the secured party that ends a secured interest because the debt has been paid. [558]

term LLC An LLC that has a specified term of duration. [683]

testamentary trust A trust created by will; the trust comes into existence when the settlor dies. [1074]

testator The person who makes a will. [1061]

thermal pollution Heated water or material discharged into waterways that upsets the ecological balance and decreases the oxygen content. [942]

through bill of lading A bill of lading that provides that connecting carriers may be used to transport the goods to their destination. [999]

time draft A draft payable at a designated future date. [453]

time instrument An instrument payable (1) at a fixed date, (2) on or before a stated date, (3) at a fixed period after sight, or (4) at a time readily ascertainable when the promise or order is issued. [461]

time instrument An instrument that specifies a definite date for payment of the instrument. [487]

time note A note payable at a specific time. [454]

title Legal, tangible evidence of ownership of goods. [395]

title insurance Insurance that owners of real property purchase to insure that they have clear title to the property. [1051]

Title I of the Landrum-Griffin Act Referred to as labor's "bill of rights"; it gives each union member equal rights and privileges to nominate candidates for union office, vote in elections, and participate in membership meetings. [873]

Title VII of the Civil Rights Act of 1964 (Fair Employment Practices Act) Intended to eliminate job discrimination based on five protected classes: *race, color, religion, sex,* or *national origin.* [838]

tort A wrong. There are three categories: (1) intentional torts, (2) unintentional torts (negligence), and (3) strict liability. [91]

tort of misappropriation of the right to publicity An attempt by another person to appropriate a living person's name or identity for commercial purposes. [95]

toxic air pollutants Air pollutants that cause serious illness or death to humans. [939]

toxic substances Chemicals used for agricultural, industrial, and mining uses that cause injury to humans, birds, animals, fish, and vegetation. [944]

Toxic Substances Control Act A federal statute enacted in 1976 that requires manufacturers and processors to test new chemicals to determine their effect on human health and the environment before the EPA will allow them to be marketed. [944]

trade acceptance A sight draft that arises when credit is extended (by a seller to a buyer) with the sale of goods. The seller is both the drawer and the payee, and the buyer is the drawee. [453]

trademark A distinctive mark, symbol, name, word, motto, or device that identifies the goods of a particular business. [337]

trademark infringement Unauthorized use of another's mark. The holder may recover damages and other remedies from the infringer. [338]

trademarks and service marks A distinctive mark, symbol, name, word, motto, or device that identifies the goods or services of a particular franchisor. [709]

trade secret A product formula, pattern, design, compilation of data, customer list, or other business secret. [322] Ideas that make a franchise successful, but that do not qualify for trademark, patent, or copyright protection. [711]

transfer Any passage of an instrument other than its issuance and presentment for payment. [495]

transfer warranties Any of the following five implied warranties: (1) The transferor has good title to the instrument or is authorized to obtain payment or acceptance on behalf of one who does have good title, (2) all signatures are genuine or authorized, (3) the instrument has not been materially altered, (4) no defenses of any party are good against the transferor, and (5) the transferor has no knowledge of any insolvency proceeding against the maker, acceptor, or drawer of an unaccepted instrument. [496]

traveler's check A form of check sold by banks and other issuers. They are issued without a named payee. The purchaser fills in the payee's name when he or she uses the check to purchase goods or services. [512]

treasury shares Shares of stock repurchased by the company itself. [738]

treaties and conventions The first source of international law, consisting of agreements or contracts between two or more nations that are formally signed by an authorized representative and ratified by the supreme power of each nation. [68]

treaty A compact made between two or more nations. [9]

Treaty Clause Clause of the U.S. Constitution that states the President "shall have the power . . . to make treaties, provided two-thirds of the senators present concur." [67]

treble damages Civil damages three times actual damages may be awarded to persons whose business or property is injured by a RICO violation. [109]

trespass to land A tort that interferes with an owner's right to exclusive possession of land. [97]

trepass to personal property A tort that occurs whenever one person injures another person's personal property or interferes with that person's enjoyment of his or her personal property. [98]

trial briefs Documents submitted by the parties' attorneys to the judge that contain legal support for their side of the case. [35]

trier of fact The jury in a jury trial; the judge where there is not a jury trial. [35]

trust Established when a person (trustor) transfers title to property to another person (trustee) to be managed for the benefit of specifically named persons (beneficiaries). [628, 1072]

trust corpus The property held in trust. [1027]

trustee The holder of legal title of the real property in a deed of trust and note transaction. [531, 1072]

trustor The owner-debtor in a deed of trust and note transaction. [531]

Truth-in-Lending Act (TILA) A federal statute that requires creditors to make certain disclosures to debtors in consumer transactions. [924]

tying arrangement A restraint of trade where a seller refuses to sell one product to a customer unless the customer agrees to purchase a second product from the seller. [970]

UCC Statute of Frauds A rule that requires all contracts for the sale of *goods* costing $500 or more and lease contracts involving payments of $1,000 or more to be in writing. [267, 386]

UCC statute of limitations A rule that provides that an action for breach of any written or oral sales or lease contract must commence within four years after the cause of action accrues. The parties may agree to reduce the limitations period to one year. [426, 446]

Ultramares **doctrine** A rule that an accountant is liable only for negligence to third parties who are in *privity of contract* or a *privity-like relationship* with the accountant. Provides the narrowest standard for holding accountants liable to third parties for negligence. [883]

ultra vires **act** An act by a corporation that is beyond its express or implied powers. [741]

unauthorized signature A signature made by a purported agent without authority from the purported principal. [498]

unconditional Promises to pay and orders to pay must be unconditional for them to be negotiable. [459]

unconditional promise or order to pay requirement A negotiable instrument must contain either an *unconditional promise to pay* (note or CD) or an *unconditional order to pay* (draft or check). [458]

unconscionable disclaimer A disclaimer that is so oppressive or manifestly unfair that it will not be enforced by the court. [443]

unconscionability A doctrine under which courts may deny enforcement of unfair or oppressive contracts. [239]

undisclosed agency An agency that occurs when the third party is unaware of either (1) the existence of an agency or (2) the principal's identity. [611]

undue influence Occurs where one person takes advantage of another person's mental, emotional, or physical weakness and unduly persuades that person to enter into a contract: the persuasion by the wrongdoer must overcome the free will of the innocent party. [255, 1069]

unenforceable contract A contract where the essential where the essential elements to create a valid contract are met, but there is some legal defense to the enforcement of the contract. [188]

unfair advantage theory A theory that holds that a merger may not give the acquiring firm an unfair advantage over its competitors in finance, marketing, or expertise. [969]

unfair competition Competition that violates the law. [321]

Uniform Commercial Code Comprehensive statutory scheme that includes laws that cover aspects of commercial transactions. [182, 378]

Uniform Computer Information Transactions Act (UCITA) A model act that provides uniform and comprehensive rules for contracts involving computer information transactions and software and information licenses. [350]

Uniform Consumer Credit Code (UCCC) A code proposed by the National Conference of Commissioners on Uniform State Laws that establishes uniform rules to regulate the entire spectrum of consumer credit. [929]

Uniform Franchise Offering Circular (UFOC) A uniform disclosure document that requires the franchisor to make specific presale disclosures to prospective franchisees. [705]

The Uniform Limited Liability Company Act (ULLCA) A model act that provides comprehensive and uniform laws for the formation, operation, and dissolution of LLCs. [678]

Uniform Negotiable Instruments Law (NIL) The predecessor of the UCC developed by the National Conference of Commissioners of Uniform Laws; used from 1886 until 1952. [451]

Uniform Partnership Act (UPA) Model act that codifies partnership law. Most states have adopted the UPA in whole or in part. [638]

Uniform Probate Code (UPC) A model law promulgated to establish uniform rules for the creation of wills, the administration of estates, and the resolution of conflicts in settling estates. [1071]

Uniform Securities Act An act that has been adopted by many states it was drafted to coordinate state securities laws with federal securities laws. [891]

Uniform Simultaneous Death Act An act that provides that if people who would inherit property from each other die simultaneously, each person's property is distributed as though he or she survived. [1068]

unilateral contract A contract in which the offeror's offer can be accepted only by the performance of an act by the offeree; a "promise for an act." [183]

unilateral mistake When only one party is mistaken about a material fact regarding the subject matter of the contract. [248]

unilateral refusal to deal A unilateral choice by one party not to deal with another party. This does not violate

Section 1 of the Sherman Act because there is no concerted action. [964]

uninsured motorist coverage Automobile insurance that provides coverage to the driver and passengers who are injured by an uninsured motorist or hit-and-run driver. [1050]

unintentional tort or negligence A doctrine that says a person is liable for harm that is the foreseeable consequence of his or her actions. [98]

union shop An establishment where an employee must join the union within a certain number of days after being hired. [869]

United Nations An international organization created by a multilateral treaty in 1945. [73]

unprotected speech Speech that is not protected by the First Amendment and may be forbidden by the government. [55]

unqualified indorsement An indorsement whereby the indorser promises to pay the holder or any subsequent indorser the amount of the instrument if the maker, drawer, or acceptor defaults on it. [474]

unqualified indorser An indorser who signs an *unqualified indorsement* to an instrument. [474]

unreasonable search and seizure Any search and seizure by the government that violates the Fourth Amendment. [153]

unsecured credit Credit that does not require any security (collateral) to protect the payment of the debt. [527]

U.S. Constitution The fundamental law of the United States of America. It was ratified by the states in 1788. [47]

U.S. courts of appeals The federal court system's intermediate appellate courts. [22]

U.S. Department of Agriculture A federal agency empowered to inspect and grade meat and poultry consumed by humans. [916]

U.S. district courts The federal court system's trial courts of general jurisdiction. [21]

U.S. Supreme Court Court created by Article III of the U.S. Constitution. The highest court in the land. It is located in Washington, DC. [21, 23]

usurp an opportunity When an agent appropriates an opportunity for him- or herself by failing to let the principal know about it. [606]

usurping a corporate opportunity A director or officer steals a corporate opportunity for him- or herself. [765]

usury law A law that sets an upper limit on the interest rate that can be charged on certain types of loans. [233]

utilitarianism A moral theory that dictates that people must choose the action or follow the rule that provides the greatest good to society. [163]

valid contract A contract that meets all of the essential elements to establish a contract; a contract that is enforceable by at least one of the parties. [188]

variance An exception that permits a type of building or use in an area that would not otherwise be allowed by a zoning ordinance. [1035]

venue A concept that requires lawsuits to be heard by the court with jurisdiction that is nearest the location in which the incident occurred or where the parties reside. [28]

verdict Decision reached by the jury. [36]

vertical merger A merger that integrates the operations of a supplier and a customer. [968]

vertical restraint of trade A restraint of trade that occurs when two or more parties on *different levels of distribution* enter into a contract, combination, or conspiracy to restrain trade. [962]

violation A crime that is neither a felony nor a misdemeanor that is usually punishable by a fine. [139]

voidable contract A contract where one or both parties have the option to avoid their contractual obligations. If a contract is avoided, both parties are released from their contractual obligations. [188]

voidable title Title that a purchaser has if the goods were obtained by (1) fraud, (2) a check that is later dishonored, or (3) impersonating another person. [404]

voidable transfer An unusual payment or transfer of property by the debtor on the eve of bankruptcy that would unfairly benefit the debtor or some creditors at the expense of other creditors. Such transfer may be avoided by the bankruptcy court. [570]

void contract A contract that has no legal effect; a nullity. [188]

void title A thief acquires no title to the goods he or she steals, nor does the buyer or lessee of stolen goods. [403]

voir dire Process whereby prospective jurors are asked questions by the judge and attorneys to determine if they would be biased in their decision. [35]

voluntary dissolution A corporation that has begun business or issued shares can be dissolved upon recommendation of the board of directors and a majority vote of the shares entitled to vote. [741]

voluntary petition A petition filed by the debtor; states that the debtor has debts. [565]

voting trust The shareholders transfer their stock certificates to a trustee who is empowered to vote the shares. [751]

waiting period A period of time that begins when the registration statement is filed with the SEC and continues until the registration statement is declared effective. Only certain activities are permissible during the waiting period. [798]

warehouse company A bailee engaged in the business of storing property for compensation. Owes a *duty of reasonable care* to protect the bailed property. [996]

warehouse receipt A written document issued by a person who is engaged in the business of storing goods for hire. [998]

warranties of quality Seller's or lessor's assurance to buyer or lessee that the goods meet certain standards of quality. Warranties may be expressed or implied. [434]

warranty A buyer's or lessee's assurance that the goods meet certain standards. [433] A representation of the insured that is expressly incorporated in the insurance contract. [1054]

warranty against infringements A seller or lessor who is a merchant who regularly deals in goods of the kind sold or leased automatically warrants that the goods are delivered free of any third-party patent, trademark, or copyright claim. [434]

warranty against interference The lessor warrants that no person holds a claim or interest in the goods that arose from an act or omission of the lessor that will interfere with the lessee's enjoyment of his or her leasehold interest. [434]

warranty disclaimer Statements that negate express and implied warranties. [441]

warranty of fitness for a particular purpose A warranty that arises where a seller or lessor warrants that the goods will meet the buyer's or lessee's expressed needs. [440]

warranty of good title Sellers warrant that they have valid title to the goods they are selling and that the transfer of title is rightful. [433]

warranty of no security interests Sellers of goods warrant that the goods they sell are delivered free from any third-party security interests, liens, or encumbrances that are unknown to the buyer. [433]

waste Occurs when a tenant causes substantial and permanent damage to the leased premises that decreases the value of the property and the landlord's reversionary interest in it. [1029]

water pollution Pollution of lakes, rivers, oceans, and other bodies of water. [940]

wetlands Areas that are inundated or saturated by surface water or ground water that support vegetation typically adapted for life in such conditions. [942]

white-collar crimes Crimes usually involving cunning and deceit rather than physical force. [145]

will A declaration of how a person wants his or her property distributed upon death. [1061]

will or inheritance If a person dies with a will, his or her property is distributed to the beneficiaries as designated in the will. If a person dies without a will, his or her property is distributed to the heirs as stipulated in the state's intestate statute. [1014]

will or inheritance A way to acquire title to property that is a result of another's death. [987]

Williams Act An amendment to the Securities Exchange Act of 1934 made in 1968 that specifically regulates all tender offers. [782]

winding-up Process of liquidating the partnership's assets and distributing the proceeds to satisfy claims against the partnership. [654] The process of preserving and selling the assets of the LLC and distributing the money and property to creditors and members. [697]

winding-up and liquidation The process by which a dissolved corporation's assets are collected, liquidated, and distributed to creditors, shareholders, and other claimants. [743]

wire fraud The use of telephone or telegraph to defraud another person. [146]

withholding delivery The act of the seller or lessor purposefully refusing to deliver goods to the buyer or lessee upon breach of the sales or lease contract by the buyer or lessee or the insolvency of the buyer or lessee. [419]

workers' compensation acts Acts that compensate workers and their families if workers are injured in connection with their jobs. [824]

work product immunity A state statute that says an accountant's work papers cannot be used in a court action in that state; federal courts do not recognize this statute. [892]

work-related test A test to determine the liability of a principal; if an agent commits an intentional tort within a work-related time or space, the principal is liable for any injury caused by the agent's intentional tort. [617]

World Trade Organization (WTO) An international organization of more than 130 member nations. [77]

World Wide Web An electronic connection of millions of computers that support a standard set of rules for the exchange of information. [353]

writ of certiorari An official notice that the Supreme Court will review one's case. [24]

written order A stop-payment order that is good for six months after the date it is written. [515]

wrongful disassociation Occurs when a member withdraws from (1) a term LLC prior to the expiration of the term or (2) an at-will LLC when the operating agreement eliminates a member's power to withdraw. [696]

wrongful discharge   The discharge of an employee in violation of a statute, an employment contract, or public policy, or tortiously. As a result, the employee can recover damages and other remedies. [822]

wrongful dishonor   Occurs when there are sufficient funds in a drawer's account to pay a properly payable check, but the bank does not pay the check. [515]

wrongful dissolution   When a partner withdraws from a partnership without having the right to do so at that time. [650]

wrongful eviction   A violation of the covenant of quiet enjoyment. Also called unlawful eviction. [1027]

wrongful termination   Termination of a franchise without just cause. [716] The termination of an agency contract in violation of the terms of the agency contract. The nonbreaching party may recover damages from the breaching party. [599]

zoning commission   A local administrative body that formulates zoning ordinances, conducts public hearings, and makes recommendations to the city council. [1035]

zoning ordinances   Local laws that are adopted by municipalities and local governments to regulate land use within their boundaries. Zoning ordinances are adopted and enforced to protect the health, safety, morals, and general welfare of the community. [1034]

Case Index

Cases cited or discussed are in roman type
Principal cases are in **bold type**

Subject Index